ACTS
AN EXEGETICAL
COMMENTARY

ACTS
AN EXEGETICAL COMMENTARY

VOLUME I

INTRODUCTION

AND 1:1–2:47

CRAIG S. KEENER

Baker Academic

a division of Baker Publishing Group
Grand Rapids, Michigan

Published by Baker Academic
a division of Baker Publishing Group
P.O. Box 6287, Grand Rapids, MI 49516-6287
www.bakeracademic.com

Printed in the United States of America

Library of Congress Cataloging-in-Publication Data
Keener, Craig S., 1960–
    Acts : an exegetical commentary / Craig S. Keener.
        p.   cm.
    Includes bibliographical references.
    ISBN 978-0-8010-4836-4 (cloth)
    1. Bible. N.T. Acts—Commentaries. I. Title.
BS2625.53.K446 2012
266.6′077—dc22   2011048744

Unless noted otherwise, all translations of Scripture are those of the author.

12   13   14   15   16   17   18   7 6 5 4 3 2 1

To Dr. Médine Moussounga Keener,
French and history professor,
researcher in African
and African-American women's history,
and mentor to her students;
former refugee in the Congo;
my friend of many years;
my colleague;
and my beloved wife

CONTENTS

INTRODUCTION

Contents

COMMENTARY

The bibliography and indexes for this volume may be found on the enclosed CD-ROM.

ACKNOWLEDGMENTS

I am grateful to Baker Academic for welcoming and fully supporting this manuscript when Hendrickson Publishers sold most of its academic titles. I am grateful to both of them for believing in this manuscript when it was orphaned the first time. Those who are aware that the manuscript was originally planned with yet a different publisher, which felt unable to produce the manuscript when it realized the length,[1] may recognize that my gratitude goes particularly deep. At more than 2.5 million words when Hendrickson accepted it (and still more when Baker Academic accepted it), this commentary is at least three times the size of my two-volume John commentary. Had I put this material instead into 350 nonoverlapping twenty-page articles or 35 two-hundred-page monographs (with at least one on each chapter of Acts), this research might have sold more copies but cost readers many times more. The way much scholarship works today, some might have cited the 35 monographs (and certainly 350 articles) far more often than citing this single work. But I have preferred to provide this material as thoroughly as possible as a single work, and I owe my publisher an immense debt of gratitude for accepting this work at its full length.

I wish to express particular gratitude to those who have worked hard on this manuscript. At Baker, this includes Tim West, Brian Bolger, and Jim Kinney, all of whom have given the work their full support. Tim, the immediate project editor, is one of the most diligent, accurate, and patient editors I have worked with. Likewise, Bobbi Jo Heyboer and all those involved in marketing, design, and other divisions have impressed me with their effectiveness and support. At an earlier stage, I am grateful to my supportive team at Hendrickson, especially Shirley Decker-Lucke and Allan Emery, with also help from Mark House, Phil Frank, and Sara Scott.

Last but not least, I must thank the editor who spent more time on the manuscript besides anyone except myself, namely, Joseph Carey, who copyedited this massive work. Because of problems with the compatibility with Greek fonts, this job included reentering all the Greek, and the same compatibility problems required the deletion of some of the Hebrew. He clearly spent much time conforming the bibliography to a standardized style as well. Although I usually do not request a specific copyeditor, my experience with Joe's detailed work led me to request his services for this, my most significant academic work.

---

1. I originally closed these acknowledgments with "Pentecost 2007"; the shift in publishers accounts for the new date of (almost) Pentecost 2008. The publisher kindly allowed me to continue to update the work where I could as the subsequent process progressed.

I am grateful to Palmer Theological Seminary (formerly known as Eastern Seminary) of Eastern University for a sabbatical leave in the spring of 2005, which allowed me time to update research for the earlier draft of this manuscript, and for subsequent support of my labor to finish a work that took much longer than expected. I am also thankful to the libraries that assisted me, especially to Palmer's library staff for securing for me virtually every source I requested. I also wish to thank the institutions that have allowed me to teach Acts: Palmer; the Center for Urban Theological Studies in Philadelphia; and Hood Theological Seminary in Salisbury, North Carolina; and Palmer also for allowing me to teach the Gospel of Luke for several years (without which Acts cannot be properly understood) and a course in the life of Paul.

I am grateful to colleagues and friends for their encouragements to continue when the magnitude of the task began to feel overwhelming. These include pastor John Piippo, fellow scholar Michael Brown, novelist Anne Rice, many of my students, and too many other dear scholar friends and prayer supporters to name individually. I also want to thank my many patient and helpful colleagues at Palmer, among them administrators (including Elouise Renich Fraser, Christopher Hall, Colleen DiRaddo, and Willette Burgie-Bryant) who were sensitive to my need for significant blocks of time.

I am grateful to those who helped with the Scripture index.

I am grateful to my wife Médine for her often unexpected insights from a different (African) cultural location, and for trying to keep our apartment usually relatively quiet so that I could work undistracted. Finally, I wish to thank our son, David, for enduring my need for quiet and the temporary reduction in bedtime stories at the project's height.

A Bibliographic Note

The commentary was written as a cohesive work keyed to the bibliography. Circumstances of publication have, however, required its release in successive volumes. The publisher therefore is providing for the users of each volume the current working bibliography for the entire work, as well as the indexes for this volume, on the accompanying CD-ROM, but the final volume will contain the final hard-copy bibliography and indexes.

Craig S. Keener
Pentecost 2008

ABBREVIATIONS

Ancient Sources

Note: Works are listed under their traditional authors for the sake of locating them, not to stake a position regarding authorship claims.

General

abs.	*absoluti,* acquitted
amb.	*ambusti,* undecided
ap.	*apud,* in (quoted in)
Bk.	Book
damn.	*damnati,* condemned
DSS	Dead Sea Scrolls
ed. princ.	*editio princeps*
epil.	epilogue
ext.	external
frg(s).	fragment(s)
intro.	introduction
LCL	Loeb Classical Library
LXX	Septuagint
MS(s)	manuscript(s)
MT	Masoretic Text
Murat. Canon	Muratorian Canon
NT	New Testament
Or.	*Orations* (except in *Sib. Or.*)
OT	Old Testament
par.	parallel
pr.	*principium*
praef.	*praefatio*
pref.	preface
prol.	prologue
Q	Quelle (hypothetical common source for Matthew and Luke)
rec.	recension
Sp.	Spell
Sup.	Supplement(s)
v./vv.	verse/verses

Old Testament

Gen	Genesis
Exod	Exodus
Lev	Leviticus
Num	Numbers
Deut	Deuteronomy
Josh	Joshua
Judg	Judges
Ruth	Ruth
1–2 Sam	1–2 Samuel
1–2 Kgs	1–2 Kings
1–2 Chr	1–2 Chronicles
Ezra	Ezra
Neh	Nehemiah
Esth	Esther
Job	Job
Ps(s)	Psalm(s)
Prov	Proverbs
Eccl	Ecclesiastes
Song	Song of Songs/Song of Solomon
Isa	Isaiah
Jer	Jeremiah
Lam	Lamentations
Ezek	Ezekiel
Dan	Daniel
Hos	Hosea
Joel	Joel
Amos	Amos
Obad	Obadiah
Jonah	Jonah
Mic	Micah
Nah	Nahum
Hab	Habakkuk
Zeph	Zephaniah
Hag	Haggai
Zech	Zechariah
Mal	Malachi

New Testament

Matt	Matthew
Mark	Mark
Luke	Luke
John	John
Acts	Acts
Rom	Romans
1–2 Cor	1–2 Corinthians
Gal	Galatians
Eph	Ephesians
Phil	Philippians
Col	Colossians
1–2 Thess	1–2 Thessalonians
1–2 Tim	1–2 Timothy
Titus	Titus
Phlm	Philemon
Heb	Hebrews
Jas	James
1–2 Pet	1–2 Peter
1–3 John	1–3 John
Jude	Jude
Rev	Revelation

Septuagint (LXX)

1–4 Kgdms	1–4 Kingdoms
Ode(s)	Ode(s)

Old Testament Apocrypha

Add Esth	Additions to Esther
Bar	Baruch
Bel	Bel and the Dragon
Ep Jer	Epistle of Jeremiah
1–2 Esd	1–2 Esdras
Jdt	Judith
1–4 Macc	1–4 Maccabees
Pr Man	Prayer of Manasseh
Sir	Sirach/Ecclesiasticus
Sus	Susanna
Tob	Tobit
Wis	Wisdom of Solomon

Old Testament Pseudepigrapha

OTP	*The Old Testament Pseudepigrapha.* Edited by James H. Charlesworth. 2 vols. Garden City, N.Y.: Doubleday, 1983–85.
Ahiq.	*Ahiqar*
Apoc. Ab.	*Apocalypse of Abraham*
Apoc. Adam	*Apocalypse of Adam*
Apoc. Elij.	*Apocalypse of Elijah*
Apoc. Ezek.	*Apocalypse of Ezekiel*
Apoc. Mos.	*Apocalypse of Moses*
Apoc. Sed.	*Apocalypse of Sedrach*
Apoc. Zeph.	*Apocalypse of Zephaniah*
As. Mos.	*Assumption of Moses*
Asc. Is.	*Ascension of Isaiah*
2–4 Bar.	*2–4 Baruch*
1–3 En.	*1–3 Enoch (2 En.* has recensions A and J)
Gr. Ezra	*Greek Apocalypse of Ezra*
Hist. Rech.	*History of the Rechabites*

Jan. Jam.	*Jannes and Jambres*
Jos. Asen.	*Joseph and Aseneth*[1]
Jub.	*Jubilees*
L.A.B.	Pseudo-Philo *Biblical Antiquities*
L.A.E.	*Life of Adam and Eve*
Lad. Jac.	*Ladder of Jacob*
Let. Aris.	*Letter of Aristeas*
Liv. Pr.	*Lives of the Prophets*[2]
Mart. Is.	*Martyrdom of Isaiah*
Odes Sol.	*Odes of Solomon*
Pr. Jac.	*Prayer of Jacob*
Pr. Jos.	*Prayer of Joseph*
Ps.-Eup.	*Pseudo-Eupolemus*
Ps.-Phoc.	*Pseudo-Phocylides*
Pss. Sol.	*Psalms of Solomon*
Sent. Syr. Men.	*Sentences of the Syriac Menander*
Sib. Or.	*Sibylline Oracles*
Sim.	*Similitudes of Enoch*
Syr. Men. Epit.	*Epitome of the Syriac Menander*
Test.	**Testament of**
Ab.	*Abraham (recensions A and B)*
Adam	*Adam*
Ash.	*Asher*
Benj.	*Benjamin*
Dan	*Dan*
Gad	*Gad*
Iss.	*Issachar*
Jac.	*Jacob*
Job	*Job*[3]
Jos.	*Joseph*
Jud.	*Judah*
Levi	*Levi*
Mos.	*Moses*
Naph.	*Naphtali*
Reub.	*Reuben*
Sim.	*Simeon*
Sol.	*Solomon*
Zeb.	*Zebulun*
Tr. Shem	*Treatise of Shem*

Dead Sea Scrolls and Related Texts

DSSNT	*The Dead Sea Scrolls: A New Translation.* By Michael Wise, Martin Abegg Jr., and Edward Cook. San Francisco: HarperSanFrancisco, 1999.
1Qap Gen^ar	*Genesis Apocryphon*
1QH^a	*Hodayot* or *Thanksgiving Hymns*
1QpHab	*Pesher Habakkuk*
1QM	*Milḥamah* or *War Scroll*
1QS	*Serek Hayaḥad* or *Rule of the Community* or *Manual of Discipline*
1QSa	*Rule of the Congregation* (Appendix A to 1QS)
4Q285	*Sefer ha-Milḥamah*
11QT	*Temple Scroll*
CD	Cairo Genizah copy of the *Damascus Document*

1. The citations give double enumerations where the *OTP* translation (listed first) and the standard Greek text differ.

2. The citations first give the *OTP* reference, then the enumeration in Schermann's Greek text.

3. Where editions diverge, I cite the enumeration in both Spittler (in *OTP*) and Kraft.

Josephus and Philo

Jos.	**Josephus**
Ag. Ap.	*Against Apion*
Ant.	*Antiquities of the Jews*
Life	*Life*
War	*Jewish War*
Philo	
Abr.	*On Abraham*
Agr.	*On Husbandry/Agriculture*
Alleg. Interp.	*Allegorical Interpretation (1–3)*
Cher.	*On the Cherubim*
Conf.	*On the Confusion of Languages*
Contempl.	*On the Contemplative Life*
Creation	*On the Creation*
Decal.	*The Decalogue*
Dreams	*On Dreams, That They Are God-Sent (1–2)*
Drunkenness	*On Drunkenness*
Embassy	*Embassy to Gaius*
Eternity	*On the Eternity of the World*
Flacc.	*Flaccus*
Flight	*On Flight and Finding*
Giants	*On the Giants*
Good Person	*Every Good Person Is Free*
Heir	*Who Is the Heir of Divine Things?*
Hypoth.	*Hypothetica*
Jos.	*Joseph*
Migr.	*The Migration of Abraham*
Mos.	*Life of Moses (1–2)*
Names	*On the Change of Names*
Plant.	*Concerning Noah's Work as a Planter*
Posterity	*On the Posterity of Cain and His Exile*
Prelim. St.	*Preliminary Studies*
Prov.	*On Providence (1–2)*
QE	*Questions and Answers on Exodus (1–2)*
QG	*Questions and Answers on Genesis (1–4)*
Rewards	*On Rewards and Punishments*
Sacr.	*On the Birth of Abel and the Sacrifices Offered by Him and His Brother Cain*
Sobr.	*De sobrietate/On the Prayers and Curses Uttered by Noah When He Became Sober*
Spec. Laws	*Special Laws (1–4)*
Studies	*On Mating with the Preliminary Studies*
Unchangeable	*Unchangeableness of God*
Virt.	*On Virtues*
Worse	*That the Worse Is Wont to Attack the Better*

Targumic Texts

Tg.	*Targum (+ biblical book)*
Tg. Jon.	*Targum Jonathan*
Tg. Neof.	*Targum Neofiti*
Tg. Onq.	*Targum Onqelos*
Tg. Ps.-J.	*Targum Pseudo-Jonathan*
Tg. Rishon	*Targum Rishon*
Tg. Šeni	*Targum Šeni*

Mishnah, Talmud, and Related Literature

Soncino	*The Babylonian Talmud.* Edited by Isidore Epstein. 35 vols. London: Soncino, 1935–52.
b.	Babylonian Talmud

bar.	baraita (with rabbinic text)
m.	Mishnah
t.	Tosefta
y.	Jerusalem (Yerushalmi, Palestinian) Talmud
'Ab.	*'Abot*
'Abod. Zar.	*'Abodah Zarah*
'Arak.	*'Arakin*
B. Bat.	*Baba Batra*
B. Meṣi'a	*Baba Meṣi'a*
B. Qam.	*Baba Qamma*
Bek.	*Bekorot*
Ber.	*Berakot*
Beṣah	*Beṣah (= Yom Ṭob* [in the Tosefta]*)*
Bik.	*Bikkurim*
Demai	*Demai*
'Ed.	*'Eduyot*
'Erub.	*'Erubin*
Giṭ.	*Giṭṭin*
Ḥag.	*Ḥagigah*
Ḥal.	*Ḥallah*
Hor.	*Horayot*
Ḥul.	*Ḥullin*
Kelim	*Kelim*
Ker.	*Kerithot*
Ketub.	*Ketubbot*
Kil.	*Kil'ayim*
Kip.	*Kippurim*
Ma'aś.	*Ma'aśerot*
Ma'aś. Š.	*Ma'aśer Šeni*
Mak.	*Makkot*
Makš.	*Makširin*
Meg.	*Megillah*
Me'il.	*Me'ilah*
Menaḥ.	*Menaḥot*
Mid.	*Middot*
Miqw.	*Miqwa'ot*
Mo'ed Qaṭ.	*Mo'ed Qaṭan*
Naz.	*Nazir*
Ned.	*Nedarim*
Neg.	*Nega'im*
Nid.	*Niddah*
'Ohal.	*'Ohalot (Ahilot in the Tosefta)*
'Or.	*'Orlah*
Parah	*Parah*
Pe'ah	*Pe'ah*
Pesaḥ.	*Pesaḥim*
Qidd.	*Qiddušin*
Roš Haš.	*Roš Haššanah*
Šabb.	*Šabbat*
Sanh.	*Sanhedrin*
Šeb.	*Šebi'it*
Šebu.	*Šebu'ot*
Šeqal.	*Šeqalim*
Soṭah	*Soṭah*
Sukkah	*Sukkah*
Ta'an.	*Ta'anit*
Tamid	*Tamid*
Ṭehar.	*Ṭeharot*
Tem.	*Temurah*
Ter.	*Terumot*
Yad.	*Yadayim*
Yebam.	*Yebamot*
Yoma	*Yoma*
Zabim	*Zabim*
Zebaḥ.	*Zebaḥim*

Other Rabbinic Works

'Abot R. Nat.	'Abot de Rabbi Nathan (recensions A and B)
Der. Er. Rab.	Derek Ereṣ Rabbah
Der. Er. Zuṭ.	Derek Ereṣ Zuṭa
Deut. Rab.	Deuteronomy Rabbah
Eccl. Rab.	Ecclesiastes (Qoheleth) Rabbah
Esth. Rab.	Esther Rabbah
Exod. Rab.	Exodus Rabbah
Gen. Rab.	Genesis Rabbah
Jer. Tg.	Jerusalem Targum
Lam. Rab.	Lamentations Rabbah
Lev. Rab.	Leviticus Rabbah
Mek.	**Mekilta (ed. Lauterbach)**
Am.	Amalek
Bah.	Bahodesh
Besh.	Beshallah
Kaspa	Kaspa
Nez.	Nezikin
Pisha	Pisha
Shab.	Shabbata
Shir.	Shirata
Vay.	Vayassa
Midr. Pss.	Midrash on Psalms (Tehillim)
Num. Rab.	Numbers Rabbah
Pesiq. Rab.	Pesiqta Rabbati
Pesiq. Rab Kah.	Pesiqta de Rab Kahana
Pirqe R. El.	Pirqe Rabbi Eliezer
Ruth Rab.	Ruth Rabbah
S. Eli. Rab.	Seder Eliyahu Rabbah
S. Eli. Zut.	Seder Eliyahu Zuta
Sem.	Semaḥot
Sipra	
A.M.	'Aḥarê Mot
Behuq.	Behuqotai
Emor	Emor
Mes.	Mesora
Neg.	Neg'aim
par.	parashah
pq.	pereq
Qed.	Qedošim
Sav	Sav
Sav M. d.	Sav Mekhilta deMiluim
Sh.	Shemini
Sh. M. d.	Shemini Mekhilta deMiluim
Taz.	Tazria
VDDeho.	Vayyiqra Dibura Dehobah
VDDen.	Vayyiqra Dibura Denedabah
Sipre Deut.	Sipre on Deuteronomy
Sipre Num.	Sipre on Numbers
Song Rab.	Song of Solomon Rabbah
Sop.	Soperim
Tanḥ.	Midrash Tanḥuma
Yalquṭ Isa.	Yalquṭ on Isaiah
Yalquṭ Pss.	Yalquṭ Psalms

Apostolic Fathers

AF	The Apostolic Fathers: Greek Texts and English Translations of Their Writings. Translated by J. B. Lightfoot and J. R. Harmer. Edited and revised by Michael W. Holmes. 2nd ed. Grand Rapids: Baker, 1992.
Barn.	Epistle of Barnabas
1–2 Clem.	1–2 Clement
Did.	Didache
Diogn.	Epistle to Diognetus
Herm.	Shepherd of Hermas
Mand.	Mandates
Sim.	Similitudes
Vis.	Visions
Ign.	Ignatius of Antioch
Eph.	Epistle to the Ephesians
Magn.	Epistle to the Magnesians
Phld.	Epistle to the Philadelphians
Pol.	Epistle to Polycarp
Rom.	Epistle to the Romans
Smyrn.	Epistle to the Smyrnaeans
Trall.	Epistle to the Trallians
Mart. Pol.	Martyrdom of Polycarp
Poly. Phil.	Polycarp Letter to the Philippians

Patristic and Other Early Christian Sources

ANF	Ante-Nicene Fathers: Translations of the Writings of the Fathers down to A.D. 325. Edited by A. Roberts and J. Donaldson. Revised by A. Cleveland Coxe. 10 vols. Grand Rapids: Eerdmans, 1975.
FC	Fathers of the Church
NPNF	Nicene and Post-Nicene Fathers. Edited by Philip Schaff. 14 vols. 1886–89. Repr., Peabody, Mass.: Hendrickson, 1994.
Ambrosiaster	
Comm.	**Ambrosiaster Commentary on Paul's Epistles**
Aphrahat Dem.	**Aphrahat Demonstrations**
Arator Acts	**Arator On the Acts of the Apostles**
Aristides Apol.	**Aristides the Philosopher Apology to Hadrian**
Athanas.	**Athanasius**
Fest. Let.	Festal Letters
Inc.	On the Incarnation
Vit. Ant.	Vita Antonii/On the Life of Anthony
Athenag. Plea	**Athenagoras A Plea for Christians**
Aug.	**Augustine**
Bapt.	De baptismo contra Donatistas
C. du. ep. Pelag.	Contra duas epistulas Pelagianorum/Against Two Letters of the Pelagians
City	City of God
Conf.	Confessions
Ep.	Epistles
Harm. G.	Harmony of the Gospels
Retract.	Retractations
Serm.	Sermons
Tract. Jn.	Tractates on John
Basil	**Basil of Caesarea (the Great)**
Holy Sp.	On the Holy Spirit
Hom. Hex.	Homilies on the Hexaemeron
Chrys.	**John Chrysostom**
Hom. Acts	Homilies on Acts
Hom. 1 Cor.	Homilies on the First Epistle of Paul to the Corinthians
Hom. 2 Cor.	Homilies on the Second Epistle of Paul to the Corinthians
Hom. Gen.	Homilies on Genesis
Hom. Jn.	Homilies on John

Hom. Matt.	Homilies on Matthew
Hom. Rom.	Homilies on Romans
Clem. Alex.	**Clement of Alexandria**
Instr.	Instructor
Misc.	Miscellanies
Protr.	Protrepticus
Strom.	Stromata
Cyprian Ep.	**Cyprian Epistles**
Cyril Jer. Cat. Lect.	**Cyril of Jerusalem Catechetical Lectures**
Ephrem Syr. Hom.	**Ephrem the Syrian Homily on Our Lord**
Epiph.	**Epiphanius**
De mens.	De mensuris et ponderibus
Her.	Refutation of All Heresies/Panarion
Euseb.	**Eusebius**
Chron.	Chronicle/Chronicon
Comm. Is.	Commentary on Isaiah
H.E.	Historia ecclesiastica/Ecclesiastical History
P.E.	Praeparatio evangelica/Preparation for the Gospel
Firm. Matern.	
Math.	**Firmicus Maternus Matheseos libri VIII**
Greg. Naz. Or.	**Gregory of Nazianzus Orations**
Greg. Nyssa Greg.	
Thaum.	**Gregory of Nyssa Vita Gregorii Thaumaturgi**
Hippol. Ref.	**Hippolytus Refutation of Heresies**
Iren. Her.	**Irenaeus Against Heresies**
Jerome	
Comm. Gal.	Commentary on the Epistle to the Galatians
Dial. Pelag.	Dialogues against the Pelagians
Ep.	Epistles
Ruf.	Adversus Rufinum
Vigil.	Adversus Vigilantium
Vir. ill.	De viris illustribus/On Famous Men
Vit. Hil.	Vita S. Hilarionis eremitae/Life of St. Hilarion
Justin Martyr	
1–2 Apol.	1–2 Apology
Dial.	Dialogue with Trypho
Exhort.	Exhortation to the Greeks
Lact. Div. Inst.	**Lactantius Divine Institutes**
Mac. Magn.	
Apocrit.	**Macarius Magnes Apocriticus**
Malalas Chronogr.	**John Malalas Chronographia**
Mart. Just.	**Martyrdom of Justin**
Mart. Pion.	**Martyrdom of Pionius**
Origen	
Cels.	Against Celsus
Comm. 1 Cor.	Commentary on 1 Corinthians
Comm. Matt.	Commentary on Matthew
Comm. Rom.	Commentary on Romans
Hom. Exod.	Homilies on Exodus
Hom. Luke	Homilies on Luke
Orosius Hist.	**Paulus Orosius Historiarae adversus paganos**
Pass. Perp.	**Passion of Perpetua and Felicitas**
Pelagius	
Comm. 2 Cor.	Commentary on 2 Corinthians
Comm. Rom.	Commentary on Romans
Photius Bibl.	**Photius Bibliotheca**
Ps.-Clem.	**Pseudo-Clementines**
Hom.	Homilies
Rec.	Recognitions

Ps.-Const. Rom.	**Pseudo-Constantius The Holy Letter of St. Paul to the Romans**
Sulp. Sev. Chron.	**Sulpicius Severus Chronica**
Tatian Or. Gks.	**Tatian Oration to the Greeks**
Tert.	**Tertullian**
Adv. Jud.	Adversus Judaeos
Apol.	Apology
Bapt.	On Baptism
Cor.	De corona militis
Fasting	On Fasting, against the Psychics
Fug.	De fuga in persecutione/On Flight in Persecution
Marc.	Adversus Marcionem
Mart.	Ad martyras/To the Martyrs
Nat.	Ad nationes/To the Heathen
Pall.	De pallio
Pat.	De patientia
Praescr.	De praescriptione haereticorum/Prescription against Heretics
Scap.	Ad Scapulam
Scorp.	Scorpiace
Spec.	De spectaculis/The Shows
Test. an.	De testimonio animae/The Soul's Testimony
Wife	To His Wife
Theodoret	**Theodoret of Cyrrhus**
Comm. 1 Cor.	Commentary on 1 Corinthians
Comm. 2 Cor.	Commentary on 2 Corinthians
Hist. Rel.	Historia religiosa
Interp. Rom.	Interpretation of Romans
Theoph.	**Theophilus of Antioch To Autolycus**

Nag Hammadi Texts

NHL	The Nag Hammadi Library in English. Edited by J. M. Robinson. San Francisco: Harper & Row, 1977.
Hyp. Arch.	Hypostasis of the Archons
Orig. World	Origin of the World
Sent. Sext.	Sentences of Sextus
Zost.	Zostrianos

New Testament Apocrypha and Pseudepigrapha

Acts John	Acts of John
Acts Paul	Acts of Paul
Acts Pet.	Acts of Peter
Acts Phil.	Acts of Philip
Acts Thom.	Acts of Thomas
Ap. John	Apocryphon of John
Apoc. Paul	Apocalypse of Paul
Apoc. Pet.	Apocalypse of Peter
Apost. Const.	Apostolic Constitutions
G. Eb.	Gospel of the Ebionites
G. Nic.	Gospel of Nicodemus
G. Pet.	Gospel of Peter
G. Thom.	Gospel of Thomas
G. Jms.	Gospel of James
Paul Thec.	Acts of Paul and Thecla
Prot. Jas.	Protevangelium of James

Other Greek and Latin Works and Authors

Ach. Tat.	**Achilles Tatius** *Leucippe and Clitophon*
Ael. Arist.	**Aelius Aristides**
Def. Or.	Defense of Oratory
Leuct. Or.	Leuctrian Orations
Or.	Orations
Panath.	Panathenaic Oration
Sacr.	Sacred Tales
Aelian (Claudius Aelianus)	
Farmers	Letters of Farmers
Nat. An.	Nature of Animals
Var. hist.	Varia historia
Aeschines	
Ctes.	Ctesiphon
Embassy	False Embassy
Tim.	Timarchus
Aeschylus	
Ag.	Agamemnon
Eum.	Eumenides
Lib.	Libation-Bearers (Choephori)
Pers.	Persians
Prom.	Prometheus Bound
Seven	Seven against Thebes
Suppl.	Suppliant Women
Alciph.	**Alciphron**
Court.	Courtesans
Ep.	Epistulae/Letters
Farm.	Farmers
Fish.	Fishermen
Paras.	Parasites
Amm. Marc.	**Ammianus Marcellinus** *Res gestae*
Anacharsis *Ep.*	**[Ps.]-Anacharsis** *Epistles*
Andocides *Myst.*	**Andocides** *De mysteriis*
Ant. Diog. *Thule*	**Antonius Diogenes** *Wonders beyond Thule*
Antiph. *Her.*	**Antiphon** *Murder of Herodes*
Ap. Rhod.	**Apollonius of Rhodes** *Argonautica*
Aphth. *Progymn.*	**Aphthonius** *Progymnasmata*
Apoll. K. Tyre	**Apollonius King of Tyre**
Apollod.	**Apollodorus**
Bib.	Bibliotheca/Library
Epit.	Epitome
Appian	
Bell. civ.	Bella civilia/Civil Wars
Hist. rom.	Historia romana/Roman History
Apul.	**Apuleius**
Apol.	Apology
De deo Socr.	De deo Socratis
Metam.	Metamorphoses
Aratus *Phaen.*	**Aratus** *Phaenomena*
Arist.	**Aristotle**
Breath	On Breath
Const. Ath.	Constitution of Athens/Athēnaiōn politeia
E.E.	Eudemian Ethics
Gen. Anim.	Generation of Animals
Heav.	On the Heavens
Hist. An.	History of Animals
Mem.	Concerning Memory and Recollection
Mete.	Meteorology
Mir. ausc.	De mirabilibus auscultationibus
N.E.	Nicomachean Ethics
Parv.	Parva naturalia
Poet.	Poetics
Pol.	Politics
Rhet.	Art of Rhetoric
Soul	On the Soul
V.V.	Virtues and Vices
Aristob.	**Aristobulus** *Fragments* (in Eusebius *H.E.*)
Aristoph.	**Aristophanes**
Acharn.	Acharnians
Birds	Birds
Ec.	Ecclesiazusae
Frogs	Frogs
Lys.	Lysistrata
Plut.	Plutus/Rich Man
Thesm.	Thesmophoriazusae
Wasps	Wasps
Arius Did. *Epit.*	**Arius Didymus** *Epitome of Stoic Ethics*
Arrian	
Alex.	Anabasis of Alexander
Ind.	Indica
Peripl.	Periplus maris Euxini
Artem. *Oneir.*	**Artemidorus Daldianus** *Oneirocritica*
Athen. *Deipn.*	**Athenaeus** *Deipnosophists*
Aul. Gel.	**Aulus Gellius** *Attic Nights*
Aur. Vict. *Epit. Caes.*	**Aurelius Victor** *Epitome de Caesaribus*
Babr.	**Babrius** *Fables*
Caesar	**Julius Caesar**
Afr. W.	African War
Alex. W.	Alexandrian War
C.W.	Civil War
Gall. W.	Gallic War
Sp. W.	Spanish War
Callim. *Epig.*	**Callimachus** *Epigrammata*
Callistr.	**Callistratus**
Descr.	Descriptions
Dig.	In Digest of Justinian
Cato	**Dionysius Cato**
Coll. Dist.	Collection of Distichs
Distichs	Distichs
Cato E.	**Cato the Elder**
Agr.	De agricultura (De re rustica)
Catull. *Carm.*	**Catullus** *Carmina*
Char. *Chaer.*	**Chariton** *Chaereas and Callirhoe*
Cic.	**Cicero**
Acad.	Academica
Ag. Caec.	Against Caecilius
Agr.	De lege agraria
Amic.	De amicitia
Arch.	Pro Archia
Att.	Letters to Atticus
Balb.	Pro Balbo
Brut.	Brutus, or De claris oratoribus
Caecin.	Pro Caecina
Cael.	Pro Caelio
Cat.	In Catilinam
Clu.	Pro Cluentio
De or.	De oratore
Deiot.	Pro rege Deiotaro
Div.	De divinatione
Fam.	Epistulae ad familiares/Letters to Friends
Fat.	De fato
Fin.	De finibus
Flacc.	Pro Flacco
Font.	Pro Fonteio
Handb. Elec.	Handbook of Electioneering
Inv.	De inventione
Invect. Sall.	Invective against Sallust

Leg.	*De legibus*		Timocr.	*Against Timocrates*
Leg. man.	*Pro lege manilia*		Zenoth.	*Against Zenothemis*
Lig.	*Pro Ligario*		**Dig.**	**Digest** of Justinian
Marcell.	*Pro Marcello*		**Dio Cass.**	**Dio Cassius** *Roman History*
Mil.	*Pro Milone*		**Dio Chrys.** *Or.*	**Dio Chrysostom** *Orations*
Mur.	*Pro Murena*		**Diod. Sic.**	**Diodorus Siculus** *Library of History*
Nat. d.	*De natura deorum*		**Diogenes** *Ep.*	[Ps.-]**Diogenes** *Epistle*
Off.	*De officiis*		**Diog. Laert.**	**Diogenes Laertius,** *Lives of Eminent*
Opt. gen.	*De optimo genere oratorum*			*Philosophers*
Or. Brut.	*Orator ad M. Brutum*		**Dion. Hal.**	**Dionysius of Halicarnassus**
Parad.	*Paradoxa Stoicorum*		1–2 Amm.	*1–2 Epistle to Ammaeus*
Part. or.	*De partitione oratoria*		Anc. Or.	*On Ancient Orators*
Phil.	*Orationes philippicae*		Ant. rom.	*Antiquitates romanae/Roman Antiquities*
Pis.	*In Pisonem*		Demosth.	*Demosthenes*
Prov. cons.	*De provinciis consularibus*		Din.	*Dinarchus*
Quinct.	*Pro Quinctio*		Epid.	*On Epideictic Speeches*
Quint. fratr.	*Epistulae ad Quintum fratrum*		Isaeus	*Isaeus*
Rab. Perd.	*Pro Rabirio Perduellionis Reo*		Isoc.	*Isocrates*
Rab. Post.	*Pro Rabirio Postumo*		Lit. Comp.	*Literary Composition*
Resp.	*De re publica*		Lysias	*Lysias*
Rosc. Amer.	*Pro Sexto Roscio Amerino*		Pomp.	*Letter to Gnaeus Pompeius*
Rosc. com.	*Pro Roscio comoedo*		Thuc.	*Thucydides*
Scaur.	*Pro Scauro*		**Epict.**	**Epictetus**
Senect.	*De senectute*		Diatr.	*Diatribai*
Sest.	*Pro Sestio*		Encheir.	*Encheiridion*
Sull.	*Pro Sulla*		**Epicurus** *Let. Men.*	**Epicurus** *Letter to Menoeceus*
Top.	*Topica*		**Euhemerus** *Sacr.*	
Tull.	*Pro Tullio*		*Hist.*	**Euhemerus** *Sacred History*
Tusc.	*Tusculan Disputations*		**Eunapius** *Lives*	**Eunapius** *Lives of the Philosophers and*
Vat.	*In Vatinium*			*Sophists*
Verr.	*In Verrem*		**Eurip.**	**Euripides**
Colum.	**Columella**		Alc.	*Alcestis*
Arb.	*De arboribus/On Trees*		Andr.	*Andromache*
Rust.	*De re rustica/On Agriculture*		Bacch.	*Bacchanals*
Corn. Nep.	**Cornelius Nepos** *Generals*		Cycl.	*Cyclops*
Cornutus *Summ.*	**Cornutus** *Summary of Greek Theology*		Dict.	*Dictys*
Crates *Ep.*	**Pseudo-Crates** *Epistles*		El.	*Electra*
Demet. *Style*	**Demetrius Phalereus** *On Style/De*		Hec.	*Hecuba*
	elocutione		Hel.	*Helen*
Demosth.	**Demosthenes**		Heracl.	*Children of Heracles*
Andr.	*Against Androtion*		Herc. fur.	*Hercules furens/Madness of Heracles*
Aphob. 1–3	*Against Aphobus*		Hipp.	*Hippolytus*
Aristocr.	*Against Aristocrates*		Hyps.	*Hypsipyle*
Aristog. 1–2	*Against Aristogeiton*		Iph. Aul.	*Iphigeneia at Aulis*
Boeot. 1–2	*Mantitheus against Boeotus*		Iph. Taur.	*Iphigeneia at Tauris*
Chers.	*On the Chersonese*		Med.	*Medea*
Con.	*Against Conon*		Oed.	*Oedipus*
Cor.	*De corona/On the Crown*		Orest.	*Orestes*
Ep.	*Epistulae/Letters*		Phoen.	*Phoenician Maidens*
Ep. Philip	*Epistula Philippi/Letter of Philip*		Rhes.	*Rhesus*
Epitaph.	*Epitaphius/Funeral Speech*		Suppl.	*Suppliants*
Eub.	*Euxitheus against Eubulides*		Tro.	*Troades/Daughters of Troy*
Exord.	*Exordia (Prooemia)*		**Ezek. Trag.** *Exag.*	**Ezekiel the Tragedian** *Exagōgē*
Fals. leg.	*De falsa legatione/False Embassy*		**Florus** *Carm.*	**Florus** *Carmina*
Lacr.	*Against Lacritus*		**Frontin.** *Str.*	**Frontinus** *Strategemata*
Leoch.	*Against Leochares*		**Fronto**	**Marcus Cornelius Fronto**
Lept.	*Against Leptines*		Ad am.	*Ad amicos*
Mid.	*In Midiam/Against Meidias*		Ad Ant. imp.	*Ad Antoninum imperatorem*
Navy	*On the Navy-Boards*		Ad Ant. Pium	*Ad Antoninum Pium*
Neaer.	*Against Neaera*		Ad M. Caes.	*Ad Marcum Caesarem*
Olymp.	*Against Olympiodorus*		Ad verum imp.	*Ad verum imperatorem*
Olynth. 1–3	*Olynthiaca 1–3*		Bell. parth.	*De bello parthico*
Pant.	*Against Pantaenetus*		Eloq.	*Eloquence*
Philip. 1–3, [4]	*Philippic Orations 1–3, 4*		Ep. graec.	*Epistulae graecae*
Steph. 1[–2]	*Against Stephanus 1–2*		Fer. als.	*De feriis alsiensibus*
Theocr.	*Against Theocrines*		Nep. am.	*De nepote amisso*
Tim.	*Against Timotheus*		Pr. Hist.	*Preamble to History*

Gaius	
Dig.	In *Digest* of Justinian
Inst.	Institutes
Galen *N.F.*	**Galen** *On the Natural Faculties*
Gorg. *Hel.*	**Gorgias** *Encomium of Helen*
Gr. *Anth.*	**Greek Anthology**
Grattius *Cyneg.*	**Grattius** *Cynegeticon*
Hdn.	**Herodian** *History*
Hdt.	**Herodotus** *Histories*
Heliod. *Eth.*	**Heliodorus** *Ethiopian Story*
Heracl. *Hom. Prob.*	**Heraclitus** *Homeric Problems*
Hermog.	**Hermogenes**
Inv.	Invention
Issues	Issues
Method	Method in Forceful Speaking
Progymn.	Progymnasmata
Hesiod	
Astron.	Astronomy
Cat. W. E.	Catalogues of Women and Eoiae
Sh. Her.	Shield of Heracles
Theog.	Theogony
W.D.	Works and Days
Hierocles	**Hierocles (the Stoic)**
Fatherland	On Duties: How to Conduct Oneself toward One's Fatherland
Gods	On Duties: How to Conduct Oneself toward the Gods
Love	On Duties: On Fraternal Love
Marr.	On Duties: On Marriage
Parents	On Duties: How to Conduct Oneself toward One's Parents
Hippocr.	**Hippocrates**
Aff.	Affections
Airs	Airs, Waters, Places
Aph.	Aphorisms
Barr. Wom.	On Barren Women
Dis.	Diseases
Ep.	Epistles
Epid.	Epidemics
Fleshes	Fleshes
Glands	Glands
Nat. Man	Nature of Man
Pl. Man	Places in Man
Progn.	Prognostic
Prorr.	Prorrhetic
Reg. Ac. Dis.	Regimen in Acute Diseases
Superf.	On Superfetation
Hom.	**Homer**
Il.	Iliad
Od.	Odyssey
Hom. *Hymns*	**Homeric Hymns**
Hor.	**Horace**
Ars	Ars poetica
Carm. saec.	Carmen saeculare
Ep.	Epistles
Epodes	Epodes
Odes	Odes
Sat.	Satires
Iambl.	**Iamblichus Chalcidensis**
Myst.	Mysteries
V.P.	De vita pythagorica/On the Pythagorean Life/Life of Pythagoras
Iambl. (nov.)	
Bab. St.	**Iamblichus (novelist)** *Babylonian Story*
Isaeus	
Apollod.	Estate of Apollodorus
Aristarch.	Aristarchus

Astyph.	Astyphilus
Ciron	Ciron
Cleon.	Cleonymus
Demes.	Against the Demesmen
Dicaeog.	Estate of Dicaeogenes
Eumath.	On Behalf of Eumathes
Euphil.	On Behalf of Euphiletus
Hagnias	Hagnias
Hagnoth.	Against Hagnotheus
Menec.	Menecles
Nicost.	Nicostratus
Philoct.	Philoctemon
Pyrr.	Pyrrhus
Isoc.	**Isocrates**
Ad Nic.	Ad Nicoclem/To Nicocles (Or. 2)
Antid.	Antidosis (Or. 15)
Areop.	Areopagiticus (Or. 7)
Demon.	To Demonicus (Or. 1)
Ep.	Epistles
Nic.	Nicocles/Cyprians (Or. 3)
Panath.	Panathenaicus (Or. 12)
Paneg.	Panegyricus (Or. 4)
Peace	On the Peace (Or. 8)
Soph.	Against Sophists (Or. 17)
Julian Ap.	**Julian the Apostate**
Let.	Letters
Or.	Orations
Justin.	**Justinian**
Cod.	Codex
Dig.	Digest
Inst.	Institutes
Juv. *Sat.*	**Juvenal** *Satires*
Libanius	
Anecdote	Anecdote
Comp.	Comparison
Declam.	Declamations
Descr.	Description
Encomium	Encomium
Invect.	Invective
Maxim	Maxim
Or.	Orations
Refutation	Refutation
Speech in Character	Speech in Character
Thesis	Thesis
Topics	Common Topics
Livy	**Livy** *Ab urbe condita*
Longin. *Subl.*	**Longinus** *On the Sublime*
Longus	**Longus** *Daphnis and Chloe*
Lucan *C.W.*	**Lucan** *Civil War*
Lucian	
Affairs	Affairs of the Heart/Amores
Alex.	Alexander the False Prophet
Amber	Amber, or The Swans
Anach.	Anacharsis, or Athletics
Astr.	Astrology
Book-Coll.	The Ignorant Book-Collector
Career	The Dream, or Lucian's Career
Carousal	The Carousal (Symposium), or The Lapiths
Charid.	Charidemus
Charon	Charon, or The Inspectors
Cock	The Dream, or The Cock
Critic	The Mistaken Critic
Cynic	The Cynic
Dance	The Dance
Dem.	Demonax
Demosth.	In Praise of Demosthenes
Dial. C.	Dialogues of Courtesans

Dial. D.	Dialogues of the Dead
Dial. G.	Dialogues of the Gods
Dial. S-G.	Dialogues of Sea-Gods
Dipsads	The Dipsads
Dion.	Dionysus
Disowned	Disowned
Downward Journey	Downward Journey
Eunuch	The Eunuch
Fisherman	The Dead Come to Life, or The Fisherman
Fly	The Fly
Fun.	Funerals
Hall	The Hall
Harm.	Harmonides
Hermot.	Hermotimus, or Sects
Hipp.	Hippias, or The Bath
Hist.	How to Write History
Icar.	Icaromenippus, or The Sky-Man
Indictment	Double Indictment
Judg. G.	Judgment of the Goddesses
Lex.	Lexiphanes
Lover of Lies	The Lover of Lies
Lucius	Lucius, or The Ass
Men.	Menippus, or Descent into Hades
Nero	Nero
Nigr.	Nigrinus
Oct.	Octogenarians
Par.	The Parasite: Parasitic an Art
Parl. G.	Parliament of the Gods
Patriot	The Patriot (Philopatris)
Peregr.	The Passing of Peregrinus
Phal.	Phalaris
Phil. Sale	Philosophies for Sale
Portr.	Essays in Portraiture
Portr. D.	Essays in Portraiture Defended
Posts	Salaried Posts in Great Houses
Prof. P.S.	A Professor of Public Speaking
Prom.	Prometheus
Prom. in Words	To One Who Said "You're a Prometheus in Words"
Runaways	The Runaways
Sacr.	Sacrifices
Sat.	Saturnalia/Conversation with Cronus
Ship	The Ship, or The Wishes
Slander	Slander
Slip	A Slip of the Tongue in Greeting
Soph.	The Sham Sophist, or The Solecist
Syr. G.	Syrian Goddess
Tim.	Timon, or The Misanthrope
Tox.	Toxaris, or Friendship
True Story	A True Story
Tyr.	The Tyrannicide
Z. Cat.	Zeus Catechized
Z. Rants	Zeus Rants
Lucret. Nat.	**Lucretius De rerum natura**
Lycophron Alex.	**Lycophron of Chalcis Alexandra**
Lysias Or.	**Lysias Orationes**
Macrob.	**Macrobius**
Comm.	Commentary on the Dream of Scipio
Sat.	Saturnalia
Manetho Aeg.	**Manetho Aegyptiaca**
Marc. Aur.	**Marcus Aurelius Meditations**
Mart. Epig.	**Martial Epigrams**
Max. Tyre	**Maximus of Tyre Orationes**
Men. Rhet.	**Menander Rhetor (of Laodicea) Treatises**
Min. Fel. Oct.	**Minucius Felix Octavius**

Modestinus Dig.	**Herennius Modestinus in Digest of Justinian**
Mus. Ruf.	**Musonius Rufus**
Musaeus Hero	**Musaeus Hero and Leander**
Nicolaus Progymn.	**Nicolaus the Sophist Progymnasmata**
Nin. Rom.	**Ninus Romance**
Orph. H.	**Orphic Hymns**
Ovid	
Am.	Amores
Ars	Ars amatoria
Con. Liv.	Consolatio ad Liviam
Her.	Heroides
Metam.	Metamorphoses
Pont.	Epistulae ex Ponto
Parth. L.R.	**Parthenius Love Romance**
Paulus	**Julius Paulus**
Dig.	In Digest of Justinian
Sent.	Sententiae/Opinions
Paus.	**Pausanias Description of Greece**
Pers. Sat.	**Persius Satires**
Petron. Sat.	**Petronius Satyricon**
Perv. Ven.	**Pervigilium Veneris**
Phaedrus	**Phaedrus Fables**
Philod.	**Philodemus**
Crit.	On Frank Criticism
Household	On Household Management
Piety	On Piety
Philost.	**Flavius Philostratus (the Athenian)**
Ep.	Epistulae/Love Letters
Ep. Apoll.	Epistles of Apollonius
Hrk.	Heroikos
Vit. Apoll.	Vita Apollonii/Life of Apollonius
Vit. soph.	Vitae sophistarum/Lives of the Sophists
Philost. Elder	
Imag.	**Philostratus the Elder Imagines**
Philost. Younger	
Imag.	**Philostratus the Younger Imagines**
Pindar	
Dith.	Dithyrambs
Isthm.	Isthmian Odes
Nem.	Nemean Odes
Ol.	Olympian Odes
Pyth.	Pythian Odes
Plato	
Alcib.	Alcibiades (1–2)
Apol.	Apology
Charm.	Charmides
Clitophon	Clitophon
Cratyl.	Cratylus
Ep.	Epistles
Epin.	Epinomis
Gorg.	Gorgias
Hipp. maj.	Hippias major
Hipp. min.	Hippias minor
Hipparch.	Hipparchus
Lach.	Laches
Laws	Laws
Menex.	Menexenus
Parm.	Parmenides
Phaedo	Phaedo
Phaedr.	Phaedrus
Phileb.	Philebus
Pol.	Politicus/Statesman
Prot.	Protagoras
Rep.	Republic
Soph.	Sophist
Symp.	Symposium

Theaet.	*Theaetetus*	*Fort. Rom.*	*Fortune of Romans*
Theag.	*Theages*	*Galba*	*Galba*
Tim.	*Timaeus*	*Gen. of Soul*	*Generation of the Soul in the "Timaeus"*
Plaut.	**Plautus**	*Gk. Q.*	*Greek Questions*
Bacch.	*Bacchides*	*Isis*	*Isis and Osiris*
Cas.	*Casina*	*L. Wealth*	*Love of Wealth*
Men.	*Menaechmi*	*Lect.*	*On Lectures*
Miles glor.	*Miles gloriosus*	*Love St.*	*Love Stories*
Most.	*Mostellaria*	*Luc.*	*Lucullus*
Rud.	*Rudens*	*Lyc.*	*Lycurgus*
Truc.	*Truculentus*	*Lys.*	*Lysander*
Pliny	**Pliny the Younger**	*M. Ant.*	*Marc Antony*
Ep.	*Epistles*	*M. Cato*	*Marcus Cato*
Panegyr.	*Panegyricus*	*Mal. Hdt.*	*Malice of Herodotus*
Pliny E. N.H.	**Pliny the Elder** *Natural History*	*Many Friends*	*On Having Many Friends*
Plot. *Enn.*	**Plotinus** *Ennead*	*Marc.*	*Marcellus*
Plut.	**Plutarch**	*Mor.*	*Moralia*
Adv. K. Well	*Advice about Keeping Well*	*Nat. Phen.*	*Causes of Natural Phenomena*
Aem. Paul.	*Aemilius Paulus*	*Nic.*	*Nicias*
Ag. Pleasure	*Against Pleasure (frgs.)*	*Numa*	*Numa*
Ages.	*Agesilaus*	*Obsol.*	*Obsolescence of Oracles*
Alc.	*Alcibiades*	*Old Men*	*Old Men in Public Affairs*
Alex.	*Alexander*	*Or. Delphi*	*Oracles at Delphi No Longer Given in Verse*
Apoll.	*Letter of Consolation to Apollonius*	*Otho*	*Otho*
Arist.	*Aristides*	*Par. St.*	*Greek and Roman Parallel Stories*
Borr.	*On Borrowing (That We Ought Not to Borrow)*	*Pel.*	*Pelopidas*
		Per.	*Pericles*
Br. Love	*On Brotherly Love*	*Phil. Power*	*That a Philosopher Ought to Converse Especially with Men in Power*
Br. Wom.	*Bravery of Women*		
Bride	*Advice to Bride and Groom*	*Phoc.*	*Phocion*
Brut.	*Brutus*	*Plat. Q.*	*Platonic Questions*
Busybody	*On Being a Busybody*	*Pleas. L.*	*Epicurus Actually Makes a Pleasant Life Impossible*
C. Mar.	*Caius Marius*		
Caes.	*Caesar*	*Poetry*	*How the Young Man Should Study Poetry*
Cam.	*Camillus*	*Pomp.*	*Pompey*
Cat. Min.	*Cato Minor*	*Praising*	*Praising Oneself Inoffensively*
Chance	*Chance*	*Profit by Enemies*	*How to Profit by One's Enemies*
Cic.	*Cicero*	*Progr. Virt.*	*How One May Become Aware of One's Progress in Virtue*
Cim.	*Cimon*		
Cleverness	*Cleverness of Animals*	*Publ.*	*Publicola*
Cleom.	*Cleomenes*	*Pyrr.*	*Pyrrhus*
Comm. Conc.	*Against the Stoics on Common Conceptions*	*R. Col.*	*Reply to Colotes*
Comp. Alc. Cor.	*Comparison of Alcibiades and Coriolanus*	*Rom.*	*Romulus*
Comp. Arist. Cato	*Comparison of Aristides and Marcus Cato*	*Rom. Q.*	*Roman Questions*
Comp. Lys. Sull.	*Comparison of Lysander and Sulla*	*S. Kings*	*Sayings of Kings and Commanders*
Comp. Thes. Rom.	*Comparison of Theseus and Romulus*	*S. Rom.*	*Sayings of Romans*
Compliancy	*On Compliancy*	*S. Sp.*	*Sayings of Spartans*
Consol.	*Consolation to Wife*	*S. Sp. Wom.*	*Sayings of Spartan Women*
Contr. A.	*On the Control of Anger*	*Sert.*	*Sertorius*
Coriol.	*Coriolanus*	*Sign Soc.*	*Sign of Socrates*
Crass.	*Crassus*	*Solon*	*Solon*
Demetr.	*Demetrius*	*St. Poets*	*Stories and Poets*
Demosth.	*Demosthenes*	*Statecraft*	*Precepts of Statecraft*
Dial. L.	*Dialogue on Love*	*Stoic Cont.*	*Stoic Self-Contradictions*
Dinner	*Dinner of Seven Wise Men*	*Sulla*	*Sulla*
Div. V.	*Delays of Divine Vengeance*	*Superst.*	*Superstition*
E Delph.	*E at Delphi*	*Table*	*Table Talk*
Eating Fl.	*Eating of Flesh*	*Ten Or.*	*Ten Orators*
Educ.	*On the Education of Children*	*Themist.*	*Themistocles*
Envy	*On Envy and Hate*	*Thes.*	*Theseus*
Eum.	*Eumenes*	*Tib. Gracc.*	*Tiberius Gracchus*
Exile	*On Exile*	*Tim.*	*Timoleon*
Face M.	*Face on the Moon*	*Uned. R.*	*To an Uneducated Ruler*
Fame Ath.	*Fame of the Athenians*	*Virt.*	*Virtue and Vice*
Fate	*On Fate*	*W.V.S.C.U.*	*Whether Vice Is Sufficient to Cause Unhappiness*
Flatt.	*How to Tell a Flatterer from a Friend*		
Fort. Alex.	*On the Fortune or the Virtue of Alexander*		

Polyb.	Polybius *History of the Roman Republic*	Servius *Comm. in Verg. Aen.*	Maurius Servius Honoratus *Commentarius in Vergilii Aeneida*
Porph.	Porphyry	Sext. Emp.	**Sextus Empiricus**
Abst.	*De abstinentia*	Eth.	*Against the Ethicists*
Antr. nymph.	*De antro nympharum*	Math.	*Adversus mathematicos/Against the Professors*
Ar. Cat.	*On Aristotle's Categories*		
Isag.	*Isagoge sive quinque voces*	Pyr.	*Outlines of Pyrrhonism*
Marc.	*To Marcella*	Sil. It.	**Silius Italicus *Punica***
Porphyry's	*Porphyry's Against the Christians: The Literary Remains.* Edited and translated by R. Joseph Hoffmann. Amherst, N.Y.: Prometheus, 1994.	Soph.	**Sophocles**
		Ajax	*Ajax*
		Antig.	*Antigone*
		El.	*Electra*
V.P.	*Vita Pythagorae/Life of Pythagoras*	Oed. Col.	*Oedipus at Colonus*
Prop. *Eleg.*	**Propertius *Elegies***	Oed. tyr.	*Oedipus the King*
Ps.-Callisth. *Alex.*	**Pseudo-Callisthenes *Alexander Romance***	Philoc.	*Philoctetes*
		Wom. Tr.	*Women of Trachis*
Ps.-Chion *Ep.*	**Pseudo-Chion of Heraclea *Epistulae***	Soranus *Gynec.*	**Soranus *Gynecology***
Ptolemy		Stad.	***Stadiasmus maris magni***
Geog.	*Geography*	Statius	**Statius**
Tetrab.	*Tetrabiblos*	Ach.	*Achilleid*
Publ. Syr.	**Publilius Syrus *Sentences***	Silv.	*Silvae*
Pyth. Sent.	***Pythagorean Sentences***	Theb.	*Thebaid*
Quint.	**Quintilian**	Stob.	**Stobaeus**
Decl.	*Declamations*	Anth.	*Anthology*
Inst.	*Institutes of Oratory*	Ecl.	*Eclogae*
Quint. Curt.	**Quintus Curtius Rufus *History of Alexander***	Flor.	*Florilegium*
		Strabo	**Strabo *Geography***
Res gest.	***Res gestae divi Augusti***	Suet.	**Suetonius**
Rhet. Alex.	***Rhetorica ad Alexandrum***	Aug.	*Augustus*
Rhet. Her.	***Rhetorica ad Herennium***	Calig.	*Caligula*
Sall.	**Sallust**	Claud.	*Claudius*
Catil.	*War with Catiline*	Dom.	*Domitian*
Ep. Caes.	*Epistulae ad Caesarem/Letters to Caesar*	Galba	*Galba*
Invect. M. Tull.	*Invective against Marcus Tullius*	Gramm.	*Grammarians*
Hist.	*Historiae*	Jul.	*Julius*
Jug.	*War with Jugurtha*	Nero	*Nero*
Mith.	*Mithridates*	Rhet.	*Rhetoricians*
Philip.	*Speech of Philippus*	Tib.	*Tiberius*
Pomp.	*Letter of Gnaeus Pompeius*	Tit.	*Titus*
Sp. Caes.	*Speech to Caesar*	Vergil	*Vergil*
Sp. G. Cotta	*Speech of Gaius Cotta*	Vesp.	*Vespasian*
Sallustius *Gods*	**Sallustius *On the Gods and the Universe***	Vit.	*Vitellius*
		Tac.	**Tacitus**
Sen. E.	**Seneca the Elder**	Agr.	*Agricola*
Controv.	*Controversiae*	Ann.	*Annals*
Suas.	*Suasoriae*	Dial.	*Dialogus de oratoribus*
Sen. Y.	**Seneca the Younger**	Germ.	*Germania*
Ag.	*Agamemnon*	Hist.	*History*
Apocol.	*Apocolocyntosis*	Terence	**Terence**
Ben.	*On Benefits*	Andr.	*Lady of Andros*
Clem.	*De clementia*	Brothers	*The Brothers*
Consol.	*Consolation to Marcia*	Eun.	*Eunuch*
Const.	*De constantia*	Moth.	*The Mother-in-Law*
Dial.	*Dialogues*	Phorm.	*Phormio*
Ep. Lucil.	*Epistles to Lucilius*	Self-T.	*Self-Tormentor*
Herc. fur.	*Hercules furens*	Themistius *Or.*	**Themistius *Orationes***
Herc. Ot.	*Hercules Otaeus*	Theod.	**Theodotion**
Ira	*De ira*	Theon *Progymn.*	**Aelius Theon *Progymnasmata*** (citing the Butts edition except where otherwise noted)
Med.	*Medea*		
Nat. Q.	*Natural Questions*		
Phaed.	*Phaedra*		
Phoen.	*Phoenician Women*	Theon of Smyrna	
Prov.	*De providentia*	Exp. Rer. Math.	*Expositio rerum mathematicarum*
Tranq.	*De tranquillitate animi*	Theophr.	**Theophrastus**
Troj.	*Trojan Women*	Caus. plant.	*De causis plantarum*
Vit. beat.	*De vita beata*	Char.	*On Characters*

Thucyd.	Thucydides *History of the Peloponnesian War*
Ulp. *Dig.*	Ulpian in *Digest* of Justinian
Val. Flacc.	Valerius Flaccus *Argonautica*
Val. Max.	Valerius Maximus *Memorable Deeds and Sayings*
Varro	
L.L.	*On the Latin Language*
Rust.	*De re rustica*
Veg. *Mil.*	Vegetius *De re militari*
Vell. Paterc.	Velleius Paterculus *Compendium of Roman History*
Vett. Val.	Vettius Valens *Anthology*
Virg.	Virgil
Aen.	*Aeneid*
Catal.	*Catalepton*
Ecl.	*Eclogues*
Georg.	*Georgics*
Priap.	*Priapea*
Vit. Aes.	*Vita Aesopi/Life of Aesop/Aesop Romance*
Vitruv. *Arch.*	**Vitruvius *On Architecture***
Xen.	**Xenophon**
Ages.	*Agesilaus*
Anab.	*Anabasis*
Apol.	*Apologia Socratis*
Cav. Com.	*Cavalry Commander*
Cyr.	*Cyropaedia*
Hell.	*Hellenica*
Lac.	*Constitution of Lacedemonians*
Mem.	*Memorabilia*
Oec.	*Oeconomicus*
Symp.	*Symposium*
Xen. Eph. *Anthia*	**Xenophon of Ephesus *Anthia and Habrocomes***

Other Ancient and Medieval Sources

ANET	*Ancient Near Eastern Texts Relating to the Old Testament.* Edited by James B. Pritchard. 2nd ed. Princeton: Princeton University Press, 1955.
ARMT	*Archives royales de Mari: Transcriptions et traductions*
ARS	*Ancient Roman Statutes.* Translated by Allan Chester Johnson, Paul Robinson Coleman-Norton, and Frank Card Bourne. Austin: University of Texas Press, 1961.
BCH	*Bulletin de correspondance hellénique*
Bede *Comm. Acts*	Venerable Bede *Commentary on the Acts of the Apostles*
BGU	*Ägyptische Urkunden aus den Königlichen Staatlichen Museen zu Berlin, Griechische Urkunden.* 15 vols. Berlin, 1895–1983.
Book of Dead	*Book of the Dead* (Egyptian)
Bray, *Corinthians*	*1–2 Corinthians.* Edited by Gerald Bray. ACCS: New Testament 7. Downers Grove, Ill.: InterVarsity, 1999.
Bray, *Romans*	*Romans.* Edited by Gerald Bray. ACCS: New Testament 6. Downers Grove, Ill.: InterVarsity, 1998.
CAGN	*Collected Ancient Greek Novels.* Edited by B. P. Reardon. Berkeley: University of California Press, 1989.

Cat. Act.	*Catena in Acta ss. apostolorum.* Edited by J. A. Cramer. Oxford: E Typographeo Academico, 1838 (Martin, *Acts: Catena on the Acts of the Apostles*).
Cat. Cor.	*Catenae in sancti Pauli epistolas ad Corinthios.* Edited by J. A. Cramer. Oxford: E Typographeo Academico, 1841 (Bray, *Corinthians: Catenae on Paul's Epistles to the Corinthians*).
CER	Origen. *Commentarii in Epistulam ad Romanos.* Edited by T. Heither. 5 vols. New York: Herder, 1990–95.
CMG	Corpus medicorum graecorum
CSEL	Corpus scriptorum ecclesiasticorum latinorum
Cod. theod.	*Codex theodosianus*
Confuc. *Anal.*	Confucius *Analects*[4]
Corp. herm.	*Corpus hermeticum*
CTH	*Catalogue des textes hittites.* By Emmanuel Laroche. Paris: Klincksieck, 1971.
Cyn. Ep.	*The Cynic Epistles: A Study Edition.* Edited by Abraham J. Malherbe. SBLSBS 12. Missoula, Mont.: Scholars Press, 1977.
Diehl	*Anthologia lyrica graeca.* Edited by E. Diehl. 2 vols. Leipzig: Teubner, 1925.
Düring	*Chion of Heraclea: A Novel in Letters.* Edited by Ingemar Düring. Göteborg, Sweden: Wettergren & Kerber, 1951.
ENPK	*Ein neuer Paulustext und Kommentar.* Edited by H. J. Frede. 2 vols. Freiburg im Breisgau: Herder, 1973–74.
Epicurea	*Epicurea.* Edited by H. Usener. Leipzig: Teubner, 1887.
Eshn.	Laws of Eshnunna
Eustath. *Com. Il.*	Eustathius of Thessalonica *Commentary on Iliad*
FIRA	*Fontes iuris romani antejustiniani.* Edited by S. Riccobono et al. 3 vols. 2nd ed. Florence: Barbèra, 1940–43.
Gilg.	Epic of Gilgamesh
GBP	*The Greek Bucolic Poets.* Translated by J. M. Edmonds. LCL. Cambridge, Mass.: Harvard University Press; London: Heinemann, 1912.
GGM	*Geographi graeci minores.* Edited by C. Müller. 3 vols. Paris: Didot, 1855–61.
Gnom. Vat.	*Gnomologium Vaticanum*
GVSGM	*Geographiae veteris scriptores graeci minores.* Edited by John Hudson. 4 vols. Oxford: E Theatro Sheldoniano, 1698–1712.
Hamm.	Code of Hammurabi
Incant. Text	Incantation text from *Corpus of the Aramaic Incantation Bowls.* By Charles D. Isbell. SBLDS 17. Missoula, Mont.: Scholars Press, 1975.
Just, *Luke*	*Luke.* Edited by Arthur A. Just Jr. ACCS: New Testament 3. Downers Grove, Ill.: InterVarsity, 2003.
KUB	*Keilschrifturkunden aus Boghazköi*
LSAM	*Lois sacrées de l'Asie Mineure.* By Franciszek Sokolowski. Paris: E. de Boccard, 1955.
LSCG	*Lois sacrées des cités grecques.* By Franciszek Sokolowski. Paris: E. de Boccard, 1969.

4. Chai's enumeration followed parenthetically by the original enumeration.

MAMA — *Monumenta Asiae Minoris antiqua.* Edited by William M. Calder et al. Manchester, U.K.: Manchester University Press; London: Longmans, Green, 1928–.

Martin, *Acts* — *Acts.* Edited by Francis Martin, with Evan Smith. ACCS: New Testament 5. Downers Grove, Ill.: InterVarsity, 2006.

MOT — *The Montanist Oracles and Testimonia.* Edited by Ronald E. Heine. Macon, Ga.: Mercer University Press, 1989.

Oden and Hall, *Mark* — *Mark.* Edited by Thomas C. Oden and Christopher A. Hall. ACCS: New Testament 2. Downers Grove, Ill.: InterVarsity, 1998.

Pauluskommentare — *Pauluskommentare aus der griechischen Kirche.* Edited by K. Staab. Neutestamentliche Abhandlungen 15. Münster: Aschendorff, 1933 (Bray, *Corinthians*, and Bray, *Romans*: *Pauline Commentary from the Greek Church*).

Petav. — Synesius. *Opera quae extant omnia.* Edited by Dionysius Petavius (Denis Pétau). 2nd ed. Paris: D. Bechet, 1640.

PG — *Patrologia graeca.* [= *Patrologiae cursus completus: Series graeca*]. Edited by J.-P. Migne. 166 vols. Paris: J.-P. Migne, 1857–86.

PL — *Patrologia latina* [= *Patrologiae cursus completus: Series latina*]. Edited by J.-P. Migne. 217 vols. Paris: J.-P. Migne, 1844–46.

Pleket — H. W. Pleket, ed. Texts on the Social History of the Greek World. Vol. 2 of *Epigraphica.* Leiden: Brill, 1969.

Rev. Laws — *Revenue Laws of Ptolemy Philadelphus.* Edited by B. P. Grenfell. Oxford: Clarendon, 1896 (cited in *SPap*).

RG — *Rhetores graeci.* Edited by Leonhard von Spengel. 3 vols. Bibliotheca scriptorum graecorum et romanorum Teubneriana. Leipzig: Teubner, 1853–56.

Rhet. Gr. — *Rhetores graeci.* Edited by Christian Walz. 9 vols. in 10. Stuttgart: Cotta, 1832–36.

SB — *Sammelbuch griechischer Urkunden aus Ägypten.* Edited by F. Preisigke et al. Strassburg, 1915–.

SHA — *Scriptores Historiae Augustae*

SSGF — *The Sunday Sermons of the Great Fathers.* Translated and edited by M. F. Toal. 4 vols. Swedesboro, N.J.: Preservation, 1996.

Syncellus "Temple Program" — George Syncellus *Ecloga chronographica* "Temple Program for the New Year's Festivals at Babylon"

UPZ — *Urkunden der Ptolemäerzeit (ältere Funde).* Edited by U. Wilcken. 2 vols. Berlin: de Gruyter, 1927–57.

Zonaras — John Zonaras *Epitome historiarum*

Papyri, Inscriptions, and Fragment Collections

AE — *L'année épigraphique*

CIG — *Corpus inscriptionum graecarum.* Edited by A. Boeckh et al. 4 vols. Berlin: Riemer, 1828–77.

CIJ — *Corpus inscriptionum judaicarum.* Edited by Jean-Baptiste Frey. 2 vols. Rome: Pontificio Istituto di Archeologia Christiana, 1936–52.

CIL — *Corpus inscriptionum latinarum.* Berlin: Riemer, 1862–.

CIS — *Corpus inscriptionum semiticarum.* Paris, 1881–.

CMRDM — *Corpus monumentorum religionis dei Menis.* Edited by Eugene Lane. 4 vols. Leiden: Brill, 1971–78.

CPJ — *Corpus papyrorum judaicarum.* Edited by Victor A. Tcherikover, Alexander Fuks, and Menahem Stern. 3 vols. Cambridge, Mass.: Harvard University Press for Magnes Press, 1957–64.

Diels-Kranz — Hermann Diels. *Die Fragmente der Vorsokratiker, griechisch und deutsch.* Edited by Walther Kranz. 3 vols. 9th ed. Berlin: Weidmann, 1959–60.

Eph. Ep. — *Ephemeris epigraphica: Corporis inscriptionum latinarum supplementum.* Edited by Wilhelm Henzen et al. 9 vols. Rome: Institutum Archaeologicum Romanum; Berlin: Riemer, 1872–1913.

Epid. inscr. — Epidaurus inscription

FGH — *Fragmente der griechischen Historiker.* Edited by F. Jacoby. 3 vols. in 15. Leiden: Brill, 1954–64.

GEF — *Greek Epic Fragments from the Seventh to the Fifth Centuries BC.* Translated by Martin L. West. LCL. Cambridge, Mass.: Harvard University Press, 2003.

I. Eph. — *Die Inschriften von Ephesos.* Edited by Hermann Wankel. 8 vols. in 10. Inschriften griechisher Städte aus Keinasien 11–17. Bonn: Rudolph Habelt, 1979–84.

I. Ital. — *Inscriptiones Italiae.* Edited by V. Bracco et al. Rome: Libreria dello Stato, 1931–.

IC — *Inscriptiones creticae.* Edited by M. Guarducci. 4 vols. Rome: Libreria dello Stato, 1935–50.

IG — *Inscriptiones graecae.* Berlin: 1873–.

IGBulg — *Inscriptiones graecae in Bulgaria repertae.* Edited by G. Mikhailov. Sofia: Academia Litterarum Bulgarica, 1956–.

IGLS — *Inscriptions grecques et latines de la Syrie.* Edited by L. Jalabert et al. Paris: Geuthner, 1929–.

IGRR — *Inscriptiones graecae ad res romanas pertinentes.* Edited by R. Cagnat et al. Paris: Leroux, I, 1911; III, 1906; IV, 1927.

ILS — *Inscriptiones latinae selectae.* Edited by H. Dessau. 3 vols. in 5. Berlin: Weidmann, 1892–1916.

KSB — *Koptisches Sammelbuch.* Edited by M. R. M. Hasitzka. Vienna: Brüder Hollinek, 1993–.

Nauck — *Tragicorum graecorum fragmenta.* Edited by A. Nauck. 2nd ed. Leipzig: Teubner, 1889.

OGIS — *Orientis graeci inscriptiones selectae.* Edited by W. Dittenberger. 2 vols. Leipzig: S. Hirzel, 1903–5.

P.Amh.	*The Amherst Papyri*. Edited by B. P. Grenfell and A. S. Hunt. London, 1900–1901.
P.Beatty	*Chester Beatty Biblical Papyri*. Edited by F. G. Kenyon. London, 1933–41.
P.Bour.	*Les Papyrus Bouriant*. Edited by P. Collart. Paris, 1926.
P.Cair.	*Die demotischen Denkmäler*. Edited by W. Spiegelberg. Catalogue général des antiquités égyptiennes du Musée du Caire. Leipzig, etc., 1904–32.
P.Cair.Masp.	*Papyrus grecs d'époque byzantine*. Edited by J. Maspero. 3 vols. in 6. Catalogue général des antiquités égyptiennes du Musée du Caire. Cairo: Institut Français d'Archéologie Orientale, 1911–16.
P.Cair.Zen.	*Zenon Papyri*. Edited by C. C. Edgar, O. Guéraud, and P. Jouguet. 5 vols. Catalogue général des antiquités égyptiennes du Musée du Caire. Cairo: Institut Français d'Archéologie Orientale, 1925–40.
P.Col.	*Columbia Papyri*. New York: Columbia University Press; Missoula, Mont.; and Atlanta: Scholars Press, 1929–.
P.Coll.Youtie	*Collectanea papyrologica*. Edited by A. E. Hanson et al. Bonn, 1976.
P.Duk.	Duke University papyrus collection
P.Egerton	*Fragments of an Unknown Gospel and Other Early Christian Papyri*. Edited by H. I. Bell and T. C. Skeat. London, 1935.
P.Eleph.	*Elephantine-Papyri*. Edited by O. Rubersohn. Berlin: Weidmann, 1907.
P.Enteux.	ΕΝΤΕΥΞΕΙΣ: *Requêtes et plaintes adressées au roi d'Égypte au IIIe siècle avant J.-C*. Edited by O. Guéraud. Cairo, 1931–32.
P.Fam.Theb.	*A Family Archive from Thebes*. Edited by M. El-Amir. Cairo, 1959.
P.Fay.	*Fayum Towns and Their Papyri*. Edited by B. P. Grenfell, A. S. Hunt, and D. G. Hogarth. London, 1900.
P.Flor.	*Papyri greco-egizii, Papiri Fiorentini*. Edited by G. Vitelli and D. Comparetti. Milan, 1906–15.
P.Fouad	*Les Papyrus Fouad I*. Edited by A. Bataille et al. Cairo, 1939.
P.Giss.	*Griechische Papyri im Museum des Oberhessischen Geschichtsvereins zu Giessen*. Edited by E. Kornemann, O. Eger, and P. M. Meyer. Leipzig and Berlin: Teubner, 1910–.
P.Giss.Univ.	*Mitteilungen aus der Papyrussammlung der Giessener Universitätsbibliothek*. Edited by H. King et al. 6 vols. Giessen: Töpelmann, 1924–39.
P.Grad.	*Griechische Papyri der Sammlung Gradenwitz*. Edited by G. Plaumann. Heidelberg, 1914.
P.Graux	Nos. 1–8: *Sammelbuch griechischer Urkunden aus Ägypten*. Vol. 4, nos. 7461–68. Edited by H. Henne. Heidelberg, 1931. Nos. 9–31: *Papyrus Graux*. Edited by S. Kambitsis. Geneva: Droz, 1995–2004.
P.Grenf.	*Greek Papyri*. Edited by B. P. Grenfell and A. S. Hunt. Catalogue général des antiquités égyptiennes du Musée du Caire. Oxford: Oxford University Press, 1903.
P.Gur.	*Greek Papyri from Gurob*. Edited by J. G. Smyly. Dublin: Hodges, Figgis, 1921.
P.Hal.	*Dikaiomata: Auszüge aus alexandrischen Gesetzen und Verordnungen in einem Papyrus des Philologischen Seminars der Universität Halle (Pap.Hal. 1) mit einem Anhang weiterer Papyri derselben Sammlung*. Edited by the Graeca Halensis. Berlin: Weidman, 1913.
P.Hamb.	*Griechische Papyruskunden der Hamburger Staats- und Universitätsbibliothek*. Leipzig, etc., 1911–98.
P.Heid.	*Veröffentlichungen aus der Heidelberger Papyrussammlung*. Edited by E. Siegmann et al. Heidelberg, 1956–.
P.Hib.	*The Hibeh Papyri*. Edited by B. P. Grenfell et al. London, 1906–55.
P.Köln	*Kölner Papyri*. Edited by B. Kramer et al. Opladen: Westdeutscher Verlag, 1976–.
P.Lips.	*Griechische Urkunden der Papyrussammlung zu Leipzig*. Vol. 1: Edited by L. Mitteis. Leipzig: Teubner, 1906. Vol. 2: Edited by R. Duttenhöfer. Archiv für Papyrusforschung und verwandte Gebiete, Beiheft 10. Munich: Saur, 2002.
P.Lond.	*Greek Papyri in the British Museum*. Edited by F. G. Kenyon et al. London: Printed by Order of the Trustees, 1893–.
P.Meyer	*Griechische Texte aus Aegypten*. Edited by P. M. Meyer. Berlin, 1916.
P.Mich.	*Michigan Papyri*. 19 vols. in 20. Ann Arbor, etc., 1931–99.
P.Mil.Vogl.	*Papiri della R. Universitá di Milano; Papiri della Universitá degli Studi di Milano*. Edited by A. Vogliano et al. 8 vols. in 9. Milan, 1937–2001.
P.Murabba'ât	*Les grottes de Murabba'ât*. Edited by P. Benoit, J. T. Milik, and R. de Vaux. Discoveries in the Judaean Desert 2. Oxford, 1961.
P.Oslo	*Papyri Osloenses*. Edited by S. Eitrem and L. Amundsen. Oslo, 1925–36.
P.Oxy.	*The Oxyrhynchus Papyri*. London: British Exploration Fund; Egypt Exploration Society, 1898–.
P.Panop.Beatty	*Papyri from Panopolis in the Chester Beatty Library, Dublin*. Edited by T. C. Skeat. Dublin, 1964.
P.Paris	*Notices et textes des papyrus grecs (p. par.) du Musée du Louvre et de la Bibliotheque impériale*. Edited by M. (A.-J.) Letronne, W. Brunet de Presle, and E. Egger. Paris: Imprimerie Impériale, 1865.
P.Petr.	*The Flinders Petrie Papyri*. Edited by J. P. Mahaffy and J. G. Smyly. Dublin, 1891–1905.
P.Rein.	*Les Papyrus Théodore Reinach*. Edited by P. Collart. Cairo, 1940.
P.Ryl.	*Catalogue of the Greek Papyri in the John Rylands Library, Manchester*. Edited by A. S. Hunt, J. de M. Johnson, and V. Martin. 4 vols. Manchester, U.K.: Manchester University Press, 1911–52.
P.Sakaon	*The Archive of Aurelius Sakaon*. Edited by G. M. Parássoglou. Bonn, 1978.
P.Stras.	*Griechische Papyrus der Kaiserlichen Universitäts- und Landes-bibliothek zu Strassburg*. Edited by F. Priesigke. Leipzig, 1912–.

P.Tebt. — *The Tebtunis Papyri.* Edited by B. P. Grenfell et al. London: H. Frowde, etc., 1902–.

P.Thead. — *Papyrus de Théadelphie.* Edited by P. Jouguet. Paris: Fontemoing, 1911.

P.Turner — *Papyri Greek and Egyptian.* Edited by P. J. Parsons et al. London, 1981.

P.Yale — *Yale Papyri in the Beinecke Rare Book and Manuscript Library.* Edited by J. F. Oates. New Haven, etc., 1967–.

P.Wash.Univ. — *Washington University Papyri.* Edited by V. B. Schuman, K. Maresch, and Z. M. Packman. Missoula, Mont.; Oplanden, Ger., 1980–90.

P.Wisc. — *The Wisconsin Papyri.* Edited by P. J. Sijpesteijn. Leiden; Zutphen, Neth.,1967–77.

PDM — *Papyri demoticae magicae.* Demotic texts in the *PGM* corpus as collated in *The Greek Magical Papyri in Translation, Including the Demotic Spells.* Edited by Hans Dieter Betz. 2nd ed. Chicago: University of Chicago Press, 1992–.

Pearson — *The Fragments of Sophocles.* Edited by A. C. Pearson. 3 vols. Cambridge: Cambridge University Press, 1917.

PGM — *Papyri graecae magicae: Die griechischen Zauberpapyri.* Edited by K. Preisendanz et al. 2 vols. Leipzig and Berlin: Teubner, 1928–31.

PSI — *Papiri della Società Italiana.* Edited by G. Vitelli et al. Florence, Felice le Monnier, etc., 1912–.

RECAM — *Regional Epigraphic Catalogues of Asia Minor*

SEG — *Supplementum epigraphicum graecum.* Amsterdam, etc., 1923–.

SPap — *Select Papyri.* Edited by A. S. Hunt, C. C. Edgar, and D. L. Page. 5 vols. LCL. Cambridge, Mass.: Harvard University Press, 1932–41.

SIG² — *Sylloge inscriptionum graecarum.* Edited by W. Dittenberger. 3 vols. 2nd ed. Leipzig: S. Hirzel, 1898–1901.

SIG³ — *Sylloge inscriptionum graecarum.* Edited by W. Dittenberger. 4 vols. 3rd ed. Leipzig: S. Hirzel, 1915–24.

SVF — *Stoicorum veterum fragmenta.* Edited by H. von Arnim. 4 vols. Leipzig: Teubner, 1903–24.

TrGF — *Tragicorum graecorum fragmenta.* Edited by Bruno Snell et al. Göttingen: Vandenhoeck & Ruprecht, 1971–.

von Arnim — *Hierokles: Ethische Elementarlehre (Papyrus 9780).* Edited by H. von Arnim with W. Schubart. Berlin: Weidman, 1906.

W.Chrest. — *Grundzüge und Chrestomathie der Papyruskunde.* Edited by U. Wilcken and L. Mitteis. 2 vols. in 4. Leipzig and Berlin: Teubner, 1912.

Modern Sources

General

ad loc.	*ad locum*, at the place discussed
B.C.E.	before the Common Era
C.E.	Common Era
ca.	circa
ch(s).	chapter(s)
col.	column
e.g.	*exempli gratia*, for example
ed(s).	edition, editor(s), edited by
enl.	enlarged
esp.	especially
ET	English translation
fig.	figure
ft.	foot/feet
Gk.	Greek
Heb.	Hebrew
i.e.	*id est*, that is
impv.	imperative
in.	inch(es)
inv.	inventory number
kg.	kilogram(s)
km.	kilometer(s)
lit.	literally
m.	meter(s)
mi.	mile(s)
n(n).	note(s)
n.d.	no date
n.p.	no place/no publisher/no pages
n.s.	new series
no(s).	number(s)
p(p).	page(s)
par.	parallel
pl.	plural
R.	Rabbi
rev.	revised
s.v.	*sub verbo*, under the word
sect.	section
ser.	series
sing.	singular
sq.	square
trans.	translator(s), translated by
vs.	versus

Bible Translations

GNB	Good News Bible
GOODSPEED	E. J. Goodspeed, *The Complete Bible: An American Translation*
JB	Jerusalem Bible
MOFFATT	James Moffatt, *The New Testament: A New Translation*
NASB	New American Standard Bible
NEB	New English Bible
NIV	New International Version
NKJV	New King James Version
NLT	New Living Translation
NRSV	New Revised Standard Version
RSV	Revised Standard Version
RV	Revised Version
TWENTIETH CENTURY	Twentieth Century New Testament

Journals, Series, and Other Reference Works

AAAH	Acta Academiae Aboensis, Humaniora
AAAM	American Anthropological Association Monographs
AAAPSS	*Annals of the American Academy of Political and Social Science*
AARAS	American Academy of Religion Academy Series
AARTRSS	American Academy of Religion Teaching Religious Studies Series
AASF	Annales Academiae scientiarum fennicae
AB	Anchor Bible
ABD	*Anchor Bible Dictionary.* Edited by David N. Freeman. 6 vols. New York: Doubleday, 1992.
ABIG	Arbeiten zur Bibel und ihrer Geschichte
ABPRSSS	Association of Baptist Professors of Religion Special Studies Series
ABR	*Australian Biblical Review*
ABRL	Anchor Bible Reference Library
AbrN	*Abr-Nahrain*
ABW	*Archaeology in the Biblical World*

ACCS	Ancient Christian Commentary on Scripture	ANTC	Abingdon New Testament Commentaries
ACl	*Acta Classica*	*AnthConsc*	*Anthropology of Consciousness*
ACQ	*American Church Quarterly*	*AnthHum*	*Anthropology and Humanism*
ACR	*Australasian Catholic Record*	*Anthrop*	*Anthropos*
ADPV	*Abhandlungen des Deutschen Palästina-Vereins*	*AnthrQ*	*Anthropological Quarterly*
		Antiquity	*Antiquity*
Advance	*Advance*	*Antonianum*	*Antonianum*
Aeg	*Aegyptus*	*ANZJPsyc*	*Australian and New Zealand Journal of Psychiatry*
AfCrit	*Affirmation & Critique*		
AfCS	*African Christian Studies*	ANZSTR	Australian and New Zealand Studies in Theology and Religion
AfET	*Africa Journal of Evangelical Theology (=EAfrJET)*		
		AOAT	Alter Orient und Altes Testament
Africa	*Africa: Journal of the International African Institute, London*	APAP	*Analytic Psychotherapy and Psychopathology*
AfSR	*African Studies Review*	APB	*Acta Patristica et Byzantina*
AfThJ	*Africa Theological Journal*	*Apeiron*	*Apeiron*
AGP	*Archiv für Geschichte der Philosophie*	APOT	*The Apocrypha and Pseudepigrapha of the Old Testament in English*. Edited by R. H. Charles. 2 vols. Oxford: Clarendon, 1913.
AGSU	*Arbeiten zur Geschichte des Spätjuden- tums und Urchristentums*		
		APsPSAL	*Acta Psiquiatrica y Psicologica de America Latina*
AHB	*Ancient History Bulletin*		
AIPHOS	*Annuaire de l'Institut de philologie et d'histoire orientales et slaves*	*Apuntes*	*Apuntes*
		AramSt	*Aramaic Studies*
AJA	*American Journal of Archaeology*	*ARAnth*	*Annual Review of Anthropology*
AJAH	*American Journal of Ancient History*	ArbInt	*Arbeiten zur Interkulturalität*
AJBA	*Australian Journal of Biblical Archaeology*	*Archaeology*	*Archaeology*
AJBI	*Annual of the Japanese Biblical Institute*	*ArchOd*	*Archaeology Odyssey*
AJEC	Ancient Judaism and Early Christianity	*ArchRep*	*Archaeological Reports*
AJP	*American Journal of Philology*	*Arethusa*	*Arethusa*
AJPS	*Asian Journal of Pentecostal Studies*	ArIntHI	*Archives Internationales d'histoire des idées*
AJSR	*Association for Jewish Studies Review*		
AJT	*Asia Journal of Theology*	ARJ	*Annual of Rabbinic Judaism*
Alfinge	*Alfinge*	ASAMS	Association of Social Anthropologists Monograph Series
ALGHJ	*Arbeiten zur Literatur und Geschichte des Hellenistichen Judentums*		
		ASDE	*Annali di storia dell' esegesi*
Altertum	*Das Altertum*	*AsEthn*	*Asian Ethnology*
ALUOS	*Annual of Leeds University Oriental Society*	*AshTJ*	*Ashland Theological Journal*
ALW	*Archiv für Liturgiewissenschaft*	ASNU	Acta Seminarii Neotestamentici Upsaliensis
AmAnth	*American Anthropologist*		
AmAntiq	*American Antiquity*	*ASocR*	*American Sociological Review*
AmBenRev	*American Benedictine Review*	ASP	*American Studies in Papyrology*
AMECR	*AME (African Methodist Episcopal) Church Review*	*AsSeign*	*Assemblées du Seigneur*
		ASSR	*Archives de sciences sociales des religions*
AmEthn	*American Ethnologist*	ASTI	*Annual of the Swedish Theological Institute*
AMEZQR	*A.M.E. Zion (African Methodist Episcopal Zion) Quarterly Review*		
		AsTJ	*Asbury Theological Journal*
AmJPsyc	*American Journal of Psychiatry*	ATDan	*Acta Theologica Danica*
AmJSocPsyc	*American Journal of Social Psychiatry*	*AThR*	*Anglican Theological Review*
AmPsyc	*American Psychologist*	*'Atiqot*	*'Atiqot*
AmSocMissS	American Society of Missiology Series	ATLABS	American Theological Library Associa- tion Bibliography Series
AmSocRev	*American Sociological Review*		
Anám	*Anámnesis*	ATSSWCRMPCS	Asbury Theological Seminary Series in World Christian Revitalization Move- ments in Pentecostal/Charismatic Studies
AnBib	*Analecta Biblica*		
AnBrux	*Analecta Bruxellensia*		
AnCrac	*Analecta cracoviensia*		
AncSoc	*Ancient Society*	AugCNT	Augsburg Commentary on the New Testament
ANES	*Ancient Near Eastern Studies*		
Angelicum	*Angelicum*	*AuOr*	*Aula Orientalis*
Annala	*Annala*	AUSS	*Andrews University Seminary Studies*
Annales	*Annales*	AUSt	American University Studies
ANQ	*Andover Newton Quarterly*	AYBRL	Anchor Yale Bible Reference Library
ANRW	*Aufstieg und Niedergang der römischen Welt: Geschichte und Kultur Roms im Spiegel der neueren Forschung*. Edited by H. Temporini and W. Haase. Berlin and New York: de Gruyter, 1972–.	BA	*Biblical Archaeologist*
		BAGB	*Bulletin de l'Association Guillaume Budé*
		BAIAS	*Bulletin of the Anglo-Israel Archaeological Society*
		BangTF	*Bangalore Theological Forum*
		BapRT	*Baptist Review of Theology/Revue baptiste de théologie*
AnSt	*Anatolian Studies*	BAR	*Biblical Archaeology Review*

BASOR	*Bulletin of the American Schools of Oriental Research*
BASP	*Bulletin of the American Society of Papyrologists*
BBB	Bonner Biblische Beiträge
BBR	*Bulletin for Biblical Research*
BCompAW	Blackwell Companions to the Ancient World
BCompRel	Blackwell Companions to Religion
BDAG	Bauer, W., F. W. Danker, W. F. Arndt, and F. W. Gingrich. *Greek-English Lexicon of the New Testament and Other Early Christian Literature.* 3rd rev. ed. Chicago: University of Chicago, 1999.
BDV	*Bulletin Dei Verbum*
BECNT	Baker Exegetical Commentary on the New Testament
BEFAR	Bibliothèque des Écoles françaises d'Athènes et de Rome
BegChr	*The Beginnings of Christianity: The Acts of the Apostles.* Edited by F. J. Foakes-Jackson and Kirsopp Lake. 5 vols. London: Macmillan, 1920–33; repr., Grand Rapids: Baker Book House, 1979.
BehBrSc	*Behavioural and Brain Sciences*
BeO	*Bibbia e Oriente*
BETL	Bibliotheca Ephemeridum Theologicarum Lovaniensium
BETS	*Bulletin of the Evangelical Theological Society* (later = *JETS*)
BEURU	Bibliotheca Ekmaniana Universitatis Regiae Upsaliensis
BHMTSNABR	The Bishop Henry McNeal Turner Studies in North American Black Religion
BHT	Beiträge zur historischen Theologie
BI	*Biblical Illustrator*
Bib	*Biblica*
BiBh	*Bible Bhashyam (Biblebhashyam)*
BibInt	*Biblical Interpretation*
BibLeb	*Bibel und Leben*
BIBMS	BIBAL Monograph Series
BibOr	Biblica et Orientalia
BibRev	*Biblia Revuo*
BibSham	Bibliotheca Shamanistica
BibSp	*Bible and Spade*
BibT	*The Bible Today*
BibUnt	Biblische Untersuchungen
Bijdr	*Bijdragen*
BIOSCS	*Bulletin of the International Organization for Septuagint and Cognate Studies*
BIS	Biblical Interpretation Series
BJGS	*Bulletin of Judaeo-Greek Studies*
BJPhilSc	*British Journal for the Philosophy of Science*
BJRL	*Bulletin of the John Rylands University Library*
BJS	Brown Judaic Studies
BJSoc	*British Journal of Sociology*
BK	*Bibel und Kirche*
BL	*Bibel und Liturgie*
BLE	*Bulletin de Littérature Ecclésiastique*
BK	*Bibel und Kirche*
BMedJ	*British Medical Journal*
BMik	*Beth Mikra*
BN	*Biblische Notizen*
BNTC	Black's New Testament Commentaries
BO	*Bibliotheca orientalis*
BollS	Bollingen Series

BPN	Bibliotheca Psychiatrica et Neurologica
BR	*Biblical Research*
BRev	*Bible Review*
BrillPauly	*Brill's New Pauly, Encyclopaedia of the Ancient World: Antiquity.* Edited by Hubert Cancik, Helmuth Schneider, and Christine F. Salazar. Leiden and Boston: Brill, 2002–.
BSac	*Bibliotheca Sacra*
BSClinPsyc	British School of Clinical Psychology
BSGA	Blackwell Studies in Global Archaeology
BSL	Biblical Studies Library
BTB	*Biblical Theology Bulletin*
BTCB	Brazos Theological Commentary on the Bible
BTr	*Bible Translator*
BTZ	*Berliner Theologische Zeitschrift*
BullCorrHell	*Bulletin de Correspondance hellénique*
BurH	*Buried History*
BWANT	Beiträge zur Wissenschaft vom Alten und Neuen Testament
ByF	*Biblia y Fe*
BZ	*Biblische Zeitschrift*
BZNW	Beihefte zur Zeitschrift für die neutestamentliche Wissenschaft
BZNWK	Beihefte zur Zeitschrift für die neutestamentliche Wissenschaft und die Kunde der älteren Kirche
CaÉ	Cahiers Évangile
CAH	Cambridge Ancient History
CahJos	*Cahiers de Joséphologie*
CahRB	Cahiers de la Revue Biblique
CanJBehSc	*Canadian Journal of Behavioural Science*
Cathedra	Cathedra
CathW	*Catholic World*
CBC	Cambridge Bible Commentary
CBET	Contributions to Biblical Exegesis and Theology
CBQ	*Catholic Biblical Quarterly*
CBQMS	Catholic Biblical Quarterly Monograph Series
CBR	*Currents in Biblical Research*
CBull	*Classical Bulletin*
C&C	*Cross & Crown*
CC	Continental Commentaries
CCER	*Cahiers du Cercle Ernest-Renan*
CCl	*Civiltà Cattolica*
CCRMS	Cross-Cultural Research and Methodology Series
CCSS	Catholic Commentary on Sacred Scripture
CCWJCW	Cambridge Commentaries on Writings of the Jewish and Christian World 200 BC to AD 200
CE	*Coptic Encyclopedia.* Edited by Aziz S. Atiya. 8 vols. New York: Macmillan, 1991.
CEC	The Context of Early Christianity
CGB	*Church Growth Bulletin*
CH	*Church History*
CHB	*Christian History & Biography* (formerly *Christian History*)
ChH	*Christian History* (continued as *Christian History & Biography*)
ChicSt	*Chicago Studies*
Chm	*Churchman*
ChongTJ	*Chongshin Theological Journal*
ChrÉg	*Chronique d'Égypte*

Christus	Christus
CHSC	Center for Hellenic Studies Colloquia
CHSP	Center for Hermeneutical Studies Protocol
ChuenKLS	Chuen King Lecture Series
CJ	Classical Journal
CJP	Canadian Journal of Philosophy
CJT	Canadian Journal of Theology
ClAnt	Classical Antiquity
ClassO	Classical Outlook
CMPsy	Culture, Medicine, and Psychiatry
CNS	Cristianesimo nella Storia
CNT	Commentaire du Nouveau Testament
Coll	Collationes
CollLat	Collection Latomus
Colloq	Colloquium
ColT	Collectanea Theologica
CommCog	Communication and Cognition
Commentary	Commentary
Communio	Communio
ComPsy	Comprehensive Psychiatry
ConBNT	Coniectanea biblica: New Testament Series
ConBOT	Coniectanea biblica: Old Testament Series
Concilium	Concilium
ConcJ	Concordia Journal
ConnCMon	Connecticut College Monographs
ConsJud	Conservative Judaism
CP	Classical Philology
CQ	Classical Quarterly
CR	Classical Review
CRBR	Critical Review of Books in Religion
CrisTR	Criswell Theological Review
Criterion	Criterion
CSHJ	Chicago Studies in the History of Judaism
CSHSMC	Comparative Studies of Health Systems and Medical Care
CSSH	Comparative Studies in Society and History
CT	Christianity Today
CTAfS	Christian Theology in African Scholarship
CTJ	Calvin Theological Journal
CTM	Concordia Theological Monthly
CTQ	Concordia Theological Quarterly
CTSR	Chicago Theological Seminary Register
CuadTeol	Cuadernos de Teología
CurBS	Currents in Research: Biblical Studies
CurTM	Currents in Theology and Mission
CV	Communio Viatorum
CW	Classical World
DACB	Dictionary of African Christian Biography. New Haven: Overseas Ministries Study Center. Online: http://www.dacb.org.
Dados	Dados
DaughSar	Daughters of Sarah
DavLog	Davar Logos
DBM	Deltion Biblikon Meleton
DCDBCN	The Development of Christian Doctrine Before the Council of Nicaea
DécHell	Décrets hellénistiques
DeutsArcIns	Deutsche Archäologisches Institut
DeuUn	Deutsche Universitätszeitung
DiabMed	Diabetic Medicine
Diakonia	Diakonia
Dial	Dialog
Didaskalia	Didaskalia
Diogenes	Diogenes
Discovery	Discovery

Divinitas	Divinitas
DivThom	Divus Thomas
Diwa	Diwa: Studies in Philosophy and Theology
DLNTD	Dictionary of the Later New Testament and Its Developments. Edited by Ralph P. Martin and Peter H. Davids. Downers Grove, Ill.: InterVarsity, 1997.
DNTB	Dictionary of New Testament Background. Edited by Craig A. Evans and Stanley E. Porter. Downers Grove, Ill.: InterVarsity, 2000.
Dor le Dor	Dor le Dor
DOTHB	Dictionary of the Old Testament: Historical Books. Edited by Bill T. Arnold and H. G. M. Williamson. Downers Grove, Ill.: InterVarsity, 2005.
DOTP	Dictionary of the Old Testament: Pentateuch. Edited by T. Desmond Alexander and David W. Baker. Downers Grove, Ill.: InterVarsity, 2003.
DPCM	Dictionary of Pentecostal and Charismatic Movements. Edited by Stanley M. Burgess, Gary B. McGee, and Patrick H. Alexander. Grand Rapids: Zondervan, 1988.
DPL	Dictionary of Paul and His Letters. Edited by Gerald F. Hawthorne, Ralph P. Martin, and Daniel G. Reid. Downers Grove, Ill.: InterVarsity, 1993.
DRev	The Downside Review
DSD	Dead Sea Discoveries
DSt	Dutch Studies
DTT	Dansk Teologisk Tidsskrift
DVerb	Dei Verbum
EAfrJET	East African Journal of Evangelical Theology
EAfSt	Eastern African Studies
East Asian PastRev	East Asian Pastoral Review
ÉcBib	École biblique
EcRev	Ecumenical Review
EdF	Erträge der Forschung
EfMex	Efemerides Mexicana
ÉgT	Église et Théologie
EHPR	Études d'Histoire et de Philosophie Religieuses
EHRel	Études d'Histoire des Religions
EKKNT	Evangelisch-katholischer Kommentar zum Neuen Testament
EkkPhar	Ekklesiastikos Pharos
ELKZ	Evangelisch-Lutherische Kirchenzeitung
EMC	Echos du Monde Classique/Classical Views
Emmanuel	Emmanuel
Enc	Encounter
EncJud	Encyclopaedia Judaica. 16 vols. Jerusalem: Keter, 1972.
Enr	Enrichment
EphLit	Ephemerides Liturgicae
EphMar	Ephemerides Mariologicae
ÉPROER	Études préliminaires aux religions orientales dans l'empire romain
EpwRev	Epworth Review
Eranos	Eranos
ErAuf	Erbe und Auftrag
ErIsr	Eretz-Israel (Erets-Yisrael)
ESEC	Emory Studies in Early Christianity
EspV	Esprit et Vie
EstAg	Estudio Agustiniano
EstBib	Estudios Bíblicos
EstEcl	Estudios Eclesiásticos

EtBib	Études Bibliques
Ethnology	Ethnology
Ethos	Ethos
EthRacSt	Ethnic and Racial Studies
ETL	Ephemerides Theologicae Lovanienses
ETR	Études Théologiques et Religieuses
ÉtudClass	Les Études Classiques
Études	Études
EunDoc	Euntes Docete
EurH	Europäische Hochschulschriften
EurSCO	European Studies on Christian Origins
EUSTS	European University Studies, Theology Series
EvJ	Evangelical Journal
EvQ	Evangelical Quarterly
EvT	Evangelische Theologie
Exp	Expositor
ExpBC	The Expositor's Bible Commentary
Explor	Explorations
ExpT	Expository Times
FaithFreed	Faith and Freedom
FCNTECW	Feminist Companion to the New Testament and Early Christian World
FemTheol	Feminist Theology
FF	Foundations and Facets
FIAEC	Fédération Internationale des Associations d'Études Classiques
FidHist	Fides et Historia
FilNeot	Filología Neotestamentaria
F&M	Faith & Mission
FO	Folia Orientalia
FoiVie	Foi et Vie
ForKathTheol	Forum Katholische Theologie
Forum	Forum
FourR	The Fourth R
FPhil	Faith and Philosophy
FreiRund	Freiburger Rundbrief
FRLANT	Forschungen zur Religion und Literatur des Alten und Neuen Testaments
FSCS	Faith and Scholarship Colloquies Series
FZPhTh	Freiburger Zeitschrift für Philosophie und Theologie
GBWW	Great Books of the Western World
GCAJS	Gratz College Annual of Jewish Studies
GDT	Global Dictionary of Theology: A Resource for the Worldwide Church. Edited by William A. Dyrness et al. Downers Grove, Ill.: InterVarsity, 2008.
GNC	Good News Commentaries
GNS	Good News Studies
GOTR	Greek Orthodox Theological Review
GR	Greece & Rome
GRBS	Greek, Roman and Byzantine Studies
Greg	Gregorianum
GTJ	Grace Theological Journal
HABES	Heidelberger althistorische Beiträge und epigraphische Studien
HBT	Horizons in Biblical Theology
HCPsy	Hospital and Community Psychiatry
HDBull	Harvard Divinity Bulletin
HDR	Harvard Dissertations in Religion
HekRev	Hekima Review
Helios	Helios
Hen	Henoch
Herm	Hermathena
Hermeneia	Hermeneia—A Critical and Historical Commentary on the Bible
Hermenêutica	Hermenêutica
Hesperia	Hesperia: Journal of the American School of Classical Studies at Athens
Hesperia Sup	Hesperia Supplements
HeyJ	Heythrop Journal
HibJ	Hibbert Journal
HisJBehSc	Hispanic Journal of Behavioral Sciences
Historia	Historia
HistTh	History and Theory
HistW	History Workshop
HMFT	Health/Medicine and the Faith Traditions
HNT	Handbuch zum Neuen Testament
HNTC	Harper's New Testament Commentaries
Hok	Hokhma
HolNTC	Holman New Testament Commentary
HR	History of Religions
HS	Hebrew Studies
HSCP	Harvard Studies in Classical Philology
HSM	Harvard Semitic Monographs
HSS	Harvard Semitic Studies
HT	History Today
HTKNT	Herders theologischer Kommentar zum Neuen Testament
HTR	Harvard Theological Review
HTS	Harvard Theological Studies
HTS/TS	HTS Teologiese Studies/Theological Studies
HUCA	Hebrew Union College Annual
HumDev	Human Development
HvTS	Hervormde Teologiese Studies
IBC	Interpretation: A Bible Commentary for Teaching and Preaching
IBMR	International Bulletin of Missionary Research
IBRB	Institute for Biblical Research Bibliographies
IBS	Irish Biblical Studies
IBT	Interpreting Biblical Texts
IC	Inscriptiones creticae 1-4, ed. M. Guarducci (Rome, 1939–50)
ICC	International Critical Commentaries
ICS	Illinois Classical Studies
IEJ	Israel Exploration Journal
IGSK	Inschriften Griechischer Städte aus Kleinasien
IgViv	Iglesia viva
IJAC	International Journal for the Advancement of Counselling
IJAHS	International Journal of African Historical Studies
IJComSoc	International Journal of Comparative Sociology
IJSocLang	International Journal of the Sociology of Language
IJSocPsyc	International Journal of Social Psychiatry
IKaZ	Internationale Katholische Zeitschrift
ImBSt	Immersion Bible Studies
Imm	Immanuel
IndCHR	Indian Church History Review
InnTStud	Innsbrucker theologische Studien
Interchange	Interchange: Papers on Biblical and Current Questions
Interpretation	Interpretation
IntRevMiss	International Review of Mission
ISBE	International Standard Bible Encyclopedia. Rev. ed. Edited by Geoffrey W. Bromiley. 4 vols. Grand Rapids: Eerdmans, 1979–88.
IsLN	Israel—Land and Nature
IsNumJ	Israel Numismatic Journal

IsNumR	Israel Numismatic Research	JLH	Jahrbuch für Liturgik und Hymnologie
ITQ	Irish Theological Quarterly	JLR	Journal of Law and Religion
ITS	Indian Theological Studies	JMBeh	Journal of Mind and Behavior
IVPNTC	InterVarsity Press New Testament Commentary	JMFam	Journal of Marriage and Family
		JMS	Journal of Mithraic Studies
JAAR	Journal of the American Academy of Religion	JNES	Journal of Near Eastern Studies
		JNSL	Journal of Northwest Semitic Languages
JAAS	Journal of Asia Adventist Seminary	JÖAI	Jahreshefte des Österreichischen archäolo-
JAbnPsy	Journal of Abnormal Psychology		gischen Instituts
JAC	Jahrbuch für Antike und Christentum	JPFC	The Jewish People in the First Century: His-
JAfrHist	Journal of African History		torical Geography; Political History; Social,
JAM	Journal of Asian Mission		Cultural, and Religious Life and Institutions.
JAMA	Journal of the American Medical Association		Edited by S. Safrai and M. Stern with
JAmFolk	Journal of American Folklore		D. Flusser and W. C. van Unnik. 2 vols.
JANER	Journal of Ancient Near Eastern Religions		Compendia rerum iudaicarum ad Novum
JANESCU	Journal of the Ancient Near Eastern Society of Columbia University		Testamentum 1. Vol. 1: Assen: Van Gor- cum, 1974; vol. 2: Philadelphia: Fortress,
JAnthRes	Journal of Anthropological Research		1976.
JAOS	Journal of the American Oriental Society	JPJ	Journal of Progressive Judaism
JAramB	Journal for the Aramaic Bible (now = Ara- maic Studies)	JPOS	Journal of the Palestine Oriental Society
		JPsycHist	Journal of Psychohistory
JAS	Journal of Asian Studies	JPsyTE	Journal of Psychiatric Treatment and
JASA	Journal of the American Scientific Affiliation		Evaluation
JATS	Journal of the Adventist Theological Society	JPT	Journal of Pentecostal Theology
JBL	Journal of Biblical Literature	JPTSup	Journal of Pentecostal Theology
JBLMS	Journal of Biblical Literature Monograph Series		Supplement
		JQR	Jewish Quarterly Review
JBPRes	Journal of Biblical and Pneumatological Research	JR	Journal of Religion
		JRA	Journal of Roman Archaeology
JBPsi	Jornal Brasileiro de Psiquiatria	JRASS	Journal of Roman Archaeology Supple-
JBQ	Jewish Bible Quarterly		mentary Series
JCounsDev	Journal of Counseling and Development	JRefJud	Journal of Reform Judaism
JDharm	Journal of Dharma	JRelAf	Journal of Religion in Africa
JEA	Journal of Egyptian Archaeology	JRelHealth	Journal of Religion and Health
Jeev	Jeevadhara	JRelS	Journal of Religious Studies
JerPersp	Jerusalem Perspective	JRH	Journal of Religious History
JerSJT	Jerusalem Studies in Jewish Thought	JRS	Journal of Roman Studies
JECS	Journal of Early Christian Studies	JRT	Journal of Religious Thought
JES	Journal of Ecumenical Studies	JSAlc	Journal of Studies on Alcohol
JESHO	Journal of the Economic and Social History of the Orient	JSCE	Journal of the Society of Christian Ethics
		JSHJ	Journal for the Study of the Historical Jesus
JEthS	Journal of Ethiopian Studies	JSJ	Journal for the Study of Judaism in the Per-
JETS	Journal of the Evangelical Theological Society		sian, Hellenistic, and Roman Periods
		JSNT	Journal for the Study of the New Testament
JEurPentTA	Journal of the European Pentecostal Theo- logical Association	JSNTSup	Journal for the Study of the New Testa- ment: Supplement Series
JExpPsyc	Journal of Experimental Psychology	JSocI	Journal of Social Issues
JFSR	Journal of Feminist Studies in Religion	JSOT	Journal for the Study of the Old Testament
JGES	Journal of the Grace Evangelical Society	JSOTSup	Journal for the Study of the Old Testa-
JGPsyc	Journal of General Psychology		ment: Supplement Series
JGRCJ	Journal of Greco-Roman Christianity and Judaism	JSP	Journal for the Study of the Pseudepigrapha
		JSPSup	Journal for the Study of the Pseudepigra-
JHC	Journal of Higher Criticism		pha Supplement Series
JHI	Journal of the History of Ideas	JSQ	Jewish Studies Quarterly
JHistPhil	Journal of the History of Philosophy	JSS	Journal of Semitic Studies
JHistS	Journal of Historical Studies	JSSR	Journal for the Scientific Study of Religion
JHistSex	Journal of the History of Sexuality	JS/TS	Journal for Semitics/Tydskrif vir Semitistiek
JHLT	Journal of Hispanic/Latino Theology	JTC	Journal for Theology and Church
JHom	Journal of Homosexuality	JTheol	Journal of Theology
JHS	Journal of Hellenic Studies	JTS	Journal of Theological Studies
Jian Dao	Jian Dao	JTSA	Journal of Theology for Southern Africa
Jian Dao DS	Jian Dao Dissertation Series	Judaism	Judaism
JIHist	Journal of Interdisciplinary History	JValInq	Journal of Value Inquiry
JITC	Journal of the Interdenominational Theo- logical Center	Kairos	Kairos
		Kairós	Kairós
JJS	Journal of Jewish Studies	KathKomNT	Katholischer Kommentar zum Neuen
JJTP	Journal of Jewish Thought and Philosophy		Testament

KBANT	Kommentare und Beiträge zum Alten und Neuen Testament
KEKNT	Kritisch-exegetischer Kommentar über das Neue Testament, begründet von H. A. W. Meyer
Kerux	*Kerux*
Klio	*Klio*
KuI	*Kirche und Israel*
LangSc	*Language Sciences*
LangSoc	*Language in Society*
Laós	*Laós*
Latomus	*Latomus*
Laur	*Laurentianum*
LCBI	Literary Currents in Biblical Interpretation
LCL	Loeb Classical Library
LCQ	*Lutheran Church Quarterly*
LCR	*Lutheran Church Review*
LD	Lectio Divina
LebSeel	*Lebendige Seelsorge*
LEC	Library of Early Christianity
Leš	*Lešonénu*
Levant	*Levant*
Ling	*Linguistics*
List	*Listening: Journal of Religion and Culture*
Listener	*The Listener*
LivL	*Living Light*
LNTS	Library of New Testament Studies
LOS	London Oriental Series
LouvS	*Louvain Studies*
LPSt	Library of Pauline Studies
LQ	*Lutheran Quarterly*
LRB	Library of Religious Biography
LSEMSA	London School of Economics Monographs on Social Anthropology
LSJ	Liddell, Henry George, and Robert Scott. *A Greek-English Lexicon*. Revised by Henry Stuart Jones and Roderick McKenzie. Oxford: Clarendon, 1968.
LTJ	*Lutheran Theological Journal*
LTP	*Laval Théologique et Philosophique*
LTPM	Louvain Theological and Pastoral Monographs
LTQ	*Lexington Theological Quarterly*
LumVie	*Lumière et Vie*
LUOSM	Leeds University Oriental Society Monograph
LVit	*Lumen Vitae*
MAAR	Memoirs of the American Academy in Rome
Maarav	*Maarav*
MaisD	*Maison Dieu*
Man	*Man*
Manresa	*Manresa*
MAP	Monographs on Ancient Philosophy
Marianum	*Marianum*
Mayéutica	*Mayéutica*
MBPS	Mellen Biblical Press Series
McMJT	*McMaster Journal of Theology*
MCom	*Miscelánea Comillas*
MdB	*Le monde de la Bible*
MedQ	*Mediterranean Quarterly*
MelT	*Melita Theologica*
Meroitica	*Meroitica*
MFC	Message of the Fathers of the Church
MHR	*Mediterranean Historical Review*
Midstream	*Midstream*
MilS	*Milltown Studies*
Mishkan	*Mishkan*
Missiology	*Missiology: An International Review*
Missionalia	*Missionalia*
MissSt	*Mission Studies*
MissT	*Mission Today*
MJCSL	Michigan Journal of Community Service Learning
MM	Moulton and Milligan
Mnemosyne	*Mnemosyne*
MNTC	Moffatt New Testament Commentary
Moment	*Moment*
Monist	*Monist*
Moralia	*Moralia*
MounM	*Mountain Movers*
MScRel	*Mélanges de Science Religieuse*
MSJ	*The Master's Seminary Journal*
MTZ	*Münchener Theologische Zeitschrift*
Mus	*Muséon: Revue d'études orientales*
NABPRSS	National Association of the Baptist Professors of Religion Special Studies Series
NAC	New American Commentary
NBf	*New Blackfriars*
NCamBC	New Cambridge Bible Commentary
NCBC	New Century Bible Commentary
NCCS	New Covenant Commentary Series
NCS	Noyes Classical Studies
NDST	Notre Dame Studies in Theology
NEA	*Near Eastern Archaeology*
NEAEHL	*New Encyclopedia of Archaeological Excavations in the Holy Land*. Edited by M. Stern. 4 vols. Jerusalem: Israel Exploration Society & Carta; New York: Simon & Schuster, 1993.
NEASB	*Near East Archaeological Society Bulletin*
NedTT	*Nederlands Theologisch Tijdschrift*
Neot	*Neotestamentica*
NESTTR	*Near East School of Theology Theological Review*
NFTL	New Foundations Theological Library
NHL	*The Nag Hammadi Library in English*. Edited by James M. Robinson. San Francisco: Harper & Row, 1977.
NIB	*The New Interpreter's Bible*. Edited by Leander E. Keck. 12 vols. Nashville: Abingdon, 1994–2004.
NIBCNT	New International Biblical Commentary on the New Testament
NICNT	New International Commentary on the New Testament
NICOT	New International Commentary on the Old Testament
NIDB	*The New Interpreter's Dictionary of the Bible*. Edited by Katharine Doob Sakenfeld. 5 vols. Nashville: Abingdon, 2006–9.
NIDNTT	*The New International Dictionary of New Testament Theology*. Edited by Colin Brown. Grand Rapids: Zondervan, 1978.
NIGTC	New International Greek Testament Commentary
NIVAC	NIV Application Commentary
NortCE	Norton Critical Edition
NotesT	*Notes on Translation*
NovT	*Novum Testamentum*
NovTSup	Supplements to Novum Testamentum
NRTh	*La Nouvelle Revue Théologique*
NTA	*New Testament Abstracts*

NTAbh	Neutestamentliche Abhandlungen
NTD	Das Neue Testament Deutsch
NTG	New Testament Guides
NTIC	New Testament in Context
NTL	New Testament Library
NTM	New Testament Message: A Biblical-Theological Commentary
NTMon	New Testament Monographs
NTOA	Novum Testamentum et Orbis Antiquus
NTS	*New Testament Studies*
NTT	*Norsk Teologisk Tidsskrift*
NTTS	New Testament Tools and Studies
NumC	*Numismatic Chronicle*
Numen	*Numen: International Review for the History of Religions*
NV	*Nova et Vetera*
OBT	Overtures to Biblical Theology
OCD³	*Oxford Classical Dictionary*. Edited by Simon Hornblower and Antony Spawforth. 3rd rev. ed. Oxford: Oxford University Press, 2003.
Oceania	*Oceania*
OEANE	*Oxford Encyclopedia of Archaeology in the Near East*. Edited by Eric M. Meyers. 5 vols. New York: Oxford University Press, 1997.
OiC	*One in Christ*
OJRS	*Ohio Journal of Religious Studies*
ÖKTNT	Ökumenischer Taschenbuchkommentar zum Neuen Testament
OLA	Orientalia Lovaniensia Analecta
OLD	*Oxford Latin Dictionary*. Edited by P. G. W. Glare. Oxford: Clarendon, 1982.
Or	*Orientalia*
OrChr	*Oriens Christianus*
OrChrAn	Orientalia Christiana Analecta
Orientierung	*Orientierung*
Orpheus	*Orpheus*
OTP	*The Old Testament Pseudepigrapha*. Edited by James H. Charlesworth. 2 vols. Garden City, N.Y.: Doubleday, 1983–85.
PAAJR	*Proceedings of the American Academy for Jewish Research*
Pacifica	*Pacifica*
Parab	*Parabola*
PAST	Pauline Studies (Brill)
PastRev	*Pastoral Review*
PBMon	Paternoster Biblical Monographs
PBSR	*Papers of the British School at Rome*
PCNT	Paideia Commentaries on the New Testament
PEFQS	*Palestine Exploration Fund Quarterly Statement*
PentEv	*Pentecostal Evangel*
PEQ	*Palestine Exploration Quarterly*
PerMS	*Perceptual and Motor Skills*
Personalist	*The Personalist*
PerTeol	*Perspectiva Teológica*
PFES	Publications of the Finnish Exegetical Society
Phil	*Philologus*
PhilAnt	*Philosophia Antiqua*
Philosophy	*Philosophy*
PhilPA	*Philosophy and Public Affairs*
Phoenix	*Phoenix*
PHR	*Problèmes d'Histoire des Religions*
Phronesis	*Phronesis*
PIBA	*Proceedings of the Irish Biblical Association*
PillNTC	Pillar New Testament Commentary
PJBR	*Polish Journal of Biblical Research*
PNAS	*Proceedings of the National Academy of Sciences*
Pneuma	*Pneuma*
PolSt	*Political Studies*
PopSt	*Population Studies*
POTTS	Pittsburgh Original Texts and Translations Series
P&P	*Priests & People*
P&Pres	*Past & Present*
Prism	*Prism*
ProcArisSoc	*Proceedings of the Aristotle Society*
ProcC	Proclamation Commentaries
ProEccl	*Pro Ecclesia*
ProtMon	*Protestantische Monatshefte*
PrRR	Princeton Readings in Religions
PRSt	*Perspectives in Religious Studies*
PrTMS	Princeton Theological Monograph Series
Prudentia	*Prudentia*
PSB	*Princeton Seminary Bulletin*
PSCC	Protocol Series of the Colloquies of the Center for Hermeneutical Studies
Psychosomatics	*Psychosomatics*
PsycRep	*Psychological Reports*
PsycRes	*Psychiatry Research*
PsycTRPT	*Psychotherapy: Theory, Research, Practice, Training*
PTMS	Pittsburgh Theological Monograph Series
PWSup	Supplement to *Realencyclopädie der classischen Altertumswissenschaft*. Edited by Georg Wissowa, Kurt Witte, and Wilhelm Kroll. 15 vols. Stuttgart: J. B. Metzler, 1903–80.
PzB	*Protokolle zur Bibel*
Qad	*Qadmoniot*
QC	*Qumran Chronicle*
QDisp	Quaestiones Disputatae
QF	*Quatres Fleuves*
Ramus	*Ramus*
RB	*Revue Biblique*
RBL	*Review of Biblical Literature*
RBPH	*Revue Belge de Philologie et d'Histoire*
RCB	*Revista de Cultura Bíblica*
RCT	*Revista Catalana de Teología*
RdT	*Rassegna di teologia*
REA	*Revue des Études Anciennes*
Readings	Readings: A New Biblical Commentary
REAug	*Revue des Études Augustiniennes*
REB	*Revista Eclesiástica Brasileira*
RechBib	Recherches bibliques
Reconstructionist	*Reconstructionist*
RefR	*Reformed Review*
REG	*Revue des Études Grecques*
REJ	*Revue des Études Juives*
RelBiog	*Religion und Biographie*
Religion	*Religion*
RelIntL	*Religion and Intellectual Life*
RelS	*Religious Studies*
RelSRev	*Religious Studies Review*
RésCon	*Résister et Construire*
ResQ	*Restoration Quarterly*
RevAg	*Revista Agustiniana*
RevAgEsp	*Revista Agustiniana de Espiritualidad* (= *RevAg*)
RevExp	*Review and Expositor*

ReVision	ReVision: A Journal of Consciousness and Transformation	SBLSCS	Society of Biblical Literature Septuagint and Cognate Studies
RevistB	Revista Biblica	SBLSemS	Society of Biblical Literature Semeia Studies
RevMet	Review of Metaphysics		
RevPhil	Revue de Philologie	SBLSemSup	Society of Biblical Literature Semeia Supplements
RevQ	Revue de Qumran		
RevRel	Review for Religious	SBLSP	Society of Biblical Literature Seminar Papers
RevScRel	Revue des Sciences Religieuses		
RevThéol	Revue de Théologie	SBLSymS	Society of Biblical Literature Symposium Series
RGRW	Religions in the Graeco-Roman World		
Rhetorica	Rhetorica	SBLTT	Society of Biblical Literature Texts and Translations
RHPR	Revue d'Histoire et de Philosophie religieuses		
RHR	Revue de l'histoire des religions	SBLWGRW	Society of Biblical Literature Writings from the Greco-Roman World
RivB	Rivista Biblica		
RivSAnt	Rivista storica dell'Antichita	SBLWGRWSup	Society of Biblical Literature Writings from the Greco-Roman World Supplement Series
RMPhil	Rheinisches Museum für Philologie		
RNT	Regensburger Neues Testament		
RocT	Roczniki Teologiczne	SBS	Stuttgarter Bibelstudien
RocTK	Roczniki Teologiczno-Kanoniczne (= RocT)	SBT	Studies in Biblical Theology
RomPhil	Romance Philology	ScC	La Scuola Cattolica
RQ	Römische Quartalschrift	ScEs	Science et Esprit
RR	Review of Religion	SCEthn	Series in Contemporary Ethnography
RRéf	Revue Réformée	SCHNT	Studia ad Corpus Hellenisticum Novi Testamenti
RRJ	Review of Rabbinic Judaism		
RSLR	Rivista di Storia e Letteratura Religiosa	SChrJud	Studies in Christianity and Judaism
RSPT	Revue des Sciences Philosophiques et Théologiques	SCI	Scripta Classica Israelica
		SCJ	Stone-Campbell Journal
RSR	Recherches de Science Religieuse	SCR	Studies in Comparative Religion
RSSSR	Research in the Social Scientific Study of Religion	ScrB	Scripture Bulletin
		Scriptura	Scriptura
RStMiss	Regnum Studies in Mission	Scripture	Scripture
R&T	Religion and Theology	ScrJudCr	Scripta Judaica Cracoviensia
RThom	Revue Thomiste	ScrTh	Scripta Theologica
RTL	Revue Théologique de Louvain	ScSoc	Science and Society
RTP	Revue de Théologie et de Philosophie	SE	Studia Evangelica
RTR	Reformed Theological Review	SEÅ	Svensk Exegetisk Årsbok
RuBL	Ruch Biblijny i Liturgiczny	SEAJT	South East Asia Journal of Theology
SacEr	Sacris Erudiri	SecCent	Second Century
SAJPsyc	South African Journal of Psychology	Sefarad	Sefarad
Salm	Salmanticensis	SEHT	Studies in Evangelical History and Thought
SANT	Studien zum Alten und Neuen Testaments		
SAnthM	Studies in Anthropological Method	Sem	Semitica
SAOC	Studies in Ancient Oriental Civilizations	SémBib	Sémiotique et Bible
SBB	Stuttgarter Biblische Beiträge	Semeia	Semeia
SBEC	Studies in the Bible and Early Christianity	SGRR	Studies in Greek and Roman Religion
SBET	Scottish Bulletin of Evangelical Theology	Shamanism	Shamanism
SBFLA	Studii Biblici Franciscani Liber Annuus	SHBC	Smyth & Helwys Bible Commentary
SBL	Society of Biblical Literature	SHR	Studies in the History of Religions (Supplements to Numen)
SBLABib	SBL Academia Biblica		
SBLBMI	Society of Biblical Literature The Bible and Its Modern Interpreters	SIFC	Studi Italiani di Filologia Classica
		Signs	Signs
SBLBSNA	Society of Biblical Literature Biblical Scholarship in North America	SJFWJ	Studia Judaica: Forschungen zur Wissenschaft des Judentums
		SJLA	Studies in Judaism in Late Antiquity
SBLCP	Society of Biblical Literature Centennial Publications	SJOT	Scandinavian Journal of the Old Testament
		SJT	Scottish Journal of Theology
SBLDS	Society of Biblical Literature Dissertation Series	SJTOP	Scottish Journal of Theology Occasional Papers
SBLEJL	Society of Biblical Literature Early Judaism and Its Literature	SK	Skrif en Kerk
		SkI	Skeptical Inquirer
		SLJT	Saint Luke's Journal of Theology
SBLMS	Society of Biblical Literature Monograph Series	SMedJ	Southern Medical Journal
		SNTA	Studiorum Novi Testamenti auxilia
SBLRBS	Society of Biblical Literature Resources for Biblical Study	SNTSMS	Society for New Testament Studies Monograph Series
SBLSBL	Society of Biblical Literature Studies in Biblical Literature		
SBLSBS	Society of Biblical Literature Sources for Biblical Study	SNTSU	Studien zum Neuen Testament und seiner Umwelt

SO	Symbolae Osloenses
SocAnal	Sociological Analysis
SocG	Sociologische Gids
SocRes	Social Research
Sophia	Sophia
SP	Sacra Pagina
SpCh	The Spirit & Church
SPCI	Studies in Pentecostal and Charismatic Issues
SPhilA	Studia Philonica Annual (Studia Philonica)
SPhilMon	Studia Philonica Monographs
Spiritus	Spiritus
SPNT	Studies on Personalities of the New Testament
SR/SR	Studies in Religion/Sciences religieuses
SSAMD	Sage Series on African Modernization and Development
SSCS	SUNY Series in Classical Studies
SSMed	Social Science & Medicine
ST	Studia Theologica
StanHR	Stanford Humanities Review
StBibLit	Studies in Biblical Literature (Lang)
StBibSlov	Studia Biblica Slovaca
STDJ	Studies on the Texts of the Desert of Judah
StHistMiss	Studies in the History of Missions
STJ	Stulos Theological Journal
STK	Svensk Teologisk Kvartalskrift
StMkRev	St Mark's Review
StOv	Studium Ovetense
StPat	Studia patavina
StPB	Studia Post-Biblica
STRev	Sewanee Theological Review
StSpir	Studies in Spirituality
StTheolInt	Studies in Theological Interpretation
StThSt	Stellenbosch Theological Studies
Studies	Studies: An Irish Quarterly Review
SubBi	Subsidia Biblica
SUNT	Studien zur Umwelt des Neuen Testaments
Supplément	Supplément
SUSIA	Skrifter Utgivna av Svenska Institutet I Athen
SvMT	Svensk Missionstidskrift
SVTQ	Saint Vladimir's Theological Quarterly
SWJA	Southwestern Journal of Anthropology
SWJT	Southwestern Journal of Theology
SyllClass	Syllecta Classica
TA	Tel Aviv
TANZ	Texte und Arbeiten zum neutestamentlichen Zeitalter
TAPA	Transactions of the American Philological Association
Tarbiz	Tarbiz
TBC	Torch Bible Commentaries
TBei	Theologische Beiträge
TD	Theology Digest
TDNT	Theological Dictionary of the New Testament. Edited by Gerhard Kittel and Gerhard Friedrich. Translated by Geoffrey W. Bromiley. 10 vols. Grand Rapids: Eerdmans, 1964–76.
Telema	Telema
Teresianum	Teresianum
Teubner	Bibliotheca scriptorum graecorum et romanorum teubneriana
Textus	Textus

TGl	Theologie und Glaube
Them	Themelios
Theo	Theologika
Theof	Theoforum
TheolEv	Theologia Evangelica
Théologiques	Théologiques
Theology	Theology
THKNT	Theologischer Handkommentar zum Neuen Testament
Thought	Thought
ThQ	Theologische Quartalschrift
ThTo	Theology Today
TijSW	Tijdschrift voor Sociale Wetenschappen
TJ	Trinity Journal
TJT	Toronto Journal of Theology
T&K	Texte & Kontexte
TLG	Thesaurus linguae graecae. Online: http://www.tlg.uci.edu.
TLZ	Theologische Literaturzeitung
TNTC	Tyndale New Testament Commentaries
TOTC	Tyndale Old Testament Commentaries
TP	Theologie und Philosophie
TPAPA	Transactions and Proceedings of the American Philological Association (later = TAPA)
TPQ	Theologisch-Praktische Quartalschrift
Tradition	Tradition
TranscPsyc	Transcultural Psychiatry
TranscPsycRR	Transcultural Psychiatric Research Review
Transversalités	Transversalités
TRu	Theologische Rundschau
TS	Theological Studies
TSAJ	Texts and Studies in Ancient Judaism
TSHP	Texts and Studies in the History of Philosophy
TSJTSA	Texts and Studies of The Jewish Theological Seminary of America
TTCABS	T&T Clark Approaches to Biblical Studies
TTEd	Teaching and Teacher Education
TTKi	Tidsskrift for Teologi og Kirke
TTZ	Trierer Theologische Zeitschrift
TynBul	Tyndale Bulletin
TZ	Theologische Zeitschrift
UCPLA	Unidade Científico-Pedagógica de Letras e Artes
UCPP	University of California Publications in Philosophy
UJT	Understanding Jesus Today
UltRM	Ultimate Reality and Meaning
UNDCSJCA	University of Notre Dame Center for the Study of Judaism and Christianity in Antiquity
UnS	Una Sancta
USFISFCJ	University of South Florida International Studies in Formative Christianity and Judaism
USQR	Union Seminary Quarterly Review
VC	Vigiliae Christianae
VD	Verbum Domini
VE	Vox Evangelica
VerbEc	Verbum et Ecclesia
VFVRUL	Veröffentlichungen des Forschungsinstituts für vergleichende Religionsgeschichte an der Universität Leipzig
Vid	Vidyajyoti
VitIndRel	Vitality of Indigenous Religions

VR	Vox Reformata		YJS	Yale Judaica Series
VS	Vox Scripturae		YonsJT	Yonsei Journal of Theology
VSpir	Vie Spirituelle		YonsRTC	Yonsei Review of Theology & Culture
VT	Vetus Testamentum		YPR	Yale Publications in Religion
VTSup	Vetus Testamentum Supplements		ZAC/JAC	Zeitschrift für Antikes Christentum/Journal of Ancient Christianity
WAfJES	West African Journal of Ecclesial Studies		ZAW	Zeitschrift für die Alttestamentliche Wissenschaft
WArch	World Archaeology			
WBC	Word Biblical Commentary		ZDMG	Zeitschrift der Deutschen Morgenländischen Gesellschaft
WD	Wort und Dienst			
WestBC	Westminster Bible Companion		ZDPV	Zeitschrift des Deutschen Palästina-Vereins
WJBlSt	Western Journal of Black Studies		ZECNT	Zondervan Exegetical Commentary on the New Testament
WLQ	Wisconsin Lutheran Quarterly			
WMANT	Wissenschaftliche Monographien zum Alten und Neuen Testament		Zion	Zion
			ZKG	Zeitschrift für Kirchengeschichte
WMQ	William & Mary Quarterly		ZKT	Zeitschrift für Katholische Theologie
WomSt	Women's Studies		ZKWKL	Zeitschrift für kirchliche Wissenschaft und kirchliches Leben
Worship	Worship			
WPJ	World Policy Journal		ZNT	Zeitschrift für Neues Testament
WPR	World Press Review		ZNW	Zeitschrift für die Neutestamentliche Wissenschaft
WSCM	World Studies of Churches in Mission (World Council of Churches)			
			ZPE	Zeitschrift für Papyrologie und Epigraphik
WSPL	Warwick Studies in Philosophy and Language		ZRGG	Zeitschrift für Religions- und Geistesgeschichte
WTJ	Westminster Theological Journal			
WUNT	Wissenschaftliche Untersuchungen sum Neuen Testament		ZSNT	Zacchaeus Studies: New Testament
			ZTK	Zeitschrift für Theologie und Kirche
WW	Word and World		Zyg	Zygon: Journal of Religion and Science
YCS	Yale Classical Studies		ZZ	Der Zeichen der Zeit

INTRODUCTION

PROLEGOMENON

Initial Considerations for Reading This Commentary

1. The Focus of This Commentary

I offer some introductory words about the commentary here. Because the eighteen chapters that follow compose this commentary's introduction to Acts, and because the introductory words here are too extensive for a preface (this chapter's original title), I have simply called this introduction to the commentary a "prolegomenon."

Most readers, and especially most users of reference works, give little attention to the prolegomena. For such readers, I simply note that this commentary is primarily academic, with a heavy emphasis on social and historical context (in addition to the necessary attention to Acts itself, of course). Such observations would be obvious, in any case.

Those who wish a more detailed description will find it following, primarily along these lines: the commentary's academic and social-historical emphasis; its explicit limitations; the legitimacy of a particularly social-historical approach; the legitimacy and methodology of investigating questions concerning historical understanding and reliability; my approach to the sources used in this commentary; the commentary's genre; and my use of nomenclature in this work.

2. Academic and Social-Historical Emphasis

A reader who scans this commentary will quickly perceive that it is more an academic than a popular commentary, although I have tried to make it accessible (e.g., using English rather than Greek where feasible) for less academic readers who are at least proficient enough to know what material to skip or skim. An academic reader would also note that it is, in a less thoroughgoing way, more consistently social-historical than literary (in terms of modern literary approaches),[1] although I do regularly (and must inevitably) emphasize literary connections within Luke-Acts.

I offer this observation to define the primary character of this commentary, not to diminish the importance of other audiences or approaches. I have written

---

1. For one example of the latter, cf. the detailed semiotic approach (using the methodology of A. J. Greimas) in Martin, *Lecture sémiotique*. While I respect such approaches, they stand outside my purview.

commentaries and other works on a less detailed level,[2] and because of space constraints, a greater proportion of their content was literary-theological than here.[3] Because of my years of research on the environment of Luke-Acts—information to which most readers would otherwise not have ready access without duplicating that effort—I have invested more space in conveying this knowledge than in insights that many other readers would arrive at without this commentary.

Frequent readers of book reviews recognize that some reviewers critique commentaries for not adhering to the reviewer's primary interest (e.g., literary, historical, social-historical) or ideology (e.g., conservative, critical, sacramental, antisacramental), even when commentators specify the limitations of their works. Especially for large publications, some reviewers address only a work's introduction,[4] which can be helpful when an introduction sets a work's tone but less helpful when (as often in a commentary) the introduction must devote much space to disposing of topics that cannot be treated in detail with each recurrence in the commentary.

Nevertheless, I hope that this commentary will prove useful even to those who would have preferred a different focus or different conclusions on various matters. Whatever their particular focus, most scholars recognize the relevance of how Acts would have sounded to its first audiences (insofar as we can reconstruct this meaning to a sufficiently useful degree of accuracy). Grappling with ancient sources, I endeavor, where possible, to offer fresh literary insight on texts (such as on the mission sign function of tongues and the inverted charges in the narrative of Stephen's martyrdom) and their social-historical setting (such as the meaning of Asiarchs as Paul's patronal "friends" in Acts 19:31 or ancient understanding of the fever in 28:8 or the forensic strategies in Paul's defense speeches);[5] and I highlight patterns in Acts (such as commenting on the apologetic inversion of the charges that Paul disturbed the peace and periodically citing philosophic parallels to Paul to develop Luke's implicit comparison of Paul with Stoic philosophers beyond the often-noted case in 17:16–34).[6] Likewise, in the abundant cases where my contributions accord more closely with past research, I hope that scholars will find valuable the frequently new supporting documentation (e.g., for figurative voting in 26:10).[7]

This commentary's primary focus is what the text meant to its first audience. Its primary contributions lie in often providing further documentation for, and sometimes further elaboration of, the social and historical framework in which Acts was first written, read, and heard. Many of the sources I cite inevitably overlap with previous discussions, but (as the indexes should attest) much of the primary material

2. E.g., Keener, *Corinthians*; idem, *Revelation*; idem, *Matthew* (1997); idem, *Romans*; in contrast to my heavier academic works such as *Matthew*; *John*; and *Historical Jesus*. Some complain about scholars writing too widely in the NT (cf. one response in Bird and Keener, "Generalist Scholars"), but I believe that demonstrated facility both with other NT narratives and with Paul can be useful when one approaches Acts. It would be odd if, emphasizing the necessary contexts of early Judaism and broader Greco-Roman settings for reading Luke-Acts, we neglected the particularly close context of early Christianity.

3. Pelikan rightly notes that "commentary" is a time-honored genre for theological reflection (*Acts*, 25); evident in Origen, it was widespread by the late fourth century (Gaca and Welborn, "Receptions," iii).

4. A complaint offered also by other commentators, e.g., France, *Gospel of Matthew*, 1; Das, *Debate*, xi.

5. See also Keener, "Inverted Guilt"; idem, "Tongues"; idem, "Asiarchs"; idem, "Fever"; idem, "Rhetorical Techniques." I address various historical questions relevant for genre also in, e.g., "Official"; idem, "Athens"; idem, "Plausibility"; idem, "Troops"; and engage more social-science approaches in, e.g., "Possession"; idem, "Comparisons"; to a degree in idem, "Case."

6. On Luke's apologetic for Paul, see, e.g., Keener, "Apologetic." Gentiles in Luke's audience would have understood Paul partly as a philosopher (see, e.g., Wilken, "Christians," 107–10; idem, "Social Interpretation of Apologetics"), though the biblically literate among them (the center of Luke's ideal audience) also had access to the "prophet" category.

7. See also Keener, "Vote."

referenced here has not been applied to Acts before. Biblical readers and expositors, and the scholars who serve them, may observe some basic literary themes with or without detailed aids (although often through methodological advances and observations pioneered by literary critics). Most modern students are not, however, as conversant in the contexts of the ancient sources, which help us better resonate with how an ancient audience would have heard the text. Hence I have focused special attention on this task.

Still, because Acts is a literary text, it is impossible to properly expound it without attention to literary questions, besides those related to its social context. Ancient readers themselves understood implicit rules of genre, such as using the entire narrative of a historical work to provide meaning for the ideas in such a work.[8] Moreover, because the implicit genre of Acts appears to be some form of ancient historical monograph, its literary function within its Greco-Roman context invites not only more direct questions of "theological" application but also discussions about questions of historical accuracy and verisimilitude (by the broader standards of ancient, as opposed to modern, historiography). For modern interests, such questions include examining where in the range of historical monographs Acts lies in accomplishing the purposes for which most historians composed such monographs. Thus, even while engaging contemporary discussions of the broader social context that Luke-Acts first addressed, I must broach some current discussions of literary and historical issues.

3. Limitations of This Work

My minimal employment of some methods is not intended as disrespect for those methods but merely reflects my own limitations and specialized focus, especially in view of the danger of making this work even larger than it already is. While seeking to provide a commentary of some general value, I have concentrated on areas where I believe my own research's contributions will be the most useful. One must circumscribe the task in order to keep a work's size under control—a constraint that has limited even the detail I can devote to the primary questions to which I address this commentary. As the Greek historian Polybius pleaded with his critics long ago, "A good critic should not judge authors by what they omit, but by what they relate."[9]

As noted above, whereas I have sometimes drawn on the insights of technical literary approaches that are not my focus, my use of them (apart from a holistic approach to Luke-Acts) has been restrained. Had I focused on them, I could afford less attention to other aspects of Acts study. (This does not mean that I have ignored literary dimensions of the text itself; without attention to these, even historical "context" would be meaningless, since a commentator would not know which elements of the vast ancient context were relevant.) The following are valuable areas of research to which I give much less detailed attention than I could.

a. A Broad Sweep

First, this commentary is social-historical and, in some sections, rhetorical in its focus and does not focus as much attention on lexical or grammatical details (a matter

---

8. Witherington, *Acts*, 59, following Mellor, *Tacitus*, 70.

9. Polyb. 6.11.7–8 (LCL, 2:294–95); he advises historians not to focus on what others have treated sufficiently (15.36.10).

treated adequately by a number of other works). Particularly because, after this commentary's completion, my publisher graciously titled it "exegetical" (not my original title), I must qualify what sort of "exegesis" my commentary actually involves. (The English term can involve simply "explanation" or "interpretation," though some employ it more narrowly.) A social-historical commentary on a relatively large narrative text such as Acts cannot pause to discuss the full semantic range of particular words except where those meanings are necessary for understanding the flow of thought in the passage (e.g., σωφροσύνη, for 26:25). A few reviewers disapproved of the lack of extensive treatment of grammatical and lexical details in my thousand-page commentary on Matthew, though generally appreciating the social and historical background less available elsewhere.[10]

Such basic lexical information is, however, readily available on a basic level through computer searches that put at the reader's fingertips not only the LXX and NT grammar but the vocabulary of nearly all extant Greek literature and papyri. To duplicate such information here would easily more than double the size (and, unfortunately, therefore increase the publishing cost) of this commentary. I would be depending on the same excellent resources (especially the most thorough of them all, the *Thesaurus linguae graecae* and Duke University's papyrology database)[11] as anyone else working through the Greek text.[12] Most exegesis students already have available electronic parsing, the repetition of which here seems tedious. Of course, many useful sources do offer important help choosing among lexical options and unraveling many of Luke's sentences,[13] but there are also some commentaries that, despite liberal appearances of Greek words, offer no information that a student could not have acquired from standard reference works.

While valuing all of these important works, I have chosen instead to focus more often (though not exclusively) on conceptual parallels to provide the reader what she or he would find elsewhere only with greater difficulty (i.e., by working through the various ancient sources for many years). Even here I have often simply listed in footnotes a variety of ancient texts, though originally collected laboriously in their contexts by reading through ancient literature, instead of commenting extensively on each of these sources; the latter approach, though of interest to specialists, would have required me to write books on chapters in Acts rather than a commentary on the whole.

In some cases I have elaborated points more extensively. Some of these were points where modern interest in the question invited exploration (such as the nature of the experiences often discussed in other disciplines with respect to Acts 2:4 and Acts 2:17–18). More frequently, where my own reading of ancient literature yielded particularly abundant material differing from modern cultural practices, organizing and deploying this material invited more detailed treatment, sometimes in excurses (e.g., at Acts 3:2; 8:27; 12:13; 17:18; 18:3; and hospitality in 16:15).

10. Noting the lack of grammatical and lexical focus, see, e.g., Doriani, "Review," 34.

11. *Thesaurus linguae graecae*, described online: http://www.tlg.uci.edu; *Duke Papyrus Archive*, online: http://scriptorium.lib.duke.edu/papyrus (including the Duke Databank of Documentary Papyri).

12. These are the sorts of activities some professors at more prestigious institutions might safely assign to research assistants or graduate seminars (neither of which have I had available during the writing of this commentary, apart from students I earlier hired to type my own earlier handwritten research). Nevertheless, even supervising such a project would be highly labor-intensive, just as my own approach to research has proved in its different way. I am not able to master both approaches in the years allotted to this project, though others building on this generation of work will, it is hoped, do so.

13. In addition to some of the stronger general commentaries on the Greek text (such as Barrett and Bruce, among others), note Parsons and Culy, *Acts*, focusing especially on this contribution.

b. Text Criticism

Second, although I do not neglect textual questions at necessary points, I have provided far less attention to text-critical details than would be possible (or desirable) for a commentary the focus of which was text-critical.[14] The disparity between commentaries focused and those not focused on textual issues may prove especially evident in commentaries on Acts, a book whose textual problems appear particularly problematic. (The Western text is a significant problem,[15] since it constitutes virtually a distinct recension; see the discussion below.)

Ancient critics, like modern ones, asked text-critical questions. Ancient commentators debated the wording of some lines in earlier texts (e.g., Aul. Gel. 1.21). Some ancient teachers edited their versions of Homer, thinking to correct them (Plut. *Alc.* 7.1).[16] Polybius, for example, allowed a conjectural emendation of "twice" for the text's "thrice" in Hom. *Od.* 12.105 to conform the text to the geography of his day (Polyb. 34.3.11). In one possibly apocryphal account from about the third century B.C.E., when Aratus asked Timon how to find the reliable text of Homer, Timon instructed him to find an ancient copy without all the modern "corrections" (Diog. Laert. 9.12.113). Likewise Virgil was found in different forms; Aulus Gellius (Aul. Gel. 6.20) claims that Virgil changed an earlier reading to the later one and explains the reason. Amoraim claimed (long after the temple's destruction) that scrolls could be corrected by being checked against the scroll in the temple (*y. Sanh.* 2:6, §3).[17] Some ancient (e.g., Origen), medieval (e.g., Bede), and Renaissance humanist (e.g., Erasmus) Christian scholars engaged in text criticism.[18]

Still, because the focus of this commentary is not on lexical or syntactical details but on the larger level of broader cultural connections to the ideas or customs alluded to in the text (and to a lesser extent the macrolevel of literary patterns in Luke-Acts), minor textual variants will prove less important here than in some other commentaries (especially those with a heavier lexical focus). Although my primary focus in the commentary is not text-critical, however, I must provide some general comments about the text here. The book of Acts provides perhaps the thorniest text-critical

14. For brief annotated bibliographies for those exploring this discipline further with regard to Luke-Acts, see, e.g., Green and McKeever, *Historiography*, 85–88; Jervell, *Apostelgeschichte*, 12–15; discussion in Schröter, "Actaforschung 2"; Grässer, *Forschungen*, 137–39, 157–79 (esp. 157–60). For older studies, see Mattill and Mattill, *Bibliography*, 95–121, §§1182–1560; Martini, "Tendances"; Bammel, "Text"; Grässer, *Forschungen*, 89–96; briefly, Wikenhauser, *Apostelgeschichte*, 23. For some recent studies, see those in Nicklas and Tilly, *Acts as Church History*; also Dupont-Roc, "Tradition textuelle"; for a discussion of recent perspectives, see Bovon, *Studies*, 24–26; for brief discussions, see, e.g., Weiser, *Apostelgeschichte*, 41–44; Eckey, *Apostelgeschichte*, 4–7; Marguerat, *Actes*, 30–31. Some take into account theological factors when approaching text criticism (see Schmid, "Eklektische Textkonstitution"). Research continues with new discoveries (Bethge, "Fragmenta biblica Cantabrigiensis") and critiques of the neglect or misuse of some lines of evidence (Kyrychenko, "Old Slavonic Acts").

15. After surveying various theories, Delobel concludes that the "Western" text remains "the most complicated matter in the field of New Testament textual criticism" and that there is no consensus today ("Text," 106). One approach working through the Western variants appears in the work of Rius-Camps and Read-Heimerdinger, e.g., "Readings XIV"; "Readings XV"; "Readings XVI"; "Readings XVII"; "Readings XVIII."

16. In Lucian's parody *True Story* 2.20, the protagonist asks Homer in the afterlife if he wrote the lines that earlier grammarians bracketed as interpolations; Homer says that he did. On correction of Homer, see also the discussion in Maclean and Aitken, *Heroikos*, xli, xlix–l.

17. Copying mistakes were frequent (e.g., Symm. *Ep.* 1.24). Josephus insists that no nation was as careful in copying and preserving its records as Israel was (*Ag. Ap.* 1.28–36). Niehoff, "Exegesis in Alexandria," suggests that some Alexandrian Jews practiced text criticism on Scripture the way scholia did on the *Iliad*. The rabbis may have allowed that earlier scribes made some emendations (*Gen. Rab.* 49:7; Lieberman, *Hellenism*, 28–37, but cf. esp. 47); rabbis' copying from memory was forbidden (*Gen. Rab.* 36:8).

18. On Bede, see Martin, "Introduction to Bede," xviii–xx; see also Ambrosiaster *Commentary on Paul's Epistles* (CSEL 81:169–79; Bray, *Romans*, 142).

situation in the NT; indeed, some scholars contend that "from the earliest times several, or at least two, editions of the book were in currency."[19] This state of affairs may stem from perhaps the publication of Acts by someone other than the author[20] (due to the author's death,[21] imprisonment, or other reasons), or from revisions by the author's circle, or simply from a wide perception that the book was unfinished and (for that reason or because it was not primarily about Jesus) safer to expand than a Gospel.[22] Most works unfinished at an author's death simply did not survive (as Pliny notes in *Ep.* 5.8.7), but some unfinished works circulated (see Quint. *Inst.* 1.pref. 7–8), and an important work might be published with only minor editing in its unfinished form, inviting some further attempts by others to complete elements that were perceived as missing (Suet. *Vergil* 41).

C. K. Barrett suggests that scribes may have exercised this textual freedom longer in Acts than in most narrative books ultimately accepted in the NT because it took longer for this book to be treated as canonical.[23] The second-century church's frequent ambivalence about Acts might reflect the genre confusion that persists to this day: neither gospel nor epistle, Acts did not fit expectations for the conventional "canonical" genres.[24]

Some scholars also suggest that Acts is cited only rarely before John Chrysostom because Luke's interests were rarely those of early patristic theologians and the controversies they faced; it may well have been such "relative obscurity" that "allowed a major second-century revision of Acts, namely, the Western text, to develop unchecked and without correction."[25] This so-called Western text consists primarily of expansive additions (and a few omissions) and diverges frequently from the likely earliest sources.

Despite the misnomer, the Western text does not appear geographically only in the west;[26] further, it may be attested as early as Irenaeus, although this suggestion is disputed.[27] F. F. Bruce points out that readings of the Western text appear "in versions as apparently independent of each other as the Old Latin and the Old Syriac, both of which go back to the later decades of the second century," and argues that "it appears in patristic citations" even earlier than the Alexandrian text does. Nevertheless, he concludes on the basis of internal evidence that the Alexandrian text remains more reliable on the whole.[28] Where it is longer than the Alexandrian text, the added ma-

---

19. Harnack, *Acts*, 48. Our general assurance that we have essentially the right text (e.g., Stanton, *Gospel Truth?*, 33–48) is thus more open to dispute in Acts. If one simply writes off the Western text, of course, the level of certainty is high, though lower than in the Gospel (Morton in Morton and MacGregor, *Structure*, 16).

20. Harnack, *Acts*, 48. Authors also altered texts for new editions (see Heyworth and Wilson, "Variants"; the discussion in ch. 1 on publication, below).

21. Strange, *Problem*, 189, argues that Acts, like many ancient works, was published posthumously in its unfinished draft form; Luke's editors were his earliest interpreters. Cf. also Rackham, *Acts*, l–lv. Strange contends that both the "Western and non-Western texts represent versions of a text left unedited by Luke" (*Problem*, 186); some of the Western material may derive from the author's own annotations, which the non-Western editing mistrusted.

22. Ancient teachers sometimes corrected their students' editions of Homer (Plut. *Alc.* 7.1), as already noted; such a tradition of text criticism naturally facilitated tendencies toward scribal emendation. The abrupt ending of Mark as we have it also invited expansion.

23. Barrett, *Acts*, 29, 2:xix–xxiii, lxix.

24. Ibid., 2:lxix–lxx. One wonders if the later appearance of apocryphal acts may have further compounded such perceptions (although apocryphal gospels also circulated).

25. Witherington, *Acts*, 172–73; cf. similarly Dibelius, *Studies in Acts*, 84–92; Powell, *Acts*, 23.

26. Barrett, *Acts*, 2:lxix. Its readings may influence the Eastern *Acts of Paul* (Pervo, *Acts*, 3).

27. Bruce, *Acts*³, 74, allows that the Western text may even reflect an early second-century revision, which is sometimes as accurate as the Alexandrian text. From discourse analysis, Read-Heimerdinger, *Bezan Text*, even contends that the skilled literary cohesiveness of Bezae (D) points to a text earlier than most Alexandrian manuscripts (though others might use the cohesiveness to argue the opposite).

28. Bruce, *Acts*³, 72.

terial is usually secondary, often reflecting the sort of expansions characteristic of later lectionaries or obvious glosses.[29] In effect, the Western text may constitute the oldest extant commentary on Acts.[30]

Our text of the book of Acts has roughly 5 percent fewer words and 10 percent fewer lines than the Gospel of Luke, which it closely parallels; although this is well within symmetrical range, one could argue that Acts should contain a slightly more expansive text, that is, something like the Western text. (Then again, later "western" editors might have expanded the text of Acts to fill as much of a standard-length scroll as the Gospel does.) Complicating the problem further, its expansions and paraphrases often reflect a Lukan style; one could contend that this stylistic assimilation suggests a later revision by the author himself.[31] While such a position is not impossible, however, in the final analysis arguments for Lukan style in the Western text are not compelling evidence for Lukan authorship.[32] The interpretive editors or copyist(s) may have simply employed a style they had learned by immersing themselves in Acts.[33]

Barrett and Bruce prefer an eclectic method: the accurate text tradition, standing to some degree behind both the Western and Alexandrian traditions, may sometimes turn up in either of these traditions.[34] Still, despite significant dissent, a fairly broad consensus exists among a majority of scholars that the Western text is usually later.[35] Although in some cases the Western reading may preserve the original wording[36] or, much more frequently, reflect at least accurate tradition, most studies suggest that it is mainly secondary. Scholars often argue that the Western variants frequently betray theological bias, especially in an anti-Judaic direction.[37] Many have also noted an antifeminine bias that is perhaps uncomfortable with Luke's more positive vision:

29. Ibid., 72–73, listing as examples "amplifications of our Lord's name (cf. Ac. 1:21; 2:38; 7:55; 13:33), added references to the Spirit (cf. 15:7, 29, 32; 19:1; 20:3), and an increase in phrases such as 'in the name of the Lord Jesus Christ' (cf. 6:8; 14:10; 18:8)."

30. Jervell, *Apostelgeschichte*, 61 ("der älteste Kommentar zur Apostelgeschichte"). It may have been circulating already by the time of Irenaeus (Gregory, "Reception of Acts," 63).

31. Bruce, *Acts*[3], 75, attributes this view to F. Blass and T. Zahn and notes among its contemporary defenders M.-É. Boismard and A. Lamouille. Few today, however, hold this view (see the full argument against it in Head, "Texts," esp. 420–42). Jean Leclerc proposed the idea in 1685 and "was also the first person to repudiate" it (as Pervo, *Acts*, 4, puts it; cf. also Head, "Texts," 416). In one detailed form, Delebecque, *Actes*, contends that Luke the physician (Col 4:14) authored the original text, substantially our Alexandrian text, as a draft in 62, and revised it into what became the Western text in 67 (see esp. 373–96). Given the existence of drafts and multiple editions (see ch. 1 of this introduction), I would find the argument more persuasive if not for instances in the Western text (such as its anti-Judaic elements) that seem inconsistent with the earlier version.

32. Cf. Geer, "Lucanisms."

33. See Witherington, *Acts*, 67; Barrett, *Acts*, 26–28. Strange, *Problem*, 189, suggests that both versions reflect some "Lucan traits, but neither of which is Lucan in all its readings"; it appears unlikely, however, that our non-Western text was so unfinished that Luke could not have finished its dedication to Theophilus and sent it to him (see Witherington, *Acts*, 66).

34. Barrett, *Acts*, 2:xix–xxiii; Bruce, *Acts*[3], 73–76. Cf. Powell, *Acts*, 23: "Even if the Western text is a redaction, the manuscripts used by the redactors were probably older than any available to us today."

35. See esp. the discussion in Head, "Texts." This is the opinion also of, e.g., Porter, "Comment(ary)ing"; idem, "Developments"; Talbert, *Acts*, xxix; Parsons, *Acts*, 11–12. For the lack of consensus, see again Delobel, "Text," esp. 106. Dibelius, *Studies in Acts*, 88, doubted that scholars should accept the Alexandrian text as readily in Acts as elsewhere; but (84–87, esp. 87) he also rejected the priority of the Western text with some isolated exceptions.

36. E.g., C. Williams, *Acts*, 229–30, concurs with A. C. Clark's preference for the Western reading at Acts 20:4.

37. See Epp, *Tendency*; followed by others, e.g., Conzelmann, *Acts*, xxxiv–xxxv; Bruce, *Acts*[3], 75. Because I argue that the church's view of itself as a non-Jewish entity postdates our extant first-century documents (Keener, *John*, 195–98; cf. also 198–214; idem, *Matthew*, 46–50), I am all the more inclined to concur that these signs in the Western text are late. Some, however, support its antiquity, finding its emphasis on Israel's rejecting the gospel more coherent than the Alexandrian text (where less reason is given for Israel's judgment; cf. Faure, "Mystère"); or future hope for Israel's conversion remains in the Western text, whereas the

the Western text tradition sometimes moves Aquila's name before Priscilla's; in contrast to the Alexandrian text, it applies nobility to both genders in Acts 17:12; and it omits Damaris in 17:34.[38] Some other expansions may reflect early second-century "harmonizing details and 'gossip'" meant to attract the sort of audience that soon after came to show interest in apocryphal gospels and acts.[39] That the Western text appealed to many church fathers does not guarantee its antiquity.[40] The "fuller" version of any work typically prevailed (hence the preference for Matthew over Mark and the preservation of the longer text of Ignatius); it would not be surprising if the same proved true for the longer recension of Acts.

Critics of the Western text's priority note four groups of stylistic peculiarities: (1) anti-Jewish elements, (2) a more universalist emphasis, (3) an augmentation of Luke's emphasis on the Spirit, and (4) honorary expansions of Christ's name.[41] In the case of inadvertent changes, either text tradition might reflect the earlier readings (although the Western text's expansive tendencies may make it less careful even in such cases); deliberate changes characteristic of the Western text, however, probably simply underline that tradition's peculiarities.

Yet even when Western readings are historically speculative (in contrast to when they reflect demonstrable bias, e.g., anti-Judaism), they may often prove helpful. It is likely that they sometimes reflect surmises that are more historically plausible than our own would be, because they stem from the author's ancient Mediterranean context. It is possible that some of the "gossip" even reflects genuine traditions from members of ancient Mediterranean churches who heard Luke or his colleagues elaborate his stories orally.[42] Oral retellings may use different language to recount the same substance, possibly even of written texts.[43] In a few cases, then, I provide comments on these traditions (e.g., at 19:9). There is, however, no need to duplicate here what has been done better by others.[44] Thus, as in some other standard commentaries,[45] I will not give Western variants the laudable attention they receive in Barrett and elsewhere, although I mention them periodically.

Alexandrian text's ambivalence betrays signs of revision (Faure, *Pentecôte*, 493–94, arguing on 495 that the Western text is Luke's text).

38. E.g., González, *Acts*, 12 (esp. n. 19); Witherington, "Anti-Feminist Tendencies"; idem, *Acts*, 506, 567n22; Malick, "Contribution"; Schulz, "Junia"; Kurek-Chomycz, "Tendency."

39. C. Williams, *Acts*, 49, though he dates the apocryphal gospels to the same period; Pervo, *Acts*, 3, sees this text tradition as something of "a transition between the mentality (and theology) of the canonical Acts and its apocryphal successors." Others also suggest that the Western text may preserve some plausible data, though they need not go back to Luke (Witherington, *Acts*, 68–69).

40. Pelikan, *Acts*, 33.

41. Bruce, *Acts*[3], 75, noting that because the fourth characteristic is less emphatic than in the Apostolic Fathers, Menoud thinks it earlier than the Apostolic Fathers and hence contemporary with Alexandrian text. For a judicious comparison of the portrayal of Rome in Alexandrian and so-called Western traditions, see Omerzu, "Darstellung."

42. Nock, *Essays*, 827, suggests plausibly that the individual behind much of the Western text "may well have belonged to the author's own circle and have thought of himself as doing a service to the book by removing difficulties and preserving stray fragments of tradition." If the companion behind the "we" material accompanied Paul to Rome, some in the western empire may have known him well; movement between east and west (e.g., between Corinth and Rome) was frequent in any case.

43. Dewey, "Oral-Aural Event," 157–58, noting that storytellers could also expand or abridge depending on audience response.

44. For standard text-critical discussion see Metzger, *Textual Commentary*, 259–503; it will also be some time before Barrett's text-critical comments (Barrett, *Acts*, passim) are superseded. For introductory discussions from various perspectives, see C. Williams, *Acts*, 48–53; Fitzmyer, *Acts*, 66–79 (including bibliography on 73–79); Barrett, *Acts*, 2–29.

45. E.g., Dunn, *Acts*, xi, in his case justifying this procedure broadly because he believes that the Western elaborations "do not belong to the original text," although they may reveal "how Acts was received and used within early Western Christianity."

The recognition that the later Byzantine text merits even less attention does not require much argument.[46] First attested in the fourth century and not identifiable in the first few centuries of patristic literature, the Byzantine text represents a revision combining elements of earlier text traditions.[47] Although even the Byzantine text may reflect the earliest form of the text on some occasions,[48] these cases prove the rare exception rather than anything close to the rule.

c. Social History and Social Science

Third, my contextual approach is primarily social-historical rather than social-scientific, although I have sometimes drawn on insights of social-scientific commentators on Acts.[49] (Where available and where I believe relevant, however, I have drawn on insights from traditional non-Western societies that offer a different approach to the text.)[50] Social-scientific approaches are especially helpful[51] when, lacking concrete ancient data, we must extrapolate by analogy or at least ask questions beyond those assumed by our traditional cultural perspectives, but they are best employed heuristically.[52] As one scholar points out, these methods "provide an alternative lens. . . . But they certainly do not serve as substitutes for evidence."[53] A wide range of scholars have offered similar warnings, concerned that models from some kinds of societies not be imposed on quite different ancient cultures.[54] Some have employed particular

46. As exemplified also in copies of Homer, the politics of admission into the Byzantine imperial library affected what would become a "majority" text (see Finkelberg, "Regional Texts").

47. Bruce, *Acts*³, 70.

48. Bruce, ibid., 70, 154, 358, suggests Acts 4:17; 16:13.

49. E.g., Malina and Pilch, *Acts*. As of 1998, there were, apparently, relatively few; Barton, "Sociology," notes especially Neyrey, *Social World*, and P. Esler, preferring the former approach but learning from both. For such approaches applied widely in the NT, see Esler, *Worlds*; applied to Paul, see, e.g., Barton, "Approaches"; Malina and Pilch, *Letters*; most commonly, in studies of Jesus and the Gospels, e.g., Stegemann, Malina, and Theissen, *Setting*; Geyser, "Uitgangspunte" (cf. also idem, "Metodologiese vooronderstellings"); Aarde, "Methods." Some have critiqued NT social-scientific interpreters for lack of methodological precision (e.g., regarding Luke-Acts, Lindboe, "Samfunnsvitenskapene," regarding Neyrey, *Social World*), but eclectic methodology, which is often needed, may sometimes sacrifice such precision (even if the identification of particular tools can be helpful). For valuable approaches and surveys, see, e.g., Horrell, *Approaches*; Osiek, *Saying*; for OT, Wilson, *Approaches*.

50. Although I have not participated in anthropological "field studies," I have limited "field experience" (of nearly one year altogether) in some African settings (the majority of it living with Africans) and, more important, have been able to consult regularly with my wife, who is African and a historian and who spent most of her life in Africa (in both rural and urban settings), for an "inside" perspective on how these texts could sound. Thus, although scholars will need to count our firsthand observations of traditional African life as merely anecdotal, I have sometimes cited them where they have expanded my interpretive horizons and where such observations can supplement the cultural perspectives that usually inform Western scholars' interpretive approach.

51. See, e.g., the emphasis in Adeyemi, "Approach"; for a survey of research a quarter century ago, Scroggs, "Present State" (cf. also Keck, "Ethos"). Gager, "Review" (esp. 175–77, 179), insists rigorously on the distinction between "social" and "sociological," though allowing the value of each.

52. See, e.g., the caution in Pizzuto-Pomaco, "Shame," 61. David Fraser, a sociologist conversant with biblical studies' applications of the data (and for several years my university's provost), and Marla Frederick, an anthropologist at Harvard also knowledgeable about biblical studies, have emphasized to me the importance of a heuristic approach. For one specific example of questions concerning some applications of social-scientific approaches (while remaining largely favorable), see Keener, "Review of *Windows*," 226.

53. Harland, *Associations*, 15.

54. See, e.g., cautions in Malherbe, *Social Aspects*, 11–13; Winter, *Left Corinth*, xiii; Harrison, *Grace*, 14–15, 22–23; Stanton, *New People*, 85; Hemer, *Letters*, 211; Brown, *Death*, 21; Collins, "Apocalyptic Literature," 362; also sources cited in Schnabel, "Reading Acts," 267 (Osiek, "Handmaid," 278; Sawicki, *Crossing Galilee*, 5–6, 37, 65–67; Jensen, *Antipas*, 30–34); see esp. Holmberg, *Sociology*, 145–57 (as cited in Meier, *Marginal Jew*, 1:16n15). Some writers note such a caution (e.g., Crossan, *Jesus*, 159) yet, in my mind, do not attend to it adequately. For a discussion of the meaning, use, and variety of models in social science, see Elliott, "Criticism," 3–9; Holmberg, "Methods," 267–68.

modern approaches as a grid without cultural sensitivity.[55] I have thus tried to focus on as wide a range as possible of hard data from antiquity.

I believe that the evidence often points to some general patterns in ancient Mediterranean culture, especially urban Mediterranean culture during the empire. Honor-and-shame issues are much closer to those found in modern Mediterranean and Middle Eastern societies than in, for example, dominant forms of British and North American culture. Nevertheless, extrapolations from modern Mediterranean societies[56] and, still more, from modern societies in other locations must be employed with much more caution than evidence closer in time and geography to the subject itself.

I have tried to make special use of contemporary parallels for phenomena where analogies are abundant in many cultures, including frequently researched anthropological topics such as kinship, spirit possession, and, to a lesser extent, healing and health practices. (I find such studies, drawn from a wide variety of cultures, more helpful than the particular parallels some have offered to Melanesian cargo cults.) Developing the approach of some other scholars,[57] I will also (esp. in ch. 9 below) attempt to compare modern "divine healing" claims with those in Acts, partly as a control on modern speculations about what ancient witnesses "could" have claimed. It seems inconsistent to treat as symbols or old legends healing reports in Acts (concerning signs workers who, for the most part, would have understood literally prior biblical traditions about signs) while at the same time treating in a radically different way (whether as charlatans, therapeutically helpful people of faith, gullible persons, or a combination of such) all signs workers today with analogous biblical understandings. (I hope that readers who often first peruse bibliographies of works, as I often do, will recognize that I cite popular sources at many of these points because I am making comparisons with popular religion; scholars of religious history, of popular religion, and of global religion regularly treat such works as primary sources attesting popular beliefs.)[58]

Because of space constraints and to limit the potential excesses of "comparative religions" approaches that neglect a movement's distinctiveness, I have limited much of the focus regarding miracle claims (albeit not regarding spirit possession, given the much wider range of anthropological literature available on that topic) to monotheistic movements, especially to those sharing the widest possible range of premises (such as biblical authority) with our subjects in Acts.[59] Even so, using these phenomena to help us understand the motives, intentions, and ideals of people two millennia ago, much less to interpret the content of the phenomena, is precarious, and they must be employed only cautiously, as heuristic tools. I address these questions most frequently in chapter 9 below, where the texture diverges from that of this commentary elsewhere due to the different character of the questions addressed. (I address these questions most fully in my book on miracle narratives.)[60]

55. This has been true, in the past, of some psychologizing approaches (see critiques in Stein, "Reading"; Malina and Neyrey, *Portraits*, 14–15; Malina and Neyrey, "Personality," 68), though the tide may be currently shifting in favor of more nuanced psychological approaches (see, e.g., Charlesworth, "Psychobiography").

56. See the caution in King, "Anthropology."

57. Especially Yale social historian Ramsay MacMullen (*Christianizing*, 7); for first-century Christian sources, note, e.g., discussions in Ashton, *Religion*, 32–40; Eve, *Miracles*, 357–59; Klutz, *Exorcism Stories*, 196–97.

58. I use academic sources for these comparisons where possible; but popular literature treats the subject far more abundantly, and I am comparing popular-level approaches in both eras.

59. Thus I draw heavily on studies of global Christianity, on the now-flourishing academic discipline of studies on Pentecostalism, and on other academic studies as well as much of the popular literature that is often studied in such research.

60. Keener, *Miracles*; cf. also idem, "Case."

d. Modern Secondary Literature

Fourth, my goal is not primarily to survey modern opinion on a passage or subject. Although I have cited more secondary sources than many Acts commentaries do, summarizing secondary literature is not my object, and I make no claim to be exhaustive.[61] Researchers seeking fuller bibliographic information have access to databases of journal abstracts (which I have used, though mostly in hard copy over the years), dissertation abstracts, the standard bibliographic tools for Acts study, and a variety of other resources; on these I do not hope to improve.[62] Mattill and Mattill, *Bibliography*, alone contains 6,646 entries; were my intention to be bibliographically expansive, I could expand my bibliography by simply reproducing their citations at numerous relevant points; but given that work's date, the reader should note that my bibliography overlaps only fairly rarely in proportion to the number of our respective sources. Thus there is yet more available for an interested researcher in these other resources, and the bibliography in a work such as this one could easily have been doubled.

Conversely, I have made abundant use of *New Testament Abstracts* in endeavoring to survey contemporary research and opinion for my notes.[63] I have drawn from such resources because I want to be as fair as possible by including as many scholars as possible who have published on these subjects, although detailed interaction would have been more helpful in these many cases had I had further time and space. Given the increasing access to data, those focusing on particular passages can work through much of this information in greater detail. Though giving preference to technical sources, I (like *New Testament Abstracts* and other resources) have often cited less technical ones, since scholars have sometimes offered their arguments in both forms.[64]

Providing secondary literature is not my primary agenda, however. Anyone can access these sources specifically on Acts, supplementing what this and other commentaries have done. By contrast, most scholars and students researching passages in Acts will not have time to read through a wide range of ancient primary sources, and I have therefore focused especially on providing this information.[65] Even in my use of secondary sources, I have tried to move often beyond what researchers would

61. As Pliny the Elder noted nearly two millennia ago, his discipline was too large for any single authority to cover fully (*N.H.* 3.1.1–2). Rowe, *World*, 11, is right to emphasize the need to prioritize the text over the massive volume of secondary literature.

62. See esp. Mattill and Mattill, *Bibliography* (1966); the update for 1962–84 in Mills, *Bibliography on Acts* (1986; updated in Mills, *Acts* [1996]), with a thousand more articles (cf., comparably on the Gospels, Mills, *Index*); also Wagner, *Bibliography*, 331–550 (to 1981); for 1991–2003, see Marshall, "Current Study"; Bovon, *Studies*, 19–37 (cf. idem, "Studies"; idem, "Études"); Grässer, *Forschungen*; most accessible but much more selective (for many, a helpful trait), see Powell, *Acts*; Green and McKeever, *Historiography* (they also list some bibliographies, 15–18); for Polish Lukan studies of 1986–99, Kiedzik, "Bibliografia"; for the state of research, also Flichy, "État des recherches"; with attention to some recent key works, Schröter, "Actaforschung 1, 2, 3, 4, 5, 6"; a concise survey in Anthony, "Saying." With a focus on methodology, see Penner, "Madness"; for a historical survey of views (esp. regarding history versus or plus theology), see Jáuregui, "Panorama." One particularly helpful topical bibliography in a commentary is Jervell, *Apostelgeschichte*, 9–48 (esp. 15–41).

63. Given the progress in electronic technology, one might soon hope to provide one's own abstracts by accessing all articles online and reading their conclusions (barring cost constraints), but *NTA* is useful not only for its abstracts but also for the great breadth of sources from which it draws.

64. Particularly in ch. 9, I have also used some nonacademic sources as primary sources to popular religion, as is the common practice in church history and other disciplines that study popular experience, as noted earlier.

65. Someday scholars will probably be able to scan in current commentators' references and pull up full citations in both primary and secondary literature with little effort. I hope that in critiquing the work of their predecessors, they will remember that our tasks were more tedious (just as our generation has advantages—of translations, papyri collections, and word-processing programs—that some of the remarkable scholars of the late nineteenth and early twentieth centuries lacked).

uncover were they searching only publications on Acts itself, in order to make available additional material that would be more difficult for most students of Acts to acquire without digressing from their focus.

With the rarest exceptions (nearly all as additions to existing footnotes), I can interact little with sources published after the completion of my pre-edited work (mid-2007) and should pause to note here some particularly unfortunate omissions necessitated by the publication dates of other works. I am unable to interact fully, or as fully as deserved, with several excellent commentaries on Acts because they were published too far along in the publication process of my own or because they remain forthcoming at the time of this commentary's publication.

Among the commentaries reported to be forthcoming of which I am aware is Steve Walton's commentary for the Word series; among other strengths, this work will surely interact thoroughly with the secondary literature. Among the most thorough narrative analyses will undoubtedly be Joel Green's commentary for the New International Commentary on the New Testament series, which will undoubtedly offer many insights from which the reader will profit. As in my work here, we should expect special sensitivity to the Greco-Roman context in the commentaries of both Loveday Alexander (Black's New Testament Commentaries) and Stanley Porter (New International Greek Testament Commentaries); Porter also will attend to lexical and syntactical details far more than is possible in a commentary such as mine. Although undoubtedly none of us would agree with every other commentator on all points (despite concurring on many other points), I write with appreciation for their work. Undoubtedly, many other works will emerge from which I would have profited but that I inadvertently failed to find or that were published too late for my use.

e. Early Reception History

Finally, I will not attend in nearly as much detail to the valuable ancient and medieval interpretations of Acts, although the index will reveal that I do include a range of samples from these writings.[66] This relative omission does not imply a thoroughgoing or necessary preference for dominant modern critical readings against the longer history of interpretation that preceded them (modern views, too, reflect the influence of their own historically conditioned philosophic context).[67] I simply had to limit the scope of my inquiry. My primary purpose is not engagement with secondary scholarship—ancient or modern—and so I have not pursued bibliographic questions in the same detail one would expect from scholars whose focus is the compilation of resources regarding scholarship on Acts.

But to the extent that I have engaged other commentators, I have given much greater attention to modern scholarship. This is primarily because most modern scholars expect commentaries to respond to critical questions debated today, even if these have not always been the most relevant questions for readers over a wider range of

---

66. For pre-Reformation scholarship, see the survey in Stuehrenberg, "Reformation"; more recently, see, e.g., the historical survey of Baptist scholarship in Barr, Leonard, Parsons, and Weaver, *Acts*. I have drawn on John Chrysostom's and Bede's commentaries and also extensively on the useful collection in Martin, *Acts*; many specialized studies are also useful (e.g., Müller, "Rezeption"). Pelikan, *Acts*, also helpfully collects many historical perspectives, although a range of reviewers have observed that this valuable work often reads theological reflections into Acts instead of providing commentary from the perspective of Luke's own theology (see Behr, "Church"; Daley, "Confessions"; Rowe and Hays, "Commentary"). Some specialists in other ancient texts also address their reception history; see Roberts, "Reception," and other articles in the same issue of *Classical Bulletin*.

67. For a critical survey of modern critical scholarship, see Gasque, *Criticism*, who rightly concludes (306–9) that many of the critical views before contemporary narrative criticism have proved unduly speculative.

history. Modern, like ancient, commentators write for specific contexts, and modern academic commentators are expected to write especially for a modern academic context. Similarly, the careful Catholic scholar Joseph Fitzmyer, confronted with space limitations, complained that he could interact with few sources before 1900.[68]

This limitation is not intended to minimize the value of such earlier voices; it would seem curious to exclude patristic commentators from the conversation about the text yet include modern commentators, whose language and culture are further removed from Luke's. I have therefore surveyed John Chrysostom's homilies on Acts and some other patristic sources and made use of Francis Martin's helpful collection of relevant patristic comments.[69]

To welcome earlier interpretive voices is not, however, to accord them "canonical" status in evaluating how Luke's first audience would have heard him (the goal emphasized in this commentary).[70] I note this caution for the sake of both those who would have preferred more patristic comments and those who would have preferred fewer. A small but vocal circle of scholars appears to want to use the views of patristic commentators to serve as an essential criterion for evaluating interpretations of earlier biblical texts (although most who value patristic sources employ them more critically).[71] The diversity of views within the patristic corpus itself precludes their supplying a monolithic interpretive grid, in any case.[72]

The greater proximity of the church fathers to Luke in language and culture is valuable, but does not always cause them to yield answers to our modern exegetical and historical questions. Many of them were homileticians more than exegetes, emphasizing contemporary rhetorical strategies.[73] And the extant range of their opinions sometimes differed from ideas suggested by our extant sources for the first century. Factors of historical distance that sometimes could have led patristic writers to interpret first-century Christian texts in a manner different from their earliest settings may include, among others, the prior rise of the Second Sophistic, with its atticizing rhetorical tastes;[74] the increasing dominance of Middle Platonism as over against the Stoicism more dominant in the first century;[75] many of the Fathers' more elite backgrounds compared with NT writers; the greater anti-Jewish and androcentric bias of

68. Fitzmyer, *Acts*, xiii.

69. Martin, *Acts*.

70. Studying these later sources in their own right is a valuable task, but I wish to avoid confusing that study—or the study of other secondary literature cited—with understanding the text of Acts in its first-century context. Hearing the earliest (primary) sources first before secondary commentators is an important and widely observed historiographic principle (cf., e.g., Noll, *Rise*, 138).

71. Historically, the Western church had often lacked access to such sources; only in the twelfth century did Peter Lombard's *Sentences* provide the Western church readier access to material from the authorities starting to be identified as "the Fathers" (see Evans, *Wycliffe*, 109). Some used returning to the Fathers, especially in original languages and entire contexts (as with Scripture), to challenge (rather than simply to reinforce) some inherited traditions of subsequent eras.

72. One might take, e.g., Justin, Origen, and the Eastern Fathers on free will (combating determinist philosophy involving fate; see Justin *Dial.* 141; *1 Apol.* 43; Tatian *Or. Gks.* 11; excursus on fate and free will at Acts 2:23) and predestinarian ideas dominant in thinkers such as the later Augustine (both of which viewpoints left their mark clearly on subsequent theological traditions).

73. Cf. Martin, "Introduction to Acts," xxii–xxiii: despite their strengths, the Fathers could use proof-texts against heresies and sometimes were (p. xxii) "more interested in moral exempla" for the purpose of "praise or blame."

74. Hence, e.g., their concern with the rhetorical status of the LXX. Technically, the expression "Second Sophistic" derives from Philostratus in the early third century, but he applies it to many sophists of the previous two centuries (Anderson, "Second Sophistic," 339).

75. Cf. also Pelikan, *Acts*, 192. Although Platonism influenced Alexandrian Judaism in this era (see, e.g., Wisdom of Solomon and esp. Philo), that Platonists were of far less importance in Luke's circle is clear from Acts 17:18. Some later Fathers' knowledge of the schools in 17:18 appears secondhand (so Martin, *Acts*, 215, on Bede).

their era;[76] decreased sensitivity to the ancient Jewish context of earliest Christianity;[77] the increasing valuing of sexual asceticism in late antiquity;[78] new challenges such as Gnosticism[79] and Manichaeism; new charges against Christians;[80] and the evolution of later church offices and customs to meet new circumstances.[81] That is, extant reception history is itself historically conditioned;[82] though a welcome and valuable conversation partner (including in this commentary), it is not designed to substitute for careful exploration of the first-century setting of our documents.

I offer these caveats not to diminish the value of earlier voices but merely to insist that they, too, had a historical context that was not identical with Luke's own. Nevertheless, in general, the church fathers were closer to the culture and certainly the language of Luke than are modern commentators, and they do constitute an invaluable source of wisdom on our earliest Christian texts for those who explore them.

In choosing not to focus on the matters noted above (or on some literary approaches noted below), I am not demeaning their importance but limiting this work to the issues where I believe it can advance the greatest contributions. Although I have not neglected all of these matters altogether, some colleagues will inevitably disagree with my decisions on what to include and what to omit. In such cases, I can only request their indulgence, especially in view of the already massive size of this work, hoping that they will find profitable much of what I have included.

4. The Legitimacy of Social-Historical Inquiry

Although it may surprise readers in some circles, in the wake of deconstruction not all readers today accept the value (or sometimes even the legitimacy) of social-historical questions. More commonly, scholars may accept the legitimacy of questions concerning how Acts' earliest audiences would have understood the work, but they may consider those audiences' understandings simply one set of possible contexts among a potentially infinite array. That is, they accept as legitimate yet ultimately of relatively marginal importance the question of the earliest audiences' understanding.

76. Some were more anti-Jewish in their rhetoric than others. High-status roles for women in the church became an apologetic problem for some church fathers (see the accusations in Cook, *Interpretation*, 166–67), and texts on women were applied selectively (Clark, *Early Church*, 15–16), though we should not oversimplify (cf. perspectives in Clark, *Women in Antiquity*, 139–41; Swan, *Desert Mothers*, passim).

77. Cf. also Hays, *Conversion*, 43. They vary among themselves; *2 Clement* and even Justin are closer to Judaism than some others, and Hegesippus and Jerome knew Jewish sources (cf. Diaspora Jewish influence on Cyril of Alexandria in Wilken, *Judaism*). With Latin writers, one must sometimes factor in even distance from Greek (Augustine, e.g., never mastered Greek, in contrast to modern NT exegetes); later Bede, despite his interest in historical context, lacked a wide range of ancient sources (Martin, "Introduction to Bede," xxxi, argues that he knew only Josephus and Pliny directly, knowing other classical works indirectly through Isidore and others).

78. E.g., Keener, "Marriage, Divorce," 713–14. This appears at least as early as Musonius (so Valantasis, "Musonius"; some of the ideas predate him, as in Gaca, "Technology"; in Philo, Sterling, *Ancestral Philosophy*, 216–17), but especially flourished in the second century and later (Deming, *Celibacy*; cf. Glenny, "Continence").

79. Thus Irenaeus's application of the Fourth Gospel to combat Gnosticism (see discussion in Keener, *John*, 161–69) instead of reading it as an intra-Jewish polemic, a reading probably more consistent with its origin (171–232).

80. On the accusations to which they responded, see, e.g., Cook, *Interpretation*.

81. Their interests are often homiletic, and the prevailing intellectual milieu among many philosophers encouraged the use of allegorization (although more in some schools, such as Alexandria, than in others). Some interpreters, such as John Chrysostom and often Bede (cf. Martin, "Introduction to Bede," xviii–xxi, though Bede often allegorizes), tended to approach Acts more literally than many others.

82. For the warning that extant reception history tends to preserve the perspectives of the "winners," see Ehrensperger, *Power*, 5; cf. the emphasis on distinguishing between the text and its reception history in idem, *Encouraged*, 177.

But while chronological priority need not dictate theological priority, the very use of an ancient Mediterranean text, composed in Greek and presupposing particular cultural assumptions, invites our attention to the text in the contexts that generated both it and the signs it employs (insofar as these contexts can be reconstructed from the interplay between the text and what we know of Greco-Roman antiquity). Understanding the text in its earliest general cultural context is fundamental in some sense for those subsequent readings for which a major objective remains hearing the text (again, as a collection of signs generated and most directly intelligible in a particular milieu). This approach contrasts with that of some scholars who (at the extreme) are not interested in the basic text of Luke-Acts as it stands (written in Greek and presupposing an ancient context), who simply wish to exploit "canonical" texts to attach canonical status to their own readings or those of their interpretive community.[83] Such readers do not, apart from that conferred status, in fact need these particular texts to communicate the different ideas they prefer to emphasize.[84]

By contrast, the history of subsequent readings from various social locations is a useful historical and sociological study in its own right and, at the same time, useful for critiquing interpreters' various inherited biases. It also offers clues for translating and recontextualizing the text's message to various modern audiences (especially for those whose interpretive communities find some authority in these subsequent readings). By evoking analogous responses, such approaches sometimes help readers to appreciate the significance such texts held in their earliest interpretive communities.

Even this useful enterprise differs, however, from our chosen task here, namely, reconstructing (to the fullest extent we are able) how the text would have functioned as a communication between the first author(s) and the historically likeliest sort of audiences for which the author(s) published works. Although I highly value and in my other work regularly emphasize learning from the perspectives of readers in a variety of cultures, our common basis for discussion across cultures is the text and (as best we can reconstruct it) how this text would have been heard by the audience for which its author(s) constructed it with ancient vocabulary, idioms, and cultural assumptions.

Our goal in interpretation shapes the approach we will take to it. To those for whom the earliest text is foundational (or even canonical), the production of readings (however recontextualized) somehow analogous to those most plausible to the text's ideal audience[85] or at least general first-century culture[86] will be vital and so demand careful attention to the earliest contexts. For others, antiquity remains at

83. Aryan rereadings of biblical texts to subvert their use for the Nazi cause (see, e.g., discussion in Head, "Nazi Quest"; Poewe, *Religions*, passim; Bernal, *Athena*, 1:349; Theissen and Merz, *Guide*, 163) offer an extreme example that nearly all interpreters today would censure (not least because of the cause for which the texts were exploited). Contrast helpful culturally diverse readings, e.g., Keener and Carroll, *Readings*.

84. This transfer of "canonical" status from the text to the interpreter, when performed by a rhetorical sleight of hand (rather than merely as allusive and as a recognized rhetorical device), resembles the "transfer" persuasion technique (not unethical in all its forms, but capable of being employed deceptively; cf. Bremback and Howell, *Persuasion*, 235; McLaughlin, *Ethics*, 76, 146–47). In this limited space, one cannot enter into dialogue with the ethics of radical philosophic deconstruction or its results (especially since many of its advocates would regard the ethical claims as themselves relative and subject to deconstruction). Deconstruction does offer some useful insights (such as that no texts are fully consistent, as also noted in Dio Chrys. *Or*. 52.7; on such inconsistencies in ancient narratives, see, in more detail, Keener, *John*, 38–39, 901), including the contingency of all readings. My objective in this commentary, however, is to offer historical reconstructions as responsibly as possible (given the limits of the evidence and our own horizons) rather than to discount the value of such a course simply because it cannot be perfectly achieved.

85. Admittedly, not all critics will agree with language such as "ideal audience" (as Aune, *Dictionary of Rhetoric*, 229, notes, some prefer "authorial audience" as more concrete historically).

86. Or whatever premises we can reasonably infer that the author likely shared with the ideal or authorial audience; see the discussion of relevance theory below in this chapter.

least the generative context for the text's signs, and hence is a necessary context for understanding the text. For yet others, the sense of the work in its earliest, generative context remains at least one historic reading of the text.

a. The Connection between Historical and Literary Questions

Although contemporary literary criticism and historical criticism were once often at odds (primarily because the former was responding to a traditional overemphasis on the latter), most scholars now accept the value of both.[87] The most common approach today is to focus on literary questions in Luke-Acts as a whole, without excluding historical questions.[88] Sharing literary criticism's contemporary dissatisfaction with hypothetical source reconstructions, I follow this emphasis on reading any part of Luke-Acts in light of other parts despite the limitations of my primary focus.

Many observers think of critical scholarship until the mid-twentieth century as primarily historically oriented, followed by a shift toward interest in rhetorical (persuasive) techniques in the texts.[89] Yet this contrast may be overblown at times: even earlier approaches to Acts scholarship often attended to Luke's distinctive perspective and approach,[90] and historical interests remain alive and well today.[91] Although this commentary addresses historical questions in the traditional historical-critical sense,[92] its focus is on reconstructing how an ideally informed first-century audience would have heard the book's message. This is a historical question, but one that is both inseparable from literary questions and distinct from the question of "historical reliability."

One fruitful blending of historical and literary approaches reads "texts using many of the reading and listening conventions in vogue at the time of composition."[93] Use of ancient rhetorical principles is therefore one means that contemporary scholars often emphasize and to which we give attention as a literary approach sensitive to Luke's milieu.[94] Some methods today that emphasize first-time hearers can be supplemented by taking into consideration written works that would have been read on multiple occasions. Although few members of Luke's ideal audience would have had access to (or competence to handle) personal copies of Luke-Acts, the work may have been read repeatedly in house churches, thus allowing its ideal hearers to pick up nuances and repeated themes not available to first-time hearers. (Ancient readers recognized the value of rereading a document as often as necessary to catch the main themes and subtleties.)[95]

---

87. McKnight and Malbon, "Introduction," 18; Donahue, "Redaction Criticism," 45–48; Byrskog, "History," 258–59, 283; Peterson, *Acts*, 41; Padilla, *Speeches*, 10–11.

88. Pervo, "Perilous Things," 40, calls Cadbury "the prototype" of this approach.

89. See Tyson, "History to Rhetoric," 23.

90. Ibid., 25–30.

91. Ibid., 30–31. For one recent survey of "background" approaches to Acts, see Baslez, "Monde"; for sample collections of relevant background, see, e.g., the useful works of Evans, *Texts*, 373–78; Boring, Berger, and Colpe, *Commentary* (because these sources are now readily available, I have not sought to duplicate their information in this commentary, although I will have unintentionally overlapped with it).

92. That is, exploring the degree of correspondence between Acts and its sources and between these sources and events they purport to recount. This task requires more space than most others, especially on controversial questions, and also dominates much of this introduction. It is not, however, my overall focus or this commentary's primary distinctive contribution (even were it distinctive).

93. Smith, "Understand," 48.

94. See, e.g., Penner, "Reconfiguring" (emphasizing the *progymnasmata*; these should be supplemented with reported real and model speeches from antiquity). For a more recent grammatical-rhetorical approach, see Martín-Asensio, *Foregrounding*.

95. For speeches, see, e.g., Quint. *Inst.* 10.1.20–21. Ancients also could recognize the reapplication of ancient quotations in (conspicuously) new ways (e.g., Brutus's quote of Eurip. *Med.* 332 in Appian *Bell. civ.* 4.17.130;

Questions from the broader historical context are inescapable if we concern ourselves with how ancient audiences, whose language and culture the text plainly presupposes, would have heard various passages. For example, Luke does not explicitly mention that Tarsus is in Cilicia until Acts 21:39, but this does not mean that his ideal audience (which did not necessarily include every individual first-century hearer) would have missed the connection with Saul's homeland in 6:9 (in light of 9:11) or 15:23. His ideal audience would recognize that Tarsus was in Cilicia, because this was common knowledge among even moderately culturally literate urban hearers in the eastern Mediterranean world. Insofar as modern literary theory focuses on communication (a primary purpose of texts), it indicates that "texts display not only internal reference (in relation to structures within the text itself), but also external reference (in relation to circumstances outside the text); they tacitly presuppose the entire cultural knowledge of the period."[96]

Although some current theories of literary interpretation reject the priority of the author's historical intention as the "intentional fallacy,"[97] most do not rule out the validity of this historical question,[98] recognizing the author's intention as at least one level of meaning, especially for readers with historical interest.[99] The modern objection that the author's intention is unrecoverable, though strictly speaking true with regard to attaining sophisticated levels of certainty, raises the bar too high for historical inquiry. All historical endeavor is necessarily conditioned by probability, and scholars often make probable inferences about the *implied* author from the text's literary strategies in their originating context.[100] (Even Wimsatt and Beardsley, in their widely cited seminal work against authorial intention, applied their critique only to aesthetic, poetic texts; they viewed communication as successful only insofar as readers accurately inferred authorial intention.)[101]

Writers such as Luke sought "to communicate with intended readers," and this purpose helped shape the text as we have it, regardless of how we utilize the text for

Virgil in Sen. E. *Suas.* 3.5–7; 4.4–5), and so writers sometimes used them for rhetorical display rather than for the authority of their original sense; but quotations used out of context to justify wrong behaviors could call for censure (as in Alciph. *Paras.* 20 [Thambophagus to Cypellistes], 3.56, ¶2). Speeches were deliberately designed so as to invite hearers to follow the flow of thought (Theon *Progymn.* 2.149–53).

96. Klauck, *Context*, 2; cf. Osborne, "Hermeneutics," 391–95. On the importance of recognizing the texts' ancient context, see also discussions in Malina, *Anthropology*, 153–54; idem, *Windows*, xi–xiii; cf. Spencer, "Approaches," 399.

97. Although I will emphasize the other side of interpretation, some ancient interpreters also affirmed polyvalence, especially rabbis approaching their sacred texts (Edwards, "Crowns," employing *b. Menaḥ.* 29b; cf. Driver, *Scrolls*, 550). Rabbis were not alone in presenting multiple views (Starr, "Flexibility") (some presenters of multiple views, however, critiqued others whom they thought erroneous, e.g., Porph. *Ar. Cat.* 59.4–14, then affirming the "correct" interpreters in 59.15–19). The widespread ancient approach of allegory could lend itself to such claims, but some approaches tended to prevail in particular schools.

98. For "the return of the author," see, e.g., Brown, *Communication*, 69–72 (emphasizing that the contemporary approach is more nuanced than earlier authorial approaches). Brown also notes that authorial activity functions differently in different sorts of texts; it is more prominent in "transmissive" communication (such as letters) than in more "expressive" communication (such as poetry), with narratives (e.g., Acts), which evoke a narrative world, between (75–76).

99. Burridge argues that "the purpose of the author is essential to any concept of genre as a set of expectations or contract between the author and the reader or audience" (*Gospels*, 125; cf. also, e.g., Shuler, *Genre*, 32; Allison, *Moses*, 3; Ashton, *Understanding*, 113). The classic defense of authorial intention is Hirsch, *Validity*, though the discussion has shifted since that time; for a brief discussion of this hermeneutic, see Osborne, "Hermeneutics," esp. 390–91; Meyer, *Realism*, 35–41.

100. This language, too, has invited criticism, although most recognize narrative strategies (see "Implied author," in Aune, *Dictionary of Rhetoric*, 228).

101. Hays, *Echoes*, 201n90 (citing Wimsatt and Beardsley, "Intentional Fallacy," 3, 5). Talbert, *Mediterranean Milieu*, 17, cites Hays approvingly. Vanhoozer, *Meaning*, 96n167, also distinguishes Wimsatt's original and reasonable objection in other respects from some subsequent applications of the essay.

subsequent purposes foreign to these authors.[102] How one defines "meaning" depends mainly on one's goal in interpretation, but its originating historical level, in which a writer sought to communicate content in a socially shared system of signs, cannot be ruled out as a valid inquiry.

b. Ancient Approaches

For those with historical interest, the question is not anachronistic: contrary to some modern suppositions, ancient writers were not shy about debating intention, whether regarding the actions of someone on trial or the purpose of legislators.[103] Indeed, many current literary approaches resemble ancient antecedents,[104] although not all correspond as closely to their alleged ancient analogues as is sometimes supposed.[105] Contrary to what some modern writers have opined, historical interests are not a purely modern concern limited to an Enlightenment mentality; just as the Renaissance emphasized classical learning, the Enlightenment[106] emphasis on historical context harks back to classical models.[107] Readers approach texts for various purposes, but at least one goal with which many readers approach ancient texts is to reconstruct how these texts were heard by their first audience in their ancient setting.

Ancient writers, like modern ones, could assume a degree of shared knowledge on the part of their readers.[108] The readers could examine a writer's meaning in a text based on that writer's usage elsewhere.[109] They could also take into account an earlier writer's historical context; thus, for example, when Dionysius of Halicarnassus

---

102. See Kurz, *Reading Luke-Acts*, 173, also noting the extrinsic reality of this author and audience, regardless of our ability to reconstruct them. On the importance of the rhetor's goal in modern rhetorical criticism, see, e.g., Brock and Scott, *Criticism*, 412.

103. For the actor's intention, see Hermog. *Issues* 49.9–14; 61.16–18; 67.6–8; 72.14–73.3; Quint. *Decl.* 274.8 (for a divine actor); 281.1–3; 289.2; 311.8; 373.12; Libanius *Topics* 2.1; also Robinson, *Criminal Law*, 16; cf. Cicero *Fin.* 3.9.32; Seneca *Controv.* 10.1.9; *y. Ber.* 2:1; for legislative intention, see Aeschines *Ctes.* 33; Lysias *Or.* 31.27, §189; *Rhet. Alex.* 1, 1422b.20–25; Hermog. *Issues* 40.6–19; 60.13–14; 66.12–13; 80.4–13; 82.4–5, 13–18; 83.20; 86.4–5; 91.9–13; Quint. *Decl.* 248.9; 249.3–5, 8; 251.2–3; 252.8; 274.9; 277.2; 297.8; 308; 317.9; 329; 331.3; 350.2, 6; esp. 317.2. Thus it was frequent to pit laws against each other; e.g., Quint. *Decl.* passim (e.g., 251 intro; 274 intro; 277.5; 299 intro; 303 intro; 304 intro; 304.1; 315 intro; 366 intro; esp. 304.1; 315.8). When useful for the case, however, one will play down the importance of the actor's (e.g., Quint. *Decl.* 302.3; 314.6) or legislator's (313.5–6) intention; laws should state qualifications (Arist. *Rhet.* 1.1.7, 1354a; Philost. *Vit. soph.* 2.33.628), or one must define them (Hermog. *Issues* 65.1–8), citing *implicit* exceptions (Seneca *Controv.* 9.4, passim). One's goal in the case determines whether one appeals to intention or wording (Hermog. *Issues* 40.6–19).

104. See Pogoloff, "Isocrates." Qoheleth rightly observed that nothing new is under the sun (Eccl 1:9).

105. E.g., cf. Aristotle's μῦθος and modern plot (Belfiore, "Plots"); cf. also his conception of imitation (Rollinson, "*Mythos* and *mimesis*"). On his development of *mimesis* as an aesthetic approach, particularly for poetry and music, see, e.g., Butcher, *Theory*, 121–62.

106. The postmodern emphasis on multiculturalism, although often focusing on reading texts from various modern contexts, can also highlight the importance of reading texts from a particular language and culture with cultural sensitivity. But while I emphasize cultural sensitivity, I was surprised to learn that my emphasis on ancient cultural context was viewed by one generally favorable reviewer as unduly "postmodern" (cf. O'Grady, "Review," 633)!

107. Classical influence was widespread. Cf. the influence of ancient historians on modern political theory in Fontana, "Historians"; on modern theater in Schröder, "History."

108. Sometimes this assumption is made explicit; e.g., Dion. Hal. *Isaeus* 14 assumes that his readers/students have read Isaeus's speeches on which he comments. Although we think primarily of Luke's "audience" rather than "readers," Polybius could speak (Polyb. 9.2.6) of his "readers" (though presumably among aristocratic intellectuals). Maxwell, "Audience," addresses some assumed audience knowledge and even suggests that authors may omit some information to augment audience participation.

109. E.g., Sen. Y. *Ep. Lucil.* 108.24–25, who interprets the use of *fugit* in Virg. *Georg.* 3.284 in light of Virgil's use elsewhere; so also Dion. Hal. *Demosth.* 46 (on Demosthenes's speeches); Philost. *Hrk.* 11.5 on Hom. *Od.* 18.359, using Hom. *Il.* 21.197; cf. Galen *Grief* 23b–26.

practices rhetorical criticism on Thucydides, he complains that the latter employs a style not used even in his own time (*Thuc.* 29).[110] Ancient writers might likewise note that older texts have grown less intelligible because words and customs have changed, and urge reading these texts in light of the original wording and customs (Aul. Gel. 20.1.6, on Rome's early laws).

Writers regularly alluded to situations that they did not need to state explicitly[111] because their ideal audiences shared this knowledge; being outside these ideal audiences, we sometimes find ourselves in the dark as to the precise referent of the allusion (e.g., Luke 13:1–4; 2 Thess 2:5).[112] Writers sometimes respond to interlocutors clearly enough that we understand the question (e.g., Sen. Y. *Ep. Lucil.* 68.1; 74.1; 75.1); at other times, however, we cannot reconstruct the question (e.g., 72.1).

c. The Value of the Ancient Contexts

Although most scholars today accept a range of both historical- and literary-critical approaches, as already noted, some do not. For example, Charles Talbert, then editor of the Society of Biblical Literature Dissertation Series, observed that others had criticized him for not using the form of literary criticism in vogue when he was writing.[113] Talbert responded that his research was directed toward a particular goal that the dominant approaches did not address.[114] He elsewhere points out that the society's Luke-Acts Group and Luke-Acts Seminar have often focused on setting Acts in its broad Mediterranean context.[115] Following one line of literary criticism, he is concerned with "the authorial audience,"[116] as reconstructed not only from the text but from the cultural world "in which the text was produced."[117]

Other scholars, interested in addressing the needs of philologists, have developed the text-analytical approach to specific intertextuality, which allows for authorial intention in deliberate associations between texts and their pre-texts.[118] As Andreas Bendlin points out, "The intention of the author and the unity of the transmitted text have not lost their appeal for classical philologists. Here, intertextuality, mostly in its restricted text-analytical form, is employed in analyzing the use of Greek precursors and models in Latin literature."[119]

110. Cf. also, e.g., Libanius *Maxim* 3.9 (on Demosthenes). Although Heraclitus often simply allegorizes, sometimes (as in Heracl. *Hom. Prob.* 79.8) he appeals to circumstances in the narrative world to explain a character's speech.

111. E.g., Xen. *Cyr.* 7.2.15 (alluding to the well-known Delphic oracle; cf. Hdt. 1.46–48); Phaedrus 5.10.10.

112. Elsewhere in ancient sources, e.g., Phaedrus 3.1.7; Dio Chrys. *Or.* 34.3, 10. Sometimes writers even deliberately obscured their meaning to outsiders (e.g., Nicholson, "Confidentiality"; less persuasively, Callaway, "Reflections").

113. His literary focus was ancient literary forms and motifs.

114. Talbert, "Chance," 236, 238–39, also complaining that the methods that are dominant tend to change from one decade to the next, in any case. Among approaches he judged merely temporarily fashionable was structuralism, which has indeed gone out of vogue. Many today might concur with his verdict on that point (noting its ahistorical approach, see, e.g., Kee, *Miracle*, 290–91; Sanders, *Jesus and Judaism*, 128).

115. Talbert, *Mediterranean Milieu*, 11–12. The focus is not on borrowing but on how the early audience for which the text was produced in a particular cultural framework would have understood it (16).

116. Ibid., 14–15 (citing Peter J. Rabinowitz and Hans Robert Jauss). See also Aune, *Dictionary of Rhetoric*, 229, as noted above.

117. Talbert, *Mediterranean Milieu*, 15 (distinguishing this approach from W. Iser's "implied reader," who is inferred solely from the text). Cf. Lang, *Kunst*, 56–89 (on "Textlinguistik als Rezeptionsästhetik").

118. See Bendlin, "Intertextuality," 873–74.

119. Ibid., 874 (worded in light of further personal correspondence with Prof. Bendlin, Sept. 7, 2011). For intertextuality in ancient historians, one may observe Tacitus's allusions to and transformation of Augustus's *Res gestae* (see discussion in O'Gorman, "Intertextuality," 231–33, though contrasting this on 233 with Tacitus's more explicit reference to some other earlier works).

Those who reject the value of trying to reconstruct how Luke's first audience may have heard his text, how the ideal author sought to communicate through this text,[120] or the use of social history in trying to better answer these questions ignore the implicit genre of the text as it would have been understood in the first-century Mediterranean world, which was the setting in which Luke's Greek vocabulary, syntax, and so forth made the most sense (and for which they were designed).[121] William Kurz, citing speech-act theories, notes that narratives normally occur

> in a context of communication. The writer of Luke and Acts was not merely amusing himself by doodling on papyrus or parchment but was attempting to communicate with intended readers through his written text. The key participants and factors of this act of communication are objective (extramental) realities, not figments of readers' imaginations, as some might deduce from certain forms of literary criticism. Thus the writer of Luke existed as a historical individual, whether or not we can identify him today. If there had been no writer, there would be no text.[122]

Explaining sociostylistic interpretation, Todd Klutz notes that, "like rhetorical criticism, . . . this type of stylistics assumes that the communicative force of a text's style usually has something to do with the goals of the text's producer, whose conformity to expectations of relevance normally entails that the assumed audience and situation are implied in the text itself."[123] In contrast to formalism's focus on aesthetic "properties of texts," "sociostylistics and related linguistic methods pay just as much attention to the extratextual conditions, causes, motives and effects of texts as they do to the aesthetic qualities of the texts themselves."[124]

To read the text as a whole, we must read it in light of not only the intrinsic data throughout the text but also the extrinsic data that the original communication presupposes.[125] At a minimum, this includes the language in which the text was written (without which the extant alphabetic characters become nothing more than random marks)[126] and the cultural, theological, and literary assumptions that are shared by author and audience without needing to be made explicit. Often the real author and audience also shared knowledge of a more particular situation, although this specific knowledge often eludes us secondary readers (far more than anticipated in the confident assumptions that informed some of an earlier generation's redaction-critical excesses).

120. The later "Neo-Aristotelian" "Chicago school" critics, e.g., Booth, differ from the New Critics in emphasizing the communication between writer and reader.

121. Even apparently purely intrinsic literary approaches themselves arise in particular historical and social contexts (see, e.g., Malina and Pilch, *Acts*, 3–5, noting esp. Prickett, *Origins of Narrative*). (For their plea for taking into account the original social contexts, see also Malina and Pilch, *Letters*, 5–9.)

122. Kurz, *Reading Luke-Acts*, 173; on speech-act theory, see also, e.g., Brown, *Communication*, 32–35. See the extensive theoretical reflection on texts as communicative acts (218–29) and authors as communicative agents (229–40) in Vanhoozer, *Meaning* (including Searle's speech-act theory, 243); for implications, see 240–65. As one critic suggests, "Every text, even the most elementary, implies information that it takes for granted and doesn't explain. Knowing such information is *the* decisive skill of reading" (Hirsch, *Literacy*, 112).

123. Klutz, *Exorcism Stories*, 16.

124. Ibid., 17, emphasizing "the sociocultural facet of stylistics . . . developed . . . by the British linguist Roger Fowler" as a form of "linguistic criticism."

125. With, e.g., Dunn, "Reconstructions," 296 (though cf. qualifications, 309–10). For the necessity of taking into account cultural context even in translation, see, e.g., Wendland, *Cultural Factor*.

126. See, e.g., Vanhoozer, *Meaning*, 242 (noting that reference to the author's language necessarily implies reference, on some level, to an author's intention). Thus not only idioms but even lexemes and smaller symbolic units (such as letters) depend on a shared cultural history for their meaning; even language is a facet of culture, so denying the relevance of cultural context for reconstructing a communication is naive.

One particularly helpful current approach, grounded in cognitive neuroscience and empirical study of how human communication functions, is relevance theory.[127] This theory observes that a communicator can leave some information implicit[128] because it may be inferred from the social context that the anticipated audience shares with the communicator. Where such information cannot be inferred, the communication fails. Such failure is especially a risk in secondary communication, where we interpret texts not addressed to us, particularly when they were not originally addressed even to our own social or linguistic contexts.[129] Because so much communication depends on inference, Gutt notes that the intended sense "is recoverable not in just any context, but *only in a context where the requirements of optimal processing are fulfilled*, that is, where there are adequate contextual effects, without unnecessary processing effort."[130]

I acknowledge the value of many approaches but cannot pursue them all in one commentary. If Luke authored his literary work to communicate a message to an audience, historical information that helps us reconstruct that audience can prove useful in our study of his work and (I believe) foundational to other uses of his work.

In contrast to scholars who avoid extratextual approaches for methodological reasons, some may avoid them because they recognize that they have limited expertise in such areas; such avoidance is, at least, better than pretending expertise they lack. Martin Hengel and Anna Maria Schwemer, whose expertise in the ancient sources should be self-evident, rightly warn that many NT scholars show little acquaintance with the ancient sources and that their deficiency proves particularly conspicuous in work on Acts that sometimes collapses into "completely uninhibited ahistorical speculation."[131] Such theories tend to arise in artificial vacuums: scholars too often explain away all the historical evidence that we do have, then create arguments from the silence that remains—"a radical form of criticism" that uncritically ignores the only extant sources we have "in order to make room for its own fantastic constructions."[132] When scholars offer historical judgments regarding Acts, therefore, it is important that they are well-grounded.

d. Other Purposes for Historical Inquiry

My historical interests overlap with literary ones, for my primary concern is how Luke's contemporaries would have heard his message. Literary questions about Acts' themes (hence perhaps Luke's emphases and interests) are paramount for interpreters, and knowledge of ancient customs helps inform how such themes would have sounded to ancient audiences.

127. For some relevant seminal works, see, e.g., Sperber and Wilson, "Précis"; idem, *Relevance*; Wilson and Sperber, "Outline"; idem, "Representation"; I owe these citations to Gutt, *Relevance Theory*, 77–79. For biblical studies, see, e.g., Green, "Pragmatics"; idem, "Interpretation"; "Metarepresentation"; Jobes, "Relevance Theory"; Brown, *Communication*, 35–38; Sim, "Relevance Theoretic Approach," ch. 2. For its compatibility with speech-act theory (despite the different emphases), see Brown, *Communication*, 35n16, 46–47.
128. Communication within a shared framework always leaves some information implicit, economizing language (Gutt, *Relevance Theory*, 33).
129. See further, e.g., ibid., 27; Sim, "Relevance Theoretic Approach," ch. 2.
130. Gutt, *Relevance Theory*, 28; "context" here involves the hearer's "cognitive environment" (21–22). Thus some messages cannot be communicated without background information for the speaker's original context (35, 63–68, 71–74).
131. Hengel and Schwemer, *Between Damascus and Antioch*, ix. For some, such ahistoricism permits their privileging of their scholarly tradition's hypothetical constructs of early Christianity over the probably better-informed (albeit no less perspectival) reconstruction of Luke. In view of reception history, Schnabel, "Reading Acts," 257, notes that dehistoricized readings tend to become speculative, often driven by current interpretive fashion.
132. Hengel and Schwemer, *Between Damascus and Antioch*, ix.

But historical details may also serve supplemental functions much less central to grasping much of Luke's message. For example, modern readers are often interested in other questions from antiquity, such as how Luke's first audience, familiar with ancient Mediterranean culture, might have envisioned the scenes that Luke depicts. Such questions are sometimes of interest to illustrators of books, film producers, and other small circles that serve much larger audiences. They are also of interest to many preachers who, desiring to retell biblical stories, are happy to supplement imaginative storytelling with concrete data from antiquity. They may be most widely of interest, however, to many Bible readers simply wondering how to visualize such events more concretely. (The lay reader who would tackle a commentary of this length is admittedly a special one.) A close reading of a story, entering into the narrative world, invites imaginative consideration of details even when we cannot resolve all the questions they raise (and Luke's first audience, and sometimes Luke itself, may not have resolved them).

Also, those interested in the history of early Christianity depend necessarily and often extensively on Acts,[133] and so this commentary is meant partly to supply much fodder for their research.[134] Traditional questions of historical reliability occupy significant space in this commentary primarily because the secondary literature and the amount of space needed to explore such questions demand extensive discussion if I treat these issues at all. Some recent commentators, such as Richard Pervo, have raised the question of Luke's reliability in such a way that commentaries published soon afterward, such as this one, must necessarily address it.

Although my interests lie more in Luke's message than in questions of historical reconstruction, these subjects are not as readily separated as some modern writers assume. In addition to its moralistic or propagandistic value, ancient historiography also made claims about past events that differentiated it from other genres that communicated ideas differently (see our discussion of genre in this introduction, chs. 2–5, especially ch. 2 below).

Reliability questions are thus of interest not only because of modern attention to Christian origins but because the work's genre would invite such questions from an ancient audience: given the genre of Acts as a historical monograph (specifically of a probably apologetic and perhaps ethnographic variety), sympathetic readers would assume some degree of correspondence between Luke's reports and the events they depict.[135] By contrast, a significant lack of such correspondence might militate against a "sympathetic" reading and hence would affect how an ancient audience (in this case more informed than he would wish) would read Luke's work. Historical claims were part of Luke's explicit agenda (Luke 1:1–4)—a central feature of his "message" (cf. Acts 1:21–22). I will return to these questions regarding historical reliability in a special section further below.

Exploring questions of historical reliability (which are not always easily settled, especially at a remove of two millennia), however, does not exhaust the relevance of Luke's employment of a historical genre. The historical questions in fact invite precisely literary ones, if only (for a "pure" historian) the question, noted above, of

133. Not all grant equal weight to its evidence, but most will question the arguments of those who reject out of hand all our earliest narrative evidence and then create new hypotheses, which they argue mainly from the silence that remains. With such speculative approaches, one could create virtually any scenario.

134. My PhD at Duke University was in "New Testament and Christian Origins"; in keeping with my training, I am interested in both the NT documents and the history of earliest Christianity.

135. This is not to claim that ancient historians wrote history the way modern ones do; everyone allowed them a range of rhetorical liberty in telling their story (see ch. 5 below).

how the first audience most likely construed the work. Although many readers today find history uninteresting and irrelevant, ancient historians sought to teach moral, apologetic, and political values through the ways they reported history. Their own agendas thus bring us back to many of the questions that literary critics ask when they approach these texts.

e. This Commentary's Sociorhetorical Approach

This commentary employs an approach most conveniently designated as sociorhetorical (represented in Acts studies, e.g., by Ben Witherington's commentary[136] and earlier introduced in Gospels studies especially by Vernon K. Robbins[137]).

As noted above, this approach is not precisely sociological; although it sometimes includes, where relevant, extrapolations from sociological models (e.g., in noting patterns characteristic of urbanization or population movements),[138] these extrapolations are best grounded in solid historical data wherever these are available. As one scholar warns, "Just as modern sociological studies test their hypotheses with field trials, so too New Testament sociological studies must assemble all the available extant data that literary and nonliterary sources yield, along with archaeological evidence."[139] My method is thus primarily social-historical rather than social-scientific, as valuable as the latter methods are (especially for filling lacunae in our knowledge and organizing data).

Rhetorical approaches likewise supplement social-historical ones. Except when addressing speeches (especially those later in Acts), more of my space is devoted to social-historical observations than to rhetorical ones in the narrowest sense, but the latter are quite valuable in a general sense. Rhetorical handbooks do not provide much information on historical writing per se; at the same time, they often do address narrative composition techniques.

Although rhetoric focused on orality, many ancient historical works were written by rhetoricians or their imitators.[140] Rhetorical training provided the primary disciplinary influence that shaped how elite historians composed their narratives, and it could not but influence even popular literary works composed in an urban milieu.[141] Educated audiences—the sort of people with most ready access to texts the length

---

136. Witherington, *Acts*. For a brief history of modern sociorhetorical criticism (esp. 1980s–1990s), see Robbins, "Test Case," 164–71. Rhetorical criticism of the NT more generally has a long history (see, e.g., Classen, *Rhetorical Criticism*, 8–16, 99–177; idem, "Rhetorik"; idem, "Rhetoric"; idem, "Analyse"; Peterson, *Eloquence*, 7; Thurén, "Chrysostom"; Black, *Rhetoric of Gospel*, 1–22).

137. Robbins, *Jesus the Teacher*.

138. As noted, I have also drawn, at points, on literature about, or firsthand observations of, traditional or transitional societies, which, though not at all identical with NT cultures, offer similarities at many points that seem foreign to modern (or postmodern) Western postindustrial societies. Likewise, experience of house churches, Pentecostal movements, minority or sectarian religious movements, etc., can also offer some parallels to NT experiences that seem foreign to many traditional Westerners. In all these instances, I seek to learn respectfully from these cultures and movements (to at least some degree perhaps aided by my marriage into an African family) without using the parallels to supplant hard data from Greco-Roman antiquity. (As mentioned above, I sometimes cite my wife's firsthand observations of traditional African life where they have expanded my interpretive horizons.)

139. Winter, *Left Corinth*, xiii. For analogous cautions, see, e.g., Harrison, *Grace*, 14–15, 22–23; the warning against treating texts more suspiciously than models in Freyne, "Archaeology," 69 (following Sawicki, *Crossing Galilee*, 64–67); warnings of bias in Levine, "Theory."

140. See chs. 4–5 (esp. 5) below; and note much more thoroughly, e.g., Rothschild, *Rhetoric of History*.

141. In contrast to elite historians like Tacitus and Suetonius, Luke would not have had tertiary training in rhetoric. Nevertheless, anyone who attended civic assemblies (if Luke was a citizen of a city) or listened to speakers in the market would know the basic conventions; rhetoric was the more popular and publicly employed of the two major advanced disciplines, and those communicating effectively with an urban audience would reflect its influence.

of Luke-Acts[142]—expected rhetorical conventions with which they were familiar, especially in speeches, which were pervasive in such histories. Written works were not speeches, and literature differed from rhetoric. But Greco-Roman advanced education usually focused on rhetoric (or, less often, on philosophy),[143] not on purely "literary" techniques. Ancient literary texts thus typically betray a variety of rhetorical techniques (varying according to genre and the respective skills of their authors).[144] Later historians sometimes critiqued earlier historians not only with respect to correspondence to truth (as in Polybius's assaults on Timaeus) but also for their rhetorical style (according to the standards in vogue with the critic, as is evident in Dionysius of Halicarnassus's critiques of Thucydides and others). In the most general sense, rhetorical examination involves recognizing Luke's persuasive narrative strategies, an approach helpful for discerning the message he endeavored to communicate.

What consequences should such a recognition have for a social-historical commentary's use of literary approaches? A variety of literary approaches exist, the full spectrum of which would also extend the scope of this commentary beyond its proper proportions. I have focused on those that relate to my primary concern for social and historical context, and I made some use, though less explicit, of others that are nevertheless necessary to elucidate the text. Although I have not highlighted some other literary approaches, I have emphasized ancient ones; in particular, where possible, I make explicit comparisons with ancient rhetorical techniques. In so doing, I do not assume that Luke knew the terms for such techniques (which sometimes varied even among ancient rhetoricians) but only that observing techniques prominent in the literature of his era is apt to bring us closer to his approach more often than a purely ahistorical method would.

5. Questions of Historical Reliability

My primary interest is the meaning of the text for the likeliest general first-century audience we can reconstruct for Luke. Yet this question cannot be completely divorced from the question of historical representation, since Luke's genre would invite his audience to consider claims of historical facticity.[145] By their very controversial

142. Although it was short by the standards of histories composed by elite historians, we should remember that the affordability of such works probably meant that even the minority of people who could read it could not own a copy. Those who could not read it could still hear it, but the author necessarily represents, and especially appeals at least partly to, a more educated circle that could help circulate the work. Acts is "popular" by the standards of the elite, but even popular works, e.g., most extant novels, probably presuppose a level of education beyond that available to the majority of people in Greco-Roman antiquity (cf. Bowie, "Readership," 452–53; Stephens, "Who Read Novels?," 415).

143. Hock, "Paul and Education," 204; Kennedy, *New Testament Interpretation*, 8–10; Satterthwaite, "Acts," 340–41; Townsend, "Education," 149, 151–52; Heath, *Hermogenes*, 11–12; Stamps, "Children," 198; Christes, "Education/Culture," 833; Burridge, "Gospels and Acts," 510; Kennedy, "Survey of Rhetoric," 18–19; cf. Quint. *Inst.* 2.2.1, 3; Dio Chrys. *Or.* 18.1–2, 5, 18–19; Tac. *Dial.* 34–35. Some may have even received some rhetoric at the grammar stage (Suet. *Gramm.* 4).

144. Cf. Satterthwaite, "Acts," 342; Dowden, "Narration"; Kennedy, *Art of Rhetoric*, 378–427, esp. 385; Scodel, "Drama and Rhetoric," 489–504; in speeches in novels, see, e.g., Anderson, "Second Sophistic," 347–49; in Ovid's poetry, Auhagen, "Rhetoric"; in Seneca the Younger's essays and even letters, see Wilson, "Rhetoric"; for some interaction with Roman satire, see Hooley, "Rhetoric" (with appropriate qualifications); for rhetorical influence on a range of written forms, cf. Fox, "Rhetoric," 370 (for whom the distinction between rhetoric and literature is partly anachronistic; cf. 380). The nature of rhetoric's contribution varies; among epics, its influence is far more pervasive in Lucan than in Virgil (Narducci, "Rhetoric," 382).

145. Albeit not in the way that modern readers expect it in modern historiography, since (as noted below) ancient historians were concerned with producing cohesive and instructive narrative, not simply recitation or discussion of bare information.

character, such questions will require in this commentary a proportion of space I might consider inordinate were it not required by the voluminous secondary literature on the subject.[146] Those who consider such questions uninteresting (of whom I am not one) may feel free to simply ignore them.

a. The Value of These Questions

As noted above, this work also addresses historical questions about early Christianity. Although such questions remain secondary to the question of the text's meaning, they are not entirely removed from it. Because Acts fits an ancient historical genre (see chs. 2–9, esp. ch. 3 below), the task of exploring its meaning also invites consideration of how accurately Luke fulfills the general promise of historical writing implicit in Acts' genre. (At the least it invites a consideration of what kind of history Luke's audience would have inferred from his narratives; each succeeding narrative could negotiate and nuance the reader's expectations further.) My doctoral work at Duke University was in NT and Christian origins (i.e., in ancient Christian history as well as ancient Christian literature), and I share historians' interest in the historical questions.

Commentators on ancient historians such as Thucydides, Tacitus, and less reliable authors such as Livy and Valerius Maximus regularly compare the texts of their authors with other ancient sources, and it is reasonable to expect some commentaries on Acts to do the same. For historians interested in earliest Christianity after Jesus, Acts is the only concrete extended source we have and, to the extent that it provides accurate information, sometimes offers the only concrete contemporary framework for other first-century Christian evidence that allows us to connect Jesus with the second-century church. In contrast to a fairly small minority of commentators who regularly put Luke's historical and moral reliability in the worst light possible (frequently substituting suspicion for evidence, often even with a touch of sarcasm), I believe that we should grapple as thoroughly as possible with whatever hard data Luke provides, to see what sense is best made of them before proceeding to conclusions. If nothing else, this approach has heuristic value in disciplining us to examine the story in its ancient setting as carefully as possible. It also reduces speculatively second-guessing a source that almost certainly had access to more information than we do.

Not all scholars agree on the extent of Luke's reliability, and even if such unanimity existed, Luke's purpose was not to chronicle the entire history of early Christianity but to focus on its expansion in a way that grounded the church of his day (including its Gentile members) in the story of Jesus and the history of Israel. Luke's own narrower purpose thus limits the work's value for modern historians' broader interests, as do other historical works with similarly limited scope or perspective. But because Acts is the best source we have, historians of early Christianity cannot avoid using it, although we must also supplement it and often ask questions that Luke did not design his work to answer. This commentary therefore endeavors to serve the historical quest as well as the literary-theological one, although the latter is more readily available to us, less punctuated with lacunae, and more to the primary point of any commentary on the complete text of Acts (including this one).[147]

---

146. Similarly, Lincoln's commentary on John (John, 2) notes that historical reliability is not a primary focus, yet by virtue of the shape of critical scholarship, he is compelled to devote extensive attention to it (cf. Keener, "Review of Lincoln").

147. My primary literary interest concerns its first-century context, but this remains a question of meaning and not simply an evaluation of historical accuracy. Because I focus on the setting of Acts, some critics may be tempted to dismiss the value of all literary insights in this commentary. I would urge them to keep in mind

When we test Luke's historical accuracy, it should be admitted at the outset (at least once we have surveyed the range of writings included in the genre of ancient historiography) that Luke and his contemporaries exercised more liberty in details than we would grant modern historians, although we employ (perhaps slightly anachronistically) the same term for both the ancient genre and its modern counterpart. Ancient historians were concerned with producing cohesive and instructive narrative, not simply recitation of available events or discussion of bare information. At times I will wade as imaginatively as possible into Luke's story world, asking questions that the text does not answer but to which his ideal audience, sharing his biblically informed, culturally informed eastern Mediterranean milieu, might have accepted a particular range of potential answers. I do this both to hear his text from a literary standpoint available to, as closely as I can approximate, the text's ideal audience and to raise historical questions where appropriate.

When we probe the text, Luke's presentation will normally reflect his general environment, which helps us hear what the earliest audience may have heard and envision the images that Luke's narration may have triggered. We can better evaluate the character of Luke's historiography when, in our general probing, we also find points where Luke's presentation resembles, or diverges from, not merely the general milieu but the specific settings about which he writes. Ancient historians without specific information often settled for verisimilitude in elements of their narration, and a popular ancient historian with specific information could still choose to recount it in ways most culturally intelligible to his audience (e.g., the roof tiles in Luke 5:19; contrast Mark 2:4). But comparing the reports in Luke's narrative with contemporary information can give us a basic approximation of the kind of historian he endeavored to be. (In anticipation of my argument, I can note my high respect for his historiographic interest and skill.)

b. Historical Probabilities

In offering historical reconstructions, a historian can offer only probabilities. Much historical reconstruction is speculative, and improbabilities grow cumulatively as one speculation is built upon another. At the same time, this commentary follows the principle that an educated guess is better than an uneducated one—that is, if some speculation is inevitable in historical reconstruction, the informed historian is responsible for providing criteria to help readers evaluate which speculations among their contemporaries are more plausible than others.

Throughout the commentary (and especially in the Pauline chapters, where we have the greatest ability to check Luke against primary ancient reports of the same events),[148] I try to provide some means of controlling speculation by evaluating the probabilities involved in such reconstructions. One would wish that the English language (or at least historians' specialist language) provided a better way of grading probabilities than the somewhat ambiguous expressions I have chosen, such as (in descending order of likelihood) "very probable," "probable," "more probable than not," "plausible," "improbable," "quite improbable," and "implausible."[149] But to provide,

the size of the commentary and so recognize that even if my work on Luke's internal themes and cohesiveness does not take up much of the space in the commentary proportionately, there remains, if extracted, enough for a smaller book.

148. I believe that this commentary's historical orientation makes it somewhat stronger in the Pauline sections (esp. Acts 13–28), where the texture of Luke's account changes (moving beyond Judea and probably vaguer tradition into more concrete material in a broader Mediterranean framework).

149. Others have also suggested terminology for gradations of historical likelihood—e.g., Broadhead, "Priests," 125. For the importance of degrees of probability in epistemology, see Polanyi, *Knowledge*, 31–32; Licona, *Resurrection*, 120–25.

for example, concrete percentages of probabilities would require a sort of precision even more difficult to achieve, and so I have tried to content myself with offering such vague evaluations of my and other scholars' reconstructions. Nevertheless, I am well aware of the limitations of such categories and understand that, in many cases, the discovery or application of some data I have missed would shift probabilities.

c. Common Ground for Historiography

Historical questions overlap with theological questions far more than some scholars (such as mid-twentieth-century existential critics) allowed; nevertheless, they are not the same. Many of us appreciate the biblical theology movement's quest for God's acts in history in biblical texts; but the biblical text is not solely a narration of such acts, nor does it purport to be a complete recitation of all such acts.

Even further from pure questions of contemporary theology is the sort of historical methodology that historical scholars of varying religious persuasions can use as a minimal common ground and language for dialogue. Some who write for audiences sharing their assumptions do not feel the need to limit themselves to the assumptions entailed in such broadly accepted academic methodology. Whatever our respective theological commitments, however, historical scholarship and interdisciplinary dialogue cannot proceed across theological and philosophic lines without initially appealing to such a minimal common ground; we scholars differ among ourselves in our philosophies of history; philosophies of science, nature, and religion; and so forth.[150]

Few who offer arguments from this minimalist common ground thereby claim that nothing other than this common ground may be affirmed (still less, that nothing other than this common ground historically happened).[151] But sufficient agreement exists on basic rules of evidence to allow (at least in principle, leaving aside human egos and attachment to traditions, whether ecclesiastical or academic) open discussion and consequent shifting of opinion in academic circles.

Having worked through Acts from basic and accepted criteria for historical reconstruction, I believe that I can affirm that Luke was an acceptable and responsible historian by the standards of his contemporaries, although he wrote for a more popular audience than some of his more elite colleagues would have appreciated.[152] (This introduction will discuss more fully this question of historical "subgenre" adjusted for audience; see chs. 3–5 below.) That he had agendas does not distinguish him from his contemporaries; his belief in miraculous or divine activity also appears commonly enough in ancient historians (although Luke betrays greater interest in them than most because they are more central to his subject). Where extant evidence from other ancient sources is available, I believe that it supports, rather than casts doubt on, Luke's basic portrayal of events[153] in the large majority of cases (see the survey in chs. 6–7 below) and rarely proves strongly compelling against his portrayals.

At the same time, the ancient historical genre differs in some respects from the usual modern approaches to history, and we should not read modern expectations

150. Thus, e.g., many confessional scholars doubt the common antisupernaturalism often presupposed by secular historical critics and vice versa. A level public playing field methodologically would privilege instead a more agnostic methodological approach that neither affirms nor rejects a priori such claims in given cases. See discussion on signs in ch. 9 below.

151. See discussion in Theissen and Merz, *Guide*, vii; Charlesworth, "Jesus, Literature, and Archaeology," 178; Tucker, *Knowledge*, 240.

152. Among the implications of this is Luke's greater proportionate interest in dramatic action scenes than, e.g., Polybius, who, while reporting actions, elaborates them less extensively than lengthy speeches and is more interested in events of public, political consequence.

153. It is usually events, rather than details, that we can test from external sources.

into Luke-Acts, which was meant to address questions often different from those that modern historians ask. (For example, we are more inclined to focus on different kinds of events and require either summaries of speeches or verbatim reports rather than summaries or reconstructions worded from a narrative standpoint as if they were quotations.) When we ask modern questions, therefore, we must acknowledge that this approach differs from merely asking Luke's meaning in its historical setting. Luke's historical reliability is a question raised by his work's genre, but it is not the only issue with which Luke was concerned. Thus I count exploration of Luke's historical claims as a separate and subsidiary (though important) purpose of this commentary, even though by its nature it demands a larger proportion of the space than it might otherwise receive.

6. The Question of Sources

Although a biblical commentary of limited size cannot comment on the relative value, or explain the full context, of each ancient extrabiblical reference cited, I am fully cognizant of the debates concerning such sources and have read the sources in their own contexts. But scholars examining social and historical questions often differ as to which sources to employ, and so I must comment briefly on my eclectic approach in this commentary.

a. Early Jewish Sources

New Testament scholars probably have engaged the debate about sources most often in terms of early Jewish ones. There are problems with various bodies of writings on which we draw for our information.[154] Josephus, one of our most useful historical sources, has biases shaped in part by his elite Hellenistic-Roman audience (see the discussion of Josephus in chs. 5 and 6 below). Philo is essentially a Jewish philosopher, using Middle Platonism (sometimes mixed with Stoic and other thought) in the service of his hermeneutics and apologetics; he moves at a philosophic level generally foreign to Luke (though cf. Acts 17:22–31). Most scholars date the Qumran scrolls to the relevant period, but the Scrolls reflect a particular sectarian understanding of Judaism. And rabbinic literature often reflects a particular side of Judaism and is later than the NT period.[155]

Likewise, various Diaspora Jewish sources are incomplete (inscriptions, for example, are often difficult to date and, like most sources, usually reflect only one side of ancient life). Although some documents in the amorphous collection called the Pseudepigrapha are clearly pre- and non-Christian (such as *Jubilees* and most of *1 Enoch*), some sources are debated (e.g., the Similitudes of Enoch,[156] the *Testaments of*

---

154. Cf. Keener, *John*, xxix–xxx.

155. I argued, ibid., 185–94, that rabbinic literature is nevertheless useful, especially when it is all we have to work with (some others go further than I did; e.g., Batch, "Littérature tannaïtique"). I neglected to mention there various studies arguing for correspondences with the Qumran scrolls (addressed by, e.g., Baumgarten, "Qumran Studies," 256; linguistically, cf. Wieder, "Notes"), lack thereof (e.g., Neusner, "Testimony"; Marcus, "Scrolls," 27), or some of each (e.g., Schiffman, *Law*, passim, e.g., 36; Mandel, "Exegesis"). For a much more thorough and nuanced treatment of dating rabbinic literature than I provided, see esp. Instone-Brewer, *Traditions*, who has applied to many texts the methodology developed by Jacob Neusner.

156. Despite the consensus on the date of the rest of *1 Enoch* (300–200 B.C.E.; Charlesworth, "Consensus"), the Similitudes have been thought pre-Christian (idem, *Pseudepigrapha and New Testament*, 18, 44), post-Christian (Sanders, *Paul and Judaism*, 347–48), Jewish Christian (sources in Longenecker, *Christology*, 13, 83–84, esp. J. T. Milik), anti-Christian (Jas, "Hénoch"), early second century C.E. (Hindley, "Date"), medieval (Black, "Parables"), or mostly finished by 50 B.C.E. (Bampfylde, "Similitudes"); but the majority

the Twelve Patriarchs,[157] and the *Testament of Abraham*[158]). Some are clearly later, and some either are Christian works or at least have significant Christian interpolations. Gentile philosophers and historians are usually easier to date, though even there each reflects only a portion of the relevant data (e.g., Roman politics or a particularly sectarian perspective in a wider range of ideas).

Most material that is relevant to the eastern Mediterranean Jewish Diaspora and that overlaps with Acts is later than Acts, but historians of the ancient world must reconstruct history with whatever clues we have available, even when the sources are chronologically or geographically removed.[159] (Naturally, nearer sources are preferable, but they are not always available.) Thus, if our only available source relevant to a passage in Acts is later, then (as Irina Levinskaya observes) we should accept Acts as an earlier attestation of the same idea or custom, "in accordance with the routine practice of ancient historians."[160] This practice is of course precarious when Christian influence on the document is evident (as in many gnostic sources), but otherwise seems generally increasingly safe where evidence supporting a distinctive custom appears quite similar in independent sources.

How do we evaluate whether a particular source probably reflects broader thought rather than simply an idiosyncratic reading? In reconstructing which Jewish ideas in the first century were sufficiently widely known to have informed Luke's ideal audience, T. L. Donaldson's typology is helpful: one can use "a kind of 'criterion of multiple attestation,'" testing whether an idea appears "in more than one sociological strand of Judaism" and in periods both before and after that which one is examining.[161] For this reason, I depend on a range of sources, not simply on the "critical minimum" of sources that are completely secure chronologically and geographically (though naturally preferring more widely circulated and pre-Christian sources). The latter standard is almost impossible to meet at the remove of two millennia, when the extant evidence is necessarily sporadic and illustrative rather than comprehensive.

---

do see it as non-Christian and pre-70 (see Charlesworth, *Pseudepigrapha and New Testament*, 89; idem, *Jesus within Judaism*, 39–40; McNamara, *Judaism*, 85; contesting one argument for dating, see Ehro, "Nature"). Other ancient works cited Enoch literature, although sometimes not our edition of *1 Enoch*, suggesting texts no longer extant (*Test. Sim.* 5:4; *Test. Levi* 10:5; *Test. Benj.* 9:1; *Test. Dan* 5:6).

157. Despite clear Jewish affinities and origins (for Qumran parallels, see Chevallier, *Esprit et le Messie*, 116–20) and some early Hebrew versions at Qumran (see McNamara, *Judaism*, 82, 89–90; Grelot, "Notes sur Testament," esp. 406; cf. Milik, "Testament de Lévi"), it is, in its present Greek form, a Christian work (so de Jonge, though now allowing a Jewish stage; Collins, "Testamentary Literature," 272; Daniélou, *Theology*, 14–15) or (the majority view) Jewish with Christian interpolations (Charles, "Testaments," 282; Grant, *Judaism and New Testament*, 86; Bickerman, "Date," 260; Charlesworth, "Self-Definition in Additions," 35–41; idem, *Pseudepigrapha and New Testament*, 38–39; idem, *Pseudepigrapha and Research*, 211–13; see the survey in Collins, "Testamentary Literature," 268–72). The dual emphasis on Judah and Levi might not sound like the early Christianity with which we are most familiar, but it appears in a Christian interpolation in *Test. Jos.* 19:11.

158. E.g., Davila, "Pseudepigrapha as Background" (NT scholars cannot depend on its priority); Turner, "Testament of Abraham," 220–21, who thinks that it is mostly non-Christian with Christian redactions; Charlesworth, *Pseudepigrapha and New Testament*, 42, who dates it to the late first or early second century; for works with various perspectives, see Nickelsburg, "Review." Certainly, apparently Christian elements abound (e.g., few being saved via a narrow gate; most obviously, the trinitarian benediction). On the recensions, see Nickelsburg, "Eschatology"; Schmidt, "Recensions," 65–83; Martin, "Syntax Criticism"; Kraft, "Reassessing"; some (e.g., Ludlow, "Recension"; Laws, *James*, 73) think that rec. A preceded rec. B, but both may reflect an earlier text. There may be some Semitic idioms (Turner, "Testament of Abraham," 222–23); Martin, "Syntax Criticism," 96, suggests that rec. B is more Semitic but that both reflect an earlier Semitic original. Clearly, however, the current *Testament of Abraham* reflects various Hellenistic motifs (see Allison, "Calf"; idem, "Tree").

159. See Levinskaya, *Diaspora Setting*, ix–x.

160. Ibid., 16–17 (using the example of rabbinic sources); cf. p. x.

161. Donaldson, *Paul and Gentiles*, 51; cf. Gathercole, *Boasting*, 24–26.

b. Greco-Roman Sources and Archaeology

I have followed the same general procedure for non-Jewish Greco-Roman sources.[162] Instead of supposing a single hypotext,[163] I have drawn from as wide a range of ancient sources as possible to illumine Luke's larger social world. Among ancient rhetoricians, I have noted classical Athenian orators and earlier Hellenistic handbooks (e.g., *Rhetorica ad Alexandrum*)[164] as well as Roman sources (e.g., *Rhetorica ad Herennium*, Cicero's rhetorical essays, and Quintilian's *Institutes of Oratory*), earlier atticizing writers (e.g., Dionysius of Halicarnassus), and later works reflecting the influence of the Second Sophistic (e.g., Hermogenes and Menander Rhetor).

I have not done so in ignorance of the limitations of these various kinds of sources but in recognition of the small amount of evidence that would remain if we compared Luke only to first-century Aegean writers producing popular historiography in Greek. When a rhetorical custom is attested both before and after Luke's time, in both Greek and Roman sources, I regard it as probably widespread. When it is more narrowly attested yet remains consistent with larger patterns, I regard it as at least illustrative of the sort of thinking available to rhetorically astute people in Luke's world. Of course, where a source appears unique and not consistent with larger patterns of thought, it is reasonable to suggest that it may be idiosyncratic, in which case a single parallel with Luke may represent coincidence rather than even a broad way of thinking in the milieu.[165]

Although Luke writes in Greek and (probably, in my view) for an audience in the Greek East, his interest in colonies suggests (again in my view) that residents of Roman colonies belong to his ideal audience (see the discussion of Luke's audience in ch. 12 below). If this observation is correct, Roman background, as well as Greek, will be of value, although the linguistic milieu of Luke's audience is undoubtedly primarily Greek. In Corinth, for example, many people, including much of the Corinthian church, spoke especially Greek even though the colony's official language was Latin (see the discussion at Acts 18:1–3, 12). But even resident Jews and Greeks in the city cannot have been oblivious to Roman culture, and Roman and Greek culture affected each other extensively in such locations. Although resident aliens from the East such as Lydia were primarily Greek-speaking, Philippi (which we shall suggest must be close to the heart of Luke's ideal audience) was also a thoroughly romanized city.

162. Recent years have witnessed the publication of many useful works on the Greco-Roman context of Acts, most notably the multivolume *Book of Acts in Its First Century Setting*, published by Eerdmans and Paternoster.

163. The dominant approach in, e.g., most of Dennis MacDonald's works so far, including *Imitate Homer*. Although one cannot a priori rule out the possibility of a Homeric hypotext, most critics so far, after examination, have found the theories unconvincing (see Mitchell, "Homer," on MacDonald, *Epics*; Sandnes, "*Imitatio*"; Johnson, "Imitate"; less negatively, Harstine, "Imitate"; I have profited here from dialogue with Professor Carsten Claussen of the University of Munich, who brought these sources to my attention); especially problematic are "a search for *the* hypotext" (Mitchell, "Homer," 255; cf. Johnson, "Imitate," 490, on the more proximate sources influenced by Homer), an emulation that is "not recognized" (Sandnes, "*Imitatio*," 725), and (in these works) neglect for "the OT intertextuality that is broadcast in this literature" (732). Having offered these reservations, I must nevertheless express admiration for Professor MacDonald's brilliance, and appreciation for his highlighting one important potential aspect of Luke's literary milieu. He is working on LXX intertextuality as well, which his previous work, while not focusing on it, did not reject.

164. This is merely a sample; like Aristotle's *Rhetoric* (Anderson, *Rhetorical Theory*, 41–49; Poster, "Affections," 35n20), which Aristotle directed toward his students (Clayton, "Audience"), *Rhetorica ad Alexandrum* apparently was not widely in use in our period (Anderson, *Rhetorical Theory*, 96). When taken together with a wider range of rhetorical sources, however, it often reflects more common ideas in ancient rhetorical traditions and thus serves our general purposes.

165. I have offered only samples, though I would not mind excluding some less relevant suggested backgrounds from consideration (with, e.g., Cadbury, *Acts in History*, 28, on mystery cults; I note them, but they are less central to Luke's ideal audience than, e.g., the LXX, rhetoric, or basic acquaintance with philosophic sects).

Archaeology is, in some ways, more concrete than extant manuscripts copied and recopied from ancient originals; it provides physical evidence and sometimes (especially through burial inscriptions) the "underside" of society less apt to be preserved in literary sources. Nevertheless, it too has its limitations, not least the "muteness" of stones apart from interpretive grids often provided, at least in part, by literary sources.[166] We further possess only a sample of even the possible physical remains, merely a portion of which have been excavated and only some of the excavations published;[167] thus we sometimes have chance finds confirming literary records that previously were unconfirmed by such data.[168] Some of the archaeological data and the interpretations of them for particular sites noted in this commentary will therefore undoubtedly require revision because archaeological information is always partial and open to reinterpretation when new evidence is found. I nevertheless prefer to include, where possible, current information in the hope that enough will prove representative of the surviving material.

c. Modern Sources

I must offer a brief word concerning references to secondary sources. I often cite other commentators even for matters that could be deemed common sense, although some readers would undoubtedly prefer less cluttered pages and less documentation for matters of reasoning that should be common property. I do this for two reasons. First, what often seems common sense to many is nevertheless often contravened by others (or will be), and it is helpful to summarize at least a sample of scholarly opinions. Second, I would rather acknowledge too many debts than risk failing to acknowledge enough.[169] In numerous cases, I came to conclusions independently but nevertheless cite other scholars whose conclusions I find to be similar, for the sake of propriety.[170]

In the end, however, the vastness of contemporary scholarship precludes full discovery and citation of all possible sources; even where one has come up with what one thinks a new idea, almost invariably someone has proposed something like it before,[171] yet it is not possible to survey everything written on the subject in the past two millennia. I apologize profusely in advance to scholars whose works I have failed to find; my honest desire has been to recognize everyone who has written on the subject, understanding that it is disappointing when one's labors do not prove useful to other scholars. But I must frankly confess that I have not been able to read anything close to everything ever written on the subject, and my criteria for where to look first have often left out valuable sources (as I often realize when I discover additional works). I nevertheless believe that this commentary's contribution will be valuable even to those whose works I unintentionally failed to discover.

166. Interpretation and biases can be just as involved in reading archaeological evidence as in reading literary evidence (cf. Tiwald, "Archäologie").

167. E.g., Yamauchi, *Stones*, 146–57 (developing Lapp, *Archaeology*, 83–84); McRay, *Archaeology*, 22.

168. E.g., Kent, *Inscriptions*, no. 57 (inv. 2414) (p. 57, an inscription confirming a claim in Paus. 2.4.6). Likewise, scholars have often doubted the existence of thirteenth-century Dibon (cf. Num 21:30; 32:3, 34; 33:45–46), on the basis of the lack of archaeological evidence at the expected site, but explicit Egyptian epigraphic evidence proves its existence (Kitchen, *Reliability*, 195).

169. Avoiding the charge of being insufficiently thorough also motivated some ancient writers in choosing what to include (e.g., Hermog. *Progymn.* 10, "On Ecphrasis," 23).

170. Where ideas are now common property, I am generally more concerned to provide samples of those who hold them than to trace the historical lineage of these views, interesting as that exploration would be. Many ideas can be traced in literature long before their appearance in twentieth- and twenty-first-century scholarship.

171. E.g., my first publication coincided with similar yet independent observations by a rabbinic scholar published the same year (Keener, "Heavenly Court"; Lachs, *Commentary*, 92, 94).

7. This Commentary's Genre

As noted above, this commentary, like my commentary on the Fourth Gospel, will be especially valuable for scholars, professors, advanced students, and other academic audiences. Nevertheless, I have tried to keep it more readable than my earlier academic works so that other readers may find it useful. As in earlier works, I depend on the Greek text for my own analysis but, where possible, offer my own English translations in the text for the sake of these other readers.[172] Less academic readers with the time and interest to use a commentary like this one should employ their discretion to screen out material less relevant to their interests.

a. Fresh Research

Scholars write commentaries for different audiences, and readers should take these genre differences into account. Some reviewers critique heavily documented academic commentaries for being too inaccessible to nonscholars. Others fault popular-level commentaries for not including fuller documentation, as if to begrudge nonscholars the utility of an accessible work or to imply that those who accommodate such audiences are inventing what they write.

Because the markets for such diverse kinds of commentaries often differ, they each serve important purposes. Lest it be assumed that I disrespect other forms of commentary writing, it should be noted that elsewhere I have written in both academic and popular commentary genres and have also offered several in between.[173] Some readers may wonder why I expend space to point out what to them appears obvious. My reason is that some reviewers have critiqued academic commentaries, including my own, for excessive documentation[174] and popular commentaries, including one of my own, for minimal documentation.[175] (Happily, others have affirmed the same choices in these cases.) It is thus important to reiterate this commentary's primary purpose.

As I have noted, my focus here is on reading Acts in its first-century Greco-Roman setting, and as in other works of this nature, I endeavor to provide, where possible, fresh insights into this way of reading the text (in addition, of course, to building on what others have done).[176] As will become quickly evident to one surveying commentaries, they frequently recycle the primary sources used by earlier commentators (some references appear regularly in many contemporary Acts commentaries; some

172. My focus is broadly cultural more than lexical, but it is difficult to avoid some explicit use of Greek, given the widely varying ways a given term may be translated. (Note that although I use also cognates in my lexical approach to some terms, I seek to do so cautiously, i.e., only where cognates recall some of the semantic range of the term in question.) Nevertheless, some reviewers have appeared to suppose that commentators who include minimal Greek in the text of their commentaries are unfamiliar with the language. Especially in view of word programs today easily able to insert the Greek text (even if the commentator possessed only minimal knowledge), such a supposition of academic incompetence on the basis of sparse display of Greek seems remarkable.

173. Thus, e.g., I intended Keener, *Matthew*, to be useful to advanced-level expositors and advanced students as well as to scholars. My New Cambridge Bible Commentary on 1 and 2 Corinthians (Keener, *Corinthians*) is at a more basic but still middle-range level. Keener, *John*, by contrast, is written specifically for scholars and advanced students, though of value to others who know how to find what they need there. Those who demand a popular treatment of some of the same material (specifically, the background) would find the survey version in Keener, *Background Commentary*.

174. As I have noticed in reviews complaining that I offer too much documentation (for just one example, *Regent's Reviews* 23 [spring 2004]: 9, though in a very positive and fair context).

175. Reviewers who complained that Keener, *Background Commentary*, did not provide enough documentation (e.g., Stoutenburg, "Review," 153; Brug, "Review," 238; more understandingly and positively, e.g., Starner, "Review," 175; Lanier, "Review," 96) are partly responsible for my citing so much of my documentation in my academic works.

176. This means that, wherever possible, I draw on sources outside the usual range of immediate NT scholarly training so as to provide the optimum new benefits.

of these same references also appear in nineteenth-century commentators).[177] Many commentators (whether because of the target audience, space limitations, time limitations, or other reasons) cannot afford to infuse a large amount of "new" data into discussions (although scholars often do so in journals and monographs).

Whenever more academic commentaries infuse new data into the discussion, the process often starts over again, with select new references proliferated in a new generation of commentaries and with a few reviewers (despite most commentaries' use of indexes) apparently oblivious to the difference between those attempting to introduce much new information and those attempting to interpret it for target audiences (an important but different task). (As I have already noted, some even critique these more detailed commentaries for excessive documentation or size when the commentators explicitly define the scope of their work.)

New major commentaries ignore previous scholarship only at their own peril; they, too, must be indebted to previous research. But I believe that it is valuable for at least some major scholarly commentaries periodically to offer an infusion of "new" data—or at least data not yet widely incorporated into standard commentaries. These works provide ready fodder for future commentators to mine. They also provide numerous references the expansion of which space and cost prohibit but that offer fodder for students and researchers to develop.[178]

Although I have thus followed other scholars at many points (and cited them accordingly), I have focused more on ancient sources than on modern ones (and, among the latter, often on those focused on ancient sources). Except where otherwise noted, the vast majority of the ancient references derive from my reading through the ancient sources in their own literary context. I trust that scholars studying particular passages will be able to make good use of the new data (the majority of my primary data) where I have provided it. I offer this hope recognizing that, given average human longevity, this work is likely to constitute my largest and most detailed commentary.[179]

b. Utility for Christian Believers

Some commentaries focus on applying the principles suggested in or behind the text.[180] Affirmations about the natural world in ancient texts are dated, but many

---

177. Naturally, many references will overlap simply because they are the only, or the most obvious, references in our extant sources addressing a subject, but when many such references are available and many commentators cite the same ones, it may be inferred that, in these instances at least, there is a good chance that they have followed earlier commentators rather than collected these particular references while directly reading through the primary sources. Any casual observer of commentaries will recognize that this practice is so common as to constitute a typical practice. I am not complaining here about the practice (when earlier commentators have found helpful sources, I too am ready to use them) but about reviewers who do not recognize when some scholars have in fact read through the ancient sources and offer ancient sources not previously applied to Acts. (Anyone reading works by a number of NT scholars [e.g., D. Aune, W. Cotter, D. Instone-Brewer, A. Malherbe, E. P. Sanders, G. Sterling, and C. Talbert, as a small sample among too many others to name] can recognize that they have devoted decades of attention to primary sources and offer fresh insights.)

178. Thus many chapters could have been expanded into books of their own by my spelling out in greater detail the particulars of ancient references I have only been able to list in footnotes. I trust that some will follow up these references in greater detail, including some who have told me that they never cite commentaries, though they cite the references that they find in them—a practice that has always bewildered me.

179. Because of the way I approached my research in ancient sources, I have material to write heavily academic commentaries on most of the NT, and at the private and public urging of some colleagues to make the research available, I am writing as quickly as my abilities and time constraints allow. But having written different forms of commentaries, I recognize that heavy academic commentaries such as this one take years of basically full-time work to produce, limiting my options for future publication if I assume an average longevity.

180. This approach can, if used carefully, help us to appreciate the ancient texts more, rather than less, sensitively. When reapplication is analogous, in a new cultural setting, to the function of the secondary

readers interested in history or philosophy may learn ethical principles or discover early predecessors of modern concepts from ancient philosophers and rabbis.[181]

Christian readers for whom works such as Luke-Acts are canonical have an even greater desire to learn from these texts, whether as a matter of heritage, because of their belief that God has spoken in them, or both. As Margaret Mitchell has pointed out regarding a different matter of historical research, *"It is simply a fact (whether allowed, welcomed, discouraged, or encouraged) that a major audience of this scholarship . . . is Christian believers seeking to understand their present in relation to their (reconstructed) past, and their sacred texts which mirror, embody, and sometimes challenge the cultural norms and expectations of their day"* (emphasis hers).[182]

I have written other books with this kind of focus, and other scholars have produced such works specifically on Acts, emphasizing application or contextualization for various cultural settings today.[183] This commentary does seek to identify Luke's message and on occasion provide generally brief sample hermeneutical comments on how modern readers might recontextualize this message (bridging the horizons) for their own audiences.[184] But because application is culture-, group-, and even person-specific (as well as temporally limited)[185] and because those who know their receiving culture and how to contextualize are usually able to make the appropriate connections if they have access to the ancient contexts of the text, the focus of this commentary is the text in its ancient cultural setting. Nevertheless, I focus on the ancient meaning with both the expectation and the hope that some readers will use this research to make such connections; I do so myself in my preaching and seminary teaching far more than this commentary, with its specialized focus, can reveal. Users of the commentary for historical purposes, however, will find more immediate relevance to their interests here.

---

communication's point in its original setting, such reapplication can be helpful in evoking its sense for hearers in the new setting (Gutt, *Relevance Theory*, 68–70).

181. Those teaching about other ancient texts also sometimes interest students in the viable messages of those texts (see, e.g., Newlands, "Ovid").

182. Mitchell, "Family Matters," 346; cf. similarly Meeks, "Why Study?," 167, urging in his Society for New Testament Studies address that NT scholars stay relevant to this audience; Agosto, "Publics"; Westerholm, "Introduction," 2–3; Horrell and Adams, "Introduction," 42. For reading from the vantage point of faith, see, e.g., Hays, *Conversion*, 190–201. In my own case, I was interested in Greco-Roman history and culture generally when I was an atheist, but acquired an interest in Acts only as a Christian believer (though, of course, others, e.g., Lüdemann, can have interest in Acts without personal religious connections to it).

183. See, e.g., contextual-application commentaries by González, *Acts*; Fernando, *Acts*; Miller, *Empowered for Mission*; Wagner, *Acts*; Williams, "Acts"; primarily North American applications in Allen, *Preaching*; Gangel, *Acts*; Hughes, *Acts*; Willimon, *Acts*; Yrigoyen, *Acts*; also preaching in Jacobsen and Wasserberg, *Preaching*; Green, *Word*; genre-sensitive preaching in Krentz, "Down"; my own popular-level approach in Keener, *Acts Studies* (though some of my own material was edited out and some applications that I did not write were added in); for another praxis-oriented approach, see Dormeyer and Galindo, *Apostelgeschichte*; outside the commentary genre, cf. also the useful thematic application of Acts in Green, *Thirty Years*; Keck, *Mandate*; González, *Months*; Fryer, "Congregational Renewal"; for meditative readings, e.g., Gargano, "*Lectio divina*." See, e.g., Kanyoro, "Mission," for the relevance of Acts for an African context, both for the empowerment of the Spirit and for proclaiming justice.

184. The piecemeal application of paragraphs to personal felt needs of hearers, characteristic of some modern Western preaching, says as much about us as about Luke: that was not his purpose. We can recontextualize his point, but in so doing, we ought to be careful not to forget his point.

185. For which reason Porter, "Comment(ary)ing," is mostly skeptical of the value of application commentaries. When I do illustrate how texts have been applied, I have sometimes looked to concrete historical models (including patristic sources). At times this also includes what were then new movements (on at least a sociological level, analogous to some features of the early Christian movement), including examples from new, widespread religious movements traditionally underrepresented in academia of their era (e.g., early Mennonites or Methodists or, increasingly cited in academic works, today's global Pentecostalism).

c. Further Research

The notes often mention additional resources that interested students and scholars working on a passage can develop more fully. These include especially primary sources but often also secondary sources, which themselves cite many further works that I have not; for example, each article in the *Oxford Classical Dictionary* concludes with a bibliography, often offering students entire books on matters I have mentioned merely in passing in a footnote.[186] As noted above, exploring the thousands of sources in bibliographies on Acts (e.g., Mattill and Mattill, *Bibliography*) could expand the range of conversation partners further. With other important resources such as the *Thesaurus linguae graecae*,[187] students can delve much further into the lexicography and background of texts. Even such work is, however, more time consuming and tedious than might at first appear.

A team of scholars could thus easily multiply the documentation in this commentary by simply following up the bibliographies of the reference articles cited, documenting far more articles (even though I have made abundant use of *New Testament Abstracts*, I have been selective, especially for earlier years) and word studies based on the *Thesaurus linguae graecae* (or even the *Theological Dictionary of the New Testament*). This work is not, then, comprehensive; it is, in a sense, merely scratching the surface of what could be done. I have tried to think innovatively, offering a fresh reading through hundreds of ancient writings[188] and also from some recent scholarly approaches, both to establish new lines of inquiry and to develop some current ones. Whereas databases can provide lexical parallels (a necessary task), conceptual parallels still require reading through ancient literature, and this is the service that I (like some others) have sought to provide. Again, any new work will inevitably confirm and build on much of what has come before, but it can also supplement and offer further directions.[189]

I collected research for this commentary both after and concurrent with my other research over more than two decades (some of it as a student), and the writing consumed most of seven years, not including subsequent work checking editing or indexing. Unless my editors work much faster than I can, it will be difficult for the commentary to prove up-to-date on all new publications. Nevertheless, I trust that it will prove valuable to subsequent researchers.

8. Nomenclature

Because nomenclature shifts and sometimes affords a cause for anachronistically criticizing earlier works, I offer a few comments here for those who might desire them.

186. Whenever possible, I cite the *OCD* and other articles by authors' names, even when the dictionary does so only by abbreviation, from the conviction that crediting authors whenever possible is important.

187. My focus is more broadly social-historical than lexical and hence entailed more reading through ancient sources in their entire contexts than performing computer searches. Work with the *TLG* would necessarily concentrate on verbal more than conceptual parallels; given the availability of verbal searches to other scholars I have tried to focus in most cases on the conceptual parallels. But lexicography is important, and my work could easily be vastly supplemented, especially through extensive use of the *TLG* and papyrological databases.

188. I have focused more on concepts than on words, because that is a distinctive service my commentary can offer; but of course one cannot access concepts in texts without the words that convey them. In the many cases where I do offer verbal parallels, scholars working from the *TLG* could offer more. I explored mostly classical (as well as early Jewish) works in their original contexts to see where they would lead, so as to avoid simply duplicating what work could be accomplished as readily by others with different time constraints. Those working from computer searches will naturally find more references; although this approach is of enormous benefit, scholars should not abandon inductive reading of ancient texts to learn whatever may be found there.

189. That is, I am more interested in following where the data appear to lead than in offering proposals that are merely "novel" but that I think improbable.

The use of nomenclature in this work reflects what appear to be current, conventional designations within the range of disciplines with which I am working. Such language is often in flux, quickly dating the terminology of reference works. For example, a range of works conflate "patronage" (when used strictly, a Roman custom) with Greek benefaction and even reciprocity; does one follow here technical ancient usage or academic convention (and common English usage)? I thus want to acknowledge some variations in usage. The reasons for most of my terminological choices are based on what I understand continues to be common usage, and I do not invest such choices with political significance. Were I writing a decade from now, my nomenclature would undoubtedly differ at points, reflecting the usage conventional at that time.

a. Religious Labels

Although I use expressions such as "Christianity" and "Judaism" because they are most intelligible to the widest range of commentary users, such expressions are generally anachronistic for the NT period. I certainly do not intend them as mutually exclusive categories.[190] Members of the Jesus movement were labeled "Christians" by some outsiders (see comment on Acts 11:26),[191] but it is not certain that the former had widely owned the label for themselves even by Luke's day. And—more important—modern notions of distinct religions should not be read into a first-century setting; many of Jesus's followers, even Gentile converts, probably viewed themselves as a sect (albeit the right one) within Judaism until long after Luke's day.[192] (Except when context dictates otherwise, most references to "Jewish" and "Judaism" in this commentary also refer to ancient Jewish thought and practice, not the views and practices these elements have developed into two millennia later. Although readers will mostly take it for granted, I use "Greek" and "Roman" for peoples and especially cultures in antiquity rather than today.) Even "church" carries too much traditional baggage for the average user of the term, but I have retained it for convention's sake (rather than sought some less standard designation such as "God's community," which highlights the original theological claim).

I have never accepted the labels "Old Testament" and "New Testament" as accurate designations, since in neither body of texts are the covenants simply identified with the body of texts that report them.[193] Yet apart from "Tanakh" and some cumbersome designation such as "early Christian Scripture written after Jesus's coming," I have no better way

190. See, e.g., the warnings in Horsley, "Assembly," 373, 375; Pilch, "Jews and Christians"; Eisenbaum, "Polemics"; against essentialist readings of such diverse movements, also Stern, "Limitations"; Nanos, "Judaism" (esp. 156). Even describing early Christians as a "new religious movement" (Watson, *Gentiles*, 86) can sometimes reduce to sectarianism (cf. 87–93); for definitions, see, e.g., Keener, *John*, 149–50. I most often use "Jewish" ethnically (hence including Paul and other early leaders in the Jesus movement; religious self-identification would have also included them). An increasing number of scholars are shifting the use to "Judean" (cf., e.g., Cromhout and van Aarde, "Judean Ethnicity"; Elliott, "Israelite"; Malina and Pilch, *Acts*, 2–3; cf. idem, *Letters*, 29; Elliott, *Arrogance*, 16; particularly helpfully, Mason, "Jews"); although the vast majority of first-century Jews (technically "Judahites") lived in the Diaspora, Gentiles did often view them as unassimilated "Judeans," rendering such language potentially useful (for whatever other reasons it may or may not be helpful; several writers go too far in separating modern Jewish ethnicity from ancient Judaism; note esp. the important concerns in Levine, *Misunderstood Jew*, 160–65). Nevertheless, this recent approach seems problematic for historical reasons (see Das, *Debate*, 59) as well as practical ones: because this usage renders more difficult semantic distinctions between Jewish residents of Judea and Diaspora Jews and because those distinctions are important in a book in which much of the action hinges on interchange between Judean and Diaspora followers of Jesus, I have retained more traditional usage here.

191. Notations such as "see comment on Acts 11:26" refer to comments in this commentary ad loc.

192. See Keener, *John*, 215, 226–27; idem, *Matthew*, 48–49; Saldarini, "Conflict"; idem, *Community*; Overman, *Crisis* (e.g., p. 10).

193. Cf., e.g., Keener, *Background Commentary*, 827; idem, *Corinthians*, 168.

to describe them, and thus I retain the traditional designations. Language communicates through accepted social convention; although we regularly adapt such convention, I have tried to balance the interests of usage and accuracy for the sake of communication.

Likewise, I do not attach to the terms "pagan" or "pagans" the pejorative connotations that ultimately developed, but employ the sense later used by some of the Roman Empire's polytheists.[194] Essentially, it is used here as shorthand for those who were not religiously monotheistic (at that time, mostly Jewish or Christian) and lacked a religious heritage in Israel. Given current sensitivities,[195] the usage may well (and probably should) shift, but in the first decade of the twenty-first century, this title remains the most common description (no other designation yet having become standard and widely intelligible).

b. Geographic Labels

This commentary uses the term "Palestine"[196] in the same way as standard reference works on the Levant in this era.[197] Neither with this title nor with "Israel" (for the people, historically) do I make a political statement. (Lest anyone think me overly cautious in explicitly offering such a caveat, note a reviewer of one of my earlier works: "One wonders whether, by using this anachronistic terminology [of 'Palestine'], Keener is attempting to exercise some kind of political influence.")[198]

One can define in various ways the cultural spheres on which the book of Acts touches directly. If we think of continents in the traditional Western sense of this designation (categories originally devised by the Greeks to distinguish themselves from peoples to their east and south), Luke's narrative begins in Asia, with an Asian religious movement; its first Gentile convert is from Africa (see discussion at Acts 8:27); and its mission reaches Europe. That is, it touches all three "continents" known to Luke's world.[199]

But Luke's goal for the mission is Rome not because of continental divisions,[200] which are not even explicit in his narrative, but because Rome is the heart of the empire

194. Cf. use by classicists, e.g., R. MacMullen (*Paganism*); two of J. Gager's works (*Moses*; *Anti-Semitism*); one by J. N. Sevenster (*Anti-Semitism*); the 1996 work by L. M. White (*Origins of Architecture*, vol. 1); one 2003 translation of H. J. Klauck (*Magic*; "paganism" in the title translates the German *Heidentum*, with the same associations); also in Ehrman, *Prophet*, 56. With Rowe, *World*, 14, I use it not to denigrate but "because of the lack of workable alternatives."

195. Today's pejorative usage makes the label problematic (Remus, "Paganism," preferring "polytheism," though noting its inadequacy as well). Yet some scholars note problems in viewing polytheism as the sole alternative to Jewish and Christian religion (Choat and Nobbs, "Formulae"; cf. Fürst, "Monotheistische Tendenzen"). The terminology also appears in anthropological studies of newer religions (e.g., Poewe, *Religions*, 86, 160, 173; sometimes it is a self-designation).

196. Some ancients depicted the entire land as "Palestine" in this period, but its official Roman designation as such may be later (so Müller, "Palaestina"). Although Jacobson intriguingly links the title with Jacob the "wrestler" ("Palestine and Israel"; idem, "Palestine Meant Israel"), Josephus's link with the Philistines remains the dominant connection ("Palestine" or "Palestinian" appears more than a hundred times in Josephus, usually in connection with the Philistines except when quoting outsiders, e.g., *Ag. Ap.* 1.169, 171). But the term did at least sometimes apply to the post-Philistine coastal region before the second century; cf. the brief discussion in LaSor, "Palestine," 632–33, citing Hdt 1.105; 2.104, 106; 3.5; 7.89 (followed in Jos. *Ag. Ap.* 1.171; cf. *Ant.* 1.145; 8.260).

197. E.g., Odeberg, *Gospel* (1929; repr. 1968); Belkin, *Philo* (1940); Bonsirven, *Judaism* (1950; trans. 1964); Lieberman, *Hellenism* (1962); JPFC passim (1974–76); Hengel, *Judaism and Hellenism* (1974); Sanders, *Paul and Judaism* (1977); Theissen, *Sociology* (1978); McNamara, *Judaism* (1983); Bauckham, *Acts in Setting* (1995); Ilan, *Women* (1995–96); Hanson and Oakman, *Palestine* (1998).

198. Stoutenburg, "Review," 153.

199. See also Keener, "Official"; idem, "Asia and Europe."

200. The Roman Empire's cultural sphere (extending over southern Europe, western Asia, and northern Africa) should be distinguished from the northern European civilization that laid claim to its heritage (addressed in Usry and Keener, *Religion*, 41–44). The Hellenistic East also differed much from the latinized West.

of which Judea is a part. Although Luke might at least once imply traditional Greek continental divisions (possibly portraying an "Asian" missions movement invading Europe in a reversal of Western [Roman] colonialism, to use modern postcolonial language; see comment on Acts 16:8–10),[201] the primary spheres in Luke's concern are Jewish/Gentile in every geographic location.

Some widely spread cultural traits in the later Mediterranean world, a portion perhaps due to Roman influence, also invite many scholars to speak of a "Mediterranean" culture. Past generations of Western interpreters appropriated the Greco-Roman mantle for European civilization (although it was a geographically Mediterranean culture with only limited influence from northern Europe), but now other interpreters are appropriating the Greco-Roman heritage differently. "Greco-Roman," currently the most common designation for the culture in literature from our discipline,[202] aptly defines most of the larger cultural sphere in which Luke's narrative moves in Acts, but the Greco-Roman world encompassed various local cultures, sometimes as an urban veneer over local rural traditions. Judean culture blended the heritage of ancient Israel, the larger traditional Middle Eastern culture, and Hellenistic culture; it also reflected significant influences from farther east, from Parthian Jewry and the royal house of Adiabene, along with other Diaspora influences (including from Asian and Egyptian Jewish communities).

Because language is socially defined, nomenclature changes as the needs of its users do. I am simply employing the language currently conventional in my discipline, not endorsing a permanent vocabulary.[203] I recognize that those explaining the same historical information in different cultural contexts may prefer different nomenclature. To stray too far from conventional language is to risk unintelligibility; to adopt conventional language without qualification is to risk miscommunication (hence the qualifications here). As with the valuable rise of inclusive language in the past generation, greater accuracy in language need not invite anachronistic prejudice against earlier writers who employed the only (or at least overwhelmingly dominant but not necessarily pejorative) language conventions at their disposal.

Conclusion

In this introductory chapter I have tried to define my primary approach and limitations. This commentary's primary focus is on the social, historical, and rhetorical dimensions of the text; it also seeks to examine (in view of Acts' apparent genre) the degree to which Luke's depiction of events coheres with the real world of the

201. Also my "Asia and Europe." Given traditional Greek boundaries between "Europe" and "Asia" at the Hellespont (although Ionian colonization, hellenization, and finally the empire had obliterated most such boundaries in practical cultural terms), some Greeks in Luke's day could have viewed the early Jesus movement as an Asian movement encroaching on their culture (see comment on Acts 16:8–9; Keener, "Asia and Europe"). Romans, too, often expressed xenophobic hostility toward Eastern cults (such as the ethnic religion of Judeans) invading their culture (cf., e.g., Keener, *Paul*, 140–42; further comment at Acts 16:20–21). Postcolonial readings highlight the presence of the empire (e.g., Joy, "Transitions"), which is indeed pervasive in Acts. Particular approaches vary among interpreters, often with differing sociopolitical locations (see discussion in Samuel, *Reading*, 14–34; cf. idem, "Mission," 27–28; for examples in biblical studies, see also Moore and Segovia, *Criticism*; e.g., Niang, *Faith*; Stanley, *Apostle*; the warning in Moore, "Empire," 21–23).

202. E.g., Neusner, *Christianity*; Fine, *Interaction*; Gager, *Moses*; Goodenough, *Symbols*; Ilan, *Women*; Jeffers, *World*; Sampley, *Paul*; Stowers, *Letter Writing*; *OCD* passim; *DNTB* passim; Cook, *Interpretation*; Taubenschlag, *Law of Egypt*; Danker, *Benefactor*; Aune, *Literature*; Penner and Vander Stichele, *Contextualizing Acts*.

203. Similarly, abbreviations and style guides changed even between the beginning of my work on the commentary and its completion.

periods he depicts. Likewise, although no attempt to forestall criticism will prove comprehensive, I have sought to answer in advance especially the objections to which responses to previous publications have accustomed me. I offer this work in the hope that a range of readers will find the information and at least some of the perspectives contained herein useful to their studies.

1

WRITING AND PUBLISHING ACTS

Although we lack specific information about how Acts was published, antiquity has supplied plenty of information about how works similar to Acts were published. Large narrative works such as Luke-Acts typically entailed multiple drafts and a circulation among people of some means. Examining these methods can give us a sense of how Luke may have published Luke-Acts.

1. Writing Large Narrative Works

The historical context helps us understand the reason that Acts is the length it is and how it may have been drafted (including likely revisions along the way).

a. Length

Large histories could be long, requiring many volumes. Polybius planned nearly forty volumes (Polyb. 3.32.2) and complained that others' histories were even longer and hence more difficult to follow (3.32.4). A book was approximately how much one could listen to in a comfortable sitting; on average, "a book of Herodotus or Thucydides is about 20,000 words, which would take around two hours to read. After the Alexandrian library reforms, an average 30–35 foot scroll would contain 10,000 to 25,000 words," depending on the size of handwriting.[1] Acts contains around 18,500 words (although variants can drive this estimate up or down), and so it is close to the middle of this expected range.

Authors often retained a sense of symmetry by keeping the separate books in a work to about the same length.[2] Allowing for textual variations (and normally not including the Western text of Acts), the Gospel of Luke is about 19,500 words, and

---

1. Burridge, "People," 141; idem, *Gospels*, 118. He adds ("People," 141n49) that scrolls were generally 8–12 in. high, with columns "2–4 inches wide, with 18–25 letters per line and 35–45 lines per column."
2. Witherington, *Acts*, 7, suggesting also symmetry in the periods covered in Luke's Gospel and Acts (about three decades in each).

43

Acts about 18,500,[3] within less than 6 percent of the Gospel in number of words. Matthew (nearly as long as Acts) and Luke are similar in word count;[4] Mark is said to be about 61 percent the size of Matthew, 58 percent that of Luke, and 73 percent that of John. The proximity of Acts and Matthew to Luke in size suggests that certain lengths of standardized long scrolls might have been more available than others. Some scholars have thus proffered that the larger books of the NT (Luke, Acts, and Matthew) each would fill a standard literary scroll, close to the maximum length before a scroll became unwieldy.[5]

Sometimes writers seem to have run out of space at the end of their scroll earlier than they intended, facilitating more abrupt endings.[6] On other occasions writers more effectively budgeted the lengths of their accounts to prevent this deficiency from happening.[7] Sometimes scrolls left blank space at the end;[8] Luke, however, appears to have used virtually all the space available to him. Reading a work of this length, then, like "books" in multivolume histories, would have taken about two hours.[9]

b. Drafting the Work

Most Greek and Roman historians began by composing a basic draft of the material in chronological order, to which a topical outline, speeches, and other rhetorical adjustments would be added later.[10] Jewish narrative writers in Greek likewise usually began with a rough draft.[11] This practice applied to other genres as well.[12] Aristotle recommends sketching a work's plot in outline, then expanding by inserting episodes; he illustrates this method with the *Odyssey*.[13] Similarly, although some rhetoricians preferred extemporaneity, most urged careful premeditation, arranging the material in advance, so that they needed to add only finishing touches when they began writing their speeches.[14] What held for speeches applied even more so to literary works, which were major undertakings.

3. My precise counts from the version on my computer are 19,539 and 18,496, respectively, but given textual uncertainties, even the figures provided above are rough estimates. The estimate of 19,428 words that some make for Luke, e.g., is probably closer.

4. Morton in Morton and MacGregor, *Structure*, 16, estimates that Luke and Acts are roughly the same length (cf. also p. 15); Matthew is within 1 percent of the length of either; John is within 1 percent of three-quarters this length, and Mark is close to half.

5. See, e.g., Bruce, *Books*, 12; Palmer, "Monograph (1993)," 5. Witherington, *Acts*, 6, follows an estimate that Acts was about 32 ft. long and the Gospel about 35 ft. long, close to the maximum 40 ft. scrolls; Metzger, *Text*, 5–6, estimating from a more compact writing size, suggests that each was about 31–32 ft. long, the maximum length being 35 ft.

6. Jos. *Ag. Ap.* 1.320; perhaps Dion. Hal. *Demosth.* 58. Luke may have included more resurrection material (Luke 24) than, e.g., Matthew because he had space available at the end.

7. Corn. Nep. 15 (Epaminondas), 4.6.

8. See, e.g., Diog. Laert. 7.2.38.

9. Burridge, "People," 141.

10. Burridge, *Gospels*, 203; Aune, *Environment*, 82, citing Jos. *Ag. Ap.* 1.47–50; Lucian *Hist.* 16, 48; Lucian *Dem.* Some scholars suggest that Plutarch's extant work on self-love was probably his unfinished draft (Van der Stockt, "Hypomnema").

11. Aune, *Environment*, 128. Thus Josephus fully revised an earlier draft of the *Jewish War* into better Greek (Jos. *Ag. Ap.* 1.49–50); some scholars think that the earlier version was an Aramaic draft, probably circulated among Parthian Jews (cf. Hata, "Version").

12. For a summary of the process (collecting material, producing draft versions, followed by finishing touches), see, e.g., Dorandi, "Copy," 775.

13. Talbert, *John*, 64, citing Arist. *Poet.* 17.6–11. Aristotle's interest in plot admittedly involves drama more than historiography (Butcher, *Theory*, 164–65).

14. Quint. *Inst.* 10.6.1–2. Orators should also be ready to add improvisations during a speech (10.6.5). Small, "Orator," 204–5, observes that when preparing for speeches, Pliny (*Ep.* 9.36) composed section by section in his head, after each section calling in a scribe to write it down; this practice facilitated memorization and was common until the fourteenth century C.E. (see also Quint. *Inst.* 10.6.1).

A lengthy (by ancient standards) and expensive[15] work such as Luke-Acts would invite careful forethought and arrangement to best communicate its message.[16] This is especially the case if we accept the argument that Luke intended this work as a "foundation document" for the community (cf. Luke 1:4).[17] Writing a thorough history could consume an enormous amount of time; historians thus might die before completing their works (e.g., Pliny *Ep.* 5.5.5).[18] To finish a literary project sometimes required shutting out other social demands to focus on writing (1.3.3–4).

In rhetoric, the arrangement of material[19] thoroughly informed the way that educated hearers and readers evaluated works,[20] and so a writer could hardly afford to ignore it. Some critics advised connecting episodes to provide continuity;[21] others, such as Polybius, allowed disjunctions in their narratives, though recognizing that not all historians agreed.[22]

Revision during the process of composition was standard practice. For the *Aeneid*, Virgil first composed twelve books in prose, then revised them in verse (in whatever sequence he chose; Suet. *Vergil* 23).[23] He reportedly dictated many verses in the morning, then spent the rest of the workday condensing them (*Vergil* 22). Even two centuries later, Virgil's work continued to circulate in different forms; Aulus Gellius (Aul. Gel. 6.20) notes that Virgil changed the earlier reading of a passage to the later one and explains why. In other works, too, writers often added nonessential clauses or removed important ones for the sake of better sound.[24] Although revisions can be expansive, ancient writers could employ them for abridgment. In most periods ancient rhetoric valued conciseness and brevity[25] so long as they did not lead to obscurity of expression.[26] Luke thus keeps his account moving by focusing on elements necessary for his story and omitting extraneous material.

Historians frequently followed an earlier historian in the first draft; Josephus seems to have followed his own *Jewish War* at points in his later magnum opus, the *Antiquities of the Jews;*[27] 4 Maccabees adapted material from 2 Maccabees.[28] Second Maccabees itself abridges an earlier work by Jason of Cyrene (2 Macc 2:23). Some argue that, like other Greek writers, Luke mostly follows one source at a time, at least in his Gospel,

15. The cost for taking slow dictation, plus papyrus (though scholars often overestimate papyrus's cost; see esp. Skeat, "Cheap"), without counting rough drafts or travel expenses, might be about forty denarii, or in today's U.S. equivalent, as high as four thousand dollars (see Richards, *Letter Writing*, 165–69, 231; inflation by the time of Diocletian's edict, which he cites, was significant).

16. Thus allowing such literary techniques as foreshadowing (Quint. *Inst.* 10.1.21). Editing provided the writer a chance to craft the material; Epictetus's *Diatribai*, e.g., undoubtedly bears less of Arrian's stamp than the *Encheiridion*, where he organizes and summarizes Epictetus's teachings.

17. With, e.g., Talbert, "Chance," 230; Pao, *Isaianic Exodus*, 3.

18. Some scholars have suggested that the final form of Acts remains unfinished, perhaps because of Luke's premature decease (either assuming that he wrote late in life or, assuming that he died young, against probably much later tradition regarding his longevity).

19. See esp. Wuellner, "Arrangement." Some forms of speeches did, however, allow random sequence (Men. Rhet. 2.4, 391.19–28; 392.9–14; 393.23–24).

20. See, e.g., Keener, *Corinthians*, 29–31.

21. Aune, *Environment*, 90, cites Lucian *Hist.* 55; Quint. *Inst.* 7.1.1. Cf., e.g., perhaps Mark 1:14–39; Smith, *Parallels*, 131.

22. Aune, ibid., 90, cites Polyb. 38.5.1–8.

23. Cf. the opening Virgilic lines of the *Aeneid* removed by the final editors (LCL, 1:240–41, esp. n. 1).

24. Dion. Hal. *Lit. Comp.* 9. On expanding and abridging, see at length the discussion under genre in ch. 4, sect. 2.c, below.

25. E.g., Dion. Hal. *Thuc.* 55; *Demosth.* 18, 20, 24; *Lysias* 5; Philost. *Vit. soph.* 2.4.569; for much fuller treatment, see comment at Acts 24:4.

26. Dion. Hal. *2 Amm.* 2.

27. Krieger, "Hauptquelle."

28. See Gardner, "Mqbym."

where he incorporates a large block of Q material into Mark;[29] both he and Matthew make Mark the backbone and supplement this material from other sources.[30] Some people viewed use of preexisting lines as plagiarism, others (when the incorporation was obvious) as flattering the source (Sen. E. *Suas.* 3.7).[31] (The nature of literary borrowing changed dramatically in the modern period, after England's copyright law of 1709.)[32] The gospel tradition seems to have become common property of the early church and its preaching, allowing less explicit acknowledgment of any particular documents.

2. Publishing Acts

"Publication" most often began with public readings; the well-to-do incorporated readings as entertainment following the dinner at banquets.[33] (They often had their own readers.)[34] Educated members of churches or servants of house churches' patrons probably read Luke-Acts after the Lord's Supper, a dinner (1 Cor 10:21; 11:20–34; Jude 12). Oral recitations at banquets and other social occasions provided one form of publication, but written publication included not only the reading of a work at such occasions[35] but sometimes its wider circulation.[36]

Hearers (or readers) of means who heard a reading and liked a work could have transcriptions made for their own copies, thereby further circulating the work.[37] Members of the wealthy elite could obtain copyists to "circulate" a book in this manner.[38] Because only the elite provided "access to the channels of literary reception,"[39] writers might hope for their elite friends to circulate their writings among other members of the elite.[40] One sometimes secured the favor of such an individual with a dedication (see comment on Acts 1:1) or more elaborate literary pieces.[41]

29. Aune, *Environment*, 139. Laistner, *Historians*, 83, 120, questions this common approach (with regard to Livy and Tacitus, respectively).

30. Aune, *Environment*, 65; cf. Downing, "Conventions"; idem, "Actuality"; Burridge, *Gospels*, 204–5. Agreements between Matthew and Luke against Mark in Markan material suggest that Luke felt free to adapt his dominant source in light of his larger repository of oral tradition and written information.

31. The elder Seneca lamented that even obvious, unethical plagiarism could go undetected because of the audience's negligence (*Suas.* 2.19; McGill, "Seneca on Plagiarizing"). (Material in this section has been incorporated, though greatly augmented, rearranged, and revised, from Keener, *John*, 5–7.)

32. Frye, "Problems," 275, noting the frequency of conflation before that time.

33. Burridge, *One Jesus*, 20; Alexander, "Book Production," 86, 90; Dewey, "Oral-Aural Event," 145–47; Shiell, *Reading Acts*, 117–22; Dorandi, "Publication," 185; cf., e.g., Diog. Laert. 1.122; Corn. Nep. 25 (Atticus), 14.1; Cic. *Att.* 2.1; 12.44; Sen. E. *Controv.* 1.pref. 19; Sen. Y. *Ep. Lucil.* 95.2; Statius *Silv.* 2.pref.; Iambl. *V.P.* 21.98–99; other sources in Keener, *Matthew*, 297. For public readings of *histories*, see Nicolai, "Place of History," 23.

34. Cic. *Fam.* 7.1.3. Readers and reciters in wealthy households were frequently educated slaves (see Duff and Spawforth, "Anagnōstēs," noting Cic. *Att.* 1.12.4; Corn. Nep. 25 (Atticus), 13.3; 14.1; Aul. Gel. 3.19).

35. For readings at banquets, see, e.g., Pliny *Ep.* 9.17.3.

36. See Alexander, "Book Production," 86, 90; Dewey, "Oral-Aural Event," 145–47; Winterbottom, "*Recitatio*"; cf. Iambl. *V.P.* 21.99; Starr, "Reading Aloud." On the limitations of literacy in antiquity, see the oft-cited Harris, *Literacy*. Lecturers sometimes brought copious research and hoped that their hearers would encourage them to continue reading (Sen. Y. *Ep. Lucil.* 95.2).

37. E.g., Phaedrus 4.prol. 17–19. The wealthy might also acquire copies for their personal libraries, which became a symbol of status (see Kunst, "Privatbibliotheken"; *Suda*, s.v. "Epaphroditos," in Sherk, *Empire*, §178 I, p. 238; Cic. *Fam.* 13.77.3; *Quint. fratr.* 3.4.5; *Att.* 1.4, 7; such personal libraries appear even in Egypt's nome capitals [Lewis, *Life*, 60]).

38. Cic. *Att.* 12.44. Cf. Gamble, "Literacy," 646.

39. Other writers recited their works at public festivals (e.g., Dio Chrys. *Or.* 8.9; 27.5), but with less hope of sponsorship for continued circulation (many did not want to hear them; cf. 27.6).

40. Cic. *Att.* 2.1; Statius *Silv.* 2.pref.

41. Citroni, "Patronage, literary," 1125. A noble might even dedicate a work to the emperor, apologizing for its unworthiness (Pliny E. *N.H.* pref. 6, 12).

Christians in northeastern Mediterranean house churches may have heard Luke-Acts read often, but few would have been able to read their own copies, both because of the level of literacy required for such an activity and because of the limited afford-ability of a copy. (Many scholars have estimated literacy in the empire at about 10 percent.[42] A higher estimate is possible, especially in urban areas,[43] but reading a work such as Acts required much more than basic literacy.)

a. Released in Stages

An author with especially elite connections might become more proactive, read-ing a work first to friends (a supportive audience), then to a wider public. Such oral recitations provided the benefit of feedback that permitted revisions to improve the work before its wider circulation.[44] (Oral publication might also occasionally entail the danger of plagiarism. One man with an exceptionally well-trained memory, hearing an author reciting a poem, claimed that the author had stolen the poem from him. The hearer then repeated it back verbatim, a feat that the actual author could not reproduce.)[45] Provided these oral tests proved successful, the author might publish the work or, far more often, "entrust it to a publisher who ordered the copies, assumed the production costs," and distributed the work. Cicero's friend Atticus, one such publisher, had many scribes in his workshops.[46] Scribes usually wrote documents while sitting down, writing on the sheet on their lap.[47]

Modern readers accustomed to mass printing should not overplay the distinction between circulating a draft among acquaintances and publishing a final copy.[48] To the extent that we can make such a distinction, however, subsequent editions usually supplanted their predecessors.[49]

Some works circulated in more than one form. Aristotle organized his teachings into both notes, which were popular and random, and the more formally arranged books, which remain extant today.[50] For authors with adequate resources, such works might remain continually in revision, improving the rhetorical quality of a work.[51] Authors might release these published works in various editions; thus, for example, Ovid ab-breviated his earlier five-volume edition of the *Amores* to three volumes (*Am.* prol.).

---

42. On public literacy, see, e.g., Lewis, *Life*, 61–62, 81–82. Scholars typically estimate literacy at ca. 10 percent, and not higher than 20 percent (Meeks, *Moral World*, 62; Botha, "Literacy"; Aune, *Dictionary of Rhetoric*, 276; Gamble, "Literacy," 644–45; Scholer, "Writing," 1283; see esp. discussion in Harris, *Literacy*, who is often cited by the other scholars and allows for regional variation; in Jewish Palestine, see Hezser, *Literacy*, 473, 496, as cited in Harrison, *Authorities*, 20). By "literacy" such estimates often mean the ability to read and understand texts of medium complexity.

43. See Horsfall, "Statistics" (cited in Harrison, *Authorities*, 20); Curchin, "Literacy"; Millard, "Literacy." In Egypt most metropolites (citizens of Greek-speaking nome capitals), in contrast to typical villagers, could read and write (Lewis, *Life*, 61–62). Note also the inscriptions (esp. *CIL* 4.4345, 4356, 4397, 4706–85; 7.12.18–20) cited by Franklin, "Literacy," 89–98, and noted in Harrison, *Authorities*, 20–21 (also citing Woolf, "Literacy," 48–49).

44. See, e.g., Suet. *Vergil* 33; Shiell, *Reading Acts*, 115. Winterbottom, "Recitatio," 1296, cites Pliny *Ep.* 5.12.1–2 but guesses (probably rightly) that it often generated flattery instead (Hor. *Ars* 428–31).

45. Sen. E. *Controv.* 1.pref. 19. Since Seneca knew which was the true author, he probably is accusing the other of showing off, not of plagiarism.

46. Dorandi, "Copy," 776. Some question whether the friendship between Cicero and Atticus was as ideal as has often been supposed (Marchetti, "Words").

47. Richards, *Letter Writing*, 55, noting one scribe's quip in a manuscript note that "good writing involved the cooperation of right hand, pen *and knee*"; for the diverse kinds of secretaries available, see 64–80.

48. Heyworth and Wilson, "Editions, second," 809.

49. Ibid., 812; cf. idem, "Variants." Political changes sometimes required revisions ("Editions, second," 811).

50. Cic. *Fin.* 3.3.10; 5.5.12. For papyrus and other writing substances, see Maehler, "Books."

51. Dion. Hal. *Thuc.* 24, noting that Thucydides continued revising his eight books over a twenty-seven-year period. Aune, "Publication," 389, notes two revisions of a work by Tertullian (*Marc.* 1.1).

An author might also release a prepublication copy but expect that it not be "published," that is, circulated beyond the one reader, until it had been polished. The dedicatee should then receive the first copy (Cic. *Att.* 13.21a).[52] After copyists had a book ready, it would be checked for corrections (13.23), and the writer might ask a friend to be certain that the revised copy was the one sent (13.48). One might even claim that one had written the book for a particular reader's attention, not initially circulating it (*Rhet. Alex.* pref. 1421a.27–38, 1421b.6).[53] At other times, well-meaning friends apparently circulated an author's notes or draft, provoking the author to object that the work was still unfinished.[54]

Some scholars think that Acts circulated in multiple editions, arguing that this diversity would explain some of the textual tradition. In any case, the normal process of examination and revision suggests that a significant narrative work such as Acts was not lightly composed but reflects careful composition and revision from information to cohesive narrative. It also suggests that Luke would have had ample opportunity to recognize and correct or explain some of the points that modern readers find curious had they seemed equally curious to him. Of course, no amount of revision allows one to guard against every possible misreading.

b. Pliny's Example

Pliny the Younger, who deliberately cultivated his literary reputation, provides abundant examples of the process noted above, although he wrote speeches rather than histories. He was not the first to offer readings even of his speeches, but this was not a common practice (*Ep.* 7.17.4). Readings of various other forms of literature were, however, common among the Roman upper class. In one letter, Pliny observed that most recent days had included some readings (1.13.1), and elsewhere he notes that some earlier writers (he specifies Silius Italicus) had submitted their verses to public feedback (3.7.5). Since Pliny read only speeches well, he would ask one of his freedmen to read verse (9.34.1).[55]

Pliny complains that most potential hearers of his day preferred to sit about gossiping (1.13.1–2),[56] but he attended most readings given by friends who invited him (1.13.5), and he praises other readings he appreciated (6.21.2). He praised one patron for restoring literature (8.12.1) by lending his home for such readings and attending them elsewhere (8.12.2). He also invited his own friends for his informal readings (9.34.1). He seemed pleased when, although he urged friends to come only if convenient, they showed up for two days of readings and "forced" him to continue on the third (3.18.4). One might fail to invite those whom one expected to be offended.[57]

---

52. Cf. Symm. *Ep.* 1.31. Augustus apparently wanted such a rough draft of the *Aeneid*, or at least a part of the work (Suet. *Vergil* 31), and Virgil provided him private readings of *Aen.* 2, 4, and 6 (Suet. *Vergil* 32). Earlier scholars' hypothesis of a proto-Luke (e.g., Streeter, *Gospels*, 201–22; C. Williams, *Acts*, 12–13) fits the pattern of ancient authors going through several drafts, although the suggestion that Luke subsequently discovered and added Mark suggests a more thorough revision than is likely. Morton in Morton and MacGregor, *Structure*, 35, proposed a proto-Acts to match proto-Luke.

53. This claim is probably a fiction; the writer of *Rhet. Alex.* almost certainly hoped that this detailed work would circulate beyond the reader he flatters.

54. Aune, "Publication," 389 (citing Quint. *Inst.* 1.pref. 7–8).

55. Elsewhere, however, Pliny complains that speeches do not "read" well, and hence he agrees to read his speech to his friends only on a friend's recommendation (*Ep.* 2.19.1–4). The Roman practice of public recitals of aspiring poets and of literature was common in the early empire and rooted in earlier precedents (Bloomer, "Declamation," 297).

56. A situation Pliny starkly contrasts with an earlier era (*Ep.* 1.13.3–4). He also complains about audiences too arrogant to applaud appropriately (6.17.1–6).

57. Thus Regulus failed to even invite Pliny to his attack on Rusticus (Pliny *Ep.* 1.5.4; cf. 1.5.2).

A person who liked another's reading could seek to procure a written copy to send on to a friend (6.21.7).

One reason Pliny invited friends was to secure feedback so that he could edit the works before publishing them more widely.[58] This he considered an important service to his readers (7.17.8–10). The reading likewise gave him a sense of which passages were inappropriate in front of a real audience (5.3.8). He also solicited feedback from those to whom he sent copies of his speeches,[59] sometimes at their request.[60] Occasionally he needed advice whether to even publish a work.[61] He provided the same favor to others who sent him their works,[62] and included critical feedback to improve them.[63] Such "editing" no doubt prevented many postpublication embarrassments.

Pliny's own works, at least, seem to have circulated widely. He explains that only by revising and publishing his speeches can he hope for them to survive him (5.8.6–7). His friends might help him publish a work (1.2.5). He claims that he has heard that his books are being read throughout the world, although the booksellers might simply be "flattering" him (1.2.6). He knows that his works are popular in Rome and is happy to hear that his books are being sold by booksellers in Gaul (9.11.2). He is pleased when a friend assembled copies of his speeches and sent them to him for correction (4.26.1).

Pliny also hopes for others' works to circulate. He encourages Suetonius to write more quickly so that his books will be "copied, read and sold."[64] He encourages another friend that he should at least offer readings of his work; once he felt the crowds' admiration, he might prove more inclined to publish (2.10.6). Pliny warns another that, important as revisions are, one must eventually stop revising, finish the work, and then begin another one (9.35.2). He seems annoyed, however, when his wealthy rival Regulus assembled a large audience for a reading Pliny considered frivolous. Regulus then had the memoir copied and distributed in Italy and the provinces, appealing to town councils to have it read.[65]

Such means of publication were available only to the very elite, but they offer at least some sense of how ancient works were circulated through networks interested in prominent persons' presentations. Not likely one of the elite himself, though with sufficient education to produce a popular or midlevel historical monograph with minimal rhetorical embellishment, Luke could hope to achieve wider circulation only through his Christian network. He might depend on some members of the elite to promote it within those circles (perhaps starting with Theophilus; see comment on Acts 1:1) but would have to depend especially on the interest that his content would generate.

Quotations in early church fathers suggest that for some time his Gospel (which fit an established genre category and focused on Jesus, the center of the church's attention) drew more attention than his Acts. Early Christians were interested enough, however, to preserve his work, even as a widely accepted element in the emerging

58. Pliny *Ep.* 5.3.8; 7.17.1–3, 7; 8.21.4.

59. E.g., Pliny *Ep.* 1.2.1.

60. E.g., Pliny *Ep.* 1.8.1; 2.5.2 (although here he does not send the part he is still revising, 2.5.1); 3.13.1, 5.

61. E.g., Pliny *Ep.* 1.2.5; 1.8.3. His hesitation might be feigned, inviting compliments—which he certainly doles out to others (e.g., 3.15.3).

62. Poems in Pliny *Ep.* 3.15.1–2.

63. Pliny *Ep.* 7.20.1 (to Tacitus, who was doing him the same favor, 7.20.2).

64. Pliny *Ep.* 5.10.3 (LCL, 1:367); cf. 5.10.1–2.

65. Pliny *Ep.* 4.7.2 (it was a memoir of the life of Regulus's son, who died as a child).

catholic "canon" of apostolic readings. Over the course of time, then, his work was more widely circulated than he had likely imagined possible.[66]

Conclusion

Luke may have begun by producing a rough draft of his two-volume work (or of the Gospel first, with a draft of Acts added after the Gospel was more polished). He could then receive feedback on this work through public readings at banquets (probably especially the Christian banquet that constituted part of the church's regular meetings) and revise it accordingly. An elite sponsor—or hoped-for sponsor, such as Theophilus (see comment on Acts 1:1)—could provide the work wider circulation in circles that could afford to have more copies made.

---

66. This observation refers to its virtually universal geographic range in the ancient Mediterranean world; the questions of whether such works addressed particular "communities" (ch. 12) or whether Luke self-consciously treated his work as a continuation of Israel's story (ch. 14) are discussed elsewhere in this commentary.

2

PROPOSED GENRES
FOR ACTS

Genre provides the culturally conditioned, conventional expectations according to the guidelines of which a work should be read.[1] Although, as categories, genres are fluid and overlap,[2] they are not always completely artificial; ancient writers could adapt them, but conventions did provide ranges of definition for those who chose to follow them.

Various proposals have been offered regarding the genre of Acts. Although Acts is part of a two-volume work, not all scholars define both volumes according to the same genre (see the discussion of biography in this chapter, sect. 3). This discussion will survey the following genres proposed for Acts: travel narrative, biography (at greater length), novel (at substantial length), epic (briefly), and "acts" (also briefly).

I will finally conclude, in agreement with the majority of scholars, that Acts fits the ancient genre of history (a conclusion articulated and elaborated more fully in chs. 3–8). Specifically, it is (as other scholars have noted) apologetic historiography in the form of a historical monograph and written for a fairly popular audience. Other proposals offer elements of truth or valuable perspectives (even the proposal that it is a novel correctly draws attention to Luke's literary techniques and popular audience), but the implied genre (suggested, e.g., by the use of speeches) is history, and the degree of correspondence with external historical data (even when we limit these data to the most certain cases) suits especially a work of history.

1. The Importance of Genre

Ancient readers were aware of various categories of genre;[3] indeed, technical rhetorical works often defined specific genres of letters and speeches more strictly than

1. Cf. Shuler, *Genre*, 25–28; Hirsch, *Interpretation*, 68–126. Although genre categories cannot be applied rigidly, deconstructionist dismissals of their value are also misplaced (see Eddy and Boyd, *Legend*, 318–20).

2. Aune, *Environment*, 23. In spite of elaborate classifications, mixed genres were common in the early imperial period (idem, "Problem of Genre," 10–11, 48; idem, *Dictionary of Rhetoric*, 307 [s.v. "Mixtum compositum"]; Burridge, *Gospels*, 33–34, 56–61; cf. Selden, "Genre," 39–40), and continued later as well (e.g., Rohrbacher, "Digressions," 470).

3. E.g., Quint. *Inst.* 10.1.36; Max. Tyre 26.4; 38.4. Admittedly, perhaps often not on the practical levels noticed by modern critics; see Conte and Most, "Genre." Rhetoricians distinguished various categories

an empirical survey of actual works would allow.[4] Ancient editors divided Pindar's poems according to the kinds of hymns and songs they were, thereby arranging them into books.[5] Observers recognized different genres, and of various models for genre criticism in antiquity, Aristotle's prevailed the longest.[6]

Scholars have placed Acts in various generic categories that were available in its day.[7] Many of these proposals contain an element of truth; in the end, Luke probably mixed genres, as ancient literature often did.[8] But no matter what else Luke-Acts may be, no one disputes that it is obviously a narrative (διήγησις, Luke 1:1).[9] Narratives of various sorts were useful for securing audiences' attention and had long been a standard early component of speeches.[10] And what characterizes narrative in general will also characterize Acts in particular. Whatever its particular generic elements, a larger narrative work invites readings different from those invited by occasional documents such as letters. It could be carefully conceived, especially if it was intended as a foundation document. As Charles Talbert points out,

> Foundation documents like the canonical gospels (and Acts) seem more analogous to systematic theology, albeit in narrative form. That is, they attempt to set forth the Christian position not only in light of problems present and pressing, but also real but past, and real but potential. Such narrative theology tells the story of the community's founder (and in Acts, of the early church) in a way that expresses the values of the group in a balanced way, not just in response to one or more immediate issues that clamor for attention in the community's present.[11]

General narrative considerations remain important for the primary generic category most scholars now recognize for Acts, namely, a form of ancient historiography. Even elite historians included morals for their readers in their works (see ch. 5, sect. 1, below). They also often examined "foundations" in a way that encouraged and solidified loyalties or convictions, whether in the form of Livy's valedictory history of Rome or, more to the point, through apologetic histories of marginalized peoples (by Josephus and others). To require an unimaginative choice between literary strategies and narrative cohesiveness, on the one hand, and substantial genuine information, on the other, is to impose categories unworkable in ancient historiography.

---

for literary forms (e.g., Theon *Progymn.* 2.5–33). The library at Alexandria may have played a role in emphasizing genre for library classification (see Fuller, "Classics," 189, summarizing George Kennedy's oral contribution).

4. See, e.g., examples in Malherbe, "Theorists." Different genres of speeches invited different styles (Dion. Hal. *Demosth.* 45–46);

5. Race, "Introduction," 1.

6. Burridge, *Gospels*, 27–29.

7. For another summary, see Powell, *Acts*, 9–13.

8. See Spencer, *Acts*, 13–14; Marguerat, *Actes*, 24; Parsons, *Acts*, 15. Barrett, *Acts*, 2:lxxviii–lxxix, finds similarities to history (citing Plümacher), biography, and historical monograph, incorporating also elements of apology and Hellenistic romance.

9. Later rhetorical handbooks often define διήγησις as a larger story that may include component elements (Hermog. *Progymn.* 2, "On Narrative," 4; Aphth. *Progymn.* 2, "On Narrative," 22S, 2R; the fifth-century Nicolaus *Progymn.* 3, "On Narrative," 12; cf. also Tannehill, *Luke*, 10; Aune, *Environment*, 116). By definition, ancients expected "history" to be narrative in form (Feldherr, "Introduction," 3n4, citing Isid. 1.41.1 and Lucian *Hist.* 55).

10. E.g., Dion. Hal. *Lysias* 9. Sometimes (e.g., *Or.* 7; 19) Dio Chrysostom narrates a lengthy story (with himself inside it, perhaps true) to draw in the audience, then expounds his subject. A narrative introduction can characterize even dialogues (e.g., Tac. *Dial.* 1–3).

11. Talbert, "Chance," 230; idem, *Acts*, xxv–xxvi. Others also view Acts as a "foundation story" (e.g., Pao, *Isaianic Exodus*, 3).

But beyond basic principles for interpreting narrative, pointing out that Luke-Acts is a narrative is not much more helpful than it is profound.[12] What *kind* of narrative is this work?

2. Travel Narrative

From an earlier generation, W. L. Knox suggested that Acts is a travel story. As he defines the genre, it can appear in either "true or fictitious" literature but "appealed to the popular taste by providing a variety of scenes and adventures with plenty of marvels thrown in." Thus Luke could follow the basic outline of Paul's life while spicing it up with signs and adventures.[13]

Knox offers a valuable comparison here;[14] signs and adventures would have attracted popular readers.[15] Such a popular work need not be identified with novels; Paul's own writings suggest to us that Luke could have had plenty of historical signs (2 Cor 12:12) and adventures (2 Cor 11:23–27) to draw from if he wished.[16] Knox's proposal of Acts' genre is problematic, however, because Luke's travel adventures do not cover Acts as a whole but only Paul's "missionary journeys," as they are popularly called.

A more serious problem with this category's adequacy is the question of how to define genre. Travels could be fictitious, as in the *Odyssey*, much of Philostratus's *Life of Apollonius*,[17] and ancient romances (including those by Petronius, Chariton, Heliodorus, Achilles Tatius, and Apuleius). But travels also appear in historical works. Herodotus and others could use them for history, and more significantly, the most relevant travel narratives for Luke's audience are the biblical accounts of Elijah and Elisha, which Luke, like most ancient Jewish interpreters, presumably took to be historical. Still more to the point, travel offers the literary framework for Jesus's Perean ministry in the Gospel of Luke.[18] This travel focus does not dictate historical questions; travel literature was entertaining but ranged "from the fantastic journey"[19] to

12. E.g., *Letter of Aristeas* is a διήγησις (so *Let. Aris.* 1; with, e.g., Bartlett, *Jews*, 11), and so is Josephus's historical work (*Ant.* 11.68; 12.137; 20.157; *War* 7.42, 274; *Life* 336; cf. also 2 Macc 2:32; 6:17); but the two works have fairly little in common, and Sirach employs the term for discourse more generally (Sir 6:35; 9:15; 22:6; 27:11; 38:25; 39:2). A cognate verb can apply to a novel (Char. *Chaer.* 1.1.1) or an oral narration (Char. *Chaer.* 2.2.6).

13. Knox, *Acts*, 55, citing parodies of fictitious travel literature in Lucian *True Story* 1, 3; a summary in *Peregr.* 9ff.; and true travels in Dio Chrysostom. He is not thinking of later "itineraries," which lacked such narrative interest (on these see Purcell, "Itineraries"). Cf. Smith, "Understand," 52–53. Malina and Pilch, *Acts*, 7, emphasize the ethnic (more than geographic) component of Luke's "travel" narrative.

14. Much of Luke's Gospel, too, is built around travel narratives (cf. Aune, *Environment*, 39, comparing the travels in Exodus through Deuteronomy but noting the difference of focus).

15. Pliny E. *N.H.* pref. 12–13, 16 notes (and may complain about) the popular taste for marvels rather than research.

16. Although Paul seems reticent to narrate many signs in his letters (cf. 2 Cor 12:5–6), he may have done so when the need warranted for defending his gospel (Gal 3:5; Acts 15:12), and others in his churches would have recalled especially those they saw (2 Cor 12:12).

17. Elsner, "Geography," thinks that Philostratus uses Apollonius's travel not simply as a narrative device but as part of his development into divinity. Elsner's comparison with Acts' use of Paul's travels for "hagiography," however, overstates Paul's role in the book of Acts.

18. For travels of Elijah and Elisha, often in the same territories as Jesus, see 1 Kgs 17:9–10; 18:1, 46; 19:3, 15, 21; 21:18; 2 Kgs 1:3; 2:1–8, 18, 23; 3:11; 4:8–9, 25, 38; 6:1–3, 13, 19, 32; 8:7; cf. Samuel in 1 Sam 7:16). Even if these events were dischronologized because of the uncertain placement of individual events (though Luke generally reproduces the sequence of his sources, in contrast to Matthew), Luke avers that his sources are true (Luke 1:1–4).

19. Krasser, "Reading," 554, citing Euhemerus, Iambulus, Lucian, and Antonius Diogenes.

authentic travel reports.[20] Because readers enjoyed travel narratives, Luke made good use of this mode, but it also served a historical and theological function, as a vector of missionary strategy.[21]

Further, Paul's writings attest that he did travel to most of the very locations Luke mentions, in roughly the period he mentions; minor tensions notwithstanding (e.g., Acts 17:14–16 and 1 Thess 3:1–2), the features that Luke and Paul's firsthand information share suggest that Luke adopts a form far closer to biography or history than to novelistic travel narratives. Even if Luke provides narrative structure where his sources are incomplete (as probably in the Gospel), such detailed correspondence with extrinsic sources at such numerous points (see ch. 7 below) is virtually unheard of in novels.

Does a travel narrative constitute a distinct genre like history, biography, and novel or merely a narrative device (such as Luke's use of symposia in Luke 14:1–24)?[22] To the extent that genre can be defined on the basis of extrinsic analogies, we should note that ancient writers, though often using this narrative device, did not employ it as a generic category. If we employ it, we must allow it to overlap with other generic categories, as Knox himself does.

3. Biography

More compelling and useful is the category of biography,[23] probably the most common proposal, next to history, for what genre Acts is.[24] The greatest virtue of this proposal is to retain for Acts the same genre usually assigned to the Gospel of Luke.[25] Luke, like the other extant first-century Gospels, mostly fits the category of biography, as numerous scholars have argued.[26] Graham Stanton regards as "surprisingly inaccurate" the older views of Rudolf Bultmann and others that the Gospels were not biographies;[27] the argument of Richard Burridge[28] is so compelling that one reviewer claims that it ought to end any further dissent about the matter.[29] To claim that the

20. Ibid., citing for travel reports Licinius Mucianus and periegetic texts such as Pausanias. Engels, "Geography," 546–47, notes that *periploi* (based on sailors' near voyages) served as precursors for later geographic and historical approaches. Thus Alexander, *Context*, 85, notes that one may compare Acts and novels on voyaging (the voyage may function as a plot, 70–75) so long as one keeps in mind that (85) "romance does not have a monopoly on voyage-narratives" (a point also emphasized in Marguerat, *Histoire*, 368, who thinks Acts closer to exploration narratives and narratives about settling colonies than to novels; in English, cf. Marguerat, *Historian*, 256).

21. Marguerat, *Histoire*, 368, emphasizing also its acknowledgment of the empire (*pace* many novels, which preferred earlier Hellenistic settings) and vindication of universalism. I regard as less secure his view that Luke writes in view of a decline of missionary travel in his day (368), since I believe that Luke intended his work to provide a missionary model as well as history.

22. For symposia, see, e.g., Aul. Gel. 7.13; Smith, *Symposium*, 49–56, 253; idem, "Fellowship"; Aune, *Environment*, 122.

23. See Talbert, "Monograph," 58–72; Robbins, "Prefaces" (esp. parallels in prefaces in 95–100); idem, "Prefaces in Biography"; Porter, "Genre and Ethics," 9. For parallels in prefaces, see Burridge, *Gospels*, 195.

24. See, e.g., the summary in Johnson, "Luke-Acts," 406 (although he rejects this view, 406–7).

25. As often noted, e.g., Porter, "Genre and Ethics," 8–15.

26. See Talbert, *Gospel*, passim; Kennedy, "Source Criticism," 128–34; Aune, *Environment*, 46–76; Stanton, *Jesus of Nazareth*, 117–36; Robbins, *Jesus the Teacher*, 10; Burridge, *Gospels*, 109–239; idem, "People," 121–22; idem, "Biography, Ancient"; Cross, "Genres," 402–4; Frickenschmidt, *Evangelium als Biographie*; Plümacher, *Geschichte*, 13–14; Keener, *Matthew*, 16–24; idem, *John*, 11–37; Ytterbrink, *Biography*; Crossan, "Necessary," 27. Kee, *Origins*, 144–47, argues that Luke combined Mark with Greco-Roman biography; but Mark was itself already biography.

27. Stanton, *New People*, 63–64; idem, *Gospel Truth?*, 137, reversing his own earlier skepticism in idem, *Gospels*, 19.

28. See esp. Burridge, *Gospels*.

29. Talbert, "Review," 715; cf. also Stanton, *New People*, 64.

Synoptics (and apparently John) are biographies is not to ignore the distinctiveness of their portrayal of their chief character, Jesus (that distinctiveness being sometimes the basis for denying a connection with the broader genre of ancient biography),[30] but to contend that biography is the most obvious category for an ancient audience approaching a volume about a single historical individual.[31]

Some scholars deny that Luke's Gospel is biography by asserting that it is instead a historical monograph involving one person, focusing on events such as Jesus's words and deeds rather than recounting his entire life.[32] But historical monographs involving a single person could be seen as a form of biography (e.g., Tac. *Agr.*), and biographies, like histories, often focused on words and deeds (with philosophic biographies, as in Diogenes Laertius, concentrating especially on words, and political biographies, as in Cornelius Nepos, on events and deeds).

To many scholars, extending the Gospel's genre to the second volume seems a logical step. Acts, as a continuation of Luke's Gospel, provides parallels of Peter and Paul with Jesus,[33] as one might expect in the ancient genre of parallel lives or in ancient double biographies (see the discussion of the unity of Luke-Acts in ch. 16 below).[34] Full histories, unlike biographies, sought to treat their subject exhaustively (Plut. *Alex.* 1.1–2). Luke, however, does not do this; that is, he does not reproduce all of his sources in the Gospel (Matthew includes far more of Mark's pericopes than Luke does) and perhaps is even more selective in Acts. Certainly the Gospel, and therefore Acts, falls in the correct length range for ancient biographies.[35] But length does not require us to adopt exclusively the biographic genre here; single-volume historical monographs were shorter and more focused than fuller, multivolume histories, and the length range of biographies also fits an appropriate length for such monographs.[36]

30. Biographies of divine men appear only later, probably largely because the concept of divine men is later; see discussion in ch. 9.

31. I leave aside the issue of novels, which I address separately in sect. 4 below (esp. showing their differences from Luke-Acts). For my argument regarding the Gospels as biographies, see also Keener, *Historical Jesus*, 73–84; idem, "Assumptions"; idem, "Biographies"; for my discussion regarding the character of biographies of recent figures in the early empire, see idem, "Otho." Gospel synopses yield results comparable to these biographies. Some respondents to "Assumptions" questioned whether my characterization of ancient biographies of then-recent figures would apply to biographies about miracle workers, but this question confuses genre with subject, and might possibly presuppose views about miracle-working sages that are also open to challenge (see ch. 9 of this introduction; idem, *Miracles*). Put somewhat differently, I used for comparison the only sort of biographies from the period that were of recent figures, but there is no reason to expect subject to change comparability, especially as among historical Jesus scholars Jesus is widely agreed to have been a sage (we have abundant parallels for the preservation of sages' teachings) as well as a miracle worker.

32. Witherington, *Acts*, 15–20. For history's focus on events rather than on persons, see Lucian *Hist.* 7; biographical writers sometimes sought not only to recount deeds but to sketch the protagonist's personality by his words and actions (Xen. *Symp.* 1.1). Talbert, *Acts*, 251, an advocate of biography, rightly notes that the boundary between biography and "a historical monograph about a single individual" is often difficult to discern. Collins, *Mark*, 33, notes affinities with didactic and historical biography; noting further that the distinction between historical biographies and historical monographs is a matter of degree, she prefers the latter emphasis without neglecting insights relevant to the former approach.

33. Without claiming that Acts is a biography, Klutz, *Exorcism Stories*, 13, emphasizes Luke's audacity in combining a life of Jesus with a work focused on Paul.

34. At the least, Acts bears some resemblance to a double biography (concerning Peter and Paul; Berschin, "Biography," 653.

35. Horsley, "Speeches," 613; see, on the Gospels, Burridge, *Gospels*, 118, 141, 199. For length in distinguishing genre, see, e.g., Arist. *Poet.* 24.4, 1459b.

36. We are tempted to underestimate the expense entailed in producing multivolume works in antiquity; only the truly elite could afford such works, and this qualification would eliminate the vast majority of Luke's potential audience in this period.

a. Nature of Ancient Biography[37]

Whether Luke writes two volumes with the same genre or one volume is biography and the other is history, the overlap between these genres is substantial.[38] (George Kennedy, indeed, classifies biography "as a subdivision of history.")[39] Although biographies could serve a wide range of literary functions,[40] ancient biographers intended their works to be more historical than novelistic.[41] As David Aune notes, "While biography tended to emphasize encomium, or the one-sided praise of the subject, it was still firmly rooted in historical fact rather than literary fiction."[42]

Nor were biographies generally uncritical glorifications of their subjects, although partisanship was rife.[43] Honoring subjects could, but need not, produce distortion of what a writer reported.[44] Most biographers critiqued even their heroes' shortcomings,[45] and most biographies mixed some measure of praise and blame.[46] One could tell a less than flattering story even about one's own teacher, although one was apt to report especially favorable matters about him.[47] One could also criticize some activities of other figures whom one regarded highly.[48] Granted, some teachers were regarded as exceptional and thus as meriting unmixed praise; Xenophon has only good to report about Socrates (*Mem.* 4.8.11), and it is hardly likely that the Gospel writers would find flaws in one whom they worshiped (cf. later Iambl. *V.P.* passim). But normally

37. In this section, I am adapting and considerably augmenting my summary in Keener, *John*, 12–13, 15–16 (having followed Burridge's now widely accepted view on the genre of the Gospels). Despite differences, ancient biography influenced modern forms (see, e.g., Mossman, "Plutarch and Biography").

38. Certainly, boundaries between imperial biography and history weakened by the late first century (Hose, "Historiography: Rome") because emperors, like Peter and Paul for Luke, were central to the historical action. Ancients did distinguish the genres (Feldherr, "Introduction," 3n4, citing Plut. *Alex.* 1.1–2; Corn. Nep. *Pel.* 1.1). Although especially biographies, the Gospels also include historiographic elements (Byrskog, *History*, 45, noting esp. Cancik, "Gattung"), a point now sometimes noted even for the Fourth Gospel (esp. Bauckham, *Testimony*, 19–21, 93–112; idem, "Historiographical Characteristics").

39. Kennedy, "Source Criticism," 136. Other classicists also recognize the close relationship (e.g., Bravo, "Antiquarianism," 516); the boundaries between these two genres are quite "fluid" (Stadter, "Biography," 528). For one recent examination of the level of historical content in biographies of then-recent characters, see Keener, "Otho."

40. Burridge, *Gospels*, 149–52, 185–88. For the divergence, see further Barr and Wentling, "Biography and Genre," 81–88, although I would not regard all their examples as biographies. Ps.-Callisthenes (treated below under novels) does not belong to the mainstream of this genre; Kennedy, "Source Criticism," 139, more accurately cites Plutarch and Suetonius (both from close to the Gospels' period) as the prime examples of biography.

41. For substantial overlap between the biography and history (as well as other) genres in antiquity, see Burridge, *Gospels*, 63–67. Although biographers might "tweak" their sources and select the most useful, we should not downplay their mimetic function too much (cf. the comparison with artistic representation in Kaesser, "Tweaking"). Satirical elements appear in autobiographies of satirists (Keane, "Satiric Memories").

42. Aune, "Biography," 125. On its epideictic character, see, e.g., Penner, *Praise*, 135; this was also true of Jewish apologetic historiography (229–35). Against Shuler's portrayal of the Gospels as encomiastic biography, see Collins, *Mark*, 30.

43. Ancients did, however, permit biography more freedom to be one-sided in praise than academic history (so Polyb. 10.21.8, contrasting depiction of someone in his history with an earlier biography he had written about the same person; cf. also comments about this approach to biography in Baynham, "Reception," 294).

44. Fornara, *Nature of History*, 64–65.

45. E.g., Arrian *Alex.* 4.7.4; 4.8.1–4.9.6.

46. E.g., Plut. *Cim.* 2.4–5; Corn. Nep. 11 (Iphicrates), 3.2; Suet. *Dom.* 3.2. For Plutarch, see Lavery, "*Lucullus.*"

47. Philost. *Vit. soph.* 2.21.602–3. One might be thought biased when writing about close friends (Philost. *Vit. soph.* 2.33.628), but Tacitus wrote well of his father-in-law because he genuinely believed his virtues (Tac. *Agr.*). One pupil reportedly did omit *some* of his teacher's sayings, but because they were rhetorically inappropriate (Philost. *Vit. soph.* 2.29.621).

48. Eunapius *Lives* 461 (on Iamblichus, who is supernatural in 459); Plut. *M. Cato* 5.1, 5; 12.4; for writers' style, Dion. Hal. *Thuc.* 1. One could also disagree with the dominant view of one's school (e.g., Sen. Y. *Ep. Lucil.* 117.6).

disciples respected their teachers enough to preserve and transmit their teachers' views accurately even when they disagreed with them, rather than distort their teachers' views to fit their own.[49] We should not, then, expect the respect that Jesus's disciples had for their teacher to lead them to extensively fabricate his teachings.

Nevertheless, we may note some distinctions between biographies and histories. First-century historiography often focused on notable individuals,[50] but biography focused on a single character whereas history included a broader range of characters and events.[51] History thus contained many biographic elements but normally lacked the focus on a single person and consequently displayed somewhat less emphasis on characterization.[52] (Although Luke focuses on major characters[53] such as Peter, Paul, and [sometimes implicitly] God, he is less interested in character development than in the plotline focused on spreading the good news.)[54] Biographies were less exhaustive, focusing more on the models of character they provided (Plut. *Alex.* 1.1–3).[55]

Ancient biographies differed from their typical modern namesakes. For example, they often began with their subject's adulthood[56] and were not constrained by chronological sequence.[57] (Matthew is arranged topically; Luke's Gospel follows Mark's

49. See, e.g., Sen. Y. *Ep. Lucil.* 108.17, 20, 22; 110.14, 20; Mus. Ruf. 1, p. 36.6–7 (Pythagoras's disciples differed, but this was considered noteworthy—Val. Max. 8.15.ext. 1). Occasionally pupils could even turn against their teachers (Eunapius *Lives* 493), but in such a case, they would no longer claim his authority for the source of their teaching.

50. Fornara, *Nature of History*, 34–36, 116.

51. Lucian *Hist.* 7; also Witherington, *Sage*, 339, citing Plut. *Alex.* 1.1–2.

52. See Fornara, *Nature of History*, 185, perhaps overstating the contrast. Fleshing out character traits also appears in drama (e.g., tragedians expanding on Homeric characters) and practice orations (e.g., Dio Chrys. *Or.* 61, on Chryseis). Nevertheless, characterization does appear significantly in histories (Pitcher, "Characterization," esp. 103–4, 106, 117; Vasaly, "Characterization," esp. 245, 259), though sometimes indirectly (Pitcher, "Characterization," 105, 107–10), through actions and words (110–12); speeches in Marincola, "Speeches," 119) or other characters' observations (Pitcher, "Characterization," 107–8). Likewise, character development does appear in both history (e.g., Pitcher, "Characterization," 115–17; see also, e.g., Tac. *Ann.* 6.51; cf. Tacitus's clarity on characters in Hadas, "Introduction," xiv–xv; e.g., Agrippina in Tac. *Ann.* 4.54; character changes in Vell. Paterc. 2.18.5; 2.25.3; 2.28.2) and novels (for one attempt to trace character development in Callirhoe, see Temmerman, "Beauty"; for some realism in this novel's characterization, see idem, "Revisited"; for suggested character development in a mythic narrative in Apuleius, see Morwood, "Cupid"). Characterization methods in rhetoric may be useful for narrative (see Temmerman, "Rhetoric"). Even a single writer like Plutarch could hold both static and developmental approaches to character simultaneously (see Duff, "Models," though attributing one to his philosophic and the other to his biographic approach).

53. For a discussion of some characters (especially divine and composite characters, such as God, Christ, Christians, Israel, and Gentiles), see Gaventa, *Acts*, 27–49.

54. Contrast, for example, Luke's portrayal of Peter and Paul primarily as divine agents for spreading God's word with Caesar's politically charged depiction of Ariovistus (Caesar *Gall. W.* 1.31–54; Vasaly, "Characterization," 247–51), Sallust's hyperbolic depiction of Catiline (Sallust *Cat.*; Vasaly, "Characterization," 251–55), and other characters starkly delineated as characters. Luke's interest is more in the mission than in the individuals through whom it was being executed, though they are not as flat (cf., e.g., Peter's development in Luke 5:8; Acts 10:28–29) as some of the characters (including Sallust's uniformly evil Catiline) noted above.

55. For character traits in biographies, see, e.g., Corn. Nep. 4 (Pausanias), 1.1; Feldman, "Jehoram." Sometimes biographers wrote for more leisurely, less technical audiences; see, e.g., Corn. Nep. 16 (Pelopidas), 1.1. If Luke writes both biography (the Gospel) and historical monograph (Acts), we may expect his audience to be more popular than that of some histories (but more technical than that of some biographies).

56. E.g., many political biographies (such as Plut. *Caes.* 1.1–4); the *Life of Aesop* (Drury, *Design*, 29); or Mark or (after his prologue) John.

57. Cf., e.g., the accidental repetition in Plut. *Alex.* 37.4; 56.1. This contrasts with the more chronological practice of historians (e.g., Thucyd. 2.1.1; 5.26.1), although even most historians tended to follow events to their conclusion, and not simply strict chronology (Dion. Hal. *Thuc.* 9; *Pomp.* 3); the writer of 4 Maccabees is aware that the mother's speech should occur at a certain point in his narrative, and says so (4 Macc 12:7; cf. 2 Macc 7), but chooses to recount it later. Cf. topical digressions in Vell. Paterc. 1.14.1; 2.38.1–2.40.1; 2.59.1–6 (esp. 2.59.1). Topical arrangement suited episodic narratives about a person (Hemer, *Acts*, 74), and recollections were often random (Sen. E. *Controv.* 1.pref. 4).

sequence more closely.[58] But Jewish interpreters sometimes even doubted whether the biblical story of Moses was fully chronological.)[59] Historians, by contrast, though not able to reproduce sequence at all points, laid a greater emphasis on chronology. That Luke usually follows Mark's sequence (except at rare key points such as his programmatic reworking of the Nazareth synagogue scene) might suggest that Luke views his biography of Jesus as part of his larger project of writing a history.

Like historians (see the discussion below, especially in ch. 5), biographers frequently sought to teach moral lessons from their stories;[60] one biographer claimed, indeed, that biographers focused on the virtues of their subject more than historians could.[61] Biographers also wrote at times for apologetic and polemic purposes.[62] Some ancient biographers emphasize moral lessons in their stories more than others, and some writers, such as Plutarch, vary in their moralizing even from one biography to the next.[63] (As will be evident in ch. 5, sect. 1, below, however, historians also emphasized moral lessons.)

Although extant first-century Gospels such as Luke betray LXX literary influence, it is not easy to compare them with contemporary Jewish biographies that were not Hellenistic, precisely for the reason that such biographies are hard to come by.[64] Events, rather than the public lives of leading characters, dominate Job, Ruth, Judith, Jonah, Esther, Daniel, and Tobit in the Greek Bible; hence, most do not view these works as biographies in the strict Greek sense.[65] By contrast, scholars often argue that biographic treatments in Josephus (both retaining history and adapting it in a way more intelligible and amenable to a Hellenistic audience)[66] reflect Greek literary conventions,[67] and other Hellenistic Jewish historians probably used these conventions as well.[68] (Philo's essays on biblical personalities are more philosophic yet also reflect some Greek biographic influence,[69] and the pseudepigraphic *Lives of*

58. Topical forms were much more common (Aune, *Environment*, 31–34, 63–64; Stanton, *Jesus*, 119–21), and Augustine did not expect the Gospels to be fully chronological (*Harm. G.* 21.51; for Mark, see Papias in Euseb. *H.E.* 3.39).

59. See 4Q158; Wise, "Introduction to 4Q158."

60. Burridge, *Gospels*, 150; cf. Dihle, "Biography," 367–74. One could learn from past teachers by proxy, as "disciples" of their recorded teachings (Robbins, *Jesus the Teacher*, 110–11).

61. Corn. Nep. 16 (Pelopidas), 1.1.

62. Burridge, *Gospels*, 151, 180; for apologetic autobiography, cf., e.g., Jos. *Life* 336–67; 2 Cor 11:8–33; Gal 1:11–24. Autobiographic writing in some form appears as early as ancient Egypt (Simpson, *Literature of Egypt*, 401–27), though honor conventions created some problems for it in Republican Rome (see Riggsby, "Memoir"; Cic. *Fam.* 5.12.8). For autobiography as a type of biography, often with apologetic or propagandistic purposes, see Stadter, "Biography," 530.

63. Burridge, *Gospels*, 68–69.

64. See much fuller discussion in Keener, *John*, 25–29.

65. Stanton, *Jesus*, 126; Aune, *Environment*, 37. Jewish haggadic expansions of pentateuchal characters (on which cf., e.g., Fisk, "Bible"; Harrington, "Bible") are not close. The suggestion that ancient Near Eastern models provided the later Greek emphasis on individual characters (cf. Dihle, "Biography," 366–67) is overstated. Nevertheless, this is not to deny the possible influence of ancient Near Eastern biographic forms as mediated through Judaism (cf. Collins, *Mark*, 29, on 30 also noting Dormeyer, *Evangelium*, 168–73); it is only to keep in mind that the Gospel writers, and especially Luke, apparently wrote in Greek for Mediterranean audiences.

66. See, e.g., Begg, "Elisha's Deeds"; idem, "Jotham"; idem, "Rape of Tamar"; and other sources in the bibliography.

67. See, e.g., Van Veldhuizen, "Model of Philanthropia," 215–24; Höffken, "Hiskija"; Feldman, "Jacob"; idem, "Jehu"; idem, "Joshua"; idem, "Samson"; idem, "Saul"; idem, "Solomon"; idem, "'*Aqedah*"; idem, "Concubine"; Begg, "Zedekiah"; the multiple articles by Feldman and Begg in this commentary's "Works Cited" (which lists only a sampling); and further discussion on Josephus below. Some particular adaptations are debated (e.g., Roncace, "Portraits"; Feldman, "Roncace's Portraits"; Roncace, "Samson").

68. Cf. Rajak, "Justus of Tiberias," 92.

69. Canevet, "Remarques sur l'utilisation." Philo adjusts figures to suit his idealizations of virtue (cf. Petit, "Traversée exemplaire").

the Prophets resembles Greek lives of poets,[70] drawing on not only canonical accounts but also a subsequent history of legendary developments. But Philo applies to penta-teuchal narratives the philosophic penchant for allegorizing old myths, and his focus on characters of the distant past allows him more freedom than most biographers about more recent figures.)[71]

Among Greek and Roman biographies, numerous examples exist from a few decades after the Gospels (e.g., those of Plutarch, Tacitus, and Suetonius and Josephus's autobiography), and others (e.g., Cornelius Nepos in the late second century B.C.E.) much earlier.[72] Other works related to biography appear even earlier, but the more historically oriented works, such as the biographies from roughly the Gospels' era, may provide the most fruitful comparisons regarding genre.

From a Hellenistic-Roman perspective, the Gospels (as accounts of a sage) seem most comparable in subject matter to philosophers' *bioi* (lives), which honored founders of philosophic schools and reported their teachings.[73] Charles Talbert rightly and influentially argued for biography as the Gospels' genre before this became the current consensus; not surprisingly, he is probably also the leading advocate of the position that Acts' genre is biography. That one would compare Acts to the same category as the Gospel is only logical if the second volume of Luke's work matches the same genre as the first. This matching of genres between the two volumes is what we would expect unless, as the case might be here, the evidence points in a different direction (or suggests mixed genres with different elements dominant in each volume).

b. Problems with Biography as the Primary Genre for Acts

Despite many biographic elements, however, the second volume self-evidently does not constitute a biography of a single figure.[74] In fact, it "seems less interested in sketching vivid portraits of past heroes than in tracing the spectacular development of 'the way.'"[75] Certainly Acts focuses on major characters as the Gospel focuses on Jesus, but Acts does not focus on a single character. Even Paul, its dominant and climactic example, functions as an agent of the work's driving theme, the gospel's expansion; Acts closes not with his death but with his proclamation in Rome. Despite its biographic emphases, Acts thus functions as historiography carried out partly in a biographic manner.[76]

70. See Aune, *Environment*, 41–42.

71. Biographies of recent figures could reflect substantial information. I found roughly fifty points of significant correspondence between Suetonius's biography of Otho and Tacitus's account in his history (not implying that Suetonius invented information where we cannot test him, against the evidence we do have); roughly the same figure applies to correspondences between Suetonius and Plutarch, and I found twenty-eight further points of close correspondence between Plutarch and Tacitus. If we were to expect an analogous degree of correspondences in Mark with contemporary information as we find between Suetonius and Tacitus here, given that Mark is roughly six times the length of Suetonius's essay, we might have more than 280 points of correspondence (see Keener, "Otho"; idem, "Assumptions").

72. Though Nepos is the earliest Roman biographer whose work remains extant, others wrote before him (see Pryzwansky, "Cornelius Nepos," surveying also scholarship on Nepos), and many Greeks wrote earlier (see, e.g., Collins, *Mark*, 32, following Momigliano, *Biography*, 28–30, 36–38).

73. See, e.g., Culpepper, *John*, 64–66; so also some of Josephus's biographies (see Van Veldhuizen, "Moses," 215–24). Some later examples of this form may borrow the gospel form (see Dillon and Hershbell, "Introduction," 25, who also suggest that John's Gospel may well have been available), but Peripatetics displayed special interest in philosophers' biography as early as the fourth century B.C.E. (Laistner, *Historians*, 18). "Lives" of divine men might provide the closest content, but these appear especially in the third century; they may depend on the Gospels, and the reverse cannot be true chronologically.

74. Pointed out by, e.g., Aune, *Environment*, 77; Peterson, *Acts*, 11. Many scholars contend that attempts to fit Acts into the genre of biography have not proved satisfactory (Plümacher, *Geschichte*, 1–4; Penner, *Praise*, 4).

75. Juel, *Promise*, 63.

76. Cf. Burridge, "Genre of Acts," 28: "a 'biographical monograph.'"

Ancient historians such as Livy might follow the life of a famous general or other hero (often interspersing other information where relevant chronologically), but such biographic elements did not change the basic genre from history to biography. Dionysius of Halicarnassus has biographic sections in his larger history, such as that about Tarquin (*Ant. rom.* 4.41–85), but his work remains a multivolume history.[77] The Gospel of Luke is a biography when taken by itself, but when fitted into the larger work of Luke-Acts, it also functions as a biographic part of a larger history, a history that promises to narrate events (Luke 1:1; cf. Acts 1:1).[78]

Some scholars have argued that "the Hellenistic school tradition" has a similar social matrix to Luke's, preserving "isolated anecdotes about famous teachers."[79] Yet despite Paul's probable adoption of the school model in Acts 19:9, little of Acts consists of such isolated anecdotes (which better suit the Gospel); Acts instead provides a continuous, forward-moving narrative. Talbert identifies a type of biography in which philosophic biographers[80] commented on the founder's followers after treating his life. But especially when it is more than "a simple list of successors," this feature is atypical, appearing in only six of Diogenes Laertius's eighty-two lives.[81] Talbert responds that the question is not how widespread a genre was but whether it occurred.[82] There is some truth in his objection. (As ch. 16 below will explore, the genre of parallel lives, perhaps an even closer analogy, is quite relevant to Luke's work, even though this analogous characteristic does not determine the "genre" of Acts in the larger sense.) But Diogenes Laertius's succession narratives also are often much briefer than those in Acts and difficult to compare in form.[83] They are more comparable in function, which may be Talbert's more substantial contribution here (see the discussion of succession at Acts 1:9–11).[84]

In the final analysis, Acts is not merely a continuation of a biography in Luke but a full volume in its own right.[85] Together the volumes function as something more

77. Balch, "ΜΕΤΑΒΟΛΗ ΠΟΛΙΤΕΙΩΝ," 143 (noting also, 143–44, that even Plutarch, who distinguishes history from biography in *Alex.* 1.1, elsewhere [e.g., *Comp. Thes. Rom.* 1.2] views his work as "history"). Biographic material does not make a work biography per se (Stadter, "Biography," 528–29). Although noting some typical distinctions between biography and history, Talbert, *Acts*, 251, helpfully notes that many histories contain biographic sections (citing Polyb. 9.22; 10.2.2; Dion. Hal. *Ant. rom.* 5.48.1; Diod. Sic. 17; Jos. *Ant.* 14–17; Dio Cass. 45–56; 73.11.2–4; Euseb. *H.E.* 6).

78. Aune, *Environment*, 121. If "biography" proper does not describe the work, "biographic history" may work better (see, e.g., Dormeyer, "Gattung," 461–65, 475, noting the utility of this category for parallels among figures, esp. on 464–65).

79. Alexander, "Biography," 56; cf. idem, *Context*, 43–68. On philosophic biography, see briefly Stadter, "Biography," 529–30.

80. Although Diogenes Laertius and others recount anecdotes about philosophers, Eunapius (*Lives* intro. 452–53) portrays Xenophon as rare for focusing on Socrates's deeds as well as words. Of the treatments of Socrates mentioned in Kennedy, "Source Criticism," 128–34, Xenophon's thus is closer to biographic character than the others (though not itself a biography). Schneider, "Zweck," also compares Luke-Acts with Diogenes Laertius. Later, see especially Iamblichus's *Pythagorean Life* (which involves not only Pythagoras; Dillon and Polleichtner, *Iamblichus*, xiv).

81. Chance, "Perspectives," 200 (more fully, 181–201); Aune, *Environment*, 78–79; Pervo, *Acts*, 16. (Succession narratives in general, however, are more widespread, as in the Elijah-Elisha cycle; see comments on Acts 1:8–11.)

82. Talbert, "Chance," 233–34. He also notes that the asymmetry (most succession lists or narratives are much briefer than the founder's biography, in contrast to what we find in Luke-Acts) is irrelevant to the question of genre (*Acts*, xxiii).

83. See Balch, "Genre," 6, who also contends that Luke-Acts addresses the issue of succession to promises in the Hebrew Bible, not just to Jesus, and is not focused on "individual, institutional successors of Jesus." Acts certainly does focus particularly on Peter and Paul, but Balch is right to note the disjunction of form.

84. Regarding function, Talbert's parallels to succession narratives or histories for single schools (*Acts*, xix–xx) may prove most helpful.

85. Division into volumes sometimes served literary purposes as well as limitations of space (cf. Royse, "Philo's Division").

than biographies or a biography followed by successors; as Gregory Sterling points out, "The narrative unity of Luke-Acts is far greater than the sequential lives of the individual figures of the philosophic schools in Diogenes."[86] Thus, although we may learn a great deal from Talbert's comparison, we should not use it too firmly to predict what to expect from Acts. As Talbert has also shown, "succession" material appears in various genres in antiquity,[87] a pattern certainly relevant in Luke-Acts[88] whether or not it is biography.[89] Further, the conjunction of the Gospel and Acts in a single work does at least suggest a biographic emphasis in much of the larger historical project.[90] One might even make an argument for Acts as "a biography of the early church" analogous to Dicaearchus's "On the Life of Greece,"[91] although this is not very different in practice from viewing Acts as an ethnographic or institutional historical monograph.[92] (I shall also argue below that Acts is not about the early church per se, but about the early Christian mission.)

c. The Same Genre for Both Volumes?

It is not necessary for each volume on its own to belong to the same genre.[93] When the two volumes are taken together, Luke may mix elements of two genres (such as parallel lives and historical monograph). Many scholars suggest the value of approaching Luke-Acts through the lens of multiple genres,[94] and this approach is most fruitful regarding biography and history, genres that apparently Luke has creatively synthesized in a fresh manner.[95] The popular level of most biography probably affects the popular way in which Luke writes his history, in contrast to more common models extant.[96]

Ultimately, however, the two-volume work reads most fully as history when both volumes are read as a whole, because it sets forth Jesus's life (a biography when taken by itself) and the story of the early church's mission within the broader framework of Israel's history.[97] (In contrast to Luke's preface, which promises to narrate events,

86. Sterling, *Historiography*, 319; less relevant to the genre question, he observes that Diogenes's concern is "who studied with whom" whereas Luke's is legitimacy (320).

87. Talbert, *Mediterranean Milieu*, 19–43; for its appearance in many genres, see esp. 41–43, 50.

88. Ibid., 43–50.

89. He regards biographies as the closest formal analogies (ibid., 50–55) but acknowledges that Luke-Acts, as a whole, has adapted the form that appears elsewhere primarily as units within larger works (52).

90. Burridge, "Genre of Acts," 28, notes that it is often difficult to distinguish biography, a one-volume genre, from historical monographs (cf. also 9).

91. Burridge, "Genre of Acts," 28 (cf. also 7).

92. Ibid., 28, rightly emphasizes the flexible boundaries between ancient biography and historiography.

93. See, e.g., Palmer, "Monograph (1993)," 3; Parsons, "Unity: Rethinking"; Pervo, "Same Genre?"; Parsons and Pervo, *Rethinking*, 20–44 (though overstating the case).

94. E.g., Penner, *Praise*, 59 (noting also idem, "Madness"; idem, "Reconfiguring").

95. Marshall, "Treatise," 180; Barrett, *Acts*, 2:lxxviii–lxxix (also admitting some other less dominant elements); Verheyden, "What Are We Up To?," 47 (citing Marshall; Hemer, *Acts in History*, 33–43, 63–100; Barrett, *Acts*, 2:lxxix). Penner, *Praise*, 135 (who overemphasizes encomium), suggests that "the line between history, encomium, and biography was becoming difficult to establish firmly." Dormeyer and Galindo, *Apostelgeschichte*, 19, regard it as the remains of a declining form of "biographischen, pathetischen Geschichtsschreibung." Marguerat, *Histoire*, 49, sees Acts as primarily historiography but notes that this is not easily separated from biography.

96. Admittedly, the qualification "extant" naturally favors elite over popular historiography.

97. See Moessner, "Re-reading." Stuhlmacher, "Genre(s)," carries this too far in playing down the Gospel's biographic character in arguing against Shuler, "Genre(s)." One approach that would allow Acts to remain a historical monograph while preserving the same genre for both volumes is to treat the Gospel as a historical monograph as well; in fact, some treat the Gospels as fitting the genre of history (e.g., Dihle, "Biography," esp. 379, 381; see my response in Keener, *John*, 11). Most notably, Adela Yarbro Collins assigned even Luke's primary model for his first volume, the Gospel of Mark, to this genre, arguing in part that biography focuses more on models for individual living (see, e.g., *Life of Jesus*, 40–46; idem, *Beginning*, 24–27). More recently she has offered a nuanced position that brings together insights from various approaches, and from which I

biographic prefaces typically specified that they would focus on a particular person's life.)[98] Luke appears to presuppose that his ideal audience has some grasp of this broader framework of salvation history, but he underlines it explicitly and repeatedly (e.g., Luke 24:44–45; Acts 3:18, 21–26; 7:2–53, esp. 7:52; 13:17–47; 26:22).

Whereas a biography focuses on a single individual, a "monograph concentrates on a particular situation, war, or period." A writer could mix these foci in a single book; for example, Diodorus Siculus, though generally annalistic, devotes to Alexander an entire book (Diod. Sic. 17) that has "many features of βίος."[99] Luke's Gospel offers a comparable biographic unit in a larger historical work, albeit one much briefer than that of Diodorus.

Thus Walaskay is right to observe how function controls form in this case: "Biography (Third Gospel) becomes history (Acts of the Apostles), a provincial sect grows into a world-wide mission, and the particularistic message of Jesus and the Jerusalem Jewish-Christians develops into the universalistic message of salvation for the gentiles."[100]

Jesus is one figure on whom Luke must focus; Luke could hardly ground the story of early Christian mission in Israel's story without connecting it to Jesus's story. Since a single canonical version of this story did not exist, it would have made sense to treat Jesus even if he wished to focus primarily on Paul's mission.[101] After completing Jesus's *bios*, he turns to history, albeit approaching history biographically much of the time. The focus on a few main characters made the work readable for a popular audience that liked heroes, and histories could focus on select central characters (as noted below). This focus allows us to gain considerable insight from Talbert's parallels without abandoning the more essential generic category of history for Acts.[102]

4. Novel

A substantial minority of scholars have compared Acts to ancient novels.[103] Although this genre should be rejected as an overarching classification for Acts, it does offer some

---

may differ only in emphasis; she notes useful insights in the biography analogy (*Mark*, 22–33, esp. 33), while preferring more analogies from the historiographic approach (33–42), blending Jewish and Greek cultures to envision an eschatological historical monograph (42–52). I argue below that ancient historiography also provided such models, and would argue that a historical monograph about a person would be read as a biography; but in any case ancient biography was closely related to historiography by this period, so that in a range of positions these are not very far apart.

98. Callan, "Preface and Historiography," 578 (citing Philo *Mos.* 1.1 as an obvious example).

99. Burridge, *Gospels*, 246. Also noted above is the existence of smaller, biographic sections of histories, e.g., Dion. Hal. *Ant. rom.* 4.41–85, on Tarquin.

100. Walaskay, *Came to Rome*, 59; cf. Aune, *Environment*, 77 (noting that Luke could be biography but, as part of Luke-Acts, is history). Cf. Bruce, *Acts*[3], 30: Luke writes history and "develops his theme biographically."

101. Of course, that he devotes an entire volume to Jesus's story, following the biographic form already circulating (Mark being one prior example), suggests that his interest is in Jesus's story as not solely a transitional preface to Acts but a part of Luke's story in its own right.

102. Cf. Barr and Wentling, "Biography and Genre," who appreciate generic similarities with biography without assigning Acts to that genre. They also show the wide divergence in the nature of biographies (81–88), though some examples they cite I would not count as biographies per se. One danger of Luke's biographic approach to history, analogous to that of some other historians from his era (cf. Laistner, *Historians*, 108–9, on Velleius), is the omission of other lines of causation.

103. For application of this comparison also to the Gospels, see, e.g., Mac. Magn. *Apocrit.* 2.12–15 (possibly by Porphyry); Mack, *Myth*, 11, 322–23. Fullmer cites novelistic stylistic characteristics in Luke's source Mark, such as parataxis (*Resurrection*, 15–16), episodic plot development (*Resurrection*, 17–22), and lively tempo (*Resurrection*, 22–26); but parataxis is popular Semitic (and probably Koine) style, and episodes characterize biographies (which often depended on anecdotes). Fullmer's contrast with elite literature is appropriate, but

fruitful literary comparisons.[104] Luke-Acts addresses the sort of popular readership shared with novels rather than the more rhetorically sophisticated, more elite readership of common multivolume histories, so the traditional storytelling techniques in popular novels remain relevant regardless of the difference in historical truth content.

a. Literary Comparisons

Some literary techniques were simply good writing, and whatever Acts' genre, we can learn about its storytelling techniques from various kinds of ancient narratives.[105] For this reason, scholars who do not accept the novel as the genre for Acts can still discover some useful insights in the writings of some of this view's advocates. Thus, for example, novels typically included many hardships yet a happy (often comic) ending (e.g., Achilles Tatius; Heliodorus).[106] Acts likewise concludes relatively happily (by stopping well before Paul's execution).

Novels could also employ suspense. Following a technique at least as old as Homer, Greek writers sometimes started stories in the middle and then recounted earlier happenings by means of storytelling within the stories.[107] They might reveal a bit of what happened earlier but save the full revelation for later.[108] Luke likewise interrupts his narrative at strategic points (e.g., Acts 9:30–11:25; 11:30–12:25), although this technique is part of his normal historiographic method of grouping his material (see this commentary's comments on these passages). More clearly, Luke builds suspense by foreshadowing and announcing the dangers that await Paul (20:22–25; 21:4, 11–13) and perhaps even by waiting to announce Saul's identity as Paul until 13:9, although even most of Luke's first-time, real Diaspora Christian hearers (and certainly the more informed center of Luke's target audience) had probably guessed it by that point.

Yet suspense was good rhetorical practice, hardly limited to novels.[109] For example, Polybius's history leaves off with Carthage ready to destroy Rome at the end of book 3, then shifts to an account of Greece during the same period, returning to Rome only later. Although this strategy fits the needs of chronology, it also creates suspense.[110] Similarly, foreshadowing appears in other historical works.[111]

Pervo has argued that we should examine Acts in light of the genre of the novel.[112] As noted below in this chapter, his comparisons of novelists' narrative techniques

novels are not the only works written on a popular level. Valuable literary comparisons between Mark and a novel (without asserting that Mark is one) appear in Starner, *Kingdom*.

104. For broader use to illumine NT texts' social world, see also Hock, "Why Read." Malina and Pilch, *Acts*, 3–5, argue that the broader emphasis on reading Scripture, other literary works, or human life on the analogy with (modern) novels stems from the Romantic period.

105. One should beware, however, reading some modern novelistic techniques (such as unreliable narrators) into ancient texts (see Kurz, *Reading Luke-Acts*, 169–70). Josephus may employ some storytelling devices from novels to develop his biographies of biblical characters (cf. Silver, "Moses and Birds").

106. Cf. Troftgruben, "Ending," 145, 232. On New Comedy as a possible precursor to elements of the ancient novel, see Konstan, "Invention," 9–10. Cf. perhaps even reuse of names like "Chaireas" (Menander and Chariton).

107. E.g., Homer *Od.* 9.37–12.453; Heliod. *Eth.* 1.1 (the background for this scene is not described until 5.28–33); 2.25–4.21.

108. E.g., Heliod. *Eth.* 2.11; suspending action appears also in the Hebrew tradition (cf. Gen 38, interrupting the direct account of Joseph in Gen 37 and 39).

109. E.g., Dion. Hal. *Lysias* 13; Cic. *Verr.* 2.5.5.10–11; Sen. E. *Controv.* 4.pref. 1.

110. One could object that we cannot know that Polybius arranged the material deliberately to create suspense, yet the same objection could be raised concerning our ignorance of Luke's motives where we are tempted to attribute his suspended narratives to a storyteller's suspense.

111. E.g., Vell. Paterc. 2.26.1.

112. See Pervo, *Profit*, passim; cf. also Praeder, "Luke-Acts and Novel." Given the sometimes acrimonious debates in which scholars engage, I should preface my further comments by warning that my obvious disagreement with Pervo on the question of genre should not be construed as disrespect for his extensive and

are useful for understanding Acts (though probably less so when using later derivative acts), even for the majority of scholars, who, for good reason, reject his genre
classification. He rightly observes that novels could use historical characters,[113] and
even provides some examples of historical novels[114] (though some of his suggested
examples are questionable).[115] Yet the most obvious non-Christian examples of novels
employing historical characters (Xenophon's *Cyropaedia*, much earlier than Luke;[116]
Pseudo-Callisthenes's *Alexander Romance*,[117] later than Luke; probably Philostratus's
Life of Apollonius, significantly later;[118] and some lesser-known works[119]) are considerably rarer than novels using both fictitious characters and a fictitious story line.[120] All

informed work on the subject. Nevertheless, it appears to me that despite many valuable literary features in
his commentary (*Acts*, passim), Pervo fairly often questions the plausibility of Luke's scenes by approaching
them with a default setting of suspicion so strong that it would undermine the plausibility of *most* historical
narratives. Rather than pause over every such question he raises (though I answer some indirectly through
historical parallels), we may note here that *all* narratives (including modern eyewitness reports) deconstruct
on some level because none supplies the information needed to answer every possible question. The worst
cases might simply impugn Luke's literary skill in those passages. Pervo also frequently offers his negative
opinions on Luke's theology or other perspectives (more than in typical commentaries, though no more
than Haenchen). Rather than challenge these opinions piecemeal, I simply observe here that, presumably,
some modern readers will share Pervo's opinions whereas others demur, since I doubt that close attention
to the text, by itself, necessarily confers on biblical scholars the status of the best available ethicists, political
theorists, etc. Sometimes Pervo also makes correct literary observations, but he assumes that Lukan literary
patterning is incompatible with historical substance, an assumption that does not consistently hold for ancient
historiography more generally (see our observations in ch. 16 of this introduction). See at somewhat greater
length Keener, "Review of Pervo."

113. Pervo, *Profit*, 103. One observes historical figures even in the ancient Egyptian *Tales of Magicians*
(Papyrus Westcar), concerning characters from a millennium earlier (Kitchen, *World*, 61–62). Typically,
however, novels portray historical figures anachronistically, often placing them in the wrong periods (see
examples in Morgan, "Fiction," 554; cf. also Tob 1:2–4; Jdt 1:1, 7). Novels often employ historiographic
devices for plausibility, but tongue in cheek, because "both sender and recipient recognize" that it is fiction
(Morgan, "Fiction," 555), playful rather than deceptive (556–57).

114. Pervo, *Profit*, 115–31 (including pagan examples, 115–16; Jewish, 116–21, esp. *Joseph and Aseneth*;
and Christian, 121–31, esp. apocryphal acts, 122–31); in *Acts*, 15, he even calls *Joseph and Aseneth* and Ps.-
Callisthenes "history," completely eliminating boundaries. Even works outside the narrative genre could include
historical data; e.g., *Sib. Or.* 5.1–50 recites recent history accurately from its author's conceptual standpoint
(i.e., including legends he assumes to be historical) despite some confusion (cf. 5.460–63). One could cite
here many Jewish works about biblical characters (see Keener, *John*, 25–29), but the genre differs starkly
from Luke-Acts, which is set in the "real" world, anchored in sources (at least in the Gospel), and connected
with history in Acts. Whereas some scholars have suggested that most novels adopted titular forms from
historiography (suggesting realism; cf. Xenophon of Ephesus *Anthia*; Heliodorus *Ethiopian Story*), others
contend that most novels' titles name the chief characters (e.g., Chariton *Chaereas and Callirhoe*; Achilles
Tatius *Clitophon and Leucippe*; see Whitmarsh, "Titles"). Wills, "Aesop Tradition," 224–25, rightly notes the
fictitious material in many popular lives, but his examples concern figures of the distant, often legendary past.
Granted that there is overlap of elements in many cases (Nicolai, "Place of History," 18–19), historiography
is still distinguishable from poetry (see our chs. 3–4 below).

115. Pervo broadens the category to include some works that are more historical; see Sterling, *Historiography*, 320n50. Porter, *Paul in Acts*, 15, is harsher. Marguerat, *Historian*, 29, notes, against Pervo, that historical
novels did not constitute "a literary genre in antiquity."

116. Fictitious stories about historical characters long predate Xenophon; see, e.g., Simpson, *Literature of
Egypt* ("Introduction to King Cheops and the Magicians," 13–14).

117. Bosworth, "Pseudo-Callisthenes," opines that "the historical nucleus is small and unusable"; cf.
likewise Zambrini, "Historians," 211, rightly distinguishing this "popular fiction" from Alexander histories.
The fictionalizing (or epicizing) of historic events such as we find in Lucan's *Civil War* is mainly limited to
poetry (cf. Fantuzzi, "Historical epic").

118. Using Philostratus as a source for the first century is problematic (Kee, *Miracle*, 288).

119. For two fictitious eyewitness accounts of the Trojan War, see Merkle, "True Story," 183–84; Schmeling, "Spectrum," 23. Many scholars think that Philostratus's main "source" for Apollonius's life, Damis, is a
fiction of either Philostratus (Jones, "Passage"; Klauck, *Context*, 170) or an earlier pseudepigrapher (though
cf. Conybeare, "Introduction," vii).

120. E.g., Apuleius's *Metamorphoses* (though developed from an earlier story also attested in Lucian);
Longus's *Daphnis and Chloe* (developed from an artistic representation); Chariton's *Chaereas and Callirhoe*.

these works are also significantly later than the historical characters on which they focus, in contrast to Acts (which is much closer to the events depicted even according to Pervo's later-than-usual dating). Offhand I know of no historical novels composed within a generation or two (or even a century) of the chief characters depicted in them; if they existed, there were not many.

A more important point is that "historical novels" are much rarer than the far greater number of works focused on serious (if, in some writers, sensationalized) history or genuine biography. Further, the scenes in these novels tend to be fleshed out with far more copious details than is possible in Luke's barer focus on events (excepting his speeches, which fit some primary expectations for ancient historiography).[121] As will be shown in subsequent chapters of this commentary, the vast majority of novels offer nothing close to the numerous correspondences between Luke's narrative, on the one hand, and, on the other, preexisting Jesus tradition (the Gospel) and the real world of Paul (Acts).[122]

The apocryphal acts later assigned to the NT apocrypha (Pervo's strongest examples) include "faked documentation and other devices used in ancient fiction to create an atmosphere of verisimilitude."[123] Indeed, most scholars recognize that the apocryphal acts bear various similarities to ancient novels.[124] As argued below, however, it is anachronistic to read later apocryphal acts (that may have used Acts as a prototype) into Luke's work.[125] More significantly, apocryphal gospels and acts are not comparable to "historical novels" in the narrowest sense, which would be closest to (though still quite different from) Acts. Novels using some historical characters (as the apocryphal gospels and acts do) were rare enough, but the few historical novels that drew fairly heavily on a historical story line are much rarer still and are quite different from second-century apocryphal gospels and acts. Such "apocryphal" works as these gospels and acts lack the detailed parallels with extant historical information found in Acts (see chs. 6 and 7 below for details).

Yet even if one were to limit the comparison to historical novels in the narrower sense (to a work such as Pseudo-Callisthenes's *Alexander Romance*), the detailed, concrete parallels with historical information in Acts are more appropriate in historical works than in novels, even in the few historical novels that straddle the categories. As we shall note, historians fleshed out scenes (some more than others), and many did so far more than Luke (usually because of their greater rhetorical interest and skill). Granted, Luke shares with novels a more popular audience focused on adventure, and this affects his storytelling style. The information content, however, is closer to ancient historians' elaborating and taking rhetorical liberties than to novels recycling earlier traditions while creating new stories.

121. Historical novels today (as well as some biographies), such as those of Anne Rice, likewise have detailed scenes quite different from the texture of Luke-Acts. Historical novels have their valuable place as a genre, but Acts is not written like one. Pervo, "Direct Speech," compares the high degree of direct discourse in Acts to that in novels, but novels do not normally use many orations the way that Luke and other historians do.

122. I know of no true exceptions, but it was not impossible for a novel to recycle earlier novelistic material: much of the story line found in Lucian's *Lucius* appears later in Apuleius's *Metamorphoses*.

123. Pervo, *Profit*, 130.

124. Aune, *Environment*, 151–52; Lalleman, "Apocryphal Acts," 67; Rebenich, "Historical Prose," 307–8; Bauckham, "Acts of Paul"; Keylock, "Distinctness," 210; Krasser, "Reading," 554; Hofmann, "Novels: Christian," 846–48; Perkins, "World." Pervo responds by dating Luke's Acts to the second century (though before *Acts of Paul*), but see ch. 10 below. Pervo, "Fabula," compares the apocryphal acts with the *Aesop Romance* (*Life of Aesop*).

125. For similarities and differences between Luke's Acts and the apocryphal acts, see, e.g., Bovon, "Canonical and Apocryphal Acts" (the substance of the article also appears as Bovon, "Apostelakten").

b. Limitations of Such Comparisons

The existence of some novels using historical characters hardly demonstrates that any particular work dealing with historical characters fits this generic category.[126] Mere use of historical characters is a far cry from historical research and use of sources (such as Luke's use of Mark and Q in his Gospel).[127] Indeed, most novels focused on fictitious characters[128] and, when using genuine characters, had little knowledge about events in a genuine character's life.[129]

This procedure contrasts starkly with historical works, which used real characters and events but sometimes embellished their sources (to varying degrees) with educated guesses about what was probable and with a view to what was edifying and entertaining.[130] As comparisons of Acts with Paul's epistles will demonstrate (see ch. 7 below; see also ch. 6 for other external history), Acts is far closer to history than to the novel on these points.[131]

Some elements of Acts tell us more about the social level of Luke and much of his audience than about its genre. Luke was educated but not part of the elite who produced the sort of multivolume histories still extant.[132] Novels, like Acts, "are stylistically and linguistically simple."[133] Novels include many religious themes,[134] but many Roman historians include annual lists of prodigies and some reports of supernatural phenomena. If Luke is more readable and more supernaturalistic than some historians (though he is more restrained than later apocryphal gospels and acts),[135] it probably says more about the social class of many early Christians and the

126. Instead of checking his own assertions with external data (contrast the numerous comparisons with such data in Hemer, *Acts in History*), Pervo (*Profit*, passim) often simply treats stories as unbelievable and biased—while simultaneously faulting Luke (64) for simply ridiculing his opponents!

127. Pervo separates the Gospel from Acts, an approach most scholars today find questionable (e.g., Sterling, *Historiography*, 320), though we should note that Pervo does not separate them in all respects (see ch. 16 below).

128. Porter, "'We' Passages," 550, shows that most ancient novels were not historical novels (possibly excepting Xenophon's *Cyropaedia* and Ps.-Callisthenes's *Alexander Romance*, neither of which became a standard generic model) and comments, "Thus Pervo is in danger of creating a new and unique genre for Acts."

129. Greek and Roman novels typically reflect the milieu of their ideal readers; see Wiersma, "Novel."

130. Penner, *Praise*, 136–37, notes that whereas everyone acknowledges 1 Maccabees as history, the measure of history and fiction in 2 Maccabees is debated. (Third Maccabees is, of course, agreed to be a novel; see, e.g., Johnson, "Fictions"; Hacham, "Polemic.") Penner, *Praise*, 138, suggests that many texts belong in the intermediate category of "historical novels"; while this is partly a matter of definition, the category shrinks considerably so long as one recognizes a degree of fictionalization in some history, as opposed to novelists who took a free or (in the rare cases of "historical novels") a mostly free hand. Droge, "Anonymously," 515, correctly (if understatedly) notes that "the romances do not purport to be a historical record of facts in quite the same way as Luke-Acts does."

131. Luke's claims in Luke 1:1–4 certainly fit much better in the large number of works whose authors view themselves as writing history rather than historical novels. A prologue like Luke 1:1–4 in a historical novel would appear as deliberate deception, not a literary device.

132. Ehrensperger, *Power*, 11, rightly observes that among Jews most intellectual leaders were not economically elite. Smith, "Understand," 50, also highlights the "popular" audience of Luke-Acts, connecting this with novelists. But even if elite histories were more apt to be preserved (especially in multiple volumes), popular interest in historical (or purportedly historical) figures persisted (e.g., *Life of Aesop*, though its traditions are mostly from a distant era, hence legendary; on the weakness of *Life of Aesop* as a parallel for Gospel genre, see, e.g., Wojciechowski, "Aesopic Tradition," 101–2). That is, the audience level cannot infallibly predict the genre.

133. Smith, "Understand," 49–50. Their primary readership, however, was people literate, leisured, and well-to-do enough to afford them (see Bowie, "Readership," 452–53; Stephens, "Who Read Novels?," 415). Some find evidence of rhetorical training (Fernández-Garrido, "Stasis-theory"); certainly most extant novels display some rhetorical knowledge (though works from the literate class have undoubtedly survived disproportionate to their numbers).

134. Smith, "Understand," 49.

135. Cf. Hofmann, "Novels: Christian," 847, noting the later works' "large ration of the absurd," such as "talking dogs and competitive displays of magic, sky travels and a miracle competition (Acts of Peter),

supernatural expectations of a movement whose chief hero was a miracle worker than about his works' genre.

As ancient biographies suggest, a popular historian could appeal to the same dramatic techniques that novelists did, while still maintaining the thrust of his sources (even elite, rhetorically trained historians such as Tacitus can betray significant dramatic influence when they provide more detailed scenes).[136] But novels do not reveal the research, dependence on sources, and lengthy parallels to externally attested data (such as sometimes minute correspondences with Paul's letters) that we find in Acts; few novelists would have been interested in such detailed correspondences.[137]

c. Similar Literary Features in Histories

Most generic features that Pervo and others find in novels also appear in other genres; most of his criteria are thus so broad that they also apply to most historical works.[138] As Daniel Marguerat objects, "The narrative devices that Pervo puts forward do not allow one to draw any distinctions between a novelistic writing and a historiographic one, as both of these genres use them interchangeably in Hellenistic culture."[139] Likewise, Clare Rothschild shows that features often attributed to Luke's theological adjustments fit standard historiographic rhetoric and do not call into question the historical genre of Acts.[140] And Marion Soards complains that many of, and possibly all, the "novelistic" features Pervo identifies in Acts appear in "ancient historians whom Pervo basically ignores."[141]

Among the works by scholars who have drawn parallels between Acts and ancient novels is the careful study by Abraham Smith.[142] Although the parallels he cites help his larger argument and approach (rightly attending to Luke's careful narrative design as we would to an ancient novel's), which are valuable, it must also be observed that most of these parallels also appear in histories and/or biographies.

Smith notes, for example, that novels often focus on the eastern Mediterranean world.[143] This claim is true, but most extant novels do so because they are Greek (a Roman writer such as Petronius includes the west) and by this period even Romans (at least educated Romans) had imbibed the heritage (both mythical and historical) of the Greek East.[144] Greek historians such as Polybius (often), Xenophon, Herodo-

---

obedient bed-bugs (Acts of John), baptized lions (Acts of Paul)," and "cannibals (Andrew and Matthew among the *anthropophagoi*)."

136. Already Thucydides borrowed narrative techniques from dramatists; see Finley, *Thucydides*, 322–23.

137. Exceptions might include, e.g., Lucan novelizing (or epicizing) the Roman civil war, but his poetic form and other factors reveal his generic agendas clearly instead of leading anyone to suppose that he writes historical prose.

138. See Burridge, *Gospels*, 245; Aune, *Dictionary of Rhetoric*, 285; Peterson, *Acts*, 13; cf. Porter, "'We' Passages," 551–52; for similar literary methods in various narrative genres, Penner, *Praise*, 137. Likewise, the difference between historians and poets was not their use of narrative devices, but "that historians research and present past realities" (Gray, "Narrative Manner," 342; cf. similarly Arist. *Poet.* 9.2–3, 1451b).

139. Marguerat, *Historian*, 29.

140. Rothschild, *Rhetoric of History*, 291–92. Elite readers expected proper rhetorical form for historiography (Cic. *De or.* 2.64) and expected rhetorically superior historiography to flourish (Cic. *Leg.* 1.5–7); Acts, which is on a more popular level, survived for other reasons.

141. Soards, "Review," 309; see further Eddy and Boyd, *Legend*, 337–38 (citing Soards [338]). Some reviewers do treat Pervo more favorably (e.g., Edwards, "Earliest Christianity").

142. Smith, "Understand," 49–50. He does note historiographic forms (50n14); he emphasizes novelistic travel narratives (50–53), which I addressed above.

143. Ibid., 49. For this focus (with only hints of Rome), see, e.g., Chariton, in Schwartz, "Rome in Novel."

144. A revival of the popularity of Hellenistic culture in the early second century precedes the majority of extant novels. Some Romans nevertheless continued to maintain a Western bias; cf., e.g., Pliny the Younger (engrossed in Roman public life) in Méthy, "Monde."

tus, and Thucydides likewise focus on the East when the arena of action they report occurred there.

Acts had good reason to devote most of its narrative to the East, where its likely primary audience was located and most of its action historically took place (who can deny that this was the place of the church's origin and, given the testimony of even Paul's letters, the bulk of Paul's ministry?). But Acts also climaxes and concludes in Rome, and much of its narrative (and all of its trial narrative) lies under the shadow of Rome, quite in contrast to the idealized Hellenism of most Greek novels.[145] (For that matter, Luke's setting diverges from many of these same typical Greek novels by being relatively contemporary rather than set in the classical Greek past.)[146]

Location is thus not a compelling criterion of genre. In fact, the location of some of Luke's narratives may point in the opposite direction. Novels often preferred glamorous, well-known cities or distant, exotic locations.[147] (Lucian parodies old poets and philosophers who recount wonders and myths,[148] often about places to which they had never traveled.)[149] Why would Luke, if a novelist, use several small towns in Asia's interior (and bother to travel there to get right their locations on key roads)?[150] (Conversely, it makes sense historically that Paul would start in small towns before achieving success in a major metropolis.) If Luke intended to be believed as a historian (which is how he presents himself), how could he simply exploit a recent figure for a fictitious framework yet provide such clear geographic connections for the figure as would easily discredit his work if it circulated in those regions? (Paul's letters do in fact confirm connections with most regions that Luke mentions, even leaving aside the contemporary debate about North and South Galatia.) And if Luke felt free to invent Paul's successes, why would he not have made Paul's carefully designed speech in famous Athens more fruitful, culminating in the establishment of a local church there rather than just a handful of converts (Acts 17:34; cf. 1 Thess 3:1)?[151]

Novels use "recapitulations" and "recognition scenes,"[152] but so does Genesis, which (whatever its original function) was not construed as a novel by most first-

---

145. Schwartz, "Trial Scenes," 109, 117, also notes this contrast between Acts and Greek novels. Alexander, *Context*, 8, shows that there is little concrete overlap between the toponyms in Acts and those in select novels. Whereas novelists deliberately avoided Rome, Luke offers a more "realistic political landscape," and one in which (as in Paul's letters) Roman-named locations figure heavily (111). She suggests (114) that Luke, in fact, reverses the traditional Greek perspective; Syria and Phoenicia are home, but moving into the Aegean region is exploration; the only "barbarians" are in the West (Acts 28:2), and Athenians are called superstitious (17:22). Acts, like novels, lists more coastal locations than do Paul's letters (118); but Luke includes Paul's travels, and where he focuses on planted churches, he is much closer to Paul's own topography.

146. Schwartz, "Trial Scenes," 117; Aune, *Dictionary of Rhetoric*, 320.

147. Often novels moved throughout the Greco-Mediterranean world and beyond (cf. Konstan, "Invention," 13). Even what Luke says about the African court official, however, does not fit the "exotic" information found in novels (see Keener, "Official," challenging the suggestion in Pervo, *Dating Acts*, 32).

148. Lucian *True Story* 1.2. The philosophers in 1.4 probably include Plato.

149. Lucian *True Story* 1.3 (e.g., Ctesias on India). Ctesias was distinctively noteworthy for his inaccuracy; far from being a normal historian, his mixture of imagination was often disapproved (Brown, *Historians*, 77–78, 86).

150. That there were major (albeit small) Roman colonies there does not mean that these sites were familiar to Luke's audience; Greek literature celebrated Greece, Macedonia, Ionia, and the Aegean islands, but Lycaonia was much lesser known, and its towns are much rarer in contemporary literature. E.g., whereas merchants from some other Anatolian towns of comparable size were active even in Greece and Italy, few are attested from Pisidian Antioch (Levick, *Roman Colonies*, 101).

151. Moreover, Paul must have experienced some success in starting churches; his letters suggest this success no less than Acts (e.g., 1 Cor 4:15; Gal 2:20–3:2; 4:11–14; Phil 1:5, 30; 4:15–16; 1 Thess 1:5–9), although focusing more on subsequent issues in the life of these churches. Further, even if we lacked Paul's letters, the churches were founded in this period by someone, and this tradition would likely be known to them. Why could it not be Paul, who must have gotten his reputation as a church planter somewhere?

152. Smith, "Understand," 50.

century Jewish hearers. Plutarch's double biographies may shape the story to make it cohesive and may prefer traditions that offer parallels, but they do not simply create events from whole cloth the way that novels do.[153] Novels allude to previous narrative worlds; likewise Luke depends on the LXX,[154] but so did nearly all early Jewish works (most of which, as already suggested, regarded the biblical story as historical; see esp. Josephus's *Antiquities*, an apologetic history).

Pervo sees Acts as mostly "a series of escapades, from nearly all of which the leading characters escape great danger."[155] But does not our historical information reveal that Paul did consistently face and (except on the final occasion) survive dangers of this sort (1 Cor 4:11–13; 15:32; 16:9; 2 Cor 1:4–11; 2:14–16; 4:7–16; 6:4–10; 11:23–33)? (Paul's lists, in fact, suggest that Luke omitted many "exciting" stories to keep the action moving in a way relevant to his plot; note especially 2 Cor 11:23–27.)[156] One of the most striking escapes in Acts (Paul let down from the wall in a basket, Acts 9:23–25) is independently corroborated in Paul's writings (2 Cor 11:31–33)—and Luke does not even elaborate it in a detailed way.[157] Acts even lacks the usual fare of pirates and bandits (even though Paul indeed was at risk from them, 2 Cor 11:26).[158] (Moreover, my own limited experience with the "story" value of genuine historical encounters with danger predisposes me to be very skeptical of using elements such as suspense and action to ascertain historical content.)[159]

Nearly all the features that Pervo rightly associates with novels (such as rowdy mobs)[160] also appear in historical works, from which novels borrowed many of their motifs and dangers.[161] Likewise, sea storms and shipwrecks appear in historical and

153. See Keener, *John*, 9–10; see also ch. 16 below.

154. Smith, "Understand," 50.

155. Pervo, *Profit*, 18. Witherington, *Acts*, 379, points out that Acts, far from supporting a divine-man portrayal of Paul, explicitly refutes those who hold that view in the story world (Acts 14:15; for Peter, 10:26).

156. Thus, by contrast, Lentz, *Luke's Portrait*, 107, 169, emphasizing Luke's portrayal of Paul's status, thinks that Luke probably *suppressed* some of Paul's harsh treatments. Acts may include too many Pauline sufferings to sustain Lentz's thesis and surely contains too few to sustain Pervo's (cf. also Parsons, *Acts*, 320, against Haenchen, *Acts*, 113–14). Trompf, *Retributive Justice*, 89, strikes the right balance, noting Luke's approach in the larger context of the moral emphases of Hellenistic historiography.

157. There are some important differences (see this commentary's comment on the passage), but the substance of an escape down the wall in Damascus—the heart of the "escapade" element—remains the same.

158. Although robbers on land remained, the empire had generally suppressed pirates—a fact one would not readily gather from novels, which often relished depictions of piracy (Wallace and Williams, *World*, 28).

159. Because I wrote and told fictional stories before seeking to narrate popular but true ones, I had a sense of how to select, arrange, and recount in a more intriguing way, yet without changing facts or inventing information, the true stories of my wife's survival as a refugee in the Congolese forest, on the basis of her recollections and journals. (The popular liberties we have taken in telling the story include omitting our documentation [date references from her journal, in French] and slightly recasting speech [which usually was not recalled verbatim and often had to be translated anyway] in our own words, without altering the content of the story or speech.) But given the divergent generic markers, no one is likely to confuse my earlier recounting of fiction (had I published it) with my recounting of our genuine experiences.

160. Pervo, *Profit*, 105–8, lists "typical features" of novels (without noting their presence in historical works). Cf. Pervo, "Meet Right" (contrasting "good" church meetings with uncontrolled public mobs; see comment at Acts 15:25). Without arguing that novels are the only influence on Luke-Acts' genre, Ascough, "Technique," helpfully provides comparisons for Chariton's novelistic crowd scenes; but despite the organizing use of literary conventions (which could be shared with, or borrowed by, other genres), novels at many points reflected social reality, including about crowds (on which see Rapske, *Custody*, 121–23; comment on Acts 7:54–8:1a). Whereas Ascough finds few crowd scenes in ancient biography and a limited number in political historiography, one might expect more in a work focusing on public preaching (see ch. 8 below) and its reception.

161. See Porter, "'We' Passages," 552; Aune, *Environment*, 80; Witherington, *Acts*, 377–78. The romances typically do share with Acts travel, imprisonments, storms, shipwrecks, and trials, but they also have erotic romance and typically "kidnapping by pirates, enslavement," and "attempted seduction by powerful rivals" before the separated lover and beloved are finally reunited (Fusillo, "Novel," 838).

eyewitness reports as well as in novels (although novels certainly provided a model for their elaboration in ways that interested readers).[162] The supposed literary convention of sea voyages never existed as a specifically novelistic device.[163] (Further, no source shares all the parallels Pervo finds with Acts' shipwreck narrative, many of which parallels are simply required to tell about a shipwreck.)[164]

Some other features (such as "humor, wit, irony, and pathos")[165] reflect the pervasive use of rhetoric in both Acts and novels; Acts, however, includes lengthy speeches usually more characteristic of histories than of novels.[166] Further, entertaining elements do not control Luke's plot; as Sterling asks, "Was Acts intended to entertain or to inform in an entertaining way?"[167] (Some later novels[168] were employed for purposes of religious propaganda,[169] but this function was the exception for novels,[170] the primary function of which remained entertainment.)[171]

162. E.g., Lucian *Peregr.* 43. See detailed discussion in this commentary on Acts 27.

163. See, e.g., Porter, *Paul in Acts*, 18–24, including a critique of Robbins here. See more fully the discussion on Acts 27.

164. Porter, "'We' Passages," 552.

165. These are hardly limited to novels (where e.g., Fullmer, *Resurrection*, 45–46, gives helpful examples of irony). They appear, e.g., in Paul (cf., e.g., Linss, "Humor") and, more clearly, elsewhere in letters (Cic. *Att.* 9.25.2; Pliny *Ep.* 1.21.1–2; though cf. Malherbe, "Theorists," 17), rhetoric (Cic. *Brut.* 43.158; *Or. Brut.* 26.88–90; 40.138; Rabbie, "Wit and Humor"), Cynic attention-getting (Branham, "Humor"), philosophic reasoning (Fronto *Fer. als.* 3.5), forensic speeches (Cic. *Verr.* 2.5.10.25), public debate and satire (Xen. *Cyr.* 2.2.16; Cic. *Fin.* 4.26.73; *Brut.* 93.322; *De or.* 2.58.236; 2.61.251; Plato *Sophist* passim; Dio Chrys. *Or.* 31.9–10; Plut. *St. Poets* 4, *Mor.* 1058c; Apul. *Metam.* 3.4–6; Tert. *Apol.* 40.2), and hostile interpersonal exchanges (Ach. Tat. 6.12.1); more generally, Suet. *Vesp.* 23.1–4; Pliny *Ep.* 8.21.1; "Jokes." Cicero *Brut.* 292 traces the use of irony back to Socrates's dialogues in Plato, Xenophon, and Aeschines. For Jewish examples in the Greek language, see, e.g., Jos. *Life* 340; *Apion* 1.295 (though sarcasm also had a long history in Israelite tradition, e.g., 1 Kgs 18:27). For more nuanced and detailed pictures of ancient irony, see especially Duke, *Irony*, 8–12; O'Day, *Revelation*, 12–19; Anderson, *Glossary*, 39, 108. For the frequency of pathos in ancient historiography, see Marincola, "Audiences," 21–22.

166. Witherington, *Acts*, 377–78; see also Plümacher, "Mission Speeches," 251–66; idem, "Missionsreden"; idem, "Luke as Historian," 398; Horsley, "Speeches," 613; though cf. Pervo, "Direct Speech." Novels do include speeches; note the judicial speeches in novels in Fernández-Garrido, "Stasis-theory."

167. Sterling, *Historiography*, 320; also Aune, *Environment*, 79. For the primarily entertaining focus of novels, cf. also Penner, *Praise*, 6.

168. E.g., Apuleius's *Metamorphoses*; Flavius Philostratus's *Heroikos*. Contrast earlier works such as Petronius's *Satyricon*; this growing application of narrative may reflect interests sparked by the popular influence of Christian gospels and acts.

169. Apuleius later apparently adapted the novel format for religious propaganda (although see Murgatroyd, "Ending," and others noted below), but the content is still distinctly novelistic (and often tongue in cheek) rather than historical, the point at issue here (no one would have taken seriously first-person narration here as autobiographic, given the name and the obvious revision of a known tale earlier adapted also by Lucian). Historical works could also reflect distinctive ideological perspectives (see discussion below).

170. Apuleius and the apocryphal acts differ from typical ancient romances precisely in their rejection of this world and self-sufficiency (see Perkins, "World").

171. "Escapism" was a dominant function (Fusillo, "Novel," 838). Merkelbach, *Mysterium*, emphasizes the religious dimension of novels, but many scholars contest this; that dimension is likelier in apocryphal acts (e.g., Perkins, "World of *Acts of Peter*," 305). Some today doubt it even for Apuleius's *Metamorphoses* (reading it as parody; Hofmann, "Novels: Latin," 844; Murgatroyd, "Ending"), though I think it likely there (significantly later though the work is than Acts). Aretalogies (cited as a precursor in Merkelbach, "Novel and Aretalogy," 290) did not constitute a distinct genre with fixed literary characteristics (Aune, *Dictionary of Rhetoric*, 57). As Merkelbach notes, novels could be used for religious purposes (as for philosophic or other purposes), but (against earlier scholars) they were not coded mystery texts (Hofmann, "Novels: Latin," 844); they may reflect a social function analogous to that of the Mysteries in the same milieu, evoking the Greek past (van den Heever, "Novel," 111, 114). Edwards, "Reading" (esp. 33–34, 46), suggests that novels such as Chariton's provided religious instruction by emphasizing Aphrodite's activity, but I wonder if such deities did not often function as narrative devices, based on theological assumptions, more than as theological instruction per se. Antiquity (in contrast to modern secular approaches) pervasively assumed divine activity, and (as Chew, "Focalization," 55, observes) deities in novels serve a literary function of providing narrative order and sense to the events.

Acts includes many features of action and entertainment, which it shares with novels.[172] But Josephus's *Jewish War* and *Life* are also full of movement because of their focus on a war, and dramatic elements appear regularly in historical writers.[173] Whereas novels were intended primarily for entertainment,[174] historians believed that they could entertain without abandoning historical truth.[175] (It was novels that borrowed elements from history and other earlier genres, rather than the reverse.)[176] Thus Maximus of Tyre, though believing that philosophic lectures are the most entertaining pastime at banquets, also finds history pleasurable (Max. Tyre 22.5).[177] Likewise, the author of 2 Maccabees notes that he employed many possible sources but that his document was also written in such a way as to be enjoyed and easily remembered (2 Macc 2:24–25). And Tacitus apologizes that the period he covers offers less intriguing stories than histories of earlier Rome.[178] Although some historians were quite "austere" and others lavish with fantastic accounts, most historians believed that readers merited some relief from the serious material they studied;[179] readers found various forms of pleasure in histories, whether the pleasure of knowledge or that of being able to pity others' misfortunes.[180]

Pervo is right that the Gospels and Acts reveal coherent plots and hence may be examined in light of techniques learned from studying "other narrative works shaped by plot structures—that is, novels."[181] (Acts, with its movement toward Rome, indeed exhibits a more coherent plot than the more episodic narrative of many apocryphal acts.)[182] This observation does not, however, define genre; historians also sought to provide internally consistent narrative worlds[183] and cohesive narratives with their events connected logically.[184] It was such cohesive narrative that distinguished history

172. Pervo, *Profit*, passim. Pervo, *Mystery*, 56, rightly emphasizes the lively pace of popular narrative; this observation applies to Acts regardless of its genre.

173. See Sterling, *Historiography*, 320, wondering whom Polybius would have been critiquing "had Pervo's method been recognized in antiquity"; and Keener, *John*, 10, esp. n. 76. Though drama set rules for poetic narrative and rhetorical tradition for prose, they had some influence on each other (Scodel, "Drama and Rhetoric"). *All* works with any rhetorical sophistication should provide "pleasure" (Dion. Hal. *Demosth.* 47; cf. the goal of pleasure in Gorg. *Hel.* 5).

174. With, e.g., Talbert, *Gospel*, 17. Witherington, *Acts*, 378, is probably right to think that most readers of novels had more time for leisure whereas Luke's audience needed encouragement more than entertainment.

175. Fornara, *Nature of History*, 120–33; Palmer, "Monograph (1993)," 3, 29, citing, e.g., Cic. *Fam.* 5.12.5; Polyb. 1.4.11; 3.31.13; Aune, *Environment*, 80; idem, *Dictionary of Rhetoric*, 285; cf. also Dion. Hal. *Demosth.* 47; Plümacher, "Fiktion und Wunder"; Krasser, "Reading," 554 (though including Ps.-Callisthenes's *Alexander Romance* too readily in the history category); Penner, *Praise*, 147 (see esp. sources in n. 116); though cf. the claim in Polyb. 9.2.6. For biographies, see Burridge, *Gospels*, 149–51. One can write basically factual accounts in the entertaining style of fiction current in one's day (e.g., Sterling, *Sisters*, 78, on Harriet Brent Jacobs's style; cf. likewise Emily Chubbock Judson in Anderson, *Shore*, 453, 455, 466–67; Hunt, *History and Legacy*, 208, 239).

176. Aune, *Dictionary of Rhetoric*, 321.

177. Indeed, Lucian can write some satires placed in classical Athens rather than in his own day (e.g., Lucian *Tim.*; *Charon*) because, to many intellectuals, classical Athens was of greater interest than their own day (so, e.g., Harmon, "Introduction," 395).

178. Tac. *Ann.* 4.32–33 (lowering expectations, though he elsewhere includes the sorts of intriguing details he here ascribes to earlier historians). Tacitus warns that his *Annals* will not be pleasurable, but history generally was supposed to be pleasurable (Woodman, *Rhetoric*, 183).

179. Fornara, *Nature of History*, 121; on pleasure in history in general, see 120–33.

180. Ibid., 133–34, citing Cic. *Fam.* 5.12.4. Cf. Gorg. *Hel.* 9 on suffering in others' failures through poetry.

181. Pervo, *Story*, 11. Bonz, *Past as Legacy*, 21–22, rightly points to the importance of plot and literary unity in epic poetry as well.

182. See, e.g., Aune, *Dictionary of Rhetoric*, 3. This arrangement could, however, simply reflect Luke's literary skill exceeding that of some of his imitators.

183. See Stibbe, *Gospel*, 32–34. Any travel narrative could use geographic movement to advance the plot (cf. Alexander, *Context*, 70–75).

184. Penner, *Praise*, 151, citing Polyb. 3.31.7–13. Cohesiveness is important in ancient Israelite historiography (Konkel, *Kings*, 30), which naturally would provide Luke with a model. Such concern for causal

from mere annals.[185] Luke-Acts, like Plutarch's parallel lives, is full of narrative connections among its main characters (see ch. 16 below); but Luke, again something like Plutarch, is constrained to some degree (indeed, as argued later in this commentary, to a significant degree in Luke's case) by his sources (see chs. 6–7 below). Thus, for example, neither Peter nor Paul faces a test by Satan exactly like that of Jesus (Luke 4:2–12), although both face tests (cf. 22:31–34; Acts 5:9) and encounter Satan's agents (Acts 5:3; 13:10). The end of Acts may bear slight resemblance to Jesus's passion,[186] but not to the degree an explicit death and resurrection would.

Beyond general cohesiveness, large historical works might also display something like a plot or at least an overarching unity around cohesive themes (such as a nation's providential greatness).[187] More relevant to Acts, literary unity and specific emphases characterize historical works on particular subjects, such as Quintus Curtius's *History of Alexander* and historical monographs (on which see the discussion in ch. 3 below.) Educated historians were most often trained primarily in rhetoric,[188] and readers expected cohesive narratives from them. Lucian and some other rhetoricians articulated rules about continuity in historical accounts, and Luke's earlier account fits these rules.[189] A single-volume historical monograph could achieve such unity and plot development more easily than could a multivolume history of Rome such as Livy's, although even such histories have driving theses (such as Rome's destiny).[190] The influence of popular biography would increase even more the expectation of plot unity. The popular level of Luke's work (where the literary insights of Pervo and others prove helpful) may allow for more plot cohesiveness than we expect in most extant biographies or histories, but literary connections appear even in such works (see our introduction, ch. 16).

d. Perspectives and Biases in Historiography

Whereas Pervo dismisses as inappropriate to histories Luke's perspective on "providence,"[191] it was an issue of intellectual discussion, not mere comic entertainment, in antiquity. David Balch notes that "the influential Stoic Posidonius" treated it as "a serious philosophical issue, argued with precisely the terminology found in

---

connections is also common to modern historiography. Suetonius even structures his biographies in ways that connect them (see, e.g., Power, "Galba").

185. Penner, *Praise*, 185. Penner compares (185–86, 218) this feature to plot in Arist. *Poet*. 1459a, though he notes that Aristotle distinguished history as more disjunctive (Bonz, *Past as Legacy*, 21, emphasizes Aristotle's distinctions more heavily). In Tacitus and others, history does tend to be more disjunctive than in novels, but even there persons, nations, and agendas provide connections. Cic. *Fam*. 5.12.5 complains that mere recital of events chronologically reads like "an almanac" (LCL p. 161).

186. Recounting Paul's Roman custody, which is surely historical (e.g., Phil 1:13), and a shipwreck, about the historicity of which scholars lack consensus but which cannot simply be dismissed a priori as fictitious, since shipwrecks were sufficiently frequent that Paul had already suffered them on three other occasions (2 Cor 11:25).

187. E.g., Dion. Hal. *Ant. rom*. Note also the overarching plot in Josephus *Antiquities*. The language of "plot" admittedly seems less appropriate for a history than more simply speaking of a "story" (see Schnabel, "Reading Acts," 265); cf. the concerns in Davidson, "Polybius," 136, about reading too much narrative unity into Polybius; and Aristotle's preference for the plot and narrative connections characteristic of drama rather than history (Butcher, *Theory*, 164–65), though historiography developed rhetorically beyond the form in which Aristotle knew it. Already by the time of Thucydides, however, some historical writing had plot and other discernible literary elements; see, e.g., Finley, *Thucydides*, 302–3.

188. With, e.g., Aune, *Dictionary of Rhetoric*, 218 (s.v. "Historiography," 215–18).

189. See Betori, "Strutturazione"; Dupont, "Question du plan." Polybius also advocated continuity through the chain of causes (Polyb. 3.32.2).

190. Josephus also accepts Rome's (divine) destiny, but despite loyalty to his Flavian patrons, he is more attached to his own people (see Stern, "Josephus and Empire," 78).

191. Pervo, *Profit*, 83, 123, 129.

Acts. Luke's work engages the discussion; does divine providence favor the 'growth' of the Roman empire or the 'growth of the word' of the gospel?"[192] Historians such as Dionysius of Halicarnassus and Josephus highlighted what they believed to be divine providence in history (see the discussion in ch. 5, sect. 1.f below); the topic, in fact, belonged more to ancient historiography than to ancient novels. (Chapter 5 below will treat the question of historians' *Tendenz* more fully.)

Pervo complains that Luke often ridicules his opponents by how he portrays them, noting that "this is popular theology at its most primitive level."[193] This complaint faults Luke, however, for not being more charitable to those he perceives as persecutors. Granted, some ancient historians, like most modern ones, expected their colleagues to be as evenhanded as possible; for example, one writer complains that Thucydides focuses on Athens's failings because it exiled him.[194] Ancient historians often provided antagonists who were round characters,[195] reporting, for instance, fears and motives on both sides of a conflict (to increase suspense, praise for the victor, and tragic pathos).[196] Such rounding, however, was often a dramatic technique (and often itself entailed imaginative reconstruction) and not itself necessary for a work to fit the genre of history.[197]

However impolite it might seem to educated moderns, ancient rhetors regularly employed wit, including jokes at opponents' expense;[198] the only limitation was that of dignity (rather narrowly defined)—of keeping wit from becoming ridicule, for example, at another's suffering.[199] Given the overlap between rhetoric and historical writing, those who wrote about opponents closer to their own period might include more rhetorical hostility, especially if they felt they had reason to do so. Tacitus is certainly not friendly toward Domitian, nor is Polybius toward his historiographic rival Timaeus,[200] but this does not mean that Tacitus or Polybius was writing a novel. Paul's writings reveal much genuine conflict in a period when Christians were those being persecuted (cf. Rom 15:31; 1 Cor 16:9; 2 Cor 1:8–10; 1 Thess 2:14–16; 2 Thess 3:2), and the conflict indeed seems fresher in Paul than in Luke.[201] Some scholars do

192. Balch, "Genre," 10–11.

193. Pervo, *Profit*, 64. In *Acts*, 18, he complains that Luke impugns the opposition's motives as jealousy, but this exact concern appears in other ancient biographers and historians (e.g., Corn. Nep. 14 [Datames], 5.2; 23 [Hannibal], 1.2; Vell. Paterc. 2.40.4; 2.47.2; Tac. *Ann.* 16.18) and was a common feature of ancient urban Mediterranean agonistic culture (see comment on Acts 5:17). For Livy's attribution of motives (in Livy 40.21–22), see Jaeger, "Fog," 397, 401.

194. Dion. Hal. *Pomp.* 3 (contrasting Herodotus's fairness). Polybius (who is usually evenhanded) condemned civic partisanship that could lead to misrepresentation (Polyb. 16.14.3–8); others also demanded evenhanded avoidance of malice and flattery (Dion. Hal. *Thuc.* 8), condemning one who ignored diverse sources to consistently present the least favorable interpretation (Plut. *Mal. Hdt.* 3–7, *Mor.* 855C–856B). One might even avoid including reports about friends to avoid charges of bias (Philost. *Vit. soph.* 2.33.628, who usually includes both strengths and weaknesses of each person he treats).

195. Cf. comments in Keener, *John*, 216.

196. E.g., Dion. Hal. *Ant. rom.* 3 (concerning the Roman conflict with the Albans). Often we may well wonder how the historian *knows* motives (e.g., Vell. Paterc. 2.35.2; 2.48.4), since historians, unlike poets, could not claim omniscience.

197. Polyb. 2.56.10 condemns Phylarchus for imaginatively reconstructing his characters' words (though Polybius certainly does some of this himself).

198. E.g., Cic. *Brut.* 93.322; *Or. Brut.* 40.138–39; cf. *Fam.* 7.32.1–3; Plut. *Cic.* 5.4; 27.1; 38.2–6; *Demosth.* 11.4; Philost. *Hrk.* 33.8.

199. E.g., Cic. *Brut.* 43.158; *Or. Brut.* 26.88–90.

200. Claims to be free from bias in reporting recent events may respond to the patronage system (Jos. *Ant.* 20.154–55; also Witherington, *Acts*, 49, listing as recent-event claims Tac. *Ann.* 1.1.3; Lucian *Hist.* 41.1; Polyb. 12.12.1–3), but these were not claims of *neutrality*, which was not demanded (Witherington, *Acts*, 50).

201. That neither Paul nor Luke explicitly guarded his language to prevent misappropriation of his text in a dominant Christian setting is unfortunate, but to expect this of them is anachronistic.

debate Luke's fairness in the way he writes about Judaism (see discussion in ch. 14 below). For the present issue, however, it suffices to point out that even when a writer could be charged with bias for portraying negatively those regarded as opponents, this charge did not transform the genre of the work from history to novel.

Finally, Luke presents a more rounded picture of various groups of Jews and Roman officials than Pervo's generalization about Luke's negative characterization of these groups suggests (see chs. 13 and 14 below).

e. Historiography, Inference, and Mistakes?

Ancient historiography at times included varying degrees of inference. Rhetorical tastes demanded a complete narrative and so sometimes invited historical reconstructions and hypothetical amplifications on points for which evidence was missing (e.g., the details of a speech given on some occasion). One could develop existing data into a scene based on inferences about probability and verisimilitude.

But excessive use of such amplification was deemed to violate the canons of historiography,[202] and developing a mere fiction to entertain one's readers was judged "culpable" even by ancient historical standards.[203] Ancient historical scenes' details may contain some elements that modern historians would consider fictitious,[204] but the genre of ancient historiography is a far cry from that of ancient novels, even the rarer "historical" novels.[205] Large-scale fictionalization in narratives with historical flavor was limited primarily to "fantastic tales, Homeric revisionism, tragic or romantic novels, and comic or satiric novels."[206] As already argued, none of these categories is easily confused with historical monographs, including Acts.[207]

Most scholars believe that Luke made some historical mistakes (the most often cited and persuasive cases are Luke 2:2, in the much earlier reign of Herod I,[208] and Acts 5:36–37,[209] although a minority of scholars offer arguments debating even these examples[210]). Yet such mistakes or deliberate embellishments would hardly make his

---

202. Fornara, *Nature of History*, 134–35.

203. Ibid., 136.

204. Although Luke sometimes indulges in reporting characters' thoughts (Acts 19:21; but cf. Rom 15:23–25, 31–32), we have relatively few examples, perhaps fewer proportionately than even some relatively careful, elite ancient historians (e.g., Tac. *Hist.* 2.74; *Ann.* 4.38, 39; 12.4). Cultural standards affect the definitions of genres; thus Romantics, loving poetry, tended to write prose with a higher concern for affective effects than for accuracy (Bebbington, *Dominance*, 162).

205. "Fictional amplifications" are standard fare in Ps.-Callisth. *Alex.*, e.g., 1.23 (Dowden's note in *Collected Novels*, 669n18); but this work is more historical novel than embellished history, and the ambiguity of its generic characterization is rare in comparison with works clearly identifiable as nonhistorical novels or histories focused on narrating historical events.

206. Bowersock, *Fiction as History*, 21. He argues that these works became popular especially in Nero's time (22) and may have been modeled on Christian "fabulous stories" (such as the resurrection) circulating at that time (27, 143). Whereas most NT scholars underestimate apostolic influence on the mid-first-century Roman world, Bowersock may credit it with too much.

207. Those who relate Acts to "fantastic tales" think primarily of its signs and wonders (though even Tacitus has some of these; but see ch. 9 below on "signs"), but fantastic tales usually refer to unnatural phenomena encountered in exotic (and unverifiable) geographic extremities (cf., e.g., Pliny E. *N.H.* 7.2.22–34)—quite in contrast with the geographic verisimilitude of Acts. Cf. also collections of unbelievable phenomena (see Rusten, "Paradoxographers").

208. Noted, e.g., by Hengel and Schwemer, *Between Damascus and Antioch*, 326–27; deSilva, *Introduction*, 369; Conzelmann, *History*, 30. Wiseman, "Decree," thinks that Luke's decree applied only to Roman citizens in 6 C.E. Luke may simply associate his event with a notable one from roughly the same period (cf. Reicke, *Era*, 135–36; Kodell, *Luke*, 19).

209. E.g., deSilva, *Introduction*, 375. Witherington, *Acts*, allows for the possibility of a mistake here, though offering alternative proposals (88, 238–39).

210. For scholars supporting Luke's accuracy in Luke 2:2, see, e.g., Ramsay, *Bethlehem*, x, 107–96 passim; Robertson, *Luke*, 118ff.; Bock, *Luke*, 903–9 (providing also a helpful survey of proposals, as also in Porter,

work fiction.²¹¹ Even if Luke was wrong on every point where a plausible case can be made that he was wrong (an unlikely premise, since in many or even most proposed cases, excepting the strongest obvious ones, a more plausible argument can be made that he was right), he would prove little different from Josephus in this regard, and Josephus was writing ancient historiography, not novels.

Indeed, more than Luke where he adapts Mark, biblical stories in Josephus's *Antiquities* differ from Josephus's source in Scripture at many points (and he did not seem to mind anyone noticing these obvious departures, by which he displayed his rhetorical talent). Yet we do not for this reason presume that Josephus was writing a novel, because we understand that his approach lay within the bounds of ancient historiography. Nor do we dismiss Josephus's value for reconstructing history and resort to historical agnosticism because we cannot be certain regarding his every claim. Despite his rhetorical flourishes, we can still reconstruct much of the outline and substance of the biblical record (though rarely the wording) from Josephus. In view of such comparisons, treating Acts as a pure novel and consequently inferring that early Christian history is completely unknown (and hence available for any speculation by which NT scholars might wish to reconstruct it) run the risk of appearing historically irresponsible.

The most trusted of ancient scholars sometimes misstate themselves on some points—for example, the encyclopedic²¹² elder Pliny, who schedules the Isthmian Games every four years (instead of two, *N.H.* 4.5.18), and his nephew the younger Pliny, who apparently confuses Prusias ad Mare with Prusa (*Ep.* 10.58.5; 10.81.6). As matters stand, however (and as argued more fully below, in chs. 6–7), Luke's historical accuracy fares sufficiently well compared with that of other historians of his era (and, for that matter, with modern historians and NT scholars, who also make our share of inadvertent mistakes).

Almost no one simply dismisses the ancient historians, on whose reports we largely depend for the events they treat, when they conflict on matters of detail (e.g., Tacitus and Josephus differ on some matters of fact that should have been clear, such as Felix's full name).²¹³ But even substantial historical inaccuracies would not make a writer

"Census," 167–72); Thompson, *Archaeology*, 376–77; Bruce, *Documents*, 115; Hayles, "Correct" (esp. part 2); Stuart, "Textual Criticism," 114 (due to faulty transmission of the name); Compton, "Census." Some translate πρῶτος as "before" (Turner, *Insights*, 23–24 [also cited in Sheler, *True*, 197]; Marshall, *Luke*, 104), an approach not decisive grammatically but nevertheless plausible (Porter, "Census," 173–76, 188). Some suggest that this was the "first census" under Quirinius, as opposed to the later one in 6 C.E. (Brindle, "Census"; Thorley, "Census"; Haacker, "Erst"), and his earlier post—whether he yet held his later title—may well have been in Syria (Ramsay, *Bethlehem*, 227–46; idem, *Discovery*, 238–300; cf. Danker, *New Age*, 23–24); yet many find it hard to date Quirinius's earlier possibly Syrian office to fit Luke (Stern, "Province," 373; cf. Porter, "Census," 172–73). The external data do more easily support other aspects of Luke's narrative (see esp. Porter, "Census," 187–88); even counting back from 6 C.E. by fourteen-year tax cycles (Ramsay, *Bethlehem*, 131; O'Rourke, "Law," 183; possibly seven-year cycles in this period, Bagnall, "Beginnings") might fit the time of Mary's pregnancy. Some cite micrographic evidence for Quirinius's being governor throughout the period (Finegan, *Apostles*, 5), though his arrival sounds later in Jos. *Ant.* 18.1 (perhaps since this is where Josephus will stress his role?) and current arguments based on claims of micrographic evidence are open to considerable debate. For approaches to Luke's literary purpose, see, e.g., Smith, "Caesar's Decree."

211. As often observed, e.g., Walaskay, *Acts*, 11; Marguerat, *Histoire*, 19–20, 25; idem, *Historian*, 12–13. For a comparison of dramatic episodes in Acts with those in Livy, Cleitarchus, Duris (Douris) of Samos, and Curtius Rufus, see Plümacher, *Lukas*, 80–136.

212. I employ the term in a modern way, not as an interpretation of his description of his work (see discussion in Doody, "Natural History").

213. See comment on Acts 23:24. Vell. Paterc. 2.53.4 criticizes predecessors for being five years off on Pompey's age—precisely because he wants to forestall criticism of himself erring on this minor detail. McGrew, "Argument," 598, notes that ancient historians differed over the number of Xerxes's troops when he

with historical intention a novelist, just a poor historian.[214] Those who (generally on a popular level) dismiss a writer's accuracy wholesale when they can provide clear evidence against only a small number of points, like those who refuse to acknowledge the existence of any evidence that could challenge their support of a document's reliability, may indulge in an all-or-nothing approach readily suited to vulgar and vitriolic forms of polemical religious discourse but inappropriate for the more sober evaluations expected in historiographic investigation.

The ancients recognized that differences between factual and fictional discourse should exist, even when elements of one might intrude in a work more characterized by the other. When Lucian parodies and lampoons those who claim their fiction to be true, he complains, "What did surprise me was their supposition that nobody would notice they were lying."[215] Nor would anyone mistake his parody for fact (or link incredible reports in historians, e.g., lists of portents, with such parody).[216] In *A True Story* Lucian reports that the people on the moon (1.11) tried to colonize the morning star, provoking war with the sun people (1.12).[217] He describes spiders larger than islands (1.15), mushrooms used as shields (1.16), and hands tied by spiderwebs (1.18). All moon people are male, being wives before age twenty-five and husbands thereafter; they bear children dead from their leg calves but hold them up to the wind with open mouths to bring them to life (1.22). Because they drink only air, they do not need to relieve themselves (1.23); they wear glass clothing and insert their eyes only when they need to see (1.25). Another city, in the air, has lamps loitering about (1.29).

Nor are these all of Lucian's fabulous adventures. A ship, swallowed by a whale (1.30), finds a land of hills and forests (1.31, 34) as well as hostile tribes of men-crabs and other composite creatures (1.35–36), which the heroes decimate (1.38–39). By starting a forest fire, they manage to kill the whale in thirteen days (2.1), then sail from its mouth, camp three days on top of it, and dig a cave in the frozen sea (2.2). Afterward they slide the boat across the ice as if sailing (2.2), discovering a sea of milk (2.3). In the place of the dead (2.10), they witness a war between the damned and the blessed (2.23), and punishment for a boy having an affair with Helen (2.25–26); later Odysseus secures hospitality for the travelers with Calypso (2.35). If some scholars have been inclined to appeal to *A True Story* to argue for fantastic narratives written as if true, they should instead recognize that Acts does not belong even to the sort of work that Lucian parodies.

Many experts would agree with the cautiously worded appraisal of Christopher Tuckett: "Luke is at times remarkably accurate in some of the details he records of the cities of the Empire," yet makes mistakes regarding Quirinius's chronology and some other details (e.g., when compared with Paul's letters).[218] Yet it is unfair to demand perfect accuracy of Luke or any other historian, and certainly not one in antiquity; given the passage of time between the events and Luke's narration of them, "almost

---

invaded Greece; the number of troops in the battle of Pharsalia (Caesar and Florus differ by 150,000); and other details, but no one denies that these events occurred.

214. Porter, *Paul in Acts*, 16–17.

215. Lucian *True Story* 1.4 (Reardon, 621).

216. Readers could generally recognize such fictitious work (see Ní-Mheallaigh, "Pseudo-Documentarism"). Some elements that Lucian parodies are more credible than others; e.g., Lucian's "malleable glass" (ὑαλίνη) clothing on the Moon (*True Story* 1.25) "is a punning parody on wooden clothing (ξυλίνη), *i.e.* cotton (Herod. 7, 65)" (A. M. Harmon, in *Lucian*, LCL, 1:279n1). But most of it is fantastic even before the parody.

217. The voyagers later stop at the morning star, which is being colonized (Lucian *True Story* 1.28). Inhabitants of comets, naturally, prefer long hair (1.23).

218. Tuckett, *Luke*, 30.

certainly Luke was striving for accuracy at this level; and almost certainly he may not have achieved perfection." Tuckett thus regards it as "scarcely surprising that one or two details have been accidentally confused" or that "he may have had a slightly less than perfect grasp of the relative chronology of" Quirinius and others.[219] Even if many would count up more mistakes (and some others would prefer fewer) than in this wording, probably most scholars would agree with the basic point: arguments for inaccuracy on some points do not require us to doubt Luke's historical purpose or his work's historical genre.

f. More Serious Flaws in the Comparison of Acts to Novels

Romances (one of the best-attested and most indisputable forms of ancient novels) focused on two lovers who persevered in faithfulness, with eros playing a leading role[220]—a story line that plainly contains no similarity to that of Acts.[221] This plotline appears even in apocryphal acts;[222] if Pervo claims that he appeals to less generically distinctive, nonromantic historical novels, he cannot rest much of his genre argument on comparisons with the later apocryphal gospels and acts. Other ancient novels also involved a private individual, perhaps mimicking biography but not history, whereas Acts shifts from Peter to Paul.[223] When novels did pose as history, they were nevertheless almost completely fictitious—which is incompatible with the numerous connections with extrinsic history found in Acts (see chs. 6 and 7 below). Despite its positive conclusion, Acts does not conclude with a full and happy resolution or final reunion as in most ancient novels (or even a grisly one as in *Acts of Peter*). Many characteristics of Acts can fit ancient novels (and, in nearly all these cases, other genres as well), but in the end too many standard features of novels are missing in Acts.[224]

Pervo's critics rightly complain that he too readily dismisses the argument based on Luke's historical prologue, a feature not found in novels, that Luke's work is history.[225]

219. Ibid., 30.

220. For this plot commonality, see, e.g., Fusillo, "Novel," 838–39; Konstan, "*Apollonius* and Novel," 173; see further this emphasis in Konstan, *Symmetry*. Fullmer, *Resurrection*, 50–54, rightly and helpfully emphasizes that not all ancient fictitious literature was strictly romance, but he defines almost any fictitious work as a novel (applying the label according to relation to extrinsic reality rather than a readily identifiable literary form), including testaments (a distinctly Jewish genre not closely related to Acts as a whole), and some forms attested only much later or earlier. Yet as we shall argue in chs. 6–7, Acts (which is not Fullmer's own subject) bears a quite different relation to extrinsic reality. He also includes some material in Josephus whose fictitious character is open to question; some of his novels also include romance elements besides those he so identifies.

221. Pervo, "Direct Speech," 294, recognizes the dissimilarity in content, while arguing for similarity "in the means of exposition," where the case is much more plausible. On 302 he notes that "no one has ever argued that Acts is an 'erotic novel.'" No analogy is exact, so it is valuable to explore the points at which Pervo intends the comparison with novels.

222. Even apocryphal acts and gospels often follow a romance story line, except that the women become devotees of the male teacher in chastity, devoted not to sexual love but to God's word (e.g., *Acts of Paul and Thecla* passim and *Acts John* 53–64, 73–80). Luke-Acts has nothing comparable (the brief treatment of Lydia hardly fills the same kind of role in Acts 16:14–15, and Luke does not develop his mention of women followers in Luke 8:2–3). The contrast is often noted (e.g., Eddy and Boyd, *Legend*, 338–39).

223. Balch, "Genre," 11, offers the same contrast: novels focused on individuals, but "ancient history," by contrast, "narrated social and political events, as does Luke-Acts."

224. Witherington, *Acts*, 377; Schierling and Schierling, "Influence of Romances." Liefeld, *Acts*, 15, notes that Acts, though a historical work, includes most features found in novels but lacks a heroine.

225. Porter, "'We' Passages," 550; Aune, *Environment*, 80; idem, *Dictionary of Rhetoric*, 285; Witherington, *Acts*, 381; see Callan, "Preface and Historiography"; van Unnik, "Once More Prologue"; Eddy and Boyd, *Legend*, 339. Granted, Alexander has argued that the prologue would not by itself identify Luke-Acts with history as opposed to ethnography or even a scientific treatise ("Formal Elements," 23; idem, "Luke's Preface")—though virtually no one argues, including Alexander, that the *content* of Luke-Acts is a scientific

Such prefaces fit many genres, Pervo argues, including medical writings, and prefaces also appear in novels.[226] The specific examples he cites, however, do not make his point; most are in works whose genre is obvious with or without a prologue—for example, a conspicuous parody on history (Lucian's *True Story*). In at least one case (Longus proem 1–2), the preface does not claim that the work is historical;[227] it can be read as explaining why the writer made the story up. Such prologues, which could not be mistaken for historical,[228] hardly serve the same function as Luke's (Luke 1:1–4; Acts 1:1), which mention sources (Luke 1:1–2), investigation or knowledge (1:3), and confirmation of shared information (1:4). The issue is not whether a work has a preface but whether a work has a preface indicating factual content (with no markers of parody somewhere to subvert it).

More telling, although Pervo's comparison of Luke's Acts with later apocryphal acts is critical to his argument, these later acts probably adapt the genre of Luke's Acts as their paradigm whereas the reverse is chronologically impossible.[229] In contrast to Luke's Acts, the apocryphal acts date from the period of the heyday of the Greek romances.[230] At least some of them, most obviously the *Acts of Paul*, appear dependent in content on Luke's Acts.[231] Just as later apocryphal gospels diverge further from Palestinian and Semitic traits in the early strata of the Jesus tradition, so these apocryphal acts often diverge much further from the undisputed epistles' portrait of Paul than Luke's Acts does.[232] As Stanley Porter points out, Pervo's appeal to later

---

treatise. But the language from technical treatises *does* suggest a claim to accurate handling of the tradition (idem, "Formal Elements," 24).

226. Pervo, *Profit*, 5, 144. Prefaces occasionally appear in fictitious works that pretend to be historical (e.g., *Let. Aris.* 1–8, though nothing in that proem specifically suggests the work's historical character). For one broad survey of classical parallels to Luke's preface, see Talbert, *Reading Luke*, 7–11.

227. Longus might contrast his approach with Thucydides (cf. Thucyd. 3.37–48; Cueva, "Longus and Thucydides"; Trzaskoma, "Novelist Writing 'History'"; engaging "intertextually" with Thucydides, Morgan, "Fiction," 555).

228. With Konstan, "Invention," 6, who emphasizes that Longus's work is mainly nonreferential, like other novels.

229. Bauckham, "Acts of Paul"; Witherington, *Acts*, 335n31; Bowersock, *Fiction as History*, 139n43; Cerro, "Hechos"; Aune, *Dictionary of Rhetoric*, 3. The apocryphal acts may be directed toward a more popular audience and are of lower literary quality (Conzelmann, *Acts*, xlii); still, for specific rhetorical techniques in their speeches (which are important in the romances [Hock, "Rhetoric of Romance"]; the romances may have often assumed education [Bowie, "Readership," 452–53; Stephens, "Who Read Novels?," 415]), cf. Pervo, "Rhetoric in Apocrypha," esp. 805. One should note that Pervo dates Luke's Acts to the second century; see ch. 10 below.

230. See Aune, *Dictionary of Rhetoric*, 322. Perhaps the apocryphal acts originated partly from Christians' reading romances through Christian lenses and seeing what they could make use of (see Price, "Evolution of Genres").

231. Aune, *Dictionary of Rhetoric*, 10. Pervo, "Hard Act," sees *Acts of Paul* not as a sequel to Luke-Acts (against Bauckham, "Acts of Paul") but as an attempt to correct it; clearly, it rewrites some of Acts' narratives, but this may be hagiographic development rather than rejection (see Marguerat, "Héritage"; idem, "Acts of Paul"; idem, "Actes de Paul"; cf. idem, *Histoire*, 369–91). Although some scholars think *Acts of Paul* dependent only on Galatians (Rordorf, "Conversion," 142–43, highlighting Acts' details missing in the later work), most have argued otherwise (e.g., Hills, "Acts and *Acts*"; Pervo, "Hard Act"; Bauckham, "Acts of Paul"; idem, "Sequel"; cf. Hills, "*Acts of Paul*"), especially regarding imitation of Acts' perceived primary subject (not so much its content). Bovon, "Reception," 69, contends that authors of the apocryphal acts are independent of Luke's Acts, but allows that they "may have known" it. (Cf. Elliott, "Apocrypha," 683, on NT apocrypha in general: they often imitate our first-century sources "and in most cases are imaginative writings intended to amplify the first-century events.") The particular dating of the post-Lukan acts is more problematic; their relative sequence also occasions debate (e.g., MacDonald, "Relationships," 40; Pervo, "Egging," 55; Stoops, "*Acts of Peter*," 83–84). Thomas, "Canon and Antitype," even suggests that the earliest version of *Acts of Peter* lacked direct literary dependence on now-canonical texts, and he attributes signs of dependence to a final redactor; but prehistories of extant documents tend to prove speculative. Gounelle, "État de la recherche," thinks that the eventual title of Luke's Acts may have polemicized against some of the second-century acts.

232. On Paul in the apocryphal acts, see Michaels, "Paul in Tradition," esp. 692–94. On Paul and Luke's Acts, see ch. 7 below.

"texts that are self-evidently derivative in order to assess the primary source" is "circular and anachronistic."[233]

Further, Acts more closely resembles historical monographs than it does the later fictitious apostolic acts.[234] Adolf von Harnack, a noted student of the early Christian sources, concluded after his study of Acts, "The Acts is *an historical work* that has nothing in common with the later 'Acts of the Apostles,' and is not to be judged by the standard nor criticised by the method which suits these."[235] Acts contains little hagiography compared with the later stories.[236] Luke does not substantially embroider his portrait of OT characters (see comment on Acts 7:20–22, the closest possibility) or Jesus (by elaborating Markan narratives in any typical haggadic manner), and so we have little reason to expect this approach in Acts.[237] Perhaps no less tellingly, as noted above, Acts lacks the romance theme, which provides the undercurrent for the later acts (despite their emphasis on celibacy, their understanding of chastity evokes contemporary romances).[238]

A leading Roman historian indeed argues that even the new novelistic form developed in *imitation* of the popular work Acts.[239] (If this thesis is true, it might not shed light on Acts except to suggest that ancients found its style of narration sufficiently exciting to imitate.) This proposal may be questioned, as at least a form of novel predates Luke.[240] Still, as a rule, novels were certainly more popular after rather than before Luke's time[241] (especially if Chariton's romance belongs after the mid-first century).[242] Many novels allude to customs from the second century C.E. or later, and they seem to cluster especially in the late second and early third centuries.[243] Even if all the novels existed in the first century C.E., however, they would have offered a somewhat less ready model for Luke than historiography did. Despite its length and price, the ancients apparently owned copies of Herodotus's history (predating Luke

233. Porter, "'We' Passages," 551; also Porter, *Paul in Acts*, 17. Eddy and Boyd, *Legend*, 339, also note that real early Christian audiences did not treat Luke's Acts like, e.g., *Acts of Paul* (citing here Dawsey, "Folk-Epic," 318).

234. See Hengel, *Acts and History*, 60.

235. Harnack, *Acts*, 272.

236. Aune, *Dictionary of Rhetoric*, 3 (on "stereotypical holy men"); Marguerat, *Histoire*, 62–63; cf. Allison, *Jesus*, 447–48. Gibert, "Invention," earlier supposed Luke the inventor of the hagiographic genre—with the same problem of anachronistic circularity.

237. For a survey of such haggadic techniques in early Jewish texts, see Keener, *John*, 27–28. Milikowsky, "Midrash," suggests that the rabbis themselves recognized that midrashic additions were homiletic, distinct from historical reconstructions.

238. See Hofmann, "Novels: Christian," 847–48; cf. Aubin, "Reversing Romance," 260–62 (noting the subversion of conventional gender assumptions); Thomas, "Fluidity," 277.

239. Bowersock, *Fiction as History*, 124, 139, 143 (citing especially the later appraisals of Origen and Celsus). It is not clear, however, how widely circulated Acts was in the first century. Even Bowersock's larger thesis that the gospel story led to novels as a genre fails to reckon with earlier novelistic works, "but the later ideal romances may well have drunk from the Christian spring for some of their inspiration" (Thomas, "Fluidity," 277). Tacitus and probably Suetonius do attest that the Christian story was a subject of public discussion in Claudian and Neronian Rome (Reimer, "Biography," 308), and Chariton's *"early dawn discovery of an empty tomb in which the stone has been rolled away"* (309, emphasis Reimer's) is too close to Mark's earlier story line for coincidence.

240. At least the *Ninus Romance*, now incomplete, is probably earlier (dated from ca. 100 B.C.E. to 50 C.E.; see Bowie, "Novel," 1049), but this source is less developed than the members of the genre on which Bowersock focuses. One may also cite the Roman author Petronius's *Satyricon* (mid-first century C.E., featuring homosexual romance) or Judith as moving in the direction of later romances. Jewish writers produced various fictions, such as Aristeas (Hadas, *Aristeas*, 54, doubts that its first readers would have understood it otherwise; the later historian Josephus, however, apparently did think otherwise, Jos. *Ant.* 12.100; *Ag. Ap.* 2.46–47) and *Joseph and Aseneth* (of uncertain date).

241. Witherington, *Acts*, 378, thinks novels became more frequent in the Second Sophistic than in the early empire.

242. So Bowie, "Readership," 442.

243. Ibid., 443; Stephens, "Who Read Novels?," 414.

by many centuries) as often as all novels (from all periods) put together, and they owned Thucydides (also predating Luke by many centuries) nearly twice as often as these novels.[244]

Even more important from the standpoint of genre, there is simply too much history in Acts to discount (see chs. 6 and 7 below); history is not characteristic of the vast majority of novels.[245] Novels might correctly present details of geography and local culture, but only very rarely were they as sensitive to historical details (and then not consistently).[246] One may dispute differences of detail when comparing Paul's letters with Acts, but the substantial overlap between the two sources is difficult to deny. For example, with the debated exception of Galatians,[247] Paul's letters coincide with where Acts reveals that he started churches; the chronology and itinerary coincide in the vast majority of details.[248] And Acts provides the correct titles and names (Gallio, Felix, Festus) for local officials in the appropriate years (see the commentary ad loc.).

Few novels would care to include so much accurate historical information; novels, in fact, generally reflected the milieu of their readership more than that of their characters.[249] David Konstan, a scholar who (like Pervo) has published much on ancient novels, notes, "History differs from fiction in that it is *about* what really happens or has happened, even if at times, or perhaps in the main, it gets things wrong. Herodotus may of course have been mistaken about events in the Persian War; the point is that there is something for him to have been mistaken about." Novels, by contrast, were largely nonreferential.[250] When Pervo argues that Acts was an ancient novel based on elements that some deem inaccurate, he does so by contrasting such novels with history, but his critics charge that, in so doing, he uses modern definitions of "history" and "plausibility," not ancient ones.[251]

g. Value and Weaknesses of This Approach

In the end, most scholars reject the characterization of Acts as a novel.[252] Ancient readers knew the genre of the novel but, in the overwhelming majority of cases, could distinguish between the narrative genres of history (where facts are important to the genre) and novel (where they are not).[253] Even when historical works have incorrect facts, they do not become fiction, and a novel that depends on historical information

244. Stephens, "Who Read Novels?," 415. The Attic revival consigned Hellenistic historians like Polybius to a more limited readership (see Nicolai, "Place of History," 23).

245. "Historical novels," as already noted, were a small minority, and even they often included little more than historical characters and a few events (a far cry from the heavy use of sources obvious in Luke's first volume).

246. Even the few historical novels interspersed historical characters and some events with mostly free composition, in contrast to Luke's close attention to locations, sequence, and sometimes officials; sometimes bare historical detail (usually in itineraries); and the use of either sources or eyewitness testimony (the "we" material).

247. And even this should not be debated, as classicists such as Barbara Levick and Stephen Mitchell have shown; see the discussion on South Galatia at Acts 14.

248. See the discussion in ch. 7 below; this commentary's analysis, passim.

249. See Wiersma, "Novel."

250. Konstan, "Invention," 5–6 (quote, 5). The recycling of a story line (cf. Lucian's *Lucius* and Apuleius's *Metamorphoses*) suggests limits to this distinction, but the point is that the novelist cannot be described as "mistaken" about his claims, since (far more than historians and mythographers) the novelist has control over the work's narrative world.

251. Balch, "Genre," 10.

252. See, e.g., Conzelmann, *Acts*, xli.

253. E.g., Lucian *Hist.* 12, who distinguishes proper biography from falsification and flattery; Plut. *Poetry* 2, *Mor.* 16F, who points to fabricated materials in poetry (quite different from how he describes his sources in the *Lives*). See Lendon, "Historiography," 43; Mosley, "Reporting," 26; Kany, "Bericht"; Witherington, *Acts*, 25–26.

does not become history;[254] what distinguishes the two genres is the nature of their truth claims.[255]

Yet Acts is certainly entertaining history, recounting "a dramatic and absorbing story."[256] The literary public was not large enough for political and other historians to gain an audience by simply recounting bare events. "The historian therefore had to recount in lively fashion events beyond his reach, and qualify ethically the personalities involved."[257] Interest in lively narration might be greater at a popular level, but by itself cannot identify the ancient genre. Such interest was not a matter of social class per se; even if novels were popular in style, their primary target audience may have been educated.[258] As seen later, Luke writes at a more popular (though less rhetorically elaborated) level than most elite historians, as one might expect from the biographic component in his work.

Acts is not, then, strictly speaking, a novel, but literary comparisons with novels may retain some value. Ancient historians and biographers readily borrowed literary techniques from dramas and novels, and Luke is no exception.[259] Acts is brief and focused enough to provide more narrative artistry and unity than found in historians such as Polybius or Livy.[260] Acts' percentage of asides[261] supplying information necessary to its story line is comparable to that of the romances.[262] And Luke at least twice reports conversations behind closed doors (Acts 5:34–39; 25:14–22) without clarifying whether information was leaked or whether these conversations are his summary of what must have been said to produce the known outcome.[263]

Those who compare Acts to novels are correct to recognize its sustained movement. Apart from the significant space Luke allots to the speeches, Acts continues the movement and the action with little interruption. Even the speeches, which provide theological reflection, are usually brief (Acts 7 being the most notable exception) and feature most extensively the *narratio*, that is, the speeches' narrative elements. Granted, Luke's selected stories are "edifying" action, but they are action nonetheless, meant to hold attention. We should not overexegete or allegorize the purpose of recounting action scenes.

254. Bowersock's examples of fictionalized history (*Fiction as History*, 21) are distinctly novelistic; historical fictions (e.g., Xenophon's *Cyropaedia*; Ps.-Callisthenes's *Alexander Romance*, the latter four to eight centuries after Alexander) were exceptional and fairly transparent. (The latter work was completed before its Latin translation in the early fourth century C.E. [Fusillo, "Pseudo-Callisthenes"]; Alexander died in 323 B.C.E.) In contrast to genuine Alexander histories, the "historical value" of Pseudo-Callisthenes "is negligible" (Zambrini, "Historians," 211).

255. Carson, *John*, 64–65, following Sternberg, *Poetics*, 23–35; see similarly Lendon, "Historiography," 43.

256. Rebenich, "Historical Prose," 307.

257. Ibid., 289.

258. Bowie, "Readership," 452–53; Stephens, "Who Read Novels?," 415.

259. Cf., e.g., the borrowing of style from Roman epics in Roman historiography (Rebenich, "Historical Prose," 312); some scholars find the borrowing of novelistic techniques in LXX expansions (e.g., Boyd-Taylor, "Adventure").

260. Though Polybius (3.32.2) also claims to follow a thread of continuity through his forty volumes by noting the chain of causes in history.

261. For a summary introduction of narrative asides in ancient texts, see Aune, *Dictionary of Rhetoric*, 312–14 (following esp. Sheeley, *Asides*).

262. Sheeley, *Asides*, 179; he treats asides in romances (41–56) and in Acts (119–35). Though he finds a "slightly lower percentage" in histories, it remains unclear if the difference is statistically significant; further, asides for general information better match most historical narratives (179; for histories, see 56–78).

263. The closest parallels to this procedure are most often in the brief romances rather than in the longer, technical, and documented histories (see Sheeley, *Asides*, 179). Private conversations do, however, appear in sober histories, including in Tacitus and Josephus (see comments on the Lukan passages ad loc.).

Why, for example, did Luke need to include the number of soldiers sent with Paul en route to Caesarea (23:23)? All questions of the number's specific accuracy aside (see comment ad loc.), the number is useful to Luke, whatever his source. First, it may underline the importance that Paul the prisoner has acquired in the eyes of his Roman captors; this is important to Luke's apologetic about Paul's status despite his chains. Second, it emphasizes the extent of opposition the Roman commander anticipated, and thereby builds suspense, just as we would by selecting the most interesting aspects of our own adventures or travels when recounting them today and just as, in different ways, journalists (or their editors) and the more popular historical writers of our day would.[264] Third, this detail in Acts invites Luke's audience to consider God's protection of Paul. Yet even if the information implied no "theology" in the most traditional sense (and certainly no pure logical discourse), it is part of good storytelling, whose techniques are as useful for recounting stories of actual events to a popular audience as they are for relating fictitious tales.

Further, as a selective writer, Luke probably uses models of the Hellenistic hero (as well as that of the sage and biblical models) to shape his presentation of information in Acts (e.g., 14:8–18; 17:16–34). But as Luke Timothy Johnson warns, literary artistry does not mean fiction: "All historical writing . . . demands a selection and creative shaping of materials, and all great histories have a large component of imagination."[265] Few modern historians would dismiss the historical value of Josephus or Suetonius[266] simply because they include "gossip and exaggeration"[267] or of Tacitus because he uses tragic motifs to tell his story.[268] On the other hand, *excessive* dramatization drew ancient criticism; Polybius criticized "tragic historians," who "improperly combined fictional drama with factual history."[269] (Different historians did draw lines in different places; see discussion in ch. 5.)

Thus one may disagree with Pervo's thesis without dismissing out of hand the value of his work and that of other novel-oriented interpreters. Their literary work often remains insightful, and those of us who emphasize the historical genre of Acts may profit from many of their more specific observations.

h. Closing Comments on Novels

Novels provide valuable comparisons for understanding the literary approaches used by ancient writers, especially on a popular level. In terms of genre, however, Acts much more closely fits the category of the historical monograph (see ch. 3 below) than that of the novel.

Contrary to what some scholars have claimed, such distinctions between historically substantive works and compositions relatively free from such constraints are hardly a uniquely modern, Enlightenment concern. Although interest in accurate information about the past marked the Enlightenment, it had also marked the Renaissance (and hence the Reformation) emphasis on the recovery of classical learning and

---

264. Cf., e.g., the more biographic focus typically preferred in "popular history" (e.g., McGee, *People of Spirit*, 13).

265. Johnson, *Acts*, 5–6.

266. Suetonius failed to sift his sources and includes much gossip (Cary and Haarhoff, *Life*, 272).

267. Johnson, *Acts*, 7. For one proposed case of Suetonius's source including a misinterpretation negative toward Caligula, see Woods, "Caligula." Thus Sheeley, *Asides*, 181, finding parallels with various genres, concludes that an analysis of asides cannot determine Luke's genre, because characteristics of various genres overlap.

268. Without fabricating events, Tacitus certainly stamped many of them with tragic coloring (e.g., *Ann.* 5.9). Tragic elements had a higher role in poetry (Quint. *Inst.* 10.1.64).

269. Aune, *Environment*, 84.

revisited distinctions among genres already emphasized in antiquity (see discussion in ch. 4 below).

Sometimes these distinctions served polemic or apologetic purposes, but this was precisely because many thinkers believed that the nature of foundational claims mattered. "The distinction between myth (or fiction) and history" became one crux in early Christianity's debates with its detractors. "Celsus describes the Gospels as fictions (πλάσματα) and viewed them as largely unhistorical," one scholar notes, and Christians took the same approach toward Philostratus's *Life of Apollonius*.[270] Porphyry and Julian likewise claimed that the Gospels were fictions, fabricating stories and not history,[271] and they apparently assumed "that one needs to show the falsity of the sources (e.g., the biblical literature) of the Christians' message before one can stop the religion."[272] The detractors treated these works as fiction not because the works did not make historical claims but precisely because the early Christians appealed to the claims about history found in these documents.

Ancients, like moderns, recognized that one could communicate truths through fictitious stories, whether Jewish sages' story parables, Greek fables, or philosophers' illustrations. But the stakes changed once authors made claims about history, thereby inviting falsification. Early Christians and their critics recognized the genre of the Gospels and Acts as offering public claims in the arena of history (cf. Luke 1:1–4; 2:1–2; 3:1–2; Acts 26:26) and proceeded in their debate accordingly.

5. Epics

Some scholars have also compared Acts to epics.[273] This comparison has been less common than that to novels but bears mention. Like novels, traditional epics are an essentially fictitious genre (despite typical use of past traditions, in contrast to novels).[274] Scholars often cite this proposal in connection with Marianne Palmer Bonz's comparison of Acts to Virgil's *Aeneid*, a proposal to which I shall shortly turn. First, however, I should note the work of Dennis MacDonald, who argues that Luke seeks to evoke Homer in a manner that his audience would recognize. I am mentioning separately MacDonald's work, which is always intriguing even when one disagrees with it, because his proposed allusions to Homer, the most widely read author of

270. Cook, *Interpretation*, 14. For Celsus's approach to the Gospels as unhistorical, see also 26–27 (Origen *Cels.* 2.13).

271. Cook, *Interpretation*, 336–37 (also noting Celsus again).

272. Ibid., 337.

273. The most thoroughgoing is Bonz, *Past as Legacy* (comparing Virgil's *Aeneid* and suggesting epic's influence on Acts' structure; cf. idem, "Best and Worst"). MacDonald, "Farewell," 190, goes further in suggesting "extensive echoes of the Homeric epics." Some compare Acts' Rome-ward movement with the *Aeneid* (Reardon, "Homing to Rome"), but Rome was the heart of its empire, and for immigrants and their cults alike, all roads did lead to Rome (cf. Ramsay, "Roads and Travel," 376; this commentary's discussion at Acts 1:8; 28:16).

274. Bonz, *Past as Legacy*, 15, counts Homeric epic as "historiographic" in the sense of being bound by past tradition rather than by the free composition characteristic of novels. But one needs genres to distinguish works such as Homer from works such as those of Polybius, and Bonz herself notes genre markers distinguishing epic from history (and novel; p. 21); she emphasizes plot unity (21–22), but such unity also appears in historical works focused on particular characters or agendas (e.g., Quintus Curtius *History of Alexander*) and which may borrow from the epic tradition but, as prose works, are not themselves epic. MacDonald, "Farewell," 202–3, allows that both Luke and Virgil preserve historical information, yet contends that Luke's audience would recognize his stories as "fictions crafted as alternatives to those of Homer and Vergil" (203). But quantitatively (and especially proportionate to length) Virgil offers far less historical information than does Luke. Not only is most of Virgil's ancient tradition legendary (by anyone's standards, since it belonged to the distant past); he also plays with it freely.

Greek antiquity (see comment on Acts 17:28), call for examination regardless of the question of genre on which this chapter focuses.[275]

MacDonald establishes criteria, such as density, sequence of parallels, and distinctive traits, to identify Homeric allusions.[276] But not all the features he identifies as distinctive in the NT texts he analyzes were rare enough in ancient literature to be genuinely distinctive of Homer. Moreover, nearly all of Luke's marked citations, plus many allusions, are to the Jewish Bible,[277] and none are clearly to Homer. Although Homer is part of Acts' larger Greco-Roman context, most critics find MacDonald's emphasis on a pervasive allusion to Homer unconvincing,[278] especially because of his search for a single decisive "hypotext,"[279] an emulation that is "not recognized,"[280] and in this work neglect for the more explicit "OT intertextuality" in Acts.[281] Because Hellenistic Jewish writers could draw on elements of Greek as well as traditional Jewish culture, OT and Greek intertextuality need not be mutually exclusive.[282] Nevertheless, Luke does not display Hellenistic allusions to anything like the degree found in, for example, Philo or the *Sibylline Oracles*, and so the overt Jewish-biblical echoes must count more heavily than less overt Hellenistic ones.[283]

If Homeric allusions offered at least an initially plausible hypothesis for the eastern Mediterranean, Marianne Palmer Bonz's comparison of Acts with Virgil's *Aeneid* might be relevant for a Roman audience.[284] Nevertheless, this Latin classic seems a

275. Even if MacDonald has drawn the net too narrowly by focusing on Homer, at least he has drawn it more widely than many NT scholars and helps us reconstruct one element of Luke's milieu.

276. MacDonald, *Imitate Homer*, 1–6. He emphasizes that even prose writers depended on Homer (1, 151). But while rhetoricians, grammarians, and others used Homer as a textbook, they used Homer selectively, not requiring us to suppose that all narratives, especially historic narratives, were constructed in deliberate imitation of Homeric models.

277. MacDonald, ibid., 10–12, does note clear Elijah typology (for discussion of such typology, see this commentary's comment on Acts 1:8–9), as does Pervo (*Dating Acts*, 29–35). Even in these cases, limitations in these parallels allow us to suppose that Luke adapted his material, filling it out with such models, rather than that he freely composed it without historical tradition (e.g., the difference between adapting and inventing resuscitations), especially given the appearance of Elijah parallels already in Mark.

278. See Mitchell, "Homer," on MacDonald, *Epics*; Sandnes, "*Imitatio*"; Johnson, "Imitate"; Spencer, *Gospel and Acts*, 39–41; Eddy and Boyd, *Legend*, 340–43 (on *Epics*); less negatively, Harstine, "Imitate." Carsten Claussen kindly directed me to these reviews. Sandnes, *Challenge*, 249–50, further argues that only upper social strata had sufficient Homeric education to catch such allusions, and this is not Luke's likely audience; later Christians with such audiences rewrote Scripture in Homeric style. Wittkowsky, "Zitate," doubts that even the pagan quotations reveal *direct* acquaintance with Greek sources. Sandnes, *Gospel*, develops his own approach further in a work that MacDonald, "Review," reviewed graciously (agreeing with some points and disagreeing with others).

279. Mitchell, "Homer," 255; cf. Johnson, "Imitate," 490, on nearer sources influenced by Homer.

280. Sandnes, "*Imitatio*," 725.

281. Ibid., 732.

282. MacDonald's current work takes more explicit account of OT intertextuality, which he did not actually deny earlier (as noted on Elijah above). Thus, in an oral interchange with Loveday Alexander at a meeting on Acts at the annual meeting of the Society of Biblical Literature, San Diego, November 17, 2007, MacDonald agreed that Luke's work is saturated with direct LXX quotations and that Luke uses it even at the discourse level. But (rightly) noting that the genre is more Greek, he found characterization and other elements to be more classical. His work with LXX intertextuality is forthcoming (personal correspondence, Nov. 26, 2010).

283. Even the innovative J. D. M. Derrett, never one to underestimate parallels, finds only vague allusions to Homer in the NT and not explicit quotations (Derrett, "Homer"). These more debatable allusions offer a striking contrast with the plethora of biblical quotations.

284. E.g., Horace probably evokes Virgil (see, e.g., Zarecki, "Duet," on esp. *Carmina* 4.15.32); Roman epic writers often imitated earlier Latin epics (Stover, "Apollonius"). Virgil's own imitation of Homer (e.g., Beck, "Ecphrasis") might contrast his hero (a noble precursor for Augustus) with the Homeric antiheroes Achilles and Odysseus (Shea, "Imitating," 50–51). Perhaps somewhat analogously, though probably for the sake of maintaining focus more than valorizing his heroes, Luke wastes little time with his heroes' weaknesses in Acts, at least once they are converted (Acts 8:1, 3; cf. Luke 5:8).

less obvious model for a work in Greek[285] probably addressing an eastern Mediterranean audience for whom Roman citizenship bespeaks significant status. Even in elite Roman works from the early empire that contain some language identical to phrases in Virgil, some scholars deny that these echoes (as opposed to larger quotations) are intentional. Some others accept the echoes as deliberate yet doubt that the literary allusion affects the meaning.[286] Luke's language, which often quotes and even more often evokes the LXX (especially early in the work), lacks even such clear phrases from Virgil.

Moreover, Loveday Alexander warns that Luke's prologue does not fit conventions expected in epic.[287] More significantly, the most obvious difference between Acts and ancient epics, which most clearly disqualifies the work from this category, is that it is written in prose. This difference does not disqualify us from comparing Acts, to some extent, with epics as functionally analogous "foundation documents," but it does limit the extent to which we push the comparison to epics, in contrast to a comparison to histories. That is, Luke's genre simply is not epic; Greek and Roman epics were metrical poetry, generally in hexameter verse,[288] a far cry from Luke-Acts.[289]

Epic poems could address mythical beginnings (most commonly) or the more recent, historical period (as in Lucan's *Civil War* or Silius Italicus's *Punica*);[290] the writers of the latter kind took the same literary liberties granted to all epic poets,[291] but elaborated historical rather than mythical events. Their liberties, however, suit a poetic genre to which Luke-Acts does not belong. Writers putting recent history into epic form turned it, by definition, into poetry, not simply interesting prose. Early Greek historians distinguished themselves from epic poets not only by using prose but by explicitly identifying themselves and the limits of their knowledge.[292]

Among others, Alexander has critiqued Bonz's thesis for these and other reasons. Those who call Acts an epic view it as a "prose epic," but such a genre (in the

285. The *Aeneid*'s composition in Latin is one of the objections that MacDonald, *Imitate Homer*, 8, puts to Bonz's thesis. MacDonald acknowledges the connections with Virgil that Bonz finds, but attributes them to Virgil's and Luke's independently imitating Homer (8–9)! Schnabel, "Reading Acts," 261 (noting Krauter, "Vergils Evangelium," 220), notes that only a small circle of elite readers would have been able to closely emulate the complex literary patterns in Virgil.

286. See the summary of views in O'Gorman, "Intertextuality," 233–34, concerning the use of Virgil's language (*Aen.* 2.13–16) in Tac. *Ann.* 2.61.1 (where an allusion does appear likely). She goes on (234–35) to note another approach to intertextuality that does not require intentionality (noting esp. Fowler, *Constructions*). Scholars differ regarding other allusions as well; e.g., does Tacitus recall Sallust in the opening of his *Histories*, as many think (Woodman, *Rhetoric*, 164–65), or Cicero, as Woodman thinks (165–66)?

287. Alexander, *Context*, 41; see also Schnabel, "Reading Acts," 261 (citing Diomedes *Ars Grammatica* 3; Quint. *Inst.* 10.1.51–57; Aristotle *Poet.* 23–24, 1459a17, b31; and Krauter, "Epos," 225–31). Granted that some ancients treated epics like the *Aeneid* as historical (Leigh, "Epic," 483), epics diverge sharply in style from the bulk of ancient historiography; overlap in some narrative elements and focus on the past does not obliterate clearer genre markers.

288. Although "elegiac distich" appears in early samples, hexameter prevailed for works about the distant past (Fantuzzi, "Historical epic," 410). In the imperial period, encomiastic epic completely displaced the regional form (411).

289. See also Alexander, *Context*, 167.

290. Cf. Hardie, "Epic." Silius Italicus, unlike Lucan, retained deities as characters, in keeping with his poetic model in Virgil, but he depended on Livy for the bulk of his historical information (Feeney, "Silius Italicus"). On the Greek association of epic with the distant past, see also, e.g., Nicolai, "Place of History," 15; on the rarer epics about more recent historical events (in poetic form), see Leigh, "Epic," 484–85, 488–92.

291. E.g., Lucan follows Livy and Caesar but "freely manipulates historical truth where it suits his purpose, e.g., in introducing Cicero in Pompey's camp on the eve of the battle of Pharsalus in book 7" (Anderson and Hardie, "Lucanus," 94). Whereas a slave rescues Scipio in Livy, it is his son in Sil. It. 4.466–68 (LCL, 1:202 n. *b*).

292. Alexander, "Fiction and Genre," 382–85. On epics, see, e.g., Latacz, "Epic: Antiquity"; idem, "Epic: Literature"; Courtney, "Epic." But epic is, by definition, metrical (Hardie, "Epic"), not comparable with Luke-Acts or other prose histories.

narrow, conventional sense of epic) did not exist.[293] By employing prose, one chose to write in a genre distinct from epic poetry, often retaining heroic ideology but avoiding mythology.[294] Alexander rightly notes, "At the surface levels of discourse and narrative management, Acts is not an epic, and no ancient reader would suppose that it was."[295]

If Luke created a new genre along the lines of a "prose epic" (not generically recognizable to his contemporaries, in contrast to what could be expected for a putative poetic progenitor), we might think of Acts in terms of foundation stories. Some scholars compare, for example, Luke's portrayal of the early Jerusalem community to typical ancient foundational mythologies.[296] It has also been argued that Luke employs literary strategies in key passages such as Acts 10:1–11:18 comparable to those in other foundation documents.[297]

But once we distinguish foundation stories from epic, we should no longer expect in them the poetic license characteristically attached to the poetic genre of conventional epic. Scholars who view Acts as a prose epic seem to classify it not in terms of conventional epic but according to a broader literary definition assigned to a transcultural function of a foundation story. This classification, however, is a matter of function rather than genre, and illuminating as it might be to read Acts (or earlier biblical history) alongside such epics for their analogous "foundation" functions, these analogies reveal nothing about genre or clear imitation.[298]

The comparison may thus be fruitful insofar as we think of Acts as a "foundation story,"[299] but foundation stories are identifiable more by their function than by their form; ancient audiences would not treat all foundation documents as mythical. Foundation stories do not of themselves require us to expect mythical elements—and certainly not when they appear in histories (a genre explored in chs. 3–5 below) dealing with the recent past.[300] Historiography could draw on epic literary strategies and interests.[301] Histories did not self-consciously create foundation myths the way Virgil did; Livy and Dionysius of Halicarnassus believed that they did their best to narrate truth about Rome's origins, though acknowledging that early origins were shrouded in myth because they were so many centuries in the past (see the discussion below in ch. 4). Even in the mainly mythical period of their foundation stories, the historians

293. With Alexander, *Context*, 173.

294. Ibid. (where Alexander notes that novels embraced epics' mythology while subverting heroic ideology).

295. Ibid., 9, noting fuller dependence on the LXX than on Greek or Roman epic (though allowing some hyperlinks to these, especially in Paul's final voyage). Alexander develops the critique more fully on 165–82. Note also concerns in Krauter, *Epos*; whatever indirect influence may exist, the similarities cannot negate the differences, and Krauter deems Bonz's thesis finally implausible (Krauter, *Epos*, 243). Schnabel, "Reading Acts," 260n58, adds other critics, including Breitenbach, "Epos," 100–101; Rothschild, *Rhetoric of History*, 8.

296. Moreland, "Mythmaking."

297. Wilson, "Urban Legends."

298. With Alexander, *Context*, 169.

299. Cf. Bonz, *Past as Legacy*; Pao, *Isaianic Exodus*, 3. During the empire, cities often emphasized their foundation legends (e.g., Lichtenberger, "Foundation Legends").

300. Rome's mythical "foundation stories" are normally in the distant, often archaic past ("Aetiology," 982); Livy follows sources, is more restrained than his sources, and probably has some basically true material even on sixth-century B.C.E. Rome (Laistner, *Historians*, 91–93). Many foundation legends in the earliest sources probably circulated due to regional pride and competition; see Dillery, "Roman Historians," 93. Most of the examples of "mythic" material in Weaver, *Epiphany*, 1–6, refer to the distant past (chronological distance constituting a larger factor, in my view, than "foundation" stories). The mythic patterns he notes in Thucydides's way of recounting history (1) are more relevant (especially to his parallels with prison escapes in Acts), but they reflect literary patterns, not event-creation.

301. Rothschild, *Rhetoric of History*, 88–91, warning (88, against Bonz) that historiography and epic were not opposites.

follow sources, which is why they overlap with one another heavily; the problem is simply that the sources stem from long after living memory of eyewitnesses. Still more relevant is that Josephus's and Luke's audiences regarded the biblical story as accurate and hence would not expect foundation stories to be necessarily mythical. Foundation stories were normally traditional even when mythical, not simply exercises in literary creativity. This is a significant point when we consider that Luke reports recent events, which were the domain of contemporary historiography rather than of mythography (see the discussion in chs. 4, 6 below); Luke's sources would not be shrouded in legend the way stories of many centuries past would be.[302]

Bonz and MacDonald, however, mean more than simply analogous foundational function; they mean that Luke consciously evokes Virgil (Bonz) or Homer (MacDonald).[303] Bonz's claim that literary allusion to Virgil is "an epic feature" is a non sequitur; as Alexander notes, most echoes or even quotations of Virgil "fall a long way short of genuine *imitatio*," and few who merely echoed or quoted Virgil intended to be understood as writing in the epic genre.[304] Suggestions of large-scale imitation of Virgil or Homer rightly draw attention to the prominence of these authors in Luke's world, but these theses look to models far less important to Luke and his Christian audience than Scripture was.[305]

Luke's conscious imitation of the LXX, by contrast, is widely acknowledged,[306] although scholars differ on the nature of imitation.[307] Most would include LXX influence at least in matters of style and theme and in the development of some narratives; Luke's work also abounds in marked quotations of the LXX. Early Christians valued their Scriptures as foundation narratives in a manner that was even more central than Homer was for the Greeks.[308]

302. Luke's geographic movement might evoke even an epic scope (with a goal of Rome, as in Virgil), but Luke's interests, defined explicitly in his preface, involve recent events that he believes to be historical (see discussion in chs. 6–7 below), though historians could exercise more freedom in speeches (see ch. 8 below).

303. So Alexander, *Context*, 169.

304. Ibid., 171. She also reminds readers that Luke's primary model is the LXX (172). Much more direct citations of Virgil appear in nonelite ancient graffiti (Toner, *Culture*, 140, citing *CIL* 4.1527, 4401, 9987), none of which sought to produce epic.

305. Alexander, *Context*, 181, emphasizing the LXX.

306. E.g., Plümacher, *Lukas*, 38–72 (in the mission speeches); Rothschild, *Rhetoric of History*, 293 (for archaizing style); Steyn, "*Vorlage* of Quotations"; also Pervo, *Dating Acts*, 29–35; MacDonald, *Imitate Homer*, 10–12; Pervo, "Flattery." Luke also certainly used Mark as a model (Pervo, *Dating Acts*, 35–47, not always persuasively, finds this in Acts as well as the Gospel).

307. Mimesis could include a wide range of models, not limited to a single genre or even to literature; see, e.g., Zimbrich, "Mimesis" (though noting poets' frequent imitation of Homer, p. 927); Symm. *Ep.* 1.2.2; 1.4.1. Epic writers imitated earlier epics (e.g., Stover, "Apollonius"), but historians also typically imitated the style of earlier writers; see some examples in Woodman, *Rhetoric*, x–xi, 6 (Thucydides imitating Herodotus), 127 (Sallust imitating Thucydides), 165–66 (Tacitus *Hist.* imitating Cicero), 167–68 (Tacitus *Ann.* imitating Sallust); some Roman historians may also draw on Ennius (Elliott, "Cunctator"), who adapted early traditions about Rome in epic form. Cf. also historians' allusions to poets (recently proposed cases include an allusion to Homer *Il.* 5.254 and *Od.* 21.426 in Suet. *Galba* 20.2; Power, "Taunt"). Yet even literary allusions to earlier writers can be used to characterize events rather than create them (Damon, "Rhetoric," 445, qualifying Woodman's approach [in *Tacitus*, xvii] to the use of Sall. *Jug.* 46.8 in Tac. *Ann.* 15.36). Sources constrain historians' application of these techniques in a way that they need not constrain novelists (on the special constraints of the historical genre, see also Lendon, "Historiography," 60). Even when using rhetorical models, one could work against them (see Nagel, "Lyrics").

308. Although Jews also had other writings, none of them (apart from some quasi-canonical works, e.g., Sirach and Wisdom, that circulated in some Diaspora collections) had achieved widespread cultural status the way that some works and traditions supplementing Homer did (e.g., dramatists and some historians), although this may be partly because Judaism straddled multiple dominant cultures (from the Parthian to Hellenistic-Roman spheres; e.g., *1 Enoch* seems limited more to the Semitic sphere).

6. Acts

Another possible genre is suggested by the second-century title: "Acts." An appropriate title would stem from a work's purpose or subject (Porph. *Ar. Cat.* 57.15–19). Our current title for Acts appears widely by the end of the second century,[309] and it does fit the proliferation of apocryphal acts in second-century Christianity (closely related to the novelistic genre treated above).[310] Such a correspondence with later Christian interests[311] could be thought to risk an anachronistic reading of the evidence, but conversely, we need not suppose that the second-century church completely misunderstood the purpose of Acts.

The title of Acts designates "a specific Greek literary form, a narrative account of the heroic deeds of famous historical or mythological figures."[312] Such extended narratives of deeds might function epideictically (though with greater literary value) as something like an expansion of lists of exploits or achievements,[313] or, especially for philosophers, *peristasis* catalogues (affliction lists).[314] To some degree they might overlap with aretalogies, a listing of signs that a few scholars have compared to the Gospels or their sources.[315] (As brief narrations or lists of divine acts, however, aretalogies cannot provide adequate analogies for finished literary works;[316] aretalogy was not even a clearly defined genre.)[317] Like the travel narrative, the category of "acts" can overlap with others. Fitzmyer, for example, takes this genre as fitting for a historical monograph.[318]

But whatever the value of comparing other recitations of "acts" or "deeds," the title Acts of the *Apostles* is certainly a misnomer. Even if we read Acts as biography rather than as history, it reports especially the acts of Peter and Paul; other figures who are somewhat prominent (e.g., Stephen, James, Silas, Apollos, and Priscilla and Aquila)

---

309. Pesch, *Apostelgeschichte*, 1:22–23, and Hull, *Spirit in Acts*, 13, citing the Latin version of Iren. *Her.* 3.13.3 (also 3.12.11; 3.14.1); Clem. Alex. *Strom.* 5.82.4; Tert. *Bapt.* 10.4; anti-Marcionite prologue to Luke; the Muratorian Canon (though other titles were also available).

310. Cf. Pesch, *Apostelgeschichte*, 1:22–23.

311. Certainly, writers of apocryphal gospels and other works respected the now-canonical writings, and readers of the canonical works also respected "the apocryphal legends" (Bovon, *Studies*, 301). Some scholars also suspect that the apocryphal acts, like patristic sources, contain some earlier extracanonical traditions (see Gounelle, "Réception," 205, though urging a cautious approach); Elliott, "Apocrypha," 688–89, also notes some correspondences of apocryphal acts and gospels with legends or tradition, though quite limited (nowhere comparable to what our first-century sources provide; see ch. 6 below).

312. Fitzmyer, *Acts*, 47–48, citing, e.g., Diod. Sic. 3.1.1; 16.1.1; Jos. *Ant.* 14.68; 2 Chr 12:15; 13:22; 28:26 LXX.

313. E.g., Max. Tyre 15.6, 9; *Res gestae divi Augusti* (conveniently, e.g., in Sherk, *Empire*, §26, pp. 41–52). On deeds in ancient encomia, see, e.g., Malina and Neyrey, *Portraits*, 28–33; Men. Rhet. 2.3, 385.8–9; 2.11, 420.24–25; Hermog. *Issues* 46.14–17.

314. Cf. 1 Cor 4:9–13; 2 Cor 4:8–11; 6:4–10; 11:23–33; Epict. *Diatr.* 1.11.33; 2.6.18; 2.19.18; Max. Tyre 12.10; 15.9; 34.9; see Malherbe, *Moral Exhortation*, 130, 141–43; esp. Fitzgerald, *Cracks*, passim (see esp. 59–65; for the history of research, see 7–31); idem, "Affliction Lists," esp. 16–17. Although most important to sages, such lists were not limited to them; cf., e.g., Rom 8:35–39; *1 En.* 103:9–15; *Test. Jos.* 1:4–7; Hodgson, "Tribulation Lists"; Danker, "Debt," 265; Heracles's trials (Epict. *Diatr.* 1.6.32–33; Max. Tyre 15.6); perhaps even the image of Philoctetes (Bowersock, *Fiction as History*, 55–76). Lists of afflictions can even be used to prove romantic love (Ach. Tat. 5.18.3–6) or to draw on political capital (Cic. *Cat.* 4.1.2). The key is that enduring suffering revealed nobility of character (e.g., Diog. Laert. 6.2.74).

315. Hadas and Smith, *Heroes.* Cf., somewhat more plausibly, aretalogical biographies (Wills, *Quest*).

316. Shuler, *Genre*, 15–20; cf. Talbert, *Gospel*, 12–13.

317. Burridge, *Gospels*, 18–19; Aune, *Dictionary of Rhetoric*, 57; for narrower and wider senses, see Haase, "Aretalogies," 1003. Talbert, *Gospel*, 43, cites biographies of immortals (mainly from the second and third centuries), but as he admits, the religious or mythical dimension does not affect genre (cf. Shuler, *Genre*, 21). Some argue that his evidence for specific cultic biographies (Talbert, *Gospel*, 91–113) is mainly inferential (Aune, "Problem," 37–42).

318. Fitzmyer, *Acts*, 48–49.

are not named as "apostles," and Paul (along with Barnabas) receives the designation in only one passage. The prominence of apostles in early chapters of Acts may have caused real readers to overestimate their significance for the book and thus contributed to the book's second-century title.[319]

Another objection proves more telling against the value of identifying Acts as belonging to a genre labeled "acts." Because the designation is so nontechnical, Aune complains that it fits any narratives depicting "the accomplishments of noteworthy individuals or cities (whether mythical, historical, or fictional)" and hence "offers little help in determining the genre of Acts."[320] This disagreement raises the question of how we define genre, which may be a question of semantics. At the least the category of acts helps us understand the repeated use of particular narrative techniques. These techniques also characterize novels, but Acts shares them with novels because, like novels, it is popular literature and not because it is, strictly speaking, novelistic. Yet the category of acts is too broad to guide us in what to expect in the work (the purpose for defining genres), was not a clearly accepted distinct category in the first century, and must yield to accepted ancient genres that provide more specific direction for the interpretation of Acts.

Conclusion

Various proposed genres include elements relevant for the interpretation of Acts. Like a novel, it is an entertaining work on a popular level; like epic, it may function as a foundation document; and like a travel narrative (a theme found in various genres), it contains narratives driven by the theme of travel. Far more important is that, like biography, Acts focuses on particular characters (a focus still clearer in Luke's previous volume, a biography about Jesus). Yet all of these elements may be found in ancient historiography, the most commonly proposed genre category for Acts. It is to this genre proposal that I now turn.

319. So Parsons, *Departure*, 184, stressing what he calls the "primacy effect." Against the title "acts of the apostles," see also Mount, *Pauline Christianity*, 42–43.

320. Aune, *Environment*, 78. The genre should not be confused, because of its English title, with Latin *acta*, which could be gazettes (including official events, decisions, lawsuits, and speeches) or lists of emperors' enactments (Balsdon and Lintott, "Acta"; Gizewski, "Acta").

3

ACTS AS A WORK
OF ANCIENT
HISTORIOGRAPHY

Although scholars diverge regarding Acts' more precise classification, the genre that scholars most commonly propose for Acts is some form of ancient historiography. Several factors converge in support of the thesis that Acts is a work of historiography, including the preface to Luke's first volume (Luke 1:1–4) and probably his use of speeches. If we conclude that Acts is a work of ancient historiography, its length requires us to understand it as a historical monograph (comparable to those of Sallust),[1] in contrast to the larger multivolume histories of some ancient authors. Exactly what kind of historical monograph it might be merits further exploration below.

By virtue of the limits of conventional language, I will use "history," "historiography," and their cognates in at least two distinct (though not unrelated) ways in this introduction: first, the genre of ancient historiography and, second, questions about historical facticity in the modern sense.[2] So long as the two senses of the term are kept in mind, context often should be sufficient to enable the reader to discern which use I intend in each case (often I will also explicitly distinguish the two).

After the argument in this chapter that Acts belongs to the genre of ancient historiography, subsequent chapters will explore issues raised by this claim. I must address the nature of ancient historiography (chs. 4–5) and where Acts lies within the spectrum of this historiography (chs. 6–7). Ancient historiography employed a range of literary and rhetorical strategies to communicate both historical information (ch. 4) and ideological perspectives (ch. 5). Contrary to what some modern scholars argue, ancient historians did make many claims about historical events. Examining the degree of correspondence with extrinsic data for claimed events thus accords with the expectations of the ancient genre, and ancient critics sometimes evaluated historical works on these grounds.

---

1. Sallust's monographs offer our earliest historical material from a Roman in the period of the empire, besides Livy, and imitate Thucydides (Hose, "Historiography: Rome," 423).

2. Even scholars who explicitly distinguish the two senses in their introductions and in whose work context makes clear which they mean are nevertheless sometimes criticized by others who acknowledge the viability of only the former sort of category, i.e., what people write about history (cf. here Wright, "Response," 246). Marguerat, "Wie historisch?," contends that the answer to the question of Acts' historicity depends on the definition of "historicity."

Despite some common objectives, narration in ancient historiography differed in some respects from its modern namesake, and these differences must be taken into account, especially in subsequent chapters. For example, since ancient historians treated speeches differently than modern historians do, we must explore information regarding ancient speeches (ch. 8). And since modern scholars' historical skepticism toward Acts' reliability often begins with historical suspicion toward Luke's signs claims, we must also examine them in a separate and fuller discussion (ch. 9).[3]

Even when this introduction moves to more literary questions, such as Luke's apologetic purpose, these broader questions are not easily separable from the issues raised in these introductory chapters on Acts' genre. Thus, for example, the importance of apologetic historiography for authors with minority perspectives like Luke will affect our reading of Luke's purpose and message.

1. The Historical-Monograph Thesis

The dominant view today, earlier argued by such Lukan scholars as Martin Dibelius and Henry Cadbury,[4] is that Acts is a work of ancient historiography.[5] As Johnson notes in the *Anchor Bible Dictionary*, "The reasons for regarding Luke-Acts as a History are obvious and, to most scholars, compelling."[6] One sampling of recent proposals concerning Acts' genre is instructive: two proponents for Acts as a novel, two for epic, four for biography, and ten for various kinds of history.[7] More examples could be listed in each category, but the sampling is nevertheless helpful for getting a sense of proportion: even in a list emphasizing the diversity of proposals, history appears five times as often as the novel and, together with biography, seven times as often as the novel. A similar sampling finds history the most common proposal, with eight

3. On this issue I will argue that signs claims need not be excluded from the earliest layers of tradition. That is, whatever our various philosophic or theological explanations for such phenomena, eyewitnesses could (and do) experience phenomena that they interpreted (and interpret) as signs. At greater length, see Keener, *Miracles*.

4. Dibelius, *Studies in Acts*, 123–37; Cadbury, *Acts in History*, passim.

5. For Acts (or, in some cases, Luke-Acts as a whole) as history (often including the more specific proposal of historical monograph), see Palmer, "Monograph (1992)"; idem, "Monograph (1993)"; Schmidt, "Influences," 59; Plümacher, "Luke as Historian," 398; idem, *Lukas*, 33–38 (comparing mission speeches), 137–39; idem, *Geschichte*, 1–32; idem, "Cicero und Lukas," 772–73; idem, "Monographie"; idem, "Historiker"; Fuller, "Classics," 189 (addressing George Kennedy's comments); Petersen, "Genre"; Bovon, *Theologian*, 5; Johnson, *Acts*, 3–7; Stagg, *Acts*, 17; Wall, "Acts," 12–13; Fitzmyer, *Acts*, 127; Cross, "Genres," 404–6; Tuckett, *Luke*, 29; Ehrman, *Introduction*, 133; deSilva, *Introduction*, 349–51; Schwartz, "Trial Scenes," 117; Balch, "ΜΕΤΑΒΟΛΗ ΠΟΛΙΤΕΙΩΝ," 141–42, 149–54 (political history); idem, "Genre," passim, esp. 11–19; idem, "Gospels (forms)," 948–49; Barnett, *Birth*, 195–96; Marguerat, *Histoire*, 49 (though noting overlap with biography); idem, "Pionnier"; Eckey, *Apostelgeschichte*, 20–31; Jervell, *Apostelgeschichte*, 77–78; Flichy, *Oeuvre de Luc*; idem, "État des recherches," 28–32 (reviewing recent research); Rothschild, *Rhetoric of History*, 296; Guijarro Oporto, "Articulación literaria"; Litwak, *Echoes*, 36; Kisau, "Acts," 1297; Riesner, "Zuverlässigkeit," 39; Malina and Pilch, *Acts*, 6; Peterson, *Acts*, 8–10; Shauf, *Theology* (e.g., 59–60, 82–83); Dormeyer, "Gattung" (esp. 475); cf. Hemer, *Acts in History*, 220. Sterling, *Historiography*, 318n39, lists as supporters also Conzelmann, *Acts*, xl; Hengel, *Acts and History*, 14, 36–37; Schneider, *Apostelgeschichte*, 1:122; Pesch, *Apostelgeschichte*, 1:23. For political-historical conventions, see, e.g., Balch, "Genre"; cf. idem, "Acts as Historiography." See now even Pervo, *Acts*, 15 (though warning that this says nothing about reliability and [18–19] finding parallels with fiction).

6. Johnson, "Luke-Acts," 406. Penner, *Praise*, 4, likewise summarizes that most scholars hold "the most obvious generic identification for" Acts, namely, "ancient historiographical writing." Even in 1985, Callan could write, "It has long been almost taken for granted that Luke-Acts is a historical work" ("Preface and Historiography," 576, noting that Talbert's biography proposal had reopened the question).

7. Penner, "Discourse," 66–67. The survey in Phillips, "Genre," also emphasizes historiography (and views this as the consensus, though anticipating a shift toward a more hybrid position).

examples,[8] and biography the second most common, with two examples, and lists five examples of all other genre proposals put together.[9] Many scholars most conversant in ancient historiography would also concur with Hengel and Schwemer that those who deny Acts as acceptable first-century historiography need to read more ancient historiography "and less hypercritical and scholastic secondary literature."[10]

In agreement with a majority of Acts scholars today, the *Oxford Classical Dictionary* notes that Acts displays "the influence of Hellenistic historiography and rhetorical devices."[11] But what form of history does Acts take? In terms of function, many scholars argue that Acts is apologetic historiography, perhaps of the ethnographic kind (see ch. 5 below). We will address the *form* of history here (see, more fully, sect. 2.a, "Types of History," below).

Given its relative brevity, many would call the literary form of this history a historical monograph, a work covering a specific historical topic. Acts is neither a multivolume universal history nor an annalistic history but most likely a historical monograph, focused on a particular topic. In contrast to listing events by year in annalistic fashion, ancient historians might write monographs that arranged their accounts around a main theme.[12] Eckhard Plümacher argues that Acts fits the sort of historical monograph that Cicero describes and Sallust's extant essays exemplify.[13] The historical-monograph format allows us to explain both Luke's specialized focus (hence "monograph")[14] and his consistency with historical data on many external points where he can be tested (hence "historical"). Defining Acts' genre in this way does not cancel insights from other proposals (i.e., it could also be apologetic history in its mode and another kind of history, e.g., institutional or ethnographic, in its topic), nor does it by itself reveal where Acts stands on the spectrum of dramatic freedoms or accuracy in historical works[15] (see chs. 4–7 below). But it does provide a useful step for further investigation.

a. The Value of This Proposal

Various factors support the thesis that Luke conceives of his project as primarily a history of some sort. Unlike in a novel, Luke uses sources abundantly in his first volume (usually agreed to be at least Mark and Q) and presumably in his second

8. Gilbert, "Propaganda," 235 (with, e.g., Cadbury and Plümacher; for historical monograph, Conzelmann and Hengel).

9. Ibid., 236 (including two examples for epic).

10. Hengel and Schwemer, *Between Damascus and Antioch*, 11. They complain (15) that most NT scholars cannot handle the primary sources well enough to discern accurate from inaccurate scholarship and that "it is easier to keep hawking round scholastic clichés and old prejudices pseudo-critically and without closer examination, than to occupy oneself with the varied ancient sources which are often difficult to interpret and remote."

11. Sacks, "Historiography," 716. Further on Luke's Hellenistic character, see Plümacher, *Lukas*, 30–31.

12. Rebenich, "Historical Prose," 311–12. Among Romans, Sallust (among extant sources) pioneered the use of the monograph rather than the annalistic form, though the latter continued to be used (e.g., in Tacitus; Pelling, "Historiography," 717). Sallust's lost *Histories*, in contrast to his monographs, was annalistic (Levene, "Roman Historiography," 282).

13. Plümacher, *Geschichte*, 6–9. A longer historical work could be divided into historical monographs (e.g., Diodore, who has two volumes; Plümacher, *Geschichte*, 9–13). On Acts as historical monograph, see further Plümacher, *Geschichte*, 1–32; idem, "Cicero und Lukas"; idem, "Monographie"; Palmer, "Monograph (1992)"; idem, "Monograph (1993)"; Bovon, *Theologian*, 5 (on Luke-Acts as a whole); Guijarro Oporto, "Articulación literaria" (though focusing on a proposed structure); Klauck, *Letters*, 420 ("historical monograph with some novelistic features"); and many sources noted above. See concise discussion in Eckey, *Apostelgeschichte*, 20–21 (who also addresses tragic or mimetic history, 25–28, and a theological/historical monograph, 28–30); Dormeyer, "Gattung," 457–59.

14. Specialized focus was also relevant to an introduction for a scientific or artistic topic, though these are not histories and are of varying length (Favez et al., "Isagogic literature").

15. See also Schmidt, "Influences," 59–60.

volume as well, although we cannot distinguish them clearly in Acts.[16] Luke's claim to investigate or have close acquaintance with his information (Luke 1:3) fits historical works (Thucyd. 1.22.2), and his occasional use of the first-person plural (see comment on Acts 16:10) emphasizes the involvement considered ideal for a good Hellenistic historian.[17]

Speeches, the preface (Luke 1:1–4; Acts 1:1), the employment of world history as a context, and other features support this understanding of the work's genre. Most argue that Luke's extensive use of public monologues in Acts plainly fits the conventions of ancient histories, some scholars observe, but not of biographies or novels.[18] (Indeed, in Acts they may cumulatively consume a larger proportion of the work than in Thucydides or Sallust, although Luke's speeches are individually shorter than typical speeches in the multivolume histories; see ch. 8 below.) Richard Pervo has offered a detailed and significant comparison with direct speech in novels, arguing that novels reflect a proportion of direct speech closer to that of Acts.[19] The high proportion of direct speech in novels is not surprising; although historians also invent direct speech not likely preserved in their sources, novelists had more freedom to do so and interest in doing so. Nevertheless, the issue is not direct speech per se, but set speeches. A careful scholar, Pervo himself concedes that "Acts lacks soliloquies and has more orations than do many of the other works cited, romantic novels (including *Aseneth*) in particular."[20] Pervo recognizes that the space devoted to orations in a historical monograph of Sallust (26.7 percent) is actually higher than, but close to, many estimates for Acts.[21] Other direct speech probably does point to the more popular character of Acts, but the orations fit well Acts' role as historical monograph.[22]

Luke-Acts also includes what appear very much like the prefaces found in histories.[23] Granted, they also bear some parallels with the scientific-treatise tradition,[24] a

---

16. Johnson, *Acts*, 3–5; Hengel, *Acts and History*, 61.

17. Plümacher, "Luke as Historian," 398.

18. See Plümacher, "Mission Speeches," 251–66; as in idem, "Missionsreden"; idem, "Historiker," 3–5; idem, "Luke as Historian," 398; Horsley, "Speeches," 613. Novelists usually preferred livelier narration.

19. Pervo, "Direct Speech," notes very limited direct speech in biographies (287) and differences from historical monographs (290–92), though monographs generally contained more orations proportionate to their size than did longer historical works (292). He emphasizes the proportion of direct speech in novels (296–97; see esp. the charts on 300–301). Novels did generally include speeches; see Anderson, "Second Sophistic," 347–49, noting much more in Achilles Tatius, Apuleius, and Heliodorus than in Longus; cf. forensic speeches in, e.g., Fernández-Garrido, "Stasis-theory."

20. Pervo, "Direct Speech," 302. For example, Susanna (Dan 13 LXX) has 46 percent direct speech, yet no speeches (Pervo, "Direct Speech," 298). Pervo's argument that the high amount of direct discourse fits works with popular ideal audiences (see 303) is less objectionable; I agree with Pervo that Acts is on a more popular level than the vast proportion of extant ancient historiography. That a historical monograph of Sallust contains less direct speech outside of major speeches (290) and far more space devoted to opposition speeches (291) may indeed reflect Luke's more popular level, at least in part. My point here is that his case does not necessarily undermine the value of Luke's speeches for the work's characterization as history; Luke's actual orations remain comparable to many historical works.

21. Pervo, "Direct Speech," 290. The estimates of speech in Burridge, "Genre of Acts," 15, come to roughly 25 percent.

22. If we ask why Luke's level is popular, it may be partly because he was not rhetorically capable of a more rhetorically sophisticated work (see Padilla, "Παιδεία"), but his largely popular audience undoubtedly also played a role.

23. On Luke's prologue as fitting for historical works, see, e.g., Porter, "'We' Passages," 550; Fuller, "Classics," 189 (addressing George Kennedy's comments); Aune, *Environment*, 80; Callan, "Preface and Historiography"; van Unnik, "Once More Prologue"; Johnson, "Luke-Acts," 406–7; Penner, *Praise*, 219–22; Rothschild, *Rhetoric of History*, 93–94; Flichy, *Oeuvre de Luc*; Plümacher, "Historiker," 2.

24. Alexander, *Preface*, 42–101; idem, "Preface"; Le Cornu, *Acts*, 2. Luke's preface resembles scientific prefaces in structure and similar linguistic usage, although some other features lack parallels in the scientific-preface tradition (Alexander, *Preface*, 147).

tradition that, not surprisingly, overlaps in some of its features with those of works of history more narrowly defined (but not novels).[25] But some proposed parallels with scientific prefaces are questionable,[26] and although Luke's preface could fit this tradition stylistically (and most kinds of prefaces share some similarities),[27] the stylistic criterion is inadequate without attention to the more important matter of content.[28] Aune points out that Luke-Acts "is obviously not a scientific or technical treatise";[29] moreover, its prefaces do speak of historical matters (Luke 1:1; Acts 1:1). Aune has also shown that historical prefaces can share the same elements found in the "scientific" (technical) treatise tradition.[30]

Loveday Alexander, who originally pointed out the parallels in technical treatises, has clarified her understanding of the value of these parallels. She agrees that Luke is not writing a technical scientific work; her appeal to such parallels in prefaces was not intended to delineate Acts' genre.[31]

> Nor was I claiming that Luke did not intend his work to be read as "history," if by that we mean a reliable account of events in the recent past. In fact (paradoxically enough), casting Luke as a sober, pragmatic, writer of "scientific prose" might give us a much more secure handle on his reliability. It is certainly evident (as I have made clear all along) that the preface shows a strong interest both in "reliability" and in the preservation of authentic tradition.[32]

Alexander acknowledges that she may have earlier formulated the question too narrowly, but she is reluctant to claim (with Sterling and Aune) that many characteristics simply transcend genres. She contends that the conventions she cites cluster in some genres more than others; where they appear in historiography, they appear "in marginal authors working on the edges of the Greek cultural tradition (including Jewish writers)."[33] Their dominance in technical treatises could also be consistent with the background that one line of Lukan scholarship proposes for the author (i.e., as a physician) or reveal that Luke had a more factual, less rhetorical, interest than some of his more elite contemporaries.[34] On the basis of his preface, Alexander argues that

25. To modestly suggest Luke's scientific background (see ch. 11 below) or that Hellenistic schools provide an important type of setting for reconstructing Luke's usage (Alexander, *Preface*, 211–12) is not problematic on the thesis that Acts is a historical work. Genuine technical treatises did seek to deal in information, not fiction (cf. idem, "Formal Elements," 23–24). They were not very restricted in topic (covering medicine, physics, sports, oratory, ethnography, and other topics; see Sallmann, "Technical Literature").

26. Adams, "Preface," 177–78, warns that given the scarcity of extant examples, the scientific prefaces we have might not be representative. Moreover, Adams argues (181–83) that Alexander's argument from preface length depends on Thucydides as representative for history whereas Luke's falls within the usual historical prefaces (as a proportion of the entire work).

27. Aune, *Dictionary of Rhetoric*, 371, points out that parallels are equally close, including some specific wording, in Plutarch *Dinner of Seven Wise Men*, which is *not* scientific.

28. With Callan, "Preface and Historiography," 577. For topics in prefaces, see Alexander, *Preface*, 31–34.

29. Aune, *Dictionary of Rhetoric*, 370.

30. Aune, "*Prooimion*" (though focusing more narrowly on Plutarch *Dinner of Seven Wise Men*).

31. Alexander, *Context*, 16.

32. Alexander, ibid., 12–13 (though she believes that Acts also contains fictional elements that ancients would have recognized as such, p. 13). She does not believe that the preface, by itself, must identify Luke-Acts as historiography, though it certainly distinguishes it from genres such as epic (21–42).

33. Ibid., 17–18. This observation would fit Sterling's observations about minority apologetic historians.

34. Luke lacks annalistic dating as in many historians; this may be a sign of his popular audience, but it need not indicate lack of interest in genuine information. In contrast to those with access to annals, most of Luke's information is oral and hence less apt to provide dates (on the general exclusion of dates from eyewitness recollection in memory studies, see Bauckham, *Eyewitnesses*, 333).

Luke is clearly not writing rhetorical history or epic history;[35] if Acts is history, it is, she contends, the sort of history where scientific and historical traditions "intersect, i.e. on the more scholarly, less rhetorical side of history . . . , and perhaps especially where the author and/or subject is non-Greek."[36]

If Alexander debates whether Luke's preface is appropriate exclusively to history, nevertheless the majority of scholars argue that, in the most important respects, this preface is consistent with, or even points to,[37] historiography. As Terrance Callan notes, a good introduction should summarize what is to follow (Quint. *Inst.* 4.1.34),[38] and in Luke 1:1, 3, the summary of what will follow is explicitly historical—"an orderly narrative of the things fulfilled among us." Likewise, his explicit purpose is to confirm what Theophilus has learned about such events (1:4). "Given this statement of the question, it is almost obvious that the preface of Luke-Acts most resembles the prefaces of histories."[39] Luke focuses on "a narrative of events," as Herodotus "writes of 'the great and marvellous deeds done by Greeks and foreigners' (1.1)."[40]

Just as Luke's purpose is to confirm truth (Luke 1:4),[41] Lucian (*Hist.* 7–14) emphasizes that history's distinctive commitment is to truth (also *Hist.* 39–40).[42] Callan argues that after the fourth century B.C.E., usefulness becomes a dominant purpose for writing history[43] but in the first century B.C.E. some historical writers stopped emphasizing utility as their purpose and emphasized instead that they simply would write a "true account of something."[44] Luke's purpose expressly fits this category, revived as early as one of Sallust's historical monographs.[45] Whether we can distinguish between histories committed to truth and those committed to usefulness as clearly as Callan suggests is questionable, but Luke's interest in the former is clear in his preface. That Luke also sees his work as useful (Luke 1:4) would not conflict with this goal;[46] the tradition of emphasizing a work's usefulness never died out, as is clear from Lucian in the second century C.E. (*Hist.* 53). Given Luke's clear statements, especially in view of parallels to such claims in historical works, Luke-Acts would easily enough appear as a historical work (especially in view of the following narratives) to a first-century audience.

35. Alexander, *Context*, 41–42.

36. Ibid., 41. For Luke's training in technical or scientific approaches, see also Padilla, "Παιδεία," 435–36.

37. E.g., Rothschild, *Rhetoric of History*, 93–94; Penner, *Praise*, 219–22, and others noted above.

38. This is a conventional expectation; see also *Rhet. Alex.* 29, 1436a.33–39; Polyb. 3.1.3–3.5.9 (esp. 3.1.7); 11.1.1–5; Dion. Hal. *Lysias* 24; *Thuc.* 19; Cic. *Or. Brut.* 40.137; Virg. *Aen.* 1.1–6; Sen. E. *Controv.* 1.pref. 21; Dio Chrys. *Or.* 38.8; Aul. Gel. pref. 25; Soranus *Gynec.* 1.intro. 2; 1.1.3; Philost. *Vit. Apoll.* 7.1; 8.1.

39. Callan, "Preface and Historiography," 577; cf. similarly Hemer, "Alexandria Troas," 98.

40. Callan, "Preface and Historiography," 577.

41. This is "Luke's own explicit statement of purpose" (Aune, *Environment*, 136).

42. Callan, "Preface and Historiography," 578, also noting that Herodotus just says that he wrote so that the past may be remembered (Hdt. 1.1); Thucydides does not specify (Thucyd. 1.1.1). For the quest for truth in historical works, see also Adams, "Preface," 186, and sources he cites.

43. Callan, "Preface and Historiography," 579, citing Polyb. 1.1; Livy pref. 10; Sall. *Jug.* 4.1–6; Diod. Sic. 1.1–2; Dion. Hal. *Ant. rom.* 1.1–2; 1.2.1; 1.6.4; Jos. *Ant.* 1.3–5, 9, 14; perhaps Tac. *Hist.* 1.3; also (curiously, since it is hardly history) *Let. Aris.* 2, 5, 7–8.

44. Callan, "Preface and Historiography," 579–80, citing Sall. *Catil.* 4.2–3; Jos. *War* 1.6 (cf. *Ant.* 1.3–4); Tac. *Ann.* 1.1; Arrian *Alex.* pref.; Dio Cass. 1.2; Hdn. 1.3. Cf. even Jos. *Ag. Ap.* 1.3.

45. Chronological typology cannot afford to be as strict as Callan seems to suggest, with works of Sallust falling into both "categories." Both reporting truth and being useful constituted important purposes for histories; Luke states the former, but the genre of Luke-Acts probably also implies the latter. In the second century C.E., Lucian advises that historical prologues note the usefulness of the work (*Hist.* 53).

46. A writer could have more than one objective (e.g., Jos. *Ant.* 1.4, citing two objectives). Thus 2 Maccabees abridges a larger work (2 Macc 2:23, 26, 28) to provide a more pleasurable narrative (2:24–25; cf. 2:27) and to profit readers (2:25).

Moessner shows that Dionysius of Halicarnassus, writing perhaps a century before Luke, "*combines three technical terms that Luke will employ in his short prooemial period (Luke 1.1–4)*" and that they share also four other key terms.[47] He argues that Luke compares the arrangement of his narrative with that of his predecessors and gives special attention to the beginning, end, and divisions of his story, as Dionysius expected in historical works.[48] Rothschild cites as common in historical prologues various elements, the following of which appear relevant to Luke's preface: claims to truth; accuracy; narrative (διήγησις), often "from the beginning"; ordering of the sources (καθεξῆς); and autopsy (eyewitness evidence).[49] Penner likewise notes comparisons of Luke's stated purposes to those frequent in historical prefaces: the comparison with earlier works; thorough acquaintance with the story; the claim to accuracy (ἀκριβῶς); the claim to an orderly (καθεξῆς) narrative; and the intention to be useful.[50] Although not all these characteristics are limited to historiography (e.g., other writers distinguished themselves from their predecessors in a discipline, including in architecture and dream interpretation), the conjunction of various features in historiography is significant.

Likewise, when possible, Luke sets his events in the context of world history, just as historians (and almost exclusively historians) did in their histories (Luke 2:1–2; 3:1–2; Acts 18:12).[51] Further, neither a biography (Talbert) nor a romance (Pervo) should end in the way that Acts does, because they would focus on Paul the character (and hence perhaps his death or release). But if Acts is a historical work, it can chronicle the "spread of the gospel" and the movement it generated, especially from Jerusalem to Rome.[52] Some scholars have even found in Luke specific stylistic echoes of Polybius and his successors in Hellenistic historiography, suggesting that Luke imitates not only the LXX but also the style of eastern Mediterranean historians.[53]

As noted above, details of local color[54] do not necessarily make a work's genre historical,[55] but Luke's consistent accuracy on many events that can be checked with other sources—including some events where Luke reports Paul's "adventures" (cf., e.g., 2 Cor 11:32–33)—supports the thesis that Acts belongs to the historical genre, whatever individual details may remain in dispute. Ancient novels valued local color but do not betray the sort of careful research or use of historical sources suggested in the case of Acts both by extrinsic evidence in general (see ch. 6 below) and, most frequently, Paul's letters in particular (see ch. 7 below).

A more specifically Jewish approach could point in the same direction. After surveying Luke's use of OT historiography, Brian Rosner notes that Luke's use of analogous features "strongly suggests that Luke was writing what he conceived to be a historical

47. Moessner, "Arrangement," 158, emphasis his.

48. Ibid., 159–63. These elements may be common rhetoric and less strictly distinctive to historiography.

49. Rothschild, *Rhetoric of History*, 67–69 (among the elements found in various historical prologues; I have listed those relevant to Luke, that is, most of them).

50. Penner, *Praise*, 219–21.

51. With, e.g., Johnson, "Luke-Acts," 406; Meier, *Marginal Jew*, 1:383. In a different form, legal documents could also be dated by rulers' period of rule (e.g., P.Tebt. 104.5–8).

52. Witherington, *Acts*, 808–9.

53. See Mealand, "Historians and Style." Although Luke shares some LXX verbs, the stylistic level of his verbs falls between a high level of Koine and Dionysius's atticizing (idem, "Verbs").

54. Cited by Bruce, *Acts*[3], 33, and others. Local color is worthy of note in the commentary because of its cumulative effect for a historical estimation but also for its rhetorical effect (relevant whatever its genre).

55. On local color not guaranteeing historicity, see also White, "Oration," 62n2. Visiting orators would appeal to local color in a well-known city (95). Vividness likewise does not guarantee historicity, being a common rhetorical activity; to make vividness demonstrate reliability is to fall into the "referential fallacy" (see Aune, *Dictionary of Rhetoric*, 399).

work."[56] Some scholars even argue that Luke sought to write salvation history as he knew it from the OT.[57] Certainly, Luke cites the LXX far more than any other source, and it is indeed the only extant historical source (apart from Mark) that he quotes (and one that he regularly quotes with marked citations). Nevertheless, as in the case of Josephus's *Antiquities*, biblical models would not prevent him from writing Hellenistic history at the same time.[58] Jewish historical writing by this period employed Hellenistic conventions; thus Shaye J. D. Cohen lists among Jewish works of history owing "more to Herodotus, Thucydides, and Hellenistic historiography than to Kings and Chronicles" both 2 Maccabees and Josephus.[59]

b. Boundaries between Novel and History?

As noted above, not every feature of Acts claimed for a historical genre is decisive in its favor. For example, novels as well as historical works could strive for precision "in matters of local color and detail,"[60] although good novels would be more apt to err more often than good histories would (especially regarding details beyond common knowledge about the location). Further, proposed discrepancies with Paul on points of detail could be cited against the historical genre (although the points of commonality are, as will be argued, much more striking).[61] But even if we accept all proposed discrepancies, similar discrepancies appear regularly in ancient historians.[62]

History was conceived, however, as primarily factual (see ch. 4 below) and, in most cases, was readily distinguishable from conventional fiction. Lucian writes that good biographers avoid flattery that falsifies events (*Hist.* 12) and only bad historians invent data (e.g., *Hist.* 24–25). By his criticism, Lucian shows us, first, that some historians did fabricate data (or at least could be so accused by those who disagreed with them)[63]

---

56. Rosner, "Biblical History," 81, after noting (65–81) the common features. See discussion of historiographic tendencies in the LXX in Meiser, "Tendenzen" (though the LXX is translation literature, 77).

57. Jervell, "Future," 110–11; idem, *Apostelgeschichte*, 78–79, 104–5; on Luke-Acts as salvation history, see also Thielman, *Theology*, 113–16. Whatever scholars' evaluation today, Luke would surely have regarded the OT historical narratives as historically reliable—at least in the sense that Greco-Roman historiography was. Other Jews in Hellenistic environments distinguished their Scripture from myth (*Let. Aris.* 168; Philo *Creation* 1–2, 157; Jos. *Ant.* 1.15; on Philo, see also Feldman, "Death of Moses"), in contrast to the evaluation of pagan critics (Cook, *Interpretation*, 129); though some Jews employed "myth" in a neutral sense (*Sib. Or.* 1.33), more rejected it (*Sib. Or.* 3.226; *Let. Aris.* 137). Some Greeks thought myth acceptable so long as it honored deity (Diod. Sic. 4.8.3–5; though truth did this better, 1.2.2; cf. Max. Tyre 4.3–5) or depicted true values (Theon *Progymn.* 3.2; Hermog. *Progymn.* 1, "Fable," 2; Aphth. *Progymn.* 1, "On Fable," 21S, 1R; Nicolaus *Progymn.* 2, "On Fable," 6); but others insisted on truth rather than gossip (Polyb. 3.20.1–5). And edifying myth remained myth, distinct from claims to truth (Trigg, "Tales"). By this period, when hearers considered the credibility of old stories, the label "myth" could be used to challenge an account's reliability (cf. Bettini, "Mythos").

58. Even if we were to accept Conzelmann's scheme of epochs, some Romans schematized Rome's history accordingly (in Sen. E., historical frg. 1, on the analogy with human life stages).

59. Cohen, *Maccabees*, 194; cf., in general, Attridge, "Historiography," 326; cf. Eisman, "Dio and Josephus." Egyptians and Babylonians likewise sought to present their history in Greek in the period of Hellenistic cultural dominance (Bartlett, *Jews*, 7). For some suggested differences (related to Jewish literature's apologetic interests) relevant to Acts, see Padilla, *Speeches*, 237–40. For specific comparisons with 1–2 Maccabees, see Schwartz, "Maccabees and Acts."

60. Johnson, *Acts*, 5.

61. That is, authorial agendas and problems in the transmission of reports may account for many differences, but the similarities, which are too great to be attributed to coincidence, indicate a significant quantity of information and a significant interest in utilizing information.

62. Johnson, *Acts*, 6–7.

63. Others, including Hayden White, recognize history as "factual truths . . . handled 'rhetorically' in the sense of 'dramatically,'" but Woodman, *Rhetoric*, 199, warns that even this approach does not sufficiently credit the role of free invention. Penner, *Praise*, 107, notes that A. J. Woodman and T. P. Wiseman have argued that ancient historians invented even events (though conceding the resistance of most classicists to

and, second, that most historians agreed that the practice was unacceptable, at least for events (rather than, e.g., details of conversations or emotions).[64]

Yet the boundaries of genres were not always clearly defined. Many ancient readers questioned the veracity of particular historians, and some historians used the trappings of history to recount fanciful tales.[65] Cicero opined that Xenophon's story of Cyrus was meant to teach about proper government, not to present history about Cyrus (Cic. *Quint. fratr.* 1.1.8.23).[66] Most scholars allow that works such as Xenophon's *Cyropaedia* and Pseudo-Callisthenes's account of Alexander are exceptions to the usual division between histories and novels, since they are novels about historical personages, sometimes employing known traditions.[67] Boundary problems are not related only to such works, however; some ancient writers' statements suggest that even some true histories fell short of the ideal standard. Plutarch complains that some writers added details missing elsewhere—for example, composing a proper tragic finale for Alexander's life (*Alex.* 70.3).[68] Even Arrian, one of the more dependable Alexander historians, can subordinate information to the value of moral instruction.[69]

Rhetoricians were permitted to "adjust stories" to provide cohesiveness to their narrative; if Coriolanus died one way and a rhetorician was paralleling Themistocles to him, the rhetorician could make use of a parallel account, already invented by others, of the latter's death. One could do this, Cicero claimed, knowing full well that the parallel account was not solid history (Cic. *Brut.* 11.42). C. W. Fornara complains that the view that Cicero here allows rhetors to "distort history" misreads his Latin; rather, Cicero simply speaks of rhetors using historical illustrations in their speeches.[70]

such claims; one might also wonder what group of scholars better than classicists would be most qualified to judge this case). The statement may be true in some cases, but our evidence suggests that it was hardly the norm. Both approaches to ancient historiography—rhetorical studies of the documents themselves and mining them for some historical information—remain represented today (Marincola, "Introduction," 3–4). They need not be played off against each other as if one precludes the other (see Feldherr, "Introduction," 8). I provide a ten-page chart in Keener, "Otho," comparing some information in Tacitus, Suetonius, and Plutarch, and demonstrating in some detail that despite differences, such writers depend extensively on prior information.

64. Thus Dibelius, *Studies in Acts*, 136–37, compares Luke's freedom on details with that of other ancient historians. Woodman, *Rhetoric*, 93, 199, gives rhetorical *inventio* a heavy role in ancient historiography, but Damon, "Rhetoric," 440, distinguishes *inventio*, which demands plausibility, from pure invention. *Inventio* had to be plausible and believable even in forensic speeches, because opposing speeches would be heard (441); likewise, the danger of refutation constrained writers of contemporary histories (442–43).

65. Alexander, "Fiction and Genre," 385–91.

66. W. Miller, "Introduction," viii, also takes Xenophon's *Cyropaedia* as historical romance, including history but allowing "many liberties with the facts of history," yet (p. x) he notes that it provides much valuable history and culture.

67. Bosworth, "Pseudo-Callisthenes," opines that genuinely historical material in Ps.-Callisthenes's *Alexander Romance* is minimal, though some of his fictitious material precedes him; so also Zambrini, "Historians," 211. Virtually no informed reader would see Pseudo-Callisthenes as historical in the way normal Alexander histories were, despite their normal historiographic liberties (cf. the distinction also in Zambrini, "Historians," 211).

68. His own romantic description of Darius's death (Plut. *Alex.* 43.2) is missing in Arrian *Alex.* 3.21–23 but was evidently not his own invention (Bernadotte Perrin in *Plutarch: Lives*, LCL, 7:352n1, cites Quint. Curt. 5.13, 28; Diod. 17.73).

69. See McInerney, "Arrian and Romance." Moralistic agendas in historiography were common; see ch. 5 below. Nevertheless, Arrian is clearly adapting history, not simply composing fiction about historical characters; unlike Luke, he also writes about a character several centuries earlier.

70. Fornara, *Nature of History*, 136–37n57. Nevertheless, Dio Cass. 1.1.1–2 does complain that some of his predecessors have compromised accuracy for rhetorical style. Woodman, "Cicero," and idem, *Rhetoric*, 76–98, even argues that Cicero welcomed rhetorical invention in historiography (citing *De or.* 2.51–64); he contends (*Rhetoric*, 77) that *De or.* 2.51–54 distinguishes a "hard core" from elaboration. But Northwood, "*De Oratore*," warns against misinterpreting this passage (esp. 2.63). See the further critique in Lendon, "Historiography," 50–53.

The context, however, at least suggests that Cicero expected some speakers to select their accounts on utilitarian grounds, that is, for what worked best rhetorically in their speeches. At the same time, Cicero was speaking about speeches depending on biography, not about Greek historiography, and Luke's parallels are more modest: Paul is not crucified, and although Peter may have been historically crucified by the time of Luke's writing,[71] Luke does not retroject this event (which he probably would have known) back into his narrative.

As Loveday Alexander points out, "fact" and "fiction" are not genres themselves, and factual markers can be subverted. As in the case of the more modern *Gulliver's Travels*, "fantasy can use the 'documentary' technique to frame a narrative of the frankly unbelievable."[72] Yet early Greek historians distinguished themselves from epic poets not only by employing prose but by explicitly identifying themselves and the limits of their knowledge.[73] Greek novels often focused on ethnographically or geographically remote subjects not easily checked; this allowed the appearance of greater plausibility.[74] Some novels were realistic,[75] but many were inconsistent or uninterested in local color.[76]

What bearing do these factors have on Acts? Alexander points out that Acts, like novels, draws on distant past oracles of a barbarian people (the LXX), "barbarian place-names," and so forth.[77] Still, in contrast to novelistic expectations, Luke provides no fantasy landscape for Palestine but an urban setting that parallels most of the rest of the Mediterranean world.[78] Further, Luke's Scriptures are genuine documents, although Alexander thinks that Greek readers would not know this.[79] She argues that the first volume's preface (Luke 1:1–4) fits the pattern for technical treatises and other "factual" writings (a claim we discussed in ch. 2).[80] The work contains supernatural events and other matters about which historians tended to use caution (see the discussion of signs, ch. 9 below) but is set realistically in the Mediterranean world and without "a fantasy happy ending." The earliest readers would, she notes, decide such issues on the basis of factors extrinsic to the text itself.[81]

Though concurring with most of Alexander's points, I believe the case for defining Luke's historical character is still stronger than her limited argument here suggests. Alexander doubts that Luke's Greek readers would know Luke's "exotic" Scriptures;

---

71. See *1 Clem.* 5.4; for Peter's stay in Rome, probably Ign. *Rom.* 4.3. Tradition claims that he was crucified (Tert. *Scorp.* 15; Euseb. *H.E.* 2.25.5–8), probably upside down (*Acts of Peter*; Origen according to Euseb. *H.E.* 3.1; for crucifixion in this posture, see also Sen. Y. *Consol.* 20; references from Talbert, *John*, 262).

72. Alexander, "Fiction and Genre," 381. In antiquity, Lucian particularly perfected this technique (although in a way that no one would mistake for history). Alexander accepts Acts as a work of historiography, but she believes that it contains some elements that ancient readers would have viewed as fictitious (*Context*, 12–13).

73. Alexander, "Fiction and Genre," 382–85.

74. Ibid., 392–94. Many novels used known centers such as Ephesus or Tyre, but much of (later) Heliodorus's *Ethiopian Story* and Antonius Diogenes's *Wonders beyond Thule* fits Alexander's point here. Of course, such exotic claims appear in some widely read histories (e.g., the gold-digging giant ants in Dio Chrys. *Or.* 35.23–24 probably allude to Hdt. 3.102–5).

75. E.g., Longus is a countryman who knows the correct fauna of Lesbos, though much of his knowledge would apply to any eastern Mediterranean setting (and he apparently lacked firsthand acquaintance with trapping techniques; Arnott, "Realism," 211).

76. E.g., on cities (Saïd, "City," noting that some novels that were interested in cities used widely known information).

77. Alexander, "Fiction and Genre," 394–95.

78. Ibid., 396.

79. Ibid., 396–97.

80. Ibid., 397. Casting the net more widely, one may compare the *exordium* of speeches (cf. Klauck, "Rhetorik: Exordium").

81. Alexander, "Fiction and Genre," 398–99.

as we note later, Luke's ideal audience appears to possess a working knowledge of Scripture.[82] Further, even when historical works embellished their story in a manner that modern historians would consider fictional, they were bound by the prior story in a way that novelists were not.[83] Moreover, where we can check Luke against extrinsic data, his claims fit the data far better than do novels set in the past, such as Chariton's romance or Judith. After 70 C.E., information about Palestine circulated widely, if not always accurately (see Tac. *Hist.* 5.5); given the networking of early Christian communities (see ch. 6, sect. 2.e, below), it is also likely that many post-70 congregations outside Palestine included Judean immigrants who could verify the plausibility of many of the Palestinian settings. An ideal audience in, for instance, Macedonia and Achaia, already informed on many matters that Luke was confirming for them, would thus have every reason to trust the ideal author's access to information.

Merely arguing that Acts was ancient historiography as opposed to fiction does not resolve all our questions about its character, since there was a wide range of historical writing. This is not to say that we cannot locate various aspects of Acts at particular places along that range but to suggest that simply defining the genre does not by itself fully resolve our questions vis-à-vis modern historical standards. For one clear example of the breadth of range of genre included in ancient historiography, Acts, as a single-volume work on a more popular level, contrasts starkly with Josephus's multivolume Hellenistic Jewish historical writing, which is on a more technical and rhetorical level.[84] This chapter therefore simply introduces arguments for Acts as fitting the genre of ancient historiography, and later chapters (esp. chs. 6–9) will explore more specific classifications of Luke's historiography (especially with regard to historical accuracy).

c. Modern versus Ancient Historiography

Although it should go without saying, we must be careful to distinguish ancient historiography from modern historiography.[85] When we claim that a biblical (or other ancient) work fits the genre of history or of letters, modern readers often make the facile assumption (happily, more difficult for apocalyptic texts) that we are talking about the same genres as modern history or modern letters.[86] Granted, there are considerable similarities, the ranges overlap, and modern analogies evolved from these ancient forms. But conventions differed, and only those who have done little reading in the ancient sources will simply equate ancient and modern historiography.

It is anachronistic to assume that ancient and modern histories share all the same generic features (e.g., the way speeches should be composed) merely because we employ the same term today to describe them. Thus those who evaluate Acts' historical details only according to modern standards, whether to defend or to condemn them, themselves risk distorting the historical task.[87] Barring supernatural inspiration to write

82. Alexander, *Context*, 251, also recognizes the heavy influence of the LXX on Luke.

83. Marguerat, *Histoire*, 19–20, 25; idem, *Historian*, 12–13. The comparison in Lendon, "Historiography," 57, to the contrast between a respected newspaper and a modern novel, may be hyperbolic, but it highlights the excesses of extreme relativism; genre does matter.

84. See Pervo, *Profit*, 5.

85. As is often noted, e.g., Marguerat, *Histoire*, 19–20. Biblical scholars, including conservative scholars, also note this caveat concerning ancient Israelite history (e.g., Dillard and Longman, *Introduction*, 23–25; Arnold, *Samuel*, 23; cf. Konkel, *Kings*, 30, 328).

86. On the divergence of ancient genre categories from their modern namesake descendants, see, e.g., Hunter, "Genre."

87. Often they assume that Luke's historical purpose must be identical to ours, an assumption rendered unlikely by an examination of other ancient historical works. Judge, *First Christians*, 249–51, explains that

according to as-yet nonexistent historical conventions that no one in antiquity expected (even when assuming such inspiration), we should not demand ancient historians to conform precisely to modern historiography. Ancient historians sometimes fleshed out scenes and speeches to produce a coherent narrative in a way that their contemporaries expected but that modern academic historians would not consider acceptable when writing for their own peers. This contrast reflects the different interests of ancient and modern historiography: ancients emphasized a cohesive narrative more than simple recitation of facts; moderns value exactness in details much more than the rhetorical flow of the narrative for their audience. Ancient historical writers varied in the degree of cohesiveness and attention to bare facts, just as modern historical writers do, but on the whole, the ancient range of historical writing was far more concerned with fleshing out missing details for cohesive narratives than modern ones are. (See further, in chs. 5 and 8 below, the discussion of historians' *Tendenz* and composition of speeches.)

This difference does not mean that Luke or most other historians (including popular historians, such as himself) made up "events." It does mean that, where necessary, they had the generic freedom to fill in a missing detail to make sense of their sources, to flesh out a speech (cf. the discussions at Acts 5:36–37; 25:14–27), and so forth.[88] In such situations, plausible and probable inferences were acceptable.[89] Having noted this general caveat, however, we do have good reason to believe that Luke had sources for the events in most of his scenes (especially in Paul's ministry), wrote reasonably close in time to the events he narrates, and was as careful as possible according to the standards expected for popular historiography, especially regarding the events of early Christianity, in which he was deeply interested.

No one would have viewed the occasional filling in of scenes such as Acts 25:14–27 on the basis of plausible inference as deceptive or erroneous; nor, given contemporary expectations about genres, would Luke have imagined a charge of deception being leveled against him on such grounds. Viewing such elaboration as deception is anachronistic because ancients expected such elaboration, often even much more than Luke provides (compare the much longer speeches in most histories). The arrangement of material in his Gospel fits the same pattern; although he may have been creative in suggesting symposia (extended meal scenes with dialogue) or arranging events in his travel narrative, he nevertheless follows the sequence of his sources (where it is possible to check him, especially with respect to Mark) more conservatively than was expected of biographers. Luke also resembles other ancient historians in his omission of material that did not concern him, as well as his editorial asides (e.g., people being "full of the Spirit" and virtues, 6:3, 5, 8; 7:55), which are not as characteristic of modern historiography.

---

rhetorical conventions shape the publications of modern historians no less than ancient ones, but we must recognize what the rhetorical conventions of a given era are when we interpret the work.

88. Cf. Tac. *Agr.* 10, where Tacitus assumes that his predecessors embellished details precisely where they lacked accurate information. This approach to writing about history is not defective, just different from our own; modern historians simply take account of it when reading ancient historians, so as to reproduce their essential information in ways more amenable to modern approaches. As Witherington points out, although Luke normally edits genuine sources, Acts 25:14–27 is "not the sort of material Luke would likely have access to"; thus he "may be following the advice of his predecessors in making the speakers say what was appropriate to the occasion" (*Acts*, 119–20).

89. Josephus can infer (or guess) what was said in private on the basis of what happened in public (e.g., *War* 2.319). Sometimes historians report characters' thoughts and emotions (Dewald, "Construction," 97). Even Tacitus, perhaps the historian of the early empire most respected today, sometimes indulges in reporting characters' thoughts and fears (e.g., *Hist.* 2.74); he probably does so more often than Luke, precisely because Tacitus is more rhetorically sophisticated than Luke. For plausibility and probability, as well as accuracy, as criteria for good ancient history writing, see Rothschild, *Rhetoric of History*, 62; cf. Damon, "Rhetoric," 440.

Matters that have invited question today are mainly points at which we would expect Luke to have less information from his Christian sources (e.g., private conversations[90] and some events most geographically and chronologically remote); questions on such points should not be used, however, to ignore Luke's record on the many other points where we can expect him to preserve the best evidence (just as we would not ignore the value of other historians' best evidence on account of their more questionable material). Indeed, in such places (e.g., details in the "we" narratives) difficulties of this sort are much harder to find. Divergences from Paul's letters on matters of history are minor whereas correspondences are often significant and legion (see ch. 7, esp. sect. 6, below).

d. Ancient History as Nonhistory?

Ancient historical works constituted a recognizable genre, in their normal form conspicuously distinct from the romances. Granted, their treatment of speeches, details, and theology (see esp. chs. 5–8 below) might diverge from modern historians' expectations, but they formed a distinct genre that provides the most complete and necessary resource for modern historical treatments of antiquity. They developed many of the critical methodologies further refined and used by historians today (see the discussion on historians and critical thinking in ch. 4 below). As Klaus Meister notes, some of the ancient historians whose works have had the greatest effect, including Herodotus, Thucydides, and Polybius, "raised and discussed many methodological, theoretical, and ideological questions which have had influence up to modern times and are still intensely debated today."[91] Although ancient historiography differs from modern historiography, it was its direct ancestor and is closely related to it.[92]

Many scholars thus go too far in holding ancient historians to a standard of precision that few of them could meet. Some have done so in order to defend a particular understanding of how Luke should have written; others use such standards to discredit Acts.[93] Both groups approach ancient historians, including Luke, in an anachronistic manner in this regard.

Yet some scholars, in rightly emphasizing the differences between ancient and modern historiography, have overstated the case.[94] For example, no less a careful scholar than Todd Penner[95] warns, "Although Luke appears to don the mantle of an ancient historian in the composition of Acts, oversimplified suggestions or tacit assumptions that the appellation 'historian' means something about historical accuracy

90. In the disputed case of Acts 21:38, Luke was not present, and discourse material, in any case, could invite greater creativity. The case of 5:36–37, more often cited, is of a conversation that took place much earlier and to which none of the Jerusalem church would have been privy (though one could argue that Paul would have known the content of the speech). Acts 25 is the strongest case for assuming Luke's reconstruction of a scene based on inference and plausibility.

91. Meister, "Historiography: Greece," 421.

92. For one discussion of modernity's frequent dependence on ancient thought, see Judge, "Ancient Beginnings," esp. 482. For the influence of ancient historians on modern political theory, see Fontana, "Historians."

93. Cf. Lüdemann, Acts, 22, 218, 363, although he manages to critique Acts without greatly changing the nature of ancient historiography.

94. Hengel and Schwemer complain (Between Damascus and Antioch, 6–7) that in modern NT scholarship, "the real danger in the interpretation of Acts (and the Gospels) is no longer an uncritical apologetic but the hypercritical ignorance and arrogance which—often combined with unbridled fantasy—has lost any understanding of living historical reality." For another argument against the usual unreliability of ancient historiography, see, e.g., Eddy and Boyd, Legend, 330–34 (noting, 333, that most of the critiques offered against ancient historians apply to modern historians as well).

95. I elsewhere draw on his useful insights in approaching the use of rhetoric in history.

and veracity in presentation are misguided."[96] Although such a statement rightly critiques "oversimplified" views, its apparent skepticism that the genre "means something about historical accuracy" is worded far too strongly if it invites a less careful reader to allow no distinction between history and novel. Although the genre does not guarantee historicity in all details, it certainly offers expectations of some ideal standards.[97]

It is true that ancient historians wrote from locations of class and political and ethnic bias,[98] that they supplied (and historians cannot help but supply) interpretive grids in how they constructed their narratives,[99] that ancient historians, especially elite historians, made abundant use of rhetoric, including epideictic rhetoric,[100] and that historical intention does not guarantee the accuracy of one's sources.[101] But shall we simply dismiss all historical value in Tacitus, Suetonius, or Josephus, as if they wrote something historically only on the level of novels about historical characters? Such a sweeping claim, if pressed fully, could easily eradicate most of what we claim to know about first-century history. I am not suggesting that Penner himself identifies history and novels; his fuller presentation nuances such statements.[102] (He also recognizes that other readers from different reading locations will sort the same historical data differently than he does.)[103] Nevertheless, scholars less familiar with ancient historical authors could gain the wrong impression.

An even more astonishing claim is that Luke's interest lay purely in foundation mythology: "The historical kernel is really quite beside the point for Lukan *historia*."[104] Such a claim not only redefines the ancient historical enterprise in a manner unrecognizable to ancient historians appealing to wider standards but also contradicts a wealth of evidence where Luke's historical accuracy, corroborated on a range of details, suggests careful research or information. Granted that Luke's accuracy is disputed on some points, it is demonstrable on numerous others where it can be tested. Luke's sole purpose (and that of any ancient historian) was not simple recitation of data from

96. Penner, "Discourse," 72–73 (critiquing Witherington and the historic approach of Fornara; other NT scholars have also made much use of Fornara, e.g., Collins, *Mark*, 25n63, 35–37, 39n172, 40, 41n183). He argues rightly that ancient *historia* was *paideia*, meant to teach citizens about proper citizenship (Penner, "Discourse," 73–77); yet most historians sought to offer their edifying lessons based on existing stories. Similarly, he treats some historiography as "pure panegyric" (idem, *Praise*, 175); yet even Phylarchus and Timaeus apparently deal in real events, however embellished! He claims that the "real dividing line" between history and novel is not accuracy but "function," in that the latter cared only about pleasure (6); yet what the former cared about surely includes some information!

97. If Penner means such statements in their fullest sense, Bock, *Acts*, 10, is right to critique him for creating "false oppositions" between creativity and historical information.

98. As Penner points out (*Praise*, 77–78), historians reinforced power grids of society, reflecting political philosophy. But while this was true of elite historians, apologetic historians such as Josephus could seek to advance the cause of their minority (in his case, his fellow Jews, though with special sympathy for other aristocratic males).

99. Penner, *Praise*, 179, views ancient historians' narratives as an interpretive, "intentional literary creation."

100. Penner, ibid., 217, correctly emphasizes the centrality of plausibility and arrangement, but he goes too far when (179) he suggests that "completely fabricated accounts may in fact be better *historia*" than accurate ones, insofar as they fulfilled their rhetorical function. The genre included a factual as well as a rhetorical component and could be judged by both standards. A modern historian may ask, "How far from the truth does truth-like take us?" (Damon, "Rhetoric," 440); the answer may vary by author, sources, and distance from events.

101. Dibelius, who regarded Acts' author as a historian and even Luke the physician, felt that Luke had little to work with except popular stories (summarized in Neil, *Acts*, 38–39).

102. Penner, *Praise*, 179, recognizes that "some historians like Thucydides may have attempted to reflect actual occurrences and personages to a higher degree than other writers such as Josephus or Livy" (although even here, Josephus and Livy were not so much creating events or persons as embellishing them).

103. Ibid., 335.

104. Penner, "Discourse," 103. In view of his more guarded statements, I may be pressing too much rhetorical force into this one.

the past, but it is difficult to explain why he expended considerable effort to ensure accuracy on so many points (not only those that were common knowledge) if accurate information was not at least part of his goal (a goal he seems to claim in Luke 1:1–4).

One writer defines history as socially constructed "imaginative narration."[105] Although this definition is indeed true as far as it goes, by itself it does not address how the historical genre differs from other genres. Both ancient and modern historians can and typically do select from and present real data, no matter how tendentious they and their sources might be in their selection. As I shall argue at greater length in chapter 4, an opposition between creative, narrative construction and historical information represents an unnecessary dichotomy.

In stark contrast to such claims, Gerd Lüdemann appears to imply that such watering down of the factual historical demands of ancient history represents modern apologists' attempt to *rescue* Acts by lowering historical standards.[106] He regards Acts as unreliable by ancient standards, claiming that it included legend along with history,[107] although he acknowledges that much of Acts' "content is historically reliable and provides information about Primitive Christianity."[108] Claims that ancient historians wrote history so differently from today that one cannot hold Luke to a high standard "are irrelevant, deceptive, or as false as the occasionally advanced claim that the ancients were not concerned about false attribution of writings"; the ancients did care about "what really happened."[109] "To say that the great Roman historians did not write what actually happened does not mean—as Ernst Haenchen seems to imply—that they could write almost anything."[110]

I believe that Lüdemann also goes too far, albeit in the opposite direction from Penner. For example, although Luke's chronology, like that of other ancient historians, required some compromises to follow his story in different locations, I regard Luke's chronology as likelier than Lüdemann's hypothetical construct about Pauline chronology based on what I would consider more limited evidence than Luke would have had available. (To test Luke's chronology where we possess concrete information, see the discussion of Paul's itineraries in ch. 7 below.) Nevertheless, Lüdemann issues a legitimate warning here: ancient historians chose the historical genre to write about actual events, even when they selected, arranged, and sometimes indeed amplified these events for praise or blame.

Thus when Josephus portrays Agrippa's death according to tragic conventions and uses the owl as an omen (*Ant.* 19.346),[111] he takes his liberties as a rhetorical historian (much more interested in Hellenistic rhetorical and tragic conventions than

105. Shauf, *Theology*, 66–84, as summarized and critiqued in Bock, *Acts*, 4. Despite my response to this phrase, Shauf himself does not rule out all historical information. Rather, "The historian selects and shapes material from the scraps that remain of the past" and frames them together as a story fitting the historian's perspective (Shauf, *Theology*, 74), an agenda quite different from free creation as in most novels.
106. Lüdemann, *Acts*, 22. Of course, ad hominem arguments about motives are risky in academic discourse, especially when Lüdemann, too, has agendas (Lüdemann [p. 383] condemns the fanaticism of Christianity, which, in his reading, has led to perhaps twenty million deaths; Christian apologists like Dinesh D'Souza have returned the charge against atheism).
107. Lüdemann, *Acts*, 363; on this mixture, see also idem, "Impropriety."
108. Lüdemann, ibid., 397 (regarding especially the chronological framework as less reliable than the one he believes he has reconstructed solely from Paul's letters).
109. Ibid., 22.
110. Ibid., 218.
111. One may well wonder about the frequency of nocturnal woodland creatures in large public theaters during daylight! Because this omen provides a probable connection with Jos. *Ant.* 18.195, it could easily be Josephus's addition to provide cohesiveness to his narrative, the way Luke, who usually follows Mark's sequence, departs from it for his Nazareth pericope.

Luke is); but he does not invent Agrippa's death on that occasion. Clare Rothschild offers a fairly balanced, centrist assessment: historians, who, like orators, claimed that they placed truth over style, varied in their preferences but mostly dealt both in information and in its persuasive presentation.[112]

Amherst classics professor Cynthia Damon likewise suggests that whatever the degree of rhetorical elaboration, "the basic narrative" provided by Roman historians is authentic and discernible. Ancient audiences were experienced in discerning this narrative and its enjoyable elaboration, and sometimes knew rival narratives.[113] One criterion for evaluating recent history was whether the author could have had access to the information. Even much of Caesar's self-serving narrative meets this criterion, although other elements reflect inferences or commonplaces, and some elements cannot be tested. Little is simply obviously invented.[114]

To claim that "the goal of providing a historically reliable account (in the modern sense) was not an ancient objective"[115] for ancient historians is tenable only if one places a heavy emphasis on "the modern sense." Most novels are completely fictitious, with a few using historical characters; ancient historical works on the whole constituted a genre completely distinct from the sort of mixture we find even in the rarer novels about historical characters. Although nearly all ancient historians exhibited both a degree of literary freedom and edifying agendas unacceptable to many modern (albeit perhaps less so to postmodern) historians, denying that most of the events they report derive from their sources is easily refuted by comparing them with their extant sources where both cover the same ground (e.g., Luke using Mark; see further p. 106). Historians could exercise flexibility on details to provide a coherent rhetorical presentation, but such flexibility did not normally entail the wholesale creation of events (and not necessarily even of all details when details were available).

Using ancient historians' practice of "adaptation" to deny them any historical value may read our contemporary (here postmodern) milieu's agendas of radical perspectivalism into the ancient writers no less than the pure "historicizing" approach does.[116] In a sense, it allows the rejected historicist paradigm to continue to set the agenda: if a text does not correspond at *all* points with history as strictly defined today, it is unreliable as a substantial historical source. Perspectives shape the selectivity of modern history

112. Rothschild, *Rhetoric of History*, 69.

113. Damon, "Rhetoric," 446.

114. Ibid., 450.

115. Moreland, "Mythmaking," 294 (lumping virtually all narrative genres together: "histories, epics, biographies, and novels"). Many acknowledge that Acts contains both historical and imaginative elements (cf., e.g., Hummel, "Factum et fictum"; Francis, "Truthful Fiction"), but it is important to use terms such as "history" and "fiction" consistently. Despite variations in some subgenres, ancients knew the difference between history and fantasy and valued accuracy in history (with, e.g., deSilva, *Introduction*, 350).

116. Penner, *Praise*, 107, prefers postmodern critics' approach to the traditional classicist approach, which he complains has been too resistant to the postmodern critique (perhaps because of the discipline's "conservative and traditional nature"). For one postmodern reading of Roman historians, see Batstone, "Theory." While postmodernists may be correct that written histories are imaginative constructs, the material from which they are constructed differs from pure imagination without substantial historical referents (cf., e.g., Dewald, "Construction," 90–91, 101; Porciani, "Enigma," 333); indeed, most postmodern historians' challenge involves frameworks more than individual facts. For a critique of the radical postmodern skepticism regarding historiography (without rejecting all its elements), see Eddy and Boyd, *Legend*, 15–24; see also Licona, *Resurrection*, 71–89 (noting that most historians are critical realists, 79, 86, 89); especially Tucker, *Knowledge*, 254–62 (cf. idem, "Future"); Lendon, "Historians." (Somewhat impatiently, Lendon also suggests [42] reading the postmodern skeptics by the same standards they apply to ancient authors.) Earlier, Laistner, *Historians*, 36–37, differentiated between merely contending that Caesar's works "were composed from Caesar's point of view" and maintaining "that they deliberately falsified history" (though Caesar may not be the best example of this principle).

and its sources as well, but this does not mean that the particular configuration of facts produces political fictions in the same sense in which novels are fictitious.[117] The genres remain discrete even when some exceptional texts (such as historical novels) straddle the categories. Whatever other approaches may yield useful insights, those who read ancient historians *primarily* as novelists, dramatists, and the like fail to read them as what they identified themselves as: tellers "of true tales about the past."[118]

Hard comparisons among ancient biographers and historians illustrate the degree of overlap among them far more clearly than do sweeping generalizations. When I wrote *The Historical Jesus of the Gospels*, I wrongly wrote as if most of my audience had read enough ancient historians to recognize the difference between historical genres and novels.[119] In a subsequent article I remedied this deficiency by comparing two ancient biographies and an ancient history, with a summary chart roughly ten pages long.[120] Here I will simply list some shared features in these authors' accounts of Otho's death, taken from that article.

His soldiers were not ready to give up the war (Suetonius *Otho* 9.3), and initially refused to believe the report that they had experienced a defeat (10.1)	His soldiers were not ready to give up the war (*Hist.* 2.46)	The soldiers with him pledged their continuing loyalty (Plutarch *Otho* 15.1–3)
Otho wanted to spare his followers further suffering on his behalf (Suetonius *Otho* 9.3; 10.1; cf. 10.2–11.1)	Otho wanted to spare his followers further suffering on his behalf (*Hist.* 2.47)	Otho wanted to spare his followers further suffering on his behalf (Plutarch *Otho* 15.3–6)
Otho's final instructions, summarized (Suetonius *Otho* 10.2)	Otho's final speeches and instructions (*Hist.* 2.47–48)	Otho's final speech and instructions (Plutarch *Otho* 15.3–17.2)
Otho gave final instructions for the safety of several people whom he addressed, including his nephew (Suetonius *Otho* 10.2)	Otho consoled his nephew Salvius Cocceianus, noting that Otho had spared Vitellius's family, hence mercy should be expected, and warning him to remember neither too much nor too little that Otho had been his uncle (*Hist.* 2.48)	Otho consoled his nephew Cocceianus, noting that Otho had spared Vitellius's family, hence mercy should be expected, and warning him to remember neither too much nor too little that Otho had been his uncle (Plutarch *Otho* 16.2)
Otho destroyed any letters that could incriminate his friends to Vitellius (Suetonius *Otho* 10.2)	Otho destroyed any letters that could incriminate his friends to Vitellius (*Hist.* 2.48)	—
He distributed money to his servants (Suetonius *Otho* 11.1)	He distributed money, though frugally (*Hist.* 2.48)	He distributed money to his servants, but carefully rather than lavishly (Plutarch *Otho* 17.1)
Those beginning to leave the camp were being detained as deserters, but Otho prohibited harming them, and met with friends until late (Suetonius *Otho* 11.1)	He urged his friends to depart and provided means (*Hist.* 2.48); the soldiers tried to prevent those departing, requiring his harsh intervention, and he met with those departing until late (*Hist.* 2.49)	Otho persuaded his friends, especially those of rank, to depart (Plutarch *Otho* 16.1–2), and provided means for their departure (17.2); the soldiers threatened to kill them unless they remained, forcing Otho to intervene harshly (16.3)

117. Otherwise, we would have to relinquish attempts at historical claims, unable to arbitrate, e.g., between genuine histories of the Nazi Holocaust and the unfounded and dangerous claims of Holocaust deniers. Deconstruction underscored the limitations of language, but while language is incomplete, anthropological studies (Grunlan and Mayers, *Cultural Anthropology*, 75, 95, citing Chomsky, *Structures*) show that it is *adequate* for communication. Likewise, historical understanding may be incomplete without being completely vacuous.

118. Lendon, "Historians," 41; cf. 60: "what the historians themselves thought they were doing, narrating events that really happened in the past."

119. Keener, *Historical Jesus*, 71–125.

120. Keener, "Otho."

At a late hour Otho quenched his thirst with cold water (*gelidae aquae*, Suetonius *Otho* 11.2)	Near evening Otho quenched his thirst with cold water (*gelidae aquae*, *Hist.* 2.49)	That evening, Otho quenched his thirst with some water (Plutarch *Otho* 17.1)
Otho chose the sharper of two daggers to place under his pillow (Suetonius *Otho* 11.2)	Otho chose the sharper of two daggers to place under his head (*Hist.* 2.49)	Otho chose the sharper of two daggers to place under his head (Plutarch *Otho* 17.1)
Otho then slept soundly one more night (Suetonius *Otho* 11.2)	Otho then spent a quiet night, reportedly even sleeping some (*Hist.* 2.49)	Otho then slept so deeply for the rest of the night that his attendants heard his breathing (Plutarch *Otho* 17.1)
At dawn he stabbed himself to death (Suetonius *Otho* 11.2)	At dawn he fell on his weapon (*Hist.* 2.49)	Just before dawn Otho fell on his sword (Plutarch *Otho* 17.3)
People rushed in when he groaned, as he was dying from a single wound (Suetonius *Otho* 11.2)	People rushed in when he groaned, as he was dying from a single wound (*Hist.* 2.49)	Hearing his groan the servants hurried in (Plutarch *Otho* 17.3, leaving the implication that the single blow was sufficient to end his life)
He was quickly buried at his request (Suetonius *Otho* 11.2)	He was quickly buried at his request, to prevent disfigurement by his enemies (*Hist.* 2.49)	Plutarch implies that he was buried quickly (Plutarch *Otho* 17.3–4)
Many soldiers killed themselves in mourning by his bier (Suetonius *Otho* 12.2)	Some soldiers killed themselves in mourning by his bier (*Hist.* 2.49)	Some soldiers killed themselves at his funeral pyre (Plutarch *Otho* 17.4)
He died in his thirty-eighth year (Suetonius *Otho* 11.2)*	He died in his thirty-seventh year (*Hist.* 2.49)	He lived thirty-seven years (Plutarch *Otho* 18.2)

*Differences between Suetonius and the others here could reflect differences between inclusive and exclusive means of reckoning years. On inclusive reckoning, see Helmut Koester, *Introduction to the New Testament* (Philadelphia: Fortress, 1982), 2:102.

Comparisons among the accounts do yield differences, which the article also addresses,[121] but the degree of overlap among the accounts is striking. Overall (not limited to the death accounts), I discovered in Suetonius's work of perhaps twenty-eight paragraphs nearly fifty correspondences with each of the other two works (a history and another biography) with which I compared it. My point in these comparisons is not to resolve questions of sources; one of the three accounts could have served as one of the sources for the other two, although this assumption is not necessary (they could all depend on earlier sources). What is clear, however, is that these authors are not engaging in free invention the way novelists typically would; at least two of these authors are bound to their sources, and they at least assume that the same is true of the third. Where we can test them, biographies and histories of recent figures plainly adhere to different conventions than novels (despite their common narrative form). Actual empirical comparisons would temper many of today's claims on both the right and the left: ancient historiography is neither identical with modern historiography nor is it mostly novelistic.

At the same time, one cannot simply lump all ancient historiography together with respect to historical accuracy; even among historians, there were degrees of reliability, with some historians valuing accuracy more than others. Luke, as a "popular" historian, is more interested than many historians in the personal adventures of his main protagonist (although he hardly need have invented them, 2 Cor 11:23–33) but exhibits less class bias than some of his contemporaries did. His sources for some earlier periods in Acts may be less complete than for his later narratives, but he writes closer even to the events as a whole than many of his contemporaries did and probably with comparable access to oral sources for recent events.

Where Luke can be checked against other known history, we find more proposed signs of literary freedom especially in the places where we would expect them in an

121. Keener, "Otho," 338, 348–51.

ancient history (e.g., in Gamaliel's private speech at Acts 5:36–37), but substantial accuracy in the places where we would expect to find more of it in ancient histories (e.g., the correct titles of officials in various localities and an itinerary that corresponds well with that found in the Pauline letters). (See fuller discussion in chs. 6 and 7 below.)

2. What Kind of History?

The precise nature of Luke's history eludes consensus.[122] Proposals include ethnographic, institutional, tragic, and other sorts of history. Some proposals are compatible and address different sorts of questions. For example, "apologetic" history addresses motive; labels like "ethnographic," "political," or "military" history address focus; and "tragic" or "dramatic" history refers to style. One could thus write a dramatic, ethnographic apologetic history, for instance.

a. Types of History

Greek historiography developed over the course of many centuries and, in the broadest sense, subsumed a range of smaller identifiable categories.[123] Following earlier theorists, Fornara suggests five genres within the broader category of ancient historiography. Although many scholars today regard these categories as artificial and anachronistic,[124] they may at least help us to survey the range of works often included in ancient historiography in the most general sense. The first category he treats is "genealogy or mythography," which "records heroic tradition and seeks to bring coherence to the sometimes contradictory data of legend, myth, and aetiology."[125] Such works tend to treat the distant, mythical past, which most historians recognized was less easily documented than history closer to their own period.[126] Ancient writers sometimes noted that poets had greater license to use myth (and analogous language for writing about gods) than did historians and prose writers.[127] The primary criterion for distinction among the narrative categories "mythical," "historical," and "lifelike" was verisimilitude.[128] (Noting the importance of verisimilitude does not, of course, prove that a plausible narrative was fabricated.)[129]

Another kind of writing often classified under this larger rubric was ethnography; lacking a general name for this category, Greeks titled specific ethnographies according

122. For a helpful bibliographic survey of philosophic debate on the nature of historical representation in general, see Green and McKeever, *Historiography*, 91–94.

123. For earlier forerunners of such historiography, see Frahm, Jansen-Winkeln, and Wiesehöfer, "Historiography: Ancient Orient." Although distinct from historiography more generally, collections of antiquarian facts also circulated (Bravo, "Antiquarianism," 516), such as Varro's work (524).

124. Felix Jacoby established these modern categories, but his developmental sequencing of them has invited serious criticism (see Marincola, "Introduction," 5–7; Rood, "Development," 147–48).

125. Fornara, *Nature of History*, 1–2. For detail, see 4–12; this approach was "demythologizing" in the sense of trying to reconcile contradictory traditions of genealogies (6).

126. Cf. ibid., 9; Bowersock, *Fiction as History*, 1–2; Laistner, *Historians*, 79, 91; on the association of epic with the distant past, see also, e.g., Nicolai, "Place of History," 15; for myth in the early period of local histories, see, e.g., Harding, *Androtion*, 4, 78. See further, e.g., Dion. Hal. *Ant. rom.* 1.8.1; information in Keener, *Matthew*, 19; idem, *John*, 20–21. Distinguishing between purely mythical elements and legends is not always possible at this remove, though ancient historians had better sources for the early republic than for Rome's origins (Lintott, *Romans*, 15).

127. So Men. Rhet. 1.1, 333.31–334.5. Cf. Pliny *Ep.* 6.21.5: poets should praise virtue but need not stay with facts.

128. Fornara, *Nature of History*, 10; cf. Woodman, *Rhetoric*, 26–28. This criterion did not guarantee truth; invective, for example, preferred plausibility to accuracy (Watson, "Invective"; cf. Arena, "Invective," 158).

129. See Rothschild, *Rhetoric of History*, 81.

to the localities they addressed, such as Berossus's *Babyloniaca*.[130] Ethnographies provided a primary model for monographs in the early empire.[131] But ethnographers, unlike most extant historians of Luke's period, could publish even unconfirmed accounts of incredible events, especially when writing of exotic places too distant to confirm;[132] not truth per se but that the report had been supplied by an informant was the critical matter.[133] As will be noted in chapter 5 below, ethnographic histories written by members of the peoples concerned (e.g., Josephus's *Antiquities*) could prove more dependable and historically oriented (by our narrower definition of history) despite their sometimes apologetic intent. They fall under the narrower definition of ancient "history" below.

Focus on a specific people (which can be history proper) differs from ethnographic explorations of various peoples.[134] Although Acts covers a great deal of geographic ground, its focus is not on narrating exotic customs of foreign peoples; in fact, it often takes knowledge of localities for granted.[135] Thus it is closer in genre to the model of history proper (treated in chs. 4–5 below), even if Luke writes history with an ethnographic focus. But is Luke's focus ethnographic, or is this at most a secondary element? That is, is Luke writing especially about the church as a people or about God's mission extended to all peoples?

Just as historians sometimes focused on the histories of specific peoples, some scholars argue that Luke may extend the biblical account of God's people in his account of early Christians in the empire.[136] Acts may be like an ethnographic history to the extent that[137] it resembles the history of a people (the remnant within Israel),[138] but the history of the church is not its focus so much as the deeds of some primary heroes and, still more, their driving mission (although histories that focused on a particular people could also include their divine mission).

Others argue that Luke is writing institutional history, in this case that of the early church[139] (if one views the church as an institution rather than as a people), but this

---

130. Fornara, *Nature of History*, 12–16, esp. 12. For the sometimes ambiguous relationship to the category of "local histories," see, e.g., Harding, "Local History," 186–87. Although ethnography predates Herodotus, his influence brought this approach into the discipline of historiography (Dench, "Ethnography," 493–94, 499).

131. See Rebenich, "Historical Prose," 296, focusing on Arrian's *Indica*.

132. Though not their primary focus, *Persica* (accounts of Persia) written by Greeks, for example, sometimes included "sensational tales" (Lenfant, "Historians," 208; cf. 204); Ctesias's tales of India (in his *Indica*) quickly earned him the reputation of a liar (Lenfant, "Historians," 203; Brown, *Historians*, 77–78). Pliny E. *N.H.* 5.1.12 complains that, when traveling, he discovered that some popular equestrian opinion had passed on spurious information about locations instead of the equestrians admitting ignorance.

133. Fornara, *Nature of History*, 15. Then again, a "pure" historian or biographer such as Suetonius (and, to a lesser extent, Tacitus) is happy to report any negative accounts he has of the despised Nero or Domitian.

134. Witherington, *Acts*, 28–29, 35, emphasizes that in contrast with typical ethnic histories, Luke specifically emphasizes that his story crosses ethnic boundaries.

135. Its focus is not even on the known places it relates; epideictic travel narratives praised (or reproached) locales (see Men. Rhet. 1.2–3, 346.26–367.9). See also our discussion in ch. 17 below.

136. Aune, *Environment*, 139–40. To the extent that this is true, Greeks would view this as "Asian historiography" (with Balch, "ΜΕΤΑΒΟΛΗ ΠΟΛΙΤΕΙΩΝ," 152–53, 186).

137. Various categories of history could borrow from the others, while remaining basically discrete (Fornara, *Nature of History*, 2).

138. It also resembles peoples' apologetic for themselves and their antiquity vis-à-vis the larger society; see the argument of Sterling, *Historiography*, in the discussion of apologetic historiography in ch. 5 below.

139. Cancik, "Institutions"; idem, "Institutionsgeschichte" (comparing, e.g., Pythagoras's school on 531–32); this is denied by Jervell, "Future," 110–11; also by Reasoner ("Theme"), who stresses the focus on divine necessity rather than on an institution; parallels with histories of philosophy also prove limited (as noted by Heil, "Arius Didymus"). One could argue (in conjunction with foundation stories noted in ch. 2, above, under "Epics") for a history of beginnings, as some have (Marguerat, *Histoire*, 50–53); but this is a *function*, not a genre per se (51). Marguerat, "Pionnier," views Eusebius as the church's first extant institutional historian, and Luke as historian of the movement's beginnings (cf. idem, *Actes*, 29).

perspective of Luke's focus on the church suffers from the same limitations as the ethnographic focus. If Luke had intended to write a history of the church instead of focusing more narrowly on its cross-cultural expansion through select leaders, we would have a very different book.

Returning to Fornara's classification, another category is local history, what the Greeks called ὡρογραφίαι (horography).[140] One kind of local history was local cult history, preserved at times in inscriptions.[141] Romans traditionally cast their local history in the form of annals, a year-by-year narration form that Roman historians such as Tacitus later applied also to history proper.[142] Many have argued that early Roman historians tended to be annalists, starting with early history and progressing to their own era;[143] chronicles based on the *pontifex maximus*'s records (which included prodigies, religious and military events, etc.) were called *annales maximi*.[144] This category need concern us no further, since Luke-Acts is clearly neither local nor annalistic, and neither Luke's purpose nor his sources would have permitted such an approach.

Still another kind of history in the general sense was chronography, "a system of time-reckoning, international in scope, permitting the calibration of events taking place in different parts of the civilized world."[145] Historians traditionally dated events in part by the appropriate year in the magistracy in which they fell, although less recent history sometimes required a larger scheme.[146] Despite some chronological indicators (Luke 2:1–2; 3:1–2), Luke-Acts clearly does not fit this approach.

Finally, there is "history" proper.[147] This category in its most basic sense described human "'deeds,' or *praxeis* (Aristotle *Rhet.* 1.1360A 35)"; it entailed "'the narration of deeds' (Quintilian 2.4.2)."[148] That early Christians called Acts by this title (πράξεις) is significant (and need not be based on later "acts"; see the discussion in ch. 2 above);

---

140. Fornara, *Nature of History*, 16–23. Although epics made use of such local history and more than three hundred authors are known to have written local history, mostly only fragments remain (Meister, "Local chronicles," 783), of which the *Lindian Chronicle* is an example (Meister, "Lindian Chronicle," 607). The category appears fairly diverse (see Harding, "Local History," 187, citing, e.g., idem, *Androtion*, 8–51; for Attic histories, see, e.g., *Androtion*, 1, 3; for its chronological arrangement, 7), but is relevant to ancient historiography (Bravo, "Antiquarianism," 516, 520).

141. Dillery, "Sacred History." Philost. *Hrk.* passim suggests the oral preservation of various local cultic traditions. Acts is not written in either manner but would be a "sacred history" more in the style of the LXX or providential histories such as those of Dionysius of Halicarnassus or Josephus.

142. Fornara, *Nature of History*, 23–28, esp. 27. For annals, see briefly Cornell, "*Annales maximi*"; idem, "Annals." Thucydides took it seasonally, occasioning later rhetorical critics' disapproval. Brown, *Historians*, 5, warns that (against Jacoby) not all local history was in the form of chronicles.

143. See Kierdorf, "Annalists"; Laistner, *Historians*, 24–29 (noting their historical value). Ancients also accepted kinds of history that were not annalistic, year-by-year reports (Aul. Gel. 5.18.6–7). The division between Roman "history" and "annals" can be arbitrary (see Marincola, "Introduction," 8), and the basis in Cic. *De or.* 2.51–53 is now often questioned (Beck, "Roman Tradition," 261); for one discussion of the "prehistory" of Roman historiography, see Wiseman, "Prehistory." Sallust wrote an annalistic history (Levene, "Roman Historiography," 282), but Cato had already moved beyond pure annals (Gotter, "*Origines*," 121).

144. Kierdorf, "Annales maximi." This source was extremely limited, lacking developed literary form (Cic. *Leg.* 1.6). At the same time, Livy's details of events by year suggest dependence on an annalistic source, however much the fuller literary units may have been embellished (Lendon, "Historiography," 45–46). Some argue for various memory traditions in the Republic alternative to written history (Flower, "Alternatives"); moreover, some Roman traditions that appear in Roman writings only later are attested earlier in Greek sources about Rome (cf. Dillery, "Roman Historians," 77).

145. Fornara, *Nature of History*, 2.

146. See further Grafton, "Time-reckoning," 1528. Despite synchronized dating in Luke 2:1–2 and 3:1–2, this is far from Luke's usual form; dating by rulers also appears in biblical prophets (e.g., Isa 1:1; 6:1; Jer 1:2–3; Ezek 1:2; Hos 1:1; Amos 1:1; Mic 1:1; Zeph 1:1; Hag 1:1) and history (e.g., 1 Kgs 6:1; 14:25; 15:1, 9, 25, 28, 33; 2 Chr 13:1; 15:10; 16:1, 12, 13; 17:7; Ezra 1:1).

147. See Fornara, *Nature of History*, 29–46. For a survey of first-century C.E. Roman sources, see Hose, "Historiography: Rome," 423.

148. Fornara, *Nature of History*, 1–2.

its focus on deeds places it in this category, and even the Gospel of Luke (which is biography), when conjoined with Acts, fits this historical genre (Acts 1:1).[149] Histories in the narrow sense traditionally included war monographs such as Thucydides; Hellēnika, or histories of Greece; and universal histories.[150] (In Luke's day, universal histories were probably more common, at least among histories written in Greek.)[151] Histories could be written as monographs, focus on contemporary events, or seek to narrate the history of the world; what they held in common was describing human actions.[152] But whereas the other related categories "collect data and report them," history alone "is mimetic."[153] It provides a realistic and coherent narrative.

Greek historians preferred to write about places other than their own city-state whereas, for Romans, history was, above all, "the deeds of the Roman people," a source for patriotic lessons.[154] Because Acts chronicles the genesis of a social-religious movement, it resembles the political approach of many histories, as in Dionysius of Halicarnassus, and some of Plutarch's interests.[155] Thus Dionysius and Josephus both treat changes in their respective national subjects' "constitutions" after the deaths or departures of their "founders," just as Luke is concerned with the church after Jesus's departure.[156] But as noted above, Acts' focus is not a history of the church (neither ethnographic nor institutional in a narrower sense) but the expansion of its message to the heart of the empire. Although some passages highlight the political element, the narrative's larger thrust concerns especially the mission. That is, despite many valuable analogies, there are also important ways in which Luke's interests differ from those of most extant historians. Luke's monograph has a distinctive focus because of its distinctive topic, limiting the need for defining it by means of tighter classifications within historiography.

b. Overlap with Biographic Approaches

Perhaps more relevant for Acts, given its focus on leading characters (e.g., Peter rather than all the Jerusalem apostles), is Fornara's discussion of histories that emphasize "leading individuals" (see comments on the biographic genre in ch. 2 above),[157] a natural emphasis given history's focus on notable deeds.[158] This approach moved historiography in a more biographic direction; thus "the Greco-Romans of the first century, chiefly prompted by the Roman habit of thinking in terms of models, . . .

149. See Rebenich, "Historical Prose," 306–7.

150. Fornara, *Nature of History*, 29–32 (war monographs), 32–34 (*Hellēnika*), and 42–46 (universal histories). Polybius complains about the narrowness of typical war monographs (Rood, "Monograph," 148–53), though he sometimes appears to demean alternatives to better market his own work. On continuous histories, see Tuplin, "*Hellenica*" (questioning the appropriateness of the title); on so-called universal histories, see Marincola, "Universal History."

151. Meister, "Historiography: Greece," 420 (although Dionysius, whom he lists, focused more on Rome). On the development of (Greek-centered) universal histories in the Hellenistic period, see Sacks, "Historiography," 715; for the first extant universal historian, see Meister, "Ephorus"; Laistner, *Historians*, 3. Despite Ephorus's lack of historical insight, he preserves useful information (Brown, *Historians*, 114).

152. Fornara, *Nature of History*, 3.

153. Ibid., 29. Cf. Gray, "*Mimesis*."

154. Fornara, *Nature of History*, 41.

155. Balch, "ΜΕΤΑΒΟΛΗ ΠΟΛΙΤΕΙΩΝ," 149–66; on the definitions, see esp. 149–54.

156. Ibid., 146n23 (citing Dion. Hal. *Ant. rom.* 4.41–85; 6.22–8.62; Jos. *Ant.* 6.31–67).

157. Fornara, *Nature of History*, 34–36, contending that this genre started with Alexander of Macedon. In fact, Theopompus already had constructed a history around Alexander's father Philip (Laistner, *Historians*, 4). The Jewish work *Biblical Antiquities* of Ps.-Philo focuses on "major figures" (a feature D. J. Harrington compares with Luke-Acts; "Pseudo-Philo," 867).

158. Fornara, *Nature of History*, 29–46. Homer, too, focused on characters rather than major events (Hermog. *Method* 33.450, citing Homer *Il.* 24.725–803).

extended the definition of history by adding the life and character of famous men to speeches and deeds as the proper subject of history."[159] Some scholars distinguish this approach from pure biography in terms of their distinct purposes.[160] (In light of the discussion in ch. 2 above, the primary distinction here is not biographic focus but whether the work is limited to a single character.)[161]

Such histories often tended to be "encomiastic," magnifying heroes.[162] This approach does not of course make them fictitious; even in biographies, most writers felt free to record negative as well as positive features of their protagonists when appropriate.[163] Thus, for example, although Suetonius's *Vespasian* is mostly adulatory (a striking contrast to his biographies of Caligula, Nero, and Domitian), he reports Vespasian's *pecuniae cupiditas*, love of money.[164] He also reports Nero's good deeds first "to separate them from his shameful and criminal deeds, of which I shall proceed now to give an account."[165] That Suetonius did not praise everyone also indicates that he did not view his task as the bestowal of indiscriminate praise but as the assignment of praise and blame on what he viewed as the preponderance of positive and negative actions; that is, he based his opinion of individuals on an interpretation of, rather than the free creation of, information.

Some historical novelists, such as Pseudo-Callisthenes (whom some modern writers prefer to classify as a novelistic historian-biographer), were more interested in rhetorical effect and praising their protagonist, but this was hardly the desired norm for history (see ch. 4 below).[166] Yet Pseudo-Callisthenes differs significantly from genuine Alexander histories and biographies, for example those by Arrian or Plutarch, despite the liberties such ancient narrators took.[167] (It should also be noted that Pseudo-Callisthenes wrote somewhere between 460 and 760 years after Alexander's death—a situation quite different from Luke's.)

Ancients were well aware that their affection or respect for a person could bias their judgments, but also recognized that such affection could be based on sound evaluations (Pliny *Ep.* 3.3.5). This is likely the case in Tacitus's encomiastic biography of his father-in-law, Agricola; certainly, bias would influence presentation if one was

159. Fornara, *Nature of History*, 116; noting this focus in Sallust, Tacitus, and Suetonius, see Laistner, *Historians*, 55 (also 59 on Sallust; 81 on Livy; 108 on Velleius). For overlap between biography and history in this period, see, e.g., Ash, "Tacitus," 434.

160. Fornara, ibid., 185, distinguishes primarily by noting that biography used only the features of history relevant to expounding character whereas "characterizing anecdotes . . . were unsuitable to history." Cf. also some typical distinctions in Talbert, *Acts*, 252–53. Biography became more like history in early second-century works such as Tacitus's *Agricola* and Suetonius's *Lives* (Fornara, *Nature of History*, 186). For helpful comparisons between portrayals of ideal leaders in Luke and the *Agricola*, see Lang, "*Dux*."

161. By the third century c.e., some philosophic "biographies" included information on lives of a philosopher's disciples as well as himself, but this may have followed Christian models (Dillon and Hershbell, "Introduction," 25–26), such as Luke-Acts.

162. Fornara, *Nature of History*, 36. At times this approach could produce distortion, but it need not do so (64–65).

163. E.g., Arrian *Alex.* 4.7.4; 4.8.1–4.9.6; Plut. *Cim.* 2.4–5; Corn. Nep. 11 (Iphicrates), 3.2; much more fully, see Keener, *John*, 16 (cf. idem, *Matthew*, 51n157).

164. Likewise, Suet. *Jul.* 52 (like much of the work) is full of scandal about Julius, but *Jul.* 53 praises him. After recounting his noble deeds (e.g., *Jul.* 73–75), Suetonius concludes that his negative actions "so turn the scale, that it is thought that he abused his power and was justly slain" (76.1 [LCL, 1:99]).

165. Suet. *Nero* 19.3 (LCL, 2:115).

166. See Fornara, *Nature of History*, 64–65, 72.

167. Distinguishing Pseudo-Callisthenes from genuine historical works, see, e.g., Zambrini, "Historians," 211; Bosworth, "Pseudo-Callisthenes." Though no longer extant, sources extant in antiquity concerning Alexander included works by "actual eyewitness historians (like Ptolemy, Aristobulus, Chares, Nearchus, and Onesicritus)" and historians such as Cleitarchus who probably interviewed some of his companions, as well as "imaginative romance and politically oriented fictitious pamphlets" (Baynham, "Barbarians," 289).

praising an emperor's virtues, even if one avoided telling any untruths (e.g., Pliny *Ep.* 6.27.1–2). Naturally, a writer would omit negative perspectives if he genuinely viewed the protagonist favorably (mostly the case in Tacitus's *Agricola*) or even as divinely authoritative (the Gospels; later, Iamblichus's *On the Pythagorean Life*). These emphases and omissions are normally cases of perspective, however, rather than of deliberate distortion (see ch. 5 below).

c. Acts' Type of History

Although Luke is interested in the story of the church as a movement (hence the parallels with political histories and perhaps ethnographic or institutional histories) and in some leading individuals (hence the parallels with more biographic approaches to writing history), the thread of his narrative is ultimately the mission laid out in Acts 1:8. We can compare this interest with the use of divine providence in histories to support a variety of other interests (e.g., Dionysius's political interests or Josephus's apologetic, ethnographic ones), but the centrality of the mission of Spirit-empowered, cross-cultural expansion seems to be a contribution from Luke's distinctively Christian worldview. In other histories Rome had a divine mission, ambitions drove various individuals, and so forth; Luke defines the goal differently and (though constrained somewhat by the length of his monograph, the demands of the genre, and the adventure-loving character of his ideal audience) never moves far from it.

Probably we can learn from several of the above proposed historical approaches; the very range of diverse interests among ancient historians permitted Luke to go his distinctive way with his own pattern.[168] If writers could mix larger genres (as noted in ch. 2 above), they could certainly mix subgenres. Acts may include elements of political, institutional, or ethnographic histories without these elements constituting Luke's central purpose; his history of the movement's expansion from "Jerusalem to Rome" need not belong to any of the more common subtypes by topic.[169] Thus these categories provide some helpful analogies without exhausting or defining Luke's own approach. That Luke employs his history, whatever its particular form, for apologetic purposes like some other writers (notably Josephus) is quite probable. (For further discussion of apologetic history, see chs. 5 and 13 below).

No extrinsic requirement compels us to limit our analogies to a single subgenre of history; just as Luke feels free to weave together biography (his Gospel) and history (Acts) into a single work, he would not feel constrained by external limitations of genre any more than many of his contemporaries. Although Acts is closest in form to a historical monograph, Luke does not focus on the usual political or military events "but trials, jail episodes, missionary encounters, a farewell speech, and a sea voyage with a requisite shipwreck scene."[170] Paul's letters attest that his life indeed did fit this pattern, but by including so much of this pattern, Luke provides a more intriguing and readable work.

In addition to considering the focus of various common topics in ancient historiography, one can also distinguish works of history (in the narrower sense) by their

---

168. Others also note Luke's distinctive approach (e.g., Heil, "Arius Didymus"). Ancients recognized that history could be written in a range of different styles (Fronto *Ad verum imp.* 1.1.2).

169. See also Phillips, "Genre," against narrowing the categories of historiography too far.

170. Richard, "Author," 18. An episodic approach to history, highlighting crucial scenes of dramatic incidents more than larger historical context, fits Livy's adaptation of his sources and a particular kind of historiography (Plümacher, "Griechischer Historiker," 255–61 [esp. 257–58]; idem, *Lukas*, 80–136 [esp. 111–26]; as noted in Shauf, *Theology*, 75–76). Fitting its apologetic emphasis, Acts includes more trial scenes than the five "canonical" Greek novels put together (Schwartz, "Trial Scenes," 118).

narrative modes. Scholars have sought to distinguish various "types" of historiography in the Hellenistic period although these categories were always fluid: rhetorical histories (e.g., those authored by Ephorus, Theopompus, and Anaximenes);[171] "tragic" historiography (striving for realism but often devolving into sensationalism); and "pragmatic" historiography (Polybius).[172] (Chapter 4 below discusses some of these tendencies more fully.)

Some scholars have suggested that Acts is "a particular type of Hellenistic historiography here, the style of the tragedy/pathos-centered historiography."[173] Acts is a fairly popular work, full of adventure and fast-moving action,[174] yet it does not at all fit Polybius's negative stereotype of "dramatic" history. Luke includes scenes with some pathos (e.g., Acts 20:36–38; Luke 19:41–44; 23:27, 48), but nothing of the sort Polybius complained about in Timaeus's work: no bloody depictions, graphic descriptions, or even (in contrast to rhetorical historians or even Polybius) extensively described scenes (see the discussion in ch. 4 below). Luke lacked the space required to be so expansive, even if he wanted to be. Nevertheless, his history is at a fairly popular level, lacking both the rhetorical flourish of some writers and the careful documentation of sources or acknowledgments of academic skepticism found in some others. Scholars debate whether Acts is at a popular or a literary level;[175] which designation proves more accurate, however, surely depends on the standard of comparison. Against such works as the *Life of Aesop*, apocryphal acts, and Mark's Gospel, Luke-Acts is a highly literary work; when compared with Polybius, Dionysius of Halicarnassus, or Tacitus, however, it is quite popular.[176] Luke writes for an educated urban audience (see ch. 12 below) but not for the true social elite.[177] Thus I have chosen to call Luke's historiography "popular" because of the standard I have chosen for comparison (the elite form of literary history, which is the dominant and nearly only kind to have survived to our day, although it was not necessarily numerically dominant in antiquity).[178]

Luke writes a historical monograph with an apologetic purpose (among other aims), narrating the spread of the "word" from Jerusalem to Rome. This focus is closely enough related to the history of the movement itself to allow close comparisons with political and ethnographic history (the latter often coinciding with apologetic historiography, as in Josephus's *Antiquities*). Nevertheless, as noted above, such categories do not exhaust its content, since Luke narrates the expansion of the "word" more than that of an institution per se. It is the story of a people (ethnographic), however, insofar as it grounds the Gentile mission in the story of Israel, so that the narrative

171. Interestingly, Dio is more impressed with Thucydides's style than Theopompus's (which he rates second), and he finds Ephorus's style tedious (despite his useful information; Dio Chrys. *Or.* 18.10).

172. Meister, "Historiography: Greece," 419. In fact all elite historiography employed rhetoric and emotion; it is simply that some believed that others used them in excessive ways (Marincola, "Audiences," 22).

173. Plümacher, "Luke as Historian," 400; idem, "Fiktion und Wunder." But Luke does not "fit into a single type of Greco-Roman historiography" (idem, "Luke as Historian," 401).

174. Trobisch, "Narrative Welt," rightly notes that Luke produced a readable, *literary* account, not a diary or annals. Pervo, *Mystery*, 56, rightly emphasizes the lively pace of popular narratives, including Acts.

175. Tyson, "History to Rhetoric," 37–38, summarizes views of Acts ranging from a popular work (including L. Alexander and R. Pervo) to a literary work with deliberate echoes of other literary works (a larger number of the contributors in Penner and Vander Stichele, *Contextualizing Acts*).

176. Most extant histories come from the elite, but even most novels may have circulated among fairly educated clienteles (Bowie, "Readership," 452–53; Stephens, "Who Read Novels?," 415).

177. As often noted, Acts provides a window into nonelite perspectives rarely available in most extant literary sources; see, e.g., Toner, *Culture*, 170.

178. In contrast to the situation of some other genres, the preponderance of elite works in the genre of historiography probably would have overwhelmed most competition. As some others have noted, however, Luke may blend features of genres, in the sense that he writes a historical monograph (a genre proper, focused on historical content, as illustrated in our introduction, chs. 6–7) with a popular, less rhetorical approach.

movement of Acts is the movement from heritage (epitomized in Jerusalem) to mission (epitomized by Rome).

Conclusion

Acts is history, probably apologetic history in the form of a historical monograph with a narrow focus on the expansion of the gospel message from Jerusalem to Rome. Luke's approach focuses on primary characters and their deeds and speeches, as was common in the history of his day (allowing overlap with the biographic genre noted in ch. 2 above). Stating that Acts is history rather than a novel affects how we should read it. The following chapters examine the character of ancient historiography more generally and of Acts in particular.

4

THE CHARACTER
OF ANCIENT
HISTORIOGRAPHY

Determining that Acts is a historical monograph is of little value for helping us understand more about this book unless there are some defining features of the genre that provide otherwise missing clues for how an ancient urban Mediterranean audience would have approached Acts. What does the genre into which Acts fits suggest to us about the nature of Luke's work?

Chapter 5 will explore the pervasiveness of theological, political, or other agendas among ancient historians and in their use of sources. This chapter, however, investigates two sides of ancient historiography that modern scholars sometimes play off against each other, although both were in fact important (in varying degrees) to most ancient historians. The latter were concerned both for historical information and for rhetorical presentation of this information; contrary to some modern assumptions, these two goals are not inherently incompatible. Most historians valued historical accuracy regarding events where they could achieve it; they often displayed critical thinking regarding sources (as often, though not always, exemplified in Polybius); and they recognized that sources closer to the events were more apt to be accurate. But they also used rhetoric, and although Luke is not as sophisticated in rhetoric as many elite historians were, he employs some conventional features of historical rhetoric. Historians knew how to expand and abridge sources as needed, and Luke could have followed the same sort of practices.

1. Concerns for Historical Information

Chapters 5 and 8 will examine historians' relative freedom in speeches and the moralistic adaptations in historiography.[1] Here we examine the more "conservative" side of ancient historiography, in that historians did not normally invent "events" in their sources. (Even those who accused others of extensive embellishment rarely accused them of inventing battles, deaths, etc.) Rhetorical adaptation (in which some histori-

---

1. It is to such elements that those who object to the historical value of ancient historians often point. These factors must be (and will be) noted, but they should not be used to ignore evidence for historians' interest in sources. Neither the historical nor the rhetorical element need exclude the other.

ans, e.g., Josephus, apparently took great pride) was not novelistic composition from scratch, and events tended to appear consistently in different writers even as interpretations of these events varied. Not surprisingly, Luke's writing provides sufficient evidence of interest in historical concerns,[2] and it is likely that authentic historical traditions would still be available to Luke. In line with this, Paul's letters suggest that the earliest Christians were interested in the apostles and their advance of the gospel.[3]

a. Historians' Concern for Accuracy?

As mentioned above, contrary to what some scholars have argued, ancient historians generally had concerns for accuracy regarding events.[4] Although historians, especially elite historians, were also concerned with rhetorical presentation (see sect. 2 below), they did not consider factual and rhetorical goals incompatible so long as rhetoric was kept within appropriate bounds (what they considered appropriate admittedly varying from one historian to another).[5] Many historians did not achieve common ideals of accuracy, but accuracy remained an ideal by which other historians evaluated their work.[6]

In a seminal study a generation ago, A. W. Mosley examined the claims and practices of various ancient historians and concluded that some (he includes both Herodotus and Thucydides) followed their material as carefully as they could whereas others (he includes Strabo and Plutarch) were much less careful.[7] Among Romans, Tacitus proved a more critical historian, but many were not.[8] Moses Hadas provides a balanced evaluation: an ancient historian such as Tacitus did not share modern historians' interest in reproducing speeches or details of battles to a high degree of accuracy,[9] but

> with allowance made for rhetorical embellishment customary in his day, and within the limits of distortion which his own views of morality and politics made inevitable, Tacitus never unconsciously sacrifices historical truth. He consulted good sources, memoirs, biographies, and official records, and he frequently implies that he had more

2. Fitzmyer, *Acts*, 56–60.

3. See, e.g., Morgan-Wynne, "Traditionsgrundlage."

4. See, e.g., Mosley, "Reporting," 26; Hemer, *Acts in History*, 63–70; Byrskog, *History*, 179–84; see, e.g., Jos. *Ant.* 20.156–57; cf. *Life* 336–39. On how history was written, see also Keener, *John*, 17–25, much of which I have also incorporated into the larger discussion here. Relevant material in my *Historical Jesus*, chs. 6–8, which overlaps with material in this Acts introduction (chs. 4–6), is adapted from the Acts commentary (the basic draft of which was completed earlier) rather than the reverse.

5. See Byrskog, *History*, 213, 223; esp. Rothschild, *Rhetoric of History*, passim.

6. Of course, they did not define accuracy at all the points the way modern historians do; they wrote what they thought were probable inferences into their narratives (instead of identifying them as possible reconstructions, as we do today) and allowed rhetorical considerations in composition that are foreign to modern historiography (see, e.g., chs. 5, 8, below). But on matters of historical events, they did indeed value such accuracy.

7. Mosley, "Reporting," 12–14; on Strabo and Plutarch, 16; for Greek historians in general, see 11–18.

8. Ibid., 20–22 (cf. Tac. *Ann.* 4.10–11; 13.20; in Pelling, "Historiography," 716; cf. also Laistner, *Historians*, 121); among Romans in general, see Mosley, "Reporting," 18–22. Roman historians often appear less careful with facts than Greeks (Cary and Haarhoff, *Life*, 263) and sometimes focused more on "trends" than details (Fornara, *Nature of History*, 88–89), but Luke, writing Greek in the eastern Mediterranean, undoubtedly is nearer the Greek model.

9. Hadas, "Introduction," xvi–xvii. Woodman, *Rhetoric*, 89, emphasizes that battle descriptions were standard in later rhetorical training. Reflecting a common rhetorical curriculum, battle scenes were similar in most ancient historians, but of course ancient battles did have similar characteristics (Laistner, *Historians*, 57, 95), and some historians (such as Thucydides, vs. Livy, on the siege of Syracuse; Caesar, vs. average historians; and sometimes Sallust) could get even military details quite accurate (ibid., 58).

than one source before him. He requested information of those in position to know. . . . He exercises critical judgment.[10]

Long before Tacitus's era, Cicero treated as common knowledge the expectation that historiography should avoid falsehood, include truth, and remain impartial.[11] Others similarly defined facticity (in terms of events' substance) as a key feature of history's genre that distinguished it from other genres.[12] Historians, who regularly drew on the work of earlier historians, took for granted this expectation of the genre.[13]

History was supposed to be truthful,[14] and historians harshly criticized other historians whom they accused of promoting falsehood, especially when they exhibited self-serving agendas.[15] To a lesser extent, they critiqued those who unknowingly made factual errors.[16] More seriously, a writer who consistently presented the least favorable interpretation, ignoring the diverse views of his sources, could be accused of malice.[17] Even biographers, who had somewhat more freedom to be one-sided,[18] might evaluate sources' or witnesses' motives; thus Antiphon's report about Alcibiades was suspect, Plutarch opines, because Antiphon hated him (*Alc.* 3.1).

10. Hadas, "Introduction," xviii. Tacitus normally follows annals and earlier histories (sometimes specified only when they became notorious, e.g., Tac. *Ann.* 4.34–35), but he also consulted personal memoirs from perhaps half a century earlier (*Ann.* 4.53). By contrast, Woodman, *Rhetoric*, challenges the accuracy of both Thucydides (9–47) and Tacitus (160–96), though once inferences are subtracted, the difference is largely a matter of degree (i.e., as to the size of the "core"). Damon, "Rhetoric," 444–45, notes that even with the limited sources that Woodman allows Tacitus, Tacitus still provides substantial information; fictional elements remain "quite limited" (445).

11. Cic. *De or.* 2.62 (elaborating further on proper literary elements of ancient historiography in 2.63–64). Historians traditionally read *De or.* 2.62–64 as affirming truth value in history (Laird, "Rhetoric," 200–201, citing among others Grant, *Historians*; Momigliano, "Rhetoric," 56–59; Brunt, "Cicero and Historiography," 313, 318). Woodman, who challenged the usual reading of Cicero among other scholars (e.g., P. G. Walsh and P. A. Brunt in Woodman, *Rhetoric*, 81, or Brunt and K. J. Dover on 197), treats this as merely avoiding bias (*Rhetoric*, 82). Others, however, retort that the problem with bias was its departure from facts (see Marincola, "Audiences," 18), and the lack of Cicero's explicit use of *inventio* here might be significant (Laird, "Rhetoric," 202; *pace* Woodman, *Rhetoric*, 93, 199). Many have criticized Woodman's interpretation, not least for ignoring some of what Cicero claims; see Lendon, "Historiography," 50–51 (citing many other critics, including Marincola, *Authority*, 160–62; Blockley, "Truth"; Leeman, "Antieke," 238; Morgan, "Review," 35–36; Bosworth, "Historians and sources," 169). Lendon, "Historiography," 51–52, argues that Cicero wanted history to belong to oratory, but recognized plainly that it did not (*De or.* 2.55–58, 62, 64). Modern readers might consider Cicero's interests interdisciplinary (in *De or.*, Laird, "Rhetoric," 202, notes Cicero's interest in orators learning philosophy and law).

12. Feldherr, "Introduction," 3n4, cites to this effect also Polyb. 2.56.11–12; Livy praef. 6–7; cf. Marincola, "Audiences," 18. Feldherr, "Introduction," 7, notes Woodman's argument that historians preserved only a "hard core" of facts, but notes (8) that the evidence suggests more than this. Note also the stark distinction between history and fictitious drama in Quint. *Inst.* 2.4.2 (cited in Collins, *Mark*, 35).

13. Lendon, "Historiography," 54. I have suggested that the reliance of Matthew and Luke on Mark suggests their similar expectation, better informed by contemporary knowledge than our modern guesses could be, that Mark was considered reliable biography (Keener, "Otho," 354; cf. idem, "Assumptions").

14. E.g., Jos. *Ag. Ap.* 1.26; Dion. Hal. *Thuc.* 8.

15. Jos. *Life* 336–39; Diod. Sic. 21.17.1; Lucian *Hist.* 24–25; see esp. discussion of Polybius below. Those who claimed the superiority of their own works, however, could risk the charge of impudence from detractors (Jos. *Life* 359); the charge of falsehood served polemical agendas well.

16. Diod. Sic. 1.37.4, 6. Some depictions considered errors in ancient accounts are more historically plausible than previously accepted (see, e.g., Jones, "Cocktail," on Pliny *N.H.* 9.119–21), but this is not always the case.

17. So Plut. *Mal. Hdt.* 3–7, *Mor.* 855C–856B (though, in defense of Herodotus, Plutarch's other extant sources may have followed a *favorable* bias; Plutarch may have his own bias because of Herodotus's critique of Boeotia, Plutarch's homeland). Penner, *Praise*, 169, notes that Plutarch resented Herodotus's "pro-barbarian" approach. Perhaps more plausibly than Plutarch, cf. Dion. Hal. *Pomp.* 3, on Thucydides's grudge against Athens.

18. Polyb. 10.21.8; but see discussion on biographies in ch. 2, above.

Aristotle notes that the difference between "history" and "poetry" is not their literary style (for one could put Herodotus into verse if one wished) but that the former recounts what actually happened whereas the latter recounts what might happen.[19] Cicero contrasts the objective of entertainment in mythical poetry with the objective of truth in historiography (*Leg.* 1.5).[20] Likewise, even the most rhetorical historians recognized that historical inquiry required not merely rhetorical skill but research,[21] and those thought guilty of inadequate research or firsthand acquaintance in their reports were likely to be doubted (Arrian *Ind.* 7.1). In the early empire, Tacitus warned against comparing his sober history to implausible rumors and fictions (*Ann.* 4.11).

In the imperial period, the perspectives of Pliny the Younger, a public figure who never found leisure to write history yet valued it,[22] are helpful. Ideal subjects for history offer original and interesting material, he opines, but only provided that the material is based on genuine facts (Pliny *Ep.* 8.4.1).[23] In contrast to some other genres, history's primary goal was truth and accuracy rather than rhetorical display (7.17.3), and accuracy was praiseworthy (5.5.3; 5.8.5).[24] (See sect. 2 below on the role of rhetoric in historiography.) Historians would insist that their duty was to present facts accurately, though acknowledging that some individuals discussed in their histories viewed the facts (and the political perspectives informing the presentation of facts) quite differently (9.19.5).

Still, contemporary political exigencies could affect the telling of current history;[25] eager to appear in Tacitus's history, his friend Pliny reminds him of one of his own noteworthy deeds (*Ep.* 7.33.1, 3), although the incident, the prosecution of one bad governor (narrated in 7.33.4–9), is barely worthy of mention. Tacitus can increase Pliny's fame, the latter urges, but of course he ought not to go beyond the facts, Pliny allows, since history must attend only to the truth (7.33.10).[26]

Pliny's interest in appearing in a contemporary history, fitting the Roman value of glory, might reflect the earlier example of Cicero, who offers a similar suggestion about his own acts' inclusion in a history (*Fam.* 5.12).[27] Cicero recognizes that history, as understood in his era, must contain facts that are not only accurate but

19. Arist. *Poet.* 9.2, 1451b; thus poetry is more philosophical, conveying general truths, whereas history conveys specific facts (9.3, 1451b). See also discussion in Butcher, *Theory,* 163–64, explaining that for Aristotle, poetry was thus nobler and more universal than mere collections of historical information (also 190–91). Pliny *Ep.* 9.33.1 notes that historians, unlike poets, care about the authority of their sources. Some (like Lucan) wrote epics on historical subjects, but with much greater freedom than characterized normal historiography. Poets spoke largely through their characters (Vell. Paterc. 1.3.2). Against their accuracy, see, e.g., Libanius *Refutation* 1.1–3, 12; 2.1; *Invec.* 7.2; favoring it, on account of inspiration, *Confirmation* 1.1; 2.1–2.

20. I am grateful to Andreas Bendlin for bringing this source to my attention. In this passage, Cicero treats his standard for factual content in historiography as higher than that of Herodotus or Theopompus (see discussion in Laird, "Rhetoric," 199–200). For possible rhetorical reasons for the flow of topics in the context (1.1–5), see discussion in Krebs, "Conversation."

21. Dion. Hal. *Ant. rom.* 1.1.2–4; 1.4.2.

22. As is clear, e.g., in his correspondence with Suetonius and especially Tacitus.

23. For the emphasis on facts in ancient historiography, see also Byrskog, *History,* 179–84.

24. Even rhetorical historians writing essays on earlier historians' rhetoric might emphasize the importance of truth-telling (Dion. Hal. *Thuc.* 55).

25. Even outside historiography proper and recent history, imperial ideology shaped historical memories (see, e.g., Sumi, "Monuments").

26. Likewise, eager to have his own account of Vesuvius in Tacitus's work, he even writes in historic style in Pliny *Ep.* 6.16, 20 (so Augoustakis, "*Nequaquam*"). As it turns out, we know far more about Pliny from his own letters than any other source (except a biography) could have provided.

27. *Fam.* 5.12 is LCL letter 22. Pliny's request could also be independent of Cicero's, both reflecting a common interest. Love of glory is explicit, especially in Cic. *Fam.* 5.12.1, 9; elsewhere, as well, Cicero also treats positive figures' glory (praise) as appropriate to historiography (*De or.* 2.63). I am grateful to Andreas Bendlin for highlighting the significance of this letter for me.

also politically significant, yet insists that the facts about himself are noteworthy and their appropriate treatment as praiseworthy will honor also the historian, Lucceius.[28] Political and personal pressures may not have freely rewritten facts, but they certainly shaped the way that historians selected and framed them. The lavish praise of Tiberius in Velleius Paterculus (passim, e.g., 2.94.2–3; 2.129.1–130.5), as opposed to later authors, is presumably not unrelated to Tiberius's reigning at the time of writing (e.g., 2.94.3).

In general, it is possible that Greek historians may have followed such rules of research more than Romans, because the latter were often interested in history more for collections of moral examples than for its own sake (although both Greeks and Romans valued both uses for history). Thus, because Livy valued history for its examples, he sometimes failed to research alternative perspectives on the character of those about whom he wrote.[29] But even among Romans, although some may have written something like fiction, "such excess . . . for which there are enough modern parallels, was a gross evasion of the rules of historical responsibility."[30] Thus where we can test Livy himself against one of his sources, Polybius, he does not engage in much imaginative creation; he largely follows his source.[31] Likewise, free creation would have led to competing versions of Roman history among ancient authors, whereas the basic story instead remains consistent throughout.[32] In the first century B.C.E., Cicero noted that everyone expected historians to avoid falsehood and bias.[33] Accuracy was not always achieved, but the desire for it distinguishes the conventions of historiography from those for novels or epic.

Fornara argues that despite the failures of some writers, objectivity remained the goal in history. For this reason, modern scholars dispute which direction Sallust leaned; he produced "a designedly neutral text," "concealed his predilections," and, "for the sake of historical truth, he repressed his loyalties and took (or tried to take) an objective view."[34] "Honesty and objectivity" were part of the genre, Fornara contends, part of "the contract between author and reader."[35] He concludes, "On balance, therefore, tendentiousness, though an omnipresent danger, probably threatened the integrity of historiography no more than in present times."[36] Fornara very likely plays

---

28. See *Fam.* 5.12.6–7 (in 5.12.7 comparing a glorious portrayal of himself with an accurate painting of Alexander). Granted, Cicero also urges Lucceius to do him a favor and show enthusiastic interest in the events even if Lucceius does not view them as very significant (*Fam.* 5.12.2–3). We should note, however, that Cicero views this as a singular exception to the normal historiographic practice (5.12.3), and also that this is simply feigned modesty to allow another reason for reinforcing the request. In Cicero's case (unlike Pliny's), the events proposed for inclusion ("the domestic conspiracy," 5.12.2 [LCL p. 157]; "from the beginning of the plot down to my return from exile," 5.12.4 [LCL p. 159]) were in fact politically significant. Where Cicero especially requests a favor (offering supporting reasons) is for the account about him to be set off from the rest of the flow of events (hence given more attention), rather than narrated merely wherever it would appear in the sequence (5.12.6–7). He offers to supply notes narrating the events that Lucceius may then polish into acceptable literary form (see 5.12.10).

29. Fornara, *Nature of History*, 116–19. Laistner, *Historians*, 85–87, argues that Livy was in fact quite critical (citing, e.g., Livy 8.40.4; 37.48.7), even if not consistently so.

30. Fornara, *Nature of History*, 135; cf. also Laistner, *Historians*, 16.

31. Lendon, "Historiography," 44; cf. 60. Lendon also notes that Livy's use of Polybius is our best case ("the sole case where we can see a Latin historian using his sources," 53).

32. Lendon, "Historiography," 44.

33. Fornara, *Nature of History*, 138–39, citing Cic. *De or.* 2.15.62–63. Cf. Laistner, *Historians*, 33–34, citing Cic. *Fam.* 5.12; *Att.* 2.1.2.

34. Fornara, *Nature of History*, 72. Others do regard Sallust as biased (e.g., Laistner, *Historians*, 45–48, 55–56, 63). Xenophon was mostly evenhanded in his history (Brown, *Historians*, 93–94), except for fully crediting his enemy Epaminondas (ibid., 97).

35. Fornara, *Nature of History*, 100. See further discussion below.

36. Ibid., 104. If a history was too biased, it was probably the weakness of the particular historian (91).

down tendentiousness too much (see the discussion in sect. 2 of this chapter and further in ch. 5 below); but he is surely correct to the extent that historians did not normally feel free to invent events but only to interpret them. They were not always objective, but blatant fabrication of persons and events violated the rules of their genre, inviting severe criticism. Interests shaped the telling of history, but they did not allow anything close to the same degree of freedom from facts that they normally afforded novels and epics.

As one sample of a range among earlier Greek historians, we may contrast Herodotus and Thucydides, perhaps the two most widely read historians in antiquity.[37] Ancients recognized that Herodotus wrote more for his audience's pleasure than Thucydides did;[38] his charm consisted especially in making a reader feel that they were reading stories rather than history (Dio Chrys. *Or.* 18.10). Thucydides, however, had a reputation for notably accurate history writing (Jos. *Ag. Ap.* 1.18).[39]

Herodotus employed but sometimes misunderstood his oral sources in his travels, and could not read other nations' written sources.[40] Yet even Herodotus, who was pioneering[41] the sort of ethnographic research he undertook, was a genuine ancient historian. His depiction of the eastern Mediterranean coastal regions fits what we know of these regions from other sources.[42] One faction of modern scholars has made him out to be "a mere 'arm-chair scholar' who only feigned his journeys, his personal observation and his sources," but Meister judges this view an "aberration" that has been refuted yet really merits little refutation. It is unbelievable, he argues, that Herodotus simply invented the vast array of citations scattered throughout his work.[43] Granted, Herodotus does not work from the consensus methodology of critical scholarship laid down after his time, in that he offers little attempt to evaluate his sources, but he does not invent them.[44] Herodotus also displays far less Hellenic bias than we might

---

37. At least insofar as we may infer from the number of copies preserved in Egypt; see Stephens, "Who Read Novels?," 411, 415–16. Josephus was sufficiently familiar with Thucydides to imitate him in *Ant.* 17–19 (Kennedy, "Source Criticism," 145–46).

38. See, e.g., Cueva, "Longus and Thucydides."

39. Woodman, *Rhetoric*, 23, thinks that Thucydides disclaimed myth to dissociate himself from Herodotus, and (45–47) that Thucydides's style has misled modern readers into treating his work like modern historiography, an error that Woodman doubts (47) that ancient readers would have made. Although Thucydides was not writing modern historiography, Woodman's language may overstate the gap between modern scholars and ancient readers like Josephus.

40. On Herodotus's method, see Meister, "Herodotus," 267 (including his personal observation and interviews with informed locals; cf. Hdt. 2.28.1; 125.6; 4.76.6; 8.65.6); for his dependence on oral sources, see, e.g., West, "Rhampsinitos," 327; Brown, *Historians*, 40. Herodotus did recognize that historical data were inseparable from the discourses that transmitted them (Byrskog, "History," 279).

41. At least as early as Cicero (*Leg.* 1.1.5), people viewed Herodotus as the first historian and Western narrative writer (Meister, "Herodotus," 269). The literary influence of Homer on Herodotus (Woodman, *Rhetoric*, 4) does not change this perception. Some scholars have compared Herodotus to the Pentateuch (Van Seters, "Primeval Histories"; cf. idem, *Search*); but the differences are considerable (Blenkinsopp, *Pentateuch*, 39–41; he suggests [42] that Israelite historiography may have anticipated Herodotus), and narratives earlier than 1–2 Kings may have earlier parallels in the Greek heroic tradition.

42. Rainey, "Herodotus' Description." Surprisingly, archaeology has often confirmed Herodotus's claims regarding Scythians and Persians (Yamauchi, *Persia*, 77–78, 96, 100, 141, 153, 160–61, 190).

43. Meister, "Herodotus," 267–68. On some of Herodotus's documentary sources, especially inscriptions, see Rhodes, "Documents," 57–58 (noting also misinterpretations, including in one case where the inscription remains).

44. Meister, "Herodotus," 268, notes Herodotus's "methodological principle": "I am obligated to report that which is reported, but I am not obligated to believe everything" (Hdt. 7.152); Herodotus often reports conflicting traditions without passing judgment either way; cf. Schepens, "History," 46; Rhodes, "Documents," 56 (citing 3.115.2; 3.123.1; 4.195.2; 7.152.3). For the interpretive level of Herodotus's discourse, see Darbo-Peschanski, "Origin," 30 (contrasting Thucydides, 32); but for his anchoring in data as accurately as possible, see Schepens, "History," 42; for his pursuit of the most original sources, see Schepens, "History," 43–47.

expect.[45] Ancient historians' frequent use of sources is not simply an anachronistic supposition (see ch. 6 below for some explicit evidence for their use of sources).

b. Historians and Critical Thinking

Although there were plenty of cases of historical credulity[46] and ancient historians were less critical of their sources than are their modern successors,[47] most historians and biographers were capable of critically evaluating their sources.[48] For example, Plutarch disputes a claim of Herodotus (Hdt. 9.85) on the basis of the numbers and an extant inscription (Plut. *Arist.* 19.5–6; others also cite inscriptions, e.g., Vell. Paterc. 2.25.4). Elsewhere he tries to distinguish more accurate from less accurate sources on the basis of reason (Plut. *Themist.* 25.1–2)[49] and questions a later source that includes information missing in an allegedly primary source (Plut. *Alex.* 20.4–5).

Such concerns are hardly rare. Livy discounts an event in his source because it did not appear in the older histories and it suspiciously honored the source's ancestral line (Livy 7.9.5).[50] Elsewhere he opines that some numbers he found in early "annals" may be exaggerated and simply concludes that, in any case, the slaughter was great (Livy 3.8.10; for historians and numbers, see comment on Acts 2:41). So, too, Tacitus recounts the views of the majority and most reliable historians but then mentions another view (*Ann.* 4.10), which he goes on to refute logically (4.11) despite its utility for his perspective.[51] The geographer Pausanias complains that many think that Theseus instituted democracy, despite the inconsistency of such a notion with the claim that he was in fact a king. Then he adds, "There are many false beliefs current among the mass of mankind, since they are ignorant of historical science and consider trustworthy whatever they have heard from childhood in choruses and tragedies."[52] On the basis of historical plausibility, the Jewish historian Josephus similarly argues against various claims (*Ant.* 19.68, 106–7).

45. See fully Meister, "Herodotus," 268–69.

46. E.g., Val. Max. 1.8.7, which Valerius justifies as believable because it is in his sources (important for our discussion, however, is that he does not invent the story). Some cases of supposed credulity fail to recognize that historians sometimes simply recounted sources without intending to approve them (Schepens, "History," 46). For the special case of "signs," see ch. 9 below.

47. See, e.g., Meister, "Historiography: Greece," 421. Certainly, Suetonius, who was in many other respects a good historian, failed to sift his sources and includes much gossip (Cary and Haarhoff, *Life,* 272).

48. Cf. Lendon, "Historiography," 53, who notes that historians sometimes paused to correct their predecessors, citing Livy's corrections of Valerius Antias more than twenty times (citing Oakley, *Commentary,* 1:89–91) and Tacitus's correction of sources (citing Mendell, *Tacitus,* 199–214). Sometimes they remained uncertain about a source even when they lacked alternative accounts (Lendon, "Historiography," 54, citing Livy 37.48.7; cf. Tac. *Hist.* 2.37); such statements communicated verisimilitude (cf. Sen. Y. *Nat. Q.* 4.3.1) only if most presumed them usually sincere (Lendon, "Historiography," 54). Lendon, "Historiography," 55, suggests that historians competed with each other not only in style but also in seeking to correctly recount the facts (Livy 1.pref. 2), yet in this period considered their accounts close enough to received tradition that they wrote with confidence that they would be believed. Had historical writing contained defenses of each point, it would have read much more like forensic rhetoric than it does; a writer was expected to narrate history rather than demonstrate it (Quint. *Inst.* 10.1.31). Of course, critical historians with poor sources could be less accurate than less critical historians with better sources (cf. the observation in Woodman, *Rhetoric,* 205–6, that critical attitudes need not mean historical reliability, citing Tac. *Hist.* 1.1.2 against Tacitus).

49. Cf. also Philost. *Vit. soph.* 1.21.516.

50. Damon, "Rhetoric," 443; the discounted source is Licinius Macer. She also notes (ibid.) that Livy doubts a rumor that he cannot confirm, though he includes it because he does not find a clear motive for its creation (Livy 37.48.1–7).

51. Despite disapproval of Tacitus's biases, Laistner, *Historians,* 132–34, commends his "candor" for often including information contrary to his own biases.

52. Paus. 1.3.3 (LCL, 1:15, 17).

Dionysius of Halicarnassus,[53] himself a rhetorician, critiques not only Thucydides's style[54] but also his failure to achieve the expected standard of historical accuracy. "Art," the rhetorician opines, "does not excuse history from such exaggeration."[55] Yet Thucydides himself was hardly oblivious to the need for critical evaluation. He recognizes (Thucyd. 1.3.2–3) that Greeks were not called "Hellenes" before the Trojan War, since Homer, writing long after that war, does not yet use the term.[56] He refuses to dismiss Mycenae's past splendor on the basis of limited remains in his day, noting that cities of his own day might hold power without impressive physical structures (1.10.1–2).[57] When a distinction between accurate and inaccurate sources proved impossible, writers often simply presented several different current opinions on what had happened.[58] A writer might simply admit that he did not know how something happened.[59]

Even Herodotus's methodology of reporting a range of sources without evaluating their accuracy[60] did not thereby assume or pronounce judgment in their favor; the audience would be duly warned to, or would understand that they were obligated to, make their own decisions. Thus Lucian advised that the historian should report a myth found in one's source without committing oneself to it: "Make it known for your audience to make of it what they will—you run no risk and lean to neither side."[61]

Polybius recognizes that myth may be helpful for bringing pleasure (Polyb. 34.4.3) and suggests that the *Odyssey* mixes myth with truth (34.4.1), but argues that the goal of history is purely truth (34.4.2).[62] Dionysius of Halicarnassus warns that history is

53. Dionysius could regard as inauthentic speeches that reflected conditions that did not fit the alleged author's time (here, "before his prime")—e.g., Dion. Hal. *Din.* 11. He used stylistic criteria to evaluate authenticity when other factors were not compelling (*Lysias* 11; cf. *Demosth.* 57).

54. E.g., that Thucydides fails to evoke the full horror of war at points (Dion. Hal. *Thuc.* 15), in contrast to the more rhetorical historians. But Dio Chrys. *Or.* 18.10 rates Thucydides first, above Theopompus and far beyond Ephorus.

55. Dion. Hal. *Thuc.* 19 (LCL, 1:512f); see Thucyd. 1.1.1–2; 1.21.2; 1.23.1–2. For some other cases of hyperbole in historical writing, see Thucyd. 8.96.1 (cf. 2.94.1); Polyb. 1.4.5; Tac. *Hist.* 1.2; cf. also, less surprisingly for us, in epic treatments of history (Sil. It. 9.183; cf. Josh 10:14), in prosecutorial rhetoric (Cic. *Verr.* 2.5.72.189), and in fiction (Xen. Eph. *Anthia* 1.1; Philost. *Hrk.* 24.2). Dionysius elsewhere notes that where it is clear that the author was not present, one may examine whether a speech fits the speaker and setting (*Thuc.* 41; Damon, "Rhetoric," 446), presumably at least for rhetorical plausibility. For rhetoricians judging historians according to standards of factual accuracy, see Lendon, "Historiography," 53–54 (citing Cic. *Rep.* 2.27; *Off.* 3.113; *Brut.* 42–43; *Leg.* 1.5; Quint. *Inst.* 10.1.75; and others).

56. Likewise, Homer does not speak of "barbarians" because Greeks had not yet distinguished themselves from others in this manner (Thucyd. 1.3.3). Velleius recognizes anachronistic language in earlier writers regarding the names of Thessaly (Vell. Paterc. 1.3.2) and Corinth (Vell. Paterc. 1.3.3, noting Homer *Il.* 2.570; 13.664). Theopompus rejected the authenticity of a treaty because it used the Ionian rather than the earlier local Athenian alphabet appropriate to its era (Rhodes, "Documents," 62).

57. Rulers also favored property claims that could appeal to ancient inscriptions and poetry (Tac. *Ann.* 4.43).

58. E.g., Diog. Laert. 1.23: "But according to others"; 6.1.13; 8.2.67–72; Vell. Paterc. 2.4.6; 2.27.5; 2.48.4; Plut. *Lyc.* 1.1; Tac. *Ann.* 2.67; 3.16, 18; 4.10; 14.51 (though happy to report negative views of Nero), 58–59; 15.38, 54; 16.3, 6 (though expressing his view); Philost. *Vit. soph.* 1.21.516; 2.5.576; y. *Soṭah* 9:13, §2. Thucydides comes across as more of an expert, however, by omitting interpretations divergent from his own, opinions that have not survived (Brown, *Historians*, 49).

59. E.g., Sall. *Jug.* 67.3; Tac. *Ann.* 4.57. Certainly, one could admit ignorance of motives (e.g., Tac. *Ann.* 15.36).

60. See Meister, "Herodotus," 268, on Hdt. 7.152.

61. Lucian *Hist.* 60 (LCL, 6:71).

62. Sophists made a pastime out of noting logical and chronological problems in Homer (e.g., Maclean and Aitken, *Heroikos*, l–li, citing Philost. *Hrk.* 23.5–6; 25.10–13). Saïd, "Myth," 85, notes Polybius's refusal to recount myth (see, e.g., Polyb. 2.16.13–15; 4.40.2; 9.2.1; 12.24.5), though he reports critically some local legends connected with myth (4.43.6) and accepts some historical basis behind legends (34.2.4, 9–11). Many spoke pejoratively of myths (or particular myths) as untrue, e.g., Plato *Rep.* 2.377C–383C; Cic. *Nat. d.* 2.28.70 (a Stoic); Val. Max. 4.7.4; Lucian *Amber* 3, 5–6; *Sacr.* 5; Philost. *Vit. soph.* 2.1.554; *Hrk.* 34.4; 50.1–2;

concerned with truth rather than legends and that one should pursue facts, "neither adding to nor subtracting from" them.[63] (Even if these historians underestimated the role of an author's presuppositions, the value of facticity they articulated for historiography is not a standard easily applied to novelistic or purely mythical narrative forms.) Herodian criticizes earlier historians for preferring rhetorical style to truth (Hdn. 1.1.1–2) and emphasizes that he never depends on unconfirmed information (1.1.3).[64] Historians could report unflattering accounts of individuals they generally respected.[65] Historians might recognize exaggerations in an account, though averring that genuine historical tradition stood behind it,[66] or might regard an account as too implausible altogether.[67]

c. Polybius's High Ideal Standard

Although not all historians shared Polybius's more rigorous standards, his work provides special opportunity to explore these questions because he raises them so frequently in his writing.[68] Polybius's invective against the excessively rhetorical historian Timaeus (Polyb. 12.3.1–12.15.12) provides an example of the standards by which historians might be judged. Granted, Polybius's peer review of Timaeus seems hardly objective itself; he impugns Timaeus's motives (12.7.6) while opining that Timaeus warrants such harsh treatment because he has been harsh with others (12.4a.1).[69] Fornara rightly questions the fairness of Polybius's critique: he polemicized "against Timaeus, by our standards an indefatigable and enterprising scholar," because the latter merely collected books rather than traveled.[70] (Lucian similarly uses hyperbole as part of his wit in satirizing "bad" historians.) Although bias may have been more acceptable and hence more pervasive in antiquity than it is today, it was probably not commonly as severe or malicious as accusers (and perhaps competitors) such as Polybius suggest. (However harsh some modern reviewers may be, modern scholars may be grateful that they did not write two millennia ago.)

Iambl. *V.P.* 32.218; Libanius *Anecdote* 3.27; Syncellus p. 73 (discussing Manetho *Aeg.* frg. 2.3). For others, myths communicated truth in pleasurable ways (Diod. Sic. 1.2.2; Max. Tyre 4.5–6). Early Jewish apologists condemned associating their biblical narratives with mythology (see comment in ch. 3, 97n57; also Philo in Feldman, "Death of Moses").

63. Dion. Hal. *Thuc.* 8 (LCL, 1:478–79); this is an ideal, not the writer's exceptionless practice.

64. My point is not that Herodian achieved this ideal (certainly, he did not strive for chronological precision; see Whittaker, "Introduction," xxxix–xl) but that it was in fact the ideal.

65. E.g., Philost. *Vit. soph.* 2.21.603 (of his own teacher, 2.21.602); the biographer Eunapius *Lives* 461 (of Iamblichus, whom Eunapius considered supernatural, 459–61).

66. E.g., Livy 3.8.10.

67. Aul. Gel. 10.12.8–10. Some could also caution readers not to be too skeptical of something that otherwise appeared implausible (Sall. *Catil.* 3.2; Plut. *Cam.* 6.4).

68. Polybius's moralistic agenda (emphasized, e.g., in Penner, *Praise*, 145; see ch. 5 below on historians' *Tendenz*) need not require fabricating events. Penner (157) shows how Timaeus's critique of Aristotle, who is useful as a positive moral model, invites Polybius's enmity (noting Polyb. 12.7.2–6; 12.8.1–2).

69. Cf. Penner, *Praise*, 118, who notes, "If every historian who accuses another of being a dramatic and rhetorical historian is doing so to garner support for his or her own version of events, then the line dividing a Polybius from an Ephorus, Theopompus, Ctesias, or Phylarchus is much thinner than one might be led to believe from the initial comments." Polybius "condemns tragic history but then resorts to it himself." Still, we should note that even in our extant sources, the level of rhetorical embellishment appears to be a matter of degree (as Penner [p. 179] also acknowledges). Polybius does what Timaeus does, but he apparently does not do it nearly as much as Timaeus. As Marincola, "Audiences," 22, observes, concern for stimulating emotion was widespread in ancient historiography; only some employed it in excess.

70. Fornara, *Nature of History*, 48; see even more fully the defenses of Timaeus's scholarship in Schepens, "History," 51–54; Vattuone, "Historiography," 196–99; cf. Marincola, "Speeches," 124–26; Brown, *Historians*, 151, 164. Others suggest that Timaeus defended Western Greeks' contributions to Greek civilization, providing an "apologetic edge" that Polybius felt compelled to challenge (Sterling, "Historians," 502). Note problems with Timaeus's chronology in Dillery, "Roman Historians," 87.

Nevertheless, Polybius's critique illustrates the demands for accuracy to which ancient historians could be subjected and the public consequences of leaving oneself open to the criticism of having failed to achieve such accuracy.[71] Polybius complains that Timaeus's work reveals that he was unacquainted with Africa, about which he writes (12.3.1–2); that Timaeus's errors are hardly surprising, since he failed to do sufficient investigation (12.4c.2–5) and, even when he did visit places and consult witnesses, he got his facts wrong (12.4d.1–2); and that when covering matters treated properly by other historians, Timaeus elaborates excessively and confuses the information that is there (12.28.12).

Polybius is not above assuming that he can infer Timaeus's motives. Timaeus's problem, Polybius argues, is not ignorance but prejudice; he is more concerned with epideictic rhetoric (praise and blame) than with proper history (12.7.1).[72] One could forgive historians who err, but Timaeus's errors are intentional lies (12.7.6). Polybius charges that Timaeus slanders people by presenting them in a worse light than is appropriate (12.15.12). This criticism may well unfairly impugn Timaeus's motives for his perspective and may simply inform us that Polybius evaluated the data differently. One could not easily avoid rivals' criticisms, but from Polybius's description, it appears likely that Timaeus did at least exaggerate.

More broadly, Polybius condemns authors who sensationalize their story to make it more graphic and provide cohesiveness (15.34.1); Polybius himself might permit a little of this to tie the narrative together, but (he contends) not very much.[73] He condemns those who make up or pass on hearsay about distant lands that cannot be verified (3.38.3). Polybius accuses Timaeus of fabricating sources where he fails to name them (12.9.1–12.11.7). (This accusation is probably unfair, reflecting simply different approaches to style or different target audiences.)

Yet on a more general level, the standards Polybius cites are not simply his own but are shared with Timaeus himself, however well or poorly he may live up to the standard in a given instance.[74] Timaeus admits that falsehood is the worst vice in writing history, and that those who write falsehood should find a different name for their book than history (Polyb. 12.11.7–8). Timaeus would also agree with Polybius that the truth of a book's content, rather than its style or length, confirms that a work is history (12.12.1–3).[75]

Likewise, Polybius feels compelled to explain why he himself depends on Aratus rather than the often-contradictory accounts of his contemporary Phylarchus (2.56.1–2).[76] He contends that the latter "makes many random and careless

71. Likewise, when Josephus thinks the perspective of some other historians distorted, he criticizes them for failing in their objective to write history properly (*War* 1.7); they undoubtedly responded polemically in kind. Vell. Paterc. 2.53.4 criticizes predecessors for being five years off on Pompey's age—precisely because he wants to forestall criticism of himself for erring on this minor detail.

72. These rhetorical techniques are certainly in common use by Luke's era, although (again) even orators could use such techniques without inventing "facts." Penner, *Praise*, 235–47, argues that epideictic techniques were common in Jewish apologetic historiography.

73. He reports graphic bloodshed (Polyb. 15.33) but claims that unlike some other writers, he avoids amplifying it for sensationalism (15.34). By Luke's day, both Polybius's "critical" approach and the "sensational" approach had left a mark on historiographic practices (see Rothschild, *Rhetoric of History*, 93–95).

74. Cf. Davidson, "Polybius," 129 (following Marincola, *Authority*; Walker, "*Enargeia*"), who argues that Polybius's standards largely followed those of Hellenistic intellectual culture, though most of it has not survived. He also finds some of these features in the Roman historiographic tradition preceding Polybius (Davidson, "Polybius," 129–30, following Marincola, *Authority*, 188–95, esp. 192).

75. A number of other historians also insisted on avoiding bias, a claim that their contemporaries understood seriously (see Cic. *Fam.* 5.12.3, on a preface in one of Lucceius's histories).

76. Penner, *Praise*, 153–55, complains that Polybius uses an ethnic plausibility criterion against Phylarchus: by evoking sympathy for the dishonorable Mantineans against the honorable Achaians, Phylarchus violates

statements" (2.56.3), and promises to offer just the most relevant examples (2.56.4). Polybius complains that Phylarchus records tragic scenes of women, children, and the aged wailing as they are enslaved; he objects to this portrayal (even though we can suspect that it is a historically likely inference) because it is meant to arouse pity, that is, pathos used for entertainment value (2.56.7).[77] The historian should not, Polybius opines, "try to thrill his readers" with exaggeration or with tragic poetry endeavoring "to imagine the probable utterances of his characters" (2.56.10).[78] A tragic poet should entertain and settle for verisimilitude, he contends, but a historian should stick with facts (2.56.11).[79]

Historians of the early empire maintained such standards as the ideal; Tacitus declares that history should cater to leaders neither by flattering nor by attacking them (*Hist.* 1.1).[80] Although political pressure might require some adjustments for current monarchs or dynasties (or even influence the selection process by which historians survived and published and by which their works remained extant), this pressure did not permit wholesale invention of facts (nor ought we to imagine Luke constrained by such political pressures from his protagonists).[81] Historians who invented events (far more than sensational or rhetorical historians merely embellishing relevant details) risked refutation and serious denunciation, and their works were unlikely to survive their patrons.[82]

---

probability. Sympathetic portrayal of opponents appears commonly in ancient epics (the Trojans in the *Iliad*; Dido in the *Aeneid*), and rhetorical historians use it to heighten tragic pathos (cf., e.g., Dion. Hal. *Ant. rom.* 3; 9.39.1–6; Livy 21.1.3; cf. discussion in Keener, *John*, 216–17); indeed, Lucian criticizes historians who praise their own leaders while slandering the other side as engaging merely in panegyric (*Hist.* 7). But it is clear that Polybius has his ethnic biases; cf. similarly Plutarch's *Malice of Herodotus*. Ancient and modern judicial rhetoric do infer probability based on past behavior; ancient and modern historians do the same, except that modern historians would be explicit about their inferences instead of simply writing them into their narratives. We would agree with Polybius that historical reconstruction necessarily includes inferred probabilities; we might prove more critical of the ethnographic basis for some of his assumptions, but this is why we must take into account ancient (or modern, whether with ethnographic, political, military, or other historiography) historians' perspectives. It is not inference from probability that differs but the way we narrate those inferences and the particular assumptions (based on differing perspectives) that inform those inferences.

77. Cicero recognized that readers of histories enjoyed the feeling of pitying others' past sufferings (*Fam.* 5.12.5), yet he writes in a context that involves actual and not imagined sufferings (5.12.4–5).

78. No one, however, will ensure that Polybius's own speeches are verbatim recollections.

79. The entire digression against Phylarchus starts in Polyb. 2.56.1–16 (including criticism for excess accommodation of tragic conventions, 2.56.1–11), followed by examples of his sensationalism in the matter at hand in 2.57.1–2.63.6. Poetic treatments of historical events (e.g., Silius Italicus; Lucan) enjoyed more freedom of expression (cf. Pliny *Ep.* 8.4.1). Even generally reliable rhetorical historians, however, could infuse scenes with pathos when the *events* they reported allowed this (e.g., Tac. *Ann.* 3.1; 4.62–63; 5.9; 16.30–32); for pathos in Acts, see comment on Acts 20:37–38. Seeking to communicate the *spirit* of the times as well as the specific events, Velleius complains that "no one has even been able to deplore the fortunes of this whole period with such tears as the theme deserves" (Vell. Paterc. 2.67.1). On the propriety in ancient historiography of generating emotion, provided it was appropriate and helped readers better share the experience of the events depicted, see Marincola, "Audiences," 21–22 (citing Cic. *Fam.* 5.12.4–5; Sempronius Asellio in *FRH* 12 F 2).

80. Cf. similarly Jos. *Ant.* 20.154, criticizing some of his contemporaries. Hellenistic historians may have rarely met Polybius's standard, but most of our surviving examples remain rooted in genuine events. Moreover, Thucydides (also a careful historian by our standards) remained a primary model (see Marincola, "Speeches," 123–27; Croke, "Historiography," 567–68).

81. Ecclesiastical pressures were, presumably, not a major factor; he portrays the Jerusalem church mostly favorably (despite Acts 20:21), yet in his location and probably in his era, the Jerusalem church could not exert ecclesiastical pressure (or could exert, at most, the pressure of heroic memories). Dio Cassius later faced much more severe constraints about the present of his era (Hose, "Cassius Dio," 462–63).

82. Perhaps the long-reigning Augustus offers an exception; but later Suetonius and Tacitus are critical even regarding Augustus, and rival views did survive. Acknowledging that he goes against the usual standard of historiography, Josephus justifies his passion and lamentation in his work (see Chapman, "Josephus," 324, noting *War* 1.9, 11); but Josephus's account was plainly controversial vis-à-vis those of his rivals.

d. Earlier versus Later Sources

The question of how soon Luke's sources derive after the events that he reports is essential to the discussion of his potential reliability. Ancient as well as modern historians valued firsthand sources most highly (all other factors being equal) and, after that, those closest in date to the events reported.[83] On this count Luke fares better than many historians; many of the events he reports are relatively recent (at most, his reports about Paul are less than a generation old on the usual dating),[84] and some (see comment on Acts 16:10) reflect eyewitness testimony.

Ancient historians were especially happy, when reporting recent events, to include oral tradition from eyewitnesses.[85] The second best source after the author himself being an eyewitness was the author's use of others as eyewitnesses;[86] eyewitnesses who participated in events were considered ideal.[87] Josephus concurs with Gentile historians in preferring this practice.[88] Whether because of bias[89] or because of memory lapse,[90] however, even eyewitnesses did not always agree on details, which required some weighing of individual testimony.[91] (Among logical principles deemed useful

83. E.g., Tac. *Ann.* 15.73 (citing sources of the time described). Historical distance multiplied the possibility of gratuitous errors, such as 4 Macc 4:15 (Antiochus Epiphanes was Seleucus's younger brother rather than his son, though the mistake is readily understandable). Of course, modern historians also prefer reports closer in time to the events recounted (e.g., Robeck, *Mission*, 293–94, 296).

84. Indeed, even Luke's first volume is fairly soon after most events it narrates; as W. D. Davies points out (*Invitation*, 115–16), probably only a single life span "separates Jesus from the last New Testament document" (cf. similarly Sanders, *Tendencies*, 28; Benoit, *Jesus*, 1:33).

85. E.g., Xen. *Apol.* 2; *Ages.* 3.1; Dion. Hal. *Thuc.* 7; Plut. *Demosth.* 11.1; Arrian *Alex.* 1.pref. 2–3; 6.11.8; Corn. Nep. 23 (Hannibal), 13.3; 25 (Atticus), 13.7; 17.1; cf. Philost. *Hrk.* 7.9; 8.2, 6–7; Sen. Y. *Nat. Q.* 3.25.8; 4.3.1. Cf. Xen. *Hell.* 6.2.31 (refusing to believe a report until an eyewitness was available); Tac. *Ann.* 3.16 (reporting an unlikely account, though not committed to it, because he received it from the previous generation). Aune, *Environment*, 81, cites for this also Hdt. 2.99; Polyb. 12.27.1–6; 20.12.8; Lucian *Hist.* 47 (and Polybius's somewhat self-serving view that participants made the best historians, 3.4.13; 12.25g.1; 12.28.1–5); Alexander, *Preface*, 34, notes that one recurrent claim was "that the best history was written on the basis of personal experience." Historians today are apt to trust eyewitness knowledge even in otherwise questionable ancient historians (e.g., Brown, *Historians*, 142, 146; in more recent history, see, e.g., Wigger, *Saint*, 363).

86. Jervell, "Future," 118.

87. Byrskog, *History*, 153–57. Although some earlier modern historians treated personal involvement as permitting bias (19–22; less today, cf. 23–26), oral historiography allows greater appreciation for participation (153; for its wider use today, see, e.g., Moniot, "Historiography," 50). To exclude such sources could undermine any historical reports by eyewitnesses in any traumatic or otherwise emotionally invested situation in history (wars, the Holocaust, etc.; see Eddy and Boyd, *Legend*, 397–98; despite limitations of war testimony noted in Woodman, *Rhetoric*, 18–22). On the use of, and methodologies for, oral history in historiography, see Byrskog, *History*, 26–33; on its use in NT scholarship, see 33–40. Whereas modern oral history focuses on "low people" excluded from traditional Western history, ancient historians focused on whatever sources gave them best access to the events important to them (305).

88. See Jos. *Life* 357; *Ag. Ap.* 1.45–49, 56; *War* 1.2–3. Romans also valued narrating events from one's era, including those in which one participated and those that could honor a friend (see Cic. *Leg.* 1.8).

89. Byrskog, *History*, 176–79, notes that ancient historians were aware that eyewitnesses could be biased, and tried to take this into account (sometimes through the grid of their own biases).

90. Cf., more recently, e.g., divergent versions of the same event in 1980 (differing in details while communicating the basic substance) evaluated in Jackson, *Quest*, 72–74.

91. Thucyd. 1.22.3. For gist generally being reliable in memory even where details are not, see Bauckham, *Eyewitnesses*, 333–34 (citing memory studies); cf. also Woodman, *Rhetoric*, 11–12 (although on 12 he also uses the weakness of one witness to question even the gist, but this witness may be more questionable than usual, even if he did not confuse different occasions). Historians themselves often quoted their sources from memory, and hence could get correct the gist while being confused on some details (Marincola, "Introduction," 2). Although interchanges likely occurred, two individuals' memories of events that both persons experienced, recalled over the span of six decades, can overlap considerably in substance (cf., e.g., Braun, *Way*, with Braun, *Here*; or informally, family recollections); many points are forgotten and shaded, but events perceived as significant, and often associated feelings, especially when the events generated intense feelings or are often recalled, can persist without deliberate intention for decades. Those responsible for retelling the information will tend to recall it in the usually retold form, but it becomes part of long-range memory.

then as today, witnesses were considered most dependable shortly after the events they purported to attest.)[92]

Because oral traditions were most reliable in the generation they recounted, Greek historians liked to travel to compile oral sources from the generation of the current events they reported. Thus "the historians of each generation establish the record of their own time" most effectively.[93] Nevertheless, sources committed to writing often held a special authority;[94] even an eyewitness might cite another eyewitness source written before his own work had been committed to writing.[95] Writers often recognized that whereas oral tradition could be modified over time, written sources were fixed.[96]

When the historian himself was an eyewitness, he usually noted this point (see comment on Acts 16:10).[97] Readers naturally would give special credence also to writers whose works bore the approval of eyewitnesses. Josephus emphasizes that he wrote his autobiography while witnesses remained alive who could verify or falsify his claims (*Ant.* 20.266), and he complains that Justus, one of his rivals, waited twenty years to publish, till after the eyewitnesses were dead (*Life* 359–60).[98] Josephus contends that Justus should be less believable than himself, whose work is known to the eyewitnesses and never contradicted by them (*Life* 361–66).[99]

Josephus condemns Greek historians willing to write about events where they were not present and for which they could not depend on those with firsthand knowledge (*Ag. Ap.* 1.45). Some, he complains, wrote about the war without having been there, which was inadequate research for appropriate histories (1.46).[100] By contrast, Josephus says, he was present (1.47) and he alone understood the Jewish refugees and wrote the information down (1.49); his accusers did not *know* the Jewish side of the story (1.56). Justus was not present when the events he describes took place in Galilee, and those who could have supplied Justus with such information perished in the siege of Jerusalem (*Life* 357).[101]

92. In a forensic setting, see, e.g., Lysias *Or.* 20.22, §160.

93. Fornara, *Nature of History*, 48. For accuracy in certain kinds of ancient Mediterranean oral traditioning over the span of one or two generations, see Keener, *Matthew*, 27–30; idem, *John*, 54–65; idem, *Historical Jesus*, 139–61; but for failure to learn accurately from purported travels, see Strabo 2.5.10; Hengel, "Geography of Palestine," 31.

94. Eunapius *Lives* 460. Suetonius depends more heavily on older written records than on interviews of more recent persons (Rolfe, "Introduction," xviii). The Greek method preferred interviews, but even Romans could write about contemporary figures (e.g., Pliny *Ep.* 9.19.5); even some Greek writers like Ephorus and Timaeus critically emphasized written sources, though Polybius appreciated the former and attacked the latter (Schepens, "History," 50–51).

95. Xen. *Hell.* 3.1.2; those who attribute the Gospel of Matthew to one of the Twelve yet accept its dependence on Mark (e.g., R. Gundry; see his *Matthew*, 609–22) could adduce that case as a further example.

96. Eunapius *Lives* 453; for anthropological confirmation, see Lord, *Singer*, 138.

97. E.g., Xen. *Symp.* 1.1; Jos. *Ag. Ap.* 1.45–47. Todd, "Introduction," 376, is skeptical about Xenophon's claim because Xenophon nowhere places himself in the narrative (Kennedy, "Source Criticism," 135, notes that most scholars are skeptical), but this argument is questionable; Todd concurs that the characters and discussion match external evidence ("Introduction," 376–78). This is also Xenophon's style, since he does not report his presence in the *Anabasis* until it is relevant to the narrative.

98. Criticizing someone should best be done while they remain alive or, if they have died, only shortly afterward (Pliny *Ep.* 9.1.3–4). Bede *Comm. Acts* pref. (L. Martin, 5) contends that Luke wrote while eyewitnesses remained alive.

99. This also suggests that if Josephus embellished his story with some details, the eyewitnesses accepted that embellishment as relatively minor, fitting acceptable historical canons. Undoubtedly, the portrayal was also not to their detriment; Josephus was careful to praise surviving political figures such as Agrippa and any member of the Flavian dynasty.

100. Naturally, Josephus would be happy to enforce a criterion that excluded his competitors but not himself. Yet Josephus hardly invented this criterion, useful as it proved in his case.

101. Josephus is not above depicting a scene, such as the suicide of the Sicarii at Masada, where he lacks potential eyewitnesses (unless we think of the two women who escaped), but he might have protested that this represented a special scene rather than a consistent pattern.

As will be argued in chapter 10 below, Luke wrote after 70 and hence more than four decades after the events described in the Gospel, albeit while some eyewitnesses may have remained alive; this date, however, allows that he wrote much sooner after the later events described in Acts, which is especially likely if (as also will be argued) he was one of the eyewitnesses of some of those events himself.

The critical sensitivity of ancient historians in general applied especially to the remote past. Ancient historians were less accurate when they wrote about people of the distant past than when they wrote about recent events (as Luke does),[102] and they were themselves aware of this difference.[103] (Conversely, the advantage of writing about ancient history was that one could simply collect what earlier historians said, whereas writing about recent matters could lead to offense.)[104]

Ancient historians, like their modern successors, generally preferred writers closer in time to the events reported rather than later sources.[105] Following the same principle, many ancient writers pointed out the obscurity of reports from centuries earlier but expected a much higher standard of accuracy when handling reports closer to their own period.[106] Most recognized that the earliest period was shrouded in myth,[107] even if they sometimes found the myths' basic outline acceptable.[108] They were also aware that propaganda helped create legend (Arrian *Alex.* 4.28.1–2).

Sources about characters of centuries past often conflicted, a conflict that inadvertently attests to a proliferation of written historical sources no longer extant (see esp. ch. 6, sect. 2.a, below). When writing about characters of the distant past, then, historians would have to sort through legendary as well as actual historical data[109] and might well have difficulty ascertaining which was which.[110] Sometimes they simply repeated apparently incredible information and warned readers to use discretion;[111] often, however, they sought to "demythologize" their reports.[112] Thus for example

102. See, e.g., Mosley, "Reporting," 26.

103. E.g., Diod. Sic. 1.6.2; Cic. *Leg.* 1.4. See further Kennedy, "Source Criticism," 139, on the mythical character of "early history," citing Quint. *Inst.* 2.4.18–19 and Livy's repeated qualifications in his first ten books. Note also Marincola, "Audiences," 19, on the higher ideals for historians writing concerning events of their own time.

104. Pliny *Ep.* 5.8.12–13 (considering earlier times more praiseworthy); Tac. *Ann.* 4.33. Thus some, like Callisthenes, composed excessively encomiastic tributes—which posterity condemned as flattery (Brown, *Historians*, 125). Obviously Tacitus and Suetonius could not have portrayed Nero or Domitian so negatively during their reigns (often observed, e.g., Vout, "Emperor," 261).

105. E.g., Livy 7.6.6; 25.11.20; Plut. *Mal. Hdt.* 20, *Mor.* 859B. This is true in spite of the fact that "modern insights" (such as bloodletting!) might be preferred to ancient ones (Sen. Y. *Ep. Lucil.* 95.22).

106. E.g., Thucyd. 1.21.1; Livy 6.1.2–3; 7.6.6; Diod. Sic. 1.6.2; 1.9.2; 4.1.1; 4.8.3–5; Dion. Hal. *Ant. rom.* 1.12.3; *Thuc.* 5; Paus. 9.31.7; Jos. *Ag. Ap.* 1.15, 24–25, 58; cf. Bowersock, *Fiction as History*, 1–2. Some ancients also considered the earlier period qualitatively different because of divine activities (Hesiod *W.D.* 158–60, 165; Arrian *Alex.* 5.1.2); by contrast, others mistrusted its reports precisely because of such unusual events (Thucyd. 1.23.3).

107. Dion. Hal. *Thuc.* 5–7; cf. Plut. *Thes.* 1.3; Keener, *John*, 20. At least, the early period was regarded as unusual (Thucyd. 1.23.3).

108. E.g., Thucyd. 1.21.1 (complaining in 1.21.2 that people make ancient events greater than they were); again, see Keener, *John*, 20.

109. They often tried to distinguish between accurate and inaccurate sources when a consensus view was available (cf. Livy 1.1.1). Interestingly, archaeology occasionally and incidentally confirms even some information behind etiological explanations once deemed mythical; see, e.g., Egelhaaf-Gaiser, "Sites," 212.

110. Historians might recognize exaggerations in an account, while averring that genuine historical tradition stood behind it (Livy 3.8.10), or might regard an account as too implausible altogether (Aul. Gel. 10.12.8–10). Some sources, such as the *Life of Aesop*, may simply string together all available popular traditions into a narrative; these traditions had grown over six centuries (see Drury, *Design*, 28–29).

111. E.g., Livy 4.29.5–6; 23.47.8; cf. (more skeptically) Lucian *Hist.* 60.

112. See, e.g., Thucyd. 1.21.1–2; Dion. Hal. *Ant. rom.* 1.39.1; 1.41.1 (cf. 1.84.4); *Thuc.* 6; Philost. *Vit. soph.* 2.1.554. See also examples in Saïd, "Myth," 81–88.

Plutarch, when he writes about Theseus, who reportedly lived more than a millennium before him, proposes to purify "Fable, making her submit to reason and take on the semblance of History" by determining what is probable and credible.[113] This means that when it was depending on historically remote sources, ancient historiography sometimes had to settle for historical verisimilitude rather than high probability (by modern standards) concerning the events that ancient historians reported.[114]

Their criteria for distinguishing what was credible from what was not were often inadequate, but they illustrate ancient intellectuals' recognition of the problem and their critical intentions.[115] Sometimes writers employed a criterion of coherency with other evidence,[116] such as known customs of a report's day;[117] other historical context[118] (including chronological data);[119] coherence with documentary sources;[120] consistency of reported behavior with a person's other known behavior (something like form critics' criterion of coherence);[121] and even material remains.[122] Following the probability argument standard in the law courts (see the comments at Acts 24:11; 26:8), Dionysius of Halicarnassus challenges an event recounted in earlier histories because of intrinsic improbabilities in their accounts.[123] Arrian often evaluates various reports by comparing them; he notes that one story too prominent to ignore is not reported by any of the eyewitness writers and so is likely unreliable.[124]

Historians' generally more cautious approach to early sources contrasts with their greater trust in more recent material. We respect Thucydides, Polybius, and (closer to Luke's era) Josephus as contemporaries of much of what they report (regardless of rhetorical embellishments). We depend heavily on writers of the early empire, such as Tacitus and Suetonius, who report relatively recent events (of the past century to century and a half, with accuracy increasing further later in that period); despite their biases, they provide an invaluable source for understanding the early empire (see the discussion in ch. 6 below on evaluating degrees of historical reliability).[125]

---

113. Plut. *Thes.* 1.3. Arrian accepts, but explains on rationalistic grounds, some old legends (*Alex.* 2.16.6).

114. See Dio Cass. 62.11.3–4; Aune, *Environment*, 83; Fornara, *Nature of History*, 134–36; Woodman, *Rhetoric*, 26–28.

115. Ancients noticed tensions in regularly read sources just as we do; even mythographers might note chronological and other tensions within a text (Maclean and Aitken, *Heroikos*, xlix–l, citing Philostratus *Hrk.* 23.5–6; 25.10–13).

116. Polyb. 3.32.4.

117. Dion. Hal. *Ant. rom.* 9.22.1–5.

118. Polyb. 3.20.1–5; 3.32.5. Polybius insisted on providing the longest-range historical context possible, both early (3.6.1–3.7.3, e.g., 3.6.10) and subsequent (9.2.5).

119. Plut. *Themist.* 27.1, though admitting uncertainty. Thucydides sought to take into account the relative dates of his sources (Thucyd. 1.3.2–3); with some sense of relative chronology, Tac. *Dial.* 16 dates Ulysses and Nestor (purportedly early thirteenth century B.C.E.) about a millennium before Alexander and Demosthenes (fourth century B.C.E.).

120. Polyb. 3.33.18; Plut. *Alex.* 46.2; *Demosth.* 5.5; Philost. *Vit. soph.* 2.1.562–63.

121. Arrian *Alex.* 7.14.4–6; Dio Cass. 62.11.3–4; cf. Athen. *Deipn.* 5.215–16, 219ab. The same criterion could apply, however, in fictitious composition or historical reconstruction based on plausibility (cf. Arist. *Poet.* 15.4–5, 1454a; Theon *Progymn.* 1.46–52; 2.79–81; 8.2–3); in myth viewed as history, Libanius *Confirmation* 2.18–20.

122. Thucyd. 1.10.1–2, evaluating the *Iliad*.

123. Dion. Hal. *Ant. rom.* 4.6.1. Cf. also Tac. *Ann.* 15.53; 16.6; Paus. 9.31.7; Plut. *Isis* 8, *Mor.* 353F; and Theon's reasons for thinking the account of Medea murdering her children implausible (*Progymn.* 5.487–501; cf. 3.241–76, 4.112–16, 126–34).

124. Arrian *Alex.* 6.28.2. Hearsay without eyewitness testimony is much less credible (Arrian *Ind.* 15.7). Arrian does exhibit pro-Alexander bias (Bosworth, "Pursuit," 447; Baynham, "Quintus Curtius," 428), though it can be overstated (Bosworth, "Pursuit," 452–53).

125. Woodman, who criticizes even relatively contemporary writers (and has been criticized for it; note the summary in Damon, "Rhetoric," 439–40), himself recognizes the principle that contemporary sources are more reliable (or less unreliable) than later ones (Woodman, *Rhetoric*, 204).

Barring convincing evidence to the contrary (such as much greater divergence from primary sources than we find in such historians), we should regard Luke in the same manner. Luke writes about events fulfilled within the past century, mostly (depending on when we date Luke) within the past half century or so. He grows more detailed in the Pauline material in Acts and especially the "we" material in Acts 20–28, the most recent material and that on which he appears most fully informed.

2. Concerns for Rhetorical Presentation

Claiming that historical writers used sources (as in ch. 6 below) and were concerned about genuine historical information does not mean that they did not place their own "twist" on the material. To the contrary, it was customary for writers to do so, and the more rhetorically sophisticated the expected audience, the greater the expectations of such displays of rhetorical prowess. (See also ch. 5 below on historians' ideological *Tendenz*.)

Because time has, naturally, preserved mostly the rhetorically respected historians of the elite class (who also had the most leisure and resources to publish their histories), these histories are typically more rhetorical (and certainly usually include fuller speeches) than Luke-Acts is.[126] Nevertheless, this emphasis on rhetoric shows that ancient historiography was more reader-driven (better, hearer-driven) than its typical modern academic analogue, and we must take this factor into account when reading ancient historical works, including Acts. Luke was writing ancient, not modern, historiography.

a. Historians and Rhetoric

Some traditional modern approaches to the Roman historians were interested especially in mining them for facts about Roman history; some newer approaches focus on the historians' rhetoric with little interest in evaluating the sources of information on which they may have drawn. Although some scholars in either camp still insist on one approach to the exclusion of the other, others recognize that both historical information and rhetorical or literary presentation are legitimate objects of inquiry. Indeed, it is problematic to try to isolate the former from the latter. One cannot access much information on which a historian draws without reading the historian's presentation.[127]

Rhetorical techniques were pervasive in ancient historiography, and the presence of such elements does not militate against the assignment of a work to the genre of history.[128] Although Herodotus probably improved the literary character of writing

126. Some estimate that barely 2 percent of Greek histories have survived, apart from fragments and summaries (Schepens, "History," 54, citing Strasburger, "Umblick"). Because he writes at a more popular level, Luke may have less polished rhetoric and more adventure. Again, this is not to suggest that Luke or his contemporaries fabricated events, but the narrative tastes of Luke's audience were, no doubt, an important factor in his selection and presentation of events.

127. See, e.g., Laird, "Rhetoric," 211–12. Feldherr, "Introduction," 7–8, suggests that now that interest in rhetorical presentation is more widely accepted, newer approaches should return to ancient historians' stated interest in representing the past accurately. Such representation is always a matter of degree. Biblical scholarship has experienced the same fruitful synthesis of historical and literary approaches, after passing through a period of mutual polemic (see, e.g., McKnight and Malbon, "Introduction," 18; Donahue, "Redaction Criticism," 45–48; Byrskog, "History," 258–59, 283; Peterson, *Acts*, 41; Padilla, *Speeches*, 10–11).

128. See Rothschild, *Rhetoric of History*, passim, esp. her conclusion, 291. Penner, *Praise*, 137, observes the influence of the *narratio* on all prose writing. Laistner, *Historians*, 8–9, shows the historical influence of rhetoric on all prose narrative, including historiography.

beyond his predecessors, it was Isocrates who most placed a rhetorical stamp on subsequent historiography. His orations preserved praise and blame concerning politics, and, as a later rhetorical historian points out (Dion. Hal. *Isoc.* 1), his students included historians.[129] Polybius, by contrast, criticized undue rhetorical influence, challenging especially Isocrates's student Theopompus.[130]

Like other literary works, many histories were apparently designed for oral performance.[131] Even apart from this expectation, elite historians would have drawn on their rhetorical training, both consciously and unconsciously, to satisfy elite audiences. Ancient writers used rhetorical techniques to make their histories persuasive.[132] Greek historians knew how to present their material in an artistic way,[133] and rhetorical conventions helped shape the telling of good history.[134] This was especially true during the empire, when rhetorical style marked not only speeches but even Roman literature.[135] Romans not only continued the Greek emphasis on argumentative history with an "interpretive superstructure" for the information; they also mixed it far more deliberately with rhetoric.[136] Pliny the Younger declares that one orator's histories are as charming as the writer's speeches, though more concise (*Ep.* 1.16.4).[137] Even Tacitus, one of the most respected Roman historians and our principal source for the early empire, was a powerful orator in his own right (Pliny *Ep.* 2.11.17). Although Greek historians, on the whole, maintained a standard of accuracy in the events they told, rhetorical principles did influence the ways they told their stories and how they conceived historical verisimilitude.

As Clare Rothschild notes, historians were interested not only in accuracy but also in plausibility and probability,[138] as in rhetoric more generally.[139] They might claim to prefer truth over style, but so did orators; such claims merely show that they dealt with information as well as style.[140] The measure of each of these elements varied from one historian to another, but historians in general both appealed to the tradition of historical research and sought to represent the past persuasively.[141] Historians could draw on epic literary strategies and interests in how they told their narratives.[142]

Although some historians sought restraint in the use of rhetoric, no one opposed it entirely.[143] "Pleasure and beauty" remained important purposes for any work (Dion. Hal. *Demosth.* 47).[144] Not only Thucydides (Thucyd. 1.1) but even the

129. Laird, "Rhetoric," 198–99, naming "Ephorus, Theopompus, and Philistus." Theopompus appears as a student of Isocrates in Cic. *De or.* 2.57, 94; *Orat.* 157.

130. Laird, "Rhetoric," 199, citing Polyb. 8.8.10–11.13.3.

131. Marincola, "Audiences," 13 (citing, e.g., Cic. *Fin.* 5.51); Laird, "Rhetoric," 206–7, 209. Marincola, "Audiences," 14, notes that many rhetorical curricula included histories and that rhetoricians urged the knowledge of history (Cic. *De or.* 1.158; *Orat.* 120; Quint. 10.1.34; 12.4.1–2), sometimes for style (suggested in Quint. 10.1.101–4) as well as examples.

132. Rothschild, *Rhetoric of History*, 65–66, arguing that they treated their histories as cases to be defended, though not as actual defense speeches.

133. Observed, e.g., by Meister, "Historiography: Greece," 421; Laistner, *Historians*, 3, 8, 30–31, 44.

134. See most fully Rebenich, "Historical Prose." Roman historiography varied stylistically (312).

135. Winterbottom, "Rhetoric."

136. Penner, *Praise*, 129.

137. History was a form of discourse distinct from others (e.g., forensic rhetoric or philosophy; e.g., Philost. *Ep. Apoll.* 19).

138. Rothschild, *Rhetoric of History*, 62; cf. Penner, *Praise*, 217.

139. Rothschild, *Rhetoric of History*, 62–64.

140. Ibid., 69. One should observe, however, that there is a difference in degree, as already noted (see, e.g., Pliny *Ep.* 7.17.3; 8.4.1).

141. Rothschild, *Rhetoric of History*, 69–70; cf. similarly Nicolai, "Place of History," 21.

142. Rothschild, *Rhetoric of History*, 88–91.

143. Witherington, "Addendum," 29–31; idem, *Acts*, 41–42.

144. LCL, 1:418–19. *Let. Aris.* 322 claims that it should provide greater pleasure than "mythographers" do.

methodologically insistent Polybius could succumb to the temptation to exaggerate the unique importance of his subject matter (Polyb. 1.4.5; 39.8.7).[145] Rhetorical conventions also appeared in ancient biography, though more so in rhetorical biographers such as Isocrates.[146] If for no other reason, the prominent role of speeches in ancient histories (see ch. 8 below) made the heavy use of rhetoric inevitable.

Some ancient historians allowed rhetoric more control over their presentation of history than others. As Rothschild points out, ancient historians debated "not about *whether*, but about *how* methods of argumentation should be used": should the orator persuade by logical appeal or by "inferior means (obsequy, amusement, sensationalism)"?[147] By Luke's day, historians imitated and mixed the various types of earlier historical approaches, including "epic, tragic and scientific approaches." Some "sacrificed standards of critical research for the immediate gratification of their audiences," using especially epic and tragic techniques; "others catering to more critical audiences imitated the more subtle argument strategies of Herodotus and his tradents"; most mixed techniques to some degree to reach the widest possible audience.[148]

We should not, however, use the rhetorical element to summarily dismiss all historical value in ancient historical writers; if Theopompus's rhetoric spoiled his history,[149] that of the orator Tacitus did not spoil his.[150] Writers fall at various places on a spectrum of rhetorical license. Even the best historians employed standards of rhetoric, but they used more restraint in rhetorical embellishment.[151] Moreover, although historians even as early as Herodotus employed rhetorical strategies, history was written quite differently "from poetry, drama, oratory, and forensic argument."[152] Most historians recognized that historical inquiry required not merely rhetorical skill but research.[153] The historian's moral or political aims could weigh more heavily than literary artistry, and neither such aims nor rhetorical presentation meant that historians simply "'revised' the past to serve their own purposes."[154] Whereas some modern interpreters debate the genus of rhetoric (e.g., deliberative or epideictic) dominating various historical works, historians themselves do not define their own narratives in these terms.[155]

145. For Thucydides, the *uniqueness* of events established their significance (Grene, *Political Theory*, 83).

146. See Burridge, "Biography." But biographies were rarely as partisan as forensic speech, where a primary object was legal victory (e.g., Dion. Hal. *Lysias* 8).

147. Rothschild, *Rhetoric of History*, 93.

148. Ibid., 95; for Herodotean echoes in Arrian, see in Bosworth, "Pursuit," 447. The function of audience is significant here: Luke's audience did not expect extensive rhetorical elaboration and pathos to the degree one finds in more dramatic historians (see discussion below), although his audience was apparently more comfortable with abundant signs claims than the audiences of many elite historians (see ch. 9 below). Many prefer eclectic approaches to ancient historiography in understanding Luke's work: Dormeyer, "Gatung," 475, views Acts as a pathetic, biographic universal history in rhetorical style with a great variety of critical-pragmatic sympathies, particularly in the speeches (my paraphrase).

149. Even Theopompus's weaknesses should not be exaggerated; he performed genuine research (Meister, "Theopompus"; Laistner, *Historians*, 4–5). Because views diverged concerning him already in antiquity and his work is no longer extant, forming solid judgments on his work today is difficult (Brown, *Historians*, 115). On the rhetoric of Theopompus, see Flower, *Theopompus*. More questionable among early figures is Cleitarchus in the third century B.C.E. (Laistner, *Historians*, 7).

150. For Tacitus's general accuracy, see, e.g., Laistner, *Historians*, 129 (noting archaeological corroborations, despite his own annoyance with Tacitus's biases on 131–39); Mosley, "Reporting," 20–22. Tacitus complained of the decline in imperial historiography but ranked himself with the earlier, superior historians (Marincola, "Tacitus' Prefaces"); for annotated bibliographies on Tacitus, see, e.g., Benario, "Recent Works" (688 sources between 1974 and 1983); Benario, "Work" (709 sources between 1994 and 2003).

151. Witherington, "Addendum," 29–31; cf. also 23–32.

152. Rothschild, *Rhetoric of History*, 81; cf. Lendon, "Historians," 41.

153. Dion. Hal. *Ant. rom.* 1.1.2–4; 1.4.2.

154. Litwak, *Echoes*, 37, noting what he is not implying.

155. Lendon, "Historiography," 52; Laird, "Historiography," 202. Lendon, "Historiography," 53, notes that Quintilian treated the rules of history and oratory as significantly "different in purpose and style (*Inst.*

Some writers explicitly criticized those more interested in showing off rhetorical skill than in historical truth.[156] Lucian expresses this concern in a particularly emphatic manner, heavily criticizing those who overemphasize rhetorical embellishment in histories (*Hist.* 22–23). In his essay *How to Write History*, Lucian summarizes the expectations of at least the more stringent historical critics (the standards by which other historians could expect to be evaluated).[157] He complains about writers who want to praise their rulers and generals (thereby attesting to the excess of epideictic interests among some historians; hence our discussion on "historians and rhetoric") and emphasizes that true history must not include any lies, unlike encomia (*Hist.* 7).[158]

Such writers, Lucian warns, must recognize that history employs rules "different from poetry and poems," which can blame their excesses on inspiration (*Hist.* 8).[159] "This . . . is the one thing peculiar to history, and only to Truth must sacrifice be made"; the writer of history must ignore all other concerns (*Hist.* 40).[160] Flatterers work for the present; historians preserve truth for the future (*Hist.* 40).[161] History's purpose, he opines, should not be to give pleasure but only to be useful, "and that comes from truth alone" (*Hist.* 9).[162] As particular models of good historians, he offers Xenophon and Thucydides (both contemporaries of the events they report), who would not let personal bias make them change facts; "public interest" and truth take priority over personal enmity or friendship (*Hist.* 39). Of course, not all ancient historians agreed with Lucian, who is among the most critical writers in this regard; Dionysius of Halicarnassus, by contrast, emphasizes rhetoric in the writing of history.[163] Josephus, too, is heavily rhetorical;[164] indeed, Dionysius was his Hellenistic model.[165] Josephus's free composition of some speeches is apparent,

10.1.31–34; cf. 2.4.2)." But cf. observations concerning different sorts of rhetorical strategies in Laird, "Rhetoric," 209.

156. E.g., Jos. *Ag. Ap.* 1.24–25; see discussion of Polybius's standard in sect. 1.c in this chapter.

157. We should, of course, take into account that Lucian is writing satire (Rothschild, *Rhetoric of History*, 81–86, esp. 81; Rothschild, "Irony"). But while Lucian's essay may have often been ironic (Rothschild, "Irony," e.g., 281), and he may have regarded historiography's ideals as now debased (289), need this mean that he regarded truth as elusive in history (290)? Or may not the heart of Lucian's irony be satirical exaggeration of some contemporary excesses? From examining ancient historians themselves, Rothschild herself questions the overemphasis on a "decline" from classical Greek models, noting that despite sensational elements, Hellenistic and Roman historians also retained the critical ideal (291).

158. Lucian does not rule out praise and blame or moral evaluation; rather (*Hist.* 59 [LCL]), "eulogy and censure will be careful and considered, free from slander, supported by evidence, cursory"—"not in court" (and hence not forensic exaggerations). The rhetorical historian Theopompus, by contrast, "impeached nearly everybody in a quarrelsome spirit," so "that he was a prosecutor rather than a recorder of events." For deliberate exaggeration in encomia, see, e.g., Libanius *Anecdote* 1.10.

159. LCL, 6:13.

160. LCL, 6:55.

161. One must, Lucian emphasizes, tell the truth, no matter how offensive to one's own contemporaries; thus one would win praise in future generations (*Hist.* 61–62).

162. LCL, 6:15. Rejecting history's entertainment value altogether—contrary to most of his own (nonhistorical) works—is a stringent standard not shared by all historians (as their pleasant readability suggests), but Lucian affirms history's edifying value, i.e., moral lessons, which flow from truth (e.g., *Hist.* 59). Usefulness and pleasure were not mutually exclusive objectives.

163. See Fox, "Dionysius." Xenophon appears less critical than Thucydides, writing history in a different way (Rhodes, "Documents," 60; cf. Dewald, "Construction," 95–96).

164. Cf. Botha, "Rhetoric and Josephus." Even Josephus's *War* may contain Greek tragic allusions (see Forte, "Echoes Revisited"), e.g., in maternal cannibalism during the siege of Jerusalem (see Chapman, "Cannibalism," 422–24, on *War* 6.199–219). As we have noted, tragedy did influence the writing of history (for discussion of the complex relationship, see esp. Rutherford, "Tragedy"), as it influenced many genres (Rutherford, "Tragedy," 513). Poetry and prose each affected the other (see Hutchinson, "Instructions").

165. Kennedy, "Source Criticism," 145 (noting that Dionysius also uses twenty books). Still, Josephus seems to follow the model of Thucydides at points in *Ant.* 17–19 (Kennedy, "Source Criticism," 145–46).

and a comparison of his *Antiquities* with the LXX reveals the degree of his rhetorical adaptation (see ch. 8 below).[166]

Was Luke heavily or only mildly influenced by models of dramatic rhetorical history writing? Luke's preface indicates some concerns shared with rhetorical historiography; his emphasis on an "orderly" account suggests that he valued persuasive arrangement.[167] But Luke is not on the rhetorical level of Dionysius or Josephus, as may be illustrated by his failure to elaborate scenes rhetorically. Osvaldo Padilla has demonstrated particularly fully that Luke probably lacked tertiary training in rhetoric, though he allows for his exposure to a secondary level of literate training.[168] Those schooled in rhetoric at a tertiary level learned various literary competencies, such as classics, Attic style, and the composition of elaborate speeches.[169] Padilla offers detailed examples of how Luke does not fit this.[170]

In particular, Padilla's observation that Luke lacks rhetorical elaboration is appropriate.[171] Vividness was an important element of rhetorical style in general,[172] and so it is hardly surprising that some measure of it usually appears in ancient narratives, including Acts.[173] Yet one goal in rhetoric was to make hearers feel as if they witnessed events with their very eyes (cf. Gal 3:1),[174] and historians often sought to achieve this goal (e.g., Vell. Paterc. 2.89.5–6, explicitly). Luke, by contrast, is quite selective in his vividness (limited mostly to speeches and a few scenes). Luke generally provides more detail in the "we" material, especially in the later chapters of Acts, but even here the details surround the narrative's key events, with little attention to, for example, the descriptions of local scenery characteristic of rhetorical display. In contrast to rhetorically lavish scenes designed to elicit pathos, Luke omits Paul's martyrdom, narrating mourning over Stephen only concisely (8:2) and over Paul briefly in advance (see comment on 20:37–38).

166. While usually maintaining the biblical story line, he occasionally augments it with subsequent traditions and often reshapes it for apologetic purposes.

167. Penner, *Praise*, 220; cf. Moessner, "Poetics," 97–112. Earlier writers like Bultmann, Dibelius, and Schmidt, who treated the Gospels and Acts as low-class literature, underestimated their rhetorical level (Padilla, "Παιδεία," 416, seeing the approach of Blass and Debrunner as much more balanced).

168. Padilla, "Παιδεία" (suggesting on 417 that Parsons, Rothschild, and some writers in Penner and Vander Stichele's volume overestimate Luke's rhetorical abilities).

169. Padilla, "Παιδεία," 421–24 (addressing knowledge of the classics on 421–22; Atticism on 422–23; and elaborate speeches on 423–24). Progymnasmata were relevant at the tertiary level (417). On Luke's speeches, see ch. 8 of this introduction. Some debate currently continues as to the degree to which Atticism dominated in speeches in various locations in this period.

170. Padilla, "Παιδεία," 424–34. Luke's few possible classical allusions (see further comment ad loc. in the commentary) reflect a more basic level of education (425–30).

171. Padilla, "Παιδεία," 417–18.

172. Dion. Hal. *Lysias* 7; Cic. *De or.* 2.45.189; Hermog. *Inv.* 3.15.166–68. On vividness (esp. ἐνάργεια and the more specific ἔκφρασις) and related forms, see also Anderson, *Glossary*, 34–35, 40, 43, 72–73; Hermog. *Progymn.* 10, "On Ecphrasis," 22–23; Aphth. *Progymn.* 12, "On Ecphrasis," 46–49S, 37–41R; Nicolaus *Progymn.* 11, "On Ecphrasis," 67–71; and classicists cited in Maclean and Aitken, *Heroikos*, 1:xiii, n. 86.

173. Woodman, *Rhetoric*, 27, notes the vividness of one of Thucydides's battle scenes, although he attributes this vividness especially to Thucydides's literary construction (while allowing for some eyewitness information).

174. Arist. *Rhet.* 2.8.14, 1386a; 3.11.1–2, 1411b; *Rhet. Her.* 4.55.68; Cic. *Or. Brut.* 40.139; Quint. *Inst.* 9.2.40; Theon. *Progymn.* 7.53–55; Longin. *Subl.* 15.2; Hermog. *Progymn.* 10, "On Ecphrasis," 22–23; Aphth. *Progymn.* 12, "On Ecphrasis," 46S, 36–37R; Nicolaus *Progymn.* 7, "On Commonplace," 45; *Progymn.* 11, "On Ecphrasis," 68; Anderson, *Rhetorical Theory*, 162; Gibson, "Notes," 141, 143, 427; in speeches, Cic. *Sull.* 26.72; Sen. E. rhetorical frg. 1; *Controv.* 1.6.12; Quint. *Inst.* 8.3.65; Jos. *Ant.* 20.123; Mus. Ruf. frg. 48, p. 140.19; Quint. *Decl.* 281.3; 291.7–8; 306.15; 314.20; 329.14, 17; 337.7; 347.9; Libanius *Topics* 1.8–11, 31; 2.11, 23; 3.14; 5.13; *Descr.* 1.2; 2; Hermog. *Method* 15.432 (on Demosth. *Fals. leg.* 192–95); in a letter, Pliny *Ep.* 5.6.40 (cf. 2.18.3); Fronto *Ad Ant. imp.* 1.4; in history, Polyb. 2.56.8 (critiquing the practice; but cf. Dion. Hal. *Lit. Comp.* 18; *Lysias* 7). Matters "passing before the eyes" could apply to imagining them (Cic. *Fam.* 14.3.2; Quint. *Inst.* 6.1.31; Sil. It. 10.584–86; 11.114–16; 12.547–49; Plut. *Demosth.* 18.2; Tac. *Dial.* 16; Lucian *Dance* 63; Philost. *Hrk.* 10.5; Xen. Eph. *Anthia* 1.5; 3.5; cf. Symm. *Ep.* 1.84).

It is significant that the more detailed rhetorical exercise of elaborately describing scenes is missing in Luke-Acts; Acts uses rhetoric, as all literary works did, but is not intended as anything like an epideictic showpiece.[175] (In its extreme forms, the practice of vivid description also earned critics, who might insist on praising virtue rather than topography.[176] Lucian suggests that such rhetoricians fixate on irrelevant details because they lack matters of importance on which to discourse.)[177]

As later rhetoricians defined it (but earlier writers practiced without the terminology), ekphrasis (rhetorical description) could "describe both persons and things, occasions and places, dumb animals and, in addition, growing things."[178] Yet even the shortest sort of ekphrasis (e.g., Thersites being "bandy-legged, lame in one foot")[179] is missing in Luke's work. Luke depicts action and itineraries, but hardly graphically; he offers physical descriptions of neither places[180] nor people, as all those who wish they knew what Jesus or Paul[181] looked like are well aware.[182]

Homer's detailed depiction of Achilles's shield (*Il.* 18.468–608) offered the standard for descriptiveness, and other writers (e.g., Aeschylus *Eum.* 39–59; Eurip. *Ion* 82–183) used such accounts long before ekphrasis is attested as a rhetorical exercise in the Second Sophistic;[183] Latin forms followed Greek ones in this practice.[184] Rhetors demanded more graphic scenes providing visual horror;[185] but some historians protested if narration of such scenes exceeded necessary details of history.[186] That Luke, though reporting several martyrdoms, avoids all mention of gore places him toward the more restrained end of this continuum.

Second Sophistic orators appreciated the work of earlier rhetorical historians, such as Sallust, who painted a vivid picture of details and feelings (Fronto *Ad Ant. imp.* 2.6.4–15), and thought that historians ought to describe the countryside (2.6.6). Luke never does either to any extent worth comparing to more rhetorical historiography. (This is true even in the "we" material, where Luke is most vivid and detailed. There is nothing, for example, about the famous hundred-petaled roses around Philippi.) But even most writers concerned with rhetoric noted that nice-sounding words were less important than words appropriate to a subject.[187] In

175. Ekphrasis (with sorts of set-piece descriptions nowhere found in Luke) does appear in narrative works (Rusten, "*Ekphrasis*"; Bowie, "Second Sophistic," 1377).

176. Dio Chrys. *Or.* 32.37–38.

177. Lucian *Hist.* 20; cf. 56. He ridicules an extensive, Homer-like description of the emperor's shield (*Hist.* 19) and other such "tasteless" flaunting of rhetoric (*Hist.* 57). Anderson, "Second Sophistic," 341–42, observes that some ekphrasis simply recycles commonplaces useful for extemporaneous delivery.

178. Aphth. *Progymn.* 12, "On Ecphrasis," 46S, 36–37R (Kennedy, 117). Ekphrasis may appear in Jewish works as early as Ezekiel the Tragedian (Heath, "Visuality," on Ezek. Trag. *Exag.* 243–69); it often appears in ancient fiction (see, e.g., Shea, "Stage," 70). On ekphrasis, see further, e.g., Cunningham, "Ekphrasis"; Rifkin, "Ekphrasis"; other articles in the same issue as Cunningham and Rifken (*Classical Philology* 102 [1, 2007]); Chinn, "Eyes"; Francis, "Maidens"; a late example in Gibson, "Tychaion" (allowing a work's dating).

179. Hermog. *Progymn.* 10, "On Ecphrasis," 22 (Kennedy, 86).

180. A standard practice; see, e.g., Aphth. *Progymn.* 12, "On Ecphrasis," 47–49S, 39–41R. Chance, *Acts*, 16, notes that Luke accords with Lucian's advice (*Hist.* 19, 56–57) by avoiding elaborate depictions of locations.

181. See the discussion of Paul's putative appearance in ch. 7 below.

182. But appropriateness was important; flowery subjects merited flowery speech whereas "dry" topics invited "dry" speech (Hermog. *Progymn.* 10, "On Ecphrasis," 23).

183. Fantuzzi, "Ekphrasis," 873; e.g., Lucian *Hipp.* 8.

184. Reitz, "Ekphrasis"; for Virgil *Aen.* 1.441–94 following Hom. *Od.* 8, see Beck, "Ecphrasis."

185. Dion. Hal. *Lit. Comp.* 18. Dion. Hal. *Thuc.* 15 complains that Thucydides often portrays successfully the abject cruelty and sufferings of war but at other times fails to evoke the appropriate horror. In art, cf., e.g., Mart. *Epig.* 3.35.

186. Polyb. 15.34.1.

187. Dion. Hal. *Demosth.* 18. That Dionysius was a historian as well as a rhetorical critic is significant in weighing his testimony here.

contrast to Dionysius of Halicarnassus, some subsequent historians such as Appian and Dio Cassius largely neglected classicizing language, leading to their neglect among scholars studying the Second Sophistic.[188] And Luke, surveying the gospel's movement from Jerusalem to Rome in a single monograph, appears to emphasize a different rhetorical virtue: conciseness.[189]

I thus differ from the scholars who see Acts as "dramatic" history in terms of such elaborations.[190] Still, Luke is "dramatic" in other ways—for example, by including numerous "signs" reports.[191] Plümacher sees miraculous elements as more dominant in "tragic-pathetic" history,[192] yet Luke is readier to report signs than to develop specifically tragic-pathetic elements at any length.[193] Popular literature often developed tales of exotic distant lands, unusual "natural phenomena," divine interventions, and wonders;[194] Luke's lands belong to the real world, and he focuses on only the unusual phenomena (miracle reports) relevant to his story. Such features suggest not that he wrote tragic-pathetic history but that he wrote in a manner more consistent with an audience immersed in Scripture (which reported many such signs) than in elite Greco-Roman rhetorical conventions and that he wrote more about miracle workers (whose role he hardly invented; cf. 2 Cor 12:12).

Care in composition, however, entailed not just the choice of words but also larger structural issues, such as arrangement.[195] Movement and changes of scene are also important in history as well as in other sorts of narratives. Thus one ancient critic prefers Herodotus to Thucydides: the former, though long, addresses diverse events whereas the latter wearies the reader with his narrow focus and tedious detail.[196] Varying literary forms within a work made it more palatable for its audience (e.g., Pliny *Ep.* 6.33.7–10).

That historians and novelists alike share such features reveals the dependence of both on standard rhetorical expectations. The pervasiveness of rhetorical elements in ancient sources warns against facile genre assignments based on such elements. At the

---

188. Gowing, "Tradition," 332–33.

189. With Parsons, "*Progymnasmata*," 53–55. On the ancient appreciation for conciseness, see this commentary's comment on Acts 24:4; Keener, *John*, 19; in narratives, see, e.g., Theon *Progymn.* 5.39–43, 52–53; Phaedrus 2.prol. 12–13; 3, 2.epil. 8–9; 4.epil. 7–9; Philost. *Hrk.* 29.6. Of course, some writers (such as Sallust) deployed considerable rhetoric even in monographs.

190. This is not to deny any kind of dramatic elements; for a comparison of dramatic episodes in Acts with those in Livy, Cleitarchus, Duris (Douris), and Curtius Rufus, see Plümacher, *Lukas*, 80–136. But Livy is the supreme extant example of the rhetorically lavish historian (Byrskog, *History*, 207). Laistner, *Historians*, 14–16, argues that criticism of third-century b.c.e. tragic/dramatic historians has been overplayed, since it is a matter of degree; on 18 he also questions the association of this approach with Peripatetics, who did careful research.

191. Probably partly because of his subject matter: he writes partly about miracle workers (such as Jesus and Paul). Scholars often include both the dramatization of events and the "enriching" of them with miraculous elements in Hellenistic and Roman historiography (e.g., Krasser, "Reading," 554, though drawing the genre a bit more widely than I would). "Signs" certainly do appear in histories (Plümacher, *Geschichte*, 33–84).

192. Plümacher, *Geschichte*, 33–84. See discussion on this thesis in Dormeyer, "Gatung," 452–56 (incorporating its insights on 475); in idem, "Historii," he notes that the preponderance of signs aligns Luke more closely with Israelite than Hellenistic historiography on this point.

193. Pathos does appear; see, e.g., comments on Acts 20:19, 31, 37; some scholars also argue that Israel's failure to respond is viewed as tragic (so Tannehill, "Rejection," esp. 98–99, 101; cf. idem, "Tragic Story"). But such occasions are minor compared with sources more steeped in Greek tragic conventions (even some descriptions in Tacitus are more "tragic-pathetic," e.g., *Ann.* 5.9; 12.47; cf. Rutherford, "Tragedy," 512; Vell. Paterc. 2.53.3) and come nowhere close, e.g., to a Phylarchus. Although tragic elements predominate more in some historians than others, there was no specific "school" of tragic historiography (see Rutherford, "Tragedy," 513–14, following Walbank, "Tragedy" = *Papers*, 241; Hornblower, "Introduction," 44; Marincola, "Audiences," 22).

194. Penner, *Praise*, 134.

195. Dion. Hal. *Lit. Comp.* 2–4. See discussion of expansion and abridgment, sect. c, below.

196. Dion. Hal. *Pomp.* 3.

same time, we should not obliterate the distinctions between pure rhetoric and the use of rhetoric in historiography (outside its speeches). Pliny the Younger points out that, for all their commonalities, history and oratory are different disciplines: rhetoric focuses on trivial narratives, and history on famous deeds (5.8.9); style, vocabulary, rhythm, and subject matter all differ (5.8.10–11).[197]

Various ancient historians indicated the careful balance they often sought. Polybius recognizes the epideictic function of historical writing (see ch. 5 below). He opines that historians must render judgments about whether peoples or individuals "are worthy of praise or blame" (Polyb. 3.4.1 [LCL]). Moral judgments and rhetorical artistry, however, do not require abandonment of historical responsibility; a history is not a speech (epideictic or otherwise).

Thus Polybius warns that he would depart from his earlier comments about a person that were offered in an encomium. There he provided a "somewhat exaggerated account of his achievements," but "the present history, which distributes praise and blame impartially, demands a strictly true account and one which states the ground on which either praise or blame is based" (10.21.8 [LCL]).[198] In a later period, Dio Cassius emphasizes that he has given attention to both tasteful literary style and historical accuracy in his narrative (Dio Cass. 1.1.1–2). Suetonius, though more disposed to credit scandals about some of his subjects than about others, avoided embellishment and would not easily be classified a "rhetorical" historian[199] in spite of his considerable interest in rhetoric.[200] But his contemporary Tacitus, a renowned orator who also wrote about oratory (*Dialogus de oratoribus*),[201] was no less careful a historian (and in some respects was more so). On average, modern readers will invest greater confidence in more concise historical works that summarize information than in those that indulge rhetorical elaboration, such as Tacitus;[202] yet a comparison of Tacitus with other extant sources suggests that he followed the story line of his sources for recent history.[203] It seems clear where Luke's concise narrative and speeches rank him by these standards.

197. On the distinction between rhetoric and history in Cicero, see Nicolai, "Place of History," 21. Pure rhetoric, not bound by historical or other truth-telling conventions, can employ fabrications (Gorg. *Hel.* 11, 13).

198. Of course, even orators praising the emperor claimed objectivity; e.g., Fronto *Ad Ant. imp.* 2.2 declares that it was not his praise of the emperor but the emperor's virtues that had produced admiration. Nor is Polybius always objective in his history. But the point is that Polybius sought to be substantially more objective in history than in pure epideictic. Indeed, historians often praised both sides in a war, thereby amplifying pathos and the credit due the victor.

199. Rolfe, "Introduction," xix.

200. See, e.g., Suet. *Rhet.* passim. Penner, *Praise*, 137, contrasts the epiphany in Suetonius's account of Caesar crossing the Rubicon with Caesar's own account; but more than a century and a half (from 49 B.C.E. to the early second century C.E.) is sufficient time for legends to grow (perhaps as much as four times the period we estimate between the opening scene of Acts and its composition), and Suetonius's dependence on such sources does not require his own fabrication. Thus in an earlier version (ca. 30 C.E.) Vell. Paterc. 2.49.4, while making the Rubicon the boundary, allows its crossing without fanfare; for discussion of possibly the earliest version, see Rondholz, "Rubicon." Most writers subsequent to Caesar seem to have preferred the account of his contemporary Asinius Pollio to Caesar's (see Damon, "Rhetoric," 442); Pollio is earlier than Velleius, but while Pollio is cited in Suet. *Jul.* 30, it is not clear that his account remains in view in 32, where the report of the apparition (attributed to multiple but unnamed witnesses) appears.

201. On Tacitus's rhetorical prowess, see Moore, "Introduction," ix (citing Pliny *Ep.* 2.1.6; 2.11.17). Tacitus certainly does develop dramatic scenes and dialogues (see Hadas, "Introduction," xx–xxi).

202. Woodman, *Rhetoric*, 204, preferring Velleius Paterculus on this point. In general, scholars have been more ready to accept T. P. Wiseman's skepticism about the early Republic than A. J. Woodman's skepticism toward "authors of contemporary or near-contemporary history" (Damon, "Rhetoric," 439–40), but Woodman himself apparently recognizes that likelihood increases with proximity.

203. See Keener, "Otho"; if Tacitus is the source for Suetonius and Plutarch (despite their omission of his added speeches), at the least we can say that they believed Tacitus to be accurate.

Samuel Byrskog, in emphasizing that ancients narrativized their history (i.e., told it as story),[204] underlines the influence of rhetoric on ancient historiography,[205] but points out that rhetoric did not eradicate the goal of historical truth.[206] Granted, some historians distorted facts, but it was generally considered that the most effective persuasion rested on facts and *"persuasion and factual credibility were supplementary rhetorical virtues, not contradictory."*[207] Historians had a factual "core" that they developed in narrativizing history, in telling "history by means of a story."[208] Thus one cannot easily separate history's story/narrative from its extratextual, factual past.[209] Ancient historiography allowed for flexibility in recounting the information, but mainstream historiography differed greatly from the writing of novels.

b. Luke's History and Rhetoric

As we have already been emphasizing, Luke was no rhetorical historian like Theopompus; he was certainly not even as rhetorically trained as Tacitus or Suetonius, leading Roman historians and biographers trained first of all in rhetoric. Most historians by Luke's day mixed the various approaches of their predecessors—both rhetorical and dramatic elaboration, on the one hand, and critical research, on the other—though many gravitated closer to one side or the other, depending on their audiences.[210] Luke, too, offers an eclectic combination of elements, in this case characteristic of early Christian circles. Less rhetorically sophisticated and with only two volumes to work with, he lacks the rhetorical elaboration or detailed scene descriptions of, for instance, Josephus, yet he also appeals to an audience prepared for a hardier diet of miracles than most elite historians would provide (see ch. 9 below).

Modern scholars evaluating Luke-Acts in terms of Greco-Roman rhetoric come to strikingly different conclusions—perhaps depending on which part of Luke-Acts they are reading. On the one hand, Philip Satterthwaite correctly argues that classical rhetorical conventions deeply influenced Luke's literary techniques in Acts.[211] On the other hand, Pervo argues that Luke's literary level would be considered low to educated Greeks, in contrast to refined Hellenistic history.[212]

Both perspectives have some value, depending on the foil with which Acts is contrasted. As noted above, Luke does seem to write for a more popular audience than most elite historians did.[213] A style differing from that of elite historians does not mean that Luke was not writing history, however; there were no "professional

204. See Byrskog, *History*, ch. 5, "History Entering into Story: Autopsy Narrativized," 199–253.
205. Ibid., 203–13.
206. Ibid., 213. Byrskog's conclusions resemble those of Rothschild, noted above (e.g., Rothschild, *Rhetoric of History*, 88–91); and Nicolai, "Place of History," 21.
207. Byrskog, *History*, 223; emphasis his.
208. Ibid., 223. Byrskog means "core" in a much fuller sense than A. J. Woodman (see p. 184), believing that ancient historians cared about facts (179–84). Others have also expressed concern that Woodman's "core" is too narrow (Feldherr, "Introduction," 8; cf. Marincola, "Audiences," 18; Lendon, "Historiography," esp. 45–46, 50–61). Cf. similarly Eddy and Boyd, *Legend*, 330–34. The extensive overlap in ancient reports (see, e.g., Keener, "Otho") underlines the extent to which even historians with differing perspectives depended on what they believed to be prior information.
209. Byrskog, *History*, 253. The criticisms of Matthews, "Review," concern not so much Byrskog's analysis of ancient historiography (which I cite here) but his application of this category to the Gospels. Yet as I have argued, Luke was writing ancient historiography.
210. Rothschild, *Rhetoric of History*, 93, 95.
211. Satterthwaite, "Acts," 337 (summarizing the conclusions of his chapter). Cf. also the positive evaluation in Bultmann, *Tradition*, 366; Parsons, *Acts*, 9 (on Luke's speeches).
212. Pervo, *Profit*, 6, citing Julian *Letter* 36.423d, who lists Luke with Matthew as inferior.
213. Cf. similarly Barrett, *Acts*, 2:xxxv (with Plümacher): Acts is a popular kind of history, using biographic and episodic narration. Most early Christians were probably "urban, lower middle class," lacking much formal

historians" in his day (most were politicians, philosophers, rhetoricians, and soldiers).[214] Luke surely did not belong to the elite like the historians of the Roman senatorial class or of the order of the *equites*. Most Hellenistic historians had formal rhetorical training;[215] it is not clear that Luke received such training. From the preface in Luke 1:1–4, Loveday Alexander suggests that if Luke writes history, he writes it from the more scientific, less rhetorical side of historiography.[216] Patristic writers were often embarrassed by the poor Greek and the lack of rhetoric in the NT (though this may be partly because they wrote after the rise of, and hence may have been influenced by the standards of, the Second Sophistic).[217]

Luke's ability to write a lengthy and cohesive work demonstrates significantly more education than was common among nonelites, but this does not mean that he displays advanced training in rhetoric. Osvaldo Padilla has rightly shown that while Luke may well have had secondary training, he did not have tertiary training in rhetoric.[218] I began my study of Acts and Paul with the assumption that Luke (whose Greek is sometimes excellent) was rhetorically proficient and Paul (contrary to Luke's portrait of him) was not. Further study has invited me to reverse these views, especially in light of the respective genres in which they wrote: rhetorical flourishes were far more common in historians' reports of speeches than they were in letters, but I find considerably more of them in Paul than even in Luke's speeches.[219] Although Luke expresses excellent Greek when it is called for (e.g., Luke 1:1–4), the speeches in Acts are not extraordinarily sophisticated.[220]

Members of the elite class expected histories to conform to the appropriate historical style.[221] Readers noticed when the pre-Lukan Roman historian Sallust regularly displayed rhetorical tropes in his historical writing (Fronto *Ad Ant. imp.* 2.6.1–2). A history written in a style between the normal historical and discursive styles could sell well among the rhetorically trained elite (Pliny *Ep.* 5.5.3). Later elite writers shaped by the Second Sophistic averred that historians should write in the "grand" style (*splendide*, Fronto *Ad verum imp.* 2.1.14), which is not Luke's preferred style.[222] The initial influence of the Second Sophistic was already, in some sense,

education but familiar with pervasive rhetorical conventions (Fuller, "Classics," 185, summarizing Kennedy's remarks).

214. Rebenich, "Historical Prose," 289.

215. See ibid., 288. Polybius, in fact, opined (presumably against his competition) that most historians lacked proper qualifications (Polyb. 12.25e.2). (On historical investigation as distinct from mere compositional interest in Polyb. 12, cf. Siegert, "Vérité.")

216. Alexander, *Context*, 41. For Luke's scientific background, see also Padilla, "Παιδεία," 435–36.

217. See here Judge, *First Christians*, 711, 713. Most educated Greeks found first-century Christian writings in general vulgar (Townsend, "Education," 148–49, citing late second-century c.e. Tatian *Or. Gks.* 26–30). This would create a problem for those for whom inspiration demanded also good rhetoric (Dion. Hal. *Thuc.* 34, though acknowledging that Thucydides was a good historian; cf. Philost. *Hrk.* 25.4, 8, who praises Homer's inspiration yet critiques his accuracy [24.1–2; 25.10–17]).

218. Padilla, "Παιδεία," 436 (suggesting instead Luke's "scientific" training). Fernández-Garrido, "Stasis-theory," suggests that major novelists had rhetorical training.

219. See, e.g., Keener, *Corinthians*, passim (e.g., 24–28, 32, 131, 234). Still, though Paul wrote well, he did not seek to write elegantly (see Caragounis, "Dionysios Halikarnasseus").

220. Admittedly, the rhetorical strategies become more recognizable with Paul addressing Gentiles than with his predecessors addressing Judeans (a rhetorically appropriate distinction); the legal strategies in Acts 22–26 are significant but could reflect the "we" narrative's closer dependence on the speaker's own forensic rhetoric (on 24:10–21, see, e.g., Keener, "Rhetorical Techniques").

221. Cadbury, Foakes-Jackson, and Lake, "Writing History," 13.

222. On the grand style, see, e.g., Dion. Hal. *Demosth.* 15; Cic. *Or. Brut.* 5.20–6.21; Pliny *Ep.* 3.13.4; 6.33.7–8; 7.12.4; 9.26.1 ; 9.26.10; Aul. Gel. 6.14; Longinus *Sublime*; Fronto *Ad M. Caes.* 3.16.2; Men. Rhet. 1.1, 335.21–22; 2.1–2, 368.9; 2.1–2, 369.8–9; 2.6, 399.21–22; 400.7–9; Keener, *John*, 48–49; Cronjé, "Περὶ ὕψους." In Latin, use of the grand style for historiography continues as late as Ammianus Marcellinus (Kelly, "Forge Tongues," 474).

under way when Luke wrote, although it had probably not yet affected members of his social circle.[223] Even in the first century B.C.E., however, some writers were already advocating the literary use of Old Attic Greek rather than Koine,[224] by which standard Luke generally falls short, though less so than most other first-century Christian writers.

Luke lacks the apology for poor Greek that some provided when they expected to fall short of the highest rhetorical standards.[225] The lack of an apology may be not because Luke's Greek is better than that of, for example, Josephus (far from it) but because his audience would not hold such critical expectations of him as elite readers might for Josephus. (With his royal patrons, Josephus could also afford considerable scribal help.) Further, Luke does not take rhetorical conventions as far as many of his contemporaries who wrote for more elite audiences.[226] Most historians in the period of the empire followed the approach of the earlier rhetorician Isocrates in (1) stressing the moral purpose of histories (providing *exempla*, such as models relevant for virtue); (2) pursuing encomiastic or epideictic aims by praising persons, as in biography; and (3) the "excessive use of declamation, moralizing digressions, the display of rhetorical virtuosity for stylistic effect," and the use of wonders primarily for entertainment. Sociorhetorical critic Ben Witherington argues that Luke made little use of these practices,[227] and he is certainly correct regarding the sort of "moralizing digressions," elaborate scene descriptions, and lavish displays of epideictic prose more characteristic of some elite works (see discussion above). Luke plainly avoids the rhetorical bombast of those derided as "Asianists" (*Asiani*).[228] He does not even seek to vary style in speeches as much as one would expect of some rhetoricians; for example, the address ἄνδρες ἀδελφοί (men, brothers) appears frequently throughout Acts (but not the Gospel) regardless of the speaker (Acts 1:16; 2:29, 37; 7:2, 26; 13:15, 26, 38; 15:7, 13; 22:1; 23:1, 6; 28:17).

At the same time, Luke shows himself a master of classical rhetoric where he finds the need for it (e.g., Luke 1:1–4; Acts 17:22–31), including in periodic sentences (Luke 1:1–4; Acts 15:24–26; cf. Luke 3:1–2).[229] He employs the same rhetorical authentication techniques found in many of the more elite historians.[230] The ability to

223. Bowie, "Second Sophistic," 1377; idem, "Sophistic," dates it to the period ca. 60–230 C.E., though some scholars begin it later and some of its initial influence may precede this period as well.

224. See, e.g., Kennedy, "Survey of Rhetoric," 18; Rowe, "Style," 156.

225. E.g., Cic. *Att.* 1.19; *Sest.* 2.4; Aul. Gel. 11.8.3 (though Cato suggested simply avoiding Greek composition, 11.8.4); Sir prol.; Jos. *Ant.* 1.7; 20.263; *Ag. Ap.* 1.27, 50; cf. (as a literary fiction) Anacharsis *Ep.* 1.1–6. In some cases, this disclaimer aimed at lowering audience expectations (for this rhetorical strategy, see, e.g., Lysias *Or.* 2.1, §190; 12.3, §120; 19.1–2, §152; Isaeus *Astyph.* 35; *Aristarch.* 1; Isoc. *Panath.* 3; *Rhet. Alex.* 29, 1436b.33–34; Cic. *Quinct.* 1.1–4; 24.77; 26.80–27.85; Sall. *Jug.* 85.31; *Sp. G. Cotta* 4; Quint. *Inst.* 4.1.8–9, 11; cf. Suet. *Titus* 7.1; Tac. *Hist.* 4.73), used often enough by Dio Chrysostom (*Or.* 1.9; 32.39; 46.7; 47.1, 8; cf. also 42.1, if that is from Dio).

226. The vast majority of extant ancient historians wrote especially for elite audiences; see, e.g., Marincola, "Audiences," 12–13 (though noting on 13 that they expected other auditors as well).

227. Witherington, *Acts*, 44–45. Clearly, Luke does provide moral *exempla* (e.g., the contrast between Barnabas and the Ananias family in Acts 4:36–5:11) and theological speeches, but he employs most overt rhetorical features with restraint.

228. For a brief discussion of the style so characterized (including, in Latin, Cicero), see esp. Calboli, "Asianism"; cf. idem, "Atticism," 325; Aune, *Dictionary of Rhetoric*, 68.

229. Blass, Debrunner, and Funk, *Grammar*, §464; Aune, *Dictionary of Rhetoric*, 347; cf. Cadbury, "Commentary on Preface"; see further comment on Acts 15:24–26. Luke 1:1–2 also includes five π-words, like Plutarch, who employs seven of them in *Dinner* pref. 146C (Aune, *Dictionary of Rhetoric*, 33); divided in two parts, Luke's prologue employs "three matching phrases" (idem, *Environment*, 116–17). For another long-sentence prologue, cf. Sirach.

230. See Rothschild, *Rhetoric of History*, passim.

vary style, even in a single speech, was rhetorically important;[231] variation was useful even in vocabulary.[232] Even if speakers in Acts often sound the same, Luke sometimes varies the speeches (see ch. 8 below). He fairly often employs the rhetorically clear technique of "inflection," but this was apparently one of the more basic exercises.[233] More significantly, Luke makes use of prose rhythm (based on vowel rhythm), which is otherwise rare in the earliest extant Christian documents.[234] The cumulative effect of ancient rhetorical patterns appearing in speeches in Acts suggests that Luke knew various rhetorical strategies and devices.[235]

More problematic is the question of linguistic register. Although an educated person did not need to invariably employ Atticism, a prestige dialect utilizing the old Attic Greek, an uneducated person could not have competently employed it; that Luke sometimes does so suggests his education.[236] Still, Luke "is basically no Atticist in his style" and proves uninterested in rhetoric inappropriate to the form of history he is writing.[237] He clearly did not write for a typical elite Greco-Roman audience. Despite classicizing passages mentioned above (esp. Luke 1:1–4), his Koine style elsewhere reflects his primary ideal audience[238] and their appreciation for the sometimes semitizing rhythms of the LXX.[239] God-fearers, even of moderately high social status, would recognize language from the LXX that might sound offensive to elite ears schooled merely in rhetoric. Some scholars have even plausibly suggested that Luke's appeal to "biblical," LXX style at times serves the archaizing, "classicizing" function for his audience that Attic style served for elite Greek audiences of other works.[240]

231. E.g., Pliny *Ep.* 2.5.7; 3.13.4; 4.14.3; 6.33.7–8; 7.9.7; 8.21.1; 9.29.1–2; Cic. *Or. Brut.* 46.156; 47.157; *Fam.* 13.27.1.

232. Aul. Gel. 1.4; Max. Tyre 21.4; Lee, "Translations: Greek," 776–77; Anderson, *Glossary,* 53–54, 71, 114; see further Keener, *John,* 325.

233. Parsons, "*Progymnasmata,*" 56–61 (esp. 61, citing the much later Nicolaus *Progymn.* 4, "On Chreia," 18–19).

234. Aune, *Dictionary of Rhetoric,* 382 (noting that Aug. *De doctrina christiana* 4.41 also observes its rareness in the NT). On prose rhythm, see briefly Dihle, "Prose Rhythm."

235. Parsons, "*Progymnasmata,*" 43–44, further arguing (44–63) that Luke probably had learned from the sort of rhetorical exercises preserved for us in the handbooks. Cf. further the high evaluation of Luke's rhetorical skill in Asso, "Raconter."

236. Alexander, *Context,* 250. Scholars employ similar methods for determining the academic training of other ancient authors (see Hock, "Curriculum").

237. Witherington, *Acts,* 43, listing as exceptions only the optative (Acts 8:31; 17:18, 26, 29) and 17:22–31 (43n155). Even during and after the Second Sophistic, critics derided excessive (Lucian *Hist.* 21) or inappropriate (Philost. *Vit. Apoll.* 8.6) Atticism. Alexander, *Context,* 18, points out that Luke's level is the high Koine that is characteristic of technical treatises, rather than the Atticism characteristic of histories; this apparent genre difference, however, may be resolved if we admit (with Aune, Barrett, and others) that Acts is *popular* historiography.

238. Even Cicero used common language when writing letters (though, presumably, not for a history; *Fam.* 9.21.1). Simple, unadorned language could also be preferable (Dion. Hal. *Demosth.* 5–6), although this varied according to one's rhetorical school (the so-called Asiatic style was portrayed as bombastic) and period (Atticism dominated by the early second century).

239. See Hanson, *Acts,* 52–53. Steyn, "*LXX-Sitate,*" finds a particularly Semitic form of the LXX; in any event, all recensions of the LXX retain many Semitisms (though some parts, such as the Pentateuch, are more literal than others). Of course, some parts even of the LXX reflect some Greek rhetorical conventions (cf. Aitken, "Rhetoric"; Lee, "Translations: Greek").

240. Alexander, *Context,* 250–52, suggesting that "biblicism" functioned as a prestige dialect among many Jews and Christians (also idem, "*Septuaginta,*" 21); Padilla, "Παιδεία," 436–37; Aune, *Environment,* 117; Witherington, *Acts,* 44. Alexander, "*Septuaginta,*" 17–19, treats this as a sort of intensive "intertextuality" (17), a living "Jewish Greek" (19) that exceeded mere LXX imitation. This is not "low register" (17) but a social dialect (23), providing cultural cohesiveness (26). Others also observe Luke's pervasive LXX language (e.g., Mielcarek, "Język").

Luke does not use the "grand" style or bombast; he appears to take a mediating approach rhetorically,[241] with a literary style of educated Koine.[242] Luke lays less emphasis on rhetorical technique than on the story he must recount; he avoids the "excessive use of declamation" that characterized many ancient historians.[243] (Of course, rhetoricians in general usually preferred a plain, rather than flowery, style in narratives,[244] although the nature of this plain style might depend on the topics addressed.)[245] Although Luke is not Josephus nor his audience the Flavian household, neither is he Mark.[246] Aune offers a balanced conclusion: "Luke-Acts is a popular 'general history' written by an amateur Hellenistic historian with credentials in Greek rhetoric."[247]

c. Expanding and Abridging Accounts

Ancient writers freely expanded or abridged accounts without any thought that their contemporaries might find this practice objectionable. Contrary to early form-critical studies of the Gospels, which supposed that the tradition's tendency was always expansive, it is impossible to predict whether the passage of time would lengthen or shorten accounts.[248] Expansion sometimes resulted from the passage of time and the consequent growth of tradition;[249] in other cases, lengthy stories were sometimes progressively abbreviated in time.[250]

Among Aelius Theon's rhetorical exercises is the practice of "expanding" and "condensing" fables:[251] "We 'expand' by lengthening the speeches-in-character in the fable, and by describing a river or something of this sort. We condense by doing the opposite."[252] When applied to other kinds of narratives, this approach need not tamper with historical substance; aside from adding details known from other sources and adding some description that is either implicit in the narrative or inherently probable in itself, Theon's example for expanding a *chreia* (anecdote) does not substantially

241. Shiell, *Reading Acts*, 45–46, 169–70 (noting, 170, that even the most exciting scenes in Acts could be delivered in middle style).

242. See Alexander, *Context*, 18, 250 (noting as an exception Luke's archaizing, "biblicist" style at points). Shiell, *Reading Acts*, 170, notes that Luke uses mostly good Greek grammar, lacking many unusual constructions. Most strongly, Judge, *First Christians*, 710–11, emphasizes that the Greek of the NT is not that of the papyri, but rather "the professional prose used by technical writers of the time," "the contemporary Greek of educated people." He notes (711) that Atticism was only coming again into widespread vogue.

243. Witherington, *Acts*, 44–45.

244. Rowe, "Style," 155–56; cf. also more conversational types of speeches (Men. Rhet. 2.4, 393.21–22).

245. A loose style, e.g., was most appropriate to informal conversation (Rowe, "Style," 151).

246. That Luke is of higher literary quality than the other extant first-century Gospels is generally recognized (e.g., Dibelius, *Tradition*, 161; Witherington, "Editing," 326, 328; Burridge, "Gospels and Acts," 526–27; Kilpatrick, "Style"). Luke includes even a few classical references (some suggest Acts 5:39; 9:5, 12; 19:35; 26:14; see Renehan, "Quotations," 22–23), though too few to satisfy an elite audience.

247. Aune, *Environment*, 77 (though I would doubt that Luke's "credentials" included tertiary training in rhetoric). That advanced education focused on rhetoric rather than on history, as he goes on to note, does not imply that historians would not learn techniques from reading other historians. For Acts as a "popular" history, see also Barrett, *Acts*, 2:xxxv; Verheyden, "What Are We Up To?," 55 (citing also Barrett, "First Testament," 101; *Acts*, 2:li); Pervo, *Acts*, 18 (though defining history loosely).

248. See Sanders, *Tendencies*, 19, 46–87, 88–189, 272; cf. Stein, "'Criteria,'" 238–40.

249. In Jewish sources, cf., e.g., 'Abot R. Nat. 7, §21 B (for a pseudonymous claim to have personally witnessed something that earlier tradition simply reports). For a halakic example, cf. Hoenig, "Kinds of Labor." Amplification and embellishment are thus more characteristic of the apocryphal gospels than of the earlier, canonical ones (Carmignac, "Pré-pascal").

250. Cf. Blomberg, "Thomas," 195, esp. on the *Gospel of Thomas* (whose additions primarily reflect apparently gnostic themes); it was especially abbreviated to streamline. (Cf. different discussions by DeConick, *Recovering*; Perrin, *Tatian*.) Likewise, Matthew frequently abbreviates Markan pericopes.

251. Theon *Progymn.* 4.37–42.

252. Theon *Progymn.* 4.80–82. Even oracles, which were considered divine utterances, could be expanded; see Aune, *Prophecy*, 58.

change its basic meaning.[253] Likewise, Longinus explains amplification (αὔξησις) as adding more and more phrases to bring home the point with increasing force.[254] In rhetorical exercises one can elaborate a *chreia* by offering an encomium on a character, then paraphrasing, then explaining, and so forth.[255]

Hellenistic Jewish historians followed this practice. Josephus, for example, often follows accurately the sequence and substance of the biblical account, at the same time expanding some biblical narratives;[256] many Jewish readers would have readily recognized the additions. Second Maccabees openly claims to be a careful abridgment of a five-volume work by Jason of Cyrene (2 Macc 2:24–25), noting that the author has followed the rules of abridgment (2:28). Most Synoptic scholars likewise believe that Matthew (and less frequently Luke) abridges Markan accounts. Few stylistic critics would have complained about abridgments. Greco-Roman writers and rhetoricians appreciated conciseness in a narrative, provided that it did not impair clarity or plausibility.[257] Perhaps more important for many readers, longer works were not only more expansive but also more expensive.

Many of the changes that writers made in their sources were matters of arrangement, which was of great importance to those trained in rhetoric.[258] Both poets and prose writers sometimes added clauses nonessential to the meaning or removed essential ones simply to make the arrangement sound better (Dion. Hal. *Lit. Comp.* 9). Perhaps relevant for Luke's Gospel, inserting sayings from sayings collections into narratives, or narratives into sayings, was considered a matter of arrangement, not a matter of fabrication.[259] One matter reminding the narrator of another was a common rhetorical technique for transition.[260]

Even writers intending to write accurate history could "spice up" or "enhance" their narratives for literary, moralistic, and political purposes.[261] Again, this is not to say that good historians fabricated events (sometimes, in fact, they simply repeated their sources);[262] but they did often alter or add explanatory details to

253. Theon *Progymn.* 3.224–40. In 2.115–23, Theon compares elaborations in earlier historical sources. Elaboration (ἐργασία) was especially useful for rebuttal (1.172–75).

254. Longin. *Subl.* 11.1; cf. Men. Rhet. 2.3, 379.2–4. For a more detailed discussion of amplification, see Anderson, *Glossary*, 26–29 (with full reference to the sources); briefly, Gibson, "Notes," 43. For developing sample narratives in rhetorical exercises, see Hermog. *Inv.* 2.1.108–9; 2.7.120–24; examples typically involve rewording, not fabrication (2.7.120–21). Hypothetical declamations could invent new situations in history (e.g., Hermog. *Inv.* 2.4.115), but this is not the setting relevant for Acts, since Luke was not working from hypothetical exercises, since everyone knew that the exercises were hypothetical, and since declamations usually used *classical* (not recent) history.

255. Hermog. *Progymn.* 3, "On Chreia," 7; Aphth. *Progymn.* 3, "On Chreia," 23S, 4R; 4, "On Maxim," 9–10.

256. E.g., Begg, "Blanks," on Jos. *Ant.* 9.29–43 and 2 Kgs 3:4–27.

257. Theon *Progymn.* 5.39–43, 52–53; Phaedrus 2.prol. 12–13; 3.epil. 8–9; 4.epil. 7–9; Philost. *Hrk.* 29.6; in speeches, e.g., Diog. Laert. 7.1.20; Dion. Hal. *Thuc.* 55; *Demosth.* 18, 20, 24; *Lysias* 5; Philost. *Vit. soph.* 2.4.569. One could, however, be too brief at times (Phaedrus 3.10.59–60; Dion. Hal. *2 Amm.* 2).

258. Cf., e.g., Dion. Hal. *Lit. Comp.* 2–4. For one clear example of rearrangement in the Gospels, cf. Matt 21:12–13, 19–22; Mark 11:13–25. For stylistic as well as halakic and ideological editing in the compilation of the Mishnah, see Kulp, "Patterns."

259. Theon *Progymn.* 4.73–79, on adding narrative to a fable or the reverse (although the narrative is added as a parallel, not as a setting, for the fable). Maxims could be added to narratives (5.388–425), or preexisting narratives could be combined to relate two or more of them at once (5.427–41). The alternative to such arrangement was to simply recite narrative episodically; most readers found it acceptable, though it did not conform to more elite fashions (Drury, *Design*, 30; cf. Smith, *Magician*, 109).

260. Quint. *Inst.* 9.2.60–61. Cf. the discussion of catchwords in Gerhardsson, *Memory*, 145–49, 153; in the Gospels, cf. Bultmann, *Tradition*, 325–26.

261. See esp. Lyons, *Autobiography*, 29–32. Lyons advises reading such texts critically rather than completely rejecting their historical value (66).

262. Often later biographers simply repeat what earlier biographers said (e.g., Dion. Hal. *Lysias* 1).

events.[263] Given the importance of vividness for rhetorical style,[264] it is not surprising that some writers added details to augment dramatic effect (Plut. *Alex.* 70.3). Orally oriented cultures would be less troubled by variations than modern Western critics are.[265]

Some writers were more careless or tendentious than others. Asinius Pollio, Caesar's contemporary, complained that he was careless with the truth, sometimes accepted too readily his subordinates' reports, and preferred higher estimates of enemy casualties than did Pollio.[266] None of this is surprising in Caesar, who has obvious political agendas and does not conceal his own pursuit of glory. Even Caesar, however, apparently did not compose so freely as to be accused of having fabricated significant contemporary events such as battles.[267]

Authors differed among themselves as to how much variation in detail they permitted, but some writers who wanted to guard the historical enterprise from distortion had strong feelings about those who permitted too much (see sect. 1, esp. 1.c, of this chapter). Thus the second-century rhetorician Lucian objected to historical writers who amplified and omitted merely for literary or encomiastic purposes (i.e., to make the character look better).[268] Herodian shares this criticism (Hdn. 1.1.1–2) despite his own rhetorical adjustments.[269] The complaint appears even in mythography;[270] we may expect that the practice was more common there.

Palestinian Jewish haggadah permitted greater amplification than Hellenistic historiography,[271] but it may be comparable to Greek mythography.[272] (A significant difference between the historical and the mythical was often perceived as that between recent historical figures and remote characters of the mythical or legendary past.)[273] The process was probably often incremental, preserving earlier legendary accretions and speculations.[274] Writers used amplification to answer questions posed by a narrative,[275] to heighten the praise of God or the protagonist[276] (sometimes by

263. Aune, *Environment*, 82. Even with regard to human memory in general, details are not always reliable, although the gist tends to be (see Bauckham, *Eyewitnesses*, 333–34, citing memory studies); Bauckham applies this to the consistency of the gist of Peter's denial among varying Gospel accounts despite "variation in inessential detail" (344–45).

264. E.g., Cic. *De or.* 2.45.189; Dion. Hal. *Lysias* 7.

265. Dunn, *Perspective*, 112; Eddy and Boyd, *Legend*, 429–30.

266. Suet. *Jul.* 56.4, with comment by Damon, "Rhetoric," 442.

267. Damon, "Rhetoric," 444, notes that most or all clear fictions that T. J. Wiseman found in ancient historiography appear in or derive from speeches or orators rather than historical narratives.

268. Shuler, *Genre*, 11–12; cf. Bowersock, *Fiction as History*, 1–27. See esp. Lucian *Hist.* 7–13; in *True Story* 1.4, he complains that novelizers failed to recognize how obvious their "lies" were.

269. Cf. Whittaker, "Introduction," xxxviii–xxxix.

270. Cf. Philost. *Hrk.* 24.1–2.

271. Such haggadic adaptation appears in both midrash and folk literature (Wright, "Midrash," 129). Penner, *Praise*, 247–60, contends that Jewish historians rewrote the past, as may be seen in their treatment of the exodus tradition.

272. Cf. Greek elaboration of sacred stories in Maclean and Aitken, *Heroikos*, li–lii.

273. See discussion in sect. 1.d of this chapter. Nevertheless, Hellenistic historians such as Josephus remain closer to the biographic literary model even for older figures, while nevertheless incorporating old legends and expansive techniques. Polyb. 34.4.1–3 argues that the *Odyssey* mixed history and myth, but notes (34.4.2) that the goal of history, unlike myth, is truth.

274. Some scholars argue that even scribes adapted texts they copied, considering the needs of their audience with an oral mentality (Person, "Scribe as Performer," noting 1QIsaᵃ).

275. E.g., Demetrius the Chronographer (third century B.C.E.) frg. 5 (Euseb. *P.E.* 9.29.16); *Jub.* 4:1, 9; 12:14; 13:11; 27:1, 4–5 (Esau and Jacob vs. Isaac and Jacob); *y. Ketub.* 12:4, §8 (fanciful midrash).

276. 2 Macc 2:1–8 (expanding Jeremiah's mission); *Jub.* 29:14–20 (rhetorically contrasts Jacob's respect for his parents with Esau's disrespect); *Test. Job* 9–15 (see *OTP* 1:832); *Test. Jos.* 3:1; cf. Josephus's expansion of Philistine casualties (*Ant.* 6.203; cf. 1 Sam 18:27, though the LXX reduced them). Cf. Jael in *L.A.B.* 31 (Burnette-Bletsch, "Jael").

fanciful midrash),[277] or to improve the story.[278] Sometimes they added names,[279] which at times were arrived at midrashically or for symbolic value.[280] One could emphasize a theme already present in a source by reiterating it where it appeared and occasionally adding it elsewhere.[281] Similarly, negative incidents could be toned down,[282] omitted,[283] or justified[284] in the character's favor. But while such traditional techniques may have influenced Hellenistic Jewish historians and particularly their sources, they did not characterize the genre of history per se.

Luke follows Greek historiographic conventions rather than a haggadic approach (cf. comment on Acts 7:20–22); even apart from his own Hellenistic setting, the haggadic approach may have been known but not favored in the Pauline mission (cf. 1 Tim 1:4; Titus 1:14).[285] What may therefore be more relevant is the degree of variation among Hellenistic Jewish works concerning historical traditions, such as 2 Maccabees and 4 Maccabees[286] or, perhaps more closely, the historian Josephus.[287]

But even here one does not expect as free a treatment of recent characters (the sort covered in Luke or Josephus's report of the Jewish War) as of those of the distant past, where audience expectations for accuracy of details were less (see sect. 1.d above). Moreover, as noted above, Luke did not write on the rhetorical level of Josephus,

277. *Pesiq. Rab Kah.* 4:3 ("the rabbis" on Solomon); *Gen. Rab.* 43:3; *Exod. Rab.* 10:4; *Pesiq. Rab.* 49:5; cf. Artapanus on Pharaoh's behavior toward Moses in light of 1 Sam 18:17, 21–25 (Euseb. *P.E.* 9.27.7). Genre conventions also could dictate amplifications; *Joseph and Aseneth*, a Hellenistic romance, incorporates features ideal in such romances.

278. *Jub.* 11:14–15; 13:18, 22; possibly 4Q160 3–5, 7; *Tg. Ps.-J.* on Gen 50:26; on Exod 13:19.

279. *Jub.* 11:14–15; *Liv. Pr.* 19 (Joad) (§30 in Schermann's Greek text); Jos. *Ant.* 8.231; *L.A.B.* 40:1 (in *L.A.B.* in general, cf. Bauckham, "Liber antiquitatum," 67; in Jewish sources more generally, Pilch, "Naming"); cf. Plut. *Alex.* 20.4–5 (questioning Chares's report).

280. See Rook, "Names," on patriarchal wives in *Jubilees.* (Names are sometimes, however, the elements of tradition most resistant to change; cf., e.g., the observation of Bernal, *Athena*, 2:337.)

281. As *L.A.B.* does in its polemic against idolatry (Murphy, "Idolatry").

282. *L.A.B.* 12:2–3 (Aaron's sin with the golden calf). *Test. Job* 39:12–13 (*OTP*)/39:9–10 (Kraft) and 40:3/40:4 seem concerned to soften God's letting Job's children die for his test.

283. *Jub.* 13:17–18 (conflict between Lot's and Abram's servants); 14:21–16:22 (omitting Sarah's problems with Hagar, though they surface in 17:4–14); 29:13 (omits Jacob's fear); *Test. Zeb.* 1:5–7 (Zebulon did not act against Joseph). In *Jubilees* (e.g., Abram passing off his sister as his wife), see Wintermute, "Introduction," 35–36; in Josephus, cf. Aune, *Environment*, 108; in Greco-Roman literature, see Shuler, *Genre*, 50 (following Cic. *Part. or.* 22). The same tendency of tradition may be noted in the Chronicler's omission of David's and Solomon's sins reported in Samuel-Kings (cf., e.g., Williamson, *Chronicles*, 236). On the golden calf in Josephus, see comment on Acts 7:41–43.

284. CD IV, 20–V, 3 (David's polygamy, behavior that the Qumran community otherwise disapproved; also 11QT LVI, 18); *Jub.* 19:15–16 (Rebekah, in light of current morality); 27:6–7 (how Jacob could leave his father); 28:6–7 (Jacob's sororal polygyny); 30:2–17 (Simeon and Levi), 41 (Judah and Tamar both made more innocent, especially Judah); 1Qap Gen^{ar} XX, 10–11 (Sarah, rather than Abraham, proposes the pretense that she is his sister); *Jos. Asen.* 23 (Levi and Simeon); *Test. Jud.* 8–12 (whitewashing Judah and, to a lesser extent, Tamar, though Judah confesses it as a lesser sin; cf. the improvement of both in *Tg. Neof.* 1 on Gen 38:25; *Tg. Ps.-J.* on Gen 38:25–26); *Test. Iss.* 3:1 (cf. Gen 49:15); *Tg. Ps.-J.* on Gen 49:28 (all twelve patriarchs were equally righteous).

285. Cf., e.g., Charles, *Jubilees*, lxxxv; Lock, *Pastoral Epistles*, 8–9; Scott, *Pastoral Epistles*, 8 (though others see a mixture of Jewish and gnostic elements, e.g., Kelly, *Pastoral Epistles*, 44–45; Dibelius and Conzelmann, *Pastoral Epistles*, 17). Naturally, Greeks also used myths in oratory (Gangloff, "Mythes") and had mythical genealogies (Meister, "Genealogy"; Men. Rhet. 1.1, 333.18–21, 27–29; 334.11–12; 340.1–30; 2.6, 400.32–401.19); these could invite critique as well both from Gentile sages (Plato *Rep.* 2.377C–383C; Cic. *Nat. d.* 2.28.70; Philost. *Vit. soph.* 2.1.554; Iambl. *V.P.* 32.218; cf. Val. Max. 4.7.4) and from Jews (*Let. Aris.* 137).

286. See Anderson, "4 Maccabees," 555; though even here Luke is not writing philosophy the way the writer of 4 Maccabees is. Scholars differ whether 2 Maccabees is a novel or dramatized history (Penner, *Praise*, 136–37, noting that all agree that 1 Maccabees is history); I believe it belongs closer to the latter, at least insofar as the intention of the author (who was abridging another source; 2 Macc 2:24–25) is concerned. Parker, "Campaigns," even argues that 2 Maccabees is more plausible than 1 Maccabees at points, meriting more respect.

287. Even this parallel is imperfect; while Josephus's interests were less philosophic than Philo's or 4 Maccabees', he had obligations to elite rhetorical and literary interests that Luke, for the most part, lacked.

who needed to impress the Greek and Roman elite with his rhetorical skills; whatever Luke's education, he clearly did not have at his disposal the resources available to Josephus. But what Luke lacks in elite rhetoric, he makes up for in the cohesiveness of his more popular and concise narrative. He does not have sensational scene descriptions, but he does include adventures and signs that would nevertheless hold attention (as argued later, Luke abridges, rather than expands, the adventures and signs available to him; cf. 2 Cor 11:23–12:9; 12:12; Rom 15:19).

Conclusion

The broad genre of ancient historiography allows us the flexibility to explain most of the phenomena we find in Luke-Acts. Historians were interested in genuine historical information (and ready to critique rivals whom they accused of misrepresenting this information). At the same time, historians were deeply concerned with how they presented their information; they were not mere chroniclers but narrative writers. In Acts, then, we should expect to find a blending of historical (informational) and literary (rhetorical, moral, and theological) interests. By ancient standards of composition, one could at least in principle accomplish each objective without harm to the other. Writers varied, however, in their amount of rhetorical expansion and adaptation.

The following chapter examines the question of the *Tendenz* and moral, political, and "theological" agendas of ancient historians (preparing for a later discussion of Luke's purpose in writing Acts). Chapters 6 and 7 offer a preliminary evaluation of the sort of historical information we might expect Luke's work to preserve and evidence for that information in Luke's own narratives.

5

HISTORICAL PERSPECTIVES, *TENDENZ*, AND PURPOSE

Most ancient historiography showed both an interest in information and an interest in pleasing rhetorical presentation (see ch. 4 above). In histories, however, rhetorical presentation was meant not merely to entertain but also to convey particular perspectives. This chapter examines perspectives in ancient historiography and Acts, as a prelude to a discussion of Acts' purpose and theology (chs. 13–15 below). After establishing the importance of perspective, we will return in the next two chapters to the other ancient historiographic issue posed here, namely, Luke's use of genuine information in Acts.

To contend that Luke wrote ancient historiography (chs. 3–4, 6–7) does not imply that he wrote without particular values or perspectives (chs. 13–15).[1] All historians, ancient and modern, write from systems of values and perspectives, whether these systems reflect the larger culture, conventions of their guild, or minority or idiosyncratic perspectives.[2] More than most historians today, ancient historians generally also wrote for cultural or moral edification (which often included nationalistic themes).

Just as most historical writers today also have particular interests (e.g., women's history, African-American history, and modern military history),[3] an ancient historical monograph could include a particular focus. After demonstrating the perspectival character of ancient historiography, later in this chapter I will survey one approach to Luke's own agenda (sect. 3), in preparation for our later chapters on Luke's purpose (chs. 13–14) and the related discussion on Luke's theology (ch. 15).

1. See discussion in, e.g., Frey, "Fragen," 16–17, 26; Schröter, "Stellung," 25, 36–41, 47 (concluding that Luke's movement from Jesus's witnesses to Paul in Rome remains intelligible in the context of Greco-Roman historiography). Some of this section employs material from Keener, *John*, 14–16, albeit greatly augmented and rearranged.

2. As often noted (e.g., Marincola, "Introduction," 3; Ehrman, *Introduction*, 133; Enns, *Problem*, 66). Ancient historians used history to shed light on their own times, as many do today; Aune, *Environment*, 62, cites esp. Isoc. *Nic.* 35; *Demon.* 34; Polyb. 1.1.2; Livy 1.pref. 10–11; Plut. *Aem. Paul.* 1.1; Lucian *Dem.* 2.

3. General textbooks on (human) "world history" would be excluded from this principle of focus, but even introductory textbooks focusing on such broad topics as "Western civilization" or "Asian history" implicitly accept the legitimacy of focusing on a theme or people in historical study.

1. History and Agendas

Ancient historians could write from particular overt moral or religious perspectives.[4] Indeed, it was an "interpretive superstructure"[5] that distinguished history as a literary work from mere chronicles. Ancient historians themselves recognized that they investigated their subjects according to interpretive grids;[6] for example, Polybius noted that one must have some understanding of the nature of events to be "able to pose the right questions" rather than simply express rambling, random thoughts.[7] Whatever the boundaries between history and novel, modern traditional boundaries between history and theology are far less applicable to ancient texts.[8] And what is true of ancient texts in general proves true also of Luke-Acts in particular. If we define the "theology" of Luke-Acts broadly as the message of the text (not limiting "theology" to its strict etymological definition as the study of God or to traditional medieval theological categories),[9] every passage in Luke-Acts is "theological" in that it contributes to the overall emphasis on pertinent themes.

No historians, including modern ones, are disinterested reporters;[10] historians select the events they report on the basis of what they find to be of greatest interest or of greatest relevance to their focus (which, too, relates to interest).[11] (Interest shapes even journalists' reports and the editing of these reports for popular consumption.) Ancient historians, however, had less strict peer review pressure in the direction of objectivity or in the direction of consensus within the academic guild than is usual today. No less than biblical historians, Hellenistic historians "selectively reported the past in order to accomplish larger goals."[12] The exemplary use of history found in ancient authors dominated historiography well into modern times; our modern historicist approach, emphasizing the distinctive social context of past events, did not take full shape until early nineteenth-century German Romanticism.[13]

Though affirming the truth of their own perspectives, ancients also recognized the danger that biases (typically others' biases) can distort the historical enterprise. Thus Josephus complains about contemporary historians who distort Nero's reign either from favor, because they benefited from it, or from malice, because

---

4. See at length, e.g., Hemer, *Acts in History*, 79–85; see also, e.g., Mason, *Josephus and New Testament*, 63; Grant, "Introduction to Tacitus," 10, 13.

5. I borrow the phrase from Penner, *Praise*, 129 (cf. also the idea, 179).

6. Byrskog, *History*, 186–90. The historian's own participation was thus valuable (188).

7. Ibid., 187.

8. Historically, it was existential theology that produced prejudice against Lukan historiography (see Shauf, *Theology*, 14–17). Some scholars regard Acts as history with theological interpretation or theology grounded in history (Hotze, "Zeugen"); for Luke's historical and theological agendas, see also Marshall, *Historian and Theologian*.

9. The narrower sense of "theology" was the term's original usage (see, e.g., Men. Rhet. 2.17, 438.14; 443.2; Iambl. *V.P.* 28.145–47), but I employ the term here in the broader sense used in modern "New Testament theologies." Nevertheless, the picture of God (whose salvation-historical purposes Luke wishes to unveil) is vital for Luke; see esp. Gaventa, *Acts*.

10. Current historians generally associate the denial of historians' presuppositions with long-outdated approaches; see, e.g., Wigger, *Saint*, 411; from a more overtly subjective angle, see Hart, *Delusions*, ix–x.

11. See, e.g., Marshall, *Historian and Theologian*, 47, critiquing Perrin for his outdated understanding of historiography. Thus, e.g., Cicero's depiction of Dionysius (*Tusc.* 5) probably is shaped partly by his concerns for Caesar's rise (Verbaal, "End of Liberty").

12. Litwak, *Echoes*, 37 (noting that it is impossible in any era to write history without a perspective). All ancient historiography was interpretive (Byrskog, *History*, 256–65).

13. Roller, "Past," 214–16. Although the historicist approach may sometimes provide access to information more objectively, its reconstructions can also be speculative and erroneous at times (229). This is not to deny ancient interest in historical context (see comments in the prolegomenon to the commentary, 4.b).

they suffered under it (*Ant.* 20.154). He charges that such historians fail to avoid bias even when reporting earlier eras (20.155), because they do not care about truth (20.156). Because his interest is in truth, he insists, he writes with greater accuracy (20.157). One may well dispute Josephus's accuracy at points, but this does not negate the ideal that he expects his audience to embrace: that bias should be avoided. That Josephus could appeal to such an ideal while straightforwardly writing with an explicit focus and from a distinct vantage point should caution us not to confuse perspective-shaped history with novels. Perspectives and interests are to be expected, but the prospect of criticism based on ideal historiographic expectations should engender some sense of accountability to fairness regarding the substance of events and set some limits on how much bias is acceptable in a public forum.[14]

a. Political and National Agendas

Historians often wrote to inculcate "good citizenship,"[15] and so they usually displayed, in varying measures, national or ethnic biases. Polybius, for example, exhibits a pro-Roman *Tendenz* (e.g., Polyb. 36.9.1–17).[16] Thucydides, though a participant in the Peloponnesian War, proves surprisingly impartial, yet even he has his biases.[17] Livy claims that history teaches a nation's greatness and what one may imitate (Livy 1.pref. 10); naturally, he has especially the greatness of Rome, his subject, in view. One also thinks of Josephus's apologetic attempt to whitewash his people of excess complicity in the revolt while he simultaneously appeals to the dignity of his Roman readership.[18]

Historians whose information was largely factual might also include stories that first circulated as imperial propaganda;[19] politics also shaped summary perspectives on when peace and order were restored.[20] Claiming that the emperor was compelled by public demand to accept his position (e.g., Vell. Paterc. 2.89.4–5) is also propaganda, though (importantly for our questions) it reflects the earliest sources (e.g., *Res gest.* 6.35).

14. When Cicero requested that an author set aside normal historiographic impartiality to narrate Cicero's story in another genre, he recognizes existing expectations for historiography (Laistner, *Historians*, 33–35). While Caesar wrote from his own perspective, he did not likely deliberately falsify evidence (ibid., 36–38). Regarding the public forum, Luke's primary audience is undoubtedly Christian, but his appeals to the public forum suggest that he wishes his history to be at least acceptable to outsiders (cf. Acts 26:26).

15. Penner, "Discourse," 73–77.

16. Cf. Momigliano, *Historiography*, 71–73. Polybius's biases may extend beyond Rome; despite his stated ideal of avoiding prejudice for one's country (1.14.4–5), he later suggests that historians should be partial to their countries (16.14.6; Woodman, *Rhetoric*, 42). Many suggest that he also shares his peers' lack of affection for Aetolians (Laistner, *Historians*, 6, 95; for discussion and nuancing, see Champion, "Aetolia," esp. 357–62). For Polybius's appreciation for history's political value, see Fornara, *Nature of History*, 113. Determining exact political loyalties is sometimes more difficult. On the ambiguity of some of the evidence, see Connolly, "Virtue," 192–93; by contrast, Tacitus's anti-Jewish bias is unquestionable (see Feldherr, "Tacitus' Jews").

17. On those biases, cf. Wade-Gery, "Thucydides," 1519, adding, "Perhaps no good historian is impartial." Dion. Hal. *Pomp.* 3 thinks Thucydides more biased (in his case, against Athens, which had exiled him) than Herodotus was; but he accuses him of focusing on Athens's failings, not of inventing them.

18. Often noted, e.g., Mason, *Josephus and New Testament*, 60–71, 77–81; cf. 196–98; Crossan, *Jesus*, 93; for Josephus's pro-Flavian propaganda, see Saulnier, "Josèphe"; but for nuancing, see Chapman, "Josephus," 323–24, and sources cited there. Partisan agendas were not limited to politics, also appearing among schools of thought; cf., e.g., Eshleman, "Sophists," on biographies of sophists.

19. See, e.g., Vell. Paterc. 2.80.3, on a putative event some sixty-six years earlier.

20. E.g., Vell. Paterc. 2.89.3; see discussion of the *Pax Romana* at Acts 10:36.

Although most history may be written by the victors,[21] triumph[22] or national loyalties did not always dictate bias even in ancient epic. Historians often reported sympathetically both sides of a conflict.[23] Herodotus, one of the earliest writers, often regards Egyptians and others as superior to his fellow Greeks (e.g., Hdt. 2.4, 32, 50, 58, 77, 82) and describes other peoples fairly objectively; he criticizes Greek failings and praises both Spartan and Athenian virtues.[24] Biographers, too, included both "flat" and "round" characters.[25] Lucian complains that historians who praise their own leaders while they slander the other side are engaging merely in panegyric (*Hist.* 7).[26] A historian who focuses on what is negative about a character can be accused of malice unless this approach is necessary for the telling of the story (Plut. *Mal. Hdt.* 3, *Mor.* 855C).

Political and ethnic agendas were not, however, the only agendas in ancient historiography. In Luke's case, political interests are probably not his dominant agenda even though he exhibits political perspectives,[27] as in his generally pro-Roman *Tendenz* (see sect. 3 below) and his occasional contrast between Caesar and Christ (Luke 2:1, 11;[28] cf. Acts 17:7). Historians had moral and theological biases as well as political ones (political, moral, and theological categories indeed sometimes overlapped). Although we cannot draw a clear line between nationalistic and moralistic agendas (patriotism was generally viewed as a moral virtue itself, particularly by other members of one's own people), broader moral lessons sometimes took precedence over nationalistic agendas. Despite Polybius's pro-Roman *Tendenz*, for example, he notes that he often praises both Romans and Carthaginians but only so that he can set before statesmen

21. Thus Xenophon, largely accurate in what he reports, proves biased in what he omits of Thebes's greatness (Brownson, "Introduction to Hellenica," ix–x; Brown, *Historians*, 97), though our "best authority" for the period (Brownson, "Introduction to Hellenica," xi), and for the most part surprisingly neutral on larger questions (Brown, *Historians*, 93–94). For history "written by the winners" among Roman historians, see, e.g., Feldherr, "Translation," 390; for Pompeians as negative examples, see Melchior, "Pompey." But not all in the early empire were positive even about Augustus (see Davis, "Evaluations"); cf. losers in Xen. *Anab.*; Jos. *War.*

22. Cf. the respective roles of Pompey and Caesar in Lucan's *Civil War* passim (even Homer portrayed the Trojans appealingly enough for Romans to latch on to the Trojan line as their own).

23. E.g., Albans in Dion. Hal. *Ant. rom.* 3; plebeians and patricians in 9.39.1–6; Romans and Carthaginians in Livy 21.1.3; Mithridates in Vell. Paterc. 2.18.1; and (outside history) the evenhandedness of Homer's portrayal of Greek and Trojan heroism in the *Iliad*, which allowed such later works as Euripides's *Trojan Women* and the Roman adoption of Aeneas (e.g., Virgil's *Aeneid*); cf. also the speeches noted in Marincola, "Speeches," 119. Historians did not always report sympathetically, and Pervo, *Acts*, 17, seems right to observe that Luke did not usually do so (Padilla, *Speeches*, 237–40, contrasts Luke's Jewish approach with Greek historians); but even Luke, though a popular historian, does this sometimes (see, e.g., comment on Acts 5:34 regarding his nuanced portrait of Pharisees; some also detect tragic pathos in Israel's response).

24. Meister, "Herodotus," 268. This approach did not commend him to everyone (cf., e.g., Plut. *Mal. Hdt.*).

25. Burridge, *Gospels*, 182–84. So also characters in history, e.g., Marcius as the greatest general of his era yet with fatal character flaws (Dion. Hal. *Ant. rom.* 8.60.1–2; 8.61.1–3). Laistner, *Historians*, 56, however, views Sallust's characters as too stark.

26. Such poetic descriptions are inappropriate within history (Lucian *Hist.* 8), though praise is permissible within careful bounds (*Hist.* 9). On the genre of prose panegyric, see (for Rome) Rees, "Panegyric." Callisthenes (though an eyewitness) reported only Alexander's heroism, and hence was dismissed by posterity as a flatterer (Brown, *Historians*, 125). For another example of epideictic historiography (though it certainly remains historical narrative), see Velleius Paterculus's adulation of Tiberius in Gowing, "Republic," 412–17. Nevertheless, Velleius otherwise fairly consistently unveils tragic weaknesses, errors, or misdeeds in otherwise strong characters (2.1.1–3; 2.3.1–2; 2.4.4; 2.6.1–2; 2.7.1; 2.33.2, 4; 2.46.2; 2.88.2; 2.91.2; cf. 2.98.2–3) and often positive traits in weak characters (2.24.2, 5); or characters changing (Vell. Paterc. 2.18.5; 2.25.3; 2.28.2).

27. See Gilbert, "Propaganda," 236. Walaskay argues that Luke defends Rome (cf. Josephus); see ch. 13 below.

28. See the discussion in Danker, *New Age*, 24; cf. Flender, *Theologian*, 58–59; imperial propaganda's use of "savior" and "peace" in Gilbert, "Propaganda," 237–42.

proper models for conduct.[29] Even if one views the church as a "people," Luke writes not primarily a history of the early church (although this interest is not altogether absent) but a history of its mission. "Political" interests are among his concerns, but are not his only or most dominant concerns.

b. Moral Agendas in Other Genres

Most ancient historians felt answerable to certain standards of historical accuracy (whether or not they achieved them), but they also felt responsible to arrange their histories in such a manner as to provide moral lessons. In general, respectable members of ancient society reflected similar concerns in a variety of genres; for example, in letters about honorable people, writers could praise past figures' virtues as models inviting imitation (Pliny *Ep.* 3.5.20, on his late uncle).[30] Morals were characteristic of ancient fables, whether the former were stated explicitly (at the beginning[31] or the end[32]) or they were inferred and added later.[33] Some writers even believed that classical Athenian drama displayed characters' vices and virtues so that viewers could avoid the former and imitate the latter.[34]

The emphasis on imitating ancestral wisdom and learning from both positive and negative historical examples is at least as old as classical Athenian rhetoric (Aeschines *Embassy* 75–76; Lysias *Or.* 2.61, §196) and remained important in Roman rhetoric (Cic. *Sest.* 68.143). Rhetoricians regularly used examples (including historical examples) and selected them on the basis of which best supported the point concerning which they sought to persuade others.[35] Thus, if one wishes to procure allies, one may provide historical examples of how Athens won by allies (*Rhet. Alex.* 8, 1429.1–6); if one wishes to demonstrate that small numbers can overpower larger ones, one cites historical examples to this effect (8, 1429b.6–22). Even during the empire, examples were often drawn from fifth-century B.C.E. Greek history (see, e.g., Max. Tyre 6.5); later orators also used Plutarch's *Lives* this way (Men. Rhet. 2.4, 392.28–31). As the

29. Polyb. 9.9.9–10. Statesmen were also a primary audience for Roman historians (Marincola, "Audiences," 12–13).

30. In other genres, cf. morals in Aesop's *Fables* (e.g., 172); in rabbinic stories, see Pearl, *Theology*; elsewhere, cf. 3 Macc 2:5; Pindar *Encomia* frg. 121; Theophr. *Char.* proem 3; Philost. *Vit. soph.* 2.1.554; Athen. *Deipn.* 1.10e, on what could be done with Homer.

31. E.g., Phaedrus 1.4.1; 1.5.1–2; 1.8.1–3; 1.9.1–2; 1.10.1–3; 1.11.1–2; 1.12.1–2; 1.13.1–2; 1.15.1–3; 1.16.1–2; 1.17.1; 1.18.1; 1.19.1–2; 1.20.1–2; 1.21.1–2; 1.23.1–2; 1.24.1; 1.25.1–2; 1.26.1–2; 1.27.1–2; 1.28.1–2; 1.29.1–3; 1.30.1; 1.31.1–2; 2.2.1–2; 2.5.1–6; 2.6.1–3; 3.1.7; 3.5.1; 3.7.1; 3.8.1; 3.9.1; 3.16.1–2; 4.1.1–3; 4.5.1–2; 4.8.1–2; 4.9.1–2; 4.12.1–2; 4.20.1; 4.23.1; 5.5.1–3; 5.7.1–3.

32. E.g., Phaedrus 1.1.14–15; 1.7.4–5; 1.14.18–19; 1.22.10–13; 2.1.11–12; 2.3.7; 2.4.25–26; 2.6.14–15; 3.2.1; 3.3.1–3; 3.6.10–11; 3.11.7; 3.12.8; 3.14.12–13; 3.17.13; 4.3.5–6; 4.4.12–13; 4.6.11–13; 4.7.25–26; 4.10.4–5; 4.11.14–21; 4.17.7–8; 4.24.3–4; 4.25.23–25; 5.2.14–15; 5.3.11–13; 5.4.7–12; 5.6.7; 5.8.6–7; 5.9.5; 5.10.10. At the beginning *and* the end, Phaedrus 3.10.1–8, 51–60; 4.13.

33. For later redaction, e.g., Phaedrus 2.2.2; 2.3.4; 3.3.14–17; 3.6.10; 3.19.1. Most ancient parables, too, had explicit interpretations, contrary to frequent expectations of NT scholars who read other NT scholars more than ancient sources (see Judg 9:16–20; 2 Sam 12:7–9; Johnston, "Interpretations," 561–62, 565–67, 637–38; Vermes, *Religion*, 92–99; Stern, *Parables in Midrash*, 24; see further discussion in Keener, *Matthew*, 381–82).

34. Lucian *Anach.* 22; this moralizing interpretation may have truth, although tragedies often stress the randomness of fate.

35. See the treatment of examples in rhetoric in *Rhet. Alex.* 8, 1429a.21–1430a.13; cf. also Hermog. *Inv.* 2.2.110; 3.11.161; Anderson, *Glossary*, 86–88; Kennedy, "Survey of Rhetoric," 21; Demoen, "Paradigm"; Nicolai, "The Place of History," 19–20; *exempla* in Roman declamations in van der Poel, "Use"; historically, see the influence of Isocrates in Laistner, *Historians*, 9. Pliny cites a report favorable to himself, noting that whether or not true, it is useful for its moral lesson (*Ep.* 9.13.25). Philosophers, too, used history, though sometimes adapting it for ideological purposes (note Lucretius's adaptation of Thucyd. 2.47–54, 71–78 in Foster, "Rhetoric"). Some poets also inscribed historical events in the larger social memory (Meban, "Eclogues").

leading academic discipline preparing for public life, rhetoric naturally affected the presentation of history as well.[36]

In contrast to rhetoricians, the generally connected nature of the events on which historians focused limited their range of examples to those in the period they covered, and they often offered examples that could be used to argue a variety of points. Historians might even feel obligated to reject accounts that suited their moral or political purposes yet seemed to them less plausible than other versions.[37] In most cases, however, they expected lessons to be drawn from the history they recounted.

c. Historians' Moral Agendas

Contrary to what some modern interpreters suppose, moral agendas characterized ancient historiography far more often than they characterized novels. The moral agenda constituted a paramount element for historians; one taught history not simply to memorize the past but to draw lessons from it.[38] Thus some of them felt that historians should choose a noble subject so that their work would contribute to good moral character as well as provide information (e.g., Dion. Hal. *Ant. rom.* 1.2.1). No less a careful ancient historian than Polybius begins his multivolume history by observing its utilitarian value: people "have no more ready corrective of conduct than knowledge of the past" (Polyb. 1.1.1 [LCL]). As Fornara points out, Polybius "treasured history as a sound inferential basis for present and future political activity"; his "rationalistic bias" did not obscure for him history's "hortatory value."[39]

Likewise, Tacitus, one of our most reliable historical sources for the early empire, emphasizes that the study of history promotes virtue (*Agr.* 1); without claiming to have invented events, he notes that he freely omitted material not of value to history's primary, moral objective (*Ann.* 3.65). Tacitus himself felt no constraint to avoid editorial statements at times (e.g., 4.33); often lamenting the decline of traditional Roman values, he was (like his contemporaries) "a moralist, who regards it as his duty to hold vice up to scorn and to praise virtue."[40] Lucian, a stickler for historical accuracy, as already noted, allows for history's edifying value, that is, moral lessons (although not mere entertainment), provided they flow from truth (e.g., *Hist.* 59).

Valerius Maximus was not the most careful historian, but his perspective on the utility of historical examples is representative: it is helpful to know history "so that a backward look . . . may yield some profit to modern manners" (Val. Max. 2.praef.

---

36. See our earlier discussion (ch. 4, sect. 2); and, most extensively, Rothschild, *Rhetoric of History*, passim (and summary, 291–92). On rhetoric as the key advanced discipline (along with, but more prominent than, philosophy), see, e.g., Townsend, "Education," 149, 151–52; Porter, "Paul and Letters," 534–35; Stamps, "Children," 198.

37. See Hadas, "Introduction," xviii–xix, on Tacitus.

38. On the hortatory value of history in Roman historians, see Judge, *First Christians*, 249–50; Fornara, *Nature of History*, 115–16; Woodman, *Rhetoric*, 42; extensively, Roller, "Past"; for history providing models for living, see fully the thorough work of Lang, *Kunst*, 7–13, 97–167 (especially note problem-solving strategies in Sallust and Tacitus, 108–37). For moralizing elements in ancient historiography, Marguerat, *Histoire*, 28–29, cites examples from Dionysius, Livy, Sallust, and Plutarch. See, e.g., Livy's use of the legendary Romulus as an example (Stem, "Lessons"); also historians' use of traditions about Alexander to illustrate both positive and negative qualities (Baynham, "Reception," 290–91), or Greek imperial historians' use of Camillus (Gowing, "Tradition").

39. Fornara, *Nature of History*, 113, noting (115–16) that Romans emphasized this even more.

40. Moore, "Introduction," xiii; cf. similarly Hadas, "Introduction," xvii–xix (noting the popular model of Livy); Laistner, *Historians*, 113–14 (citing *Ann.* 2.65.1; 4.33.2), 123, 131–39 (criticizing his tendentiousness); Williams, "Germanicus" (addressing Tacitus's perspective in one work). In other cases, the ways Tacitus reports the accounts reveal his opinions as well as explicit asides would have revealed (e.g., *Ann.* 5.1–2; 14.39).

[LCL]). The intellectual orator Maximus of Tyre opines that history preserves the memories of humanity and so "guards its virtues" (Max. Tyre 22.5 [Trapp]). Historians frequently included even moralizing narrative asides to interpret history's meaning more directly for their readers, to illustrate the fulfillment of prophetic utterances, or to provide the author's perspective.[41] Jewish historiography was certainly no less interpretive.[42]

d. The Value of Moral Examples

What such historians often meant by the instructive value of history was the positive and negative moral examples provided by other persons' behavior. Whereas an individual's life was too short to use his or her own experience to guard against all faults, the collective memory of humanity offered greater wisdom. Historians generally believed that if it was understood why events happened,[43] not merely historians but also statesmen[44] and orators[45] (both of which some of them were) could use these events as precedents (παραδείγματα).[46]

Dionysius of Halicarnassus lists three purposes for writing history: first, that the courageous may gain "immortal glory" that outlives them; second, that their descendants may recognize their own roots and seek to emulate their virtue; and finally, that he may show proper goodwill and gratitude toward those who provided him training and information.[47]

Jewish people understood the Bible's narratives as providing moral lessons in the same manner: the writers recorded examples of virtue and vice for their successors to emulate or avoid.[48] Writers could likewise employ postbiblical models as examples of virtues (e.g., 4 Macc 1:7–8). Because Josephus repeats so much of the biblical narrative in the *Antiquities*, one can readily[49] observe the way he adapts biblical characters to accentuate their value as positive (Lot,[50] Isaac,[51] Joseph,[52] Moses,[53] Ruth and

41. E.g., Polyb. 1.35.1–10; Diod. Sic. 31.10.2; Dion. Hal. *Ant. rom.* 7.65.2; Vell. Paterc. 2.75.2; Dio Cass. 1.5.4; Arrian *Alex.* 4.10.8; Corn. Nep. 16 (Pelopidas), 3.1; Tac. *Ann.* 16.15; characterizing asides throughout Velleius Paterculus (e.g., 2.41.1–2; 2.66.3–5; 2.72.1–2; 2.91.2–3; 2.98.2–3). For narrative asides in histories and biographies, see Sheeley, *Asides*, 56–93; for Herodotus's judgments (e.g., 1.34; 2.123.3; 4.205; 9.120), see Dewald, "Construction," 95; for Xenophon, ibid., 98; for Tacitus's (Laistner, *Historians*, 139, unhappily); for "parenthesis" as a rhetorical technique, see Rowe, "Style," 147; Black, "Oration at Olivet," 87, citing Quint. *Inst.* 9.3.23; Anderson, *Glossary*, 89–90.

42. See, e.g., Dobbeler, "Geschichte"; van der Kooij, "Death of Josiah"; Reinmuth, "Zwischen Investitur und Testament"; Bergren, "Nehemiah"; Borgen, "Reviewing and Rewriting."

43. See, e.g., Polyb. 2.56.13; 3.32.2. Ancient historians did not, as some scholars contend, ignore lines of cause and effect (Rajak, *Josephus*, 102).

44. Dion. Hal. *Ant. rom.* 5.56.1; Polyb. 3.31.11–13.

45. For παραδείγματα to make moral points in speeches, see Dion. Hal. *Ant. rom.* 6.80.1; *Rhet. Alex.* 8.1429a.21–1430a.13; Cic. *Sest.* 48.102; cf. also Kennedy, "Survey of Rhetoric," 21.

46. On such historical "paradigms," see also Diod. Sic. 37.4.1; Hdn. 3.13.3. The Roman use of *exempla* reflects earlier Greek use of *paradeigmata* (Gowing, "Tradition," 333–34). Although people most often appealed to the past for examples, Velleius points out that even the present could supply some (Vell. Paterc. 2.92.5).

47. Dion. Hal. *Ant. rom.* 1.6.3–5; cf. Diod. Sic. 15.1.1; 37.4.1.

48. Philo *Abr.* 4; Jos. *Ag. Ap.* 2.204; 1 Cor 10:11. On Abraham as *exemplum* in Philo and Josephus, cf. Reed, "Construction" (contrasting *Test. Ab.*)

49. One should perhaps add "normally," since the direction of adaptations and their reasons are sometimes disputed for individual characters. The general degree of adaptation and its frequent apologetic thrust is not, however, disputable.

50. See Avioz, "Lot."

51. For a more detailed study of Josephus's adaptation of Isaac, see Feldman, "Isaac."

52. See Feldman, "Joseph."

53. See Feldman, "Moses." Hata, "Moses within Anti-Semitism," emphasizes the apologetic value of Josephus's portrayal of Moses against anti-Semites.

Boaz,[54] Samuel,[55] Hezekiah,[56] Jehoshaphat,[57] Josiah,[58] Daniel,[59] Nehemiah[60]), negative (Jeroboam,[61] Ahab[62]), or intermediate moral models.[63]

e. The Role of Praise and Blame

Historians narrated accounts with a view to praise or blame.[64] Some historians might criticize other historians for getting the mixture wrong, but no one doubted that history provided moral lessons. Thus Polybius, who insists on the appropriate distribution of praise and blame (Polyb. 3.4.1), criticizes some historians for praising Philip, noting that his actions warrant censure (8.8.3–6); he finds it appalling that Theopompus praises Philip while depicting his despicable deeds.[65] Polybius notes that he himself does not praise or blame prominent people in his prefaces but always while recounting their behavior; that, he avers, is the appropriate place to express one's views (10.26.9). Nor was Polybius alone in viewing praise and blame as important elements in selecting moral examples. History writing preserves for immortality the fame of those who deserve it, Pliny opined (*Ep.* 5.8.1–2), and hence offers incentive for noble deeds.

Historians' interest in these matters reflected the broader value assigned to imitating moral examples in antiquity. Thus rhetoricians invited hearers to learn from both positive and negative examples in history.[66] Classical orators, for example, had long praised those who imitated their ancestors' valor in battle (Lysias *Or.* 2.61, §196) and summoned their hearers to imitate their ancestors' wisdom (Aeschines *Embassy* 75). When reading ancient historians, modern historians can

54. See Levison, "Ruth."
55. See Feldman, "Samuel."
56. See Jos. *Ant.* 10.24–35; Begg, "Illness"; Feldman, "Hezekiah."
57. See Jos. *Ant.* 9.1–17; Begg, "Jehoshaphat"; Feldman, "Jehoshaphat."
58. See Begg, "Josiah"; Feldman, "Josiah."
59. See Feldman, "Daniel."
60. See Feldman, "Nehemiah."
61. See Feldman, "Jeroboam."
62. See Feldman, "Ahab."
63. Noah appears positive, but Feldman, "Noah," thinks that Josephus reduced his role because he was ancestor of the Gentiles (though Josephus does not transfer Noah traditions to Moses the way later rabbis did). In idealizing characters into various types, Josephus may have also used standard Hellenistic typologies for women characters (Sarah as the good wife, Potiphar's wife as evil, etc.; Amaru, "Women").
64. See, e.g., Trompf, *Retributive Justice*, 51; Feldherr, "Introduction," 5 (citing Tac. *Ann.* 3.65); Marincola, "Audiences," 19–21 (on 19–20 noting that the practice had continued since the fourth century B.C.E., and on 20–21 that the practice was meant to teach moral values). Explicit editorial comment often appeared in death notices (Marincola, "Audiences," 20), which do not appear in Luke-Acts, but epideictic factors were not limited to such editorializing. Plümacher thinks the historical monograph ideally suited for propagandistic tasks such as Luke's. Cicero felt that historical monographs were ideal for glorifying their subjects, and Plümacher includes a work of Cicero's and 2 Maccabees as examples of monographs fulfilling this function (Plümacher, *Geschichte*, 15–32; idem, "Cicero und Lukas," 772–73). Inviting a historian to recount events surrounding Cicero's exile and return, Cicero emphasizes the historian's skill in properly assigning praise and blame, implying that the historian will paint Cicero in a positive light (*Fam.* 5.12.4). Naturally, the practice of praise and blame is also a dominant element in biography (Penner, *Praise*, 135).
65. He insists that one may forgive historians who are slightly wrong but not those driven by severe bias (Polyb. 8.8.8–9); fairness is the standard (8.8.7). He sometimes digresses in asides to give lessons related to the events narrated (1.35.1–10). But while Theopompus was one of the major "rhetorical" historians, he did genuine research (Meister, "Theopompus"). The standard of fairness remained in first-century B.C.E. Roman historiography; thus Cicero took seriously the claim in Lucceius's preface that Lucceius was impervious to bias (*Fam.* 5.12.3). He also emphasized the moral and epideictic function of proper historiography (*De or.* 2.63) alongside its impartiality and avoidance of falsehood (2.62).
66. Aeschines *Embassy* 75–76. Thus some objected to (Dio Chrys. *Or.* 7.119; Philost. *Vit. Apoll.* 4.2) or even censored (Val. Max. 2.6.7b) immoral mimes that could teach wrong values by imitation; most mimes were vulgar (Friedländer, *Life*, 2:92).

take epideictic factors into account, but we do not, for such reasons, discount the value of their evidence.[67]

f. Historians' "Theology"

Historians' moral illustrations, social commentary in speeches, and political interests often reveal their distinctive philosophic and theological perspectives.[68] For example, many writers dwelled on violations of temples (see comment on Acts 19:37) and other offenses against the gods that warranted judgments.

Most important for understanding Acts, most ancient historians also sought to interpret the divine will in some patterns in history.[69] Oracles and omens were said to reveal Rome's divine destiny.[70] Some deity helped the Greeks escape, Xenophon decides (Xen. *Anab.* 5.2.24). Despite Herodotus's occasional rationalism, he reports dreams, omens, and other signs of divine activity, his ideal audience's consensus on the reality of which he seems to assume.[71] Israelite historians also sought to interpret from a divine perspective the events they recited.[72] Although postmodern critics may view history as usable for agendas, the thought that it included objectively recognizable patterns seems odd to both modern and postmodern readers; yet this was the dominant perspective in many other eras (albeit a perspective that could not preclude diverse opinions concerning what constituted those patterns).[73]

From a broader perspective, Hellenistic historians saw providence in history, so that Diodorus could describe "historians as 'ministers of divine providence' who arrange their accounts in the light of their understanding of providence in human events."[74] Dionysius of Halicarnassus includes among history's lessons the virtue of piety toward the gods (Dion. Hal. *Ant. rom.* 8.56.1). Luke's understanding of God's providential guidance of the early Christian movement closely fits the programmatic role of providence found in Hellenistic historians such as Dionysius and Josephus (see, further, comment on Acts 2:23).[75] Josephus is often explicit about providence

---

67. Most scholars take this nuanced approach to Josephus (e.g., Curran, "War"). Historians can offset biases by comparing multiple sources (e.g., Laistner, *Historians*, 131). One may compare the similar problems encountered in studying nineteenth-century historiography. Suiting biographic standards of their era, the biography of William Wilberforce by his sons selects information that would present their father in the best light (Tomkins, *Wilberforce*, 15–16), and rewords matters to suit their own high-church preferences (16); nevertheless, it often depends on records (16) and recollections heard from their father and his friends (16–17).

68. E.g., some Socratic ideas appear in Xenophon's Cyrus (e.g., *Cyr.* 3.1.17; Xenophon's other works reveal his admiration of Socrates), though *Cyropaedia* is not a true historical work or biographic work in the later sense (Cic. *Quint. fratr.* 1.1.8.23 argues that *Cyropaedia* was intended to teach proper government, not primarily to report historical truth). Cf. causation by Fortune or deities in Tacitus in Tac. *Ann.* 3.18; Hadas, "Introduction," xvi; Fortune in Polybius in Walbank, "Fortune."

69. Cf. Sen. E., historical frg. 1, who divided Rome's history into ages corresponding to human maturation. Contrary to some modern interpretations of ancient historiography, some ancient historians did think in terms of cause and effect, though not all of these were divine (e.g., Polyb. 2.56.13; 3.6.1–3.7.3; 3.31.11–13; 3.32.2).

70. E.g., the interpretation of a head found beneath Rome (Dion. Hal. *Ant. rom.* 4.59.2; 4.61.2; Plut. *Cam.* 31.4; Dio Cass. frg. in Zonaras 7.11). Perhaps the diggers inadvertently struck part of an old burial site (though our sources claim a freshly severed head), but their interpretation became the dominant memory.

71. Meister, "Herodotus," 269. The line between "objective" (Herodotus, Thucydides) and "confessional" (OT; Luke) historiography may often be thinner than one would surmise from Marguerat, *Histoire*, 42.

72. With, e.g., Konkel, *Kings*, 328.

73. Frei, "Apologetics," 56, notes that this view was also influential in eighteenth-century England.

74. Squires, "Plan," 38, citing Diod. Sic. 1.1.3.

75. See Squires, *Plan*, 15–17, on Dionysius; 18–20, on Josephus; and 20–36, on Luke; for the nature of providence in Hellenistic history, see 38–46; in Josephus, 46–51; in Luke-Acts, 52–77 (where see also Brawley, *Centering on God*, 86–106); for tempering divine determinism with free will, see Squires, *Plan*, 154–60, on Hellenistic historians; 160–66, on Josephus; and 166–85, on Luke-Acts. See also Marguerat, *Histoire*, 36–37; for Luke's interest in providence, 59–61. Hellenistic historiographers of Rome seemed less emphatic about the divine plan for Rome's destiny and the empire's benefit to other peoples than were some Romans

in human affairs, sometimes using it to justify reporting apparently supernatural phenomena (*Ant.* 17.353; cf. 17.350–52). (Hebrew Scripture likewise affirmed God's providence in all events, even in acts of disobedience to God.)[76]

Thus it should not surprise us that Luke is explicit in presenting his primary protagonists as models for virtue. Just as Jesus provided a model for his followers in his farewell address (Luke 22:27), so does Paul in his farewell address (Acts 20:35).[77] But Luke was not interested in only human models. Like other historians (see above in this section), Luke would not have thought theology incompatible with history. Those who find in Luke's obviously prosaic work some less accurate "poetic history" because of his depictions of God's activity ignore the theological perspectives of many ancient historians. They additionally beg several theological questions (if one does not rule out God's existence and nature a priori, one need not a priori claim that God did not act as Luke claims). Moreover, one can hardly exclude from history all reports of events that cannot be easily disentangled from the theological framework in which eyewitnesses supply the reports, such as Paul's conversion.[78]

That one could learn theology from history would certainly be assumed by early Christians, who inherited Jewish Scripture;[79] even most Hellenistic Jewish intellectuals viewed most of Scripture as historically as well as theologically true.[80] In the context of a Jewish covenant understanding of history as the framework for God's revelation, the earliest Christians should have been interested in the history of Jesus.[81] Even apocalypses often provide "historical reviews."[82] And even the Qumran sect, whose teacher was important but much less central than in the Christian movement,[83] preserved at least some information about its teacher.[84] Interest in history distinguishes

(Pelling, "Historians of Rome," 257–58, citing, e.g., Cic. *Rep.* 3.36; later, Plut. *Fort. Rom.* 2, *Mor.* 316E–317C; acknowledging divine protection for Rome in Dionysius, e.g., *Ant. rom.* 5.54.1).

76. Eichrodt, "Faith in Providence," 19–20.

77. See esp. here Kurz, "Models," 175–76, who also treats the Hellenistic concern for narrative models to imitate (176–85; in history, 177–82; in biography, 182–83; in other narrative genres, 183–84); cf. Lang, *Kunst*, 7–13, 97–168; see fuller comment in our ch. 15.

78. See Bock, *Acts*, 4.

79. Even in an earlier era, Israel's historical interests contrasted with many surrounding cultures' "extratemporal myths" (de Vaux, *Israel*, 272), but the contrast should not be overdrawn as if only Israelites cared about history (see Frahm, Jansen-Winkeln, and Wiesehöfer, "Historiography: Ancient Orient"; Millard, Hoffmeier, and Baker, *Historiography in Context*); cf. Van Seters, "Historiography," for some possible parallels with Greek historiography.

80. E.g., Philo *Creation* 1–2: Moses refused to invent fables; cf. also Allison, *Jesus*, 444. Philo did, however, allegorize embarrassing portions (as not literal, not just in addition to literal), and some did so more liberally than he. But an extreme circle of Alexandrian intellectuals were, undoubtedly, less representative than Josephus and others who treated (albeit flexibly) the biblical narratives as real history. The features that Acts shares with OT historical works confirm that Luke intended to write history (Rosner, "History," 81).

81. Wright, *People of God*, 426.

82. See, e.g., Venter, "Reviewing History."

83. There is some debate whether the "Teacher" refers only to the founder (Brownlee, "Messianic Motifs," 13–15) or also to his successors in an office (e.g., Aune, *Prophecy*, 132; later Qumran sources suggest this, Buchanan, "Office"); some scholars have also portrayed him as an eschatological figure (Wacholder, "Teacher" [among Karaites, Siegel, "References"]); as messianic (Allegro, "References," 175–77; the priestly Messiah, Rosenberg, "Moreh"); as not messianic (Smyth, "Scrolls and Messiah"; Brown, "Messianism," 72–75); earlier, a particular Zealot figure (Roth, "Teacher"); other particular figures (cf. Murphy-O'Connor, "Judah"); or one whose identity is unknown (Burgmann, "Lehrer"). There is today debate even as to how many other documents at Qumran genuinely derive from this sect. For Jesus's pervasive centrality in extant early Christian Christology, see Hurtado, *One God*; Keener, *John*, 289–310.

84. The Qumran sect emphasized inspired interpretation yet preserved authentic memory of their founding Teacher (Stuhlmacher, "Theme," 13; cf. Keener, *John*, 977–82, on John 14:26), albeit not at length. Historical references tend to be generalized, whether because they did not matter or because their audience understood the referents (Callaway, "Reflections").

the Christian movement[85] from both Mithraism, with its more cosmic emphasis,[86] and earlier mystery cults,[87] but fits the commitment of ancient historians.[88]

Thus, as N. T. Wright contends, the NT writers claimed to use genuine history as their evocative "myth."[89] They were far more interested in Jesus than in the history of their movement (as the greater emphasis on the canonical Gospels than on Acts in the patristic period illustrates), but this valuing of history as a vehicle for theology would allow some appreciation for Luke's enterprise as well. Part of Luke's "theology" is proclamation of God's acts in history; thus, if some modern readers reject his claim that God acted in history in Jesus of Nazareth and continues to act in the witness to those historical acts, they should be clear that they disagree with Luke's theology (and not just with his historiography). Whether God acts in history is a theological question impinging on the historical question not normally primarily in terms of the "facticity" of events (except in extraordinary cases implausible apart from supranatural explanations) but in terms of hypotheses about causation.

Luke provides both historical information and theological perspective. If Luke communicates perspectives as well as information, his approach challenges interpretive strategies that mine Acts solely for historical information. More comfortable with description than prescription, some contemporary theologians and exegetes debate whether modern Christians should derive theology from the patterns in Acts,[90] but Luke surely expected his contemporary audience to do so.[91] Reception history certainly confirms that, rightly or wrongly, readers have often approached Acts in precisely this way. Thus, for example, various Christian restoration movements through history have used the patterns in Acts to guide their own movements. This includes, for example, some monastic communities, the Pietists, the Moravians, Wesley, the Churches of Christ, and Pentecostalism.[92] Their derivation of theology from narrative simply continued a practice that had long been available, including in ancient Judaism.[93] Arguing that Luke intended to teach theology, of course, does not settle the question of what theology Luke intended to teach,[94] an important question but one that I defer for chapters 14–15 below and especially appropriate points in the commentary.

2. Is Luke's *Tendenz* Compatible with "True" History?

Modern historians, just like ancient ones, write from various perspectives, as interpreters in postmodern times in particular emphasize. (Dunn points to the varying

85. Or most of it; over-Platonized versions had other interests, and Burkitt, *Gospel History*, 289, aptly titles his ch. 9 "Marcion, or Christianity without History."

86. See Martin, "Mithraism"; cf. Mattingly, *Christianity*, 5.

87. Metzger, "Considerations," 15, 19–20.

88. With Hemer, *Acts in History*, 63–70.

89. Wright, *People of God*, 471. Some argue that the Christian theology of history provided the first serious *philosophy* of (and teleology for) historiography (Nicolai, "Place of History," 17–18).

90. Cf., e.g., the discussions in Fee, *Gospel*, 83–104; Fee and Stuart, *Worth*, 105–10.

91. See, e.g., Haenchen, *Acts*, passim; Martin, *Worship*, 202; Bruce, "Apostolic Succession."

92. See, e.g., Noll, *Rise*, 66; McGee, "Hermeneutics," 97–102, 111. Narratives are important for contemporary theology (see Hauerwas and Jones, *Narrative*), a point applicable to Acts (e.g., Willimon, *Acts*, 2–4).

93. In addition to Israelite historiography (cf. McKenzie, "Historiography," 420), Jesus communicated by means of parables, Paul derived lessons from biblical narratives (e.g., 1 Cor 10:6, 11), and rabbinic tradition communicated truth through stories (see, e.g., Pearl, *Theology*, passim; rabbis did not, however, further develop the biblical genre of historiography; see Neusner, "History").

94. See, e.g., Michaels, "Evidences," 203–4.

estimates of Winston Churchill and Margaret Thatcher today as examples.)[95] No historian can escape subjective bias, but a perspective concerning events does not make the information about the events bad history.[96] Similarly, even news outlets in different countries (and sometimes in the same country) select and spin news in different ways, but most (the vast majority of free media) are responsible enough to use genuine data.[97] All authors write from particular perspectives; we in turn tend to evaluate their perspectives (e.g., theodicy, capitalism, or globalism) from our own perspectives (e.g., Enlightenment rationalism, Marxism, or nationalism). Recognizing writers' perspectives does not, however, require us to assume that they falsified their data; another writer may select and emphasize the data differently without disagreeing, in the main, with the reliability of the specific data presented.

Like all other ancient historians, Luke wrote with specific agendas in mind; we may regard these agendas as much of what he sought to *teach*.[98] With Luke, these are less often moralistic or nationalistic than was the case among many of his contemporaries, but no less often (and in fact generally more often) theological (in the stricter sense). He was deeply invested in discerning God's purposes in history and hence, from his perspective, in endorsing the Pauline, Gentile mission that was now enjoying success in his day. Movements often have the most interest in characteristics of their founder that contributed to or produced the movement, and they hence sometimes offer our best historical source regarding the founder, whatever we might say of their biases.[99]

At the same time, Luke, like other ancient historians, executed these agendas by recounting stories that he believed to be true.[100] He was not simply writing an abstract or epideictic theological treatise, which ancient writers did often enough without resorting to the historical genre.[101] As the Jewish scholar Geza Vermes points out, "A theological interest is no more incompatible with a concern for history than is a political or philosophical conviction," and we can allow for these interests when we interpret these sources.[102] The same is true for apologetic interests (as Josephus demonstrates); thus, for example, Luke has apologetic reasons to stress Paul's higher-than-average social status, but historically such status and its generally concomitant educational level are not improbable for one with Paul's obvious argumentative skills. His status

95. Dunn, *Acts*, xvi. Laistner, *Historians*, 95, points to how it took perhaps a century for British and U.S. historians to be "fair to both sides" regarding "the American Revolution." For a survey of varied applications of the life of Francis Asbury (some quite one-sided), see Wigger, *Saint*, 405–18.

96. As is widely acknowledged, including in studies on Acts; e.g., Marconi, "Interpretation"; Levinskaya, *Diaspora Setting*, 2; Hemer, *Acts in History*, 86–90; for the postmodern critique, cf. also Eddy and Boyd, *Legend*, 398–99. Judge, "Sources," 280–81, challenges the disengaged, depersonalizing preference of much modern (as opposed to ancient) historiography as unrealistic, because "historical enquiry is inescapably personal."

97. E.g., people in the United States can often obtain a more global perspective from the BBC than from U.S. media outlets; one popular and respected U.S. newsmagazine, for example, failed to mention war in the Democratic Republic of the Congo until the estimated death toll passed three million (see my complaint in "Did Not Know"). Such omissions certainly distort perspectives for readers dependent on these sources, yet no one would accuse that newsmagazine of having deliberately fabricated whatever data it did report.

98. I distinguish agendas from assumptions in that Luke sought to inform and especially persuade about his agendas.

99. Flusser, "Love," 154, compares the case of the Jesus movement with the followers of Simon Kimbangu or Joseph Smith. The analogies are, of course, inexact; e.g., unlike Smith, Jesus left no written record, and unlike Jesus, Kimbangu did not train disciples (in the ancient Mediterranean sense). But the examples are sufficient for Flusser's point.

100. E.g., Luke's emphasis on Paul's going to the Gentiles is hardly a Lukan creation (cf. Botermann, "Heidenapostel") even if the way he recounts this going creates a characteristic pattern (cf. Rom 1:14; 11:11–14).

101. Cf. Vermes, *Jesus and Judaism*, 20. Luke's epideictic or theological interests need not eliminate his information.

102. Ibid., 19; cf. Levinskaya, *Diaspora Setting*, 2; Hemer, *Acts in History*, 79–90.

also would help explain his longevity in Roman detention (Acts 24:27; 28:30; Phil 1:7) despite the powerful forces arrayed against him (cf. Rom 15:31; 1 Cor 16:9).

When Stephen (Acts 7:2–50) or Paul (13:17–37) preaches from biblical history, his retellings are selective but substantially accurate rehearsals of the tradition; that is, they edit rather than invent their material. If this approach illustrates Luke's method and theory of history, we should expect Luke to use his sources in his narrative in the same way.[103] Elements of Luke's narrative traditionally attributed to his "theological agendas" appear commonly as rhetorical authenticating techniques in ancient historiography.[104] This observation does not mean that Luke lacks a theology; it does mean that he communicates his theological message according to the principles that guided the historical genre in which he has chosen to write.[105] As scholars today usually recognize, the traditional modern dichotomy between history and theology is inadequate.[106] Indeed, the very dichotomy is anachronistic, framed from a purely modernist Western perspective; interpreters of Acts through most of history would not have assumed it.[107]

In contrast to the view articulated in the old Tübingen school's rewriting of early Christian history, Luke does not represent what has traditionally been called "early Catholicism," whose traits are largely missing in Acts.[108] Luke does not harmonize the problems of the earliest church to make everything look pleasant: one need only remember the need to replace Judas (1:18–20); the greed of Ananias and Sapphira (5:1–10); the conflict between cultural factions in Jerusalem (6:1); the magical associations of those who sought some connection with the church (8:9–13, 18–24; 19:12–13, 18); the division over the nature of Gentile admission into the church (11:3; 15:5); the split between Paul and Barnabas (15:39); and the preacher who knew only John's baptism (18:25; cf. 19:1–3).[109] Eusebius, not Acts, invented the myth of early Christian uniformity.[110] Luke does reduce descriptions of conflicts that were no longer relevant in his day or part of his church experience, but this different emphasis would not mean that he creates a fiction to conceal the past.[111] Indeed, if Luke sought to provide paraenetic models for his audience (who undoubtedly experienced enough conflicts of their own), it did make sense to stress (rather than conceal) the conflicts as a primary interest.[112]

103. See here Scott, "Stephen's Speech."

104. See extensively Rothschild, *Rhetoric of History*, passim (e.g., 291).

105. Theology was "integrated in the enterprise of ancient historical composition" (ibid., 59; cf. also 295).

106. E.g., Strelan, *Artemis*, 22; Neil, *Acts*, 18–22; Martin, *Foundations*, 53–56; Marshall, *Historian and Theologian*; Jáuregui, "Panorama"; Green, "History/Writing"; Walaskay, *Acts*, 10–12; Eckey, *Apostelgeschichte*, passim; Marguerat, *Histoire*, 91; Rothschild, *Rhetoric of History*, 59; cf. Yoo, "Sens." Luke emphasizes providence (Marguerat, *Histoire*, 59–61) yet writes about beginnings, not the sort of hagiography dominant in the third century (62–63; cf. Allison, *Jesus*, 447–48; Keener, *Miracles*, 857–66).

107. E.g., Erasmus read Acts as historically reliable yet also applied it to his audience (Pabel, "Retelling"). Cf. Malina and Pilch, *Acts*, 6.

108. Hengel, *Acts and History*, 65 (citing, e.g., the lack of magic in the sacraments; archaic Christology; and lack of hierarchical structure); Hays, *Moral Vision*, 135 (citing the charismatic dimension of Acts). Tübingen scholars, indeed, reacted against Acts partly because it was not theological enough according to their standards of "high" theology (Hengel and Schwemer, *Between Damascus and Antioch*, 20).

109. Following Witherington, *Acts*, 127; Wright, *People of God*, 454; see also at greater length Thompson, "Unity"; idem, "Idealization" (esp. 541–42).

110. Wright, *People of God*, 454. Eusebius himself reports many heresies down to his own period, when he found himself embroiled in the Arian controversy. On the historical setting and consequences of Eusebius and other late antique, ecclesiastical historians, see Croke, "Historiography," 574–77.

111. Barrett, *Acts*, 2:xli; cf. Bruce, "Real Paul?"; Witherington, *Acts*, 171. From Luke's work, I believe that his personality is probably also more conciliatory and integrative than some other early Christian voices, but this is a subjective judgment the specific weight of which is difficult to assess.

112. Hengel, *Acts and History*, 63.

Luke may write from the perspectives of his generation and for the questions of his generation; but if, as shall be argued, Luke was a sometime companion of Paul, his generation need not have been so far removed from Paul's as the most skeptical scholars would suggest. And even if Luke wrote as much as a generation after the events he describes toward the end of Acts,[113] we form our evaluations in a much later period, with much less access to information than Luke had. We may often exercise greater critical scrutiny of the sources, but some ancient historians evaluated traditions no less critically (see earlier comments on their critical approaches in ch. 4, esp. sect. 1.b, above), and we do both Luke and ourselves a serious disservice to assume that we can reconstruct the first three decades of the church better than he did. Instead we must endeavor to discover his emphases from how he tells his story, even though we usually (in the absence of information from Paul's letters) cannot know what details he chose to leave out.

Some specific themes will be mentioned later (see chs. 14 and esp. 15 below). Additionally, I believe that Luke intended Acts as a model, in some respects, for Christian missionaries after Paul, who might likewise use signs, debate, and even awkward legal situations as opportunities for public proclamation. To equip his audience for awkward legal situations, however—especially members of churches in Corinth and Philippi who were Roman citizens—Luke also provides a model for public apologetics.[114] Apologetics could include debating Jewish scribes or Athenian philosophers, but in the cities of the empire (and especially colonies) it especially involved demonstrating that one's faith did not subvert the Roman order.[115] Luke presents the church and its leaders as a public group, unafraid of debate and certainly not the sort of subversive and secretive sect that the Romans deplored.[116]

3. Apologetic Historiography

Most scholars concur that one of the primary functions of Luke-Acts is apologetic. Chapter 13 below, "The Purpose of Acts," will address this function more fully. This question cannot be considered properly, however, apart from a discussion of apologetic historiography in general, which is best introduced here in this discussion of historiography and its range of agendas. Because apologetic involves an agenda or purpose rather than a specific literary form, it can overlap with various other types of historiography that are classified instead by form or topic. Nevertheless, apologetic historiography was common for works by minority authors about their peoples (or, in this case, an aspect of their movement).

Ancient historians wrote many kinds of histories, with different (though sometimes overlapping) emphases: political history, military history, and so forth.[117] Luke's many allusions to the earlier biblical story and his frequent emphasis on its fulfillment suggest

113. A gap that modern historians would still regard as small when writing of the previous generation. Even in locations in the world where more concrete documentation would be lacking, oral history about events only a few decades removed is not comparable in quality to traditions centuries old.

114. For the sermons in Acts as models that could be adapted in Christian preaching, see Bauckham, "Summaries"; cf. Tannehill, *Acts*, 329.

115. For Roman concerns about such subversion from Eastern cults, see, e.g., Balch, *Wives*, 65–80, 118; Keener, *Paul*, 140–42.

116. See Hengel, *Acts and History*, 60. Rome had long been insecure about secret gatherings unapproved by the state (Livy 39.15.11).

117. See, e.g., the observations of Polybius, who distinguishes his political history from other approaches (Polyb. 9.1.1–6; 9.2.1–5). Until the nineteenth century, elite political and military interests tended to dominate historiography (van der Laan, "Approaches," 203).

that he sees himself continuing this biblical story, writing salvation history. Others before him, such as the Chronicler, Josephus, some writers of Qumran scrolls, and possibly the authors of some of the Maccabean literature, had sought to reinterpret or update the biblical story.[118] (See ch. 14 below, which addresses Israel's story.)

But how would the broader Greco-Roman world hear such a particular story about God's people? Gregory Sterling has examined the question of ethnographic and apologetic historiography at length, providing a careful analysis of the broader generic framework into which Luke-Acts may fit, and a summary of his conclusions will prove helpful here. Many early Greek historians were ethnographers chronicling "the land, the history, the marvels, and the customs of a people," but originally from a purely Greek perspective.[119] They became more sympathetic to other peoples in a later period but still worked from Greek categories and perspectives.[120] (Tacitus, a second-century C.E. Roman historian, complained that Greek historians admired only their own culture.)[121] Inevitably, other Near Eastern peoples, especially the priests guarding their sacred traditions, felt a need to respond to Hellenism's cultural imperialism.[122] To gain a hearing, however, these peoples had to use the Greek language and Greek literary forms; in the process they created a new genre: apologetic historiography.[123]

For this project, the literary elite of these cultures could employ their local traditions, which provided both an antidote to Greek ethnocentrism and evidence of their own antiquity.[124] Often they argued that their own civilizations predated the Greeks and hence that the Greeks borrowed from them.[125] Hellenistic Jewish historians

118. See, e.g., Juel, *Promise*, 118, who thinks that Luke, like Josephus, had to address the disillusionment, generated by the post-70 C.E. situation, about God's providence.

119. Sterling, *Historiography*, 20–53; quote, 53. Herodotus was said to be the first historian to publish a universal, rather than specific ethnographic, history (Dion. Hal. *Thuc.* 5).

120. Sterling, *Historiography*, 55–102. For negative Greek views of "barbarian" intellect, see, e.g., Dion. Hal. *Ant. rom.* 5.4.3; Jos. *Ant.* 18.47; Xen. Eph. *Anthia* 3.11; Diod. Sic. 1.2.6; Epicurus in Diog. Laert. 10.117; contrast Anacharsis *Ep.* 2.1–2, to Solon; Diogenes *Ep.* 28; Jos. *Ag. Ap.* 1.15–18.

121. Tac. *Ann.* 2.88 (admitting some, but lesser, Roman bias). (Though generally positive toward Rome, Hellenistic historians depicting its history clearly did so from a Greek vantage point; see Pelling, "Historians of Rome.") Nevertheless, most Roman historians similarly focused on Rome; Pompeius Trogus was distinctive in his focus on non-Roman peoples, including (in bks. 11–40) Alexander and his successors (see discussion in Levene, "Roman Historiography," 287–88). Roman historiographic treatment of other peoples could also promote the ideology of Roman conquest (see, e.g., O'Gorman, "Politics," 384); the quintessential expression of Roman ethnography appears in Roman triumphs (Dench, "Ethnography," 502, on 501–2 also noting Caesar's conquest tracts).

122. Greek historians were part of Alexander's conquests from the start, and imposed their understanding on the peoples among whom Greek education was spreading, inviting local responses (Dillery, "Historians," 221). Some of the best known today, Berossus (authoring the *Babylonica* [FGH 680]; cf. Kuhrt, "Mesopotamia," 62–63; Dillery, "Historians," 222–25), Manetho (*Aegyptiaca* [FGH 609]; Dillery, "Historians," 225–28), and eventually Josephus (*Antiquities*) "were priests who used the records of their own people to write their histories" (Sterling, "Historians," 502). Even the first history by a Roman, Fabius Pictor, was composed in Greek and fit this tradition (Dillery, "Roman Historians," 78–84; though some see it as addressing the Roman aristocracy, Gotter, "Origines," 121).

123. Sterling, *Historiography*, 103–36 (though not all scholars explain these minority histories as primarily apologetic; see Dillery, "Historians," 228–30). For a summary of apologetic literature more generally, see Aune, *Dictionary of Rhetoric*, 51–54. Greeks had local cult histories (Dillery, "Sacred History"); non-Greeks might write their own local histories with an emphasis on their deity, but a larger-than-local ethnographic history allowed them to assert their value in a more public space.

124. Sterling, *Historiography*, 135. For the apologetic argument from antiquity, see below. Greeks themselves, however, could provide apologetic slants on history; Polybius, before writing his history, had to absolve the memory of some earlier Greek leaders to prevent the Romans from destroying their statues (Polyb. 39.3.3–11).

125. Sterling, *Historiography*, 136. Greeks themselves recognized that Egyptian culture predated and influenced their own.

followed this pattern, adapting their stories as well as possible to Greek literary and rhetorical forms to argue that their culture was older and greater than that of the Greeks.[126] Although the apologetic element is not always dominant, all extant ancient Jewish historiography was, to some degree, apologetic historiography, emphasizing especially the antiquity and superiority of Israel's religion.[127]

Josephus's retelling of sacred Jewish history in his *Antiquities* is our most massive and complete example of such Jewish apologetic historiography; Josephus seeks to demonstrate God's providence in Israel's history.[128] As Daniel Harrington notes, Josephus "reworks Jewish traditions in categories derived from and comprehensible to a Greco-Roman public."[129] Although it was particularly in his *Antiquities* that Josephus sought "to dispel the ridicule and misinformation that characterized literate Roman portrayals of the Jews,"[130] his other works also reveal heavily apologetic emphases (such as the claim in the *War* that merely a few bandits provoked the entire conflict).[131] He also seeks to vindicate the Jewish God vis-à-vis Roman gods or Fortune, showing after the loss of 70 C.E. (as did the compilers of Kings and Chronicles after the exile) that the defeat belonged to God's plan.[132] In contrast to Josephus's multivolume treatise, Jewish writers could also offer briefer monographs of apologetic history; one may argue that Philo's *Flaccus* fits this category,[133] though the work is as different from Acts as its author is from Luke.[134]

Gregory Sterling argues that Luke-Acts fits the genre of apologetic historiography, and many scholars now follow him.[135] This proposal makes good sense, although Luke goes about this apologetic historiography in his own way and, like some other ancient Jewish historical works, includes this function as only one part of his objective. Certainly Luke devotes considerable space in his narrative to refuting charges against Paul such as are found in Acts 24:5, and the Lukan purpose that such an observation suggests invites us to look for Lukan apologetic elsewhere. Apologetic historiography is a kind of historiography identified by goal, a sort of classification

126. Ibid., 137–225; see also idem, "Appropriation," 234–38. For the idea that Greeks borrowed Jewish wisdom, see this commentary's comment on Acts 17:22–31. Josephus's rival Justus probably provides one example no longer extant (see Rajak, "Justus of Tiberias," 92). For apologetic in Hellenistic Jewish narrative writers, see further Holladay, *Theios aner*, 234 and passim.

127. Wandrey, "Literature: Jewish-Hellenistic," 696.

128. Sterling, *Historiography*, 226–310. More generally, others also emphasize Josephus's apologetic objectives (e.g., Feldman, "Apologist of World"; in defending himself, Vogel, "Vita 64–69"; Lamour, "Organisation").

129. Harrington, "Bible," 245, following H. A. Attridge. For example, Josephus's story about Moses may challenge Alexandrian anti-Jewish propaganda influential in Rome (see Hata, "Moses within Anti-Semitism"). Whether Josephus was able to gain much of a non-Jewish audience is questionable, given the reluctance of the Greco-Roman world to engage ethnic minority perspectives (cf. Feldman, "Reflections on Jews"); but he does appear to be a source for Tacitus and others.

130. Mason, *Josephus and New Testament*, 71 (concluding his discussion of *Antiquities*, 65–71).

131. Ibid., 60–61; for the *Life* as a self-defense against Justus, see 73–76; his fullest apologetic, of course, was the explicit apologetic in *Against Apion* (see 77–81). Others also note Josephus's apologetic motifs (e.g., Boccaccini, *Judaism*, 241–42).

132. See, e.g., Kelley, "Perspective."

133. See Meiser, "Gattung." The discourses in *Flaccus* help support this conclusion.

134. E.g., *Flaccus* is more rhetorical and focuses on the blame aspect of epideictic, with abundant overt editorializing.

135. Sterling, *Historiography*, 311–89; also Mason, *Josephus and New Testament*, 196–97; Kee, *Every Nation*, 11–12; Johnson, *Acts*, xii. (Sterling, "Appropriation," 242, notes the irony that not rabbinic Judaism but early Christianity developed Jewish apologetic historiography, without the traditional ethnic element.) Tomson, "Counsel," 603–4, suggests that Josephus and Luke both use Pharisaism to appeal to Roman aristocrats; this is plausible, though most of Luke's audience is, presumably, on a lower socioeconomic level than Josephus's. Palmer, "Monograph (1993)," 15–18, compares Josephus *Antiquities* and critiques Sterling here, but Sterling's case, on the whole, seems stronger than the critique. For Luke's apologetic use of outsiders' speeches in a manner comparable to specifically Jewish historiography, see Padilla, *Speeches*.

not identical with classification by rhetorical level (in Luke's case, more popular than elite) or by specific content (the gospel's expansion) or form (monograph). As noted earlier, Luke is less rhetorically sophisticated than Josephus and some other extant Jewish apologists.[136] This category is thus compatible with some other suggestions about Luke's historiography.

Part of Luke's apologetic is his argument that the Gentile Christian movement, far from being a recent innovation, is an appropriate outgrowth of Israel's ancient and sacred history. Luke indeed goes beyond other Hellenistic Jewish writers, such as Artapanus,[137] Demetrius, Eupolemus, and Pseudo-Eupolemus, in his overarching promise-fulfillment schema;[138] naturally this approach reflects his theological perspective that the promised messianic era has come. It claims to unify Luke's story with Israel's earlier story in a way that these earlier writers did not claim for their own stories, suggesting that he views Luke-Acts itself as a continuation of the biblical story.[139] One embarrassment to Luke's claim that Jesus and the Gentile mission climax God's historic dealings with Israel was Israel's failure to embrace this claim.[140] This embarrassment thus invites not only Luke's emphasis on promise fulfillment and the continuity of salvation history but also a narrative explanation of why many Jewish people had not yet embraced the message.[141] Luke blames both the abuse of political power (by the Sadducean elite, now discredited after 70) and Judean hostile prejudice against Gentiles (a hostility likewise discredited after 70, especially from the perspective of Gentiles). Luke may well hope that these objects of blame would invite a positive reevaluation of the Jesus movement among fair-minded, God-fearing Jews as well as invite the approval of Gentiles.

Luke's apologetic (which qualifies his work for the category of apologetic historiography) requires a fuller discussion in chapter 13, on the purpose of Acts. After a brief discussion of other proposed purposes of Acts, that chapter will return to the theme of Acts as apologetic and then to the related questions of Luke's relation to Judaism and the OT story of salvation.

Conclusion

More than their modern counterparts, ancient historians had obvious moral and ethnic agendas, and often theological perspectives as well. Luke is no exception to this rule, though like many other minority authors he chooses a subject and theology distinct from the dominant culture. His focus on a particular movement, the theological premises of which he shares, diverges from the mainstream of elite Greco-Roman

136. Penner, *Praise*, 235–47, rightly notes the epideictic element in Hellenistic Jewish apologetic literature presenting the past. This comparison is certainly relevant to Acts, but differences in rhetorical level and function must also be accounted for.

137. Also an apologetic writer, apparently refuting Manetho's charges (see Collins, "Artapanus," 892), though some scholars do question whether Artapanus himself was Jewish (cf. Jacobson, "Artapanus"). On Manetho's early Hellenistic version of the exodus (lepers driven from Egypt), see discussion in Raspe, "Manetho on Exodus."

138. See Holladay, "Acts and Fragments" (also arguing that Acts shares with these works the heroic characterization of the central heroes). See comment below in ch. 14, sect. 2, on Luke's use of the OT.

139. To make such a claim was not to claim canonicity, although canon was apparently an open question among many Jewish groups. See the discussion of such questions in Smith, "Gospels."

140. Scholars often see this embarrassment as an invitation to Luke's apologetic (Nolland, "Salvation-History," 80; idem, *Luke's Readers*, 119–28).

141. Cf. the discussion in Johnson, *Acts*, 7–12; cf. Cunningham, *Many Tribulations*, 340; the problems here comport with those addressed by Paul in, e.g., Rom 3:3; 9:6; 11:17.

historians not only theologically (most obviously, he is not a polytheist) but, in a sense, "ethnically" (narrating the story of what Romans often viewed as an "eastern cult," he has an uphill battle for respectability no matter how ancient the faith's origins).[142] Although in form Luke's historical work is a monograph, in purpose it functions in ways analogous to other apologetic histories of peoples outside the culturally dominant Greek and Roman mainstream. This conclusion paves the way for chapter 13 below on the purpose of Acts.

142. As argued earlier (ch. 3 above), Luke does not write about a "people" in the strict sense but about early Christian mission; this difference, however, qualifies, rather than vitiates, a comparison with typical apologetic historiography.

6

APPROACHING ACTS
AS A HISTORICAL SOURCE

Granted that Acts is ancient historiography, what kind of ancient historiography is it? The question can be answered in different ways, depending on one's objective: from the perspective of form, Acts is (as argued above, following many others) a historical monograph; from the perspective of purpose and function, it is (as also suggested above, again following others) apologetic historiography and the foundation story of a people or (more precisely) a movement. Here we consider the degree of Luke's fidelity to historiographic ideals.

As already noted, most ancient historiography included both an interest in information and an interest in pleasing rhetorical presentation. This chapter investigates Luke's use of information, examining a question of great interest to modern historians of antiquity (and of significance to ancient readers of histories as well): to what extent can we trust Luke's reliability regarding the historical claims that he offers?[1]

I pose this question of reliability here in terms of the standards of ancient historiography, not modern historiography. As already argued, ancient historians expected substantial accuracy regarding events, but they did allow the construction of scenes supporting such events, sometimes based on inferences (especially regarding speech and discourse material). Yet, as also noted, there was a range of practices among ancient historians; not all proved equally reliable by either ancient or modern standards. Establishing a general range of reliability on major points for ancient histories in general does not settle where Acts lies on this range.

To better answer this more particular question, we must first survey Luke's use of sources and then turn to some specific evidence. Writing according to the constraints of ancient rather than modern historiography, Luke exercises flexibility even in his own summaries of the events he reports; he does not expect his readers to flinch when he gives accounts that diverge in some details (cf., e.g., Luke 23:50–53 with

---

1. Merely establishing that Luke wrote historiography cannot settle the question of veracity (cf. Penner, *Praise*, 5–6), even if it provides a generally narrower range than we would have without these genre markers. The question of Acts and history has long intrigued scholars (note esp. Cadbury, *Acts and History*; for this history of historical criticism of Acts, see Mattill and Mattill, *Bibliography*, 181–89, §§2430–2561). Mattill and Mattill, 189–93, §§2562–93, cite more than 30 sources addressing Acts' historical reliability (e.g., Howard, "Source") and many from the eighteenth and nineteenth centuries (Biscoe, *History* [1742, 1829]; Blunt, *Veracity*, 1829; Holtzmann, "Actes" [1868]; Howson, *Value* [1880]) and early twentieth century (e.g., Bernard, "Historical Value" [1902]; Chase, *Credibility* [1902]; Beardslee, "Inaccuracies," [1903]; Wendt, "Trustworthiness" [1913–14]; Foakes-Jackson, *Criticism* [1916]; Ayles, "Credibility" [1923–24]; Deissmann, "Value" [1929]).

Acts 13:28–29; Luke 24:40–51 with Acts 1:3–9). Taking this flexibility for granted, I instead focus in this chapter on points of likely correspondence with external history.

To some extent, however, this chapter merely introduces some issues that must also be addressed later. The next chapter will take up the genuine major test case for Luke's reliability, namely, comparison with Paul's letters. I believe that this test case will argue strongly for Luke's use of substantial historical information (and that most readers will find this evidence for Luke's use of such data persuasive).

After these discussions we will turn to the questions of speeches and signs reports in ancient historiography and in Acts (chs. 8–9 below). Because of the special problems associated with these issues, the present discussion on reliability addresses primarily nondiscourse, nonsupernatural narrative in Acts. To separate speeches and signs from other historical narrative is not to prejudge the case but to recognize that, in view of ancient (especially for speeches) and modern (especially for signs) questions, more space is required to address these issues separately.

1. Evaluating Degrees of Historical Reliability

No one believes that nothing happened in history (or even in our day-to-day lives) other than what we can prove or provide evidence for. When we discuss historical "probability," we acknowledge that some events that our methods deem probable did not happen and that others that our methods deem improbable did happen; our methods entail much educated guesswork. Nevertheless, an educated guess is apt to be correct more often than an uneducated one. When we speak of historical probability, then, we speak in terms of the principles of historiography that tend to give us more accurate answers. Normal historical methodology suggests that Paul appeared before Gallio but that no one in the Sanhedrin scene of Acts 5 should have mentioned Theudas. This methodology cannot guarantee such conclusions, but insofar as we ask questions based on extant evidence, we can offer conclusions that are probable on the basis of such evidence. This is what scholars normally mean by "historical probability." The degree to which our conclusions are tentative in a given case depends on the quality, quantity, and representative character of our extant evidence.

Although we often lack direct access to firsthand ancient sources, we can look to the ancient historical writers who still had access to such sources, then test them by means of other writers to try to determine the degree of their fidelity to those sources. Comparing different ancient historians such as Herodian and Dio Cassius turns up discrepancies but also confirms that both were employing substantial historical data.[2] Such a comparison will also reveal that such writers did not always choose to cover the same ground; thus, for example, there are many omissions in Herodian, but hints of the information suggest that he did not lack the information itself.[3]

Although ancient historians did not always have access to the best sources for earlier eras, their treatment of more recent history was generally more dependable, as suggested above (ch. 4, sect. 1.d). The Roman historian Tacitus, for instance, recorded much of the history of first-century Rome, often using imperial annals;[4] he is widely regarded as one of the most reliable sources for the history of this period. When Tacitus wrote

---

2. Whittaker, "Introduction," xlv–xlviii. Dio Cassius claims to have spent ten years collecting his research thoroughly (Hose, "Cassius Dio," 464).
3. Whittaker, "Introduction," xlviii–lii.
4. For these and Tacitus's numerous other kinds of sources, see, e.g., Hadas, "Introduction," xviii; cf. Grant, "Introduction to Tacitus," 13–14.

biography, he maintained the same standard he had upheld in writing Roman history: although his *Agricola*, a biography of his father-in-law, has a particular agenda (to praise his father-in-law while condemning the depravity of the Flavian era), it is certainly as historically reliable as Tacitus's resources allowed him to make it. Indeed, Tacitus, as Agricola's son-in-law, also had firsthand acquaintance with the data he reported.

Other historians reporting contemporary or recent events were also substantially reliable, although one must consider how critically each writer used his sources and how freely he adapted them. Suetonius's biographies of the twelve Caesars provide critical information to modern historians of antiquity; they may be less reliable than Tacitus, but where Suetonius errs, it is by depending too uncritically on his sources, not by fabricating material.[5] Collecting so much material was no mean feat or small service to subsequent historians. Other historians and biographers, such as Livy and Plutarch, took much more freedom to moralize and spice up their narratives.[6] But as noted above, even Plutarch plainly believes that it is historical data he is using to make his moral points, and his record frequently parallels other historical sources. Historians did make errors,[7] but they could expect their successors to expose their errors when discovered (Diod. Sic. 4.56.7–8).

Josephus may provide an example of a freer historian. Josephus's history and autobiography are dominated by his apologetic *Tendenz*;[8] J. D. Crossan wryly but insightfully remarks of Josephus's *War*, "Nobody from the highest aristocracy on either side is guilty of anything."[9] Even many of his adaptations of biblical accounts emphasize points pleasing to his Roman sponsors and Gentile audience.[10] He also interprets his sources for his Hellenistic audience in other ways.[11] After promising to add nothing to Moses's laws (*Ant.* 4.196; cf. 1.17), he finds among them a specific prohibition against theft from pagan temples (4.207), a prohibition against women's testimony (4.219), and the requirement of seven judges per city (4.214). Numerous studies have traced Josephus's adaptation of biblical accounts, but whereas the degree of adaptation varies from one narrative to another, it remains balanced by his general fidelity to the basic biblical account.[12] He seems to have viewed his "translation" task

5. A later historian emphasized Suetonius's "truthfulness" (*SHA, Probus* 2.7, cited approvingly in Bradley, "Suetonius," 1452).

6. Defending Livy's accuracy, however, see Laistner, *Historians*, 65–102. Much more extreme, Lucan's war poetry (more epic than historical in style, though on the larger level recounting largely historical events) played on the grotesque but impossible images of his tradition: e.g., because weapons pierced Catus from both sides, the blood did not know which way to flow (Lucan *C.W.* 3.586–91).

7. E.g., Dio Cass. 48.26.2 (see LCL note), contradicting Josephus (who was earlier; Jos. *Ant.* 14.359–69; *War* 1.268–73) and himself (Dio Cass. 49.22.6); see also Hdn. 3.4.3 (see LCL, n. 1); 3.9.3 (LCL, n. 3).

8. As often noted (e.g., Harrington, "Bible," 245; Sanders, *Judaism*, 6; on the autobiography, Mason, *Josephus and New Testament*, 41–42, 73–76). Clearly, Josephus exaggerated in his own interests, though it is less certain that (with Krieger, "Verwandter") he did not belong to the priestly aristocracy. The danger of appearing to praise oneself could make glory-seeking autobiography a more delicate exercise than other forms of epideictic biography (see Cic. *Fam.* 5.12.8).

9. Crossan, *Jesus*, 93. Josephus had too much to lose to tell the truth in all respects. Sometimes the Romans apparently accepted the excuse that a small band had forced others to resist Rome (Livy 24.47.6, in 213 B.C.E.).

10. Cf., e.g., Begg, "Amaziah"; idem, "Nahum"; idem, "Uzziah"; Feldman, "Asa"; idem, "Joseph"; idem, "Manasseh"; idem, "Pharaohs"; idem, "Ezra"; cf. also the transformation of Ahasuerus into a fully positive character in Jos. *Ant.* 11 (Feldman, "Ahasuerus"). Begg, "Gedaliah," suggests that some of Josephus's reports *may* also reflect influence from his experience.

11. Clearly, not all stem from desire to please Rome: it is unlikely that Josephus avoids Nineveh's repentance because of Roman antiproselytism views (Feldman, "Jonah"), given his reports of many conversions elsewhere, and still less likely are some parallels drawn between the Jonah story and the Argonautica (Hamel, "Argo to Nineveh").

12. For specific examples of Josephus's adaptations, see, e.g., Begg, "Jotham"; idem, "Fall"; idem, "Putsch"; idem, "Jehoahaz" (improving the character); Feldman, "Elijah"; other articles by Feldman cited in this chapter;

as including interpretation and adaptation for his audience; Plato, Cicero, and others understood the translation task similarly.[13]

Few agree with Josephus's population estimates (see discussion at Acts 2:41); probably all that he had available in most cases were guesses. His speeches are likewise viewed as suspect (see discussion in ch. 8 below). Nevertheless, archaeology confirms that he usually gets right even many minor details unaffected by this *Tendenz*[14] (although his accuracy has exceptions).[15] Inscriptions likewise sometimes confirm his accuracy on disputed details, sometimes against other historians.[16]

Josephus retells the same event in different ways in different books, yet this practice suggests not that the event never happened but that he presents it from a different perspective.[17] While adding details and perspectives, he even retains the stories of David's sin with Bathsheba (*Ant.* 7.130–31) and Uriah's murder (7.131–46), though— perhaps with an eye toward anti-Judaic polemic such as Apion's sources—he omits the episode of the golden calf (3.95–99). Although Josephus was not striving for modern standards of historical accuracy, E. P. Sanders concludes that "wherever he can be tested, he can be seen to have been a pretty fair historian."[18] (A fuller comparison with Josephus is offered here below.)

Although we have established that historians intended the substance of their works to be historically reliable and that they accomplished this intention much more commonly with recent sources than with older ones, historians varied in their degree of reliability. Evidence examined here so far suggests that Luke writes a historical monograph; that he therefore reports events that he believes to be true (whatever the accuracy of particular details); and that given the recent nature of the events he reports (and especially the more recent ones), he is likelier than not to be largely correct in the events that he claims. But how far should we press this general principle?

For example, it is certain that Paul was publicly punished at Philippi (1 Thess 2:2; Phil 1:30), likely that he was jailed there, and reasonably likely that this happened in response to an exorcism as Luke claims. But to what degree should we press Luke on the details (such as particular conversations in that narrative or even the meal with the jailer)? Where on the range of reliability should we expect him to fall—in other words, *how* probable should we expect his reliability to be in any given case, and where does the burden of proof lie, and how heavily? And what sort of sources does Luke have for the period before Paul's ministry? From a strictly historical standpoint, such questions can be resolved historically (to the extent that a strict historical method can resolve them) only by working through the text passage by passage with

---

Gafni, "Josephus and Maccabees," 126–27. In Josephus's case, the claim not to have added or omitted anything seems, however, pure convention (Feldman, "Hellenizations: Abraham," 133).

13. Inowlocki, "Neither Adding nor Omitting."

14. E.g., Syon, "Gamla"; Cotton and Geiger, "Yyn"; Mazar, "Josephus"; Feldman, "Introduction," 45–46; Thackeray, *Josephus*, 49. Cf. also his claims concerning an Essene gate (Jos. *War* 5.142–45), in Riesner, "Gate"; Pixner, "Gate"; Pixner, Chen, and Margalit, "Zion."

15. Fischer and Stein, "Marble." Some scholars also suggest that his use of conventional forms in his suicide accounts militates against the accuracy of his battle suicides (Newell, "Forms"), but a historian might employ the same convention for an authentic event (suicide was common enough; cf. comment on Acts 16:27).

16. Cf. probably Kokkinos, "*Gentilicium*"; see comment on Acts 23:24.

17. Wright, *People of God*, 378, also comparing Luke 24:51; Acts 1:3. Cf. also the divergent details in Josephus and Philo on the same events (Theissen, *Gospels*, 149). Josephus follows but apparently modifies some literary sources (see Ben Zeev, "Reliability"); he is not always correct, but he does not normally appear to deliberately misrepresent his sources (idem, "Ambiguities").

18. Sanders, *Judaism*, 6. Many claims against Josephus's reliability are overstated; see, e.g., Rajak, *Josephus*, 9–10.

such questions in mind.[19] But we can start by laying out general observations below concerning historians' use of sources, including Luke's use of them.

2. Luke's Use of Sources

Ancients expected historians to utilize sources, whether written (most commonly), oral (for recent or local events), or their own firsthand experiences (where they were eyewitnesses). Although Luke is less apt to name his sources than most extant ancient historians (who tended to be elite historians), he clearly had sources available (e.g., Luke 1:1–2; Acts 16:10).

a. Other Historians' Use of Sources

Omniscient narrators, common in epic poetry,[20] were not common to historians. Historians, in fact, often felt constrained to indicate some of their sources,[21] especially if they depended on written sources and wrote for upper-class readers who might have access to these various works.[22] Accuracy of sources, unimportant in some genres, was known to be a concern of historians (Pliny *Ep.* 9.33.1). One could establish one's point better by naming various earlier sources supporting it (Suet. *Jul.* 9.3). A historical writer who does not include everything that has been written might need to explain that he had in fact read almost everything but did not judge it all suitable for inclusion (Dio Cass. 1.1.1–2).

That ancient historians, biographers, and anthologists depended on earlier sources is not in question; both biblical[23] and Greco-Roman traditions[24] frequently cite them.

19. Some conservative reviewers have criticized similar statements (in my view, out of context) in some of my previous books (e.g., Doriani, "Review"). But neither those statements nor this one are intended as conclusions; rather, they are transitional from one part of an argument to the next. I do not believe it appropriate to claim for an argument more than one has demonstrated or than, by the means agreed on in the form of argument, one can demonstrate. If some scholars think that establishing historical genre alone is sufficient to guarantee the reliability of whatever details ancient historians wrote, I believe that their malady would be cured by reading more ancient history (as would that of those skeptical of most of the basic substance of what ancient historians wrote).

20. E.g., Sil. It. 9.66–177; cf. also drama (e.g., the goddess Fortune providing such information in Menander *Aspis* 97–148). They could provide such insights, they believed, through inspiration (Val. Flacc. 3.15–17; Sil. It. 9.340–45; cf. also Nagy, "Prologue," xxx; Maclean and Aitken, *Heroikos*, xxxix), through which they could also reveal the divine purposes in history (Sil. It. 1.19). Pervo, *Acts*, 17, finds Acts' narration closer to this model, but I find it closer to historians (who reported private scenes no less than Luke; both reported them less than poetic works did). Of course, Luke would have believed in prophetic insight into events (e.g., Acts 27:31; cf. 2 Kgs 6:12), a practice I have also observed among African prophets. Even historians did sometimes act omniscient, reporting characters' thoughts (Dewald, "Construction," 97), though Luke rarely does this. Like Luke at times, other historians sometimes displayed confidence about motives (e.g., Vell. Paterc. 2.35.2; 2.48.4).

21. Dion. Hal. *Ant. rom.* 1.1.1; see Keener, *John*, 22–23; for historians' ideally using sources, see also Marguerat, *Histoire*, 30. Pervo, *Dating Acts*, 6–7, notes that writers did not always acknowledge their sources, as long as they rewrote the material (citing Josephus's rewrite of Exod 7:8–12 in Jos. *Ant.* 2.284–87). It is true that for reasons of style (like most modern works' avoidance of full documentation) historians did not acknowledge all their sources (Laistner, *Historians*, 51, 86), but it is rare to find elite historians who never mention their predecessors when such existed.

22. Granted, when they wrote noncontemporary history they depended primarily on earlier historians rather than other kinds of documents; they could compare these (a tedious enterprise, Pliny *Ep.* 5.8.12) and evaluated discrepancies by probability (Marincola, "Audiences," 19). Some of the historians on whom they depended, however, had written contemporary accounts.

23. E.g., Num 21:14; Josh 10:13; 2 Sam 1:18; 1 Kgs 14:19, 29; 15:7, 23, 31; 16:5, 14, 20, 27; 22:39, 45; 2 Kgs 1:18; 8:23; 10:34; 12:19; 13:8, 12; 14:15, 18, 28; 15:6, 11, 15, 21, 26, 31, 36; 16:19; 20:20; 21:17, 25; 23:28; 24:5; 1 Chr 27:24; 29:29; 2 Chr 16:11; 20:34; 24:27; 25:26; 27:7; 28:26; 32:32; 35:27; 36:8; 2 Macc 2:24–25. Rabbis, too, often emphasized citing sources for traditions (e.g., *m. ʾAbot* 6:6; *b. Nid.* 19b).

24. E.g., Dion. Hal. *Ant. rom.* 1.6.1; Arrian *Alex.* 6.2.4; Plut. *Alex.* 30.7; 31.2–3; 38.4; and further below. For details from Tiberius's time, Tacitus cites "historians of that era" (*Ann.* 5.9). Even a novelist might occasionally

(Other means of detecting them, such as different textures within a narrative, are usually less dependable.)[25] They often cite varying accounts, even when preferring one over another.[26] Arrian prefers over other sources his two earliest ones, which often agree, and he chooses between them when they diverge;[27] when sources diverge too much, he frankly complains that the exact truth is unrecoverable.[28] Likewise Philostratus notes a point where his sources diverge and his research provided no definitive resolution;[29] such a complaint hardly implies that ancient historians regularly practiced free invention.[30] At one point Plutarch names five sources for a "majority" position[31] and nine for a minority one, plus an extant letter attributed to the person about whom he writes, but he then adds that the minor divergence does not affect our view of his hero's character (the main point for him; *Alex.* 46.1–2). Valerius Maximus, a more popular and less careful writer than some others, rarely cites his sources (and often confuses his data), but he mentions them occasionally when they diverge (e.g., Val. Max. 5.7.ext. 1; 6.8.3). Occasionally historians also found ways to harmonize traditions (Diod. Sic. 4.4.1–5). Sometimes they appear to have smoothed out contradictions in their sources in their own rewriting.[32]

At the same time, we dare not assume that historians have such sources only when they cite them; as a matter of rhetorical elegance, they avoided documentation where they found it unnecessary.[33] Historians usually mentioned these sources only when they conflicted or the author disagreed or was unsure about their reliability[34] or about which sources were best.[35] Such conflicts arose more often when they were treating events of the more remote past than when they were treating the present. Luke (like the other Gospel writers) does not identify specific sources (except perhaps

---

remember to provide the story world verisimilitude by providing a source (Apul. *Metam.* 9.30). In other genres, cf. *Contest of Homer and Hesiod* 323; Parth. *L.R.* 11.1–3; 14.5. Ovid's account of Lichas's end (*Metam.* 9.225) diverges from Soph. *Wom. Tr.* 777–82; Ovid claims dependence on prior tradition, but his emphasis on metamorphoses certainly accounts for which tradition he prefers! Cf. Cook, "Plutarch's Use," for a stylistic source indicator in Plutarch; for Plutarch's range of sources, see Rhodes, "Documents," 65–66.

25. E.g., the material about Panthea in Xen. *Cyr.* 7.1.29–7.3.16 seems different from the context, but the criteria are not objective enough for certainty (witness NT scholars' continuing debates over the extent of pre-Pauline "hymns").

26. E.g., Dion. Hal. *Ant. rom.* 1.87.4; 3.35.1–4; 8.79.1; Livy 9.44.6; 23.19.17; 25.17.1–6; Appian *Hist. rom.* 11.9.56; 12.1.1; Plut. *Alex.* 31.3; 38.4; *Demosth.* 5.5; 29.4–30.4; *Themist.* 25.1–2; 27.1; 32.3–4; Apollod. *Bib.* 1.4.3; 1.5.2; 1.9.15, 19; 2.3.1; 2.5.11; Ovid *Fasti* 6.1–2, 97–100; Philost. *Vit. soph.* 2.4.570; Paus. 2.5.5; 2.26.3–7; Arrian *Alex.* 4.9.2–3; 4.14.1–4; 5.3.1; 5.14.4; 7.14.2; 7.27.1–3; Hdn. 7.9.4; 7.9.9; Corn. Nep. 7 (Alcibiades), 11.1; 9 (Conon), 5.4; *y. Soṭah* 9:13, §2; see further *Livy*, LCL, 12:320n2. Livy cites many sources (Laistner, *Historians*, 84), and cites a major source, Quadrigarius, especially where the latter's account varies from Livy's (Forsythe, "Quadrigarius," 391)—and hence may follow him at other times without citing him.

27. Arrian *Alex.* 1.pref. 1–2.

28. Arrian *Alex.* 3.3.6.

29. Philost. *Vit. soph.* 2.5.576.

30. Nor can one object that Philostratus, writing lives of sophists, was simply unaware of appropriate rhetorical conventions.

31. Thereby implying far more than the five sources he has named. On the multiplicity of first-generation Alexander accounts, now lost, see Zambrini, "Historians."

32. Cf. Damon, "Source to *sermo*," on Livy 34.54.4–8 (contrasting Tacitus's freer composition in *Ann.* 1, 14), if this redaction-critical approach proves durable.

33. Judge, *First Christians*, 379.

34. See Hemer, *Acts in History*, 65; cf. Lendon, "Historiography," 54 (citing the statement to this effect in Tac. *Ann.* 13.20); Laistner, *Historians*, 120 (for controversial matters), 127 (Tacitus reporting variations in the views of his sources, which may have been contemporary with the events narrated); for Livy's citation of Quadrigarius only when varying from his own narrative, see Forsythe, "Quadrigarius," 391. See, e.g., Val. Max. 5.7.ext. 1; 6.8.3 (though Valerius confuses sources more often than most, especially when commenting on an earlier period); Tac. *Ann.* 2.73, 88; 4.57; 13.20. Lendon, "Historiography," 54, notes writers struggling over which sources to prefer (Livy 10.9.10–12; cf. Tac. *Ann.* 14.2; *Hist.* 3.28).

35. E.g., Philost. *Vit. soph.* 2.4.570; in a different genre, cf. Ovid *Fasti* 6.1–2, 97–100.

"we" in Acts 16:10–28:16), probably in part because he discusses events of a recent generation on which sources have not yet diverged greatly.[36] A historian might also more generally refer readers interested in more detail to "other historians" (e.g., Vell. Paterc. 2.48.5), not unlike Luke's oblique reference to other authors in Luke 1:1. The Gospel writers' reticence to name sources might also follow some Jewish conventions on this point; in some early Jewish works we can identify the sources only because they are extant.[37] The more popular audience that the Gospel writers anticipated may be a more important factor in their failure to name sources; popular works of various genres were less likely to cite sources, even when they clearly depended on them. Earlier scholarly exaggerations of the contrasts between elite and popular literature aside,[38] the Gospels do not reflect an elite audience (though Luke's audience appears socially higher than the others').

Including material missing in earlier extant sources does not always betray fabrication. A writer providing information missing in some earlier historians sometimes was drawing from sources unavailable to the other historians, whether the sources were written, oral, or both.[39] Moreover, even writers who preserved their sources redacted them, even in the case of sacred cultural texts[40] and philosophic works.[41] Some scholars argue that such changes were more common at the written than at the oral level,[42] perhaps because the former reflected literary urban culture and the latter more traditional society.

Polybius complains that Timaeus failed to make appropriate use of earlier historians' works although living in Athens provided him access to them (Polyb. 12.25d.1);[43] this complaint reinforces the picture that many sources were available and that good historians were expected to consult them when possible. For Polybius, real history requires a study of documents, although this must take a third place behind visiting the locations in question and reviewing their historical context (12.25e.1, 25i.2).

We should not underestimate the research sources available to ancient writers, especially if (as in Luke 1:1) they mention the existence of such works. Clearly, an abundance of contemporary sources existed then that are no longer extant (cf. the many contemporary histories of Nero noted in Jos. *Ant.* 20.154);[44] for example, Pliny the Elder, explaining that he could not survey everything (*N.H.* pref. 18), notes that he surveyed about two thousand volumes (though using especially a hundred) and

36. Cf., e.g., Tacitus, who, naturally, does not need to cite many sources on his father-in-law, Agricola.

37. E.g., 1 Esdras blends Chronicles, Ezra, and Nehemiah with some midrash. Josephus does not state most of his extrabiblical sources (Nicolaus of Damascus being an important exception); even Livy can mention that there are many while citing only one (Livy 42.11.1).

38. Schmidt, "Stellung"; Kümmel, *Introduction*, 37; see the brief discussion in Keener, *Matthew*, 17. "High" literature influenced "low" literature, creating an overlap of style (Burridge, *Gospels*, 11, 153; Aune, *Environment*, 12, 63; Downing, "Relevance").

39. E.g., Dion. Hal. *Ant. rom.* 1.6.1, 3; sometimes earlier oral traditions probably also surface later in rabbinic literature (see, e.g., Keener, *John*, 189–90). Oral and written traditions sometimes overlapped (Jeremias in Hennecke, *Apocrypha*, 1:95). Even the vast majority of ancient histories (on which extant ancient historians could have also depended) have perished (cf. Laistner, *Historians*, 5–6; Brown, *Historians*, 107).

40. E.g., Cic. *Nat. d.* 3.16.42 (concerning Hom. *Od.* 11.600ff.; see esp. H. Rackham in *Cicero*, LCL, 19:324–25 n. *a*); Diog. Laert. 1.48 (Solon redacting Hom. *Il.* 2.557).

41. Possibly Hierocles in Stobaeus; Malherbe, *Exhortation*, 85. Jewish scribes, however, rarely practiced redaction criticism on Scripture (despite an occasional fourth-century Palestinian Amora; cf. *Lev. Rab.* 6:6; 15:2).

42. Gundry, "Genre," 102; Witherington, *Christology of Jesus*, 22; contrast the older approach of Dibelius, *Tradition*, 3.

43. For comment on this passage, see also Byrskog, *History*, 117. For Polybius's use of documents, see Rhodes, "Documents," 64–65.

44. Note that Josephus published the *Antiquities* perhaps just twenty-seven years after Nero's death.

supplemented them with other data (pref. 17).[45] Few of his sources remain extant, but we can appreciate Pliny's preservation of much of the content.

Tacitus omits reporting most of Seneca's dying words, recorded by the latter's secretaries, because in Tacitus's day they remained too well-known (*Ann.* 15.63). He elsewhere cites "historians of that era" (*Ann.* 5.9) as sources for events a century before his time.[46] He normally follows annals and earlier histories (sometimes specified only when they became subjects of history, e.g., *Ann.* 4.34–35), but also consulted personal memoirs from perhaps half a century earlier (*Ann.* 4.53).[47] Suetonius's sources include notes that he took from official "libraries and archives," and while he proved less critically discerning about his various sources than Plutarch, modern historians appreciate "his hesitation to impose his own judgments" on his material.[48] Suetonius apparently made some local inquiries for his work (*Vesp.* 1.4), and sometimes could establish his point by naming various earlier sources supporting it (*Jul.* 9.3).

One may compare sources already available to Tacitus, Suetonius, and Plutarch when writing about the short-lived Roman emperor Otho, who perished roughly half a century earlier.[49] One source that they sometimes shared might be the no-longer-extant work of Fabius Rusticus (cf. Tac. *Ann.* 13.20.2; 14.2; 15.61).[50] Plutarch consulted witnesses, including an officer who described to him what he saw while Plutarch was touring the site with him (Plut. *Otho* 14.1).[51] One of Suetonius's sources concerning Otho is explicit: his own father Suetonius Laetus was a tribune serving under Otho, and shared with him information about Otho's character and actions (*Otho* 10.1).[52] By ancient standards, these writers, like Luke, were writing a fairly brief time after the events, within living memory of eyewitnesses. Indeed, on the majority view of the dating of Acts, Luke writes closer to most of his events than these historians wrote to the time of Otho.

b. Luke's Prologue in the Quest for Sources

Luke's original prologue (Luke 1:1–4) probably introduces the entire two-volume work,[53] although not necessarily every statement covers every section of his work equally. (This commentary investigates some aspects of his prologue in further detail at Acts 1:1.) At least for his Gospel, Luke claims the availability of many[54] written documents covering the same ground he covers (Luke 1:1). Some of these may have constituted sources for him to investigate;[55] certainly, they were not all written at once,

45. Similarly, Dio Cassius had to defend his omission of some material by explaining that he had in fact read almost everything but did not judge it all suitable for inclusion (1.1.1–2).

46. He often mentions both the verdict of "the majority" of historians from the earlier era noted and dissenters from that consensus (e.g., *Ann.* 4.57). Various historians could also refer readers more generally to "other historians" (e.g., Vell. Paterc. 2.48.5; cf. Luke 1:1).

47. For Tacitus using sources (and fairly critically), see Laistner, *Historians*, 121; for historians' use of documents (legal documents, inscriptions, and the like), see Rhodes, "Documents" (though they did not always cite them; Laistner, *Historians*, 51).

48. Kennedy, "Source Criticism," 141.

49. See discussion in Keener, "Otho."

50. Cf. Martin, "Tacitus," 1470.

51. In this case Plutarch confesses that he does not know why the scene was as his witness described it (bodies gathered and piled up at a temple; *Otho* 14.2). Plutarch also visited Otho's tomb at Brixillum (Plutarch *Otho* 18.1). For Plutarch's range of sources, see Rhodes, "Documents," 65–66.

52. Not to be confused with Suetonius Paulinus, a prominent general of the time.

53. The majority view (so Fitzmyer, *Acts*, 59).

54. Fuller, "Classics," 182, notes G. Kennedy's observation that the plural (rather than the dual) requires minimally three writers and, grammatically, each of these writers produced his own narration.

55. Aune, *Environment*, 121, doubts the certainty of this premise, given the conventionality of the statement; but other historians who used this convention did have sources (even if "many" could be hyperbolic)—i.e.,

and those he mentioned wrote before him, although we cannot say how early the first narratives were.[56] Did Luke more frequently find such sources trustworthy or suspect?

Ancient historians often cited inadequacies in earlier writers as reasons for writing,[57] although some explicitly disclaimed such reasons.[58] Some rhetorical critics also offered this claim of unique superiority for select historians before their time.[59] Many scholars think that Luke thus finds fault with the work of his predecessors; ἐπιχειρέω appears elsewhere in Acts for futile or mistaken efforts (Acts 9:29; 19:13), and an adjective cognate to ἀσφάλεια in Luke 1:4 addresses distinguishing truth among "competing claims" (Acts 21:34; 22:30; 25:26).[60]

Luke's language, however, is far less harsh than that of writers who genuinely criticized their predecessors, and it certainly need not imply that he is claiming that they lacked eyewitness sources that he has.[61] Some ancient writers noted that they simply had a fresh perspective to add to the work of their predecessors.[62] Another writer could claim to prefer even his predecessors' style to his own but to regard his own selectivity as an improvement,[63] or could note that he has nothing new to add in terms of information but offers it in a different way.[64]

Luke departs from the work of his predecessors not primarily in terms of accuracy of information but instead in terms of rhetorical superiority:[65] he promises to write καθεξῆς, that is, with the proper sequencing of events in terms of cause and effect, necessary to an accurate account. Smaller accounts within the larger one (e.g., 1:21–22; 26:4–5) and historical retrospectives in speeches serve to reinforce this purpose.[66] The term need not specify chronological order but refers rather to logical and persuasive order;[67] for a history, however, logical order would include as much chronology as

the convention is not a fiction. Hellenistic prefaces often mentioned predecessors (90); for the mention of sources in prefaces, see Alexander, *Preface*, 32–34; mention of many sources can also occur after concluding a discussion (as in Diog. Laert. 4.1).

56. Kennedy, "Source Criticism," 134–35, suggests as early as 45 C.E. on the basis of Euseb. *H.E.* 2.14–15, but Eusebius's tradition here seems questionable. More plausibly, Theissen, *Gospels*, 203–34, esp. 220–21, 230–32, dates Q (though not necessarily a narrative, it might fit Luke's term) in the 40s, though this is uncertain. Certainly, we cannot rule out even some early Palestinian written sources, given evidence for sufficient literacy there (Millard, *Reading and Writing*, esp. summary in 227–29); scribes (cf. 168, 176) could also be paid to take dictation. Others give lower estimates of literacy, but none exclude it altogether.

57. E.g., Jos. *War* 1.1–2, 7; *Ant.* 20.154–57 (cf. 20.262); Wardle, *Valerius Maximus*, 67, cites Livy pref. 2; Sall. *Hist.* frgs. 3, 7; Tac. *Hist.* 1.1.2–3; *Ann.* 1.1.2 (comparing also Hecataeus frg. 1; Cato E. *Origins* frg. 77; Asinius Pollio frg. 4). Outside history, see, e.g., Longin. *Subl.* 1.1.

58. E.g., Val. Max. 1.pref. Only after praising his predecessors does Quintilian note that he will differ from them on some points (*Inst.* 3.1.22). Vell. Paterc. 2.53.4 criticizes predecessors for being five years off on Pompey's age, not to criticize them, he claims, but because he wants to forestall criticism of himself erring on this minor detail.

59. E.g., Dion. Hal. *Thuc.* 5.

60. Mason, "Chief Priests," 127, following Sterling, *Historiography*, 343–45; Parsons, *Luke*, 47.

61. Robbins, "Claims of Prologues," 73–75, 83, arguing that Luke instead intends to provide a continuous account "from the beginning to Rome." Aune, *Dictionary of Rhetoric*, 371, also doubts that Luke criticizes his predecessors' accuracy.

62. Xen. *Apol.* 1–2 (though citing, for this new emphasis, a specific informant, *Apol.* 2).

63. Aul. Gel. pref. 10 (preferring their style), 11–12 (preferring his selectivity). Cf. also this explanation (of greater selectivity) in 2 Macc 2:24–25 (conciseness was a narrative virtue, Theon *Progymn.* 5.39–40).

64. Nicolaus *Progymn.* 1.pref. 1.

65. One could refute sources on the basis of rhetorical criteria (e.g., Theon *Progymn.* 3.241–44) and claim superiority in arrangement over one's predecessors (Artem. *Oneir.* 3.pref.).

66. Moessner, "Poetics," 97–112.

67. Danker, *New Age*, 4 (comparing Ovid *Metam.* 7.520); Tannehill, *Luke*, 9–10; Penner, *Praise*, 220; Parsons, "*Progymnasmata*," 52 (noting arrangement for clarity in Theon *Progymn.* 87.13; Quint. *Inst.* 4.2.83; but also acknowledging preference for exact sequence in *Rhet. Alex.* 30.28–31; *Rhet. Her.* 1.9.15, and Theon's disapproval of accidental confusion of sequence in *Progymn.* 80.26–29). Certainly, historical prefaces were supposed to promise that they would be easy to follow (Lucian *Hist.* 53).

possible. Because Luke's sources, whose sequence he usually follows meticulously in his Gospel, control his arrangement there but are probably not entirely chronological, Luke's purposeful sequencing of a continuous narrative is probably more effective chronologically in Acts.[68] In contrast to some other genres,[69] history should be written sequentially (Pliny *Ep.* 1.1.1),[70] though with the flexibility to allow for completing narratives begun at different times (cf. the problem in Acts 11:30; 12:25).

Other elements of Luke's prologue may point to either rhetorical or factual excellence. Balch argues that some historians (including Polybius, Dionysius of Halicarnassus, and, in his view, Luke) felt that their readers would be dissatisfied with an epitome containing almost exclusively deeds (e.g., 2 Maccabees or Mark);[71] they wanted to hear the reason for events, and so the historians provided narratives more ἀκριβῶς, fully, hence including speeches that explained events.[72] He contends that ἀκριβῶς in Luke 1:3 modifies γράψαι and means to write fully rather than to follow accurately.[73]

Although this reading of 1:3 is possible (it might better fit the contrast with earlier writers in 1:1–2, and it may accurately depict the situation with speeches [see below]), Luke's own use of ἀκριβῶς elsewhere could suggest accuracy instead of, or *in addition to*, completeness; accuracy was also part of the term's nuance (e.g., Diod. Sic. 1.4.4; 1.6.2). In most Lukan texts, one could interpret the term either way (Acts 18:26; 22:3; 23:15, 20; 24:22; 26:5), but Acts 18:25 seems to imply primarily "accuracy" (possibly implying the same for 18:26, but 18:26 may play on the other nuance of the term), and the texts about Pharisaic scrupulousness (22:3; 26:5; cf. 18:25–26) probably specify "accuracy," in view of similar descriptions of Pharisaic learning in Josephus (*Ant.* 17.41; 19.332; *War* 1.110; 2.162; *Life* 191).[74] The phrase can suit an "exact" account elsewhere.[75]

68. Most of Acts is chronologically arranged, and the Gospel, with very few exceptions, follows the sequence of Mark and (probably) Q (on his sequential approach to putative sources, cf. also Morton and MacGregor, *Structure*, 27; Perry, *Sources*, 19–20).

69. Biography need not be chronological (see Görgemanns, "Biography"; Stanton, *Jesus*, 119–21; cf. even 4Q158; Aug. *Harm. G.* 21.51; for Mark, see Papias in Euseb. *H.E.* 3.39); cf., e.g., the accidental repetition in Plut. *Alex.* 37.4; 56.1. See the somewhat more detailed discussion in Keener, *John*, 12–13.

70. Thucyd. 2.1.1; 5.26.1 (although even most historians tended to follow events to their conclusion and not simply strict chronology; Dion. Hal. *Thuc.* 9; *Pomp.* 3). Cf. "from the beginning" (ἀπ᾽ ἀρχῆς) in Diod. Sic. 4.8.5 (on recounting Heracles's acts); John 15:27; for the beginning of the period in question, cf. *Test. Ab.* 15:14 A; 4:13 B. Cf. "handing down from the beginning" in Iambl. *V.P.* 1.1. Not only rhetoricians (e.g., Anderson, *Glossary*, 116; cf. Arius Did. *Epit.* 2.7.7, pp. 42–43.13) but philosophers (Mus. Ruf. 8, p. 62.19; Arius Did. *Epit.* 2.7.5b.2, pp. 14–15.15; 2.7.5k, p. 34.1; 2.7.5l, pp. 36–37.4; 2.7.11i, pp. 78–79.14–15; Diog. Laert. 3.103–4 [though cf. 2.130]; Lodge, *Ethics*, 65) and moralists (Cic. *Off.* 1.40.142; Plut. *Table* 1.2.4, *Mor.* 617B; Dio Chrys. *Or.* 33.48; cf. Mitchell, *Rhetoric of Reconciliation*, 174–75) preferred "order" (rhetorical, social, or moral) to disorder.

71. He sees Mark as possibly "the Lukan congregations' original Gospel" (Balch, "Ἀκριβῶς," 238), a reasonable surmise. Brief historical epitomes include that of Livy (see Gärtner and Eigler, "Epitome," 1154–55).

72. Balch, "Ἀκριβῶς," 229–39. Significantly, Dionysius of Halicarnassus (*Ant. rom.* 3.18.1) promises to seek "accuracy" (ἀκρίβεια) in recounting each incident; Penner, *Praise*, 163, associates this claim not merely with investigation but with "exactitude" in supplying a complete interpretive picture, including causes and effects.

73. Balch, "Ἀκριβῶς," 239, against Moessner.

74. For other groups with "accurate" interpretation, see, e.g., Jos. *Ant.* 12.49, 104; perhaps *Ant.* 1.14; *Ag. Ap.* 2.144, 149; for non-Jewish laws, *Ag. Ap.* 2.227, 257. Josephus's clearest parallel to Luke might be 2.287, but by itself this could be interpreted either way.

75. E.g., Alciph. *Court.* 13, frg. 6, ¶19; in a history, Diod. Sic. 1.6.2 (writing as accurately as possible given his subject's antiquity). Similarly, Herodian employs μετὰ πάσης ... ἀκριβείας to his careful research—though we do not consider Herodian particularly precise (Whittaker, "Introduction," xxxix–xl); Josephus, too, promises to treat everything with accuracy (ἀκριβῆ, *Ant.* 1.17; cf. 1.214), though we may think this an exaggeration; he also promises to narrate with accuracy in contrast to those whose histories are falsified (*War* 1.2, 6, 9, 22; *Life* 358, 360, 365, 412); cf. his favorable view of Thucydides (*Ag. Ap.* 1.18). Josephus surely concurs that Scripture speaks accurately (*Ant.* 1.82; cf. *War* 1.17; *Ag. Ap.* 1.29). That Luke is at least concerned for precision

Luke's rhetorical superiority to earlier Gospels of his day (though not to elite historians) is likely: as a comparison with our other extant Gospels may confirm, his Gospel is far closer to the general vein of extant Greco-Roman historiography. Nevertheless, his research and arrangement did not lead him to depart substantially from the *facts* of his predecessors; he saw his purpose as confirmatory (Luke 1:4). Their proximity in basic substance may reflect the relatively recent nature of the events they report.

c. Luke's Use of Sources

Luke has more information available than he recounts, and sometimes this information is already known to his ideal audience (see, e.g., Luke 1:4). Thus he sometimes recounts a matter as if his audience already knows it, when in fact he has not mentioned it (e.g., Acts 9:39; 17:6). The large majority of scholars hold that Luke used Mark in writing his Gospel, and most also hold that he shared a common source with Matthew;[76] some even suggest a common source or sources with John.[77] Some have also used Semitisms to suggest Semitic sources behind some of his work (esp. Luke 1–2), although these may simply display Luke's skill at writing "biblical" Greek.[78] Luke is well informed about the first-century c.e. history of Judea's rulers (e.g., Luke 3:1; Acts 23:24; 24:27; 25:13), including plausible events not recorded elsewhere (e.g., Luke 13:1).[79] This suggests that he found records or memories of Judean events available; neither he nor Josephus (who was not alive during the period reflected in the earlier accounts in his *War*) composed histories from thin air.[80]

Luke may avoid naming specific sources in part because he writes on a more popular level[81] than most extant works, which tend to reflect elite circles. Elite circles were more concerned about plagiarism,[82] though it seems to have been fairly common. Pliny the Elder notes that he begins his first volume by listing his sources—even though most of them had not done their predecessors the same favor (*N.H.* pref. 21).[83] "For

---

is suggested by his caution with estimates (e.g., Acts 25:6; "about" in 4:4; 5:7, 36; 10:3, 9; 13:18, 20; 16:25; 19:7, 34; 22:6; 27:27; Luke 3:23; 8:42 [vs. Mark 5:42]; 9:28 [cf. Mark 9:2]; 22:41, 59; 23:44; 24:13).

76. I have argued elsewhere for a high degree of reliability in the Synoptic tradition (Keener, *Matthew*, 16–36, esp. 24–32; idem, *John*, 29–34). I will not repeat that argument here specifically for Luke's Gospel, since some commentators on that Gospel (e.g., Fitzmyer, *Luke*; Marshall, *Luke*; Bock, *Luke*; Nolland, *Luke*) have already offered fuller arguments than I would have space for here.

77. For possible dependence of John and Luke on related oral traditions (but not John on Luke), see Myllykoski, "Luke and John," 115–56, esp. 152. Some of the proposed agreements between Acts and John (Cribbs, "Agreement") are unpersuasive (the prophet-like-Moses allusions, p. 55, are hardly limited to Luke and John), but parallels in the passion narratives may be significant. Boismard and Lamouille, *Actes*, 1:15, think that Luke and John share some common tradition from what Origen knew as "Peter's memoirs." Many scholars believe that the Fourth Gospel preserves reliable tradition at points, especially in its narratives (see summary in Keener, *John*, 40–47).

78. See this commentary's introduction to Acts 1, pp. 642–45.

79. Luke writes as if the event is known; he also lacks reason to fabricate it (especially given the allusion's brevity). Cf. also his allusion to the "assassins" in Acts 21:38, though it is not quite clear that even the speaker in the story world has all of the details straight. The details were better understood in hindsight (as with Josephus), but Luke's report (or source) may be either slightly confused or based on the officer's inaccurate assessment at the time of the occasion depicted, before hindsight was available.

80. Many scholars concur that Luke had good sources (e.g., Riesner, "Zuverlässigkeit," 39–40).

81. One must expect a fairly popular level if his audience for Acts is the same as that for the Gospel (cf. Acts 1:1), since biographies tended to appeal at a lower level than histories (Corn. Nep. 16 [Pelopidas], 1.1)—though biographies, too, could list sources, especially when their subjects were not recent.

82. Genuine plagiarism was despised but not illegal (Schmitzer, "Copyright," 778). At the least, it seemed courteous to mention predecessors (e.g., Vitruv. *Arch.* 7.pref. 10–17), although not everyone did so. Cf. discussion of the sense in Martial in Mira Seo, "Plagiarism."

83. Pliny the Elder's entire first volume of the *Natural History* consists of an extensive table of contents, with a bibliography of sources for each point. At least his nephew became sensitive to the use of bibliographies; Pliny *Ep.* 3.5.1–6 provides a friend a bibliography of Pliny the Elder's works in chronological order. Indeed,

you must know," he warns, "that when collating authorities I have found that the most professedly reliable and modern writers have copied the old authors word for word, without acknowledgement" (pref. 22); how petty, he charges, to prefer theft to repaying one's loan (pref. 23). While Luke does not identify his sources, however, both Luke 1:1 and the Gospel's internal evidence make clear that he used sources.[84] If Luke has reworked them, often adapting their wording and making them his own, most ancient circles would not count this as "plagiarism."[85]

But if Luke avoids naming sources for literary reasons, his ethical justification may be simply that he, like his predecessors, depends on recent and communal memory ("accomplished among *us*," Luke 1:1). The earliest Christian biographers and historians were not bound to written works the way that historians and biographers narrating the distant past were. (Thus, for example, as we have mentioned, Tacitus does not need to cite sources in his biography of his father-in-law, Agricola, the way Plutarch does for Alexander of Macedon.)[86] The Gospel reflects the shared, recent memory of the community, of things "accomplished among us" (1:1), passed down orally from many leaders "to us" (1:2), and already widely known (1:4).

Luke does use written sources (cf. 1:1) in his Gospel, surely Mark and likely Q (and very possibly others as well), but these sources themselves depended on the shared tradition of the community of which they had become an important part. The matter appears even more clear-cut in Acts: the sources here are probably entirely oral (reports heard and interviews) or based on firsthand acquaintance (see the fuller discussion on authorship and esp. comment at Acts 16:10), which made for history writing in the best of the Hellenistic historiographic tradition.

Even in elite circles, if a writer alluded to well-known works that the hearers might recognize, the thought was not plagiarism but literary sophistication;[87] if he could assume his audience's knowledge, he did not need to state the source of his quotes. Luke's audience knew some gospel tradition, which seems to have been "common property" of the early churches (cf. Luke 1:4). If Luke's preferred written sources, supplemented with oral ones (cf. 1:2–3), were recognizable and common property, we might also not expect him to feel the need to identify them.[88] (Naming sources is not in itself a question of genre, since elite mythographers also can name their sources.[89]

despite adaptations, ancient historians depended heavily on their predecessors' works for content about the past (see Marincola, "Universal History," 178–79, citing esp. Bosworth, "Historians and sources").

84. Despite some scholarly dissent (e.g., Bruggen, *Narratives*, 66), most today recognize Luke 1:1–4 as a preface for both volumes (see Fitzmyer, *Acts*, 59; cf. discussion in Wolter, "Proömien"), though we may doubt that others had yet written apostolic acts. Few have been persuaded by those who argue for free composition in the Gospel (on the basis of a very limited number of sources; e.g., Drury, *Design*, passim). Since the concern about borrowing words was directed at the theft of another's rhetorical labors, borrowing Mark's more common wording probably would have caused more offense for rhetorical weakness than for plagiarism (Luke often upgrades it).

85. Certainly, Livy reworked much of earlier historians, and Pliny E. *N.H.* did the same. Biographers had a limited number of sources they could use; they tended to name sources most when they conflicted. Sometimes storytellers reworked earlier, probably familiar stories (e.g., the story in Lucian's *Lucius* is similar to Apuleius's *Metamorphoses* [Macleod, "Introduction to *Lucius*," 47, 50, follows Photius in thinking that Lucian probably followed the lost work of Lucius, also adapted by Apuleius]; Alciphron's *Letters of Courtesans* might reflect familiarity with Lucian's *Dialogues of Courtesans*). More formal works tended, however, to identify their sources.

86. Likewise, though lamenting that historians often neglect current personages (2.92.5), Velleius Paterculus eschews detail on the most recent sixteen years as superfluous for his readers (2.126.1).

87. Sen. E. *Suas.* 3.7. Lucian expected his audience to recognize the literary works he satirized (*True Story* 1.2).

88. This practice may have been more common for Jewish religious texts in other genres; cf., e.g., 2 Peter's use of Jude, or the borrowing in *Sib. Or.* 2.56–148 from Ps.-Phocylides.

89. E.g., Apollod. *Bib.* 1.4.3; 1.5.2; 1.9.15, 19; 2.3.1; 2.5.11. With a historical person, Philostratus (*Vit. Apoll.* 1.2) claims that he gathered information from cities (i.e., local, century-old traditions), from others' accounts and from his letters, and also (1.3) from Damis's memoirs.

The practice of naming sources when it was relevant to do so simply illustrates that prose writers about the past typically built on what preceded them instead of freely inventing in the way dramatists or novelists far more often did.)

Scholars devote volumes to the "Synoptic Problem" and to how (in the most common view) Luke has used Mark and the material he shares with Matthew (commonly called Q). I have entered this fray elsewhere[90] and here simply summarize my agreement (to a reasonable degree of probability) with the general consensus of scholarship on this question. I have also argued that, as with other ancient Mediterranean literature reporting on past events (e.g., Paus. 1.23.2), we should allow for a considerable range of other sources, written and especially (for events this recent) oral, which are no longer extant.[91]

If one works through the Lukan texts from a synopsis of the Gospels, one will note both that he exercised considerable freedom in adaptation (such as the construction of symposium scenes) and that much of the Gospel is tightly bound to its sources in depicting events, sayings, and even many of the details of these events. It seems reasonable to assume that if Luke, in most cases,[92] follows his sources closely where we can test him, he follows a similar approach with his sources that are no longer extant.

d. Sources in Acts

That Luke used sources in Acts, as in the Gospel, is likely. The general uniformity of style in Acts no more counts against the use of sources there than the stylistic similarities between Acts and the Third Gospel count against sources in the latter.[93] Likewise, Luke's usually fairly consistent style cannot count against his use of sources any more than Josephus's rewriting biblical narratives in his own style should lead us to think that he did not follow biblical accounts. Historians typically rewrote sources in their own style.[94]

Most often, however, Luke's sources for Acts were probably oral reports.[95] If Luke's sources were mostly oral (except for the travel journal in the "we" sections), we should expect even less stylistic indication of sources than in Josephus. Whereas many had

90. See Keener, *Matthew*, 8–10; idem, *John*, 31; for others, see further, e.g., Tuckett, *History*, 34–39; Davies and Allison, *Matthew*, 1:73–74.

91. See further my discussion in Keener, *Matthew*, 27–31; and idem, *John*, 23, 43. More often than in Matthew (who follows Mark and Q more frequently), some sections of special L material might reflect independent written sources, but Luke probably often supplements with oral tradition. The countless allusions to other stories in Homer (e.g., the voyage of the Argonauts in *Od.* 12.69–72) lent themselves to later development, but they clearly refer to fuller stories that Homer's works did not record and that we have in forms developed from such traditions. In the case of the Gospels, the writers themselves assume knowledge of traditions about Jesus not recorded in their Gospels (e.g., Acts 20:35; John 20:30).

92. In some others, such as Luke 19:12–27 if it is really a parallel to Matt 25:14–30 (unclear, since Jesus himself, like many sages, may have employed multiple versions of the same story line on different occasions), the extreme divergence may stem from pre-Lukan tradition rather than from radically different uses of Q (in view of much closer wording elsewhere). On Luke's relatively minimal editing of Mark, see, e.g., Ramsay, *Luke the Physician*, 47; Marshall, *Luke*, passim; Bock, *Luke*, 9–14.

93. With Witherington, "Editing," 324–25. For Luke's valuable early sources and his dependence on them, see Riesner, "Zuverlässigkeit."

94. Johnson, "Luke-Acts," 406, cites here Jos. *Ag. Ap.* 54. Some Josephus scholars now focus on the intratextual dynamics in Josephus, doubting supposed tensions in the text as a mark of sources (Mason, "Contradiction"; though others still seek to identify different sources on the basis of style, e.g., Bellemore, "Josephus, Pompey, and Jews").

95. With, e.g., Knox, *Acts*, 16–39 (esp. 39), allowing only written documents possibly for Acts 1–5 (minus the speeches) and 9:32–10:48; cf. Byrskog, "History," 259–79; the variety of sources in Bottini and Casalini, "Informazione." That Luke knew Paul's letters is possible, but that he used them (given some tensions between the sources and frequent omissions) is unlikely (see ch. 7 below).

written accounts of Jesus (Luke 1:1; of which pre-Lukan sources at least Mark remains extant today), Luke's second volume was probably breaking new ground that apparently failed to be understood even in the mid-second century.[96] Because we lack the sort of overlapping documents Matthew and Mark provide for the Gospel, we also have no hard evidence for reconstructing sources in Acts, and this reduces most arguments about them to speculation. Trying to reconstruct the sources of Acts is akin to trying to reconstruct Mark if all that we had available was Luke.[97] Few source-critical reconstructions agree,[98] and whatever sources Luke may have had he rewrites in his own style.[99] Thus most scholars today are content to admit that Luke has sources in Acts but that we cannot reconstruct them.[100] As Beverly Gaventa reminds us, "Whatever Luke's sources may have been, they are no longer available."[101]

Despite our inability to reconstruct them, Luke's use of oral sources remains probable (see the discussion below). In this case, what should we expect of such oral sources? Many studies of human memory approach memory as reconstruction more than copy, with a recollection of components rather than of wholes.[102] Such reconstruction has constraints; the reconstruction approach to memory explains inaccuracies in eyewitness reports, but constraints explain "the relative accuracy and the broad element of stability."[103] Interpretive elements color both one's initial experience and the recollections; although these do not necessarily distort the content, the result is "more like a painting than a photograph."[104] Among elements of experience most apt to support

96. On the second-century church's reception of Acts, see, e.g., Barrett, *Acts*, 48.

97. With C. Williams, *Acts*, 8.

98. For such reconstructions, see, e.g., Pesch, *Apostelgeschichte*, 1:45–51; Fitzmyer, *Acts*, 80–89; Boismard and Lamouille, *Actes*, 1:4. For some source-critical works before 1965, see Mattill and Mattill, *Bibliography*, 157–65, §§157–65; before 1990, see T. Smith, "Sources"; through the early 1990s, see Green and McKeever, *Historiography*, 109–12; in greater detail (though earlier), see Dupont, *Sources*, on the single-source hypothesis (17–32), the parallel-source hypothesis (33–50), complementary sources (51–61), and the Antioch source (62–72). Older scholars cited doublets (e.g., Klausner, *Jesus to Paul*, 215), but scholars now usually see this as deliberate literary parallels (see discussion of unity below). Pervo, *Dating Acts*, wants to include Mark (35–47) and Paul's letters (51–147) as sources of literary motifs and information.

99. With, e.g., Dibelius, *Studies in Acts*, 201; Jervell, "Future," 119; idem, *Unknown Paul*, 69; idem, *Apostelgeschichte*, 67; Fitzmyer, *Acts*, 80–89. Neil, *Acts*, 24, thinks that what appear to be sources may simply represent Luke's own editing and revision over time. Cadbury, Foakes-Jackson, and Lake, "Writing History," 7–15, argue that Luke reworks his sources (at least in the Gospel) far less than one would expect of a Greek writer (less even than Josephus) but far more than older Jewish sources, e.g., the Chronicler.

100. E.g., Dupont, *Sources*, 166; Jervell, *Unknown Paul*, 69; Bruce, *Commentary*, 29; Arrington, *Acts*, xliii; Johnson, *Acts*, 3–5; idem, "Luke-Acts," 406; Marshall, *Acts*, 37–39; Witherington, *Acts*, 165–73; Kea, "Source Theories"; Strelan, *Artemis*, 21; Bock, *Acts*, 20; Shillington, *Introduction*, 17; with a few concessions, Knox, *Acts*, 16–39; cf. Brodie, "Imitation of Texts," 37.

101. Gaventa, *Acts*, 178 (cf. also 119).

102. Bauckham, *Eyewitnesses*, 325–26.

103. Ibid., 327; on variations, cf. Allison, *Jesus*, 1–13, 24, 28–30, 374, 455; Kirk, "Memory," 166–72. In contrast to Pervo, *Dating Acts*, 352, who dismisses Witherington's approach "as fantastic," doubting any correspondence with eyewitness-type narratives in Acts, Bauckham's approach to gospel narratives (*Eyewitnesses*, 472–508) may prove more helpful (some of the particular questions raised in Tuckett, "Review," including regarding names corresponding to sources, are legitimate, but Bauckham's overall case for eyewitness tradition should move discussion in a direction more sensitive to ancient sources). Neil (*Acts*, 22–23) is among those who have thought that Acts sounds like "a vivid piece of first-hand reporting," with greater detail and realism in the "we" parts.

104. Bauckham, *Eyewitnesses*, 330. Gist may be accurate even where details are not (333–34); on interpretive structuring, see also 335–36. Memory studies show that (*pace* older form critics) "forms" or narrative structures precede even an eyewitness's first telling (350–51). Redman, "Eyewitnesses," warns that eyewitnesses' memories may lapse over time; Bauckham's model does, however, allow for memory's imperfection. Professors who teach courses multiple times recognize that frequent retelling of material, as would have been expected of Jesus's eyewitnesses, provides a firmer grasp on more of the material. For limits on memory, see Allison, *Jesus*, 1–10, 30; for significant recall or gist, 8–9n46, 11–13, 24, 28–29, 374, 455.

the preservation of the sorts of memories common among Luke's likely informants are distinctive and consequential events[105] and frequent retelling.[106] Narrative structures used as a grid to interpret these components of memory may be borrowed from narrative structures in the larger culture.[107] (Chapter 8 below addresses memory more fully.)

The kinds of oral reports that Luke might have had available (beyond the "we" narratives, where, I argue, despite the skepticism of many, the evidence is far more convincing than not that Luke was present; see the much fuller discussion at Acts 16:10) are not hard to conjecture. If the author spent months traveling with Paul, his memory of Paul's occasional anecdotes would provide a sufficient oral source for many of the reports in Acts (Acts 9:1–30; 11:25–30; 13–20);[108] Philip (whom Luke could have interviewed or listened to at 21:8–10) could provide material about the Hellenists (Acts 6–8) and about ministry in Caesarea (8:40; 10:1–48); Jerusalem sources would cover most of the rest of the book, and Luke apparently had up to two years for any interviews with Judeans in Judea, though probably only a minimum of that in Jerusalem proper (see 21:15; 24:27; 27:1).[109] If the author was, as many scholars think, a Gentile[110] (see the discussion on authorship in ch. 11), Luke's *direct* access to Jerusalem sources may have been somewhat limited (cf. 21:18), and Galilean sources would have proved even less available;[111] but he would likely have had abundant access to accounts of those who had settled in Caesarea (cf. 21:8) and perhaps some familiarity with the coastal cities (cf. 8:40; 9:32–43). Luke had less concrete material for the earlier chapters and hence fleshed them out "with summaries, speeches, and vivid descriptions."[112] Once his narrative reaches Acts 13, Luke appears to possess more "substantial and reliable" data, an observation consistent with the view that Paul could have been an oral source.[113] The reports seem most complete in the "we" narratives, an observation consistent with the view that the author may have been present on the occasions mentioned.[114]

How much would Luke have adapted his sources? Certainly Luke, like other Greco-Roman writers, feels free to vary details, since he does so even when retelling

105. Bauckham, *Eyewitnesses*, 331–32.

106. Ibid., 334–35. Bauckham (341–46) applies these and other criteria to memories about Jesus among his disciples.

107. Ibid., 336–37.

108. For an example of Pauline corroboration of basic outlines of Luke's story (albeit from a clearly independent perspective), see comment on Acts 9:23–30.

109. Some others also suggest such oral sources, e.g., Knox, *Acts*, 39; C. Williams, *Acts*, 11–12; Blaiklock, *Acts*, 17–18; Chance, *Acts*, 6. Witherington, *Acts*, 166, suggests that Luke's interest in lodgings may be to point to the early Christian network for transmitting the traditions; he mentions (168) Luke's two years in the Levant, and he argues (169) for use of blocks of sources (such as above but also including Peter, Acts 1–5; 9:32–12:23) as in the Gospel; Luke added summaries but retained the existing blocks.

110. Especially if he accompanied Paul on the collection mission. One could object that some of Paul's companions, such as Timothy (Acts 20:4), were legally Jewish (16:1–3), so that the point of the representatives is that they hailed from the Diaspora, not that they were Gentiles; but then, why not have taken more Diaspora Jewish believers, who would have been more welcome? Note also Rom 15:27.

111. Rural Jewish Galilee was probably not a friendly place for a foreign Greek-speaking Gentile (see ch. 11, sect. 2.a, below) to go exploring by himself ca. 60 c.e. Biblically informed, Luke might have passed for merely a hellenophone Diaspora Jew, but probably would not have ventured into rural Galilee on his own even if he already planned his book.

112. Johnson, *Acts*, 4. This was appropriate rhetorical practice for expanding stories (see, e.g., Theon *Progymn.* 4.37–42, 80–82; Longin. *Subl.* 11.1; cf. Men. Rhet. 2.3, 379.2–4; Talbert, *John*, 64, citing Arist. *Poet.* 17.6–11), and it could be performed without fabricating material (Theon *Progymn.* 3.224–40 [cf. 2.115–23]). Johnson, *Acts*, thinks that even if the Sanhedrin persecuted the apostles (1 Thess 2:14–15), Luke may have created the scenes of the hearings (Acts 4–5); though this contention is possible, we lack sufficient historical evidence to prove or disprove it.

113. See Johnson, *Acts*, 4.

114. See here also Riesner, *Early Period*, 413; Johnson, *Acts*, 4.

the same event in his finished narrative work, yet in such cases he preserves the basic core of the account.[115] In the Gospel he preserves the basic substance of his sources where we can compare them.[116] Luke's editing of Mark is most often stylistic,[117] eliminating historical presents and less appropriate imperfects;[118] some scholars argue that he might be even more conservative with Q.[119] (Mark presumably employed historical presents for vividness,[120] but some other writers employed them only sparingly,[121] and some ancient critics complained of inconsistency in verb tenses.)[122] Luke also edits to adapt details of the tradition for his Diaspora audience; for example, in a parable he transforms a Palestinian wadi into a river, and in a narrative he transforms men digging through a thatched Palestinian roof into men removing roof tiles, as in the northern Mediterranean region.[123] Luke's practice on this point fits what we expect for rhetorical adaptation of narratives (outlined, e.g., in Aelius Theon's *Progymnasmata*).

Martin Dibelius observes that Luke was "more bound by his material in the Gospel," so that there he acted as editor but in Acts "as an author."[124] This view underestimates Luke's authorial role in shaping his Gospel but may nevertheless reflect a genuine difference between the two works. Because no predecessors had (so far as we know) established a pattern for a Christian work such as Acts, Luke may have exercised somewhat greater freedom in selecting and retelling his oral sources than he could have done in a Gospel. (This observation warns us against arguing from silence that Luke, in contrast to other ancient historians, must have invented material wherever we cannot reconstruct his sources.)

At the same time, where we can test him, Luke does not indulge this freedom recklessly; even the three fairly free retellings of Paul's conversion in Acts (9:1–18; 22:5–16, 21; 26:12–18) preserve the basic substance.[125] Luke remains a historian,

115. On variation in Luke's three accounts of Paul's conversion, see, e.g., Dunn, *Acts*, 117 (though the core does not change and the words of dialogue remain identical each time; cf. p. 121). See, perhaps more relevant, the recapitulation of Luke 24 in Acts 1:2–11 (see comment there), with changes even of Jesus's wording but the same substance (probably what he had available in his source or sources for this occasion).

116. See my argument in Keener, "Luke-Acts and Historical Jesus"; idem, *Historical Jesus*, 85–94.

117. Cf., e.g., Burkitt, "Use of Mark." Like Matthew, Luke often abbreviates Mark's pericopes, following the rhetorical virtue of conciseness (Parsons, "*Progymnasmata*," 54–55). Nevertheless, Frye, "Problems," 268–71, provides historical analogies for a later writer putting more sophisticated language into the vernacular.

118. Only one historic present remains from 151 in Mark, and Luke usually changes Mark's imperfects to aorists; Witherington, "Editing," 326, 328; Burridge, "Gospels and Acts," 526–27. On verb tenses in Acts more generally, see discussion in Victor, "Wechsel der Tempora."

119. Witherington, "Editing," 332–35. See Marshall, "Luke and 'Gospel.'" Sayings may have invited more verbal care than narratives.

120. See regularly in Caesar *C.W.*, e.g., 1.22, 25, 33, 41, 59; 2.21, 25, 26, 30 (while Caesar's narrative seems unadorned, however, he may employ sophisticated rhetorical strategies; see Kraus, "Account"); in other genres, heavy in the narrative of Virgil's *Aeneid* (Pinkster, "Present Tense"); cf. the grammatical shift in Philost. *Vit. Apoll.* 8.1–2. Osburn, "Historical Present," argues that Mark's use of the historical present resembles those in Xenophon, Plato, and the LXX.

121. E.g., Cic. *Quinct.* 4.14; 5.20. But the historical present is more common in classical and atticizing Greek (Aune, *Dictionary of Rhetoric*, 215 [s.v. "Historical present"]).

122. Dion. Hal. *2 Amm.* 12.

123. Blomberg, *Gospels*, 162 (citing the analogous practice in many modern translations). On oral as well as written sources in the gospel tradition, see, e.g., Baum, "Sources."

124. Dibelius, *Tradition*, 3; see also idem, *Studies in Acts*, 2–4, 185; note especially the difference between collections of Jesus's sayings in the Gospel and full speeches in Acts (184); cf. Pervo, *Acts*, 14. For the integrity of Luke-Acts as a literary whole, see esp. Tannehill, *Luke*; idem, *Acts*.

125. See, e.g., Witherington, "Editing," 335–44; this commentary's comments ad loc. Witherington concludes, "Luke appears to be rather more like a Thucydides or a Polybius, and the character of his work like what Lucian said *ought* to be the character of the work of one who seeks to do history writing, rather than say a Livy" (344). Few would quibble over insignificant detail (such as word order, e.g., Acts 15:20, 29; 21:25).

not a novelist or tragic poet. Indeed, the reports in Acts may be viewed as even closer to firsthand sources than those in the Gospel.[126]

Although it is not implausible that Luke's Palestinian informants for earlier parts of Acts might account for his Semitisms, such supposed linguistic evidence has not proved widely convincing. Some scholars have found Semitic sources in the early sections of Acts (often as far as Acts 15)[127] as in the Gospel (Luke 1–2).[128] Today scholars more often attribute this apparent characteristic to Luke's semitizing or archaizing[129] style in these passages rather than to discrete sources that he employed. Luke removes Semitisms from Q less often than he edits Mark's grammar; often he elsewhere adds Semitic constructions, perhaps by imitating the LXX.[130] Some think that the LXX reflected or generated a sort of "Jewish Greek."[131] Others find such constructions in Koine,[132] possibly reflecting the bilingual Eastern milieu in which Koine evolved.[133]

The currently dominant opinion is that many of these characteristics reflect Koine, even if knowledge of a Semitic language (or imitation of the LXX) may have generated some "peculiarities" in individual writers.[134] Where Luke's style is especially Semitic, however, it may reflect biblicizing idiom from the more literally rendered (hence semitizing) parts of the LXX, as distinct from his usual style elsewhere.[135] Luke's editing of Mark shows that he controls the style in his narrative; he replaces loanwords in Mark and "restyles Mark's simple paratactic sentence structure into participial and relative clauses that are more in keeping with the higher literary language."[136]

126. With Witherington, *Acts*, 165. As became obvious working on a writing project with my wife, I have full command of the material when recounting my own past, but needed to lean heavily on my wife's written source material and consult her regularly because the material was not part of my own memory. The "we" material is the most detailed material in Luke-Acts. Witherington also suggests that had Luke engaged in free composition, he would have provided more information on other apostles (170). In view of the parallels among figures, however, this argument is weaker than some others.

127. E.g., Payne, "Semitisms," 134–50; Torrey, *Composition*, 3ff.; Martin, "Evidence," 59. But see Wilcox, *Semitisms of Acts*; see further discussion in the introduction to Acts 1, pp. 642–45.

128. E.g., Farris, "Semitic Sources"; Laurentin, "Traces d'allusions"; Wenham, "Source Criticism," 145 (tentatively); Jung, *Language*. See further discussion in the introduction to Acts 1, pp. 642–45.

129. Preference for atticizing style (albeit more dominant in the second century) may have contributed to appreciation for archaizing styles, on which see concisely Aune, *Dictionary of Rhetoric*, 57 ("Archaism, literary and linguistic"); many scholars suggest that this affected Luke's adoption of "biblical" style at points (idem, *Environment*, 117; Witherington, *Acts*, 44; Alexander, *Context*, 250–52). Many note Luke's archaizing style, possibly modeled on the LXX (Plümacher, *Lukas*, 72–78; Rothschild, *Rhetoric of History*, 293). Epics employed archaizing style because they depicted the distant past (Nicolai, "Place of History," 15), or because they imitated earlier epics.

130. Knox, *Acts*, 5–8, suggesting that Luke seeks to evoke a sort of "holy language," perhaps echoing some traits already present in the gospel tradition; also Hanson, *Acts*, 52–53.

131. E.g., Alexander, "*Septuaginta*," 19–26 (noting that objections to defining it as a dialect would work equally against Atticism, p. 21); Horton, "Semitisms," 23; following Nigel Turner (see, e.g., Turner, "Thoughts," 46–47; cf. Nock, "Vocabulary," 138–39).

132. Horsley, *Documents*, 5:5–40 (not disputing Semitisms or other features of bilingualism but the existence of a distinct dialect, pp. 6, 40).

133. Languages can influence each other in contact situations (Gippert, "Language contact," 215), and more relevant here, interference becomes common when minority linguistic groups adopt the dominant language (Binder, "Language switching," 222).

134. Porter, "Greek of New Testament," 430. Some earlier interpreters, e.g., Jerome (*Commentary on Isaiah* 3, 6, 9, 10) and later Bede (*Comm. Acts* pref. [L. Martin, 4]) argued for Luke's greater education and eloquence in Greek than in Hebrew.

135. Jervell, "Future," 119, notes that 90 percent of Luke's language appears in the LXX (cf. idem, *Apostelgeschichte*, 74–75); on the pervasiveness of LXX language, see also, e.g., Mielcarek, "Język."

136. Koester, *Introduction*, 1:108. Even Matthew reduces Mark's parataxis (Burridge, "Gospels and Acts," 526), though not to this degree.

Luke is, as is widely acknowledged,[137] quite capable of varying his style, a skill appreciated in his rhetorically astute milieu. Such variations in style have led to questions about more than one work's authorship,[138] so it is not surprising that it would lead some scholars to suspect non-Lukan sources behind Luke's narrative. If Luke composed his own semitizing passages, he was also capable of more stylish, classical rhetoric, as in Luke 1:1–4.[139] Even the most skilled rhetoricians employed different styles in different settings;[140] adapting one's style to the setting in the narrative was regarded as rhetorically appropriate. It is Luke's careful modulation of his style that renders doubtful most source theories and his retention of a "we" from a source not written by him.[141] (See the discussion of the "we" material especially at Acts 16:10.) This conclusion does not rule out the possibility that informants shaped the use of some Semitisms early in Acts, but it reduces the likelihood of identifying them.

e. Investigation and Thorough Knowledge (Luke 1:3)

How reliable were Luke's sources? I have argued elsewhere, based on a broad range of parallels from Mediterranean antiquity, that the gospel traditions would have been preserved mostly reliably for the generation or two (usually estimated at ca. thirty-five to sixty-five years) necessary to reach our written Gospels.[142] This would have been even more the case with the more recent events toward the end of Acts (by our dating, at most twenty years), though these may have been of less thoroughgoing interest to the churches. It also appears that Luke undertook to examine extant sources for his gospel narrative firsthand in a manner no longer available to us, by interviewing some survivors closest to the events described.

For the Greeks, the very term used for research or investigation, ἱστορία (historia), left "no doubt possible about what was early considered the defining characteristic of the genre. . . . The method . . . consisted basically of the interrogation of witnesses and other informed parties" and then weaving their responses into a cohesive narrative.[143] Even if some writers failed to travel to all the places their narratives covered, travel was apparently a familiar component of historical research. Herodotus initiated this emphasis on research (Hdt. 1.1), traveling widely; Thucydides, who cross-examined his sources, assumed this approach as the standard (Thucyd. 1.22.2; 5.26).[144] Diodorus

137. E.g., Johnson, "Luke-Acts," 406; Kodell, *Luke*, 23; Pervo, *Acts*, 7–8.

138. See, e.g., the defense of Lucian's authorship of *Syrian Goddess*, despite its archaizing preference for an Ionic dialect as opposed to Lucian's usual Attic (A. M. Harmon, in *Lucian*, LCL, 4:337n); by contrast, some doubt Seneca's authorship of tragedies (Kohn, "Plays"). Whatever the merits of these particular cases, educated ancients were expected to be able to write in multiple styles (e.g., Pliny *Ep.* 3.13.4; 4.14.3; 9.29.1–2; cf. Dion. Hal. *Demosth.* 45–46; Rowe, "Style," 151, 155).

139. E.g., Aune, *Dictionary of Rhetoric*, 33, 347; Marshall, *Luke*, 39–41, 51; see also the rhetorical observations of Witherington, *Acts*, 45–46.

140. Cic. *Fam.* 9.21.1; Albucius in Suet. *Rhet.* 6.

141. It also leads some scholars to suspect that where the style remains unpolished (see Barrett, *Acts*, 524, for examples), it stems from the work's being left unfinished (cf. Harnack, *Acts*, 48). The same is likely true of Thucydides's work (Wade-Gery, "Thucydides," 1517–18), though the lack of speeches in the later part might also stem (1518) from an experiment, as Cratippus suggests.

142. Keener, *Matthew*, 16–36, esp. 24–32; idem, *John*, 29–34, 40–47; idem, *Historical Jesus*, 139–61; idem, "Otho." Accepting ancient reports concerning events of the prior one to two generations (up to a century) is not uncommon methodology (see, e.g., Downing, *Cynics*, 52).

143. Fornara, *Nature of History*, 47. See also Aune, *Environment*, 81–82, noting the interview of eyewitnesses (Polyb. 4.2.2); other sources when the writer traveled to the scenes in question (Hdt. 2.52; Polyb. 3.48.12; 4.38.11; 10.11.4); and reading accounts of eyewitnesses (Polyb. 28.4.8; 38.4.8). The practice weighs more than the terminology; Schepens, "History," 39–40, notes this concept of *historia* (see also 47), but on 41–42 notes modern disagreements about it.

144. Fornara, *Nature of History*, 47–48; Schepens, "History," 47–48. Thucydides notes that he procured (and investigated) reports of speeches from others who heard them (Thucyd. 1.22.1–2) and that he sometimes

Siculus claims to have visited the sites of his history in Asia and Europe, complaining that even some of the best historians err when they do not visit the sites in question (Diod. Sic. 1.4.1).[145] Appian (*Hist. rom.* pref. 12) claims to have checked out his reports by traveling to Carthage, Spain, Sicily, Macedonia, and elsewhere. Likewise, the later historian Herodian insists that he accepted nothing secondhand without tracking down all the facts (Hdn. 1.1.3). Although most of Philostratus's sophistic subjects were long deceased, he interviewed some who still lived, even on multiple occasions (*Vit. soph.* 2.23.606).[146] According to later tradition, even mythographers traveled from one city to the next gathering their various oral traditions (Philost. *Hrk.* 48.11).[147]

Polybius avers that investigation is "the *most* important part" of writing history (Polyb. 12.4c.3).[148] His proposed method for conducting investigation, given the limitations of space and time, was to interview people, critically evaluate reports, and accept the most reliable sources (12.4c.4–5).[149] He severely criticizes Timaeus for neglecting travel to the locations about which he writes (12.25e.1), complaining that written sources alone are not sufficient (12.25e.7) or even the most critical part of historical study (12.25i.2). Although interviews were impossible when one was dealing with the distant past,[150] writers preferred them when living witnesses remained available.[151] Greek historians often traveled to the locations of events and consulted those who were considered reliable oral sources.[152] Condemning writers who sought to make guesses sound plausible, Polybius notes that in his research he also came across documentary evidence.[153] Probability is one helpful test, but visiting a location and interviewing witnesses there is much better (12.9.2).[154]

Greek historians had their weaknesses, but primary research was one of their strengths. Klaus Meister observes,

had to evaluate conflicting claims of eyewitnesses (1.22.2–3). Woodman, *Rhetoric*, 26, warns that more of Thucydides's work depends on reports of others than on his own. (If the view is accurate, it might be relevant, as an illustration of the value placed on intellectual travel, that some scholars have even connected the Roman practice of meditative walking with the philosophic ideal of traveling for knowledge; O'Sullivan, "Mind.")

145. He also claims to have consulted records (Diod. Sic. 1.4.4–5). Though granting Diodorus's travels to some locations, Oldfather, "Introduction to Diodorus Siculus," xiii, doubts that Diodorus visited either Mesopotamia or Athens; his skepticism concerning Mesopotamia is plausible (though certain only with respect to Nineveh), but his argument regarding Athens is from silence (i.e., what Diodorus does not mention).

146. On other occasions Philostratus's research came up empty, but he incidentally confirms that he had done some (*Vit. soph.* 2.5.576).

147. Consultation with Odysseus's ghost (Philost. *Hrk.* 48.12) underlines that the depicted investigation was fictitious; it draws, however, on known research methods. Philostratus may have drawn on a variety of local traditions (Maclean and Aitken, *Heroikos*, xc–xci). Likewise, Artem. *Oneir.* 1.pref. emphasizes gathering oral reports in addition to reading all the works of his predecessors.

148. LCL, 4:316–17. Polybius's emphasis on investigation appears throughout Polyb. 12.4c.1–5.

149. It was possible, however, to visit places, consult witnesses, and still prove mistaken (Polyb. 12.4d.1–2, on Timaeus). Like a historian researching recent events, a prosecutor preparing a case would carry out research, such as tracking down eyewitnesses (e.g., Lysias *Or.* 23.2–8, §§166–67).

150. Even here, ancients sometimes found local oral sources that purported to have survived over the centuries (e.g., Paus. 1.23.2). Nevertheless, it is not without reason that scholars today often question the local oral information from a much earlier period (Pretzler, "Pausanias and Tradition").

151. E.g., Philost. *Vit. soph.* 2.23.606 (who unsuccessfully tried to evaluate conflicting reports this way in 2.5.576), in contrast to his lack of interviews for earlier information.

152. Aune, *Environment*, 81, citing Hdt. 2.52; Polyb. 3.48.12; 4.38.11; 10.11.4; for travel research, see also Diod. Sic. 1.4.1 (though he certainly did not visit Nineveh).

153. Polyb. 3.33.17–18 (citing here a bronze tablet of Hannibal). For appeals to inscriptions and the like, see also Vell. Paterc. 2.25.4; Plut. *Arist.* 19.5–6; sources noted in Lendon, "Historiography," 45 (citing the claim concerning Licinius Macer).

154. Also Plut. *Demosth.* 2.1–2. Urban centers tended to provide better access to documentary sources and those whose memories preserved events (2.1). For plausibility and probability as criteria in ancient historical writing, as in ancient rhetoric more generally, see Rothschild, *Rhetoric of History*, 62–64; cf. also discussion at Acts 26:8.

Although Greek historians usually referred to only one or two predecessors and quoted them uncritically (an "unscholarly" practice according to modern understanding), their primary research was often superior to that of modern historians: they relied to a large degree on "autopsy" and their own experiences, collected and examined the oral transmission, questioned eyewitnesses and sources, and visited the scenes of events in order to gather their information on the spot.[155]

In practice, not all historians in this period traveled.[156] Romans focused on Roman history, most of which was available locally through armies and legates sending word back to the senate. Thus Roman historians sometimes simply collected information without field research;[157] they nevertheless expected accuracy in their writing.[158] Was Luke more like a typical Greek or like a typical Roman historian on the matter of travel? If, as many contend (including myself; see discussion at Acts 16:10), the author of Acts also authored the "we" source, Acts stands much closer to the Hellenistic mold. Luke would not have traveled as widely as Polybius,[159] but he would be acquainted firsthand with material and locations in his more detailed "we" material, including Philippi, Jerusalem, and especially Caesarea. Given Luke's Greek style and his focus on events in the Greek East, those who contend that Luke was primarily a "Hellenistic historian" rather than a Roman one are undoubtedly correct, in any case.

Luke informs his audience that he "was thoroughly familiar with" the matters about which he writes (Luke 1:3). The verb παρακολουθέω does not specifically denote investigation or research, "although both these activities might be required in the process";[160] but it does indicate *thorough* acquaintance by one means or another.[161] In view of other ancient prologues using the same language, Luke's use of παρηκολουθηκότι (1:3) suggests that he has a thorough familiarity with reports (λόγων, 1:4) and that he is able to evaluate their accuracy.[162] This was a "stock term from discussions of poetics and possibly also from rhetorical handbooks," used to affirm one's "impeccable credentials" for writing and advertise the writer's reliability.[163]

How extensive was Luke's firsthand acquaintance and/or his investigation? As already noted, Roman historians typically consulted records; Greek historians in the

155. Meister, "Historiography: Greece," 421. For the preference for oral sources, see also the discussion in Aune, *Environment*, 81. Thucydides could supplement interrogation of others with his own eyewitness experience more than Herodotus, but continued to depend also on the former (Schepens, "History," 47).

156. Consulting distant records would be even more difficult (cf. Ben Zeev, "Capitol"), though this is different from consulting people orally when one traveled to a region, as I argue that Luke did.

157. Fornara, *Nature of History*, 56. Second-century sources (Aul. Gel. 11.17; 13.20.1; Fronto *Ad M. Caes.* 4.5) might suggest that in libraries slaves brought books to the scholars instead of scholars' searching for the works themselves (Houston, "Library"). Apart from Athens (Aul. Gel. 7.17.1–2), Rome, (later) Ephesus, and (earlier) Alexandria (e.g., 7.17.3), however, the majority of libraries were private (Aune, *Dictionary of Rhetoric*, 273–75). By its nature, earlier (rather than recent) history necessarily depended on earlier historians (Pliny *Ep.* 5.8.12).

158. Fornara, *Nature of History*, 61, citing Suet. *Caesar* 56. Nevertheless, the overlap in content and approach between Greek and Roman historians in the imperial period is significant; see Gowing, "Tradition," 332.

159. Nor does he pretend to have; Luke includes the "we" sparingly, not pervasively or even commonly.

160. Alexander, *Preface*, 128.

161. See ibid., 128–30. The term ἄνωθεν could also mean "thoroughly," but here it presumably means "from an early point," paralleling "from the beginning" (Bauckham, *Eyewitnesses*, 123); "from the beginning" appears in histories to claim the presence of eyewitnesses from the start (119–22).

162. Moessner, "Poetics," 85–97. Cf. also Hemer, *Acts in History*, 322 (noting that Cadbury thought that this involved even participation, a reasonable surmise only in Acts, not in the Gospel).

163. Moessner, "Poetics," 97; idem, "Prologues," 413. The closest parallel is Jos. *Ag. Ap.* 1.54, 213ff., where Josephus uses the same language to underline that he is thoroughly immersed "in the events, traditions, and reports" and hence can evaluate the various claims.

tradition of Polybius traveled and consulted with witnesses.[164] Luke's travels allowed him to confirm many of the oral traditions circulating (1:2), traditions already known to his audience (1:4).[165] Presumably, for the Gospel, this would have at least included interviewing Jerusalem followers of Jesus who could confirm and augment the stories circulating among Diaspora Christians.[166] Luke's appeal to αὐτόπται ("eyewitnesses")[167] fits the appreciation for research in Hellenistic historiography and has parallels in some histories.

The specific term αὐτοψία (mentioned by Meister, above) is a rare one, but the convention of appeal to such sources is much more widespread.[168] Although the term may not be common, the emphasis on visual observation that it implied was;[169] both Greek[170] and Roman[171] historians emphasized it. The ideal for ancient historians was to have seen events themselves;[172] since this was not always possible, they often had to depend on oral sources.[173] When they needed to defend their work, historians typically showed their reliance on oral sources and autopsy, from Polybius through

164. Witherington, *Acts*, 27. Witherington (27, 32–34) places Luke closer to a Polybius than to many other historians. Still, most writers would not have the resources to travel as much as Polybius, and the limitations of the "we" narratives suggest that Luke's travel, too, was limited, though this section specifies only the period that Luke was with *Paul* during the events he narrates.

165. Witherington, ibid., 59, following Nock, *Essays*, 828, suggests from Luke 1:3 that Luke may have also had contact with the Christian movement before the "we" narratives begin.

166. As Bruggen, *Narratives*, 65–66, notes, it does not require Luke to have been an eyewitness for the events of the Gospel.

167. BDAG cites for this sense Dion. Hal. *Pomp.* 6.3; Max. Tyre 16.3h; Jos. *Ant.* 18.342; 19.125; *Ag. Ap.* 1.55; Papias 2:2; 12:2; and Luke 1:2. The original apostolic tradents implied in Luke 1:2 knew Jesus's entire public ministry (Acts 1:21–22; cf. Gerhardsson, *Memory*, 280–88). Although the term here would include the Twelve, it is broader than them alone (Acts 1:21–22; Bauckham, *Eyewitnesses*, 389). For the recent trend in a number of studies affirming eyewitness tradition in the Gospels, see Riesner, "Rückkehr." Collins, "Eyewitnesses," 450–52, argues that what they witnessed was the written "word," i.e., a document. Although the term has a broad semantic range, in Luke's ninety-seven uses it normally means oral words, the vast majority for an oral message; early Christians could speak of seeing it (1 John 1:1), as visionaries could "see" the prophetic word (Jer 23:18; cf. Ezek 13:6; other "seeing" in Wis 2:17). All Collins's own examples of "autopsy" (451) refer to something firsthand, and in Josephus *War* 3.432 it refers to the bringer of an eyewitness report; in 6.134, as one who watches firsthand; and in the more historiographic sense in *Ag. Ap.* 1.55, it refers to Josephus's firsthand observation that supplemented his participation. Collins (451) insists that their observation of the word was simultaneous with their serving it, and hence insists that Luke refers to the period of *reception*; but even if one insists on simultaneity, the gospel tradition suggests that witnesses preached from the start (Mark 6:12; Luke 9:2; 10:9), and early Christian tradition could employ the phrase "from the beginning" to the witnesses' early connection with Jesus himself (John 15:27; 1 John 1:1; see esp. here Acts 1:22). While "even as" (1:2) can be used for identical matters, it can also be used for comparison (Acts 22:3), such as adding eyewitness experience to oral reports (Luke 2:20); and if the observers of Luke 1:2 were merely identical with the writers of 1:1, Luke's opening lines would be repetitious.

168. Alexander, *Preface*, 34–36 (on the convention of αὐτοψία, see 34–41). Herodotean history uses the word this way more than Thucydidean history does (38; cf. Adams, "Preface," 189) and often with an emphasis on distant locations (Alexander, *Preface*, 121; as Judea would have seemed to Luke). Alexander suggests that the use for the author's presence at events in Jos. *Ag. Ap.* 1.55 depends on Polyb. 3.4.3 (against Polybius's normal usage). (In principle, at least, Luke could depend on the same passage as Josephus, but in reality, he probably was less apt to know Polybius.)

169. Byrskog, *History*, 48–49 (noting [49] that Alexander focuses too much on the term whereas leading classicist experts on autopsy in ancient historiography emphasize the centrality of the *practice*).

170. Byrskog, ibid., 49–53, addresses Heraclitus and others; 53–57, Herodotus; 58–59, Thucydides; 59–62, Polybius (note esp. [p. 60] Polyb. 4.2.1–2); 62–63, Josephus (noting *Ag. Ap.* 1.47).

171. Byrskog, *History*, 63, noting Livy as the exception, most following the Greek preference. Byrskog notes that Dion. Hal. *Ant. rom.* 1.6.2 "praises Fabius Pictor and Cincius Alimentus . . . for relating with great exactness only the events at which they themselves had been present."

172. Byrskog, *History*, 93–94.

173. Ibid., 94 (for its not always being possible, Byrskog cites Polyb. 12.4c.4). Byrskog deals (94–98) with the use of oral sources in Herodotus, Thucydides, and Xenophon; he notes (98) the more unusual defense of some that oral sources were even better than autopsy (Isoc. *Panath.* 150; Strabo 2.5.11) but suggests (98–99)

the first century.[174] Tacitus sought information from witnesses where possible (and otherwise had access to imperial annals for numerous points).[175] When the term is used, it normally indicates "those with personal/first-hand experience: those who know the facts at first hand."[176] Luke emphasizes eyewitness attestation not only in his preface, but commonly enough to reinforce the preface's claim.[177]

That Luke's research serves a primarily confirmatory purpose (Luke 1:4) suggests that Luke in the end does not arrive at conclusions far distant from his sources.[178] Ancient rhetoricians often appealed to common knowledge to make a point; although this information may have sometimes been gossip, it seems unlikely that it was normally simply a rhetorical deception.[179] Appeals to common knowledge suggest that the knowledge was in fact widespread and hence that what Luke reports in his Gospel (and, to a lesser extent, in Acts) was already in wide circulation at the time of his writing, probably within the lifetime of some who had known Jesus's public ministry.

Many stories that Luke includes in his Gospel were probably widely disseminated, and other information may have also been broadly disseminated among many churches. The early churches throughout the empire were already informally networked long before Luke wrote[180] and certainly long before the more explicit network of bishops that we recognize by the early second century. In Mediterranean antiquity in general, travelers regularly carried news from one location to another,[181] residing especially with members of their own social group, such as Jews or Christians or resident aliens from their homeland (see also "Travel and Geography in Acts" in ch. 17, esp. sect. 1.e, below). In the cosmopolitan cities of the eastern Mediterranean world, such as Alexandria, Antioch, Jerusalem, Ephesus, and Corinth, one regularly found people who had moved there from various kingdoms.[182] When one learned of someone traveling near a place where friends resided, one might prepare and send a letter.[183]

Even during Paul's years of planting churches, urban Christians traveled (1 Cor 16:10, 12, 17; Phil 2:30; 4:18) carrying letters (Rom 16:1–2; Phil 2:25), relocated to other places (Rom 16:3, 5; perhaps 16:6–15), or sent greetings to other churches (Rom 16:21–23; 1 Cor 16:19; Phil 4:22; Col 4:10–15). In the first century, many churches knew what was happening with churches in other cities (Rom 1:8; 1 Cor 11:16; 14:33; 1 Thess 1:7–9), and even shared letters (Col 4:16). Missionaries

that more commonly they were appreciated as supplementing autopsy. For documents' use of eyewitnesses in historians, see 149–53.

174. Byrskog, *History*, 122 (excepting Livy). Of course, Dionysius of Halicarnassus and others covering long periods of history could not depend on immediate oral history for most of it, as they themselves recognized. For apologetic use of autopsy (as in Josephus), see 214–22.

175. Ibid., 63–64, citing Pliny *Ep.* 6.16 (esp. 6.16.22); 6.20. For the *Annals*, Tacitus would have access to witnesses starting in the period of Nero's later years (64).

176. Alexander, *Preface*, 120. Historians considered this the best evidence (Aune, *Environment*, 81, citing Hdt. 2.99; Polyb. 12.27.1–6; 20.12.8; Lucian *Hist.* 47).

177. Most extensively, see Rothschild, *Rhetoric of History*, 213–90, noting this authenticating technique.

178. As Maddox, *Purpose*, 21, 186, emphasizes, "confirmation" is a primary purpose of Luke-Acts; ἀσφάλειαν is the climactic, final word of the Gospel's preface (Luke 1:4).

179. E.g., Isaeus *Pyrr.* 40; Dion. Hal. *Ant. rom.* 7.43.2; Jos. *Ag. Ap.* 2.107; cf. 1.50–52, 56; see comments on Acts 24:8; 26:5; and 26:26.

180. Cf. also Willis, "Networking"; on the network that Acts also reveals, see esp. Alexander, "Mapping"; (also in idem, "Ἐκκλησιολογία").

181. Eurip. *El.* 361–62; Demosth. *Ep.* 5.1; Cic. *Att.* 2.11; Sen. Y. *Ep. Lucil.* 47.1; P.Oxy. 32; Apul. *Metam.* 1.26.

182. Even in Tarsus in *Apoll. K. Tyre* 8 (though this is a novel, it likely presupposes social reality on this point).

183. E.g., Cic. *Att.* 1.10, 13; 4.1; 8.14. This method could be quick; a letter from Caesar in Britain reached Cicero in less than a month (Cic. *Quint. fratr.* 3.1.8.25). Despite a modern postal service, those of us traveling to and from many parts of Nigeria, Kenya, and Cameroon in recent years have still carried mail for acquaintants.

could speak to some churches about other churches (Rom 15:26; 2 Cor 8:1–5; 9:2–4; Phil 4:16; 1 Thess 2:14–16) and send personal news by other workers (Eph 6:21–22; Col 4:7–9). Although different locations might have their own struggles or theological emphases, the idea that the early, geographically distinct Christian communities were theologically and socially isolated from one another is a fiction created by modern scholarship on the basis of inferences incompatible with the hard evidence.

Even scholars who, such as Haenchen, doubt that the author of Acts was well acquainted with Paul can suggest that Luke could have either traveled to major Pauline centers (e.g., Philippi, Corinth, Ephesus, Antioch) or depended on informants who did so.[184] Yet given the level of detail of Luke's knowledge of Paul at many points (albeit in Lukan style), we would expect an even stronger acquaintance than this.[185] Luke knows some centers' histories (e.g., Philippi) in greater detail than others (e.g., Corinth, Antioch) but is, of course, most detailed in the "we" narratives (which include, e.g., Philippi but not Corinth or Antioch). See the discussion at Acts 16:10 for the likelihood that Luke did not simply travel after Paul but traveled with him at some points. (See also ch. 7 below, against the traditional claim that Luke could not be acquainted with the real Paul, a claim often based on a misleading modern Protestant interpretation of Paul.) In any case, the quality of Luke's research seems evident from the volume of information in Acts that can today be confirmed as accurate from other sources,[186] especially Paul's letters; his contradictions of other historical sources are relatively few, certainly, by widely accepted ancient standards.

f. Comparison with Josephus

As a Hellenistically educated monotheist steeped in Palestinian Judaism but writing history for a Diaspora audience,[187] Josephus may invite comparison to Luke.[188] The comparison is less complete than one might initially suppose; since both adapt broader Greco-Roman writing conventions (which spanned a range of forms) and since Luke addresses a less sophisticated, more popular audience than does Josephus, one cannot simply reason from Josephus's methods to Luke's. Luke's historiographic method may still be closer to that of Thucydides and Polybius, as some have argued:[189]

184. Haenchen, *Acts*, 86 (he dates Acts ca. 75 C.E., a reasonable estimate; this would, he notes, allow sufficient communal memories about Paul to remain extant). He even suggests that this is where Luke may have acquired the travel diary (87). Other examples of more skeptical critics who nevertheless believe Acts often depends on historical sources include Lüdemann, "Acts as Source."

185. With Hemer, "Alexandria Troas," 96–97.

186. For such information, see Hemer, *Acts in History*, 101–58; and this commentary's comments ad loc.

187. Vermes, *Jesus and Judaism*, 139, opines that Josephus produced Judaism's "*best* historiography"; certainly, he is our main source for postexilic Jewish history (Hengel, *Acts and History*, 7); he was also known to early Christians (e.g., Iren. frg. 32). Much has been written on early Jewish historiography; see, e.g., Mor and Rappaport, *Bibliography*. Suet. *Vesp.* 5 speaks of Josephus's influence (probably ultimately dependent on Josephus on this point).

188. Indeed, until the nineteenth century, Christians employed Josephus as the most important extrabiblical source for understanding the NT (Krieger, "Priester").

189. Meyer, *Ursprung*, 1:2–3 (as cited in Bruce, *Acts*³, 27); Bruce, *Acts*³, 28; Witherington, "Editing," 344; for Herodotus, Thucydides, and Polybius and Luke's location among them, see the discussion in Molthagen, "Geschichtsschreibung" (esp. 181). Josephus is closer to the model of Thucydides and Polybius in the *War* than in the later *Antiquities*, where he follows the more rhetorical model of Dionysius (Attridge, *History in Josephus*, 44–50; followed by Newell, "Suicide Accounts," 285). Some modern readers show a bias against Josephus as a participant observer that they do not apply to his models in Thucydides and Polybius (Chapman, "Josephus," 323). For participant observation in modern anthropology, see the discussion in Tedlock, "Observation"; in sociology, cf., e.g., Covell, "Foreword," x.

certainly they did exert continuing influence,[190] and Thucydides was widely read.[191] Or Luke may have gone his own way, in eclectic fashion. (Luke's preface, at least, owes little to any specifically Jewish literary conventions,[192] and his use of Scripture was too common in the early Christian movement to require other specifically Jewish literary models.)

Nevertheless, Josephus provides one among several possible analogies for Luke's historical objectives, one we cannot afford to neglect. This is especially true because of Josephus's analogous apologetic interests. Such shared interests need not require shared historical methodology, given the vast rhetorical distance between the two writers, but at the least they suggest the possibility of shared rhetorical techniques and invite further exploration here.

Clearly Josephus both preserves and adapts prior material. Josephus does not uncritically affirm all his sources; he can note that some make a particular claim (*Ant.* 19.60), and refuse to decide himself the cause of some events, diplomatically leaving final decisions to the reader's discretion (19.61, 108);[193] he can also question a source's bias (e.g., 16.183–84). Yet we can best test Josephus's reliability where he is reproducing accounts to which we have ready access, most often biblical accounts.[194]

As indicated above, Josephus, like some other Jewish writers,[195] dramatizes, adds speeches, omits what appears counterproductive, and inserts his own apologetic slant.[196] Sometimes Josephus apparently "corrects" or adjusts biblical accounts on the basis of other biblical passages.[197] This practice may not represent his method everywhere; he may strive for greater rhetorical sophistication in his magnum opus, the *Antiquities* (where we have most of his overlap with Scripture), than in his earlier *War*.[198] But even here Josephus tends to adapt events in his sources, not create them.[199]

Even when Josephus adds extrabiblical events to biblical accounts (such as Moses's exploits as an Egyptian prince), our sources often confirm that he is following earlier

190. Sacks, "Historiography," 715. Some argue that subsequent historians such as Livy had forsaken Polybius's principles (Weeden, *Mark*, 15–16; though cf. my comment on 281 below); but while many never followed such principles (e.g., many Roman historians did not travel), they remained interested in historical information, and many (e.g., Tacitus) did have access to annals and substantial historical data.

191. From sources in Egypt, one might guess that readers owned copies of Thucydides—despite his work's level, length, and consequent expense—nearly twice as often as all Greek novels combined and nearly twice as often as Herodotus (and more than half as often as Demosthenes, though only about an eighth as often as Homer); see Stephens, "Who Read Novels?," 411, 415–16. Thucydides continued to offer a model in this period (Marincola, "Speeches," 123–27; Croke, "Historiography," 567–68).

192. Alexander, *Preface*, 147–67, esp. 165. She does, however, suggest that it allows a marginal social location as found among Jewish writers (idem, *Context*, 41–42).

193. Somewhat like Luke, Josephus cites his sources directly far less often than did many other extant historians.

194. Cohen, "Josephus and Scripture," argues that Josephus exercises more freedom and stylizes more in *Ant.* 1–5 than afterward. Comparing Josephus's *War* and *Antiquities* where they overlap also reveals some of his rhetorical freedom, a freedom he was happy to display publicly to lavishly meet Greek rhetorical standards.

195. Sometimes Ps.-Philo *Biblical Antiquities* dramatically rewrites an account (e.g., Begg, "Ceremonies"), but usually it depends on the biblical text for events. Feldman, "*Antiquities* and *Antiquities*," 76, argues that in narrative style, *Biblical Antiquities* is closer to Acts than to Josephus.

196. See, e.g., Penner, *Praise*, 113. Josephus explicitly excuses himself from the usual standard of dispassionate, objective historiography (highlighted by Polybius) on the grounds of his experience of his and his people's suffering (*War* 1.9, 11; see Chapman, "Josephus," 324); one may thus expect amplification of pathos.

197. See Höffken, "Reichsteilung."

198. Cf., e.g., Attridge, *History in Josephus*, 44–50; followed by Newell, "Suicide Accounts," 285. Even in the *War*, Josephus may write for Rome's elite, who would recognize Greek tragic allusions in *War* 1 (so Forte, "Echoes Revisited").

199. For sample analyses of many of his accounts, see the many works (not all are listed) by L. Feldman and C. Begg on this subject in this commentary's "Works Cited" (also noted above on biography, since many of them resemble biographic adaptation as well).

extrabiblical traditions, not composing from his imagination. For postbiblical as well as biblical events, Josephus also clearly depends on sources,[200] such as the work of Nicolaus of Damascus (e.g., *Ant.* 12.127),[201] although he critiques what he sees as Nicolaus's bias (14.9; 16.183–84).[202]

Like other historians whose works have survived, Josephus affirms his intention to write truth in contrast to historians who he thinks are unconcerned with it (20.156–57, 260, 262, 266).[203] This claim recalls the standard that historians demanded but does not resolve the extent to which Josephus fulfills it. (He specifically condemns a rival historian for lack of accuracy [*Life* 336] and compares him to a forger of contracts [*Life* 337–39]. In this instance, however, for all we know, Josephus might be the one lying.)[204] He condemns those who wrote about events without any firsthand knowledge, contrasting these writers with his own knowledge of the Judean-Roman war (*Ag. Ap.* 1.45–49). Not only was he an eyewitness of much that he claims (e.g., 1.48–49); he claims to have even taken notes (1.49), receiving reports also from deserters from the city (1.50).

Yet whether because of conflicting sources,[205] careless composition, or neglecting to explain information that would resolve some of the tensions, Josephus sometimes contradicts himself, even in some of his most rhetorically refined material and closest to his own lifetime. (Sometimes the apparent mistakes might instead betray deliberate literary connections,[206] but this approach does not explain all of them.) At one point (*Ant.* 20.16) he appears to claim not only that Herod, brother of Agrippa I, removed a high priest but that the authority to remove high priests continued among his descendants, whereas elsewhere Josephus is clear that Agrippa II (Agrippa's son, not Herod's) ultimately assumed this role.[207] Josephus sometimes forgets to include information; although promising to recount more about Helena's and Izates's benefactions during Jerusalem's famine (20.53), he never returns to the subject (at least not in this extant volume).[208]

How does Josephus usually fare in his reports of the postbiblical period? Scholars on Josephus range from skepticism to appreciation, generally depending on the aspects of his historiography on which they focus their attention. On a number of points he fails to impress[209]—for example, in his speeches (which ch. 8 below will address).[210]

---

200. Bellemore, "Josephus, Pompey, and the Jews," suggests that Josephus depended on more Roman sources and fewer Jewish sources in the later *Antiquities* than in the *War*. He may employ genuinely Iranian material (whether originally accurate or not) in Jos. *Ant.* 18.314–70 (cf. Herman, "Motifs").

201. Josephus probably depends on Nicolaus as his main source from Antiochus IV through Herod I (e.g., Stern, *Authors*, 1:229).

202. Josephus also writes from a Jewish perspective that differs from Nicolaus's Greco-Syrian one (Wacholder, "Nicolaus"). Josephus sounds less favorable to Herod in *Antiquities* than in *War*.

203. That the historians he had in mind probably made the same claims need not have troubled him; though reporting various perspectives as a rhetorical technique, ancient authors rarely reckoned with the multivalence of perspectives the way postmodernists would today. Josephus sometimes legitimates his own historical work (vis-à-vis that of other historians) by citing tradition (Gillet-Didier, "*Paradosis*").

204. Josephus's claim not to have added anything may be conventional (Feldman, "Hellenizations: Abraham," 133, citing Dion. Hal. *Thuc.* 5, 8; Lucian *Hist.* 47) and certainly does not fit his adaptation of biblical narratives in his *Antiquities* (see articles by Begg and Feldman listed above).

205. But cf. Mason, "Contradiction."

206. See the argument in Sievers, "Name."

207. Perhaps Josephus meant only that the right continued among Herod's *relatives*, though his ἀπογόνοις here normally means "descendants." Herod replaces priests in Jos. *Ant.* 20.103; Agrippa II does so in 20.179, 196, 203.

208. Josephus provides only a later summary of what he already recounted, in *Ant.* 20.101.

209. His account of Caligula's death reflects a source different from, and impossible to harmonize with, Suetonius's (Scherberich, "Sueton und Josephus").

210. Josephus, like Herodotus, fared much better on narrative than on speeches by our standards (cf. Mosley, "Reporting," 11–22); he is heavily influenced by rhetoric (see Botha, "Rhetoric and Josephus").

Most historians today also argue that Josephus's population estimates are unreliable and that he is sometimes mistaken on distances.[211] Since it is unlikely that Josephus actually counted people or measured distances, such matters do not otherwise affect the substance of what he reports about events. He occasionally makes mistakes on even his most public information,[212] although this appears to be the exception rather than the rule.[213]

Josephus's biases are, despite his claims of straightforwardness, difficult to miss. He is probably more accurate in his general narration of events than in his summaries; he does not fabricate events, but he puts his slant on them. Indeed, his overarching summaries[214] and apologetic perspectives[215] sometimes conflict with the information he himself reports. He presents the Judean-Roman war as virtually an accident in which incompetent governors and a few Jewish "bandits" forced Judea into unwilling conflict with Rome.[216] He likewise defends Titus; after all, he was writing under the patronage of the Flavian dynasty. His perspective is that of an aristocrat favoring Jewish aristocrats;[217] in some of his work he favors Pharisees, one of whom he had allegedly been;[218] he may also exaggerate Jewish privileges in the empire (albeit based on genuine precedents) to further his apologetic on his people's behalf; and he presents Jewish sects in terms of Greek philosophic ideals.[219] Josephus's biases do not, however, significantly hamper our use of his work for historical reconstruction. "These biases are to be expected" and are usually easy enough to recognize. "With proper allowance made for his special interests and recognition that he was sometimes misinformed, the reader will find Josephus on the whole reliable."[220]

If we leave aside examples of bias (including in summaries), speeches, and difficult estimates, however, Josephus proves generally accurate on matters of historical detail. As noted above, whereas archaeology has challenged some of Josephus's claims, it has vindicated him on many detailed points.[221] Apart from distance estimates, Josephus proves generally reliable on geographic matters,[222] and archaeology confirms most of his observations about Jerusalem, which he knew well: here, despite some errors, he is often accurate in even quite minute details, such as the measurements of

211. Safrai, "Description in Works," esp. 320–21. On population estimates, see further the comment on Acts 2:41.

212. Cf., e.g., Jos. *Ant.* 18.206, which, at least in the text as we have it, misconstrues Germanicus's relationship to Tiberius.

213. Sometimes there is considerable debate, e.g., surrounding Felix's full name (see comment on Acts 23:24).

214. For proposed problems in Josephus's summaries, see, e.g., McLaren, "Josephus' Summary Statements"; further discussion at Acts 2:41–47.

215. He defends both Rome to his people and his people to Rome (as widely noted, e.g., Neusner, *Politics to Piety*, 2; Crossan, *Jesus*, 93).

216. Nearly three centuries before this time, an Italian city used the same excuse of being forced by a few troublemakers (in that case, their leaders), and escaped punishment (Livy 24.47.6). Experiences and observations in northern Nigeria have given me more respect for the possibility of a few extremists' ultimately provoking wider conflict.

217. Cf., e.g., Pastor, "Strata."

218. Although some scholars think that he emphasizes the Pharisaic connection because of the changed political landscape. Williams, "Josephus on Pharisees," attributes to Josephus the full force of his anti-Pharisaic passages (by denying them to Nicolaus of Damascus); he may have followed much of Pharisaism without having officially joined (Mason, "Was Josephus a Pharisee?").

219. With, e.g., Ferguson, *Backgrounds*, 387.

220. Ibid., 387.

221. See, e.g., Syon, "Gamla"; Cotton and Geiger, "Yyn"; Mazar, "Josephus and Excavations"; Safrai, "Education," 995; Feldman, "Introduction," 45–46; Thackeray, *Josephus*, 49; Riesner, "Gate"; Pixner, "Gate"; Pixner, Chen, and Margalit, "Zion."

222. Safrai, "Description in Works," esp. 320–21.

columns.[223] One of Herod's three towers remains, 66 feet square and 66 feet high—just as Josephus claims (*War* 5.166).[224]

Outside Jerusalem, the Caesarea Ancient Harbor Excavation Project has largely confirmed Josephus's description of Caesarea's harbor, despite some omissions in his description.[225] Josephus appears to confuse the directions of the theater and amphitheater from Caesarea's harbor but supplies many correct details.[226]

As one Israeli archaeologist emphasizes regarding the physical data (where Josephus fares better than when we critique his fairly blatant biases or rhetorical distortions):

> Before archaeological excavations, it was the vogue among historians—very serious historians—to argue that Josephus in many places relates sheer nonsense, that he is not historical, that he exaggerates, and so forth. But the more we dig in Jerusalem and at Masada and at Herodium and in [Herodian] Jericho, the greater respect we—both archaeologists and historians—have for the accuracy of Josephus. He is one of the greatest historians. Of course he had his own prejudices. But show me any historian without them. Josephus is accurate not only for his own period but for previous periods as well, for example, the Hellenistic period.[227]

Despite reservations, scholars normally accept Josephus's main outline of events as accurate.[228] As Mosley points out,[229] Josephus not only claims accuracy[230] (itself no guarantee of it) but presented copies of his work to Vespasian, Titus, Herod of Chalcis, and Agrippa—and so dared not seriously misrepresent the events known also to them (*Ag. Ap.* 1.50–51)[231] (particularly not to their detriment!).

How does Luke compare with Josephus? Luke's adaptation of Mark generally sticks close to Mark's stories and (with very rare exceptions)[232] even his sequence. If this is representative of his use of written sources, Luke may stay closer to his sources than Josephus stays to the Bible in his *Antiquities*. How each adapts oral sources (probably more to the point in Acts) is harder to discern, but the use of written sources is the best guide to the question we have, and so at the very least we should not think Luke less attached to his sources than is Josephus. As argued above, Luke is not primarily a "rhetorical" historian; by contrast, Josephus in his *Antiquities* (more than in his *War*), following the model of Dionysius and Isocrates,

223. Feldman, "Introduction," 45–46; Mazar, "Josephus and Excavations," 325–29; Charlesworth, *Jesus within Judaism*, 118–19.

224. McRay, *Archaeology*, 117–18.

225. Ibid., 140.

226. Ibid., 144 (noting esp. Jos. *War* 1.415; *Ant.* 15.341; cf. 18.57; *War* 2.172).

227. Yigael Yadin in Shanks, "BAR Interviews Yadin," 19.

228. Thackeray, *Josephus*, 49; Mosley, "Reporting," 23–24. Broshi suggests that the sources for much of Josephus's accurate information included Roman military commentaries ("Credibility of Josephus"; see esp. Jos. *Life* 348, 352; *Ag. Ap.* 56 [p. 381]). Newell, "Suicide Accounts," argues for conventional forms in Josephus's suicide accounts, the battle suicides probably simply following the form; the evidence may not be sufficient to verify this suggestion, but Josephus does use tragic pathos like other rhetorical historians. Given his own experience, it is not surprising that he digresses to lament (e.g., *War* 5.19), though quickly returning to the subject with the notice that the rules of history prohibit such lamentation (5.20).

229. Mosley, "Reporting," 23–24, noting that Josephus composed speeches freely, but he has many firsthand sources (e.g., *Ant.* 14.144–45, 189, 219, 224, 228).

230. Jos. *Ant.* 1.17; 20.154–57, 260–62; *War* 1.9–12, 30; 7.454–55; *Ag. Ap.* 1.47; *Life* 65.

231. Just as, we may note, Luke could not have easily avoided criticism if he fabricated new events contradicting those known to Theophilus (Luke 1:4). On appeals to common knowledge, see, e.g., comment on Acts 26:26; this appeal is a higher-order appeal than some, since it encompasses a range of data.

232. Most notably, for literary purposes Luke brings the Nazareth pericope forward and makes it programmatic (Luke 4:16–30; Mark 6:1–4).

often is.[233] If we frequently depend on Josephus, despite his *Tendenz* and literary freedom, for historical information where he is our primary source, we ought not hesitate to grant the same courtesy to Luke.

g. Chronology?

Chronology was important to history and, where possible, to some other genres.[234] Military historians such as Polybius and Thucydides could provide careful chronology because they or their sources had annals or notes available;[235] the same was not true when one's sources depended on oral recollections.[236] Thus, for example, Seneca the Elder promises to recall events of the past so long as he need not do so in sequence;[237] Papias reports that Mark recounted Peter's reports but not in order.[238] Biographies (such as the Gospels) were even less constrained by chronology than history was;[239] having surveyed Augustus's life, Suetonius promises, "I shall now take up its various phases one by one, not in chronological order, but by classes, to make the account clearer and more intelligible."[240] Thus Suetonius would summarize either the positive or the negative minority of an emperor's acts before focusing on the good or evil that characterized him.[241] Only if one specified chronology (and in the process contradicted other historical sources) did one open oneself for criticism.[242] Sometimes historiography also required one to backtrack or advance into the future, to keep to a train of thought or a geographical region.[243]

Luke's Gospel follows the sequence of Mark[244] except in a few places (most obviously the programmatic scene of Luke 4:16–30; cf. Mark 6:1–5) necessary for his own literary structure; but Mark's Gospel itself need not be chronologically arranged, and there can be no guarantee of chronology for Luke's other sources in his Gospel. The nature of events over the greater length of time covered in Acts allows for better estimates of sequencing there, and Luke's fairly consistent following of Mark's sequence may suggest that his chronology in Acts is fairly reliable. Yet even in Acts,

233. In the *War*, Josephus is closer to the model of Thucydides and Polybius (Attridge, *History in Josephus*, 44–50; followed by Newell, "Suicide Accounts," 285).

234. In general, see *Rhet. Her.* 1.9.15. An author, if following other than a chronological outline of material, may need to justify arranging it as he has (Vitruv. *Arch.* 2.1.8). Synchronizing local chronologies to produce a standard sequence could be difficult; see discussion in Feeney, "Time."

235. E.g., Thucyd. 2.1.1; 5.26.1. For one's personal notes or diaries in the Roman tradition of the *commentarius*, see Rebenich, "Historical Prose," 313–14; Pelling, "*Commentarii*." *Commentarii* were originally minutes of civic authorities or councils, normally in a series, but by the late republic, they included lecture notes, speech drafts, etc. (Rüpke, "Commentarii," 628), and personal or business diaries (idem, "Ephemeris"). Others filled notebooks with their thoughts (Pliny *Ep.* 1.6.1, 3).

236. Even in oral performance of standard stories, performers often can rearrange the sequence (Eddy and Boyd, *Legend*, 433–35). For weaknesses in chronology, see, e.g., Sallust's historical monographs (Laistner, *Historians*, 58–59); different reckoning methods in Livy's sources confused his chronology (Laistner, *Historians*, 94–95).

237. Sen. E. *Controv.* 1.pref. 4. Allison, *Jesus*, 5, notes memories' sequential limitations.

238. Euseb. *H.E.* 3.39. Early Judaism also recognized the need to rechronologize some OT accounts; see 4Q158; Wise, "Introduction to 4Q158," 199–20.

239. Ancient biographies were not expected to be in chronological order (Görgemanns, "Biography"; Stanton, *Jesus*, 119–21).

240. Suet. *Aug.* 9 (LCL, 1:133). For Suetonius's thematic approach, see also Matthews, "Emperor and Historians," 292.

241. See, e.g., Suet. *Calig.* 22.1 (after positive acts in *Calig.* 13–21).

242. See Suetonius's criticism of Pliny in *Calig.* 8.3. Later rabbis doubted that the Torah was chronologically arranged (originally to resolve potential contradictions; see Kaunfer and Kaunfer, "Time and Torah").

243. E.g., explicitly in Jos. *Ant.* 18.194 (though he does this elsewhere without noting it, e.g., placing Pilate's recall in 18.89 before Philip's death in 18.106).

244. Also sometimes the material that he shares with Matthew, who, however, otherwise does not share the same interest in chronology, rearranging Mark and, presumably, the material shared with Luke as well.

he must sometimes restructure the chronology to retain a cohesive narrative (cf., e.g., Acts 11:30; 12:25).

When a historian was using episodic narrative "woven . . . around the impact of a personality," similar to biography, a topical arrangement was appropriate.[245] Even in history more generally, chronology could be negotiable. Dionysius of Halicarnassus complains that Thucydides's chronological style breaks up his flow of thought and obscures his narrative whereas Herodotus more naturally follows the flow of events.[246] Debates about the chronology of Acts sometimes center on Paul's activity in Tarsus and Antioch, of which Luke tells us little; but Paul's letters correspond closely to Luke's itinerary for him in the places where Luke's narrative is detailed (see ch. 7 below). We may not know how precise Luke's chronology is in Acts, but were it less than fully precise, this would not count against Luke as a historical writer.

h. Omissions

Scholars are sometimes troubled by Luke's omissions of matters stated in Paul's letters.[247] Given the tension between Luke's space and the length of the period he covers, however, numerous omissions are not surprising, and Luke is a rhetorically strategic writer who uses only what serves his purpose (which may help explain the work's preservation). Thus, for example, if he wishes to report positive precedents from Roman officials, he may have cause to omit the reasons for which Claudius expelled Rome's Jewish community: if the dominant interpretation of Suetonius is correct, Christians may have been involved in the dissension in Rome (see comment on Acts 18:2). Acts may likewise omit some early Christian controversies no longer relevant to Luke's own audience; the rhetorical principle of τάχος allowed Luke to omit some details to reserve "more space for the truly momentous controversies that changed the shape of the early church."[248]

We can hardly deny an ancient writer's status as a historian because of deliberate omissions, whether due to his focus (a necessary constraint in all history) or, less acceptable today, his bias.[249] Historians often did omit some events[250] and did not regard it as a criticism when someone else testified to the accuracy of what they reported but offered to supply additional information.[251] Sometimes hints of information suggest that a historian who omitted it did not lack the information itself.[252] For that matter, ancient historiographers demanded selectivity and sometimes made this characteristic

245. Hemer, *Acts in History*, 74. Cf. one element of Suetonius's topical approach in Thorburn, "Tiberius."

246. Dion. Hal. *Pomp.* 3. Thucydides went so far as to divide his narrative by summers and winters, distorting continuity so inappropriately that later historians avoided this method (Dion. Hal. *Thuc.* 9; LCL, 1:485n8, mentions one partial exception).

247. For one example of Luke's selectivity, he omits many of Paul's sufferings (Lentz, *Luke's Portrait*, 169; although Pervo, *Profit*, 18, may think that Luke includes too many!).

248. Witherington, *Acts*, 440; see further 436–38. E.g., the conspicuously concise summary in Libanius *Narration* 27 highlights only key points, years apart.

249. As a notorious example of the latter, see Josephus's omission of the golden-calf episode (*Ant.* 3.79–99), though even Josephus rarely omits such a critical event. Some accuse even Tacitus of bias in his omissions (Laistner, *Historians*, 132); likewise Xenophon (Brown, *Historians*, 95–97, though regarding Xenophon as otherwise mostly evenhanded, 93–94).

250. E.g., Jos. *Life* 339; *Ag. Ap.* 1.60–66; Dio Cass. 1.1.1–2 (though Dion. Hal. *Ant. rom.* 7.66.5; 11.1.1–6 emphasizes accuracy over brevity). In novels as well, retellings could omit some uncomfortable details (e.g., Chaereas's kick in Char. *Chaer.* 2.5.10–11). Noting omissions concerning Paul's life in Acts, Chrys. *Hom. Acts* 21 (Martin, *Acts*, 112) explains that "the historian, for conciseness, often omits incidents and condenses the times." (Bede *Comm. Acts* 9.26 explains the same omission simply by Luke's lacking reason for interest.)

251. Jos. *Life* 365–67 boasts that Agrippa II testified to the accuracy of his work but offered to supply additional information.

252. Whittaker, "Introduction," xlviii–lii, on Herodian.

a major distinction between "history" and "chronicles."[253] Sound historical method thus did not require the inclusion of all available information but merely prohibited the creation of events.

By modern standards, ancient writers can be accused of bias in their selectivity. Thus a modern historian who recognizes that most of what Xenophon's *Hellenica* reports is accurate nevertheless considers him inaccurate for what he fails to report.[254] So fond is Xenophon of Sparta that he omits its failures and the greatness of its rival, Thebes.[255] But while ancient readers were willing to charge some authors with bias motivated by malice (e.g., Plut. *Mal. Hdt.*),[256] standard rhetorical practice did allow them to select what they considered most essential for their purposes.

Thus one ancient rhetorical critic warned good historians not to focus too much on what was unimportant or to neglect what was important.[257] Tacitus frankly admits that he does not treat all senate business, but only that of moral value for his audience (*Ann.* 3.65). The historian Polybius complains that some writers focus too much of their narrative on matters that others have treated sufficiently or on matters that would not be helpful to their readers (Polyb. 15.36.10). That Luke omits some themes to dwell on others is not surprising. Polybius insists that he must omit some matters about Roman customs (6.11.4–6), pleading with his critics that they should evaluate writers by what they recount, and assume that omissions are due to ignorance only when what they recount is found to contain errors (6.11.7–8).[258]

Hengel observes that Luke omits what is unnecessary and sometimes "abbreviates some events so much that they become almost incomprehensible," elaborating and combining as needed.[259] Likewise, he argues that Luke knew Palestine's geography well in some places (especially Jerusalem, Caesarea, and the coastal plain he would have traveled in Acts 21–24) but poorly in others (namely, Samaria and Galilee)— though like any outsider entering the land would.[260] Getting geography as right as possible was important; some ancient historians could critique other historians harshly for erring in their geography.[261] But Tacitus, whose interest was rhetoric,

---

253. Ibid., li–lii, citing Lucian *Hist.* 4–6, 27.

254. Brownson, "Introduction to *Anabasis*," ix; he concedes (xi) that the work remains "the best authority we have for the half century which it covers." As noted earlier (ch. 5, sect. 2), some observers today challenge even some brief media reports that lack sufficient context to produce the interpretations the observers consider balanced.

255. Ibid., x. Likewise, Arrian or his source omits one story damaging to Alexander's reputation, possibly deliberately (Baynham, "Quintus Curtius," 428), although he includes some others.

256. *Mor.* 854E–874C; cf. Philost. *Hrk.* 24.1–2 (on Homer). In fact, it may be Plutarch who displays the malice, because Herodotus criticized Plutarch's native Boeotia. In other cases, he evaluates various historical sources by noting their relational or political biases (e.g., Plut. *Themist.* 32.3–4; *Alc.* 3.1).

257. Dion. Hal. *Thuc.* 13, expounding this point more fully in *Thuc.* 13–17; see further Satterthwaite, "Acts," 345, who cites in this respect Lucian *Hist.* 56–57; Cic. *De or.* 3.27.104–5; 53.202–3; Quint. *Inst.* 8.4; Longin. *Subl.* 11–12; cf. Lucian *Hist.* 6). Narrators should pass over quickly matters that would disturb the audience (Theon *Progymn.* 5.52–56)—probably one reason for the brevity of Jesus's baptism in the canonical Gospels.

258. Polybius is not equally gracious in his criticisms, complaining that some historians' narrow focus requires them to exaggerate and focus on irrelevant matters (Polyb. 7.7.1–8).

259. Hengel, *Acts and History*, 61. For one example with an external referent, Luke's δῆμος (Acts 12:22) abbreviates fuller information on which Josephus's picture of Agrippa's death in the theater is also based, but one would not know this without knowing such information.

260. Hengel, *Jesus and Paul*, 97–128, responding to those who have regarded Luke's knowledge of Palestinian geography too negatively. One would not expect even a Jerusalemite such as John Mark to know Galilean geography (idem, "Geography of Palestine," 33n19). Because visiting the temple was common piety for Jews and God-fearers, however, knowledge of Jerusalem's topography does not prove that Luke visited *as* Paul's *companion* (Theissen, *Gospels*, 17–18). Neither Luke nor the other Gospel writers were interested in geography the way sources such as Josephus were (see Freyne, "Geography," 79–80).

261. Lucian *Hist.* 24 attacks one for inaccuracies concerning the geography of Syria—especially for placing Lucian's native Edessa in Mesopotamia instead of Roman Syria!

politics, and morals, also is obscure and even inaccurate in his geography of Britain.[262] Luke's geographic obscurity at points[263] thus hardly disqualifies his work from the genre of history.

> All this can also be found in the secular historians of Greek and Roman antiquity. On the other hand, one can hardly accuse him of simply having invented events. . . . He is not just an "edifying writer," but a historian and theologian who needs to be taken seriously. His account always remains within the limits of what was considered reliable by the standards of antiquity. That means that the author's assurance in Luke 1:3 is more than mere convention; it contains a real theological and historical programme, though this cannot be measured by the standards of a modern critical historian.[264]

By the standards of modern historiography, the real problem is not that "Luke simply invented whatever he needed," a premise for which we have no clear supporting evidence. Rather, the primary historiographic problem is "that he often passed over in silence things he thought were either unpleasant or secondary."[265] But it is important that we avoid anachronistically judging Luke by modern criteria; by the historiographic standards of his day such as those found in Dionysius of Halicarnassus and Lucian—and the criteria by which we evaluate the usefulness of ancient historians for reconstructing history—Luke was a good historian.[266] As Loveday Alexander notes, Luke's adaptation of Mark falls within the range of adaptation acceptable in ancient works; a first-century audience "would have found the reality of Luke's work well within the range of the expectations aroused by the preface."[267] Likewise, W. C. van Unnik notes that Luke follows most of the rules that generally characterize ancient historiography, such as lively movement and appropriate speeches.[268]

3. Luke-Acts as a Historical Source

Arguing that Acts is a historical monograph allows us to make some statements about historical intention but does not clarify the nature of Luke's historical endeavor in the way that modern historians of antiquity would like. Ancient historiography was a broad overarching genre providing a wide range of historical works; not every historian proved equally fit for the task or even understood the nature of the task in precisely the same terms. Some modern interpreters grow impatient with historical questions, but historical questions are also literary questions: if the genre of Acts is

262. Hutton, "Introduction," 156–58 (comparing, in more recent colonial times, the memoirs or biography of a British imperial officer in India, 159–60). *Most* ancient historians were inaccurate on topography (Laistner, *Historians*, 58, 95; on Tacitus, ibid., 130), even when visits to a location could have acquainted them with it better (ibid., 58–59).

263. At other points, however, Luke or his sources, like the other Gospels, reveal remarkable acquaintance with Galilean geography (Aviam, "Topography," provides examples from all the Gospels).

264. Hengel, *Acts and History*, 61; also Patzia, *Emergence*, 87. Early Christians believed that biblical history was accurate history (cf. Allison, *Jesus*, 444); thus Bruce, "Record or Reconstruction?" may be right to argue that even Luke's theology would invite good historiography.

265. Riesner, *Early Period*, 413. Omitting or playing down a subject's mistakes was acceptable rhetorical practice (Gibson, "Notes," 195).

266. See Fitzmyer, *Acts*, 124; Hemer, *Acts in History*, 43–49; van Unnik, "Book and Historiography"; Bruce, "First Church Historian."

267. Alexander, *Preface*, 207–8.

268. Van Unnik, "Book and Historiography." Bock, *Acts*, 2n4, observes that Marguerat (*Historian*, 14) finds Luke deficient in only two of van Unnik's ten rules, and Bock explains these in terms of Jewish historiography. Marguerat, *Actes*, 26, recognizes in Acts a confluence of Hellenistic and traditional Jewish historiography.

history, what did this genre entail, and how well did Luke conform to the general expectations that his implicit genre initially invited?

Historically, a great deal more is at stake than students of Acts itself sometimes recognize. Although the stakes should not dictate the outcome of the exploration (this approach would invoke a functionally utilitarian epistemology that could distort the historiographic enterprise as modern historians ideally practice it),[269] they should be taken seriously by those who dismiss available sources too readily because (for equally utilitarian reasons) they do not think they will need them. Scholars often note that Acts provides some of the most complete evidence available for first-century eastern Mediterranean life from a nonaristocratic perspective.[270] For some eastern Mediterranean cities in the mid-first century, Acts "provides the sole literary insight" from antiquity.[271] Classicists recognize the various weaknesses of their sources, but they nevertheless find them more practical than modern alternative reconstructions offered without any extant evidence.[272]

Although Luke-Acts is merely valuable for reconstructing some features of ancient Mediterranean life, it is indispensable for understanding the life of early Christianity. Luke may have his agendas, but without Acts we lack sufficient information to say much, beyond modern speculation about the first three and a half seminal decades of the early church as the Christian movement exploded across the empire sufficiently to provoke even the emperor's attention. Its unique role in supplying much information about this period makes Acts indispensable for historians interested in the early church.[273]

Those who reconstruct early Christian history on the basis of a very selective reading of Acts, such as the Tübingen school, are likely to read it in light of their own biases (in that case, Hegelian dialectic); those who exclude Acts altogether may be forced to reconstruct Christian origins almost by arguing from silence after they have eliminated the clearest concrete sources.[274] (This practice becomes obvious, for example, in the case of many wildly divergent interpretations of Paul, often according to scholarly fashions dominant at the time, often evident among those who rule out any use of Acts and depend entirely on Paul's letters.)[275]

a. Plausibility Structures

More skeptical scholars sometimes dismiss the historical value of Acts on the basis of historical implausibilities that they believe they find there, but plausibility structures are often socially constructed entities. Classicists, on the whole, seem far more ready to make use of Acts as a historical document than NT scholars are.[276] This may be because

269. Pervo, *Mystery*, 5, is correct when he implies that relying on Acts simply because we lack other relevant sources is not by itself a historical argument.

270. Blaiklock, "Document."

271. Gill and Gempf, "Preface," xiii.

272. See, e.g., Foster, "Introduction," xxxi, who argues that though Livy is sometimes uncritical, he is our only source, and hence our best source, "for long stretches of Roman history." Likewise, Josephus is, for all his weaknesses, our best source for postexilic Jewish history (Hengel, *Acts and History*, 7). The work of Megasthenes may be imperfect, but "it is the best we have" on its subject (Brown, *Historians*, 151).

273. Larsson, "Apostlagärningarna"; Green, *Thirty Years*, 7; Wallace and Williams, *Acts*, 1; cf. Lüdemann, "Acts as Source," 121; Strelan, *Artemis*, 23. Thus, e.g., by excluding Acts and considerable other evidence, Crossan, *Birth*, can say little about early Christianity beyond speculation (cf. Wright, "Birth"; Doherty, "Figure").

274. Cf. my complaints about Burton Mack's historical reconstructions in Keener, *Historical Jesus*, 26–31, 61–66, 352–55. Against such arguments from silence, see also Brown, *Death*, 7–8.

275. Hengel and Schwemer, *Between Damascus and Antioch*, 119 (noting Paul the pure Hellenist and Paul the complete non-Hellenist).

276. See Baugh, "Paul and Ephesus," 12–13 (citing A. N. Sherwin-White and others); Winter, *Left Corinth*, xiv; cf. Nobbs, "Historians" (on Sherwin-White, 285–87; on A. H. M. Jones, 287–88; on Fergus Millar, 288);

NT scholars study Acts in more minute detail, noticing narrative inconsistencies and rhetorical adaptation in details, areas where Luke, like other ancient historians, could exercise more literary freedom than in the substance of events. But it seems noteworthy that those who work closely with other ancient historical productions tend to find Acts a useful source (even if some would be skeptical of supernatural claims in both Luke and other historians). Such external controls put Acts in context and support its utility for historical reconstruction and have generally pointed classical scholars toward respect for Acts. New Testament scholars raise questions on matters of detail; classicists appreciate Acts as a source on a par with comparable ancient sources.

Thus, more than a century ago, in the heyday of NT criticism's historical skepticism shaped by Tübingen's academic orthodoxy, William Ramsay advocated a second-century date for Acts and viewed it as an imaginative work. It was, however, his archaeological investigations of specific localities[277] that led him to a first-century date and trust in Luke as a historian. In 1921 Alfred Wikenhauser compared Acts with secular sources and found few divergences;[278] later the respected specialist in Roman law A. N. Sherwin-White found that Acts fit the civic structures and laws of the early empire, showing a writer well informed on details in the way that a later writer could not have been.

Our respective perspectives are also shaped in part by our perception of our pedagogic and scholarly task. New Testament professors often emphasize Acts' "unreliability," using modern history as the foil and seeking to wean modern students from their traditional assumptions that fail to distinguish events themselves from the narration of them. By contrast, those who use ancient historiography as the foil generally respect Acts much more highly because Acts fares well by the standards of ancient historiography. As noted above, Luke wrote in the genre of ancient historiography, not in the as-yet nonexistent genre of its modern successor. Although debunking anachronistic genre assumptions of students may be a noble task, the very comparison with modern historiography, if unqualified, runs the serious risk of playing into these anachronistic assumptions.[279]

How important is internal consistency as a historical criterion? From a literary perspective, we should not press our demands for consistency beyond what could work for other historical sources; even apart from some legitimate insights that deconstruction provides concerning the limitations of any narrative, some of what appears inconsistent is often a deliberate portrayal of weaknesses or narrative tensions.[280] In historical works, some apparent inconsistencies stem from incomplete reporting or the blending of equally incomplete sources.[281]

---

see, e.g., the works of B. Levick and S. Mitchell on Asia Minor; also Paul's letters, in Judge, *First Christians*, 554. For examples of those who use Acts in other disciplines related to the study of Mediterranean antiquity, see Jonge, "New Testament," 42; also the critique of more skeptical Acts scholarship's subjectivity in Stark, *Cities*, 15–17.

277. Especially in Phrygia, because his ship landed in Turkey instead of Greece (Finegan, *Apostles*, 3–4). My examples here are from ibid., 3–5.

278. Wikenhauser, *Geschichtswert* (Münster: Aschendorff, 1921); also idem, *Apostelgeschichte* (cited in Finegan, *Apostles*, 4).

279. Hengel and Schwemer (*Between Damascus and Antioch*, 10–11) argue that from the Tübingen school forward, arguments against Luke have been primarily ideological (e.g., Tübingen presupposed a romantic and dialectic reality obscured by Luke's tendentiousness, or judged Luke by Pauline standards). They also argue (20) that Tübingen advocates, Bultmann, and others dismissed historical information as uninteresting and irrelevant, preferring only the "highest" (by their standards) theology, history remaining "theologically . . . largely irrelevant and at the same time almost 'inferior,' because it was only relative" and not certain.

280. This has also been argued, e.g., with regard to Josephus (e.g., in Sievers, "Name").

281. When taking notes on my wife's randomly remembered accounts of her refugee experiences, I gained confirmation from other eyewitnesses but often had to clarify apparent inconsistencies in dialogue with her—something much more difficult to do with ancient texts.

But granted such limitations, ancients themselves recognized that historical accounts should fit the other historical data available.[282] Thus Polybius challenges a claim of Fabius as implausible, reasoning from undisputed historical evidence.[283] He subsequently allows that Fabius may be right sometimes, but demands that critics evaluate his claims by examining the facts.[284] Even the "purest" of historical reports may contain some events that seem implausible, but they are likely to fare much better (and are expected to fare much better) than carelessly fabricated or novelistic reports. Yet provided we allow for the sort of inconsistencies (real or apparent) and reports of supernatural phenomena (or claims of such phenomena) that characterize most ancient historians,[285] plausibility remains a useful criterion for historical inquiry.[286] We should be able to test Acts in one of the ways that Polybius and others suggest we evaluate historians, namely, by examining the plausibility of accounts.

This commentary will pursue the question in specific passages, but we should note here that plausibility proves not necessarily an account's accuracy but Luke's ability to write cohesive historical narrative;[287] this is, first of all, more a literary than a historical question. Indeed, a poor writer with good sources could produce an implausible narrative yet preserve much accurate information, just as a skilled writer could make fiction sound plausible (a skill that orators employed both in law courts and in encomia). Nevertheless, in general, it counts more in favor of a narrative's accuracy if a writer fairly consistently provides internal cohesiveness and plausibility than if he or she generally writes implausibly. We would expect Luke to meet this criterion more readily where he writes at greater length and in more detail (especially in "we" material) than where he offers primarily summary reports enlivened with speeches.

b. Scholarly Views

On the whole, scholars seem more appreciative than not of Acts as a legitimate source for historical reconstruction, but this appreciation appears far from unanimous.[288] Some scholars are fairly skeptical regarding the historical reliability of Acts,[289] especially voices from the Acts Seminar, successor to the notorious, self-selected[290]

282. See Polyb. 3.47.6–9 for demands for internal consistency and plausibility in accounts.

283. Polyb. 3.8.1–11 (even given Carthage's pride, which Polybius does not take into account, his critique here is undoubtedly accurate).

284. Polyb. 3.9.1–5.

285. See ch. 9 below. Although I, along with most others, would disregard many signs and "prodigy" reports from antiquity, some reports can be explained on naturalistic grounds (prodigies such as ashes or stones from the sky, whether at the eruption of Mount Vesuvius or, more commonly, unattributed in our sources), and even the a priori exclusion of the possibility of any genuine divine activity is necessarily a philosophic premise rather than a conclusion from an inductive, strictly historical examination.

286. Ancients also would employ plausibility as a criterion for evaluating (or discrediting) a position (Hermog. *Progymn.* 5, "On Refutation and Confirmation," 11; Aphth. *Progymn.* 5, "On Refutation," 27–28S, 10R; Nicolaus *Progymn.* 6, "On Refutation and Confirmation," 30).

287. E.g., Euripides was known for attending to plausibility (Dio Chrys. *Or.* 52.11); everyone recognized fables as fictitious (cf. Nicolaus *Progymn.* 4, "On Chreia," 22), but to be effective, they needed to be plausible, i.e., resembling truth (Hermog. *Progymn.* 1, "Fable," 2; cf. Aphth. *Progymn.* 1, "On Fable," 21S, 1R; Nicolaus *Progymn.* 2, "On Fable," 6).

288. For a survey of views on the historical reliability of Acts, see Marguerat, *Histoire*, 12–18; idem, *Historian*, 2–7.

289. E.g., Erlemann, Heiligenthal, and Vouga, "Urgemeinde" (treating reliance on Acts for history as naive); Smith, "Rewriting." See further discussion in ch. 2, sect. 4, above, concerning novels. Many who reject Acts' historicity prefer some earlier, reconstructed portrait of a "pristine" Christianity once sought in Acts itself (Walsh, "Reconstructing").

290. In a sense, academia, as a whole, is "self-selecting"; I mention this feature of the Jesus Seminar only in contrast to the popular assumption outside the academy that its conclusions spoke for Jesus scholarship as a whole (note the critique in Johnson, *Real Jesus*, 41).

Jesus Seminar.[291] Many studies today[292] welcome discussions of "history" and Acts (hence Acts' historical context) but reject questions of its historical reliability as representing an older era's approach.

Although the current emphasis on historical context is paramount for interpreting Acts, rejection of reliability questions altogether seems to me inconsistent with Acts' genre: if Luke writes as an ancient historian, he makes claims about history. We cannot hold him to the standards of peer-reviewed modern historiography, but neither can we isolate his narrative world from the earlier real world he emphatically claims (Luke 1:3–4) that it emulates. He is not writing about mythical characters but about Peter, Paul, Agrippa I, Gallio, Felix, Festus, Agrippa II, and so forth.

It is therefore legitimate to investigate the degree of correspondence between Luke's portrait of the events and what can be reconstructed of the events (where they can be reconstructed at all)—that is, to ask where on the broader continuum of ancient historiography Luke fits. Granted, we cannot reconstruct historical details with certainty, but many literary interpretations of the works likewise remain debated. That a task cannot be completed perfectly is not necessarily reason to abandon it; otherwise we would have to abandon inquiry about ancient history altogether.

Because Luke's narrative, where we can compare it with external data, corresponds with the real world far more often than not, scholars who focus on these data are impressed with his carefulness. In contrast to some earlier generations, many scholars today have grown in their appreciation of Luke's historiography.[293] Hengel thus opines that "Luke is no less trustworthy than other historians of antiquity."[294] Michael D. Goulder, comparing numerous details in Acts with Paul's letters (see ch. 7 below on this subject), argues that Acts is a work of ancient history and points out, "One may get other matters wrong, and one may tell the story with a spin on it, but one cannot be repeatedly accurate unless one is well informed."[295] Or as Luke Timothy Johnson puts it:

> Taking into consideration his use of the one source we can check [i.e., Mark], his general accuracy in matters we can otherwise confirm from archaeological or documentary sources, and the overall agreement between his account of Paul and that in the letters, we can conclude that Luke is accurate in what he tells us, certainly by the standards of Hellenistic historiography (Hengel 1979). The phrase "in what he tells us," however, is critical. Luke writes selectively.[296]

C. K. Barrett notes that we lack certainty at many points but that the story must have happened in much the way Luke tells it, to yield the outcome that history reveals that it did.[297]

291. On the Acts Seminar, see Smith, "Acts Seminar"; for voting tabulation, see, e.g., "Voting Records"; "Records 2002"; Smith, "Meeting 2006"; idem, "Meeting 2007"; idem, "Fall 2007"; idem, "Spring 2008"; idem, "Fall 2008"; idem, "Spring 2009." Unfortunately, this group may present themselves to the media, as the Jesus Seminar sought to do, as representing a scholarly consensus. A larger number of the leading commentaries on Acts currently in the process of publication, however (excepting especially Pervo), point in a different direction. In the final analysis, of course, "majority scholarly opinion" (which changes over time) has no necessary bearing on truth.

292. See, e.g., the summary in Tyson, "History to Rhetoric," 39–40. White, "First Christians," views both Acts' pre-Lukan information and Luke's adaptation of his material as legitimate goals of study.

293. See Stenschke, "Hinweise"; cf. Casalini, "Nuovi commenti."

294. Hengel, *Acts and History*, 60.

295. Goulder, *Competing Mission*, 223.

296. Johnson, "Luke-Acts," 406. (Johnson is citing Hengel, *Acts and History*.)

297. Barrett, "Historicity." Cf. also Parsons, *Acts*, 7–8: Luke seeks "to get the story straight"; this does not guarantee accuracy in every detail, but "neither is Luke free simply to 'make stuff up.'"

Many scholars thus argue for Luke's general dependability as an ancient historian,[298] judged by the criteria that we use for other ancient (rather than modern) historians. They conclude this even if most of these scholars also allow that Luke (like other historians) reported some historical inaccuracies (most often found in Luke 2:2 and Acts 5:36–37). Given Luke's freedom to rewrite details in passages such as Luke 24:39–52 (esp. 24:47–52) and Acts 1:3–12 (or even the slight differences among Paul's conversion accounts), Luke clearly does not work from a modern perspective and would hardly be as disturbed by questions about the rarer proposed exceptions (e.g., Acts 5:36–37) as some of his subsequent readers have been.[299]

To judge Luke's integrity by modern assumptions of how he should have written, rather than by his objectives and standards as a Christian Hellenistic historian, disrespects Hellenistic historians in general, violating our own historical canons against anachronism. All extant ancient historians contradict others at some points.

Some scholars defend Luke even at Luke 2:2[300] and Acts 5:36–37,[301] but if evidence allows us to accept Luke's accuracy in at least most cases, this is sufficient to keep the burden of proof where it belongs: except where one has compelling reason to believe otherwise in particular instances, Luke's reports about events should normally be respected.[302] Provided we also apply other tests at our disposal in relevant cases, we expect Luke to usually reflect events in his sources if he does so where we can test him. Apart from the more extreme postmodernists who are skeptical about most ancient history, detractors against this position apply a skepticism that they would not apply in normal historiography. (When scholars treat what has become Scripture as a special case, they may reflect a canonically determined bias, even if in their case the bias is against the material.)

No one regards the speeches as verbatim, but few scholars would regard Luke's speech summaries as less historical than the fleshed-out speeches of other historians of his time. (Indeed, he might fare generally better than Josephus; see below). I believe that the evidence probably argues against the usual "conservative" chronology of Acts 15 and Gal 2, but this is a problem for one scholarly position, not for the historical nature of Acts. In the Gospel, the divergences from Mark and possibly from material shared with Matthew are all within the expected literary freedom of ancient writers.

---

298. E.g., Rackham, *Acts*, xliv–xlvii; Sherwin-White, *Society*, passim; Gasque, "Acts and History"; Munck, *Acts*, xli; Ehrhardt, *Acts*, 12; Hemer, *Acts in History*, 43–49; Larsson, "Synpunkter"; Marshall, "Luke and 'Gospel,'" 273–92; D. Williams, *Acts*, 7–10. This is true even of Harnack, *Acts*, 298, though he complained that his brilliant pupil William Ramsay (for all "his great learning") tried to salvage too much (302). For a survey of views on the historical reliability of Acts, see again Marguerat, *Histoire*, 12–18; idem, *Historian*, 2–7.

299. Cf. Massey, "Disagreement," 54–55. Memory studies show that memory generally preserves gist even where details vary (Bauckham, *Eyewitnesses*, 333–34); in the Gospels (e.g., Peter's denial), this helps explain variation in detail while the essential story remains basically stable (344–45); cf. Allison, *Jesus*, 11–13.

300. Ramsay, *Bethlehem*, x, 107–96 passim; Robertson, *Luke*, 118ff.; sources mentioned in ch. 2 of this introduction; see discussion in Porter, "Census."

301. See discussion ad loc.

302. Talbert, *Mediterranean Milieu*, 216, notes Lüdemann's way of posing the problem: is Luke's work true unless proved false, or false unless proved true? In contrast to Lüdemann, I think it more nuanced to reframe the question thus: do the data suggest that Luke is usually right or usually wrong where we can check him? Since Luke could not predict what evidence would survive, his usual pattern where we can test him should shape our basic default approach elsewhere. We also need to take into account where he is accurate; e.g., if we found Luke accurate on narratives but not on speeches, this would adjust the burden of proof for these kinds of genre. On burden-of-proof issues (as applied to Gospels studies), see Eddy and Boyd, *Legend*, 364–71 (for the range of views among both historians in general and NT scholars, see 366–69); Goetz and Blomberg, "Burden of Proof." (I use "burden of proof" here not to imply that claims will always prove right or wrong, but simply as how the evidence we do have should shape our expectations where tests are not possible.) Public claims, such as inscriptions, are usually accepted as valid (though slanted) sources of information in the absence of contrary evidence (Yamauchi, *Persia*, 144, following Frye, *Persia*, 86).

The radical skepticism of the old Tübingen school retains few advocates today; indeed, on the whole, extreme critical approaches have proved too subjective to yield consensus.[303] (Even Haenchen's skepticism is too severe, applying a standard of suspicion under which even Polybius and Thucydides would fare badly.[304] Contrary to the views of some modern critics, the NT writers knew more about their subjects than we modern critics can at our remove.)[305] Although radical views such as those associated with nineteenth-century Tübingen have not vanished, scholarship today is divided especially between those who argue for a high degree of Acts' historical reliability and those who allow that it is at some times reliable but that this is not Luke's focus.[306] Most scholars today would probably concur with Fitzmyer: the genre and external corroborations of many points in Acts do "not guarantee, of course, the historicity of every Lucan statement or episode, but" they do reveal "that what is recounted in Acts is substantially more trustworthy from a historical point of view than not."[307]

By many modern standards, Luke may have taken significant literary liberties to produce a coherent narrative rather than a documented chronicle. Even for his own day, Luke provides less "documentation" of his sources than the generally longer and more rhetorically sophisticated histories of his day. But Luke is accurate where it counts for popular historical writing of his day: he probably participated in some of the events he narrates; relevant for more of his narrative, he interviewed eyewitnesses where possible and wrote of relatively recent events. So long as we recognize and take into account that Acts is a single-volume, popular-level apologetic history, we should give Luke the same courtesy of trust for historical events that we accord other competent ancient historians discussing recent events.[308]

When all has been examined, a number of scholars rank Luke among the more accurate historians, such as Polybius, Thucydides, and Tacitus,[309] though others would view this verdict as excessive. We must note again that Luke's rhetorical techniques reflect the fact that he writes for a somewhat less demanding, more popular audience than such historians (but, on the other side of it, less interested in rhetorical flourishes and other rhetorical expectations). Yet even most of the scholars who are more skeptical accept that Acts has historical value.[310]

---

303. For a summary of his historical survey and critique, see Gasque, *Criticism*, 306–9. While not all "conservative" approaches to Luke's historical reliability (in the modern sense of that phrase) are equally plausible, they share the common value of a disciplined attempt to explain the text rationally before cavalierly dismissing it. If employed heuristically, such an approach helps us grapple more carefully with the text in its context, and may be comparable to a helpful approach toward classical sources (cf., e.g., Green, "Diodorus," on Diodorus as a "reasonably competent" [363], though second-tier, ancient historian).

304. With Gasque, *Criticism*, 247.

305. Cf. esp. Brown, *Death*, 7–8, commenting on the Gospel writers; Sumney, *Opponents*, 86, commenting on the matter of Paul's opponents.

306. See earlier the summary of scholarship in Wilson, *Gentile Mission*, 255–57; Wilson himself holds a mediating position (267). Barrett, "History," however, argues that modern NT scholars have simply shifted Baur's view of the later conflict between Jewish and Gentile Christians back into the NT era.

307. Fitzmyer, *Acts*, 127; similarly Dunn, *Acts*, xvi–xviii; Barrett, *Acts*, 2:xxxiii–lxii, esp. xxxiii–xliii.

308. By "popular" history, I mean only that much of Luke's audience (and, correspondingly, his rhetoric) need not be elite; we do not seek to evoke K. L. Schmidt's contrast between grand writings and a folk literature that evolved haphazardly (cf. Keener, *Matthew*, 17; Burridge, *Gospels*, 11, 153; Aune, *Environment*, 12, 63).

309. Ehrhardt, *Acts*, 12 (following E. Meyer); Witherington, "Editing," 335–44; idem, *Acts*, 27, 32–34 (following Fornara, *Nature of History*, 25ff., 49); Bruce, *Acts*[3], 27 (following Meyer, *Ursprung*, 1:2–3). Harnack moved from skepticism to increased respect for Luke over time (noted, e.g., by his student Ramsay, *Luke the Physician*, 4–5; for Ramsay's own view, see, e.g., 80).

310. Bornkamm, *Paul*, xix; though uncertain which elements are historical, Bornkamm is most optimistic where scholars "find least traces of obviously legendary embellishment" (a potentially subjective criterion), "of the overriding interests of the book," and, perhaps most debatable (since telling a story in an artistic way does not make it untrue), "of the literary activity of its author."

c. Evaluating Luke's Usefulness as an Ancient Historical Writer

Despite some scholars' reservations, it seems most logical to presume that Luke's standards of reliability where we cannot test him are roughly equivalent to his standards where we can. This is the same procedure we would apply to establish (more narrowly than genre alone permits) the relative burden of proof for the factual accuracy of any ancient historian; writers could not know what information would remain extant, even in the unlikely event that they wrote only for future generations; thus the burden of proof rests heavily on interpreters who expect the degree of reliability to decline precipitously where we cannot test it. Of course, while it is not our focus here, the test also cuts the other way: the evidence will suggest that Luke has considerable information, increasingly detailed in later chapters, but he also takes the ancient historian's storytelling liberties to narrate the story in a cohesive, interesting, and edifying way.[311]

We can test the historical accuracy of Acts by noting its relatively conservative use of sources and the likely reliability of these sources (as noted above). We can also test its reliability by comparing it with other sources that cover the same material and then determining which sources most consistently represent the likely consensus of ancient evidence. Paul's letters, as a primary source, provide the most significant test case for Acts,[312] as Q and Mark do for Luke's reports about Jesus in the Gospel; here, however, the issues are significant enough to merit a separate chapter on Paul and Acts (ch. 7 below). We must also compare Acts with its extratextual setting wherever the opportunity arises. I shall survey such correspondences here, but this more detailed task belongs especially to the commentary that follows. First I mention some of the other evidence, though I will treat most of it in detail only under the requisite passages.

Leaving aside places where we cannot test the work, external evidence corroborates Luke's accounts at many points.[313] One area of interest here is Luke's accuracy in titles for local officials, which changed from one locale to the next and sometimes within a locale from one decade to the next. Whereas Agrippa I and II are rightly "kings," Antipas is a tetrarch (in contrast to Mark 6:14; cf. the correction also in Matt 14:1); Philippi's magistrates are praetors with rod-bearing lictors; Thessalonica has its "politarchs"; Asia has its "Asiarchs"; and "the chief municipal officer of Ephesus is the 'town clerk.'"[314] Long ago Cadbury observed that just as one can evaluate a person's

> knowledge of modern Oxford and Cambridge by his ability to name correctly the presiding officer of each college whether as Master, Principal, Provost, Warden, rector, President or Dean, or one's knowledge of old Germany's political constitution when more than three hundred territorial sovereignties existed within the Holy Roman Empire ruled by kings, electors, and princes, counts and counts palatine, dukes and grand dukes, landgraves, margraves and all the rest, so one may test Luke's knowledge of municipal institutions in Aegean cities. His language fully meets the test.[315]

311. Perhaps most fully in the earliest chapters. A popular historian may tell stories more freely in one way, a rhetorical historian more freely in a different way, each with his own conventions (though the more rhetorical works probably follow more explicitly defined conventions).

312. E.g., Acts fits well most of the itinerary suggested in Philippians, 1 Thessalonians, and 1–2 Corinthians; we would, then, expect it to provide useful information where we cannot check it as well (deSilva, *Introduction*, 350; cf. 375–80).

313. See Fitzmyer, *Acts*, 125–26; see discussion of individual texts in the current commentary. Since Luke could not know which external evidence would be preserved for future readers, we must take these correspondences as a representative sampling.

314. Bruce, *Acts*[3], 32; deSilva, *Introduction*, 369, 375, among many others.

315. Cadbury, *Acts in History*, 40–41.

Charles Talbert notes that congruence with the period depicted does not by itself establish historicity,[316] but he also notes that the "points at which the contemporary color of Acts can be challenged . . . are few and insignificant compared to the overwhelming congruence between Acts and its time and place."[317] Likewise, he contends that the sequence of events in Acts fits external history and Paul's letters fairly well (except Gal 2:1–10).[318] External sources confirm numerous points.

Colin Hemer provides a massive list of such correspondences,[319] including (for a small sampling of his examples):

- The Sergii Paulli are attested (Acts 13:7).[320]
- Iconium was ethnically Phrygian rather than Lycaonian (14:6).[321]
- Unlike most towns where Paul traveled, Lystra would have people speaking a local language (14:11).[322]
- Zeus and Hermes are particularly paired in this area (14:12).[323]
- Coming from the Cilician Gates, one would reach Derbe before Lystra (16:1).[324]
- Philippi was a Roman colony (16:12).[325]
- Thyatira was a center of dyeing (16:14).[326]
- Amphipolis and Apollonia allow for the journey from Philippi to Thessalonica to be divided into realistic travel legs (17:1).[327]
- Thessalonica, as a "free" city, had a δῆμος (17:5).
- A major congregating place for Athenian Stoics (17:18) was near the Areopagus (17:19).[328]
- The two-part form Ἄρειος πάγος appears often "in many inscriptions of the period" (17:19).[329]
- The specific quotations in 17:28 might derive from authors and contexts fitting either Paul's background in Tarsus (Aratus) or his "unknown deity" allusion (Epimenides),[330] perhaps implying that Luke or his source abbreviates a lengthier Pauline speech in Attica.
- Acts 18:2 fits the likeliest period of Claudius's expulsion.[331]
- The timing of Paul's appearance before Gallio fits precisely (18:12).[332]

316. Talbert, *Mediterranean Milieu*, 201; idem, *Acts*, 237 (though also citing Gasque's argument that the level of correspondence fits history, not novel; Gasque, *Criticism*, 193n94).

317. Talbert, *Mediterranean Milieu*, 201; idem, *Acts*, 236. He notes (*Mediterranean Milieu*, 200–201; idem, *Acts*, 236) lack of congruence (e.g., in Acts 5:36–37; Luke's weaker acquaintance with noncoastal Palestinian geography) and (*Mediterranean Milieu*, 198–200; idem, *Acts*, 235) more examples of congruence.

318. Talbert, *Mediterranean Milieu*, 202–6; idem, *Acts*, 237–41. For a discussion of correspondences and differences between Acts 15 and Gal 2:1–10, see this commentary's comment at Acts 15.

319. Hemer, *Acts in History*, 108–220, esp. 108–92 and most fruitfully 108–58.

320. Ibid., 109.

321. Ibid., 110.

322. Ibid.

323. Ibid., 111.

324. Ibid.

325. Ibid., 113. This datum would, however, have been well known.

326. Ibid., 114.

327. Ibid., 115.

328. Ibid., 116, also noting the proximity of many idols (but these were pervasive).

329. Ibid., 117; likewise the form Ἀρεοπαγίτης in Acts 17:34 (p. 119).

330. Ibid., 118.

331. Ibid., 119, 167–68.

332. Ibid., 119, 168–69.

- The title γραμματεύς is precisely the title for Ephesus's chief officer (19:35).[333]
- The unusual title ἡ θεός appears frequently for Artemis in inscriptions from Roman Ephesus.[334]
- Ἀγοραῖοι fits the custom in Roman Asia of the governor periodically holding court in the capitals of the nine assize districts, of which Ephesus was one (19:38).[335]
- The form Βεροιαῖος fits that attested on local inscriptions (20:4).[336]
- The itinerary in 20:13–17 and 21:1–8 closely fits known geography.[337]
- The penalty for Gentiles entering the temple was death (21:28).[338]
- The Roman cohort in the Antonia remained ready to quell disturbances in the temple (21:31).[339]
- The staircase by which the soldiers descended to the temple's outer court is well attested (21:35, 40).[340]
- The tribune mentions the Egyptian Jewish false prophet, whose activity was recent from the standpoint of the narrative world.[341]
- The nomen Claudius (23:26) fits recent acquisition of citizenship under Claudius, under whom the grant was frequent, and cheaper toward the end of his reign (22:28).[342]
- Ananias is the correct high priest for the narrative date (23:2).[343]
- Felix's tenure fits the narrative date (23:24).[344]
- Antipatris is the correct military stop from Jerusalem to Caesarea; the road is documented; it was also the correct location (in more Gentile territory) where the infantry could be dismissed (23:31).[345]
- Felix might have deferred a case to another governor, except that Paul was from Cilicia, which was, precisely in this period, under his own superior officer (23:34).[346]
- Drusilla, perhaps about nineteen at the time depicted in the narrative, was married to Felix at this time (in contrast to her and his earlier marriages; 24:24).[347]
- The name and timing of Porcius Festus (24:27) are correct.[348]
- The presence of Berenice with Agrippa II fits this period (rather than the times that she was married; 25:13).[349]

333. Ibid., 122.
334. Ibid. (citing, e.g., *I. Eph.* 27.12–13).
335. Ibid., 123. He also compares the "regular" assembly to *I. Eph.* 27.468–69 (also p. 123).
336. Ibid., 124.
337. Ibid., 125–26.
338. Ibid., 126 (citing *CIJ* 1400).
339. Ibid. (citing Jos. *War* 5.244).
340. Ibid. (citing Jos. *War* 5.243).
341. Ibid. (citing Jos. *War* 2.261–63; *Ant.* 20.169–71, and noting that where the figures diverge, Luke's more modest figures should be preferred, since Josephus is known to inflate figures).
342. Ibid., 127, 170.
343. Ibid., 128, 170–71.
344. Ibid., 128, 171.
345. Ibid., 128.
346. Ibid., 128, 172.
347. Ibid., 172–73.
348. Ibid., 130.
349. Ibid., 173.

- The itinerary, weather conditions, and sailors' actions are correct down to minute details in most of 27:1–28:15.[350]

Not all of these examples are equally compelling,[351] but the cumulative weight of the best of them should be sufficient to dispel any notions that Luke is writing a novel rather than ancient historiography or that Luke is a careless historian unconcerned with detail. Hemer also notes numerous internal correspondences that suggest consistent information on which Luke never capitalizes for his narrative—for example, "we" leaving off and resuming at Philippi (16:17; 20:5–6) and again in Jerusalem (21:18; 27:1) or the assumption of Paul's personal possession of funds (21:24; 24:26; 28:30).[352]

Some scholars have simply dismissed such historical correspondences as (in the case of Hemer, though not Cadbury or Talbert) the work of a "conservative" scholar (academic shorthand in some circles for a work that does not come to the appropriate conclusions and hence may be dismissed as closed-minded). This is, however, an ad hominem label rather than an argument. Hemer provides abundant data, more often than not data difficult to contest.[353] Such correspondences do not prove that everything Luke wrote is factual,[354] but they do indicate that he had access to solid information; he may have adapted it, but he was not ignorant of it. And serious historical interest would limit the degree of adaptation in a way that a primarily novelistic approach (or very careless historiography) would not.

4. Examples Where Acts' Accounts Are Historically Probable

As already noted, it was an ancient historical work, rather than an ancient novel (despite some displays of local color), that would be typically confirmed on incidental matters by external data. Such a description certainly suits Acts. The key test is Paul's letters (see ch. 7 below), but other extrinsic data provide helpful tests as well.

Although we should not expect any two ancient historians to agree on every detail, we find for Acts numerous confirmations of substance that fit the mainstream of historical but not of novelistic works. For example, Josephus and Luke concur that Agrippa died after accepting public adulation in Caesarea (Acts 12:19–23). Moreover, some objections to Luke's reliability are ill founded. Whereas Haenchen complains that Gentile soldiers were not stationed in Judea during Agrippa's reign,[355] Josephus explicitly tells us otherwise (*Ant.* 19.357; though we cannot be sure the Cornelius episode happened during Agrippa's reign, in any case). Following are examples in support of Luke's usual accuracy (some overlapping with those offered by others above).

350. See ibid., 132–56.

351. Some of these details may have been widely known. A writer would not easily have known so many details over a wide geographical range, however (and especially lesser-known areas), unless he had traveled to many of the places in addition to his own region. Getting the right associations during the appropriate range of years in such cases (e.g., with Drusilla and Berenice) is also probably more than coincidence.

352. Hemer, *Acts in History*, 190–93 (for these particular examples, 192).

353. This is not to say that one must concur with all Hemer's conclusions, such as the work's date, which need not all follow from his data.

354. See the caution about Hemer's approach in, e.g., Lentz, *Luke's Portrait*, 6.

355. Haenchen, *Acts*, 360, speaks of "Roman soldiers," which is technically true, since these would have been auxiliaries. But his point in the context appears to be Gentile soldiers in general, since the objection is to these troops being stationed there during the reign of Agrippa I, to 44 c.e. He counts this presence of soldiers against the narrative's historicity. Against this position, see Keener, "Troops."

a. Accurate Local Color

Although accurate local color does not prove reliability, obviously it is consistent with it, especially when Luke would have had to travel or depend on informants to obtain detailed information (i.e., where it was not simply common knowledge). As Richard Wallace and Wynne Williams, both classicists, observe, "It is the accuracy over quite obscure details which is striking."[356]

Luke gets correct the local color in Ephesus; for example, Ephesus did sometimes publicly defend the Artemis cult, Asia Minor's cities had many riots and much unrest in this period, and economic concern for the Artemis temple was at a peak in precisely these decades. In addition, Luke's portrayal of Ephesians calling Artemis both ἡ θεά and ἡ θεός fits local Ephesian usage (rare outside Ephesus). Even what we can reconstruct of the progress of the riot in his account (admittedly hypothetical, given uncertainties over some of our archaeological data there) appears to fit the local topography of Ephesus.

Far more impressively, Luke correctly describes details of the Anatolian interior (such as geography; key sites, occurring often on known roads and in the right sequence; and the greater than usual linkage of Zeus and Hermes), yet these are not (and appear before any) "we" narratives and Luke makes no claim to have traveled to these locations.[357] Nor had most of his Aegean contemporaries; it is unlikely that Luke relies on a (non-Pauline) source for his geography here. Today, as another commentator notes, "even skeptical critics" are impressed with Luke's accuracy on "geographical, social and political minutiae," but "reference works that would make such research possible did not exist in the first century."[358] The relative inaccessibility of such information suggests that, to acquire it, either Luke would need very reliable information from someone who traveled or he himself would have had to travel in the period described—with or without Paul. Yet he does not write himself into narratives in the Anatolian interior and elsewhere (as someone seeking to validate a fiction might).[359] (This commentary treats most of these correspondences in the comments on the specific passages where they appear, but some scholars have documented such information at much greater length.)[360] Likewise, Jerusalem in Acts becomes increasingly dominated by nationalism in precisely the decades for which Josephus reports its growth, yet Luke neither draws attention to this shift (as he might if deliberately

---

356. Wallace and Williams, *Acts*, 27. They note that (28) one can evaluate Luke's historical accuracy by "comparison with other sources," by assumptions that "particular elements 'must have' been invented," and by "*a priori* assumptions that certain kinds of event cannot have occurred," noting that only the first approach is objective enough to "yield secure results."

357. Everyone acknowledges that Luke knows the coasts of Asia Minor better than the interior (see, e.g., Bechard, *Walls*, 345–52); although I think Luke's information regarding the interior normally accurate where he does report it, he includes far less detail than on the coastal itinerary.

358. Larkin, *Acts*, 22; for a more skeptical critic impressed with Luke's accuracy on minutiae Larkin cites Koester, *Introduction*, 2:50. Other examples of more skeptical critics who nevertheless believe Acts often depends on historical sources include Lüdemann, "Acts as Source."

359. Would Luke care enough about accuracy to travel to out-of-the-way locations simply in order to create a purely fictitious narrative (less detailed than in the "we" narratives)? And if Luke carried out such research for a fiction, why not write himself into the narrative fictitiously, if this was what he supposedly did with the "we" in the "we" narratives (as some scholars opine)? Is it not more probable that Luke did not travel to these locations but had genuine information about Paul's mission there? (The mission certainly happened; the churches were founded early by someone, and Paul was an early church founder with a reputation for founding churches, presumably for good reason. See also this commentary's comments on the sections in question.) Genuine tradition best accounts for the correspondence of these incidental details to features of the region less widely known outside.

360. See Hemer, *Acts in History*, 101–58; on the Anatolian interior, see esp. works by Stephen Mitchell (cited in our commentary loc. cit.).

trying to highlight his realism) nor obscures this reality (as a novelist pursuing free composition undoubtedly would).

Other elements may contribute to an impression of historical accuracy. Detail by itself does not; it appears in poetry and drama as well as history,[361] and in poetry and drama it is a sign of invention. But Luke provides far more detail in the "we" narratives, where he was present (or, in some views, had an eyewitness source), than he does elsewhere, a pattern consistent with what we would expect of genuine reminiscences. Likewise, he provides more historical detail where his sources are better (more recent events known to Paul) than in the early chapters of the book.[362] This conforms to what we would expect of a fairly conservative historical method, not the relatively free composition of a novelist.

Luke's narrative arena in Acts contains real geography (often known to his audience, especially in the Aegean region) in quite recent history, in contrast to novels. Such settings demanded more accuracy than the distant times or exotic locations sometimes featured in other kinds of works. When Luke speaks of Paul's conflicts in synagogues of specific locales, or the behavior of local authorities, or the founding of local churches, he reports matters that may well be preserved in local memories at the time of his writing. Local churches could dispute his assertions; synagogues could treat what they heard of his reports in the way they responded to and generated other polemic. Luke could not afford to get his basic facts wrong if he wished a wide readership, especially in the regions on which his narrative focuses. And it seems likely that just as Luke is disposed to quote biblical texts accurately, he would also wish to communicate accurately the history of his community. Although the former belonged to the community's common repository of information, it appears that some of the latter did as well (Luke 1:4).

Gospel scholarship has discovered over time that the criterion of dissimilarity works effectively only in a positive way (affirming material), not a negative one (excluding it).[363] This is because we should not expect the historical Jesus to have differed on every point with either his environment (whose language and imagery we would in fact expect him to use) or his followers (who, as disciples, would in fact be expected to respect, preserve, and propagate much of his teaching). The criterion of Palestinian environment thus effectively cancels out that of dissimilarity fairly often. In the case of Acts, we cannot exclude a claim's accuracy merely because it fits what we know of early Christian beliefs; we dare not assume that what was useful to Luke (whose Christian faith was undoubtedly nurtured in the setting of early Christianity) could not have also happened in early Christianity. Historians often selected historical material that strengthened their case, but no one supposes that whatever fits their case must therefore be fabricated. Thus, as with the Gospels, the criterion proves more useful in its positive form. Some apparently non-Lukan material, or material embarrassing to later Christians (such as Paul's split with Barnabas), is unlikely to have been invented.

361. Brodie, "Imitation of Texts," 38; Aune, *Dictionary of Rhetoric*, 399; Pervo, *Acts*, 11.

362. See Johnson, *Acts*, 4; Riesner, *Early Period*, 413.

363. For discussion, see, e.g., Keener, *Historical Jesus*, 156–57; Meier, *Marginal Jew*, 1:173; Brown, *Death*, 19; Stanton, *Gospel Truth?*, 143; Young, *Jewish Theologian*, 257; cf. Mealand, "Dissimilarity Test"; Mack, *Lost Gospel*, 193; Sanders, "What We Know," 60n12; idem, *Jesus and Judaism*, 16, 145; Theissen and Merz, *Guide*, 11, 115; Ehrman, *Prophet*, 92 (though using the criterion in a limited manner); Holmén, *Covenant Thinking*, 20–31, esp. 29–30; idem, "Introduction," 2; idem, "Doubts about Dissimilarity"; Kazen, "Son of Man," 87; Broadhead, "Priests," 125; Dunn, *Perspective*, 57–78 (esp. 58); Stein, *Messiah*, 48; Tuckett, "Sources," 133; Levine, "Introduction to *Historical Jesus*," 10–11; Borg, *Conflict*, 20–23; Bird, "Quest."

b. The Jerusalem Church

Although Luke's sources for Paul's life, especially in the "we" material, are more thorough, many scholars believe that Luke also preserves genuine traditions about the early Jerusalem church.[364] He portrays some of the information as being well known in Judea (Luke 24:18; Acts 10:37; 26:26); although we could accuse him of fabricating this portrayal, such fabrication would have been riskier in his own day when presumably some people remained—especially scattered refugees from Judea—who could have discounted such claims (cf. Luke 1:2, 4). More concretely, his Pentecost narrative seems to presuppose, regarding the festival, some Jewish Christian theologizing on which he himself fails to capitalize; perhaps the Christology and more clearly the imminent end expectation portrayed in Acts 3:12–26 may also suggest some knowledge of ideas that circulated in an earlier period of the Jerusalem church, ideas that Luke would not, apart from his historian's mantle, feel as much need to emphasize.

Luke's portrayal of Pharisaic tolerance (e.g., 5:34–39) fits much of what we know of first-century Pharisees outside the gospel tradition. Likewise, we would probably not expect Luke to invent the complaint of the widows in 6:1 and then work to soften the charge. Nor would he likely invent the account of Philip's ministry to the African court official, an account that seems in tension with the church's official account of Cornelius (which Luke also approves). His information regarding the official fits ancient historical accounts of Meroë better than it fits ancient fictional ones.[365]

The Hellenists' mission in Antioch in 11:19 is incidental to Luke's focus on major characters such as Barnabas and Paul (who arrive only afterward) and hence probably reflects pre-Lukan information too widely known to ignore. Luke's tradition about the origin of the title "Christians" in Antioch (11:26) is also likely, since Luke himself prefers different titles for Jesus's followers (and "Christians" does not appear complimentary when employed in this period). Although a global famine (11:28) may be Lukan hyperbole (a not uncommon ancient device), many data corroborate widespread famine conditions during much of Claudius's reign (though this reign was admittedly probably still often remembered in Luke's day).[366]

Luke's report of Peter's escape, often considered legendary, fits both the timing of Agrippa's brief reign and archaeological data for Jerusalem's topography (see comment ad loc.). Luke's report of James's death in 12:2 appears incidental to his focus on Peter's story and is historically likely. Because the house of John Mark's mother is spoken of as well known, Luke probably is drawing on authentic local tradition for it.[367] Luke's narrative seems to presuppose knowledge of John Mark (12:12) and James the Just (12:17), suggesting that Theophilus had heard somewhat more than (or at least a fuller version of) the gospel tradition itself (Luke 1:4). That some degree of leadership would pass to James the Lord's brother (Acts 12:17; 15:13–22; 21:18) would fit Middle Eastern kinship expectations (although Luke does not specify the sibling connection, which appears in Gal 1:19; 2:12).

Agrippa's death in Caesarea agrees, on the essentials, with Josephus's account, and Agrippa's personality in Acts (see esp. comment on Acts 12:1, 3) fits the more

364. For details in this paragraph, see comments in this commentary on the relevant passages.
365. See Keener, "Official."
366. A severe famine in Egypt, the primary grain source for the eastern Mediterranean world, is well attested ca. 45–46 C.E., with repercussions beyond Egypt in the years immediately following. Josephus indicates that the dearth struck Judea forcefully (see comment on Acts 11:28).
367. Conzelmann, *Acts*, 94 (Luke has "factual support" for it). Such information would have been available during his visit to Jerusalem (Acts 21:15–18).

negative side of his personality in Josephus. Although each source mentions and emphasizes points the other omits and hence neither is likely dependent on the other,[368] the overlap is considerable:

Josephus *Ant*. 19.343–50	Acts 12:19–23
Agrippa was in Caesarea (19.343)	Agrippa was in Caesarea (12:19)
Setting of games in the theater in honor of Caesar; no mention of the embassy (19.343–44)	Mention of the embassy, with no description of the setting of the event (except that he was at a βῆμα [12:20] and that his hearers included a δῆμος, the citizen body of Caesarea [12:22])*
Mentions Agrippa's glorious robe as a cause for praise (19.344)	Mentions his royal apparel, though without details that would explain why this mention is important (12:21)
No mention of Agrippa's speech before he is struck, but a rhetorically apt one is composed for him afterward (19.347)	Agrippa is speaking when he is praised (12:21)
Flatterers acclaim Agrippa as divine (19.344–45)†	Flatterers acclaim Agrippa as divine (12:22)
Agrippa struck just afterward (19.346–48)	Agrippa struck just afterward (12:23)
Because he did not rebuke the acclamation (19.346–47)	Because he did not defer the glory to God (12:23)
He suffered stomach pains for five days (19.348–50)‡	He was eaten by worms (12:23)§
He died (19.350)	He died (12:23)

*A theater was a natural meeting place for the δῆμος, as would be games.
†They also plead for mercy ("Be propitious to us," Jos. *Ant*.19.345 [LCL, 9:378]), which might fit Luke's context of at least the embassy (Acts 12:20).
‡Eusebius treats Josephus's account here as corroborating Acts (*H.E.* 2.10.10; Witherington, *Acts*, 390n112).
§That the duration is unspecified may fit the nature of Luke's tradition or interests (cf. Acts 9:23).

c. The Pauline Mission

Much of Paul's ministry in Paphos fits external evidence. One Lucius Sergius Paullus is "the only senator attested from this generation of the family" and hence, the classicist Stephen Mitchell concludes, surely the one Paul met in Cyprus.[369] Acts 13 and the inscription in question both fit together well with the way senatorial careers usually proceeded in this era and could indicate the same individual.[370] Given the rareness of the name and the normal pattern of a senatorial career, Mitchell is also convinced that this would be the same Sergius Paullus who became *consul suffectus* in 70 C.E. (*CIL* 6.253).[371] Various rulers depended on magicians or similar sorts of advisers, and Sergius Paullus, who was a Roman from southern Anatolia, grew up surrounded by Eastern culture and perhaps was more open to it than most Roman officials would have been; for what it is worth, evidence also suggests that there may have been other Jewish magicians in Cyprus. Perhaps most significantly, the Sergii Paulli, though Italian by descent, "were native to Pisidian Antioch,"[372] which fits historically the next location of the team's ministry even though Luke never clarifies the connection.

That Luke mentions only Perga (Πέργη, normally transliterated outside the NT as Pergē) at Acts 13:13 and only Attalia on the departure of Paul and Barnabas at 14:25 fits historical reality, since Perga was the appropriate goal if they wished to reach the Via Sebaste for travel into the inland highlands whereas Attalia was the more appropriate

---

368. The unclear role of Blastus suggests Luke's abridgment of a source besides Josephus (see Barrett, *Acts*, 589).
369. Mitchell, *Anatolia*, 2:7.
370. Nobbs, "Cyprus," 287.
371. Mitchell, *Anatolia*, 2:6; cf. also Levick, *Roman Colonies*, 112.
372. Mitchell, *Anatolia*, 2:7. On the Caristanii, see also Levick, *Roman Colonies*, 111–13.

goal for a departure port.[373] Most of Luke's portrait of events in Pisidian Antioch fits what we know of the town, as does Paul's interest in evangelizing there (for details, see commentary loc. cit.). Even some non-Lukan midrash in Paul's speech there appears to be pre-Lukan[374] (also comporting well with Pauline language there), although we do not know Luke's source (unless it was, if anyone, probably Paul himself and probably orally), and it is tenuous to automatically infer that something being "pre-Lukan" necessarily makes it what Paul must have said on an occasion.

Moreover, in view of Paul's ministry in prominent locations such as Corinth, who would invent ministry in such out-of-the-way towns as Iconium and Lystra?[375] As mentioned above, the pairing of Zeus and Hermes is well attested at Lystra,[376] and it seems unlikely that Luke acquired such information by visiting this site personally; other elements of local color are also dominant (see comment ad loc.). Luke's compressed account there also suggests traces of prior information (such as mention of "the gates," without clarifying what these gates are, 14:13).

James's speech in 15:13–21, like some other speeches to Jewish audiences in Acts, seems to imply Jewish exegetical arguments that Luke himself only summarizes and nowhere develops[377] (for a more concrete argument for the Jerusalem Council itself, see ch. 7 below). The conflict between Paul and Barnabas (15:37–39), as something Luke probably would not have invented, meets the criterion of embarrassment; so, most likely, does Luke's implied portrayal of Mark. This embarrassment leads to another: the new mission initially appears to wander aimlessly now that Paul lacks Barnabas's help and has pressed beyond the previous sphere of ministry (16:6–9). It is not the sort of report Luke would likely invent about his hero.

The known timing of both Gallio's governorship and particularly explicit anti-Jewish sentiments (though the latter could have also occurred at other times) fits Luke's description in Acts 18 well.[378] Paul's letters indicate his friendship with Prisca and Aquila; Luke's additional specification that Aquila hails from Pontus (which neither is important to his narrative nor reflects a particularly high-status location in this period) makes little sense except as historical tradition. Given the relatively low status of artisans, Luke is unlikely to have invented such activity for Paul, Priscilla, and Aquila (18:3) in a document dedicated to a person of status (Luke 1:3; Acts 1:1).

373. Attalia's more heavily trafficked harbor, directly on the sea, provided the better port for a return voyage to Syrian Antioch (Acts 14:25–26; Campbell, "Paul in Pamphylia," arguing from this information and the asymmetry of Luke's references in Acts 13:13–14 and 14:24–26 for the virtually assured historical accuracy of Luke's itinerary here).

374. Especially the use of *gezerah shevah*; note also implicit links presumably present in Luke's source but omitted in his more compressed account.

375. The exception might be if Luke's primary audience was located there—which is extremely unlikely. Wallace and Williams, *Acts*, 27, emphasize Luke's accuracy regarding "Derbe and Lystra, neither of them well known cities."

376. Mitchell, *Anatolia*, 2:24, arguing from this for "the historical precision of the famous episode in Acts."

377. James's choice of *text* justifying an eschatological perspective is plausible enough in Judea. The Amos quotations used by him here and by Stephen in Acts 7:42–43 are among those used in a key Qumran document to define that sect's own identity; James's quotation may even diverge from the traditional LXX reading in favor of the Hebrew at various points despite Luke's normal dependence on LXX versions. This correspondence need not imply a literal translation of a verbatim transcript, but it could suggest that Luke depends on a very specific oral tradition. Given the importance of the meeting (and probably others like it), we need not even rule out the possibility that a summary transcript or notes existed.

378. A novelist would not dare fabricate the precedent about a recent figure, nor would a novelist research the details that Luke has accurately provided. Luke would hardly dare invent an official hearing before a named proconsul in recent memory. Indeed, if he was simply fabricating an account many years after the fact, how would he even know in what years to place Paul in Corinth (see Sherwin-White, *Society*, 104–5)? Moreover, had Luke been freely inventing precedents, we might expect him to have granted Paul a full acquittal instead of portraying a case as being dismissed out of either anti-Jewish prejudice or procedural issues.

The riot in Ephesus also likely indicates historical tradition. Luke plays the events of this section for all they are worth dramatically, but he would not likely invent them. To invent a riot associated with Paul's activity would weaken the apologetic case Luke so carefully cultivates in much of his work against the charges that Paul stirs riots (see comment on Acts 24:5); he is at such pains to explain Paul's innocence (here and on other occasions) that creating the problem to begin with makes little sense. Given his apologetic considerations, it is far more likely that Luke toned down the repercussions of the incident than that he created it.[379] That Luke could not deny Paul's involvement suggests that there were people who recalled that the unrest there related to his missionary activity (cf. Acts 21:27–28). That Paul later avoids Ephesus (although Luke provides a less suspicious reason) suggests that Paul experienced more decisive hostility there than in most other locations. Luke also appears to assume knowledge of a wider body of information than he reports, mentioning Alexander the Jew and Paul's relation to the Asiarchs as if they were known (19:31, 33–34).

As mentioned above, Luke gets the correct local color for Ephesus. More specifically, local elements of the account reflecting the spirit of Ephesus include the following:

1. On two other known occasions, Ephesus as a city publicly defended the Artemis cult; the city had never taken lightly insults to the Artemis cult (cf. the execution of forty-five Sardians in *I. Eph.* 2).[380]
2. A century after Paul's ministry there, Ephesus's city council, with the proconsul's backing, acted to make certain that the month of Artemision remained sacred to Artemis (*I. Eph.* 24).[381]
3. Asia Minor's cities had many riots and much unrest in this period.[382]
4. Economic concerns for the temple were of special concern in this period (see comment on Acts 19:25).
5. Luke's use of ἡ θεά and ἡ θεός in the mouths of the Ephesians fits local Ephesian usage and was extremely rare outside Ephesus (see comment on Acts 19:27, 37).[383]
6. The silversmiths' shops (Acts 19:24–25) may have been located on the road from the harbor to the theater (or perhaps near the busy market) and were probably relatively close to the theater (see comment on Acts 19:29).

Cumulatively, such details have persuaded many scholars that Luke displays considerable accurate information, at least about Ephesus. As the *Oxford Classical Dictionary* points out, Luke here "gives a vivid picture of the Artemisium's religious and economic importance for the Roman city."[384] Historian Fergus Millar observes, concerning Luke's report of this incident, "No text illustrates better the city life of the Greek East, its passionate local loyalties, its potential violence precariously held in check by the city officials, and the overshadowing presence of the Roman governor."[385]

379. Cf. Conzelmann, *Acts*, 164 (citing Pauline evidence); Dunn, *Acts*, 263; Johnson, *Acts*, 351–52. See this commentary's comment on Acts 20:17.
380. Trebilco, "Asia," 331; Horsley, "Inscriptions of Ephesos," 155–56; see esp. Sokolowski, "Testimony on Cult."
381. Trebilco, "Asia," 332.
382. Ibid., 338.
383. See esp. Baugh, "Phraseology and Reliability."
384. Calder et al., "Ephesus."
385. Millar, *Empire and Neighbours*, 199; quoted in Gill and Gempf, "Preface," xiii. In the same passage, Millar compares an "inscription from Ephesus of a few years earlier."

Thus many scholars, though stressing Luke's style, affirm that he depends on a report of an authentic event.[386] Nevertheless, taken by itself, local color could reflect mere knowledge of Ephesus rather than of the events reported; what carries more weight is the testimony of Paul's letters (see ch. 7 below).

The careful itinerary in 20:13–15 and 21:1–3 and their contexts, belonging to "we" material, serves no overt theological purpose, yet as one early twentieth-century scholar remarked, "the narrative portion of the twentieth chapter of Acts is full and correct enough for a guide-book."[387] Moreover, as Barrett notes, Paul's passing Ephesus and meeting the elders in Miletus poses the sort of problem that Luke (who was present on the voyage, 20:15) would not "voluntarily concoct."[388]

Likewise, the Tyrian prophecies in Luke's "we" narrative (21:4) meet the criterion of embarrassment: given the mistrust of failed prophecies or of those that contradicted other sources of knowledge, Luke presumably would not have invented a prophecy worded as if prohibiting Paul from doing what he in fact did (potentially allowing less sympathetic readers to infer that, against Luke's character portrayal of Paul, Paul's disobedience to prophecy led him into his trouble with Rome). Although we might assume that narrators would clean up such tensions,[389] such narratives probably reflected the ambiguities of genuine charismatic experience (1 Cor 13:9–12; 14:29; 1 Thess 5:20–22).[390]

d. Paul in Roman Custody

In one letter written from Corinth, Paul expected trouble in Judea (Rom 15:31), and we next meet him in Roman custody (e.g., Phil 1:13; Phlm 1, 9). Romans normally did not arrest people without either catching them in a subversive act or receiving accusations from locals. Yet local accusers probably would not have gently handed Paul over to Romans on the charge of violating the temple (which, our evidence suggests, at least a sufficient number of them would have been prepared to avenge more directly); more clearly, Luke would not have missed the opportunity to parallel Paul and Jesus if the Sanhedrin arrested Paul and handed him over to the governor (cf. Acts 24:6). A mob scene such as Luke describes in his "we" narrative is therefore plausible. While it makes for good adventure, it also supports the charges of stirring riots (24:5) that Luke is at pains to refute in his own narratives by blaming Paul's enemies. Luke would hardly invent a situation that could be construed as supporting the very charges for which he frames his apologetic narrative.

The one offense for which Jerusalemites could automatically kill an offender, even (Josephus claims) a Roman citizen, was desecration of the temple; this is precisely the most plausible charge if we grant that Paul was nearly lynched in the temple (for stronger corroborative support from Paul's letters, see ch. 7 below). That the report[391] "came *up*" (ἀνέβη) to the chiliarch in charge of the garrison (21:31), that the soldiers "ran *down*" (κατέδραμεν, 21:32), and the later mention of "stairs" (ἀναβαθμοί, 21:35,

386. Conzelmann, *Acts*, 164–65 (noting that Alexander remains unexplained in the narrative); Selinger, "Demetriosunruhen"; Lampe, "Acta 19."

387. Burkitt, *Sources*, 16.

388. Barrett, *Acts*, 960 (also observing that although he might have invented a speech in Ephesus, he lacked reason to invent one to Ephesians in Miletus).

389. Uncomfortable with the ambiguity of a true prophet misleading another in 1 Kgs 13, Josephus turns him into a false prophet (*Ant.* 8.236–45).

390. Luke even uses a correct term for the smooth "beach" outside Tyre (αἰγιαλόν, Acts 21:5). This description fits local topography (Bruce, *Commentary*, 422n6; Bruce, *Acts¹*, 385); see further Strabo 16.2.25.

391. Even the crowd's confusion (Acts 21:34), which serves Luke's narrative purpose, is not implausible, at least no more than in some other histories (e.g., Corn. Nep. 3 [Aristides], 1.4; Dion. Hal. *Ant. rom.* 7.15.4).

40)—all these details fit the topography of the temple.[392] Once Rome had intervened and taken Paul into its custody, however, he could be condemned only after a proper investigation. The portrayal of subsequent political influence and legal corruption in Paul's custody arrangements is certainly believable; ancient reports abound with these factors (see comment on Acts 24:26), and legal "justice" functions this way against the politically weak in many parts of the world today. Of course, these are matters of plausibility rather than of external corroboration.

Though appearing in conversation, even the relative citizenship and status claims of Paul and Claudius Lysias fit the period in question better than Luke's own. Dio Cassius indicates that Claudius bestowed citizenship freely and almost indiscriminately (Dio Cass. 60.17.5). His successor, Nero, cracked down on cases of corruption in the previous administration's imperial favors (e.g., Tac. *Ann.* 14.50), suggesting that Luke's portrayal of Lysias's acquiring citizenship fits the narrow window of time during Claudius's rule (41–54 C.E.).[393] The tribune's name, "Claudius Lysias" (Acts 23:26), supports this picture.[394] "Lysias" is a Greek name, suggesting that he was born in the East. The name "Claudius" reveals that he became a citizen between 41 and 54 C.E.; new citizens normally took the name of the emperor under whom they were enfranchised.[395] That Luke nowhere draws the connection between this incident and the tribune's name (reported in a separate location in Acts) and that the tribune's name would be preserved in the court's official documents suggest that Luke's information here is historically dependable. The verbal exchange that Luke reports (for which Paul could have been the source)[396] might even reflect the shift during Claudius's reign: early in that reign, Lysias had to pay a high price for citizenship; thus he could wonder whether Paul was one of the newer citizens who had obtained the franchise cheaply toward the end of Claudius's reign (Dio Cass. 60.17.6).

Luke would have hardly gone to the trouble of securing precise names for the governors of Judea, in the right sequence, for his period if he were writing a novel; the roles (and characterization) of Felix and Festus, on the other hand, fit well a work of history. Even Felix's question of Paul's province (Acts 23:34) and his immediately subsequent decision to decide the case himself (23:35) fit Paul's lifetime better than a period after 70 C.E. and especially substantially afterward. Cilicia Pedias, like Judea, was in precisely this period part of the larger Roman province of Syria-Cilicia (cf. Gal 1:21).[397] Cilicia became a separate province again only under Vespasian in 72 C.E.;[398] it was thus separate again when Luke was writing, on the post-70 dating assumed in this commentary. Because Paul belonged to the very administrative sphere in which Felix worked, transferring the case was less appropriate. Like many other points in Acts, this detail reflects a situation much more relevant to Paul's day than to Luke's, with Luke having nothing to gain even in credibility by so presenting it (since much of his audience would not have known

---

392. Soldiers could run down two pairs of stairs into the outer court from the Antonia if they needed to intervene during festivals (Jos. *War* 5.243–44). That the soldiers could and did intervene at times during this period of tension reinforces the plausibility of Luke's account (cf. Johnson, *Acts*, 382).

393. Cf. Sherwin-White, *Society*, 154–56; Gasque, "Acts and History," 57.

394. See also Jones, *Empire*, 288.

395. E.g., Pesch, *Apostelgeschichte*, 2:237; Hemer, *Acts in History*, 127, 170; Johnson, *Acts*, 392.

396. Although the "we" is not present on this occasion, it is surely nearby and hence soon after again in contact (Acts 21:17–18; 27:1–2).

397. As is generally noted (Jones, Seyrig, Sherwin-White, and Liebeschuetz, "Syria," 1464; Cadbury, "Law and Trial," 310; Gasque, "Acts and History," 57; Täuber, "Cilicia," 330; Green, "Syria and Cilicia").

398. Fitzmyer, *Acts*, 729; Hemer, *Acts in History*, 172. They were separate provinces in Cicero's day (*Sest.* 25.55), though their adjacent position entailed military implications for both (*Fam.* 15.4.4); they shared a border in Strabo 16.2.1.

this detail). Thus Luke likely reflects accurate historical information about a real conversation at this point.

The portrait of Paul's final trials also comports well with external data. Acts approximates so closely the procedure of Roman law, indeed, that many Roman historians have treated it as the clearest illustration of how governors in the provinces conducted such trials.[399] A. N. Sherwin-White, the one Roman historian who has written on the matter at length and with particular expertise, has adequately demonstrated the legal accuracy of many features of Luke's accounts, sufficiently challenging the unwarranted skepticism of Haenchen and others.[400] Haenchen is characteristically skeptical about the substance of Paul's defense speeches, not distinguishing them from other kinds of speeches in the book, but they fit what one expects for records of official proceedings, which would have been available to the defendant and were normally summaries of roughly the length Luke provides.[401]

The emperor to whom Paul appeals in Acts 25:10–12 is Nero, yet to Paul's detriment at some later hearing, Nero turned out to be vicious against Christians in 64 C.E. In 54–59, however, Nero remained under the moderating influence of Seneca the philosopher and Burrus the praetorian prefect.[402] This distinction fits the historical context of Paul's time better than the perspective dominant when Luke was writing, by which time Nero's repression of Christians would have dominated Christian thinking about Nero. Would Luke have invented an appeal that could have made Paul appear foolish or lacking in prophetic insight?

Even apart from this portrayal, there is no compelling reason to doubt Paul's appeal. Roman citizens would have been sent to Rome for trial more frequently than other persons;[403] thus later the Christians whom Pliny detained and who were Roman citizens he sent to Rome for trial (Pliny *Ep.* 10.96.4) instead of simply executing them as he did the others (10.96.3). One could counter that Festus could have sent Paul to Rome even without the appeal that Luke here describes, but such an approach would fail to explain the coincidence between Paul's destination in Rome while in Roman custody and his explicit earlier hope to visit Rome after Jerusalem (Rom 15:23–28). This "coincidence" more readily supports the thesis that Paul may have had something to do with his Roman destination (albeit with the procurator's cooperation), just as depicted in Luke's narrative (Acts 25:10–11).[404]

A cover letter concerning Paul's case would surely have been sent to Rome with him,[405] from which Luke might infer the sort of favorable verdict he reports in 26:30–32 (although not the exact words). Had Agrippa thought Paul guilty, Festus surely would have handled the matter in a more politically advantageous manner instead of sending him on to Rome and increasing the imperial committee's workload. Paul's citizenship explains why he is also not handled in a manner more politically expedient vis-à-vis his high-status local accusers.[406] On the usual first-century datings of Acts, Agrippa II

399. Sherwin-White, "Trial," 101.

400. Sherwin-White, *Society*, 48–70.

401. Winter, "Official Proceedings," 307n7, challenging Haenchen, *Acts*, 656.

402. With Bruce, *Commentary*, 479; Witherington, *Acts*, 726. Paul may have also heard of Seneca's influence and might know that Seneca was brother of Gallio, who dismissed the case against Paul in Acts 18:14–16.

403. For a defense of Paul's Roman citizenship, see comment on Acts 16:37.

404. As noted above and as emphasized in ch. 7, below, that Paul expected trouble from Judeans (Rom 15:30–31; and elsewhere had conflicts with some leaders of his own people, 2 Cor 11:24; cf. 1 Thess 2:15) and we next find him in Roman custody (Phil 1:13) also independently coheres with Luke's narrative.

405. Available to the defendant or at least cited at the hearing if there was one.

406. Luke is happy to lay blame for the real accusation at the feet of some Asian Jews who did not appear for the hearing, but he does not omit the more prominent local accusers who carried the case (and without whom it would have been dropped for lack of accusers); see Acts 24:1, 19.

remained alive and respected at the time of initial publication, so that Luke would hardly have dared to misrepresent Agrippa's interest (which even in Acts is more a matter of neutrality than commitment; see comment on Acts 26:28).[407]

Scholars have often noted the detailed correspondence of weather and topography patterns between Paul's voyage to Rome and what is known from subsequent mariners' testing (27:1–28:14). These connections are developed in greater detail in the commentary; here it is sufficient to say that the account must reflect the observations of an eyewitness, not unbridled imagination.[408] Minimalists could excise from this account the participation of Paul, but one should note that they can delete this element precisely because it is the only element not available for external testing. Yet it seems intrinsically likelier that Luke recounts a genuine experience on this voyage (which Paul certainly undertook, traveling from the east to Rome) than that he discovered another genuine storm account that coincidentally shared the same itinerary taken by Paul and the other members of his "we." (It would not have been Paul's first storm, 2 Cor 11:25.)

Where we can test Luke most fully, however, is where his testimony overlaps with Paul's letters (ch. 7 below explores these connections at much greater length; the exploration is even more detailed in the commentary on the relevant passages).

e. Perspectives

The twentieth century's most renowned historian of Greco-Roman antiquity, Eduard Meyer, opined that Luke was a great historian and that Acts, "in spite of its more restricted content, bears the same character as those of the greatest historians, of a Polybius, a Livy, and many others."[409] Some interpreters have criticized Meyer and other historians of antiquity for depending on Acts, complaining that they write outside their specialization.[410] But the questions of how first-century readers would have understood, and how historians of antiquity best evaluate, Acts' historical claims are in fact questions not of theology but of ancient historiography, especially when Luke's overarching perspectives are no more pronounced than those of other ancient historians. Whose specialization is better to offer such analyses than specialists in Greco-Roman historiography?[411] Indeed, as one historian notes, where the details can be checked, Luke is, on the whole, "marked by carefulness" far more than Josephus is.[412] Josephus provides us more historical information concerning the period in general, but where we can check them (especially by using Paul's letters), Luke is proportionately more often correct in the limited details that he chooses to report.

407. Writers hoping to gain a hearing could not afford to misrepresent matters of public interest on which they could be readily challenged (see, e.g., the comments of Judge, *First Christians*, 379–80, regarding the Gallic Romans publishing their own version of Claudius's speech).

408. This conclusion does not rule out the use of traditional language from storm scenes in epic tradition, as is likely, especially prominently at some points (e.g., Acts 27:41).

409. Meyer, *Ursprung*, 1:2–3, as cited in Bruce, *Acts*³, 27. (Meyer does not specify Luke's location on the implied range of good historiography; most would regard Polybius as more careful than Livy.) F. F. Bruce, a classicist by training, argued that Luke follows the historiographic approach of Thucydides, noting Luke's contrast with his predecessors and his use of synchronisms (28). These particular elements, however, were hardly uniquely Thucydidean. He also notes (29–30) that Luke fares well according to Lucian's standards (*How to Write History*), setting out his theme (the gospel from Jerusalem to Rome, Acts 1:8) and following it through.

410. Vielhauer, "Paulinism," 50n37.

411. With Bruce, *Acts*³, 28, himself a classicist before he became a NT scholar, as already noted.

412. Hemer, *Acts in History*, 219 (Hemer also began as a classicist and became a NT scholar). As much as it may embarrass some within our guild, I believe that an open-minded reader of Hemer may discover that this conclusion follows fairly from the evidence he presents. Those inclined to doubt this statement should survey his voluminous evidence before dismissing it.

Historians read their sources critically but regard some sources as more useful than others. As historical sources go, Acts is an extremely valuable one, offering serious evidence of dependence on considerable eyewitness testimony. Ancient historians could strive merely for verisimilitude where their details were incomplete,[413] and so one arguing for substantial historical testimony in Acts need not suppose that Luke has tradition for every detail. But the contrary supposition, that Luke simply invents a novel about the early church and Paul, runs counter to the numerous correspondences between Paul's letters and Luke's portrayal (see ch. 7 below). These external correspondences with the Pauline portion of Acts, indeed, appear more often, in proportion to Acts' size, than external correspondences for most first-century historians or biographers and their subjects (though this is partly because most biographic subjects left no epistolary corpus). Having written detailed commentaries on both Matthew and John, I am far more impressed with Luke's historical interest and acumen, which are in keeping with Luke's use of this genre.[414]

These observations do not of course make him a modern historian who reports taped words verbatim or who may neglect some kinds of rhetorical, moralistic, and literary concerns. But it does mean that we should be readier to lend the benefit of the doubt to Luke than to the sort of modern hypotheses of Christian origins that dismiss our only concrete historical source and then argue from the silence that remains.[415] Such hypotheses are all too common, yet they prove speculative, subjective, and impossible to verify or falsify; occasionally they gain respect through repeated citation, but otherwise they merely compete with other equally speculative scholarly proposals. Writing when eyewitnesses could still be consulted,[416] two millennia closer to the events he reports than we are, Luke remains, for reconstructing Christian origins, a source that we neglect only to our historiographic peril. Whatever limitations we might attribute to him, Luke knows more about his subject than we do.

Scholarship on these issues sometimes divides into partisan camps instead of examining each issue on its own terms. Often (although not always) this approach has prejudged conclusions and led to ignoring the work of scholars in different camps (not to mention reviews fixated more on these categories than on the broader contents of the books being reviewed).[417] For example, some Acts scholars have a tendency

413. This principle does not, however, prove that historians regularly invented freely (Rothschild, *Rhetoric of History*, 81).

414. Perhaps because Luke, probably far more than the more Greco-Jewish biographies Matthew and John, employs forms of Hellenistic historiography (more amenable to modern historiographic tastes than are less hellenized Jewish biographic forms of that period). Although Luke may make use of the genre's flexibility at times (e.g., compare perhaps Luke 24:4 with Mark 16:5), I have discovered concrete signs of this freedom less than in Matthew and much less than in John.

415. Many others have complained about such cavalier approaches to ancient evidence (e.g., Moody, "Chronology," 240).

416. A point not lost on some ancient Christians, such as (seventh century) Bede *Comm. Acts* pref. (L. Martin, 5).

417. Some reviews, including some reviews of my Matthew and John commentaries (Keener, *Matthew*; idem, *John*), focus mostly on whether works on NT topics or books are as "critical" or as "conservative" as the reviewers, sometimes considering other views less thoughtful or "orthodox" or even "warning off" their constituents from reading a work. (The faulty assumption of some that only two "sides" exist, self-identified as "conservative" and "critical," suits binary thinking but fails to reckon with the genuine range of positions and the range of issues on which diverse positions are held.) Although reviews should identify works' general historical and theological orientation, it is unfortunate when they ignore elements more intrinsic to a work's broader value for readers. In my own works, the examples I know best, a few of the reviewers, preoccupied with these issues, virtually ignored my commentaries' strength, the marshaling of thousands of citations from ancient sources not cited before so as to enable readers to better hear the works in their first-century setting. Yet a reader who bracketed out the historical conclusions with which she or he disagreed would still have most of the commentary left over to work with. (Analogously, a reader interested in Luke's theology

to ignore Ramsay's archaeological work as unduly "conservative," whereas Anatolian archaeologists depend heavily on this research, which subsequent study has more often than not confirmed.[418] Sometimes a work is judged "critical" on the basis of conclusions adhering to scholarly consensus rather than of the breadth or depth of research. Worse, it is sometimes judged "critical" (regardless of scholarly consensus) only if it agrees with the critic's measure of historical skepticism (as if no amount of evidence or analysis could lead to a different conclusion)—a rigid, doctrinaire approach that represents its own kind of "fundamentalism."

On the range of scholarship publishing for a wide range of readers, my conclusions on matters of Luke's historiography will be viewed as fairly "conservative" (though on many or most points fairly mainstream):[419] I contend that Acts is a historical monograph, affirm genuine eyewitness presence in the "we" narratives, and find frequent external corroboration of Luke's claims. Taking into account the conventions of ancient historiography, I have high respect for Luke's reliability. I believe that this is where the strongest evidence points, and I make no apology for this claim.

At the same time, the evidence does not always support a partisan line for some common conservative conclusions: for example, against many (though not all) conservative scholars, I do believe that the evidence favors identifying the Jerusalem Council with Gal 2:1–10 rather than with an earlier famine visit (I prefer the "late" date for Galatians, though the difference is not great here: the late date is less than a decade later than the "early" date). Likewise, ancient historiography often handled speeches and details differently than we do (see ch. 8 below); although Luke may have been more faithful to his sources than were some of his contemporaries, it is neither necessary nor feasible to suppose that Luke followed modern rather than ancient historiographic conventions, conventions that did not yet exist. As even most conservative biblical scholars today recognize, Luke and other ancient historians had theological, moral, political, and literary/rhetorical agendas in how they shaped their accounts. Ancient historians allowed such factors, especially the literary concern for a complete narration, far more play than modern historians would.

With some other fairly conservative commentators (such as Bruce and Witherington) but in contrast to a number of others, I think that our current form of Acts was published after 70 C.E. (though exactitude in dating in either direction is admittedly impossible, given the limited data from which we draw our inferences; see ch. 10). For a particular issue in a matter of detail, I cannot imagine (as some scholars have argued) that Josephus and Luke each had in mind a separate revolutionary leader named Theudas. In sum, hearing Luke's voice in its first-century setting cannot always be fitted into predetermined conclusions; impartial historical investigation will not always yield the results expected by traditional schools of thought. Nevertheless, many scholars of varying persuasions value the fair quest of truth, even when it requires

---

can approach the story without addressing most historical questions [Gaventa, *Acts*, 213], though as we have argued, historical questions do matter.)

418. The leading classicists publishing on southern Anatolian colonies more often than not concur, decades later, with his conclusions. Thus his publications appear forty times in the bibliography of Levick, *Roman Colonies*, 231–40; although Levick lacks an author index, Ramsay is cited, always respectfully and usually in agreement, on 10, 18, 21, 23, 27, 29, 32–35, 37, 40, 44, 45, 49, 52, 53, 66, 72, 78, 83, 86, 88, 93, 112ff., 121, 124–25, 128, 153–55, 183, 189, 193, 197, 211, 212, 222. His work is no less pervasive in Mitchell, *Anatolia*, passim. Although, naturally, subsequent discoveries have reversed some of his minor archaeological judgments, more have stood the test of time.

419. I have been labeled variously by others to my "right" or my "left" but would self-identify myself as "conservative" with respect to Luke's historiography (as defined here) because I believe it is where the evidence strongly points.

some adjustments in their paradigms, and most do not uncritically adopt all ideas of one school. I have done my best to be honest with where I think the evidence points.

Conclusions regarding Luke's Historiography

At this point it is helpful to summarize not only this chapter but where past chapters on Acts' genre have brought us and where subsequent chapters must take us. Our first chapter on genre noted that arguments offered for most proposed genres for Acts include elements of truth that shed light on how Luke tells his story. These include Luke's interests in key individuals (as in biography or, in this case, a biographic approach to history), literary features (such as cohesiveness, plot, and entertainment value, often noted in novels), and a foundation story (as in some epics). Luke, as an ancient writer, could draw from literary techniques found in a variety of genres without such genres defining his work.

The most suitable ancient category for Acts, however, is the historical monograph. Luke's interests are far too historical to classify Acts as a novel and more thematic (focusing on the gospel mission to all peoples) than one would expect in biographies about single individuals. Ancient historiography differed from its modern namesake, but an examination of Luke's historical reports and his use of sources lands Acts squarely among ancient historical works.

Because Acts' genre is historical, it is fair to include historical questions when examining its literary meaning. Given the work's genre, Luke's first audience would expect him both to find meaning in the events he narrates and to narrate what he believed to be genuine events. Although all historians used rhetorical principles to tell their story and provide speeches, the more rhetorical historians tended to be lavish with detailed description in a manner that Luke is not. Ancient historians did create speeches and construct more detailed scenes based on inference, where necessary, to flesh out cohesive narratives; but readers expected them not to create events, and the best of them (for the purposes of modern historians, in any case) were generally reworking information genuinely at their disposal.

Although at this remove we cannot test Luke's historical reliability as well as his contemporaries might have, the extrinsic historical question remains a legitimate one (alongside, not instead of, more intrinsic literary concerns). If Luke implicitly purports to write historical narrative, we can ask how well he achieved his purpose that this genre promises (by the criteria by which that enterprise was defined in his milieu).[420] First we should define what we mean by "historical reliability" for an ancient historian in general and for Luke in particular. Insofar as the evidence that has so far been examined here for ancient historiography generally can offer clues, Luke, like other historians, should have been free to construct speeches, infer private scenes, fill in dramatic details, and so forth, although reconstructing them in the most plausible (as well as compositionally satisfactory) manner consistent with what was known. (How much was known will have varied from one historian to another and one case to another.)

Yet ancient historians such as Luke would not invent major events (such as Paul's abuse in Philippi or, in my opinion, Lydia's conversion there) and certainly not major, pivotal matters such as Paul's Roman custody in Judea and transfer to Rome (which

---

420. In terms, i.e., of Greco-Roman historiography in general and especially what this would have looked like at the more popular level (though elite sources by prominent statesmen tend to dominate in what remains extant).

also appears in detailed "we" material). Had Luke invented such material, we might well be highly tempted to view Acts as a novel rather than a historical monograph, little as the work seems to fit the characteristics of the former genre.[421]

These judgments from ancient historiography provide merely a range of options; they do not by themselves tell us where on the accuracy scale of ancient historians Luke appears nor decide for us how often Luke's details reflect prior historical tradition. Granted that Luke writes history, where on the continuum of historical reliability (by either ancient or modern standards for history) does his work lie? When we examine more concrete evidence not pertinent to historians in general but specific to Luke's treatment of various issues that we can test, in the strong majority of cases we find Luke a reliable reporter of events. It is especially our comparison of Paul's letters with Acts' claims about Paul that will confirm this expectation in greater detail. That Luke was a masterful narrator is not in question; that what he narrated was historiography rather than a novel most scholars concur; that his historical work is useful for modern historical understanding of early Christianity should, I believe, likewise be granted.

Where we can test him, Luke is as accurate as, or more accurate than, many historians contemporary with him (perhaps partly because, although he employs rhetoric, his audience expected less rhetorical embellishment than was demanded by some more elite contemporaries). At the same time, he is a popular, rather than elite, historian, and this must be taken into account when one notes the ways he tells his story, with its emphasis on adventures, signs, continuous action, and a tightly cohesive plot.

The genre (and general evidence for how Acts fits this genre) also suggests what we should expect where Luke reports events. In the absence of external evidence supporting or rendering suspect a particular Lukan claim, we ought to give Luke the same benefit of the doubt that we would grant other historians writing about ancient events, especially when extrinsic data so often confirm his claims.[422]

Some scholars would grant this principle for the most part but except from it supernatural claims, although these appear in other historians as well as in Luke. Chapter 9 below will discuss this caveat separately not because the issues are unrelated but because they require special attention (regarding both Acts and other authors) and at least a cursory, nonjudgmental comparison between the general worldview presuppositions of antiquity and those of modernity. The question of speeches, which might consume even more space in Acts than signs, is also extensive enough to require separate treatment (ch. 8 below). Regarding most kinds of events, however, I believe that the evidence above and especially in the following chapter, on Paul, are already sufficient to invite confidence and assign the usual burden of proof to those skeptical of Luke's claims.

---

421. Even if Luke designed the programmatic scene in Luke 4:16–30 with no other tradition except what remains to us extant elsewhere (a skepticism that presumes too much knowledge about Luke's possible sources), we know from Mark that Luke did not invent Jesus's teaching in the Nazareth synagogue, the hearers' amazement, their unbelief, or Jesus's saying about a rejected prophet. And this scene is one of the few places where Luke departs from Mark's sequence, probably indicating a special literary design here rather than Luke's usual practice.

422. Along with granting the benefit of the doubt regarding events, we should allow the same skepticism toward any modern verbatim notion of Luke's speeches as we grant to those of other ancient historians. From ancient historians' perspective, however, this would not be skepticism but rejection of the unfair imposition of a standard culturally different from the expectations of their own contemporaries. See ch. 8 below.

7

ACTS AND PAUL

Comparing Luke's Pauline information with what scattered details are available in Paul's letters highlights some contrasts between the two sources (often related to the character of their genre as well as their respective emphases in particular settings) but often underlines their common information.[1] Both the contrasts and the randomness of the correlations suggest that Luke was not simply deriving his Pauline information from Paul's letters but that both sources independently attest to the historical figure of Paul that stands behind them.[2]

Although Luke and Paul write in different genres and usually have different interests, these sources mostly agree where they treat Pauline chronology[3] and the locations where Paul founded churches. The correspondences between Acts and Paul's letters are, indeed, so many that Acts must fit ancient history or biography, not the expected conventions of a novel.[4] One would not expect a novelist (e.g., the later author of the *Acts of Paul*) to preserve so much historical information. The basic events of Paul's life fit well where we can test them, by ancient historical standards; to infer that Luke's standard of accuracy is approximately equivalent[5] on such basic events where we cannot test him is logical (an inference the sometimes cavalier dismissal of which is correspondingly illogical).

This observation is not meant to claim that the sources coincide in every detail, but they fall well within the expectations of careful ancient historians treating recent personages. Because this chapter belongs to a commentary introduction and does not constitute a monograph, the treatment here cannot be exhaustive, but it should be sufficient to illustrate the point offered. How Luke filled out the

1. For contrasts, see, e.g., Pervo, *Mystery*, 32 (I concur with at least five of the eight differences).

2. For a survey of views on Acts and Paul through 1978, see Mattill, "Value"; for more recent work, see esp. discussion in Porter, *Paul in Acts*; idem, "Portrait"; also Phillips, *Paul and Acts* (too recent for my full interaction).

3. Especially the sequence of the Pauline mission (see comments below, esp. Campbell, "Journeys"). This observation omits the large areas where they do not touch on the same information because of incidental gaps in either source. Alexander, "Chronology," finds that Acts and Paul fit closely except on two points where Luke lacked full data. Phillips, *Paul and Acts*, 63–65 (who does not interact with Campbell, Alexander, or Riesner), emphasizes the differences more heavily, though especially the special case of Acts 15 (see 74–82), where I believe the parallels are more significant than the differences (cf. our discussion of Acts 15 ad loc.). Scholars today appear increasingly ready to employ all the earliest Christian sources rather than just Paul's undisputed letters in reconstructing Pauline chronology (Edo, "Cronologías").

4. Even the rare historical novel would not be expected to have so many close correspondences; if it did, it would be "almost" history, and I know of none that was so close to history as Acts is.

5. I refer to analogous events, not to the sort of details, such as the content of speeches on particular occasions, for which we lack sufficient external corroboration in some cases to demand analogous accuracy in others.

details may be debated, and this commentary treats such questions according to the genres or issues relevant to the individual particulars involved (some in ch. 8 below; others in ch. 9 below;[6] and yet others simply in the comments on passages where they appear) if any evidence exists for an informed historical judgment in either direction.

This chapter first treats Acts' perspective on Paul (Luke's apologetic approach, his sources, and his lack of interest in physically describing his protagonist). It then turns to the scholarly debate about how accurately Luke represents Paul in general. After briefly introducing the competing scholarly views regarding Acts' treatment of Paul, the chapter turns to what not to expect in comparisons between Acts and Paul's letters (in view of the incompleteness of extant information and the need to allow for the divergent perspectives and emphases of the different sources). It argues that scholars should not simply consistently privilege Paul as a source over against Acts; it does so by comparing other letter collections with histories and biographies and taking into account the limitations of Paul's letters. Despite the differences between Acts and Paul's letters, some scholars argue that Luke knew and used Paul's letters. I argue (with most scholars) that Luke did not use them in Acts (whether or not he knew of them).

The bulk of the chapter focuses on correspondences between Luke and Paul, which cumulatively support Luke's extensive knowledge of Paul's ministry. Because some scholars think that Luke's Paul is too distant theologically from the epistolary Paul for Luke to have known him well, the chapter also addresses theological differences, both real and imagined; some of the alleged contrasts reflect the traditional Protestant misreading of certain Pauline letters, and other differences reflect divergent emphases without, however, providing a real argument against Luke having genuine information about Paul on these various points.

1. Luke's Perspective on Paul

Much of this chapter addresses the congruity of Acts and Paul for the purpose of examining Luke's historiography. First, however, I will offer preliminary observations regarding Luke's treatment of Paul.

Although Paul is not the only "hero" or protagonist in Acts, he is the climactic one, and he receives more comment than any other nondivine characters[7] (with Peter coming second). He is also of special concern to Luke, who either was (as I and many others argue; see comment on Acts 16:10) Paul's traveling companion or (as others argue) presents himself or his source as such. Some scholars think that Luke wrote partly to defend Paul or Pauline Christianity for his generation.[8] Although I was for a time more skeptical of this approach, after working through especially the defense speeches (but also the rest of the Pauline part of Acts), I now concur that this is

6. Some scholars, though conceding that Luke knew basic events, would insist that he must have sensationalized and fictionalized these events with "signs" claims. Yet such claims appear as a frequent part of evangelism in patristic and even modern sources, sometimes citing eyewitnesses; one may explain such phenomena in various ways, but to relegate all of them to a process of legendary accretion ignores actual data to favor modern Western assumptions of how early Christian "heroes" should have acted (see ch. 9 below).

7. Gaventa, *Acts*, 43, notes that God's activity stands behind even Paul's apparent prominence. For Paul's prominence in Acts, see also Kurichianil, "Paul."

8. Cf., e.g., Trocmé, "Beginnings of Historiography." Georgi, *Opponents*, 319, thinks that Luke's effort to promote Paul vis-à-vis his opponents proved successful.

indeed part of Luke's apologetic objective (though not his only purpose).[9] Ancients could certainly propagandize for or defend their heroes.[10] Thus the apologetic issue is briefly treated here, but chapter 13 below addresses Luke's purpose (including its apologetic element) in significantly more detail.

a. Apologetic for Paul

Whether or not Luke (or others) originally collected responses to charges against Paul for a legal brief, most scholars rightly doubt that Acts, as it currently stands, is such a brief. Nevertheless, concerns about Paul seem to have persisted, whether among Roman authorities, among Jewish detractors, among believers, or, more probably, some combination of the above (e.g., Christian concerns raised by Jewish detractors, of relevance to their own current situation vis-à-vis Rome).[11] The charge of stirring unrest (Acts 24:5) was a serious one, and Luke takes it so seriously that his narrative includes both incidents that could be cited against Paul and evidence that in none of these cases did Paul cause the trouble. Luke as an apologist would hardly have cited so many suspicious incidents to begin with if accusations of stirring unrest did not remain too much of a live issue for him to evade.

Passage	Luke's Perspective	Jewish Involvement?
Acts 9:23–25	Opposition in Damascus	Jewish opposition
13:12	Positive response from the proconsul	Despite a Jewish opponent
13:50	Aristocrats in Pisidian Antioch driving them out (perhaps forgotten by now)	Jewish instigation
14:5	Mob in Iconium	Jewish instigation
14:19	Mob in Lystra nearly killing Paul	Jewish instigation
16:22–23	Beaten in Philippi but vindicated (16:37–40)	Because of anti-Semitism
17:10	Paul's escape without responding to charges (but these expired once the politarchs left office)	Jewish instigation
17:14	Chased out of Beroea	Jewish instigation
17:32–34	Acceptable response in Athens	No trouble from synagogue
18:12–17	The governor's rejection of the charges against Paul as purely religious	Jewish legal opposition
19:23	The riot in Ephesus	No Jewish instigation, but it embarrasses the Jewish community
21:28	Riot in the Jerusalem temple	Jewish instigation

Wherever Roman officials appear (before Felix), they are favorable, and the legal precedents positive (18:12–17; cf. 13:12); intellectual dialogue also demonstrates the potential respectability of the movement's best arguments (17:32–34; 19:9–10).

9. See more fully Keener, "Apologetic." Even modern scholars in various disciplines often become fond of and "defend" their subjects; e.g., scholars of Stoicism may want to help students appreciate Stoicism, and they hence answer some of the objections against it (e.g., Oksenberg Rorty, "Faces," 243; cf. also Irwin, "Stoic Inhumanity," 238); a classics professor may become fond of Herodotus (Cartledge, "Herodotus"); and some modern Pauline scholars rally to Paul's defense on various points. But Luke's apologetic is generally more intense than this. Even Luke's portrayal of the love and loyalty Paul's associates had for him (e.g., Acts 20:36–38) serves Luke's apologetic purpose, though it is also consistent with Paul's letters (e.g., 1 Thess 3:6), underlining Paul's kind and generous character against the counterportrayals of Paul circulating elsewhere (e.g., Rom 3:8; 2 Cor 6:8; Phil 1:14–17; cf. 2 Tim 1:16); see further discussion ad loc.

10. Cf. the function of royal spinmeisters in Philost. *Hrk.* 31.5 and presumably behind 1–2 Samuel (in the context of ancient Near Eastern royal apologies, see Long, "Samuel," 270); probably also the apologetic for Socrates in Xenophon and Plato. Josephus's autobiography is apologetic (with, e.g., Lamour, "Organisation").

11. Concerns about Paul persisted, albeit without interest in his Roman execution, in later decades; Judge, *Athens,* 62–63, cites as non-Pauline sources *Shepherd of Hermas* (numerically rivaling Paul's letters among the papyri), the *Didache,* and *Barnabas* (though neglecting *1 Clement,* Polycarp, and Ignatius).

But Jewish instigation appears in the vast majority of the above instances where trouble occurred.[12]

Luke's account is clearly ironic on this point: it is Paul's opponents (i.e., those who would be viewed as allied with his accusers) who stirred the riots rather than Paul himself.[13] (For the conventional rhetorical approach of shifting guilt to the accusers, see comment on Acts 24:19.) Meanwhile Paul had some legal precedents in his favor, especially the Achaian governor's dismissal of frivolous, merely religious charges brought by local synagogue leaders. Such precedents could be concretely documented, and Luke, like Josephus writing apologetic history on behalf of his people, is eager to trot out this information. Luke undoubtedly responds to genuine charges against Paul, and his manner of defense suggests that genuine unrest occurred (though we know that historically Jewish unrest regarding Jesus was not limited to Paul's mission; see Suet. *Claud.* 25.4 and comment on Acts 18:2).

Luke includes an apologetic for Paul on another level, for which the Gospel and the first part of Acts prepare (in addition to their other functions). The extensive parallels with Jesus and the Jerusalem Christian leaders (where possible; see ch. 16 below) reveal that those who respect Jesus, Stephen, and Peter should also respect Paul. If he suffered the humiliation of Roman custody and execution, he simply followed the steps of his Lord. (The material on Luke's apologetic in ch. 13 below and, especially, relevant passages in the commentary develop this observation more fully.)[14] One may also offer connections such as in Acts 26:16: Paul is "servant" and "witness" just like Jesus's original apostles in Luke 1:2 (despite the different wording).

b. Pauline Material in Acts

The Pauline section of Acts also provides a special case study because of its distinctive character. At least in Acts,[15] Luke's sources appear most complete when he is treating Paul. Although he has done an admirable job of filling in earlier narratives (supplementing them with a greater proportion of speech material), his details for the earlier period tend to be sketchier than when he writes about Paul (especially concerning his later missions and, in greatest detail, the "we" narratives, including Paul's Roman custody). The transitional Hellenists (Acts 6–8) provide vindication for Paul's mission, connecting him to the earlier protagonists, especially to Jesus and Peter.

Of greatest concern here, Paul's writings also provide the clearest basis for external comparison with Acts, compared with the relative paucity of Petrine material (and absence of any early Christian material attributed to Stephen or the evangelist Philip). As a methodological observation, the comparisons I offer here include all the early Pauline literature but with less emphasis on the Pastorals. Although the personal

12. Paul's own letters testify of conflicts with his own people (2 Cor 11:24, 26), although he had them with Gentiles as well.

13. See Keener, "Apologetic." Mauck, *Trial*, 83–84, also insightfully notes narrative countercharges against Paul's opponents, such as the Sanhedrin flogging innocent persons (5:40), some opponents supporting perjury (6:11), some supporting or attempting murder (7:58; 9:23; 21:31; 23:12–14), and so forth. Although Luke is emphatic that Paul did not stir unrest, he also avoids associating him with the culturally shameful vice of cowardice; Paul is prepared to sacrifice his life for his divine mission (20:24; 21:13; cf. 9:16), a Lukan portrait reflecting Paul's genuine commitment (2 Cor 4:10–11; 11:23–27; Phil 1:20–24; 2:17; cf. Rom 15:25, 31; 1 Cor 15:30–32; 1 Thess 2:8).

14. Some proposed apologetic for Paul, however, is implausible—e.g., Luke's attempt to dissociate Paul from Gnosticism (Lüdemann, *Paul*, 15–16, citing Acts 20:29–30, which reveals no particularly gnostic concerns). Gnosticism is too late for relevance here (see Yamauchi, *Gnosticism*; Smith, *Gnostic Origins*; Keener, *John*, 164–69) and too peripheral to Luke's concerns, in any case.

15. Numerous other reports of, and written documents about, Jesus's life and teaching were already circulating (Luke 1:1), and so, in his Gospel, Luke needed merely to supplement and edit those.

allusions in 2 Timothy[16] incline me to respect the case for Pauline authorship of the Pastorals more than critical scholars commonly do,[17] the matter is too disputed[18] (especially in view of the obviously divergent and apparently incompatible style)[19] for me to argue any position in this commentary without a lengthy excursus. Although a majority of scholars may be skeptical of Pauline authorship, most do allow for Pauline tradition, which is the essential point for comparison in this commentary.[20]

c. No Physical Description of Paul

Given his interest in Paul, why does Luke omit a physical description of his appearance, such as is later found in *Acts of Paul and Thecla*? Ancient biographies commonly provided descriptions of their heroes,[21] especially physically magnificent ones.[22] Praise of physical beauty was also a welcome aspect of Greek epideictic.[23] Some ancients also thought that they could discern one's personality or future through physiognomy.[24] Perhaps Paul's appearance was unpleasant.[25] Unpleasant appearance and especially physical deformity invited ridicule, just as did weakness in rhetorical gestures.[26] But ancient writers often did not hesitate to present weaknesses in their heroes' appear-

16. Such personal notes can appear in purely pseudepigraphic texts (Brox, "Notizen"), but not usually so extensively.

17. See, in favor of Pauline authorship, e.g., Jeremias, *Briefe*, 4–5; Kelly, *Pastoral Epistles*, 3–33; Lock, *Pastoral Epistles*, xxv–xxxi (very tentatively); Fee, *Timothy*, xx; Mounce, *Pastoral Epistles*, cxviii–cxxix; Ellis, "Authorship"; idem, *Paul and Interpreters*, 49–57; idem, "Pastoral Letters"; McRay, "Authorship"; Montague, *Timothy*, 16–23; cf. Johnson, *Writings*, 381–89; idem, *Timothy*, 4; Witherington, *Titus, Timothy, John*, 49–64. The story presupposed in the Pastorals is internally consistent.

18. For their pseudonymity (though many allow for Pauline tradition), see, e.g., Scott, *Pastoral Epistles*, xvi–xxiii; Dibelius and Conzelmann, *Pastoral Epistles*, 1–5, 16; Zmijewski, "Pastoralbriefe"; Cook, "Fragments"; Maloney, "Authorship"; Verhoef, "Pseudepigraphy"; idem, "Paulines."

19. Certainly, the style is quite different (Harrison, "Hypotheses"; Grayston and Herdan, "Authorship"; Mealand, "Extent"; though cf. Metzger, "Reconsideration"; Barr, "Scale"; idem, "Dependence"; Aune, *Dictionary of Rhetoric*, 453; esp. Richards, *Letter Writing*, 141–47; written vs. oral style in Baum, "Variation," esp. 291–92); less relevant and compelling in my opinion are purported theological differences (e.g., Allan, "Formula"; Dunn, *Jesus and Spirit*, 347–50).

20. Recognizing various arguments and Pauline materials but rejecting Pauline authorship in the strictest traditional sense, see esp. Marshall, *Pastoral Epistles*, 57–92 (noting [92] that the Pastorals "may well have been produced in a group which included Timothy and Titus themselves"; see also idem, "Pastoral Epistles," 122; cf. Witherington, *Titus, Timothy, John*, 25); cf. evenhanded discussion in Quinn and Wacker, *Letters*, 18–23.

21. E.g., Suet. *Jul.* 45.1; *Tib.* 68.1–2; *Nero* 51; Tac. *Agr.* 44. Some such descriptions probably display the historians' interests and may both help illuminate and be illuminated by comparisons with surviving portraiture; see discussion in Vout, "Emperor," 263–74.

22. E.g., 1 Sam 9:2; Plut. *Alex.* 60.6. I do find, however, considerably more comment in fiction than in biographies and histories (e.g., Philost. *Hrk.* 10.1–4, esp. 10.3; 26.4, 13; 29.2; 33.39–40; 48.1; 49.3).

23. E.g., Men. Rhet. 2.5, 398.14–18; see further Anderson, *Glossary*, 125 (citing *Rhet. Her.* 4.63; for ridicule, Cic. *De or.* 2.266).

24. Cf. texts practicing divination through physiognomy (e.g., 4Q561; on zodiacal physiognomy in 4Q186 [see esp. 1 II, 5–8], see Schmidt, "Astrologie"; Böck, "Commentary"; Popovic, "Physiognomic Knowledge"; but by contrast, 4Q303 3 may not address physiognomy [Lange, "Physiognomie"]) or believing that physiognomy correctly predicted the future (Suet. *Tit.* 2). On physiognomy, see further Sassi, "Physiognomy"; in Stoicism, see Ramelli, *Hierocles*, 51n37 (citing *SVF* 2.10a from Dio Chrysostom *Or.* 33.53–55).

25. Some scholars have seen his description in *Acts of Paul and Thecla* in this way, but see Malherbe, "Physical Description" (also idem, *Philosophers*, 165–70; comparing descriptions of Augustus, Heracles, and Agathion), and the stature of Odysseus (Hom. *Il.* 3.193–94). Malina and Neyrey, *Portraits*, 100–152, offer a physiognomic perspective on *Acts of Paul*.

26. See Marshall, *Enmity*, 62, 64–65; Suet. *Jul.* 45.2; for gestures (which probably *were* relevant to Paul; cf. 2 Cor 10:10), Marshall, *Enmity*, 62, 65–66; on gestures more generally, see Hall, "Delivery," 224–27; Hurschmann, "Gestures"; Lateiner, "Gestures." Against some commentators, Gal 4:14–15 does not refer to an unsightly eye disease (as in Cic. *Att.* 7.14; 8.12–13; 10.14; 14.4.6); Gal 4:15 reflects a common idiom (Callim. *Hymns* 3 [to Artemis], lines 210–11; Petron. *Sat.* 1; Catull. *Carm.* 3.5; 14.1–3; 45.11–12; 48.1; 82.1–4; *Sipre Deut.* 313.1.4; perhaps Sen. E. *Controv.* 1.4.10; Sil. It. 10.637; see Keener, "Eyes").

ances, whether in epics' statements about Odysseus or in historical memories of Socrates's snub nose.[27] Some scholars even propose that Luke more generally subverts physiognomic conventions in his work.[28]

Further, such descriptions were far from mandatory in biographies and were uncommon in histories. Whereas Aristotle stresses physical description, Xenophon mentions it rarely; Plutarch and Diogenes Laertius include it in only some of their biographies; Tacitus's *Agricola* provides it only briefly.[29] Luke provides no physical description of Jesus either, whether before or after the resurrection; this omission hardly plays down the importance that Jesus had for Luke. Philosophically minded reporters felt that describing a teacher's soul was far more important than describing his body (Max. Tyre 1.10); external appearance and false opinions lead to harm for the soul (Sen. Y. *Ep. Lucil.* 94.13).[30] Luke prefers to depict even Paul's character indirectly through his actions and speeches rather than through narrative asides.

2. Scholarly Views

Most of this chapter must respond to the historical question of how accurately Luke represents Paul. Before examining the evidence, we should note contrasting views on the relationship between Acts and Paul that explain why we should explore the question at some length.

Some NT scholars remain skeptical of Acts as a historical source regarding Paul.[31] Erwin Goodenough provides an extreme example, comparing Luke with those Paul cursed as preachers of a false gospel (Gal 1:8): "For no one in the Galatian or Corinthian churches would have recognized in the pages of Acts the Paul they had heard preach or had read in his letters."[32] The classic statement of the case, however, comes from Philipp Vielhauer and Haenchen.[33] Often such scholars are more skeptical than historians would be of most other histories or biographies from antiquity, and certainly more skeptical than historians would normally be of other historical works plausibly purporting to describe events that had transpired within the memory of some living witnesses. Historians can disregard some traditions in their sources without dismissing wholesale their value as historical sources.

27. For Socrates's nose, see, e.g., Max. Tyre 1.9; cf. also Aesop's physical deformities in *Vit. Aes.* 1. Some criticisms of Odysseus's appearance admittedly derived from his enemies (Philost. *Hrk.* 34.5).

28. E.g., by showing short Zacchaeus's hospitality in Luke 19:3, 8–10 (see Parsons, *Body*, 97–108), though Luke's mention of Zacchaeus's height (to explain his climbing the tree) is incidental to the point of his repentance from sin.

29. Stanton, *Jesus of Nazareth*, 124.

30. Against judging by appearance, see also Eunapius *Lives* 472–73; 2 Cor 5:16; John 7:24. Arius Did. *Epit.* 2.7.5b.4, pp. 18–19.8–14, compares physical and moral beauty (but not on the assumption that they correspond in the same person). But whereas κάλλος appears fifty-four times in the LXX (e.g., often in Judith and Sirach; also five times in *Psalms of Solomon*), it does not appear in the NT (in contrast to the related καλός, ninety times in the NT and more than two hundred times in the LXX).

31. E.g., Sandmel, *Genius of Paul*, 13 (placing Paul and Acts in the same canon, in fact, "neutralizes" Paul's radical character, p. 155). For the history of the division between scholarship connecting the Paul of Acts with the epistolary Paul, and contrasting them, from the skeptical approaches of F. C. Baur to (esp.) John Knox and Philipp Vielhauer, see helpfully Phillips, *Paul and Acts*, 30–49. Mount, *Pauline Christianity*, 172–80, concludes that Luke and his successors generated Paul's importance as an individual figure in Christian memory; but what of Paul's own view of his role in 1 Cor 4:15; 9:5–6; 15:5–10; Gal 1:16–20; 2:1–14?

32. Goodenough, "Perspective of Acts," 58.

33. Vielhauer, "Paulinism"; Haenchen, "Acts as Source Material." Vielhauer is followed by, e.g., Theissen, *Writing and Politics*, 85; cf. others, e.g., Schille, *Apostelgeschichte*, 49–50.

By contrast, a large number of NT scholars prove less skeptical than Vielhauer and Haenchen and affirm that Acts does reflect valuable tradition or personal knowledge about the genuine historical Paul.[34] Many today also argue, against earlier contrary claims (which often failed to account for differences in genre and purpose), that even the content of Paul's speeches in Acts genuinely comports well with the Paul of the letters by the standards of ancient historical writing.[35] The speeches may be Luke's compositions (see ch. 8 below) yet preserve some knowledge about authentic Pauline preaching. Given my earlier discussion of the genre and the expectations that this issue raises for readers of Acts (chs. 3–6), it will not be surprising that I share this higher estimate of Acts' portrayal of Paul. Before proceeding, however, it must be established what is meant here by a "higher estimate" of his reliability. Luke undoubtedly used his storyteller's liberty to the extent used by popular historians about recent persons, but, as in the case of these other historians, this freedom does not imply that he "created" events.[36] Luke is not just our best available historian covering Paul's life (nor simply the only one whom we have) but also (as argued above and further here) a good ancient historian.[37]

3. What Not to Expect in Comparisons

Paul's letters provide the major test case for Acts,[38] as Q and Mark do for Luke's reports about Jesus in the Gospel. In designing this test, however, some interpreters lay too much weight on the kinds of differences that show us little about Luke's sources. It is reductionist to assume that differences between Luke's and Paul's perspectives and style militate against Luke's use of the historical Paul, or informants close to him, as a genuine source. We do not doubt that Josephus knew the biblical story of Isaac simply because he expresses it so differently in his *Antiquities*.[39]

Paul's readers have reapplied him as a model in various ways through history—for example, as a virtuous model (John Chrysostom) or one struggling with the flesh (Augustine)[40]—not because they lacked access to shared information about Paul (in this case, Acts and the letters) but because their questions and interests differed.[41] Luke certainly has more information about Paul than do many of his successors, even

34. E.g., Jervell, *Unknown Paul*, 68–76; Bruce, *Acts¹*, 34–40. Marguerat, "L'image de Paul," notes both points that comport well with Paul and points that he believes fit a later generation.

35. See, e.g., Haacker, *Theology*, 143–44; Baum, "Paulinismen," esp. 414–35.

36. For Luke as a "popular" historian, see the discussion on genre in ch. 2, above (cf. also ch. 5); he did not cite his various sources even in his first volume, where he clearly acknowledges knowledge of them (Luke 1:1–2). Elite historiography (a class distinction not so relevant to novels) was far more apt to survive, so Luke-Acts is one of our few examples of popular historiography; interpreters must thus adjust historiographic expectations in light of some popular conventions, usually by substituting some storytelling expectations for elite rhetorical ones. Nevertheless, the many external correspondences to Acts that confirm Luke's historiographic genre also confirm that he followed that genre's expectations for narrating genuine events.

37. Points shared in common by independent portraits might be accepted as a least common denominator (Ael. Arist. *Def. Or.* 78, §25); but even for such a minimalist approach to Paul, we possess from an early period virtually only Acts and his letters, and a less minimalist approach must take into account the caveats below.

38. With also Bruce, *Acts³*, 46–47.

39. See the discussion in Gempf, "Speaking," 293–94. For similar ideas expressed differently, see, e.g., O'Toole, "Notion of 'Imitators.'"

40. See Mitchell, "Palimpsests."

41. Keck, "Images," argues that various portraits of Paul (he distinguishes Acts, Paul's letters, and deuteropaulines) may all contain historical foundations, just as each (including Paul's own writings) contains exaggerations; Paul's successors each sought to claim his legacy.

though, according to the vast majority of scholars—both those who think Luke knows Paul well and those who question this judgment—Luke probably did not use Paul's letters (see sect. 5 below).

a. Incomplete Information

Comparing Acts with Paul does not mean that we should seek to find every aspect of the epistolary Paul in Acts, only that what we do find should be compatible with him.[42] When Polybius omits some matters, he warns potential critics that they should not evaluate his performance by what he omits, as if he were unaware of matters he omits. (Here he defends himself against potential charges not even of error but merely of ignorance.) Rather, if they find no errors in what he does recount, they should allow that he omitted other details deliberately, presumably because they did not suit his purpose (Polyb. 6.11.4–8).[43]

Further, we should not assume that our own knowledge of Paul is complete; Paul the letter writer alludes to entire aspects of his public ministry, such as miracle working (Rom 15:19; 2 Cor 12:12) or private mystic experiences (1 Cor 14:18; 2 Cor 12:2–4),[44] that must have consumed a significant part of his time, yet they consume little space in his letters. Some of what we often think we do know is a caricature of Paul, frequently based solely on two letters where he addresses the law most thoroughly (Romans and Galatians) and on the Corinthian correspondence.[45] (Indeed, harmonizing even Romans with the more polemically framed Galatians has challenged many modern interpreters.) Bultmann and his followers unfavorably contrasted Luke as a salvation historian with the epistolary Paul, whom they regarded as an existentialist—a view of the historical Paul no longer compelling.[46] Even the old liberal scholar Harnack was quick to point out that "St. Paul was not so 'Pauline'—if I may venture the word—as his biographers would have us think."[47]

The genre differences between letter and history are significant, but more detailed genre differences also come into play. All Paul's letters are to churches or Christians, and so we must expect Paul's approach there to differ from his evangelistic speeches in Acts (though we do find parallels in his own allusions to his evangelistic preaching; compare, e.g., Acts 14:15 with 1 Thess 1:9).[48] The one speech in Acts that most closely approximates Paul's paraenetic instruction in his letters (Acts 20:18–35) is, not coincidentally, the only speech attributed to him in Acts that addresses Christians.[49] (This speech also appears in the context of "we" material.)

---

42. Arguments against authenticity that are based on omissions employ fallacious reasoning: (1) It is possible to recount everything significant about Paul; (2) an author is obligated to recount everything (that we would count) significant about Paul; (3) we have a right to critique these omissions because, possessing some of Paul's sample letters, we know more than Luke does; (4) if Luke does not know and recount what we know, the information that he does recount is not dependable.

43. Einhard claims to have witnessed many events surrounding Charlemagne yet never quotes him directly (Frye, "Problems," 274); a witness need not recall or supply all information. For a philosopher's complaint about the logic of argument from omissions, see McGrew, "Argument," 598 (noting also that in law, "minor discrepancies among witnesses," far from discrediting their testimony, challenge the likelihood of collusion).

44. That 2 Cor 12:2–4 refers to Paul's own experience (cf. 12:1, 7) is fairly certain (see Keener, *Corinthians*, 237–38); cf. 2 Cor 5:13.

45. Donfried, *Thessalonica*, 90–96, critiques Vielhauer for ignoring Paul's earlier letters, especially 1 Thessalonians (though Donfried dates it at least half a decade earlier than I would).

46. See Wilckens, "Interpreting," esp. 75, 77, for critique of this old Bultmannian approach.

47. Harnack, *Acts*, 300. Paul's Jewish-Christian theology may be less distinctive, vis-à-vis that of other Jewish Christians, than is often assumed on the basis of Galatians and Acts 15 (see Wright, *Founder*, passim).

48. Scholars of other ancient works often note that competent authors composing in different genres employed correspondingly different styles; see, e.g., Woodman, *Rhetoric*, 126.

49. See Witherington, *Acts*, 433–34; at length, Walton, *Leadership*.

b. Different Perspectives

Even Paul's major polemical letters have internal tensions among them; to think that all his companions would have characterized him as we find him in these letters is to assume more than we actually know about him.[50] (We may forgive Jacob Jervell's exaggeration in thinking that Paul is so diverse in his own writings that it is almost harder to harmonize Paul with Paul than with the flatter portrait in Acts.)[51] Some scholars suggest that if Luke traveled with Paul only during the "we" sections, he may have had much of his Pauline material secondhand[52] (although if, as I think, Luke was also Paul's companion en route to Rome and had already been researching for his work, he could have obtained this material from Paul himself).[53]

Luke at times may present perspectives on events different from Paul's without misrepresenting the events themselves.[54] Likewise, he may justify the Gentile mission differently than Paul does (13:46; 18:6; 28:28), without this meaning that he is ignorant of Paul's approach (cf. the compatible Rom 11:11); certainly for Luke no less than for Paul, Paul is an appointed ambassador to the Gentiles (Acts 9:15; 21:19; 22:21; 26:17, 20, 23); and for Paul no less than for Luke, Paul's mission to Gentiles was inseparable from his love for Israel (Rom 11:13–14).[55]

Luke may not have even grasped the detailed nuances of Paul's theology as it appears in some of his letters. (Indeed, some commentators suggest that probably most first-century readers did not understand Paul's letters well;[56] cf. 2 Pet 3:16.) The difference in genre may further facilitate this impression: one cannot write narrative theology (or even summaries of speeches) the way one writes a detailed argument. But even if Luke understood Paul's theology completely differently than Paul intended (and this is unlikely, whatever may have been his apprehension of some theological nuances), this would not imply that the factual information Luke does possess is wrong.[57]

Time and individual development may account for some shifts. Arguing for the possibility that the Evangelists Mark and Luke were Pauline traveling companions, Adela Yarbro Collins suggests that "if they were young men when they had contact with Paul and wrote fifteen or more years later, after exercising their own leadership in the movement and experiencing individual and communal change and development,

50. Jervell, *Theology*, 2–3, following Räisänen, *Paul and Law*, on the tensions in Paul's letters. Hurd, "Chronology and Theology," warns against harmonizing either Acts or the epistles, citing in the latter case the need to attend to theological development.

51. Jervell, *Unknown Paul*, 56–57. Although extreme conservative approaches to the Gospels gave "harmonization" a bad name, more moderate approaches to harmonization are, in fact, used in trying to reach the truth behind differing historical documents—e.g., differing biographies of Lincoln—and even news reports today (see Eddy and Boyd, *Legend*, 423–25, noting, e.g., the experiment of J. P. Holding). Unless historians find some variation, they often suspect dependence or forgeries (425). But harmonization of any sorts of historical records usually involves speculation precisely because we lack so much information.

52. C. Williams, *Acts*, 22. Dibelius, *Studies in Acts*, 136–37, suggests that those who think Acts too erroneous to have been written by Paul's companion exaggerate "both the proximity to Paul and the number of errors" (he also doubts that Luke would have felt obligation to report as precisely as modern historians expect, in any case).

53. Others also recognize Paul as a possible source (e.g., Chance, *Acts*, 6). Autobiographic sections in Paul's letters make it likely that he talked about his life when he spoke, and a young admirer would undoubtedly have listened happily to such stories on lengthy voyages.

54. See, e.g., Jervell, *Theology*, 4, on their different applications of the decree in Acts 15; see further discussion in this commentary under Acts 15.

55. Porter, *Paul in Acts*, 190–93, arguing against Haenchen on this and other points (e.g., God's call supreme in both Acts 26:14 and 1 Cor 9:16; Rom 9–11). For the close compatibility between Acts 28:16–31 and Rom 11, see esp. Litwak, "Views"; idem, *Echoes*, 241–48.

56. C. Williams, *Acts*, 22–23.

57. With Witherington, *Acts*, 59. Differences of emphasis are not necessarily conflicts (cf. Lodge, "Salvation Theologies"), though even conflicts do not disprove acquaintance.

such differences would be not only explicable but expected."[58] One need only compare possibly different pictures of Paul entertained by his close associates with what many students, even long-term students, take away from a teacher's classes,[59] to recognize that association or even appreciation over a period of time does not guarantee which features of the teacher's personality or agenda will become foremost in the minds of others. A student who reads my commentary and writes a report will also approach me from a very different standpoint than my son or wife or even my own student would; for that matter, someone could probably read my personal journal (for the years that I kept one) without much awareness that I spend much of my day writing commentaries. One who knew the missionary Paul personally would not write of him with the same emphases as one who merely read his surviving letters.

As Porter observes, "These are merely the kinds of differences that one could expect to find between virtually any two different yet accomplished authors when writing about the same events."[60] This factor is the same for ancient authors as it is for modern ones. Two collections about Musonius Rufus, for example, present quite different portraits of him.[61]

As noted more fully in chapter 8 below, the speeches in Acts do not offer, for the most part, a helpful stylistic comparison with Paul's letters.[62] Stylistic comparisons are difficult because Luke writes mostly in his own style (historians usually wrote or rewrote the speeches in their works, though sometimes reflecting genuine subjects of historical speeches; see ch. 8 below). But even were this not the case, we should not expect Paul's letters to sound precisely like his speeches. As Cicero puts it, noting that he used everyday language in his letters, "I don't always adopt the same style. What similarity is there between a letter, and a speech in court or at a public meeting?" (Cic. *Fam.* 9.21.1 [LCL, 2:261]).[63]

c. Different Emphases

Further, Luke does write for his own era, which (by the dating accepted here) is post-Pauline (even if only by a few years). Despite the attention devoted to the Jerusalem Council (ca. 49 C.E.), Luke would not write with the same perspective toward the conflict as the author of Galatians (accepted here as dating to the 50s); many issues were already settled, at least in Luke's circle of churches (cf. Phil 3:2).[64] That he reserves the title "apostles" almost exclusively for the Twelve and applies it sparingly to Paul (only in Acts 14:4, 14) is a stylistic matter; it hardly means that Luke disparages his hero's apostleship. Possible debates over the character of Paul's apostolicity (2 Cor 3:1; 11:12–13, 23; Gal 1:1; 2:6) and issues such as the collection (especially if the latter failed to accomplish what the epistolary Paul hoped) were no

58. Collins, *Mark*, 5. She argues that these Evangelists were the companions bearing those names in Col 4:10, 14 (5); she views that letter as pseudonymous but probably containing authentic information, some of it independently confirmed in Acts (6, esp. on Col 4:10).

59. Further, students have multiple teachers and (especially including written sources) multiple conversation partners, which also provide a grid through which they select what is most meaningful in our presentation. As Chance, *Acts*, 3, notes, "Paul, though admired, need hardly have been the author's only source of theological thinking." Hengel, *Peter*, 80, 85, suspects that Luke's time in Judea with Paul (Acts 21–27) helped reshape his Paulinism. Even individuals are not always consistent; see Allison, *Jesus*, 91–92, 103–4.

60. Porter, *Paul in Acts*, 206.

61. Lutz, "Musonius," 12–13.

62. See esp. Porter, *Paul in Acts*, 109–15.

63. Still, Bernard, "Discours," contends that the rhetorical level even in this letter mediates between normal letter style and forensic speech. Because Paul's letters have more argumentation than most letters do, they probably do recall much of his preaching material, but this connection should not be pressed too far.

64. See, e.g., Bruce, "Real Paul?"; Witherington, *Acts*, 171.

longer of critical importance by Luke's day.[65] To argue for Luke's inaccuracy on the basis of these omissions is both to argue from silence and to ignore the accuracy of what he does say.[66]

Luke's emphasis can differ from Paul's without necessarily departing from facts. For example, Luke, in contrast to Paul, portrays Paul's high status (including his Roman citizenship) for apologetic reasons, but had Paul historically lacked some form of status, Luke probably would have needed to explain his summary execution rather than his years in Roman custody (Acts 24:27; 28:30; cf. Phil 1:7). Detention until trial could be lengthy, but given the forces ranged against Paul (cf. Rom 15:31; 1 Cor 16:9) and the normal use of custody merely as temporary detention until trial or execution,[67] Paul probably would have faced death more swiftly. Paul's letters avoid boasting about his social status, but that he did reach some people of status and that his letters betray a much higher level of education than was common, except among the elite, should be admitted as significant factors in this discussion. (See further discussion at Acts 16:37.)

4. Why Not to Privilege Paul against Luke

Modern scholars are quick to prefer writings by Paul over writings about him,[68] but the need for this preference becomes self-evident only if Luke did not know Paul and wrote long after him. Certainly, Paul would know his own thoughts better than Luke would (cf. 1 Cor 2:11), but Paul's letters were also more situation-oriented than Acts is,[69] giving less of a coherent and global summary of his ministry and character than a companion with some advantage of hindsight (and possibly greater objectivity) could provide.

a. Comparing Other Histories and Letters

Against the traditional critical assumption that biographies would be less helpful for historical reconstruction than a person's own letters, some scholars have recently resorted to more objective comparisons of various ancient letter collections with biographies about the people who wrote the letters. Far from the biographies proving uniformly biased,[70] they exhibit varying degrees of tendentiousness or accuracy. Thus one cannot claim before examining them that Acts and Paul will contradict each other; they may prove complementary.[71] Roman historians make comparable use of both Cicero's letters and Sallust's "only slightly later history" describing the Catiline rebellion; also of Favorinus's corpus and the discussions by his "contemporary, Gellius, and a later writer, Philostratus; and the much later case of the use of the letters of Julian and the history of Ammianus."[72]

---

65. With Witherington, *Acts*, 436–38. Porter, *Paul in Acts*, 196–97, also responds to Luke's use of "apostle" as differing from Paul's. Those who challenged his apostleship in his letters were his competitors; Luke, by contrast, is his very favorably disposed biographer.

66. For objecting to arguments based on what Luke does not say, see also Porter, *Paul in Acts*, 200–203.

67. E.g., Aeschines *Tim.* 16; Cic. *Cat.* 4.4.7; Appian *Bell. civ.* 1.3.26; Plut. *Cic.* 20.3; 22.2; Caird, *Revelation*, 35; Aune, *Revelation*, 166 (citing *Dig.* 48.19.8.9; 48.19.35); Rapske, *Custody*, 12–13; idem, "Prison," 827–28.

68. E.g. (among extreme examples), Hurd, "Reflections," 133, suggests that "the letters must be treated first and treated as though Acts did not exist," though one can then consider what Acts might add.

69. As is often observed, Paul wrote his letters not as a systematic but as a pastoral theologian, a pastor and missionary (on the latter point, cf., e.g., Grams, "Mission Theologians").

70. Biographies proper were not intended to be fictitious; see Aune, "Biography," 125; Witherington, *Sage*, 339; Keener, "Otho"; idem, *Matthew*, 18–20; for the overlap among genres, cf. Burridge, *Gospels*, 63–69.

71. See Hillard, Nobbs, and Winter, "Corpus."

72. Winter, *Left Corinth*, xiv.

Acts is obviously more direct and complete in its portrait of Paul than the letters are, and may include elements of the historical Paul that we would miss when reading merely his occasional letters.[73] Pauline scholars must make some use of Acts if they wish to do more than comment on his theology or on isolated data such as his relations with particular churches. Just as we would not a priori exclude either the letters by, or biographies about, any other ancient figure whose life we sought to reconstruct, students of Paul cannot afford to dispense with everything that Acts contains; his letters alone do not provide historians sufficient material.[74] Even if some scholars find difficulty matching all elements of Acts, which does not include all of Paul's life, with Paul's chronology,[75] an attempt to construct a Pauline chronology on objective data entirely apart from Acts is nearly hopeless. Apart from three sequences, scholars who attempt to construct outlines from Paul's letters without using Acts produce widely different portrayals.[76]

In the same way, we could compare with Paul's letters the epistles in Cicero's collection *Letters to Friends*; historians can use these epistles as primary documents for the civil wars (e.g., official letters from consuls to Marc Antony).[77] While they flesh out and personalize the broader narratives of Roman historians who covered this period, they are much more intelligible to us in the context of the connected narratives of the historians, who wrote with access to fuller data than we possess (just as Luke's many incidental correspondences to Paul's occasional letters, very probably without dependence on them, suggest that he had access to data that we do not possess). Acts and Paul's letters are works of Mediterranean antiquity, and NT scholars should not treat Acts more skeptically than historians would treat comparable works.

b. Limitations of Paul's Letters

Is it difficult to reconcile some features of Acts with some features of Galatians or other letters? Witherington, pointing to rhetorical forms and strategies in Paul's letters, argues that all of them, including Galatians (I would suggest, *especially* Galatians), are tendentious; many or perhaps even most of his autobiographic remarks are apologetic.[78] Another scholar observes that, like Acts, Galatians uses "history to make theological points. Therefore neither source deserves markedly to outrank the other."[79] In his letters, Paul's "comments are ad hoc, occasional, selective, and often highly rhetorical." Further, though Paul is obviously an eyewitness to his own life, his autobiographical remarks are "often indirect or in passing."[80] And as Riesner notes, many "contradictions" are not between Acts and Paul's letters themselves but between our interpretations of these documents.[81] Many, indeed, appear in interpretations of Paul's letters themselves, for example, between Romans and

73. For suggestions of such elements, cf. Larsson, "Paul: Law and Salvation."

74. Jervell, *Unknown Paul*, 15; Hemer, *Acts in History*, 19–21.

75. Donfried, *Thessalonica*, 72, suggests that Luke's theological agenda may interfere with precise chronology. Yet we would expect reasonable chronology in a history, and Luke lacked theological incentive to place Paul's travels after the Syrian ministry (Donfried places some of Paul's travels earlier, e.g., 74, 99–117; so also others, e.g., Campbell, "Attestation" [relying on a reconstructed text]), if that was not how he thought it happened.

76. See Riesner, *Early Period*, 30, 231; cf. also Witherington, *Acts*, 87. For a chronology that accepts Acts where it fits the letters, see Jeske, "Luke and Paul on Paul."

77. E.g., Cic. *Fam.* 11.1–2.

78. Witherington, *Acts*, 87, 307–8, 430–31; cf. Talbert, *Mediterranean Milieu*, 205–6.

79. Hall, "Inference," 320.

80. Witherington, *Acts*, 86–87, 307–8; see also Riesner, *Early Period*, 29–30. For autobiographic elements that do appear in Paul, see esp. (on Galatians) the careful work of Lyons, *Autobiography*.

81. Riesner, *Early Period*, 30.

Galatians.[82] (Some current Romans scholarship finds it compatible with Luke's "very Jewish Paul.")[83]

Jervell argues that Paul's letters are too occasion-oriented to give us a balanced picture of him; Acts gives a broader, more "balanced" perspective of Paul's ministry as a whole. Thus, as in Acts 16:3, 18:18, and 21:26, the historical Paul was himself Jewish (cf. also Rom 3:31; 9:3–5; 11:1) and should not be "Paulinized" wholly in light of Galatians (via the later construct of Luther and some modern scholars).[84] Jervell's warning on this matter is apropos and can apply to other aspects of Luke's presentation as well. Paul and Luke often offer different kinds of information; both reflect perspectives that must be taken into account when they are being used for purposes of modern historiography.

5. Could Luke Have Known Paul's Letters?

A minority of scholars attribute Luke's knowledge about Paul not to independent sources but to Paul's letters themselves; in this case, Luke's coincidences with the letters do not suggest his access to further information but only to mostly the sources we already have (depending on the range of Pauline letters available to Luke).

Scholars articulate a variety of views as to whether Luke knew and used Paul's letters.[85] Some believe that Luke used Paul's letters in writing his own story of Paul[86] or even that he wrote Acts as an introduction to Paul's letter collection.[87] John Knox admits that there is no clear evidence that Luke used Paul's letters (Luke certainly does not cite them), but thinks it a priori likely that they were important in the church.[88] Certainly, Paul's letters were being circulated by the date that Knox gives for the final edition of Luke-Acts (ca. 125 C.E., as a reaction to Marcion's abuse of Luke and Paul),[89] but this date is highly unlikely for the work (unless one thinks of some later text traditions as the "work"). Most scholars today recognize Knox's reconstruction as highly speculative.

But one need not date Luke-Acts so late as to think that he would have had access to Paul's letters. Certainly, if Luke wrote in the late 80s or 90s, he should have known

---

82. For differences between these letters, see, e.g., Tobin, *Rhetoric in Contexts*, 43–46, 418; Cohen, *Maccabees*, 167; cf. Hays, *Echoes*, 176; Udoh, "Views on the Law." Boers, *Justification*, 223–24, contends that their message is compatible on the level of deeper structures.

83. See esp. Nanos, *Mystery*, 18; also 4, 21, 240 (noting [338] consistency with Acts' portrait).

84. Also Haacker, *Theology*, 146, concurring with Jervell. Cf. Barnett, *Birth*, 192: "An eyewitness of good memory and judicious perception may be an equal or better source of information than the subject himself."

85. For one useful survey, see Walker, "Pauline Letters," listing works arguing that Luke did not know them; that he did know some but did not use them; and that he knew and used some.

86. E.g., Pervo, "Dating Acts"; idem, *Dating Acts*, 51–147 (citing often even detailed turns of phrase); idem, *Mystery*, 4 ("near certainty that Luke used Paul's letters"). Goulder, "Letters," argues that Luke knew 1 Corinthians and 1 Thessalonians (98), but his evidence is not impressive. Pervo's detailed comparisons are commendable, but they admit of other possible explanations. If Luke moved in the Pauline circle, could he not have picked up "Pauline" phraseology (or both picked up similar language in those circles)? Some of his comparisons, such as the correspondence of the three elements of Luke 18:11 with three of the eleven elements of the vice list in 1 Cor 6:9–10 (pp. 64–65), may, at most, reflect Pauline language. Some others, such as "anxiety" appearing in both 1 Cor 7:32–35 and Luke 10:40–41 (p. 67), simply press too much into common use of widespread vocabulary to be plausible. We should note, however, that Pervo, *Dating Acts*, 146, is not claiming that Luke, though using Paul's letters, lacked other sources.

87. See Knox, "Acts and Corpus"; Walker, "Acts and Corpus Reconsidered." Although Polycarp may have written his letter to the Philippians partly to introduce a letter collection (Poly. *Phil.* 13.2), he also had other purposes in writing (cf., e.g., 11.1, 4).

88. Knox, "Acts and Corpus," 282–83.

89. Ibid., 286.

of some of Paul's letters or perhaps even the collection of them. Allusions in Clement of Rome, Ignatius of Antioch, Polycarp of Smyrna, 2 Pet 3:15–16, and, later, Marcion's canon suggest that at least the bulk of the letters had been collected and were being referred to by the end of the first century.[90] Unless Luke depends on Josephus, however (and as ch. 10 below notes, the arguments for this are quite weak), there is no reason to date Acts in the 90s; scholars who argue that Luke was a companion of Paul, in fact, usually date his work to the mid-80s at the latest. The premise that Luke uses Paul's letters rests on prior assumptions about the work's date (on which see our introduction, chs. 10–11).

Most scholars doubt that Luke knew Paul's letters;[91] some argue that he probably did not know them because they probably had not yet been collected.[92] It does indeed appear likely that Acts was composed (see ch. 10) before Paul's letters were collected. More concretely, most cite the minor discrepancies with Paul's letters and the relatively few echoes of them (possibly excepting Acts 9:20, 13:38–39, and some of 20:18–35) in his speeches.[93] On the basis of the "we" narratives, Luke (or his eyewitness source, in this view) would not have been present during the writing of Paul's letters before his Roman (or Caesarean) imprisonment.[94]

Fitzmyer suggests that Luke could have had access to the letters if Paul had kept copies with him, but he doubts Luke's access on the grounds that he wrote as much as two decades later.[95] One need not date Acts this late, however, to conclude that Luke would not have had access to many of the letters by means of Paul. Scribes would have made second copies of his long letters, but these would have remained with the sending churches; it is highly unlikely, for example, that Paul would have carried (and undoubtedly lost in his serial misfortunes) a bag of used scrolls from one place to another.[96] Luke would have known where to find letters (e.g., at Corinth) had he needed them, but (in my view of the "we" narratives) he probably regarded his personal acquaintance with Paul and his circle as sufficient for his purposes. When historians did use documents such as letters for earlier persons, they frequently displayed their documentary research (or invention at times) by citing them; Luke's failure to do so is conspicuous.

One could argue that Luke knew, and that his work reflects, some of Paul's letters without having access to the entire collection. For example, M. D. Goulder argues that "Luke knew 1 Corinthians and 1 Thessalonians."[97] He seeks to establish this position on the basis of clusters of words found both in Luke's redaction in the Gospel and in these letters, but with a few possible exceptions,[98] his connections are not distinctive enough to be convincing.[99] To the extent that any possible echoes appear, they

90. See Witherington, *Acts*, 171, who, however, does not date Acts this late; also Pervo, *Dating Acts*, 53 (who does date it in the second century).

91. E.g., Deissmann, *Light*, 246; Maddox, *Purpose*, 68; Barrett, "Acts and Corpus"; Wallace and Williams, *Acts*, 11; Porter, *Paul in Acts*, 206; Walton, *Leadership*, 14–17; Langner, *Hechos*, 35.

92. Bornkamm, *Paul*, xx.

93. Fitzmyer, *Acts*, 133, though noting many correlations (134–36) alongside the differences (136–37); O'Neill, *Theology*, 101–2; Johnson, *Acts*, 3–5.

94. Witherington, *Acts*, 170.

95. Fitzmyer, *Theologian*, 16.

96. On second copies, see, e.g., Cic. *Att.* 9.11, 13a, 14; 10.3a; 13.29; *Fam.* 3.3.2; 7.25.1; 11.11.1; *Ad Brut.* 3.1 (2.2.1); Sen. Y. *Ep. Lucil.* 99.2–32; Pliny *Ep.* 1.1.1; Fronto *Ad M. Caes.* 5.26; cf. also Richards, *Letter Writing*, 217 (citing Cic. *Att.* 13.6.3); Schmidt, "Letter," 437.

97. Goulder, "Letters," 98.

98. Especially Acts 15:20 reflecting 1 Cor 8–10 (Goulder, "Letters," 104).

99. See his summaries in Goulder, "Letters," 111–12. Other connections that are more concrete than the suggested verbal ones are more apt to depend on common information than on a common document.

may reflect the influence of Pauline preaching (not surprising if Luke was a traveling companion or even simply belonged to a Pauline church) rather than his letters per se.

Other scholars believe that Luke could have known some of Paul's letters but need not have used them;[100] certainly, if Luke was near Philippi about 50–58 C.E., he should have known Philippians.[101] But unless Paul's letters were collected by the time Luke wrote Acts (and they probably were not), Luke would have had access, at most, to a few of them—and perhaps not thought it necessary to consult even these. Granted, historians sometimes appended, quoted, or even invented letters as documents (Luke certainly resists the temptation to compose a Pauline letter in Acts). Biographers sometimes did cite literary epistles by their protagonists when these epistles were among the prominent material still available about these persons (Philost. *Vit. soph.* 2.33.628). But in contrast to these writers, Luke nowhere cites such documents as authorities, and if Luke had enough to say about Paul without the letters, he had little reason to depend on them or consult them.

Because of their later canonical status, readers of Paul's letters today often attribute to the letters a function out of proportion to their historical role in Paul's larger ministry. (Even early post-Pauline readers of Acts often felt the natural impulse to connect Acts with Paul's letters.)[102] Granted, the Corinthian correspondence had a major impact on Paul's relations with the Corinthians while he was away from them. But given Paul's year and a half among them in person (Acts 18:11), which Luke surveys in merely a few paragraphs in Acts 18, we ask too much if we expect Luke to expend space merely on these letters.

Indeed, if Luke knew much about Paul's ministry, he would have little reason to refer much to the letters. That he appears to contradict them on some points of detail (Acts 17:14–16; 1 Thess 3:1–2) or emphasize very different points in the same stories (Acts 9:23–25; 2 Cor 11:32–33)[103] reinforces the likelihood that he did not invent stories based on them and that where his accounts agree with Paul's letters (e.g., the majority of elements in these same passages), they do so independently of the letters.[104] Luke presumably knew that Paul wrote letters, and may have known some of these letters, but they were less important to him than the living memory of Paul himself.

If Luke knew and depended on Paul's letters, some features of Acts are difficult to explain. Why are incidental details so often confirmed (as will be noted below) when Luke omits most of the heart of the Corinthian correspondence (such as the names of most persons there; the collection and all but the barest mention of the Achaian trip connected to it; and conflict over status, spiritual gifts, etc.)? Why does Romans

100. Contrast Pervo, *Dating Acts*, 54, who suggests that lack of letter-writing in Acts probably suppresses knowledge of Paul's letter-writing. Yet one wonders how successfully Luke's silence would suppress their influence (especially if they were as widely known in the Pauline circle as Pervo apparently thinks they were). In my view, Acts does not mention his letter-writing because it was of far less interest than his personal visits and sufferings (though Luke does not focus even on his teachings in person); it fits neither Luke's purview nor his era. Only in a later generation, when his living memory faded, would such letters come to the fore. Pervo (100) recognizes that "direct contact with Paul and/or some of his associates" would explain the data as well as would dependence on Paul's letters, but thinks that Luke so misrepresents Paul (e.g., by subordinating him to the Jerusalem apostles—if one finds this example persuasive) as to make this unlikely. I address Luke's supposed misrepresentation of Paul later in this chapter.

101. See also Fitzmyer, *Theologian*, 16 (contrast Fitzmyer, *Acts*, 133).

102. Cf. the postscript inserted at Acts 28 in Ethiopic versions (Uhlig, "Pseudepigraphischer Actaschluss").

103. Luke omits major elements of the letters and focuses, e.g., on different elements of the Jerusalem Council.

104. See also Fitzmyer, *Acts*, for differences (136–37) and correlations (134–36); Lüdemann, *Christianity*, 7–8. Ancient historians also could demand coherency with other accounts or evidence (Polyb. 3.32.4–5).

leave no direct trace (with Phoebe at Cenchreae, Prisca and Aquila explicitly back at Rome, and the Roman church struggling with Jewish-Gentile issues)? Why do we not read of "Galatians" rather than of that province's towns more specifically mentioned in Acts? Why do key elements of these letters' theology appear only sporadically, though in appropriate settings (e.g., Paul addresses justification by faith with a synagogue audience and uses "natural theology" when addressing some Gentiles)? Had Luke drawn on Galatians, as some have argued, we should not expect such ambiguity as to fuel the long-standing debate as to whether Acts 15 does (as I think) or does not reflect the events also reported in Gal 2:1–10. Even if Luke knew some of Paul's letters, they seem to have interested him far less than Paul's life.

Sometimes those who argue that Luke depended on Paul's letters also criticize him for misunderstanding the Pauline theology we infer from the same letters, but it is hard to have it both ways. While I argue that some scholars have exaggerated the differences between Luke's Paul and the letters' Paul, I believe that the former would look much more like the latter if Luke had Paul's letters as a significant (and probably most direct) source. If Luke drew from Paul's letters, he must have done so mostly unconsciously, having forgotten most of what he read (yet remembering some obscure historical details)! Other constructs appear much likelier than the thesis that Luke depended on Paul's letters.

As an aside, we may note that some scholars also believe that Luke participated in the production of the Pastoral Epistles,[105] which many scholars also hold to include at least a significant deposit of Pauline tradition.[106] Luke's itinerary for Paul, however, does not fit the itinerary of the Pastorals; they can be reconciled if (plausibly) Paul was released, traveled further, and was again imprisoned in Rome at a later date, but the return to Ephesus implied in the Pastorals (1 Tim 1:3) does not fit easily with Acts 20:25 (though see comment there). In my view, the content of the Pastorals is thus not fitted closely or deliberately to the narrative in Acts. (Moreover, against some scholars, use of an amanuensis[107] should not be ruled out, whoever wrote the works; the uneducated used scribes because they needed them,[108] and the well-to-do because they could afford them.) Although Luke's involvement in the Pastorals remains possible (see esp. 2 Tim 4:11), it is not certain.[109]

---

105. Most thoroughly, for Luke as full author, Wilson, *Pastoral Epistles*, marshaling considerable evidence; for Luke as Paul's amanuensis for the Pastorals, C. F. D. Moule, followed by others (e.g., Knight, *Sayings*, 149–50); quite plausibly, Lukan redaction (Feuillet, "Affinités"). History is so distinct from nonnarrative genres (Pliny *Ep.* 5.8.7–11) that the correspondences we do find (often noted; e.g., Aune, *Dictionary of Rhetoric*, 339) appear more significant; some of these may simply represent educated (especially Stoic) vocabulary, but given the limited Pauline circle we know (a serious limitation), perhaps no one seems likelier than Luke. For medical imagery in the Pastorals, see Malherbe, *Philosophers*, 121–36; pseudepigraphy also seems to have flourished in medical circles (e.g., the expansive Hippocratic corpus; cf. Aune, *Dictionary of Rhetoric*, 165, 323).

106. Besides those affirming Pauline authorship, e.g., Bornkamm, *Paul*, 86; Harrison, "Hypotheses"; Rogers, "Pastoral Epistles"; Zmijewski, "Pastoralbriefe." Cf. Quinn, "Volume," who suggests (70–75) an epistolary appendix for Acts, like the three letters ending Diogenes Laertius's life of Epicurus; but in view of the homogeneity of the texture of Acts, I believe that this proposal goes too far.

107. E.g., Rom 16:22; Cic. *Fam.* 16.14.1–2; 16.22.1 (the scribe is also an interpreter for the copyists); Dio Chrys. *Or.* 18.18; Corn. Nep. 18 (Eumenes), 1.5; Suet. *Horace* 2 (a more creative secretary); Fronto *Ad M. Caes.* 5.26. See further Ukachukwu Manus, "Hypothesis"; Longenecker, "Amanuenses," 282–89; esp. Richards, *Letter Writing*, 64–80, 92–93, 143.

108. E.g., P.Tebt. 104.40; P.Lond. 1164 (h), line 30; P.Oxy. 269.17–18; 1206.24; 1636, lines 45–46; *BGU* 405.23–24.

109. One could even postulate that Timothy and Titus had received instructions from Paul such as those in these letters but, lacking surviving copies of the original letters (cf. Heb 13:23), secured help from someone (perhaps Luke, who had been with Paul), who could reconstruct the substance of Paul's message; or one could postulate that those who heard the letters' substance from them sought to reconstruct them.

If one argues for dependence on Paul's collected letters, one must ask how he comes by his other early information (confirmed by other external sources), many unusual deviations from the reports in Paul's letters, silence about those letters (and key elements in them), and the strong divergence from the itinerary in the Pastorals' traditions (see the excursus "Acts and the Pastorals" at Acts 20:25). The apologetic for Paul also likely reflects charges fresh in the minds of Luke's ideal audience.[110] Most works after Paul's letters do not hew to Pauline chronology and so forth the way that Acts does (see sect. 6 below).

6. Correspondences between Luke and Paul

Here and hereafter, for the purposes of this commentary, I will use most of Pauline literature as a backdrop for the "epistolary Paul," with whom I will compare the Lukan portrait of Paul.[111] Paul's letters correspond with Acts substantially in their treatment of events and chronology.[112]

Luke often names people also named by Paul, yet he does this without depending on Paul's letters, as is shown by his use of less formal names (e.g., Prisca and Priscilla).[113] Luke's itinerary for Paul's journeys in the "we" narrative is accurate, as well as titles of officials (such as "politarchs") in various locales. Someone could argue that Luke simply traveled, learned local color, knew when Gallio was proconsul of Achaia, and knew the names of Paul's colleagues in ministry (presumably without, as noted above, knowledge of his letters), then simply invented stories about Paul. But accuracy in so many details is not typical of fiction,[114] and Paul's letters confirm many details about the founding of the churches, the order in which Paul evangelized them, and so forth. Would Luke coincidentally prove accurate on information that happens to remain extant, yet fictionalize everywhere else?

One might then object that the broad contours of Luke's history are most accurate but that his accounts of Paul as miracle worker—most objectionable to modern Western tastes—are Lukan creations. Some scholars have argued that the epistolary Paul, in contrast to Luke's Paul, was not much of a miracle worker.[115] Although Paul's miracles do not have reason to come up more often than other aspects of his initial evangeli-

---

110. See Keener, "Apologetic."

111. I will treat Ephesians and Colossians as Pauline; even if they are Pauline at one remove, nearly all their language and thought remain compatible with some earlier Pauline passages. By contrast, as noted in sect. 1.b above, this commentary will not assume the language of the Pastorals as Pauline. Even if their substance is from Paul (which I believe is significantly likelier than many concede), the language differs so starkly from Paul's undisputed letters that even supporters of Pauline authorship usually attribute much of the language to an amanuensis; hence most would agree that the language (the issue in question in some of our discussions) is not indisputably Pauline. Because their authorship is a debate to which we cannot attend in a commentary on Acts, it seems better to make the case for the biblical academy from documents that are more widely accepted there. I will, however, draw on the Pastorals periodically for their deposit of information about Paul, which most, regardless of views on date and authorship, at least date significantly earlier than the fictitious apocryphal *Acts of Paul*.

112. Bruce, *Acts*[3], 47–52 (who concludes, 52–59, that Luke's portrayal of Paul is genuine); idem, "Paul"; deSilva, *Introduction*, 375–79; cf. Alexander, "Chronology"; Chance, *Acts*, 20–21.

113. Hemer, *Acts in History*, 206.

114. Ps.-Callisthenes's *Alexander Romance* may follow the general itinerary of Alexander's conquests, but the itinerary was well known and published and therefore difficult to contravene. The case of Paul's itinerary differs. If we argue that both simply followed geography, Luke's narrative includes far more details corresponding to Paul's own than would be necessary for simply postulating movement westward.

115. Williams, *Miracle Stories*, 6–9, counters this skepticism, pointing out that Luke portrays Paul's sufferings (as Paul does) and Paul mentions his own miracles (as Luke does). Emphasis may differ (probably partly on account of the differing genres in which they write), but their information is coherent.

zation activities (e.g., 1 Thess 1:9; 1 Cor 2:1–5; Gal 4:13–14), they do appear quite significant to his evangelistic activity when they are mentioned. Paul recounts these as an integral part of his ministry (Rom 15:19; 2 Cor 12:12; cf. Gal 3:5), sometimes even in locations where Luke omits them (2 Cor 12:12; cf. 1 Cor 1:22); he has other supernatural experiences (1 Cor 9:1; 14:18, 37; 15:8; 2 Cor 12:1–4, 7; Gal 1:15–16) and expects such experiences in his churches (1 Cor 12–14; Gal 3:5; 1 Thess 5:20).[116]

If we cannot attribute the agreement with Paul's letters to dependence on Paul's letters (and we probably cannot), the agreement probably indicates dependence on eyewitness tradition about Paul or on contact with Paul himself.[117] As the commentary will illustrate and some recent essays have demonstrated, events in Paul's life depicted in Acts comport well with those in Paul's letters.[118] For example, his letters reveal a Paul concerned to reach both Jews and Gentiles with his message, as in Acts (e.g., Acts 9:15; Rom 1:14–16).[119]

a. Earlier Lists of Correspondences

Various scholars have provided lists of correspondences. Long ago Harnack concluded that the agreements are so substantial where Luke can be checked that doubting him where he cannot be is wildly speculative.[120] In an excursus, he noted thirty-nine cases where Paul's letters corroborate Acts; the most persuasive are listed here:[121]

1. Jerusalem, not Galilee, was the starting place (Gal 2).
2. Christian groups elsewhere in Judea are mentioned (1 Thess 2:14; Gal 1:22; Acts 9:31).
3. Judean churches faced persecution (Acts passim;[122] 1 Thess 2:14).
4. Judean churches obeyed the law (Acts 15:1ff.; 21:20; Gal 2:12), and Paul was not sure how they accepted him (Rom 15:31).[123]
5. The Twelve led this church (Acts 1:13; 6:2; Gal 1:17; 1 Cor 15:5).
6. Barnabas was an apostle, in addition to the Twelve (Acts 14:4, 14; 1 Cor 9:5–6; 15:7).
7. Peter and John "stand out" among the Twelve (Acts 3:1ff.; 8:14ff.; Gal 2:9).
8. Peter is the chief head (Acts 2:37; Gal 1:18; 1 Cor 15:5).
9. Peter made journeys for his mission (Acts 9; Gal 2:7–8, 11).
10. The Lord's brothers are mentioned as "a group side by side with the Apostles" (Acts 1:14; 1 Cor 9:5).[124]
11. James headed the Lord's brothers and was a "pillar" no less authoritative than Peter and John (Acts 12:17; 15:13ff.; 21:18; 1 Cor 15:7; Gal 2:9, 12).

---

116. See the discussion of signs in Luke's theology in ch. 15 of this introduction, sect. 6, below; from a historical and social standpoint, ch. 9 below; on gifts, see further Keener, "Gifts"; idem, *Gift*, 102–35. Porter, *Paul in Acts*, 193–94, also responds to Haenchen's contrast here, but he plays down Paul's miracles in Acts too much.

117. See Porter, *Paul in Acts*, 206; cf. also Emmet, "Tradition."

118. See esp. Wenham, "Corpus," more extensively than here; also Hemer, *Acts in History*, 181–90; Witherington, *Acts*, 445–49.

119. Porter, *Paul in Acts*, 167.

120. Harnack, *Acts*, 272: "The agreement which in these numerous instances exists between the Acts (chaps. i.–xiv.) and the Pauline epistles, although the latter are only incidental writings belonging to the later years of the Apostle, is so extensive and so detailed as to exclude all wild hypotheses concerning those passages of the Acts that are without attestation in those epistles." The logic is the same as arguments that a source unreliable where it can be checked should be assumed unreliable elsewhere (cf., e.g., Ehrman, *Interrupted*, 110, on Papias).

121. Harnack, *Acts*, excursus 1, pp. 264–74.

122. See esp. Acts 7–8.

123. See here also Acts 21:21.

124. Harnack, *Acts*, 267.

12. Barnabas is portrayed "as the most important of the missionaries to the Gentiles together with St. Paul," working together with him (Acts 9:27; 11:22ff.; 13–14; Gal 2:1ff.; 1 Cor 9:6).
13. Barnabas belonged to (Acts 4:36–37), or felt loyalty to (Gal 2:13), the Jerusalem church.
14. Mark is connected closely with Barnabas (Acts 15:37ff.; Col 4:10).
15. Silas was a companion of Paul, with Timothy more subordinate (Acts 15:40ff.; 16:1ff.; 1 Thess 1:1; 2 Thess 1:1; 2 Cor 1:19).
16. There were many members of the Jerusalem church even at the earliest period (Acts 2:41; 4:4;[125] 1 Cor 15:6).
17. Baptism was used for entrants into the community (Acts 2:38, 41; 8:12–13; Rom 6:3–4; Gal 3:27).
18. Signs and wonders accompany apostleship (Acts 2:43; 14:3; 2 Cor 12:11–12).
19. Paul persecuted Christians (Acts 9:1ff.; Gal 1:13–14; 1 Cor 15:9; Phil 3:6).
20. Paul is on a par with Peter and other apostles (the parallelism in Acts; Gal 2:7ff.).
21. Paul was converted near Damascus by a revelation of the Lord (Acts 9:2–9; Gal 1:12, 17; 1 Cor 15:8).
22. Paul escaped Damascus in a basket from the wall (Acts 9; 2 Cor 11:32).
23. Paul went to Jerusalem afterward (Acts 9:26; Gal 1:18–19, specifying the time).
24. Paul ministered in Jerusalem (Acts 9:28–29; 23:11; Rom 15:19).
25. The cities of Paul's ministry in Acts 13–14 fit 2 Tim 3:11.
26. Paul teaches justification by faith in Acts 13:38–39.

Not only does Luke get correct many data in the first (and most disputed) half of Acts; his record also fits the sequence of Paul's missionary work, as noted by Thomas H. Campbell more than half a century ago:[126]

- Persecution (Gal 1:13–14; cf. Acts 9)
- Conversion (Gal 1:15–17a; cf. Acts 9)
- To Arabia (Gal 1:17b; not in Acts)
- To Damascus (Gal 1:17c; cf. Acts 9)
- To Jerusalem (Gal 1:18–19; cf. Acts 9)
- To Syria and Cilicia (Gal 1:21; cf. Acts 11:25)
- To Jerusalem after fourteen years (Gal 2:1–10; Acts 11 or 15?)
- Antioch (Gal 2:11; Acts 15:30–35)
- To Philippi (1 Thess 2:1–2; Phil 4:15–16; cf. Acts 16)
- To Thessalonica (1 Thess 2:1–2; cf. Acts 17)
- To Athens (1 Thess 3:1–3; cf. Acts 17)
- To Corinth (2 Cor 11:7–9; cf. Acts 18)
- To Ephesus (1 Cor 16:8–9; cf. Acts 19)
- To Troas (2 Cor 2:12; not in Acts)

125. Better for the Pauline parallel, Acts 1:15.
126. Campbell, "Journeys," 87 (for the chart; in greater detail, 81–84; Campbell starts with Damascus, but I have augmented the outline). Talbert, *Mediterranean Milieu*, 203–4, regards this article as significant and cites the concurrence of Kümmel and Fitzmyer. Cf. the similar concurrence of itineraries in Trebilco, "Itineraries"; more briefly, Wallace and Williams, *Acts*, 26–27; other agreements in Riesner, "Zuverlässigkeit," 41–42.

- To Macedonia (2 Cor 2:13; 8–9; cf. Acts 20)
- To Corinth (2 Cor 9:4; 7:5; cf. Acts 20:2b–3)
- To Jerusalem (Rom 15:22–25; cf. Acts 21)
- To Rome (Rom 15:22–25; cf. Acts 28)

As for areas where Paul is silent in contrast to Luke, Paul's "from Jerusalem as far as Illyricum" implies that he worked in more places than he records.[127] No novel known to us from antiquity betrays such detailed correspondences with external, incidental information. Moreover, no ancient author would have worked so hard to extract such information from occasional documents, then failed to cite them.[128]

Charles Talbert draws attention to the work of both Harnack[129] and Campbell[130] and challenges the skepticism of many scholars who have paid inadequate attention to such correspondences. The assumption that Acts is a later secondary source less reliable than Paul's letters, he warns, merits "careful reconsideration given the nature of autobiography in antiquity."[131]

Goulder may explain the source of Luke's information differently than we would, but he helpfully lists the following points of agreement between some of Paul's undisputed letters and Acts (with an emphasis on 1 Corinthians and 1 Thessalonians):[132]

- Paul and Barnabas were co-pastors in Antioch (Acts 11:25–26; 13:1; Gal 2:1–14).
- Their policy was distinct from that of the Jerusalem missionaries (Acts 13–14; 1 Cor 9:6).[133]
- The founders of the Corinthian church were Paul, Silas, and Timothy (Acts 18:1, 5; 2 Cor 1:19).
- They first founded the Thessalonian church in Macedonia (Acts 17:1–9; 1 Thess 1:1).
- They faced hostility there (Acts 17:5–9; 1 Thess 1:6–7; 2:14).
- Paul began the Corinthian mission before others arrived (Acts 18:1–4; 1 Thess 3:1, 6).
- He ministered briefly in Athens en route (Acts 17:15–34; 1 Thess 3:1).
- He earned his living in Corinth (Acts 18:3; 1 Cor 1:9 [sic; cf. 4:12; 9:6]).
- One early convert "was a man of note called Crispus" (Acts 18:8; 1 Cor 1:14).
- Apollos followed him and was like-minded (Acts 18:24–28; 1 Cor 1:12).
- Paul afterward stayed for a long time in Ephesus (Acts 19; 1 Cor 16:8–9).
- The final visit to Corinth was via Macedonia (Acts 20:1–2; 2 Cor 1–2).

A number of other examples could be added, among the most important being the occasion of the Jerusalem Council in Acts 15 and Gal 2:1–10; although this correlation

127. Campbell, "Journeys," 85.
128. If Luke used them but then "suppressed" them by silence, as Pervo, *Dating Acts*, 54, has suggested, why not also suppress the version of Paul's ministry (including this itinerary) they contained?
129. Talbert, *Mediterranean Milieu*, 207–8.
130. Ibid., 203–4.
131. Ibid., 205; Talbert, *Acts*, 240. He notes that first-person narrative was often apologetic and tendentious (*Mediterranean Milieu*, 206; *Acts*, 240).
132. Goulder, *Competing Mission*, 223. He also thinks that the hearing before Gallio is likely, as also the link with Priscilla and Aquila, and the mention of Sosthenes.
133. This point appears less clear to me.

has often been disputed, the connections are significant (see discussion at Acts 15). The following section explores some of these other correlations (besides some over-lapping with observations above).

b. Pauline Correlations with Acts

Many scholars have offered lists of Pauline correspondences; my brief treatment here will necessarily overlap with some of them. Nevertheless, because these correspondences are so critical to the argument about Acts and the particular character of Luke's historiography, I cannot complete the discussion of my earlier chapters regarding Acts' genre without addressing this issue or by simply footnoting other important studies. Although the commentary proper provides more detailed comparisons, I will compare here some of Paul's letters, usually undisputed ones.

In most of the following examples, differences in detail suggest that Luke is not depending on Paul's letters or seeking to impress those with access to them. Nevertheless, the areas of coincidence are so many that we may conclude that Luke clearly reports genuine historical events. That is, Luke is writing history, not a novel, and he does not invent events even if he may elaborate at points (most obviously, the behind-the-scenes dialogue of Festus with Agrippa and Berenice, Acts 25:14–22), as historians often did (maintaining a narrative rather than explanatory genre). Even some of the divergent details below could be explained as historically reliable, but comment regarding these questions must be reserved for the relevant commentary passages.

i. Paul's Early Years and Companions

The respective accounts of Paul's conversion, for example, focus on different details (and Luke emphasizes the theophanic element more than in other disciples' resurrection encounters, a point not clear in, though neither clearly contradicted by, Paul's letters). Nevertheless, Luke and Paul overlap at some significant points: Paul was converted through a revelation of Jesus Christ (Gal 1:12), presumably meaning a revelation the content of which was Jesus Christ (1:16); this interpretation fits the context (1:15–16) and other Pauline passages (1 Cor 9:1; 15:8). Paul did not solicit the revelation; it came freely by divine grace (Gal 1:15). It came in the context of his call to preach among Gentiles (Gal 1:15–16; Acts 9:15; 26:20). This call occurred somewhere near Nabatean Arabia, near Damascus (Gal 1:17), and in the period when he was persecuting Christians (1:13). Paul himself claims to have experienced a "revelation" of Christ (1:12, 16) and (more explicitly than Acts 9:3–8; 22:6–7; 26:13–14; but see 9:17; 22:14–15; 26:16) to have seen Jesus (1 Cor 9:1) in a sort

Event	Acts	Paul
Paul was converted through a revelation of Jesus Christ, presumably meaning a revelation the content of which was Jesus Christ	Acts 9:3–6; 22:7–10; 26:13–15	Gal 1:12, 15–16; 1 Cor 9:1; 15:8
Paul did not solicit the revelation; it came freely by divine grace	Acts 9:3–5; 22:6–7; 26:9–14	Gal 1:15; 1 Cor 15:8–9
It came in the context of his call to preach among Gentiles	Acts 9:15; 26:20; cf. (diplomatically) 22:15	Gal 1:15–16; cf. 1 Cor 15:8–9*
This occurred somewhere near Nabatean Arabia, near Damascus	Acts 9:3; 22:6, 10–11; 26:12, 20	Gal 1:17; cf. 2 Cor 11:32
It occurred in the period when he was persecuting Christians	Acts 9:2, 4; 22:4, 7–8; 26:9–15	Gal 1:13; cf. 1 Cor 15:8–9
Paul counts the beginning of his ministry in Jerusalem (though he was in "Arabia" earlier)	Acts 9:26, 28; 26:20	Rom 15:19; cf. Gal 1:17

*Paul also employs ἀφορίζω with respect to his calling (Rom 1:1; Gal 1:15); cf. Acts 13:2.

of belated resurrection appearance (15:8). As in Acts, Paul apparently starts with his own people (cf. Rom 1:16), including in Jerusalem (15:19).

No matter how Luke may have adapted this account in retelling it as a coherent narrative (cohering also with his larger work), he is clearly not writing imaginative fiction but develops genuine pre-Lukan information. If this is the case where we can test him, we ought to infer that it is also the case where we cannot test him. This case regarding Paul's conversion is all the more significant in that it occurs before the "we" narrative, though it was probably also one of Paul's more frequently retold stories.

We may also compare the accounts of Paul and Luke regarding Paul's first escape from Damascus; although they diverge on the identity of his opponents, they otherwise tell the same story:

Acts 9:23–25	2 Cor 11:32–33
Jews plotted to kill Paul (9:23)	The *ethnarch* tried to seize Paul (11:32)
Jews were watching the gates (9:24)	The *ethnarch* was guarding the city (11:32)
Let down in a basket from the wall (9:25)	Let down in a basket from a *window* in the wall (11:33)

Again, Paul speaks of his visit to Jerusalem as involving Cephas and James, not the other apostles, whereas Luke more generally summarizes Paul as spending time with "the apostles"; in other respects, however, they clearly report the same event:

Acts 9:26–30	Gal 1:18–19
Paul went from Damascus to Jerusalem (9:25–26)	Paul went from Damascus to Jerusalem (1:17–18)
Barnabas made the introduction to the disciples (9:26–27)	(Missing, but Paul's letters attest Barnabas's prominence)
Paul met the apostles (9:27)	Paul met Cephas and James (1:18–19)
Paul continued in association with the apostles (9:28)	Paul stayed with Cephas fifteen days (1:18)
Paul's stay was apparently relatively brief (9:29–30)	Paul's stay was brief (1:18)

Although the absence of Titus from Acts seems particularly curious,[134] Luke knows many of the major figures from Pauline tradition, including Peter, John, James, Barnabas, Silas, Timothy, and Aquila and Priscilla as well as some of the less prominent characters, such as Mark (Acts 12:12; Col 4:10; Phlm 24; cf. 2 Tim 4:11), Aristarchus (Acts 19:29; 20:4; 27:2; Col 4:10; Phlm 24), Tychicus (Acts 20:4; Eph 6:21; Col 4:7; cf. 2 Tim 4:12; Titus 3:12), Sopater (Acts 20:4; Sosipater in Rom 16:21), Crispus (Acts 18:8; 1 Cor 1:14), and Trophimus (Acts 20:4; 21:29; cf. 2 Tim 4:20).[135] Unless we postulate dependence on Paul's letters (which again fails to explain the incongruities), Luke is extremely well informed about Paul's immediate circle (see table on p. 243).

Luke's travel narratives also comport well with Paul's letters. Both Paul's letters and the rapid growth of eastern Mediterranean Diaspora churches that later claimed him as one of their founders testify that Paul did undertake such travels. Despite the incompleteness of both Acts and Paul's letters, we know from Paul's letters (as scholars cited earlier have pointed out) that Paul did in fact minister in most of the cities and regions that Luke mentions, and did reach them (where our sources overlap) in the same sequence. By contrast, neither source portrays Paul visiting prestigious major centers such as Alexandria or Seleucia on the Tigris (half of the empire's four largest cities). A novel need not have followed the events of Paul's ministry so carefully; a

134. The omission of Demas (Col 4:14; Phlm 24) may make sense in view of 2 Tim 4:10. As for Luke (Col 4:14; Phlm 24; perhaps Rom 16:21; cf. 2 Tim 4:11), see ch. 11 below.

135. Perhaps also Jason (Acts 17:5–9, in light of Rom 16:21) and probably Sosthenes (Acts 18:17; 1 Cor 1:1).

Name	Acts	Pauline Literature
Peter/Cephas	Acts 1–12 passim; 15:7	1 Cor 1:12; 3:22; 9:5; 15:5; Gal 1:18; 2:7–11, 14
John	1:13; 3:1–11; 4:6, 13, 19; 8:14; 12:2	Gal 2:9
James	12:17; 15:13; 21:18	1 Cor 15:7; Gal 1:19; 2:9, 12
Barnabas	9:27; 11:22, 30; 12:25–15:38	1 Cor 9:6; Gal 2:1, 9, 13; Col 4:10
Silas/Silvanus	15:22–18:5	2 Cor 1:19; 1 Thess 1:1; 2 Thess 1:1
Timothy	16:1; 17:14–15; 18:5; 19:22; 20:4	Rom 16:21; 1 Cor 4:17; 16:10; 2 Cor 1:1, 19; Phil 1:1; 2:19; Col 1:1; 1 Thess 3:2, 6; Phlm 1; etc.
Aquila and Priscilla	18:2, 18, 26	Rom 16:3; 1 Cor 16:19; 2 Tim 4:19
Mark	12:12, 25; 15:37, 39	Col 4:10; Phlm 24; 2 Tim 4:11
Aristarchus	19:29; 20:4; 27:2	Col 4:10; Phlm 24
Tychicus	20:4	Eph 6:21; Col 4:7; cf. 2 Tim 4:12; Titus 3:12
Sopater/ Sosipater	20:4	Rom 16:21
Crispus	18:8	1 Cor 1:14
Trophimus	20:4; 21:29	2 Tim 4:20

proper history, by contrast, might exercise freedom to fill in details but would not invent events such as the founding of Paul's churches.

ii. Paul's "Missionary Journeys"

Many classical historians find Acts one of the most valuable sources (even "most valuable of all") because it is one of our few sources for travel conditions for "the plain civilian or merchant" in this period.[136] I trace here some further samples from Acts 13–28, in roughly the sequence in which they will appear in the commentary. Paul's Letter to the Galatians is consistent with the knowledge that Antioch was a base for both Paul and Barnabas (Gal 2:11, 13), so that decisions there could affect Galatia's churches (hence the potential magnitude of 2:11–14).[137] If one accepts the South Galatian hypothesis, which seems to fit better with the whole of our evidence and is probably now the majority view (see this commentary's introduction to the fifteenth chapter of Acts), Paul's letters also suggest, in at least a general way, the evangelization reported in Acts 13–14.

Paul's letters do not lay out his missionary strategy, but Luke's portrayal of his ministry as starting in synagogues (e.g., Acts 13:5) comports well with what the letters do reveal. Paul's understanding of salvation history gives priority for the Jew first and then the Gentile (Rom 1:16; 2:9–10). He explicitly claims to have adapted himself to reach Jews as well as Gentiles (1 Cor 9:20) so that all might be saved (9:22); no place in the Diaspora was better suited for religious discussion with gathered Jews (and even God-fearers) than the synagogue. Even contexts emphasizing Paul's mission to the Gentiles (e.g., Rom 11:13; 15:16, 18) reflect deep concern for reaching his own people (11:14). He would hardly have been disciplined in synagogues (2 Cor 11:24) if he remained uninvolved in them. Paul's letters also presuppose a measure of biblical literacy in most of his churches, which in turn might presuppose (in such young churches) some Jewish believers or God-fearers there (albeit in some churches more than others). (See fuller discussion at Acts 13:5.)

Paul's stoning in Lystra in Acts fits his own report. Lest we suppose Luke's narratives too dramatic in such cases as this, Paul records sufferings far more extensive in his own writings (1 Cor 4:9–13; 2 Cor 1:4–10; 4:8–12; 6:4–10; 11:23–28), including far more

---

136. Charlesworth, *Trade Routes*, 85–86.
137. Cf. Riesner, *Early Period*, 271.

beatings and shipwrecks than Acts records (2 Cor 11:23–25).[138] Paul attests that he faced dangers both from his fellow Jews[139] and from Gentiles (11:26 mentions both). Most relevant of all, he explicitly notes that he was once stoned (11:25). That Paul and Barnabas would return to cities where they had begun churches (Acts 14:21b) also fits what we know of the historical Paul. He continually carried concern for his churches (2 Cor 11:28–29; 1 Thess 3:5–7) and made plans to visit when possible (1 Cor 4:18–21; 16:3–7; 2 Cor 12:20–13:2; Phil 2:24; Phlm 22).

The Jerusalem Council in Acts 15 betrays several significant points of contact with Paul's own account in Gal 2:1–10. (For reasons offered at Acts 15, I find this correlation far more convincing than the proposed correlation with Acts 11:30.) Acts 15 reports decrees sent only as far as Syria-Cilicia, that is, Antioch's (and Tarsus's) province (15:23, 41).[140] This limitation suggests that Luke accurately reports a period in which the "Judaizers" opposed in Paul's Letter to the Galatians have not yet reached Galatia (although no one doubts that Luke writes after Paul wrote Galatians). Numerous commonalities are evident:

Commonalities	Acts 15:6–22	Gal 2:1–10
The same basic object	15:5	2:4
The same basic outcome	15:19–21, 28–29	2:5–6
Paul's mission is recognized	15:12	2:2
Leaders agree that Gentiles need not be circumcised	15:19–20	2:7–9
Peter was involved	15:7–11	2:9
James was involved	15:13–21	2:9
James holds special rank in the assembly	Cf. 15:19 (and 12:17)	2:9 (listing him first among the pillars)
James is apparently associated with conservatives	15:13–22*	2:12

*James's words appear to carry weight with them here; he belongs to the group that interprets the conservative faction's concerns in Acts 21:18–25.

Differences in the details included (such as the agreement that Paul should care for the poor, Gal 2:10) and in perspective must be factored into our evaluation of Luke's historiography, but these were to be expected among ancient (and, to a different extent, all) historians. What is clear is that Luke deals here in real events, not novelistic fabrication, however much he (like other historians) defines his own focus and approach.

On the historical level, Paul was publicly shamed in Philippi (1 Thess 2:2; Acts 16:22–23), and the rest of his welcome in Macedonia seems to have been no more hospitable.[141] Likewise, there can be no question that the hostility was severe in Thessalonica and that it also continued after Paul left (Acts 17:13). Paul writes that the believers there received the word amid affliction (1 Thess 1:6) and that he had preached

138. Paul's "brand marks of Jesus" (Gal 6:17) probably also implies that the beatings left marks (with Ramsay, *Galatians*, 472; Ridderbos, *Galatia*, 228; though others take them solely figuratively, Betz, *Galatia*, 324). Cf. further his theology of apostolic "tribulation," in the comment on Acts 14:22.

139. Cf. also, for Judea, 1 Thess 2:14–16; Rom 15:31; Gal 6:12 (but this last text probably represents Paul's Christian opponents' non-Christian peers in Jerusalem, not in Asia Minor). Luke emphasizes local Jewish opposition in each location where he finds it, whereas Paul summarizes more the widespread unbelief of his people (Rom 9:3–6; 9:27–10:3; 10:19–21; 11:7–32).

140. Although the decree was reported in southern Galatia orally (Acts 16:4), this region was not specified in the decree.

141. For further discussion on Philippi (material appearing in conjunction with the "we" narrative), see comment on Acts 16 ad loc. Because Luke provides more detail there, proportionately less of it affords detailed parallels in Paul's letters than in, e.g., Acts 17:1–9, but it appears in conjunction with the "we" narrator's presence. Paul's citizenship claim there, perhaps the specific element challenged the most often, is more plausible than its detractors allow (see comment on Acts 16:37).

there in the face of hostility (2:2). In Luke's report of Paul's Thessalonian ministry (Acts 17:1–9), the most significant differences from 1 Thessalonians are Luke's emphasis on Jewish opposition;[142] that Paul seems to presuppose a longer stay in Thessalonica than Luke reports; and the details of who stayed behind.[143] These instances may reveal a degree of flexibility in details, though no more than one expects in other historians. The points of commonality, however, are too striking for a mere novel:

1 Thessalonians	Acts 17:1–9
The church knows Silvanus and Timothy (1:1)	Luke implies the presence of Silas (17:10, 14) and Timothy (17:14)
Converts turned from idols (1:9)	Converts included Gentiles (though many were already God-fearers; 17:4)
Paul preached eschatology (1:10; cf. 3:13; 4:13–5:11, esp. 5:2), possibly including the kingdom (1 Thess 2:12; cf. 2 Thess 1:5) and a royal parousia (1 Thess 2:19; 3:13; 4:15;* 5:23; cf. 2 Thess 2:1, 8)	Paul was accused of preaching "another king," Jesus (17:7)
Paul came to Thessalonica from Philippi, where he suffered shame (2:2)	They left Philippi under duress (16:40) and, after traveling through two other towns en route, reached Thessalonica (17:1)
Paul spoke boldly but faced much opposition (2:1–2), perhaps accused of being a charlatan (2:3–11)†	They encountered opposition (17:5–9), including false accusations of being politically subversive (17:6–7)
The Thessalonian believers became like the Judean churches, suffering from their fellow Macedonians as Judean churches did from Judeans (2:14); this apparently began while Paul was with them (2:13–14)‡	The church had to suffer publicly (17:7, 9), though Paul's situation was more severe (17:10)
Some Jewish people have proved hostile to the Gentile mission (2:16)	Paul faced Jewish opposition (17:5)
Satan thwarted Paul's return (2:18); it was safe for Timothy to return, but not Paul (3:1–2)	The politarchs' decree against Paul made his return dangerous until they left office (17:8–10)
Unemployment was a major local problem (4:11–12; cf. 2 Thess 3:6–12)	Unemployed men from the marketplace constituted a local problem (17:5)

*The connection with "meeting" in 1 Thess 4:17 confirms the likelihood of this sense of parousia (Best, *Thessalonians*, 199; Bruce, *Thessalonians*, 102; idem, *Books*, 68–69; Marshall, *Thessalonians*, 131; see further comment at Acts 28:15).
†See here Malherbe, "Gentle as Nurse."
‡It *might* even relate to some dying (1 Thess 4:13), though this is questionable. For this passage's probable authenticity, see comment on Acts 17:5.

Riesner's comparisons are even more detailed and more optimistic than mine here. Of twenty-five details in Acts, most (eighteen to nineteen) of them "are either directly or indirectly confirmed by 1 Thessalonians." Luke has some independent details, of which "four can be checked" by external means and two are possible; if one uses minimalist criteria, four of his details appear questionable "or one-sided," but "none of them is impossible. On the whole, these are quite admirable findings for an ancient historian."[144]

142. Even here the digression in 1 Thess 2:14–16 makes the best sense if connected with some Jewish hostility in Thessalonica, though the "countrypeople" of 2:16 would be mostly Gentiles. Moreover, no opposition is reported in the synagogues in Acts 17:10–12, 17 (cf. also 16:12); such local variations in Luke's pattern probably indicate that Luke, like other historians, looks for and then highlights patterns in his historical sources without conforming every instance in his sources to fit the pattern. The significant Gentile component in the church is apparent in 1 Thess 1:9, but Paul's free use of Jewish eschatological imagery suggests that he anticipated a Jewish component as well. Nevertheless, Luke fairly often emphasizes the Jewish side of Paul's opposition.

143. Although the differences in sequence are not irreconcilable, they are clearly independent. Ancient historians did not share our insistence for precision on all details they considered secondary (in contrast to accuracy about basic events). See comment on Acts 17:15.

144. Riesner, *Early Period*, 366–67. For Paul and the Thessalonian church, see Milligan, *Thessalonians*, xxvi–xl.

We can also place Paul's Thessalonian ministry securely in the larger context of the sequence of this "missionary journey" reported by Luke:[145]

Public beating in Philippi	1 Thess 2:2	Acts 16:22–23
Successful but persecuted ministry in Thessalonica	Phil 4:15–16; 1 Thess 1:1, 5–6	Acts 17:1–10
Paul in Athens	1 Thess 3:1	Acts 17:15–34
Paul in Achaia with his companions	2 Cor 1:19; cf. 1 Thess 3:6	Acts 18:1–18, esp. 18:5

Historically, we know that Paul traveled to Thessalonica after Philippi (1 Thess 2:2) and that he went soon after to Athens (1 Thess 3:1; Acts 17:10–15),[146] and probably we can add that he went to Corinth afterward (2 Cor 11:7–9).[147] Of course, even if we lacked these details, the fact that Paul evangelized these areas would lead us to expect this basic sequence on the basis of geography, in a world where travel was much slower than for much of the world today.

Luke presents Paul as founder of the Corinthian church, as do Paul's letters (1 Cor 3:6; 4:15; cf. 1:16; 16:15). The agreements between Acts and Paul's letters regarding his Corinthian ministry are substantial, including the following details:[148]

- Aquila and Priscilla were a married ministry team (Acts 18:2, 26; Rom 16:3).
- They made their home available for the Lord's work (Acts 18:3; Rom 16:5) and were known to the Corinthian believers (1 Cor 16:19).
- They had connections with Rome (Acts 18:2; Rom 16:3) and Ephesus (Acts 18:18–19; cf. 2 Tim 4:19).
- Paul supported himself by means of a trade while in Corinth (Acts 18:3; 1 Cor 4:12; 9:6).
- Crispus was converted and baptized (Acts 18:8; 1 Cor 1:14).
- The participation of Timothy is mentioned (Acts 18:5; 1 Cor 4:17; 16:10–11; 2 Cor 1:19).
- The participation of Silas is mentioned (Acts 18:5; 2 Cor 1:19).
- Paul began the Corinthian mission before Silas and Timothy arrived (Acts 18:1–4; 1 Thess 3:1, 6)
- He ministered briefly in Athens en route (Acts 17:15–34; 1 Thess 3:1).
- Possibly the same Sosthenes is mentioned, especially if he was later converted (or it is a Greek name for Crispus; Acts 18:17; 1 Cor 1:1).
- The Corinthian congregation probably included a Jewish element (1 Cor 1:22–24; 9:20; 10:32; 12:13; 2 Cor 11:22).
- Later Apollos followed (Acts 18:24–28; 1 Cor 1:12; 4:15), and he belonged to the same circle (Acts 18:26–27; 1 Cor 16:12).
- Paul afterward visited Ephesus at length (Acts 18:19; 19:8–10; 1 Cor 15:32; 16:8; cf. 2 Cor 1:8).

145. Cf., in further detail, Witherington, *Acts*, 446–47.

146. Paul's letters indicate that he stopped in Athens but do not report that he spoke before the Areopagus. Historians could compose speeches for their characters, but Luke's lack of overwhelming triumph at the conclusion (Acts 17:33–34), the plausibility of a new speaker in town being briefly evaluated by the Areopagus council, and the prominence of Stoic language in Paul's letters all warn against a facile dismissal of even this scene.

147. Riesner, *Early Period*, 233.

148. Esp. Witherington, *Acts*, 537. I have added several to his list (including some from Goulder, *Competing Mission*, 223) and omitted his weaker connection of fear in both (Acts 18:9; 1 Cor 2:3; a connection also in Dunn, *Acts*, 243–44).

III. Paul's Collection and Roman Custody

Paul's travel plans reported in Acts 19:21 fit Lukan theology (cf. Luke 9:51), but the thoughts that Luke attributes to Paul here were authentically the historical Paul's. Paul certainly had plans to go both to Jerusalem (Rom 15:25; 2 Cor 1:16; cf. 1 Cor 16:3) and (afterward) Rome (Rom 1:11, 13; 15:23–24; cf. 2 Cor 10:16). Paul also carries out these plans both in Acts and in the record in his letters. This is one of the few parts of Paul's life where his letters provide a secure sequence, and the sequence here in Acts and in following chapters fits Paul's letters precisely where there is overlap. Neither source includes every detail found in the other (if they did, we would need to suspect dependence), but they confirm each other on the points where they overlap (see table on pp. 248–49).[149]

Paul does not mention the Ephesian riot (and cannot do so in the letters in question, which precede the time when the event would have occurred, near the end of his stay there). But he speaks of public conflicts with people hostile to his ministry in Ephesus (1 Cor 15:32; 16:8–9; 2 Cor 1:8);[150] such letters suggest that, if anything, Paul suffered much worse in Ephesus than Luke indicates (a suspicion not diminished by Acts 20:16). Luke's central point (Paul's persecution for his successful ministry in Ephesus) is confirmed by Paul's letters, regardless of how much Luke may have dramatized the event. (Moreover, as noted previously, Luke has no reason to invent riots involving Paul, given the apologetic problem to which he was responding; see comment on Acts 24:5.)

Paul's traveling companions mentioned in 20:4 overlap with Paul's letters. These include Sopater of Beroea,[151] probably called Sosipater in Romans; Aristarchus appears with Paul in his later imprisonment (Phlm 24; Col 4:10); Tychicus, Trophimus, and particularly Timothy all appear in letters attributed to Paul. That the agreement of Gal 2:1–10 would have been discussed on the occasion of Paul's meeting with the Jerusalem leaders, as in Acts 21:25, is likely historically, since, despite Luke's silence about the matter, this was the occasion when Paul brought the collection (Rom 15:26–31), and the collection (or something like it) was part of the original agreement (Gal 2:10).

That some Jewish opposition led to Paul's detention by Romans in Jerusalem fits Luke's narrative pattern but is also historically likely. Paul expected opposition in Jerusalem (Rom 15:31), and we know that he was detained by the Romans sometime after this (see Phil 1:7, 13, 14, 17; Col 4:3, 18). Why would the Romans just happen to detain Paul in Judea, especially given their stronger economic ties with Asia and Achaia? Unless Paul were caught by Roman authorities in an apparently illegal act, Rome normally depended on local accusations for arrests.

Even the original temple charge (though formulated in clearly Lukan language) gains plausibility as pre-Lukan information based on Pauline literature. Luke's report of the temple charge, though part of a larger pattern in Acts, also dovetails well with tradition independently preserved in Ephesians (although many scholars attribute it to one of Paul's disciples rather than to the apostle himself). Whether the implied setting is fictive or not (I myself am inclined to argue that it is not), the implied author Paul writes from detention (Eph 3:1; 6:20), reminding Asian Christians of the

149. See Riesner, *Early Period*, 233, here adapted and expanded; Witherington, *Acts*, 447–49; cf. also Dunn, *Acts*, 262; more briefly Hemer, *Acts in History*, 187; Fitzmyer, *Acts*, 652. Cf. the complementary use of both sources in Haacker, "Paul's Life" (and comments on Acts 19–20).

150. Contrary to some other proposals, the likeliest source of affliction in 2 Cor 1:8 is "severe persecution" (Thrall, *2 Corinthians*, 116–17).

151. The form for "Beroean" fits exactly the evidence of local inscriptions (see Hemer, *Acts in History*, 124).

Paul's Letters	Acts
Paul taught the "Galatians" about the collection (1 Cor 16:1)*	Paul strengthened "the disciples" throughout Galatia and Phrygia (18:23)
Paul's ministry in Ephesus (1 Cor 16:8)	Paul's ministry in Ephesus (19:1–20)
Many events while Paul was in Ephesus (1 Cor 16:8) a. Visitors: members of Chloe's household (1 Cor 1:11); Stephanas, Fortunatus, Achaicus, with a gift (16:17); someone (probably Stephanas's group) with a letter (7:1) b. The writing of 1 Corinthians c. Probably his second painful visit to Corinth (briefly alluded to in 2 Cor 2:1; 12:14; 13:2)†	Paul's stay in Ephesus lasted more than two years (19:8, 10; 20:31) The summaries are brief (esp. 19:10), with a few examples added that are germane to Luke's points about the gospel spreading (19:10–20) and persecution (19:23–20:1). Luke has addressed the Corinthian church's inner life too little for us to expect him to comment on Paul's Corinthian correspondence from Ephesus; Luke is not interested in Paul's letters. That Paul remained in contact before visiting, however, seems safe to assume.
Apollos was known to the Corinthians as a strong preacher and was with Paul in Ephesus (1 Cor 16:12)	Apollos earlier left Ephesus for Corinth, where he preached for a period of time (18:24–28)
Paul planned to visit a. Macedonia (1 Cor 16:5),‡ b. then Achaia (16:5–6; cf. 4:18–21), c. Judea (Rom 15:25; 2 Cor 1:16), d. and finally Rome (Rom 1:11–13; 15:23–25; cf. 2 Cor 10:16)	Paul planned to visit a. Macedonia, b. Achaia, c. Judea, d. Rome (in that sequence; 19:21)
At some point while they were in Ephesus (1 Cor 16:8), Paul sent Timothy to Corinth ahead of himself (4:17; 16:10);§ Timothy was later with Paul in Corinth (Rom 16:21)	While in Ephesus, Paul sent Timothy and a companion into Macedonia (19:21); Timothy is next mentioned leaving Corinth (or just possibly Macedonia) with Paul (20:3–4)
The situation in Corinth a. At one point Paul considered sailing to Corinth before Macedonia (2 Cor 1:15–16),‖ but the plans did not materialize (1:17), partly because of conflict with the Corinthian church (2:1–3) b. At some point rival Jewish Christian missionaries (2 Cor 2:17; 4:2) with letters of recommendation (3:1) and self-commendations (10:12–18; 11:18) entered Corinth, exacerbating the tension with Paul (11:4, 12–15, 19–23) c. Paul sent Titus to Corinth with a sorrowful letter (2 Cor 2:13)	In a section already compressed, Luke omits conflicts with the Corinthian church, which would not serve his purpose.
Paul visits Troas (2 Cor 2:12)	This is implied as a normal part of the journey through Macedonia, the simplest route between Asia and Greece, 16:11; 20:5–6
Events in Macedonia a. Anxious about the Corinthians' response and not having heard from Titus, Paul left Troas for Macedonia (2 Cor 2:13; 7:5; cf. 1 Cor 16:5) b. Offerings in Macedonia (2 Cor 8:1–5; 9:2) c. Paul probably made a visit to Illyricum (Rom 15:19), though some scholars place this closer to Acts 17:10 (less likely)# d. Titus, returning from Corinth, met Paul in Macedonia with good news that the Corinthians had disciplined the offender (2 Cor 7:6–7, 13) e. Paul wrote 2 Corinthians and sent it with Titus, in preparation for the collection to be ready when he arrived (2 Cor 8:6, 16–19, 22–23; 9:3–5; cf. 1 Cor 16:2); he expressed confidence in the Corinthians (1 Cor 8:24; 9:2)	Paul visited Macedonia (20:1–2) Again Luke omits details of the conflict with the Corinthians. They provide little narrative action, do not advance Luke's apologetic point, and may have been forgotten or remembered only painfully by Luke's audience (who may have been Greeks and Macedonians) after Paul's death.
Despite his delay (2 Cor 1:16–17; 2:1), Paul planned to visit Corinth (13:1) with traveling companions from other cities (9:4)	Paul visited Achaia (20:2–3); soon afterward he is mentioned with traveling companions from various cities (20:4)
Paul finished his collection in Macedonia and Achaia (Rom 15:26) and wrote Romans from Corinth, sending it by a church leader from Cenchreae (16:1)**	Paul stayed in Achaia for three months (20:2–3)

Paul's Letters	Acts
After leaving Macedonia and Achaia (Rom 15:26), Paul presumably carried through his plan to visit Jerusalem (15:25)	Paul visited Jerusalem (21:17)
Paul was aware that Jerusalem might prove dangerous (Rom 15:31); his next letters are from Roman captivity (least disputed, Philippians; Philemon)	Paul was arrested in Jerusalem and detained by the Romans (22:24–23:30)
Paul apparently ended up in Rome, though not necessarily by the means he had originally planned (Phil 4:22; cf. Rom 15:23–24)	Paul used his Roman citizenship to have his case transferred to Rome (25:10–12)

*He writes as if the Corinthian Christians knew of this journey.

†Riesner, *Early Period*, 299, appears to think of Paul's second letter as a surrogate visit, taking 2 Cor 2:1 figuratively in its context of abandoned travel plans. Given Luke's summary of "two years" in a verse in Acts 19:10 (though adding afterward an anecdote), however, we should not count Luke's silence against an interim journey noted only in 2 Corinthians.

‡For a planned Macedonian visit, cf. also Phil 2:24; but unless this was written during an Ephesian imprisonment (which I doubt; cf. the likeliest sense of 4:22), it involves later plans (as also 1 Tim 1:3).

§These may represent two comings of Timothy (based on the aorist indicative in 1 Cor 4:17 and the aorist subjunctive in 16:10), but if he writes from his own chronological standpoint (Timothy's future arrival but past sending), Timothy might be part of the party bearing the letter (perhaps with others in 16:17–18). Paul plans to send Timothy to Macedonia in Phil 2:19, but unless he writes from an Ephesian imprisonment (I think 4:22 points more easily to a Roman one; even a Caesarean provenance is more likely for Philippians than an Ephesian one), this is later.

‖This was probably discussed either in his letter of reproof (2 Cor 2:4; 7:8), in which case the coming may have been a threat (cf. 1 Cor 4:18–21; 2 Cor 13:2) and was delayed so that Paul would not have to carry it out (2 Cor 2:1–4), or in an earlier letter, in which case the letter of reproof (2:4) temporarily substituted for his presence. Although some scholars defend the identification of 2 Cor 10–13 with this "tearful letter" (e.g., Watson, "Painful Letter"; Talbert, *Corinthians*, xix), most doubt it (Thrall, *2 Corinthians*, 13–18; Bruce, *Corinthians*, 167–68; Sumney, *Opponents*, 126; Scott, *Corinthians*, 6; Amador, "Revisiting," 95–98; Kreitzer, *Corinthians*, 23–25; Best, *Corinthians*, 2–3).

#That section of Acts details Paul's movements fairly specifically whereas omissions of detail are far more to be expected in Acts 20:1–3; see comment on Acts 17:10.

**A Corinthian provenance for Romans is also likely because he has finished the collection (Rom 15:25–26; Riesner, *Early Period*, 233–34) and because of the status and perhaps high proportion of Roman names among his colleagues (Rom 16:22–23; cf. 1 Cor 1:14); though these arguments might also fit Philippi, Acts (if it is not circular to admit its evidence here) suggests a much briefer stay in Philippi (Acts 20:3, 6); cf. also discussion of Erastus (Rom 16:23) at Acts 19:22. The connection with Cenchreae in Rom 16:1 is most important; the ending of Romans is generally accepted today as part of the original letter (Hunter, *Romans*, 128–29; Lönnermark, "Frågan"; Donfried, "Note on Romans 16"; Stowers, *Diatribe*, 183; *Letter Writing*, 155; Drane, "Romans," 223; esp. Gamble, *Textual History*; *pace*, earlier, e.g., Manson, "Letter"; Richards, "Chronological Relationship," 30; McDonald, "Romans XVI"). Most today accept a Corinthian provenance for Romans (e.g., Bruce, *Commentary*, 405; Hemer, *Acts in History*, 188; Barrett, *Acts*, 947).

unity of Jewish and Gentile believers[152] in 2:11–13; 3:1–8.[153] Most relevant is that Paul emphasizes the unity of Jew and Gentile through the image of a new temple (2:19–22) with a shattered dividing barrier (2:14).[154] Paul is a prisoner for the sake of the Gentiles (3:1, 13) in this new temple (2:19–22).[155] If Luke's account is, as I would suggest, accurate in its essentials, the Christians of Asia would know from their agents (Acts 21:29; cf. 20:4) and perhaps also from their enemies (21:27) that the charge of violating the Jewish-Gentile partition in the temple was the cause of Paul's detention. This background would make Ephesians' use of the temple and dividing barrier all the more meaningful.

Other sources (Eph 6:20; Col 4:18; 2 Tim 1:16) also note Paul's chains (Acts 26:29; 28:20), hardly a normal source of boasting, much less epideictic invention, in antiquity. Paul himself (or, in many others' views, Pauline tradition) calls Aristarchus his "fellow captive" (Col 4:10). Another captivity letter also attests that Aristarchus, along with Luke, remained with Paul during his (probably Roman) detention (Phlm 24).

152. Potentially a live issue in and around Ephesus (Acts 19:17).

153. Cf. also the "us" and "you" in Eph 1:3–14. I do not mean to play down differences between the emphases about Paul in Acts and Ephesians (on which see, e.g., Sterling, "Apostle," viewing both as late first century; Acts and a wider range of Pauline interpreters in Marguerat, "Réception").

154. By contrast, 4Q174 1 II, 1, 4 emphasizes the eschatological exclusion of foreigners (Schnabel, *Mission*, 113); cf. Zech 14:21.

155. Cf. Keener, "Reconciliation," 118–21.

Such Pauline correlations with Acts render probable Luke's other information about Paul; his accuracy in these cases must represent a fair and unbiased sampling, since he could not have known what sources would remain extant. That is, we cannot attribute Luke's accuracy on these cases to coincidence or argue from silence that Luke was accurate on such a high proportion of points where we can check him, yet erred promiscuously wherever we cannot. If Luke has accurate information in greater detail in the "we" material, the traveling companion of Paul indicated in that material could also have supplied not only such detailed accounts but also earlier stories about Paul, reasonably accurate though less detailed. It is intrinsically likely that those who heard Paul in person knew some of his earlier stories; thus, for example, though Paul's companions in starting the Corinthian church were Silas and Timothy (2 Cor 1:19), he expects the Corinthians to know about Barnabas (1 Cor 9:6), having apparently mentioned their work together. Luke is confirming widely circulated information (Luke 1:4), not writing a novel.

7. Paul's Theology in Acts

Scholars who question the reliability of Acts' portrayal of Paul turn particularly to the more subjectively debatable and often debated questions of his theology. Although Luke does seem acquainted with Paul's theology[156] (see ch. 8, sect. 3.e.iii, below, for a discussion of some Paulinisms in the speeches), some regard the differences as so striking as to be incompatible with a writer who genuinely knew Paul. The classic statement articulating this skepticism is Vielhauer's:

> To summarize: the author of Acts is in his Christology pre-Pauline, in his natural theology, concept of the law, and eschatology, post-Pauline. He presents no specifically Pauline idea. His "Paulinism" consists in his zeal for the worldwide Gentile mission and in his veneration for the greatest missionary to the Gentiles. The obvious material distance from Paul raises the question whether one may really consider Luke ... as the author of Acts.[157]

As noted in chapter 8 below, Luke wrote the speeches mostly in his own style and emphasized the elements relevant to his audience, as other historians did. But Vielhauer's point is not only the presence of Luke's theology (which hardly anyone disputes) but what he argues is the absence of Paul's.

a. Critiquing Vielhauer's Critique

Scholars have pointed to serious weaknesses in Vielhauer's critique.[158] Paul's letters and Acts present not only different (yet not necessarily contradictory) emphases but even different genres; Vielhauer's stark contrasts are not evenhanded comparisons but

156. With, e.g., deSilva, *Introduction*, 379–80. Perspectives, of course, differ; thus Luke may be more optimistic than Paul, and different emphases shape their common approach to justification (note these examples in Pervo, *Mystery*, 34).

157. Vielhauer, "Paulinism," 48, stressing further Luke's distinctive theology.

158. See, e.g., Donfried, *Thessalonica*, 90–96 (noting that Vielhauer virtually ignores Paul's early works, such as 1 Thessalonians); Marshall, "Luke's View of Paul"; idem, *Acts*, 42–44; Porter, *Paul in Acts*, 189–206 (contending, 187–89, also that the older German line of scholarship represented by Haenchen and Vielhauer never really grappled with the critique of W. Ramsay that influenced British scholarship); Litwak, "Views" (esp. 229–31); Bock, *Acts*, 15–19 (esp. 16–17); Riesner, "Zuverlässigkeit," 42. For a survey of critiques of Vielhauer and Haenchen, see Walton, *Leadership*, 6–12. As Powell, *Acts*, 35, observes, "Vielhauer's essay has had a controversial reception."

compare "apples and oranges."[159] Certainly, he exaggerates the non-Pauline character of Paul's speeches in Acts.[160] Vielhauer complains that the Paul of Acts offers few christological statements aside from Acts 13:13–43 and 26:22–23 and that these few match only pre-Pauline material in Paul's letters (Rom 1:3–4; 1 Cor 15:3–4).[161] But Paul's letters do not tell us how much attention he gave to Christology in evangelistic sermons to Gentiles (possibly not much; cf. 1 Thess 1:9, probably from the primary period that more of Paul's evangelistic sermons in Acts represent), and Christology is not an equally explicit focus of all his writings (nor does he emphasize the same christological categories in each—contrast, e.g., the "new Adam," "wisdom," and "Christ" categories). Further, contemporary literary criticism reminds us that if Paul includes "pre-Pauline" material, he does so because he agrees with it; Paul was not against the "pre-Pauline" theology that some identify in his own letters.

Much alleged incompatibility between Paul's letters and Luke's portrayal of Paul follows from such overstrict comparisons. For example, though the natural theology of Acts 17:24–27 differs from that in Paul's writings, including his version of natural theology in Rom 1:19–23, they are not incompatible. They are no more different than one would expect for one writer summarizing another's views or (less relevantly) even for the same philosopher (e.g., Seneca) in different passages at different times addressing different concerns in the wide spectrum of natural theology. This appears especially to be the case when one takes into account that Luke's Paul and Romans 1 address different situations and that Paul's own presentation varies from one passage to another (e.g., humanity's "fall" through idolatry in Rom 1:21–25 vs. its Adamic fall in 5:12–21).[162] Paul also addresses pagans' knowledge of God elsewhere (e.g., 1 Cor 1:21).[163] In both Acts 17 and Rom 1:18–25, Christian writers have adapted standard Hellenistic Jewish models that reflect especially Stoic influence (directly or indirectly)—for example, in Rom 1:19–20.[164] Contrary to common assumptions that Acts 17 exaggerates Paul's Stoic connections to fit the setting, I have found far more Stoic connections in 1 Corinthians (though admittedly partly because it is longer) than in Acts 17, and I believe that scholars who work with Greco-Roman moralists and philosophers will find even more echoes of these philosophers in the historical Paul than in Luke's summary portrait of him.[165] As Mikeal Parsons notes, "Given the strikingly different contexts, the similarities are more remarkable than the tensions."[166]

On some points Vielhauer finds legitimate contrasts, but he makes too much of them; granted, Paul did not author his own portrait in Luke-Acts, but neither is it one he would have denounced as misrepresenting him. On other points, Vielhauer has misread Paul on the basis of traditional theological assumptions. Vielhauer's complaint that the Paul of Acts fails to replicate the epistolary Paul's antithesis between

159. Cf. Barnett, *Birth*, 196.

160. See the critique, e.g., in Fitzmyer, *Acts*, 145–47; Hemer, *Acts in History*, 245–47; cf. Ware, *Synopsis*.

161. See the critique in Porter, *Paul in Acts*, 200–203.

162. Some scholars find Adam in Rom 1; see Hooker, "Adam"; Barrett, *Adam*, 17–19; against, see, e.g., Scroggs, *Adam*, 75–76n3; O'Rourke, "Rom 1,20," esp. 305. I am not convinced of the need to read the Rom 5:12–21 fall narrative into Rom 1; but Paul is Jewish and alludes to human creation, and so further allusions to male and female (Rom 1:27) and God's image (cf. 1:19–20, 23) are likely (cf. Hooker, "Adam," 305).

163. Fitzmyer, *Acts*, 147.

164. Cf. Sen. Y. *Ep. Lucil.* 117.6; Epict. *Diatr.* 1.6.7, 10; cf. Cic. *Tusc.* 1.13.30; *Nat. d.* 2.54.133–2.61.153. See further Porter, *Paul in Acts*, 145–50, 167–70; Bruce, "Paul and Athenians"; this commentary's comments ad loc.

165. See Keener, *Corinthians*, passim (I hope to publish further information in later Pauline commentaries); see also Malherbe, *Philosophers*. I do not believe that the pattern that Engberg-Pedersen, *Paul and Stoics*, finds in Paul is uniquely Stoic, but he is certainly right to offer comparisons and to contend that the Stoic dimension of Paul's letters has been underexplored.

166. Parsons, *Luke*, 136.

law and Christ rests on a misreading of Paul, as contemporary Pauline scholarship has increasingly shown.[167]

If Vielhauer charges that the Christology of Luke's Paul is "adoptionist" and his soteriology neglects the cross, Luke's emphasis differs primarily in what he omits. Paul's letters do, in fact, emphasize the resurrection, though also noting the cross;[168] also, there is not enough information to argue from silence that Luke's Paul has only adoptionist Christology (as if this were Luke's preferred christological construct), especially when Peter affirms Jesus's deity in Acts' first evangelistic speech (Acts 2:21, 38). Even the Paul of the letters could be construed as adoptionist if we had only the wording in Rom 1:3–4 (which, whether pre-Pauline or not, is certainly used by Paul).[169] If Vielhauer complains that Luke focuses on history, removing the centrality of eschatology, this focus, too, is a matter of emphasis. Luke does not *oppose* eschatology (cf. Acts 1:6–7; 3:19–21; 10:42; in a Pauline speech, 17:31). Luke does not therefore contradict Paul here but selects features most germane to his own vision and needs. Paul's view of history is, in fact, similar to Luke's (Rom 9–11).[170]

Peder Borgen, examining Vielhauer's critiques, rightly concludes, "Even though there are differences at some points between the Pauline and the Lucan theologies, the theology of Luke must to a great extent be considered a further development of elements occurring in Paul's letters. Luke hardly ever uses the letters, but he is partly dependent on traditions from and concerning Paul, and both Luke and Paul are partly dependent on the same early Christian traditions."[171] Luke's portrayal of Paul is selective, but this selectivity no more rules out his being a companion of Paul than students' selective memory and presentation of their teachers rules out their having been students of those teachers.

b. Other Alleged Incompatibilities

Haenchen adds his theological critique of Luke, complaining that "Luke was no longer able to grasp theologically, as Paul had, the legitimacy of the mission to the Gentiles free of the Torah."[172] Acts does present Paul as a good Jew, but this does not suggest that Luke's Paul "compromises" with Jewish practices in ways that the epistolary Paul would not have (cf. Acts 16:3; 18:18; 21:26; Gal 2:3).[173] For modern

---

167. From various perspectives (but all contradicting Paul's supposed opposition to the law), e.g., Longenecker, *Paul*; Fuller, *Gospel*; Reicke, "God of Abraham," 191–93; Rhyne, *Faith*; Schreiner, "Works of Law"; Dunn, *Theology of Paul*, 716–22; Engberg-Pedersen, *Paul and Stoics*, 8; cf. Moule, "Obligation." See Gasque, "Acts and History," 66: Vielhauer's critique of Luke's Paul rests "more on his rigorous Lutheran understanding of the antithesis of law and gospel in Paul than on a careful exegesis of the letters of Paul" (cf., e.g., Vielhauer, "Paulinism," 42: though Luke knew that Paul taught justification by faith, he did not know its "central significance").

168. For Paul's gospel narrative in 1 Cor 15:1–11 and Luke's own passion and resurrection traditions being comparable, even where Luke modifies Mark, see Borgen, "Paul to Luke," 179–80.

169. Many scholars regard this affirmation as pre-Pauline (e.g., Hunter, *Predecessors*, 24–25; Beasley-Murray, "Romans 1:3f"; Betz, *Jesus*, 94–95) or even view this premise that it is pre-Pauline as unanimous (Hengel, *Son*, 59), but not all concur; the premise is, at best, unproved (Anderson, *Rhetorical Theory*, 207n45), and the supposed creed could be Paul's composition using traditional vocabulary (Poythress, "Romans 1:3–4").

170. Borgen, "Paul to Luke," 170–82, esp. 170–74, shows the similarity to Rom 9–11; both treat the Gentile period as an interim (more clearly than in Mark, p. 182).

171. Borgen, "Paul to Luke," 181.

172. Haenchen, "Acts as Source Material," 265. For Luke's Paul as pro-law, countering Marcion, see Tyson, "Wrestling" (esp. 25–27); but Luke's portrait of Paul need be contemporary with Marcion to be used to challenge it no more than John's portrait of Jesus (addressing an esp. Jewish setting) need be contemporary with Irenaeus's gnostics.

173. See Porter, *Paul in Acts*, 190–93, for a critique of the supposed incompatibility of Paul and Acts regarding Paul's Jewish fidelity; he notes that the "New Perspective" on Paul (E. P. Sanders, J. D. G. Dunn, and others) would eliminate this supposed conflict if one held it (though he does not). Cf. also the critique

readers to suppose that because Paul differed with most Jews on some points, he must have renounced his Judaism is an anachronistic reading into which one can fit neither the Dead Sea Scrolls nor various other ancient Jewish protest literature.[174]

The Paul of the letters no less than the Paul of Acts is a good Jew[175] who simply refuses to impose uniquely Jewish customs on the Gentiles (1 Cor 9:21). Paul's epistles that address the issue present him as faithful to his biblical heritage (e.g., Rom 3:21, 31; 9:31–32)[176] and indicate that he remained within synagogues long enough to incur many beatings there (2 Cor 11:24).[177] Genuine apostates such as Tiberius Alexander might have known Scripture but would hardly have quoted it as authoritative the way that Paul did; what Paul offered was not apostasy from Judaism (see comment on Acts 21:21; not everyone, however, would have agreed with Paul's perspective) but a distinctive interpretation of Judaism in light of Jesus's identity and work and hence his complete efficacy as savior. Paul was clearly ready to identify with his Jewish heritage not least for the sake of building evangelistic bridges to his community (1 Cor 9:20),[178] was supremely concerned with the salvation of his people (Rom 9:1–3; 10:1; 11:14), and probably cited his heritage in preaching to the Jewish community, as in Acts (Rom 11:1; 2 Cor 11:22; Phil 3:5–6).[179] Likewise, rejection of Paul's gospel by fellow Jews is not a Lukan construct but figures prominently in Rom 9–11 (esp. 11:7–17, 28–32) and elsewhere (e.g., Rom 15:31; 1 Thess 2:14–16, esp. 2:16).[180]

The complaint that Luke's Paul is less eschatological than Paul's writings does rightly suggest Luke's emphasis on realized eschatology but misses the diversity even in Paul's letters; certainly, the eschatology of 2 Cor 4:16–5:10 is less end-time oriented than that in 1 Thess 4:13–5:11[181] (Philippians[182] includes some of both forms; compare

in Franklin, *Interpreter*, 57–61 (though he contrasts Luke's contextualization of Paul for his generation with the "real" Paul; e.g., p. 161); Parsons, *Luke*, 137–38 (noting esp. Wilson, *Luke and Law*, 61–65).

174. Cf. the comments on Matthew in Davies and Allison, *Matthew*, 3:695.

175. Albeit a Diaspora Jew at least somewhat effective in Greco-Roman rhetoric; but this is also true of Acts' Paul, where Paul speaks and not just writes eloquently. For the Jewish fidelity of Paul in most current reconstructions, see, e.g., Nanos, "Paul's Judaism"; Harrington, "Paul the Jew"; Frankemölle, "Apostol Pawel"; Tomson, "Tradycje"; Reiser, "Heiden"; Uchelen, "Halacha"; Bieberstein, "Freiheit"; Neuhaus, "Rencontre"; Roetzel, *Paul*, ix; Bachmann, "*Verus Israel*"; Zetterholm, "Judar"; Stegner, "Jewish Paul"; idem, "Jew, Paul the"; Kessler, "Paul the Jew"; many earlier, e.g., Davies, *Paul* (esp. note 216); Sanders, *Paul and Judaism*, 1; for Jewish perspectives, see, e.g., Langton, "Identity"; idem, "Myth"; Segal, "Studying; idem, "Exégètes juifs"; Denaux, "Visie"; Reinmuth, "Perspektive."

176. See, on Rom 3:31, e.g., Gerhardsson, *Memory*, 287 (but this is not necessarily technical rabbinic language; see Rhyne, *Faith*, 73–74; Thompson, "Background"); Nanos, *Mystery*, 22, 176, 180–81; esp. Rhyne, *Faith*, passim; for Rom 9:31–32, see Fuller, *Gospel*, x–xi. Many scholars today take τέλος in Rom 10:4 as "goal," "aim," or "purpose" (see, e.g., Howard, "End," 336; Kaiser, "Matters," 177; Cranfield, *Romans*, 2:520; Rhyne, "*Nomos*"; Donaldson, *Paul and Gentiles*, 130; Haacker, *Theology*, 86–87; Johnson, *Romans*, 170, 175; Hays, *Echoes*, 76; pace, e.g., Käsemann, *Romans*, 282–83). For Pauline exegesis in both letters and speeches, cf. Bruce, "Paul's Use of Old Testament."

177. Sanders, *Law and People*, 192; Donaldson, *Paul and Gentiles*, 306; Witherington, *Corinthians*, 245; Thrall, *2 Corinthians*, 737.

178. For the relevance of 1 Cor 9:19–23 for Paul's missionary strategies, see, e.g., Gasque, "Acts and History," 69; Krentz, "All Things"; Reid, "Model"; Theobald, "Allen" (in relation to 1 Corinthians itself, see Chadwick, "All Things"). But one suspects that it was his adaptation to Gentiles rather than to his own people that took the greater adjustment (cf. Hort, *Judaistic Christianity*, 110–11; Jervell, *Unknown Paul*, 58). Paul's accommodation also may have had Jewish (Daube, *New Testament and Judaism*, 336ff.; despite Bornkamm, "Missionary Stance," 195) as well as Gentile (see, e.g., Mitchell, "Accommodation," 208–14; idem, "Many-Sorted Man"; Glad, "Adaptability"; other sources in Keener, *Corinthians*, 81) models.

179. See also Witherington, *Acts*, 434–36.

180. See, e.g., Fitzmyer, *Acts*, 147; see further the discussion of Acts and Judaism in ch. 14 below.

181. Cf., on the former, Aune, "Duality." The contrast should not, of course, be overstated; compare, e.g., 2 Cor 4:14 with 1 Thess 4:14 (see further Plevnik, "Destination").

182. On the likely assumption of unity or, at the *least*, that constituent letters derive from the same period in Paul's ministry.

Phil 1:21–24 with 3:20–21).[183] That Paul should climax his speech in Athens with a future day of judgment (Acts 17:31) might seem almost too eschatological in view of Paul's sensitivity to his audience![184]

It cannot be denied that Luke glorifies Paul's rhetorical skills whereas Paul plays them down.[185] But Paul's abundant use of rhetorical devices, especially in the context of his denials (e.g., 1 Cor 2:1–3; 2 Cor 11:6),[186] shows that he was able to play the Corinthians' status game when he needed to, albeit by his own rules.[187] (All this in spite of the fact that letters were not speeches and that rhetoricians frowned on excessive rhetorical devices in letters.)[188] Even Paul's probably earliest extant letter, 1 Thessalonians, is very carefully crafted.[189]

Without using the explicit designation, Acts portrays Paul as an educated rhetor of some social station and familiar with philosophy,[190] but so do Paul's letters, again without making this explicit claim.[191] Despite Haenchen's contrast between a rhetor and a letter writer, some quite well-known ancient figures engaged in both pursuits (most prominently Cicero). Further, although Paul plays down his rhetorical ability (emphasizing God's power perfected in his weakness; e.g., 1 Cor 1:18; 2:4–5; 2 Cor 13:4), Paul's rhetorical weaknesses were mainly in delivery and apparently especially when judged by well-to-do Corinthians (since they are mentioned only in letters to

183. See also the critique of Vielhauer here in Porter, *Paul in Acts*, 203–5 (who also compares with Acts the sort of eschatology in Phil 1:20–24; 2:16–17; 3:11–14).

184. Paul does climax 1 Corinthians with future eschatology (1 Cor 15), though he presses the matter less starkly in 2 Corinthians, and in both cases, he addresses those already converted. Still, at least in his earlier ministry, eschatology was at the heart of what he taught new believers (1 Thess 1:9–10).

185. See, e.g., Johnson, *Function*, 39. Luke occasionally provides Paul a prose rhythm missing in his letters (Aune, *Dictionary of Rhetoric*, 382); nevertheless, his brief speeches lack the rich rhetorical devices in Paul's letters.

186. Rhetorical devices in 1 Cor 1:18–20, 26; 2 Cor 11:22–29 include rhetorical questions, antithesis, a *peristasis* catalogue, and especially various forms of repetition (see, e.g., Keener, *Corinthians*, 27–32, 233). Noticeable devices appear throughout the correspondence (e.g., 1 Cor 15:42–49, 53–56, on pp. 131–34; 2 Cor 6:4–10, on p. 188). Classen, *Rhetorical Criticism*, 29–40 (esp. 30–31, 34–36), argues even for Paul's familiarity with some rhetorical terminology.

187. For various views of Paul's use of rhetoric in 1 Corinthians, see, e.g., Pogoloff, *Logos*; Winter, *Philo and Paul*; Mitchell, *Rhetoric of Reconciliation*; Litfin, *Theology*; Reid, "Strategies" (suggesting dependence on a Rhodian tradition).

188. Cic. *Fam.* 9.21.1; Sen. Y. *Ep. Lucil.* 75.1–3; further discussion in Keener, *Corinthians*, 3–4, 29; Anderson, *Rhetorical Theory*, 114–27, 280–81; Classen, *Rhetorical Theory*, 6, 23; Reed, "Epistle"; Porter, "Paul and Letters," 541–61, esp. 562–67; idem, *Paul in Acts*, 106–7; Stamps, "Rhetoric," 958; Weima, "Theory," 329; idem, "Letters," 644; idem, "Aristotle"; Bird, "Rhetorical Approach"; cf. also Demet. *Style* 229 (in Garland, *1 Corinthians*, 19); even Kennedy, *Classical Rhetoric*, 109. But this need not exclude all rhetoric from letters (cf. Dio Chrys. *Or.* 18.18; 73 [in view of 73.10]; Fronto *Ad Ant. imp.* 2.5; Philost. *Ep. Apoll.* 19), especially those that, like Paul's, employed argumentation (cf. Forbes, "Comparison," 151) and were meant for oral public delivery (Danker, *Corinthians*, 108–9). Rhetoric may thus have use for analyzing Paul's style, though not his structure (Anderson, *Rhetorical Theory*, 127; Reed, "Epistle," 191; Porter, "Paul and Letters," 567–68, 585; Malherbe, "Theorists," 17); it is noteworthy, however, that through much of church history, scholars did use rhetorical categories to analyze Paul (cf. Classen, "Rhetoric"; idem, "Rhetorik"; idem, "Analyse"; Harvey, *Listening*, 22–23). That elements paralleled in formal rhetoric appear in Paul's argumentation is clear enough to anyone familiar with both rhetoricians and Paul, and they are clearly Greco-Roman, not the sort of Galilean rhetoric that dominates the Jesus tradition.

189. See Harvey, *Listening*, 259–76.

190. Cf., e.g., Malherbe, *Philosophers*, 150–54. Parallels among several of Paul's speeches may portray him as the ideal speaker (Quesnel, "Paul prédicateur"). Talbert, *Patterns*, 129, finds this philosophic model even for Jesus, but Maddox, *Purpose*, 16, is undoubtedly right to view "this analogy" as "at best a very remote one. . . . Luke is no Philo." I do not claim here that Luke presents Paul as having tertiary rhetorical training, only that he appears as an effective speaker.

191. See, e.g., Witherington, *Acts*, 432–33; on philosophy, Malherbe, *Philosophers*, passim. In Acts, see Brawley, *Luke-Acts and Jews*, 61–62, noting that this portrayal of Paul could help establish status (citing Demosth. *Cor.* 258; Jos. *Life* 2.8–9; Cic. *Brut.* 306–21); cf. also his complete Jewish "status" in Acts (Brawley, *Luke-Acts and Jews*, 68–83, esp. 83). Grant, *Paul*, 11, thinks that many of Paul's perspectives in 1 Corinthians "confirm the picture of him in Acts, where he is proud of being a Roman citizen by birth."

them; 1 Cor 2:3; 2 Cor 10:10).[192] One finds in Paul's letters, in fact, far more rhetorical devices than would be possible in the brief summaries of Acts,[193] devices such as climax or sorites (Rom 5:3–5; 8:30; 10:14–15),[194] anaphora (1 Cor 1:12, 26; 15:42–44),[195] antistrophe (1:27–28; 13:11),[196] antithesis (Rom 5:12–21; 1 Cor 15:42–49; 2 Cor 6:8–10),[197] irony (1 Cor 4:8; 2 Cor 11:8, 19–21; 12:13),[198] *peristasis* catalogues (1 Cor 4:11–13; 2 Cor 4:8–11; 6:4–10; 11:23–29),[199] and vice[200] and virtue[201] lists (Rom 1:29–31; 1 Cor 5:11; 6:9–10; Gal 5:19–23).

192. On ridicule for weakness in gestures, see Marshall, *Enmity*, 65–66; on the importance of delivery and gestures, see, e.g., Cic. *Brut.* 17.55; 37.141; 43.158; 66.234; 82.283; 91.316; *Rhet. Her.* 3.11.19; Plut. *Demosth.* 7.2–3; 11.2–3; Pliny *Ep.* 2.3.9; 2.19.2–4, 6; 5.20.3; 6.11.2; Suet. *Claud.* 30; 41.2. On voice intonation, see, e.g., Dion. Hal. *Lit. Comp.* 11; Val. Max. 8.7.ext. 1; on theatrical gestures, e.g., Cic. *Brut.* 55.203; *Rosc. Amer.* 32.89; Suet. *Jul.* 33; Tac. *Dial.* 39; Lucian *Prof. P.S.* 22; Philost. *Vit. soph.* 1.25.537–38, 541–42; Hall, "Cicero and Quintilian"; some studied with actors to improve their delivery (Plut. *Cic.* 4.3). Hall, "Delivery," 230, notes that orators could learn from actors regarding voice training (citing as relevant Quint. *Inst.* 11.3.19; perhaps Suet. *Aug.* 84) and gestures (*De or.* 1.251; Plut. *Cic.* 5; Macrob. *Sat.* 3.14), but avoid being associated with their nonaristocratic bearing (229–30, citing *Rhet. Her.* 3.26; Cic. *De or.* 3.220). Porter, *Paul in Acts*, 194–96, also responds to Haenchen on this point. For orators disclaiming skills, see Keener, *Corinthians*, 34.

193. For some samples, see Aletti, "Rhetoric," 244–46.

194. *Rhet. Her.* 4.25.34–35; Demet. *Style* 5.270; Cosby, "Language," 214 (citing esp. *Rhet. Her.* 4.25.34; Quint. *Inst.* 9.3.54–55, 62); Rowe, "Style," 130; Porter, "Paul and Letters," 579; Anderson, *Rhetorical Theory*, 224; idem, *Glossary*, 57–58; Aune, *Dictionary of Rhetoric*, 102, 446–47; for examples, see Demosth. *Con.* 19; Fronto *Ad M. Caes.* 1.6.4; Max. Tyre 16.3; Philost. *Ep. Apoll.* 33; Porph. *Marc.* 14.244–45; 24.378–79; Wis 6:17–20; *Sipre Deut.* 161.1.3; *y. Šeqal.* 3:3; *b. 'Abod. Zar.* 20b, bar.; *Ber.* 61a.

195. See Cic. *Or. Brut.* 39.135; Aune, *Dictionary of Rhetoric*, 34; Anderson, *Glossary*, 19; Rowe, "Style," 131; cf. Demet. *Style* 5.268; for examples, see Mus. Ruf. 14, p. 92.35–36; Fronto *Ad Ant. imp.* 2.6.2; *Ad M. Caes.* 2.3.1, 3; 3.3; Anderson, *Rhetorical Theory*, 170; Porter, "Paul and Letters," 579; Lee, "Translations: Greek," 779; Black, "Oration at Olivet," 86.

196. See Rowe, "Style," 131; Anderson, *Glossary*, 54; idem, *Rhetorical Theory*, 163; Porter, "Paul and Letters," 579; Lee, "Translations: Greek," 779; Black, "Oration at Olivet," 86.

197. *Rhet. Alex.* 26, 1435b.25–39; Dion. Hal. *Lysias* 14; Cosby, "Language," 216; Rowe, "Style," 142; Black, "Oration at Olivet," 87; Anderson, *Glossary*, 21–22. In 1 Cor 15:42–44, we also have symploche (on which see Rowe, "Style," 131–32; on the passage, see Harvey, *Listening*, 174); for other examples of repetitive antithesis, see, e.g., Max. Tyre 3.4. With 2 Cor 6:8–10 compare the antithetic parallelism in, e.g., Cic. *Phil.* 8.5.16; *Scaur.* 16.37; Sen. Y. *Ep. Lucil.* 95.58; Max. Tyre 36.2; Marc. Aur. 2.11; Oxford Geniza Text Col. A + 1Q21.

198. See *Rhet. Alex.* 21, 1434a.17–32; Cic. *Or. Brut.* 40.137; Walde, "Irony"; Anderson, *Glossary*, 39–40, 108; Rowe, "Style," 128–29 (in rhetoric; for philosophy, see Erler, "Irony"; more generally, Duke, *Irony*, 8–17; Ray, *Irony*, 34–49; in Scripture, Ray, *Irony*, 11–27, including Luke-Acts, 53–66). Cf. its use in forensic polemic (*Rhet. Alex.* 35, 1441b.24–28; Cic. *Phil.* 13.2.4; *Verr.* 2.1.6.17; 2.2.31.76; 2.5.10.25; *Sest.* 37.80; Plut. *Cic.* 27.1; Ael. Arist. *Leuct. Or.* 5.4–5; Libanius *Declam.* 36.12); sarcasm (Cic. *Sull.* 24.67; *Phil.* 8.5.16; *Fam.* 5.2.8; *Att.* 9.7; Jos. *Ag. Ap.* 1.295; *Life* 340; Dio Chrys. *Or.* 31.9–10; 47.25; Pliny *Ep.* 8.23.3; Ach. Tat. 6.12.1) and sarcastic challenges (Sil. It. 11.254–55; Marc. Aur. 2.6; *Sib. Or.* 3.57–59); parody (Athen. *Deipn.* 15.698A–699C); dissembling in Socratic dialogues (Fronto *Ad M. Caes.* 3.15.2); and haggadic farce (Kovelman, "Farce"). Stoics complained about dissembling and sarcasm (Arius Did. *Epit.* 2.7.11m, pp. 88–89.10–13) and were sometimes objects of it (Plut. *St. Poets* 4, *Mor.* 1058c). For the rhetoric of 1 Cor 4:9–13, including irony, see further Fitzgerald, *Cracks*, 131–32.

199. See most fully Fitzgerald, *Cracks*; idem, "Affliction Lists"; discussion in ch. 2, above.

200. For vice lists, see Ptolemy *Tetrab.* 3.13.14–15; Lucian *Posts* 4; *Charon* 11, 15; *Tim.* 28; *Nigr.* 17; Philost. *Ep. Apoll.* 43; Wis 14:22–27; *Test. Levi* 17:11; 4Q477 2 II, 4. They appear often in rhetoric (Cic. *Pis.* 27.66; *Cat.* 2.4.7; 2.5.10; 2.10.22; Cic. *Invect. Sall.* 6.18; Dio Chrys. *Or.* 1.13; 3.53; 4.126; 8.8; 32.28, 91; 33.23, 55; 34.19; Fronto *Nep. am.* 2.8; Max. Tyre 5.7; 36.2); also among philosophers (Plato *Laws* 1.649D; Arist. *E.E.* 2.3.4, 1220b–1221a; Philo *Sacr.* 32; *Posterity* 52; Diogenes *Ep.* 36; Iambl. *V.P.* 17.78), especially Stoics (Sen. Y. *Dial.* 9.2.10–12; Epict. *Diatr.* 2.8.23; Arius Did. *Epit.* 2.7.5b, pp. 12–13.2–12; 2.7.10b, pp. 58–59.32–36; 2.7.10b, pp. 60–61.1–7; 2.7.10e, pp. 62–63.15–19; 2.7.11e, pp. 68–69.17–20; Diog. Laert. 2.93). In negated form (hence functioning as a virtue list), Cic. *Mur.* 6.14; Mus. Ruf. 3, p. 40.17–22; Max. Tyre 25.6. For antithetical lists of virtues and vices, e.g., Ezek 18:5–9; Arist. *V.V.* 1249a–1251b; Cic. *Cat.* 2.10.25; *Cael.* 22.55; *Phil.* 3.11.28; 8.5.16. "Eschatological" vice lists also appear (e.g., Hesiod *W.D.* 181–201; cf. Lucian *Men.* 11), though mostly in Jewish and Christian eschatological texts (cf., e.g., 1QS IV, 9–11; *Sib. Or.* 2.255–82; *Did.* 5.1–2). See further Charles, "Vice Lists"; Engberg-Pedersen, "Vices."

201. For virtue lists, see, e.g., *Rhet. Alex.* 36, 1442a.11–12 (adjacent to vices in lines 13–14); *Rhet. Her.* 3.2.3; Pliny *Ep.* 6.11.2; 6.26.1; Lucian *Portr.* 11; Max. Tyre 3.1; 18.5; among Stoics, Sen. Y. *Ep. Lucil.* 66.6; Mus. Ruf. 14, p. 92.31–33; 16, p. 104.18–24, 32–35; 17, p. 108.11–22; Arius Did. *Epit.* 2.7.5b.17–24; 2.7.11e, pp.

Some scholars find Luke's claim of Paul's Roman citizenship dubious in view of Paul's failure to mention it in his letters.[202] But in which of the extant letters would we expect Paul to have mentioned it? When Paul boasts about himself to the Corinthians, he boasts in matters of low status to invert their values (1 Cor 4:9–14; 2 Cor 11:23–12:10); when he compares himself favorably with other Jews, he emphasizes his Jewish credentials (2 Cor 11:22; Gal 1:13–14; Phil 3:5–6). Still, the epistles are compatible with the possibility of his citizenship (see, more fully, comment on Acts 16:37). The frequency of Roman names in Roman Corinth suggests that the church contained a fair number of Roman citizens,[203] who, despite some complaints (notably about Paul's artisan work and rhetorical skill), seem to have been comfortable enough associating with him from the start as a respected teacher. This observation suggests only a respectable status, not necessarily his citizenship, but it does comport well with Luke's picture. Christians in another Roman colony, whose citizens were thus Roman citizens, apparently felt that in some way Paul was on trial for their future as well as his own (Phil 1:7). Most important, though Roman names do not necessarily indicate Roman citizenship, the name "Paulus" normally appears only for citizens (see comment on Acts 16:37).

On another point, Porter notes that the Paul of Acts, like that of the letters, argues from Jesus's resurrection and displays "incredible complexity and argumentative skill. When the character of Paul as seen in Acts is compared with the Paul of history (so far as he can be known), and compared with the kind of person he must have been to have written and accomplished what he did, perhaps the lines of demarcation fade even further."[204] Despite the abridgment in Acts, Paul's approach is compatible in both sources. This compatibility does not prove that Acts reports the same Paul as the epistles, but neither can the comparatively minor differences prove the opposite.[205]

As Hengel and Schwemer point out, if Luke differed from Paul in some theological perspectives, this does not reduce the likelihood that he was Paul's "travelling companion and eyewitness." If Luke spent two years in Judea, allowing "contact with the bearers of the specific Palestinian Jesus tradition," he probably synthesized what he learned from the various sources. He could still know and love Paul, even remaining more loyal to his thought than scholars often do to their teachers.[206] In such a case, Luke would naturally emphasize the points he himself found most significant and useful in Paul's teaching, given the genre of Acts (see ch. 5 above) and Paul's positive role within Luke's work. One grid for selection of Paul's teachings might be their con-

---

68–69.12–16; 2.7.11i, pp. 78–79.12–18; 2.7.11m, pp. 88–89.1–8. In negated form, see Dio Chrys. *Or.* 32.37. We often encounter lists of Aristotle's four cardinal virtues (e.g., Mus. Ruf. 4, p. 44.10–12; this commentary treats these more fully at Acts 24:2 and esp. 26:25).

202. E.g., Goodenough, "Perspective of Acts," 58.

203. Although not all would have been citizens, the preponderance of Roman names (in a Roman colony) is significant: Aquila and Priscilla (Acts 18:2; 1 Cor 16:19), Titius Justus (Acts 18:7), Crispus (18:8; 1 Cor 1:14), Gaius (Rom 16:23; 1 Cor 1:14), Fortunatus and Achaicus (1 Cor 16:17), Quartus (Rom 16:23), and Tertius (Rom 16:22).

204. Porter, *Paul in Acts*, 171; against Haenchen's attribution of resurrection preaching to Acts' Paul at the expense of the epistles' Paul, see 197–99.

205. Ibid., 170–71. For compatibility on mission vision and practice, see Schnabel, *Missionary*, passim.

206. Hengel and Schwemer, *Between Damascus and Antioch*, 9. Melanchthon's approach to theology differed considerably from Luther's (cf. Bergendoff, *Church*, 112–14), but he was clearly influenced by him. Scholars often differ from their mentors, despite the mentors' influence (cf., e.g., Bruce Metzger and Bart Ehrman). Wallace and Williams, *Acts*, 11, compare the varied perceptions of Socrates in Plato and Xenophon. The analogy should not be overpressed, of course; the latter was not as closely acquainted with Socrates as the former, though the former (focused on discourse) probably took greater "historical" liberties. One could even go so far as to allow that "the author could have been an inaccurate eye-witness, or a highly accurate non-eye-witness" (Tuckett, *Luke*, 16), although we have considerable evidence for Luke's accuracy.

sonance with that of the Jerusalem apostles, since Luke writes not simply a biography of Paul but a history of the early Christian movement's mission.

Not all of Paul's companions shared his views on every point (note Barnabas in Gal 2:11–14); being a companion of Paul hardly makes one his "mouthpiece."[207] Disciples learned their teachers' words and behavior and passed them on for posterity[208] (sometimes adding that they disagreed but almost always reporting the teachings respectfully).[209] Luke appears as a traveling companion, not a disciple, so he might not have memorized Paul's teaching the way Jesus's disciples probably sought to recall and rehearse his.[210] No "disciples" of Paul are reported after Acts 9:25, but it is nevertheless likely that Paul, as a teacher, would have expected his associates to remember accurately his teachings (though different disciples naturally gravitated toward and reported different teachings on the basis of their individual predilections).[211] If Luke was a traveling companion of Paul, we should expect him to report genuine information from his own perspective. But "his own perspective" constitutes a highly selective interpretive grid, one that differs from aspects of Paul that those steeped in his now-extant letters would emphasize.

As F. F. Bruce concludes, Luke's Paul "is the real Paul viewed in retrospect by a friend and admirer, whose own religious experience was different from Paul's, who expresses a distinctive theological outlook, who writes for another constituency than that for which Paul wrote his letters."[212]

Conclusion

Acts and Paul's letters are both important sources for informing us about Paul's life. On the (often incidental) elements where they address the same issues, the vast number of correspondences (despite the differences) indicate that Luke clearly knew much about Paul. He was writing a work of history, not a novel.

---

207. DeSilva, *Introduction*, 299; cf. Chance, *Acts*, 3.

208. See Keener, *John*, 57–60, and sources cited there (including for teaching, Aul. Gel. 7.10.1; Socrates *Ep.* 20; *Sipre Deut.* 48.1.1–4; for behavior, Philost. *Vit. Apoll.* 5.21; *b. Ber.* 62a).

209. See, e.g., Sen. Y. *Ep. Lucil.* 108.17, 20, 22; 110.14, 20; Mus. Ruf. 1, 36.6–7 (Pythagoras's disciples differed, but this was considered noteworthy, Val. Max. 8.15.ext. 1). Occasionally pupils could even turn against their teachers (Eunapius *Lives* 493; Luke 22:47–48), but in such a case, they would no longer claim his authority for the source of their teaching. See further Keener, *John*, 16–17.

210. For this difference, see, e.g., Porter, "Portrait," 137.

211. Compare the quite divergent portrayals of Socrates among his followers. Traveling with Paul, Luke probably knew him better than Xenophon knew Socrates (though Xenophon's prosaic portrait is probably less slanted than Plato's "Platonized" one).

212. Bruce, *Acts*[3], 59.

8

SPEECHES IN ACTS

We have noted the importance of rhetoric to historiography; it was in speeches, however, that historians displayed their rhetorical skills most freely.[1] Most students of ancient historiography would agree with F. W. Walbank when he points out that modern historians would not feel comfortable inserting into their historical works "versions of speeches delivered, or reputedly delivered, by historical characters. But this practice is almost universal among ancient historians, who regarded it as an important part of their work."[2] Of one scholar's examples of alleged historical inaccuracies in ancient historians, nearly all originated in speeches or from orators rather than in historical narrative.[3]

Once we have classified Acts as a work of ancient historiography, the speeches[4] require special attention because ancient history-writing practice diverges sharply from its modern descendant on this matter.[5] Historians did not typically treat speeches as conservatively as they did narrative,[6] but fleshed them out more fully (and could also compose them, provided they were appropriate to the occasion).[7] Ancients could either adapt existing sources or completely invent speeches, and one cannot predict, simply on the basis of historical genre, which practice characterizes the speeches of a given author or relates to a given speech within an author.[8] This observation raises questions for our study: To what extent has Luke followed this typical historiographic practice of his day?[9] Moreover, in light of other historians' use of speeches, what is the purpose and function of speeches in Acts?

1. With, e.g., Laird, "Rhetoric," 204.
2. Walbank, *Speeches*, 1 (excepting Cratippus and Pompeius Trogus). This recognition is widely shared, e.g., Feldherr, "Introduction," 2.
3. The observation of Damon, "Rhetoric," 444, regarding the examples in Wiseman, *Historiography*. Even A. J. Woodman's broader critique of narratives based on inferences is limited in its reach (Damon, "Rhetoric," 445–46).
4. For a systematic and historical review of scholarly approaches to Acts' speeches, see esp. Soards, *Speeches*, 1–11.
5. Often noted, e.g., Judge, *First Christians*, 380. Historiographic speech-writing customs vary in different periods; thus, e.g., it was customary in the nineteenth century to reword verb tenses throughout the entire speech (Tomkins, *Wilberforce*, 225).
6. This practice regarding speeches differs from Jesus's sayings in the Synoptics, the wording of which tends to be preserved more carefully than that of the narratives (see discussion below concerning the transmission of sayings, as opposed to entire speeches).
7. Even where they had existing speeches available, failing to rewrite them made historians appear rhetorically deficient, at least those writing for elite audiences.
8. The exception would be speeches for which there were no surviving witnesses (clearly invented) or for which the writer's sources remain extant.
9. To put the matter differently, what does it mean for Luke to be a good ancient historian when we study the question of speeches? To try to make him a good *modern* historian is to force his work into a genre that,

1. Luke's Speech Material

Despite some overarching rhetorical principles (such as typical forensic arguments in the defense speeches), Luke's speech material is not as rhetorically sophisticated as we would expect in elite historians. His speeches are much more compact, suiting the one-volume character of his work. Nevertheless, his speeches consume a high proportion of his narrative, befitting works of history (but perhaps more than usual even in histories because, for Luke, proclamation is the narrative's chief subject and action).

Although categories overlap, the book's primarily "evangelistic" speeches tend to be deliberative; the book's later defense speeches are forensic (though even there Paul is not above deliberatively seeking conversion, Acts 26:27–29). Historians could use speeches to interpret the surrounding narrative; Luke undoubtedly uses them to keep the focus on the gospel message that his protagonists are proclaiming throughout his account.[10]

a. Elite Rhetoric versus Acts' Speeches

Speeches in histories were rhetorically significant; this would be the case especially in readings for educated audiences. Lectors of histories presumably orally performed speeches (as they also did other parts of the works) with dramatic gestures and intonation appropriate to the content.[11] Rhetorical scholar George Kennedy has argued that the speeches in Acts do not fit classical Greek orations and has suggested that Jewish rhetorical conventions influenced them.[12] But while some sermons (esp. 13:16–41) naturally show parallels with synagogue homilies and the greater (though not exclusive) Semitic penchant for parallelism (cf. the long chiasmus in 2:22–36) is present at places, Diaspora Jewish orators probably used Hellenistic oratorical principles at least outside the synagogues and probably, to some degree, even in their homilies.[13] (For that matter, even very old and traditional Jewish interpretive techniques were analogous to, and probably rooted in, Greek argumentative rules.)[14] Later speeches in Acts, including notably Paul's defense speeches, do display characteristics indicating familiarity with rhetorical conventions.[15]

---

in its current form, could not yet exist. Nevertheless, the most nuanced approach allows us to identify a range of speech-composition practices in ancient historiography and to ask where in this range Luke falls (or where particular speeches fall; e.g., most scholars quickly conclude that Luke 6:20–49 hews close to its source [cf. esp. Allison, *Jesus*, 309–51] but that the conversation in Acts 25:14–27 represents free composition).

10. For studies of Luke's speeches, see Grässer, *Forschungen*, 99–115, 254–70; before 1965, see also Mattill and Mattill, *Bibliography*, 165–73, §§2220–2338.

11. See Shiell, *Reading Acts*, 102–36 (esp. 133). Literary cues would signal proper changes in vocal inflection (see in detail 83–89, addressing such cues as indignation, irony, ridicule, flattery, or other emotionally evocative tones and postures).

12. Kennedy, *Classical Rhetoric*, 129. See more specific parallels in Ellis, "Midrashic Features"; Bowker, "Proem and Yelammedenu Form." I do recognize that conventional Jewish rhetoric predominates in some early Christian material (emphasized in Keener, "Study of Rhetoric").

13. See Wills, "Form of Sermon"; and esp. the response in Black, "Form of Sermon"; in Christian preaching, see Bauckham, "Summaries," 191–204 (Ascension of Isaiah) and 204–9 (Ignatius).

14. As is widely recognized (Lieberman, *Hellenism*, 47–82; Hengel, *Judaism and Hellenism*, 1:80ff.; Levine, *Hellenism*, 113–16); for Hillel's seven rules, cf. Cic. *Inv.* 2.40.116 (Stambaugh and Balch, *Environment*, 103; Hengel, *Judaism and Hellenism*, 1:81). E.g., with *qal vaomer*, compare Arist. *Rhet.* 2.23.4–5, 1397b; gematria has Greek roots (Sambursky, "Gematria"); notarikon may have Babylonian origins (Cavigneaux, "Herméneutique"); even the later pilpulistic hair-splitting of the rabbis resembles sophistic discussion (Diog. Laert. 2.30). Naturally, this was especially obvious regarding allegory (with, e.g., Sandmel, *Judaism*, 113; Mickelsen, *Interpreting*, 27).

15. See Keener, "Rhetorical Techniques"; Neyrey, "Forensic Defense Speech"; and other sources cited loc. cit.

Kennedy's observation that Acts' speeches differ from those of classical orators is worth noting. Yet one cannot soundly critique these speeches for rhetorical inadequacy, since they are mere summaries of speeches.[16] Clearly, Luke himself expects his audience to understand that these speeches are abridgments (see 2:40; cf. 4:3); orators could be quite long-winded (see, more fully, comment on Acts 24:4), and the audience reactions do not fit the brevity of the speeches Luke provides. Cicero, for example, complained that a first-century B.C.E. law had limited defense speakers in a court to only three hours apiece.[17] Pliny the Younger suggested a positive reception to a seven-hour oration he gave (*Ep.* 4.16.2). Even the speeches in Thucydides, which are much longer than those of Luke, are "quite compressed," compared with actual speeches given.[18] In any case, Luke is more interested in his content than in eliciting praise for rhetorically sophisticated speech composition, and even rhetoricians could recognize such divergent purposes. The ancient rhetorical critic Dionysius of Halicarnassus regarded Plato's writing style, in general, as tasteless (*Demosth.* 23), particularly because Plato seems proud about his style (*Demosth.* 25); nevertheless, he regarded Plato as one of the finest writers of philosophy (*Demosth.* 41).

Seeking to portray what happened with optimum verisimilitude, most historians applied rhetorical principles to compose full speeches[19] for their characters; Luke, however, has provided instead brief overviews of their arguments. The contrast with other ancient historians is stark enough to have been widely noticed[20] and may suggest that Luke did not follow the standard practice of rhetorically fleshing out his tradition. Perhaps because Luke is not writing a multivolume work or primarily seeking to display his rhetorical prowess, he prefers to summarize many samples of the apostolic message rather than include just a few long ones. That much may be missing rhetorically does not mean, however, that we cannot examine the speeches' structure and arguments in light of rhetorical strategies of the day.[21]

Kennedy suggests that Luke "is a reasonably skilled writer of speeches," though he regards Paul and the Fourth Gospel as more eloquent.[22] In rhetorical style for his speeches, Luke seeks an effective middle road (if we take into account that their brevity precludes ornateness). No less a rhetorical purist than Dionysius of Halicarnassus advises that speeches whose audience includes both the educated elite and the "ignorant masses" should avoid the extremes of both "the plain and the grand style," going down the middle (Dion. Hal. *Demosth.* 15 [LCL]).[23] Whereas sections of Paul's letters abound with some rhetorical devices (e.g., Rom 5:3–5; 1 Cor 4:8–12; 15:42–44; 2 Cor 6:4–10; Gal 1:8–9; 4:20), the speeches in Acts are generally much plainer (though it is letters that most ancient critics would have expected to be plain). This style may have suited some ancient critics who preferred a plain style without excessive metaphors or unusual words.[24] In normal speech (as

16. Barrett, *Acts*, 2:lxxx; Porter, *Paul in Acts*, 124.

17. Cic. *Brut.* 93.324.

18. Kennedy, "Survey of Rhetoric," 15. Porciani, "Enigma," 333–34, suggests that Thucydides may have actually condensed some available materials for his speeches.

19. Not, of course, several hours in length. They could be condensed (Pliny *Ep.* 1.16.4), but Luke's are unusually brief.

20. E.g., Soards, *Speeches*, 141.

21. See, e.g., Neyrey, "Forensic Defense Speech"; Keener, "Rhetorical Techniques."

22. Kennedy, *New Testament Interpretation*, 115. I agree in Paul's case (though not, perhaps, John's); most of Paul's letters are carefully crafted (see, e.g., Harvey, *Listening*, passim).

23. Dion. Hal. *Isoc.* 2, 3, 12 critiques Isocrates for piling up ornate rhetorical devices generating needless words. For his Atticist purity, see, e.g., Dion. Hal. *Lysias* 2; also Rebenich, "Historical Prose," 292–93.

24. Dion. Hal. *Lysias* 3. When simply illustrating a point, a rhetorician could articulate simply for clarity (Hermog. *Inv.* 1.1.94–95), a point relevant to Luke's mere speech summaries.

opposed, perhaps, to the riddles of an Eastern sage such as Jesus in the Gospel), clarity is preferable to obscurity;[25] certainly Paul's speeches in Acts are clearer than his letters, though the occasional obscurity of the latter is probably inadvertent (2 Pet 3:16).[26] Length, however, is a primary issue in the speeches in Acts; actual speeches could be hours in length (see comment on Acts 24:3), and Luke does not expect us to regard his speeches as more than summaries. The speeches in Acts are simply too concise for us to expect them to display the sort of eloquence typical of the elite historians' speeches.

b. Quantity of Speech Material

Speeches constitute a large percentage of Acts, larger than expected in most historical works. Estimates of the particular percentage vary greatly, depending on whether one counts only lengthy speeches, all direct discourse, or some amount in between, and whether one counts the narrative contexts.[27] Some estimate that the speeches compose one third of the book, indicating their importance for it.[28] Paul Schubert estimates that Luke's speeches and their contexts together make up nearly three-quarters of the book. By including their contexts, one simply counts all stories that contain speech material, but as we have noted, this characterization appropriately fits a story about the spread of God's message, as Schubert emphasizes.[29] Acts must include a significant proportion of material including speeches because proclamation is the focus of his work. Soards gives one of the highest estimates, higher than G. H. R. Horsley's; this estimate is probably too high from the standpoint of the work's genre because ancient historians would distinguish sayings and even dialogue from speeches proper.[30]

Whatever the precise parameters for speeches in Acts, the percentage remains high, and many argue that it is higher than in most other historians.[31] Scholars regularly cite Horsley, who provides figures that are many times as high as other ancient historians—twice the amount in Herodotus or Tacitus's *Annals*, four times Josephus's *War*, eight times Thucydides, and sixteen times Polybius (despite the length of their speeches).[32] Exact figures are disputable, but mainly because they depend on what one counts; in the end, most scholars have concurred with Horsley's essential point.

What one counts is significant. Thus Aune estimates that "speeches occupy 24 percent of Thucydides, and 25 percent of Acts."[33] He estimates that half of the *Iliad* and more than half of the *Odyssey* (which often surveys past events through the

25. Dion. Hal. *Lysias* 4.

26. On the sometimes obscure style of Paul's letters, see Anderson, *Rhetorical Theory*, 280–81.

27. E.g., Borgman, *Way*, 11, counts 19 major speeches; Dibelius, *Studies in Acts*, 150, counts 24 speeches; Eckey, *Apostelgeschichte*, 30–31, counts 26; Aune, *Environment*, 124–25, counts 32.

28. Smith, *Studies*, 9, 40.

29. See Schubert, "Final Cycle"; he believes that this does not fit Thucydides's approach. Cf. Martinson, "Ending," 316, viewing Acts as proclamation (though incorrectly counting this as Acts' "unique" *genre* rather than distinctive focus); Penner, "Discourse," 84 (though exaggerating in seeing the speeches as so central that Luke lacks interest in historical narrative). Pervo, "Direct Speech," 302, acknowledges the widespread attribution of Luke's focus on speeches to his proclamation theme, but himself attributes it to the popular genre instead.

30. Soards, *Speeches*, 183n3, estimates higher than Horsley because Horsley counts "only . . . the major speeches"; but presumably he counts only those in other historians as well. It may well be because Pervo counts all direct speech and not simply orations that his figures for novels run much higher than for history (note the concession in "Direct Speech," 302).

31. Horsley, "Speeches," 613. Laird, "Speech presentation," rightly emphasizes the prominence of direct-discourse monologues in ancient narratives but curiously plays them down in ancient historiography; Pervo, "Direct Speech," does the same, taking the highest count for Acts and the lowest for ancient historians generally.

32. Horsley, "Speeches."

33. Aune, *Environment*, 125.

protagonist's retelling) are direct speech.[34] In Hellenistic histories, speeches made up, on average, "20 to 35 percent of the narrative," which compares well with the "25 percent" he finds for Acts.[35] But he notes that when "the narrative frameworks" are taken into account, the picture changes: in Acts, in contrast to Thucydides, the speeches together with their contexts may compose "74 percent of the narrative."[36] Acts' percentage is high, not so high as to bring its genre into question[37] but merely to reinforce, as Schubert argues, the centrality of preaching in the work.[38] Luke's work is shorter than multivolume histories, but he includes the same proportion of speeches and a necessarily greater proportion of stories concerning preaching, given his focus.

Scholars propose various reasons that Acts includes so many speeches. Johnson, for example, suggests (probably rightly) that speeches function as a narrative filler in Acts 1–7, where Luke has less information from his sources; they constitute "fully half the narrative to that point."[39] Others suggest that speeches fill a stylistic concern to break up and move the narrative,[40] and certainly, ancients did alternate the nature of their content to supply variety to their speeches or writings (Dion. Hal. *Isaeus* 3) and could use speeches to supply variety to their histories (Diod. Sic. 20.2.1).[41] Others suggest that the speeches are simply a historiographic convention to instruct and please the reader.[42]

But by themselves, such individual proposals can be reductionist if viewed as the entire picture. The speeches may fulfill several functions, and different speeches sometimes fulfill different functions.[43] Although different speeches probably do fulfill different functions and elements of several approaches are undoubtedly correct, the overall amount of speech material does suggest an overarching purpose that allows for this distribution. This observation brings us back to the centrality of preaching in Acts.

If, as I will argue concerning Luke's purpose, Acts provides in part a model for missions, then its speeches may further provide something like apologetic and missionary models for Luke's audience,[44] as the later speeches in John probably serve for John's audience.[45] This is not to suggest that Luke would expect others to reproduce his speeches directly; rather, the speeches explore the kinds of responses that could strengthen the spread of the gospel in the Roman world. Although the sayings material in Luke's Gospel is of a very different kind (sometimes with figures recognizable

---

34. Ibid., 91, offering other examples as well. Also Aune, *Dictionary of Rhetoric*, 139; although Homer's poetic genre differs, it became the model for subsequent narratives (447). Ancients understood that poets composed speech material freely (Vell. Paterc. 1.3.2–3).

35. Aune, *Environment*, 124–25. Ehrman, *Introduction*, 133, suggests "nearly a quarter" for the average history. On indirect and direct speech in Polybius (the former often giving way to the latter), see Usher, "Oratio Recta."

36. Aune, *Environment*, 125.

37. It does not fit drama at all (with, e.g., its staging, choruses, poetic lines, and barely any narrative) whereas most other genres have *less* speech material.

38. With others in addition to Schubert, e.g., Witherington, *Acts*, 118, 665.

39. Johnson, *Acts*, 10 (citing Acts 1:4–8, 16–22; 2:14–40; 3:12–26; 4:8–12, 24–30; 5:35–39; 7:2–53; apart from 1:4–8, these are evident).

40. Horsley, "Speeches and Dialogues"; cf. Cadbury, *Making*, 184.

41. Biographers regularly wove sayings and stories together; e.g., Philost. *Vit. soph.* 2.5.574; see more fully Keener, *Matthew*, 33–36; Burridge, *Gospels*, 203; cf. the large amount of speech material in Iambl. *V.P.* 8–11. In Roman histories after Sallust, following Thucydides's model, see, e.g., Cary and Haarhoff, *Life*, 263. For rhetorical instructions concerning how to insert sayings into narratives, see Theon *Progymn.* 4.73–79; cf. 5.388–441.

42. For one brief survey of the discussion, see van Unnik, "Storm Center," 26; still more briefly, Powell, *Acts*, 30–31. Contrast here Witherington, "Addendum," 24, 28–29; idem, *Acts*, 48, 117, 455.

43. Soards, *Speeches*, 9–11; Porter, *Paul in Acts*, 127–28.

44. Cf. Tannehill, *Acts*, 329; Bauckham, "Summaries." Cf. Bruce, "Apostolic Succession," who applies the apostolic preaching in Acts as a model for modern ministers.

45. On John, cf. Keener, *John*, 53–80, esp. 69.

to Greek as well as traditional Jewish rhetoric, but often discrete sayings rather than speeches), the large amount of speech material in the second volume might also provide a partial parallel to the first. Most important, the quantity of speech material reflects again the centrality of preaching in the story that Luke recounts.

c. Kinds of Speeches

Most ancient rhetoricians formally divided speeches into three categories: forensic (judicial, courtroom), epideictic (ceremonial, containing praise or blame), and deliberative (seeking to persuade someone to adopt a course of action).[46] Some rhetoricians divided speeches differently,[47] but even the dominant tripartite classification was not followed strictly, except perhaps in the practice declamations of the schools. Some speeches fell into none of the three categories.[48] Different genres of speeches required different styles (Dion. Hal. *Demosth.* 45–46).[49]

To the extent that speeches in Acts and other ancient literature conform to such categories, speeches of significant length in the first part of the book are largely deliberative (7:2–53 combines this purpose with a forensic setting and conclusion), seeking converts; Acts 20:18–35 exhorts especially Christians; and Paul's later speeches are especially forensic.[50] Naturally forensic elements dominate the speeches in courts (even if a deliberative purpose is included; e.g., 26:29); even Stephen's speech, which in some sense aims to persuade, seems more intent (in forensic fashion) on answering and then reversing the charges, convicting his accusers (7:51–53).

Yet public speeches could straddle various categories and even shift from one to another in their different parts. Most evangelistic speeches in Acts will be largely deliberative, calling for conversion, but the christological praise in these speeches involves an epideictic element (e.g., Acts 2:22; 3:13–16; 10:36–41).[51] Mixtures thus appear, as in some other ancient speeches.[52]

The most basic outline for speeches (especially of the forensic variety) was (1) prologue, (2) narrative, (3) proof (sometimes further divided into confirmation of one's view and refutation of the opponent's), and (4) epilogue.[53] Speeches also commonly included a proposition. Scholars may examine speeches by elite persons in elite histories according to standard principles of ancient rhetoric.[54] Not surprisingly, completed

46. E.g., Dion. Hal. *Isoc.* 20; Theon *Progymn.* 1.74–76; Diog. Laert. 7.1.42 (on Stoics); Hermog. *Issues* 34.21–35.2; Men. Rhet. 1.1.331.4–9; Nicolaus *Progymn.* 1.pref. 3; discussion in Anderson, *Rhetorical Theory,* 97; Calboli, "Genera." In greater detail, see Kennedy, *Art of Rhetoric,* 7–18, for forensic; 18–21, for deliberative; and 21–23, for epideictic oratory.

47. See, e.g., Aune, *Environment,* 91 (classifying speeches in the *Iliad*).

48. Garver, "Aristotle," noting that they did not all fit these categories even in Aristotle's time.

49. Ancients recognized the diversity of style among artists (Fronto *Ad verum imp.* 1.1.1), poets (1.1.2), philosophers (1.1.3), and others.

50. With Watson, "Speech," 184. In my view less convincingly, he places Acts 20:17–38 in the epideictic category because it is a farewell speech (190–91); but though it may praise Paul for Luke's readers (191; but farewell speeches normally praised the place being left, not the speaker), its function in the story world appears more deliberative. Not surprisingly, "the vast majority of historiographical speeches" were deliberative (Marincola, "Speeches," 127; for Livy, also Laistner, *Historians,* 96), with many forensic cases as well (Marincola, "Speeches," 128).

51. True epideictic was typically elaborate and sometimes rhythmic, however (Hermog. *Inv.* 1.5.106–8; 4.1.171; Fronto *Ad M. Caes.* 3.16.1), so it fits better some christological passages in the Pauline corpus (often viewed, perhaps inappropriately, as hymns) rather than speeches in Acts.

52. Mixed rhetorical genres were common (Aune, *Dictionary of Rhetoric,* 419).

53. Heath, *Hermogenes,* 9–10; *Rhet. Her.* 1 (for judicial speeches); 3.7–9 (deliberative); 3.11–15 (epideictic); Diog. Laert. 7.1.43 (among Stoics); Nicolaus *Progymn.* 1.pref. 4; 11, "On Ecphrasis," 69–70; for examples, see Dion. Hal. *Lysias* 9; Tac. *Dial.* 19.

54. See, e.g., Laird, "Rhetoric," 204–6.

speeches in Acts generally conform to such a basic outline,[55] though often they are interrupted after the *narratio*, the narrative component that readers of the larger narrative work would seem most readily disposed to appreciate. As is the case with speeches in other historians, Luke's speeches derive especially from major characters, with a smaller number from minor ones.[56]

Although some professors of rhetoric (who naturally emphasized preparation) held a low opinion of the improvisation entailed in extemporaneous declamation,[57] many hearers on a more popular level appreciated the ability to declaim on short notice,[58] and some preferred this practice to prepared speeches.[59] That preachers regularly preach extemporaneously in Acts (e.g., 2:14; 3:12; 4:8; 14:14–15; 17:19–22; probably 13:16) underlines their dependence on the Spirit (Luke 12:12; 21:15) and would augment the appreciation of Luke's audience.

Delivery was also important in a speech; thus a later critic complained that Isocrates's written speeches could not "accommodate inflection, expression or animated delivery" (Dion. Hal. *Isoc.* 13 [LCL]).[60] Despite Paul's and some of his hearers' protestations of his inadequate delivery style (1 Cor 2:3; 2 Cor 10:10; though rhetors sometimes used such statements merely to lower expectations),[61] he appears as a competent rhetorician in Acts (cf., e.g., stretching out his hand in Acts 13:16; 26:1). The problem noted in Paul's letters was not Paul's argumentative style but his delivery (2 Cor 10:10); many rhetors despised those whose rhetoric was much stronger in letters (which could depend on forethought) than in person.[62] Apparently, whereas Paul chose to emphasize his weakness in some of his letters (1 Cor 2:1–3; 2 Cor 11:6; Gal 4:13–14), Luke chose to emphasize the side that many of Paul's other followers saw, the intellectual hero for a moving (true) story.

d. Purpose and Function of Speeches

For modern readers, lengthy discourses interrupt narrative and are tedious; ancient hearers, however, may have been most accustomed to hearing the entire works, narratives included, in oral form.[63] Speeches could fulfill various purposes.[64] Historians could employ speeches, no less than narrative, to entertain as well as to inform, though these purposes are not mutually exclusive.[65] Speeches may have also offered an opportunity for characterization, in which ancient historians were sometimes reticent to engage as explicitly as some historians today.[66] Historians today also believe that

55. See, e.g., Rodríguez Ruiz, "Discurso misionero." Naturally, there is the risk of imposing too much of the taxonomy of classical ideals on genuine texts (Black, *Rhetoric of Gospel*, 21); flexibility was intrinsic to good rhetoric (Cic. *Quinct.* 10.35).

56. Horsley, "Speeches," 609.

57. Quint. *Inst.* 10.7.21.

58. E.g., Pliny *Ep.* 2.3.1–3. Hermog. *Method* 17.433, thus advises feigning this approach for jurors; commenting, Kennedy adds Quint. *Inst.* 10.6.6.

59. See Winter, *Philo and Paul*, 205–6.

60. On the importance of delivery, see, e.g., Cic. *Brut.* 17.55; 37.141; 43.158; 66.234; 82.283; 91.316; *Rhet. Her.* 3.11.19; Plut. *Demosth.* 7.2–3; 11.2–3; Pliny *Ep.* 2.3.9; 2.19.2–4, 6; 5.20.3; 6.11.2; Suet. *Claud.* 30; 41.2.

61. E.g., Isoc. *Panath.* 3; Cic. *Quinct.* 1.1–4; 24.77; 26.80–27.85; Sall. *Jug.* 85.31; *Sp. G. Cotta* 4; Quint. *Inst.* 4.1.8–9, 11; cf. Ovid *Metam.* 13.137; Pliny *Ep.* 8.3.3; Suet. *Tit.* 7.1; Tac. *Hist.* 4.73. It is used often enough by Dio Chrysostom (*Or.* 1.9; 32.39; 46.7; 47.1, 8).

62. See Winter, *Philo and Paul*, 205–6.

63. Laird, "Rhetoric," 206–7.

64. On ancient distinctions among purpose, theme, speaker, and form of speeches in terms of types of causes in Aristotle's *Physica*, see Poster, "Affections," 35n20.

65. See, e.g., Dunn, *Acts*, xvii–xviii. Varying genres within a work aided its reception (Pliny *Ep.* 6.33.7–9).

66. Laird, "Rhetoric," 207.

ancient historians employed speeches in a way that applied the earlier issues to the issues of the ancient historians' day.[67]

Speeches could help hold narratives together. Dionysius of Halicarnassus could use speeches to provide continuity to the flow of history.[68] In OT historical works, writers could employ speeches, as Rosner puts it, "to introduce or sum up the theme of a unit or to serve as a transition to the next unit." Some speeches and prayers in Acts function in the same way (e.g., Acts 4:24–30 puts events in perspective the way that 1 Kgs 8:22–53 does).[69]

Historians also used speeches as interpretive events, which suggests that Luke's speeches will offer us clues to his theology of history.[70] Speeches in ancient narratives often provided the writer's clues to the meaning of the historical narrative[71] (or at least a rhetorical display of competing views, each argued eloquently) as well as the writer's best reconstruction or, when sources were lacking, best guess of what the speaker may have said. (Speeches also could function to show off the writer's polished rhetoric,[72] but those in Acts are clearly too brief to display an interest in this function.)[73] Thucydides plainly acknowledges that he provides speeches in his narrative at points where he knows that they occurred, and uses them to expound critical issues.[74] Likewise, the invented speeches of the rhetorical historian Dionysius of Halicarnassus shed light on his narratives.[75]

Herodotus offers an example of the freedom with which historians could create speeches; he sometimes provides various accounts of events, but never of speeches, which he composed freely.[76] Thus Cadbury can assert that "the ancient writers and their readers considered the speeches more as editorial and dramatic comment than as historical tradition."[77] The person to whom a narrative attributes speech is important; some voices (such as divine ones) are more significant than others (Libanius *Maxim* 1.3). As in Greco-Roman historiography, some Palestinian Jewish haggadic works used the speech of reliable characters to illumine the narrative's significance; for example, speeches in *Jubilees* often interpret the events they accompany.[78] Presumably, speeches in narratives often fulfilled this function regardless of the degree to which the narrator possessed a historical tradition regarding the speech's key content.

67. Laird, "Rhetoric," 208–9. One may compare how preachers apply biblical texts to their audiences, although some ancient historians may have been more creative.

68. See Plümacher, "Missionsreden." For a comparison of the function of Acts' mission speeches with the function of the speeches in Dionysius and Livy, see idem, *Lukas*, 33–38.

69. Rosner, "Biblical History," 76. For the interpretive function of OT speeches, see also Konkel, *Kings*, 23.

70. Most scholars think that Luke uses speeches to advance his purpose (e.g., Strelan, *Artemis*, 23). We examine Luke's theology in both speeches and narrative more extensively in ch. 15 below.

71. Lindner, "Geschichtsauffassung"; Attridge, "Historiography," 326; Marincola, "Speeches," 119. Israelite historical works, like Acts, often used speeches to summarize a unit or move the narrative forward to the following unit (Rosner, "Biblical History," 76).

72. Cadbury, *Making*, 184.

73. Despite brief hints that some of the speeches should be understood as more rhetorically proficient, as in, e.g., Acts 17:22–31; 24:10–21.

74. Thucyd. 1.22.1; Satterthwaite, "Acts," 355–56. Speeches in Thucydides provide his estimate but not primarily his personal views; rather, they expound "what Thucydides thought would have seemed to him the factors in a given situation, had he stood in the place of his speakers" (Finley, *Thucydides*, 96); they function in connection with the rest of the work (100).

75. Plümacher, *Geschichte*, 109–26, comparing Luke.

76. Aune, *Environment*, 91. On Herodotus's special liberties, see Kennedy, *Classical Rhetoric*, 110; he was "the first [known] historian to use direct speech for dramatization" (Aune, *Dictionary of Rhetoric*, 448).

77. Cadbury, *Making*, 185.

78. Endres, *Interpretation*, 198–99.

Each speech will be addressed in detail at its juncture in the commentary, but suffice it to say here that Luke's speeches function ideologically (for Luke I would say theologically), as do speeches in most other ancient historical works. If Luke uses speeches as interpretive devices, his speeches emphasize his theology of history as salvation history. This theology includes the history of promise through David climaxing in the fulfillment of Jesus (Acts 13; see the discussion of promise fulfillment in ch. 14 of this introduction) and the current era of the Spirit (2:17–21). It also includes the history of Israel's rejection of their divinely appointed leaders (7:2–53; 28:25–27), which helps explain Israel's current failure to embrace Jesus. Luke offers samples of OT interpretation dispersed among various speeches, and not only the "law" (the most widely quoted part of Scripture in ancient Judaism). He addresses the "writings" (cf. Luke 24:44), for example, through Elijah and Elisha (Luke 4:25–27); the Psalms (Acts 2:25–35; 13:33, 35); and overviews of salvation history (with a Mosaic emphasis in 7:19–44 and with a Davidic emphasis in 13:22–23, 34–36; cf. 2:25–34). He closes with quotations from the prophets in 7:49–50 and 13:41, 47 as well as in his final speech in 28:26–27. Such examples flesh out the global citations in other speeches (e.g., 3:18, 24; 26:22).

Many speeches also explain salvation and provide a model for preaching the gospel from various starting points to different groups of people, such as salvation history (as noted) for Israel (2:14–39; 3:12–26; 7:2–53; 13:16–41) and God the Creator for Gentiles (14:15–17; 17:22–31). Since Luke's central audience probably consists especially of believers in Jesus, these models are relevant, but his Pauline message for believers to watch out for false teachers who exploit the flock could also play a particularly strategic role (20:18–35). Perhaps Luke faced a setting in which false teaching and rejection of Paul (see ch. 7 above) were real threats (as in the Pastorals; see, e.g., 2 Tim 1:15; cf. 1 Tim 1:19–20; 2 Tim 2:17–18; 3:6–8).

Scholars sometimes also note that the speeches in Acts fulfill a special function less shared with other histories, since the focus of Acts' history is on the expansion of the gospel message.[79] As noted earlier, the speeches themselves are part of the action and convey the substance of the message the spread of which Luke reports.[80] This may be the reason that Christian proclaimers' speeches in Acts share common themes and interests more than do the speeches in most histories (see the discussion on the unity of the speeches below). Nevertheless, in principle Luke does what other historians do, albeit with a different subject. Though writers used speeches to explain events, the speeches (especially of political and military leaders) were themselves historical events that played a role in history, sometimes as causes of subsequent events.[81]

Although many of Luke's speeches are deliberative, many (and especially those in forensic settings) serve an apologetic purpose.[82] The speeches thus substantially advance the apologetic aim of the overall work (see the discussion of apologetic in chs. 5 above and 13 below), especially vis-à-vis the Roman administration (esp. Acts 24–26). Even those that ground the Gentile mission in the heritage of Israel can serve

79. Cf. Schubert, "Final Cycle"; Martinson, "Ending," 316.
80. See, e.g., Ferreira, "Plan."
81. Gempf, "Speaking," 261. This can remain true in political history (cf. the prominence of speeches' historic role in the British Parliament in, e.g., Metaxas, *Grace*, passim).
82. See, e.g., Bruce, *Commentary*, 24. Besides speeches with a deliberate apologetic function in the narrative world, Luke seems to employ most outsiders' speeches apologetically, in a manner comparable to other Jewish narrative (including historiographic) works (see esp. Padilla, *Speeches*). Emphasizing apologetic elements pervasive in the speeches, Mauck, *Trial*, 62–64, argues that most speeches reveal that the Christian movement is genuinely Jewish or that the Christians are evangelists rather than subversives.

an apologetic function with regard to Rome by emphasizing that the Jesus movement is thoroughly Jewish and hence not a disrespectable new cult. Paul's evangelistic preaching, too, functions apologetically, though often in a manner different from the forensic speeches. It commends apostolic teaching by presenting it in terms of the highest ideals that pagan audiences often respected in worshipers of a supreme deity, including in ethical monotheism.[83] Although Luke goes beyond such attempts to find common ground (14:15; 17:29–31), there can be no question that he does seek to establish this ground (14:17; 17:22–28).

In most narratives that desired even basic respectability, whatever their actual level, speeches included at least some rhetorical techniques.[84] Rhetorical devices in several of Luke's speeches[85] suggest that Luke was familiar with rhetoric,[86] though his speeches are too brief for him to display it the way most elite historians would. (In some respects, he adds rhetorical skill to Paul as a speaker,[87] but in some other respects, Paul's letters display more rhetorical techniques than Luke has space to employ, given his focus on the message; see ch. 7 above.) In contrast to most speeches in elite histories, though, Luke does not avail himself of the opportunity to demonstrate his rhetorical prowess. This is one point, at least, where his speeches differ sharply from those in many other extant histories.

e. Some Compositional Issues

Here we will survey questions about the speeches' settings, the use of narrative devices (specifically Luke's preference for speeches over extensive dialogue, and the technique of interruption), and some unusual aspects of Luke's speeches.

i. Settings of Speeches

Speeches should be appropriate to their settings (Cic. *Fam.* 9.21.1),[88] a principle that Luke seeks to follow. Although some scholars argue that Acts' speeches are less related to the circumstances that prompt them than is the case in most historical works,[89] it may be only the continuous emphasis on the gospel message (which Luke undoubtedly found appropriate to a focused, one-volume monograph as well as to his religious purpose)[90] that produces this relative independence. Otherwise, Luke seems "well versed in and quite capable of composing speeches appropriate to the occasion and the audience,"[91] as rhetoricians expected.

83. See esp. Downing, "Pagan Theism and Speeches," comparing common arguments in Josephus and Dionysius.

84. See those in the later apocryphal acts in Pervo, "Rhetoric in Apocrypha."

85. See, e.g., Watson, "Speech"; Veltman, "Defense Speeches"; Neyrey, "Forensic Defense Speech"; Keener, "Rhetorical Techniques."

86. So Parsons, "*Progymnasmata*," 43–44 (arguing further [44–63] that he probably had learned from the sorts of rhetorical exercises in the handbooks); Asso, "Raconter" (though some would critique his emphasis on Aristotle for this period).

87. E.g., probably occasionally prose rhythm (Aune, *Dictionary of Rhetoric*, 382).

88. Thus, e.g., the Italian Sallust composes a letter for Mithridates that is more anti-Roman than what Pompeius Trogus, a Gaul, composes (Adler, "Anti-Roman").

89. Soards, *Speeches*, 142–43. Penner, "Discourse," 84, thinks that Luke as historian is so interested in speeches that much of the narrative simply sets the stage for them and that hence Luke is not much interested in history; I would argue, however, that Luke's emphasis on speeches fits the normal generic expectations for history, and especially histories the focus of which included substantial speaking roles (see discussion in chs. 3–4 above).

90. As noted in ch. 3, a historical monograph would involve a specific focus. Historians desired compositional unity, including in the speeches (Polyb. 3.32.2; Diod. Sic. 20.1.5–9). Nevertheless, most included more presentation of varied perspectives than Luke does (though cf. Acts 5:34–39; 19:24–27, 35–40).

91. Burridge, "Gospels and Acts," 520.

Philip Satterthwaite notes, "Classical historiography and epic, in spite of their basically narrative structures, contain many speeches; and the material in the speeches is almost always of especial significance in its context." This was true of Thucydides, Livy, Tacitus, and others.[92] Diodorus of Sicily, indeed, severely criticizes those who compose speeches inappropriately, thus interrupting their audience's interest (Diod. Sic. 20.1.1) and failing to provide the sort of speech required for a designated setting (20.1.3–4).[93] Plümacher contends that Luke, like the better histories, also uses speeches at major junctures in his narration and in manners relevant to their context.[94] Comparing the use of some evangelistic speeches in Acts with those in Dionysius of Halicarnassus, Plümacher concludes that Luke follows conventional forms for Hellenistic history (as opposed to biographies or novels).[95]

Luke may have composed and inserted the speeches, as we have them, at a different stage in constructing his work than he did some of their settings. Historians normally composed their rough draft first, apparently adding speeches at the final stage.[96] This practice fits the sequence of narrative composition more generally. Although writers followed their sources more closely in their drafts, they took care to cast their entire work, including all their sources, in their own words at the final stage.[97]

Only works shaped by the author's own style were compositionally satisfactory. Some writers even collected synonyms so that they could most effectively paraphrase older writers (Fronto *Eloq.* 3.5). Such compositional practices remained relevant whether or not writers had sources available for speeches. Paraphrasing even revered sayings was standard rhetorical practice, as evidenced by the school exercises in which it features prominently.[98] Such paraphrase provided a degree of rhetorical freedom and, in the case of familiar lines, would prove more aesthetically appealing than verbatim repetition.[99] Sayings were sometimes also redacted in collections, rather than recited verbatim.[100] Thus Phaedrus feels free to adapt Aesop for aesthetic reasons, meanwhile seeking to keep to the *spirit* of Aesop (Phaedrus 2.prol. 8). (See further discussion below on speech composition and traditions.)

II. Speeches and Narrative Devices

Although occasionally Acts provides opposing speeches (Acts 24:2–21) or something like them (cf. 5:29–39; 15:5–11; 19:24–27, 35–40), it includes no debates

---

92. Satterthwaite, "Acts," 355–56, citing many supporting references.

93. History must remain unified like a living being (Diod. Sic. 20.1.5–9); one should use suitable words in speeches (20.2.2).

94. Plümacher, *Lukas*, 33–38; for English summary, see Soards, *Speeches*, 137–38, but note his disagreement, 142–43.

95. Plümacher, "Mission Speeches"; idem, "Missionsreden."

96. Aune, *Environment*, 127, citing Lucian *Hist.* 47–48 and Jos. *Ag. Ap.* 1.49–50 on rewriting, and the absence of speeches in "unfinished" parts of Thucydides (Thucyd. 5.10–83; 8) and Herodian (Hdn. 5–8). The lack of speeches in part of Thucydides, however, may stem from an experiment, as Cratippus suggested (Wade-Gery, "Thucydides," 1518).

97. Cadbury, Foakes-Jackson, and Lake, "Writing History," 13–14.

98. E.g., Theon *Progymn.* 1.93–171; Libanius *Anecdote* 1.4; 2.3; *Maxim* 1.2–5; 2.3; 3.2; Hermog. *Method* 24.440; cf., e.g., Epict. *Diatr.* 1.9.23–25 with the Loeb note referring to Plato *Apol.* 29C, 28E (Oldfather, LCL, 1:70–71). On paraphrase in secondary education, see also Hock, "Paul and Education," 202–3.

99. Contrast tedious repetition in some earlier literature, e.g., Hom. *Il.* 8.402–8, 416–22 (except the change from first to third person). Some Palestinian Jewish sources also employed paraphrase (e.g., 4Q422, a homiletic paraphrase of Genesis; Elgvin, "Section").

100. Cf., e.g., the redactional structure of *m. 'Abot* 2:9, where Johanan ben Zakkai asks five disciples a question in positive form, commending the answer of the fifth; when he repeats this in negative form, he again receives mainly the same answers in negative form and again commends the fifth.

(even less than in, e.g., Luke 20:21–39; John 8:12–58).[101] That Acts focuses more on speeches than on dialogue (with some notable exceptions) fits the general Greek and Roman preference in rhetoric.[102] Luke is fond of direct discourse, which better holds attention in narrative than indirect discourse would; thus, although ancient writings used both direct and indirect discourse, the speeches in Acts "are almost entirely in direct discourse."[103]

The technique of speech interruption in Acts (Acts 2:37, on which see comment; 10:44) is not unusual, though it is noteworthy.[104] It appears in other ancient narratives,[105] but we should pause to consider that it probably also occurred frequently in the sort of real-world speech settings that narratives sought to imitate. Interlocutors commonly interrupted speakers with both genuine questions and criticisms, and sometimes as hecklers.[106] The diatribe style with its fictive interlocutors' objections partly mimics this pattern.[107] In Acts, however, it normally appears at strategic points in the speeches, after a speech has expanded the content of the apostolic message or communicated what is needed to contribute to the narrative's overall message. This pattern, where it occurs, offers Luke an efficient way to communicate the point of the speech concisely while reproducing the realism of the ancient rhetorical situation.

III. UNUSUAL ASPECTS OF LUKE'S SPEECHES

Although Luke's speeches, in most respects, parallel those of other Greco-Roman historians of his era, they do exhibit some distinctive features. Soards and Witherington summarize some of these (sometimes adjusting Plümacher's earlier list).[108] First and perhaps most obviously, the speeches in Acts are much

101. See Dibelius, *Studies in Acts*, 150–51; Pervo, "Direct Speech," 291; Padilla, "Παιδεία," 432–34. For speeches in John, including dialogues, see Keener, *John*, 53–80. Opposing speeches offered historians an opportunity to display rhetorical skill (Protagoras may have offered the philosophic foundation for that approach; cf. Aune, *Dictionary of Rhetoric*, 36), which may be one significant reason that Luke barely includes them.———

102. Cf., e.g., Lévy, "Conversation"; Pernot, "Rendez-vous"; though for the dialogue form, see Keener, *John*, 61–62, 65–66.

103. Aune, *Environment*, 127. Aune, 91, follows W. C. West in counting 52 direct speeches in Thucydides in addition to 85 in indirect discourse. Pervo, "Direct Speech," 303, attributes Luke's preference for a high proportion of direct discourse to his work's popular genre; for other suggestions, not necessarily incompatible with this one, see sect. 1.b above.

104. Horsley, "Speeches and Dialogues," thinks that it occurs in eight of ten speeches to conceal the speeches' brevity.

105. See ibid. This is not to mention the more common literary forms of dialogue and imaginary interlocutors.

106. E.g., Cic. *Prov. cons.* 8.18; Caesar *C.W.* 2.33 (positively); Mus. Ruf. 3, p. 38.25–26; Plut. *Demosth.* 6.3; 8.5; *Lect.* 11, *Mor.* 43BC; Dio Chrys. *Or.* 15.26–32; Pliny *Ep.* 9.13.19; Lucian *Dem.* 14; Aul. Gel. 8.10; 18.13.7–8; 20.10.1–6; Diog. Laert. 7.1.19; ʾAbot R. Nat. 6 A; t. Sanh. 7:10. Often in court settings, e.g., Plut. *Cic.* 16.3; Pliny *Ep.* 3.9.25; 3.20.3 (in the senate); Philost. *Vit. soph.* 2.30.623; in church, perhaps 1 Cor 14:34–35. Crowd interaction was normal (Lucian Z. Rants 41; contrast Aeschines *Tim.* 35); lack of interaction was rude (Pliny *Ep.* 6.17.1–4; cf. Eunapius *Lives* 460), but so was excessive interruption (Plut. *Lect.* 4, *Mor.* 39CD; 18, *Mor.* 48AB; cf. Sen. E. *Controv.* 3.pref. 4–5). For instructions how to handle interruptions, see *Rhet. Alex.* 18, 1432b.35–40; 1433a.14–18; Cic. *Or. Brut.* 40.138 (less seriously, Lucian *Prof. P.S.* 20).

107. For imaginary interlocutors, see, e.g., Demosth. *Philip.* 3.15; Cic. *Rosc. com.* 3.8–9; *Verr.* 2.3.20.50–51; *Tusc.* 3.23.55; Sen. Y. *Dial.* 3.6.1; *Ep. Lucil.* 42.2; 66.40; 92.14; 94.32; 102.8–10, 18; Mus. Ruf. 4, p. 46.13; 12, p. 86.20; 15, p. 98.18, 26; Jos. *Life* 340; Epict. *Diatr.* 1.1.23–25; Dio Chrys. *Or.* 50.9; Pliny *Ep.* 7.17.5; Fronto *Ad M. Caes.* 3.12; Max. Tyre 3.5; 25.4; 27.8; y. Sanh. 6:1, §1; Pesiq. Rab. 13:7. On rhetorical conventions regarding this and related figures, see *Rhet. Her.* 4.23.33 (cf. 4.16.23–24); Cic. *Or. Brut.* 40.137; Anderson, *Glossary*, 14, 18, 33, 51–52, 58, 108, 124; Stowers, *Diatribe*, 128–29. For examples in Epictetus, see Tobin, *Rhetoric in Contexts*, 93.

108. Soards, *Speeches*, 141–42; Witherington, *Acts*, 46.

briefer than the usual speeches in ancient histories.[109] They are not, strictly speaking, merely outlines,[110] but Luke's failure to fill them in more fully may imply that he has engaged in free composition less than some of even the most careful Hellenistic historians,[111] perhaps because he writes for an audience with less elite rhetorical expectations.

Second, they usually defend a single point of view instead of being balanced with counterspeeches offering divergent perspectives. Third, some scholars note that whereas Thucydides uses speeches to explain events, Acts uses them far more often as part of the action.[112] Luke's speeches may do both, but Luke's focus on preaching the message about Jesus gives his speeches a role out of proportion to the usual function of speeches in military and even political histories. Soards thinks that the content of Acts' speeches differs significantly from that of other historians, being less related to the situation that prompts the speech.[113] Not all proposed differences command consensus; in contrast to Plümacher, who allowed for no deliberative and little epideictic rhetoric in Acts, Soards finds these elements (he seems obviously correct with regard to deliberative rhetoric). Further, Soards finds more stylistic differences among speakers than Plümacher allows[114] (again perhaps correctly, though the differences seem relatively minimal[115] and may stem from Luke's use of prosopopoeia).

We can explain the brevity of most of the speeches and the presence of relatively few counterspeeches partly on the basis of Acts' short length compared with most of the histories in question; the others are multivolume works.[116] In his speeches Luke also shows less interest in displaying his rhetorical skills than in communicating their consistent message. But the most decisive factor in all the differences Soards cites is Luke's consistent concern for the apostolic message, a concern that surfaces in most of our earliest Christian writings. This was the same factor earlier noted above as most decisive in the dominance of speech material in the book.

Historians were to focus on features most important to their narrative (Dion. Hal. *Thuc.* 13–17). For Luke, what is most important is the apostolic witness narrating and explaining the story of Jesus, particularly his resurrection. (See the section below on the unity of Acts' speeches.)

109. Cf., e.g., Polyb. 9.28.1–31.6; 9.33.3–39.7.

110. Rather, "cameos" (Dunn, *Acts*, xviii), "abstracts" (Hemer, *Acts in History*, 427), or "synopses" (Gasque, "Speeches," 249).

111. See Witherington, *Acts*, 46. Others did sometimes abbreviate speeches found in their sources (Aune, *Environment*, 82, cites here Tac. *Ann.* 11.23–25; Jos. *Ant.* 12.417–18), and *Rhet. Alex.* 22, 1434b.11–18 provides directions for how to abbreviate speeches (circumstances also could dictate abridging some sections, e.g., Men. Rhet. 2.3, 379.2–4); but the speeches in Acts are often no more than précis.

112. Witherington, *Acts*, 46. Sometimes they help explain (e.g., Acts 7), but this is far less common than in even the Fourth Gospel (see Keener, *John*, 69–70). Perhaps fitting Luke's popular audience, the speeches themselves include action, the narrative element predominating. Helping translate somewhat analogously for modern audiences, a dynamic equivalent video rendering of Acts could keep the action moving by including clips of the actions that the speeches narrate.

113. Soards, *Speeches*, 143. This is not to deny Luke's interest in settings; Witherington, *Acts*, 46, contends that Luke gives more space to the speeches' narrative settings than appears in Thucydides.

114. Soards, *Speeches*, 142, cites Stephen's antitemple language and justification in Acts 13:39 (also, e.g., Munck, *Acts*, xliv); Plümacher, by contrast, cites Peter's "Pauline" language in 15:7–11.

115. As one must expect if one allows even that the speeches are not verbatim transcripts but rendered in Luke's own style, and in view of his likely sources having usually preserved, at most, a summary or random details of most speeches.

116. Even the reports in other histories do not represent full speeches, considering that most orations in the empire were limited to two hours (earlier speeches were not limited; Tac. *Dial.* 38; see comment on Acts 24:4). Counterspeeches do appear in Acts 19:25–27, 35–40; 24:2–21.

2. "Authenticity" of the Speeches

Because Acts is a historical monograph, modern readers who accept this classification often expect the speeches to be as "historical" (in the modern sense) as the narrative. Ancient historiography, however, employed speeches in a manner different from modern usage; although the event of the speech might be historical, the degree to which the content of a speech conformed to the actual speech delivered on that occasion varied according to the writer, his sources, and the extent to which any accurate memories of a speech existed. We turn, therefore, to one of the more hotly disputed questions in the study of Acts as ancient historiography.

The language of "authenticity," however, is the language of modern scholarship.[117] For ancients, a speech in keeping with a speaker's character and with what the speaker was likely to have said on an occasion would be authentic whether any memory of the speaker's exact words on that occasion were available or not. Even the most conservative historians wrote in a milieu where their audience expected a cohesive narrative fleshed out with action and speeches, constructed as plausibly as possible, rather than much of the sort of modern academic discussions of probabilities of what may have been said or done (often replete today with footnotes). Historians writing for more elite audiences would be evaluated by both how plausible and how rhetorically sensitive their speeches were to both the speakers and situations that they depicted. Especially in view of the divergence from modern practice, the question merits further exploration.

a. Historians Creating Speeches

Martin Dibelius established the major contour of the modern debate about the historical authenticity of speeches in Acts by arguing that Luke, like other ancient historians, composed his speeches.[118] Dibelius is correct that ancient historians composed their speeches; whether some of them did this at times partly by developing historical tradition or eyewitness memory where it was available is a separate question addressed in more detail below.[119]

Modern interpreters can better grasp the issues being debated if they recognize that the question of the speeches in Acts is not one of the "reliability" of Acts but of the genre—it is good ancient history, which, though related to its historical successors, is not exactly the same genre as modern history. Thus Henry Cadbury argues that ancient readers were accustomed enough to historians creating speeches that they read them "more as editorial and dramatic comment than as historical tradition."[120] He further notes, "If, as seems to me at present more likely, they are mainly the evangelist's own composition, they illustrate, as do the speeches and letters, how the author conforms to the customs of his literary inheritance—customs often quite different from our own."[121] Some historians may have drawn on actual speeches (and I shall take

117. See Judge, "Sources," 278–79, though observing on 280 the biblical origins of the valuing of authenticity that informs modern historiographic practice. Modern historians' generalizing summaries offer a functional equivalent to the more detailed speeches of ancient historians (279).

118. Dibelius, *Studies in Acts*, 3, 138–85; idem, *Tradition*, 16; Luke could develop materials as a historian writing literature, but he was an evangelist as well as a historian (*Studies in Acts*, 185). Dibelius did recognize, like Dodd, that the sermons' structure followed the ancient kerygma (*Tradition*, 16–18). Nock, *Essays*, 828–29, appreciated Dibelius's recognition of the difference between the character of narrative and speeches in ancient historiography.

119. Cf., e.g., the critique of C. Williams, *Acts*, 37–38.

120. Cadbury, *Making*, 185.

121. Ibid., 192–93. Ancient historical speech-writing, though different from modern practice, is not bad; we simply must understand its function (see Laistner, *Historians*, 16; cf. ibid., 42).

this practice into further account below), but even in these cases, many emphasized rhetorical appropriateness as a key element in their approach.[122]

I. Divergent Reports of Speeches in Antiquity

In view of this practice, it is not surprising that different historians often gave similar reports of events but widely diverging speeches, while preserving their basic message.[123] The most obvious case is the version of a speech of 48 C.E. that Tacitus, a mainly reliable historian, composed for his *Annals*, placing it in the mouth of the emperor Claudius; we have the original, and although it addresses the same subject (more, it might be noted, than some commentators allow for the speeches in Acts), Tacitus's report is his own composition.[124] This may have been Tacitus's common practice.[125]

Likewise, we possess different versions of the emperor Otho's final speech (despite agreements in narrative)[126] and Caesar's speech to his soldiers.[127] Still more tellingly, in terms of what ancient authors expected their audiences to accept, Josephus reports a well-known speech from 1 Maccabees differently from that well-known source[128] and even composed speeches for the same occasion differently in his various works.[129] Josephus is known for his rhetorical embellishment, but he is hardly alone.[130] Cadbury and his colleagues point out:

> When Livy follows Polybius for the facts of his narrative he almost regularly makes a change in the occasion and form of his speeches. So Plutarch and Tacitus agree very closely in their account of Otho but give entirely different reports of his last address. Josephus, who has occasion in his parallel works to deal twice with the same situation, puts two different speeches in the mouth of Herod. The speech of Caesar to his soldiers in Dio Cassius is very different from the brief address reported by Caesar himself on

---

122. So Walbank, *Speeches*, 19.

123. Cadbury, *Making*, 186–87.

124. With, e.g., Walbank, *Speeches*, 19; Woodman, *Rhetoric*, 13; Hadas, "Introduction," xvi; Judge, *First Christians*, 379–80. Laistner, *Historians*, 129, notes that he retains the substance of Claudius's speech and even some elements of his style, but the speech is largely in Tacitus's own style, deletes material that Claudius borrowed from an earlier speech, rearranges material, and even adds some observations.

125. Tacitus includes many speeches for which we cannot expect exact words to have been preserved (e.g., *Ann.* 2.71–72, 76, 77; 6.48; 11.7; 12.48; 13.21; 16.22), including private conversation (4.7, 52, 54, 68–69; 12.65); indirect speech also appears at events where we cannot be certain that scribes would have kept records (e.g., 12.2; 14.53–54, 55–56; 15.51). Even public speeches to the emperor or senate (e.g., 2.33, 37, 38; 3.33–36, 58, 69; 4.34–35, 37–38; 12.6, 37; 14.43–44; 16.28, 31; perhaps 13.42) will not have been preserved verbatim (though the substance would, presumably, appear in official records). Some speeches are even summaries of what people more generally (rather than an attributed individual) were saying (indirect but at length, in 3.17, 40; 14.20; 15.59; 16.25; more briefly, 4.64; 16.4, 29). Sometimes, however, sources close to the event may report conversation we would otherwise disregard (15.63, which Tacitus regards as too well known to repeat; 15.67, for which Tacitus seems to have exact words though they were not so widely published; cf. possibly 13.20). Probably, Tacitus often reports the substance of his sources, even when we suspect that the claims could have arisen originally from gossip or rumor (e.g., 14.9, 59). Tacitus elaborates speeches where contemporary biographers omit them (*Hist.* 1.29–30) or merely mention them (*Hist.* 1.15–16 with Suet. *Galba* 18.3; Plut. *Galba* 23.2), but sometimes includes the same point as in their summary (Tac. *Hist.* 1.83–84 with Plut. *Otho* 3.8; Tac. *Hist.* 2.47–48 with Suet. *Otho* 10.2; Plut. *Otho* 15.3–17.2; cf. Tac. *Hist.* 1.37–38 with Suet. *Otho* 6.3).

126. Talbert, *Mediterranean Milieu*, 211, cites Plut. *Otho* 15 and Tac. *Hist.* 2.47; but note comment above. For agreements in the narrative cf. Keener, "Otho."

127. Talbert, *Mediterranean Milieu*, 211, cites Caesar *Gall. W.* 1.40 vs. Dio Cass. 38.36–46.

128. Jos. *Ant.* 1.279–84 vs. 1 Macc 2:50–68 (Talbert, *Mediterranean Milieu*, 211).

129. Herod's speech to soldiers in Jos. *Ant.* 15.127–46 vs. *War* 1.373–79 (Talbert, *Mediterranean Milieu*, 211).

130. For rhetorically trained historians, reproducing speech sources verbatim may have smacked of something of the odium we attach to blatant plagiarism (except that the issue was one's reputation for rhetorical creativity, not one's integrity in crediting sources).

the same occasion. When the actual speech had been published the historian usually mentions the fact as a reason for omitting any speech of his own.[131]

Although these differences should not be exaggerated (as noted below), neither should they be underestimated by those who want to claim for Luke a degree of verbal accuracy in his speeches that was not part of his contemporaries' expectations for the ancient historical genre. One who wishes to ignore principles of the ancient genre may as well ignore that the work was written in Greek or by an author in the first century.

II. Pseudepigraphic Speech Composition in Other Genres

Greek orators regularly composed forensic speeches for their clients, even eliciting critics' remarks on the most effective ways to help them (e.g., Dion. Hal. *Lysias* 8). These rhetorical practices were too conventional to raise any ethical questions about "pseudepigraphy" in such cases. Orators could also create fictitious dialogues to address topics,[132] sometimes even between historical characters—for example, between Philip of Macedon and his son Alexander (Dio Chrys. *Or.* 2). (Justin's *Dialogue with Trypho* fits the same format, though it is not impossible that it recalls, albeit not fully accurately, elements of some actual dialogue[s] that Justin had.)[133] One could spice up one's subject matter by placing it in the literary form of an extensive dialogue (e.g., Cic. *Brut.* 3.10–96.330; *Fin.* passim; Plato passim).[134] That fictitious dialogues were a recognized literary form (not a deliberate deception) is clear from the fact that various friends of Cicero wanted their names used as characters in some of his (Cic. *Att.* 12.12).[135] Although these examples belong to a different genre from

131. Cadbury, Foakes-Jackson, and Lake, "Writing History," 13–14, comparing Plut. *Otho* 15 with Tac. *Hist.* 2.47; Jos. *War* 1.373–79 with *Ant.* 15.126–46; Dio Cass. 38.36–46 with Caesar *Gall. W.* 1.40; and for omissions of speeches, Sall. *Catil.* 31; Tac. *Ann.* 15.63. Cf. Toynbee, *Thought*, 179–80; Whittaker, "Introduction," lix. Plutarch, Livy, and Josephus are notoriously less careful with speeches; perhaps not all representatives would fare equally poorly.

132. E.g., Dio Chrys. *Or.* 15, between two highly literate Athenians. Dio uses dialogues in *Or.* 21, 23, 25, and 26 (though in *Or.* 25 Dio takes over speaking after initial interchanges); *Or.* 23 is in the form of a dialogue with one of his students (J. W. Cohoon in LCL, 2:301, suggests that *Or.* 23 might recall Dio's genuine pedagogic interactions).

133. Although the "dialogue with Jews" form developed a long history (Hulen, "Dialogues"; Bokser, "Justin and Jews," 98) and even Justin's conversion account seems stylized (Wilken, "Social Interpretation of Apologetics," 443; Osborn, *Justin*, 7; Kaye, *Apology*, 13–14; Chadwick, "Defence," 280), it might reflect genuine dialogue. Thus, for example, Trypho does not convert (Justin *Dial.* 142; see Schneider, "Reflections," 173, 175); some of his objections seem stronger than Justin's own case (e.g., *Dial.* 27, 55–56); and some of Justin's arguments (e.g., *Dial.* 46) may support a genuine debate in the mid-130s, though later elaborated with every subsequent argument he could find (see Barnard, *Justin Martyr*, 23–24, 39–40; Williams, *Justin Martyr*, xi–xix; cf. Osborn, *Justin*, 7; Kaye, *Apology*, 13–14; Chadwick, "Defence," 280; perhaps drawing on debates with various Jewish disputants: cf. *Dial.* 50; Aune, "Use," 184). Though we cannot isolate the source, Justin betrays some knowledge of postbiblical Jewish beliefs (Barnard, "Old Testament," 401, 406; idem, *Justin Martyr*, 45–46; Williams, *Justin Martyr*, xxxii–xxxiii, 80n4; Shotwell, *Exegesis*, 80, 89; Schneider, "Reflections," 168–69), though he also clearly misunderstands or misrepresents Judaism at points (see, e.g., Schneider, "Reflections," 169; Higgins, "Belief," 304–5; Bokser, "Justin and Jews," 112). Traditions like the hidden Messiah (Higgins, "Belief," 300; Williams, *Justin Martyr*, 18n2; Barnard, *Justin Martyr*, 46–47; Shotwell, *Exegesis*, 72) and apparent use of "Man" as a divine circumlocution (*Dial.* 59.1; *Eccl. Rab.* 2:21, §1; 8:1, §1; *Pesiq. Rab.* 14:10; Marmorstein, *Names*, 65–67) parallel rabbinic sources; by contrast, his dialogue offers some unsupportable claims, such as the one that the rabbis do not challenge belief in the Messiah's deity (cf. *Dial.* 63; Higgins, "Belief," 305; see *b. Men.* 110a; *Sanh.* 38ab; *Pesiq. Rab* 21:6).

134. In *Brutus*, Cicero employs real characters who knew him, and he may include some of their actual ideas; but this is hardly a verbatim presentation. (For a higher estimate of some of Cicero's and others' sources for dialogues, cf. Kennedy, "Source Criticism," 136).

135. Poets, of course, felt free to compose words for their characters, even if their story renders it impossible for surviving human witnesses to have recounted the words (e.g., Prop. *Eleg.* 3.7.57–64). Though citing epic and dialogue, Hermog. *Method* 20.436 freely attributes oaths contained therein to the composers (Homer *Od.*

historiography, they reflect the sort of rhetorical practices that Greek and Roman historians knew and probably made use of.

Some other kinds of pseudepigraphic works could be produced for a variety of motives, sometimes to invoke authority, sometimes to offer plausible guesses of the sort of work the attributed author would have created, and sometimes simply as a rhetorical exercise.[136] Thus some Jewish writers wrote works in the names of ancient heroes, such as *1 Enoch*, *4 Ezra*, and *2 Baruch*.[137] Roman writers sought to distinguish, for example, genuine from spurious plays of Plautus.[138] This is not to mention cases of deliberate deception, that is, forgeries.[139] But speeches in histories were not viewed as forgeries or pseudepigraphic works; they were an expected literary convention.

Sophists practiced creating speeches for earlier Greek heroes.[140] Older Greek works about historical personages employed such conventions widely. Dionysius complains that Plato's *Apology* for Socrates, while purporting to be Socrates's defense speech, "never saw even the threshold of a law-court or an open assembly"; it defies the genre of a true oration (Dion. Hal. *Demosth.* 23). (It would not therefore meet a historian's plausibility criterion.) Writers could invent speeches for opposing generals even when preserved historical tradition must have often been slender (e.g., Xen. *Cyr.* 3.3.43–45),[141] in addition to providing speeches for considering different sides of an argument (5.1.9–12).[142] Speech composition for other narrative genres inevitably affected historiography.[143]

III. Historians Composed Speeches

Historians also composed speeches, usually employing appropriate rules of rhetoric (see comment on historians and rhetoric in ch. 4 above).[144] Lacking verbatim reports

20.339; Plato *Gorgias* 489E). Xenophon countered Plato's *Symposium* and *Apology* with more realistic versions (though Plato knew Socrates better and they share some common, probably historical, tradition, e.g., Xen. *Symp.* 8.12; for a helpful evaluation of historical tradition, see Marchant, "Introduction," ix–xv, esp. x–xiv); Xenophon composes narrative better, but Plato dialogue.

136. This exercise apparently continued even into the Islamic period (Cook, *Dogma*, 51).

137. Brin, "Uses," thinks that the author of the *Temple Scroll* (esp. col. XLVIII) sought to imply for it Mosaic authorship; cf. elsewhere, e.g., Abegg, "Pseudo-prophets." Cf. Egyptian attribution of new works to Thoth (Frankfurter, *Religion in Egypt*, 240).

138. Aul. Gel. 3.3.

139. E.g., Polyb. 5.42.7; 5.50.11; Livy 40.55.1; Jos. *Life* 356; Pliny *Ep.* 6.22.3–4; 10.58.3; 10.65.2; Arrian *Alex.* 6.12.3 (though this work turned out to be genuine); Apul. *Metam.* 4.16; Philost. *Vit. Apoll.* 7.35; Iambl. *V.P.* 1.2; cf. Suet. *Vesp.* 6.4; for Roman laws regarding forgery, see Robinson, *Criminal Law*, 36–39 (cf. Quint. *Inst.* 5.5.1; sometimes addressing forged wills, e.g., Suet. *Aug.* 33.2; *Claud.* 9.2; 15.2); on ancient understanding of forgery, see, e.g., Judge, *Athens*, 75–76. A minority take this approach to documents believed pseudepigraphic in the NT (see Verhoef, "Pseudepigraphy"; idem, "Paulines"; idem, "Impact"); certainly, the patristic era rejected documents that were thought pseudepigraphic (Carson, "Pseudonymity," 860–63), though such works (e.g., the Cynic Epistles) were known among contemporaries. Cf. the distinctions between forgeries and propagandistic pseudepigraphy in Görgemanns, "Epistolography," 1146. Common though pseudepigraphy was, it was often viewed negatively (see Aune, *Dictionary of Rhetoric*, 388; Ehrman, *Forged*, views pseudepigraphy even more negatively).

140. Maclean and Aitken, *Heroikos*, xlix. Of less relevance here, some created fictitious attributions for speeches to give them authority while protecting the real authors from harsh retribution (Tac. *Ann.* 5.4).

141. Supposedly, deserters reported the substance to Cyrus (Xen. *Cyr.* 3.3.48), but this is a plausibility measure in a narrative that integrates fiction with history in a way rarely followed by successors. Although Xenophon may have woven in earlier anecdotes, he reports in direct speech the lengthy boyhood conversations of Cyrus (e.g., 1.3.2–18). For skepticism about generals' speeches, see Marincola, "Speeches," 128.

142. Though this does relate to the following narrative (Xen. *Cyr.* 5.1.18), it clearly ends with the wisdom of the more reliable character (5.1.12). As noted in ch. 2, Xenophon's *Cyropedia* is probably largely fictitious.

143. Penner, *Praise*, 208–11, compares with historians' speech composition the practice in rhetorical handbooks and the tragic conventions in Aristotle's *Poetics*.

144. E.g., Eckey, *Apostelgeschichte*, 32–34. Witherington, "Addendum," 24, 28–29, argues that this practice stemmed from particular historians and was never a "convention." He may define "convention" more narrowly than most do.

(and varying in the information available), historians offered speeches with as much verisimilitude for the speaker and occasion as possible.[145] Ancient authors wished to accommodate the expectations of their audiences, who appreciated speeches as a way to enliven narratives.[146] Most scholars (albeit with a significant dissenting minority) argue that Luke, as historian, would have followed this same practice.[147]

Some dissent, contending that NT scholars argue for such free composition by historians only to absolve Luke from the charge of dishonesty.[148] Thus Gerd Lüdemann objects, "Historians of ancient Greece and Rome did not consider themselves free to weave the speeches of important figures (the only kind they would report) out of the thread of their own imaginations."[149] But the sources that Lüdemann cites are limited,[150] and it is difficult to imagine that the long speeches of most historians reflect pure memory (far more difficult even than imagining the same for Luke's shorter reports). Although the extent to which they push their claim is problematic, Lüdemann and others are probably right to an extent: historians undoubtedly used traditions and sources where they had them available (often giving the substance of speeches given on particular occasions or at least thought to have been so given).

Claiming that historians composed full speeches does not normally mean that speeches did not occur on such occasions or even that the historians invented the speech's subject matter when the actual subject was known or earlier reported differently. Historians sought plausible verisimilitude, which often meant drawing on what was in fact known of the occasion, the subject, and the speaker's style.[151] Where they lacked material, however, plausible rhetorical constructions sufficed, and where they possessed it, they augmented and adjusted it according to rhetorical convention and plausibility.

Kennedy notes that as early as Herodotus, speeches (or a debate) could be created "to summarize in a vivid way the characteristics of monarchy, oligarchy, and democracy as he understood them."[152] Ancient writers were aware of this practice. Thus Dionysius comments on a speech "which Herodotus puts into the mouth of Xerxes" (Dion. Hal. *Demosth.* 41 [LCL]). Herodotus seems to have reacted against the narrower approach of Thucydides; Polybius, in turn, reacted against the free compositional approach of Herodotus and his successors, though this approach remained common.[153]

145. With, e.g., Horsley, "Speeches," 609; Ehrman, *Introduction*, 133–34. Some disciples sought to preserve as much as possible of the style and content of their teacher (Epict. *Diatr.* 1.pref., perhaps in contrast to Plato), but this would be more difficult for individual speeches.

146. Pliny E. *N.H.* pref. 12 complains that his *Natural History* is not a highly literary work, for it lacks "digressions, . . . speeches or dialogues" as well as striking incidents "interesting to relate or entertaining to read" (LCL, 1:9). For its readers, however, see, e.g., Symm. *Ep.* 1.24.

147. E.g., Dibelius, *Studies in Acts*, 138–85; Plümacher, "Luke as Historian," 398–99; Johnson, "Luke-Acts," 409; Talbert, *Acts*, 28–30.

148. Lüdemann, *Acts*, 24, avers that, at the very least, Luke freely composed a key speech of Jesus (Luke 4:18–27) from Mark 6:2. Historians could, in fact, expand on such a nugget as Mark 6:2, but we cannot prove that Luke did so in this case or regularly. First, our lack of a direct source for the speech in Luke 4 does not mean that Luke must have lacked such a source. But second and, in my opinion, more important, Luke's inaugural scene is a special one; this is one of only two significant places where he diverges from Mark's chronology, and it does not reflect a typical habit of his.

149. Lüdemann, *Acts*, 24.

150. He cites only Thucyd. 1.22.1 and Fornara, *Nature of History*, 154–55.

151. They might well depend for this on the known claims of earlier historians (whose own sources might ultimately be accurate or themselves freely composed). Laistner, *Historians*, 17, thinks that the basic picture the speeches conveyed was true, even if the words were invented.

152. Kennedy, *Classical Rhetoric*, 110, referring to Hdt. 3.80–83. In contrast to some later historians, Herodotus seems to have used an epic model (Pohlenz, according to C. Williams, *Acts*, 36–37).

153. Aune, *Dictionary of Rhetoric*, 448.

Nor did the practice of speech composition in histories end with the early Greeks. For example, Quintus Curtius in the first century offers speeches for the Persians that no one would expect to reproduce what was said on such occasions; they might be plausible or even reflect his sources, but the likelihood of their reflecting authentic eyewitness tradition is minimal.[154] Just a few decades after Luke, Pliny, whose standards for historical accuracy are normally high, praises an orator-historian who provides his characters speeches as excellent as his own, though more concisely (*Ep.* 1.16.4). Certainly, as late as Herodian, historians continued to invent speeches, though insisting that they should be historically plausible.[155] Diodorus Siculus opines that there is nothing wrong with historians seeking to display their rhetorical skills in speeches, composing "public discourses and speeches for ambassadors, likewise orations of praise and blame and the like; for by recognizing the classification of literary types and by elaborating each of the two by itself, they might reasonably expect to gain a reputation in both fields of activity" (Diod. Sic. 20.1.2 [LCL]). Though criticizing those who provide speeches inappropriate to their setting (20.1.1–4), he refuses to ban speeches from historical works completely, "since history needs to be adorned with variety . . . so that, whenever the situation requires either a public address from an ambassador or a statesman, or some such thing from the other characters, whoever does not boldly enter the contest of words would himself be blameworthy" (20.2.1 [LCL]).

As Aune notes, even those who published inscriptions of decrees failed to copy exactly the wording "of the originals . . . deposited in archives" but were satisfied to communicate the "gist" of those decrees. "If public inscriptions of official documents conveyed only the general substance," Aune asks, "why should historians aim at slavish imitation?"[156] As suggested above (sect. 2.a), some scholars cite as an example Claudius's rambling speech preserved as a transcript in an inscription (*ILS* 212 = *ARS* 175) versus the concise and rhetorically sensible version in Tacitus (*Ann.* 11.23–25, esp. 11.24).[157] Edwin Judge suggests that Tacitus "probably never saw the original, but developed his own version from an official digest of it, or from a summary in one of his predecessors."[158]

This example reveals that even Tacitus composed speeches for his history.[159] On the other hand, it also shows that he did so on the basis of a historical core of what Claudius said on the occasion (see discussion, in the next subsection, of capturing the gist).[160] As Conrad Gempf is careful to point out, Tacitus gives "the general sense" and even retains elements of Claudius's style, while greatly condensing.[161] Certainly,

---

154. Quint. Curt. 4.14.9–26 (a prebattle speech of Darius); 5.8.6–17; note also the advice speech of one of Darius's officials, 5.9.3–8; note esp. 3.2.11–16, where the speaker (3.2.17) and primary auditor die soon afterward. Naturally, Quintus Curtius also supplies speeches for the Greeks (4.14.1–6; 6.3.1–18; 6.8.15–6.9.24), including an impromptu defense speech (6.10.1–37).

155. Whittaker, "Introduction," lix (noting the requirement for plausibility in Thucyd. 1.22 and appropriateness in Lucian *Hist.* 58).

156. Aune, *Environment*, 82.

157. Ibid.

158. Judge, "Rhetoric of Inscriptions," 819.

159. Cf. also Tac. *Ann.* 15.63, where he plainly says that he does not need to reproduce Seneca's words exactly (Talbert, *Mediterranean Milieu*, 210). Laistner, *Historians*, 128, contends that as Tacitus matured his speeches grew more concise, with greater "individual characterization and more contrast between the speakers."

160. Compare Arrian's summary of his teacher Epictetus's teachings in *Encheiridion* with the more rambling *Diatribai*, which preserves even Epictetus's style through Arrian's more detailed notes.

161. Gempf, "Speaking," 284. A core could prove, not surprisingly, much shorter than rhetorical historians' (as opposed to Luke's) elaboration of speeches; even in recent history, extant notes for a genuine, three-and-a-half-hour speech may be read aloud in three minutes (Tomkins, *Wilberforce*, 80, 84).

Tacitus made no effort to deceive readers into thinking that he provided verbatim reports; everyone knew that historians composed speeches based on a basic knowledge, when available, of what was said.[162] Tacitus's contemporaries also knew him as a particularly outstanding orator (Pliny *Ep.* 2.11.17); his historical composition dared not waste his rhetorical talents without risking compromise to his reputation.

Balch argues that some historians felt that their readers would be dissatisfied with an epitome containing almost exclusively deeds (e.g., 2 Maccabees or Mark); they wanted to hear the reason for events, and so the historians provided narratives more fully, hence including speeches that explained events.[163] He concludes that "historians, including Luke, composed speeches that were not verbatim reports, but that like adverbs modify the verbal events of the narrative."[164] The speeches would thus be idealizations, even when based on earlier traditions about the apostolic message.

iv. The Ideal of Capturing the Gist

Historians regularly composed or "freely adapted" the speeches in their sources, but at least those who most valued the known models of Thucydides and Polybius tried to base their speeches on historical ones.[165] That is, the ideal was to capture the gist[166] but in their own words, wherever sufficient information to supply the gist was available. Ancients might evaluate some historical speeches only for appropriateness, but they would expect more substance if, for example, the author was present or heard them from those who were.[167] Ancient historians' freedom in composition did not require them to fabricate new speech events; often, as we shall observe below, they simply adapted what was available. As Aune notes, to omit "discourse material in their sources" was "usually unthinkable"; yet transcribing them without modification was "almost unthinkable" (for rhetorical reasons), and so most changed the language of what they found in their sources.[168] Gist was not objectionable; ancients relied on their memory to retrieve and arrange information because the standard for accuracy was the "gist."[169] Memory often preserves the gist of matters even when details remain more obscure or inaccurate.[170]

Scholars today often debate the specific meaning of Thucyd. 1.22.1, which provides that author's rationale for using speeches. Classicists themselves have interpreted his statement in various ways, but the majority read Thucydides as providing to speakers

---

162. Cf. Tacitus's qualifications regarding Galba's speech: "according to the report," he "spoke to this effect" (*Hist.* 1.15 [LCL, 1:27]); he "spoke further to the same effect" (1.16 [1: 33]); and "people report" the soldiers' response (1.17). On historians sometimes explicitly disavowing their reports being verbatim, see further Marincola, "Speeches," 120, citing, e.g., Polyb. 18.11; Sall. *Cat.* 50.5; Livy 37.45.11; Arrian *Anab.* 5.27.1; Tac. *Hist.* 1.15–16; *Agr.* 29.4, and noting that emphasis on verbatim quotes was rare and dealt with short lines (e.g., Tac. *Ann.* 14.59.4; 15.67.4). The only historian who offered verbatim speeches was Cato, and the speeches were his own (Woodman, *Rhetoric*, 13).

163. Balch, "Ἀκριβῶς," 229–39.

164. Ibid., 244.

165. Aune, *Environment*, 93, and sources he cites. Idem, *Dictionary of Rhetoric*, 448, seems to exempt only Thucydides and Polybius from sourceless speech composition (cf. Plümacher, "Luke as Historian," 398–99, perhaps not even exempting Thucydides), but (given our limited data) this verdict seems too narrow; for Arrian, see Hammond, "Speeches," and for even Livy, see discussion below.

166. As often noted, e.g., deSilva, *Introduction*, 351.

167. Thus Dion. Hal. *Thuc.* 41 would examine speeches only for appropriateness when he could infer from the narrative that Thucydides was neither present nor dependent on those who were (see Damon, "Rhetoric," 446).

168. Aune, *Environment*, 125.

169. See Small, "Memory." In ancient schools, see, e.g., Alexander, "Memory," 143.

170. So Bauckham, *Eyewitnesses*, 333–34 (citing memory studies), noting also variation in detail among the different Gospels, which nevertheless preserve the essential substance of events (such as Peter's denials, 344–45). See also Allison, *Jesus*, 11–13; Eddy and Boyd, *Legend*, 275–85, and the many memory studies they cite.

what it was expected that they should have said, "sometimes at least on the basis of what Thucydides or his sources remembered."[171] Thus he might recount a speech of Pericles that he himself heard, with the final product, however, being Thucydidean as well as Periclean.[172] Political speeches were rarely published until after Thucydides's day, and so he often had to depend on τὰ δέοντα, what fit the situations he depicted.[173] That is, he provided the most plausible historical reconstruction he could, instead of offering little or no reconstruction (an approach that, for an ancient audience, would have itself seemed a violation of the narrative's plausibility).[174]

But on what basis could Thucydides define and construct that which would be historically plausible? No one questions that the speeches are written in Thucydides's own style, but are they purely imaginative? Some scholars take ἡ ξυμπᾶσα γνώμη as the speech's "general intention" in the sense that Thucydides reconstructed the speeches solely on the basis of knowing the speech's situation and the speaker's political inclinations.[175] But another phrase of Thucydides in this passage might warn against such a free understanding of that phrase: τῶν ἀληθῶς λεχθέντων, "what in truth was said." Thucydides acknowledges that speeches' hearers would not recall them verbatim, so that he can merely give the general purport and reconstruct from the situation. Yet it is also clear that, where possible, he worked from genuine sources, seeking to balance available truth with rhetorical suitability.[176] One may doubt the precision of a number of his sources,[177] but his words suggest the approach that he considered the ideal.

In 1.22.1–2 Thucydides notes that he heard some speeches and that he had informants; that he cannot remember them in the same way that he recalls events; and that he has sought to represent plausibly the sorts of things the speakers would have said. He also claims (1.22.2) that this approach in the speeches contrasts with his more painstaking investigation of all the events he reports. Beyond such general contours, the precise sense of Thucydides's wording is probably more debatable on several points than either side in the argument has been willing to acknowledge.[178] Thucydides seems to be suggesting that he simply did the best he could, on the basis of whatever information he possessed plus historical imagination, to construct the speech close to the way it should have been spoken.[179]

171. C. Williams, *Acts*, 37, contrasting this common and mediating view with the extremes; cf. Witherington, "Addendum," 24–25.

172. See Zimmern, *Commonwealth*, 199 (as cited in Pelikan, *Acts*, 255).

173. Kennedy, "Survey of Rhetoric," 15. Marguerat, *Histoire*, 32–34, contends that Thucyd. 1.22.1 requires verisimilitude and appropriateness.

174. Thucydides probably did not use the speeches as an opportunity to show off his rhetorical skill; see the critique of this defect by the rhetorical historian Dionysius (Dion. Hal. *Pomp.* 3, cited by Fitzmyer, *Acts*, 105; Witherington, *Acts*, 48). Dionysius appears more interested in Thucydides's rhetorical inappropriateness than in his fictionalizing speeches (Marguerat, *Histoire*, 34).

175. A view noted in Walbank, *Speeches*, 3, as accepted by many German scholars in the mid-twentieth century. Woodman, *Rhetoric*, 11–12, argues (probably rightly) that Thucydides claims to recount only the gist, but on 12–13 argues (based esp. on memory studies, addressed below) that even the gist may have often been unavailable; he questions the degree of Thucydides's reliability on 9–47 (e.g., questioning his personal experience for the geographic digressions [15–16] and his claims to exclude myth and legend [16, 23]).

176. See Walbank, *Speeches*, 4. For this balance between fidelity and invention, see also Marincola, "Speeches," 121–22, noting further that (122) "his inability on occasion to learn the actual words spoken will have necessitated a certain amount of imaginative reconstruction." Porciani, "Enigma," 333–34, allows for an interpretive framework but argues against mere creation of passages based on imagination.

177. False information came into many ancient histories through their dependence on funeral eulogies, which often included falsified information (Woodman, *Rhetoric*, 91, citing Cic. *Brut.* 62; Livy 8.40.4–5).

178. See Porter, *Paul in Acts*, 110–12; idem, "Thucydidean View?"

179. Lest anyone question the use of historical imagination: even in Thucydides, the speeches are long and fleshed out. Woodman, *Rhetoric*, 13, suggests that Thucydides formed long speeches to rival Homer.

Thucydides's plan regarding speeches provided an important model for his successors, both Greek and Roman. Nevertheless, Thucydides's immediate successors often failed to share his interest in τῶν ἀληθῶς λεχθέντων.[180] Where did the average historian exercise the greatest freedom to develop his sources regarding speeches? C. W. Fornara, a specialist in Greco-Roman historiography, remarks: "The rhetorical formulations, the sometimes profound and sometimes elegant analyses, belong to the historians; so does the organization of the material in accordance with rhetorical principle. Everything was heightened, made precise, given point and relevance from foreknowledge of events."[181] Others allow that historians could invent speeches to enliven the narrative, but also contend that historians such as Thucydides sometimes had a précis containing recollections of a speech.[182]

In general, the more distant in time the reported speech, the greater the necessity for the historian's imagination to reconstruct it. Sometimes historians must have even merely inferred, rather than known, that a speech was delivered at a given event.[183] Yet this was not always the case. Even if Fornara exaggerates the frequency with which the ideal was attained (as some other scholars suggest, probably rightly), at least his arguments warn against hastily dismissing the possibility of historians' composed speeches ever preserving the gist of historical speeches: "But these imperfections in the practice of the historians should not detract from the basic integrity of their approach, even if that approach substantially differs from our own, and it is therefore reasonable to assume that we possess the core of the speeches as well as the record of the deeds of the Greeks from (at least) the end of the sixth to the first century B.C."[184] A reasonable guess of the sort of speech given on an occasion, though highlighting the author's interests, would not be welcome in a modern history textbook. That the subject and perspectives of such speeches were, to most historians' knowledge, often based on as much knowledge as possible of the speeches' historical substance (or at least their primary agenda) brings us closer to modern historical interests but still differs from the way we write history. Ancient history was in this respect a somewhat different genre from its modern successor, with somewhat different rules.[185]

These caveats do not fully resolve the nature of historical tradition in speeches from one historian to the next. Although different historians recording the same events followed rhetorical convention in composing different speeches and, further, employed speeches to entertain, Cadbury and others note that the more serious historians still set limits and preserved, where available, the basic message of the speeches.[186] Normally, Greek historians, while filling out the contents of speeches,

180. Walbank, *Speeches*, 4. Yet Marincola, "Speeches," 123–27, shows that Thucydides's model remained an ideal; Croke, "Historiography," 567–68, shows that he was most read and probably the prime model.

181. Fornara, *Nature of History*, 167.

182. Horsley, "Speeches," 609.

183. Fornara, *Nature of History*, 167–68.

184. Ibid., 168. Even Roman reports of speeches (less relevant to a discussion of Luke-Acts) apparently are "substantially trustworthy from the time of the Second Punic war to the end of the fourth century A.D." (168). Of course, even where writers may have adapted a speech from earlier sources, the earliest source in the chain could have composed the speech more freely; subsequent preservation and the ideal of historical fidelity do not by themselves guarantee historical veracity in the modern sense. I am thus less optimistic than Fornara, though I acknowledge that the gist may have been preserved in many cases.

185. Ibid., 142. Many modern readers, indeed, would prefer at most a summary of the speech's thrust and effect to its plausible reconstruction, just as some of my students, accustomed to fast-action television, prove bored with the long speech of Stephen in Acts 7:2–53.

186. Cadbury, *Making*, 186–87; Hanson, *Acts*, 36; Gempf, "Speaking," 264, 299. See especially the balance in Marincola, "Speeches," 121: "in almost every historiographical speech there will have been a mixture of what was actually known and what could be surmised."

did not invent the actual events or occasions of the speeches. Such events were historical events no less than battles,[187] even if one could merely guess what was spoken on many occasions of the distant past.

Thus the better[188] Greek historians would include the substance of what was spoken if this were available to them (this much, at least, seems implied in Thucyd. 1.22.1). The range of speech-writing practices among ancient historians (from the general fidelity of Thucydides and Polybius to the often-blatant fabrications of Josephus) makes it impossible to predict a priori Luke's accuracy purely on the basis of any historiographic "convention" of speech writing.[189]

v. Criticisms of Inappropriate Creativity

Despite some differences between ancient and modern history, ancient historians were capable of asking the same critical questions that we are asking today. Dionysius grants that Thucydides was often present, participating in what he reports (Dion. Hal. *Thuc.* 6). But from what Thucydides himself says, he was an exile in Thrace during a later part of his book and could not have heard a speech reported elsewhere (*Thuc.* 41). We could respond that Thucydides maintained contact with his friends and hence would have had access to the basic contents of the speech, but Dionysius is more skeptical. Arguing that we must evaluate whether the dialogue he composed fits the known facts and character of the delegates, he doubts whether Thucydides lived up to his introductory promise in Thucyd. 1.22 to stick to the basic point of what was said in some parts of the speech (Dion. Hal. *Thuc.* 41).

Likewise, Polybius proves quite critical, at least in the standards he uses to evaluate his apparent nemesis, Timaeus. (That Polybius expects his readers to be outraged just as he is probably implies the normal historiographic expectations of his day, at least in his circles.)[190] He complains that Timaeus neither quotes speakers nor provides their general sense but supplies what he thinks they *should* have said, using their speeches as an occasion to display his rhetorical skills (Polyb. 12.25a.4–5). This approach, Polybius insists, violates the particular purpose of writing history, which includes discovering the words originally spoken (12.25b.1); by introducing his own rhetorical practice rather than dealing with the genuine speeches, Timaeus "destroys the peculiar virtue of history" (12.25b.4 [LCL]). As a crowning blow, Polybius complains that on top of all this, Timaeus is rhetorically inept as well (12.25k.8; 12.26.9)!

We should not press Polybius's demand for accurate speeches in any modern verbatim sense. Even Polybius cannot avoid introducing some generals' speeches—for example, supplying both those of Roman officers and those of the Carthaginian Hannibal.[191] He could well have had access to, and passed on the substance of, the Roman speeches (and possibly even some Carthaginian ones), but he reports them as direct speech, not merely the summaries that, at best, he had.

---

187. Cf. Gempf, "Speaking," 264: "Just as a writer was expected to represent faithfully the strategies, tactics and results of a battle . . . so a writer was expected to represent faithfully the strategies, tactics and results of a speech, without necessarily recording the exact words used on the day."

188. That is, from our perspective and their own; their detractors, naturally, would have differed in such estimates.

189. Gempf, "Speaking"; cf. also his dissertation (idem, "Appropriateness"); also Witherington, "Addendum," 24, 28–29; idem, *Acts*, 48, 117, 455; Hemer, *Acts in History*, 75–78.

190. Gempf, "Speaking," 272. Polybius may exaggerate Timaeus's failure here; cf. Marincola, "Speeches," 125.

191. E.g., Polyb. 3.63.3–13; 3.64.5–8; 3.108.6–109.12; 3.111.3–10. For other speeches, see, e.g., 9.28.1–31.6; 9.33.2–39.7; 11.4.1–7.8; 11.28.3–29.13. Walbank, *Speeches*, 12, argues that Polybius does have military speeches in his sources; although this may well be the case, Polybius undoubtedly develops them. Other historians also use speeches of opposing leaders, not likely preserved in significant detail (e.g., Tac. *Ann.* 14.35; 15.1, 2).

Some historical writers during the empire may reveal careful memory of speech material. Seneca the Elder reports that he remembered details of speeches from his school days (*Controv.* passim), though his memory was exceptional. Indeed, sometimes a writer would provide only the purport of a known speech, refraining from trying to reproduce it because his source could recall only the gist (Eunapius *Lives* 484).[192] We must revisit the question of memory and speeches further below (sect. 2.c).

VI. THE ACTUAL PRACTICE OF LIVY

Ancient historiographic theory allowed a writer to put a speech in his own words, provided he did not invent the content.[193] Thus, for example, some scholars argue that Arrian abbreviated and adapted to his own words the speeches in his sources but faithfully followed their gist.[194] In practice, most historians seemed to recognize that their fellow historians did retain the essential substance of speeches that they found in their sources.[195] Granted, this does not tell us how reliable their sources were, but it suggests that there was a conservative as well as a creative rhetorical element in historians' treatment of speeches when they had sources for these speeches.

A critical test case for this principle is Livy; as a *rhetorical* historian, he, if anyone, would adapt speeches. Yet where Livy covers the same speeches as Polybius, he retains the gist, despite "liberties with content and staging," instead of inventing something new; that is, he is basically reliable regarding the gist. Some of his minor alterations of the history may reflect other prior sources; in any event, "he substantially reproduced the source-content of the speeches he inherited from others."[196] As one expert points out, "Livy treats the speeches in his sources with some respect, reproducing the content while changing the form, and almost always adding to the length of the speech considerably, without thereby adding fictitious topics, and what additions are there can often be chalked up to the attempt to give a convincing character study."[197] Indeed, another historian observes that even Pompeius Trogus, with the worst excesses, avoids "free fiction."[198]

Speech writing became problematic only when Roman historians tried to write "ancient" history for which they no longer had oral traditions (e.g., writing during the empire about "the monarchy and the early republic").[199] Even regarding ancient speeches, historians often resorted to older historians' reports of such speeches (whatever the source of these older reports). These sources continued to circulate during the empire, and some speakers used them for oratorical practice (Dio Chrys. *Or.*

---

192. That writers could choose to omit some passages from speeches (Philost. *Vit. soph.* 2.29.621) assumes that they did have copies of the speeches (by this period, often published).

193. Fornara, *Nature of History*, 143–54. Cf. Gempf, "Speaking," 264: "Woe betide the historian if the speech is not *faithful* to the alleged situation and speaker."

194. Esp. Hammond, "Speeches."

195. Fornara, *Nature of History*, 154–68.

196. Ibid., 160–61; also Witherington, *Acts*, 40. For Livy's selection and adaptation of earlier sources, see Luce, *Livy*; Forsythe, *Livy* (cited in Forsythe, "Quadrigarius," 396). For Livy's composition of speeches to provide characterization for the speakers, see Laistner, *Historians*, 96. Though unwilling to extrapolate to other speeches, Laistner, *Historians*, 97, notes that Livy is less rhetorically attentive when reproducing Polybius's speeches closely.

197. Gempf, "Speaking," 283 (based on comparison of such speech reports as Polyb. 3.62ff.; 11.28ff.; 15.6.4ff.; 21.19ff. with Livy 21.42–43; 28.27ff.; 30.30; 37.53–54; noting Walsh, *Livy*, 231). Historians would adapt their predecessors' speeches when they reported the same speech occasions (rather than composing speeches for different occasions, as they also did), but they felt bound to their basic content (Marincola, "Speeches," 129, giving as examples Livy's reworking of Polybius and Tacitus's of Claudius).

198. Fornara, *Nature of History*, 161. Regarding excesses, Laistner, *Historians*, 16, notes that modern historiography also has pockets of excess (citing "economic determinists").

199. Fornara, *Nature of History*, 166–67.

13.14–15; 18.18–19).[200] Further, when historians invented these ancient speeches, comparing other sources indicates that they at least sometimes reflected kernels of historical information.[201]

VII. THE QUESTION OF ACTS

How does Luke fare in these terms? Most scholars regard historians such as Thucydides as much more careful than Livy (who had a much longer period of history to cover and more compelling literary interests). But as Fitzmyer observes, "Thucydides and Luke," unlike Livy, "were recording events that were more or less of their own times." One would expect them more often to have access to, and provide the nonverbatim substance of, the speeches they report.[202] (And even Livy, as we have observed, has a conservative element.) It is true that Josephus writes about events close to his own time as well, but it is difficult to question that Luke shows far more rhetorical restraint (or modesty about his more limited skills) in his summary speeches than does Josephus.[203]

To claim that historians had wide latitude in speech composition is not to claim that each of them exploited this latitude to the same degree as others or equally in all of their speeches; hence it does not establish the degree of freedom that Luke took in all his speeches. It merely establishes the outer limits of freedom that Luke could have pressed while remaining a writer of ancient historiography. The parameters on the other side—namely, how faithfully Luke might have reported speech material—must be explored by other means (here the historian may investigate Luke's access to such information, correspondence with extrinsic data, etc.). Unified style is a less useful criterion, since it establishes only that the material is Lukan, not that it cannot be Luke's selection and adaptation of prior material from his own perspective.

A major factor in historians' creativity in speeches was the display of rhetorical prowess in constructing entire speeches intended to plausibly represent what could best be imagined to have been said on an occasion. Although Luke presumably does follow this general approach of plausible construction (and it is virtually certain that he does so in Acts 25:14–22), he provides mere summaries, not entire speeches; in contrast to most models under discussion, he shows no interest in rhetorical expansion. Thus Charles Talbert, after pointing out the compositional practices of ancient historians noted above,[204] comments, "The brief speeches in Acts . . . bear no resemblance to the rhetorical compositions of Josephus," which might allow "that some or all of the speeches in Acts are a digest or summary of what was actually said."[205]

Luke certainly is willing to report the gist rather than strive for (or even wish to appear to be striving for) a verbatim report, as is evident from occasions where he repeats a report in varied words (e.g., compare Luke 24:47–49 with Acts 1:4–8; Acts 10:4–6 with 31–32; and 10:14 with 11:8). Ancients valued literary variation.[206] The frequently recurring themes in Luke's speeches (see discussion in sect. 3 below)

200. In Dio Chrys. *Or.* 13.14–15, Dio refers to a speech of Socrates. This may be spurious; but it is earlier than Dio, and he believes it to be such a speech. In 18.18–19, he refers to written speeches in Xenophon.

201. Cf. the examples (e.g., Quint. Curt. 9.6.13–15 with Arrian *Alex.* 6.13.4–5) in Quintus Curtius (who invents most of his speech material) in Baynham, "Reception," 297–99.

202. Fitzmyer, *Acts*, 105.

203. See, e.g., Dudley, "Speeches," who also ranks Luke closer to Thucydides than to Livy or Josephus.

204. Talbert, *Mediterranean Milieu*, 210–11.

205. Ibid., 211–12; cf. Marshall, *Acts*, 41. Talbert, *Mediterranean Milieu*, 211, also notes Polybius's complaint about Timaeus (Polyb. 12.24–25).

206. E.g., Aul. Gel. 1.4; Cic. *Or. Brut.* 46.156–57; *Fam.* 13.27.1; Max. Tyre 21.4; cf. Cic. *Brut.* 91.316; Anderson, *Glossary*, 53–54, 114; Trapp, *Maximus*, 182n9; Nock, "Vocabulary," 137; Lee, "Translations of OT," 776–77; Keener, *John*, 324–25. One should merely take care to avoid "improper" synonyms (Rowe,

also suggest that Luke's own theological interests help shape how he reports these speeches.[207]

Still, one might hope that Luke, given his sources (e.g., Luke 1:1–3; Acts 16:10), had better access to the basic gist of what was spoken than did those who wrote about events long past. Luke produces a more monolithic tract than most historians writing larger works with literary ambitions, but he also exhibits less desire to display his own rhetorical skill and preserves much shorter speeches. Luke's speeches are usually rhetorically weaker than some other parts of his work, and whereas other historians often lengthened their "gist," Luke's concise speeches may summarize rather than expand (cf. Acts 2:40).[208]

These factors support the possibility that historical tradition stands behind many of his speeches. That Luke writes about recent, rather than distant, events allows him to take the approach of historians such as a Thucydides more readily than that of a Livy, as I note elsewhere.[209] Certainly, where Luke adapts Jesus's speech in Mark (e.g., Mark 13:5–37 in Luke 21:8–36), his adaptations leave in place the essential substance of a speech (even if Luke's perspective is considerably more historicized). This comparison, admittedly, should not be pressed too far: in Acts, Luke is usually not dealing with the sayings of the Lord (apt to be most carefully preserved and transmitted) and probably not with written sources.[210] Moreover, for the Jerusalem church, Luke may have better information about the kind of preaching that flourished there than about the points of particular speeches on the occasions he reports;[211] the ancient historian's task of verisimilitude, even at its best, required no more than that he construct such speeches as plausibly as possible from his tradition.

As already noted, Acts on occasion may report conversations to which Luke and his sources would not likely have been privy (Acts 25:14–22). In such cases one would not be surprised if Luke composed the account according to what he deemed probable rather than according to an oral or written source; in so doing, he would simply have been following the procedure expected for ancient historians.[212] But in many

---

"Style," 123–24); for ancient discussion of synonyms, see, e.g., Porph. *Ar. Cat.* 68.5–27. In some writers, a more consistent sense obtained, but this was unusual (Aul. Gel. 2.5.1).

207. That Luke uses speeches as theological commentary on his narrative is likely; some scholars have also suggested that the narratives illustrate the themes articulated in the speeches (Hinkle, "Preaching," 100).

208. With T. Smith, "Sources," 75.

209. See ch. 4, sect. 1.d; also, e.g., Keener, *Historical Jesus*, 102–5 and notes 95–150 on 445–48; Fitzmyer, *Acts*, 105.

210. As noted by Bruce, *Acts*³, 35; cf. Aune, *Dictionary of Rhetoric*, 326. There is also debate as to whether Luke expands Jesus's inaugural speech (we cannot discount the possibility that Luke possessed sources in addition to Mark 6:1–4; see Luke 1:1), but this case may be a special one, since it is Luke's programmatic scene and one of the very rare occasions where he diverges from Mark's sequence.

211. Cf. Marshall, *Acts*, 41, noting that, in general, the evidence for tradition is "insufficient to demonstrate that all the speeches were actually delivered on the occasions specified—a point which probably lies beyond historical proof in any case." Hengel, *Peter*, 85, suggests that, given Peter's prominence in the gospel tradition and even more as leader of the early apostolic movement, Luke could have had genuine Petrine tradition available for his Petrine speeches.

212. With, e.g., Witherington, *Acts*, 119–20. In epic genres, one could invoke inspiration to make up for one's lack of knowledge (Keener, *John*, 116; cf. Philost. *Hrk.* 43.6; Nagy, "Prologue," xxx–xxxiv; Maclean and Aitken, *Heroikos*, xliii, xlix-l); not all expected such inspiration to prevent all error or bias (cf. Philost. *Hrk.* 24.1–2; 25.2–17; also Ramelli, *Hierocles*, 98, on Hierocles *Gods* criticizing Hom. *Il.* 9.497 in Stob. *Ecl.* 1.3.53; less relevantly, cf. Lucian *True Story* 2.32; Libanius *Refutation* 1.1–3, 12; 2.1; *Invective* 7.2), but it certainly was often thought to help (cf., e.g., Libanius *Confirmation* 2.1–2). (Gentiles did approach Homer differently than the way that Jewish people approached the Torah; see Rives, *Religion*, 28.) But while Luke might have allowed biblical prophet-historians this possibility (cf., e.g., 2 Kgs 6:12), it is not part of the Polybian or Thucydidean historiographic tradition; then again, Josephus's view of his prophetic ability shows that it need not have been incompatible with Jewish historiographies.

more cases, especially for Pauline speeches, Luke could have had genuine sources, often eyewitness reports or summaries (for Luke's or his source's possible access to Paul, see ch. 11, sect. 3.a, below, and esp. comment on Acts 16:10).

Dibelius was right that historians neither expected nor desired verbatim quotation of speeches, but we should also take very seriously the criticism that Dibelius's late dating of Acts caused "him to underestimate an ancient historian's desire to include, so far as possible, in the speeches recorded the 'general sense' of what was said or would have been said on each occasion, so far as Luke or his informants remembered."[213] The length of most historians' speeches, one factor that leads us to suppose most historians' creativity, is much greater than that of the speeches in Acts.

Thus Luke may have developed historical traditions about the topics of speeches on given occasions with other traditions about the way these speakers or parts of the church, in general, taught (see discussion of prosopopoeia below). He undoubtedly developed this material further to produce coherent speeches, but given his speeches' unusual brevity, he apparently developed his material less thoroughly than did most other historians.

b. Prosopopoeia

Scholars have found primitive Christology in some of the speeches (e.g., "God appointed Jesus as Christ"; "servant"; "holy one").[214] Although not all these scholars' arguments are fully persuasive, those features they identify that may genuinely reflect primitive Christology need not reflect tradition on the precise words used on a particular occasion but might fit the practice of προσωποποιία (prosopopoeia)[215] or, by a number of ancient rhetoricians' narrower and more technical definitions, ἠθοποιία (ethopoeia).[216] Most rhetoricians applied the term προσωποποιία to any kind of personification whereby one provides speech for whatever or whoever is clearly not speaking (e.g., a country or one's ancestors).[217] Those using this device nearly always identified the speaker.[218]

As noted below, where no report of a specific speech's contents was available, historians might compose what they thought the speaker would have said, aiming for verisimilitude; this practice resembled composing speeches "in character."[219] Lucian

213. C. Williams, *Acts*, 37–38. For a similarly nuanced perspective, written long before Dibelius, on ancient historians regarding both gist and attempted accuracy, see Abbott, *Acts*, 15, from 1876.
214. E.g., Knox, *Acts*, 75; Zehnle, *Pentecost Discourse*, 56–60; Robinson, "Primitive Christology."
215. Some have suggested Luke's skill in this exercise (Kennedy, *New Testament Interpretation*, 114–40; Burridge, "Gospels and Acts," 520; Aune, *Environment*, 125). It also appears in diatribe (Stowers, *Diatribe*, 90–91; Tobin, *Rhetoric in Contexts*, 93, citing Epict. *Diatr.* 1.4.28–29; 1.9.12–16; 1.26.5–7, 10, 20–22, 26–49; 3.24.68–70, 97–102); see further Anderson, *Glossary*, 106–7; Rowe, "Style," 144; Tobin, *Rhetoric in Contexts*, 227 (citing, e.g., Theon *Progymn.* 2.117.6–32; Quint. *Inst.* 4.1.28; 6.1.25–27; 9.2.29–30). (It is probably implied also in Lucian *Dance* 65.) At a more advanced level, declamations integrated speeches-in-character exercises with other basic rhetorical exercises (Bloomer, "Declamation," 299).
216. Many rhetoricians technically limited "prosopopoeia" to personified things, using "ethopoeia" for real persons (e.g., Hermog. *Progymn.* 9, "On Ethopoeia," 20; Aphth. *Progymn.* 11, "On Ethopoeia," 44–46S, 34–36R, esp. 44–45S, 34R; Nicolaus *Progymn.* 10, "On Ethopoeia," 64–65). Cf. also the application of "prosopopoeia" to nonhuman things and *sermocinatio* to humans in Rowe, "Style," 144 (citing, for the former, Demosth. *Fals. leg.* 119; Cic. *Cat.* 1.7.18 and, for the latter, Demosth. *Fals. leg.* 235; Aug. *Ep.* 108.17); for *sermocinatio*, see also Porter, "Paul and Letters," 582 (citing 1 Cor 1:12); see further Anderson, *Glossary*, 33 (citing Dion. Hal. *Thuc.* 37; *Rhet. Her.* 4.65; Quint. *Inst.* 9.2.31); an example in Tzounakas, "Peroration." Ethopoeia was a form of what was more generally called prosopopoeia (Anderson, *Glossary*, 60–61).
217. E.g., Demet. *Style* 5.265 (he cites [5.266] an example in Plato).
218. Aune, *Dictionary of Rhetoric*, 383, citing Quint. *Inst.* 9.2.37. Naturally, this would always be the case in historical narrative.
219. Cf. Aune, *Environment*, 93, 125; Johnson, *Acts*, 53; Penner, *Praise*, 211–12.

advised using prosopopoeia by letting the speaker's language fit the person and the subject, though he permitted rhetors the freedom to use the opportunity to display their own eloquence;[220] this was, Lucian expected, the procedure for a true historian.[221]

Writing speeches in character for various characters of the past was a common rhetorical exercise (Theon *Progymn.* 8), and it could include what some other rhetoricians called "ethopoeia," speaking in the *ēthos*, or character, of a person.[222] One might, for example, write about "What Words Niobe Might Say When Her Children Lie Dead,"[223] or even a (mock) defense for Phaleris, who sent Delphi a tainted gift.[224] One should retain what suited the person and the situation—for example, what fit an older versus a younger man or a rejoicing person versus a mourning one.[225] Dio Chrysostom commonly invented "appropriate" speeches for characters; for example, he creates a fictitious dialogue between Alexander the Great and Diogenes the Cynic as a way to illustrate a theme (Dio Chrys. *Or.* 4).[226] Some created fictitious dialogues to emulate the styles of particular classes of people.[227] Such created speech also appears in first-century Stoic diatribe,[228] and even the early Stoic philosopher Chrysippus employed this technique (προσωποποιεῖν, Fronto *Eloq.* 1.15). Cicero, for example, demonstrates his command of various philosophic systems by supplying suitable lines for each of the speakers in *De finibus* and other dialogues.[229]

Ancient rhetorical critics were sensitive to matters of individual style and did practice stylistic criticism; thus, for example, though none of the elements of Demosthenes's style are exclusive to him, they are characteristic of him and cumulatively help distinguish him from others (Dion. Hal. *Demosth.* 50). Many also emphasized realism in speeches; thus Pseudo-Longinus criticizes writers of tragedies who employ bombast in speeches even though they do not sound like real speeches (Longin. *Subl.* 3.1).[230]

Appropriateness in composition was important.[231] Rhetors should be sensitive to local color and values (Quint. *Inst.* 3.7.24) and should address different kinds of assemblies (e.g., forensic speech for juries, usually deliberative for political assemblies,

220. Johnson, *Acts*, 53, citing Lucian *Hist.* 58 (also cited in Talbert, *Mediterranean Milieu*, 211).
221. Hengel, *Acts and History*, 61. Some rhetorical exercises included "impersonation" (Lucian *Dance* 65).
222. See Butts, *Progymnasmata of Theon*, 459n; cf. Maclean and Aitken, *Heroikos*, xlix; for its importance in later antiquity, see Gibson, "Notes," xxi. Greek students also learned to imitate the style of famous authors (Oldfather, "Introduction to Epictetus," xiv; cf. Aune, *Environment*, 31).
223. Later in Aphth. *Progymn.* 11, "On Ethopoeia," 45–46S, 35–36R; Libanius *Speech in Character* 8. Niobe is a mythical example; both mythical and historical examples were used (Gibson, "Notes," 355).
224. Lucian *Phal.* passim (though most rhetorical exercises of writing in character were *not* tongue in cheek, as noted by A. M. Harmon in *Lucian*, LCL, 1:1).
225. Hermog. *Progymn.* 9, "On Ethopoeia," 21, associating ἦθος (*ēthos*) with the speaker and πάθος (*pathos*) with the emotional situation involved. Some characterizations focused on emotion and others on character (Aphth. *Progymn.* 11, "On Ethopoeia," 44–45S, 35R; Nicolaus *Progymn.* 10, "On Ethopoeia," 64).
226. Dio notes that Diogenes was an exile (Dio Chrys. *Or.* 4.1), and compares himself with him (4.3). Many of Dio's speeches involve dialogues of Diogenes (*Or.* 4; 6 [partly describing, partly quoting]; 8; 9; 10) or Alexander (with Philip, *Or.* 2; with his superior Diogenes, *Or.* 4); cf. also "Pheidias's" speech about graven images (taking up much of *Or.* 12).
227. See, e.g., Alciphron *Letters of Fishermen*; *Letters of Courtesans*; Aelian *Letters of Farmers*; cf. Maclean and Aitken, *Heroikos*, xlix.
228. Tobin, *Rhetoric in Contexts*, 93 (citing Epict. *Diatr.* 1.4.28–29; 1.9.12–16; 1.26.5–7, 10, 20–22, 26–49; 3.24.68–70, 97–102).
229. Cicero is rhetorically superior to Plato on this point, presupposing a more careful study of various alternative systems of thought.
230. An example in Longin. *Subl.* 3.2 is Gorgias of Leontini calling Xerxes the "Persian Zeus."
231. See Black, "Oration at Olivet," 88 (who cites esp. Arist. *Rhet.* 3.2, 1404b–1450b; Cic. *Or. Brut.* 75–121; *De Or.* 3.9.37–39; 3.52.199; Quint. *Inst.* 1.5.1; 8.1–11). A rhetorical speech in the mouth of a non-rhetorician's character could even denounce rhetoricians (Quint. *Decl.* 268.16–20).

and epideictic for festivals) differently (Dion. Hal. *Lysias* 9).[232] Greek historians frequently used archaizing language when representing the speech of ancients, and so Luke might have deliberately utilized earlier christological titles in some of the early speeches.[233]

This archaizing would suggest, however, that if Luke did not have access to the exact words spoken on those occasions, he was, at the least, aware of the christological language believed to be employed in earlier times and how it differed from current dominant usage.[234] Socrates's successors differed in their interpretation of him, and their reports of his specific words differ substantially; but all reproduced his lofty style (Xen. *Apol.* 1) and often shared common topics.[235] This practice could suggest that even where a historian like Luke may lack historical tradition about the wording of a particular speech, he could make use of historical tradition about the kinds of speech typically used by the speaker or those like him on such occasions, and hence offers the most reasonable suggestion about a particular speech (for which tradition may have supplied the setting and thrust). Such factors could prove helpful for historians' hopes to create "plausible" history.

c. Preserved Speeches

Jervell argues that tradition would have preserved the teaching of the apostles as well as that of Jesus. He notes that Paul's letters present as already known to the churches the preaching of apostles and Jerusalem leaders (see, e.g., 1 Cor 1:12; 9:5; 15:5, 7; Gal 1:18–19; 2:7–14); the churches also remembered Paul's ministry and preaching (e.g., 1 Thess 1:5–9).[236]

Still, although these arguments suggest that the church preserved the apostles' *message*, they fail to demonstrate that it preserved their individual speeches. The apostolic message was foundational (Eph 2:20; 3:5), but it is doubtful that Christians had the same interest in preserving their sayings, apart from their witness to the gospel tradition, as in preserving those of their Lord. Even Jesus's sayings can appear in different settings in different Gospels, fitting biographers' freedom to rearrange their material, which was not typically preserved as discrete speeches.[237] Precisely because Jesus and the apostles spoke so much, recalling particular speeches out of the many that were surely offered probably happened only for particularly dramatic occasions.[238]

Although such arguments for preserving early apostles' individual speeches are thus not compelling, neither are arguments that all such speeches would have been forgotten. If modern Westerners can recall the major thrust of some very significant or famous speeches over the course of several decades, it is all the more likely that ancient hearers, more familiar with oral traditioning, could have done so. Moreover,

232. Thus rhetoricians criticized dramatists who used bombast in character's speeches, because it failed to resemble genuine speech (Longin. *Subl.* 3.1–2). One might praise a rhetor who used a more diverse array of arguments, ideas, and presentation, though many failed in this (Dion. Hal. *Lysias* 17; *Isaeus* 3).

233. Soards, *Speeches*, 140, following Plümacher, *Lukas*, 72–78. Romans also used deliberate archaisms "to impart solemnity" (Holford-Strevens, "Archaism").

234. Likewise, although Luke's Gospel often calls Jesus "Lord," raising the suspicions of some (e.g., Sandmel, *Judaism*, 369), until the resurrection, the vast majority of nonvocative uses of this title by mortals are from the narrator himself, not participants in the story (Moule, "Christology of Acts," 160).

235. The parallels probably stem not from imitating competing writers but from the historical Socrates (see Marchant, "Introduction," ix–xv).

236. Jervell, *Theology*, 9.

237. For a treatment of Johannine speeches, see Keener, *John*, 53–80; these might resemble the use of speeches in ancient historians (Keener, *John*, 68–76; Bauckham, "Historiographical Characteristics").

238. Such occasions could potentially include some of Luke's speech settings, such as the Olivet discourse, or Pentecost or the healing in Acts 3. For Luke 6, see Allison, *Jesus*, 309–51.

the author of the "we" source (which I argue was Luke himself) was near Paul during later speeches and could have had access, as some scholars have argued, to written notes and even court summaries. Thus, while some speeches in Acts may derive from Luke's inferences (again, most obviously, Acts 25:14–22), others may reflect genuine summaries of what was said on the occasions in question.

That those who held particular speeches to be important could preserve them is clear from the example of Dio Chrysostom, many of whose speeches were preserved, sometimes even with apparent speaker feedback to audience responses. Dio himself sometimes repeated to other hearers speeches that he gave before the emperor (*Or.* 57.10–12), though he would likely adapt some of the wording for a new audience.[239] Speeches themselves were, in such perspectives, events meriting recital. How common were such practices, and how relevant would they be to the situation in Acts?

I. Speakers' Notes and Manuscripts

Most speeches depicted as given in Acts were extemporaneous rather than prepared (cf. Luke 12:11–12; 21:14), and given by preachers rather than professional orators, so that speakers' notes or manuscripts are unlikely. Nevertheless, in the interest of thoroughness, we should examine the practice of notes on speeches, which may be relevant for some of the court speeches later in Acts.

Professional orators usually wrote out and published their speeches after delivery, in the process often improving on their original product.[240] Some, after improving their speeches, might offer them at public readings (Pliny *Ep.* 7.17.5), even though readings lost some of the dynamic of genuine oratory (2.19.2, 4). They might also condense to summaries less interesting parts of their oral speeches.[241] At other times, the improved written speech proved considerably more elaborate than its delivered form.[242] Such written versions could be sent to friends or openly published;[243] Pliny corresponds with those who read his speeches.[244] Of course, speakers' polished sermons published after delivery would not be relevant to the speeches in Acts, none of which were delivered by professional rhetoricians. Speakers' notes from before delivery, however, might be a different matter.

Speakers often used written speeches or notes.[245] For example, even though Cassius Severus was known especially for his improvisations and extemporaneous speeches, he always used notes (Sen. E. *Controv.* 3.pref. 4–6); indeed, in contrast to some whose notes were merely outlines,[246] he wrote out most of his speeches whenever possible (3.pref. 6). Some speakers did not use notes, though generally not for reasons that would affect the defense speeches in Acts: one writer cites the bad example of Marcus Antonius the orator, "who used to say that he never put a speech in writing so that if something said at an earlier trial would damage a subsequent client he could deny having said it" (Val. Max. 7.3.5 [LCL]). Another had such an exceptional memory

---

239. On this last point, see Crosby, "Introduction."

240. E.g., Cic. *Brut.* 24.91 (remarking on the laziness of those who fail to write them out); Pliny *Ep.* 2.5.1–2; 5.8.6; 5.20.3 (noting that the reception of written speeches was less subject to chance); 7.17.5.

241. So Pliny *Ep.* 1.20.7–8 (countering a contrary view mentioned in 1.20.6).

242. Pliny *Ep.* 3.18.1 (referring to his *Panegyricus*).

243. E.g., Pliny *Ep.* 3.13.1; 4.5.3.

244. E.g., Pliny *Ep.* 4.26.1–3; Pliny expects to hear from another when that person sees Pliny's published version (4.5.3).

245. *Rhet. Alex.* 36, 1444a.16–28; Sen. E. *Controv.* 1.pref. 17. Probably also implied in Eunapius *Lives* 494. Notes of declamations could include instructions to provide vivid descriptions of events (Sen. E. *Suas.* 3.2).

246. As we have noted, even in recent history, extant notes for a genuine, three-and-a-half-hour speech may be read aloud in three minutes (Tomkins, *Wilberforce*, 80, 84).

as to obviate his personal need to preserve his speeches in writing (Sen. E. *Controv.* 1.pref. 18).

Although speakers' notes would not be relevant to the extemporaneous speeches in much of Acts, they could be relevant to Paul's forensic speeches at the end. (Another proposal, the use of official documents,[247] could even account for the use of such sources after the shipwreck, but the "we" source's careful itinerary in Acts 27 might suggest that even something of the writer's own notes survived; see the discussion at Acts 27:43–44.) Further, secretaries could well have recorded the substance of significant speeches in assemblies (as in Acts 15); official bodies often maintained such notes.[248]

II. NOTE-TAKING BY HEARERS

No method allowed a verbatim record of ancient speeches (apart from access to some speakers' own manuscripts, though even these would be altered during delivery).[249] No system of Greek shorthand existed in the period of the great Hellenistic historians; it began to be introduced in the first century B.C.E. and became prominent in the second century C.E.[250] In Luke's day shorthand existed and was widespread geographically,[251] but it was not a common or widely available practice. A sign could mean any of several words; hence its conversion "into longhand required, as it does today, some recall on the part of the stenographer," and one reader would not necessarily understand another's shorthand (Cic. *Att.* 13.32).[252] Although this time range allows the possibility for some verbatim recording of speeches in Luke's era, it is very unlikely that he or his informants for most speeches would have been trained in it, and virtually impossible that informants for all his speeches would have been trained in it.[253]

Although transcriptions can be ruled out, we cannot a priori exclude the possibility of some notes. Haenchen found incredible the proposal of F. F. Bruce that Luke may have had access to notes of the speeches, but it is significant that Bruce was the classicist, with a much stronger background in Greco-Roman sources than Haenchen possessed. Quintilian mentions such taking of notes, even while emphasizing the use of memory.[254] Our collection of discourses from Musonius Rufus appears to depend on the writings of one of his students;[255] other sources also indicate that students took notes.[256] Most settings in Acts do not invite this practice, but it could stand behind

247. Winter, "Official Proceedings," 307; idem, "*Captatio benevolentiae*," 526–28.

248. See Rüpke, "Commentarii," 628. Associations, like cities, could have secretaries keeping minutes of business meetings.

249. Even had verbatim recording been possible, elite audiences would have dismissed such reports as rhetorically inept, because they expected historians to be more creative, just as we expect writers to compose in their own words and not plagiarize their sources.

250. Maehler, "Tachygraphy," 1468. Richards, *Letter Writing*, 67–68, points out that Latin shorthand precedes Paul by at least a century (Plut. *Cat. Min.* 23.3–5; Euseb. *Chron.* 156); Richards's argument (68–69) that the use of Greek terms in Cicero, the alleged Latin originator, suggests an earlier Greek practice, is less certain (since Plutarch, who preserves the tradition, writes in Greek).

251. Richards, *Letter Writing*, 65–72. That shorthand appears even in the desert in P.Murabba'ât 164 suggests that it was widespread by the time of the Second Judean Revolt (pp. 71–72).

252. Richards, *Letter Writing*, 73 (who concludes that it is unlikely that Paul had access to shorthand secretaries, 73–74).

253. From a modern historical standpoint, we should also be clear that even firsthand notes may contain mistakes at times. Anyone who has been part of a group reviewing minutes from a previous meeting will recognize that the group's memory may sometimes correct notes from a month or season before.

254. Gempf, "Speaking," 299, citing Haenchen, *Acts*, 590; and Quint. *Inst.* 11.2.2, 25.

255. Lutz, "Musonius," 7, 10.

256. Sen. Y. *Ep. Lucil.* 108.6. Cf. evidence in Millard, *Reading and Writing*, esp. 199–208 (in Jewish circles, see 204–8). For personal notebooks as diaries, see Rüpke, "Ephemeris."

some other speeches, particularly in the "we" material. Although I doubt that Luke used notes for most speeches, Haenchen's peremptory dismissal of any possibility neglects considerable ancient evidence of which he seemed unaware.

(1) Academic Note-Taking

Orality and literacy coexisted in Mediterranean school settings.[257] Those with sufficient education knew how to take notes well enough to capture the gist of speeches. Disciples of advanced Greek teachers, both in philosophy and rhetoric, very often took notes during their teachers' lectures.[258]

From an early period, those who took such notes sometimes published them. For instance, the notes (ὑπομνήματα) of rhetorical lectures by the fifth-century B.C.E. teachers Corax and Tisias, made by themselves or by their students, were published.[259] The practice is attested far closer to the NT era by Arrian, a disciple of Epictetus; his accounts of Epictetus's teaching in Koine are so different from Arrian's own atticizing diction in his other writings[260] that he feels it necessary to apologize for the rough style of the *Diatribai* (*Discourses*): "Whatever I heard him say I used to write down, word for word, as best I could, endeavouring to preserve it as a memorial, for my own future use, of his way of thinking and the frankness of his speech."[261]

Quintilian, the famous Roman teacher of rhetoric, inadvertently attests the potential accuracy of such a practice. Some of the boys who were his students had published in his name their notes on his lectures. He attests that their notes were fairly accurate, though he indicates that he wishes that he had had the opportunity to polish them for publication; his own published work overlapped with what they had written.[262]

Although Jewish disciples may have taken fewer notes and emphasized orality much more highly, they also were able to take notes and use them as initial mnemonic devices to recall larger blocks of material.[263] At least some Palestinian Jews could write.[264] But Acts' speeches are not academic lectures.

(2) Note-Taking on Speeches

If students of rhetoricians took notes at their lectures, the habit might well carry over to noteworthy speeches. Hearers of speeches sometimes took notes to capture the gist of the speeches,[265] including school declamations (Sen. E. *Suas.* 3.2), although

257. See Gamble, "Literacy," 646; cf. Millard, *Reading and Writing*, esp. 184–209. Although some have argued against overplaying the orality/literacy divide (Malina, "Criticism," 98, as cited in Botha, "Cognition," 37), some others warn against playing it down too much (Botha, "Cognition").

258. Cf. Sen. Y. *Ep. Lucil.* 108.6; Arius Did. *Epit.* 2.7.11k, pp. 80.36–82.1; Lucian *Hermot.* 2; see also Kennedy, "Source Criticism," 129–31 (with favorable evaluations in Meeks, "Hypomnēmata," 159–60; Fuller, "Classics," 178–79); Stowers, "Diatribe," 74, on Arrian's notes on Epictetus; Lutz, "Musonius," 7, 10, on notes from Musonius's pupils; cf. Iambl. *V.P.* 23.104; Hippol. *Ref.* 1.15. Cf. the brief discussion of Plutarch's notebooks in Cherniss, "Introduction," 398–99. Notes could derive from other sources as well; an intellectual might in several days fill five notebooks with extracts from sixty "books" (including brief speeches; Fronto *Ad M. Caes.* 2.10.2). I am reusing and augmenting here some material from Keener, *John*, 55–56.

259. Kennedy, *Classical Rhetoric*, 19.

260. Oldfather, "Introduction to Epictetus," xii–xiii. Even in the *Encheiridion*, where Arrian organizes and summarizes his master's teaching, Epictetus's character dominates.

261. Epict. *Diatr.* 1.pref. (LCL, 1:4–5). He might employ γράφω in contrast to συγγράφω, "compose" (the latter perhaps recalling the treatment of Socrates in Plato and Xenophon [LCL, 1:4–5n1]); one may be tempted to compare Luke 1:3, but Luke uses γράφω in the sense of "write to" rather than "write down."

262. Quint. *Inst.* 1.pref. 7–8 (LCL, 1:8–9). Other teachers also had problems with people pirating their books and publishing them before they could nuance them properly (Diod. Sic. 40.8.1). When recounting such exploits to my students, I often add facetiously, "Don't do that to me!"

263. Gerhardsson, *Memory*, 160–62; cf. Safrai, "Education," 966.

264. See Millard, "Literacy"; Head, "Note on *Reading*."

265. Gempf, "Speaking," 299, citing esp. Quint. *Inst.* 11.2.2.

some speakers wanted their hearers too spellbound to be able to take notes.[266] Again, these practices would not affect most speeches in Acts, particularly those whose setting was spontaneous. Note-taking is more plausible for formal meetings (as in Acts 15:7–21), Paul's defense speeches in forensic settings, and speech material in the "we" narratives (esp. 20:18–35).[267]

(3) Other Personal Notes

One could also takes notes[268] from which to later arrange material for a composition, again guarding memory (cf. Cic. *Fin.* 3.3.10; 5.5.12). Thus Aulus Gellius notes that whenever he came across information worth remembering, he jotted down notes as an aid to memory (Aul. Gel. pref. 2); he was very selective, though working through innumerable scrolls (pref. 11–12), and ended up with twenty books of notes (pref. 22).

Is it possible that Luke or anyone else close to Paul took notes about speeches? Whether Luke had advanced rhetorical training or not, he would have had sufficient education to take notes on the occasions when he was present, and if he already had historical interest, he had all the more reason to write. But even granting this possibility (and that the author was a traveling companion of Paul), he would have been present for, at most, the speeches in Acts 20; 24–26 and smaller discourse material (which would not require notes) in Acts 27–28. We could then expect these speeches to reflect greater familiarity with actual words (rather than general themes) uttered on the occasions, though we cannot be certain whether he took notes on these occasions (or perhaps from Paul's recollections of these and other occasions).

Indeed, Luke's sources for the essential substance of the speeches of Acts 24–26 are probably quite reliable, and this could be the case even if he were not present at the actual trials and whether or not he took notes. Unlike most earlier speeches in Acts, the substance of these speeches would have been preserved in writing, probably in the same sort of summary fashion in which he presents them. Court transcripts, in the form of brief minutes summarizing trials, are quite common in extant papyri. Against Haenchen's skepticism about Luke's speeches here, records of official proceedings were roughly the length Luke provides, and all these records were simply summaries.[269] There also survive some apparent court briefs prepared for litigants' orators.[270] Again, however, such claims do not cover all the speeches.

III. The Potential for Oral Memory

Speeches in Acts do not represent a relatively controlled academic setting such as that of Jesus training his disciples; the skills of memory acquired in any ancient learning context, however, would also prove useful in other settings. Although we should not expect extensive memory of individual apostolic speeches heard or even necessarily extensive content distinctive to specific speeches, except at most on unusually memorable occasions, familiarity with ancient memory allows us to consider whether some features may have been preserved.

266. Zeno in Diog. Laert. 7.1.20.
267. Although we cannot prove that Luke planned to write a historical work when he traveled with Paul, the detailed travel itinerary strongly suggests that the narrator did take some notes.
268. Cf. Montanari, "Hypomnema," on *hypomnemata* as notes or memory aids (though after the Hellenistic period they often represent a running commentary on texts, 72); Kennedy, "Source Criticism," 136–37.
269. Winter, "Official Proceedings," 307n7. Forensic speeches typically employed a plain, unadorned style compared to the grand style of much epideictic (Fronto *Ad M. Caes.* 3.16.1); yet they could be impassioned (so, e.g., Pliny *Ep.* 7.9.7), as opposed to the more reasoned style of deliberative rhetoric.
270. Winter, "*Captatio benevolentiae*," 506.

(1) Oral Cultures?

By Luke's day, some of the Mediterranean world was literate as well as oral,[271] but only a minority could read, especially on a formal level, and orality remained an important part of the larger culture. Memory cultivation is important in oral cultures.[272]

Many cultures orally pass on information for centuries, maintaining accuracy in the central points transmitted.[273] (Even in the transmission of Balkan ballads, where this has been disputed, the basic story is fixed at the oral stage long before the words are fixed at the written stage.[274] These cases involve poetry or poetic devices, however, which aid memory.)[275] In oral cultures the point of recall tends to be thematic rather than verbatim, but the substance of epics considered hopelessly long to modern Western audiences can be recalled.[276] Variation is to be expected in oral performances, perhaps explaining a number of variants in our gospel tradition as well.[277]

Not all societies are equally careful, but oral history can thus supplement written records in both orally skilled and unskilled societies.[278] Oral historiography has therefore come into its own as a discipline,[279] although it is more useful (for historical information) when applied to figures in the recent memory of the informants[280] than when investigating the legendary past.[281]

Like some other societies, the ancient Mediterranean world highly prized oral memory.[282] Bards recited Homeric epics and other poets from memory, though in-

271. For the coexistence of literacy and orality, see the example in Aune, *Dictionary of Rhetoric*, 325: "Greek schoolchildren who used to memorize from written texts of the poets in order to recite them without the written text" (Plato *Prot.* 325E). Byrskog, *History*, 111–12, stresses Plato's preference for memory over texts.

272. Byrskog, *History*, 110–11; cf. examples in Allison, *Jesus*, 29, 374. Oral history approaches memory more optimistically than the dominant contemporary emphasis in psychology and sociology (Eddy and Boyd, *Legend*, 280). For one discussion of the issues in psychological memory studies, see Bauckham, *Eyewitnesses*, 325–41. For one useful survey of orality studies with respect to the Gospels, see Iverson, "Orality."

273. Lewis, *History*, 43; Vansina, "Afterthoughts," 110; cf. Yamauchi, "Homer," on very general historical events behind Homer; also Redman, "Eyewitnesses," 191, though specifying (as we normally should also for Greco-Roman antiquity) content rather than verbatim wording.

274. Lord, *Singer*, 138.

275. Redman, "Eyewitnesses," 191–92.

276. See Harvey, *Listening*, 41; the Hindu child in Noll and Nystrom, *Clouds*, 129. On the retention of "gist" in eyewitness memory even when details are inaccurate, see Bauckham, *Eyewitnesses*, 333–34.

277. Dunn, *Perspective*, 112 (with 110), 122; cf. Kirk, "Memory," 170–72. Most Roman literature in this period was orally performed, affecting its shaping (Schmidt, "Public recital"); nevertheless, our knowledge of how gospel tradition was orally performed in the eastern Mediterranean remains quite limited (cf. Gerhardsson, "Performance Criticism"). On the frequent lack of verbatim recall, and often re-creation, see, e.g., Moniot, "Historiography," 56–57; performances are adapted to new audiences (Bazin, "Past," 70–71). The variation is typically greater in prose than in verse (Kennedy, "Source Criticism," 143).

278. Cf., e.g., Hoeree and Hoogbergen, "History"; Aron-Schnapper and Hanet, "Archives"; on rote memorization in traditional Quranic education, cf. Wagner and Lotfi, "Learning." Limitations do, however, exist, especially over time (e.g., Iglesias, "Reflexoes"; Harms, "Tradition"; Raphael, "Travail"). For a recent and well-documented case for the potential reliability of oral transmission of gospel materials in light of more general knowledge about oral transmission, see Eddy and Boyd, *Legend*, 239–68 (esp. 252–59).

279. Used in academic African historiography since the 1950s (Moniot, "Historiography," 50), needed to reconstruct practices before modern influences (Horton, "Possession," 14). Westerners' prior neglect often reflects ethnocentric prejudices (Chrétien, "Exchange," 77).

280. With, e.g., Eddy and Boyd, *Legend*, 395 (on events no older than 80–150 years), citing various sources.

281. Henige, "History," 103, rightly warns of the fanciful excesses caused by using theory to interpret evidence in reconstructing history behind oral tradition. Eddy and Boyd, *Legend*, 260–64, suggest that even folklore traditions about historical characters may often preserve more of the substance than Western critics have often assumed, but their focus is more recent history.

282. Ancient theories on how memory worked varied (see Arist. *Concerning Memory and Recollection*; Plato *Meno* 81CD; Philost. *Vit. soph.* 1.22.523); Cicero expounded on mnemonics (*De or.* 2.351; Olbricht, "Delivery and Memory," 163). Philo (Boccaccini, *Judaism*, 192–94) and Ps.-Aristeas (Boccaccini, *Judaism*, 194–98) stress memory, blending Greek language with Jewish memorial traditions concerning God's historic acts.

tellectuals generally regarded these bards as low-class, engaging in an elementary exercise.[283] (That is, ancient emphasis on memory was not limited to those with a literate education, as some have wrongly assumed.) Centuries before Luke, the best professional reciters could recite all of Homer by heart (Xen. *Symp.* 3.5–6); in Luke's era, Dio Chrysostom even reports a people who no longer were able to speak Greek well but most of whom knew the *Iliad* by heart (*Or.* 36.9).[284] Many poems remained fluid, but the *Iliad* remained textually constant because it became canonical for Greek culture.[285]

In the ancient Greek world, some writers felt free to add information from centuries-old oral traditions that did not appear in their written sources.[286] Jewish storytellers also passed on traditions informally over long stretches of time, ultimately contributing to many of the documents now collected as "Pseudepigrapha."[287] Such oral tradition is difficult to guarantee,[288] but within the first generation or two, within living memory of the eyewitnesses, one would expect more of the widely circulated oral sources to remain accurate than would be the case in a later period.[289] Even Jesus's disciples were apparently not trained "professionally" in rigorous memory practices the way ancient bards would have been, but they probably had significantly better memories to work with than modern Western people do.[290]

(2) Academic Memory

In contrast to many oral cultures today,[291] in the ancient Mediterranean world, memorization was the most pervasive form of education.[292] Memorizing sayings of famous teachers was a regular school exercise at the basic level;[293] students at various levels also memorized examples.[294] Although it was the youngest who learned by rote memorization at the elementary level,[295] higher education (after about age 16) included memorizing many speeches and passages useful for speeches[296]—though the ultimate goal was both understanding and remembering (Isoc. *Demon.* 18). Even at the stage of advanced education, which focused on rhetoric, students especially

---

283. Cf. West, "Rhapsodes." The frequency of literary fragments scattered throughout the papyri (cf. Avi-Yonah, *Hellenism*, 248) attests to the commonness of their usage.

284. Although we cannot confirm this report, the culture that Dio reports apparently did exist (cf. *CIG* 2.2077 in J. W. Cohoon, LCL, 3:447n2).

285. See Finkelberg, "*Cypria*" (doubting that texts always develop from fluid to rigid); cf. Yamauchi, "Homer."

286. E.g., Paus. 1.23.2; cf. also Maclean and Aitken, *Heroikos*, xc–xci. Cf., e.g., Xen. *Cyr.* 1.2.1 for an example of long informal traditioning by storytelling and song. Scholars often have misgivings about Pausanias's oldest oral information (cf. Pretzler, "Pausanias and Tradition").

287. See Charlesworth, *Pseudepigrapha and New Testament*, 1–3; cf. Bailey, "Tradition." For stories passed on in Mediterranean households, see Pizzuto-Pomaco, "Shame," 38.

288. Eunapius *Lives* 453 (writing it down fixed it and prevented further changes). Even first-century writers recognized that centuries of oral transmission could produce variations in ancient documents (Jos. *Ag. Ap.* 1.12).

289. For example, other factors being equal, we would normally prefer Velleius Paterculus's contemporary account to that of Tacitus, writing roughly a century later (Woodman, *Rhetoric*, 204).

290. Redman, "Eyewitnesses," 192–93 (cf. also the concession on 179).

291. Moniot, "Historiography," 56–57, notes that "formal instruction" in traditions is rare today.

292. See, e.g., Quint. *Inst.* 1.3.1; Plut. *Educ.* 13, *Mor.* 9E; Mus. Ruf. frg. 51, p. 144.3–7; Diog. Laert. 6.2.31; Eunapius *Lives* 481; Watson, "Education," 310, 312; Heath, *Hermogenes*, 11; further Carr, *Writing* (esp. 111–73).

293. Mus. Ruf. frg. 51, p. 144.3–7 (though it is misattributed or, more likely, Musonius recycled an earlier saying of Cato [144.10–19]).

294. Theon *Progymn.* 2.5–8.

295. On their learning, see Quint. *Inst.* 2.4.15; Jeffers, *World*, 256; memorizing poets in Aune, *Dictionary of Rhetoric*, 143.

296. Jeffers, *World*, 256. Historians frequently quoted other historians from memory (Marincola, "Introduction," 2; cf. Laistner, *Historians*, 77), a practice that, in biographic form, might also help explain some variants in the gospel tradition.

"memorized model speeches and passages" for their own use,[297] skills that would have enabled them to preserve the gist of other speeches.

Most important for our point, they memorized what their professors taught them. As noted above, students in advanced academic settings continued to take notes on what their teachers said (e.g., Sen. Y. *Ep. Lucil.* 108.6). But one philosopher reportedly reproved a friend who lamented losing his notes, "You should have inscribed them . . . on your mind instead of on paper."[298] Lucian portrays an excellent philosophic student as rehearsing each of the points of the previous day's lectures in his mind (*Hermot.* 1). One need not always agree with one's teacher,[299] but respect for teachers was paramount,[300] and in such a setting we would expect respectful preservation of teachings even when the transmitter registered disagreement.

Some schools were known for practicing particularly diligent training of students' memories, especially in stories about the Pythagoreans (e.g., Philost. *Vit. Apoll.* 1.14; 2.30). In one fictitious account, a disciple memorized all that his teacher taught (1.19); as a method of training their memories, the Pythagoreans reportedly would not rise from bed in the mornings until they had recited their previous days' activities.[301] (Pythagorean emphasis on repetition for memorization[302] reflects a relatively effective method of preserving long-term memory.)[303]

Although legendary Pythagorean disciples were particularly famous for their memories,[304] memorization characterized advanced education more generally. Sayings attributed to founders of Greek schools were transmitted by members of the school from one generation to the next;[305] the practice seems to have been encouraged by the founders of the schools themselves.[306] Disciples had to be attentive; thus the philosopher Peregrinus rebuked an equestrian who seemed inattentive and yawning.[307]

Although the emphasis lay on memorizing teachings, students also cared about and learned teachers' behavior, an object of their study and emulation.[308] They also transmitted it; thus, for example, Eunapius learned a story about Iamblichus from

297. Jeffers, *World*, 256.

298. Antisthenes in Diog. Laert. 6.1.5 (LCL).

299. See, e.g., Val. Max. 8.15.ext. 1; Sen. Y. *Ep. Lucil.* 108.17, 20, 22; 110.14, 20; Mus. Ruf. 1, 36.6–7; Philost. *Vit. Apoll.* 7.22. Especially among rabbis, correcting a teacher was rare (*'Abot R. Nat.* 1 A); against striving with one's teacher, see *Num. Rab.* 18:20; against offering legal decisions in front of one's teacher, y. *Šeb.* 6:1, §8 (it merited death, *Sipra Sh. M. d.* 99.5.6; b. *'Erub.* 63a; *Tem.* 16a; *Lev. Rab.* 20:6–7).

300. E.g., *'Abot R. Nat.* 25 A; y. *Bik.* 3:3, §9; *Gen. Rab.* 22:2; for rank for esteemed Jewish sages, see, e.g., t. *Mo'ed Qat.* 2:17; *Sanh.* 7:8; b. *Hor.* 13b, *bar.*; y. *Sanh.* 1:2, §13; *Ta'an.* 4:2, §§8–9. If a pupil needed to point something out to the teacher, even this should be done respectfully (e.g., Fronto *Ad verum imp.* 2.3); a pupil who contradicted a teacher might need to be reconciled to him (Philost. *Vit. Apoll.* 5.38). Later, one who despised a rabbi despised one's help (b. *Šabb.* 119b) or risked losing eternal life (*Pesiq. Rab.* 11:2); by stinginess toward rabbis (b. *B. Bat.* 75a) or speaking ill of them after their death (b. *Ber.* 19a), one might inherit hellfire; offending rabbis might yield deadly judgment (cf. b. *B. Qam.* 117a; *B. Meṣ.* 84a; *'Erub.* 63a; *Tem.* 16a).

301. Diod. Sic. 10.5.1; Iambl. *V.P.* 29.165; on their memories, see further 20.94; 29.164; 35.256. On memorization techniques, cf. *Rhet. Her.* 3.22.35; see further Kennedy, *Classical Rhetoric*, 98.

302. Iambl. *V.P.* 31.188.

303. Cf., e.g., Thompson, Wenger, and Bartling, "Recall," 210 (noting that it becomes unnecessary beyond a certain point; this source was supplied to me by M. Bradley, then a student at Duke).

304. Iambl. *V.P.* 35.256; Philost. *Vit. Apoll.* 3.16. Certainly, their handing teachings down secretly only by memory (Iambl. *V.P.* 32.226) is portrayed as unusual.

305. Culpepper, *School*, 193; Alexander, "Memory," 141; Aul. Gel. 7.10.1; Socrates *Ep.* 20. Some schools emphasized memorizing texts, others, memorizing the teacher's words (Culpepper, *School*, 177).

306. Diog. Laert. 10.1.12, on Epicurus; on followers of Pythagoras, cf. Culpepper, *School*, 50. All schools emphasized memory, though Epicurus more than Plato (Alexander, "Memory," 133, 138).

307. Aul. Gel. 8.3.

308. See, e.g., Philost. *Vit. Apoll.* 5.21; Jos. *Life* 11; Xen. *Mem.* 1.2.3; Sen. Y. *Ep. Lucil.* 108.4; b. *Ber.* 62a; Liefeld, "Preacher," 223; Robbins, *Jesus*, 64; the apparently contrary statement of Eunapius *Lives* intro. 452–53 refers in context to casual activities only (cf. Xen. *Symp.* 1.1). For rabbinic behavior establishing legal precedents,

Eunapius's teacher Chrysanthius, who learned it from Aedesius the disciple of Iamblichus himself (Eunapius *Lives* 458); Philostratus has oral information about a teacher two generations earlier through an expert from the previous generation (Philost. *Vit. soph.* 1.22.524).

Jewish education emphasized memorization of Torah (through repeated reading and recitation).[309] Thus a rabbi might praise a student who, instead of trying to learn on his own, merely preserved his teacher's wisdom, like a good cistern (R. Akiba in *Sipre Deut.* 48.2.6).[310] Josephus stressed memorization regarding the Torah;[311] it was part of regular Jewish education in the home and of the basic school education all Jewish youths were to receive.[312]

This practice was all the more intense for those studying to be teachers of Torah.[313] Some scholars have complained (technically correctly) that all the rabbinic evidence is late, but it is hardly likely that this evidence would be discontinuous with all other Jewish and Greco-Roman evidence, especially given the particular focus on it in our later extant sources. Some scholars curiously exclude all samples of evidence for oral tradition, voluminous though they are, and the closest analogies available: rabbinic evidence because it is late, Greek or Roman evidence because it is Gentile, uneducated bards because they sang poetry, and orators and philosophers because they were educated (though not all philosophic students were), and so forth. Individually, each of these reservations is accurate, but they seem problematic when used to explain away the cumulative direction of the bulk of surviving evidence. To what nearer ancient parallels should we look? Having classified away the majority of possibly relevant ancient evidence, despite its abundance, variety, and often independence, such scholars assume that they have vindicated traditional scholarly skepticism about the Gospels and Acts. Instead, I believe they inadvertently simply preserve New Testament scholarship in a vacuum impervious to insights from appropriately cognate disciplines.[314] For those interested in drawing on all evidence from antiquity, rabbinic evidence, like other strands of surviving evidence, should remain a legitimate subject of inquiry, provided it remains balanced with the other surviving evidence.

Rabbis lectured to their pupils and expected them to memorize their teachings by laborious repetition.[315] In both Tannaitic and Amoraic literature, there is much emphasis on careful traditioning.[316] At the same time, teachings could be condensed

---

see *t. Pisha* 2:15–16; *Sipre Deut.* 221.1.1; *y. B. Meṣi'a* 2:11, §1; *Demai* 1:4 [22b]; *Nid.* 1:4, §2; *Sanh.* 7:2, §4; *Yebam.* 4:11, §8.

309. Watson, "Education," 312.

310. Traditional Israelite learning had emphasized the transmission of wisdom while also allowing individual learning (cf. Shupak, "Learning Methods").

311. Jos. *Life* 8; *Ag. Ap.* 1.60; 2.171–73, 204. Josephus's statements on Jewish literacy, like that in *m. 'Abot* 5:21, may reflect the literate elite, with much of the population learning Torah orally (Horsley, *Galilee*, 246–47); but there were, undoubtedly, reasons others considered Judeans a "nation of philosophers" (Stern, *Authors*, 1:8–11, 46–50; Gager, *Anti-Semitism*, 39), and "the synagogue was a comparatively intellectual milieu" (Riesner, "Synagogues in Jerusalem," 209). The illiterate learned Torah orally (Kirk, "Memory," 157–58).

312. See Riesner, "Education élémentaire"; idem, *Jesus*.

313. See Gerhardsson, *Memory*, 124–25. For Gerhardsson's right point, see Kelber, "Work," esp. 191–94.

314. Cf. Keener, "Assumptions," 40–48; "Reply," 117. Given the scarcity of surviving evidence from antiquity, historians of antiquity routinely draw on and compare a range of evidence, even when attestations outside the document one is analyzing may be later or from a different location; note Levinskaya, *Diaspora Setting*, ix–x, 16–17; Donaldson, *Paul and Gentiles*, 51; and discussion in this commentary's prolegomenon.

315. *Sipre Deut.* 48.1.1–4; Goodman, *State*, 79; cf. *Sipre Deut.* 4.2.1, 306.19.1–3; *b. Ber.* 38b; *y. Meg.* 4:1, §4; Gerhardsson, *Memory*, 113–21, 127–29, 168–70; Zlotnick, "Memory."

316. E.g., *t. Yebam.* 3:1; *Mek. Pisha* 1.135–36; *Sipre Deut.* 48.2.6; *'Abot R. Nat.* 24 A; *Pesiq. Rab Kah.* 21:5; *b. Sukkah* 28a; *y. Šeq.* 2:5; cf. *m. 'Ed.* 1:4–6; *Sipra Behuq. pq.* 13.277.1.12; see further Moore, *Judaism*, 1:99;

and abridged,[317] and the very emphasis on the tradition could lead rabbis to portray their teaching as merely amplifying what preceded[318] or to attempt harmonizations of earlier contradictory opinions attributed to a given rabbi.[319] Thus both faithfulness to, and adaptation of, oral sources characterize early rabbinic use of earlier tradition.[320]

Of Christian leaders in Acts, only Paul is said to have had actual "disciples," and then only in the early period (Acts 9:25), perhaps before he learned that some others in the apostolic movement ascribed the role of "rabbi" to Jesus alone (cf. Matt 23:8). But the apostles in general would have had many hearers learning from them and eager to preserve their behavior and general teachings (cf., e.g., Acts 2:42; 5:12–16). Patterns in the broader culture would have cultivated an interest in learning well.

(3) Sayings Traditions

Sayings of famous teachers could be passed on orally to a remarkable degree of accuracy, especially in the first generation or two while the teacher's disciples (and perhaps the disciples' disciples) remained his primary spokespersons.[321] Teachers passed on (παραδίδωμι) their teachings (e.g., Lucian *Alex.* 61), language that could also be used for the transmission of information through written histories (Dio Chrys. *Or.* 18.10).[322] Both attributed and unattributed maxims were memorized and passed on for centuries even in elementary educational settings.[323]

Still, although this observation is helpful for how we approach Luke's preservation of Jesus's sayings in his Gospel, it is not so helpful for explaining the more extended speech material in Acts. At most, we could expect this method of transmitting a sage's sayings to preserve a few of the apostles' individual sayings, not connected speeches. There are at least three reasons that this process is not very helpful for understanding speeches in Acts. First, whereas Jesus often uttered succinct proverbial statements and quips that shamed his opponents[324] and sometimes taught in easily memorized forms,[325] this differed from most of what we know of the teaching style of the one apostle whose works are best attested, namely, Paul.[326]

Second, even if such brief sayings of the apostles (as opposed to summaries or memories of their message) were preserved and transmitted orally in the way Jesus's

---

Urbach, *Sages*, 1:68; Gerhardsson, *Memory*, 122–70; idem, *Origins*, 19–24; Riesenfeld, *Tradition*, 14–17. When the proper attribution was unknown, this was sometimes stated (*y. Ter.* 8:5).

317. Gerhardsson, *Memory*, 136–48, 173; Goulder, *Midrash*, 64–65. Similar sayings thus could appear in different words (*m. Šabb.* 9:1; *ʾAbod. Zar.* 3:6).

318. Simeon ben Azzai in *Sipra VDDen. pq.* 2.2.3.1, 3.

319. *y. Soṭah* 5:6, §1; cf. *y. Ketub.* 3:1, §4. Of course, the rabbi may have issued several different opinions on a subject in his lifetime; cf. *y. B. Qam.* 2:6, §3. Sometimes rabbis also seem to have told stories as fictitious homiletic illustrations instead of wishing to be understood as drawing on previous traditions (cf., e.g., *Sipre Deut.* 40.7.1).

320. Davies, "Aboth," 156. Cf. communal memory's selectivity for relevance (Kirk, "Memory," 168).

321. See, more fully, my comment in Keener, *John*, 62–65; esp. idem, *Matthew*, 25–31, where the topic is far more relevant than in Acts.

322. For this verb in passing on information in early Christian circles, cf. Luke 1:2; Acts 16:4; 1 Cor 15:3.

323. Cf. Hermog. *Progymn.* 4, "On Maxim," 8–10. (By the strictest definition, "maxims" might be unattributed; cf. the later Nicolaus *Progymn.* 5, "On Maxim," 25.) On boys learning these and *chreiai*, see also Anderson, *Glossary*, 126–27 (citing Sen. Y. *Ep. Lucil.* 33.7). While historians did not reproduce entire speeches verbatim, they could reproduce brief sayings in this manner (Marincola, "Speeches," 120, cites Tac. *Ann.* 14.59.4; 15.67.4; and compares a saying in Arrian *Anab.* 4.12.5; Plut. *Alex.* 54.6).

324. See documentation in Keener, *Matthew*, 25–26; more fully Stein, *Method and Message*; Tannehill, *Sword*.

325. See documentation in Keener, *Matthew*, 25–29. Greek and Roman philosophers also could do the same (Philost. *Vit. soph.* 1.22.523), even using poetry to reinforce their teaching for early students (Sen. Y. *Ep. Lucil.* 108.9–10), though not advanced ones (108.12; poetry and song involved memorization, Apollod. *Bib.* 1.3.1; Sen. E. *Controv.* 1.pref. 2, 19).

326. Though letters are indeed different from lectures, Paul's letters, if anything, may point to a diatribe lecture style.

teachings were, which is questionable, they would not have functioned as a core for the sort of speeches preserved in Acts. One might find Petrine themes in Peter's speeches here or there, but Acts' speeches are too cohesive to reflect a simple linking of isolated sayings.

Third and more important, although the early church preserved collections of apostolic letters, it appears to have been interested in preserving the individual sayings only of Jesus.[327] The early church's demonstrated capacity for, and interest in, memory, though not inviting us to think of verbatim recall of sayings, do lead us to expect that they preserved the basic ideas of their early leaders (just as they preserved Paul's letters); thus it is reasonable to surmise that Luke had access to elements of the "primitive" apostolic message.

(4) Oratorical Memory

One of the most essential tasks of an orator was the memorization of his speech.[328] Pliny the Younger praises a rhetorician so skillful that he could repeat verbatim speeches that he had delivered extemporaneously (Pliny *Ep.* 2.3.3).[329] Rhetorical students practiced declamation, offering their practice speeches "from memory."[330] Orators who developed such skills with their own speeches would naturally be able to recognize and recall elements of others' speeches as well.

One rhetor memorized his speech as he was writing it out, never needing to read it again (Sen. E. *Controv.* 1.pref. 17); he could remember every declamation he had ever delivered, word for word, making books unnecessary (1.pref. 18). But whereas orators would memorize their speeches—even speeches of several hours' duration[331]—ordinary hearers' memorizing of long speeches while hearing them is difficult to attest.[332] Still, at least rhetorically trained hearers could recall elements of speeches, even some they considered inferior, with memory strong enough even to supplement written sources (Eunapius *Lives* 494).[333] Likewise, a deceased teacher's former disciples might also collectively remember bits and pieces of speeches, sewing them together (Philost. *Vit. soph.* 1.22.524), a process relevant to communal memory.

(5) Ancient Mnemonics in Other Settings

Ancients especially reported those whose memories were so exceptional as to function as oral repositories of a generation of their own speeches (Sen. E. *Controv.* 1.pref. 17–18) or to recall preserved memories of ancient teachers (Eunapius *Lives* 481).[334]

---

327. See also Bruce, *Acts*[3], 35.

328. See, e.g., Heath, *Hermogenes*, 7; Olbricht, "Delivery and Memory" (esp. 159, 163, citing *Rhet. Her.* 1.3; Cic. *De or.* 2.351); Russell, "Rhetoric, Greek," 1313; Satterthwaite, "Acts," 344; Walde, "Mnemonics" (citing Cic. *Inv.* 1.9; *Rhet. Her.* 3.28; Quint. *Inst.* 3.3.1); cf. Eunapius *Lives* 502. Ancient rhetoricians praised memory earlier (Aeschines *Embassy* 48, 112), and it became part of rhetorical and other pedagogy by Cicero's day (see Gaines, "Handbooks," 167, citing Cic. *De or.* 1.142).

329. For other praises of orators' memory, see, e.g., Pliny *Ep.* 6.11.2.

330. Watson, "Education," 310.

331. Quint. *Inst.* 11.2.1–51.

332. Among rhetorically trained hearers, the particularly adept might memorize lengthy speech material (e.g., Sen. E. *Controv.* passim, below), but most hearers would not fit this category.

333. Naturally, this would be easier for a speech heard recently; thus Lucian *Peregr.* 3 (LCL, 5:5, 7) promises to repeat verbatim, as best he can, the words of a Cynic he heard the previous day. Knowing Cynic style may have helped him with memorization. People (including myself) can often vividly recall scenes that stick in their memories though neglected in their notes at the time (e.g., Grindal, "Heart," 67, supplementing his anthropological notes with vivid memories).

334. For other examples of exceptional mnemonic skills, see, e.g., Sen. E. *Controv.* 1.pref. 19. Despite some (rarer) modern mnemonic feats that render many accounts credible, not all the ancient claims appear plausible (e.g., those in Pliny E. *N.H.* 7.24.88).

Rhetoricians believed that artificial memory, augmented by discipline and training, could move far beyond natural memory (*Rhet. Her.* 3.16.28).[335]

The elder Seneca was able to recount long sections of numerous declamations that he heard in his youth (*Controv.* passim),[336] though he was admittedly exceptional.[337] Difficult as it may seem to most readers today,[338] the elder Seneca testifies that in his younger days he could repeat back two thousand names in exactly the sequence in which he had just heard them or recite, in reverse, up to two hundred verses given to him (*Controv.* 1.pref. 2). Even if his recollections of youthful prowess are exaggerated, they testify to an emphasis on memory that far exceeds standard expectations today. He also reports that another man, hearing a poem recited by its author, recited it back to the author verbatim (facetiously claiming the poem to be his own). And he also recalls the famous Hortensius, who listed back every purchaser and price at the end of a daylong auction, his accuracy attested by the bankers (1.pref. 19).

Even if the early church altogether lacked individuals with such exceptional memories (and it seems likely it may have had *some* with exceptional memories), far less exceptional *communal* memory was required to preserve the basic substance of what was preached on the few noteworthy occasions reported in Acts. Communal memory is relevant where a group of hearers could remind one another of various points, with those whose memory was most exceptional taking the lead (Philost. *Vit. soph.* 1.22.524). Whereas "chain" transmission might depend on a single person's memory, "net" transmission of a community could help guarantee larger amounts of tradition.[339]

IV. Relevance for Acts?

Comparing other ancient sources, Hillard, Nobbs, and Winter note that it is possible for Luke to be more accurate at points than has often been assumed: "The careful reporting by Gellius of Favorinus' speeches either *verbatim* or in indirect speech should alert us to the fact that it may not always be apposite to evaluate all or some of the speeches of Acts in what New Testament scholars popularly perceive to be the 'Thucydidean' tradition."[340] It is of course doubtful that Luke would have had

---

335. For ancient memory techniques, see, e.g., Small, *Wax Tablets*; idem, "Orator" (including as a key element in rhetorical training, 196); Walde, "Mnemonics"; Byrskog, *History*, 163–65. Note Quintilian's heavy emphasis on memory in *Inst.* 11.2 (see also Small, "Orator," 196–97). Small, "Orator," 202–3, notes that one would memorize a longer work piece by piece (Quint. *Inst.* 11.2.27); practice and then test oneself to ensure getting it correct (11.2.34–35); and repeat one's lines aloud (11.2.33). Further, she notes, literate persons memorizing written material helped their memories by seeing it (11.2.32) and engaging it by marking it up (11.2.28–29). As modern studies also show, a night's rest after memorizing helps retention (11.2.43).

336. Kennedy, "Source Criticism," 143, argues that given the ancient emphasis on memory and the use of commonplaces in declamations, Seneca's recollection of declamation pieces is more credible than some critics have allowed.

337. Tacitus also claims to remember long dialogues years later (*Dial.* 1), but to some degree, this is a literary device (cf. Justin *Dialogue with Trypho*, though some elements also suggest that some genuine dialogues may stand behind this work; see 273n133 above); although such a dialogue may have occurred, "Maternus" in the dialogue speaks for Tacitus's own views. Contrasting modern weak memory, Eddy and Boyd, *Legend*, 283, cite the reported mnemonic feats of ancient and medieval cultures (e.g., Josephus and Thomas Aquinas). Exceptionally trained memories exist today but (esp. in the West) appear far more isolated.

338. Although some consider Seneca's ability exaggerated, it is noteworthy that ancient mnemonics expert Small, "Orator," 204, does accept the reports of Seneca and also the elder Pliny; on 205–6 she contrasts the mnemonic deficiencies of modern Western society. Some mnemonic claims from much earlier periods (Val. Max. 8.7.ext. 16: Cyrus's knowledge of all his troops' names, or Mithridates's of the twenty-two languages of his subjects), does appear less credible (these and also Lucius Scipio's memory of all the Roman people's names appear also in Pliny E. *N.H.* 7.24.88).

339. See Dunn, *Perspective*, 43, 114–15. Traditional Middle Eastern culture values communal memory (45–46, citing Bailey's decades of observations). Weeden, "Theory," critiques Bailey, but Dunn provides a sound response in "Theory." Cf. communal religious memory in Allison, *Jesus*, 29, 374.

340. Hillard, Nobbs, and Winter, "Corpus," 212.

access to anything close to verbatim reports of early speeches in Acts; Peter, not a professional rhetorician, would not have written out his speech afterward, and for a different reason Stephen could not have done so. Nor does one normally carry notes in preparation for speeches uttered spontaneously. Given the most likely meaning of the "we" narratives, Luke was present, at most, during Paul's exhortation to the Ephesian elders in Acts 20:18–35 and during Paul's later trials.

But again, if Luke authored the "we" section, he had (as argued above) access to eyewitness tradition for many (perhaps even most) of the cases where he was not present. Certainly, in the case of Paul's speeches, a companion of Paul would have had access to his recollections.[341] (Indeed, R. P. C. Hanson plausibly opines that the Pauline language at 13:38–39 and 20:18–35, which is not from Paul's letters, likely derives instead from Luke's personal acquaintance with Paul himself.)[342]

Beyond speeches where he was present, like Thucydides "or any historian of recent events,"[343] Luke would often have to depend on the memories of his oral sources. Even if Luke depended on only one source for each speech, we would expect him to report the speech because he believed he had acquired at least the gist of it; unlike some historians, he clearly does not create speeches merely to show off his rhetorical skills.

Studies of long-term memory show the character of information preservation by informal, untrained eyewitnesses in modern Western culture.[344] Typically, informal memory will include components rather than the whole and lack the chronological framework[345] (thus, e.g., various claims of Peter on different occasions could easily have been linked in memory reconstructions). Memories frequently conform new experiences to a schema, or interpretive grid.[346] Memory changes over time, and memories may be shaped by talking with others who participated in events, a process likely among Jesus's early followers, who presumably discussed their experiences among themselves.[347] Such collective memories tend to be more stable than merely individual memories;[348] an individual's error can be introduced into group memory,[349] but group memory might also correct such errors.[350] Although memories can be imperfect, there are limits to this imperfection (i.e., they do not ordinarily involve the free composition of events); even when some details are inaccurate, the "gist" is usually accurate.[351] The

341. With, e.g., Robertson, *Luke*, 228.

342. Hanson, *Acts*, 21–27, 38.

343. Aune, *Environment*, 125.

344. Presumably, memory works in roughly similar ways in all cultures; my point in noting the cultural difference is simply that we would not expect an oral culture's eyewitness memory to be *less* dependable than modern Western memory. Cultures that inculcate memory tend to develop it more strongly than in the West.

345. Bauckham, *Eyewitnesses*, 326, 333, 344. Thus estimates of numbers and related figures (such as height or weight) appear more easily forgotten, although timing is often remembered where it fits schematic expectations (Redman, "Eyewitnesses," 182). Similar memories blend (Kirk, "Memory," 166).

346. Redman, "Eyewitnesses," 180–81.

347. Ibid., 185. Inaccuracies can arise even in the first few weeks after an event (196); Redman also notes that early Christians' faith introduces bias, though I wonder why faith is considered more a bias than any other expectation.

348. Ibid., 186.

349. Ibid. Even among individuals, errors, once introduced into memory, tend to be preserved there (187–88).

350. Westerners tend to choose among conflicting individuals' memories, but more group-oriented cultures tend to find ways to combine them ("compromise memories," ibid., 187).

351. Bauckham, *Eyewitnesses*, 327, 333–34, 345. Eyewitnesses may differ on matter of detail, e.g., the recollections of John and Charles Wesley regarding the Holy Club (Tomkins, *Wesley*, 33–34), whether because at least one forgot earlier incidents or because they evaluated the relevance of incidents differently. Cf. also the problematic recollection in Tuttle, *Wesley*, 115n6.

reconstruction and arrangement of memory do involve interpretive structures, but such structures would also be involved even in the initial hearing.[352]

Studies of long-term memory also show the sorts of information apt to be preserved by eyewitnesses. These include, among other elements, unusual events,[353] consequential events,[354] events in which the eyewitness "is emotionally involved,"[355] "vivid imagery,"[356] and "frequent rehearsal."[357] It is difficult to doubt that hearers at some seminal speeches in the early church would have remembered and retold elements of, and what they interpreted as the heart of, such speech events. The dramatic results of Peter's preaching in Acts 2, 3, and 10 certainly qualified these speeches as unusual, consequential, and emotionally charged events; such events would be frequently retold (cf. 11:15; 15:7), and hearers of the retellings might well retell them as well.

If speeches were given on these occasions, Luke could well have had oral information about some of what was said on these occasions, and some of it could well have been accurate regarding the substance. As a historian, Luke had the freedom to construct plausible speeches based on whatever was known or believed about the earliest Christian preaching. The point in the suggestions about oral memory, however, is that some of what was believed about early Christian preaching may well have been accurate, although we have it through the interpretive grid of hearers' memories and Luke's overarching narrative schema.

d. Expanding Speeches

"Amplification" (αὔξησις) normally referred to a rhetor's expanding on an important point in a speech,[358] but the techniques of amplification might also allow historians to expand briefer summaries or notes about speeches in their sources. Not all the techniques would work in Acts. One could, for example, lengthen speeches by recapitulating points (*Rhet. Alex.* 20, 1433b.29–1434a.17; 22, 1434b.5–11), but

---

352. Bauckham, *Eyewitnesses*, 330, 334–38, 350.

353. Ibid., 331. Reports of surprising details that violate observers' expectations are unlikely to have arisen from the frequent process of memories adjusting details to fit the schema (Redman, "Eyewitnesses," 181–82). Redman does warn on 182 that this observation does not guarantee their accuracy; one might add, however, that it improves the likelihood. Apart from particularly noteworthy, surprising details, in cases where some information fits the preexisting schema and other information does not, what fits the schema has the better chance of being recalled accurately (181).

354. Bauckham, *Eyewitnesses*, also Redman, "Eyewitnesses," 183 (on events that one considers significant).

355. Bauckham, *Eyewitnesses*, 331–32; Elliott, *Feelings*, 44–45 (citing, e.g., Izard, "Relationships," 22). Redman, "Eyewitnesses," 184, emphasizes these emotionally intense experiences, which produce "flashbulb memories—memories that are especially vivid and appear to be frozen in time, as though in a photograph." She considers eyewitness experiences of Jesus's miracles and the like as fitting this category; while these are among the most accurate of memories, they may develop in the first week through consultation with other witnesses and deteriorate over time; for reconstructive errors there, see Allison, *Jesus*, 7n40. The partial exception to the greater accuracy of intense memories may be experiences so intense that they produce temporary sensory overload, as on battlefields (see Woodman, *Rhetoric*, 18–22).

356. Bauckham, *Eyewitnesses*, 332. But see here Allison, *Jesus*, 7n40.

357. Bauckham, "Eyewitnesses," 334; Redman, "Eyewitnesses," 189 (noting that also with stories, elements retold most often were quickly stereotyped and remembered). Given the degree of overlap in information between Bauckham and Redman, Redman's conclusion (based on information similar to Bauckham's) that Bauckham's emphasis on eyewitnesses does not really increase the probability of accuracy significantly (193, 196–97) is surprising, and may reflect a misunderstanding of Bauckham's primary argument. Although all remembering includes distortion (194), it surely retains more information than not remembering, and eyewitnesses are still generally more reliable than nonwitnesses. Redman recognizes that Bauckham was not really claiming verbatim transmission of Jesus's words (do any scholars claim that?), yet supposes (195–96) that he wants to trust generally trustworthy witnesses fully, whereas in fact even they do not recall everything accurately. Bauckham was not, however, claiming to trust them on every point; rather, he regards eyewitness material as more likely accurate than other material, a thesis that, on average, should still hold true.

358. See Heath, "Invention," 95; Anderson, *Glossary*, 26–29.

because this procedure was especially helpful in long speeches (22, 1434b.1–5), it would probably not be very useful in short summaries of speeches (and hence, not surprisingly, is rare in Acts' speeches).

Ancient historians often augmented kernels of tradition, filling in outlines with what seemed historically plausible (which to them might seem to provide more historical verisimilitude than simply recounting an outline that was obviously much briefer than what was said on the occasion). Diodorus Siculus allowed limited "rhetorical embellishment" in composing speeches for historical works.[359] Historians could also abridge their sources. Those responsible for recording a previous generation's speeches could omit passages that had been poorly expressed rhetorically (Philost. *Vit. soph.* 2.29.621); they could also reshape them: a writer praises a sophist who not only "received" instruction as a disciple accurately but also "passed it on" eloquently (2.29.621). Some apparently even deleted from, and added to, predecessors' speeches as a rhetorical exercise (Pliny *Ep.* 7.9.5).

That most of Luke's speeches (apart from Stephen's) are much shorter may suggest that Luke failed to "fill in" his speeches as much. In addition, his audience probably held lower rhetorical expectations than those of most other extant historians' audiences (see discussion in chs. 2 and 4 above).[360] Despite such expectations, Luke's brevity was unusual, and scholars have noticed this distinction. Horsley, for example, suggests that Luke used the device of interruption to conceal this brevity.[361]

e. Comparing Hellenistic Jewish Speeches

Soards compares to Acts Hellenistic Judaism's blending of the forms of Greco-Roman historiography with Jewish content, especially from the LXX.[362] That the speeches in Acts resound with Septuagintal allusions renders plausible the suggestion that Luke, steeped in the LXX, might have its speeches in mind at various points. One could compare the longer speeches in the LXX, such as those of Samuel (1 Sam 12:1–25), Joshua (Josh 23:2–16; 24:2–27), and (throughout Deuteronomy) Moses.[363] Historians in the Greco-Roman period often deliberately imitated the speeches of classical literature, and so it would not be surprising that some speeches in Acts would deliberately evoke the LXX.[364] But there are, as Soards notes, some differences demanded at least by the different setting; the LXX speeches normally lack controversy settings and hence mostly lack an apologetic dimension.[365]

The LXX probably also affects Luke's "biblical" style at points, especially in recounting the early Jerusalem church. Scholars debate whether a "Jewish Greek" ever existed[366] or alleged Semitic elements simply reflect Koine Greek in general.[367] Because Hel-

---

359. Diod. Sic. 20.1–2; Aune, *Environment*, 93; idem, *Dictionary of Rhetoric*, 449.

360. The idea of composite collections of speech material is not new; John Calvin, trained as a humanist, allowed that the Gospel writers might have arranged some of Jesus's sermons from independent sayings (as cited in Blomberg, *Reliability of John's Gospel*, 52). On anthologies, see, e.g., Schwindt, "Anthology."

361. Horsley, "Speeches and Dialogues." See comment on Acts 2:37.

362. Soards, *Speeches*, 160.

363. Ibid., 156, noting also the heavy use of 2 Esd 19 in Acts 7; Kurichianil, "Speeches," comparing the farewell speeches in Acts 20:18–35 and 1 Sam 12:1–25. Various prophetic discourses (e.g., Jer 14:2–15:9) function as entire speech units, though this does not mean they fit Greco-Roman patterns (Gitay, "Criticism," 13–24).

364. Van der Horst, "Parallels to Acts," 56; Soards, *Speeches*, 139–40, both following Plümacher, *Lukas*, 38–78.

365. Soards, *Speeches*, 156–57; idem, "Speeches in Relation to Literature." The exception might be if one thinks of them answering accusations from Israel (cf. 1 Sam 12:3; but there does not seem to be actual controversy [cf. 12:4]).

366. In favor, cf., e.g., Turner, "Thoughts," 46–47; Nock, "Vocabulary," 138–39.

367. More common today, e.g., Horsley, *Documents*, 5:5–40; Porter, "Greek of New Testament," 430.

lenistic urban civilization in the eastern Mediterranean often imposed its Greek over previously dominant Aramaic language structures, it is reasonable to suppose that "Jewish Greek" is part of a wider phenomenon of eastern Mediterranean linguistic interchange that affected Koine in general. This principle probably extended to syntax as well. Philo and some Hellenistic Jewish intellectuals may have felt at home with periodization or syntactic subordination, but most of the apocrypha and pseudepigrapha reflect the more popular-level parataxis that also appears in the translation Greek of much of the LXX.[368] Although Luke significantly diminishes Mark's parataxis, he probably writes for a target audience that knows the LXX and will not be put off when he adopts a consciously semitizing style (as, e.g., in Luke 1–2).[369] (Ability to vary one's style was held to be praiseworthy; e.g., Cic. *Fam.* 9.21.1.)

Other early Jewish speeches may augment their sources. Pseudo-Philo's *Biblical Antiquities* freely adapts biblical speeches and composes new speech material for biblical characters.[370] While acknowledging that both Acts and Hellenistic Jewish historians used history for apologetic, Soards emphasizes the differences in the character of the speeches. He correctly observes that most Hellenistic Jewish works are fragmentary and Josephus's speeches (which are not fragmentary) are quite different. He may overemphasize the differences between Acts' speeches and those in 2 Maccabees, however, given the difference of purpose between the two works.[371] Where Acts is most distinctive from other works, he argues, is in its repetition of key themes.[372] Schubert's explanation for the dominance of speech material probably applies to the repetition of themes as well: the speeches in Acts are mostly kerygmatic, summarizing the apostolic message.

f. Comparing Josephus

Josephus offers our most extensive example of Hellenistic Jewish historiography. He tends, however, to be a more "rhetorical" historian than Luke could even pretend to be, and part of this rhetorical versatility includes extensive speech composition (admittedly, not all of it of the highest quality).[373]

I. SKEPTICISM ABOUT JOSEPHUS'S APPROACH

Although scholars have found many historical details where Josephus is reliable, most are skeptical about the historical authenticity of his speeches.[374] He seems to have taken fuller advantage than many of his contemporaries of the historians' liberties to create speeches *for rhetorical purposes at will*; that is, he is closer to the rhetorical historian Dionysius than to Thucydides or Polybius.[375] Of more than a

368. Anderson, *Rhetorical Theory*, 281, commenting on Paul's style.

369. See discussion on Luke's sources in Acts in ch. 6, esp. sect. 2.d, above; see also discussion in this commentary's introduction to Acts 1.

370. Bauckham, "Liber antiquitatum," 68, though doubting that this practice would apply so "readily to historical figures who were remembered as authoritative teachers and whose teaching was preserved."

371. Soards, *Speeches*, 157–60.

372. Ibid., 161; Soards allows that 2 Maccabees employs repetition, but contends that Acts uses it more (159–60).

373. On Josephus and rhetoric, see, e.g., Runnalls, "Rhetoric"; on the rhetoric in some of his forensic speeches (the same occasions but rewritten between the *War* and the *Antiquities*), see Saddington, "Rhetoric."

374. His work is full of them, including speeches to encourage for battle (e.g., Jos. *War* 1.373–79), to dissuade from war (2.345–401), to reject Zealots (4.162–92), and to surrender (5.375–419). By contrast, Nicolaus's defense of Archelaus (Jos. *Ant.* 17.240–47) may reflect a more reliable source, probably Nicolaus's own writings. Josephus probably follows his sources more closely in the *War* than in the later *Antiquities* (Newell, "Suicide Accounts," 285–86), where rhetorical interests (to produce a greater literary work) are stronger.

375. See, e.g., Mosley, "Reporting," 24; Hemer, *Acts in History*, 76–78; Attridge, "Historiography," 326; Mason, *Josephus and New Testament*, 192–94; Rajak, *Josephus*, 80; cf. Gempf, "Speaking," 299, who regards

hundred speeches in his *War*, "all are uniformly cast in the author's language and style" (not in itself uncommon among other historians), "all are deliberative or advisory, and all are vehicles for his personal viewpoint."[376] Many also reflect typical rhetorical uses of his time.[377] Although they are generally plausible, they repeat the same themes throughout (for reasons different from Acts).[378] Given the apologetic nature of his work, apologetic elements in the speeches are not surprising, even where they show up in relatively unexpected places.[379]

Although a few of his speeches may approximate what was said and some others are so linked to their occasion that we likely get their gist, there are also many literary "'set' speeches inserted and invented for the turning points."[380] For example, in one speech Josephus has Titus exhort his soldiers publicly by talking about the Jewish God (*War* 6.39–41).[381] Elsewhere Josephus presents one speech for a particular occasion in his *War* but provides a completely different one for his *Antiquities*; Josephus thus seems to presuppose that his readers would accept or at least pardon this practice.[382]

One may also illustrate Josephus's penchant for free composition by comparing his *Antiquities* in its early chapters with its primary written source. For example, Josephus considerably expands God's words of reproof to Adam in Gen 3 (*Ant.* 1.46). He also invents a bold speech for Moses during the challenge of Korah (4.25–34) and a seductive speech for the Midianite women (4.134–38). And in flat contradiction to Exodus (Exod 4:10, 14–16), he claims that Moses was skillful in speech making and spoke loudly (*Ant.* 4.25). Even prophets such as Samuel sound like rhetoricians in a Hellenistic history (6.20–21), and Josephus continues his rewriting in the material he derives from 1 Maccabees.[383]

II. Composing Speech without Witnesses

Following the common historical practice of inserting speeches to keep the narrative graphic, Josephus reports private conversations in direct discourse (Jos. *Ant.* 19.78–83; cf. Acts 25:14–22; Tac. *Ann.* 12.65). Elsewhere he reports accurate information selectively. Thus Claudius's edict to Alexandrians in Jos. *Ant.* 19.280–85 is a reaffirmation of Jewish rights there; historically, however, we know (P.Lond. 1912) that Claudius reproved the Jewish residents *as well as* affirmed their rights. The preserved decree does affirm their rights, but it also warns them not to agitate

---

Josephus as exceptional. With respect to compositional standards, however, Price, "Failure," argues that Josephus's careful composition meets Thucydidean standards.

376. Aune, *Environment*, 107. For his speeches' deliberately revealing his distinctive theology and perspectives, see Lindner, "Geschichtsauffassung" (summarizing Lindner's dissertation; addressing speeches in *War* 2, 5, and 7); Josephus uses his allies' speeches to advance his own position (Rajak, *Josephus*, 180), these allies functioning as reliable characters. He does supply some opposing speeches.

377. Aune, *Environment*, 108; Bünker, "Disposition der Eleazarreden."

378. See Rajak, *Josephus*, 81; for their function in denouncing rebels, see Rajak, *Josephus*, 81–82.

379. See Kelley, "Perspective."

380. Gempf, "Speaking," 289–90.

381. Ibid., 290. See also Jos. *Ant.* 10.7 (which echoes 2 Kgs 18:25); Josephus omits the more directly affirmed divine causation in 2 Chr 35:21–22 (*Ant.* 10.75–76; also missing in 2 Kgs 23:29).

382. Jos. *War* 1.373–79; *Ant.* 15.126–46; often noted, e.g., Gempf, "Speaking," 290; Cadbury, Foakes-Jackson, and Lake, "Writing History," 13–14; Dunn, *Acts*, xviii. (Woodman, *Rhetoric*, 176–79, suggests what could be an analogous change from Tacitus's *Histories* to his *Annals*, though we should not presume that Tacitus lacked other sources, and hence details, no longer extant.) Luke varies wording in two versions of a speech in his two-volume work (Luke 24:47–49; Acts 1:4–8) but without changing the basic sense.

383. Mosley, "Reporting," 24n2, illustrates by comparing 1 Macc 2:50–68 and Jos. *Ant.* 12.279–84; Aune, *Environment*, 82, by comparing 1 Macc 8:23–32 with Jos. *Ant.* 12.417–18 (where Josephus reduces the speech nearly by half). Still, Gafni, "Josephus and Maccabees" (esp. 126–27), emphasizes that even in the speeches, Josephus tends to *adapt* 1 Maccabees for his Hellenistic audience, not to create.

for more, and Josephus has not only omitted this inconvenient information but clearly elaborated on the decree abundantly (albeit within the spirit of the affirmation element).[384]

Eleazar's final speech for the Sicarii at Masada is clearly Josephus's own composition, his "greatest masterpiece" rhetorically.[385] Archaeology confirms much of Josephus's report about Masada, but the speech is implausible.[386] As Tessa Rajak observes, this speech fits the long-standing tradition, found, for example, in Tacitus, "of putting stirring and even anti-Roman words into the mouths of defeated enemies."[387] One could claim that the only two survivors of the mass suicide (two women who hid)[388] might have eavesdropped and reported the speech's substance, but what is the likelihood that two Sicarii women would have had sufficient Greek rhetorical and philosophical understanding to recount such a speech?[389]

Worse yet, it is difficult to imagine the leader of the Sicarii expounding philosophically on the soul's immortality (Jos. *War* 7.344–57), adding analogies (7.349–50) and foreign examples (7.351–57) for not being afraid of dying, and the consequent moral propriety of their suicide.[390] Josephus's readers would recognize that Josephus was practicing his rhetorical and philosophic hand, not reporting what Eleazar said.[391] Of course, Josephus may invent more freely when no witnesses remain than when, for example, Agrippa is known to have publicly advised a particular course on a particular occasion.[392]

III. JOSEPHUS NOT THE STANDARD

Josephus was hardly an ideal standard for historical speech writing. He is more emotionally committed to his material than most other historians because he has a personal stake in the matters about which he writes, the other side of the advantage of his being an eyewitness. Thus he includes three of his own orations and others by his allies, all of which advance his position and denounce his own position's critics

---

384. The only element of reproof sounded appears in Jos. *Ant.* 19.290, warning Jewish people not to look down on other nations' practices, but even this is put in Jewish terms, filtered through Josephus's perspective. It sounds much less explicit than Claudius's warning that they should stop agitating for citizenship (P.Lond. 1912, col. 3, lines 88–89)!

385. Sanders, *Judaism*, 6.

386. Cohen, "What Happened at Masada?" But some scholars do suggest that there remain historical reminiscences beneath his hellenized reworking (cf. Bauernfeind and Michel, "Beiden Eleazarreden").

387. Rajak, *Josephus*, 80–81. For the "noble barbarian" tradition, cf. this commentary's introduction to Acts 8:26–40; briefly, Keener, *Matthew*, 105n96.

388. Unless Josephus invented them as literary informants; but given the conspicuousness of Josephus's free composition, this is unlikely.

389. Granted, some women studied philosophy (Diog. Laert. 1.89–90; 2.72, 86; 4.1; 8.1.42–43; Iambl. *V.P.* 36.267; Lefkowitz and Fant, *Life*, 160, §168), including well-known examples such as Hipparchia (Diog. Laert. 6.7.96–98; Diogenes *Ep.* 3; Crates *Ep.* 28–29) and later Sosipatra (Eunapius *Lives* 466–69); for the Stoic ideal, see, e.g., Mus. Ruf. 4; Ward, "Musonius," 288; among Jewish scholars, Beruriah (cf. Adler, "Virgin"). Others were also well educated (e.g., Sall. *Catil.* 25.2; Quint. *Inst.* 1.1.6; 4 Macc 18:11–19; Jos. *Life* 185; *Sipre Deut.* 307.4.1; *Sop.* 18:5; cf. Blomqvist, "Chryseïs"; Brooten, *Women Leaders*, 5–33; Blank, "Texts"). But the training was sometimes limited (Mus. Ruf. 4, p. 46.8–23; Ilan, *Women*, 190–204; Swidler, *Women*, 104–11) and was much rarer than with men (Gamble, "Literacy," 645; Scholer, "Writing," 1283; Safrai, "Education," 955; Goodman, *State*, 74; Wegner, *Chattel*, 161–62; Swidler, *Women*, 97–104; Davies, *Rhetoric*, 252).

390. Sanders, *Judaism*, 7, thinks that Josephus portrays the Sicarii here more nobly than he dare elsewhere (and that he authentically portrays their spirit). Ladouceur, "Josephus and Masada," argues (plausibly) that Josephus views the speech and suicide negatively rather than heroically or as justified by Stoic notions of suicide as a choice.

391. See more fully Luz, "Masada" (especially his comparisons with Greek philosophic rhetoric). Cf. Paetus's poetic dying lamentations in Prop. *Eleg.* 3.7.57–64—to which there were obviously no witnesses.

392. But Josephus may have created even Agrippa II's speech (in the form in which it appears in *War* 2.345–404) as commentary revealing his views (Roduit, "Discours").

among the rebels.[393] Few Greek or even Roman historians "would have praised or endorsed the clumsy and inappropriate speeches of Josephus," though many (e.g., Lucian) allowed more freedom with speeches than with narrative.[394] We cannot infer too much from Josephus except that some historians took great latitude in speech composition and that they trusted their audience not to complain. We should not, however, assume that all historians made equal use of this rhetorical liberty. Luke is certainly less interested in providing his audience with full rhetorical speeches, even had he felt capable of doing so.

3. Unity among the Speeches?

One important literary issue in Luke's speeches is the question of their theological and (often) verbal unity. Clearly, the speeches in Acts reflect the work of the single author; because historians often used speeches to voice significant perspectives in their works, the theological unity of these speeches is essential for reconstructing the theology and message of Acts (including its apologetic thrust). These are the questions that will be of greatest importance for most readers of Acts.

Yet scholars have also traditionally asked whether such literary unity has a bearing on the question of historical authenticity. This scholarly debate, potentially more speculative and less fruitful for theological purposes, is nevertheless important for historical reconstruction. It is also important to those for whom the theology of the apostolic church, and not just the theology of Luke, is important. Because this question has consumed much scholarly ink and demands considerable space, it is our focus below; chapter 15 (esp. sect. 2) below will comment (albeit not at such length) on some of the theology of Luke's speeches.

a. Unity and the Authenticity Question

The answer to the question whether a significant degree of literary unity has a bearing on the question of historical authenticity depends partly on how we define "authenticity." If by "authenticity" we mean *ipsissima verba*, it is clear that Luke has not preserved the apostles' "very words"; probably he lacked access to them, and he probably also lacked interest in reporting them in that form.[395] If by "authenticity" we mean the basic substance of the speeches, Luke's selectivity and use of his own wording would have no bearing on whether he had authentic tradition, and therefore the speeches' unity would have little bearing on the authenticity question. Indeed, some scholars argue that there is sufficient variety in these speeches to suppose that Luke did preserve this much.

In most cases, we lack sufficient comparative material to make an objective comparison, but some evidence is stronger. Luke's speeches of Paul, for whom we have the most comparative authentic material (his letters), do contain some distinctive Paulinisms (such as "Son of God" and justification by faith).[396] This does not mean that Luke had a transcript of these speeches, but at the very least, it suggests that Luke was familiar enough with some of Paul's teaching that he could provide a sample of the sort of ideas that Paul would have articulated on such occasions (see comment on prosopopoeia, above).

393. Rajak, *Josephus*, 80–82, 180.
394. Gempf, "Speaking," 290.
395. So, e.g., Guthrie, *Introduction*, 381 (although he does believe [p. 382] that Luke preserves genuine reminiscences).
396. See extended comment at Acts 13:38–39, including the table comparing Pauline phraseology. One can also compare Paul's preaching against idolatry and even (against some) the approach to natural revelation (despite differences; see comment on Acts 17:22–31).

I do believe that it is reasonable to suppose that Luke had more than this minimum of information, but this suggestion is based especially on the case for the author as Paul's traveling companion (argued esp. at Acts 16:10), not on the internal evidence of the speeches treated here. Because I believe that the author was Paul's traveling companion (travel permitted much time for talking, and Luke, likelier than not, already had some historical interests at that time), I believe that Luke could have heard from Paul summaries of his message that Paul gave on particular significant occasions.[397] At the very least, however, we can say that Luke knows enough Pauline preaching to summarize the sort of preaching that Paul gave on such occasions, though in Luke's own words and reflecting what interested Luke in that message.

b. Literary Unity of Speeches

The narrative element of some speeches in Acts rehearses the story of Israel but also, at times, the outline of the gospel story also found in Luke (e.g., Acts 10:37–42). The evangelistic message in the speeches often reflects common themes that recur in the preaching of diverse speakers, showing that, as Luke saw it, there were common elements in the preaching of leading figures in the early Christian mission. Paul shares the same basic kerygma as the Twelve.[398]

Scholars have long noted structural similarities among speeches in Acts.[399] Eduard Schweizer's influential essay, in particular, underlined the very clear similarities in structure among the speeches in Acts and their compositional unity.[400] Differences, he noted, were far more often adaptations for different audiences than for different speakers.[401] (Adapting one's speeches for different audiences was considered good rhetorical practice; see, for example, Cic. *Fam.* 9.21.1.)[402] Subsequent studies have confirmed and developed the structural patterns in the speeches in Acts.[403]

I. Reasons for Similarities?

But what should we make of this unity? The structural unity in the way the speakers preached may be more impressive than the less surprising theological unity. When Paul preaches to a Jewish audience in Acts 13, most of his message sounds very much like Peter's earlier sermons to Jewish audiences.[404] (Others opine [less plausibly; cf. Acts 16:3; 18:18; 21:26] that Luke provides Paul a more "Gentile theology" than appears in his epistles.)[405]

Yet it would not be surprising if the early Christians' evangelistic preaching shared many common elements.[406] To some extent, these similarities in Acts' speeches may reflect the common gospel preached by early Christians not only in Acts but in most

---

397. Cf. also Robertson, *Luke*, 228.

398. See Pichler, "Anliegen," 742–43. According to the count in Borgman, *Way*, 11, Peter and Paul each deliver seven speeches.

399. E.g., Knox, *Acts*, 16–39.

400. Schweizer, "Davidic 'Son,'" 208–16. For structural similarities between Peter's first two sermons, see Zehnle, *Pentecost Discourse*, 19–24.

401. Schweizer, "Davidic 'Son,'" 214. For audience adaptation in good rhetoric, see, e.g., Dion. Hal. *Lysias* 9; Quint. *Inst.* 3.7.24.

402. One should also adapt one's style for the different genres of speeches (Dion. Hal. *Demosth.* 45–46).

403. See Via, "Moses and Meaning"; followed by Puskas, "Conclusion: Investigation," 42–43. Many of these components are, admittedly, self-evident elements of narrating a speech.

404. Dibelius and Kümmel, *Paul*, 11; Goulder, *Type and History*, 83. The classic statement of the non-Pauline character of Paul's speeches in Acts is Vielhauer, "Paulinism," but he clearly overstates his case (cf. Fitzmyer, *Acts*, 145–47; and ch. 7 above).

405. Cf. Barrett, "Acts and Corpus."

406. Dodd and Dibelius found in these patterns "reproductions of the apostolic preaching," but Wilckens thought otherwise (see *Missionsreden*); see van Unnik, "Storm Center," 26.

of our earliest Christian sources (see 1 Cor 15:1–11, esp. 15:11; Gal 1:7–8; 2:7–8);[407] although early Christians differed over matters such as circumcision and the place of Gentiles, they recounted the same basic passion outline (cf. 1 Cor 11:23–25; 15:3–7).[408] Their unity may thus simply reflect a standard early Christian kerygmatic pattern, resembling Mark 1:14–15 and found in some early Christian epistles.[409]

Evangelistic speeches to pagans (Acts 14:15–17; 17:22–31) follow a pattern attested in 1 Thess 1:9–10. Granted, no such pattern is attested for evangelistic speeches to Jews outside Acts, but this could be precisely because we lack early Christian speeches outside Acts and the sorts of sources that would supply us this kind of information.[410] Thus Luke's basic kerygma might reflect less his distinctive theology than an accurate reflection of the standard pattern of apostolic preaching. Those who believe early Christians used *testimonia*, or at least a common tradition of exegesis, will also not be surprised at recurrent patterns of biblical exegesis, especially in apologetic passages.[411]

Still, although the speeches normally echo the common gospel of the early church, they do not reflect the full range of diverse emphases found in other parts of the apostolic witness (e.g., the sacrificial value of Jesus's cross is emphasized less frequently than in some other early Christian sources, e.g., Rom 3:25; 5:9; 8:3; Heb 10:10–14; 1 John 2:2). Despite similarities with other NT documents, the apologetic themes and the ways the speeches develop them reflect more similarity among the speeches themselves than with literature outside Luke-Acts. This suggests that Luke at least pared the preaching down to elements he considers most relevant to his story.

II. Value of Repetition

Soards finds the repetition in the speeches one of their most distinctive elements vis-à-vis those of other Hellenistic histories. He argues that this repetition of common themes is part of Luke's specific literary plan; the repetitions create analogies and hence an "*emphasis* so that the speeches articulate a distinct worldview."[412] He believes that the standard topics in the sermons, which recur even when not directly relevant to the situation at hand, are (1) the christological kerygma; (2) the resurrection, especially of Jesus; (3) repentance and/or forgiveness; (4) "the universal significance of God's salvation"; and (5) the Holy Spirit. These are themes that Luke wishes to emphasize.[413] (Some of these suggested elements in the speeches, such as the resurrection, are considerably more pervasive than others, such as the Holy Spirit.)

---

407. Even Paul's first-century opponents apparently "distorted" the "gospel" not by denying the resurrection but by undermining Paul (2 Cor 11:4–6) or requiring circumcision for salvation (cf. Gal 1:6–7; contrast the "pillars" in 2:2, 7, though Paul feels that Peter compromises the gospel's implications in 2:14).

408. See Bruce, *Commentary*, 277, comparing Acts 2 with Acts 13; cf. also Peterson, "Extent"; Nanos, *Mystery*, 354, 358n45. Marshall, "Resurrection," 92–107, argues that the resurrection preaching in Acts derives from the earliest Christian sources. For some of the common elements in Acts' preaching, see Dodd, *Preaching*; and, e.g., in Petrine speeches, D'Souza, "Sermons of Peter." Dibelius himself allowed that the sermons followed the ancient kerygma also found in 1 Cor 15 (*Tradition*, 16–19).

409. As often affirmed since Dodd (*Preaching*); e.g., D. Williams, *Acts*, 10–11; deSilva, *Introduction*, 352–53 (noting parallels in 1 Peter).

410. Given the paucity of first-century Christian sources overall, one must avoid arguing too much from this silence. See here Bruce, *Acts*³, 37, also arguing that the use of Scripture in these speeches (with, e.g., "it was fulfilled") is not characteristic of Luke's own narrative and hence may reflect an earlier "apostolic" method in speeches (following Harris, *Testimonies*, 2:80).

411. Bruce, *Commentary*, 277, comparing Acts 2 with Acts 13; for Acts and Paul, cf. Bruce, "Paul's Use of Old Testament."

412. Soards, *Speeches*, 182–83 (quote, 183), though some speeches are more to advance the narrative than to put forward a view. But on stylistic unity see also my pp. 302, 308.

413. Ibid., 203–4.

Granted, they are also part of the preaching of the early church reflected elsewhere, as Luke correctly communicates. But they are Luke's selection, not, for example, Paul's or John's or that of the author of Hebrews.

The recurrent emphasis is surely deliberate; as Cicero observes, a good orator "will treat the same subject in many ways, sticking to the same idea and lingering over the same thought" (*Or. Brut.* 40.137 [LCL]). Yet even orators lingering over a single idea in one speech should employ different arguments in their various speeches; Dionysius praises Lysias for varying his arguments in the introductions of his two hundred forensic speeches but complains that many orators repeat the same commonplaces even in a few speeches (Dion. Hal. *Lysias* 17). Luke is clearly interested in continuity more than in expected rhetorical diversity. Soards draws attention to the analogous pattern of similarities in the speeches of Moses, Joshua, and Samuel, which most OT scholars believe provide coherence to the Deuteronomistic History in its current form.[414] Unity of the message is paramount.

c. Unity versus Historical Tradition?

The speeches in Acts must, at the least, reveal Luke's compositional artistry because "what we have in almost every case is a précis or edited summary of a speech, and not an entire speech."[415] Luke made no attempt to conceal the stylistic unity of his speeches; one may compare even the obvious opening addresses of speeches in Acts, most of which include ἄνδρες ("men") and many of which include ἄνδρες ἀδελφοί ("men, brothers") regardless of the speaker (Acts 1:16; 2:29, 37; 7:2, 26; 13:15, 26, 38; 15:7, 13; 22:1; 23:1, 6; 28:17).

I. STYLISTIC UNITY AND AUTHENTICITY?

Luke's style is fairly uniform in his narrative as well, where we can be relatively positive about his use of historical information.[416] Almost no one disputes that Luke used sources in his Gospel (Luke 1:1–4), but Luke writes the narrative in his own style (significantly editing Mark's grammar). He certainly edits Mark according to literary principles more acceptable among the highly educated, removing "barbarous" loanwords and transforming Mark's simple parataxis into more complex sentence structures.[417] Thus, even if Luke had sources, he, like other Greco-Roman historians, made them his own.[418]

Nevertheless, although the undeniable stylistic unity of Acts' speeches, which indicates the work's overall literary unity, indicates Lukan composition, scholars often note that this unity need not exclude historical tradition.[419] Acts 17:22–31 may be the most careful literary composition among the speeches, suggesting the most Lukan work, but even in this case one need not suppose that Luke lacked historical tradition about the event and essential substance (especially if, as argued above, he knew Paul and would thus have had access to Paul's own retellings of the events).[420]

414. With, e.g., Munck, *Acts*, xliv; Soards, *Speeches*, 12–13. Rosner, "Biblical History," 76, finds in Acts and the Deuteronomistic History analogous methods of periodization.

415. Witherington, *Acts*, 46; cf. idem, "Addendum," 31; Acts 2:40.

416. Cf. Dibelius, *Studies*, 2, 184–85, 201; Dupont, *Sources*, 166.

417. Koester, *Introduction*, 1:108. Rhetoricians knew (cf. Anderson, *Glossary*, 39) but did not favor such paratactic style.

418. Witherington, *Acts*, 117.

419. Hanson, *Acts*, 37; Lüdemann, *Christianity*, 47–48; Hengel, *Acts and History*, 61; Aune, *Environment*, 126; Fitzmyer, *Acts*, 105–6; Witherington, *Acts*, 117–19; Porter, *Paul in Acts*, 130.

420. Bruce, *Commentary*, 354, claims that classicists tend to find it authentic (citing Cadbury, "Speeches," 406n1); Bruce, *Apostle*, 244.

11. Stylistic Unity in Other Historians

As a comparison with other ancient sources indicates, stylistic unity does not by itself count against the presence of tradition. Thucydides and other ancient historians also lacked significant stylistic divergence in their speeches;[421] indeed, purely stylometric analysis cannot distinguish the speeches in Tacitus from his narrative.[422] Likewise, even on the level of thematic unity discussed above, Polybius repeats many themes in speeches by different figures, probably in part because some of these themes were common themes in speeches on issues relevant to the period in question.[423] It should hardly surprise us, then, if apostolic preaching of the kerygma in Acts repeats common themes when many of these themes are attested elsewhere in early Christian preaching.

Thus Porter warns, "This pattern is consistent with other historians of the ancient world. Common practice was to reshape one's sources, so that the original source was closely conformed to the author's own style."[424] Aune likewise concludes, "In epic, tragedy, comedy, and Herodotean history, characterization does not include linguistic individualization; direct speech uniformly reflects the author's style."[425] This is not to deny that orators, even highly praised orators, had their individual styles (see Cic. *Brut.* 56.204); rather, it means that historians felt no obligation—and probably, in many cases, had no means[426]—to reproduce an individual speaker's style in their writings, beyond some basic characteristics known to be distinctive to that speaker.

Hengel argues that Luke, though promoting his agendas in the speeches, mostly does so by using "older traditions. . . . Once again, this is the procedure which Lucian requires of the true historian: the words of the speaker should match his person and his concern."[427] Aune believes that in the speeches, Luke likely "combined research and memory with free composition."[428] But he rightly observes:

> While most historians imposed their own style on speeches (e.g., Thucydides, Polybius, and Dionysius of Halicarnassus), there are important exceptions (e.g., Herodotus). Writing speeches in styles appropriate to various speakers was widely practiced by

421. McCoy, "Shadow of Thucydides," 15–16; Witherington, "Addendum," 31; Laistner, *Historians*, 86 (uniform style in Thucydides and other historians); Porter, *Paul in Acts*, 130–31; Aune, *Dictionary of Rhetoric*, 448 (though allowing that some of these are inauthentic). This practice could, of course, occasion the complaint of a rhetorical historian (Dion. Hal. *Pomp.* 3.20, cited by Fitzmyer, *Acts*, 105); on memorizing or rewording speeches in earlier written material, see Dio Chrys. *Or.* 18.18–19. Thucydides's speeches do not resemble extant speeches actually delivered in his period but follow rhetorical handbooks from the era (Walbank, *Speeches*, 3), further suggesting that he has composed them (though not demanding that they are bereft of accurate information; see Walbank, *Speeches*, 4).

422. Wharton, "Tacitus' Tiberius" (noting that this conclusion does not resolve whether Tacitus used official sources).

423. So Walbank, *Speeches*, 13–15; see esp. 13: "If a point is valid, it may be made twice, and if all fourth-century speeches which mention the services of Athens against the Persians were to be branded as rhetorical forgeries, we should have few pro-Athenian apodeictic speeches left." Polybius might have composed such points freely; the point here is that we *need* not assume that he did so on the basis of modern content criticism.

424. Porter, *Paul in Acts*, 130–31.

425. Aune, *Environment*, 91, giving as an example the savage Cyclops's "'inappropriately' elegant speech" in Hom. *Od.* 9.447–60.

426. When it was available, sometimes they did reproduce the style, even when it was not rhetorically pleasant (e.g., Epict. *Diatr.* 1.pref. [see comments in Oldfather, "Introduction to Epictetus," xii–xiii]; the claim in Philost. *Vit. Apoll.* 8.6). Probably for reasons suggested above, Luke seems to underline this unity in the speeches far more than his elite contemporaries. Because prosopopoeia invited composing in varied styles, Luke appears less rhetorically sophisticated than some of his contemporaries (despite Semitic coloring in early chapters, Paulinisms, etc.).

427. Hengel, *Acts and History*, 61, citing Lucian *Hist.* 58 and also Thucyd. 1.22.

428. Aune, *Environment*, 125.

Hellenistic writers (Lucian, *History* 58; Theon, *Progymnasmata* 10). If one argues that speeches reflecting the historians' style are not authentic, the speeches of Thucydides would fail the test (dubious), but if one argued that speeches exhibiting stylistic variety are authentic, the speeches of Herodotus could be judged historical (equally dubious).

He concludes that "Luke's speeches stand between these two extremes, and no historical judgment is possible based on stylistic criteria alone."[429]

d. The Speeches: Accurate or Invented?

As will be argued below, the stark choice between claiming that the speeches were accurate and claiming that they were invented is a false dichotomy; indeed, many of the scholars surveyed below in fact represent not one position to the exclusion of the other but various positions on a continuum.

Virtually no scholars publishing in mainstream academic circles argue that the speeches in Acts are verbatim.[430] Verbatim reproduction of speeches was not possible, expected, or necessarily even desirable in ancient historiography (which, as already noted, differed in some respects from modern expectations for historiography). All scholars agree that the speeches are Luke's compositions, regardless of their views of the degree to which the speeches may also reflect traditional elements about the speakers' theology more generally or even words on those occasions.[431]

Indeed, Luke's own compositional method in Acts itself refutes any misplaced expectation of verbatim quotations: although multiple accounts of the same event often repeat verbal elements verbatim, they can also rephrase them differently (compare, e.g., Acts 9:5–6 with 22:8, 10; 9:15–16 and 22:10 with 26:16–18; 10:5–6 with 11:13–14; compare also 9:4 with 26:14; 1:4–5, 7–8 with Luke 24:47–49). Other arguments may also point in this direction: if we compare the contents of the speeches, in matters of detail, with external historical data, Luke generally fares quite well, but most scholars doubt this to be the case in the notorious reference to Theudas and Judas, in a speech behind closed doors. Here many would argue that in Acts 5:36–37 Luke simply mentions the best-known revolutionary movements for Gamaliel, whose exact words would not likely be known or recalled even if (via Paul or another) his gist was known (or could be inferred from the outcome).[432] Indeed, on the basis of the way speeches were composed, it is plausible that Luke would not need to have Paul's Areopagus speech before him to provide a genuinely "Pauline" Areopagus speech for that occasion; he could have known well enough the substance of Paul's preaching on such occasions (cf. Rom 1:19–20; 1 Thess 1:9) to represent him appropriately.[433] (Focusing on differences

429. Ibid., 126 (Aune does not believe that Thucydides succeeded in his goal of accuracy regarding speeches in every case [p. 92], but remains even more skeptical of Herodotus [91]).

430. Cf., e.g., the insistence of Marshall, *Acts*, 41–42, on genuine Lukan compositional freedom alongside tradition (also idem, "Acts," 516). Despite the prejudicial stereotype among some of their detractors, the vast majority of conservative biblical scholars do not even claim verbatim reports (or something like exact translation) for Jesus's sayings in the Gospels, which plainly vary in wording (cf. Stagg, *Acts*, 26; Wenham, *Bible*, 92–95; Feinberg, "Meaning," 299–301 [the exact voice, but not words, of Jesus]; Bock, "Words," 75–77); "minor variations" in Paul's conversion stories likewise show lack of interest in verbatim retellings (Stagg, *Acts*, 26–27; Abbott, *Acts*, 111; Witherington, *Acts*, 311; Dunn, *Acts*, 117). Recognizing the literary genres involved, even the strictest models of inspiration would not ascribe to personages mentioned in, e.g., the book of Job the poetic discourses attributed to them (Metzger, "Forgeries," 22). The use of speeches in the genre of ancient history may likewise be taken into account.

431. See Powell, *Acts*, 32.

432. Presumably, most of Luke's ideal audience had never heard of Theudas, but perhaps some had.

433. This is one approach; other alternatives are composition without even attempting to imitate Paul (rhetorically improbable); insufficient information to imitate Paul well; and Luke's (or his source's) knowledge, from Paul, of the gist of what he said on that occasion. See this commentary's comment ad loc.

between Paul's presentation of natural theology in Romans and that in his speeches in Acts, scholars sometimes underestimate the points of commonality.)[434]

To claim that the speeches are not verbatim, however, no more means that none of them may preserve the essential substance of the message of speeches than to make the same claim for sayings in the Jesus tradition.[435] (Even the Jesus Seminar, which represents a relatively skeptical segment of North American Jesus scholarship, accepts some genuine tradition among sayings attributed to Jesus!)[436] I have already noted that early Christians would not have preserved apostolic sayings in the same way that they preserved those of Jesus; here, however, we examine what Luke did with what he had available. If Luke has accurately preserved many of Jesus's sayings in his Gospel—and comparison with other extant Gospels, where he can be checked, does suggest that he did—we would not expect him to prove careless in Acts with the apostolic tradition available to him.[437] Witherington seeks to quantify this approach; when following Mark, Luke adapts wording in the narratives but "reproduces about 53 percent of Mark's exact words." He suggests that the same would be likely in the apostolic tradition.[438] Because it is doubtful that Luke possessed written documents for more than a handful of his speeches in Acts, I believe that this figure is too optimistic. Nevertheless, the analogy with Luke's use of Mark does suggest Luke's basic conservatism (appropriate for historians) with the substance of his sources.

Luke and his sources likely treated sayings of the church's Lord differently from others' speeches.[439] Yet given the respect he shows Paul and the Twelve, his respectful way of preserving Jesus material at least suggests that he would also respectfully preserve relevant elements of the apostolic message where he had them available. Luke is not an aristocratic rhetorical historian interested in displaying his own rhetorical talent in the speeches (if he were one, he apparently expended most of his rhetorical skill in his Gospel preface and had little left over afterward).

In 1942, F. F. Bruce argued, continuing the more conservative (and historically dominant) tradition, that the speeches in Acts were not verbatim reports but provided the gist of what was said on each occasion.[440] The view that speeches in Acts provide at least the gist of what was said continues to be widely defended.[441] Many thus contend that Luke sought to report the speeches accurately.[442]

434. See, e.g., Porter, *Paul in Acts*, 145. The approach in these texts is not, of course, exclusively Pauline; from Philo to Augustine, monotheists challenged pagan natural philosophy (Miller, "Idolatry").

435. Others have also offered this comparison; e.g., Dodd, *Preaching*, 18; Ridderbos, "Speeches of Peter," 9; Hemer, *Acts in History*, 78–79.

436. I treat the issue of Jesus's sayings in more detail in Keener, *Matthew*, 24–32; idem, *John*, 29–34; idem, *Historical Jesus*, chs. 13–15.

437. E.g., Smalley, "Christology of Acts"; Munck, *Acts*, xlii; Longenecker, *Exegesis*, 82.

438. Witherington, "Editing," 326–27 (quote, 326).

439. Correctly, e.g., Liefeld, *Acts*, 63.

440. Bruce, *Speeches in Acts*, passim; cf. idem, "Speeches Thirty Years After"; for OT use, idem, "Paul's Use of Old Testament."

441. E.g., Ridderbos, "Speeches of Peter," 9; Munck, *Acts*, xliv; Longenecker, *Exegesis*, 80–82; Gasque, "Speeches," 248–49; idem, "Acts and History," 58–63; Fitzmyer, *Acts*, 105–6; Witherington, *Acts*, 117; Dudley, "Speeches in Acts."

442. Of course, it is precarious to define "accuracy" and "gist" too narrowly, since what Luke had available may have varied from one speech to the next, and even in Luke's Gospel, many scholars argue that he may take more liberty in constructing the Nazareth synagogue pericope than with most other scenes. At the very least, the gist would normally be the subject of the speech given on an occasion, along with whatever could be reconstructed of how it was developed on the basis of tradition regarding the speech, regarding the speaker, or (where the least would be available) regarding the era. Such a definition allows Luke literary flexibility but also allows him to draw on substantial tradition where he had it available. Given the brevity of the speeches, Luke probably does not need to flesh out his sources much.

From the standpoint of other Greco-Roman literature, this contention is certainly plausible and (so long as phrased in terms of gist) even probable in speeches where Luke had access to what was said on an occasion. What some (though not all) of its advocates have failed to do, however, is address the literary unity of the speeches in Acts. The speeches' literary unity has been a major factor in persuading the majority of critical scholars, following especially the argument earlier established by Dibelius, to view the speeches as Lukan compositions.[443] Some also point to language from Luke's day in even the earlier speeches.[444] On the basis of such arguments, many thus doubt that Luke sought to report the speeches accurately.

But as noted above, not all scholars accept a forced choice between the speeches' compositional unity as we have them and the historical tradition behind them. The extremes of such mutually exclusive positions, each citing substantial evidence, might bring scholarship to an impasse, but the extremes of these positions conflict much more than does the evidence cited as support for either of them. Many scholars (especially those who argue for the gist) recognize both that Luke reports something of the substances of speeches, where he has them available (which should have been often, especially for major Pauline speeches), and that he has freely reworked them to fit the overall literary and theological purpose of his work.

e. Historical Tradition in the Speeches?

Many scholars who do not believe that all the speeches contain pre-Lukan material nevertheless find it in some of them. Richard Zehnle, for example, argues that Luke freely composed "a rhetorical masterpiece" in Acts 2, but finds elements of early source material in Acts 3 or in 10:34–43.[445]

One can agree that the speeches mostly reflect Luke's style, yet find some elements that not only are not characteristically Lukan but that better fit the language of an earlier period or other voices in NT theology. Certainly, it is reasonable to hope that in Acts Luke wishes to recall the earliest kerygma, insofar as possible, especially given his willingness to portray rather than cover over the misunderstandings of the earliest church regarding the Gentile mission (10:14, 28; 11:3) and eschatology (1:6).[446]

I. SEMITISMS AND "PRIMITIVE" CHRISTOLOGY

Max Wilcox seeks to isolate pre-Lukan tradition by means of stylistic criteria (particularly Semitisms); Jewish Christian elements predating Luke's more metropolitan Greco-Roman milieu; comparison of speeches with writers (e.g., Paul) outside Acts; and points where a speech does not fit its context well.[447] Thus, for example, scholars find some Semitisms in the early speeches.[448] These make Luke's Greek style more

---

443. Dibelius, *Studies in Acts*, 138–85; Townsend, "Speeches"; Wilckens, *Missionsreden*; Schweizer, "Concerning Speeches."

444. E.g., Jones, "*Christos* in Luke-Acts"; for theological unity, Townsend, "Speeches."

445. Zehnle, *Pentecost Discourse*, passim (e.g., p. 37 on the "masterpiece"; 43 on Acts 10:34–43). Lüdemann, *Christianity*, 48, thinks that elements of Acts 2 (such as 2:21, 34–35) are pre-Lukan.

446. Despite Luke's portrayal of other aspects of the earliest church as ideal or pristine (cf. Acts 2:44–45). Granted, he can use the apostles as a foil for God's work (as in the gospel tradition), but (as again in the gospel tradition) enemies might have made better foils than the church's "heroes" if it did not happen much as Luke suggests.

447. Wilcox, "Foreword to Speeches."

448. Dodd, *Preaching*, 19–20, following Torrey, *Composition*, who viewed most of the first half of Acts as Aramaic material; cf. Martin, "Evidence," 59; Payne, "Semitisms"; Ehrhardt, *Acts*, 1. Torrey underestimated the extent to which Koine, Semitic (or aramaized Greek), and translation Greek overlap (cf. LXX; *Jos. As.*; cf. Turner, "Thoughts," 46; Nock, "Vocabulary," 138–39; though, for Rome, contrast Leon, *Jews*, 92), but it is

awkward than is customary for him,[449] when one would expect his speeches to be, if anything, more polished.[450]

Many scholars point to elements of "primitive" Christology in early speeches in Acts—the speeches, in fact, with which we would have expected Luke to have had the least personal acquaintance.[451] W. L. Knox doubts that Christians of Luke's generation would have spoken of God *making* Jesus Lord and Christ (2:36) or of a "man" appointed (2:22); Stephen calls Jesus "Son of Man" (7:56), a title elsewhere in the NT found almost exclusively on Jesus's own lips.[452]

Although Luke would not have disagreed with the theology of the earlier speeches, neither was it the common language of his day. Knox notes that only after Paul's conversion do we find "anything which corresponds to the later and more developed Christology of the Pauline Epistles."[453] Knox finds in Luke's failure to harmonize the earlier language with the language of his own day "a striking testimony to Luke's fidelity to his sources and to their reliability."[454]

J. W. Doeve finds traditional Jewish methods of argumentation in both Acts 2 and Acts 13, though suggesting that the latter is closer to rabbinic style than the former, as one might have expected from their purported authors. Doubting that Luke would be as familiar with these methods as Peter and Paul would be, Doeve suggests that these factors indicate pre-Lukan tradition.[455] One might object that Luke could be familiar enough (like Doeve himself) to situate Paul or Peter appropriately within their milieu; yet Luke does not usually betray sophisticated knowledge of Jewish exegetical practices. Nevertheless, although this argument may suggest pre-Lukan tradition, it need not guarantee that such words were said on the specific occasion depicted; one could argue that Luke had genuine sources suggesting that Peter, Paul, or another early interpreter sometimes employed these exegetical maneuvers, without one presuming that the speaker must have employed them on this particular occasion.

ii. Need for a Balanced Appraisal

Several factors somewhat temper this analysis. First, Luke may deliberately "archaize" language for the early sermons[456] (though his ability to archaize presupposes his knowledge of earlier Christian language, making his effort more conscious than most critics suppose). Second, "high" Christology does appear even in the earliest speeches (see comment on Acts 2:38), though Luke's employment of the language of his day need not obliterate some "primitive" language retained from his sources as well.[457] Third, Paul's own extant letters begin less than two decades after Pentecost, and so the period of development in terminology assumed by this model is relatively

---

true that apparent Semitisms predominate in the early chapters. Proposed Semitisms must be examined on a case-by-case basis.

449. Gasque, "Speeches," 248–49; Bruce, *Acts*[1], 18.

450. At least—for the sake of verisimilitude—in Paul's speeches. But that is, in fact, what we find for Paul's speeches (see discussion below).

451. C. Williams, *Acts*, 47–48; Moule, "Christology of Acts"; Smalley, "Christology of Acts," 358; idem, "Christology Again"; Robinson, *Studies*, 139–53 (regarding the Christology of Acts 3:12–26 as more primitive than that in 2:14–39).

452. Knox, *Acts*, 75–76.

453. Ibid., 77.

454. Ibid., 78. One may of course unintentionally echo one's sources at points; thus, for example, some echoes of the voices of my interviewees remain in my reports of their words in *Miracles* (esp. in 264–599, 712–59, passim) despite editing by myself and other editors.

455. Doeve, *Hermeneutics*, 176. Cf. examples I note in comment on Acts 20:18–35.

456. C. Williams, *Acts*, 44; Soards, *Speeches*, 140. This may reflect deliberate septuagintalizing (Hengel, *Acts and History*, 62; De Zwaan, "Greek Language") to fit the character of his speakers.

457. For christological language from Luke's own day in Acts, see, e.g., Jones, "*Christos* in Luke-Acts."

brief. Fourth, some elements that have been cited as "early" (such as God enthroning Christ) also appear in later documents (Eph 1:20; Heb 1:13).[458]

Although these factors exclude some evidence and diminish the importance sometimes attached to the rest, the use of some titles only in earlier speeches in Acts does seem to reflect a knowledge that the preaching in Jerusalem differed from Paul's preaching, pointing in the direction of tradition (at the least concerning the language and ideas of the earlier church). Although Luke emphasizes unity and continuity in the apostolic message, he is not willing to sacrifice verisimilitude to this end. His narratives, including his description of Jerusalem Christians worshiping in the temple and making inroads even into the priesthood, indicate that, in the words of R. P. C. Hanson's Oxford commentary, Luke "knew very well what Christianity was like during the period roughly A.D. 50–60. It is unlikely that such a man knew nothing about the preaching and teaching of the primitive church."[459]

III. Petrinisms, Paulinisms

Scholars often compare speeches in Acts to writings attributed to the purported authors of the speeches.[460] This is the sort of an argument that could have carried some weight with ancient stylistic critics, who recognized that particular writers might employ their language in distinctive ways.[461] Thus, for example, some find distinctly Petrine material both in Peter's speeches in Acts and in 1 Peter.[462]

More substantially (given the broader and less disputed base of evidence), scholars also find parallels between the Paul of the letters and Paul's speeches in Acts[463]—for example, "Son of God" (Acts 9:20) and justification by faith (13:38–39). Correspondences are, however, especially notable with 20:18–35. Even those who regard the speech as largely Lukan composition often recognize its overwhelmingly Pauline elements, so that the speech reflects imitation of Paul's actual way of speaking: "This is surely not Stephen or Peter delivering the speech. It is unmistakably Paul."[464] Because this is the only speech in Acts addressed to a Christian audience, it is the one case where we can best test similarities with Paul's letters, which also exhort Christian audiences.[465]

---

458. It does, after all, reflect the language of Ps 110:1 (Heb 1:13). The source of enthronement is less specific in Heb 1:3; 8:1; 10:12; 12:2; 1 Pet 3:22.

459. Hanson, *Acts*, 37–38.

460. E.g., Hengel, *Acts and History*, 61; Munck, *Acts*, xliv; Kistemaker, "Speeches in Acts"; Williamson, *World of Josephus*, 290, as quoted in Yamauchi, *Stones*, 97; D. Williams, *Acts*, 11.

461. E.g., Philost. *Hrk.* 11.5 (on Hom. *Od.* 18.359, using *Il.* 21.197); Dion. Hal. *Lysias* 11–12; *Demosth.* 50. But sometimes the same speaker employed different styles in different genres of writing (e.g., Cic. *Fam.* 9.21.1; Philost. *Vit. Apoll.* 7.35), and so even lack of similarities would not necessarily prove different authors.

462. E.g., Selwyn, *Peter*, 33–36; D. Williams, *Acts*, 11; Smalley, "Christology Again" (though I doubt that "Petrine" Christology is that distinctive). Some themes recur in Peter's speeches, though these are adapted for different settings (cf. Tannehill, "Functions of Peter's Speeches"). Kistemaker, *Acts*, 9–11, finds some convoluted Greek in Peter's speeches (Acts 3:16; 10:36–37) comparable to 1 Pet 4:11; 2 Pet 3:5b–6, though convoluted Greek appears elsewhere. He also parallels appeals to God's foreknowledge (Acts 2:23; 1 Pet 1:2) and references to the judge of the living and the dead (Acts 10:42; 1 Pet 4:5), but one might compare also non-Petrine texts such as Rom 8:29; 2 Tim 4:1. For prophecy in Petrine sources, see now Himes, "Peter."

463. E.g., Baum, "Paulinismen," esp. 414–35, on Paul's mission speeches; see more detailed discussion in this commentary on relevant passages. Some appeal is also made to unusually distinctive local color in locations that Luke is not likely to have visited himself (e.g., Porter, *Paul in Acts*, 139, following esp. Breytenbach, "Zeus und Gott"). Some speeches to Jewish audiences also imply midrashic techniques in Luke's sources that he does not develop and may not have recognized (see comments esp. on Acts 2, 3, 13, and 15).

464. Johnson, *Acts*, 367; cf. Hemer, "Ephesian Elders"; Stanton, *Jesus of Nazareth*, 111; Witherington, *Acts*, 171.

465. Walton, *Leadership*, 1, noting that it is "widely recognised as paralleling the language and ideas of the Pauline epistles."

The articulation of ministry principles here[466] fits the practical pastoral concern of the Paul of the letters.[467] This speech employs language familiar from philosophers and moralists,[468] just as Paul's letters do.[469]

Simon Kistemaker lists several parallels:[470]

Acts 20:18–35	Letters
Serving the Lord with all humility (20:19)	Serving the Lord (Rom 12:11)
Serving the Lord with all humility (20:19)	With all humility (Eph 4:2)
So I may complete the race (20:24)	I have completed the race (2 Tim 4:7)
Finish the ministry I received from the Lord (20:24)	Fulfill the ministry you received from the Lord (Col 4:17)

Unfortunately, only one of these parallels is from a letter universally agreed to be from Paul; the others, however, are, at the least, from the distinctively Pauline circle.

Some other scholars have provided more abundant parallels. Steve Walton's extensive study of parallels between this speech and just one of Paul's letters, 1 Thessalonians (probably his earliest extant letter), turns up numerous parallels.[471] Although some other parallels might be added,[472] Stanley Porter provides an extensive list of even verbal parallels in the Pauline corpus (including numerous ones from the less disputed letters):[473]

- Serving the Lord (Acts 20:19; Rom 12:11)[474]
- "With all humility" (Acts 20:19; Eph 4:2)[475]
- "Jews and Greeks" (Acts 20:21; Rom 3:9; 1 Cor 1:22, 24; 10:32; 12:13)[476]
- "Complete the course" (Acts 20:24; 2 Tim 4:7)[477]
- Complete his service (Acts 20:24; Col 4:17; 2 Tim 4:5)
- The service received from the Lord (Acts 20:24; Col 4:17)

466. See, e.g., in Barnes, "Finishing," 240; Gilliland, "Missionaries," 260–70.

467. On which see, e.g., Malherbe, "Paul as Pastor" (esp. on 1 Thess, 126–28). Paul's own ministry style was flexible, reflecting both the compassion and the sternness of a parent (e.g., 1 Cor 4:14–21; 2 Cor 12:14; 1 Thess 2:7, 11; cf. the thesis of Joubert, "Shifting Styles," even if one might differ on the examples).

468. Malherbe, *Philosophers*, 152–54.

469. See ibid., passim (e.g., on 1 Thess, 49–66; but esp. 67–77, even if Malherbe's conclusion [77] may be overstated).

470. From Kistemaker, *Acts*, 11–12. Parallels also appear in the speech summary in Acts 14:22, again addressed to believers (see comment ad loc.).

471. Walton, *Leadership*, 140–85; he also shows (203–12) that these parallels reflect dependence not on 1 Thessalonians but on authentic Pauline tradition. He observes (186–92) some parallels with Ephesians but notes that they are far less close than with 1 Thessalonians.

472. Hanson, *Acts*, 203, includes recalling the past (Phil 1:5; Col 1:6; cf. also, e.g., 1 Cor 2:1–5; Gal 4:13–14), tears (2 Cor 2:4; cf. also Phil 3:18), and protesting innocence (1 Thess 2:3–11; 2 Cor 7:2). Dunn, *Acts*, 271, adds others, most notably "profitable" (Acts 20:20; 1 Cor 6:12; 10:23; 12:7; 2 Cor 8:10; 12:1).

473. Porter, *Paul in Acts*, 117. Four of these also appear in Kistemaker, *Acts*, 11–12.

474. The verb δουλεύω appears elsewhere in Acts only at 7:7 (though in the Gospel at Luke 15:29; 16:13); it appears sixteen times in Pauline literature, in this sense in Rom 14:18; Eph 6:7; Col 3:24; 1 Thess 1:9; cf. Rom 7:25.

475. The exact match appears only in Eph 4:2 in the NT; the term ταπεινοφροσύνη is also mostly from Paul's later years (Eph 4:2; Phil 2:3; Col 2:18, 23; 3:12; elsewhere in the NT only 1 Pet 5:5). Cognate evidence is more ambiguous; the cognate adjective appears three times in Paul (against once in Luke); the verb only once more in Paul than in Luke.

476. It is also Lukan (Acts 14:1; 18:4; 19:10, 17), though in the Diaspora, Pauline, section of Acts. As a Hellenist in Jerusalem, Paul probably naturally thought in these terms.

477. More general athletic imagery, including running, is common in Paul, as among other Diaspora teachers (1 Cor 9:24, 26; Gal 2:2; Phil 2:16; 3:12–14; see more fully Pfitzner, *Agon Motif*).

- The grace of God (Acts 20:24, 32; passim)[478]
- Church of God (Acts 20:28; passim)[479]
- Watch for yourselves (Acts 20:28; 1 Tim 4:16)
- Consider (Acts 20:31; 1 Cor 16:13; Col 4:2; 1 Thess 5:6, 10)
- "Build up" (Acts 20:32; Rom 15:20; 1 Cor 8:1, 10; 10:23; 14:4, 17; Gal 2:18; 1 Thess 5:11)[480]
- The inheritance among saints (Acts 20:32; Col 1:12)
- Hands working (Acts 20:34–35; 1 Cor 4:12; Eph 4:28)
- "Repeated language of earnestness (Acts 20:31; 1 Thess 2:7–8)"

One could add other examples. As in Acts 20:24, the Paul of the epistles also resolved to face death for the gospel's sake (1 Cor 15:31–32; 2 Cor 4:10–11; 6:9; 11:23; Phil 1:21; 2:17; 3:10–11). As in Acts 20:31, "admonish" (νουθετέω) is common in Paul's letters (Rom 15:14; 1 Cor 4:14; Col 1:28; 3:16; 1 Thess 5:12, 14; 2 Thess 3:15); it appears nowhere in the NT except Paul and here. The pairing of "day" with "night" was fairly familiar in ancient language (see comment on Acts 20:31), but it may be noteworthy that Paul applies it to his ministry, as in Acts 20:31 (1 Thess 2:9; 3:10; 2 Thess 3:8). As in Acts 20:33–35, the epistolary Paul also worked to distance himself from charlatans, sometimes in conventional ways (2 Cor 2:17; cf. 1 Thess 2:3–7).[481] The working with his hands in Acts 20:34–35 also becomes an example for others, as in Pauline epistolary exhortation.[482] The purpose of having enough in Acts 20:35 was to "help" the weak; Paul spoke of helping the weak in 1 Thess 5:14, and the same purpose for work appears in Eph 4:28.

In addition to these verbal parallels are biographic information (e.g., Paul's reluctance to burden churches; Acts 20:33–34; 1 Cor 9; 2 Cor 11:7–11; 1 Thess 2:9–12) and theological similarities (cf. perhaps "blood of his own" in Acts 20:28; for debates about the textual status and meaning of the phrase, see comment ad loc.). Porter remarks that Luke's desire to add "an authentic Pauline stamp," held by most scholars, works here only if Luke knew either Paul's letters or Paul himself.[483] (The former option is, as noted in ch. 7 above, unlikely.) Nor are "Paulinisms" the only grounds for suspecting genuine reminiscences in this speech. Indeed, in one of the most interesting turns, a conglomeration of undeveloped allusions to Ezek 33–34 (and related passages in Ezekiel) may suggest a larger midrashic homily behind the preserved Pauline speech in Acts 20 (see comment on Acts 20:26–28). That a fuller original lay behind Luke's speech may also be suggested by the conclusion on the subject of sacrificial giving, since we know that Paul was journeying to Jerusalem to bring the collection (Rom 15:26–27; 1 Cor 16:1–2; 2 Cor 8–9), a point that Luke mostly omits. Any controversy

478. Eleven times in Pauline literature, most of them undisputed references; four other times in Luke-Acts (one in a summary of Pauline speech, Acts 13:43), with four other uses in the NT. "The grace of the Lord" or "our Lord" appears twice in Luke-Acts (Acts 15:11, 40) and eleven times in Paul (mostly undisputed; with only one other use in the NT).

479. Seven times in Paul (six undisputed).

480. Mainly Pauline in this sense, though see also Acts 9:31; perhaps 1 Pet 2:5, 7.

481. One of Paul's letters written a year or two before this journey cites his own example, explaining why he works rather than accepts patronage (1 Cor 9:1–18).

482. He worked hard with his hands night and day (cf. Acts 20:31) so that he could preach to the Thessalonians freely (1 Thess 2:9). He did this, as here, as an example (2 Thess 3:8–9; cf. 1 Cor 4:12, 16); they too should work (1 Thess 4:11; 2 Thess 3:10–12; Eph 4:28), as here (Acts 20:25). Likewise, he emphasized to the Corinthians that he had worked (1 Cor 9:3–18) to avoid hindering the gospel (9:12).

483. Porter, *Paul in Acts*, 117–18.

surrounding the risks of Paul's journey (cf. Acts 20:23; Rom 15:31) may have made his discussion of the mission's importance (and hence the collection) paramount.

But this is one of the few speeches in the eyewitness "we" sections and also represents virtually the only speech where Paul exhorts believers, as in his letters. Although, in general, Paul's speeches in Acts do comport with the theology of his letters much better than critical scholarship has sometimes allowed,[484] we should not expect to find as many specific parallels in his other speeches in Acts as in Acts 20:18–35, both because they are not addressed to the same sorts of audiences as Paul's letters and because they do not even purport to be firsthand eyewitness material (and hence less apt to preserve the speakers' actual language as well as their subjects). (Chapter 7 above treats the relationship between the Paul of the letters and the Paul in Acts in more detail.)[485]

Unfortunately, some of the individualistic elements that scholars identify are not at all distinctive of the extra-Lukan authors they identify (especially in the case of Peter, where the evidence for Peter's distinctive theology outside Acts is quite limited). Relatively distinctive material does remain (e.g., Pauline language in 9:20; 13:39; 20:31), but outside Acts 20 one could explain this material on the basis of prosopopoeia (treated above, sect. 2.b).

On the other side again, successful use of prosopopoeia would suggest that Luke knew something of Paul's distinctive language (easily acquired through the sort of acquaintance with him that the "we" sections suggest). That is, Luke presumably acquired his knowledge of Paul's style at such points either from his letters or from hearing Paul; on a first-century date, the former source is problematic (and would also fail to explain the cluster in Acts 20 in contrast to earlier speeches), but in a straightforward reading of the "we" narratives, the latter is in fact likely.

If one finds consistent patterns like these in the speeches, one could make a case for pre-Lukan tradition. But as already noted, we should not be optimistic (outside 20:18–35) about finding a great deal of evidence based on style. Although "the style of the speeches is not uniform," Aune notes, "it is consistent with the author's general style."[486] Hengel rightly warns: "The style-critical method of separating redaction and tradition . . . can only be used with the greatest caution in the case of Luke, since like all ancient historians who used existing material he did not simply copy out his original sources, where these were not authoritative sayings of Jesus, but reshaped them according to his own style."[487] Nevertheless, Hengel is optimistic that the speeches do preserve earlier tradition.[488]

There are some differences among the speakers appropriate to their respective characters. All the speeches are in Luke's wording; all the speakers emphasize the resurrection; yet we can hardly imagine Peter giving the Areopagus discourse or crafting the more rhetorically skilled defense speeches of Acts 24–26. At the very least Luke has considered rhetorical appropriateness and knows at least something about the figures who participate in his narrative.

IV. WEIGHING CRITERIA

Ward Gasque argues for pre-Lukan material on the basis of Semitisms and other non-Lukan features that Luke "presumably . . . failed to edit out." Gasque holds that,

484. With, e.g., Haacker, *Theology*, 143–44.

485. Although I will argue that they are not incompatible, the case for Acts' reliability about Paul rests on correlations with reports of historical incidents more than on stylistic or linguistic parallels.

486. Aune, *Environment*, 125–26.

487. Hengel, *Acts and History*, 61–62 (suggesting that Luke treated Jesus's sayings differently because he treated them like biblical quotes; cf. Acts 20:35).

488. Hengel, *Acts and History*, 61.

had Luke merely created these speeches to display his own theology or rhetoric, they should reflect his best literary skills, of the sort displayed in Luke 1:1–4, yet, especially in the early chapters, the grammar in his speeches does not accord with these literary skills.[489]

This analysis, though ably offered, is open to some criticism, at least on the level of rhetoric. Since historians sought to make their speeches appropriate, Luke would hardly provide Peter with classical rhetorical skills to demonstrate his own prowess (the extensive chiasmus in Acts 2:22–36 is quite sufficient), Josephus's Eleazar at Masada notwithstanding. Some of Acts' speeches do employ a higher level of rhetorical skill than his narratives[490] (though admittedly more later in Acts, where the setting demanded superior rhetorical prowess in its established Greco-Roman form). Of course, a rhetorical historian would still want to offer better rhetoric (and fuller speeches) than Luke does. As noted earlier, Luke does not write to display his rhetoric, yet this disinterest need not mean that he lacked theological agendas.

Further, Gasque's skepticism toward the proposal that the Semitisms in the earlier chapters might represent Luke's imitation of the LXX rather than the use of sources[491] is open to serious challenge, given rhetoricians' ability to vary style according to content. Still, Gasque's basic point demands attention: were Luke intent on simply demonstrating his skills, one would expect a higher rhetorical polish than we find and longer speeches as in most other historians. Moreover, Luke is apparently well informed regarding the Semitic and less rhetorical style of earlier speeches and is probably aware of their message as well. Thus these observations do not dismiss the fundamental value in Gasque's proposal, but its weaknesses make the proposal more difficult to quantify, in any given case, as an authenticity criterion.

Criteria such as Gasque's and Wilcox's can be helpful, but only if we can agree that the pre-Lukan elements intrude frequently enough in the right places to reveal whatever tradition might stand behind Luke's text. In view of the work's literary unity, the focus on the common kerygma, Luke's use of prosopopoeia (including adopting semitizing style where relevant), and even the cumulative effect of such elements do not constitute a *certain* proof of historical tradition in most given cases (and certainly, their absence can never be used to prove its unreliability). (Again, there are exceptions—for example, Acts 20:18–35—but this most striking exception is in Luke's "we" material.)

The process of isolating traditions in a literary work as cohesive as Acts is difficult. An analogy helps illustrate the conundrum: reconstructing sources in Luke's Gospel if we lacked Mark and parallel material in Matthew would probably produce highly speculative, widely divergent, and usually mistaken results. What these scholars' efforts on Acts cumulatively could suggest is that the narrative unity does not appear to obliterate all traces of underlying tradition; they therefore remind us that one does not need to choose between narrative unity and the existence of tradition, even if they cannot easily prove the use of such tradition for particular occasions.

f. Conclusions regarding Historical Tradition

That Luke both preserves and varies some of his direct-discourse material when he repeats it indicates that Luke himself made no secret that he was not reporting speeches verbatim (compare Acts 9:5–6 with 22:8, 10; 9:15–16 and 22:10 with

489. Gasque, "Speeches," 248–49 (quote, 249); see similarly Bruce, *Acts¹*, 18.

490. Witherington, *Acts*, 44 (citing Aristides *Ars Rhetorica* 1.13.4 on the greater need for rhetorical skill in speeches than in narratives).

491. Gasque, "Speeches," 249.

26:16–18; 10:5–6 with 11:13–14; compare also 9:4 with 26:14; and especially 1:4–8 with Luke 24:47–49).[492] (He makes clear that he used summaries [Acts 2:40; Luke 3:18].) That ancient history is a genre that differs in this respect from modern history should also lay to rest any attempt of modern readers to anachronistically demand of Luke a kind of writing that he does not claim to offer. Following the practice of the best ancient historians, Luke could employ (and would probably have needed to employ) at least some more freedom in his speeches than in his narrative (likely the opposite of the situation in his Gospel, given the parallel material in Matthew).

Further, the speeches in Acts display the sort of literary unity that characterized the speeches of ancient historians in general. Yet historians also sought to provide speeches appropriate to the speakers, and elements distinctive to particular speakers in Acts may represent the ancient rhetorical practice of borrowing elements of speakers' style or language deemed appropriate to them when writing speeches for them.

At the same time, it is reasonable to argue that although Luke authored the speeches in their current form, he also preserved their gist when he had this information available, like many other historians. At the very least, he seeks to preserve the authentic theological message and traits of the speakers, albeit selectively and adjusted to fit his larger work; one cannot consciously borrow distinctive elements of a speaker's style or message unless one has some familiarity with that style or message. Further, I have argued above that Luke has oral eyewitness sources for most of the events recorded in Acts (sometimes, I will argue, Luke himself). The sources that provided the events in his narrative could also have supplied him with the gist of speeches given on significant occasions, which were themselves "events" (especially in view of his work's focus precisely on the spreading of the gospel message). Although clues are not pervasive, enough elements of early tradition may appear to suggest that Luke was familiar with the theology, argumentation, and sometimes even style of some early Christian preachers, the strongest case among them being for Paul.

Long ago C. H. Dodd suggested that the author "apparently used to some extent the liberty which all ancient historians claimed (after the example of Thucydides), of composing speeches which are put into the mouth of the personages of the story."[493] But he further concluded (though not always on the most objective grounds) that Luke apparently used "his historian's privilege with considerable restraint"; he argued that the speeches reflected pre-Lukan Christian tradition of the apostolic kerygma.[494] It may be relevant that, for all the first-century debates about circumcision and the role of Gentiles (cf. Gal 2:2–5), there seems to have been consensus between Paul and the Jerusalem apostles on the basic apostolic message of the resurrection (1 Cor 15:1–11; cf. Gal 2:7–8). Unity of a core message is not Luke's invention, though it may serve his literary and theological purposes and receive more emphasis than some other elements that he could have included.

Such conclusions accord well with a centrist position adopted by many NT scholars regarding the speeches in Acts. From a literary standpoint, those who claim that the speeches are Lukan compositions are correct. From a historical standpoint, however, Luke could well have generally preserved the substance of what was said on the various occasions (and other "primitive" material in apostolic tradition plausible for the speakers), when this information was available to him. Virtually no mainstream scholars have argued that the speeches, especially those early in Acts, are verbatim

---

492. That these examples are relatively brief makes the verbatim reporting of longer speeches all the less plausible.

493. Dodd, *Preaching*, 17.

494. Ibid., 18–19.

compositions. But many argue that these speeches do preserve the gist of what was said on the occasions.[495] At minimum, many of the speeches preserve genuine reminiscences and reflect traditions about earlier Christian preaching.

Of course, scholars continue to debate how much of the speeches as we have them represents the original gist and which speeches might reflect prior traditions. Beyond the secure information that Luke had, he could have employed the freedom of the genre of ancient history to present what could plausibly be inferred from what was known. He could have developed the sort of argument expected for particular speakers, filling in with details like those that the speakers were reported to have sometimes used or at least were of the kind that they would have probably used. Thus Dunn argues that Acts' speeches reflect Luke's summary of speakers' views as best he can reconstruct them; ancient readers would not expect more than this.[496]

In the final analysis, I have provided only a basic generic context for the discussion here; those who look for form-critical signs of underlying tradition must examine one speech after another, and even such detailed analysis can yield at most probabilities in historical terms. Given our limited historical data, the historical method is limited in its results, restricting the potential conclusions we can articulate on historical grounds here. Although I will pause at some points to interact with previous scholarship and to note Pauline parallels where these prove relevant for particular speeches, my focus in the commentary proper will be on matters on which historical study can speak with fuller probable results—namely, the speeches in their context in Acts and their function for a late first-century Greco-Roman audience.

495. With, e.g., Munck, *Acts*, xliv; Fitzmyer, *Acts*, 105–6; Bruce, *Speeches in Acts*; idem, Bruce, *Acts¹*, 21; Smalley, *John*, 164; Porter, *Paul in Acts*, 125; Hemer, *Acts in History*, 415–27; Dunn, *Acts*, xvii–xviii; Gasque, "Speeches," 248–49; idem, "Acts and History," 58–63; Dudley, "Speeches in Acts."

496. Dunn, *Acts*, xvii–xviii; "Luke's impression" of early Christian theology (based on probabilities available to him) as he has interpreted it (p. xviii); cf. Puskas and Crump, *Introduction*, 109; Allison, *Jesus*, 455. Witherington, *Acts*, 119–20, also admits that Acts 25:13–22 may be Luke's best reconstruction.

9

SIGNS AND
HISTORIOGRAPHY

Some scholars who grant that Acts is a historical monograph containing considerable accurate historical information in its narratives find the miracle reports in these same narratives problematic. This apparent inconsistency in approach stems not from a change in genre but from philosophic assumptions about what is possible for intelligent people in other cultures and eras to believe they have seen.[1]

Signs consume as much as a fifth of Acts. Luke claims that eyewitnesses and participants saw what they and Luke believed were miracles. Moreover, some of these claims appear in "we" material (Acts 20:9–12; 28:8–9), usually attributed to an eyewitness. Scholars can explain most such incidents in either naturalistic or supernatural terms, depending on their assumptions, but reducing them to novelistic flourishes or legendary accretions (as is usually the case for the nonhistorical, later apocryphal acts) requires reading them in a way different from much of the rest of Luke's narrative.

This chapter therefore addresses two distinct issues. The first, which I believe this chapter will establish to most readers' satisfaction, regardless of their philosophic assumptions, is that the kinds of healing reports in Acts are generally plausible historically. Similar claims, often from convinced eyewitnesses, circulate widely today, and there are no a priori reasons to doubt that ancient eyewitnesses could have made analogous claims. One may agree that such recoveries occur without attempting to explain all of them. The second, which challenges a worldview and hence will not likely persuade all readers,[2] is that we are not obligated to begin with the a priori assumption that none of these events could involve intelligent, suprahuman causation.

My primary concern is to persuade readers of my first, less controversial point, since that is where any challenge to Luke as an ancient historian would lie. The second point, however, a philosophic issue, will be important for readers also concerned with

1. This is the sort of skepticism noted (but not endorsed) in Talbert, *Acts*, 248; Achtemeier, *Miracle Tradition*, 136–37; Parsons, *Acts*, 52. Others, who grant the reports but question only Luke's interpretation, work from philosophic assumptions about what is possible that differ from Luke's; in practice, they tend to accept reports about healings and exorcisms that they can explain psychosomatically, but would be more skeptical of, e.g., the nature miracles in Luke's Gospel (not relevant to Acts).

2. I hope that those who are not persuaded will at least appreciate the valiant and academically legitimate nature of my attempt. Worldviews do not crumble easily, although I am convinced that thoroughgoing antisupernaturalism should be dismantled (while allowing abundant room for methodological naturalism in the appropriate spheres and cases).

Luke's theology, since Luke attributes these miracles to divine causation. Because of this commentary's social-historical focus, however, I concentrate much more on the former point than the latter, which I suggest, more than argue, here.

My book on miracles addresses these questions, especially the latter one, in far greater detail than is possible here.[3] That book grew originally from this chapter, and in an effort to reduce duplication, I have removed about half of this chapter (including scores of healing reports and interviews from around the world, and some 270 secondary sources) and simply refer interested readers to that book, more sophisticated and now nearly a thousand pages longer than this chapter would have been.

1. The Problem

Previous chapters have established Acts' genre as a work of ancient historiography; we cannot leave this topic without examining the modern question of miracle claims in predominantly accurate historical reports. A section in chapter 15 below will examine Luke's theology of signs,[4] but here we must address the historical question, which, because of the complex philosophic, comparative, social, and theological questions involved in it, must consume a larger proportion of space. Studying this question, we must examine non-Christian miracle accounts from Luke's era as well as the historic context of ancient and modern philosophic skepticism toward miracles. Finally (and at some length), we must confront the question of how modern Western readers can relate to such claims; I will suggest that many other cultures (and some religious subcultures within our culture) provide better paradigms for a sympathetic reading of Luke's claims than do our dominant Western academic paradigms.[5]

Historians of this period often include miraculous or other supernatural elements in their works (as was also the case earlier in much of ancient Israel's historiography),[6] and so acknowledging the presence of such claims does not shift the genre of Acts away from ancient historiography. Yet Luke reports signs more often, given the amount of space available, than typical extant historians from his period (though in a proportion comparable to certain sections of Israelite narratives and perhaps with a lower concentration than parts of the Elijah-Elisha cycle). Indeed, even among the earliest Christian sources, Acts emphasizes signs to a greater degree than usual. It portrays them as more unambiguously positive than the way that they appear in Mark or John and as more central than they appear in Paul's letters (though the difference in the latter case may be one of genre).[7]

---

3. Keener, *Miracles*. The philosophic issue predominates especially in chs. 4–6, 14; see also Keener, "Case." Cf. more briefly Keener, "Comparisons."

4. The biblical tradition of "signs" was less interested in their "supernatural" character (cf., e.g., Gen 9:12–17; 17:11)—the dichotomy between "natural" and "supernatural" stemming from modern philosophy—than in their attesting God's activity (see Meier, "Signs," 758). God's "mighty acts" were not violations of a natural order but expected signs of the faithfulness of nature's ruler; they were not proofs of God's existence (which was not disputed) but demonstrations of God's covenant faithfulness (Ross, "Miracle," 50–56). Likewise, if by "supernatural" one means "divinely empowered," at least some circles in early Christianity averred that believers should live in the "supernatural" sphere continually (e.g., Rom 8:2–9; Keener, "Spirit Perspectives"). For a pre-1965 bibliography on signs (thaumatology) relevant to Acts, see Mattill and Mattill, *Bibliography*, 303–5, §§4241–70.

5. With, e.g., Roschke, "Healing"; Jenkins, "Reading," 72.

6. See, e.g., Krasser, "Reading," 554; Plümacher, *Geschichte*, 33–84.

7. E.g., James clearly expects divine healing (Jas 5:14–16; cf. McKnight, *James*, 440–42), but one would not be aware of this expectation without a single paragraph in which he raises the issue; Paul raises the issue more often (e.g., Rom 15:19; 1 Cor 12:9, 28–30), though over a longer course of letters. Early Christian narratives, however, include more signs (esp. the Gospels; cf. even Rev 11:5–6).

Thus although many or most ancient historians mentioned paranormal phenomena, they rarely dwelled on them as Luke does. Yet most other extant historians were writing about political or social events, not the early history of a miracle worker and a "charismatic" movement known in that period for its signs. And as argued below, there is little reason to doubt that the first Christians (like some revival movements since that time) believed that signs were occurring among them, and that they could offer first-, second-, or thirdhand testimony to such events.

This chapter addresses only the questions specific to signs (comparing ancient sources, modern analogies, and the philosophic question behind the historiographic one), not questions about Luke's historiography treated here earlier. That is, one may affirm that events such as these can occur, or even grant that they may sometimes occur supernaturally, but this does not mean that every purported case of a sign in history happened, still less that it happened supernaturally. Historical analysis cannot guarantee that Luke's oral sources did not blur or exaggerate details over time. Moreover, even in eyewitness material, Luke presumably shaped the story to sharpen it for literary purposes, as historians normally did. But these are questions concerning Luke's historiography more generally, addressed above, and hence will be addressed here only rarely. (Claims of dreams and visions, less often disputed, are treated in this commentary's excursuses at Acts 2:17–18 and 16:9.)

2. Some Introductory Questions

Today, as in the first century, scholars can offer historical reconstructions on the basis of testimony, sometimes artifacts, and, frequently, critical evaluation based on intrinsic probability and the weighing of evidence. Two problems thus confront a discussion of miracles in earliest Christianity: the limitations of the evidence (some testimony; no first-century artifacts) and (for the probability argument) the long-standing (albeit declining) Western philosophic a priori denying the possibility of miracles (or at least raising the bar of skepticism so high that no individual miracle claim could ever be accepted). This second problem does not always translate into a denial that witnesses claimed to see phenomena that could be interpreted in such terms, but it has sometimes done so. We will return to the second problem below, but we focus at present on the first. Because much discussion has been centered on Jesus's miracles and because Luke's first volume is devoted to Jesus, I include here elements surrounding that discussion, deeming them relevant to this discussion of signs in Acts as well.

a. Evidence for Jesus's Miracles

The former problem, namely, the limitations of kinds of evidence available, is not as serious as it might first appear; although the evidence is limited concerning most particular miracles, all of the many ancient sources that comment on the issue agree that Jesus and his early followers performed miracles: Q, Mark, special material in Matthew and Luke, John, Acts, the Epistles, Revelation, and non-Christian testimony from Jewish and pagan sources.

Most scholars today thus accept the claim that Jesus was a healer and exorcist.[8] The evidence is stronger for this claim than for most other specific historical claims

---

8. For summaries of this consensus, see Blackburn, "Miracles," 362; Eve, *Miracles*, 16–17; Welch, "Miracles," 360. Ehrman, *Prophet*, 197–200, notes that scholars can accept Jesus as an exorcist and healer without passing judgment on whether he acted supernaturally.

that we could make about earliest Christianity; miracles characterized Jesus's historical activity no less than his teaching and prophetic activities did.[9] If followers would preserve his teachings, how much more would they (and especially those who experienced recoveries) spread miracle reports?[10] Because miracle claims attach to a relatively small number of figures in antiquity (itinerant or not), there is little reason to suppose that Jesus would have developed a reputation as a wonder-worker if he did not engage in such activities.[11] As Gerd Theissen and Annette Merz put it, "Just as the kingdom of God stands at the centre of Jesus's preaching, so healings and exorcisms form the centre of his activity."[12]

Among non-Christian sources, the rabbis[13] and Celsus are clear, and Vermes also argues that the miracle claim in Jos. *Ant.* 18.63 is authentic, on the basis of Josephus's style.[14] Josephus calls Jesus a σοφὸς ἀνήρ, a wise man, who also "worked startling deeds" (παράδοξα; cf. Luke 5:26), a term by which Josephus also depicts the miracles worked by the prophet Elisha (*Ant.* 9.182). (Many later non-Christian sources attribute the miraculous works to sorcery, which probably constitutes the earliest anti-Christian explanation for Christian miracles.)[15] This unanimity is striking given the conversely unanimous silence in Christian, Jewish, and even Mandaean tradition concerning any miracles of respected prophetic figures such as John the Baptist.[16]

Thus most scholars today apparently grant the claim for Jesus, regardless of their philosophic assumptions about divine activity in miracle claims. E. P. Sanders regards it as an "almost indisputable" historical fact that "Jesus was a Galilean who preached and healed."[17] Using traditional historical-critical tools, John Meier finds many of Jesus's miracles authentic.[18] Raymond Brown notes that "scholars have come to realize that one cannot dismiss Jesus's miracles simply on modern rationalist grounds, for the oldest traditions show him as a healer."[19] Otto Betz regards it as "certain" that Jesus was a healer, a matter that "can be deduced even from the Jewish polemic which

9. See, e.g., Twelftree, "Miracles"; idem, *Miracle Worker*. The Third Quest is more respectful toward the Gospels' miracle tradition than the so-called First and Second Quests were (Meier, "Third Quest"). Scholars who treat Jesus as prophet and miracle worker appear to remain in the mainstream (see, e.g., Meier, "Quest"; Tan, *Zion Traditions*, 237; Flusser, "Love," 154; Theissen and Merz, *Guide*, 113, 281–315; Kee, "Quests"; Pikaza, "Jesús histórico"; Rusecki, "Kryteria"); this paradigm is not intrinsically opposed to Jesus as sage (Oyen, "Criteria"), just as sages and mystics were not incompatible (Sterling, *Ancestral Philosophy*, 99–113).

10. Wright, "Seminar," 114 (suggesting that the reports would rapidly assume a standard form, as they were told and retold).

11. Theissen and Merz, *Guide*, 113. Miracles are also not widely attached to messianic figures or to the majority of prophets. Using criteria of coherence and dissimilarity, Eve, *Miracles*, 386, argues for the authenticity of Jesus's distinctive ministry of healing and exorcism.

12. Theissen and Merz, *Guide*, 281 (see more fully 281–315).

13. Yamauchi, "Magic?," 90–91, cites *b. Sanh.* 43a; *t. Ḥul.* 2:22–23; cf. Vermes, *Jesus the Jew*, 79.

14. Vermes, "Notice"; idem, *Jesus the Jew*, 79; see also Meier, *Marginal Jew*, 2:621; Theissen and Merz, *Guide*, 74 (arguing that Josephus seeks to report about Jesus with the same neutrality he used concerning John and James); Van Voorst, *Jesus*, 102.

15. Cf. *b. Sanh.* 107b; in paganism, Cook, *Interpretation*, 36–39, 138. Although rabbinic sources do not recite the charge before the late second century (Flusser, *Judaism*, 635), Sanders, *Jesus and Judaism*, 166, rightly notes that the charge concerning Jesus must be early: "Why answer a charge that was not levelled?" (see Matt 12:24; cf. John 8:48).

16. See Stauffer, *Jesus*, 10–11; the Mandaean and Islamic evidence he cites, however, is too late for actual relevance. For Jesus as a worker of miracles (attributed by his detractors to magic), see, e.g., Qur'an 5.110; 61.6. The issue never arises clearly in Paul (except with respect to his own miracle working), though cf. Wenham, "Story," 307–8.

17. Sanders, *Jesus and Judaism*, 11. Certainly, the Gospels portray Jesus's miracles as "an essential part of that ministry" (Filson, *History*, 105).

18. Meier, *Marginal Jew*, 2:678–772; for historical evidence supporting Jesus as a miracle worker, see 2:617–45; see also Twelftree, *Miracle Worker*; Blomberg, *Gospels*, 127–36.

19. Brown, *Death*, 143–44.

called him a sorcerer";[20] the miracles are central to the Gospels, and without them, most of the other data in the Gospels are inexplicable.[21] Even Morton Smith similarly argues that miracle working is the most authentic part of the Jesus tradition,[22] though he explains it along the magical lines urged by Jesus's early detractors.[23]

If such signs characterized Jesus, there is no reason to doubt that they could have also characterized those viewed as his successors. Perhaps Jesus even trained his disciples as his successors (as teachers normally trained their disciples to be), expecting them to be able to perform the same activity that he did (cf. Mark 9:18–19, 28–29; 11:23; Luke 9:40–41; 17:6). Indeed, most of the signs claimed in Acts, as in the Gospels, are healings and exorcisms[24]—precisely the claims Christian sources in later centuries also offered from contemporary eyewitnesses.[25]

Seeking to distinguish tradition from redaction in Acts' miracles, Benjamin Williams compares Luke's redaction of Markan miracles, identifying consistent redactional patterns relevant to Luke's portrayal of miracles.[26] Williams's approach should follow, in a general way, from the logical premise that Luke would value historical tradition in his second volume (a historical monograph) no less than in his first (on its own terms, a biography). For example, while retaining the substance of Mark's accounts, Luke feels free to compose audience reactions of astonishment, fear, and so forth if Mark lacks these (though one might well infer such reactions from human nature), and especially adds acclamations of praise to God.[27] Luke nowhere adds discourses to his miracle stories, though he could abbreviate, "improve the vocabulary, or even omit discourses altogether."[28]

What we cannot be certain of, however, is the nature of Luke's sources in the second volume; in contrast to many of his sources in the Gospel, many of his sources in Acts were probably oral, altering the character of the "editing."[29] At the same time, we might expect his historical interests in the second volume to remain analogous to those in the first and hence expect him, as Williams argues, to continue to shape, rather than begin to fabricate, his miracle stories in his second volume.[30]

20. Betz, *Jesus*, 58.

21. Ibid., 60.

22. Smith, *Magician*, 16. There are both Jewish and Greek parallels, but not regarding roughly contemporary teachers or philosophers (characters of the distant past, such as Enoch and Noah in *1 Enoch*, were special candidates for traditional embroidery).

23. Neusner, "Foreword," xxvii; idem, *New Testament*, 5, 173, offers perhaps the harshest critique of Smith's magical thesis.

24. In contrast to, e.g., commanding bedbugs to leave, as in *Acts John* 60–61.

25. The explanation for those claims will vary in part according to one's view of nature, but this is a theological and philosophical matter, not a question of history per se. Contemporary examples illustrate that people may believe that they have witnessed such phenomena (see discussion below).

26. Williams, *Miracle Stories*, 13, 35–54. E.g. (52), Luke exercises the greatest redactional liberty in reformulating the conclusion of Markan miracles; Luke reshapes Markan crowd reactions thoroughly (e.g., in Luke 5:15, 26; 6:11; 8:47), allowing overlap with Mark only in "individual words." Their readily memorable form makes miracle stories one of early Christian tradition's most recognizable narrative forms (15). Still, Weissenrieder, *Images*, 336–37, suggests that there may be differences between the approaches to healing in the Gospel and in Acts.

27. Williams, *Miracle Stories*, 53.

28. Ibid., 54.

29. The exact wording of discourse was probably also fluid in oral traditions behind any written accounts even in the Gospels, with the exception of some carefully remembered sayings of Jesus. On the special question of speech material, see ch. 8, above.

30. Because some forms of miracle stories (particularly exorcisms and a form of raising-the-dead story) characterized their Middle Eastern origin more than Hellenism (Williams, *Miracle Stories*, 22–26, 32), Williams hopes to identify in the Jewish missionary movement's expansion into the Hellenistic world the period from which some characteristics derive (32–33). Far from being primarily late forms, "the bulk of these stories

More tellingly, some of his miracle reports appear in eyewitness material much closer to Luke than his Gospel sources were (Acts 20:9–12; 21:11; 27:21–26; 28:3–6, 8–9). Luke is clearly convinced that miracles occur; Paul is likewise convinced that they happened through his ministry (Rom 15:19; 2 Cor 12:12); modern scholars are also usually convinced that Jesus and many early Christians (e.g., second-century exorcists) were believed to perform miracles. If Jesus and his first followers believed that they experienced miracles firsthand, how can modern hearers relate to these claims?

b. Methodological Questions

This evidence raises two kinds of questions from a modern perspective. First, although early Christian literature emphasizes an abundance of miracle workers not attested to this degree in other first-century movements, miracle claims were abundant in antiquity. How do the bulk of the Christian claims compare with analogous claims? Should all be explained psychosomatically, as deception, as misinterpretation, or in other nonsupernatural terms? Are some claims likelier than others, and in which circles?

Second, if modernist assumptions are incompatible with supernatural claims, does this incompatibility obligate us to a priori rule out the possibility of such activity? Or should we reevaluate some assumptions of modernity and hence leave open at least the possibility of nonnatural (in this case, most often theistic) explanations? Whatever answers we give to the second set of questions will not satisfy everyone, but we cannot address the historical question fully without at least raising them; the veracity of the events aside, the question of explanatory models remains a legitimate subject of historical inquiry, and causation (albeit, generally, human causation) is a common historical concern. Nevertheless, for purely historical purposes, in the final analysis, the question of whether eyewitnesses claimed such phenomena does not depend on the explanations or models proposed for these phenomena. Scholars may debate whether history as a discipline may ask questions of causation beyond the human level, but definitions of historiography technically belong to philosophers of history and are historically conditioned, arbitrary disciplinary boundaries. One may limit the focus of one's inquiry, excluding questions of supernatural causation, without thereby declaring those questions illegitimate or out-of-bounds for other disciplines. Thus, although the questions may overlap when interpreters address causation, in principle these questions may be (and sometimes are) treated separately.

3. Ancient Miracle Accounts outside Early Christianity

Luke reports signs more often, given the amount of space available, than typical ancient historians did. This greater proportion of miracle reports in Luke-Acts may stem from various factors, such as greater skepticism among other extant historians' elite readers (who, naturally, account for the bulk of their audiences). It especially reflects, however, Luke's focus: he writes not just general history but the history of a charismatic movement, especially its missions thrust (with which he particularly associates signs and wonders). Nevertheless, belief in, and reports of, miracles were widespread.

---

mirror the needs and convictions of Christians in the first three or four decades of the new movement, during which they essentially took shape" (168).

a. Gentile Greco-Roman Miracle Accounts

Belief in miracles was alive and well in the Roman imperial period.[31] Most ancient "supernatural" healing accounts, especially in the first century, appear to involve particular healing sanctuaries, but we also have reports of pagan miracle workers.

I. Healing Sanctuaries

Deities such as Asclepius and Serapis, who were believed able to provide practical benefits such as healings, often supplanted more traditional deities in popular devotion.[32] Many ancients believed that Serapis brought healing dreams daily in Alexandria;[33] he was also known for healing through dreams in his Corinthian sanctuaries.[34] Some identified Serapis with Asclepius, since both specialized in healing (Tac. *Hist.* 4.84).[35] Isis, associated with Serapis, was known as a healing deity.[36] Late antiquity also honored other deities[37] and heroes[38] associated with healing powers. The Epidaurus inscriptions[39] suggest that Apollo was honored alongside Asclepius;[40] Apollo was also a deity traditionally associated with healing.[41]

According to the usual version of the ancient myth, Asclepius was originally a mortal who was struck dead for raising too many fellow mortals (or for raising particular mortals) from death.[42] But Asclepius was widely said to now continue to heal the

---

31. Strelan, *Strange Acts*, 26 (following Theissen, *Miracle Stories*, 274), though noting that the models are Elijah and Elisha and the closest parallels in Hellenistic Jewish sources (Strelan, *Strange Acts*, 27–28). For a collection of sources, see Cotter, *Miracles*, 35–47 (for Hellenistic heroes; for biblical miracle workers, see 47–53; more briefly, idem, "Miracle Stories"); Cotter rightly warns (*Miracles*, 7) against abusing the collection in a way that looks for genetic sources rather than a cultural framework for understanding. More briefly, see the survey in Achtemeier, *Miracle Tradition*, 205–9.

32. See Grant, *Gods*, 38, 54, 66–67; Nilsson, *Piety*, 171; Kee, *Miracle*, 104. On healing deities, see Graf, "Healing Deities"; Martins Terra, "Milagres"; in ancient Egypt, Jansen-Winkeln, "Healing Deities"; in Roman Egypt, Frankfurter, *Religion in Egypt*, 46–52; for a collection of sources, see Cotter, *Miracles*, 11–34 (Heracles, Asclepius, and Isis). On Asclepius and his healing cult, see Klauck, *Context*, 155–68; Ferguson, *Backgrounds*, 173–76; Wickkiser, "Asklepios"; Martin, *Religions*, 50–52; Kee, "Self-Definition," esp. 129–33; idem, *Miracle*, 78–104.

33. Dio Chrys. *Or.* 32.12.

34. Engels, *Roman Corinth*, 105. Not all Serapis healing dreams materialized favorably (see Toner, *Culture*, 41). Some healing reports today remain associated with dreams (e.g., Shorter, *Witchdoctor*, 153–54; Bush and Pegues, *Move*, 51, 61).

35. But sometimes Egyptians were said to identify Asclepius instead with an ancient king with medical skills; Manetho *Aeg.* frg. 11 (from Syncellus p. 104); also frg. 12a (from Syncellus p. 106), and frg. 12b (Armenian version of Eusebius's *Chronicle*). The primary healing deity was a hybrid, Imouthes-Asclepius (P.Oxy. 11.1381, lines 32–52, in Frankfurter, *Religion in Egypt*, 238), the local Imhotep (Imouthes) being identified with Asclepius (Lewis, *Life*, 99). For some possible (but uncertain) evidence for an earlier Egyptian healing deity, see Kaiser, "Pantheon," 94.

36. E.g., Diod. Sic. 1.25.2–3. Note also healings at the sanctuary of Isis and Serapis at Delos (Heyob, *Isis*, 65), an island especially associated with Apollo.

37. Cf. perhaps the cult of Diana at Philippi (Abrahamsen, *Reliefs*, 119–21); also the sanctuary at Eleusis (Burkert, *Mystery Cults*, 20). Cf. Asclepius's association with Hygieia (Hygeia) in Kent, *Inscriptions*, no. 64 (plate 7, inv. 877 = Meritt, *Inscriptions*, no. 118; *SEG* 11.88); esp. Engels, *Roman Corinth*, 100.

38. E.g., Philost. *Hrk.* 4.10; 16.1; 28.5; Paus. 6.11.9. On Amphiaraus, see, e.g., Ferguson, *Backgrounds*, 173. Priests at Egyptian sanctuaries were also reputed to perform magical healings (Dunand, *Religion en Égypte*, 125); for magic and healing, see also *PGM* 18b.1–7, 1–2.

39. Archaeologists have found these, but inscriptions at the sanctuary are also mentioned in Paus. 2.27.3.

40. Klauck, *Context*, 160. Asclepius's healing gift derived from his being Apollo's son (Philost. *Vit. Apoll.* 3.44).

41. E.g., Hom. *Il.* 5.446–48; 16.526–31; Hor. *Carm. saec.* 62–64; Ovid *Fasti* 3.827; Ps.-Tibullus 3.10.1–12; Dio Chrys. *Or.* 32.56–57. Narrative necessity sometimes dictated different outcomes; Apollo could not raise a dead maiden he loved (Ovid *Metam.* 2.617–18; cf. the sun god's inability to heal a beloved in 4.247–49).

42. Panyassis frg. 5, in Sext. Emp. *Math.* 1.260; Lucian *Dance* 45; on his raising the dead, see also Paus. 2.26.5. Supposedly, the Muses taught this son of Apollo both healing and prophecy (Ap. Rhod. 2.512).

sick,[43] often through dreams in his temples.[44] People expected him to be able to cure even blindness, and hence they might suggest that a blind person spend the night in Asclepius's temple.[45] Some traveled to Asclepius sanctuaries to entreat deities even to heal others.[46] Like other deities, however, Asclepius could also exact judgment; a person who ordered this deity's sacred grove cut down to build ships was killed.[47]

Asclepius sanctuaries were most often situated near healthy springs.[48] Because of its warmth, Epidaurus's water had long been associated with healing (Xen. *Mem.* 3.13.3). Aelius Aristides credited a well in Asclepius's temple for bringing him healing (*Or.* 39.14–15). (Entirely apart from healing sanctuaries, therapeutic springs were widely appreciated,[49] including in Palestine.)[50]

Asclepius's cult was widespread. Strabo praises Asclepius's healing power at Epidaurus, Cos, and Tricca (Strabo 8.6.15). Pergamum in Asia Minor was the leading cult center for Asclepius in the period of the empire.[51] Its massive Asclepius temple was 425 by 360 feet,[52] and it was known for the snake associated with Asclepius;[53] like other sites, it featured healing through dreams.[54] The sanctuary at Cos was also significant and renowned.[55]

Closer to a center of the Pauline mission, near Corinth, the sanctuary of Asclepius at Epidaurus (Paus. 2.26.1–2.27.6) was also well known. The Epidaurus cult claimed that Asclepius was born at that sanctuary.[56] Romans claimed that Asclepius at Epidaurus cured a Roman plague, and the Romans enticed the god to come to Rome.[57] Epidaurus continued to be associated with successful healings.[58]

Not far from Epidaurus,[59] Corinth's Asklepieion, built near the city's northern wall, was one of that city's more prominent cult sites,[60] situated so as to have its own water

43. Soph. *Philoc.* 1437–38 (sent by the now-deified Heracles); Suet. *Claud.* 25.2; Max. Tyre 9.7.

44. Paus. 2.27.2; Ael. Arist. *Or.* 2.30–36, 74–76; Philost. *Vit. soph.* 1.25.536; 2.4.568; Iambl. *Myst.* 3.3; Hdn. 4.8.3. Modern readers approach these accounts from various angles; for a psychoanalytic approach, see Rousselle, "Cults."

45. Aristoph. *Plutus* 410–11, 620–21. Isis was also among deities supposed to be able to heal the blind (Heyob, *Isis,* 65).

46. Lucian *Dem.* 27 (for a son).

47. Val. Max. 1.1.19.

48. Vitruv. *Arch.* 1.2.7.

49. E.g., Vitruv. *Arch.* 8.3.4; Pliny E. *N.H.* 31.31.59–61; Plut. *Sulla* 26.3. For hot springs more generally, e.g., Men. Rhet. 1.2, 349.30; Eunapius *Lives* 459; Philost. *Hrk.* 23.30; cool springs were thought less healthy (Pliny *Ep.* 2.8.2). For hot water for health more generally, e.g., Val. Max. 2.4.5.

50. For the hot springs of Tiberias, see, e.g., Jos. *War* 2.614; 4.11; *Life* 85; Pliny E. *N.H.* 5.15.71; *Pesiq. Rab Kah.* 11:16; *Eccl. Rab.* 10:8, §1 (cf. more general mention in Jos. *Ant.* 18.36; *y. Ber.* 2:7, §3; *b. Sanh.* 93a; 108a; *Šabb.* 40b; 147a; *y. Ned.* 6:1, §2; *Gen. Rab.* 76:5); in Palestine elsewhere or more generally, see Jos. *War* 1.657; Pliny E. *N.H.* 2.95.208; 5.15.72; Hirschfeld and Solar, "Hmrhs'wt"; idem, "Baths"; Dvorjetski, "Healing Waters."

51. Klauck, *Context,* 157; Fronto *Ad M. Caes.* 3.9.1; for its importance, see also Statius *Silv.* 3.4.23–24; Tac. *Ann.* 3.63; Paus. 2.26.9; Lucian *Icar.* 24; Philost. *Vit. Apoll.* 4.11, 34; *Vit. soph.* 2.25.611. It had long been famous (Hom. *Il.* 5.446–48).

52. McRay, *Archaeology,* 271 (and for further details on the sanctuary).

53. Statius *Silv.* 3.4.25; also evident on coins and other representations from there (Ramsay, *Letters,* 286; Koester, *Introduction,* 1:182; Hemer, *Letters,* 84–85). The snake is also associated with Epidaurus, though that one was allegedly transferred to Rome (Val. Max. 1.8.2). The connection of snakes with healing is Eastern and pre-Greek (Kaiser, "Pantheon," 42–43).

54. E.g., Hdn. 4.8.3; Philost. *Vit. soph.* 1.25.536.

55. E.g., Pliny E. *N.H.* 20.100.264; Tac. *Ann.* 4.14; cf. Grant, *Religions,* 4–6. For its architecture, see Owens, *City,* 120.

56. Klauck, *Context,* 158. Pausanias appears convinced (2.26.8).

57. Val. Max. 1.8.2.

58. Ovid *Pont.* 1.3.21.

59. As often noted (e.g., Pliny E. *N.H.* 4.5.18); Epidaurus is included with Corinth in Paus. 2.26.1–2.27.6 (under the title "Corinth"), unlike the rest of Achaia (reserved for Paus. 6). For Epidaurus in Corinth's inscriptions, see West, *Inscriptions,* 57, on no. 71. Cf. the sanctuary in Paus. 2.10.2.

60. Rothaus, *Corinth,* 42 (for its later history, see 47); esp. Roebuck, *Asklepieion* (for the sacred precinct, see 23–64). It adjoined the gymnasium (Biers, *Bath,* plate 56; cf. Engels, *Roman Corinth,* 151; Paus. 2.4–5).

supply.[61] It was not comparable to the great Asclepius sanctuaries at Epidaurus, Cos, or Pergamum but resembled those at Troezen and Athens.[62] For this reason, it is likely that it was used mainly for locals; it did not house supplicants from far distances for sometimes months at a time as the great sanctuaries did.[63]

The Asclepius sanctuary in Ephesus venerated Asclepius and Hygieia.[64] Apparently, at Dor an Apollo temple became an Asclepius temple before its later transformation into a Byzantine basilica.[65] Asclepius also was said to reveal himself in dreams at his sanctuary at Aegae in Cilicia;[66] he had also long had a sanctuary at Agrigentum in Sicily[67] and eventually had a very popular shrine on Mount Ida in Crete.[68]

Various records of cures in the Epidaurus inscriptions were stylized into standard forms for posterity.[69] The introductory notes that are present in discrete accounts at Epidaurus and in the Talmud would be dropped when miracle stories were incorporated into connected narratives like those we find in the Gospels.[70]

The most basic format of a miracle story is, as one would expect, a description of (1) the circumstances of the healing, (2) the healing itself, and (3) its confirmation or effects on the audience.[71] The exact format varies somewhat, depending on the situation addressed by a particular collection's editors. A sampling of Epidaurus inscriptions, for instance, could yield the following steps in description:[72]

1. Statement of the suppliant's original infirmity (sometimes including the infirm person's name and home city, probably for documentation).
2. The suppliant comes to the sanctuary.
3. (Optional: the suppliant sometimes mocks the cures listed in the inscriptions.)
4. (Usually) the suppliant sleeps in the sanctuary.
5. (Usually) Asclepius appears to the suppliant in a dream.
6. When day arrives, the person emerges cured.

Some features, such as the suppliant coming to the sanctuary and the practice of incubation (sleeping in a deity's sanctuary to receive a dream),[73] specifically characterize a local healing shrine as opposed to a traveling miracle-working teacher.[74]

61. See Roebuck, *Asklepieion*, 1, 3, 96–99.

62. Ibid., 25.

63. Engels, *Roman Corinth*, 100–101.

64. Aurenhammer, "Sculptures," 266–67. For Asclepius worship in Ephesus, see *I. Eph.* 105, 1253–54 (though this is far less prominent than Zeus—*I. Eph.* 1239–43—and about as prominent as Dionysus or Demeter).

65. Dauphin, "Apollo and Asclepius."

66. Philost. *Vit. Apoll.* 1.7, 10.

67. Cic. *Verr.* 2.4.43.93.

68. Philost. *Vit. Apoll.* 4.34.

69. See Dibelius, *Tradition*, 170.

70. Theissen, *Miracle Stories*, 128–29.

71. Aune, *Environment*, 50. For people marveling after miracles, see, e.g., Philost. *Vit. Apoll.* passim. In the opening story of Luke, e.g., note fear (Luke 1:12, 64–65), astonishment (1:12, 29), praise (1:42), and joy (1:58). The audience response may characterize a conventional way to report the story, but it would not be surprising in most cultures (cf., e.g., Hickson, *Heal*, 120–21, 129).

72. Drawn from the sampling in Grant, *Religions*, 56–58. Paus. 2.27.3 notes that the inscriptions list the names of the healed, their disease, and how they were cured. Cf. also records of healings in Horsley, *Documents*, 2:21–25.

73. Grant, *Gods*, 66–67; Ael. Arist. *Or.* 2.30–36, 74–76 (Grant, *Religions*, 53–55). This practice of incubation was already in vogue probably for at least two millennia before our period; note "The Tale of Aqhat" (*ANET* 149–55), AQHT A (i), 150; less relevant, "The Legend of King Keret" (*ANET* 142–49), KRT A (i), 143; cf. Gen 15:12; 1 Sam 3:3–15; 1 Kgs 3:4–15. For its continuance in early Christianity, see Markschies, "Schlafkulte."

74. Aelius Aristides attests that Asclepius sometimes healed away from the shrine as well (Grant, *Gods*, 66). On other sanctuary-based healing cults, see Ferguson, *Backgrounds*, 173–77 (Amphiaraus); Asclepius

Recourse to such sanctuaries did not entail rejection of physicians.[75] Whereas Epidaurus has turned up votive tablets announcing miraculous cures, Asclepius's shrine on Cos turned up medical instruments, suggesting that no barrier separated physicians from divine activity.[76] Pliny the Elder even records an antidote for venomous bites preserved on the wall of the Asclepius temple at Cos (*N.H.* 20.100.264). Doctors trained at Asklepieia.[77]

II. PAGAN MIRACLE WORKERS

Probably more relevant for Acts than healing sanctuaries, but less often documented for this period, are stories of individual wonder-workers in Greek tradition. One may take as an example the later fictitious account of an Egyptian prophet-magician who performs a resuscitation of someone dead.[78]

The widely recited powers of Asclepius before (as well as after) his apotheosis[79] refute in advance any possible suggestion that pagans had no pre-Christian stories of healers.[80] Certainly, stories of the distant past abounded with regular divine interventions in heroes' lives; compare, for instance, the *Argonautica* of the second-century B.C.E. poet Apollonius Rhodius. But apart from their shared supernaturalist worldview and belief that divine activity could be mediated through human agents (more common than not among human societies in general), such stories about the mythical past offer weak parallels for historical works about recent persons. In virtually contemporary sources, perhaps the best example of healing through a divinely blessed person included two cures attributed to Vespasian;[81] although these may reflect genuine cures (albeit utilized for political propaganda), Vespasian was not a miracle worker per se (such reports do not recur).

By contrast, the most significant pagan parallels to Christian miracle-worker stories (such as the extant literary account of Apollonius of Tyana) first appear in third-century literature,[82] after Christian miracle stories had become widely known and Christian and pagan expectations had influenced each other more generally. The older "divine man" hypothesis for Jesus has fallen on hard times, primarily because the combination of traits that scholars once found in this composite category were blended together only in much later sources, which were potentially influenced by

---

at Cos (Grant, *Religions*, 4–6); possibly Diana at Philippi (Abrahamsen, *Reliefs*, 119–21); healing miracles were also attributed to Eleusis (Burkert, *Mystery Cults*, 20) and were associated with Apollo (Hor. *Carm. saec.* 62–64). A Jewish version delegates authority over illness to Raphael (*1 En.* 40:9, Sim.; cf. *Test. Sol.* 18).

75. Because most people could not afford physicians, however, folk cures may have predominated. Because perhaps 70–90 percent of treatments in cultures such as Taiwan and the United States occur on a popular, rather than medical, level (Eve, *Miracles*, 356, following Kleinman, *Healers*, 50), it seems reasonable to suppose no smaller a proportion in antiquity (Eve, *Miracles*, 356).

76. Goppelt, *Theology*, 1:141; cf. Klauck, "Ärzten"; Markschies, "Schlafkulte." Even at Epidaurus, rather than rivalry, each sphere had its place (Klauck, *Context*, 166–67). Ancients did not distinguish medicine from religion as we do today; traditions linked Hippocrates with the "sons of Asclepius," physicians at healing shrines (Kee, "Hippocratic Letters," 498–99).

77. Engels, *Roman Corinth*, 101.

78. Apul. *Metam.* 2.28. This tale is probably meant to parody the telling of such tales more generally.

79. The myth appears in, e.g., Achtemeier, *Miracle Tradition*, 205 (citing, e.g., Apollod. *Bib.* 3.10.3.5–4.1; Xen. *Cynegeticus* 1.1–6; following Edelstein and Edelstein, *Asclepius*, 1:3, 9, 54, 56).

80. Price, *Son of Man*, 21, 131, thinks these the best parallels to some miracles attributed to Jesus. Yet they belong to a distant past era, and it is unlikely that Jesus's first Jewish followers (particularly disciples, normally charged with accurately representing teachers) would invent such stories without a basis in the tradition (see, e.g., Keener, "Otho"; idem, "Assumptions," 39–57). (It is inconceivable that within a generation, they would so thoroughly embellish the tradition about him that healings and exorcisms would pervade every stratum of the tradition, but Price is not addressing healings and exorcisms here.)

81. Tac. *Hist.* 4.81 (citing surviving eyewitnesses); Suet. *Vesp.* 7.

82. Blackburn, "ΑΝΔΡΕΣ," 199–204.

Christianity, were not likely to have influenced early Christianity, and were still less likely to have influenced the historical Jesus and his immediate Galilean followers.[83] This problem is discussed further below.

(1) Magical Associations

Not everyone viewed all of these wonder-workers in a positive vein; although miracle working tended to be public and magic secretive, miracle workers in the Greco-Roman world could easily be understood as sorcerers.[84] Magicians were generally feared and usually detested[85] (hence the antimagical apologetic in Acts 8:9–11; 13:8–11; 19:13–19).[86] The Pythagorean Empedocles reportedly "performed magical feats" (γοητεύοντι)—a term that generally had unpleasant connotations.[87] Ferguson is probably right that "behind Philostratus are two older views of Apollonius—as a magician and charlatan or a wonder-worker";[88] the magical character of some of the deeds still frequently surfaces in Philostratus,[89] although he is trying to clear Apollonius of the charge.[90] Apollonius is discussed further below.

(2) The "Divine Man"

Many scholars have interpreted the NT accounts of Jesus's miracles, and sometimes those of his agents, in light of a Hellenistic category they call the "divine man."[91] The title did not make the person a deity per se but drew attention to the person's divine qualities.[92] To a lesser extent, this category might be applied to miracle-working leaders in Acts.

Yet, as some other scholars point out, structural similarities between Christian and pagan tellings of miracles hardly make the NT accounts representatives of divine-man ideology.[93] This is true for two reasons. First, the applicability of the very category "divine man" to first-century miracle workers is a matter of considerable dispute. Second (as will be explored below), Judaism already had a miracle-working tradition in the Elijah-Elisha cycle, a tradition that it did not accentuate for Hellenistic apologetic; this relative indifference in Judaism diminishes the likelihood that the Gospels, which are less hellenized than some of our other Jewish sources, would have appealed to divine man ideology. The supposed connections between aretalogies and divine men are also inadequate.[94]

In the past, many scholars have argued that the divine man was a composite type in antiquity with specific characteristics,[95] but most scholars now recognize that the

---

83. See the critique of the "divine man" hypothesis in earlier NT scholarship in Holladay, *Theios aner*; Gallagher, *Divine Man*; Pilgaard, "*Theios aner*"; Blackburn, "ΑΝΔΡΕΣ"; Tiede, *Figure*; Theissen and Merz, *Guide*, 305; and other scholars and discussion cited in Keener, *Spirit*, 66–67; idem, *John*, 268–69. Individual pagan miracle workers arose especially in the first-century East and thereafter developed in competition with early Christianity (Frateantonio, "Miracles," 53).

84. Harvey, *History*, 105.

85. See the extensive excursus on ancient magic and views concerning it, at Acts 8:9–11.

86. Each of these accounts concludes with God's word spreading (Acts 8:12; 13:12; 19:20). Accusations against Christians for using magic (e.g., *Eccl. Rab.* 1:8, §4) made such apologetic all the more imperative.

87. Diog. Laert. 8.2.59, citing Satyrus's citation of Gorgias, who claimed to be a witness.

88. Ferguson, *Backgrounds*, 306.

89. E.g., Philost. *Vit. Apoll.* 4.43; 6.43; cf. also Evans, "Apollonius," 80–81.

90. Smith, *Magician*, 87; Klauck, *Context*, 169. See further Reimer, *Miracle* (below).

91. Reitzenstein, *Religions*, 207; Bultmann, *Theology*, 1:130; Koester, *Paul and World*, 120; Mack, *Lost Gospel*, 66. I have taken much of the material in this section from Keener, *John*, 268–70.

92. Strelan, *Strange Acts*, 20 (noting even application of "divine" to Isaiah in Jos. *Ant.* 10.35 and to Moses in Philo *Mos.* 2.188). Some have also linked this divine man with Jesus's title, "son of God," a title explored briefly in this commentary's excursus at Acts 9:20. For application to apostles in Acts, see, e.g., Pervo, *Acts*, 25.

93. Kingsbury, *Christology*, 39.

94. Gallagher, *Divine Man*, 173–74; cf. Gundry, "Genre," 107.

95. Cf. Talbert, *Gospel*, who relates men who achieved immortality (26–31) to *theioi andres*, while noting that not all *theioi andres* became immortal (35–38). Aune, "Problem of Genre," 19, is more skeptical of Talbert's differentiation between "eternals" and "immortals."

various characteristics derive from many diverse sources and have been unified in a single type only by the creativity of modern scholarship.[96] The ancient use of the phrase is too broad to delineate a specific type; it can refer to a literal "divine man," an "inspired man," a man somehow related to deity, and an "extraordinary man."[97] The sense in which such a phrase appears in the third-century *Life of Apollonius* by Philostratus did not yet exist in the first century.[98]

Thus earlier scholars blended too many disparate features in pictures of the "divine man."[99] The individuals who fit the category best are Pythagoras (of whom relatively little is known historically), Apollonius (for reports of whom we are largely dependent on third-century C.E. Philostratus),[100] and Empedocles[101] (like the other two, associated with Pythagoreanism). Although Pythagoras and Empedocles lived centuries before early Christianity, the attribution of wonders to them apparently derives from long after their own lifetimes.

Significant differences must be taken into account; magical texts and Philostratus provide little "historical evidence for events reported by writers of the first century, who were operating within a very different life-world."[102] Healing accounts had already become more detailed and began to appear in literary texts in the imperial period, a period in which magic also began to acquire greater prominence.[103] "Fantastic tales" and other fictitious elements in works with historical settings apparently grew popular, especially beginning in the literary revival of Nero's reign.[104] Nevertheless, such ideas are more characteristic of third-century sources.[105]

That third-century miracle narratives are much more complete than accounts in earlier historians probably suggests that pagan propagandists suited their accounts to existing Christian parallels.[106] Thus parallels between first-century Christian stories of Jesus raising the dead and third-century accounts of first-century Apollonius of Tyana[107] doing the same may tell us more about Christian influence on paganism in late antiquity than about the reverse.[108]

---

96. See Tiede, *Figure*, 99 (cf. 14–29, on Pythagorean conceptions; 71–97, on Heracles); Gallagher, *Divine Man*, 173; Shuler, *Genre*, 18; Blackburn, "ΑΝΔΡΕΣ," 188–91; Kingsbury, *Christology*, 34; Martitz, "Υἱός," 8:339–40; Betz, *Jesus*, 64. The "type" is especially inappropriate for the first century, when many of its features are not yet documented.

97. Holladay, *Theios aner*, 237.

98. Kee, *Miracle*, 37.

99. See Klauck, *Context*, 177.

100. In Philost. *Ep. Apoll.* 48, Apollonius claims that the gods have publicly attested him as a "divine man."

101. Klauck, *Context*, 176.

102. Kee, *Miracle*, 288; cf. 52. Kee contends that the "divine man" type is nonexistent (297–99; cf. idem, *Origins*, 61–62).

103. Theissen, *Miracle Stories*, 269–71, 274.

104. Bowersock, *Fiction as History*, 22 (attributing some of this to the influence of the Jesus tradition, 27, 143; but would it have exercised such influence on Rome's aristocracy by Nero's reign?).

105. See Kee, *Miracle*, 288; cf. Klauck, *Context*, 170.

106. See Lown, "Miraculous." Philostratus has a story resembling the raising of the widow's son in Luke 7:11–17, but Luke's version is earlier. Luke's Gospel locates the miracle at Nain, an insignificant village, does not report the young man's revelations about the afterlife, and is otherwise similarly unadorned, favoring authenticity over later, embellished pagan parallels (Harris, "Dead," 299). Note further comment below.

107. Anderson, *Philostratus*, 121–239, argues for the antiquity of the Apollonius traditions; Bowie, "Apollonius," 1653–71, and idem, "Philostratus," 181–96, argues for their lateness (cf. also Bowersock's views on the priority of the Christian stories, in *Fiction as History*). Reimer, *Miracle*, 20–22, summarizes Anderson and Bowie and concludes that even if one rejects the narratives' antiquity, they can "illuminate shared cultural data" relevant to an earlier period (23, following Anderson, *Philostratus*, 121). I agree on this level and use Philostratus accordingly in my work.

108. Pélaez del Rosal, "Reanimación," may well be right that Philostratus read Luke; against Theissen, *Miracle Stories*, 277; cf. Price, "Easters," who reads some gospel signs in light of Philostratus and analogous sources. For significant contrasts between Philostratus and Luke here, see Harris, "Dead," 301–3. Narrative

(3) Philostratus's Claims about Apollonius

As suggested above, some sources—possibly the majority—before Philostratus associated Apollonius with magic.[109] Philostratus seeks to counter this accusation in his portrayal. The antimagical apologetic in Philostratus resembles that in Acts and other sources: ethical and communal criteria were important in distinguishing benevolent miracles from harmful magic.[110] Thus, for example, magic could seek to manipulate the divine for personal advantage.[111] For Apollonius (Philostratus *Vit. Apoll.* 1.34), various criteria distinguish magic from miracle working, but most important among them is the issue of greed; the most effective answer to miracle workers' critics was to keep using miraculous power without seeming to desire it or to be greedy.[112] Good intermediaries might also put themselves in danger to benefit others.[113] Such beliefs about ancient magic probably helped shape both Luke's and Philostratus's apologetic.

Philostratus's own portrait suits a second- or third-century setting (i.e., his own) much better than a first-century setting (i.e., Apollonius's); his accounts of Apollonius even resemble reports from Christian gospels, though especially of the "apocryphal" variety.[114] By the fourth century, pagan writers used Apollonius as an alternative to Jesus, claiming that the pagan world offered its own healers.[115]

Use of stories about Apollonius and others as rivals to Jesus invited Christian apologetic responses,[116] though it may be noted that the most significant apologetic on a popular level may have been the reports of continuing miracle workers among Christians (see discussion below). Although scholars today often doubt the nineteenth-century view that Philostratus tried to offer Apollonius as an alternative to Jesus (apart from the cases of the strongest parallels),[117] it seems clear that Christian stories at least were among the serious influences on his storytelling approach (offering literary fodder for miracle stories).[118]

Thus, for example, Apollonius stops a bier and raises a dead girl (Philostratus *Vit. Apoll.* 4.45)—like Jesus (Mark 5:41–42; Luke 7:14–15). His exorcisms reflect a different understanding of demons from that found in the Gospels and Acts (cf. excursus

techniques in 1 Kgs 17:17–24 influenced Luke's composition (cf. Pélaez del Rosal, "Reanimación"; Brodie, "Unravelling"; Hill, *Prophecy*, 53), but he did not simply compose it from this source (Harris, "Dead," 299–301; Witherington, *Women*, 76; against Drury, *Design*, 71).

109. Klauck, *Context*, 169.

110. Reimer, *Miracle*, 249.

111. Ibid., 250.

112. Ibid., 246; cf. 139, 252. People viewed magicians as deviant, outside the religious community (248). But social marginalization was necessary and desirable for miracle workers to avoid charges of ambition (139–41, noting the apostles and, still more, Apollonius and other exotic sages in Philostratus). For early miracle workers' asceticism, see Frateantonio, "Miracles," 53.

113. Reimer, *Miracle*, 85, comparing the apostles.

114. Klauck, *Context*, 170. Admittedly, stories of Jesus as miracle worker are limited in extant apocryphal gospels (Achtemeier, *Miracle Tradition*, 177–78; cf. Remus, *Healer*, 92–95), but miracle stories are abundant in apocryphal acts (Achtemeier, *Miracle Tradition*, 179–88; cf. Remus, *Healer*, 102–3).

115. Klauck, *Context*, 170; Conybeare, "Introduction," xi–xii.

116. See, e.g., "The Treatise of Eusebius, the Son of Pamphilus, against the Life of Apollonius of Tyana written by Philostratus, occasioned by the Parallel drawn by Hierocles between him and Christ" (in Philostratus, *Life of Apollonius*, LCL, 2:484–605); Eusebius notes (ch. 1) that Celsus had already required such refutation by Origen. See further Cook, *Interpretation*, 250–76, esp. 266–68.

117. E.g., Borzì, "Accostamento" (not Philostratus himself but other ancient writers). See further Klauck, *Context*, 170–71, himself arguing that the case should be left open.

118. Note also that in Nero's day, Apollonius leaves Rome for Spain (Philost. *Vit. Apoll.* 4.47)—like Paul (Rom 15:24). Philostratus *possibly* borrows Apollonius's offering wisdom to Vespasian before he becomes emperor from Josephus's earlier story (cf. also Johanan ben Zakkai), in a setting that detests the bloodshed of the Judean war (*Vit. Apoll.* 5.27–28).

at Acts 16:16) and are more dramatized, but some similarities appear here as well. Response to Christian claims is likely in Apollonius's promise to his disciple that he will meet him at a designated location alive though, in the disciple's view, risen from the dead (Philostratus *Vit. Apoll.* 7.41). When he appeared to followers in a distant location (8.10–11) and they supposed him a ghost, he urged them to take hold of him and see that he was not a ghost, and they embraced him (8.12; cf. Luke 24:39). Some other elements are quite different—for example, getting a formerly mad dog to lick the wound it had inflicted, thereby healing the boy (*Vit. Apoll.* 6.43), and even incantations in some of the above stories. Yet it is interesting that the parts of the story most apt to be confirmed by Apollonius's letters[119] exhibit the least parallels with the Gospels.

(4) Jewish "Divine Men"?

Against the contentions of some scholars, it does not appear clear that Hellenistic Jewish writers accentuated the miraculous for Hellenistic audiences. Jewish sources do not consistently portray Moses as a divine man;[120] he is a miracle worker in Artapanus and a philosopher for Philo and Josephus, but the two ideas are not brought together under a single category.[121] Although some Diaspora Jewish writers emphasized the miraculous powers of historic Jewish heroes,[122] they do not seem to have heightened miracle-working motifs for Hellenistic consumption. Thus Philo seems to diminish Moses's miracles, and Artapanus's embellishments of Moses do not focus on miracles.[123]

So different are the Jewish portraits of past heroes from Philostratus's third-century picture of Apollonius of Tyana that one is forced to question "just how attractive the miracle-worker motif was to pagans" in the first and second centuries, a fact that "may explain why this aspect of the Jesus tradition is non-existent in the apostolic fathers"[124] and why emphasis on miracle working tends to decrease as sermons in Acts become more Hellenistic.[125]

Jewish miracle workers, magicians, and fortune-tellers[126] were not "divine men." Carl Holladay, who has written in detail on the divine-man question, warns that the divine-man approach "obscures" clearer connection with OT models and Jewish eschatology.[127] By dramatic contrast to the lack of clear allusions to any specific Hellenistic miracle workers, in Luke's narrative, allusions to the exodus traditions and Elijah-Elisha cycles recur throughout the Gospel miracle narratives. The expression "divine man"

---

119. Regardless of the letters' authenticity (it may be doubtful), they predate Philostratus's story. The letters focus on Greek cities where Apollonius indeed probably traveled (not the lands of the Ethiopians, Indians, etc., where Philostratus's most fanciful tales transpire).

120. *Pace* Georgi, *Opponents*, 122–64; cf. also 390–409.

121. Tiede, *Figure*, ch. 2, "Images of Moses in Hellenistic Judaism," 101–240. Moses was "divine" in the sense that he was affected by the deity (Jos. *Ag. Ap.* 1.279). Cf. the probability that Josephus presents Jesus as both teacher and miracle worker (*Ant.* 18.63; as noted above, Josephus employs the same term, παράδοξα, for the miracles worked by the prophet Elisha, in 9.182; cf. 2.267, 285; 10.28, 235; 13.282; 15.379).

122. See Hengel, *Judaism and Hellenism*, 1:241 (citing Jos. *Ag. Ap.* 1.176–83); Collins, "Artapanus," 893, following Tiede, *Figure*, 166–74.

123. Holladay, *Theios aner*, 238–39.

124. Ibid., 238. It should be admitted, however, that many of the extant Apostolic Fathers aim at a philosophical, rather than popular, audience whereas the Gospels do not.

125. Ibid., 239, comparing Acts 2:22; 10:38; 17:22–31 (although the last passage, again, is directed toward a philosophical audience; contrast the absence in 13:23–31; but cf. 1 Cor 1:22).

126. See, e.g., Lucian in Stern, *Authors*, 2:221–23 (citing Lucian *Lover of Lies* 16; *Alex.* 13; *Tragodopodagra* 171–73); see also Juv. *Sat.* 6.542–47.

127. Holladay, *Theios aner*, 239. Cf. similarly Kee, *Origins*, 62; Betz, *Jesus*, 64. For a survey of especially OT healing theology (in its ancient contexts), see esp. Brown, *Healer*; for a survey of texts about healings, see Warrington, "Healing."

never appears in the LXX or NT and is rare in any Jewish sources.[128] (Josephus's single use of the term may be roughly equivalent to "man of God";[129] Philo's use is closer to a Stoic conception but is unrelated to miracles.)[130] If anything, hellenization may have made Jewish conception of a "*divine* man" more, rather than less, problematic.[131]

Application of the title to Jesus is problematic, despite suggestions of some scholars that Mark addresses this image. It is not impossible that the crowds in Mark followed Jesus because he was a wonder-worker and that Mark opposes reducing Jesus's ministry to such terms, insisting that the suffering aspect of his ministry must also be taken into account. Although Mark is himself charismatic rather than anticharismatic,[132] it is possible that he opposes a Christology or, more likely, a pneumatology that emphasizes Jesus's miracles above his passion. The term θεῖος ἀνήρ, however, is too broad to designate such a category helpfully.[133] It is no more appropriate in Luke-Acts.

b. Early Jewish Miracle Workers

As noted above, Jewish parallels to early Christian miracles appear to offer closer models than most Gentile analogies.[134] Jewish people, after all, attributed healing to the one true God (Exod 15:26) and prayed to God regularly for healing Israel's sicknesses.[135] Some pre-Christian Jewish parallels, especially those in the OT, likewise resemble the miracle forms used in the Gospels.[136] Some miracle stories in Acts display clear intertextual links with OT accounts[137] (see, e.g., comments on Acts 9:36–42). It is intrinsically more likely that even the most hellenized of Gospel writers, Luke, would have looked to the LXX for his primary model for recounting Jesus's miracles (he knew its contents and style thoroughly, and he cites it regularly in explicitly marked quotations) than to inscriptions at a healing shrine or to oral reports of magicians or polytheistic miracle workers.

Granted, some analogies resemble the common model that ancients often attributed to sorcery, a model available in many Jewish circles. Jewish magicians (with whom some of early Christianity's detractors polemically associated it) became common in the Diaspora (see comments on Acts 8:9–11; 13:8), especially through their supposed access to the secret name of God (secret names were considered powerful in

128. The count is from Holladay, *Theios aner*, 237–38.

129. See the discussion of the passage, Jos. *Ant*. 3.180, in Meeks, *Prophet-King*, 138.

130. Tiede, *Figure*, 123, 240; cf. Philo *Names* 125–28.

131. Holladay, *Theios aner*, 238.

132. I believe that Boring, *Sayings*, 201–2, is wrong to suggest that Mark opposes charismatic excesses in Q; Mark draws on Q at places (e.g., in his abbreviated introduction; in Mark 3:22–30). But Boring is correct to note that as a charismatic, Mark could oppose charismatic excesses (*Sayings*, 203). Kümmel, *Introduction*, 93, rightly observes against Weeden that Mark does not deny Jesus's role as a wonder-worker; the signs are clearly positive (Rhoads and Michie, *Mark*, 105; Kingsbury, *Christology*, 76–77), even if they must be read in view of the cross.

133. Vander Broek, "Sitz," 131–89. Lane, "*Theios anēr*," 160, thinks that the view might be attributable to the crowds. Weeden, *Mark*, 52–69, thought Mark's opponents followed a θεῖος ἀνήρ Christology like the one some attribute to Paul's opponents in 2 Corinthians. The term "opponents" may be too strong, and θεῖος ἀνήρ too ambiguous (although they may hold "a triumphalist theology characterized by . . . miraculous acts," p. vii).

134. With, e.g., Koskenniemi, "Apollonius"; Strelan, *Strange Acts*, 27 (following Weiss, *Zeichen*, 22–39, who supplies considerable material). I use here material esp. from Keener, *John*, 255–57.

135. The eighth benediction of the Amidah, including both spiritual and physical sicknesses (Bonsirven, *Judaism*, 131).

136. Blackburn, "ΑΝΔΡΕΣ," 199–204. Resuscitation stories appear; cf. the claim for Empedocles in Diog. Laert. 8.2.59; *4 Bar*. 7:19–20 (a resuscitation "in order that they might believe" [my translation]); rabbis in *b. B. Qam*. 117a; Abraham in *Test. Ab*. 14:11–14; 18:9–11 A; 14:7 B.

137. See Brucker, "Wunder."

magic; see comment on Acts 19:13). Although the rabbis were officially opposed to magic,[138] magical practices infiltrated even rabbinic circles.[139] By and large, however, the teachers of the law who addressed signs in a positive way emphasized miracles wrought by God for the pious, eschewing what they or others considered magic.

Judaism knew of both biblical and postbiblical miracle workers. Some biblical prophets, such as Elijah and Elisha, were particularly emphasized as healers;[140] some others, such as Isaiah, might heal occasionally (Isa 38:21);[141] and Jewish sources continued to link miracles with many of the biblical prophets.[142] According to third-century Palestinian tradition, Abraham had the gift of healing.[143] Other miracle workers, such as Hanina ben Dosa, appeared closer to the contemporary period, healing, according to tradition, the sons of Johanan ben Zakkai and Gamaliel II.[144] The Jewish historian Geza Vermes goes so far as to suggest that holy men such as Hanina ben Dosa dominated first-century Galilean religious experience more than the priests or scribes did;[145] although this suggestion certainly goes too far, it rightly emphasizes the popular nature of charismatic leaders and the degree to which they could become influential in first-century Galilee.

Josephus is more interested in (though disparaging of) purported eschatological-sign prophets, some of whose promised activities may evoke Moses, in their attempts to secure eschatological deliverance.[146] (Signs and wonders were often associated with Moses,[147] who used "wonders and signs" to withstand kings.)[148] Many Jewish people probably not only expected significant signs before the final deliverance and special miracles at the end[149] but also pondered the promised signs of the messianic era offered by Isaiah, Ezekiel, and other biblical prophets. Consistent with such images, later rabbis taught that signs offered by biblical signs prophets anticipated the signs that would take place in the messianic era.[150]

138. E.g., *m. Sanh.* 7:11; *y. Ḥag.* 2:2, §5; *Roš Haš.* 3:8, §1; *Sanh.* 7:13, §2. Note also Wis 17:7; Ps.-Phoc. 149; *1 En.* 65:6 (Similitudes); *Asc. Is.* 2:5; *2 Bar.* 60:2; 66:2; *Test. Reub.* 4:9.

139. See Goldin, "Magic"; Neusner, *Sat*, 80–81; *b. Sanh.* 65b; 67b; cf. *ʾAbot R. Nat.* 25 A (on R. Eliezer ben Hyrcanus); Basser, "Interpretations."

140. For Elijah and Elisha as examples of healing miracles in Josephus, see Betz, "Miracles in Josephus," 219–20; as models among signs sages, see Galley, "Heilige."

141. With Cohen, *Maccabees*, 200. Eve, *Miracles*, 385, argues that the only miracle directly attributed to Isaiah in the account was the shadow going up, but Isaiah does play a role in the healing here.

142. E.g., Sir 48:13; *Liv. Pr.* 2:3 (on Jeremiah, in *OTP* 2:386–87; Schermann, 81–82, §25).

143. *Gen. Rab.* 39:11, R. Levi; later R. Huna amplified this tradition.

144. *B. Ber.* 34b. Later reports also apply to later rabbis (cf., e.g., Rosenfeld, "Simeon b. Yohai").

145. Vermes, *Jesus and Judaism*, 5. By contrast, most reports of rabbinic miracles, probably fitting the predominantly halakic character of rabbinic literature, are "rule miracles," i.e., signs to demonstrate the truth of one's legal teaching (Theissen, *Miracle Stories*, 106–12).

146. See Keener, *John*, 270–71; Eve, *Miracles*, 115–16, 324. On these sign prophets, see initially Barnett, "Prophets"; and now esp. Gray, *Figures*, 112–44. Gray contends, probably rightly, that (137) only the cases of Theudas and the Egyptian genuinely evoke the exodus and conquest traditions; but even these two examples offer sufficient evidence to suggest that such views circulated in first-century Judea (whether already in Jesus's day or perhaps even evoking some early views about him). Philo's miracles focus especially on "the distant Mosaic past" (Eve, *Miracles*, 84), like most early Jewish miracle reports (377, though noting that they were not cessationist).

147. *Jub.* 48:4; *L.A.B.* 9:7; *Sipre Deut.* 9.2.1; 4Q422 III, 4–5; see further Meeks, *Prophet-King*, 162–63; Eve, *Miracles*, 244. But some sources such as Ben Sira may associate miracles more with prophets subsequent to Moses (Eve, *Miracles*, 115–16).

148. Wis 10:16.

149. E.g., Sir 33:1–8/36:1–8. Eve, *Miracles*, 263–66, 379, notes that early Jewish sources could connect miracles with eschatology (citing 4Q521; *Jub.* 23:23–31), but warns (266) that the association was not "automatic."

150. *Pesiq. Rab Kah.* 9:4, Amoraic; cf. related ideas in Marmorstein, *Names*, 175.

Jesus's reported miracles accord well with the Q allusion to Isa 35:5–6 (Matt 11:5// Luke 7:22), which could suggest an eschatological interpretation of his miracles as blessings of the future kingdom in the present.[151] This conception of an eschatological renewal of signs suits the way Luke identifies the Christian movement from Pentecost forward (Acts 2:17–18). Most scholars recognize that in the Gospels Jesus's miracles function as signs of the kingdom (also Matt 12:28//Luke 11:20).[152]

c. Comparison of Early Christian and Pagan Miracle Accounts

Among Luke's social circle in early Christianity or among God-fearers steeped in the LXX, Luke's supranormal claims would hardly seem implausible. Elite historians might well despise his historiographic approach on this point as sensationalistic, given the unusual abundance of miracles and divine communications (which we would expect to this degree only in works, historical or otherwise, concerning miracle workers, works such as Luke-Acts); but this was a price Luke would have to pay to remain faithful to the sources (such as Mark) and traditions that he considered normative. Modern Western readers usually concur with elite historians' negative estimate of popular historiography concerning wonder-workers' signs and portents, but this preference may partly reflect a coinciding of our cultural bias with theirs.

Some scholars, pointing to the parallels between early Christian and other ancient miracle accounts, have suggested that both are fabricated.[153] While the conclusion need not follow from the premise—either because both kinds of accounts could sometimes be true or because similar form could reflect cultural options for expression rather than identical activity—the premise itself may be open to some question. Parallels are clear, but observers must also take account of the differences among the various kinds of miracle stories, including the Christian miracle stories. That all the accounts strike many modern Western readers as very similar may stem partly from our cultural assumptions, in view of which all miracle reports diverge starkly from our construction of reality.

Distinctive as well as more common features characterize most of the miracles in our earliest Christian sources.[154] An analysis of the miracle stories collected by Theissen[155] shows that some motifs (especially those intrinsic to miracle narrations in any setting) were widespread. At the same time, such an analysis will reveal that some other NT miracle motifs exhibit rare, perhaps only coincidental, parallels. Likewise, some repeated accounts of pagan miracle workers (albeit in sources much later than the objects of their comment) have few early Christian parallels; for example, Musaeus, Calais, Zetes, Abaris,

---

151. Cf. Harvey, *Jesus*, 115, although taking matters too far; Witherington, *Christology*, 171; Sanders, *Figure*, 167–68. Other Jewish pietists adapted similar Isaianic language for the eschatological inversion (1QM XIV, 6), praying for an eschatological miracle (4Q176 1–2 I, 1). Qumran also may have combined the very texts to which Jesus alluded here, which perhaps suggests a Palestinian tradition (Evans, "Messianic Apocalypse," 696 [on 4Q521]; Le Cornu, *Acts*, 1388; though cf. Kvalbein, "Wunder"; idem, "Wonders").

152. See Blackburn, "Miracles," 372–74; Evans, *Fabricating Jesus*, 141; see further Twelftree, *Miracle Worker*, passim.

153. Some earlier scholars also committed parallelomania; cf., e.g., Bultmann, *Tradition* (1963), 222: "H. Jahnow has shown the probability . . . that the removal of the roof in Mk. 2⁴ goes back to an exorcist custom" forgotten or changed during transmission.

154. If some critics would (by means of an ad hominem argument) charge the acknowledgment to "apologetic" motives (i.e., impugning motives), denying it can be charged to a reductionism that looks at parallels without appreciating distinctions among them. ("Apologetic" activity, in the sense of defending a thesis, is pervasive in scholarship, with no necessary correspondence to religious convictions.) Bias can occur in either direction, either the agenda of reducing or that of augmenting NT miracles' distinctiveness (cf. Strelan, *Strange Acts*, 11). If it is fair to examine analogous elements, we must also note the many great distinctions.

155. See Theissen, *Miracle Stories*, 47–72.

and a Hyperborean magician in Lucian could fly,[156] but the only possible early Christian parallel (Acts 8:39; see comment there) apparently specifically borrows biblical language (drawing on Ezek 8:3; 11:1, 24, where, however, the experience was visionary).

Similarly, one account reports that Pythagoras taught in two places at the same time.[157] Love magic,[158] a continual fast,[159] a fifty-seven-year nap,[160] magicians' self-transformation into animal forms,[161] and revealing golden thighs[162] are among other sorts of miracles unparalleled in the Gospels, which generally stress healings and exorcisms as benevolent acts of compassion (see the section on signs in ch. 15 below).[163] Some scholars also emphasize "matter-of-fact restraint" rather than amplification in most miracle stories in the canonical Gospels,[164] though this may be partly because there are so many of them to narrate in so little space!

Nor does Luke write like a typical epic poet or mythographer; in contrast with Virgil's *Aeneid*, Luke offers no scenes explaining "what God is thinking or how God views the events unfolding in the human realm."[165] Luke does not report fictions about exotic lands,[166] does not report internal workings of divine courts, and does not report monsters or other fabulous creatures.[167] He does report healings and prophecies, but we know from Paul's own writings that early Christians truly believed that these events were genuinely occurring in their time (Rom 15:19; 1 Cor 12–14; 2 Cor 12:12; Gal 3:5; 1 Thess 5:20), just as probably the majority of Christians in most parts of the world believe they are occurring today. (The same texts reveal that Paul did not believe this claim in some theoretical sense but believed that he and, in some passages, the churches participated in the actual experience of such phenomena.)

Moreover, although pagans naturally understood Jesus's works as those of a (possibly malevolent) magician (Mark 5:15–17),[168] Jesus's miracles have little in common with magic as normally defined, especially the magic elaborately documented for us in the third-century magical papyri. (Part of the debate about magic and Jesus's miracles turns on one's definition of "magic,"[169] but to the extent that "religion" and "magic" are distinguished, the normal criteria readily distinguish Jesus's reported activity from magic.)[170] Pagan magicians typically sought to coerce deities or spirits

---

156. Blackburn, "ΑΝΔΡΕΣ," 190. For the text conveniently, see also Cotter, *Miracles*, 191.

157. Blackburn, "ΑΝΔΡΕΣ," 190.

158. The Hyperborean (ibid., 191).

159. Abaris (ibid.).

160. Ibid.

161. Periclymneus, Nectanebus (ibid., 190, 193).

162. Pythagoras, Alexander of Abonuteichos (ibid., 193). This is the closest these texts come to Jesus's transformation (Mark 9:2–8), a narrative far more evocative of Moses's transformation on Mount Sinai (cf. Bultmann, *Tradition*, 229; Glasson, *Moses*, 70–71; Davies, *Sermon*, 20–21; some commentators appeal more to general apocalyptic images).

163. Contrast also many of the supernatural acts in traditional religions, e.g., in Mbiti, *Religions*, 258. On comparisons with Greek heroes, see further Blomberg, *Gospels*, 115–19; like Blackburn and others, he notes (116) that most Greek prodigies are unparalleled in the Gospels.

164. Gundry, *Use*, 190; Witherington, *Christology of Jesus*, 161–62.

165. Alexander, *Context*, 179.

166. See Keener, "Official."

167. Many of these elements were common in popular literature (cf. Penner, *Praise*, 134).

168. See Keener, *Matthew*, 287–88, and sources cited there. Although Morton Smith's citation of the charge against Christians in Tac. *Ann*. 15.44.3–8 as "a charge appropriate to magicians" (Smith, *Magician*, 51–52) is unhelpful (pagans charged the Jewish people with the same "hatred of humanity"), he has probably correctly identified the way the earliest Gentile witnesses of Jesus's miracles would have perceived him (as well as Jesus's opponents in Mark 3:22 par.).

169. Cf. Aune, "Magic," 1557; Blomberg, "Reflections," 449.

170. Kee, *Miracle*, 214–15; Meier, *Marginal Jew*, 2:537–52; Twelftree, *Exorcist*, 190–207; Goergen, *Mission*, 173–75; Vermes, *Religion*, 6.

by incantations; Jesus simply commanded as God's authoritative agent.[171] (Of course, pagans could also articulate such a difference when it served their interests;[172] Jewish rabbis also had to seek to distinguish the two.)[173] I have already addressed comparisons with Apollonius above.

Clearly, the Galilean sage and prophet Jesus moved in an environment quite different from the Hellenistic environment that formed the magical papyri.[174] Nevertheless, his detractors accused him of magic (Mark 3:22, probably also in Q Matt 12:24//Luke 11:15),[175] the easiest charge to bring against wonder-workers. Luke is eager to absolve early Christians as well as Jesus from the charge, by way of contrast with those who misunderstood or opposed them (see comment on Acts 8:9–11; 13:6–8; 19:11–19).

One may also note differences between the kinds of sources claiming the performance of various miracles. After carefully comparing the accounts of Jesus's miracles with those of others, Meier concludes that "the early dating of the literary testimony to Jesus's miracles, i.e., the closeness of the dates of the written documents to the alleged miracles of Jesus's life, is almost unparalleled for the period."[176] His conclusions for the Gospels' testimony to Jesus would apply a fortiori to Acts, which reports some miracles even roughly thirty years after Jesus's public ministry, possibly within fifteen years before Luke wrote (Acts 28:8–9).

d. Comparison of Early Christian and Jewish Miracle Accounts

The miracles of Jesus and his followers in Luke-Acts resemble especially those of Elijah, Elisha, and Moses in the Hebrew Bible (see, more extensively, comment on Acts 1:9–11),[177] and the use of such patterns was probably deliberate (for Jesus, for those who reported the tradition orally, and for those who recorded the pattern in the Gospels and Acts). This comparison does not, however, affect the question of authenticity if one grants that the miracle workers themselves could have looked to the earlier biblical accounts for examples (the early Christians would have viewed the correspondences as favorable and, certainly, as counter to the magic charge). Jesus and his early followers, like some other Jewish wonder-workers,[178] may have deliberately emulated these models. Unlike other models that some propose, these biblical examples are clearly earlier than our early Christian accounts and were clearly known to Jesus, his audience, and those who told, wrote, and heard about him.

Nevertheless, we turn to some other comparisons.[179] In some respects, comparisons of Jesus's miracles with those attributed to the rabbis are more difficult than even comparisons with some Greco-Roman accounts because of striking differences in genre in the sources that report them. Some writers have debased rabbinic miracles as more magical than Jesus's;[180] but despite some activities whose only parallels occur

---

171. Drane, "Background," 122–23; cf. similarly Theissen, *Miracle Stories*, 296; Yamauchi, "Magic?," 133; Twelftree, *Exorcist*, 172–73.

172. E.g., Apul. *Metam.* 3.21–25 (by magic, reversed by Isis in *Metam.* 11).

173. See Urbach, *Sages*, 1:102–3.

174. With, e.g., Theissen and Merz, *Guide*, 306–7.

175. According to the Two Document Hypothesis, agreements between Matthew and Luke against Mark in the pericope (esp. Matt 12:28//Luke 11:20) suggest a common source additional to Mark. See discussion in Keener, *Spirit*, 104–9; Stanton, "Magician," 174–80; cf. discussion on John 7:20 in Keener, *John*, 714–16.

176. Meier, *Marginal Jew*, 2:624; see further 2:536, 576–616; Clark, "Miracles," 207.

177. See also, e.g., Strelan, *Strange Acts*, 27; cf. Eve, *Miracles*, 377.

178. As models among signs sages, see Galley, "Heilige."

179. Honi the Circle-Drawer and Hanina ben Dosa probably followed Elijah's model but, normally, different aspects of it (such as rainmaker) than Jesus (though many of his Galilean followers may not have made such distinctions).

180. Alexander, *Possession*, 59.

in magic, not all rabbinic miracles were magical. Although Morton Smith somewhat exaggerates the contrast between the gospel tradition's interest in a miracle worker and the rabbinic tradition's interest in teachers,[181] he is correct that the two kinds of accounts describe different kinds of characters and communicate different sorts of information about them. (At least some rabbinic miracle stories are simply homiletic illustrations.) The differences between the two kinds of accounts are considerable. Correspondingly, miracle stories are common in early Christian texts but proportionately quite rare in rabbinic texts.[182]

The genre difference is critical. Generally, accounts of rabbis who wrought miracles were related by rabbis to make a homiletic point concerning a teaching; the Gospels and Acts recount miracles of Jesus and his followers primarily to validate Jesus's person and mission rather than just a particular teaching.[183] (By implication, this pattern about signs focusing on Jesus and his mission in the gospel tradition also applies to the Gentile mission in Acts, which perpetuates Jesus's ministry to the outsider.)[184] Moreover, most of the leading protagonists in the Gospels and Acts (Jesus, his apostles, and some others) are miracle workers; the rabbinic protagonists who appear most often in rabbinic literature are not miracle workers, especially not in the earliest sources about them.

Although genre affects the focus of miracle stories, their content also offers another specific contrast. Although first-century Christian texts recount other miracles (most of which also function as benevolent acts helping those in need), they especially claim healings and exorcisms. Rabbinic stories, by contrast, address the procurement of rainfall more often than healing.[185] (Miracles are not even constrained by such biblical models. In the Mishnah, God even temporarily expands space in the temple to accommodate prostrated worshipers.)[186] Later Jewish stories often recognize the particular association of healing miracles with Christians.[187]

Indeed, when one surveys Jewish tradition in general, it provides few parallels to the characteristic ways Jesus and his followers healed; perhaps the closest parallel is Jesus's relatively rare use of saliva.[188] A. E. Harvey points out that at least eight of Jesus's reported cures involved the deaf, mute, blind, or lame but that such miracles, though noted at pagan healing shrines, are absent in Jewish accounts.[189]

---

181. Smith, "Tradition," 173–74.

182. With Smith, *Parallels*, 84.

183. With, e.g., Eve, *Miracles*, 285–86. Somewhat similarly, Dibelius, *Tradition*, 150–51, notes that rabbinic accounts extol saintly men and the Gospels narrate the epiphany of God's power through his agent Jesus.

184. See, e.g., Acts 9:34; cf. Warrington, "Healing Narratives."

185. Harvey, *History*, 100; followed also by Blomberg, "Reflections," 450–51. See, e.g., Jos. *Ant.* 14.22; *m. Ta'an.* 3:8; *t. Ta'an.* 2:13 (an anonymous man but resembling Honi); *'Abot R. Nat.* 6 A; *b. Ta'an.* 8a; 19b–20a (Naqdimon ben Gurion); 23ab (including Honi and others in 23a and not only Abba Hilkiah but his wife in 23b); 24a–26a; *y. Ta'an.* 1:4, §1; 3:9, §§6–8; 3:11, §4; cf. Jos. *Ant.* 8.343–46; 14.22; Empedocles in Diog. Laert. 8.2.59–60; Aeacus's prayer in Paus. 2.29.8; further information in Vermes, *Jesus the Jew*, 70, 76; for morals in the stories, cf. Schofer, "Cosmology." For the link with corporate piety, see *1 En.* 101:2; *Pss. Sol.* 17:18; *Gen. Rab.* 13:14; *Lev. Rab.* 34:14; 35:10; *Num. Rab.* 3:12; cf. *b. Ta'an.* 19b; on the miraculousness of rain (included in the benediction of the resurrection), cf. *b. Ber.* 29a; 33a; *Ta'an.* 2b; 7a; *y. Ta'an.* 1:1, §2; *Gen. Rab.* 13:6; *Deut. Rab.* 7:6. Rainmakers are prominent in many cultures (e.g., Mbiti, *Religions*, 89, 234–37). More generally, for gods and heroes controlling wind and sea, see Cotter, *Miracles*, 131–65.

186. *M. 'Abot* 5:5; cf. Segal, "Few Contained Many."

187. Cf. Herford, *Christianity*, 50–51, 54–56, 211–15; Bagatti, *Church*, 95–96, 106–7; Manns, "Jacob." *Y. Šabb.* 14:4, §3, may be an example but is uncertain; cf. magic in *Eccl. Rab.* 1:8, §4.

188. Vermes, *Jesus the Jew*, 65; cf. Cangh, "Miracles"; Harvey, *History*, 100n10. But cf. even here Bourgeois, "Spittle," 32–33.

189. Harvey, *History*, 115; in pagan accounts, see Blackburn, "ΑΝΔΡΕΣ," 192.

The most detailed Jewish comparisons and contrasts to date have been those of Eric Eve, who concludes that Jesus's healing and exorcistic ministry, though exhibiting some parallels to its general Jewish framework, differs in serious respects from other early Jewish models.[190] As he notes, most of the miracles in non-Christian early Jewish sources differ in *kind* from those reported in early Christian sources.[191] Eve notes that most of the types of miracles in Josephus differ from those in the Gospels and Acts, with little interest in healings;[192] meanwhile, stories of postbiblical miracles are not very common outside Josephus,[193] and healings are particularly rare.[194] Apart from some works, such as *Lives of the Prophets*, most early Jewish sources display only limited interest in miracles, far less than in our earliest Christian sources.[195]

The miracles that most interested Jewish people were miracles of national deliverance, which are not the category of miracles most often associated with Jesus's ministry.[196] Meanwhile, some of the sign prophets that emerged in the decades following his ministry[197] could each announce a major eschatological sign, but they did not perform it.[198] Unlike them, Jesus "healed and exorcized, but seems not to have promised a particular spectacular sign."[199]

Although Honi the Circle-Drawer (Onias the Righteous) was undoubtedly known for obtaining answers to prayer regarding rain (Jos. *Ant.* 14.22),[200] most of the details we hear about him surface only in Amoraic tradition—perhaps half a millennium after he lived.[201] At the very least, much of the rabbinic characterization of Honi is later.[202] Eve contends, against Vermes, that it is not clear that Honi represents a class of people beyond himself.[203]

Hanina ben Dosa is usually assigned to the first century[204] and, like Jesus, was Galilean, though he is the only other Galilean we know of to whom signs are

190. Eve, *Miracles*, passim. Cf. similarly Avery-Peck, "Charismatic," 164, especially focusing on the date of the sources.

191. The only parallels Eve finds are in Christian sources or some isolated depictions of an antichrist figure (*Miracles*, 244–45); I suspect that the latter are late, like much antichrist material (cf. Keener, *Matthew*, 573–75).

192. Eve, *Miracles*, 52 (concluding his discussion of miracle in Josephus, 24–52). Like Josephus, Philo overlaps with the Gospels primarily in miracles of provision (84–85).

193. Ibid., 244. They do appear more in later Amoraic haggadah.

194. Ibid., 253, 378. Eve acknowledges some exorcists but questions whether they were common (378). (Given the different focus of most of the other surviving first-century documents, it is hard to be sure.) He also notes rightly that some exorcists have magical associations (378).

195. Ibid., 243.

196. Ibid., 377.

197. Eve, ibid., 324, emphasizes that those reported by Josephus are apparently all later than Jesus.

198. Theissen and Merz, *Guide*, 308–9. Many scholars have built on the category of "sign prophets" (see early Barnett, "Prophets"). Eve, *Miracles*, 296–325 (esp. 324), thinks them a disparate group despite Josephus's lumping them together, but he might underestimate common factors.

199. Eve, *Miracles*, 385 (noting that healings and exorcisms were "not that essential to the prophetic role," since even most OT prophets did not perform them). On these sign prophets not performing miracles, especially healings and exorcisms, see also p. 321.

200. Cf. ibid., 277–78, arguing that Josephus's focus is not on this but on his role on the war (given Josephus's focus on the war). Rainmaking is the only miracle common to both Honi and Hanina and is absent from Jesus's ministry (Blackburn, "Miracles," 378–79).

201. The only Tannaitic account is *m. Ta'an.* 3:8 (Eve, *Miracles*, 274–75), and W. Scott Green and Neusner both deny reliable information even there (275–77).

202. Thus, e.g., we do not know if Honi the Circle-Drawer in fact drew a circle around himself, as in the rabbinic legend (but not Josephus), or merely prayed for rain; one could use drawing a circle for an ultimatum (Livy 45.12.5; Val. Max. 6.4.3; Vell. Paterc. 1.10.1–2; for drawing circles in the ground more commonly, see Hermog. *Inv.* 4.8.195).

203. Eve, *Miracles*, 274.

204. Eve, ibid., 281, notes that this date is uncertain (conceding [282], however, that he was probably from the Second Temple period). Amoraic traditions place him in the first century (see 287–88).

attributed.[205] He appears several times in Tannaitic sources,[206] where he could tell, when he prayed, whether or not the sick would recover (*m. Ber.* 5:5) and where a lizard who bit him as he prayed died (*t. Ber.* 3:20). Amoraic material about Hanina is much more abundant but was transmitted and developed over the course of three or four centuries.[207] Moreover, even if the tradition is reliable, it differs from Jesus: whereas Jesus was itinerant, people came to Hanina for prayer, and few of the divine interventions mentioned included healing.[208] In their respective sources, Hanina was a petitioner of numinous or divine power whereas Jesus was its bearer.[209] We cannot know much about other Galilean folk healers, but Jesus was no ordinary one.[210]

Thus, Eve concludes, early Jewish parallels do not advance beyond the closest parallels to Jesus's signs: the biblical models of Elijah, Elisha, and (for the sea and feeding miracles) at least some links with Moses.[211] He argues that the evidence "leaves Jesus as unique in the surviving Jewish literature of his time as being portrayed as performing a large number of healings and exorcisms," and especially as a *bearer* (not just a mediator or petitioner) of divine power.[212]

Eve is not alone in his observations. Theissen and Merz appear representative of many scholars today in concluding that although Jewish wonder-workers offer closer parallels than do pagan ones, they differ significantly from Jesus (especially in working only through prayer and lacking eschatological miracles).[213] No other source reports as many miracles concerning an individual as the Gospels do regarding Jesus,[214] and Jesus stands alone among prior miracle workers in using miracles, in his case healings and exorcisms, to indicate the coming of the eschatological order.[215]

None of this rules out the relevance of these parallels in helping us understand how Palestinian Jews would have viewed Jesus or his first disciples; Vermes has clearly shown that one need not look to more geographically distant Gentile healing traditions for the historical Jesus. Moreover, the Jewish activity of Elijah is an early source, and in view of Mal 4:5–6, it can be construed as a valid model for an eschatological prophet as well. Jesus may have combined relevant elements from models followed by any other claimed signs workers and eschatological prophets. Nevertheless, the evidence suggests that Jesus (and his followers who emulated him) were also distinctive in many respects.[216] Ideally, critical historiography observes individuals' distinctive characteristics as well as those identifying them with their context.

205. Blackburn, "Miracles," 378.

206. Eve, *Miracles*, 280–81, cites *m. Ber.* 5:5; *Soṭah* 9:15 (= *t. Soṭah* 15:5); *'Abot* 3:10–11; *t. Ber.* 3:20; *Mek.* on Exod 18:21.

207. Eve, *Miracles*, 282–83 (four centuries, on the Babylonian Talmud); Blackburn, "Miracles," 378 (three centuries, on the Jerusalem Talmud).

208. Eve, *Miracles*, 285. None included exorcism (294).

209. Ibid., 289, 295. Eve also argues (292–93) that the Mishnah's category for Hanina, "men of deed" (*m. Soṭah* 9:15), need not specify miracle workers, noting that the semantic range of "deed" is much broader than "miracle."

210. Eve, *Miracles*, 357–59, 379, compares Mexican folk healer Pedrito Jaramillo, who stood out above other folk healers of his era.

211. Ibid., 377. (I suspect that the Mosaic emphasis in the feeding miracle may be stronger than Eve recognizes; he tends to downplay these, e.g., 324–25.)

212. Ibid., 378. Eve argues from this both the likely authenticity of the Gospels' consistent portrait of Jesus and a Christology implicit in his activities no less than in his sayings (386).

213. Theissen and Merz, *Guide*, 307–8; Blackburn, "Miracles," 379 (who notes that Jesus rarely is said to pray before working a miracle).

214. Theissen and Merz, *Guide*, 290.

215. Ibid., 309.

216. See again Eve, *Miracles*, 384–86, esp. 386.

e. Parallels and the Authenticity Question

Parallels in form (or even function) need not imply the inauthenticity of the accounts in the Gospels and Acts, as some scholars have argued;[217] ancient healing stories usually share the same form because they necessarily follow the same course. As Pierre Benoit asks, "Is there any other way of relating a miracle?" He concludes that "it is not the literary form which distinguishes one from the other; it is the substance, the external authentication, the internal probability."[218] (For that matter, many suppliants at ancient healing shrines probably did recover, a point that I will briefly revisit below.)

The nature of the accounts is not altogether the same. As our survey of ancient pagan accounts above suggests, most pagan claims fall into one of several categories: healings at healing shrines, often involving dreams; direct intervention of deities; mythographers' tales regarding the semi-prehistoric past; secretive magic; and, at most, perhaps occasional reports of the traveling sage-healer, a form not clearly dominant till the third century (and perhaps affected in part by the growing challenge of Christian claims by that period).[219] Nor in the case of healing sages is healing necessarily the sage's dominant supernatural activity to the extent found in the Gospels and Acts, and where it appears to be, some of the accounts clearly reflect the literary influence of the Gospels and Acts (as noted above). Although we have some dream revelations and direct intervention of the deity in first-century Christian sources, by far the vast majority of Christian "parallels" in the texts are with the last and (outside Christian sources) rarest category.

It is possible that this model (along with exorcism) was more dominant in the East in this period than our extant sources alone would suggest; although most Jewish parallels are later, traditions about Honi (or perhaps the Jewish exorcist in 4Q242 1–3 4) are suggestive. (Certainly, Elijah's model predates Jesus and was widely known among Jewish people.)[220] But our extant evidence does not support the claim that the Gospels and Acts imposed a preexisting pagan model on the Jesus movement's founder and early leaders.

In fact, the primary "parallel" between the earliest Christian sources and the dominant pagan models here is that both envision "supernatural"[221] activity, a premise unobjectionable and not very distinctive for most societies in history. The "parallel" seems striking to modern Western culture only because it is foreign to us, yet it is our culture that is most distinctive in this regard; we hardly dare assume genetic links among supernatural claims in all cultures that offer them. In all cultures people need health, healing, and so forth, and most cultures seek suprahuman assistance for these needs. Those reputed as miracle workers or healers of some sort would be popular in most cultures (except rare ones such as much of Western academia) because such figures meet a central felt need. The need is transcultural, and anthropological studies

217. Concurring with Taylor, *Formation*, 128; against Bousset, *Kyrios Christos*, 101–3; Jeremias, *Theology*, 88–92. Jeremias's use of parallels to question the authenticity of these miracles or to attribute them to psychosomatic activity (88–92) rests on his premise that modernity rejects the miraculous (89). For this section, see Keener, *John*, 260–61.

218. Benoit, *Jesus*, 1:34.

219. The pervasive influence went both ways, as becomes obvious by the increasing dominance of, e.g., Egyptian Christian exorcists, but this point is not relevant to the matter under consideration (because these sources are significantly later than Luke-Acts).

220. Eve, *Miracles*, 377, though skeptical of some early Jewish analogies to Jesus, readily accepts Elijah's model.

221. For that matter, pagan healers do not all claim to act in the name of a deity (though often they have innate divinity in the generalized Greek sense); "supernatural" is a catchall phrase reflecting again modern Western assumptions (not altogether compatible with modern physics) about a closed continuum of nature.

show that such figures (e.g., shamans) arise in cultures without any necessary external influence.

When one moves beyond such generalities, NT stories of Jesus and the apostles have more in common with earlier Elijah and Elisha stories (models available for Jesus and the apostles to imitate) than with later stories of Philostratus and others. This observation does not rule out all value in the latter comparisons, but it certainly does invite us to keep them in perspective.

Benoit contrasts the miracle stories of the canonical Gospels with some pagan accounts (such as the woman, pregnant for five years, bearing a five-year-old at Epidaurus,[222] though this is an exceptional case), many Jewish accounts (a reported conversation between God and the angel of the sea), and most accounts in the apocryphal gospels[223] and acts.[224] Of course, these other accounts are not all of a kind; some reports do come closer to resembling the dominant examples in the Gospels and Acts. But Benoit is correct that even if we argue for parallels in narrative methods of recounting miracles, this literary form has no bearing on the authenticity of the events it reports.[225] In contrast to Benoit, however, who rejects the authenticity of the pagan accounts, many early Christians, though monotheistic, would have accepted the reality of many of the pagan healing claims (cf. 1 Cor 10:20; 2 Thess 2:9; Rev 13:13; Did. 16.3–4).[226] Dunn is probably right that the Jewish accounts of Honi and Hanina are probably also rooted in genuine tradition.[227]

By purely historical means, we cannot a priori exclude the possibility of some eyewitness claims of sudden, unexpected recoveries that the beneficiaries believed were caused by deities (indeed, both inscriptions and votive offerings of body parts at some Asclepius sanctuaries indicate that many people did believe this). We might reject the usual ancient interpretation of such an event, but this rejection involves a theological rather than a historical judgment. The distinctiveness of Christian accounts is, indeed, noteworthy, but this does not by itself rule out the more general observation that others also made some healing claims attributed to "supernatural" agencies.

4. Antisupernaturalism as an Authenticity Criterion?

While granting that most ancient historians included supernatural claims, modern critics often use supernatural elements as a criterion for distinguishing what is genuinely

---

222. Boring, Berger, and Colpe, *Commentary*, 65, compare this possibly fourth-century c.e. legendary embellishment of an earlier account here with the gospel tradition, but the differences, such as lapse of time and the continuance of eyewitnesses for the gospel tradition, mitigate the force of the comparison. The original votive tablet depicts only a "fantasy pregnancy," upgraded to a real one in the later interpretation (see clearly Klauck, *Context*, 161–62).

223. Benoit, *Jesus*, 1:34. The conversation between God and the angel that Benoit mentions is a homiletic illustration, not historical in genre.

224. Fabulous elements include "talking dogs" and "sky travels" (as in *Acts of Peter*), "obedient bed-bugs (*Acts of John*), baptized lions (*Acts of Paul*)," etc. (Hofmann, "Novels: Christian," 847). Apocryphal acts marshal all traits of their narrative, including miracles, to amplify divine glory (Bovon, *Studies*, 253–66). Cf. "Miracles, Miracle-workers," 54: the apocryphal gospels and acts, which "sought to respond in a folkloric or novelistic way to the needs of Christian circles for entertainment, edification, and glorification of the heroes of the faith, magnified miracles to the point of exuberant fabulousness." But miracle stories are much more common in the apocryphal acts than in the apocryphal gospels (Achtemeier, *Miracle Tradition*, 177–88). For miracles as propaganda in the romances, see Kee, *Miracle*, 252–89.

225. Benoit, *Jesus*, 1:33.

226. Cf. further 1 Cor 12:2; 1 John 4:1–3; *Herm.* 43.2–4.

227. Dunn, "Demythologizing," 291. On Onias (Honi) in Josephus (where some aspects of his depiction resemble Elijah), see Gray, *Figures*, 145–47.

historical in ancient histories from what is not. For example, some earlier scholars, eager to underline the greater historicity of the later chapters of Acts where Luke himself was an eyewitness, sought to do so in part by emphasizing that angels and signs dominate the first part of Acts much more than the Pauline portions (excepting Acts 27:23), just as they appear rare in Paul's epistles.[228] These scholars' simple method of counting pericopes neglects the shorter span of time covered by later chapters and the level of detail devoted to the defense speeches; signs remain central in Paul's later ministry both in Acts (19:11–12; 28:6–9) and his epistles (somewhat in the content of his teaching, 1 Cor 12–14; but especially in descriptions of his ministry, Rom 15:19; 2 Cor 12:12; cf. Gal 3:5).[229] Luke devotes more space to describing visible signs of the Spirit's work than does Paul, but this hardly means that they were less significant in the latter's evangelistic ministry; this difference is largely a question of narrative versus occasional genre.[230]

a. Ancient Skepticism toward Miracles

Some ancient writers shared modern critics' concerns about undue interest in the paranormal, though not for exactly the same (radical Enlightenment) reasons.[231] Although lacking knowledge of empirical science,[232] some ancient writers came up with naturalistic alternatives for explaining natural phenomena, alternatives that differed from traditional religious explanations in polytheism. Thus, for example, some viewed the winds as divine;[233] others presented them as under divine or angelic authority;[234] but still others viewed them as purely natural phenomena.[235] Likewise, many thought that violent winds created thunder and lightning;[236] others, that wind is air flowing in a single direction.[237] (Compare further the naturalistic explanations for earthquakes mentioned at Acts 16:26.) Naturally, such explanations among ancients could go only so far from the perspective of modern knowledge—for example, the views that the planets and stars cause rain,[238] that the fire from stars falling into clouds causes lightning storms,[239] or that wind can be caused by the stars moving in a direction opposite to that of the earth.[240]

Yet skepticism applied not only to supernatural interpretations of what we would call natural phenomena; it often applied to paranormal phenomena. Such skepticism

---

228. Harnack, *Acts*, 148–49; Knox, *Acts*, 91–93.

229. Cf. here also Jewett, *Romans*, 911; Byrne, *Romans*, 438; Talbert, *Romans*, 329; Parsons, *Luke*, 126–27. For Paul on signs, cf. further Twelftree, "Signs"; idem, "Healing." Moreover, claims of diminishing signs throughout the book (or a later portrait supplanting an earlier one; cf. Hickling, "Portrait in Acts 26") neglect that Luke may have already successfully made his point; Luke earlier emphasizes the Spirit on Jesus in Luke 3:22; 4:1, 14, 18, but no one claims that the Spirit declines for him later (Dollar, "Theology of Healing," 47).

230. Cf. Bovon, *Theologian*, 198–238, esp. 238.

231. I say "radical Enlightenment" to distinguish the perspective from some early Enlightenment thinkers more open to supernatural reports, at least those in Christian Scripture. Much of this section derives from Keener, *John*, 261–63.

232. If unrestrained, winds would blow away the universe (Virg. *Aen.* 1.58); Helen was carried to Egypt by winds (Philost. *Hrk.* 25.10); winds carry along the sun and moon chariots (*1 En.* 72:2, 5); winds hold up the heavens (18:2–5; *Jos. Asen.* 12:2/3).

233. Fronto (Naber, 211, §7); personified, at least, in Plut. *Bride* 12, *Mor.* 139DE.

234. E.g., Val. Flacc. 8.322–27; *1 En.* 4:3; *Tg. Jon.* on 1 Kgs 19:11–12; probably angels in *Apoc. Mos.* 38:3.

235. See Sen. Y. *Nat. Q.* 5.16.1–5.17.2; for ancient "scientific" theories on weather, see Pliny E. *N.H.* 2.39.105–6.

236. Pliny E. *N.H.* 2.38.104.

237. Sen. Y. *Nat. Q.* 5.1.1; Pliny E. *N.H.* 2.44.114.

238. Pliny E. *N.H.* 2.39.105–6 (by contrast, Pliny offers a much more accurate explanation in 2.42.111).

239. Pliny E. *N.H.* 2.43.112.

240. Pliny E. *N.H.* 2.45.116; cf. 2.6.32–33, where the planets move in a direction opposite the world. More plausibly, gusts from the earth, solar heat, and irregularities in the mountains also produce winds (2.44.114–15).

appears both among characters in fiction and in historical writing. Ovid makes some of his characters more believable by having them doubt the supernatural, while others affirm that deities can do anything,[241] before they are all changed into bats for disbelieving in Bacchus.[242] Unlike most authors, Hermippus suspected that Pythagoras was a phony;[243] Diognetus taught Marcus Aurelius not to believe miracle workers, magicians, and exorcists.[244] Pliny the Elder emphasized that the wisest people rejected the efficacy of incantations, but complained that mostly everyone else accepted them.[245] Cicero, though a member of "the priestly college of augurs" (presumably for political reasons), regarded such practices as superstitious, although probably only a small minority of people shared his skepticism.[246] Even Philostratus accommodates some of the skepticism of his day, perhaps to refute associations with magic.[247]

Various writers satirized gullibility and tall tales,[248] and one deliberately generated some. Lucian reports that he embellished stories of Peregrinus's death with fabulous claims to have fun at the expense of his unlearned hearers, discovering that some not only believed his report but went out claiming to have witnessed such phenomena (*Peregr.* 39–40). In histories Lucian approves of reporting potential myths so long as one does not affirm them, but he leaves their veracity to the audience to decide (*Hist.* 60).[249] The most thoroughgoing critique of including paranormal events in histories, however, comes from the historian Polybius, whom I noted (in ch. 4, sect. 1.c, above) as a particularly critical historian.

1. Polybius's Critique of Sensationalist Historians

Polybius complains about historians who focus too much on marvels (πολλήν τινα διατέθεινται τερατείαν) or prodigies (σημεῖα) and use tragic coloring (Polyb. 7.7.1).[250] In view of the existence of such writers, Plümacher contends that Luke follows this sensational form of historiography with the goal of stimulating readers' pleasure and passion; it was a recognized form of history, but one that, though interested in what happened, was not interested in that alone.[251] (This suggestion is addressed below.) Some reports of signs serve such functions; for example, Valerius Maximus reports many *miracula*, simply as collections of unusual phenomena (Val. Max. 1.8.praef.;

241. Ovid *Metam.* 4.272–73.

242. Ovid *Metam.* 4.402–15. Elsewhere when recounting something incredible (ghosts terrorizing Rome, *Fasti* 2.551–54), Ovid notes that he can hardly believe it himself (2.551).

243. Diog. Laert. 8.1.41.

244. Marc. Aur. 1.5; C. R. Haines in LCL, 4–5n6 (citing *Dig.* 50.13.1, §3; Justin 2 *Apol.* 6; Tert. *Apol.* 23; Iren. *Her.* 2.6, §2; Lact. *Div. Inst.* 5.21), may be correct that the exorcism comment applied especially to Christians, but Philostratus and third-century magical papyri suggest that it need hardly apply to them alone.

245. Pliny E. *N.H.* 28.3.10. Yet Pliny feels constrained to respect ancestral practice (28.3.12–13) and leaves such matters open to his audience to decide (28.5.29).

246. Klauck, *Context*, 180, citing Cic. *Div.* 2.83.

247. Theissen, *Miracle Stories*, 284–85. Like a good sophist, Philostratus sometimes provides rationalistic explanations (Maclean and Aitken, *Heroikos*, l–li, citing Philostr. *Hrk.* 48.11–13; 50.1, 7–11; cf. also p. lxiv on Dio Chrys. *Troikos* [*Or.* 11] 54, 70); cf. Philostr. *Hrk.* 33.6; restrained language in 4.2; sympathy for skeptics in 51.11; distinction between eyewitness testimony and hearsay, rendering the former more credible (8.8); and the progressive persuasion of the open-minded skeptic in 3.1; 7.9, 11; 8.2, 8; the skeptic believed as a child (7.10).

248. Petron. *Sat.* 62–63; Lucian *True Story* 1.2–4; Lucian *Dial. D.* 446–47 (9/28, Menippus and Tiresias 2–3); *Lover of Lies* 15, 32; Apul. *Metam.* 2.28.

249. Others followed this practice, e.g., Pliny E. *N.H.* 28.5.29.

250. He also objects to historians who create such implausible obstacles that they require a *deus ex machina*, as in the tragic dramatists, to nevertheless yield the known historical outcome (Polyb. 3.48.7–8), inventing divine apparitions (3.48.9) not found in their sources. Menander *Theophoroumene* frg. 5 may parody the *deus ex machina* convention.

251. Plümacher, "ΤΕΡΑΤΕΙΑ"; cf. Plümacher, *Geschichte*, 33–84.

1.8.1–2; 1.8.ext. 1–19); he justifies one report as believable simply because it appears in his sources (1.8.7). (The dangers of magic also added intrigue to novels.)[252]

Polybius's complaint about historians who focus on unusual phenomena is part of his longer complaint about those who focus on such a narrow range of events that they must exaggerate and focus on irrelevancies rather than on important characters (Polyb. 7.7.1–8). This is partly Polybius's way of again distinguishing and marking the superiority of his work, which covers a broader span of history and geography. (That Thucydides covers a shorter span yet is a careful historian may escape Polybius's notice, but Thucydides also eschews the fantastic.)

Many elite historians proved skeptical of the paranormal, including Thucydides, Polybius, and usually Tacitus. Thucydides, in fact, promises to include fewer accounts "of the fabulous" than poets who focus on myths; he prefers, he claims, to deal with probable events, namely, the sorts of events that are historically repeatable (Thucyd. 1.22.4 [LCL]).[253] One orator opines that poets could use mythical language because they wrote about the gods, but historians, who wrote about people, had to keep close to their sources (Men. Rhet. 1.1, 333.31–334.5). Pliny the Elder apparently believed that stories of marvels would sell better than his dry research treatise could (N.H. pref. 12–13).

II. Signs in Critical Historians

Surely, however, not all the historians whom Polybius characterizes as sensationalist would have agreed with his description. By the imperial period, historians often included "miraculous and fantastic elements,"[254] and not every writer who included paranormal events was generally "sensationalist." Whereas Lucian and Polybius are skeptical, many Greek and Roman historians reported curiosities in their sources, ambivalent "between skepticism and credulity."[255] Others allowed both natural and divine factors side by side.[256]

Livy is among the writers after Polybius who chronicle reports of unusual events (prodigies) for each year;[257] some of these we would regard as natural phenomena and others as originally fabricated, but they undoubtedly stemmed from Livy's sources.[258]

---

252. E.g., Heliod. *Eth.* 6.14.

253. Thucydides admitted that some earlier descriptions of hardships and natural disasters, dependent on oral tradition, had been rendered credible by the more recent events he was describing (Thucyd. 1.23.3), but he portrays his own account as unique. He offered an effective model of restraint to many of his successors (see Remus, *Conflict*, 36–37).

254. Krasser, "Reading," 554 (citing Livy, Appian, Plutarch, and others). Judge, *First Christians*, 420–22, doubts that ancient audiences, accustomed to prodigies, would have balked at the reports in Acts.

255. Hemer, *Acts in History*, 428–29; more fully, 428–43. Sophists employed "rationalistic explanations" where possible (Maclean and Aitken, *Heroikos*, l, lxiv); also of astrological phenomena such as eclipses (Philost. *Hrk.* 33.5–6; see comment on Acts 2:20). See, e.g., Tac. *Germ.* 3. Some phenomena could be attributed to coincidence, though with divine involvement in the timing (Remus, *Conflict*, 45–47).

256. Remus, *Conflict*, 42–44; cf. 45–47. Herodotus speaks of gods but not of their intervening regularly in the narrative as "in Homer and the Attic drama" (McDonald, "Herodotus," 86); although Luke reports much divine activity, God appears directly only very rarely, as in Luke 3:22; 9:35 (though the risen Jesus appears in Acts). For Herodotus, divine powers are viewed differently among different peoples; he does not treat divine intervention "in anthropomorphic terms" (McDonald, "Herodotus," 86). Herodotus views both divine and human activity as within the natural order (88–89); where he reports traditions of miracles, "he regularly indicates his reservations" (87), unlike Luke. Xenophon is unapologetic in his belief in gods and their activity (Brown, *Historians*, 97).

257. Among other writers, see, e.g., Val. Max. 1.6.5; Appian *Bell. civ.* 1.9.83; 2.5.36; 2.10.68; 4.1.4; for other prodigies, see Cic. *Verr.* 2.4.49.108; Pliny E. *N.H.* 17.38.241–45; Tac. *Ann.* 12.43, 64; 14.32; 15.22, 47; 16.13; Suet. *Jul.* 81.3; Aul. Gel. 4.6.2; Arrian *Alex.* 4.15.7–8. In exaggerated, fictitious form, Lucan *C.W.* 1.529–63 passim; Phaedrus 3.3.4–5. See further discussion in Keener, *Matthew*, 568–69. In contrast to Livy, subsequent writers like Tacitus associated prodigies more closely with the emperor; see Feeney, "History," 140–41.

258. E.g., Livy 21.62.1–5; 24.10.6–11; 24.44.8; 25.7.7–9; 26.23.4–5; 27.4.11–14; 27.11.2–5; 27.37.1–6; 29.14.2; 32.1.10–12; 32.8.2; 33.26.7–8; 34.45.6–7; 35.9.2–4; 35.21.3–6; 36.37.2–3; 40.45.1–4; 41.13.1–2;

Livy often warns, however, that many of the reported prodigies may have been accepted too readily by their contemporaries;[259] the more that such reports were believed, the more that further reports of this nature were generated.[260] Still more reliable historians also provide reports of such phenomena (such as of signs attesting Vespasian in Tac. *Hist.* 4.81; Suet. *Vesp.* 7.2–3)[261] or signs surrounding Jerusalem's fall (Tac. *Hist.* 5.13, possibly following Jos. *War* 6.288–310),[262] though they may do so with distancing sufficient to retain the appearance of objectivity.[263] Sometimes the reports include a preceding generation's events about which most of us today would be skeptical; Tacitus avers that dignified historians ought not "to collect fabulous tales" merely to "delight" their readers, but "cannot . . . dare to deny the truth of common tradition."[264] (Tacitus himself apparently did believe at least in gods and in sacrificing to them.)[265]

Although Diodorus Siculus accepts some major supernatural feats, he often prefers nonsupernatural accounts and "demythologizes" them, depicting how he thinks such accounts were reworked into mythical ones.[266] Eunapius recounts a barely believable event only with hesitation, noting that none of the supposed eyewitnesses had written anything down.[267] Although Arrian accepted the possibility of divine interventions (*Alex.* 5.1.2), he was not extremely gullible; he complains that some writers tell of various wonders at the ends of the earth (ants that mine gold for the Indians, and water monsters and griffins also in India) only because they can get away with inventing entertaining stories about matters that their readers cannot check.[268] Plutarch accepted some reports but could also exercise critical discretion and reject a tale as incredible.[269] He cautiously reports various views about the activities of statues, noting the frequency of the reports (Plut. *Cam.* 6.1–4) and concluding that one should avoid either believing too much (superstition) or disbelieving too much (irreligion; 6.4).[270]

41.21.12–13; 42.2.4–5; 43.13.3–6; 45.16.5. For discussion of Livy's sources, see Rosenberger, "*Nobiles*," 294. Justifying Livy's supernaturalism, see Laistner, *Historians*, 69 (though what he attributes to possible Stoic thought on 69–77 could simply reflect popular religion).

259. So Livy 21.62.1.

260. Livy 24.10.6. We should keep in mind, however, that cultural expectations shaped the attention that anomaly reports received; thus roughly half of prodigies reported occurred in Rome, and most of the rest in Italy (Rosenberger, "*Nobiles*," 297), fitting the contours of the sources interested in reporting them. Reports did not become prodigies until officially declared such (in the republic, this was by the senate; see Orlin, "Religion," 60).

261. Cf. also Vespasian's vision in Tac. *Hist.* 4.82; modern scholars often contend that such stories originated as imperial propaganda (cf. Domitianic propaganda in Luke, "Touch"), but they do not for that reason disqualify Tacitus as a critical (ancient) historian.

262. On signs surrounding Jerusalem's fall, see fuller discussion in Keener, *Matthew*, 584.

263. Thus Tacitus's account in *Hist.* 4.81 is somewhat naturalistic, and both here and esp. in Suet. *Vesp.* 7.3, Vespasian is convinced only against his own expectations.

264. Tac. *Hist.* 2.50 (LCL, 1:243), reporting an omen; he treats as foolish those who ignore omens (*Ann.* 15.7–8).

265. See Pliny *Ep.* 9.10.1, where Tacitus has urged Pliny to sacrifice to Diana as well as Minerva (and Pliny replies that he has not enough boars). Tacitus's suggestion could be facetious but probably rests on a genuine belief. For the action of deities as well as humans as acceptable fodder for ancient historiography, see Davies, "Religion," 167; for the possible influence on Tacitean historiography of his role as priest, see 175.

266. E.g., Diod. Sic. 4.47.3–4; cf. Plut. *Alex.* 35.5–6.

267. Eunapius *Lives* 460 (the alleged event occurred two generations earlier with but one oral link).

268. Arrian *Alex.* 5.4.3.

269. Plut. *Isis* 8, *Mor.* 353F. After narrating some extraordinary events related to an oracle several centuries earlier (*Cam.* 5.4), Plutarch admits that this may sound "mythical" (5.5). For other paranormal phenomena in Plutarch, see, e.g., *Sulla* 27.2 (a creature taken as a satyr); for his suspicions of, or lack of, commitment to some reports, see also, e.g., *Alex.* 35.5–6. Mackay, "Plutarch," 108–9, opines that Plutarch could have accepted most of the miracle stories in the NT except the resurrection and the incarnation (and that he would have also found Christianity's particularity problematic).

270. Aristotle's principle of the mean served Plutarch in this case. Most ancients understood then, as we do today, that statues were inactive (e.g., Diogenes *Ep.* 11), but many made exceptions for unusual phenomena (a few of the references are listed in Keener, *Revelation*, 351–52, 362; cf. Rev 13:15).

Many historians sometimes qualified reports with "It is said" or similar caution-ary devices.[271] Freely reporting wonders in their sources, they nevertheless distanced themselves from seeming too credulous by warning readers to evaluate the veracity of such reports for themselves.[272] Yet despite a higher level of skepticism fashion-able among the intelligentsia than among many others, ancient historians were not products of the radical Enlightenment.

Although this practice means that the most careful historians by other standards were also sometimes the least credulous, we should note that the differences also usually correspond to the expectations of the audiences for which they wrote, the epistemological presuppositions of which are not a matter of historical research per se. Most were critical of some reports while accepting the possibility of others (i.e., they did not a priori decide the possibility of all paranormal events). Early Christians, as followers of a miracle worker, members of a charismatic movement, and usually not members of the Greco-Roman elite, were more open to miracle claims than were most elite historians. While Plümacher does not rank Luke among "sensationalist" historians lightly, critical historians were not averse to signs; Luke records more be-cause he writes about miracle workers and follows an Israelite and Jewish tradition, not because he follows a sensationalist Hellenistic one. Moreover, an emphasis on signs in such works need not lead to a particular assignment of genre (and certainly not to all the particulars often associated with it).

III. Ancient Plausibility Structures

Certainly, not all ancient intellectuals were skeptical of "supernatural" phenomena. Thus, for example, Stoics (despite their disdain for immoral mythology) were known for defending the gods and divination;[273] thinkers influenced by the Pythagorean tradition clearly affirmed tangible, divine supernatural activity.[274]

Hellenistic histories often included portents as signs of divine action, just as Luke did.[275] Paranormal events could be viewed as the occasional activity of divine persons or heroes (and hence no less repeatable than those of mortals). Arrian notes that the early stories about Dionysus are difficult to believe but that what would normally be improbable cannot be dismissed when one is dealing with a divine element.[276]

These writers normally employed signs "not solely for entertainment value, but as illustrations of divine guidance."[277] We may choose to dispute the veracity of their reports, but this dispute would not suggest that they simply invented the reports rather than derived them from sources. This observation is true also of early Chris-tian reports. Celsus and other later critics of Christians sought not to deny their miracles but to challenge the value of these phenomena by questioning their source (sorcery) or the social status of Christians.[278] Lucian was more skeptical, accusing Christians of "believing" without evidence and hence being easily exploited financially

---

271. Witherington, *Acts*, 221–22 (citing Jos. *Ant.* 1.108). Cf. similarly Ovid *Fasti* 2.551. Cf. even one novel's nods to objectivity (e.g., τι in Philost. *Hrk.* 4.2; the selective claims of 8.8; Philost. *Vit. Apoll.* 4.45).

272. E.g., Pliny E. *N.H.* 28.5.29; Aune, *Environment*, 134 (citing Hdt. 2.123; 5.45; Dion. Hal. *Ant. rom.* 1.48.1); cf. Paus. 1.26.6 (on a statue that supposedly fell from heaven).

273. Klauck, *Context*, 181. See further comment at Acts 17:18.

274. See the discussion of Apollonius above.

275. See esp. Squires, *Plan*, 78–84; further, 89–101 for Luke-Acts; 78–89 for other historians.

276. Arrian *Alex.* 5.1.2. Cf. some philosophers who pointed out that all things were possible for the gods (Iambl. *V.P.* 28.139, 148; cf. Luke 1:37). Sall. *Catil.* 3.2 fears that some will dismiss his accounts because they report characters nobler than those the reader would expect.

277. Squires, *Plan*, 102.

278. Hemer, *Acts in History*, 428–29; Cook, *Interpretation*, 39.

by charlatans (*Peregr.* 13), but his account also thereby appears to confirm our other sources' reports that Christians were associated with (and did not simply invent for literary purposes) such paranormal phenomena.[279]

In contrast to some elite Hellenistic historians, Jewish sources not composed for Greek intellectual consumption usually show no reticence about reporting wonders.[280] (Popular second-century Christian accounts and later rabbinic accounts depict spectacular miracles even more lavishly.)[281] Josephus, writing for a more Hellenistic audience, sometimes follows the cautious conventions of his Greek contemporaries, adding a noncommittal remark after reporting biblical miracles (e.g., *Ant.* 1.108; 2.348; 3.81, 322; 4.158).[282] He plays down Elijah's miracles[283] and some other miracles.[284] Nevertheless, Josephus did believe in miracles and wanted his audience to do so also.[285] Among "signs" (σημεῖα) he also used portents.[286] It appears that Josephus, like some Greek and Roman historians (as well as more than a few modern NT scholars), approved of belief in some paranormal phenomena but, in writing about them, mostly acceded to the conventions long established for the historical genre.[287]

Luke, writing for Christians who believe in a powerful and historically active Deity, is not reticent at all to report miracles. He is, however, sensitive enough to some critics' skepticism that he distinguishes his own claims for Jesus's resurrection from more incredible popular stories by citing "proofs" (Acts 1:3) and acknowledging that some find the resurrection claim unbelievable (26:8).[288] Likewise, Luke does not seek to report all sorts of wonders and prodigies; his focus is signs (*sēmeia*)—"signs, that is to say, of the inbreaking of the kingdom of God (cf. Luke 11:20)."[289] Luke's story focuses on miracle workers along the lines of Elijah and Elisha; he also writes for a community that, in contrast to some readers of elite histories, already believed that Luke's protagonists performed signs. Luke thus diverges from the norm of elite histories by reporting miracles more lavishly than they do. Nevertheless, to link these miracles with a wider range of exotic reports in "sensationalist" historiography and then to further attribute all the wider traits of that historiographic category to his

279. In Lucian *Peregr.* 11, Peregrinus learned the "marvel-wisdom" (θαυμαστὴν σοφίαν) of the Christians, perhaps wisdom related to signs-working, marvels. Lucian noted that some after Peregrinus's death would probably attribute miracles to his spirit (*Peregr.* 28, *perhaps* influenced by Christian healing in Jesus's name).

280. E.g., 4Q422 III, 4–5 (Moses); 4Q176 1–2 I, 1 (eschatological); wonders in *1 En.* 24:4–25:6; 27:1–4; *Let. Aris.* 99; throughout the LXX. For a survey of healing theology among OT writers and their ancient Near Eastern contexts, see Brown, *Healer*, passim.

281. For apocryphal collections of "acts" as almost aretalogies, see Aune, *Environment*, 147.

282. Aune, *Environment*, 109; Squires, *Plan*, 84–89; Betz, "Miracles in Josephus," 212–13, who also notes that Josephus limited them mostly to the past (218). He follows Greek historiographic convention (Aune, *Environment*, 134, cites Lucian *Hist.* 60; Hdt. 2.123; 5.45; Dion. Hal. *Ant. rom.* 1.48.1).

283. Feldman, "Elijah."

284. Feldman, "Hellenizations: Abraham," 150.

285. Betz, "Miracles in Josephus," 212–13; Eve, *Miracles*, 52. Betz thinks that Josephus did not expect them in the present ("Miracles in Josephus," 218); if Betz is right on this caveat, Josephus must have excepted prophecy (for others, *War* 1.78–80; 2.159; for himself, Isaacs, *Spirit*, 48; Hill, *Prophecy*, 26–27, on Jos. *War* 3.351–54; see also Jesus ben Ananias in *War* 6.300–309; Noack, *Jesus Ananiassøn*; Gray, *Figures*, 158–63).

286. Betz, "Miracles in Josephus," 231–33. For this language for portents, see also Plut. *Demosth.* 19.1; Philost. *Hrk.* 16.5; 17.4; 18.2; 31.5.

287. Greek influence may have contributed to Josephus's rationalizing, but the Jewish belief in miracles reflecting God's power contributed the more dominant influence (MacRae, "Miracle," 142).

288. Luke is also restrained in an eyewitness report (Acts 20:12). Moule, "Classification," 242, thinks that "Luke has a sort of rationalization (though demonstrably misconceived)" in Luke 23:45 because he attributes darkness to an "eclipse" (BDAG there has "cease to shine" but notes that "Luke's diction is standard for description of an eclipse," citing Thucyd. 2.28; 7.50.4; Xen. *Hell.* 1.6.1; *FGH* 239 B 16; Plut. *Pel.* 31.3; Sir 17:31; Philo *Mos.* 2.271). Yet well-timed eclipses were hardly explained only naturalistically (see comment on Acts 2:20).

289. Bruce, *Acts*[3], 31.

work, neglecting OT models, collapses too many categories.[290] The subject of Luke's history, rather than elaborate rhetorical license, drives his accounts.

Many ancient thinkers' determination to exercise critical judgment in particular cases (whether their conclusions were usually right or wrong) contrasts with the few ancient thinkers and many modern ones who a priori reject supernatural phenomena wholesale.[291] It also contrasts with some modern readers' skepticism that eyewitnesses or sources ultimately dependent on them can offer miracle claims.

b. Modern Skepticism toward Supernatural Phenomena

Modern scholars sometimes treat wonders as fictitious elements in ancient historiography, including in Acts.[292] We should recognize, however, that ancients with different plausibility paradigms may well have experienced genuine events that modern Western interpreters would simply attribute to different causes.

Moreover, and more to the point in this section, modern Western interpreters who are skeptical of all such events or must read all of them through a purely naturalistic paradigm are hardly "neutral" in their assumptions.[293] Antisupernaturalism emerged from specific historical circumstances no less than did ancient or modern, Western or non-Western, supernaturalist approaches. This is not to say that it must therefore be logically wrong; it is to say that we need not assume antisupernaturalism as an a priori[294] and, even more important from a literary standpoint, that we must beware of simply assuming its unsympathetic reading of ancient texts, so different from how the first audiences would have heard them.[295] It is a bias that can hinder us from entering Luke's narrative world as fully as his first audience could.

Thus this section will survey the historical context of modern Western philosophic assumptions regarding supernatural phenomena. We will deal afterward with miracle claims in the modern world and some of their varied interpretations in the Majority World and in the West. A purely naturalistic paradigm that a priori excludes the possibility of divine causation is not the only interpretative approach to reality held by intelligent people, nor is it self-evident to observers in all cultures.

1. Our Cultural Limitations

Assumptions about reality are often culturally formed, and events that function as "reality" by the criteria of one culture can shape its history even if these assumptions are foreign to other cultures.[296] Ramsay MacMullen, a noted historian of Greco-Roman antiquity, warns that history proper does not pass judgment on whether ancients believed rightly or wrongly about their miracle claims; history proper simply describes

290. Chapter 4, above, has already argued that Luke-Acts cannot readily fit the category of tragic-pathetic historiography.

291. E.g., Philo accepts both natural laws and biblical testimony to miracles (Wolfson, *Philo*, 1:347–56). A later Neoplatonist (albeit one given to credulity) charges that thoroughgoing skepticism itself reflects unproved presuppositions: since the gods are powerful, it is imprudent to dismiss marvelous claims where they might be involved (Iambl. *V.P.* 28.148; cf. 28.139).

292. E.g., Plümacher, *Geschichte*, 33–84; similarly, regarding the earlier Elijah cycle, Gordon, *Near East*, 222.

293. See, e.g., Swinburne, *Miracle*, 71.

294. The history of ideas, including in scientific paradigms (cf. Kuhn, *Structure*), shows that the same data may be interpreted through diverse interpretive grids after paradigm shifts; interpretive models often control our perspectives on what is possible.

295. Likewise, Wink, "Write," 6, notes that scholars whose background is either "rationalistic, scholastic religion" or a rigid dogmatism will not easily "enter empathetically into the spontaneity and boundary-shattering milieu of the early church."

296. See Achtemeier, *Miracle Tradition*, 137, and the sources he notes. Remus, *Healer*, 112–13, observes (citing one anthropological study) that traditional healers can be effective if a society believes in them even if the healers are skeptical themselves. A healer's confidence might augment this effect.

these beliefs. "To doubt their account of what they saw—to doubt that [the West African prophet William Wadé] Harris, or any saint, or Jesus himself truly suspended the laws of nature—could only be theology, good or bad. To doubt that Asclepius worked miracles back then would likewise be theology."[297]

Scholars today sometimes emphasize the importance of cultural sensitivity to the differences between ancient and modern medicine for avoiding ethnocentric evaluations of ancient perspectives.[298] Likewise, taking into account the differences between our modern Western critical perceptions about miracles and those of the first century can help broaden our understanding of what appears "realistic" in a given epistemological framework.[299] Numerous examples of a different cultural and philosophic understanding are addressed below.

Ancient historians' perceptions of paranormal events that they reported are a different question from the perceptions of modern historiography, but one that is legitimate to ask. If some individuals are tempted to despise ancient Mediterranean historiography as significantly inferior to our own genre simply because it defines its task differently than we do, however, we should remain cognizant of our own philosophic and existential horizons: aside from the susceptibility of such a methodological bias to some scholars' postmodern critique,[300] it is historically naive when elevated from a working assumption to an ontological affirmation.

It is difficult for those working from a Western Enlightenment paradigm to appreciate ancient claims of paranormal events, and all the more so when such claims are attributed to supernatural causation. Yet if we are to read Luke sympathetically, entering imaginatively into his narrative world and understanding the presuppositions that he shared with his ideal audience, it will be helpful for us to find other models for reading his texts than the modern radical Enlightenment paradigm.[301]

As Peter Berger notes, true relativism must allow for the possibility of the supernatural.[302] In the wake of postmodernity, the collapse of traditional Western paradigms has led to the reevaluation of a number of long-held interpretations of reality. As noted below, readers in many cultures (perhaps especially those least trained in Western paradigms) approach Luke's reports of signs not as problems but as a model for ministry. I suspect that this wider, global Christian reading is closer to that of Luke's ideal audience than is our usual Western approach.

After examining the context of modern skepticism about miracles, we will sample some perspectives from other worldviews. From the historical standpoint, the issue is simply whether eyewitnesses can claim such events (for which the decisive answer must be "Yes"), rather than resolving the nature of causation. Nevertheless, putting in context our culturally informed interpretations of causation helps us to read the ancient interpretations more sympathetically, and historians do often explore questions of causation.

297. MacMullen, *Christianizing*, 24. Likewise, some sociologists of religion contend that sociologists can report their subjects' miracle claims but cannot as sociologists rule on the possibility of the subjects' claims of supernatural activity (Miller and Yamamori, *Pentecostalism*, 153; cf. 104).

298. Pilch, *Healing*, 1–4. Cf. varying cultural perceptions, e.g., of schizophrenia (Furnham and Wong, "Comparison"). For Pilch's social-scientific approach to healing in Luke-Acts, see also Pilch, *Healing*, 89–117; idem, "Healing."

299. Cf. esp. Anderson, Ellens, and Fowler, "Way Forward," 249.

300. Cf. Berger, *Rumor*, 52, 120–21. One should not confuse this critique with postmodern historiography in general, which tends to affirm historical truth in ancient historians less than modern scholars of ancient history do (cf. Lendon, "Historiography," critiquing postmodern approaches).

301. As Roschke, "Healing," 471, suggests, paralleling his entering into another culture, "Do we want to observe Luke's worldview as an outsider—as The Other—or are we willing to enter into this Word ...?" Cf. Wink, "Write," 6.

302. Berger, *Rumor*, 52, 120–21. Cf. the nuanced approach in Berger, *Relativism*.

We should pause to distinguish among some terms. The usual modernist prejudice is against what is "supernatural," but this way of defining the question may bias the case, since the ancient worldview allowed for suprahuman activity that was nevertheless part of the natural order.[303] (In an Israelite worldview, only the Creator was supernatural.) "Paranormal" activity is that which is inexplicable in terms of current knowledge of the natural order, but it need not presuppose the activity of suprahuman personal entities (such as divine activity) and hence is a wider term than "suprahuman." (I use it in a broad sense, not the frequent, narrower popular sense of "occult.") By "suprahuman" I mean, more narrowly, the claim for divine activity or for that of other intelligent entities as allowed for in many ancient and modern religious and ancient philosophic systems.[304] Because what is at issue today is especially encompassed in the term "supernatural," however, I often accede to this language in my discussion.

II. SHOULD WE PRIVILEGE OUR WORLDVIEW?

Charles Talbert notes that some scholars, such as Gerd Lüdemann, rule out any historical core of miracle stories because miracles are assumed not to happen.[305] By contrast to such approaches, some writers question whether a priori dismissal of all claims for evidence of supernatural activity is a genuinely open-minded, objective approach.[306] As Talbert notes, the question as to whether miracles are possible reflects the understanding of possibility in one's worldview, and "worldviews are highly resistant to disconfirmation. The materialistic worldview, represented by Lüdemann, dictates that the world was and is ruled by iron physical laws that not even God could or can bend." This is, however, a worldview, not an argument.[307] Scholars differ in their evaluations of what is possible, evaluations that in turn shape "their evaluations of the historicity of Acts."[308]

Nearly all ancient historians report some phenomena (or at least relate others' reports of such phenomena) that most of us would find dubious. No one seriously dismisses the wholesale value of these works simply because they stem from writers whose philosophic (or religious, political, or moral) perspectives differ from our own. Perhaps more telling with regard to our presuppositions, what we tend to dismiss is the

---

303. Jews and Christians allowed for beings of intermediary rank between God and humans (see the excursus on spirit possession at Acts 16:16); Greeks allowed gods and demigods (sometimes subordinate to a supreme deity, to nature, or to fate).

304. One could define the term more broadly to include any beings, physical or nonphysical, more intelligent than (or equally intelligent but more powerful than) humans, the existence of which is unproved but need not be ruled out a priori. But this definition exceeds what is relevant for the matter under discussion.

305. Talbert, *Mediterranean Milieu*, 215; idem, *Acts*, 248–49. Lüdemann, *Acts*, 23, contends that "one ought not to begin with the assumption that miracles occur." But a truly "neutral" assumption would be that they *might* occur; one must test evidence. Technically, though, Lüdemann, 22–23, claims that he does not presuppose the rejection of miracles; only that (23) one cannot presuppose God or gods and should reject the miracle explanation unless no other is available. This limitation may effectively exclude all evidence in practice and bias the investigation (since one could always find *some* naturalistic explanation, even if it is less plausible than suprahuman intelligent causation in some cases). Nevertheless, Lüdemann is more precise and honest about his assumptions than are many.

306. The question is well put by Gardner, *Healing Miracles*, 165, a physician who claims considerable evidence for paranormal healings.

307. Talbert, *Mediterranean Milieu*, 215; on the resistance of worldviews to disconfirmation, see also Wink, "Stories," 212. For a critique of the materialist worldview from the standpoint of modern physics, see Barr, *Physics and Faith* (e.g., 256). Reacting against the completely materialist view of the mind, see, e.g., 167–252, esp. 225–26; Beauregard and O'Leary, *Brain* (the latter supporting dualistic connections with a universal cosmic consciousness). One need not, however, reject a materialist view of the mind to distinguish between a material universe and a source of its structure (i.e., information content) external to it.

308. Talbert, *Mediterranean Milieu*, 216. Talbert allows that experiences of healings can shape believers' faith in a particular direction (*Matthew*, 323).

credibility of those reports not susceptible to alternative (i.e., in this case, naturalistic) explanations. In general, our suspicions are undoubtedly well founded, grounded as they are in a fuller understanding of scientific reality and the "ordinary" course of events than was available to our ancient counterparts.[309]

Yet before one dismisses all possibility of suprahuman intervention, one must make explicit and evaluate the presupposition on which such a wholesale dismissal would be based. If we take into account the historically conditioned presuppositions favored in antiquity, we must also consider those of modern academia; these too constitute a context of the discussion and will be taken into account by subsequent interpreters of current scholarship if the worldview of our own era proves as transient as those of its predecessors. We cannot evade being explicit concerning presuppositions informing much traditional modern historiography if we are to hear the ancient narratives sympathetically, and much less can we do so if we are to honestly examine the possibility that any ancient miracles could reflect genuinely suprahuman causation.

Modern Western interpreters typically ground our critique of supernatural phenomena in a modern Western worldview, but unexamined assumptions provide questionable criteria for claiming authoritative metanarratives. As children of the Western Enlightenment, many Western biblical scholars reject all reports of supernatural activity out of hand without critically examining the philosophic prejudices they themselves bring to the table. Despite postmodern critiques of the radical Enlightenment's approaches to dominant perspectives and other cultures' challenges to the hegemonic assumptions of Western tradition, some scholars equate "critical thinking" with dismissing other societies' worldviews without even evaluating the bases for their own.[310]

Some critics may simply dismiss without consideration challenges to examine their worldviews (and they may perhaps likewise dismiss parts of this chapter), but I believe that most such critics act this way on the basis of historically conditioned a prioris that they have never seriously examined personally and that some hold inflexibly. If those in circles where purportedly supernatural experiences are unknown or even ridiculed charge with bias those who take some such claims seriously, those in whose circles such occurrences are believed to occur will be no less apt to return the charge, undercutting any basis for cross-cultural and cross-philosophic dialogue.

Thus some sociologists whose field studies noted extensive claims of miracles, many from purported eyewitnesses, warn that their research might feel threatening

309. Science's traditional "methodological naturalism" offers useful rigor in exploring patterns of cause and effect. But the early Western scientists who founded most scientific disciplines as we know them conceived this objective and achieved the same practical effect from their premise of order in creation rather than from denial of divine design or causation. They denied that the Creator was bound by his own laws (Brooke, "Science," 9; cf. also Wykstra, "Problem," 156; Sharp, "Miracles," 11; Force, "Dominion," 89, 91; idem, "Breakdown," 146–50). That is, their naturalism was theistic and presupposed a different philosophic metanarrative than the paradigm dominant today. Before the rise of deism ("a new religion"; see discussion in Spickard and Cragg, *Global History*, 242), they examined the normal natural order without denying the possibility of exceptional divine activity outside that norm. For the struggle between deism and Christianity regarding miracles, see Cragg, *Reason*, 160–67.

310. In light of my historical methodology in most of this commentary, it should be self-evident that though citing this postmodern critique, I welcome many Western or Enlightenment methodological contributions. Although objective knowledge may not be perfectly attainable in many areas, pursuing it as evenhandedly as possible offers common ground for academic discussion whereas refusal to share such a common objective can readily devolve into competing factions in which political strategy and power count more highly than free enquiry. On various points, however, including the matter at hand, I believe that Western perspectives can be much improved through the input of other cultures. Certainly one may not pretend open-minded inquiry while dismissing other approaches without allowing them on the table.

to Western scholars "who live out their existence within the shelter of the academy, where everything but faculty politics operates on assumptions of rationality and empirical verifiability."[311] They suggest that, for all scholars' talk about willingness to challenge the status quo, a real challenge to the dominant paradigms of academia would be to allow consideration of such phenomena, for which the "supernatural" explanation is sometimes the most "parsimonious."[312]

Similarly, NT scholar Walter Wink notes that he once thought that his intellectual integrity was alienating him from the world he found in the book of Acts, when in fact it was merely his materialist assumptions about reality.[313] Later he observed what he believed were divine healings, incompatible with the antisupernaturalistic assumptions he now rejected; these included a large uterine tumor disappearing apparently immediately after prayer.[314] "Because of that, and many similar experiences with spiritual healing, I have no difficulty believing that Jesus actually healed people, and not just of psychosomatic diseases."[315] Scholars who would deny the truth of his story to defend their worldview, he charges, do so "not on historical grounds, but on the basis of their" materialistic worldview.[316]

Wink claims that "historical research depends on analogy" to evaluate the plausibility of accounts about the past but that our limited experiences can unfairly constrict the analogies with which we work. "People with an attenuated sense of what is possible will bring that conviction to the Bible and diminish it by the poverty of their own experience."[317] Not only medical research regarding mind and body connections but especially the new physics have expanded the range of what is now considered possible.[318] Others also point out how cultural or other experiential limitations sometimes compromise the usefulness of the analogy argument for historiography, since history is full of apparent anomalies.[319] As noted below, however, the analogy argument today makes miracles more, rather than less, plausible.[320]

III. Modern Objections Considered

The assumption that suprahuman activity is impossible is an interpretive grid, not a demonstrated fact; contrary to what appeared to be the case to many intellectuals one or two centuries ago, history does not support a linear evolution of all cultures toward this position.

A limited methodological naturalism—interpreting phenomena as natural when possible and plausible (with or without possible divine providence at work) and

311. Miller and Yamamori, *Pentecostalism*, 158.
312. Ibid. (following Smith, *Animals*, 109). The principle of parsimony follows Occam's razor.
313. Wink, "Write," 4; cf. idem, "Stories," 214.
314. Wink, "Write," 6.
315. Ibid.
316. Ibid. In Wink, "Worldview," he challenges a reductionist materialism (20–21); Murphy, "Social Science," 32–33, values Wink's critique of reductionism but regards it as difficult to classify philosophically. The issue is ultimately not materialism except insofar as it excludes a divine entity beyond nature. Ancient Stoics emphasized the materiality of the cosmos, yet distinguished from this the intelligence (materialists today might prefer the language of information content) that structures matters.
317. Wink, "Write," 6.
318. Wink, "Stories," 213.
319. McClymond, *Stranger*, 83, recounting the story that the king of Siam, hearing from Dutch visitors about riding horses on top of rivers that became so cold they became hard like stone, "knew that the men were liars." (Cf. Silvoso, *Perish*, 101–2, comparing the incomprehensibility of Mexico City's smog in rural Greenland.) Likewise, Blomberg, *Gospels*, 111, argues that the real problem is not with lack of analogies (since one from a warm region might lack analogies for ice) but with analogies to what is unhistorical (e.g., UFO sightings have so often "turned out to be air-balloons" and other such phenomena).
320. See, e.g., Theissen and Merz, *Guide*, 310.

looking for natural causes and effects—is useful heuristically. This tool should not, however, be confused with a thoroughgoing philosophic naturalism[321] that a priori rejects the possibility of activity reflecting suprahuman intelligent activity,[322] including the possibility of some claims that might be empirically verified or falsified.

(1) Some Historic Philosophic Obstacles

As many scholars note, antisupernaturalism is little more than a presupposition, rarely actually argued and rarely marshaling evidence.[323] Seventeenth- and eighteenth-century rational philosophy, rather than any specific evidence, is mainly responsible for the usual summary dismissal of belief in supernatural phenomena in the modern academy.[324] Spinoza argued that miracles are self-contradictory, because, on the basis of his monistic identification of God with the natural order, he saw "laws of Nature" as identical with God or God's will.[325] Ironically, much subsequent thought has assumed Spinoza's thoroughgoing naturalism while rejecting his pantheism. It was metaphysical presuppositions, not empirical evidence, that drove scientism in a reductionistically naturalistic direction.[326]

One of the most influential voices was the eighteenth-century philosopher David Hume, usually regarded as the starting point for modern discussion of miracles.[327] Hume provided the basis for most Enlightenment arguments against miracles.[328] Indeed, those who claim that science or historiography denies the possibility of miracles are actually repeating not scientific but philosophic premises stemming from Hume.[329] Scientists are experts about the *normal* happenings of nature, but when asking whether something outside the norm happens, they no longer speak as scientists per se because this is a philosophic question. Likewise, the question of whether there can be exceptions to natural law "is a philosophical rather than a narrowly scientific issue."[330]

321. Distinguishing metaphysical from methodological naturalism, see, e.g., Tennant, *Miracle*, 25; Plantinga, "Science," 100–101; Evans, *Narrative*, 158–61; John Polkinghorne in Frankenberry, *Faith*, 344; Davies, "Preface," xi–xii.

322. Supporting the possibility of fine-tuning, and hence at least a degree of cosmological design, see, e.g., McGrath, *Universe*; Spitzer, *Proofs*, 13–74; Flew, *God*, 95–154; Tennant, *Theology*, 2:1–126.

323. E.g., Torrance, "Probability," 249–50; Kee, *Miracle*, 3–12; Gregory, "Secular Bias"; deSilva, "Meaning," 13–18; Sabourin, *Miracles*, 14; Stein, *Messiah*, 18–23; Marsden, *Outrageous Idea*, 29, 74; also Pannenberg, *Jesus*, 109 (cited in Licona, "Historicity of Resurrection," 93; idem, *Resurrection*, 133); and the other scholars cited below. Eddy and Boyd, *Legend*, 372–73, note that many scholars skeptical about the gospel tradition are on record as presupposing that miracles do not happen.

324. Benoit, *Jesus*, 1:39; see Kee, *Miracle*, 3–12; Dembski, *Design*, 49–69. For two lengthy responses to this worldview (too recent for me to cite as pervasively as I otherwise would), see Eddy and Boyd, *Legend*, 39–90; Licona, "Historicity of Resurrection," 93–138.

325. See Tonquédec, *Miracles*, 10; Léon-Dufour, "Approches," 15; van der Loos, *Miracles*, 11; Dunn, *Remembered*, 29; McGrew, "Miracles" (3.1.1); Dembski, *Design*, 55. Many theistic thinkers today cite the major infusion of complex information and order into the big bang theory's closed system of a finite universe and/or theorizing about the cosmic anthropic principle to argue against identifying Creator with creation. Whether or not one agrees, monism's appeal is now more culturally negotiable (see, e.g., Barr, *Physics and Faith*, esp. 118–57; Spitzer, *Proofs*, 13–74; McGrath, *Universe*, particularly 111–42).

326. See Dembski, *Design*, 82–85. Some seventeenth-century scientists gained cultural prestige for scientific epistemology by demonstrating its utility for religion (hence inadvertently "modernizing" religion), but the social power situation has now reversed, with scientific epistemology, not surprisingly, holding greater cultural prestige (Harrison, "Miracles," 510). The politics of knowledge, rather than incompatibility between science and faith for many ordinary scientists and believers, drove the dichotomy between science and faith (see Poewe, "Rethinking," 253–54).

327. Williams, *Miraculous*, 19, 24; Twelftree, *Miracle Worker*, 39–40; cf. Johnson, *Hume*, 76–78.

328. Houston, *Miracles*, 3; in theology, 102. Thus, e.g., Lüdemann, *Two Thousand Years*, 4: "Those actions are unhistorical which presuppose that the laws of nature are broken."

329. Houston, *Miracles*, 4. Hume echoed deists (Burns, *Debate*, 70–95, 141).

330. Ibid., 123. On the respective domains of science and philosophy here, cf. also Flew, *God*, 89–90.

Hume regarded miracles as a violation of natural law,[331] in contrast to some earlier thinkers.[332] But even granting this definition, a substantial part of Hume's argument depends on his conception of natural law,[333] and these ideas of natural law are now recognized as outmoded in view of more recent developments in physics.[334] Thus J. Houston, in a recent Cambridge monograph, challenges Hume on two fronts: first, his claim "that the evidence for the relevant law(s) of nature is . . . undeniably relevant to an assessment of the probability" of alleged miracles;[335] second, his claim that the general improbability of events in a particular class of event prejudges "the probability of the truth of an actual report of the event."[336]

Hume's first argument is not neutral as to the possibility of supernatural or divine activity; it a priori excludes the possibility and hence prejudges the conclusion.[337] A theistic response need not (as Hume poses as the alternative) exclude a basic regularity in the universe (hence abandoning the value of analogy and experience);[338] one can postulate a *normal* order in the universe yet allow the hypothesis of "a characteristically order-giving yet occasionally miracle-working god" or other supernatural agent.[339] That is, one need not postulate a forced choice between a deistic/atheistic orderly universe and a universe without order, ignoring alternative views even held by the majority of the founders of modern science themselves.[340] In a truly neutral starting point, one does not have to presuppose the existence of a deity to allow the *hypothesis* of a deity's action; one need only not *rule it out*.[341] Yet this is precisely what Hume's argument must effectively do. "It is only by presupposing a conclusively justified *atheism*, or presupposing belief in a non-miracle-working god . . . that you are entitled to adduce with any cogency" natural laws against miracles.[342] Presupposing without

331. Houston, *Miracles*, 103. Ashe, *Miracles*, 13 (cf. 26), thinks "miracle" an advanced concept because it depends on natural law, but this refers to only a modern Western concept of "miracle," and not necessarily the most current form.

332. Houston, *Miracles*, 104, notes that Augustine and many others spoke of miracles as *above*, rather than *against*, nature. In contrast to Hume, John Locke did believe that miracles were compatible with reason (33–48); Hume's echoes of Locke suggest that he was dialoguing with Locke's position (50).

333. Williams, *Miraculous*, 20.

334. See, e.g., ibid., 204–5; Pannenberg, "History," 65; Gilman, "Miracles," 478; Griffith, "Miracles," 35; Collins, *Beginning*, 53–54; Meier, *Marginal Jew*, 2:519–20; Charlesworth, "Resurrection," 170–71; "Origin," 227; Blomberg, *Gospels*, 105–6 (and sources he cites). Cf. discussions in Twelftree, *Miracle Worker*, 51 (following Larmer, *Water*, 52–56, and others); Barr, *Physics and Faith*.

335. Houston, *Miracles*, 133 (developed on 133–50). Hume's claim here by definition excludes miracles held to contravene such laws and hence uses a definition to fix the argument so that miracles cannot happen. Many philosophers today reject the logic of Hume's argument; see, e.g., the challenge to Hume's approach in his essay in Johnson, *Hume*; Taylor, *Hume*; Swinburne, *Miracles*; Beckwith, *Argument*; Ward, "Believing"; idem, "Miracles and Testimony"; Earman, *Failure*; idem, "Bayes"; idem, "Hume"; Eddy and Boyd, *Legend*, 61–63; for historical context, see Burns, "Hume and Miracles." For one of the defenses of Hume, see Fogelin, *Defense*.

336. Houston, *Miracles*, 133 (developed on 151–68). Prejudging likelihood by classification also depends on the reliability of the classification and the likelihood one assigns to it. Again, since an event that was ordinary would not be defined as miraculous, ruling out extraordinary events not only rules out much of actual history but also seems designed to create a "default setting" that excludes the probability of miracles.

337. Ibid., 133–34; Twelftree, *Miracle Worker*, 41 (cf. also 44, against the argument of Alastair McKinnon).

338. As in a worldview where capricious spirits dominate causation. But we must also reckon with the limitations of reported experience—and Hume's a priori exclusion of the experience of irregular events.

339. Houston, *Miracles*, 141; cf. Collins, *Language of God*, 50–53; Tonquédec, *Miracles*, 11.

340. E.g., Christians such as Galileo; Johannes Kepler; Antony van Leeuwenhoek (in microbiology); Robert Boyle (in chemistry); Andreas Vesalius (in anatomy); William Harvey (in physiology); and Gregor Mendel, a monk (in genetics). Isaac Newton, who was theologically Arian, argued for design in the universe.

341. Houston, *Miracles*, 148, 160.

342. Ibid., 162. Houston notes that if one presupposes atheism methodologically, so that one's conclusions must be atheistic, no argument could satisfy the position's demands (168). Some would argue that one might even start with a premise of theism if other grounds warranted (cf. Evans, "Naturalism," esp. 205). Hume recycled many deist arguments; see Burns, *Debate*, 141; see also 9–10, 70–95.

argument that there can be no intelligent agency elevates "ontological economy to a supremacy which not even Occam accords it."[343]

Interestingly, Hume[344] cites strong testimony for some miracle reports, then uses the very strength of this testimony to argue that even strong testimonies are useless in favor of miracles, since (he asserts without argument) these particular miracles may be dismissed! Others have noted the circularity of his denial of these reports of miracles (particularly among Jansenists), which he offered on the basis that miracles cannot happen.[345]

Hegel, with his long-standing influence in German thought, followed by David Strauss and other Hegelians, was particularly effective in redirecting the course of modern Western thought, stressing his antithesis "between ancient religion" and nineteenth-century "intellectual sophistication."[346] This vantage point solidified into an uncontested consensus until relatively recent times[347] without an adequate impartial, massive empirical investigation into diverse miracle claims. Modern Enlightenment thought has often identified "scientific" as "true" and "unscientific" as false; its simultaneous a priori "exclusion of the supernatural from the domain of science" taints supernatural approaches with the suspicion of "falsity and irrationality." Yet such identifications unfairly load the deck epistemologically.[348]

Many scholars complain that the common reduction of what is real to what is material is not empirical science per se but a philosophic construct;[349] much of the argument comes down to simple assertions based on plausibility structures dominant in the era in which they originated.[350] Much of the empiricist refutation of earlier supernaturalist worldviews rested on philosophic premises that have since been abandoned in light of subsequent scientific and philosophic developments.[351] Thus, as physics professor Stephen Barr observes, a century ago physics was entirely materialistic and deterministic and faulted religion for suggesting that the physical universe was not "causally closed." Unexpectedly, however, "that determinism did in fact give way in the face of new discoveries," and it was traditional religion instead of the physics of the era that made the successful prediction about the nature of the universe.[352]

343. Houston, *Miracles*, 195. The majority of philosophers publishing on philosophy of religion actually argue for rather than against God's existence (Smith, "Metaphilosophy," 197), so theism can hardly be dismissed a priori (apart from hegemonic fiat).

344. Hume, "Miracles," 41–48.

345. Gaskin, *Philosophy*, 125 (regarding Hume's denial as "obscurantist"); Lewis, *Miracles*, 102 (often cited to this effect); Wright, *Miracle*, 51–52, 80; Brown, *Miracles*, 88; Larmer, *Water*, 106; Gardner, *Healing Miracles*, 39–40; Licona, "Historicity of Resurrection," 100 (citing Lewis, and Gregory, "Secular Bias," 137–38); Ruthven, "Miracle," 548; cf. Lawton, *Miracles*, 58; Holder, "Hume," 57; deSilva, "Meaning," 14–15. For Jansenist claims, see Kreiser, *Miracles*, 78–95, 122–23.

346. See Kee, *Miracle*, 14–16. On the influence of Strauss on modern academic treatment of miracles, see further Twelftree, *Miracle Worker*, 32–33.

347. On the historical-critical method (by which Kee intends especially its reductionist, antisupernaturalist form) to recent times, see Kee, *Miracle*, 12–41. For the philosophic history of theological antisupernaturalism, see Hamilton, *Revolt*.

348. O'Connor, *Healing Traditions*, 15; cf. also 16 and, more generally, all of ch. 1, "Defining and Understanding Health Belief Systems," 1–34.

349. See, e.g., Houston, *Miracles*, 123; Williams, *Miraculous*, 204. Macklin, "Yankee," 74 (an anthropology professor), contends that scientism thus functions as religion rather than as science (cf. similarly, e.g., Barrington-Ward, "Spirit Possession," 464).

350. See Williams, *Miraculous*, 34.

351. Ibid., 137–57, 205. Williams offers a philosophic challenge to antisupernaturalism, 158–202 (though I do not find all of Williams's own explanations satisfying).

352. Barr, *Physics and Faith*, 253. The success or failure of predictions is essential in the scientific testing and revision of hypotheses. The claims that the universe is finite and had a beginning fall into the same category (against earlier naturalism); cf., e.g., Collins, *Language of God*, 66–84. On an uncritical bias toward materialism in many traditional circles, see, e.g., Beauregard and O'Leary, *Brain*, 93–94; cf. Peat, "Science."

Science as science concerns repeatable events and cannot as science pronounce judgment on specific, unique events in history, such as miracles by definition would be.[353] Some philosophers of science have pointed out that "the action of agency (whether divine or human) need not violate the laws of nature; in most cases it merely changes the initial and boundary conditions on which the laws of nature operate."[354] That is, human or divine agents can also function as causes.[355] Theistic religion and science overlap in interests, though often asking different questions.[356]

Some define "history" in such a manner as to exclude the possibility of genuine miracles in history,[357] but on a popular level this definition risks collapsing two meanings of "history," namely, history as a limited methodology that *as history* cannot pronounce judgment concerning claims of supernatural causation,[358] and history as "events" that may have actually happened.[359] Such a confusing of meanings further risks (and sometimes produces) the assumption that history as a discipline rejects the possibility of miracles. History *as* history does not pass judgment on whether an occurrence (such as the resurrection) was a *miracle* (a theological judgment involving philosophic questions about God's existence and activity). As history, it can attempt to address only whether an event literally happened.[360] If an event happened, it can be subject to historical investigation.[361] To a priori deny that such events happen is to prejudge the conclusion before doing objective investigation—and this is a philosophic issue, not a historical one.

Miracles are unique events, but history (unlike science) is full of events that are unique in some respects.[362] Were historians to begin excluding unique or unusual events, they would have to rule out much of history; in 1819, one scholar demonstrated that one could explain away a large measure of Napoleon's life by this method.[363] Some argue that miracles are too unique, belonging to a category that differs too much

353. Charlesworth, "Resurrection," 170. If one avers the existence of an ultimate creator and/or infinite being, that being would not be subject to natural "law" and could constitute a far "freer" agent of intelligent causation than are humans.

354. Meyer, "Scientific Status," 167; cf. Colwell, "Defining Away" (among sources that Meyer notes).

355. Cf. also Blomberg, *Gospels*, 106; for the analogy between human and divine intelligent causation, see also Hesse, "Miracles," 41–42.

356. See further, e.g., Polkinghorne, *Belief*; idem, *Faith*; idem, *Quarks*. The biblical tradition and science both affirm the natural order, but whereas science analyzes its data, theistic perspectives explore what can be inferred from the data about nature's Creator (McGrath, *Dialogue*, 208–9; idem, *Science and Religion*, 53–54).

357. E.g., Ehrman, *Prophet*, 193; Price, *Son of Man*, 19–20, 131 (appealing, he claims, not to metaphysical presuppositions but to the argument from analogy).

358. Ehrman, *Prophet*, 196–97, notes that many historians, as people of faith, believe that miracles did happen but they at these times speak "not in the capacity of the historian, but in the capacity of the believer." Yet one wonders if the methodology is neutral if historians *as historians* must be committed to atheistic/deistic presuppositions even if evidence suggests stronger alternative explanations.

359. Thus even some thinkers who do not rule out the possibility of divine intervention exclude such events from "history" by using a definition of "history" that excludes the supernatural (e.g., Meier, "Reflections," 106). Although such a difference is a matter of definition and hence ultimately semantic, abuse of the definition risks reinforcing a traditional Enlightenment philosophy of history that is open to challenge, since some have used the narrow definition as license for excluding an event not only from their methodological purview but, by simple definition rather than argument, from possibility as a genuine event.

360. Habermas, *Evidence*, 25; challenging the neutrality of secular bias in some historiographic approaches, see Gregory, "Secular Bias." This approach would offset the force of the argument in Ehrman, *Prophet*, 193, that history concerns only "events that are accessible to observers of every kind." Still, Ehrman is right in that because miracles are irregular events, we do not take miracle reports simply at face value, without some evidence.

361. Habermas, *Evidence*, 25.

362. Ehrman, *Prophet*, 195; Wright, *Resurrection*, 685; cf. Tucker, *Knowledge*, 240–53; further, Popper, *Historicism*.

363. Whately, *Doubts*, cited in Brown, *Miracles*, 146–47; Blomberg, *Gospels*, 110.

from normal experience to ever be deemed probable.[364] Yet this appeal to analogy and experience today is more apt to cut the other way than when it was formulated,[365] since (as argued at some length in this chapter) claims about extranormal events reflect the widespread experience of much of humanity today.[366]

(2) The Shift in the Western Worldview

The particular arguments once used by Spinoza, Hume, and others to form the modern consensus against miracles made sense only on the philosophic and scientific presuppositions of their era, not those of our own.[367] The assumption that only atheistic or deistic approaches can be objective (i.e., epistemologically neutral) presupposes that atheism or deism is self-evidently true; it does not prove them, and it is certainly not neutral.[368] Christian philosopher William Lane Craig contends:

> The presupposition of the impossibility of miracles should, contrary to the assumption of nineteenth and for the most part twentieth century biblical criticism, play no role in determining the historicity of any event. . . . The presupposition against the possibility of miracles survives in theology only as a hangover from an earlier Deist age and ought to be once for all abandoned.[369]

Other scholars have become less and less comfortable with such unproved postulates of the Enlightenment era; as Leonhard Goppelt remarks regarding the assertion that miracles are historically impossible, critical reflection must question this proposition because "there is no such thing today as a complete and generally accepted philosophical understanding of reality."[370] "History" in the sense of "what happened" may be distinguished from "history" in the theoretical sense of "what can be explained by natural causes without recourse to supernatural causes."[371] Marcus Borg also rightly points out:

> The primary intellectual objection to it [supernatural activity] flows from a rigid application of the modern worldview's definition of reality. Yet the modern view is but one of a large number of humanly constructed maps of reality. It is historically the most recent and impressive because of the degree of control it has given us; but it is no more an absolute map of reality than any of the previous maps. All are relative, products of particular histories and cultures; the modern one, like its predecessors, will be superseded.[372]

Indeed, theoretical science has already abandoned "the modern worldview in its popular form."[373]

364. Ehrman, *Prophet*, 196. Ehrman contends that no matter how credible the witnesses are, their credibility is less probable than our knowledge that miracles do not happen. Yet such "knowledge" is hardly universally conceded and is, in fact, the point under debate.

365. So also Theissen and Merz, *Guide*, 310; Wink, "Write," 6.

366. See, e.g., Jenkins, *Next Christendom*, 107, 122–31; De Wet, "Signs"; Lambert, *Millions*, 109–20; Khai, "Pentecostalism," 268–70; Grazier, *Power Beyond*; Gardner, *Healing Miracles*; idem, "Miracles"; Harris, *Acts Today*; Rumph, *Signs*; Chavda, *Miracle*; Eddy and Boyd, *Legend*, 67–73, 82–83; cf. Berger, *Rumor*, 1–34.

367. Meier, *Marginal Jew*, 2:519–20; cf. also Wink, "Stories," 213; Polkinghorne, *Belief*. See, for further arguments for the possibility of concrete divine activity in history, the essays in Geivett and Habermas, *Miracles*.

368. A majority of philosophers of religion addressing theism today in fact argue for it (so Smith, "Metaphilosophy," 197; Smith is not a theist himself).

369. Craig, "Miracles," 43, concluding his discussion in the study. Cf. Boyd, *Sage*, 113–28; Wink, "Stories," 211 (regarding "materialism"); on the dominance of theistic rather than atheistic approaches today in philosophy of religion, see Smith, "Metaphilosophy," 197 (not himself a theist, as noted above).

370. Goppelt, *Theology*, 1:145.

371. France, "Authenticity," 105–7.

372. Borg, *Vision*, 33–34.

373. Ibid., 34.

Charles Talbert notes that the antisupernaturalist, materialistic worldview is less dominant today, not because "of new evidence" but because of "shifting evaluations of what is possible."[374] Acts scholar Rick Strelan also notes that scholars are moving beyond the old paradigms and becoming more open to examining supranormal-phenomena claims in early Christian sources, albeit most often in exclusively scientific (e.g., neurophysiological) terms.[375] Scholars increasingly reckon with their own "post-Enlightenment Western" worldview in seeking to grapple with miracle and magic claims in ancient sources foreign to our understanding.[376]

Some scholars point out that utterly paranormal events occur that cannot be attributed to the Christian God. Thus Eduard Schweizer notes a documented case of a guru who allowed his heart to be stabbed, without dying, on more than one occasion.[377] First-century Christians might have explained such an occurrence in supernatural but not divine terms, on the basis of biblical precedents (cf., e.g., Exod 7:12; Acts 13:6–10);[378] others might prefer other explanations. The minimal point on which there should be agreement here, however, is that some paranormal events do occur in reality and not merely in fiction.

Some older modern theologians, such as Bultmann, declared that "mature" modern people do not believe in miracles and that "no one can or does seriously maintain" the NT worldview.[379] Yet as John Meier points out, a 1989 Gallup poll showed that 82 percent of the people in the United States believe in miracles today, with only 6 percent categorically rejecting this view.[380] Although numbers would be lower in some regions, such as Europe, they would be higher in some other regions, such as most of Africa and Latin America. Orthodox Jews, Christians, and Muslims, as well as followers of traditional tribal religions, spiritism, and, in fact, most worldviews not derived from Western rationalism (including its specifically atheist versions), affirm the reality of supernatural phenomena.[381]

Indeed, a more recent, 2006 Pew Forum survey of Christians in ten nations estimated the percentage who believe they have *witnessed* healings; translated into hard numbers, this is well more than 300 million persons and does not even include figures

374. Talbert, *Mediterranean Milieu*, 216.

375. Strelan, *Strange Acts*, 9.

376. E.g., Reimer, *Miracle*, x.

377. Schweizer, *Parable*, 44. For a variety of non-Christian paranormal claims, see the sources cited in my *Miracles*, 205, 242–49.

378. Though most Christians would also deny that the sphere of God's love and activity is limited to Christians, probably most would also regard the above feat as exhibitionistic rather than as a demonstration of divine love.

379. Bultmann, "Mythology," 4 (noting [5–6] that modern beings presuppose all as coming from ourselves, not from alien powers, even deity, and forcing a choice [9] between accepting and rejecting the entire NT worldview). Bultmann allows that God acts existentially in ways communicated by mythical language (32; idem, "Demythologizing," 110), but uses the presence of miracles as a criterion of inauthenticity in Jewish texts (idem, *Tradition*, 58); he denies that the historical continuum may be "interrupted" by supernatural interventions (e.g., idem, "Exegesis," 147; cf. "Demythologizing," 122; Perrin, *Bultmann*, 86; Thiselton, *Horizons*, 292) and affirms as "myth" whatever involves supernatural forces (Bultmann, "Demythologizing," 95; cf. "Mythology," 9; Perrin, *Bultmann*, 77; Poland, *Criticism*, 11). Although now arguing against the dominant culture, cf. similarly the antisupernaturalism of Mack, *Myth*, 51, 54, 76, 209–15.

380. Meier, *Marginal Jew*, 2:11, 520–21; see also Woodward, *Miracles*, 21; Johnson and Butzen, "Prayer," 249; cf. Matthews, *Faith Factor*, 4. Pilch suggests that 90 percent of the world today accepts both "ordinary reality and non-ordinary reality," the latter including God and spirits (*Visions*, 17). Indeed, complementary use of spiritual therapies is fairly common even in more secular regions (Molassiotis et al., "Medicine").

381. See, e.g., Abogunrin, "Search"; Mbiti, *Religions*, 253–57; Hollenweger, *Pentecostals*, 129; Nanan, "Sorcerer"; Ashe, *Miracles*, 26–27; McClymond, *Stranger*, 82–83 (citing the views of "billions of people," probably without exaggeration). The kinds of questions one asks about miracles also vary in different cultural contexts (e.g., Arowele, "Signs").

from many of the nations with particularly abundant claims, such as China.[382] Yet Bultmann's position summarily dismissed such worldviews—easily the majority of the world's population—as not part of the modern world.[383] Such summary dismissal of the supernatural without appeal to satisfying contemporary philosophical arguments or concrete scientific data may have succeeded among those who shared the assumptions held by Bultmann's mid-twentieth-century Western academic setting but apparently does not satisfy most of those outside that elite subculture.

By defining modernity ethnocentrically in terms of a mid-twentieth-century academic Western elite, Bultmann simply restated as universal his own philosophic presuppositions, many of which are no longer fashionable in the academy.[384] Some have observed that Bultmann was obsessed with a now out-of-date worldview, one that Anthony Thiselton attributes to Bultmann's neo-Kantian roots.[385] Regardless of how fashionable in some circles the consensus may remain that genuine supernatural activity by a deity, deities, or spirits may simply be dismissed, it is uncritically naive, in today's multicultural world, for otherwise critical scholars to accept and propagate this consensus without inductively examining data.[386]

In view of current trends, some postmodern observers may well accept claims of supernatural phenomena without moral judgments on their sources[387] (e.g., neither the early Christian claim that Jesus's miracles were from God nor the opposing claims that they were works of sorcery would be a priori privileged). Whether or not one approves of such cultural trends, the days when supernatural phenomena can be dismissed without discussion may well be numbered. This trend toward greater openness will probably continue and grow in light of the larger context of global thought (see discussion below). Philosophic approaches from the Majority World will bring to the table many interests, but the Western Enlightenment antipathy to suprahuman activity will not likely be among them.

Western academia has hardly been neutral in its worldviews;[388] those who a priori rule out any "supernatural" claims effectively deny the worldviews and religions held

---

382. Pew Forum on Religion and Public Life, "Spirit and Power: A 10-Country Survey of Pentecostals" (October 5, 2006), n.p. Online: http://pewforum.org/surveys/Pentecostal; accessed Jan. 4, 2009 (including over a third of noncharismatics). A Pew Forum survey suggests that 34 percent of Americans claim to have witnessed or experienced divine healing; see also the June 2008 *U.S. Religious Landscape Survey*, 11, at http://religions.pewforum.org/pdf/report2-religious-landscape-study-full.pdf; accessed Dec. 2, 2008.

383. For a critique of Bultmann's demythologization program and its theological consequences, see Bockmuehl, *Theology*, 9–76, esp. 70–74.

384. E.g., the greatest influence on his thought is the early Heidegger (Perrin, *Bultmann*, 15; Hasel, *New Testament Theology*, 85), whom Bultmann thought discovered a picture according with what Bultmann found in the NT ("Mythology," 23–25; Thiselton, *Horizons*, 178–79, 226, 232, 262). Bultmann saw existential understanding not as a bias but a necessary perspective, like any other approach to history ("Exegesis," 149; cf., e.g., idem, *Word*, 11). Old liberalism (despite Bultmann, "Mythology," 12–13; Poland, *Criticism*, 26–27, 29) also influenced him; for influences from earlier NT scholarship and his approach to miracles as "mythology," see Twelftree, *Miracle Worker*, 33–37.

385. See Thiselton, *Horizons*, 260–61.

386. We need working assumptions, but they must be open to revision on the basis of evidence, not calcified in academic traditions. Paradigm shifts do not come easily (Kuhn, *Structure*); when investigators approach topics, even they tend to be laden with traditional assumptions (and concerns for respectability within the guild; cf. Yancey, *Compromising*, 59, 64, 66, 98–101, 116–19, 142, 153–54, 173).

387. For one objective anthropological investigation that takes a similarly morally neutral approach, see, e.g., Goodman, *Demons*.

388. Indeed, historians have documented the early twentieth-century power struggle in which the ultimately dominant side deliberately promoted antireligious agendas in U.S. academia (see, e.g., Smith, "Secularizing Education," 103, 152–53), in some cases funded by some of the robber barons (Marsden, *Soul of University*, 279–84, 332–33; Smith, "Rethinking Secularization," 74–77) and ultimately leading to a climate of antireligious prejudice in many sectors of the academy (Marsden, *Soul of University*, 396, 429–30, 437–40).

by the majority of the world's population. We may regard this assumption as right or wrong, but as a starting assumption, it is hardly neutral. On atheistic or deistic premises, divinely driven supernatural phenomena cannot exist; on the premises of many faiths, they must exist; on the agnostic premises from which critical intellectual inquiry claims to begin, one must investigate the evidence to determine, if possible, whether they do exist. This "neutral" starting point does not mean that those who engage in the discussion do not already have some personal views, but for the purpose of academic dialogue, they agree to suspend judgment (or at least to listen respectfully), while considering and presenting evidence. The point here is simply that we must be honest with ourselves and our students about the philosophic grid through which we sift the evidence. We must not confuse our presuppositions with the evidence, nor dare we confuse them with "neutrality."[389]

c. Majority World versus Modernist Western Assumptions

Scholars sometimes opine that miracle reports such as those in Luke-Acts must depend on later legend or a writer's imagination,[390] but this premise rests on culturally and intellectually narrow assumptions that read much of the world's experiences through the nonexperiences of much of our Western academic culture.[391] Many other cultures (as well as much of Western culture historically) have worked from other assumptions, and the labels traditionally employed by Western modernity to denigrate those assumptions are no longer suitable in an emphatically multicultural, postmodern world. For this reason, some NT scholars today argue, for example, that comparisons with shamans (and how analogous figures functioned in the first century) would be more helpful in understanding Jesus's miracles than anachronistic modernist readings of Western skeptics.[392]

Elsewhere I survey a much larger range of miracle claims in the Majority World, in the premodern West, and in popular culture in the West as well.[393] I will not seek to repeat all of that survey here. Nevertheless, the claim that no one in the modern world believes in miracles (once seriously offered by some scholars as an answer to the question of miracles, as noted above) can no longer be seriously entertained. I mention only a few sources here. Although I give greater attention to academic sources, some of my "primary" sources are popular, as is usual in the academic study of popular religion. (A fuller comparative study would also examine the massive number of modern non-Christian supernatural-activity claims,[394] but given that this

389. Except to the extent that our working premise is open to the most plausible readings of the evidence. And even there we must be open to redefining our understanding of "plausibility" if sufficient evidence so demands.

390. Cf. Dibelius, *Studies in Acts*, 24, regarding as characteristic of "legend" "a miracle related in naïve style" (cf. 17–18, 20); also the sort of approach noted in Achtemeier, *Miracle Tradition*, 136–37.

391. Polybius opined that "as nothing written by mere students of books is written with experience or vividness, their works are of no practical utility to readers" (Polyb. 12.25g.2 [LCL]).

392. See Craffert, "Healer"; cf. Berends, "African Healing Practices," 285–86; Borg, *Conflict*, 73, 230–31, 305, 373; Malina and Pilch, *Acts*, 211–13; idem, *Letters*, 366–68; also Eve, *Miracles*, 354 (following Kleinman, *Healers*, 71–82, 139–40, 366), though noting differences. Some compare prophetic healers in what they view as analogous colonial settings (cf., in detail, Davies, "Prophet/Healer"; idem, *Healer*). Though recognizing theological differences between the two, Miller and Yamamori, *Pentecostalism*, 24, note that Pentecostalism "resonates culturally" where shamanism is practiced and observe functional analogies between them.

393. Keener, *Miracles*, chs. 7–12; more concisely, see idem, "Case"; briefly, "Comparisons." My volume on miracles originally grew from research for this chapter. It was written after this commentary but has been published before it. I have revised this chapter in light of it.

394. E.g., Peters, *Healing in Nepal*, 51–53, 61, 63, 65–68 (though cf. the shaman's selective reservations, 73–74); Narayanan, "Shanti"; Winkelman and Carr, "Approach"; Arai, "Spirituality"; Crawford, "Healing," 34–35; Finkler, "Religion," 51 (and sources cited there); Grundmann, "Healing," 27; Umeh, *Dibia*, 203–27;

discussion already strays beyond the usual contours of NT scholarship and that the material included below should be sufficient to flesh out the basic analogy I am making, I have restricted my focus. Many of the non-Christian claims are also less analogous to those in Acts, though also less potentially derivative.)

1. Many Miracle Claims Today

Even if they are outside the experience of most scholars, today's world is full of firsthand claims to have witnessed miracles (some sincere, others not), and there is no reason to suppose that the ancient world was any different. One may readily dispute observers' explanations for such experiences, but when some scholars deny that such experiences ever belong to the eyewitness level of historical sources, they ignore the social reality of a sizable proportion of the world's population, and millions of intelligent but culturally different people will feel compelled by their own experience, or that of others close to them, to dismiss such scholarship as an experientially narrow cultural imperialism.

Thus Theissen and Merz, although reluctant to attribute the phenomena to purely supernatural causes,[395] point out that the plausibility principle of analogy used in historiography "obliges us to recognize the possibility of healings and exorcisms. For in many cultures there is an abundance of well-documented analogies to them—and even in the 'underground' of our culture, although that may be officially denied."[396] The principle of analogy, traditionally used against miracle reports in the wake of the radical Enlightenment, now favors their probability.[397]

(1) A Multicultural Approach

As Justo González remarks in his commentary on Acts, the frequent denial of narratives' historicity on account of miracle reports employs a questionable epistemological criterion. Bultmann denies that modern people who use scientific inventions can believe in miracles, yet "what Bultmann declares to be impossible is not just possible, but even frequent." Miracles are, González points out, affirmed in most Latino churches despite the influence of the mechanistic worldview from much Western thought.[398]

Turner, *Experiencing Ritual*, passim; idem, *Hands*; idem, *Healers*; idem, "Actuality"; Krippner and Achterberg, "Experiences"; Evans-Pritchard, *Religion*, 308; Firth, "Foreword," xiii–xiv; cf. many essays in Barnes and Talamantez, *Teaching*; Rosny, *Healers* (though not focusing primarily on a supernatural element); Ashe, *Miracles*, 26–27 (attributing such phenomena to anything "Other," not necessarily deities). The paranormal approach of Turner and others of similar persuasion has often received a respectful scholarly hearing (cf. Barnes, "Introduction," 19–20; Strelan, *Strange Acts*, 51).

395. Theissen and Merz, *Guide*, 310–13; cf. Ashe, *Miracles*, 26–27.

396. Theissen and Merz, *Guide*, 310; cf. also Price, *Son of Man*, 20–21; Allison, *Jesus*, 23n94. Theissen and Merz, *Guide*, 310, employ the same analogy principle to discount nature miracles, which they think written in light of the resurrection (301–4; but then, so is everything in the Gospels!); contrast Allison, *Jesus*, 23n94. Yet this differentiation normally assumes antisupernaturalism (cf. Moule, "Classification," 240), and as we have noted elsewhere, there are also many modern reports of "nature miracles" (again, whatever their explanation), though far fewer than healing and exorcism claims (e.g., Heim, *Transformation*, 195–98; Yung, "Integrity," 174; McGee, "Miracles," 253; Wigger, *Saint*, 193, on Asbury's perspective; Kinnear, *Tide*, 92–96; Khai, "Pentecostalism," 268; Dayhoff, "Barros"; Lindsay, *Lake*, 48–49; Harris, *Acts Today*, 66–67, 80; Bush and Pegues, *Move*, 54–55, 59, 64, 192; Koschorke, Ludwig, and Delgado, *History*, 223–24). Some people I know have offered me eyewitness reports, e.g., Dr. Emmanuel Itapson (Nigeria), April 29, 2008; Sandy Thomas (Congo), Aug. 26, 2008; Dr. Paul Mokake (Cameroon), May 13, 2009; Dr. Ayo Adewuya (Nigeria), Dec. 14, 2009.

397. Note here also Wink, "Write," 6.

398. González, *Acts*, 84–85; cf. Martell-Otero, "Satos," 31–32. Although González is speaking more broadly, some estimate that 28 percent of all Latino Christians in the United States identify with Pentecostal or (especially among Catholics) charismatic movements (Espinosa, "Contributions," 124); naturally, these would be included among those agreeing with González's statement.

Western scholar Philip Jenkins notes that, in general, Christianity in the global South is quite interested in "the immediate workings of the supernatural, through prophecy, visions, ecstatic utterances, and healing."[399] Referring to the different issue of hostile suprahuman forces, John S. Mbiti, a scholar of African religion, complains that most Western scholars "expose their own ignorance, false ideas, exaggerated prejudices and a derogatory attitude" that fails to take seriously genuine experiences pervasive in Africa.[400] Asian theologians like Malaysian Methodist bishop Hwa Yung have also critiqued Western Enlightenment approaches toward claims beyond Western expectations.[401]

Regardless of how we interpret miracle reports and other supernatural claims, their frequency in today's world indicates that large numbers of intelligent, sincere people believe that such cures are occurring today, including through their own prayers. How much more likely would this be in a culture generally less skeptical than is common in the modern Western world? There is no intrinsically *historical* reason to think that Luke had to invent such miraculous claims (especially in the eyewitness "we" material, Acts 16:18; 20:10; 28:4–6, 8–9; cf. 21:4, 11, 19)[402] or for us to attribute them to deception.

The danger of reading biblical narratives through the grid of solely modern Western assumptions is not a merely theoretical one. Traditional Western academic approaches to other cultures have often proved ethnocentric,[403] including through derogatory Western assumptions about "religion."[404] If research is guilty of ethnocentric assumptions when addressing cultures contemporary to us, we run an even greater risk of compounding this ethnocentrism with anachronism when we study ancient cultures. This danger seems particularly relevant in academic approaches to miracles, which have traditionally been shaped by Enlightenment philosopher David Hume. One of his arguments against miracles was that most reports stemmed from what he derided as "ignorant and barbarous nations."[405]

By contrast, following an approach more consistent with the rise of global awareness and the increase in voices from the Majority World,[406] postmodernity rejects the privileging of Western cultural assumptions.[407] In an example of the trend toward cultural openness, medical anthropology now rejects "medicocentrism," the

399. Jenkins, *Next Christendom*, 107, who also complains that Westerners too often contest the legitimacy of such perspectives. Versus early missionaries, Africans embraced such ideas (e.g., Eshete, *Movement*, 89).

400. Mbiti, *Religions*, 253; cf. also Uzukwu, "Address," 9; on the supernatural, Eya, "Healing," 51–52. Another African scholar notes that miracle workers, both Christian and non-Christian, are an authentic part of African culture (Ukachukwu Manus, "Miracle-Workers"). Another writer with experience in Africa suggests that African culture offers better foundations for understanding such texts (Roschke, "Healing").

401. Yung, *Quest*, 7, 230, 238–39; idem, "Integrity," 173–75.

402. Baur, indeed, cited the presence of miracles against the genuineness of eyewitness claims in the narratives (as noted in Campbell, *We Narratives*, 9) purely on the philosophic assumption that miracles are implausible.

403. See, e.g., the critique in MacGaffey, "Epistemological Ethnocentrism" (cf. also idem, "Ideology"); Vansina, "Knowledge" (passim, but esp. 39–40); Chrétien, "Exchange," 77.

404. MacGaffey, "Epistemological Ethnocentrism," 43–45.

405. Hume, "Miracles," 37. Hume's language is consistent with his ethnocentrism elsewhere; see Ten, "Racism"; Taliaferro and Hendrickson, "Racism"; cf. also Keener, "Case."

406. Unfortunately, sometimes these voices are still publicly filtered through Western academia, since only by accepting its implicit political rules can one gain a hearing.

407. Valuing culturally diverse voices need not constitute a blanket endorsement of all ideas frequently associated with postmodernity (which other cultural shifts will, in any case, likewise presumably supersede). For one discussion of the postmodern emphasis on difference and a post-postmodern response underlining human solidarity, see Min, *Solidarity*, 47–64 and 65–88, respectively; on postmodern theology, see, e.g., Vanhoozer, *Postmodern Theology*. Apart from specifically postmodern assumptions, other domains have long valued multicultural approaches (e.g., Taylor, *Missiology*).

ethnocentric view that maintains that only current Western views of sickness and healing are authentic and that disputes the many claims to cures outside Western views.[408] Medical anthropology, John Pilch argues, "could help the exegete to adopt a transcultural stance."[409] (Indeed, some physicians now partner with some "spiritual healers" because of the observed effectiveness of some of the latter, regardless of views of the causes.)[410]

Similarly, cross-cultural anthropological studies suggest that people in a variety of cultures experience visions or other altered states of consciousness and that vision reports in Acts therefore would appear perfectly plausible to much of the world's population both at the time of Acts and today.[411] As noted above, there has also been a shift away from dogmatic antisupernaturalism, so that even the interpretation of such claims (as well as the existence of the phenomena themselves) is more open to discussion than in the past.

Some modern critics have complained that early Christianity spread by claiming signs and wonders, playing on the fears of superstitious people.[412] Yet most Christians in the Majority World, less shaped by the modern Western tradition of the radical Enlightenment, find stories of miraculous phenomena far less objectionable than do their Western counterparts.[413] These other cultures offer a check on traditional Western assumptions; as Yale scholar Lamin Sanneh points out, it is here that Western culture "can encounter . . . the gospel as it is being embraced by societies that had not been shaped by the Enlightenment" and hence are closer to the milieu of earliest Christianity.[414]

(2) Collecting Reports

As is elaborated further below, many of these Majority World voices, in fact, can recount reports (including at times their own eyewitness testimony) of phenomena, both associated with Christianity and not associated with it, that seem difficult to explain, if taken at face value, without recourse to the activity of suprahuman entities. Hundreds of millions of sincere people around the world believe that suprahuman

408. See Pilch, "Sickness," 183. As we have observed, one of Hume's arguments against miracles was that most reports stemmed from "ignorant and barbarous nations" ("Miracles," 36; also noted in Meier, "Signs," 760); his ethnocentrism contributed to his further failure to critically evaluate the influence of his own culture in suppressing reports of such experiences.

409. Pilch, Healing, 35 (for medical anthropology in general, see 19–36; for application to Jesus research, see idem, "Anthropology"). We may not believe in being moonstruck or struck by the evil eye, but anthropologists recognize these as "folk-conceptualized disorders" (19). Social scientists note accounts of miracle cures in many cultures (McClenon, Events, 131); for some anthropological approaches to local healing traditions, see, e.g., Scherberger, "Shaman," 59–64; McClenon and Nooney, "Experiences," 46–48.

410. Remus, Healer, 114–15 (noting recent medical research, esp. Harpur, Touch). Western Christians have also sometimes collaborated with traditional healers (e.g., Seale, "Collaboration"; cf. Kyomo, "Healing," 146–47), although they are generally more open to their more "naturalistic" methods (such as herbs) than to their competing supernatural approaches (Seale, "Collaboration," 316–17).

411. Pilch, Visions, passim (see also the excursus on spirit possession at Acts 16:16). Pilch notes (158–59) that such phenomena have continued despite attempts of the Enlightenment to discredit the earlier experiences throughout history.

412. Critics sometimes address the Christian exorcists in late antiquity who, like other practitioners of their era, responded to the pervasive sense of demonization in that period. Others regard this as a form of culturally sensitive adaptation to local psychological needs (cf. observations concerning the continuity and discontinuity in Frankfurter, Religion in Egypt, 273–77; on this period, see also Lewis, Life, 98; for anthropological assessments of the therapeutic aspects of exorcisms, see the excursus on spirit possession at Acts 16:16). In either case, these claims are far more pervasive than those offered in Acts.

413. Jenkins, Next Christendom, 122–31; cf. also Richards, "Factors," 95–96; Eddy and Boyd, Legend, 67–73, 82–83 (also noting, 71–73, the shift among [and citing] "many western ethnographers" and anthropologists who have grown increasingly respectful toward other cultures' approaches to the supernatural).

414. Sanneh, Whose Religion?, 26.

forces are at work or that they have experience with miraculous healings;[415] whether one likes it or not, it is neither charitable nor plausible to simply dismiss the existence of such claims, however one chooses to explain them. By analogy, it is plausible that many ancient claimants also sincerely believed that they reported such experiences accurately, rather than that they simply invented them for the purposes of propaganda.

Even should volumes of such claims be collected by researchers (which would not be difficult), the collection would not prove that any given claims to miracles in the past were authentic (we have evidence and other reasons to affirm that many claims, in fact, are inauthentic), but such research at least empirically refutes the claim that such experiences cannot be sincerely reported by eyewitnesses.[416]

My primary purpose is to highlight the fact that eyewitness claims to healings are widespread; secondarily, I hope that some examples will support the plausibility of a theological explanation for some miracle claims. In the latter case, I hope that the number and geographic range of claims available today will give pause to those who think that by challenging the authenticity of a few miracle claims, they can readily dismiss all of them. Granted, many claims prove false, and in many other cases the medical evidence cannot render a conclusive verdict whether claims involve supernatural activity (since remissions do occur without prayer). But it is a logical fallacy to rule out the paranormal authenticity of *all* miracle claims based on either point; one cannot inductively prove a negative (a weakness in Hume's argument), but a single, certain positive case would refute a claim that miracles cannot happen.

Even some readers who reject all nonnaturalistic explanations may have difficulty explaining some of them on purely naturalistic terms. Nevertheless, although I will venture comments about potential explanations later, scholars can agree that claims are firsthand without needing to agree about explanations. What is more critical from the historical standpoint of our discipline is to note that such experiences are widely claimed by firsthand sources and hence that it is not necessary, whatever the proposed explanations, to deny the possibility of firsthand claims for such experiences in the first century. The next subsection offers as examples a small number of Majority World claims and then surveys a few proposed explanations for the claims.[417]

II. Majority World Voices

Luke's claims of signs and attendant church growth (notwithstanding his attendant reports of skeptical resistance to such signs) seem much less "novelistic" in parts of the world where such claims and attendant church growth occur today. If its accounts of dramatic signs make Luke-Acts a foreign and foreboding work to segments

415. If one goes beyond those who claim to have experienced or witnessed such phenomena to those who believe that they sometimes occur, the numbers are exorbitant. Pentecostal and charismatic Christians alone may constitute half a billion people (see, e.g., Sanneh, *Disciples*, 275; Cox, "Miracles," 88; Noll, *Shape*, 22; higher, Johnson, Barrett, and Crossing, "Christianity 2010," 36; Johnson and Ross, *Atlas*, 102), though this may be a high estimate (for discussion of the figures, see Anderson, *Pentecostalism*, 11); with the majority of Christians, Muslims, and various other groups added, it is clear that antisupernaturalists are a minority of the world's population. This observation does not make antisupernaturalism wrong, but it does make it arrogant to simply dismiss all other worldviews by claiming one's assumption as self-evident.

416. Modernist antisupernaturalists can question the interpretation of such reports, but even in this case, they do not attempt to demonstrate the claim that genuine miracles do not happen. (I am raising here not so much an objection as an observation, since it is impossible to inductively prove a negative. But as noted above, the traditional antisupernaturalist deductive assumptions no longer fit many of our contemporary worldviews, including in the physical sciences.)

417. The fuller treatment of the philosophic issues involved, the claims, and the proposed explanations appears in Keener, *Miracles* (respectively chs. 4–6, 7–12, and 13–15).

of modern Western academia,[418] it is nevertheless a work welcome in many of the dynamic churches (including, though not limited to, those of the Pentecostal and charismatic varieties)[419] of Africa, Latin America, and Asia, which claim to share its experiences. (This observation is relevant beyond the question of miracle reports. Although willing to study other sorts of sociological analogies, scholars often fail to consider the experiences of those who have lived in many situations most similar to those described in Luke's narratives, such as experiencing boldness during persecution; cf. comment on Acts 4:8. Out of deference to Western scholarly practice, I will rarely draw such analogies here, but I do suspect that we sometimes neglect too quickly the value of some popular readings within potentially analogous frames of spiritual experience.)[420]

(1) Learning from Other Cultures

Some scholars have complained how quickly Western commentators have tended to pass over signs claims in Acts, often in embarrassment.[421] Dissatisfaction with this state of affairs has propelled many to look to other eras and cultures for helpful parallels.

When MacMullen compares with Christian claims in the Roman Empire Simon Kimbangu's healings from 1921 in the Belgian Congo, he warns against extrapolating too much from anthropological parallels. Nevertheless, he believes that Kimbangu's "story might alert us to points in the evidence from antiquity which deserve special attention."[422] Although the movement changed over time, even Kimbangu's earliest followers affirmed that he "raised the dead, caused the paralyzed to stand upright, gave sight to the blind, cleansed lepers, and healed all the sick in the name of the Lord Jesus."[423] MacMullen contends that rapidly expanding movements such as Kimbangu's[424] and William Wadé Harris's healing ministry in West Africa (starting in 1914)[425] can be helpful in expanding the parameters of Western readers unaccustomed to think

418. As Wink, "Write," 4, notes was once the case with himself.

419. For Pentecostalism in Africa and the African Diaspora, see Yong, *Spirit Poured*, 59–80; in Asia, 45–58; in Latin America, 33–45; cf. also Petersen, "Latin American Pentecostalism"; for the role of healing in Pentecostal missiology, see, e.g., Hodges, *Indigenous Church*, 50–51; York, *Missions*, 155. Pentecostalism has tended to adapt readily to address the supernatural interests of traditional Majority World societies (e.g., Martin, "Christianity," 79). Its theology is hardly monolithic, but Pentecostal and charismatic beliefs are, by definition, incompatible with antisupernaturalism. Now the subject of studies by major university presses, movements grouped together by sociologists as Pentecostal-like may include more than half a billion people; see, e.g., Johnson and Ross, *Atlas*, 102; Johnson, Barrett, and Crossing, "Christianity 2010," 36; Sanneh, *Disciples*, 275. On its rapid growth, see also Tomkins, *History*, 220, 245; Berger, "Faces," 425; Mullin, *History*, 211.

420. Of course, popular readings often lack the scholarly rigor of careful attention to literary and social context. Yet the insights of (or concerning) house-church believers regarding the dynamics of house churches, the insights of (or concerning) first-generation converts regarding the dynamics of conversion within non-Christian kin and other social networks, and so forth can allow for the more precise framing of questions that may not occur to readers with less analogous experiences.

421. Ashton, *Religion*, 174–75, 177, noting that MacMullen differs from most NT scholars here. Field, "Possession," 10, has compared her observations of West African apostolic "Holy Spirit" sects with Acts.

422. MacMullen, *Christianizing*, 7; cf. also the comparisons with Kimbangu (and their limitations) noted in Eddy and Boyd, *Legend*, 155–57; Flusser, "Love," 154.

423. Koschorke, Ludwig, and Delgado, *History*, 260, quoting an early document of the Kimbanguist Church.

424. See further Brockman, "Kimbangu"; Etienne, "Diangienda"; Rabey, "Prophet"; Jenkins, *Next Christendom*, 49–50; Cox, *Fire*, 252–53; Yates, *Expansion*, 173; Ndofunsu, "Prayer"; specifically on healings drawing attention in African Independent Churches (including Kimbanguism), see De Wet, "Signs," 99–100. Kimbangu also influenced Daniel Ndoundou, a leader in the 1947 revival in Congo-Brazzaville (see Keener, "Ndoundou").

425. MacMullen, *Christianizing*, 23–24. See further Shank, "Prophet"; Haliburton, *Harris*; Walker, "Harrist Church"; idem, *Revolution*; Isichei, "Soul of Fire"; Bediako, *Christianity in Africa*, 91–93, 103–4, 204; Barrington-Ward, "Spirit Possession," 467; Jenkins, *Next Christendom*, 48–49; Robeck, *Mission*, 272; Yates, *Expansion*, 170; Kalu, *African Pentecostalism*, 20, 31, 36–38; Noll and Nystrom, *Clouds*, 65–79 (esp. 74–75).

in terms of such experiences. Into the same category might fall the African Christian prophet Garrick Braide, who healed the sick and caused rain to fall in the name of Israel's God, until the colonial authorities arrested him in 1916 for cutting into their liquor profits in West Africa.[426]

Other scholars have compared the documented successes of the "'mad monk' Rasputin," which affected the course of Russian history and thus cannot be omitted from historical inquiry.[427] Still others have compared Don Pedrito Jaramillo, a Mexican folk saint active from 1881 till 1907, who achieved more notoriety than other healers of his era.[428] One critic of Western commentators' embarrassed silence about miracles has compared literature about shamans from around the world.[429] Despite often significant differences among the objects of comparison, the comparisons do highlight the contrast between beliefs about suprahuman enablement in most of the world (not limited to Christian systems, despite our focus here)[430] and the Western Enlightenment assumptions that help make these texts so foreign to us.

Global experience challenges the Western academic prejudice against the sort of experiences that the West traditionally construed as supernatural activity.[431] Thus, for example, Michael Green (at the time of his writing, a senior research fellow at Wycliffe Hall, Oxford) reports that a disabled minister in Malawi, unable to walk, asked him to pray for healing. Reluctant but unable to avoid the challenge, Green prayed for him, and "the man got up and started dancing around, just as the Lystra cripple is recorded as doing."[432] The parallel to Acts is not coincidental; missionaries in various contexts continue to look to Acts for a model of miraculous ministry and power encounters.[433]

(2) Majority World Claims Widespread

Elsewhere I follow the lead of MacMullen and these other scholars in such examples[434] but seek a wider array of examples in view of the long history of claims of

426. Sanneh, *West African Christianity*, 181–83; Yates, *Expansion*, 170, 172; Brockman, "Braide"; Koschorke, Ludwig, and Delgado, *History*, 223–26; Kalu, *African Pentecostalism*, 31, 36, 38–39. Kalu, *African Pentecostalism*, 31, suggests that such indigenous African prophetic movements prefigured the contemporary Pentecostal emphasis in African Christianity.

427. McClymond, *Stranger*, 83 (following Jong, *Rasputin*, 136–42). Noting his effects in history is not to equate him with Kimbangu; many viewed the mystic Rasputin as unscrupulous and contributing to his royal benefactors' decline.

428. Eve, *Miracles*, 357–59 (following Romano, "Folk-Healing"), arguing that he achieved this status especially by claiming divine authorization, offering unique cures, and (fitting cultural expectations for such healers) renouncing himself. Eve, *Miracles*, 360, 379, compares aspects of Jesus's ministry.

429. Ashton, *Religion*, 32–40 (including in his discussion also the sixth-century ascetic Theodore of Sykeon, 34–36). For shaman analogies, cf. also, e.g., Klutz, *Exorcism Stories*, 196–97; Craffert, "Healer." For other comparisons (and especially contrasts) of shamans with ancient Mediterranean seers, see Brown, *Israel and Greece*, 81–117.

430. Most non-Western worldviews accept a variety of suprahuman phenomena (e.g., Wright, *Process*, 74–114, esp. 85–88, 95–98; Turner, *Experiencing Ritual*, passim). Others have tried to explain NT miracles by analogy to "paranormal" telepathy, clairvoyance, and precognition (Montefiore, *Miracles*); although the differences, again, are significant (NT accounts suggest divine dependence rather than innate abilities), the analogy represents another attempt to go beyond typical Western assumptions.

431. With Eddy and Boyd, *Legend*, 67–73; cf. again Keener, *John*, 266–67; note also presentations by African scholars, e.g., Chinwokwu, "Localizing."

432. Green, *Thirty Years*, 104. Green offers his eyewitness accounts of healings in southeast Asia in Green, *Asian Tigers*, 8 (cf. also other accounts in 9, 56, 90, 97–100, 104, 110). Green, an Anglican, has also been adviser in evangelism to the archbishops of Canterbury and York.

433. E.g., Pettis, "Fourth Pentecost," 252–53; Green, *Thirty Years*, 9–10.

434. Keener, *Miracles*, chs. 7–9, 12. Although MacMullen's primary focus is a period subsequent to Acts, others also have regarded his portrayal of popular Christian expansion as appropriate, in this sense, to Acts (Alexander, *Context*, 203–4).

such experiences throughout the past and their pervasiveness today. Because such analogies remain unusual in commentaries, I refer the reader to that other publication and offer merely a very brief summary below. Yet even my fuller treatment, which cites hundreds of examples, many from firsthand interviews, offers merely samples of a much wider sphere of experience.

In contrast to the period when many of the plausibility structures for modern critical NT scholarship were defined, Two-Thirds World Christians are now the majority; moreover, expectation of healings is common among many Majority World churches.[435] Likewise, estimates of global figures even for specifically charismatic and Pentecostal Christians (groups traditionally known for expecting healings) are in the hundreds of millions (projected by some as approaching even half a billion), making the charismatic branch of Christendom second in size only to Roman Catholicism (with which it overlaps).[436] Historian Robert Bruce Mullin observes that already by the end of the twentieth century, there were "more Pentecostals worldwide" than mainline Protestants.[437]

Most of these Christians are economically poor, and they are not as widely represented among academicians as their numbers might otherwise suggest, but they do represent a significant voice. These Christians do not represent a single theological approach to the miraculous,[438] but the majority of them do affirm miraculous phenomena. Popular sentiments cannot define scientific or historical plausibility, but charity toward others' worldviews can invite us to at least reevaluate the primacy of old philosophic assumptions that we have often taken for granted without consideration.

(3) Examples in the Majority World

Supernatural phenomena are compatible with most African worldviews,[439] and reports of miraculous healings are frequent in Africa, especially where normal medical resources are difficult to come by.[440] Some standard reference works on global

435. Moreland, *Triangle*, 166–67, cites sources regarding a dramatic growth of "evangelical" Christianity around the world (possibly even a 1,000 percent increase in three decades), up to 70 percent of it "intimately connected to signs and wonders." Already before those three decades, Christiaan De Wet, writing a thesis on "signs" involved in church growth around the world, surveyed more than 350 theses representing most of the world and interviewed countless missionaries. He complained, "My research has turned up so much material on signs and wonders that are happening and churches that are growing, that it is impossible to use all of it" ("Signs," 92).

436. Johnson, Barrett, and Crossing, "Christianity 2010," 36, estimate 614 million; see further Johnson and Ross, *Atlas*, 102; more cautiously, Anderson, *Pentecostalism*, 11. See also Jenkins, *Next Christendom*, 122–31; various essays in Dempster, Klaus, and Petersen, *Globalization of Pentecostalism*, including Klaus, "Global Culture"; Robeck, "Charismatic Movements," 150–54.

437. Mullin, *History*, 211; cf. similarly Noll, *Shape*, 32.

438. Some Western observers note with understandable concern the proliferation of "health and wealth" teaching in Africa (though definitions vary; cf. Kalu, *African Pentecostalism*, 255–63), and so I pause here to note the denominational and theological diversity of my examples, most of which are *not* associated with that teaching (cf. discussion of other more socially engaged streams of Pentecostalism in Miller and Yamamori, *Pentecostalism*). The link between healing and prosperity was not part of early Pentecostalism, emerging only "well into the twentieth century" (Curtis, *Faith*, 206).

439. See, e.g., Abogunrin, "Search"; Mbiti, *Religions*, 253–57. Many African indigenous Christian movements "expected to experience miracles in everyday life" (Kalu, *African Pentecostalism*, 98). For the relevance of miraculous power in Africa, see also Gräbe, "Discovery."

440. Cf. some claims in, e.g., Mensah, "Basis," 177–79; Hanciles, *Beyond Christendom*, 329; Stinton, *Jesus of Africa*, 65–71; Kalu, *African Pentecostalism*, 96; Ranger, "Dilemma," 352–53. De Wet also cites a number of sources for Africa; in one African Catholic church, see Jenkins, *New Faces*, 118–19. For a range of African healing claims, see (especially for the twentieth century), e.g., Akinwumi, "Babalola"; idem, "Idahosa"; Brockman, "Kimbangu"; idem, "Kivuli"; Dayhoff, "Marais"; Etienne, "Diangienda"; Fuller, "Tsado"; Hexham, "Shembe"; Keener, "Ndoundou"; Larbi, "Anim"; Lygunda li-M, "Pelendo"; Manana, "Kitonga"; idem, "Ndaruhutse"; Menberu, "Mekonnen Negera"; Millard, "Duma"; Nsenga, "Fuisa"; Odili, "Osaele"; idem, "Agents"; Akinwumi,

Christianity indicate the pervasiveness of healing claims, from Catholic to Pentecostal, in Latin America.[441] Researchers offer many reports on signs and church growth in Latin America;[442] because of the limits of most of my current sources,[443] I will focus, for concrete examples, especially on evangelicals and Pentecostals here. Already a generation ago healing campaigns were catalyzing evangelical-church growth in Latin America.[444] One of the most common factors in persons' joining Pentecostal churches in Latin America is the experiencing of healing after prayer.[445] When urban migrants in one Argentinian church were interviewed, 37.7 percent of them claimed that healings had led to their accepting the gospel message; among the ailments they reported healed were blindness, cancer, deafness, heart disease, paralysis, and tuberculosis.[446] In another study, 86.4 percent of Brazilian Pentecostals claimed that they had experienced divine healing,[447] and one scholar has reported that every Colombian Pentecostal she interviewed claimed miraculous experiences.[448] Ninety percent of Ecuadorian Pentecostals in another study claimed to have been miraculously healed.[449]

Reported miraculous healings have abetted church growth in much of Asia,[450] including India, where two sociologists of religion note that "healing was viewed as commonplace."[451] For example, it is said that church growth among the Nishi tribals began when an important official's son was raised from death after an experimental prayer to Jesus, leading to hundreds of conversions.[452] Likewise, Thomas Mathews of Kerala and his coworkers in the Filadelfia movement witnessed significant church growth in Rajasthan through healings and other anomalous experiences.[453] Even in the nineteenth and early twentieth centuries, indigenous Indian revival movements (often challenging missionary control) included claims of supernatural phenomena.[454]

"Orimolade" (not suggesting that all the oral traditions are authentic); idem, "Oschoffa"; Buys and Nambala, "Hambuindja"; idem, "Kanambunga"; Baker and Baker, *Miracles*, 7–8, 39, 43, 57, 78, 108, 114, 137, 152, 163, 170, 172, 180, 183, 192–93; idem, *Enough*, 65, 76, 157, 169, 171–73; Chevreau, *Turnings*, 142.

441. See Rivera-Pagán, "Transformation," 193–95.

442. E.g., Castleberry, "Impact," 112–13, 143; for other healing claims in Latin America, see, e.g., Petersen, *Might*, 100–101; Lehmann, *Struggle*, 197; Sánchez Walsh, *Identity*, 43–44; Norwood, "Colloquium," 24–26; earlier, De Wet follows about fifteen major sources for Latin America.

443. Catholic miracle claims would also be numerous (e.g., Rivera-Pagán, "Transformation," 193–94; cf. Durand and Massey, *Miracles*, 45–66; MacNutt, *Healing*, 26–27); unlike some Protestants (reacting against what they considered Catholic excesses), Catholic and Orthodox theology never adopted a "cessationist" stance (e.g., Mullin, *Miracles*, 133; Kselman, *Miracles*, 197).

444. Marostica, "Learning"; McGee, "Radical Strategy," 89–90; Read, Monterroso, and Johnson, *Growth*, 323; Castleberry, "Impact," 106–8, 112, 151, 166–68; on signs and church growth in Latin America, see further De Wet, "Signs," 100–108.

445. Chiquete, "Healing," 480–81. He notes (481) that many of those who are not healed also join these churches because of the churches' care and concern for their wholeness.

446. De Wet, "Signs," 103–4 (following Larson, "Migration," 312).

447. See Chesnut, "Exorcising" (for particular accounts, see, e.g., idem, *Born Again in Brazil*, 81–82).

448. Bomann, *Faith in Barrios*, 62 (for particular accounts, see, e.g., 62–63).

449. Castleberry, "Impact," 166.

450. E.g., Yung, "Integrity," 173–75; Khai, "Pentecostalism," 268–70 (in Myanmar); Wiyono, "Timor Revival," 277, 288; Williams, "Answer," 114–16; Filson, "Study," 150–51, 154; Knapstad, "Power," 78; De Wet, "Signs," 108–23; Daniel, "Labour," 160; Ma, "Encounter," 135–37; idem, "Vanderbout," 130–32; Kim, "Influence," 30–31; Kwon, "Foundations," 187, 227–32; Bush and Pegues, *Move*, 62–64.

451. Miller and Yamamori, *Pentecostalism*, 152; see also Bergunder, *Movement*, 163–65, 232–33; idem, "Healing," 109–11; further examples in Devadason, "Missionary Societies," 189; Bergunder, *Movement*, 152.

452. De Wet, "Signs," 110–11 (following Cunville, "Evangelization," 156–57).

453. E.g., Thollander, *Mathews*, 84, 87–90; cf. other signs, 3, 125, 128–30; beyond Rajasthan, see Pothen, "Missions," 189–90. I know personally Thomas Mathews's son-in-law, Finny Philip, an Indian NT scholar who affirms the veracity of Thollander's book.

454. McGee, "Revivals in India" (esp. on 1860–ca. 1881 and 1905–7); Satyavrata, "Perspectives," 205 (on 1860); Burgess, "Pandita Ramabai," 194–95; George, "Beginnings," 235.

A Korean missiologist with the Oxford Center for Mission Studies observes that Pentecostal Christians in northern Luzon in the Philippines experience healings as in Acts.[455] One Western researcher in the Philippines interviewed people who were prayed for, to see if any felt better, and was astonished to learn "that 83% of them actually reported that they had experienced some dramatic healing from God in their bodies."[456] Healing has also characterized Korean Christianity since the Korean revival of 1907.[457]

Many scholars have noted the emphasis on, and many testimonies of, healing and exorcism in the Chinese church;[458] although more overt in the house churches, it also appears in Three Self churches.[459] "In fact," one researcher notes, "according to some surveys, 90% of new believers cite healing as a reason for their conversion."[460] Other estimates are more conservative, at roughly 50 percent,[461] but either estimate suggests a remarkable proportion. Such testimonies are so common that it is said that even a number of government officials recognize that many become Christians in response to claims of prayers resulting in healings.[462] Some reports concern even raising of the dead (see comment on Acts 9:40). Miracle claims spurred the growth of indigenous Chinese churches in the early twentieth century,[463] including the famous ministry of Dr. Shang-chieh Song (Dr. John Sung), who engaged in the sort of apostolic evangelism portrayed in Acts.[464] Such examples appear to reflect the Lukan evangelism paradigm in a manner foreign to traditional modern Western approaches.

d. Premodern and Earlier Modern Miracle Reports

The "West" (and areas it counts in its heritage, many of which are technically in Asia and Africa) has a long supernaturalist tradition of its own. (Rather than retrace in detail my work elsewhere,[465] I merely offer several examples and sources here.) More noteworthy for the purposes of our treatment of Luke's historiography is the observation that modern historians writing for major university presses have increasingly been reporting historical healing claims without expressing prejudice against those claims.[466] That is, historians today can allow that such claims often rest on genuine observations without feeling the need to arbitrate their interpretation.

Luke's claims about signs and attendant church growth hardly seemed novelistic to most Christian readers in history, including most believers on a popular level after the

455. Ma, "Manifestations."
456. De Wet, "Signs," 119–21; cf. a significant Filipino example in Jenkins, New Faces, 114.
457. See, e.g., Kim, "Influence"; Shaw, Awakening, 44–46; Kim, "Re-enchanted," 273–74. German theologian Jürgen Moltmann shares his own experience with Korean healing ministry in Place, 351.
458. E.g., Oblau, "Christianity in China," 414, 421; Währisch-Oblau, "Healthy," 89, 93–94, 97; Zhaoming, "Chinese Denominations," 450–51; Jenkins, New Faces, 114; Yamamori and Chan, Witnesses, 10–11, 37, 42–48, 59–60, 70; Lambert, Millions, 109, 113–18; Wesley, Stories, 37, 84–85, 133; idem, Church, 42, 47, 53.
459. Tang, "Healers," 481. Hunter and Chan, Protestantism, 151–52, note that the government expects Three Self pastors to downplay healing; although they may pray for it, they normally do not openly claim success. I cite more reports from house-church circles because more are readily available, but most accounts from either group of churches are not possible for me to verify (or falsify).
460. Tang, "Healers," 481, noting that "this is especially true in the countryside," where medical treatment is less available.
461. Währisch-Oblau, "Healthy," 87 (from the official China Christian Council).
462. Lambert, Millions, 112, 117.
463. Zhaoming, "Chinese Denominations," 440; for one specific example, see, e.g., Lambert, Millions, 112.
464. For healing claims, see, e.g., Sung, Diaries, 2, 4, 23, 27, 28, 32, 36, 40–41, 43–44, 48–49, 52, 56, 61, 74, 76, 87, 91, 93–94, 99, 104, 106, 109, 111, 116, 121, 134, 135, 140, 145, 152, 153, 155, 158, 161, 162. He was not associated with Western missionaries. Cf. Noll and Nystrom, Clouds, 214–29 (esp. 224–25).
465. Keener, Miracles, ch. 10.
466. See, e.g., Mullin, Miracles; Porterfield, Healing; Opp, Lord for Body; Curtis, Faith.

Enlightenment.[467] Our tendency is to regard most cultures in history and in today's world as "precritical" without so much as undertaking a critical analysis of any of their claims.[468] Yet such disdain for vast numbers of claims from other cultures, purely on the basis of unproved presuppositions, risks the charge of ethnocentric elitism. Most reading communities in history could accept Luke's signs as authentic indications of divine activity, and many sincere eyewitnesses claimed to see such activity. There is thus no transcultural reason to suppose a priori that Luke must have either fabricated his miracle stories or depended on sources that must have done so.

Rabbinic sources associated some Christian contemporaries with healing miracles.[469] Before the 300s, exorcisms proved to be a major factor in the spread of Christianity;[470] in the 300s, exorcisms and miracles are the most explicit cause of conversion to Christianity mentioned in early Christian sources.[471] Christians appealed to them for evidential value in public discourse. Thus Origen, arguing against Celsus and addressing pagans, in the first half of the third century claimed that Christians were still expelling evil spirits and performing cures and that he had seen some of these incidents (*Cels.* 1.46, 67).[472] Similarly, Athanasius in the 350s (*Vit. Ant.* 80) portrays Anthony confronting skeptics by challenging them either to cure these demoniacs with their ideas and idols or to just observe Christ's power; Anthony himself then cured them.[473]

Far from being merely incredulous about a distant and unverifiable past,[474] various church fathers noted that miracles and healings continued in their own day.[475] Cyprian noted that Christians were sometimes cured by baptism (*Ep.* 75.15); Tertullian

467. Successive centuries of Christians continued to report miracles (see, e.g., Irvin and Sunquist, *Earliest Christianity*, 145–47; McGee, "Strategy," 50–52; idem, "Miracles and Mission," 146–48; through history, Gardner, *Healing Miracles*, 67–92). In contrast to my work in ancient Jewish and pagan sources, I depend mainly on secondary sources to survey patristic and later Christian opinion, yet the survey should at least prove sufficient to underline the central point I am arguing.
468. Davies and Allison, *Matthew*, 2:62–65, cite various eyewitness claims through history and today and contend that such claims cannot be dismissed as merely "antique naïveté."
469. Christians healed in the name of Yeshu (*t. Ḥul.* 2:22–23; see also Urbach, *Sages*, 1:116; Herford, *Christianity*, 103–11; Klausner, *Jesus of Nazareth*, 40; Pritz, *Nazarene Christianity*, 96–97), though the rabbis often associated Christians' powers with magic or fakery (e.g., *y. 'Abod. Zar.* 2:2, §3; Urbach, *Sages*, 1:115–16; Herford, *Christianity*, 115–17; Lachs, *Commentary*, 178; cf. Deut 13:1–5). In some apocryphal stories, holy rabbis destroyed miracle-working Christians with greater magic (see Herford, *Christianity*, 112–15).
470. MacMullen, *Christianizing*, 40–41, 60–61. Cf. also Brown, *Late Antiquity*, 55, as cited in Jenkins, *Next Christendom*; "Miracles, Miracle-workers," 54.
471. MacMullen, *Christianizing*, 61–62. On the patristic church's ministry in healings and exorcisms and on its growth thereby, cf. also Burgess, "Proclaiming"; MacNutt, *Crime*, 82–88; Cho, "Foundation," 31–35. Even in Justin *Dial.* 35.8, signs perform an authenticating function. Culture apparently influenced, to a degree, the form taken by such signs (as also more recently; see, e.g., McGee, "Miracles and Mission"). Miracle reports grew from the mid-third century, in conjunction with saint veneration ("Miracles, Miracle-workers," 54; cf. analogous pagan hero veneration in the same period).
472. Kelsey, *Healing*, 136; further on Origen, see Woolley, *Exorcism*, 20–23. Kelsey notes (*Healing*, 137–38) that Origen added "that there were many instances he could set down from his own experience" (*Cels.* 1.46).
473. MacMullen, *Christianizing*, 112. On illness and healing in Athanasius, see Barrett-Lennard, *Healing*, 167–96.
474. The modern theological argument that excludes all postbiblical miracles (while accepting biblical ones; often for anti-Catholic reasons) rests on theological a prioris and philosophic inconsistency (see Ruthven, *Cessation*, 83–92; cf. 35–40, 64–71; cf. Jaki, *Miracles and Physics*, 38). The principle of historical uniformity shattered cessationism's historically arbitrary barrier between biblical and postbiblical miracles, each evaluated by different rules (and facilitating Hume's polemic against modern miracles): now people usually denied both or accepted both (Mullin, *Miracles*, 30; Lawton, *Miracles*, 58).
475. Woolley, *Exorcism*, 13–25 (here esp. 13); see evidence arranged topically in Frost, *Healing*, 71–110; Kelsey, *Healing*, 149 (citing Quadratus *Apology* frg.; Justin *2 Apol.* 6; *Dial.* 30, 39, 76, 85; Theoph. 1.13; 2.8; Tert. *Scap.* 4; *Test. an.* 3; *Spec.* 26, 29; *Apol.* 23, 27; *The Soul* 57; Tatian *Or. Gks.* 17–18, 20). Kelsey, *Healing*, 135–99, addresses claims of healing in the early Fathers; on related matters, see Kydd, *Gifts*. More briefly, De

named prominent pagans who had been cured from evil spirits and became grateful to Christians (*Scap.* 4).[476] Irenaeus offers the fullest list of signs, almost the same range as in Acts, noting that such signs were converting pagans.[477] We have no means to verify such reports today, but they do illustrate continuing belief in miracles and, in many cases, first- or secondhand claims to having witnessed them. On a popular level, Coptic texts report a range of Christian cures in Egypt.[478] Most of these are believable even from a purely naturalistic perspective, since people naturally recover from many ailments, though some appear potentially more dramatic.

Augustine initially sounded as if he thought that miracles had ceased, but he later retracted this way of putting his view. True, he said, not everyone today speaks in tongues when hands are laid on at baptism, nor are the sick *always* healed; but even when he had written his apparent denial, he knew of a blind man healed by approaching martyrs' bodies, and countless other miracles.[479] In *City of God*, Augustine noted that a depository of documents recording miracles in Hippo had been established only two years earlier, that it already had more than seventy published documents, and that he knew of many miracles not recorded among these. Another shrine in the area, having kept records longer, had a much larger collection.[480] Augustine recounts numerous healings, including some where he was an eyewitness.[481] Previously more skeptical, he had grown in his openness to continuing healings.[482] Although I abbreviate here, such reports continued through the centuries.

Documentation is more abundant in recent centuries. Despite the radical Enlightenment's influence on both deism and cessationism,[483] healing claims continued to abound—for example, those surrounding Valentine Greatrakes (1628–83)[484] and the Wesleyan revival in Britain;[485] Dorothea Trudel in Switzerland (1813–62);[486]

Wet, "Signs," 62–70, addresses sources in the period 100–400 C.E.; also Wimber, *Power Evangelism*, 157–65; bibliography in Ruthven, *Cessation*, 18–19; more generally, Porterfield, *Healing*, 43–65.

476. Kelsey, *Healing*, 136–37; on Cyprian's healing reports, further see 151. Cf. also Min. Fel. *Oct.* 27.

477. Kelsey, *Healing*, 150–51 (citing Iren. *Her.* 2.6.2; 2.10.4; 2.31.2; 2.32.4–5; 3.5.2); cf. also Woolley, *Exorcism*, 14–15; much more fully, Barrett-Lennard, *Healing*, 89–135 (on possession and exorcism in Irenaeus, see 137–65). *Apost. Const.* 8.16 contains prayers that presbyters be filled with both healing and teaching gifts (Dawson, *Healing*, 147).

478. Godron, "Healings," 1212–13. From fourth-century letters, see Barrett-Lennard, *Healing*, 44–86.

479. Houston, *Miracles*, 9; Kelsey, *Healing*, 185 (citing Aug. *Retract.* 1.13.7 [PL 32:604–5]); *On the Advantage of Believing* 16.34; *Conf.* 9.7.16). On healing through relics (perhaps as points of contact for faith), see, e.g., Gardner, *Healing Miracles*, 78–81 (others find these more theologically problematic; e.g., Saucy, "View," 116; but cf. Bulgakov, *Relics*, 1–40; Deere, *Power of Spirit*, 74); already in Scripture, unusual means of healing appear (cf. 2 Kgs 13:21; Acts 19:11–12). On the expectation of gifts, including prophecy and tongues, during confirmation and other initiation rites, see McDonnell and Montague, *Initiation*, 314.

480. Aug. *City* 22.8 (Bettenson, 1043). Kelsey, *Healing*, 185; Ruthven, *Cessation*, 30; cf. Gardner, *Healing Miracles*, 136.

481. Kelsey, *Healing*, 185; Ruthven, *Cessation*, 30; cf. Gardner, *Healing Miracles*, 136; MacMullen, *Second Church*, 65; Herum, "Theology"; for a translation, see Bettenson and Knowles, *City of God*, 1043. In *City* 22.8 he claims to have been an eyewitness to some of these supernatural healings.

482. Kelsey, *Healing*, 186–88; Gardner, *Healing Miracles*, 135–37; earlier, see Murray, Gordon, and Simpson, *Healing*, 174–76.

483. See, e.g., Ruthven, *Cessation*, 35–40, 71; cf. MacNutt, *Crime*, 145–52; Noll, *History*, 166. I highlight below some claims in Protestant circles because it was Protestants who often denied continuing miracles; for abundant Catholic claims (often with accompanying documentation), see, e.g., the scholarly study of Duffin, *Miracles*.

484. Rose, *Faith Healing*, 41–42; Robertson, "Epidauros to Lourdes," 187–88; he was "rediscovered" by late nineteenth-century healing advocates (Mullin, *Miracles*, 284n30).

485. Rack, "Healing," 145–50; Wesley, *Journal*, May 10, 1741; Dec. 25, 1742; Sept. 22 and Oct. 3, 1756; Tomkins, *Wesley*, 60, 72, 98, 106; Kelsey, *Healing*, 235; cf. Mullin, *Miracles*, 89. For the late seventeenth and early eighteenth century, see also Kidd, "Healing" (esp. 162).

486. Mullin, *Miracles*, 89; Kydd, *Healing*, 142–53; Curtis, "Character," 31–32; Hardesty, *Faith Cure*, 17–19.

and Johann Christoph Blumhardt in Germany (1805–80).[487] They proliferated still more abundantly in evangelical Holiness and interdenominational circles in the late nineteenth-century United States.[488] Such signs also appeared in Christian movements outside the West in the late nineteenth and early twentieth centuries.[489]

e. Modern Western Perspectives

Although I have been arguing here especially concerning perspectives of the non-Western world (i.e., the majority of the world) and the premodern world (i.e., most of the world's history to date), it should be observed that a significant subculture even in the twentieth-century West[490] continued to dissent from antisupernaturalistic assumptions, emphasizing paranormal phenomena and interpreting them with reference to theological or other spiritual causes.[491] From a sociological perspective, Peter Berger several decades ago challenged many religion scholars' views that the modern world no longer harbors much belief in the supernatural.[492] Thus the "lack of contemporary analogies" used to rule out supernaturalism restricts the source of "acceptable" human experience not simply to the West but (as Paul Eddy and Gregory Boyd put it) "to the *secular academic subculture within this single culture*."[493]

i. Supernaturalist Christian Claims in the Twentieth-Century West

Some Western academicians may sometimes tend to discount and ignore miracle claims not only for cultural reasons but also, unconsciously, for class reasons.[494] Many of the Western claims, especially in the first half of the twentieth century (before the spread of the charismatic movement in the mainline denominations), come from the very poor. This is not surprising, since the poor have less access to medical care[495] and are less influenced by Western academic philosophic presuppositions of antisupernaturalism; education was also less widely available in the larger culture

487. See extensive eyewitness accounts in Ising, *Blumhardt*. Karl Barth criticized Bultmann for uncritically rejecting Blumhardt's stories (Kelsey, *Healing*, 236–37), describing Blumhardt as one of his mentors (Barth, *Letters*, 251); some other German theologians also cite Blumhardt's influence favorably (Moltmann, "Blessing," 149; Heim, *Transformation*, 173–74). For the nineteenth-century healing movement generally, see Alexander, *Healing*, 8–63.

488. See Chappell, "Healing Movement," 1–80 (esp. 58–86), 192–283; Hardesty, *Faith Cure*, 27–50; Alexander, *Healing*, 18–23; Curtis, *Faith*, 1–12, 64–65, 96–97; idem, "Lord for Body"; idem, "Houses of Healing"; Opp, *Lord for Body*, 46–47; cf. further Brown, "Tent Meetings"; Baer, "Bodies"; McGee, "Radical Strategy," 74, 90–91.

489. For a Ghanaian respected for healing powers who lived 1834–1917, see Jenkins, "Reindorf"; Nigerian Anglican minister Emmanuel Moses Lijadu was associated with healings, especially during the 1895 influenza epidemic in Nigeria (Kalu, "Lijadu").

490. Some examples below are not restricted to the West (such as Hickson's global activities), but most originate in the West.

491. See esp. Eddy and Boyd, *Legend*, 74–78, and the numerous sources they cite; besides many examples below, see also Shaub, "Analysis," 118–19.

492. Berger, *Rumor*, 1–34. Religion itself has flourished despite earlier secular predictions (Cladis, "Modernity"; Butler, "Theory," 54, 60–61; Haught, *Atheism*, 58–59; Ammerman, "Sociology," 76–77).

493. Eddy and Boyd, *Legend*, 75 (emphasis theirs); see examples of miracle claims in Wilson, "Miracle Events"; most doctors affirm miracles ("Science or Miracle").

494. Cf. Hardesty, *Faith Cure*, 142–44; Cox, "Foreword," xix; Storms, *Convergence*, 29.

495. Some scholars contend that in the Western world today, dependence on legitimate medical means of recovery (which all should affirm as beneficial) has rendered us less apt to depend on the divine or supernatural intervention that many other peoples see as their only access to recovery (Winckley, "Healing," 178–79). Chevreau, *Turnings*, 16–17, emphasizes that around the world, miracles are far more common among the poor; this observation would certainly fit Lukan theology (cf. Luke 4:18–19).

at that time.[496] Many of us academicians tend to view the apostles as academically "rational" (or rationalistic) people like us; yet in some respects,[497] the Twelve, in contrast to elite leaders such as the Sadducean high priests, may have been more like leading figures in some popular healing movements appealing especially to the socially disenfranchised.

Indeed, such claims of widespread healings commanded the attention of much of U.S. popular culture at various times in the past century.[498] Likewise, in British Anglican circles, healings were associated with Dorothy Kerin[499] and James Moore Hickson.[500] Not surprisingly, early Pentecostalism, birthed in a context of Holiness and other evangelical circles praying for healings, augmented the quantity of healing testimonies.[501] By the mid-twentieth century, a significant proportion of pastors in mainline churches reported incidents that they attributed to divine healing.[502] Even popular magazines cited medical documentation for paranormal recoveries associated with prayer,[503] and some doctors provided medical verification of organic changes.[504]

II. SUPERNATURALIST CHRISTIAN CLAIMS IN RECENT DECADES

Such claims have continued in recent decades, including among the well educated.[505] Other writers have collected so many claims, albeit often on a popular level, that I

---

496. Moreover, earlier studies of vernacular health beliefs tended to focus on "marginal" nonconventional populations whereas "the enormous extent of recourse to vernacular healing strategies among educated, thoroughly acculturated, 'mainstream' groups has only recently begun to be recognized" (O'Connor, *Healing Traditions*, 18, and the numerous studies cited there).

497. I refer here to healings and exorcisms. Paul was highly educated, and we may approach him in connection with the intellectual milieu of his day; as historians or those with literary interests, many of us can identify also with Luke.

498. See, e.g., Warner, *Evangelist*, passim (e.g., 160–61, 180–81); McGee, *People of Spirit*, 83, 138, 198–99, 206, 243, 266, 275, 337–38, 358; MacNutt, *Crime*, 185–97; for a popular survey of twentieth-century healing claims, see Wimber, *Power Evangelism*, 175–85. In my own research in Keener, *Miracles*, chs. 7–12, I place greater trust in individuals' testimonies after their cure than in spontaneous claims in public healing meetings, but I mention evangelists partly because of the availability of published sources.

499. Gusmer, *Healing*, 13; Rose, *Faith Healing*, 105; Maddocks, *Ministry*, 101–2; Kerin, *Touch*, 12–15, 28–40.

500. See Hickson, *Heal*, passim (reproducing letters especially from Anglican bishops and clergy who witnessed the healings), e.g., 29, 65–66, 74–76, 87–88, 118, 121, 123, 124, 128, 129, 130, 134, 135, 141, 151, 152–53, 159, 162, 183, 191, 196, 212–13, 218, 220, 226; see further comment at Acts 9:18, 34. Local newspapers in South Africa followed up and confirmed a number of the cures in 1922 (122–23, 129–30, 134–35). Cf. more diverse opinions in Mews, "Revival," 299, 303–5, 312–19, 322–23, 328–31.

501. See, e.g., Opp, *Lord for Body*, 157–59, 193; Blumhofer, *Sister*, 83, 160–61, 171–74, 213; Gardner, *Healing Miracles*, 98–101; McGee, *People of Spirit*, 83, 138, 198–99, 206, 243, 266, 275, 337–38, 358; cf. Reyes, "Framework," 67–90. On John G. Lake, see his popular biography, Lindsay, *Lake*, though others have cited "exaggerations" (noted in Kalu, *African Pentecostalism*, 55); the reports of T. L. and Daisy Osborn run to more than twenty volumes (Osborn and Osborn, *Evangelism*, passim).

502. Braden, "Study," 225–31; cf. also Oursler, *Power*, 129–32.

503. See "Miracle Woman," 62.

504. See Casdorph, *Miracles*, passim (e.g., 25–33); Warner, *Kuhlman*, 132–34; Buckingham, *Daughter*, 185–89, 229–31. On the other side, see Nolen, *Healing*, 41–102 (esp. 99), though note responses in Buckingham, *Daughter*, 211–12; esp. Casdorph, *Miracles*.

505. See, e.g., the sociological analysis of Lewis, *Healing* (first brought to my attention by Prof. Peter Davids); regarding the same circles, see, e.g., Best, *Supernatural*, 29, 56, 77–78, 79, 88, 94–95, 101n7, 108, 124, 125, 126, 127–28, 129; Jackson, *Quest*, 13, 50, 59, 100, 116–17. For medical documentation, see recently Brown, Mory, Williams, and McClymond, "Effects." A significant proportion (more than a quarter) of my own colleagues at Palmer Seminary reported experiences of healing, either their own or of those close to them; in addition to those noted in Keener, *Miracles*, 324, 327, 351, 440–41, 444–45 (including an apparent raising), 594, 746, I received a surprising account from my dean, Christopher Hall, about a dying friend healed after two minutes of prayer in Colombia (shared with the author, May 10, 2011). I focus on reports fairly close to me in 751–56 (evaluating the statistical unlikelihood of mere coincidence in 757–59). Other reports have come to me after that book (e.g., Manohar James, Sept. 4, 2011, Nicholasville, Kentucky; Vincent, "Sociology"; Brandon Walker, Dec. 9, 2011; Lee Schnabel, Dec. 15, 2011; Alice Kirsch, April 11–13, 2012).

can refer readers to them only in passing here.[506] As historians of popular religion recognize, most sources for popular religion remain nonacademic; many are also anecdotal[507] (though the latter can be employed as case studies).[508] The work of Rex Gardner, a physician, recounts numerous healings verified by eyewitnesses, some with significant medical documentation.[509] An increasing number of sociological studies with major university presses are examining global healing movements.[510]

Though one might explain some such claims as reflecting psychosomatic elements, others—such as raisings from the dead;[511] the immediate and nonmedical healing of a child's medically attested broken neck;[512] the healing of broken bones;[513] instant and visible changes such as a withered arm growing out,[514] or more commonly the immediate disappearance of goiters[515] or other lumps;[516] and the healing of irrevers-

506. See, e.g., Warner, "Still Healed"; idem, "Living by Faith," 3; Grazier, *Power Beyond* (esp. 95–97, 125–27); Shaub, "Analysis," 118; Bush and Pegues, *Move*, passim (e.g., 51–52, 61); Neal, *Smoke*, 21–28; Reed, "Case History," esp. 39, 43; Harris, *Acts Today*, passim; Rumph, *Signs*, passim (e.g., 173–81); Pullinger, *Dragon*, 73, 123, 142, 171, 201–2, 230 (Miller and Yamamori, *Pentecostalism*, 99–105, came to unexpectedly favorable conclusions about Pullinger's activity); Chavda, *Miracle*, passim; MacNutt, *Healing*, passim (e.g., 35–36); Wimber, *Power Evangelism*, 63; idem, *Healing*, 131–32, 201; Wagner, *Acts*, 475–76; O'Connor, *Movement*, 162–63; Storms, *Convergence*, 49; idem, "View," 213; Deere, *Power of Spirit*, 31, 127–28, 145–46; Chevreau, *Turnings*, 35–36, 105–6, 142–44, 166–67, 181–82, 214; Wilkerson, *Beyond*, 139, 149–51. The official Assemblies of God archives website (http://www.ifphc.org) affords access to more than 200,000 pages of Pentecostal periodicals; a search for the word "healing" generated 7,309 sources (information courtesy of Darrin Rodgers).

507. One wider academic collection that is taking note of a number of miracle claims in Africa (where relevant to the subjects) is the *Dictionary of African Christian Biography* (*DACB*), produced by Overseas Ministries Study Center in New Haven (e.g., Negash, "Demelash"; further examples above).

508. Cf. Southall, "Possession," 232 (on anthropological studies of spirit possession); Ashe, *Miracles*, 165, 178–79. Wink, "Stories," 212, complains that "materialists" dismiss as "anecdotal" all supramaterial healing claims "however well documented."

509. Gardner, *Healing Miracles*, passim (e.g., 20–21, 31–35, 202–5); idem, "Miracles." For other physicians' claims, see, e.g., White, "Lady," 72–75, 79–84; Stegeman, "Faith"; Glew, "Experience," 81–83; physician-evaluated cases in, e.g., Heron, *Channels*; note especially Lourdes (see discussion in Marnham, *Lourdes*; Cranston, *Miracle*; treated briefly in, e.g., Nichols, "Miracles," 706–8) and other investigations approved by the Catholic Church (see Duffin, *Miracles*). Some individuals have also provided me medical documentation for healing reports (e.g., Michael McClymond, Jan. 5, 2011).

510. See esp. Brown, *Global Healing*.

511. E.g., Miller and Yamamori, *Pentecostalism*, 151–52; Ma, "Encounter," 137; Jenkins, *New Faces*, 114; De Wet, "Signs," 110–11; Khai, "Pentecostalism," 270; Zhaoming, "Chinese Denominations," 451; Kim, "Pentecostalism," 32; Sánchez Walsh, *Identity*, 43–44; Chesnut, *Born Again in Brazil*, 86; Gardner, *Healing Miracles*, 138–40; Crandall, *Raising*, 1–5 (and interviews by author, May 28, 30, 2010); Bush and Pegues, *Move*, 52, 57–60; Harris, *Acts Today*, 98–99, 101–3; Chevreau, *Turnings*, 53–56; Baker and Baker, *Enough*, 74–76; idem, *Miracles*, 89, 169; Anderson, *Pelendo*, 69–70; Antoinette Malombe, interview by author, Dolisie, Congo, July 12, 2008; Jeanne Mabiala, interview by author, Brazzaville, Congo, July 29, 2008; Elaine Panelo, interview by author, Baguio, Philippines, January 30, 2009; Iris Lilia Fonseca Valdés (Aug. 11, 2010); Yusuf Herman, interviews by author, July 10; Aug. 7, 2011 (including a follow-up phone interview with Dominggus Kenjam, translated by Yusuf, Aug. 7, 2011); see, further, comment on Acts 9:40. Some claims concern even those dead for two days or more (Bush and Pegues, *Move*, 118–19; Chevreau, *Turnings*, 54–56; Wilkerson, *Beyond*, 81; cf. Tari, *Wind*, 76–78; Miller and Yamamori, *Pentecostalism*, 152).

512. Rumph, *Signs*, 119–24; cf. healing of the functions of a severed spinal cord, attested by Dr. Douglass Norwood, interview by author, Philadelphia, June 6, 2006.

513. E.g., Williams, *Signs*, 140–41; Moreland and Issler, *Faith*, 136; cf. Casdorph, *Miracles*, 30–32; Jackson, *Quest*, 256; Lambert, *Millions*, 115–16.

514. Rumph, *Signs*, 110–11; cf. analogous extraordinary reports in Hickson, *Heal*, 85, 218; Moreland, *Triangle*, 169; over the course of several days, a disabled leg measurably growing several inches in MacNutt, *Power*, 51–54.

515. E.g., Ma, *Mission*, 65–66; Sung, *Diaries*, 58; my interview with Gebru Woldu (May 20, 2010); personal correspondence from Bruce Kinabrew (June 24, 2008); Dwight Palmquist (Feb. 2, 2009); cf. Ma, "Encounter," 136. Overnight, see Ma, "Vanderbout," 130.

516. E.g., Kim, "Prominent Woman," 205; Brown, "Awakenings," 363; Llewellyn, "Events," 256–57; Sithole, *Voice*, 58; author's interviews with Bill Twyman (Nov. 11, 2007); Eleanor Sebiano (Jan. 29, 2009); Iris Lilia Fonseca Valdés (Aug. 11, 2010); earlier, Duffin, *Miracles*, 37.

ible organic damage in a baby[517]—require different explanations. To summarize, such claims are plentiful, and in some of these cases the evidence supporting them is substantial.

Such reports do not compel scholars to adopt a uniform interpretation of them; they do, however, require us to allow, following the usual historiographic principle of uniformity, that dramatic recoveries may have occurred in the first century in the context of prayer and that early Christians might well associate these with divine activity. It is, of course, precarious, for a variety of reasons, to compare the apostles in Acts to many modern ministers emphasizing healing, even when we restrict the discussion solely to claims of healings.[518] But since we lack access to contemporary, extrabiblical accounts concerning the first-century apostles, modern analogies at least provide an additional, minimal sociological control that can be checked with modern sources.[519]

On the basis of such analogies, we can aver at the least that probably a number of people in apostolic times found themselves cured. If some others did not, these negative cases would not dampen the spreading movement's enthusiasm over the cases that were accepted and recited. Since Paul expects that apostles exhibit signs (2 Cor 12:12) and he also seems to have anticipated signs in local congregations (1 Cor 12:8–10; 14:24–26), many undoubtedly offered eyewitness claims of healings, and Luke offers only a summary of what he probably could have reported.

f. Proposed Explanations

Some scholars will accept those paranormal claims in early Christian sources for which we have analogies today (such as healings and exorcisms), yet reject those that they regard as unparalleled and that cannot easily be explained purely naturalistically, such as raisings from the dead.[520] (We do, however, have a significant number of modern claims for resuscitating dead persons; in addition to several sources sampled above, see comment at Acts 9:36–42.)[521] Such scholars' approach by analogy is sufficient to allow the possibility that most of the miracle reports in Acts could be based on eyewitness sources.

i. Natural Explanations

Because historians normally ask questions about causation, however, and theological interpreters are interested in Acts' implications of divine causation, we should note the range of possible explanatory options. Virtually everyone will regard some miracle claims as fallacious, sometimes through deception.[522] But extrapolating from a number of fraudulent claims to the conclusion that all miracle claims are fraudulent

517. Gardner, *Healing Miracles*, 25–27 (note the healing of lung scarring); a malformed epiglottis in Rumph, *Signs*, 49–52.

518. Certainly, the biblical apostles did not "specialize" in healing, but in the theology of Acts, the signs that God performed through them were meant to confirm the Lord they proclaimed.

519. On a different point (orality, literacy, and colonialism), cf. Draper, "Orality," 2: "The study of ancient cultures in the light of cognate contemporary cultures provides a useful yardstick against which to judge claims about what might have happened in antiquity."

520. Borg, "Disagreement," 232 (rejecting the uniqueness of Jesus or the first apostles); cf. similarly Price, *Son of Man*, 19–21, 131; Ehrman, *Prophet*, 196; Theissen and Merz, *Guide*, 310.

521. See also Keener, *Miracles*, ch. 12.

522. Jos. *Ant.* 20.167–68; Robertson, "Epidauros to Lourdes," 188. Also cf. the comparison of faith-healing quacks and medical quacks in Frye, "Faith Healing," 16–17; some non-Christian practitioners (Hunter and Chan, *Protestantism*, 147).

would entail a logical fallacy.[523] Some recoveries may be due to merely positive suggestion or the placebo effect.[524] In some cultures "indigenous folk-healers" offer a higher cure rate than Western medical practitioners there, especially in treating the many mental causes of ailments.[525] Nevertheless, this analogy is, at best, of limited relevance for many ailments reported cured in the NT and which cannot usually be merely psychosomatic (such as immediate cures of leprosy or most cases of paralysis and blindness). The accounts in the Gospels and Acts also do not easily allow time for the sort of "folk psychotherapy" attested in these other accounts.[526] Some writers who favor theological explanations further warn that attributing *all* medically unexplained recovery claims to exclusively psychological causes risks reductionism.[527]

Avoiding a reductionist approach, one recent academic work in the sociology of religion notes that some of the reports of miracles that the authors collected could involve spontaneous remission, psychosomatic illnesses, or exaggerated rumors, yet others defied such naturalistic explanations and would be regarded by believers as supernatural.[528] They allow that many cases may permit "*complementary* explanations"—both social and theological, both human and suprahuman elements.[529]

Although we cannot hope to reconcile such competing perspectives here, we should note that the broader approach is the one that allows all the evidence to be heard. Those who rule out miracles today based on Hume's epistemology must follow him in dismissing miracles partly on the grounds that no credible witness claims miracles; yet hundreds of millions of people claim to be witnesses, so it seems odd to dismiss their testimony (rather than critically sifting it) based on what is essentially a circularly argued presupposition. Hume's approach demands "overwhelming evidence" before accepting the validity of a miracle, but at such a rigorous level of skepticism that if applied consistently it would necessarily exclude even most nonmiraculous historical events.[530] Many scholars employ an antisupernaturalistic interpretive grid that may well dismiss significant evidence.[531] Thus one supposedly objective study in 1925, still sometimes cited as authoritative,[532] dismissed as exaggerated or deceptive 350 Pentecostal healing claims. Yet historian James Opp has recently shown the severe bias that pervaded the study, which did dismiss significant evidence for medically inexplicable

523. See Jenkins, *New Faces*, 122–23. Dr. Candy Gunther Brown offers psychological reasons that people tend to extrapolate from isolated cases of fraud to generalize about cure claims in general (personal correspondence, Jan. 1, 2011).

524. See, e.g., Ludwig, *Order Restored*, 141–59, 183; Pennington, "Relationship," 160–61; Kelsey, *Healing*, 243–77; Hirschberg and Barasch, *Recovery*, 307; Rose, *Faith Healing*, 119–34, 176; Robertson, "Epidauros to Lourdes," 188 (though cf. also 189). For religion's positive role generally, see, e.g., Matthews, *Faith Factor*; Koenig, *Medicine*; Benson, *Healing*. Many ailments may lack organic causes (Frye, "Faith Healing," 18; Markle, "Body," 16–17; Baroody, "Healing," 87–88); for the placebo effect, see, e.g., Remus, *Healer*, 110–13; Droege, *Faith Factor*, 15–33 (esp. 23–26); Hirschberg and Barasch, *Recovery*, 277–78; Beauregard and O'Leary, *Brain*, 144–50; also Beecher, "Placebo" (though some of his work has subsequently generated controversy). For the helpful insights of psychoimmunology and psychogenic illnesses, see Pilch, *Healing*; Capps, *Village Psychiatrist*; applied to the Gospel accounts, see Davies, *Healer*, 70–72; Capps, *Village Psychiatrist*, 8, 57–80.

525. Eve, *Miracles*, 354 (citing Kleinman, *Healers*, 71–82, 139–40, 366).

526. Eve, *Miracles*, 355–56.

527. Gardner, *Healing Miracles*, 29–31.

528. Miller and Yamamori, *Pentecostalism*, 152–53. They critique Durkheim's approach as too reductionist ("or at least a bit arrogant," p. 219).

529. Ibid., 158–59; cf. also 219–20.

530. Hesse, "Miracles," 40.

531. As warned by, e.g., Wink, "Write," 6.

532. Anderson, *Vision*, 93–94; followed by Hunter and Chan, *Protestantism*, 146.

cures.[533] Moreover, even some investigators who use the most stringent criterion (i.e., of no possible alternative natural explanation) have noted a few cases that meet it.[534]

The discussion "is complicated," one scholar notes, "by the simple fact that the historian must work with historical probabilities, while miracle stories are concerned by definition with the occurrence of historical improbabilities."[535] It is also limited, as noted above, by the interpreters' presuppositions. "The assessment of probability," another scholar points out, "is in no small measure a function of one's epistemic base."[536]

Those who are committed to an antisupernatural worldview can find alternate explanations for virtually any purportedly suprahuman phenomenon (and virtually everyone, including those who affirm suprahuman intervention in human affairs, recognizes that natural explanations are the more plausible ones in many cases). What I do not believe is intellectually legitimate is to simply dismiss the sincerity of all those who claim to have witnessed such phenomena or to insist that such claims could arise only gradually in legend or through a writer's imagination. Such insistence flies in the face of an extraordinary amount of evidence, denying voluminous and cross-cultural testimony[537] on the basis of a dogmatic theory forged in a very different era and context (one dependent on a much narrower range of evidence as well as on now questioned epistemological and cosmological assumptions). In view of such extensive evidence, I would consider such insistence (or the insistence that "no one in the modern world believes in miracles") as impossibly naive and misinformed.

Collections of limited firsthand observations are, technically, "anecdotal,"[538] but those who insist that they have *seen* some unusual dramatic recoveries immediately following prayer are surely no more biased than are those who, not having seen them, deny that anyone else could have seen them either. Their a priori skepticism appears plausible when forged in contexts where such phenomena are not observed, but it seems less than charitable when they presuppose universal nonexperience on the basis of their own. Whatever the value assigned to testimony in some disciplines, historiography would be impossible without it.

II. Suprahuman Explanations?

One can evaluate Luke as historian without engaging theological and philosophic disputes about the possibility of miracles, but engaging Luke as a theologian also invites the question as to whether we can agree with his interpretation of his reports. The primary critique here has been against those who deny that credible eyewitnesses can report paranormal events, not against those who simply reduce the question to one of interpretation of the observations.[539] Yet if we do turn to the interpretation of such events, the denial of suprahuman causation is, as we have noted, no more neutral a premise than its affirmation.

533. Opp, *Lord for Body*, 176–86. The committee attributed genuine recoveries to mass hypnosis (180), a favored approach of that era (166–69), or it dismissed them as the result of a prior misdiagnosis, without citing contrary evidence (187). Cf. discussion of the epistemological issues in *Lord for Body*, passim, e.g., 208–10.

534. E.g., Hirschberg and Barasch, *Recovery*, 113–15, 137 (in the latter case noting that the hematologist feared the prejudice of his colleagues).

535. Williams, *Miracle Stories*, 143.

536. Torrance, "Probability," 259.

537. Again, for the sake of space, the reader is referred to Keener, *Miracles*, especially chs. 7–12, and hundreds of sources cited there. These represent only a sample of the sources that researchers could collect.

538. By virtue of definition, paranormal events do not fit the expected "regularity" of nature and hence seem most amenable to a case study approach (cf. Ashe, *Miracles*, 165, 178–79).

539. For the latter, compare many anthropological accounts that nonjudgmentally report unusual phenomena (see the excursus on spirit possession at Acts 16:16).

The radical Enlightenment (as opposed to early Enlightenment thinkers such as Locke) excluded even the hypothesis of divine intervention from consideration in explaining the data of even the best-attested miracle claims. But should we not regard as culturally elitist an approach that simply dismisses from consideration the credibility of traditions stemming from most cultures and eras in history, on the basis of a presupposition for which those who hold it rarely seek to offer evidence? Granted, as noted, many individual claims (especially those far removed from eyewitnesses) are inauthentic or misinterpreted, but critical thinking does not require an all-or-nothing approach. Science and history address whether some people genuinely recovered; they do not need to rule out the question of why they recovered or the option of divine causation, although this theological question remains distinct from those normally asked in their own disciplines.[540] Some cases noted above are difficult to explain on naturalistic grounds currently known.

If theism is not a neutral assumption, neither is its exclusion; in fact, the vast majority of philosophers of religion addressing the question in scholarly literature today write in *support* of theism.[541] Contrary to the belief of some outside academic philosophy, theism remains an acceptable subject of discussion in that discipline;[542] simply dismissing this hypothesis as an option on the basis of uninformed antisupernaturalistic assumptions is thus intellectually questionable. Historical evidence for particular miracle claims should thus be admitted as possible instead of being dismissed as a priori impossible.[543] Likewise, Luke's theology should be engaged respectfully, whatever the interpreter's own starting assumptions.

5. Approaching Luke's Miracle Claims

Chapter 15 below will briefly examine some aspects of Luke's theology of signs; this chapter has focused on the question of healing claims and Luke's historiography. Following the approach of some recent social studies of early Christianity, this commentary will, on occasion, offer further analogies with claims of signs, exorcisms, and power encounters in various cultures today to illustrate that such claims are fairly common where such events are expected. To acknowledge the frequency of such claims is not to pass judgment on their accuracy, but it does at least bring into question some traditional critics' suppositions that any such claims reflect a lengthy period of legendary accretion; most of the claims cited above are from sources claiming to represent eyewitnesses or voices at most one remove from eyewitnesses.

Often Luke simply summarizes that many miracles were performed and reports explicitly only the most extraordinary or significant among them (Acts 5:12–16; 19:11–12).[544] For Luke to keep his Gospel and Acts to manageable size required that he include only a portion of the accounts undoubtedly available to him (just as, e.g., he does not include all of Mark or Q). There is no reason to assume that Luke invents Paul's miracles; his accounts cohere well with Paul's claims, which seem to

---

540. Not because they exclude the question of causation or personal agency but because, following Kant's dichotomy, questions about superhuman agency become delegated to theologians and philosophers of religion.

541. So Smith, "Metaphilosophy," 197, although himself not sharing a theistic view.

542. See, e.g. (among many others), Plantinga, *Minds*; Davies, *Physics*; Davis, *Proofs*; Dembski, *Inference*; Gale and Pruss, "Argument"; idem, *Existence*; Koons, *Realism*; Oderberg, "Argument"; Manson, *Design* (for both sides); Swinburne, *Existence*; Nowacki, *Argument*; O'Connor, *Theism*.

543. Cf. Swinburne, *Miracle*, 33–51.

544. On Luke's summary statements in general, see comment on Acts 2:41–47.

point to miracles pervading Paul's public ministry (cf. Rom 15:19; 2 Cor 12:12).[545] In fact, given Paul's own claims that such signs characterized his evangelizing of new areas, we have greater reason to believe instead that Luke selects only a few incidents and periods in Paul's life in which to describe miracles, from a much broader base of tradition available to him.

Whereas Luke does not describe miracles in Corinth, Paul reports these as a dramatic and observable part of his ministry there (2 Cor 12:12). Luke mentions miracles in fewer locations than Paul seems to believe that they occurred, since the latter seems to believe that miracles happened virtually wherever he preached (Rom 15:18–19). If some modern critics must attribute all descriptions of allegedly supernatural phenomena to fabrication, they ought to attribute them to Luke's sources—such as Paul, who claims to have been present and personally involved in the events—rather than to Luke himself. Despite the opportunity to parallel Paul's experience in a storm with that of Jesus, who stilled one (Luke 8:24–25), Luke does not bring a miraculous end to the storm, though he does recount that all miraculously survived it (Acts 27:24–26, 44).

If one counters that most of the signs that Paul claims are more plausible historically because they might have been effected psychosomatically or coincidentally, one could, if one wished, provide the same response for most of those that Luke reports about Paul.[546] But one should note that the expectations of both authors concerning signs (Rom 15:19) seem to have exceeded those of their non-Christian contemporaries,[547] with the possible exceptions of any signs prophets or magicians underlying the later depictions of Apollonius of Tyana and others like him.[548] That Paul anticipated noticeable miraculous phenomena in the Christian communities (1 Cor 12:9–10, 28–30; Gal 3:5) distinguishes these communities from other synagogues and religious associations in antiquity (as distinct, e.g., from temples of Asclepius, where healings were expected).[549] If modern critics have a problem with the supernatural, the same reservations cannot be attributed to early Christians.

Granted, accounts of unusual phenomena can grow over time; even a third-generation oral tradition with exact attributions could report dramatically paranormal events such as apparitions.[550] But most scholars do not date Luke this much later

545. See Caird, *Apostolic Age*, 64; Williams, *Miracle Stories*, 6–9; at length, Jervell, "Paul in Acts: Theology"; esp. idem, *Unknown Paul*, 77–95 (*pace* Bruno Bauer's sometimes uncontested 1850 claim). Schmithals's denial (without evidence) of the normal biblical sense of "signs and wonders and miracles" in 2 Cor 12:12 should not be seriously entertained (see Borgen, "Paul to Luke," 175–76, noting also that a meaning intelligible to the "super-apostles" is necessary here). Unlike later apologists using signs to validate Christianity in general, Paul often had to validate his own (see Kelhoffer, "Paul and Justin").

546. Skeptical observers and those who claim healing often differ over whether supernatural causes are at work (though some do not completely rule out the alternate explanation, e.g., *Science Digest* contributing editor William Nolen in "Woman," 36–37, addressing accurate prediction of the remission of a spontaneous tumor).

547. At least of those about whom reports remain extant. Signs workers drew dramatic attention, but usually only elite writings have survived (which means that names in philosophic schools, which were propagated by their followers, are better attested than names of typical signs workers; Jesus's movement, as a genuine movement founded by a miracle-working sage, is distinctive).

548. Most of our evidence for Apollonius is later, as already noted; Josephus's sign prophets are from a more relevant period, but they do not perform healings or, as far as Josephus is concerned, even their promised signs. For a cross-cultural approach to folk healers, see Pilch, "Sickness," 193–94.

549. For healing deities and aretalogies, see, e.g., Stambaugh and Balch, *Environment*, 43; Grant, *Gods*, 54. But as already noted, these differ from human agents of healings such as we find in the Gospels, Acts, and Philostratus's accounts of Apollonius.

550. Eunapius *Lives* 459–60. Eunapius (born ca. 345 C.E.) idealizes Neoplatonists "to compete with the biographies of Christian saints" (Matthews, "Eunapius," 569) and hence does not provide strong background for Luke's period.

than Paul,[551] and certainly, on the view of authorship suggested in chapter 11 below, a three-generation duration of transmission will not suffice as an explanation for Luke's accounts in Acts.

In the climate of current scholarship, one might do well to merely write like Josephus, urging caution with particular miracle claims while leaving open the possibility that some could occur. Several statements, however, are possible and, it is hoped, widely agreeable:

1. Most ancients believed that miracles occurred, and early Christians believed that many among their own number witnessed miracles on a regular basis.
2. Modern scholars may entertain a range of interpretations concerning such events yet regard some of them as genuine experiences for those who claim them. (That many others were fraudulent, of course, no scholar in antiquity or today would deny.)
3. The a priori modernist assumption that genuine miracles are impossible is a historically and culturally conditioned premise not shared by all intelligent or critical thinkers and, notably, not by many non-Western cultures. The assumption is an interpretive grid, not a demonstrated fact; contrary to what appeared to be the case to many intellectuals one or two centuries ago, history does not support a linear evolution of all cultures toward this position.
4. Even the vast majority of those who always reject suprahuman interpretations of ancient miracle reports do not uncritically otherwise reject the value of ancient historians who include them.
5. Without prejudice based on one's views regarding the possibility of divine causation, we must recognize that enormous numbers of eyewitnesses claim to have witnessed such phenomena, and hence many such claims (certainly regarding cures during prayer) can belong even to the eyewitness level of our sources and need not be attributed to imagination or a long process of oral development.

Whether or not in the end one shares the early Christian worldview concerning signs, it is ethnocentric to simply despise it. And whether or not in the end one despises it, one cannot objectively expunge from the record the clear evidence that early Christians (and many people since then) believed that they experienced or witnessed these phenomena.

Oxford scholar G. B. Caird long ago remarked,

> Luke has often been accused of credulity because he has packed his narrative with signs and wonders, but it would be more in keeping with the evidence to commend him for his faithful reproduction of one of the major constituents of early Christianity. For the Epistles bear their concurrent witness that the preaching of the Gospel was everywhere accompanied by exorcisms and healing and by other forms of miracle.[552]

---

551. Strauss had to date the Gospels implausibly late to maintain his view that the miracle stories were mythical; most scholars today who hold his conclusion seem unaware of his premise, which few of them share (Sabourin, *Miracles*, 64; Bernard, "Miracle," 392). These stories were undoubtedly recounted as miracles from their first telling (Dunn, *Remembered*, 672).

552. Caird, *Apostolic Age*, 64, citing Rom 15:19; 1 Cor 12:9–10, 28–30; 2 Cor 12:12; Gal 3:5; and, I believe, less clearly, Heb 2:4.

10

DATE

B ecause works were sometimes released in different drafts, as already noted, the question of Acts' date may be more complicated than that of most modern writings; that is, when we speak of Acts' date, which draft of Acts do we have in mind? For our purposes, we are interested in the author's final completed form of Acts, which is similar to the form to which we have access today (as best we can reconstruct it despite its complicated subsequent textual history).

Views on the date of Acts range widely, and scholars should be charitable in their disagreements here. Scholars have argued for various positions, and it should be clear that I respect the arguments of those with whom I disagree. Indeed, various proposals enjoy varying degrees of certainty (e.g., the approximate date I suggest could be raised or lowered a decade without conflicting very significantly with the strongest evidence I offer). Some scholars have assigned others to partisan "camps" to concisely and effortlessly dismiss their position rather than considering their arguments seriously. Aside from the fact that many scholars do not fall predictably into "camps" on every issue, "camps" often hold particular views because of a conglomeration of beliefs that rest on prior arguments or assumptions. In this case, views about date cannot be separated completely from views about authorship, views about the degree to which Luke's reports cohere with extant sources besides Luke, and the like.

No particular proposed date for Acts (among those between 64 and 90) is absolutely compelling, though the weight of evidence might incline us more toward one date than another.[1] One cannot separate the question of date entirely from the question of authorship, since one who attributes Acts to a companion of Paul would need to date Acts within the lifetime of a companion of Paul.[2] Still, a companion of Paul could have written as late as three decades after Paul's death, as some scholars have, in fact, come close to arguing.[3] Historical precedent certainly allows a substantial delay in writing; Xenophon wrote a vivid enough account of the Greek retreat from the heart of Persia long after the events he narrates, undoubtedly on the basis of notes he took during the

1. For older studies of authorship, date, and provenance, see Mattill and Mattill, *Bibliography*, 147–52, §§1940–2028.

2. If Acts merely pretends to be by a companion of Paul, the dramatic date of the narrator's world could differ from the actual date of composition (as probably in the case of Tacitus's *Dialogus de oratoribus*; see Kennedy, "Survey of Rhetoric," 33); but as I argue elsewhere, this is unlikely.

3. Fitzmyer, *Luke*, 1:53–57 (dating Luke to ca. 80–85 and Acts afterward). (Pervo, *Dating Acts*, 24, meanwhile, dates Acts long after Luke, while allowing the same author.)

events.[4] Because we do not know the author's age, the question of authorship is not absolutely decisive for the date (apart from excluding the rarer second-century proposals, which Acts' reliability on numerous key points might also exclude). Unfortunately, neither are any of the other factors (in terms of certainty).

Nevertheless, having worked through Acts examining patterns that suggest what Luke desires to emphasize, I believe that a date after 70 is likelier than an earlier date. Because charges against Paul and his death in Roman custody appear to remain a live apologetic issue (see the discussion of apologetic for Paul in ch. 7 above), however, I am also inclined to date Acts much sooner after 70 than are some other scholars. I believe that the value of Paul's legacy (and not merely its content) remained in dispute especially in the years immediately after his death.[5]

Of the four positions surveyed below, the centrist position (70s–80s), which I hold, has by far the most adherents (perhaps four times as many adherents as supporters of a second-century date); probably the early date (60s) is second in number of adherents (Pervo cites more than thirty scholars); a date in the 90s ranks third; and the second century (clustering toward its beginning) boasts the fewest adherents.[6] To my knowledge, no one dates Acts outside these ranges; the conclusion of Luke's narrative precludes an earlier date, and textual and patristic evidence a later one.

Various factors support the first-century date, and in my opinion a date closer to 70 rather than later. First, as I have mentioned, authorship by a companion of Paul is, given ancient usage, by far the most natural way to construe the "we" citations in Acts, despite the reluctance of many NT scholars to grant this observation (see comment on Acts 16:10). Second, the massive correspondences between Acts and first-century historical events, shown by Talbert and others, reflect early memory (or at least heavy reliance on early sources).[7] Third, the Pauline apologetic in Acts responds in detail to memories of fairly detailed local charges, memories that would have mattered most in the early period.[8] As pointed out in chapter 6 of this introduction, to have produced such detailed charges merely for entertainment would have undercut Luke's apologetic for Paul.

4. Brownson, "Introduction to *Anabasis*," 234–35, allowing that it might have been written shortly after his return to Greece (394 B.C.E.) but not published till ca. 370 B.C.E. (since his *Hellenica* in 380 B.C.E. must refer to another's work on the same subject).

5. Luke may have proved one of the compelling Diaspora Christian voices in his support if the dispute was serious enough to threaten it (cf. 2 Tim 1:8, 15–16; earlier, Phil 1:14–17).

6. See the extensive survey of views in Pervo, *Dating Acts*, 359–63 (following Hemer on some of them), which lists roughly thirty-one in the 60s, forty-eight in the 70s–80s, twenty in the 90s, and eleven for ca. 100 or any decade thereafter. Hemer focused on earlier sources and Pervo on later ones, though later dates remain fewer even in Pervo's list. More conservative scholars with early dates could be added, but undoubtedly, the list of those with later dates could also be amplified. I use Pervo's survey merely to illustrate the range of views, with roughly 10 percent after 100, almost twice that number (18 percent) for the 90s, almost three times that number (28 percent for the 60s) and more than four times that number (nearly 44 percent) for the 70s–80s. Tyson, "Dates," and idem, *Marcion*, ix, uses three categories: early (60s); middle (70–100); and late (ca. 110–20); with most scholars, I fall in his "intermediate" range. Others prefer the three categories of early (60s), middle (70–90), and late (95–100, based on use of Josephus; e.g., Gangel, *Acts*, 2).

7. If one argues instead for dependence on Paul's collected letters, one must ask the source of Luke's other early sources, many unusual deviations from the reports of those letters and silence about those letters (and key elements in them), and (if one thinks of a full collection) why the strong divergence from the itinerary in the Pastorals' traditions. Most works after Paul's letters do not hew to Pauline chronology and so forth the way that Acts does. See discussion in ch. 7, sect. 5, of this introduction.

8. See Keener, "Apologetic." From my examination of Luke's apologetic arguments in ibid., I would argue that the memories of civic disorder surrounding Paul's ministry are far too concrete and localized to fit a setting half a century after Paul's death (*pace* the milieu that Pervo, *Mystery*, 7, envisions for Acts).

1. In the 60s

Many scholars have argued for an early date, before Paul's death.[9] This position has sometimes been advanced even by scholars skeptical of some of the contents of the book; for example, late nineteenth- and early twentieth-century liberal scholar Adolf von Harnack gradually recognized the appeal of this position,[10] and Erwin Goodenough (much more skeptical of Acts' content) also dated it early.[11]

a. Argument from Acts' Ending

Usually scholars arguing for a pre-70 date contend that Acts ends where it does because the events had unfolded only this far at the time of Luke's writing, that is, about 62 C.E. Why else would Luke devote a quarter of Acts to Paul's trial and appeal yet not record the outcome?[12] Some ancient interpreters came to the same conclusion.[13]

Although this argument seems convincing on the surface, it is open to considerable challenge. An argument from the abrupt ending in Acts need not mean that Luke knew no more about Paul, any more than Mark's abrupt ending (Mark 16:8) means that Mark knew no more about Jesus's resurrection appearances (cf. 1 Cor 15:5–8).[14] Some ancient writers criticized historians who ended their accounts prematurely, but these very criticisms confirm that the practice was known. No less renowned a historian than Thucydides, who lived to see the conclusion of the twenty-seven-year Peloponnesian War, ends his account of the war five years before its conclusion.[15] Valerius Maximus ends his work abruptly with no genuine conclusion (Val. Max. 9.15.ext. 2). Herodian ends his history suddenly at the accession of Gordian III (*Hist.* 8.8.8), but he does not leave off at this point simply because he is writing then; *what* he writes he would not have dared write until after Gordian's fall.[16] Second Maccabees, though written after 1 Maccabees, both starts and ends at a period earlier than 1 Maccabees (and ends on a happy note); clearly, it did not bring events up to its author's day.

Granted, if Luke recorded Paul's Roman hearings in Jerusalem and Caesarea for use at a trial before Caesar, this material was clearly compiled before Paul's death. One can, however, affirm such a purpose for this material and yet deny an early date of our book of Acts; Luke undoubtedly incorporated considerable earlier material into a later, final finished product. Also, this material, in its current literary (as opposed

9. This has been argued perhaps most thoroughly and convincingly recently by Mittelstaedt, *Historiker* (who dates the bulk of the work to Paul's Caesarean custody in 57–59 C.E.).

10. Harnack, *Acts*, 293 (although he ultimately maintains the likelihood of a later date, 296–97).

11. Goodenough ("Perspective of Acts," 58) dates it to the early 60s, when controversies about Paul remained alive (cf. Phil 1:16–18), though he ascribes little historical value to much of Acts (51–59).

12. Supporting the early date, see, e.g., C. Williams, *Acts*, 18–19; Clark, *Acts*, 390; Munck, *Acts*, liv; Mattill, "Date and Purpose"; Blaiklock, *Acts*, 16; Bruce, *Acts¹*, 11, 481; Finegan, *Apostles*, 6; Arrington, *Acts*, xxxiv–xxxvi (tentatively); Hemer, *Acts in History*, 365–410; Robinson, *Trust*, 72–74; idem, *Redating*, 90; Le Cornu, *Acts*, xxviii–xxix; Gangel, *Acts*, 2; Bock, *Acts*, 25–27 (tentatively); Freedman and MacAdam, "Witness"; Mauck, *Trial*, 41–45; Delebecque, *Actes* (for Luke's first draft, essentially our Alexandrian text); particularly extensively, Mittelstaedt, *Historiker* (for composition before Paul's death, 219–21); cf. Moberly, "Planned and Shaped" (mostly completed before the story ended).

13. See Euseb. *H.E.* 2.22.1–8 (Martin, *Acts*, 319).

14. Fitzmyer, *Acts*, 52. For the appropriateness of Mark ending at 16:8, see Boomershine and Bartholomew, "Techniques"; Hooker, *Message*, 119; discussion at Keener, *Matthew*, 702n295. Abrupt endings were common, whether for literary works (e.g., Ps.-Philo, *Biblical Antiquities*; Thucyd. 8.109.1; Val. Max. 9.15.ext. 2; Lucan *C.W.* 10.542–46; Plut. *Fame Ath.* 8, *Mor.* 351B; Men. Rhet. 1.3, 367.8) or for speeches (Isaeus *Pyrr.* 80); see further discussion at Acts 28:30–31. Farmer, *Verses*, however, argues from internal (79–103) and external (3–75) evidence that the discussion for the inclusion of Mark 16:9–20 should remain open.

15. Dion. Hal. *Thuc.* 12 complains that Thucydides promised in his introduction to recount the entire war (he actually makes the promise in Thucyd. 5.26).

16. See Whittaker, "Introduction," xii–xv.

to purely forensic) form, could remain valuable in the years immediately following Paul's execution, especially if it had been associated with a broader persecution of Christians on similar charges or if Paul's reputation had been challenged in some circles (see comment on Acts 24:5).

Further, Luke could have suppressed explicit mention of Paul's death (even if his audience shared knowledge of the event) because it did not suit his larger narrative purpose. Martyrdom would not match the pattern of vindication in Roman courts that he has provided (like Josephus's focus on favorable precedents), the triumphant progress characterized in his narrative, or the parallel with Jesus's resurrection. Or (on a different view) perhaps he omitted it because the imprisonment itself parallels Jesus's passion in his Gospel but Luke and his audience knew that Paul was released at the end of two years. The period in which the story in Acts breaks off does not provide decisive evidence for when Luke finished writing it.

Thus although the arguments supporting a date before Paul's death are stronger than most other specific arguments for dating Acts, they are hardly compelling by themselves.[17] In fact, if we are correct that Acts is a historical monograph rather than a biography (see ch. 3 above), Luke is under no obligation to narrate Paul's execution; his climax is the gospel reaching the heart of the empire.[18]

Luke seems to specify a period of "two years" at the end of his record (Acts 28:30) because he and his audience share knowledge that something happened at the end of the two years—whether Paul's death or his release, to one of which his narrative points. Luke also seems aware that Paul did in fact appear before the emperor (27:24).[19] Some scholars also think that 20:25 predicts Paul's death, leaving the reader to understand that it will follow in the narrative world, just as the *Iliad* predicted, without narrating, Achilles's death (Hom. *Il.* 20.337; 24.538–40);[20] if Acts 20:25 does not predict Paul's death, it at least warns that he will not return to Ephesus.[21]

Luke probably could not have extended Acts much beyond its current length if the symmetry between his two volumes is deliberate; the number of Greek words in Acts is nearly the figure for the Gospel, which may have been the fullest length for Luke's normal scrolls. Although some writers may have completed more volumes and then revised them,[22] usually each volume in a multivolume work was complete at the time of its "publication" (Pliny *Ep.* 5.5.5). Narrating Paul's death would fit the parallel with Jesus minus the resurrection—an omission that would not end Acts on the triumphant note of the gospel's progress, consistently portrayed earlier in Acts. Luke thus need not narrate it regardless of the date assigned to his work.

b. Other Arguments for a Pre-70 Date

Scholars supporting a pre-70 date have also advanced other arguments favoring this position, drawn especially from the setting the book seems to address. One

---

17. See arguments against the early date in Witherington, *Acts*, 807. Most of these counterarguments are reasonable except the claim that Luke 1:1–4 and Acts 1:1 suggest "some time and distance" from the events; they could suggest distance from Jesus's ministry without suggesting distance from Paul's. In any case, for whatever it is worth, most scholars do place Acts after Paul's death (e.g., Conzelmann, "Luke's Place," 299).

18. See Witherington, *Acts*, 61; cf. Trompf, "Death of Paul" (emphasizing Luke's divine-retribution theme). Whatever the reasons (possibly his own failing health or death), Livy's failure to narrate Augustus's death does not mean that Augustus did not predecease Livy, who outlived him by three years (Laistner, *Historians*, 80).

19. Witherington, *Acts*, 807.

20. A view noted in Bruce, *Acts*³, 12–13n6.

21. So ibid., 13–14 (doubting the relevance of 1 Tim 1:3).

22. The last volume in Thucydides's work has been thought unfinished, though this is debated (Wade-Gery, "Thucydides").

argument is based on Luke's failure to describe the temple's destruction as past;[23] but Luke certainly implies Jerusalem's destruction (past or not; Luke 19:43–44; 21:20–24), and this omission is a weak argument from silence for a narrative that ends well before the time of the temple's destruction. (As Pervo rightly maintains, such an approach would require us to date James Joyce's *Ulysses* before World War I, since it does not mention the war.)[24]

At greater length than most, Richard Longenecker, known for his expertise in early Judaism as well as the NT, notes the following:[25]

1. Acts portrays Jews "as being both a spiritual and political power who had influence with Roman courts," a situation unlikely to obtain after 70.
2. It seems unlikely that Luke would associate Christianity with Judaism as a *religio licita* (see the discussion of Acts as apologetic in ch. 13 below) after 70.
3. Expectation of Roman justice would be unlikely after the Neronian persecution of 64–65.[26]
4. Acts employs the language of the earliest church, is correct on geographic titles, and so forth.
5. Acts betrays "no knowledge of Paul's letters," with differences from Galatians (and 1 Thessalonians).

Some of these arguments are stronger than others, though I would argue that none of them is completely compelling. First, Luke's portrayal of the influence of the Jewish elite within the narrative world need not reflect his own era; but even if it does, it does not necessarily support a pre-70 date. Judaism did apparently retain influence in some cities in Asia and presumably Greece after 70 (Rev 2:9; 3:9);[27] further, Paul usually escapes Jewish accusations in Roman courts, which one could argue reflects the very post-70 setting that Longenecker doubts (though for other reasons I believe that this picture primarily reflects Luke's historical information). Indeed, the very hostility of a number of Jewish opponents makes sense after 70 as an apologetic to Roman readers (though it was also historically true at an earlier period; see 1 Thess 2:14–16; 2 Cor 11:24; Gal 1:13; Phil 3:6).

Second, the association of Christianity with Judaism reflects historical reality, and it would profit Christians in some parts of the empire even when it might not help them in others; Revelation, in the 90s, probably offers the same association.[28] By representing the Christian movement as a pacifist form of "true Judaism," Luke could

23. This line of argument is most commonly associated with Robinson, *Redating*; cf. also Mattill, "Date and Purpose," 341–48; Igenoza, "Hypothesis" (noting that Africans, in view of their traditional context, find successful predictive prophecy less troubling than Westerners).

24. Pervo, *Dating Acts*, 337.

25. See Longenecker, *Acts*, 31–34; several of these arguments also appear in Bruce, *Acts¹*, 11; for the favorable Roman setting, see esp. Bruce, *Commentary*, 22–23; for issues current in view of Paul's approaching trial, see Vine, "Purpose and Date." Bruce, *Acts¹*, 11, claims that Jewish-Gentile relations, a focus of Acts, were less of an issue after 70 C.E., but aside from the need of Acts to record foundational history, the Johannine literature shows that the issue continued to be a live one well into the Domitianic era.

26. Kistemaker, *Acts*, 23, following Parker, "Treatise," doubts that Acts could end with such optimism after Nero's persecution. But Achaia probably escaped this persecution, and we cannot say whether Macedonia had martyrs at that time; Luke's "optimism" may also relate to his apologetic.

27. In a later period, see esp. the Sardis synagogue (e.g., Hanfmann, "Campaign"; Mitten, "Sardis," 61–62; Bonz, "Approaches"; Botermann, "Synagoge"; esp. Seager and Kraabel, "Synagogue"; Trebilco, *Communities*, 37–54).

28. The lampstands, symbols of the churches (Rev 1:20), traditionally symbolized Judaism (*CIJ* 2:117, §890; 2:128, §910; 2:131, §918; 2:137, §932; 2:142, §943; 2:147, §956; 2:149, §961; 2:165, §980; 2:234–35, §1197; 2:235, §1198); in the Diaspora (especially Asia), see *CIJ* 2:12, §743; 2:32, §771; 2:38–39, §781; 2:40,

retain the most positive associations with Judaism while dissociating the movement from negative ones. (Luke also has salvation-historical interests relevant to teaching even a largely Gentile church, like the church in Philippi, about its heritage.)

Third, expectation of Roman justice might be difficult during Nero's persecution but not necessarily afterward in stabler parts of the empire (e.g., Greece and Asia). Fourth, Acts may be accurate without being so early, especially if Luke did research and recorded it (Luke 1:1–4). Finally, Paul's letters were not collected and circulated in his churches immediately after his death and probably not until some time after 70; postulating a date before the collection of Paul's extant letters does not therefore require a pre-70 writing date. (For that matter, even if they were available, Luke, possessing other information, might not feel compelled to use them.) Luke would not have needed to depend on the letters at any date so long as he himself had known Paul (and hence lacked reason to depend on mere letters).[29]

Other scholars point to the careful detail in some narratives as a sign of an early date, but such detail might mean only that Luke kept good notes (or, in some more skeptical scholars' views, where extrinsic comparative data is lacking, had a vivid imagination). In favor of an early date, one might also argue that Luke speaks of the Beautiful Gate (Acts 3:2) and the synagogue of the *Libertini* (6:9) as if both remained standing; the present participles fit other continuing geographic realities (1:12). But they could be present simply in terms of the main verb (cf. 1:3, 6; cf. also the same passive participle in 8:6; 27:11; 28:24).

The pre-70 date is not the exclusive domain of "conservative" interpreters. Goodenough, who thinks Luke's portrait of Paul largely fictitious, nevertheless dates the argument of Acts to the early 60s because Luke would need to argue this way for Paul's greatness only in a period when there was a controversy about him.[30] But the nature of Paul's legacy continued to be disputed long after the 60s, and it would be no less possible, in any case, for Luke to use Paul as a ministry model because he was widely accepted by Luke's time than it would be that he would idealize and defend him.

c. After Paul, before 70

Some scholars have suggested a date after Paul's death but before the fall of Jerusalem. T. W. Manson argued in 1944 that Luke distinguished Christianity from Judaism because most Gentiles in the empire associated Judaism with the revolt that began in 66; such a distinction, he thought, would prove less needful after 70 C.E.[31]

One wonders, however, if Manson's observation might not be stronger than the conclusion he draws from it here; given the special tax on Jews and lingering suspicions of them in the Flavian period (some of which Josephus writes to counter), Luke would still have reason to distinguish the two groups after 70. But in light of intensified demands for civic participation in the imperial cult in some Asian cities, probably presupposed in some passages of Revelation,[32] the reverse temptation, to identify with

§783; 2:42, §785; 2:43, §787; 2:43–44, §788; 2:45, §790; 2:46, §792; 2:47, §794; 2:50, §798; 2:52, §800; 2:53, §801; 2:94–95, §855; 2:100, §862; 2:108, §873); for scores of other references, see Keener, *John*, 133–34.

29. If Luke ever visited Philippi again, he would at least know Paul's letter to the Philippians, and given his likely company in Caesarea and Rome, he was, presumably, with Paul when he wrote it. But he lacked reason to show much interest in Paul's letters, which become paramount only after the memory of Paul and his direct teaching to churches had faded.

30. Goodenough, "Perspective of Acts," 58.

31. Manson's view is summarized in C. Williams, *Acts*, 13–14; cf. perhaps similarly Marshall, *Acts*, 48 ("towards AD 70"). Usually, however, scholars date Acts either before 64 or after 70 (e.g., Kent, *Jerusalem to Rome*, 15–16).

32. E.g., Keener, *Revelation*, 36–38; Cuss, *Cult*; Price, "Man and God."

Jews exempt from the cult, might prove more likely after 90. Manson's suggestion could then point us toward a date anywhere between 66 and 90, less promising for narrowing the range of dating than Manson undoubtedly hoped. (Luke's emphasis on the Christian movement's continuity with its biblical heritage is even less helpful in pinpointing a date, since theological and apologetic reasons could account for this regardless of the date.)

Because Luke writes when Christians and the imperial authorities could have positive relations, some argue that the best range is between 70 and 90.[33] Although this conclusion is probable, it should be frankly admitted that reconstructing the date from the setting of the implied audience is precarious, especially when conditions varied from one location to another even in the same period (see, e.g., Rev 2–3).

2. After 70

Some scholars insist that Acts contains too much legendary material to stem from apostolic times,[34] but as I have argued in addressing historical questions, this premise is not only difficult to demonstrate but undoubtedly mistaken. Nevertheless, more defensible reasons than this exist for dating Acts after 70.[35]

a. Based on Mark and Luke 21

A stronger argument for a date after Paul's death follows from the usual premise that Mark wrote before Luke. Papias reports that Mark wrote what he had heard from Peter; if this language suggests that their relation is past, it probably points to a date after Peter's death.[36] If Luke wrote after using Mark, he presumably would be writing after Peter's death as well and presumably after Mark's Gospel had begun circulating among churches in urban centers. One could respond by positing again a form of proto-Luke, but without Mark it would not even have the current Gospel's structure. Lukan priority, though proposed,[37] has so far attracted few advocates. One could date Mark before what Papias suggests or date Peter's death before what early Christian tradition suggests, but then one is dispensing with the limited evidence we do have, in support of a hypothesis extrapolated from Acts' ending, which can be explained in other ways. Luke's dependence on Mark thus suggests a date after the deaths of Peter and Paul, that is, probably after the Neronian persecution.

At the same time, one should not use Luke's dependence on Mark to press for a very specific range of dates in the post-70 era. Luke need only write at a time after Mark had become widely circulated (at a minimum, several years later), and one cannot easily

---

33. Witherington, *Acts*, 793, following Walaskay, *Came to Rome*, 64.

34. Windisch, "Tradition," 310.

35. A number of "conservative" scholars (including Witherington, *Acts*, 61; D. Williams, *Acts*, 12–13; Bruce, *Acts*³, in contrast to his earlier work) date Acts after 70. I note this to respond in advance to the suspicion that dating a book a decade later than some others might bring into question the orthodoxy of one's argument (cf., e.g., Doriani, "Review," 35). I am hoping that those who date the book just a decade earlier (or later) will not ignore my entire commentary on that account!

36. Brosend, "Means," 358 (using Papias frg. 3.15). On Peter's martyrdom, see, e.g., John 21:18–19; *1 Clem.* 5.4; later, Tert. *Scorp.* 15; Euseb. *H.E.* 2.25.5–8; 3.1. Even were we to think that Mark writes under Peter's tutelage, it would have likely been toward the end of Peter's life in Rome (1 Pet 5:13; cf. Col 4:10; Phlm 24). Of course, not all scholars accept Markan priority (Farmer, *Synoptic Problem*; cf. Longstaff, *Conflation*, 218; Murray, "Conflator"; for proto-Matthew, see Lowe and Flusser, "Theory"), though not all proposed solutions for the "minor agreements" between Matthew and Luke challenge that hypothesis (see, e.g., Friedrichsen, "Agreements"). I discuss these issues more fully in Keener, *Matthew*, 8–10 (favoring Markan priority).

37. For something like Lukan priority, see Lindsey, *Jesus*, 84; Young, *Parables*, 129–63.

assign Mark a date late in the first century. Mark had to write early enough that Matthew would use his work extensively well before Matthew became the favorite of the second-century church. Indeed, Luke's dependence on Mark does not by itself require us to date Luke long after 70. Possible association of Mark with Roman persecution under Nero, and an apparently fresh memory of Claudius's attempt to set himself up in the temple for worship, could support dating Mark before 70. The close connection between the temple's demise and Jesus's parousia also suggests a date within a few years of 70. Mark could easily have been available for Luke's use in the early 70s.

Most scholars believe that Luke 21 (e.g., Luke 21:20; cf. 23:29–31) reflects the accomplished fall of Jerusalem and argue that Luke wrote Acts after completing his Gospel.[38] Granted, most of the discrete elements in Luke 21 could date from before the war of 66–70; various Jewish figures predicted judgment on Jerusalem and its temple before its demise,[39] and the language recycles Septuagintal descriptions of Jerusalem's earlier sufferings.[40] Certainly, Jerusalem's judgment was in view as early as Q, almost certainly before 70 c.e. (Luke 11:50–51; Matt 23:35–36).[41] The description does, however, more closely resemble the details of events in 66–70 than the description found in Mark (Mark 13:14–23).[42] The wars and disturbances (Luke 21:9) might be those following Nero's death, since 21:7 sounds less eschatological than the parallel texts in Matthew and Mark; certainly in 21:20, Luke clarifies Mark's "abomination" (Mark 13:14) by inserting Jerusalem's being surrounded. Granted, an eschatological section (Luke 21:25–28) seems to follow this, but the gap between Jerusalem's fall and the end (and consequently the duration of the Gentile era in 21:24) remains indefinite.

One could argue that assumptions in such a description might seem inevitable, once Roman armies surrounded Jerusalem, for someone who accepted Jesus's prophecies of judgment; hence one could date Luke to the period after 66 yet before 70. The mention of Jerusalemites being carried away captive among the nations (21:24), however, though echoing the OT, may suggest specific knowledge that the parousia did not occur when Jerusalem fell. In view of Luke's use of earlier biblical language, this argument for dating Luke-Acts after 70 is not certain, but it is more secure than most of the other arguments.

C. S. C. Williams suggests that if Acts was written after 70, it (like Luke) would surely mention Jerusalem's fall.[43] But Jerusalem's fall may be a critical presupposition of Luke's plot development in Acts (culminating in the temple establishment's rejection of Paul and his message of embracing Gentiles).[44] Paul's repudiation in the temple

38. E.g., Windisch, "Tradition," 310; van der Waal, "Temple in Luke"; Goulder, *Type and History*, 112–15; Tiede, *Prophecy*, passim; Gaventa, *Acts*, 51; Langner, *Hechos*, 35, 40–41.

39. See, e.g., *Test. Mos.* 6:8–9; Jesus son of Ananias in Jos. *War* 6.300–309; further sources and discussion in Keener, *Matthew*, 561. Cf. the difficulty of knowing how Tacitus treats the Jewish War in view of this section of his work being lost (Feldherr, "Tacitus' Jews," 316).

40. Cf. Dodd, "Fall"; Robinson, *Redating*, 13–30; Mattill, "Date and Purpose," 341–48; see now esp. Mittelstaedt, *Historiker*. Aune, *Prophecy*, 396–97n39 (to p. 176), accepts a post-70 date for Luke but remarks at how little Jesus's prophecies have been transformed to suit the new setting. Robinson, *Redating*, 28, argues that even Jerusalem's being surrounded by armies (apparently Lukan redaction) is not a prophecy after the event.

41. Cf. Theissen, *Gospels*, 203–34, esp. 220–21, 230–32, for a date for Q in the 40s; *pace* Mack, *Myth*, 84. Whether or not the correct date is the 40s, I believe that Q predates Mark (explaining several of Matthew's and Luke's agreements against Mark as simple dependence on Q where Mark abbreviated it).

42. Nor does Luke make the issue of the second coming explicit in Luke 21:7 (though paraphrasing Mark 13:4, in a context anticipating both) as Matthew does in Matt 24:3.

43. C. Williams, *Acts*, 15. Already in 1876, Abbott, *Acts*, 14, dated Acts before 70 because it does not mention Jerusalem's destruction. For data on the war of 66–70, see, e.g., Cornfeld, *Josephus*; Mendels, "Revolt" (and bibliography there).

44. Of course, Luke could presuppose his readers' knowledge of the event from Luke 21, even if not from extratextual knowledge.

(Acts 21–22) parallels Jesus's arrest for his act in the temple (although that arrest differed by its conspicuously private character, Luke 19:47–48; 22:2–6) and has the same function in the unified work.[45] If Luke writes after 70, his concluding quotation from Isa 6 (Acts 28:26–27) seems particularly appropriate: Isaiah's prophecy (Isa 6:9–10) stands in the context of Isaiah's call (6:1–8) and the announcement of Israel's judgment and devastation (6:11–13). This context might highlight two approaches, one leading through Jesus to the Gentile mission, the other leading to resistance against Rome without divine sanction, and the holy city's devastation.[46]

F. F. Bruce, who in earlier editions of his Acts commentary argued for a pre-70 date, shifted to a post-70 date in his final edition. While conceding that not all prophecies that come true are composed after the fact (e.g., those of the Dominican reformer Savonarola were not), he points to Luke (Luke 21:20) recasting Mark's "abomination" (Mark 13:14) in terms of Jerusalem's being surrounded by armies, arguing that the form in which Luke recasts prophecies of Jerusalem's demise (Luke 19:41–44; 21:20–24; 23:28–31) "presupposes their fulfilment."[47]

Luke seems to understand Jesus's prophecies of Jerusalem's fall as akin to Jeremiah's prophecies and views Jerusalem's destruction against the historical template of the Babylonian captivity (a template widely shared among Jews and Christians alike).[48] The terrible fate of Jerusalem stands behind not only Luke 21 but also 19:42–44, and probably also the warnings in 13:1–5 and perhaps also 11:50–51 with 13:34–35 (though Luke has not clarified this meaning as much as Matthew did).[49] This commentary at some passages (e.g., Acts 22:22–23) will suggest that its shadow also stands behind Acts. It is therefore difficult to argue that Luke lacks interest in these events. He simply cannot narrate them as past because they remain future within his narrative world.

Further, would Luke relate a true story about a young man who betrayed a plot in Jerusalem when this story could endanger the young man (Acts 23:22)? Perhaps Luke knew that the young man left Jerusalem before Luke left for Rome with Paul; otherwise, however, the account makes better sense after 70 or at least after the flight of Jesus's followers from Jerusalem, usually estimated to have been around 67.

b. Acts before Luke?

A few scholars argue that Acts was written before the finished version of the Gospel and hence date the completed Gospel after 70 but Acts before Paul's martyrdom.[50] Such a view requires either an earlier proto-Luke Gospel (missing Luke 21 or at least

---

45. Perhaps the fall of Jerusalem even provided Luke an additional incentive to reiterate Paul's appeal to a different path of relations with Gentiles, the rejection of which had now led to tragedy.

46. Cf. Taylor, "Jerusalem Temple," who contrasts post-70 desires to rebuild the temple with Luke's summons to seek the restoration of the divine presence through turning to Christ.

47. Bruce, *Acts*[3], 16 (see also 17). The description in Luke 19:41–42 fits both OT prophecies and what one expects generally at cities' fall (Aune, *Prophecy*, 176, citing B. Reicke and others), but Aune also thinks (176) that Luke applied it to Jerusalem's destruction. Luke 13:35 may also be relevant (Matt 23:38, at least, clearly refers to the temple, in context; Luke is less explicit about the interpretation, but it is probable).

48. Cf. Rome as Babylon (conqueror of Israel) in 1 Pet 5:13; Rev 14:8; *Sib. Or.* 5.143, 159–61 (though it refers back to literal Babylon in 5.434–46); perhaps Bar 1:1; *2 Bar.* 67:7; 77:12–79; 80:4; *4 Ezra* 3:1, 28, 31; 4Q163 6–7 II, 4–5; frg. 8–10. Many in the Roman Empire believed that literal Babylon was now ruined (Pliny E. *N.H.* 6.30.121–22), though others differed (Philost. *Vit. Apoll.* 1.25), and "Babylon" could still be employed figuratively for Parthia (Lucan *C.W.* 1.10). Among the rabbis, cf. the four kingdoms (e.g., *Sipre Deut.* 317.4.2; 320.2.3; cf. Dan 2:37–45; 7:3–8; *2 Bar.* 39:7; *Sib. Or.* 8.6–11).

49. It may also stand behind Luke 19:45–46 and 23:45 (see, e.g., comment in Keener, *John*, 524–27; idem, *Matthew*, 686–87; Kingsbury, *Christology*, 132; Matera, *Kingship*, 139).

50. C. Williams, *Acts*, 14–15. See also discussion in Bouwman, "'Livre' et date."

the historically accurate divergences from Mark 13) or that Luke wrote the Gospel later, adding the connection between volumes (Acts 1:1–12, esp. 1:1) only to a later edition of Acts. But although one might add one's introduction only to one's finished work, it seems strange that Acts would sit for nearly a decade before being sent to the dedicatee. (Then again, Luke could have sent him the various editions, as ancient writers sometimes did.) The consistent length of the two volumes also tentatively argues against their finished composition at radically different times. Occam's razor (the principle of logic that favors the simpler solution) also argues against it, though some have rightly warned that Occam's razor is too dull for cases where evidence is too slender.

c. Majority Range

Most scholars today suggest dates between 70 and 85, with some as late as 90.[51] This range of dates in the early Flavian period, before Josephus's publications but when works similar to those of Josephus (and his competitors) were flourishing, is not unreasonable as a guess. Harnack originally suggested a composition date in the time of Titus or early in Domitian's reign.[52]

Many scholars who maintain that a companion of Paul wrote Acts nevertheless hold that he wrote after Jerusalem's destruction, hence within this range.[53] Fitzmyer is among the scholars who prefer a date in the 80s, although his explicit arguments specifically support only a post-70 date.[54] Witherington thinks that Luke depends on fresh eyewitness sources but that Acts also reflects the benefit of sufficient hindsight, and hence he suggests a date in the 70s or early 80s.[55] Dunn suggests a date in the 80s; although he believes a former companion of Paul wrote Acts, he dates it after the Gospel and the Gospel after Mark, which he dates in the late 60s or early 70s. He also believes that Acts reflects "concerns of the post-Pauline generation."[56]

d. Soon after 70

If we date Mark before 70,[57] however, and if Luke would have had early access to this Gospel in Greece or Rome, we need not date Luke's Gospel much after 70; the church was not so large that a work such as Mark would necessarily take long to circulate, once it achieved some popularity. (Matthew, probably writing in Syria

51. For a consensus date in the 70s–80s, see, e.g., Zwiep, *Ascension*, 168; Puskas and Crump, *Introduction*, 149; cf. Chance, *Acts*, 5. Powell, *Acts*, 37, suggests that "the great majority of scholars date Acts somewhere around A.D. 80–85, with the admission that this cannot be established with precision."

52. Harnack, *Acts*, 290–97 (sometime after 78 C.E.; he does allow [296–97], however, as early as the beginning of the 70s).

53. E.g., Faw, *Acts*, 19; Ehrhardt, *Acts*, 4; Polhill, *Acts*, 27–31; Jervell, *Apostelgeschichte*, 86; and scholars listed below.

54. Fitzmyer, *Acts*, 54–55 (adding in favor of his specific date in the 80s only the observation that many opt for 80–85, and he finds no reason to reject that). A date in the 80s is most common (e.g., Juel, *Promise*, 7; Sterling, *Historiography*, 329–30), sometimes alongside an insistence on trustworthy sources for the 40s and 50s (Martin, *Foundations*, 66).

55. Witherington, *Acts*, 165–72. Bruce offers the same suggested range (*Acts*[3], 18). Hengel, *Peter*, 91, suggests 75 to 85.

56. Dunn, *Acts*, xi. Wayne Meeks and others think that Luke fictitiously raises Paul's status to fit a later generation, but Paul's own letters show sufficient contact with the elite to question this premise (e.g., Rom 16:23; see Gill, "Élites," 105–18, esp. 109–12, 117–18).

57. Noting that he fails to distinguish as clearly as his successors, especially Matthew, between the temple's desolation and the Son of Man's return. A dating of Mark to ca. 64 (Bruce, "Date of Mark," 78) or around the outbreak of the war (Anderson, *Mark*, 26) allows sufficient time, though we cannot know Mark's date with certainty. Because Mark seems to expect the Romans to erect an image of the divine emperor on the site of the temple, Collins, *Mark*, 14, dates the work before 70 (albeit just barely before 70).

a few years after Luke, had access to many of the same sources.) Nor need we allow a great lapse of time between Luke's Gospel and Acts, especially if Luke had been collecting notes for several years. Hengel and Schwemer argue that Luke mediates between Paul "and the supporters of the earliest [Jerusalem] community" (cf. Gal 2:9–12); this would hardly be necessary "long after 70."[58]

Theissen suggests that the historicizing language about Jerusalem's fall in Luke 21 addresses the false eschatological expectations that surrounded Jerusalem's fall (cf. Luke 21:8–9; Mark 13:14, 21). Thus he dates Luke's Gospel to shortly after 70. Because he, curiously, reads Luke's prologue as claiming to belong to the third generation after Jesus (in fact, it suggests instead that eyewitnesses remained available for Luke's investigation), however, his "shortly" would be longer than ours: Theissen suggests that the Gospel should be dated in the 80s or 90s.[59] Without this unusual reading of the prologue, however, Theissen's own evidence could point us to a date in the early 70s, in the very wake of Jerusalem's destruction.

Luke probably writes after Nero's death and publishes shortly thereafter—after the war had begun and, in my view, probably after 70. This would make sense of the emphasis on Jewish (as opposed to Roman) rejection of the message; although Luke emphasizes continuity with Israel's heritage, a distinction from current Judean politics would be helpful in a largely Gentile setting after 70. Granted, Luke's notes were probably available much earlier, and the work probably went through various "editions" (originally of one or a few copies each) with the feedback of audiences (fitting the normal process of "publication"), some of them possibly before 70. Nevertheless, we lack evidence that compels us to accept a completed, published work before 70.

Luke favors more realized eschatology than some other early Christian authors, such as Paul, Matthew, or the author of Revelation (see ch. 15, sect. 4). Nevertheless, *pace* Conzelmann's view of Luke's eschatology, Luke might believe that Jesus's generation will see the end (Luke 21:31–36); one might speak of the generation remaining so long as some were still living (as some presumably were; cf. the beloved disciple in John 21:23; perhaps also Luke 9:27, but like Mark, Luke applies this saying to the transfiguration). Luke appears to expect the prophesied events fairly soon after the temple's destruction (Luke 21:5–28, esp. 21:20–28), which would fit dates proposed for his work between 66 and 75 c.e. His approach appears different from that of Matthew (see the clear differentiation of questions in Matt 24:3), who may be writing later. Nevertheless, Luke's "captive among the nations" (Luke 21:24) suggests a date after 70 or 73. A date in the mid-70s thus seems reasonable.

Given Luke's emphasis on Jerusalem's judgment, his portrayal of the large Jerusalem church vis-à-vis Paul's mission, and various other elements treated in the commentary, I am inclined to think that the destruction of 70 is past but well remembered. More important for dating, Luke's strong apologetic for Paul (see ch. 7, sect. 1.a) makes most sense when his memory burned most brightly yet remained most susceptible to challenge—that is, not many years after his death or after the Neronian persecution, with which it was likely connected. I thus view Haenchen's estimate that Luke prepared Acts about 75 c.e.[60] as a reasonable one, give or take a few years.

---

58. Hengel and Schwemer, *Between Damascus and Antioch*, 10, adding, "At the time Luke wrote, it was still well known who Peter, John, James, Stephen, Paul, Philip, Barnabas or even Mark had really been. Around 110 or 120 this was no longer the case in the same way."

59. Theissen, *Gospels*, 280.

60. Haenchen, *Acts*, 86 (this is his date for preparing Acts, not necessarily its publication or circulation).

3. After 90

Those who date Acts after 90 usually do so because they argue for dependence on Josephus.[61] Thus, for example, Acts' depiction of Paul employs some apologetic motifs also found in Josephus[62]—though these are conventional enough apologetic motifs to undercut any need for dependence.[63] It would be difficult, however, for Luke to have made direct use of Josephus; Josephus's *Antiquities* probably was issued about 93/94,[64] and the copies of its twenty books would have been quite expensive and not readily available soon after their publication to nonelite persons.

In the final analysis, it is highly unlikely that Luke depends on Josephus. The strongest argument for dependence is Luke's citation of Theudas and Judas. Yet it seems unlikely that Luke would have read Jos. *Ant.* 18–20, used barely any of it, and then gotten wrong the one point most likely drawn from it, if he was dependent at all.[65] The other matters that he could have taken from Josephus were widely known.[66] Josephus did not compose his reports of Theudas or Judas from thin air, and oral or written reports about these leaders would have been available to Luke as well as to Josephus. Josephus completed his *Antiquities* no earlier than 93 C.E., but Luke's sometimes positive portrayal of Roman administrators probably would make less sense in the later years of Domitian's reign.[67]

Bornkamm dates Acts in the 90s because it is later than Luke, which is later than Matthew and Mark, which, he avers, are both post-70.[68] But even if Mark is post-70 and Luke is the latest of the Synoptics (I prefer a pre-70 date for Mark and think that Matthew, like John, addresses a Jewish Christian situation slightly later than Luke), this sequence provides us no exact chronology for pushing Luke-Acts so late.[69] If, as many commentators (including myself) believe, Luke was a companion of Paul, a date before 90 is more likely (though a post-90 date would not be rendered impossible).[70]

61. E.g., Pervo, "Dating Acts"; idem, *Dating Acts*, 149–99 (esp. 152–60, on Theudas and Judas); idem, *Mystery*, 4 (a "very strong probability"); idem, *Acts*, 12. Against this position, see, e.g., Fitzmyer, *Acts*, 52; Barrett, *Acts*, 2:xliii; Ehrhardt, *Acts*, 2–4; also Conzelmann, *Acts*, xxxiii (though he dates Acts to 80–100).

62. Gnuse, "*Vita apologetica*," noting their shared experiences of education, shipwreck, and dream-revelation. Yet Paul's own letters do imply education and clearly speak of shipwrecks (2 Cor 11:25) and revelations (2 Cor 12:1–7)!

63. *Any* such details would count for honor in an apologetic biography *insofar* as they were true. Thus, e.g., Paul (Phil 3:5) and Josephus are both Pharisees; but only Josephus is a priest (Paul was from a different tribe; Rom 11:1; Phil 3:5). By 90, Paul's legacy was probably also more secure, requiring less apologetic (*1 Clem.* 5.5; 47.1; Ign. *Eph.* 12.2; *Rom.* 4.3; Poly. *Phil.* 3.2; 9.1; 11.2–3; Papias 28.1).

64. With, e.g., Wandrey, "Iosephus."

65. Pervo concedes that a mistaken citation of Theudas, who acted more than a decade after the speech's "dramatic date," could have occurred as early as the 60s (*Dating Acts*, 310).

66. With C. Williams, *Acts*, 19–22; Bruce, *Acts¹*, 24; Packer, *Acts*, 13, 48. Luke often conflicts with Josephus where they address the same topic (Bruce, *Acts¹*, 25; Hemer, *Acts in History*, 95; Gempf, "Speaking," 288).

67. On probable Christian suffering in at least some locations during Domitian's reign, see, e.g., Söding, "Widerspruch"; Jones, *Empire*, 323–24; Hemer, *Letters*, 7–11; Keener, *John*, 178–79; cf. Dio Cass. 67.14.1–2; Euseb. *H.E.* 3.17–18. Contrasting Luke's vision of the empire with John's, cf. Kim, *Caesar*, 180–90.

68. Bornkamm, *Paul*, xx.

69. D. Williams, *Acts*, 12, notes against a late date that Luke's Christianity remains spontaneous and Spirit-led, not very institutional. This may be right, but it is not clear that the church had become stratified everywhere by the 90s; Johannine literature betrays no sign of such stratification (though some think that Diotrephes in 3 John 9 claimed a hierarchical role; see the summary of this position in Brown, *Epistles*, 733–34, although Brown disagrees with it), in contrast to Ignatius a few decades later.

70. Aged people could write memoirs with accuracy; see, e.g., Seneca the Elder (esp. *Controv.* 1. pref. 2–4; 9. pref. 1); for other elders with sharp minds, see, e.g., Cic. *Brut.* 64.229; Val. Max. 8.7.1; 8.7.ext. 5, 9–13; Philost. *Vit. soph.* 1.9.494; 2.21.604; Eunapius *Lives* 482 (also Keener, *John*, 102–3, for numerous examples). My most regular correspondent, and one of the sharpest, at the time of this book's editing is in her nineties.

4. Second Century

A smaller minority of scholars date Acts to the second century, sometimes as late as the mid-second century.[71] Some do so because they believe that Luke depends on, or was writing a preface for, Paul's collected letters, but this premise is unlikely and would not, in any case, necessarily demand a second-century date (see ch. 7 above). J. C. O'Neill thinks that Luke's presuppositions place him in the generation of Justin Martyr[72]—a view that I believe either underestimates the continuity with Judaism in Luke (see ch. 14 of this introduction) or overestimates it in Justin. John Knox thinks that Marcion shortened the earliest form of Luke whereas our present Luke-Acts (which he dates after Marcion) expanded it.[73]

Such arguments have not, however, persuaded many,[74] and such a late dating hardly seems likely. In addition to the relevance of arguments already lodged against a date in the 90s above, one would hardly expect a mid-second-century work to recollect so many historical details (such as first-century offices in various locations) so accurately, especially in a period that produced many novelistic acts rather than historical monographs.[75] C. K. Barrett observes that Acts reflects the character of the provinces in the first rather than the second century; the early second-century church may not have known what to make of Acts, but it did know the work.[76] Luke's very probable independence from Matthew is also difficult to explain with a second-century date, when Matthew flourished as the most popular Gospel.[77] Luke's lack of emphasis on a number of Pauline theological themes (see the discussion in ch. 7 above) that must have become widely known once Christians began collecting Paul's letters (cf. allusions in *1 Clement*; 2 Pet 3:15–16), his pre-Ignatian

71. E.g., Townsend, "Date," 58; Pervo, "Dating Acts"; Price, *Son of Man*, 33; Parsons, *Acts*, 3, 17 (ca. 110 C.E.); Walker, "Portrayal" (anti-Marcionite); for a post-Marcionite date, Tyson, "Date of Acts" (though on some approaches to Marcion this thesis might date Acts close to a period when Irenaeus, writing perhaps three decades after Marcion, was defending the four Gospels!).

72. O'Neill, *Theology*, 175. Justin opposed Marcionite teaching, although this part of his polemical work is now lost; see Efroymson, "Connection," 105; Chadwick, "Defence," 290; cf. Stylianopoulos, *Justin*, 20–32. Justin allows for more continuity with the Torah than in Barnabas or Marcion (see Osborn, *Justin*, 5, 160–61), but by prioritizing some parts of the law over others (Stylianopoulos, *Justin*, 51–52, 58–68, 74) and presenting Christ as a new law (*Dial.* 11).

73. Knox, "Reflections," 112. Because he believes that Marcion's date is unknown, Knox requires the finished product of Luke-Acts to be dated no later than 125 C.E. ("Acts and Corpus," 286). Yet the "formidable" nineteenth-century history of interpretation that Knox (followed by Tyson and others) cites in support of his approach to Marcion and Luke-Acts may depend on Knox's misreading of the sources (see Roth, "Marcion's Gospel").

74. See the summary in Bruce, *Acts³*, 18–19n21. The nearly mid-second-century position is rare enough for Powell, *Acts*, 36, to attribute it to "an occasional scholar." For one careful yet firm response to the thesis that Luke expands Marcion's Gospel, see Hays, "Marcion." But although the second-century view remains a distinctly minority position, it has been growing in some scholarly circles especially since recent arguments by Pervo and Tyson.

75. In contrast to Roman historians, Luke had no annals and perhaps, in Acts, no prior written sources from which to draw.

76. Barrett, *Acts*, 30–48, esp. 48; cf. also lxix. C. Williams, *Acts*, 2, finds allusions in 2 Tim 3:11 and the gnostic *Gospel of Truth*; Conzelmann (*Acts*, xxvii–xxxii), by contrast, finds attestation in the Apostolic Fathers but not in the Pastorals. Most patristic allusions (e.g., Justin *1 Apol.* 39.3; 50.12; *2 Apol.* 10) need not, however, establish a first-century date for Acts; Luke uses Mark (and acquaintance with Paul) without a fifty-year gap. (But cf. earlier *1 Clem.* 2.1, unless it independently attests the agraphon in Acts 20:35.)

77. Theissen and Merz, *Guide*, 32. Against those who argue that Luke depended on the completed version of Matthew (as opposed to a proto-Matthew much like other scholars' Q), material like the tensions between the infancy narratives and the two authors' divergent treatments of Judas's death (Matt 27:3–10; Acts 1:18–19) make such dependence well-nigh impossible.

ecclesiology, his lack of interest in Gnosticism, and other factors also militate against a later date.[78]

In the first drafts of this commentary, I ended my cursory treatment of second-century proposals here, focusing on the primary views of pre-70, 70–90, and the 90s, since very few scholars today date Acts in the second century. Since that time, however, two noted Acts scholars (Richard Pervo and Joseph Tyson) have published monographs, roughly simultaneously, arguing for a second-century date.[79] They are themselves aware that they are defending a relatively rare position; Tyson considers 70–100 the "consensus dating" of Acts scholars, complaining that few scholars today bother to question or defend it "except among those who would favor a date in the sixties."[80] Although this view attributing Acts to the second century remains relatively rare and just a few years ago could have been viewed as relatively idiosyncratic outside this circle of scholars, a view is not rendered incorrect simply by virtue of being rare, and hence it merits at least some concise engagement here.[81]

Some scholars draw attention to patristic evidence and date Acts no earlier than its first attestation in those sources. Admittedly, extant sources before Irenaeus (and, more fully, John Chrysostom) make little use of Acts;[82] Barrett attributes Acts' neglect in the second century to its apparent irrelevance until the Marcionite controversy.[83] Tyson, by contrast, believes that it was not simply irrelevant until Marcion but became relevant to that controversy because it was written directly to meet the Marcionite challenge.[84] Reconstructing dates based purely on reconstructed external situations is usually hazardous, although understandably often hazarded; as noted above, few have been persuaded by the anti-Marcionite position, and (I believe) with substantive reason. (It is interesting that some patristic writers, such as Tertullian, seem to have almost avoided Acts in their conflicts with Marcionites.)[85] Because I have mentioned the Marcionite case above,[86] I will focus here on Pervo's arguments based on patristic evidence.

The earliest argued piece of patristic evidence that may attest knowledge of Acts comes from Poly. *Phil.* 1.2:

78. With Witherington, *Acts*, 61–62 (also arguing from the "we" passages that Luke sees his own time as a continuation of Acts); cf. Wallace and Williams, *Acts*, 11 (contending for a date before Paul's letter collection, on which Ignatius drew).

79. Pervo, *Dating Acts*; Tyson, *Marcion*; cf. Pervo, "Dating Acts"; Tyson, "Dates."

80. Tyson, *Marcion*, ix; the survey of views, 1–23 (though focusing on those who support a second-century dating).

81. Views also change over time; Pervo, *Dating Acts*, 2, is aware that an antithesis against a previous consensus tends to readjust the resulting center or synthesis.

82. Jones, "Rejoinder," thinks that the Jewish Christian source of *Ps.-Clem. Rec.* 1.27–71 comments on—and seeks to supplant—the imagery in Acts. Our extant material, however, appears later than Irenaeus. For a full survey of possible references or allusions to Acts in the first six centuries, see Bovon, "Reception"; most relevant here are his observations regarding Irenaeus's sources (68), the mid-second-century *Epistula apostolorum* (69), the Muratorian Canon and Western text (70), and some other possibilities that some have suggested (71–72).

83. As noted by Pervo, *Dating Acts*, 331.

84. Tyson, *Marcion*, 50–78 (see esp. 73, 76–78); idem, "Wrestling" (emphasizing the pro-law Paul of Acts). Although one can read Acts this way, it is not the only way, and it makes Luke's accuracy on much earlier matters of testable detail remarkable. He suggests that a pre-Marcionite Gospel of Luke began with Luke 3:1; Marcion's version of this Gospel followed; then the author of Acts created the present canonical Luke (adding 1:1–2:52 and other material) and later wrote Acts, publishing the work as an entirety ca. 120–25 C.E. (Tyson, *Marcion*, 119–20). Without positing a definitive date, Gregory, "Reception of Acts," 64, observes that the theological affinities discerned might mean not that Acts was *written* in the early second century but that it was read then.

85. From an index of Scripture citations in Tertullian, I estimate that several of Tertullian's works cite the Gospel of Luke about twice as often, and Matthew about three times as often, as Acts. Yet Tertullian cites Luke closer to sixteen times his Acts citations in his anti-Marcionite work.

86. Tyson, *Marcion*, xi, 76–77, is explicit that his views echo those of Knox, who was his mentor.

Poly. *Phil.* 1.2	Acts 2:24
ὃν ἤγειρεν ὁ θεός	ὃν ὁ θεὸς ἀνέστησεν
λύσας τὰς ὠδῖνας τοῦ ᾅδου	λύσας τὰς ὠδῖνας τοῦ θανάτου

The language is unusual and not found in this form before Polycarp except in Acts, another early Christian document.[87] Unless one supposes that Luke and Polycarp draw on a common tradition here (which is possible but, against the principle of Occam's razor, introduces an unnecessary level of complexity), we have a likely allusion to the language of Acts in the early second century. Pervo accepts this as a possible but not certain allusion;[88] because he will date Acts about 115, an allusion in Polycarp would not necessarily undercut his proposed date.[89] Beyond these connections, at a very early date *1 Clem.* 17.1 and Polycarp *Phil.* 6.3 apparently betray knowledge of Acts 7:52, which also mentions prophets foretelling Jesus's first "coming" (using ἔλευσις, a term that is, apart from minor textual variants, a NT hapax).[90] It would be difficult to demand patristic sources earlier than these, since these are among the earliest.

Perhaps also relevant, because the longer ending of Mark betrays familiarity with Luke's Gospel,[91] it seems fair to look for allusions to ideas in Acts as well. Of these, several are probable or possible (cf. esp. Mark 16:20 with Acts 14:3; perhaps Mark 16:18a with Acts 28:3–6; perhaps Mark 16:19 with Acts 1:11).[92] Some date this ending to the period 100–140 C.E., which would provide quite early evidence for allusions to Acts.[93] Certainly the longer ending of Mark circulated by the late second century, used in Tatian's harmony of the Gospels (ca. 170) and attributed by Irenaeus to Mark (ca. 180).[94] The *terminus a quo* for this addendum to Mark is, however, uncertain, making the allusions less decisive than certainly early sources such as Clement and Polycarp.

Some scholars, however, who favor a second-century date are more impressed by lack of evidence, which they interpret as negative evidence. Pervo argues, for example, that Eusebius cites Papias regarding only Mark and Matthew, not Luke or John.[95] Given our small corpus of Papian material, however, this could well be coincidence and is surely an argument from silence. Pervo contends that Papias

87. The conjunction of the verb ἔλυσας and the noun ὠδῖνας in Job 39:2 LXX is hardly comparable, and the correspondence here is close.

88. Pervo, *Dating Acts*, 17–20.

89. Though a date so early should render Tyson's Marcionite approach untenable, Tyson could counter that this part of Acts belonged to a pre-Marcionite version. Occam's razor, however, prefers fewer necessary conjectures, the multiplication of which could be used to defend most hypotheses.

90. Charles E. Hill pointed this likelihood out to me in personal correspondence (Jan. 18, 2010). There is also a possible but not necessary conceptual allusion in *Ep. Diogn.* 9.1 to the idea in Acts 14:16; 17:30 (Hill, *Polycarp*, 148), which Hill believes may well be the work of Polycarp (ibid., 97–165). Because the longer ending of Mark betrays familiarity with Luke's Gospel (cf. Mark 16:9 with Luke 8:2; Mark 16:12–13 with Luke 24:13–35), it may well allude to ideas in Acts as well (cf. esp. Mark 16:20 with Acts 14:3; perhaps Mark 16:18a with Acts 28:3–6; perhaps Mark 16:19 with Acts 1:11; the tongues of Mark 16:17 may be more general—see comment on Acts 2:4 and McDonnell and Montague, *Initiation*, 314). The *terminus a quo* for this addendum to Mark is, however, uncertain, making the allusions less helpful than definitely early sources.

91. Cf. Mark 16:9 with Luke 8:2; Mark 16:12–13 with Luke 24:13–35. For other connections, see, e.g., France, *Mark*, 686.

92. France, *Mark*, 687, suggests that Mark 16:17–18 alludes to signs in Acts and 16:20 summarizes Acts. The tongues of Mark 16:17 may reflect knowledge of more general practice (see comment on Acts 2:4 and early Christian tradition in McDonnell and Montague, *Initiation*, 314).

93. Bratcher and Nida, *Handbook on Mark*, 506, noting that it may have been known by Justin (*1 Apol.* 45) and dating Tatian's *Diatessaron* to 140 C.E. Scholars usually date the *Diatessaron* later, however.

94. Anderson, *Mark*, 358.

95. Pervo, *Dating Acts*, 20.

either did not know Acts or disagreed with it, "for he twice contradicts it."[96] The "contradictions" do not, however, amount to much, by the standards of the Apostolic Fathers. First, Papias frg. 3 differs from Acts and Matthew regarding Judas's death.[97] Yet the early fathers certainly knew Matthew, whom Papias's account also contradicts; Papias simply had more traditions from which to choose than the two preserved in the NT.

The second "contradiction" proves even less compelling. Papias frg. 11.3[98] claims that the Jews killed both James and John the evangelist—fitting Mark 10:35–40, Pervo reasons, but not Acts 12:2. Yet that Jewish people authored the persecution fits Acts 12:2 more clearly than it fits Mark 10:35–40, and Papias, who is merely being summarized, does not specify that the two died together. Arguing from Papias's failure to cite Acts is thus an argument from silence, since Papias was heir to multiple traditions of the apostles and preferred oral to written sources (frg. 3.4; 7.2). Moreover, Papias's knowledge of Justus Barsabbas (Acts 1:23; Euseb. *H.E.* 3.39.9–10) probably either reflects Acts or, if derived from Philip's daughters, as Eusebius says, provides independent support for tradition reported in Acts.

Pervo also points out that Hegesippus (ca. 110–80) reflects no knowledge of Acts though he is interested in the early bishops of locations (for which Eusebius cites him) and was in Rome about 160–170.[99] Against making so much of the silence here, we have primarily Eusebius's citations of Hegesippus, and Eusebius need not rely on Hegesippus to provide information that he already has in Acts! Even for some time afterward, church fathers were more interested in the Gospels, especially Matthew, and Paul's letters than in Acts.[100] This interest indicates a preference for use, however, rather than identifying exhaustive knowledge of relevant works.

Pervo might be correct about Justin's failure to cite Acts,[101] but the evidence here is ambiguous. Haenchen finds possible echoes of Acts in Justin *1 Apol.* 39.3 (recalling the idea, though not the words, of Acts 4:13), 49.5 (alluding to Acts 13:48), and 50.12 (using Luke 23:49; 24:25, 44–45 and wording from Acts 1:8).[102] Acts is not Justin's favorite book, but he may know of its content, directly or indirectly.

96. Ibid.

97. Ibid., 378n52. Too recent for engagement here, MacDonald, "Papias," suggests Luke's dependence on Papias.

98. Pervo, *Dating Acts*, 378n52. My edition (Lightfoot, Harmer, and Holmes) identifies it as frg. 5.1.

99. Pervo, *Dating Acts*, 20. Others date his sojourn in Rome slightly earlier.

100. See, e.g., Dibelius, *Studies in Acts*, 88–89.

101. Pervo, *Dating Acts*, 20–22.

102. Haenchen, *Acts*, 8. Pervo doubts the allusion to Acts 1:8 ("power" appears in Luke 24:49; but "receiving power" does sound as if it draws on Acts 1:8; moreover, unless one accepts Pervo's separation of Luke from Acts [Pervo, *Dating Acts*, 24], Justin's knowledge of the Gospel would likely presuppose the existence, sometime not many years after it, of Acts). For uncertain but not impossible allusions to Acts (3:14; cf. 26:29), see Justin *Dial.* 8; 16. Justin seems more interested in Jesus's sayings (see Bellinzoni, *Sayings*), which he may quote from memory (see Kaye, *Apology*, 104–8). (He might also know a harmony [Osborn, *Justin*, 126–28], testimonia [115–17], Parkes, *Conflict*, 99; Chadwick, "Defence," 282; Barnard, *Justin Martyr*, 74], postcanonical material derived from the Synoptics [Bellinzoni, *Sayings*, 139; cf. 21, 140], Barnabas [Williams, *Justin Martyr*, xxi–xxii], and some source shared with the *Pseudo-Clementines* [Kline, "Sayings"]). He has much less interest in Paul (though some find Paulinisms [Stylianopoulos, *Justin*, 96] and contacts with 2 Thessalonians [Barnard, *Justin Martyr*, 63]). Even Justin's complete silence about Acts would not, however, argue that Acts did not exist. For an analogy: apart from the logos (similar to John's, Justin *Dial.* 128; *Apol.* 2.13; Holte, "Logos Spermatikos"; Barnard, *Justin Martyr*, 85–100), which Justin could have developed independently (Bauer, *Orthodoxy*, 156; Barnard, "Study," 160; against dependence even on Philo, see Barnard, "Logos Theology," 137; Osborn, *Justin*, 73–74; Chadwick, "Defence," 296–97), Justin alludes to the Fourth Gospel rarely (Chadwick, "Defence," 283; cf. Bauer, *Orthodoxy*, 208–12), probably only to John 3:3 (*Apol.* 1.61; Osborn, *Justin*, 137, attributes this instead to a baptismal liturgy, but Barnard, *Justin Martyr*, 60–62, thinks that the cumulative weight of parallels suggests allusions). Nevertheless, earlier gnostic use and $\mathfrak{P}^{52}$ make clear that the Fourth Gospel was already in circulation.

Pervo concludes that Irenaeus, writing about 180, "remains as the earliest certain witness to the existence of Acts."[103] Pervo recognizes that Luke's Gospel is attested as early as Marcion and hence was in use by 110 or 120,[104] but he separates Acts from Luke and thinks it unclear that Marcion knew Acts.[105] The vast majority of scholars today view Luke-Acts as a unity and would view evidence for the Gospel's date as an indicator of a near date for its second volume (although Acts can be later).

But is dating a document no earlier than its first clear attestation in later sources a fair criterion, in any case?[106] Should we date Luke's Gospel decades before Acts and Matthew, the patristic church's favorite Gospel, before Mark? Taking the latest possible date of a document as its most probable actual date would radically reshift the dates assigned to many of our ancient sources. Irenaeus hardly adopted precisely these four Gospels randomly, especially given his emphasis on church tradition; and is it an accident that he chose the four Gospels more reflective of first-century Judean traditions than our other extant gospels (the "apocryphal" gospels and gnostic sayings treatises)?

In my view, the correspondences with the external Roman world of the first century (such as the correct titles of officials such as Gallio or Festus in the correct years), especially in the Pauline portions of Acts, would be highly unlikely for a second-century author unless Luke had available some fairly accurate written sources (more than I have argued as likely).[107] Certainly a novelist (in Pervo's view) would not have gone to the trouble of locating these details. Second-century apocryphal acts lack the connections we have in Luke's Acts, a historical monograph; the genre differs.

Moreover, patristic use (and Irenaeus's confidence of unanimity among the "orthodox") makes it difficult to date any of the four Gospels as late as the mid-second century (the Fourth Gospel, the best candidate, cannot be so dated because a manuscript fragment dated earlier than this period exists).[108] But Acts certainly comes from the same author, at least, as Luke's Gospel, whatever one's view of their unity.[109]

More concretely, Pervo cites Acts' dependence on Paul's letters,[110] but as we have noted, most scholars reject this dependence (and ch. 7 above has given reasons for favoring this rejection). He also cites dependence on Josephus,[111] which is also addressed

---

103. Pervo, *Dating Acts*, 23. For Irenaeus as the first clear citation, see Gregory, *Reception* (who finds the first certain use of Luke's Gospel in the mid-second century, and Acts a bit after that), but he is not arguing that Acts was *written* this late.

104. Pervo, *Dating Acts*, 25.

105. Ibid., 24. Could it be the pro-Pauline, pro-Gentile stance of Acts that made much of Luke's Gospel acceptable to Marcion? Given Pervo's date of ca. 115, however, his view would not necessarily suffer by allowing Marcion's knowledge of Acts.

106. In a public response to discussion after his paper (Gregory, "Irenaeus"), Gregory emphasized that we lack 85 percent of works that one writer *names* as existing then and also that Greco-Roman writers often are quoted in *extant* works only later. Gregory, "Reception of Acts," 64–65, warns against arguing from silence based on when works are first explicitly attested. One might note that most scholars believe that a fragment of John's Gospel demonstrates its circulation probably earlier than its attestation in Justin. Meanwhile, Tyson, who refuses to date Acts before its explicit citation in extant sources, infers Luke's actual use of Josephus and Paul's letters without explicit citations of them.

107. Because I have argued that Luke's sources in Acts are primarily oral, his accuracy on such points cannot be compared with that of, e.g., Tacitus, who writes long after many events described by him yet has annals and other written sources from which to draw.

108. On 𝔓⁵², see, e.g., Roberts, *Fragment*; Metzger, "Papyri," 40. The fragment is virtually identical to the passage in John's Gospel (Dibelius, *Jesus*, 13).

109. A unity contested on one level (that of purpose more than of authorship) by Parsons and Pervo, *Rethinking*.

110. Pervo, *Dating Acts*, 51–147; idem, "Dating Acts"; cf. also several others, e.g., Walker, "Acts and Corpus Revisited."

111. Pervo, *Dating Acts*, 149–99. Despite his commendable detail, I do not find his appeal to dependence on Josephus convincing.

above. Less concretely, he cites anachronisms that he believes require a later date for Acts,[112] for example, Peter supposedly speaking of Jerusalem's residents and telling them of a field called something in their language.[113] Most readers, however, recognize these words as simply the narrator's digression (see comment on Acts 1:19).

Pervo compares Acts with writings from "the first third of the second century."[114] Yet one also can compare Luke with first-century sources,[115] though extant first-century sources are fewer in number, and explain second-century parallels as the common growth of a Christian language stemming from earlier usage. Moreover, Pervo's date for Acts would place it fairly close to Pliny the Younger's letter to Trajan (*Ep.* 10.96), which portrays a state of affairs quite different from the one to which Acts responds.

5. The Date of Acts

Because I believe that the arguments are compelling in favor of the author having been one of Paul's traveling companions (probably for a brief time as early as ca. 48 C.E.), I would restrict any date estimate I would offer to within the probable lifetime of such a companion. Such a limitation does not necessarily preclude any first-century options, since we know neither the author's age when he first traveled with Paul nor the extent of his longevity.

The date of Acts is uncertain, but my best guesses, for reasons that follow, are in the early 70s, with dates in the 80s and 60s still plausible, and a date in the 90s not impossible. The arguments limiting the range between 70 and 90 (the majority view) seem to me stronger than the alternatives; because I also favor the tradition of Lukan authorship and because I find a strong apologetic for Paul engaging a range of concrete accusations about his involvement in specific local riots (see ch. 7, sect. 1.a), accusations that would seem less relevant in later years, I am inclined to suggest a date in the early 70s rather than a later time. Luke the apologist would hardly invent a history of local riots surrounding Paul, yet unable to deny them, he must explain them, at a time when the local memories of such riots remained alive and Paul's legacy remained contested (see more fully ch. 7, sect. 1.a; ch. 13, sect. 3.a.i).[116] Yet though I believe this argument strongly favors a date fairly soon after Paul's ministry, to an extent any suggested date is merely an educated guess, and as I have noted one need not date Acts so early to maintain eyewitness authorship. If Luke was about thirty (he could have been younger or older; if one accepts the tradition that he was a physician, he was probably at least twenty)[117] when he traveled with Paul about 50 C.E. (Acts 16:10), he would be in his early fifties by the early 70s and in his early sixties by the

112. Ibid., 309–17.

113. Ibid., 310.

114. Ibid., 201–57 (quote, 257). Pervo uses other comparisons with the Apostolic Fathers (259–308) to establish a date most likely (307) ca. 110–120 (hence ca. 115, p. 346). He argues that social and legal issues resemble those found in second-century apologists (327–28), e.g., "a willingness to ridicule polytheistic practices" (327)—yet such ridicule occurs commonly in earlier Jewish sources, including Isa 46 (see fuller comment on Acts 14:15–17)! On Acts and the apologists, see also Pervo, "Apologists."

115. Certainly, Luke's Gospel fits better with Matthew and Mark than with later gnostic "sayings gospels" or even the apocryphal gospels. Parallels with Acts are so many as to suggest to me Luke's substantial knowledge about Paul (though Pervo would argue that most of this derives from Paul's letters).

116. Cf. also, e.g., Stagg, *Acts*, 22 (shortly after the Judean-Roman war); Polhill, *Acts*, 27–31. For Luke responding to still-concrete memories of riots associated with Paul, see Keener, "Apologetic."

117. Then again, because apprenticeship ended younger, it is not surprising to know of one physician perhaps aged seventeen (Lewis, *Life*, 153–54, citing P.Giss. 43 = *SB* 10630; for physicians less than twenty in Asia Minor, he cites *Phoenix* 36 [1982]: 271). Some of Paul's other putative traveling companions were younger than Paul, probably adolescents at the beginning of their work with him (John Mark and Timothy).

early 80s (or in his seventies in the 90s if one dates Acts so late). If the author was as young as twenty ca. 50 C.E., he would be only seventy years old ca. 100 C.E.[118] Paul's memory remains fresh, Diaspora churches are establishing their identity distinct from local synagogues, and the troubles of the later Domitianic era have not yet arisen.

That Luke names Theophilus, a person of status, and provides an optimistic legal apologetic might suggest that his audience is facing neither Nero's persecution (albeit perhaps relevant only in Rome) nor the local persecutions that occurred in some cities under Domitian.[119] Even under Nero (cf. Tac. *Ann.* 15.44), it is not clear that the Corinthian Christians, though Corinth might emulate Rome, experienced direct persecution. By contrast, Christians in Philippi may well have (Phil 1:28–30); in any case, Christians in Roman colonies would certainly have known of persecution in Rome and have had reason for concern.[120] If Philippi is a major center of Luke's audience, this might suggest a date after Nero, though his policies could appear more rational to distant colonies than in the capital (by the time of his demise, Nero was discredited at least among the Roman aristocracy). Further, as best one can reconstruct the implied audience from the data available, Theophilus may belong to a church that knows and appreciates the Pauline mission, but he and many others may have become believers since Paul's own work there.

All such dating, however, is at best educated guesswork, given the inadequacy of our data; we cannot even reconstruct the period on the basis of the setting without also knowing the location. Nevertheless, given my arguments for authorship, a first-century date, at least, should be regarded as secure. This commentary assumes a post-70 date (within, however, living memory of Paul). If this premise is mistaken, it will bring into question some of my interpretive judgments at key points (such as Paul's speech in Acts 22:3–21 as constituting a final public invitation to the people of Jerusalem to turn from their anti-Roman course before Jerusalem's destruction).[121] Such a misjudgment would, however, affect only a relatively small portion (less than 1 percent) of the commentary proper, and I still think this dating likelier than not.

Further, even if the author of Acts is identified with Luke the physician in Colossians, we cannot be certain that the medical training preceded his initial voyage with Paul (Acts 16:10–12).

118. Given average post-childhood longevity and a median guess of an age of twenty-five to thirty when he first traveled with Paul, we might prefer a date before 85 C.E., but only as an estimate.

119. These did not affect every locality: among the seven central churches of Asia, persecution appears only in Rev 2:9–10, 13; 3:9; see Keener, *Revelation*, 37–39, esp. 39.

120. Later, in the period of the Apostolic Fathers, the Corinthian church apparently continued to struggle with prosperity (cf., e.g., *1 Clem.* 13.1; 38.2; 59.3); while this temptation also existed for some in Philippi (Poly. *Phil.* 2.2; 4.1, 3; 5.2; 6.1; 10.2; 11.1–2), they may also risk persecution (Poly. *Phil.* 8.2; 9.1–2; 12.3). The persecution in Philippi seems less obvious than in Paul's day, however (Phil 1:28–30; 1 Thess 2:2).

121. Although one could read the narrative thus simply in view of Luke 21, the point would be much stronger for a Diaspora audience after 70.

11

THE AUTHOR OF LUKE-ACTS

Today almost all[1] scholars acknowledge that Luke and Acts share the same author. Although there are differences of language between the two works, these differences by themselves do not require distinct authors, and the similarities are compelling.[2] (Chapter 16 below discusses the narrative unity of Luke-Acts; although narrative unity has been questioned more than common authorship, it also remains the strong consensus.)

Beyond this general agreement, a majority of (but not nearly all) scholars agree that Luke was a Gentile, writing for a largely Gentile (or, perhaps more accurately, mixed Gentile and Jewish) Diaspora audience. A much smaller number, though probably still the majority, argue that the author was at least a short-term companion of Paul. This is the most important of the authorship claims (in terms of Luke's fulfilling the contract of Acts' implicit genre), but the bulk of my argument for this observation is deferred until Acts 16:10, at the introduction to the "we" narratives. (Deferral of full discussion until the first textual occurrence of "we" allows this introductory chapter to be more concise than some others.)

Less important, but worthy of investigation, is the question of who this traveling companion may have been. Of possible candidates in Pauline literature who fit this description, Luke the physician (Col 4:14) is the likeliest candidate historically and also the one supported (despite his relative obscurity) by subsequent Christian writers who claimed access to earlier sources no longer available to us.[3] Although nothing within Luke-Acts requires us to suppose that the author was a physician, the evidence is consistent with this tradition, and some knowledge of ancient physicians may thus illumine Luke's profession for those who (like myself) think him the likeliest candidate for author.

---

1. Cf. Powell, *Acts*, 6: "virtually everyone."
2. With, e.g., Beck, "Common Authorship." Knox, *Acts*, 100–109, responds to A. C. Clark's linguistic arguments for different authors and shows that these need not follow. Granted, one author *could* pick up precisely where another has left off, without providing notification to this effect (Xen. *Hell.* 1.1.1, starting where Thucydides stopped), but this was hardly the norm (and any stylistic differences between Luke and Acts are minuscule compared with those between Xenophon and Thucydides). Cf. differences between two works of Hecataeus (noted in Brown, *Historians*, 11).
3. Some object that those who agree with early Christian tradition on this or other points reflect a bias toward the tradition. The tradition need not always be correct, but Westerners in the age of television underestimate oral memory, and the frequent tendency of NT scholars to distance themselves from the tradition exerts no less a bias, especially tempting to those of us who value being perceived by our peers as critical. I do not accept all traditional authorship claims, but in the case of Luke believe that this ascription is where the evidence points, and am certainly in much good company here. Classicists are more ready to start with external evidence than NT scholars typically are (Kennedy, "Source Criticism," 147).

1. Questions about Authorship

The issue of authorship was among the standard questions ancient critics, as well as modern ones,[4] asked. Ancients recognized that forgery (e.g., of letters and legal documents) occurred and they sometimes suspected it.[5] By contrast, literary pseudepigraphy was more common for literary works; pseudonymity was an established and possibly often acceptable literary practice of the day both in broader Greco-Roman[6] and in some Jewish circles[7] though, when used for some kinds of works, it could be viewed as forgery.[8] Ancient literary critics sometimes sought to distinguish genuine and spurious works attributed to an author (e.g., Aul. Gel. 3.3, on plays of Plautus) or at least make note of which works were disputed.[9] Thus, for example, some attributed the *Epigoni* to Homer, but Herodotus (Hdt. 4.32) and a scholiast (on Aristophanes, frg. 1) doubted this attribution.[10]

Sometimes even declamations could be "forged" (*falsi*) within a generation (Sen. E. *Controv.* 1.pref. 11);[11] thus later rhetoricians would, when other evidence (such as coherence with the period they depict) was lacking, use stylistic criteria to evaluate the authenticity of a speech (Dion. Hal. *Lysias* 11–12; *Demosth.* 50).[12] When rejecting speeches' authenticity (e.g., Dion. Hal. *Din.* 13), however, one would offer more reasons than when accepting them (*Din.* 12).[13] Given that works were probably authentic more often than not, this principle is a logical one. Acts claims no author by name, though Theophilus and, presumably, the first ideal audience as a whole knew him, and so pseudepigraphy is irrelevant to Acts, in any case.[14]

2. The Author's Probable Background

The author may have been a Gentile God-fearer who spent time with Paul especially during part or all of his Roman custody.

4. For older modern studies of authorship, date, and provenance, see Mattill and Mattill, *Bibliography*, 147–52, §§1940–2028.

5. E.g., Arrian *Alex.* 6.12.3; Livy 40.55.1; Quint. *Inst.* 5.5.1; Jos. *Life* 356; Suet. *Vesp.* 6.4; Philost. *Vit. Apoll.* 7.35; Iambl. *V.P.* 1.2; cf. 2 Thess 2:2; 3:17.

6. E.g., most of the "Cynic Epistles"; cf. Maloney, "Authorship"; discussion in Metzger, "Forgeries." Sometimes its function (as perhaps in some secondary works of Plato) was mere stylistic imitation for rhetorical practice. In the Byzantine period and later, see, e.g., Cook, *Dogma*, 51. Some cases may be part of the fiction, and hence relevant only to fiction.

7. E.g., *1 Enoch*; *4 Ezra*; *2 Baruch*; 4Q537; cf. Jos. *Ant.* 8.51–55. The *Temple Scroll* (11QT XLVIII) may have sought to imply its Mosaic authorship (Brin, "Scroll").

8. See Carson, "Pseudonymity," 858–63; Ehrman, *Forged* (rejecting the frequent modern view that the practice was sometimes accepted); Witherington, *Homilies*, 29–37; e.g., Jos. *Ag. Ap.* 1.3.

9. E.g., Arrian *Alex.* 5.6.5; Jos. *Ag. Ap.* 1.221; Dion. Hal. *Demosth.* 23, 57; Sen. Y. *Ep. Lucil.* 88.40; Suet. *Vergil* 19; *Gramm.* 7; 14.

10. West, "Introduction," 10.

11. Sometimes it was also hard to know if sayings were always correctly attributed, especially after the passage of time (e.g., Pliny *Ep.* 6.29.5). By definition, declamations were mock speeches (Bloomer, "Declamation," 298), but even declamations could be misattributed.

12. Others proved less skeptical than Dionysius of Halicarnassus (*Lysias* 12), and in some cases probably rightly so. He always held a speech to the rhetor's highest standards, but the rhetor had fallen short of that standard, especially in his early development. For coherence with the purported author's time and life, see also Dion. Hal. *Din.* 11.

13. One also had to beware of inauthenticity claims motivated by malice (Dion. Hal. *Isoc.* 18). Usher, "Introduction to *Dinarchus*," 246–49, notes that librarians at Alexandria and Pergamon had been most interested in distinguishing authentic from spurious works until Dionysius of Halicarnassus's time in the first century B.C.E.

14. To make Luke's "we" a pseudepigraphic literary device, when the author is not even named, would contend for implicit pseudepigraphy—for which I am aware of no parallels in antiquity (there cannot have been many).

a. Jewish or Gentile Christian?

On the basis of internal evidence, scholars debate whether the author was either a Gentile Christian (for whom the Gentile mission in Acts is a matter of life and death) or a (Diaspora) Jewish Christian who was part of the Hellenist mission to the Gentiles. Plausible arguments have been offered for both positions.

Scholars often opine that the author was a God-fearing Gentile. From his geographical competence and his interpretation of Judaism, it is certain that he was not a Palestinian Jew. Granted, Palestinian Judaism had imbibed much of the Hellenism with which it had interacted for centuries, though typically to a lesser extent than Judaism in eastern Mediterranean cities outside the Holy Land.[15] But Palestinian Judaism also included significant elements with which Luke appears less familiar than, for example, John or Matthew was.[16] He may have been a Diaspora Jew with interests in the Gentile mission, but given his relationship to Judaism and perspectives, many scholars prefer the idea that he was a Gentile. Scholars who, on other grounds, identify the author with the Luke mentioned in Col 4:14 will likely also conclude that he was a Gentile.[17]

Luke's excellent Greek and presumably Hellenistic education no more require him to be a Gentile than those of Josephus and Philo make them Gentiles; this would be especially the case in the Diaspora.[18] Although the external tradition may be construed as supporting a Gentile (Col 4:11, 14), the internal evidence more easily favors someone immersed in Diaspora synagogue Judaism.[19] This might seem to support someone who was raised in a Jewish home.

On the other hand, if (as shall be argued; see esp. comment on Acts 16:10) Luke traveled with Paul to Jerusalem as a representative of the Gentile churches (Acts 20:4–5; cf. Rom 15:27; 2 Cor 8:23), he was probably ethnically Gentile.[20] If Luke was a Gentile Christian,[21] however, he was probably either a God-fearer—an adher-

---

15. See, e.g., Lieberman, *Hellenism*; Tcherikover, *Civilization*; Avi-Yonah, *Hellenism*; Hengel, *Judaism and Hellenism* (esp. 1:103ff., 252); idem, "Hellenismus"; Simon, "Synkretismus"; Jacobson, "Kings"; Engberg-Pedersen, "Introduction"; Sterling, *Ancestral Philosophy*, 11–32; Wallace and Williams, *World*, 41–70; for Roman law, see Cohen, *Law*. This is not to say that Palestinian Judaism, especially in all its strata, was completely hellenized (cf. cautions in Sandmel, "Theory"; Feldman, "Hellenism"; Vermes, *Jesus and Judaism*, 26; Wasserstein, "Non-hellenized Jews"; Chancey and Meyers, "Jewish"; Chancey, "Milieu"); some regions were more hellenized than others (Meyers, "Judaism and Christianity," 77–78), and Palestine achieved maximum hellenization only in the third century C.E. (Meyers, "Challenge").

16. But compare Luke 11:44 with Matt 23:27; Luke 11:42, 45–46 with Matt 23:13–29.

17. Nevertheless, the grammar of Col 4:11 does not compel all interpreters to view this Luke as a Gentile (see, e.g., Deissmann, *Light*, 438; Martin, *Colossians*, 135–36 and sources cited there). Against weighting Rom 16:21 the other way, that passage may refer to a different person. Admittedly, just about 0.3 percent of attested Greeks in antiquity held this name (Richard Fellows, personal correspondence, June 7, 2007); it is, however, one of the most common Latin names (Stambaugh, *City*, 94; Fellows suggests that 21 percent of Roman citizens held this name), and these names are disproportionately represented among Paul's companions (especially in a colony such as Corinth, to which Rom 16:21 refers). Moreover, Paul spells the name differently in Rom 16:21 than in Phlm 24 and Col 4:14, which usually leads scholars to differentiate them (e.g., Fitzmyer, *Romans*, 748; Moo, *Romans*, 934; Schreiner, *Romans*, 807; Witherington, *Romans*, 399; Jewett, *Romans*, 977; though cf., e.g., Stuhlmacher, *Romans*, 255; Dunn, *Romans*, 909; entertaining the possibility, Origen *Comm. Rom.* on 16:21).

18. Sterling, *Historiography*, 327–29.

19. Sterling, "Legitimation," 217, suggests a Diaspora Jew able to draw on traditional Diaspora Jewish models justifying life outside the sacred land. Many others concur (e.g., Shillington, *Introduction*, 10).

20. Timothy (Acts 20:4) would be viewed as Jewish (16:1–3), but the majority of the delegates are probably Gentiles (see Rom 15:27).

21. E.g., Pesch, *Apostelgeschichte*, 1:27 (probably); Hotze, "Zeugen"; Doohan, *Acts*, 14–15 (noting the "majority"); Pervo, *Acts*, 7. A later rabbi doubted that names such as "Luke" were used for Jews (*b. Giṭ.* 11b, cited by Le Cornu, *Acts*, 5), but some Jews bore it ("Lucius" in *CIJ* 1:111, §155). "Luke" was sometimes a hellenized variant (Judge, *Rank*, 36n19) or shortened form (Deissmann, *Light*, 435; Ramsay, *Discovery*, 370–84,

ent of a synagogue before becoming a Christian[22]—or a long-standing member of the Hellenistic Jewish Christian movement.[23] Whether Jewish or devout Gentile, he probably traced his spiritual heritage to the Hellenist Jewish Christian movement of Acts 6; he, far more than Paul, would have found himself an outsider in his visit to Judea in Acts 21–26.

If Luke was a Gentile, he was nevertheless one with considerable experience of Judaism. Although he could have acquired much of this knowledge as a Christian, it is reasonable to suggest, as some scholars have, that he may have been a God-fearer with a long-standing knowledge of the Diaspora synagogue. Nevertheless, we should beware of reading too much about the author's background (or audience) into his use of the OT.[24]

Although we can say that the author was at least probably a God-fearer before becoming a Christian, early Christians continued the Jewish practice of teaching Scriptures at their meetings, which in time would allow Gentile converts to learn the Bible, just as it does today. His immersion in the LXX, however, is considerable; if he did not grow up with it, he must have acquired it long before and thoroughly, for he knows how to write Greek with a "biblical" or "Jewish accent," so to speak.[25]

Unless we accept the early Christian tradition that he was from Syria, however, we need not assume that he was competent in Aramaic.[26] Some of his variants in handling Q vis-à-vis Matthew may reflect an Aramaic original,[27] but Luke need not have translated the Aramaic himself; immersion in the LXX could explain his heavily Semitic sections (such as most of Luke 1–2), and heavy dependence on urban Hellenists may explain his focus on Hellenists in Acts (perhaps as early as 2:9–11) and his topographic limitations in Judea.

b. After Jerusalem

The implied narrator traveled to Rome with Paul (Acts 28:14, 16) and, assuming (on the basis of the argument in this chapter and at Acts 16:10) that our companion of Paul is the Luke mentioned in Paul's epistles, remained with him (Col 4:14; Phlm 24; cf. 2 Tim 4:11).[28] If Mark wrote to Christians in Rome (or if some Christians migrating to Rome, as many apparently did, brought Mark's Gospel there), Luke would have had access to Mark's Gospel there, allowing him to arrange his earlier

---

esp. 384) of "Lucius," which was a common Roman praenomen (Stambaugh, *City*, 94); the Lucius in Rom 16:21 is surely Jewish, so that many dispute the identification with Luke in Col 4 (e.g., Danker, *New Age*, xii).

22. For a Jewish author, see, e.g., Denova, *Things Accomplished*, 230–31; Malina and Pilch, *Acts*, 7; for a Jew or God-fearer, e.g., Jervell, *Theology*, 5; idem, *Apostelgeschichte*, 50–51; Sterling, *Historiography*, 328; for a God-fearer, e.g., Tuckett, *Luke*, 63; tentatively, Ray, *Irony*, 165–70.

23. Perhaps he had somehow become an adherent of the Jesus movement before joining Paul in Acts 16:10; perhaps he migrated from the Christian community in Antioch, though the tradition favoring this may not be accurate.

24. E.g., Denova, *Things Accomplished*, 230–31, thinks that Luke was probably "a Jew" seeking "to persuade other Jews." Assuming that he must have been a God-fearer before his conversion follows the same logic; it seems likelier than not, but we should not underestimate one's ability to learn Scripture after conversion. For example, I myself acquired all my knowledge of Scripture (though not all my knowledge of Greco-Roman literature) after conversion from my previous condition as a biblically illiterate atheist.

25. See Alexander, *Context*, 251–52.

26. Indeed, even in Antioch he could have been hellenophone.

27. E.g., Matt 5:48 vs. Luke 6:36; Robinson, *Trust*, 32.

28. I am treating the narrator as the work's author, which some would regard as a conflation. But as argued in the comment at Acts 16:10 (against many scholars), the narrator of the "we" narratives is surely the book's author, unless the author at this one point becomes inept. One can distinguish authors and narrators, but this was not the usual expectation in antiquity (see Keener, *John*, 111–12, for further discussion). Du Plooy, "Author," treats characteristics of the implied author of Luke-Acts.

research around it. (Although he also had other sources [Luke 1:1], he generally follows Mark's sequence, with two major obvious exceptions.)

It is possible, though by no means certain (and not necessarily probable), that Luke himself was imprisoned and, like Timothy, released about 67–68 C.E.[29] Conversely, Luke may have evaded detention, but in any case he likely would not have published this work during the Neronian persecution; the conditions of that persecution would militate against its circulation, and no internal evidence suggests the kind of apocalyptic mistrust of Rome that one would expect under such circumstances (cf. Mark and Revelation).

Luke may then (as argued in ch. 10 above) have been able to complete and publish Luke-Acts by the early 70s,[30] viewing the destruction of Jerusalem as the tragic (albeit temporary) end that Israel's rejection of Jesus and his messengers had produced. I offer this suggestion merely as one of the more plausible scenarios from our available evidence, but ultimately any such reconstruction contains an element of historical speculation.

3. The Likeliest Author

Unfashionable as it is in some circles to come to any conclusions supporting the existence of eyewitness material in the NT, if we treat Acts the way we treat analogous historical works from its era we should accept the work's eyewitness claims as authentic indications of the author's presence. Internal evidence points strongly to a Christian who accompanied Paul on a small number of his travels and should have become well acquainted with him especially on the journey to Jerusalem and Rome. Although the external evidence is less important, it strongly points to Luke "the physician" (Col 4:14) as the author, a claim that tradition is not likely to have invented (given Luke's relative obscurity). The external and the internal evidence are compatible, making Luke the likeliest author.

The primary reason for many scholars treating "we" in Acts differently than they would in most other ancient historical works is the argument that a genuine traveling companion of Paul cannot have so misunderstood him. I do not judge this reason sufficiently plausible to overturn our normal expectation for first-person pronouns in ancient historical literature. Aside from the question of whether most of Paul's modern interpreters have understood him well enough to pass judgment on some of Luke's interpretations (see discussion in ch. 7, esp. sect. 7, of this introduction), the argument betrays inadequate familiarity with ancient historians. If Luke frames his material about Paul (especially in the speeches) in light of what Luke wants to say, he simply acts like many other ancient historians did. Material from ancient authors sometimes remains extant alongside biographic reports about them, and the range of perspectives between the epistolary and Lukan Pauls is no greater than the presentations in these other sources.[31] When we factor in the popular level of Luke's

29. On my understanding of Timothy's situation in Heb 13:23. Another reasonable solution, given the viciousness of Nero's persecution, would be that the author was martyred under Nero, hence Acts' lack of a suitable conclusion and of finishing rhetorical touches (Rackham, *Acts*, l–lv); but its conclusion is not as deficient as some claim, and arguments for a completed account after Jerusalem's fall (unless a later writer redacted the Gospel) work against this solution.

30. A writer with good notes could publish memoirs years after the events described (e.g., Xenophon's *Anabasis*); some (e.g., Sen. E. *Controv.* passim) published memoirs based on memory. See Rebenich, "Prose," 313–14, on *commentarii*, private records, especially as used by Romans.

31. See the careful study in Hillard, Nobbs, and Winter, "Corpus" (esp. remarks on 211). One must read both Cicero's self-portrayal and Sallust's portrayal of him critically, considering the genre and purposes of each source and using the sources together (Hillard in 185–96). Ammianus's portrait of Julian (composed about

historical writing, the assumption that Luke never knew the historical Paul because he uses him for his own rhetorical purposes (influenced by Paul but also by other early Christian sources) becomes untenable.

Although I feel that the evidence strongly points toward a companion of Paul, I recognize that on this question I cannot speak as though there is a consensus even to the extent that I can speak of a fairly strong majority opinion about Acts' basic genre. Despite firm confidence in the direction in which Luke's "we" material points, I pause to acknowledge my respect for other positions. As noted regarding questions of Luke's date, scholars sometimes dismiss other scholars' work by categorizing them into particular "camps" and remarking, "That is the view one expects for someone in that camp." An approach that better suits the most open-minded and finest liberal tradition in scholarship is to consider other arguments and disagree respectfully where we cannot agree.

a. A Companion of Paul

A large number (probably the majority) of English-speaking commentators believe that the author was a companion of Paul, as the "we" narratives suggest.[32] Although there remain some significant detractors to this position,[33] the bulk of the evidence points in this direction, and it is our most secure available observation regarding authorship.

This observation (rather than the specific identification with Luke the physician, which is consistent with, but need not follow from, it) is the most important observation we could make about authorship, but it will not be treated in detail here. Because it follows from the interpretation of the "we" narratives, I reserve the full survey of approaches and extensive comment (as well as responses to objections) for the introduction to those narratives at Acts 16:10, comment on which I depend here. Likewise, discussion of the supposed inconsistencies between Luke and Paul appears in chapter 7, section 7, above. Nevertheless, a few points are briefly summarized below.

When historians include "we" in their histories, they almost always mean that they were present at those points. Scholars often cite the observation of Harvard classicist Arthur Darby Nock, who noted that, apart from some minor stylistic lapses (excluded in Acts by the geographic consistency of the "we"), "I know only one possible parallel for the emphatic use of a questionable 'we' in consecutive narrative outside literature which is palpably fictional. . . . Since on stylistic grounds the hypothesis of a redactor is excluded, I think we must take these statements at their face value."[34] Examples could be multiplied. For instance, when Philostratus suddenly introduces "we" and

---

events that occurred during the former's lifetime) complements Julian's picture of himself (Nobbs in 206–10). The portrayals of Favorinus by Gellius and Philostratus diverge, with the former being less tendentious and more consistent with Favorinus's orations (Winter in 196–205). On Ammianus's probable pagan biases, see Kelly, "Ammianus Marcellinus," esp. 358–60.

32. E.g., Abbott, *Acts*, 131–34; Ramsay, *Luke the Physician*, 26; Rackham, *Acts*, xvi; Lenski, *Acts*, 14–15; C. Williams, *Acts*, 22–30; Arrington, *Acts*, xxxii; Spencer, *Acts*, 12–13; Dunn, *Acts*, x; Fitzmyer, *Acts*, 50; Le Cornu, *Acts*, xxvii–xxviii; Chance, *Acts*, 4; Parsons, *Luke*, 8; Hemer, *Acts in History*, 312–34; Peterson, *Acts*, 1–4, 17 ("most scholars"); also, beyond Anglophone scholarship, cf. Fusco, "Sezioni-noi"; Botermann, "Heiden-apostel"; Riesner, "Zuverlässigkeit," 38–39; Thornton, *Zeuge*; Jervell, *Apostelgeschichte*, 66, 82.

33. E.g., Barrett, "Acts and Corpus"; see further discussion at Acts 16:10. Most accept at least an eyewit-ness as the source of the "we" material; Boismard and Lamouille, *Actes*, 1:21, curiously suggest Silas (which would explain the Macedonian connection, 1 Thess 1:1), though he is named both in the "we" narrative (Acts 16:19, 25, 29 though, admittedly, the explicit "we" ends at 16:17) and outside it (15:22, 27, 32, 40; 17:4, 10, 14–15; 18:5).

34. Nock, *Essays*, 827–28, skeptical of a fictitious "we." Cf. discussion in Dupont, *Sources*, 167–68; Hanson, *Acts*, 23; as an autobiographic narration technique, see Baum, "Wir und Er-Stellungen."

"us" (in his *Vit. soph.* 2.21.604) for students of Proclus of Naucratis, it is because he himself *did* study with him (2.21.602).

Historians mention their presence to emphasize their historical credentials and because they belonged to the action; Luke was undoubtedly no less present at the points he claims than they were.[35] As Dupont, in his study of Acts' sources, concluded, "Comparison with ancient texts which present the same peculiarity makes the significance of the procedure clear—the author wishes it to be understood that he has personally taken part in the events he is recounting."[36] New Testament scholars who deny Acts' author the same privilege as other ancient historical writers, against all our expectations from ancient sources, do so mainly because of supposed incompatibility with Paul (or the assignment of Acts to a genre other than history), not because it is the most obvious approach to an ancient text.[37] (Despite obvious differences between Paul and Luke, however, the proposal of actual incompatibility with Luke having known him appears strained, as argued in ch. 7, sect. 7, above.)

If the author simply wished to insert himself into the narrative, it would be surprising that he does so infrequently and at places of less theological import than one would expect. Instead of claiming to be an eyewitness to most events in Acts, the author merely traveled with Paul on some occasions, especially the final period (which is accordingly recorded in much greater detail than the rest of the work).[38] Further, the first-person narration breaks off in one city and resumes at the same place later, suggesting its authenticity (Acts 16:16; 20:5; cf. similarly 21:18; 27:1).[39] Finally, Luke demonstrates more knowledge in the "we" accounts, which he often treats at greater length.[40] Paul's comparatively brief sojourn in Philippi seems to warrant more detail than his lengthy stay in Corinth or most of his time in Ephesus; the greatest detail is given for Paul's voyages to Jerusalem and Rome and for his Roman custody in Acts 21–28.

Scholars offer other solutions, addressed in this commentary at Acts 16:10. For example, some argue for a fictitious literary device; but such devices appear elsewhere almost exclusively in fictitious narratives (where they appear pervasively), not historical ones, and a deliberate deception would not (as noted above) appear only at such minor points in the narrative, with a mere walk-on role.[41] Others suggest that

---

35. See also Cadbury, "We in Luke-Acts"; Fitzmyer, *Acts*, 103; Dunn, *Acts*, x; Spencer, *Acts*, 12–13. For the value placed on historians being present, see, e.g., Dion. Hal. *Thuc.* 6; cf. Polyb. 29.21.8; Corn. Nep. 25 (Atticus), 13.7; 17.1; Jos. *Life* 357; *Ag. Ap.* 1.45–49, 56; Aune, *Environment*, 81; Meister, "Historiography: Greece," 421; Byrskog, *History*, 153–57; cf. Plümacher, *Geschichte*, 85–108.

36. Dupont, *Sources*, 167.

37. This is to agree with Neil, *Acts*, 23, against some frequent critical theories, that the author's presence is the "obvious conclusion" and the alternative solutions "put a premium on critical ingenuity at the expense of common sense." Cf. Dibelius, *Studies in Acts*, 136: probably the author introduced "we" to the existing narrative "in order to indicate when he was present" (cf. also p. 105).

38. Chance, *Acts*, 16, compares Luke's only occasional and implicit eyewitness claim to Lucian's demand that good historians avoid "exaggerated" eyewitness claims (*Hist.* 28–29). Indeed, among historians, some narrators such as Xenophon intrude less frequently than others, such as Herodotus and Thucydides (Dewald, "Construction," 98); but Luke does so even less frequently.

39. With others, e.g., Dibelius, *Studies in Acts*, 136; Fitzmyer, *Theologian*, 11–16. Note also the fluctuation in other members of the "we" group (Kurz, *Reading Luke-Acts*, 114–20).

40. Riesner, *Early Period*, 413; Neil, *Acts*, 22–23.

41. Against the literary fiction interpretation, see, e.g., Porter, *Paul in Acts*, 24–27; Porter, "'We' Passages," 560; Fitzmyer, *Acts*, 100–102. I borrow the phrase "walk-on role" from Plümacher, "Luke as Historian," 398. One specific suggestion is a convention of "we" in sea voyage narratives (Robbins, "We-Passages and Voyages"; idem, "Land and Sea"), but "we" also appears on land in Acts (16:10, 12–16; 20:7–8; 21:7–17; 28:14–16) and scholars have subjected the alleged convention to heavy criticism (Barrett, "Paul Shipwrecked"; Fitzmyer, *Theologian*, 16–22; Hemer, "First Person Narrative"; esp. Praeder, "First Person Narration," 210–18).

the author borrows the narrator's "we" from a travel journal; while use of a travel journal is quite possible, Luke does not retain first-person pronouns from his other sources. Would he become an inept editor at this point and only this point?[42] One must take recourse to these or other solutions only if it is implausible for the author to have been Paul's traveling companion.

As noted above, those who argue against the author's having been a companion of Paul generally stress the differences between Paul's letters and the portrayal of Paul in Acts.[43] These differences should not be overemphasized, however, as scholars who think Luke a traveling companion of Paul emphasize.[44] Paul's letters provide a sample of Paul's thought when dealing with various issues in particular churches; there is variation even among the undisputed letters (certainly between, e.g., the eschatological depictions in 1 Thessalonians and those in 2 Corinthians).[45] Paul is harsher toward the law in Galatians than in Romans; he touches the issue only briefly and on occasion in 1 Corinthians.

That, according to my view, the author occasionally traveled with Paul and noted carefully Paul's legal situation does not mean that the author was intimately acquainted with details of Paul's theology as expressed in the sample letters of Paul today extant.[46] Nor, if he were so acquainted, would he (having a broader sample than we do) necessarily choose to emphasize these aspects of Paul's life and thought or need to express his own theology in the same terms as Paul's occasional letters.[47]

Even if Paul were the author's source for his accounts of Paul's missions, Acts is not, nor is it intended to be, an autobiography. Other ancient biographies provide the same kinds of challenges when compared with the subject's extant letters.[48] Correspondences between the Paul of Acts and the Paul of the epistles (not based on the author's knowledge of Paul's letters, given the differences) support the possibility that, in fact, the author did know Paul (at the very least, he knew sources close to him).[49] (See further discussion in ch. 7 above.) Arguments that the author was a companion of Paul in the "we" sections seem to me still more compelling (see esp. discussion at Acts 16:10), and given the comparison with first-person claims elsewhere in ancient historiography, I find extremely dubious the arguments against this claim. Paul often was accompanied by coworkers (e.g., Rom 16:21; 2 Cor 8:23; 12:18; Phil 4:3; Phlm 24; Col 4:7–11; perhaps Gal 1:2), and, applying the same approach we apply to other ancient historical works, we have far more reason to accept the author's claim to have been one of them than to question it.

42. The style of these sections appears Lukan (with Fitzmyer, *Acts*, 99–100; Dibelius, *Studies in Acts*, 104, 136; Droge, "Anonymously," 507; contrast, however, Porter, "'We' Passages").

43. E.g., Barrett, *Acts*, 2:xxvii–xxx; Windisch, "Tradition"; Marguerat, *Actes*, 19; see discussion in ch. 7, sect. 7. Pervo, *Acts*, 5, argues from the date of 115 c.e., which he assigns to Acts (against most scholars).

44. E.g., Fitzmyer, *Luke*, 47–51; Martin, *Foundations*, 67–68; D. Williams, *Acts*, 4–5.

45. On this point, see esp. Jervell, *Theology*, 2–3 (citing Räisänen, *Paul and Law*).

46. Nock, *Essays*, 828, indeed suggests that Luke need not have been intimate with Paul, though traveling with him, and if he "failed to understand Paul's theology, he was not alone in that." He follows Dibelius in suggesting that Luke may have lacked "literary plans" when he was with Paul; although I would suggest otherwise (why else record his itinerary in the "we" narrative?), if the literary plans arose later, this would demand a greater dependence on memory. Regarding historical details, Paul speaks of companions (including Luke, Phlm 24), not chroniclers per se; thus some propose that Luke could have conceived of the project (apart from his travel notes) afterward (e.g., Chance, *Acts*, 3).

47. Against Vielhauer, Fitzmyer, *Luke*, 47–51, attributes Luke's presentation of Paul to a lay imprecision of language rather than to ignorance. Luke also lacked Paul's Jerusalem exegetical training.

48. See Hillard, Nobbs, and Winter, "Corpus."

49. E.g., Emmet, "Tradition."

b. Luke the Physician as the Author?

Both later Christian tradition and the coherency of Pauline evidence with the narrator's being Paul's traveling companion en route to Rome support the likelihood of Luke as the author.

I. PATRISTIC EVIDENCE

Classicists normally start with the external evidence, the most concrete evidence we have.[50] If the author was a companion of Paul, the tradition that this companion was "Luke," a physician (Col 4:14), is a reasonable one.[51] This tradition appears in the *Anti-Marcionite Prologue* to Luke, where it is quite specific: Luke, the doctor from Antioch, disciple of the apostles, remained unmarried and died in Boeotia at age eighty-four.[52]

How much of the tradition found in the *Prologue* is dependable? One of the least likely lapses in early Christian memory would be the name of the author of two major works (Luke and Acts), especially the widely circulated Gospel,[53] but on other details, not all of this tradition is probable. The Antioch connection probably stems from an improbable inference from Acts 13:1 (connecting the author with Lucius of Cyrene; see comment there); Luke's information about Antioch is also sketchier than his report of Paul's travels (especially the "we" material), despite its significance for the early Christian mission and for Paul himself.[54] The name of his place of origin could also be a case of a prominent locale claiming a prominent figure for itself.

Other aspects of the *Prologue*'s tradition are of questionable weight. The author's occupation in the tradition could be inferred from Col 4:14, given the tradition of his name. That he was a disciple of the apostles could represent a reasonable surmise or apologetic move or even a general statement about his generation; that he remained unmarried might reflect the rising tide of sexual asceticism in the church.[55] The date of this prologue is also uncertain. The Muratorian Canon claims that Luke is author

---

50. Emphasized by Kennedy, "Source Criticism," 147 (noted even more forcefully in Fuller, "Classics," 176; acknowledged respectfully by Fuller, "Classics," 176–78, 183). But Kennedy ("Source Criticism," 147–51) may accept elements of Papias's tradition too uncritically (cf. Meeks, "Hypomnēmata," 170).

51. For the tradition, see, e.g., Pesch, *Apostelgeschichte*, 1:25; esp. Fitzmyer, *Luke*, 35–41. Fitzmyer, *Theologian*, 1–26, treats Luke as Paul's occasional companion because of second-century traditions, Luke being in Macedonia, and the Letter to the Philippians. Some attribute the church's tradition of a Pauline companion to the desire to have an eyewitness (e.g., Langner, *Hechos*, 34); but the claim to be present is, as we have noted, explicit in the narrative itself.

52. C. Williams, *Acts*, 1, also noting the eighty-four years in the sixth- or seventh-century Coptic inscription from Egypt; Witherington, *Acts*, 56; Eckey, *Apostelgeschichte*, 9; Arrington, *Acts*, xxxii.

53. The titles of the four Gospels each seem to preserve earlier tradition, being themselves early enough and accepted enough to have been unanimous and unchallenged throughout the ancient church (Hengel, *Mark*, 81–82; cf. Aune, *Environment*, 18). Since all four titles were probably bestowed simultaneously, given their identical form, they were probably composed to circulate with the collection of four Gospels, presumably before both Irenaeus and Tatian's late second-century *Diatessaron* and definitely before the late second-century 𝔓[66]. Some scholars have doubted that the titles themselves predate 180 C.E. (Sanders, *Figure*, 64–66), but if this is the case, the unanimity across a wide geographic range seems difficult to explain. Others favor a period much earlier in the second century (Aune, *Environment*, 18, and Witherington, *Wisdom*, 11, suggest ca. 125 C.E.). But Acts was early detached from Luke. In Chrysostom's day, Acts was accepted as Scripture, yet not widely preached on (Chrys. *Hom. Acts* 1.1).

54. A significance recognized by Luke and probably also in Gal 2:11. Even if the tradition were accurate, the Greek language in Eusebius may suggest only that Luke was of "an Antiochan family," not that he hailed from there (Ramsay, *Luke the Physician*, 66–67, citing analogous language in, e.g., Arrian *Ind.* 18).

55. On rising asceticism, see, e.g., Keener, "Marriage, Divorce," 713–14. Although it appears earlier (e.g., Valantasis, "Musonius"), it especially flourished in the second century and later (Deming, *Celibacy*; cf. Glenny, "Continence"). On the other hand, some of these traditions may be correct: Luke was, presumably, unmarried for the years he traveled with Paul, and he may give hints of valuing singleness (e.g., Luke 2:37; some interpretations of 20:35). Fitzmyer, *Luke*, 41–47, argues that Luke was a Semitic Gentile, ethnically Syrian,

of the Gospel (lines 2–8) and Acts (lines 34ff.), but although traditionally assigned to the late second century, its date is now in dispute. A very minor textual variant at Acts 20:13 appears to support Lukan authorship, but again this source is of uncertain date.[56]

Probably more helpful are some other commonly cited sources. Irenaeus (ca. 180 C.E.) also attributes Acts to Luke (*Her.* 3.1.1; 3.13.3; 3.14.1).[57] The same tradition appears in Clement of Alexandria (*Strom.* 5.12), Tertullian (*Marc.* 4.2), Origen (in Euseb. *H.E.* 6.25), and others.[58] At least equally important, 𝔓[75] (175–225 C.E.) calls the Gospel the "Gospel according to Luke."[59] Our earliest external evidence unanimously supports Luke's authorship. Given his relative obscurity, this is probably not coincidence.

II. Companions in Pauline Literature

Even if the tradition is based on an inference from early Christian evidence, we might make a similar inference ourselves (based on the likely slighter evidence available to us). As Mark Powell notes, "If it could be established that the third gospel and the book of Acts were written by one of Paul's coworkers, most scholars would agree that Luke is as likely a candidate as any."[60] Paul[61] names most of his associates during his Roman custody; given the risks they ran in identifying with a prisoner, this honor would have been deemed appropriate. It is unlikely that one who voyaged to Rome with Paul and remained with him for some time there would remain anonymous when Paul seems to name the candidates exhaustively (Col 4:10–14; Phlm 23–24).

Among these named candidates, the author does not seem to be Paul's fellow prisoner Aristarchus, though he accompanied Paul to Rome (Col 4:10; Phlm 24); Aristarchus is distinguished from the author en route to Rome in Acts 27:2 as well as earlier in 20:4–5 (and by implication in 19:29). Those who argue that the author is a Gentile may rule out several of Paul's companions, including Aristarchus (Col 4:10–11); the author's lack of interest in the Lycus Valley might rule out Epaphras (1:7; 4:12). Meanwhile, Demas (4:14; Phlm 24) may not have persevered long enough to write the work (if 2 Tim 4:10 reports accurately).[62]

A more likely proposal is Titus, who was a close companion of Paul yet, surprisingly, does not appear in Acts even when Paul's epistles indicate his activity (Gal 2:1–3; 2 Cor 2:13; 7:6–8:23; 12:18).[63] But given Titus's greater prominence in Paul's letters than Luke, why would the tradition have unanimously settled on Luke?[64] The same

---

rather than Greek. I think that Luke's worldview fits the Hellenism of Achaia, Macedonia, or Asia better, though the external evidence favors Syria.

56. "The O. Syr. (perhaps representing the original δ text)" (Bruce, *Acts¹*, 374; cf. p. 5 and his comments on an Armenian commentary, following Conybeare's comments in Ropes, *Text*, 442); R. Williams, *Acts*, 17, dates the variant to ca. 120 C.E., but this seems unduly optimistic.

57. Irenaeus also appeals to the "we" narrative for Luke as Paul's companion in *Her.* 3.1.1; 3.14.1.

58. C. Williams, *Acts*, 2; some also cite as secondary evidence the Western text of Acts 11:28 (placing the author in Antioch) and the Armenian variant on 20:13. Later, see the consensus in Jerome *Vir. ill.* 7 (Pelikan, *Acts*, 30).

59. Witherington, *Acts*, 56.

60. Powell, *Acts*, 33. (Of course, as Powell notes, not all accept this premise.)

61. Or, according to some views of Colossians, the Paulinist; but Philemon, which also names Luke (though not his profession), is usually regarded as a genuine Pauline captivity letter.

62. C. Williams, *Acts*, 3.

63. Some argue that Titus remains anonymous because he was Luke's "brother" in 2 Cor 8:18 (which Ramsay very tentatively suggests might mean "cousin"; cf. *Luke the Physician*, 18, including n. 1); but this is only one possible guess. "Brother" may be a fictive kinship label (cf. comment on Acts 9:17).

64. With C. Williams, *Acts*, 3–4. The proposal of Titius Justus (Acts 18:7) does not solve the lack of Titus's mention in Acts 20, though the abbreviation of the narrative might. Nor can Titus be the same companion elsewhere named Luke if we accept the tradition in 2 Tim 4:10.

might be said if one argues (less plausibly) for Timothy.[65] Yet Luke does, in fact, fit our narrow list of possible candidates. Early sources indicate that Luke was with Paul in Rome (Col 4:14; Phlm 24; cf. 2 Tim 4:11).[66]

Luke was not otherwise prominent in tradition, and so the unanimous support for his authorship in the tradition is noteworthy.[67] We would not expect anyone to have invented a non-apostle and non-eyewitness of Jesus's ministry; indeed, Irenaeus can be construed as sounding almost defensive about Luke as the author.[68] Moreover, it is unlikely that a work the size of a Gospel would have circulated anonymously in the churches;[69] the oral tradition remained strong in the early second century, and the tradition would likely preserve the author's name (surely known to the first audience; cf. "I" in the prefaces) more readily than nearly any other detail. Some writers object that the authors of certain works, such as the *Epistle to Diognetus*, are unknown;[70] but Theophilus surely knew Luke personally, and a work the size of Luke-Acts would not easily lend itself to the same fate as works whose authors were forgotten.

Thus many scholars accept Luke as the author of Acts.[71] For example, renowned classicist Arthur Darby Nock confessed that he had long been unable to view the author as "Paul's friend, the physician, the beloved. The objections remain formidable, but I am now inclined to agree with Cadbury and Dibelius that he was a companion of Paul and with Dibelius that the traditional name may be used."[72] Indeed, as one scholar notes (accurately for at least Anglophone scholarship at the time of his writing), this "traditional view of its authorship, unquestioned till the end of the eighteenth century, but seriously challenged in the nineteenth, is once again generally accepted now."[73] Although such historical judgments lack absolute certainty, the arguments in favor of Luke's authorship seem to me to outweigh those against it or for alternative figures.

---

65. If Timothy composed the Pastorals from memory of Paul's words and also wrote Acts, this would explain similarities between each type of work; historians might use the first-person but recount their participation in the narrative's activity in the third person (see comment on Acts 16:10). But apart from Acts 16:1–3, Timothy does not "participate," and if Timothy were involved in Luke's "we," we would expect a "we" at 17:14–15, 18:5, 19:22, and 20:4. Moreover, early Christian tradition would hardly replace well-known Timothy with obscure Luke.

66. The Lucius of Acts 13:1 (not part of a "we" narrative) is undoubtedly different, as is probably the Lucius of Rom 16:21 (cf. also Danker, *New Age*, xii), as noted above. "Lucius" was one of the most common Latin names (Stambaugh, *City*, 94).

67. E.g., Danker, *New Age*, xii; Marshall, *Acts*, 44–45; idem, *Luke*, 33–34; Longenecker, *Acts*, 34–36. Cadbury, "Tradition," notes that the tradition is unanimous but questions whether it may depend on the Muratorian Canon, which may have invented an answer that it lacked.

68. Witherington, *Acts*, 56.

69. Of Aune's reasons for anonymity claims in ancient documents (*Dictionary of Rhetoric*, 35), we may rule out fear of recrimination. Luke's use of personal pronouns probably rules out the document as purely communal property; this leaves his second explanation (that the original recipients know the author's identity) as most likely here. Anonymity might follow OT models for emphasizing the content over the author (Baum, "Anonymity"). But sometimes, as with Xenophon's works, authorship was known or even "an open secret" though not specified in the work itself, but available to later generations only through ancient traditions (Brown, *Historians*, 91).

70. Cf. C. Williams, *Acts*, 3.

71. E.g., Knox, *Acts*, 1–15; Rackham, *Acts*, xv–xvii; Emmet, "Tradition"; Knowling, "Acts," 7; Dibelius, *Studies in Acts*, 135–37; Delebecque, *Actes*; Blaiklock, *Acts*, 13–15; Stagg, *Acts*, 24; Bruce, *Acts¹*, 1–8; Guthrie, *Introduction*, 113–25; Fitzmyer, *Luke*, 35–53; *Theologian*, 1–26; *Acts*, 50; Finegan, *Apostles*, 1–2; Arrington, *Acts*, xxxii; D. Williams, *Acts*, 2–5; Hertig and Gallagher, "Introduction," 4–5; Peterson, *Acts*, 1–4; Wenham and Walton, *Guide*, 313–14; apparently also Collins, *Mark*, 5. Cf. Boismard and Lamouille, *Actes*, 1:42–43, for the second redactional stage; they also believe him an eyewitness of some of the events he narrates (ibid., 1:17).

72. Nock, *Essays*, 827, basing his evaluation especially on the "we" narrative and Luke 1:3.

73. Hull, *Spirit in Acts*, 13. If the view that this is "almost unchallenged" (Gangel, *Acts*, 1) is too optimistic (presumably counting primarily conservative scholarship), the contrary position can likewise probably claim a majority only by emphasizing disproportionately its own advocates.

Indeed, some scholars even argue that Luke, who was said to be present with Paul to the end (2 Tim 4:11), wrote the Pastorals for him, on the basis of similarities in style.[74] Stylistic differences are to be expected, of course, when an author composes in different genres.[75] (Thus, for example, if Lucian genuinely authored *Gout*,[76] the style would nevertheless differ significantly because of its poetic form.)[77] The Pastorals may share more Stoic ethical vocabulary with Luke than with any other specific NT writer outside Pauline literature, so that Luke seems the likeliest candidate we know of (a significant qualification) in Paul's circle. Still, one does not wish to hang a case for Lukan authorship of Luke-Acts on the mention of Luke's presence in 2 Tim 4:11; in my opinion, defending common authorship of Acts and the Pastorals requires considerable ingenuity in harmonizing their respective Pauline itineraries.[78] It seems safest not to count Lukan parallels in the Pastorals too heavily in favor of Acts' authorship.

Some scholars today would be anxious to avoid the association with Luke, since, as Fitzmyer notes, it has become fashionable for scholars to display critical "objectivity" by denying early traditions about authorship.[79] (Dibelius offered a similar complaint when he contended for Lukan authorship in an earlier generation.)[80] As much as I would like to be fashionable, however, I am among those who believe that scholars have a greater responsibility toward seeking to discern and articulate what they genuinely believe is true than remaining innocuous in terms of academic politics. Although I acknowledge that many other scholars deny Lukan authorship for sincere and honorable reasons (especially those who genuinely believe Acts incompatible with a traveling companion of Paul), I honestly believe that this is where the best (though limited) evidence points.

In short, against many NT scholars, I continue to maintain that "we" in Acts as in other ancient historical narratives nearly always constituted a claim that the narrator was present. There is little possibility that the narrator is distinct from the author; distinguishing an unidentified narrator from the author was not normal practice in ancient histories, and nothing in Luke's narration suggests it.[81] Moreover, Luke would

74. Most thoroughly, for Luke as full author, Wilson, *Pastoral Epistles*, marshaling considerable evidence; for Luke as Paul's amanuensis for the Pastorals, C. F. D. Moule, followed by others (see, e.g., Knight, *Sayings*, 149–50); quite plausibly, Lukan redaction (Feuillet, "Affinités"). Cf. also others (e.g., Witherington, *Homilies*, 57–61; idem, *Acts*, 807n104; noting commonalities, Aune, *Dictionary of Rhetoric*, 339). Boismard and Lamouille, *Actes*, 1:42–43, attribute the penultimate redactional stage of Acts to the author of the Pastorals, whom they hold to be Luke. Even if one accepted this view, it still would not need to make the Pastorals anything like a "third volume" for Luke-Acts (*pace* Quinn, "Volume," 70–75; see Witherington, *Acts*, 807n104). Chapter 7, above, also discusses questions of the Pastorals' authorship.

75. Cf., e.g., Suet. *Rhet.* 6; Keener, *John*, 128–31; Peterson, "Introduction," 5. History is quite distinct from nonnarrative genres (Pliny *Ep.* 5.8.7–11), and even within a work, one should vary style at times (3.13.4; 6.33.7–8; 9.29.1–2).

76. So Macleod, "Introduction to *Gout*," 319–20.

77. The Pastorals also employ some metaphoric medical imagery (see Malherbe, *Philosophers*, ch. 8, "Medical Imagery in the Pastoral Epistles," 121–36), though medical metaphors were common (see, e.g., Keener, *Matthew*, 298, on Matt 9:12) and appear even in earlier Pauline texts (Lohse, *Colossians*, 121–22, although this is not technical language).

78. See the excursus at Acts 20:25. Cf. Schröter, "Paulusrezeption," for a comparison of the reception of Paul in Acts and the Pastorals.

79. Fitzmyer, *Acts*, 50 (himself nevertheless maintaining Lukan authorship).

80. Dibelius, *Studies in Acts*, 136; his view "is completely opposed to the one which was known to the generation of our teachers (with the exception of Harnack) as the 'critical' view," which complained that Acts "could not have been written by Luke, Paul's companion." Dibelius supports Luke's authorship (*Studies in Acts*, 104, 135–37).

81. On potential distinctions between authors and narrators (esp. in modern texts), and my argument against this occurring in the Fourth Gospel, see Keener, *John*, 111–12, 917–18, 1154–55. The distinction appears in fiction, but not (or at best rarely) in historical narrative; pseudepigraphic devices like unreliable narrators were much less common in antiquity than today (Kurz, *Reading Luke-Acts*, 169–70).

hardly have left a source's "we" as a deliberately deceptive marker (at least Theophilus and probably a wider circle of hearers already knew his identity) or as an accident (given the compositional unity of his work and the location-specific recurrence of the marker). Once we grant that the author was a traveling companion of Paul during specific periods, several known candidates are possible, but the strongest case is for Luke. In this instance, I believe that the tradition got the attribution correct.

c. Physicians and Luke

Nothing in the text of Luke-Acts requires us to suppose that the author was a physician. If, however, external evidence leads us to suppose that Luke the physician is in fact the likeliest individual candidate for author, the text of Luke-Acts is consistent with such a premise. Examining evidence for physicians in antiquity may give us a better sense of the sort of background "Luke the physician" may have had.

The language of Luke-Acts is consistent with the tradition that a physician (Col 4:14) wrote it,[82] including the use of language characteristic of scientific treatises.[83] Long ago William Kirk Hobart (as the extreme example) argued for an abundance of medical terminology in Luke, both where this language is missing in parallel passages of Mark and Matthew[84] and where Mark and Matthew omit the accounts altogether.[85]

We should, however, be clear that, apart from the tradition, such language is plainly not sufficient to indicate that the writer is a physician. The same language, for example, also appears in other historians.[86] Matthew and Mark seem no less interested in healings than Luke is,[87] and despite Luke's sometimes more sophisticated language, Kirsopp Lake and Henry Cadbury long ago showed that his supposed medical terminology actually appears in ancient texts far more broadly than in medical writers. Indeed, more than 80 percent of Hobart's supposed medical terms appear in the LXX, sometimes frequently; three-quarters also appear in Lucian (and 90 percent in Lucian, Josephus, and Plutarch combined); and the other Gospels sometimes include medical language that Luke lacks.[88] As detractors of the medical-language argument long ago pointed out, "The fact that a word is found in a medical book proves nothing as to the profession of another writer who uses it, if it be also used elsewhere."[89] Moreover, Luke employs both nautical and legal

82. Cf., e.g., Eckey, *Apostelgeschichte*, 14–15. Luke's interest in sickness and healing extends to concepts, not just vocabulary or "word analogies" (see esp. Weissenrieder, *Images*, esp. concluding observations, 365–66). In the NT, only Luke uses παραχρῆμα (at once, immediately) with reference to health; this ancient pharmacological usage does not, by itself, identify him as a physician, of course (Fabricius, "Παραχρῆμα").

83. Alexander, *Preface*, 176–77. For language resembling technical treatises, see further Alexander, "Preface"; for Luke's scientific background, see also Padilla, "Παιδεία," 435–36. Luke-Acts does not fit the genre of scientific treatise, but similarities in prologue language would be consistent with the tradition about Luke's background (Witherington, *Acts*, 14–15). Nevertheless, technical treatises involved a range of other topics (including oratory, ethics, mathematics, and ethnography; see Sallmann, "Technical Literature").

84. Hobart, *Medical Language*, 54–85 (conclusion, 85).

85. Ibid., 86ff.

86. See Schmidt, "Influences," 59.

87. *Pace* Harnack, *Acts*, 133 (emphasizing healings in the "we" sections). The claim that Luke, as a physician, had special reason to omit Mark's judgment in Mark 5:26 is also questionable (as also noted by Pilch, *Healing*, 95); Matthew likewise omits it, and medical writers themselves admitted that physicians sometimes made sicknesses worse (Hippocr. *Aff.* 13). Eve, *Miracles*, 357, suggests that these may be "folk-healers."

88. See W. Clarke, "Septuagint," 83; A. Clark, *Acts*, 405–6. Admittedly, our corpus for each of these noncanonical sources is substantially larger than for Luke.

89. Cadbury, Foakes-Jackson, and Lake, "Subsidiary Points," 355. Most scholars today rightly follow the argument of Cadbury (against specifically medical language) rather than the contrary argument of Hobart, T. Zahn, or Harnack (e.g., Schille, *Apostelgeschichte*, 28).

language without his being a sailor or jurist; the breadth of his vocabulary simply illustrates that he was well educated.[90]

Nevertheless, the language is *consistent* with that of a physician if we have other reasons to believe this was Luke's profession.[91] Not all the arguments for this position are compelling. Because Luke claims that the Maltese highly honored "us" (Acts 28:10), for example, some have argued that Luke (i.e., Luke the physician of Col 4:14) practiced his medical art alongside Paul's supernatural healing.[92] Although we cannot rule out such medical practice, nothing in the text of Acts necessarily suggests it. Better arguments exist for Luke's familiarity with medicine. Thus Annette Weissenrieder has recently argued, based on a detailed study, that it is certain that the Gospel's author "had some knowledge of ancient medicine."[93] Evidence favoring Luke the physician as author (on the basis of inference from Paul's letters and early Christian tradition) invites us to consider this possibility.

The profession of physician would certainly not count against Luke's writing as a historian. The ancient world had no "professional historians" but merely politicians, philosophers, orators, and others who wrote histories.[94] Physicians were known among the intelligent professions (Diog. Laert. 6.2.24),[95] and at least some were rhetorically skilled.[96] Certainly, our author is a cultured historical and theological writer comfortable with the LXX and Hellenistic Jewish Christian tradition.[97] Some philosophers concerned themselves with medicine; accounts claim that Pythagoreans had traditions of medical knowledge that they applied.[98]

With his likely good Greek education, Luke as a physician might also be well equipped for other intellectually stimulating tasks. Although moralists were not usually physicians nor physicians moralists, both were respectable professions and one could not complain if compared to the other. Ancient writers regularly compared physical sickness to moral or intellectual sickness,[99] and physical health to that of the soul;[100] some argued for healing for the soul alongside, and as more essential than, healing for the body.[101] Thus physicians became a metaphor for many kinds of help,

90. Powell, *Acts*, 24, on Cadbury, *Making*, 219–20. For Luke's language betraying some education and rhetorical knowledge, cf., e.g., Langner, *Hechos*, 34.

91. Witherington, *Acts*, 779n129, noting that Horsley, *Documents*, 2:20ff., §2, favors reopening the case for the author's being a doctor; also Robertson, *Luke*, 90ff.; Bruce, *Acts*[1], 29. In the late twentieth century, more scholars have shown appreciation for potential medical language (Roschke, "Healing," 463–64). Parsons, *Luke*, 6, also rightly points to Cadbury's caveat that his argument against using pervasive medical language to prove that the author was a physician was not meant to exclude the claim that the author was a physician.

92. Ramsay, *Luke the Physician*, 16.

93. Weissenrieder, *Images*, 335 (summarizing an important result of her study).

94. Rebenich, "Prose," 289.

95. See further Watson, "Education," 311, including comments about the use of Greek (though cf. Galen) and the usual study of texts alongside apprenticeship. Cf. Galen's philosophic orientation in Gill, "Galen and Stoics."

96. Cf. Hippocr. *Ep.* 23.1 and the comments of Aune, *Dictionary of Rhetoric*, 323 (s.v. "Novelistic Letters"); Galen *Grief* 24b–26. One well-known earlier Hellenistic physician, Ctesias, was also a historian, albeit not a very good one (Brown, *Historians*, 78–79).

97. Pesch, *Apostelgeschichte*, 1:27.

98. Iambl. *V.P.* 29.163–64; 34.244. In a later period, cf. Christian monks in Arab cultures (Irvin and Sunquist, *Earliest Christianity*, 201–2).

99. E.g., Plato *Rep.* 4.444E; *Rhet. Alex.* 1, 1422b.33–36; Cic. *Tusc.* 3.3.5; 3.10.22; 4.13.28; Epict. *Diatr.* 4.8.29; Pliny *Ep.* 4.22.7; Max. Tyre 7 passim, esp. 7.7; 25.5–6; 28 passim, esp. 28.4; Diog. Laert. 10.138; Porph. *Marc.* 31.480–83; Arius Did. *Epit.* 2.7.10e, pp. 62f.20–21, 27–28; 2.7.11k, pp. 82–83.9–11.

100. E.g., Plut. *Virt.* 3, *Mor.* 101B; Arius Did. *Epit.* 2.7.5b.4, pp. 16–17.32–35; pp. 18–19.1–14; cf. *Rhet. Alex.* pref. 1421a.16–17.

101. E.g., Philost. *Ep. Apoll.* 23; cf. 3 John 2.

including rulers who directed the state[102] and (most commonly, at least in moralist literature) teachers and moralists who helped the human soul.[103] Occasionally orators compared orators to physicians,[104] and historians compared historians to physicians.[105] Philosophers were like physicians, opined Dio Chrysostom; the wise advice of both went unheeded (*Or.* 27.7).[106] Naturally early Christian workers could be compared with physicians as well.[107] Colossians 4:14 is not, however, in a context that would suggest a figurative interpretation.

The idea that Paul sometimes experienced illness (Gal 4:13) might also suggest why a physician might be especially welcome to travel with Paul.[108] Perhaps this, rather than status associations, would explain Paul's explicit mention of Luke's profession in Col 4:14. Their friendship might, then, be less than surprising; a prominent person's physician was often among the person's closest friends and confidants.[109]

Excursus: Ancient Physicians

On the view that Luke may have been a physician, it may be useful to explore briefly what could be relevant to Luke in the information we have about physicians in antiquity. This material is in an excursus, however, because I am not confident that much of this information, interesting though I find it, sheds light directly on the text of Acts itself.

1. Physicians and Their Limitations

Ancient medical knowledge being what it was, we cannot be sure when Luke's medical training would have helped Paul (and others) and when it could have hurt them.[110]

102. E.g., Aeschines *Ctes.* 225; Dion. Hal. *Ant. rom.* 9.53.3; Plut. *Cam.* 9.2; Philost. *Vit. soph.* 1.15.500; Iambl. *V.P.* 30.172; cf. military strategists in Quint. Curt. 5.9.3.

103. See Xen. *Mem.* 4.2.5; Cic. *Tusc.* 4.27.58; Livy 42.40.3; Philo *Good Person* 12; Sen. Y. *Ep. Lucil.* 40.5; 72.6; 75.6; 85.36; Mus. Ruf. 1, p. 32.8–12; p. 34.3; 2, p. 36.27–32; 3, p. 42.19–21; 5, p. 50.3–8, with 5, pp. 48.1–50.3; 6, p. 52.10, 27; 8, p. 66.16–18; 16, p. 100.20–21, 27; p. 104.9–10; Epict. *Diatr.* 2.14.21; Dio Chrys. *Or.* 1.8; 8.5; 13.32; 32.17–18; 33.44; 34.26; 38.7; Pliny *Ep.* 5.16.10; Philod. *Crit.* frgs. 7; 39; 59.9; 63; 64; 69; 86 (= 90 N); column 17 a; also Tablet 12 M; Lucian *Phil. Sale* 8; *Dem.* 7; *Nigr.* 38; Lucian *Hipp.* 1; Anacharsis *Ep.* 9; Crates *Ep.* 17; Diogenes *Ep.* 49; Diog. Laert. 2.70; 6.1.4; 6.2.30; Diod. Sic. 12.13.4; Philost. *Vit. Apoll.* 7.26; *Ep. Apoll.* 1; probably also Mus. Ruf. frg. 36; Philod. *Crit.* Tablet 12, end; Max. Tyre 1.2–3; 4.2; 22.7; Mark 2:17. Reason itself is a doctor in Max. Tyre 10.3–4. For harsh Cynics claiming to be healers, see Malherbe, *Philosophers*, 135; for the metaphor for philosophers generally, see Nussbaum, *Therapy*. In Judaism, see, e.g., *'Abot R. Nat.* 23 A; *y. Ketub.* 7:7, §3.

104. Ael. Arist. *Def. Or.* 247–49, §76D; Tac. *Dial.* 23, 41.

105. Polyb. 3.7.5; 12.25d.3–5.

106. The image often applied to Diogenes the Cynic, who may have been among its early users (e.g., Dio Chrys. *Or.* 8.7–8; 9.2; Diog. Laert. 6.2.30).

107. Cf. discussion in Bazzana, "Missionaries as Physicians."

108. Cf., e.g., Witherington, *Acts*, 57; more elaborately, Wagner, *Acts*, 391 (suggesting that Luke joined him in Galatia when he was ill; this does not fit Acts). Itinerant doctors were not uncommon (Horsley, *Documents*, 2:19–21, §2), and some teachers regarded them as helpful (e.g., Socratics *Ep.* 32). It is unlikely, however, that 2 Cor 12:7 refers to sickness (see Keener, *Corinthians*, 240); Gal 4:13, by contrast, likely does involve sickness, though not of the eyes (see idem, "Eyes").

109. E.g., Polyb. 5.56.1–6; Val. Max. 1.7.1; Tac. *Ann.* 4.3; 15.64, 69.

110. Medicine could be combined with astrology (Ptolemy *Tetrab.* 1.3.15). But in this period, Greeks rarely mixed magic with medicine (Yamauchi, "Magic?," 113–15; he argues this point even in the majority of cases in earlier Egypt [107–10]).

Seneca, a contemporary of Paul, opines that earlier physicians lacked the knowledge available to those of Seneca's time, having been ignorant of techniques such as bloodletting and bandaging extremities to draw strength from the middle of the body.[111] One parody praises physicians for helping the glutton vomit and draining most of his blood, so preventing his death from his gluttony.[112] Medical malpractice was often dangerous, sometimes fatal.[113]

The profession's activities in antiquity would have entailed serious risks even if the state of medical knowledge had been more accurate. Although the papyri reveal that medical books were widespread, no structures existed to provide certification or even an examination for physicians. Many would have learned their trade through apprenticeship under physicians or in the urban medical centers.[114] But competing schools of physicians existed—for example, those in the Hippocratic tradition at Cos and the Ctesian tradition at Cnidus.[115] Some rejected "modern" medicine and preferred natural herbs (e.g., Pliny E. *N.H.* 25; 26.7.12–26.9.20).[116]

a. Medicine and Superstition

Peasants experimented over the centuries, and treatments that coincided with recoveries became traditional, though only some of them were genuinely empirically effective.[117] It was said that Marcus Cato, rejecting Greek physicians, used only home remedies, costing the lives of his wife and child.[118] Sometimes a genuine medical treatment can appear in the context of magical incantations.[119] Superstitious traditions sometimes affected even more empirical forms of medicine, such as Galen's approach.[120] Some cures, happily, were so difficult to procure that they were not falsifiable![121] For example, urine from a wild boar's bladder, placed a bit at a time in one's drinks, was

111. Sen. Y. *Ep. Lucil.* 95.22.

112. Alciph. *Paras.* 4 (Hetoemocossus to Zomecpneon), 3.7 (¶2). Cf. the use of purgatives to remove sickness (Cic. *Fam.* 16.10.1; cf. Plut. *Cam.* 9.2). On bloodletting and other "cures," see Stambaugh, *City*, 136–37. For cases of fraud, see Paul of Aegina, Appendix to Book 5, *On Feigned Diseases and their Detection*, as cited in Toner, *Culture*, 40.

113. E.g., Xen. *Anab.* 6.4.11; Heraclitus *Ep.* 6; Paulus *Sent.* 5.23.19; cf. Hippocr. *Aff.* 13; making matters worse, Plut. *L. Wealth* 2, *Mor.* 523E. On other occasions, they simply could not help (e.g., Mark 5:26; Tob 2:10; Athen. *Deipn.* 15.666A; also *CIL* 2.4314 in Sherk, *Empire*, 217) and sometimes, because of greater exposure, themselves died in larger percentage (Thucyd. 2.47.4; for the image of the sick physician, see Luke 4:23; Philost. *Vit. soph.* 1.15.500; *Gen. Rab.* 23:4; *Lev. Rab.* 5:6; *Babr.* 120.6–7; cf. Pliny E. *N.H.* 7.37.124; Max. Tyre 8.3; Marc. Aur. 3.3.1; 4.48; Nolland, "Parallels to 'Physician'"; Renehan, "Quotations," 19). Despite reports of miracle cures at Asklepieia, Koester, *Introduction*, 1:174, reckons that a larger number of unreported cases went uncured.

114. Lewis, *Life*, 153. Indeed, perhaps most learned under fathers or on their own, though a minority traveled to study (Nutton, "Training," 840).

115. E.g., Aune, *Dictionary of Rhetoric*, 323 (s.v. "Novelistic Letters").

116. On the medical use of various plants, see Touwaide, "Medicinal plants."

117. Lewis, *Life*, 152. Cf. herbal remedies in Pliny E. *N.H.* 25 (rejecting the "guesswork" of those who neglected herbs, 26.7.12–26.9.20), even for bad breath (25.110.175). One supposed Ethiopian plant cured dropsy (24.102.163); another induced hallucinations leading to suicide (24.102.163; 27.1.2; 27.3.11–12); some plants from the Asian interior could pacify beasts (24.102.162–63); some soils had healing properties (Philost. *Hrk.* 28.5). For treatments for snakebites, see comment on Acts 28:5. Novelists could write of herbs resuscitating the dead (Apul. *Metam.* 2.28).

118. Plut. *M. Cato* 23.3–24.1.

119. E.g., *PDM* 14.574–85 (using oil in the throat, alongside an incantation, to dislodge a bone). On magical cures, see also Llewelyn, *Documents*, 6:190–96, §28 (R. A. Kearsley). For ancient Egyptian medicine as a mixture of genuine observation and magic, see also Jordan, *Egypt*, 157.

120. Boudon, "Marges."

121. E.g., "To produce conception, give, as hot as possible, inkfish roasted over a flame, very hot and half-cooked, to nibble. Grind Egyptian nitre, coriander, and cumin, make small balls and insert in the vagina" (Hippocr. *Epid.* 2.6.29).

a reported cure for dropsy.[122] More accessibly, mixing a cow's brain with one's food might help one's eyelashes to grow;[123] binding a frog to the back of a baby's head as an amulet could cure the baby's illness.[124]

Some of the rabbis appear to have been familiar with Hippocratic traditions, including those about climate and health;[125] some scholars argue that they sometimes surpassed the best Greek medicine, avoiding excessive reliance on theory.[126] Nevertheless, they still faced the limitations of medical knowledge available in their era. One rabbi who was a physician explained the proper approach to bloodletting.[127] Some concluded, for example, that a suppressed discharge led to dropsy or that holding in urine produced jaundice.[128] The rabbis reported various folk formulas meant to cure ailments;[129] some of the medicine bordered on magic.[130]

b. Sounder Medicine

Some ancients, however, provided useful empirical observations about anatomy and physiology.[131] Occasional recommendations of exercise were beneficial,[132] as were, undoubtedly, some dietary recommendations.[133] Some medicines worked (or at least coincided with recovery).[134] Some physicians also rejected many of the same remedies that we would consider superstitious;[135] Soranus, for example, claims that the ancients did not realize that their "blood-drawing suppositories" did more harm

122. Pliny E. *N.H.* 28.68.232. Among more magical remedies (30.31.105) was the application of dogs' vomit to one's abdomen.

123. Pliny E. *N.H.* 29.37.115. Happily, mad cow disease was first reported in 1986.

124. Pliny E. *N.H.* 32.48.138.

125. Newmyer, "Climate."

126. Newmyer, "Medicine."

127. An Amora in *b. Šabb.* 129b. For bloodletting, see also Fronto *Ad verum imp.* 2.6; in the rabbis, *y. Ber.* 2:7, §3.

128. *B. Bek.* 44b, bar.

129. *M. Šabb.* 6:9; *b. Šabb.* 108b; *y. Šabb.* 6:9, §2. Even scorpions were used for curing some ailments (*b. Giṭ.* 69a; this apparently worked [Amitai, "Ash"]).

130. E.g., *b. Šabb.* 66b–67a; *Giṭ.* 68b. For magical cures, see further, e.g., Levene, "Heal"; for some that would appear to us as sympathetic magic but not to ancients, see Bar-Ilan, "Magic and Religion." Most Jewish pietists frowned on genuinely magical medicine (*1 En.* 7:1; 8:3). Nevertheless, Jewish women often wore an amulet to ward off miscarriages (*t. Šabb.* 4:2; Safrai, "Home," 764–65); one could also tie a hen to the mother, though shutting windows to block out demons was forbidden (Safrai, "Home," 766, citing *t. Šabb.* 6:4 and other sources). Burying the afterbirth helped warm the newborn (Safrai, "Home," 766, citing *t. Šabb.* 15:3).

131. See discussion in Vallance, "Anatomy." For earlier forms of medicine, see, e.g., Weeks, "Medicine"; in various regions, see Avalos, "Medicine." One digested faster lying on one's right side (Pliny E. *N.H.* 28.14.54).

132. See, e.g., Pliny E. *N.H.* 11.117.283–11.118.283; 28.14.53; Plut. *Demosth.* 6.2; Soranus *Gynec.* 1.5.25; 1.7.32; Libanius *Invective* 5.16; cf. sunshine in Pliny E. *N.H.* 28.14.53, 55. Exercise was widely valued (e.g., Xen. *Cyr.* 1.6.17; *Lac.* 1.4; Isoc. *Demon.* 14; Plut. *Cic.* 4.3; 8.3; *Table* 4.1.3, *Mor.* 662F; Pliny *Ep.* 3.1.7–8; Fronto *Pr. Hist.* 11; Philost. *Vit. soph.* 2.17.598; *Hrk.* 12.4; 33.14–18; Char. *Chaer.* 1.1.5), including by many philosophers (e.g., Xen. *Mem.* 1.2.4, 19; *Symp.* 2.17–19; Plato *Lach.* 182A; Mus. Ruf. 6, p. 54.10–11; 18B, p. 120.2–5; Diog. Laert. 6.2.70; 7.1.123; Iambl. *V.P.* 21.97; Crates *Ep.* 20), though it could also double as an analogy for practice in intellect (Sall. *Ep. Caes.* 10.2), virtue and philosophy (Cic. *Or. Brut.* 3.14; Sen. Y. *Ep. Lucil.* 80.3; *Dial.* 4.15.2; Mus. Ruf. 6 passim, e.g., p. 52.15–17; Diog. Laert. 7.1.8), or oratory (Dio Chrys. *Or.* 18.6; Eunapius *Lives* 495). Many valued study over physical exercise but approved both (e.g., Plut. *Educ.* 11, *Mor.* 8CD; cf. Isoc. *Demon.* 40).

133. E.g., eating in moderation and avoiding gluttony (Pliny E. *N.H.* 28.14.56); for food, rest, and exercise, see also Plut. *Adv. K. Well, Mor.* 122B–137E. For the value of milk (despite cultic connections), see Laskaris, "Mothers" (cf. other connotations in Keener, "Milk"). Even some of these recommendations were exaggerated; Pliny the Elder deals with foods used to cure ailments (*N.H.* 20), e.g., vision and stomachaches (20.39.98). Pythagoreans preferred dietary remedies to medicine (Iambl. *V.P.* 34.244).

134. Diod. Sic. 17.31.6.

135. E.g., Soranus *Gynec.* 3.4.29.

than good (*Gynec.* 3.1.12).[136] Whereas some Hippocratic works claimed that one could predict the baby's gender on the basis of physical phenomena in the mother,[137] Soranus rejected this supposition.[138] Not all physicians felt comfortable doing surgery, but Galen apparently expected most to be able to perform some of the essential, basic operations.[139] Many doctors trained at Asklepieia, where they observed many sick persons firsthand.[140] At the very least, the training would have taught physicians, probably including the Luke whom Paul mentions, to observe sicknesses carefully.

Some scholars have suggested that Luke's interest in pneumatology might also be consonant with the pneumatic school of thought gaining increasing attention among physicians in this period,[141] but one should not read much into this by itself, since more critical salvation-historical reasons for Luke's emphasis on the Spirit existed.[142] Although other factors are undoubtedly at work in Luke's generally positive view of women (see ch. 18 below), a medical profession would be consistent with this; the profession of physician was one that was open to both genders[143] (even if women physicians were often midwives),[144] although women were a minority.[145]

2. Physicians' Status and Background

Physicians were frequently slaves.[146] One scholar observes that "it is astonishing how often the name of a doctor shows him to have been a Greek freedman."[147] In medical matters, masters were known to submit to slave physicians.[148] Whether slave or free, they would be educated and of higher status, in most important respects, than nominally free peasants.[149] A physician lacking local competition could acquire considerable substance (Dio Chrys. *Or.* 77/78.8). The most reputable physicians could make large salaries;

136. Temkin, 139. A pregnant woman who was bled might well miscarry (Soranus *Gynec.* 1.19.65, citing Hippocr. *Aph.* 5.31). But cf. fasting during a part of the pregnancy (Soranus *Gynec.* 1.15.48–50; though cf. 1.16.54). Cf. also fasting and purgatives to get rid of sickness (Cic. *Fam.* 16.10.1).

137. Hippocr. *Aph.* 5.42, 48; *Epid.* 2.6; *On Barren Women*; *On Superfetation*.

138. Soranus *Gynec.* 1.13.45. He also addressed (1.19.60) the allegedly Hippocratic technique of jumping so as to discharge the seed.

139. Singer and Nutton, "Surgery," 1457.

140. Engels, *Roman Corinth*, 101.

141. See Marx, "Physician," who also notes other correspondences with physicians. They were influenced by Stoicism (Vallance, "Pneumatists") but remained a less prominent school (idem, "Medicine," 949), and the use of *pneuma* in both arteries and nerves goes back several centuries (see Staden, "Erasistratus"; Vallance, "Pneuma"). Another school was the "Methodists" (Touwaide, "Methodists").

142. Despite some overlap between Greek and Jewish usage, Luke's pneumatology is Jewish, especially biblical, not Greek (see Keener, *Spirit*, 7–8; also the excursus on the background of Luke's understanding of the Spirit in ch. 15 below).

143. For women's equivalent roles, see Flemming, "Women and Medicine"; cf. Reden, "Work," 743. Some professions, but a minority, were open to both genders (cf., e.g., Lindner, "Frau und Beruf").

144. Sherk, *Empire*, 223–24 (citing *ILS* 7802–3); Friedländer, *Life*, 1:171; Gardner, *Women*, 240. In Jewish Palestine, see, e.g., Jos. *Life* 185 (Josephus might mention it with a negative slant, but given his misogyny elsewhere this would not surprise us).

145. See discussion in King, "Gender roles: Medicine," 745; Flemming, "Women and Medicine." One list of more than ninety physicians includes only one woman, though Pleket lists five more (Horsley, *Documents*, 2:16–17, §2). For a more complete listing, see Lefkowitz and Fant, *Life*, 27, 161–62 (including *CIL* 6.7581 = *ILS* 7804; *CIL* 6.6851; 6.9614, 9615, 9617, 9619); for midwives, 162–64. Twenty-five appear in *Corpus inscriptionum latinarum* (King, "Midwives").

146. E.g., the inscriptions in Sherk, *Empire*, 150 (*FIRA* 1.73), 223–24 (*ILS* 5152; 7812); Friedländer, *Life*, 1:167–68; Stambaugh, *City*, 136; Meeks, *Urban Christians*, 57; Martin, *Slavery*, 7; cf. Diog. Laert. 6.2.30.

147. Charlesworth, *Trade Routes*, 95.

148. Diog. Laert. 6.2.30.

149. Thus, e.g., P.Col. 27.1.25–28 specifies among its six witnesses a physician (1.26) alongside a village scribe (1.28).

the wealthy might have their own doctors (slave or free) for their estates.[150] Physicians were normally considered honorable, which made a dishonorable one all the more unexpected (Lucian *Alex.* 60), though some could ridicule physicians as unable to accomplish anything (Athen. *Deipn.* 15.666A). A physician could argue that everyone needed doctors, one of the most useful professions (Quint. *Decl.* 268, esp. 268.2).

Some scholars argue that the author of Acts reflects a view of artisans characteristic of artisans themselves (rather than of the upper class),[151] though this suggestion appears difficult to quantify on the basis of our limited evidence in Acts. If "Luke" is a Greek version of the Latin name "Lucius,"[152] it would allow the suggestion that Luke had been a Greek slave for a Roman and received the master's name when freed.[153] If this were the case, Luke would also be a Roman citizen, perhaps explaining his interest in the synagogue of freedpersons (Acts 6:9) and the privilege accorded him in accompanying a citizen prisoner to Rome (27:2).[154] This is speculation (nothing, for example, indicates that Aristarchus, who also joined that voyage, was a citizen), but we do know that citizenship was a reward occasionally given to physicians (Pliny *Ep.* 10.5.1) or even to their relatives (10.11.1).[155] As a Latin praenomen, "Lucius" need not imply citizenship, and the contraction *Loukas* will not appear among cognomina in official documents since it is a nickname.[156]

Luke would have been welcome in Rome. Most physicians in Rome were foreigners,[157] and they were among the most prized foreigners in the city.[158] Thus a century earlier Julius Caesar had granted citizenship to doctors and teachers in Rome to increase the city's attractiveness to these trades (Suet. *Jul.* 42.1).[159] Despite positive incentives for competent physicians, however, Roman texts sometimes parody the uncertain attempts of physicians who could offer little certain help.[160]

Many physicians were Greeks; some earlier traditional Romans refused to trust them for this reason, but this mistrust had probably dissipated by the first century.[161] On the whole, Greek physicians from Asia Minor had the best reputation;[162] although we cannot be sure where Luke originated, it might be of interest that he seems to have joined Paul in urban Greek Asia (Acts 16:10).

150. Friedländer, *Life*, 1:172 (cf. also Tac. *Ann.* 4.63); specialists, especially surgeons (Friedländer, *Life*, 1:171), also existed. It was known that emperors had personal physicians (e.g., Jos. *Ant.* 19.134); physicians were normally available only to people of means (Malina and Rohrbaugh, *Gospels*, 84); poor people, by contrast, might obtain medical care simply from their barber (Stambaugh and Balch, *Environment*, 71). For doctors' ample income in *t. B. Bat.* 10:6, see Goodman, *State*, 60.

151. Witherington, *Acts*, 55.

152. Cf. Judge, *Rank*, 36n19: "Loukas ('Luke') may be a hellenised variation of Lucius." On the identity of the names, cf. further Ramsay, *Discovery*, 370–84; Deissmann, *Light*, 435.

153. Jeffers, *World*, 194. Jews could bear this name (e.g., *CIJ* 1:111, §155).

154. Though, even as a citizen, he probably would not have been granted the favor apart from the relatively light custody, based on the presumption of Paul's innocence by those who sent him.

155. Pliny's examples include the intervention of the emperor. Other rewards could be given (Dio Chrys. *Or.* 77/78.11, referring to Darius's time).

156. Judge, *First Christians*, 561, 563.

157. Friedländer, *Life*, 1:168.

158. See esp. Suet. *Aug.* 42.3, where doctors and teachers were the least dispensable foreigners there. Augustus honored his physicians (*Aug.* 59).

159. Cf. Vespasian's favor toward them in Sherk, *Empire*, 127–28.

160. See Stambaugh, *City*, 136–37, and sources there.

161. Plut. *M. Cato* 23.3–4; 24.1. The Greek physician in Dio Chrys. *Or.* 77/78.10 proves more successful than his Egyptian colleagues (Dio is, not surprisingly, Greek). The argument in Quint. *Decl.* 350.12 might presume that some persons mistrusted some prescriptions. Trust invested in physicians could make them potentially more dangerous if they wished harm (e.g., Libanius *Topics* 3).

162. Charlesworth, *Trade Routes*, 95. We read of a highly praised one in Corinth, though the patient in question apparently died (Kent, *Inscriptions*, no. 300, line 7 [p. 117]).

3. Paganism, Judaism, and Physicians

If Luke learned medical practice in pagan circles, he was likely closely exposed to Asclepius, patron deity of pagan physicians.[163] Cult sanctuaries of Asclepius were not only for the poor; they charged fees, and inscriptions show the mixed background of supplicants.[164] Because no surgical instruments have been recovered from Epidaurus (in contrast to Asclepius's sanctuary at Cos), some scholars suggest that many people drew help from the power of suggestion together with baths and nourishment.[165] (On the Asclepius cult, see, more extensively, ch. 9 above.)

Jewish people recognized that God was ultimately the healer,[166] and sought God's help in prayers.[167] Opinions differed on the role that physicians played in healing; a popular ancient sage declared that God's word, not medicaments, heals,[168] and some Jewish traditions preferred trusting God instead of physicians.[169] By the late second century, R. Judah mentions physicians among socially proscribed professions; although this may be partly a matter of class division, he assigns the best of them to Gehinnom.[170] Were such views widespread, Luke might have done well to keep his professional background to himself when in Jerusalem.[171]

At least some Palestinian Jews with a more cosmopolitan education, however, made use of physicians (Jos. *Life* 404), and a sage whose wisdom circulated widely in the first century praised physicians and their medicine as instruments of God (Sir 38:1–9).[172] The school of the second-century R. Ishmael held that God could work through physicians;[173] even Galilean physicians could earn a great deal.[174] Some thought that one should not reside in a city lacking a physician.[175]

163. E.g., *ILS* 2092. Asclepius figures prominently in Galen (Grant, *Gods*, 60). In larger towns, many physicians would be attached to the local cult of Asclepius (Friedländer, *Life*, 168–69; traditions associated Hippocrates with these Asclepiads [Kee, "Hippocratic Letters"]); public physicians were common (Horsley, *Documents*, 2:10–19, §2). For such physicians as "sons of Asclepius," Ἀσκληπιάδαι, see, e.g., Men. Rhet. 2.1–2, 375.14; Libanius *Common Topics* 3.5; for the association of medicine with Asclepius, see, e.g., Ach. Tat. 4.17.1; for "the gods" as originators of medicine, see Quint. *Decl.* 268.21; Libanius *Common Topics* 3.4.

164. Klauck, *Context*, 167.

165. Ibid., 166.

166. E.g., Exod 15:26; Wis 16:12; *b. Pesaḥ.* 68a (Raba). Sickness was often associated with sin (Gen 20:7, 17; Job 42:8; Sir 38:9–10; Jas 5:14–16; *Gen. Rab.* 97, NV; *Lev. Rab.* 18:4; *Pesiq. Rab.* 22:5; cf. 4Q560 in Naveh, "Fragments"). In a possibly first-century document, Raphael is assigned over diseases, wounds, and (apparently) healing (*1 En.* 40:9); angel invocation could drive away the spirits causing infirmity in *Test. Sol.* 18.

167. A prayer in Incant. Text 42.12 of the Aramaic incantation bowls (Isbell, *Bowls*, 101); Sir 31:17; 38:9; Jas 5:14–15; *m. Ber.* 5:5; *b. Ber.* 60b; *Gen. Rab.* 53:14; cf. synagogue prayers, especially the eighth benediction when applied to physical infirmities (cf. *y. Ta'an.* 2:2, §7; *Song Rab.* 7:2, §3). This appears to be a transcultural phenomenon; see Mbiti, *Religions*, 55.

168. Wis 16:12.

169. 2 Chr 16:12; *Test. Job* 38:7–8 (*OTP*)/38:11–13 (Kraft); cf. Job 13:4. Nevertheless, physicians in ancient Judah probably had more medical knowledge than we often assume (Wright, *Archaeology*, 171).

170. *M. Qidd.* 4:14; cf. *'Abot R. Nat.* 36 A.

171. This is especially the case if he was a Gentile (*m. 'Abod. Zar.* 2:2).

172. Cf. also Sir 10:10. Sir 38:15 could be directed against physicians, but in context probably is directed only against sickness. For the positive view of physicians in Sirach, see McConvery, "Ancient Physicians"; idem, "Praise." Kraemer, "Doctor," treats Sirach as transitional between the usually negative biblical tradition and the more open talmudic approach.

173. *B. Ber.* 60a (though many voices in the text attribute healing only to God).

174. Goodman, *State*, 60, cites *t. B. Bat.* 10:6. Negatively, cf. perhaps Mark 5:26, diplomatically omitted by Matthew and Luke.

175. So *y. Qidd.* 4:12, §2. "Honor your physician before you are sick" was a proverb for praying before trouble comes (*Exod. Rab.* 21:7).

Medical help was normally sought only as a secondary line of defense,[176] and one who needed to go to a physician was to pray for God's healing.[177] Given the mixing of magic with scientific elements in some Jewish folk medicine,[178] as noted, this may have been an especially good idea. Although Galilean physicians probably lacked formal Greek training, they adopted some Greek medical practices.[179] As also noted above, Galilean physicians, like Greek ones, mixed genuine medical knowledge[180] with what we would regard today as superstition.[181]

---

176. Goppelt, *Theology*, 1:142.

177. *B. Ber.* 60a, anonymous opinion.

178. See Urbach, *Sages*, 1:101; Safrai, "Home," 764–66; *b. Bek.* 44b; *Pesaḥ.* 111ab; *Giṭ.* 68b–70b; *Šabb.* 66b–67a; 108b–111a; cf. perhaps Vermes, *Jesus the Jew*, 63; *1 En.* 7:1; 8:3; Brayer, "Psychosomatics." The rabbis were, apparently, familiar with and sometimes surpassed some Greek medicine (cf. Newmyer, "Medicine"; idem, "Climate"); many ancient health practices were superstitious, but others, such as food, rest, and exercise (Plut. *Adv. K. Well, Mor.* 122B–137E), were prudent. Mixing magical and medical counsel was standard in antiquity, e.g., in Egyptian medicine (Jordan, *Egypt*, 157).

179. Goodman, *State*, 60, includes anatomical details (such as "the number of limbs," *m. 'Ohal.* 1:8; cf. also *t. 'Ed.* 2:10; *'Abot R. Nat.* 16 A; *Pesiq. Rab Kah.* Sup. 3:2; *Gen. Rab.* 69:1; *Lev. Rab.* 12:3; *Tg. Ps.-J.* on Gen 1:27).

180. Goodman, *State*, 60, lists *m. Pesaḥ.* 2; *t. Šabb.* 12(13):10–11 and cites skilled operations (*m. Bek.* 8:1; *Ker.* 3:8; *t. B. Qam.* 6:20; *'Ed.* 1:8; *'Ohal.* 2:6).

181. Goodman, *State*, 60, lists *m. Yoma* 8:6; *t. Šabb.* 4(5):9. See comments above on this topic.

LUKE'S AUDIENCE

The question of Luke's particular audience is less pressing today than it was in the heyday of redaction criticism. Increasingly scholars are recognizing that large narrative works probably addressed wider audiences than the local "communities" that scholars have often constructed.[1] Writers composed such works with more of an interest in them as enduring literature than as simply occasional documents.[2] Nevertheless, it is usually possible to locate an ideal target audience, generally one that the writer also expected to be most receptive.[3]

1. Of High Status and Educated?

Luke's ideal audience was probably, on average, of higher education than many others, with a wide knowledge of the northern Aegean Greek culture and a familiarity with the LXX. This observation probably also supports the likelihood that it was more economically stable than, say, rural peasants in Galilee or Egypt, and some were probably better off than the average artisan (Theophilus perhaps much better).

a. Theophilus and Marks of Status

The frequent scholarly suggestion that Luke's audience was wealthier and more highly educated, on average, than that of the other Gospels is a reasonable one.[4] Luke

---

1. Stanton, "Communities"; idem, *New People*, 50–51; Talbert, *John*, 63; esp. the essays in Bauckham, *Gospels for Christians*, particularly idem, "Gospels," esp. 48; Burridge, "People," 113–45; Alexander, "Book Production," 90; Parsons, *Acts*, 20.

2. Talbert, "Chance," 230.

3. For the latter assumption in the case of Josephus's audience, see Mason, "Value for Study," 597. See further Burridge, "People," 143, who compares Gospel audiences with "market niches" or "target audiences"; Barton, "Audiences," 194, though skeptical of "communities," thinks it appropriate to look for "the Gospel *audiences* and their social location(s)." Roman historians probably also had both a primary audience (the Roman elite) and secondary audiences (others) in mind; see Marincola, "Audiences," 12–13. For secondary audiences, one might consider the claim of Cic. *Fin.* 5.19.51 (cited in Laird, "Rhetoric," 207) that "even artisans" enjoyed history (although I suspect this may have taken a more popular form than Livy's 140 volumes noted by Laird, op. cit.).

4. E.g., Karris, "Poor"; Witherington, *Acts*, 63. We should note, however, that urban eastern Mediterranean Jews, in general, may have commanded a significant knowledge of recent history (cf. the ideal reader in *Sib. Or.* 5.1–50). For a survey of some views regarding the wealth of Luke's audience, see Donahue, "Decades on Rich and Poor."

dedicates his work to a "most excellent" Theophilus (Luke 1:3), a title suggesting that Theophilus was probably a person of prestige and rank in society (cf. Acts 26:25).[5]

Although Theophilus is an explicit "narratee,"[6] no ancient audience would assume that the dedicatee was necessarily socially representative of Luke's ideal audience. One might dedicate a work to a patron who would be of higher rank than the clients who heard the work read, for example, at one of the banquets sponsored by the patron. Nevertheless, by addressing Theophilus as at least a part of his audience, Luke appeals to a person with some status in the larger society.[7] Luke further emphasizes many people of status following the Way (e.g., Luke 8:3; 23:50–51; Acts 13:12; 17:4; 28:7); likewise, he portrays Paul's status as relatively high,[8] a point of interest to any ancient hearer but perhaps especially to another person of status.

Although his Gospel contains the most sweeping condemnations of the accumulation of wealth (e.g., Luke 3:11; 12:13–21, 33; 14:33), his very emphasis on this issue might suggest an audience that can afford to be challenged in the area of generosity.[9] (It also suggests that, like biblical prophets or Cynic sages, he was willing to confront those whose responsibility was greatest rather than simply curry favor.)[10] Luke's emphasis on the poor, prominent especially in his Gospel, does not tell us anything about Luke's own background; although Sirach emphasizes care for the poor, its author belongs to the elite (e.g., Sir 38:25–39:4).

Finally, an educated audience would best appreciate the elements of classical rhetoric alongside the appropriate stylistic variations for different settings. Whereas, in a work such as the *Infancy Gospel of Thomas*, Jesus refuses to learn the Greek alphabet, Jesus reads Scripture in Luke (Luke 4:16), and Paul quotes Greek poets (Acts 17:28) and had special academic training (22:3).[11]

b. Limitations of Such Inferences

At the same time, we should not press the connection with either Theophilus or elite converts in the text too far. Though Theophilus is of significant status and Luke emphasizes the high status of many characters, this need not mean that Luke's audience is entirely or mostly of high status. Even today groups marginalized from society are often eager to point to isolated high-status members or precedents that show them respectable with the dominant culture, a culture that otherwise tends to dismiss or ignore them. Religious persons attending secular schools hostile to their faith may cite the existence of some professor or scholar at *any* school who shares their beliefs; those who attend religiously minority congregations of mostly low-status

---

5. See comment on Acts 1:1.

6. Emphasized, e.g., by Creech, "Narratee," 110–11. For Luke's writing with Theophilus in view, cf. also Garrison, *Theophilus*, reasonably positioning Theophilus as a pro-Roman Gentile who knew the Gospel of Mark (cf. Luke 1:4); Parsons, *Acts*, 27.

7. Nock, *Essays*, 825–26, warns that dedications reveal simply that a book was in published form; they did not obligate the dedicatee in any respect.

8. See Neyrey, "Location of Paul"; Lentz, *Luke's Portrait*. Apologetic literature often emphasized the reception of one's claims by "respectable" people (Jos. *Ag. Ap.* 1.176–212; see Witherington, *Acts*, 295). Although Luke's emphasis, this is not his fabrication; thus he may emphasize Paul's sojourn in honorable cities such as Ephesus (Neyrey, "Location of Paul," 273) and Corinth (273–74), but Paul's letters leave no question that this sojourn happened (1 Cor 15:32; 16:8; cf. 1 Tim 1:3; 2 Tim 1:18).

9. Luke 14:15–24 directly challenges the assumptions of the elite (Rohrbaugh, "Pre-industrial City," 146). Some scholars see an emphasis on social subversion in Luke's narratives in Acts (Thomas, "Upside-Down").

10. Luke is ready also to attribute special responsibility for injustices to leaders that act unjustly or lead others in doing so (e.g., Acts 3:17; 4:26; 13:27; 14:5).

11. Robbins, "Location," 326. For Paul's status, see esp. comment on Acts 22:3; also comments on 16:37; 21:39.

workers might seek to validate their faith to dominant-culture outsiders by mentioning a socially respectable member, for example, a doctor or attorney.[12] Whatever its members' status, Luke's audience might appreciate "respectable" examples, provided it was an ignored, rather than a persecuted, minority.[13]

What we *can* possibly conclude from this is that Luke's target audience is relatively stable (and hence not hostile to the culture); Luke is positive toward the culture without needing to sound polemical against separatism from it. That Luke's ideal audience is of higher-than-average status and educational attainment is, however, likely, but for a different reason: Luke's literary level and his presupposition of significant cultural literacy (both Jewish, in knowledge of the LXX, and Greek, in geographic knowledge). It is not the audience of an elite multivolume history, but it is culturally literate enough to appreciate his work. Luke's audience is not of elite status, but neither are they agrarian peasants; they are not too put off by manual labor (9:43; 18:3; 20:34; Luke 5:2), so the median target may have been artisans, with persons of higher and lower means included in the audience.[14]

c. Status and Surmounting Status

Rank and status were crucial issues in Mediterranean society.[15] Epitaphs suggest that those of lower rank could still celebrate their status within their group of peers,[16] though some scholars have found here "a marked feeling of inferiority and . . . a pathetic desire for self-assertion."[17] Social mobility was uncommon[18] except among freedpersons and newly wealthy urban merchants.

There were also challenges to class and status divisions,[19] in line with the Greek (but not Roman)[20] ideal of equality (not always fulfilled in practice).[21] Despite

---

12. Apul. *Metam.* 11.10. Similarly, in antiquity, cultic groups often achieved mainstream status through benefaction or patronage (White, *Origins of Architecture*, 1:58–59).

13. In the latter case, an apocalyptic worldview celebrating distance from the culture would more often take hold.

14. Even mostly illiterate urban people could produce graffiti repeating lines from their cultural canon, albeit with spelling irregularities; see Toner, *Culture*, 140, on Virgilian graffiti "in a brothel, an iron-mongers and a gladiators' barracks" (*CIL* 4.1527, 4401, 9987).

15. See, e.g., Xen. *Cyr.* 5.5.34; Pliny *Ep.* 9.5.3; Apul. *Metam.* 3.11, 15; 4.23; at length, Friedländer, *Life*, 1:98–206; Llewelyn, *Documents*, 6:132–40, §17; in architecture, Vitruv. *Arch.* 6.5.1–3; in dream interpretation, Artem. *Oneir.* passim, e.g., 4.26. For the social pyramid, see further Lewis, *Life*, 18–36, 66; Rohrbaugh, "Pre-industrial City," 133; in Judaism, *t. B. Qam.* 9:12; Applebaum, "Social Status," 707 (though Israelite law, in contrast to Mesopotamian and Roman law [e.g., *Dig.* 47.21.2; Paulus *Sent.* 5.23.14.19], lacked most class distinctions). This determined propriety in relationships (e.g., Sir 13:2; Polyb. 26.1.1–3; Livy 41.20.1–3), behavior (Phaedrus 1.3; Apul. *Metam.* 10.23; Sherk, *Empire*, §35, p. 62), and even the legality of marriage interests (Paulus *Sent.* 2; *Dig.* 23.2.42.pr. 1; both in Lefkowitz and Fant, *Life*, 193, §196). Greeks were also somewhat familiar with the Indian caste system (Arrian *Ind.* 11.1–7).

16. On status consistency in general, see Lenski, "Status Crystallization."

17. Nock, *Conversion*, 212.

18. Malina and Neyrey, *Portraits*, 175.

19. Cf., e.g., Xen. Y. *Ep. Lucil.* 47.16; Dio Chrys. *Or.* 7.115; Philost. *Ep. Apoll.* 97. The ideals of friendship (see Keener, *John*, 1008–9, citing, e.g., Plato *Laws* 8.837AB; Arist. *E.E.* 7.9.1, 1241b; Diog. Laert. 5.31; Iambl. *V.P.* 29.162; 30.167; *Let. Aris.* 228; Jos. *Ant.* 19.317) and sometimes table fellowship (Xen. *Cyr.* 2.1.30; *Mem.* 3.14.1; Pliny *Ep.* 2.6.3–5; Plut. *Table* 1.2.3, *Mor.* 616E; Lucian *Carousal* 43; Athen. *Deipn.* 1.12C; Heraclitus *Ep.* 9; for the Lord's table, Theodoret *Comm. 1 Cor.* 236–37) sometimes evoked equality; Saturnalia afforded status inversion for Romans momentarily (Lucian *Sat.* 13, 17–18); also cf. equality before God in Jewish thought (*m. Bik.* 3:4; *t. Bik.* 2:10).

20. Cf., e.g., Pliny *Ep.* 2.12.6; 9.5.3. Exceptions might be influenced, e.g., by Stoicism and Greek ideals (Marc. Aur. 1.14).

21. E.g., Xen. *Cyr.* 1.3.18; Dion. Hal. *Ant. rom.* 10.1.2; Mus. Ruf. 4, p. 48.9; Lucian *Dial. D.* 433 (30/25, Nireus, Thersites, Menippus 2); 436 (8/26, Menippus and Cheiron 2); *Hermot.* 22; Men. Rhet. 1.3, 363.6–7. Among Greek-speaking Jews, e.g., *Let. Aris.* 257, 263, 282. Many intended only equity, according to each person's

fixed roles for various status groups in the larger society, Eastern cultic associations sometimes surmounted such barriers.[22] But even in an association such as the four-hundred-member second-century Dionysiac *thiasus* at Tusculum, where senators and clients met together, "only the senators' immediate clients" were part of it,[23] suggesting a continuation of some degree of the standard relationships in this case. Stoic philosophy also challenged assumptions about the importance of rank[24] although, even when a Stoic emperor sat on the throne, it did little to change them.

d. Likely Status of Audience

Luke portrays Paul with images drawn from popular philosophy and rhetoric. Although in practice, different members of the real audience would have caught the nuances of his narrative with varying levels of accuracy, his ideal audience would have caught the allusions.

Luke's ideal audience appears to be urban, Greek, and perhaps in officially romanized cities such as Corinth and Philippi and would be familiar with some measure of education and with public orations, Jewish religion, and (at least through banquet lecturers and philosophic orators) some philosophic ideas. Even if they did not have formal training, rhetorical techniques probably filtered down to urban audiences accustomed to hearing speeches.[25]

2. Jewish, Gentile, or God-Fearing?

The question as to whether Luke's audience is largely Jewish or Gentile may be, in one sense, a forced dilemma. By this period the Greek churches included a sizable number of Gentiles; Philippi had never had a large Jewish population to begin with (see comment on Acts 16:13). At the same time, most of these churches grew from synagogues (Acts 17:10–12; 18:4–8; 19:8–10) or at least Jewish prayer groups (16:13) and would include a sizable number of Jewish people and Gentile synagogue adherents, who would have necessarily constituted the initial teaching nucleus for the congregations. (To the extent that one can define the ethos of a broad audience, "God-fearers" might thus be central.)[26]

Joseph Tyson provides a likely portrait of the ideal readers of Luke-Acts presupposed in the text. Some elements—for example, the knowledge of public figures, such as emperors—could be taken for granted, but among his most significant characteristics of these readers are the following:

"worth" (Arist. *N.E.* 8.7.3, 1158b; *Pol.* 3.7.2, 1282b; 5.1.7, 1301b; Arius Did. *Epit.* 2.7.5b.1, pp. 12f.19–20; 2.7.5b.2, pp. 14f.8; 2.7.5b.5, pp. 18f.34–35; cf. Pliny *Ep.* 2.12.6).

22. Cf., e.g., Evans, "Sanctuaries"; Mylonas, *Eleusis*, 282; Pomeroy, *Goddesses*; Klauck, *Context*, 49 (citing P.Lond. 2710), 66; Gager, "Class," 102–3.

23. Gager, "Class," 107–8.

24. E.g., Matheson, *Epictetus*, 13.

25. See, e.g., Kennedy, *New Testament Interpretation*, 8–9; Litfin, *Theology*, 124–26, 130; Burridge, "Gospels and Acts," 510. Even edicts reflected rhetorical conventions (cf. Fronto *Speeches* 12), and the basic grammatical level of urban education included some exposure to rhetoric (Suet. *Gramm.* 4). Cf. rhetorical influence on Philo (Conley, "Philo"), Josephus (Runnalls, "Rhetoric," 737–54, esp. 753–54), and even the LXX (Lee, "Translations: Greek," esp. 781), though rhetoric would be foreign to most Galilean Jews (Goodman, *State*, 73). Rhetoric continued to shape expectations even among illiterate audiences in Byzantine times (Cunningham, *Faith*, 69).

26. Cf., e.g., Arai, "Stephanusrede." Reiser, "Heiden," sees God-fearers as a primary audience for Paul's letters, many of which presuppose some biblical literacy.

1. They are well educated, basically familiar with eastern Mediterranean geography (and more familiar with the better-known provinces).[27]
2. Luke could expect them to know only Greek (also, he uses Greek coin titles, etc., suggesting that they are probably a Diaspora audience).
3. They are attracted to Judaism and know the LXX and much about Judaism, though less about some areas of it.
4. They know much about pagan religion and are put off by it.

Tyson thus infers that the implied readers are probably like the God-fearers in Acts.[28]

Presumably, much of the teaching nucleus of the church came from those who already knew the LXX well. Most Gentile Christians in this period still saw themselves as converts to a form of Judaism (Rom 2:29; 11:17–24; Gal 3:29; 1 Thess 4:5; 3 John 7; cf. 1 Cor 10:32);[29] with his emphasis on the continuity of salvation history, Luke continues to embrace this idea even in the wake of 70 C.E. Certainly his work is laced with quotations from, and allusions to, Scripture, far more than his occasional explicit classical reference.

The more specific relationship with Judaism is debated (see ch. 14 below). Some envision a Jewish or partly Jewish audience. Thus Jacob Jervell argues that Luke writes to persuade Jewish Christians to welcome Gentile Christians fully. He observes that Luke shows the faithfulness of Jewish Christians to the law and demonstrates that Gentile converts are of the kind already acceptable to synagogues, namely, God-fearers.[30] Robert Brawley argues that Luke "responds to Jewish antagonism apologetically and proffers conciliation." Paul's rejection in synagogues explains why he turned to the Gentiles.[31]

Loveday Alexander also suggests that the apologetic audience seems primarily Jewish.[32] Only one of the final defense speeches addresses specifically a Roman;[33] although other speeches do address pagan religion or philosophy (Acts 14:15–17; 17:22–31), most address Judaism (e.g., 3:12–26; 7:2–53; 13:16–41).[34] Luke gives more space to Paul's custody than to his missionary journeys,[35] but even when addressing Roman officials, Paul is answering Jewish issues, and he continues to address Jewish issues (and a Jewish audience) in his final speech in Acts.[36] Acts concludes not with legal vindication but with God's faithfulness to his people.[37] All these observations are

27. Luke's assumed eastern Mediterranean geographical literacy for his audience is not, however, demanding by the standards of some others, such as Philostratus (see Maclean and Aitken, *Heroikos*, xc).

28. Tyson, *Images of Judaism*, 35–36; followed by Barrett, *Acts*, lxxix–lxxx (from whom I have abbreviated the summary); Tyson, *Luke, Judaism, and Scholars*, 145 (summarizing his *Images of Judaism*, ch. 2; and idem, "Reading as Godfearer"); tentatively, see also Ray, *Irony*, 165–70.

29. This remained true in works that I deem later; see Keener, *Matthew*, 45–51; idem, *John*, 172–75.

30. Jervell, "Church," 20. Le Cornu, *Acts*, xxix, postulates a Jerusalem audience, which requires a pre-66 date; but whereas she doubts that the emphasis on Jerusalem and Caesarea would be of relevance to a Diaspora audience (xxx), one may counter that it would be of interest to Diaspora Jewish believers and therefore to the majority of Gentile believers in this period who recognized themselves as adherents to a Jewish messianic movement. Most interpreters do presume a Diaspora audience (e.g., Langner, *Hechos*, 36).

31. Brawley, *Luke-Acts and Jews*, 155–56; he argues that "ends of the earth" in Acts 1:8 vindicates Paul's Gentile mission (28–50).

32. For Acts as apologetic, see Alexander, *Context*, 183–206.

33. Ibid., 200. Against Alexander, I would count three, since Festus is part of the audience in Acts 26, but the Jewish element in Acts 22 and 26 cannot be minimized.

34. Alexander, *Context*, 204. Of course, speeches to Gentiles can become relevant within the narrative world only once the mission moves among them.

35. Ibid., 204–5.

36. Ibid., 205.

37. Ibid., 206.

important, but Luke would have had to address Jewish accusations in any case if, in fact, these were an issue vis-à-vis local and Roman governments.[38] Luke's pervasive apologetic for Paul (see ch. 7, sect. 1.a; ch. 13, sect. 3) suggests a concern for what Rome thought of accusations that Paul, a leader of the Diaspora Christian movement, stirred unrest. These accusations often come from Paul's Jewish detractors, but Luke's concern seems less what the Jewish community thinks of Paul than what Roman officials think of Jewish (and other) accusations.

Although apologetic responses to Jewish objections appear in biblical arguments in some of the book's apologetic speeches, especially in its closing scene, this apologetic does not guarantee a direct unbelieving Jewish audience any more than the apologetic concerning riots (see comment on Acts 24:5) guarantees the book a direct audience of Roman officials. Rather, Luke is providing a biblically literate Christian audience (composed of both Jews and Gentiles) a response to objections that concern them. That is, an apologetic *for* a group is not necessarily an apologetic directly *to* that group.

Although I do not agree that Luke writes primarily for a Jewish audience to secure Gentile admission into the church, I do believe that Luke may write with one apologetic eye on the larger Jewish community, both those who complain that Christians are discontinuous with Israel's heritage and those who remain uncommitted for or against the faith. A few decades before Luke writes, Paul confronted Jewish Christians tempted to "Judaize" Gentile converts (Gal 2:3; 5:2–6) to make them acceptable for the more conservative audience in Jerusalem (5:11; 6:12). Writing after 70 c.e. to Diaspora Christians, Luke might deal with Jewish communities on the whole less conservative and more likely to accept God-fearers.[39] In any case, Gentile Christians were by now a fact of life rather than a new threat.

From my investigation of Acts, it seems to me that Luke assumes an audience in which Gentiles are numerically predominant, as we might expect to be the eventual case with the churches in the Pauline mission that he depicts. The foundation of the churches is Jewish, and his ideal audience is conversant with Scripture. Their knowledge of Judaism encompasses not Palestinian Judaism (although they are apparently aware of aspects of it, such as differences between Pharisees and Sadducees) but a biblically based Diaspora Judaism. They know the Bible far better than they know postbiblical Jewish traditions (though at least Luke is familiar with some traditional Hellenistic Jewish apologetic). Although the churches' foundations are Jewish, they also know the larger Greco-Roman culture, and not with the sense of a minority as second-class resident aliens. A sense of integration into the larger culture would fit some Jewish communities in Asia Minor, but it does not fit as easily the smaller Jewish communities in Philippi or possibly Corinth (see discussion of the geographic range of the audience below). It might fit many God-fearers even there and could certainly fit Gentiles who might expect their uncircumcised monotheism, for all its Jewish basis, to be viewed as distinct from participation in a foreign, ethnically based cult.

Studying the Gospels of Matthew and John in my earlier works,[40] I concluded in favor of primarily Jewish audiences (an urban Syrian Jewish Christian one for Matthew and perhaps a sectarian Jewish Christian one in Asia Minor for the Fourth Gospel). For Luke-Acts, however, I tend to favor a mainstream Greco-Roman audience in Macedonia and Achaia, with Jewish founders (not least Paul), a mixture of Gentile and Jewish members, and considerable Jewish and God-fearing didactic input.

---

38. Which seems to be the case even later in some settings, such as Rev 2:9; *Mart. Pol.* 13.1; 17.2; 18.1.

39. On the question of the salvation of God-fearers in various forms of early Judaism, see Donaldson, *Paul and Gentiles*.

40. Keener, *Matthew*, 40–42, 45–51; idem, *John*, 142–232.

3. Geographical Range of Audience

Where is Luke's audience geographically? Regardless of Theophilus's influence, it is unlikely that Luke would produce such a polished two-volume work merely for a single house church.[41] Presumably, he would expect the work to find a receptive audience along the entire circuit of urban churches in the eastern Mediterranean world. This probably broad, hoped-for audience does not, however, diminish the likelihood that Luke had a narrower target audience, churches that he knew directly and particularly expected to resonate with (and perhaps help circulate) the accounts he had selected.

a. Rome?

Some scholars think that Luke addresses especially congregations in Rome,[42] where the churches probably still spoke especially Greek.[43] This suggestion has some merit; after all, in Acts the climax of the gospel's spread is Rome, and in it Roman Christians would receive a report of the gospel's spread from the beginning until it reached them.[44]

The problem with limiting this interest to Christians in Rome is that everyone in the cities of the empire thought of Rome as the heart of the empire and would regard this destination as strategically significant, whether or not they lived there (cf. Rom 1:8; though cf. also 1 Thess 1:7–8). This would especially be true of Christians in Roman colonies such as Corinth and Philippi, who would directly profit from any favorable precedents in the capital (cf. perhaps Phil 1:7). Indeed, Luke omits some major items of interest to the Roman church, such as Prisca and Aquila's presence in Rome by this period (Rom 16:3–5);[45] more significantly, he omits even mentioning in his narrative other friends and coworkers of Paul who eventually migrated there (16:5–15, esp. 16:7). That Acts leaves the narrator in Rome at its conclusion would demand a Roman provenance only if one must assume that the narrator wrote shortly after the close of Acts, and even then his place of writing would still not decide his intended audience.[46]

b. Corinth or Ephesus

Although the ultimate goal of Paul's mission may be Rome, the focus of his public ministry recorded in Acts is Asia, Macedonia, and Achaia, that is, mostly in the Aegean region.[47] By comparison, Rome itself receives only a few paragraphs and an

41. See esp. considerations raised in many of the essays in Bauckham, *Gospels for Christians*.

42. Foakes-Jackson and Lake, "Internal Evidence of Acts," 202–4 (provenance).

43. See, e.g., Paul's Letter to the Romans; but also cf. the dominance of Greek in Jewish inscriptions from Rome (Leon, *Jews of Rome*, 75–92, esp. 75–76; Noy, "Writing"; Lung-Kwong, *Purpose*, 105; Stambaugh, *City*, 95). Some Aramaic occurs (Chilton, "Epitaph"), but it is minimal compared with Greek.

44. See Kilgallen, "Rome." Based on Luke 12:55, Theissen, *Gospels*, 252–54, argues for a Western perspective, or at least a certainly non-Palestinian, non-Syrian one. He (probably rightly) thinks (258) that Luke likely visited Palestine but was not from there.

45. With most scholars today, we can take for granted the Roman destination of Rom 16 (see Gamble, *Textual History*, widely followed; Donfried, "Note on Romans 16"; Lönnermark, "Frågan"; Lung-Kwong, *Purpose*, 24–35), against some earlier hypotheses (e.g., Manson, "Letter"; Richards, "Romans and Corinthians," 30; McDonald, "Romans XVI"). Admittedly, Luke does introduce and depict earlier (Acts 18:2–3, 18, 26) this couple known to Rome's Christians—but they were well known not only in Rome but in Achaia and Asia (1 Cor 16:19; cf. 2 Tim 4:19).

46. The historic traditional view of a provenance in Antioch (Foakes-Jackson and Lake, "Internal Evidence of Acts," 201) would connect with the emphasis on Antioch (Acts 6:5; 11:19–30; 13:1–3; 14:26–15:2; 15:22–23, 30, 35; 18:22); but Paul's letters also presuppose Antioch's role (Gal 2:11), and the preferred text of Acts does not associate Luke specifically with Antioch.

47. Polhill, *Acts*, 31–32, notes that Philip Esler, working from clues in the text for the social setting addressed, also suggests the urban Roman East. Others have also opted for Achaia (e.g., Leaney, *Luke*, 11).

essentially unfinished ending. Despite our considerable knowledge of persons in the Roman church (Rom 16:3–15, many of them migrants from the east), individuals in eastern Mediterranean churches are the ones named in Acts (Acts 16:14–15, 40; 17:5, 34; 18:8; 19:29; 20:4). Christians in Greece would have more freedom and public posture than Roman churches in this period.

Of specific local congregations, Corinth is one of the most likely options;[48] Christians there seem to have coexisted peacefully with their society.[49] Paul's Corinthian correspondence addresses concerns of wealth, status inversion, and equality, as does Luke; he also addresses a congregation that emphasizes charismata (although in a less mission-oriented way than does Luke, 1 Cor 12–14) and apostles' ministry signs (cf. mission-oriented signs in 2 Cor 12:12). Emphasizing an apostolic decree about sexual immorality and idol food (Acts 15:20, 29) would publicly reinforce Paul's earlier teaching on these subjects (1 Cor 6–10).[50] Luke might also have reason to stress the unity of Peter, Paul, and Apollos against Paul's detractors (1 Cor 1–4).[51] The theology of persecution in Acts could call charismatics to contemplate suffering as part of their mission, an emphasis the Christians in Corinth might still need (1 Cor 1:17–23; 2:2, 8; 4:9–16; 15:30–32; 2 Cor 1:4–10; 2:14–16; 4:7–5:8; 6:4–10; 11:23–33; 12:7–10; 13:4).[52] Still, Luke records few details of Corinth (considering the length of Paul's stay, Acts 18:11), presumably because his information there was only secondhand.

Another plausible audience is Ephesus,[53] but there are problems with viewing this as the most probable audience. Although Luke devotes more space to Paul's ministry to the Ephesians (most of 18:18–19:41; 20:17–38) than to any other part of his ministry, few church members there are named (though one could argue that Luke's audience knows of Alexander; cf. comment on Acts 19:33); when they are, they are named as if not known (21:29). (Indeed, even Apollos, who preached successfully in Ephesus and Corinth, is introduced as if unknown [18:28], but probably some of the audience had heard of him.) Luke's scenes in Ephesus are brief except for the dramatic riot, which would be a matter of some apologetic concern. Luke devotes so much space to Ephesus because it constitutes the climax of Paul's precaptivity ministry; the length of time Paul spent in Ephesus and the achievements of his ministry there[54] are sufficient cause for this attention.

The assumed geographic knowledge is wide (though less than, e.g., in Philostratus; see Maclean and Aitken, *Heroikos*, xc).

48. Goulder, "Letters," 110, suggests that Luke settled there after Paul's death (although the connections he proposes [p. 111] do not strike me as persuasive). Another possibility often defended is Ephesus (see discussion below).

49. I first noticed the correspondences mentioned here between Acts and the Corinthian letters, January 10, 1990, when I inclined toward that destination for Luke-Acts. "Theophilus" is attested as a citizen name in Corinth (Kent, *Inscriptions*, 24, 28, both before Luke's period), but this name is not very unusual (see comment on Acts 1:1).

50. Cf. also the favorable view of virginity in Acts 21:9; 1 Cor 7:25–38.

51. Luke's baptismal theology (e.g., Acts 2:38; 22:16) differs from the emphasis in 1 Cor 1:13–17, but the baptismal situation that Paul addressed there does not appear in 2 Corinthians and may have been resolved.

52. *First Clement* suggests that many issues that Paul addressed in Corinth remained at the end of the first century. I also suspect that Hebrews was written to the sort of congregation taught by those educated in a Hellenistic synagogue setting, possibly (though not necessarily; cf. perhaps Heb 13:24) Corinth, which explains some similarities.

53. See, e.g., Pervo, *Acts*, 5–6, emphasizing local knowledge of Ephesus; idem, *Mystery*, 8, emphasizing the Pauline circles there in the early second century, when he dates Acts.

54. As also suggested in Ephesians and 1 and 2 Timothy (perhaps also Ign. *Eph.* 12.2; but this is less clear than, e.g., Polycarp's allusions to Paul's Philippian ministry in *Phil.* 3.2; 11.3; probably 9.1). The elements of

c. Philippi

Corinth is probably included in Luke's target audience,[55] but it is even more likely that he also includes Philippi, a church where the narrator himself stayed at some length (Acts 16:12–17; 20:5–6) and whose founding he describes in special detail.[56] Luke mentions Jason in nearby Thessalonica without introduction as if Luke is either ineptly abbreviating a source (which would be uncharacteristic of him) or, more likely, his audience already knows of Jason (17:5–6).

If a major part of Luke's audience includes Philippian Christians who know him well, he probably writes some time after the end of Nero's persecution; Macedonian Christians all suffered far more than those in Achaia (Phil 1:29–30; 1 Thess 1:6; 2:14; 3:3–4; cf. perhaps Poly. *Phil.* 9.1–2; 12.3). Paul's execution or other negative reports about Rome would not help their situation, but Acts seems too positive toward Rome, in general, to be simply suppressing critical information; for Luke, Nero's era may seem like an exception rather than the rule. If Claudius's anti-Judaic decree (Acts 18:2) may have adversely affected Christians in Macedonia (see comment on Acts 16:20–21), Nero's policies (generally popular in Greece as a whole) surely would have done so.

Undoubtedly, most Jewish and Christian groups scrambled to distinguish themselves from Judean revolutionary movements in the Flavian period, perhaps complete with recriminations against eschatologically oriented sectarians (as Christians would appear). Suspicions about Christians probably took a greater toll in Macedonia than in Achaia or Asia (cf. Phil 1:28–30; 1 Thess 1:6; 2:14; 3:2–4), though specifically Jewish hostility, as opposed to concern for Roman-Philippian disdain for Paul's execution, was not likely a factor in Philippi. But we may guess that even Christians in Philippi need not have found Luke's usually positive reports of Roman precedents unrealistic. In any case, they, even more than the Corinthian churches, would have found these reports encouraging.

One problem with proposing an audience especially located in Greece and Macedonia is Luke's complete silence about Titus (unless he is Titius Justus or, in contrast to 2 Tim 4:10–11, Luke himself).[57] Given Luke's report of other persons less critical to the later Pauline mission, the omission would appear almost deliberate. Perhaps the Macedonian or Achaian Christians later experienced conflict with Titus (in contrast to the earlier period in 2 Cor 7:6–8:23; 12:18). Or perhaps troubles arose with Titus after his role known to us in extant sources (cf. perhaps 2 Tim 4:10), making him controversial. One can only speculate the reasons for omitting such a prominent coworker of Paul.

A problem with presupposing an audience primarily in Philippi would be that it lacked a large Jewish community (see Acts 16:13), whereas Luke's ideal core audience is biblically informed, perhaps from a background in the synagogue. Nevertheless, the Philippian church had now existed for many years and, undoubtedly, had plenty of instruction from someone with such a background if Luke had long sojourned there. Moreover, some of the other churches in the region (Thessalonica in Macedonia and

---

known truth in Acts 19:26–27 might not go over well in a document meant for primary circulation in Ephesus (if nonbelievers might hear it), despite Demetrius's role as a demagogue.

55. Writers would rarely devote such a monumental work with a target audience of only a single house church or a network of such churches in only one city; see again the essays in Bauckham, *Gospels for Christians*.

56. Luke could, of course, focus on Philippi because he knows it best, yet write to churches elsewhere. But I am arguing that he writes with the Christians he knows best in mind, not that he intended only Christians in Philippi to read his work. As a person of status, "Theophilus" is probably not Philippian, since most persons of status there would probably go by their Roman names.

57. Another suggestion has been Luke's brother. An author might avoid praising those closest to him to avoid the charge of bias (Philost. *Vit. soph.* 2.33.628).

especially Corinth in Achaia) included some Jewish elements, whose presence and teaching may have influenced other churches in the region. Since women had more freedoms in Macedonia (see comment on Acts 16:13–15), it is also plausible that Lydia and other God-fearing women in her circle (16:13) helped to instruct that church (cf. Phil 4:2–3). A church with fewer Jewish members might also require additional instruction in its Jewish heritage.

Probably Philippi is not the book's only destination, as noted above, and as Luke's interest in Jewish matters could further suggest. But while I believe that Luke sought an audience throughout Macedonia and Achaia (including Corinth) and would have welcomed one elsewhere (including Ephesus and Rome), the church he knew best seems to be Philippi. This church, like some of the others, was by now a significant community, and was among those that remained strong several decades later (see Polycarp's letter to the Philippians).

d. Ancient Writers' Geographic Assumptions

Writers could expect educated readers to appreciate descriptions of various locations.[58] During the imperial period, knowledge of geography (within the limits of the empire) was important for educated people.[59] Even in small towns, people with education and means could have some knowledge about major locations and distances and the relative location of provinces.[60] What they did not know they might be interested to learn because such knowledge displayed their cultural competence within the sphere of the empire. Diaspora Jews also may have prided themselves in such competencies,[61] although, inevitably, they, like others, were sometimes wrong about their information.[62]

Authors took for granted such knowledge on the part of their ideal audience, even if such assumptions would have stretched the competencies of some of their real readers. Our earliest Greek literature, rooted in widely circulated oral traditions, evokes a wide range of geographic awareness.[63] A highly educated orator such as Dio Chrysostom adapted his speeches to each locale's character, and readers of his collection would be able to appreciate enough of this local sensitivity to appreciate his intellect. Thus in *Or.* 34 he addresses Tarsus's hostility to philosophers (34.3) and a problem with registers (34.10);[64] in *Or.* 31 he plainly knows about Rhodes and expects his reading audience to share such information.[65] Likewise, Marcus Aurelius expects his teacher to understand his mention of various plants growing in different parts of the empire (Fronto *Ad M. Caes.* 2.5). Pliny the Younger insists that people in Rome were more interested in wonders in Greece and Asia than in Rome itself (*Ep.* 8.20.2).[66] Likewise, when Philostratus writes of India in *Life of Apollonius*, he either verifies claims (albeit usually wrongly) or reinforces beliefs already held about it; when he writes of locations in Asia, he describes famous temples of various cities

---

58. We think, e.g., of Polybius's scenes, not simply the idyllic landscapes of poets (on the latter, see Hardie, "*Locus amoenus*").

59. Talbert, "Geography," 776.

60. See Talbert, "Small-Town Sources."

61. E.g., (outside the empire but later) the cultural influences on Judaism as expressed in the synagogue at Dura-Europos; Goodenough, *Symbols*, vols. 9–11 (summary in 12:158–83).

62. E.g., the apparent assumption that all consuls were Caesars (*Sib. Or.* 11.265–67).

63. See fully Purcell, "Geography," and sources noted there.

64. Neither of these situations is understood today.

65. E.g., Rhodes's military triumphs (Dio Chrys. *Or.* 31.19) would be well known.

66. This is not to suggest that Roman Christians in the same period would be equally interested in Greek churches. That is, the focus on the East in Acts' narrative probably suggests an Eastern audience.

that he visited (temples also mentioned elsewhere). Philostratus appears to assume that his ideal reader is familiar with and interested in such topics.

Historians also assumed a wide range of geographic knowledge, though, where their audience lacked it, they provided it. Polybius provides as many concrete local descriptions as possible, as part of his approach of putting history in context (Polyb. 5.21.7–8) but also to acquaint hearers with these places (5.21.9). He recognizes that some of his readers will not have sufficient geographic knowledge, but he prefers educating them instead of leaving out matters that his more conversant ideal audience will readily grasp (3.38.4). Some apparently expected even more detail, so that Polybius has to defend himself by insisting that excessive details about exotic locations would distract from his main narrative (3.57.1–9).[67] (For discussion of travel and geography in Acts, see further ch. 17 below.)

e. Luke's Geographic Assumptions

Luke's Gospel begins and ends in Jerusalem; Acts begins in Jerusalem but ends in Rome. This contrast suggests a reorientation of mission and strategy, a transformation of the historical geographic orientation in previous salvation history (though not without precedent; see Acts 7). The focus relocates from the heart of salvation history to the heart of the empire, from the center of the world for the Jewish people to the center of the world for Gentiles[68]—and thus from heritage to mission (see ch. 15, sect. 3, and esp. ch. 13, sect. 2.a).

Luke, less concerned with liberally educating his audience about geography than is Polybius, does not include digressions of purely geographic interest. He does, however, presuppose some geographic knowledge and interest on the part of his educated audience. Long ago scholars pointed out that Luke alludes "to more than one hundred towns and cities," often with "characteristically different experiences in different places."[69] It is unlikely that he alludes to such a range of information solely for his own entertainment.

How likely is it that he could expect his audience to share familiarity with some of this information? In a maritime center such as Corinth, knowledge of Aegean ports would be fairly widespread, at least among the congregation's elite members and, undoubtedly, also those who lived and worked in Cenchreae, Corinth's port city (Rom 16:1; see comment on Acts 18:18).[70] Certainly people knew of the sites mentioned in their cultures' epics, even when they knew them primarily orally.[71] People in this region had long exhibited knowledge of current news (e.g., about conquests), readily exchanging it when various cities came together for events such as the Isthmian Games, hosted by Corinth.[72] Likewise, Philippi and the nearby Aegean port town of Neapolis were in contact with and knowledgeable about the rest of the Aegean region.

67. He digresses to address this problem more fully in Polyb. 3.57.1–3.59.9. He would also consider direct experience of these places paramount for himself as a writer (12.25g.1–2), condemning historians who did not travel (12.25g.3–4; see Polybius's emphasis on this point in our comment on historians investigating their subjects, ch. 6, sect. 2.e).

68. That is, from the standpoint of an audience within the empire (Parthians, Nubians, Germans, and farther peoples in India, China, and elsewhere would have certainly demurred if this claim were pressed literally!).

69. Abbott, *Acts*, 13–14.

70. For Corinthian inscriptions mentioning Alexandria and cities in Asia Minor, see, e.g., Kent, *Inscriptions*, nos. 136 (p. 64), 138 (pp. 64–65), 303 (pp. 118–19), and 370 (p. 143).

71. In the West, even mostly illiterate urban people could produce graffiti repeating lines from their cultural canon, albeit with spelling irregularities; see Toner, *Culture*, 140, on Virgilian graffiti "in a brothel, an iron-mongers and a gladiators' barracks" (*CIL* 4.1527, 4401, 9987).

72. So, e.g., Polyb. 18.46.1–2. Diaspora Jewish sources in late first- to early second-century Alexandria presume some knowledge of recent Mediterranean history on the part of readers (*Sib. Or.* 5.1–50, which is reasonably accurate for recent centuries; but cf. the confusion in 5.460–63).

Most of the locations that Luke mentions in the Aegean were familiar to those who knew Greek history, myth, and literature—that is, to those who prided themselves on being literate. Because Luke's ideal audience (probably only a portion of his real audience) had ample familiarity with many of the cities mentioned, it is helpful for what is known about some of these cities to be noted for modern readers of commentaries. Of course, patron deities or famous temples in cities mentioned only in passing in Acts (some merely to designate the progress of Paul's journeys) are nowhere close to being as central to Luke's "meaning" as narrative parallels in Luke-Acts or background directly illumining the narrative.

Such information does, however, give us a better feel for Luke's real world and the narrative world most likely inferred by his first audience than what modern readers tend to infer after a history of Christendom. Knowing the world first confronted by the apostolic church, chiefly the Pauline mission, also helps modern Christians to reappropriate the text in a post-Christendom setting and in areas with many first- and second-generation converts.

When the commentary cites ancient comments about these places, this is not to imply that Luke's audience consciously considered allusions to such background simply because Paul traveled there; rather, the citations seek to illustrate how recognizable such sites were to Luke's contemporaries who were cultured or aspired to appear as such and how deeply their histories resonated with the shared cultural heritage of much of Luke's audience.

Conclusion

Our knowledge of Luke's real audience is limited, and conclusions here must be tentative. Scholars have offered reasonable cases for various positions; I have attempted merely to offer the best reconstruction I can. Probably Luke's ideal audience consists of mixed but predominantly Gentile congregations. Although he welcomes other listeners, his target audience seems to be Aegean, especially Roman colonies with strong Pauline churches like Corinth and Philippi; of these, the author has the most direct personal knowledge of Philippi. His audience is acutely aware of the larger Roman Empire and developing attitudes toward the Christian movement. Negative public views toward their executed founder Paul constitute a matter of shame, perhaps especially in the Roman colony of Philippi but elsewhere as well, inviting Luke's apologetic.

13

THE PURPOSE OF ACTS

Although I employ the title "The Purpose of Acts" out of deference to a traditional category of Lukan scholarly inquiry, "Purposes of Acts" might be more apropos.[1] The question of the "purpose" of Acts' implied author is inseparable from the question of his work's implied "theology" or, in a broader sense, his themes and emphases. Examining Luke's themes leads to the question of why he emphasizes what he does; as noted in chapter 5 above, ancient historians wrote from deliberate perspectives. To ask *why* Luke writes what he does invites inevitably (if somewhat more speculatively) the historical question of reconstructing, as best we can, the situation that prompts him to write.[2] I will discuss at greater length the historical setting of his apologetic emphasis. But whereas the earlier chapters of this introduction focused more on historical questions, the chapters on Luke's purpose (ch. 13 below), his story's relation to the story of Israel (14), its themes (15), and its overarching narrative unity (16) focus on the more "theological" questions, although historical and narrative questions in Acts are not fully separable.

My extended discussion of genre closed (in ch. 5 above) with a discussion of apologetic histories and Luke's place in this category of literature.[3] Scholars have frequently (and correctly) emphasized Luke's apologetic purpose, and this chapter will devote substantial attention to this proposal. Just as speakers in Acts provide apologetic arguments through historical retrospectives (most notably in Acts 7), Luke himself does so through his entire narrative.

Before addressing Luke's apologetic intentions in further detail, however, I must survey other proposed purposes for Luke-Acts. Not all of these are mutually exclusive;[4] even Josephus probably had other purposes in addition to his apologetic objectives.[5]

---

1. With, e.g., Powell, *Acts*, 13 (who offers [13–19] a fuller survey of proposed purposes for Acts than here). For older studies on Luke's purpose, see Mattill and Mattill, *Bibliography*, 152–57, §§2029–96.

2. That is, "purpose" is more bound up with the question of authorial intention (or what we can infer of the plan of the ideal author) than with merely themes we infer by their prominence and repetition in Luke-Acts. As a secondary level of inference, the question of purpose entails more subjective judgments than does discerning Acts' "theology" per se.

3. Most historically oriented Diaspora Jewish works displayed a significant apologetic interest (Wandrey, "Literature: Jewish-Hellenistic," 696).

4. Stagg, *Acts*, 5–18, surveys various proposed purposes, focusing on "unhindered" (Acts 28:31) and the expansion of the Jesus movement beyond the ethnic confines of Judaism (esp. 12–17).

5. See, e.g., Aune, *Dictionary of Rhetoric*, 253. That at least one purpose of historiography is to say something about the past has already been argued (ch. 4 above) and need not be repeated here, where we focus on more particular ideological emphases (see ch. 5, above, for how ancient historiography's past material was often ideologically framed).

(For example, Luke's emphasis on the Gentile mission of the past is surely an encouragement to continue in, and a model for, carrying out this mission in his own day; some of these issues will be introduced in this chapter but developed more fully in the discussion of some of Luke's themes, in ch. 15 below.) After returning to the question of the apologetic function of Acts, I will turn, in the following chapter, to the closely related issues of the book's relation to the ancient story of Israel.

1. Some Proposed Purposes for Acts

Scholars have proposed various purposes for Acts (or, more broadly in some cases, Luke-Acts). One purpose that is explicit in Luke's prologues is the communication of historical information (Luke 1:1–4; Acts 1:1), a purpose inseparable from the work's genre (see discussion in chs. 2–6 above).[6] But as noted in chapter 5 above, ancient works of history had other purposes than simply communicating information for information's sake. These other purposes helped shape what information was presented and how it was presented.

As a sample of traditional scholarly views, one may take C. S. C. Williams's survey of proposals roughly a half century ago.[7] Several of these views include an apologetic emphasis and hence will recur later in this chapter. First, some (e.g., B. S. Easton in 1936) believe that Acts presents Christianity as the true Judaism, hence protected under Roman law. Second, others (e.g., W. G. Kümmel) believe that Acts was also intended to build up Christians. Third, yet others (e.g., J. I. Still in 1914) see Acts as Paul's trial defense. Fourth, the Tübingen school (now largely abandoned) saw Acts as a synthesis of Judaistic and Pauline Christianity.[8] Finally, Dibelius argued that Acts emphasized theology by showing how *God* helped the message spread.

This survey of views illustrates the problem of isolating a single purpose in the narrative of Luke-Acts; in fact, multiple themes are likely at work, and it is not a foregone conclusion that all these emphases represent the same purpose.[9] Although probably written after Paul's death (and hence not for his trial, even if it includes strategies prepared for that trial),[10] Acts is heavily apologetic (and some of its strategies might help later Christians on trial). (For the emphasis on an apologetic for Paul, see ch. 7, sect. 1.a, above, as well as discussion below.) Although Acts is no mere synthesis of traditional Jewish Christianity and Pauline thought, it illustrates the diversity of early Christianity without choosing to focus on the conflicts that occurred as consensus was growing. Acts, like Luke, is intended to edify Christians both by placing them in a broader historical perspective and by providing teaching and moral examples. Acts also emphasizes God's activity, implies that this activity continues, and invites the church of Luke's day to continue to follow the models for mission and evangelism the book provides.

6. With Bruce, *Acts*[3], 22, who also (22–27) sees Luke as an apologist (cf. idem, *Message*, 50–51); see also Maddox, *Purpose*, 21, 186 (noting Luke's emphasis on ἀσφάλειαν, the final word of the Gospel's preface, Luke 1:4). As noted above, these elements combine in apologetic historiography.

7. C. Williams, *Acts*, 15–18.

8. One reason for abandoning this position, besides the obsolescence of its philosophic underpinnings, is the increased recognition of Paul's Jewish heritage; see, e.g., Davies, *Paul*; Sanders, *Paul and Judaism*; Longenecker, *Paul*; Donaldson, *Paul and Gentiles*.

9. See, e.g., Dunn, *Acts*, xi–xiii; Liefeld, *Acts*, 30–32. One proposal that has generated little support and is not likely is that it is an antignostic polemic, well as Luke's concrete historical theology might work for that (see Talbert, *Luke and Gnostics*, passim).

10. Cf. Mattill, "Date and Purpose," 350, for Acts as an "apology for Paul and the world mission." Some others also view it as partly (though usually not primarily) an apology for Paul's apostleship, challenged by others (Bruce, *Commentary*, 24).

Posing alternatives may be an unhelpful method of investigating the purpose for Luke-Acts. Rarely do writers today, or did writers then, have only a single agenda in mind when producing a literary work; even Paul's letters to particular congregations often treat multiple issues in the congregations despite some pervasive themes (e.g., 1 Corinthians; 1 Thessalonians). If Acts provides apologetic material, it thereby supplies also a model for how its readers should respond to persecutors, including members of the Roman government when they are on trial.[11] Luke wants to avoid unnecessary conflict posed by Christian hostility toward the state; he expects that Christians can usually function within the society that he knows. Luke's historical perspective answers Jewish objections about the Way's departure from Jewish tradition and consequent (or potential) Roman suspicions that the Way has abandoned any proper claim to be part of a protected ethnic religious heritage.[12]

One could add other views to Williams's summary of proposals; for example, some argue that Acts is evangelistic—that is, that Luke seeks to commend Christianity to Theophilus's circle.[13] At least if adapted slightly, this proposal has much to commend it: Theophilus himself has been instructed (Luke 1:4), but Theophilus could use Luke-Acts for public readings at banquets that include non-Christian social peers and clients.

The problem with this proposal as a primary purpose is that Luke's ideal audience is steeped in the LXX, which would not be the case with most of Theophilus's social peers (though it could be for some of his clients if Theophilus is or has been patron or benefactor for a synagogue association, such as a "father of a synagogue" often was).[14] Although Luke may have been happy or even eager for his work to be used in such evangelistic settings, it seems doubtful that non-Christians constitute his primary audience for the work. Luke, presumably, wants to encourage others in what they have been taught, just as he does Theophilus (1:4).[15] That Luke has a major interest in evangelism, however, can hardly be questioned.

2. Salvation History and Mission

Even if Acts is not primarily directly evangelistic, Luke has a major interest in historically validating the Gentile mission, which had already been proved successful, and, likely also, in providing models for continuing mission. Acts focuses on the mission of bringing witness to all peoples (Acts 1:8). The focus of Acts is not simply church history in the mold of Eusebius but the expansion of the Christian message through pivotal agents.[16] In view of such agents, it might even be titled "From Jesus to Paul."[17]

11. Cf. Tannehill, *Acts*, 329, on Acts 26: it "provides both a defense of Paul against his detractors and a model for the later church."

12. Even in a significantly later period, churches faced Roman intolerance because they lacked the excuse of belonging to a separate national religious tradition (Judge, *Athens*, 56).

13. E.g., Larkin, "Recovery of Luke-Acts," 410–12; cf. Liefeld, *Acts*, 31; against the centrality of evangelism in Luke's purpose, see, e.g., Maddox, *Purpose*, 20. Stanton, *Jesus of Nazareth*, 29–30 (on Luke 1:4), thinks that Luke seeks Theophilus's conversion, but this is unlikely: Theophilus had already been "instructed" deeply enough to know much of the gospel tradition (1:4).

14. For "fathers of synagogues," see, e.g., CIJ 1:66, §93; 1:250f, §319; 1:360, §494; 1:372–73, §§508–10; 1:393, §533; 1:398, §537; 1:505, §694; perhaps 1:397, §535; 1:462, §645; 1:463, §646; 2:9, §739. The title is sometimes connected with benefactions (e.g., CIJ 1:520, §720, here "father of the people"). See also the survey in CIJ 1:xcv–xcvi.

15. See, e.g., Liefeld, *Acts*, 24. Admittedly, Luke's purpose may not be clear from prologues alone (cf. Brown, "Prologues").

16. See, e.g., Bovon, *Theologian*, 238; Kistemaker, *Acts*, 33–34.

17. Hengel, "Geography of Palestine," 36; this title is more accurate than "Acts of the Apostles," since, apart from Peter, it focuses on those whom Luke rarely (Paul) or never (Stephen) calls apostles.

Because the mission to all nations, after the early chapters, concerns especially the Gentile mission, many scholars see the Gentile mission (or a Diaspora mission with a Gentile agenda) as Luke's central theme (including myself; see comments on Luke's theology in ch. 15 below). Some think that Luke is defending the Gentile mission for a largely Jewish Christian audience,[18] but given our ethnic reconstruction of Luke's audience (despite its Jewish base), it is more likely that he is encouraging especially Gentile Christians despite non-Christian Jewish opposition.[19] Then again, the responses of the broader synagogue community may have generated both apologetic replies and Gentile Christians' need for encouragement that they were genuinely accepted without circumcision. Issues raised by some Jewish leaders about Paul's involvement in unrest also threatened to taint the legacy of his Gentile mission, and hence many of his churches, especially after his execution.

Although we may view mission and apologetic as distinct purposes, for Luke they were closely intertwined. Luke's apologetic was a concrete expression of mission in his own context, and it was often mission that generated the need for the apologetic.

a. From Heritage to Mission

Luke's largest agenda in Luke-Acts itself is to place the mission of Jesus and the church in its place in salvation history.[20] Like good ancient writers, Luke is happy to start a story in the middle, providing the background as he proceeds: although he opens the story with Jesus's coming, biblical quotations and allusions point to the implicit prequel.[21]

Acts likewise points to an unfinished mission of taking the gospel to the ends of the earth; by planting it in Rome, Paul has laid a solid foundation for continuing outreach and provides a model for the continuing mission of the church until Jesus returns (1:8–11). Jesus is thus the centerpiece and climax of history, and his apostles illustrate how Luke's audience should continue his mission.[22] As Stephen (Acts 7) and Paul (Acts 13) preach from what Luke treats as key themes in biblical history, Luke provides clues for his more specific agendas in the themes he emphasizes while recounting the history of Jesus, the Jerusalem church, and Paul.

Because Luke's narrative, though situated in the metanarrative of salvation history, spans a more limited (albeit focal) period, it invites us to focus our attention further. The Gospel begins (Luke 1:9) and closes (24:52) in Jerusalem (indeed, in the temple, 1:9–10; 24:53), grounded in the heritage of the OT. Acts, however, begins in Jerusalem (Acts 1:4) but proceeds to Rome (28:16), the sample of (more particularly, the symbolic, strategic center and stepping-stone for) "the ends of the earth" most relevant for Luke's readers in the empire.[23] Although this mission to the "ends of the earth" is rooted in Scripture (cf. 13:47, quoting Isa 49:6) and begins in

18. See Donfried, "Christology and Salvation." This is my view of Matthew's version of the Gentile mission (Keener, *Matthew*, 719–20).

19. See Maddox, *Purpose*.

20. Cf. Wright, *People of God*, 373–75. Larkin, "Recovery of Luke-Acts," rightly speaks of Luke-Acts as "grand narrative," hence a metanarrative that provides cohesion for individual stories. Miller, *Empowered for Mission*, 42–43, 82, sees Acts' purpose as missiological.

21. Many ancient epics presuppose a broader cycle of widely known oral stories to which allusion was made (e.g., allusions to the voyage of the Argo in Hom. *Od.* 12.69–72; cf. also Acts 20:35); further, most people heard such epics multiple times and hence could approach the story with the necessary preliminary story in mind. On Luke-Acts as a continuation of the biblical story, see ch. 14, sect. 2.d, below.

22. Cf. Karris, *Invitation*, 15. Goppelt, *Times*, 9, rightly notes that Luke connects Jesus and the development of the church in terms of redemptive history.

23. Despite the geographic shift and the emphasis on the Gentile mission (Acts 28:28), the Jewish people remain prominent (28:17–28).

Jerusalem, its fulfillment and goal are eschatological (even in the Isaiah texts as they were understood) rather than the heritage in which this future goal is grounded. God's agents work toward the goal in continuing history, but its final boundary is the end (Acts 1:6–8).

Thus Luke-Acts seeks to continue the biblical story by pivoting it, albeit in a way predicted and prefigured earlier in the story (Acts 13:17–41; also 7:2–53). Without denigrating the foundational story of Israel, Luke-Acts redirects the focus *from heritage to mission*.[24] Many observe the geographic pattern, in Acts, of Jerusalem to Rome,[25] an observation emphasized earlier by B. H. Streeter,[26] who titled Acts "The Road to Rome."[27] Whereas Luke's Gospel is framed with scenes of worship in the temple (Luke 1:9; 24:53), his second volume begins in Jerusalem but ends in Rome. Indeed, even Paul's custody experience, which constitutes the climactic section of Acts, proceeds from Jerusalem to Rome, recapitulating the geographic progression of the book as a whole. I believe that the theological function of this geographic shift in Acts is the movement of the community's focus from heritage to mission.

This redirection from heritage (epitomized in Jerusalem) to mission (exemplified in Rome) would challenge even most of Diaspora Judaism in its focus on Jerusalem,[28] a historic centrality that had undoubtedly caused ideological crisis after 70 C.E.[29] Moreover, before that time Christians even in the Pauline circle continued to cede a special authority or relevance to Jerusalem (Rom 15:19, 25–27; Gal 2:1) or to Jerusalem leaders or other "authentic" Jewish Christians (2 Cor 11:22; Gal 1:17, 22; 2:9; Phil 3:5; cf. 1 Cor 1:12; Col 4:11; 1 Thess 2:14).

Even former pagans might be accustomed to privilege Jerusalem; as pagans, they had been familiar with particular sites holy to certain cults, deities, or heroes or even with cities dedicated to special patron deities.[30] Pagans might question the power of the Christian deity, since his holy city was destroyed by Rome, but Luke shows that God himself judged Jerusalem (Luke 19:44; 20:16, 19; 21:22; 23:28–31) for rejecting both Jesus (9:22; 17:25; 18:31; 20:17) and his messengers of reconciliation toward Gentiles (Acts 22:21–22). The people of Jerusalem preferred Barabbas, an anti-Roman revolutionary, depending on human power (Luke 23:18; Acts 3:14), to Jesus, their divinely promised leader, who heeded the pleas of a Roman officer (Luke 7:9–10).

If Luke wrote Acts just before or after 70 C.E. (cf. Luke 21:25–28), he may have considered Paul's ministry as itself fulfilling the prerequisite for the end stipulated in Christian tradition, taking the gospel to the ends of the earth (Luke 21:12–15 [cf. 12:11–12]; Acts 1:6–8; Mark 13:10; Matt 24:14; Rom 11:25).[31] But the indeterminate period of the "times of the Gentiles" implied after 70 (Luke 21:24) allows for a continuation of history beyond that tragedy and hence suggests that Paul's ministry, like the Diaspora Jewish hearers in Acts 2:5–11, fulfilled that mission only proleptically.

After 70, believers might readily see a connection between Jesus's call to Diaspora mission and his warning of Jerusalem's impending destruction (Luke 19:43–44;

24. Cf. similarly others, e.g., Green, "Demise of Temple"; Bowe, "Birth."

25. E.g., Neil, *Acts*, 27; Packer, *Acts*, 2; Eckey, *Apostelgeschichte*; Judge, *Athens*, 50 (noting that the title "Acts of the Apostles" distracts from this theme).

26. Streeter, *Gospels*, 531–32.

27. Ibid., 532.

28. For Jerusalem-centeredness in a broad range of ancient Jewish sources, see Keener, *John*, 613–14; and especially comment on Acts 1:8.

29. Tiede, *Prophecy*, thinks that Luke explains the sufferings of 70 C.E. especially to Jewish Christians. I have argued that he responds apologetically to questions about it but do not see it as his primary purpose.

30. See, e.g., Maclean and Aitken, *Heroikos*, lxxxviii, xc.

31. Cf. Col 1:23; perhaps 1 Thess 1:8; Rom 15:19–24; probably 2 Pet 3:9, 15.

21:6–24); worldwide mission, rather than the heritage in Jerusalem, must be their focus. Thus the pre-70 Diaspora mission, with Paul as a key voice, now assumed an importance that parts of the church had not recognized in advance. Subsequent history vindicated the Spirit-driven movement from heritage to mission, and Luke chronicles this movement in his historical monograph, as an invitation to participate until the end.

b. Model and Apologetic

As noted in chapter 5, section 1, above, ancient historical writers sought to provide moral instruction or ethnic, civic or national pride for their own generation through the lessons of the past. Luke's record and adaptation of Jesus's teachings in the Gospel should be enough to alert us to Luke's interest in praxis and not mere information for its own sake. Luke-Acts offers patterns that are prescriptive, not merely descriptive.[32] Luke looks not only to the past but to the church's continuing witness through the Spirit.[33]

The expectation of models for imitation in ancient biography and historiography more generally would prime Luke's first, ancient Mediterranean audiences to look for models also (see ch. 5 above on historians' agendas). More concretely in his work, the parallels among characters (see ch. 16 below) suggest consistent patterns that not only serve a potential apologetic value (e.g., vindicating Paul for those who respected Jesus; see ch. 7, sect. 1.a) but also provide a norm (or, better, a template) recognizing God's continuing activity.

In this case, Jesus (in the Gospel) and the evangelizers and church planters (in Acts) provide a missiological model for Luke's audience as they continue the task. Why else emphasize that the Spirit is given for mission (Acts 1:8) and also available to all subsequent generations of believers in addition to the first (2:38–39)? Luke thus encourages his audience to expect continuing signs and wonders (the primary method for securing attention for the message in Luke-Acts, as a simple survey of Acts will show), preaching, church planting, persecution, and the growth of the Way in the face of opposition (see, e.g., ch. 15, sects. 3, 6, below). By this observation I do not imply that Luke offers all these models for every individual (as individualistic Western readings might be tempted to suppose). Rather, he offers them for the Christian movement as a whole (though with some features applicable to some individuals, e.g., key missionaries, doing work analogous to that of figures in Acts).

Luke writes history, but ancient historiography includes paradigms and lessons for the audiences of the historians' own era. Since patterns in Jesus's ministry are replicated in the ministry of the Jerusalem church and then in the Gentile mission (the latter still carried on in Diaspora churches of Luke's era), it is difficult to evade the conclusion that the repetitive features in Luke's portrayal of the early church are deliberate and paradigmatic. If the mission continues till the end of the age (see Acts 1:8), Luke's history of the positive prototypes for this mission suggests how the church should continue to carry it out. Some modern readers might seek to evade this conclusion partly by distinguishing conspicuously supernatural activity, such as signs and wonders, from potentially "natural" activity, such as preaching the gospel, arguing

---

32. With, e.g., Walton, "Acts," 30 (noting that elements of conversion indicated in Acts 2:38–42 recur in subsequent narratives, albeit in varying sequence). While acknowledging some exemplary value (esp. 20:35), Barrett, "Imitatio," 262, does not view it as central, contrasting it with a historical emphasis on Jesus as savior and apostles as witnesses. But a forced choice between historical events and models would not make sense in ancient historiography (see ch. 5, above, regarding historians' agendas).

33. With, e.g., O'Day, "Acts," 306.

that only the latter is a model. This criterion for dividing Luke's material, however, is anachronistic, distorting Luke's purpose in the service of accommodating Enlightenment rationalism (see ch. 9 above). For Luke and the apostolic church, preaching the gospel was no less supernatural than the signs and wonders that followed it (hence "the word of the Lord" throughout Acts; cf. also 1 Thess 2:13); to persuade without the Spirit's power might produce religious converts like those of any other cult, but this approach to proselytization was less than the apostolic ideal portrayed in our early Christian documents (1 Cor 2:4–5; 1 Thess 1:5; 2:13).

Chapter 15 below will investigate some of these concepts more fully, addressing especially the central Gentile mission and, at greatest length, the more controversial issue of "signs." The relationship between Judaism and the Jesus movement, and between Jewish and Gentile believers, is also addressed to some degree in chapter 14 below.

The move away from Jerusalem may not only help Luke explain and defend the existence of a mixed Diaspora church against Jewish detractors. It may also offer his audience an apologetic against Gentile detractors who complain about a movement whose initiating center has been destroyed, apparently abandoned by Israel's own God. Among Luke's purposes, his entire narrative offers an explanation for Jerusalem's destruction (Luke 19:42–44; 21:20–24, esp. 21:22) and reveals that God had long before demonstrated his freedom from the temple (see comment on Acts 7) and his commitment to reaching the Diaspora, including (most strikingly) Gentiles there. Thus the Christian movement should retain what pagans respected most about Judaism (such as its ethical monotheism and ancient roots) while remaining free of what annoyed pagans most about Judaism (especially its perceived ethnic separatism).

Many scholars have proposed that Acts is an apologetic; the continuity of salvation history (addressed further below) could be part of this apologetic. I turn now to the apologetic functions of Acts, including its potential apologetic audiences, the question of legal tolerance for particular cults, ancient appeals for Roman toleration, and arguments from antiquity in the service of apologetic. The following chapter will turn to the closely related matters of the relation of Luke and his narrative world to first-century Judaism, and subsequently to some sample themes that illustrate Luke's theology. Each of these subjects is related to the purposes of Acts, which are likely too diverse to be summarized under a single rubric.

3. Acts as Apologetic

Scholars generally regard Luke-Acts as at least partly an apologetic work.[34] Some do demur, pointing to Roman officials rejecting the gospel,[35] but even the least favorable officials (e.g., Acts 24:27) do not condemn Paul despite the request of often high-status accusers; they are not Paul's primary enemies, and often they protect

34. E.g., Hengel, *Acts and History*, 60; Kent, *Jerusalem to Rome*, 17; Downing, "Law and Custom" (Christians as religious in the most respectable ways); Bruce, "Apologetic and Purpose" (Christians as not subversive, for Rome); idem, *Acts*[3], 23–25; idem, *Message*, 52; Puskas and Crump, *Introduction*, 143–46. Lüdemann views Luke's apologetic treatment of the Roman government as serious distortion ("Tale"; cf. "Impropriety"), but Luke was no more tendentious than most historians of his own day and some in ours. Rothschild, *Rhetoric of History*, 65–66, says that historians often treated their histories as cases to be defended.

35. Gaventa, *Acts*, 48; cf. Davies, *Gospel and Land*, 281; Maddox, *Purpose*, 95 (who nevertheless accepts apologetic as a subsidiary purpose).

him.[36] Even before an examination of Luke's work in greater detail, the presence of numerous apologetic speeches (esp. 7:2–53; 22:3–21; 24:10–21; 26:2–29) and of "apologetic"[37] and accusatory[38] language appears to support this premise.

But why does Luke need an apologetic? Probably not to impress Roman officials *directly*; few today take Acts (in its finished form) as a legal brief.[39] Further, some elements in Acts would, in fact, work against the favor of Roman courts if presented to Roman officials—which makes it unlikely that Luke intended the entire book to function in this way.[40] Luke authored his two-volume work not primarily for outsiders but to legitimate and confirm faith (Luke 1:4).[41] Likewise, whatever Jewish apologists' intentions for their works,[42] it is doubtful that they received a large hearing outside Jewish circles; despite Judaism's probable numeric strength in the empire, most were not widely read by Gentile audiences.[43] This was probably the case with most minorities.

Apologists may write for sympathetic audiences, providing them a more direct apologetic than is possible for hostile ones. If Acts provides models for Christian mission (see below), it also provides raw material for implementing this mission successfully, including biblical apologetics for Luke's hearers to use with Jewish objectors, and legal precedents to use in Roman lawcourts (cf. Luke 21:12–15; 1 Pet 3:15).[44] It refutes the treason charge against Jesus; when Jesus was arrested, the disciples had swords (Luke 22:36), but only to number Jesus as a transgressor (22:37); further, the swords

36. A case was considered very strong when one could appeal it to even otherwise unfavorable judges (Pliny E. *N.H.* pref. 10); Luke shows that objective, or even negatively biased but not hostile, critics will not repress the faith. This observation does not imply the *invention* of data, which could undermine one's case; for the consistency of Acts with Pauline evidence for positive relations (esp. Rom 13:1–7), see discussion in Bruce, "Powers." For God's sovereignty over rulers in Luke-Acts, see brief discussion in the excursus at Acts 2:23.

37. The verb ἀπολογέομαι appears eight times in Luke-Acts (all forensic, including the six in Acts; Luke-Acts provides 80 percent of the NT uses; it appears once in the Apostolic Fathers, in *Mart. Pol.* 10.2, and just three times in the LXX [Jer 12:1; 38:6 [31:6 ET]; 2 Macc 13:26]); the noun ἀπολογία twice more (Acts 22:1; 25:16; only one-quarter of NT uses, but these, like most of the others, are forensic; in the LXX, it appears only in Wis 6:10, and never in the Apostolic Fathers).

38. The verb κατηγορέω appears thirteen times in Luke-Acts (almost 60 percent of NT usage; in the LXX only at 2 Macc 10:21; in the Apostolic Fathers, only in *1 Clem.* 17.4), and the noun κατήγορος four times (every NT usage [in the LXX, only at Prov 18:17; 2 Macc 4:5; in the Apostolic Fathers, Ign. *Magn.* 12.1], though Rev 12:10 employs κατήγωρ). Luke does not employ κατηγορία, which appears three times in the NT (never in the LXX or the Apostolic Fathers).

39. Mattill, "Purpose"; idem, "*Naherwartung*," is exceptional. More recently, and well argued, see Mauck, *Trial*, noting that Acts ends with Paul in prison and rightly noting how Luke's portrait absolves Paul of charges of fomenting unrest (ix); Mauck rightly underlines Luke's provision of narrative arguments throughout Acts (34–40; for documents potentially used at the hearing, see 194–96). Yet the function as a trial brief depends on his dating the work to roughly 61–62 C.E. (see pp. 41–45), and the current narrative of Luke-Acts neither fits the form of a trial brief (esp. one suited for busy Roman judges) nor can be completely explained by that purpose alone.

40. See Cassidy, *Society*, 145–55, noting the disciples' defiance (Acts 4:19–20; 5:29 [p. 154]; though cf. my comment ad loc.) and the Zealot (Acts 1:13; Luke 6:15 [p. 155]). Cf. the tension in the NT more broadly in Bryan, *Caesar*.

41. Marshall, "Luke and 'Gospel,'" esp. 291; Schneider, "Zweck" (noting how Luke emphasizes the community's connection back to Jesus). Also Witherington, *Acts*, 37, 63, who accepts it as apologetic, but for insiders rather than outsiders. Stoops, "Riot," 90, suggests that happy as Luke may have been for Roman authorities to read the work, he would not assume this audience likely and that, rather, he encouraged Christians, establishing self-definition and providing "political apologetic."

42. E.g., the *Letter of Aristeas* is commonly viewed as an apologetic, but some think that it is meant to keep Jews and others in Egypt on friendly terms and to justify residence there (Hacham, "*Aristeas*") or is propaganda to make Jews more open to Greek education (Tcherikover, "Ideology," 83).

43. See Feldman, "Reflections on Jews." For a survey of sources, see Stern, *Authors*.

44. For applicability of the apologetic for Luke's audience, cf. deSilva, *Introduction*, 355. Roman magistrates before Nero usually seem to have distinguished Christians from politically sensitive Jewish messianic movements (see Bacchiocchi, "Rome and Christianity")—though cf. comment on Acts 17:7; 18:2.

were few (22:38), and Jesus opposed their use (22:51). Instead of portraying Jesus as sanctioning the use of weapons, the narrative immediately provides a countercharge against those who arrested him (22:52–53).[45] Pilate repeatedly declares Jesus innocent (23:4, 14, 22), condemning him only for non-Roman political considerations (23:20, 23). The leader of the Roman execution squad further declares Jesus's innocence after his execution (Lukan redaction in 23:47).[46] Likewise, Luke also responds at great length (Acts 21–28, not including passages that predict or foreshadow it) to Paul's detention, which became an issue of some discussion even in the Roman church (cf. Phil 1:15–17; 2 Tim 1:16) and may have remained so after his execution.

Such an apologetic approach is not incompatible with Acts as a model for ministry; successful examples in Acts may encourage witnesses that they, too, may obtain a hearing in the Greco-Roman world.[47] Readers wishing to reapply Luke's point in today's world might look for ways to provide apologetic and engage with their culture today, although the specific ways to implement this approach would vary from one culture to another.

a. Potential Apologetic Audiences

Rome plays a crucial role in Luke-Acts from beginning (Luke 2:1) to end (Acts 28:16),[48] and Acts climaxes in Rome as a culminating vindication for the Gentile mission.[49] Scholars have proposed various apologetic audiences for Acts, some of which involve Rome: in some views, Luke defends Rome to Jesus's followers; in others, Luke defends Jesus's followers directly to Rome; in yet others, Luke offers Jesus's followers a defense and confirmation that they can use as needed. (One could nuance the list in greater detail by noting other variations on these views, and some overlap between the second and third proposals.)

Some suggest that Luke presents Rome positively to offer an apologetic supporting Rome to his audience.[50] This goal does appear in ancient histories: Josephus pragmatically defends Rome to his people[51] (probably also expanding distinctions between

---

45. For the use of countercharges in ancient forensic rhetoric, see comment on Acts 24:19.

46. Luke's omission of the cursing of the fig tree (Mark 11:14, 20), however, is unrelated to concerns about property damage; he includes the destruction of the swine (Luke 8:32–35; though one might attribute this damage to the demons).

47. See "unhindered" as the final word in Acts (Acts 28:31) and compare Jos. *Ant.* 16.41, 166 for apologetic value.

48. Cf. Plümacher, *Geschichte*, 168. It should be noted, however, that in these cases Rome provides part of the backdrop for specifically Jewish encounters.

49. Cf. ibid., 135–69.

50. Walaskay, *Came to Rome*, 64, may go too far in arguing that Luke wrote to defend Rome "to his church" (removing most anti-Roman sentiments in his sources), but his insights retain value. One might contrast several reasonably fair officials (by standards that provincials might expect) in Acts with Apuleius's portrait of a soldier trying to steal a poor man's animal and having the man, who resists him, killed (*Metam.* 9.39–42; for other cases of soldiers' abusing the right of requisition, see Livy 43.7.11; 43.8.1–10; Hdn. 2.3.4; 2.5.1; P.Lond. 3.1171; *IGLS* 5.1998 = *SEG* 17.755 in Sherk, *Empire*, 89, 136; *PSI* 446). Most scholars position themselves in a more nuanced way between Cassidy's and Walaskay's poles on whether Luke is anti- or pro-Roman (Chen, *Father*, 239); Luke's approach varies (Walton, "State," 33–35), offering "a strategy of critical distance from the empire" (35), with elements both appealing to Rome and indicating political reversal (Kelber, "Imperialism," 143–44; cf. Omerzu, "Apologetik"; Burrus, "Acts," 152–53; Talbert, *Romans*, 297). One should make good use of positive relations (cf., e.g., Acts 25:16) but be prepared for negative ones (Navone, "Empire"). (One could employ the categories of empire even for resistance literature; cf. deSilva, "Tools," on 4 Maccabees.) On Luke's attitude toward the Roman state in his Gospel and Acts, see also Horn, "Haltung" (addressing also Herod's family and Christian apologetic). Scholars vary also on Tacitus's views toward the empire (see Laistner, *Historians*, 117–20, questioning Tacitus's consistency; doubting also his consistency on religion, 115–17).

51. See Spilsbury, "Josephus on Rise"; cf. Neusner, *Politics to Piety*, 2. For the positive view of Rome's imperial activity in 1 Macc 8, see Hidal, "Rombilden." Josephus's apologetic does not mean that he always

Pharisees and overlapping elements of populist resistance).[52] Likewise, historians from the East during the Roman Empire portrayed Rome positively, "regarding Roman rulership as necessary and legitimate."[53]

Although Luke does want to prevent Christians from antagonizing Rome and apparently works in a region and a period in which severe persecution (such as under Nero in 64 C.E.) is not the rule, the book contains too much defense of Christians before authorities for his *primary* interest to be the defense of authorities. As noted in chapter 5, section 3, above, apologetic historiography often defended minority peoples against the criticism of the elite; Josephus also provides many precedents defending his people vis-à-vis Rome. More commonly, scholars believe that Luke sought to provide an apologetic supporting Christians in the Roman Empire. Some argue that Luke wrote Acts, or at least the accounts of Paul's hearings and experiences in Acts 22–28,[54] for Paul's defense in Rome.

That Paul and Luke would have prepared earlier precedents in this way is not unlikely, but they would hardly expect a representative of the emperor to listen to the entire work Luke-Acts. Few scholars today see the entire work as a trial brief;[55] naturally, the majority who date Acts after Paul's death cannot do so. More than likely, Luke expects the work's direct audience to be Christians who need confirmation in what they have already heard (much like Theophilus, Luke 1:3–4).

Such confirmation does not exclude apologetic concerns, however: the truth in which Luke wishes to confirm his audience could well include the truth about Jesus, despite the charge on which he was crucified under Pilate, as well as the truth about Paul, the Gentile mission's most prominent advocate, despite the charge on which he was executed under Nero.[56] The audience may need to be equipped to respond to misrepresentations of their faith lodged against them by the gossip or even policies of outsiders.

Some argue that Acts' apologetic audience seems primarily Jewish.[57] Only one of the final defense speeches addresses specifically a Roman;[58] Luke affords more space to Paul's custody than to his missionary journeys,[59] but even when addressing Roman officials, Paul is answering Jewish issues, and he continues to address Jewish issues (and a Jewish audience) in his final speech in Acts.[60] Acts concludes not with legal vindication but with God's faithfulness to his people.[61]

---

distorted his accounts (e.g., Leoni, "Wishes"; idem, "Incendio," argues that Titus did not order the temple's burning).

52. Although Josephus dissociates Pharisees from "Zealots" (*War* 2.118, written in the wake of the war), even he confesses that Zealots shared most Pharisaic views (*Ant.* 18.23; and Pharisaic influence, 18.4, 9); certainly, there was some cooperation at times (18.4), and they shared some common mistrust of Rome (cf. probably *m. 'Abot* 1:10; 2:3) and (at least in an earlier period), at the very least, an ideal of civil disobedience (*War* 1.648–55). Cf. Sanders, *Judaism*, 13–14, 408–11; Horsley and Hanson, *Bandits*, xv, 194, 198; Witherington, *Christology of Jesus*, 83–84; Simon, *Sects*, 44.

53. Meister, "Historiography: Greece," 420. Romans, of course, naturally glorified Rome also (e.g., Livy 1.28.11).

54. E.g., Bammel, "Activity," 364n26. Early Christian apologies such as those of Athenagoras and Justin did take the form of ambassadorial appeals to the emperor, following a Jewish apologetic form in material in Josephus and Philo (see Schoedel, "Ambassadorial Activities").

55. Against the trial brief hypothesis, see, e.g., Munck, *Acts*, lviii–lix; Kent, *Jerusalem to Rome*, 17; Witherington, *Acts*, 14; Liefeld, *Acts*, 31.

56. That Paul's kerygmatic language could be construed in political ways (Donfried, "Rethinking") may have made an apologetic on his behalf more urgent.

57. For Acts as apologetic, see Alexander, *Context*, 183–206.

58. Ibid., 200. Against Alexander, I would count three, since Festus is part of the audience in Acts 26; but the Jewish element in Acts 22 and 26 cannot be minimized.

59. Alexander, *Context*, 204–5.

60. Ibid., 205.

61. Ibid., 206.

All these observations are important, but Luke would have had to address any accusations against Paul, a founder of his movement, if, in fact, these were an issue vis-à-vis local and Roman governments.[62] Luke is probably interested in answering Jewish objections of concern to his audience both because of their own relationship with local Jewish communities (and probably sometimes relatives) and because of the effects of such accusations on Christians' standing with regard to Rome.

1. Emphasizing Paul's Innocence

Acts, as a whole, functions as a highly refined literary apologetic useful in addressing various external—including Roman—concerns. The very amount of space devoted to Paul's custody (Acts 22–28, plus briefer earlier custodies) indicates this interest.[63] Luke often signals by repetition the points he wishes to emphasize. For example, he underlines the Gentile mission by three times repeating the Cornelius narrative (Acts 10–11; 15) and three times repeating the account of the conversion of the apostle to the Gentiles (Acts 9; 22; 26). In the same way, he reports three Roman hearings concerning Paul's final custody, none of which supplies any conclusive evidence against him.[64]

Although our present book of Acts is not a trial brief, parts of it focus so fully on Paul's (or others') innocence that one must wonder if some of this material was not originally collected for such a purpose. Paul as an executed convict of Rome could also become an apologetic issue for Luke's era if slanders survived him (cf., e.g., 21:21; Rom 3:8; 2 Cor 6:8); it was far easier to simply dissociate from Paul's memory than from Jesus's (cf. Phil 1:17–18; 2 Tim 4:10, 16), but not so easily if he was father of the Gentile mission. The truth that should have vindicated Paul the first time might need to be reapplied for the sake of the defense of his gospel.[65] I have just mentioned Paul's defense speeches, but we can examine also the riots that followed Paul's ministry. Undoubtedly, a significant and potentially deadly charge against Paul was that he stirred unrest (Acts 24:5); followers of one "Chrestus" had already been charged with stirring unrest in Rome's Jewish community under Claudius (Suet. *Claud.* 25.4), and Nero certainly branded them as seditious (Tac. *Ann.* 15.44).[66]

In this light, Luke's reports of the riots following Paul's ministry take on more serious overtones than for scholars who (like Pervo) view them primarily as entertainment. Unrest followed Paul's preaching in most places where he went, and Luke cannot easily deny this. But Luke can provide explanations that defend Paul and return charges against the accusers (a conventional forensic strategy; see comment on Acts 24:19). Thus Jewish rabble-rousers (the kind Rome particularly despised after 66 C.E.) often started the trouble (Acts 9:23; 13:50; 14:2–4, 19; 17:5–8; 18:12); or vested economic interests vied against Paul, as when some falsely denounced him as non-Roman because he was forced to cast out a demon (a benevolent act; 16:18–21); or when a rabble-rouser in Ephesus accused him of hurting local interests (19:25–29).

---

62. Which seems to be the case even later in some settings, such as Rev 2:9; *Mart. Pol.* 13.1; 17.2; 18.1.

63. See my fuller discussion in Keener, "Apologetic." Acts may include more trial scenes than the five standard Greek novels put together (Schwartz, "Trial Scenes," 118).

64. See Witherington, *Acts*, 73. Cf. officials' vindications of Jesus's innocence in the Gospel (Luke 23:4, 14, 22; cf. also 23:41, 47), as noted above.

65. Cf. Luke-Acts as an apologetic for Paul in Wasserberg, "Lk-Apg als Paulusapologie." This may not exhaust Luke-Acts, but it seems an important function, especially given the final quarter of Acts.

66. Cf. Suet. *Nero* 16.2; Tert. *Apol.* 5.3–4; cf. later Sulp. Sev. *Chron.* 2.29 (in Barrett, *Documents*, 17). Others blamed the fire completely on Nero (Suet. *Nero* 38; Dio Cass. 62.16.1–18.1, esp. 62.16.2), though Rome (e.g., Tac. *Hist.* 1.2; Suet. *Aug.* 30.1; *Claud.* 18.1; *Tit.* 8.3–4), like other locations (e.g., Pliny E. *N.H.* 28.4.19; 28.5.26; Pliny *Ep.* 10.33.1–3; 10.39.4), suffered many fires and some scholars doubt Nero's complicity (e.g., Bohm, "Nero").

Just as Josephus must show that Tiberius's expulsion of Jews from Rome (see comment on the later expulsion in Acts 18:2) stemmed from a lone exploiter, and the Judean-Roman war from irresponsible governors and a few Jewish bandits, Luke must show that Paul's enemies, not Paul himself, caused the unrest of which he was accused.[67]

Yet Roman courts and important officials (people with the kind of status that weighed in Roman courts)[68] exonerated him (16:36–39; 18:14–15; 19:37–40)! Even so, Luke's historiographic sensitivity does not allow him to paint every official the same way, and he cannot suppress some tension (e.g., 4:27; 24:27).[69] Moreover, some close calls (17:10) suggest that just behind the surface of Luke's apologetic were serious challenges against Paul; chains, imprisonment, and execution were shameful in the empire, and Luke had an important but difficult job in exonerating Paul. Association with one convicted of a crime could be used in courts to imply guilt by association, so that some would seek to dissociate themselves from one's memory or legacy (e.g., Quint. *Decl.* 307.6).

Toward the end of Paul's life and soon afterward, his prisoner status was problematic even for some Christians (cf. Phil 1:17; 2 Tim 1:8, 12, 16); the prominence of this concern in Philippians (Phil 1:7, 12–20; 2:17) could have made it a very relevant issue for Luke's own immediate setting (at least for non-Christian critics there; cf. Phil 1:28–30), especially if we have correctly situated the work's provenance (based on the frequency of the "we" in Philippi; see above, ch. 12, sect. 3.c). How does one honor the founders of one's movement, hence the movement itself, when they are vilified by a world that values the verdicts of corrupt courts and human status? Showing that such condemnations were aberrations rather than appropriate precedents would also better equip other Christians to defend their position vis-à-vis Rome.

Further, Luke (much like Josephus for Diaspora Jews) multiplies various official outcomes and expressions of favor that could function as legal precedents against persecuting early Christians as subversives (Acts 13:12; 16:38–39; 17:32–34; 19:38–40; 24:20–27; esp. 18:14–15; 26:30–32). Herod Antipas, Pilate, and a centurion all pronounce Jesus's innocence toward the end of the first volume (Luke 23:15, 22, 47).[70] Luke often portrays the disorder accompanying the spread of Christianity as due to hostility from fellow Jews (or, on two occasions, "vested property interests").[71]

---

67. Stoops, "Riot," 73, argues that Luke here employs "a pattern of apologetic argument developed among diaspora Jews. The argument ran: 'Because our opponents riot our rights ought to be confirmed'" (citing [pp. 79–80] Philo *Embassy* 335–36; Jos. *Ant.* 14.244–46; 16.58–60; 19.284–85; *War* 2.487–98; 7.107–11). Jewish people had learned that demonstrating their opponents to be at fault in riots led to reaffirmation of Jewish rights but failure to do so led to their mistreatment (79). The same principles could apply to Christians as a Jewish sect (81). We may add Josephus's arguments on how unjust repression of Jews helped spark the tragic war (e.g., *Ant.* 20.183).

68. Minority cults depended on sponsors of status to achieve more mainstream status (White, *Origins of Architecture*, 1:58–59), and the words of people of rank weighed much more heavily in courts (Gaius *Inst.* 4.183; cf. Jas 2:6; Winter, *Welfare*, 111–13; idem, *Left Corinth*, 60–64; Rapske, *Custody*, 56–62), although this may have been more fully formalized legally in the second century (Garnsey and Saller, *Empire*, 115–16; Krause, "Honestiores"; Callistr. *Dig.* 47.21.2) and many complained about wealth protecting the guilty (Cic. *Verr.* 1.1.1; 1.3.8; 1.5.13; Libanius *Declam.* 36, e.g., 36.8–9; cf. *'Abot R. Nat.* 20, §43 B). For the Jewish apologetic use of outsiders' speeches affirming Jewish identity, see now Padilla, *Speeches*, 42–105 (applying this research insightfully to comparable outsiders' speeches in Acts, 106–32).

69. E.g., Maddox, *Purpose*, 95; Davies, *Gospel and Land*, 281 (probably going too far).

70. So does a condemned criminal (Luke 23:41), though this would not impress the more elite members of Luke's audience.

71. Bruce, *Commentary*, 20–21 and 21n16 (though Bruce in this earlier work still applied this claim to a life setting before Nero's persecution, p. 22). For some causes of hostility to Christians and their message, see, e.g., Green, *Thirty Years*, 17–24 (esp. 20–24, for Gentiles).

Granted, it was never safe for public documents to challenge the Roman authorities or portray them in a hostile light, least of all for a sect whose founder was a provincial executed on a cross.[72] But the accumulation of precedents in Acts (see ch. 7, sect. 1.a, above) is probably no more a coincidence than are the analogous precedents in Josephus (see sect. 3.c.ii below). Further, some of the primary accusations that Christians had to counter after the middle of the first century included charges of subverting family structures and so threatening Roman authority (e.g., 1 Tim 5:15; 6:1; Titus 2:5, 8, 10).[73] Acts emphasizes both genders, all classes, and, when possible, the conversions of households in response to that of the *paterfamilias* (e.g., Acts 10:2, 24, 44; 16:31–33).

I noted above that Paul had detractors in the churches as well as outside them (Phil 1:7, 12–20; 2:17; 2 Tim 1:8, 16; 4:16). Paul's final hearing before Nero's court—whether culminating the detention narrated in Acts 28:16–31 or a subsequent detention—ended with his execution and probably affected more than Paul. In keeping with his calling to preach to kings (Acts 9:15; cf. Luke 21:12), Paul probably used the occasion to offer his message in some form to the emperor and/or his court (cf. 2 Tim 4:16–18; perhaps earlier Phil 1:13), as Luke apparently implies (Acts 23:11; 27:24). Some members of the churches were ashamed of his testimony (cf. 2 Tim 1:8), and preaching could exacerbate persecution, at least for those already detained (cf. Phil 1:17). Luke thus has reason to provide samples of Paul's earlier preaching while in Roman custody (22:1–21; 24:10–21; 25:10–12; 26:2–29), revealing that he offered no objectionable teaching.

Likewise, if some believed that Paul's final, bold testimony inflamed Nero's persecution more fully, Luke has already shown that the ultimate outcome of such events was positive. Jesus's death scattered his disciples, but God soon empowered them. Persecution in response to Stephen's preaching (explicit in 11:19) scattered the church, but in so doing spread the gospel (8:1–4; 11:19–21). Paul carries on Stephen's role as witness (22:15, 20–21), and believers should not despise his legacy. The long-range benefit to the kingdom outweighed the short-term suffering.

II. Radical but Not Subversive

Although Jesus's teachings in the Gospel are socially transformative through those who embrace them (cf. Luke 12:33; 14:33; 18:22) and Jesus does challenge the Sadducean elite (20:13–18), Luke is careful to avoid any suggestions of political subversion. Luke (3:12; 5:27–30; 7:29, 34; 15:1; 18:10–13; 19:2) includes more tax gatherers than Mark (Mark 2:15–16); their fairly positive role may help counter any associations with Judean nationalism epitomized in the revolt of 66–73. "Render to Caesar" is an obvious case in point (Luke 20:25).[74] Whereas most of Luke's audience may not have caught the allusion to the tax revolt in Luke 2:2,[75] contrasts with

---

72. Witherington thinks that Acts is positive toward Roman authorities because it was not safe to be otherwise in the Flavian period (*Acts*, 62–63, citing Tac. *Agr.* 2, but this probably has only Domitian in mind), but antigovernment tracts would be considered subversive at any time in the period of the empire.

73. For how such charges were viewed as subverting Roman authority, see Keener, *Paul*, 140–42; for the family as a microcosm of the state, see Malherbe, *Social Aspects*, 51; Meeks, *Moral World*, 21; cf. Cic. *Off.* 1.17.54.

74. Talbert, *Acts*, 113, uses Luke 20:25 to help explain both Luke's usually positive attitude toward the state and his hostility toward ruler worship in Acts 12:22–23. That Luke can describe Paul "calling on" Caesar (25:11) as well as on Christ (22:16; cf. 2:21; the same verb) does not suggest a rigid incompatibility of kingdoms.

75. The census would evoke taxation, but a connection between Judas the Galilean and a revolt under Quirinius was probably not widely remembered. Luke might know something of it, given the reference to "peace" in Luke 2:14.

revolutionaries in Acts 5:36–37 and 21:38 are obvious enough.[76] Far more explicitly than in the other Gospels, the expected kingdom involves peace (Luke 1:79; 2:14; 19:38; Acts 10:36; though cf. Luke 12:51), dissociated from Jerusalem's revolt (Luke 19:42). Mentions of "Caesar" are hardly incidental. Charges of sedition against Caesar (Luke 23:2; Acts 17:7; cf. 25:8) are fabrications, as is clear to Luke's audience (Luke 20:22, 25); Paul proves so confident that he has not dishonored Caesar that he appeals to him for vindication (Acts 25:11; 28:19; cf. 25:12, 21; 26:32; 27:24).

The challenge belongs to the future (1:6–7; 3:19–21; Luke 21:25–28, 31), not so much the present.[77] Even with reference to the future, Romans at the beginning of the empire looked for a future golden age. Christ supplants Caesar in that vision, and Christian monotheism could not brook Caesar worship in the present (cf. Luke 20:25; Acts 12:22–23); but Luke suggests this fundamental disagreement in as conciliatory a manner as possible. Although it is certainly true, as some scholars have argued, that the eschatological vision of a just and caring community (cf., e.g., Luke 18:22–30; Acts 2:44–45) and a greater kingdom lend themselves readily to challenge societal injustice and the mores of Roman imperialism, this is not an application that Luke would dare offer explicitly. Luke does not address a democracy that welcomes political participation, nor can he count among his audience the elite that controlled the political order (which then included and could include few Christians). His kingdom movement is a minority sect that can, at most, transform the world for the better on a local scale countless times over, proclaiming good news and spreading what ought to be the ideal, eschatological community. His alternative kingdom belongs to an eschatological dimension that transforms society instead of challenging Rome politically in the present.[78]

III. Apologetic Elements

Many components in Acts have apologetic potential. Visions and revelations could provide convincing evidence to outsiders (cf. Acts 23:9; 26:19),[79] just as accounts of signs and wonders could (for the propagandistic value of signs, see ch. 15, sect. 6.c, below). Clearly, many of the speeches in Acts function apologetically for various audiences, such as Israel (7:2–53), philosophers (17:22–31), and Roman authorities (Acts 24–26).[80] Luke makes use of outsiders' speeches for apologetic purposes as well: Gallio (18:14–15); Ephesus's town clerk (19:35–40); Festus, Bernice, and Agrippa (26:31–32); and so forth.

I argued in chapter 7, section 1.a, that Acts includes (probably in addition to its general apologetic) an apologetic for Paul, defending his legacy against the charges surrounding his custody and (on a post-Pauline date) his execution.[81] Some scholars

---

76. Still, one of Jesus's disciples is a "zealot" (Luke 6:15; Acts 1:13); whatever this title may have meant originally, it probably carried more revolutionary connotations after 70 C.E.

77. Cf. discussion in Kim, *Caesar*, 156–57.

78. The goal of contextualizing Luke's models in societies allowing political participation is important, but we should also recognize the limitations of Luke's context and not anachronistically judge him as falling short of our construct for a different kind of society. That is, we should not take Luke out of his context, but may find Lukan principles, including political ones, that would need to be applied differently in different contexts. Cf. the helpful balance in Rowe, *World*: because religion and politics were inseparable (9), Luke's vision of Christianity challenges pagan culture, yet without sedition (4–7, 51; for the challenge, esp. 17–51; for the innocence, 53–89); also Kim, *Caesar*, 200–201: we cannot expect a struggling minority sect to safely challenge political structures; cf. also Harrison, *Authorities*, 43, regarding Paul: Paul had to articulate the right balance, avoiding alienating the authorities or compromising Christ's Lordship (cf. also 7).

79. Munck, *Acts*, lx–lxi.

80. See, e.g., Bruce, *Commentary*, 24.

81. See also Keener, "Apologetic."

also argue that Acts includes a defense of Paul against his detractors in parts of the church (cf. Phil 1:15–17); this may be especially relevant for some Jewish followers of Jesus still uncomfortable with the Gentile mission.[82] The precedents for Roman toleration in Acts suggest that this is not Luke's only concern, but it is plausible as a part of it.[83]

Certainly, Paul had some opponents in conservative Jewish Christian circles (Acts 21:21; Rom 3:8; 2 Cor 11:22; Gal 2:4; cf. Rom 15:31). Luke emphasizes Paul's monotheism, sometimes in contrast to that of his Jewish detractors (Acts 14:14–19; 19:26–27, 33–34); his otherwise shameful sufferings gain respectability by being linked, in the work's structure, to those of Jesus and the apostles before him. One side of Luke's work may answer (perhaps in advance) Jewish detractors of Paul. Some may have emphasized his Diaspora origins, forcing Luke to emphasize Paul's orthodox Palestinian upbringing (22:3), though, for Luke's own audience, Paul's Diaspora background was a virtue (for which reason Luke also stresses this).

To reiterate a point emphasized in chapter 12, Luke's primary apologetic audience need not be Jewish. Although apologetic responses to Jewish objections appear in biblical arguments in some of the book's apologetic speeches, especially in its closing scene, this apologetic does not guarantee a direct unbelieving Jewish audience any more than the book's apologetic concerning riots (see comment on Acts 24:5) guarantees a direct audience of Roman officials. Rather, Luke is providing a biblically literate Christian audience (composed of both Jews and Gentiles) a response to objections that concern them. That is, an apologetic *for* a group is not necessarily an apologetic directly *to* that group.

Yet Jewish opinions of the Diaspora Christian movement (and Paul, its apostle) would be relevant not only for their own sake. If Roman magistrates were to accept Christianity as an ethnic religion, a sect within Judaism, Paul's relationship with Judean Judaism could also become an apologetic concern toward Roman law. Although Plato reveals various agendas in writing, some of his works focused on Socrates's greatness, a matter that would convey some status importance to his adherents despite his execution.[84] But Socrates's virtue may have been less controversial by the time that Plato wrote than Paul's was in some circles of Luke's day.

Luke's apologetic directed toward Rome in Acts often does emphasize that Rome understood Christians as a socially harmless sect or party within Judaism.[85] This may be one reason that Luke ties Jesus and his movement into the larger history of Israel (see discussion on Luke and the OT in ch. 14 below), although he certainly has other historical reasons to stress the solidarity as well.[86] If Judaism was a permitted religion (see subsection b below), then Christians should be likewise; the two groups shared a common appeal to an argument from antiquity (see subsection d below).[87]

---

82. See esp. Jervell, "Church," 20; idem, *Luke and People of God*, 198–99. Le Cornu, *Acts*, xxx, argues that a primary purpose of Acts is "to explain the relationship between the Jewish and gentile segments of the early community." Lüdemann, *Paul*, 16, thinks that Luke portrays the Jerusalem church leaders as accepting Paul, to head off criticisms that Paul deprecated the law; Lüdemann may have a genuine observation about Luke's apologetic here, though he is too skeptical about Luke's information.

83. Cf. Bruce, *Acts*[3], 25, accepting this as a possible secondary reason.

84. Cf. also *Theages*, probably by an early Platonist imitator (Lamb, "Introduction," 345).

85. See McGrath, "Apologetics." Apologetic interests might also motivate Luke's reduced (albeit not absent) emphasis on the parousia.

86. See Wright, *People of God*, 373–75.

87. E.g., Winter, "Imperial Cult," 98; Wright, *People of God*, 376.

Identification with Judaism could also exempt early Christians from civic pressure to participate in the imperial cult.[88]

b. A religio licita?

So long as the Jesus movement remained a part of Judaism, it would remain entitled to any legal privileges that Judaism had in the Roman Empire.[89] Although Luke obviously has strong theological reasons (not the least of them his appropriation of Jesus's and Paul's Jewish canon and history) to emphasize the continuity of Israel and the Jesus movement, he likely has apologetic reasons as well (see ch. 14 below).

A long line of scholarship argues that Judaism was a *religio licita*, based on privileges conferred by Julius Caesar and confirmed by Augustus.[90] Others deny that Judaism fit this category or argue that the category of *religio licita* did not formally exist.[91] The phrase, in fact, first appears in Tertullian (*Apol.* 21.1), not in Roman law.[92] Some maintain that Romans always treated foreign cults ad hoc.[93]

Despite these reasonable objections to the phrase, evidence indicates that some groups were generally tolerated. Indeed, if the term *religio licita* first appears in Tertullian, he used it with good reason; *collegia licita* is attested earlier,[94] which would be relevant to Jewish groups in the empire.[95] Precedents could help indicate which groups had earned and retained such toleration. Although rulers and provincial officials were not bound by precedent,[96] they respected precedent and used it as a guide.[97] Rome's respect for ancestral religions provided a means of arguing for political legitimation.[98] Christians might not find protection under the umbrella of Judaism as a "legal religion," but they could find it within Judaism as an *ancient* religion.[99] In practice, this might amount to virtually the same thing.

c. Appeals to Roman Toleration

Traditional Palestinian Jewish works often displayed mistrust of the rulers and portrayed them as persecutors rather than defenders (e.g., *1 En.* 103:14–15).[100] Authors

88. See Winter, "Imperial Cult," 99–100; Keener, *John*, 177–79, esp. 179; idem, *Revelation*, 38–39; Selwyn, *Peter*, 51–52.

89. With, e.g., Bruce, *Acts³*, 23. This concern might prove all the more urgent if, with Judge, *First Christians*, 431–36, we suppose that Romans distinguished Christians from the Jewish community from the start. Luke's apologetic apparently never convinced Roman officials: Christians lacked the protection of Judaism in subsequent Roman policy (see ibid., 435–41). Granted, Christians appealed to Israel's history, and hence an argument from antiquity; but this largely fell on deaf ears (Judge, *Athens*, 114). For many, the earliest Christian movement, lacking cult and loosening ethnic moorings, would not have even qualified easily as "religion" (idem, *First Christians*, 404–5; cf. Rives, *Religion*, 23–28, 47–49).

90. E.g., Smallwood, *Jews*, 539; Reinhold, *Diaspora*, 74; Goppelt, *Times*, 107. Jews notably mourned Caesar's decease (Suet. *Jul.* 84.5).

91. Rajak, "Charter"; Maddox, *Purpose*, 91–93; Koester, *Introduction*, 1:365; Esler, *Community*, 211–14; Tuckett, *Luke*, 66; Das, *Debate*, 185–90; cf. Ben Zeev, "Position"; Rabello, "Condition," 703–4.

92. Parkes, *Conflict*, 8; esp. Rajak, "Charter," followed by others, e.g., Witherington, *Acts*, 542.

93. See Esler, *Community*, 214–17.

94. See Aune, *Revelation*, 1:170; Levinskaya, *Diaspora Setting*, 6.

95. As an ethnic community, "the Jews formed a 'collegium' rather than a 'religio'" (Parkes, *Conflict*, 8). On the banning of some clubs as *collegia illicita*, see Smith, *Symposium*, 97.

96. E.g., Ferguson, *Backgrounds*, 50–51.

97. E.g., Cic. *Att.* 6.1; Pliny *Ep.* 10.66.1; Tac. *Ann.* 4.37.

98. Esler, *Community*, 214–17.

99. Witherington, *Acts*, 541–44. In contrast to synagogues, however, churches eventually became multiethnic, making their analogy to a national institution appear more subversive (see Judge, "Toleration").

100. Cf. Adinolfi, "Autorità romane," who contrasts the positive portrayal of Paul's relations toward Rome in Acts with a condemnation of Rome in Jewish apocalyptic circles (e.g., 1QpHab III, 4–5). Even works that present Rome as hostile may emphasize Israel's innocence (e.g., *y. Sukkah* 5:1, §7).

of Hellenistic Jewish works, however, had provided flattering portrayals of benevolent Ptolemaic rulers (e.g., *Let. Aris.* 24), and some such writers also gave Rome generally high marks (cf. Jos. *Ant.* 14.188–240).[101] Diaspora Judaism often experienced and viewed Rome as a protector, especially in troubled areas such as Alexandria, where their minority rights were regularly challenged.[102]

1. Roman Tolerance toward Various Cults

One way to provide apologetic with Roman official policy in mind was to cite precedents of Roman toleration. When codified, Roman law noted the differences between particular legal systems (such as Roman law) and universal law (Gaius *Inst.* 1.1); particular legal systems applied only to particular peoples.

Rome generally accommodated local cults so long as they provided no threat to public order; it preferred to keep all deities well disposed toward the Roman state.[103] In Rome itself foreign cults remained suspect during some periods[104] but could be regulated and in time accepted.[105] After all, as polytheists, most inhabitants of the empire could accept the existence of the deities whose cults were in dispute, if not always the decorum of their followers. Thus Rome welcomed the cult of Ceres (Demeter), using Greek priestesses so that she would feel at home but providing her Roman citizenship so that she would help Rome (Cic. *Balb.* 24.55). When the Romans besieged towns, Roman priests would invoke local deities, promising them greater worship by the Romans if they would abandon the besieged towns under their protection (Pliny E. *N.H.* 28.4.18).

Exceptions were usually extreme cases, such as the Druids of Gaul and Britain, accused of practicing human sacrifice.[106] New cults also had to beware of fitting Romans' stereotypical fears that they might subvert Roman family values;[107] the memory of second-century B.C.E. excesses of the Dionysiac cult was never far from the surface.[108]

101. For the apologetic (and missionary) nature of Hellenistic Jewish literature, see, e.g., Sabugal, "Exégesis de Aristábulo." Not all Hellenistic Jewish works are identical in purpose; unlike Philo, Wisdom of Solomon may presuppose, rather than seek to reconcile, Judaism and Hellenism (Isaacs, *Spirit*, 23–24).

102. See Meeks, *Urban Christians*, 38. Claudius's edict of toleration for Jews in Alexandria (41 C.E.; the most favorable part is P.Lond. 1912.82–88; cf. Jos. *Ant.* 19.280–85, 302–11) has been much discussed; see Feldman's bibliography in *Josephus*, LCL, 9:429–31.

103. See, e.g., Stambaugh and Balch, *Environment*, 45; Georgi, "Socioeconomic Reasons," 35; Caird, *Revelation*, 22.

104. Especially during the republic; see Dion. Hal. *Ant. rom.* 3.35.2; Livy 4.30.9–11; 25.1.11–12; 39.15.2–3; Val. Max. 1.3.2, 4; second-century B.C.E. Jews in Val. Max. 1.3.3; cf. in Massilia (Val. Max. 2.6.7b). For an incident in 58 C.E. in Tac. *Ann.* 13.32.2, see Stuhlmacher, *Romans*, 195.

105. See O'Rourke, "Law," 178; Koester, *Introduction*, 1:364–65. Rome temporarily crushed the Isis cult in Rome, reportedly in response to a scandal (Jos. *Ant.* 18.79; more fully, 18.64–80; but cf. Moehring, "Persecution in A.D. 19"; Heyob, *Isis*, 22, 118). Augustus banned Egyptian cults from the *pomerium*, though some argue that this was simply to demarcate Roman from foreign (Orlin, "Boundaries"). A few select ancient cults were welcomed (Suet. *Aug.* 93; Nock, "Developments," 499), but these were exceptional (Suet. *Claud.* 25.5); during the early empire, most were viewed as competition against state religion (see Garnsey and Saller, *Empire*, 170–71) and viewed unfavorably (Val. Max. 7.3.8; Petron. *Sat.* 16–26; Suet. *Tib.* 36; *Nero* 56; Apul. *Metam.* 8.29; 9.9–10). Official disfavor did not prevent their spread (Salles, "Société interculturelle"; Grant, *Gods*, 33–34).

106. Mattingly, *Christianity*, 18. Rome tried to regulate, but not to obliterate, local Egyptian religion (Frankfurter, *Religion in Egypt*, 198).

107. See Keener, *Paul*, 140–42, and documentation there, esp. Plut. *Bride* 19, *Mor.* 140D; Meeks, *Moral World*, 22; cf. Petron. *Sat.* 16–26; Apul. *Metam.* 8.27–30; 9.9–10. On Juv. *Sat.* 6.540–41, 548–50 (cf. 14.100–103), see further Carcopino, *Life*, 131; Juvenal's "filth of the Orontes" (*Sat.* 3.62) might allude to Polyb. 5.59.11.

108. See Livy 39.15.11; 39.18.9; Val. Max. 1.3.1; esp. Grant, *Paul*, 82–84; Shelton, *Romans*, 394–96; cf. Nagy, "Superstitio"; concerns about Livy's presentation in Laistner, *Historians*, 86. Judaism had been confused with Dionysus worship (e.g., Plut. *Table* 4.6.2, *Mor.* 671DE, 672A; cf. Tac. *Hist.* 5.5; Leon, *Jews of Rome*, 213–15) and treated as a superstitious mystery (Juv. *Sat.* 14.100–103; cf. Tac. *Hist.* 2.4), comparable to

11. Josephus's Appeal to Favorable Decrees

Jewish apologists were more than happy to appeal to this precedent of basic Roman tolerance where it supported their cause.[109] Josephus notes that each nation should observe its own laws properly rather than critique those of other nations, as the anti-Semite Apion does (*Ag. Ap.* 2.144).[110] Specifically, Romans did not force peoples to break the laws of their own cultures (2.73). Josephus appeals to Roman decrees to show the Jewish people's loyalty to Rome (2.61), an idea much in dispute in the decades after 70; Augustus himself, he notes, defended Diaspora Jews' religious rights (*Ant.* 16.162–65).[111] None of the Caesars sought to reduce the privileges that Alexander of Macedon bestowed on the Jewish people (Jos. *War* 2.488). In his *Antiquities*, Josephus cites various Jewish rights repeatedly established in the Diaspora, which E. P. Sanders summarizes as follows:[112]

1. To assemble (*Ant.* 14.214–16, 227, 235, 257–58, 260–61)[113]
2. To keep the Sabbath (14.226, 242, 245, 258, 263–64)
3. To keep to their "ancestral" food (14.226, 245, 261)
4. To decide their own affairs (14.235, 260)
5. To contribute money (14.214, 227)

More generally, they could exercise the right to pursue their own customs (14.213–16, 223, 227, 242, 245–46, 258, 260, 263).[114] These rights probably varied from place to place—Josephus normally cites local precedents[115]—but cumulatively, they provided a strong argument from Roman and many local traditions for tolerance.

Josephus may select only favorable decrees (and only the most favorable parts of such decrees),[116] but their limited yet public and falsifiable nature, in a work submitted to potential imperial examination, among other factors, indicates that he did not simply invent such precedents.[117] (That an occasional precedent might have been fabricated before him and unknown to him is not impossible; in some less cosmopolitan locations, at least some governors' edicts were suspected of

---

Cybele worship (Pers. *Sat.* 5.179–84 with 5.185–88; cf. Ovid *Fasti* 4.236) or despised Egyptian cults (Suet. *Tib.* 36). Jews could employ the name (*CIJ* 2:445, §1538) and some symbolism (*Let. Aris.* 70) but were quite different (2 Macc 6:7).

109. Political expediency figured more highly than either anti-Judaism or Jewish antiquity in the empire's response to its Jewry (Garnsey and Saller, *Empire*, 169–70).

110. Josephus likewise notes that God's law forbids accusing others' laws or mocking their gods (*Ag. Ap.* 2.237); for Jewish apologetic against the charge of robbing others' temples, see comment on Acts 19:37.

111. For one discussion concerning this edict's date, see Eilers, "Date of Edict."

112. Sanders, *Judaism*, 212.

113. The right to assemble had to be explicitly stated, since Rome regulated and normally forbade this right (Rabello, "Condition," 719); Sanders, *Judaism*, 212, regards this right as virtually unique to Jews (citing Jos. *Ant.* 14.215–16; Suet. *Jul.* 42.3; Philo *Embassy* 311), though this was their primary special privilege (see Ben Zeev, "Position").

114. Sanders, *Judaism*, 212. For a full discussion of Jewish privileges, see Kraft, "Judaism on World Scene," 88–90; Whittaker, *Jews and Christians*, 92–105; Tajra, *Trial*, 14–21; Applebaum, "Legal Status," 420–63.

115. See here esp. the emphasis in Rajak, "Charter," 112–14.

116. This is the case with Claudius's decree to the Alexandrians, a copy of which survives: Josephus does, in fact, cite a genuine decree, but only the portion that interests him and serves his purpose (i.e., the favorable part). Luke may sometimes follow a similar procedure (contrast Acts 18:2 with Suetonius's statement about "Chrestus," and note common suggestions about Acts 20:16).

117. See Winter, *Left Corinth*, 289–90; Rhodes, "Documents," 65 (citing *Ant.* 14.187–88 about documents in the capitol, and noting that most today accept most of Josephus's documentary appeals); and most thoroughly Ben Zeev, *Jewish Rights*, passim. Ben Zeev, "Ambiguities," admits Josephus's errors and some of his tendentiousness but contends that he mostly represents genuine material.

being of dubious authenticity.)[118] The idea of appealing to precedents was hardly limited to Josephus.[119] Rome had to choose between persecuting Jews and making exceptions for them that others would count as privileges; usually it chose the latter course.[120]

III. Luke's Appeal to Precedent

That Luke would provide a similar (albeit necessarily more limited) appeal to precedents (noted above) is not surprising. Still, Luke's apologetic remains distinct from that of Josephus. Josephus is less apt to emphasize the conversion of Romans; Jewish proselytism had provoked considerable Roman hostility.[121] Acts, like some Diaspora Jewish literature,[122] values conversion too highly to omit it.

But if (as most scholars think) Luke writes after Nero's persecution, Christians have a negative precedent against them.[123] Provincial governors' decrees could normally serve as precedent, but an imperial decree could ratify or annul any policies based on such decrees (Pliny *Ep*. 10.108.1–2).[124] Governors' precedents would be of limited value to Luke if Nero later established new *imperial* precedent—but they were all that Luke had. Distancing from Nero would help; although he was loved in the Greek East,[125] including by some Jewish people,[126] his memory was hateful to the Roman aristocracy[127]—that is, the class that would supply further governors' decrees.

Unlike some of his successors in church history, however, Luke does not emphasize that it was just a "bad emperor" who began the persecution;[128] nor does he appeal to the apparent affection for the Jewish community held by Nero's mistress Poppaea[129] as a reason for persecution of Christians (happily, since we lack clear reason historically to believe that there was any connection there). He prefers the safer route of emphasizing entirely positive precedents.

118. Pliny *Ep*. 10.65.2 (though those so suspected seem to have been a minority).

119. E.g., precedents in law (*Rhet. Alex*. 1, 1422b.20–25); previous honors conferred that are listed in city encomia (Men. Rhet. 1.3, 365.10–18).

120. Parkes, *Conflict*, 9.

121. Gager, *Anti-Semitism*; Tajra, *Trial*, 21–24; see comment on Acts 16:20–21.

122. E.g., *Joseph and Aseneth*, if it is not influenced by Christian perspectives.

123. On the post-70 date favored in this commentary, Nero's persecution was over; but Christians were now a known and vilified entity, and the precedent of controlling them was now available (see, later, Pliny *Ep*. 10.96–97; Lucian *Peregr*. 12–14).

124. In the instance cited here, Trajan benevolently appeals to what the local laws already are (Pliny *Ep*. 10.109).

125. E.g., IG 2².3277 (Sherk, *Empire*, §78A, p. 115); IG 7.2713 (Sherk, *Empire*, §71, pp. 110–12); he was popular enough for "revived" Neros to circulate for a time (Dio Chrys. *Or*. 21.9–10 [most favorably]; Tac. *Hist*. 1.2; 2.8; Suet. *Nero* 57.1–2; Lucian *Book-Coll*. 20; Dio Cass. 66.19.3; cf., sometimes unfavorably, *Sib. Or*. 4.137–39; 5.33–34, 137–54, 361–85). This does not appear to have endured (e.g., Epict. *Diatr*. 1.1.19–20; 1.25.22; 4.5.17; Plut. *Div. V*. 32, *Mor*. 567F; Dio Chrys. *Or*. 3.134; 21.6, 9; Paus. 10.7.1; Lucian *Nero* 10; Dio Cass. 61.2.1–63.4; Philost. *Vit. Apoll*. 4.35, 38–44; 5.8–9). On Nero's philhellenism, see Griffin, *Nero*, 208–20.

126. Some Jewish views of Nero were more favorable than those among Romans (e.g., *b. Giṭ*. 56a [discussed also in Cohen, "Meir"; Bastomsky, "Nero"]), but this should not be exaggerated (Jos. *Ant*. 20.153; *War* 2.250–51; cf. *Sib. Or*. 12.78–94).

127. E.g., Juv. *Sat*. 4.136–39; 8.211–30; Tac. *Hist*. 1.72; Suet. *Nero* passim; *Tit*. 7; Pliny *Ep*. 1.5.1; 3.5.5; 3.7.3; 5.5.3; 6.31.9; 8.6.17; Marc. Aur. 3.16. It is said that in Nero's day, the Roman aristocracy hated him, but not the masses (Tac. *Hist*. 1.4); but the celebration by the masses at his death (Suet. *Nero* 57) may suggest this was an exaggeration.

128. Cf. Tert. *Apol*. 5.3–4; *Acts Paul* 11.3–6; Euseb. *H.E*. 2.25; Sulp. Sev. *Chron*. 2.29 (in Barrett, *Documents*, 17); *Sib. Or*. 8.68–72. Later suspicions that Jewish complaints contributed to Nero's treatment of Christians, however, probably represent polemic (Hare, "Relationship").

129. Jos. *Ant*. 20.195; *Life* 16; cf. further Williams, "Θεοσεβής." On Poppaea as Nero's mistress, see, e.g., Tac. *Hist*. 1.13; he reportedly kicked her to death while she was pregnant (Suet. *Nero* 35.3; the story is probably independent of the earlier tyrant Periander, Diog. Laert. 1.94).

d. Arguments from Antiquity

Respectable people esteemed and appealed to antiquity, the ultimate form of precedent. Thus, for example, in epideictic rhetoric it was easier to praise a more ancient city than a newer one.[130] A rhetor had to dismantle the argument from antiquity before challenging the esteemed Plato.[131] Another writer, a rhetorical historian, defends his right to critique Plato by appealing to the fact that others (starting with Plato's famous pupil, Aristotle) have done so.[132] One rhetorician contends that if two laws conflict, one should prefer the older one.[133]

For Romans, any discussion of their own religion and customs must start with their ancestors (Val. Max. 1.1.1). In underlining the heinousness of Verres's temple robberies, Cicero often stresses the antiquity of the sanctuaries he desecrated.[134] Even when anxious to obliterate the depraved Bacchic cult from Rome, Romans left the oldest altars, which they believed stemmed from a less corrupted period of Bacchic worship (Livy 39.18.7). Romans respected Greeks because of their antiquity and their influence on the origins of civilization (e.g., Pliny *Ep.* 8.24.2–3). Greek and Jewish respect for antiquity was one reason for locating the Sibylline prophetess in the distant past.[135] Antiquity could also become a matter of apologetic importance. Augustus accepted only those foreign rites (such as those at Eleusis) the antiquity of which was undisputed, but treated Egyptian and Judean cults as superstition unfit for Romans (Suet. *Aug.* 93).

I. EGYPTIAN AND JEWISH ARGUMENTS

Seeking to establish their own claims to significance, Egyptians emphasized the special antiquity of their tradition.[136] (Romans made some concessions to Egyptian culture on account of its antiquity,[137] but Egypt's critics, especially many Greeks, were not so readily persuaded.)[138]

To compete with Egyptians, Phoenicians, and (more easily) Greeks, early Jewish apologetic historians had to date Jewish beginnings as early as possible. Thus Eupolemus suggests that Jews introduced use of an alphabet; Artapanus goes further, crediting them with "all important aspects of civilization."[139] Despite a very different impression gained from a straightforward reading of Genesis, Josephus declares that the Jewish people are five thousand years old and not derived from anyone else (*Ag. Ap.* 1.1). Many doubt their antiquity because Greek historians fail to mention them

130. E.g., Men. Rhet. 1.2, 354.1–8; 355.2–11.

131. Ael. Arist. *Def. Or.* 1 (1D)–12 (4D).

132. Dion. Hal. *Pomp.* 1, end; he also appeals to Aristotle in defending a rhetorical observation in Dion. Hal. *Lit. Comp.* 25 (citing Arist. *Rhet.* 3.8.4–7).

133. Hermog. *Issues* 87.2–9.

134. E.g., Cic. *Verr.* 2.4.45.99; 2.4.46.102.

135. Parke, *Sibyls*, 8.

136. Manetho *Aeg.* frg. 1.6 (rulers that could be traced back to the original gods and demigods); Egyptians interpreted old traditions in Greek, but for an anti-Greek connection with their past (Frankfurter, *Religion in Egypt*, 244, 250). (Some modern Afrocentric writers have followed this Egyptian apologetic, but all scholars today recognize, of course, that Egyptian civilization was, in fact, much more ancient than Greek regardless of the degree of the former's influence on the latter.)

137. Frankfurter, *Religion in Egypt*, 14.

138. Lucian *Sacr.* 14 mocks the Egyptians for claiming some foolish myths, which they claimed had been inscribed on their temples thousands of years earlier. In Philost. *Vit. Apoll.* 6.20, one sage defends Egyptian customs against Apollonius on the grounds of their antiquity (rather than logic), but he fails to persuade Apollonius.

139. Ferguson, *Backgrounds*, 349; see also Hengel, *Judaism and Hellenism*, 1:93. Some, however, doubt that Artapanus was Jewish himself (cf. Jacobson, "Artapanus").

(1.2), and so Josephus introduces further evidence (1.3–29), emphasizing that the Greeks themselves are less ancient (1.7).[140]

Josephus may title his magnum opus *Antiquities of the Jews* to recall Dionysius's *Roman Antiquities*; the preface of each work promises to cover the respective nation's "ancient history and political constitution" (Jos. *Ant.* 1.5; Dion. Hal. *Ant. rom.* 1.8.2).[141] The emperor Claudius defended Jewish rights to maintain their "ancient" customs (Jos. *Ant.* 19.283, 290). Thus Josephus may open his most explicitly apologetic work, *Against Apion*, by specifying that he has already established the great antiquity of his people in his *Antiquities* (*Ag. Ap.* 1.1). (Josephus apparently writes especially for interested Gentiles,[142] hence more apologetically and more for an "outside" audience, in contrast to Luke's probably believing primary audience.)[143]

In the first book of his polemic against Apion, Josephus repeatedly returns to the antiquity of Judaism (1.215–18, 227), for example, that of Jerusalem (1.196); he indicates that the point of book 1, indeed, was to demonstrate this antiquity (2.1). Moses was, he claims, the most ancient lawgiver (2.154–56, 279), and Josephus claims he has demonstrated that, contrary to anti-Jewish slanders, many authors do mention his people and that they are very ancient (2.288). Josephus's line of argument was time-honored in more ways than one; though contending that many Jewish customs were dishonorable, even Tacitus had to admit that some must be defended on the basis of their antiquity (Tac. *Hist.* 5.5).

Second-century Christian apologists continued this line of argument. Justin contended (rightly) that Moses was more ancient than all Greek writers—and (wrongly) that Plato (in *Rep.* 10) derived material from Moses (Justin *1 Apol.* 44). Tertullian argued that Christians had the true mysteries, of which others were poorer copies; he further insisted (with Scripture in view) that the Christian mysteries were older (Tert. *Apol.* 47.14).

ii. Part of Ancient Judaism

The earliest Diaspora followers of Jesus endured most of the challenges faced by Judaism, but in addition, they could be scorned for their lack of antiquity if they were regarded as a new sect that had broken from Judaism. Thus Luke, like Josephus regarding Judaism, must demonstrate the antiquity of his movement's message.[144] By grounding the Christian movement as a fulfillment of biblical prophecies, Luke "would have given Greek-speaking Christians the chance to appeal to an argument from antiquity."[145] Of course, early Christians believed that they were not a new religion but the fulfillment of biblical prophecy (cf., e.g., Mark 1:3–4; Rom 3:21; 1 Pet 2:4–10); Luke did not *invent* this conception for apologetic purposes. The question here is not whether they viewed themselves as continuous with Judaism but how Luke's emphasis on this continuity serves his larger apologetic.

140. Josephus charges that "barbarian" nations have preserved history more fairly than the Greeks (*Ag. Ap.* 1.58), and that one can testify of his people's antiquity from foreign writings (1.59); Egyptian records, he claims (misinterpreting data), show Jews long before Greeks (1.103–5).

141. E.g., Twelftree, "Jesus in Traditions," 292–93, also noting that Josephus follows Dionysius's division into twenty books. Josephus (*Ag. Ap.* 2.145–46) and Acts both present their communities in ideal political terms that would appeal to the broader culture (see Penner, "Discourse," 89–100, here esp. 91).

142. See Höffken, "Überlegungen."

143. Cf. Luke 1:4 and discussion in ch. 12, above.

144. Mason, *Josephus and New Testament*, 198. The antiquity argument may also have additional appeal in a rapidly changing world (cf. Backhaus, "Hörsaal").

145. Peterson, "Enterprise," 539. Most scholars acknowledge the apologetic value of solidarity with Israel's heritage in Acts; e.g., Foakes-Jackson and Lake, "Internal Evidence of Acts," 183–84; Haenchen, *Acts*, 100; Aune, *Environment*, 137; Bock, "Scripture and Realisation," 42.

That this movement included uncircumcised Gentile converts might seem problematic, although not dramatically so, to outsiders: other Jews did accept (usually) circumcised converts and uncircumcised sympathizers, and much of the Roman elite disapproved more of circumcision than of less overt displays of sympathy.[146] By accepting foreigners into their house churches, Lukan Christians might appear to be behaving differently from Moses's and even Jesus's customs (cf. the charges in Acts 6:11–14). Luke must show that this movement does in fact accord with "the ancient founder(s), in this case, Moses and Jesus."[147] (Luke manages to accomplish this continuity within the bounds of his historical genre and information.)[148]

Arguments for antiquity worked not only in apologetics directed toward Gentiles, but also in intra-Jewish debates. The Pharisees, for example, defended their traditions on the basis of their antiquity, though they did not elevate their traditions to the level of Scripture as the Essenes did.[149] The intra-Jewish debate over the status of the Jesus movement could remain a threat to the Gentile world's perception of the movement's Jewish identity and hence to its appeal to an ancient precedent for rejecting the world's gods. If in time Gentile converts predominated, outsiders (or even insiders) might doubt the movement's connection with its ancient heritage and hence view it as a new religious aberration that without acceptable cause despised the empire's patron deities and challenged the stability of the social order.

e. The Value of Precedents

Whether discussing rhetoric or religion, Greeks and Romans regarded precedent as important. If arguments from antiquity were helpful, arguments by precedent might also carry weight with conservative Roman courts and magistrates. Precedents might not be ancient, but they were, in any case, older than the current decisions; decisions were thus normally best guided by the past unless one had good reason to depart from such precedents.

This sense that decisions established legal tradition was ancient and pervasive. In classical Athens, for example, a rhetor might declare that by shaping the city's attitudes, the jury metaphorically functions as lawmakers (Lysias Or. 14.4, §139).[150] Legal interpreters could argue on the basis of not only the lawgiver's intention but also the court's interpretations of the law that reinforced it (Rhet. Alex. 1, 1422b.20–25). In the Roman Republic, "practices sanctioned by custom" could become formal laws.[151] Even the emperor Augustus excused his rejection of a plea on the basis that

---

146. On common Roman hostility toward circumcision, see Gager, Anti-Semitism, 56–57. It was sometimes associated with castration (Plut. Cic. 7.5; Pesiq. Rab Kah. 3:6), though this did not affect policy before Hadrian (Robinson, Criminal Law, 51–52; I think that Cordier, "Circoncision" dates the association with mutilation too late). This Roman perspective proved problematic for other peoples also (Lewis, Life, 92).

147. Balch, "ΜΕΤΑΒΟΛΗ ΠΟΛΙΤΕΙΩΝ," 140. Balch argues (174–80) that whereas founders change constitutions in Plutarch, Dionysius, with a more apologetic end, emphasizes continuity instead, and he concludes (180–83) that Luke's believers, distinct from both Romans and kosher-keeping Jews, must emphasize continuity.

148. Luke does not invent new pro-Gentile sayings for Jesus and even omits the Syrophoenician woman (Mark 7:24–30), though including the centurion (Luke 7:1–10; Matt 8:5–13). But Luke emphasizes Jesus's acceptance of outsiders—already in the tradition—and Jesus's use of the Scripture to support the Gentile mission (Luke 24:46–47; Acts 1:8; a postresurrection commission predates Luke in the tradition [associated with the Spirit, cf. John 20:21–22] and independently stresses proclamation to other peoples [Matt 28:19; cf. Mark 16:15]).

149. Sanders, Judaism, 424, citing Baumgarten, "Pharisaic paradosis," for the Pharisaic argument from antiquity. Claims about the value of "oral Torah" grew in time (see sources in Keener, John, 356).

150. A reader is reminded that this is merely metaphor by Lysias Or. 15.9–10, §145, where Lysias reminds jurors that their duty is to enforce, not to write, laws (15.9), though again their activity sets precedent (15.10).

151. O'Rourke, "Law," 170.

he did not like to make exceptions and break custom.[152] Early in Vespasian's reign, law officially rooted his powers in those of Augustus (*CIL* 6.930).[153] This preference for dependence on precedent probably hardened further over time. One later body of Roman law admonishes the judge especially "not to depart from the statutes, imperial pronouncements, and custom" (*ne aliter judicet, quam legibus aut constitutionibus aut moribus proditum est*).[154]

Provincial Roman officials were not bound to follow Roman *ordo*, legal precedents, or local customs; Roman policy gave such officials discretion to decide cases on their own merits (through *cognitio*, examination).[155] Nevertheless, they would follow precedent more often than not.

Luke had a risky, two-pronged apologetic. First, the Jesus movement was securely grounded in Israel's history and hence merited the toleration accorded ancient and ancestral religions.[156] This was true despite the massive influx of Gentiles; their presence was not the denial but the logical development of the ancient faith. It was, in fact, no more problematic than that of Gentile God-fearers in the synagogues (problematic as this appeared to some Romans). Second, the movement was not nationalistic or subversive and was not to be associated with the revolutionaries who led the Judean revolt of 66 C.E. (cf. Acts 5:36–38; 21:38–39; Luke 20:25; 23:2–4).

Although Luke's apologetic did not prevent persecution in the Roman Empire, it may have reduced it in some circles. What we can say more certainly is that second-century Christian apologists picked up and developed further the same conciliatory sort of approach toward Greek and Roman culture. Some may have gone further than Luke would have appreciated (Clement of Alexandria embraces Greek philosophy far more than does Acts 17), but many Christians' conciliatory approach to the empire likely helped gain Christians toleration in some parts of the empire.

f. Contextualizing Luke's Apologetic

How can modern interpreters, often concerned to derive applicable principles from Luke-Acts, make use of such themes? One way to understand Luke's apologetic more fully is to seek modern analogies similar to Luke's agenda.

Part of Luke's apologetic is that the apostolic movement posed no threat to Roman order; the apostles proclaimed the kingdom but waited for God himself to establish it. To translate such an apologetic into today's cultures might entail demonstrating to authorities in countries where Christians are repressed for their faith that Christians pose no threat to, but rather offer a benefit to, their societies.[157]

Of course, Luke, who emphasizes moral concerns (e.g., care for the poor), would not carry this so far as to strip Christians of a moral voice (especially in societies that welcome the voice of all citizens). But by virtue of their own historical situation, the earliest churches (like postexilic Israel before the Hasmonean era) offer more straightforward models for minority churches in sometimes hostile environments than for Christian discipleship in the midst of Christendom. Since the vast majority of today's

---

152. Inscription in Sherk, *Empire*, 7, §3 (despite his wife Livia's favor).

153. Ibid., 124–25, §82.

154. Justin. *Inst.* 4.17.intro. (Birks and McLeod, 142–43).

155. Ferguson, *Backgrounds*, 50. Despite careful collection of precedents, cases often had to be decided without precedents available (cf. Meeks, *Moral World*, 63).

156. Of course, Luke's interest in this question is not solely apologetic; the apparent inner contradiction of a movement with many Gentiles that held Israel's Scriptures demanded consideration.

157. This "service" approach to contextualization could come at a price for some Western Christians, who might have to divest their faith of the cultural trappings of dominant Western civic religion or state churches that sanctify particular sets of social values.

governments are secular, Islamic, or atheistic and practicing Christians are minorities in most of the world's cultures, Christians in most societies may find some value in Luke's apologetic. Here, as at many other points, modern Christian interpreters are tempted to proof-text or ignore sections of Luke-Acts without understanding it first on its own terms, but careful study suggests that Luke offers some fruitful directions we have rarely pursued. Even the most clearly historically conditioned elements of his apologetic reflect careful strategies that may also offer wisdom in other settings if the new settings are taken into proper account.

Conclusion

Luke probably has more than one agenda in Luke-Acts. One of them appears to be vindication for the mission to uncircumcised Gentiles (and hence for its leading advocate, Paul), probably with implications for how the Spirit will continue this mission in Luke's own day. As will be suggested in chapter 15 (sect. 3.a), Acts probably offers the apostolic model for the church's continuing mission rather than only a recitation of past history vindicating the church's foundation.

More commonly emphasized is the work's function as apologetic historiography, vindicating the Christian movement with the larger Roman world. Romans generally tolerated Judaism because it was an ancient, ethnic religion; although the Christian movement now included many Gentiles (and some Romans despised Roman conversions to Eastern cults), Luke argues for his movement's continuity with biblical history to indicate that it should be tolerated. Many would not be convinced by Luke's argument for toleration, but it was the best and, from the vantage point of first-century Christianity, perhaps the most authentic one available.

14

ISRAEL'S STORY

L uke grounds the story of the Gentile mission in the story of the Jewish Messiah Jesus, and the story of Jesus in the story of Israel. For Luke, to follow Jesus was, in short, to follow Israel's promised leader, who welcomed Gentiles into covenant obedience to himself even if much of Israel failed to obey. Luke's emphasis on continuity with the biblical heritage was important to a movement that claimed ancient Israel's Scriptures as their own as well as for a world that made antiquity a basic criterion of authenticity.

If Luke grounds his story in Israel's story, appropriating the LXX, how can he be accused of anti-Judaism? As many later gnostics showed, it was possible to salvage something of a Jewish religion while rejecting its Jewishness;[1] more to the point, later "orthodox" Christians showed a second option of which Luke is likelier to be accused, namely, that of accepting Israel's history without accepting Israel, by replacing Israel with the church. Neither option, however, seems justifiable in light of Luke's overall record. If Luke regards those faithful to Israel's true king as the righteous remnant of Israel, his thinking remains in continuity with the prophets. Like other ancient Jewish renewal movements, this one would seek Israel's restoration (cf. Luke 22:30// Matt 19:28; see comment on Acts 1:26). The critical difference is that he affirms the welcoming of uncircumcised Gentiles into Israel; it is the genius of his story that he seeks to do so in a way that both affirms new revelation about the uncircumcised Gentile mission (throughout Acts) and grounds it in Israel's story (and especially the prophecies of Isaiah).

1. Acts and Judaism

If one of Luke's primary purposes is apologetic (as argued above) and if Luke seeks to defend the Christian movement, even in its Gentile form, on the basis of antiquity, he must ground the movement's story in the ancient story of Israel.[2] That the majority of the Jewish people had not committed themselves to the distinctive beliefs of this

---

1. On Gnosticism and Judaism, see sources in Keener, *John*, 166–68, but now esp. the perspective of Smith, *Gnostic Origins*.
2. Many studies address Acts and Judaism, e.g., Müller, "Entscheidung"; Brawley, *Luke-Acts and Jews*; also Jervell, *Luke and People of God*; Sanders, "Salvation of Jews"; for a survey of recent discussion, see esp. Schröter, "Actaforschung 4."

sect and that some Jewish people opposed it raised a new apologetic issue for Luke to address (just as Paul had to address the question earlier in Rom 3:3; 9:6; 11:1–2).[3]

As noted in chapter 12 above, Loveday Alexander, who emphasizes Luke's apologetic, also notes the dominance of its Jewish element.[4] Only one of the final defense speeches addresses specifically a Roman;[5] although other speeches do address pagan religion or philosophy (Acts 14:15–17; 17:22–31), most address Judaism (e.g., 3:12–26; 7:2–53; 13:16–41).[6] Luke gives more space to Paul's custody than to his missionary journeys,[7] but even when addressing Roman officials, Paul is answering Jewish issues, and he continues to address Jewish issues (and a Jewish audience) in his final speech in Acts.[8] Acts concludes not with legal vindication but with God's faithfulness to his people.[9] Although all these observations are important, Luke would have to address Jewish accusations whether or not his audience was Jewish if, in fact, their accusations could raise issues for local and Roman governments.[10] That is, an apologetic involving Judaism would not be relevant only to a Jewish audience.[11]

At the same time, as argued above regarding audience, Luke's biblically informed target audience probably contained both some Jewish and some God-fearing elements not easily distinguished at our remove. Moreover, other members were likely in contact with nonbelieving Jewish people and their objections.

a. Anti-Judaism in Acts?

Some scholars contend that Luke polemicizes against Judaism.[12] Many of these scholars would regard Acts as representing a triumphalist view of Gentile Christians against Judaism;[13] Samuel Sandmel, indeed, goes so far as to claim that Acts presents Jewish people as "villains."[14]

Jack Sanders is one of the most consistent voices supporting this position,[15] but some of his arguments are tendentious and overstated. For example, he argues that Jesus's followers are to stay in Jerusalem only until empowered and that the commission

3. With others, e.g., Ray, *Irony*, 172.

4. For Acts as apologetic, see Alexander, *Context*, 183–206.

5. Ibid., 200. Against Alexander, I would count three, since Festus is part of the audience in Acts 26; but the Jewish element in Acts 22 and 26 cannot be minimized.

6. Alexander, *Context*, 204. Of course, speeches to Gentiles can become relevant within the narrative world only once the mission moves among them.

7. Ibid., 204–5.

8. Ibid., 205.

9. Ibid., 206.

10. Which seems to be the case even later in some settings, such as Rev 2:9; *Mart. Pol.* 13.1; 17.2; 18.1.

11. Conversely, some scholars think that Luke emphasizes the church's Jewish roots to counter a rejection of these (such as later appears in Marcion's time; Tuckett, *Luke*, 69–70, following Houlden, "Purpose"); in my opinion, this proposal does not account for the apologetic noted here as well as it accounts for the continuity with Judaism in Acts. Some first-century Gentile Christians did need reminders of their Jewish heritage (Rom 11:18–24), but this does not appear to be the primary purpose of Luke's apologetic.

12. See, e.g., Slingerland, "'Jews' in Pauline Portion" (in later part of Acts); Matera, "Luke 23,1–25" (on Lukan redaction of Mark in Luke 23). Tyson, *Marcion*, 128, thinks that Luke "elevates Moses and the prophets" while denigrating "most ancient and contemporary Jews"; this fits his reconstruction of a second-century Lukan Acts both combating Marcionites and avoiding Judaism. (His reconstruction of Marcionite views [24–49, 128–31] appears conveniently more modern and pleasant.) The anti-Judaic tendency of the Western text, of course, is widely accepted (see Epp, *Tendency*).

13. E.g., Hare, "Rejection in Gospels and Acts," 27 (though he applies this charge especially to Matthew).

14. Sandmel, *Anti-Semitism*, 100 (perhaps following the language of Harnack, *Acts*, xxiv–xxv); cf. Klausner, *Jesus to Paul*, 229, who suggests that Acts' central theme is "that the Jews are the source of evil." Such opinions from previous generations of Jewish scholars are understandable given the history of Christian anti-Judaism. Strangely, Sandmel in *Judaism*, 363–39, instead finds in Luke's Gospel comparatively little anti-Semitism.

15. E.g., Sanders, "Salvation of Jews"; idem, "Who Is a Jew?" For his more general discussion of early Jewish-Christian relations, see idem, *Schismatics*.

continues to the Gentiles by way of continual Jewish rejection.[16] But although Acts may suggest that Christians were too slow to disperse for evangelism, Paul himself in Acts affirms the piety and legitimacy of the Jerusalem church (Acts 21:23–26). Likewise, although Jewish rejection commonly appears and does provide a reason for going to the Gentiles, the rejection is not wholesale, and it *needs* to provide justification for going to the Gentiles only because the message is for the Jew first. (If one wonders where Luke received his understanding of Jewish privilege and the idea that Gentiles obtained only what Jewish people first rejected, one might consider the theology of his hero, Paul.)[17]

As Rosner points out, "If the same standards were applied many of the Hebrew prophets would be branded anti-Jewish."[18] (Compare, for example, Amos's rejection of Israel's festivals in Amos 5:21.) That a different standard is applied to earliest Christian writings probably reflects our modern knowledge of the subsequent division of Judaism and Christianity and later Christian anti-Semitism, but it is historically anachronistic to read this later division into first-century documents, just as it is anachronistic to read it into the Qumran scrolls or the Hebrew prophets.[19]

Other scholars argue that Acts portrays Christians as the true heirs of Israel's heritage and as good citizens, but Jews as seditious.[20] The chief priests accused Paul of stirring riots (Acts 24:5), and in good forensic fashion, he essentially returns the charge against his original accusers (though stopping short of doing so explicitly and of accusing the high priests; 24:18); Luke suggests that assassins whom the Romans wished to suppress (21:38) expected the cooperation of some of these same high priests (23:14–15). That Luke sometimes offers such contrasts is true enough, but it is easy to overgeneralize such a picture, anachronistically ignoring both Luke's diverse portrayals of Judaism and the substantial overlap between the categories "Christian" and "Jew" (most major protagonists are, in fact, both).[21]

b. Conflict Reports

Luke's reports do include a measure of polemic, but a polemical motive for selecting information need not mean that one is inventing the information.

I. EMPHASIZING OR DE-EMPHASIZING CONFLICT?

Whether based in fact or in fiction and whether balanced by nonpolemical elements or not, some measure of polemic is clear. Whether this polemic is viewed as intra-Jewish or external, it could serve apologetic interests: most of Christians' conflicts with Rome in Acts stem from false accusations from segments of the Jewish community.[22] After 70

16. Sanders, "Salvation of Jews," passim and summary, 117. For the pattern of initial Jewish acceptance followed by rejection, see more fully Tyson, "Jewish Public."

17. See Rom 11:11–15, 19–20; cf. Rom 1:16. Cf. also the Jesus tradition (Mark 7:27–29).

18. Rosner, "Biblical History," 71; cf. (more selectively) Hare, "Rejection of Jews," 35; on Matthew's Gospel, see Davies and Allison, *Matthew*, 3:260–67.

19. Against essentialist definitions that make "Christianity" and "Judaism" mutually exclusive categories, see, e.g., Eisenbaum, "Polemics."

20. Wills, "Depiction of Jews."

21. Faure, *Pentecôte*, 493, sees the Alexandrian text as more ambivalent than is the Western text, because the former revised the latter, more consistent text. Israel remains elect in the Western text, and through the end of Acts hope remains for Israel's future conversion, whereas the Alexandrian text allows for a future parousia, with its resurrection and last judgment but without a need for Israel's conversion. As noted in our prolegomenon, however, most scholars consider the Western text later and many regard it as more anti-Jewish.

22. See, e.g., Mason, *Josephus and New Testament*, 201–2; Agouridis, "Δεσμὰ τοῦ Παύλου." Cunningham, *Many Tribulations*, 340, suggests that Luke is not anti-Jewish but that he is forced to address why most of Israel rejects Jesus and most persecutions were Jewish.

C.E., such pleas might play well[23] but, while reporting truth, remain selective at best: if Rome detested Jewish proselytism, it probably would also be uncomfortable with Christians even apart from Jewish accusations. (Jewish separatism would not be a cause of accusation against Gentile Christians who did not keep Sabbath or food laws, but their shared monotheism would prevent participation in domestic and civic cults.)[24]

Some scholars think that Luke may, in fact, play down Jewish persecution against Christians, simply hoping to induce the Romans to restrain such persecution.[25] In light of other early Christian sources, this is not impossible.[26] Paul, at least, is known to have persecuted Christians (1 Cor 15:9; Gal 1:13, 23; Phil 3:6) and could not have accomplished much single-handedly. He reports other persecution of Christians in Judea (1 Thess 2:14–16), his own suffering for Christ from synagogue leaders on multiple occasions (2 Cor 11:24, 26), and the expectation of hostility in Judea (Rom 15:31). Far from displaying an anti-Jewish agenda, Luke does not even recount Paul's synagogue beatings (2 Cor 11:24). But neither does he recount the shipwrecks that Paul mentions (11:25);[27] publication was expensive, and Luke had only so much space in his volume to work with.

Yet if Luke plays down the conflicts between Jewish and Gentile Christians (Acts 15:25),[28] he might also play down the conflict between Judean leaders and Judean believers in Jesus; most people still viewed Christians as a Jewish sect, and highlighting the conflict might have done as much harm as good. Because we do not have access to many first-century sources to test the assumption, it is unclear whether Luke emphasizes or plays down such conflicts more frequently.[29] Noting the pattern of Jewish instigation in many cases of unrest in which Paul is involved (see ch. 7 above; comment on Acts 24:5), Luke at least emphasizes Jewish involvement where he probably responds to Jewish accusations that Paul stirred unrest (24:5). That anti-Judaism also stirs such unrest, however (16:20–21; cf. 19:26, 34), warns against the hasty assumption that Luke simply creates all such incidents to fit a pattern.

II. Genuine History of Conflict

What is clear is that Luke did not create the reports of conflict. Rightly embarrassing as the history of conflict is to most Jews and Christians today (and a much larger stretch of history stands as an embarrassment to subsequent Christians than to Jews), the conflict is inescapable in first-century sources. Some scholars have argued

23. The Flavians emphatically celebrated Jerusalem's demise not only in Judea but in other provinces and in Rome (see Zarrow, "Coins").

24. For the domestic conflicts created by converted wives in polytheistic households, see, e.g., Balch, *Wives*, passim.

25. Bammel, "Activity," 357.

26. That Paul faced genuine hostility from some fellow Jews is difficult to deny in the face of his own reports (Barclay, "Paul among Jews," 115); Acts essentially confirms the picture in Paul's letters on this point (115–16).

27. These shipwrecks preceded the shipwreck depicted in Acts 27:39–44, but one nighttime shipwreck, in which Paul spent part of a night and day in the sea (risking hypothermia; 2 Cor 11:25), was more dramatic than the brief time in the water in Acts 27:43–44 (though the storm was undoubtedly shorter). Luke's shipwreck occurs at a better juncture in the story and merits more description because the story's author was an eyewitness at that point.

28. Although Luke does report serious conflict (Acts 15:5; indeed, the views of the Judeans in 15:1 may be harsher than those of Paul's rivals in Galatia) and may have had the language of the apostolic decree, he cannot match the tone of suspense about the council's outcome offered by an affected participant (Gal 2:2). He and Paul each mention different compromises (Acts 15:20; Gal 2:9–10).

29. Certainly, in second-century sources (e.g., Justin *Dial.* 16), it became more common to employ rhetorical amplification of persecution (Flannery, *Anguish*, 28); "atrocity stories" are a common method of rhetorical retribution (Bailey, *Peasant Eyes*, 75–77; e.g., Cic. *Sest.* 35.77; Val. Max. 9.2.1; *b. Giṭ.* 57a; *y. Sukkah* 5:1, §7), as in later rabbinic reports of the slaughter at Bethar (*y. Taʿan.* 4:5, §10; *Lam. Rab.* 2:2, §4; 3:51, §9).

that conflicts were later falsely retrojected into the life of Jesus;[30] even if this were so (I am not of that opinion), whoever retrojected them was experiencing conflict, and that within the first century; one can postpone reckoning with the reality of the conflict only so long.[31]

The same goes for arguments that later reports of hostilities were interpolated into 1 Thess 2:14–16.[32] If one follows this view, perhaps Paul alone had expressed hostility toward Christians before he became one (1 Cor 15:9; Gal 1:13; Phil 3:6), making the convert the only former persecutor. Yet such optimism requires revisionism in our sources without explaining them. (Paul associates his persecution of the church with his former life and advancement in Judaism in Gal 1:13–14;[33] this probably suggests that some others approved of Paul's actions.)

Dunn rightly notes that even if Luke developed Jewish communities' opposition to Paul, "he assuredly did not invent it, since Paul himself recalls such trials and tribulations, including Jewish involvement, on what must have been several occasions (II Cor. 6.4–5; 11.23–27)."[34] That Paul received synagogue beatings so frequently (five times by the middle of his ministry; 2 Cor 11:24) testifies to his continued participation and ministry in the synagogue despite severe opposition. It also indicates that a number of synagogues proved hostile enough to his preaching to prescribe corporal punishment.

III. Intra-Jewish Conflict

What should be realized in any of these cases, however, is that neither Jesus nor Paul was a Gentile Christian; historically, there is not the slightest doubt that they were Jews in conflict with some fellow Jews over the meaning of true Judaism. This was, moreover, a conflict certainly experienced also by a host of other first-century Jews, be they Pharisees, Essenes, social bandits, or others. Some other Jews before 70 C.E. spoke even of judgment on the temple.[35] Not only in intra-Jewish strife nearly two centuries earlier (during the civil war during Alexander

---

30. Sanders, *Jesus to Mishnah*, 95–96; idem, *Figure*, 217. But Pharisees were not primary enemies of Jesus's followers in the 40s through the 60s (Theissen, *Gospels*, 230–31), and Mark's conflict accounts clearly reflect pre-70 material (see Witherington, *Christology of Jesus*, 60). Moreover, our earliest Christian mention of Pharisees specifies at least one Pharisee involved in persecuting Jesus's followers (Phil 3:5–6). Multiple attestation supports the thesis that Jesus did have Sabbath conflicts (Borg, *Conflict*, 139–43; Witherington, *Christology of Jesus*, 66). They appear in Mark (e.g., Mark 2:23–28), independently in John (John 5:1–9), and perhaps independently in special Lukan material (Luke 13:10–17; Q provides few narratives). On Jesus's conflicts with other teachers, see Holmén, *Covenant Thinking*, 90–106, 221–51; Keener, *Historical Jesus*, 223–37.

31. See further Keener, *Matthew*, 351–53; idem, *Historical Jesus*, 223–37; for a somewhat later period, idem, *John*, 65–68, 194–207. See esp. and at greatest length Holmén, *Covenant Thinking*, passim.

32. For an interpolation, see Bruce, *Thessalonians*, 49–51; Setzer, *Responses*, 16–19; against it, see Collins, "Integrity"; Donfried, *Thessalonica*, 198–99; Witherington, *End*, 101; Stowers, *Rereading of Romans*, 177 (citing esp. Hurd, "I Thess. 2:13–16"); Watson, *Gentiles*, 80 (noting Ps 68:23–24 in Rom 11:9–10, an irenic context). There is no textual evidence for an interpolation, and so the interpolation proposal appears suspiciously like "content criticism"; the passage may reflect pre-Pauline tradition later reported in the Synoptics (see Wenham, "Apocalypse," 361–62; Donfried, *Thessalonica*, 203).

33. Similarly, the zeal that motivated Paul's persecution of Jesus's followers in Phil 3:6 is associated with ancestral traditions in Gal 1:14; although this does not guarantee that his colleagues interpreted the ancestral traditions the way he did, interpretation within the academy (implied by his "advancing" in 1:14) was normally a corporate activity.

34. Dunn, *Acts*, 225; cf. Barclay, "Paul among Jews," 115–16.

35. E.g., Jos. *War* 6.301. The *Testament of Moses*, which accuses priests of polluting the altar (5:4), prophesies judgment against the temple (6:8–9), and because the Roman ruler destroys only part of the temple in the oracle, the prophecy undoubtedly predates 70 C.E. 1QpHab IX, 6–7 warned (rightly, it turned out) that the Kittim (by whom is meant the Romans) would carry off the Jerusalem priesthood's wealth.

Jannaeus's reign)[36] but also in the recent war with Rome, Judeans massacred fellow Judeans of rival parties.[37]

Josephus faced life-threatening opposition from rivals within his own social class (e.g., Jos. *Life* 272–75, 302–3), and both the passages just noted and the history of other early Jewish groups such as the Essenes (violent conflicts with the priesthood, e.g., 1QpHab VIII, 8–12; IX, 4–7; XII, 5; 4QpNah 3–4 I, 11)[38] and Pharisees[39] indicate the pervasiveness of intra-Jewish strife. Social-conflict theory illustrates that conflicts become most severe among groups most closely connected.[40]

To make the actions of some Jews against other Jews a "problem" for modern Jewish-Christian relations is to retroject subsequent categories onto ancient texts in a manner that is historically irresponsible.[41] Conflict (and the variety of motives, both noble and ignoble, that help produce it) is endemic to human nature, and it should not surprise us to find it in our sources. In most kinds of societies, new religious movements (e.g., the early followers of Muhammad or of Joseph Smith) have faced persecution. In ancient Mediterranean culture, people commonly expressed their strong opinions and partisan allegiances in opposition to others;[42] not all disagreement resulted in abuse, but all ancient histories show that it sometimes did (nor are such incidents difficult to document today, especially in societies with less emphasis on tolerance or dialogue). This was not a specifically Jewish problem or even a specifically first-century Mediterranean problem. Nor was the conflict with all Jews; even in Acts, the Pharisees sometimes support the Jesus movement (Acts 5:34–39; 23:6–9; cf. 15:5; Jos. *Ant.* 20.200–203).

c. Genuinely Anti-Jewish Polemic in Antiquity

Genuinely anti-Jewish literature was often quite harsh. In the early Hellenistic period, Manetho's alternative version of the exodus was that Egypt expelled the unclean

36. Le Cornu, *Acts*, 388, cites 4QpNah 3–4 I, 6–8; Jos. *Ant.* 13.372ff.; *War* 1.88ff., 96–98.

37. Of course, those familiar with the most recent Roman civil wars would recognize that strife was pervasive, not limited to a single people. I emphasize intra-Jewish conflict here only because of the specific issue under discussion.

38. For harsh persecution from the Jerusalem high priest in the Qumran scrolls, Le Cornu, *Acts*, 388, cites 1QpHab I, 13; V, 9–10; VIII, 8, 16; IX, 2, 9–10; XI, 4–5; XII, 2–3; 4Q171 II, 18–19; IV, 8. The "Wicked Priest" has been identified with Jonathan (Rost, *Judaism*, 163), John Hyrcanus (Brownlee, "Messianic Motifs," 13–15), and "the false priesthood of the Temple at any time between the Maccabean period and the fall of the Hasmonean dynasty" (Fritsch, *Community*, 83–84). Some have identified the "Young Lion" of 4QpNah 3–4 I, 5 with Alexander Jannaeus (Allegro, "Light," 92; Eisenman, *Maccabees*, 35); others have maintained that a specific identification is impossible (Rowley, "4QpNahum"); yet others have even identified him with Pontius Pilate (Thiering, *Gospels and Qumran*, 70, with little support). As the original Teacher of Righteousness became a model for the future one (CD VI, 10–11) and the title probably applied to all his successors (Buchanan, "Office"), the identity of the original "Wicked Priest" may have applied to the priesthood in perpetuity. Overman, *Crisis*, 224 cites 4QMMT as a sample of halakic debates at Qumran.

Some scholars find clues of Essene antagonism toward Pharisaism (Roth, "Subject Matter of Exegesis," 65; idem, "Reference"; Dupont-Sommer, *Manuscrits*, 33) or of Pharisaic or rabbinic opposition to the Essenes (Lieberman, "Light," 396–400). The rabbis nevertheless reflect legal or cultural traditions often shared with Qumran, though reasons for these parallels are debated (e.g., Baumgarten, "Qumran Studies," 256; Neusner, "Testimony"; Schiffman, *Law*).

39. Conflicts with Sadducees, e.g., Jos. *Ant.* 18.17; *m. Yad.* 4:7; *t. Ḥag.* 3:35; *Nid.* 5:3; *'Abot R. Nat.* 5 A; 10 B; *b. Nid.* 33b; *Sukkah* 48b.

40. Stanton, *New People*, 98–102.

41. Nor is the argument always productive from a pragmatic standpoint, although that is not the issue in question here: in the Majority World, where Jewish-Christian dialogue is often minimal (in some places, far surpassed by Muslim-Christian dialogue) but where the Bible is often widely available, the view that the text is anti-Jewish could be used to support, rather than to repudiate, anti-Judaism.

42. Among urban aristocrats in Rome and its colonies, see, e.g., Marshall, *Enmity*, passim.

Jews for leprosy.[43] Apion's blood libel against Jewish people (Jos. *Ag. Ap.* 2.89–111)[44] resurfaced in more dangerous forms in later centuries.[45] Such slanders eventually found their way into more mainstream sources—thus, for example, Diodorus's report that Antiochus Epiphanes found a statue of a man on a donkey in the holiest place (Diod. Sic. 34.3). Authorities with genuine anti-Judaic sentiment often mistreated Jewish people (see, e.g., Philo *Embassy* 349–65; *Flacc.* passim).

It is difficult to think that Luke's contemporaries would have seen as anti-Judaic his attempt to lay claim to the Jewish heritage for a Jewish movement that included uncircumcised Gentile converts; even Jews who viewed the movement as a dangerous schism presumably would have viewed such Gentile Christians as runaway God-fearers seeking to usurp proper Jewish privileges, not as potential persecutors. They did not, of course, have the vantage point of the experience of nearly two millennia of Christian anti-Semitism from which to read the text. I would argue that such a modern reading is an anachronistic counterreading of Acts, though it is an understandable one from the social location of its subsequent readers.

One may helpfully contrast the language of Luke with that of Justin Martyr, who writes in the mid-second century.[46] Although Justin affirmed continuity with Israel's Scriptures,[47] he claimed them for the church and no longer for Israel (at least in a polemical context).[48] In fact, he viewed the church as "the true, spiritual Israel."[49] Many of his views continue those found in first-century Christian apologists,[50] but he surpasses them with such explicit claims, writing as a Gentile Christian in a time when the divide between ethnic Israel and the church has grown. Justin does not go so far as Apion or even some later Gentile Christian writers,[51] but he goes considerably beyond anything we see in Luke-Acts.[52]

43. See, e.g., discussion in Raspe, "Manetho on Exodus."

44. Jacobson, "Apion and Sacrifice," thinks that Apion applied Euripides's *Iphigeneia at Tauris* to the Jews. Vogel, "*Contra Apionem*," approaches the work differently. Cf. Parkes, *Conflict*, 16.

45. See, e.g., Roth, *Encyclopedia*, 92–93; Grayzel, *History of Jews*, 314–15, 452; Flannery, *Anguish*, 98–101, 182; on a more popular level, Dimont, *History*, 234–35; Brown, *Blood*, 61–63.

46. Although disclaiming knowledge of Judaism before his adulthood (Barnard, *Justin Martyr*, 39), Justin was born in Palestine, in a Gentile area in Samaria (*1 Apol.* 1; Chadwick, "Defence," 276n3; Osborn, *Justin*, 6; Williams, *Justin Martyr*, ix). Some think he intended his dialogue with Trypho for a Gentile Christian audience (Chadwick, "Defence," 278), others a Gentile audience wavering between Christianity and Judaism (Nilson, "Addressed"), and others a Jewish audience (Stylianopoulos, *Justin*, 17–18, 33–44, 169–95).

47. Frend, "Old Testament," 149–50.

48. Justin *Dial.* 29.

49. Justin *Dial.* 11, 123, 135; cf. *Barn.* 13. See further Richardson, *Israel*, 9–14; Osborn, *Justin*, 171–85, esp. 175–78; Bokser, "Justin and Jews," 99, 208; Schoeps, *Argument*, 29. Christians were the people promised to the patriarchs (Justin *Dial.* 119–20). Justin recognized that some Jews excluded other Jews from consideration as Jews (*Dial.* 80).

50. Physical Jewish descent does not itself provide salvation (Justin *Dial.* 140); the ancient righteous under the law are also saved through Christ (*Dial.* 45); the spirit of prophecy was proof that Christians were God's people (*Dial.* 82; just as earlier prophets were filled with the Spirit, *Dial.* 7).

51. A trajectory probably also evident in Qur'an 4.154; 5.12–13, 78. Comparing Justin favorably with others, see Barnard, *Justin Martyr*, 40; Williams, *Justin Martyr*, xxvi; most favorably, Schoeps, *Argument*, 88 (the most positive written dialogue for the next fifteen centuries).

52. For strongly negative views of Justin, cf. Williamson, "Tradition," 273, 283, 292; Bokser, "Justin and Jews," 101–2, 211–12. Trypho can appear in a positive light, e.g., intelligent (*Dial.* 1) and open-minded (10), and he and Justin become friends (8–9, 142). Nevertheless, the *Dialogue* draws on established anti-Judaic polemic (cf. also Chadwick, "Defence," 286–87). Although treating the spiritual Sabbath as eternal (*Dial.* 12; cf. *1 Apol.* 67), he envisions circumcision as a sign to mark the Jewish people for suffering (*Dial.* 16.2, in Williams, *Justin Martyr*, 32). His language can be harsh (*Dial.* 12); he assumes that Jewish disbelief is willful (17, 68, 108, 112, 115; for his emphasis on human responsibility vs. determinism, see *1 Apol.* 43; cf. *Dial.* 141); he equates the scribes and Pharisees with all the Jewish people (17). He views Hadrian's slaughter of Judeans as fulfillment of messianic prophecy (*1 Apol.* 47; cf. *Dial.* 16), insensitive to one of the most terrible memories of ancient Jewish history (cf., e.g., Hadrian in *Gen. Rab.* 10:3; 28:3; 65:21; 78:1; *Exod. Rab.* 51:5;

d. Intra-Jewish Polemic?

Some subsequent readings of Acts in later historical settings may have been anti-Jewish, but it is unlikely that informed readers in Luke's first circle of churches would have construed the text in this manner. The polemic within Luke-Acts, like the polemic of the generation that preceded it, is primarily intra-Jewish.[53]

The expression "Jews" is employed in a number of ways in Acts—sometimes, though not nearly always, in a pejorative way.[54] The negative uses, however, correspond to the negative uses sometimes found in other Jewish texts about fellow Jews.[55] The picture as a whole is complex, but it does make a difference to what degree Luke's portrayal represents what at least Jewish Christians would have viewed as intra-Jewish polemic and to what degree it represents what they would have viewed as a Gentile attacking Judaism.

i. Was Luke's Audience Jewish?

Some scholars think that Luke addressed especially Jewish Christians.[56] Jervell argues that Luke's language reflects not only the LXX but also descriptions of the law at home in Hellenistic Judaism.[57] He also believes that contrary to usual modern views, Gentile Christianity did not become dominant until the second century and that Acts bears this out.[58] Marilyn Salmon thinks that Jack Sanders is correct in his survey of events in Luke-Acts but mistaken in his perspective, since a narrative approach suggests that Luke is an insider rather than an outsider to Judaism.[59]

Some scholars believe that Luke writes after a full schism with the synagogue;[60] others, that Luke sees the schism but wants "to *prevent* any final schism," noting that many Jews believe (Acts 13:43; 14:1; 17:4, 11–12; 18:8; 19:9; 20:20; 28:24).[61] Some argue that Luke writes after the schism but accurately represents the law piety of the previous generation of Jerusalem Christians to emphasize that the breach between Judaism and Christianity stemmed from the non-Christian Jewish side.[62] I have argued elsewhere that the communities in the NT books typically accused of the harshest anti-Jewish polemic (Matthew, John, and Revelation) were precisely those that most saw themselves as part of Judaism and engaged in intra-Jewish polemic.[63]

Lev. Rab. 18:1; *Deut. Rab.* 3:13; *Lam. Rab.* 3:23, §8; 3:58–60, §9; *Ruth Rab.* 3:2; *Eccl. Rab.* 2:17, §1). When hard-pressed for an argument, Justin appeals to Jerusalem's destruction as proof (*Dial.* 51) in a manner irrelevant to the question.

53. Many scholars conclude that Luke's polemic is intra-Jewish, e.g., Evans, "Prophecy and Polemic," 210. Hare, "Rejection in Gospels and Acts," 35–38, compares some of it with the prophets and considers much of the rest of it intra-Jewish.

54. Barbi, "Use and Meaning," 140–42, arguing that normally it is *not* pejorative but those so described do emerge as adversarial especially toward the end of Acts.

55. Saldarini, *Community*, 34–36; Keener, *John*, 217–18; cf. Tomson, "Israel."

56. E.g., Juel, *Promise*, 118–19; Donfried, "Christology and Salvation"; Jervell, *Theology*, 4–5 (thinking, I believe correctly, that Jewish Christians remained strong after 70 C.E.).

57. See Jervell, *Luke and People of God*, 136–37.

58. Jervell, *Unknown Paul*, 13–21 and esp. 26–51. He argues that most converts in Acts in the mass conversions were Jewish (15), but only a few of the many texts he cites in support of this contention come from Paul's Gentile mission.

59. Salmon, "Insider," 81–82. This might be true even if he is a Gentile "God-fearer."

60. Juel, *Promise*, 118–19.

61. Mason, "Chief Priests," 152.

62. Hengel, *Acts and History*, 63–64. It should be noted, however, that law-observant Jewish Christianity continued in the second century, though in a polarized environment increasingly marginalized, on the one side, by Gentile Christians and, on the other, by rabbinic Judaism (see Pritz, *Nazarene Christianity*; cf. Justin *Dial.* 47).

63. Keener, *Matthew*, 45–51; idem, *John*, 172–75, 194–228; idem, *Revelation*, 38–39, 115–16, 118–19.

As mentioned in chapter 12, I believe that Luke's audience contained a Jewish and God-fearer nucleus (which would have been the teaching center for the first generation of converts) but that Gentile converts who viewed themselves as converts to Israel's true faith were now numerically dominant. Yet whether Luke's audience contained more Jewish Christians or Gentile Christians, it apparently saw itself as following Israel's faith and certainly Israel's true king.

Pervo argues that after Acts 9:22 Luke employs "the Jews" only for Jewish people who reject Jesus, indicating two distinct communities. He believes that this fits a Lukan setting outside Judaism and that Luke wrote to make Jews appear bad and to make Christians look innocent.[64] This perspective fails on several counts. First, although "Jews" are hostile in 12:3; 13:45, 50; 14:2, 19; 16:3; 17:5; 18:12, 14, 28; 20:3, 19; 23:12, 20, 27; 24:9, 27; 25:2–10, 15, 24; 26:2, 7; and 28:19, the later and more abundant and pervasively hostile references involve specifically "Judeans" (note Paul's use of the term for Judeans in 28:19, where he addresses Roman Jews, 28:17). More obviously, the designation applies more broadly in 11:19; 13:5, 43; 14:1; 17:1, 10–11, 17; 18:4–5, 19; 19:10, 17; 20:21; 22:12; 28:17; and it applies to servants of Christ in 16:20; 18:2; 21:20–21.

Second, any sectarian group within Judaism would also distinguish its community from others, as scholars have generally recognized since the discovery of the Qumran scrolls.[65] One thus cannot assume that Luke writes after schism with the synagogue simply because he identifies Jesus's followers as a movement distinct from larger Judaism. Because the Diaspora churches were ethnically mixed and less ethnically focused than synagogues, it made sense to identify them differently from the Jewish community. To outsiders, however, a movement that shared Jewish morality, Jewish Scripture, and the Jewish God would appear more Jewish than not, and Luke makes no attempt to conceal these connections.

Finally, with reference to claims about persecution or innocence (the moral issue behind Pervo's criticism), not only in Paul's day but even still in Luke's, the Jesus movement was by far the smaller minority and with far less power than the rest of the Jewish community.[66] One might thus wonder whether it is not Luke but Pervo who writes only from a postseparation perspective.

I am among those who think that full schism happened at different places at different times and in many places would not yet have occurred for all Christians in a synagogue community.[67] I do, however, think that the churches in places such as Corinth and especially Philippi (see comments on audience in ch. 12), though rooted in the ethos and culture of synagogue Judaism, were now primarily ethnically Gentile. Thus they would share both a Jewish religious and moral ethos, on the one hand, and often an experience of past Gentile worship and behavior, on the other. Acts does

64. Pervo, "Gates."

65. Early Christianity fell far short of the form of sectarianism generally suggested for the Essenes (cf. Jos. *War* 2.119–61).

66. Again, Christians have been responsible for massive atrocities against Jewish people throughout subsequent history, and Jewish people (who lacked political power) have engaged in few if any against Christians. But in the founding years of the Christian movement (particularly while it remained part of Judaism), early Christians faced persecution from some Jews in much the way that some other radical movements within Judaism had faced persecution. Persecution should not be exaggerated, but first-century cultures governed by local elites did not value tolerance the way we emphasize it in the modern West.

67. See Keener, *John*, 195–98, 208–14; Saldarini, *Community*; Overman, *Crisis*. Zetterholm, "Judar," argues that the Jesus movement viewed itself as a Jewish sect with Gentile adherents until the Jewish War (for Paul's continuing identity within Judaism, cf., e.g., Dahl, *Studies*, 19; Neuhaus, "Changement"; Bieberstein, "Freiheit"; Bachmann, "*Verus Israel*"; Frankemölle, "Apostoł Pawel"; Harrington, "Paul the Jew"; Stegner, "Jewish Paul"; Roetzel, *Paul*, ix). The danger is anachronism regarding categories (Dunn, *Partings*, 143).

indicate breaks from the synagogue in Corinth (18:7) and Ephesus (19:8–9), though with churches that included a Jewish and God-fearing nucleus.

ii. Partly Jewish Self-Identity

Probably Jervell is right to the extent that Gentile Christians still saw themselves as converts to the true form of the biblical Jewish faith, Israel's heritage.[68] Luke is no Marcion,[69] nor is he from an era when Gentile Christians could claim to have "replaced" Israel.[70] The valuing of Israel's heritage guarantees friendly dialogue with other synagogues, however, no more than their common biblical heritage rendered Sadducees, Pharisees, and Essenes on friendly terms. Certainly, Jervell is correct that Jewish Christianity remained vibrant.[71] For example, second-century Gentile apologists who condemned Ebionites for their low Christology continued to affirm the Nazarenes, whom they regarded as faithful Christians as well as Jews.[72] Lucian speaks of the Christians' "priests and scribes in Palestine."[73]

What is at least clear—and most significant—is that Luke can conceive of Christians remaining in the synagogue for extended periods of dialogue until finally being forced out (e.g., Acts 18:26; 19:8–9), even if he himself was no longer part of the synagogue. For Luke, faith in Jesus does not necessitate separation from the synagogue or from Israel, from the *Christian* side. Luke certainly emphasizes the church's heritage in Israel's biblical piety and presents the Jerusalem church's continuance in this heritage positively (2:46; 21:20); though Gentile anti-Semitism sometimes harms Paul's opponents (18:14–17; 19:33–34), it also works against Paul (16:20–21).

As mentioned, scholars debate exactly during what period Gentile Christians became dominant in the church; this process may have varied from one location to another, and some churches may have remained more attached to their Jewish roots than others were.[74] In any case, by the time Luke is writing, many Jewish people have been rejecting the early Christian message, whereas many Gentiles have been embracing it. Luke welcomes the Gentiles, but may now be forced to address a theological and apologetic problem that appears as early as Paul's Letter to the Romans (e.g., Rom 3:3, 29; 4:10; 9:14; 11:1, 11): is the dominant Jewish view of Paul's contemporaries correct, in which case Gentile Christians are not fully members of God's people, or has salvation history experienced an irreparable breach with a rejection of Israel?[75] Luke rejects both these alternatives; his emphasis on fulfilled prophecy points to the Gentile influx being part of God's predicted plan from the beginning, even if most Jewish people had not recognized it.

---

68. See, e.g., Jervell, *Unknown Paul*, 16; Donaldson, "Riches," 98; cf. Rom 11:17–18; 1 Cor 10:1, 32; Eph 4:17; 1 Thess 4:5; 3 John 7. Even outsiders recognized Christianity's Jewish roots well into the third century (cf. Wilken, "Christians," 119–23). Brawley, "Commonwealth," sees Gentiles as gathered into the eschatological commonwealth of Israel.

69. With his "Christianity without History" (so Burkitt, *Gospel History*, 289). Marcion's use (rather, mutilation) of Luke is a counterreading.

70. See Dahl, "Abraham," 151, perhaps even too cautiously.

71. Jervell, *Unknown Paul*, 19–20.

72. See esp. Pritz, *Nazarene Christianity*.

73. Lucian *Peregr.* 11 (LCL, 5:13).

74. See more fully Keener, *John*, 195–98, 208–14. The Christian movement eventually developed its distinctive more fully than, say, the Qumran sectarians did (if one may judge by the distinctly "sectarian" works in their respective libraries; Stökl Ben Ezra, "Weighing"), but the evidence for this comes from later than our period.

75. Johnson, *Acts*, 8, though perhaps importing too much of the thought of Romans. Cf. similar apologetic questions in Witherington, *Acts*, 64–65; Brawley, *Luke-Acts and Jews*, 158–59. Cf. Haenchen, *Acts*, 100, who attributes the breach to Gentile failure in law-keeping.

However we reconstruct Luke's audience, the polemic within the narrative itself (a much less speculative question) is mainly intra-Jewish. No invective in Acts is stronger than Stephen's speech, but this speech is explicitly intra-Jewish polemic from a Hellenist Jew to other Hellenist Jews, and its harshest words are quotes or allusions from the prophets.[76] Stephen's preaching sounds much like the polemic of other pre-70 C.E. Jewish sects (e.g., the Essenes) who regarded themselves as the true remnant of Israel.[77] No Gentile Christians in Acts engage in harsh rhetoric toward anyone Jewish.

Throughout this discussion, I am employing terms in relatively conventional ways (to remain as intelligible as possible to my larger audience), but the categories themselves are anachronistic.[78] Judaism was extremely diverse in its beliefs both in Palestine and in the Diaspora,[79] and the supposition that the fall of the temple immediately conformed all Jews to one standard is naive. Further, Rome often treated Judaism as an ethnic entity (hence the need for tolerance) rather than a religious entity probably until the end of the first century.[80] "Christianity" as an entity is also a later construct; Jewish Christians saw themselves as proponents of the true faith of Israel, and early Gentile Christians saw themselves as converts to it.[81] I accommodate the language of subsequent history simply because one must use familiar language, however imperfect, to communicate; but much that is traditionally associated with this usage is anachronistic.

e. Diverse Jewish Roles in Luke-Acts

Although conflicts between Jesus's followers and Jewish leaders existed, as noted above, Luke also reports diversity in Jewish responses (e.g., Acts 2:41, 47; 4:4; 6:7; 13:43; 14:1–2; 17:10–11; 18:6–8; 19:9; 21:20; 23:7; 28:24).[82] Such diversity was a disappointment to those expecting the conversion of all Israel, but it was certainly not wholesale rejection, either.

I. LAW-OBSERVING PROTAGONISTS

Likewise, Luke portrays significant protagonists, such as Mary, Jesus, Peter, and Paul, as faithful Jews (e.g., Luke 2:21–24, 27, 39; 9:30–31; 10:26; 24:44; Acts 10:14; 16:3; 18:18; 21:23–26); those in supporting roles, such as Simeon and Anna, Jairus, and the poor widow with two coins, also present in a very positive light at least a significant remnant within Jewish piety.[83] As C. K. Barrett remarks, "A book whose main actors—Peter, Stephen, Paul, James, not to mention Jesus (mainly off stage)—are

76. Spencer, *Acts*, 81, also noting that excepting Acts 7:52, "no uniquely 'Christian' elements appear anywhere else in the speech."

77. Donaldson, "Sectarian Nature."

78. As often observed, e.g., Horsley, "Assembly," 373–75; see further discussion in our prolegomenon, sect. 8.

79. E.g., Porton, "Diversity"; Groh, "Jews and Christians," 87–89; Boccaccini, "Multiple Judaisms"; Luke, "Society Divided"; Keener, *John*, 181–85. This is not to deny considerable commonality on central concerns (Sanders, *Jesus to Mishnah*, 255–56).

80. See Goodman, "Nerva." This is not to say that the Jewish status of God-fearers remained unclear (Levinskaya, *Diaspora Setting*, 3, against Goodman).

81. For this view in Acts, see esp. Squires, "Acts 8.4–12.25"; for Gentile believers as "proselytes" already in Paul, see Donaldson, *Paul and Gentiles*, 236–47; idem, "Riches," 98. This is the usual perspective of "Messianic Judaism" today, but this phrase is also anachronistic for the first century because the Jesus movement was not the only messianic movement, though it was the only one that demonstrated longevity (and has "risen again").

82. For more detail, see, e.g., Brawley, *Luke-Acts and Jews*, 133–54; idem, "Borderlines" (applying Acts' "open-ended" conclusion also to the Jewish response); also Jervell, *Luke and People of God*, 44, 49; Nanos, *Mystery*, 268–69. Because of this diverse response, O'Toole, "Treatment of Jews," warns that it is unfair to depict Luke's negative approach specifically toward the hostile respondents in terms of modern anti-Judaism.

83. See, e.g., Rosner, "Biblical History," 71; Jervell, "Paul in Acts: Theology."

all Jews cannot easily be judged anti-Jewish (still less anti-Semitic—Acts shows no interest in race as such)."[84]

In Acts Paul experiences widespread opposition not limited to Judaism.[85] Indeed, in Luke's skillful irony, the same Paul who faces conflict from the Jewish community in some cities faces conflict elsewhere because he is a Jew (Acts 16:20; cf. 19:34), and even what he suffers from Jews is for the sake of Judaism (26:6; 28:20). (This is reported from the vantage point of Paul, but as a reliable character, he normally reveals the Lukan perspective.)

On other occasions, it is precisely Paul's fidelity to Judaism that creates friction with less faithful Jews. Immediately after he exhorts pagan crowds against polytheism (14:15–18), Jewish opponents incite them to stone Paul (14:19). Much of the synagogue in Ephesus seeks to distance itself (19:8–9, 33–34) from his monotheistic preaching in that city (19:26–27). The opposition to Paul's Gentile associations (cf. 21:27–29) may be based on principle (cf. 15:5) but, in practice, opposes what was becoming the most successful single program in history to recruit Gentiles for the worship of Israel's one God. These observations apply not only to Paul: when the earliest apostolic church faces opposition from the priestly authorities, it also associates such hostility with "the Gentiles" (4:25–27), who supplied the governor who condemned Jesus.

We may also note Paul's solidarity with Jewish customs in Acts (16:3; 18:18; 21:23–26; cf. 15:29–31),[86] a fact that has troubled some scholars as incompatible with Paul's own epistles (I believe partly because we have too often read Paul from a traditional post-Reformation Protestant lens; see ch. 7 above). Paul offers no condemnation to the law faithfulness of Jerusalem's Christians, which is presented in a favorable light in Acts so long as it is not imposed on Gentiles (21:20–26). Brawley argues that in addition to producing apologetic, Luke is irenic. He points out that the second half of Acts employs various "conventional legitimating techniques" to show that Paul and his Gentile mission pose no threat to the true Jewish message and heritage despite Jewish opponents and "sympathetic Christian" schismatics.[87]

Certainly, Luke does not oppose Jewish Christians; he honors law-keeping (e.g., Luke 1:6, 9–10; 2:21–24), and so his portrayal of Jerusalem Christians devout in the law is a positive one (Acts 21:20). He does object to the ethnocentrism of some Jerusalem Christians (11:3; 15:5; 21:21) but portrays the leaders of the movement positively and Jerusalem Christians as generally open to learn from God's ways (11:17–18; 15:7–21).[88]

II. Characterization

Claudia Setzer rightly notes both favorable and unfavorable Jewish attitudes toward Jesus throughout Acts, though she believes the latter predominate, especially in the

84. Barrett, *Acts*, 2:xcvii, though noting (xcviii) that many Jewish people were rejecting Jesus's messiahship in this book.
85. Cassidy, "Opponents."
86. See, e.g., Jervell, *Theology*, 4; Botermann, "Heidenapostel"; cf. Jankowski, "Messianische Realpolitik?"
87. Brawley, "Paul in Acts," 143–44; Jervell would agree with much of this. Against expectations of a dichotomy, Bovon, *Studies*, 31, notes that of early Christian documents, Luke-Acts is the most positively disposed both to Israel and to the Gentile mission.
88. Most scholars recognize that Luke does not condemn believing Jews (e.g., Salmon, "Insider," 81–82). By contrast, Tyson, "Problem," 137, thinks that the Jerusalem Christians function in the narrative especially as Paul's enemies.

later section. To reduce Luke's presentation to a single perspective is to oversimplify; Luke includes both.[89]

Some argue that ancients may have lacked the modern interest in exploring subjective individuality; certainly, they often show interest in broader character types and in moral explorations.[90] Yet in contrast to some modern expectations about them, ancient readers preferred narratives spiced up with round, realistic characters, though some flat characters were also acceptable. Both dramatists and historians were concerned with characterization.[91]

Luke uses a standard ancient narrative technique of contrasting characters, presenting Jewish believers in Jesus positively but the nation's religious leaders negatively and blaming the latter for the division.[92] The division, however, is between believer and unbeliever, not between Jew and Gentile, though Luke seems to emphasize greater responsibility for those who had greater knowledge of God's law (Luke 12:52–53; cf. 12:47–48). The division repeatedly cuts its swathe through the Jewish community itself (e.g., Acts 14:1–2; 18:6–8; 19:9; 28:24), so that the complaint is not that no Jews believed but that God's people, as a whole, did not do so.[93]

III. Diverse Groups' Responses

Not all groups in Acts respond the same way. In the early twentieth century, even Harnack, who complained that "the Jew is in a sense the villain in this dramatic history," also noted that Luke differentiates Pharisees from Sadducees and reports favorable information (e.g., Gamaliel's speech and the conversion of Jerusalem priests and Beroean Jews). "This impartiality of the narrative, in a point where there was such an extraordinary temptation to partiality, is a valuable proof of the careful sense of justice of the historian St. Luke."[94]

Luke also provides diverse pictures of the non-Christian Jewish community, including the Pharisees (who appear almost entirely negatively in the post-70 Jewish Christian Gospels Matthew and John).[95] Luke sometimes presents the Pharisees as a composite character clueless about Jesus's real mission,[96] but he also presents

---

89. Setzer, *Responses*, 44–82. Cf. Foakes-Jackson and Lake, "Internal Evidence of Acts," 183; for positive as well as negative Jewish responses, see, e.g., Brawley, *Luke-Acts and Jews*, 156.

90. Gill, "Character." Theophrastus provided an entire essay delineating (often in humorous ways) various character types. Many ancients viewed character as inborn, not changed, e.g., Pindar *Olympian* 13.12; also 11.19–20; Eurip. *Alcmeon in Corinth* frg. 75 (Stob. 4.30.2); *Antigone* frg. 166 (Stob. 4.30.1); *Archelaus* frg. 232 (Stob. 4.29.44); *Dictys* frg. 333 (Stob. 4.30.5); *Meleager* frg. 520 (Stob. 4.22.131); *Phoenix* frg. 810; also frg. 1027; 1067 (Stob. 4.29.47); 1068 (Stob. 4.30.3); frg. 1113 (Stob. 4.29.35); Lucian *Nigr*. 37; cf. Arius Did. *Epit*. 2.7.11k, p. 80.26–31; 82.5–18; Quint. *Decl*. 268.6. Others, however, recognized that character changed (Val. Max. 6.9.pref.–6.9.9; cf. 2 Chr 24:17–22), or accepted both nature and nurture (some Stoics in Arius Did. *Epit*. 2.7.11m, p. 86.21–34).

91. For characterization in modern literary theory, see Gowler, *Host, Guest*, 29–75; in ancient narratives, see 77–176. For plausible character development in a narrative, cf. Herod in Josephus (though some of this may reflect his accurate source, Nicolaus of Damascus).

92. Thompson, "Contrasting Portraits," 343–44. On contrasting characters, see further Shuler, *Genre*, 50; Keener, *Matthew*, 97; in fuller detail, idem, *John*, 916–17, 966–69, 1183–84. They could, of course, be "rounded" (discussion in *John*, 216–17).

93. Gaventa, "Comment(ary)ing," also contends that the theme of "resisting" God is not limited to Jewish leaders but applies to Gentile leaders such as Felix and sometimes even to the church (e.g., Ananias and Sapphira; and even Peter himself in the Cornelius narrative). In this approach, the divide is not just between believers and unbelievers but ultimately between God and humanity.

94. Harnack, *Acts*, xxiv–xxv, regarding Luke as more anti-Jewish than Paul (Rom 11:25–32) but less than other writers.

95. *Pace* Jack T. Sanders, "Redaction in Luke XV.11–32"; idem, "Parable and Anti-Semitism"; cited by E. P. Sanders, *Jesus and Judaism*, 386n31, as the basis for his own claim of Luke's "anti-Pharisaism" (180).

96. See esp. Darr, *Character Building*, 85–126.

them as respecting Jesus, fighting him only verbally, and sometimes even trying to protect him from those who wished to kill him (Luke 13:31).[97] The Pharisees and Jesus clash over law observance, but it is the Sadducees who engineer his execution (e.g., 22:2–4, 52, 66; 23:10; 24:20).[98]

Brawley finds Luke's view of the Pharisees positive in Acts, and in the Gospel more positive in his redaction than in his tradition.[99] For example, Luke uses them to legitimate Jesus in the Gospel and, to some extent, Paul in Acts (see, e.g., Acts 5:35–39; 23:6–9).[100] In one of the most thorough studies of the Pharisees in Luke-Acts, David Gowler demonstrates Luke's diverse characterizations of the Pharisees in his narrative.[101] He argues that Luke presents them more favorably in Acts than in the Gospel, as positive legitimators; even the Christian Pharisees who take the wrong position in Acts 15:5 seem to accept the church consensus in 15:22.[102] In Acts, the Pharisees continue to be the Jerusalem Christians' closest influential allies (5:34–39; 23:9); one can be both Pharisee and Christian (15:5); and Paul is comfortable identifying himself with Pharisaism, as far as it goes (23:6).[103] For Luke, one commentator notes, Paul is "the ideal Jew."[104] (See, further, comment on Acts 5:34.)

By contrast, the chief priests are enemies of the church fairly consistently throughout Luke-Acts.[105] The cornerstone image suggests special judgment on the leaders (Luke 20:17; Acts 4:11). Given the negative portraits of them in other contemporary Jewish sources, however, one cannot regard Luke's perspective as anti-Jewish; the Jewish Christians were not the only ones who experienced the Sadducean aristocracy's power as abusive.[106] Luke can hardly be charged with anti-Semitism for opposing the same Sadducees who were hated by Pharisees and Essenes.

Some patterns are fairly consistent in Luke-Acts:

1. "The people,"[107] left to themselves, loved Jesus and his apostles—not only in Galilee but even in Jerusalem (e.g., Luke 21:38; 23:27; 24:19; Acts 2:47; 5:13).
2. Jerusalem's leaders feared Jesus's and the apostles' appeal to the people (Luke 19:47–48; 20:6, 19, 26; 22:2, 6, 53).[108]
3. Jerusalem's leaders charged that Jesus was misleading the people (Luke 23:5, 14).

---

97. Mason, "Chief Priests," 134–42.

98. Tyson, "Opposition in Luke" (also noting the improved image in Acts). Hakola, "Pharisees," also notes that the Pharisees appear more favorably in Acts, noting that there they are *relatively* positive because of new standards of comparison; Hakola helpfully grounds the apparent inconsistency in the consistency of social identity theory (see 194–200).

99. On this redactional improvement, see also Ziesler, "Luke and Pharisees."

100. Brawley, *Luke-Acts and Jews*, 84–106, esp. 105–6. Instead of reading Acts primarily in light of the earlier negative portrait (so Darr, *Character Building*, 43, as summarized in Spencer, "Approaches," 404), we should thus also read earlier material in light of Acts (as in the shift in focus from heritage to mission).

101. Gowler, *Host, Guest*, 177–296.

102. Ibid., 301–5. (Though, against the view that he portrays Pharisees favorably to legitimate Christianity, see Kingsbury, "Pharisees in Luke-Acts.")

103. Marmorstein, "Attitudes," 383–84, tendentiously accepts all the early Christian evidence for positive relations (e.g., Acts 5:34–39) but doubts all evidence for persecution—mainly because he argues in terms of Jews and Christians, not (more specifically) Sadducees and messianic Jews.

104. Bruce, *Acts*[3], 26, citing Acts 24:14.

105. Mason, "Chief Priests," 142–47; Brawley, *Luke-Acts and Jews*, 107–32.

106. See, e.g., Jos. *Life* 216; 1QpHab IX, 4–5; Keener, *Matthew*, 613; more fully, comment on Acts 23:2.

107. Luke's first four uses of λαός (Luke 1:10, 17, 21, 68) appear in four different cases; this fits an oratorical method for emphasizing a key term (Parsons, "*Progymnasmata*," 60).

108. Granted, this is not an exclusively Lukan concern (Mark 11:12, 18, 42; 14:2), but Luke emphasizes it; e.g., Mark mentions fear of the people (Mark 11:32), but Luke adds the concern for stoning (Luke 20:6; this is a familiar, though not exclusively, Lukan image, 13:34; Acts 7:58–59; 14:5, 19; cf. John 8:5–7, 59; 10:31–33; 11:8).

Far from being anti-Jewish, Luke's narrative, as a whole, suggests that Jerusalem might have embraced the message about Jesus had the corrupt authorities not thwarted this outcome (cf. Acts 2:47; 4:3–4; 5:12–18). Luke is not anti-Jewish; he is against the authorities who once ruled Jerusalem.[109] (Perhaps Judea's function in his narrative also includes an element of theodicy, explaining the holy city's destruction by showing the elite's rejection of Israel's rightful spiritual leadership.)[110]

If Luke could expect some other Jewish people after 70 C.E. to share this perspective of the pre-70 Jerusalem Jesus movement, his argument may have had some appeal. Israel's exploitive leaders, who proved corrupt and whom the Pharisees and other Jewish groups disliked, directed public opinion against the early Jesus movement. Had it not been for the obstinacy of this class, Luke may imply, Judaism as a whole might have believed, and salvation history might have been consummated in the first generation (without a prior large influx of Gentiles).[111]

f. Pro-Judaism in Acts?

Jervell's argument in 1972 shifted the consensus of scholarship, which had previously viewed Luke as mostly negative toward Judaism.[112] Others have developed a more positive approach from a variety of diverse angles, but with the basic sense that Luke viewed "the rise of the early Jewish church as itself the locus of the fulfillment of hopes for Israel's restoration," through Jesus's "ascension to the eternal throne of David and gift of the Spirit."[113]

i. Arguments for Luke's Pro-Judaism

Many scholars see Luke as pro-Jewish rather than anti-Jewish.[114] One may take, for example, the positive portrayal of much Jewish observance in Luke-Acts, from key figures in the infancy narratives[115] to Paul (Acts 16:3; 18:18; 20:16; 21:26)[116] and others (e.g., 22:12).[117]

---

109. With, e.g., Danker, *New Age*, 228; cf. George, "Israël." Luke charges Jerusalem's elite, not all Jews, with Jesus's unjust execution (see further comment at Acts 2:23; 3:17; and esp. Weatherly, *Responsibility*; Matera, "Responsibility for Death").

110. Cf. Josephus's similar theodicy in explaining the Judean-Roman war and the temple's destruction, or the similar explanations of Samuel-Kings and the Chronicler regarding the first temple's destruction and Israel's exile.

111. Paul views this rejection as God's providential plan to provide Gentiles a chance for life (Rom 11:11, 30–31), but in Paul's theology, God could appoint rebellious human agents precisely to accomplish his purposes (9:17).

112. Jervell, *Luke and People of God*; for earlier sources, see idem, "Israel und Heidenvölken"; for his summary of the current state of the question, see idem, "Faithfulness." Some warn that today's correct emphasis on Acts' Greco-Roman context risks obscuring its Jewish setting, which Luke himself finds so central (Tyson, "History to Rhetoric," 38–39, 41); this is a potential danger even in a commentary such as this one, which addresses Luke's Diaspora context at length (because it requires more exposition for modern readers) yet treats his central theology (without neglecting it) in less detail.

113. Turner, *Power*, 307–8.

114. E.g., Jervell, *Theology*, passim; Danker, *New Age*, 228. Cazeaux, *Actes* (e.g., 338–39), offers a very different approach, suggesting that Paul, unlike Peter in the first half of the book, rejects Israel in favor of the mission to the nations and comes to the right approach only at the end of the book. (He connects this with the overemphasis on the resurrection at the expense of the passion, the passion being emphasized in the first part of the book, e.g., 339.) While Cazeaux is right to see emphases on both heritage and mission in Acts, however, I believe that the portrayal of Paul's mission is much more favorable (cf. 13:47) and that Luke supports even his appeal to Caesar (cf. Keener, "Apologetic").

115. Carras, "Observant Jews," 704–5.

116. Ibid., 697–703.

117. Ibid., 708, compares the characterization of observant Jews in Josephus.

Some of the indications of Luke's loyalty to Judaism that scholars have proposed would not sound as pro-Jewish to many modern Jewish hearers as among many NT scholars. Thus, for example, the claim that Luke has not rejected Israel sounds welcome, but scholars typically demonstrate this claim by appealing to Luke's continuing evangelistic interest toward Israel, which runs counter to most modern Jewish groups' rejection of "Christian proselytization."[118]

Likewise, Luke's emphasis on continuity with biblical Israel, demonstrated by portraying Gentile Christians as grafted into God's people (to borrow a Pauline metaphor), can be read anachronistically in light of later Christian claims to have "replaced" Israel. But while these topics constitute issues of conflict in contemporary Jewish-Christian dialogue, NT scholars can view them as pro-Jewish insofar as we read Acts against the theological agendas of Luke's own generation, which is our historical interest here. We need only consider that most Gentiles were polytheists and many resented Judaism; by contrast, those who see Luke as pro-Jewish can note that his Christian Gentiles worshiped Israel's God, used Israel's Bible, and refused to relinquish their solidarity with Israel's heritage in the face of opposition.

Some who see Luke as pro-Jewish point to the sequence of events:[119] in honor of their favored ancestors, God offered Israel blessings first (3:25–26); Paul always began with the synagogues (13:5, 14; 14:1; 17:1, 10, 17; 18:4, 19; cf. 16:13); thus there is continuity on God's part, even if Israel did not embrace it.[120] There is a sense in which Luke sees positive continuity on Israel's part, too, even in the act of rejection, since Israel's history reveals many rejections of God's divine plan without God's ever repudiating the people as a whole (Acts 7).[121] Some scholars suggest that Luke presents the story of rejection in such a way as to evoke pathos, as in ancient tragedy, though Luke still had hope for a greater Jewish response in his day.[122] The element of tragic fate is not missing in Josephus (e.g., *Ant.* 20.257). Similarly, narrative irony may connect his themes of prophecy fulfillment with frequent Jewish rejection.[123]

118. See a nuanced discussion in Talbert, *Romans*, 269–74. The status of Messianic Judaism has remained a critical sticking point in Jewish-Christian dialogue, but Messianic Judaism may resemble most closely the earliest Jesus movement's situation vis-à-vis Israel's heritage and offers a potential alternative to the impasse in dialogue between those who insist that everyone should consider their truth claims about Jesus and those who, in light of intervening centuries of Jewish-Christian conflict, view the acceptance of such premises as ethnic and religious suicide. In a sense, it may offer both groups a chance for dialogue by revisiting the original schism through a group that bridges the most essential commitments of both camps. For some more positive Jewish perspectives on the movement, see, e.g., Harris-Shapiro, *Messianic Judaism*, 166–89; Cohn-Sherbok, *Messianic Judaism*, 169–213 (esp. 174, 203–13); more concisely, idem, "Introduction," xiii–xiv.

119. For the possible significance of sequence, cf. Luke 1:3–4; but scholars debate whether Luke intends order in this sense.

120. Johnson, *Acts*, 9. Moessner, "End(s)ings," 219, thinks that Acts' conclusion marks the inauguration of the "times of the Gentiles" (Luke 21:24), allowing the Gentile mission without requiring one to start with Israel (he argues [p. 218] that the narrative's conclusion ushers in a new situation, as in the conclusion of Diodorus Siculus's *Library of History*).

121. Cf. Foakes-Jackson and Lake, "Internal Evidence of Acts," 183. This is not to imply that Luke would necessarily, in an ideal situation, attribute more obstinacy to Israel than to others; presumably, he shares Paul's belief in general human depravity (Rom 1–3; cf. Acts 14:16; 17:27, 30), which is revealed in special ways among those with greatest exposure to the standard of truth (Rom 2:12–29).

122. Tannehill, "Rejection," esp. 98–99, 101; idem, *Story*, 105–24; cf. idem, "Tragic Story." Against this reading, see Cook, "Mission," 122–23 (citing Luke 11:50; 20:17; Acts 4:11); Sanders, "Jewish People," 74–75 (who, unfortunately, sees them as villains); Tuckett, *Luke*, 61 (arguing that readers will sympathize more naturally with Luke's protagonists).

123. Ray, *Irony*, passim (introduced, 8–9). Ironically, "it is the Jewish rejection of the divine plan that actually brings about its accomplishment" (9); note his comments on Acts 13:27 (155–58). From a different approach, Dawsey, *Voice*, addresses irony in Luke's Gospel (especially in the characters' voices' differing from that of Jesus and the narrator, but see Padilla, *Speeches*, 11).

Scholars usually concur that Luke argued for Christianity as "a legitimate development of Judaism," whether or not he fully explained his reasons.[124] Jervell argues that
Luke's primary interest "is to demonstrate the church as the one and only true Israel,
the unbroken continuation of the people of God in the time of the Messiah-Jesus."[125]
Some argue that Luke sees the promises of Luke 1–2 fulfilled in Acts 15; this emphasis
would fit a situation in which the Jewish Christians were still in competition with
other Diaspora Jews for the title of Israel.[126] Others would argue that Acts 15, like
other events in Luke's work, offers merely a prelude to Israel's future restoration (cf.
3:19–21 and comment loc. cit.)

If some scholars' language such as "true Israel" is too strong or anachronistic, at
least the language of the continuation of the remnant (which, through most of Israel's
history, welcomed Gentiles) is clear in Luke-Acts (this is what many scholars mean
by the language "true Israel," in any case).[127] As already noted, however, the language
is much stronger in Justin Martyr and later writers (see comments in sect. 1.c above)[128]
than in the NT (cf. Rom 2:29; 11:17–18; Gal 3:29; 1 Thess 4:5). Indeed, many Jewish
people expected widespread apostasy in Israel in the end time,[129] and some seem to
have viewed their own group as the true elect remnant of Israel.[130]

Such language may sound offensive today after a long history of Christian anti-
Semitism,[131] and sound interpretation must prevent the exploitation of such texts
in the service of subsequent anti-Jewish traditions. But for first-century Christians,
such language constituted a means of establishing their distinctive identity within
Judaism and their solidarity with salvation history.[132] Some scholars understandably
complain that Luke's language of Judaism is more favorable than his content, since
the promises now do not apply to ethnic Jews without conversion.[133] But apart from

124. Cohen, *Maccabees*, 167.

125. Jervell, *Theology*, 4–5; idem, *Apostelgeschichte*, 92, 629. Le Cornu, *Acts*, xxx, argues that a primary
purpose of Acts is "to explain the relationship between the Jewish and gentile segments of the early community." Some connect Luke's use of "epochs" in salvation history to his appropriation of elements of the Jewish
symbolic world to provide identity for Christians (Wolter, "Epochengeschichte," 284); some also portray
Christology as a key factor in constituting God's people, hence welcoming Gentiles (cf. Schröter, "Heiden").

126. Turner, *Gifts*, 56.

127. E.g., Stowers, "Synagogue in Theology of Acts": God-fearing Gentiles who follow the minimal Noahide
laws (Acts 15:20) join Israel's remnant, supplanting only the unbelieving portion of Israel. The remnant of Israel
is called to bring the rest of Israel back to the Way (13:47; cf. Isa 49:5–6; Moessner, "Fulfillment," 46–50).

128. Later rabbis polemicized against some Gentiles who claimed to be the true Israel (e.g., *Song Rab.* 7:3,
§3; *Pesiq. Rab.* 5:1) and against some "schismatics" who called Israel apostate (*b. Yebam.* 102b); cf. Herford,
Christianity, 247–51, 290–91; Neusner, *Beginning*, 12. Cf. *b. Sanh.* 44a, where the rabbis must argue that
Israel's election can never be revoked.

129. E.g., 1Q20 XV, 9; 1Q22; 4Q163 6–7 II, 4–5 (possibly); 4Q390 1 7–9; 4Q501, line 3; *1 En.* 91:7;
93:9; *3 En.* 48A:5–6; *4 Ezra* 5:1–2; 14:16–18; *Test. Iss.* 6:1; *Test. Dan* 6:6; 7:3 MSS; *Test. Naph.* 4:1; *Mart. Is.*
2:4; Matt 24:12; 2 Thess 2:3; 1 Tim 4:1; *Sipre Deut.* 318.1.10; *Pesiq. Rab Kah.* 5:9.

130. Cf. 1QM XVII, 6–8. Thus most scholars believe that Qumran sectarians regarded themselves as the
true Israel (Jeremias, "Qumran Texts," 69; Fritsch, *Community*, 74; Vermes, *Jesus and Judaism*, 117; Flusser,
Judaism, 49; Gärtner, *Temple*, 13; with careful nuancing, cf. Sanders, *Paul and Judaism*, 242–49; idem, *Law and
People*, 175–76). This has been claimed (e.g., Jeremias, *Jerusalem*, 246, 248; idem, *Theology*, 171–72; Goppelt,
Judaism, 33, 52–53) and disclaimed (esp. Sanders, *Paul and Judaism*, 152ff.) for the Pharisees; it was surely
true of the Samaritans (Bowman, *Documents*, ii).

131. On which see, e.g., Flannery, *Anguish*; Parkes, *Conflict*; Tyson, *Luke, Judaism, and Scholars*, 1–11. The
greatest risk, however, comes in de-Judaizing earliest Christianity, a tool that Nazi theologians used to justify
anti-Semitism (see Heschel, "De-Judaization").

132. Meeks, "Birth," 19, suggests that even "the *adversus Ioudaeos* literature" of early church fathers "looks
much uglier when transposed from a minority group that sees itself under attack into a triumphant church
backed by imperial power."

133. Räisänen, "Redemption," 94–114; cf. Sanders, "Who Is a Jew?" Marshall, "Acts," 600–601, summarizes
Jervell, *Apostelgeschichte*, 628, as thinking that Acts rejects a Rom 11–style eschatological conversion of Israel;
Schneider, *Apostelgeschichte*, 2:419, and Pesch, *Apostelgeschichte*, 2:310, as allowing for individual conversions;

the intervening centuries that lend plausibility to the accusation of this perspective supporting anti-Judaism, one could level the same charge against the Dead Sea Scrolls, where most of Israel remained followers of Belial (e.g., as the "congregation of Belial," 1QH^a X, 22–23).[134] In the first century, as Dunn notes, *the key categories were not yet fixed"* (emphasis his); not only the meaning of "Christian" but that of the terms "Jew" and "Judaism" were understood differently by different communities.[135]

That this continuity with the biblical remnant necessarily portrayed the rest of their people as breaking covenant with God (a matter for which biblical history also provided them numerous precedents) mandated evangelism as a sign of concern for their people. Thus some scholars think that Luke's emphasis on a continuing witness to Israel despite many rejections shows the continuing loyalty of early Christians to their Jewish roots.[136]

II. DIVISION, NOT WHOLESALE REJECTION

When Acts concludes, Jewish people continue to respond as well as reject (Acts 28:24),[137] though for Luke, as for Paul, the failure of Israel as a *whole* to embrace the Messiah is unacceptable (3:19–26; Rom 11:7, 25); the remnant is not yet "Israel as a whole" (Rom 11:26).[138] As in the prophets, God "contends" with Israel, summoning his people to repentance, but never finishes with them or rejects them.[139] Already twice after promising to turn to the Gentiles and doing so, Paul keeps preaching to synagogues elsewhere (Acts 13:46; 18:6).

Thus Paul's final recorded rebuke to a local, divided Jewish community (28:25–28) is just that—it simply continues the pattern in which Paul rebukes a Jewish community in a particular locale but continues to go to the Jewish people first.[140] (This passage is, indeed, less explicit about turning from Jewish hearers than the previous two references, after neither of which did Paul abandon the mission to Israel. See fuller discussion in the commentary at Acts 13:46; 18:6; 28:25–28.)

The frequent (though not consistent) repetition of Jewish rejections reinforces Luke's point, which is not final Jewish rejection (an idea that would make inexplicable the continuing repetition of preaching first to Israel; see comment on Acts 13:46; 28:28) but, rather, the availability of the gospel also to the Gentiles.[141] Probably in Lukan as in Pauline eschatology, had Jewish people embraced the message, God would have fulfilled the promises by consummating the kingdom, and the Gentiles would have missed an opportunity to hear (3:19–21, 25–26; Rom 11:11, 25, 30–32). As Jesus sought out the marginalized, including the morally marginalized ("sinners"), in Luke's Gospel, so the theme of ironic, eschatological inversion carries over into

---

Barrett, *Acts*, 1246 (cf. also 2:xcvii–xcviii), as viewing the data as complex; and Marguerat, *Historian*, 221–30, as viewing it as deliberately ambivalent.

134. Cf., e.g., 1QS I, 22–24; CD IV, 13, 16; XIX, 14.

135. Dunn, *Partings*, 143.

136. Tannehill, *Acts*, 3 (though Tannehill personally denies the need to continue this mission today).

137. Moessner, "End(s)ings," 219, thinks that this divided Jewish reaction (Acts 28:25) marks a shift in Luke's narrative toward the future, an improvement over previous hostility; but cf. the division in 19:9.

138. Tyson, "Problem," 137, rightly holding that Luke is dissatisfied with partial acceptance, also thinks (I believe, incorrectly) that even the Jerusalem Christians are Paul's enemies and that by Acts 28 the Jewish mission has failed. For the close correspondence between 28:16–31 and Rom 11, see Litwak, "Views."

139. See Tiede, "Glory," 33–34; cf. idem, "Contending." For God's not rejecting Israel permanently in Luke's Gospel, see also Chen, *Father*, 214.

140. See Witherington, *Acts*, 73–74; Soards, *Speeches*, 206; cf. Le Cornu, *Acts*, xxxv, 1522.

141. Johnson, *Acts*, 250. Watson, *Gentiles*, 344, suggests that Paul discovered the Gentile mission through uncircumcised God-fearers' receptivity and Jewish rejection in the synagogues. This pattern does fit Acts and Paul, though I believe that the God-fearers' very receptivity (and Jewish hostility) suggests a prior, distinctive pro-Gentile element already in the Christian Paul's message.

Acts in the mission to the Gentiles.[142] Acts' ending, like the ending of the parable of the elder brother (Luke 15:32, addressing Judean religious experts in 15:2), is open-ended, an invitation.[143]

In the same conclusion, Paul continues to affirm his own solidarity with, and love for, his people (Acts 28:19–20) and to reason from the Jewish Scriptures as God's word (28:23, 25–27).[144] Some scholars even read this final scene as defending Paul against the charge of betraying Judaism (cf. 28:19).[145]

Moreover, the movement of the Gospel from Jerusalem to Rome is not so much a matter of moving away from Jerusalem as it is of moving toward a more strategic base for mission.[146] As Luke Timothy Johnson notes, "Each movement of the Gospel away from Jerusalem also circles back to it (see 8:14; 11:1–18, 29–30; 12:25; 15:2; 18:22; 19:21; 20:16; 21:13; 25:1)"; Luke seems at pains to emphasize that the expansion of the Christian movement was effected in continuity with the Jerusalem Christians.[147] Jerusalem remains the eschatological focus of promise (compare Acts 1:9–11 with Zech 14:4; cf. also Acts 1:6; 3:21–26; the temporal limitation in Luke 13:34–35; 21:24; probably 22:30).

In light of expectations apparently posed in the Gospel, Israel's promised restoration (cf. Luke 1:68–78; 2:25, 32, 38; 19:9; 21:24, 28; 22:30; 24:21) would not be abandoned in Acts any more than the promised Gentile mission is; it is simply deferred. Acts does not reiterate this point often, given its different focus on mission to the nations,[148] but it reiterates it often enough (see commentary on Acts 1:6; 3:19–21; cf. also 26:6–7; 28:20). Mission may cause heritage to be reconceived; it does not abolish it.

2. Acts and Israel's Scripture

Discussion of the use of the OT in Acts[149] is necessarily relevant for, though different from, the question of Acts and Judaism. Whatever Luke's approach to Israel more generally, he certainly affirmed Israel's Scripture; in this period, that affirmation probably also suggests that he values Israel as well. Although Gentile Christian anti-Semitism eventually made it possible for writers to claim the OT while remaining hostile to the Jewish people,[150] we lack evidence (or logic) for any Gentiles' rejecting the OT yet supporting the Jewish people. We also lack evidence in our first-century Jewish documents for the later Christian anti-Jewish synthesis.[151]

142. Talbert, *Mediterranean Milieu*, 172–73, arguing that this is not anti-Judaism.

143. Some scholars view it as ambivalent—no longer clear that all Israel's people will turn yet inviting them (Marguerat, *Histoire*, 333; idem, *Historian*, 152–54, 230). See further discussion at Acts 28:17–31.

144. See also, e.g., Brawley, "Promises and Jews," 296.

145. See Tannehill, "Story of Israel," 339, arguing that Paul's anguish in Acts 28 is also Luke's anguish. One view relatively rare today is that God *temporarily* rejected Israel during the Gentile period (Luke 21:24), Acts being a transitional period between dispensations (Frost, *Revelation*, 60).

146. Theologically, Luke moves from heritage to mission but does so in such a way that he seeks to retain the centrality of heritage (hence explaining, based on Isaiah, even the closing scene of Israel's division, Acts 28:25–27).

147. Johnson, *Acts*, 11.

148. Even mission to the nations never excludes Israel (e.g., Acts 9:15; 26:20, 23).

149. For a literature review up till 1983, see Bovon, *Theologian*, 78–108 (with a chronological bibliography, 78–83); for a more recent but briefer survey of scholars' treatment of Luke's use of Scripture, see Pao, *Isaianic Exodus*, 5–17 (with a focus on Isaiah, 10–17).

150. This anti-Judaism became most virulent in its gnostic forms, sometimes including a rejection of the OT. For comments on genuinely supersessionist vs. nonsupersessionist approaches to Israel's Scripture (viewing Paul as the latter), see Hays, *Conversion*, 176.

151. Although it has often been identified in Matthew, John, and Revelation toward the end of the first century and these works include much harsher polemic than Luke-Acts, they are also more pervasively Jewish.

Whatever the other literary influences on Luke (other than his direct sources), the most obvious would be Scripture, the authoritative heritage he shares with his audience and apparently expects them to recognize. Acts contains at least twenty explicit quotations from the LXX[152] and, perhaps more demanding for the audience, a host of allusions (e.g., to Isaiah in Acts 1:8; to Elijah in 1:9). As C. K. Barrett rightly puts it, "The influence, whether literary or theological, of the Old Testament upon the Lucan writings . . . is profound and pervasive."[153]

a. Expected Level of Biblical Literacy

Luke's level of biblical sophistication is lost on most modern readers but would not have been lost to nearly the same extent on Luke's ideal audience. Naturally, not all Luke's real hearers were biblically literate, but his ideal audience was, and the latter must have constituted enough of his anticipated real audience (at least among those who might hear the work multiple times) to merit the consideration lavished on his work.[154] Luke himself appears so immersed in biblical language (or at least the sort of eastern Mediterranean, Jewish language matrix of which biblical language was a part) that it pervades much of his work.[155]

i. Greek and Biblical Allusions

That both biblical and Hellenistic culture inform our understanding of Luke-Acts should not surprise us.[156] Diaspora Jews would know both the Scriptures and the surrounding Gentile culture, and early Christians learning within such a Diaspora Jewish matrix (whether by synagogue or church) would naturally develop the same flexibility. That Luke could freely incorporate both kinds of influences seems to represent an emerging consensus among scholars.[157]

Like other biblically focused Diaspora Jews and early Christians, however, Luke would have rooted his theological worldview especially in Israel's salvation history.[158] Whereas the Dead Sea Scrolls and other "sectarian" literature demonstrate the diversity of interpretations of Scripture available in early Judaism, most Jews were united around a central canon (even if some of its outer boundaries—e.g., in the case of what we call "apocryphal" works, or perhaps Esther at Qumran—were still being defined in various circles; the Torah and prophets were not in dispute).

I addressed some of these questions at greater length in, e.g., Keener, *Matthew*, 45–51, 535–36, 612–16, 670–71; idem, *John*, 171–232 (esp. 214–27); idem, *Revelation*, 115–16, 118–19.

152. With, e.g., Pao, *Isaianic Exodus*, 4. Steyn, *Septuagint Quotations*, 26–31, lists twenty-five introductory formulas introducing twenty-seven quotations, in addition to nine quotations without introductions (not including allusions). For classification by degrees of usage (summary references; citations; indirect citations, esp. in Acts 7 and 13:17–25; allusions; echoes; typical LXX language), see Marshall, "Acts," 518–19; for classification by function (history; promise and fulfillment; pattern and type; principles; characterization), see 519–20.

153. Barrett, "Luke/Acts," 231 (as cited in Marshall, "Acts," 513).

154. Cf. the extensive biblical literacy presupposed for Paul's implied audience, treated, e.g., in Hays, *Conversion*, 23, 49.

155. See Alexander, *Context*, 251–52.

156. The traditional scholarly dichotomy between Judaic and Hellenistic influences was used in the service of anti-Judaism or sometimes for Christian apologetic (see Meeks, "Birth"; Martin, "Dichotomy"); today it is probably maintained more often only as a result of overspecialization in NT scholars' training. For Luke's Hellenistic context, see, e.g., Plümacher, *Lukas*, 30–31.

157. For the consensus, see Schmidt, "Influences," 60.

158. Jervell, "Future," 104–9. Luke's (and other extant first-century Christian writers') *literary* "canon" was the Jewish Scriptures (see Wall, "Intertextuality," 544). Thus even many scholars working especially with Hellenistic sources recognize that most NT authors' primary cultural sphere was Jewish; e.g., for Paul's contemporaries, "the cultural authorities Paul appeals to [esp. Moses] would be sufficient to identify him as 'Jewish'" (Alexander, "IPSE DIXIT," 127).

Luke can expect most of his ideal audience to pick up his more obvious Hellenistic literary or cultural allusions (e.g., Acts 14:11–12; 17:19),[159] and we will explore these allusions wherever possible in this commentary. These allusions could be important for those for whom Greek history, mythology, and legend were an important and emotional part of their heritage, not readily severed from their background. For such an audience, Paul's ministry at "Troas" (perhaps recalling nearby Troy) or as a new Socrates in Athens allowed them to redeem or salvage, as it were, part of their own cultural heritage.[160] (Luke, admittedly, does not carry out such a plan with the sort of sophistication expected of one for whom connection with Hellenistic learning was a major goal.)[161]

Still, though I comment on and affirm such probable associations for Greek hearers, the far more explicit, marked references to the LXX suggest a different *primary* world and interpretive theological grid. Most obvious and central for Luke is his explicit grounding of Jesus and the Gentile mission in the story of Israel. As in the case of most other extant first-century Christian writings, biblical quotations are quite frequently explicitly marked; other possible allusions (including non-Jewish ones) are usually unmarked and hence are rendered most plausible when a significant accumulation of evidence for a multiplicity of them offers greater cumulative confidence that some are present.

The bulk of Luke's quotations occur in the first half of Acts, especially in speeches to Jewish audiences (i.e., in the sort of speeches found in the first half of Acts).[162] Since most biblical quotations in Luke's first volume also occur in discourse material (especially from Jesus)[163] and since speeches are adapted to their audiences, this distribution is what we would expect. Nevertheless, Luke also closes with a strategic, paradigmatic text from Isaiah (Acts 28:26–28), matching the function of some earlier paradigmatic prophetic texts at key points (Luke 4:18–19; Acts 2:17–21; see comment on Acts 1:8). The Gentile cultural allusions predominate especially during the Diaspora mission, but it is Scripture and Israel's heritage that frame and provide the more consistent, explicit subtext for the narrative.

II. RANGE OF BIBLICAL LITERACY

Luke's real audience certainly exhibited, and he presumably expected, a range of cultural literacy and interpretive competence, so that he included allusions that only some could be expected to comprehend fully.[164] Sometimes these allusions might involve intertextual echoes from the context of Luke's marked quotations;[165]

159. These were surely more often literary topics or themes, or sometimes allusions to a particular celebrated character (e.g., Socrates in Acts 17:19 and perhaps 4:19; 5:29), than to specific Greek texts, though the latter cannot be ruled out a priori.

160. Cf. allusions to Greek literature even in the rabbis (even, at times, to Homer; Manns, "Source de l'aggadah"). Collins, *Mark*, 1, suggests that Mark may have also assimilated Jesus to Hellenistic heroes and philosophers.

161. Contrast, e.g., the sort of clear allusions found in Philo *Plant.* 129; *Sib. Or.* 3.814 (referring to Circe, Hom. *Od.* 10.210; Virg. *Aen.* 7.19–20); even in matters of Greek style, e.g., a Homeric phrase in Jos. *Ant.* 1.222. Cf. also the allusion to Diomedes's capture of the Palladion in a cameo from Jerusalem (Rahmani, "Cameo").

162. Marshall, "Acts," 513 (citing Steyn, *Septuagint Quotations*, 230).

163. Marshall, "Acts," 527.

164. Cf. the similar comments of Koester, "Spectrum," esp. 14–15, on the Fourth Gospel. Comic dramatists could cite and parody tragic plays of their era, evoking common recognition (e.g., Menander *Aspis* 426–29, 432).

165. Cf. Hays, "Category or Methodology" (on Isaiah, see esp. Pao, *Isaianic Exodus*, passim, mostly quite persuasively); for a definition of "echoes," see Hays, *Echoes*, 25–33; Aune, *Dictionary of Rhetoric*, 395. Some others doubt that ancient hearers would have recognized contexts (on Paul's audiences, Tuckett, "Paul and Ethics"; cf. discussion in Stanley, "Pearls"; cf. also the response in Abasciano, "Diamonds"). The text-analytical approach to intertextuality, sensitive to the needs of philologists, focuses on marked and deliberate "relations

astonishing as this seems to some modern Western readers overloaded with access to a vast range of texts, many people in various largely oral cultures can achieve significant familiarity with, and competence in, a single narrow canon (such as the Torah or Qur'an). Since few would have their own copies of biblical scrolls and hence most would depend on oral memory and recitation, they might prove most familiar with narratives (the sequence of which provides ready contextual recall), psalms (if recited in worship), and the Torah (used regularly for legal and ethical teaching).

Since Luke also values quotations from the prophets,[166] sometimes using them as climactic complements to Torah citations like readings from the prophets following the Torah in synagogue services (Acts 3:24; 7:49–50; 13:40–41, 47), he apparently presupposes a biblically literate ideal audience (though he, undoubtedly, welcomes other hearers and would remain mostly intelligible to them).

Perhaps Luke merely wishes that his audience will have such familiarity, but that he typically displays it himself (despite some apparent minor lapses in the biblical stories in Acts 7) renders plausible his expectation that some of his audience will possess it. There was nothing unusual or elitist about writers' expecting specialized levels of knowledge among their readers; these expectations allowed them to produce readable specialist works uncluttered with the excessive examples or explanations that valiantly monumental attempts to be comprehensive can sometimes produce.[167]

Luke does not anticipate specialist sophistication (he does not engage in detailed, rabbinic-style argumentation like some passages in Paul's letters),[168] but he does expect an audience rooted in the biblically informed piety of synagogues and churches. On a more popular level, Greek writers assumed their audience's basic knowledge at least of Homer and often of other quotations and allusions that functioned as part of their cultural "canon" (see comment on Acts 17:28).[169] (Greek writers sometimes used these to lavishly display their learning[170]—expecting their audience to recognize and admire the use of allusions—or, probably more relevant to Luke, to connect with the audience on a deeper level through common background stories.) But less culturally literate readers need not have caught even such allusions to follow and enjoy a popular work.[171]

Some of Luke's ideal audience probably knows the OT well enough to follow his arguments; after all, Luke himself does (despite some apparent confusion in, e.g.,

---

between a text and literary pre-texts" (instead of opening the text to infinite associations; Bendlin, "Intertextuality," 873–74).

166. Cf. Luke 24:44; Acts 3:18, though these, presumably, include the narratives of "prophet-historians" outside the Torah.

167. So Dion. Hal. *Demosth.* 46; *Isaeus* 14.

168. Only the wealthiest members of his audience would have had the leisure to share a fully literary education (cf. Gray, "Class and Classics"). Probably, Paul expected at least some Jewish Christian teachers in the congregations (especially in Rome; cf. Rom 16:3–5, 7) to understand, but it is not surprising that some people encountered his teaching as obscure (2 Pet 3:16).

169. See, e.g., Trapp, *Maximus*, xxxv–xxxviii (the index to Trapp's translation of Maximus of Tyre includes about three columns of Homer, two of Plato, and three of others put together, and Maximus was a Middle Platonist); Maclean and Aitken, *Heroikos*, lxxxvii–lxxxix; multiple allusions in Lucian *Men.* 1 (where the dialogue makes clear that the allusions are expected to be recognized). Lucian *True Story* 1.2–3 declares that he expects his audience to recognize the unnamed authors he parodies.

170. Explicit in Lucian *Fisherman* 6. In contrast to biblical exegesis but presupposing no less familiarity with the text, critiquing and emending Homer "became a kind of 'literary sport'" by the early empire (Maclean and Aitken, *Heroikos*, xli, xlix–l, lx–lxxvi).

171. Pervo, *Profit*, 84, noting Homeric allusions in Chariton. The principle extends beyond novels to other nontechnical works.

7:16; he probably had no scrolls in front of him as he worked,[172] but could often depend on communal memory for corrections during early readings of the work).

b. Sources for Luke's Quotations

Luke's biblical quotations are most prominent in speeches, especially those addressed to Jewish audiences (and hence more common in Acts 1–15; but also cf. 23:5; 28:26–27).[173] Scripture citations typically serve the same function as other authority citations in Greco-Roman speeches,[174] albeit with a more defined and authoritative canon.[175] The periodization of history in the speeches resembles OT models.[176]

i. Septuagint Use

Most or all of Luke's quotes are from the popularly used LXX (in some of its variant forms)[177] rather than from his own or other translations of the Hebrew.[178] Although Greek-speaking Jews even in Jerusalem would have used the LXX, some scholars have been troubled by the implications of LXX quotations in the mouth of Jesus or Aramaic-speaking apostles, instead of seeing them as simply reflecting a fresh translation of their words. But while the form of such quotations could suggest that Luke (and Mark, who also uses the LXX) has added quotations himself, it could also simply suggest that he and many other Diaspora Christians transcribed or standardized their quotations according to the forms in which they were accustomed to hearing them.[179] In either case, it may be significant that none of Luke's Scripture quotations (in contrast to those, e.g., in Hebrews) must depend solely on the LXX for their sense.[180]

Some scholars suggest that Luke and some other early Christians may have used Jewish or Jewish Christian collections of texts.[181] Some Jewish interpreters collected lists of biblical proof-texts (as in 4Q176), possibly for later use in exhortation or apologetic.[182] They could also compose their own thematic midrashim (as in 4Q177).[183] Luke could depend on such a collection of texts from the LXX, but the collection

172. Though some house churches (cf., e.g., 1 Tim 4:13), like many early synagogues (cf., e.g., Acts 13:15; 2 Cor 3:14; Jos. *Ag. Ap.* 2.175), perhaps including house synagogues, probably did acquire some scrolls.

173. Fitzmyer, *Acts*, 91–92.

174. Black, *Rhetoric of Gospel*, 128. On the citation of ancient texts as authorities, see, e.g., Anderson, *Glossary*, 67. Greco-Roman authors tend to cite Homer the way Paul cites Scripture (Stanley, "Paul and Homer"); that neither Paul nor Luke does so suggests the narrower primary canon whose authority they and their audiences share.

175. Homer was the foundation of the Greek literary "canon"; see comment on Acts 17:28. The focus on select primary texts of antiquity fostered their intertextual comparison (Aune, *Dictionary of Rhetoric*, 234 [s.v. "Intertextuality," 233–34]).

176. Rosner, "Biblical History," 76, noting Van Seters's location of this in the Deuteronomistic History (1 Sam 8:8; 10:18–19; 12:8–11).

177. The variants are many (with, e.g., Barr, "Paul and LXX"), but I speak of the LXX "family" of readings here and elsewhere because of the problem's complexity. Marshall, "Acts," 516, notes that the consensus is that Luke's usual form is close to Alexandrinus, diverging mainly in the Psalms (perhaps because of liturgical adaptations); he may have sometimes "cited loosely from memory."

178. Witherington, *Acts*, 123–24; and esp. Fitzmyer, *Acts*, 91, following E. Richard and *pace* M. Wilcox.

179. Hanson, *Utterances*, 78–89, argues that Luke took most OT material directly from his sources (probable with regard to his use of Mark; not necessarily in Acts).

180. Bock, *Proclamation*, 271. It has been argued differently for Acts 15:17, but see our comment on that passage for the basic sense there.

181. Kilpatrick, "Quotations in Acts," for at least seven passages.

182. Cf. Hatina, "Consolations"; Stanley, "4QTanhumim." Many see in Qumran *testimonia* a confirmation of J. Rendel Harris's *testimonia* theory or of something like it (Allegro, "References," 186–87, though noting that 4Q175 was more eschatological than messianic; Fitzmyer, *Essays*, 59–89, esp. 88); 4Q175–177 is eschatological but 4Q175 has only about two messianic texts. For messianic *testimonia* in rabbinic literature, cf. Urbach, *Sages*, 1:686; for classical quotations, see comment on Acts 17:28.

183. Cf. Williams, "Catena."

might be oral, might simply reflect favorite preaching texts of the early church, or might be gathered in part from his own study of Scripture.[184] If Luke can expect his audience to recognize the sources and sometimes the context of his quotations, it would not be startling if he knew Scripture well enough to find these quotations himself.[185] Others suggest that if Luke expected his audience to recognize without explanation the function of these citations, then many of them must have already been in prior Christian use.[186]

II. Parts of the Canon Emphasized

Luke derives his primary texts from a number of locations in Scripture. For example, for Luke, the Davidic promise is critical for Jesus's role,[187] as exemplified in the infancy narratives, in the use of "Davidic" psalms such as Ps 110, and in some synagogue preaching (Acts 13:22–36). More dominant at key points in Acts' structure is Isaiah.[188] David Pao suggests that the primary scriptural grid "is none other than the foundation story of the Exodus as developed and transformed through the Isaianic corpus."[189] Although this claim may limit Luke too much to a single "primary grid," the use of Isaiah in various programmatic texts (Luke 3:4–6;[190] 4:18–19;[191] Acts 13:46–47;[192] 28:25–28[193]) makes a strong case, as do the clear allusions in Luke 24:46–47[194] and Acts 1:8.[195] Certainly, Isaiah proves to be the most critical grid for the narrative's movement to Gentiles, making Pao's contribution one of the most helpful recent studies on Acts.[196]

Isaiah does not, however, provide Luke's only narrative subtext. Although Isaiah supplies most of the programmatic statements,[197] one of Luke's key programmatic texts in Acts clearly derives from the briefer prophet Joel (Joel 2:28–32 in Acts 2:17–21); it may be secondary to Acts 1:8 in import but is a more explicit citation. Such various statements prove programmatic for different themes: 1:8 is programmatic for the church's Spirit-empowered mission (the primary theme for Acts), and 2:17–18 for

---

184. For challenges to *testimonia* elsewhere in the NT, see, e.g., Stendahl, *School of Matthew*, 207–17; cf. Lindars, *Apologetic*, 13–14; Longenecker, *Exegesis*, 89–90; Ellis, "New Testament Uses Old," 201.

185. Since Luke probably wishes to teach hermeneutics in speeches such as Stephen's, filling in the summaries in tantalizing verses such as Luke 24:27, 44, it will not do to simply assume that Luke and his audience shared familiarity with the same testimony books (although they undoubtedly shared familiarity with the more commonly used texts, such as Ps 2 or Isa 53).

186. Marshall, "Acts," 518, citing (apparently favorably) the position of Albl, *Scripture*, 198–200, and suggesting that most of Luke's Scripture arguments thus reflect earlier Christian tradition. Because Jewish exegetical techniques and contextual associations in quoted texts left implicit by Luke appear in various speeches (e.g., 13:16–41; 20:18–35), I do believe at least that he often depends on prior material, summarized in his work.

187. See esp. Strauss, *Messiah*.

188. In addition to Isaiah's usefulness, it could appeal to wider cultural usage, at least among prophetic movements. Fabry, "Jesaja-Rolle," views Isaiah as one of Qumran's favorite books; writing earlier, Fritsch, *Community*, 45, considered it the most widely attested book at Qumran, even more than the Pentateuch and Psalms.

189. Pao, *Isaianic Exodus*, 5; cf. 93–95.

190. See ibid., 37; on Isa 40:1–11 (esp. 40:3–5), see 37–69.

191. See the discussion in Pao, *Isaianic Exodus*, 70–84.

192. Ibid., 96–101.

193. Ibid., 101–9.

194. Ibid., 84–86.

195. Ibid., 91–96.

196. Pao (ibid., 111) also mentions Isaianic themes he finds prominent in Acts, some of them stronger than others: Israel's restoration (found elsewhere, but the allusions do point especially to Isaiah's influence; he treats this topic further, 111–46), God's word (this theme is pervasive in Scripture and hence less clear by itself), anti-idol polemic (very likely), and salvation offered to the Gentiles (certainly).

197. Ibid., 109. On Luke's application of OT and especially Isaianic "Spirit" passages, see also Ma, "Empowerment," esp. 40 (Jordan May brought this article to my attention).

the work's emphasis on Spirit-empowered speech (more explicitly than in 1:8) and charismatic guidance;[198] 13:47 applies the witness commission of 1:8 to Paul and his colleagues, who carry forward the Gentile mission; and 28:25–28 interprets the response of the Jewish community that further (as well as retrospectively) justifies turning to Gentiles.

Luke offers samples of biblical interpretation dispersed among various speeches. He does not leave us to merely wonder what sorts of texts in the Law, Prophets, and Writings Jesus explained to the disciples in Luke 24:27, 44. Luke offers examples from biblical narrative, for example, the behavior of Elijah and Elisha (Luke 4:25–27); and overviews of salvation history (with a Mosaic emphasis in Acts 7:19–44; with a Davidic emphasis in 13:22–23, 34–36; cf. 2:25–34); he draws on the "Writings" (cf. Luke 24:44) with various psalms (Acts 2:25–35; 13:33, 35).[199] As in good synagogue expositions (as best we can reconstruct them), he closes with quotations from the prophets in 7:49–50 and 13:41, 47 as well as in his final speech in 28:26–27. Such examples flesh out the global citations in other speeches (e.g., 3:18, 24; 26:22).

Besides explicit quotations, Luke employs the literary template of some biblical stories, especially in pre-Pauline portions of Acts (where his hard information seems less complete), such as the Elijah-Elisha succession as a model for the succession narrative in 1:9–11 (with the gift of the Spirit in 1:8, although 1:8 has a more direct allusion to Isa 49:6 and Isaiah's context), or the foreigners and eunuchs of Isa 56:3–6 in Acts 8:27. This does not mean that Luke invents the events—he could have made the parallels closer, more frequent, and more conspicuous had he wished, and the tradition of Jesus's ascension is reported elsewhere in the NT (see comment on Acts 1:9–11).[200] But Luke expects the reader (already familiar with Elijah and Elisha parallels in his Gospel) to recognize in the allusions a repeated salvation-historical pattern. If one accepts earlier biblical revelation, Luke seems to indicate, Jesus and the movement eventuating in the mixed Diaspora churches are consistent with, and hence are the true continuation of, God's workings of old.

c. Luke's Promise-Fulfillment Schema

By various means, biblical quotations in Luke-Acts establish continuity with the larger story of Israel and God's plan.[201] One of these means appears in the theme of promise and fulfillment.[202] In addition to his other approaches (e.g., typology; see below and comment on Acts 7:9–16), Luke often draws on direct biblical prophecies;

---

198. As well as gender inclusion and "all flesh" including Gentiles who would receive the Spirit (via the Isa 57:19 allusion in Acts 2:39), hence the gift going beyond the original witnesses.

199. Although "typological application" is treated below, I do not find many striking parallels with Moses or David in Luke's narratives (in contrast, e.g., to Matthew; see Allison, *Moses*). Parallels with Elijah and Elisha (Luke 4:25–27) seem more compelling (see discussion at Acts 1:6–9); such parallels fit Luke's "parallel lives" approach (see ch. 16 below).

200. Likewise, no one thinks that Luke invented Pilate or Herod to fulfill Ps 2:1–2, by which Luke interprets them in Acts 4:25–26.

201. E.g., Soards, *Speeches*, 201 (emphasizing their rhetorical function); Tomson, "Scriptures." Just as Luke has in mind the broader story in Isaiah (Pao, *Isaianic Exodus*, 251), he reads in light of the broader canonical story. Although Luke's work cannot strictly constitute an epic (not being poetry; see ch. 2, sect. 5), it is a foundation story, and its open ending shares with epics a connection to a larger story (see Troftgruben, "Ending," esp. 187, 220–21, 232–44). Later generations of Christians (as attested in patristic sources) may have embraced Acts as canonical precisely because it connected the stories of Israel, Jesus, and the apostolic church so effectively (see helpfully Smith, "Structure").

202. For various approaches to the fulfillment of promises in Acts, see Powell, *Acts*, 40–42. Some even find affirmation of biblical fulfillment in Luke's narratives in Luke's preface (Mallen, *Reading*, 164, 195), though the verb in Luke 1:1 is not the typical one for this function. In a very different sort of way, Polybius emphasized the importance of continuity through linking causes (Polyb. 3.32.2).

fulfillment of prophecy plays a larger role in Luke's use of the OT than many have recognized.[203]

As noted above, both Jewish and Gentile literature in Luke's era regularly affirmed both divine necessity in history and its partial revelation to humanity by oracles; hence the theme of fulfillment would have been amenable to most ancient audiences.[204] Such patterns are evident in both Dionysius of Halicarnassus and Josephus (see, further, comment on Acts 2:23).[205] That the patterns also appear in Josephus suggests that rigid dichotomies between Greek and Jewish cultural heritages on this point are unhelpful.[206]

Various early Jewish writers approached their Bible from different perspectives, and so the extent and function of this theme varies among them. Carl Holladay's study (focusing on fragmentary authors) contends that Luke's prominent promise-fulfillment theme is foreign to other Hellenistic Jewish works despite their diversity among themselves in most respects.[207] By contrast, N. T. Wright (focusing on Josephus) argues that Josephus presents his *War* as the fulfillment of biblical prophecy, comparable to Luke-Acts.[208] Surveying a larger range of literature, William Kurz concludes that the theme of promise and fulfillment, connecting contemporary stories with the larger story of Israel, appears elsewhere in Hellenistic Jewish narratives. Various communities may have laid claim to this approach, he points out, precisely because they were competing for the title to Israel's heritage.[209]

There is a difference in degree, however, between Luke and a minority of Jewish writers, on the one hand, and the majority of Jewish writers, on the other, a difference related to their divergent eschatological perspectives. Certainly, some Jewish authors envisioned fulfillment of biblical promises in their own time; even more commonly, they understood biblical history's patterns as normative for all times (and completed in the eschatological time). "The very premise behind reading history as involving promise and pattern is divine design and the constancy of God's character as he saves in similar ways at different times. Jewish imagery reusing Exodus motifs or new creation language shows how Judaism accepted this view of history."[210] In these ways, Luke's approach resembles that of his contemporaries (see discussion on Luke's typological approach below). For the most part, however, Luke is arguing for

203. See Bock, *Proclamation*, 275–77; Ray, *Irony*, 69–91. Talbert, "Promise and Fulfillment," similarly argues that promise and fulfillment constitute a major theme in Luke-Acts, though not (*pace* some scholars) the major one. Prophecies often concern Jesus's passion and the Gentile mission (Ray, *Irony*, 83–91), key issues for which Luke must also (given the view of Luke's apologetic already articulated) offer special apologetic support. Müller, "Reception," finds more direct prediction in Luke-Acts than in Matthew, though unnecessarily inferring from this a second-century date for Luke's work.

204. See esp. Peterson, "Fulfilment and Purpose" (whose view of Luke's theme rightly includes both OT and contemporary prophecies); also Squires, "Plan," 38. On the divine-necessity theme in ancient writers, see comment on Acts 2:23.

205. See Squires, *Plan*, 15–17; Balch, "Acts as Historiography." Ancestor stories may prefigure or foretell a coming king in Dionysius (idem, "Genre," 14–16).

206. For Josephus, see Squires, *Plan*, 18–20, 46–51, 61–66; Josephus often followed models such as Dionysius of Halicarnassus (see Attridge, *History in Josephus*, passim). Balch, "Acts as Historiography," critiques Schmidt, "Historiography of Acts," for focusing on Deuteronomic historiography. Most today allow both; see Schmidt, "Influences," 60.

207. Holladay, "Acts and Fragments," though contending that they (as well as Acts) share a common heroic characterization of central biblical heroes.

208. Wright, *People of God*, 373–75 (comparing the focus on Jesus's death in Luke-Acts to Jerusalem's fall in Josephus).

209. See Kurz, "Promise and Fulfillment."

210. Bock, "Scripture and Realisation," 47. On divine necessity's role, see also Peterson, "Fulfillment and Purpose."

a degree of current, climactic eschatological fulfillment not found in most ancient Jewish writers. An obvious exception is the pesher interpretive technique in the Dead Sea Scrolls because the Qumran community after its first generation also apparently embraced a degree of realized eschatology because of their presumed vantage point near the end of the age.[211]

Whatever the degree of, and purpose for, its differences, in any case, Luke uses the promise-fulfillment motif in competition with other visions of Israel's faith. In Greco-Roman rhetoric, different parties would argue lawgivers' intention in laws, each to his own advantage (e.g., Hermog. *Issues* 60.13–14). Jewish Christians and other Jews would have argued the same ways.[212]

It may be relevant here that whereas the opponents of Jesus and his movement sometimes challenge them with arguments that presuppose an understanding of Scripture (Luke 6:2, 7; 13:14; 14:1; cf. Acts 6:9–10; 19:8–9), they are barely reported as quoting any Scripture in the narrative (cf. Luke 20:28).[213] Although, presumably, some offered such arguments, Luke gives them little explicit voice, especially in Acts. Far and away, Jesus is the primary expositor of Scripture in the Gospel (e.g., 4:4, 8, 12, 18–19; 7:27; 8:10; 13:35; 18:20; 19:45; 20:17, 37, 42; 22:37; 23:30, 46; 24:27, 45). In Acts, Peter (Acts 1:20; 2:17–21, 25–28, 34–35; 3:23, 25), Peter and John (4:11), the Jerusalem church (4:25–26), Stephen (7:3, 7, 18, 28, 32, 34, 37, 40, 42–43, 49–50),[214] Paul (13:33–35, 41, 47; 23:5; 28:26–27), and James (15:16–18) quote Scripture.[215] Even before the Sanhedrin, those quoting Scripture are the Jerusalem apostles (4:11), Stephen (7:2–53), and Paul (23:5)—not the Sanhedrin itself. In Acts, then, Jesus's movement carries the primary voice of Scripture, for its adversaries fail to mount convincing arguments from it or accurately hear God's voice in it (28:26–27).

d. Extending Biblical History

Through his promise-fulfillment motif, Luke presents "his story of Jesus and of Christian beginnings" as "a prolongation of biblical history."[216] Kenneth Litwak contends, "Luke ties his narrative to the Scriptures of Israel. Luke-Acts forms the continuation of the history of God's salvific acts and the outworking of the divine plan, to which the Scriptures of Israel witness."[217] Stephen's speech in Acts 7 is the longest survey of salvation history in Luke-Acts, and offers insight into Luke's agenda: Jesus and the experience of the church (7:37, 51–52) continue and climax earlier biblical experience, a living experience of God's activity in the present (cf. 2:17–18).

Many elements of Luke's style suggest some continuity with biblical history, but some of these may simply characterize the salvation-historical reporting style of

211. On its realized eschatology, see Aune, *Cultic Setting*.

212. For extant, though post-Lukan, evidence for such polemic, see the discussion in Keener, *John*, 194–214.

213. The initial and dominant voice of opposition quoting Scripture starts, in fact, with the devil's out-of-context use in Luke 4:10–11 (contrasting with Jesus's contextual use in 4:4, 8, 12). Granted, a scribe can quote Scripture wisely (10:27), but he is not really antagonistic (cf. 10:28); crowds quote it, but as the adulation of disciples (19:37–38).

214. Philip is not cited as quoting in Acts 8:32–33, but he explains it (8:35).

215. Beyond this are all the Scripture arguments that are mentioned but not directly quoted, e.g., those of Apollos (Acts 18:28) and Paul (28:23) and global citations (e.g., 3:18, 21, 24; 10:43; 13:27; 24:14; 26:22, 27).

216. Johnson, *Acts*, 12; also Smith, "Gospels," 8–14. Litwak, *Echoes*, in fact, argues that (32) Luke's primary application of Scripture was not proof from prophecy "but to show continuity between the events recorded in the Scriptures and the events surrounding Jesus and his first followers."

217. Litwak, *Echoes*, 206. Some earlier Greek historians (like Thucydides and Xenophon) envisioned their narratives as picking up where their predecessors left off (Darbo-Peschanski, "Origin," 33–34; Brown, *Historians*, 91–92; see comment regarding later historians below).

someone steeped in the LXX.[218] The promise-fulfillment motif, by contrast, might suggest that Luke places on the biblical level the events he narrates—primarily in Jesus but also in the apostolic mission (e.g., Acts 1:16–20; 2:16–21; presumably he anticipates this continuing in the church's activity until Christ returns).[219] Likewise, some scholars contend that he takes up OT themes to complete, in a sense, the OT story.[220] If "complete" sounds too strong (as if implying the exclusion of other compatible stories [cf. Luke 1:1] that might also complete the biblical metanarrative), scholars today generally at least agree that Luke embeds the Pauline story in Jesus's story, and both in the story of Israel.[221] As Rosner puts it:

> Whether or not Luke saw himself as writing Scripture, the evidence of this chapter indicates that Acts is integrally related to the Scriptures regarded by Jews as normative and not simply a document brought into an artificial relation with the Old Testament by the later Christian Church.[222]

The Dead Sea Scrolls show that not everyone accepted the idea of a "closed canon,"[223] and some early Christian writers may have believed they were continuing the OT story in authoritative ways for their particular audiences. This does not necessarily mean that Luke sees himself as writing Scripture in the sense that he would anticipate all Christians accepting his work as "canonical."[224] It is not at all clear that he would have regarded his work or a select group of works including his as the final word (a new "closed canon") on the matters he covers. (It is likewise not surprising that some later Christian historians, like Luke, whom they emulate, start their local salvation histories where the currently accepted canonical histories leave off.[225] Yet such extensions of biblical history in no way necessarily implied extending the canon.)

Nevertheless, he undoubtedly did envision his work as true, authoritative, and useful as a history for the parts of the church where it would circulate, as perhaps the most useful of many efforts (cf. Luke 1:1–3). Given his pervasive emphasis on the Spirit's empowerment to present the gospel (e.g., Acts 1:8), he probably also believes that he is writing inspired history like earlier biblical historians.[226] And

218. E.g., the retellings within Luke-Acts; see Maloney, *Narration of Works*, 190 (see, e.g., the sample report in Luke 24:33–35 [pp. 37–41]).

219. More often, however, events of the interim time simply reflect patterns and principles: prophesied persecution of Jesus (Acts 4:25–28) was applicable also to his agents (4:29); Jesus's mission as the servant (8:32–33; cf. Luke 4:18) is applicable to his agents (Acts 13:47); rejection of the word continued to apply (7:51; 28:25–27).

220. Rosner, "Biblical History," 82.

221. See, e.g., Green, "Problem of Beginning"; Moessner and Tiede, "Introduction," 2; Moessner, "Poetics," 114; Gaventa, *Acts*, 51; and esp. Kurz, "Promise and Fulfillment"; for a survey of views, see Green and McKeever, *Historiography*, 45–46.

222. Rosner, "Biblical History," 82. Although doubting that Luke sees himself as writing Scripture, Walaskay, *Acts*, 6–7, suggests that Luke imitates "biblical Greek" in much of his work to draw attention to the events he narrates that fulfill biblical promises.

223. 1QM XV, 5–6 may use a scriptural quotation formula for an extrabiblical text, but this is uncertain (the text is reconstructed).

224. See the cautions in Witherington, *Acts*, 35–39, who emphasizes Acts' genre as Hellenistic history.

225. See, e.g., James, "God Came to England," 18 (on Bede); Smith, "Wide Angles," 20 (on medieval chroniclers). Luke did not begin this practice; centuries before him, Xen. *Hell.* 1.1.1 shows that one historian could pick up where another left off.

226. On "inspired histories," see esp. Hall, *Histories*, 171–208. Gentile historians, too, could claim to write at divine initiative (Dio Cass. 73.23, in Matthews, "Emperor and Historians," 295). For a more detailed argument than here, cf. Keener, *John*, 115–22, on the probability that the writer of the Fourth Gospel believed that work to be a form of inspired historical biography. Polyb. 29.21.7, 9 speaks of a treatise so accurate that it was prophetically inspired, but this may be hyperbole.

he sees the events he describes as the climax of salvation history to which other events pointed.

Luke's use of Scripture allows him to emphasize the antiquity of the faith (i.e., the true faith of Israel proclaimed by prophets and apostles) and hence serves the apologetic function noted above in chapter 5.[227] It also allows him to justify, from Israel's heritage, ideas controversial among his Jewish contemporaries, especially that of moving beyond that heritage (7:48–50) and bringing salvation for the Gentiles (cf. 2:17, 39; 13:47).[228] Complaints of Luke's antinomianism, though less frequent than complaints about Paul's, are equally misplaced in both cases (see comment on Acts 16:3; 18:18). The new phase in salvation history invites a new approach to the law's intention, not a rejection of its value.[229]

e. Luke's Typological Application

Luke rereads Israel's history in a manner that differs starkly from many readings of his contemporaries. Luke's "revisionism," however, develops elements within the biblical tradition itself. Although Luke favorably views some patriarchs,[230] he mostly avoids whitewashing their faults in the biblical record,[231] and he sometimes emphasizes a history of often rejecting God's commandments[232] and deliverers that makes the rejection of Jesus more understandable.[233]

i. Finding Narrative Patterns

One primary approach to biblical application in Luke-Acts is typological.[234] Indeed, if the arguments offered in Acts are an indication (see esp. Acts 7), patterns in salvation history probably constituted a major part of the tradition of biblical interpretation that Luke claims the apostolic church received from Jesus (Luke 24:27, 32, 44–45).

Typological patterns need not imply allegorization of earlier biblical narratives in the modern sense of "allegory."[235] In fact, most ancient "allegory" did not assume the radical polyvalence of narratives. Usually allegory did assume that selected narratives

227. See also Witherington, *Acts*, 44.

228. Cf., e.g., Steyn, *Septuagint Quotations*, 243, 248; Pervo, "Heritage and Claims," 142–43.

229. For Luke and the law, see, e.g., the discussion in Bovon, *Studies*, 59–73.

230. As Dionysius offers encomium on ancestors (Balch, "Genre," 16).

231. Compare the haggadic whitewash at some points in works such as *Jubilees* and *Testaments of the Twelve Patriarchs* (see the discussion of haggadic whitewash in ch. 4, sect. 2.c).

232. Already present in the text (e.g., Lev 26:43; Judg 2:17; 2 Kgs 17:13–15; Neh 9:29, 34; Jer 44:10; Ezek 5:6; 20:13, 16, 24; Amos 2:4; Zech 1:6; Mal 3:7).

233. Such an approach to history does not mean that Luke invents the stories in Acts to fit the patterns (*pace* some of Goulder's arguments), any more than he invented the OT accounts where he finds the patterns. Rather, he shapes them in light of shared elements, as he shaped his Gospel's passion narrative while evoking biblical parallels (with, e.g., Marshall, "Acts," 525). Had Acts been primarily an extended midrashic composition, we would not find the abundant historical connections we do, and the genre involved would resemble some traditional Jewish works unlike Luke's Greco-Roman historiography (see Keener, *John*, 25–29). Luke-Acts rewrites the history of Jesus and part of his movement in light of patterns he finds in Scripture; he is not simply rewriting Scripture and inventing new stories to do so (Marshall, "Acts," 525, with Evans, "Function," 70n4).

234. I am not using this term in the narrower sense of Bock, *Proclamation*, 50, who distinguishes between analogy and typology. Especially if one reads the term "typology" as being a deliberate foreshadowing or prophecy, "typology" may not offer the ideal description for the patterns that Luke presents.

235. Jeremias, *Parables*, 69, thinks Luke "more restrained in his use of allegory" in parable interpretations than is Matthew (though *pace* Jeremias they are not secondary; see Johnston, "Interpretations," 561–62, 565–66, 638; Vermes, *Religion*, 92–99; Keener, *Matthew*, 381–84; cf. Stern, *Parables in Midrash*, 24; Snodgrass, *Stories*, 34–35). Allegory is missing in Luke's range of interpretive approaches (Marshall, "Acts," 520). Also relevant for Luke's narrative patterns, Roman historians saw patterns in history; see, e.g., Schnabel, "Reading Acts," 261 (citing Tac. *Ann.* 6.51.2); more extensively, Trompf, *Historical Recurrence*; and our introduction, ch. 16. Biblical allusions and patterns need not imply fictionalization (Allison, *Jesus*, 389).

were mythical representations of moral or natural truths,[236] but sometimes interpreters "allegorized" simply by drawing principles from patterns in their texts.[237] Apart from the question of "allegory," writers often drew analogies with known texts for rhetorical, illustrative, or explanatory purposes.[238] Sometimes historians used earlier figures in their narratives to foreshadow later ones.[239]

Noting patterns within a cohesive literary work is simply sound narrative analysis. Ironies in the book of Esther, for example, appear too clear to be accidental:

Xerxes divorces Vashti for refusing to come (Esth 1:12, 19)	Xerxes forgives Esther for coming unbidden (Esth 5:2)
Vashti lost favor at a banquet (1:3, 12)	Esther was installed at one banquet (2:18) and received favor at another (5:6)
Haman is hanged on Mordecai's gallows (7:10; 8:7)	Mordecai obtains Haman's job (8:2, 7, 15; 9:4)

(For examples of patterns in pentateuchal texts, see the commentary's discussion of Acts 7.) Where ancient readers approached the text differently from modern ones was by treating all of Scripture as a cohesive work and sometimes by viewing the patterns as normative (or at least suggestive) for subsequent events. Writers of Israel's Scripture themselves often followed earlier patterns in Scripture or tradition as models; for example, crossing the sea in Exod 14 "provides the pattern that structures" the Jordan crossing in Josh 3–4, as Josh 3:7 makes explicit.[240]

Finding such patterns did not, however, mean that most Jewish interpreters (even Philo) treated biblical narratives as pure symbols, the way some Stoics salvaged Homer.[241] Historians also extrapolated lessons from historical narratives, as already noted, without thereby assuming that the narratives they recounted (with the occasional exception of the distant past) were purely mythical codes without genuine historical merit. Most Jewish interpreters accepted most of biblical history as authentic history (some educated Diaspora Jews excepting some embarrassing passages)[242] even while preaching from patterns they found there. The earliest Christian writers seem to have followed suit (e.g., 1 Cor 10:6, 11; Gal 4:24),[243] and we would expect the same from Luke, who provides morals in his story yet presents it as historical narrative.

236. On ancient allegory, see, e.g., *Rhet. Her.* 4.34.46; Cancik-Lindemaier et al., "Allegoresis." Especially among philosophers, e.g., Plato *Laws* 1.636CD; 2.672BC; 7.822AC; 10.899E–900; 12.941B; Cic. *Nat. d.* 2.28.70 (Stoics); Sen. Y. *Ep. Lucil.* 88.5; Cornutus *Summ.* 19 (Lang, 33, line 14), in Grant, *Religions*, 78–79; Porph. *Marc.* 33.515–16; as well as among orators with philosophic inclinations (e.g., Dio Chrys. *Or.* 1.62–63; 8.33; 60.8; Max. Tyre 4.5–8; 26.8–9; 38.4); see also gnostics (e.g., Iren. *Her.* 1.18). Some Jews also used it (esp. Philo, e.g., *Worse* 15; *Posterity* 7; *Plant.* 36, 129; *Good Person* 82; *Dreams* 1.102; *Names* 255; *Jos.* 148; *Alleg. Interp.* 1–3; Wolfson, *Philo*, 1:87–163; Kamesar, "*Endiathetos*"); it was less emphasized among the rabbis (cf., e.g., *Gen. Rab.* 53:10; 64:9); among medieval rabbis, cf. Jacobs, *Exegesis*, 2, 13–14.

237. Cf. Max. Tyre 26.5, 9; the range of usage in Anderson, *Glossary*, 14–16. Even Gal 4:24 may be closer to what we call "typology" (cf. Hays, *Echoes*, 56, 116, 166; Tronier, "Spørgsmålet"; or even sarcasm, Anderson, *Rhetorical Theory*, 177–79); for the distinction, see Thiselton, *Corinthians*, 730.

238. E.g., Dion. Hal. *Lit. Comp.* 4; *Anc. Or.* passim. Cf. Soards, *Speeches*, 201–2, who argues that many biblical quotations in Acts' speeches are not cited as predictions but to "clarify the meaning of the present in terms of God's own purposes."

239. For Dionysius of Halicarnassus, see Balch, "Genre," 14–16, esp. 16.

240. Hays, *Echoes*, 101.

241. E.g., Murray, *Stages*, 202; Ferguson, *Backgrounds*, 98. Jews also recognized this function of Greek allegory (Jos. *Ag. Ap.* 2.255).

242. Philo complained about those who went too far, especially in abandoning literal practice of the kashrut (see, e.g., Hay, "Extremism," on Philo *Migr.* 89–93; Wolfson, *Philo*, 1:57–68). Rhetoricians also warned against excessive use that obscured clarity (Dion. Hal. *Demosth.* 5), and some patristic exegetes tended toward the literal approach (Pelagius *Comm. 2 Cor.* 3; especially most Antiochene patristic exegesis, as in, e.g., Kepple, "Analysis").

243. Apart from a midrash of Gen 14:18–20 based on Ps 110:4, even Hebrews restricts typology mainly to the tabernacle (cf. Philo *Mos.* 2.76), on the basis of an older Jewish interpretive tradition and an assumed

Luke, like his Jewish and Christian contemporaries, understood biblical narratives as well as more explicit prophecies as prophetically inspired.[244] If the biblical prophets pointed to Israel's ultimate hope of restoration especially with regard to the messianic era (Acts 3:18), one could justify reading the biblical story as leading toward that goal. Thus Luke does not simply provide proof from direct prophecy; he uses the Scriptures to provide theological context for the events he narrates.[245] Patterns that revealed consistent ways that God had dealt with Israel and Israel had often dealt with God, the sorts of deliverers God used, and so forth, could all suggest the way the ultimate and ideal deliverance would take place.

Some scholars even suggest that Luke draws parallels between how reliable characters interpret Scripture in his two volumes. Charles Talbert suggests seven such parallels:[246]

Jesus as Interpreter in the Gospel	Believers as Interpreters in Acts
Scripture predicts John as preparing the way (Mal 3:1, in Luke 7:27)	Scripture predicts John as preparing the way (18:24–28)
Jesus fulfills biblical promises (e.g., 4:18–19; 20:17)	Jesus fulfills biblical promises (e.g., 3:22–26; 4:11; 10:43; 13:23; 17:2–3, 11; 28:23)
Jesus's death and exaltation fulfill Scripture (e.g., 9:22; 18:31–33; 22:37; 24:7, 25–27, 32, 44–49)	Jesus's death and exaltation fulfill Scripture (e.g., 2:25–28; 3:18; 8:32–35; 13:27, 33–35; 17:2–3; 26:22–23)
Jewish rejection fulfills Scripture (20:17)	Jewish rejection fulfills Scripture (4:11; 13:27, 40–41; 28:25–27)
Scripture had promised the Spirit (24:46, 49; Acts 1:4, 8)	Scripture had promised the Spirit (2:16–21)
Scripture promised the Gentile mission (24:46–47; cf. 4:25–27)	Scripture promised the Gentile mission (13:47)
Scripture promises that the dead will be raised (20:37)	Scripture promises that the dead will be raised (24:14–15; 26:6–8)

In fact, Acts 18:24–28 (and even 13:24–25) does not tie John to Scripture fulfillment. Although the other examples have better textual support, it is not clear whether Luke deliberately connects Jesus's interpretation with his followers' interpretation in any one-to-one correspondence; he may simply raise the themes pervasively, whenever possible. Nevertheless, the line of continuity is clear, since it is Jesus who, after the resurrection, helped his followers to understand these promises in Scripture (Luke 24:25–27, 32, 44–49).[247]

II. Comparing Pesher and Character Types

Understanding these texts retroactively in light of the events that the early Christians had experienced (Luke 1:1; Acts 2:16–18; 10:43; 26:26) would have seemed no more unusual than earlier Israelites' so understanding prophecies they believed fulfilled in their day; or the Qumran sect with its pesher interpretations; or Josephus's understanding the abomination of desolation as having occurred in his era. On the premise that the events they narrated (especially the deliverer's resurrection) had

---

exegesis of Exod 25:9 (which could have made sense in the ancient Near East; cf. Harrelson, *Cult*, 4–5; Clifford, "Tent," 226; though cf. Spieckermann, "Stadtgott"). Later the *Epistle of Barnabas* is far less restrained. "Allegory" (cf. Gal 4:24) could include simpler comparisons as well as reduce narratives to symbols (cf. the range of usage in Anderson, *Glossary*, 14–16).

244. See sources in Keener, *Spirit*, 13; and some additional sources in comment on Acts 2:17–18.
245. See Arnold, "Use of Old Testament in Acts," 321; Evans, "Prophecy and Polemic," 209–11.
246. Talbert, *Acts*, 77–78.
247. With Talbert, *Acts*, 78.

taken place,[248] a retroactive christological hermeneutic for the prophets and salvation history made sense.[249] Luke's christological hermeneutic is more grounded in the biblical story's actual salvation-historical patterns (see discussion on Acts 7:37 and passim in Acts 7) than the sometimes wildly allegorizing christological hermeneutic of some later patristic and medieval interpreters, but it is christological nonetheless.[250] Early Jews and Christians apparently shared similar procedures for reading; it was not usually techniques that differed but the "interpretive grid."[251]

If some offered pesher readings based on the presence of the time of eschatological fulfillment (see, more fully, comment on Acts 2:16), Jesus and his first followers who believed that they stood on the threshold of the time of eschatological fulfillment may have responded accordingly. That the Messiah had already come would be a controlling exegetical presupposition for those who believed it; one could read the promise in light of the fulfillment.[252] We should remember, however, that Luke's thematic use of Isaiah shows that even when he uses types or prophecies, Luke is interested in the broader story.[253]

Educated ancient readers were familiar with the notion of literary character types (see, e.g., Theophrastus's *Characters*), and Luke uses some obvious ones. He often uses the OT narrative pattern of the rejected prophet, for example, in Stephen's ministry.[254] He uses various earlier biblical models for Jesus's ministry and (by his parallel-lives structure; see ch. 16 below) makes Jesus an important grid for the Jerusalem church at Pentecost, for Stephen, and, more fully, for Peter and Paul.

Some ancient Jewish hermeneutical approaches seem arbitrary to most modern readers[255] and often appear anachronistic and lacking in historical perspective.[256] Some of these conventional interpretive methods, such as *gezerah shevah*, appear only rarely

248. Jervell, *Unknown Paul*, 122–37, sees Jesus's death and resurrection as the climax, for Luke, of "all" that the prophets had spoken.

249. Some today argue that the practices of the interpretive community can justify approaches such as Luke's (cf., e.g., McCracken, "Interpretation").

250. Luke's approach is not surprising; historians in general could use earlier figures to foreshadow later ones, including a king (Balch, "Genre," 16).

251. See Bock, "Scripture and the Realisation of Promises," 43–44. Enns, "Interpretation," also sees a "Christocentric" hermeneutic in light of Jewish interpretive conventions of the era. Today, cf., e.g., the nuanced but theologically grounded "hermeneutic of trust" in Hays, *Conversion*, 190–201.

252. Cf. Longenecker, *Exegesis*, 95, for messianic presence as an exegetical presupposition; Black, "Christological Use," for Qumran's pesher hermeneutic as a background for NT christological interpretation. Indeed, the point of all midrash was "to make yesterday's text (which is the word of God for all time) meaningful and nourishing for today" (Wright, "Midrash," 133–34). Alexander, "This Is That," argues that Luke reads Scripture flexibly, as through the grid of Christian experience in the Cornelius narrative. Luke also sometimes reads ecclesiocentrically, an approach also fitting a perspective of eschatological fulfillment (on ecclesiocentric readings in Paul, albeit dependent on his Christology, see, e.g., Hays, *Conversion*, 187).

253. Pao, *Isaianic Exodus*, 251.

254. See Denova, *Things Accomplished*, 162, 167–68.

255. This could include differentiating parallel lines (*m. 'Abot* 4:1; *Sipre Deut.* 313.1.4; cf. Keener, *Matthew*, 491); harmonizing, even earlier rabbinic opinions (*y. Sukkah* 4:6, §1); and reading "sons" as either masculine or inclusive, depending on the interpreter's needs (e.g., *y. Ber.* 2:2, §5). When two passages contradict, a third can be invoked to arbitrate (*Beraita de Rabbi Ishmael pq.* 1.7; cf. *Gen. Rab.* 15:2). These later rabbis believed that there was greater meaning in the Torah than was available in the text itself (Levine, "Letters," on *b. Menaḥ.* 29b; cf. Sandmel, *Judaism*, 247–48). The strong contrast between literal and "deeper" senses, though, becomes explicit only in medieval texts (Reif, "Review," 157–58), and sometimes rabbis preferred the literal sense (e.g., *Gen. Rab.* 53:10). For some comparisons (and contrasts) with earlier Qumran exegesis, see, e.g., Mandel, "Exegesis"; Slomovic, "Understanding"; Vermes, "Interpretation"; for comparisons with patristic exegesis, see Hruby, "Exégèse"; comparisons with the NT abound (e.g., Miller, "Targum"; Longenecker, *Exegesis*, 32–38).

256. E.g., the ancient Sanhedrin (*y. Sanh.* 7:5, §5; *Tg. Ruth* 4:1, 4; *Tg. 1 Chr.* 18:17; *Tg. Qoh.* 2:10; *Tg. Rishon* on Esth 2:21); synagogues (*Lam. Rab.* proem 2); patriarchs keeping hours of prayer (*b. Yoma* 28b); ancient heroes as rabbis with disciples (*b. Mak.* 23b; *Num. Rab.* 15:16). Cf. Patte, *Hermeneutic*, 67–68.

in Luke's work and may reflect his sources (see comment on Acts 13:34).[257] But while this method, usually used to connect key words, is rare in Luke's narratives, his method of connecting characters is more characteristic of his interpretive activity; see discussion at Acts 7, especially 7:9–16. (One might compare also the fairly free handling of biblical texts in Josephus and other Hellenistic Jewish writers, as noted briefly in ch. 4 above.[258] Such writers commonly reframed the biblical message in a context more intelligible to hellenized readers. But Luke seems to adapt the stories far less than Josephus; see, for example, comment on Acts 7:20–22.)

Conclusion

Far from being anti-Jewish as some have argued, Luke respects the Jewish people and maintains hope for their future. Nevertheless Luke, like Paul, expresses dismay that large numbers of Jewish people have rejected what he regards as God's current agenda in salvation history.

Particularly relevant for understanding Luke's theological perspective is his approach to Scripture. In arguing that the Gentile mission was a legitimate extension of Israel's faith, Luke presents the biblical heritage positively, emphasizing continuity with this heritage wherever possible. He finds discontinuity only where necessary and where confirmed by clear divine sanction (from the biblical God of Israel), such as the divinely arranged meeting between Philip and the African treasurer or the corresponding visions to Cornelius and Peter. Luke finds in Israel's Scripture both promises and patterns fulfilled in his own day. For him, the ministry of Jesus, the Jesus movement, and the Gentile mission climax and continue the biblical story in his own day.

257. On *gezerah shevah*, see comments in Keener, *John*, 305, 1184; on *qal vaomer*, see Keener, *John*, 716–17, 742, 829, 931, 1184.

258. E.g., Borgen, "Reviewing and Rewriting"; the many articles by Feldman, Begg, and others (see this commentary's "Works Cited" for a sample).

15

SOME LUKAN EMPHASES

Most scholars agree that Luke was theologian as well as historian, regardless of where their own primary academic interests or emphases lie.[1] Indeed, these approaches must overlap considerably in Luke-Acts, since Luke's theology is a narrative theology depicting a God who acts in history. As noted in chapter 5 above, ancient historiography typically included various agendas, which could be moral, political, and/or theological, among others. In Acts Luke chooses the form of a historical monograph to articulate his theology and articulates it (as any writer or speaker must do) in language- and history-specific ways. But we can also isolate a significant number of Lukan themes, emphases that, by emphatic language or repetition, emerge in the larger context of Luke-Acts.

The themes that commentators emphasize often reflect the interests of the era in which they write as well as those that dominate in the texts on which they comment. When I teach Luke-Acts, I focus on Lukan themes that recur most frequently, raising them as we first come to them in the text. Because this is a commentary, I will also reserve most comment on Luke's theology for some of the texts that highlight this theology. (In some cases such comment will require extended treatment in an excursus, where the subject has commanded recent interest or involves many sources; in other cases I will simply emphasize the many Lukan texts addressing the theme.) Some other themes I have had to address elsewhere in the introduction; for example, although this chapter addresses Luke's theology of signs, much material about signs was necessarily relegated to chapter 9 above, on signs and historiography. Likewise, discussion of Luke's theology is inseparable from discussion of Acts' purpose, to which chapters 13 and 14 were devoted. Here I will not repeat most of the work covered elsewhere in this introduction, allowing this chapter to be more concise than it might otherwise be.

In introducing some of Luke's emphases here, however, I am focusing not so much on themes that are merely dominant but on those that seem to me to require special

---

1. E.g., Marshall, "Luke as Theologian"; idem, *Historian and Theologian*; Strelan, *Artemis*, 22; Neil, *Acts*, 18–22; Martin, *Foundations*, 53–56; Tuckett, *Luke*, 13–14; Arrington, *Acts*, xxxvii; Green, "History/Writing"; Hotze, "Zeugen"; Marguerat, *Histoire*, 28–29, 36–37, 42, 59–63, esp. 91; Miller, *Empowered for Mission*, 34–38; Eckey, *Apostelgeschichte*; Rothschild, *Rhetoric of History*, 59, 295; Osborne, "History and Theology" (on the Gospels); Shauf, *Theology*; Schröter, "Stellung," 47. Likewise, in a context of accusations against the Christian movement, Luke's legal apologetic would necessarily include theological interests (see Mauck, *Trial*, 22). For recent bibliography on Luke's theology, see now Schröter, "Actaforschung 5," and studies, noted below, surrounding particular aspects of this theology; see also sources in Grässer, *Forschungen*, 128–33, 270–85.

comment yet are not addressed more fully under one of the texts in which they appear.[2] I have treated some themes already, such as Luke's perspective on salvation history (through the story of Israel and Jesus) and the relationship between the Gentile mission and the heritage of Israel (the Gentile mission is addressed in other respects below). Because this commentary's focus is on social-historical context (albeit not exclusively), the approach where it can make the fullest distinctive contribution, I will try to approach the theological questions with this context as well.

Luke's distinctive, frequent interests that this commentary treats elsewhere include, for example, the participation of women in his narrative (see ch. 18 below); prayer (see comment on Acts 1:14); themes such as possessions and care for the poor and marginalized (see discussion esp. at Acts 2:44–45, and brief treatment below on Luke's introduction to the Gentile mission, sect. 3.a.i; some background at Acts 3:2); baptism and repentance (see comment on Acts 2:38); worship and community (see comments on Acts 2:42, 46–47); the church (see comments on Acts 2:41–47; 12:12–13);[3] the role of the temple and the land (comments on Acts 2:46; Acts 6–7); and divine deliverance (passim). This chapter, however, is reserved mostly for important themes not treated so extensively at these other points (such as the Gentile mission, the Spirit, and signs). (Readers interested in particular subjects may scan the index, though a commentary is not intended, and by its nature is not equipped, to provide a full-orbed Lukan theology.)

1. What Is Lukan "Theology"?

As noted in chapter 5 above, the *Tendenz* of ancient documents reveals a range of ideological commitments, including "theological" (in the narrower sense) and "political" elements. Commentators who look for themes generally seek to explore the range of these perspectives, whether "theology" in the narrower sense, or "ideology" or "perspectives" more broadly (what scholars often mean by texts' "theology"). The broader use of "theology," of course, includes the narrower sense, but it is important to be clear about which we have in mind. (This chapter surveys some of both.)

If by "theology" we mean Luke's understanding of God,[4] there is not a pericope that, in light of the whole work that forms its context, fails to exude this concern. If

---

2. By not devoting more space to "theology" in this introduction, I am not diminishing its importance. For many, including myself, Luke's work is part of the canon of Scripture, and even for those with purely historical interest, one cannot claim to study any ancient writer purely philologically while ignoring his or her message. This is, however, especially a social-historical commentary, not a thematic summary of Luke's message, and I include in the introduction primarily the global issues that inform the reading of the text from those perspectives. Informed readers of Acts as Scripture (including myself) will read and reread Acts, absorbing its themes; in my role as a preacher and a teacher of seminarians, I focus on such themes. But others have summarized and elaborated these themes extensively elsewhere (see esp. Marshall and Peterson, *Witness*) or offered commentary from that perspective (e.g., Gaventa, *Acts*, for which I expressed appreciation in Keener, "Review of Gaventa"; cf. also Peterson, *Acts*, and my favorable review in Keener, "Review of Peterson"). I have focused on making a contribution that is not easily possible for those who have not specialized in ancient extrabiblical sources, and hence even my treatment of Luke's themes generally addresses this context.

3. For more focused studies on areas of Lukan ecclesiology that I have not treated, see, e.g., Villemin, "Ecclésiologie"; Thompson, *Church*; Leonardi, "Ecclesiologia"; Peterson, *Acts*, 92–97; Twelftree, *People*; for earlier studies relevant to ecclesiology in Acts, see Mattill and Mattill, *Bibliography*, 283–88, §§3941–4007; 294–96, §§4100–4141. A major "ecclesiological" issue for earliest Christian ecclesiology (in contrast to the later Gentile Christianity) was the question of the relationship of Gentile converts to the remnant of Israel (see discussion at Acts 15, including 15:20).

4. This was also the pre-Christian Middle Platonic and later Neoplatonic sense of "theology" (cf., e.g., Philo *Creation* 12; *Mos.* 2.115; *Rewards* 53; Men. Rhet. 2.17, 438.14; 443.2; Iambl. *V.P.* 28.145–47; cf. Jos.

we define theology in the broader, traditional Christian way as examining particular traditional categories of Christian beliefs, however, we run the risk of forcing Luke's evidence into molds not designed for it.[5] That is, the contours of Luke's message examined inductively do not coincide precisely with such traditional categories. This is not to say, for example, that Luke has no interest in, or relevance for, "hamartiology"; from Judas to Ananias and Sapphira to the enemies of the gospel, the vested economic interests of Philippian slaveholders and cultic artisans profiting from Ephesian paganism, and the corrupt, bribe-seeking governor Felix, the narrative is full of examples instructive for hamartiology.

But if we look for Luke's own themes inductively, highlighted at foundational points (e.g., Acts 1:8) or defended by him citing Scripture, we will more readily emphasize, for example, the Gentile mission, a matter crucial for salvation history but less obvious through the lens of traditional medieval categories. "Possessions" are a crucial theme in Luke-Acts[6] yet do not belong to one of the traditional categories. Definitions are therefore important.

a. Theology Proper

Luke parallels Jesus, Peter, and Paul (and to a lesser extent Stephen), though obviously not on the same level (Jesus trains Peter and converts Paul, and they act in his name). But throughout Acts, the dominant character behind the scenes (and frequently in them) is God.[7] God even has speaking parts, though often the message is conveyed through Jesus, angels, prophecy from the Holy Spirit, or the recitation of God's message in the gospel.[8] Elsewhere he often remains the silent presupposition unspoken in the background, driving the plot that, of all the characters, only he comprehends in full detail, perhaps like a sort of implicit omniscient narrator active within the story.[9]

Ag. Ap. 1.78, 225, 237). Those who offered hymns in the imperial cult were apparently also called "theologians" (Deissmann, *Light*, 348–49; Smith, *Symposium*, 117), a tradition preserved also in its Christian form in patristic sources (Deissmann, *Light*, 349, esp. on Euseb. *H.E.* 5.28.5).

5. Lukan scholars readily recognize that Luke is not writing systematic theology (e.g., Jervell, *Apostelgeschichte*, 91; Malina and Pilch, *Acts*, 10). For one thoughtful discussion of the meaning of documents' "theology" and the applicability to a historical work like Acts, see Shauf, *Theology*, 38–53, 285. Part of Acts' "theology" or message, for example, is its presentation of Paul (ibid., 290); cf. our discussion of an apologetic for Paul in this introduction, ch. 7, sect. 1.a.

6. See most fully Johnson, *Function*; idem, *Sharing Possessions*.

7. See Gaventa, *Acts*, 27–44 (esp. 28–31); Wall, "Acts," 18–20; Walton, "Acts," 30–31; idem, "Acts of God"; Bock, *Acts*, 33–34, 769; Wenham and Walton, *Guide*, 307–8; on "the God of Acts," see, e.g., Doohan, *Acts*, 87–93; Karris, *Saying*, 49–58; Langner, *Hechos*, 47; Chhuanliana, "Theocentricity" (including an example of contextualization); extensively Marguerat, *Histoire*, 119–48; Bock, *Theology*, 108–28. Schwartz, "Maccabees and Acts," 129, compares 2 Maccabees' portrayal of God's involvement (in contrast to 1 Maccabees). For one recent careful study on Luke's understanding of God (God's fatherhood in Luke's Gospel), see Chen, "Father"; idem, *Father*. She notes that in response to Dahl, "Factor," NT theology has somewhat redressed its prior neglect of the subject of God (Chen, *Father*, 1, 240; but see also the survey she cites in Bovon, "Studies").

8. The OT and early Christian texts regularly employ the masculine pronoun for God (perhaps partly for linguistic reasons; masculine was a default grammatical gender for mixed plurals, and by now the Jewish traditional divine pronoun, and so we need not infer much theological weight from the selection of a particular gender by those writing in the Hebrew or Greek language). In following this use descriptively for Luke's divine language (partly because avoiding pronouns for God is cumbersome and the alternatives raise additional problems), I am not implying that I think that readers today should imagine God in gender-specific (hence biological) terms or even that Luke would have made such an assumption.

9. Burridge, "Genre of Acts," 15, warns that God is the subject of "only 3% of Acts' verbs," and that is after including Jesus and the Holy Spirit (cf. also 13–15). God appears as grammatical subject primarily in proclaimers' speeches. Nevertheless, Luke does emphasize some of his key theological themes in the speeches.

I. The God of All Humanity

Luke portrays a God active in challenging human biases and promoting the Gentile mission.[10] Thus, for example, God arranges for the witness to the African court official through an angel, the leading of the Spirit, the providential reading of the witness of appropriate Scripture, and an open heart (Acts 8:26–34). He arranges a persecutor's conversion, confirms Paul's calling to Gentiles, and mandates the acceptance of an uncircumcised Roman officer's purity through double, coinciding visions (9:3–16; 10:3–20).

More explicitly, God shows no ethnic partiality (10:34, adapting a common ancient theological theme). Unlike idols, God is a "living God" (14:15; 17:29), whom pagans should recognize as Creator and benevolent sustainer of creation (14:15–17; 17:24). In contrast to the practices of pagan religion, God does not need temples or anything from humans, who are themselves his creation, like other creatures (17:24–25). (Ironically, Israel also needs this reminder [7:48–50].)

God is gracious in Christ; his message of salvation is a message of grace, of unearned benefaction (20:24, 32; cf. 2:39).[11] God loves Israel and keeps his promises to his people (3:25–26; 24:14–15; 26:6–8; earlier, 7:17). God has not left humanity to wander in its ignorance but made them in his image, to be his children; he has therefore blessed them with the message of Christ as an opportunity to turn to him (17:27–30). Nor is God unconcerned with their response; he summons humanity to turn to him (14:15; 17:30; 20:21; 26:20).

God graciously (i.e., generously) turns many to him unexpectedly, so that others recognize this turning as God's generous grace (11:19–23, esp. 11:23) and his gift (11:17–18); the way of Christ is the way of God's grace (13:43; 20:32). God opens the hearts of those who will embrace his message (16:14) and adds new believers to the church (2:47; cf. 5:14).[12] God graciously chooses even those who will be the witnesses (10:41), and his grace equips them (14:26; 15:40; 26:22). Sometimes he grants even more than what they need for their mission (27:24). The fruits of apostolic ministry are ultimately about what God himself has done (19:11), as the apostles themselves testify (14:27; 15:4, 12; 21:19).

God has acted to bring Gentiles into his people. He knows the hearts of all (1:24; 15:8), yet he confirms his acceptance of Gentiles (15:8), making no spiritual distinction between Jew and Gentile (15:9; cf. 10:34). God makes clear his guidance for the mission along the way (8:29; 16:10).[13]

II. The God of Salvation History[14]

Most obviously, God acts in history, climactically in relation to the mission of Christ. Although Stephen's speech in Acts 7 mentions multiple human characters, the pervasive protagonist is God (θεός appears sixteen times in the speech proper); Paul

10. God actively drives the Gentile mission in Acts, often in the face of his people's resistance, no less than in the book of Jonah. The books differ completely in plot and structure, but the relation between God and a Gentile mission drives the plot in both.

11. God showed benefaction earlier as well, as is characteristic of him—to Joseph (Acts 7:9), to David (7:46), and most generally to Israel (7:34, 45; 13:17)—but God also shows favor to Gentiles (10:4, 31) who respect him (10:2, 35). God's gift is clearly unearned and unpurchasable (8:20).

12. Some sectors of ancient Judaism accepted both God's sovereignty and human free will (see, e.g., Jos. *Ant.* 13.172–73; *Pss. Sol.* 9:4; *Sipre Deut.* 319.3.1; in more detail, Keener, *John*, 572–73); Acts likewise proclaims both God's sovereignty and his summons to repentance and obedience. To read later theological paradigms into the text is therefore not helpful; this is a case of both-and rather than either-or.

13. God overcomes human hostility and weaknesses; cf. Scholtus, "Problemas."

14. For scholars' approaches to God's control of history, see Powell, *Acts*, 39–40 (especially, but not exclusively, commenting on O'Toole, *Unity of Theology*).

emphasizes that David died after he fulfilled God's purpose for him for his generation (13:36).[15] God is the one who continues the work, despite his individual human agents' limitations and mortality.

For Luke, as for other early Christians, God was ultimately active especially in Christ. God was with Jesus in his benevolent ministry of healing and deliverance to humanity (10:38; Luke 4:18); Jesus is also the chief agent of grace (Acts 15:11). Christ's suffering was part of God's plan (2:23); his God is the God of earlier Scripture, who foretold these things (3:18, 21; cf. 13:23). God raised and exalted Christ (2:24, 32–36; 3:13; 5:30–31; 10:40; 13:30, 33), appointed him as judge for humanity (10:42; 17:31), and authorized him to pour out God's own Spirit (2:33).

To reject God's testimony is to put him to the test (15:10), as Israel of old had done; testing God or lying to him can have terrible consequences (5:4–5, 9–10). God can hand transgressors over to their own madness (7:42) or send other judgments (8:20–21). He can punish terribly those who usurp his role (12:22–23) and is angry with hypocrites who speak falsely in his name (23:3). The appropriate response to God's acts is praise (3:8–9; 4:21; 10:46; 21:20; cf. 15:3; 16:25; 28:15) and faith (16:34); those in need pray to him (12:5) and can trust his words (27:25, 35). God must also be obeyed (4:19; 5:29); humanity's rightful ruler, he summons obedience through the message of the kingdom (his rule), which will eventually be consummated (e.g., 1:3; 8:12; 19:8; 28:23, 31).

In this narrow sense, theology is a pervasive theme of Luke-Acts;[16] even when God is not speaking directly through the Spirit, God is at work behind the scenes to accomplish the divine purpose (see our discussion on theological perspectives in ancient histories, esp. in ch. 5). The very gospel is God's message (4:31; 6:2, 7; 8:14; 11:1), and the mission (5:39), including the Gentile mission (10:15, 28; 11:9, 17–18; 15:14, 19; see below), is God's agenda. Acts is thus God's book, though readers may identify more with the dominant human characters[17] through whom God often accomplishes the mission.

b. Emphases beyond Traditional "Theological" Categories

Use of the term "theology" can complicate our enterprise here if it risks semantic confusion with traditional "theological" categories. Luke's "theology" can refer narrowly to his teaching specifically about God. Biblical and systematic theologians, however, generally use the term "theology" more widely, the former for key emphases in a biblical writer or book and many of the latter for conventional theological categories established from medieval times (though today often for a broader range of categories).

Biblical theology can proceed by inductively seeking a biblical work's themes. If, closer to much NT theology than to most systematic theologians, we use the expression "theology" for the message that the implied biblical author communicated to the implied first-century audience, we are defining our quest for Luke's theology more in terms of inductive analysis of Acts than in terms of more standardized general

---

15. Whom God chooses to carry out a task is up to God (Acts 15:7; 22:14); whether one can fulfill one's plans is also up to God (18:21; though this is traditional language, in a deity-fearing world it was normally sincere). Those who promoted themselves rather than Jesus became false prophets (5:36–37; 8:9; 20:30; cf. Luke 21:8).

16. In Acts, note the special attention that Gaventa, *Acts*, regularly grants this important theme.

17. Apart from Scripture quotations, visions, and prophecies, these characters hold far more speaking parts, suiting the usual historiographic (or biographic) genre. The dominant actors in most scenes are human, but different actors cluster in different sections (e.g., Peter in Acts 1–5; 9–12; Paul in Acts 9; 13–28), with God as pervasively and consistently sovereign behind and above the scenes.

theological rubrics. Although Luke does display interests that fit within the confines of traditional theological categories, we must begin by acknowledging that such categories can by no means contain his interests.[18]

1. LUKE AS HISTORIAN

Luke's theology is not a traditional systematic theology; it may be understood, however, as a work of narrative theology. As noted in chapter 5 above, ancient Mediterranean historians had a *Tendenz* and often even communicated a picture of God active in history. (For some comments on Luke's theology of history, see this commentary's introduction to Acts 7.) At the same time, we must allow for what is distinctive to their genre, even if some modern existential scholars (in contrast to the salvation-historical approach) have considered such historical material relatively unimportant.

Luke is not always clear theologically or in other details. Scholars sometimes complain that Luke nuances theological debates less carefully than does Paul or Matthew (see comment on Acts 15:1). Some sayings that are clear in a Jewish setting in Matthew (e.g., Matt 23:26) become more obscure in Luke (e.g., Luke 11:41).[19] Sometimes he appears less clear on the nature of the Pharisees (16:14),[20] though his comments about them in 11:38, 45 seem more nuanced than the parallels in Matthew. But Luke writes biographical history, not a theological treatise; he argues by example rather than detailed linear argument, and his more generalized language at points does not detract from the point of his presentation.

Some of Luke's interests are primarily aesthetic and historical; often he provides geographic and chronological details of little direct relevance to modern homiletic or theological concerns. Modern interpreters may, of course, consider what we can learn "theologically" from such interests. His aesthetic interests may teach us, for example, that Luke appreciates good communicative strategies; his historical interests affirm that God acts in the concrete arena of time, space, and human flesh, where people live.

Some of Luke's geographic details evoke the world of his audience's Scriptures; others evoke the geographic horizons of the Greek world of their own or their host culture's ancestors. Luke contextualizes his message again within their world and blends the horizons of biblical history and contemporary response. (To some extent, the need to take this approach was predetermined by, as well as served by, the historical genre he chose.) In the very process of abstracting these principles, modern interpreters sometimes risk silencing, to a degree, Luke's own communicative strategies.[21]

We cannot separate Luke's theology from his historiography as easily as modern scholars are sometimes apt to do. The pure "theology" found among later Neoplatonists is ahistorical,[22] but it is a far cry from anything found in Luke-Acts (except,

18. Still less can Luke's interests always satisfy many modern congregational settings that evaluate sermons solely by their relevance to the hearers' personal existential states. Luke was certainly relevant to his own contemporaries, but those who wish to understand his message today must recognize that just as we must translate from his Greek to modern languages, we must take into account the historical and cultural divide when we grapple with how to hear that message.

19. See Black, *Aramaic Approach*, 2; Burney, *Aramaic Origin*, 9; Keener, *Matthew*, 552–53. Luke 11:44 may be a more original form of the saying in Matt 23:27, but Matthew's (or his tradition's) adaptation is fully intelligible in a Jewish milieu (Keener, *Matthew*, 553).

20. Though their leisure for study may suggest that other Pharisees, in addition to Gamaliel, belonged to Jerusalem's elite. Perhaps Luke's theology (against wealth) and historical tradition (about many Pharisees as being well-to-do, even if it is an exaggeration to make them a retainer class) blend here.

21. Nevertheless, modern interpreters will recognize that this distortion is sometimes the price of translation and application, which are necessary to evoke equivalent responses and help modern readers to appreciate any ancient text's message by seeking to bridge the horizons.

22. Cf., e.g., Men. Rhet. 2.17, 438.14; 443.2; Iambl. *V.P.* 28.145–47.

perhaps, in Acts 17:24–25) or much of the rest of first-century Christian literature. If one part of Luke's purpose is to recount what happened among God's people (as he emphasizes in his first volume's proem, Luke 1:1–4), then communicating salvation history is part of his theology. The biblical tradition, explicit citations and clear allusions to which pervade Luke's work, informed his approach to salvation history; God's acts continued in recent times as in earlier biblical times, and Luke was continuing the biblical story (as noted in ch. 14 above, on Luke and Israel, and esp. Luke and Scripture).

Most Jewish people not immersed in Greek philosophy found in such a story God's acts in history; reciting God's acts honored God and was deeply theological, albeit by reflecting on God by recounting his acts rather than by philosophic abstractions. As suggested above, scholars today would call it "narrative theology." Paul, for example, writes with significant christological assumptions but constantly rehearses Jesus's death and resurrection; even the earliest Christian creeds focused on Jesus's "work" as well as on his "person." But all Greco-Roman historians advanced agendas and emphases through their concrete examples (as noted in ch. 5, sect. 1, above), and Luke-Acts is no exception.

II. Apologetic Emphases

For an example already addressed above in chapter 13, a major emphasis in Acts is Luke's political apologetic, arguing that, contrary to accusations (Acts 17:7; 24:5), Christians were not a subversive movement out to undermine the state. (Luke may undermine the larger society's values and gods, but any public disorder in his narrative is blamed on the Christians' enemies.) Those who study Luke as a guide for modern Christian faith and praxis (rather than for purely historical interests) may find more of a model here than traditional theological categories might lead us to expect: Luke offers a sort of church-state model for his culture (where Christians were a tiny minority). Political cultures vary too greatly (e.g., secular democracies, Islamic states) to simply import Luke's model wholesale into different systems. Nevertheless, his apologetic strategies provide a well-thought-through model of contextualization relevant for those constructing appropriate models for various respective cultures.

What of the details that Luke supplies because his chosen genre of apologetic historiography demands them? His point in including some names and details may be the same as that of other historians in including names and details: their historical enterprise demanded it, though political or theological agendas may have guided their selection and arrangement of, and slant on, their materials. If some modern theological readers are tempted to dismiss such details as irrelevant to their theological enterprise, they should not therefore assume that these details were irrelevant to Luke's "message."

Luke's historical method is itself important theologically precisely because it reveals that he affirmed that verifiable history could not only serve other historians' political agendas but reveal God's acts. Just as Luke appeals to apologetic eyewitness claims within speeches (Acts 2:32; 3:15; 5:32; 10:39–41; 13:31; 22:15; 26:16), he implies their value for his narratives (e.g., Luke 1:2; Acts 1:8, 22; 4:33).[23] Although some modern readers may doubt his claim that such events occurred in history, they should not pretend that such a claim is not part of Luke's message, that is, what we

---

23. Cf. also the "we" narratives, though here a special debate is involved (see comment on Acts 16:10).

commonly call his theology. Although Luke's theology is prominent in Acts, one can divorce it completely from his narrative only at a steep price.[24]

Having posed the problem of definition, I will focus below on several of Luke's recurrent interests in the book that are usually considered "theological." Luke's theology can be (and often has been) explored in much greater detail, but I focus here on several recurrent themes most easily introduced at this point. I revisit these themes and a larger number of others at appropriate locations within the commentary proper. Because this commentary, by its nature, focuses on the text's ancient meaning and works through each passage in some detail, a more integrative treatment of the themes is better suited to a separate study. That being said, the themes and literary unity of Luke-Acts are presupposed in each passage that the commentary explores.

2. Some Theological Themes

Luke's speeches and narratives are full of themes and emphases through which Luke (as one expects for an ancient historian) is teaching about various subjects, including God.

a. Introductory Comments

One place to look for Luke's theology would be the "standard set of topics" in the speeches in Acts, often repeated even when not directly relevant to the situation at hand.[25] That is, they remain a fixed part of the preaching of the good news for various settings. C. H. Dodd listed elements he found central in the apostolic preaching in Acts:

1. The "age of fulfilment has dawned."
2. This has occurred "through the ministry, death, and resurrection of Jesus," as Scripture says.
3. On the basis "of the resurrection, Jesus has been exalted at the right hand of God," as Messiah, king of Israel.
4. The present activity of "the Holy Spirit in the Church is the sign of Christ's present power and glory."
5. Christ's return will soon consummate this interim era.
6. "Finally, the *kerygma* always closes with an appeal for repentance, the offer of forgiveness and of the Holy Spirit, and the promise of 'salvation,' that is, of 'the life of the Age to Come.'"[26]

Soards gives the following, similar list:[27]

1. The christological kerygma
2. The resurrection (especially of Jesus)
3. Repentance and/or forgiveness
4. "The universal significance of God's salvation"
5. The Holy Spirit

24. This is not to deny the value of distilling some of his themes or of exploring their contemporary applicability, but the themes of greatest interest to modern readers do not always include all parts of Luke's message.

25. Fernando, *Acts*, 32–38, provides a thorough table comparing which section of those that he surveys includes which points.

26. Dodd, *Preaching*, 21–23. Others (e.g., Michael Green) are more flexible here.

27. Soards, *Speeches*, 203–4.

Some of these themes are more pervasive than others, but their distribution within Acts is appropriate. Most evangelistic speeches mention the resurrection, and other speeches may do so as well (Acts 1:22; 2:24, 31–32; 3:15; 4:2, 10, 33; 5:30; 10:40; 13:30, 33–37; 17:18, 31–32; 23:6; 24:15, 21; 26:8, 23).[28] By contrast, the Holy Spirit appears in speeches to Jewish audiences and, when to Gentiles, to Gentile Christians (1:5, 8, 16; 2:17–18, 33, 38; 5:32; 7:51; 10:38; 11:12, 15–16; 15:8, 28; 20:23, 28; 28:25); most non-Christian Gentiles would not understand the Jewish and Christian meaning of the Spirit without explanation.[29]

But Luke's narrative teaches "theology" no less than the apostolic message announced by his reliable protagonists, and hence repetition of divine works may teach us there as well. After all, Luke's first volume, his own Gospel, develops in greater detail some of the basic elements of the kerygma encapsulated above. Narrative diversifies the "normative" patterns—for example, the pattern for receiving the Spirit in Acts 2:38–39 (e.g., 8:15–17; 10:44–47).

Here I treat only selected themes in Acts, treating others at greater length under one of the early passages where they occur in the commentary (e.g., prayer, at Acts 1:14; or God's sovereignty, especially at 2:23; or faith, which is mentioned roughly fifty times, at Acts 3:16) or as they appear at various points in the text (e.g., the theme of persecution). If we define "theology" broadly as not simply Luke's perspectives about God but his message more generally, it could include such themes as Christians' uprightness before Roman law (see above in ch. 13, on apologetic) and the integrity of Paul's message. Further, although the "theology" of Luke-Acts may be its message, shaped to some degree by its purpose, Luke may have held other theological convictions shared among early Christians or Jewish people that he did not need to articulate in his work.[30]

As already noted, the question of definition is necessary to limit the range of a "theological" investigation, and writing a theology of Luke-Acts is beyond the purpose of this work, in any case (though it is hoped that the passage-by-passage insights in light of the whole could contribute to such a work). But here I introduce (in relatively cursory form) several themes, namely, Christology (treated further under, e.g., Acts 2:21, 34–36); salvation (cf. comment on Acts 27:20); briefly, eschatology (treated in greater detail at Acts 1:6–8); much more extensively, the Gentile mission (also treated, with other aspects, under Acts 1:8); the Spirit (although different aspects of this are treated under Acts 1:8; 2:17–18); and signs. Because this is a social-historical and rhetorical commentary, my emphasis here is to put these themes in their late first-century context, and so the survey of secondary literature on these subjects will be necessarily limited.

b. Jesus as God's Agent of Salvation

The theme of Jesus as God's saving agent is too pervasive and central to warrant detailed treatment in one place;[31] I will simply survey it here. (For background on

---

28. I do not treat the resurrection here as a discrete topic, treating it instead in the commentary at Acts 1:3. It is, however, central to Luke's story; whereas he apparently accepts the same understanding of atonement in the cross as many early Christian writers (see comment on Acts 8:32–33), his focus is on the resurrection (for this focus, see extensively Anderson, *Raised*; cf. Marguerat, "Resurrection," for one discussion of the various forms of resurrection testimony in Acts). This may stem partly from Luke's genre in the speeches, which are more designed to proclaim the basic event to new hearers than to explain the theological mechanics (an interest more characteristic of Paul).

29. See Keener, *Spirit*, 7–8; see discussion below in the excursus "Background for Luke's View of the Spirit," sect. 1.

30. Cf. Marshall, "Theology," 14–15.

31. For Luke's Christology, see esp. O'Toole, *Christology* (emphasizing both the variety and its coherency); Buckwalter, *Christology*; briefly, Jervell, *Apostelgeschichte*, 93–97; Doohan, *Acts*, 93–101; Peterson, *Acts*,

Jewish Christology and further comment on Luke's, see, e.g., comment at Acts 2:21, 34–36). Since Luke's first volume, as a whole, deals with "all that Jesus began to do and to teach" (Luke 1:1), one might rehearse this entire Gospel here. Luke's second volume repeatedly summarizes this mission, which will be merely highlighted here. Epideictic rhetoric permitted one to highlight the centrality of one's main character (e.g., Libanius *Encomium* 2.24), but Jesus's role for early Christianity was foundational, and hence warranted *distinctive* focus and praise.

Jesus is the central focus of proclamation in Acts (highly significant given the prominence of the speeches; even in Acts 17:22–31, Jesus is the climax in 17:31). Luke often shows that Jesus is the object of proclamation or "preaching good news" (e.g., 5:42; 8:5, 35; 9:20; 11:20; 17:3; climactically, 28:31), the equivalent of preaching the kingdom (8:12; 19:8; 20:25; 28:23; especially 28:31) and the "peace" it includes (10:36; cf. Isa 52:7). As already noted above (sect. 2.a), the speeches in Acts summarize elements of how God used and exalted Jesus in the first volume. God was with Jesus, having anointed him to perform benefactions of healing and deliverance for Israel (Acts 10:38). God gave him these signs to attest him to Israel (2:22). Nevertheless, some of his people rejected and murdered him (2:23; 7:52) according to God's plan (2:23; 3:18; 4:28); the leaders held special responsibility (3:17; 4:10, 26–27; 5:30; 13:27).

But God raised him up (2:32; 3:15; 5:30) and enthroned him at his own right hand, as the psalmist's "lord" (2:33–35; 5:31). He is also the coming "Son of Man" (7:56; cf. Dan 7:13), "standing" at God's right hand (Acts 7:56), perhaps as the true judge. Most important, he is "Lord" (e.g., 9:1, 10, 11, 17, 27, 28; 11:16;[32] 22:10; 23:11; 26:15),[33] often as "the Lord Jesus" (e.g., 4:33; 8:16; 9:17; 11:17, 20; 15:11, 26; 16:31; 19:5, 13, 17; 20:21, 24, 35; 21:13; 28:31); he appears in the form of divine glory (9:3–5; 22:7–8; 26:14–15).[34] His resurrection and exaltation grant him this public status, in accordance with the proclamation of Psalm 110 (Acts 2:34–36).

Jesus's lordship applies to him traditionally divine language. In antiquity in general, "Lord," when not used in the vocative,[35] could function especially as a divine title.[36] "Lord" is clearly used as a divine title also in Acts (Acts 2:34, 39; 5:9; 8:22, 24, 39; 9:31; 13:2; 16:14), especially when referring to OT citations (2:20–21; 3:22; 4:26; 7:31, 33, 49; 13:47; 15:17, 18) or employing OT phrases such as "angel of the Lord" (5:19; 8:26; 12:7, 23), "hand of the Lord" (11:21; 13:11), and "name of the Lord" (2:21; applied to Jesus in 8:16; 9:28; 19:5, 13, 17; 21:13).[37] As just noted, this title

---

56–60; for a survey of studies, see Powell, *Acts*, 42–45; for numerous earlier studies, see Mattill and Mattill, *Bibliography*, 274–81, §§3814–81.

32. "Word of the Lord" is also a familiar OT idiom for God's message; cf. Acts 8:25; 13:48, 49; 15:35–36; 16:32; 19:10, 20. This phrase is equivalent to "message of God" (e.g., 4:31; 6:2, 7; 8:14; 11:1), but as the message about the Lord Jesus (or even from him, 11:16; Luke 22:61; cf. 1 Thess 4:15), it might also relate to Luke's conception of Jesus's deity (so Bowman and Komoszewski, *Deity*, 161).

33. Probably also Acts 9:35, 42; 14:23; 16:15; 18:8, 9, 25; 20:19; perhaps 11:21, 23, 24; 13:12; 14:3; 15:40. Many other references that are ambiguous might refer to either Christ (his more common usage in Acts) or the Father, and Luke probably does not object to the ambiguity because, in practical terms, they act together.

34. Cf. perhaps Acts 7:59–60 (depending on the status of the variant reading), where Jesus would hear prayers for forgiveness and receive the dying, as the Father had done for him.

35. Usually meaning "Sir"; applied even to a relative of higher rank, e.g., P.Oxy. 1231, 26; *SPap* 1:338–39, lines 1, 24; P.Giss.Univ. 21.11.

36. See especially its use in Judaism (e.g., Hurtado, *Lord Jesus Christ*, 108–18; Keener, *John*, 297–98). Sometimes it was used for Caesar (P.Fouad 8 [Sherk, *Empire*, §81, p. 123]; *Mart. Pol.* 8; Deissmann, *Light*, 351–55); whether the NT includes a contrast with imperial usage is debated (in favor, e.g., Cullmann, *Christology*, 228; against, e.g., Nock, *Christianity*, 34).

37. Cf. also, e.g., "serving the Lord" (Acts 20:19); "turning to the Lord" (11:21); with even Hellenistic divine parallels, "the Lord's will be done" (21:14).

often applies specifically to Jesus (e.g., 1:21; 2:36; 4:33; 8:16; 9:5), including in a foundational context that applies a programmatic text to Jesus (see 2:21 with 2:34, 36, 38; cf. also Luke 3:4). Jesus is also designated as "Lord of all" (Acts 10:36), again normally a divine title. There can be no question that Luke accepts Jesus's divinity in at least some sense; this is not surprising if he was in Paul's circle (which uses some divine language for Jesus),[38] though it appears much more widely in first-century Christology than advocates of traditional hypotheses demanding a slowly evolving Christology have been prepared to acknowledge.[39]

Because Jesus is God's Christ, he will also rule his people in the future era (3:20–21) and is already the rightful Lord (2:34–35). In the present, he is the one who pours out the Spirit (2:33; Luke 3:16), a divine role (Acts 2:17). We even read of the divine Spirit as "the Spirit of Jesus" (16:7). God offers Israel and others forgiveness and the gift of the Spirit in Jesus's name (2:38; 5:31). Jesus is the only means of salvation (4:12; 15:11) and is Israel's rightful leader and only savior (5:31; 13:23).[40] It is in his name that those turning to God must be baptized (2:38; 8:16; 19:5). He, like God, is the appropriate object of faith (11:17; 16:31; 20:21; 28:31), glorification (19:17), and proclamation (11:20; 28:31); preaching can be done in his name (9:28).

Jesus fulfills what Moses only started (3:22–23; 7:37) and what all prophets fore-told (3:24) and deliverers foreshadowed (7:9–37); he suffered rejection from God's own people, as did deliverers such as Joseph (7:9) and Moses (7:35). He is the Son of David, who fulfills God's promise to David and David's aspirations for his line (2:25–30).[41]

Jesus is God's servant (3:13, 26) and obeyed God even to the death (8:32–33, an observation relevant to Jesus's servant role especially if we may assume the immediate Isaian context). He is the truly holy and righteous one (3:14; 7:52), the prince of life (3:15).[42] He is the psalmist's rejected but exalted cornerstone (4:11).

God had chosen particular witnesses who would testify about Jesus. They needed to know the entire story since John the Baptist (1:21–22), but they especially testified about the key issue (in terms of salvation-historical significance), Jesus's resurrection (2:32; 3:15).[43] It was the resurrection that vindicated Jesus after the cross, confirm-ing him as God's agent; this was the climax of God's acts, one that, being naturally incredible, required special attestation. The Spirit also attests Jesus's exaltation, both as a present reality (2:33) and as a witness (5:32).

Jesus is not only the primary subject of proclamation in the speeches; he remains also a dramatic actor in the second volume's narrative, intervening by direct revela-tions (9:3–6, 10–16; 16:7; 18:9–10; 22:7–8, 10, 18–21; 23:11; 26:14–18). Jesus is also the one who continues to work in the book of Acts, because it is his name that produces healings (3:6, 16; 4:10; cf. 19:13); he stands behind all action done genu-inely "in His name" (see 9:34).

---

38. See, e.g., Keener, *John*, 300–302. On early Christian Christology in its Jewish context, see more fully Hurtado, *One God*; Longenecker, *Christology*; Bauckham, *Crucified*.

39. See, e.g., again, Longenecker, *Christology*; Hurtado, *One God*; Bauckham, *Crucified*.

40. In the context of Israel, the LXX portrays God as Israel's savior (e.g., Deut 32:15; 1 Sam 10:19; Isa 12:2; 17:10; 45:15, 21; 62:11; Mic 7:7; Hab 3:18; Jdt 9:11; Wis 16:7; Sir 51:1; Bar 4:22; 1 Macc 4:30; cf. 3 Macc 6:29, 32; 7:16), though the title is also used for God's agents (Judg 3:9, 15; Neh 9:27).

41. For discussion of this motif, see, e.g., Strauss, *Messiah*. Jesus fulfills multiple biblical models (as Luke 24:44 would lead his audience to expect).

42. For discussion of those designations, including "righteous one" possibly reinforcing the contextual allusion to Isaiah's servant, and discussion of the semantic range of the term summarized here as "prince," see comments ad loc.

43. And, by corollary, Jesus's exaltation (Acts 5:32).

Jesus remains in fact no less central to Acts than to Paul or Revelation, though Luke is no longer writing a biography of Jesus as in his first volume. The subject of Luke's first volume (Acts 1:1), Jesus remains directly central in the opening scene of Acts, where he instructs the disciples, ascends, and remains the subject of angelic discourse (esp. 1:11). Yet even after the ascension, Jesus is never far from the action. He is the promised one whose betrayal thus commands significance in 1:16–20, and for whom the number of witnesses must be completed (1:8, 20–23). He is the one who gives the Spirit in chapter 2 (see 2:33), and thus the subject of Peter's preaching (2:22–38). He is the one in whose name the lame man in chapter 3 is healed (3:6, 13, 16; 4:10), and thus again the subject of Peter's preaching (3:13–26), and the subject of the prophets' discourse (3:18–26; cf. also 2:25–30). The apostles' proclamation of Jesus is the occasion of their arrest (4:2), and the apostles preach Jesus again to the council (4:10–12); their very behavior marks them as exhibiting the model of Jesus (4:13). Warned no longer to speak for Jesus (4:18), the apostles find such wicked threats foretold in Scripture (4:26–30; cf. 5:40) and continue preaching Jesus (4:33; 5:30, 42). Stephen preaches Jesus as the rejected deliverer, following earlier biblical models (ch. 7); Philip, as the true great one of God (in contrast to magical claims, 8:10–12) and the suffering servant (8:32–35).

Jesus himself converts and calls Paul directly (9:3–6; 22:6–10; 26:13–18; cf. 20:24), sends Ananias as his confirming and healing agent (9:17), becomes the subject of Paul's proclamation (9:20, 22, 27), and heals through Peter (9:34) and others (14:3). As the subject of Peter's preaching (10:36–43), he is the reason that Gentiles receive the Spirit (11:17), the basis of their salvation (15:11). Those who spread the word beyond Palestine also preach Jesus (11:20), who remains the subject of Paul's message (13:23–39; 14:21); risking one's life for Jesus's honor attests one's fidelity to what the movement is about (15:26; cf. 21:13). Jesus continues to guide the mission (16:7) and remains the basis for exorcism (16:18) and salvation (16:31); he is promised in and proclaimed from Scripture (17:3; 18:28; 26:22–23; 28:23; cf. 18:4–5). He remains the clear subject of proclamation (19:4–5; 20:21, 35; 24:24; 28:31), even when hearers misunderstand or twist the message (17:7, 18; 25:19). The real Jesus cannot be manipulated by magical formulas but works only through his chosen agents (19:13–17). He continues to speak to his servants about their mission (18:9–10; 23:11) and to guide the action (22:17–21; cf. 23:11; 27:23). Jesus thus remains central in Acts, as in most of earliest Christian literature.

c. Salvation

Luke is interested in what we call salvation history, from God's promise to Israel to the consummated salvation of the resurrection and Israel's restoration under its true king. Discussion is limited here to the particular term σῴζω and its cognates; other aspects and terminology are treated in key passages. Other scholars have surveyed this theme much more thoroughly,[44] and I will not simply repeat the surveys here. For how Luke's use compares with ancient usage of the terminology in general, see comment at Acts 27:20, 34. One should note, however, that Luke employs the nouns (with the exception of 16:17)[45] especially in a Jewish context.

44. E.g., O'Toole, *Unity of Theology* (passim, perhaps esp. 33–61); Powell, "Salvation"; Green, "Salvation"; Buckwalter, "Saviour"; Stenschke, "Need for Salvation"; Witherington, "Salvation"; idem, *Acts*, 821–43; Peterson, *Acts*, 65–70; Matera, *Theology*, 68–75; Twelftree, *People*, 45; in ancient texts generally, see also, briefly, Keener, *John*, 627–28; for a survey of views, see Powell, *Acts*, 47–50; for earlier studies of soteriology in Acts, see Mattill and Mattill, *Bibliography*, 282–83, §§3931–40.

45. This verse's mention of the "Most High" is not specifically Jewish or God-fearing. Presumably, this proclamation underlies the jailer's question about how to be saved (Acts 16:30).

The verb σῴζω is the least theologically specific of the set of cognates bearing its wide range of Greek meanings. Most basically, it can mean "rescue."[46] In the Gospel, it includes the Lord bringing physical wholeness (Luke 7:50; 8:48, 50; 17:19; 18:42; cf. 6:9) and deliverance from demonization (8:36); Acts occasionally applies the verb to physical restoration (Acts 4:9), which can also come through faith (14:9). Luke can use such healings as portraits of the wider salvation God brings for individuals who trust in Christ and ultimately for Israel as a whole (cf. the use in 4:9, 12). Those who believe in Jesus may be saved (Luke 8:12);[47] those who offer their lives for Christ will save them (9:24); those who sacrifice all may enter the kingdom someday (18:25) and hence be saved (18:26). Only a minority are being saved (13:23), but Jesus came to "save" what was lost in Israel (19:10).

In Acts, whoever calls on the Lord's name will be saved before the eschatological day of judgment (Acts 2:21); in context, this requirement is fulfilled through baptism in Jesus's name (2:38). Peter exhorts people to "save" themselves from a generation headed for destruction (2:40). Luke refers to those "who were being saved"; the present participle may refer to the continuing conversions but, in any case, does not depict salvation as taking place only in the future. One is saved from destruction by coming to Christ; but one who has believed can return to the path of destruction by abandoning Christ (cf. Luke 8:12–14; Acts 8:13, 20–22; 14:22; 20:26–30), making salvation secure (from the standpoint of human experience) only in the end. Jesus is the only way of salvation (Acts 4:12), and those who receive the message are saved (11:14); salvation is not through circumcision (15:1) but through Christ's grace (15:11), through faith (16:31).[48]

Salvation (σωτηρία) is Israel's expected deliverance from its enemies (Luke 1:71) and from its sins (1:77) through the promised Son of David (1:69); salvation rightly belongs to descendants of Abraham (19:9). Moses was God's earlier agent of deliverance (Acts 7:25). Jesus is humanity's only way of salvation (4:12), and through Israel's savior, God brings salvation also to the Gentiles (13:47).[49] Σωτηρία also refers to physical deliverance or safety; this general usage could be due more to the Greek term's semantic range than to a deliberate theological application on Luke's part, though such deliverance was also the gift of God (or, among pagans, gods). In view of the overall story (and Luke's play on different senses of cognate language in 4:9–12), however, this other usage might reflect more than lexical coincidence.

Jesus is the savior (σωτήρ), the messianic Lord of David's house, in Luke 2:11; he is Israel's savior who brings them forgiveness (Acts 5:31) and fulfills the Davidic promise (13:23). Given the premise of Luke's divine Christology, "Savior" may support this usage (as in Luke 1:47), in view of its use in the LXX.[50] (An LXX background is most likely, given Luke's application of the title "Savior" to specifically Jewish contexts; Acts 5:31; 13:23.) For other points, see comment on the relevant passages (e.g., 2:38, on repentance).

46. Acts 27:20, 31 (though divinities were trusted to do this, the term has a wider semantic range). Cf. Luke 23:35, where Jesus's enemies debase the notion of his "saving" or bringing deliverance to others; 23:37, 39, where they debase the notion of him as Israel's Messiah and savior.

47. The verb for deliverance here is aorist passive subjunctive; "believe" is an aorist active participle.

48. The man who asks how to be "saved" (Acts 16:30) may depend on the proclamation that these servants of God bring a message of salvation (16:17), but his question follows the form of other questions for eternal life (Luke 3:10 with 3:9; Acts 2:37 with 2:38), perhaps modeled on the question in Luke 18:18 (cf. Mark 10:17).

49. This is true of the cognate σωτήριον; as Simeon saw God's salvation (Luke 2:30), so would "all flesh" (3:6; cf. Acts 2:17, 21), and this salvation was sent to the Gentiles (Acts 28:28).

50. Deut 32:15; 1 Sam 10:19; Pss 23:5 (24:5 ET); 24:5 (25:5); 26:1, 9 (27:1, 9); 61:3, 7 (62:3, 7); 64:6 (65:6); 78:9 (79:9); 94:1 (95:1); Isa 12:2; 17:10; 45:15, 21; 62:11; Mic 7:7; Hab 3:18; Jdt 9:11; Wis 16:7; Sir 51:1; Bar 4:22; 1 Macc 4:30; elsewhere, cf., e.g., 3 Macc 6:29, 32; 7:16; Odes 2:15; 4:18; 9:47. But the title is also used for his agents (Judg 3:9, 15; Neh 9:27).

I earlier commented on the theme of God's purpose, foreshadowed by both biblical and contemporary oracles and repeatedly fulfilled in the narrative. Aune regards this theme of divine guidance (along with that of the mostly Jewish rejection and mostly Gentile acceptance of the new prophets) as the major plot-moving device in Luke-Acts.[51] Some scholars have developed this and related themes in detail.[52]

d. Suffering

Throughout Acts, God's plan advances through suffering. Because I elsewhere treat the persecution theme[53] under some passages where it appears, I summarize here some of the ways first-century hearers might have viewed it. Jewish piety emphasized the value of suffering for doing good (e.g., Tob 1:17–20; 2:7–10); by the first century, some Jews viewed martyrdom as having atoning value (4 Macc 6:27–29; 17:21–22).[54] The theme of meritorious suffering became prominent in early and rabbinic Judaism (see comment at Acts 9:16; on martyrs and atonement, see comment at Acts 7:60). At the same time, some apparently held the contradictory notion that martyrs suffered justly yet martyrs were innocent,[55] perhaps best resolved by recognizing their innocence before people and the fact that none are innocent before God.

Acts does not, however, speak of martyrs' atoning deaths (even where the best opportunity presents itself, Acts 7:60), probably because Jesus's death holds pride of place in this regard (cf. comment on Acts 8:32–33). Nor does it connect martyrs' deaths with their sins; rather, martyrs die through others' sins (7:60).[56] Like Paul, however, Luke does connect sufferings with the mission, and does so repeatedly (see commentary on the respective passages).

Some have compared the lists of Paul's sufferings in his writings to the traditional catalogues of philosophers' "labors" or sufferings (1 Cor 4:11–13; 15:30–32; 2 Cor 4:8–11; 6:4–10; 11:23–29).[57] Given the view here that Luke portrays Paul as a model philosopher for his Greco-Roman audience (see comment on Acts 19:9), it seems likely that Luke would narrate some of Paul's sufferings with a goal similar to that of Paul's suffering lists, despite the different (narrative) literary form.

3. The Gentile Mission

The Gentile mission was addressed briefly under proposed purposes for Acts, but it can be addressed more fully here. Most scholars recognize that the Gentile mission (i.e., more accurately, a "universal" mission) is one of the central themes (if not *the* central theme) in the book of Acts.[58]

51. Aune, *Environment*, 131.
52. See esp. Squires, *Plan*.
53. On the persecution theme, see Dehandschutter, "Persécution"; Mittelstadt, *Spirit*, 12–20; Twelftree, *People*, 101–9; at greater length, esp. Cunningham, *Many Tribulations* (summary, 337–40); in conjunction with Luke's emphasis on the Spirit, see Mittelstadt, *Spirit*; Warrington, "Suffering."
54. Cf. 2 Macc 7:37; 4 Macc 9:24; *Test. Mos.* 9. See further discussion of ancient atonement ideas in Hengel, *Atonement*.
55. Avemarie, "Aporien."
56. This is not to suppose that Luke affirmed martyrs' past sinlessness but simply to argue that Luke never connects this kind of suffering with punishment. One could argue for a relationship in Acts 9:16, but if 9:16 connects Paul's future with his past, it is in terms of understanding the cost, not punishment.
57. See Alexander, "Biography," 59–60 (citing Sen. Y. *Ep. Lucil.* 104.27–33); and esp. Fitzgerald, *Cracks*, passim; idem, "Affliction Lists."
58. E.g., Cadbury, *Making*, 316; Dupont, *Salvation*, 11–33; Wilson, *Gentile Mission*; Maddox, *Purpose*, 56; Dahl, "Abraham," 151; Senior and Stuhlmueller, *Foundation for Mission*, 255–79; Matson, *Conversion*

Clearly, the focus of Acts is not church history in general but tracing the expansion of the early Jesus movement from Jerusalem to the heart of the empire.[59] Whereas Luke's first volume opens and closes in or near Jerusalem, his second volume moves from Jerusalem to Rome—from heritage to mission.[60] Luke recounts a variety of the sorts of obstacles that the Christian mission faced, and he shows how, by the power of God's Spirit, the mission successfully surmounted these barriers "unhindered" (Acts 28:31; cf. 8:36; 10:47; 11:17).[61] The final section of Acts recapitulates this theme as Paul proceeds to Rome after being dramatically and continuously rejected in Jerusalem (Acts 21–28).

The prominence of evangelism in this focus may be observed by noting, with David Matson, that "next to the speeches, conversion stories may represent the most important formal grouping in Acts, comprising just over one-fourth of its narrative material."[62] Some aspects of A. J. Mattill Jr.'s proposed setting for Acts are debatable, but he could be correct in contending that Luke authored Acts (at least in part) "to expedite an essential part of the apocalyptic plan, the evangelization of the world in his generation."[63]

a. Luke's Emphasis on the Gentile Mission

When we speak of the "Gentile mission," we speak only about what is distinctive in Luke's (and much of the early Christian movement's) vision; Paul's continuing ministry to Diaspora Jewish communities shows that the mission is never exclusively to Gentiles but simply includes them. Thus, for example, the strategic Diaspora church in Antioch reaches both Jews and Gentiles; its missionaries reach both Jews and Gentiles in the Diaspora. That is, the mission is for all people; the overall pattern is therefore mission, not specifically the Gentile mission.

It was Gentiles' inclusion, however, that was controversial to Jesus's early movement in Jerusalem, and hence it warrants Luke's special emphasis. If we may gather insight from a similar emphasis in Matthew (Matt 1:3–5; 2:1–2; 3:9; 4:15; 8:11, 28; 10:15; 11:21–22; 12:39–42; 15:21–22; 24:14; 25:32–33; 27:54; 28:19), the issue may have remained controversial in some circles even well past the close of Paul's ministry. Matthew sought to motivate his audience to embrace controversial cross-cultural mission to culturally undesirable people; Luke may seek recognition for the

---

Narratives, 184 (stressing household evangelism); Mangatt, "Believing Community"; Richard, "Experiences"; idem, "Pluralistic Experiences"; Talbert, *Mediterranean Milieu*, 161–73; Eckey, *Apostelgeschichte*, 598–600; Gruchy, "Mission"; Peterson, *Acts*, 79–83; Langner, *Hechos*, 45; Park, "Barriers"; Keathley, *Mission* (esp. 3–62, finding the same emphasis in Paul in 65–113); Murphy, "Perspectives" (esp. 481); Cazeaux, *Actes*, 339 (though viewing the Pauline mission partly as a negative rejection of Israel); Eisen, *Poetik* (justified by most of Israel's rejection); survey of other views in Powell, *Acts*, 67–72. This may be combined with ministry to others who are marginalized, as in the Gospel (Green, "Repentance and Forgiveness"; see also below). Even if the theme is central in all of Scripture (Wright, *Mission*; in Acts, 514–21; in Paul, 522–30), its prominence in Acts is particularly noteworthy.

59. Kent, *Jerusalem to Rome*, 17; Bovon, *Theologian*, 238. The movement from Jerusalem to Rome is clearer than the proposed chiasmus in Wolfe, "Structure."

60. That other first-century Christians (as well as later ones) noted the tension between Jerusalem and Rome—at least after the latter destroyed the former—seems evident from Revelation's contrast between the New Jerusalem and Rome as "Babylon" (e.g., Keener, *Revelation*, 41, 369, 381, 405–7, 491, 496; Minear, "Cosmology," 30). Rome's prestige earned it priority throughout the empire; e.g., Nasrallah, "Cities," 556, compares the later Panhellenion's retention of Athens's traditional importance while underlining the greater significance of Rome.

61. See Stagg, "Unhindered Gospel"; idem, *Acts*, 12–17; Jackson, "Churches," 1.

62. Matson, *Conversion Narratives*, 11. On conversion in Acts, see further Talbert, *Mediterranean Milieu*, 135–48.

63. Mattill, "Date and Purpose," 350 (though he also sees Acts as an apology for Paul, then awaiting trial).

mission on which the Pauline circle of churches is based, as well as encouragement for continuing mission.[64]

1. Preparing for the Gentile Mission

Acts, as a whole, develops the announcement of the Gentile mission in Luke 24:47, which is interpreted in the language of Acts 1:8 as a fulfillment of Isaiah's vision for the Gentiles.[65] But Luke prepares for this theme long before the conclusion of his Gospel. The birth narratives foreshadow it.[66] Likewise, Jesus's programmatic mission statement in Luke 4:18–27 includes ministry to the Gentiles: though Isa 61 speaks primarily of the marginalized within Israel, Jesus's examples are Elijah's and Elisha's ministry (fitting Luke's emphasis on Jesus as prophet greater than Elijah; see discussion on Acts 1:9–11) to a Gentile leper and a possibly Gentile (or at least Diaspora) widow (Luke 4:26–27). Thus Luke prepares the reader for a theme to be taken up in his second volume.

Although the Gospel of Luke suggests ministry to Samaritans (Luke 9:52; 10:33; 17:16; cf. Acts 8:1, 5, 25)[67] and Gentiles (Luke 2:32; 24:47),[68] especially illustrated by foreign soldiers in Palestine (e.g., 3:14; 7:2–10; 23:47; cf. Acts 10:1),[69] it also omits some of Mark's examples that it could have used, such as the Syrophoenician woman (Mark 7:24–30, which would have well fit Luke 4:26), the crucial "for all nations" in Mark 11:17 (cf. Luke 19:46), and Mark 13:10 (perhaps because of Luke's emphasis on the events surrounding 70 C.E.; cf. Luke 21:24–25). It seems that Luke reserves most of his explicit emphasis on the Gentile mission for his second volume, for the period following Jesus's explicit command to evangelize all nations (Luke 24:47; Acts 1:8). Conscious of his role as a historian, Luke certainly does not invent examples of ministry to the Gentiles for his Gospel![70]

Luke prepares the way for the Gentile mission, however, by showing in the Gospel how Jesus welcomes other powerless or needy groups, such as lepers, other infirm people, women, the poor, and especially "sinners" (e.g., Luke 5:32; 7:22, 34; 14:21; 15:1–2).[71] Sacrificial ministry to the poor continues in the second volume (Acts

---

64. The theme appeared widely in early Christianity; cf. Keener, "Matthew's Missiology"; idem, "Sent"; idem, "Temple"; idem, "Power."

65. See esp. Pao, *Isaianic Exodus*, 84–95, 226; for Luke's christocentric exegesis consistently supporting the Gentile mission, see Meek, *Mission*. Roetzel, *Paul*, 52, suggests that the LXX translators of Isaiah had a deliberate universalist agenda, advocating "the inclusion of Gentiles in the people of God."

66. See Luke 2:32; Radl, "Beziehungen," 305–6.

67. See Lane, *Gentile Mission*, 47–48. Jesus's parable in Luke 10:25–37 reflects a brotherly love emphasis in Luke's work (Oegema, "Gebot," 510–13).

68. See Lane, *Gentile Mission*, 43–47. Many scholars suggest hints in the mission of the seventy-two (Lane, *Gentile Mission*, 85–130; Matson, *Conversion Narratives*, 29–38; Luke 10:1; Jeremias, *Theology*, 234n3; Lignée, "Soixante-douze"; Marshall, *Luke*, 415; Ladd, *Theology*, 114; cf. *3 En.* 30:2), which becomes even more persuasive if one accepts the variant reading "seventy" (for this possibility see Metzger, "Seventy," 306); cf. the "seventy nations" in, e.g., *Jub.* 44:34; *3 En.* 2:3; 29:1; *Pesiq. Rab Kah.* 28:9; *b. Sukkah* 55b; *Gen. Rab.* 39:11; *Lev. Rab.* 2:4; *Tg. Ps.-J.* on Gen 11:8; *Tg. Rishon* on Esth 2:22; based on Gen 10. The seventy elders plus two in Num 11:16–17, 26 may account for the variant (Danker, *New Age*, 125; Wilson, *Gentile Mission*, 45–47), but seventy-two in the LXX of Gen 10 is also a possibility. An allusion to the seventy-two translators of the LXX (Jellicoe, "Seventy(-Two)," 321) seems less probable.

69. The soldiers in Luke 3:14 might be Jews working for Herod; see Jos. *Ant.* 18.113–14. They could be Jewish "police" who accompanied tax collectors (Jeremias, *Theology*, 48n3), or they could be Syrian auxiliaries (Manson, *Sayings*, 254 [possibly]; Reicke, *Era*, 140), perhaps initially sent to investigate John's activity (Danker, *New Age*, 47).

70. Cf. Tuckett, *Luke*, 54: "For Luke then the Gentile mission is prefigured in the Gospel; but it is not written back into the pre-Easter story." Indeed, historically, some of Jesus's activity did prepare for the Gentile mission (see Schnabel, "Beginnings," passim, esp. 58; Bird, *Gentile Mission*, passim, esp. 3, 172).

71. Dollar, *Exploration*, 57–81; Lane, *Gentile Mission*, 48–57; Tannehill, "Ethics," 120; Mallen, *Reading*, 132; on the theme of the poor in Luke's Gospel, see also Hoyt, "Poor in Luke-Acts," 97–212.

2:44–45; 4:32–35; 6:1–3; 11:28–30; 24:17), though in a different way,[72] and women continue to play prominent roles (e.g., 1:14; 2:17–18; 8:3, 12; 9:2; 16:13; 17:4, 12; 22:4). Lepers disappear (perhaps because of the geographic shift), but Jesus's name continues to heal the sick.[73]

The most noticeable difference is that "sinners" (a term that appears nearly twenty times in Luke) do not appear by that title in Acts.[74] Likewise, the morally marginalized of Israel (the "lost" who must be saved, Luke 19:10) give way to the morally marginalized nations, those outside Israel.[75] But the principle of inversion continues from the Gospel into Acts; as in the entire gospel tradition, those who feel most secure with power, including among God's people, are most susceptible to the blindness that power brings. The marginalized, by contrast, are most ready to depend on Christ the healer, liberator, and savior.[76]

Many scholars regard the debate over the necessity of circumcision and, consequently, law-keeping in Acts 15 as the theological center of Acts. Most Jews accepted the possibility of Gentiles' becoming part of Judaism, but the vast majority of Jews would have required them to be circumcised if these Gentiles wished to belong to Israel fully (not simply as righteous God-fearers attending the synagogue). What makes Paul's Gentile mission distinctive is that it welcomes Gentiles as genuine converts, spiritual peers of Jewish Christians, with whom they can have table fellowship (cf. the different approach in 11:3; 15:20).[77] A strict reading of the covenant (cf. Gen 17:10–14) might seem to disallow this practice, but some believers might justify it on the basis of half-measures already accepted for Gentiles (see comment on Acts 15:20) and biblical interpretation about the new eschatological situation (Acts 15:15–19). What is clear is that God has led the church to this discovery (15:7–14). To "trouble" the Gentiles now (15:19) is tantamount to opposing God (cf. 11:17; 26:14), a proposition doomed to failure (5:39).

II. REASONS FOR THIS EMPHASIS

Scholars debate the reason for emphasizing the Gentile mission. Some believe that the Judean church of Luke's day remained skeptical of the Gentile mission and that Luke writes to encourage it otherwise.[78] Others, especially those who (including myself) date Acts after Jerusalem's destruction, find dubious the notion that the Judean church's views would remain so critical for Diaspora churches, especially in a document clearly addressed to a Diaspora audience. (One could use this argument to date Acts before 70, but see ch. 10 above.) The contrary formulation, that Acts presents as necessary for the church's mission its rupture, accomplished through the insights of Paul, from what Luke is supposed to have viewed as the bondage of

72. Because the theme is no longer center stage in the second volume, it either takes a second place to the Gentile mission in the work as a whole (Bergquist, "Good News to Poor") or appears as another aspect of the same gospel to the needy (with different kinds of need).

73. For the παράδοξα (extraordinary matters; cf. Luke 5:26) involved in the healings, see Grassi, *Laugh*, 44. For the term, cf. relevant examples in Jos. *Ant.* 9.182; 18.63.

74. Cf. also Roth, *Blind, Lame, Poor*, 207, on the disappearance of some marginalized groups in the Gospel. Some scholars emphasize the social outcast status of "sinners" (e.g., Pienaar, "Sondaars"; Jeremias, *Parables*, 132), although it must have meant more than this (cf. Sir 12:4, 7; *1 En.* 100:7–9; *Pss. Sol.* 2:34; 13:1; 14:6–7; *Sib. Or.* 3.304; *Tg. Jon.* on Judg 3:10; *Tg. Qoh.* 6:6; discussion in Keener, *Matthew*, 294–96).

75. On the connection, cf., e.g., Talbert, *Mediterranean Milieu*, 172–73. On Luke's negative portrayal of Gentiles' preconversion spiritual state, see Stenschke, *Gentiles*.

76. As noted earlier, the ideological commitments of ancient documents could be political as well as "theological" in the narrower sense. We need not always separate these elements.

77. For Paul's centrality in articulating pro-Gentile theology, see, e.g., Turner, "Paul and Globalisation."

78. Jervell, *Unknown Paul*, 24; Donfried, "Christology and Salvation."

contemporary Judaism,[79] is still less likely. Would a work that includes the apologetic focus of connecting Christians with their (officially tolerated) Jewish ancestry seek to articulate precisely the opposite position?

Many scholars believe that Gentile Christians, now joining the Jewish Jesus movement and learning from a Jewish Bible, needed encouragement that God himself had welcomed them as part of his people.[80] Moreover, in keeping with the partly apologetic purpose for Acts described above, underlining the connection of the Gentile church with its ancient Jewish roots would provide a response to "pagan and Jewish detractors."[81] The church's commitment to Gentiles also serves a public apologetic purpose, in view of common propaganda against Judaism (especially in the wake of Judea's revolts); for example, while discussing circumcision (cf. Acts 15), Tacitus complains that those converted to Judaism follow the Jewish practice of rejecting gods, country, parents, and other family (*Hist.* 5.5). While maintaining Judaism's theological exclusivism, the Christians rejected ethnic exclusivism and hence could combat negative perceptions attached to many other Jews.[82]

Carrying out the Gentile mission connects with some other themes in Luke-Acts, especially the Spirit's empowerment (see, e.g., Acts 1:8; 2:4–11; 8:29; 10:19, 45–47; 11:16–18; 13:2, 4, 9; 15:28; 16:6–7; discussion below; and, further, comment on Acts 1:8),[83] signs and wonders (see discussion below), prayer (see comment on Acts 1:14), God's purpose and guidance (see comment on Acts 2:23 and passim), and suffering, which proved inseparable from the mission.[84]

III. A MODEL FOR MISSION

Some of these solutions (including affirming Gentile Christians and apologetic purposes) seem to me to represent valid aspects of Luke's purpose, although I doubt that any by itself is the entire solution. I believe that Luke intends Acts not merely as a historical record (although it is that) but also as a model for the continuing work of his own day. Granted, the gospel message had reached Rome in Acts 28, following the same pattern (Jewish division, some Gentiles accepting) as earlier in the book. But this pattern suggests the continuance of the mission "to the ends of the earth" (1:8). This universal mission is prefigured in Jerusalem (2:5–11; cf. 2:39); the conversion of the first Gentile, who was from "Ethiopia" (8:27); the conversion of a representative of Rome (10:1); and, finally, the gospel in the heart of the empire itself (28:17).

As we argued in chapter 5, historiography and biography regularly employed their accounts as positive or negative models; early Christians were also accustomed to reading inspired narrative in this manner (1 Cor 10:11). For Luke, many models in his book are prescriptive; he provides models for the church's continuing cross-cultural mission, which he believed to be the natural expression of the Spirit's empowerment (1:8). Because the Spirit means to empower, the apostolic witness (1:8) is to be shared

---

79. O'Neill, *Theology*, 75; cf. Ladd, *Theology*, 354. O'Neill treats Acts as the story of how the church "discovered its true nature" (*Theology*, 178) and argues "that Luke was writing at a time when events had made it clear that the Church's future lay principally with the Gentiles, and that the remaining Jewish Christian congregations would have to live with this fact" (133).

80. See Maddox, *Purpose*.

81. Aune, *Prophecy*, 191.

82. Luke does include Jesus's teaching about putting Jesus above family (Luke 9:59–62; 18:29) and Paul's denunciations of idolatry (Acts 14:15; 17:29–30), but like Paul he avoids nationalism, the feature most discredited (probably even for many northern Mediterranean Jews) in the wake of the Judean revolt.

83. For emphasis on the Spirit's empowerment for missions and/or the Gentile mission, see, e.g., Hull, *Spirit in Acts*; Stronstad, *Charismatic Theology*; Shelton, *Mighty in Deed*; Kim, "Mission," 41–42; Philip, *Pneumatology*, 204–24.

84. On the persecution theme, see esp. Cunningham, *Many Tribulations* (summary, 337–40).

among all believers in all places (2:39), including (deliberately) among Samaritans (8:15–17) and (more surprisingly) among Gentiles (10:45–46), and Luke anticipates that all believers, including his audience, should share this empowerment. Because this empowerment is for mission, all new believers and churches must become not merely objects of mission (their initial status) but indigenous partners in mission.

Clearly, much of Acts is intended as a model.[85] Paul's speech to the Ephesian elders (20:18–35) offers a warning for the future, presumably included because relevant for Luke's generation. This passage makes much of Paul's apostolic example of sacrificial ministry (20:18–21, 31, 33–35). Because Luke includes Paul as an example in discourse material (which authors could employ to underline their emphases), it seems likely that Paul also functions as a model in Luke's narrative. Chapter 5 above has already discussed the paradigmatic function of much ancient historiography in general.

It is thus not surprising that contemporary missiologists and others interested in contextualization find in Acts important models for mission.[86] Many of the growing churches in the global South and East are using Acts as a model for their present mission and empowerment.[87] Acts addresses the conflicts of shifting cultures and provides models for contextualization,[88] and readers who so use it are rediscovering an approach to Acts that appears in keeping with the work's own emphases.

In speaking of missions, however, I should emphasize that I am using modern language to communicate something different from much of the modern concept. It is anachronistic to view Paul's "missionary" work through the postcolonial lens that often intertwines Western missions with colonialism[89] (an understanding more applicable to some missionaries' work in the 1700s–1900s than to others),[90] especially in view of the dominance of Majority World missions movements today.[91] In Paul's day, the Romans (not the apostles) were the oppressive colonialists;[92] Paul

85. Cf. Rosenblatt, *Paul the Accused*, passim (who sees Paul in Acts as a model for how others should face suffering for the Christian mission); Rosner, "Progress," 232–33 (Acts' incomplete ending invites readers to participate in spreading the gospel); Menzies, "Sending," 92, 112; Hernando, "Function," 264. Cf. obvious narrative contrasts such as Luke 18:18–23; 19:2–8; Acts 4:36–5:11.

86. See, e.g., Wagner, *Acts*, passim; Kuck, "Preaching"; Hertig and Gallagher, "Introduction," 2; Rogers, *Ministry*; on an exegetical level, see Köstenberger and O'Brien, *Salvation*, 111–59; cf. Keck, *Mandate*, 83–102, esp. 98. Harun, "Überschreitung," sees it as a model for spreading the gospel in a pluralistic society.

87. E.g., Green, *Thirty Years*, 9–10; Noll, *Shape*, 24, 33–36, 123; for application for indigenous Indian evangelism in the face of hostility in some locations, see, e.g., Meagher, "Paul's Experience."

88. See, e.g., Flemming, *Contextualization*, 25–88. On a more general level, addressing the interface between missiology and biblical interpretation, see Keener, "Foundation."

89. For such questions in Acts studies, see, e.g., Shillington, *Introduction*, 86–101.

90. E.g., colonial authorities often opposed missionaries, e.g., Turaki, "Legacy"; Isichei, *History*, 233; Usry and Keener, *Religion*, 26. In fact, free-church missionaries (in British colonies, those not aligned with the Anglican church) were usually not closely tied to colonialism (Bebbington, *Dominance*, 113–14). For a survey of some ambivalent perspectives, cf., e.g., Dinwiddy, "Missions" (esp. 441).

91. See, e.g., Park, "Survey"; Pothen, "Missions," 18–45; in modern India, see 69–237; Devadason, "Missionary Societies," 27–42 (esp. 32–42); for some Indian perspectives on missiology, see, e.g., Samuel and Joseph, *Remapping*, esp. Joseph, "Remapping." As of 1988, Indian Christians (Pothen, "Missions," 315–16) "had 10,243 missionaries working with 194 mission agencies," most emphasizing both evangelism and social ministry. Current theological paradigms (Ott and Netland, *Globalizing Theology*) and historical perspectives (e.g., Irvin and Sunquist, *Earliest Christianity*; Spickard and Cragg, *Global History*; Sanneh, *Whose Religion?*) are increasingly sensitive to the range of cultures, and modern missiology has long emphasized this sensitivity (recently, see, e.g., Pocock, Van Rheenen, and McConnell, *Face*).

92. Indeed, many philosophic underpinnings for modern colonialism were originally formulated by Stoic philosophers for the Roman Empire; see Erskine, *Stoa*, 181–204, esp. 181. As Willimon puts it (*Acts*, 191), "To call Luke-Acts 'triumphalistic,' as some have done . . . , is to ignore Luke's intended audience—a persecuted minority fighting for its life." Or as Marguerat, *Historian*, 40, notes, the gospel spreads through *sufferings*: "Rather than a triumphal path, the route of the heralds of the Word is the road of the cross." This is usually the case for the spread of Jesus-discipleship in new cultures through history and today.

belonged to a suppressed people in Asia, but he contextualized the gospel for others and brought them a message that urged a new, multicultural unity without any one people's dominance.[93] (Cultural-sensitivity concerns should also be distinguished from a priori philosophic objections to Paul's monotheistic message.)[94]

Earlier I argued that Luke is not anti-Jewish; rather, he affirms the importance of the mission to all the nations (citing Isaianic precedent) as over against any lethargy or resistance to expansion. There is therefore a sense in which Luke's concern about the Judean elite involves religious elites more generally. Initially even the leaders of the Jerusalem church unconsciously echo the complaints of Jesus's Pharisaic detractors when God invites them to accept the Gentile mission (Acts 11:3; cf. Luke 15:2). Long before the Judean-Roman war would scatter Judeans, God forces the church to decentralize (8:4; 11:19–20), and the apostles catch the vision afterward (8:14, 25; 9:26–28; 11:22–24). As often in history, however, nationalism and local concerns came to obscure the divine imperative for expansion (cf. 21:20– 21).

b. Comparing the Social Context

Despite Jesus's teaching on the subject in the narrative (Acts 1:8),[95] many Jerusalem Christians probably took little more interest in a Gentile mission than did their Judean contemporaries. Gentiles were not, after all, part of their everyday lives the way they were for Jewish communities in the Diaspora. Most segments of Judaism welcomed proselytes,[96] but it is doubtful that seeking them was uppermost on most Jerusalemites' minds. For Gentile offspring of the Gentile mission, however, the issue was central to their own faith and practice; they had to reconcile their faith with the centrality of the Jerusalem church before 70 and the Judeocentric history that they received in the LXX, which was now their Scripture.

i. Judaism and a Gentile Mission?

Although Judaism did not send missionaries (see discussion at Acts 1:8), most Diaspora Jews welcomed converts, and some went out of their way to seek them. Concern for positive relations with Gentiles, as well as the interest of some in converting interested Gentiles, helped generate an apologetic tradition that early Diaspora

---

93. See helpfully Muthuraj, "Mission"; cf. also Xavier, "Faith"; Paul as missionary from Asia in Keener, "Asia and Europe." Without the early Gentile mission, Christianity probably would not have survived.

94. Some today would condemn as *religious* imperialism the early Christian insistence on one rightful Lord and king of all humanity, especially when it is linked with Israel's heritage and Scriptures. Those who have experienced religious truth claims closely connected with political force are, understandably, anxious about the former, but again, it is anachronistic to read this connection into the mission portrayed in Acts, where the missionaries represented a tiny persecuted minority. (Indigenous expansion in a free society likewise is methodologically antithetical to conquistadors' force; cf., e.g., Sung, *Diaries*, 62.) An insistence on a supreme Lord was a necessary corollary of monotheism (indeed, an absolute egalitarianism among sentient beings, as opposed to merely one among humans, is impossible in a universe with deities as they are normally conceived). First, denouncing as imperialistic the insistence on submission to a deity assumes that the existence of such deities is a purely subjective notion lacking knowable correspondence with reality (fitting modernity's association of faith with subjectivity, but purely a presupposition nonetheless). Second, it insists that religious claims of universal import (and perhaps any other claims of universal import, sometimes excepting scientific claims) are, by nature, hegemonic (although this very insistence itself constitutes a claim about religious matters), but such a criticism could be leveled against any truth claims in any discipline. Truth claims enforced politically are hegemonic, but when those offered in academic dialogue or by oppressed minorities are dismissed in the same terms, one suspects that the accusation of "hegemonic dialogue" has been abused in a hegemonic manner.

95. Though many scholars are skeptical that Jesus historically advocated a mission to the Gentiles. See, e.g., Sanders, *Jesus and Judaism*, 220 (applying Matt 8:11 to the Jewish Diaspora; but differently, see Keener, *Matthew*, 269–70; Glasson, *Advent*, 149–50). It is probably not coincidence that Matthew, Luke, and apparently the long ending of Mark all report Jesus urging a mission to other peoples.

96. For various positions, see esp. Donaldson, *Paul and Gentiles*, 52–74.

followers of Jesus could readily develop in their own expanding mission. It is thus useful to consider the Jewish setting for the early Christian mission to Gentiles.

(1) Views regarding Gentiles

Many Diaspora Jews had already grappled with the relationship between Jew and Gentile and had arrived at various solutions. Jewish views of Gentiles varied widely, from more positive Diaspora perspectives (as in *Letter of Aristeas*) to less positive sectarian Palestinian ones (as in 1QM).[97] Most Diaspora Jews welcomed (and believed that God welcomed) the interest of Gentiles.[98] Rabbis also believed in showing Gentiles kindness for the sake of peace.[99] The emphasis toward helping Gentiles eventually predominated against the more negative approach.[100]

Given Israel's sufferings at the hands of foreign empires, some Jewish texts reflecting mistrust of Gentiles are not surprising. Some Jewish people believed that the nations were worthless, like spittle.[101] Most later rabbis did accept the possibility of some "righteous Gentiles,"[102] often those who kept the Noahide laws.[103] Most teachers believed that righteous Gentiles could be saved without formal conversion to Judaism.[104] Nevertheless, the vast and representative majority of Gentiles were morally untrustworthy.[105] (By even the basic standard against idolatry in the Noahide laws and elsewhere, this was undoubtedly true.)

Clearly, Jewish people held a range of views regarding the fate of Gentiles.[106] Many early Jewish texts indicate the damnation of the Gentiles in the end time.[107] Later

---

97. See Boccaccini, *Judaism*, 251–65; Donaldson, *Paul and Gentiles*, 52–74; in *Letter of Aristeas*, see Boccaccini, *Judaism*, 176–79.

98. See, e.g., Hadas, *Aristeas*, 225 (on *Let. Aris.* 316); van der Horst, "Pseudo-Phocylides," 569. Rost, *Judaism*, 124–25, addresses 4 *Ezra* as transcending limits of nationalism.

99. E.g., *m. Giṭ.* 5:9; *b. Ber.* 17a; *Eccl. Rab.* 11:1, §1; Poulin, "Loving-Kindness." See even CD XII, 6–8; though cf. Bonsirven, *Judaism*, 154, for qualifications of this principle. The principle was a widespread one; Isoc. *Ad Nic.* 22 stresses the obligation to treat foreigners well for reputation's sake. Ps.-Phoc. 39–40 may be directed toward just treatment of Alexandrian Jewry rather than toward witness to Gentiles.

100. Urbach, "Self-Isolation," 278–84, esp. 283–84.

101. *L.A.B.* 7:3; 12:4; 4 *Ezra* 6:56; 2 *Bar.* 82:5. They are Israel's enemies (*Jub.* 1:19; 1 Macc 5; *Gen. Rab.* 80:7), wicked (4QpNah 3–4 I, 1; *Jub.* 23:24; *Sipre Deut.* 213.1.1; cf. *Jub.* 15:34; 24:25–33), idolaters (*Jub.* 1:9; 22:16–18, 20–22). To some, even their sacrifices might prove unacceptable (*y. Ter.* 1:1; 3:8; *Pesiq. Rab.* 48:1).

102. E.g., *b. 'Abod. Zar.* 64b; some viewed Job as such (*b. B. Bat.* 15ab; *Gen. Rab.* 57:4; cf. *Exod. Rab.* 1:9); some Gentiles could also show wisdom (e.g., *Gen. Rab.* 34:10). Martyrdom for Israel or Torah could bring righteous Gentiles into the coming world (*Sipre Deut.* 307.4.2). God had lower standards for Gentiles (*Sipra A.M. par.* 6.187.1.1).

103. *Mek. Bah.* 6.90ff.; *Sipre Deut.* 343.4.1; *b. Yebam.* 48b; *'Abod. Zar.* 64b ("the Sages"); *Sanh.* 56ab, bar.; 59a (purportedly Tannaitic tradition); 74b; *Gen. Rab.* 26:1 (Tannaitic); 34:14; *Exod. Rab.* 30:9; *Deut. Rab.* 1:21; *Pesiq. Rab Kah.* 12:1; cf. Urbach, "Self-Isolation," 275–78; Moore, *Judaism*, 274–75. See fuller discussion at Acts 15:20.

104. *Let. Aris.* 279; *t. Sanh.* 13:2; *Sipre Deut.* 307.4.2. Naturally, idolatry and sexual immorality excluded most Gentile men from the broadest Jewish definition of "righteous"; nevertheless, individual righteous Gentiles do appear (e.g., *Sipra A.M. pq.* 13.194.2.15; *b. Ḥul.* 92a; *Lev. Rab.* 1:3; cf. also a third-century C.E. Phrygian inscription praising one who "knew the law of the Jews," *CIJ* 2:34, §774). See further Donaldson, *Paul and Gentiles*, 65–69.

105. E.g., *m. 'Abod. Zar.* 1:2; *b. Bek.* 11b; *y. 'Abod. Zar.* 2:1, §3; cf. also *Jub.* 30:7–11; *Test. Naph.* 4:1. In CD XI, 14–15, they are apparently defiling (see discussion at Acts 10:23, 28); for their moral responsibility, see 1Q27 I, 9–11. For example, nursing a Gentile baby merely nurtures it for idolatry (*m. 'Abod. Zar.* 2:1; *t. 'Abod. Zar.* 3:3; contrast Samaritans in *t. 'Abod. Zar.* 3:1), and one should be cautious with a Gentile barber (*t. 'Abod. Zar.* 3:5); an Israelite who kills a Gentile is not liable (8:5); they are suspected of bestiality, fornication, and murder (*m. 'Abod. Zar.* 2:1). On Gentiles' usual sinfulness, see Sanders, *Judaism*, 266–70.

106. For a survey of ancient Jewish texts' diverse positions on the lostness of the Gentiles, see Sanders, *Paul and Judaism*, 206–12; Bonsirven, *Judaism*, 66–70; Donaldson, *Paul and Gentiles*, 52–74; for a broad sampling of rabbinic texts on Gentiles, see Montefiore and Loewe, *Anthology*, 556–65.

107. E.g., 1QM XI, 12–13; XIV, 7; XV, 1–2; XVII, 1–2; apparently *Jub.* 15:26; cf. 1 *En.* 99:4; other texts in Bonsirven, *Judaism*, 65–68; Donaldson, *Paul and Gentiles*, 52–54. Some of these texts include in the judgment the wicked of Israel as well.

rabbis, too, often believed that most Gentiles would ultimately be lost.[108] Yet others believed that the Gentiles would bring tribute[109] or in some traditions even be converted wholesale by God in the eschatological time.[110] After dividing ancient Jewish views regarding the eschatological fate of Gentiles into six categories, E. P. Sanders argues that Gentiles' "deserved punishment" increases after 70 C.E.[111] Terence Donaldson breaks down the categories of views concerning Gentiles as follows:

1. Hopelessly lost (e.g., *Jubilees*; *4 Ezra*)[112]
2. Proselytes welcomed, saved[113]
3. Natural law "proselytes" (Jos. *Ant.* 20.41; *Sib. Or.* passim; Philo)[114]
4. According to many (e.g., some Tannaim; those who accepted Gentile sacrifices in the temple), some righteous Gentiles existed[115]
5. Eschatological pilgrims[116]

Though Christians became universalistic ethnically, they proved "less willing to recognize the possibility of salvation for nonbelievers, be they Jews or Gentiles," than most other segments of early Judaism.[117] (For a discussion of God-fearers, see comment on Acts 10:2.)

(2) Approaches to Proselytes

Some individual Jewish people even sought proselytes,[118] and some provided apologetic to support Gentile interest; sometimes Judaism's success (deliberate or not) at attracting sympathizers and converts generated a backlash (as apparently in Rome).[119] Abraham (and often Sarah) became not only the model convert but the

108. E.g., *t. Sanh.* 13:2; *Sipre Deut.* 311.3.1; 315.1.1; 333.5.2; *b. Ber.* 8b; *Roš Haš.* 17a; *Šabb.* 104a; *Lev. Rab.* 13:2; 21:4; 33:6; *Num. Rab.* 19:32; *Eccl. Rab.* 1:9, §1; *Song Rab.* 8:8, §1; *Pesiq. Rab Kah.* 6:2; *Pesiq. Rab.* 10:5; 11:5.

109. E.g., 4Q504 1–2 IV, 8–12. Bhayro, "Status," argues that *1 En.* 6–11 includes two perspectives (the earlier, a future promised only to Jews; the later, allowing subjugated Gentiles). Fuller, *Restoration*, 111–84, carefully elaborates the defeat of the nations as the dominant approach (whether by Israel's army, as in 1 Maccabees or 1QM, 117–48; divine intervention, 148–62; or the warrior king of *Psalms of Solomon*, 162–69).

110. 1QH^a XIV, 12–14; 1QM XII, 14 (in both texts, the nations' conversion's function is to exalt Israel's eschatological glory); *Sib. Or.* 3.710–26 (second century B.C.E.; perhaps also 1.129); *Test. Zeb.* 9:8 (textually uncertain); *t. Ber.* 6:2; *Num. Rab.* 1:3; perhaps 4Q464 3 I, 8–9; *Song Rab.* 7:5, §3. In *Pss. Sol.* 17:30, Gentiles survive under Messiah's yoke; for the close relationship between Gentile conversion and subjugation in many early Jewish texts, see Fuller, *Restoration*, 126–33. For surveys of the diverse opinions on the lostness of the Gentiles in ancient Jewish texts, see Sanders, *Paul and Judaism*, 206–12; Bonsirven, *Judaism*, 66–70; and Donaldson, *Paul and Gentiles*, 52–74.

111. Sanders, *Jesus and Judaism*, 214–15. By contrast, Urbach, "Self-Affirmation," 278–84, attributes the predominantly negative attitude toward Gentiles to the period before 70 C.E., suggesting that rabbis at Yavneh (Jamnia) amended it to avoid profaning God's name. Jeremias, *Promise*, 40–41, suggests that the negative view (which he may overemphasize) climaxed in such statements as that of R. Eliezer ben Hyrcanus, ca. 90 C.E.: "No Gentile shall have a part in the world to come." But Moore, *Judaism*, 2:385–86, cites texts indicating that R. Eliezer was believed to have changed his mind; see Sanders, *Jesus and Judaism*, 215, for a critique of Jeremias on this point.

112. Donaldson, *Paul and Gentiles*, 52–54.

113. Ibid., 54–60.

114. Ibid., 60–65. Philo seems to allow *spiritual* circumcision (63–64).

115. Ibid., 65–69.

116. Ibid., 69–74.

117. Boccaccini, *Judaism*, 265.

118. See esp. Jos. *Ant.* 20.34–48; also see *Ag. Ap.* 2.210; *Ant.* 18.81–83; *m. ʾAbot* 1:12; *b. Šabb.* 31a (purportedly Tannaitic); *Sanh.* 99b; *Gen. Rab.* 39:14; 47:10; 48:8; 84:8; 98:5; *Num. Rab.* 8:4; *Eccl. Rab.* 7:8, §1; *Pesiq. Rab Kah.* Sup. 1:6; *Pesiq. Rab.* 14:2; 43:6. For further discussion, see Bamberger, *Proselytism*, 13–19 (OT period), 19–24 (intertestamental period), 222–25 (early rabbis), 225–28 (the royal house of Adiabene), 267–73 (on Matt 23:15); Urbach, *Sages*, 1:549–54 passim; Flusser, "Paganism," 1097; cf. the information in Georgi, *Opponents*, 83–164, although his conclusions go too far.

119. See, e.g., Stern, "Greek and Latin Literature," 1157; esp. Gager, *Anti-Semitism*, passim.

model convert maker.[120] Nevertheless, Judaism did not send out formal "missionaries" to make proselytes.[121] Although formal "missionaries" were not employed, those who spread the message were deeply committed to it.[122]

Undoubtedly, many Jews, like members of various other religious groups, spread their faith when they traveled (see comment on Acts 8:4); their relative theological marginalization (as monotheists in a polytheistic society) could have made their efforts seem a part of survival. Yet Paul's mission and the model that it provided for Luke's audience were an element distinctive to the Christian movement in the ancient Mediterranean world.

I suspect that Gentile converts would have been less welcome in some times and places than in others—for example, in Jerusalem in the years immediately preceding the Judean revolt (cf. Acts 21:20–25; 22:21–22). Nevertheless, they were often welcome.[123] The OT ger, or stranger, was entitled to the same justice as the native,[124] and ger came to be understood as "proselyte" in many early Jewish texts.[125] Proselytes were to be treated well,[126] for they had a favorable standing before God.[127] Just how great a measure of status could be attributed to proselytes may be illustrated by later rabbis' common identification of Abraham as a model proselyte[128] and by the tradition that Shemayah and Abtalion were descendants of proselytes.[129] Proselytes could become disciples of the sages.[130]

Despite social disadvantages to the first-generation proselyte, a proselyte's spiritual status was, in theory, equal to that of an Israelite. Some rabbis taught that although

120. See, e.g., *Song Rab.* 1:3, §3; Safrai, "Abraham und Sara"; Hayward, "Abraham as Proselytizer"; Bamberger, *Proselytism*, 176–79. Cf. also Job (Jacobs, "Motifs").

121. Levinskaya, *Diaspora Setting*, 19–33; Donaldson, *Paul and Gentiles*, 59; Cohen, "Missionize." See further discussions at Acts 1:8 and 10:2.

122. Hoenig, "Conversion," 49; Lake, "Proselytes," 75; Sevenster, *Anti-Semitism*, 203; Talbert, *Mediterranean Milieu*, 147–48n33. Feldman, "Conversion," suggests massive numbers of proselytes even without missions. Active proselytizing may have imitated Hellenistic models (cf. Goodenough, *Church*, 9; Culpepper, *School*, 117) and may have been stifled by the wars with Rome (Applebaum, *Jews and Greeks in Cyrene*, 343; Gager, *Kingdom*, 137; for other perspectives, see, e.g., Cohen, "Conversion").

123. Because the strong majority of early Jewish literature relevant to the subject is rabbinic, I draw on it here despite its later date, though generally listing Tannaitic sources before Amoraic ones.

124. For a summary of the OT data, see Moore, *Judaism*, 1:330–31; De Ridder, *Discipling*, 46.

125. Cf. *Sipra Qed. par.* 4.206.1.2; *Sipra Emor par.* 7.223.1.1, *pq.* 19.243.1.12; *Sipra A.M. par.* 7.190.1.1, *pq.*11.191.1.1; *Pesiq. Rab Kah.* 3:16; *Pesiq. Rab.* 12:9; also Montefiore and Loewe, *Anthology*, 566. It probably still means "foreigner" in CD VI, 21, where it is conjoined with the poor as those needing aid; Ohana, "Prosélytisme," argues from targumic usage that the identification is later. But the identification had already begun in the LXX; see Blauw, *Missionary Nature*, 56; Lake, "Proselytes," 84.

126. *Mek.* on Exod 22:20 (in Smith, *Parallels*, 104–5); *Sipra Qed. pq.* 8.205.1.4, 6; *Sipre Num.* 78.3.1, 5.1; *b. B. Meṣiʿa* 59b; *Pesiq. Rab.* 42:1. These passages especially stress not reminding the proselyte of his or her former life; see comment below.

127. Jos. *Ant.* 20.89–91; *y. Sanh.* 6:7, §2; *Exod. Rab.* 27:5; *Lev. Rab.* 1:2; 2:9; 3:2; *Num. Rab.* 8:1, 2, 9; 13:15–16; *Ruth Rab.* 3:5; *Eccl. Rab.* 7:8, §1; the thirteenth benediction of the Amida (in Oesterley, *Liturgy*, 65). Cf. *t. Peʾah* 4:18, which extols the piety of Monobases, king of Adiabene. Like Israelites, proselytes have accepted the covenant (*Sipra VDDen. par.* 2.3.3.1) and must keep the Law (*Sipra Qed. pq.* 8.205.1.5; *Sipre Num.* 71.2.1); because the proselyte could not depend on ancestral merits, his or her part in the world to come would have been acquired through his or her own merit entirely (*Num. Rab.* 8:9; cf. *2 Bar.* 42:4–6; *Exod. Rab.* 19:4). Proselytes would testify against the nations on the day of judgment (*Lev. Rab.* 2:9; *Pesiq. Rab.* 35:3).

128. *Mek. Nez.* 18.36ff. (Lauterbach, 3:140); *b. Sukkah* 49b; *Gen. Rab.* 39:8; *Num. Rab.* 8:9; cf. Bamberger, *Proselytism*, 175–76; Torrance, "Origins," 170. But although there was never consensus, many Tannaim forbade proselytes to call Abraham their father (see Cohen, "Fathers").

129. *B. Yoma* 71b; *Giṭ.* 57b; cf. also Bamberger, *Proselytism*, 222–23. Cf. the eminent descendants of Rahab the proselyte in *b. Meg.* 14b; similarly, on Ruth in *Gen. Rab.* 88:7 (implied in Matt 1:5).

130. *Sipre Deut.* 253.2.2; *Pesiq. Rab.* 14:2 (purportedly Tannaitic); *Eccl. Rab.* 7:8, §1 (purportedly Tannaitic). Aquila, who made the extremely literal Greek translation, was said to be a disciple of the sages, though he was a proselyte; *Gen. Rab.* 70:5; *Exod. Rab.* 19:4.

proselytes from particular peoples could not marry directly into Israel in the first generation, according to one understanding of the Torah, they also could not marry pagans because, in regard to them, they were of Israelite status.[131] Justin also testifies to the mid-second-century Jewish belief, apparently widespread, that the proselyte is "like one who is native born."[132]

This is not to say that there were not certain restrictions on proselytes, especially regarding whom they should marry.[133] They also ranked below other members of Israel in social standing[134] and would more quickly be accused of sin.[135] Sincerity was absolutely essential for proselytes; Judaism despised false proselytes,[136] with later texts explicitly demanding fear of God as the proper motive for authentic conversion.[137] Some second-century rabbis rejected proselytes who balked at so much as a single obligation of Torah.[138]

After a thorough review of the evidence, however, Bernard Bamberger concludes that the halakah is overwhelmingly friendly toward converts[139] and that rabbinic texts are mostly favorable toward them.[140] Sidney Hoenig is more convinced of this for the Tannaitic period than for the Amoraic period,[141] but for our purposes, the Tannaitic evidence is more relevant (closer to the era in question), in any case.

The early Christian emphasis on mission not only has a historical setting (such as Jewish interest in proselytes) but provides part of the backdrop for events that have played a major role in subsequent history. The book of Acts reflected, and probably contributed to, the missions focus of early Christianity,[142] a focus that, in turn, has

131. *Y. Yebam.* 8:2, §7 (purportedly Tannaitic), attributed to Akiba and his circle. Rabbi Joshua, cited in the majority opinion against R. Gamaliel II, argued the case that Ammonite proselytes should be accepted (*b. Ber.* 28a), which has implications for how Deut 23:3 came to be read by the rabbis.

132. Justin *Dial.* 123.1; see Barnard, "Old Testament," 403; Williams, *Justin Martyr*, xxxii. On the "newborn child" status, see the more extensive treatment in Keener, *John*, 543–44.

133. *Sipre Deut.* 253.2.2; *y. Yebam.* 8:2, §7; *Pesiq. Rab Kah.* 16:1, for specific kinds of proselytes. In general, they were restricted only from marrying into priestly families (Stern, "Aspects," 623; cf. Keener, *Marries Another*, 56–61), although the second generation was only restricted, if ever, if both parents were proselytes (*m. Qidd.* 4:7; *b. Yebam.* 77a; cf. *b. Qidd.* 73a–74b), and marrying proselytes could be discouraged (*b. Pesaḥ.* 112b); but an Amora, citing tradition purportedly from Hillel, advocates the intermarriageability of all classes in Israel, including proselytes (*b. Yebam.* 37a). The prohibition against proselytes' marrying priests perhaps reflected rabbinic distrust of Gentiles' virginity after the age of three years and one day, taken together with the Torah's requirement that priests marry virgins or the widows of priests (*b. Yebam.* 60b; *Qidd.* 78a, both purportedly Tannaitic). On the other side, however, strangulation, the more lenient form of punishment, could be applied to a proselyte not native-born, as opposed to one born into Israel of a proselyte mother (*m. Ketub.* 4:3).

134. *M. Hor.* 3:8; *Num. Rab.* 6:1; perhaps CD XIV, 4; cf. Derrett, *Audience*, 47; Jeremias, *Jerusalem*, 272, 323. They would be excluded from the eschatological sanctuary in Qumran, and this exclusion probably reflected some broader Jewish conceptions of their social inferiority; see Baumgarten, "Netinim"; Blidstein, "4QFlorilegium."

135. *B. Šabb.* 33b–34a; *Lev. Rab.* 27:8; *Pesiq. Rab.* 23:4. In *b. Pesaḥ.* 91b, however, because proselytes do not know the law well enough, they may err by being *too* strict.

136. E.g., Jdt 11:23; *Test. Jos.* 4:4–6; *Sipre Deut.* 356.5.7; *b. 'Abod. Zar.* 3b; *Šabb.* 33b; *Pesiq. Rab.* 22:5.

137. E.g., *b. Qidd.* 62a; *Yebam.* 24b; 47a; *y. Giṭ.* 1:4, §2; *Qidd.* 4:1, §§2–3; *Num. Rab.* 8:4, 9; cf. Urbach, *Sages*, 1:387–88, on *b. B. Meṣi'a* 72a. Some did allow that proselytes from impure motives might still have some status before God (cf. *y. Sanh.* 6:7, §2). Neusner, "Conversion," 66, argues that political factors may have partially motivated the conversions of Helena and Izates, though their conversions were sincere.

138. *T. Demai* 2:50; cf. *Num. Rab.* 5:3.

139. Bamberger, *Proselytism*, 145.

140. Ibid., 149–61; for the few unfavorable ones, 161–65; and mixed opinions, 165–69. Converts are as dear to God as born Jews (149–54), or dearer (154–56); Israel's dispersion was God's way to increase proselytes (156–58); converts were protected by (mainly Tannaitic) laws against harm from Jews (158–61). Bamberger argues that this favorable attitude carries through the whole talmudic period, although at times the popular prejudices did affect the rabbis (277–78). Proselytes had no place in the land, but neither did priests (66–67); there is also some evidence that some people were proud to trace their ancestry from converts (230).

141. Hoenig, "Conversion," 43.

142. It also appears in more heavily Jewish Christian works such as Matthew (see Keener, *Matthew*, 719–20) and, to a lesser extent, perhaps John (cf. idem, *John*, 627, 1204–6; but cf. 149–52).

contributed to the survival of Christianity (in its plethora of post-Lukan forms) to this day.[143]

ii. Pagan "Universal" Ideals

Imperial propaganda worked hard to produce a united empire out of many diverse peoples, as Alexander's or Persia's or other earlier empires had done.[144] (As in most empires, some ethnic conflicts remained under the surface, sometimes for centuries.[145] But trade, cultural interchange, the use of Greek in the East, and geographic mobility had created a degree of cultural unity among urban citizens of the eastern empire, especially in Asia, Macedonia, and Greece.)[146] In contrast to the forced mixing of human empires, Luke instead[147] emphasizes that Israel's God is humanity's God,[148] and advocates a unity composed of diverse ethnic elements under the true Lord, Christ.[149]

Christians were not the only ethnically and socially "universalistic" cult in the empire; some foreign cults, such as that of Isis, sought to make converts among Romans and others,[150] and some other Mysteries lacked class barriers.[151] Nevertheless, the combination of Christians' ethnic universalism and their (much rarer) theistic particularism made conversion of others an imperative. (Although some streams of Judaism were more universalistic than others,[152] Judaism, in general, remained more of an "ethnic" faith than the Pauline movement was.)[153] Although Luke presents this ethnic universalism as God's call and ideal, his narrative also addresses the church's early struggles as it grappled with the cross-cultural implications of its mission.[154]

iii. Gentile Multiculturalism

Educated people recognized that cultures varied considerably in their preferences (e.g., Max. Tyre 21.6). Naturally, Skeptics, who reduced all arguments down

143. As Wayne Meeks points out, of the many religions in the Roman Empire, the only two that transformed themselves sufficiently to persist into the present were rabbinic Judaism and Christianity, both of which grew from earlier Judaism (Meeks, "Foreword," 9).

144. Witherington, *Acts*, 439, 459; for the unity of humanity in ancient thought, see Judge, *First Christians*, 588–94. For Alexander, see, e.g., Quint. Curt. 6.6.4, 7, 9 (noting his Macedonians' resistance); Sen. Y. *Ep. Lucil.* 94.63; Plut. *Alex.* 45.1–3; 47.3; Dio Chrys. *Or.* 4.49; *Num. Rab.* 13:14; for Persians, perhaps Ps.-Callisth. *Alex.* 1.23; for Rome, e.g., Polyb. 39.8.7; Vitruv. *Arch.* 1.pref. 1; Dio Chrys. *Or.* 3.6–7; Men. Rhet. 2.12, 422.22–23; less favorably, Rev 13:7; for the ideal, e.g., Fronto *Ad M. Caes.* 4.1. For earlier empires, see, e.g., Plut. *Themist.* 27.2–3; 3 Macc 6:5. War had also united the legendary Trojans and their allies (Hom. *Il.* 4.437–38).

145. E.g., Philost. *Vit. soph.* 1.24.529 (addressing a seven-century-old local conflict in the second century C.E.).

146. Like Roman imperialism outside Rome, Hellenism was universalistic in its cultural outlook (Theissen, *Sociology*, 88).

147. For contrasts between Caesar and Christ in Luke-Acts, see, e.g., Luke 2:1, 14 and comments on it by Danker, *New Age*, 24.

148. Fontana, "Opera."

149. Witherington, *Acts*, 439, 459.

150. Cf., e.g., the Isis cult (Apul. *Metam.* 11.10, 15; Grant, *Gods*, 69–70); cf. the Serapis cult's making converts (Klauck, *Context*, 63–64). This is not to say that all cults could make converts; Greeks rejected Mithraism, e.g., as too Persian (148).

151. E.g., Gager, "Class," 102–3; but for all its openness (Mylonas, *Eleusis*, 282; Klauck, *Context*, 99; Evans, "Sanctuaries"), Eleusis accepted only Greek initiates (cf. Lucian *Dem.* 34).

152. See, e.g., Segal, "Acts 15," who traces Paul's universalism to this source. For one discussion of particularism and universalism in the OT, see Park, *Jew or Gentile*, 12–16; in early Jewish texts, 16–20.

153. Although Paul probably viewed Gentile converts as proselytes (see Donaldson, *Paul and Gentiles*, 230–47; idem, "Riches," 98), lack of mandatory circumcision reduced the boundaries (on the tensions this generated, cf., e.g., Ravens, *Restoration*, 247–49). On Gentiles in Acts being gathered into the commonwealth of Israel, cf. Brawley, "Commonwealth." Pao, *Isaianic Exodus*, 217–48, fruitfully grounds Luke's view of Gentiles'/nations' status in Isaiah.

154. On the cultural tensions between heritage and mission, cf., e.g., Pantelis, "Etnias e iglesias"; for one application from Acts 6–12 to an Indian context, see Vadakkedom, "Work."

to cultural differences, emphasized this recognition, using it to relativize the differences.[155] But since Herodotus's travels, Xenophon's reports of Persia, and Alexander's conquests, Greeks (while generally maintaining their own cultural superiority) in general recognized differences that extended beyond their traditional dichotomy of "Greeks" and "barbarians."[156] Some historians even warned readers not to judge other peoples' customs by their own cultural standards (Corn. Nep. pref. 2–3; 15 [Epaminondas], 1.1).[157]

Sensitivity to local customs and mores became a widespread strategy of communication and relating to local cultures;[158] Rome also did not bind the provinces by most Roman customs (Pliny *Ep.* 10.68–69). G. W. Bowersock notes that the development of novels focused on anything exotic or foreign; the empire and the form of eastern Hellenism dominant in the imperial period had begun to embrace multiculturalism instead of simply "asserting the superiority of Graeco-Roman culture. The old standard of Hellenism broke down in the second and third centuries [with some tendencies in the first], and in doing so it made way for a new kind of Hellenism, an ecumenical Hellenism that could actually embrace much that was formerly barbaric."[159]

Most Greeks were interested, however, primarily in Mediterranean geography; even Strabo (whose geographic interest is wider than Pausanias's) showed no interest, for example, in European peoples to the north.[160] Garnsey and Saller observe that "from Strabo to Cassius Dio . . . the cultural elite of the empire drew a firm line between what they saw as the Mediterranean core of the empire and its barbaric periphery. In particular, the conquest of the North did not in their view produce a broader cultural unity."[161]

Luke's purview also remains the empire, especially the eastern Mediterranean, which was his home. Because of the faith's Jewish identity, "strange" Asian Palestine receives greater attention than in traditional Hellenistic sources. But Luke gives only sample attention to the spread of the message to the south (Acts 8:27) and even less to its certain spread into Jewish Parthia;[162] his audience in the empire would have been most interested in their gospel reaching the heart of the empire. But given this setting, Luke shows the same sort of awareness of cultural dynamics that characterizes minority cultures within a dominant culture. This sensitivity of minorities also characterized Diaspora Judaism in the empire, which provided Paul's original context and earliest Christianity's cultural bridge to the Gentiles. Like Paul (1 Cor 9:20–21), Luke emphasizes the need for sensitivity to local cultures within the larger universal church (Acts 11:3–18; 15:19–21; 21:20–25).

155. Sext. Emp. *Pyr.* passim, e.g., 3.198; cf. 1.2.5–6; Sen. Y. *Ep. Lucil.* 88.44; Epict. *Diatr.* 1.27.2, 15; Aul. Gel. 11.5.1–8; Lucian *Indictment* 15, 25; *True Story* 2.18; *Phil. Sale* 27; Diog. Laert. 9.11 passim, e.g., 9.11.74, 79, 90, 101–2.

156. E.g., for distinctive views about Africans from the classical through the patristic period, see esp. Snowden, *Blacks in Antiquity*; idem, *Color Prejudice*; idem, "Black-White Relations."

157. For various cultural differences, see, e.g., Corn. Nep. pref. 5–7.

158. In rhetoric, Quint. *Inst.* 3.7.24; Eunapius *Lives* 495; also recommended by some rabbis, *Exod. Rab.* 47:5 (an older saying about acting according to customs where one visits); more generally, Ap. Rhod. 2.1017; Plut. *Alex.* 45.1–3; *Alc.* 23.4–6; Corn. Nep. 7 (Alcibiades), 11.2–6; Max. Tyre 21.6; Diog. Laert. 2.66.

159. Bowersock, *Fiction as History*, 53; more fully, 29–53. This reverted, in a sense, to Alexander's attempted cultural fusion, more limited by his successors.

160. Garnsey and Saller, *Empire*, 14–15, noting that even Ael. Arist. *Or.* 26 (*To Rome*) reveals "firm Hellenocentricity."

161. Garnsey and Saller, *Empire*, 19. For Roman imperial unification as subjugation of (at least initially) peripheral peoples, see, e.g., *Res gest.* 5.26; for conquering via conquered, see Lopez, "Visualizing," 88.

162. Cf. Bauckham, "East Rather Than West."

4. Luke's Eschatology

Although eschatology is not a major emphasis in Acts, it has generated considerable discussion.[163] Since the commentary addresses the question more thoroughly at Acts 1:6–7, it is introduced only briefly here. Some scholars have played down eschatology in Luke-Acts. Luke is, after all, a historian, and those with a view to history's long-range verdicts are not generally those who emphasize an imminent end of the age.[164] Further, some scholars think that the delay of the parousia caused early Christians to shift their interest, whether this hope was surrendered or merely deferred indefinitely.[165] Haenchen, for example, thinks that although Luke preserved the hope of the parousia, he denied its imminence and simply called his audience to spread their message until Christ's return.[166]

Others, however, are skeptical that we can safely read so much into Luke's use of the historiographic genre.[167] Groups could show interest in their history while maintaining future eschatology; the Qumran community preserved the teachings of their founder both when they expected the end in their generation and when they were forced to defer this expectation temporarily.[168] Luke also maintains future eschatology (e.g., Luke 13:25–30; 17:20–18:8; 21:20–36), even in the apostolic preaching to Gentiles at points (Acts 10:42; 17:31), though more clearly to Jewish audiences (1:6–7; 3:19–21). Scholars are thus certainly not unanimously skeptical of Luke's future eschatology. Some, indeed, have found eschatological anticipation in Luke's eucharistic material[169] or even proposed that Luke wrote Acts to hasten the fulfillment of the Gentile mission and its role in God's end-time plan.[170] Because many divine promises are fulfilled within the narrative of Luke-Acts (including the promise of the Spirit in Acts 1:4–5), Luke presumably expects us to infer that the promise of Jesus's coming (1:11) will also be fulfilled.[171]

Nevertheless, Luke does not emphasize imminent future eschatology the way that Mark or Matthew does. Though less than in John, Luke's focus is realized eschatology, as Jesus's answer to his disciples' eschatological question in Acts 1:6–8 makes clear (see also comment on Acts 2:2–4, 17–21).[172] At the same time, the eschatological structure of Jesus's Palestinian Jewish kingdom message differs from contemporary Gentile expectations. Although poets and propagandists of the early Augustan period saw in their time the dawning of a new era, by the early second century (reflecting on events of Luke's era), Roman historians (e.g., Tacitus) pes-

---

163. For studies of eschatology relevant for Acts before 1965, see Mattill and Mattill, *Bibliography*, 301–3; for one more recent survey of views, see Powell, *Acts*, 58–62.

164. See, e.g., Cic. *Att.* 2.5, more concerned for his reputation six centuries hence than in his own day.

165. E.g., Case, *Origins*, 179–80. See further discussion at Acts 1:6–7.

166. Haenchen, *Acts*, 95–96.

167. Van Unnik, "Storm Center," 24, 28–29.

168. For the coexistence of present and future eschatology at Qumran, see Aune, *Cultic Setting*, 29–44. Even apocalyptic literature often includes summaries of previous history to set the stage for eschatological suffering and triumph (cf., e.g., Frost, "Apocalyptic," 144). Most historians in Greco-Roman antiquity lack eschatology in the Jewish sense precisely because they were not Jewish (usually the case) or because they were very hellenized or wrote for hellenized audiences (e.g., Josephus and Alexandrian Jewish writers). Nothing in the genre demands these assumptions, however, and so they should not be presupposed for a document from early Christianity, birthed as an eschatological movement (cf. Collins, *Mark*).

169. Kee, *Origins*, 117. See esp. Luke 22:16, 18.

170. See Mattill, "Date and Purpose," 350. We should note, however, that Luke omits Mark 13:10.

171. With Gaventa, *Acts*, 67 (citing idem, "Eschatology Revisited," 37; Carroll, *Response to End*, 126–27).

172. Cf., e.g., Maddox, *Purpose*, 145 (recognizing future eschatology but focusing on the present); Luke 17:20–21. For Luke's emphasis vs. Paul's on this and some other points, see Lodge, "Salvation Theologies." Contrast Luke 21:6–7 (and Luke's source here, Mark 13:2–4) with Matt 24:2–3.

simistically regarded their civilization as in decline and viewed the past nostalgically. Luke instead views the new era in Christ as good news, part of the inbreaking of the future kingdom.[173]

Hans Conzelmann tried to fit Luke-Acts into a tripartite division of salvation history, but subsequent scholarship has severely critiqued his perspective (see comment on Acts 1:6–8). More helpfully, one critic opines that in Luke's perspective, "the same story keeps repeating, but in different keys and with a definite sense of escalation toward a climax represented by the parousia."[174]

Playing down all future eschatology in Luke may appeal to modern interpreters more than to first-century Christians, who could allow multiple elements to stand side by side.[175] The rejection of future eschatology has often characterized modern Western attempts to "translate" biblical teaching into a noneschatological worldview, though it is likely that the early Christians, even had they understood our culture, would have viewed such "translation" as distorting their message.[176] Thus Bultmann views the real point of eschatology as realized in preaching, both in the past and in the present.[177] He deliberately reinterprets Johannes Weiss's and Albert Schweitzer's approaches to apocalyptic eschatology in terms of Martin Heidegger's existentialism.[178] Yet it has been argued that Bultmann works from a fairly narrow layer of NT writings, interpreting them "in a way which carries him quite close to the gnosis of the second century."[179]

The Gentile mission (treated above) probably plays a role in Luke's eschatology (cf. Luke 21:24, "times of the Gentiles"). If Luke understands Isaiah as saying that the period of welcoming Gentiles lasts until Israel's repentance and restoration,[180] then the very hardness of Israel justifies the Gentile mission, against Jewish objections. When Israel turns to the king whom God appointed for them, God will bring about the end (Acts 3:19–21). Acts 1:6–8 might imply that the mission to the Gentiles is a prerequisite for the end (cf. Matt 24:14; Rom 11:25–26). All these matters are discussed more fully under Acts 1:6–8.

5. The Holy Spirit

Despite the brevity of this treatment of Luke's theology, we cannot forgo at least a brief discussion of the Spirit in Luke's theology (and presumably the experience of the Pauline churches of which he was a part).[181] (Because this is the most appropriate location to discuss the early Jewish context of Luke's pneumatology, also included here is a more extensive excursus on the Spirit in early Judaism.) The Spirit is central

173. See Witherington, *Acts*, 12.

174. See Nolland, "Salvation-History," 70–76, esp. 70; for the infancy narratives' contradicting Conzelmann's scheme, see p. 72.

175. Even the Fourth Gospel, which strongly emphasizes realized eschatology (Käsemann, *Testament*, 15–16; Dodd, *Preaching*, 75; Schweizer, *Jesus*, 164–68), has some future elements (see Kümmel, *Theology*, 294–95; Lindars, *Behind*, 66; Barrett, *John*, 68–69; Moule, "Factor," 159; Kysar, *Maverick Gospel*, 87, 110; Burge, *Community*, 115).

176. Had Jesus's earliest followers desired noneschatological forms for expressing their faith, such options existed in the Sadducees (Goldingay, "Expounding," 354), and still more in much of Diaspora Judaism.

177. Bultmann, "History and Eschatology," 16.

178. Perrin, *Kingdom*, 115.

179. Rordorf, "Theology," 361. Some of Bultmann's successors have appealed more directly to gnostic documents as if these provide an earlier picture of the Jesus movement than do more eschatological sources.

180. "To make them jealous," as Deut 32:21 and Paul (Rom 10:19; 11:11, 14) put it.

181. A number of scholars have shown concern for the spiritual experience behind the text (e.g., Dunn, *Jesus and Spirit*; Fee, *Paul, Spirit, and People*; idem, *Presence*).

in Luke's theology (Acts has even been titled "the Gospel of the Holy Spirit"),[182] and the subject has invited considerable scholarly comment.[183] If one counts all possible references to the Spirit in Acts (59), these constitute nearly a quarter of NT references to the Spirit; no other NT book has even half as many.[184] Even Luke's Gospel has nearly three times the references to the Spirit found in Mark (about half its length) and about 1.4 times the references to the Spirit found in Matthew (of equivalent length).[185]

Luke presents the Spirit as necessary for the success of the church's mission (Acts 1:4–8).[186] This centrality of the Spirit is made clear by the fact that in both volumes, Jesus's final words to his disciples before his ascension include the promise of the Spirit (Luke 24:49; Acts 1:4–8). Indeed, the major programmatic texts of both volumes concern the Spirit's empowerment for the mission of God's agents (Luke 4:18–19; 24:48–49; Acts 1:8; 2:17–18); any treatment of Acts that minimizes either the Spirit or the Diaspora mission misses a central point in the work. It was not without reason that John Chrysostom called Acts "the Gospel of the Holy Spirit," the record "of what that 'other Paraclete' said and did."[187]

a. Empowerment by the Spirit

Luke's Gospel is full of references to the Spirit, with each aspect of the Spirit's work there reappearing in Acts.[188] For Luke, as for other early Christians, emphasis on the

---

182. Cf. Chrysostom's title "Gospel of the Holy Spirit" noted below.

183. For surveys of Acts texts about the Spirit, see, e.g., Haya-Prats, *Believers*; Warrington, *Discovering*, 51–74 (for the Gospel, 23–34); Lampe, "Spirit in Luke"; Neil, *Acts*, 52–60; Trocmé, *Esprit-Saint*, 19–44; Stalder, "Geist"; Bruce, "Presentation of the Spirit"; Mangatt, "Spirit and Church"; Neves, "História e Espírito"; Edanad, "Spirit and Community"; Gaventa, *Acts*, 35–39; Karris, *Saying*, 105–17; Doohan, *Acts*, 101–8; Coleman, "Dynamic" (with an application emphasis); Thomas, "Charismatic Structure" (for its centrality); Fitzmyer, "Role of Spirit"; Marguerat, *Histoire*, 149–74; Dumais, *Communauté* (especially in relation to the community); Allen, *Preaching*, 71–87 (with an application emphasis); Jervell, *Apostelgeschichte*, 97–99; Eckey, *Apostelgeschichte*, 617–22; Dormeyer and Galindo, *Apostelgeschichte*, 21–22; Rogers, *Ministry*, 58–88; Bruni, "Spirito"; Walton, "Beginning," 464–65; Robinson and Wall, *Called*, 121–30; Hamilton, "Theology of Spirit"; Puskas and Crump, *Introduction*, 135–37; Peterson, *Acts*, 60–65; Langner, *Hechos*, 275–76; Keener, "Luke's Pneumatology." Mattill and Mattill, *Bibliography*, 270–74, §§3764–74, cite a number of earlier studies (e.g., Allen, *Pentecost*; Baer, *Heilige Geist*; Dana, *Holy Spirit*; Bonnard, "Esprit Saint"), including unpublished theses and studies from the nineteenth and early twentieth centuries. For a survey of views about receiving the Spirit, see Turner, "Significance of Receiving"; for a survey of views about the Spirit in Luke-Acts, see esp. Bovon, *Theologian*, 198–238 (for a chronological bibliography, see 198–201); much more briefly, Powell, *Acts*, 50–56. Stagg, *Acts*, 5–9, contends that the Spirit is not Acts' primary focus (although a prominent one, 8) because it is not mentioned everywhere, but it is far more pervasive than Stagg's genuinely helpful "unhindered" emphasis!

184. Hull, *Spirit in Acts*, 12. This emphasis is even clearer if we restrict consideration to the exact phrase, "holy Spirit" (Haya-Prats, *Believers*, 3–5). Presence or absence of the article is not conceptually significant; although Haya-Prats, *Believers*, 13–16, 22–28, follows O. Proksch in allowing a general pattern of differentiation, it is not very consistent, and he charts more relevant grammatical patterns on 22–26. Turner, *Grammatical Insights*, 18, suggests that the anarthrous use in Acts 2:4 but articular use in 2:33, 38 fit usage for "the definite article with proper names," treating the Spirit as "a divine person"; in my opinion, though, his approach leads to absurd results in classifying Luke's pneumatological references (17–22). Turner, "Spirit Endowment," classifies seventy-five references to the Spirit in Luke-Acts in six categories (though one could classify the references by various other criteria). The Western text amplifies this emphasis on the Spirit even further (Bruce, *Acts*³, 75).

185. Marshall, *Historian and Theologian*, 91, noting that most references to the Spirit not found in the other Gospels concern testimony to Jesus at his birth (and noting the Gospel's use as fitting the dominance of the Spirit in Acts).

186. Mangatt, "Spirit and Church"; Edanad, "Spirit and Community"; Miller, *Empowered for Mission*, 62, 69 (noting [133] that although Luke focuses on just key episodes, many of these include empowerment by the Spirit); Cheum, "Spirit and Mission," 3–12.

187. Chrys. *Hom. Acts* 1.5, cited in Bruce, *Acts*³, 61n3; Bock, *Acts*, 36. In more recent times the phrase has been attributed to Ehrhardt, "Construction and Purpose," 67 (as cited in Powell, *Acts*, 50).

188. Stronstad, *Charismatic Theology*, 34–48, with special emphasis on prophetic inspiration.

Spirit underlined dependence on God's power and activity. As Richard Hays points out (commenting on Acts 2), "The idea that Acts sanctions a pallid and stultifying 'early catholicism' can only have been promulgated by academics utterly oblivious to the lure of the Spirit's power. This text is, if anything, an expression of 'early Pentecostalism,' not 'early catholicism.'"[189]

1. The Spirit Mandatory for Mission

In an inaugural scene of Jesus's ministry in the Gospel, Jesus, whose empowerment by the Spirit in the Gospel prefigures that of the church in Acts,[190] declares that he is empowered with the Spirit in connection with his mission (Luke 4:18–19). That this passage is the "programmatic" text for Luke's Gospel[191] and that it goes on to prefigure the Gentile mission (4:25–27) make it all the more ideal as a prototype for the church's empowerment to reach the Gentiles (Acts 1:8).[192] Many regard Acts 2:17–18 as the key programmatic text of the second volume; here (as in 1:8, which must count as Acts' thesis statement if it has one) the emphasis on the Spirit's empowerment is paramount.

R. E. O. White also emphasizes the degree to which the mission in Acts depends on the Spirit:

> It is difficult to convey at all adequately the place of the Spirit in Luke's conception of the church without rewriting his entire book. The New Age is the age of the Spirit, the church is above all else the *locus* of the Spirit, her origin, direction, authority, expansion, and development are directly the Spirit's concern, and her members are those upon whom the Spirit has "fallen" or "been poured."[193]

For Luke, baptism in the Spirit offers more than the optimum results of human obedience by adding an obviously divine dimension. Whereas Paul associates the Spirit especially with ethical empowerment and also particular gifts for ministry, Luke focuses on the Spirit's empowerment for, and the Spirit's guiding the church in, cross-cultural evangelism (his theme, 1:8; see comment there).[194]

As noted above, the Spirit, sent fundamentally to empower the apostolic witness (1:8), is democratized in subsequent narratives among all believers in all places (2:39), including Samaritans (8:15–17) and Gentiles (10:45–46). Luke thus anticipates that all believers, including his audience, should share this empowerment. Because this empowerment is for mission, all new believers and churches must become not merely objects of mission (their initial status) but indigenous partners in mission. Such an understanding and experience of the Spirit undoubtedly fueled earliest Christianity's

189. Hays, *Moral Vision*, 135 (using conventional academic, not denominational, parlance). Keck, *Mandate*, 51, likewise points out that one problem with relating to Luke's perspective on the Spirit is "that the churches we actually know often seem bereft of the Spirit," often dependent on bureaucracy, investments, etc. (today we might add marketing).

190. See, e.g., Stronstad, *Charismatic Theology*, 51; Talbert, *Patterns*, 16; further comment on Acts 1:5.

191. E.g., Wilson, *Gentile Mission*, 40; Marshall, *Historian and Theologian*, 91; extensively, Schreck, "Nazareth Pericope." With regard to its significance, cf. also the possible chiasmus in the passage (Bailey, *Poet*, 68; Tiede, *Prophecy*, 35).

192. For Jesus's role in Luke 4:16–30 as paradigmatic for his followers, see, e.g., Brawley, *Luke-Acts and Jews*, 24–25.

193. White, *Initiation*, 189.

194. "Power" in Luke-Acts connects with Jesus's and the church's mission (Luke 1:17, 35; 4:14; 24:49; Acts 1:8; 4:33; cf. Luke 21:27) and often with attesting "signs" (Luke 4:36; 5:17; 6:19; 8:46; 9:1; Acts 3:12; 4:7; 6:8; 10:38). Luke, like Paul (Rom 1:4; 15:13, 19; 1 Cor 2:4; Eph 3:16; 1 Thess 1:5; cf. 2 Tim 1:7), often couples the Spirit with power, especially in key texts (Luke 1:17, 35; 4:14, 36; Acts 1:8; 10:38). Cf. Strelan, *Strange Acts*, 59–63, associating "spirit" with power more generally.

phenomenal growth rate (a growth rate paralleled in some Christian movements today, most commonly in the Majority World, that have appropriated the same ideal).[195]

II. Spirit Baptism and Diverse Experiences

One key text is John's prophecy about the coming one's baptizing the righteous in the Spirit and the wicked in fire (Luke 3:16).[196] This promise of baptism in the Spirit (Acts 1:5) is identical with the "gift" (2:38; cf. 8:20) and "promise" (1:4; 2:33, 39; Luke 24:49) of the Spirit, clearly identified with the experience in Acts 2 (Acts 2:33, 39 show the fulfillment of the "promise" in 1:4). The identification is also clear because the Spirit as "gift" (2:38; 8:20; 10:45; 11:17) is the Spirit as "promise" (they are identified in 2:38–39). As gift and promise, the Spirit further reflects God's benevolence, not a resource people can buy (8:20) or earn (cf., similarly, Rom 5:5; Gal 3:2–5). This perspective contrasts with the idea in one stream of Jewish tradition that the Spirit is reserved only for the very pious (or would be so reserved, had the generation not been unworthy).[197]

The phrase "baptism in the Spirit" must include what all believers experience; in Luke 3:16 John's wording refers to an eschatological outpouring on all the righteous in contrast with the eschatological fire baptism of the wicked. It includes the entire sphere of the Spirit's work, into which conversion initiates the believer. Nevertheless, Acts is clear that believers do not all experience every aspect of the Spirit upon conversion (cf., e.g., Acts 4:8, 31).[198] (See discussion at Acts 1:4–5; 8:15–16.) Luke emphasizes the Spirit's activity especially in empowerment for ministry, and in his narrative these experiences do not always occur precisely at conversion (though the anticipated norm for his ideal, evangelistic church was that it occur very close to that time).

In Paul (and apparently even in Luke's theology, 2:38), empowerment for ministry belongs to the entire sphere of the Spirit's activity initiated in the believer's life

---

195. For one discussion of the earliest movement's growth rate, see Keener, "Plausibility."

196. For this interpretation of the Q saying, see my argument in Keener, *Matthew*, 127–28; cf. Menzies, *Development*, 137–44; the careful treatment in Bock, *Theology*, 213–18.

197. See, e.g., *Mek. Besh.* 7.135ff. For few being worthy and the generation unworthy, see *t. Soṭah* 13:3–4; *y. 'Abod. Zar.* 3:1, §2; *Hor.* 3:5, §3; *Soṭah* 9:16, §2; *Song Rab.* 8:9, §3; the same is said of the Shekinah (e.g., *'Abot R. Nat.* 14 A; *b. Sanh.* 11a, bar.; *Soṭah* 48b). But elsewhere a good deed or a pious life can merit the Holy Spirit (*m. Soṭah* 9:15; *t. Soṭah* 13:2; *'Abot R. Nat.* 11, §28 B; *b. Sukkah* 28a, bar.; *Exod. Rab.* 5:20; *Lev. Rab.* 35:7; *Song Rab.* 1:1, §9) or the Shekinah for oneself (*Sipre Deut.* 173.1.3; *'Abot R. Nat.* 28, §57 B; *b. B. Bat.* 10a) or for Israel (*Num. Rab.* 12:21) or can merit prophets (*Sipre Deut.* 176.1.1; 176.2.2) or prophecy (*b. Sanh.* 39b). Similar statements about worthiness appear elsewhere in the rabbis (e.g., *t. Sanh.* 4:7; cf. *3 En.* 2:4). But the "gift" of the Spirit is not unusual Jewish language (e.g., Wis 9:17; cf. *Sib. Or.* 4.46, 189–90; cf. Wisdom in Sir 1:10; Wis 8:21).

198. So also various authors (e.g., Stronstad, *Charismatic Theology*; Keener, *Gift*, 157–68); Yong, *Spirit Poured*, 119, sees the baptism in the Spirit as including both salvation and empowerment, at different levels (cf. Atkinson, "Luke-Acts"). Wenk, *Power*, 315–16, also denies the distinction between "prophetic" and "conversion." I would concur that a distinction between the Spirit in conversion and afterward is not Lukan (Luke shows little interest in sequence unless it is to rid us of emphasizing it); to contrast prophetic and conversion categories is to mix functional and temporal categories. In my view, John the Baptist's original phrase encompasses the entire sphere of the Spirit's eschatological work; nevertheless, Luke plainly emphasizes the empowerment dimension (see Acts 1:8). The Holy Spirit certainly is eschatological, associated with restoration (as I have argued earlier; Keener, *Gift*, 145–46), but the manifestations in Luke-Acts are *especially* (though not exclusively) prophetic (see Acts 2:17–18), as one can see easily enough by simply surveying all the passages in Acts referring to the Spirit's activity. The association with conversion occurs at the theological level (as in 2:38), but in narratives, even when the Spirit is received at conversion, this reception is often expressed in a charismatic-prophetic way (10:44–48). That Luke's emphasis on the Spirit is on prophetic empowerment rather than on salvation or sanctification is clear enough at the textual level; see, e.g., Haya-Prats, *Believers*, passim (esp. xvii, 138, 192, 237), who notes that salvific features are instead focused on Jesus (192). Nevertheless, H. Gunkel overstates the contrast with Paul (who emphasizes salvation or sanctification, but also includes charismatic empowerment; cf. Stonehouse, *Areopagus*, 72, 86).

through conversion.[199] Luke, however, readily departs from this neat schema in his narrative, suggesting that early Christian experience was fairly diverse.[200] Despite the common temptation to read Paul's theology into Acts, it seems fairly clear that, in Acts, believers could experience the Spirit at faith but before baptism (10:44–48), immediately after baptism (19:5–6) or somewhere close to that time (9:17–18), clearly subsequent to baptism (8:12–17), and on multiple occasions (compare 2:4 with 4:8, 31; 9:17 with 13:9).[201] Interpreters often regard up to two-thirds of Luke's examples as "exceptions" to what they view as his ideal pattern, but it seems more prudent to suspect that Luke invites his audience to recognize that the pattern varied in practice.[202] It should be remembered, however, that Luke only rarely focuses explicitly on the Spirit's role in conversion and that he focuses most often on the prophetic-empowerment dimension[203] of the Spirit's activity. Thus Luke allows for a particular dimension of Christian experience subsequent to faith and repentance but is not distinguishing conversion from the latter. The gift, apparently, technically begins at conversion in principle but, in terms of Luke's emphasis on its prophetic-empowerment dimension for mission, may be experienced in this prophetic form subsequent to conversion (and on multiple occasions).[204]

III. Prophetic Empowerment

The portrayal of God's agents as filled with the Spirit may serve multiple theological purposes. One of these may be as apologetic toward Judaism: the end-time Spirit (Acts 2:17) earmarks the true community of God's Messiah.[205] The apostolic leaders of this community are also led by God as the prophets of old were, including in their outreach to Gentiles (cf. Luke 4:25–27; 6:23). Because pagans also respected some mystic sages, the narrative might serve an apologetic function even toward them; for an analogy, Philo may have an apologetic purpose in portraying Moses as having a continuous prophetic experience of being filled with divine spirit.[206] But the specific setting for Luke's theological language about the Spirit is distinctively Jewish and Christian. His thoroughgoing emphasis on the Spirit also suggests a genuine theological belief that God's direct prophetic empowerment enables the church to carry out God's mission and that this mission is not possible apart from the Spirit (cf. Acts 1:4 and Luke 24:49, forbidding the mission to begin without this empowerment).

Certainly, Luke associates the Spirit with prophetic proclamation, as the vast majority of Lukan scholars agree.[207] According to the early Jewish model, prophetic

199. Paul often portrays ministry in terms of spiritual gifts, which he views in terms of members of Christ's body, a status achieved at conversion. For χαρίσματα as "ministries," see Aker, "Gifts."

200. In addition to preserving accurately the diverse experiences of early Christianity (even at the expense of his own schema in Acts 2:38), Luke may find some theological import, reporting these variations on the pattern to demonstrate God's sovereignty as well as to offer literary variety in his narrative. Many scholars note the variation (see comment at Acts 8:15–16).

201. That is, the primary issue of import is not a "second" experience per se but *multiple* experiences of empowerment as needed, alongside a continuous state of being "full" of the Spirit in some passages. See, e.g., Keener, *Gift*, 166–68; also Carson, *Showing Spirit*, 160.

202. In the same way, Luke's portrayal of prophecy is far less "neat" than modern theological interpreters might like; cf. Acts 21:4.

203. As broadly conceived: the empowerment that ancient prophets experienced, including, for those following the Elijah/Elisha model (on which see comment on Acts 1:8–11), signs and wonders.

204. Some even see Acts 2:38 as making conversion merely the prerequisite for receiving the Spirit in the dominant Lukan sense—i.e., for empowerment. See comment on Acts 2:38.

205. Cf., e.g., 4Q504 1–2 V, 15; 4Q504 4 5; 4Q506 131–32 11.

206. Sterling, *Ancestral Philosophy*, 171–80, esp. 180.

207. Some scholars associate the Spirit almost exclusively with empowerment for witness (esp. Menzies, *Empowered*; Stronstad, *Prophethood*, esp. 121–22; Haya-Prats, *Believers*, 31, 34, 192); most scholars who feel

inspiration could include not merely verbal inspiration (although this is its most common focus) but also activity like that of the prophets (cf. the model of Jesus in Luke 24:19).[208] The Spirit provides power for confronting those hostile to the message (e.g., Acts 4:8; 5:32; 7:55; 13:9), most obviously in Paul's defense speeches in Acts 22–26 (see Luke 12:11–12). The Spirit also inspires the content of the message, "the word of the Lord" or "the word of God," which throughout Acts represents most often the good news about Christ (particularly his resurrection and attendant offer of life). To summarize the content of the protagonists' speeches in Acts is also to summarize the sort of message Luke expects the Spirit to inspire: bold preaching of, and argument for, Christ.

b. A Survey of Some Other Themes about the Spirit in Acts

We will explore the following texts in considerably greater detail in the commentary proper and pause only to survey them briefly here (using this introduction to survey more fully key elements of the understanding of God's Spirit among Luke's contemporaries).[209] Even aside from the abundant passages discussing the Spirit in Luke-Acts, the Spirit plays a central role in the pivotal conclusion of the Gospel of Luke and its recapitulation in Acts (Acts 1:4–8); introductions typically laid out main themes. The Spirit is an essential prerequisite for all the disciples' ministry in and beyond Jerusalem, and they dare not begin this ministry without the Spirit (1:4). This empowerment was apparently necessary to fulfill testimony to all the nations as the prerequisite for the kingdom (1:6–8).

i. Realized Eschatology

Baptism in the Spirit is realization of the eschatological promise (2:17), perhaps again by bringing many to call on the Lord before the fullness of the kingdom (2:21).[210] Paul, too, associated the experience of the Spirit with realized eschatology (e.g., Rom 8:11, 23; 1 Cor 2:9–10; 2 Cor 1:22; 5:5; Gal 6:8; Eph 1:13–14), and so this perspective is appropriate for a writer in the Pauline circle of Christianity. Because some Jewish circles believed that the Spirit had been suppressed (at least in the sense of inspiring full prophets),[211] it was natural to link the Spirit with eschatology even more (e.g., Isa 44:3; 59:21; Ezek 36:27–28; 37:14; 39:29; Joel 2:28–3:1). Some other Jewish circles apparently believed that the Spirit's activity among them represented the proximity of the end time.[212]

---

that this first group of scholars sometimes overstates the case nevertheless associate the Spirit in Acts *primarily* with this emphasis (e.g., Walton, "Acts," 29, citing also Dunn and Turner; Cho, *Spirit and Kingdom*, 136, citing "most scholars," including myself). Read, "Spirit," notes four connected pneumatological emphases in Acts (including the prophetic element). Levison, *Filled*, 425–26, notes Luke's emphasis on inspired speech but also his valuing of sober intellect.

208. On Jesus as prophet in Luke's Gospel, see esp. Stronstad, *Prophethood*, 35–53. (Croatto, "Prophet," also emphasizes Jesus's prophetic role in Luke-Acts, though contrasting this too much with a messianic approach.) On Luke's portrayal of prophetic themes (associated with Jesus's movement) versus conventional priestly hostility, echoing Israel's earlier history, see helpfully Phillips, "Prophets."

209. As Hur, *Reading*, 274, observes, the Spirit appears "at every plot-stage" in Acts.

210. One may note that Luke employs the language of "promise" both for the Spirit (Luke 24:49; Acts 1:4; 2:33–39) and earlier promises to Israel (7:5, 17; 13:23, 32–33), a promise climaxing concretely in the eschatological resurrection of the righteous (26:6–7).

211. See discussion in the excursus at Acts 2:17.

212. Aune, *Cultic Setting*, passim (especially on Qumran). The association of the Spirit and the end time in the rabbis is mostly late and peripheral (cf. Menzies, *Empowered*, 94–98, who suspects that the association was not dominant in first-century Judaism; cf. also 232–43). Wenk, *Power*, 56–111, traces the connection between the Spirit and covenant renewal in early Jewish sources.

II. Cross-Cultural Empowerment

Cross-cultural empowerment by the Spirit (see discussion of the Gentile mission, above) is essentially a *new* mission. This cross-cultural empowerment is marked initially by other peoples' tongues (Acts 2:4) reflecting the wide range of peoples directly known to those present (2:5–11); that Luke also mentions other tongues on two subsequent occasions (10:46; 19:6) underlines just how important this gift's function is in communicating Luke's emphasis on the cross-cultural element of the Spirit's empowerment.

Although Luke explains this phenomenon in terms of biblically sanctioned inspired speech (2:17–18), the cross-linguistic character of tongues speaking is new and points to the distinctively new character of cross-cultural ministry to the Gentiles. In seeking to underline the Spirit's empowerment to witness to all peoples (1:8), to what more obvious sign could Luke appeal in the inaugural Pentecost narrative than Spirit-generated worship in other people's languages?[213] (Although Luke also views this experience as a turning point in salvation history, he grounds the eschatological ministry to the Gentiles in Isaiah's prophecy of the Gentile mission; see comment on Acts 1:8.)[214]

The Spirit empowers cross-cultural evangelism in the rest of the book (8:29; 10:19–20; 11:12), pointing out where (or where not) to evangelize at a given time (16:6–7) and even snatching Philip away so that he will keep preaching to other strategic places (8:39–40). The Spirit sends Paul and Barnabas out (13:2, 4), as demonstrated by the Spirit's power in 13:9, providing a Spirit-empowered paradigm for the rest of their mission (as with Jesus's ministry in Luke 4:1, 14, 18), even though Luke does not mention the Spirit explicitly at every turn.[215] Ultimately, the goal of cross-cultural evangelism is the multicultural church;[216] addressing cross-cultural conflicts, the Spirit guides believers to cross-cultural *unity* (Acts 15:28).

III. For All Believers

Luke's focus is on key leading agents of the mission, demonstrating continuity between the apostolic ministries of Peter (for the circumcision) and Paul (for the uncircumcision; cf. Gal 2:8). Despite Luke's narrative focus, however, he affirms that the Spirit is for all believers (Acts 2:17) and hence participation in the mission extends beyond the original "witnesses" (1:8) to all believers (8:4). This empowerment continues to be offered to all believers (2:38), including later generations of Gentile Christians (like much of Luke's audience; 2:39).

The Jerusalem church expected the Spirit always to follow in churches that were in spiritual continuity with the apostles (8:14–17; 9:17; 10:44); the signs of continuity could be that later groups received the Spirit "just as" the first believers did (10:47; cf. 11:15; 15:8). New churches join in the mission, empowered by the same Spirit. God was readier to accept the later groups than were the apostles, and confirmed his acceptance of them by this gift (10:44–48; 11:15; cf. 13:52). The Spirit corroborates

---

213. See Keener, "Tongues."

214. For this theme, see esp. Pao, *Isaianic Exodus*. On the Spirit and the Gentile mission, see, e.g., Philip, *Pneumatology*, 204–24; briefly, Langner, *Hechos*, 287.

215. Aletti, "Testimoni" (focusing on the parallel with Jesus's passion) points out the lack of emphasis on the Spirit in Acts 22–26. In view of the promises in Luke 12:11–12 (cf. 21:13–14), however, we must assume the Spirit's activity in the defense speeches; other texts show that the Spirit was active during (Acts 20:22–23; 21:4, 11) and after (28:8) this period in Paul's life.

216. Paul's establishment of faith communities rooted in Diaspora Judaism but including uncircumcised Gentiles clearly exerted an influence on Luke and perhaps on many other streams of early Christian thought as well (cf. Rev 5:9; 7:9).

such members as God's people (15:8),[217] again performing the literary function of connecting believers from all peoples (and all generations, including those subsequent to that of Pentecost; cf. 2:39).

IV. GOOD NEWS FOR THE SOCIALLY MARGINAL

Although Acts emphasizes the Spirit's connection with evangelism and other prophetic speech more than with acts of compassion and justice, the two cannot be totally separated. The Gospel's concern for the marginalized continues in Acts, and while in Acts this emphasis figures predominantly in terms of the Gentile mission, the Gospel's theme of justice for the poor is nowhere repudiated.[218] Indeed, it remains, albeit usually in the background, as part of the ideal community that the good news of the kingdom is meant to produce (e.g., Acts 6:1; 24:17), and is connected with outpourings of the Spirit on the community (2:44–45; 4:32–35).

This theme fits Jesus's inaugural statement in Luke's Gospel, where the Spirit anoints Jesus to bring good news to the poor and liberation to the captives (Luke 4:18–19). Although Luke probably envisions this liberation initially especially with regard to hostile spiritual powers (Acts 10:38), Jesus's concern is for the literal poor (Luke 6:20; 7:22; 16:20; 21:2–3), whom the new community must serve (14:13, 21; 18:22; 19:8; Acts 4:34), and for the literal blind, whom he literally heals (Luke 4:18; 7:21–22; 18:41–43; Acts 9:18) and the community must serve (cf. Luke 14:13, 21). Healing is connected to God's "power" in Luke-Acts (see comment on Acts 1:8), which is in turn connected with the empowerment of the Spirit to bear witness to the truth of Christ's exaltation and gracious character (Acts 1:8).

In contrast to some traditional Christian approaches, however, the Spirit's relation to social concern in Luke-Acts involves not only compassion but *empowerment*. Christ not merely helps but heals and restores the broken. Likewise, he welcomes the marginalized not simply to receive charity but to become partners themselves in the fellowship of the new community (see discussion of κοινωνία and κοινός at Acts 2:42, 44)—not objects but participants.[219] The Spirit's empowerment obviates gender and age barriers (2:17–18) and, throughout Acts, cultural and ethnic boundaries; all these groups become themselves sharers in the Spirit (2:17–18; 8:17; 10:45; cf. 2:39) and hence participants in the mission (cf. 1:8). This means that Luke connects the Spirit not just with acts of justice (by themselves potentially paternalistic) but with the creation of a new community of people equally dependent on Christ and committed to one another (hence the climax of the Pentecost narrative in the formation of the ideal community, 2:41–47; cf. 4:31–35).

V. OTHER ACTIVITIES

The Spirit is related to prophecy in 11:28, probably 13:2, 4, and especially in the programmatic quotation of 2:17–18 (for the Spirit and OT prophecy, see 4:25; 28:25).[220] Trustworthy leaders could be "full of the Spirit" (Luke 4:1; Acts 6:3, 5; 7:55; 11:24),

217. Cf. also, e.g., Hur, *Reading*, 276.

218. Cf., e.g., O'Toole, *Unity of Theology*, 109–48. Just as Luke moves from heritage to mission in Acts yet does not wish to repudiate heritage (in which his entire story is grounded), and as "kingdom," appearing roughly forty-five times in the Gospel yet mentioned only rarely (eight times) in Acts, remains an important concept (featured in Acts 1:3 and 28:23, 31, thus framing Acts). For the centrality of concerns for justice and the poor in Lukan theology, see, e.g., Cassidy, *Politics*; Ringe, *Liberation*; Green, "Good News"; Langner, *Hechos*, 45; discussion at Acts 2:44–45.

219. Among theologians today, this emphasis on shared ministry appears in, e.g., Sanders, *Margins*; cf. idem, *Ethics*, 115.

220. The Spirit also brings christocentric prophecy in Luke 1:41, 67; 2:25–27. For the christocentric aim of the Spirit, see Twelftree, *People*, 205–6 (as in John 15:26–16:15).

and the Spirit appoints leaders to guide the local churches (Acts 20:28); perhaps this means that they were appointed through the Spirit's direction, perhaps in prophecy as in 13:2–4 (though this was confirmatory; cf. 1 Tim 1:18; 4:14; 2 Tim 1:6).[221] The Spirit also gives leaders discernment (Acts 5:3).

The Spirit empowers believers to witness for Christ even against rulers (4:8, 31; 5:32; 7:51; cf. Luke 12:11–12) and other opposition (Acts 6:10); the Spirit provides boldness to speak for God even in the face of death (7:55). The Spirit is related to the power of signs (6:3, 8; cf. 4:33), a topic explored at greater length below (in sect. 6; in addition to ch. 9 above).

The Spirit figures in Luke's Christology: this outpouring is proof of Jesus's enthronement (2:33),[222] and by pouring out God's Spirit, Jesus takes on a clearly divine role (cf. Luke 3:16).[223] Some scholars have argued that the locus of Luke's treatment of the Spirit is personal holiness;[224] but although some early Christian writers do emphasize the activity of the Spirit in moral purification,[225] Luke's primary focus is power for mission. It does seem likely that Luke sometimes associates the Spirit with salvation (cf. Luke 3:16; Acts 2:38–39), but the prophetic emphasis tends to be dominant even in these very contexts (cf. Acts 2:17–18).[226]

The emphasis on God's presence and covenant renewal also appears, especially in the Pentecost narrative,[227] though it is expressed in Acts especially in a prophetic way.[228] Acts 1:8, a programmatic text, places Spirit-inspired speech (there "witness") in the context of Isaiah's restoration promises (i.e., covenant renewal). The promised (eschatological) prophetic Spirit is indeed a sign of God among his people and serves

221. Subsequent analogies in charismatic traditions could be multiplied. One may compare for example the prophecies that led two Pentecostals to go to a certain "Para"—of which neither had heard but which they learned was a state in Brazil—which resulted in the founding of a major segment of Brazilian Pentecostalism, altogether now tens of millions strong; see Anderson, *Pentecostalism*, 71–72.

222. See discussion on Acts 2:32–36, esp. work by Max Turner. Tremolada, "Gesù e lo Spirito," notes the conjunction of Christology and pneumatology at Luke 1:35; 3:21–22 and (in a different way) Acts 2:32–36.

223. Apart from its christological context, one could read Luke 3:16 as promising that the coming one was God himself (Keener, *Matthew*, 130). Naturally for Luke and early Christians, such a distinction was not strictly necessary.

224. Strelan, *Strange Acts*, 53, citing 1QS IV, 21; IX, 3–4 (apparently without recognition that this Qumran view represents a relatively isolated stream of Jewish expectation; cf. Keener, *Spirit*, 8–10).

225. See, e.g., Keener, *Spirit*, 135–89.

226. Cho, *Spirit and Kingdom*, 136, cites for salvation Luke 1:35 but notes that (138) this involves the broader issue of salvation history and that (138–40) the same context associates the Spirit even more often with prophecy (Luke 1:15, 17, 67; 2:25–27). Luke connects the Spirit with proclamation, not (in contrast to Paul) with kingdom blessings such as sonship (160–95; idem, "Spirit and Kingdom").

227. Wenk, *Power*, argues (against Menzies) that Luke associates the Spirit not just with prophecy but with covenant renewal (see 118, 252–53); I would argue that, despite such associations in early Judaism (Wenk, *Power*, 56–111), the *dominant* emphasis in both early Judaism and Luke-Acts is prophetic (fitting Menzies's point; cf. Keener, *Spirit*, 10–13), though Wenk is, of course, correct about the larger sign of God's presence, of which even prophetic renewal is a part. (Wenk himself is not denying the prophetic element [see, e.g., *Power*, 316], simply insisting on the ethical component also.) For the Spirit manifesting Christ, see rightly Robichaux, "Incorporation."

228. The Holy Spirit certainly is eschatological, associated with restoration; Luke contemplates the entire sphere of the Spirit's eschatological activity, as I have argued earlier (Keener, *Gift*, 145–46), but the manifestations in Luke-Acts are *especially* (though not exclusively) prophetic. I undertook my dissertation (Keener, "Pneumatology") independently of (and, at the time, entirely ignorant of) the current debate and tried to categorize the data only after collecting them by reading through ancient literature. Because inspired wisdom and knowledge overlapped with prophecy and other activities associated with prophets in the OT, I grouped them as one large category, and texts concerning moral purification as the other, much smaller one; although prophetic material appears throughout the literature, I found the emphasis on purification especially in Essene-type circles, which also included the prophetic element (see excursus just below). I was working on John's Gospel, where both emphases occur; but in Luke-Acts, the predominant category is that associated with prophetic activity, and this is what the programmatic Joel quotation explicitly emphasizes.

an apologetic purpose to this effect. But when one compares Luke with Paul or John, it is difficult to evade the conclusion that Luke's emphasis on the *practical* activity of the Spirit is overwhelmingly prophetic, even if placed in a broader covenant framework. This broader covenant framework helps us evaluate the theological importance of this empowerment, however, in terms of Luke's reading of the new community as part of God's larger story of salvation history (see ch. 14 above).

c. The Spirit and God

As in the rest of early Judaism, we cannot speak of God's Spirit in Luke-Acts without thinking of God.[229] In 5:3–4, lying to the Spirit is lying to God. At the same time, like some other early Christians, Luke may go beyond the traditional Jewish understanding of the divine Spirit at times. Although Luke does not write to provide answers for later trinitarian debates, his language at many points (e.g., Acts 1:16; 5:3, 32; 7:51; 13:2, 4; 15:28; 16:6; 20:23, 28; 21:11; 28:25) is not inconsistent with the view that the Spirit acts as a person.[230] Paul seems to presuppose a prototrinitarianism already in his letters,[231] and Luke portrays the Spirit carrying on Jesus's ministry[232] and even as an actor throughout Luke-Acts.[233] As Gaventa points out, the Spirit sometimes acts as "the initiator of events" and sometimes is "resisted"; in such cases, "it is exceedingly difficult to disentangle the Spirit from God."[234]

But even if we may assume that Luke was usually unlikely to contradict Paul (his protagonist and in whose circle of churches he moved), Luke is hardly explicit in portraying the Spirit as a distinct divine identity.[235] Whatever else he may have believed, Luke includes nothing like John's Paraclete sayings; rather, his emphasis is on the Spirit's power for evangelism, continuing the OT idea of God's Spirit providing prophetic empowerment to speak for him. The Spirit speaks, as to the prophets of old; given Luke's focus, it is not surprising that he emphasizes this activity particularly in connection with cross-cultural evangelism (8:29; 10:19; 11:12; 13:2; 16:6–7). It is on this aspect of the Spirit's work, therefore, that this commentary must focus. See, more fully, comment on Acts 1:4–5; 2:4, 17–18.

229. For the Spirit as an aspect of God, sometimes treated anthropomorphically, already in Isaiah, see Ma, *Spirit*, 208; for God's Spirit on the analogy with human spirits in the OT, see, e.g., Keener, "Spirit," 485–86.

230. Shepherd, *Narrative Function*, 255–56, stressing Luke's portrait of the Spirit, in narrative-critical language, "as a character" (but cf. the church as a "character" in Thompson, *Church*, esp. 241–48); cf. Haya-Prats, *Believers*, 93, noting that Acts moves in this direction; cf. Turner, *Grammatical Insights*, 18, arguing from a grammatical peculiarity, but not (in my opinion) persuasively. Later, and thus taking narrative analysis further, Hur, *Reading*, 129–80, notes that the Spirit appears both like and unlike a person, "as an enigmatic *divine* character," usually characterized indirectly (178); emphasizing the Spirit's personality, sometimes at the expense of other characteristics, cf. also Choi, "Personality," 101–222. Fitzmyer, "Role of Spirit," 177–79, concurs that Luke sometimes personifies the Spirit beyond the OT (the Spirit "speaks," "testifies," "snatches," is "lied to," etc.). Bonnah, *Spirit*, 97–98, highlights appearances of the Spirit with Jesus and God. Strelan, *Strange Acts*, 63–65, notes personal references to the "spirit" (e.g., as an angel) in Jewish sources (see, in more detail, Keener, *John*, 957–71) but thinks (65) that Luke may refer to multiple kinds of "spirit" (God's spirit, spirit of Jesus, etc.; I would instead view these phrases as reflecting different aspects of the one divine Spirit placed on Jesus; cf. Acts 2:33). Witherington, *Acts*, 72, is correct that Luke's focus is on events more than on persons (even divine ones), but given the biographic character of Luke's Gospel (focusing on Jesus), Luke must hope that his readers will focus on the divine activity in the narrative.

231. See esp. Fee, *Presence*, 839–42; Watson, "Identity"; cf. Talbert, *Matthew*, 313; in Paul, esp. 1 Cor 12:4–6; 2 Cor 13:14; Eph 4:4–6. Levison, *Filled*, 229–31, cites a range of OT and early Christian texts in which the Spirit may act somewhat personally.

232. See Quesnel, "Critère," especially for Acts 1–2. This is more explicit, of course, in John (John 14:16, 26; 16:9–10, 14–15; see Keener, *John*, 962–69; idem, "Pneumatology," 218–65, esp. 254–65).

233. Shepherd, *Narrative Function*, passim.

234. Gaventa, *Acts*, 38 (citing Acts 5:3; 7:51).

235. See Turner, *Power*, 41–44.

Excursus: Background for Luke's View of the Spirit

Although I will focus in this excursus on less-familiar elements of Luke's context, his most significant backgrounds for portraying the Spirit in his work are early Christian experience and understanding of Scripture. In his Gospel, Luke retains most references about the Spirit from Mark and Q and adds others.[236] Most of Luke's themes about the Spirit derive (whether through the gospel tradition or directly) from the OT.[237] This is significant because the Spirit marks out believers as the restored people of God, in continuity with the biblical remnant, those who keep God's covenant (cf. Isa 32:15; 42:1; 44:3; 59:21; 61:1; Ezek 36:26–27; 37:14; 39:29; Joel 2:28–29; Zech 12:10).[238] More particularly, Luke develops the biblical theme of the Spirit who empowered the prophets to speak (and sometimes to act, with signs and wonders) for God.[239] Although Luke does not focus on prophetic empowerment exclusively, there is a wide consensus that he focuses especially on prophetic inspiration and witness.[240]

Early Judaism[241] would recognize most of these themes, but its emphasis differed from what biblically illiterate Gentiles would readily comprehend.[242] Because Luke's themes about the Spirit already appear in his Bible (although the pervasiveness of pneumatic and prophetic experience among believers is especially an eschatological amplification of the earlier experiences, following Joel 2:28–29), I will not belabor early Jewish perspectives (which mostly develop the same biblical material) at undue length. Nevertheless, we must at least survey this material because it offers a context for how many of Luke's contemporaries would have understood both his text and the earlier experiences that his text describes. This introduction, rather than the main text, is the appropriate place to survey some thoughts about the Spirit in early Judaism relevant to Luke-Acts (other points specifically relevant to Acts 2:17–18, relating

---

236. See the list in Stronstad, *Charismatic Theology*, 35.

237. Ibid., 14–27; for the influence of the LXX, see Fitzmyer, "Role of Spirit," 168–70. For the Spirit in the OT, see, e.g., Lys, *Rûach*; Wright, *Spirit through Old Testament*; Fee, *Presence*, 905–10; Keener, "Spirit," 484–87; the survey of sources in Ma, *Spirit*, 20–25; in Isaiah, see Ma, *Spirit*, passim.

238. See Jervell, *Unknown Paul*, 96–121; cf. Turner, *Power*, 300–301; Wenk, *Power*. Lövestam ("Apostlagärningarnas ärende") also addresses the Spirit's creating God's new people across ethnic boundaries. On the Spirit's association with ethics and covenant renewal in the OT, see Wenk, *Power*, 56–65; in Palestinian Jewish literature, 66–82; in Hellenistic Jewish literature, 83–97; and in the Qumran scrolls, 98–111.

239. See Keener, "Spirit," 486, 489 (treated less extensively here because I have addressed it elsewhere); Menzies, *Empowered*, 106–228; idem, *Development*, 205–77 (on Acts); Cho, *Spirit and Kingdom*, 162–95; Kremer, *Pfingstbericht*, 84 (prophecy, tongues, and miracles); Bonnah, *Spirit*, 206; in early Jewish thought, Menzies, *Empowered*, 49–101; idem, *Development*, 53–112; idem, "Power"; Turner, *Power*, 86–104; Keener, *Spirit*, 10–13, 31–33; in the OT, Wright, *Spirit through Old Testament*, 63–86; briefly, Keener, "Spirit," 486–87; and further below in this excursus. Likewise, Cho, *Spirit and Kingdom*, 10–51, argues that early Jewish sources associate the Spirit with prophecy rather than with life-giving wisdom. Although sources occasionally do associate the Spirit with wisdom (see Keener, *John*, 961–64; idem, "Pneumatology," 254–57), my own research for my 1991 dissertation basically concurs with Cho.

240. Turner, "'Spirit' as Power," 327–48 (esp. 333–37); idem, *Power*, 333–46 (esp. 318); idem, *Gifts*, 38–40; idem, "Empowerment"; cf. also *Gifts*, 46–55 (though Turner associates the gift of the Spirit more closely and consistently with conversion than I think the narratives warrant; cf. 46–55; idem, "'Spirit' as Power," 339–47; idem, "Challenge"). Turner, "Work," notes that the majority perspective today on Lukan pneumatology focuses on prophetic empowerment separate from conversion (though himself treating them together).

241. For surveys of the Spirit in early Judaism, see, e.g., Isaacs, *Spirit*; Büchsel, *Geist*; Menzies, *Empowered*, 49–101; Keener, "Pneumatology," 58–114; idem, *Spirit*, 6–48.

242. See Keener, *Spirit*, 7–8; for exceptions, see, e.g., Dion. Hal. *Ant. rom.* 1.31.1. Connections between Luke's pneumatology and the pneumatic school of Greek medicine (Marx, "Physician") appear ingenious but tenuous. Turner, "Authoritative Preaching," is skeptical that even the early Jewish understanding played a role (focusing on Christian experience).

early Jewish pneumatology to eschatology and prophetism, will be surveyed in the commentary on that passage).[243]

1. Gentile Backgrounds?

Although some scholars have suggested a Persian background for the Spirit (more plausible for the "holy spirit" phrase than for the content),[244] scholars have appealed to Greek usage more frequently. Yet even the non-Christian Greek range of usage for πνεῦμα differs considerably from the Jewish range for what we translate as "Spirit" (with reference to the divine Spirit). Max-Alain Chevallier summarizes its Gentile Greek usage as follows:[245]

1. Breath, wind
2. A personal power—a good or bad δαίμων
3. Anthropologically, dualistically opposed to the body
4. Not the divine spirit in the sense found in Jewish literature[246]
5. Psychological dispositions

Although there is considerable overlap with the usage of רוח (*ruakh*) on points 1–3, Chevallier finds little overlap on points 4 and 5.

a. Spirit and the Divine

The image of the divine spirit varied in Greco-Roman literature. Quintilian, for instance, observes that some think that god (*deum*) is a spirit (*spiritum*) "permeating all things" (*omnibus partibus immixtum*), whereas others, such as Epicurus, think god has a human form.[247]

The Stoics and those influenced by their language[248] sometimes associated πνεῦμα with the divine,[249] but hardly in the Jewish or Christian sense. "Spirit" in Stoicism was an impersonal cosmic substance, "the finest form of matter,"[250] a mixture of fire

---

243. I am drawing here from Keener, *Spirit*, 7–13 (with notes, 27–33), which I have abridged and supplemented at a few points.

244. The Persian parallel suggested by some writers (e.g., Finegan, *Religions*, 90, 93; Ringgren, *Word*, 170; Fritsch, *Community*, 70–73) is more verbal than conceptual ("holy spirit" as the Good vs. the Evil Spirit in Zoroastrianism [Olmstead, *Persian Empire*, 94, 96, 104; Yamauchi, *Persia*, 437]) and not particularly related to prophecy (though cf. Olmstead, *Persian Empire*, 96), and the Persian sources are difficult to date certainly and are, by this period, culturally remote; see, e.g., Scott, *Spirit*, 46, for relevant observations on this point (cf. Yamauchi, *Persia*, 466).

245. So Chevallier, *Ancien Testament*, 37–39.

246. See esp. Isaacs, *Spirit*, 18–19; apart from the Stoics, the references in Greek literature to this are rare. Thus the view that the Spirit concept in the Gospels is hellenized (Leisegang, *Ursprung*, esp. 140–43) may be open to correction; for critics, see the sources in Hur, *Reading*, 34n67; see Isaacs, *Spirit*, 115–16, on Bultmann's improper use of Dalman's data. Πνεῦμα in Hellenistic Judaism, except when it refers to wind, normally is of divine origin (Isaacs, *Spirit*, 59–64), if Isaacs is right to understand the human spirit also in this way.

247. Quint. *Inst.* 7.3.5 (LCL, 3:84–85).

248. E.g., the Middle Platonist Max. Tyre 4.8 adapts Poseidon from being the breath in the sea (as in early Stoics) to being the cosmic breath altogether. For gnostic texts, undoubtedly betraying Christian influences, see Wilson, "Spirit"; Chevallier, *Ancien Testament*, 74–76.

249. Isaacs, *Spirit*, i.

250. So Lake, "Spirit," 103; see Klauck, *Context*, 353–54; Scott, *Spirit*, 52–53; on non-Jewish approaches, including Stoicism, see Strelan, *Strange Acts*, 55–58. For Stoics, anything that truly existed consisted of substance (Nolan, "Stoic Gunk"; Vogt, "Brutes"); only material things truly existed (Arius Did. 2.7.5a.5–6; 2.7.5b.7, p. 20.28–22.1; Hierocles *Elements of Ethics* 1.14–15); some others concurred with the physicalist approach

and air[251] that interpenetrated all other matter and was like the soul of the universe.[252] It was not central to Stoicism's ethics but to its physics and metaphysics, conceptualized in terms of Stoic monism.[253] As Arthur Darby Nock points out, the Stoics knew πνεῦμα ἱερόν (sacred spirit) but not πνεῦμα ἅγιον;[254] the Stoic concept is thus quite different from the traditional Jewish concept.[255] It is part of early Stoicism's monistic pantheism.[256]

b. Spirit and Inspiration

There is, however, one context in which Greek discussion of divine spirit overlaps somewhat with Jewish interests. Greeks and Romans understood the notion of divine inspiration, a concept that pervades their literature (see comment on Acts 2:17–18). Usually this inspiration is attributed to particular deities, such as Apollo or the Muses (see comment on Acts 2:17–18), but given the discussion of the divine spirit above, it is not surprising that some texts would also speak of inspiration by the divine spirit.[257]

Some ancients claimed that inspiring vapors possessed the Pythian priestess (see comment on Acts 16:16) and other mantics to speak for local deities (Pliny E. *N.H.* 2.95.207–8).[258] Yet in the formative period of Jewish and Christian usage, such inspiration only rarely emphasized divine πνεῦμα.[259] Hans Leisegang can cite texts associating "spirit" with the inspiration of the Pythoness,[260] but apart from Strabo, most of his sources are late enough to betray Christian influence. A stronger case can be made with Plutarch's[261] late first-century use of πνεῦμα as a source of inspiration.[262] But the concept of "spirit" here has more to do with Stoic-like conceptions of a pervasive substance, or with exhalations from the earth such as those affecting the Pythian priestess at Delphi (the standard view earlier held by Plutarch), than with a spirit

(see, e.g., Gill, "Galen and Stoics"). The Spirit could also be portrayed in somewhat materialistic language in rabbinic sources; see Abelson, *Immanence*, 212–23.

251. Long, *Philosophy*, 155–58; cf. Chevallier, *Ancien Testament*, 41–42. For different views of the basic elements, with air and fire emerging among the four conventional ones, see, e.g., Vitruv. *Arch.* 8.pref. 1.

252. Long, *Philosophy*, 171; cf. Schweizer, *Spirit*, 29; Sext. Emp. *Pyr.* 3.218.

253. Büchsel, *Geist*, 45–49, esp. 47.

254. Nock, *Christianity*, 51; also Büchsel, *Geist*, 52–53.

255. Some argue, however, that Philo may have merged the two (Dodd, *Interpretation*, 222). Yet Scott, *Spirit*, 58–59, and Isaacs, *Spirit*, 19, point out some clear differences that Philo maintained against the Stoa in his use of πνεῦμα, apparently due to antecedent Jewish usage. Chevallier, "Souffle," 43–46, esp. 45–46 (on Wisdom of Solomon), observes that Hellenistic Jewish sources retain OT perspectives but also evince an infusion of ideas from the Hellenistic world, especially Stoicism. Though often helpful in his insights elsewhere, Engberg-Pedersen, "Spirit," is too ready to read Stoic materiality into Paul's conception of *spirit*.

256. Klauck, *Context*, 353–54.

257. For the popular Greek (as well as Jewish) association of πνεῦμα with irrational, enthusiastic inspiration, see, e.g., Jewett, *Romans*, 73 (also mentioning miracle working).

258. Thus Men. Rhet. 2.4, 390.23–24, writing in the third or fourth century, speaks of Apollo "filling [ἐπλήρου] prophets with the mantic spirit [μαντικοῦ (τοῦ) πνεύματος]." In the second century, Max. Tyre 8.1 speaks only of a δαιμόνιον filling the Pythoness and other oracular personnel.

259. Isaacs, *Spirit*, 15; the most noteworthy exceptions are Eurip. frg. 192 and Plato *Phaedr.* 265B (against his standard usage); cf. also Dion. Hal. *Ant. rom.* 1.31.1, but here the expression is δαιμονίῳ πνεύματι. Πνεῦμα was probably not associated with ecstasy in the Mysteries; cf. Büchsel, *Geist*, 104. Chevallier, *Ancien Testament*, 39–40, cites Euripides and the inspiration of the Delphic Pythoness, Sibyls, and bacchants, noting that by the NT era, when πνεῦμα, as a term, came to be applied to inspiration, it had become current to speak of the "mantic spirit," but he does not document this last remark; he notes (40–41) Plato's use of ἐπίπνοια rather than πνεῦμα for poetic inspiration but argues that this is equivalent to Plutarch's (much later) use of πνεῦμα.

260. Leisegang, *Ursprung*, 32, citing Suidas, Origen, and John Chrysostom.

261. Plut. *Obsol.* 41, *Mor.* 432F–433A. For comments on the spirit in Plutarch, see Büchsel, *Geist*, 49–52.

262. The Greek is λεπτύνειν τὸ πνεῦμα; the word "prophecy" does not occur, but this is implied by the context.

associated *particularly* with inspiration.[263] As Aune observes, "While Greco-Roman writers certainly had a concept of inspiration, they did not normally associate that conception with *pneuma*."[264] The rare occurrence of possible exceptions contrasts starkly with the abundance of sources in early Judaism (see discussion below).

In other cases, earlier Jewish usage may have even occasionally influenced Greek usage, given strong Jewish influences in Greco-Roman magical practices.[265] The LXX's rendering of רוח (*ruakh*) as πνεῦμα probably influenced "subsequent Greek literature."[266]

2. The Spirit of Purification in Early Judaism

One could divide the evidence of early Jewish pneumatology in a variety of ways,[267] but I have chosen to divide it into two categories. This is because some usages (such as praise) seemed too rare to merit their own large category (unless it is "other"); some applications (such as to the Messiah)[268] often overlapped with other categories (such as prophecy);[269] some usages (such as prophecy and knowledge) are more distinguishable (and hence could, in fact, justify separate categories) but overlap considerably; miracles[270] were normally performed by prophets in biblical tradition, and so the few examples of this association also may be subsumed here. The two most readily distinguishable streams appear to be purification and prophetic empowerment, although the latter is a much broader category, and more widespread in early Judaism, than the former.

Beyond these two larger rubrics, the Spirit of God anoints God's servants for a variety of functions in the OT, including wisdom for craftsmanship,[271] and physical prowess and strength.[272] Such usages continue in early Jewish texts, although rarely (except for the

263. Parke, *Oracle*, 22–24; Isaacs, *Spirit*, 15, 50; Schweizer, *Spirit*, 30; Aune, *Prophecy*, 34. In Dio Chrys. *Or.* 72.12, she "filled herself with the breath of the god" (LCL, 5:186–87); Cic. *Div.* 1.36.79 notes that the power of the earth *incitabat*, "aroused," the Pythian priestess, in contrast to the Sibyl's inspiration, but in 2.57.117 it is said (against the Stoic view) that the subterranean exhalations that once inspired her no longer work. Cary and Haarhoff, *Life*, 317, observe that "mephitic vapours" did not, in fact, exist in the temple; see also Klauck, *Context*, 187; Lehoux, "Drugs" (though contrast recently McGinnis, "Faults").

264. Aune, *Prophecy*, 34.

265. Nock, *Christianity*, 51: the references to the "holy spirit" in magical texts may be due to Jewish influence, although this similarity may have contributed to further development of Christian pneumatology.

266. Isaacs, *Spirit*, 17. Fitzmyer, "Role of Spirit," 168–70, rightly sees the LXX as a major influence on the portrayal of the Spirit both in Acts and in Jewish literature in Greek.

267. See, e.g., Turner, *Power*, 86–104 (helpfully treating prophecy, inspired wisdom, revelations, and praise).

268. Ibid., 114–18.

269. Discrete discussion of the Messiah's empowerment seems to me to constitute a category in a list of objects of empowerment rather than in one of the nature of empowerment. That is, the Messiah (a key object of empowerment) might receive, among other gifts, prophetic empowerment (a mode of empowerment). Rather than compare apples and oranges (objects and nature), I have chosen to focus exclusively on categories about the nature of empowerment here. Nevertheless, the messianic application is certainly relevant for passages associating Jesus with the Spirit (see esp. Turner's comments addressed in the commentary at Acts 2:33).

270. Turner, *Power*, 105–14, offers the limited evidence. He is right to note that associating the Spirit with prophecy does not rule out also associating the Spirit with miracles (118). (On the association being fairly rare, cf. also Menzies, *Development*, 57.)

271. Exod 31:3; cf. 1 Kgs 7:14, where the writer omits reference to the Spirit.

272. Judg 13:25; 14:6, 19; 15:14; cf. 16:20; 1 Sam 11:6; cf. 18:2 (an evil spirit acting similarly). In most of these cases, however, the power was also related to the fact that God's servants functioned as leaders in Israel; cf. Judg 3:10; 6:34 (on the Spirit and leadership in the OT, see Ma, "Empowerment," 31–33; idem, *Spirit*, 29–30). The Pauline use of strengthening by the Spirit may be related to this, especially where it may connote doing battle with spiritual powers, as in Ephesians, but the ethical sense (below) probably contributes more to the usage in the Pauline literature. The Spirit is also related to God's creating work (see Wright, *Spirit through Old Testament*, 13–34).

spirit of revelatory wisdom), compared with more dominant uses. Thus one could be clothed with the Lord's spirit, the spirit of power, for battle,[273] though reference to this function of the Spirit of God sometimes[274] occurs in the expounding of the OT texts that speak of it.[275] Some other occasional usages, such as praise and miracles, are treated below under the spirit of prophecy, since they are not common and can be related to the broader categories of inspiration and activity associated with biblical prophets.

More common, however, are references to the Spirit of God or Holy Spirit as the Spirit that purifies.[276] This usage also has biblical roots, perhaps in the image of prophetic empowerment also transforming character,[277] but especially in the image of eschatological cleansing by God's Spirit portrayed as water.[278] The spirit of purification appears less frequently than the spirit of prophecy in early Judaism, more limited to Essene-like circles.

In the Qumran scrolls, the "Holy Spirit" can refer to the "spirit of holiness" genuinely emphasizing holiness, whether the Spirit of God who purifies (e.g., 1QH^a VIII, 20; 4Q255 2 1; 4Q257 III, 10) or the human spirit (e.g., CD V, 11; 4Q266 3 III, 5; 4Q270 2 II, 11; 4Q418 8 4) that has been set apart to God.[279] Thus the "holy spirit" in 1QS III, 7 and IV, 21 is characterized as the spirit that cleanses or purifies from sin, with a possible background in passages such as Ezek 36:25–27;[280] 1QS IV, 21 compares the spirit of holiness to purifying waters[281] poured out on the chosen at the time of the end; and III, 4, 8–9 speaks of a ritual immersion upon initiation into the community. In some of these contexts, especially that of IV, 21, the Spirit is associated with the spirit of truth in contrast with the spirit of error, along with a number of

273. *L.A.B.* 27:9–10 (referring to the OT period).

274. Not always: cf. the Spirit and strength for battle (possibly figurative) in 1QH^a XV, 6–8. Some Qumran references to being sustained by the Spirit's strength, especially in several of the *Thanksgiving Hymns*, are probably related to the Spirit's teaching function (see G. Johnston, "Spirit," 38), on which see discussion below.

275. So the Amoraic interpretation of Judg 13:25 in *y. Soṭah* 1:8, §3, where the Spirit of God becomes "the Holy Spirit." In view of Isa 11:2, we may also consider *Pss. Sol.* 17:37, speaking of the Messiah being δυνατόν in the Holy Spirit and wise (for the specifically messianic associations of the Spirit in some texts, see Chevallier, *Esprit et le Messie*, 125–43).

276. Coppens, "Don," 211–12, 222; Puech, "Esprit"; Hur, *Reading*, 230; Keener, "Pneumatology," 65–69 (I applied it soteriologically, 162–84; idem, *Spirit*, 146–51, 162; idem, *Questions*, 31–34; idem, *Gift*, 137–46). This is similar to the ethical and covenant renewal emphasis in Wenk, *Power*, 56–111, esp. 98–111. Against my treatment, Bennema, *Wisdom*, 47, 92, does away with purification as a separate category (in contrast to some who tend to overcategorize references to the Spirit) but rightly emphasizes (as I did elsewhere) the soteriological aspect of the Spirit (Bennema, *Wisdom*, 51–99 passim), though I believe going too far (defining "soteriological necessity" too broadly and imposing this Christian theological category too much on early Jewish sources; also sometimes coalescing the Spirit, wisdom, and salvation in some texts on the basis of others). Despite the usual portrayal of his position, Menzies, *Empowered*, 71–82, acknowledges soteriological significance at Qumran. Cho, *Spirit and Kingdom*, 10–51, is correct, however, that (51) "soteriological pneumatology" is emphasized less widely than "non-soteriological," prophetic activity.

277. E.g., 1 Sam 10:6–7, again in the context of anointing for leadership of God's people. Thus the good spirit from God departs from Saul to David, and an evil spirit from God torments Saul, when David is anointed king, in 16:13–14.

278. Particularly Ezek 36:25–26; Isaiah uses the water image for the Spirit as a symbol of fertile restoration and blessing (Isa 44:3–4), and Joel retains the connection between the outpoured Spirit of God and the spirit of prophecy (Joel 2:28–29; 3:1–2 MT).

279. Chevallier, *Ancien Testament*, 52–57, summarizes the main uses of רוח in the Qumran scrolls: wind or breath (52), invisible powers of a personal character (spirit of truth or of error, 52–53), the interior dispositions of a person (54), the "spirit of holiness" (1QH^a XVI, 2, 3, 7, 12, p. 55), the last including the use for purification (56–57).

280. Johnston, "Spirit," 40. Chevallier, "Souffle," 40, says that the purifying spirit in the Qumran scrolls performs a double function: purifying a person and revealing the truth to the person. These functions are, no doubt, conceptually linked. Lindars, *Apologetic*, 46, finds the background for the language of 1 Thess 4:8 in Ezek 37:14.

281. Lit. מי נדה, "waters of impurity," as in 1QS III, 4.

other adjectival genitive constructions.[282] God's "Holy Spirit" similarly has moral associations in 1QH[a] XVII, 32, although here it is also linked with the truth-teaching function of the Spirit.[283] In 4Q444 1 I, 1, the Holy Spirit enables the righteous to do good, withstanding the ways of evil spirits (1 I, 2–4).

Some texts warn against defiling one's own spirit (CD V, 11–12; VII, 3–4).[284] Although these texts do not refer to God's Spirit, they do illustrate that the language of "holy spirit" could be applied easily enough to moral holiness,[285] possibly related to the Qumran purification baths.[286] Other texts are not clearly connected to this concept, although a possible relationship cannot be ruled out. The *Testaments of the Twelve Patriarchs*, for instance, of less certainly pre-Christian date, can associate the Spirit of God with doing good, as in *Test. Sim.* 4:4.[287]

These are not a large number of texts, but outside rabbinic literature, our references to the Spirit of God acting on humans are not abundant to begin with; John Pryke has suggested that of ninety-seven texts definitely referring to Spirit "in the four main documents of Qumran," there are only seven clear references to God's Spirit and seventy-two referring to the human spirit.[288] Whether or not this estimate is accurate,[289] it is clear that of the Qumran texts referring to God's "Holy Spirit," a significant portion do refer to the purifying Spirit.

Jubilees also shares the general outlook of much of the Qumran literature and may reflect the same circles that authored the sectarian documents. *Jubilees*, after a warning against the spirit of Beliar, who leads into sin (*Jub.* 1:20), notes that God will "create a pure heart and a holy spirit"[290] for Israel, purifying it to obey his will (1:21, 23). The language echoes that of Ezekiel, who also associates Israel's new heart and new spirit, as well as God's own Spirit, with Israel's restoration and obedience. Interestingly, some early Christian writers also emphasize this imagery from Ezekiel (e.g., John 3:5).[291] Yet even the Qumran scrolls associate the Spirit with revelation more often than with purification.

3. The Spirit of Knowledge and Prophecy in Early Judaism

Early Jewish sources often associate the Spirit with inspiration (usually of a prophetic nature)[292] and divine illumination or revelation in wisdom or knowledge. The

282. In *Texte Aus Qumran* (ed. Lohse), 10, 14.

283. Ibid., 148; Hymn P in Dupont-Sommer, *Writings*, 233. Cf. similarly Wis 1:5: "For the holy spirit of instruction [παιδείας] will flee deceit."

284. One may compare Sus 45, in which God raised up Daniel's τὸ πνεῦμα τὸ ἅγιον to defend Susanna.

285. On the Holy Spirit as purifier from sin in the Dead Sea Scrolls, see, e.g., Bruce, "Spirit in Qumran Texts," 52–54.

286. Suggested in passing by Johnston, "Spirit," 33.

287. Cf. *Test. Benj.* 8:3 (*OTP* 1:827; Greek, p. 225, counting as 8:2), although this could well be part of a Christian interpolation (like, potentially, much of *Testament of Benjamin*); for filling with an evil spirit, cf. *Test. Ash.* 1:9. The early Christian ethical function of the Spirit (which predominates in Paul with the indwelling Spirit/Christ) may also testify to the continuance of this usage.

288. Pryke, "Spirit," 345. On the human spirit in the Scrolls, see also Johnston, "Spirit," 27–36 passim.

289. A survey of Johnston's references to the Spirit ("Spirit," 38–40) would at least suggest that the matter is open to dispute; the scrolls made available since Pryke wrote have also increased the number.

290. Probably the pure heart and the holy spirit are meant to be identical.

291. See Keener, *John*, 546–55, esp. 551–52; idem, *Spirit*, 143–46.

292. As Menzies, *Empowered*, 102, puts it, "The literature of intertestamental Judaism consistently identifies experience of the Spirit with prophetic inspiration." He acknowledges exceptions, and some other scholars emphasize the exceptions more; but most scholars recognize the frequent connection with prophetic activity in the sources.

Qumran scrolls emphasize especially the spirit of wisdom and knowledge, and the rabbis especially prophecy, but there is enough overlap between inspired insight and inspired predictions, pronouncements, and so forth for us to associate them together (for our purposes) in a more general category. (The alternative approach would be quite viable, but the points of overlap would be significant.)[293]

a. Early Judaism in General

Those who assign the connection of the Spirit with prophecy almost exclusively to rabbinic Judaism[294] have missed much of the evidence (not least the OT antecedents).[295] The association appears in Jewish literature written or preserved in Greek. Josephus, for example, notes that when the divine Spirit (τοῦ θείου πνεύματος) first came to David, he "began to prophesy," a point not found in the biblical text here.[296] Philo similarly speaks of "the Divine Spirit of prophecy," commenting on Num 11:16 (*Flight* 186).[297] In Sir 48:24 Isaiah foresaw the future by means of a great spirit.[298] In *Test. Job* 48:3 (though its pre-Christian nature is not beyond doubt)[299] we read that as Job's daughter Hemera spoke ecstatically, "the Spirit" was written on her cloak.

The association also appears in early Palestinian Jewish literature. When Isaac was to bless Jacob's sons in *Jubilees*, "a spirit of prophecy came down upon his mouth,"[300] and the Spirit also functions as the spirit of prophecy in the fifth book of *1 Enoch* (*1 En.* 91:1). The Holy Spirit inspired the prophets also in the Qumran scrolls,[301] although texts about the present are more apt to stress the Spirit's role in granting insight to God's mysteries.[302] In a later work, a "holy spirit" (*spiritus sanctus*) moved someone to ecstasy and he prophesied (*L.A.B.* 28:6). Likewise, Ezra is inspired to write many books through the Holy Spirit (*4 Ezra* 14:22). It is further worthy of note that some early Christian texts carry over the same concept and language.[303]

293. For the Spirit and wisdom, cf., e.g., Harris, *Origin*, 38; Keener, "Pneumatology," 59, 255–57; idem, *John*, 963–64; Bennema, *Wisdom*, 58, 65; cf. Levison, *Filled*, 118–53 (emphasizing inspired knowledge on 178–201).

294. E.g., Aune, *Prophecy*, 200.

295. The Spirit of Yahweh is commonly associated with prophecy already in the OT; cf., e.g., Chevallier, *Ancien Testament*, 27–29; Wright, *Spirit through Old Testament*, 63–86; Ma, *Spirit*, 30–32, 202–3, 206–7; Keener, "Spirit," 486–87. In early Judaism more generally, see, e.g., Menzies, *Empowered*, 49–101; Menzies, *Development*, 53–112; Turner, *Power*, 86–104 (including inspired wisdom and praise); Keener, *Spirit*, 10–13, 31–33.

296. Jos. *Ant.* 6.166 (LCL, 5:248–49); cf. *Ant.* 6.56, 222–23; 8.408. Isaacs, *Spirit*, 47–48, provides a number of other examples that illustrate Josephus's association of πνεῦμα in the LXX with prophecy, and prophecy in the LXX with πνεῦμα. Best suggests that Josephus almost always uses θεῖον πνεῦμα only for the spirit of prophecy and oracular speech ("Pneuma," 222–25); the one exception he comes upon is Jos. *Ant.* 1.27 (= Gen 1:2, too important to change), and he finds the usage restricted to the biblical period. For a more recent survey of Josephus's adaptations about the Spirit, see Levison, "Interpretation."

297. See also Philo *Heir* 265; *Moses* 1.175, 277; 2.265; *Decal.* 175; *Laws* 4.49; further, Isaacs, *Spirit*, 47.

298. In Sir 39:6, the righteous person is filled with the spirit of understanding (συνέσεως) when God wills.

299. E.g., Spittler ("Introduction," 834; but not mentioned in idem, "Testament of Job") sees Montanist redaction in the final chapters.

300. *Jub.* 31:12 (*OTP* 2:115); see likewise *Jub.* 25:14.

301. 1QS VIII, 16; 1Q34bis 3 II, 7; 4Q381 69 4; cf. CD II, 12; perhaps 4Q266 2 II, 12; 4Q270 2 II, 14. On the issue of the Spirit of prophecy in the DSS, see also Bruce, "Spirit in Qumran Texts," 51 (although he cites only CD II, 12); Johnston, "Spirit," 36–37, in more detail. One should also consider references (following the sort of prophetic tradition one finds in Daniel) to the Holy Spirit's illumining the secrets of God; see Johnston, "Spirit," 33–35, 39–40. Daniel, "Prophètes," 59–64, believes that the Essenes called themselves "seers" and practiced prophecy; although the thrust of his article may be mistaken, the evidence in Josephus for Essene prophets suggests that they would emphasize the prophetic.

302. E.g., 1QS IX, 3; 1QHᵃ V, 24–25; XX, 11–13; 4Q213a 1 I, 14; 4Q504 4 5. For the Spirit and charismatic wisdom, see also Turner, *Gifts*, 8–10 (esp. his citation of Sir 39:6; Philo *Mos.* 2.265; *4 Ezra* 14:22); in the Qumran scrolls, also Menzies, *Development*, 84–87.

303. E.g., *Did.* 11.7–9; Justin *Dial.* 32–34; *1 Apol.* 31, 44, 47, 63; Athenag. *Plea* 7; Theoph. 2.33; cf. also Irenaeus's *Proof of the Apostolic Preaching* in Williams, "Christianity," 25.

535

In other early Jewish texts, the Holy Spirit also revealed or inspired in other ways besides prophecy in the strictest sense. The Spirit revealed matters in dreams (to biblical characters in *Test. Ab.* 4:7–8 A; *L.A.B.* 9:10). Similarly, the Spirit could be associated with singing a spontaneously created song,[304] which would have been associated with inspiration in antiquity.[305] One could also "see," in the sense of prophetic perception, by the Spirit.[306] Prophetic associations were the most common for the Spirit in early Jewish texts.

b. In Rabbinic Literature

What was true of early Judaism in general became even more emphatic in rabbinic literature (which, though later than many of our other sources, by its sheer volume provides more abundant examples). For example, the Tannaim could associate the Spirit with prophetic revelation and insight.[307] Thus the people of Israel knew Pharaoh's plans against them through the Holy Spirit that rested on them.[308]

The later Amoraim follow this tradition as well: the Spirit gives correct knowledge about persons or events,[309] foretells the future,[310] is associated with visions,[311] and is generally associated with prophecy.[312] It appears as "a divine power" for prophecy, praise, and so forth in the Targumim;[313] in the Targumim, "Holy Spirit" and "Spirit of Prophecy" are functionally interchangeable, the differences mandated by style.[314] It is therefore not surprising that modern students of rabbinic texts often comment on the association of the Spirit with prophecy there.[315]

---

304. *L.A.B.* 32:14. Cf. *Mek.* on Exod 14:31 (cited in Smith, *Parallels*, 64); *y. Soṭah* 5:4, §1; and later, *Pesiq. Rab.* 9:2; *Tg. Jon.* on 1 Sam 19:23.

305. E.g., Ap. Rhod. 1.22; Virg. *Aen.* 9.525–29; Plut. *Table* 1.5.2, *Mor.* 623B; Philost. *Hrk.* 7.5–6; *Sib. Or.* 3.489; 1 Sam 10:5; 1 Chr 25:1–3; 1 Cor 14:15, 26; Eph 5:18–19; poetry in Plut. *Poetry* 1, *Mor.* 15E. Music could also initiate inspiration (Iambl. *Myst.* 3.9; 2 Kgs 3:14–16; cf. 1 Sam 16:16; at Mari, cf. Huffmon, "Prophecy," 112).

306. *L.A.B.* 28:6; cf. *Test. Job* 52:9 (*OTP* 1:868)/52:4 (Kraft, 84) for the prophetic vision of Job's charismatically endowed daughters; cf. *Lev. Rab.* 9:9; *Num. Rab.* 14:5; *Eccl. Rab.* 10:8, §1, for perceiving by the Holy Spirit.

307. *Sipre Deut.* 22.1.2; *t. Pisha* 2:15. Hillel allegedly associated the Spirit with Israel as a whole and said that its people were disciples of the prophets (*t. Pisha* 4:14).

308. *Mek. Shir.* 7.17–18 (Lauterbach, 2:55). For another reference to the spirit of prophecy, cf., e.g., *Mek. Pisha* 1.150ff. (Lauterbach, 1:14).

309. E.g., *b. Ber.* 31b; *B. Bat.* 122a; *Yoma* 73b.

310. E.g., *y. Hor.* 3:5, §2; *Num. Rab.* 21:9; *Eccl. Rab.* 7:23, §1.

311. In *y. Šeq.* 3:3; *Lev. Rab.* 9:9; *Num. Rab.* 9:20; *Tg. Ps.-J.* on Gen 37:33; 45:14; cf. Ezek 8:3; Joel 2:28; perhaps Dan 4:9; *L.A.B.* 28:6; *Test. Job* 52:9 (*OTP*)/52:4 (Kraft).

312. E.g., *Pesiq. Rab Kah.* 1:8; 4:3; 11:16; *Gen. Rab.* 91:6; *Exod. Rab.* 5:20; *Lev. Rab.* 1:3; *Num. Rab.* 13:20; 14:5; 18:8; *Ruth Rab.* 4:3; *Eccl. Rab.* 10:8, §1; *Tg. Ps.-J.* on Gen 27:42; *Tg. Ps.-J.* on Num 11:25, 28–29; *Tg. Neof.* 1 on Num 11:26, 28–29; *Tg. Jon.* on Judg 3:10; *Tg. Isa.* 40:13. Rabbi Meir's revelation sight in *Lev. Rab.* 9:9 (in *Deut. Rab.* 5:15, through Elijah) was mentioned above.

313. McNamara, *Targum*, 113. For prophecy, see, e.g., *Tg. Ps.-J.* on Gen 31:21; 35:22; but in Exod 35:31, the MT's "spirit of wisdom" becomes "a spirit of *holiness from before the Lord*" (*Tg. Neof.* 1 on Exod 35:31).

314. See the data in Schäfer, "Geist," 306–7: *Targum Neofiti* and the Fragment Targum always have "Holy Spirit," *Targum Onqelos* always has "Spirit of Prophecy" (except in one instance), and *Targum Pseudo-Jonathan* uses both about equally; though Schäfer observes that "Holy Spirit" has a broader range of meaning than "Spirit of Prophecy." Schäfer elsewhere (*Vorstellung*, 135–39) seeks to trace the origin of the term to "Spirit of the Sanctuary" (critiqued by Reif, "Review," 158), but the standard usage, not the etymology, is our concern here. For a collection of some of the significant targumic texts, see Schäfer, *Vorstellung*, 23–26.

315. E.g., Moore, *Judaism*, 1:237, 437; Abelson, *Immanence*, 238–67; Marmorstein, *Names*, 99–100; Sandmel, *Judaism*, 174–75; idem, *Genius of Paul*, 78; Davies, "Spirit in Mekilta," 98; Bonsirven, *Judaism*, 57; Jeremias, *Theology*, 78; Horwitz, "Ru'ah," 365. New Testament scholars less known for a rabbinic focus tend to follow (e.g., Ellis, "Christ and Spirit," 274; Bruce, "Spirit in Apocalypse," 337; Boring, *Sayings*, 63; idem, "Oracles," 518; Bultmann, *John*, 575).

The rabbis, who focused heavily on the Torah, especially often associated the spirit of prophecy with the inspiration of books of the Bible.[316] Given the Spirit's association with prophecy, such a usage naturally appears also in nonrabbinic Jewish texts,[317] but it becomes far more prominent in Tannaitic[318] and Amoraic[319] texts and pervasive in the *Midrash Rabbah*[320] and *Pesiqta Rabbati*.[321]

This information may suggest that rabbinic Judaism not only developed the concept of the Spirit as the prophetic Spirit, almost to the exclusion[322] of other possible models, but also developed this role particularly with regard to the supremacy of the Scriptures that the rabbis interpreted. This is a natural development, since the rabbis' primary attention as legal scholars was to the biblical texts. Further, this strategy provided an epistemological guard against strongly pneumatic movements (e.g., the intensely charismatic early Jesus movement). For further comment on prophecy and the spirit of prophecy, see the excursus at Acts 2:17–18.

Another matter of interest as background for Luke's pneumatology was the widespread view that prophets had ceased (see full discussion in the excursus on Acts 2:17–18). Although most Jewish people believed that prophecy and revelation continued, the specific title "prophet" is usually granted (e.g., in Josephus, Philo, Qumran, and rabbinic sources) only to figures of the biblical era. Some (like most rabbis, for whom our sources postdate Luke) believed that the Spirit (which they associated especially with inspiration) had been quenched; others (like the Qumran sectarians) believed that they possessed the Spirit, yet do not seem to emphasize an association of the Spirit with the present activity of "prophets" (and perhaps in the present only with inspired insight). Likewise, even Josephus, when mentioning prophecy in the present, does not mention the Spirit as he does for prophecy on occasion during the biblical era (*Ant.* 6.166, 222; cf. 8.408). Luke's unapologetic mention of full-fledged prophets (e.g., Acts 11:27–28; 13:1; 21:9–11) is a dramatic departure from the norm, emphasizing his view that Jesus has inaugurated the era of the Spirit (2:17–18, 33).

6. The Function of Signs

As noted in chapter 9 above, Luke exhibits a particularly heavy emphasis on signs;[323] he reports signs more often, given the amount of space available, than typical extant

316. For the association of the Spirit and the Scriptures in Acts, see Bonnah, *Spirit*, 210–66.

317. 1QS VIII, 16: "what the prophets revealed by his Holy Spirit"; Jos. *Ag. Ap.* 1.37; *4 Ezra* 14:22; *1 Clem.* 47.3; *Barn.* 9.2; 14.2, 9; *Herm.* 43.9; Justin *Dial.* 25. In the Apocrypha and Pseudepigrapha in general, see Büchsel, *Geist*, 57–58.

318. E.g., *Sipra VDDen. par.* 1.1.3.3; 5.10.1.1; *Sipra Sh. M. d.* 94.5.12; *Sipra Behuq. pq.* 6.267.2.1; *Sipre Deut.* 355.17.1–3; 356.4.1 (repeating 355.17.2). See further, e.g., Isaacs, *Spirit*, 51; Foerster, "Geist," 117.

319. E.g., ʾAbot R. Nat. 4 A; *b. Ber.* 4b; *Pesaḥ.* 117a; *Meg.* 7a (attributed to R. Eleazar and R. Akiba); *y. Soṭah* 1:9, §1; cf. *Pesiq. Rab Kah.* Sup. 5:1.

320. *Gen. Rab.* 63:14; 80:8; 91:5; 92:9; 93:7; 97 (NV); *Exod. Rab.* 8:1; 15:17; 27:9; 33:5; 48:6; *Lev. Rab.* 3:6; 4:1; 5:5; *Num. Rab.* 10:2; 11:1; 19:15; 20:18; *Esth. Rab.* 10:5; *Lam. Rab.* 2:20, §23; 3:58–60, §9; *Eccl. Rab.* 1:1, §1; 3:16, §1; *Song Rab.* 1:1, §§5–6, 9–10; 2:1, §3; 7:12, §1.

321. *Pesiq. Rab.* 10:2; 11:2; 20:1; 30:1; 33:2–3; 34:1; 35:1; 50:1, 4. In the rabbis, see also Moore, *Judaism*, 1:238–39, 247–48. Later also in the Targumim, e.g., *Tg. Qoh.* 1:4; 3:11; 4:15; 9:7; 10:7, 9.

322. In ʾAbot R. Nat. 34 A, the Holy Spirit involves only prophecy and obscure speech.

323. Surveys of signs in Acts include De Wet, "Signs," 41–51; Davids, "Miracles," 746–50; "Signs," 1094; Hamblin, "Miracles"; for Luke's Christology and signs, see Avemarie, "Acta" (use of Jesus's name, 551–56; Jesus's connection with the Spirit, 557–61); cf. Jackson, "Churches," 170–74, 312–13; for healing in Luke-Acts, see Pilch, *Healing*, 89–117; Davids, "Healing," 436–37; for more studies on miracles in Acts, see Grässer, *Forschungen*, 234–35. There are numerous studies from various approaches (e.g., Neirynck, "Miracle Stories").

historians from his period. Signs are more unambiguously positive in Acts than in Mark or John[324] and are far more prominent than in Paul's letters (though the difference may be one of genre).[325] (When I say they are "unambiguously" positive, I refer to the standpoint of the informed audience,[326] not to all characters within the narrative world.)[327] Signs appear frequently in Acts, especially drawing attention to the message; they are even solicited in public prayer, probably for the purpose of supporting the message (Acts 4:29–30). Nevertheless, many Western commentators on Acts have given but scant attention to this Lukan emphasis, perhaps in part because of our own cultural discomfort with such claims.[328]

Like speeches, signs consume extensive space in Acts. The function of signs is not, however, mere exhibitionism, miracles pointing only to themselves.[329] "Signs," by their definition, "signify" something; they draw attention to the message in Acts and hence serve an evangelistic and missiological function.[330] Yet signs do not point to those who work them, as if to honor their own "power or reverence" (Acts 3:12); rather, they exalt Jesus's name as an object of trust (3:16) and attest the content of the apostolic message about God's generosity in Jesus Christ (14:3). Signs confirm the Gentile mission[331] and also enable Christ's followers within the narrative world to draw attention to the gospel, which often provides physical as well as ultimate "benefaction" and "salvation" (4:9–12; 10:38).[332] Signs also fit Luke's promise-fulfillment schema, connecting the Jesus movement with earlier biblical prophets (especially Moses) and prophecies (especially Isa 35:5–6; Joel 2:28) as well as demonstrating the eschatological activity of the Spirit that confirms Jesus's messiahship.[333]

324. I have argued that signs function more ambiguously in John (Keener, *John*, 275–79), but I find their role mostly positive in Acts; John often does build narratives around seven key signs, but for their centrality in Lukan theology, see discussion below.

325. E.g., James clearly expects miracles (Jas 5:14–16), but one would not know this without a single paragraph in which he raises the issue; Paul raises the issue more often, though over a longer course of letters. Early Christian narratives, however, include more signs (esp. the Gospels; cf. even Rev 11:5–6).

326. All activity that Luke characterizes as "signs" or attributes to the mediation of reliable characters is positive.

327. Marguerat, *Histoire*, 175–203, treats magic and healings in Acts and the "risk" of miracles in evangelization (177–85); he notes the possibilities of misunderstanding (178–79), especially the confusion of human and divine (180–82). Miracles are decisive in evangelization, but there was always the risk of syncretistic misunderstanding in light of paganism (185); thus the Pythoness calls them "servants of Most High God" (189–90), and Luke reports conflict with magic (192–202). Marguerat concludes that Luke requires his hearers to hold together miracle, word, and faith: miracle provides assurance of the message, and without it, the word is hollow; without the word, miracle is dangerously ambiguous (203). "Supernatural" activity can be positive or negative, but this category is a modern one. Ancients might distinguish positive from negative supernatural activity on the basis of those who performed them (see Reimer, *Miracle*; discussion of antimagical apologetic at Acts 8:9–11).

328. See the criticism by Strelan, *Strange Acts*, 12–13.

329. Robinson and Wall, *Called*, 62, note that signs in Acts do not create faith, which instead comes through the proclaimed message; rather, signs invite attention to message.

330. Pervo, *Acts*, 58, also compares the pattern with later apocryphal acts (which, I have argued, use Luke's Acts as a model). Wilkinson, *Healing*, 178, is correct that they do not function merely as propaganda but, in playing down their evangelistic function, underestimates this function in Luke's missiological perspective.

331. Sometimes for those within the narrative (Acts 10:45–48; 15:12) and especially, on the narrative level, for Luke's ideal audience.

332. For the close connection of signs to preaching and the importance of the latter to faith in Luke's theology, see Williams, *Miracle Stories*, 180–82.

333. Lampe, "Miracles," 172, compares Luke's signs to OT foundation stories; he notes (173) the connection with the "prophetic hope" in Acts 2:19.

a. Expecting Continuing Signs

Luke reports signs in Acts especially to confirm that the Holy Spirit is with the Gentile mission that he narrates (see esp. Acts 15:12; cf. 15:4, 8).[334] Yet I suggested earlier (ch. 13, sect. 2; cf. ch. 5, sect. 1) that Luke is interested in models for mission as well as apologetic. Thus signs' overwhelming abundance in a variety of forms also constitutes a pattern of how Luke expects God to work in the continuing Gentile mission. Luke believes that the active, intervening God of Israel's earlier Scriptures is even more active in his day after Pentecost and that believers continue to live in the "biblical" era.

Luke does not envision that the Spirit poured out on Pentecost will be poured back (whether permanently or for some sort of temporary interim era, had he been able to imagine that). The outpouring is for the "last days" (2:17, Luke's emphatic adaptation of Joel's "afterward"), the era of salvation (2:21), the time of Christ's reign until all enemies are subjugated beneath his feet (2:34–35). That is, the Spirit remains active since the day of Pentecost, and the signs-and-wonders activity depicted in Acts should be normative for the entire duration of the church's mission until Jesus's return.[335]

Despite Luke's focus on Peter and Paul, signs and wonders are not limited in Acts to Paul's circle and the Jerusalem apostles (note Stephen, 6:8; Philip, 8:6, 13; and Ananias, 9:12, 17).[336] In fact, the prophetic, Elijah-like anointing applies to all Christians (see comment on Acts 1:8–11; 2:17–18), though Luke, like Paul, does not seem to expect each Christian to experience this empowerment in the same ways. Prophecy, visions, and dreams are a regular part of the church's normal experience (2:17–18), especially on the cutting edge of evangelism (1:8).

To argue that Luke expects signs to cease after Acts 28 is to argue from silence (since we have no Acts 29) and to ignore Luke's narrative pattern.[337] Readers today may disagree with Luke's perspective on the era of the prophetic Spirit and signs, but we should not distort what he says. Many Majority World Christians involved

334. Thus we should neither expect him to record the absence of signs on some occasions nor make too much of his silence on issues that were not his focal concern. On the Spirit and miracles (to confirm the message) in Luke-Acts, see Shelton, *Mighty in Deed*, 74–84.

335. That is not to suggest that Luke need have envisioned them with equal intensity in every time and place, but to suggest that they, like the mission they accompany, belong to the interim era of Jesus's enthronement before his parousia. The inaugurated eschatological character of Pentecost inevitably and decisively refutes approaches suggesting that Luke would have regarded gifts (to borrow Paul's language) such as tongues as ceasing before Christ's return (Paul also expects such gifts to cease only at Christ's return, 1 Cor 13:8–12; see, e.g., Carson, *Fallacies*, 76–77; idem, *Showing Spirit*, 66–77; Fee, *Gospel*, 7–8, 77; Grudem, *Prophecy*, 210–19; Elbert, "Face to Face"; *pace* Rogers, "Tongues"; Hodges, "Tongues"; Johnson, "Tongues"; Toussaint, "Tongues"; Thomas, "Tongues"). On Luke's narrative as a theological model including signs, see, e.g., Menzies, "Paradigm."

336. In these cases, the purpose still relates to the expansion of the gospel or equipping those who will carry it. This focus fits Luke's theme; we cannot expect him to tell us much outside his focus.

337. The supposed reduction of signs that some have suggested in Acts' later chapters ignores Acts 20:9–12; 27:23–25; and 28:5, 8–9 and that Paul's captivity dominates 21:33–28:31 (Jesus does not work many signs during the passion narrative either). Those theologically committed to a full cessation of signs may always find arguments for their case, but I believe that they must either force the evidence or let their case die the death of a thousand qualifications (Moreland, *Triangle*, 174, notes cessationism's decline among Christian scholars). For a more moderate cessationism, see Sawyer and Wallace, *Afraid* (moderate cessationists might be able to accommodate most of the signs recounted in ch. 9 above); for the cessationist approach in general, see, e.g., Robertson, *Word*; Gaffin, *Perspectives*; idem, "View"; MacArthur, *Chaos*; for noncessationist responses, e.g., Fee, *Gospel*, 75–77; idem, *Paul, Spirit, and People*, passim; Turner, *Gift*, 286–302; Grudem, *Theology*, 355–75; Ruthven, *Cessation*; Deere, *Power of Spirit*; Elbert, "Themes"; Morphew, *Breakthrough*, 169–82; Keener, *Gift*, 89–112; Green, *Holy Spirit*; Shogren, "Prophecy"; Snyder, "Gifts," 332–34; Gardner, *Healing Miracles*, 130–54; in Acts in particular, see Twelftree, *People*, 153–63. For multiple views, see Grudem, *Gifts*.

in groundbreaking evangelism today expect signs[338] because they believe that they still live in "Bible times" and/or in the "end time." Luke manifestly believed both.

Signs constitute a major, or perhaps the major, means of inviting attention to the message throughout Luke-Acts, both for the audience within the narrative world and for Luke's own. As noted above, the apostles performed many signs, but signs were not characteristic only of apostles (despite Luke's narrative focus). They frequently accompany the proclamation of the message. Although educated speakers such as Paul, Apollos, and apparently Stephen engage in public debates, Paul and Stephen also join the majority of leading figures in Acts (educated or uneducated) in drawing attention to their message through signs (e.g., 2:43; 3:12–13; 5:12; 6:8; 8:6; 9:34–35, 41–42; 13:12; 14:3; 19:11–20). This observation does not imply that Luke expected every individual believer to do what these leading figures did, but that Luke does anticipate God confirming the message through signs in a way not strictly limited to the Twelve (or, more arbitrarily, the Twelve plus Paul). The church apparently prayed for signs to confirm its message (4:30) and to grant them boldness (4:29). Such signs displayed the Lord's own confirmation of his message concerning grace (14:3). They belong to Luke's theology of "power" for evangelism (see comment on Acts 1:8).

Luke employs the term "wonders" (τέρατα) only alongside "signs" (σημεῖα) and only in Acts (2:19, 22, 43; 4:30; 5:12; 6:8; 7:36; 14:3; 15:12);[339] "sign" has a broader potential semantic range, but Byzantine lexicographers treated "wonder" as roughly synonymous with "sign" when the latter applied to extraordinary phenomena.[340] The coupling of these terms so often in the opening section (2:19, 22, 43) hints at their significance: Jesus's "signs and wonders" (2:22) fulfill Joel's heavenly "wonders" (2:19), and the apostles continue this ministry (2:43). Not only Jesus (2:22; cf. 10:38), but Moses (7:36) prefigures this activity of signs and wonders. The phrase "signs and wonders" surely derives from LXX usage, nearly always concerning the period of the exodus.[341] That is, Luke is emphasizing not so much healing gifts as expressed within

338. See discussion in ch. 9, above.

339. In the Gospel, the term σημεῖον by itself carries a different range of meaning (Luke 2:12, 34), such as a heavenly (11:16) or an eschatological sign (21:7, 11, 25); Jesus refuses such signs (11:16, 29–30) and also signs at Herod's request (23:8; cf. 4:3–4). In Acts, the term means "miracle" even when not attached to "wonders" (Acts 4:16, 22; 8:6, 13). Josephus describes miracles rarely as δυνάμεις (in contrast to the Synoptics) or παράδοξα (Luke 5:26) but typically as σημεῖα, sometimes conjoined with τέρατα (MacRae, "Miracle," 143–44), though Jos. *War* 1.28, 377 and 6.295 refer more to prodigies than to anything through human agents and *Ant.* 20.168 refers to false prophets.

340. See Remus, *Conflict*, 48 (citing *Suda*, s.v. τέρας). Extrabiblical terminology for signs (such as *semeion* or *teras*) is often interchangeable (Remus, "Terminology," 535–51); rhetorical repetition could reinforce a point. Repetitious reinforcement is likelier here than Origen's suggestion that miraculous "signs" point to the future, in contrast to wonders (*Comm. Rom.* on 15:19; *CER* 5:218; Bray, *Romans*, 362). The different sense of σημεῖα in rhetoric, as a form of proof (Anderson, *Glossary*, 108–9; cf. Libanius *Invect.* 6.3), might at least be relevant for Luke's evidential use of signs in his apologetic; divine σημεῖα were also sought in divination (Arius Did. *Epit.* 2.7.11s, pp. 98–99.18).

341. Exod 7:3, 9; 11:9–10; Deut 4:34; 6:22; 7:19; 11:3; 26:8; 29:3; 34:11; Pss 77:43 (78:43 ET); 104:27 (105:27); 134:9 (135:9); Jer 39:20–21 (32:20–21); Wis 10:16; Bar 2:11. On signs in the Pentateuch, see Meier, "Signs." See also others, e.g., Dunn, *Romans*, 868; Bock, *Acts*, 230; early Jewish treatment of miracles, while not cessationist, focuses especially on the exodus (Eve, *Miracles*, 244, 377). Strelan, *Strange Acts*, 28, acknowledges this as the dominant source but does note the terms together representing prodigies and portents in Plut. *Alex.* 75.1; Appian *Bell. civ.* 2.36; 4.4 (following Weiss, *Zeichen*, 18–22); cf. also in Josephus (*War* 1.28, 377; *Ant.* 6.295). In Dan 4:2 (not in the standard LXX), "signs and wonders" refers back to God's deliverance of the three Israelites in Dan 3. Lampe, "Miracles," 172, argues that Luke views his miracles as akin to those in OT foundation stories. Although relating such signs to the exodus may connect them to special periods of divine activity, it hardly follows that Luke would not expect such signs to often accompany new evangelism settings (*pace* Peterson, *Acts*, 86–87), which are themselves salvation-historical events (unless we think "to the ends of the earth" completed at the end of Acts); if this is not part of the model that Luke offers (problematic as it feels to us Westerners), then it is difficult to know what model we should expect from him.

the church (1 Cor 12:9; Jas 5:14–15), valuable as those are,[342] as dramatic salvation-historical activity expanding the frontiers of the kingdom and carrying out the mission of Acts 1:8.[343] Luke would expect this salvation-historical activity to persist so long as the mission of 1:8 continues. (That is, for Luke, salvation history climaxed in Jesus's exaltation but did not end there.)

These "signs and wonders" characterize the Jerusalem apostles (2:43; 5:12); Stephen (6:8); and the missionaries carrying out the Gentile mission (14:3; 15:12).[344] Whether through the Jerusalem apostles, Stephen, or Paul and Barnabas, all these references to "signs and wonders" occur in the context of proclaiming the message of Christ. The church prays for such signs (4:30), and the signs attest not only Jesus (2:22) but his message (14:3).

b. Signs in the Context of Luke's Missiology and Other Themes

Luke connects the Spirit with the Gentile mission and also points to the Spirit as the source of signs. Other aspects of the Spirit's activity in Luke-Acts are discussed above (see also fuller discussion at Acts 1:4–5; 2:4, 17–18), but Luke (like other authors; see, e.g., Rom 15:19; 1 Cor 12:8–11; Heb 2:4; Matt 12:28) sometimes links the Spirit with reports of signs and wonders (cf. Acts 2:43; 4:30–31; 6:5, 8, 10).[345] Allison Trites suggests, "According to Luke, the witness of the Spirit frequently takes the form of signs and wonders which are evidence of the Spirit's activity."[346] That Luke sometimes offers such a connection (though far less often than with prophecy per se) is hardly surprising, given the frequent association of the Spirit with the prophets in biblical and early Jewish thought,[347] along with the frequency of biblical prophets (especially in the Elijah-Elisha tradition) working signs.[348]

Thus God empowered Jesus with the Spirit to perform healings and exorcisms as acts of benevolence (Acts 10:38; cf. Luke 4:18). God answers the prayer of the church's members for boldness through healings and signs (Acts 4:29–30) by filling them again with his Spirit, so that they speak with boldness (4:31). The Spirit enables Paul to pronounce judgment, with immediate results (13:9–11); the Spirit is probably connected with Stephen's working of signs (6:5, 8, 10). This is compatible with other streams in early Christian theology, which aver that believers live in the life of the Spirit (e.g., Rom 8:9–16, 23, 26–27; 14:17; 1 Cor 12:3–13; Gal 5:16–23; John 14:16–17; 1 John 3:24; Jude 19–20), sometimes linked with signs (Rom 15:19; Gal

342. Whether or not those healed are already believers in Jesus is not so much the issue (cf., e.g., Acts 9:17–18, 36, 40; 20:9–12) as that this activity functions as a sign to secure attention for the gospel. Gifts of healing could thus function as signs, but they do not do so always (because the sign value is not the sole purpose for the gift).

343. One of my academic mentors, Ben Aker, brought this distinction in usage to my attention (cf. the particularly evangelistic function of "signs" in Paul, Rom 15:19; probably also 1 Cor 1:22; 2 Cor 12:12). Although I have not emphasized the new exodus much in Acts, perhaps those who envision a Lukan new exodus, even through the lens of Isaiah, might be able to develop further here the salvation-historical connection between Acts and earlier biblical narrative.

344. As already noted, "signs" also characterize Philip (Acts 8:6, 13) and others (9:17–18, though not employing the term), but I limit the references here to those explicitly using "signs and wonders." Probably the only difference in the adding of "wonders" is so Luke can evoke the exodus era more explicitly; having made the point by adding "wonders" explicitly on some occasions, Luke then feels free to use the abbreviated expression "signs" on others.

345. For the connection, see, e.g., Turner, "Spirit and Miracles"; cf. Marguerat, *Histoire*, 163–65.

346. Trites, *Witness*, 149–51 (quote, 149); because of realized eschatology in Luke's pneumatology, Trites also connects signs with the messianic age (149; cf. Jos. *Ant.* 20.168).

347. See, e.g., Keener, *Spirit*, 10–13, 31–33; and in our excursus on background for Luke's view of the Spirit in the present chapter (sect. 3); more fully, Menzies, *Empowered*, 49–101; idem, *Development*, 53–112.

348. Cf. Luke 24:19; for connections with Elijah, see comment on Acts 1:8–11.

3:5). Believers thus live in God's presence and power (a sort of "supernatural" existence), where what is "normal" (in principle) would often appear utterly abnormal to those attached only to natural existence. The possibility of signs follows easily enough from such a "supernatural" existence.

Yet the point of "signs" in the biblical tradition that Luke utilized is not their manifestly "supernatural" character. The dichotomy between obviously "supernatural" and potentially merely "natural" activity is a purely modern one, unknown to ancients, especially to Jews, who affirmed God's sovereignty. "Miracles" in the modern sense would be signs, but a "sign" of God's activity could be a rainbow (Gen 9:12–13, 17) or circumcision (17:11).[349] In Luke-Acts, "signs" tend to be compelling confirmations of divine activity, especially healings, but their primary function is to attest God's activity, not a "supernatural" worldview per se (which was not then in question). Like the emphasis on the Spirit or faith, signs emphasize dependence on the Lord who is their obvious and only source.

Because Luke's focus on signs is on their attesting function (even when he offers them as a model for the continuing spread of the gospel in new regions), we should not look to him to answer questions that would inevitably rise, whether in antiquity (cf. 2 Tim 4:20)[350] or in modern times, about those not healed (cf. Luke 14:13; or about various other questions he does not address). Luke has not set out to provide a complete theology of healing (or suffering); rather, he focuses in Luke-Acts on the signs that he can claim, signs that most clearly reveal divine confirmation. To argue that Luke would never have asked or addressed the question elsewhere is to argue from silence, though he does not appear to address it in a significant way in his two-volume work.

i. Signs and the Gospel

Haenchen suggests that Luke uses miracles to demonstrate divine sanction for the Gentile mission;[351] certainly, they proved strategic in that mission.[352] In contrast to the sometimes ambivalent function of signs in the Fourth Gospel,[353] in Luke-Acts they invite people to faith.[354] They attest Jesus (Acts 2:22) and fulfill God's plan for the new era of salvation (Luke 4:18; Acts 10:38).[355]

If Elijah and Elisha and their signs provide the prophetic model for Jesus's ministry as prophet in the Gospel of Luke (Luke 1:17; 4:25–27; 9:8, 19, 54, 61–62; cf. 24:19; Acts 1:8–11; 9:39–41), it is not surprising that the prophetic Spirit in Acts would often be expressed in signs and wonders.[356] These signs are worked not only by apostles (e.g., Acts 2:43; 3:6–8; 4:33 [probably]; 5:12–16; 9:34, 40) but also by some other witnesses of Jesus (Luke 10:17; Acts 6:8; 8:7; 9:12–18), though these other witnesses are not Luke's primary focus. That is, they are primarily intended to

---

349. Meier, "Signs," 758.

350. Bede *Comm. Acts* 28.8 (Martin, *Acts*, 314) explained the lack of healing in 1 Tim 5:23 and 2 Tim 4:20 by arguing that physical healing was a benefit especially for those lacking inner life.

351. Haenchen, "Acts as Source Material," 265, though overstating the claim that only miracle stories could validate this for Luke's generation.

352. See Dollar, "Theology of Healing," 10. From Luke, one might anticipate them especially in cases of groundbreaking evangelism (cf. Solomon, "Healing," 364).

353. On which see, e.g., Keener, *John*, 275–79.

354. See Tannehill, *Luke*, 86; Achtemeier, "Perspective on Miracles," 553–56 (cited in Tannehill; Achtemeier finds Luke less critical than some of his colleagues).

355. Tannehill, *Luke*, 96 (on the Gospel).

356. Turner, "Spirit and Miracles," uses the Spirit's association with signs against Menzies's limitation (Menzies, *Development*, 53–112) of the Spirit to prophecy, but one may understand "prophetic" as referring more broadly than to merely prophecy (as Turner also argues, e.g., *Gifts*, 6; is some of the debate semantic?). Menzies, "Power," responds to Turner, "Authoritative Preaching."

attest the message of Christ's grace (Acts 14:3) and hence remain as part of Luke's model for how mission should be carried out. (The old dichotomy between an earlier, charismatic stage of the church and a later, institutional one is based on a misunderstanding of Max Weber, for whom the former could continue alongside the latter.)[357]

It is noteworthy that although the message itself is central, the primary method for drawing attention to the message is signs and wonders.[358] Hellenistically educated speakers also spread it through debates in public forums—whether in public settings in Jerusalem (Acts 6:9–10; 9:29), in synagogues (9:20, 22; 13:5, 14–16; 14:1; 17:1–3, 10–12, 17; 18:4, 19, 26, 28; 19:8), or in philosophic settings (17:18–34; 19:9). Apologetic speeches before courts also provide opportunities to expose the elite to the message, countering their misperceptions in a world where the elite determined what would or would not threaten public order. It is significant, however, that those without a Hellenistic education do not engage in such debates or apologetic speeches (although they do respond to charges in the Sanhedrin). Signs appear more widely.

In the narratives themselves, signs and wonders represent the primary method of drawing attention to the message among both highly educated and relatively uneducated agents of the message about Christ.[359] Having noted this pattern in passing, we may survey it with more concrete examples here. Disciples speaking in tongues (2:4) provided the attention (2:12, 16–18) that led to three thousand conversions at Pentecost (2:41). Among the factors in the church's continued growth (2:47; 5:13–14) were apostolic signs (2:43; 5:12, 15–16). The healing of a man unable to walk from birth raised the number of Judean believers significantly higher (4:4).

Luke reports that the Samaritans heeded Philip's message specifically because of his signs (8:6–7). Other large populations in Judea were converted through signs (9:34–35, 40–42); so were a Roman governor (13:9–12) and probably the Philippian jailer (16:29–30). Clarifying the difference between Paul's signs and magic led to a large number of conversions (or of marginal Christians committing themselves fully) in Ephesus (19:11–20). Although Paul arrived on Malta a refugee and captive, his ministry in healing (28:8–9) led to public honor (28:10) and hence, presumably (albeit not explicitly), also to some responding with faith. Even judgment miracles spread respect for God's message (5:5, 10–11; cf. 12:23–24).

Luke's approach to signs resembles, and has undoubtedly helped to shape, some subsequent Christian approaches.[360] Later Christian movements emphasizing signs and wonders have often located them in the context of evangelism, typically reporting that signs lead to conversions.[361] This is true, for example, of earlier Christian missionaries such as Willibrord and Boniface[362] and of early twentieth-century Pentecostals.[363] Some

357. See Kee, *Miracle*, 52–54 (not intending "charismatic" in its common theological sense today).

358. Some modern readers have viewed this theme as prescriptive for contemporary Christian evangelism (see Wimber, *Power Evangelism*). Though many believers in Acts work signs, however, not *all* do.

359. With also Alexander, *Context*, 203, who regards this as the dominant apologetic in Acts (distinct from the primarily philosophic approach of second-century apologists, p. 204).

360. For a survey of various denominational views, see, e.g., De Wet, "Signs," 52–61; for a brief history of signs in the context of mission, see McGee, "Miracles and Mission"; for the past two centuries, cf. idem, "Dilemma," 53–59.

361. Associating signs with evangelism, Severus of Antioch in *Cat. Act.* 10.44 (Martin, *Acts*, 140) averred that signs were no longer necessary, the gospel having been widely spread. Such an approach today would expect signs to predominate in less evangelized regions.

362. Kelsey, *Healing*, 230; Neill, *History of Missions*, 75; Latourette, *To A.D. 1500*, 348; cf. others in 344; Finlay, *Columba*, 173; Young, "Miracles in History," 115.

363. See, e.g., Warner, *Evangelist*, 161; Opp, *Lord for Body*, 157–59, 193–94; discussion in Keener, *Miracles*, ch. 10.

signs claims surface even in relatively neglected nineteenth-century missions reports.[364] Consistent with this function of signs, many of the most extraordinary cures in subsequent times have been reported by evangelists among non-Christians,[365] confirming the expectation of some Christian readers based on their reading of "signs" in Acts.[366]

Sometimes signs drew a crowd's attention to the apostles, but the crowd wrongly understood the signs in light of their own religious or magical assumptions (14:11; 19:13; 28:6; cf. 19:18). Because signs were difficult to ignore, when they did not invite attentiveness, they provoked persecution (5:16–17; 6:8–12; 16:18–19; cf. 14:19; 19:24–29). One way or the other, they raised the stakes and made neutrality difficult. Signs also encouraged those who preached God's word to continue doing it boldly (4:29–31; 14:3), even in the face of persecution (4:24–29; cf. 14:2; cf. 7:55–57). Like Jesus's ministry of healings and defense of the marginalized in the Gospel, such healings also constituted benefactions (4:9; 10:38), which helped needy believers even if no unbelievers were present to be evangelized (20:10–12).

If, as argued in the commentary, Luke portrays Paul as a sage (see comment on Acts 19:9), his portrayal of Paul as a signs worker is significant. Although this combination of characters became common in a period after Christian documents such as Acts and the narrative Gospels were widespread, this does not seem to have been common yet in the period in which Luke wrote.[367] As one scholar summarizes, "Cultured authors in the wise man tradition tend to reject the miraculous [but] Luke-Acts synthesizes the two traditions so that the miraculous stands in close proximity to appeals to the cultured."[368] Parallels among the miracles of various figures, especially Jesus, Peter, and Paul, are also significant here (see the discussion of "parallel lives" as an approach to Acts in ch. 2 above).[369]

II. Signs and Promise Fulfillment

The early Christians believed that they lived in the era of OT fulfillment, and hence they expected continuity with OT miracles and revelations. Paul's concluding argument in his climactic speech in 26:19–23 rests on the continuity between OT prophetic experience and his own experience; if one accepted the doctrine of the resurrection, how could one rule out that the risen Jesus actually appeared to and commissioned Paul?

Early Christians believed that they continued to live in "biblical" times (renewed by the Spirit's outpouring in Acts 2), expecting analogous phenomena. (These experiences today tend to be reported especially among Christian renewal movements

---

364. See McGee, "Miracles and Mission," passim (e.g., 146, noting Mason, *Ko Thah Byu*, 160). Cf. also the early twentieth-century Shandong (Shantung) Revival reported by Southern Baptists (Oblau, "Healing," 309; Bays, "Revival," 173; McGee, *Miracles*, 191; Crawford, *Shantung Revival*).

365. A minister present at British Anglican James Moore Hickson's 1921 meetings in China reported that many more nonbelievers than Christians were healed, just as reported earlier in India, perhaps because non-Christians came "in simple, childlike faith that they will be healed" (Hickson, *Heal*, 76). Out of an estimated ten thousand at one meeting in South Africa where 70 percent were not Christians, phenomenal cures are reported: thirty-six "cases of blindness alone being cured . . . two of the blind people who were cured had been born blind" (Hickson, *Heal*, 141). For some other signs among non-Christians that led to testimony and/or conversion, see, e.g., Pullinger, *Dragon*, 123, 142.

366. Ammonius in *Cat. Act.* 28.9 (Martin, *Acts*, 314) notes that "miracles are mostly performed among and for unbelievers" (cf. Bede *Comm. Acts* 28.8; Martin, *Acts*, 314).

367. See Tiede, *Figure*, passim. This refutes an overreliance on the θεῖος ἀνήρ concept sometimes attributed to Luke-Acts (e.g., Weeden, *Mark*, 74–75; Haenchen, *Acts*, 246); contrast also those who prefer the apologetic Paul to the miracle worker (cf. Hickling, "Portrait in Acts 26").

368. Brawley, *Luke-Acts and Jews*, 54. The combination of sage and sign prophet probably goes back to the example of the historical Jesus (see Keener, *Matthew*, 53–58, and sources discussed there).

369. See, e.g., Fenton, "Order of Miracles"; Goulder, *Type and History*, 106–7; on miracles in Acts, see also, e.g., Witherington, *Acts*, 220–24.

that expect continuing revelations because they believe that they continue to live in "biblical" times and do not relegate biblical experiences to a past era.[370] This approach seems to reflect the growing dominant trend in global Christendom today.)[371]

III. DEMONSTRATING DIVINE COMPASSION

Although signs' primary function in Acts is to draw attention to the gospel, the particular character of most of the signs reported reveals something about the character of that gospel. After all, explosions in the sky would have served just as well to draw attention (Luke 21:11; cf. Acts 2:19), but the most common signs in Luke-Acts involve healing the sick or delivering those oppressed by demonic forces. That God's compassion is in view is made still clearer by instances where Luke evokes pathos concerning those who are helped (e.g., Luke 7:12; Acts 9:39).

This character of the miracles is informed by Jesus's ministry in the Gospel, which displays compassion (e.g., Luke 7:13) and mercy (e.g., 17:13; 18:38–39).[372] Jesus's compassionate activity in relieving suffering sometimes stands in stark contextual contrast with the nitpicking scholastic approach of his spiritually powerless critics (6:7, 11; 13:14; 14:1–6).[373] His ministry to the afflicted coheres with his ministry to the poor, the socially marginalized, and those without social power, in contrast to his frequent conflicts with the elite. In Acts, it is Jesus who continues to heal (Acts 3:6; 9:34), and so the same compassion would remain in view. Although Luke's focus in this second volume is on the church's carrying on Jesus's ministry, rather than on specifying again the motivation for such ministry, it may be assumed to be the same motivation already expressed in the Gospel.[374] This also fits God's activity in ancient Israelite theology; the purpose of miracles was not to prove God's existence (which was not in doubt) but to demonstrate his faithfulness.[375]

One should not infer from Luke's reports of healings that Luke expected healing in every case (cf. Luke 14:13); even if we employ the strictest reading of his narrative and the earliest possible date assigned to his work, Luke was well aware that many first-generation followers of Jesus had died (cf. also Luke 14:13). Nevertheless, when

370. They are more consistent with the early Christian view of salvation history (despite the ambiguities of revelatory experiences in both eras; cf. comment on Acts 21:4) than are thoroughgoing cessationists, who attribute "biblical" activities to a bygone era, generally with postbiblical (or very tenuous biblical) explanations. The Protestant cessationist apologetic for lack of signs developed in the Enlightenment era, and the circles in which it was forged, resemble the perspectives of some Greek and Roman historians who accepted the mythological past as of different character than the present (see our ch. 4, sect. 1.d). (Others accept ebbs and flows of signs associated with events in salvation history, with the apostolic era naturally being a "flow"; still, Paul and probably Luke expected the "apostolic" era of the Spirit and accompanying signs to continue uninterrupted until the parousia, just like the mission [Acts 1:8] for which the Spirit empowered God's agents and that signs attested. Undoubtedly, they did not expect centuries' delay preceding the parousia.)

371. As noted by Wagner, *Acts*, 51; Wagner writes from the perspective of a charismatic missiologist and church growth specialist. See further discussion in ch. 9, above; also in Keener, *Miracles*, ch. 7.

372. I suspect that Majority World Christians more often appropriate healing gifts than Westerners in part because they cannot afford to speak as glibly about physical needs as we sometimes may be tempted to do. Those who dismiss miracles' value as being only for those of immature faith rarely report experiencing them; this evaluation might betray its presuppositions.

373. Thus the biblical principle of compassion takes precedence even over the biblical principle of the Sabbath; those who might apply the principle of the emergency Maccabean Sabbath exception to rescue their animal yet did not understand the daily suffering of fellow humans missed a deeper biblical principle (Luke 13:15–16; 14:5). Luke here reflects earlier Jesus tradition (see Matt 12:11–12; cf. Mark 3:4).

374. The same may be said for the sharing of possessions in Acts 2:44–45, which carries over a theme from the Gospel.

375. Ross, "Miracle," 50–56 (noting that such divine acts did not violate a natural order but were "natural" in the sense of expected on the basis of God's character and covenant); the point was God's character (60).

signs did occur, they did not merely attest and garner attention for a noteworthy message; they also underlined its character as good news of "salvation" motivated by God's compassion.

IV. SIGNS AND LUKE'S AUDIENCE

To whom would reports of miracle working most appeal? Granted that reports of miracle working do not offer the most compelling criterion for determining audience location, in this instance they cohere well with our other evidence that seems stronger. Given the geographic distribution of claims for miracle workers (as opposed to simply prodigies) in this period, an audience in the eastern Mediterranean is plausible.[376] Philostratus reports Apollonius's miracles in many cities of the East; although this source is much later than Acts and possibly influenced by it on some points,[377] Theissen may well be right that urban audiences were just as open to believing in demons and other suprahuman forces as were rural ones.[378] Thus these reports could appeal to the kinds of cities on which the Pauline portion of Acts focuses, namely, the locations already judged in chapter 12 above most likely for Luke's primary ideal audience.

More objectively, we can say that Luke's reports of signs would have appealed to the early Christian movement, which celebrated the stories of Jesus's signs and invoked such claims in its own evangelistic work.

c. Signs for Authentication

Luke's use of signs for authentication was not unique to his work. Aside from aretalogies and mythography, Luke's emphasis on signs appears heavier than that of most of his contemporaries (in the first century, though not later eras), but recounting signs for edifying purposes was not unusual. Charles Talbert distinguishes three basic functions of miracle stories in antiquity: legitimation (e.g., Vespasian's alleged miracles), evangelization (Lucius's conversion to the cult of Isis after his restoration, in Apul. *Metam.* 11), and an opportunity for behavioral instruction (e.g., Wis 16:26; Aelian frg. 89).[379] Especially since the Hellenistic period, aretalogies had used miracles as propaganda for competitive cults, not only for Greek cults such as Asclepius but for imports such as Isis and Serapis.[380]

Ancient writers and storytellers often used miraculous works to authenticate deities or, more often, mortal individuals.[381] Such signs demonstrated that the person indeed possessed numinous authority to justify his[382] claims. Patristic sources continued to use miracles and particularly exorcisms as proofs verifying their claims.[383]

---

376. See more fully Theissen, *Miracle Stories*, 253–54.

377. Ibid., 247, cites not only Tarsus (Philost. *Vit. Apoll.* 4.43), Athens (4.20), and Rome (4.45) but also Ephesus (4.10) and other cities where Paul performed miracles (Lystra, Philippi, and Troas), suggesting that this particular work by Philostratus reflects knowledge of the Acts traditions and may not be the most reliable independent source here.

378. Theissen, *Miracle Stories*, 247; cf. Acts 19:12–19.

379. Talbert, *John*, 162, finding parallels for each of these in John's Gospel. For the legitimating function of Suetonius's report about Vespasian (*Vesp.* 7.2–3), see discussion in Spahlinger, "Sueton-Studien II."

380. Versnel, "Miracles." Cult officials collected them and intensified the miraculous dimension for propaganda purposes (Klauck, *Context*, 161, 166); they need not, however, constitute a distinct literary genre (Aune, *Dictionary of Rhetoric*, 57), and they differ in genre from NT healing narratives, which belong to broader narratives rather than to lists (Klauck, *Context*, 167; for other contrasts, 168).

381. I used this material also in Keener, *John*, 272–74.

382. In the vast majority of cases, they were men, although we do encounter exceptions such as the later Sosipatra.

383. Lampe, "Miracles," esp. 215–17. For how patristic theology handled this, see also Wiles, "Miracles."

I. PAGAN MODELS

When applied to deities, as in the case of the healing list at Epidaurus, testimonies of miracles were meant to persuade people to trust for themselves to be healed;[384] this especially applies to Asclepius's healing of skeptics.[385] Similarly, Mark's reports of healings encourage his hearers to trust their risen Lord to do miracles for them; disciples are reproved if their own faith for miracles is inadequate (Mark 4:38–40; 8:14–21; 9:18–29; 11:20–25).[386] (Mark's promises for faith, as in 11:20–25, however, are substantially greater than those of the Epidaurus inscriptions; the former virtually made all believers "holy persons" with direct access to God, whereas the latter sought to "cushion disappointments" as well as "increase expectations.")[387] Miracles came to possess such propagandistic value that Romans could employ miracle claims of the Isis cult for political propaganda.[388]

Ancient writers report the healings attributed to Vespasian before the inauguration of his Flavian dynasty—undoubtedly a form of propaganda meant to authenticate his claim to rule.[389] Any common idea of miracle-working sages, however, normally (in contrast to Acts) applied only to "divine" sages[390] and developed only over time. First-century philosophers emphasized the divine wisdom of true sages rather than miraculous authentication; by the second century, writers such as Lucian contested the growing popular ideal of such authentication; by the third century, many thinkers had capitulated to the popular ideal, portraying the intellectual heroes of the past as wonder-workers as well. (This trend increased as astrology, magic, and other customs from the East supplanted some of the traditional reliance on the more rationally oriented cultus of Roman religion and the like.)[391]

II. BIBLICAL AND EARLY JEWISH MODELS

The OT reported both miracles performed directly by God and those performed through his agents, certain kinds of prophets;[392] Jewish hopes for both kinds of miracles continued in the period of Christian beginnings. On a popular level, miraculous answers to prayer probably authenticated Hanina ben Dosa,[393] Honi the Circle-Drawer, and the other teachers Vermes has called "charismatic rabbis."[394] (As with Jesus and his apostles in Luke-Acts, a primary model behind ancient portrayals of some of these signs sages, such as Hanina, was Elijah.)[395] Because Honi was before God like

---

384. Also Dibelius, *Tradition*, 170; cf. Grant, *Gods*, 66. Compare the translation of some of these accounts in Grant, *Religions*, 55–58.

385. Inscriptions 3 and 4 in Grant, *Religions*, 56, 57.

386. Signs are positive if inadequate in Mark; see Rhoads and Michie, *Mark*, 105; Kingsbury, *Christology*, 76–77. Divine or supramundane activity elicits human praise, as, e.g., in *1 En.* 24:4–25:7; *Let. Aris.* 99.

387. On this function of the Epidaurus inscriptions, see Theissen, *Miracle Stories*, 283–84.

388. Kee, *Miracle*, 128–31.

389. Tiede, *Figure*, 91, citing Tac. *Hist.* 4.81; Dio Cass. 65.8; Suet. *Vesp.* 7. On Suetonius's report (*Vesp.* 7.2–3), see more fully Spahlinger, "Sueton-Studien II."

390. Greek biographers, in Aune, *Environment*, 34.

391. Tiede, *Figure*, 99. Fate, astrology, and magic became increasingly pervasive by the third century (cf. *PGM* passim; Frankfurter, *Religion in Egypt*; Murray, *Stages*).

392. See Kee, *Miracle*, 147.

393. Cf. Moore, *Judaism*, 1:377; Strack, *Introduction*, 110, for his miracles in *b. Ber.* 33a; 34b; *Ta'an.* 24b; and that he was contemporary with Johanan ben Zakkai (*m. 'Abot* 3:9, 10; *Mek.* on Exod 18:21).

394. On Honi and Hanina, see, e.g., Daube, "Enfant"; on Hanina, see Vermes, "Hanina"; for examples of Jewish miracle stories in general, see Montefiore and Loewe, *Anthology*, 339ff. Bokser, "Wonder-Working," suggests that Palestinian tradition stressed God's protection of the pious man whereas Babylonian stressed such a man's responsibility to others.

395. See Galley, "Heilige."

a special son to a father, he was said to be able to change God's mind on matters.[396] Hanina was so highly respected that it was said, "'When Haninah ben Dosa died there were no workers of miracles left.'"[397] These signs authenticated those who performed them; a holy man had power to make things happen, because he was holy.[398] This trajectory developed lavishly in medieval Christian hagiographic tradition and still later Hasidic tales.[399]

In similar traditions, perhaps more relevant for Acts, signs could attest one's message.[400] Some halakists, such as R. Eliezer and R. Joshua, also reportedly performed miracles to validate their halakah (although this story is clearly a homiletic one).[401] Such stories not only glorified the signs worker but also offered a more widely applicable moral. Most accounts of such miraculous works by past rabbis, though sometimes hagiographic, made a point about piety or impiety; God hears the pious and punishes those who disregard proper teaching of the law, especially those who would not believe without miracles.[402]

iii. Rabbinic Mistrust of Miracles

Most later rabbis, however, carefully subordinated miracles[403] and even the heavenly voice[404] to tradition in halakic interpretation. Prophets must be attested by signs, some later rabbis insisted, but elders as interpreters of the law may be accepted without signs.[405] Vermes thinks that charismatics such as Hanina sometimes flouted rabbinic law, and although the rabbis dared not discipline these charismatics because of their divine power,[406] rabbis became generally wary of supernatural proof when formulating legal decisions.[407] These rabbis clearly subordinate the status of miracle workers to that of halakists like themselves.[408] Thus later rabbis could complain that even Honi's prayers were delayed, and explain that this was because he failed to approach God *humbly*.[409]

If such reluctance to depend on miracles circulated in Luke's day (cf. Luke 11:15–16), predecessors of these later rabbis would have rejected Peter's appeal to subjective visions (even two coordinated ones to separate individuals to defend eating with Cornelius; Acts 11:5–14; cf. 11:15–17; 15:7–11), including his "heavenly voice" (11:7–10). Likewise, they would have rejected Paul's appeal to his own signs authenticating his Gentile mission (15:12; cf. Rom 15:18–19). (By contrast, probably many other Jewish people were more open to such attestation.)

Some scholars argue that the rabbis' earlier respect for rule miracles (miracles confirming particular legal interpretations) diminished further in response to the much greater Christian use of authenticating miracles.[410] Christian miracles authenticating

---

396. *Y. Ta'an.* 3:10, §§61–63.

397. Moore, *Judaism*, 1:378, citing *m. Soṭah* 9:15, "a late appendix."

398. *Y. Ta'an* 3:11, §4; cf. *b. 'Abod. Zar.* 18a (on R. Meir); *Me'il.* 17b (R. Simeon ben Yohai); *Sukkah* 28a (Jonathan ben Uzziel). Cf. *b. B. Meṣi'a* 86a in Neusner, *Sat*, 77–78, where signs are recorded to glorify Rabbah b. Nahmani.

399. See Keener, *Miracles*, appendix C.

400. *Y. Sanh.* 6:6, §2, about a man sent to Simeon ben Shetah.

401. *B. B. Meṣi'a* 59b, where Joshua, instead of losing the debate, finally declares that halakah is not settled by miracles; see esp. Baumgarten, "Miracles," for the importance of miracles confirming halakah.

402. Cf. also Dibelius, *Tradition*, 145–46; Urbach, *Sages*, 1:108–9.

403. E.g., *t. Yebam.* 14:6, "the rabbis" to R. Meir.

404. E.g., *b. Ḥul.* 44a; *Pesaḥ.* 114a; *y. Mo'ed Qaṭ.* 3:1, §6.

405. *Y. Sanh.* 11:4, §1.

406. Vermes, *Jesus the Jew*, 80–81, appealing to *m. Ta'an.* 3:8; *y. Ta'an.* 67a; *b. Ta'an.* 23a.

407. Cf. also *b. B. Meṣi'a* 59b (cited in Longenecker, *Paul*, 4n17).

408. Dibelius, *Tradition*, 149–50 and references.

409. *Y. Ta'an.* 3:9, §3.

410. Theissen, *Miracle Stories*, 107; cf. Guttmann, "Miracles."

Jesus were problematic for later rabbis; Ephraim Urbach suggests that this may be why the rabbis stressed that one should depend on the God of Abraham, not on Abraham as a miracle worker himself.[411] From Paul's letters[412] through rabbinic literature,[413] Christians and outsiders alike continued to perceive early Christianity as confirming itself with signs like those of Jesus.

IV. Who Is Authenticated?

Unlike some other ancient writers, Luke uses signs to attest not the miracle workers themselves (except in the case of Jesus) but primarily their message (or, in a sense, the name of Jesus, which they bear). This message is no mere, particular halakic point but the saving claim of Jesus. Nevertheless, in one sense, Luke does suggest that the signs even in Acts continue to attest to their ultimate worker; it is Jesus's name that heals (3:6; 4:7, 10, 30; 16:18; 19:13, 17; cf. 14:3; Luke 9:49; 10:17), and so the Jesus who healed in the first volume continues to perform the signs in the second through his agents (cf. esp. Acts 9:34).[414] The use of signs for authentication also carries on in some later Christian sources.[415]

Conclusion

This chapter has merely sampled some Lukan themes, examining them, where possible, in the light of their broader cultural framework. These themes have included, in particular, the Gentile mission, the Spirit, and the function of signs, as well as briefer perusal of some other topics. For the most part, however, I address other themes simply when they arise in the text of Acts (since commentaries are not NT theologies per se, though they may supply raw materials for them).

Even the sample themes that have been briefly treated, however, should suffice to illustrate that Luke did not offer primarily a haphazard collection of unrelated historical details but, rather, a cohesive narrative work emphasizing some major points he sought to communicate. This observation leads to a discussion of a major feature of Luke's narrative unity, namely, conspicuously parallel characteristics in his portrayals of various characters.

411. Urbach, *Sages*, 1:117.

412. Aune, *Prophecy*, 194, cites as examples Gal 3:5; Rom 15:19; 2 Cor 12:12; 1 Thess 1:5; 1 Cor 2:4 for Paul's picture of himself as a miracle worker; Paul clearly also believed such activities characterized the early Christian communities (1 Cor 12:8–10, 28–31).

413. Christians healed in the name of Yeshu ben Pandira (*t. Ḥul.* 2:22–23; see also Urbach, *Sages*, 1:116; Herford, *Christianity*, 103–11; Klausner, *Jesus of Nazareth*, 40; Pritz, *Nazarene Christianity*, 96–97), though the rabbis often associated their powers with magic or fakery (e.g., *y. ʾAbod. Zar.* 2:2, §3; Urbach, *Sages*, 1:115–16; Herford, *Christianity*, 115–17; Lachs, *Commentary*, 178). In some apocryphal stories, holy rabbis destroyed miracle-working Christians with greater magic (see Herford, *Christianity*, 112–15).

414. On the idea of agency and representatives, see Keener, *John*, 310–15. For a related discussion of the relationship between healing in the two volumes, see Warrington, "Healing Narratives"; Shelton, "Used to Be?" Rightly underlining parallels between Jesus and the disciples but noting that disciples do not emulate Jesus's *messianic* ministry, Warrington emphasizes healing's christological function ("Healing Narratives," 195) and that healings reveal his presence (217); he argues that Jesus's healings are not paradigmatic for individual followers (Warrington, *Healer* 160–62; cf. idem, "Response"). Shelton, who responds to Warrington, also seems right to affirm that Jesus's healings are also paradigmatic for the church ("Used to Be?," 221–22, 224), if we take that as the church as a whole (through some who are gifted). On Jesus's exorcisms as a model in Luke-Acts, see esp. Twelftree, *Name*, 130–37.

415. E.g., Justin *Dial.* 35.8.

16

THE UNITY AND
STRUCTURE OF LUKE-ACTS

O ne of the most important insights offered by the past century of scholarship
into the interpretation of Luke-Acts is that we should read the two volumes
together.[1] Although scholars have been interpreting Luke and Acts together more
deliberately in recent decades, earlier interpreters also recognized this historical
connection, despite their early separation in the canon.

Sir William Ramsay, frequently cited in connection with the archaeological evidence he collected in support of Luke's usual historical accuracy, also recognized
that Acts "was understood by the author as the Second Book of his history; and the
reader will best understand it if he studies it in this way. It was probably at some time
in the second century that the Second Book was separated from the First" so that the
first could be included among the other approved Gospels.[2] Richard Rackham, still
more clearly, spoke of the "architecture" of Luke's history, finding structural parallels between the two volumes.[3] But it was Cadbury's work that brought the unity of
Luke-Acts most clearly to the attention of scholars.[4]

Most current Luke-Acts scholars build on this insight, emphasizing the literary
unity of the two volumes. By telling a single story that includes both the Gospel and
Acts, Luke connects the Gentile mission with, and grounds it in, Israel's heritage.[5]
Joseph Verheyden, noting that the vast majority of scholars now read Luke and Acts
together, rightly concludes, "This means that the Gospel is the introduction to Acts
and the basis upon which Acts is built, but also that the Gospel, in a sense, needs
Acts and calls for the continuation in which its message is realized in the world, and
consequently that Luke and Acts together constitute one work."[6]

1. With, e.g., Gasque, Criticism, 308; Pesch, Apostelgeschichte, 1:24–25.

2. Ramsay, Pictures, xv. Cf. Bruce, Commentary, 15.

3. Rackham, Acts, xlvii (comparing the waiting period in Luke 1–2 and Acts 1; baptism in the Spirit in
Luke 3 and Acts 2; then active ministry and finally suffering; see more fully pp. xlvii–xlix). Shauf, Theology,
1n1, notes that Bacon, Introduction (esp. 218), already spoke of Luke-Acts and treated the works together.

4. See Cadbury, Making, esp. 10–11 (where he treats Luke and Acts as two volumes of a single work, like
Samuel-Kings, which constitutes a multivolume work in the LXX).

5. See, e.g., Clark, "Role," 185–89; Marshall, "Theme in Parts"; Richard, "Author," 25–27; cf. Pervo, "Heritage and Claims," 142–43. See also our discussion on Luke's portrayal of Israel's story and of the Gentile
mission in chs. 13 and 14.

6. Verheyden, "What Are We Up To?," 56. Verheyden (ibid., 52–53) credits especially the pioneering
work of C. H. Talbert, and also W. Radl, G. Muhlack, and F. Neirynck.

1. Unity

The vast majority of scholars today recognize and work from the premise of the literary unity of Luke and Acts.[7] In the past some denied even common authorship,[8] but such arguments are rare today. As Arnold Ehrhardt already put it long ago, "It can also be stated that stylistically the Third Gospel and the book of Acts correspond so closely to each other, that we can without reserve ascribe the two books to the same writer."[9] (Xenophon in *Hell.* 1.1.1 shows that one historian could pick up where another left off; but this practice was not common, and the differences in style between Xenophon and Thucydides, whose work he continues, are blatant.)

Luke advertises the unity of his work openly. The Gospel and Acts share a common theme and vocabulary.[10] More important, the story line provides a narrative unity.[11] Perhaps most obvious, our finished version of Acts opens with the author pointing the dedicatee to his former book (Acts 1:1) and then picking up with the very story where his first volume left off.[12] Both the recapitulation of the Gospel's conclusion in Acts' introduction and the second preface's mention of the first volume have sufficient ancient analogies (see comments ad loc.) to leave no room for doubt that we should view Luke's Gospel and Acts as two volumes of a single work.

a. Considering Objections to Unity

This claim to unity does not imply that no differences exist between the two works, especially in sources, texture, and emphasis.[13] For example, although Luke uses Hellenistic devices, such as symposia, in the Gospel, one does not write the biography of a Palestinian sage, especially one many of whose sayings remained in wide circula-

7. E.g., Boismard and Lamouille, *Actes*, 1:8; Pesch, *Apostelgeschichte*, 1:24–25; Schneider, "Zweck"; Marguerat, *Actes*, 17–18; idem, *Histoire*, 65–92; idem, "Unité"; Green, "Reaffirmation"; Peterson, *Acts*, 7–8; Tyson, "Source Criticism," 38–39; Hemer, *Acts in History*, 3–33; Arrington, *Acts*, xxxi; Witherington, *Acts*, 4–8; Marshall, "Theme in Parts"; idem, "Reading"; Bergholz, *Aufbau* (extensively); Richard, "Author," 25–27; Mekkattukunnel, "Proof for Unity" (with some detailed comparisons); Pate et al., *Story*, 177–87; Jervell, *Apostelgeschichte*, 91; Verheyden, *Unity*; idem, "Unity of Luke-Acts"; idem, "Unity"; Flichy, *Oeuvre de Luc*; Rothschild, *Rhetoric of History*, 115–16 (a table); Borgman, *Way*; Hamm, *Acts*, 5–8; Chance, *Acts*, 19; Puskas and Crump, *Introduction*, 105, 111–13; cf. some examples of continuity in Maddox, *Purpose*, 6. Marguerat calls the work "un diptyque" (*Histoire*, 65, 91; idem, "Unité," 80). Talbert, *Patterns*, 96, emphasizes unity through the succession from Jesus to the Twelve (then to Paul and to the Ephesian elders).

8. Clark, *Acts*, 408. Even then most favored authorial unity, e.g., Knowling, "Acts," 3–4; Carter and Earle, *Acts*, i–ii; R. Williams, *Acts*, 15. Today, see Walters, *Unity*, citing stylistic differences (with careful observations on 43–136, 149–89), which she contends exceed what would be expected for a single author (147). (Some features more characteristic of one volume, however, such as archaizing, also appear at appropriate points in the other volume.) She questions the probability of Luke's extraordinary literary versatility (praised by Cadbury, Talbert, and others) and is not satisfied with Dibelius's argument (which I find very probable) that Luke depended on more traditional material in his first volume. Possibly editorial help was available for one volume, or Luke's rhetorical skills improved over time, or (most likely) much of the second volume (freer from tradition and a Judean setting) afforded a setting more conducive to Hellenistic rhetorical techniques.

9. Ehrhardt, *Acts*, 1; he notes that others sometimes completed famous works, making stylistic analysis necessary, but here the analysis is conclusive.

10. Boismard and Lamouille, *Actes*, 3:14–16.

11. See esp. the parallels in Goulder, *Type and History*; Talbert, *Patterns*; Tannehill, *Luke*; idem, *Acts*; for some particularly concise surveys, see Aune, *Environment*, 119; Perkins, *Reading*, 265; Dunn, *Acts*, xiv; Talbert, *Acts*, xxiv–xxv, xxviii.

12. See Marshall, "Treatise."

13. See, e.g., Marguerat, *Histoire*, 66–70 (recognizing dissonances); earlier, Dibelius, *Studies in Acts*, 3–4, 103. Dreams and visions are much less frequent in the Gospel than in Acts (and angelic revelations mute during Jesus's ministry), presumably because Jesus does not need them (Koet, "Divine Communication," 756–57). For observations regarding unity and diversity in speeches, miracle counting, and meal reports in Luke's double work, see Lindemann, "Einheit." Yet Luke would not be the only writer to take a different approach in different volumes (see, e.g., Hecataeus in Brown, *Historians*, 11).

tion, in exactly the way one would compose a typical Hellenistic history. Jesus used a Palestinian Jewish teaching style; Paul used Greco-Roman rhetoric, which is distantly related but often quite different.

Some scholars doubt the unity of the two volumes, though more often in terms of purpose than of authorship.[14] Some question even the common style,[15] but while some vocabulary and stylistic features are limited to one or the other volume,[16] these are not the sorts of differences that a common author writing at somewhat different times or on somewhat different subjects could not betray.[17] Some scholars suggest that despite their relationship (Acts 1:1), Luke and Acts tell distinct stories at the discourse level.[18] But while one may grant that Luke's source material prevents him from offering only detailed parallels, Luke selects and shapes much of this source material toward a common goal. Josephus, some object, clearly tells us to expect more volumes, yet Luke does not.[19] But not all ancient writers announced their future volumes, and 1:1 is a perfectly clear allusion to the previous volume.

1. Reception History

Other scholars argue, plausibly, that the early reception history of the Gospel and Acts argues against unity;[20] this division seems especially clear from the interposition of John in the arrangement of the canon[21] and Acts' textual history, which suggests canonization later than the Gospel.[22] (Some of the second-century evidence, however, could point toward their unity.)[23] But while these factors do suggest that many second-century readers separated the two (a point not easily dismissed, given their mostly shared culture and language with Luke), they do not prove that Luke's first audience would have shared that conviction.[24]

Even some scholars who emphasize the works' divergent reception in the second century acknowledge that Luke-Acts itself allows us to infer its authorial design as a

14. The best-known objections appear in Parsons and Pervo, *Rethinking*. Among others, Litwak, *Echoes*, 37–47, critiques their skepticism, objecting that they fail to define narrative unity and that they overlook many cues for the narrative's purpose. For one survey of the current discussion, see Bird, "Unity," 426–39.

15. See Dawsey, "Questions of Style."

16. The same vocabulary can appear in different ways, e.g., κολλάομαι in Luke 10:11; 15:15; Acts 5:13; 8:29; 10:28; 17:34); cf. καθίστημι in Acts 7:10; 17:15; perhaps λαμπρός in Luke 23:11; Acts 10:30. In the Gospel, προσδοκάω is usually positive and theological, but less so in Acts; ὁμοθυμαδόν is common in Acts, in contrast to the Gospel. Different subject matter, sources, genre, or even mood could account for such differences.

17. E.g., Josephus's use of παράδοξος seems broader in his *Antiquities* than in his *War*; a more thorough examination could find many other such differences.

18. Parsons and Pervo, *Rethinking*, 45–83. Pervo, *Acts*, 20, though denying that Luke necessarily planned Acts when he wrote the Gospel, does allow that the former may have been written as a "sequel." Some ancient authors' views apparently changed in the course of writing longer works (e.g., Livy in Woodman, *Rhetoric*, 126). For various views on the nature of unity (or disunity) between the works, see Powell, *Acts*, 6–9.

19. See Parsons, "Unity: Rethinking," 41–45.

20. Parsons, "Unity: Rethinking," 48–51. Rowe, "Hermeneutics," 132–48, likewise explores the reception history, though he does not draw from it inferences for Luke's authorial purpose. For other discussions of this early reception history, see Kany, "Warum"; Mount, "Investigation" (noting that even the separate titles obscure the connection [380], though the prefaces internally "impose a unity" on the volumes [382]); for Acts as a canonical bridge between Gospels and Letters, see Goswell, "Order," 232–34 (citing also Childs, *Canon*, 219–25; Wall, "Canonical Context").

21. Parsons, "Unity: Rethinking," 48.

22. Ibid., 49. Parsons also cites the production of apocryphal acts to show that they were read separately (51).

23. Gregory, "Reception and Unity," 461–63, finds clues (such as application of the Gospel's preface to Acts) that cumulatively convince him that Irenaeus (and [p. 463] the witness of the Muratorian Fragment) read Luke both with Acts and as part of the fourfold Gospel. Later writers could also treat Luke and Acts together (e.g., Bede *Comm. Acts* pref. [L. Martin, 4–5] cites Luke 1:1, 3 for understanding Luke's writing in Acts).

24. Johnson, "Literary Criticism," 159; Gregory, "Reception and Unity," 463–66 (esp. 466).

unity.[25] Although ideal readers are not the same as real readers,[26] Luke presumably knew his target audience better than we do, a target audience earlier by roughly a century than most voices cited as reading the volumes separately. What factors may account for the shift in the reading approach to Luke?

By the mid-second century (and probably much earlier),[27] "gospels" constituted a distinctive, identifiable genre; for apologetic and other reasons, the church in this century came to focus on its four Gospels as the heart of its post-Tanakh canon (cf. Irenaeus's emphasis on the fourfold Gospel). Readers rightly distinguished John from the Synoptics; sharing the gospel genre does not mean identity in all characteristics. Yet that Gospel's shared biographic genre appeared clear enough. Luke's Gospel was likewise classified by its apparently biographical (and certainly "gospel") genre, not by its explicit linkage with Acts (Acts 1:1). But Acts 1:1 suggests that Luke's first audience, which did not find the first volume in a Gospel "canon," received the works together, or received Acts as the sequel to the Gospel, from the same author; they would have begun with different presuppositions about the unity of the works.

I strongly agree with those who argue that Luke and Acts are more than merely authorially and theologically united; they represent a narrative unity, telling a consistent story.[28] But even those who argue against Luke-Acts as a literary unity find pervasive theological themes in both volumes because of probable authorial unity.[29] And even those who emphasize unity must recognize some differences, differences that Luke's sources made inevitable.

II. Distinct Genres?

A clearer objection to one kind of unity is that common authorship, audience, and even a common story would not necessarily demand common genre.[30] The analysis of genre earlier in this introduction lends some support to this question; although I regard the work as a whole as history (following probable cues in the Gospel's preface), the Gospel, taken by itself, would be read more naturally as biography. While this observation would be true for any biographic volume in a larger history (as noted in ch. 2 above), it seems especially true for a work cognizant of other works focused on Jesus (Luke 1:1).

But it is precisely for this reason that the Gospel must not be taken *only* by itself but as a biographic segment belonging to a longer history: otherwise, some primarily historical cues in the preface would point *only* to the second volume. Ancients

---

25. So Rowe, "Reception History," 451; cf. idem, "Hermeneutics," 152–53. Unlike Parsons and Pervo, Rowe ("Reception History," 452) simply contends that such authorial unity does not address how they were read in an ancient context and (in "Hermeneutics," 153) that the different reading of early Christians allows us other interpretive options (see also here Bockmuehl, "Let Acts Be Acts," esp. 163). Since I am writing a commentary on Acts (and not on Luke-Acts), I must grant at least some weight to this observation despite my heavy emphasis on the narrative unity of Luke's work!

26. Conceded by Gregory, "Reception and Unity," 466. Like Gregory, Johnson, "Literary Criticism," 161, emphasizes that Luke's *ideal, intended* reader will treat the volumes together. Rowe, "Reception History," 452, denies that such observations (with which he agrees) address his point about real readers.

27. The similarity of Luke to the other Gospels shows that he himself followed this category (presumably introduced by Mark or a writer no longer extant), but whereas Luke and his peers were writing proclamatory "lives" of Jesus (identifiable as biographies), their "canonical" status had solidified a distinctive way of reading them by the late second century. Had Irenaeus been alone in his opinions about the fourfold Gospel, it is highly questionable that the opinions of the bishop of Lyons alone would have swayed the "orthodox" writers of the eastern empire, where the church was strongest, and beyond. Tatian's *Diatessaron* in Syria is probably earlier evidence than Irenaeus. For the Gospel canon, see Hill, *Gospels*.

28. E.g., Tannehill, *Luke*, xiii.

29. Parsons and Pervo, *Rethinking*, 84–114, 123–26.

30. See Pervo, "Same Genre?"; Parsons, "Unity: Rethinking," esp. 45–48; see also Bird, "Unity," 440.

sometimes mixed genres, and historical biography and history that are focused on significant individuals' words and actions are closely enough related that distinctions based on our theoretical classifications (and those of ancient writers) may break down in practice at this point. It is, in fact, the blending of these genres that displays Luke's distinctive genius: Luke grounds his story of Paul and the Gentile mission in the emerging gospel genre, an "audacious move of conjoining a βίος about Jesus and a volume whose dominant concern is the reputation of Paul."[31] Luke might intend this move partly to rehabilitate Paul for some Christians who viewed his custody and execution as having discredited him (see ch. 7 above).

b. Unity from an Ancient Perspective

Some scholars object that ancient readers would not have thought of approaching works with such "modern" premises as literary unity.[32] Although ancient readers may not have emphasized literary unity or authorial style to the extent to which modern biblical scholars do, ancient rhetorical critics regularly commented on ancient writers' style, even using this criterion to evaluate claims to authorship.[33] While casual readers today may miss the connections, they would not be lost on ancient audiences who heard the oral recitation multiple times and lived in a culture where people listened for such connections. Audiences could hear important works multiple times.[34]

Nor should we suppose that they applied this literary approach only for the sake of observation (and the Greek penchant for classification), to the exclusion of interpretation. Seneca understands *fugit* with time figuratively in one passage in Virgil (*Georg.* 3.284) precisely because this was Virgil's consistent usage elsewhere (Sen. Y. *Ep. Lucil.* 108.24–25). As to unity, even some ancient genres that were less cohesive than a story demanded careful connections and construction, like a fine robe.[35] Moreover, as should be evident below, ancient "parallel" narratives most certainly did emphasize the sort of narrative parallels that critics explore under the title of "unity."

Charles Talbert has also defended his earlier thesis on the unity of Luke-Acts by pointing out that the same approach worked with other ancient documents. He in fact borrowed his method of "architecture analysis . . . from classicist Cedric Whitman of Harvard, who used such detection of large patterns to argue, with success, for the unity of Homer's work against its detractors."[36]

Luke and Acts are each roughly the length of the longest standard scroll, between thirty-two and forty feet.[37] By writing two volumes of roughly equal length (the Gospel has roughly 5 percent more words than the standard version of Acts), Luke emphasizes his plan to match the two volumes. Ancient writers by no means demanded symmetry in the size of volumes; in length, one of Sallust's monographs (which might have consumed two shorter scrolls) is almost double the other (which would have fit on a

---

31. Klutz, *Exorcism Stories*, 13.

32. Aune, *Dictionary of Rhetoric*, 315 (s.v. "Narrative criticism," 315–17) argues that ancient literary critics were not concerned with narrative unity (following Heath, *Unity*), which he finds also problematic for modern historical critics (following Merenlahti, *Poetics*, 25) and not important in nonbiblical literary criticism (Merenlahti and Hakola, "Reconceiving"; Merenlahti, *Poetics*, 28).

33. E.g., Dion. Hal. *Lysias* 11–12.

34. Hermog. *Method* 13.428.

35. See Fronto (Naber, 211; LCL, 1:41, on eulogies and epideictic speeches). Cf. also the repetitive character of "oral" narratives in Dewey, "Oral-Aural Event," 148–49.

36. Talbert, "Chance," 233; idem, *Acts*, xv; see esp. idem, *Patterns*, 67–70, for classical analogies and 70ff. for Middle Eastern analogies. As in the broader culture, such patterns served especially aesthetic purposes (120).

37. Ferguson, *Backgrounds*, 94; Aune, *Environment*, 117 (who suggests that, given average dimensions of papyrus sheets, the Gospel may have been 35 ft. long and Acts, 32 ft.).

single scroll).[38] Parallel volumes, however, were usually of roughly equal length—for example, the two volumes of Josephus's apologetic *Against Apion*.[39] Although Luke may well have completed the second volume a significant length of time after the first,[40] he may intend even the comparable length of each volume to reinforce his intention that they be read as a pair. Practical considerations such as standard scroll lengths dictated division into books, but such division also served literary purposes.[41]

c. Narrative Parallels between Luke and Acts

In view of early Christian commands to imitate Christ (1 Cor 11:1; Eph 5:2, 25) and the culture's wider expectations of divine imitation,[42] it is not surprising that second-century Christians drew parallels between their heroes and Jesus; thus the captain of the police arresting Polycarp is called Herod (*Mart. Pol.* 6.2; 8.2; 17.2; 21.1); Polycarp has something of his own triumphal entry (8.1), and his martyrdom explicitly follows Christ's pattern (19.1). It seems uncontroversial that some first-century writers may have also sought parallels between the lives of Jesus and some of his followers.[43]

i. FROM UNDER TÜBINGEN'S SHADOW

In the past, however, a few scholars were reticent to find parallels among characters in Luke-Acts[44]—perhaps for apologetic reasons. The now largely discredited nineteenth-century Tübingen school argued that Acts paralleled Peter's and Paul's deeds, creating a reaction against the view in some circles.[45] Yet one need not agree with the speculative aspects of that school's explanations (grounded in Hegelian dialectic and other perspectives of the era) to appreciate its more objective observation about the parallels.[46]

Thus even some writers justly suspicious about the old Tübingen approach have found the parallels difficult to evade. Harnack, for example, cautiously opines that

---

38. Palmer, "Monograph (1993)," 5.

39. Aune, *Environment*, 117–18, also cites Diod. Sic. 1.29.6; 1.41.10. Admittedly, writers did not always plan the lengths of their volumes well; the first scroll's ending seems to catch Josephus by surprise (*Ag. Ap.* 1.320; Mason, *Josephus and New Testament*, 79).

40. Aune, *Environment*, 117: "Ancient historians occasionally published books separately" (Dion. Hal. *Ant. rom.* 7.70.2), especially if expecting them to be long.

41. In Philo, cf. Royse, "Philo's Division."

42. Many in antiquity urged imitation of God; see Keener, *Matthew*, 205. Many Greco-Roman (Xen. *Cyr.* 6.2.29; Cic. *Tusc.* 5.25.70; Sen. Y. *Dial.* 1.1.5; 7.8.4; Mus. Ruf. 8, p. 64.14; 17, p. 108.8–22; frg. 38, p. 136.5; Heraclitus *Ep.* 5; Dio Chrys. *Or.* 3.82; Plut. *Borr.* 7, *Mor.* 830B [somewhat demurring]; Epict. *Diatr.* 2.14.12–13; Max. Tyre 35.2; Eunapius *Lives* 498; cf. Rutenber, *Doctrine*, chs. 2–3; Russell, "Virtue"), Greco-Jewish and Christian (*Let. Aris.* 188, 190, 192, 208–10, 254, 281; Philo *Creation* 139; *Spec. Laws* 4.73; *Alleg. Interp.* 1.48; 4.188 [rulers, as often in *Letter of Aristeas*]; *Virt.* 168; *Decal.* 98, 100; Eph 5:1; Matt 5:45, 48; *Test. Ash.* 4:3; *Sent. Sext.* 44–45), and later Jewish (*Mek. Shir.* 3.43–44; *Sipra Qed. par.* 1.195.1.3; on the rabbinic doctrine of imitating God in Tannaitic and Amoraic texts, see further Vermes, *Religion*, 201–4; cf. idem, *Jesus and Judaism*, 52; Shapiro, "Wisdom"; Veghazi, "Imitación"; Meirovich, "Crisis"; in a broad Mediterranean context, Crouzel, "Imitation") teachers also acknowledged the principle of imitating God. For disciples' imitating teachers, see also Jos. *Life* 11; *b. Ber.* 62a; Kirschner, "Imitatio"; Abrahams, *Studies* (2), 138–54; Xen. *Mem.* 1.2.3; Sen. E. *Controv.* 9.3.12–13; Lucian *Peregr.* 24; Philost. *Vit. Apoll.* 5.21; 1 Cor 4:16; Fiore, "Exemplification," 233–34.

43. E.g., regarding martyrdom, see Acts 7:56–60. Barrett, "*Imitatio*," 262, doubts that imitation of Christ or others plays a central role in Luke-Acts, but ancient auditors accustomed to find models for imitation in historical and biographic works would undoubtedly have thought otherwise (see ch. 5, above, on historians' agendas). For Jesus as an ethical model in Luke-Acts, see Buckwalter, *Christology*.

44. E.g., Knowling, "Acts," 15–16.

45. On Baur's thesis, see also discussion in Frey, "Fragen," 4–5. More recently, Tyson, *Marcion*, 62–63, has used the parallels to support something like Baur's thesis. Gibert, "Invention," has argued that Luke invented the genre of hagiographic history, promoting its protagonists as imitators of Christ. Playing Paul off against the other apostles goes back to Marcion (Räisänen, "Marcion," 302, 304–5).

46. Cf. C. Williams, *Acts*, 89 (on Acts 5:15).

the comparison between Peter and Paul in Acts "was certainly not created by St. Luke, but by History herself"[47]—a conclusion that, despite being perhaps framed apologetically vis-à-vis the Tübingen school, has some early support in Paul's own letters (Gal 2:7–9). Certainly, Luke would have agreed: he finds patterns in the way God used individuals earlier in salvation history (see esp. Acts 7:37),[48] and locating similar characters in a new stage of salvation history is a central part of Luke's agenda.[49]

Today most scholars recognize the parallelism between Luke and Acts and among their various major characters.[50] Most also recognize that Luke uses these parallels in part to underline the unity between Israel's heritage and the Gentile mission.[51] In addition to providing the narrative with cohesiveness,[52] the selective repetition in these narratives reinforces the repeated themes and conveys to Peter, Paul, and others the authoritative sort of character attached to Jesus, the biblical prophets, and Moses.[53] Given the role of examples in ancient history and biography, the parallels also serve the paraenetic function of showing how all followers of Christ should follow the model of his life, making these followers' patterns also paradigmatic for others (cf. 1 Cor 11:1).[54]

Granted, most details in Luke lack parallels in Acts, and vice-versa; although Luke unites them in a common plot,[55] they are two different smaller stories, and their material was transmitted in Luke's sources in two different ways. Luke's Christology also demands some limitations. Thus, whereas Jesus sends disciples ahead of him (Luke 10:1), Paul does not do so in quite the same way (Acts 19:22 and 20:17 are somewhat analogous yet differ) because Paul is not the object of proclamation (cf. 2 Cor 4:5).[56] But these contrasts do not negate the many clear parallels that exist.

II. EARLY PARALLELISMS IN THE GOSPEL

Luke's opening allusion to his previous work (Acts 1:1) would invite readers to keep that work in mind when reading Acts. Luke introduces us to his method of comparing figures from the start of his two-volume work, by obvious comparisons of Jesus and John the Baptist, the births of both of whom were announced by Gabriel.[57]

---

47. Harnack, *Acts*, xix. For important historical commonalities despite tensions between them, see, e.g., Dillmann, "Begegnungen."

48. Narrative criticism has isolated some patterns in the canonical sources on which Acts 7 draws; see comment on Acts 7:9–16, 19, 21.

49. Ancient historians generally believed that they discovered patterns in history, not that they created them out of whole cloth (see discussion on historians' "theology" in ch. 5, above; in the present chapter, see esp. sect. 1.f below).

50. E.g., Ehrhardt, *Acts*, 12–13; Boismard and Lamouille, *Actes*, 2:26; O'Toole, "Parallels between Jesus and Disciples"; Verheyden, "What Are We Up To?"; Malina and Pilch, *Acts*, 181–84; recently and in significant detail, Clark, *Parallel Lives*.

51. E.g., Clark, "Role," 185–89; Foakes-Jackson and Lake, "Internal Evidence of Acts," 182. Clark, *Parallel Lives*, offers particularly detailed comparisons between the Jerusalem apostles (especially Peter) and Paul, underlining (as Gal 2:7–9 does) the unity between the Jewish and the Gentile missions. Tyson, *Marcion*, 62–63, finds this the very evidence that led to Baur's thesis, and believes it supports a second-century date, but Galatians shows that the issues existed even during Paul's lifetime.

52. Tannehill, *Acts*, 76; Aune, *Environment*, 119.

53. Tannehill, *Acts*, 74–75. Writers could link skills or miracles of teachers and their disciples; see, e.g., Iambl. *V.P.* 28.135–36; and comment on succession narratives on Acts 1:9–11.

54. Cf. O'Toole, "Parallels between Jesus and Disciples"; Karris, *Invitation*, 15; Syreeni, "Paradigms," 36 (following Räisänen, *Mutter*).

55. Penner, *Praise*, 151, 185–87, 218, discusses the cohesiveness and "plot" of ancient historical works in connection with Aristotle's approach to other narrative genres.

56. On Jesus's continuing unique role despite the parallels, see, e.g., Kee, *Miracle*, 190.

57. For correspondence between Jesus and John, see Goulder, *Type and History*, 120–24, esp. 120; more fully, Tannehill, *Luke*, 15–44, esp. 15–20; on John's temporal priority yet subordination in Luke's Gospel, cf.

Luke 1:12: the vision's recipient troubled	Luke 1:29: the vision's recipient troubled
1:13: do not be afraid	1:30: do not be afraid
1:13: reason for miracle	1:30: reason for miracle
1:13: child's name (John)	1:31: child's name (Jesus)
1:15: child will be great	1:32: child will be great
1:15: filled with the Holy Spirit from the womb	1:35: conceived through the Holy Spirit*
1:16–17: mission	1:32–33: mission
1:18: question	1:34: question
1:19–20: proof or explanation	1:35–37: proof or explanation
1:20: Zechariah muted for unbelief	1:38, 45: Mary praised for faith
1:80: child grows	2:40, 52: child grows†

*For the contrasting role of the Spirit in John's and Jesus's prenatal experience, see Tatum, "Epoch," 188–89.
†I have omitted less obvious parallels such as circumcision (Luke 1:59; implicit in 2:21) or "favor" for both Elizabeth (1:25) and Mary (1:30). Flender, *Theologian*, 29, helpfully views the contrast between Mary and Zechariah in light of a series of contrasts, often between religious insiders and others, in the Gospel (Luke 7:36–50; 10:29–37; 14:15–24; 15:24–32; 18:9–14; 20:45–21:4).

That the narrative portion of this two-volume work opens with such clear parallelism would alert hearers to be sensitive to such parallels later in the work as well. Luke's literary model here is not merely Hellenistic rhetorical and biographic *synkrisis*, but also biblical narrative (from the literary canon he particularly shares with his ideal audience). Although the story of Zechariah and Elizabeth echoes that of Abraham and Sarah, the contrast between Zechariah and Mary might evoke to some degree that between Eli and Hannah in 1 Sam 1. This suspicion becomes more likely in view of Mary's echoes of Hannah in this context:

1 Samuel 2:1–10	Luke 1:46–55
God exalts lowly (2:1, 4–5, 8)	God exalts lowly (1:48, 52–53)
I rejoice in your salvation (2:1)	I have rejoiced in God my savior (1:47)
No one holy like the Lord (2:2)	Holy is his name (1:49)
Proud brought down (2:3–5)	Proud brought down (1:51–53)
Humble exalted, proud brought down (2:4–5)	Humble exalted, proud brought down (1:52–53)
Celebration of God's sovereignty in such reversals (2:3, 6–9)	Celebration of God's sovereignty in such reversals (1:51–53)
Barren given children (2:5)	(Context: Elizabeth's pregnancy)
Poor vs. rich (2:7–8)	Rich empty-handed (1:53)
Hungry vs. full (2:5)	Filled the hungry (1:53)
Poor displacing nobles (*dunastōn*, 2:8)	Brought down rulers (*dunastas*, 1:52) [same term]
Raises up from death (2:6)	(Implicit Lukan subtext?)
Shift from personal deliverance to God's anointed king (2:10)	Shift from personal deliverance to Israel's deliverance

Although other echoes may appear also (Ps 111:9 in Luke 1:49; Ps 89:10 in Luke 1:51; perhaps God doing "great things" in Deut 10:21; 11:7; cf. 34:12), even here one allusion echoes the context of Hannah's song (1 Sam 1:11 in Luke 1:48). Luke's use of biblical models for *synkrisis* at the beginning of his Gospel[58] suggests that

---

Robinson, *Problem of History*, 70–71. The kinship connection between John and Jesus unique to this Gospel also prevents rivalry (Malina and Neyrey, "Honor and Shame," 53).

58. Luke's contemporaries would not expect verbatim sources for speeches, especially a full generation before Jesus's public ministry. They would expect him to reconstruct material with sensitivity to the appropriate setting, in this case drawing on the most relevant biblical models to produce what he would regard as the likeliest sort of texture for these birth annunciation scenes in which the God of Israel acts. This observation concerning ancient historical writing does not rule out Luke's possible use of Mary (cf. Brown, *Birth*, 33) or her son James as possible sources (see esp. Byrskog, *History*, 82–91; historical interest in Daniélou, *Infancy Narratives*), but is simply meant to note that, in general, historians will expect more from recent traditions

Luke	Acts
Luke 3:21: Jesus praying before his baptism and the descent of the Spirit	Acts 1:14: the disciples praying before being baptized in the Spirit
3:21–22: Spirit on Jesus	2:1–4: Spirit on church
4:14–21: inaugural mission speech	2:14–39/13:16–41: inaugural mission speeches
4:40; 5:17; 8:46: healing many, power going forth unexpectedly	5:14–16/19:11–12; 28:9: healing many, power going forth unexpectedly
5:17–26: healing a paralytic	3:1–10/14:8–11: healing paralytics
5:29–6:11: opposition from Jewish leaders	4:1–8:3; 12:2–3/23:2, 15: opposition from Jewish leaders
8:40–56: raising the dead	9:36–41/20:9–12: raising the dead
7:1–10: God-fearing centurion	10:1–48: God-fearing centurion (cf. 27:1–3)
7:11–17: widow's son raised	9:36–43: widow raised (cf. the youth in 20:9–12)
5:30; 7:36–50; 15:2: pious criticism of fellowship with sinners	11:3: pious criticism of fellowship with sinners (cf. Paul's Gentile mission inviting hostility)
9:51: Jesus's journey to Jerusalem	19:21: Paul's journey to Rome
13:33: warned of dangers in Jerusalem	20:23; 21:12: warned of dangers in Jerusalem
19:11, 28: determined to go	20:24; 21:15, 17: determined to go
19:36–38: triumphal entry to Jerusalem	21:17–20; 28:15: triumphal entry to Rome, a lesser one to Jerusalem*
19:45–48: enters temple	21:26: enters temple
20:27–39: hostile Sadducees reject resurrection	4:1–2/23:6–9: hostile Sadducees reject resurrection
22:15–38: Jesus's farewell speech†	20:18–35: Paul's farewell speech
22:66–71: arraigned before the Sanhedrin	6:8–15/22:30–23:10: arraigned before the Sanhedrin
22:69: provocative announcement of Son of Man at God's right hand	7:56: provocative announcement of Son of Man at God's right hand
23:34, 46: committing his spirit and praying for forgiveness of the persecutors	7:59–60: committing his spirit and praying for forgiveness of the persecutors
23:47: centurion recognizes God's attestation of Jesus's innocence	27:31–32, 43: centurion recognizes God's attestation of Paul's innocence
Jesus's four hearings (before a governor and, only in Luke, Herod)	Paul's four hearings (before Roman governors and before Herod Agrippa II)
Luke emphasizes the fulfillment of Scripture, pointing to a mission to the nations (24:44–47)	Luke emphasizes the fulfillment of Scripture, continuing a mission to the nations (28:25–28)

*Some points, including this one, represent my own adaptations.
†Because the passage includes disciples' discussion, scholars may define its boundaries differently.

these are important in his thinking (one may compare the parallels among biblical characters in Stephen's speech in Acts 7; on Luke's speeches, see discussion in our introduction, ch. 8).

III. Luke-Acts Parallels

Luke 6:40 permits us to expect such parallels between Jesus and the church. Likewise, in Acts 20:33–35, Jesus's teaching (20:35) functions as a basis for Paul's behavior (20:33–34), suggesting that the church in Acts, when at its best, will exemplify Jesus's teachings reported in the Gospel of Luke. Jesus models the baptism in the Holy Spirit that he will afterward bestow (Luke 3:16, 21–22).[59] Jesus's teaching on, and promise of, baptism in the Holy Spirit are also fulfilled in the church, including in Peter (Acts 2:4; 4:8, 31), Stephen (6:5; 7:55), and Paul (9:17; 13:9). It is likewise transmitted through Peter (8:15–17; cf. 10:44), Paul (19:6), and others (9:17), suggesting its continuity (explicit in 2:38–39).

---

than older ones. The material in Acts is more recent. The early scenes in the Gospel, however, clearly reveal Luke's interest in narrative parallels.

59. The connection already appeared in Mark 1:8–10 (see Keener, *Spirit*, 49–90) and probably in the Q material that Luke also follows.

It is therefore not unexpected that many strong parallels among the ministries of Jesus, Peter, and Paul appear. Scholars today point to recognition of the parallels between Peter and Paul at least as early as 1841.[60] In the early twentieth century, F. J. Foakes-Jackson and Kirsopp Lake noted that Luke "obviously schematizes the stories of Jesus, of Peter, and of Paul as to bring out the parallelism between them" for the purpose of rooting the church in the larger history of Israel.[61] The helpful attention that narrative criticism has focused on the text has made such parallels still more obvious today.

Scholars include the parallels listed in the table on page 558, among others.[62]

As will be evident in the commentary, these examples are only some of the more obvious of many likely deliberate parallels among the major characters in Luke-Acts.

iv. Goulder's More Detailed Parallels

On the whole, the parallels drawn by Charles Talbert and Robert Tannehill are well conceived and rarely objectionable. The larger structural parallels that Goulder earlier found in broad units of text are sometimes more subjective, but their very elaborate and extensive character invites special examination here.[63]

Goulder finds four sections of Acts, which each provide parallels with events in Luke's Gospel. As an example of his occasionally subjective treatment, he sometimes isolates "parallels" that could be found more closely elsewhere and are chosen simply because they appear in the right place in his structure. Some parallels are weak (including those he finds for the resurrection). Nevertheless, his careful attention to many parallel elements of Luke-Acts is, more often than not, illuminating:[64]

Choosing a new minister (Acts 1:15; 6:1; 10:9; 13:1)	Electing and coming of Jesus (Luke 1–2)
Descent of Spirit (2:1; 8:14; 10:44; 19:1)	Baptism of Jesus and descent of Spirit (Luke 3)
Kerygma (2:14 [3:12]; 8:26; 10:34; 13:16 [17:22; 28:17])	Nazareth sermon (4:18–27)
Mighty works (3:1; 6:1; 11:27; 14:8)	Jesus's mighty works (4:31)
Persecution (4:1; 6:8; 12:1; 14:19)	Persecution (5:17)
Gathering of church (4:31; [8:14]; 11:1; 15:1)	Prayer (5:16)
Confounding of false disciple (1:16; 5:1; 8:18; 12:20; 13:8 [23:1])	Judas (Luke 22)
Passion and death (5:17; 6:11; 12:3; 21:27)	Jesus's passion and death (Luke 22–23)
Resurrection (9:1, 32, 36)	Jesus's resurrection (Luke 24)

Presented differently, his thesis appears as seen in the first table on page 560.[65]

Again, some of the links are far-fetched, and even despite his adjustments and selection, Goulder's sequence does not always work. But his analysis does illustrate that many themes recur in the lives of Jesus and his leading followers.

Though sometimes pressing minor comparisons too far (while leaving large areas of text unparalleled), Goulder does offer intriguing parallels in different cycles in the

60. Schneckenburger, *Apostelgeschichte*, 52–58, noted in Brawley, *Luke-Acts and Jews*, 43n26, and Bruce, *Peter*, 23–24n24. Praeder, "Parallels," surveys the past two centuries of approaches to these parallels, showing, however, the diversity of conclusions.

61. Foakes-Jackson and Lake, "Internal Evidence of Acts," 182.

62. Aune, *Environment*, 119; Perkins, *Reading*, 265; Dunn, *Acts*, xiv; Talbert, *Acts*, xxiv–xxv; for the church in Acts imitating Jesus, see also Varickasseril, "Prayer." Lane, *Gentile Mission*, 69–72, provides parallels between Jesus and Peter (69–70), Stephen (70), and Paul (70–72); see also Pervo, *Mystery*, 75–82.

63. Powell, *Acts*, 117, notes that Goulder's typological approach follows Farrer, *Matthew and Luke*.

64. Goulder, *Type and History*, 72–74. In the Gospel column, I have sometimes included only his primary sample verse or verses whereas Goulder also suggests others.

65. See ibid., 74.

Gospel	Apostles	"Deacons"	Peter	Paul
Choosing (Luke 1–2)	Acts 1:1, 12	Acts 6:1	Acts 10:9	Acts 13:1
Descent of the Spirit (3:22)	2:1	8:14	10:44	19:1
Kerygma, baptism (4:16)	2:14; 3:11 (Jerusalem)	(8:26)	10:34	13:16
Mighty works (4:33 and passim)	3:1	6:1 [6:8; 8:6–7]	(11:29)	14:8
Persecution (5:21 and passim)	4:1	6:8	12:1	14:19
Gathering of church (6:12)	4:23	(8:14)	11:1	15:1
Confounding of false disciple (22:3; Acts 1:16)	5:1	8:18	12:20	13:8; 23:1
Passion (22–23)	5:17	7:54	12:3	27:1
Resurrection (Luke 24)	5:18	9:1, 32, 36	12:7	Acts 28

book's sections, parallels that he believes advances cyclically.[66] We may survey as an example his comparisons in Acts 1:1–6:7 (some of which appear strong but others quite tenuous):[67]

Acts 1:1: Christ's ascension after forty days	3:1: a man crippled for forty years	—
1:12: gathering of the church	—	4:23: gathering of church
2:1: all filled with the Spirit	—	4:31: all filled with the Spirit
2:14: apostle's sermon	3:11: Solomon's Portico and Peter's sermon	5:12: Solomon's Portico
—	4:1: arrest of Peter and John	5:17: arrest of the Twelve
2:27: 3,000 converted	4:4: many converted, 5,000 strong	—
—	4:5: Trial: Peter's defense; 4:23: apostles released	5:19: release by angel; 5:39: Gamaliel's speech
2:42–47: summary, including signs; communal sharing; many added to the church	4:34: communal sharing; 5:1: miraculous death; 5:12: summary with many added	5:42: summary; 6:1: charity; 6:7: summary with the disciples multiplied

Danger escalates as the narrative progresses, heightening suspense. Some elements, such as the gathering of the church, may be coincidence; the number forty probably is. Other elements, such as the parallel trial accounts (again with escalating stakes), are often noted and difficult to doubt, although historical information (selected and arranged to highlight the parallel) is probably also a factor here. Many scholars find Goulder's observations overly subtle, noting that the recurrence of Luke's themes need not indicate such intricate structures.[68] Still, though Goulder's painstaking analysis is not always accurate, it does repay attention for the way it highlights recurrent themes and the key sorts of events (emphasized through their repetition) reported in Acts.

v. Goulder on Jesus and the Church

The connections appear somewhat stronger when one compares Jesus's ministry in Luke as a whole with the church and its agents in Acts as a whole. As Goulder acknowledges, whether Peter, Paul, or the church parallels Christ, the important point is that Christ's life is shown in his body (cf. Jesus identifying with his church in Acts 9:4).[69] The early parallel between Jesus receiving the Spirit at his baptism (Luke

---

66. Ibid., 14–33. Goulder argues (46, not fully persuasively) for three brief cycles under the apostles in Jerusalem (see the table below), then a fuller one running from Stephen through Saul's conversion, another in which Peter reaches Gentiles, and four concerning Paul.

67. Ibid., 22.

68. Powell, *Acts*, 27 (noting Houlden, "Review").

69. Goulder, *Type and History*, 61–62.

3:21–22) and the church's baptism in the Spirit (Acts 1:4–5; 2:4), often noted, is very strong.[70] Goulder lists some of the overarching parallels that he finds as follows:[71]

Gospel of Luke	Acts
Incarnation (Luke 1–2)	Ascension (1:9–11)
Jesus baptized in water (3:21)	Church baptized in Spirit (Acts 2)
Jesus's message rejected in πατρίς; attempt to do away with Jesus (4:24, 28–30)	Church's message rejected in Jerusalem; attempt to do away with apostles (Acts 3–5)
Galilean ministry (4:31–39)	(parallels distributed)
Feeding of 5,000 (9:10)	Feeding of widows (6:1)
Three see Jesus in glory (9:28)	Stephen sees Jesus in glory (7:55)
Samaritan village (9:51)	Philip in Samaria (8:5–25)
Mission of seventy (Luke 10)	Mission of seven (Acts 6–8)
First half of journey; condemns Israel (Luke 10–13)	Church leaves Israel behind to turn to Gentiles (Acts 8–13)
Herod intends to kill Jesus (13:31)	Herod attempts to kill Peter (Acts 12)
Second half of journey: gospel to outcasts (Luke 14–18)	Gospel to Gentiles (Acts 13–20)
Jesus's long journey to Jerusalem (Luke 9–19)	Paul's journey to Jerusalem (Acts 19–21)
Jesus's passion and four trials (Luke 20–23)	Paul's passion and four trials (Acts 21–26)
Jesus's death (Luke 23)	Paul's "death" (Acts 27)
Jesus's resurrection and ascension (Luke 24)	Paul's "resurrection" and arrival at Rome (Acts 28)

Not all of these parallels are persuasive, but some others are valuable, especially if the link to the sequence is broken. Although Paul certainly does not die and rise at the end of Acts, its conclusion is "comic" (in the sense of an upturn, as opposed to tragic);[72] Paul's being sent on to Rome is the best "passion" narrative Luke can offer while reporting a happy ending without fabricating Paul's (historically untrue and implausible) resurrection. On the level of detail, many more parallels can be found if Goulder's interest in parallel sequence is abandoned.

VI. PETER-PAUL PARALLELS

Some scholars have long contended that, against the misnomer "Acts of the Apostles," Luke's second volume instead contains something like "Acts of Peter" and "Acts of Paul" (albeit not to be confused with the later "apocryphal" works by these titles).[73] Scholars have offered a number of parallels between Peter and Paul in Acts, as seen in the first table on page 562.[74]

Paul repeats most miracles cited for Peter earlier in Acts.[75] Although sequence is not a necessary component for the parallels, the sequence is frequently close enough to reinforce the picture. (Only by citing parallels very selectively, however, can one conform the sequences so fully as to argue that Luke was unduly concerned with parallel sequence to the extent of either inventing events or changing his narrative.)

---

70. Ibid., 54; widely accepted, e.g., in Karris, *Invitation*, 15.

71. Goulder, *Type and History*, 61. Some, such as the feedings of Luke 9:10 and Acts 6:1, remain quite weak; the graphic asymmetry of parallels between a verse in Luke (e.g., Luke 13:31) and chapters in Acts also stems from Goulder's desire to keep the parallels in sequence where possible. He admits that some significant events in Acts (e.g., Paul's conversion; the Jerusalem Council) lack parallels with Luke but insists (wrongly) that anything in Luke which could have a parallel in Acts does (62).

72. I borrow these categories from ancient drama as applied by Via, *Kerygma and Comedy*.

73. Bruce, *Peter*, 23–24.

74. E.g., Perkins, *Reading*, 264; Dunn, *Acts*, xiv. Cf. also parallels with Stephen: analogous charges in Acts 6:13–14; 21:20–21; 25:8, and stoning expanding the mission in Acts 6:8–8:4 and 14:19–23 (Perkins, *Reading*, 264).

75. See Witherington, *Acts*, 221; Stronstad, *Prophethood*, 110. Fenton, "Order of Miracles," even finds six miracles each of Peter and Paul arranged sequentially to form three chiastic structures. Still, one doubts that most ancient readers (like most modern ones) would have recognized this pattern.

Peter	Paul
Sermon (Acts 2:22–39)	Sermon (Acts 13:26–41)
Healing of paralytic (3:1–10)	Healing of paralytic (14:8–11)
Sermon following healing, denying apostles' power (3:12–26, esp. 3:12)	Sermon following healing, denying apostles' power (14:15–17, esp. 14:15)
Filled with the Spirit in ministry (4:8)	Filled with the Spirit in ministry (13:9)
Healings through apostles without direct consent (5:15)	Healings through apostles without direct consent (19:12)
Defended by a Pharisee in the Sanhedrin (5:34–39)	Defended by Pharisees in the Sanhedrin (23:9)
Appoints leaders through laying on hands (6:1–6)	Appoints leaders through laying on hands (14:23)
People receive Spirit through his hands (8:17)	People receive Spirit through his hands (19:6)
Confronting and superseding false prophets (8:18–24)	Confronting and superseding false prophets (13:6–11; 19:13–20)
Raising the dead (9:36–41)	Raising the dead (20:9–12)
Befriends centurion (10:24–48)	Befriends centurion (27:1–44)
Rejects Gentile worship (10:26)	Rejects Gentile worship (14:15; cf. 28:6)
Defends Gentile mission in Jerusalem (11:4–17; 15:7–11)	Defends Gentile mission in Jerusalem (15:4, 12; cf. 21:21–26; 22:21)
Imprisoned at a Jewish festival (12:4–7)	Imprisoned at a Jewish festival (22:24; cf. 20:16)
Miraculous release from prison (5:19; 12:6–11)	Miraculous release from prison (16:25–34)

Other literary patterns also repeat in Acts—for example, cycles of ministry outside the community, followed by both positive and negative reactions, and the peaceful life of the church afterward:[76]

Miracle and preaching	Acts 2:1–39	3:1–26	5:12, 15	6:8
Favorable response	2:40–41	(4:4)	5:13–14, 16	—
Opposition	—	4:1–23	5:17–42	6:9–8:3
Community life	2:42–47	4:32–5:11	6:1–6	— (perhaps 9:31?)

In view of the rhetorical tendency to compare major figures, it is not surprising that comparisons between Peter and Paul persisted (see *1 Clem.* 5, especially 5.4–7).[77] These two figures may have already emerged as the leading ones for the wider church (cf. 1 Cor 1:12), or the pairing might reflect early influence from Acts.

d. Parallels versus Historical Tradition?

Did Luke "adjust" his historical traditions and genre to fit parallels, or did he simply frequently include and highlight whatever traditions proved amenable to making parallels? Biblical scholars traditionally regarded similar reports repeating key features as doublets of the same event.[78] In view of contemporary emphasis on Luke's deliberate patterning, the idea that such "doublets" reflect different sources' approaches to identical events or traditions becomes less compelling. But does this mean that Luke lacked sources regarding analogous events?

This question is examined below, but no conclusion to this question of how Luke constructs parallels or narrative unity would necessarily call into question the genre of Acts as ancient historiography.[79] Certainly, when Luke recapitulates the close of his

76. Satterthwaite, "Acts," 363.

77. Whatever the precise date of *1 Clement*, it is noteworthy that 5.1 speaks of Peter and Paul as belonging to the writer's own "generation" (though opposed to the "ancients," the language is curious if Peter and Paul are not within living memory of the author).

78. E.g., Klausner, *Jesus to Paul*, 215. Sometimes a writer may have forgotten that he already recounted a story, thereby inadvertently creating a doublet (probably in Plut. *Alex.* 37.4; 56.1; the work is lengthy).

79. Penner, *Praise*, 151, 185–87, 218, discusses histories' cohesiveness and "plot," noting Aristotle on other narrative genres. Cf. biblical patterning without fictionalizing in Allison, *Jesus*, 389.

first volume in the introduction to his second or provides obvious parallels between the works, he expects his audience to notice the connection, without supposing that they will, on this basis, reassign the genre of his work. Indeed, some scholars argue that Thucydides, Polybius, and Josephus all employ patterns of historical recurrence as an authenticating technique;[80] Israelite historiography does likewise (e.g., with Moses and Joshua, or Elijah and Elisha).[81]

1. Goulder's Skepticism

The more objective literary approach to parallels can suggest its own historical questions.[82] Goulder suggests that (emphasis his) *"where there are no types, Acts is intended to be factual"*; conversely, *"the thicker the types, the less likely is the passage to be factual."*[83] But if Luke is not interested in writing history throughout (see chs. 3–4 above), why does he include so much traditional material and not simply engage in parallels throughout? Although we can and do identify numerous parallels, a simple reading through Luke's Gospel will reveal that *most* details do *not* have clear parallels in Acts. For example, Paul tells no story parables; likewise, Acts has no grainfields on the Sabbath, although it does have religious (apparently even apostolic) critics of God's activity (cf. Acts 11:1–3). The attempt to find parallels for many of these details would require literary gymnastics, and an attempt to find parallels for other details could not be made to appear compelling even with such gymnastics. Rather, given the existing genre of parallel lives, one can consciously look for and select parallel materials from a much larger body of available material.

As one who has also written and spoken in nonacademic genres, I am skeptical of the view that one must choose between historical content and literary arrangement; because my purposes incline my interest toward certain kinds of stories, telling my own or my wife's "history" would involve selection from a much larger body of information and considerable repetition of particular kinds of elements, a repetition that could become more highly developed as I retold the stories, noticed the most rhetorically suitable elements, and both highlighted and structured them for their greatest evocative impact in my setting. Yet I would certainly bristle at any implication that this process of selection and emphasis required me to fabricate my information!

In his work on Matthew, Goulder rightly observes that in midrashic exposition later material in a source can be glossed onto an earlier, similar account, creating two parallel accounts.[84] But whereas Matthew may employ some forms of midrashic

---

80. Rothschild, *Rhetoric of History*, 97 (in rhetoric, see 99–141). She notes that the parallels help pave the way for those appreciating the first volume to hear the second favorably (122), an emphasis that might prove particularly useful if, as some (including myself) think, Paul's legacy needs any defense among some of Luke's audience. Further on literary recurrence in ancient historical narratives, see Trompf, *Historical Recurrence*. Though noting Thucydides's incompleteness, Hornblower, "Thucydides," 636, also recognizes his literary, Homeric-like "comparisons" across the span of his history "by using similar phrasing"; cf. also the observation of repetitive patterns in Finley, *Thucydides*, 301. Note also patterns in Appian's *C.W.* 1 (Bucher, "Evaluation," 458–59).

81. See, e.g., Hays, *Echoes*, 101, on Josh 3–4; Cotter, "Miracle," 102; for Elisha's miracles evoking Elijah's, see, e.g., Levine, "Twice." In a contrasting manner, cf. Ahab in 2 Chr 18:33 with Josiah in 35:23.

82. Pervo, *Mystery*, 73, illustrates that novels could parallel characters. This practice appears in various genres, including history and biography, so parallelism in Acts does not by itself specify the work's genre. The common rhetorical technique of comparison made such interests inevitable in a variety of genres.

83. Goulder, *Type and History*, 181 and 182, for the respective quotes. Pervo, *Acts*, 9–11 (esp. 11), views Luke's employment of patterns as the main problem for "treating Acts as simple history," although he concedes that historians do look for patterns and often ignore other data. (One might concede Luke's work as historiography while questioning whether "simple history" describes any ancient historical work—or perhaps any modern one for that matter.)

84. Goulder, *Midrash*, 36. I find his work on Matthew less convincing than his work on Acts, but for other reasons.

techniques, Luke the Hellenistic historian betrays little interest in them. He does use "types" in his exposition of the OT, but his use of the OT, in fact, illustrates the point that a writer may highlight patterns without fabricating information. Luke never invents new persons nor characteristics nor acts of persons in his rehearsals of OT narratives by attributing the characteristics or acts of others to them. Yet this is precisely what Goulder's model would demand at this point; and if not with Luke's typology of the OT, why for more recent sacred history?[85]

Most important, a comparison with parallel lives in other ancient literature (see below) calls Goulder's skepticism into question: the writer normally demonstrated literary genius by finding parallels among the available traditions, not by simply inventing them. This is, at least, what our extant writers claim, and given the fact that the sources to which they appeal could well have been available to their audiences, I believe that we are wiser to normally take them at their word (i.e., except in cases where concrete evidence provides compelling reason to do otherwise).

Luke does extend his use of narrative parallels further in Acts than in the Gospel.[86] He recounts Cornelius's and Paul's conversions three times each in Acts (Acts 9–11; 15:7–9; 22:4–11; 26:9–18) and repeats from the Gospel both the list of disciples (Luke 6:14–16; Acts 1:13, minus Judas Iscariot, of course) and Jesus's commission and exaltation (Luke 24:47–51; Acts 1:4–11). Whereas the Gospel (where Luke may have had to pare down material that he had) usually avoids parallel scenes, Acts develops repetition for emphasis in the narratives, just as it does in the speeches.

II. Unity and Tensions

Although scholars offer a wide range of views on Luke's historical reliability, most do not force one to opt for either literary parallels or historical information at the expense of the other, as if the options were mutually exclusive.[87] Some who view Luke as historian note that he does not invent figures; he does harmonize, mediate, "'tone down' conflicts and pass over much that was unattractive," yet the conflicts remain evident enough.[88] In the same way, Luke can highlight "parallel" features, as Plutarch and others did, by drawing on, rather than replacing, historical tradition.[89]

Luke's emphasis on the unity of major figures does play down differences, but differences in the early church over circumcision and other controversies do remain. The subject of such controversies was historically not, however, the radical differences about Jesus that some modern scholars discern by reading in unattested controversies and unattested views held by imaginary communities. (Such are the fictions that some radical scholars create by explaining away all extant textual evidence, then

85. If one argues that the more recent traditions remained more fluid than the earlier canonical ones, one is confronted with the closeness of Luke's story to Mark's. If one argues that only the post-Jesus traditions in Acts were fluid, one has basically eliminated all comparative evidence, since it is for Acts alone that we lack other sources (though it is likely that Luke did have some more freedom in Acts). Naturally, we do have minor adjustments in both Luke and Acts (such as the centurion's verdict in Luke 23:47 vs. Mark 15:39), but no wholesale creation of events.

86. See Cadbury, "Features," 88–89.

87. See, e.g., Harnack, *Acts*, xix.

88. Hengel and Schwemer, *Between Damascus and Antioch*, 10. Such an approach is common in movements' early histories; cf., e.g., the Hutterite *Chronicle*'s idealized view of that movement's early unity (Williams, *Radical Reformation*, 674).

89. With Bruce, *Acts*[3], 26: Luke draws parallels between Peter and Paul, but "it does not follow, as F. C. Baur and others supposed, that the parallels were invented by the author in order to minimize the difference between the two men; rather, the author selected from the record of events accessible to him those which best subserved the aim he had in view in composing his work." This was the ideal of parallel biographers, as already noted.

creating new "communities" on the basis of silence and speculation.) Paul and his predecessors were united on the basic gospel message (1 Cor 15:1–12);[90] we lack any evidence, except for secondary scholarship reflecting speculation, for "Jesus communities" that did not affirm Jesus as Messiah (and hence King and Lord) or that denied his resurrection. (That such views existed in the spectrum of Jewish opinion is inherently likely, but they are never attested in any extant first-century sources as any part of the earliest Jesus movement, not even in these sources' polemic against Christian detractors.)[91]

Moreover, historians might adjust details, but only at significant risk to their reputations would they fabricate events; whatever one might propose about Luke's conforming details of figures to each other, he does not invent parallel events, though he is happy to recognize parallels where they appear available. Thus, for example, Paul is not executed at the end of Acts to parallel Jesus (even though in this instance Luke would not have been inventing, since he probably knows of his execution); the closest parallel for Jesus's passion that scholars often find at the end of Acts is Paul's suffering and deliverance at sea. Even there, if Luke were simply creating parallels to fit the Jesus tradition, he missed the opportunity to have Paul still a storm (Luke 8:24). Further, some parallels between Luke and Acts could be explained in terms of persons in Acts deliberately imitating their Lord (e.g., Acts 7:59–60), given the importance of imitation noted above. Some other parallels, such as the mention of an upper room in connection with a corpse in 9:37 (cf. 1 Kgs 17:19), may reflect a not uncommon practice;[92] Luke could make the detail explicit to highlight the parallel, but such a parallel is not in itself particularly unexpected or profound.

Benjamin Williams observes that scholars have approached apparent parallels among Lukan miracles of Jesus, Peter, and Paul in different ways. On account of the parallelism, Gerhard Schneider doubts that the paralleled miracles in Acts derive from sources or any historical (or pre-Lukan) foundation.[93] By contrast, Plümacher suggests that these parallels reflect the sorts of events recounted, doubting that Luke even intended parallels.[94] Williams prefers the latter approach, noting that "certain kinds of stories can be told in only certain ways."[95] He points out that where the parallelism appears strongest (between Acts 3:1–10 and 14:8–10), Haenchen attributed the similarities to the character of the stories, not to Luke's agenda.[96] "It is no coincidence," Williams argues, "that those who argue for Jesus-Peter-Paul parallels have neglected form critical analysis of the stories, and the form critics have usually ignored any supposed 'parallelism.'"[97]

90. As noted by many, e.g., Peterson, "Extent." Many support the pre-Pauline character of much of 1 Cor 15:3–5 (e.g., Fuller, *Formation*, 10; Webber, "Note"; Haacker, *Theology*, 108–9; Satake, "1Kr 15,3"; Tobin, *Rhetoric in Contexts*, 163; cf. Wenz, "Fatale Argumentation").

91. *Possibly* excepting the late 1 John 2:22. From 1 Cor 15:12, 2 Thess 2:2, and 2 Tim 2:18, we learn of groups that denied a future resurrection, but even these groups appear (esp. in 1 Cor 15) to have accepted Jesus's resurrection. Reading later conflicts (such as Petrine Pseudo-Clementine literature vs. a catholic compromise) into first-century sources is fraught with anachronism. It ignores major changes between the eras, such as the Jewish-Gentile schism, the theological division between "Nazarenes" and "Ebionites" in second-century sources, and too many other shifts away from earliest Christianity.

92. Though either an upper or a lower room would render the other unclean (see comment on Acts 9:39).

93. Schneider, *Apostelgeschichte*, 306n7.

94. Plümacher, "Acta-Forschung," 144. Williams, *Miracle Stories*, 4, observes that one has only so many options, even G. Theissen providing "only about eight categories" of miracle stories.

95. Williams, *Miracle Stories*, 5.

96. Citing Haenchen, *Acts*, 430. Williams, *Miracle Stories*, 175, argues that most correspondences are "motifs which are *characteristic of almost all of Luke's miracle stories*."

97. Williams, *Miracle Stories*, 5.

I believe that the parallels are stronger and indicate Lukan shaping more than Williams's approach appears to allow;[98] nevertheless, his basic point is well taken. Luke could well have accounts of Jesus, Peter, and Paul healing persons unable to walk (a common and serious disability in their era); he may have selected and shaped the material accordingly, but he need not have *invented* the basic events in Peter's or Paul's ministry simply to parallel that of Jesus. One could simply select reports that did offer parallels; Paul and probably the others would have *many* stories of healings to choose from (Rom 15:19).[99]

A word of caution is also in order here, relevant not only to the historical question but also to our literary observations about narrative parallels in Luke-Acts more generally. We can test observable parallels in some modern historical works, where the historical data remain available for testing. Noticing parallels and contrasts between two incidents in one modern institutional history, I queried whether the author paralleled them deliberately. To my surprise, the historian replied, "I did not have a conscious intention to make them parallel." He suspected instead that the similar incidents reflected the kind of occurrences that exhibit similar social dynamics.[100] Likewise, I consulted a friend regarding a set of parallel events in his popular autobiography. In this case the literary parallel was deliberate (and explicit) and in his correspondence with me he described the process that led to this structured narration; he did not, however, invent the details.[101] Undertaking more such comparisons in modern historical works might chasten some of our assumptions about which parallels in ancient works were deliberate and what we should make of those that were. Luke might have even appreciated some of our observations about parallels and contrasts in his work without having had them consciously in mind as he wrote.

Most important, an obvious test case is Luke's use of a source still extant: he (or his sources) finds parallels among some major characters in Israel's history in Acts 7—but he does not invent them. It is not difficult to deliberately highlight parallel features in genuine accounts if one's specific criterion for selecting many features is that they have parallels; this is so easily illustrated[102] that it requires little specific elaboration.

e. Where Luke *Omits* Parallels for Acts

Although it is not our purpose here to highlight *non*-parallels, purely free composition to fabricate parallels would not explain the numerous events that lack obvious parallels (even, for example, Paul's failure in Acts 27 to *still* the storm as Jesus did in Luke 8:24–25); as a historian, Luke is still bound to his subject matter. Anyone skeptical of this point could easily satisfy their skepticism by trying to parallel all the stories in Luke-Acts. Here, however, I draw attention to specific cases where we know that Luke *could* have offered a parallel yet for some reason did not do so.

98. In fact, Williams, ibid., 176, does allow for deliberate parallelism in "gazing," "leaping," faith, and a "pathos-heightening" "from his mother's womb"; he disallows it for such factors as "a certain man," rising up, and crowd response. The parallels he does allow are significant; his point is that Luke reshaped, not invented, the basic stories.

99. For the plausibility of multiple miracle claims associated with particular persons, see briefly ch. 9, above; more extensively, Keener, *Miracles*.

100. Kenneth Kinghorn, personal correspondence, Aug. 17, 2011. I had written concerning incidents in chs. 7 and 17 of Kinghorn, *Story*.

101. The parallel appears in Kopaska and Liston, *Afterburn*, 106. In personal correspondence with me (Sept. 2, 2011), he notes that the events took place, but that he "connected the dots," noticing the importance of parallel features of them only over time as he shared his story. That is, retelling key features of a story may provide it structure without requiring the teller to invent the details.

102. For example, I could do it randomly with significant details in my life and that of my wife, despite our different backgrounds; one could isolate connections in almost any substantive biography.

In a comparatively small number of cases, Mark or Q provides potential parallels for Acts that are omitted in Luke's Gospel. Some are as follows:[103]

- Mark 4:12; Acts 28:25–27 (but cf. Luke 8:10)
- Mark 6:17–29; Acts 24:24–26
- Mark 7:18–19; Acts 10:15
- Mark 14:58; Acts 6:14

Clear parallels among figures in Luke-Acts (such as do not appear merely coincidentally in other ancient works) are too numerous proportionately to call into question the approach of seeking parallels. Nevertheless, these omissions appear inconsistent with Luke's parallelisms elsewhere and invite us to ask why they occur.

Scholars often argue that Luke intended to pick up these omissions in Acts and had them in mind when he wrote his Gospel.[104] This solution is possible; he also omits some information in Acts 22:17–20 that he will retell more fully a few chapters later in Acts 26.[105] What plausible motive, however, distinguishes why Luke in some cases explicitly highlights parallels and in other cases suppresses them? One could speculate that Luke used those completely deferred to Acts (as opposed to those occurring in both places) to invent stories for Acts and that Luke was unwilling to use such material twice when it appeared in his sources only once. This speculation, however, would be no more helpful than other guesses; it would not even explain why Luke would feel compunction about duplicating his material if he did not mind inventing stories based on it. Such free invention of stories based on nuggets in Mark characterizes neither standard Greco-Roman historiography (in contrast to some forms of haggadic elaboration) nor what we characteristically find in Luke's Gospel pericopes.

If Luke was very familiar with Mark or Q, however, he may have written the second volume with them in mind without remembering in every case whether he had recorded that detail in his Gospel, even if he worked over the Gospel several times. Sometimes writers promised to revisit a topic in detail later and never managed to do so (e.g., Jos. *Ant.* 20.144, 147);[106] they might also refer back to a reference they thought they had included but that, in fact, they had not (e.g., 18.54).[107] Luke certainly remembered more than most writers today would, and we cannot fault him if he missed a few opportunities: checking each point in a scroll is far more time-consuming than using the "Find" function in one's word-processing program. Luke knew a great deal more of the Jesus tradition than he could record in his Gospel (cf. Acts 20:35). Moreover, Luke condensed his material so frequently in Acts (as I have repeatedly observed in working through the commentary), omitting elements in the narrative that obscure some of what he reports, that it is entirely plausible to imagine that Luke sometimes condensed out something he thought he had included. Some of these omissions due to oversight might be caught and restored during later public recitations, but Luke may not have caught them all.

103. See, e.g., Dunn, *Acts*, xv.

104. See, e.g., Lane, *Gentile Mission*, 72–73.

105. As noted by Dunn, *Acts*, xv.

106. Likewise, Jos. *Ant.* 20.53 (only a later summary appears in 20.101); if Josephus fulfilled these promises in a later work, it is not extant.

107. It is barely possible that the corresponding materials in Josephus are simply missing from our surviving manuscript tradition, but if so pressed, one might argue the same for Luke-Acts.

f. Parallel Lives in Ancient Biography and History

Although many scholars have followed Conzelmann's schema of neatly segmented salvation history for Luke-Acts (see discussion on eschatology in ch. 15 above), the parallels in major characters suggest a greater continuity and development than his model presupposes. Luke's first audience would likely have recognized the parallels, since comparing characters was standard practice and parallel lives even emerged as a distinctive subgenre of biography. Many recognize that Luke draws on the literary convention of parallel lives used in Hellenistic historiography and biography.[108]

Probably Luke has more in mind in these parallels than a mere literary technique; he may think in terms of succession narratives (as with Moses-Joshua or Elijah-Elisha parallels in the OT; see comment on Acts 1:9–11). His theology also may motivate this approach to showing that even when he narrates significant works of Peter, Paul, and others, it is Jesus, the protagonist of his first volume, who stands behind them (cf. Acts 9:34). Thus even when Peter or Paul appears heroic, the auditor, remembering the conversion of Peter and Paul by Jesus and Jesus's model and empowerment for their ministries, recognizes Jesus as the true and ultimate hero. In this respect the separation of Luke's Gospel and Acts has serious theological consequences. Whatever scholars conclude about the specific reasons for the parallels, it seems clear that Luke does underline some significant parallels and that these are consistent with the paralleling of characters already found in some other ancient biographies and histories.

i. Ideal Types?

Long ago Dibelius claimed that in portraying Peter and Paul as "types" of the ideal "Christian missionary," Luke was "following the practice of historians of antiquity, who did not aim at all at portraying the personal characteristics and special activities of their heroes, but who were more commonly concerned with what was *typical* and *general* and *ideal*."[109] Dibelius was correct that Luke employs Peter and Paul as models, but he greatly exaggerated the extent of idealization in Greek and Roman historians.

Some ancient writers were satisfied with writing about ideal types (what we would call "flat characters"), but rhetorically educated writers sought to diversify their portrayals (with what we would call "round characters").[110] Lucian criticizes historians who praise their own side's leaders while slandering those of the enemy; such behavior belongs properly to panegyric, not to history (Lucian *Hist.* 7).[111] Most historians did, in fact, seek to "humanize" both sides in a conflict, adding tragic pathos to their narrative.[112]

Some scholars suggest that Luke, like a good rhetorician, would conceal his persuasive artistry by using the narrative itself, rather than asides, to characterize his

---

108. E.g., Kee, *Miracle*, 190.

109. Dibelius, *Studies in Acts*, 132. For an often humorous classification and characterization of various kinds of personality, see especially the thirty character types in Theophr. *Char.* passim.

110. Style critics also pointed out weaknesses in good writers (often where a writer fell short of his own standards); they did not assign them binary categories of good and bad (e.g., Dion. Hal. *Thuc.* 1).

111. Lucian opines that one must avoid such poetic descriptions in history (*Hist.* 8) and that although praise is permitted, one should keep it within bounds (*Hist.* 9).

112. See, e.g., Dion. Hal. *Ant. rom.* 3; comments in Keener, *John*, 216. Luke, writing only two volumes, does not expend space to develop his opponents so sympathetically, but he does portray some groups, such as the Pharisees, with more complexity and ambiguity (see comment on Acts 5:34).

protagonists.[113] Luke has mixed characters (e.g., Gamaliel and Sergius Paulus), and even his protagonists are "round": Peter stumbles in the Gospel and even in Acts must learn God's agenda (Acts 10:14, 28; 11:8).[114] Paul seems generally "flatter" and more uniformly positive after his conversion (though we might find implicit hints of his growth in terms of strategies, e.g., in 19:9), but the account of the division between him and Barnabas (15:39) probably does not flatter either of them.[115] Luke is less interested in developing his characters and, using his limited space, even more focused on using them as models than some of his contemporaries; but they are not "flat" enough to fit Dibelius's caricature of Greek and Roman historians.

II. Parallels in History

If Dibelius's model is exaggerated, what models are available? Perhaps for Thucydides, the *uniqueness* of events provided a gauge for their significance;[116] but most historians were happy to look for parallels. Greco-Roman historians and biographers alike drew attention to patterns that they found in history, patterns that they typically attributed to divine design.[117] For example, Appian, writing a providentialist history of Rome, was happy to note a Roman victory that paralleled, in many details, an earlier Roman defeat, demonstrating (in his view) that God had granted the Romans recompense for their defeat (Appian *Hist. rom.* 7.8.53). Such historians' approaches helped define Luke's task and approach:

> An obvious *literary* function of schemes of correspondence is to unify the composition. A *historical* function of such schemes is to demonstrate that history itself has a pattern. For both these reasons, ancient historians often sought to elicit patterns of historical recurrence in their narratives. Appian (ca. A.D. 95–165) saw historical parallels between the Roman defeat at Cannae and the defeat of Hasdrubal the Carthaginian.[118]

But "whereas Greco-Roman historians often paused to note the recurring pattern of events" explicitly, Luke is less intrusive, expecting the reader to discern the patterns.[119] Nevertheless, it seems that Luke has made the patterns obvious enough for readers to discern easily the clearest examples. Luke's biblical models (such as 1 Samuel, noted above) offered parallels among characters, as Luke expects his ideal, biblically informed audience to recognize (as fleshed out in Acts 7; see examples cited there). Even the seminal exodus narrative depends on the irony of narrative connections and contrasts: for example, in retribution for Egypt drowning Israel's babies in the Nile (Exod 1:22), God turned the Nile to blood (Exod 7:17), slew Egypt's firstborn (Exod 12:29–30), and drowned Egypt's army (Exod 14:27–28).

---

113. See Satterthwaite, "Acts," 376, noting the rhetorical admonition of Quint. *Inst.* 4.1.57; 4.2.58–59; 4.5.5; 9.4.147.

114. For Peter as a "round" and complex character in Luke-Acts, see Brawley, *Centering on God*, 139–47.

115. See my comment ad loc. Brawley, *Centering on God*, 148–58, finds Paul to be complex and ambiguous, like Peter: he defies easy classification (158). In the narrative logic of Acts, God, rather than other characters, guides the events (see 86–106).

116. Grene, *Political Theory*, 83; cf. similarly Polyb. 39.8.7.

117. On views of divine design in history, see Squires, *Plan*; for historians seeking patterns or cycles in history, see Trompf, *Historical Recurrence*, 78ff., 170ff. (cited in Witherington, *Acts*, 423); in Acts, see also Brawley, *Centering on God*, 86–106. Nonhistorians also linked events (e.g., Philost. *Hrk.* 7.6).

118. Aune, *Environment*, 119 (citing the same text in Appian as above). Historians today can note ancient historians' tendencies or reasons for writing without dismissing historical tradition behind their presentation (e.g., Laistner, *Historians*, 97). Velleius Paterculus uses characteristics of earlier figures to prepare his audience for Tiberius (Gowing, "Republic," 412–13). On "rhetorical unity" in Plutarch's biographies, see Stadter, "Biography," 537). Suetonius arranges Tiberius's biography meaningfully (Thorburn, "Tiberius").

119. Aune, *Environment*, 119.

III. The Technique of Comparison

Scholars tracing Luke's techniques for creating unity in volumes based on some-times diverse sources often note the effects of redundancy[120] and the rhetorical tech-nique of σύγκρισις, or comparison.[121] Comparison of various figures was a standard narrative technique (Theon *Progymn.* 2.86–88, commenting on this rhetorical practice in Demosthenes).[122] This technique was too widespread for writers in a Greco-Roman setting not to have known it.[123] In his rhetorical handbook, Theon devotes a chapter to comparison (Περὶ συγκρίσεως, *Progymn.* 10), noting that though one could compare either characters or subjects (10.3–4), characters can embody virtues and provide opportunity for comparing both (10.4–7).

Rhetoricians recognized contrasts among characters in Homer—for example, the rage of both regal Agamemnon and passionate Achilles versus the wisdom of aged Nestor (Max. Tyre 26.5), and adulterous and cowardly Paris versus the sober hero Hector (26.6).[124] Philo, who often writes about biblical characters, also employs the full range of rhetorical techniques for σύγκρισις.[125] Such comparisons allowed one to teach virtue and admonish vice;[126] rhetors used such examples to teach proper speak-ing and writing.[127] Comparison was effective in political propaganda; thus Herodian propaganda compared Herod I with David.[128]

That Paul receives more space in Acts probably reflects partly the quality of Luke's sources, but in view of additional factors, it probably also signifies that Luke compares Paul favorably with Peter, of whom he also thinks highly.[129] The comparison is not, however, unfriendly competition from Luke's perspective. The Jerusalem apostles, who provide the largest narrative link between Jesus in the Gospel and Paul in the second half of Acts,[130] appear mostly favorably. Although they misunderstand the sequence of kingdom eschatology (Acts 1:6–7) and learn only slowly to approach Gentiles (10:20, 28–29, 34; 11:5–18, esp. 11:18), Luke portrays them positively. A work's opening typically helped foreshadow its direction, and Luke does not open

120. E.g., Marguerat, *Histoire*, 80–82. On Luke's techniques for achieving unity more generally, see 73–86.
121. Ibid., 82–83; Rothschild, *Rhetoric of History*, 118–19.
122. In practice, see, e.g., Philost. *Hrk.* 37.2; 38.1; as a rhetorical technique, see generally Marshall, *Enmity*, 348–53; Anderson, *Glossary*, 110–11 (citing Quint. *Inst.* 9.2.100–101 [cf. 2.4.21]; *Rhet. Her.* 2.45; Theon *Progymnasmata* (*RG* 2:112, lines 19ff.); Gärtner, "Synkrisis"; later, Hermog. *Progymn.* 8, "On Syncrisis," 18–20; Aphthonius *Progymn.* 10, "On Syncrisis," 42–44S, 31–33R; Nicolaus *Progymn.* 9, "On Syncrisis," 59–62; Hermog. *Inv.* 4.14.212. We do not, however, think of a sequential, point-by-point comparison as in Men. Rhet. 2.3, 381.31–32; 386.10–13; 2 Cor 11:21–23. Cf. the use of "detailed discourse" to heighten contrasts (Anderson, *Glossary*, 70).
123. With Forbes, "Comparison," 150, on Paul; for its common use in the NT, see, e.g., 150–60; Aune, *Dictionary of Rhetoric*, 110. Hock, "Paul and Education," 213, critiques Malina and Neyrey for assuming that σύγκρισις appears this early in encomium; but even if it was not yet emphasized in encomium, it certainly existed this early.
124. On the use of antitheses in the rhetorical historian Sallust, cf. Fronto (*Ad Ant. imp.* 2.6.1), but he speaks only at the sentence level. Some of Homer's comparisons were intended as good and better, not bad and good (e.g., *Il.* 22.158; pointed out also in Men. Rhet. 2.10, 417.10–11, which quotes it; interpreting Homer *Il.* 2.768–69, see Libanius *Encomium* 3.23 [applying it differently, cf. 1.16; 2.1]).
125. See Martin, "Philo's Use."
126. See our section above on history and moral lessons (ch. 5, sect. 1.b–d).
127. E.g., Dion. Hal. *Pomp.* 1–2, 6.
128. Ilan, "King David." By contrast, Matthew compares Herod with Pharaoh (Matt 2:16; Keener, *Matthew*, 102, 107–8; Allison, *Moses*, 146), and his intended victim, Jesus, with Moses (see Allison, *Moses*, passim).
129. Ancients sometimes used length of "air time" as a clue to someone's significance (Philost. *Hrk.* 14.2), relevant to Jesus's receiving more space than Peter and Paul put together. That matched arguments often finished on the preferred side (e.g., paired declamations in Max. Tyre 15–16; 23–24) is less relevant; chronology determines Luke's sequence, from Israel through Jesus and Paul's mission.
130. The speeches emphasize that Paul carries on Jerusalem's basic message (cf. Borgen, "Paul to Luke," 176–78, esp. 178).

Acts with Peter's denial or with disciples sleeping at Gethsemane or debating about greatness during their final meal with Jesus.[131]

Writers could use comparisons to denigrate others, sometimes as part of deliberate invective or self-exaltation at others' expense;[132] but this was far from comparison's only use. Comparisons between various characters (whether Peter and Paul in Acts or the beloved disciple and Peter in the Fourth Gospel) need not disparage any of them. In epideictic orations and elsewhere, one might be careful to praise someone in comparison with another without demeaning the latter; comparing an honorable person favorably with another honorable person yielded more praise for the former than would comparing the former with a dishonorable person.[133] One could compare one's subject with famous people of the past to increase the subject's status;[134] one could likewise compare cities with great cities.[135]

Though some writers felt that competition was injurious to friendship,[136] ancient texts more commonly allow for competitive comparisons between friends.[137] (Friends sometimes even used rivalry to spur one another on to achievement; see Pliny *Ep.* 3.7.15.) Later rhetorical handbooks are explicit that comparison can be between equals at times, just as it can be at the expense of one party at other times.[138] One could even compare bride and groom in a wedding speech, to praise each, intending to denigrate neither.[139]

The Greek historian Polybius compared the Roman general Scipio with the Spartan lawgiver Lycurgus, as a means of articulating Scipio's character more clearly (Polyb. 10.2.8–13).[140] Likewise, the Roman rhetorician Quintilian compared the most famous Greek epic poet, Homer, with Virgil, his Roman analogue (Quint. *Inst.* 10.1.85). Some writers developed such comparisons between Greek and Roman figures into an entire genre, using the rhetorical technique of comparison to target the ways that they would recount their "lives."

IV. PARALLEL BIOGRAPHIES

Even more plainly, Plutarch offers biographies of paired Greek and Roman figures, specifically selected because their stories proved comparable in some ways (allowing

131. See Parsons, *Departure*, 182.

132. See, e.g., Cic. *Brut.* 93.321–22; *Phil.* 3.6.15; *Pis.* 22.51; *Ag. Caec.* 12.37; Tac. *Hist.* 1.30; Marshall, *Enmity*, 52–55. On invective, see, e.g., Arena, "Invective."

133. See Dion. Hal. *Demosth.* 33; Fronto *Ad Ant. imp.* 1.2.4; Men. Rhet. 1.2, 353.9–10; 2.1–2, 376.31–377.2; 2.3, 380.21–22, 30–31; 2.10, 417.5–9, 13–17; Hermog. *Progymn.* 8, "On Syncrisis," 19–20; Aphth. *Progymn.* 10, "On Syncrisis," 43–44S, 32–33R, pp. 114–15; more fully, Keener, *John*, 916–17, 966–69, 1183–84; Anderson, *Glossary*, 121; Gibson, "Notes," 321. When one did not wish a comparison with a good person to benefit one's subject, one might say so (Cic. *Verr.* 2.4.54.121). Contrast the less challenging method of merely competing for honor within a small and less esteemed circle (2 Cor 10:12), though comparing oneself out of one's league is hubris (cf. *Sent. Syr. Men.* 340–44; also Hom. *Il.* 7.111, cited by way of illustration in Nicolaus *Progymn.* 5, "On Maxim," 28).

134. E.g., Men. Rhet. 2.10, 416.2–4. Some even achieved fame by being considered rivals of those who were truly their superiors (Eunapius *Lives* 493–94). By contrast, one could compare one's subject with something smaller to magnify it by comparison (*Rhet. Alex.* 3, 1426a.27–32).

135. E.g., Men. Rhet. 2.12, 422.11–12; 2.14, 426.30; 2.14, 427.1–4.

136. Iambl. *V.P.* 22.101; 33.230.

137. E.g., Philost. *Hrk.* 27.3; 13.3–4; cf. Pliny *Ep.* 10.100. Orators also compared bride, groom, and their families (Men. Rhet. 2.6, 402.26–29; 403.26–32; 404.5–8), and novelists wrote of lovers competing in affection for each other (Xen. Eph. *Anthia* 1.9); some writers competed with earlier writers to develop skill (Pliny *Ep.* 7.9.3). One could even compare one's work favorably with one's own earlier work (6.33.1; cf. Cic. *Fam.* 9.14.6).

138. Hermog. *Progymn.* 8, "On Syncrisis," 19.

139. Men. Rhet. 2.6, 403.26–32; 404.5–8; comparing their families, 2.6, 402.26–29.

140. He also compares the final leaders of Greece and Carthage who brought their nations to ruin before Rome (Polyb. 38.8.14–15).

Plutarch to demonstrate his skill in σύγκρισις)—the statesman Pericles with Fabius Maximus, the rhetor Demosthenes with Cicero, the conqueror Alexander with Caesar, and so forth. Thus he announces his intention in writing about Theseus, "the founder of lovely and famous Athens the counterpart and parallel to" Romulus, "the father of invincible and glorious Rome" (Plut. *Thes.* 1.2 [LCL]; cf. *Comparison of Theseus and Romulus*).[141] As one would expect in light of the emphasis on comparison in rhetoric, Plutarch was not alone in comparing historical figures.[142]

Some works did admittedly bend stories to conform them to each other. Cicero permitted historians to choose (though not to fabricate) traditions according to which ones best fit the parallels that they sought to articulate (e.g., the account of Themistocles's death that best fit the author's intended parallel to Coriolanus, regardless of other criteria for evaluating the most likely end for Themistocles; Cic. *Brut.* 11.42). Pseudo-Plutarch's *Greek and Roman Parallel Stories* (Plut. *Mor.* 305A–316B) presents paired stories so similar that they must either be doublets of the same tradition or be deliberately assimilated by the writer.[143] Plutarch complains that some writers added details missing elsewhere—for example, composing a proper tragic finale for Alexander's life (*Alex.* 70.3).[144]

Plutarch himself, however, who provides our strongest extant examples of the genre, generally was more careful (though more flexible than modern historiography).[145] He opines that nature itself supplies sufficient events for observers to find parallels if only they are sufficiently attentive (*Sert.* 1.1 [LCL]):

> It is perhaps not to be wondered at, since fortune is ever changing her course and time is infinite, that the same incidents should occur many times, spontaneously. For, if the multitude of elements is unlimited, fortune has in the abundance of her material an ample provider of coincidences; and if, on the other hand, there is a limited number

141. After his individual paired biographies (e.g., of Lucullus and Cimon), Plutarch typically provides works that directly compare the two (*Comparison of Lucullus and Cimon* [*Lives*, LCL, 2:610–21]).

142. Cf. the unmerited comparison of Julius Caesar with Alexander in Appian *Bell. civ.* 2.21.149 (with Vell. Paterc. 2.41.1 even preferring Caesar, for his discipline); cf. paired speeches (in Livy; Laistner, *Historians*, 96; Laird, "Rhetoric," 207–8). Some comparisons are rooted in the sources; Caesar is said to have compared himself with Alexander. Likewise, people compared newer figures with earlier ones, e.g., various emperors with Romulus (Vell. Paterc. 2.60.1; Suet. *Aug.* 7.2; *Calig.* 16.4; cf. Livy 5.49.7; Plut. *Cam.* 1.1; Haley, "Hadrian"; cf. Kearsley, "Octavian"); others with Alexander (Men. Rhet. 2.14, 426.23–24); or some later emperors with predecessors (Pliny *Ep.* 1.5.1; Suet. *Tit.* 7); and so forth (Cic. *Piso* 17.39; Lucan *C.W.* 9.15–18; 1 Cor 15:45; Rev 17:11). There were also impostors claiming the mantles of Alexander (Lucian *Book-Coll.* 20), Philip (Polyb. 36.10.1–7; Vell. Paterc. 1.11.1; Lucian *Book-Coll.* 20), or Nero (Tac. *Hist.* 1.2; 2.8–9; Suet. *Nero* 57.2; Lucian *Book-Coll.* 20; Dio Cass. 66.19.3; cf. Dio Chrys. *Or.* 21.9–10; *Sib. Or.* 4.137–39; 5.33–34, 137–54; 361–85; 8.68–72, 139–50). Parallel lives comparing Romans with Greeks grew from an emphasis already found during the Roman Republic, including in the first-century B.C.E. biographer Cornelius Nepos (Stadter, "Biography," 533, though noting that Nepos adds little to our knowledge base). In the epic genre, Virgil's Aeneas may function as a type for Augustus (Krauter, *Epos*, 238).

143. Frank Cole Babbitt, the Loeb translator, thinks this work stylistically inept; it is almost certainly not from the biographer Plutarch. As a rhetorical exercise, this method may have accelerated the transfer of traditions about one person to another (e.g., Philost. *Vit. soph.* 1.485 with LCL note; Alexander, "IPSE DIXIT," 121).

144. His own romantic description of Darius's death (Plut. *Alex.* 43.2) is missing in Arrian *Alex.* 3.21–23 but was evidently not his own invention (Bernadotte Perrin, in *Plutarch: Lives*, LCL, 7:352n1, cites Quint. Curt. 5.13, 28; Diod. 17.73).

145. Clark, *Parallel Lives*, 92–93, does suggest that Plutarch sometimes depended on his imagination for details (though noting that what can be proven is rearrangement of chronology; selection and omission for the sake of parallels; and sometimes even transference of actions to different characters—the sort of characteristics also encountered in midrash). Certainly, some of Ovid's stories introduce the element of metamorphosis to earlier myths simply to highlight his unifying theme; but Ovid's *Metamorphoses* belongs to a different genre. On Plutarch's likely methods (and their limitations by modern standards), see Pelling, "Plutarch's Method in Roman Lives."

of elements from which events are interwoven, the same things must happen many times, being brought to pass by the same agencies.

Likewise, he believed that the similarities he was able to find were due to the divine power's making people alike in many respects (*Demosth.* 3.2).[146]

Still, Plutarch tells distinctive stories about individuals he compares, noticing contrasts (e.g., *Comp. Alc. Cor.* 3.1). Even when Plutarch says that two people are so much alike that it is difficult to discern the differences between them (*Comp. Arist. Cato* 1.1), the claim plainly exaggerates because he does go on to point out differences (5.1, 3–4; 6.1). (Naturally the lives of statesmen will provide some parallels and contrasts with other statesmen, and even modern readers would understand such comparable features as often part of the nature of social reality, though not necessarily finding as many parallels as Plutarch.)

Plutarch did not try to simply invent parallels. He claims that he looked hard for the right people to compare with each other (*Cim.* 3.1–3). When appropriate, Plutarch sometimes concluded his comparison with a contrast (a sort of antithetic parallel) instead of conforming the subjects to each other: "Sulla won the more successes, while Lysander had the fewer failings"; the one is greater "in self-control and moderation . . . the other, in generalship and valour" (*Comp. Lys. Sull.* 5.5). If rhetoricians emphasized the importance of selectivity,[147] available parallels with another notable character could simply provide a criterion for selecting relevant points to record.[148] One did not have to invent parallels to discover them; anyone can find "parallels" among various characters in history (or between two persons conversing and looking for common ground). Limiting such parallels mostly to what one's sources provided displayed special skill that mere fabrication of such details would not. Many ancient writers were happy to advertise their skill in this genre.

Luke, like Plutarch, seeks to observe some limits, following patterns he believes were already present in history.[149] His sources are recent and his traditions, hence his potential parallels, are limited.[150] Paul is not crucified at the end of Acts; and though Peter may have been crucified historically, Luke neither carries Acts to this point chronologically nor retrojects this later event into an earlier place in his account. (Of course, even had he done so, Jesus's resurrection would have been more difficult to duplicate.)[151]

v. Biblical Models

The principle of linking characters "typologically" in biblical history is not one that Luke originated; nor would his source for such an approach necessarily be solely Hellenistic. Old Testament literature often structured narratives in parallel patterns as well. "Whereas scholarship of previous generations tended to explain many of these cases as doublets due to the combination of two or more sources, a more recent tendency has been to see such similar patterning as a deliberate authorial strategy

---

146. Polybius himself believed that his task as a historian was merely to report how Fortune had designed history, observing the causal connections that were her marks (cf. Polyb. 1.4.1–3).

147. E.g., Men. Rhet. 2.4, 393.25–30; see comment at Acts 24:4 on brevity.

148. Ancient hearers would also not find repetition of key themes in various parts of a work unexpected (in some kinds of speeches, see, e.g., Men. Rhet. 2.3, 384.25–27).

149. For historians' interest in patterns, see again Squires, *Plan*.

150. Thus, e.g., Luke can parallel healings of paralytics through Jesus, Peter, and Paul, yet he lacks lepers to be healed in his second volume. Likewise, he uses "sinners" to prepare the way for Gentiles in the second volume but lacks many examples of Gentiles for his Gospel (and omits one available example, that of the Syrophoenician woman, which he possesses from Mark).

151. At best, Luke could foreshadow it in a proleptic way (cf., e.g., Acts 26:6–8).

which invites the reader to read one incident in the light of the other."[152] Similarly, the prophets' picture of a new exodus (e.g., Isa 12:2; 40:3; Jer 31:32–33; Hos 2:15; 11:1, 5, 11) evoked its prototype.[153] Indeed, even the Jordan crossing in Josephus deliberately echoes the sea crossing at the exodus.[154] Later Jewish historians and storytellers also recounted their narratives along patterns from earlier salvation history, believing that God had objectively authored these patterns in history.[155] Jewish eschatological literature even uses the *Urzeit* as a prototype for the *Endzeit* (especially Eden).[156] I have mentioned other examples above; Luke's own interests are evident particularly in Acts 7 (see my discussion there).

2. Structure of Acts

Breaking a long work into smaller sections, each with its own openings and conclusions, might retain interest (Pliny *Ep.* 9.4.1–2). But while Luke certainly does divide his work, contemporary scholarship lacks consensus on the structure of Acts.[157] Although even some kinds of speeches required no particular structure,[158] this is probably not the reason for different possible approaches to Acts. Appropriate arrangement of material was a primary concern for those who were rhetorically sensitive,[159] and the strengths of some divergent yet valuable structural proposals for Acts seem to suggest that Luke provided various structural clues allowing for different related approaches, instead of lacking structure.[160]

a. Summary Statements

Summary statements appear throughout Acts (Acts 2:41, 47; 4:4; 5:14; 6:7; 9:31, 42; 11:21; 12:24; 13:48; 16:5; 19:20; 28:31) and clearly are Luke's own editorial work.[161] Scholars widely recognize these, though not all believe that Luke intended them as structural indicators.[162] Narrowing these statements to the clearest summaries of the gospel's expansion (6:7; 9:31; 12:24; 16:5; 19:20) provides many scholars with six "panels" in Luke's story:

1. 1:1–6:7: the church in Jerusalem
2. 6:8–9:31: Judea and Samaria (cf. 1:8)

---

152. Satterthwaite, "Acts," 363. On such patterns, see discussion regarding Luke and the OT in ch. 14; also the discussion at Acts 7. In some cases a writer might rewrite one incident in light of another, without fabricating the incident; compare a detail surrounding Josiah's death in 2 Chr 35:23 with one surrounding that of Ahab in 18:33, with a parallel in 1–2 Kings only in 1 Kgs 22:34 (not at 2 Kgs 23:29–30; cf. Williamson, *Chronicles*, 411), though we do not know the Chronicler's range of sources (cf. 2 Chr 35:26–27; cf. Williamson, *Chronicles*, 408).

153. Kugel and Greer, *Interpretation*, 46–47.

154. Hays, *Echoes*, 101.

155. Jacobson, "Visions of Past," citing 1 Maccabees, 3 Maccabees, and Judith and Tobit (cf. also Daniel the official as following the model of Joseph). The contrast he draws with Hellenistic historians, however, seems unfortunate.

156. Kugel and Greer, *Interpretation*, 47; cf. *4 Ezra* 8:52–54; 9:5–6; on the *Endzeit* and the *Urzeit*, see discussion at Acts 3:21.

157. For surveys of views, see Betori, "Ricera"; Witherington, *Acts*, 74–76.

158. See Men. Rhet. 2.4, 391.19–28; 392.9–14; 393.23–24.

159. See esp. Wuellner, "Arrangement," 51–87.

160. On structuring devices in Acts, cf. also Longenecker, "Aversion."

161. See the excursus on summary statements at Acts 2:41; esp. Acts 6:7. Some question the historical value of the summary statements (Cadbury, "Summaries"); this concern seems reasonable, since Josephus proves least reliable in his summary statements, but see discussion on Acts 2:41–47 (esp. the disputed numbers of 2:41). Luke is a less rhetorical historian than Josephus, and his summaries cohere better with his overall narrative.

162. Liefeld, *Acts*, 41–42.

3. 9:32–12:24: to Gentiles (a nongeographic category)
4. 12:25–16:5: Asia and the shift to emphasizing the Gentile mission
5. 16:6–19:20: urban centers in Europe (returning also to Ephesus)[163]
6. 19:21–28:31: to Rome[164]

This outline depends on the summary statements, however, whereas some other statements in Acts are analogous (e.g., 2:47; 9:21).[165] It is helpful, like some other outlines, in revealing the narrative progress of the gospel among different groups (though Luke would probably prefer readers to hear all the summary statements that way).

b. Geographic Plans

A simple geographic plan follows the four geographic regions explicit in Acts 1:8 (see further comment there): Jerusalem, Judea, Samaria, and the ends of the earth.[166] This is a perspective that would have made sense to the Jerusalem apostles more than to Luke's audience; virtually the entire Pauline mission and more than half the book of Acts constitute the final category (cf. 13:47), whereas Judea and Samaria (which may constitute a single step in 1:8) together take up only a few chapters.[167] But whether proportional to the book's contents or not, this outline does show the general geographic direction of the narrative and is explicit in the texts.

James Scott structures the book, even less symmetrically, according to the world-view of ancient Jewish geography: the missions to Shem (2:1–8:25), Ham (8:26–40), and Japheth (9:1–28:31).[168] Although no such divisions are explicit in the text, some passages (esp. 2:5–11; perhaps 1:8) do suggest Luke's familiarity with the table-of-nations tradition.[169] In Scott's view, these missions meet in the circle of Stephen and are in varying stages of completion (with the Shem mission mostly completed and the Ham mission only begun).[170] Whatever the particulars, the structure should comport with the work's plotline, following the gospel's expansion from Jerusalem to Rome.[171]

c. Characters and Action

Another perspective from which to view the book's structure, and the one particularly relevant to the discussion on parallelism above, is its penchant for parallels

---

163. Luke has interest in Roman colonies such as Corinth and Philippi here (but also strategic free cities such as Thessalonica and free cities of symbolic import such as Athens); colonies appeared in Acts 13–14 also, but their status may have been less obvious to Luke's audience.

164. E.g., in Witherington, *Acts*, 74 (who provides other possible analyses, 74–76); also Bruce, *Commentary*, 131; Arrington, *Acts*, xliv–xlv; and MacGregor in Morton and MacGregor, *Structure*, 40–41 (all following C. H. Turner); Hernando, "Function," 245; similarly but slightly differently, Peterson, *Acts*, 36. Moody, "Chronology," 227, develops C. J. Cadoux's approach in connecting these panels with five-year periods, but ancient historiography did not work this way (Luke does not date events in Acts). O'Neill, *Theology*, 72, provides five sections, of which only Acts 19:21–28:31 (asymmetrical for any scheme) agrees with the six-section scheme; cf. also five parts in Zeigan, "Wachstumsnotizen."

165. Puskas, "Conclusion: Investigation," 67; Puskas and Crump, *Introduction*, 125; Morton and MacGregor, *Structure*, 41 (though finding C. H. Turner's outline useful).

166. See comment on Acts 1:8. Note further the fivefold division in O'Neill, *Theology*, largely developing Menoud, "Plan des Actes" (see Powell, *Acts*, 117).

167. This asymmetry could reflect Luke's rhetorical commitment to write appropriately for the situation, or it could suggest that the wording in Acts 1:8 reflects historical tradition.

168. Scott, "Horizon," 531.

169. Ibid., 525–30.

170. Ibid., 544.

171. Thus, e.g., Jervell, *Apostelgeschichte*, 52–55, divides the work into the Jerusalemite mission (Acts 1:1–8:40), the beginning of the Gentile mission (9:1–15:35), the Pauline Diaspora mission (15:36–21:26), and the trial against Paul (21:27–28:31).

among its primary characters. This parallelism appears most objectively in the twofold division between Acts 1–12 and Acts 13–28 (although the Paul material begins in the first division). Parallels between Peter and Paul and other elements recur between these sections and are undoubtedly deliberate, as was noticed by scholars at least as early as the early nineteenth century.[172] We have explored some of these parallels above.

d. Various Outlines Possible

Because Luke's story contains overlapping chronological, geographical, and cultural components and markers, we can "outline" Acts in more than one way. Not all of these approaches necessarily point to a conscious structuring of the material by Luke as carefully as we might suppose,[173] but they do reflect objective markers in the text pointing to the progress of the gospel toward Rome, which is the story that he narrates.

We focus on the clearest indicators of structure, that is, those supporting Luke's purpose for the expansion of the gospel from Jerusalem to Rome. A purely geographical structure (cf. 1:8) does, to be sure, invite overlap (and considerable asymmetry, with Judea and Samaria functioning transitionally in 8:1–11:18, esp. the summary in 8:1). But Luke is not Aristotle, nor can one structure historical works as tightly as an argument; various approaches to structure offer helpful clues to the narrative progress of the book, which is what is most at issue.

e. A Sample Partial Outline

Acts lacks clear breaks concluding the preface and at many other points; Luke likes to create smooth transitions. Ancient writers did not always work according to hierarchical outlines, as modern scholars often do.[174] Such an outline therefore is necessarily forced at points, allowing diverse, equally plausible proposals from various commentators. Nevertheless, structure was an important feature of rhetorical and literary composition,[175] and even general outlines from antiquity (often as tables of contents)[176] do exist for some works.

The following is one attempt to reflect something of the work's narrative structure within the confines of a hierarchical outline. It differs at points from the commentary outline because at numerous points I needed to incorporate more or less information in that outline, depending on how much background was available or necessary for a section. Sometimes I have also sacrificed elements of structure for symmetry; for example, 4:31–5:42, as a whole, parallels the preceding unit (3:1–4:22), but the chronologically later section contains more paragraphs that need to be separated. Likewise, units are often transitional and hence can belong in more than one location; for example, although in many respects the prayer of 4:23–30 belongs more naturally with the following effects of the prayer, I have kept it with the preceding section to highlight some narrative connections. If one builds the outline from individual pericopes, it will come out differently than a top-down outline from major units because the major units (and their subunits) are of very uneven length; in this commentary

---

172. Brawley, *Luke-Acts and Jews*, 43, and Bruce, *Peter*, 23–24, both citing Schneckenburger, *Apostelgeschichte*, 52–58 (1841). These parallels are widely accepted today (e.g., Kistemaker, *Acts*, 30; Arrington, *Acts*, xliv; Pervo, *Acts*, 21).

173. Cf. Arrington, *Acts*, xliv (arguing that in keeping with the work's genre, Luke's *primary* structure is, whatever else may be added, chronological). For Luke's use of overlapping models, see rightly Pervo, *Acts*, 20–21.

174. Note a similar warning in Stowers, *Rereading of Romans*, 231, regarding imposing paragraph divisions on Paul.

175. On the concern for arrangement in rhetoric, see Wuellner, "Arrangement."

176. E.g., Pliny E. *N.H.* pref. 33; *N.H.* 1 (the entire volume).

I have tried to compromise between the two objectives, working from a top-down outline (which produces asymmetry in sections) but including also independent, briefer units for readability. No outline is perfect, and every outline must admit criticisms from those who highlighted different connections. Nevertheless, this sample should illustrate that Luke composed a cohesive work, not simply lumping together disparate material.

I. The First Outpouring of the Spirit (1:1–2:47)
   A. Introduction and Recapitulation (Transition from Jesus to the Church; Awaiting the Promise) (1:1–11)
      1. Preface (1:1–2)
      2. Promise of the Holy Spirit (1:3–8)
      3. Ascension (and Promise to Return) (1:9–11)
   B. Preparation for Pentecost (1:12–26)
      1. Praying Together (1:12–14)
      2. Establishing Leaders and Their Testimony for the Future (1:15–26)
   C. The Event of Pentecost (2:1–13)
      1. Signs of Pentecost (2:1–4)
      2. Responses to Signs (2:5–13)
   D. Peter's Call to Repentance (2:14–40)
      1. Response to Drunkenness Charge (2:14–15)
      2. Biblical Basis for the Event (2:16–21)
      3. Narration about Jesus's Death and Resurrection (2:22–24)
      4. Biblical Explanation for Jesus's Resurrection (2:25–36)
         a. Psalm 16 (2:25–28)
         b. Not David (2:29–31)
         c. Appeal to Apostolic Witness (2:32) and Their Own Witness (2:33)
         d. Not David, Psalm 110 (2:34–35)
         e. Conclusion of Argument (2:36)
      5. Demanded Response (2:37–40)
   E. The Empowered Community (2:41–47)
II. Apostolic Leadership in Jerusalem (3:1–5:42)
   A. Healing of the Paralytic and Its Aftermath (3:1–4:31)[177]
      1. Power of Jesus's Name (3:1–10)
      2. Offer of Restoring Israel's Kingdom If Israel Receives Its King (3:11–26)
      3. Confronting the Elite (4:1–22)
      4. Prayer for More Boldness (4:23–30)
   B. Results of Second Outpouring of the Spirit (4:31–5:16)
      1. Immediate Impact of Prayer (4:31)
      2. Sacrificial Sharing of Believers (4:32–35)
      3. Positive Example: Joseph Barnabas (4:36–37)
      4. Negative Example: Ananias and Sapphira (5:1–11)
      5. Apostles' Honor and Signs (5:12–16)
   C. More Persecution (5:17–42)
      1. Arrest, Release, Arrest (5:17–26)
      2. Confronting the Elite Again (5:27–33)
      3. Gamaliel's Counsel (5:34–40)

---

177. Because 4:31 is transitional and the following paragraph is closely connected with what precedes, I mention it here, though treating it more in the next section.

1. Charges against Paul (24:1–9)
2. Paul's Defense (24:10–21)
3. Felix's Procrastination (24:22–27)
4. Paul's Appeal to Caesar (25:1–12)
   a. Authorities in Jerusalem Denounce Paul (25:1–5)
   b. Paul Defends Himself before Festus (25:6–9)
   c. Paul Appeals to Caesar (25:10–12)
5. Festus Discusses the Case with Agrippa (25:13–22)
6. Paul before Agrippa (25:23–26:32)
   a. Introducing the Hearing (25:23–26:1a)
   b. Proem and Paul's Background (26:1b–11)
   c. Paul's Divine Commission (26:12–18)
   d. Paul's Gospel (26:19–23)
   e. Paul's Desire to Convert His Audience (26:24–29)
   f. The Verdict (26:30–32)
D. Voyage to Rome (27:1–28:15)
   1. The Voyage Begins (27:1–8)
   2. Ignoring Paul's Warning (27:9–13)
   3. Disaster at Sea (27:14–20)
   4. Paul Shares the Angel's Message (27:21–26)
   5. Paul's Leadership as They Approach Land (27:27–38)
   6. Reaching Land Safely (27:39–44)
   7. Ministry in Malta (28:1–10)
      a. Paul Survives a Snakebite (28:1–6)
      b. Healings and Hospitality (28:7–10)
   8. Final Voyage to Rome (28:11–15)
E. Continuing Ministry in Rome (28:16–31)
   1. Paul Meets Jewish Leaders (28:16–22)
   2. Recalcitrance of God's People Prophesied (28:23–28)
   3. Continuing, Unhindered Ministry (28:30–31)

17

GEOGRAPHIC
BACKGROUND

Some issues relevant for social-historical study of Acts require discussion too extensive for the main text of the commentary and hence are treated here: travel, geography, and the frequent divide between rural and urban populations in the empire. These factors are relevant especially for Paul's travels in the second of the book's two major sections.

1. Travel and Geography in Acts

Travel is important for Luke, both as an organizing principle for an interesting narrative[1] and because the geographic movement in his narratives corresponds to following God's will (cf. Acts 19:21; 21:13–14). In Acts believers must travel to fulfill Jesus's commission (1:8), and Paul, like Jesus, is drawn to his destiny in Jerusalem (and, for Paul, beyond that to Rome). The shorter travel report in Mark (Mark 10:1–52) is expanded to cover one-third of Luke's Gospel (Luke 9:51–19:44), perhaps in part to provide symmetry with the travels in Acts.[2]

Understanding facets of ancient travel[3] (the nature of which Luke's ancient audience would likely have been able to take for granted) is helpful for visualizing what Paul endured. His sufferings for the gospel included both long journeys and the various sufferings attending them (2 Cor 11:26). Paul, both in Acts and in his letters, was nothing if not a traveler. Jack Finegan estimates that the travels in Acts alone covered at least "12,000 miles (20,000 kilometers)," not including later travels claimed by early Christian tradition.[4] Despite his emphasis on Paul's status, Luke explicitly depicts Paul's land travels as on horseback only in captivity (Acts 23:24),

---

1. On Luke's attention to locations as scenes for his narrative's action, see, e.g., briefly, Mazich, "Geography." Geography and history were in fact closely intertwined disciplines in antiquity (Engels, "Geography," 540–46, following, e.g., Marincola, *Authority*, 12–19; idem, "Genre"; Clarke, *Geography*).

2. Pao, *Isaianic Exodus*, 1, notes that Luke offers frequent reminders of the destination (Luke 9:51, 53; 13:22, 33; 17:11; 18:31; 19:11, 28, 41). The connection with "the Way" (Pao, *Isaianic Exodus*, 2) and (with M. Strauss) Isaiah's exodus (12) appear to me more forced, though perhaps I have simply not explored these connections adequately.

3. See, e.g., Ramsay, "Roads and Travel"; Charlesworth, *Trade Routes*; Casson, *Travel*; Kreitzer, "Travel"; Wallace and Williams, *Worlds*, 15–29; Reynier, "Voyages"; Patella, "Travels."

4. Finegan, *Apostles*, xix, noting that these would add a further "3,000 miles (5,000 kilometers) or more."

suggesting that he usually traveled on foot.[5] Although we moderns, who cover long distances in cars or planes, may miss the point, Luke's audience would have recognized that such travels must have consumed much of his time in ministry. Ancients recognized the need for time when traveling; when Pliny must make a round-trip journey of 150 miles (plus some business when he arrives there), he asks leave for a month (Pliny *Ep.* 10.8.6).[6]

a. Geographic Information

Chapter 12 above addressed the probable geographic assumptions of Luke's audience; here we turn to other geographic issues relevant for Paul's travels. (For comments on Hellenistic and Roman imperial "multiculturalism," see ch. 15, sect. 3.b.)

Geographic knowledge and often even maps were fairly accurate when their focus remained within the Roman Empire.[7] The elder Pliny contends that geography was very advanced by this period, and Augustus built a portico "containing a plan of the world" based on Marcus Agrippa's research (Pliny E. *N.H.* 3.2.17). Romans had *itineraria*, somewhat like road maps, for military but also civilian use (and useful especially to merchants); these listed roads, rest stops, distances between sites, and even some topography.[8] They were not always accurate,[9] but they represented significant progress beyond what was available earlier. Although pictorial maps were available, descriptive, verbal, "mental" maps were much more common than the pictorial kind.[10] Elite citizens who could afford to travel for leisure knew much about the Mediterranean world,[11] but so did those who listened to sagas or orations, most of which either contain or presuppose significant geographic knowledge.[12]

Acts is full of geographic knowledge and often presupposes that members of its ideal audience would recognize the names of various cities and their general proximity to one another. Acts reflected their real world. As one classicist points out regarding ancient sources for travel in Asia Minor, "The evidence found in the Acts is perhaps most valuable of all because it indicates the ordinary voyages and the conditions that the plain civilian or merchant would have to face."[13]

Many in the first century were interested in travel narratives, whether as adventure novels or as illustrations of sages' ability to address people in all places.[14] The movement in Acts would thus hold attention. Travel narration is not, of course, the primary focus of Acts: travel narratives and geographies often employed the rhetoric of praise and blame in describing places,[15] whereas Acts fails to linger over the particular

---

5. Ibid. For fuller sources on Paul's travels and travel more generally, see Hvalvik, "Stadig."

6. Presumably this duration allows plenty of cushion, not only travel time.

7. See Charlesworth, *Trade Routes*, 13; Casson, *Mariners*, 70, 80; Purcell, "Maps"; see further Dilke, *Maps*; Talbert, "Cartography." For a sample map, see Gold, "Mosaic Map," 67–70.

8. Burian, "Itinerare," 1023; cf. Le Cornu, *Acts*, 709. *Itineraria* included especially "the road network and its stations, with" approximations of "the respective distances" (Burian, "Itinerare," 1024).

9. Burian, "Itinerare," 1024, notes one particularly useful *itinerarium*, "even though some of its details contain inaccuracies, mistakes and other errors."

10. See Sundwall, "Ammianus Geographicus." Some may have disliked maps (Hermog. *Inv.* 1.2.102, but this is hypothetical declamation).

11. For tourism in the empire, see Friedländer, *Life*, 1:323–428; note especially the resorts in Greece, the Greek islands, and Asia Minor (340–49).

12. E.g., also Philost. *Hrk.* 1.3 (on the presupposed competence of this work's implied audience, see Maclean and Aitken, *Heroikos*, lxxxvii–lxxxix).

13. Charlesworth, *Trade Routes*, 85–86, contrasting the elite, who appear most prominently in our sources.

14. Cf. Marguerat, "Voyageurs" (comparing the centrality of travel in Acts). See the "travel narrative" proposal in ch. 2, above.

15. See Men. Rhet. 1.2–3, 346.26–367.9; cf. Dio Chrysostom's local orations and esp. Aelius Aristides's orations to Rome (*Or.* 26) and Athens (*Or.* 1).

places where Paul travels. The theological significance of travel in Acts focuses on the expansion of the apostolic message.

An even more obvious contrast with some fictitious travel narratives is that Acts comes nowhere close to collections of wonders about exotic locations too distant to check;[16] it is part of the real world of Luke's audience.[17] Thus one may contrast exotic tales of India's gold-digging ants larger than foxes[18] or of some of its rivers carrying gold.[19] Pliny the Elder offers reports (without commending them) about suicidal Hyperboreans who ultimately tire of their great longevity,[20] a king with just one eye (*N.H.* 6.35.195), Indians with backwards feet (7.2.22) or dogs' heads (7.2.23), and a woman who birthed an elephant (7.3.34). In his *Life of Apollonius*, Philostratus is fairly accurate within the boundaries of the empire, but he depends on earlier authors and generally departs from reality in Mesopotamia and India.[21]

Despite Acts' different focus, however, informed members of Luke's audience probably knew something about many of the places Luke mentions. Luke is particularly careful to document locations during Paul's Aegean travels, especially when he (on the view of authorship articulated in ch. 11) is traveling with Paul (Acts 16:11–12; 20:13–15; 21:1–2; 27:7). Such documentation is not limited to the Aegean,[22] but it is concentrated there because this is the phase of Paul's ministry on which Luke offers the most detail, next to Paul's final custody.[23] Elsewhere, such as in the interior of Asia, Acts proves accurate on abundant details (see commentary on Acts 13–14), although it is not clear that Luke had visited there or that his audience was very familiar with that region. Yet Luke goes into less detail on the itinerary there than in the "we" narratives.

b. Cultic Associations of Locations

Most educated Christians in Philippi would know something of the history not only of Macedonia but also of the entire Aegean region through epics about ancient heroes from various locations and stories of more recent times. Paul traveled to evangelize locations with which Luke's ideal audience was often familiar, connecting their new faith with their ancestral cultural heritage. These unarticulated nuances available to Luke's ideal audience are generally lost on the modern reader.

Such details are worth noting because they help us to hear more of the resonances that these stories could have had for Gentile members of Luke's first audiences, rather than simply reading our modern or postmodern (as well as Christian or post-Christian) perspectives into the texts. Whether or not Luke's audience regularly knew of particular deities and cults associated with particular cities (deities and cults are

16. Where armchair reporters could pontificate most freely (cf. the disgust in Pliny E. *N.H.* 5.1.12; Lucian *True Story* 1.3). Apocalyptic geography also included striking elements (e.g., *1 En.* 17–18; 21:7; 77:8 [Knibb]/77:9 [Isaac]). Studious intellectuals also entertained notions of waters that turned sheep various colors (Pliny E. *N.H.* 2.106.230; in this case, all in known regions).

17. Errors happened even for such a nearer world, of course; e.g., *Sib. Or.* 11.265–67.

18. See Dio Chrys. *Or.* 35.23–24; Hdt. 3.102–5.

19. Quint. Curt. 8.9.18. India's pearl divers would also have been astonished had they heard that the sea simply deposited pearls and precious stones on the shore (the view in 8.9.19). Ctesias's tales of India (in his *Indica*) quickly earned him the reputation of a liar (Lenfant, "Historians," 203).

20. Pliny E. *N.H.* 4.12.89, uncertain whether the reports are accurate.

21. See Jones, "Passage."

22. Though Luke's travel comments are hardly exclusive to the Aegean when other points belong to the same itinerary (Acts 21:3) or his narrative (27:1–6; 27:8–28:1; 28:11–15).

23. This is true, to some extent, even outside the "we" narratives; Corinth (Acts 18:1–18), Ephesus (18:19–21; 19:1–41; 20:17), and even, if we count the speech, Athens (17:15–34) receive more attention than Paul's probably lengthy ministry in Antioch (11:26, 30; 12:25–13:3; 14:26–15:2; 15:30, 35). Nasrallah, "Cities," reads Paul's itinerary in Acts in the context of contemporary perspectives on the empire's cities.

mentioned periodically in the commentary when treating those sites), they knew that their environment was largely polytheistic. Often they even knew the cultic reputations of various locations; certainly most educated urban hearers knew of Artemis of Ephesus, but also of other famous local cults. They were utterly conscious, in a way that our readings after Christendom or in largely monotheistic environments often are not, that the apostles whom Luke portrays as boldly preaching were articulating a perspective then held by a tiny minority, not a dominant culture.[24]

Romans believed that the gods provided safety in travel by road or sea (Fronto *Ad M. Caes.* 3.9.2); Acts implies that God protected Paul in his travels (for potential dangers, see 2 Cor 11:25–27). Jewish people who traveled prayed for God to provide safety.[25] Monotheistic travelers such as Paul could not, however, have avoided being confronted regularly with signs of the more common pagan travelers' religion. Sacred monuments alongside roads often were devoted to Hermes, deity of travelers (cf. Acts 14:12), so often that later rabbis mention them.[26]

c. Safety and Hardship of Travel

Seneca the Younger appreciated travel as useful for learning and inquiry but was ambivalent about it in some other respects.[27] Many people regarded travel as a hardship to be avoided whenever possible (e.g., Firm. Matern. *Math.* 53.50).[28] Travel by sea could be dangerous, and those who undertook it looked to various patron deities to protect them, especially Castor and Pollux (see comment on Acts 28:11). Many Greeks historically looked to Apollo as protector on journeys in general (e.g., Aeschylus *Ag.* 1080, 1086). Those who played the odds seem to have calculated a significant mortality rate on long journeys, naturally compounded for frequent travelers.[29] Robbers (cf. 2 Cor 11:26; Luke 10:30) were dangerous especially in the mountains ("where roads were not carefully guarded"), but travelers could encounter danger anywhere.[30] Bands of highwaymen were common,[31] though such robbers were widely hated[32] and cruelly

24. The earliest Christian mission had, and could have had, nothing in common with cultural imperialism. (Many outsiders would have viewed it instead as a troublesome little cult, one among many, in this case a particularly radical form of Judaism.)

25. *M. Ber.* 9:4 (cited in Le Cornu, *Acts*, 790).

26. Le Cornu, *Acts*, 708, citing *merculis* (sing.) in *m. Sanh.* 7:6; *'Abod. Zar.* 4:1; *t. 'Abod. Zar.* 6[7]:13; *b. Sanh.* 64a; *'Abod. Zar.* 50ab.

27. See Montiglio, "Travel."

28. MacMullen, *Social Relations*, 97; for hazards, see further Wallace and Williams, *World*, 27–29.

29. See the calculations, based on oracular answers, for the dangers of travel, in Toner, *Culture*, 48, estimated at perhaps 20 percent cases of serious danger by the time inquirers were anxious enough to ask.

30. Robbers were probably especially frequent on smaller roads in difficult provinces (Stambaugh and Balch, *Environment*, 38), possibly explaining some Galilean towns' location away from roads (Freyne, *Galilee, Jesus*, 153); they are well attested in Egypt (P.Ryl. 125; P.Oxy. 1408.11–21; P.Gur. 8; cf. Xen. Eph. *Anthia* 3.12; for burglary, see Lewis, *Life*, 77) and would endanger Paul in the mountainous interior of Asia Minor (Ramsay, "Roads and Travel," 392; Liefeld, "Life," 12). Some innkeepers may have stolen guests' possessions (*b. Ta'an.* 21a; *Gen. Rab.* 92:6); grave robbery was a particularly heinous offense (cf. Iambl. *Bab. St.* 7; Xen. Eph. *Anthia* 3.8; *Apoll. K. Tyre* 32). Of course, thieves could break into homes even if one was not traveling (see Lucian *Lucius* 16; Robinson, *Criminal Law*, 27; Schiemann, "Furtum"; further discussion in Keener, *John*, 803–4).

31. E.g., Horace *Ep.* 1.2.32–33; Phaedrus 4.23.16; Jos. *Ant.* 20.113; *Tr. Shem* 6:1; 7:20; *b. A.Z.* 25b; *B. Qam.* 116b, bar.; *Gen. Rab.* 75:3; *Exod. Rab.* 30:24; *Pesiq. Rab Kah.* 27:6; further discussion in Friedländer, *Life*, 1:294–96; MacMullen, *Enemies*, 255–68; Shaw, "Brigandry." In novels, see Ach. Tat. 3.9.3; Xen. Eph. *Anthia* 2.11; for massive bands (though in novels), see Xen. Eph. *Anthia* 4.1; 5.2; Lucian *Ship* 28.

32. E.g., Apul. *Metam.* 8.17; Max. Tyre 5.7; *Lev. Rab.* 9:8. Social bandits (see comment on Acts 21:38; excursus on Zealots at Acts 1:13) may have commanded some local support (cf. Jos. *Ant.* 20.124, 160), but most ancient sources despise robbers (cf. the devastation of villages in Jos. *Ant.* 20.185; cf. discussion in McGing, "Bandits"). In a few cases brigandage appeared a romantic lifestyle (Lucian *Ship* 28), but most believed that brigands would have preferred a better means of income (Sen. *Ben.* 4.17.4; Libanius *Progymn.* Invective 6.11; cf. Alciphron *Fishermen* 8 [Eucolymbus to Glaucê], 1.8).

treated if caught;[33] many also expected divine judgment against them.[34] Robbers were a particularly grave danger at night,[35] even within cities,[36] and sometimes highwaymen even killed their victims.[37] The rich traveled in large and well-guarded caravans, and so, ironically, poor travelers probably suffered more from robbers than did the rich.[38] MacMullen summarizes:

> No one should build his farmhouse near a main road "because of the depredations of passing travelers." That was the advice of a man who knew Italy well, at the height of its peace; while the advice of a contemporary in Palestine was, if one stopped the night at a wayside inn, to make one's will. Both warnings came to the same thing. Away from centers of population, one risked being robbed or killed.[39]

Still, travel was generally easier and safer in this period than in the past; Rome maintained its roads, and guards protected the *stationes* on the way.[40] Although sea travel was faster, storms were less dangerous by land and the season was less important.[41] Although Rome had suppressed the worst of piracy by this period,[42] some fear of pirates may have persisted.[43] Travel by road was very common.[44] Roman roads were rarely more than twenty feet wide, but they were carefully designed; in mountainous country, for example, the roads followed paths least endangered by avalanches.[45] Roman roads through the empire were superior to most roads in most of Europe until 1850.[46]

33. Most approved of harsh punishment (*Rhet. Alex.* 1, 1422b.5–8); Roman officials often executed them (Jos. *Ant.* 20.5, 161; cf. Robinson, *Criminal Law*, 26; Schiemann, "Furtum," 626) and were praised for suppressing them (Cic. *Quint. fratr.* 1.1.8.25; Vell. Paterc. 2.126.3; Plut. *Cic.* 36.4–5). One resisting a robber might kill him (Cicero *Mil.* 21.55), intervening to protect another against robbers was valued (Diod. Sic. 1.77.3, suggesting that failure to do so was a capital offense in Egypt), and a villager who caught a thief might recruit fellow villagers to aid in beating the man (Alciphron *Farm.* 16 [Pithacnion to Eustachys], 3.19, ¶¶1–2; this happens at times in Africa). Custom may have barred a past thief from public speaking (Sen. E. *Controv.* 10.6.intro). Tolls helped support desert police (Lewis, *Life*, 141); governors might deploy even military means such as armies to destroy large bands of robbers (Fronto *Ad Ant. Pium* 8; in a novel, Xen. Eph. *Anthia* 5.2–3).

34. E.g., Lucian *Dialogues of Dead* 450 (24/30, *Minos and Sostratus* 1); Sir 20:25; *b. Sanh.* 108a; *Tg. Neof.* 1 on Gen 6:11, 13); some also viewed experiencing robbery as judgment (*m. Ber.* 1:3; *b. Ber.* 11a), but other people viewed it as not one's fault (Quint. *Decl.* 320.12; for piracy, Llewelyn, *Documents*, 6:82–83, §12).

35. Catull. *Carm.* 62.34–35; Tibullus 1.2.25–28; cf. the compound word translated "night robberies" in *Sib. Or.* 3.238, 380.

36. Stambaugh, *City*, 201; Stambaugh and Balch, *Environment*, 119; cf. Ebner, "Latrocinium"; Cic. *Quint. fratr.* 1.1.8.25 regarded urban robbers as a graver threat to order than rural ones. The wealthy apparently traversed Rome's streets at night only with bodyguards (Jeffers, *World*, 61).

37. E.g., *Gr. Anth.* 7.310, 516, 581, 737; Lucian *Lucius* 27; Xen. Eph. *Anthia* 4.3; *Gen. Rab.* 80:2; 92:6.

38. Ramsay, "Roads and Travel," 392 (noting two soldiers granted as an escort to a rich man in Lucian *Alex.* 55). By contrast, Dio Chrys. *Or.* 7.9–10 doubts that robbers will waste effort on the poorest.

39. MacMullen, *Social Relations*, 4, citing Colum. *Rust.* 1.5.7 and the Jerusalem Talmud; for the danger of thieves, cf. Jos. *War* 2.125; Weeber, "Travels," 869–70; in more detail, MacMullen, *Enemies*, 255–68.

40. See Liefeld, "Preacher," 7–11. For routes and methods of travel, see ibid., 16–19; on travel, cf. also Rapske, "Travel and Trade."

41. Casson, *Travel*, 176. For the widespread presumption of sea travel's dangers, see, e.g., Quint. *Decl.* 257.2 and comment at Acts 27. On the relative speeds of land and sea travel, see Friedländer, *Life*, 1:280–87.

42. See, e.g., Vell. Paterc. 2.32.4–6; *Res gest.* 5.25; Souza, "Pirates"; Tröster, "Hegemony"; Lintott, *Romans*, 62. Caesar, held by pirates, later slew them (Suet. *Jul.* 4; Plut. *Caes.* 1.4; 2.4). Armies during the Roman Republic also practiced seaborne raids (see discussion of some purposes in Bragg, "Raids").

43. Quint. *Decl.* 257 intro; 342 intro; 388 intro; Libanius *Progymn.* Invective 5.4–5; *Thesis* 1.28; Iambl. *V.P.* 27.127. Earlier, 1 Esd 4:23–24; Vell. Paterc. 2.73.3; Charlesworth, *Trade Routes*, 227.

44. On land travel, see Casson, *Travel*, 176–96; Friedländer, *Life*, 1:287–99; on the roads, see Casson, *Travel*, 163–75.

45. Cary and Haarhoff, *Life*, 138. Milestones marked distances.

46. Ibid. Chinese engineers also built great roads in this period, though their lack of paving prevented their survival (Casson, *Travel*, 174).

Romans learned their hydraulic-engineering techniques from the Etruscans, which allowed for proper draining, especially important for streets in the cities.[47]

d. Speed of Travel and Stopping Places

Those whose business was urgent preferred sea travel to land, at least during passable seasons for the former. With favorable winds (e.g., from Egypt to Rome or the reverse during appropriate seasons) ships could travel a hundred miles in a day. Meanwhile, on Roman roads "the imperial messenger service, using fresh horses at regular intervals," may have averaged, like vehicles, only twenty-five to thirty miles (thirty-eight to forty-five kilometers) per day, though under duress people could travel more than forty miles (sixty kilometers).[48] But even the time needed for travel by sea was uneven, potentially delayed by ships' loading or off-loading their cargoes; likewise, "winds and waiting for a connecting ship easily lengthened a journey, quite apart from seasonal delays."[49]

On land the average distance between *mansiones* (inns), which were spaced according to how far people could travel in a day, was about thirty to thirty-six kilometers (some eighteen to twenty-three miles); soldiers could march this far (Veg. *Mil.* 1.9), but if the marching continued for several weeks, about thirty kilometers (less than twenty miles) a day was a maximum. On long journeys, then, a strong but ordinary traveler could probably traverse fifteen to twenty miles per day (twenty to thirty kilometers).[50] On such journeys, Jewish travelers (such as Paul and Barnabas) would lose a day of travel each week for the Sabbath;[51] the obligations of hospitality could also significantly slow a traveler's journey (cf. Acts 20:16),[52] although probably not as much in a region where one was a first-time visitor introduced only by letters.

Moving from estimates to actual travel figures (based on papyri where the dates of sending and receipt are marked), "letters traveling relatively short distances seem to follow the pattern of approximately 15–20 miles per day. Longer journeys were less standard." Given their dependence on travelers' itineraries, some letters traveled ten miles a day, though another might travel fifteen miles a day and yet another a mere four miles a day.[53] Given their mission (and often their desire to stay ahead of their enemies), Paul and his companions probably traveled closer to the higher estimates, especially in their younger days.

The *mansiones* provided numerous rooms for eating and sleeping, as well as provision for travel animals.[54] "At more frequent intervals, perhaps every ten miles or so, were *mutationes*, smaller stations where official couriers could change horses and where ordinary travelers could find something to eat and a bed."[55] Inns had, however, poor reputations for their amenities and moral suitability (given the prevalence of prostitution there), rendering them less than suitable for aristocrats and most pious

47. Casson, *Travel*, 163.

48. Jeffers, *World*, 37 (for the imperial service, 25–30 miles); Riesner, *Early Period*, 310 (for vehicles, 25–30 miles, and estimating 38–45 km; and nearly 40 miles or roughly 60 km for exceptional speed). The mile and kilometer estimates (esp. from Riesner) diverge from the standard conversion because both figures, especially the miles, are rounded.

49. Richards, *Letter Writing*, 197.

50. Jeffers, *World*, 37 (15–20 miles); Riesner, *Early Period*, 311 (15–20 miles or 20–30 km).

51. Richards, *Letter Writing*, 191.

52. Ibid., 192.

53. Ibid., 198, from the Zenon papyri.

54. Stambaugh and Balch, *Environment*, 38. On inns in general, see discussion at Acts 16:15.

55. Stambaugh and Balch, *Environment*, 38.

Jews.[56] (For inns, see further comment at Acts 16:15.) Towns offered a greater variety of restaurants, baths, and accommodations (from converted "luxurious villas" to bug-infested beds).[57]

Typical roads of the Roman period in the Near East were between two and four lanes in width; some discovered in the Judean wilderness were as wide as a modern highway of five lanes.[58] People commonly transported goods by land in carts drawn by several oxen; the heaviest supplies traveled by a form of large wagon that could hold up to 1,500 Roman pounds.[59] Paved roads might include an unpaved lane about two feet wide on which pedestrians and pack animals traveled.[60]

Nevertheless, although Roman roads were suitable for "pedestrians and pack animals," "their stiff gradients" often made hauling heavier goods difficult.[61] Though some could afford donkeys, horses, or (most expensive) camels, most travelers made their journey on foot.[62] Some sorts of travelers had more experience with traveling than others did. Merchants were known for their travels and diversity of experience.[63] Those who traveled extensively also included the military, entertainers, and wandering sophists.[64] During the empire, people of means also traveled as tourists.[65] Those who traveled much would often be considered experienced and wise (Sir 31:9–12).

e. Travel and Companions

That early Christians, like others, traveled and hence carried news with them and networked the churches is almost certain, despite the almost inexplicable assumption of some NT scholars that Christian groups developed in isolation from one another in various parts of the empire.[66] Sages traveled;[67] landless Cynics were thought to travel throughout Greece, often seasonally to accommodate the weather (Max. Tyre 36.5). More commonly, merchants often unofficially spread their religion when they traveled,[68] and the same is likely for early Christians in general (Acts 8:4); that Paul's focus was on evangelism does not rule out his being also a leatherworker or tentmaker (18:3).

---

56. See Friedländer, *Life*, 1:290–93; Casson, *Travel*, 206–7, 215–18; Malherbe, *Social Aspects*, 66 (citing Kleberg, *Hôtels*, 197–218); Ramsay, "Roads and Travel," 393; cf., e.g., Cic. *Div.* 1.27.57; Sherk, *Empire*, 210–11 (including *ILS* 6036–37, 6039; *Copa* 1–6 [in *Appendix Vergiliana*]; *IG* 14.24; *CIL* 4.1679).

57. Stambaugh and Balch, *Environment*, 38.

58. Dorsey, "Roads," 432.

59. Dorsey, "Carts," 434.

60. Le Cornu, *Acts*, 708.

61. Cary and Haarhoff, *Life*, 138; for the nature of the traffic, see also Friedländer, *Life*, 1:299–303.

62. Stambaugh and Balch, *Environment*, 38; Lohse, *Environment*, 211 (adding wagons for the travel of the rich). For what travelers carried and wore, see Casson, *Travel*, 176–78.

63. See Liefeld, "Preacher," 21–22 (cf. the diverse places of origin of gifts in Mart. *Epig.* Bks. 13–14); for commercial intercourse, see Friedländer, *Life*, 304–16; Charlesworth, *Trade Routes*, 76–96 (in Asia Minor); cf. further Pleket, "Elites and Business"; and (for the transition to the medieval period) Whittaker, "Roman Trade."

64. For military travels, see, e.g., Liefeld, "Preacher," 20; for government, 20–21; intellectual or literary pursuits, 23; entertainers, 23–25; mendicant priests, 26; and sophists, 26–32.

65. See Friedländer, *Life*, 323–428; Wallace and Williams, *Worlds*, 17–18; for what interested the tourists, see esp. Friedländer, *Life*, 367–94.

66. Here I agree with, e.g., Stuhlmacher, "Theme," 16; Bauckham, "Gospels," 33–44; Thompson, "Internet," 49–70. Against the idea that Christian groups were developing in theological isolation (articulated notably by Burton Mack), see warnings in, e.g., Keck, "Ethos," 448–49; Witherington, *Sage*, 211–12. One may view eastern Mediterranean cities in the early second century in terms of a "network" (see Doukellis, "*Panhellenion*").

67. Including in fictitious texts (cf. Elsner, "Geography," though historically Apollonius surely did travel).

68. See Liefeld, "Preacher," 21–22, 26, 151; Bowers, "Propaganda," 320; Klauck, *Context*, 63–64; see comment on Acts 8:4. For the receptivity of Mediterranean antiquity to, and the mobility of, the new religions, see Stambaugh and Balch, *Environment*, 41–46.

When traveling, people often looked for suitable companions for discussion (for safety reasons, it was important to have fellow travelers).[69] Some pious Greeks would talk about the gods as they walked (Eunapius *Lives* 458). Pious Jews sought to avoid traveling with Gentile caravans traveling to idolatrous festivals (*t. 'Abod. Zar.* 1:16). Many people sought intellectual stimulation as they traveled, and so conversation was very important.[70] Sea voyages provided an easier venue for conversation and certainly for reading and writing than could travel on foot.[71] Acts includes both kinds of travel, and ancient readers would have assumed that Paul and his traveling companions probably engaged in long discussions of Scripture and, presumably, other matters as well.[72]

We can guess that Luke (the question of whether he was a physician aside!) might have recognized one positive side benefit of travel (or other physical labor) as its contribution to health, despite the dangers. Most Greeks and Romans recognized the value of exercise for health.[73] Nevertheless, "exercise" can hardly be a major factor in Luke's reports or Paul's travels. Luke provides little detail to satisfy our modern interest in this aspect of apostolic travels, except what we gain by inference.

2. Urban versus Rural Life

Although Luke's overt geographical schema in Acts leads from Jerusalem to Rome, the work also narrates the growth of a movement from culturally marginalized, rural roots in Galilee (Jesus's primary world) to urban Jerusalem (the first apostles' primary sphere of ministry)[74] and then on to prestigious urban locations in the empire (Luke's primary world), by far the most prestigious of which was the heart of the empire.[75] Luke's theological movement is from heritage to mission, but his history also reveals a sociological movement from rural to urban.[76]

Paul targeted cities, particularly significant ones such as Roman colonies (Troas, Philippi, and Corinth) and other important or strategic sites (such as Thessalonica,

69. Hock, *Social Context*, 28, cites Epict. *Diatr.* 4.1.91, for the greater safety that travel companions provided; see also *Eccl. Rab.* 3:2, §2.

70. Hock, *Social Context*, 28, cites for this Dio Chrys. *Or.* 10.1; 36.7–17; Aul. Gel. 12.5; 16.6.1; Diogenes *Ep.* 2; he also cites texts for rhetorical practice (Philost. *Vit. soph.* 618), reading (Philost. *Vit. soph.* 488; Aul. Gel. 9.4.1–5; 19.1.14), and letter writing (Sen. Y. *Ep. Lucil.* 48.1; 72.2).

71. Hock, *Social Context*, 28 (citing Aul. Gel. 2.21.1–2; Philost. *Vit. Apoll.* 6.19), who suggests that some subjects became standard on such voyages (Epict. *Diatr.* 2.19.15–16; Philost. *Vit. Apoll.* 4.15).

72. For Torah study on journeys, cf. *b. Ḥag.* 12a; 14a; *'Erub.* 54b (Talbert, *Acts*, 76). For Torah as the ideal focus of devout Jewish conversation, see, most fundamentally, Deut 6:7; cf., e.g., Sir 9:15; *m. 'Abot* 3:2–3; *'Abot R. Nat.* 26, 29 A; 32, §68 B; *y. Ta'an.* 3:11, §4; *Lev. Rab.* 12:1; Safrai, "Education," 968–69.

73. E.g., Plato *Lach.* 182A; Xen. *Cyr.* 1.6.17; *Mem.* 1.2.4; *Symp.* 2.17–19; Isoc. *Demon.* 14; *Ep.* 84.1; Plut. *Cic.* 4.3; 8.3; *Table* 4.1.3, *Mor.* 662F; Soranus *Gynec.* 1.5.25; Fronto *Pr. Hist.* 11; Crates *Ep.* 20; Diog. Laert. 6.2.70; 7.1.123; Philost. *Vit. soph.* 2.17.598; *Hrk.* 33.14–18; Char. *Chaer.* 1.1.5.

74. Luke mentions Jerusalem twice as much "as any other Gospel writer" (Rohrbaugh, "Pre-industrial City," 148; though his writings also have 60 percent of NT uses of χώρα [Oakman, "Countryside," 151]). Sepphoris and Tiberias were urban but much smaller (see, e.g., Reed, *Archaeology*, 96).

75. Cf., e.g., Schmeller, "Weg der Jesusbotschaft"; Osiek, "City." For a Roman audience, Jesus's life in Galilee (Judea's "frontier") and his execution through corrupt priests in Jerusalem would seem insignificant; the geographic action was in Rome (cf., e.g., Philost. *Vit. Apoll.* Bks. 7–8, the climax of the work, as Apollonius goes to Rome). Luke thus can make Paul's arrival in Rome climactic (though omitting the trial that Philostratus later emphasizes for Apollonius's "passion").

76. For urban and rural life (and their interdependence) in the NT (and early Christianity), see recently Carter, *Empire*, 44–63. Cf. discussion of cities in Millar, *Empire and Neighbours*, 81–103. Narrative movement itself was not unusual (cf., e.g., 1 Maccabees, as opposed to 2 Maccabees, in Schwartz, "Maccabees and Acts," 121–24).

Athens, and Ephesus).[77] Ambitious sophists or rhetoricians would have done the same, and for them, as for Paul, there was no more influential geographic goal to reach than Rome itself.[78] In contrast to the degree of change in some urban environments,[79] most rural communities proved conservative and their values resilient; poverty was too endemic to risk social experimentation.[80] That cities were more open to change provided Paul a more natural inroad into them with the gospel[81] (though once christianization did take hold in rural areas,[82] it proved particularly tenacious there).[83] Interpreters in the Roman Empire would have naturally understood this: Paul and Silas "pass through the small towns and hurry to the biggest," Chrysostom observes, "since the word was to flow to nearby cities as from a source."[84]

That Luke highlights urban centers (including Jerusalem) probably gives some indication of the cultural presuppositions of his implied audience. Luke writes Acts from an urban Mediterranean perspective, with an urban ideal audience in view.[85] Historians who wrote in urban centers, where more books and oral sources were available, had an advantage over those from smaller towns (Plut. *Demosth.* 2.1–2). Just how steep was the chasm between urban and rural perceptions in antiquity?

a. Urbanization and Cultural Chasms

Urbanites were limited to about a thousand towns and cities, the collective population of which may have constituted only 10 percent[86] or 15 percent[87] or 20 percent[88] of the empire's population. Outside the Greco-Roman cities, rural culture often reflected the persistence of earlier local cultures (such as those with Syrian and Middle Eastern roots).[89] Still, small towns and villages in Greece may have experienced little isolation

---

77. As often noted, e.g., Mitchell, *Anatolia*, 2:8; with consideration of particular texts, Klauck, "Urbane Frömmigkeit"; Baird, *Corinthian Church*. Earlier, see John Chrysostom in *Cat. Act.* 17.1 (Martin, *Acts*, 211), who notes that Paul targeted the largest cities, which would exert the greatest influence. Missiologists sometimes employ Paul as a model for urban church planting (e.g., Greenway, "Success," 192).

78. Mitchell, *Anatolia*, 2:8. (This focus on Rome contrasts starkly with many novels; cf., e.g., Schwartz, "Rome in Novel.")

79. For cultural mixing in cities, see, e.g., Libanius *Comparison* 5.16.

80. MacMullen, *Social Relations*, 27. For rural (and urban) poverty, see the discussion at Acts 3:2.

81. Christians still were having an impact mainly on the cities into the early second century (Judge, *Pattern*, 60–61).

82. Pliny the Younger complains that this is already occurring in Bithynia (*Ep.* 10.96.9).

83. Also observed in most situations of dramatic urbanization today; see Grigg, *Urban Poor*, 10–11; Greenway, "Urban Church Planting," 15–16.

84. John Chrysostom in *Cat. Act.* 17.1 (Martin, *Acts*, 211).

85. As others recognize (cf., e.g., Botha, "Community"). Luke's knowledge of Palestine is likewise especially of Caesarea and Jerusalem (see Hengel, *Jesus and Paul*, 97–128; Witherington, *Acts*, 227; cf. Hengel, "Geography of Palestine," 32–33); if he was a Gentile, he probably could not travel alone as safely in the interior of Judea ca. 60 C.E. He may apply the title πόλις too freely, especially in the Gospel (see Oakman, "Countryside," 170; but cf. the comments of Judge, *Pattern*, 14), but his usage is hardly unusual (see, e.g., Hierocles *Elements of Ethics* 11.16–17).

86. Malina, *Anthropology*, 72–73; cf. Horsley and Hanson, *Bandits*, xii (following Sjoberg, *Preindustrial City*, 110). Rohrbaugh, "Pre-industrial City," 133, even suggests 5–7 percent (for cities). Cary and Haarhoff, *Life*, 103, speak of "thousands" of towns but doubt that most had more than 50,000. MacMullen estimates that outside perhaps ten major cities, most "cities" averaged perhaps 20,000 (*Social Relations*, 57).

87. Toner, *Culture*, 3 (speaking only of the majority nonelite there).

88. Jeffers, *World*, 48. Suburbs tended to function as an extension, or population spillover, from city walls rather than as rural or intermediate areas (for Rome, see Witcher, "Extended Metropolis"). Perhaps 80 percent of Mediterranean antiquity's population worked in agriculture (Reden, "Work," 740, extrapolating from early modern societies).

89. Rajak, "Location," 11–13; Jeffers, *World*, 49. See comments on local languages at Acts 14:14; for similar dynamics between the two hellenized cities in Galilee and the majority population there, see Horsley, *Galilee*, 163; Freyne, *Galilee, Jesus*, 146–47; cultural differences between towns and cities in *m. Meg.* 1:3.

from knowledge of the larger Roman world.[90] Numerous scholars, in fact, argue that many of the rural peasants worked estates owned by absentee (often urban) landlords.[91]

When traditional societies with extended kin networks face rapid urbanization, the contrast between the two models of life (and often between two generations in the cities) is stark and the demands on urban support systems overwhelming. For example, many first-generation urbanites in Africa maintain primary ties with their village kin networks and are expected to provide extensive support to those in the villages and to house younger extended kin who come to seek education in the cities (demands that sometimes limit the advancement of the urbanites unless they indulge in forms of corruption). The growth of shantytowns, inadequate waste disposal, shortages of drinkable water (and sometimes other water as well), electricity (today), and other resources become part of normal life, and tribal or clan loyalties can be imported (for at least a generation).[92]

The first-century Mediterranean world probably differed, however, from the modern societal chasm spawned by urbanization in many respects.[93] For example, Roman historians' reports of census records (cf. comment on Acts 28:16) render questionable whether the pace of urbanization was so dramatic in most places (although it was quite dramatic in places such as second-century Ephesus); further, extended kin networks, though more important than in the modern West, were less significant than in much of Africa and Asia.[94]

Nevertheless, sources do suggest massive migration to cities in antiquity as well[95] (its population effects perhaps offset somewhat by high mortality). These modern phenomena illustrate the sharp contrast that could exist between urban and rural societies, especially once urbanites grew separate from rural norms and values over the course of several generations. Peasants who moved to the cities as artisans "lost the status and protection of their previous connections," including the land and extended-kin support.[96] The census records of antiquity that are mentioned above suggest much higher population figures[97] than modern estimates based on water supplies; this may be because ancient city dwellers lived on less water than we deem feasible today.[98]

90. Cf. Apuleius's *Metamorphoses* (second century C.E.) (as noted by Millar, "World of *Ass*").

91. E.g., Lee, "Unrest," 127. For a discussion of rural peasants and their economic situation, see comment at Acts 3:2.

92. On urbanization, cf., e.g., Linden, "Cities"; Wallace, *Urban Environment*, 126–27; Bakke, *Urban Christian*, 35–36. On the centrality of kin networks in anthropological analyses, see, e.g., essays in Radcliffe-Brown and Forde, *Systems*; Graburn, *Readings*; Needham, *Rethinking*; various articles, e.g., Yalman, "Structure"; Tyler, "Context"; Cunningham, "Categories"; Lucas, "Influence"; Frisch and Schutz, "Analysis"; Petersen, "Kin Research"; Kitaoji, "Structure"; Schusky, *Manual*; Bieder, "Kinship"; Kuznecov, "Typology"; Tzeng, Osgood, and May, "Differences"; Lewin, "Implications." Kinship structures can maintain a degree of continuity (e.g., Pinson, "Kinship"; Hecht, "Kinship," 65; Hammel, "Change"; limited change in Foster, "Continuity") but also change, due to urbanization, modernization, and other factors (Ember, "Descent Groups," 577; Pasternak, "Atrophy"; Heiskanan, "Structure"; Taylor, "Family," 302; Vatuk, "Trends," 306; Kottak, "Adaptation," 141–44; Banks, "Kinship"; McGaffey, "Structure"; Hilton, "Family."

93. Extrapolations from modern sociology have some benefit but are limited, given potential differences among societies; see, e.g., Malherbe, *Social Aspects*, 11–13; Stanton, *New People*, 85; Winter, *Left Corinth*, xiii; Harland, *Associations*, 15. There remain also continuing debates among various ideological grids for the sociology of Greco-Roman antiquity (e.g., Morrall, "Marx and Weber"; Wood, "Marxism and Greece"; Oakes, "Weber's *Sociology*").

94. Though extended families had significance (Saller and Shaw, "Tombstones"; Martin, "Slave Families," 208–13), epigraphic evidence indicates that nuclear families were more prominent, including in Rome (Garnsey and Saller, *Empire*, 129; Stambaugh, *City*, 158; Rawson, "Family," 7), Roman Asia (Martin, "Slave Families," 208), and Galilee (Goodman, *State*, 36). Also problematic for modern studies is the difficulty of reconstructing ancient kinship patterns, given limited extant evidence; see, e.g., Allen and Richardson, "Reconstruction"; Bryce, "Terms."

95. See Onken, "Rural exodus."

96. Rohrbaugh, "Pre-industrial City," 127–28 (quotation, 128).

97. For Rome, see discussion at Acts 28:16.

98. In addition to being smaller physically, most of those who survived childhood were perhaps able to adapt to conditions as do many in the Majority World today—with the caveat that then, as today, many proved

Although taxes, soldiers, and other forms of romanization in the West and hellenization in the East made inroads even into the countryside, local languages and customs persisted.[99] An urban traveler to the countryside might find difficulty in making himself understood, apart from rich villas.[100] "Many inhabitants of the empire had little experience or conception of Rome."[101] The division in society was clear:

> Roman civilization was an urban phenomenon, built on the agricultural surplus from the countryside. Not only did the cities exploit the countryside to feed and clothe their residents, but the urban dwellers, a small minority of the whole population, were also contemptuous of the masses as "rustics," who were unacquainted with the sophisticated culture of urban life and often literally spoke a different language.[102]

As for immigrants to the cities, some cultures could remain permanently alienated resident aliens, though in some cities (e.g., in Roman Asia) their children might become more acculturated and a part of civic life. In "language and nomenclature, diet and lifestyle, cults and patterns of authority," villagers in Asia Minor inhabited a different world than townspeople; urban people often despised rural people, and some urban authorities apparently extorted from villagers.[103]

The largest cities, such as Rome, subsisted heavily on the produce derived from the countryside.[104] Population density was probably as high in Rome as in modern Calcutta,[105] and life expectancy was lower there than in the countryside ("because of the poor sanitation, the dirt and the noise, and the general lack of medical care").[106] Urban overcrowding affected not only physical but also mental health.[107] Given the cosmopolitan knowledge presupposed in Acts, Luke's audience was undoubtedly urban and not rural.

b. Urban Disdain for Rural Life

MacMullen notes that the urban Roman world regarded inhabitants of the countryside as "clumsy, brutish, ignorant, uncivilized," and the rural Roman world regarded those who lived in cities "as baffling, extortionate, arrogant."[108]

---

more susceptible to disease. On the inequities of water distribution today, see, e.g., "Politics of Thirst"; "Wars over Water?"; "Water: Medicine"; "Clean Water."

99. Garnsey and Saller, *Empire*, 192–94 (especially on Punic-speaking peasants in North Africa six hundred years after Rome's conquest [p. 193]).

100. MacMullen, *Social Relations*, 45–46, citing the prevalence of Punic (cf. comment on Acts 28:2), Aramaic (cf. comment on Acts 21:40), Phrygian (cf. comment on Acts 14:11), and other languages. He also notes some papyrus references in Alexandria to thrusting out Egyptian countryfolk for their speech.

101. Garnsey and Saller, *Empire*, 203.

102. Ibid., 119. For the contrasts between urban and rural life, see Ps.-Theocritus *The Young Countryman* passim (*GBP* 238–43); and at length Finley, *Economy*, 123–49. Others also remark on the mutual contempt and mistrust (Meeks, *Moral World*, 38; in some Jewish sources, see Applebaum, "Economic Life," 663–64; Neusner, *Beginning*, 24–25).

103. See Mitchell, *Anatolia*, 1:195.

104. See, e.g., Garnsey and Saller, *Empire*, 119; Polyb. 1.71.1–2; but cf. the counterbalance to this perspective in Engels, *Roman Corinth*, 131–42 (cities such as Corinth subsisted primarily on trade, not on the countryside, which could not have supported Corinth, in any case). For Rome's grain dole, see Kraybill, *Cult and Commerce*, 66, 107; Casson, *Mariners*, 207.

105. Stambaugh, *City*, 90; on difficulties of overcrowding there, see Toner, *Culture*, 129, 134. On high population density in ancient cities more generally, see, e.g., Stark, *Cities*, 27.

106. Stambaugh, *City*, 89–90.

107. See Toner, *Culture*, 64.

108. MacMullen, *Social Relations*, 15; cf. 32 (where city dwellers were viewed as natural enemies). Nevertheless, the empire could economically exploit the produce of the countryside to support the cities (MacMullen, *Social Relations*, 48–56; Garnsey and Saller, *Empire*, 119); but while this was true of Rome, it was probably not so true of cities such as mercantile Corinth (Engels, *Roman Corinth*, 131–42). Most of the empire's labor force was farmers, mostly living at subsistence level (Garnsey and Saller, *Empire*, 43–46).

From the perspective of an empire ruled from Rome, however, cities held higher status than mere communities.[109] Few of the hundreds of towns throughout the empire held more than fifty thousand residents, but urban life was probably roughly comparable with that in eighteenth- and early nineteenth-century Europe.[110] Although only a minority of people lived in the cities, urbanites exerted a broader cultural influence, and historians can argue that "the civilization of the Greeks and Romans was essentially urban."[111]

Elite intellectuals expected more education, though not always more wisdom, in the cities. One writer praised an unusual country dweller whose learning seemed more at place in Athens than in the countryside (Pliny *Ep.* 7.25.4–6). Country dwellers, like women and minors, were less culpable under Roman law because they were less apt to understand it.[112] Thus in one satire Pan, a rural deity, notes that he is not clever like urbanites.[113] Some viewed the building of cities as special signs of human reason and cooperation (Ael. Arist. *Def. Or.* 398, §135D). (Yet contrary to some modern expectations, ancient urban populations seemed no less interested in miraculous reports than were rural ones.)[114]

Perspectives varied sufficiently to allow opposing views of the importance of rural life to be a standard debating topic (Max. Tyre 23–24).[115] However urbanites might have viewed the low status and exposure of agrarian peasants, they respected their work[116] and, at least in Rome, held fond memories of a former, largely bucolic existence and its comparatively stern traditional values. Certainly in the first century B.C.E., to despise farmers did not play well in Rome, where Cicero could expect Verres's disdain for "mere" farmers to stir anger (*Verr.* 2.2.61.149).

Those converted to philosophy might be thought likely to turn against farming,[117] a stereotype with some foundation in Stoic teaching. Stoics compared worthless persons to rustics; just as rustics were unfamiliar with urban laws, so worthless people were uninformed.[118] Yet some philosophers, by contrast, felt that urban evils distracted students from learning philosophy.[119] It was said that Apollonius disliked city life because of its luxury, preferring a smaller town (Philost. *Vit. Apoll.* 1.7).

c. Rustic Simplicity

In the first century C.E., Seneca the Younger notes that his health is improving now that he has "escaped from the oppressive atmosphere of the city, and from that awful odour of reeking kitchens which, when in use, pour forth a ruinous mess of steam and soot" (*Ep. Lucil.* 104.6 [LCL]).[120] Seneca did note, though, that despite the

109. See Garnsey and Saller, *Empire*, 27–32; cf. Purcell, "Vicus." For the functions of cities, see Garnsey and Saller, *Empire*, 32–34.

110. Cary and Haarhoff, *Life*, 103, 107.

111. Ibid., 103.

112. Robinson, *Criminal Law*, 17. MacMullen, *Social Relations*, 46, notes that even laws sometimes despised country dwellers.

113. Lucian *Indictment* 11.

114. Theissen, *Miracle Stories*, 247.

115. E.g., the warrior Scythians are free, but Egyptian farmers are under others' domination (Max. Tyre *Or.* 23.4). But the opposed views clearly climax in favor of the farmers (*Or.* 24).

116. See, e.g., Dio Chrys. *Or.* 70.1. See further comment below.

117. Alciph. *Farm.* 11 (Sitalces to Oenopion, his son), 3.14; 38 (Euthydicus to Philiscus), 3.40, ¶3.

118. Arius Did. *Epit.* 2.7.11k, pp. 80–81.12–15. Such persons were also "wild" and "bestial" (lines 15–17). Nor is this purely a theoretical comparison; cities, in their function as places ruled by laws, are places of civilization (2.7.11i, pp. 80–81.1–11).

119. Mus. Ruf. 11, p. 84.10–11. Musonius also believed that rural workers were stronger than urban because of their labor (18B, p. 118.36–120.1; cf. 18B, p. 120.2–5).

120. A city could assign an orator to declaim on how Scythian life was superior to cramped and smelly city life (Philost. *Vit. soph.* 2.5.573) or how those with bad health in the plains should move to the mountains (2.5.575).

value of fleeing from society's folly, life in the countryside does not by itself make one think virtuously (94.69).[121] Others also seem to have appreciated the benefits of agricultural life (Ps.-Phoc. 161) or they suggested that the dangers of the urban environment outweigh its advantages (Babr. 108).[122]

Many in the cities, in fact, portrayed pastoral life as pristine and paradisiacal (e.g., in Longus's *Daphnis and Chloe*). In eighth-century B.C.E. Greece, Hesiod "contrasts the goodness of the village engaged in agricultural work with the evil of the city-state occupied by war and the shipping trade."[123] In the first century B.C.E., the Roman poet Horace celebrated "the Roman agrarian ideal of the late Republic"; the happiest life was on a family farm like the earliest of peoples (*Ep.* 11).[124] Paul's contemporary Seneca the Younger portrays Hippolytus as claiming rural life to be more ancient, free, and pure (*Phaed.* 483–85), imitating the days when mortals lived together with the deities (525–28). The rural cult of Silvanus became popular among the poor of the cities in the second and third centuries C.E., probably indicating nostalgia for the simpler life of the country and a longing to escape the wretchedness of ancient urban existence.[125]

Dio Chrysostom, though urban, met rural people during his time of exile under Domitian and composed an oration based (however loosely) on his association with them. A rural person could tell that Dio was from a city despite his wearing rags (Dio Chrys. *Or.* 7.8). One rural man had never been to town, and the other only twice (once as a boy and once when he was mistreated by some urban people; 7.21). The second rural person showed hospitality to someone from the town demanding tax (7.22) and then, by contrast, nearly met a sorry fate in the town (7.29–33). In Dio's idealization, the poor man in the ensuing debate tries to reason with the crowd yet misunderstands them at every turn because their concepts, especially about money, are so foreign (7.44, 48–49, 60–61).[126] Dio concludes that countryfolk, enjoying their hospitality and simple pleasures, are the happiest of people (7.65–66) and that the poor are better off than the rich (7.81).[127] This is an idealization, but it reveals the deep cultural chasm between urban and rural lifestyles.

Some ancients opined that urbanites envied the simplicity of the rustic lifestyle no less than farmers did that of city dwellers (Max. Tyre 15.1).[128] Many viewed farmers as hardworking and strong (24.6; cf. 25.1).[129] Thus Cicero, arguing that a client was not greedy, claimed that he "always lived in the country and occupied himself with the cultivation of his land"; such is a life of duty, not of avarice (*Rosc. Amer.* 14.39). Rural dwellers were also more inclined toward values like sharing with neighbors their own surpluses, values that were sometimes even translated by urban observers into the language of ideal philosophic ethics.[130] This generosity,

---

121. Seneca also opined that busy city life increased one's need for a wise counselor nearby (*Ep. Lucil.* 94.72).

122. Cf. the debate topic in Libanius *Comparison* 4–5 (for superior morality, esp. 5.5–9, 17–18); *Encomium* 7 (for superior morality, 7.5). Agriculture was central to Palestinian Jewish life (Jos. *Ag. Ap.* 1.60).

123. Oakman, "Countryside," 152, on Hesiod *W.D.* 225–47.

124. Oakman, "Countryside," 152–53 (quote, 152).

125. Klauck, *Context*, 29.

126. A countryperson might also think cities too congested (Dio Chrys. *Or.* 7.50) or learn by experience that people in cities do not greet with kisses as in the countryside (7.59).

127. Among the poor, he includes farmers, hunters, and shepherds—i.e., rural occupations.

128. On country villas, see, e.g., Cary and Haarhoff, *Life*, 101.

129. Alciph. *Farm.* passim shows that urbanites knew the hardships of farmers. Some urbanites opined that although farming should produce fruit for the farmers (Max. Tyre 25.5; 1 Cor 9:10; 2 Tim 2:6), farmers should seek merely the produce, not a profit (Max. Tyre 24.3).

130. Alciph. *Farm.* 5 (Agelarchides to Pytholaüs), 1.26, ¶1; 12 (Cotinus to Trygodorus), 3.15; 27 (Ampelion to Euergus), 3.30, ¶3; 29 (Comarchides to Euchaetes), 3.73, ¶2.

along with the utter naiveté of some about city life,[131] could render them gullible and easily exploited by urban hucksters;[132] villagers who exploited their neighbors were seen no longer as honest farmers but as urban orators.[133] Some people idealized rural dwellers as more simple, with a wisdom expressed not in rhetoric but through their very lives.[134]

Such views also affected Jewish thinkers even in urban Alexandria. The *Letter of Aristeas* opines that urban life leads to neglect of the land and to a hedonistic philosophy (*Let. Aris.* 108),[135] and laments that such has overtaken Alexandria (*Let. Aris.* 109). Although Philo is somewhat ambivalent,[136] he portrays the Essenes as preferring traditional rural values of sharing and as avoiding cities because of their sinfulness (*Good Person* 76).[137] But these are themselves urban authors lamenting the decadence of urban life.[138]

d. Despising Cities

Urban literature also portrayed rural people content with their lives and despising the cities. One novel portrays the horrible fate of a rural girl as being forced to "live in a city" (πόλιν οἰκήσει; compared to the horrible fate of sheep and goats being killed [Longus 2.22]). Elsewhere one farmer is portrayed as warning his son to avoid philosophers, who do nothing useful for humanity; he should stick to his farmwork and guarantee having sufficient food.[139]

Another artificial character protests that a woman has abandoned their way of life and Pan and the nymphs for new gods and urban life; she is becoming crazy, addicted to luxury.[140] Another pleads with her husband to stop idling away his time in the town and return to help with the farm.[141] A semidivine hero whose plot a gardener had once tilled became angry with the gardener for moving to a city and obtaining education there (Philost. *Hrk.* 4.6–10). But now, when an outsider feels that he has wrongly demeaned the gardener by characterizing him as a mere "vinedresser" (4.11), the gardener (and the hero for whom he works) values the title (4.12). A shoreline fisherman threatens to divorce his wife unless she stops running to shows in the city and learns to be content as a fisherman's wife.[142] One scholar comments,

131. Alciph. *Farm.* 17 (Napaeus to Creniades), 3.20, ¶¶2–3; 28 (Philocomus to Astyllus), 3.31, ¶¶1–2. A son beseeches his mother not to die before she has come and seen the beauty of the city (37 [Philometor to Epiphanium], 3.39).

132. Cf., e.g., Alciph. *Farm.* 5 (Agelarchides to Pytholaüs), 1.26, ¶3; 17 (Napaeus to Creniades), 3.20, ¶¶2–3. But people criticized gullibility wherever it was found, even in an emperor (Tac. *Ann.* 16.2). A country-dweller might charge that rich city-dwellers could treat rustics as exotic, like persons deformed or with different colorations (Quint. *Decl.* 298.12).

133. Alciph. *Farm.* 26 (Orius to Anthophorion), 3.29, ¶¶1–2.

134. Aelian *Farmers* 20 (Phaedrius to Sthenon).

135. Perhaps an anti-Epicurean sentiment (cf. *Let. Aris.* 223), though the sentiment can be more widespread (for its Aristotelian source, see Hadas, *Aristeas*, 143, 187).

136. E.g., contrasting the good and the evil city (Runia, "City").

137. On cities' alleged sinfulness, cf. Plato *Laws* 3.677B; in Rome, Lucian *Nigr.* 16; on Rome's distractions for philosophers, Epict. *Diatr.* 1.26.8–12. One should not, however, read Rom 1:24–32 as Paul's view of Rome specifically (as in Deissmann, *Light*, 283); it is simply a conventional vice list.

138. Third- and fourth-century Palestinian rabbis are also mostly urban and elite (Lapin, "Rabbis and Cities").

139. Alciph. *Farm.* 11 (Sitalces to Oenopion, his son), 3.14 (cf. 38 [Euthydicus to Philiscus], 3.40, ¶3). A farmer's wife pleads with her son to abandon notions of being a soldier, to prefer safety and food, and to care for his aged parents (13 [Phyllis to Thrasonides], 3.16). Likewise, a rural father disowns his son when he discovers him an urban parasite (Quint. *Decl.* 298 intro; 298.4–6), denouncing urban vices (298.10).

140. Alciph. *Farm.* 8 (Dryantidas to Chronium), 3.11, ¶¶1, 3.

141. Alciph. *Farm.* 22 (Hylê to Nomius), 3.25.

142. Alciph. *Fish.* 4 (Cymothoüs to Tritonis), 1.4, ¶4.

Introduction

Although a kind of "urbaphobia" was manifested by the urban clients (this would certainly be true of Juvenal), a smoldering hatred of the city was added by the peasants to the lengthening list of social tensions within the Empire. In part, their hatred of the city stemmed from the fact that the exploiters lived there; but more important was the fact that the city represented a specially privileged, even pampered society from which the peasants felt they had been systematically excluded. They felt totally alienated from the culture and society of the urban centers, and as more and more rights and exemptions were lavished upon these centers by the emperors—usually at the peasants' expense—their hatred of the city became more intense.[143]

Conclusion

Luke's first audience would understand the difficulties of travel in ways that we often do not, and hence would recognize the lengths to which Paul went to reach new areas. The contrast between urban and rural communities also highlights dimensions of Paul's travels and ministry; although he focused his ministry on towns and especially cities, much of the territory through which he traveled when evangelizing Phrygia was rural and foreign to his own background.

---

143. Lee, "Unrest," 128, noting that the most rural province, Egypt, was full of unrest and anti-urban sentiment. On urban unrest (especially in a later period), see more fully MacMullen, *Enemies*, 163–91.

596

18

LUKE'S PERSPECTIVE
ON WOMEN AND GENDER

Wˢhat was intended as an excursus on Acts 1:14 has grown to such length that I felt constrained to include it instead as a separate chapter within the introduction. It was impossible for me in a brief excursus to survey the background material and also provide sufficient nuance for one of antiquity's more complex topics; the ancient material is too diverse and too vast to be treated in the summary fashion I have assigned to some other topics, even if the passages that they help us understand in Luke are fewer than, for example, those focused on the Gentile mission. The discussion here, and especially the exploration of ancient sources, is meant to offer background useful not only for 1:14 but for a range of other passages, most significantly 2:17–18; 8:3, 12; 9:2; 13:50; 16:13–15; 17:4, 12, 34; 18:3; and 18:26.

1. Gender in Luke-Acts

Scholars differ considerably in their evaluation of Luke's approach to women. Is his approach "positive" or "negative"? This question is significant in contemporary discussions of Luke's theology and ethics. Although we have examined questions usually associated with Luke's historical reliability, for many interpreters today the question of Luke's approach to gender is a matter of his theological reliability, a question of greater importance to them. My approach here as in the rest of the commentary is primarily historical, but the interests of many readers invite consideration of the topic. This chapter is primarily a historical exploration to provide perspective on Luke's approaches to gender, but gender is also a topic of much theological interest today. At the same time, the topic is important with respect to Luke's historiography; historians' views toward women in their own day often helped shape the way they selected and presented the actions of women in their narratives.[1]

From a historical standpoint (the commentary's primary focus), what concerns us directly is where Luke stands among the range of perspectives in his culture. For those with hermeneutical concerns beyond the first-century meaning, the historical question remains a crucial starting point. If Luke was among the more progressive voices of his era and his foundational statements (e.g., Acts 2:17–18) are supportive

---

1. See the examples in Milnor, "Women."

of women, we might expect Luke to have been supportive also of more flexible arrangements in other cultures had the question ever been put to him and had he had opportunity to consider it. Thus interpreters interested in the counsel of respected ancient voices frequently can work from historical information to extrapolate theological or philosophic perspectives useful for their own contexts.

But before interpreters can come to such conclusions historically, they must investigate both what Luke says and what the range of views was in his culture. Given this commentary's focus on providing historical information less available to students of the NT, I will spend more space on the latter, though this will represent only a brief survey compared to the many books that have been written. I will not take time to explore the hermeneutical concerns and expand an already extensive commentary further, although I will state briefly where I think the evidence points.[2]

a. The Debate

Scholars debate Luke's view toward women; as A.-J. Levine summarizes, "Like the Gospel of Luke, the Acts of the Apostles has its feminist advocates and its feminist detractors."[3] Though some have been skeptical that Luke is positive toward women, and others are somewhat ambivalent,[4] I would argue that those who see Luke as positive toward women seem to have the better case, on the whole.[5] Part of the dispute among adherents of these views may be a matter of definition.[6] Luke may not have been a modern egalitarian (he could not have had the advantage of even exposure to that perspective), but if he is read in the context of his own time, he surely would have seen his special attention to women as supporting their cause. Jesus's support for women in Luke's Gospel (fitting the gospel tradition more generally; see, e.g., Mark 5:34; 10:11; 14:9; 15:40–41) may fit the pattern of his supporting marginalized groups; certainly, women were marginalized from the power structures of Luke's day.[7]

Scholars frequently comment on Luke's positive interest in women.[8] Luke often mentions women followers along with the central group of male followers (Luke

---

2. For the record, my own theological perspective to gender is egalitarian, and I have explored such questions in other works (e.g., Keener, *Paul*; idem, "Perspective"). My effort here, however, is to focus on providing as evenhanded a survey of the historical evidence as is possible, a survey that I hope even those who disagree (whether with my contemporary egalitarian application or my view that Luke was among the more, rather than less, progressive of first-century authors) will find helpful.

3. Levine, "Introduction to *Companion*," 1. For one survey of several approaches (esp. to Acts 6:1–7 and Luke 10:38–42), see Koperski, "Women and Discipleship"; more recent studies include Howes, "Handelinge."

4. Cf. Melzer-Keller, "Frauen" (ambivalent vs. highly positive). Beck, "Women," 281, sees Acts as more androcentric than other NT works but (300–304) also recognizes positive female role models. Ringe, *Luke*, 3, 8, 11–12, 112 (esp. 12, on Luke 24), notes both positive and negative traits, although her view appears ultimately more positive. D'Angelo, "Redactional View," thinks Luke ambiguous but more restrictive than Mark or John. Reid, *Choosing*, 205, concludes that Luke portrays women as primarily silent, so that a feminist approach must read the narrative "against Luke's intent." She acknowledges the positive side of Luke's portrayal but believes that the message is often mixed and must be recontextualized for new settings (206–7); most interpreters (whatever their view of Luke's perspective on gender roles) would concur with the importance of cultural recontextualization.

5. E.g., O'Toole, *Unity of Theology*, 118–26 (by comparison with his, not our, era, 125); Sweetland, "Luke the Christian," 60–61; Gaventa, *Acts*, 43–44; Allen, *Preaching*, 107–22; Bock, *Theology*, 344–52; cf. Kee, *Origins*, 91; Rigato, "Donna." Pelikan, *Acts*, 205, is positive (but cf. the limitation [206]).

6. Cf. Arlandson, *Women*, 117, who notes that the level of a woman's experience of oppression depended on her class (citing the contrast between plantation slaves and a female plantation owner); cf. the insights of womanist theologians, esp. here Grant, *Black Women's Jesus*.

7. Sweetland, "Luke the Christian," 60–61; see ch. 15 (sect. 3).

8. E.g., Tannehill, *Luke*, 132–39; Danker, *Luke*, 58; Flanagan, "Women in Luke"; Maly, "Women and Luke"; Witherington, *Acts*, 334–39; Kee, *Origins*, 91; cf. Langner, *Hechos*, 46.

8:2–3;[9] 23:49, 55) or as converts (Acts 16:13; 17:4, 12, 34) and includes pairings of men and women in prophecy (Luke 2:25–38; Acts 21:9–11), healing stories (Luke 8:40–56; 13:11–16; Acts 9:32–42; cf. Luke 7:11–15),[10] and parables (Luke 13:18–21; 15:4–10; 18:2–8).[11] Even in the opening chapter of his Gospel, Luke balances annunciations to Zechariah and Mary (with Mary portrayed more favorably; 1:18–20, 34–38; see ch. 16, sect. 1.c.ii, above), and both Elizabeth and Zechariah are filled with the Holy Spirit and speak for God in 1:41–45, 67–79. In contrast to Matthew's annunciation narrative (admittedly unknown to Luke), Luke focuses more on Mary than on Joseph. Mary as God's "servant" on whom the Spirit comes (1:35, 38) foreshadows the people of Pentecost (Acts 2:18) and hence becomes an ideal model for all followers of her son.

This positive interest in women characters becomes more striking when we consider the roles of women accepted in the Greco-Roman world at this time.[12] Their roles varied according to region and social class, but Luke's portraits rank among the more progressive voices of his day, even if these voices do not seem progressive when measured against the achievements of women in our own era.[13] Bonnie Thurston correctly observes that women had more freedom under Roman law than in the East, and Acts appears to presuppose an audience especially in more romanized urban centers.[14] Beverly Gaventa concludes that Luke-Acts fares well by the standards of other ancient narratives: women in Dionysius of Halicarnassus's history, *Roman Antiquities*, and Chariton's novel, *Chaereas and Callirhoe*, appear mostly in terms of their relations to male relatives, whereas the women in Acts appear in this connection fairly rarely.[15] (We do not know who constituted Lydia's "household" any more than we can answer this question for Cornelius or for the unnamed Philippian jailer.) Indeed, given Luke's emphasis on people of status wherever possible, his emphasis on women (not only those of status, though naturally his interests intersect at that point) seems remarkable.

Luke's sources may also reflect a pre-Lukan interest in gender egalitarianism that emerged in the earliest decades of the Christian movement.[16] Such an egalitarianism may have grown out of Jesus's teachings[17] but also from a shared experience,

9. The question of these disciples' gender in Luke 8:2–3 is not peripheral, since the unit follows on the heels of a woman protagonist in 7:36–50 (only their gender, not their social status, is in common). In contrast to the woman of Luke 7, however, these women are portrayed as benefactresses; contrary to later tradition, Mary Magdalene is certainly not a prostitute (see, e.g., Reid, *Choosing*, 125, 129, also rightly noting [130] that their sharing possessions fits the paradigm for discipleship in Luke-Acts).

10. Women appear in ancient healing reports (e.g., Epid. inscr. 4), but even here men normally outnumber them (see in Grant, *Religions*, 57).

11. Such balancing is often noted; e.g., Flender, *Theologian*, 9–10; Kistemaker, *Acts*, 783; Stricher, "Parallels"; Spencer, *Gospel and Acts*, 41–43. Shillington, *Introduction*, 105, estimates that women may constitute only roughly a quarter of the persons featured in the Gospel, but in Mark they are less than 15 percent and in Matthew just more than 17 percent; for comparisons with other ancient sources, see discussion below.

12. Some other ancient works also balance stories about men and women; e.g., b. *'Erub.* 53a–54a (see Valler, "Talk").

13. On gender roles in Greco-Roman antiquity, see, e.g., Keener, "Marriage," 687–91.

14. Thurston, *Widows*, 28. This fits our proposed audience, dominated by churches in Philippi and Corinth and others in their region.

15. Gaventa, *Acts*, 44; idem, "Daughters," 53–56 (noting also [55] that Luke gives little attention to female characters' appearance). For another comparison, Josephus usually plays down women's roles in Israel's history, though he accentuates Abigail (Begg, "Abigail Story"); on women in Tobit (as strong characters guarding their people), see Levine, "Women in Tobit." Luke says little about women's beauty or sexuality, major concerns of the romances, where women almost always figure heavily.

16. For suggestions of this egalitarianism see, e.g., Stambaugh and Balch, *Environment*, 55; Beavis, "Origins."

17. Sometimes Q material reveals male-female pairing (e.g., Luke 13:18–20/Matt 13:31–33; Luke 17:26–35/Matt 24:37–41; see Michaels, "Pairs and Parallels"; Flender, *Theologian*, 9–10).

among both genders, of prophetic inspiration (Acts 2:17–18; 21:9–11; cf. Luke 2:25–38).[18] Although women held patronal and other roles, rarely were they granted public-speaking roles in ancient literature. Their testimony was far less valued than men's.[19] A few women became philosophers, but only a small percentage of philosophers were women.[20] An even smaller percentage of women became rhetoricians, reflecting the other form of advanced education in the Greco-Roman world; Hortensia, known for oratory, was a rare exception.[21] The experience of the Spirit, which empowered recipients for charismatic speech, would have provided some advances for women.[22]

But given Luke's historiography in general, postulating a more liberated community that Luke has suppressed may tell us less about Luke than about our own desire for a more egalitarian pristine Christianity. If the church could not immediately surmount ethnic and cultural barriers, we should not be surprised if the earliest community developed egalitarian sensitivities only gradually and not everywhere at once.[23] Luke might even affirm the ideal of Acts 2:17–18 while largely "choosing his [cultural] battles" on the basis of different principles of urgency (such as pervasively focusing on bridging the Jewish-Gentile division), although we might wish for more emphasis on the former than he provides.[24]

b. Examples in Luke-Acts

This interest in women appears in both the Gospel and Acts but is more obvious in the former;[25] even in the latter, women normally "appear as individuals with their own names and never as types representing women's position in the church."[26] The greater emphasis in the Gospel is not surprising. Many marginalized groups in the Gospel of Luke appear never or rarely in Acts;[27] women fare better but also are affected by the shift in focus between the Gospel and Acts. This shift may reflect the

18. Reid, *Choosing*, 206, doubts that the prophetic women of Luke's opening narratives (Elizabeth, Mary, and Anna) represent "the ideal for Christian women" (linking them instead with the OT era). But the one programmatic statement of Luke-Acts that specifically mentions women, Acts 2:17–18, points toward an even greater and more paradigmatic prophetic role for women in the new era.

19. E.g., Jos. *Ant.* 4.219; Plut. *Publ.* 8.4 (on an earlier period); Justin. *Inst.* 2.10.6 (though contrast Gaius *Inst.* 2.105); *Sipra VDDeho. pq.*7.45.1.1. For a perspective that nuances such references, Maccini, *Women as Witnesses*, 63–97.

20. See discussion below; examples in Harich-Schwarzbauer, "Philosophers" (with more notable Christian examples in late antiquity on 720).

21. See Witherington, *Acts*, 336; many rhetoricians mentioned in public only women who were deceased or considered disreputable (336n38). See further discussion below.

22. Ibid., 335–36. Women could be mantic agents elsewhere in antiquity as well (see comment on Acts 16:16), but the charismatic nature of early Christianity as portrayed in Acts and Paul's epistles seems far more pervasive than the special possession of select individuals in Greco-Roman paganism (see ch. 15, sect. 5.a).

23. Scholars often argue that egalitarian sentiments declined in later parts of the NT; I believe that they declined far more in the church fathers, probably generally as the social status of the writers rose (Keener, "Woman," 1211–14).

24. Beck, "Women," 307, argues that women's status in Acts appears "both immeasureably better than their place in society and far worse than that which the church had promised."

25. Jervell, *Unknown Paul*, 157; for the contrast put more strongly, see Vander Stichele, "Gender," 312 (following D'Angelo, "Redactional View"; Seim, *Double Message*, 3, 14–15; and others).

26. Jervell, *Unknown Paul*, 155. This statement may be too sweeping; Jervell himself concedes (156) the frequent appearance of widows (Luke 2:37; 4:25–26; 7:12; 18:3, 5; 20:47; 21:2; Acts 6:1; 9:39, 41). Male-female paired stories are less common in Acts than in the Gospel, but they are also balanced in mentions (Vander Stichele, "Gender," 312, developing D'Angelo, "Redactional View," 445). Rhetoricians might alternate proper names by gender at some points (Hermog. *Inv.* 4.4.188) simply for purposes of rhetorical variation, but Luke's variation is more pervasive.

27. Roth, *Blind, Lame, Poor*, 207 (mentioning prisoners, lepers, and even the poor). Luke, right from the beginning, has a heavy emphasis on the marginalized and needy (e.g., Luke 1:7, 26–27, 48, 51–53). God also

nature of Luke's material; in the former work, he has many traditions about Jesus and, in the latter, a tighter focus on the Gentile mission.

Yet even if Mary occupies a special place in Luke's story (foundational in Luke 1–2 and appearing toward the beginning of Acts as well, in Acts 1:14), this status by itself would not necessarily imply much concerning his perspectives on women in general. A few "mythic women" attained heroic roles in Greek tragedy without thereby abolishing the system that restricted Athenian matrons to the domestic sphere.[28] To reconstruct Luke's perspective on women, one must survey a wider range of female characters in Luke-Acts—while also keeping in mind that Luke is writing a history and hence is somewhat limited by his sources (limitations on what is preserved may reflect an androcentric bias from some of his sources rather than his own perspective).

Key passages highlighting Luke's agenda are thus more instructive than his unexplained silence elsewhere. One key passage for understanding Luke's perspective on gender roles is Luke 10:38–42. Some scholars aver that Jesus here silences Martha's defense of her diaconal role while he affirms Mary's silent passivity for women.[29] Common as this approach is among respected scholars, I confess that I find it astonishing. Jesus affirms the role of *disciple* in Mary over against the traditional feminine role of homemaker. Mary's role as disciple connects with the male disciples and their ultimate evangelistic role in Acts; the role of serving tables is important yet secondary, in Luke's vision of ministry, to that of proclamation (Acts 6:2–4), but this role of serving tables, though often a feminine, domestic role in antiquity, is clearly not restricted to women in Acts 6. Mary is paradigmatic for discipleship in general, not exclusively for female discipleship.

No one would have been surprised by Martha's "feminine" role, but most Palestinian Jewish women would have been surprised by Mary's role (Luke 10:38–41).[30] The larger Greco-Roman world knew of traveling philosophers who welcomed women students,[31] but even these were a minority.[32] Training Mary in the law would not necessarily make her a teacher of it, given social realities of the era, but it did challenge social ideals. Thus, for example, in Musonius Rufus's Stoic ideals, which are among the most progressive recorded for the era, daughters should receive the same education as sons (Mus. Ruf. 4), especially where relevant for virtue (4, p. 42.31–37; p. 48.1–26). Musonius opines, however, that women need not be given technical philosophic knowledge, since they have few opportunities to use it (p. 48.21–23).[33]

Although it is difficult to miss the prominent mention of women in Luke-Acts, some scholars doubt that women exercise there any roles of public leadership or Christian proclamation.[34] Some regard Luke as less liberated than Paul,[35] since Paul mentions

---

proved to be especially near the broken in the Hebrew Scriptures (Gen 29:31; Pss 51:17; 69:33; 138:6; Isa 57:15; Zeph 3:11–12).

28. Willner, "Oedipus Complex."

29. E.g., Schüssler Fiorenza, "Criteria"; idem, "Interpretation"; Reid, *Choosing*, 158.

30. Arlandson, *Women*, 138; cf. also Witherington, *Women*, 101 (though he thinks Martha's "serving" role also surprising).

31. Arlandson, *Women*, 138. See discussion below. See further comment on Acts 17:34.

32. See discussion below.

33. Though nature has fitted women more for lighter tasks rather than for the hard labor that men do (Mus. Ruf. 4, p. 46.8–23), men and women could interchange these works in some situations (46.23–31).

34. Rook, "Women in Acts?" Certainly, they did not help "to elect Matthias" (Jeffers, *World*, 251–52), who was not, in fact, "elected" (Acts 1:26), but they were part of the prayer in the preceding context.

35. Beck, "Women," 281. Because Luke belongs to the Pauline circle (see our introduction, ch. 7), it is reasonable to suppose that he knows of women active in ministry in Paul's circle, on which see many scholars, e.g., MacDonald, "Women in Churches," 268–78; Bieringer, "Women"; Byrne, *Romans*, 450–51; Croft, "Text Messages"; Dunn, *Romans*, 900; France, "Romans," 240–42; Gerberding, "Women"; Gooder, "Women"; Hoyt, "Romans," 274; Mben, "Women"; McGinn, "Co-Workers"; Mingo, "Mujeres"; Mourlon Beernaert,

women coworkers; but even if we exclude 1 Cor 14:34–35 as an interpolation, as some do,[36] we cannot easily do the same for 11:2–16.[37] Paul, like Luke, contended with an environment holding social sensitivities that differed from our own.[38] Although I have argued elsewhere that Paul was progressive by the standards of his day, I believe that in at least some settings he also probably accepted some limitations that he considered strategic to preserve the support of more conservative elements in his milieu.[39]

In contrast to the skepticism entertained by some scholars about Luke's support for women in proclamation roles, Luke is careful to balance not only male and female models in accounts of Jesus's healings and in his parables but also male and female involvement in prophecy (Luke 2:25–38; Acts 2:17–18; 21:9–11) and, where possible, more generally, as being Jesus's followers (Luke 8:2–3; 10:38–42; 23:49, 55; 24:10; Acts 1:14; 5:14; 8:3, 12; 9:2; 12:12–13; 16:13–15; 17:4, 12; 22:4). If men hold more prominent speaking roles as prophets, this prominence could reflect Luke's sources or the results of social realities of his day rather than his own bias (see comment on Acts 21:9).[40] As Gaventa argues, although Luke does not often or at length recount women's speech, this is probably not deliberate suppression (any more than Luke suppresses Peter by his allowing Peter to disappear from the narrative, or five of the Seven disappearing from Acts after their roles are complete). Luke's focus is just salvation history.[41] We can wish that he focused more on gender or provided more information on early institutions or more biographic information on individual leaders, and so on, but although Luke does not denigrate those other interests, his focus remains on the Gentile mission.

Women become the first witnesses of the resurrection event (Luke 24:3–10); that the men emphatically disbelieve their testimony (24:11, 22–24)[42] is to the discredit

---

"Collaboratrices"; Murphy-O'Connor, "Promoter"; Omanson, "Identifying"; Osiek, "Diakonos"; Scholer, "Co-Workers"; Schüssler Fiorenza, "Women"; Smith, "Coworkers"; Venetz, "Frauen."

36. A large number of commentators (e.g., Conzelmann, *Corinthians*, 246; Murphy-O'Connor, *Corinthians*, 164; Horsley, *Corinthians*, 188–89, 196; Hays, *First Corinthians*, 246–48; Bassler, "Corinthians," 328; Snyder, *Corinthians*, 185–86; most thoroughly, Fee, *Corinthians*, 699–705) and other scholars (e.g., Bruce, "All Things," 94; Pelser, "Women," 7:100; Petzer, "Reconsidering"; du Toit, "Swyggebod"; Schulz, "Look"; Lockwood, "Exclude"; Scroggs, "Woman," 284; Meeks, *Urban Christians*, 125; cf. also Meeks, "Androgyne," 203–4), including some of the ablest and best-known text critics (Fee, *Presence*, 272–81; Ehrman, *Introduction*, 484; Payne, "Fuldensis"; idem, "MS. 88"); it does not fit the context well. But against an interpolation here, see, e.g., Wire, *Prophets*, 149–52, 230–32; Jervis, "Reconsideration," 52–59; Thiselton, *Corinthians*, 1148–50 (following esp. Ross, "Floating Words"); Collins, *Corinthians*, 516; Keener, *Paul*, 74–75; idem, "Learning," 162; Schüssler Fiorenza, *Memory*, 230; Niccum, "Voice"; Hasitschka, "Frauen"; Carson, "Silent," 142; Odell-Scott, "Dilemma"; Bryce, "Study"; cf. perhaps Aune, *Dictionary of Rhetoric*, 233.

37. Some have viewed it as an interpolation (Walker, "Paul's Views"; Trompf, "Attitudes"; Cope, "Step"), but the vast majority do not (e.g., Murphy-O'Connor, "Character," esp. 621; Blattenberger, *Rethinking*, 6–8; Mitchell, *Rhetoric of Reconciliation*, 261n417; Furnish, *Theology*, 76n1).

38. On the function of head coverings in 1 Cor 11:2–16, see, e.g., Keener, "Head coverings"; idem, *Paul*, 19–69; for other relevant background, cf. Llewellyn-Jones, *Tortoise*.

39. Keener, *Paul*, passim; cf. idem, "Subversive Conservative"; Lemmer, "Strategist." Such a strategy (which I do understand as a strategy rather than a conviction about what should be universal) becomes more explicit in the Pastorals (1 Tim 5:14–15; Titus 2:3–5; cf. 1 Tim 6:1). Even in later, probably more conservative centuries, women's roles among Christians proved a target for elite pagan critics (Cook, *Interpretation*, 166–67).

40. In Acts 21:9, it is possible that they prophesied regularly but did not prophesy Paul's impending passion, the point that Luke emphasizes in the context (21:11; cf. 20:23); the narrator may do a favor to them, to Philip, and to others by not specifying individuals (apart from himself) in 21:12, since the position articulated there differs from that attributed to the divine perspective in 21:13–14. Of course, a senior prophet such as Agabus (cf. 11:28) might command more attention for Luke's audience than would virgins anyway, given their likely age and experience (see again comment on Acts 21:9), despite the ideal regarding both gender and age in 2:17–18. This need not alter the ideal.

41. Gaventa, "Daughters," 60.

42. Cf. also Mark 16:11, though this may depend on Luke. On the disciples' disbelieving the women, cf. Vermes, *Jesus the Jew*, 40–41. For the centrality of women's testimony for Luke's account, see Bauckham, *Eyewitnesses*, 129–32.

of the men, not the witnesses, a point reinforced both by Jesus's reproof (24:25) and by the analogous situation at Peter's deliverance (Acts 12:13–15).[43] True, the women are not explicitly told to proclaim the resurrection in Luke 24:5–7, in contrast to Mark 16:7 (as well as Matt 28:7, 10; cf. John 20:17).[44] But they also turn out to be more effective witnesses than in Mark 16:8 (where they remain silent from fear), the one specific source that we know Luke had available here (though, in the resurrection narratives, the Gospel writers apparently had available a variety of sources diverging in details).[45]

Moreover, as noted above, women do appear as prophetesses (Luke 2:36; Acts 21:9), a role that illustrates the heart of Luke's programmatic message, which includes Spirit empowerment for both genders (Acts 2:17–18). This prophetic empowerment is connected with witness (1:8) and is fundamental for ministry of the "word of the Lord" in Acts (a biblical prophetic phrase applicable, in Acts, to proclaiming the good news). Jesus himself is something of a prophetic figure (e.g., Luke 7:16, 39), including in his own self-presentation (4:24; 13:33; 24:19). It appears to me that Luke is far more interested in charismatic ministry (such as modeled by Paul's mission or prophetic figures) than in institutional authority, in the cases where those forms of ministry differ. That most traveling ministers whom he could report (apart from married ones such as Priscilla) are male probably reflects the general historical reality of his sources, which probably, in turn, reflects the most common social conditions of the era.

Granted, the Twelve are all men (Acts 1:13),[46] and they instruct the congregation to select seven "men" (ἄνδρας) to direct the program for feeding widows (6:3). (See also the frequent addressing of crowds as ἄνδρες; as to whether such a designation could ever function gender-inclusively, see comment on Acts 2:14.) But at least the gender of the twelve apostles and probably the stated gender expectations of the earliest community reflect tradition rather than Luke's creativity, so he can hardly be blamed for them. Priscilla helps instruct Apollos in the way (18:26); although Luke does not include even passing mention of a woman apostle as we find in Paul (Rom 16:7), we should remember that, apart from Acts 14, Luke never shares the title "apostle" outside the Twelve, even for Paul himself.

Is it possible that just as the Spirit eventually led most Jerusalem Christians beyond their ethnocentrism (Acts 10:14–15, 19, 28; 11:18; 15:28), the promise of Pentecost in 2:17–18 suggests similar crossing of gender barriers in the future, an ideal that the earliest community about which Luke writes had not fully attained?[47] On the whole, I believe that Luke's perspective, especially as exemplified in Luke 8:2–3; 10:38–42; and Acts 2:17–18, points in this direction, though Luke has a limited body of tradition available to support this trajectory. Ultimately, however, determining Luke's perspective entails choosing which evidence in Luke-Acts we weigh most heavily.

43. Their skepticism may accommodate skepticism about women's testimony in antiquity; but historians accommodated a wide range of skepticism about miracles, and some works included a skeptical perspective only to refute it (e.g., Philost. *Hrk.* 7.9, 11; 8.2).

44. This genuine contrast was helpfully brought to my attention by Brock, "Magdalene." Of the four Gospels, Matthew may be most emphatic, including two commissions to the women, which provide the model for the commission to all disciples in Matt 28:18–20 (cf. Keener, *Matthew*, 699, 715).

45. See discussion in Sanders, *Figure*, 280.

46. Emphasized by some (cf. apparently Pelikan, *Acts*, 206) as the model for one form of Christian ministry. They were, however, also all Jewish Galileans, reflecting their contingent historical situation no less.

47. Gaventa, "Daughters," 60, suggests that as other prophecies in the narrative are fulfilled, the ideal reader should infer the ultimate fulfillment of this one as well. (Many of Luke's contemporaries may not have recognized the extent to which this was not yet fulfilled, but Luke's pairing of male and female prophetic figures may have disturbed such complacency.)

The presence of married women (cf. Luke 8:3) with other women's husbands may have posed more of a problem than the role they were playing.[48] No one objected to women speaking with other women, but people held a range of views regarding women speaking with men, especially in more traditional society. Although Jewish women attended synagogue with men, inappropriate mixing could violate widespread ancient Mediterranean mores. A gossiper might complain that some women were immoral because they talked with men (were ἀνδρόλαλοι, Theophr. *Char.* 28.3; cf. John 4:27). Men's eating with women other than their spouses would be suspicious (Isaeus *Philoct.* 21), as would be women talking with male neighbors (Quint. *Decl.* 354 intro). The presence of women in Acts 1:14 (see comment there) thus could continue a potential for scandal[49] found in Luke 8:2–3,[50] where women traveled with Jesus. Paul continued this potentially controversial activity (Acts 16:15; see comment there).

That Luke's narrative does not mention the offensive character of such behavior may stem partly from the location of Luke's Diaspora urban audience. Though genders were far more segregated in urban classical Athens[51] than in any period in Palestinian Judaism,[52] they were less segregated in Macedonia and especially in a Roman colony such as Philippi[53] (where I have suggested some of Luke's target audience lay). Nevertheless, among Greeks and even among Romans,[54] some gender-exclusive

48. Both among some Judeans/Jews (e.g., Sir 9:9; 42:12; *Test. Reub.* 6:1–2; *m. 'Abot* 1:5; *Ketub.* 7:6; *t. Šabb.* 1:14; *b. Ber.* 43b, bar.; *'Erub.* 53b; *y. 'Abod. Zar.* 2:3, §1; *Soṭah* 1:1, §7; *Ḥal.* 2:1, §10; John 4:27) and among Gentiles (Eurip. *El.* 343–44; Eurip. frg. 927; Theophr. *Char.* 28.3; Livy 34.2.9; 34.4.18 [but contrast 34.5.7–10]); in the rural Middle East more recently, Delaney, "Seeds," 43.

49. Philosophers and moralists who associated with women drew criticism (see, e.g., Liefeld, "Preacher," 239–41, citing Iren. *Her.* 1.13.1, 3; 1.23.2, 4; Lucian *Runaways* 18); the same accusation was used to discredit the Pharisees (Sanders, *Figure*, 109; Ilan, "Women to Pharisaism") and gnostics (Klauck, *Context*, 488).

50. In view of the potential scandal, it is not likely that this tradition (also Mark 15:40–41) was invented (Witherington, *Women*, 117); it was clearly unconventional (Gnilka, *Jesus*, 179; Stanton, *Gospels*, 202).

51. See Gould, "Position in Athens," 47, 50; Dover, "Attitudes," 145; Pomeroy, *Goddesses*, 72, 170; Boer, *Morality*, 243–44 (though contrast drama, in Foley, "Conception," 161; cf. Willner, "Oedipus Complex"); Lysias *Or.* 3.6, §97; Xen. *Oec.* 7.17–22; 9.5; Dio Chrys. *Or.* 6.11 (Diogenes); Plut. *Demosth.* 25.6; *Cam.* 11.2; Char. *Chaer.* 1.1.4; 5.4.10; in Hellenistic Egyptian marriage contracts, Verner, *Household*, 38. In preclassical Greece, see Hom. *Od.* 1.356–61; 18.184. For the general cultural ideals, cf. Malina and Neyrey, *Portraits*, 177–81; Giovannini, "Chastity," 67; Delaney, "Seeds," 42; the private sphere was more "honorable" for classical women (Xen. *Oec.* 7.30). But (see, e.g., Boer, *Morality*, 251) it was hardly as complete as some sources imply; e.g., for the limited architectural potential for such segregation in classical Greece, see Robertson, *Greek and Roman Architecture*, 297; cf. deSilva, *Honor*, 193; architecture offers still less potential in the Roman West (White, "*Pater familias*," 461).

52. Although an ideal of separation obtained (Wegner, *Chattel*, 18, 150–53; Ilan, *Women*, 128–29; Goodman, *State*, 37; cf. Swidler, *Women*, 119–20; Ps.-Phoc. 215–16; *Tg. Rishon* on Esth 2:7), full gender segregation was probably possible only among elites (Fiensy, "Composition," 225, citing Philo, *Spec. Leg.* 3.169; *Flacc.* 89; 4 Macc 18:7), though bathing was separated (*t. Nid.* 6:15; *Num. Rab.* 9:12; cf. Safrai, "Home," 762). Women went to the market (Verner, *Household*, 46), sometimes worked there (Safrai, "Home," 752), and enjoyed considerable contact with other women (Goodman, *State*, 37). Some Eastern women, especially Persians, were more segregated than the Athenians (Jos. *Ant.* 11.191; Plut. *Themist.* 26.3–4; *Alex.* 21.3).

53. The traditional public-male/private-female distinction (e.g., Dion. Hal. *Ant. rom.* 3.21.2; 8.39.1; cf. MacMullen, "Women in Public," 209) was never complete (e.g., Hallett, "Role," 245) and was not now rigidly observed (Hemelrijk, "Masculinity"). Indeed, Romans in the early empire allowed even mixed bathing (Balch, "Paul, Families, and Households," 268), although "honorable" women avoided it, it ultimately led to scandal (see, e.g., Pliny E. *N.H.* 33.54.153), and Hadrian banned it (Carcopino, *Life*, 258; McRay, *Archaeology*, 47–48; Massa, *Pompeii*, 115; though contrast Ward, "Baths"). Although banquets were traditionally separated (Vitruv. *Arch.* 6.7.4), this practice was beginning to break down among aristocratic Romans (Smith, *Symposium*, 208–9, 298n27; Stambaugh, *City*, 207). Romans knew that Greeks were stricter on this point (Corn. Nep. pref. 6–7).

54. E.g., Dio Chrys. *Or.* 3.70; Plut. *Bride* 9, *Mor.* 139C; 30, *Mor.* 142C; 32, *Mor.* 140D; some in Mus. Ruf. 3, p. 42.13–14. Even as late as the third century, those outside a household might not admit knowledge of a young bride's appearance (Men. Rhet. 2.6, 404.11–14).

ideals remained.[55] Luke may otherwise omit mention of the offense because it would have been obvious to his audience that at least very conservative elements among the early church's (and to a lesser extent, among Luke's) contemporaries would have taken offense. Such behavior might not provoke criticism from one's friends (cf. John 4:27), but enemies were certain to exploit it.[56]

2. Women in Antiquity

It is anachronistic to evaluate Luke's approach to gender without reference to the views of his milieu. When we evaluate the options articulated among his contemporaries, we quickly recognize that a range of options existed and that Luke's presentation is among the more favorable toward women.

Presenting this full range is somewhat precarious: some scholars focus mainly on the negative data regarding women in antiquity, and others on the positive, reacting against (and sometimes challenging the objectivity of) scholars doing the opposite.[57] Both poles of the range represent genuine views held in antiquity; unless we regard none of the literary evidence as representative, it is also not easy to say what the "majority" position was, except with respect to particular regions, eras, and classes.

Even ancient writers who were progressive by the standards of their milieu were normally not modern egalitarians, and women rarely achieved prominence in the male spheres of politics and rhetoric; rarely do they appear even as teachers of philosophy (and, as rabbis and rhetoricians, even less often—indeed, almost never). At the same time, apart from outright misogynists, actual male views toward women were often tempered by affection for mothers, sisters, wives, and daughters; even the harshest laws or wisdom sayings would therefore be qualified in practice. Some role divisions conventional among people of means were impossible among peasants or artisans,[58] where every hand was needed for the work.

a. General Observations

Depending on how one weighs the evidence,[59] one can argue either for women's being poorly treated in antiquity[60] or for their being well treated;[61] there was considerable variation even within the same period from one region to another.[62] Class also

55. E.g., some Romans still viewed public affairs as primarily male (e.g., Pliny *Ep.* 4.19.4). A generation before Luke's apostles, profaning an exclusively women's festival in Rome caused scandal (Cic. *Att.* 1.12; *Fam.* 1.9.15; Plut. *Caes.* 10.1–3, 6; *Cic.* 28.2; cf. 19.3–4).

56. Cf. Klauck, *Context*, 488; Cook, *Interpretation*, 113–14, 166–67; Osiek and MacDonald, *Place*, 221–22.

57. When studying the practices of other cultures and eras, we usually seek to balance our modern values of gender egalitarianism (which I affirm) and the importance of cultural sensitivity (essential for objective study). Some degree of tension in how we balance these factors is difficult to avoid when we seek to learn sensitively and objectively about cultures for whom modern forms of these values were not yet among their range of options (although I believe that we should advocate for justice when we are engaging cultures and not just studying them). Some perspectives are not "progressive" by our standards yet were so by the standards of their own milieu, and we need to take into full account the social context in which they functioned.

58. On rural Galilee, cf. Horsley, *Galilee*, 204; in Hellenistic society, cf. Pizzuto-Pomaco, "Shame," 74; in traditional south Lebanon, see Eickelman, *Middle East*, 194.

59. For a mediating position, see, e.g., Boer, *Morality*, 251–56; Keener, "Marriage," 687–91. The same range of opinion exists on Jewish roles; thus Witherington, *Women*, 10, urges a mediating approach.

60. E.g., Boer, *Morality*, 243–46; Lefkowitz and Fant, *Life*, 12–20; in Judaism, cf. Swidler, *Women*, 56–82; and especially negatively, Jeremias, *Jerusalem*, 359–76.

61. E.g., Boer, *Morality*, 246–51; Lefkowitz and Fant, *Life*, 11–12.

62. E.g., Boer, *Morality*, 269. For one balanced appraisal, see, e.g., Cohick, *Women*.

made a major difference;[63] an outspoken wife might be viewed as noble if she was an aristocrat working at common purpose with her husband.[64]

Intellectuals often recognized that views about gender roles varied among cultures. Thus, for example, women had more freedoms in Egypt[65] and Sparta[66] than in Athens, although none of these societies was fully egalitarian. Greeks found it strange that Ligurian women worked in the fields (Diod. Sic. 4.20). Then again, few places were as restrictive as classical Athens (and especially as conservative Athenian writers portrayed their city to be); earlier Mycenaean women probably shared more activity and status with men than did classical Athenian women.[67] Early Roman law was also more favorable than classical Greek culture;[68] Greeks recognized that, historically, women were more influential among Romans than among Greeks,[69] and in the early empire, women had much more freedom in the West than in the East.[70] Palestinian Jewish wives lacked some rights held by Greek or Roman women, but they possessed other rights that most of the latter lacked, such as the right to sue without a guardian.[71] Palestinian Jewish wives also had much mobility outside the home, going to the market or the well and conversing with other women.[72]

Roman women owned businesses and homes, and their homes, unlike aristocratic Greek homes, did not separate male and female domains.[73] Some Stoics opined that most work is, by its character, suited for either gender[74] except that physical labor was more suited for men and weaker tasks, such as spinning, for women.[75] Women were accomplished in many fields;[76] some, for example, proved successful as artists.[77] As suggested above, in many places women must have been heavily engaged in agrarian labor.[78] On women's engagement in work, see further comment at Acts 18:3.

The sphere of Roman law appears more ambivalent. In the midst of an extended verbal attack on women (Juv. Sat. 6), Juvenal complains that no legal quarrel existed that did not start with the involvement of a woman (6.242–43). Roman laws often treated

63. See Arlandson, *Women*, 117.
64. E.g., Plut. *Cic.* 20.2 (though presented less positively in 29.3); cf. Jos. *Ant.* 18.361. Even aristocrats, however, might view negatively a strong wife making demands of her husband (e.g., Jos. *Ant.* 18.246).
65. E.g., Diod. Sic. 1.27.2; Cosgrave, *History of Costume*, 14. Some suggest that adaptations in the LXX also reflect the freer environment of Ptolemaic Egypt as against the earlier Near East (Schorch, "Hellenizing Women"). Germans likewise depended on their wives prophetically, in contrast to Romans (Tac. *Germ.* 8).
66. E.g., Xen. *Lac.* 1.3–4 (contrasting Sparta with most city-states); Arist. *Pol.* 2.6.7, 1269b (complaining); Plut. *S. Sp. Wom.*, Gorgo 5, *Mor.* 240E. But Spartan women, too, obeyed fathers and husbands (Plut. *S. Sp. Wom.*, anonymous 22, *Mor.* 242B).
67. Billigmeier and Turner, "Roles," 10.
68. Frank, *Aspects*, 22–23.
69. Appian *Hist. rom.* 3.11.1.
70. Salles, "Diversité." For women's higher roles in Rome than in Greece, see, e.g., Lefkowitz and Fant, *Life*, 244–47.
71. Verner, *Household*, 45.
72. Safrai, "Home," 752. But Safrai (762) says that normally husbands went to the market.
73. Balch, "Paul, Families, and Households," 274.
74. Mus. Ruf. 4, p. 46.27–31.
75. Mus. Ruf. 4, p. 46.8–23. Even during the male activity of war, Greek women played supporting roles (cf. Loman, "No Women"), though the humor in Aristophanes's *Lysistrata* works because their role was limited.
76. See, e.g., Lefkowitz and Fant, *Life*, 21–25.
77. Pliny E. *N.H.* 35.40.147–48 (though he notes many more men and elaborates throughout 35.36.79–97 on Apelles alone).
78. Scheidel, "Women"; cf. Stambaugh, *City*, 99, 159. Yet women's work in the fields seemed strange to many Greeks (Diod. Sic. 4.20). Lower classes probably did not divide work or spheres much by gender (Reden, "Work," 743).

women more leniently, as less knowledgeable and hence less culpable than men.[79] In early Roman law, women could not make wills, though Hadrian later changed this custom.[80] Apart from some significant exceptions,[81] women's testimony, when accepted, normally carried much less weight than men's in both Roman[82] and rabbinic[83] law.

Conversely, Roman law recognized a divorced woman as emancipated from male control, and this allowed considerable freedoms.[84] Even in the late republic, a wife of a living man could own an estate.[85] We even read of several women who pleaded their own cases in court (Val. Max. 8.1–3), though one was called manly (8.3.1) and another, who could have found male advocates had she wanted them, impudent (8.3.2).[86] Although Roman law treated women as equals of men in some respects,[87] it did not do so in the majority of ways affecting public life.

b. Prominent Women

Greeks and Romans knew of prominent women in various other cultures, such as Egyptian queens[88] and the British queen Boudicca.[89] Although prominent women often achieved a category unavailable to other women, they did not always fare well. Xenophon, more appreciative of women than were many of his male contemporaries, notes that one Persian satrap's widow reigned well (Xen. *Hell.* 3.1.10–13) until her son-in-law, resolving that satrapy was a man's job, murdered her (3.1.14).

Rome, however, had its own prominent women. The most noted was the empress Livia, wife of Augustus Caesar,[90] who was known to influence him, albeit within limits.[91] But although Augustus made propagandistic use of her prominence, he maintained general social conservatism.[92] She participated alongside the next emperor Tiberius in honoring her deceased husband, as if she held great authority (αὐταρχοῦσα).[93] But when she sought to remain active in public affairs after

---

79. Robinson, *Criminal Law*, 17, 56. Roman law originally placed women under male custody because of "the weakness and light-mindedness of the female sex (*infirmitas sexus* and *levitas animi*)" (Pomeroy, *Goddesses*, 150).

80. Buckland, *Roman Law*, 288. In earlier Athenian law, adoption for inheritance could be invalidated if found to be influenced by a woman (Isaeus *Menec.* 1, 19; *Philoct.* 29–30), the legal equivalent to the testator's being declared insane (*Menec.* 19).

81. Cf. Davies and Taylor, "Testimony"; Rothstein, "Testimony."

82. E.g., Justin. *Inst.* 2.10.6 (though contrast Gaius *Inst.* 2.105); Schiemann, "Intestabilis," 875; cf. Buckland, *Roman Law*, 293. For other groups, cf., e.g., Sen. E. *Controv.* 7.5; Prop. *Eleg.* 3.6.20; for distrust of women's speech, see, e.g., Avianus *Fables* 15–16.

83. E.g., Jos. *Ant.* 4.219; *Sipra VDDeho. pq.*7.45.1.1; Wegner, *Chattel*, 120–23 (esp. 122).

84. Dupont, *Life*, 109–10. Citizen women with three children could conduct business without a guardian (e.g., P.Oxy. 1467, from 263 c.e.).

85. In Cic. *Verr.* 2.3.22.55. A wife who appeared to control her husband's money, however, became an easy target for ridicule (Petron. *Sat.* 37).

86. More commonly, women would secure a man to represent them, befitting their "female weakness" (P.Oxy. 261.12–13).

87. Cf., e.g., marital gifts (Gardner, *Women*, 74).

88. E.g., Manetho *Aeg.* frg. 10, 20–21 (from Euseb. *Chron.* 1.96); cf. Cleopatra in *Sib. Or.* 11.254–59. For Attalid queens in Asia Minor, see Polyb. 22.20 (Verner, *Household*, 65–66).

89. Tac. *Ann.* 14.31–37. She was the king's widow (14.31) and noted that Britons could fight under women (14.35); the Roman general mocks the abundance of women warriors in 14.36.

90. On her power, see Treggiari, "Jobs"; on her deification, see Flory, "Deification"; for her ambiguous status (as both feminine and imperial), cf. Jenkins, "Livia."

91. E.g., Sherk, *Empire*, §3, p. 7. Women in emperors' families often influenced them (e.g., Hdn. 5.8.10; 6.1.1, 10; Temporini–Gräfin Vitzthum, "Family," 751; Balsdon, "Women"), though Rome's emperors themselves were male.

92. See Flory, "Livia and History."

93. Dio Cass. 56.47.1. The title "Augusta" applied to new emperors' mothers (see Flory, "*Augusta*").

Augustus's death, his heir, Tiberius, warned her to stop meddling.[94] In some respects, even the publicly honored Livia was made into an exception instead of views about women in general being changed; thus Philo praises her by claiming that she became almost male in her intellectual ability.[95] Yet other women achieved or displayed unusual power without being empress, such as Germanicus's widow Agrippina[96] or Agrippa I's daughter Berenice.[97]

Wealthy benefactresses and patronesses commanded great respect and exercised considerable influence,[98] including in the Jewish community.[99] Most Roman honorary inscriptions regarding women (in contrast to their funerary inscriptions) celebrated them as benefactors rather than mothers.[100] Sometimes a woman could be patroness even of a city.[101] Yet although high-class Roman men viewed some women as peers, this perspective coexisted with the view that men were different and often superior to women.[102]

A wide range of offices in the East were held by women as well as by men.[103] Some prominent offices in the East were liturgical; that is, they primarily conferred public honor in return for substantial economic contributions.[104] This is probably true of many public offices held by aristocratic women,[105] but it is not true of all of them (see, e.g., the comment on priestesses in subsection i [Women in Myth and Religion] below). Although women do appear in civic administration, the vast majority of civic administrators were men; civic life in the eastern Mediterranean remained primarily a man's world. Women achieved prominence in some other venues—for example, a noted Jewish woman alchemist cited by Greco-Roman alchemists.[106]

c. Women's Advancement in Society

Women in classical Greek society held little power;[107] classical Athens is typically the extreme with which other ancient Mediterranean societies are compared. It is from ancient Greece that we have opinions such as those of Semonides (*On Women*) in the sixth century B.C.E., for whom women were made out of all sorts of terrible garbage and are the greatest curse of Zeus on men.[108] Greek women's situation improved in

94. Suet. *Tib.* 50.3.
95. Philo *Embassy* 319–20 (Meeks, *Urban Christians*, 24).
96. Shotter, "Agrippina."
97. See, e.g., Young-Widmaier, "Representation"; further comment at Acts 25:13. Earlier Hasmonean women became newsworthy when widowhood or other factors granted them a degree of independence from men (see Sievers, "Women in Hasmonean Dynasty," 144–45).
98. Cf., e.g., Lefkowitz and Fant, *Life*, 24, §48 (Pleket 5); 243–44, §232 (*CIL* 10.6328/*ILS* 6278); Pomeroy, *Goddesses*, 200–201; Gardner, *Women*, 239–40; Stambaugh and Balch, *Environment*, 134; White, *Origins of Architecture*, 1:81; Winter, *Left Corinth*, 199–202; Gill, "Élites," 115; cf. *Gr. Anth.* 7.728.
99. See, e.g., Brooten, *Women Leaders*, 151; Trebilco, "Communities," 565–66; Matthews, "Ladies' Aid"; Sanders, *Figure*, 109.
100. Forbis, "Image." Cf., e.g., one munificent priestess in first-century C.E. Roman Spain in Donahue, "Iunia Rustica."
101. See Hemelrijk, "Patronesses."
102. See Hallett, "*Same* and *Other*."
103. In Asia Minor, Kraabel, "Judaism in Asia Minor," 44, lists "stephanophoros, prytanis, demiourgos, dekaprotos, hipparchos, archon, gymnasiarchos, agnothetis and timouchos."
104. So, e.g., offices held by a number of younger men (Strubbe, "Young Magistrates").
105. Gardner, *Women*, 67–68. Cf., e.g., Lalla of Lycia, a "gymnasiarch out of her own resources" (Pleket 13, in Lefkowitz and Fant, *Life*, 157, §159).
106. Van der Horst, "Maria," 679 (also noting that she is the first extant source to know of hydrochloric acid).
107. See, e.g., Kraemer, "Ecstatics," 58–73. Social reality was undoubtedly more diverse, but Athenian law treated women as perpetual minors (Gould, "Position in Athens," 43–44).
108. Lefkowitz and Fant, *Life*, 14–16. No "sugar and spice" for Semonides.

the Hellenistic period[109] but did so much more rapidly in the first century C.E. under Roman influence.[110] Romans themselves had long been making gradual progress from highly chauvinistic traditions;[111] for example, not until about 396 B.C.E. did the senate rule that funeral eulogies could be said over women as well as men,[112] and it was reportedly only Caesar's behavior in 68 B.C.E. that introduced mourning over young as well as older women.[113] Roman women experienced greater advances in the first century, though not without opposition.[114] The advancements were not unilinear, of course; there was a revival of the norm of submissiveness for imperial women in the early second century,[115] perhaps mirroring the increase of philhellenism at that time.

Contributing to women's progress in Roman society was the gradual abandonment of the transfer of wives to their husbands' authority, thus leaving them under that of their fathers.[116] Because married women no longer lived with their fathers and because fathers frequently passed away in their daughters' early adulthood, this arrangement allowed women much more freedom.[117] Sometimes women's "progress" even violated norms of morality, stirring resentment.[118]

d. Gender Ideologies

Despite women's considerable progress in society, older literary models and ideologies continued to influence elite thinking and writing.[119] According to one view, women exist only to make men miserable (Eurip. *Orest.* 605–6); a misogynist might wish that women did not exist, apart from bearing children (Lucian *Affairs* 38). An example of tactlessness is for a guest to denounce women when he is invited to speak at a wedding (Theophr. *Char.* 12.6). Juvenal longs for the old days of cavewomen, before adultery had been invented (*Sat.* 6.7–8).[120] Because of their supposed immaturity, women were often linked with minors, slaves, and the like.[121] Indeed, Socrates or Thales was said to have praised fortune for not making him a woman, beast, or barbarian,[122] a saying eventually adapted into a Jewish benediction as well.[123]

Aside from such ideology, some men were simply brutal: for example, to obey the priests and not be defiled, Sulla divorced his sick and dying wife and had her carried

---

109. Tarn, *Civilisation*, 99 (though, for limits, see 100–101); Verner, *Household*, 35–39, 64–65.

110. See Pomeroy, "Women in Egypt," 318 (somewhat tentatively); Meeks, *Moral World*, 62.

111. Galilean women also seem to have acquired more freedoms (Goodman, *State*, 36), though husbands did want their wives to stay home and what little a wife earned belonged to her husband (37).

112. Plut. *Cam.* 8.3.

113. Plut. *Caes.* 5.2.

114. See, e.g., discussion in Winter, *Wives*, passim.

115. See Boatwright, "Imperial Women."

116. The *sine manu* marriage, complete by the time of Gaius *Inst.* 1.111 in the second century C.E. (Garnsey and Saller, *Empire*, 130). The *in manu* marriage entailed subordination to, and dependence on, the husband (Gaius *Inst.* 1.49).

117. Garnsey and Saller, *Empire*, 138.

118. See Winter, *Left Corinth*, 123–26; cf. already Mommsen, *History*, 548.

119. Although I have drawn my examples from various periods, this remained true in much Roman literature of the early empire, such as the portrayal of mothers (perhaps reacting against new freedoms; e.g., in Propertius, Ovid, and Statius, see Gold, "She-Wolves"; Lateiner, "Mothers"; Newlands, "Mothers").

120. See Keane, "Cave-Woman."

121. E.g., Cic. *Off.* 2.16.55–57; Ael. Arist. *Def. Or.* 130, §41D; with barbarians and uneducated persons in Sen. Y. *Dial.* 6.7.3; cf. Jewish laws in *m. Sukkah* 2:8; *Ḥag.* 1:1; cf. esp. *Sipre Num.* 39.6.1 (where women, proselytes, and slaves do not belong to Israel proper).

122. Diog. Laert. 1.33. In Plato, see Avi-Yonah, *Hellenism*, 136; Longenecker, *Social Ethics*, 70.

123. E.g., *t. Ber.* 6:18; *b. Menaḥ.* 43b–44a, bar. "Gentile" naturally replaced "barbarian." The saying is often noted (e.g., Meeks, "Androgyne," 167–68; Bonsirven, *Judaism*, 134; Lohse, *Environment*, 150; Barth, *Ephesians*, 2:655–56), although the sentiment is gratitude for the privilege of observing more commandments (with Schüssler Fiorenza, *Memory*, 217).

away while she lived.[124] Plutarch reports that when Alcibiades's good wife asked for a divorce in response to his behavior with courtesans, he dragged her home forcibly; she died soon after, while he was away (*Alc.* 8.3–4). This was not cruel, Plutarch explains, because the law requires the wife to go to court precisely so that if the husband wants her, he may take her (8.5). Abuse was sometimes sanctioned,[125] especially in earlier times,[126] though even the "ancients" had their limits.[127] Another man ordered his freedman to beat his eight-months-pregnant wife; she died in childbirth, but he was not guilty because he grieved and was not seeking her death.[128] Husbands could go too far, however. A man who was found to have killed his wife by throwing her out the window after a struggle did face death.[129]

Most regarded the natures of men and women as different;[130] Aristotle was particularly emphatic in contrasting them;[131] the male was by nature superior to, and ruling over, the female.[132] Against Socrates, he doubted the animal analogy in arguing for gender equality; lower animals, Aristotle insisted, do not have households requiring careful management![133] Others appealed to nature to show that males were superior to females.[134] Physical differences were used to justify divergent social treatment.[135] Not all allowed such distinctions to be thoroughgoing; for example, though hunting was traditionally male, Artemis had gifted some women for it (Xen. *On Hunting* 13.18). But to be shown up by a woman was considered a shameful matter.[136] Women were held to be weaker

124. Plut. *Sulla* 35.2; likewise (33.3), he ordered Pompey to divorce his wife and then gave him his daughter, already pregnant by another husband; she died in childbirth. In a fictitious work, one man, unwilling to accept the widow's refusal of his pursuit, raped her (Alciph. *Farm.* 35 [Epiphyllis to Amaracinê], 3.37).

125. Not least by Zeus's example with Hera, hanging her from Olympus (Apollod. *Bib.* 2.7.1). Augustine's mother, Monica, told wives to endure such beatings with servility (Aug. *Conf.* 9.9); Quint. Curt. 8.8.3 portrays wives having to endure husbands' beatings as a matter of course (set in Alexander's day).

126. E.g., Val. Max. 6.3.9 (where a man cudgeled his wife to death for drinking wine). A tyrant such as Periander (who allegedly killed his pregnant wife in anger, then slew his concubines for goading him on, Diog. Laert. 1.94) is, however, exceptional; the context shows Periander ready to kill men no less cheaply. People in the empire also knew of the Indian custom of widow burning (Diod. Sic. 17.91.3; Cic. *Tusc.* 5.27.78).

127. In the myth in Apollod. *Bib.* 3.15.1, the Areopagus banished a man who accidentally killed his wife.

128. Philost. *Vit. soph.* 2.1.555–56.

129. Tac. *Ann.* 4.22. Patterns of abuse may have varied by region, and textual evidence for physically abusing wives is far less abundant than that for beating children and slaves, suggesting that it may have been less acceptable.

130. E.g., Xen. *Oec.* 7.16, 22, 31. Nature fitted women for indoor existence, and men for outside (7.22–25, 30–31, 39), but both genders were equal in memory, diligence, and the potential for self-control (7.26–27).

131. See Wagner-Hasel, "Roles: Greece," 742, on Aristotle. He denied that virtues were the same for both genders, though both genders could express virtue; thus a man displays courage by commanding, and a woman by obeying (Lefkowitz and Fant, *Life*, 64, §86). Stoics would agree in principle with assigning virtue according to each entity's appropriate nature (Mus. Ruf. 4, p. 46.3–4), though their conclusions differed from Aristotle's.

132. Arist. *Pol.* 1.2.12, 1254b.

133. Arist. *Pol.* 2.2.15, 1264b. Aristotle did derive the husband-wife relationship from nature and instinct (*N.E.* 8.12.7, 1162a); virtues differed by gender (*Pol.* 3.2.10, 1277b). Deslauriers, "Difference," argues, however, that Aristotle's treatment of gender in his biological treatises differs from his treatment in the *Politics*. Some advocated marrying equals but intended this in terms of the same social class (Aeschylus *Prom.* 901–2).

134. Aelian *Nat. An.* 11.26 (among his analogies is the dragon; fortunately, not ants or bees). Xen. *Oec.* 7.33 uses the queen bee analogy for wives staying inside.

135. In Hippocratic writers, see King, "Gender roles: Medicine," 745. Soranus, by contrast, avers that the two have analogous characteristics despite differences in particulars (*Gynec.* 3.prol. 1–5; 3.12.45). For a survey of medical writers on women, see, e.g., Lefkowitz and Fant, *Life*, 85–97, 215–34.

136. E.g., Soph. *Antig.* 677–80; Virg. *Aen.* 11.734; Apollod. *Bib.* 1.8.2 (cf. 3.9.2); *Debate of a Montanist and an Orthodox* (*MOT* 125, the orthodox speaking; Bray, *Corinthians*, 106).

physically,[137] emotionally,[138] intellectually,[139] and socially.[140] Female "weakness" explained why one first-century woman could not attend court (P.Oxy. 261.12–13). Such "weakness" could mean vulnerability and might merit protection or invite sympathy.[141]

Philosophers often affirmed women's equality in principle, though as a school apparently only Epicureans achieved this ideal in practice.[142] Socrates claimed that a woman's nature was not inferior to a man's except in strength and intellect;[143] a Cynic writer more generally denies that women are worse by nature than men.[144] Although women held some prominence in Pythagorean communities,[145] a Pythagorean argued that wives should submit to their husbands (Iambl. *V.P.* 11.54). Another thinker of Pythagorean persuasion, benevolently encouraging his wife to grow intellectually, warned her to flee from what was effeminate as if she were male and to regard herself as female no longer.[146]

In the first-century Stoic ideals of Musonius Rufus, women, like men, are gifted with reason by the gods.[147] A daughter should receive the same education as a son (Mus. Ruf. 4),[148] though adapted for women's work such as spinning;[149] after all, trainers equip female as well as male dogs and horses.[150] Training in virtue is the same for all,[151] though Musonius points out that he does not mean that women should receive technical philosophic training, since they would have little occasion to use it.[152] More generally, he could point out that domestic and public welfare depend on both genders together.[153]

---

137. E.g., Xen. *Lac.* 3.4; Livy 25.36.9; 28.19.13; Cic. *Mil.* 21.55; Virg. *Aen.* 12.52–53; Mus. Ruf. 4, p. 46.17; Sil. It. 1.445; Dio Chrys. *Or.* 2.29; Aul. Gel. 17.21.33; Lucian *Dial. D.* 414 (6/20, Menippus and Aeacus 2); Heliod. *Eth.* 4.21; Aphth. *Progymn.* 5, "On Refutation," 29S, 13R; perhaps *Lam. Rab.* 4:19, §22; Quint. *Decl.* 368.3 (textually suspect). Phaedrus 4.17.6 could be either physical strength or courage. Men apparently considered such delicateness attractive (Char. *Chaer.* 2.2.2); for a major exception, see discussion on Amazons at Acts 8:27.

138. E.g., Eurip. *Med.* 928; Sen. Y. *Ep. Lucil.* 78.17; *Let. Aris.* 250; cf. *b. B. Meṣiʿa* 59a. This included reluctance to inflict punishment (Aeschylus *Prom.* 79) and softhearted love (4 Macc 15:5).

139. E.g., Cic. *Mur.* 12.27 (*infirmitatem consilii*); Livy 28.19.13; Val. Max. 9.1.3 (*imbecillitas mentis*); *Let. Aris.* 250; Philo *Good Person* 117 (nature gave women "little sense," LCL, 9:77). A good wife can manage the household so long as her husband instructs her properly (Xen. *Oec.* 3.10, 14–16; 7.10), including where to put things (9.1), especially since Greek men often married women when the latter were very young (3.13; 7.4–5). They were more easily deceived (e.g., Plut. *Bride* 48, *Mor.* 145CD; *Test. Job* 26:6 [*OTP*]/26:7–8 [Kraft]). Cf. in later Islamic thought Eickelman, *Middle East*, 205–6.

140. E.g., Aeschylus *Suppl.* 468–89 (esp. 489), 748–49; Xen. *Cyr.* 5.5.33; *Gen. Rab.* 22:6; perhaps 1 Pet 3:7. This is especially relevant in court petitions, where women claim that their weakness disposes them to greater vulnerability toward oppression (A. L. Connolly in Horsley, *Documents*, 4:131–33, §30, esp. p. 131, citing P.Flor. 1.58; P.Oxy. 34.2713; 1.71, col. 2; P.Amh. 2.141); cf. also in traditional North African society (Eickelman, *Middle East*, 243).

141. E.g., Dion. Hal. *Ant. rom.* 8.24.4–5; Livy 34.7.14; Plut. *Rom. Q.* 108, *Mor.* 289E; Quint. *Decl.* 272.3–5, 9; 338.8; see note on court petitions above.

142. Meeks, "Androgyne," 170–73 (esp. 170).

143. Xen. *Symp.* 2.9, reporting Socrates's view (if, as is likely, γνώμης involves intellect and not simply decisiveness).

144. Crates *Ep.* 28. Diogenes Laertius, however, treats women's nature as inferior in some sense in the tradition (Diog. Laert. 6.2.65).

145. See Malherbe, *Moral Exhortation*, 82–85.

146. Porph. *Marc.* 33.511–16.

147. Mus. Ruf. 3, p. 38.26–27.

148. Plato had also argued for similar education, though accepting women's natural inferiority (Meeks, "Androgyne," 170). Many note Musonius's support for women's education (e.g., Ward, "Musonius," 288), though Meeks, *Moral World*, 46, notes that we do not know of any women among his students.

149. Mus. Ruf. 4, p. 46.8–23 (and this only because nature fitted women best for this, but the roles could be interchangeable at times, lines 23–31).

150. Mus. Ruf. 4, p. 42.35; p. 44.1–4 (a good Stoic "argument from nature").

151. Mus. Ruf. 4, p. 46.31–37; p. 48.1–26; cf. 3, p. 40.6–7, 10–12, 17–35; p. 42.1–29; 4, p. 44.23–35. Aristotle argued that virtue differed by gender (Arist. *Pol.* 3.2.10, 1277b).

152. Mus. Ruf. 4, p. 48.21–23. Musonius is on the defensive here against criticisms that advanced philosophy wastes the time of women, who should attend to domestic chores (see 3, p. 42.11–17, esp. 13–15).

153. Mus. Ruf. 14, p. 92.38; p. 94.1.

Yet Seneca the Younger, another first-century Stoic, though allowing that women were capable of the same virtues as men,[154] often portrayed women as unstable and irrational,[155] and a later Stoic emperor could regard a man's soul as different from a woman's.[156] In contrast to Epicureans and Pythagoreans, Stoics had few, if any, women pupils.[157] Seneca's apparent inconsistencies come from the Stoic idea that the same virtue could be expressed differently for different settings and an understanding of equality different from today's.[158] The egalitarian trend moving beyond Aristotle's chauvinism was not meant to disrupt the hierarchical roles already existing in society.[159] Thus "Roman Stoics were egalitarian in theory but Aristotelian in practice."[160] Even Pythagoreans, who allowed women to be philosophers, accepted the basic distinction between public and private spheres, limiting military, civic, and political leadership to men and expecting women to care for their households.[161] Others had earlier contended for women's equality intellectually and morally,[162] arguing that nature had simply fitted men physically for outside life and women for inside life;[163] but this was an unusually progressive position for its time.[164]

Many people considered women more emotionally unstable, and thus less self-controlled, than men.[165] They were considered more fickle and changeable than men;[166] their instability could be expressed in anger,[167] hatred,[168] or gullibility.[169] Hysteria may have even been an accepted female outlet in that culture (in contrast to today).[170]

---

154. Sen. Y. *Dial.* 6.16.1. Some of his portrayals of women's virtue may be designed to support male virtues or challenge male vice (cf. Wilcox, "Grief").

155. See Lavery, "Never Seen"; cf. Sevenster, *Seneca*, 192–96; Sen. Y. *Dial.* 6.7.3.

156. As that of children, tyrants, and animals also is (Marc. Aur. 5.11). The image need not imply a universal; Xenophon thought that Greeks had better "souls," i.e., were better equipped for battle, than Persians (*Anab.* 3.1.23). In the mid-second century B.C.E., Stoics had begun moving away from their earlier political egalitarianism (Erskine, *Stoa*, 181).

157. Meeks, *Urban Christians*, 23. (This claim refers to disciples, not aristocratic girls in households where Stoics could be hired to teach.)

158. See Manning, "Seneca"; Arthur, "Classics," 402.

159. Meeks, *Moral World*, 60–61 (also noting that the Stoic emphasis on Stoic wisdom—which only the elite could afford to pay for—supported hierarchy of a different sort).

160. Balch, "Household Codes," 31; see further idem, *Wives*, 143–49.

161. A third- to second-century B.C.E. treatise in Lefkowitz and Fant, *Life*, 104, §107.

162. Xen. *Oec.* 7.26–27.

163. Xen. *Oec.* 7.22–25, 30–33, 39. A wife could prove more honorable in her sphere than the husband in his (7.42).

164. Xenophon was certainly not egalitarian from a modern perspective, as we shall see, but he surpassed most of his Athenian contemporaries, perhaps partly because of Spartan influence or his cultural versatility. Many male Christian writers in late antiquity and afterward viewed women as weaker intellectually or morally, grounding treatment of women in this perspective rather than in physical differences (Xenophon's basis for the domestic/external role distinction). Cf. the useful survey of data in Doriani, "History."

165. Cf. Polyb. 2.56.9 (in light of 2.56.7–8); Cic. *Fam.* 16.27.1; Livy 34.2.13–14; Dio Chrys. *Or.* 3.34; *b. Šabb.* 33b; also Seneca in Lavery, "Never Seen." Cf. Gemünden, "Passionnelle" (though the rationality/passion divide is not limited to its gender associations).

166. E.g., Virgil *Aen.* 4.569–70 (cf. 5.656–63); *Let. Aris.* 250.

167. Over petty matters (Livy 6.34.7) or regardless of consequences (Polyb. 2.8.12). Never mind that moralists could advise wives to remain silent during husbands' rage (Plut. *Bride* 37, *Mor.* 143C)! They were harder to reconcile than men because they were made from bone instead of earth (*'Abot R. Nat.* 9, §24 B).

168. E.g., the speaker in Tac. *Ann.* 3.33 (warning of vicious abuse of power). Cf. Publ. Syr. 6: they only love or hate. Through building up anger and hatred in their hearts, women often eventually go insane (Lucian *Disowned* 30).

169. Tac. *Ann.* 14.4 (believing what was appealing).

170. So Shelton, *Romans*, 301–3, esp. 301 (comparing women fainting in the Victorian era, when it invited sympathy; for discussions of gender-conceptualized "hysteria" and idealized illness in nineteenth-century life, see Curtis, *Faith*, 38–50; Capps, *Village Psychiatrist*, 15–22).

Preference for luxury or comfort, as opposed to hardship, was considered feminine;[171] in the rabbinic worldview, masculinity involved the self-discipline of Torah study, which was not a normal feminine activity.[172] Women were considered more prone to fear[173] and servility[174] as well as grief.[175] (Nevertheless, regardless of general gender stereotypes, individual women could be hailed for courage.)[176]

Although Epicurean communities tended to be among the most egalitarian, an Epicurean writer warns that women do not receive correction gladly[177] because they take it personally and suspect the reprover's personal motives;[178] they are too emotional, vain, and attached to their reputation.[179] They believe that their weaker nature should invite pity, and hence believe that those stronger than they are exploiting their weakness from contempt.[180]

Pliny the Younger's letters depict intelligent women and affectionate friendships.[181] Judith favorably portrays its heroine's intelligence (Jdt 11:21). Later rabbis take special precautions for pregnant women,[182] and some Jewish burials show equal treatment in death.[183] The rabbis recognized that girls reached majority on average a year before boys, though this was based on puberty and did not affect girls' freedoms.[184] In general, parents often preferred bearing sons over daughters.[185] Yet daughters were also important,[186] and fathers could lavish

171. E.g., Polyb. 36.15.2; Cic. *Verr.* 2.5.31.81; *Off.* 2.16.55–57; Val. Max. 9.1.ext. 1, 7; Sen. E. *Controv.* 1.pref. 8–10; Sen. Y. *Ep. Lucil.* 104.34; Mus. Ruf. 9, p. 70.11–12, 24–25; Dio Chrys. *Or.* 6.11; 62.6; 70.2; Aul. Gel. 3.1; Lucian *Anach.* 25. Cf. Plutarch's apparent portrayal of Marc Antony in terms of feminine (and Greek) traits (so Russell, "Emasculation").

172. See Satlow, "Construction of Masculinity."

173. E.g., Xen. *Lac.* 11.3; Diod. Sic. 32.10.9; Dion. Hal. *Ant. rom.* 9.7.2; 10.28.3; Polyb. 3.108.5; 6.37.11; 32.13.6–7; 32.15.9; 36.15.1–2; 38.12.9; Val. Max. 2.7.9; 9.13.praef.; Sen. Y. *Ep. Lucil.* 70.6; 96.4; *Med.* 42; Sil. It. 9.263; 13.313; Plut. *Alex.* 47.1; Philost. *Vit. Apoll.* 1.21; *Hrk.* 23.19; 45.8; Apul. *Metam.* 5.22; Ps.-Callisth. *Alex.* 1.46. Exceptions, however (e.g., Val. Max. 3.2.2, 15; 3.2.ext. 8–9; 5.4.6; Pliny *Ep.* 7.19.7; Iambl. *V.P.* 31.194; 4 Macc 16:5, 14), persuaded some that courage could be learned and was not limited to one gender (Xen. *Symp.* 2.12; Mus. Ruf. 3, p. 40.33–35); a rhetorician could argue either side (Theon *Progymn.* 10.57–59 with 10.62–65).

174. E.g., Polyb. 30.18.5–6; 32.15.7.

175. E.g., Cic. *Fam.* 5.16.6; Sen. Y. *Ep. Lucil.* 99.1–2; *Dial.* 6.7.3. See further comment on Acts 8:2.

176. E.g., Diod. Sic. 10.24.2 ("even" [κἄν] for women); Vell. Paterc. 2.26.3; 2.87.1; 2.88.3; Plutarch's *Bravery of Women, Mor.* 242E–263C; Libanius *Narration* 15. This was more common among the Gauls (Diod. Sic. 5.32.2).

177. Philod. *Crit.* col. 21b.13–14.

178. Philod. *Crit.* col. 22a.

179. Philod. *Crit.* col. 22a.9–11.

180. Philod. *Crit.* col. 22b.

181. Dobson, "Depiction." He appreciated an intelligent wife (Pliny *Ep.* 1.16.6, though wondering whether her husband cultivated her intellect or simply wrote in her name) and appreciated his own wife for her intelligence (4.19.2, as well as her housewife skills), expressed in delighting in his oratory (4.19.3–5).

182. Safrai, "Home," 764; e.g., *t. Ta'an.* 2:14. They also showed concern to protect a woman from rape (*m. Ter.* 8:12).

183. E.g., Nagar and Torgeë, "Characteristics" (but cf. the arguments for some distinctions in Peleg, "Gender and Ossuaries"). Unusual as it seems from a modern perspective, however, ancients often allowed equality as persons without providing for equality of role. Still, some ancients did not accept even equality of human worth (e.g., Eurip. *Iph. Aul.* 1393–94).

184. Wegner, *Chattel*, 36–37, suggesting that soon after puberty the girl would be married. Once she reached majority or had been married once, she was freed from *patria potestas*, and hence her consent was necessary for a betrothal (Cohen, *Law*, 298).

185. E.g., Artem. *Oneir.* 1.15; 4.10; *Sipre Deut.* 138.2.1; 141.2; *b. Ber.* 5b; praying for a son in *Pesiq. Rab Kah.* 9:2; *y. Ber.* 9:3, §6. See esp. Safrai, "Home," 750 (esp. the citation of *b. B. Bat.* 16b, bar.: those with sons are blessed, but woe to those with daughters); cf. Derrett, *Audience*, 31–32. This preference may reflect the daughter's marrying and being lost to her family of origin (*Gen. Rab.* 26:4).

186. E.g., *Exod. Rab.* 1:13. Ilan, *Women*, 44–48, argues that the birth of a daughter is a disappointment in all the Jewish sources but that Jews did not seek to reduce the number of daughters artificially as pagans did.

affection on their daughters;[187] some wrote that fathers were especially close to daughters, and mothers to sons.[188]

e. Jewish Perspectives

Ancient Israelite roles for women often mirrored those of surrounding societies.[189] Conforming to norms in their milieu, Jewish women in the Greek Diaspora were regulated by Greek, rather than Judean, practices.[190] Like Greek stories about ancient women, Jewish stories about ancient women may not reflect current social reality, yet they are instructive nonetheless. Women play important roles in the book of Tobit (Sarah, Edna, and Anna);[191] Judith subverts traditional gender roles in some respects as well.[192] Pseudo-Philo's *Biblical Antiquities* also appears to expand the roles of some biblical women;[193] *Jubilees* may improve Genesis's picture of Rebekah more than that of any other character.[194] Many midrashic texts honor biblical women such as Sarah and Miriam;[195] later than our period, Amoraim often mentioned the merit of the matriarchs.[196] Eve tended not to fare so happily in most texts.[197]

Second Temple Judaism reveals a wide range of views toward women.[198] The Qumran scrolls probably reflect more traditional patriarchal ideology.[199] Philo claims that Essenes avoided marriage because women were selfish and deceitful (*Hypoth.* 11.14–15); men bound to them become enslaved (11.16–17).[200] Josephus opines that Essenes avoided women because women were immoral (*War* 2.121). Although

---

On Greek child abandonment (probably of daughters somewhat more often than sons despite the controversy on that point), see comment on Acts 7:19.

187. E.g., Cicero's love for Tullia (*Fam.* 14.5.1; 14.18 title); her death crushed him, as he would have preferred his own death (9.11.1).

188. Plut. *Bride* 36, *Mor.* 143B.

189. Mullins, "Secular Roles"; idem, "Religious Roles."

190. Stambaugh and Balch, *Environment*, 50.

191. See Levine, "Women in Tobit."

192. See Sawyer, "Judith's Performance"; cf. Schüssler Fiorenza, *Memory*, 116.

193. So van der Horst, "Women in *Liber*" (cf. also idem, "Beobachtungen"); Burnette-Bletsch, "Jael," notes that *L.A.B.* 31 expands Jael's role (suggesting that weak Israel in the author's day would identify with Jael). DesCamp, "Women," even suggests a woman author. Still, negative aspects appear; e.g., the depiction of Tamar in *Biblical Antiquities* is androcentric (Polaski, "Taming Tamar").

194. See Endres, *Interpretation*, 194, 217–18 (cf. also 51–84). Cf. also Leah (*Jub.* 36:23).

195. See Aleixandre, "Mujeres." For Sarah, see, e.g., 1Qap Gen^ar XX, 2–8 (see also comment in Fitzmyer, *Apocryphon*, 120); *Test. Ab.* 3:5; 5:14; esp. 6:1–8 A (cf. also 6:6–13 B); *'Abot R. Nat.* 26, §54 B; *Gen. Rab.* 20:6; 41:2; 52:5, 13; *Num. Rab.* 14:11; *Pesiq. Rab.* 43:4; Urbach, *Sages*, 1:155; she is idealized in Josephus (see Amaru, "Women"). For Miriam, cf., e.g., *Sipre Deut.* 305.3.1; *b. Šabb.* 35a; *Ta'an.* 9a; *Num. Rab.* 1:2; 13:20; *Song Rab.* 4:5, §2; *Tg. Neof.* 1 on Exod 1:21; on Num 21:1.

196. E.g., *Pesiq. Rab Kah.* 11:6; *Exod. Rab.* 1:12; *Lev. Rab.* 21:11; 36:5; *Num. Rab.* 11:2; *Pesiq. Rab.* 12:5; 15:9; cf. *Pesiq. Rab Kah.* Sup. 5:2; *Tg. Neof.* 1 on Exod 17:12; *Tg. Ps.-J.* on Exod 40:8.

197. E.g., *1 En.* 69:6; Philo *Creation* 151, 167; *Sib. Or.* 1.42–45; *'Abot R. Nat.* 1 A; 9, §25 B; 42, §117 B; *y. Sanh.* 2:4, §2; *Šabb.* 2:6, §2; *Gen. Rab.* 17:8; 18:2; 21:5; *Lev. Rab.* 18:2; *Num. Rab.* 10:8; *Gr. Ezra* 2:16; see also Greiner, "Eve"; texts in Scroggs, *Adam*, 21. Pandora is assimilated to Eve at times (see, e.g., Johnston, "Interpretations," 524). Eve's portrayal in *L.A.E.* (e.g., 10:1; 18:1; 35; 38:1–2; 44:1–5) is pathetic (also the parallel *Apoc. Moses*, e.g., 11:1–2; 14; 18:5–6; 21:6; 25:1–2; 29:17; 31–32; 42); cf. her role later in Islamic tradition (Delaney, "Seeds," 40–41). But both Adam and Eve are deceived in some texts (*1 En.* 32:6; *Sipre Deut.* 323.6.2), and sometimes Eve appears favorably (*b. Sanh.* 39a); for both sides on Eve in rabbinic literature, see Gradwohl, "Frau."

198. So Ilan, "Women's Studies" (also arguing that the more radical approach of Jesus and his earliest followers can fit within early Judaism's diversity). Cf. Swidler, *Women*, 56–82, albeit with a heavier emphasis on the negative.

199. So Bengtsson, "Kvinnor."

200. The topos of a weak man who is a slave to a bad wife (e.g., unable to divorce her) appears elsewhere (e.g., Plut. *Virt.* 2, *Mor.* 100E).

later rabbis accorded mothers and fathers equal honor,[201] Qumran texts accord more to fathers.[202]

The approach toward women in Sirach is often harsh.[203] Some scholars suggest that *Testament of Job* is positive (regarding Sitis and especially Job's daughters),[204] although this has been disputed.[205] Some have argued that even rabbinic Judaism was largely patriarchal and androcentric,[206] though it was, undoubtedly, less so than most other streams of early Judaism known to us (represented, e.g., in Josephus and Philo). Tannaitic rabbis did articulate women's proper rights and often affirmed their dignity.[207] Although some have argued that Judaism became harsher toward women in the talmudic era,[208] others have argued the opposite.[209] Rabbinic law treated women as chattel with regard to their sexuality,[210] though as persons in most other respects.[211] The wife was obligated to serve her husband, and her earnings belonged to him.[212] A man's life must be saved before a woman's, but her sexuality was more vulnerable and required greater protection than a man's.[213] Women functioned as a cultic contaminant,[214] inviting the development of Levitical regulations (which also originally reflect more widespread cultural ideas).[215]

Philo is fairly negative toward women.[216] He always portrays male as superior to female, and some scholars argue that he even gives Wisdom some masculine characteristics.[217] Masculinity is closer to divinity than is femininity.[218] Philo thinks well

201. E.g., *Mek. Pisha* 1, lines 28ff. (Lauterbach, 1:3); *Mek. Bah.* 8, lines 28ff. (Lauterbach, 2:259); *Gen. Rab.* 1:15.

202. 4Q270 7 I, 13–15.

203. With, e.g., Witherington, *Sage*, 91. Although Sirach seems less hellenized than many later documents, some have attributed its "patriarchal" approach to gender to Hellenism (Cook, "Perspective on Women").

204. E.g., van der Horst, "Women in Testament of Job"; Spittler, "Introduction," 833, 835–36; cf. also van der Horst, "Beobachtungen" (also listing *L.A.E.* 15–30 as positive, which does not persuade me, though I agree with him that Sirach, Josephus, and Philo are negative).

205. E.g., Garrett, "Weaker Sex," esp. 57–58. The dating and source of this work are also still debated.

206. Ilan, "Frauen"; Swidler, *Women*, 126–30 (also for other groups, 29–55); see esp. Wegner, *Chattel*; idem, "Tragelaphos"; cf. Neusner, *Beginning*, 32. Ilan, "Women's Studies," even allows that rabbinic Judaism may have clamped down on women in response to Christianity, but Christianity showed a similar trend in the same period. Contrasting the OT period, Neusner in *Tosefta* (ed. Neusner), 3:x, suggests that, while respected, women in Qumran and the Tannaim lack significant rights.

207. See Langer, "Vermögensrecht."

208. Swidler, *Women*, 167–68. The legal genre may account for some of the impression.

209. E.g., Witherington, *Women*, 10; cf. Neusner, *Beginning*, 59.

210. Cf. *m. Qidd.* 1:1; Wegner, *Chattel*, 3–4, 20–34, 40–70, 114, 171. Women functioned as a legal hybrid (7–8), somewhat like slaves and others in Roman law.

211. Wegner, *Chattel*, 34–38, 70–95 (e.g., property ownership, 87–91). See, e.g., Babatha's retention of property (*p. Yadin* 16, ca. 127 C.E.; Cotton and Greenfield, "Property").

212. Falk, "Law," 516–17. Anything she found belongs to him (*m. Ketub.* 6:1).

213. *M. Hor.* 3:7. Restoring what is lost to the husband is also a higher priority than what is lost to the wife (*m. Hor.* 3:7; *t. B. Meṣiʿa* 2:32).

214. Wegner, *Chattel*, 148–67, esp. 162–65; cf. Swidler, *Women*, 130–39; *y. Ḥag.* 2:6, §2; dangers in *b. Pesaḥ.* 111a; pious caution in *Pesiq. Rab Kah.* 12:15. Strictest tradition prohibited eating with a menstruating woman (*t. Šabb.* 1:14). Qumran was, however, stricter (cf. 11QT XLV–XLVII; McNamara, *Judaism*, 141).

215. Walton, Matthews, and Chavalas, *Background Commentary*, 64, 130–31; cf. Gen 31:35. Some Greeks apparently believed that intercourse rendered a woman impure (Diog. Laert. 8.1.43) or led to impurity more generally (cf. Porph. *Marc.* 28.439–40; Alciph. *Court.* 1 [Phrynê to Praxiteles] frg. 3), certainly by the standards of some temples (deSilva, *Honor*, 251); for Israelites, both genders might be temporarily impure (e.g., 4Q284 1 I, 7). For Greeks, childbirth polluted because blood was shed (Clark, "Childbirth"; cf. Theophr. *Char.* 16.9).

216. On Philo, see Baer, *Categories*; Sly, *Perception*; briefly, Meeks, "Androgyne," 176–77.

217. Mattila, "Wisdom." Philo may even adapt grammatical gender to raise male over female (Baynes, "Transformation"); on his negative use of female terminology, see also Baer, *Categories*, 65–66. Male is more complete than, and superior to, female (41, citing Philo *Spec. Laws* 1.200–201); female is "an imperfect male" (41, citing Philo *QE* 1.7; *QG* 1.25); and nature places men before women (*Spec. Laws* 2.124).

218. Cf. Conway, "Gender"; Baer, *Categories*, 55–64.

of Sarah as a matriarch, but when he allegorizes her, he must masculinize her for his system.[219] Philo does view positively the female Therapeutae, but he remains fairly consistent and forestalls criticisms by emphasizing their virginity.[220] When he praises the empress Livia, he claims that her training made her virtually male in her intellect.[221] Others have argued that Philo's detractors have overemphasized his misogyny;[222] even if this is the case, his portrayals are hardly positive toward women.

Josephus is likewise negative toward women in general.[223] Josephus liked some women—especially wealthy aristocratic women—better than others (e.g., *Life* 426–27).[224] He knew and respected women patrons, aristocratic women sympathetic to Judaism.[225] He treats the matriarchs well, as he does the patriarchs, but presumably because he views them as members of the aristocratic class.[226] (Some scholars think that he decreases Deborah's role,[227] but others differ.)[228] By contrast, when the Levite's concubine was brutally gang-raped in Judg 19:24–28, Josephus claims that she died from shame, doubting that her husband would forgive her![229] Josephus believes that men who heed the folly of women merit judgment,[230] and cites approvingly the Essene suspicion of women's infidelity.[231]

f. Women and Morality

As already noted, some philosophers argued that virtue was the same for men and women, even if expressed in different ways.[232] Likewise, Jewish sages spoke of virtuous[233] as well as wicked[234] women; for some later rabbis, the wife's virtue was more influential in the family than the husband's.[235]

---

219. So Niehoff, "Mother." On Philo's negative use of the feminine in allegory, see, e.g., Baer, *Categories*, 38–44. He normally used "Eve" for "sense-perception" (LCL, 1:xxv, citing Philo *Creation* 165; *Alleg. Interp.* 2.38, 70; 3.50, 60; *Cher.* 57; cf. also Peinador, "Protoevangelio"), though "Eve" could also mean "life" (LCL, 1:xxv, citing Philo *Agr.* 95; *Heir* 52); "Adam" often stands for the mind (*Creation* 165; *Alleg. Interp.* 1.25; 2.13; 3.50, 246; *Cher.* 10, 57; *Plant.* 46; *Heir* 52; *Dreams* 2.70).

220. See Taylor, "Virgin Mothers"; cf. Kraemer, "Monastic Women" (their unmarried status made them less female for Philo); Baer, *Categories*, 98–101; Golberg, "Choruses." On virginity and asexuality, cf., e.g., *Orph. H.* 32.7, 10; 42.4.

221. Meeks, *Urban Christians*, 24, citing Philo *Embassy* 319–20; on females becoming more male, see Baer, *Categories*, 45–49, 69 (esp. 45). Similarly, Seneca praises his mother for her manliness (Grant, *Social History*, 34, citing Sen. Y. *Consol.* 16), and Porphyry encourages his wife that she can be virtually male (Porph. *Marc.* 33.511–16). It is this line of tradition, rather than a Galilean Jesus, that is echoed in *G. Thom.* 114.

222. Sterling, *Ancestral Philosophy*, 199–219.

223. See Mayer-Schärtel, "Frauenbild" (esp. on Jos. *Ant.* 15.259–60).

224. Josephus adds to the biblical text that there are many causes for divorcing women (*Ant.* 4.253; though this may be to align with the more lenient opinion of his day despite the dominance of Shammaite thought on the question in Pharisaism; see Keener, *Marries Another*, 38–40); Josephus divorced a wife for displeasing behavior (*Life* 426) after two of their three children died. He also warned of wives' power over husbands through desire (cf. *Ant.* 11.51–55).

225. Bailey, "Portrayal," 155–56.

226. Ibid., esp. 176.

227. E.g., Feldman, "Roncace's Portraits."

228. E.g., Roncace, "Portraits."

229. Jos. *Ant.* 5.146–47.

230. E.g., Jos. *Ant.* 18.252–55.

231. Jos. *War* 2.121.

232. For virtue as the same for both genders, see, e.g., Mus. Ruf. 4, p. 44.10–35; p. 48.1, 4, 8, 13; Crates *Ep.* 28 (to Hipparchia); Antisthenes in Diog. Laert. 6.1.12; on Musonius, see further Lutz, "Musonius," 30. Both have equal authority to practice self-control (Xen. *Oec.* 7.27). Conversely, Spartan boys could outdo others' women in modesty (*Lac.* 3.4).

233. E.g., Sir 7:19; 26:1–4, 13–18. Abba Hilkiah's wife was as righteous as he (*b. Ta'an.* 23b), and Abba Judan's wife was even more righteous than he (*Lev. Rab.* 5:4).

234. E.g., Sir 25:13, 16–26; 26:5–12.

235. *Gen. Rab.* 17:7.

The particular nature of feminine virtue suited a wife's situation. Thus Musonius, who emphasizes equality in virtue, opines that a virtuous, philosophically knowledgeable woman serves her husband by her own hands.[236] (That is, Musonius was progressive by the standards of his day but was not a modern egalitarian.)[237] Plato and the Stoics believed that women could display the same virtues as men did, but most ancients limited women's "wisdom" mainly to domestic activity.[238] It is not surprising that some feminine specialities in virtue emerged. Ancient writers presented as virtuous women who defended their chastity with their life;[239] a woman who slew herself rather than be dishonored sexually might be called a matron of manly soul.[240]

Not all thinkers agreed that virtues were the same for both genders. Aristotle held that even a woman or slave may be "good," but only by comparison with other women or slaves, since "a woman is an inferior thing and a slave beneath consideration."[241] Aristotle's views were less influential in the early Christian era,[242] but he was not alone in his perspectives; even in Luke's day, feminine characteristics were often considered weaker and more passionate than the strong, rational traits characterizing men.[243]

A Roman sage lamented that a woman was at her best when her evils were openly exposed.[244] In various periods, some writers portrayed women as deceptive,[245] dangerous,[246] greedy,[247] lazy,[248] in strife with other women,[249] and so forth. They were considered more prone to sexual immorality[250]—though perhaps only because most male license, which was far more prevalent, was not counted as immoral. Thus a woman was easily deceived if a man slept with her;[251] a woman who prostitutes herself acts according to her nature, unlike a man who does so.[252] Yet some also warned that men were easily seduced (positively and for a good cause in Jdt 10:7), usually warning against the dangers of women.[253] When R. Jose caught a man trying to glimpse his

236. Mus. Ruf. 3, p. 42.7–8. She even does things considered slaves' kind of work (δουλικά; p. 42.8).

237. As also noted by others (e.g., Lincoln, *Ephesians*, 359).

238. North, "Mare." Though Plato tended to be sympathetic toward women (far more than Aristotle and many others), even he generally believed women inferior to men (Pomeroy, *Goddesses*, 230).

239. E.g., Dion. Hal. *Ant. rom.* 4.66.2–4.67.1.

240. *Animi matrona virilis* (Ovid *Fasti* 2.847; cf. similarly Dion. Hal. *Ant. rom.* 4.82.3).

241. Arist. *Poet.* 15.3, 1454a (LCL, 55). Among "appropriate" characters, only a man may be brave or clever (15.4, 1454a).

242. In many respects. Cf., e.g., the post-Aristotelian shift in the use of "virtue" (ἀρετή) in the Hellenistic era (on which see Finkelberg, "Virtue").

243. Stowers, "Self-Mastery," 543; cf. Manetho *Aeg.* frg. 35.3; 36. Not all concurred with this more Stoic perspective, but it was probably widely known among intellectuals.

244. Publ. Syr. 20.

245. E.g., Hesiod *W.D.* 375.

246. E.g., Babr. 22.13–15 (perhaps a later addition); Phaedrus 2.2.1–2.

247. E.g., Apollod. *Bib.* 3.9.2 (Atalanta seduced by the golden apples; also in Ovid *Metam.* 10.560–680; Libanius *Narration* 33; 34); '*Abot R. Nat.* 3 A; *Gen. Rab.* 45:5.

248. Pliny *Ep.* 7.24.5 (on aristocratic women's idleness).

249. Tiberius in Tac. *Ann.* 4.40.

250. E.g., Theophr. *Char.* 28.3; Tac. *Ann.* 3.33–34 (including, though less harshly, the more "progressive" speaker, 3.34); Jos. *War* 2.121; *m. Soṭah* 3:4; Wegner, *Chattel*, 159–62; probably Diod. Sic. 1.59.3–4. Cf. also in traditional Islamic village perceptions in the Mediterranean region (Delaney, "Seeds," 41; Eickelman, *Middle East*, 205–6); Muslim Somalis believe women spiritually weaker and hence more susceptible to demons (Lewis, "Possession," 211).

251. Hom. *Od.* 15.419–22; Char. *Chaer.* 1.4.1–2. Thus one husband guarded his wife carefully, but at a funeral she was seduced (Lysias *Or.* 1.6–8 [*Murder of Eratosthenes*]). That the woman's greater sexual susceptibility suggests that men engaged in intercourse more casually somehow fails to generate a corresponding verdict against male immorality.

252. Aeschines *Tim.* 185.

253. E.g., Sir 25:21; 26:9; 1 Esd 4:32, 34; *Pss. Sol.* 16:7–8; *Test. Jud.* 15:5–6; *Test. Reub.* 3:11–12; 5:1–5; 6:1; Jos. *War* 2.121; *Ant.* 7.130. See further Eron, "Mastery"; Rosen-Zvi, "Bilhah"; cf. sources in Keener, *Matthew*, 187, esp. n. 82.

(R. Jose's) beautiful daughter, he cursed her: "My daughter, you are a source of trouble to mankind; return to the dust so that men may not sin because of you."[254] Though designed to experience love passively, Seneca complains, some women now match men in their passions.[255] Many Mediterranean cities elected γυναικονόμοι, officials whose role was to "control women,"[256] and in some (undoubtedly a small minority), women were not supposed to run shops or engage in other business in the market.[257]

Women were also considered talkative and prone to gossip;[258] their words were untrustworthy,[259] and some ancients said that women characteristically wasted their time in talk.[260] Before marrying a woman, a man should learn about her tongue because "a talkative woman is a hell."[261]

Although most cultures allowed that both genders practiced magic, some associated magic more with women than with men.[262] According to one rabbinic tradition, "most women practice witchcraft,"[263] though in concrete narratives only some specific women were sorceresses,[264] and the rareness of examples may suggest that the gender association reflects mostly male prejudice.[265]

One early Jewish sage warns men not to sit among women (Sir 42:12) because evil comes from them like a moth from clothes (42:13); a man's evil proves better than a woman's good (42:14). Some later rabbis complained that Satan was created along with Eve;[266] one apocalyptic writer insists that of sixty thousand souls led to destruction, only one woman was found whose good deeds even equaled her bad ones, allowing her to be kept in the intermediate state.[267]

Some writers reacted against "modern" women, who had come to share male vices.[268] Seneca the Younger complains of liberated women now engaging in men's sins of drunkenness and gluttony, which brings on the same diseases such men suffer from (*Ep. Lucil.* 95.20–21). Juvenal, whose satirical comments on women suggest

254. *b. Taʿan.* 24a (Soncino 122); cf. a woman's prayer in *b. Soṭah* 22a. Even the most virtuous man who counted money into a woman's hand so as to gaze at her was destined for Gehinnom (*b. Ber.* 16a, bar.).

255. Sen. Y. *Ep. Lucil.* 95.21.

256. Men. Rhet. 1.3, 364.1–2; although this source is from the late third to the early fourth century C.E., Winter, *Wives*, 85, reports that the office existed widely in the first century.

257. Men. Rhet. 1.3, 364.2–5 (although I wonder to what extent this prohibition would have been enforced, especially with regard to resident aliens and especially in the first century; see comment on women in business at Acts 18:3). Women were also excluded from particular festivals (Men. Rhet. 1.3, 364.5–7).

258. E.g., Aul. Gel. 1.23.7–10 (along with curious and gullible); Lucian *Prof. P.S.* 23; *Sent. Syr. Men.* 336–39; *Gen. Rab.* 18:2 (along with jealous, flirtatious, etc.); 45:5 (along with envious, greedy, etc.); 70:11; 80:5 (again with the other characteristics); *Deut. Rab.* 6:11.

259. So, e.g., Babr. 16.10; Avianus *Fables* 15–16. Women's speech was obscene, one said, because their tongues were formed from the same material as their private parts (Phaedrus 4.15).

260. Livy 6.34.6. Unable to fight like warriors, women simply chattered and contended with words (Hom. *Il.* 20.251–55).

261. *Sent. Syr. Men.* 118–21 (*OTP* 2:595).

262. E.g., Pliny E. *N.H.* 7.2.17–18; for the related issue of poisoning, cf. Livy 8.18.1–12. Cf. the curse tablets noted in Witherington, *Corinthians*, 18.

263. In *b. Sanh.* 67a; cf. also *b. Ber.* 53a; *Pesaḥ.* 110b; 111a; Moore, *Judaism*, 2:137; Murray, "Magical Female." See earlier *m. ʾAbot* 2:7, attributed to Hillel: "the more wives, the more sorceries."

264. See Lesses, "Sorceresses," arguing that these narratives are more nuanced than the claim that most women are witches.

265. Ilan, *Women*, 221–25. The association also appears in pagan sources (Lefkowitz and Fant, *Life*, 124–26, 255–58). Barred from other forms of power, women might have been more inclined to folk magic, but the preponderance of female-targeted love charms in magical papyri might argue against this, at least for those able to afford official formulas.

266. *Gen. Rab.* 17:6 (based exegetically on the first letter of his name appearing at her creation).

267. *Test. Ab.* 9:8 B. Recension A, perhaps earlier, does not report that this soul was female or 10:5–15 B's report of a wicked woman who murdered her daughter. Cf. perhaps Eccl 7:28, but the sense is not clear.

268. Indeed, such reactions are reported even for the republic (Plut. *S. Rom.*, Cato the Elder 3, *Mor.* 198D).

misogyny,[269] complains of pampered aristocratic women enjoying their leisure while having innocent slaves brutally flogged (*Sat.* 6.474–85). Such a woman governs her house cruelly (6.486) and, if she is in a hurry, may abuse and rip the hair of a slow servant woman (6.490–91).

g. Womanly Ideals

Modesty[270] and meekness[271] were among the chief virtues traditionally expected for women, although these aristocratic ideals had outlived actual practice in much of Roman society (and may sometimes reflect male nostalgia for an idealized past). Traditional Roman matrons were portrayed as submissive, supportive, and subservient.[272] In traditional Greek values, a shameless, bold woman was bad;[273] in earlier Roman times, an aristocratic woman who spoke too arrogantly could be fined,[274] and a strict husband might divorce a wife who went to the games without his knowledge.[275] Seneca the Elder advised a wife to walk around looking at the ground; if a man greeted her with too much interest, it was better for her to respond rudely than immodestly, and if she must respond to the greeting, she should act confused and blush, so guarding her honor.[276]

Yet people knew that even Augustus, who urged men to command their wives as they wished and admonish them to modesty, did not treat his wife Livia in this manner.[277] Such practices had declined further in the first century C.E.[278] but remained an ideal. Thus Plutarch urges that sensible wives wait silently for their husbands' fits of rage to subside before comforting them.[279]

h. Marriage Roles

The Greek and Roman world carefully defined gender roles,[280] especially when children reached maturity.[281] Regarding gender roles, Dio Chrysostom believed that

269. Braund, "Misogamist," suggests that Juv. *Sat.* 6, in fact, opposes marriage rather than women. Most scholars, however, view Juvenal as misogynist.

270. E.g., Thucyd. 2.45.2; Lysias *Or.* 3.6, §97; Demosth. *Mid.* 79; *Aristocr.* 141; Val. Max. 7.1.1 (*pudicitia*); Lucan *C.W.* 2.360; Plut. *Bride* 17, *Mor.* 140C. A respectable matron was ashamed to go by herself among men (Hom. *Od.* 18.184). Cf. even in the novels (Wiersma, "Novel"). In Alciph. *Fish.* 4 (Cymothoüs to Tritonis), 1.4, ¶3, modesty includes staying home with the husband rather than being with elite women; in Aelian *Farmers* 9 (Chremes to Parmenon), a hardworking farmer complains that even courtesans pretend coyness. For ancient valuing of modesty, see Winter, *Wives*, 101–2; cf. female shame in Delaney, "Seeds," 40.

271. Certainly in the classical era, e.g., Aeschylus *Suppl.* 202–3; Xen. *Lac.* 1.3 (most Greek city-states, except Sparta in 1.4); an inscription in Lefkowitz and Fant, *Life*, 11, §22; also Pomeroy, *Goddesses*, 74; Llewelyn-Jones, *Tortoise*, 165; for gentleness, see, e.g., *Jub.* 36:23. Also expected in Hellenistic marriage contracts (Verner, *Household*, 65); cf. also later rabbis (*Gen. Rab.* 18:2).

272. Hallett, "Role," 241–42.

273. So Hom. *Od.* 19.91 (on Melantho's cruelty). Later rabbis felt that a husband not angry with such a wife was a sinner (*Num. Rab.* 9:12).

274. Aul. Gel. 10.6. In the early empire, the perception of Agrippina the Elder's arrogance and ambition would prove fatal (Tac. *Ann.* 4.12).

275. Val. Max. 6.3.12. For the ancient prejudice against "'headstrong and arrogant' women," see Winter, *Wives*, 65–66.

276. Sen. E. *Controv.* 2.7.3. Spartan boys also displayed modesty by looking at the ground (Xen. *Lac.* 3.4).

277. Dio Cass. 54.16.4–5. Cicero's wife was not meek, but she acted with noble demeanor (Plut. *Cic.* 20.2).

278. See Winter, *Wives*, passim.

279. Plut. *Bride* 37, *Mor.* 143C.

280. Wagner-Hasel, "Roles: Greece"; Stahlmann, "Gender Roles"; cf. Keener, "Marriage," 687–91. Even when comedy inverted such roles, it played on them (James, "Constructions").

281. Wagner-Hasel, "Roles: Greece," 740; age seven in Rome, Stahlmann, "Gender Roles," 743. Cf. the strong differentiation in rearing boys and girls (including girls' obedience) among the Garrese in Sicily in Giovannini, "Chastity," 67.

"everyone would admit that man is stronger and more fitted to lead. Consequently, to her falls the larger share of the household tasks"; yet this does not make women's lot more fortunate than men's.[282]

Funerary inscriptions appear to attest many happy marriages.[283] Yet despite exceptions for some prominent women, funerary inscriptions also attest that the vast majority of women were honored for their roles as mothers, wives, and daughters.[284] In one fictitious letter, a man requests that his daughter may spin with the servant women to prevent the parents' shame when she would marry; this would help school her "in propriety and modesty."[285] The wife ruled the domestic sphere (caring for home, children, and, in some homes, servants) as the husband ruled in public;[286] some philosophers proposed to instruct women in the virtue of proper household management.[287] A classical Greek author could note that husbands chose wives not from lust but for childbearing and child rearing;[288] indeed, in classical Athens a bride became a γυνή (woman, wife) only after bearing her first child.[289]

Jewish women's roles in Palestine were also especially domestic (e.g., cooking and child rearing).[290] Concern for household and children was to be paramount.[291] Thus a wife's "beauty" involved the ordering of her house (Sir 26:16), and a rabbi could claim that he would endure a difficult wife so long as she kept him from sin and reared the children.[292] Early Diaspora Christians followed the same distinction between public (masculine) and private (feminine) spheres (1 Tim 5:14, addressing a Hellenistic setting), even though their biblical canon allowed considerably greater freedom (e.g., Gen 29:9; Prov 31:16, 20, 24, 31).[293]

Inscriptions also praise obedient and sacrificial wives,[294] and numerous texts show us this expectation in ancient sources. The ancient Greek expectation was of the wife's subordination and submission to her husband;[295] a truly prudent wife should

---

282. Dio Chrys. *Or.* 3.70 (LCL, 1:137).

283. Balsdon, "Women," 31. Although Romans often viewed marriage as unhappy, a happier perspective of mutual affection grew from the late republic into the empire (Stahlmann, "Gender Roles"). Unhappy marriages are the majority in some societies (e.g., Schapera, *Life*, 277).

284. See Kleiner, "Women"; e.g., *CIL* 6.10230 (= *ILS* 8394; *FIRA* 3.70; in Sherk, *Empire*, §184, p. 242); cf. Lefkowitz and Fant, *Life*, 133–47.

285. Alciph. *Farm.* 39 (Dryades to Melionê), 3.41, ¶2 (LCL, 147).

286. With, e.g., Wagner-Hasel, "Roles: Greece," 741; cf. Winter, *Wives*, 160; Reden, "Work," 743; earlier, Xen. *Oec.* 7.33, 39. For such domestic activity, see, e.g., the distaff or loom in Prov 31:19; Hom. *Il.* 3.126–27; Virg. *Aen.* 8.407–15; Ovid *Metam.* 4.35; 6.26–145; food preparation in *Test. Ab.* 4:3 B. Xen. *Oec.* 7.17–22 notes that wives do indoor tasks and husbands outdoor tasks but both are necessary.

287. E.g., Ps.-Melissa *Letter to Kleareta* (in Malherbe, *Moral Exhortation*, 83); Mus. Ruf. 3, p. 40.10; p. 42.26; 4, p. 44.14.

288. Xen. *Mem.* 2.2.4. We must weigh this, however, with Demosth. *Neaer.* 122: high-class prostitutes are for pleasure, concubines or attendants for daily needs, but wives for bearing and rearing legitimate offspring.

289. Wagner-Hasel, "Roles: Greece," 741. In some modern Mediterranean culture, see Pizzuto-Pomaco, "Shame," 48, 50–51.

290. Goodman, *State*, 37; Safrai, "Home," 761, 764; see esp. *m. Ketub.* 5:5. For washing, cf. Jeremias, *Jerusalem*, 18.

291. Perhaps even in LXX adaptation of the Hebrew (so Brayford, "Shame," though not all concur).

292. *B. Yebam.* 63ab.

293. The Pastorals' social ethics do reflect an explicit apologetic concern (1 Tim 5:14; 6:1; Titus 2:5, 8, 10; see esp. Padgett, "Rationale").

294. Horsley, *Documents*, 3:33–34, §8; indeed, she was ready to find him another wife when she could not bear (36). Cf. similarly ibid., 40, §11 (although obedience is not explicit here).

295. Cf. the common view of the virtue of wifely obedience in Plato *Meno* 71 (in Allen, *Philosophy*, 98); Quint. *Decl.* 262.8; see further Verner, *Household*, 30–33. Dibelius and Conzelmann, *Pastoral Epistles*, 47, cite the New Comedy poet Philemon: "It is a good wife's duty, O Nikostrate, to be devoted to her husband, but in subordination; a wife who prevails is a great evil." Spartan women could be viewed as exceptional (Plut. *S. Sp. Wom.*, Gorgo 5, *Mor.* 240E), but even they obeyed their fathers and husbands (*S. Sp. Wom.*, anonymous 22, *Mor.* 242B).

"yield in all things" to her husband.[296] This was certainly clear in Homer, the most widely recited of Greek poets: Telemachus reminds his mother that he holds the authority in the house and warns her to leave speaking in public to men.[297] Aristotle emphasizes that the sort of "friendship" a husband and a wife share is analogous to that shared by rulers and subjects, appropriate equity requiring the superior party to receive the greater share.[298]

Xenophon, one of the more progressive authors of his era, praised his wife for obeying even his mere word (adding that she was so skilled in managing the household that she had "a masculine mind").[299] He notes that if a wife misbehaves, it is the husband's own fault if he has not properly instructed her, just as it is the fault of one who tends animals if the animals are poorly trained.[300] Hellenistic marriage contracts granted new rights to women but reflect the older conventional expectations about wives' restrictive roles in marriage, including the wife's submissiveness.[301] In Philo's symbolism, male naturally rules female;[302] in his ethics, the wife "serves" the husband and the husband-wife relationship is comparable to father-child and slaveholder-slave relationships.[303]

Disparity in age naturally affected Greek marriages. Indeed, throughout the Mediterranean world, men married women who could be significantly younger,[304] and this "must have encouraged a psychological subordination of wife to husband."[305] Younger mothers could be viewed as still somewhat "childish";[306] their husbands would have to put up with new brides' childish antics until they matured.[307] Greek men married around thirty,[308] marrying a young woman on average about eighteen[309] but potentially much younger.[310]

296. Eurip. *El.* 1052–53 (in this case opposing Clytemnestra's killing her husband to avenge his killing of their daughter).

297. Hom. *Od.* 1.356–59; she complies with his wise saying in 1.360–61. Arthur, "Early Greece," 15, however, emphasizes the "mutual respect and affection" in the marriage of Telemachus's parents. Ajax expects his bed partner to obey "in everything" (Soph. *Ajax* 526–28), but in this case she is also his slave.

298. Arist. *N.E.* 8.11.4, 1161a.

299. Xen. *Oec.* 10.1. For Aristotle on the husband ruling, see, e.g., Lefkowitz and Fant, *Life*, 63, §86.

300. Xen. *Oec.* 3.10. She must be taught (3.14–16); once a particular man found his wife teachable (7.10), he began to teach her (7.11–22).

301. Verner, *Household*, 38, 64–65 (some as late as the first century B.C.E.). "Wives are expected to be domestic, socially retiring, chaste, and submissive to their husbands" (65). Collins, *Corinthians*, 521, cites first- and second-century B.C.E. marriage contracts that list first among a wife's duties subjection to her husband (P.Giss. 21; P.Tebt. 1.104). She could not spend a night or a day away from home without his consent (P.Tebt. 104.27–28; *BGU* 1052.25–27).

302. Baer, *Categories*, 69.

303. Philo *Hypoth.* 7.3, 14, as noted by Meeks, "Androgyne," 177.

304. Girls could marry at, e.g., thirteen (Ovid *Metam.* 9.714) or fifteen (Xen. *Oec.* 7.4–5). Soranus *Gynec.* 1.8.33 suggests that fourteen is the natural age for first intercourse (cf. also *Nin. Rom.* frg. 1, A-3); others considered it an ideal age for beauty (Xen. Eph. *Anthia* 1.2). Palestinian Jewish women apparently married initially at about twelve to eighteen (Jeffers, "Families," 134–35; Chapman, "Marriage," 186), but men often at about eighteen to twenty (*m. 'Abot* 5:21; *b. Qidd.* 29b–30a; *Eccl. Rab.* 3:2, §3; *Lam. Rab.* 3:27, §9; cf. Safrai, "Home," 748); cf. a Diaspora Jewish marriage at about twenty-two (*CIJ* 1:409, §553), but some surely married later (cf. Thornton, "Bachelors"). Girls might be betrothed virtually from birth (Cohen, *Law*, 297–98), and rabbis ideally wanted them married as soon after puberty as possible (e.g., *Pesiq. Rab Kah.* 11:6; cf. also *Test. Levi* 9:10). Some claimed fifteen for Assyria (*Nin. Rom.* frg. 1, A-3) and seven for India (Arrian *Ind.* 9.1).

305. Garnsey and Saller, *Empire*, 131.

306. Soranus *Gynec.* 2.12.19.

307. Plut. *Bride* 2, *Mor.* 138D.

308. Hesiod *W.D.* 695–97; also Wagner-Hasel, "Roles: Greece," 741; Ferguson, *Backgrounds*, 55. For a younger marriage, see Demosth. *Boeot.* 2.12; not all young women were happy with considerably older men (Alciph. *Farm.* 7 [Phoebianê to Anicetus], 1.28; *Court.* 17 [Leontium to Lamia], 2.2; *Eccl. Rab.* 11:9, §1). Some ancients appealed to astrology to decide relative ages for marriage (Ptolemy *Tetrab.* 4.5.182–83)!

309. Hesiod *W.D.* 698.

310. See, e.g., Ovid *Metam.* 9.714 and other sources above.

Although the age disparity was not as great as among Greeks,[311] similar expectations obtained in Roman society.[312] Among the aristocracy, for whom we have the most information regarding such matters, wives should be knowledgeable enough to encourage their husbands' opinions, but they were not encouraged to offer their own. "In public they were best seen—nodding in agreement or smiling appreciatively at their husbands' wit—but not heard."[313] Roman men often looked wistfully to marriages in the "good old days" of the republic or the beginning of the empire.[314] Thus Cato preferred a wife of noble birth to one who was merely rich, because the former type cared about their honor and hence would prove more obedient (ὑπηκόους) to their husbands (Plut. *M. Cato* 20.1).[315]

In the early second century B.C.E., one critic of women's advancement[316] opined that if the state eased up on women's subjection, wives would not settle for equality but even become their superiors;[317] after all, they had already gone so far as to publicly speak to other women's husbands.[318] Cato was particularly offended by their speaking in public to other women's husbands, insisting that they should have made their requests to their own husbands at home.[319] He could only imagine that these women had come to make their requests in public because they thought they were more attractive to men other than their husbands.[320] The opposing side of the debate, however, won out.[321]

Roman laws changed in the early empire as wives passed from husbands' to fathers' authority.[322] Some scholars contend that wifely subordination had even ceased to be the norm among Romans before the imperial period.[323] This is true only by way of comparison with earlier practice, however, not in the sense of modern egalitarian

311. Some scholars argue that Roman men averaged about five years older than their wives, who were usually married between twelve and eighteen (Jeffers, "Families," 134; idem, *World*, 238), and that girls usually married "in their early teens" (Ferguson, *Backgrounds*, 55; and Hopkins, "Age at Marriage," which he cites; cf., e.g., Quint. *Inst.* pref. 4). Others argue that lower-class Roman women married in their late teens and men in their mid- to late twenties, with a ten-year gap on average (larger among aristocrats; Shaw, "Age"; for men marrying at twenty-five or later, see Saller, "Age").

312. Cf. Verner, *Household*, 33–34. One woman desires to "serve" a husband as her "master" in Virg. *Aen.* 4.103, 214; the Roman matron rules the domestic sphere through obedience to her husband (Publ. Syr. 108). Val. Max. 6.7.1 even praises a wife for submissively feigning ignorance of her famous husband's affair with a slave; Cato *Distichs* 3.12, 20 criticizes a wife who is uncooperative and unsubmissive.

313. Shelton, *Romans*, 299.

314. In the first century B.C.E., Catullus noted that a wife should stay home, nodding her assent to everyone (*Carm.* 61.154–56); out of obedience to her parents, she should not strive with her husband (62.59–65). Literally or figuratively, a married woman's husband (cf. Tibullus 1.2.41, 55–56) is called her *dominus*, "lord," in Tibullus 1.2.7. Livy 34.7.12 claims that in 195 B.C.E. a male speaker argued that wives will remain subject so long as men live and that women themselves prefer it so.

315. One of his few regrets was trusting his wife with a secret (Plut. *M. Cato* 9.6). Nevertheless, he was said to be kind to his wife (20.1); he thought it terrible for a man to strike his wife and that it was better "to be a good husband than a great senator" (20.2 [*Lives*, LCL, 2:361]).

316. The issue, actually, was restrictions on well-to-do women's apparel (Livy 34.1.2–5).

317. Livy 34.3.1–3 (playing on conventional expectations of women's instability, 34.2.13).

318. Livy 34.4.18. Livy (writing shortly before the NT era) indicates that their husbands had ordered them to stay home but the wives ignored "modesty" (34.1.5).

319. Livy 34.2.9; even at home, however, they should leave business to men (34.2.10). Women were not to conduct business without a male guardian (34.2.11), but now, he complains, we have allowed them into the Forum (34.2.11).

320. Livy 34.2.10.

321. Livy 34.7.1–3.

322. See Garnsey and Saller, *Empire*, 130–31; also Gardner, *Women*, 5, who compares sons under their fathers' authority and notes that not all men would have taken all the power that the law, in principle, granted.

323. Winter, *Wives*, 113 (following Treggiari, *Marriage*, 261). Cf. Carcopino, *Life*, 84–85 (cf. also 90–95); for upward mobility among aristocrats, Meeks, *Urban Christians*, 23–24.

marriage.[324] A husband "bossed around" by, or compliant to, his wife or freedmen remained an object of ridicule.[325] A first-century Roman Stoic could insist that a virtuous, philosophically knowledgeable woman serves (ὑπηρετεῖν) her husband by her own hands, doing even servants' work.[326] In the early second century, Pliny praises his wife, noting that her devotion to him confirms her virtue.[327] An orator of second-century C.E. Rome opined that even the backward Cyclopes ruled at least their wives and children.[328] A late second-century Stoic emperor praised the gods for an obedient wife.[329] Another second-century Roman writer could present a wife promising to obey her husband.[330] One should not divorce an "obedient" wife.[331]

The ideal may have persisted more fully in the East, where a wife could call a husband "master" much later than this.[332] Josephus claims that the law of Moses regards women as inferior to men in every respect; the authority belongs to the husband, and the wife should be submissive.[333] Heeding one's wife can even merit punishment.[334] In the late first century, Dio Chrysostom regards it as common knowledge that men are stronger than women and hence more suited to lead.[335]

Likewise, Plutarch, writing in the late first and early second century, advises a wife not to cultivate her own friends or religion but to accept those of her husband.[336] Wives are praised if they "subordinate themselves to their husbands" (ὑποτάττουσαι μὲν γὰρ ἑαυτὰς τοῖς ἀνδράσιν); the husband meanwhile ought to control his wife not as one controls property but as the soul controls the body to "govern" (ἄρχειν) it lovingly without being enslaved by its desires.[337] Plutarch did advocate harmonious consent, but at the same time insisted on the husband's leadership.[338]

In the second century C.E., a writer in Asia Minor takes for granted that wives, children, and slaves should obey.[339] Aelius Aristides declares that a wife "should be

324. Certainly, we do not read of the public approving of husbands' murdering their wives for alcohol consumption in this period (as earlier in Val. Max. 6.3.9), although, in at least some regions, abuse must have continued (Aug. *Conf.* 9.9; *y. Ketub.* 11:3, §2). We may also suspect that men often did not get their ways, given the number of love spells meant to induce women to love men (e.g., *PGM* 36.69–101, 102–33, 134–60, 187–210, 295–311; some were designed to get them away from their husbands, *PDM* 61.197–216 = *PGM* 61.39–71).

325. Even an emperor (Suet. *Claud.* 25.5).

326. Mus. Ruf. 3, p. 42.7–8. Musonius, who may be guarding against antiegalitarian criticisms, lectured in basically the same era as Luke wrote.

327. Pliny *Ep.* 4.19.2. He praises a wife who would have been a model even in earlier times, always respecting her husband greatly (8.5.1).

328. Max. Tyre 15.7. He praises a wise ancient Greek who knew properly how to "run his household" (25.1).

329. Marc. Aur. 1.17.7.

330. Apul. *Metam.* 5.5. In Severian of Gabala in *Pauluskommentare* 261 (Bray, *Corinthians*, 107), woman has man over her.

331. Quint. *Decl.* 327.5.

332. Xen. Eph. *Anthia* 5.14 (probably second century C.E., though the narrative world might recall earlier mores). The title "lord" for husband appears over a wide range of sources (e.g., Gen 18:12; Hos 2:16; Virg. *Aen.* 4.214; Tibullus 1.2.7; *Test. Ab.* 5:12; 6:2, 8; 15:4 A; 4:2; 6:5 B; 1 Pet 3:6; Xen. Eph. *Anthia* 5.14; *'Abot R. Nat.* 1, §6 B), though such respectful titles also appear for others of superior rank, including in families (e.g., Gen 33:13–14; *SPap* 1:338–39, lines 1, 24; P.Giss.Univ. 21, line 11; *Test. Ab.* 2:7, 10; 3:5; 15:4; 18:4 A; 8:9; 10:1; 11:1; 12:3 B; *Jos. Asen.* 4:5/7, 9/12), or even a son of higher rank socially (P.Oxy. 123, lines 1, 26).

333. Jos. *Ag. Ap.* 2.200–201.

334. Jos. *Ant.* 1.49; 18.255; cf. similarly the emphasis in *L.A.E.* 26:2.

335. Dio Chrys. *Or.* 3.70.

336. Plut. *Bride* 19, *Mor.* 140D. Keeping to ancestral religion was a traditional value (cf. Cic. *Inv.* 2.22.65–66).

337. Plut. *Bride* 33, *Mor.* 142E (LCL, 2:323). Plutarch criticizes the Persian king for ruling others as slaves but not his own wife, of whom he should have been "master" (δεσπότης) especially (Plut. *Uned. R.* 2, *Mor.* 780C).

338. Plut. *Bride* 11, *Mor.* 139CD. And in this, Plutarch, as Garnsey and Saller, *Empire*, 134, remind us, was more benevolent than many.

339. Artem. *Oneir.* 1.24.

pleased with whatever the husband says; her place is to be 'ruled' [ἄρχεσθαι], and he will command her; she will also seek to be girded by his nature, "as a better person would treat an inferior one."[340] The second-century Stoic Hierocles agreed with the dominant perspective in placing wives over domestic and husbands over public activities but protested against making these distinctions absolute.[341] Later still, a Pythagorean writer could contend that a wife should not oppose her husband;[342] and Cynic writers (of less certain date) portrayed virtuous wives as those who carry out their husbands' wishes as an unwritten law.[343]

What is clear is that the confrontation of old and new values created tension.[344] Advancements that had occurred could provoke a backlash,[345] illustrated most readily by complaints from the early second-century c.e. satirist Juvenal: because women are always complaining and demanding more, marriage may lead to suicide (*Sat.* 6.30–37); wives contended with husbands violently (6.111–12) and bickered with husbands even in bed (6.268–85).[346] Juvenal contrasts the humble and chaste wives of the past (6.286–305). Wives, he complains, order slaves crucified, regardless of their husbands' sentiments, and change husbands frequently (6.219–24).[347]

For many ancients, however, marriage was not just about subordination. Mutual love is common in the sources;[348] not only the wife[349] but the husband[350] could demonstrate love for the spouse. Even centuries earlier, Xenophon portrayed marriage as sharing and partnership.[351] A first-century Greek author describes a wife as a partner in sharing a husband's entire life.[352] Another first-century author depicts an ideal marriage as "perfect companionship [συμβίωσιν] and mutual love"[353] and summons the husband to the same measure of fidelity as demanded for the wife.[354] A moralist from this period emphasizes that husband and wife should feel

340. Ael. Arist. *Def. Or.* 129, §41D (LCL, 1:357). He likens the husband's superiority to the wife and God's superiority to mortals, the ruler's to the citizen, and the master's to the slave (130, §41D, undoubtedly in different ways).

341. Hierocles *On Duties: Household Management* (in Malherbe, *Moral Exhortation*, 97–98).

342. Iambl. *V.P.* 11.54.

343. Ps.-Melissa, *Letter to Kleareta* (in Malherbe, *Moral Exhortation*, 83). To ground wifely submission in a general mutual submission of believers, as Ephesians does (Eph 5:21–22), was unusual and characterizes a distinctively Christian ethic of servanthood.

344. With, e.g., Verner, *Household*, 81.

345. Cf. the early second-century revival of conservative values in imperial households (Boatwright, "Imperial Women"). Women's exaltation could cause male complaints even in myth (e.g., Apollod. *Bib.* 1.8.2).

346. Even some of Juvenal's authentic examples about women (e.g., women gladiators) are extreme cases (Friedländer, *Life*, 1:249).

347. For their cruelty to slaves, see also Juv. *Sat.* 6.474–85. In the late republic, Cicero complained that a man who cannot deny his wife anything is no better than a slave (Cic. *Parad.* 36).

348. For conjugal love in general, see, e.g., Cic. *Off.* 1.17.54; Val. Max. 4.6; Philost. *Hrk.* 11.1; Dixon, *Roman Mother*, 2–3; *CIJ* 1:cxvi; particularly moving, Lefkowitz and Fant, *Life*, 12, §26 (despite the formulaic character of epitaphs [e.g., Rawson, "Family," 26], they can reflect genuine sentiment, as today).

349. For wives' love, e.g., *IG* 14.1976 (in Horsley, *Documents*, 4:35, §10); Apollod. *Bib.* 3.12.6; Val. Max. 4.6.5; 4.6.ext. 1, 3; Petron. *Sat.* 111; *CIJ* 1:118, §166; 1:137, §195; Horsley, *Documents*, 3:47–48, §14.

350. For husbands' love for wives, see, e.g., Hom. *Il.* 9.341–42; Cato *Coll. Dist.* 20; Val. Max. 4.3.3; 4.6.1–3; Pliny *Ep.* 8.5.3; Iambl. *V.P.* 18.84; *Gr. Anth.* 7.340; Ps.-Phoc. 195; *b. Yebam.* 62b, bar.

351. Xen. *Oec.* 7.18, 30. Xenophon clearly articulated distinct natures for distinct roles (7.16–42 passim), but he seems more progressive than most of his contemporaries.

352. Dio Chrys. *Or.* 3.122. But an earlier writer could emphasize their "partnership" while assigning outside work to men and indoor work to women (Xen. *Oec.* 7.30).

353. Mus. Ruf. 13A, p. 88.17–18; cf. "partnership" (κοινωνίαν) and "harmony" (ὁμόνοιαν) in Mus. Ruf. 13B, p. 90.6–8, 13–14.

354. Mus. Ruf. 12, p. 86.33–40; p. 88.1 (arguing [p. 86.39–87.1] that surely we should not expect men "to be less moral than women" [Lutz, 89]). Porph. *Marc.* 2.21 later claims that he married Marcella to be his "partner" (κοινωνόν), his sharer in life.

that they share everything;[355] the wife must supply "conversation, character, and comradeship."[356]

Even a Qumran text warns against disdaining one's wife, one's "closest companion."[357] Unlike many Greek philosophers, many rabbis emphasized husbands' sexual appreciation for their wives.[358] It was said that R. Akiba consulted his wife before accepting a position, and she gave her advice.[359] Not everyone agreed with such perspectives. Thus, for Josephus, God punished Adam for being so weak as to have heeded his wife (*Ant.* 1.49); God likewise punished Antipas for listening to a woman's talk (18.255; cf. 18.240–55). That different rabbis even in a later period retained different views is clear: one Babylonian Amora charged hyperbolically that a man "who follows his wife's counsel will descend into *Gehenna*," and another responded with the saying, "If your wife is short, bend down and hear her whisper!"[360] Some wives proved unrighteous, such as the wife who objected to her husband's generosity to the poor during famine;[361] for such circumstances, however, divorce remained an option.[362]

Later rabbis insisted that a husband must respect his wife[363] (that the reverse was also true goes without saying).[364] He could not prevent her from visiting her parents, going to the bathhouse, or visiting the grieving.[365] Mutuality is clear in the lists of marital duties, although they are mostly divided by gender and need not indicate equality.[366]

Still, Jewish women were mostly under the authority of either husbands or fathers.[367] Women do not control their lives, being under others' dominion.[368] A Qumran text reminds the husband that he holds authority over his wife;[369] he alone may govern her,[370] and he may rule her so that she lives the way he wants her to.[371] A man governed by his wife would be held miserable.[372] Philo opines that wives are under their

---

355. Plut. *Bride* 34, *Mor.* 143A (explaining what he thought to be the point of Roman law's forbidding conjugal gifts).

356. Plut. *Bride* 22, *Mor.* 141AB. They should avoid all conflicts, but especially on their marriage bed (39, *Mor.* 143E).

357. 4Q416 2 (+ 4Q417) II, 21 (trans. Abegg, 384).

358. See Satlow, "Love" (including the one-sided emphasis on the wife's beauty).

359. *Y. Pe'ah* 8:7, §3. For traditions about R. Akiba's relatively high view of women, see Finkelstein, *Akiba*, 187–91 (though cf. also Akiba's liberal divorce policy toward wives, applicable in principle if one found another woman more beautiful; *m. Giṭ.* 9:10). Rabbi Meir also was said to have virtuously heeded his wife's good counsel (*b. Ber.* 10a).

360. So *b. B. Meṣiʿa* 59a (Soncino 351); their successors harmonized the sayings by applying the harsher view to external (as opposed to domestic) matters or to religious (as opposed to secular) matters.

361. *'Abot R. Nat.* 3 A.

362. Sir 25:26 (for disobedience). But one should never divorce a good wife (7:19, 26).

363. Safrai, "Home," 763–64 (a value also in Plut. *Bride* 47, *Mor.* 144F–145A); on treatment of wives, see further Montefiore and Loewe, *Anthology*, 507–15. God cares about peace between husband and wife (*b. Ḥul.* 141a; R. Ishmael in *b. Šabb.* 116a); some later sources even attribute family conflicts to a demon (*Test. Sol.* 18:15).

364. One rabbi helped another rabbi to divorce his wife for disrespecting him (*y. Ketub.* 11:3, §2). For mutual respect or honor, see also Plut. *Bride* 36, *Mor.* 143B; *Sent. Sext.* 238.

365. Safrai, "Home," 762.

366. E.g., *m. Ketub.* 5:5–9; *y. Ketub.* 5:3–9:1 (e.g., 5:8, §1); *Gen. Rab.* 52:12; Falk, "Law," 516; Safrai, "Home," 761; Wegner, *Chattel*, 11, 74–76; Witherington, *Women*, 4. For Greek lists of reciprocal duties, see, e.g., Lewis, *Life*, 55; Verner, *Household*, 37–38.

367. Fiensy, "Composition," 225 (citing Jos. *Ag. Ap.* 2.201; *m. Ketub.* 4:4); even wealthy Babatha depended on a man for "contacts with authorities" (Fiensy, "Composition," 226). See also Chapman, "Marriage," 206–10.

368. *Sipra Qed. par.* 1.195.2.2. Some scholars argue that the rabbis held that Miriam was punished for seeking to lead (Graetz, "Miriam").

369. 4Q416 2 (+ 4Q417) III, 20–IV, 2.

370. 4Q416 2 (+ 4Q417) III, 20–IV, 6.

371. 4Q416 2 (+ 4Q417) III, 20–IV, 7.

372. *b. Beṣah* 32b, bar.; the wife having authority should be avoided (Sir 30:19).

husbands' authority and obey their commands,[373] and Josephus claims that wives should be submissive, since the Jewish law granted the husband the authority over the wife for her good.[374] Samaritans also expected wifely obedience.[375]

i. Women in Myth and Religion

Women's piety could be praised.[376] Women were often involved in religious cults in ways that, at least in traditional Greek culture, were not open to them in other aspects of life.[377] Many Roman rituals could be performed by either gender.[378] Women could become priestesses[379] both in Italy[380] and in the Greek East,[381] for example, Flavia Ammon, a first-century C.E. high priestess of a temple in Ephesus,[382] and Paulina, a fourth-century C.E. priestess of multiple mystery cults in Rome.[383] In some cases, these offices belonged to families, but in others, the woman held this office alone;[384] the primary function of many of these offices was, however, patronal rather than cultic.[385] Often priestesses were engaged in temple administration, but it remains noteworthy that priestesses usually belonged to the same class as priests, in contrast to the majority of women not found in such offices.[386] That is, these offices were open to the elite and were determined by class more than by gender. Women sometimes had their own special cults and rites;[387] men who were found invading these rites would provoke scandal.[388] (Likewise, men also had some exclusive[389] or nearly exclusive[390] cults.) On women's roles in religion, see further comment on Acts 16:13.

Moreover, although men were also involved in each of these cults, women were known for their participation in the Egyptian cult of Isis[391] and (apparently often

373. Philo *Creation* 167.

374. Jos. *Ag. Ap.* 2.201.

375. Bowman, *Documents*, 311.

376. E.g., Iambl. *V.P.* 11.55–56. For their greater inclination to many religious practices, see, e.g., Dion. Hal. *Ant. rom.* 8.39.1; Avi-Yonah, *Hellenism*, 31.

377. Even in classical Athens (Gould, "Position in Athens," 50). In modern Mediterranean culture, see Pizzuto-Pomaco, "Shame," 43–45.

378. Croom, *Clothing*, 70.

379. For a survey, see Kraemer, *Maenads*, 211–17, §§78–83.

380. Lefkowitz and Fant, *Life*, 259f, §§255–57. Farther west, e.g., Donahue, "Iunia Rustica."

381. Lefkowitz and Fant, *Life*, 157, §159; 260–62, §§258–64.

382. Ibid., 260, §258.

383. *ILS* 1259–61 in Lefkowitz and Fant, *Life*, 279f, §264a.

384. Gardner, *Women*, 67–68; Kearsley, "Asiarchs, *archiereis*"; R. A. Kearsley, in Llewelyn, *Documents*, 6:26, §1.

385. Gardner, *Women*, 68.

386. Simon, "Priestesses."

387. E.g., Cic. *Verr.* 2.4.45.102; Appian *Hist. rom.* 5.7; Plut. *Caes.* 9.3; Juv. *Sat.* 2.87–92; Suet. *Julius* 6; see further Kraemer, *Maenads*, 11–42; cf. also Kroeger, "Cults"; Pomeroy, *Goddesses*, 205–6. In some different societies, cf. Eliade, *Rites*, 79.

388. Cic. *Att.* 1.12; *Fam.* 1.9.15; Plut. *Caes.* 10.1–3, 6; Cic. 28.2; cf. 19.3–4. Men were not, of course, excluded from most goddess cults (e.g., Plut. *Rom. Q.* 3, *Mor.* 264C).

389. E.g., Strabo 14.6.3. Some festivals apparently excluded women (Men. Rhet. 1.3, 364.5–7). The Hercules cult in Rome may not have excluded women (Schultz, "Prejudice"), though Sil. It. 3.22–23 says that women and pigs were kept away. The cult of Silvanus may have welcomed both genders (Dorcey, "Women").

390. Although military interest may have skewed some results, many scholars say that Mithraism excluded women (Gager, *Kingdom*, 133; Martin, *Religions*, 114) or did so with a few exceptions (Klauck, *Context*, 141, 148); evidence for women's involvement (e.g., David, "Exclusion") seems exceptional. Women were relatively few in the Samothracian Mysteries (Cole, *Theoi megaloi*, 42).

391. Cf. Heyob, *Isis*, 81–110, and (somewhat less critically) 37–80 (see esp. 40, 52, 76, 80); Dunand, *Religion en Égypte*, 69–70; Barth, *Ephesians*, 2:656–57; see comment on Acts 18:18. In practice, women remained a minority of worshipers in the cult, though a significant one (see esp. Heyob, *Isis*, 81–83, 110); men largely dominated (also Kee, *Origins*, 91), but Isis remained a patroness for women (e.g., Horsley, *Documents*, 1:20, §2).

ecstatic) participation in the cult of Dionysus (popular in Asia Minor),[392] probably in reality[393] as well as in myth,[394] and in the cult of Cybele[395] (also associated with its origins in Asia Minor).[396] Romans were often concerned with the inroads such Eastern cults were making into dignified Roman society; the cult of Dionysus provoked scandal partly regarding women more than two centuries earlier,[397] and the cult of Isis only recently.[398] Some claimed that women were particularly susceptible to such cults.[399] Such scandals required groups like these (including Judaism and the early Christians) to respond with a careful apologetic emphasizing that they upheld traditional family values.[400]

Classical myths sometimes portray women negatively,[401] as in the story of Pandora;[402] man received woman as a punishment for receiving the gift of fire (Hesiod *Theog.* 570–612).[403] A misogynist thus might be portrayed as cursing Prometheus for making women.[404] Tiresias, who had been each gender at different times, testified that a

392. E.g., *I. Magn.* 215 (a.); *I. Eph.* 106, 1211; Harland, *Associations*, 46; Aurenhammer, "Sculptures," 267–69; Finegan, *Apostles*, 168.

393. Cf. *I. Magn.* 215 (a.) 24–40 (Lefkowitz and Fant, *Life*, 113–14, §115); *IG* 9².670 (Lefkowitz and Fant, *Life*, 252–53, §245); Diod. Sic. 4.3.2–5 (Kraemer, *Maenads*, 26); Plut. *Alex.* 2.5; *R.Q.* 112, *Mor.* 291AB; *Table* 4.6.1, *Mor.* 671C; Artem. *Oneir.* 2.37; Ferguson, *Backgrounds*, 207; cf. further Kraemer, "Ecstatics"; idem, "Ecstasy," esp. 80; idem, "Euoi," esp. 233; Burkert, *Religion*, 164–65; Otto, *Dionysus*, 142, 171–80; Henrichs, "Identities," 138–48. Women were especially dominant before the late Hellenistic period (Kraemer, "Ecstatics," 48–57).

394. In mythic texts, e.g., Soph. *Antig.* 955–65; *Hom. Hymns* 1.17 (to Dionysus); Diod. Sic. 3.64.2; 4.2.6; Plut. *Table* 1.1.3, *Mor.* 614A; Paus. 2.2.7; cf. Reniers, "Épopée" (despite the approach to matriarchal origins). In art, cf. McNally, "Maenad" (sometimes defending themselves, 107–8). At least in Euripides, however, the Bacchae are not truly liberated (Segal, "Menace," 208–9).

395. For frenzy there (though often associated with men), see, e.g., Livy 38.18.9; Catull. *Carm.* 63.4; Ovid *Fasti* 4.236, 243, 245–46; Strabo 10.3.13; Val. Flacc. 7.635–36; Sen. Y. *Ep. Lucil.* 108.7; Plut. *Dial. L.* 16, *Mor.* 758EF; Suet. *Otho* 8.3; Lucian *Gout* 30–32; *Lucius* 37; *Alex.* 13; *Orph. H.* 27.13; Burkert, *Religion*, 178. But some ancients claimed that the majority of the frenzied participants were women (Iambl. *Myst.* 3.10; cf. Lucian *Affairs* 42). Some associated this cult with that of Dionysus (Lucian *Gout* 38; also Bremmer, "Attis" [citing Catull. *Carm.* 63]). For some Roman resentment (cf., e.g., Pers. *Sat.* 5.185–89; Apul. *Metam.* 8.27–9.10; cf. the Hellenistic Pythagorean treatise in Lefkowitz and Fant, *Life*, 104–5, §107) but mostly gradual acceptance (see, e.g., Val. Max. 1.1.1; 7.5.2; Sil. It. 17.1–4), see Grant, *Gods*, 33; Klauck, *Context*, 124.

396. So, e.g., Eurip. *Bacch.* 59; Lucret. *Nat.* 2.611; Val. Max. 7.5.2; Pliny E. *N.H.* 5.41.147; *Orph. H.* 27.11–12; Apul. *Metam.* 11.4–5; Diog. Laert. 6.1.1; Lucian *Dial. G.* 233–34 (20/12, Aphrodite and Eros 1); Graf, "Asia Minor: Religion," 150.

397. E.g., Rawson, "Family," 16; Kee, *Origins*, 89. Cf., more generally, Livy 25.1.11–12; 39.15.11; 39.18.9.

398. Jos. *Ant.* 18.64–80; cf. Tac. *Ann.* 2.85; Suet. *Tib.* 36. For Roman concerns, gradually eased, see, e.g., Val. Max. 1.3.4; 7.3.8; Juv. *Sat.* 6.489, 511–29; Grant, *Gods*, 34–35; Heyob, *Isis*, 26–27, 36; Dunand, "Mystères," 38. Even much later, Isis worshipers worked hard to emphasize their loyalty to Rome and its values (e.g., Apul. *Metam.* 11.17; cf. chastity, 11.19).

399. Carcopino, *Life*, 131, citing Juv. *Sat.* 6.540–41, 548–50. Wives must follow their husbands' (Roman) religion (Plut. *Bride* 19, *Mor.* 140D).

400. Balch, *Wives*, 117–18 (cf. 65–80); Keener, *Paul*, 139–56 (more briefly, idem, "Man and Woman," 587); for explicit indicators of such concerns in the Pastorals, see Padgett, "Rationale." Some argue that Luke's apologetic aims cause him to limit women's roles (see D'Angelo, "Redactional View"; Matthews, *Converts*, 53–54); although I would not see Luke's portrait as negative against the larger backdrop of Greek culture (and he does not reduce women's testimony as perhaps 1 Cor 15:5–8 does), apologetic concerns might prevent Luke from fleshing out his ideal in Acts 2:17–18 as fully as he otherwise might have.

401. See Sussman, "Workers," 89.

402. E.g., Hesiod *W.D.* 90–95; cf. Paus. 1.24.7.

403. Thus Zeus "made women to be an evil to mortal men, with a nature to do evil" (Hesiod *Theog.* 601–2 [LCL, 123]); cf. Hesiod *W.D.* 57, cited also in Ach. Tat. 1.8.2. In Lucian *Dial. G.* 204 (5/1, Prometheus and Zeus 1), Zeus is angry with Prometheus for creating women. Or Pandora was a composite design from various deities, with the resulting mess that one expects from committees (Dio Chrys. *Or.* 77/78.25).

404. Lucian *Affairs* 9, 43. Misogynists could also revile all women (Ach. Tat. 1.8.1). Lefkowitz, *Women in Myth*, 112–32, addresses misogyny, highlighting Aristotle (for his pervasive influence later, cf. Peradotto and Sullivan, "Introduction," 3).

woman's life was much easier than a man's.[405] Yet myths often focused on women as objects of violence and abuse—common, for example, in Ovid's *Metamorphoses*.[406] Tragedies often focused on women because of their perceived weakness.[407] Some, however, objected to such portrayals. Because Clytemnestra murdered him, the deceased Agamemnon advised Odysseus never to trust a woman,[408] but Dio Chrysostom objects that the issue was not that she was a woman but that she was an evil woman.[409]

At the same time, some women achieved "heroic" status in myth[410] and could come to the fore (for good or harm) in drama in ways they did not typically in daily life.[411] Still, even such "heroic" status did not always benefit the women in question. Although the Amazons (see comment on Acts 8:27) are portrayed as powerful warriors, they are always defeated, serving as a foil for the "normal" masculine heroes of Greek narratives.

Jewish women were often actively engaged in the life of their synagogue communities,[412] although these roles varied from one location to another. Contrary to some older suppositions,[413] women held leadership roles in some synagogues in Asia Minor,[414] probably a minority approach in ancient Judaism that mirrored the social prominence of women in some of these cities.[415] Thus we read of women as synagogue rulers, for example, in Smyrna (*CIJ* 2:10, §741) and Caria (2:20, §756). In some such locations, a few women became "heads of synagogues";[416] some were apparently wealthy and probably benefactors of the synagogues, which was also how men typically achieved the same office.[417] Women account for only about 10 percent of the "synagogue head" inscriptions,[418] a percentage similar to that for women as patronesses in general, but their existence, in any case, refutes the claim that women could not fill the office.

405. Lucian *Dial. D.* 445 (9/28, Menippus and Tiresias 1) (though Lucian himself is skeptical; see *Dial. D.* 445–47, but ¶¶2–3).

406. See Curran, "Rape," 270 (also noting that the victims were usually the ones punished, 271–72). Women also appear inferior to men in Ovid (see Keith, "Lay of Land"); those who behave appropriately in Ovid belong to the domestic sphere (Bolton, "Spaces"). His portrayal of women's subordination also matches artwork from the Augustan period (Ramsby and Severy-Hoven, "Gender").

407. So Aristoph. *Lys.* 137–38.

408. Dio Chrys. *Or.* 74.18–19, developing Hom. *Od.* 11.441–43. In *Od.* 11.432–34, Clytemnestra's behavior reflects badly on her gender (even though she murdered Cassandra, too; 11.422); Odysseus observes that many perished for Helen and now others by Clytemnestra (11.436–39), without pausing to observe the vast majority of bloodshed in Homer performed by men.

409. Dio Chrys. *Or.* 74.19.

410. Willner, "Oedipus Complex."

411. Foley, "Conception."

412. See, e.g., Kraemer, "Evidence"; Safrai, "Place of Women"; Cohen, "Women"; Kraabel, "Judaism in Asia Minor," 46–48; Manns, "Femme."

413. E.g., Jean-Baptiste Frey in *CIJ* 1:lxxxix: "On ne voit jamais une femme remplir la fonction d'archonte."

414. Trebilco, *Communities*, 104–13; women also held prominent roles in pagan cults in Asia Minor, though this (unlike in synagogues) would not correlate with any higher roles in noncultic society (113–25). (Cf. Kraabel, "Judaism in Asia Minor," 44; but his supposed link between women's higher roles here and "female divinities in Anatolian religions" [p. 48] is improbable.) The Tannaim apparently did not approve of women as community administrators (*Sipre Deut.* 157.2.2).

415. Trebilco, *Communities*, 125. Horsley, *Galilee*, 237, believes that early Galilean women participated more freely than later rabbinic sources indicate, though less than in the urban Diaspora.

416. Brooten, *Women Leaders*, 5–33, noting that there is no evidence that these are purely honorific, "heads of synagogues" normally representing the synagogue communities to outsiders. At least some uses of the term, for some people, were honorific if we may infer from the title's application to an infant (Chilton and Yamauchi, "Synagogues," 1146), perhaps from a family that held the title. On the usual sense of the title, see comment on Acts 13:15.

417. Brooten, *Women Leaders*, 32–33.

418. Chilton and Yamauchi, "Synagogues," 1146, count three out of thirty.

Bernadette Brooten also notes some women in the role of ἀρχηγός.[419] Three of the five women "elders" are from one town, Venosa (and two other women are bearers of office there); though women remained the minority in leadership even there, that Jewish community appears to have provided women with more opportunity for office than was usual.[420]

j. Women's Education

Some brilliant and educated women generated respect and praise.[421] Women from wealthy households increasingly had access to education in the first and second centuries C.E.[422] We read, for example, of women poets,[423] including from the imperial period.[424] Educated mothers were valued, though perhaps particularly for the influence on their sons' eloquence.[425]

These women were, however, exceptional achievers in a system that did not tend to facilitate women's achievement. Women had far less access to education, particularly concerning public activities such as speaking, than did males of the same class.[426] Most women (i.e., outside the small percentage of the population that was well-to-do) had little education; scholars who give examples of educated women often fail to note that these cases are the exception and that even their advanced education most frequently focused on domestic activity.[427] Some estimate that "for every five or six men who could read and write, there was one woman who was fully literate."[428]

Whereas most upper-strata males could read and write, some argue that only "a small percentage of women from the same social orders could."[429] Even though such a claim probably underestimates female literacy in the upper strata of the first century

---

419. Brooten, *Women Leaders*, 35–39. Also women priests (73–99), though this title might simply specify "daughters of Aaron" (cf. Luke 1:5).

420. See Brooten, *Women Leaders*, 44; on the elder inscriptions more fully, 41–55. For another example, a fourth- or fifth-century elder inscription from Malta, see Kraemer, "Inscription from Malta." One of the few synagogue inscriptions from Crete identifies a woman elder (Sanders, *Crete*, 43).

421. Cf., e.g., Sall. *Catil.* 25.2 (though Sempronia was also evil; on Sallust's hostile view of Sempronia, see discussion in Milnor, "Women," 279–81); Plut. *Dinner* 3, *Mor.* 148CE (placed as a contemporary of Anacharsis); Pliny *Ep.* 1.16.6 (though Pliny is unsure if she is the true author). Cf. even praise for a woman's wisdom in Hom. *Il.* 13.432, though this refers to wisdom in women's matters. Shelton, *Romans*, 299, suggests that, in general, a woman's intelligence was praised for enjoying her husband's opinions, rather than for expressing her own. I adapted this material on women's education in antiquity also for an article, Keener, "Education" (meant to contrast opportunities available in antiquity with those available today).

422. Winter, *Wives*, 112–13, following Hemelrijk, *Matrona docta*, 92–96; cf. also Christes, "Education," 822; Verner, *Household*, 39.

423. See, e.g., Vivante, "Authors," 712; on Sappho, see, e.g., Grant, *Social History*, 12; Lefkowitz and Fant, *Life*, 4–6; for the view that her poetry expresses lesbian sentiments, see Stigers, "World"; Winckler, "Gardens"; Hartmann, "Homosexuality," 469 (cf. Philost. *Vit. Apoll.* 1.30). For women physicians, see the excursus on ancient physicians in ch. 11 above.

424. E.g., two in the early second century C.E. in Brennan, "Poets." Cf. Roman women poets in Hallett, "Authors" (who on 716 also notes later Roman Christian women authors, such as Faltonia Betitia Proba and Egeria).

425. Quint. *Inst.* 1.1.6; cf. Dixon, *Roman Mother*, 3. Articulate nurses were also valued for the same reason (Quint. *Inst.* 1.1.4–5; cf. Tac. *Dial.* 29; *b. Ketub.* 50a). Fathers were responsible for education (e.g., 4 Macc 18:10; *b. Qidd.* 29a; 30a; Moore, *Judaism*, 2:127; Goodman, *State*, 72; Safrai, "Education," 947, citing *t. Qidd.* 1:11; *Sipre Deut.* 46; Jos. *Ag. Ap.* 2.178; Philo *Embassy* 210), but for mothers' role in teaching children, see Plut. *Educ.* 20, *Mor.* 14B; Hdn. 5.8.10; 6.1.1; cf. Prov 1:8; 6:20; 15:20; 23:22; 31:26; 2 Tim 1:5; Barclay, *Train a Child*, 157; Verner, *Household*, 137; in a secondary way, *b. Ber.* 17a; *Soṭah* 21a; a grandmother in Tob 1:8. Women (and unmarried men) may not teach children in *m. Qidd.* 4:13, but this probably does not refer to their own.

426. Cf. Gamble, "Literacy," 645.

427. Forbes, *Prophecy*, 277 (esp. n. 57).

428. Scholer, "Writing," 1283.

429. Davies, *Rhetoric*, 252 (following Harris, *Literacy*). This is certainly true for metropolites in Egypt's nome capitals (Lewis, *Life*, 62), though there were literate women, at their parents' discretion (62–63). Even

for places such as Rome, women had far less access to education for public activity. In well-to-do families, some girls would receive elementary education along with boys from age seven, but from twelve, generally only boys moved to the second level in public, girls learning household duties at home.[430] Dio opined that gold earrings were acceptable for girls' ears, but for those of Greek boys, only education.[431]

Views on women's education differed. Although even the most progressive voices were rarely egalitarian in practice (sometimes perhaps due to social constraints), a number of voices in antiquity advocated women's education[432] and trusted women's ability to learn.[433] Around 600 B.C.E., Cleobulus advocated providing husbands with women educated in wisdom;[434] he was supporting their education but presumably upholding traditional roles (since they were being provided for husbands). Aristotle, reacting against such views, attacked general education as wasteful; it was not sensible trying to educate everyone in the same way.[435] In advocating that women be taught philosophy,[436] Musonius guarded against accusations that this learning subverted roles traditionally assigned to women by arguing that they be taught what would help them more effectively fulfill the roles that society demanded of their gender.[437] That is, it would be adapted for women's work, such as spinning;[438] women did not need technical philosophic training because they lacked opportunity to use it.[439]

Plutarch insisted that a husband, contrary to common perspectives, ought to care for his wife's learning, which will keep her from following nonsense and immorality;[440] he then chivalrously proceeded to insist that women, left to themselves, produce only base passions and folly and so they need a man's input.[441] Some argued that women were less intelligent or more susceptible to deception than men;[442] Juvenal ridicules women who try to be educated in philosophy and rhetoric.[443] Because of their gener-

in the classical period, though women were less literate than men, there is evidence for some literate women (Cole, "Read").

430. Stamps, "Children," 198; cf. Watson, "Education," 309 (allowing that some girls did receive education from twelve to fifteen). Jeffers, World, 255–56, suggests that upper-class girls' education stopped at fourteen, in time for arranged marriages, while boys would go further. The discrepancies may reflect different times and places concerned.

431. Dio Chrys. Or. 32.3.

432. See, e.g., Plato Laws 6.780–81; 7.804–6; 8.838–39, as quoted in Lefkowitz and Fant, Life, 72–75, §88; Plutarch's A Woman, Too, Should Be Educated.

433. E.g., Xen. On Hunting 13.18. Sometimes this meant the husband teaching her (e.g., Xen. Oec. 3.10, 14–16; 7.10; Plut. Bride 48, Mor. 145BC; 1 Cor 14:35), which such writers sometimes present as among the more radical options of their day.

434. Diog. Laert. 1.90. His own daughter reportedly "composed riddles in hexameters" (1.89).

435. Arist. Pol. 2.4.6, 1266b.

436. Mus. Ruf. 4.

437. Yet Musonius appears to have accepted these roles as conventional, or based on general physical traits, rather than universal.

438. Mus. Ruf. 4, p. 46.8–23 (and this only because nature fitted women best for this, but the roles could be interchangeable at times, lines 23–31).

439. Mus. Ruf. 4, p. 48.21–23.

440. Plut. Bride 48, Mor. 145C. Plutarch (or a later writer in his name) seems to have advocated women's education (A Woman, Too, Should be Educated frg. 128–33).

441. Plut. Bride 48, Mor. 145DE. Cf. Publ. Syr. 376 (LCL, 63): "A woman when she thinks alone thinks ill" (cf. similarly Publ. Syr. 365). Blomqvist, "Chryseïs," considers Dio more respectful toward intellectual women than Plutarch was.

442. Val. Max. 9.1.3; see further discussion above. Sen. Y. Dial. 6.7.3 apparently compares them to the uneducated. For "old wives' tales," see Cic. Nat. d. 1.20.55 ; Sen. Y. Ep. Lucil. 94.2; Philost. Vit. Apoll. 5.14; Vit. soph. 1.25.541; Iambl. V.P. 32.227; Jos. Asen. 4:10/14; 1 Tim 4:7; see also Dibelius and Conzelmann, Pastoral Epistles, 68; Winter, Wives, 30–31; esp. Rosivach, "Anus"; cf. Hrk. 7.10; 8.2.

443. Juv. Sat. 6.434–56.

ally lesser education than that of males of the same class, women were sometimes targeted by unscrupulous teachers, who found wealthier women particularly useful; at least, these were the claims of the teachers' detractors.[444]

Because they were so few in proportion to the vast numbers of men, women trained in philosophy drew disproportionate attention and comment in literary sources, but they are well attested.[445] The Pythagorean tradition is noteworthy in its inclusion of women.[446] After listing 218 names of the known disciples of Pythagoras, Iamblichus lists the most famous women by name, of whom he mentions seventeen.[447] This allows that 8 percent, and possibly more, of the early disciples were women, an extraordinary figure by ancient standards in general.[448]

Pythagorean tradition offers examples of learned women. Pythagoras's wife, Theano, was known for her philosophic wisdom,[449] and she authored some works.[450] Pythagoras also entrusted his writings to his daughter Damo.[451] Iamblichus reports that the pregnant wife of a Pythagorean philosopher was tortured to make her reveal the school's secrets; concerned lest her female weakness dispose her to break under torture, she bit off her tongue and spat it out.[452] In a later period, Porphyry explains to his wife that he married her partly because of her aptitude for philosophy;[453] thus he freed her from other masters and shared philosophy with her.[454]

Plato reportedly had some women disciples; later sources name among them Lastheneia of Mantinea and Axiothea of Phlius.[455] Although his other named pupils were male, among Aristippus's disciples was his daughter Arete.[456] For all of Philo's gender bias, he seems happy to portray women Therapeutae as philosophers; yet for ancient philosophers, these women's virginity insulated them from "feminine" traits.[457] Elsewhere Philo seems ready to allegorize Rebekah as a true disciple of God able to

444. Liefeld, "Preacher," 239–41 (citing polemical texts, Iren. *Her.* 1.13.1, 3; 1.23.2, 4; Lucian *Runaways* 18); 2 Tim 3:6–7; cf. Jos. *Ant.* 18.65–84.

445. E.g., note "Magnilla the philosopher," daughter and wife of philosophers, from second- or third-century Asia Minor (Pleket 30, translated in Lefkowitz and Fant, *Life*, 160, §168). That a disproportionate number of women trained in philosophy were daughters of philosophers (Diog. Laert. 2.86; 8.1.42) reinforces the perception of the social difficulties confronted in achieving such a status.

446. Pythagorean writings also included significant instructions to women (Malherbe, *Moral Exhortation*, 82, citing letters 34 and 35, i.e., Ps.-Melissa *Letter to Kleareta* [p. 83] and Ps.-Theano *Letter to Eubule* [83–85]), though some of the advice (e.g., about modesty) is conventional. It was said that Pythagoras educated boys and girls in different settings when locals so requested (Iambl. *V.P.* 9.50).

447. Iambl. *V.P.* 36.267. He lists the most prominent disciples in 35.251 and the chain of successors in 36.265–66.

448. The percentage could be lower if the women are drawn from a larger period, but since these are the most noteworthy women, the total number of women could be higher.

449. Diog. Laert. 8.1.43; cf. Lucian *Affairs* 30; Frede, "Theano"; for her reputed role as Pythagoras's partial successor, see, e.g., Euseb. *P.E.* 10.14.14 (in Inwood, "Mnesarchus"). Some held her to be another's wife but Pythagoras's pupil (Diog. Laert. 8.1.42; our sources for Pythagoras are many centuries after Pythagoras died, but there is no reason to doubt that Theano studied philosophy). She was also known for her womanly modesty (Plut. *Bride* 31, *Mor.* 142CD).

450. Diog. Laert. 8.1.43.

451. Diog. Laert. 8.1.42.

452. Iambl. *V.P.* 31.194. A freedwoman kills herself to avoid breaking under torture in Tac. *Ann.* 15.57 (praising her noble spirit); a woman who divulges information under torture is exculpated (by an advocate) on account of her weak gender in Quint. *Decl.* 272.3–5.

453. Porph. *Marc.* 3.37 (also out of friendship to her deceased husband, 3.38–39).

454. Porph. *Marc.* 3.43–45. She should not therefore concern herself with being a woman physically, since that was not why he married her (33.511–13); she should flee what is feminine and pursue a virginal soul (33.513–16).

455. Diog. Laert. 4.1.

456. Diog. Laert. 2.86 (cf. 2.72).

457. See Taylor, "Virgin Mothers."

teach wisdom to men[458] (although this process involves allegory and, as noted above, Philo knows how to make exceptions for women belonging to the elite).

As already noted, Stoics were more prone to talk about egalitarianism in virtue than to have women disciples.[459] Epicurus, however, allowed women into his communities.[460] As also noted, even among Epicureans women might face conventional prejudices,[461] but they had more opportunity there than in most schools. Over the centuries, at least eight women students of the Epicurean school are named;[462] presumably there were others, although traditions appear more apt to mention women (because of their relative rareness) than men. This would still leave women a small minority, but it left no doubt that the school, in at least much of its history, admitted women.

Lucian mentions among women trained in philosophy "Aspasia, Diotima, and Thargelia";[463] I comment more fully on Aspasia below. Hipparchia, the pupil and wife of the Cynic sage Crates, went down in history as a very rare yet genuine woman "Cynic."[464] She successfully defended her right to learn philosophy as more important than weaving.[465] Nevertheless, she apparently generated some mild detractors in a later era, who felt that she needed some special prodding.[466] Lucian mocks Cynic pretensions to allow women disciples, accusing them of group sex instead.[467]

In one Hellenistic Jewish work, it is the father who teaches his sons the Law and the Prophets (4 Macc 18:10), but the mother can certainly *quote* Scripture (18:11–19). Clearly, Jewish women had access to some learning, as is clear even in some of the more conservative literary traditions.[468] Women regularly attended synagogues,[469] although rabbinic sources, at least, portray them mainly as listening passively.[470] Some women must have gone further, actively pursuing learning. One husband complained about a wife who he thought was neglecting her household responsibilities to go hear R. Meir teach.[471]

Josephus acknowledges that women, children, and servants are permitted to hear the Law read, as adult males do, at the Feast of Tabernacles[472] and that even the women and the servants among the Jewish people affirm that God's law upholds virtuous living.[473] Rabbi Hananiah ben Teradion's wife and daughter are each able

458. Philo *Posterity* 136, esp. 151 (in Robbins, *Jesus the Teacher*, 96).

459. This may be true even of Musonius; no women are known among his disciples (Meeks, *Moral World*, 46). Our sources, however, are far from complete.

460. As often noted (e.g., Stowers, *Letter Writing*, 39; Smith, *Symposium*, 58). Some may have been fitted into traditional sexual roles, so that a courtesan is a mistress of the aged Epicurus and apparently perhaps one of his pupils in Alciph. *Court.* 17 (Leontium to Lamia), 2.2 (but this may reflect anti-Epicurean polemic).

461. Philod. *Crit.* col. 21b.13–22b.

462. Dorandi, "Epicurean School," 1075.

463. Lucian *Eunuch* 7 (Harmon in LCL, 5:339n1, suggests that Diotima, from Plato's *Symposium*, may be fictitious). For some other women, see Harper, "Women in philosophy."

464. Diog. Laert. 6.7.96–98. See further Goulet-Cazé, "Hipparchia."

465. Diog. Laert. 6.7.98; cf. Mary's "superior" role in Luke 10:42.

466. See Crates *Ep.* 28–29. By contrast, other of the Cynic Epistles praise her (Diogenes *Ep.* 3).

467. Lucian *Runaways* 18, playing on Plato's group marriage (Plato *Rep.* 5.457, 459E), mocked further elsewhere (Lucian *True Story* 2.19; *Phil. Sale* 17) and recalled in other sources (Sext. Emp. *Pyr.* 3.205). It was apparently earlier held by the early Stoic Zeno (Diog. Laert. 7.1.33, 131), and possibly practiced independently by others (as in Pliny E. *N.H.* 5.8.45); for modern cultural examples, see Mbiti, *Religions*, 166; Grunlan and Mayers, *Cultural Anthropology*, 161.

468. See, e.g., *Sop.* 18:5 in Blank, "Texts."

469. See esp. Brooten, *Women Leaders*, 140–41.

470. Safrai, "Education," 955.

471. See Brooten, *Women Leaders*, 140–41; Le Cornu, *Acts*, 991 (citing *y. Soṭah* 1:4, comparing Luke 10:39).

472. Jos. *Ant.* 4.209 (more generally, 209–11); on public reading of the law to all, including women, see also, e.g., 1 Esd 9:40.

473. Jos. *Ag. Ap.* 2.181.

to quote Scripture accurately and appropriately in one schematized story.[474] That women in rabbinic literature quote Scripture[475] does not necessarily indicate special training in Scripture, since women would hear Scripture quoted in synagogue and elsewhere, but it does suggest a degree of potential biblical literacy among Jewish women.

Most of the knowledge of Torah expressed by women in rabbinic sources, however, concerns domestic halakah (such as kosher regulations) necessary for a matron to know, what a woman learned from a family member at home, or fairly simple portions of Scripture.[476] A Torah scroll written by a woman was invalid,[477] and women were exempt from the obligation for Torah study.[478] They were exempted from many of the commandments;[479] for example, they were not required to observe tefillin.[480] Men also seem more disposed to attend festivals.[481] But in later sources, wives (or children or slaves) could recite a blessing on behalf of the male head of the household if he was unable to do it.[482]

Rabbis differed among themselves about how much Torah teaching a daughter should receive. Whereas some insisted that girls be taught the Torah,[483] especially the passage about the suspected adulteress,[484] others felt that teaching daughters Torah (whether the same passage[485] or as a whole[486]) was sexually dangerous.[487] The point may be that coeducation of girls with boys could lead to sexual immorality, which may be why girls did not attend schools, though they must have been taught the blessings and other Torah information, presumably in the home.[488]

In any case, the Tannaim required Torah learning for boys but not girls.[489] Girls could not but learn Torah in synagogues and from the home, but they were normally not schooled in it and trained to recite it as boys were.[490] An Amoraic source claims

474. *Sipre Deut.* 307.4.1. The daughter may be the same as Beruria (Moore, *Judaism*, 2:128–29) if that is not a later harmonistic tradition.

475. Though so do inanimate objects, as Le Cornu, *Acts*, 992, mentions. The woman servants in R. Gamaliel II's household reportedly knew Torah well (*b. Roš Haš.* 26b; *Meg.* 18a; *Naz.* 3a), but they were very exceptional (Moore, *Judaism*, 2:128).

476. Ilan, *Women*, 190–204 (including in this summary even rabbinic information about Beruria, 197–200).

477. *B. Menaḥ.* 42b (Amoraic and Babylonian).

478. So *b. Qidd.* 34a (perhaps because they had not been properly educated for it).

479. E.g., *m. Ḥag.* 1:1; *t. Ber.* 6:18 (lest they perform the commandments wrongly and offend the Lord); *b. Menaḥ.* 61b; *y. Ḥag.* 1:1, §7; see further Ilan, *Women*, 176–84. A husband could not force a wife to break a Nazirite vow, though he could annul it (*m. Naz.* 9:1); women are not reckoned highly with regard to *zimmun* (*b. Ber.* 45b).

480. *M. Ber.* 3:3; *Mek. Pisha* 17, lines 160–61 (Lauterbach, 1:153); *y. Ber.* 2:2, §5; *Pesiq. Rab.* 22:5.

481. Thus, for Sukkoth, Lydda was emptied "of men" (ἀνδρῶν, Jos. *War* 2.515); later rabbis exempted women from the obligation to dwell in the sukkah (*m. Sukkah* 2:8; *b. Sukkah* 2b; *y. Sukkah* 2:9). (Rabbis also exempted shopkeepers on intermediate days of festivals to obtain goods; Goodman, *State*, 55.)

482. *M. Ber.* 3:3; *t. Ber.* 5:17; *y. Roš Haš.* 3:10; cf. *Sukkah* 3:10.

483. See *m. Ned.* 4:3 (Witherington, *Women*, 6).

484. So *m. Soṭah* 3:4; *y. Ḥag.* 1:1, §1.

485. So Wegner, *Chattel*, 161.

486. Given the comparison with sexual immorality in the passage, the rabbis might be thinking particularly of stories involving immorality (especially Tamar, Potiphar's wife, and the Midianite women). But girls would hear such stories (and much of Torah) expounded eventually in the synagogue, in any case.

487. So *m. Soṭah* 3:4. Tradition said that the second rabbi, Eliezer ben Hyrcanus, preferred that the Torah be burned rather than that it be taught to a woman (*Num. Rab.* 9:48; see further Moore, *Judaism*, 2:128n4); yet his wife appears well versed (*b. Šabb.* 116ab). Concern about women's sexuality may have eventually led to "protecting" them from Torah study (see Wegner, *Chattel*, 161–62).

488. See Safrai, "Education," 955.

489. Ibid., noting that the later OT, the Apocrypha, Philo, and Josephus also support this picture.

490. On late second-century Palestinian Jewish boys' training (perhaps hyperbolic or addressing only well-to-do families), see *m. ʾAbot* 5:21 (cf. Jos. *Life* 9–12; *Ant.* 20.264–65).

that women earned merit by sending their sons to synagogue to learn Torah and their husbands to Beit ha-Midrash to learn Mishnah.[491]

We also do not read of women as formal disciples of rabbis (though cf. the learning of Beruria in talmudic tradition), as is often noted.[492] Second-century Palestinian rabbis expounded less technical moral counsel to synagogue audiences than in their schools,[493] and the same was probably true of those who taught disciples in the first century.

3. Women Speaking in Public

The classical ideal,[494] though long mitigated in practice,[495] was that the public domain was a male sphere of activity whereas the domestic domain belonged to the wife. Practice apparently shifted increasingly away from such a sharp distinction, but among Greeks and even among Romans, some gender separation remained an ideal, often for moral reasons.[496]

"Silence," one gruff warrior in a classical text informs his concubine, "makes a woman beautiful."[497] In classical Greece, precautions were taken (at least among the well-to-do who could afford this) to keep women in the private sphere and to keep them from being heard.[498] In the early first century C.E., Valerius Maximus emphasizes that ancestral custom prohibited women from speaking in a public meeting, with only the rarest of exceptions.[499] Granted, he mentions some women who pleaded cases before magistrates despite Roman custom (Val. Max. 8.3),[500] but he does so precisely because it was unusual[501] and offers only three examples. These were rare

491. *B. Ber.* 17a; *Soṭah* 21a.
492. E.g., Derrett, *Audience*, 33 (noting the exceptional picture of Jesus in the Gospels, including Luke 8:2; 10:42; Mark 15:41).
493. Goodman, *State*, 74 (and also 223n175 [to p. 74]).
494. Especially in classical Athens (e.g., Gould, "Position in Athens," 47, 50; Dover, "Attitudes," 145) but continuing in Hellenistic Egypt (see Verner, *Household*, 38); more generally, see Llewellyn-Jones, *Tortoise*, 189–90. Jewish sources also maintain the ideal (Ps.-Phoc. 215–16; Wegner, *Chattel*, 18, 150–53; Ilan, *Women*, 128–29), but in practice it was limited (e.g., Safrai, "Home," 752; Fiensy, "Composition," 225).
495. See, e.g., Hemelrijk, "Masculinity." Even segregation in banquets was beginning to break down among aristocratic Romans (Smith, *Symposium*, 208–9, 298n27; Stambaugh, *City*, 207), though Greeks were stricter (Corn. Nep. pref. 6–7).
496. E.g., Dio Chrys. *Or.* 3.70; Plut. *Bride* 9, *Mor.* 139C; 30, *Mor.* 142C; 32, *Mor.* 140D; some in Mus. Ruf. 3, p. 42.13–14; Pliny *Ep.* 4.19.4. See also examples in Paige, "Matrix," 226–31.
497. Soph. *Ajax* 293 (LCL, 1:59). Hera is silenced, though by the threat that Zeus will beat her (Hom. *Il.* 1.565–69). Wives should keep quiet even at home when the husband is in a rage (Plut. *Bride* 37, *Mor.* 143C). I have noted above the preference for women's "meekness" and "modesty."
498. See sources in Grant, *Social History*, 5.
499. Val. Max. 3.8.6 (though his wording may suggest that the "custom" was already being flouted at times). On Valerius's bias, see Milnor, "Women," 276–77. One may also contrast the male deity of speech with goddesses of silence (Dubourdieu, "Divinités de la parole"). If Tacitus did not go so far, he nevertheless resented the impropriety of women being with, and speaking to, soldiers (*Ann.* 2.55).
500. See esp. Simon, "Causes." Winter, *Wives*, 115, mentions these without noting that Valerius himself views them as exceptional (though Winter knows that they are; see idem, *Left Corinth*, 135–36). Winter, *Wives*, 176–79, mentions more on women in the courts, again without pointing out that this was exceptional.
501. Normally they needed advocates (Hermog. *Method* 21.436–37). Under duress, women sometimes pleaded before judges (e.g., *Pesiq. Rab Kah.* 15:9; *Song Rab.* 5:16, §2) and might request or win special consideration on account of their gender (P.Sakaon 36 in Horsley, *Documents*, 4:132–33, §30; P.Ryl. 114, line 5; Alciph. *Court.* 4 [Bacchis to Phrynê], 1.31, ¶4; cf. Luke 18:2–7; Lysias *Or.* 32.11–18, §§506–11; Bailey, *Peasant Eyes*, 134–35). Under such duress, women likewise pleaded with Marcius to spare Rome in Appian *Hist. rom.* 2.5.3; Plut. *Coriol.* 34.2. A woman summoned to court might weep in silence before answering (Tac. *Ann.* 16.31). As noted above, Mediterranean laws were prejudiced even against women as witnesses (e.g., Justin. *Inst.* 2.10.6; Jos. *Ant.* 4.219).

women whose feminine nature and the normal "modesty" attached to it could not make them "silent" (8.3.praef.). As noted above, one was called manly (8.3.1); another was impudent, a "monster" to be ridiculed (8.3.2).

Plutarch insists that a wife ought to reserve her speaking for her husband or speak through him.[502] Pliny the Younger praises his young wife for enjoying his readings— as she sits privately behind a curtain.[503] He also mentions an excellent speaker who publicly read eloquent letters from his wife,[504] whereas the wife herself would not make an appearance to read them. A virtuous woman in a possibly third-century novel prefers that the man accompanying her do the speaking, "for I think it proper for a woman to be silent, and for a man to make answer, before a company of men."[505] Conventional "wisdom" opined that women's words were untrustworthy.[506]

Some exceptional women emerged despite social obstacles. In an early period, Aspasia allegedly taught rhetoric[507] and numbered Socrates among those who learned from her.[508] In late antiquity, one Sosipatra married the famed philosopher Eustathius, but her wisdom was so great that it was greater than his.[509] She held a very famous chair of philosophy.[510] Allegedly, however, she did not achieve her wisdom in the conventional way, by studying with sages, but by supernatural teaching from the gods.[511] More prominent still was the late fourth- to early fifth-century C.E. philosopher Hypatia; she became leader of Alexandria's Neoplatonic school. Like some other prominent women, she was the daughter of a noted intellectual, though her father was a mathematician rather than a Neoplatonist lecturer.[512]

But Aspasia, Sosipatra, and Hypatia were notable exceptions. As noted above, only a small proportion of those trained in philosophy were women; those who became teachers were far fewer still. Whereas ancient sources often speak of women teaching their sons at home, there is little evidence for women as professional teachers in public, as sages hired by wealthy homes or as heads of rhetorical schools.[513] Indeed, although we know of women trained in philosophy, we know of few trained in rhetoric, which inevitably entailed public speaking. Even those who granted women's intellectual equality with men did not (apart from homeless, countercultural Cynics) advocate destroying the public/private partition that separated most traditionally masculine from most feminine activities. Although these barriers gave way before wealth and

---

502. Plut. *Bride* 32, *Mor.* 142D.

503. Pliny *Ep.* 4.19.4.

504. Pliny *Ep.* 1.16.6. Pliny expresses uncertainty whether the man composed the letters in his wife's name or instead developed her eloquence.

505. Heliod. *Eth.* 1.21.

506. So, e.g., Eurip. *Hippolytus Veiled* frg. 440 (from Stobaeus 4.22.180); *Danae* frg. 321 (Stob. 4.22.172); Babr. 16.10; Avianus *Fables* 15–16; Phaedrus 4.15; Fronto *Ep. graec.* 2.3 (written to a woman!); cf. Eurip. *Stheneboea* frg. 671 (men should not trust women); see discussion above.

507. Hornblower, "Aspasia," citing the *Suda*.

508. So Fronto *Fer. als.* 3.5 if this is not a rhetorical flourish. Hornblower, "Aspasia," mentions only discussions with Socrates (in Plut. *Per.* 24). Pervo, "Entführung," compares the *Life of Aspasia*, which he views as largely fictitious, with the *Life of Aesop* (*Aesop Romance*).

509. Eunapius *Lives* 466.

510. Eunapius *Lives* 469.

511. So Eunapius *Lives* 467–68. She fits the so-called "divine man" profile more widespread in her period.

512. Harper, "Women in philosophy," 1626. Christians lynched her in 415 (Mastrocinque, "Choices," 391), but Hart, *Delusions*, 45–47, argues that her politics rather than her gender or religion led to her martyrdom.

513. So Winter, *Wives*, 115–16, citing the absence of women in such posts in Philostratus's *Lives of Sophists* and in Hemelrijk's work. Aspasia and Sosipatra may be viewed as exceptions, but neither is within even a century of the early empire. We should also exclude lower-level teachers, such as instructors in rudimentary Greek in Egypt's towns, a minority of whom were women or slaves (Lewis, *Life*, 63).

patronage for certain public offices, they rarely gave way for teachers (who normally had to achieve sufficient acceptance in that role, after all, to acquire students).

Rabbinic tradition also reveals some exceptional women. Imma Shalom helped to expose an unfair judge; she was R. Gamaliel II's sister and wife of R. Eliezer.[514] In a later legend, the wife of Rabbi Simeon ben Halafta persuades him from Torah and refutes R. Judah ha-Nasi himself.[515] Much more important[516] is that Beruria entered into rabbinic disputes and once even persuaded the majority of rabbis about her position on a halakic matter.[517] But as the daughter of R. Hananiah ben Teradion and the wife of R. Meir,[518] Beruria may have had access to more learning than did some of her female contemporaries.[519] There was apparently a fair degree of fictionalizing in the talmudic portrayal of Beruria and the two other rare women (Imma Shalom and Akiba's wife, Rachel) fluent in the Torah.[520] Yet even though Beruria was probably not studying three hundred talmudic topics daily,[521] such stories were presumably told of her rather than others precisely because of her unusual Torah knowledge. In any case, some women, such as Beruria, achieved sufficient skill in Torah learning to command attention, but they remained exceptional.[522]

Men were supposed to avoid unnecessary conversation with women to guard against unchastity[523] or folly.[524] Some teachers even applied this rule to speaking with one's own wife.[525] (As noted above, however, some rabbis did support heeding wives.) As a rule, the rabbis forbade women even to teach children.[526] Some scholars note that the rabbis forbade women to read in the synagogue, from respect for the congregation;[527] others argue that they were allowed to read in synagogues until the

514. *B. Šabb.* 116ab. Rabbi Gamaliel's household seems to have hosted educated women even among the servants (Moore, *Judaism*, 2:128).

515. *Exod. Rab.* 52:3 (the characters are from the late second century).

516. Swidler, *Women*, 97–104, calls Beruria "the exception that proves the rule," noting that (104–11) other "exceptions" were not clearly learned in the Torah. Talmudic accounts of Beruria suggest the dissonance that her role created against conventions (Adler, "Virgin").

517. Safrai, "Education," 955 (citing as examples of her learning, *t. B. Qam.* 4:17; *t. B. Meṣiʿa* 1:6; *b. Pesaḥ.* 62b; elsewhere, see, e.g., *b. ʿErub.* 53b–54a); Moore, *Judaism*, 2:128–29 (and sources there).

518. Safrai, "Education," 955.

519. Both sons and daughters raised in rabbinic families stood at an advantage in knowing Torah (see Goodman, *State*, 78, citing *t. B. Bat.* 2:3; for daughters, *t. B. Qam.* 4:17; cf. also Witherington, *Women*, 195n232). The situation is analogous to daughters of philosophers, noted above. But for the ambiguous situation of rabbis' daughters, see Weisberg, "Desirable but Dangerous."

520. Ilan, "Quest for Beruriah"; Ilan, *Women*, 200.

521. See, e.g., Moore, *Judaism*, 2:129 (citing *b. Pesaḥ.* 62b).

522. Safrai, "Education," 955.

523. E.g., Sir 9:9; *b. Ber.* 43b, bar.; *Ned.* 20a; *y. Ḥal.* 2:1, §10; cf. Swidler, *Women*, 123–25. Some (attributed ultimately to a second-century Tanna) went so far as to claim that God himself avoided speaking with women (*y. Soṭah* 7:1, §2; *Gen. Rab.* 20:6; 48:20; 63:7; cf. also Urbach, *Sages*, 1:155). At least some women upheld this gender boundary (*b. ʿErub.* 53b). Certainly, no wife could be alone with a man besides her husband (*y. Soṭah* 1:1, §7).

524. E.g., God punished Antipas for heeding a woman's (in this case, his wife's) talk (Jos. *Ant.* 18.252–55).

525. *M. ʾAbot* 1:5 (with a pre-Christian attribution); *ʾAbot R. Nat.* 14, §35 B. The issue in this case may be simply public onlookers unaware of the relationship (*b. Ber.* 43b), since some rabbis certainly did approve of listening to their wives. But against confiding some things to one's wife, cf. *ʾAbot R. Nat.* 7 A.

526. *M. Qidd.* 4:13. Undoubtedly, this means children in a school, not their own children; unmarried men are also excluded. The *Gemara* may imply that this was from concern about immorality between the teacher and fathers who brought children to school (Swidler, *Women*, 114, on *b. Qidd.* 82a), though the accuracy of this interpretation is not entirely clear.

527. Le Cornu, *Acts*, 688, citing *b. Meg.* 23a; cf. Witherington, *Women*, 7. Moore, *Judaism*, 2:131, noted that she could be one of the seven readers but it was disapproved of and that no examples remain extant. Wegner, *Chattel*, 146, argues that the Mishnah's framers excluded women's public religious activity even more than in most other ancient religious groups.

time of the Babylonian Talmud.[528] At least as early as the editing of the Tosefta, rabbis disapproved of a woman's reading the Torah in public;[529] but another text from this period permits even menstruating women to read the Torah,[530] and by the early third century, a rabbi could say that women are obligated to read the Megillah.[531] In the Greek-speaking Diaspora, we have no reason to doubt that this could occur.[532] Because the evidence against the practice is more explicit and prevalent than the quite slender evidence for it,[533] however, we may gather that in most locations men were the more usual readers. In any case, women's expounding on the Torah in synagogue services does not seem to have been the norm in Jewish Palestine. Though we cannot rule it out in the cases where we have female synagogue leaders in some cities of Asia Minor (see discussion above), that women would not teach would fit the usual pattern regarding women's public teaching in Greco-Roman antiquity. One text instances a man who made a marriage covenant requiring the wife to support him financially and teach him Torah, but the text plainly presents this situation as the inversion of the norm.[534]

Inspired speech might be treated differently;[535] a tradition that acknowledged prophetesses could not well silence any form of inspired speech, although some traditions may have expected women to prophesy privately and men to relay the message.[536] (On prophetesses, see comments on Acts 2:17–18; 21:9.) But if they were expected to prophesy privately, this would simply reinforce the traditional private/public distinction between the genders, which constituted a particularly fundamental characteristic of ancient gender ideology (at least in literary sources).[537]

4. Implications for Luke's Perspective

The closest Luke comes to offering a statement of ideology about gender in Acts is his programmatic quotation of Joel about sons and daughters prophesying. That he notices the gender significance of the quotation should be beyond dispute, since he illustrates it in his narratives (with respect to Anna and Philip's four daughters).[538] I have addressed this matter more fully above, in the early part of this chapter.

Acts offers much less about marriage relations than about prophecy, and even the Gospel's clearest statements on the subject address more the priority of the kingdom

528. Safrai and Safrai, "Hkl." Horsley, *Galilee*, 237, believes that early Galilean women participated more freely than later rabbinic sources indicate, though less than in the urban Diaspora.

529. So *t. Meg.* 3[4]:11. Brooten, *Women Leaders*, 95, notes this and also that *m. Sukkah* 3:10 reluctantly permits women to read "the Hallel in private."

530. So *t. Ber.* 2:12.

531. So R. Joshua ben Levi in *b. Meg.* 4a.

532. Brooten, *Women Leaders*, 95, noting the possibility.

533. Note again ibid.: "Further, although there is no solid evidence for women having read the Torah publicly in the synagogue service, it cannot be excluded, particularly for the Greek-speaking congregations (about which we know next to nothing), that they did."

534. *T. Ketub.* 4:7 (esp. with 4:6).

535. Cf. Sigountos and Shank, "Public Roles"; sacral speech in Paige, "Matrix," 231–33. Unlike Germans, Romans did not believe women especially prophetically endowed (Tac. *Germ.* 8).

536. Cf., e.g., the Delphic Pythoness, on which see comment on Acts 16:16.

537. As Ferguson, *Backgrounds*, 57–58, points out, although many have overstated the reality of wifely seclusion, the domestic sphere remained especially that of the wife. Public activity (in the sense of politics, war, and oratory, not the market) remained especially that of the husband. See also discussion in broader cultural terms in Malina and Neyrey, *Portraits*, 177–81; on their exclusion from political life, see, e.g., Rives, *Religion*, 106.

538. In both cases, they contextually supplement male prophets (Simeon and Agabus). That is, Luke could have settled for the explicit males' prophecies to make his point (although, in Simeon and Anna's case, it fits his interest in double confirmations) had the point not included a valuing of gender balance.

over marriage than gender roles. We may, for this discussion, leave aside Luke's examples of elite women (whom society obligated everyone of lower station to respect). Moreover, that Luke includes women who work (e.g., Acts 18:3) or function as patrons (e.g., 16:15) is not surprising in light of the larger cosmopolitan culture.

More significantly, Luke's portrayal of close public association between male agents of the kingdom and women (e.g., Luke 8:2–3; Acts 16:15) does suggest that Luke favors the approach of more progressive cosmopolitan contemporaries rather than that of extreme traditionalists, even though this approach could have appeared scandalous to more traditional minds (or to those looking for excuses to attack the early Christian movement).[539] That women follow Jesus itinerantly along with male disciples (Luke 8:2–3) and some learn at his feet (10:38–42) was certainly unusual among ancient rabbis.

Luke does not address the question of women's engagement in some kinds of ministry.[540] Bringing female traveling companions was hardly practical for Paul (later stories of Thecla aside), especially on the final journey to Jerusalem, where the slightest hint of scandal would have appeared counterproductive to that mission's purpose. Likewise, Luke reports no women apostles, but we should recall that he restricts the term "apostle" almost exclusively to the Twelve and his options for recording women's roles were constrained by available historical sources about what had happened.[541] Yet he does allow Paul's allies Priscilla and Aquila to instruct the famous Apollos (Acts 18:26).

As examples above should illustrate, some ancient traditionalists (e.g., Valerius Maximus) allowed and even highlighted exceptions, yet for them exceptions proved the rule; others who were more progressive (e.g., Musonius) might use such "exceptions" to encourage further cases. Luke offers no editorial aside to explain how to interpret these examples, but that he offers multiple cases cannot, I believe, be coincidence. As elsewhere in analyzing Luke's narrative, we infer many of his points through repetition and emphasis.

What is clear is that Luke expects women (such as Anna and Philip's four daughters) to declare the word of the Lord and regards this as normative, illustrating the programmatic principle articulated in 2:17–18. The same Spirit that forces the church across ethnic and cultural barriers also breaks down gender barriers for speaking God's message. The most obvious examples are specific prophetesses, who, like specific prophets, are limited in number. But for Luke, the principle of 2:17–18 applies to all believers, since the Spirit empowers all to announce the message about Jesus, including cross-culturally (see comment on Acts 1:8).

Weighing our exploration of Luke's approach to gender with our exploration of the options in his culture does not allow us to pinpoint with precision Luke's opinion on every item that he does not explicitly address. I do believe, however, that it suffices to place him among more progressive, rather than less progressive, voices of his era.

---

539. Cf. Lucian *Runaways* 18; esp. Liefeld, "Preacher," 239–40; Klauck, *Context*, 488. The attraction of even aristocratic women to Pharisaism (cf. Jos. *Ant.* 17.41; *War* 1.110) invited criticism (see further Ilan, "Women to Pharisaism").

540. It is also possible that he omits some prominent models because of the apologetic concerns that also dominate his work, as suggested above.

541. Had he expanded the title more broadly to its Pauline usage, he still lacked opportunity to discuss Junia (if he knew of her; Rom 16:7), since he names no one in Rome and his treatment of Paul's early years is sparse. Some do affirm a historical Thecla (e.g., Albrecht, "Thecla"), though most are more skeptical.

COMMENTARY

PART 1

THE FIRST OUTPOURING
OF THE SPIRIT (1:1–2:47)

Acts 1–2 offers a strategic opening unit for Luke's second volume. Fulfilling promises by OT prophets and Jesus himself, the exalted Lord pours out God's Spirit on his witnesses, initiating cross-cultural witness and carrying on Jesus's mission.

1. Transitional Function

The *literary preface*, by ancient standards, was Acts 1:1 or 1:1–2, but this is distinguishable from an introduction connecting Acts with the previous book. This introduction may be 1:1–11 or 1:1–14, although the entire larger opening block of Acts as a whole may well extend until 2:47. Not only the introduction proper (probably 1:1–11 but possibly 1:1–14)[1] but also the opening scenes up to the first summary statement (2:41–47) address the transition from Jesus's ministry to that of the "successors" of his mission narrated in the Gospel.[2] The abridged preface (1:1) may imply this transition in "all that Jesus *began* to do and teach."[3] Jesus's promise of the Spirit to equip the

---

1. Scholars differ as to the introduction's contours (much of the summary taken from Gaventa, *Acts*, 62): Acts 1:1–2 (Krodel, *Acts*, 51; Conzelmann, *Acts*, 3–4); 1:1–5 (Lake and Cadbury, *Commentary*, 2; Bruce, *Acts*[3], 97, 102); 1:1–8 (Haenchen, *Acts*, 144–47); 1:1–11 (Johnson, *Acts*, 23–32); and 1:1–14 (Barrett, *Acts*, 61–64; Marguerat, *Actes*, 21, 33–34; Pervo, *Acts*, 34; Langner, *Hechos*, 282–83). Walton, "Beginning," 467, sees "the ends of the earth" (1:8) as the goal of the opening verses.

2. Walton, "Beginning," esp. 466, also sees all of Acts 1–2 as a bridge between Jesus's life and the church; likewise others (Luke 24:44–53 and Acts 1:1–11 as a bridge between the Gospel and Acts, e.g., Mallen, *Reading*, 79). In some genres, "prologues" could prove quite lengthy (Zimmermann, "Prologue," 2–3). On the role of "succession" in Luke-Acts, see, e.g., Talbert, *Acts*, xix–xxv.

3. A good transition could summarize what came before while introducing what would come next (*Rhet. Her.* 4.26.35).

apostles[4] as witnesses closes Luke's Gospel (Luke 24:48–49) and opens Acts (Acts 1:4–8), in a strategic transition from Jesus's biography as he departs (1:9–11). Luke highlights this transition with motifs from the biblical account of the transition from Elijah's to Elisha's ministry.

Before the Spirit is poured out (2:1–47), the exact contours of the group of apostolic witnesses are carefully defined (1:15–26). The transition between volumes 1 and 2, then, is a transition of leadership from Jesus to the apostles (the Spirit working through both) and from Jesus's active ministry in person to his continuing ministry through his name (2:38; 3:6) and (most regularly emphasized in Acts) the Spirit (2:33). The empowerment of the Spirit is foundational for the rest of the church's mission, as is clear from the warning not to leave Jerusalem without it (1:4).

In the entire context of Acts, this transition prepares the way for another one, namely, Paul's mission to uncircumcised Gentiles and hence the transition to the multicultural church of Luke's own day. The risen Jesus remains active through the church, which continues to bear witness along the lines carefully defined by the apostles whom Jesus himself commissioned. The Diaspora mission highlighted by Jesus for the disciples in 1:8 surfaces quickly in Luke's narrative. Even on Pentecost, the witness to the nations is proleptically foreshadowed in the Jewish hearers from many regions (2:9–11).

The first two chapters of Acts introduce major themes in Acts, just as the first two chapters of Luke's Gospel introduce its major themes: Beverly Gaventa rightly notes that these include "fulfillment of prophecy, the power of the Holy Spirit, the apostolic witness to Jesus, and the formation of Christian community."[5] Signs and wonders and a foreshadowing of the gospel going out to the nations are also essential elements in this section. That such themes appear here is hardly surprising; introductions often prefigured major themes, especially in rhetoric[6] but also in other venues.[7]

2. Semitic Character?

Opening comments on this section also provide an appropriate place to comment on a stylistic feature more common to the first half of Acts, probably meant to characterize the Jerusalem church. In the early twentieth century, C. C. Torrey, a master of Semitic languages, contended for a probable Aramaic influence in the first half of Acts, especially in the speeches.[8] He then went beyond this relatively modest claim to deny that it was sufficient to regard these as merely "frequent Semitisms; the truth is that the language of all these fifteen chapters is translation Greek through and

---

4. I use the term here in its narrower Lukan sense rather than in the broader Pauline sense. On apostleship and its background, see, e.g., Keener, *John*, 310–15. For earlier studies of apostles and apostleship relevant for Acts, see Mattill and Mattill, *Bibliography*, 296–98, §§4142–73.

5. Gaventa, *Acts*, 61.

6. Both in rhetorical advice (*Rhet. Alex.* 29, 1436a.33–39; Dion. Hal. *Thuc.* 19; *Lysias* 24; Cic. *Or. Brut.* 40.137) and in actual speeches (e.g., Sen. E. *Controv.* 1.pref. 21; Dio Chrys. *Or.* 38.8; cf. Pliny *Ep.* 2.3.3). In a particular kind of speech, one could forgo normal order, but this was unusual (Men. Rhet. 2.4, 391.19–28; 392.9–14; 393.23–24).

7. This was less emphasized in philosophic argument than in rhetoric (Fronto *Eloq.* 3.4), but it appears there as well. Other good writers also introduced the points to be covered (Polyb. 3.1.3–3.5.9, esp. 3.1.7; 11.1.4–5; Virg. *Aen.* 1.1–6; Aul. Gel. pref. 25; Soranus *Gynec.* 1.intro.2; 1.1.3; 2.5.9 [25.78]; Philost. *Vit. Apoll.* 7.1; 8.1; Zimmermann, "Prologue," 2–3).

8. Torrey, *Composition*, 3ff. Cf. Martin, "Evidence," 59 (favoring Hebrew over Aramaic). In a more general, less linguistic way, Greco-Roman specialists also observe the noticeable shift from a more "Hebraistic" flavor of Acts' earlier chapters to a more "Hellenistic" flavor in its later ones (e.g., Ramsay, *Luke the Physician*, 50–51).

through, generally preserving even the order of words."[9] He argued that this Semitic character contrasts starkly with the lack of Semitic style in Acts 16–28, where the few apparent Semitisms probably simply represent Koine or occasionally Luke's having become accustomed to the translation Greek.[10]

Some others have followed Torrey's argument, doubtful that Luke's skill in imitating the LXX would be sufficient to produce such an array of Semitisms.[11] Indeed, though Torrey was by no means disposed to accept large portions of Scripture as historically reliable, his argument in this case might well lend support to those who contend that Luke has some secure historical sources for the first part of the book. Yet as I have suggested in the introduction, we have other sufficient grounds for believing that Luke has secure sources about the Judean church; his two years in the Levant (Acts 21–26) would have permitted him considerable opportunity to hear various accounts.[12] Probably most of these were oral; though some of those who recounted them to Luke may have been bilingual, providing an aramaized style at points,[13] it is not clear the extent to which recounting in such style would affect Luke's own style in reporting their words. Even if it did exert a notable degree of such influence, would it by itself produce the pervasive Semitic language often attributed to these chapters? Further, the likeliest suggested individual source for some of the early chapters, Philip (cf. 21:8–10), was a Hellenist who would have been among the least likely to be influenced by Aramaisms (6:1, 5).

Most scholars, though impressed with Torrey's considerable command of Aramaic (stronger, indeed, than that of the vast majority of his critics), have failed to find his case persuasive.[14] Some allow that some sections may have Aramaic sources (esp. in 1:1–5:16; 9:31–11:18; parts of Acts 12 and possibly 15), but feel that Torrey overstated his case.[15] In a thorough study in 1965, Max Wilcox demonstrated that although some traditional material may exist in the speeches and elsewhere, a continuous Semitic source in Acts is improbable.[16] Fitzmyer, a noted scholar in the Aramaic of the Dead Sea Scrolls (not, of course, available in Torrey's time) notes that Torrey's patterns based on later Aramaic do not fit the Aramaic of Luke's day.[17] More important, many of Torrey's "Aramaisms" are clear echoes of the LXX (which was, in the general sense, already "translation Greek").[18] Granted, Luke omits the apodictic conjunctions typical of the LXX (and Hebrew),[19] but that Luke significantly reduces parataxis in his use of Mark indicates that Luke does not favor this style in general (whether in a source such as Mark or, presumably, in his own composition).

---

9. Torrey, *Composition*, 7.

10. Ibid.

11. E.g., Ehrhardt, *Acts*, 1; Ladd, *Theology*, 313.

12. E.g., Witherington, *Acts*, 168.

13. On bilingualism influencing style, see comments on Acts 21:40.

14. See already Foakes-Jackson, *Acts*, xiii.

15. Bruce, *Acts¹*, 22 (citing De Zwaan, "Greek Language," 44ff.); Bruce, *Commentary*, 28.

16. Wilcox, *Semitisms of Acts*. Even where Wilcox argued for some genuine Semitisms apart from the LXX, he has been critiqued by others (see Horton, "Semitisms"; survey of views in Powell, *Acts*, 28–29). Wilcox has also argued strongly for a dominant bilingualism in Judea and Galilee (see Wilcox, "Influence," 1094–95).

17. Fitzmyer, *Acts*, 81–82; and passim on particular verses (e.g., p. 444, on Acts 9:32). Torrey, *Composition*, 9, does admit that knowledge of Judean Aramaic in Luke's day is scanty, but sufficient evidence remains to reconstruct the basic syntax of Semitic languages.

18. Fitzmyer, *Acts*, 81–82; see also Hengel, *Acts and History*, 62; see esp. De Zwaan, "Greek Language" (noting abundant LXX language and quotations; similarly, Clarke, "Septuagint"). The most common form of the LXX is especially "literal" in the Pentateuch.

19. Most, "Imitate Septuagint?" For earlier syntactic arguments for Aramaic sources, see Martin, "Evidence" (summary, 59).

The Semitic style early in Acts, probably modeled on the LXX, was not, of course, due to scholars' imagination.[20] Often, at least, Luke's Semitisms probably deliberately recall Septuagintal style in exclusively Jewish settings where this style would be appropriate. But rhetoricians advised varying style according to the subject matter, and Luke accordingly demonstrates his stylistic versatility by using more "biblical Greek" in Jerusalem (where his Diaspora audience would expect such style) and a more conventional Aegean style of Greek, climaxing in Acts 17, in the Diaspora.[21] This is the same method Luke employs in the first two chapters of his Gospel, a method of deliberate archaizing meant to parallel Greek writers' "atticizing" style.[22] The extent to which Luke comfortably competed in Attic style may be debated, but churches accustomed to biblical Greek readings would appreciate a style in which otherwise more sophisticated "atticizing" orators could not compete.

Even before the rise of the Second Sophistic, some (e.g., Dionysius of Halicarnassus) had long contended for a purist, Atticist approach to rhetoric;[23] this practice must have been increasing in the late first century. Some of these writers deliberately archaized their historical narratives with Atticist style.[24] A pure Attic style might make his work difficult for some of his ideal audience, and rhetoricians did recommend adapting speech styles to the audience.[25] Thus one of the most popular novels of a period after the second-century Atticist revival has a "limp" style, possibly deliberate, that seemed characteristic of novels appealing to popular, "nonelite audiences."[26] Acts is not a novel (see discussion in the introduction, ch. 2, sect. 4), but Luke's ideal audience, though probably partly elite (1:1), is not limited to the elite, and they appear less rhetorically concerned than typical recipients of works by elite writers.

Although atticizing per se might be excessive and not common in Acts, deliberate archaizing might be a different matter: The best-informed segment of Luke's target audience, schooled in Scripture in synagogues or by those who had been, might appreciate Luke's deliberate archaizing with a Septuagintal flavor when focusing on his heritage.[27] Although Quintilian warns against archaisms in rhetoric (*Inst.*

---

20. Luke uses the most familiar LXX spelling for Jerusalem in Acts 1–10 (excepting 1:4, which some scholars argue is distinctively Lukan, and in 8:1, 14, 25, which some might attribute to a special source or, more likely, to a view away from Jerusalem); he varies the spelling afterward (cf. Ross, "Spelling of Jerusalem"). This could suggest an LXX source in these chapters but probably reflects Luke's deliberate septuagintalizing of the early chapters, and the broader Greco-Roman setting of later ones.

21. With Witherington, *Acts*, 43–44.

22. Aune, *Environment*, 117; Alexander, "Septuaginta," 17–21. See discussion of Semitisms in the introduction, ch. 6, sect. 2.d; more briefly, ch. 4, sect. 2.b. Arguing for genuine Semitisms in Luke 1–2, see Farris, "Semitic Sources" (making a strong argument for translation Greek); Laurentin, "Traces d'allusions" (favoring Hebrew over Aramaic); Jung, *Language* (arguing for Hebrew sources); Wenham, "Source Criticism," 145 (tentatively); Marshall, *Luke*, 46–47 (allowing that originally Hebrew sources may have "reached [Luke] in Greek form"); Winter, "Observations," 121 (contending that Luke is often more Hebraic than the LXX here); Most, "Imitate Septuagint?" (noting that Luke's omission of apodictic καί counters the view that he imitates the LXX). Others disagree (see, forcefully, Turner, "Hebraic Sources"), countering that Luke imitates LXX style here (Stanton, *Gospels*, 162; Aune, *Environment*, 117); for numerous parallels with the Judean *Psalms of Solomon* in Luke 1:6–79, see Knox, *Jerusalem*, 90 (much less convincingly, Aalen, "Chapters," suggests a relation between Luke's Gospel and *1 En.* 91ff., possibly even [p. 13] that Luke was its Greek translator!). Either translation Greek or Greek with Aramaic interference might fit interviews with Judean sources.

23. For this approach in the first century B.C.E., see Rowe, "Style," 156; in the mid- to late second century C.E., see, e.g., Trapp, *Maximus*, xxxiv; and works on the Second Sophistic.

24. See, e.g., Calboli, "Atticism," 325 (imitation went from Lysias to Thucydides to archaizing more generally).

25. On adaptation to audience tastes, see, e.g., *Rhet. Alex.* 22, 1434b.27–30.

26. Dowden, "Callisthenes," 651. Others believe that novels did appeal to the elite; their style, in any case, remains popular, like Luke's.

27. Aune, *Environment*, 117; Witherington, *Acts*, 44; Alexander, *Context*, 250–52; for Luke's LXX imitation and his archaizing style, see also Plümacher, *Lukas*, 38–72 and 72–78, respectively. Alexander, "Septuaginta,"

2.5.21; cf. 8.3.60; 12.10.42), Latin writers could archaize deliberately to elevate the language, such as in prayers or official documents.[28] (See some further discussion of Atticist versus the more bombastic, so-called Asianist style of rhetoric at Acts 17:22.)

3. Title

Our current title for Acts (Πράξεις ἀποστόλων, "Acts of Apostles") appears widely by the end of the second century.[29] The title's first element, "Acts," is not inappropriate, given other works such as Valerius Maximus's *Memorable Deeds and Sayings* (see the discussion of the ancient genre of "acts" in the introduction, ch. 2, sect. 6). This correspondence need not, however, suggest that Luke issued the book with such a title on the outside of the scroll; πρᾶξις is not a frequent Lukan term, especially in this sense (Acts 19:18; Luke 23:51), and this title, "Acts of the Apostles," fits the era of the proliferation of apocryphal acts in second-century Christianity.[30] In contrast to "Acts" (see introduction, ch. 2), the second element, "of the Apostles," is less accurate. The emphasis on the "apostles" (by which Luke means especially the Twelve) hardly carries through the book, but their role at the beginning of the narrative apparently led real readers to overestimate their centrality to the narrative.[31]

This later title distracts from the work's primary theme exemplified in the shift from Jerusalem to Rome.[32] Acts continues the story of Jesus in the Gospel of Luke, and the stories of both volumes are embedded in Luke's broader understanding of salvation history rooted in the LXX. Acts traces this continuing story through the Jerusalem church (exemplified especially in Peter) and the mission as far as Rome, particularly through Paul, Luke's prime agent in the Gentile mission. If Luke's first volume was "all that Jesus began to do and teach" (Acts 1:1; see comment there), his second volume might be titled "What Jesus's Followers Continued to Do and Teach" (cf. the emphasis on apostolic teaching in 2:42),[33] with a special focus on Peter and Paul. The two volumes together might thus be called "Deeds and Sayings" or "Acts and Teachings," with the speeches representing the direct teachings of the second volume. But because the primary characters of the work as a whole are not the Twelve, the title as we have it is not what Luke would have titled the work. What Luke himself might have wished the work to be called, we can at most speculate.

17–19, treats this as a sort of intensive "intertextuality" (17), a living "Jewish Greek" (19) that exceeded mere LXX imitation. This is not "low register" (17) but a social dialect (23), providing cultural cohesiveness (26). Roman historians sometimes borrowed the style of Roman epics (Rebenich, "Historical Prose," 312), and even sculptors often revived earlier styles (Stewart, "Retrospective Styles").

28. See Blänsdorf, "Archaism."

29. Pesch, *Apostelgeschichte*, 1:22–23; Jervell, *Apostelgeschichte*, 56; Pervo, *Acts*, 29; and Hull, *Spirit in Acts*, 13, citing the Latin version of Iren. *Her.* 3.12.11 (probably); 3.13.3 (clearly referring to our book of Acts, which is quoted repeatedly in 3.14.1); Clem. Alex. *Strom.* 5.82.4; Tert. *Bapt.* 10.4; Anti-Marcionite Prologue to Luke; the Muratorian Canon (though other titles were also available). See also Euseb. *H.E.* 3.4.6 (noted in Weiser, *Apostelgeschichte*, 26).

30. Cf. Pesch, *Apostelgeschichte*, 1:22–23. Gounelle, "État de la recherche," thinks that the eventual title of Luke's Acts may have polemicized against some of the second-century acts.

31. Parsons, *Departure*, 184, citing the "primacy effect" (what comes first affecting perceptions of what follows). Second-century readers probably also assumed Paul's apostleship, despite Luke's rare application of the title to him.

32. Agreeing with, e.g., Judge, *Athens*, 50, who thinks that Luke's own title is simply "The Second *Logos* for Theophilus" (see Acts 1:1).

33. Assuming that the "began" is not grammatically superfluous; see my comment there.

NARRATIVE
INTRODUCTION
AND RECAPITULATION
(1:1–11)

Acts 1:1–11 provides a narrative introduction to Luke's second volume, a recapitulation of the final scene of his first volume, and on the level of his narrative functions as a transition from Jesus to the church. One cannot really separate 1:1–2 (a single sentence) from 1:3–11 (beginning, "and to these," i.e., those just mentioned); the entire unit belongs to a single introduction and recapitulation. For pragmatic purposes, however, the discussion here will be divided in a manner that makes it less unwieldy.

1. Introducing Introductions

Introductions were meant to be significant, and Luke's is no exception. (For this reason, this introduction will receive more extensive comment than some other portions of Acts.)[1] Writers often introduced their main themes at the beginning of a work or section.[2] Josephus provides such a preview in *Ag. Ap.* 2.2, following his retrospective about the previous volume in 2.1; Polybius does so in Polyb. 3.1.3–3.5.9, following his retrospective in 3.1.1–2. Polybius notes that having a general view of a matter helps one learn the details, making an introductory survey important (3.1.7); he had come to prefer such surveys to prologues (11.1.4–5). Rhetorical handbooks available in the first century B.C.E. advised that introductions should summarize some of the arguments that would follow.[3] A rhetorical critic (Dion. Hal. *Thuc.* 19) thus complains about an earlier historian who failed to meet this standard in his introduction.

Granted, Luke, like some other Greek historians, does *not* provide an *explicit* summary of what will follow; this leads some scholars to doubt that Luke intends a prospective summary.[4] One did not, however, need to follow all conventions in a single introduction. Luke *does* recapitulate what preceded, and in his retrospective summary introduces major themes that set the tone for the book, including the inbreaking of the new era and especially Spirit empowerment and consequent cross-cultural witness (in Acts 1:8). His introduction thus implicitly summarizes what will follow, even if it does not explicitly identify itself as such a summary. The first two

---

1. I followed the same methodology (though to a greater extent) in discussing John's prologue at much greater length than other Johannine pericopes (Keener, *John*, 331–426).
2. See, e.g., Virg. *Aen.* 1.1–6; Aul. Gel. pref. 25 (introducing subject matter in chapter headings at the beginning, whether Gellius's or an editor's; see LCL, 1:xxxviii–lxiii). See fuller discussion in note above.
3. See, e.g., *Rhet. Alex.* 29, 1436a.33–39; Dion. Hal. *Thuc.* 19; *Lysias* 24; later, Hermog. *Method* 12.427 (where Kennedy adds Dion. Hal. *Comp.* 23; Quint. *Inst.* 9.2.106).
4. Palmer, "Monograph (1993)," 22.

chapters of Acts provide "a sort of theological prologue" to the book of Acts, as Luke's infancy narratives do for the Gospel.[5] The opening paragraphs, however, introduce Luke's agendas most concisely.

As if to make absolutely clear that his second volume is a continuation of the first, Acts 1:2–11 provides a recapitulation of the narrative conclusion of Luke's first volume (Luke 24:47–51).[6] Other narrative works sometimes (though not always) included such recapitulations, especially at the beginning of another volume (e.g., Jos. *Ag. Ap.* 2.1; Char. *Chaer.* 5.1.1–2).[7] (Some also cite the repetition of Cyrus's edict in 2 Chr 36:22–23 and Ezra 1:1–3, though it remains unclear whether Ezra's author intends it as a sequel to 1–2 Chronicles.)[8] Authors had other ways to connect volumes. Sometimes the close of one volume would also introduce the content of the following book (Diod. Sic. 16.95.5, introducing Diod. Sic. 17) or some future treatise developing the subject in greater detail (Dion. Hal. *Demosth.* 58). Writers sometimes presupposed their audience's knowledge of some events or personalities,[9] but Luke here refers us back to the Gospel for most of the postbiblical information his narrative presupposes.

2. Luke's Recapitulation

J. Bradley Chance offers one comparison between the close of Luke's first volume and the opening of the next, focusing on elements in Acts 1 that match or fail to appear in Luke 24 (see table on p. 648).[10]

Not all the connections are precise recapitulations, but there are enough of these to make clear that Luke is, indeed, repeating key themes from the close of his Gospel.

Although Luke recapitulates the events of Luke 24:39–53 at the beginning of his new book, he does so with some differences. Scholars suggest different reasons for these variations. Often Greek historians reported divergent accounts of an event, sometimes noting which version they thought most likely but at other times deferring the determination to the reader's discretion. Some scholars have suggested that Luke's paired accounts may function in the same way.[11] The substantial degree of overlap between Luke's two versions, however (as well as his silence concerning the versions and his failure to place them side by side in the same book), suggests that literary freedom plays a larger role here than variant tradition.[12] That Luke feels free

5. Zehnle, *Pentecost Discourse*, 128–29 (quote, 128), except that he compares not the infancy narratives but the programmatic scene in Luke 4:16–30 (which we would compare with Peter's speech; cf. also Zehnle, *Pentecost Discourse*, 130).

6. E.g., Pesch, *Apostelgeschichte*, 1:61, 72 (with Luke 24:50–53); Miller, *Empowered for Mission*, 56–60; in detail, Goulder, *Type and History*, 16–17; cf. Longenecker, "Aversion"; Borgman, *Way*, 249–52. For other transitional themes, cf. Zehnle, *Pentecost Discourse*, 103–4.

7. Aune, *Environment*, 90, 117, citing Polybius, Strabo, Diodorus (Diod. Sic. 1.42; 2.1.1–3; 3.1.1–3; 18.1.1–6), Josephus, and Herodian, while also noting their absence in many places; Marguerat, *Actes*, 36. Although Luke may well have presented Theophilus with the first volume earlier, one cannot infer this conclusion *primarily* from the recapitulation here (as Witherington, *Acts*, 107, seems to do). Writers sometimes recapitulated the prior work and surveyed the present book in a preface (Aune, *Dictionary of Rhetoric*, 368, citing Hdt. 1.42; 2.1.1–3; 3.1.1–3; 8.1.1–6).

8. Fitzmyer, *Acts*, 194.

9. Brownson, "Introduction," x.

10. Chance, *Acts*, 34. I have adapted it only slightly, especially by noting "power" in both. For briefer lists of comparisons, see, e.g., Langner, *Hechos*, 285; Wolter, "Proömien," 492.

11. Aune, *Environment*, 135, citing Hdt. 3.3; 4.11, 179; 7.150, 167, 214; Polyb. 1.36.4; Dion. Hal. *Ant. rom.* 4.2.1.

12. Cf. Parsons, *Departure*, 189–90; Marguerat, *Actes*, 48; on the narrative function of redundancy in Luke-Acts (explaining the overlap), see Parsons, *Departure*, 191–93; for the function of variations, see 193–98.

Acts 1	Luke 24
Jesus teaches the disciples through the Spirit (1:2)	Jesus teaches the disciples after the resurrection, including explicit times (24:25–27, 32, 44–48)
Jesus offers many proofs of his risen state (1:3a)	Jesus demonstrates his risen state (24:13–32, 34, 36–40)
Jesus appears for forty days (1:3b)	Missing in Luke 24*
Jesus speaks of the kingdom (1:3b)	Not explicit in Luke 24, but cf. biblical exposition in Luke 24:27, 45–47†
Jesus eats with his disciples (1:4a)	Cf. Jesus eating in their presence (24:41–43)
Jesus orders them not to leave Jerusalem (1:4b)	Jesus orders them to stay in Jerusalem (24:49b)
Jesus instructs them to wait for the Father's promise (1:4b)	They must stay in the city until they receive the Father's promise (24:49)
Disciples expect the kingdom's restoration to Israel (1:6)	Cf. a similar notion expressed by other disciples, who expected Jesus to redeem Israel (24:21)
Jesus promises the Spirit and that they will be witnesses (1:8)	They are witnesses and will receive promised power (24:48–49)
They will receive power (1:8)	They will be clothed with power (24:49)
Jesus ascends (1:9–11)	Jesus ascends (24:51)
The disciples leave Mount Olivet for Jerusalem (1:12)	They leave Bethany (24:50; this is near the Mount of Olives, 19:29) and return to Jerusalem (24:52)
They pray in the upper room (1:13–14)	They worship in the temple (24:53)‡

*Some period of time is assumed, however, to accommodate the appearances; this would be even more if we figure in Galilean appearances (known to Luke's audience from Mark). As Parsons, *Acts*, 34, notes, including the extended period in Luke 24 would have undermined the rhetorical effectiveness of that passage.

†Given Luke's larger theology of the kingdom in his Gospel, Luke 24:46–49 would imply the kingdom message.

‡Luke probably expects us to suppose that they met both in homes (here, the upper room) *and* in the temple (as in Acts 2:46).

to paraphrase the same substance in different words should warn interpreters not to press his speeches as verbatim reports; clearly, he did not intend them this way.[13] Rhetorical custom emphasized stylistic variation in retelling a matter.[14]

It was also customary for material to overlap in recapitulations (Lucian *Hist.* 55),[15] though Luke may find some elements more useful for a book's closing than for its opening (hence the raised hands for a blessing in Luke 24:50 do not recur in Acts 1).[16] Like Luke, Josephus retells the same event in different ways in different books; this does not mean that either historian invents the events in question but, rather, that they each used their literary freedom to present varied perspectives on the event.[17]

The retelling also provides information missing earlier; for example, whereas Luke 24 telescopes events as if they might have all happened in one day (Luke 24:1, 13, 28, 36, 50), Acts presents a longer period (as suggested also by Matt 28:16; John 20:26;

13. See our introduction, ch. 8. Josephus even composes different speeches for the same incident in different works; compare Jos. *War* 1.373–79 with *Ant.* 15.126–46; cf. possibly the adaptation of a scene in Tacitus suggested in Woodman, *Rhetoric*, 176–79. Cf. the importance of variation, alongside sometimes verbatim agreement, in the "recitation composition" characterizing rhetorical culture (Robbins, "Writing," 146–55; cf. Dewey, "Oral-Aural Event," 148–49). Even eyewitness accounts are more consistent in the gist than in most incidental details (Bauckham, *Eyewitnesses*, 333–34, 344–45), and so Luke's approach is more realistic than the expectations of some modern readers.

14. Witherington, *Acts*, 107; cf. Blomberg, *Gospels*, 157–58; for Luke's practice of variation here and elsewhere, see Mussies, "Variation."

15. Witherington, *Acts*, 107.

16. Parsons, *Departure*, 197, probably correctly (unless our conception of appropriateness is influenced by subsequent liturgical use of the Aaronic benediction [Num 6:22–27; cf. lifting hands for blessing people in Lev 9:22; Sir 50:20–21] for closure). Many scholars see in the lifting of hands here an allusion to the priestly blessing (e.g., Danker, *New Age*, 24; Stempvoort, "Interpretation of Ascension," 34; particularly fully, Mekkattukunnel, *Blessing*), although not all agree (e.g., Bock, *Luke*, 1945). Litwak, *Echoes*, 148, associates it with OT blessings such as Gen 49; Deut 33.

17. Wright, *People of God*, 378.

21:1; 1 Cor 15:5–8).[18] By providing a different version that includes some new information, Luke also alerts the reader to look for new information in the retelling of other accounts in Acts (especially the conversions of Paul and Cornelius).[19]

3. Preface (1:1–2)

We must examine Luke's own prefaces (Acts 1:1–2; Luke 1:1–4) in special detail, since they provide crucial information concerning the purpose and audience he was addressing. I will not, however, rehearse in significant detail material covered in the introduction, chapter 6, section 2.b (i.e., the relevance of Luke 1:1–4 for the nature of Luke's historiography).

a. Prefaces

A preface normally did not consume the entire introductory section of a work. Thus, for example, Polybius has an opening preface, but the entire first two volumes of his work (which originally was thirty-nine volumes) constitute his introduction (Polyb. 2.71.7).

Although scholars have inferred various genres for Luke's work on the basis of the language of the preface (and most of its features could cover several genres),[20] the genre characteristics most closely fit those expected in a work of history (especially the "events" among us, Luke 1:1).[21] (See a more complete discussion in chs. 3 and 6 of the introduction.)

Prefaces by educated authors follow typical rhetorical conventions.[22] Greek historians reused themes from prefaces in Herodotus and Thucydides, including "the praise of history, the claim of impartiality and the permanent value of the subject."[23] They typically used some of the following stock topoi in their prefaces, some of which Luke also uses:[24]

1. "Requests and dedications"[25]
2. Apology for substandard style[26]
3. Discussion of history's usefulness
4. Brief discussion of predecessors (often negatively)
5. Claim to be impartial
6. Discussion of, and claim to, using proper methods
7. Reasons for having selected the topic

18. Witherington, Acts, 107–8; cf. Wright, People of God, 378. Tannehill, Acts, 10, sees this conflict as an example of Luke's penchant for variation going too far (also Acts 9:7 with 26:14).

19. See Perkins, Reading, 255–56.

20. See, e.g., Robbins, "Prefaces"; Alexander, "Luke's Preface." Alexander, Context, 16, notes that "scientific" prefaces do not identify genre and that Luke-Acts is not a technical scientific work.

21. See Aune, Environment, 121 (cf. 89–90, 120–21); idem, "Prooimion"; Callan, "Preface and Historiography"; van Unnik, "Once More Prologue"; Schmidt, "Influences"; Moessner, "Arrangement," 158–63; idem, "Synergy" (comparing Luke's approach with that of Dionysius); Witherington, Acts, 11. Contrast Pervo, Profit, 5, 144 (treated earlier). Alexander, Context, 12–13, notes that she never denied that Luke intended his work as "history," but contends (17–18) that the preface resembles those of technical treatises rather than histories, perhaps suggesting the kind of history Luke intends.

22. For a comparison between 4 Macc 1:1–12 and Luke 1:1–4 and ancient speeches, see Klauck, "Rhetorik: Exordium."

23. For this list, see Aune, Environment, 89–90; in general, see Earl, "Prologue-Form in Historiography."

24. This list is from Aune, Environment, 90.

25. For this convention (though not pervasive), Adams, "Preface," 183–84, cites Plut. Rise and Fall of Athens 1.1; Jos. War 1.16; Ag. Ap. 1.1; and the implications of Dion. Hal. Ant. rom. 1.4.3. Pervo, Acts, 35, doubts the convention, regarding Josephus as its earliest example.

26. See Aul. Gel. pref. 10; Apul. Metam. 1.1; Jos. Ant. 1.2–3, 7; cf. Jos. War 1.3; Ant. 20.263 (conclusion).

Luke shows some of these features: he apparently includes a dedication (Luke 1:3; Acts 1:1) and his purpose for writing, and for writing on this subject (albeit not on the value of history, which anyone steeped in Jewish Scripture would have to accept), and he mentions his predecessors (though he does not severely critique them).[27] Luke also specifies his appropriate methodology, emphasizing his careful investigation (Luke 1:3).[28]

Rhetorical prefaces served three primary functions (Lucian *Hist.* 53):[29]

1. Securing audience favor
2. Securing their attention
3. Preparing them to receive instruction

Luke undoubtedly seeks to fulfill all three functions with his prefaces.

Historians could omit full prefaces when the subject matter was sufficiently familiar to the ideal audience to require no detailed explanation (Lucian *Hist.* 52); historians should also omit the request for a favorable hearing characteristic of oratory. Yet even historians were to note their topic, assert its usefulness, and also declare that their exposition of it will be easy to follow (*Hist.* 53). Luke offers each of these three points in his two-volume work's preface ("the matters accomplished among us," Luke 1:1; the subject's usefulness, 1:4; and its clear presentation, 1:3) but only in the preface to the whole of Luke-Acts (1:1–4), not in Acts itself.

It thus seems reasonable to read the brief preface of Acts 1:1 in the light of the longer preface in Luke 1:1–4, which probably introduces the entire work and not the Gospel only;[30] the preface to a two-volume work could cover both volumes (e.g., Philost. *Vit. soph.* pref. 479).[31] "Secondary prologues," however, were common in new volumes of multivolume works, as here.[32] Sometimes later volumes opened with an explanation as to why they had been added to the earlier volumes (Artem. *Oneir.* 3.pref.); at other times they simply made explicit the transition they were making (Pliny E. *N.H.* 3.1.1; 9.1.1). Luke follows good rhetorical practice (Lucian *Hist.* 55) in keeping his prologue shorter in the second volume and in summarizing the first volume's contents.[33] Ancient writers generally preferred brief prefaces (2 Macc 2:32, in name if not in practice; Artem. *Oneir.* 1.pref.).

b. Luke's Own Preface in Acts (1:1–2)

Prefaces differed from one another,[34] and Luke's prefaces reveal distinctive features. Luke's preface in Acts refers back to the first volume, making the first preface relevant (to at least some extent) for the entire work of Luke-Acts.

27. On Luke's approach toward his predecessors, see below; cf. also Massey, "Disagreement," esp. 71–72.
28. On this, see Thucyd. 1.22.1–2; and our introduction, chs. 2–8, esp. here chs. 3 and 6.
29. Aune, *Environment*, 90; see further Heath, "Invention," 103. For the emphasis on securing the audience's favor, see also Gärtner, "Prooemium," 16–17; much fuller comment at Acts 17:22.
30. With Fitzmyer, *Acts*, 193.
31. The first preface in a multivolume work was usually the most important (Aune, *Dictionary of Rhetoric*, 368).
32. Witherington, *Acts*, 105.
33. Johnson, *Acts*, 28, citing as an example Jos. *Ag. Ap.* 1.1 and 2.1. Some scholars continue the preface beyond Acts 1:1 (certainly the sentence does not end there; Palmer, "Monograph [1993]," 23), but Luke is simply smoothing his transition to the narrative, as rhetoricians advised (Sen. E. *Controv.* 1.1.25; also Hanson, *Acts*, 57, citing Lucian *Hist.* 55; cf. Anderson, *Glossary*, 70–71).
34. Conventions that were common were not therefore mandatory for every preface. Polybius claimed that prologues were useful to focus readers' attention on the correct agenda (Polyb. 11.1.1–2), but since prologues

1. Relation to Volume One (1:1)

Writers often summarized or referred back to their previous volumes, especially at the start of a new one (e.g., Polyb. 2.1.1; 3.1.1–2). (As in the case of Luke 24:47–53, the end of one book could also announce the topic of the next [e.g., Diod. Sic. 19.110.5; 20.113.5].) One could also refer to former works that were not part of the same enterprise for which one was currently writing. Thus Josephus allows himself to omit details in his autobiography because he recounted other details in the *Jewish War* (*Life* 412), freeing him to add other material not in the *War* (*Life* 413). Yet a reader might expect comment especially if a writer was deliberately pairing two essays, as in Philo *Good Person* 1 (LCL, 9:11): "Our former treatise [πρότερος λόγος],[35] Theodotus, had for its theme 'every bad man is a slave' and established it by many reasonable and indisputable arguments. The present treatise is closely akin to that, its full brother, indeed, we may say its twin, and in it we shall show that every man of worth is free." One might also announce a forthcoming volume or volumes.[36]

A few scholars have argued, on the basis of the strictest sense of πρῶτον in Acts 1:1, that the Gospel was not the former of two but, rather, the first of several planned volumes.[37] In this case, perhaps Luke proved unable to complete his work (explaining the unfinished character of parts of Acts and the slowness of the church to pay more attention to it). Most scholars, however, find this inference unwarranted, often pointing out that the Greek term was probably used as loosely at times as modern speakers employ the superlative in English.[38] The classical distinction between "first" and "former" no longer widely obtained; despite our technical exception from Philo above (*Good Person* 1), papyri show that πρῶτος mostly superseded πρότερος in the popular Koine.[39] Some point to Luke's usage elsewhere to confirm that the term simply means "former," which also makes the best sense of our current two volumes.[40] Perhaps a strict Atticist would have objected to Luke's usage, but most readers would have understood Luke's point perfectly well, and his lack of Attic purity elsewhere does not suggest that he wrote especially for antiquarian purists.[41]

Scholars have debated what Luke means by ἤρξατο ("began"). Some argue that it is simply a Semitic pleonasm, which is possible where Luke uses sources (Luke 3:8 with Matt 3:9) and especially with verbs of speaking (Luke 4:21; 5:21; 7:15, 24, 49; 11:29; 12:1; 13:26; 20:9; 23:2, 30; 24:47; with other verbs, see 7:38; 13:25; 14:9).

---

were neglected in his day (11.1.3), he preferred to provide introductory summaries instead (11.1.4–5), except in his first six books.

35. By calling his first volume "word" (λόγον), Luke probably does expect us to see his gospel story as part of the larger divine "word" or "message" that his writings often mention (e.g., Luke 1:2; 4:32, 36; Acts 2:41; 4:4; and passim), but as this parallel with Philo indicates, it was also a normal way to describe one's earlier account.

36. As Lucian *True Story* 2.47 does, but only in jest (LCL, 1:357n1: "The biggest lie of all, as a disgruntled Greek scribe remarks in the margin!").

37. E.g., Ramsay, *Traveller and Citizen*, 27–28; idem, *Teaching*, 370.

38. Johnson, *Acts*, 24 (comparing Philo *Good Person* 1; Jos. *Ag. Ap.* 2.1); Barrett, *Acts*, 65; Carter and Earle, *Acts*, 1; Knowling, "Acts," 49; Arrington, *Acts*, 4. Although one might not expect such loosened sense in atticizing introductions, Koine employed superlatives less often than classical Greek (Dana and Mantey, *Grammar*, 39–40), and a comparative adjective may function like a superlative (Wallace, *Grammar*, 111, 299–300); cf., e.g., Matt 5:19; 22:36, 38.

39. Lake and Cadbury, *Commentary*, 2; Bruce, *Acts*[1], 65; Bruce, *Commentary*, 32n12; Moulton and Milligan, *Vocabulary*, 557; Blass, Debrunner, and Funk, *Grammar*, 34, §62; Parsons and Culy, *Acts*, 2.

40. C. Williams, *Acts*, 54; Schille, *Apostelgeschichte*, 66. Whereas Luke never uses πρότερος (only eleven times in the NT), he uses πρῶτος ("first") frequently, and there can be no question that sometimes it simply means the first of two, e.g., Acts 7:12–13 (though the brothers came again in Genesis, "first" is contrasted with "second" here); 12:10.

41. Luke might prefer more classical usage in his primary preface (Luke 1:1–4) without requiring it here (Acts 1:1).

This Semitic construction is also familiar from the LXX, in which Luke and his ideal audience are steeped.[42] Luke may well use this wording "to achieve a rhythmically impeccable sequence of words, which could not have been attained with a simple imperfect or aorist."[43]

Conversely, with other verbs (and sometimes verbs of speaking) it more often makes good sense with reference to beginning an action rather than completing it (Luke 9:12; 11:53; 12:45; 14:29–30; 15:14, 24; 19:37, 45; 21:28; 22:23; 23:5).[44] Also, pleonasms are less likely in a preface where higher literary style was expected, and here it refers to the beginning of Jesus's ministry, as in 3:23 and Acts 1:22; 10:37.[45] Thus others suggest that it probably means that the second volume addresses what Jesus continued to do and teach, presumably by his name and the Spirit through the disciples.[46] This would make Jesus the "paradigm for the church's ministry"[47]—a pattern that certainly fits Luke's plan elsewhere.[48] The syntactical evidence, on the whole, may favor reading "began" as a stylistic flourish, but the context of Luke's theology (and parallelism between Jesus in the Gospel and key figures in Acts) could support the sense that Acts continues Jesus's works, especially given the attention that Luke as a competent writer would devote to his preface.[49] Certainly, Jesus's agents act in his name (e.g., Acts 3:6, 16; 4:7, 10, 30), and Jesus continues to actively stand behind the miracles (esp. 9:34).[50]

The former volume recounted Jesus's "words and deeds." (Most of Jesus's "speaking" in the Gospel should be understood as synonymous with the "teaching" mentioned here.)[51] Jesus's "deeds" included his signs, which Luke emphasizes heavily.[52] In Luke's larger work, others had also recognized (not long before) that Jesus was a prophet "powerful in deed and word" (Luke 24:19) just as Moses had been (Acts 7:22). This approach fits a Gospel,[53] but also characterizes historical works more generally. His-

42. Widely noted, e.g., Carter and Earle, *Acts*, 23; Lake and Cadbury, *Commentary*, 3; Witherington, *Acts*, 10.
43. Haenchen, *Acts*, 137n4.
44. Its pleonastic use is rarer in Acts than in the Gospel (Acts 2:4; 11:4; 24:2), but so is its normal sense, though it does occur in some texts, most referring to speech (8:35; 11:15, in view of 10:44; the cases of 18:26 and 27:35 could be argued either way). Other texts could also use "begin to" with verbs of speech deliberately (e.g., *Sib. Or.* 3.560, ἄρξονται . . . κλήζειν).
45. See also Johnson, *Acts*, 24.
46. E.g., Bruce, *Acts¹*, 66 (regarding it as "emphatic"); idem, *Acts³*, 21; Blaiklock, *Acts*, 49; Reicke, "Lord and Church"; Hays, *Moral Vision*, 112, 120; Burridge, "Genre of Acts," 28; cf. Barrett, *Acts*, 2:lxxxv, who holds it as probable but allows that "even if he did not intend it Luke would not have disagreed." Cf. similarly Chrys. *Hom. Acts* 1 (*NPNF* 11:7): "The Gospels, then, are a history of what Christ did and said; but the Acts, of what that 'other Comforter' said and did."
47. Hays, *Moral Vision*, 120–22.
48. Goulder, *Type and History*, 63–64, pointing to the parallels in Acts (see further discussion in ch. 16 of our introduction). "The whole book is an exposition of this sentence" (64).
49. Hull, *Spirit in Acts*, 179–80, notes that syntactically it could simply reflect comprehensiveness but, in view of Luke's theology, probably means that the second volume carries forward this subject matter of the first.
50. See Gaventa, *Acts*, 63, 162, noting also that Jesus's apostles are his "witnesses" (Acts 1:22; 2:32; 3:15; 5:32; 10:39; 13:31).
51. Jesus's speech in Luke is regularly connected with teaching (Luke 4:15, 31; 5:3, 17; 6:6; 11:1; 12:12; 13:10, 22, 26; 19:47; 20:1, 21; 21:37; 23:5). Acts likewise emphasizes apostolic teaching (Acts 5:21, 25, 28; 11:26; 18:11; cf. 21:21, 28) and connects it explicitly with preaching (4:2, 18; 5:42; 15:35; 28:31; also other verbs of speaking, 18:25; 20:20).
52. Higgins, "Preface and Kerygma," 91, argues from Acts 1:1 that the kerygma in Acts (like its detailed account in Luke's Gospel) includes not only preaching but miracles *demonstrating* the preaching; this would fit Luke's emphasis on signs (on which see ch. 9 in our introduction). On "deeds" in encomia, see, e.g., Malina and Neyrey, *Portraits*, 28–33 (citing Menander Rhetor and esp. Aristotle).
53. Probably already a generation later, Mark's recitation of Peter's recollections appears in similar words (Papias frg. 3.15, in Euseb. *H.E.* 3.39.1; cf. here Kurzinger, *Apostelgeschichte*, 9). Papias's language could possibly reflect the influence of Acts 1:1, but given the completely different wording might simply reflect broader usage.

tory focused on words, that is, speeches (λόγοι), and deeds, or actions (e.g., Polyb. 2.56.11; deeds in Arist. *Rhet.* 1, 1360 a35; Val. Max. 1.pref., first sentence; Quint. *Inst.* 2.4.2).[54] Thus Valerius Maximus often links words and deeds to reinforce the title of his work.[55] Observers also tested the consistency of the actions of moral teachers and others with their words (Matt 23:3; Rom 2:21–22; Jas 1:22; 1 John 3:18).[56] Writers could even use such consistency to seek to vindicate a teacher's innocence or integrity.[57] In view of their reversal in Luke 24:19, one should not argue from word order here that Jesus's deeds take *precedence* over his words; ancients recognized that when word sequence varied randomly in different passages of an author's writing, the author attached no significance of priority to the sequence.[58]

Claiming that the first volume recounted "*all* of Jesus's words and deeds" was the sort of overstatement (contrast John 21:25, a different kind of overstatement)[59] characteristic of ancient rhetoricians[60] (and of Luke in some other settings, e.g., Luke 2:1; Acts 19:10). Still, it also implies comprehensiveness, which ancient historians sought to provide.[61]

II. DEDICATIONS (1:1; LUKE 1:3)

The custom of dedicating works to others to show respect or affection was ancient and common in both Greek and Roman literature.[62] It functioned as a symbolic way of presenting the work to the dedicatee[63] and was meant to honor the dedicatee.[64] In contrast to some other kinds of works, narrative works (including epics and historiography) usually lacked dedications until "the imperial period, when dedications

54. Fornara, *Nature of History*, 1–2, 116, 185; Witherington, *Acts*, 10–11 (who provides some of these references); Aune, *Environment*, 91. The special form of novelized history in Xen. *Cyr.* 5.1.1 also claims to recount what Cyrus and his allies ἔπραξάν τε καὶ ἔλεξαν in *Cyr.* Bk. 4.

55. See Wardle, *Valerius Maximus*, 66 (citing esp. Val. Max. 4.1.12; 6.2.pref.; 7.2.pref.; 7.3.pref.; 9.3.pref.; 9.11.pref.; 9.11.12).

56. E.g., ancient thinkers typically coupled deeds with words (in Jewish sources, see Sir 3:8; Wis 1:16; *Test. Ab.* 9:4 A; *Test. Gad* 6:1; Jos. *Ag. Ap.* 2.169, 292), e.g., Hesiod *W.D.* 710; Aeschylus *Suppl.* 515; Xen. *Cyr.* 5.1.1; *Hell.* 6.3.12; *Mem.* 1.5.6; 4.4.10; Aeschines *Tim.* 30; Isaeus *Menec.* 32, 38; Isoc. *Nic.* 61 (*Or.* 3.39); Theophr. *Char.* 1.1; 14.1; Ap. Rhod. 3.81; Polyb. 3.111.10; 31.29.11; Catull. *Carm.* 76.8; Val. Max. 1. pref.; Sen. Y. *Ep. Lucil.* 20.1–2; Epict. *Diatr.* 1.25.11; 2.9.13; Pliny *Ep.* 10.3A.3; Ael. Arist. *Def. Or.* 279, §87D; *Panath.* 403, in 320D; Lucian *Runaways* 15; *Hipp.* 1; Max. Tyre 15.6; Diog. Laert. 6.2.64; 6.3.82; Iambl. *V.P.* 2.10; 8.35; Men. Rhet. 2.4, 394.20–21; Hdn. 1.2.4; Eunapius *Lives* 495. Such advice was an ancient commonplace (Demosth. *Olynth.* 3.14; *Philip.* 2.1; 3.15; Diod. Sic. 9.9.1; Dion. Hal. *Ant. rom.* 7.33.3; 9.10.3; 9.47.4; 11.1.4; 11.58.3; Cic. *Fam.* 13.6a.4; Quint. *Inst.* 1.pref. 14; Mus. Ruf. 1, p. 36.4–5, 9–12; 8, p. 64.11; Aul. Gel. 17.19; Max. Tyre 25.1–2; Porph. *Marc.* 8.142–43; 14.237–39; 16.277–78). For coupling of "word" and "deed" elsewhere, see, e.g., *Rhet. Alex.* 9, 1430a.14–21; 36, 1442a.16–18; 38, 1445b.30–34; Fronto *Ad verum imp.* 2.8; Philost. *Hrk.* 32.1; Iambl. *V.P.* 24.108; 33.232.

57. See Robbins, *Jesus the Teacher*, 63. Some early readers used the sequence of "do" and "teach" to support doing before teaching (John Cassian *Conferences* 14.9 [Martin, *Acts*, 3]). Jewish teachers taught "deeds" as well as words (Gerhardsson, *Memory*, 185), and their behavior could even constitute halakic precedent (*t. Piska* 2:15–16; *Sipre Deut.* 221.1.1; *y. B. Meṣiʿa* 2:11, §1; *Demai* 1:4; *Nid.* 1:4, §2; *Sanh.* 7:2, §4; *Yebam.* 4:11, §8).

58. E.g., Dion. Hal. *Lit. Comp.* 5; *Mek. Pisha* 1.28 (Lauterbach, 1:3); *Gen. Rab.* 1:15; *Pesiq. Rab.* 23/24:2.

59. Also common in ancient writers; see Keener, *John*, 1241–42, citing, e.g., Hom. *Od.* 3.113–17; Lysias *Or.* 2.1, §190; Diod. Sic. 16.95.5; 1 Macc 9:22; 2 Macc 2:24–25; Philo *Abr.* 1; *Spec. Laws* 4.238; *Song Rab.* 1:3, §1; *Pesiq. Rab.* 3:2; Iambl. *V.P.* 28.135.

60. Witherington, *Acts*, 9 (citing Thucyd. 2.65.2, 9). Pervo, *Acts*, 35, suggests more specifically that it also characterized prefaces.

61. Witherington, *Acts*, 9 (citing Lucian *Hist.* 55; Diod. Sic. 16.1, and contrasting biographies). In contrast to an attempted universal history, however, a historical monograph would focus on a particular topic and cover merely this in detail; Conzelmann, *Acts*, 3–4, sees monograph characteristics here.

62. Citroni, "Dedications," 438.

63. Aune, *Dictionary of Rhetoric*, 123.

64. Cf. Pliny the Elder's criticism of Apion's immodesty in claiming that his dedications bestowed immortality on their recipients (*N.H.* pref. 25); cf. Josephus's lavish praise of Epaphroditus in *Ant.* 1.8.

were extended to historiographical works."[65] Ancient writers often dedicated literary works to friends who were equals (especially if the writer was himself a person of means) or sometimes "friends" who were patrons.[66] Among dedications within one's class, Antonius Diogenes opens his novel by dedicating it to his sister (*Thule* 110a–111b). For examples of superiors, Plutarch dedicates his work on the sayings of kings to the emperor Trajan (*S. Kings* pref., *Mor.* 172BC). By dedicating his work to the emperor Titus, Pliny the Elder feared (or feigned fear) that he risked presumption (*N.H.* pref. 6, 12). Occasionally writers might also use such dedications to encourage literary patrons or sponsors to fulfill their promised obligations quickly (e.g., Phaedrus 3.epil. 8–21).[67]

One might pause at various intervals in one's work to honor one's dedicatee with further mentions (Plut. *Isis* 1, 3, *Mor.* 351C, 352C), especially when moving from one book to another,[68] as here. One could mention the dedicatee toward the end of a book as well as toward the beginning.[69]

Sometimes a writer would dedicate a work to the person who urged him to investigate the subject (cf. Dion. Hal. *1 Amm.* 2), a point that might be relevant to Theophilus's apparent curiosity (Luke 1:4).[70] One might write a work to fulfill another's request to know more about a particular subject;[71] one might also dedicate a work to others' interest, even if it seemed likely that one had provoked that interest oneself (cf. Jos. *Ag. Ap.* 2.296; *Ant.* 1.8).

Not all dedicatees, however, were necessarily as interested as others.[72] Phaedrus addresses book 3 to one Eutychus, entreating him with arguments why he should invest the time to read the work (Phaedrus 3.prol., which is sixty-three lines). Sometimes a writer dedicated a work probably with the goal of securing a patron for its publication, that is, so that the person would be flattered enough to have it read at some of his banquets (see introduction, ch. 1).

Patrons could prove very influential in works, whether or not they had invited the writer to treat a topic. A writer might set aside one project for another one if the patron so desired (Dion. Hal. *Thuc.* 1), and might arrange an essay in such a manner as to make it easiest for the dedicatee to follow (Dion. Hal. *2 Amm.* 2). At the same time, an author is responsible to give the truth to his patron even if this is less apt to please him (Dion. Hal. *Thuc.* 55).

Like other matters involving elite social relations, appropriate honor protocol demanded careful attention with regard to book dedications. Cicero complains that his friend should not have published (i.e., circulated to a reader) a copy of his work in its unrevised form; he needed to polish the work, and then the dedicatee would receive

65. Citroni, "Dedications," 439.

66. For this distinction, see Keener, "Friendship," 381–82; idem, *John*, 1006–9; for Roman dedications and the patronage system, see Citroni, "Dedications," 438; idem, "Patronage, literary," 1125.

67. Since authors normally received nothing from booksellers (Citroni, "Patronage, literary," 1125), patronage was especially important.

68. E.g., Cic. *Fin.* 1.1.1; 3.1.1; 3.2.6; Jos. *Ag. Ap.* 1.1; 2.1; Quint. *Inst.* 4.pref. 1; Artem. *Oneir.* 3.pref.; often in the historical work of Vell. Paterc. (1.13.5; 2.7.5; 2.49.1; 2.65.3; 2.96.2; 2.101.3; 2.104.2; 2.113.1; 2.130.4). Hermog. *Inv.* 3.1.126 offers one in his third book but not the first two.

69. Dion. Hal. *Demosth.* 58; Jos. *Life* 430; *Ant.* 20.266; *Ag. Ap.* 2.296; Plut. *Demosth.* 1.1; 31.4.

70. Often writers claimed that the task of writing was difficult but undertaken out of duty to fulfill the dedicatee's request (Citroni, "Dedications," 438, mentions *Rhetorica ad Herennium* and some of Cicero's works on rhetoric as examples).

71. Dion. Hal. *2 Amm.* 1; Cic. *Or. Brut.* 1.1 (who also emphasizes his affection for Brutus, his dedicatee); Quint. *Inst.* 6.pref. 1.

72. Connections between the dedicatee and the work's content may be minimal in genres such as satire and elegy (Citroni, "Dedications," 439).

the first copy (Cic. *Att.* 13.21a). Receiving a book dedication was an honor, a matter of great importance at least for the politics of the urban elites; Cicero complained that Varro "promised to dedicate a great and important work to me" but two years later had still not written it (*Att.* 13.12 [LCL]). Likewise, a certain Caelius encouraged Cicero, should he ever have some free time, to "compose and dedicate to me some sort of *brochure*, to make me feel that you take an interest in me," as a way of recalling their friendship to many future generations (Cic. *Fam.* 8.3.2 [LCL]).

"O" (ὦ) as part of an address can appear as exalted rhetoric[73] but need not tell us about the addressee's status (see exclamations in Rom 2:1, 3; Gal 3:1; Jas 2:20); in Luke-Acts it is usually employed with some degree of reproof (Luke 9:41; 24:25; Acts 13:10; 18:14; 27:21), although that is not the case here. More important, Theophilus's title, "most excellent" (κράτιστε, Luke 1:3), probably implies status (Acts 23:26; 24:3; 26:25).[74] It was considered appropriate to flatter a book's addressee; Artemidorus, for example, writes for "the greatest orator ever to come before the public" (Artem. *Oneir.* 1.pref.; White, 14).[75] But it was also appropriate to select a person of status as the dedicatee; thus Josephus dedicates both his autobiography and his apology to "most excellent Epaphroditus" (*Ag. Ap.* 1.1, κράτιστε; *Life* 430; *Ant.* 20.266), apparently his patron; Dionysius addresses κράτιστε Ἀμμαῖε, honorable Ammaeus (Dion. Hal. *Anc. Or.* 1.1).[76] We need not assume that such titles were "merely" honorary; it is more likely that those who could do so would dedicate their works to persons of status who would read and, it was hoped, commend to others their works, publishing them at their banquets.

Because a client was part of his patron's extended household, a writer could dedicate a work to a "friend" for use in educating his son (Quint. *Inst.* 1.pref. 6) or dedicate the work directly to a member of that household.[77] Dionysius dedicates a book to an adolescent as a gift to him—but the youth is the *son* of Dionysius's "friend," presumably meaning his patron (Dion. Hal. *Lit. Comp.* 1).

Not all dedicatees were patrons, though dedicatees were often people of status. Philostratus dedicates a massive work to a consul (Philost. *Vit. soph.* pref. 479). Pliny dedicates his collection of epistles to the friend who had urged him to collect them (*Ep.* 1.1.1–2). One could also address a letter-essay to a wealthy admirer who had challenged the author on some point, prompting an essay in response (Dion. Hal. *Pomp.* 1). Catullus dedicates a book to one of his readers who had appreciated his "humble" work before others did (*Carm.* 1.3–4). Cicero dedicated, on Atticus's advice, a book to Brutus (*Att.* 13.21a); some other books to Varro and to Brutus

---

73. Cf., e.g., in Fronto *Ad M. Caes.* 2.3.1, in Latin.

74. See discussion in Robbins, "Location," 321–22. Some scholars think that it could mark Theophilus as an equestrian, though acknowledging that it could also function as a courtesy title (as with Felix in Acts 23:26; so, e.g., Bruce, *Message*, 51n1); Danker, *New Age*, 4, suggests a Roman official (believer or not); Montefiore, *Gospels*, 2:362, more simply concludes "that he was in a high station." Citing more general usage in this period, Wallace and Williams, *Acts*, 32, suggest that we can claim him only of higher status than Luke. Ramsay's guess (*Bethlehem*, 64–65) that he was a Roman citizen is plausible, but his arguments are not at all compelling. The wide Greek usage does not necessitate anything more than a polite address (see BDAG, noting its frequency in dedications), but Luke's own usage elsewhere probably does imply status here.

75. If his addressee is Maximus of Tyre, the latter is indeed a famous orator. See also (more realistically) Statius *Silv.* 2.pref.; 2.2.

76. Similarly Avianus *Fables*, introductory letter, line 1 ("most excellent Theodosius").

77. Marcellus was the "truest of friends" (LCL), a relationship that would establish a household relationship between the two families regardless of patronal connections; see comments on guest friendship in Keener, *John*, 913 (esp. Hom. *Il.* 6.212–31; Cic. *Fam.* 13.34.1).

(13.23); and his *De senectute* (also called *Cato Major*) to Atticus himself (*Att.* 14.21; cf. *Senect.* 1.1). Writers sometimes also dedicated poetic lines to praising a friend.[78] Many scholars suppose that Theophilus was, or likely was, Luke's patron.[79] This proposal is certainly possible; if historians lacked other means of independent support, they might depend on a patron,[80] and dedications to patrons were common.[81] It seems doubtful that Theophilus sponsored Luke during his travels with Paul when he did his "field research," but it is certainly possible that he sponsored his writing project and its publication.[82] More clearly, he could help promote the work once it was out, and his name would lend to the work the status and credibility of a respected member of society. Churches may have made their own copies as word about the book caught on, but possibly Luke hopes that Theophilus, as a person of status, will sponsor the work by circulating it among members of his own class.[83] (This was begun, as noted in ch. 1 of the introduction, especially by public readings at banquets;[84] the well-to-do could also lend their homes as venues for other public readings.)[85] Given Theophilus's special status, this seems fairly likely, though, as we have noted, not all dedicatees were patrons.

What we can say about Theophilus certainly is that he is "an 'overt narratee'"—the one person who can be certainly assumed in Luke's audience.[86] Then again, this does not necessarily help us to construct even Luke's ideal audience:[87] a dedicatee might be named precisely because his status was higher than that of many other members of the audience; his name would then honor the manuscript, as well as the reverse.[88] Conversely, Luke would probably not have worked to produce the quality of Greek he produced in some parts of his work had he not intended (or hoped for) an audience that included at least some persons of status and education. It is possible that Luke strikes so forcefully at the dangers of wealth precisely because many in his audience face this temptation.[89]

No one, however, intended the dedicatee to be the only reader of a published work;[90] in fact, Dionysius writes one work because his dedicatee found insufficient two previous works he had written on the subject—one to the current dedicatee but the other to a different one (Dion. Hal. *2 Amm.* 1). Dionysius thus attests that the work

78. E.g., Mart. *Epig.* 10.19, praising Pliny and quoted by the latter on the former's death in Pliny *Ep.* 3.21.5. Some question the ideal friendship suggested in Cicero's dedication in *Amic.* (Marchetti, "Words").

79. Aune, *Environment*, 77; Witherington, *Acts*, 13–14 (arguing that "most excellent" functions this way in Jos. *Ag. Ap.* 1.1; cf. 2.1); more tentatively, Fitzmyer, *Acts*, 195; Barrett, *Acts*, 65. The hypothesis that he was a Roman official for whom Luke was arguing Paul's case (Mauck, *Trial*, 22), connected with taking Acts as a trial brief, is rarer and more difficult.

80. Aune, *Environment*, 77; Witherington, *Acts*, 55. For patronage of poets, see Schmidt, "Circles, literary."

81. Besides the sources above, see Horace's dedications to Maecenas (*Ep.* 1.1.1–3; *Sat.* 1.1.1–3; *Odes* 1.1).

82. Richards, *Letter Writing*, 170, suggests that a patron's sponsorship would have aided Luke considerably in view of the substantial cost of producing even the first copy of Luke-Acts (which he would estimate as more than $4,000 in today's currency; cf. 167–69).

83. See Dunn, *Acts*, xi; cf. the discussion of publication methods in Scholer, "Writing," 1283 (following Gamble, *Books and Readers*); also ch. 1 of our introduction, above.

84. See ch. 1 of our introduction, our initial chapter on publication.

85. E.g., Pliny *Ep.* 8.12.1–2 (though the noteworthiness of this example suggests that it was not common).

86. Tannehill, *Acts*, 9; Creech, "Narratee," 110–11; "the ideal reader" in Klauck, *Magic*, 4.

87. Cadbury, *Acts in History*, 138, notes that Luke wrote for a wider circulation than Theophilus and that his work's "effect on Theophilus himself was not the main concern of the author."

88. It could serve an apologetic function; some outsiders may have shared Celsus's later disdain for Christians' effective appeal to "the socially objectionable classes" (Cook, *Interpretation*, 84–85). Cultic groups could achieve mainstream status through the help of patrons (White, *Origins of Architecture*, 1:58–59).

89. For a survey of some views regarding the wealth of Luke's audience, see Donahue, "Decades on Rich and Poor."

90. Mason, *Josephus and New Testament*, 198, notes that Josephus is explicit on this matter.

addressed to the other person had been circulated and was part of the background he could assume in writing for a different dedicatee now.

Other sources also indicate that a writer recognized that there would be other readers besides a patron and therefore had to take into account that audience as well (Dion. Hal. *Thuc.* 2). Thus, for example, though Dionysius dedicates his *Literary Composition* to a particular reader, his opening and closing suggest a wide literary audience (the splendid epideictic of *Lit. Comp.* 1 includes notable *paronomasia*, with five words ending in -ῆμα).[91] Josephus urges Epaphroditus to accept the dedication of his apology but implies a wide audience: "To you, who are a devoted lover of truth, and for your sake to any who, like you, may wish to know the facts about our race" (*Ag. Ap.* 2.296 [LCL]).

III. WHO IS THEOPHILUS?

Some scholars have suggested that Luke uses θεόφιλος, "loved by God," symbolically rather than as the dedicatee's real name;[92] not surprisingly, this approach was common in an earlier era that valued allegory.[93] From a very early period, Greek could use "beloved by God" as an adjective: thus in Homer, Achilles is Διίφιλε, loved by Zeus (Hom. *Il.* 1.74), as is Apollo (1.86). A classical writer could speak of soldiers victorious in battle as θεοφιλεῖς (Xen. *Cyr.* 4.1.5). Philosophers could call divinely inspired persons, such as poets or lawgivers, "beloved by the gods" (Mus. Ruf. 11, p. 80.26; 15, p. 96.24), or apply the adjective to the wise soul (Porph. *Marc.* 14.238), wise deeds (15.260), or a wise person (16.281). Good people were "loved by the gods" (θεοφιλεῖς, Dio Chrys. *Or.* 31.58).[94] Some Jewish people also spoke of lovers of learning as θεοφιλεῖς (*Let. Aris.* 287) and similarly of Abraham (Philo *Abr.* 89) or Moses (Philo *Conf.* 95).

If the name were used symbolically, it could represent all hearers loved by God, but this interpretation would entail an unusual use of a dedication.[95] Conversely, it could be applied symbolically to a person of rank who would risk too much by being named.[96] But it made little sense to dedicate a work to someone yet conceal the dedicatee's name; this would neither honor the dedicatee nor secure the endorsement value of his status for the work. Granted, Luke would hardly name him if he wrote for Roman Christians shortly after Nero's fire, but our introduction (chs. 10–12) suggests that Luke probably wrote somewhat later and, still more probably, in a region lacking overt, life-threatening persecution.

Given the attached title ("most excellent") in Luke 1:3, "Theophilus" is almost certainly a real name.[97] The name was quite common in antiquity and (in contrast

---

91. On Luke's likely wide audience, see further Ferguson, *Backgrounds*, 94.

92. E.g., Klauck, *Magic*, 4 (although he accepts Theophilus as both a historical person and "the ideal reader," whose name fortuitously has symbolic value). Usually we lack external means to identify the named recipients of ancient letters (e.g., Dillon and Polleichtner, *Iamblichus*, xvii).

93. Origen *Hom. Luke* 1.6 (Just, *Luke*, 4); Bede *Comm. Acts* 1.1 (trans. L. Martin, 9; Martin, *Acts*, 2).

94. Many other texts likewise apply this to a blessed state of favor with the gods (e.g., Men. Rhet. 1.3, 361.17–22; Philost. *Hrk.* 58.1); cf. application to a city in Libanius *Encomium* 5.2. For cognate terms in Philo, see Bekken, *Word*, 102–6.

95. In contrast to the common character of the name, symbolic dedications are not well attested (Alexander, *Preface*, 132–33, 188; Gaventa, *Acts*, 50, 62–63).

96. Fellows, personal correspondence, June 5, 2007. Marx, "New Theophilus," even suggests that it is Agrippa II (Acts 25–26), with Luke hoping to convert him (Acts 26:28). Although Josephus addresses such prestigious patrons, Luke's literary level might not appear sufficient for one of this rank.

97. Barrett, *Acts*, 65–66; Alexander, *Preface*, 188; Marshall, *Acts*, 55–56; Morris, *Luke*, 66; Bock, *Acts*, 52. Luke's simple designation (like that of many dedications in antiquity) is adequate, since Theophilus's circle would know his identity.

to the title) does not indicate much about the possessor's status or ethnicity.[98] It became a common Jewish name in the Diaspora, like others compounded with roots such as εὐσεβ- or σαββάτις.[99] Along with other *theo*-compounded names, it appears frequently in Jewish papyri from Roman Egypt.[100] Although "Dositheos" is apparently "the only theophoric name . . . used in the Hellenistic period almost exclusively by Jews," theophoric names such as "Theophilos" were quite common among Egyptian Jewry.[101] An Alexandrian Jewish novel applies it to a Palestinian Jewish sage (*Let. Aris.* 49), and it appears as the name of a high priest's father (i.e., a Greek-speaking Judean aristocrat) in Jos. *Ant.* 20.223 in the time of Agrippa II.

Theophilus was almost certainly a Christian,[102] since he was already well instructed in the gospel tradition (Luke 1:4). As argued in the discussion of audience in chapter 12 of the introduction, Theophilus was probably a Gentile God-fearer but certainly someone knowledgeable in the LXX (possibly from many years in the church). Since Theophilus would not represent the entire audience, however, some of these reconstructions (such as Gentile God-fearers) could apply to others without applying to him; what is certain is that he had been instructed in the accounts, especially the gospel tradition and some basic knowledge of the apostolic church, of which he was a part (1:4).

c. Luke's Preface to Volume One (Luke 1:1–4)

Because Luke's second preface abbreviates but refers back to the first,[103] it is valuable to survey briefly some elements of Luke's preface for both volumes in Luke 1:1–4. Even if this preface serves primarily Luke's first volume, it is intended to introduce the work as a whole. This is the only literary preface among the canonical Gospels.[104] I will not investigate this passage in detail here because chapter 3 in the introduction has already treated Luke's prologue at some length, and other elements (such as the identity of Theophilus) are addressed above.

Luke may contrast his work with those of his predecessors (Luke 1:1). Historians and other authors often contrasted their works with those of their predecessors, explaining why they needed to write this work and why their own work, when competing with others, should be read. Some ancient writers evaluated their predecessors no more charitably than some modern dissertations that denigrate earlier works on their subject in order to emphasize their own distinctiveness. Others managed to articulate the need for their works without critiquing others.

Thus, for example, Artemidorus denigrates previous writers with whom he contrasts his own work (*Oneir.* 1.pref.; 3.pref.), as do some other nonhistorical writers;[105]

---

98. "Theophilus" appears as the name of a gymnasiarch in Ephesus (*I. Eph.* 1944), but it appears across the social spectrum. Marcus Antonius Theophilus was one of two duumvirs in Corinth in (apparently) 29/28 B.C.E. (Kent, *Inscriptions*, 24); Q. Cispuleius Q. f. Theophilus received an honorary aedileship there under Tiberius (28). "Theophilos" was also a wise Alexandrian, apparently a philosopher, in Dio Chrys. 32.97.

99. See *CIJ* 1:lxvii; 1:83, §119. Cf. θεοδωρ- and θεοδοτ- names in *CIJ* 1:24, §30; 1:25, §31; 1:504, §693; 1:522, §722; 2:40, §783; 2:62, §818; 2:111, §879; 2:113, §882; 2:133, §922; 2:188, §§1027–28 (in Semitic letters); 2:266, §1265; 2:267, §1266; 2:268–69, §§1269–72; 2:333, §1404; 2:445, §1537; also θεοδουλ- names, 1:515, §713.

100. *CPJ* 2:117.

101. *CPJ* 1:xix; *CIJ* 1:lxvii. Nearly one-third of the Greek names of Jews in Ptolemaic papyri related to military matters are theophoric (*CPJ* 1:148); for examples of θεο- compounded names in Egyptian Jewish papyri, see *CPJ* 3:176–78.

102. *Pace* Stanton, *Jesus of Nazareth*, 29–30. That he was a Jewish aristocratic priest (cf. Rius-Camps, "Confrontación") is unduly speculative.

103. Most scholars regard Luke 1:1–4 as the prologue for both volumes (Fitzmyer, *Acts*, 59).

104. As noted by, e.g., Filson, *History*, 84.

105. E.g., Longin. *Subl.* 1.1; for critiquing earlier theories at the beginning of arguments, cf. Arist. *Heav.* 3.7–8, 305a 33–307b 24; 4.2, 308a 34–b3.

among historians, Polybius, for example, does likewise (Polyb. 3.32.4–5).[106] The preface of *Rhetorica ad Alexandrum* explains that previous works have never attained full accuracy on the subject, which this work's author will now attempt (pref., opening, lines 1–12). Dio Cassius contrasts himself with some writers who have compromised historical truth in the interests of rhetorical style (Dio Cass. 1.1.1–2);[107] Josephus accuses some of his own predecessors of falsehood.[108] Diodorus of Sicily criticizes the information of his predecessors more charitably, conceding that some were good historians but explaining that they lacked access to the particular information he cites (Diod. Sic. 1.37.4, 6).[109] Pseudo-Hermogenes sets out to try to clarify what none of his predecessors have managed to explain clearly (*Inv.* 3.4.133). Still others deny that they are offering any criticism of predecessors.[110]

Some distinguished themselves from predecessors without explicit disapproval of them, simply by emphasizing their comprehensiveness or (by contrast) their selectivity.[111] Diodorus provides his reasons for offering a new work, distinguishing his work from that of predecessors (1.3.1) by noting that most of them focused on single issues or peoples whereas he is endeavoring to produce a comprehensive history of the world (1.3.2). (Aulus Gellius, by contrast, thinks his own work better than that of his predecessors because he is more selective; Aul. Gel. pref. 11–12!)[112] Aelius Aristides distinguishes his praise of Athens from earlier panegyrics on the city because his will endeavor to praise all of Athens's greatness, a task that they did not dare attempt (*Panath.* 4, 152D). Quintilian observes that he had many distinguished predecessors and hence wrote only because so urged by his friends (*Inst.* 1.pref. 1–2); his predecessors did not find early education a suitable topic for rhetorical display (1.pref. 4), but Quintilian believes it necessary to address it (1.pref. 5).

Distinguishing one's more complete approach from the earlier efforts of others was not the same as censuring them, a sometimes rude behavior[113] that one writer attributes to the historical prefaces of Anaximenes and Theopompus (Dion. Hal. *Ant. rom.* 1.1.1).[114] Vitruvius notes that it is good to acknowledge one's predecessors (and sources) when writing on a topic (*Arch.* 7.pref. 10–17) and distinguishes himself

---

106. So also Justus, according to Jos. *Life* 357–59 (critiqued by Josephus). For Polybius's hostile approach to some other historians, see our introduction, ch. 4, sect. 1.c.

107. Like the authors listed below who emphasize their selectivity, he also claims that he read nearly all the earlier extant histories but preferred to include only what was most suitable (Dio Cass. 1.1.1–2). Herodian also criticizes his predecessors for preferring rhetorical style to truth (Hdn. 1.1.1); Tacitus does so more gently: they embellished some things only because they lacked sufficient information (*Agr.* 10).

108. Jos. *War* 1.1–2, 7; *Ant.* 20.154–57; he emphasizes that no one else could have written his subject as well as he (*Ant.* 20.262). For critiques of predecessors, Wardle, *Valerius Maximus*, 67, cites Livy pref. 2; Sall. *Hist.* frg. 3, 7; Tac. *Hist.* 1.1.2–3; *Ann.* 1.1.2.

109. Many failed to write successfully, he notes, because they did not visit the sites in question (Diod. Sic. 1.4.1; though his own travels may have been limited, as Oldfather, "Introduction to Diodorus Siculus," xiii, argues); he checked out records as well (Diod. Sic. 1.4.4–5). Tacitus also notes that his able predecessors lacked access to the current information he has (*Agr.* 10).

110. E.g., Val. Max. 1.pref. Quintilian starts by listing various views of a matter, offering his own only later (*Inst.* 5.pref. 1–3); more to the point, only after praising his predecessors does Quintilian note that he will differ from them on some points (3.1.22).

111. Comparison need not denigrate (e.g., Men. Rhet. 2.1–2, 377.1). Noting that the discipline he is addressing is too vast for any single authority to treat comprehensively, Pliny E. *N.H.* 3.1.1–2 promises not to criticize anyone.

112. Cf. 2 Macc 2:24–25.

113. Historians critiquing other historians could be charged with envy (Sall. *Catil.* 3.2). Avoiding rudeness, Arrian *Alex.* 1.pref. 3 manages to compare his work favorably to that of his predecessors without being explicit, by inviting anyone questioning his reason to write to compare his work with that of his predecessors.

114. Rhetoric even recommended praising one's subject by contrast with one's predecessors *without criticizing* the predecessors (Men. Rhet. 2.3, 378.18–26).

from them merely by noting that most of them were Greeks, whereas he thought it important that a Roman such as he would write (7.pref. 18).[115] If one genuinely wrote to critique the work of one's predecessors, at least for some writers the critique might well show up elsewhere in the work, sustaining the contrast in one's favor (e.g., Hermog. *Issues* 74.16–75.10).[116] In the end, Luke's note about his predecessors serves a popular purpose in prefaces: he must explain, as Frederick Danker puts it, why he is "adding yet another work to a long list of publications on the same subject."[117]

The "handing down" of information from the eyewitnesses (Luke 1:2) probably evokes the technical language of traditioning.[118] Such oral transmission could prove much more accurate than modern Western societies would expect (see discussion in ch. 8, sect. 2.c.iii, of the introduction).[119] The appeal to common knowledge in 1:4 (common, at least, to the writer's and Theophilus's circle) matches other such rhetorical appeals in Acts, not surprisingly in speeches (Acts 10:37; 26:26). Other writers sometimes also appealed to what was already known.[120] Because Mark and other Gospels were circulating (Luke 1:1), it is not surprising that Theophilus would already know much of the information in the Gospel.[121] Luke's second volume is probably more distinctive, although reports about Paul (cf., e.g., 1 Thess 1:8–9; negatively, Rom 3:8) and other apostles (1 Cor 9:5–6; Gal 2:11–14) had circulated, at the very least orally.

d. Jesus's Orders until His Taking Up (Acts 1:2)

If Jesus's "taking up"[122] ends the period of time described in Acts 1:2, it might contrast with the period after his suffering in 1:3. In this case, the "taking up" might refer to his death.[123] Significantly more likely, Jesus's "taking up" refers to his ascension (1:9–11, with ἀναλαμβάνω appearing in 1:11 as here and thereby framing the pericope), since this is the event on which the first volume closes (Luke 24:51).[124] The cognate noun in Luke 9:51 could refer either to his death or to his exaltation

---

115. Others might distinguish their work simply by saying that they offered a distinctive arrangement, though nothing truly new (Nicolaus *Progymn.* 1.pref. 1).

116. The only possible instance of this behavior in Luke's work would be his treatment of John Mark (Acts 13:13; 15:37–38)—but only on the assumption (more plausible than some allow) that he and his audience knew this Mark to be the author of a popular Gospel, and even then we could not be certain that he was critiquing him as a predecessor, since Mark's failure concerned Paul, not the Jesus tradition. A Luke and a Mark in the Pauline circle may have even worked together (Col 4:10, 14; Phlm 24; cf. 2 Tim 4:11).

117. Danker, *New Age*, 3; cf. Marshall, *Luke*, 39.

118. E.g., Jos. *Ant.* 13.297, 408; Sen. Y. *Ep. Lucil.* 40.3; Lucian *Alex.* 61; Socratics *Ep.* 20; Philost. *Vit. soph.* 2.29.621; Iambl. *V.P.* 28.148–49; 32.226; see further sources in Klauck, "Presence," 61–62 (Plut. *Stoic Cont.* 9, *Mor.* 1035AB; *Alex.* 7.3; Theon of Smyrna *Exp. Rer. Math.* 1; Cic. *Tusc.* 1.29); Alexander, "IPSE DIXIT," 120; van der Horst, "Cornutus," 168–69; Metzger, "Considerations," 17–18n84. The language also applied to what historians "handed on" (Dio Chrys. *Or.* 18.10) or to practices passed on from ancestors (Thucyd. 1.85.1). For receiving through a chain of tradition mentioning only the original source, see, e.g., *m.* '*Ed.* 8:7; '*Ab.* 1:1; '*Abot R. Nat.* 25 A; *b. Šabb.* 108a, bar.; *Pesaḥ.* 110b; *Meg.* 19b; *Naz.* 56b; perhaps 1 Cor 11:23.

119. See also Keener, *Historical Jesus*, 139–61; idem, "Assumptions"; and sources cited there.

120. E.g., Isaeus *Pyrr.* 40; Dion. Hal. *Ant. rom.* 7.43.2; Jos. *Ag. Ap.* 2.107.

121. See discussion on Luke's use of sources in our introduction, ch. 6, sect. 2.

122. Bruce, *Documents*, 24, suggests that the clause about taking up probably was added for clarity when Luke and Acts were severed to add Luke to the collection of Gospels.

123. Tannehill, *Acts*, 11 (basing his argument on Luke 9:51). The "suffering" undoubtedly refers to Jesus's death (for the cognate noun πάθος as suffering applied to death elsewhere, see, e.g., Philost. *Hrk.* 2.9; 9.2; 20.3; 21.2; 31.7; 48.10; 12.1—though it can be used for experience, as in 7.9; 8.6; 33.6; suffering more generally in 18.5; 25.15; 46.2). First Peter uses the verb eleven times for Jesus and his followers; Luke-Acts applies it especially to Christ's suffering (Luke 9:22; 17:25; 22:15; 24:26, 46; Acts 1:3; 3:18; 17:3; for Paul in Acts 9:16).

124. This is probably the term's sense also in Acts 1:22; though Luke uses it in a variety of ways, it can refer to being taken up to heaven also in 10:16.

but probably refers to the entire process with an emphasis on the latter, since the exaltation is the pivot on which Luke-Acts turns.[125]

Before his "taking up" (probably his ascension, Acts 1:11, as noted), Jesus gave his disciples orders by the Holy Spirit (1:2).[126] Certainly, Jesus acted by the Spirit (Luke 4:18; Acts 10:38); emphasizing this point here allows Luke to connect Jesus's speaking by the Spirit with the impending empowerment of Jesus's followers for speaking by the Spirit (Acts 1:5, 8).[127] The same connection would apply if we read the syntax differently (the apostles *chosen* by the Spirit, i.e., in prayer in Luke 6:12–13),[128] though this reading seems less likely contextually (the Spirit is not mentioned in Luke 6:12–13).[129] This demonstrates, from the very beginning of the volume, the parallel between Jesus and the church, between what he did in the Gospel and what he continues to do through the disciples (cf. comment on Acts 1:1, the sense of which is in dispute).

Jesus's "orders" here must include at least waiting in Jerusalem (Acts 1:4 [see comment there]; Luke 24:49; elsewhere in Acts, one is told to wait for further instructions or empowerment, Acts 9:6; 10:5–6). It should also include their call to announce the good news (1:8, although the key verb is technically indicative; 4:19–20; 5:28–29; 10:42; Luke 24:47–48). The particular verb (ἐντέλλομαι) recurs again in Acts 13:47 with reference to the mission to the nations (a mission soon addressed in this context, 1:8).[130]

The choosing (ἐκλέγομαι) of the apostles points back to Luke 6:13, when Jesus first selected the Twelve (6:14–16); the context there does not mention the Spirit, although it mentions that Jesus spent the night in prayer beforehand (6:12), suggesting his dependence on divine guidance. The verb soon recurs in Acts 1:24 for the divine choice (by lot) of the twelfth witness to replace Judas and in 15:7 for God's choice of Peter to officially introduce the Gentile mission. It also applies to Jerusalem believers choosing seven leaders of the social ministry in 6:5 and to the Jerusalem church's selection of representatives to confirm for Diaspora Christians the Jerusalem decree (15:22, 25). That Luke uses it for God's choice of Israel (13:17) and the Messiah (Luke 9:35, according to the likeliest reading) may provide some theological background to Luke's usage here (on the relationship between the Twelve and Israel, see Luke 22:30; comment on Acts 1:15–26).

---

125. Dion. Hal. *Thuc.* 10–12 emphasizes that one should begin a narrative at the most natural starting point. Historically, the events of this "pivot" probably occurred in 30 C.E. (Nisan 14 or 15 may have fallen on a Friday then, April 7; see Witherington, *Acts*, 78; esp. and extensively, discussion favoring 30 or 31 C.E. in Jeremias, *Eucharistic Words*, 36–41; for 30, see also Blinzler, *Trial*, 72–80; Brown, *Death*, 1373–76; Meier, *Marginal Jew*, 1:402; Riesner, "Pauline Chronology," 11; but for the tenuousness of astronomical dating, in view of potential early Jewish observational mistakes, see Sanders, *Figure*, 284). The alternative date of 33 C.E. (Jewett, *Chronology*, 29) seems less probable (though see Duriez, *AD 33*, 219–25, and sources he cites, 245).

126. The most likely grammatical connection; see Fitzmyer, *Acts*, 196; Barrett, *Acts*, 69; Parsons and Culy, *Acts*, 3; Peterson, *Acts*, 103. This dependence on the Spirit in teaching apparently continues until the ascension (see Dunn, *Baptism*, 46; cf. Rom 1:4; 1 Tim 3:16; 1 Pet 3:18–19, cited in Dunn, *Acts*, 6).

127. Cf. also Dunn, *Acts*, 6.

128. Johnson, *Acts*, 24, suggests both (cf. Gaventa, *Acts*, 63). But Luke's ambiguity here may stem from lack of care (despite being in his introduction) instead of being deliberate; only the larger context of his theology can help resolve the question at this remove.

129. Another suggested reading of the syntax is that Jesus chose the apostles *because* they would eventually receive the Spirit (Kilgallen, "Chose"); although this proposal makes excellent sense of the context, one would normally expect the accusative πνεῦμα (which does not appear with διά in the NT) if this were the intended meaning (with the genitive, the construction appears three times in Acts, all referring to prophetic activity, Acts 4:25; 11:28; 21:4).

130. Luke's other use, Luke 4:10 (from Q, Matt 4:6), is not relevant. The cognate ἐντολή appears once in Acts (at Acts 17:15), for (in contrast to 1:2) *not* delaying.

That the apostles are "chosen" is significant also for Luke's view of the Twelve. We cannot know how varied the theological perspectives of Luke's day were, but we can be certain that he expected the church to conform to the norm of apostolic teaching. Although anyone in the church might prophesy (Acts 2:17–18), it was the apostles who had been with Jesus from the baptism of John through the resurrection (1:21–22) who guaranteed continuity with Jesus's ministry and teaching. Luke highlights this continuity by narrating at length (1:15–26) God's choice (1:24–26) of a final apostolic witness,[131] a section bracketed between the promise and the coming of the Spirit (1:4–8; 2:1–4) and an emphasis on the "founding" believers' unity (1:14; 2:1).

For Luke, however, this apostolic norm is interpreted through God's continuing, sovereign work, not any intrinsic superiority of the apostles themselves (3:12). His narrative emphasizes that God thrust the Gentile mission on the church and that Paul was called as its leading exponent; Paul, too, is "chosen" (9:15) as a "witness" (22:15; 23:11; 26:16). Although these witnesses were foundational (cf. similarly Eph 2:20), from the standpoint of Luke's theology, such choices did not exalt the individuals chosen *as* individuals (hence the emphasis on their backgrounds, e.g., Luke 5:8; 22:34; Acts 8:3); rather, these choices highlighted God's sovereign plan to fulfill the mission effectively. (Peter, for example, is kept by Jesus's prayers and not his own virtue and must likewise strengthen the others [Luke 22:32].) God continued to make "choices" among them for particular tasks (Acts 15:7), but apart from Jesus, all the protagonists would be like David, who passed from the scene after fulfilling God's purpose in his generation (13:36).

4. Promise of the Holy Spirit (1:3–8)

Luke first summarizes Jesus's postresurrection appearances to the Twelve and his teaching to them, which concerns especially the "kingdom" (1:3). He then elaborates in more detail the promise of the Spirit, God's empowerment for the witnesses' mission from Jerusalem to the ends of the earth. This empowerment is the implicit (and often explicit) driving force behind the narrative's movement from Jerusalem to Rome, from a culturally comfortable city representing the church's heritage to a culturally and religiously dissonant city representing its mission and future.[132]

a. Summary of the Forty Days (1:3)

Although Luke will provide one or two (composite) detailed scenes (1:4–11), he first summarizes Jesus's appearances and his explanations about God's kingdom (1:3). The forty days of appearances provide convincing proofs as well as his teaching.

God's "kingdom" is similarly the focus of many other summaries (e.g., 8:12; 14:22; 19:8; 20:25; Luke 4:43; 8:1, 10; 9:2, 11, 60; 10:9; 16:16). This includes two teaching summaries that frame the concluding message of this book (Acts 28:23, 31), just as the kingdom dominates discussion in 1:3, 6. Kingdom teaching thus frames the book of Acts, connecting the movement's message with that of Jesus in Luke's Gospel. The more detailed scene that follows the present summary will flesh out the nature of his teaching about the kingdom, including the promised eschatological Spirit (1:4–8).

131. I am using "apostle" here in its narrower, usual Lukan sense, in contrast with the broader usage in Paul and even Acts 14:4, 14.

132. Cf. the somewhat different use of the two cities in Revelation, where Babylon represents the world system epitomized in Rome and the new Jerusalem represents the eschatological future (as well as continuity with Israel's heritage; discussion in, e.g., Keener, *Revelation*, 313, 379, 405–6, 412–13, 434, 486).

I. Appearances, Proofs (1:3)

Some Gentiles in Luke's audience might think of various general analogies to the activities that Luke describes here, but would also think of differences. Greeks would be familiar with the evidential category of epiphanies, which could include a deity's "appearances."[133] Hellenistic historiography provides examples of divination and epiphanies for divine guidance.[134] Even the sober Roman historian Tacitus claims that Vespasian saw an apparition of a person who was in fact eighty miles away (*Hist.* 4.82).

Thus it is not surprising that Celsus compares resurrection appearances of Jesus to Hellenistic epiphanies, with attestation and powers, in seeking to undermine Christian claims.[135] But while ancients commonly reported apparitions of deceased persons[136] or deities[137] and hence occasionally those of persons who had become immortal (e.g., Plutarch's reports of Romulus more than half a millennium earlier),[138] these are not *resurrection* appearances.[139]

Even the appearance of Apollonius of Tyana, which exhibits some parallels with the Gospel accounts (Philost. *Vit. Apoll.* 8.31),[140] is not an exception. This story appears in a third-century source, after Christian teaching on the resurrection had become widely disseminated; further and more to our present point, Apollonius proves that he has not died, not that he has risen.[141]

Such apparitions could imply a sort of divinity or at least an exalted status,[142] neither of which would have troubled Luke's audience in Jesus's case (cf. 2:33–39), but

133. See, e.g., Henrichs, "Epiphany."

134. Squires, *Plan*, 103–8; for Josephus on divination and epiphanies (e.g., dreams), see 108–12; for Luke-Acts (including appearances and visions), 112–20.

135. Origen *Cels.* 3.23–24 (Martin, *Acts*, 165–66); Remus, *Conflict*, 8 (citing Origen *Cels.* 2.55; 3.26, 32–33); Cook, *Interpretation*, 58–59 (noting that Origen concedes these but attributes them to demons).

136. E.g., Apul. *Metam.* 8.8; 9.31; '*Abot R. Nat.* 40 A. One supposed divine apparition turned out to be a conjured ghost of a gladiator (one of low class; Eunapius *Lives* 473). Likewise, although the biblical tradition reported only apparitions of angels in dreams, both pagan (e.g., Hom. *Il.* 23.65, 83–85; Eurip. *Hec.* 30–34, 703–6; Virg. *Aen.* 1.353–54; 2.268–97, 772–94; 4.351–52; 5.721–23; Ovid *Metam.* 11.586–88, 635, 650–73; Apul. *Metam.* 8.8; 9.31; Plut. *Br. Wom., Mor.* 252F) and Jewish ('*Abot R. Nat.* 40 A; *Pesiq. Rab Kah.* 11:23; *y. Ḥag.* 2:2, §5; *Ketub.* 12:3, §7; *Sanh.* 6:6, §2; cf. *Acts Paul* 11.6) dreams often included apparitions of deceased persons.

137. Ovid claims to be terrified in his depictions in *Fasti* 1.95–98; 6.19–20, but these are poetic and may be a literary device. For comment on deity appearances, see comment on Acts 9:3; on those of Castor and Pollux, see comment on Acts 28:11.

138. In Talbert, *Gospel*, 41; cf. Plut. *Cam.* 33.7; Weiser, *Apostelgeschichte*, 61, cites Livy 1.16. Boring, Berger, and Colpe, *Commentary*, 163–64, cite Romulus's apotheosis appearance to Proculus Julius in Livy 1.16.2–8; Plut. *Rom.* 28; *Numa* 11.3; Ovid *Fasti* 2.500–509, and notes that Justin *1 Apol.* 21 made an apologetic comparison between Jesus's resurrection appearances and pagan understanding of imperial apotheosis.

139. For this discussion, see esp. Keener, *John*, 1185–88. See Wright, *Resurrection*, passim, for historical evidence supporting the claim of Jesus's resurrection and its distinctiveness and especially the point that "resurrection," by its Jewish definition, involved the body (what did not involve the body was something else; see 85–206, brought to my attention by C. L. Blomberg; for resurrection in Second Temple Judaism, see also Anderson, *Raised*, 48–91; for some earlier Israelite antecedents, see Raharimanantsoa, *Mort*, 378–47; for one survey of early and late evidence, arguing for a decisive shift with 2 Macc 7, see Bauer, "Tod"). For various approaches to the subject of Jesus's resurrection, see Davis, Kendall, and O'Collins, *Resurrection*.

140. Sanders, *Jesus and Judaism*, 320.

141. Blackburn, "ΑΝΔΡΕΣ," 193. In another third-century C.E. work by the same author, the hero Protesilaus appears to people and lives on; he is said to have "come back to life," though he refuses to explain the nature of this claim (Philost. *Hrk.* 58.2). But whatever else his "return" from death might claim, it does not involve bodily resurrection: his body remains buried (9.1). (He visits both Hades and the world of the living [11.7] but visits his wife only in Hades [11.8]. Others also returned from Hades without immortality [e.g., Ant. Diog. *Thule* 109ab].) Even claims like this one made for Protesilaus do not predate the rise and spread of Christianity. See Bowersock, *Fiction as History*, 108–13; even his mid-first-century parallel does not indicate a bodily resurrection (it may simply mean "a brief tryst with his wife," 112, as in earlier sources; see Petron. *Sat.* 129.1).

142. See the discussion of Talbert, "Concept of Immortals"; and other sources in comment on Acts 1:9–11, below. More recently, cf. the discussion of apotheosis in Talbert, *Matthew*, 317–20 (also acknowledging distinctives on 319–20).

the forms of these apparitions differ from the circumstances that Luke depicts here. Deities periodically "manifested" themselves to mortals in Greek tradition, sometimes in sleep and sometimes as apparitions.[143] Paul's language in 1 Cor 15 applied in the LXX especially to revelations of God or angels (cf. Bar 3:37; *Sib. Or.* 1.200).[144] Many "apparitions" were simply "signs" in general; thus, when a comet appeared for seven nights during games honoring Caesar, people believed this to be his soul (Suet. *Jul.* 88). From the late Hellenistic age, "epiphanies" of Greek gods usually meant the activity of a deity rather than its appearance;[145] it is primarily these that witnesses attest,[146] though appearances in personal dreams and visions occur.[147] Appearances of deities visible to large numbers of people normally belonged to an era many centuries earlier than the writings.[148]

Early Christian portrayals of Jesus's resurrection appearances differ from some modern reconstructions of what is supposed to have taken place. Very little evidence suggests the plausibility of other successive and mass, *corporate* visions (see esp. 1 Cor 15:5–7).[149] Conditions in first-century Judea and Galilee were not those that produced the seventeenth-century messiah Sabbatai Zevi, many of whose followers failed to be deterred by his apostasy[150] and some even by his death.[151] Aside from different social conditions, knowledge of the Christian belief in Jesus's resurrection and redefinition of messiahship could provide later messianic movements a model for redefining the messianic mission in a manner that did not exist before Jesus.[152]

There are some claims of more public "appearances" that are more difficult to explain along the above sorts of lines (though these seem to appear at a distance, not personally interacting with those who knew the person). Thus among prodigies reported before Jerusalem's fall were armies clashing in the skies and a voice declaring the "gods'" departure from the temple (Tac. *Hist.* 5.13).[153] Tacitus follows Josephus (*War* 6.297–99), who reports that people saw heavenly chariots moving through the clouds and surrounding cities (cf. 2 Kgs 6:17; 2 Macc 3:24–26; 4 Macc 4:10–11; *Sib.*

143. E.g., Eurip. *Bacch.* 42, 53–54; Plut. *Cic.* 14.3; Ael. Arist. *Or.* 48.41; Apul. *Metam.* 11.3; Ach. Tat. 7.12.4; Char. *Chaer.* 2.2.5; 2.3.5; Philost. *Hrk.* 2.8; 18.1–2 (see further Maclean and Aitken, *Heroikos*, xxvi); reports in Grant, *Religions*, 9–13, 123; Rives, *Religion*, 102; in unrelated cultures, see Wolf, "Virgin of Guadalupe"; Mbiti, *Religions*, 105–12 passim; for more concrete effects of angelic manifestations in Hellenistic Jewish tradition, see Tob 12:19, 22; 2 Macc 3:24–26 (cf. God in 2 Macc 3:30).

144. See further Bartsch, "Inhalt."

145. Nilsson, *Piety*, 106; the inscription of 324 C.E. in Grant, *Religions*, 123; Diod. Sic. 5.62.4; 11.14.3–4 (providential lightning); Dion. Hal. *Ant. rom.* 8.56.1–3 (including a statue speaking). Cf. the apparition of God in 2 Macc 3:30 (referring to the apparitions in 3:24–26).

146. Cf. Grant, *Gods*, 66, 54–55, 64–65.

147. E.g., PDM 14.74–91, 95, 98–102, 169; probably Dio Chrys. *Or.* 32.12, 41.

148. So, e.g., Plut. *Coriol.* 3.4 (writing of the time of Tarquin, 3.1); or, less dramatically, the appearance of the Dioscuri's stars (Plut. *Lys.* 12.1; 18.1); perhaps 2 Macc 3:24–26. Sometimes they might be just a century and a half earlier, like Suetonius's report of an apparition publicly urging Caesar to cross the Rubicon (*Jul.* 32), perhaps originally political propaganda from Caesar's faction.

149. E.g., Schweizer, *Jesus*, 48–49; see especially Licona, "Historicity of Resurrection," 136n196, 346–47; idem, *Resurrection*, 484–85, 573–74; personal correspondence, April 25, 2010; but cf. also the qualified approach in O'Connell, "Hallucinations," 75–83 (noting differences on 87–105).

150. Grayzel, *History of Jews*, 516; Bamberger, *Story*, 240.

151. Scholem, *Sabbatai Sevi*, 920; Greenstone, *Messiah*, 225–30.

152. See discussion in Keener, *Historical Jesus*, 153, 343. Price, *Son of Man*, 29, offers this figure as a comparison, but its value is limited.

153. Such reports of visions of heavenly armies appear in other war reports (Pliny E. *N.H.* 2.58.148). Similarly, people more recently have claimed to see, e.g., a cross in the sky (Sung, *Diaries*, 106, reporting the claims of some others; similar celestial phenomena in Wacker, *Heaven*, 93). But given the mutability of clouds, reports of shapes in the sky are not the same as corporate visions of a person before them on the ground.

Or. 3.805–8), and priests heard voices in the temple.[154] Horsley and Hanson regard these as collective fantasies,[155] but they could also be (1) authentic appearances of something related to Jerusalem's fall (which I would deem highly unlikely but which a post-Enlightenment theological perspective need not simply dismiss); (2) the sun playing tricks on eyes at dusk; (3) propaganda to justify Jerusalem's fall after the event, which Josephus has accepted;[156] or (4) Josephus's own propaganda (he is the only extant witness concerning witnesses apart from sources dependent on him).[157]

One of the final two views seems most likely. In fact, Josephus, as a highly rhetorical historian, may be following a standard sort of report of such events as portents of destruction.[158] Some writers engaged in poetic license,[159] such as a giant Fury stalking the city and shaking the snakes in her hair;[160] others were more sober historians citing reports for particular years. Portents included events such as we might regard as natural phenomena today, such as physical deformities at birth, lightning striking temples, and comets,[161] but also included visions of celestial figures or armies.[162] The armies were sometimes heard rather than seen;[163] sights that were seen were often acknowledged as divine illusions rather than objects physically present;[164] and the apparitions of armies did not draw near anyone.[165] Such reports were normally not verified by citing witnesses, and the historians who report them sometimes express skepticism concerning their value, at times allowing for imagination in their production[166] and at times pointing out that such reports fed on each other among the gullible.[167] Some of what was genuinely seen at a distance may have been misconstrued; thus, for example, the report of two suns and light at night may reflect an aurora.[168]

In any case, this phenomenon is quite different from meeting again and talking with a person one has personally known, which Luke stresses. There is also a difference between accumulating prodigies portending a dramatic event, on the one hand,

154. For signs portending the temple's destruction, see Jos. *War* 6.293–96; *b. Yoma* 39b; *y. Yoma* 43c; cf. Tac. *Hist.* 5.13, noted in Dibelius, *Tradition*, 195 (although he thinks the tradition circulated only after 70; ibid., 195n3).

155. Horsley and Hanson, *Bandits*, 182–84.

156. Somewhat similarly, Saulnier, "Josèphe," suggests that Josephus borrows the tradition from Flavian propaganda.

157. Tac. *Hist.* 5.13.2–7 likely depends on Jos. *War* 6.288–315.

158. E.g., Aul. Gel. 4.6.2.

159. E.g., Lucan *C.W.* 1.526–57; most obviously, who reported on Charybdis (1.547–48)?

160. Lucan *C.W.* 1.572–73. Lucan writes epic poetry about historical events, not history proper.

161. E.g., many of the portents listed in Livy 21.62.5; 24.10.7–10; 25.7.7–8; 26.23.4–5; 27.4.11–14; 27.11.2–5; 29.37.1–5; 29.14.3; 32.1.10–12; 33.26.7–8; 34.45.6–7; 35.9.2–3; 35.21.3–6; 36.37.2–3; 40.45.1–4; 41.21.12–13; 43.13.3–6; 45.16.5; Lucan *C.W.* 1.562–63.

162. E.g., Livy 21.62.4–5; 24.10.10; 42.2.4; Plut. *Themist.* 15.1; Hdn. 8.3.8–9.

163. Appian *Bell. civ.* 4.1.4 (43 B.C.E.); one of the portents in Livy 24.44.8 (213 B.C.E.); Caesar *C.W.* 3.105; Philost. *Hrk.* 56.2.

164. E.g., Livy 24.10.11; 24.44.8. If I correctly interpret Livy's summaries, in some cases some reported seeing figures at another location when those present at that location could not confirm them. Sometimes what the apparition supposedly portended did not occur (Plut. *Cic.* 14.3).

165. Livy 21.62.5. Contrast Josh 5:13–15 (cf. 2 Kgs 6:17)!

166. E.g., Livy 21.62.1; Hdn. 8.3.8 (though he concludes that it is credible, 8.3.9). One fictitious or amplified, after-the-fact claim (e.g., Lucian *Peregr.* 39–40) was also sufficient rumor to provide grist for such a report, in contrast to what would be necessary to supply the multiple attestation for Jesus's resurrection claims in Paul and the Gospels.

167. Livy 21.62.1; 24.10.6; 27.37.2; 29.14.2.

168. See the LCL, note on Livy 29.14.3; some discussion in Stothers, "Objects"; idem, "Optics." Flames seen in the sky (e.g., Livy 32.8.2), showers of "stones" (36.37.3), a rainbow in a clear sky (41.21.12), meteors (e.g., 43.13.3), a comet shining for seven nights (Suet. *Jul.* 88), and many other phenomena are also plausible in this manner. Some reports, of course, were simply fabricated by someone.

and citing eyewitnesses committed to the veracity of a central, dramatic event, on the other (as already in Paul, 1 Cor 15:3–8).

But the difference between the early Christian accounts and other appearance accounts again concerns the *resurrection*. To most ancient Mediterranean peoples, the concept of corporal resurrection was barely intelligible; to Jewish people, it was strictly eschatological. Yet if one grants, from a neutral starting point, the possibility of a bodily resurrection of Jesus within past history, the appearances would likely follow such an event naturally with or without parallels. In a Jewish framework, Jesus's resurrection within history must also signify the arrival of the eschatological era in some sense (e.g., Acts 1:3–6; "from among the dead ones," Rom 1:4; 1 Cor 15:20; Gal 1:4; Heb 6:5).

Later Platonists doubted that gods could become visible, though they affirmed that lower angels or demons could do so (Iambl. *Myst.* 2.10). Others warned that one could not always distinguish the individual phantoms of past heroes who appeared (Philost. *Hrk.* 21.1, third century C.E.);[169] it is thus important for Luke to emphasize that Jesus is no mere ghost (Luke 24:37–43). Some who doubted whether apparitions really occurred might prove willing to believe if convinced by an eyewitness or even by someone who had heard an eyewitness (e.g., Philost. *Hrk.* 7.11; cf. 2.8).[170] The notion of appearances was thus intelligible in the broader culture, but recognition of this general intelligibility should not allow us to obscure genuine differences.

II. CONVINCING PROOFS (1:3)

Novels often included resuscitations, but normally only after *apparent* deaths.[171] Because the idea of apparent deaths was growing in literature of the imperial period, it may have been all the more important for Luke to make clear that Jesus was actually dead (just as he had to emphasize, on the other side, that he was no mere phantom). Nor was this merely the magical revivification of a corpse (cf. Ant. Diog. *Thule* 110b). Perhaps most important, as noted above, Luke emphasizes that this was no mere phantom or subjective experience.

Although Greek commonly employed τεκμήριον as evidence generally (and as an obvious symptom in medical writers), it bore a stronger and more specific sense for rhetors seeking to prove a case in a courtroom (relevant in Acts; cf. Acts 1:8; 22–26). When rhetoricians spoke of τεκμήρια, they meant that the proofs were irrefutable, with conclusions that followed inevitably.[172] In a court, one might offer a strong claim "by many proofs" (ἐκ πολλῶν τεκμηρίων, Isaeus *Aristarch.* 6 [LCL]). The phrase "many proofs" appears especially frequently in Hellenistic historiography.[173]

The particular evidences in view are fleshed out in Luke 24:39–43, including Jesus eating;[174] Luke merely mentions them again in summary fashion here.[175] Some of these

169. In Philost. *Hrk.* 21.5, the gardener initially fails to recognize even Protesilaus.

170. This work probably dates to the early third century C.E. Cf. Iamblichus's disciples who reportedly doubted other evidences but were persuaded by something indisputably supernatural (Eunapius *Lives* 459–60).

171. E.g., Xen. Eph. *Anthia* 3.5–8; Apoll. K. Tyre 25–26; Iambl. (nov.) *Bab. St.* 3–4 (Photius *Bibl.* 94.74b), 5 (74b), 6 (75a). People also entered and left the underworld (e.g., Ant. Diog. *Thule* 109ab).

172. Lake and Cadbury, *Commentary*, 4; Witherington, *Acts*; Johnson, *Acts*, 25; Anderson, *Glossary*, 44, 108–9, 116–17 (some citing Arist. *Rhet.* 1.2.16–17, 1357b; Dion. Hal. *Lysias* 19; Quint. *Inst.* 5.9.3–7; cf. *Rhet. Alex.* 7, 1428.19–23). The term is a NT hapax legomenon but cf. the Hellenistic Jewish works Wis 5:11; 19:13; 3 Macc 3:24 (the only uses in the LXX).

173. See Mealand, "Many Proofs"; Witherington, *Acts*, 108, citing Jos. *Ant.* 3.317–18; Diod. Sic. 3.66.4.4; Dion. Hal. *Ant. rom.* 1.90.2.2. Cf. Jos. *War* 1.638 (Nicolaus's prosecution of Antipater); Philo *Good Person* 1.

174. Arator *Acts* 1 (Martin, *Acts*, 3) understood this as evidencing Jesus's true humanity.

175. Cf. also John 20:17, 20, 25–27; much more briefly, Matt 28:9.

may diverge from contemporary expectations. Some Jewish traditions imply that just as angels did not need food or drink,[176] so glorified humans would lack desire for it (2 En. 56:2, of uncertain date).[177]

That Greek readers would need assurance of such proof indicates that Luke does not believe he describes mere appearances of a phantom or ghost, which were already commonly accepted in their tradition.[178] Hellenistic mythology includes numerous cases of wraiths that only seem to be the person whose image they represent.[179] Thus, for example, deities also sent phantom images made only of cloud.[180] Mythographers analogously spoke of Iphigeneia only appearing to be sacrificed; in reality, a deer was clandestinely substituted for her.[181]

Nor would doubts be limited to Luke's audience; the disciples' own initial doubts appear in some Gospels (Matt 28:17; John 20:25; cf. Mark 16:11, 13–14), including Luke (Luke 24:23–25, 37, 41). Luke had promised to confirm Theophilus's faith (Luke 1:4) and frequently emphasizes both physical evidence (3:22; 24:38–40) and apologetic dispute (Acts 9:29; 17:3; 18:4, 19; 19:8–9; 28:23).[182] Some scholars cite Hellenistic examples for demonstrations of apparitions' physicality (esp. Philost. Vit. Apoll. 8.12),[183] though, given their date, these authors may have derived the idea from the Christian resurrection accounts widespread by their time. Likewise Philostratus, probably influenced by gospel tradition, speaks of a divine hero allowing embraces when he appears.[184] The novelist also offers scars and footprints as marks of the divine hero.[185]

Less relevant for our consideration here would be the observation that Greeks could not even be certain, when dealing with the divine, that the images they saw in other settings were authentically the entities that they appeared to be. Greek folklore assumed that deities took on various familiar shapes to communicate with people or to disguise themselves or escape,[186] or concealed or transformed the appearance

---

176. Test. Ab. 4:9–10 A (cf. 6:5); 'Abot R. Nat. 1 A; b. Yoma 75b; Gen. Rab. 48:11, 14; Exod. Rab. 32:4; Lev. Rab. 34:8; cf. Goodman, "Angels." Greeks (whose deities subsisted on nectar and ambrosia) could describe as mortals those who ate grain (Hom. Il. 13.322).

177. Cf. Philost. Hrk. 11.9, where the hero's ghost is never observed eating, yet the food is instantly consumed.

178. E.g., Lucan C.W. 1.11; Plut. Caes. 69.5, 8; Pliny Ep. 7.27.1–16; Max. Tyre 9.6–7; Dio Cass. 42.11.2–3; Johnston, "Dead, Cult of," 114; Dubourdieu, "Dead, Cult of," 115–16; in the ancient Near East, see Scurlock, "Ghosts." On wraiths or false apparitions, see, e.g., Hom. Il. 5.449–53; the parody in Lucian Dial. D. 402–3 (11/16, Diogenes and Heracles 1–2).

179. E.g., in Hom. Il. 5.449–53; cf. Ovid Fasti 3.701–2 (allowing Caesar's snatching up to heaven despite his apparent death, 3.703–4); the angel arrested in Moses's place in y. Ber. 9:1, §8 (third century C.E.). The docetic idea of a wraith as substituted for Jesus on the cross (critiqued in Iren. Her. 1.24.4), followed in the Qur'an (cf. Cook, Muhammad, 79), apparently derives from this approach.

180. Helen in Euripides's Helen (following Stesichorus's Recantation) and Apollod. Epit. 3.5; Ixion's cloud in Apollod. Epit. 1.20.

181. Lycophron Alex. 190–91; Apollod. Epit. 3.22. Euripides and others had tamed the ferocity of Homer's tale at this point.

182. Johnson, Acts, 25.

183. Theissen, Miracle Stories, 67.

184. Philost. Hrk. 11.2–3 (Maclean and Aitken, Heroikos, 35n39, contrasts the vanishing ghosts of Hom. Il. 23.65–101; Od. 11.204–22, 390–94).

185. Philost. Hrk. 12.4; 13.2–4. The spirit appears in the same form and age in which he died (Hrk. 10.2).

186. Hom. Il. 4.86–87, 121–24; 5.127–28, 177, 183, 191, 461–62, 604, 784–85; 7.58–59; 13.43–45, 69, 215–16, 356–57; 14.136; 16.715–20, 788–89; 17.71–73, 322–26, 551–55, 582–83; 20.79–81; 21.284–86, 599–611; Od. 1.420; 2.267–68, 382–87, 399–401; 6.21–22; 7.19–20; 8.8, 193–94; Virg. Aen. 1.314–15, 402–6, 657–60; 5.618–20, 645–52; 7.415–16; 9.646–52, 657–58; 12.784–85; Georg. 4.405–14, 440–42; Ovid Metam. 1.676; 11.241–46, 633–43; 14.765–71; Paus. 3.16.2–3; Ach. Tat. 2.15.4; Apollod. Bib. 2.4.8; 3.8.2; 3.10.7; 3.12.6; 3.13.5; Sil. It. 7.422–25, 435; Eunapius Lives 468; for ghosts, cf. Philost. Hrk. 21.1. They could also disguise the appearance of mortals (e.g., Hom. Od. 13.397–99) and become invisible (Il. 5.845).

of their favorite mortals;[187] Jewish hearers might think especially of the disguises of angels.[188] In view of such traditions, some hearers might misinterpret Luke's reports of people's not initially recognizing Jesus (Luke 24:16, 31; cf. John 20:14), inviting Luke's clarification.

In most cases, however, Jewish sources include revelations of the supernatural person's true identity. Tobias could not tell that Raphael, who claimed to be a son of one Anania known to Tobias's father (Tob 5:12), was an angel (5:4–6; 9:1–5); he explains the "vision" in 12:19. In the Hebrew Bible, God himself sometimes came unrecognized at first (Gen 18:9–13), especially as the angel of the Lord (Judg 6:22; 13:20–23). Jewish traditions also speak of God or others changing the appearance of some persons in the biblical narrative.[189] Luke's "many proofs" demonstrate to his audience that the Jesus who appeared to the apostles after the resurrection was the same one they had known before.

III. Forty Days (1:3)

In Luke (in contrast to John 20:19–23), a significant period separates Jesus's resurrection and the coming of the Spirit.[190] Although Jesus's resurrection and ascension are theologically connected (Acts 2:32–33; Phil 2:8–9; 1 Pet 3:22), none of our narrative accounts suggests that Jesus left the disciples immediately after the resurrection.[191] Luke, wishing to stress the objective certainty of the resurrection, has particular reason to underline the time Jesus spent with his disciples; this time reinforces the certainty of their testimony that he was again alive. Similarly, Luke's emphasis on the bodily character of the resurrection (Luke 24:39–43) suggests the importance of a clear point of demarcation for the ascension, distinguishing Jesus's resurrection appearances from the mere nonbodily apparitions of Greek belief.

The forty days serve a narrative function in filling much of the period between Jesus's resurrection and Pentecost (fifty days; 2:1).[192] Other sources also suggest that Jesus continued with his disciples for a period of time before parting from them (Matt 28:16; John 20:26; 21:1), though they do not specify the particular duration of this period.[193] The period that Paul assumes in 1 Cor 15:5–8 may represent more than a few days because it must allow for other apostles (perhaps Luke's seventy; Luke 10:1)[194] to have joined the Twelve after the latter's first encounter with Jesus (1 Cor 15:5, 7; cf. 15:9), as well as for other appearances.

Some later writings cite even longer periods for the glorified Jesus's revelations (eleven years in the gnostic tract *Pistis Sophia* 1),[195] but Luke's period coheres more reasonably with our other early data. Some scholars think that, in contrast to such

---

187. E.g., Hom. *Od.* 13.189–93; 16.454–59; Ovid *Metam.* 8.851–54, 872–74; cf. perhaps Jdt 10:7; see further Keener, *John*, 773–74.

188. See Gen 18; Tob 5:4–6, 12; 9:1–5; Philo *Abr.* 114; *Sipre Deut.* 38.1.4; *y. Pe'ah* 3:8, §3; Heb 13:2; cf. Luke 24:16, 31. Also Satan in *Test. Job* 6:4; 17:2 (*OTP*)/17:1 (Kraft); 23:1; cf. *Pesiq. Rab Kah.* 26:2.

189. *L.A.B.* 12:1; 61:9; 64:4. *Sipre Deut.* 47.2.8 speaks of the righteous as sometimes unseen, but not in the sense of disguised (perhaps intended corporately).

190. See comment in Robinson, *Studies*, 166.

191. Although the summary account in *Barn.* 15.9 connects both the resurrection and ascension with Sunday (cf. comment in Schille, *Apostelgeschichte*, 68), it is not clear that the same day must be in view.

192. With Fitzmyer, *Acts*, 202.

193. Witherington, *Acts*, 107–8.

194. John 20:24 reports that Thomas joined the group later, but because our lists count him as one of the Twelve (Mark 3:18; Matt 10:3; Luke 6:15; Acts 1:13; as in John 20:24), this may be a different and unrelated tradition.

195. Johnson, *Acts*, 25, citing also "the *Epistula Apostolorum, The Apocryphon of James* (550 days)"; cf. Schille, *Apostelgeschichte*, 68, noting also eighteen months in Iren. *Her.* 1.3.2; 30.14. Gnostic "postresurrection" sayings often take the form of oracular dialogues (Aune, *Dictionary of Rhetoric*, 126–27).

traditions, Luke may use the "forty days" especially to limit the period of Jesus's revelation to his apostles.[196] Some other scholars today think that the appearances must have continued longer than forty days because Paul lists resurrection appearances continuing as late as his own conversion, which they date up to two years later (1 Cor 15:6–8).[197] Some opine that Luke plays down resurrection appearances after Pentecost because he prefers simply defined epochs.[198]

Nevertheless, although Luke may prefer such epochs, it is not continuing appearances that Luke himself denies (Acts 9:4); he distinguishes such a later experience as Paul's, however, from Jesus *remaining* on earth with the disciples.[199] A single appearance on the road to Damascus and subsequent visions (18:9; 23:11) differ at least quantitatively from disciples touching and eating with Jesus (Luke 24:41–43). Paul himself presents Jesus's appearance as a divergence from the normal pattern of time (1 Cor 15:8).[200] Further, if Luke's interest is limiting revelations, he would be more concerned to limit the recipients or the content of revelations than their timing. Any revelations in the first few years would have predated later mystics' claims, in any case, and even during the first forty days more than the Twelve were present (Acts 1:15).

Dunn points out that Paul cites multiple appearances, including one to five hundred persons (1 Cor 15:6), which Dunn believes suggests that by that point the movement had grown beyond the 120 of Acts 1:15 (a number he apparently accepts more readily than the forty days).[201] But is it not likelier that shortly after the feast Jesus appeared to more of his Galilean followers, most of whom then returned to their homes in Galilee while the smaller number remained in Jerusalem?[202]

Nevertheless, the issue of Jesus's instruction is an important one. Forty days allows enough time for the disciples who will carry on his mission to receive enough teaching.[203] (Since Luke's Gospel is full of teaching, perhaps it would be better to say here that they received sufficient postresurrection clarification of his earlier teaching, fleshed out in Acts' speeches as the kerygma in light of Scripture; cf. Luke 24:25–27, 44.) Jesus's time with his disciples after the resurrection would also offer hearers an explanation for how Jesus's followers learned what happened to Jesus in their absence, such as during the trial, when they slept in Gethsemane, or earlier, at the temptation.[204]

---

196. Zwiep, *Ascension*, 170–75, esp. 174.

197. Perkins, *Reading*, 255; cf. Hengel and Schwemer, *Between Damascus and Antioch*, 26 (arguing that Luke here sides with the Jerusalem church against Paul).

198. Dunn, *Acts*, 12–13, also citing the danger of unlimited revelatory claims based on indefinitely continuing appearances, as in later gnostic documents.

199. For Luke's distinction between these resurrection appearances and mere visions, see discussion in O'Collins, "Closing of Appearances"; ὀπτανόμενος (Acts 1:3) refers to visibility, and the verb was not limited to visions (Lake and Cadbury, *Commentary*, 4, citing esp. 3 Kgdms 8:8 LXX; P.Paris 49.33; P.Tebt. 24.5; *PGM* 4.3033ff.).

200. See Keener, *Corinthians*, 125 (here perhaps as something like a *post*mature birth). The LXX normally employs Paul's term for "abortion" here figuratively (with Hollander and van der Hout, "Abortion"). Some scholars even take Paul's language to mean that he was the final apostle (Jones, "Last Apostle"), but in view of his more general use of "apostle" elsewhere (e.g., Rom 16:7; 1 Cor 15:5–7; Gal 1:19), this position seems too extreme. Some others take the language as implying Paul's rejection (Mitchell, "Aborted Apostle") or that his acts of persecution had contradicted the purpose for which he was born (Nickelsburg, "*Ektrōma*").

201. Dunn, *Acts*, 3–4, who speculatively links "all the apostles" (1 Cor 15:7) with the Hellenist expansion (Acts 8:4; 11:19–21).

202. In Luke's version; even the Twelve apparently returned to Galilee historically for at least a short period (Mark 14:28; 16:7; Matt 16:32; 28:7, 10, 16; John 21:1).

203. See Parsons, *Departure*, 195; idem, *Acts*, 35.

204. In Philost. *Vit. Apoll.* 3.27, Apollonius provides such unknown information to his disciple Damis. Damis may well be fictitious (appropriate to the genre in which Philostratus writes), but his role here illustrates the concern to identify a potential source for the writer's information. On Gethsemane see Allison, *Jesus*, 415–19.

As a background for Luke's specific number of days here, scholars sometimes cite forty days of seeking revelation from God in apocalyptic literature.[205] These texts, however, depend on the biblical traditions of forty days of seeking revelation associated with Moses (Exod 24:18; 34:28; Deut 9:9, 11, 18, 25; 10:10)[206] and (also dependent on the Moses story) Elijah (1 Kgs 19:8).[207] But these are the same periods of time associated with Jesus's ministry in the wilderness,[208] which is close to the foreground of what Luke can presuppose for what his audience knows (Luke 4:2).[209] As Jesus was tempted for forty days before his public ministry, now he spends forty days with his disciples before theirs. Whatever else we may suspect about reasons for emphasizing this interim period, the particular number of days probably echoes the period of Jesus's temptation, signaling a prelude to new ministry.

b. Jesus's Teaching about the Kingdom (1:3)

Luke's summary of Jesus's postresurrection teaching exhibits significant continuity with Jesus's preresurrection teaching in Luke's Gospel. Before his ascension, Jesus continued teaching his disciples about the kingdom (Acts 1:3). This teaching about the kingdom informs the realized eschatology of Luke's pneumatology in 1:6–8 and 2:17. Though explicitly mentioned in Acts mostly in summaries of preaching (because it is treated more thoroughly in Luke), the kingdom remains important to Luke, with Jesus's and Paul's teaching on it providing one inclusio around the book (1:3, 6; 28:23, 31, accounting for one-half of the references).[210]

We may surmise that Luke is content to provide us with merely this summary that Jesus taught about the kingdom because Luke has provided a fuller exposition of this teaching in the Gospel (the "teaching" of which is mentioned in Acts 1:1).[211] Nearly all references to the kingdom in Acts are summary reports about preaching (8:12; 14:22; 19:8; 20:25; 28:23, 31), presupposing the content outlined in the Gospel.[212] The Gospel includes summaries of Jesus's preaching of the kingdom as well. Jesus preached about the kingdom (Luke 4:43; 8:1; 9:11), promising it to the poor (6:20), little ones (18:16–17; cf. 12:32), and the radically obedient (9:62; 16:16); by contrast, it would be difficult for the rich (6:24–25; 18:24–25). Jesus also sent his disciples to preach the kingdom (9:2, 60; 10:9, 11), a mission relevant for their proclamation in Acts (Acts 8:12; 19:8; 20:25; 28:23, 31).

205. Cadbury, "Eschatology," 309. But many ancients recognized that forty days without food could precipitate starvation (Diog. Laert. 8.1.40; for a much lower estimate, Pliny E. *N.H.* 11.118.283).

206. Naturally recalled in later literature as well (e.g., *Jub.* 1:4; 4Q364 frg. 15.2; frg. 26bi.10; frg. 26bii + e2; Philo *Dreams* 1.36; *Mos.* 2.69–70; Jos. *Ant.* 3.95, 99; *b. Šabb.* 89a) and emulated by others (Adam in *L.A.E.* 6:1; cf. 17:3; *4 Ezra* 14:23, 36, 43–45; *3 Bar.* 4:14).

207. Johnson, *Acts*, 25; Talbert, *Acts*, 5–6. Cf. here also the time the spies surveyed the land (Num 13:25; 14:34). Pelikan, *Acts*, 38, suggests that the combination of "commanded" and "forty days" in Acts 1:2–3 is an allusion to Sinai's Torah; this is possible, but Luke appears to make less of this association than Matthew does.

208. Again echoing Moses and/or Israel in the wilderness; for a discussion, see, e.g., Keener, *Matthew*, 136; Sanders, *Figure*, 112–13.

209. With, e.g., Perkins, *Reading*, 255; Spencer, *Acts*, 25; Pervo, *Acts*, 37.

210. For the inclusio (and summary), see Chrupcala, "Disegno." Although an inclusio usually appears around smaller units (e.g., Luke 15:24, 36; Hom. *Od.* 1.1–2, 10; Catull. *Carm.* 52.1, 4; 57.1, 10; Pliny *Ep.* 3.16.1, 13; Harvey, *Listening*, 102–3), it also occasionally appears around some books (e.g., trial scenes in Char. *Chaer.*; John 1:1, 18; 20:28; Rom 1:5; 16:25; see esp. Harvey, *Listening*, 67, 111–12, with Hom. *Il.* 1; 24).

211. For the Jewish setting of Jesus's teaching on the kingdom (and a survey of some secondary scholarship), see, e.g., Keener, *Matthew*, 68–70. For the kingdom teaching here (Acts 1:3) providing continuity with the Gospel, see also Dunn, *Acts*, 7. For the kingdom in Luke-Acts as one unifying theme, see del Agua, "Evangelization."

212. The specific construction περὶ τῆς βασιλείας appears here and in Luke 9:11 (Jesus); Acts 8:12 (Philip); 19:8 (Paul).

The Gospel also articulates in greater detail the message of the kingdom that Luke presupposes here. Although people should yearn for the kingdom (Luke 11:2; 12:31; 23:51), part of the message was that it was present in a hidden way (13:18–21), currently available for those willing to receive it (8:10).[213] Perhaps through the impending Gentile mission (see below on Acts 1:8), the kingdom would spread and pervade the world before its ultimate consummation (Luke 13:18–21).[214] Jesus's followers could enter the kingdom and find there a role greater than John's (7:28; 16:16).[215]

The kingdom was near (Luke 10:9, 11; 11:20; 17:20–21), but in the sense that Jesus would go away to "receive" it and return (19:11–15; cf. the application of Ps 110 in Luke 20:42–43), apparently receiving it after the cross (Luke 23:42–43). It would be "near" again in the future when Jesus's return was near (21:31). The hope of the kingdom in Luke's eschatology includes a future kingdom with the restoration of Israel (1:33; 22:29), although scholars debate in what form Luke intends this; it included the expected future banquet with Abraham (13:28–29; 22:16, 18, 29–30; cf. 14:15), would be preceded by great tribulation (17:22–18:8; Acts 14:22), and included great reward (Luke 18:29–30). Following Mark, Luke seems to regard the transfiguration of Jesus in glory as a foretaste of the future kingdom (Luke 9:27 in the context of 9:26–36; cf. Mark 9:1–8).

What the disciples had not fully understood in Jesus's kingdom teaching earlier, however, was especially that Jesus would go and then return (Luke 19:12),[216] equipping them with the Spirit in the meantime to carry out the mission (Acts 1:8–11). Jesus's explanation to them about the interim period provokes their obvious question as to the time of the consummation in 1:6 (though he has already explained that they will not know the time; Luke 17:20–30; 21:9).

Excursus: God's Kingdom in Early Jewish and Christian Teaching[217]

The Hebrew, Aramaic, and Greek terms here translated "kingdom" usually signify the concept "reign" or "authority" or "rule."[218] Like the OT (e.g., Isa 6:5), Jewish teachers could speak of God's present rule (especially among the people who obeyed his law).[219] But Jewish people also looked for the kingdom as God's future rule, when God would

213. It is present in Luke 11:20; 17:21 (though conjoined with future material in 17:22–37); 18:17 (cf. future material in 18:7–8); future in 1:33 (if distinguished); 11:2; 13:28–29 (cf. present material in 13:18–21); 19:12; 22:29–30; perhaps 6:20; 12:32.

214. This is not, however, "triumphalism"; it would come through sufferings (Marguerat, *Historian*, 40).

215. The kingdom appears as both present and future in Luke-Acts (see Nolland, "Salvation-History," 68–70; Ellis, "Fonction de l'eschatologie"), and Acts 1:3 is comprehensive, encompassing all Jesus's teaching on the subject (Nolland, "Salvation-History," 70).

216. The historical model for Luke 19:12 could be Herod or Archelaus; see comment on Acts 2:35.

217. *Pace* the surprisingly poorly researched claims of Mack at this point (Mack, *Myth*, 70–73; idem, *Lost Gospel*, 126), the kingdom is a pre-Christian Jewish concept (e.g., Meier, *Marginal Jew*, 2:243–69; Vermes, *Religion*, 127–28); even if one discounted all other sources, the teachings about God's kingdom in the Hebrew Bible and the LXX are certainly pre-Christian (see, e.g., Meier, *Marginal Jew*, 2:243–47; discussion of Daniel, below).

218. Frequently acknowledged, e.g., Dodd, *Parables*, 34; Perrin, *Kingdom*, 24; Betz, *Jesus*, 33; Boring, Berger, and Colpe, *Commentary*, 54; see esp. Meier, *Marginal Jew*, 2:240–43; but contrast Aalen, "Reign."

219. E.g., *m. Ber.* 2:2; *Sipra A.M. pq.* 13.194.2.1; *Sipra Qed. pq.* 9.207.2.13; *Sipre Deut.* 313.1.3; 323.1.2; *t. B. Qam.* 7:5; see Bonsirven, *Judaism*, 176; cf. Pss 145:2; 146:10. Reciting the Shema accepted this yoke (*m. Ber.* 2:2; *b. Ber.* 61b; *Deut. Rab.* 2:31).

reign unchallenged,[220] as attested in regular Jewish prayers.[221] Because "heaven" was a common Jewish periphrasis for "God,"[222] some other Jewish texts use "kingdom of heaven" as a periphrasis for "kingdom of God" (e.g., *Sipra Qed. pq.* 9.207.2.13; *y. Qidd.* 1:2, §24; Matthew, passim).[223] Sometimes they also seem to use "kingdom" as a periphrasis for the divine name.[224]

Jesus's picture of the kingdom, as well as of the Son of Man, may derive especially from Dan 7, a passage less frequently mined by Jesus's followers than in the Jesus tradition itself.[225] With its collocation of language such as "mystery" about God's "kingdom," "son of man," and God's kingdom ending worldly empires, Daniel provided the most fertile (and immediate) background for Jesus's teachings about the kingdom.[226] Daniel's kingdom intervened at the climax of all earthly kingdoms, in the time of the fourth human kingdom, which ancient interpreters (at least in the Roman period)[227] understood as the Roman Empire.[228]

Because virtually every stratum of gospel tradition testifies that Jesus regularly announced the kingdom, there should be no doubt that this was a characteristic emphasis of Jesus's teaching.[229] Scholars have sometimes debated, however, whether Jesus emphasized a present or a future kingdom. More clear evidence seems to favor Jesus announcing a future (impending) kingdom.[230] Yet many have noted an emphasis on the presence of the kingdom in the Gospels, especially in the kingdom parables and in sayings such as the one about entering the kingdom as a child (e.g., Luke 13:18–21; 18:17; Mark 4:26–32; 10:15).[231]

220. E.g., Isa 9:6–7; 24:23; 52:7; Zech 14:9; Wis 5:16 (even despite its Hellenistic approach); *Jub.* 1:28; *Pss. Sol.* 17:5; *2 Bar.* 73:1; *Sib. Or.* 3.767; 4Q246 II, 5; 4Q554 2 III, 14–21, esp. 20–21; *Test. Mos.* 10:1; *Mek. Shir.* 10.42–45; *Sipra Behuq. pq.* 8.269.2.3; *Tg. Isa.* 40:9. *Pace* Crossan, this kingdom belongs more to an apocalyptic than to a sapiential frame of reference (Freyne, *Galilean*, 136–37). For further data, cf. Moore, *Judaism*, 1:423; 2:309; Bonsirven, *Judaism*, 176–77; Laurin, "Immortality"; Young, *Parables*, 193; *Tg. Ezek.* 7:7, 10 in Boring, Berger, and Colpe, *Commentary*, 53; for the present and future aspects, see also Ernst, "Reich."

221. See, e.g., Oesterley, *Liturgy*, 65, 70.

222. E.g., Dan 4:26; 3 Macc 4:21; *1 En.* 6:2; 1QM XII, 5; Rom 1:18; Luke 15:18; *m. 'Ab.* 1:3; *t. B. Qam.* 7:5; *Sipra Behuq. pq.* 6. 267.2.1; 79.1.1.

223. This is commonly pointed out both by scholars of Judaism (e.g., Bonsirven, *Judaism*, 7; Marmorstein, *Names*, 93; Moore, *Judaism*, 1:119) and by those of the NT (e.g., Goppelt, *Theology*, 1:44).

224. E.g., *Test. Ab.* 8:3 A; *Tg. Isa.* 40:9.

225. Witherington, *Christology of Jesus*, 242.

226. With, e.g., Niskanen, "Kingdoms"; Witherington, *Christology of Jesus*, 242; Evans, "Daniel's Visions."

227. Some scholars view the fourth beast as Greek but Rome as partaking in it (Caragounis, "Culture"), but the view held may depend on the interpreters' period. Cf. the Kittim, who in at least the earliest Qumran scrolls might be pre-Roman enemies (Rowley, "Kittim"; Avi-Yonah, "War," 5; Treves, "Date," 420; Michel, *Maître*), though many take the Scrolls' Kittim as Romans (Rabin, "Jannaeus"; Burrows, *Scrolls*, 123–42; idem, *More Light*, 194–203; Dupont-Sommer, *Writings*, 167–68; Charlesworth, *Pesharim*, 109–10; Bolotnikov, "War"; Vermes, "Elements"; cf. the redactional approach in Eshel, "Sny"), quite plausibly (cf. 4QpNah 3 + 4 I, 3; 1QpHab III, 11; 4Q161, frg. 8–10; 4Q491 8–10 II, 8–12; 13 5); some take them more generally (Carmignac, "Kittim" [though *originally* Macedonians]; North, "War," 86–87; Van der Ploeg, *Rouleau*, 24–25; Gaster, *Scriptures*, 388), most plausibly (1QM I, 2, 4, 6; XI, 11; XV, 2; XVIII, 2–3; perhaps 1QpHab II, 12–14; III, 4, 9; IV, 5). The meaning could vary among documents depending on their date (Yadin, *Scroll of War*, 25).

228. On the four kingdoms, see 4Q554 2 III, 14–21; *2 Bar.* 39:5–7; *4 Ezra* 12:11; *Sib. Or.* 8.6–11; *Sipre Deut.* 317.4.2; 320.2.3; *Pesiq. Rab Kah.* 5:2; *y. Ta'an.* 2:5, §1; *Song Rab.* 7:1, §1; *Midr. Pss.* 40, §4; Collins, "Eschatologies," 330–31; for early Christian readings, note esp. Pfandl, "Interpretations." Cf. the similar Hellenistic-Roman perspective in Mendels, "Five Empires"; and, more relevant, four ages of metals from Hesiod to Persian sources and Daniel (Lucas, "Origin").

229. Sanders, *Jesus and Judaism*, 139–40. Cf. also others, e.g., Giesen, *Herrschaft*.

230. With, e.g., Sanders, *Jesus and Judaism*, 146–48, 151–54, 231–32; Allison, "Eschatology"; Meier, *Marginal Jew*, 2:289–397; cf. Burkitt, *Sources*, 69; Schweitzer, *Quest*, 223–397.

231. So, e.g., Dodd, *Parables*; Jeremias, *Parables*; Young, *Parables*, 221; Vermes, *Religion*, 147–49; Borg, *Conflict*, 249; see also Meier, *Marginal Jew*, 2:398–506.

If one examines the entire evidence available in the Gospels, the kingdom appears to be both present and future, as is widely recognized today.[232] It was only natural for Jesus and his first followers, once they recognized that Jesus would need to come again to establish his kingdom fully, to recognize that the anticipated kingdom would arrive in two stages corresponding to Jesus's first and second coming. If one does not arbitrarily exclude either set of evidence by posing a contradiction that the first generations of disciples would not have recognized, both sets of evidence fit together adequately. If Jesus implied his messiahship[233] and spoke of a future Son of Man, we may thus assume that when he announced the kingdom, he undoubtedly announced God's imminent rule in the final sense (rather than simply God's providential rule over creation or over Israel through the law). But his claim also suggests that he expected to play a role in the kingdom,[234] already active in a hidden way in the present (Luke 13:18–30).

Early Christians (most notably in the Pauline circle) continued the present and future tension in eschatology required by a Messiah who had not yet visibly completed Israel's eschatological hopes. As Jesus's resurrection is the first installment on the future resurrection of the righteous, guaranteeing that it will occur (1 Cor 15:20), so Jesus's demonstrations of God's rule at his first coming would foreshadow the completed revelation of God's rule when he returns. In the interim, according to the distinctive perspective probably shared by most early Christians, believers enjoy the Spirit as the "down payment" of their future hope (Rom 8:23; 2 Cor 1:22; 5:5; Eph 1:13–14; Heb 6:4–5). The present significance of the future kingdom in early Christian teaching was thus that God's people in the present age were citizens of the coming age, people whose identity was determined by what Jesus had done and what they would be, not by what they had been or by their status in the world.[235]

Some contemporary scholars, who maintain that Jesus's future kingdom is an unrealistic hope for modern people, label the kingdom a myth and translate it into existential language more appropriate for their own academic circles of thought.[236] But other scholars respond that their position presupposes modern contempt for apocalyptic thought rather than a detailed historical argument.[237] Further, a future

232. E.g., Stein, *Method and Message*, 60–79; Ladd, *Theology*, 70–80; Aune, *Cultic Setting*, 3–4; Dunn, *Jesus and Spirit*, 89; Harvey, *History*, 91; Perrin, *Kingdom*, 73–74 (noting the modification in Dodd's own approach); Davies and Allison, *Matthew*, 1:389; Allison, *Jesus*, 103–4, 107; Witherington, *End*, 51–74; Meier, *Marginal Jew*, 2:10, 289–506; Stanton, "Message and Miracles," 57–61; Theissen and Merz, *Guide*, 275; cf. Young, *Parables*, 193. Sanders, *Figure*, 177–78, grudgingly concedes this possibility but remains doubtful that any authentic passage clearly teaches the kingdom's presence. But especially odd here is Mack, *Lost Gospel*, 126, who thinks that the authentic kingdom sayings in Q simply match the Cynic use of a philosopher reigning as king (in contrast to the LXX and other Jewish traditions of the reign of Israel's one God!); *pace* Mack, though the kingdom is not dominant in early Jewish texts, it is frequent (see Meier, *Marginal Jew*, 2:240–69; cf. Vermes, *Religion*, 127–30; Neusner, "Kingdom," acknowledging its subordinate function).

233. See, e.g., Brown, *Death*, 473–80; Keener, *John*, 289–90; Witherington, *Christology of Jesus*, 104, 116; cf. kingship in Sanders, *Jesus and Judaism*, 234, 307–8; messianic-type associations in Charlesworth, *Jesus within Judaism*, 139. Most scholars agree that Pilate had Jesus executed as a king (this fits the criterion of embarrassment) and that the disciples after the resurrection viewed him as the Messiah; a common source is far likelier than the possibility that the disciples obtained the idea from Pilate.

234. Historically, in the larger context of his ministry, Jesus's preaching of the kingdom has implications for his role (see Beasley-Murray, "Kingdom," 27–32; Sanders, *Jesus and Judaism*, 234, 307).

235. Some scholars also note that the ideals of this kingdom challenged worldly political powers (such as that of Antipas); see, e.g., Freyne, *Galilean*, 148–49; Malina, *Social Gospel*, 1, 71. God's kingdom was technically a theocracy (with, e.g., Malina and Pilch, *Acts*, 22, 215), though this excluded other governments in its future, rather than its present, form (see discussion in our introduction, ch. 13, sect. 3.a.ii).

236. E.g., Bultmann, *Theology*, 1:24; Perrin, *Kingdom*; Tannehill, *Sword*, 56; Borg, *Conflict*, 248–63 (see esp. 257, 261); cf. Bultmann, "Science," 137–38.

237. See Sanders, *Jesus and Judaism*, 7, 27, 125–27; cf. also Meier, *Marginal Jew*, 2:242; somewhat less helpfully, Scott, *Parable*, 57.

kingdom hardly appears irrelevant to the persecuted and oppressed, who nurture hope that God's justice will ultimately triumph and vindicate them.[238] Finally, on the historical level, whatever modern readers' application, it would be naive to presuppose that the members of the early Jesus movement shared modernity's noneschatological perspective; had they wanted a noneschatological mode for expressing their convictions, Sadducees and much of Diaspora Judaism offered such options.[239]

c. The Promise of the Spirit (1:4–5)

Whereas Acts 1:3 summarizes Jesus's appearances and preaching about God's kingdom (similar to the closing summary of Paul's preaching in 28:31), in 1:4–11 Luke provides one or two[240] scenes of Jesus's final preascension communications in more concrete detail. The events in Luke's material here presumably did not all happen at once; 1:4a probably suggests table fellowship, but Luke has identified the scene of the ascension as near Bethany (Luke 24:50), on Mount Olivet (Acts 1:12). Despite its potentially disparate chronology, however, all of the material that Luke portrays is thematically connected:[241] the Spirit is the foretaste of the kingdom and the empowerment to prepare a people for it. The Spirit thus enables the witnesses to carry on Jesus's mission after his ascension, just as Elisha received a double portion of the Spirit to carry on Elijah's work after his ascension. Although the coming of God's reign included fire for the wicked, it would be realized in the lives of the repentant through the Spirit (Luke 3:16).

i. A Final Gathering (1:4)

Presumably, "sharing salt" (συναλιζόμενος) here functions as a metonymy for "sharing a meal,"[242] which Luke clearly affirms Jesus did with his disciples after the resurrection (Luke 24:30, 35, 41–43; Acts 10:41), probably including on this occasion.[243] Thus one character in a story "shared salt" (ἁλῶν ἐκοινωνοῦμεν) with his fellow travelers.[244] (Early versions, including Coptic, Latin, and Syriac, also understood this expression with reference to eating together.)[245]

238. Cf. also Thompson, *Debate*, 95; Thurman, *Disinherited*, 20–27.

239. Goldingay, "Expounding," 354. Borg, *Conflict*, 11–12, questions Perrin's use of "apocalyptic" for a concept that is not in fact apocalyptic.

240. One scene if the aorist participle συνελθόντες in Acts 1:6 refers to the same gathering implied in 1:4; two if it does not. But Luke's depiction is likely a composite, in any case.

241. The Spirit is connected with the kingdom; cf. Smalley, "Spirit, Kingdom, and Prayer." See esp. Cho, *Spirit and Kingdom*, who rightly notes that whereas, for Paul, the Spirit actualizes in believers' lives what the Synoptics would call God's reign (cf. 52–109; note also Dunn, *Romans*, 822), Luke's connection is considerably more modest (Cho, *Spirit and Kingdom*, 162–95, connects this to proclamation; also in idem, "Spirit and Kingdom").

242. For various interpretations in addition to what is provided here, see BDAG. Some scholars understand the term as simply "coming together" (i.e., equivalent to συνελθόντες in Acts 1:6). For metonymy in ancient rhetoric, see *Rhet. Her.* 4.32.43; more fully, Rowe, "Style," 126 (including the sharing of salt in Demosth. *Fals. leg.* 189); Black, "Oration at Olivet," 85.

243. Fuller, *Formation*, 109, 125; Tannehill, *Luke*, 291; Dunn, *Acts*, 7–8; Johnson, *Acts*, 25. Lake and Cadbury, *Commentary*, 5, allow this interpretation, though they prefer (following the tendency toward emendation more common in their era) to view it as an orthographic variant for συναυλιζόμενος, a frequent confusion in Greek literature. Black, *Aramaic Approach*, 141, also prefers "dining together" to proposed Aramaisms here. Sharing salt with strangers was a necessary and expected part of hospitality (*Pesiq. Rab Kah.* Sup. 4:1); banqueters might use salt at dessert to arouse thirst for the drinking party to follow (Smith, *Symposium*, 30, citing Plut. *Table* 4.4, *Mor.* 669B).

244. Lucian *Lucius* 1; LCL, 8:53n1, suggests, "I.e. became friends and ate together."

245. Cullmann, *Worship*, 16.

This final meal would provide continuity between Jesus's ministry that preceded (Luke 5:29; 7:34, 36; 9:16–17; 11:37; 14:13; 15:2; esp. 22:14; 24:30) and the church's life that follows (Acts 2:42, 46; 16:34; 27:35; cf. Luke 10:7; Acts 9:19). It may also suggest an emphasis on realized eschatology, if Jesus now eats and drinks with his disciples "in the kingdom" (Luke 22:16–18), but it must prefigure future eschatology as well (13:29; 14:14–15; the likelier sense of 22:16, 18). If Luke indicates eating here, he alludes to a scene where he has offered a more concrete sample of this activity, namely, in 24:41–43. Since a spirit probably would not eat (cf. 24:37),[246] this scene emphasizes the corporeality of Jesus's resurrection.

Table fellowship invited covenant relationship among those who shared it.[247] For example, those who have eaten together should behave as friends and avoid slandering each other (Aeschines *Embassy* 22, 55). Injuring or slaying those who had eaten at one's table was a terrible offense from which all but the most wicked would normally shrink;[248] such behavior was held to incur divine wrath.[249] The language of "salt" may evoke this image of covenant relationship even more explicitly (cf. Lev 2:13; Num 18:19; 2 Chr 13:5);[250] in the semitized Greek of the East (and perhaps Luke's informants), it may be more significant that an Aramaic verb etymologically involving eating salt had also come to mean simply eating together (cf. Ezra 4:14).[251] The Greek verb can, however, simply refer to coming together, the one element of meaning here that is most clear.[252]

ii. Waiting in Jerusalem (1:4)

Although Jesus gave various commands before his crucifixion[253] and presumably after his resurrection (Acts 1:2), Luke explicitly states only one postresurrection command here (and, by implication of its consequence, another in 1:8): they must *wait* for the Spirit so that they can fulfill their mission (1:4; also emphasized in Luke 24:49).[254] (By implication, the command probably also includes their promised witness to the nations in Acts 1:8; cf. the same verb in 10:42, though Luke employs it in various ways elsewhere.) That Luke emphasizes the necessity of this empowerment

246. E.g., Lucian *True Story* 2.12. In Jewish sources, angels do not normally eat (*Test. Ab.* 4:9 A; 'Abot R. Nat. 1 A; *Gen. Rab.* 2:2; cf. *2 En.* 56:2; evil spirits in *1 En.* 15:11), though they might do so on earth (*Exod. Rab.* 47:5).

247. See, e.g., *Jub.* 35:27; 45:5; discussion in Keener, *John*, 913; hospitality created friendly ties even with strangers (Eurip. *Cycl.* 125) and could even reconcile enemies (Plut. *Cic.* 26.1). See comment on Acts 10:23; 11:3.

248. E.g., Hom. *Il.* 21.76; *Od.* 4.534–35; 11.414–20; 14.404–5; Hes. *W.D.* 327; Eurip. *Cycl.* 126–28; *Hec.* 25–26, 710–20, 850–56; Ap. Rhod. 3.377–80; Ovid *Metam.* 1.144; 10.225–28; Livy 25.16.6. This principle included providing protection from other enemies (Ovid *Metam.* 5.44–45; Corn. Nep. *Gen.* 2 [Themistocles], 8.3).

249. Hom. *Od.* 21.26–28; Livy 39.51.12. Nevertheless, some warned that too much trust even of friends could prove dangerous (Hes. *W.D.* 370–72).

250. Commentators cite Greek and Arabic parallels; Wenham, *Leviticus*, 71; Herr, "Salt," 286; Pollard, "Covenant"; earlier, also Gane, "Leviticus," 292 (including here Ezra 4:14). The LXX uses ἁλίζω for seasoning offerings with salt (Lev 2:13; also Mark 9:49) or (apparently) rubbing it (Ezek 16:4); it probably applies to food in Matt 5:13.

251. See Le Cornu, *Acts*, 9 (and comparison with rabbinic comments on table fellowship).

252. See BDAG, second meaning (citing Jos. *War* 3.429; *Ant.* 8.105; Petosiris frg. 33; Herodotus's *Histories*). None of the objections to this view are compelling.

253. The verb applies, however, only to specific settings (Luke 5:14; 8:29, 56; 9:21).

254. When a teacher or other person of superior status sent off a social inferior, their roles invited the teacher to give parting advice (Men. Rhet. 2.5, 395.8–12); Jesus's status elevates the parting words to a command. Acts does not emphasize Jesus's teaching (cf. Strange, "Jesus-Tradition") as much as Luke's Gospel does, but Luke still regards his teaching (Acts 1:4–5; 11:16; 20:35) and story (1:21–22; 10:36–42) as important.

both in the conclusion to his Gospel and in the introduction to Acts reveals how pivotal it is for Luke's theology of the divine mission.[255]

The importance of this command comports with Luke's approach elsewhere. Just as Jesus did not begin his public ministry before receiving the Spirit around age thirty (Luke 3:22–23; 4:1; Acts 10:38),[256] the disciples were not to attempt their mission on their own strength; to do so, in fact, would be disobedience. Jesus praised Mary and made her a model of discipleship for waiting at Jesus's feet instead of engaging in direct activity (in contrast to Martha, Luke 10:38–41);[257] likewise, it is only after prayer and fasting that the Spirit sends out Barnabas and Saul for the work to which they were already called (Acts 13:2).

The disciples could not generate the Spirit or spiritual experience; "waiting" for the "promise" entailed faithful dependence on God.[258] Certainly Luke emphasizes dependence on God's power to fulfill tasks assigned by God.[259] Luke's pneumatology emphasizes especially the Spirit's empowering the church for mission.[260] (This connection of the Spirit with apostolic evangelism was widespread in early Christianity—for example, 1 Thess 1:5; 1 Pet 1:12; Mark 13:11; John 15:26–27; Rev 19:10.)

That the original apostles stay in Jerusalem much longer than necessary for evangelizing Jerusalem (Acts 15:2–6, 22–23; 16:4; though not as late as 21:18) may imply their misunderstanding (cf. 1:6; 10:14, 28). Jesus tells them to stay there only until they receive the Spirit (Acts 1:4; Luke 24:49), with the mission to the nations (Acts 1:8; Luke 24:47) demanding that they go beyond Jerusalem, from which they initially venture only in response to others' example (Acts 8:14–25) or under duress (12:17). Peter exemplifies a pattern closer to Luke's ideal in 9:32–11:1, but the other "apostles" are not with him physically (11:1) and, probably at that point, theologically (11:1–3; cf. 10:28–29).

Luke is probably not, however, accusing them of deliberate *disobedience*. The Twelve are mostly reliable characters in Acts, and hence they may have seen themselves as supervising the expansion while remaining in a headquarters (their imminent capital) in Jerusalem (cf. 8:1, 4), guaranteeing the connection with Israel's heritage. If they understand Jesus's words as referring to Diaspora Jews[261] (which is not the most natural way to construe them but perhaps the only way conceivable to them), perhaps they think that shepherding the Hellenist Jews among them fulfills their call, at least initially (though some scholars think that they delegate this responsibility in 6:3–6). They might also construe the Isaiah allusion in 1:8 in light of Isaiah's words about the

---

255. With Miller, *Empowered for Mission*, 62, 69; Hernando, "Function," 247–48.

256. Rackham, *Acts*, xlvii, notes that there was a waiting period before both Jesus's and the church's anointing (Luke 1–2; Acts 1).

257. Martha's activity is not negative (cf. Luke 4:39) but only by contrast with Mary's (as in 14:26); discipleship takes precedence over traditional gender (or other) roles (cf., e.g., 9:59–62; 18:29–30). Given the following context (11:1–13), Mary's model also is appropriate for those seeking the gift of the Spirit (11:13). See comment on Acts 6:2–4.

258. Cf. discussion in Keck, *Mandate*, 52–56, esp. (here) 52.

259. Paul (e.g., Rom 5:5; 7:6; 8:4–16, 23, 26; 1 Cor 2:12; 3:16; 6:19; 12:3–13; 2 Cor 1:22; 3:3–18; 5:5; Gal 3:2–5, 14; 4:6, 29; 5:5, 16–25; 6:8) and John (John 3:5–8; 4:23–24; 7:39; 14:17, 26; 15:26; 16:13–15; 20:22) likewise speak of the Christian life and ministry as completely dependent on the Spirit; the view was probably widespread among early Christians (see further, e.g., Fee, *Paul, Spirit, and People*; Keener, "Spirit"; cf. Dunn, "Gospel According to Paul," 148–51, on the Spirit as the defining mark of believers).

260. See, e.g., Hull, *Spirit in Acts*; Stronstad, *Charismatic Theology*; Shelton, *Mighty in Deed*; Penney, *Missionary Emphasis*; Hur, *Reading*, 275; Haya-Prats, *Believers*, 97–108, 192; though cf. Turner, *Gifts*, 38–55; idem, "Every Believer as Witness?" Outside Johannine and Pauline literature, God's Spirit provided moral empowerment especially in the Dead Sea Scrolls and circles related to them (e.g., 4Q444 1 I; Keener, *Spirit*, 8–10), and in a way different from Paul and John.

261. Cf., e.g., Bock, *Acts*, 66.

eschatological gathering of God's people to the Holy Land. This understanding would not require them to relocate; Jerusalemites believed that people from the ends of the earth were already coming to them for worship (Jos. *War* 5.17). More likely, they want to complete the Jerusalem phase of the mission before moving on to the next phase (a logical plan), which would signify misunderstanding but not disobedience.

In view of Luke's (and perhaps their) eschatology, they may have seen themselves as seeking to turn Israel to repentance, the final prerequisite for Christ's return (Acts 1:6–11; 3:19–20). In Luke's perspective, Jerusalem's final rejection of the mission to the Gentiles (22:21–22) may have effectively sealed Jerusalem's fate (Luke 11:49–50; 13:34; 19:42; 21:20–24), ending most of the Jerusalem mission until the time of the Gentiles would be fulfilled (21:24; cf. Rom 11:25–26).[262] In this case, the mission that occasioned their prolonged stay might appear to prove futile from the standpoint of a longer range of history, the immediate future lying with the Gentile mission. But in Luke's perspective, borrowed from the prophets, a currently "futile" mission might be nevertheless a legitimate one (cf. Luke 8:10; Acts 28:27; Isa 6:9–10; 30:10–11).

The Twelve do not ultimately prove hostile to the Diaspora mission (though they at first receive news of the successes among Gentiles, and apparently in Samaria, with concern or caution; Acts 8:14; 11:3, 22). They learn more about the mission from others who already have cultural bridges beyond the Jewish people (8:25), and by the time of Paul's visit in Acts 21, they themselves no longer seem to be in Jerusalem.

III. The "Promise"

Luke expects his audience to be able to fill in details surrounding the promise by remembering what they have already learned in Luke 24:49. There Jesus promises the believers[263] "power" for their mission, which probably includes signs and wonders that would confirm their powerful message (see comment on Acts 1:8; cf. Acts 4:29–30; 14:3). In that passage Jesus also speaks of being "clothed" with this power, an image that might evoke a range of associations among ancient hearers.[264] We read elsewhere of garments of wisdom and a belt of knowledge[265] or of being "clothed" with righteous qualities.[266] Pseudo-Philo's *Biblical Antiquities* even claims that Kenaz "was clothed with the spirit of power" before he went out to battle.[267] Special eschatological clothing also appears in early Jewish texts (cf. 1 Cor 15:53).[268]

---

262. Cf. perhaps the implication of a final turning of Jerusalem to salvation in Rev 11:2, 13 (Keener, *Revelation*, 287–89, 296–97), though the probability of this interpretation rests on the connection with the other passages (the city coalesces in other aspects with Babylon, Sodom, and Egypt, representing the evil world that Revelation often epitomizes in Rome).

263. According to Luke 24:33, the eleven, those who were with them, and the two whom Jesus had met on the road (one being Cleopas, possibly Luke's source for the previous scene).

264. In view of the more general Elijah allusion in the context, Litwak, *Echoes*, 147, compares Elijah's mantle (2 Kgs 2:13). (In Mark 1:6, John's belt evokes that of Elijah in 2 Kgs 1:8, but Luke omits this description, despite Luke 1:17; see further discussion of Luke's Elijah typology below.)

265. *L.A.B.* 20:2–3.

266. E.g., 4 Macc 6:2; *Apoc. Mos.* 20:1; perhaps *'Ab.* 6:1, bar.; *Pesiq. Rab.* 1:2; clothed with evil in 4 *Ezra* 3:26. But clothing with some quality was a frequent metaphor (e.g., Philost. *Vit. soph.* 2.10.590). Esther was clothed with the Holy Spirit (*b. Meg.* 14b); Israel is clothed with God's strength (*Exod. Rab.* 8:1).

267. *L.A.B.* 27:10; in 27:9, he is "clothed with the Spirit of the Lord."

268. Jerusalem "puts on" eschatological "clothes of glory" (*Pss. Sol.* 11:7; i.e., glorious raiment, signifying restoration; cf. Isa 52:1; 61:10); the righteous could eschatologically don "garments of life" and glory (*1 En.* 62:15–16, possibly first century C.E.; later, like angels, *2 En.* 22:8; cf. 22:9–10); cf. further *Odes Sol.* 25:8; *Apost. Const.* 8.6.6. (But cf. "garments of glory" or "honor" for Adam and Eve in *Tg. Neof.* 1 on Gen 3:21, *Tg. Ps.-J.* on Gen 3:21, and *Tg. Onq.* on Gen 3:21.) Many later rabbis thought that someone buried clothed would return clothed (*Gen. Rab.* 95:1; 100:2). For putting off an old robe and donning a new one at conversion, see *Jos. Asen.* 14:12; some views concerning Eph 4:24.

Of early Christian writers, Luke alone uses the distinctive phrase "the Father's promise" (though some other early Christian writers describe the "promise" of the Spirit; see Gal 3:14; Eph 1:13; cf. Hag 2:5); in the NT documents, it appears only here, in Acts 2:33, and in Luke 24:49. Luke probably connects it with the earlier biblical eschatological promise of Israel's inheritance (Acts 7:17), hence the resurrection (13:32–33; 26:6–7) and the messianic era (13:23), perhaps as a sort of foretaste of that inheritance (part of the sense of the promise of the Spirit in Gal 3:14; Eph 1:13).[269] Certainly, the prophets promised the coming of the Spirit (Isa 44:3; 59:21; Ezek 36:26–27; 37:14; 39:29; Joel 2:28–29; perhaps Zech 12:10),[270] but Jesus may also refer to his own current (Acts 1:5) promise and/or an earlier promise of the Spirit to his disciples, guaranteed by the Father's words and character (see esp. Luke 11:11–13).[271] (The pattern of Jesus's words being fulfilled is larger than this promise; many of Jesus's words in the Gospel are fulfilled in Acts.)[272]

For Luke, the "promise" here is not only a matter of historical interest concerning Jesus's first witnesses; it is paradigmatic for all Christians. This is clear from the fact that the promise is later reiterated for all who will repent (Acts 2:38), including the "far off" Gentiles (2:39). Although versions vary, diverse early Christian sources confirm that the disciples believed that Jesus promised them his continuing presence (Matt 18:20; 28:20; John 14:16–26)[273] and that they experienced the expected prophetic Spirit in a dramatic way (John 20:22; cf. Rom 2:29; 7:6; Phil 3:3; see the introduction to Acts 2).

IV. Baptized in the Spirit (1:5)

The promise here evokes John's prophecy about Jesus's mission in Luke 3:16: Jesus is the eschatological bestower of the Spirit.[274] Luke omits here the parallel description of Jesus bringing "fire" because judgment is not immediately relevant in this context (see discussion at Acts 2:3).[275]

The Spirit, promised in the Prophets and in the Gospel of Luke, provides an important "thematic link" between the two volumes.[276] Though Luke parallels Peter and Paul with Jesus in his second volume, it is clear from the introductory framework that it is the Spirit working through disciples that carries on the activity that the Spirit had also empowered Jesus to do.[277] Jesus (Luke 4:24; 13:33–34), his disciples (Luke

---

269. For the Spirit as an eschatological foretaste, see also the Spirit as ἀρραβών (2 Cor 1:22; 5:5; Eph 1:13–14), ἀπαρχή (Rom 8:23); also 1 Cor 2:9–10; probably Rom 14:17; Heb 6:4–5. On Luke's use of the promise to encompass eschatological blessings, see Haya-Prats, *Believers*, 69.

270. On this future promise in the prophets, see Wright, *Spirit through Old Testament*, 121–56. Witherington, *Acts*, 109, suggests that Luke grounds the new experience in history for apologetic motives; on the function of antiquity for apologetic, see our introduction, ch. 13, sect. 3.d.

271. Tannehill, *Luke*, 239, argues that the "promise" and the "gift" of the Spirit in Acts naturally look back to Luke 11:13, where the Father "gives" the Spirit. Stronstad, "Baptized," 167, notes multiple promises of the Spirit by Jesus: Luke 11:13; 24:49; Acts 1:4–5, 8 (fulfilled on Pentecost); and Luke 12:12 and 21:14–15 (though the latter is not explicit; fulfilled in texts like Acts 4:8 and 6:10).

272. See, e.g., Lane, *Gentile Mission*, 74–76; compare Luke 21:12–15 with Acts 25:23–26:29.

273. For discussion of the implications of such claims in an early Jewish context, see Keener, *Matthew*, 455–56, 718; idem, *John*, 951–82.

274. Marguerat, *Histoire*, 75–76, observes that the outpouring of the Spirit in Acts 2 fits the unity of Luke-Acts by fulfilling a fundamental promise made as early as Luke 3:16.

275. Luke also omits here the context that explains this sense of "fire," in contrast to Luke 3:9, 17. Matthew, the only other source (undoubtedly following Q) to report the fire saying, likewise supplies the context (Matt 3:10–12) whereas Mark and John mention only baptism in the Spirit and omit the discussion of fire in the context.

276. Menzies, *Development*, 198.

277. For the Spirit's continuing Jesus's activity in Acts 1–2, see, e.g., Stravinskas, "Role of Spirit." For the Spirit's empowering Jesus, see Luke 3:22; 4:1, 14, 18; Acts 10:38.

24:19; Acts 3:22–24; 7:37; cf. Acts 7:52), and others (Luke 7:16, 39; 9:8, 19) saw his ministry as prophetic;[278] his Spirit-filled ministry (Luke 4:18; Acts 10:38) thus functions as a paradigm for the prophetically inspired ministry of his followers in Acts (Acts 4:8; 6:5; 7:55; 9:17; 10:44; 13:9; 19:6).[279] (On the disciples as prophets in the broader sense, see also Luke 6:23; Acts 2:17–18; the prophetic "word of the Lord" throughout Acts refers to the good news about Jesus.)[280]

The parallelism between Jesus's and the church's receiving the Spirit is clear in Luke's narrative and, given Luke's additions in the Gospel, surely deliberate:

1. Both are praying (Luke 3:21; Acts 1:14; contrast Mark 1:9; Matt 3:13–15).
2. The Spirit descends (Luke 3:22; Acts 2:33; also in Mark 1:10; Matt 3:16; John 1:32).
3. The Spirit looks like something physical (Luke 3:22, using ὡς; Acts 2:3, using ὡσεί).[281]
4. The ensuing public ministries open with sermons that introduce themes for the rest of the book (Luke 4:18–27; Acts 2:14–40).[282]

Jesus's promise of baptism[283] in the Spirit here reiterates John's promise and is central to Jesus's promised mission (Luke 3:16), though not fulfilled in Luke's first volume. If much can be read into the imperfect ἔλεγεν in Acts 11:16 (admittedly, this possibility is debatable), Jesus probably reiterated this promise on more than one occasion. Given the deliberate parallels between John and Jesus in Luke's infancy narratives (see ch. 16, sect. 1.c.ii, of the introduction), it is not surprising that Luke would emphasize the continuity between their messages on this point.[284]

Because the promise is first uttered by John (as any of Luke's audience familiar with the rest of the gospel tradition would know, even had they missed his first volume; cf.

278. One could be *more* than a prophet without thereby compromising prophetic status (Luke 7:26).

279. Brawley, *Luke-Acts and Jews*, 24–25; cf. Russell, "Anointing." Turner, "Jesus and Spirit in Perspective," and idem, *Gifts*, 35, argues from Jesus's high Christology (the exalted Jesus as Spirit giver) that Jesus's experience of the Spirit is not paradigmatic; but this wrongly assumes a forced choice between Jesus's functions as earthly paradigm and as heavenly Lord. Turner's "Messianic" category for the Spirit (Turner, *Gifts*, 17–18) depends on the categories in which he divides the evidence (it overlaps with the prophetic category).

280. For "word of the Lord," see Acts 8:25; 11:16 (a saying of Jesus); 12:24; 13:48, 49; 15:35, 36; 16:32; 19:10, 20. For "word of God," see 4:29, 31; 6:2, 7; 8:14; 11:1; 13:5, 7, 44, 46; 17:13; 18:11. For "word" otherwise, see, e.g., 2:41; 6:4; 8:4; 10:36; 11:19; 13:26; 14:3, 25; 15:7; 16:6; 17:11; 18:5; 20:32. Distribution shows that these phrases are equivalent despite sometimes identifying Jesus as "the Lord." Cf. the use of "word" in the Gospels and Acts in Millanao T., "Comprensión"; Pauline usage in Pahl, "Gospel."

281. Cf. Luke 22:44; Luke often employs these expressions (Luke uses ὡς 111 times, compared with Mark's twenty-one times and John's thirty times; and ὡσεί fourteen times, compared with Mark's use of it once and John's not using it at all).

282. With minor adaptations, this set of parallels is from Talbert, *Patterns*, 16; Stronstad, *Charismatic Theology*, 51. The objection some raise against the parallels, that the Spirit is Jesus's gift (Acts 2:33; Turner, *Gifts*, 35), forces a choice between earthly paradigm and heavenly giver that Luke would not likely have envisaged.

283. Some insist on employing only the verb cognate because Luke-Acts uses only the verb; I consider the distinction in this case unduly pedantic (Luke plainly uses the noun cognate to cover the same semantic range as the verb, e.g., regarding John's baptism, as a noun, Luke 3:3; 7:29; 20:4; Acts 1:22; 10:37; 13:24; 18:25; esp. 19:3–4, which has both forms), but those who object to the noun form are welcome to treat it as verbal in all my uses if they wish.

284. For John as Jesus's "precursor" in Luke-Acts (and presence of this idea in the tradition before Luke developed it), see Fitzmyer, *Theologian*, 86–116; in this instance, also Dunn, *Acts*, 9. Other early Christians schematized the continuity between John's message and Jesus's (Matt 3:2; 4:17), though behavioral contrasts were clear (Matt 11:19//Luke 7:34; perhaps overstated in Sanders, *Jesus and Judaism*, 92). John was greater than other prophets (Luke 7:26a) because he introduced Jesus, but the least in the kingdom proclaim a fuller revelation than John (cf. 7:26b; 10:23–24). The transition from indirect to direct discourse in Acts 1:4 was not unusual (see Conzelmann, *Acts*, 6, citing 23:22; Luke 5:14; Jos. *War* 1.76; *Ant.* 1.100; Arrian *Alex.* 5.11.4).

Mark 1:8; John 1:33; Matt 3:11), it is to that opening passage about Spirit baptism that we must look to understand what Luke's audience would first assume. John's water baptism foreshadows Jesus's greater baptism in fire and the Spirit.[285] Whereas John summarizes Jesus's "mission" toward the wicked as a baptism of fiery judgment (Luke 3:9, 16–17), his mission toward the righteous is baptism in the Spirit (3:16).[286] The immediate context thus guarantees the gift to all the righteous and hence is theologically part of salvation (as in the Q material Luke here reflects).

At the same time, in context in Luke 3, this promise must include power to fulfill one's mission in the face of great opposition. Jesus receives the Spirit at his baptism (Luke 3:21–22) and thus becomes the model for the Spirit-baptized life, immediately afterward led by the Spirit in the face of testing (4:1–2).[287] Jesus declares that God has anointed him with the Spirit for mission (4:18; cf. Acts 10:38). Although Luke retains the tradition in which baptism in the Holy Spirit includes the entire sphere of the Spirit's activity to which God's servants are introduced at conversion,[288] his own special emphasis in his narrative usually lies on the more particular dimension of empowerment for mission.

Because the promise of the Spirit in Acts 1:4 refers to Jesus's promise of the baptism in the Spirit in 1:5, the promised gift of the Spirit in 2:38–39, which refers to Jesus's followers' experience on Pentecost (2:33), is a paradigmatic expression of baptism in the Spirit. Though Acts speaks again of being "baptized" in the Spirit only in connection with Cornelius's household (11:16),[289] that experience is also called "receiving" the Spirit (10:47; cf. 1:8; 2:33, 38),[290] which also applies to the experiences of the new disciples in Samaria and Ephesus (8:15, 17; 19:2).

It appears that in Luke's theology, as in Paul's, "receiving" the Spirit is connected with conversion (2:38–39; 11:16–17; cf. Luke 3:16);[291] but Luke's narrative sometimes distinguishes them chronologically (Acts 8:12–17; cf. 2:4; 9:17; 19:5–6).[292] This apparent dissonance could be because Luke emphasizes a particular dimension of

285. The connection between John's lesser and Jesus's greater baptisms may imply an unstated premise, namely, that John's baptism foreshadowed the coming baptism of Jesus; incomplete syllogisms are common in Luke, including in characters' speech (Vinson, "Enthymemes," 119–22, 131; on various definitions of enthymemes, cf. Anderson, *Glossary*, 44).

286. For discussion (including various views) on the Q material, see, e.g., Menzies, *Development*, 137–44; Keener, *Spirit*, 94–96 and notes; idem, *Matthew*, 127–28.

287. For discussion, see Keener, *Spirit*, 49–90, esp. 50, 70–71 (on Mark 1:8–12). For a broader theological approach, see Issler, "Prototype."

288. Ideally, in a baptism of repentance (see comment on Acts 2:38), although Luke's narrative displays varied scenarios. On this tradition of Spirit baptism as spiritual purification and initiation (like physical proselyte baptism), see, e.g., Keener, *Gift*, 138–46, 152–57, esp. 152–53; idem, *Spirit*, 135–89. Johanson, "Alternative View," also finds in the term both conversion and empowerment (44; though he distinguishes especially the complementary approaches of John the Baptist [8–27] and Jesus [27–43]); encompassing both conversion and subsequent experience, cf. Osborne, *Matthew*, 119.

289. This later occurrence renders it doubtful that Luke intends the phrase to cover only the church's experience on Pentecost (Brown, "'Baptism' and 'Baptism'"; Green, *Spirit*, 172–78). Robinson, *Studies*, 167, argued for the "one baptism" of Pentecost as merely represented ritually in subsequent baptisms; by contrast, Kim, "Mission," 49–62, esp. 53–62, argues for multiple outpourings in Acts as a model of repeatability.

290. On various synonyms, see, e.g., Stronstad, *Charismatic Theology*, 49–50; cf. Witherington, *Acts*, 133. Orators preferred to vary their terminology rather than repeat significant terms too frequently in a given context; see, e.g., Hermog. *Method* 4.416–17 (citing Hom. *Il.* 11.269–77; *Od.* 19.205–8; Thucyd. 1.1, 6, 8). Cf. also Lee, "Translations: Greek," 776–77; but Anderson, *Rhetorical Theory*, 162, 170–71, defines μεταβολή differently.

291. See Dunn, *Baptism*, passim (cf. idem, "Baptism"); Turner, "'Spirit' as Power," 339–47; idem, *Gifts*, 46–55; idem, *Power*, 348 (stressing the "norm" of Acts 2:38–39 and that 8:16 is anomalous); idem, "Challenge." But there is some debate; see further comment on Acts 2:38.

292. For the Spirit's coming variously before or after baptism in Acts (in contrast to Paul), cf. also Bruce, "Holy Spirit in Acts"; Haya-Prats, *Believers*, 148–52. See comment on Acts 8:16 for further arguments and supporting sources.

pneumatology (prophetic empowerment; cf. 1:8; 2:17–18; see our introduction, ch. 15, sect. 5.a.iii; and comment on Acts 2:17–18), sometimes almost to the exclusion of other elements.[293] For Luke, empowerment to tell others about Christ is central, not peripheral, to the Spirit's activity with believers. If Luke focuses on this element, he is not obligated to depict every activity of the Spirit (in contrast to some other early Christian writers, Luke does not explicitly associate the Spirit with, or even employ the language of, regeneration) but does so most often with occasions of prophetic empowerment. He can affirm that all Jesus's followers receive access to the sphere of the Spirit in a broader sense, yet he can focus on an empowerment dimension that sometimes appears subsequent to conversion in his narratives. His narratives (see comments ad loc.) usually appear to reserve the language of "receiving the Spirit" for his focus on empowerment for mission (whether experienced at or after conversion), which, for Luke (who emphasizes the Spirit's activity in mission), is central to the church's life.

Thus without (in the view presented here) denying that those who were delayed in receiving the Spirit (i.e., this aspect of the Spirit's activity) were "converted," Luke allows that, in some cases, people experienced this prophetic-empowerment dimension[294] shortly after, or (from a different perspective) as a later stage in, their conversion process.[295] Instead of reading his apparently ideal theological paradigm (2:38) into the narrative evidence, Luke allows for a diversity of pneumatic experience (8:12–17; 10:44–48; 19:5–6) and presumably invites his audience to show the same courtesy.[296]

Members of Luke's informed audience, who presumably know that Pentecost was fifty days after Passover (Lev 23:15–16; cf. 1 Cor 16:8) and can subtract the forty days

293. See Haya-Prats, *Believers*, 192; esp. Menzies, *Empowered*, 106–228; idem, *Development*, 205–77 (though I believe that this approach can be taken too far; cf. esp. probably Luke 3:16; Acts 2:38); more nuanced, Cho, *Spirit and Kingdom*, 136, 162–95; for further discussion, see our introduction, ch. 15, sect. 5.

294. Menzies, *Empowered*, 230, notes that "subsequence" is problematic only if the experience is assumed identical with conversion and read in Pauline terms. (Various Pentecostal scholars have admitted the theological unity of the experience in Paul while pointing to the more varied character of Luke's narrative; e.g., Hodges, *Theology of Mission*, 41.) Whereas those who deny subsequence often dismiss advocates of subsequence as biased, the assumption that Luke must employ phrases in the same manner as Paul seems to me to be a frequent bias in the argument against subsequence in Luke's narratives. Virtually no one excludes subsequent "fillings" (e.g., Acts 4:8, 31; 13:9), which makes the issue here somewhat a semantic one (cf. Oss, "View," 243–44; Keener, *Gift*, 147–49).

295. See more fully Keener, "Spirit," 491–92; idem, *Gift*, 157–68 (noting also that this is my understanding of Luke, not of all NT writers). Reception history is interesting here, perhaps reflecting both readers' location and legitimate observations about the text. Some scholars make some of the narrative examples' subsequence paradigmatic: in addition to the sacramental version (confirmation), note the second experience of Puritan and Reformed Sealers (assurance; see Lederle, *Treasures*, 5; Dayton, *Roots*, 37; for later Reformed versions, see Curtis, *Faith*, 7–8), Wesleyan-Holiness movements (perfected love), the Keswick movement (power for service, which fits the emphasis in this passage), and classical Pentecostalism (Lederle, *Treasures*, 5; on Keswick, see also Alexander, *Fire*, 73; cf. also A. B. Simpson in Simpson, *Church*, 17–32); on empowerment, see also Bebbington, *Dominance*, 210–11. For a survey of views, see, e.g., Lederle, *Treasures*, passim; for subsequence in various traditions (including Wesleyan, Anglican, and Catholic traditions), see Dayton, *Roots*; Gresham, *Doctrine*; Synan, *Movement*, 18–21; Hollenweger, *Pentecostals*, 21, 26n2; Bruner, *Theology*, 76, 323–41; McGee, "Hermeneutics," 101; Keener, "Holy Spirit," 164–65; cf. perhaps Baptist A. J. Gordon in Barr, Leonard, Parsons, and Weaver, *Acts*, 119. For the meaning of baptism in the Spirit in various theological traditions, see, e.g., Brand, *Perspectives* (including Del Colle, "Baptism"; Dunning, "Perspective"; Hart, "Baptism"; Horton, "Baptism"; Kaiser, "Baptism"); Macchia, *Baptized*; McDonnell and Montague, *Initiation*, 23–41; Wessels, "Doctrine" (noting the priority of Acts in Pentecostal interpretation, 185–202, 337); Wheelock, "Spirit Baptism" (for classical Pentecostalism, 149–240; also in Protestant [241–78] and Catholic [278–301] charismatic circles); Yun, "Baptism."

296. With respect to distinctions between Paul's and Luke's terminology, it should be noted that many in antiquity did not require the same terminology even in the same work. Plato and some of his successors rejected the pedantic attachment to consistent terminology reflected by some other philosophers (Max. Tyre 21.4; Trapp, *Maximus*, 182n9, cites also Arius Didymus in Stob. *Ecl.* 2.6.3, 2.21.11ff. [Meineke]). Rigorous consistency (in the sense in which many seek it) is more often the domain of dogmatics than of exegesis.

of Acts 1:3, will understand that the fulfillment was due in "not many days" (1:5),[297] a phrase that distinguished this occasion of the promise from others (Luke 3:16; Acts 11:16). Although the timing of eschatological events such as Israel's restoration might be indefinite (Acts 1:6–7), the coming of the Spirit was imminent and its time plainly marked out.[298]

d. When the Kingdom? (1:6–7)

Jesus was teaching the disciples both about the Spirit (1:4–5) and about the kingdom (1:3), and the disciples would have every reason to understand these two themes as inseparably linked.[299] The sourcebook for much of Jesus's postresurrection teaching was the Bible (Luke 24:27, 44), including what he taught them about their impending mission as his witnesses (24:45–47) and presumably about their reception of the Spirit (24:49).

The prophets had regularly linked God's pouring out his Spirit with the time of Israel's restoration,[300] and so any talk about the Spirit's outpouring was de facto eschatological in character. Indeed, in their contexts, the primary Spirit texts alluded to in all of Luke's programmatic statements concern Israel's restoration. For example, the program for Jesus's mission in the Gospel appears in Luke 4:18–19, which quotes Isa 61:1–2; this passage refers explicitly to the comforting good news, which in context is the good news that God is restoring his people (Isa 40:1, 9; 41:27; 49:13; 51:3, 12; 52:7, 9; 54:11; 57:18; 60:6; 66:13).

Luke indicates that Jesus's pre-ascension teaching to his disciples during this period reflected significant attention to the Scriptures (Luke 24:44–45); Luke presumably offers us samples of the content of Jesus's midrash in apostolic sermons that expound Scripture (esp. in Acts 2:16–39; 7:2–53; 13:17–47) but even more explicitly in biblical allusions in his final instructions to the disciples. The primary allusion in Luke 24:49 (power "from on high," ἐξ ὕψους) is probably to Isa 32:15 LXX (the Spirit "from on high," ἀφ' ὑψηλοῦ), which refers to Israel's restoration (32:16–18; cf. 34:16–35:10).[301] Luke's parallel text in his second volume, Acts 1:8, might also evoke Isa 32:15 (given its use of ἐπέρχομαι with πνεῦμα)[302] and alludes to Isaiah's passage about the Spirit's empowering Israel as God's witnesses in the end time (Isa 43:9–12; 44:3, 8–9; on which see in more detail below). Indeed, the coming of the Spirit in

297. The phrase is acceptable Koine (Mealand, "Not Many Days"; pace Lake and Cadbury, Commentary, 7, who saw it as an Aramaism resembling Exod 2:23; 4:18 LXX; Torrey, Composition, 24, saw ταύτας as an aramaized "redundant demonstrative"; Bruce, Acts¹, 69). This is an example of litotes or meiosis (Mickelsen, Interpreting, 193), for which see Rhet. Her. 4.38.50; Anderson, Glossary, 20–21 (s.v. ἀντεισαγωγή); Rowe, "Style," 128 (citing Lysias Or. 12.22 [Against Eratosthenes]; Cic. Cat. 3.7.17); Porter, "Paul and Letters," 579 (citing Rom 1:16); examples in Hermogenes Method 37.455–56 (citing Homer Il. 1.330; 15.11).

298. For early Jewish hopes for a very near restoration or judgment, see, e.g., 4Q385 3 4–5; 4 Ezra 4:44–50; 6:18; 8:61.

299. Elsewhere in early Christianity, the link is explicit in Matt 12:28 (probably Matthean redaction; see Keener, Matthew, 364; Gundry, Matthew, 235; Schweizer, Matthew, 287; Witherington, Christology of Jesus, 201; Davies and Allison, Matthew, 2:340; Allison, Moses, 237; pace Rodd, "Finger"; Haya-Prats, Believers, 32; Dunn, Jesus and Spirit, 45–46; Menzies, Development, 186–89); John 3:5; Rom 14:17.

300. E.g., Isa 42:1; 44:3; 59:21; Ezek 36:24–28; 37:14; 39:29; Joel 2:28–3:1; for some discussion, cf., e.g., Ma, Spirit, 212–13; see discussion below. The Spirit's eschatological connection may remain in Irenaeus's Proof of the Apostolic Preaching (see Williams, "Christianity," 25).

301. See esp. Turner, Power, 300. The slightly different Greek expression in Luke does appear in the LXX (2 Sam 22:17; Pss 17:17; 101:20; 143:7; Lam 1:13; Sir 16:17), but these cases do not concern the Spirit and are less relevant. The "pouring" of the Spirit in Isa 32:15 provides a natural midrashic link for Joel 2:28.

302. Marshall, "Acts," 528 (following Pao, New Exodus, 528); see also Haya-Prats, Believers, 5. Elsewhere in the LXX, these terms are conjoined only at Num 5:14, 30; Job 4:15; and Wis 1:5, none of which is as relevant. Without the compound form, Haya-Prats, Believers, 5, cites further Ezek 2:2; 3:24; Wis 7:7.

Isaiah is often associated with Israel's restoration (42:1; 44:3; 59:21; cf. 11:1–10; the new exodus material in 63:10–14). This is also the case with Joel 2:28–29 (quoted in Acts 2:17–18), which appears in the context of Israel's eschatological restoration (Joel 2:27; 2:32–3:1).

Thus the disciples ask what seems, from their solely future eschatological perspective,[303] the obvious question: When will Jesus restore the kingdom to Israel?[304] Some view their question as shortsighted, but this context specifies that the problem is with timing (Acts 1:7), not with content. After all, "Luke's own story forthrightly declares at the outset that Jesus will occupy the throne of his father David (Luke 1:32–33)."[305] Nor are they the first to draw a wrong temporal inference from Jesus's teaching about the kingdom.[306]

Their question presupposes a theology of Israel's restoration that is indeed affirmed in some texts in the Gospel (Luke 1:32–33, 54–55, 68–74; 2:32, 38; 22:15–16, 30; cf. 24:21)[307] as well as occasionally in Acts (Acts 3:21, 25–26; probably 15:15–17).[308] Luke does share this restoration eschatology in some form with the Israelite prophets[309] and with Paul (e.g., Rom 11:15–26;[310] cf. also Matt 23:39).[311] Indeed, the restoration hope was widespread; long after Rome destroyed the temple in 70, many Jewish people continued to expect even the ten "lost" tribes to return in the end time.[312]

303. Parsons, *Departure*, 181, thinks that the implied reader will likely identify with the disciples and their question and hence be challenged by Jesus's response. Whenever we date Acts, however, Luke's ideal audience will know that the parousia did not follow immediately. Nevertheless, Parsons may be right that they will identify with the disciples and regard the question as a perfectly logical one (cf. similarly John 14:5).

304. Though Vermes, *Jesus the Jew*, 51, associates their question with Zealot-like expectations of Galileans, even the most sectarian Jews shared this hope (e.g., 1QpHab V, 1–2 in Silberman, "Unriddling," 342; 4Q385 3 3); cf. also *Sib. Or.* 2.174–86 (the more so if this material belongs to the Christian interpolation in the context). For political eschatologies, including Hellenistic influence on Jewish expectations of the four kingdoms, see Collins, "Eschatologies," 330–31. On the expected restoration of the twelve tribes, see comment on Acts 26:7.

305. Gaventa, *Acts*, 65. Kayama, "Israel," helpfully emphasizes reading all of Luke's programmatic "Israel" passages sequentially (though this might not resolve the question of where to lay emphasis).

306. In Luke 19:11, after Jesus has talked often about the kingdom and recently about salvation "today" (19:9), people expect the kingdom to appear when he reaches Jerusalem.

307. Bede *Comm. Acts* 1.6 helpfully compares the disciples' hope in Luke 24:21 with the hope expressed by the apostles here.

308. Luke's interpretation of this theology undoubtedly differed from that of many of his contemporaries (see below), but their views also differed widely among themselves.

309. E.g., Isa 60:1–3; Jer 31:27–40; Hos 14:4–7; Amos 9:11–15; examples could be multiplied. For this hope in early Judaism, see, e.g., Sanders, *Jesus and Judaism*, 96–98.

310. Luke's eschatology is closer to Paul's than has often been allowed; see in greater detail Giles, "Present-Future Eschatology"; Litwak, "Views," 241–48; Baum, *Gospel*, 167. For proposals concerning the literal Jewish people's restoration in some sense in Rom 11, see, e.g., Das, *Paul and Jews*, 96–111; Tobin, *Rhetoric in Contexts*, 423; Munck, *Israel*, 136; Goppelt, *Judaism*, 164; Rissi, *Time*, 130; Ladd, "Israel"; Nanos, *Mystery*, 240. (The argument that Rom 11:26 refers only to spiritual "Israel" [as in, e.g., Ponsot, "Israël"] requires a sudden change of word usage in the context; but cf. application to the present era's remnant in Horne, "Phrase.") For the proposal of a temporal use of εἰς τέλος in 1 Thess 2:16, hence limiting the period of judgment, see Donfried, *Thessalonica*, 207–8. Various Christian interpreters through history also expected Israel's restoration (e.g., Humbert, "Objections"; Wolffe, "Dismantling," 38), although, in the second century, we have only Justin (Stylianopoulis, *Justin*, 42).

311. On the latter, see discussion in Allison, "Matt. 23:39 = Luke 13:35b"; Keener, *Matthew*, 558–59; the position in Luke 13:35 is not so clearly future from Luke's standpoint as it is in Matthew's placement. Cf. also Rev 11:1–2, 13, on which I remarked earlier.

312. E.g., *Test. Benj.* 9:2 (if not a Christian interpolation); *Pesiq. Rab Kah.* 24:9; *Sup.* 5:3; *Gen. Rab.* 98:9; cf. *4 Ezra* 13:40–43; contrast the minority view in *m. Sanh.* 10:5; *t. Sanh.* 13:12; *b. Sanh.* 110b. Earlier, e.g., Bar 4:37; 5:5; Tob 13:6; 2 Macc 2:18; cf. *Pss. Sol.* 17:28; 1QM II, 2–3, 7–8; III, 13; V, 1; 11QTᵃ XVIII, 14–16 (some of these from Sanders, *Jesus and Judaism*, 96–97). See the more nuanced elaboration of approaches in Fuller, *Restoration* (the historic regathering in the Hebrew Bible, 15–23; the future regathering as a return of the Diaspora, e.g., in Tobit and Sirach, 25–48; a regathering from Israel, e.g., CD and *1 En.* 85–90 and *4 Ezra*,

But (like Paul) Luke also allows for an interim period before Israel's final repentance and restoration, in which Gentiles are converted,[313] perhaps to provoke Israel's response (cf. Paul's view in Rom 10:19; 11:11–14). He emphasizes realized eschatology more than Matthew or Mark (though less than John); like Paul (Rom 8:11, 23; 14:17; 1 Cor 2:9–10; 2 Cor 5:5; Gal 5:5; 6:8; cf. Eph 1:13–14; 2 Thess 2:13; Heb 6:4–5) and John (John 4:23–24; 7:37–39; 14:17–18; 16:13–16), he emphasizes realized eschatology through pneumatology. Like the Baptist, the disciples did not understand that the king would come twice, hence bringing the kingdom in two stages (Luke 3:16–17 with 7:19–20). The disciples' lack of understanding (suggested again in Acts 1:11) provides a suitable transition from their character as learners in the Gospel to their mission in Acts.[314]

The disciples by now understand that Jesus is the Messiah (Luke 24:46) but have not yet understood the implications for the present meaning of the kingdom. Luke-Acts portrays Jesus as heir to David's throne, but the nature of his royalty is not immediately a "political, this-worldly restoration" or "re-establishment of the monarchy," dramatically affecting the empire's political situation.[315] It redefines their hope and especially their immediate focus.

The disciples' question is important enough to warrant more detailed discussion here. As noted above, writers often put essential ideas up front in their introductions. In this case, eschatology frames the transition from Jesus's presence to the disciples' mission: they ask about the time of Israel's restoration (Acts 1:6), and angels declare the bodily character of Jesus's future return (1:11).[316]

1. Views concerning Luke's Eschatology

Conzelmann set much of the tone for the past half century of discussion of Lukan eschatology by claiming that Luke responded to the parousia's delay by leaving the parousia as a distant hope[317] and instead emphasizing three epochs: the OT era, Jesus's ministry, and the era of the church (cf. Luke 16:16).[318] Haenchen also thinks that Luke denied the parousia's imminence (while accepting that it would happen), seeking to shift the focus to the present mission, which must be fulfilled before the Lord's return.[319]

48–84; and Philo's spiritual journey, 84–101); Fuller can use this range to support his understanding of the distinctively Lukan shape of restoration.

313. Adapting Isaiah's eschatological vision; see Pao, *Isaianic Exodus*, 229. On Isaiah in Luke-Acts, see also Mallen, *Reading*.

314. Especially during oral performance, hearers may have identified with the disciples' confusion here; cf. audience identification in Dewey, "Oral-Aural Event," 152–53 (citing Plato's use of *mimesis* for emotional identification with characters). Goldingay, "Comic Acts?," may also be correct that Luke allows some humor at the disciples' expense (and even later in Acts, in 12:12–17; cf. 23:9–10).

315. Tuckett, "Christology," 162.

316. Both the Scriptures (e.g., Isa 9:1–7; 11:1–11; Jer 23:5–6) and early Judaism generally (e.g., Luke 24:21; 4Q252 V, 3–4; *Pss. Sol.* 17:23; *2 Bar.* 30:1; 39:7; 72:2; *4 Ezra* 12:32; *Tg. Hos.* 14:8) associated Israel's restoration with the Messiah's coming, though some allowed for an interim period (*Sipre Deut.* 34.4.3; 310.5.1; *Pesiq. Rab Kah.* 3:16; 27:5). Frequent prayers linked the two hopes together (*Pss. Sol.* 17:21; Fitzmyer, *Acts*, 205, cites Shemoneh Esre 14; Kaddish 2).

317. Theissen, *Gospels*, 279–80, may be correct that the war of 66–70 C.E. "awakened eschatological expectations," which now seemed less imminent, until Jesus would appear (Luke 21:28).

318. Conzelmann, *Theology of Luke*, 95–136. For Conzelmann, Luke's church replaced most immediate interest in the parousia. Luke could employ a transition of epochs in grounding the church's identity in Israel's history (Wolter, "Epochengeschichte," 284). For studies of eschatology relevant for Acts before 1965, see Mattill and Mattill, *Bibliography*, 301–3 (including Borgen, "Eschatology"; Smith, "History").

319. Haenchen, *Acts*, 95–96. Conzelmann's approach to Luke and the parousia is only one among several major lines of interpretation; see the survey in Faure, *Pentecôte*, 43–46. For one recent discussion of the problem of the parousia in Acts, see Grässer, *Forschungen*, 48–58, 292–320.

Conzelmann's neat schema, however, is problematic. It cannot accommodate, for example, the positive portrayal of Jewish Christians valuing the law (Acts 21:20–26; cf. Luke 16:17). Moreover, the schema contradicts its key verse, Luke 16:16, in which the era of salvation starts with John's ministry, not with his execution.[320]

Many (and probably most) scholars have disagreed with the premise that Luke abandons imminent hope in the parousia, relegating it only to a distant future; Luke may allow for delay (certainly more than the disciples hoped for), but he also allows for the possibility of a nearer end.[321] After all, Luke portrays the church's experience of the Spirit and mission as the "last days," the eschatological era (Acts 2:17).[322]

The delay of the eschatological time remained a problem not only for early Christians but for other Jewish thinkers as well (e.g., 4 Ezra 4:33–37); some believed that God was being patient toward sinners.[323] The Qumran scrolls evidence some theological grappling with delays in eschatological expectation.[324] Others opined that the delay was meant to inculcate faithful waiting on God (b. Sanh. 97b). Many counted up eras to suggest various schemes for the time of the end;[325] others cursed the very notion of trying to calculate it (also in b. Sanh. 97b). In some traditions, God depended on Israel to be righteous and hence precipitate the end (Pesiq. Rab. 31:5). Probably some earlier revolutionaries acted expecting their zeal (cf. comment on Acts 22:3) to help precipitate the end as well.

Yet others have contended that the importance of the parousia's delay for early Christian thought has probably been overstated.[326] Jesus and Paul may have spoken only of potential imminence, which would reduce the tension between promise and fulfillment.[327] Indeed, the delay of the parousia did not by itself create even Gnosticism, although it probably strengthened it.[328]

Although realized eschatology and eschatological fervency could remain two divergent responses to the parousia's delay, the continuing eschatological fervency reduces the probability of the need for the parousia's delay as an explanation for realized eschatology in some other sources.[329] Certainly Revelation, probably authored somewhat later than Luke, has not lost any eschatological fervor (although it represents a very different stream of early Christian thought). Indeed, the expectation remains quite fervent in the most pneumatic and evangelistic sectors of Christendom today

320. Hill, Prophecy, 43, comparing Luke's portrayal of this ministry in Luke 3:1–18; 7:26.

321. Wilson, "Lukan Eschatology"; Nielsen, "Purpose," esp. 88; Giles, "Present-Future Eschatology"; Gaventa, "Eschatology Revisited"; Bayer, "Eschatology in Acts 3:17–26"; Tuckett, Luke, 36–43; Nolland, "Salvation-History," 65–67; Turner, Power, 300; cf. also Ellis, Eschatology, passim; idem, "Fonction de l'eschatologie." For a survey of responses to Conzelmann, see Bovon, Theologian, 25–29 and esp. 29–74, and cf. 1–8 (who also argues that Luke's salvation-history approach reflected much of early Christianity, not his own invention; 26, 74–77).

322. See Hiers, "Problem of Delay."

323. 4 Ezra 7:74; Gen. Rab. 67:4; cf. 2 Pet 3:9; more generally, 2 Bar. 24:2; Let. Aris. 187–88; Sipre Deut. 43.14.1; y. Ta'an. 2:1, §11; Pesiq. Rab Kah. 7:10; Eccl. Rab. 7:15, §1. On delays of divine vengeance, cf. also Plut. Div. V. passim, Mor. 548A–568A.

324. 1QpHab VII, 7–8, 11–14; Vermes, Jesus and Judaism, 24. Reicke, Epistles, 179, suggests that such delay was felt as a problem even to OT prophets (citing Hab 2:3; cf. also Zech 1:12). Later movements also addressed skeptics about the coming judgment; see, e.g., Qur'an 34.3; cf. 14.42.

325. On 2 Baruch, see, e.g., Roddy, "Two Parts" (though 2 Baruch's calculations were doubtless less precise).

326. See discussion in, e.g., Aune, "Delay." The "problem" interested their critics far more (Mac. Magn. Apocrit. 4.1–7).

327. Witherington, End, 48. Apocalyptic embraced both imminence and continuance (Allison, Jesus, 94).

328. Nock, "Gnosticism," 271. Cf. the connection between Gnosticism and realized eschatology in Talbert, "Delay"; Aune, "Delay," 99–100 (although one need not agree with this background for 2 Peter; cf. Bauckham, Jude, 153; by contrast, Bruce, Message, 94–95, finds the issue of delay highlighted there).

329. See, e.g., Flusser, "Salvation."

(as well as in a number of other now-old millennial and apocalyptic religions and sects).[330] Some scholars even contend that, for Luke, the parousia's delay invited all the more urgency in expectation.[331]

Granted, Luke is a historian with historical, not just eschatological, interest, but these interests are not logically mutually exclusive, and the historical genre does not a priori predict the theological predispositions of those who used it. More significant in predisposing us to doubt Luke's eschatology, he is a *Hellenistic* historian; but not all Diaspora Jews and God-fearers were equally hellenized in all respects, and Paul, despite his Diaspora mission, apparently maintained an imminent eschatology (e.g., 1 Cor 15:52; Phil 3:20–21), though it admittedly dominates more in his earlier writings (esp. 1–2 Thessalonians), before he contextualized for Greeks as fully as he would.[332] Luke's emphasis is on inaugurated eschatology (perhaps more than Paul's yet less than John's),[333] but he affirms future eschatology (see remarks in the introduction, ch. 15, sect. 4).

Haenchen and Conzelmann certainly advance some correct ideas regarding Luke's emphasis in the current passage. One need not accept Conzelmann's neat chronological scheme or the textual basis he provides for it to recognize that Luke embeds the story of the church's mission (sampled in Acts) in the story of Jesus (presented in the Gospel) and this story, in turn, in Israel's history. Further, Luke occasionally adapts Mark's wording to shift emphasis from eschatological details to the fulfilling of the church's mission.[334] More crucial is that the Spirit's empowerment enables the church to witness to all nations, which probably functions here (on the analogy of some other early Christian sources, esp. Matt 24:14; Rom 11:25–26; 2 Pet 3:9, 15) as a prerequisite for the end.[335] As Cullmann understands this passage, no one knows when the kingdom will come, "but there is one thing the disciples can be sure of: that they must proclaim the Gospel to all the world, until that 'day' comes."[336] Yet Luke may have believed that the church could complete this task of universal witness in his generation (cf. Col 1:23), just as Christians in many subsequent generations have believed they could;[337] there is no reason, then, to suppose that he thought the parousia a necessarily distant event.

II. LUKE'S FUTURE ESCHATOLOGY

Just as various texts warn about some events that must precede the "imminent" end,[338] so Luke 21 warns that before Jesus will really return (Luke 21:8), Jerusalem will fall

---

330. I intend only an analogy; comparison of early Jewish movements, including Christianity, with geographically and chronologically distant Melanesian cargo cults and modern millenarianism (e.g., Gager, *Kingdom*, 20–37) is often rightly cited as an example of imprudent application of sociological models (e.g., Collins, "Apocalyptic Literature," 362).

331. Cf. Carroll, *Response to End*, passim.

332. Boismard and Lamouille, *Actes*, 1:28–29, think that Paul eventually abandoned the idea of a political restoration of Israel; but the apparent decline in his future eschatology may simply reflect better contextualization for a Gentile audience. His restoration theology in Rom 11:26 may not be explicitly political, but those who read it in light of the OT prophecies would take it that way (though Paul differed from the usual scenario, presenting Gentile converts as full proselytes, belonging to the covenant people).

333. On Johannine eschatology, see, e.g., Keener, *John*, 320–23.

334. Hays, *Moral Vision*, 129–31; I do not find most of his examples here persuasive, but the emphasis on the past events of 70 C.E. in Luke 21:20, 24 seems to be.

335. With, e.g., Witherington, *Acts*, 110.

336. Cullmann, "Eschatology and Missions," 416–17.

337. E.g., the late nineteenth-century Student Volunteer Movement (Neill, *History of Missions*, 393–94; Howard, *Student Power*, 91).

338. E.g., Mark 13:14, 29–30; 2 Thess 2:3–4, especially if taken in light of 1 Thess 5:2 (I take 2 Thessalonians to be authentic because I find the composition of 2 Thess 2:4 after 70 C.E. to be inconceivable and pure

(21:24). Beginning with the fall of Jerusalem, the end is "near" (21:28–32), but the duration of the interim remains undefined;[339] after this indefinite period, there will be heavenly signs (21:11, 25–26) and the Son of Man's return (21:25–27).[340] Jesus in the Gospel emphasizes that the timing of the kingdom is unknown (17:20–21); it will surprise the world unexpectedly (17:22–37). Although the disciples know the kingdom's mysteries (8:10), they do not know its timing. Elsewhere in Luke-Acts, the plural expressions "times" or "seasons" can refer to the past era of Gentile ignorance (Acts 17:30), the present "times of the Gentiles" (Luke 21:24), or the future era of restoration (Acts 3:20–21); these nouns, however, are not limited to, and do not necessarily specify, these examples. In a more general manner, they signify especially that God is in control (cf., e.g., Acts 14:17; 17:26).

Contrary to the later Gentile church's de-Judaized way of reading Scripture, Jesus does not deny that Israel's restoration will come.[341] Rather, he merely warns the disciples that it is not their place to know the *times* (1:7),[342] the sort of detailed chronological map offered in some apocalyptic documents;[343] instead, they must focus on their mission (1:8, which may function as a prerequisite for the end).[344] This warning coheres both with Luke's eschatology elsewhere (i.e., leaving the interim period indefinite) and with the Jesus tradition (cf. Mark 13:32; Matt 24:36).[345] (Indeed, as one might infer from Luke's description, a saying of the historical Jesus very likely stands behind the close verbal parallel about unknown "times and seasons" in 1 Thess 5:1, which occurs in a section pervaded by Jesus tradition.)[346] Although the time of

pseudepigraphy to be unlikely in the brief interim between Paul's death and 70). Jewish eschatology can also balance an unknown time of the end with preceding signs (e.g., Bonsirven, *Judaism*, 53).

339. Luke 21:24, probably Luke's redaction, provides for such an undefined interim (Glasson, *Advent*, 72–73).

340. For a survey of source- and redaction-critical perspectives on Luke 21, see Verheyden, "Source(s) of Luke 21."

341. Cf., e.g., Tannehill, *Acts*, 15; McLean, "Correct View of Kingdom?" (though focusing on an ethnic, national entity); Dunn, *Acts*, 10; Witherington, *Acts*, 110n24; Franklin, *Interpreter*, 106; cf. the political reading in Buzzard, "Acts 1:6"; idem, "Eclipse"; *pace*, e.g., Barrett, *Acts*, 78–79. Parsons, "Place of Jerusalem," 168, plausibly argues that its place as "the beachhead for the Gentile mission" exhausts Jerusalem's promised eschatological role; but while it certainly prefigures it (cf. also the Mount of Olives in Acts 1:12; Zech 14:3–5), Jesus's mere evasion of the temporal question suggests that it does not *exhaust* it.

342. Sages could advocate knowing the time (Sir 4:20; Eph 5:16), but this counsel probably involved recognizing its character (cf. Gal 1:4); less relevant here is that particular times (in terms of calendrical precision) could exemplify God's commandments (*Jub.* 23:19). Ultimately God alone knew "the times and the years and the days" (*1 En.* 75:3 [Knibb, 175], regarding astronomical phenomena) and controlled the "times" (*2 Bar.* 48:2; cf. 1QM XIV, 4–5).

343. E.g., *1 En.* 89; *b. Sanh.* 97b–98a; cf. *Test. Levi* 17 (Jubilee periods; perhaps Christian redaction); the Samaritan Chronicle (Bowman, *Documents*, 43, 46–47); perhaps Dan 11 passim; cf. Frost, "Apocalyptic," 144. Others acknowledged that the final time remained secret (e.g., *Pss. Sol.* 17:21; 1QpHab VII, 12–14). Later rabbis debated whether Israel's repentance could hasten the end (*b. B. Bat.* 10a; *B. Meṣiʿa* 85b; *Deut. Rab.* 6:7; *Song Rab.* 2:5, §3; 5:2, §2; 8:14, §1; cf. 2 Pet 3:12; *2 Clem.* 12.3–6; perhaps already *Jub.* 23:26–27) and delay it through sin (*b. Nid.* 13b, bar.; *Sanh.* 97b) or whether God has established that time (e.g., *Exod. Rab.* 25:12; *Lev. Rab.* 15:1; probably *Pss. Sol.* 17:21), or whether it is a combination of both (*Pesiq. Rab.* 31:5). See the survey of rabbinic views in Moore, *Judaism*, 2:350–51.

344. As Luke Timothy Johnson notes, Luke believes in Israel's restoration but expects the universal mission to the ends of the earth to precede it (*Acts*, 29). Johnson (26) associates the "restoration" with Elijah's role as "restorer" (Mal 3:23 LXX, alluded to in Luke 1:17; cf. Sir 48:10); although this may be part of it (cf. Mark 9:12), Elijah restores families and is associated in Luke 1:17 with John rather than with Jesus; Acts 3:21 carries the restoration image much further.

345. Soards, *Speeches*, 24, sees this as "Luke's version of a Synoptic logion not found in Luke's Gospel (see Mark 13:32 and Matt 24:36)," but the wording is too close to 1 Thess 5:1 for coincidence. Others also compare all these sources (e.g., Weiser, *Apostelgeschichte*, 51; cf. Kurzinger, *Apostelgeschichte*, 10).

346. See Keener, *Matthew*, 565–66; Waterman, "Sources"; Ford, *Abomination*, 22; esp. Wenham, *Rediscovery*. My rough, preliminary comparison of parallels between the Thessalonian correspondence and Jesus

Israel's restoration (ἀποκαθιστάνεις, Acts 1:6) is unknown, it presumably happens when the Christ comes "for" them (Acts 3:20), a coming promised at the close of this section (1:11). The "restoration" (ἀποκαταστάσεως) that the prophets announced (3:21) is plainly Israel's (as in 1:6).[347] Other promises within Luke's narrative are fulfilled (including, in this context, baptism in the Spirit); there is no reason to doubt that Luke expects the promise of Jesus's coming (1:11) to turn out the same way.[348]

Jewish traditions also comment on how the future time is unknown.[349] Just as Jewish thinkers experienced a tension between the future time's being divinely fixed and the need for human obedience to facilitate it,[350] Luke notes both the fixed times of Israel's restoration (1:6–7) and the period of the Gentile mission, of indeterminate duration, that will precede it (1:8; cf. 1:11).

Because Luke views Gentile Christians as grafted into Israel's heritage (to borrow Paul's language in Rom 11:17–24), they are a welcome part of Israel's restoration; that is, the church is part of eschatological Israel, and the restored remnant of Israel will also belong to the church.[351] (Even the Jewish people least optimistic about Gentile salvation would have expected sincere proselytes to share Israel's eschatological salvation,[352] and most further allowed for some righteous Gentiles outside this schema, as probably in Acts 15:17, 20. Naturally, they did not expect Gentile adherents to overwhelm Jews numerically, in contrast to the possible proportions in, and hence expectations of, Luke's audience.) Israel's end-time repentance and an end-time ingathering of Gentiles belong together in Isaiah and make good sense as part of Jesus's own teaching.[353] Israel's repentance (3:19) would lead to the fulfillment of end-time promises on Israel's behalf (3:19–21) and the completion of the Gentile era (Luke 21:24). Whether Luke expects more than a remnant of Jewish people to turn to Christ after Acts 28 (and, more critically, after Jerusalem rejects the prophet Paul in Acts 22:22[354] and faces the judgment of 70 C.E.; cf. Luke 13:34–35) continues to be debated, but on the whole, it seems very likely; see discussion in our introduction, chapter 14, section 1.f.

---

tradition, on the one hand, and these parallels and those in the far more vast body of Jewish eschatological sources, on the other (see Keener, *Historical Jesus*, 361–71), led me to the conclusion that the possibility of mere coincidence in the densely packed former parallels is, for practical purposes, virtually nil. Dan 2:21 speaks of God changing "times and epochs," revealing wisdom about future kingdoms and the kingdom; this is less close than 1 Thess 5:1 but may ultimately stand behind the dominical saying.

347. See also Tannehill, *Acts*, 16.

348. Gaventa, *Acts*, 67 (citing idem, "Eschatology Revisited," 37; Carroll, *Response to End*, 126–27). On prediction as an authentication method in ancient historiography, see Rothschild, *Rhetoric of History*, 142–84.

349. See, e.g., *2 Bar.* 21:8; *b. Pesaḥ.* 54b, bar.; *Sanh.* 97a; *Num. Rab.* 5:6; *Tg. Qoh.* 7:24; Moore, *Judaism*, 2:231; Daube, *New Testament and Judaism*, 289–90; Le Cornu, *Acts*, 16. Others noted signs (e.g., *2 Bar.* 27:15 [but *ambiguous* signs]; *Lam. Rab.* 1:13, §41) or virtually set dates (see, e.g., rabbis in *b. Sanh.* 97ab; *Lam. Rab.* proem 21; Bonsirven, *Judaism*, 178; Morris, *Apocalyptic*, 46–47; cf. *Test. Ab.* 7:12 B; *Gr. Ezra* 3:3–4). For imminence more generally, see, e.g., 4Q385 3 3–5; *4 Ezra* 4:44–50; 6:18; 8:61–62; cf. Knibb, *Esdras*, 211.

350. Some viewed the time of redemption as conditional on Israel's merit (e.g., *b. Sanh.* 94a; *B. Bat.* 10a; *B. Meṣiʿa* 85b; *Nid.* 13b, bar.; *y. Taʿan.* 1:1, §7; *Deut. Rab.* 6:7; *Song Rab.* 2:5, §3; 8:14, §1; Manson, *Paul and John*, 23–24; cf. *Jub.* 23:26–27; *2 Clem.* 12); others, as fixed (e.g., *Lev. Rab.* 15:1); for a survey of both conditional and fixed views in the rabbis, see Moore, *Judaism*, 2:350–51; Urbach, *Sages*, 1:669. Some harmonized: God's timing and Israel's repentance were interdependent (*Pesiq. Rab.* 31:5); Israel's repentance could hasten the time that had been scheduled beforehand (*Exod. Rab.* 25:12); but the fixed dates had passed, so only merit could hasten the redemption (an Amora in *b. Sanh.* 97b).

351. Cf. Wolter, "Israel's Future and Delay," 323.

352. See discussion in our introduction, ch. 15, sect. 3.b.i. For a survey of Gentile views about salvation, see esp. Donaldson, *Paul and Gentiles*, 52–74.

353. See further Bird, *Gentile Mission*, 26–29, 177. Schmidt, "Abkehr," believes that the Diaspora mission in Acts supplants the need for an eschatological gathering in Jerusalem.

354. Paralleling Jesus's rejection in Luke 19:41–45.

e. Power for Testimony to the Nations (1:8)

Most scholars recognize that the primary activity of the Spirit emphasized in Acts is the empowering of witnesses for their mission.[355] As noted below, the witnesses specifically addressed in this verse are the Twelve, but their commission becomes paradigmatic for other, later witnesses (e.g., Paul, whom Luke especially emphasizes). They, too, are empowered by the Spirit, a gift for all believers (Acts 2:38–39).

Nevertheless, the consensus is not unanimous. Max Turner, a noted scholar of Lukan pneumatology, is skeptical that the Spirit's primary function in Acts is to empower Christians for mission. He admits that the gift of the Spirit for all Christians (Acts 2:38–39) involves the Spirit of prophecy (2:17–18), that only eight Spirit texts in Acts do not immediately fit prophetic categories in the OT, and that even these can ultimately fit those categories.[356] Yet remarkably, he argues that "with the exception of Paul (Acts 9) there is barely any evidence for the view that Luke thinks the Spirit is given to converts as empowering for mission."[357] He doubts that Acts portrays the Spirit "primarily (Shelton) or ... exclusively (Menzies)" as "empowerment for mission."[358] Turner objects that Luke's summary passages "speak of a variety of aspects of church life" and emphasize only the witness of apostles, not ordinary disciples.[359]

This objection, however, misses the mark: the focus of Acts is on certain leaders (particularly Peter; Stephen and Philip; and Paul and his companions) despite the appearance of "ordinary" disciples at points. Where such ordinary disciples do appear, however, they sometimes carry out similar tasks (e.g., 9:10–17; 22:12), including evangelism (8:4; 11:19–21; cf. the growth of churches, e.g., 2:47, and note moreover that the Seven and, in the Gospel, the Twelve began precisely as ordinary disciples).[360] The primary leaders are both representative of, and paradigmatic for, the mission of the church as a whole. The particular language of "witness" is more often restricted to the apostles, but it is paradigmatic for the entire church's cross-cultural evangelistic mission (see discussion below).

The promise of empowerment for mission is given directly to the apostles (1:8), but that the same power is promised to all the church at Pentecost (2:38–39) implies that all Spirit-empowered believers will contribute to the same task (albeit in diverse ways). The summaries do portray some other important aspects of church life, but the *direct* consequence of the Spirit's empowerment, which Luke explicitly connects with this empowerment, is speaking for Christ, whether for leaders (4:8; 13:9) or for the entire community (4:31). Although the Spirit is also an eschatological gift

---

355. For emphasis on the Spirit's empowerment for missions, see, e.g., Hull, *Spirit in Acts*; Marshall, "Significance of Pentecost"; Stronstad, *Charismatic Theology*; Shelton, *Mighty in Deed*; Penney, *Missionary Emphasis*; Bovon, *Theologian*, 198–238; Meagher, "Pentecost Spirit"; Klaus, "Mission," 574–75; cf. Bruce, "Holy Spirit in Acts"; Russell, "Anointing"; Wyckoff, "Baptism," 448–49; Robinson and Wall, *Called*, 122; Keener, "Power"; missions and evangelism in Haya-Prats, *Believers*, 97–108; prophetic empowerment in Acts 2 in Kremer, *Pfingstbericht*; the church's mission in Bonnah, *Spirit*, 267–390, and esp. 394, 401–2. For the emphasis on mission in early Christianity, see esp. the massive and carefully researched Schnabel, *Mission*; more briefly, idem, "Mission" (on Acts, 766–67).

356. Turner, *Power*, 349–52.

357. Ibid., 348.

358. Ibid., 399; cf. Turner, "Empowerment." Turner, "Work," treats nonsalvific prophetic empowerment as the majority view; while allowing the importance of the Spirit of prophecy, he connects that also with soteriology.

359. Turner, *Power*, 399. He does correctly note (402–4) that although missions is paramount, many mentions of the Spirit in Acts lack *direct* missiological significance (Acts 5:3, 9; 6:3; 11:28; 20:23, 28; 21:4, 11).

360. On earliest Christian evangelism, see Lim, "Evangelism"; Green, *Evangelism*; Beck, "Evangelism."

associated with Israel's restoration (as Turner rightly emphasizes and I comment on at Acts 1:6–8; 2:17–18),[361] the aspect that Luke emphasizes more in his narratives in Acts is empowerment for the mission that must precede that restoration (e.g., 1:8; 2:17–18; 4:8, 31; 7:51; 8:29, 39–40; 10:38; 11:12; 13:2, 4, 9; 16:6–7). The other aspects that Turner notes are real, but they are not Luke's primary narrative focus in most of his work. The immediate function of the Spirit within the narrative world is to empower eschatological mission; the larger function of the Spirit for Luke's audience is as a sign of eschatological restoration; to make these two functions mutually exclusive (which Turner himself does not) is to confuse categories, mixing proverbial apples and oranges.

1. "Power" (1:8)

Luke is emphatic in his promise of "power," repeating it in both Luke 24:49 and Acts 1:8 (though some other elements, including explicit mention of the Spirit, do not appear in both; cf. also Acts 4:33). With most scholars, the power here is directly connected with the task that Acts 1:8 specifically mentions and hence is power to be witnesses among the nations. It is no coincidence that not only this passage but the other dominant programmatic biblical texts in Luke-Acts (Luke 4:18–19; 24:45–48; Acts 2:17–18) refer to the Spirit's empowering God's agents for mission.

The OT and Jewish tradition sometimes spoke of the Spirit's giving people physical strength (Judg 14:6, 19; 15:14; perhaps 1 Sam 11:6–7),[362] and occasionally the Spirit is even called "the spirit of power."[363] But physical strength is not the dominant association here, and in this instance, Luke's own usage elsewhere points in a different direction, one also attested in the OT. Power had other associations with the Spirit; for example, God sometimes gave prophets his Spirit as his power to boldly stand against false prophets (Mic 3:8).[364]

The range of ancient sources about "power" is enormous, whether referring to divine power[365] or power in general.[366] For example, in one tradition, God called Noah (and, by implication for later chapters, Israel) to "grow strong" to subdue the earth.[367] Likewise, God "renews the faithful in his strength."[368] But not all of these sources are as relevant as those above; demanding an explicit connection with the Spirit reduces our data about "power" to more workable proportions. God's "power" is sometimes

---

361. Turner, *Power*, 300, 404–5, citing also Luke 1–3 (but while the Spirit empowers John and Jesus to minister to Israel [Luke 1:15–17; 4:18–19], this foreshadows the Gentile mission in Acts, Acts 2:17; Luke 4:25–27). Turner is surely correct (300), however, about the allusion to Isa 32:15 LXX in Luke 24:49 (// Acts 1:4, 8).

362. Cf. also Elijah in 1 Kgs 18:46, but because the language is absent, we should not envision a deliberate Elijah allusion here.

363. *L.A.B.* 27:10; *Tg. Jon.* on Judg 13:25; 14:6, 19.

364. On Mic 3:8, cf. also Wessels, "Empowered." Cf. Isa 11:2 for the Spirit's power for the Messiah's leadership (similarly, and derivatively, *1 En.* 49:3; *Pss. Sol.* 17:42). Also God's Spirit could help Israel's leaders accomplish their people's restoration, impossible by human power (Zech 4:6–7). Cf. also *1 En.* 68:2; 71:11; cf. *2 Bar.* 85:7; less relevant, *1 En.* 60:15–16.

365. For God's power, cf., e.g., Deut 9:29; Wis 1:3, 5; *1 En.* 1:4; 1QS XI, 19–20; 4Q176 12–13 I, 14; the second paragraph of the Amidah associates this power with resurrecting the dead (e.g., *m. Roš Haš.* 4:5; Sandmel, *Judaism*, 148; cf. Rom 1:4; 1 Cor 6:14).

366. Sometimes "power" referred to political or social power (Dio Chrys. *Or.* 3.62, 89; 38.31; Philost. *Hrk.* 4.1–2; 33.25; Eunapius *Lives* 462), military power (*Jub.* 38:1; 1 Macc 1:4; 2:66; 10:19), or even rhetorical power (Sir 21:7) or magical power (Arnold, *Power*, 34–36, 73–74; cf. Rood, "Christ comme *dynamis*"); for Greek and Roman conceptions of power, see, e.g., Corrington, "Power"; Peradotto and Sullivan, "Introduction," 3.

367. *Tg. Neof.* 1 on Gen 9:1.

368. 4Q521 2 II, 6 (*DSSNT* 421); cf. Isa 40:29, 31; *Test. Job* 4:11; *Pesiq. Rab Kah.* 25:1.

associated with the Spirit (Zech 4:6),[369] sometimes filling individuals to act for God (Mic 3:8, noted above).[370]

Like Paul (Rom 1:4; 15:13, 19; 1 Cor 2:4; Eph 3:16; 1 Thess 1:5; cf. 2 Tim 1:7),[371] Luke elsewhere pairs the "Spirit" with "power" (in addition to here, Luke 1:17, 35; 4:14), sometimes focusing on Jesus's ministry to work miracles as benefactions (Acts 10:38). Particularly distinctive, Luke regularly associates "power" with miraculous healing (Luke 5:17; 6:19; 8:46; 9:1; Acts 6:8; 10:38),[372] although this power is not a permanent possession of Jesus's agents but only of Jesus's name, which they rightly carry (Acts 3:12; 4:7, 10). (One may also compare the potential semantic link to δυνάμεις as "miracles.")[373] The witnesses of Jesus—both the original ones and subsequent ones (14:3)—would bear witness backed by the Spirit's power, which quite often would be expressed in miracles confirming their testimony (14:3). Not surprisingly, signs and wonders (especially healings and exorcisms) constitute the major means of drawing attention to the gospel in Acts (see the discussion in the introduction, ch. 15, sect. 6.b).

II. "Witnesses" (1:8)

"Witness" or "testimony" was a widespread motif in early Christianity; the terms μαρτυρέω, μαρτυρία, μαρτύριον, and μάρτυς appear in the NT 167 times.[374] The clearest evidence in the Jesus tradition applies it to Christians' expected testimony for Christ when tried in court for their faith (Mark 13:9), but multiple sources also indicate that his followers believed that Jesus urged such "testimony" in broader settings as well (Matt 24:14; Luke 24:48; John 15:27).

Jesus tradition is surely relevant here; there is considerable evidence that the distinctive emergence of the Gentile mission in this particular Jewish sect is no coincidence but relates to various elements in the Jesus tradition.[375] More important for the saying in question, multiple sources, varying considerably in individual detail, share the common claim that the risen Christ sent his disciples to proclaim salvation through him (Matt 28:19–20; John 20:21–23; cf. Mark 16:15).[376] (Whether by several of Jesus's

---

369. E.g., Philo *Alleg. Interp.* 1.37, 42. The collocation of terms in Philo *Creation* 131 refers merely to the force of the wind, as in Wis 5:23. Wisdom of Solomon 11:20 refers to "breath of power" but may be more relevant.

370. Cf. Jos. *Ant.* 8.408.

371. For Paul's association of the Spirit with power, see, e.g., the comments of Fee, *Presence*, 35–36.

372. Cf. here Chrys. *Hom. Jn.* 86 (Martin, *Acts*, 10): "And they did become witnesses by their miracles"; Bagalawis, "Power," esp. 2–5. For the association of "power" with miracles, see also Ambrosiaster *Comm.* on Rom 1:16 (CSEL 81:35; Bray, *Romans*, 29); Pelagius *Comm. Rom.* on 15:19 (de Bruyn, 148; Bray, *Romans*, 362). Cf. also Jervell, *Apostelgeschichte*, 115; Hekman, "Power" (including comparison to Native American conceptions); Pervo, *Acts*, 42 ("thaumaturgic and charismatic"); Keener, "Power," 49–50; Haya-Prats, *Believers*, 31–34. The suggestion that Luke introduces "power" to reduce associating the Spirit with miracles (cf. Matt 12:28; Luke 11:20; Menzies, "Power," responding to Turner, "Authoritative Preaching") may go too far (see Acts 10:38; Luke 1:35); miracles constituted a "prophetic" activity.

373. The term usually translated "miracles" is δυνάμεις, which (despite its now conventional usage; see BDAG) might easily be associated with its sense in the singular form, δύναμις (cf., e.g., Luke 10:13; 19:37; Acts 2:22; 8:13; 19:11; again see BDAG). For exorcism and related ideas, see Luke 9:1; cf. 10:19; for "power" and miracles in Paul, see Rom 15:19; though it more often is associated with the "weak" miracle-working message itself (Rom 1:16; 1 Cor 1:18, 24; 2:4–5; Phil 3:10; 1 Thess 1:5; cf. 2 Tim 1:8).

374. Fifty-seven of them in the Fourth Gospel and Johannine epistles, nineteen in Revelation, and thirty-four in Luke-Acts, though this count encompasses various senses of the terms. Textual variants could adjust counts slightly.

375. See Schnabel, "Beginnings," passim, esp. 58; at greatest length, Bird, *Gentile Mission*, passim, esp. 1–3, 172. Bird argues that (in contrast to the developed picture in Paul and Acts) Jesus treated ministry to the Gentiles as simply part of the ongoing Jewish mission, without addressing freedom from Torah (172, 177). He notes that even the "Judaizing" mission competing with Paul accepted a "Gentile mission" more generally (6).

376. See also, e.g., Guillet, "Récits évangéliques"; *pace* Héring, *Second Corinthians*, 110–11. Evidence for preresurrection mention of a Gentile mission is more debatable; see Sanders, *Jesus and Judaism*, 220, on Matt 8:11–12; but in favor, cf. Keener, *Matthew*, 269–70.

words reported *ipsissima verba* in Acts 1:8 or by an extrapolation from his words like those in this verse, it is possible that Jesus was also a source for Paul's understanding of his own mission as being to the ends of the earth; see Rom 15:24, 28.)[377] Jesus also taught them to depend on the Spirit's help for their testimony, not only in Luke (Luke 12:11–12; 21:13–15) but also in the broader Jesus tradition (Mark 13:10–11; John 15:26).[378] The very language of eschatological "witness" probably existed already in the Jesus tradition before Luke's adaptation,[379] although Luke presumably shapes the tradition as needed.

Witness is also a central motif in Luke-Acts (especially Acts).[380] Soards summarizes this motif as applying to five groups in Acts:[381]

1. Apostles (Acts 1:8, 22; 2:32; 3:15; 5:32; 10:39, 41; 13:31)
2. The Holy Spirit (5:32)
3. Paul (22:15; 26:16)
4. Stephen (22:20)
5. *False* witnesses (6:13; 7:58)

(1) Background of Witness Here

The language attributed to Jesus in this verse stems from what scholars often call "Second Isaiah" (esp. Isa 43:9–12; 44:8–9).[382] An emphasis on Isaiah (and an assumption that it will be recognized) is not at all surprising, given its prominent use in this period.[383] The disciples would understand this eschatological Isaiah allusion as relevant to their question about Israel's restoration (Acts 1:6)[384] and recognize its relevance as well to the nations (Luke 24:47) and ends of the earth (Acts 1:8).

In Isaiah, God promised to bring his dispersed people back from among the nations in a new exodus (Isa 43:1–7, 16–19), including from east and west, north and south (43:5–6; cf. Luke 13:29) and from the ends of the earth (as here; Isa 43:6). God would summon the nations to himself at that time and invite them to produce their own witnesses before his court (43:9; 44:9), something they could not do;

---

377. The potential echo in Rom 15 (given views about Spain being at the ends of the earth) might count in favor of the wording "ends of the earth" being close to what Jesus spoke, but Luke 24:47 could suggest that Luke was not particular with the wording; for views regarding Luke's creativity in his first volume's programmatic scene, for example, see esp. Schreck, "Nazareth Pericope." One could argue that "end of earth" here renders a Semitic original, confusing "end of the age" (*'olam*, עוֹלָם; cf. Matt 28:20), but Luke's own wording seems more likely.

378. Cf. also, e.g., Lofthouse, "Spirit in Acts and Fourth Gospel"; Keener, *John*, 1022–24. Some scholars think that John derived his version from the Synoptics (Lincoln, *John*, 394); others see it as independent tradition confirmed by the test of coherency.

379. The eschatological "witness" in Matt 24:14 does not appear in Mark 13:10, but Matthew has probably not simply invented it. "Witness" in Matt 8:4 stems from Mark 1:44 (cf. Luke 5:14); Matt 10:18 is more positive than Mark 6:11 (Luke 9:5), but might borrow its language; yet "testimony" appears probably independently in Luke's eschatological discourse (Luke 21:13).

380. See esp. Soards, *Speeches*, 192–200; cf. also Bovon, *Theologian*, 367–70; Weiser, *Apostelgeschichte*, 72–75; Taylor, "Witness." For the overlap with evangelism (and a focus on Paul), see Aletti, "Evangelizzare."

381. Soards, *Speeches*, 197.

382. See Bruce, *Commentary*, 39; Johnson, "Jesus against Idols"; Penney, *Missionary Emphasis*, 57–58; Turner, *Power*, 300–301; Köstenberger and O'Brien, *Salvation*, 126. At least some Tannaim emphasized this Isaian witness theme for Israel (see Moore, *Judaism*, 2:103–4; cf. 1QS VIII).

383. Fabry, "Jesaja-Rolle," views it as one of Qumran's favorite books; Fritsch, *Community*, 45, considered it the most widely attested book at Qumran, even more than the Pentateuch and Psalms. See especially Mallen, *Reading*, 29–59.

384. Pao, *Isaianic Exodus*, 111–46, shows at length that Luke sees Israel's restoration especially through the lens of Isaiah. Mallen, *Reading*, 98–101, emphasizes Luke's reliance on Isaiah's vision of salvation (cf. 131–32 for Luke's specific emphasis on particular elements of this vision).

their idols could not foretell the future (41:22–24; 42:8–9; 44:6–11; 46:9–10). God's saved people, however, would be his own witnesses in that day (43:10–12; 44:8). This would be the time when God would equip his people with his Spirit to speak for him in order to bring justice to the earth (42:1; 44:3; 48:16; 59:21; 61:1).

Isaiah refers to the return of scattered Israelites, whom God would vindicate against the nations in that time. Many of the Gentiles, their gods vanquished, would honor and serve Israel, turning to their God and to their king and looking to their holy land (49:22; 52:10; 60:3–5, 11, 16; 61:6, 9–11; 62:2; 66:12, 18–20). Other Gentiles would be destroyed (54:3; 60:12; 64:2).[385] But for Luke, eschatological Israel included the Gentile converts[386] made while Israel was scattered among the nations, together with only part of ethnic Israel, the righteous remnant who truly followed God. Luke and his theological sources could have drawn on many passages in Isaiah to support their understanding (Isa 49:6; 52:15; cf., by inversion, 63:16; 65:1); Gentiles were welcome to join the Jewish dispersion and would receive an eternal name better than those of ethnic Jews who did not obey the covenant (56:3–8). Early in Luke's Gospel, John was already announcing a widespread eschatological salvation, and the kingdom was, in some sense, soon to follow (cf., e.g., Luke 3:4–6, quoting Isa 40:3–5 LXX).[387]

If an ideal Lukan reader might infer similar knowledge on the part of Jesus's disciples in the narrative world and hence that they understood the allusions to Isaiah, these disciples might well still misunderstand the sequence of events to follow. In principle, an ancient hearer could approach Isaiah itself as a unity from various interpretive perspectives (various passages could be cited as pointing in various directions). Perhaps Israel would need to be saved and restored *before* the conversion of the nations, or perhaps the apostles were to be witnesses only *against* the nations (cf. Mark 6:11) instead of seeking their conversion (cf. the competing testimony of Israel and idolaters in Isa 43:9–12; 44:6–11). They might establish Jerusalem and expect the remnant of their people to return to Jerusalem, with righteous Gentiles coming there to worship, as in Isaiah.

Only gradually (e.g., Acts 10:28, 45–48; 11:18) will the apostles begin to realize that because their own salvation as God's people has begun, the time for their Gentile mission also has begun. Luke's realized eschatology in the context helps set the stage for this reading of the prophets: the eschatological Spirit signals the "last days," the era of salvation for *all* humanity who call on the Lord (2:17), including those far off (2:39). The fall of Jerusalem in 70 C.E. and further scattering of Judeans (Luke 21:24) would finally vindicate this alternative eschatological plan of glorifying God among the nations. The two stages of the kingdom meant that the disciples should occupy themselves with their eschatological mission but leave the time of Israel's restoration to God (Acts 1:6–8).

385. Various strands of early Judaism followed these diverse visions (see Donaldson, *Paul and Gentiles*, 52–74), including these views: (1) Gentiles were hopelessly lost (*Jubilees*; *4 Ezra*, 52–54; I would add 1QM); (2) proselytes would be welcomed and saved (54–60); (3) there were natural-law "proselytes" (Jos. *Ant.* 20.41; *Sib. Or.* passim; Philo, allowing spiritual circumcision) (60–65); (4) there were some righteous Gentiles (some Tannaim; Gentile sacrifices accepted in the temple) (65–69); (5) there were eschatological pilgrims (69–74). On welcoming God-fearers, cf. also (for the Amoraic period) Hirshman, "Rabbinic Universalism."

386. Pao, *Isaianic Exodus*, 246, notes that Jewish texts link the Gentiles' pilgrimage with Israel's restoration (Tob 14:6; *Pss. Sol.* 17:31; *Test. Sim.* 7:2) but that (p. 247) they are not "equal partners" (*Pss. Sol.* 17:31; *1 En.* 90:30; the greater equality in Philo *Spec. Laws* 1.51–52; 1.309 applies to converts). By contrast, he argues (247–48), Luke accepts Gentiles *as* Gentiles; Pao fruitfully grounds (217–48) Luke's view of Gentiles'/nations' status in Isaiah. Roetzel, *Paul*, 52, thinks that even the LXX translators of Isaiah universalized, advocating "the inclusion of Gentiles in the people of God."

387. The LXX mention of all flesh seeing salvation is consistent with Isaiah's themes; elsewhere the ends of the earth witness it (52:10).

Jesus summons his followers to be witnesses to "the ends of the earth" (1:8), again echoing the range of Isaiah's testimony to God's saving glory (Isa 41:5, 9; 43:6; 45:22; 52:10).[388] (Luke deliberately weaves an allusion to Isa 52:10 into his new exodus quotation in Luke 3:4–6, adding to both Isa 40:3–5 and Luke's Markan source.) The disciples may have understood this witness "to the ends of the earth" as part of their mission in the Jewish Diaspora, since in Isaiah it was scattered Jews who would be witnesses for far-flung places when God saved and vindicated them (Isa 43:10–12; 44:8). In this light, the Gentile mission in Antioch (Acts 11:20–21) may not have seemed inappropriate (before questions about noncircumcision of converts arose); they could have treated it as analogous to Jews welcoming and making proselytes of interested God-fearers. Yet Jesus's first apostles in this passage seem committed to their vision of converting Jerusalem before evangelizing the Diaspora; it is others (many of them presumably bicultural Hellenists already) who therefore precede them in the latter (8:1, 4).

Yet in Acts it is ultimately Paul's deliberate mission to the Gentiles that gives an explicitly different understanding to the Isaiah passage (13:47) as an intentional mission to all peoples.[389] Although others undoubtedly had engaged in such ministry before (and Luke's mention of Isaiah in Acts 8:32–33 suggests that he does not begrudge them this role as forerunners), it is Paul's mission to which Luke gives center stage as a model for subsequent mission to follow. Instead of the mission summoning the righteous to Jerusalem, they must scatter (8:4; 11:19; language reapplied from Diaspora Judaism to Jesus's followers already in 1 Pet 1:1) to win Gentiles to obedience to Israel's God.[390] Retroactively, such an interpretation is easy to miss.[391]

The term "witness" often functioned in a legal context.[392] In such settings, it mattered whether the witness was reliable or unreliable.[393] In classical Athens, witnesses were a more important source than documents, but over time documentary evidence grew more prominent (cf. Justin. *Cod.* 4.20.18);[394] outright mistrust of witnesses, however, belongs only to the later empire.[395] In Judaism, one who was able to testify firsthand yet withheld the testimony could be viewed as liable before God.[396] In the LXX, the term indicates an appeal to objective evidence,[397] and it frequently appears in lawcourt or controversy imagery.[398]

Other uses may have been originally metaphoric extensions,[399] but the metaphor was common enough that the originally figurative use had become by this period

388. God's signs also extended to the ends of the earth (Ps 65:8), as would faith (65:5).

389. For the radical distinctiveness of Paul's activity even in a Greco-Roman context, see esp. Bowers, "Propaganda," 318–19. Paul probably drew on Isaiah to understand his own role in Israel's restoration and in extending "that salvation to the Gentiles" (Wagner, *Heralds*, 29–33). Luke probably knew of missions of the Jerusalem apostles (cf. 1 Cor 9:5; 1 Pet 1:1) but focuses on Paul (see Porter and Westfall, "Cord," 114–15).

390. Ladd, *Young Church*, 93–94, contrasts the building of new relationships, implicit in this mission (e.g., Acts 19:31), with the Qumran model of monasticism.

391. Ironically, although later generations of Christians were effective in promoting Israel's God, they often combined it with anti-Semitism, undermining the strategy that Paul and possibly Luke envisioned (cf. Rom 10:19; 11:11, 14.)

392. E.g., Aeschines *Tim.* 89; Lysias *Or.* 3.14, §97; 3.20–21, §98; 3.27, §98; *Rhet. Alex.* 15, 1431b.21; cf. Casey, "Μάρτυς," 30–31.

393. *Rhet. Alex.* 15, 1431b.22–23; Hermog. *Issues* 45.10–20.

394. Todd, "Evidence," 579. Romans did not have a legal preference for witnesses (Nicholas, "Evidence").

395. Nicholas, "Evidence."

396. Le Cornu, *Acts*, 117, citing *t. Šebu.* 3:2; *b. B. Qam.* 55b–56a.

397. Trites, *Witness*, 16–19.

398. Ibid., 20–47, esp. 35–47 on witness for God in Isa 40–55 (cf. also Cothenet, "Témoignage"). On other Jewish texts, see Trites, *Witness*, 48–65 (Philo bridges the gap between the OT and Hellenistic use); in rabbinic literature, see 231–39.

399. Casey, "Μάρτυς," 30–31.

part of the term's standard semantic range.[400] A Stoic philosopher, for example, could claim that good persons are among God's servants and his μαρτύρων (Epict. *Diatr.* 3.26.28) and that God summons wise people to testify (μαρτύρησόν) concerning what he expects from them (1.29.47). Although the legal setting does not therefore delimit the term's use, we should note that it sometimes functions in this way in Luke-Acts, especially given the frequent setting of persecution and lawcourts (Luke 21:12–15; Acts 22–26).[401]

At the same time, the importance of the term is that it involves verification; Luke writes not a court brief but a historical monograph that, like a legal brief, can be verified or falsified by testimony (Luke 1:2). Personal testimony implied firsthand knowledge (usually historical[402] but occasionally revelatory).[403] Naturalists regarded eyewitness observations of phenomena as particularly noteworthy (Sen. Y. *Nat. Q.* 3.25.8); likewise, a general might refuse to credit a report until confirmed by an eyewitness (Xen. *Hell.* 6.2.31). But most relevant to Luke's genre, historians reckoned eyewitness evidence particularly reliable.[404] Writers could cite other authors as if witnesses in a courtroom; Josephus thus produces historians as "witnesses" for his claims (*Ag. Ap.* 1.4), and Plutarch claims that Homer testifies (μαρτυρεῖ) in support of his view (Plut. *Or. Delphi* 22, *Mor.* 405A). Thucydides, recognizing the dangers of oral tradition, focused primarily on contemporary history, where sources could be cross-examined;[405] "Polybius (e.g., Polyb. 4.2.3), pays at least lip service to Thucydides's views on evidence, but the question did not apparently worry Roman writers."[406] Luke himself, who has examined at least some eyewitnesses (Luke 1:2–3; Acts 16:10), naturally follows the historiographic tradition of the Greek East, using testimonies as part of his own case for his hearers, just as do the witnesses in his narrative world.

(2) Who Are Luke's Witnesses?

Luke applies the term "witness" especially to the eyewitnesses of the gospel story that he recounts in his first volume (Acts 1:21–22). The apostles had to bear witness to Jesus's resurrection in a variety of settings (2:32; 3:15; 4:33; 5:32; 10:39, 41; 13:31).[407] Jesus had performed miracles as a testimony (Luke 5:14; Mark 1:44; cf. Acts 2:22) and earlier sent his disciples and commanded them to provide testimony against those who rejected their message (Luke 9:5, presumably effective in the day

400. See, e.g., Arist. *Rhet.* 1.15.13, 1375b; 1.15.17; Plut. *Apoll.* 14, *Mor.* 108E; *Or. Delphi* 22, *Mor.* 405A; *Nic.* 6.3; Libanius *Maxim* 3.3; Jos. *Ag. Ap.* 1.4; *Jub.* 1:12. Trites, *Witness*, 4–15, shows that they were used in both legal and nonlegal (e.g., historiographic) contexts to establish data. "Witness" could be linked with "evidences," "sign," and "example," as Hermog. *Method* 4.417 finds in Thucyd. 1.1, 6, 8.

401. Cf. also Trites, *Witness*, 129–33; Soards, *Speeches*, 199.

402. Cf. Aune, *Environment*, 81, citing Hdt. 2.99; Polyb. 12.27.1–6; 20.12.8; Lucian *Hist.* 47 (on αὐτοψία, eyewitness knowledge). Luke's specific term in Luke 1:2 is not limited to historiographic contexts (see Collins, "Eyewitnesses," 450) but normally does involve firsthand experience (including in the examples that Collins cites; in history, see Jos. *Ag. Ap.* 1.55, distinct from participation but describing direct acquaintance).

403. E.g., *1 En.* 104:11; 105:1; cf. Aune, *Prophecy*, 115. The language of "testimony" can also apply to disciples' accounts of their teachers' supernatural exploits (συνεμαρτύρουν; Eunapius *Lives* 459). Those skeptical of secondhand supernatural testimony sometimes proved more receptive if the testimony was from an eyewitness (e.g., Philost. *Hrk.* 7.9; 8.2, 6–7, though this is a novel).

404. Aune, *Environment*, 81 (citing, e.g., Polyb. 12.27.1–6; 20.12.8; Lucian *Hist.* 47); also Xen. *Ages.* 3.1; see further discussion in our introduction, ch. 4, sect. 1.d. See Trites, *Witness*, 136–39, for Acts' emphasis on the *eyewitness* character of its testimony.

405. More than witnesses in an Athenian lawcourt from the same period (Todd, "Evidence," 579)!

406. Ibid., 579 (though overstating the case through excessive dependence on Livy and Cicero *De or.* 2.62; *Brut.* 42; see our introduction, ch. 3, sects. 1.b, 2.a).

407. Cf. Turner, "Every Believer as Witness?"; Köstenberger and O'Brien, *Salvation*, 126–27. Even in the immediate context, however, the witnesses extend beyond the eleven to all who were present for the events (Luke 24:33, "those who were with them"; see Dillon, *Eye-Witnesses*, 291).

of judgment; Mark 6:11); in the Gospel the wicked also were said to testify against themselves (Luke 11:48; cf. 4:22; paradoxically, 22:70–71).

But just as the supernatural empowerment was not for the first witnesses alone (Acts 2:39), neither is the commission to testify about what one has seen, which applied to both Paul (22:15, 18; 23:11; 26:16, 22; cf. 20:26) and Stephen (22:20). Others, too, would "see and hear" dramatic events about which they could bear witness (2:33; 8:6; and esp. 22:15; for the original disciples, see Luke 10:24; Acts 4:20; for others before the disciples, Luke 2:20; 7:22).[408] The prophets "bore witness" before Jesus's coming (Acts 10:43; cf. 1 Pet 1:11–12),[409] and so the role of witness was never *limited* to the Twelve.[410]

Further, Acts does not report (as later tradition does) the dispersal of the original witnesses to the nations, despite Luke's commitment to the Gentile mission (and the probability of at least some trips, 1 Cor 9:5). Yet witness to the "ends of the earth" fulfills an eschatological prerequisite (rooted in the restoration of Israel texts in Isa 41:5, 9; 43:6, 10; 45:22; 52:10) that in Luke's day remained incomplete. Although the commission as witnesses thus refers, in the first instance, to the eyewitnesses of Jesus's public ministry (Acts 1:21–22), it functions paradigmatically for the mission of the church in its Gentile mission.[411] Luke's narrative will thus fill out what they were to expect in the course of being witnesses, especially in terms of sufferings.[412]

(3) Content of Witness

In view of Luke 24:46–48, the parallel passage in the Gospel that informs this one, the disciples are to bear witness concerning the gospel story (with an emphasis on Jesus's passion and resurrection), to which they are eyewitnesses. Because this story is a microcosm of Luke's own Gospel (especially in its expanded form implied in Acts 1:21–22), Luke probably sees his own mission as reporter in similar terms, providing a detailed narrative based on his consultation with witnesses (Luke 1:2). The focus of the gospel story is Jesus's suffering and resurrection on the third day, according to the Scriptures (24:46–47; the "these things" of 24:48; cf. 1 Cor 15:3–4); the appropriate response to the proclamation is repentance (Luke 24:47).

Although the focus of the testimony's content is the gospel story (especially given Luke's emphasis on narrative), Luke's wording also implies the relevance of Christology here (cf. Acts 2:36). That Jesus calls them to be "*my* witnesses" (1:8; not mentioned in Luke 24:48 but perhaps implied in 24:46–48) evokes the language of "my witnesses" in Isaiah, but there it is God speaking (Isa 43:10, 12; 44:8).[413] Although Luke's narrative does not articulate an understanding of Jesus's deity in the early Jerusalem church, he presumably can take for granted this belief in his circle of churches (cf. Rom 9:5 for possible use of the language;[414] for clearer use of the idea in some

408. For Luke, Isa 6:9–10 sets the tone for the failure of some to see and hear (Luke 8:10, 18; Acts 28:26).

409. On the prophets as "witnesses" in *Jub.* 1:12; 4Q216, see Steck, "'Zeugen' und 'Tora-Sucher.'"

410. Using the image of character witness (Acts 6:3; 10:22; 16:2; 22:5, 12; 26:5), God himself bore witness to his servants (13:22), including the Gentiles who accepted him (15:8), but especially to the message of his generosity (14:3).

411. Cf. Gebauer, "Mission und Zeugnis"; Bolt, "Mission" (Acts invites readers to follow its own model of propagating the message of the apostolic witnesses).

412. Cf. Rosenblatt, *Paul the Accused*, passim, who rightly argues that Luke uses Paul as a model for others who will also suffer for the Christian mission.

413. For the image of divine activity in Acts 1:8, see also Mallen, *Reading*, 82.

414. Many scholars favor the probability (e.g., Sanday and Headlam, *Romans*, 233–38; Cullmann, *Christology*, 313; Fahy, "Note"; Longenecker, *Christology*, 138; Schlatter, *Romans*, 202–3; esp. Cranfield, *Romans*, 2:467–68; Harris, *Jesus as God*, 143–72), though others disagree (e.g., Hunter, *Romans*, 90; Johnson, *Romans*, 157; cf. Hunter, *Gospel according to Paul*, 62–63). That this expression occurs in praise (so, e.g., Burridge and Gould, *Jesus*, 94) suggests functional, rather than dogmatic, interest.

sense, 1 Cor 8:6; Phil 2:6–7).[415] The exegesis of Joel 2:32 suggested in Acts 2:21 and 2:38 reinforces the likelihood that Luke intends 1:8 to suggest a divine Christology.

The rest of Acts provides frequent examples of the Spirit-filled speech that this passage predicts (e.g., 2:4; 4:8, 31; 13:9).[416]

f. Jerusalem to the Ends of the Earth (1:8)

The mission summarized here represents the theme of Acts (the Gentile mission), which moves from heritage to mission (see introduction, ch. 13, sect. 2.a).[417] Acts marks an obvious geographic shift from Jerusalem to Rome,[418] theologically underlining the movement of the narrative (and ideally of the community's focus) from heritage to mission. Even here in the introduction, the focus shifts from Israel's promised restoration (1:6) to the Gentile mission (1:8), likewise appropriate to the eschatological era.[419] Jesus's words about the mission are stated as a promise rather than as a command,[420] and this mission will be successful because "the most reliable of characters" has promised it.[421]

Ancient critics sometimes expressed annoyance with those who, having expressed a subject, digressed from it.[422] Luke, however, maintains his newly stated focus on the Gentile mission throughout this volume. (Contrary to first impressions, he even prefigures it in his Gospel; see the comment on the Gentile mission in our introduction, ch. 15, sect. 3.a. See also comment on Acts 1:8 as an outline for Acts, below.) The mission's expansion here is expressed geographically, but Acts develops it ethnically as well, so that the gospel crosses all barriers; we blandly call this the "Gentile mission" but could also call it the "universal mission."[423]

Early Christian supporters of the Christian mission (including Matthew, John, and Paul as well as Luke) needed to articulate their understanding of the mission carefully partly because their activity was so distinctive.[424] Traveling merchants, preachers, and even priests spread their religions as they traveled; Jews

415. See, e.g., Witherington, *Corinthians*, 198; Bauckham, *Crucified*, 38, 52–53; Longenecker, "Contours," 126–28; Hooker, *Preface*, 84. For Paul on Christ's deity more generally, see, e.g., Wright, *Founder*, 63–72; Howell, "Interchange"; for Christ's preexistence in Paul, see, e.g., Byrne, "Pre-existence"; *pace* Dunn, *Theology of Paul*, 266–93.

416. See Soards, *Speeches*, 44. On the Spirit and the Gentile mission, see, e.g., Philip, *Pneumatology*, 204–24; on the Spirit and witness, see Haya-Prats, *Believers*, 97–103; on the Spirit and evangelism, 103–8.

417. On the mission's centrality in Acts, see, e.g., Mangatt, "Believing Community"; Bovon, *Theologian*, 238; see further ch. 15, sect. 3, in my introduction.

418. E.g., Streeter, *Gospels*, 531–32 (titling Acts "The Road to Rome," 532); Neil, *Acts*, 27; Packer, *Acts*, 2; Eckey, *Apostelgeschichte*. This pattern also fits the work as a whole, since the Gospel begins and ends in Jerusalem (Marguerat, *Histoire*, 93; idem, *Historian*, 65). Although most scholars have viewed the two cities as antithetical, Luke embraces both (Marguerat, *Histoire*, 115–18; idem, *Historian*, 82–84; cf. Bovon, *Studies*, 31).

419. Both grounded in Isaiah's eschatology (see Pao, *Isaianic Exodus*, 229) but shifting the focus from God's activity (Israel's restoration) to what Luke's audience could help bring about (evangelizing all peoples).

420. Gaventa, *Acts*, 175. On every other occasion in Luke-Acts, the second future middle indicative (as well as all plural future middle indicatives) of εἰμί is a prediction rather than a command (Luke 1:20; 5:10; 6:35; 11:19; 12:52; 13:30; 14:14; 17:34–35; 21:11, 17, 25; 23:43; Acts 13:11; 22:15). But in the two most relevant cases, the prediction may welcome participation (Luke 5:10; Acts 22:15); cf. thus Pervo, *Acts*, 41, regarding "the implicit imperative."

421. Parsons, *Departure*, 155.

422. E.g., Philost. *Hrk.* 25.13 (though eager, in any case, to critique Homer).

423. A more accurate designation, since the "Jewish mission" continues. On the mission's including the ethnic as well as the geographic element, see, e.g., Stagg, *Acts*, 10–11, 36 (although playing down Luke's geographic framework, from Jerusalem to Rome, too much).

424. Mission in the Christian sense was distinctively Christian in this period (Heimgartner, "Mission"), though later also Manichaean and Islamic (Heimgartner, "Mission," 63; Toral-Niehoff, "Mission: Islam").

also welcomed proselytes.[425] All of this religious zeal occasionally drew xenophobic Roman ire when it converted Romans in Rome, though the Romans were generally legally *tolerant* of such activity even in the capital.[426] But Paul's mission went considerably beyond most contemporary models. Ancient cults provided propaganda, but this was typically limited to public ceremonies and inscribed testimonies.[427] In pagan circles, traveling teachers carried their messages, but we lack evidence for their "sense of vocation deliberately to attempt a geographically-defined expansion," or a systematic mission like Paul's.[428]

Despite some Jewish people who may have actively sought proselytes (like a traveling merchant in Jos. *Ant.* 20.34–48), Judaism did not send formal "missionaries."[429] (Nor, given their pervasive presence in the Diaspora, would Jewish people have needed to do so; they had simpler, less confrontational, ways to win Gentiles to their faith.[430] Some scholars envision a concerted Jewish mission to the Gentiles;[431] they are right in recognizing some Jews' interest in making proselytes,[432] but the evidence does not support any centralized effort, which is what many mean by a "missions" movement.) For the early Christians, what was especially unique was their message, not their method, yet the current state of scholarly discussion suggests that the methodology of Paul and his circle was also distinctive to a considerable degree in that era.

1. Jerusalem

For those who knew it especially through their Bible, Jerusalem evoked a rich plethora of images surrounding Israel's heritage, from David's time forward.[433] (Luke often employs the indeclinable Septuagintal name for Jerusalem, Ἰερουσαλήμ,[434] as in Acts 1:8, but sometimes, as in 1:4, the declinable Ἱεροσόλυμα,[435] which in Greek presumably evokes the thought of the ἱερόν, the temple.[436] He usually prefers the familiar Septuagintal spelling for the city in Acts 1–10,[437] reinforcing the premise that he evokes a "biblical" milieu in the early chapters of Acts.) Apart from the gospel story, Luke's ideal audience would have known more about Jerusalem than Galilee,

425. Most often they apparently attracted them through their behavior (McKnight, "Proselytism," 842–44).

426. Cf. Juv. *Sat.* 3.60–63; Gager, "Class," 107; idem, *Anti-Semitism*; Keener, *Paul*, 140–42; Nilsson, *Piety*, 185.

427. Stambaugh and Balch, *Environment*, 43.

428. Bowers, "Propaganda," 318–19.

429. See ibid., 320–21; Murphy-O'Connor, "Jewish Mission?"; McKnight, *Light among Gentiles*; Cohen, "Missionize"; see some related discussion under the Gentile mission's background in our introduction, ch. 15, sect. 3.b.

430. See, e.g., Donaldson, *Paul and Gentiles*, 59. Some later rabbinic advocacy of winning proselytes may react to Christian successes in converting pagans (Goodman, "Proselytizing"). I believe that Matthews, *Converts*, 3, is correct to allow for Jewish "mission" if we understand it to mean that some Jews actively pursued proselytes. (It does not seem to be deliberate geographic relocation, although it might resemble Paul's activity: traveling merchants could proselytize [Jos. *Ant.* 20.34–48], and Paul could work.)

431. E.g., Paget, "Proselytism"; Ker, "Missionary Activity"; Rokéah, "Proselytism." For Abraham as a model missionary in later sources, see Hayward, "Abraham as Proselytizer."

432. Hence the reaction against proselytization in Rome; Diaspora Jewish literature sensitive to Gentile concerns (and welcoming interested proselytes, e.g., *Joseph and Aseneth*); and so forth.

433. Dunn, *Acts*, 2, regards Jerusalem as a theological as well as geographic starting point, emphasizing the heritage that informs the mission throughout (even as late as Acts 28:20).

434. Seventy-four times in the NT; 790 times in the LXX (including the Apocrypha except 2 Maccabees); Luke uses this title sixty-two times (thirty-six times in Acts).

435. Sixty-two times in the NT; thirty-two times in the LXX, but all are in the Apocrypha, mostly in the Maccabean literature, esp. 2 Maccabees.

436. Klauck, *Magic*, 4–5. Pliny the Elder notes that Bambyx in Syria was called Hierapolis, "Holy City" (*N.H.* 5.19.81; cf. a town named Hiero, "Holy," on the Black Sea, 6.5.17).

437. Cf. Ross, "Spelling of Jerusalem."

both because of their biblical heritage and the relative fame of urban Jerusalem (even before 70 C.E. and certainly afterward).[438]

Although Luke, who employs Mark extensively in his Gospel, must have been aware of the widespread tradition that Jesus spent time with his disciples in Galilee after the resurrection (Mark 14:28; 16:7; Matt 26:32; 28:7, 10, 16; John 21:1), he simplifies the movement in his narrative by mentioning only the disciples' experience in Jerusalem (compare Luke 24:6 with Mark 16:7), which also seems to be part of the tradition of resurrection appearances (John 20:1–29).

Some scholars have thought that Jesus's Judean and Galilean resurrection appearances are incompatible; Marxsen, for example, thinks that Mark emphasized a parousia in Galilee (Mark 14:28; 16:7) and was followed by later traditions in Matt 28 and John 21 whereas Luke and John had Judean appearances.[439] But both kinds of appearances appear early in the tradition; it made little sense to invent Galilean appearances, despite Mark's favoritism toward Galilee, and it is difficult to account for Luke's certitude in Acts without a Judean apostolate, despite his theological use of Jerusalem (see further comment below).

Sanders suggests that when Luke's Jerusalem center is taken into account, the most plausible scenario is that the disciples "fled to Galilee and then returned to Jerusalem,"[440] where Galileans often traveled in any case.[441] Yet some of Luke's details require an appearance in Jerusalem before the flight to Galilee. Luke indicates that Jesus left two Judean disciples about sundown (Luke 24:29, 31), and the disciples hurried immediately to Jerusalem (24:33), where Jesus greeted all the disciples together (24:36).

That the closest disciples remained in Jerusalem immediately after the Passover despite fears of persecution (cf. John 20:19) makes sense, since they would be in mourning for their master, who had just been buried. This mourning period normally lasted seven days.[442] The disciples would naturally be continuing in their most intense mourning period at this time; later rabbinic traditions suggest that such mourning included sitting on the ground without shoes and abstaining from working, washing, anointing, and even study of Torah.[443] One might expect them not to travel during this time. Mark's Galilean emphasis explains why Jesus promises an appearance to the disciples in Galilee (Mark 14:28; 16:7). But since the disciples were from Galilee and had families and fellow disciples there (who would have returned after Passover if they had come to Jerusalem and who would need to hear about the Lord's resurrection), it is also historically likely that they did return there (again, even if one were skeptical of resurrection appearances there). Interestingly, the author of John 21 does not treat the Galilean appearance as incompatible with a prior Judean appearance such as in Luke (John 21:1).[444]

Thus it is possible that the disciples met Jesus in Jerusalem, then followed him again to Galilee, after the need to mourn had vanished,[445] and then were sent back

438. After the loss of Jerusalem, later rabbinic tradition increasingly idealized it (e.g., *m. Šeqal.* 8:1; *'Abot R. Nat.* 35; *b. Pesaḥ.* 19b).

439. Marxsen, *Mark*, 82–83. For Marxsen, Luke prefers Jerusalem because of its centrality in biblical history (as already noted, this centrality would be relevant to his audience's interests); a return to Galilee (where Mark's community still expected the parousia, in Marxsen's view!) would be a regression (109).

440. Sanders, *Figure*, 278.

441. Jerusalem functioned as a symbolic center for Galileans as well; see Freyne, "'Servant' Community," 109.

442. Sir 22:12; Jdt 16:24; cf. *L.A.E.* 51:2; *Apoc. Mos.* 43:3; *b. Ketub.* 8b and sources in Sandmel, *Judaism*, 201.

443. See Safrai, "Home," 782.

444. On the majority view, the author would know that he was appending the account to John 20; I have argued elsewhere that there is good reason to suppose that both "authors" are in fact the same author (Keener, *John*, 1219–22).

445. By John's chronology, the initial Jerusalem stay requires at least ten days after the crucifixion (John 20:26).

to Jerusalem well before Pentecost. Even the journey to Galilee was not undertaken overnight, however, and so it seems easier for us not to suppose that the "forty days" (Acts 1:3) all transpired in Jerusalem; it could thus be after the disciples had returned to Jerusalem that Jesus gives his command to remain there, perhaps a week or so before Pentecost.[446] If Jesus and his disciples arrived in Jerusalem several days, perhaps as much as a week, early for Passover (Luke 19:28; 21:37; 22:7), it is not incredible that the disciples would have arrived perhaps a week or more early for Pentecost, even had they lacked specific instructions concerning their mission there.

Although Luke has reason to emphasize Jerusalem's centrality, he does not *invent* it: historically, it was the center of the apostolic mission (Rom 15:19, 25–26, 31; 1 Cor 16:3),[447] and the pre-Pauline apostles remained there for some time (Gal 1:17–18; 2:1). To argue otherwise is to extrapolate a permanent return to Galilee from the Gospels' mention of disciples returning there temporarily, while ignoring earlier and more explicit textual evidence suggesting that the movement began in Jerusalem.[448] Nor does Luke explicitly rule out any Galilean appearances, as if he polemicizes against a competing Galilee tradition. Luke is not anti-Galilean (e.g., Luke 1:26; 2:39; 4:14; Acts 1:11; 9:31; 10:37; 13:31), though both his focus on the church's Judean heritage and his own urban Aegean cultural sphere render him much more enthusiastic about the biblically familiar and urban Jerusalem.

More important, the readers who knew enough of Pentecost (Acts 2:1) to know that it was a biblical pilgrimage festival would readily infer that many Galilean Passover pilgrims would have normally returned to Galilee and then returned to Jerusalem later for Pentecost.[449] Again, Luke does not rule out Galilean appearances that he does not narrate; we do not need to exclude historical evidence that could be complementary rather than contradictory. (Jesus's command to remain in Jerusalem in Luke 24:49 and Acts 1:4 occurs, according to Luke's chronology, in connection with the ascension *after* forty days of appearances and hence would not exclude any *prior* return to Galilee.)[450] But by omitting intervening Galilean appearances and focusing exclusively on Jerusalem, Luke clarifies his focus on Jerusalem, the theological (as well as historical) location of the mission's beginning.[451]

The theological priority of Jerusalem could explain Luke's invention if it were such, but in light of all the evidence, it explains the disciples' historical relocation to Jerusalem even better. The earliest Christians may well have accorded the location

446. I estimate a week because the forty days would begin with resurrection appearances, which sources suggest began on the day of the resurrection. Forty could be a round number, but if Jesus chose it (as he did the twelve disciples) for symbolic value, he may have stayed with them for a full forty days to communicate the point; see comment on Acts 1:3.

447. On Jerusalem as "sacred center" for Paul, see, e.g., Stowers, *Rereading of Romans*, 131; cf. Bornkamm, *Paul*, 53.

448. Skarsaune, *Shadow*, 147–48; *pace* Watson, *Gentiles*, 68. This evidence also undermines attempts to attribute the Jerusalem church's centrality to mythmakers there opposed by Paul (*pace* Smith, "Jerusalem Church"); Paul knows the pillars in Jerusalem (Gal 1:17–19; 2:9–10), and Luke would hardly exalt them at the expense of his hero Paul.

449. Some Diaspora Jews who had traveled from a farther distance (and hence made pilgrimage rarely) might well remain for the entire period (see comment on Acts 2:9–11), but Galileans (with business to attend to at home) probably would not. Luke's audience is probably familiar with the festivals (cf., e.g., Acts 20:6).

450. The claim, based on Luke 24:49, that the disciples spent the entire time "waiting" in Jerusalem (Dunn, *Acts*, 3), neglects Luke's subsequent clarification of a forty-day interim before that command (Acts 1:3–4), to which no geographic location is specifically attached. Given the distance, the disciples could have gone to Galilee and back even several times during that period had they wished (although there is no reason to suppose such movement) before returning.

451. See Dunn, *Acts*, 3–4. This provides a neater conjunction between chronology and geography (Luke 24:6; Acts 10:37; 13:31).

eschatological significance (cf. Acts 1:6);[452] Luke's mention of Olivet in 1:12 may suggest that he himself recognized such significance in view of Zech 14:4. Jerusalem was for Judaism the theological center of the world;[453] many Jews viewed it as the center literally (cf. Ezek 5:5; 38:12).[454] Thus texts might portray judgment beginning at the temple (Ezek 9:3–7; 10:18–19; 11:22–23) or in Jerusalem (Jer 25:17–26), and the center of future eschatological hope as Jerusalem (Isa 2:3; Mic 4:1–3).

Although, for most Greeks and some others influenced by them, the world's "navel" was Delphi,[455] most of the empire saw the political center of their world as Rome; Rome even included one monument measuring distances to major cities in the empire, with another monument to its north, the Umbilicus Romae, as the symbolic center of the Roman world.[456] Greek novels set in a past era might omit Rome,[457] but Luke, writing about events in the recent real world of the empire, could hardly do so.

A mission from Jerusalem to Rome (as far as the book of Acts carries us) moves from the heart of salvation history to the heart of the empire, hence from heritage to mission (in contrast to the Gospel, which begins and ends in Jerusalem). In his Gospel, Luke gives little play to Jesus's Markan journeys in Gentile territory (except in Luke 8:26–39),[458] just as Luke reserves his emphasis on the Gentile mission especially for his second volume.

One should not think that these interests are mutually exclusive chronologically (whatever Luke's alleged penchant for dividing time into eras; cf. Gal 2:7–9). Just as a Jewish mission remains in effect concurrent with the Gentile mission (e.g., Acts 13:46; 18:6; 19:8–9; 28:28),[459] the Jerusalem church was flourishing in 21:20 and presumably continued to flourish for several more years until the beginning of the Judean-Roman war of 66–70 C.E.

452. See further Taylor, "Jerusalem and Temple."

453. E.g., for its centrality in Josephus (without his emphasizing it eschatologically), see Feldman, "Importance." For John 7:37–38, see Keener, *John*, 722–30.

454. *Jub.* 8:12 (for Zion's role in *Jubilees*, cf. Sulzbach, "Geography"); *Sib. Or.* 5.249–50 (probably late first to early second century C.E. Egypt); *b. Yoma* 54b. Cf. also Scott, "Horizon," 526; Alexander, "Imago mundi"; Paczkowski, "Ombelico" (including its influence on later Christian conceptions); Davies, *Gospel and Land*, 7. *Let. Aris.* 83 (cf. 115, μέση for seaports, also) places the center in the midst of Judea, as does Jos. *War* 3.52. *1 En.* 26:1 may place the middle of the earth in Jerusalem (26:2–6). This view may have reacted polemically against the Delphic claim (Alexander, "Omphalos"; see below). For the temple as the center, see *Jub.* 8:19; *b. Sanh.* 37a; *Num. Rab.* 1:4; *Lam. Rab.* 3:64, §9; *Pesiq. Rab.* 10:2; 12:10; cf. Hayman, "Observations"; Schäfer, "Schöpfung"; Goldenberg, "Axis"; for its foundation stone, *t. Kip.* 2:14; *Lev. Rab.* 20:4; *Num. Rab.* 12:4; *Pesiq. Rab Kah.* 26:4; cf. Böhl, "Verhältnis"; for the Sanhedrin, *b. Soṭah* 45a; perhaps *Song Rab.* 7:3, §1 (in light of Soranus *Gynec.* 1.17.57–59). For a "navel" *within* a city, see Pindar *Dith.* 4, frg. 75 (possibly on a prominent altar within Athens); cf. Paus. 10.16.3.

455. Eurip. *Med.* 667–68 (ὀμφαλὸν γῆς); *Orest.* 591 (μεσομφάλους); Pindar *Pyth.* 4.74; 8.59–60; 11.10; *Paeans* 6.17; 21, frg. 54 (in Strabo 9.3.6); Varro *L.L.* 7.2.17 (*umbilicus*); Livy 38.48.2; Ovid *Metam.* 10.168; 15.630–31; Lucan *C.W.* 5.71; Men. Rhet. 1.3, 366.29; see further Schachter, "Omphalos"; cf. McGinnis, "Center." Scott, "Horizon," 485, cites Hdt. 4.36 and Arist. *Mete.* 2.5.362b.13; cf. Geroussis, *Delphi*, 6; Nikopoulou-de Sike, *Delphi*, 5–6. Scott, "Horizon," 486, cites later Greek writers who made Rhodes the center (Agathemerus *Geographiae informatio* 1.5). While Philost. *Hrk.* 29.9 applies the phrase "belly of earth" literally to an oracular chasm, he probably intends a parallel to the Delphic use. Harrelson, *Cult*, 36, may also be correct in citing Mesopotamian parallels, though even unrelated cultures could see their own land as the world's center (e.g., China; Kantowicz, *Rage of Nations*, 45).

456. McRay, *Archaeology*, 344. Rome is central in the Peutinger map (*Tabula Peutingeriana*) (Jewett, *Romans*, 912); for early Roman ideology about Rome's centrality, see Dillery, "Roman Historians," 94–95. Most peoples saw themselves as in the world's middle (e.g., Pliny E. *N.H.* 2.80.190; likewise, although Pliny viewed the earth as spherical [2.65.161–65], he was certain that the cosmos was geocentric [2.69.176]). For a symbolic imperial shift of center, see Bexley, "Rome."

457. Cf. Schwartz, "Rome in Novel."

458. See Hengel, "Geography of Palestine," 32–33.

459. See, e.g., Jervell, "Israel und Heidenvölken"; and discussion in our introduction regarding Israel.

Acts 1:8 is a paradigm based on salvation-historical priority, and Luke does not provide a clear indication of how his own audience should adapt it. Presumably, they, like the apostles, would start their mission at their own location.[460] The geographic pattern of Paul's ministry in 26:20 closely follows the paradigm of 1:8 (cf. Luke 24:27), except that it appropriately starts where Saul found himself just after his conversion, and when it returns to Jerusalem, it returns to his home (cf. Acts 8:1). Yet Luke's primary audience in the sphere of the Pauline mission will most identify not with Jerusalem (or starting there) but with the fact that they are part of those carrying on the mission to the "ends of the earth" (on which see discussion below).

II. Judea and Samaria

Instead of the τε that precedes Ἰερουσαλήμ being pleonastic in view of the following polysyndeton (the three occurrences of καί that follow), we might translate, "not *only* in Jerusalem but also . . ." Because one feminine definite article covers both the Greek words for Judea and Samaria, we should think of them together as the next stage of the mission (thus we read of more of the Judean mission in 9:32–43, *after* the Samaritan mission of 8:5–25).[461] Thus we may have not four geographic sections of Acts[462] but three.

Luke may occasionally employ the title "Judea" for the entire province under the governor (i.e., Judea and Samaria without Galilee; Luke 3:1); sometimes he employs it for all Palestine (Luke 1:5; 7:17; 23:5; Acts 10:37), but most often for the Jewish land (what "Judea" means) minus Samaria, Galilee, and perhaps even Caesarea.[463] Sometimes Luke also distinguishes Judea from Jerusalem (Luke 6:17; Acts 1:8; 8:1);[464] the meaning here might be, "the rest of the Jewish homeland inhabited by Jews" as opposed to Gentiles and Samaritans. Thus the disciples are to start with the ancestral capital, spread to the rest of Jewish Palestine, and then (shifting from primarily topographic to primarily cultural distinctions) to Samaria. The "ends of the earth" could then mean everything else, whether Diaspora Jews or Gentiles or both.[465]

III. Background for the Phrase "Ends of the Earth"

When Luke provides his basic thesis for Acts in 1:8, he also has in mind the programmatic passage he will provide in 2:17–21 (parallel to the Isaiah text's role in Luke 4:18–19). There salvation will come to "all humanity" (Acts 2:17; cf. Luke 3:6), by which Luke (as likely opposed to Peter, the speaker in the narrative world) implies Gentiles as well as Jews (cf. Acts 2:39); there, as in this context (1:6–8), this will be accomplished in the "last days" by the Spirit's enablement (2:17–18). But whereas Joel provides some of the backdrop, themes from Isaiah constitute the foreground.

---

460. For applications starting locally, see, e.g., Kanyoro, "Mission," 62. Jerusalemites believed that people from the ends of the earth were already coming to them for worship (Jos. *War* 5.17). Subsequent narratives in Acts retain the salvation-historical priority of starting with the Jewish people (see comments on Acts 13:5), but not a repetition of the first church's geographic priority.

461. Though cf. the microcosm of the mission in Acts 8:1–39, suggested in Thornton, "End of the Earth" (Judea in 8:1–4; Samaria in 8:5–25; the ends of the earth in 8:26–39). Melbourne, "Acts 1:8," however, counters that the mission to the "ends of the earth" continues through Paul (13:47) to Rome.

462. As in, e.g., Goulder, *Type and History*, 68.

463. Hengel, "Geography of Palestine," 32 (citing Luke 4:44; 5:17; Acts 1:8; 9:31; 11:29; 12:19; 15:1; 20:10; 26:20; 28:21).

464. Hengel, "Geography of Palestine," 32. He suggests that Luke is still influenced by the biblical territory of Judah (Luke 1:39; cf. the Judahite hill country, 1:65; 2:4; 21:21).

465. Even many Syrian Jews were sufficiently hellenized that Josephus labels Jews in Greek cities "Greeks" (as opposed to "Syrians" in the countryside); see Rajak, "Location," 1.

Just as Acts 1:8 alludes to Isaiah for "my witnesses," it also alludes to Isaiah for the geographic range of the testimony of God's salvation (Isa 41:5, 9; 42:10; 43:6; 45:22; 48:20; 49:6; 52:10; 62:11). That Luke depends on Isaiah's language here is clear: although mention of the ends of the earth is common in ancient literature, Luke's complete and exact phrase ἕως ἐσχάτου τῆς γῆς appears four or five times in the LXX (Isa 8:9; 48:20; 49:6; 62:11; also *Pss. Sol.* 1:4) and only twice in the NT (Acts 13:47 and here); it also appears in Christian writings dependent on Isaiah or Acts but "nowhere else in the immense range" of literature in the *Thesaurus linguae graecae* (TLG).[466] Most important for the interpretation of the phrase in Acts 1:8, Luke's other use of the phrase, 13:47, specifically quotes Isaiah (Isa 49:6).[467] More generally, "ends of the earth" is a common Septuagintal "phrase for distant lands, especially in the prophets . . . without any conscious reference to any one place."[468] Most scholars do recognize the allusion to 49:6 in Acts 1:8.[469] It is not surprising that Acts 1:8 appears to allude to Scripture, since the passage it recapitulates (Luke 24:47–48) is explicitly grounded in Scripture (24:44–46).[470]

The "ends of the earth" thus includes the entire Gentile mission (Acts 13:47), even though Luke's narrower goal for his own narrative in Acts will be Rome because it is the heart of the empire,[471] the world known directly by his audience.[472] (Rome's conquests had deliberately forced all its empire to focus on Rome, as was widely acknowledged.)[473] If some prophecies in the Gospel are fulfilled in Acts and some prophecies in both remain future (Luke 21:25–28; 22:16–18; Acts 1:6–7; 3:19–21), there is no reason to assume that the end of Acts closes off further fulfillment of this opening statement.[474] Thus Paul's ministry in Rome exhausts neither the Gentile mission nor the "ends of the earth."[475] Instead it predicts this mission's completion in a proleptic way, just like the presence of Diaspora Jews at Pentecost (Acts 2:5) or the first conversion of a Gentile, who, not coincidentally, comes from a region Greeks regarded as at the literal southern ends of the earth (8:27).

Paul seems to have taken such proleptic symbolism seriously himself, claiming that his mission was preaching the gospel fully to all the earth (Rom 15:18–19; cf. Col 1:6), though, for him, his remaining goal was Spain (the western border) by way of Rome and Jerusalem (Rom 15:23–25, 28). His interest in Spain (and in every people under heaven; cf. Rom 15:11; 16:26; Gal 3:8; Col 1:23) may presuppose an early logion like this or Matt 24:14 (though cf. the less contextually explicit Mark 13:10).

---

466. Tannehill, *Acts*, 17; followed also by Pao, *Isaianic Exodus*, 94. For the less complete "ends of the earth" in LXX, in addition to Isaian references, see LXX Deut 28:49; Ps 134:6–7 (ET 135:6–7); Jer 6:22; 10:13; 16:19; 27:41; 28:16; 32:32; 38:8; 1 Macc 3:9; cf. *Pss. Sol.* 1:4; 8:15; cf. also 1QM I, 8. Besides more closely verbal LXX parallels, some compare Jesus's unending kingdom in Luke 1:33 and even Virgil *Aen.* 1.278–79 (Bonz, *Past as Legacy*, 133, cited in Krauter, "Epos," 236), but Dan 7:14 would be clearer (Krauter, "Epos," 236).

467. Tannehill, *Acts*, 17; Dupont, *Salvation*, 18; Arrington, *Acts*, 9; Moore, "End of Earth."

468. Lake and Cadbury, *Commentary*, 9; cf. Bruce, *Acts*[1], 71; Bruce, *Commentary*, 39n30.

469. See Pao, *Isaianic Exodus*, 92; e.g., also Mallen, *Reading*, 81.

470. Luke 24:46–47 does not specify the text, but it is clear from Acts 1:8 (and 13:47; Pao, *Isaianic Exodus*, 85). Acts 26:23 alludes to the same passage (86). Not only modern readers (e.g., Borgman, *Way*, 249–52) but inevitably even some ancient ones did connect Luke 24:44–49 with Acts 1:8 (see, e.g., Cyril of Alexandria *Comm. Luke* 24, in Just, *Luke*, 389).

471. Given the centrality of Rome for all the empire, an allusion to Aeneas's Rome-ward journey (Reardon, "Homing to Rome") seems too narrow.

472. For Luke, the mission to the "ends of the earth" vindicates also Paul's Gentile mission (see Brawley, *Luke-Acts and Jews*, 28–50).

473. Dion. Hal. *Anc. Or.* 1.3.

474. See also Brawley, *Luke-Acts and Jews*, 39.

475. Agreeing here with, e.g., Tannehill, *Acts*, 17; Jervell, *Apostelgeschichte*, 116; Klauck, *Magic*, 5; Gaventa, *Acts*, 65–66; Melbourne, "End of Earth," esp. 11–14; Bock, *Acts*, 65.

IV. WHERE WERE THE "ENDS OF THE EARTH"?[476]

Most ancients held that the river Oceanus encircled the world;[477] to go beyond it was to reach the literal ends of the earth.[478] Usually, when they spoke of the ends of the earth, however, they meant the lands before Oceanus, such as Spain in the west and Ethiopia in the south. Still, in the time that Luke was writing, Rome was pressing "beyond the limits of Ocean"; Claudius had added Britannia to the empire in 43 C.E.[479] Elsewhere in the north, some knew about Ireland.[480] For many, exotic places such as "Thule" (possibly Iceland or Norway) were at the ends of the earth;[481] a first-century writer calls Thule the farthest of lands (Sen. Y. *Med.* 379).[482]

For Pliny the Elder, the ocean surrounded the western limits of the world (beyond Spain); in the north, some had sailed from north of Germany around Jutland (Denmark) and as far as very cold Scythia.[483] Pliny placed the Caspian Sea on the northeast end of the world (*N.H.* 2.67.167). Some had reportedly sailed from Spain south past Mauretania all the way to Ethiopia (2.67.169); if true, and if by "Ethiopia" they meant the region most often so designated in antiquity, they had circumnavigated Africa. (But some might have regarded the dark-complexioned West Africans as "Aethiopians," since many ancients would not have limited the title to Meroë; see comment on Acts 8:27.)

The phrase could epitomize distance (Catull. *Carm.* 11.2–3). Some employed the phrase poetically; hence Ovid complains that his place of exile is the very end (*extremum*) of the earth (Ovid *Tristia* 4.9.9).[484] Someone wandering in exile might depict his travels as going to the furthest part of the earth.[485] Cicero complains that Mithridates seeks to gather troops in the northeast, *in ultimis terris* (*Agr.* 2.19.52). Cicero also praises Rome's glory as known to peoples in the most distant parts of the world (*Verr.* 2.5.64.166).[486] The phrase appears in a hyperbolic mission statement in a pseudepigraphic letter attributed to Crates of Thebes, writing to Hipparchia: "And seek wise men, even if you have to go to the ends of the earth [ἐπ' ἔσχατα γῆς]."[487]

Distant peoples to the east included Scythians (Sen. Y. *Med.* 483) and Indians (*Med.* 484). Likewise, ancient writers sometimes spoke of India as in the eastern ends of the earth.[488] Thus one could pair Spain as the western and India as the eastern

476. Le Cornu, *Acts*, 21, briefly entertains the phrase referring to the boundaries of Eretz Israel but rightly concludes that Luke uses "land" more broadly than this elsewhere and that no part of Israel would be called "the remotest part." For one survey of ancient views of the "ends of the earth," see Romm, *Edges* (cited in Pervo, *Acts*, 44).

477. Sen. E. *Suas.* 1.4; Pliny E. *N.H.* 2.67.170 (also noting the Mediterranean dividing the world); 2.112.242; Jos. *Ant.* 1.38; Plut. *Alex.* 44.2; probably 1QM X, 13; Fronto *Ad M. Caes.* 2.6.3.

478. E.g., Philost. *Hrk.* 8.13; cf. *1 En.* 33:2–3. Cicero can figuratively describe the ends of the Roman Empire as Oceanus (accurate on the west, at least, beyond Spain; *Verr.* 2.3.89.207). Oceanus is the limit of earth (γῆς τέρμα) in Glycon, quoted in Sen. E. *Suas.* 1.11.

479. Gill and Gempf, "Preface," ix.

480. See Todd, "Hibernia."

481. See Warmington and Millett, "Thule"; Todd, "Thule."

482. Pliny E. *N.H.* 4.16.104 similarly designates it the land farthest north.

483. The Scythia normally so called would be inaccessible by the northern sea; Pliny assumed that the Caspian had a northern outlet in the ocean that circled the continents (H. Rackham, LCL, 1:302 n. *b*).

484. Ovid also called the place Scythia (*Tristia* 1.3.61; 3.3.46; 3.4.49; 4.6.47; 4.9.17); for many in the Mediterranean world, Scythia did, in fact, represent the extreme northeast (Aeschylus *Seven* 728, 817; Cic. *Nat. d.* 2.34.88; Ptolemy *Tetrab.* 2.3.60; Pliny E. *N.H.* 2.67.167; cf. Goldenberg, "Scythian-Barbarian"), and "civilized" Greeks and Romans viewed Scythians with both curiosity and fear (see further discussion of Scythians at Acts 8:27). The cold of the extreme north invited mythological speculation (e.g., *1 En.* 34:1–2).

485. Dio Chrys. *Or.* 13.9 (ἐπὶ τὸ ὕστατον ἀπέλθῃς τῆς γῆς).

486. Cf. also *Verr.* 2.3.89.207.

487. Crates *Ep.* 31 (*Cyn. Ep.* 80–81).

488. Earlier, Pompey's conquests between the Pontic and the Red Seas seemed to extend to the ends of the earth (Diod. Sic. 40.4; Le Cornu, *Acts*, 23).

sides of the world.[489] After the conquests of Alexander of Macedon, whose successors held territory even near the Punjab for a time,[490] some Greek thinkers were in contact with Indian thinkers.[491] Much was rumored and known about India[492]—for example, that they were the world's most numerous people,[493] that they had "naked" philosophers,[494] and that a widow might be burned on her husband's funeral pyre.[495] Not only mercantile ties[496] (e.g., in ivory,[497] pearls,[498] or other expensive substances[499]) but also philosophical and religious ties[500] existed. It was said that India sent envoys to Augustus.[501] Trajan's conquests in the early second century expanded Roman influence to India's borders.[502]

Proposed examples of connections between Jewish and Indian texts[503] appear to be coincidental, based on shared themes and images from a somewhat related milieu. But some Jews were apparently even engaged in, or knew directly of, trade with India.[504] A mid-first-century c.e. guidebook for the Red Sea has survived, and it reports the African coast as far south as Dar es Salaam,[505] then the voyage to the mouth of the Indus River and especially the profitable Malabar Coast of India.[506] Many Roman gold and silver coins have been recovered in southern India, especially from the times of Augustus and Nero.[507] By the late second century, mariners reached Annam (today's Vietnam), and others "traded with Malaya and Java."[508]

489. Strabo 1.1.8; Sen. Y. *Nat. Q.* 1.pref. 13; Juv. *Sat.* 10.1–2.

490. Casson, *Travel*, 119. For early Hellenistic rulers and India, see Jakobsson, "Founded."

491. Pyrrho (ca. 360–270 b.c.e.; Diog. Laert. 9.11.61); allegedly Apollonius of Tyana (Philost. *Vit. Apoll.* 2–3 [LCL, 1:117–229, 2:231–345]); cf. Finegan, *Religions*, 149, on archaeological confirmations of such reports; for possible influence on Hellenistic thought, see Scott, "Attitudes." Apparently, however, only the Greeks who traveled to the east knew much about Indian religion (Delaygue, "Grecs").

492. Cic. *Tusc.* 5.27.78; Strabo 15.1.11–13ff. (LCL, 7:14–19ff.); Xen. *Cyr.* 2.4.1–8; Val. Max. 2.6.14; 3.3.ext. 6; cf. Hor. *Ep.* 1.6.6; *Odes* 1.12.56; 1.31.6; 3.24.1–2; 4.14.42; *Jub.* 8:21. Some of the information was clearly speculative (e.g., Ach. Tat. 4.5.1; Philost. *Vit. Apoll.* 2.8–9; 3.40). See more fully Avi-Yonah, *Hellenism*, 164–66; Nock, *Conversion*, 46–47.

493. Lucian *Runaways* 6.

494. E.g., Val. Max. 3.3.ext. 6; Philost. *Vit. soph.* 2.5.572; Ps.-Callisth. *Alex.* 3.5; cf. Pliny E. *N.H.* 7.2.22; Lucian *Runaways* 7; Hippol. *Ref.* 1.11, 21.

495. Val. Max. 2.6.14 (the LCL note cites also Cic. *Tusc.* 5.78).

496. E.g., Petron. *Sat.* 38; *Poem* 18; Paus. 3.12.4; Xen. Eph. *Anthia* 4.1; cf. *Sib. Or.* 11.299; Wheeler, *Beyond Frontiers*, 115–71; Drexhage, "India"; Casson, *Travel*, 124; idem, *Mariners*, 199, 204–6; Koester, *Introduction*, 1:86; Bauckham, *Climax*, 353, 358, 360; Aune, *Revelation*, 999. Cf. Ceylon (modern Sri Lanka) ties with Rome in Pliny E. *N.H.* 6.84–85 (in Sherk, *Empire*, 32); cf. ch. 4, "The Sea Route to India and Ceylon," in Charlesworth, *Trade Routes*, 57–73; on Greek and Roman knowledge of this island, see Karttunen, "Taprobane." The trade declined in the later empire, though some Christian missionaries traveled there (Karttunen, "India," 772).

497. See, e.g., Catull. *Carm.* 64.48; Pliny E. *N.H.* 8.4.7–8 (noting the greater size of Indian elephants, 8.11.32; though cf. 8.13.35); Dio Chrys. *Or.* 79.4; Schneider, "Ivory."

498. E.g., Pliny E. *N.H.* 9.54.106–9; 12.41.84; Philost. *Vit. Apoll.* 2.24; 3.57.

499. For precious stones, e.g., Mart. *Epig.* 4.28.4; for ebony, e.g., Pliny E. *N.H.* 12.8.17; for spices, e.g., Ovid *Fasti* 3.720; Statius *Silv.* 2.1.160–61; 5.1.212.

500. Juv. *Sat.* 6.585. The Indian emperor Aśoka reportedly sent representatives of Buddhism to Egypt in the third century b.c.e. (Finegan, *Records*, 67).

501. *Res gest.* 5.31; Suet. *Aug.* 21.3. See also discussion in Lintott, *Romans*, 1–5.

502. Sherk, *Empire*, 177–78, §136.

503. E.g., in Stehly, "Upanishads," although Gispert-Sauch, "Upanisad," thinks that it is possible.

504. See Steiner, "Laissez-*passer*." Traditions speak of Christian missionaries from an early period (Irvin and Sunquist, *Earliest Christianity*, 93–95; more confidently, Thapar, *History*, 134–35; esp. and most helpfully, Schnabel, *Mission*, 881–95), and the Christian movement is well documented there in the second half of the first millennium (Irvin and Sunquist, *Earliest Christianity*, 308–10).

505. Casson, *Mariners*, 203, on the *Periplus maris Erythraei*.

506. Ibid., 204. For the sea route from Arabia to India, see Pliny E. *N.H.* 6.26.100–101; from Egypt to India, 6.26.101–6; on the Red Sea and the Persian Gulf, see 6.28.107–11.

507. Casson, *Mariners*, 205.

508. Ibid.

Like India, China was known to be far away.[509] The empire also had trade ties with China, although, because of its greater distance, it was not known as well as India.[510] A well-known item of the China trade was silk;[511] one late third-century C.E. source rates a pound of silk as the price of a pound of gold.[512] What is known as the Silk Road already linked these two great empires by the first century.[513] China knew of Rome (by the name Daqin), again primarily as a source of foreign treasures.[514] Some Roman voyagers may have reached Canton; in 226 C.E., after a Western merchant came to Vietnam by ship, Chinese records indicate that he "was sent on to the emperor at Nanking" and report "a large and expensive gift that a group from the West brought the emperor in 294."[515]

Some ancients wrote of Spain (especially Gades) as the ends of the earth;[516] even for those in Rome, it was "the west" (Sil. It. 3.325). One thought of the east and the west together as "both abodes of the sun" (Ovid Her. 9.15–16 [LCL]). That Spain formed one boundary of the ends of the known world undoubtedly informed Paul's desire to go there (Rom 15:24, 28; 1 Clem. 5.5–7)[517] despite obstacles he would face there,[518] though it is not explicitly part of Luke's horizon.[519] Parts of Spain were quite romanized,[520] though some earlier elements persisted in local culture.[521] Spain was well known in the empire;[522] Roman merchants had regular ties with Spain,[523] and Spain had figured prominently in recent generations' history.[524] Because of the chief

509. E.g., Pliny E. *N.H.* 12.1.2. Although at least some Christians must have arrived earlier, early sources from China document the Christian movement there at least as early as 635 (Blaiklock, *Archaeology*, 76–77; esp. Irvin and Sunquist, *Earliest Christianity*, 315–19). For comparative studies on China and Greece, see Tanner, "China."

510. E.g., Pliny E. *N.H.* 12.1.2; 12.41.84; Bauckham, *Climax*, 359; Aune, *Revelation*, 999.

511. E.g., Casson, *Mariners*, 198, 206; Bauckham, *Climax*, 355; on Jewish knowledge of silk, e.g., *2 Bar.* 10:19; for the history of the silk trade, see, e.g., Frye, *Heritage*, 153–57. Even if some thought that it grew on trees (Bauckham, *Climax*, 355), Romans knew of the silk moth (Pliny E. *N.H.* 11.25.75; 11.26.76). The best silk was from China, but it was also being produced in Roman Asia (e.g., *N.H.* 11.27.77; Cary and Haarhoff, *Life*, 96).

512. Croom, *Clothing*, 22 (citing *SHA, Aurelianus* 45.5).

513. Herbert, "Silk Road." Aune, *Revelation*, 999 (following Charlesworth, *Trade Routes*, 97–111), thinks that this trade flourished especially 90–130 C.E.

514. Ying, "Ruler."

515. Casson, *Mariners*, 205. Chinese ties with Europe go back to the second millennium B.C.E., but the sea route is certain only by the second or third century C.E. (so Brentjes, "China").

516. Strabo 1.1.5, 8; 3.2; Sen. Y. *Nat. Q.* 1.pref. 13; Sil. It. 1.270 (*extremis . . . terris*); 15.638; Pliny *Ep.* 2.3.8; Gr. *Anth.* 4.3.84–85; cf. "at the ends of Europe" (τῶν ἐσχάτων τῆς Εὐρώπης) in Arrian *Alex.* 2.16.6. Riesner, *Early Period*, 305, cites also Lucan *C.W.* 3.454; Juv. *Sat.* 10.1–2; Strabo 2.5.9; Sil. It. 17.637. This must also be the view in *1 Clem.* 5.5–7 (Grant, "Christian and Roman History," 16).

517. Cf., e.g., Aus, "Plans."

518. It is not clear that Spain yet had a Jewish community (first clearly attested there in the third century; Bowers, "Communities"; but cf. the suggestion of earlier residence in Stern, "Diaspora," 169–70); moreover, Paul would need to use Latin there (Ramsay, *Pictures*, 276; Garnsey and Saller, *Empire*, 186; cf. Untermann, "Hispania"). For an examination of the later tradition of Paul's presence (cf., e.g., *Murat. Canon* 38–39), see Latourette, *First Five Centuries*, 96–97; Meinardus, "Traditions." Philostratus claims that the danger of preaching in Rome under Nero led to Apollonius's voyage to Spain (*Vit. Apoll.* 4.47), but this "parallel" may be based on Paul.

519. A few scholars do think of Spain in Acts 1:8, e.g., Davies, *Gospel and Land*, 279–80; Ellis, "End of Earth."

520. Cf., e.g., Donahue, "Iunia Rustica"; Olshausen, "Incorporation"; Garnsey and Saller, *Empire*, 186; esp. the survey of archaeological work in Keay, "Work."

521. E.g., Graf, "Hispania," 397 (focusing on religious elements). For places with mixed Phoenician and Roman influence, see, e.g., Mierse, "Architecture."

522. On ancient Spain and ancient views of Spain, see Barceló, "Hispania," esp. 388, 391.

523. On Spain, see Pliny E. *N.H.* 3.1.6–3.3.30. Rome imported from there, e.g., dyes (Vitruv. *Arch.* 6.7.2; Pliny E. *N.H.* 16.12.32), silver (Polyb. 34.9.8–9; Pliny E. *N.H.* 33.31.96), mercury (Pliny E. *N.H.* 33.32.99–100), gold (Polyb. 31.22.3), black wool (Pliny E. *N.H.* 8.73.191), and horse breeding (8.67.166). On the mines in Roman Spain, see 4.20.112; Orejas and Sánchez-Palencia, "Mines." On the harsh conditions of these mines, see, e.g., Forbes, *Technology*, 7:223.

524. E.g., Cic. *Fam.* 3.8.10; 6.18.2; 8.16.3; 9.9.2; *Att.* 9.2a. Although important to Rome, it could require a significant journey (see Ramsay, "Roads and Travel," 392).

trade routes, ancient maps depict east-west distances on a larger scale than north-south ones;[525] this made the westernmost known land a natural "end" of the earth.

More relevant is that Nubia stood at the southern ends of the Mediterranean world's earth (see comment on Acts 8:27). The African court official's conversion proleptically symbolizes the future completion of the mission to the southern ends of the earth.[526] Homer's view of Ethiopians had great influence; Strabo refers to his view that "Ethiopians live at the ends of the earth, on the banks of Oceanus . . . at the end of the earth."[527] Mythographers were happy to speculate on the cosmology of the four ends of the earth (e.g., *1 En.* 35:1–36:2), reporting (unverifiable) marvels at the earth's "ends."[528] In the distant north, for example, dwelt the mythical Hyperboreans.[529]

Many scholars cite *Pss. Sol.* 8:15 to argue that some viewed Rome as the ends of the earth, a view that, as they note, fits well the place where Acts concludes (Acts 28:14–31).[530] *Psalms of Solomon* refers to Pompey, but since, historically, Pompey came from many years of warfare in Spain,[531] it is not completely clear whether the author and his audience would think of Rome. The matter is disputed, however; unless the ideal audience of *Psalms of Solomon* were well informed concerning events in the west more than a century earlier, they might well think of Pompey as simply coming from Rome, since he was a Roman.[532] Some Jewish documents could refer to Italy as the "west" (δυσμῶν, *Sib. Or.* 4.102–3). In the first century B.C.E., Rome and Spain were both in the far west from a Judean perspective, but they would be far more readily distinguished for a first-century C.E. Greek audience.

Despite this possible reference to Rome, Rome was not what most people in the eastern empire thought of when they heard "ends of the earth." For most, the peoples of the ends of the earth would have been "Germans, Scythians, Indians and Ethiopians,"[533] as well as Britons. Dio Chrysostom can use such a phrase to mean "everywhere" (*Or.* 13.9).[534] Greeks by this period lacked a single standard conception of the world and what constituted its ends.[535] But more important for Luke, as already noted, the LXX as a whole and Isa 49:6 in particular (which Luke quotes in his other clear use of the phrase, in Acts 13:47) invite a very broad reading of the phrase.

Rome thus serves the function of the ends of the earth for Luke, but only in a proleptic way, as already noted, like the Diaspora Jews at Pentecost (Acts 2:5–11) or the African court official (8:27). Barrett thinks that Rome is in view but in a sense that also looks beyond it: if one can evangelize Rome, one can also evangelize the rest of the world. Thus it likely means "Rome, but to Rome not as an end in itself but as representative of the whole world."[536]

525. See Jewett, *Romans*, 912.

526. Martin, "Chamberlain's Journey"; Keener, "Aftermath of Eunuch." For Ethiopia as the end of the earth for Acts, cf. Thornton, "End of the Earth"; in a proleptic way, Gaventa, *Acts*, 145.

527. That is, ἔσχατοι . . . ἔσχατοι, Strabo 1.1.6 (LCL); cf. Hom. *Od.* 1.23; Hdt. 3.25.

528. E.g., in the north in Ant. Diog. *Thule*, passim, e.g., 110b, 111a. Antonius Diogenes claims to derive these stories from earlier sources, while admitting that he fabricates them.

529. E.g., *Epigoni* frg. 5 (so Hdt. 4.32) and in Hesiod frg. 150.21 M.-W. (so *GEF* 59); Pliny E. *N.H.* 4.12.89.

530. Fitzmyer, *Acts*, 206–7; Barrett, *Acts*, 80. One could note that the Roman Empire is *Luke's* world (Luke 2:1), but Acts 8:27 does show his interest in "ends of the earth" beyond that.

531. Rosner, "Progress," 218.

532. Barrett, *Acts*, 80.

533. Hengel, "Geography of Palestine," 36. For the world's extent in the LXX, see Scott, "Horizon," 502–3.

534. Johnson, *Acts*, 26–27.

535. See Scott, "Horizon," 484–87, esp. 487; for Roman conceptions, see 487–92; for Jewish conceptions, 492–522. Early Palestinian Jews did have some knowledge of Hellenistic geography (cf. *Jub.* 8:12 and esp. *OTP* 2:72 n. i, Wintermute).

536. Barrett, *Acts*, 80.

Therefore it seems likely that Luke's "ends of the earth," while prefigured at various stages (including his own conclusion), looks beyond the close of his work to the continuing mission.[537] The "open end" of Acts invites Luke's audience to participate in this universal mission.[538] Ultimately, context determines meaning; the ends of the earth meant different things in different contexts, but the LXX uses the phrase to emphasize universality.[539] Thus there is, in a real sense, no outline after Samaria; the mission "reaches beyond the end of Acts."[540]

v. An Outline for Acts?

Much to the dismay of modern NT commentators (whose suggested outlines often conflict with those of their peers), most ancient writers did not produce, and many of their works do not readily fit, hierarchical outlines. Good Hellenistic and Roman writers did, however, offer thoughts in some organized sequence (cf. Luke 1:3), and some works even contain explicit and detailed outlines at the beginning of their books (though none of these appears in the NT). Those who did not offer outlines often provided previews of main themes, sometimes sequentially.

Some scholars complain that Luke violates convention by not giving a preview for his second volume, but most agree that Acts 1:8 fulfills this function.[541] Most see the text as a programmatic statement for Acts;[542] Martin Hengel calls the geographical range in 1:8 "a mere table of contents for Acts."[543] Certainly, it includes the major themes of Acts: the Spirit's power for the worldwide mission (see introduction, ch. 15, sects. 3.a, 5.a). Even skilled rhetoricians did not always fulfill their introductory promises,[544] though ancient critics sometimes expressed annoyance with those who, having expressed a subject, digressed from it.[545] Luke, however, keeps to the point.

Some writers also stated a thesis or hypothesis that they then developed in their work; although Luke has not offered anything so technical here, such devices do illustrate that forethought to questions of introduction was common. By usual definition, a *thesis* offered a theoretical topic whereas a *hypothesis* offered a concrete topic with particulars.[546] Orators often stated their theses or topics toward the beginning of a

---

537. Hengel, "Geography of Palestine," 36; Rosner, "Progress," 218.

538. See Rosner, "Progress," 232–33; Marguerat, *Historian*, 230.

539. Johnson, *Acts*, 26–27 (citing Deut 28:49; Ps 134:6–7; Isa 8:9; 48:20; 49:6; 62:11; Jer 10:12; 16:19; 1 Macc 3:9; though he uses Acts' context to emphasize Rome); Lake and Cadbury, *Commentary*, 9.

540. Tannehill, *Acts*, 18; cf. Hengel, "Geography of Palestine," 36.

541. Tannehill, *Acts*, 9; Witherington, *Acts*, 106; Marguerat, *Actes*, 20 (following P.-H. Menoud); cf. Molthagen, "Geschichtsschreibung," 166. For examples of this convention, see Jos. *Ag. Ap.* 2.2; Polyb. 3.1.3; yet it was hardly universal.

542. See Klauck, *Magic*, 5; O'Day, "Acts," 305; Gangel, *Acts*, 10; Kisau, "Acts," 1300; Schröter, "Stellung," 47; esp. Parsons, *Departure*, 155.

543. Hengel, "Geography of Palestine," 35 (comparing also the church's missionary program in the Gospels; *1 Clem.* 42.3–4; *Herm. Sim.* 8.3.2; Aristides *Apol.* 15.2; Justin *1 Apol.* 31.7; 39.1ff.); cf. Dupont, *Salvation*, 12–13; Ridderbos, "Speeches of Peter," 6; Stendahl, *Paul*, 118; Weiser, *Apostelgeschichte*, 27–28; Hamm, *Acts*, 9; Schmidt, "Abkehr"; Kurichianil, "Orderly Account." Contrast van Unnik, "'Acts' and Confirmation," 39; Brawley, *Luke-Acts and Jews*, 39.

544. E.g., the promise of Dio Chrys. *Or.* 25.1 in the rest of *Or.* 25.

545. E.g., Philost. *Hrk.* 25.13 (though eager, in any case, to critique Homer).

546. Theon *Progymn.* 1.60; 2.91–104; 11.2–6, 240–43; Hermog. *Progymn.* 11, "On Thesis," 24–25; Aphth. *Progymn.* 13, "On Thesis," 49S, 41R; Nicolaus *Progymn.* 12, "On Thesis," 71–72; see further Anderson, *Glossary*, 63–65 (esp. on Quint. *Inst.* 3.5.5–18; Cic. *Or. Brut.* 125; for the use of *thesis* in first-century school exercises, Quint. *Inst.* 2.4.24–32; Theon *Progymnasmata* (*RG* 2:120, lines 12ff.); on *hypothesis*, Cic. *De or.* 2.133–47; *Top.* 80; *Or. Brut.* 45–46); more briefly, Aune, *Dictionary of Rhetoric*, 459–60; Schenkeveld, "Philosophical Prose," 247; Mitchell, *Rhetoric of Reconciliation*, 198–99; Gibson, "Notes," 509 (cf. also xxi, noting that thesis may have been one of the less dominant exercises in late antiquity). For developing a hypothesis (a sample declamation theme) see, e.g., Hermog. *Inv.* 1.1.93–100.

speech (e.g., Dio Chrys. *Or.* 1.11; 38.5–6); a rhetorical argument was to begin with a proposition.[547] Other skilled writers likewise often stated their topic at the beginning of books;[548] Paul, for example, probably uses a thesis or hypothesis in his most polished extant letter (Rom 1:16–17).[549] (Because philosophers proposed theses for discussion, their proposals were generally not self-evident statements.)[550]

Not only terse thesis statements but preliminary summaries were common (e.g., Dio Chrys. *Or.* 38.8; see our introduction to 1:1–11). Cicero opines that a good orator "will announce what he is about to discuss and sum up when concluding a topic" (*Or. Brut.* 40.137 [LCL]). It was considered appropriate, as here (Jerusalem; Judea and Samaria; ends of earth), to divide one's material into a small number of topics,[551] then treat them in succession.[552] Many writers would offer such brief outlines of their material at strategic points.[553] It is thus no surprise that a historian could outline material to cover before elaborating it (e.g., Vell. Paterc. 2.129.1, explicitly).

Thus Seneca the Elder notes that Latro would, before his speech, "set out the points at issue in the *controversia* he was to declaim," but Seneca also notes that orators do not always do this because this practice makes it obvious if they leave anything out (*Controv.* 1.pref. 21). Many writers provided outlines at the beginning of what they would cover, albeit far more explicitly than Luke does here.[554] Few went so far as Pliny the Elder, who provided a table of contents so thorough that it consumes the entire first book of his *Natural History*.[555] Perhaps most relevant is that a good historical preface should show causes of events and outline "the main events" (Lucian *Hist.* 53).[556]

That Luke's advance summary comes in an oracle of Jesus is appropriate from a literary standpoint. Oracles provided a useful literary means to announce what would come, without digressing from the narrative world into an aside. Oracles often functioned as plot-moving devices (e.g., Apollod. *Epit.* 5.10; see further comment on Acts 2:23); in a very general way, Jesus's words here provide an outline for the geographic plot of Acts.[557]

If Luke briefly outlines the rest of the book here, why does he focus on geographic divisions? Most obviously, Luke's focus on the gospel's expansion invites geographic

547. Quint. *Inst.* 4.4.1–2.

548. E.g., Thucyd. 1.23.6; Pliny E. *N.H.* 8.1.1; 18.1.1; 33.1.1; 34.1.1; 36.1.1; 37.1.1; Philost. *Vit. Apoll.* 7.1; 8.1. Dion. Hal. *Thuc.* 10–11 critiques Thucydides for inadequate arrangement (Moessner, "Arrangement," 161).

549. E.g., Tobin, *Rhetoric in Contexts*, 104; Johnson, *Romans*, 26; Aune, *Dictionary of Rhetoric*, 430 (as the πρόθεσις); Jewett, *Romans*, 135. Others are less certain here (Keck, "Pathos," 86; Elliott, *Arrogance*, 17).

550. Schenkeveld, "Philosophical Prose," 247.

551. Three in Men. Rhet. 2.1–2, 375.7–8; four in 385.8; three or four in Gorg. *Hel.* 6 (developed in *Hel.* 6, 7, 8–14, and probably 15–19; summarizing again in 20).

552. Men. Rhet. 2.1–2, 375.8ff.; 385.9–386.10; see discussion in Hermog. *Inv.* 3.1.126–29.

553. E.g., Arius Didymus in Stob. *Ecl.* 2.7.5; again, 2.7.5a.6–7, preparing for lines 7–15. This somewhat resembles the rhetorical practice of διαίρεσις (Men. Rhet. 2.1–2, 375.7–8; 385.8; Porph. *Isag.* 1.6–7; *Marc.* 24.376–84; cf. Iambl. *V.P.* 30.168–69; though cf. the different technical definitions in Anderson, *Glossary*, 32–33; Rowe, "Style," 134; Aune, *Dictionary of Rhetoric*, 125; cf. the later use of κεφάλαιον in Anderson, *Glossary*, 67–68; the idea in Fronto *Eloq.* 3.4). For sectioning a work for the convenience of readers, see, e.g., Pliny *Ep.* 9.4.1.

554. E.g., in rhetoric, *Rhet. Alex.* 29, 1436a.33–39; Dion. Hal. *Lysias* 24; Cic. *Or. Brut.* 40.137; Sen. E. *Controv.* 1.pref. 21 (noting that not all orators did so); Dio Chrys. *Or.* 38.8; in other sorts of works, Soranus *Gynec.* 1.intro. 2. For smaller sections or arguments within a work, e.g., 1.1.3; 2.5.9 (25.78); Pliny *Ep.* 6.29.1–2; Philost. *Vit. Apoll.* 7.1; 8.1. For others' summaries of books, cf. Galen *Grief* 29–30.

555. Pliny E. *N.H.* 1; cf. Pliny's explanation in *N.H.* pref. 33; see also Aul. Gel. pref. 25.

556. Failure to include this could be cause for censure by Hellenistic rhetorical critics (Dion. Hal. *Thuc.* 19). This could also be used for other narrative works (e.g., Virg. *Aen.* 1.1–6). Within a history, see Polyb. 3.1.3–3.5.9, especially the explicit explanation in 3.1.7; 11.1.4–5.

557. Johnson, *Acts*, 12, points out that Acts 1:8 is merely the most obvious of several such programmatic prophecies in Acts.

as well as chronological development. Other suggestions may provide further context for this approach. Witherington suggests that Luke follows the geographic form of arranging history established by Ephorus and, "like Ephorus and Polybius before him, divides the world into geographical regions and proceeds to discuss what is happening in each one at a time."[558] This practice would help explain a historian focusing on geography but leaves unanswered the reason for Luke's specific outline. James Scott makes a case for a traditional Hellenistic Jewish division of nations. There is here a threefold mission relating to Jewish geography, built on the table of nations tradition:[559] "*Shem* (Acts 2:1–8:25), *Ham* (8:26–40), and *Japheth* (9:1–28:31)."[560] Some Hellenistic Jewish authors divided the world into three continents: Asia (Jos. *War* 2.358–59, 366), Libya (2.363, 383), and Europe (2.358).[561] Although Luke's own world does not require (or his sources permit) equal treatment of each of these sections, it is not unlikely that Luke had such broad divisions in mind at least in part (see comment on the transition between Asia and Europe in Acts 16:9–11).

Although this is an outline for Acts, it does not provide a very clear (and certainly not a very symmetrical) structure; other structural analyses will be more fruitful for those concerns (see introduction, ch. 16, sect. 2). At the same time, this is an explicit outline for the mission that Luke gives us, and it constitutes one starting point for recognizing the book's development.

VI. Geographic Knowledge

Can Luke really expect much of his audience to follow intelligently the geographic movements in his work? Some ancient writers assume a high degree of geographic knowledge for their audience, as Maclean and Aitken point out:

> As one might expect in a dialogue in which a major characters [sic] is a Phoenician merchant who sails the Aegean and the Black Sea, the *Heroikos* is replete with geographical references. Like the merchant, the audience is expected to recognize the names of cities, regions, islands, mountains, and rivers where associated with the biographies, exploits, and sanctuaries of the heroes, their sanctuaries or where supernatural marvels are to be found. The majority of these are in the northern Aegean, the Hellespont, and the Troad, but the world circumscribed by the dialogue extends from India to Spain and from Ethiopia to the banks of the Danube.[562]

The primary geographic horizons of Acts (the locations where Luke focuses the greatest detail, apart from Jerusalem) are very similar except that Luke presupposes less detailed knowledge.[563] (Indeed, Luke's knowledge of the Aegean Islands and coastal cities is stronger than his knowledge of Galilean geography[564] despite the subject of his Gospel and Polybius's admonition for historians to visit all the places they wrote about.[565] But Luke was admittedly not alone; numerous writers confused locations

---

558. Witherington, *Acts*, 34–35, 159n107 (citing Fornara, *Nature of History*, 45).

559. See Scott, "Horizon," 525–27; for this tradition more fully in Second Temple Judaism, see 507–22. Roughly, nations to the south represented Ham; to the east, Shem; and to the west, Japheth.

560. Scott, "Horizon," 531.

561. Ibid., 493n33; the same three divisions appear in Philo *Embassy* 283–84 (497n47). For the historic division between Europe and Asia and possible relevance to Acts, see Keener, "Asia and Europe."

562. Maclean and Aitken, *Heroikos*, xc.

563. Of the seventy-four place names found in both the LXX and the NT, Acts uses fifty-three (72 percent) of them (Scott, "Horizon," 524).

564. See Hengel, *Jesus and Paul*, 97–128; even Jerusalemites probably knew little of the topography of Galilee, a rural backwater (see idem, "Geography of Palestine," 33n19).

565. Hengel, "Geography of Palestine," 78, notes that Luke probably never saw a map of Palestine, and he warns that modern scholars would be more generous to him if ever forced "to give an accurate description

in Palestine,[566] including Jewish writers.)[567] When Luke mentions, for example, the regions the Spirit did not allow Paul to enter (Acts 16:6–7) or the landmark Samothrace (16:11), Luke expects his ideal audience to understand the allusions as more than a set of unfamiliar names. As mentioned in the introduction, chapter 12, section 3, this suggests an audience in the Greek East, probably in the Aegean rim.

That the earliest churches looked to Jerusalem for leadership (Gal 2:1–10)[568] and, still more, for spiritual heritage (Rom 15:25–26) and symbolic centrality (Rom 15:19; Gal 1:17–18; 4:25–26) is not surprising. Many cults were local, so that people far from Ephesus might still worship the *Ephesian* Artemis (see comment on Acts 19:27) or someone far from Pharos could worship Isis of Pharos.[569] But just as Jerusalem's destruction led most of Judaism to consider precedents for a nonsacrificial faith (especially from the exilic period), it must have led Christians to look for precedents in which the churches did not need to look to Jerusalem (e.g., the Antioch mission; Acts 11:19–30; 13:1–3; Gal 2:11). The Romans could feel threatened by loyalty to Jerusalem, in any case;[570] witness the *fiscus judaicus* imposed on all Jews in the empire as a result of Jerusalem's revolt.[571]

Cultural interchange, by this period, had been sufficient for urban populations to recognize the need to respect (albeit sometimes mainly in the sense of "tolerate") differences among cultures.[572] This did not eliminate cultural disdain—for example, Greeks against (an often slightly modified definition of) "barbarians" (see comment on Acts 28:2) or, less consistently, Roman disdain for outsiders (especially in Rome itself).[573] But cross-cultural evangelism would be easier in the relatively tamed nationalisms and ethnocentrisms of the empire than in the more hostile intertribal conflicts that existed in many locations before and outside it.

5. Jesus's Ascension and Promise to Return (1:9–11)

The promise of Jesus's return in this passage (implicitly associated with the time of the kingdom's restoration, Acts 1:6) is to be regarded as no less certain than the promise of the Holy Spirit's coming just treated in 1:3–8 (and fulfilled in 2:4).

---

of the geography of the outer suburbs of our home towns or even to put on a blank map of Palestine those places the location of which Luke knew" (such as Antipatris and Caesarea).

566. Ibid., 29–30 (citing Strabo 16.2.16–46, esp. 16.2.21, 28–29, 34; Pliny E. *N.H.* 5.66–73; Tac. *Ann.* 12.54.2; Ptolemy *Geog.* 5.15.1–7 [5.16.1–10 in Nobbe]).

567. Most of the Jewish writers were from the Diaspora, like Luke (Hengel, "Geography of Palestine," 29–30, citing here *Let. Aris.* 115–18; Ps.-Hecataeus in Jos. *Ag. Ap.* 1.196–97; Philo *Prov.* 2.107 = Euseb. *P.E.* 8.14.64); but even Josephus erred sometimes—surprisingly, most often when he was present! First and Second Maccabees and a military source in Polyb. 5.61.3–62.6; 66.1–72.12 tend to be much more accurate.

568. Some might add 2 Cor 11:5, 22; but cf. Keener, *Corinthians*, 227, 233.

569. See Frankfurter, *Religion in Egypt*, 97–144, esp. 102.

570. Cf. Nero's consideration of massacring Gauls living in Rome lest they join the Gallic revolt from the province of Gaul (Suet. *Nero* 43.1).

571. See *CPJ* 1:80–81; 2:119–36, §§160–229; Suet. *Dom.* 12.2; Dio Cass. *R.H.* 65.7.2; Hemer, "Ostraka"; Carlebach, "References." Appian *Hist. rom.* 11.8.50 claims that Jews paid a higher poll tax because they rebelled so often; Romans had never been happy about the temple tax, in any case (Cic. *Flacc.* 28.66–67). Note also the wide distribution of *Judaea capta* coins and their minting in the empire (Zarrow, "Romanisation").

572. For the need for Greeks to respect Asian (Persian) culture, e.g., Plut. *Themist.* 27.2–3; *Alex.* 45.1–3, esp. 45.3; for Greek and Roman cultural differences, e.g., Corn. Nep. pref. 5–7. But for Greek cultural solidarity, cf. Martin, "Anti-individualistic Ideology." On universalist cults and tendencies, see the discussion of "pagan 'universal' ideals" in our introduction, ch. 15, sect. 3.b.ii–iii.

573. See Keener, *Paul*, 140–42. But most Roman disdain for Greeks stemmed from the first century B.C.E. (e.g., Cic. *Quint. fratr.* 1.2.2.4; but contrast 1.1.9.28; *Att.* 1.15), when the efficacy of Greek cultural imperialism was a threat rather than a fait accompli.

Jesus's "taking up" is critical for Luke, predicted in the major turning point of Luke's narrative, Luke 9:51,[574] and introduced in a way that frames Jesus's departure in Acts (Acts 1:2, 11). It forms the narrative basis for Luke's theology of Christ's exaltation (Acts 2:33–36). It also provides the imagery of his return;[575] because Jesus will return the same way he left (1:11),[576] his departure in a cloud (1:9) fits the image of his return (Luke 21:27).[577]

a. Succession Narratives

As addressed at much greater length in the introduction (ch. 16, sect. 1), ancient biographers often used other lives that they believed providence had paralleled with their subject as a criterion for selecting the most relevant anecdotes (e.g., Plut. *Thes.* 1.2). The better ancient biographers believed that they discovered parallels already in history, rather than simply invented them (Plut. *Sert.* 1.1; *Cim.* 3.1–3; see introduction). Though more restrained and usually attempting to be more comprehensive, historians also looked for parallels because they believed in a divine pattern in history.[578]

Some scholars have compared Luke-Acts to a particular form of ancient biography that functioned as a succession narrative.[579] Though the examples of entire biographies modeled this way are, at best, relatively few,[580] they do illustrate the importance of succession and could form a more explicit link than most parallel lives (on which see introduction, ch. 16, sect. 1.f). To the extent that this model is relevant to Luke-Acts, it applies most securely to the pivot where the transition of leadership occurs, namely, the passage presently under discussion.[581]

Succession could prove a messy matter when no successor was designated beforehand.[582] According to one line of tradition, the struggles for Alexander's kingdom after his death stemmed from his willing the kingdom "to the best man" (Arrian *Alex.* 7.26.3 [LCL]). Solomon's succession to David was accomplished safely only by a formal coregency (1 Kgs 1:32–40). Jesus, however, clearly designates his "successors" (or, more in line with Luke's pneumatology, his agents).[583]

i. Passing on Ministry

Jubilees presents Jacob as Abraham's successor for a blessing to the nations (*Jub.* 19:17). Second-century rabbis spoke of disciples of prophets who waited on them

---

574. See also Talbert, *Patterns*, 112.

575. The claim of some (e.g., Goppelt, *Times*, 18) that Luke's exaltation coincides with the resurrection as in Paul mistakes theological unity with chronological unity (as in our discussion of Luke's narrative presentation of Spirit baptism, in our introduction, ch. 15, sect. 5.a.ii; and at Acts 1:4–5; 2:38; 8:15–17).

576. Cf. also the comment on the Mount of Olives in Acts 1:12.

577. On parousia imagery in the ascension, see, e.g., Flender, *Theologian*, 93.

578. E.g., Appian *Hist. rom.* 7.8.53; *Bell. civ.* 2.21.149.

579. Talbert, *Mediterranean Milieu*, 19–43, notes many types of figures and texts (although these normally do not compose double volumes like Luke-Acts) and that it is "not genre specific" (41–42); he finds the succession principle also in Luke-Acts (43–55). But Talbert views Luke-Acts as biography, and the closest parallels (to succession narratives rather than lists) are in biography. See further idem, *Acts*, xix–xxv (esp. for examples of histories of schools, xix–xx).

580. Aune, *Environment*, 78–79, notes only six of Diogenes Laertius's eighty-two lives (7 or 8 percent). With or without parallels, the subject of succession is a natural one in cases of leadership transition (e.g., on a popular level, Lindsay, *Lake*, 41–52, with also an Elijah allusion: Lake's "mantle" fell on Letwaba).

581. Cf. Brodie, "Emulation," 85.

582. Cf. the similar legal problem with heirs of one who died intestate or whose will might be disputed; Pliny *Ep.* 10.84; Gaius *Inst.* 2.156–60; Garnsey and Saller, *Empire*, 137; for detailed Roman laws on succession, see Buckland, *Roman Law*, 365–404. Some were confident, however, that others would complete their work if they died beforehand (Polyb. 3.5.7–8).

583. For Jesus designating his successors, see, e.g., Luke 6:13; Acts 1:2; on Luke 22:29–30, see Talbert, *Acts*, xxi.

and became prophets in their own right, such as Joshua with Moses and Elisha with Elijah (*Mek. Pisha* 1.150–53, מתלמידי הנביאים).[584] Later rabbis spoke of an unbroken chain of tradition from Moses to Joshua to the elders to the judges to the prophets and then to the sages of old (*'Abot R. Nat.* 1 A; 1:2 B). A probably Amoraic tradition contends that just as God replaced Moses with Joshua and Eli with Samuel, so, when one great rabbi (e.g., R. Akiba) died, another (e.g., R. Judah ha-Nasi) was born.[585] Then again, some opined that whatever one could pass on, its strength could diminish over the generations.[586]

The closest background here is that of Elijah's passing on his ministry to Elisha—described as passing on the firstborn's portion of the Spirit that was on him (2 Kgs 2:9, 15; cf. Sir 48:12).[587] Moses likewise imparted the Spirit to Joshua, so that he was filled with the Spirit of wisdom (Deut 34:9; cf. Acts 2:4; 6:3, 10).[588] Although both may form part of the background, however, the transfer of the Spirit from Elijah to Elisha is most relevant, for it is part of the OT's only explicit ascension scene (to which the passing on is explicitly connected; 2 Kgs 2:10, 13; cf. Sir 48:9, 12).[589] Plainly, in view of both these earlier biblical models, Jesus is passing on his prophetic ministry and empowerment to his disciples.[590]

In Acts, granted, the Spirit carries on Jesus's ministry in a sense (cf. Acts 9:5, 34).[591] But it seems closer to the heart of Luke's emphasis to say that the disciples carry on Jesus's ministry and that the Spirit anoints[592] or empowers both for their tasks (Luke 4:18; Acts 2:17–18; 10:38).

II. ELIJAH IN LUKE-ACTS

Because the Elijah-Elisha succession is by far the most relevant as background for Acts 1:9–11, it is helpful to note Luke's comparisons and contrasts between Jesus and Elijah elsewhere. But it may be helpful to survey other early Christian comparisons between Jesus and Elijah.

584. Joshua also appears as Moses's *successor* (Latin in *Test. Mos.* 1:7; 10:15; διάδοχος in Sir 46:1). Later rabbis viewed prophets' disciples on the analogy with rabbinic academies (e.g., *Tg. Jon.* on 1 Sam 19:23; 2 Kgs 6:1; 9:1, 4); likewise, CD VIII, 20–21 assimilates Jeremiah's Baruch to Elisha's Gehazi. On Moses-Joshua succession in the sources, see Talbert, *Mediterranean Milieu*, 33–35; he also notes the Saul-David succession, citing 1 Kgs 16–18 LXX (this is actually the subtext of much of 1 Samuel), and the succession from David to Solomon (35). Of the many succession narratives, the closest analogies are in the LXX (51).

585. *Gen. Rab.* 58:2; *Pesiq. Rab.* 51:2, bar.

586. Rabbi Nehemiah claimed that God drove off marauders in response to the prayers of a pious sage; God later did the same for his disciple, though the disciple's hand withered; God neither drove off marauders nor withered a hand in response to the prayers of the disciple's disciple (*y. Ta'an.* 3:8, §2; *Pesiq. Rab Kah.* 24:18).

587. With, e.g., Green, "Repetition," 292. Elisha's miracles also evoke those of Elijah (Levine, "Twice"). Elijah provided a model for hagiographic portrayals of signs workers from Hanina ben Dosa to Anthony of Egypt (Galley, "Heilige"); for Shenoute and other Egyptian saints, see Frankfurter, *Religion in Egypt*, 20. Talbert, *Mediterranean Milieu*, 53, compares also the Spirit coming "on" them as on Elisha (though this is familiar OT and Lukan terminology).

588. The Elijah story imitates that of Moses at some clear points (compare 1 Kgs 19:8 with Exod 3:1; 24:18; 34:28), just as Elisha's recapitulates that of Elijah at points; thus we should expect diverse OT connections when we find any.

589. Despite Scripture's explicit claim that Moses died (Deut 34:5–6; cf. 1 En. 89:38; 2 Bar. 17:4; m. 'Ab. 5:9; Tg. Neof. 1 on Deut 33:21), there are postbiblical reports of Moses's survival (e.g., one view mentioned in *Sipre Deut.* 357.10.5; *b. Soṭah* 13b; cf. Mark 9:4; Rev 11:6) as well as later polemic against such a perspective (e.g., *Deut. Rab.* 11:10). Everyone acknowledged that Moses's death was unusual at the least (cf., e.g., Philo *Sacr.* 8–10; *Test. Mos.* 11:8; *'Abot R. Nat.* 12 A).

590. Johnson, *Acts*, 30; Stronstad, *Charismatic Theology*, 20–21.

591. E.g., Quesnel, "Critère." This idea is, however, much more prominent in the Fourth Gospel (see John 14:16–17, 26; 16:13–15; Keener, *John*, 966–69); but even in John, compare 15:27 with 15:26.

592. Although Luke (unlike some other early Christian writers, 2 Cor 1:21; 1 John 2:20, 27) reserves "anoint" for Jesus, associated with his title as the Christ (Acts 4:27).

In Mark, followed and articulated more explicitly by Matthew, John is the new Elijah, the Lord's promised forerunner (Mal 4:5; Sir 48:10; Mark 9:13; Matt 17:12–13). For John's Gospel, the Baptist is neither Elijah nor the Mosaic prophet (John 1:21, 25);[593] although some rightly recognized Jesus as a prophet, he is not *merely* a prophet (4:19; 6:14; 7:40). For Revelation, the church apparently subsumes the roles of Elijah and Moses (Rev 11:6, 12).[594] Other early Christians viewed Elijah as a model of faith in general (Jas 5:17); in later centuries, Shenoute and some other Egyptian Christian saints were portrayed according to the model of Elijah.[595]

In Luke-Acts, however, Jesus occasionally and John more often (Luke 1:17) fill the role of Elijah; most significant are the passages where Jesus is like Elijah but much greater than he.[596] Jesus heals leprosy (5:12–13) like Elisha (2 Kgs 5:14; Luke 4:27; cf. perhaps Moses in Num 12:13–15) and does other works that are applied exclusively or especially to these prophets. Many of these comparisons are most explicit in Luke 9 and 10. In Luke 8–10, Jesus sometimes resembles Elijah, though not all the proposed connections here are clear. He raises the dead (7:14–15; 8:54–55), sometimes in relative privacy (8:51; but already Mark 5:40; 1 Kgs 17:19–23; 2 Kgs 4:33); the life of the child returns (Luke 8:55; 1 Kgs 17:22; cf. 2 Kgs 4:35; not explicit in Mark 5:42); compare also the "upper room" as the scene for a raising from the dead in Acts 9:37–39 (1 Kgs 17:19, 23; 2 Kgs 4:10, 21, 32).[597] Jesus multiplies food (Luke 9:16–17) as Elijah and Elisha did (1 Kgs 17:16; 2 Kgs 4:3–7, 42–44). Power flowing from Jesus involuntarily (Luke 8:46) might resemble Elisha in 2 Kgs 13:21. Jesus's command to his disciples to greet no one because of the urgency of their mission (Luke 10:4; missing in Matt 10:10) echoes Elisha in 2 Kgs 4:29. The most explicit connection appears in Luke's special programmatic scene in the Nazareth synagogue, where Jesus compares his own ministry with those of Elijah and Elisha (Luke 4:25–27; see table on p. 715).

The contrasts, however, are more explicit; yet these are contrasts not because Jesus is unlike Elijah but because, though much like him, he is by far his superior. Jesus appears in Luke 9:8 as a reported new John, Elijah, or prophet (moved from Mark 6:15). But Jesus *counters* this perception (Luke 9:19) by inviting his disciples to recognize his messiahship (9:20). Jesus is no mere Elijah but one with whom

593. Cf. discussion in Keener, *John*, 434–37.

594. Thus many commentators, including Keener, *Revelation*, 289–93; Bowman, *Drama*, 71; Hill, *Prophecy*, 89; Bauckham, *Climax*, 166, 273–75; Michaels, *Revelation*, 138–39; Talbert, *Apocalypse*, 45–46; Aune, *Revelation*, 631; Beale, *Revelation*, 572–75; Mounce, *Revelation*, 218; Reddish, *Revelation*, 211–12. This couple balances the two evil figures of Rev 13:1, 11, one of which is also a *redivivus* figure (a new Nero).

595. Frankfurter, *Religion in Egypt*, 20 ("an identification apparently often made for charismatic Christian figures in this period"). This may carry Luke's parallels to a logical conclusion, insisting that the continuity from the OT through the apostolic era continued afterward.

596. Many scholars note Elijah-Elisha typology in Luke-Acts; see, e.g., Brodie, "Emulation"; Stronstad, *Charismatic Theology*, 44. Certainly, Luke takes at least some of this material, and probably more, from tradition (cf. Achtemeier, "Perspective on Miracles," who doubts that Luke so shaped the material). Bostock, "Elisha," suggests that Jesus (as John/Elijah's successor) views himself as Elisha. Elijah is far more prominent in sources of this period, but Josephus increases the prominence of Elisha (whom he associates with political agendas; Höffken, "Elischa"). Some even view the historical Jesus in terms of the eschatological Elijah (e.g., Meier, "Quest"). Brodie, *Interpreter*, is thus right in observing connections with the Elijah-Elisha narratives, but he errs in viewing Luke as creatively "rewriting" them; rather, Luke rewrites his sources about Jesus and some of his movement in light of the connection tradition supplied about Elijah (with, e.g., Marshall, "Acts," 525; Evans, "Function," 70n4).

597. The term is not common in the OT, but upper rooms were natural places to keep corpses during preparation for burial. The term ὑπερῷον appears twenty-two times in our conventional LXX, four of them in these texts (1 Kgs 17:19, 23; 2 Kgs 4:10–11), or about 18 percent of the uses; the NT uses of this term (though cf. Mark 14:15; Luke 22:12) are only Acts 1:13; 9:37, 39; 20:8 (hence 75 percent appear in a resuscitation narrative).

Activity	Jesus	Elijah	Elisha or others
Heals leprosy	Luke 5:12–13	—	2 Kgs 5:14; cf. Num 12:13–15
Raises the dead relatively privately	Luke 8:51	1 Kgs 17:19–23	2 Kgs 4:33
Child's life returns	Luke 8:55	1 Kgs 17:22	2 Kgs 4:35
Upper room as scene for raising	(Peter in Acts 9:37–39)	1 Kgs 17:19, 23	2 Kgs 4:10, 21, 32
Multiplies food	Luke 9:16–17	1 Kgs 17:16	2 Kgs 4:3–7, 42–44
"Greet no one"	Luke 10:4	—	2 Kgs 4:29
Explicit comparison	Luke 4:25–27	—	—

Elijah and Moses speak respectfully (9:30, 33–35).[598] In "special" Lukan material, the disciples want to call down fire (9:54) as Elijah did (1 Kgs 18:37–38), but Jesus rebukes them (Luke 9:55). A prospective disciple wants to follow Jesus according to the rigorous standards by which Elisha followed Elijah (9:61; 1 Kgs 19:20), but Jesus demands more (Luke 9:62; cf. 1 Kgs 19:19, 21).[599]

For Luke, John is explicitly the new Elijah; he will go in his "Spirit and power" (Luke 1:17) because, like him, he is filled with the Holy Spirit (1:15).[600] In a sense, John, like Elisha, has received Elijah's mantle (2 Kgs 2:12–13); both Elisha (2:9) and John (Luke 1:17) receive the Spirit of Elijah.[601] His mission of turning fathers to children refers to the role of the Lord's forerunner in Mal 4:5, reinforcing Luke's subtle hints at a divine Christology.[602] John's mission as a new Elijah is to Israel (Luke 1:15–17), but Elijah's mission, as Jesus declares in his programmatic statement, extended to Gentiles (4:25–27); thus it prefigures the church's Gentile mission in Acts. Because John follows the model of Elijah by being "filled with the Spirit" (1:15), the church, soon to be filled with the Spirit (Acts 2:4), will do the same.[603] The exalted Jesus is much greater than the ascending Elijah (see table on p. 716), and he gives the church, his "successor," a greater measure of the Spirit than Elijah passed on to Elisha (2:33).

III. ELIJAH TRADITIONS IN EARLY JUDAISM

Jewish tradition naturally developed the image of Elijah in multiple directions.[604] It elaborated the promise of Elijah's return in Mal 4:5–6 (MT 3:23–24), a development that surfaces as early as Ben Sira (Sir 48:10). Later rabbis seized particularly

598. That he should be heeded (Luke 9:35) may recall Deut 18:18, about Moses (cf. Bock, *Luke*, 874; Mauser, *Christ in Wilderness*, 114; Davies, *Sermon*, 24; Lane, *Mark*, 321; Bruce, *Time*, 40; Longenecker, *Christology*, 36; Gundry, *Matthew*, 343; Young, *Jewish Theologian*, 211).

599. The parallel (Q) pericope in Matthew (Matt 8:19–22) omits this anecdote, possibly implying Lukan composition; yet if it is pre-Lukan (more in line with my view of Luke's historiography), this is a logical place to insert it.

600. Elijah's "Spirit and power" functions as a hendiadys, hence "Spirit of power"; this suggests (at least in part) miracle-working power, as in the comment on Acts 1:8 (though Luke cannot attribute miracles to John; cf. John 10:41). For one discussion of the Spirit in Luke 1–2, see Turner, *Power*, 140–65.

601. Luke's addition of "power" to the Spirit (certainly not from 2 Kgs 2:16 LXX; Wis 5:23) is typically Lukan (Luke 1:35; 4:14; Acts 1:8; 10:38) and not surprising to one in the Pauline circle (Rom 1:4; 15:13, 19; 1 Cor 2:4; Eph 3:16; 1 Thess 1:5; 2 Tim 1:7). For OT precedent, cf. 1 Sam 11:6; Mic 3:8; Zech 4:6; see also Wis 11:20.

602. In this case, following Mark (Mark 1:2–3), though Luke, following Q (cf. Matt 11:10), uses the Malachi part of Mark's reference only in Luke 7:27. On divine Christology in some Lukan passages, see comment on Acts 2:21.

603. That the disciples can rejoice in their miraculous ministries (Luke 10:17) shortly after John's demise (9:7, 9; more clearly connected in Mark 6:13–30) casts the shadow of suffering forward over their ministries as successors of John's successor.

604. I have adapted material here from Keener, *John*, 435–36.

Elijah or Elisha	Jesus
(Elijah honors him, Luke 9:30–35)	Jesus repudiates idea that he is a new Elijah (Luke 9:8, 19–20)
Elijah calls down fire (1 Kgs 18:37–38)	Jesus refuses to call down fire (Luke 9:54–55)
Elijah permits Elisha to bid farewell to his family (1 Kgs 19:19–21)	Jesus's demands are higher than Elijah's (Luke 9:61–62)
—	John rather than Jesus is the new Elijah, forerunner for the Lord (who is Jesus; Luke 1:17)

on this feature of eschatological expectation, although they developed it in very different ways from nonrabbinic streams of thought.[605] That Elijah remained alive was safely assumed from the biblical text (2 Kgs 2:9–12; Mal 4:5–6; cf. 1 Macc 2:58; Sir 48:9), and later rabbis continued to work from this assumption.[606] In these later rabbis, however, his role in the present period before the final time became more prominent than his eschatological function, perhaps due, in part, to the de-emphasis of messianic eschatology after the sufferings under Hadrian. (The rabbis also tended to view the prophets as protoscribes.)[607] Like other biblical prophets, Elijah became a master halakist, often sent to settle rabbinic disputes;[608] also sometimes described with a role comparable to that of angels,[609] the rabbinic Elijah often was sent on divine errands to miraculously aid rabbis.[610]

Other rabbinic evidence, however, does point to Elijah's eschatological role. The rabbis were clearly aware of Malachi's prophecy and anticipated Elijah returning at the end of the age,[611] destined to appear alongside rabbinism's other eschatological figures.[612] Elijah would also exercise an eschatological halakic role,[613] especially (in line with the rabbinic interpretation of Malachi) in determining proper lines of descent

605. Diversity of perspectives on Elijah extended even to interpretations of biblical narratives; cf. Zeller, "Elija."

606. E.g., b. Mo'ed Qaṭ. 26a; Sanh. 113b, although such texts may reflect differing implications as to whether (perhaps 'Abot R. Nat. 38, §103 B, till the Messiah comes) or not (cf. Pesiq. Rab Kah. 9:4) he would die. Josephus's words are more guarded (Ant. 9.28), perhaps accommodating Hellenistic skepticism.

607. See Keener, Spirit, 20–22; Sipra Sh. M.D. 99.5.6; also Tg. Jon. on 1 Sam 19:23; on 2 Kgs 6:1; 9:1, 4.

608. 'Abot R. Nat. 2 A; b. 'Abod. Zar. 36a; Ber. 3a; Giṭ. 42b; Ḥag. 9b; Qidd. 79a; Menaḥ. 32a; y. Ber. 9:2, §3; Ter. 1:6 (it is unclear here whether the activity in this text was in ancient Israel or during the rabbinic period); Pesiq. Rab Kah. 11:22; Elijah conversed with rabbis about unspecified or nonhalakic issues in b. B. Meṣi'a 85b; Sanh. 113b; Yoma 19b–20a. Cf. his settling of questions pertaining to himself in b. Ketub. 106a (instructing R. Anan as he wrote Seder Eliyahu Rabbah and Seder Eliyahu Zuta); Gen. Rab. 71:9. Elijah already appears as "greatly zealous for the law" in 1 Macc 2:58.

609. E.g., b. Ber. 4b; he appears as an executor of judgment against a sacrilegious man in b. Ber. 6b; as a bearer of news to a rabbi in b. Šabb. 33b (Simeon ben Yohai); Deut. Rab. 5:15 (Meir); Tg. Rishon on Esth 4:1 (to Mordecai). For his knowledge of what God does, cf. b. B. Meṣi'a 59b; he wakes the deceased patriarchs for prayers in b. B. Meṣi'a 85b.

610. E.g., b. 'Abod. Zar. 17b; Ta'an. 21a; y. Ketub. 12:3, §6; Kil. 9:3, §4; Pesiq. Rab Kah. 18:5; Gen. Rab. 33:3. Other miracle workers may have been associated with Elijah (cf. Vermes, Jesus the Jew, 72, 76–77, whose case is probable though not certain). His appearances to Jewish teachers seem to begin in the second-century sources (Bamberger, "Prophet," 308).

611. Sipre Deut. 41.4.3; 342.5.2; b. Menaḥ. 63a; at the redemption of the new exodus in Exod. Rab. 3:4; he would punish the Gentiles in Gen. Rab. 71:9; involved in the resurrection in m. Soṭah 9:15; y. Šeqal. 3:3. Ford, Revelation, 179, cites also Pirqe R. El. 43, 47; S. Eli. Rab. 25ff.

612. E.g., the four craftsmen and comments on the seven shepherds of Mic 5:4 in b. Sukkah 52b; Pesiq. Rab Kah. 5:9; Song Rab. 8:9, §3; Pesiq. Rab. 15:14/15 (one may compare the priest anointed for war—and perhaps the two messiahs—in these texts with earlier Qumran expectation). In late texts of varying date and opinion, he is associated with the Messiah (Lev. Rab. 34:8; Deut. Rab. 6:7; Song Rab. 2:13, §4), preceding him (b. 'Erub. 43b; Pesiq. Rab. 35:4), coming with him (Exod. Rab. 18:12), knowing something about the time of his coming (b. B. Meṣi'a 85b); he is also protective of his coming reign (Gen. Rab. 83:4); or Elijah is Phinehas the high priest (Tg. Ps.-J. on Exod 6:18; cf. L.A.B. 48:1).

613. Primarily in Amoraic texts, e.g., b. Ber. 35b; B. Bat. 94b; B. Meṣi'a 3a, 30a; Menaḥ. 45a, bar.

(Israelites versus proselytes, etc.).[614] Although the bulk of this evidence derives from the more numerous Amoraic texts, some of it is also Tannaitic.[615]

The evidence for Elijah's eschatological role is hardly limited, however, to later rabbinic evidence.[616] Aune finds reference to him as forerunner in *1 En.* 90:31;[617] *4 Ezra* 6:26 assumes him among historic figures with special roles at the end of the age (among those who never died);[618] and Matthew (Matt 17:10) unhesitatingly follows Mark (Mark 9:11) in presupposing that this role was widely known in Jewish circles. Sirach's portrayal of Elijah as a restorer and forerunner of the end time (if not explicitly of the Messiah) is very close to this.[619]

Comparing these traditions with Luke may highlight the contrast more than the similarities, apart from the expectation of his return. Luke follows the biblical narrative model of Elijah, especially applicable because of the biblical promise of Elijah's eschatological activity; it is not clear whether he knew of other Jewish traditions about Elijah. The allusion to Elijah in the ascension narrative, along with widespread expectation of Elijah's eschatological role, may reinforce the emphasis on inaugurated eschatology in this context.

b. Ascension in Its Ancient Setting

Ancient literature includes many ascension narratives, although the closest background for Luke's is the early biblical account of Elijah's ascension, connected with Elisha's receiving a double portion of his spirit.[620] How would ancients have understood such narratives? What implications does this understanding have for discovering what Luke sought to communicate to his first-century audience through this narrative? Finally, if we find significant evidence for pre-Lukan tradition (and we do), how can modern readers grasp or (for Christian readers) assimilate a tradition so foreign to our contemporary cosmology?

1. Ascension Narratives

Ascension narratives were common in ancient literature;[621] what is most distinctive about that of Jesus is his bodily resurrection, not his relocation. Most of these

614. M. *'Ed.* 8:7; t. *'Ed.* 3:4; cf. *Song Rab.* 4:12, §5.

615. E.g., m. *'Ed.* 8:7; *Soṭah* 9:15. Milikowsky, "'Lyhw,'" cites *Seder 'Olam* as an early source for Elijah as the Messiah's forerunner (although the source's date may be debated).

616. See the many references (especially the nonrabbinic ones) in Teeple, *Prophet*, 4–8. Cf. also *Sib. Or.* 2.187–89; but because its context is a Christian interpolation, we cannot date it early with much assurance; 4Q382 frg. 31 may be eschatological (in a context about Elijah, frg. 1, 3, 9). Justin's view that Elijah precedes Christ (*Dial.* 8.4) fits the evidence (cf. Williams, *Justin Martyr*, 18n5), but that he would anoint the Messiah (*Dial.* 8; 49) lacks other attestation (see Schneider, "Reflections," 169; the parallel in Williams, *Justin Martyr*, 18n6, is inadequate).

617. Aune, *Prophecy*, 124–25; cf. Brown, *John*, 1:47. This is relevant even if rabbinic evidence for Elijah's role as forerunner (b. *'Erub.* 43ab, bar.) is later (as contended by Faierstein, "Elijah" [see esp. 86]; Fitzmyer, "Elijah"; contrast Allison, "Elijah").

618. Enoch, Moses, "and possibly Ezra, Baruch, and Jeremiah" (Longenecker, *Christology*, 33).

619. Teeple, *Prophet*, 106, is probably wrong, however, in identifying Elijah in this text with a prophet-king Messiah.

620. "Double portion" is the right of the firstborn son (Deut 21:17). Although Elijah's spirit (2 Kgs 2:9, 15) probably refers to the Spirit of the Lord (cf. 2 Kgs 2:16; Deut 34:9), if one extends it figuratively to include a sense of Elijah's presence, this could apply in a much fuller sense to Jesus (Acts 3:6; 9:34).

621. E.g., Talbert, "Myth" (emphasizing Hellenistic Jewish sources); idem, *Acts*, 2–4; Strelan, *Strange Acts*, 42–47; Eckey, *Apostelgeschichte*, 57–60; Boring et al., *Commentary*, 309 (citing Dio Cass. 56.46 for Augustus's ascension, according to one witness); Diod. Sic. 4.38.3–5 for that of Heracles; Romulus in Ovid *Fasti* 2.500–509 and Plut. *Numa* 11.3; ironically implied for Peregrinus in Lucian *Peregr.* 39; for emphasis on witnesses for Greek ascensions, Aune, *Revelation*, 626–27; for some sense for kings (at death) in ancient Egypt, cf. Davis, "Ascension-Myth"; *ANET* 18. If one counts others snatched up (like Ganymede), one could add further examples; see Aune, *Revelation*, 689–90. Van der Horst, "Macrobius," 225, cites Macrob. *Comm.* 1.9.9.

claims addressed the mythological past and appeared more often in dramatists and mythographers than in historians (except for the universal histories that treated the very ancient and disputed periods acknowledged to be uncertain).[622] Thus Heracles vanished (ἠφανίσθη) from among people after his ascension (Lysias *Or.* 2.11, §191). Dionysus seized his mother, Semele, from Hades and both ascended to heaven (Apollod. *Bib.* 3.5.3). Zeus took Polydeuces to heaven (3.11.2). Romans claimed that Romulus was translated to heaven (Sil. It. 5.145). When Iphigeneia disappeared, some assumed that she was taken up among the gods.[623]

Usually ascension narratives apply to heroes who had a divine parent anyway, but sometimes writers claimed that heroes were able to ascend because they merited it. Thus, for example, Hercules was taken into heaven (*caelo receptus*) to reward his "virtue" (*virtutem*) (Phaedrus 4.12.3).[624] Alexander's evil deeds nearly prevented his ascension to heaven.[625] Josephus's Moses, perhaps because of his humility, does not want anyone to think that he ascended because of special virtue (*Ant.* 4.326). Elijah, by contrast, was taken up (ἀνελήμφθη) as far as into heaven (εἰς τὸν οὐρανόν) because of his great zeal for the law (1 Macc 2:58).

In Jewish narratives, God[626] or angels[627] could go up to heaven again. Sometimes these provide formal parallels to Luke's description (though some such parallels merely reflect the common theme of ascension in both); the ascent of divine wisdom might provide an especially fruitful theological comparison, although the evidence is limited and is figurative rather than epic.[628] But these differ in content from Luke's emphasis on a human's being raised to heaven at the end of his earthly ministry. (Angels descended from heaven[629] and ascended there again precisely because many were thought to normally live there. The common denominator of ascension stories is simply a cosmology that places the suprahuman in heaven.)[630]

Early Jewish rapture stories often developed OT accounts (Elijah)[631] or possible hints (Moses,[632] Enoch),[633] though sometimes they were transferred to other char-

---

622. But there are exceptions, such as the ex-praetor who testified that he saw Augustus's form ascending to heaven after his cremation (Suet. *Aug.* 100.3–4, esp. 100.4). Supposedly divine beings started the fire at Caesar's pyre (Suet. *Jul.* 84.3).

623. Eurip. *Iph. Aul.* 1608, 1614, 1622; *Cypria* 8 (the no-longer-extant epic, but summarized in Proclus *Chrestomathia*, which the editor supplements by Apollod. *Epit.* 3.1–33; *GEF* 75). For another case of readily bestowed immortality, here for Odysseus's family, see *Telegony* 4 (from Proclus; *GEF* 169). These examples do not include hypothetical or figurative claims of mortals ascending to find deities (as in Char. *Chaer.* 3.2.5; 3.3.7).

624. Heracles's "virtue" included his heroism and a highly allegorical reading of his behavior that would not fit any likely Jewish or Christian readings of his morality in classical texts.

625. Val. Max. 9.3.ext. 1, who apparently thinks Alexander's ambitious conquests merited his ascension anyway.

626. In *Jub.* 32:20, Jacob watches God's ascent (cf. 32:21, where an angel descends).

627. Luke 2:15; Judg 13:20; Tob 12:20 (ἀναβαίνω); *Test. Ab.* 4:5; 8:1; 9:7; 15:11 A (ἀνελθών; in 9 A, also λάβε and ὕψωσον, on a cherubim chariot); 4:4 B (ἀνελήφθη; as in ἀναλημφθείς, Acts 1:11); *Test. Ab.* 8:2–3 B (ἀνῆλθεν); *L.A.E.* 43:4; *Jos. Asen.* 17:8, some MSS (absent from Philonenko, 190, for 17:6; with a chariot of fire comparable to Elijah's); 3 *Bar.* 3:1.

628. Wisdom descended from heaven to save Israel (Wis 18:15), and no one could ascend to grasp it (Bar 3:29).

629. E.g., *Jub.* 32:21; 2 *Bar.* 6:5; 4 Macc 4:10; 4Q537 frg. 1, introductory line; Gal 1:8; Rev 10:1. On the ascent and descent of angels (together in, e.g., Gen 28:12; *Jub.* 27:21), especially the sometimes divine angel of the Lord, see further Talbert, *Gospel*, 57, 62.

630. E.g., Mark 13:32; 1 *En.* 97:2; 104:1; 106:12–13.

631. 1 Macc 2:58.

632. See Zwiep, *Ascension*, 64–71; cf. Meeks, *Prophet-King*, 156–58, 205–9, 241–46. Some rabbis apparently believed that Moses did not, in fact, die (*Sipre Deut.* 357.10.5; cf. Rev 11:6); cf. also Moses's earlier ascension to receive the Torah (e.g., *Sipre Deut.* 49.2.1). Some scholars connect Moses's ascension with older myths of heavenly invasion (Halperin, "Ascension"), though I am not persuaded.

633. For Enoch ascension traditions, see, e.g., Sir 49:14; Heb 11:5; *Tg. Ps.-J.* on Gen 4:24; Zwiep, *Ascension*, 41–51 (and cf. 51–58); Luke, "Enoch's Ascension." Ancient interpreters differed in their understanding of

acters as well (Ezra).[634] Josephus believed that Enoch went to God (*Ant.* 1.85); that Elijah did as Enoch (9.28);[635] and that Moses wrote of his apparent death only to prevent people from thinking that he went to God (4.326).[636] These Jewish stories form almost the closest repository of motifs from which Luke can draw.[637]

Yet without doubt, the closest parallel, one carrying over from the impartation of the Spirit in the context (Acts 1:8), is the biblical account of Elisha's succession of Elijah.[638] Luke 24:51 and Acts 1:9–11 both echo 2 Kgs 2:11.[639] Luke's repetition of ἀναλαμβάνω for the ascension (Acts 1:2, 11) fits the use (also repeated) in 4 Kgdms 2:9–11.[640] Elisha received the firstborn's portion of the Spirit who was on Elijah, precisely because he was with him at his ascension (2 Kgs 2:10); this underlines the importance of the disciples' presence with Jesus at his ascension in the present passage. (The clouds, which do not appear explicitly in 2 Kgs 2, probably evoke Dan 7:13, as in Luke 21:27; Mark 14:62.)[641] That they *saw* Jesus ascend into heaven might evoke Elisha witnessing Elijah ascend,[642] which validated Elisha's succession because he remained with Elijah long enough to witness it (2 Kgs 2:15–18). Zwiep's conclusion here is certainly correct:

> Luke's primary source of inspiration was the biblical story of Elijah's ἀνάλημψις into heaven and his expected return at the end time (2 Kings 2:1–18; Mal 3:22–23; Sir 48:9–12; 1 Macc 2:58). Luke's terminology to describe Jesus's ascension (ἀναλαμβάνομαι, Acts 1:2, 11, 22; ἀνάλημψις, Luke 9:51) and the nature of his eschatological activity (ἀποκαθίστημι, Acts 1:6; ἀποκατάστασις, Acts 3:21) are clear echoes of the language traditionally used in connection with Elijah. The stress on the visibility of Elijah's departure to heaven (2 Kings 2:10), the subsequent passing of the spirit from Elijah to Elisha as a means of empowerment for his future task (2 Kings 2:9–10), and the promise of his eschatological return "to restore all things" (cf. Mal 3:23; Sir 48:12) are themes which, each in their own way, have put their imprint upon . . . the opening chapters of Acts.[643]

Enoch (cf., e.g., Luciani, "Sorte"); many rabbis, perhaps polemicizing against the Enoch tradition, denigrating him, claimed that he died for wickedness or before he could become wicked (*Gen. Rab.* 25:1; cf. Wis 4:10–11). Prerabbinic sources portray him favorably (e.g., Sir 44:16; Ps.-Eup., via Alexander Polyhistor, in Euseb. *P.E.* 9.17.8–9; *Jub.* 10:17; *1 En.* passim, e.g., 83:8; 106:7; 4Q227; 4Q530 II, 21–23; 1Qap Gen^ar II, 19–25; V; Philo *Abr.* 17–19; *Test. Dan* 5:6; *Test. Jud.* 18:1; *Asc. Is.* 9:9; cf. VanderKam, "Traditions," 245) and as escaping death (*Jub.* 4:23; *Test. Ab.* 11:5 B). Enoch literature circulated widely (cf., e.g., *Test. Sim.* 5:4; *Test. Naph.* 4:1), and his name was used by some later Jews (*CPJ* 3:40, §478; 3:98, §509).

634. For Ezra, see, e.g., (later) *Gr. Ezra* 5:7. See Aune, *Revelation*, 625–26; Zwiep, *Ascension*, 71–74. Cf. Baruch in Zwiep, *Ascension*, 74–75.

635. Although, as the LCL note here points out (R. Marcus, LCL, 6:16–17), Josephus plays down the miraculous element of Elijah's ascension proper.

636. Cf. Begg, "Disappearances of Enoch" (who cites Moses's humility in Jos. *Ant.* 3.212). Josephus probably employs the appealing language of deification while maintaining a strict monotheism; but as noted in our introduction (ch. 6, sect. 2.f; ch. 8, sect. 2.f), he writes for a more sophisticated audience than Luke, one less tolerant of future eschatology (cf. Josephus's approach to the Pharisaic doctrine of the resurrection, *Ant.* 18.14; esp. *War* 2.163).

637. See Palatty, "Ascension" (emphasizing also Tob 12:16–22).

638. With Zwiep, *Ascension*, 59–63, 194; Witherington, *Acts*, 112; Litwak, *Echoes*, 149; Marshall, "Acts," 527; Pervo, *Acts*, 45. Bede envisions a contrast with Elijah here, since he doubts that the latter genuinely ascended to heaven (*Comm. Acts* 1.11).

639. Brodie, "Emulation," 83 (noting "*came to pass*," "*parted*," "*carried up*," and "*heaven*"). Compare possibly walking and talking together in Luke 24:32 (cf. 24:14–30) with 2 Kgs 2:11, although Luke 24:32 precedes the ascension narrative proper.

640. Litwak, *Echoes*, 150; cf. Parsons, *Acts*, 27. Note also the noun cognate in Luke 9:51, which undoubtedly shares in the Elijah allusion (the connection to Isa 53:8 in Feuillet, "Deux references," is improbable).

641. Also Witherington, *Acts*, 112.

642. Cf. similarly Johnson, *Acts*, 31.

643. Zwiep, *Ascension*, 194.

Still, early Christians also found, in Jesus's ascension, fulfillment of Ps 110:1 (explicit in Luke 20:42; Mark 12:36; Matt 22:44; Heb 1:13),[644] exemplified also in this context (Acts 2:33–34; cf. 7:55–56).[645] They cited the authority of Jesus for the use of this text (Mark 12:36; 14:62),[646] and in Luke's story Jesus is also the source for the early Christians' biblical theology surrounding his exaltation (Luke 20:42; 22:69). See comment on Acts 2:33–36 for Luke's use of this key to approaching the ascension's theology.

ii. The Meaning of Jesus's Ascension

Jesus's exaltation is important for Luke, connecting Jesus's resurrection with his messianic enthronement (see Acts 2:25, 30–36). Jesus remains exalted at the Father's right hand (7:55–56; Luke 22:69) until his return (Acts 2:35; Luke 21:27), though he also remains active among his people (e.g., Acts 9:3–5 [esp. "from heaven," v. 3], 34; 16:7; 18:9–10).[647] Some sources extrinsic to Luke's direct narration can also shed light on how he understands the ascension narrative. Certainly, Luke interprets the ascension in light of Ps 110:1; Jesus as exalted Lord imparts his Spirit.[648] Further, the backdrop in the succession narrative of Elijah and Elisha indicates that, for Luke, Jesus is passing his mission to the church as exemplified in its leading representatives.

Often ascension involved apotheosis, transformation into divinity or immortality.[649] A cloud took Heracles to heaven, making him immortal (Apollod. *Bib.* 2.7.7), as he was taken from one place to another (μεταστάντος) to the gods (2.8.1).[650] At Heracles's funeral pyre, he left his human nature (ἀνθρωπείας φύσεως, Philost. *Hrk.* 28.1).[651] When Romulus was taken up, his mortal body was dissolved (Ovid *Metam.* 14.824–28); after a star from heaven burned up his wife, changing her mortal body, she was reunited with him as a goddess (14.846–51). After a voice called Empedocles up to heaven, his followers decided that he had become a god and that they should now sacrifice to him (Diog. Laert. 8.2.68). Some ancients apparently thought that Apollonius ascended to heaven (Philost. *Vit. Apoll.* 8.30). Some scholars have also compared imperial apotheosis after death (though, naturally, without bodily

644. Allusions further appear in Acts 2:33; Luke 22:69; Mark 14:62; Matt 26:64; Mark 16:19; Rom 8:34; Eph 1:20; Col 3:1; Heb 1:3; 8:1; 10:12; 12:2; 1 Pet 3:22.

645. Most NT writers who refer to the ascension do so only by way of Ps 110:1 (see Boismard and Lamouille, *Actes*, 3:35).

646. On the basis especially of the antinomy regarding Davidic descent in Mark 12:35–37, many contend that this pericope reflects authentic Jesus tradition; see Jeremias, *Theology*, 259; France, *Matthew*, 321.

647. Sleeman, *Geography*, 257 (and passim), argues that the ascension narrative shapes the texture of all of Acts 1–11.

648. This model differs from that of Jesus as prototype for the Spirit-filled life (cf. Turner's emphasis on the exalted Lord versus the prototype; e.g., "Jesus and Spirit in Perspective"), but Luke does not treat them as incompatible.

649. See, e.g., discussion in Scott, "Ascent," 447–48. On Greek deities' mortal sons who suffer, are taken to heaven, and become saviors, see Strelan, *Strange Acts*, 46 (following van Tilborg and Counet, *Appearances*, 235); in accord with Greek perspectives on the body, these do not include bodily resurrection. For more general Greek conceptions of deification, see also the data in Keener, *John*, 298–99 (cf. 178–79, 292–93).

650. Apollodorus uses the same word (μεθίστημι) for heavenly relocation in *Bib.* 3.11.2. Widely seen sculptures (e.g., in Athens's agora) celebrated Heracles's apotheosis (*Athenian Agora*, 47).

651. Burning away mortal elements of infant demigods also appears (Apollod. *Bib.* 3.13.6); whether this is related to sacrificing infants (cf. Lev 18:21; 20:2–5; 2 Kgs 23:10; Jer 32:35; Lycophron *Alex.* 229; Arrian *Alex.* 1.5.7; Tert. *Apol.* 9.2; Glueck, *Rivers*, 61; Albright, *Biblical Period*, 17; idem, *Yahweh*, 152; Rundin, "Pozo Moro"; especially, nearly a hundred infant skeletons in Ashkelon's Roman-period sewers in Stager, "Eroticism at Ashkelon") is unclear. (On human sacrifice in general in antiquity, in myth or history, see, e.g., Hom. *Il.* 23.175–76; Aeschylus *Ag.* 205–26; Soph. *El.* 530–45; Cic. *Resp.* 3.9.15; Apollod. *Bib.* 2.5.11; Appian *Bell. civ.* 1.14.117; Sen. Y. *Troj.* 360–70; Plut. *Par. St.* 35, *Mor.* 314CD; *Cic.* 10.3; *Themist.* 13.2–3; Suet. *Aug.* 15; Lucian *Sacr.* 13; Xen. *Eph. Anthia* 2.13; Ritner, *Mechanics*, 162–63; Mitchell, "Archaeology," 185; Dandoy, Selinsky, and Voigt, "Celtic Sacrifice"; Euskirchen, "Celts: Religion," 98).

resurrection intervening!), which functioned as political legitimation.[652] (On the deification of emperors at their death, see comment on Acts 12:22–23.) Perhaps most relevant is that some Greco-Egyptian Jewish sources viewed Moses's putative ascent to heaven as an apotheosis.[653]

Some scholars therefore point out that even uninformed Gentiles would see in this text at least hints about Jesus's current divinity and immortality.[654] Granted, to read the account as a narration of Jesus's "deification" violates an intrinsic reading of Luke-Acts (see discussion below); nevertheless, this Greek perspective is helpful in recognizing the extent to which Jesus's ascension is also his exaltation to a new public status.

Yet it is not the entire picture. Since Luke's ideal audience is knowledgeable in the LXX and the rest of Luke-Acts, suggestions of "deification" here are overstated. Monotheistic rapture accounts (e.g., of Elijah, Enoch, or Moses) do not generally connote deification or the conferral of immortality for virtue.[655] Jesus was already God's Son (Luke 1:32, 35; 3:22; 4:41; 8:28; 9:35; 10:22; 22:70) and, more important, had already exchanged his mortal body for an immortal one at the resurrection (24:31–43). The exaltation is Jesus's public investiture, but Aune contends that a purely pagan Greek reading without taking into account Luke's report of the resurrection is inadequate: "The ascension tradition of Luke-Acts, while it has external similarities with Graeco-Roman conceptions of *ascensio*, has two important material differences: (1) The ascension tradition . . . does not change the *status* of Jesus, only his *location* and *mode of presence*. (2) The ascension tradition is intimately connected with the resurrection tradition."[656] Jesus's status as God's Son is not new; his public status, enthroned at God's right hand, is new but, even for Luke, one of the more Hellenistic writers in the NT, it rests on Ps 110, not on anything resembling Greek apotheosis.[657] Luke undoubtedly invested special attention in the introductory section to Acts as he did the first two chapters of his Gospel, in which he would seek to connect with the entire range of his audience. But despite foreshadowings of his Diaspora milieu (esp. in 2:9–11), Acts 1–2 still moves in the Judean world of Luke's Gospel. It shares the biblically informed ideal audience also addressed through the first two chapters of the Gospel.

III. How Can Modern Interpreters Approach This Narrative's Cosmology?

Although many scholars feel comfortable with the narrative's theology, they are less comfortable with its historical value; some naturally question both, especially

---

652. Gilbert, "Propaganda," 242–47, esp. 243. Although early Christians naturally drew this comparison (as noted Gilbert, "Propaganda," 247, citing Justin *1 Apol.* 21), Gilbert too readily plays down the more relevant comparison with Elijah (p. 246). On imperial apotheosis as ascent, see further Herz, "Emperors," 314.

653. Scott, "Ascent," 448–50 (citing Ezekiel the Tragedian's *Exagōgē*, especially the heavenly enthronement in Ezek. Trag. *Exag.* 68–89; Philo *Mos.* 1.158; possibly 4Q491 [4QMᵃ] 11 I, 11–18); cf. 4Q374 in Fletcher-Louis, "4Q374." Some suggest that 4Q491 11 I, 8–24 may also allude to a heavenly enthronement-deification of the Teacher of Righteousness (Laansma, "Mysticism," 731).

654. See Talbert, "Concept of Immortals"; idem, *Gospel*, 39; Witherington, *Acts*, 109.

655. See Zwiep, *Ascension*, 194–95. The more hellenized versions may, however, apparently move more in this direction (Scott, "Ascent," 448–50, noted above; cf. Fletcher-Louis, "4Q374"), but certainly these concepts are missing in the biblical accounts that are Luke's clearest model.

656. Aune, "Problem of Genre," 47–48; ancient Judaism did not link resurrection with enthronement (Allison, *Jesus*, 248, following Eskola, *Messiah*, 248). Strelan, *Strange Acts*, 47, also notes that Luke's ascension account is theologically connected with Jesus's parousia.

657. Borgman, *Way*, 257–58, intriguingly contrasts Jesus's ascent with the Spirit's descent. Unfortunately, neither text mentions a "descent"; the closest possible cases are the Spirit's being "poured out" or "falling on" persons, but Luke does not take advantage of the possibility of a contrast between ascent and descent imagery, though it was available to him in Mark 1:10 (cf. Matt 3:16; Eph 4:9–10; in baptism, also *Herm.* 93.4, 6).

those who reasonably expect a historical basis for theological premises presented as historical narrative.

One approach is to view the ascension account as purely visionary.[658] But although one could postulate such an explanation for the original experience behind the account, it is difficult to read Luke on these terms.[659] The verb ἀτενίζω need not point in this direction,[660] nor are angels confined to visions;[661] nor, in view of Acts 8:39, does Luke seem to question whether God could physically relocate his servants, even when he echoes biblical visionary language from Ezekiel.

Lüdemann, not surprisingly, rejects the historicity of the account, rightly noting that it is "rooted in the conceptions of the time."[662] Certainly, modern science renders beyond credibility literal ascensions into "heavens" in the forms assumed by ancient cosmology (see esp. comment on "heaven" in Acts 1:11). Nevertheless, if Luke's tradition reports an event of Jesus being taken from the disciples after his resurrection, one could allow and even expect Luke and/or his sources to understand and describe it in the cosmological language of his day, without denying that he reports a tradition concerning an event. Luke communicates his message for a context where his audience was familiar with deities' residence in heaven (19:35) and Jewish language about heaven (cf., e.g., Isa 66:1 in Acts 7:49; Ps 110:1 in Acts 2:34; and the allusion to Isa 14:12 in Luke 10:15, 18).

Many scholars suggest the theological significance of Luke's language, while not sharing (as in fact virtually no one today does) the cosmological presuppositions that appear to inform his language.[663] Thus Dunn notes that we may accept the ascension while weighting more heavily than Luke's own audience would the metaphoric nature of its description.[664] Benoit argues that early Christians had different traditions about the ascension and hence that the best view is that Christ entered the new, spiritual world, opening it and being exalted on the day of his resurrection.[665] John A. T. Robinson views the ascension as not spatial but as emphasizing Christ's ascendancy over creation.[666] These interpretations appear more plausible if "heaven" not only could function as a location but also "stood analogically for the spiritual world above."[667]

658. Strelan, *Strange Acts*, 38–39; cf., carefully, Pilch, *Flights*, 168–71.

659. One would probably not also think of a collective vision rather than individual ones, given the rareness of collective visions, unless they are experienced supernaturally. See discussion in Licona, "Historicity of Resurrection," 136n196, 346–47; idem, *Resurrection*, 484–85, 573–74; personal correspondence, April 25, 2010; though for the possibility, see O'Connell, "Hallucinations," 75–83.

660. Strelan, *Strange Acts*, 39, cites this usage; but apart from Acts 10:4; 11:6 and possibly 7:55 (we should not think the Sanhedrin experiences a vision in 6:15), the other uses are not visionary; many of the others are in miracle contexts, but this is not the case for Luke 4:20; 22:56; or Acts 23:1. The parallel with Acts 7:55 might help, however, since Stephen is the only person present to see the exalted Son of Man.

661. Strelan, *Strange Acts*, 39–42, connects the angels to visions. An angel appears in a vision in Acts 10:3, but in 12:9 Peter thinks that his experience with an angel is merely visionary, yet is proved wrong; the claim that the women at the tomb saw a "vision of angels" in Luke 24:23 comes from the mouths of skeptical reporters in the narrative world. Thus one may conclude at most that this is one possible way to read the text (as well as the history behind it).

662. Lüdemann, *Christianity*, 30.

663. For one sample application, see, e.g., Mulloor, "Ascension."

664. Dunn, *Acts*, 13.

665. Benoit, *Jesus*, 1:209–53; as already noted, this exaltation on the same day does not leave enough time for the sorts of intimate encounter provided in the Gospels' resurrection narratives.

666. Robinson, "Ascendancy." Transcending a heavenly/earthly dichotomy, cf. Sleeman, *Geography*, drawing on Edward W. Soja's conception of thirdspace. Green, "Acts," 737, cites "visions of enthronement." Although these might appear esp. in the apocalyptic genre, there is no reason in principle to exclude descriptions of apocalyptists' visionary experiences in historical narrative (few other historical narratives have occasion to depict mystics and apocalyptists).

667. Lincoln, *Ephesians*, 20; cf. Lincoln, *Paradise*.

Although Luke often means only "sky" (e.g., Luke 4:25; 8:5; 9:58; 12:56; 13:19; 17:24; 21:11; Acts 2:19; 10:12; 11:6), he at least sometimes follows earlier usage, well documented in early Judaism, for "heaven" as a circumlocution for God (Luke 15:18, 21) or in association with God (11:13) or his realm (15:7; 19:38), associated also with a hope for the righteous (6:23; 10:20; 12:33; 18:22). See further discussion under the heading "Heaven (1:11)" below.

Such "demythologization" dare not be pressed too far, as if we may privilege modern philosophical approaches to ancient texts in disregard of Luke's genre. Luke uses his standard historiographic style here rather than writing as a knowing mythographer.[668] Given Luke's treatment of his sources (such as Mark) where we can check him, it seems likely (at least to myself) that Luke believed that his sources reported that some had seen Jesus ascend, albeit probably quickly, as Elisha saw Elijah ascend quickly. One could affirm that Luke had such a tradition or affirm even the event's historicity yet view the event's spatial imagery as a divine accommodation to the culture's dominant cosmology. Still, Luke has shaped the event in his own language.[669]

Lüdemann rejects the plea that it was a literal event described symbolically, noting (correctly) that we do not make the same claim for other ascension accounts of the day.[670] This conclusion, however, may press too much into the comparison with the other accounts: few of the other accounts appear as recent events in historians who regard them as certain; most, in fact, are legendary descriptions from the distant past.[671] There exist only so many ways of reporting people's watching a person's disappearance to another realm (assuming that such a disappearance might occur), and none of these ways determines the genre of the report.[672] Further, divine or heroic figures could disappear without visibly ascending,[673] diminishing any need to report an ascension as a necessary element of Jesus's departure, though the visible ascent was naturally the most dramatic way to report such a disappearance (e.g., Tob 12:20–22).

If we make an allowance for Luke's use of contemporary cosmology, it seems more appropriate for critics who discount all such reports (including Luke's) to affirm explicitly, instead of merely implying, that such events cannot or do not occur. Usually such denials stem from antisupernaturalistic presuppositions, though one could, in principle, deny the possibility of some kinds of supernatural events without denying

668. Cf. Stempvoort, "Interpretation of Ascension," 38. Marguerat, *Actes*, 50–51, notes that early iconography interpreted Luke's graphic depiction literally. Historians often included what they recognized as myths, but from the primeval past and often with remarks about their skepticism (see discussion in our introduction, ch. 9).

669. One might argue that he has done this especially to bring out the parallel with Elijah; but to this argument it could also be objected (on the basis of Luke's preference for John as Elijah, above) that this parallel stems from Luke's material itself, as reported by Jewish Christians who had long contemplated the event's significance.

670. Lüdemann, *Christianity*, 30. Lüdemann's response may rightly counter convenient suggestions that Luke would not care "what actually happened" (Strelan, *Strange Acts*, 35, though right that Luke's *interpretation* is more significant); such lack of concern might fit a foundation myth whose sources were obscure and ancient, but not a recent event.

671. This is true even when they occur in historians, e.g., in Dion. Hal. *Ant. rom.* (on which see, e.g., Balch, "ΜΕΤΑΒΟΛΗ ΠΟΛΙΤΕΙΩΝ," 162).

672. Cf., e.g., the view among traditional Shilluk that their hero-founder "disappeared" into immortality (Mbiti, *Religions*, 250).

673. E.g., Eurip. *Iph. Aul.* 1608, 1614, 1622; Plut. *Cam.* 33.7; Eunapius *Lives* 468. Deities could come in disguise, then vanish (Virg. *Aen.* 9.657–58; perhaps Gen 18:33); Greek deities also could cause invisibility (e.g., Aristoph. *Acharn.* 390; Soph. *Inachus* frg. 8, 26 [*SPap* 3:24–25]; Apollod. *Bib.* 2.4.2), and when they did so, mortals could not make themselves visible again until the deities wished (Virg. *Aen.* 1.579–81, 586–87; cf. Hom. *Od.* 7.143; 13.352; 16.167–79).

all of them. (For a brief critique of antisupernaturalism as a necessary paradigm, see introduction, ch. 9.)

More objective (less presuppositional) grounds could exist to question Luke's report. First, the account coheres well with Luke's theology and includes OT "types" such as the forty days and the Elijah succession narrative.[674] To this we may respond that everything Luke reports fits his own theology and style; this observation need not undermine Luke's use of sources (among which we would include Mark and Q in his Gospel). Further, the types could just as easily belong to Luke's sources as be his invention; his Elijah typology in the Gospel portrays John more explicitly than Jesus as the new Elijah, and Luke was not the only writer capable of Elijah typology.[675] Characteristically, Matthew plays on forty days for Moses/Israel typology even more plainly than does Luke's Gospel (Matt 4:1–2; cf. 2:15, 18, 20).[676] Jesus himself may have chosen to emulate Elijah, as did some other ancient figures.[677]

Second, why would other sources not provide eyewitness reports of something as dramatic as the ascension?[678] But these grounds are much less substantial than they might first appear, since the other Gospels stop their narration before this point: Mark probably ends even before the promised resurrection appearances (Mark 16:8), though the longer later ending, possibly dependent on Luke, narrates the ascension (16:19).[679] Matthew prefers to end on Jesus's commission and the promise of his continuing presence with the disciples (Matt 28:18–20). John also ends his Gospel with resurrection appearances and no mention of Jesus's departure in the narrative; but he does explicitly *predict* that departure, and as an ascension (John 20:17; cf. 3:13; 6:62).[680] Other first-century Christian writers accept it theologically and consequently—given ancient cosmology—probably historically; see 1 Tim 3:16;[681] Eph 4:8–10; Heb 4:14; 7:26; 8:1; 9:24; and 1 Pet 3:22.[682] Many more texts place Jesus in heaven, whether they are describing his current reign (cf. Ps 110:1; e.g., Rom 8:34; Eph 1:20; Col 3:1–2; Heb 1:3; Rev 5:6–14; 6:16; 7:9–10, 17) or his future parousia from heaven (e.g., Phil 3:20; 1 Thess 1:10; 4:16; 2 Thess 1:7; Rev 19:11–16; cf. Phil 2:9–10).[683] It might be

---

674. Goulder, *Type and History*, 182–83.

675. E.g., the ascensions of Moses and Ezra in some Jewish traditions depend heavily on the explicit biblical ascension account of Elijah.

676. See, e.g., Keener, *Matthew*, 137; Teeple, *Prophet*, 75–76; Dunn, *Baptism*, 30; Riesenfeld, *Tradition*, 76; Albright and Mann, *Matthew*, 36; Collins, "Temptation"; Meier, *Vision*, 59–61; Gundry, *Matthew*, 53; France, *Matthew*, 98; Stegner, "Temptation Narrative." On Matt 2, Keener, *Matthew*, 107–9; on Moses analogies in Matthew, see esp. Allison, *Moses*.

677. For sign prophets, see discussion in, e.g., Galley, "Heilige"; cf. also biblical models in Eve, *Miracles*, 115–16, 324. The rabbinic rainmaking sages, Honi and Hanina, also seem to have followed Elijah's example (cf. 1 Kgs 18:44–45); Elijah also served as a model for some subsequent Christian miracle workers (see Frankfurter, *Religion in Egypt*, 20).

678. Goulder, *Type and History*, 182–83.

679. Cf. Zwiep, *Ascension*, 189–90, rightly doubting whether this source antedates Luke. Naturally, later sources recount the ascension (e.g., *Gr. Anth.* 1.19).

680. See Keener, *John*, 1192–95. Similarly, Homer's *Iliad* predicts Achilles's death without narrating it (e.g., 21.110; 23.80–81; for other examples of this literary technique, see Keener, *John*, 1194–95).

681. Zwiep, *Ascension*, 189, doubts the relevance of 1 Tim 3:16 and (more reasonably) Rev 12:5 because "ascension language is often used in the context of the resurrection-exaltation paradigm, which for this reason cannot be taken as evidence." But this doubt is circular; would not the claim of Jesus's exaltation itself constitute "evidence"? Rev 12:5 may allude to Jesus's exaltation by way of the cross (John 12:31; 14:30; 16:11).

682. Also in second-century writers, e.g., *Barn.* 15.9; Papias frg. 3.10.

683. Cf. also the tradition that Jesus originally came from heaven (Rom 10:6; 1 Cor 15:47; cf. Eph 4:9; John 3:13). On the ascending-descending motif in early Christology, see Longenecker, "Christological Motifs," 542–44; *Christology*, 58–62; cf. Keener, *John*, 561–63 (cf. 162–63). For Jesus's enthronement and exaltation in early Christianity, see, e.g., deSilva, "Exaltation"; Allison, *Jesus*, 247–51.

difficult for ancient hearers to envision this location for Jesus without inferring an ascension. The criterion of multiple attestation produces unexpected support to Luke's basic claim at this point.[684]

Those who did not narrate the ascension surely did not omit it out of believing that Jesus remained among them in the same way as before. Did they believe that Jesus continued to converse and eat with his followers on earth as he did before his death or in the initial resurrection appearances? He did, after all, cease to appear among them except in isolated cases, such as Paul's or (more typically) pneumatic visions. Did the appearances simply stop (for the most part), or was their stopping marked by a climactic resurrection appearance in which the disciples witnessed Jesus parted from them?[685] And if the disappearance was not witnessed, at the least the risen Jesus's physical absence would have to be noticed. Given Luke's emphasis on the concreteness of Jesus's resurrection appearances—or, more accurately, the disciples' continuous experience of the risen Christ—implied in Luke 24:3, 23, 37–43 and Acts 1:3, an ascension would have to follow at least for Luke.[686] The physically resurrected Christ was obviously not living and reigning from some undisclosed location on earth.

Zwiep's study of Jesus's ascension recognizes pre-Lukan components for the narrative, as well as Lukan design. Zwiep suggests that Luke wove together earlier building blocks of the ascension tradition, such as the close of the special period of resurrection appearances, but used Jewish ascension narratives (Elijah, Enoch, Moses, etc.) as a model to help him construct these traditions into a cohesive narrative.[687] In addition, one might suspect that early Christian expectation of believers' future gathering to Jesus, exemplified especially in 1 Thess 4:15–17, may have also helped shape the imagery, given the promise that Jesus would return in the "same manner."

Most scholars who reject altogether historical tradition in the narrative do so because of their critical orientation; most scholars who accept earlier tradition behind it (including myself) can do so because of different epistemological presuppositions. Meanwhile most scholars critiquing the other scholars' works do so on the basis of the assurance that their own presuppositions are superior to the others'. Those more skeptical of the narrative's historicity, however, should at least acknowledge the qualitative difference between Luke's potential dependence on recent eyewitnesses and the reports of some ascensions surrounding legendary characters of many centuries past. (And scholars ought not, as some scholars in the past were sometimes wont to do, simply to dismiss the academic credibility of scholars who work with different premises, as if the critics themselves lack identifiable presuppositions.)

c. Signs of Glory: Cloud, Angels, Heaven, and Return (1:9–11)

The details of the narrative are important for its interpretation. Angels explain Jesus's departure, just as they explained his resurrection (Luke 24:4–7). Not only the angels (cf. Luke 9:26) but the mention of the cloud and heaven fit predictions of Jesus's return, as well as signs of divine glory in the Scriptures.

---

684. Similarly Larkin, *Acts*, 38; Witherington, *Acts*, 112 (adding Justin *1 Apol.* 50). For various views regarding pre-Lukan tradition and redaction in the ascension narrative, see Bovon, *Theologian*, 170–77.

685. Cf. Goppelt, *Times*, 18, who views the ascension as "basically the symbolic conclusion of one appearance which stood for the end of the Easter appearances."

686. Talbert, *Patterns*, 113, rightly observes Luke's emphasis on corporeality (whether or not one accepts antidocetic polemic there, as also in idem, *Luke and Gnostics*; arguing for the polemic in Luke's Gospel, see also *Patterns*, 116–19).

687. Zwiep, *Ascension*, 192–93.

1. The Cloud (1:9)

The physical impossibility of clouds holding a person's weight was no more lost on ancient critics than modern ones (Mac. Magn. *Apocrit.* 4.1–7).[688] Most ancient writers would, however, allow special properties or activities of cloud-like vapors generated by deities or the deity for special purposes.

Sometimes deities hid in a cloud[689] or hid someone else in a cloud while removing them[690] or taking them to heaven.[691] Since mist was the only way the ancients knew to hide in open sight, it is not surprising that it often appears. Occasionally, Jewish sources also report clouds as vehicles for ascensions.[692] Josephus claims that Moses disappeared in a cloud, Moses writing that he died lest people assume that he was taken to God (*Ant.* 4.326).[693] In some texts a human agent of God could fly on, or be moved by, clouds (*1 En.* 14:8; 39:3).[694] Scholars also note that heavenly ascents and descents in ancient texts were sometimes effected in clouds.[695] (Haenchen, indeed, distinguishes Luke's account from contemporary accounts because Luke does not mention the cloud lifting Jesus;[696] but this distinction probably makes too much of a few parallels.) Apparently borrowing conventional Canaanite or West Semitic imagery,[697] the Hebrew Scriptures sometimes portray Israel's God coming in the clouds (Pss 97:2; 104:3; Isa 19:1; cf. Dan 7:13).

Luke's ideal audience would undoubtedly think particularly of two clouds from his first volume: the cloud of God's glory at Jesus's transfiguration (Luke 9:34–35),[698] which compares Jesus favorably with Moses (who was earlier glorified, Exod 34:29)[699] and Elijah (Luke 9:30–31, 35), and the cloud in which Jesus would return in glory (Luke 21:27; see comment on Acts 1:11).[700] Elijah ascended with a whirlwind (2 Kgs 2:11), which some texts regard as a cloud.

688. Likely from Porphyry; see Hoffmann, *Porphyry's Against Christians*, 68.

689. Sil. It. 9.488; cf. Job 22:14; Ps 18:11.

690. Sil. It. 9.484–85; cf. Plut. *Cam.* 33.7. Also, a deity could shroud one in a frightening cloud to terrify enemies (Hom. *Il.* 18.205–6).

691. Apollod. *Bib.* 2.7.7. Parsons, *Acts*, 27, adds other texts for a cloud in ascensions.

692. *2 En.* 31:1–2 J (probably much later than Acts). Also the late *Gr. Ezra* 5:7, where a cloud (νεφέλη) snatched (ἥρπασεν) Ezra up to heaven. Johnson, *Acts*, 27, cites Enoch in *2 En.* 3:1; the new Moses and Elijah of Rev 11:12; and Jesus in *Epistula apostolorum* 51. Parsons, *Acts*, 27, adds *Test. Ab.* 8:3; 10:2; 12:1, 9 (but these appear only in the possibly later B recension).

693. Also noted by others in connection with Acts 1:9; e.g., Cadbury, "Eschatology," 309 (who also emphasizes it as parousia imagery from Dan 7:13 forward); Lake and Cadbury, *Commentary*, 9; Johnson, *Acts*, 27; Le Cornu, *Acts*, 27; Marguerat, *Actes*, 47. Moses is elsewhere associated with the cloud of glory (Exod 19:9; 20:21; 24:15–18; 33:9; 40:35; Ps 99:7; 1 Cor 10:2; 4Q377 1 II, 10); concealment of one's taking to heaven appears later in *2 En.* 67:1–3.

694. Also *Test. Ab.* 9:8–10:1 A; 8:3; 10:2; 12:1 B. God controls clouds like the way he controls lightning in Enochic theology (cf. angelic names in *1 En.* 6:7; 41:3); *Pesiq. Rab.* 1:3 claims that someday clouds will carry Israelites to Jerusalem every Sabbath; God's host (probably angels) could be compared with clouds (1QM XII, 9). Stempvoort, "Interpretation of Ascension," 38, thinks Luke's description refers not to "a fog cloud hiding a mystery but a royal chariot" (though he doubts a connection to Elijah's ascension in a chariot in 2 Kgs 2:9–12 because it lacks a cloud).

695. Lake and Cadbury, *Commentary*, 9 (citing 2 Kgs 2:11; Dan 7:13; *1 En.* 39:3; 1 Thess 4:17; Rev 1:7; Mark 13:26; 14:62; and esp. Jos. *Ant.* 4.326).

696. Haenchen, *Acts*, 149 (citing only Livy 1.16.1; *1 En.* 39:3).

697. Albright, *Yahweh*, 125; see, e.g., *ANET* 130 (Baal III AB A), 131, 132, 137.

698. See also Parsons, *Departure*, 172, noting that both occurred on mountains (Luke 9:28; Acts 1:12); Arrington, *Acts*, 11. Note also the two men, Elijah and Moses, there (Ehrman, *Introduction*, 137).

699. For Moses motifs in the transfiguration, see Moses, *Transfiguration Story*, passim, e.g., 84–85; Davies and Allison, *Matthew*, 2:695; Keener, *Matthew*, 435–37. Comparison with Moses's glory was a key biblical allusion for early Christians (see, e.g., Keener, *John*, 405–26; idem, *Corinthians*, 168–70).

700. See Flender, *Theologian*, 93; Cadbury, "Eschatology," 309.

One should probably think here of a cloud of glory associated both with the Lord (Exod 16:10; 24:16; 40:34–35; Num 16:42; 1 Kgs 8:11; 2 Chr 5:14; Isa 4:5; Ezek 10:4)[701] and with the son of man (Dan 7:13; hence Luke 21:27 via Mark 13:26).[702] God's dwelling was associated with his glory (e.g., 1QM XII, 2, כבודכה).[703] In later Jewish tradition, God's presence could be banished by sin[704] or invited by merit.[705] Here Luke offers no emphasis on God's departing presence, however, since this presence will be restored and multiplied at Pentecost a few days later (Acts 2:2–4).

That their "eyes" saw him may be emphatic (in light of Luke 2:30; 10:23) and might possibly contrast with their previous inability to recognize him (24:16, 31; cf. Acts 26:18; 28:17); Luke frequently employs ἀτενίζω (gaze).[706] Some scholars argue that the angelic order to stop gazing would challenge what Luke's audience would assume to be the natural reaction, implying that the disciples should stop being concerned with the event that has just occurred and get busy.[707] This proposal could also fit Acts 1:6–8, which redirects attention from theological speculation to action. Luke asks similar questions in 22:16 ("Why delay?"; cf. perhaps Luke 6:46) and especially (with regard to "gazing") in Acts 3:12, and even more clearly (with regard to looking for the risen Christ) Luke 24:5.[708]

II. THE ANGELS (1:10)

The two men[709] in white recall the men at the tomb in Luke 24:4–7, connecting the ascension and resurrection announcements (see table on p. 728).[710]

The parallel might suggest that the angels here query their hearers' behavior because they should have believed what Jesus already spoke, as the men at the tomb explicitly indicate in Luke 24:6–7. That is, the disciples should have understood and expected Jesus's ascension, in this instance because he had told them how he would return (in the clouds, 21:27), implying where he had to go before he could return from there.

701. With, e.g., Bruce, *Commentary*, 41; Minear, *Hope*, 119–21. Cf. *Test. Ab.* 9:8 A (where νεφέλην φωτός is a cherubim chariot).

702. Cf. the messianic figure who flies with the clouds of heaven in *4 Ezra* 13:2.

703. The heavens were a realm of glory (as the realm of stars, or lights, along with clouds, 1QM X, 12). Cf. God speaking through a cloud, e.g., *Test. Job* 42:3 (*OTP* 1:861)/42:2 (Kraft, 74) (cf. Job 38:1).

704. E.g., ʾAbot R. Nat. 38 A; *Sipra Qed. pq.* 8.205.2.1; par. 4.206.2.6; *Sipre Deut.* 258.2.3; 320.2.1; *b. Ber.* 5b; *Roš Haš.* 31a; *Šabb.* 33a; 139a; *Yebam.* 64a, bar.; *Yoma* 21b; *y. Sanh.* 8:8, §1; *Deut. Rab.* 5:10; 6:14; *Ruth Rab.* 1:2; cf. *Sipre Num.* 1.10.3; so with Wisdom (Wis 1:4; 6:12–25, esp. 6:23; cf. Wis 7:25–26; Babr. 126). The Shekinah was progressively banished from, and then reinvited to, earth (ʾAbot R. Nat. 34 A; *Pesiq. Rab Kah.* 1:1; *Gen. Rab.* 19:7; *Song Rab.* 5:1, §1); because of sin, his tabernacle or temple was necessary to bring his presence (*Pesiq. Rab.* 7:4). For the Shekinah's continuing with Israel even when the nation sins, see Abelson, *Immanence*, 135–42.

705. Especially on the clouds of glory in the wilderness or revealed to Moses, *Sipre Deut.* 305.3.1; 313.3.1; 355.6.1; *Gen. Rab.* 60:16; *Exod. Rab.* 45:5; *Num. Rab.* 19:20; *Song Rab.* 4:5, §2; 7:6, §1; cf. *Pesiq. Rab.* 10:2 on a later period.

706. Twelve of fourteen uses in the NT; in the Apostolic Fathers, it is similarly clustered only in *1 Clem.* 7.4; 9.2; 17.2; 19.2; 36.2.

707. Parsons, *Departure*, 182, citing the technique of "defamiliarization." Idem, *Acts*, 28, compares the mild implied reproof with that in Acts 1:7–8. González, *Months*, 15, suggests that they are redirected to their mission on earth (as in Acts 1:7–8), a contrast with the practice of some (2 Thess 3:11).

708. Perhaps such questions also recalled a relevant cultural way of expressing encouragement in these cases.

709. Their gender reflects Luke's narrative connections among these figures, as well as tradition, which might in turn reflect expectations for most angelic messengers (cf., e.g., Gen 19:1, 5; Judg 13:6, 8). Complaints against gender exclusivity here (Beck, "Women," 281) are therefore misplaced if directed primarily at Luke (see comment on Acts 1:14), since the exclusivity is rooted in a broader cultural tradition.

710. Also Tannehill, *Acts*, 19 (suggesting that in this way the apostles experience a "vision of angels" like the women in Luke 24:23). Luke might shape the account in Luke 24 to fit the present narrative; Mark 16:5 mentions just one man (Luke may have an additional source, but note at least the similarity between Mark 16:6 and Luke 24:6).

Luke 24:4–9	Acts 1:10–12
Behold, two men in flashing clothing (24:4)	Behold, two men in white clothing (1:10)
Question: "Why are you seeking the living one with the dead?" (24:5)	Question: "Why have you taken your stand looking into heaven?" (1:11a)
Explanation of Jesus's absence: "He is not here, but instead rose and is alive" (24:6)	Explanation of Jesus's absence: "Jesus has been taken from you into heaven, but will return" (1:11)
They return to the city (24:9)	They return to the city (1:12)

The men in Luke 24:4 may well also echo Moses and Elijah at the transfiguration discussing Jesus's exodus (9:30).[711] Johnson, indeed, suggests that the two men may *be* Moses and Elijah;[712] but this suggestion may press the analogy too far. If these figures were Moses and Elijah, why would Luke identify them explicitly in Luke 9 but not at their subsequent appearances (where their "propaganda" value would be no less significant)? More likely, ancient readers would see the figures at the tomb and here as angels,[713] who also make other strategic announcements in Luke-Acts (1:13, 30; 2:9–15; Acts 8:26; 10:3–7, 22; 11:13; 27:23–24); Luke makes this claim explicit for the resurrection narrative in Luke 24:23.[714]

Their garb in white (Acts 1:10) helps reinforce their identity as angels (cf. John 20:12; Rev 15:6).[715] This color was not, of course, associated exclusively with angels. People wore white or linen for a variety of reasons.[716] (Linen had long been the most common fabric for clothing in Egypt and elsewhere.[717] Dyed garments were usually heavier woolen garments; white clothes could be of wool or linen, but linen was rarely dyed and could instead be bleached white.)[718] People especially wore white or linen to enter or serve in sacred places,[719] including the Jerusalem temple.[720] Pythagoras's

---

711. Johnson, *Acts*, 27, who also thinks that this link fits the earlier ascensions of Moses and Elijah (2 Kgs 2:11–12; Philo *Mos.* 2.291; cf. Deut 34:6); cf. Ehrman, *Introduction*, 137. Some think that Elijah and Moses there stand for the Law and Prophets (cf. Origen *Comm. Matt.* 12:38; Augustine *Sermons on New Testament Lessons* (SSGF 2:63) [both in Oden and Hall, *Mark*, 119–20]; Taylor, *Mark*, 390; Montefiore, *Gospels*, 1:207), so that "hear him" (Mark 9:7; Luke 9:35) places Jesus higher than the OT, or that they function as harbingers of the end (Moule, *Mark*, 70; Young, *Jewish Theologian*, 208); most important, a new Moses and Elijah were expected (Deut 18:15–19; Mal 4:4–5), and Mark's narrative presents each (Mark 9:7, 12; cf. Matt 17:5, 12–13).

712. Johnson, *Acts*, 31; followed by Wall, "Acts," 43–44.

713. In some passages, angels could look like people (e.g., Gen 18:2 with 19:1, 15; Tob 5:4; *2 En.* 20:1–2; *Gen. Rab.* 50:2; *Pesiq. Rab.* 20:4; Rev 21:17; cf. Judg 13:6–8; Ezek 40:3), as could (in fewer texts) demons (*b. Giṭ.* 66a). Angels also functioned as God's messengers in Scripture, as they do here; they appear in pairs in Gen 19:1; John 20:12; cf. Matt 28:2–7.

714. So also Brown, *Death*, 300.

715. White or linen in *1 En.* 71:1; 87:2; 90:31–33; 2 Macc 3:26; 11:8; *L.A.B.* 9:10; Rev 15:6; *Jannes and Jambres* fragments in P.Beatty 16; clothed in glory in *1 En.* 71:1; 3 Macc 6:18. Lake and Cadbury, *Commentary*, 9, also cite 2 Macc 11:8; *Herm. Vis.* 4.2.1–5; *Sim.* 8.2–3.

716. On linen, see briefly Wild, "Linen."

717. Cosgrave, *History of Costume*, 20; on linen in Greco-Roman world, see, e.g., Pekridou-Gorecki, "Linen"; we have some apparently first-century linen from Qumran (Taylor et al., "Textiles"). On preparing flax for linen, see Pliny E. *N.H.* 19.3.16–18; on various kinds of linens, 19.4.19–21; the heavier wool was also often white (8.73.190).

718. Croom, *Clothing*, 26.

719. E.g., Paus. 9.39.8; Ovid. *Her.* 4.71 (Eleusinian rituals); Philost. *Vit. Apoll.* 8.19 (shrine of Trophonius); cf. Ramsay, *Letters*, 386; Croom, *Clothing*, 70 (for Roman togas), 71 (Isis's priests wearing linen); Eurip. *Bacch.* 112; Livy 27.37.11–12; 40.51.3; *Acts John* 38; Egyptian priests in Plut. *Isis* 3–4, *Mor.* 352C; App. *C.W.* 4.6.47; Apul. *Metam.* 11.10, 23; worshipers in Ovid *Metam.* 1.747; Paus. 2.35.5; 6.20.3; Pythagoras in Diod. Sic. 10.9.6; Diog. Laert. 8.1.33; Hipponax frg. 65; Athen. *Deipn.* 4.149d; *SEG* 11.923 in Sherk, *Empire*, 58. For clean or special garments for sacred festivals, cf., e.g., Libanius *Descr.* 29.3.

720. Jos. *War* 2.1; *Ant.* 11.327. Jos. *Ant.* 20.216–18 limits linen to the priests (against Agrippa II's allowance for Levites); priests were to wear linen to prevent sweat (Ezek 44:18). Croom, *Clothing*, 131, suggests that Judean men often wore white and notes the same (p. 132) for Egypt (though most of the evidence is from funerary settings, this preference makes good sense in a hot climate).

disciples used white and linen;[721] some deities were portrayed wearing white,[722] though those associated with death could be portrayed as wearing black.[723] Roman politicians also wore white to emphasize purity, and Romans wore white on other important occasions.[724] But the figures are certainly not priests here, are not in the temple here, and therefore better fit Jewish expectations for angels.

More generally, white could signify good, and black could signify evil or negative things (Diog. Laert. 8.1.34).[725] Black or dark colors also could symbolize death or mourning,[726] and white, life and joy,[727] which are appropriate associations here.[728] (The contrast between light being positive and dark being negative mostly reflects associations with day and night,[729] darkness being related to night,[730] not, as some have wrongly assumed, to complexion.)[731] Although these uses are broader than angelic, they do cover the angelic use of white. With the possible exception of Moses and Elijah, mentioned above, who else, supernaturally informed enough to dress for the occasion, would speak for Christ here to his own apostles?

Luke introduces them with "behold" (ἰδού, Acts 1:10) in his typical style; it appears seventy-eight times in Luke-Acts (e.g., Luke 2:10; Acts 12:7).[732] This frequency

721. Iambl. *V.P.* 28.153, 155; whether linen, as in *V.P.* 21.100; 28.149, or wool, replaced in later times with linen, as in Diog. Laert. 8.1.19.

722. Cf. Mithras in *PGM* 4.635–38; cf. 4.698–99.

723. E.g., "Black Aphrodite" (Engels, *Roman Corinth*, 97–98).

724. Croom, *Clothing*, 28.

725. Cf. Hom. *Il.* 1.103; Ovid *Metam.* 2.832; *Pont.* 2.5.37–38; Marc. Aur. 4.28; 4Q183 II, 4–8 (possibly also 4Q185 1–2 II, 6–7); 4Q544 1 10–14; 2 3–5 (both depicting the ruler of darkness); 4Q548 1 10–15; Sil. It. 11.548; Dupont, *Life*, 260; perhaps Albrile, "Colore." Black functions negatively in Aeschylus *Seven* 832–33 (a terrible, "black curse"); Ovid *Fasti* 1.58 (inauspicious); Marc. Aur. 4.28. Athenians used white ballots for acquittal, black for a death sentence (Plut. *Alc.* 22.2). Cf. the Pythagorean use of white in Iambl. *V.P.* 28.149; also 28.153 (against the laziness of sleep), 155 (even worn to funerals). But black was also used for wall decorations (Vitruv. *Arch.* 7.10.1–4).

726. E.g., Eurip. *Alc.* 216, 427; Aristoph. *Frogs* 1337; Isaeus *Nicost.* 7; Lysias *Or.* 13.40, §133; Ovid *Metam.* 8.777–78; Val. Max. 1.7.7; 2.4.5; Sen. E. *Controv.* 10.1.1, 4; Plut. *Alex.* 49.3; Apollod. *Epit.* 1.7, 10; Sil. It. 11.257–58; Tac. *Ann.* 3.2; Paus. 1.22.5; Philost. *Hrk.* 31.9; 53.9, 11, 17; Hdn. 4.2.3; *Jos. Asen.* 10:8–9/10; 14:12; cf. Dupont, *Life*, 260; Llewellyn-Jones, *Tortoise*, 306; Hurschmann, "Mourning dress." Those on trial also wore black (*y. Roš Haš.* 1:3, §27; Ramsay, *Letters*, 387); death is regularly dark (e.g., Hom. *Il.* 5.22, 47, 310; cf. *Od.* 11.32–33; death as "black" in Statius *Theb.* 4.528; the Styx in Lycophron *Alex.* 705.

727. E.g., *y. Roš Haš.* 1:3, §27; Ovid *Tristia* 5.5.8. Gregory the Great *Homilies* 21 opines that the angel came in white because of joy (Oden and Hall, *Mark*, 243). But people might prefer either white or dark wool (Sen. *Y. Nat. Q.* 3.25.4). The burial clothes of the righteous were white in Judaism (*L.A.B.* 64:6; cf. *Test. Ab.* 20:10 A; *L.A.E.* 48:1; *Apoc. Mos.* 40:1–3; *b. Ber.* 18b). Greeks also buried corpses in white (Klauck, *Context*, 72). Romans mourned in white (Plut. *Rom. Q.* 26, *Mor.* 270D) and buried in white (270DE).

728. One returning from death might be thought to wear white (Lucian *Peregr.* 40).

729. Cf. Hesiod *W.D.* 154–55; Aeschlyus *Eum.* 745 (the Furies spring from Night); Ovid *Am.* 1.8.3–8 (night as the time for witchcraft); Philost. *Hrk.* 33.6 (white associated with the sun god); Lucan *C.W.* 6.624; Philo thinks black the absence of light and white (*Creation* 29; *Abr.* 10). Ephraim Isaac, an Ethiopian translator of *1 Enoch*, points out that in *1 En.* 85:3, white suggests the image of purity in Ethiopic (*OTP* 1:63n85e; see also *1 En.* 87:2).

730. See, e.g., Walde, "Nyx," 932. Given the inability to see far and the suspicion that subversive activity or crimes that no one should see were most frequent at night, the association of evil with darkness is not surprising. On light and darkness imagery in antiquity, see Keener, *John*, 382–87.

731. White is associated positively with the spirit world in some traditional African societies (Mbiti, *Religions*, 73, 277; Isichei, *History*, 64; Beattie and Middleton, "Introduction," xxiii–xxiv; Beattie, "Mediumship," 160–61; black is for death in Shoko, *Religion*, 40). This is true also of many Islamic societies, though not always before the advent of Islam (Abdalla, "Friend," 43; there *are*, however, ethnic connections occasionally, as in Kenyon, "Zar," 111–12, on Sudanese spirits). Witchcraft is associated with night (Fape, *Powers*, 103; cf. Rosny, *Healers*). Philost. *Vit. Apoll.* 2.19 associates Indians' preference for black with their dark complexion, but is clear that this is his own guess.

732. Although familiar as a Semitic expression, it is acceptable Koine (e.g., Epict. *Diatr.* 3.24.75; 4.8.31). It appears rarely (eight times) in Paul, four times in John, seven times in Mark, but twenty-five times in the more Semitic syntax of Revelation and nearly sixty times in Matthew, who employs it most abundantly.

reinforces the probability that the expression here is pleonastic, that is, a case of emphatic superfluity.[733] The angels open their address with "Men, Galileans" (Acts 1:11), following Luke's typical rhetorical style ("men" frequently paired with a local or ethnic term, 2:14, 22; 3:12; 5:35; 13:16; 17:22; 19:35; 21:28).[734] Some scholars have taken the specific designation of "men" here as unduly gender exclusive, but whatever the use may be elsewhere (e.g., the direct address in 1:16;[735] see esp. comment on Acts 2:14), here those so designated are, presumably, literally male. "They" in 1:12–13 are specified as the apostles (i.e., the eleven; 1:2, 26), to which the "women" of 1:14 are added.

III. Heaven (1:11)

That Jesus is "received up" (a form of ἀναλαμβάνω, Acts 1:11; also 1:2, 22)[736] may offer a wordplay with the forms of λαμβάνω in 1:8 and ὑπολαμβάνω in 1:9:[737] Jesus is "received up" whereas the disciples "receive" power to carry on his mission. Nevertheless, the sense of the term here is relevant; ἀναλαμβάνω can apply to taking aboard (20:13–14) and, most relevant here, taking up into the sky (10:16).[738] The fourfold repetition of "into the heaven" is emphatic. For many ancients, heaven was the celestial and divine realm;[739] see comments on analogous instances of Lukan usage above (in the section "How Can Modern Interpreters Approach This Narrative's Cosmology?"). In some Jewish literature, it appears even as a circumlocution for God.[740]

The older cosmology was a three-tiered universe of heaven, earth, and underworld, with the vast majority of the dead in the last. From the Hellenistic period forward, many intellectuals conceived of the earth as a sphere surrounded by the planetary spheres in which the sun, moon, and planets moved.[741] In this period many thinkers, both Greek and Jewish, came to believe that unencumbered souls would rise upward to the highest heavens.[742] (Some even believed in forms of astral immortality.)[743]

733. See Black, "Oration at Olivet," 88; Anderson, *Glossary*, 102.

734. Soards, *Speeches*, 25. For the frequency of such an address ("Men . . .") in ancient rhetoric, see comment on Acts 2:14, 22. "Galileans" designates their place of origin and is not a title for Christians per se (Cadbury, "Names for Christians," 387, noting that usage only in Epict. *Diatr.* 4.7.6; Julian the Apostate).

735. Vander Stichele, "Gender," 314, notes that the women of 1:14 are framed by addresses to "men" in Acts 1:11, 16; because the public sphere was an especially male arena, Luke emphasizes male messengers (following D'Angelo, "ANHP Question," 52; cf. similarly Seim, *Double Message*, 162).

736. Predicted in the cognate in Luke 9:51; the verb probably bears this sense also in 1 Tim 3:16.

737. This is not the most common use of ὑπολαμβάνω, but Luke did not invent it for a wordplay (cf. Jos. *Ant.* 11.238 in BDAG).

738. The omission of "into the heaven" in D is probably not significant for the earliest text, given Luke's repetition of the phrase (Haenchen, *Acts*, 150; less certainly, Metzger, *Textual Commentary*, 283); in context, its omission can hardly change the sense, in any case. Certainly, the ascension belongs in the text (Zwiep, "Text").

739. E.g., Val. Flacc. 1.498; Libanius *Narration* 7.2; though classical Greek mythology (as opposed to Hellenistic philosophy) emphasized Olympus more.

740. E.g., Dan 4:26; 3 Macc 4:21; *1 En.* 6:2; 1QM XII, 5; Rom 1:18; Luke 15:18; *m. 'Ab.* 1:3; *t. B. Qam.* 7:5; *Sipra Behuq. pq.* 6.267.2.1; 79.1.1; *b. 'Abod. Zar.* 18a; *Moʿed Qaṭ.* 17a; *B. Qam.* 76a; *Pesaḥ.* 66b; *Taʿan.* 14b; Diod. Sic. 40.3.4; *Num. Rab.* 7:5; 8:4; *Ruth Rab.* 7:1; *Eccl. Rab.* 7:8, §1; 9:12. See also comment on "kingdom of heaven" in the excursus on kingdom of God at Acts 1:3.

741. Aune, *Revelation*, 318 (citing, e.g., Cleomedes 1.8–9; Ptolemy *Mathematica syntaxis* 1.3; Arist. *Heav.* 2.13, 292ab; Theon *Progymn.* 148.6–7; Philo *Conf.* 5; *Cher.* 22).

742. See, e.g. (among many other possible examples), Cic. *Tusc.* 1.19.43; 1.31.75; *Resp.* 6.14.14; 6.26.29; Cercidas frg. 1; Sen. Y. *Dial.* 11.9.3; 12.11.6; Plut. *Isis* 78, *Mor.* 382F–383A; Max. Tyre 10.2–3; Heraclitus *Ep.* 5; Aune, "Duality," 228–30; 2 Cor 4:17–18; souls were by nature (in this view) heavenly (e.g., Virg. *Aen.* 6.728–34; Mus. Ruf. 18A, p. 112.24–25; Plut. *Isis* 78, *Mor.* 382F; *Face M.* 28, *Mor.* 943A; *Exile* 17, *Mor.* 607D). Heroes would surely live in heaven (Virg. *Aen.* 9.641; *Ecl.* 5.56–57, 64; Val. Max. 9.3.ext. 1; Sil. It. 3.137; Eunapius *Lives* 469), and some others also expected to go there after death (Cic. *Resp.* 6.26.29; Virg. *Georg.* 4.226–27; Ovid *Metam.* 15.875–76; Lucan *C.W.* 9.1–9; Fronto *Nep. am.* 2.8; Plot. *Enn.* 3.4.6; Hdn. 1.5.6).

743. See, e.g., Val. Flacc. 3.378–82; Sen. Y. *Ep. Lucil.* 73.15; *Herc. fur.* 959; especially for "great" persons (Virg. *Ecl.* 9.47; Ovid *Metam.* 15.749, 843–51); cf. Plato *Tim.* 41E. Though most common in Roman sources,

Hostile spirits were sometimes thought to inhabit the lower heavens,[744] and so Jesus's ascension can function as his triumph over them in some early Christian theology (Eph 1:20–22; 1 Pet 3:22).[745] Luke does not emphasize this theological conviction as some other early Christian writers do.[746] Frequent as heavenly journeys are in Jewish apocalyptic literature, Luke offers no such imagery here.[747]

Despite numerous descriptions of heroes' ascents, ancient literature offers far more accounts of postmortem[748] and visionary[749] ascents.[750] But while these may provide useful insight into their authors' cosmology and offer parallels of language as other ascents to heaven, Luke might intend his narrative about the apostles' experiences with their bodily risen Lord to stand over against these ideas.

IV. RETURNING THE SAME WAY HE LEFT (1:11)

Because Jesus will return the same way he left (Acts 1:11), his departure in a cloud (1:9) fits the image of his return (Luke 21:27).[751] Luke probably also emphasizes the continuity of Jesus's bodily identity at his return, as Luke did for Jesus's body before and after the resurrection (24:39–40).[752] (The angels' announcement that he will return in the same way may even function as an allusion to what Jesus already spoke, as in 24:5–8.)

---

it also appears in some Jewish sources (2 Bar. 51:10; cf. 4 Macc 17:5; perhaps a play on this in 1 Cor 15:41). Although Cumont, After Life, 91–109, overemphasized astral immortality, he did not invent the notion.

744. Cf., e.g., Test. Sol. 2:3; Exod. Rab. 21:5; Eph 2:2; Bagatti, Church, 283–84; Daniélou, Theology, 191–92; such sources also attribute wings to angels and demons ('Abot R. Nat. 37 A; Pesiq. Rab Kah. 16:1; b. Ḥag. 16a, bar.; Giṭ. 68b; Num. Rab. 12:3; Deut. Rab. 6:6; cf. also 1 En. 61:1; 2 En. 1:5; 3:1; 4:2; 16:7; 19:6; 72:9; 3 En. 9:3; 18:25; 41:3; 47:4; Test. Sol. 2:3; 25:3; Incant. Text 17.2; 43.6–7; Apoc. Sed. 2:4). Literary demonology becomes more dominant in third-century and later sources, but it probably reflects some ideas circulating on a popular level earlier, especially in Parthia, Syria, and Egypt. For many of the spirits invoked in magic, see, e.g., PGM 1.179–80; 4.3043–44; 12.67; for other spirits (or departed souls) in the air, see, e.g., Plato Epin. 984DE; Stoics, in Cic. Nat. d. 2.6.17; Philo Conf. 174; Giants 9; Dreams 1.135; Max. Tyre 9.6; 10.2; 11.12; Pythagoras in Diog. Laert. 8.1.32. Cf. also the heavenly angels of the nations (comment on Acts 16:9).

745. Gr. Anth. 1.19 (late); Daniélou, Theology, 191; Barth, Ephesians, 1:170; esp. work by W. Dalton (although his presentation of Jesus as the new Enoch goes too far; Dalton, "Victory"; idem, Proclamation; "Proclamation"; "Proclamatio"; "Interpretation"). Jesus's victorious ascent might also resemble Moses's ascent to take the Torah despite angelic opposition (on which see, e.g., Schultz, "Angelic Opposition"), though again this image predominates in later sources.

746. Jesus's name is supreme over demons in Acts (Acts 16:18; 19:13–15), but Jesus expelled demons before his ascension (Luke 4:35–36, 41; 6:18; 7:21; 8:2, 29–33; 9:42; 11:14, 20; 13:11–13, 32; cf. 9:1; 10:17, 20). Luke employs the same text as in Eph 1:20–22, but in a sense, Jesus's enemies are not yet under his feet (Acts 2:35). Luke does not explicitly address Jesus's triumph over the powers through the ascension. (Luke does emphasize Christ as exalted judge; Acts 10:42; 17:31.)

747. Sleeman, Geography, 77.

748. E.g., Test. Ab. 20:12 A; 7:13 B (ἀναλαμβανέσαι; and figuratively, ἀναβαίνοντα); 14:7 B (ἦρεν); see comment above on souls ascending.

749. E.g., (later) Porph. Marc. 7.131–34; 16.267–68; 26.415–16. The Platonic tradition allowed this through contemplation of the divine (see, e.g., Philo Spec. Laws 3.1–2, 6; Plut. Isis 77, Mor. 382D; Max. Tyre 11.9–10; 26.1; 38.3; cf. Winston, "Philo's Mysticism"); cf. the goal of divine vision in Jewish mysticism (e.g., Arbel, "Understanding"). Jewish mysticism noted dangers if one was not properly prepared for the ascent (e.g., Scholem, Gnosticism, 14–15; Lieber, "Angels"; cf. earlier Egyptian postmortem dangers in Egyptian Book of the Dead [Allen, 9, Sp. 7; 123–37, Sp. 145–46]).

750. See Segal, "Ascent in Judaism" (though he employs structuralist models, 1337–40), where postmortem examples predominate.

751. The cloud is the clearest allusion to the parousia here (also found in 1 Thess 4:17; Rev 1:7; Mark 14:62); the idea of an earlier coming "alone" (so Strombeck, Rapture, 27) does not appear in the context and violates the allusion to Zech 14:5 in Acts 1:12 and the meaning of the cloud allusion (Dan 7:13; Mark 13:26; 14:62; Luke 21:27; cf. Luke 22:69).

752. Given the later gnostic and Neoplatonic challenge, it is hardly surprising that patristic sources often emphasize Jesus's bodily return, as he left bodily; so, e.g., Chrys. Hom. Acts 2; Hom. 2 Cor. 11.3; Aug. Tract. Jn. 21.13.2–4; Bede Comm. Acts 1.11B (Martin, Acts, 11–12). This emphasis could account for the inclusion of Luke 24:40 in most witnesses, although it also has early attestation.

The verse immediately after the ascension narrative proper reinforces this picture of Jesus returning the same way he left: he left from Mount Olivet (Acts 1:12), which would also be the place where the Lord would come (Zech 14:4). The implicit allusion to Zech 14 recalls a context relevant to early Christian interpretation (Zech 14:5 in Mark 8:38; 1 Thess 3:13), as Luke presumably knew (Luke 9:26).[753] Presumably, this future coming of the king (at the time when his enemies would be subdued, cf. Acts 2:34–36) would coincide with the consummation of the kingdom (1:6–7) and the completion of witness to the ends of the earth (1:8).

Other promises within Luke's narrative are fulfilled; there is no reason to doubt that Luke expects the promise of Jesus's coming (1:11) to turn out the same way.[754] Of the three promises introduced in 1:4–11, one (the promise of the Spirit) is fulfilled in 2:4, another (the witness beyond Judea) is progressively fulfilled (at least proleptically) later in Acts, and the final promise (Jesus's coming) remains future but certain.[755] Some Jewish people also seem to have expected those who ascended to return in the end time (4 Ezra 6:26).

The Jesus who would return would be the same Jesus who had risen; the emphasis might be necessary so that no one would think he would return as another (cf. Luke 17:22–24) coming merely in the "spirit" of Jesus (like John, who came as "Elijah," 1:17). Certainly the rise of impostors was a possibility (21:8).[756] But "this Jesus" may simply be emphatic proclamation, recurring in Peter's proclamation in Acts 2:32, 36 (cf. 10:36) and in Paul's proclamation in 17:3 (cf. 9:20, 22).[757]

---

753. Cf. also Zech 14:8 as one of the key elements behind John 7:37–39 (see Keener, *John*, 725–26, noting also the context in *t. Suk*. 3:18; Dodd, *Interpretation*, 350; Hunter, *John*, 84–85; Schnackenburg, *John*, 2:155).

754. Gaventa, *Acts*, 67 (citing idem, "Eschatology Revisited," 37; Carroll, *Response to End*, 126–27). The ascension confirms the certainty of the parousia (Faure, *Pentecôte*, 82).

755. Gaventa, *Acts*, 27. See discussion of Luke's eschatology, above.

756. The phenomenon was hardly unknown in antiquity; for one example from Luke's general era, Nero impostors arose in the years following his demise (Tac. *Hist*. 1.2, 2.8-9; Suet. *Nero* 57.2; Dio Cass. 66.19.3; probably Dio Chrys. *Or*. 21.9–10).

757. Cf., more negatively, "this Nazarene, Jesus" in 6:14.

PREPARATION
FOR PENTECOST:
AWAITING THE PROMISE
(1:12–26)

If 1:1–11 introduces the promise of the Spirit and provides the transition to the church's ministry, 1:12–26 concerns waiting for the promise. In 1:12–14, Jesus's followers wait in prayer for the promise; in 1:15–26, they also make preparations in faith for the renewal of their people. Parallels with the Qumran community on numerous points suggest that Luke in fact preserves early Palestinian tradition, though he freely composed the narrative in his own words and for his purposes.[1]

In Luke-Acts, fulfillment often follows predictions immediately, but the fulfillment of Acts 1:8 in 2:2–4 is interrupted by "a problem left over from the Gospel," as Johnson puts it.[2] One of the twelve witnesses must be replaced. Yet there is also a sense in which 1:12–26 is not simply a "problem" but part of the preparation for Pentecost. Not only must the disciples be praying together (1:14; often linked with the Spirit's descent [cf. Luke 3:21–22; 11:13; Acts 4:31; 8:15, 17]); the leadership structure for the righteous remnant of Israel must be restored (see comment esp. on Acts 1:26). Because the pivotal connection between Luke's Gospel and Acts reinforces the continuity between Jesus's mission, rooted in the heritage of Israel, and the Gentile mission, exemplified particularly in Paul, this transition in defining the character of God's people is of paramount importance. (A righteous remnant of varying size had always existed within the larger ethnic-national entity Israel; the question at root here is what identifies this remnant at this stage in salvation history.)

If Jesus promised that the witnesses would be empowered (Acts 1:8), the apostles must also define for the community who the authoritative witnesses of the Jesus tradition are (1:22). The rest of the book of Acts, in fact, addresses the issue of witness (see comment above on 1:8). Trusting Jesus's promise, the disciples demonstrated their faith by *preparing* for the Spirit's coming, establishing the witnesses who would carry out the mission once the Spirit came.[3]

Although this narrative has some general significance for Luke (establishing "team" leadership structures remains important elsewhere in Acts, e.g., 13:1; 14:23),[4] Luke

---

1. Johnson, *Acts*, 39, comparing twelve leaders (1QS VIII, 1; Acts 1:26), psalms applied in light of their experience (4QpPsᵃ II, 6–25 [Ps 37]; Acts 1:20), sharing possessions (1QS V, 1–3; CD X, 18–20; Acts 2:44–45), and decisions by lots (1QS V, 3; VI, 16; Acts 1:26), though other Jews applied psalms and utopian communities shared possessions.

2. Johnson, *Acts*, 38. To be sure, the prediction of Acts 1:11 cannot follow immediately.

3. Cf. David preparing in faith for the temple that could only be built by his successor (cf. 1 Chr 28:11–19; 29:1–5; 2 Chr 2:7), or Jeremiah preparing for Judah's restoration (Jer 32:6–15).

4. For various views concerning leadership structures and models in Acts, see, e.g., discussions in Zettner, *Amt*; Clarke, "Imitators"; and works cited in this commentary at relevant passages.

is also concerned for specificity concerning the apostles' number (1:20–22, 26) and identity (1:13, 26). The Spirit may inspire anyone to prophesy (2:17–18), but only the apostles chosen (1:2) by the Lord, who had been close to him in person (1:21–22), are guarantors of the Jesus tradition.

The genre of Acts suggests that Luke is interested not only in general moral applicability (common as this was in histories) but also in the *history* of the movement (most histories also were concerned with the foundations of present nations or movements). Further, he has both apologetic and theological reasons to emphasize that the apostles provided continuity with Jesus. Apologetically, this continuity underlines the accuracy of his report about Jesus and hence the movement's continuity with Israel's ancient faith. Theologically, it defines the contours of the movement that grows from the apostolic witness, contrary to others who might claim to speak for the movement. In particular, it will support the transition to the Gentile mission that the apostles approved (15:7–29).

1. Praying Together (1:12–14)

Luke connects the more detailed scenes in 1:9–11 and 1:15–26 with a summary of intervening events in 1:12–14;[5] this observation, however, does not exhaust the passage's narrative significance. After returning from the Mount of Olives, the disciples do what Jesus has instructed: they wait in Jerusalem for the Spirit (1:4). Luke names the male disciples and mentions the women (notably Mary, Jesus's mother) and his brothers (1:12–13), providing connections with the Gospel narrative that preceded in his two-volume account. Finally, he emphasizes that the believers were praying together (1:14), behavior that commonly precedes the Spirit's coming in Acts (e.g., 8:15; see esp. Luke 11:13).

a. The Setting (1:12)

At some points elsewhere, Luke tidily mentions people's return home after fulfilling some activity.[6] The disciples returned to Jerusalem as the women had after their revelation (Luke 24:9) and like Zechariah after completing the days of his priesthood (1:23) and Mary after visiting Elizabeth (1:56).

The location, the Mount of Olives (Acts 1:12), is of greater significance.[7] It proved central to Jesus's final days; this was where the crowds met him (Luke 19:37; not in Mark)[8] and where he regularly stayed (Luke 19:29; 21:37; 22:39). Jesus was arrested there (22:39), connecting his arrest and passion with his exaltation. Most significantly, however, it reinforces the thought that Jesus would return in the same way that he had left (Acts 1:11), since Luke's biblically literate audience expected the Lord's coming to that mountain at the time of the parousia (Zech 14:3–5, a passage also apparently applied to Jesus in Mark 8:38; 1 Thess 3:13; Rev 19:11–14; and Luke 9:26).[9] Although

5. See Malina and Pilch, *Acts*, 23.

6. Apparently he was too tidy in Acts 15:33, requiring editorial clarification in 15:34!

7. Because of its olive presses, the mountain also could be called "the mountain of anointing" (e.g., *b. Pesaḥ.* 14a).

8. Parsons, *Departure*, 196, notes the allusion to the triumphal entry (Luke 19:29, 37), so that here, as with Bethany in Luke 19:29; 24:50, Jesus's "Triumphal Exit" recalls his triumphal entry (though he emphasizes Luke 22:39 more).

9. Various commentators note the connection, e.g., Lake, "Ascension," 22 (who cites also a rabbinic tradition on Ezek 11:23); Haenchen, *Acts*, 150. Cf. eschatological acts at this mountain in *Test. Naph.* 5:1; other eschatological mountains in *1 En.* 24:2–3 (especially where he will judge, in 25:3); Rev 21:10. Parsons, *Acts*, 27,

most of Luke's original audience probably would not know this additional detail, apparently some other messianic figures also chose the Mount of Olives as a staging ground for establishing the kingdom, presumably in view of Zechariah's prophecy (Jos. *War* 2.262; *Ant.* 20.169).[10] (Luke and his audience may also know that Jesus gave an eschatological discourse there, though Luke does not explicitly repeat this information from Mark 13:3.)

Luke mentions the Sabbath day's journey to show their proximity to the holy city (fulfilling Luke 24:49)[11] but also to indicate that they continued to observe the law (cf. 23:54–56).[12] This may be part of the Palestinian Jewish coloring that characterizes the early chapters of Acts; it displays significant knowledge (or a knowledgeable source) for a probable Diaspora Gentile. The measurement of a Sabbath day's journey (Acts 1:12) need not imply that it was a Sabbath, but it implies that Luke's sources thought in terms of such distances. Luke might expect his audience to take the forty days as a round number ("forty" often functions this way in the OT),[13] but if he expects them to take it more precisely (hence his omission of his characteristic "approximately," Luke 3:23; 8:42; 9:14; Acts 1:15; 2:41; 4:4; 5:7, 36; 10:3, 9; 13:19; 16:25; 19:7, 34; 22:6), this is probably forty-one days after the Sabbath of Luke 23:56.[14]

A Sabbath day's journey was between one-half and three-quarters of a mile and thus not a very long walk.[15] Luke likely knows the popular measurement used also by Pharisees and reported in later rabbinic literature, namely, 2,000 cubits,[16] estimated in various commentators (on the basis of varying cubit estimates) at about 960 yards, or 1,120 meters; this fits the distance from Jerusalem to the mountain's summit, which overlooks Jerusalem (Jos. *Ant.* 20.169; *War* 5.70).[17] This measurement was more generous than the normal rule at Qumran, which was 1,000 cubits, though 2,000

notes many ancient parallels to mountains as sites for ascensions (e.g., Lucian *Hermot.* 7; Apollod. *Bib.* 2.7.7; Diod. Sic. 3.60.3), presumably because they were considered closer to heaven. Kurzinger, *Apostelgeschichte*, 11, adds to Zech 14 mention of Ezek 11:23 (in which the mountain east of Jerusalem is the next holiest site).

10. Barrett, *Acts*, 1025.

11. Luke elsewhere offers estimates of distance, e.g., "about a stone's throw" (Luke 22:41, which does not refer to the proximity of danger by slingers!).

12. Johnson, *Acts*, 33. Although passages such as this show Luke's knowledge of Jerusalem (Hemer, *Acts in History*, 108), Luke generally records distances only to make a specific point, as in Luke 24:13 (see Hengel, "Geography of Palestine," 47). For strict observance of these limits, see, e.g., *m. ʿErub.* 4:1–11. But "domains" could extend such limits; see, e.g., *t. Šabb.* 1:3; *b. Sukkah* 44b; *y. Maʿaś.* 2:3; in one later apocryphal account, one disciple learned how to include all Galilee within the Sabbath limit (*y. ʿErub.* 5:1). Some later interpreters applied the Sabbath day's journey allegorically (Bede *Comm. Acts* 1.12B; Martin, *Acts*, 13).

13. For days, e.g., Gen 7:4, 12, 17; 8:6; Num 13:25; 14:34; 1 Sam 17:16; Ezek 4:6; Jonah 3:4; Tob 1:21; 2 Macc 5:2; 3 Macc 4:15; 6:38. Elsewhere, e.g., *2 Bar.* 76:4; *3 Bar.* 4:14; *4 Ezra* 14:23, 36, 43–45; Jos. *Ant.* 14.476; 18.272; *War* 1.305; 4.56. Most relevant are Moses's forty days on the mountain (Exod 24:18; 34:28; Deut 9:9, 11, 18, 25; 10:10; 4Q364 frg. 15.2; frg. 26bi.10; *Jub.* 1:4; Jos. *Ant.* 3.95, 99; *Ag. Ap.* 2.25; Philo *Dreams* 1.36; *Mos.* 2.69–70).

14. This depended, however, on how one counted the days; see *m. Ḥag.* 2:4; cf. *b. Menaḥ.* 65a.

15. Lake and Cadbury, *Commentary*, 10; Witherington, *Acts*, 113.

16. E.g., *m. ʿErub.* 4:3; 5:7–9; *Soṭah* 5:3–14. The figures were natural extrapolations from Exod 16:29 (one must not leave one's place on the Sabbath) and Num 35:5 (identifying one's place as 2,000 cubits square; cf. Kurzinger, *Apostelgeschichte*, 11).

17. Conzelmann, *Acts*, 9 (citing Strack and Billerbeck, *Kommentar*, 2:590–94); Barrett, *Acts*, 85 (citing *Mek.* on Exod 16:29 and later sources for the Sabbath day's journey); Le Cornu, *Acts*, 29 (citing *m. ʿErub.* 4:3; 5:7; *b. ʿErub.* 51a); also *b. ʿErub.* 45a. Finegan, *Archeology of New Testament*, 96, translates as 900 meters (see also Schille, *Apostelgeschichte*, 75, for 880 meters for the Sabbath day's journey and 900 meters for Josephus's estimate of the mountain's distance from the city). The oft-mentioned divergence between the two estimates in Josephus is minimal (compare also John 11:18 with Luke 19:29; 24:50); one should not think that he or his sources measured the distance exactly, as for mile markers on Roman roads. Further, Mount Olivet is large, and one could measure the distance to more than one point on it (Hengel, "Geography of Palestine," 46).

cubits was permitted when one was pasturing animals.[18] Bethany, also mentioned by Luke as the site of the ascension (Luke 24:50), was on the eastern slope of the mountain (cf. 19:29).[19]

Excursus: The Sabbath in Early Judaism[20]

The seventh day was already important in the Genesis creation narrative, but it became still more so in later tradition (e.g., *Jub.* 2), which declared that angels kept the Sabbath and that this day was holier than any other holy day (2:21, 30).[21] Some later rabbis even said, in notoriously hyperbolic language, that the Sabbath outweighed all other commandments of the Torah.[22] A well-educated first-century Jew[23] such as Josephus could assume that Moses commanded Jewish people to assemble to learn the law together each Sabbath (*Ag. Ap.* 2.175),[24] though the law itself commanded no such thing. The same writer testifies that Jewish laws required, and even the laxer Jews of Tiberias observed, retiring to one's home for a dinner when the Sabbath began around 6:00 p.m. (*Life* 279).[25]

Thus later rabbis meticulously detailed a fence around the Sabbath law.[26] Most Jewish people allowed some exceptions, especially for saving a life. After Syrian troops slaughtered a thousand Israelites who refused to defend themselves on the Sabbath (1 Macc 2:34–38), most Jewish pietists contended that the law would permit defensive warfare on the Sabbath (2:41).[27] But any activity that could be done before the Sabbath was prohibited on the Sabbath.[28] Although matters of life and death remained exceptions and common people were probably less particular, the Pharisees probably opposed minor medical cures on the Sabbath.[29] Later rabbis

18. CD X, 21; XI, 5–6; 4Q265 7 II, 5–6; see Barrett, *Acts*, 85. Sadducees likely disagreed with the Pharisaic system of *erub* (Holmén, *Covenant Thinking*, 81).

19. Fitzmyer, *Acts*, 213. Luke 24:50 may read "over against" Bethany; cf. Carter and Earle, *Acts*, 14; Bruce, *Commentary*, 42.

20. I have adapted this material from Keener, *John*, 641–43.

21. In addition to biblical warrant in the creation narrative, later tradition provided another sign in creation, a river that flowed only on the Sabbath (e.g., *Tg. Ps.-J.* on Exod 33:10); Jewish people also kept a Sabbatic year (Lev 25:4–5; Neh 10:31; Safrai, "Religion," 825–27; probable numismatic evidence in Pfann, "Coinage"; *t. Ter.* 10:10; *y. Šeb.* 8:2, §7; Tac. *Hist.* 5.4).

22. *Y. Ned.* 3:9, §3; cf. *Lev. Rab.* 3:1. The rabbis regularly extolled the Sabbath (e.g., *Gen. Rab.* 10:9–11:10; *Pesiq. Rab.* 23:7–8); some even said the Messiah would come if all Israel kept the Sabbath together (*Exod. Rab.* 25:12).

23. Josephus affirmed Sabbath keeping and denigrated, in his narrative, Jews whom he portrayed as failing to observe it (see Weiss, "Sabbath in Josephus").

24. Second-century rabbis also expected at least some children to study Torah under a teacher on Friday evenings (Safrai, "Education," 954, cites *m. Šabb.* 1:3; *t. Šabb.* 1:12).

25. In rabbinic tradition, joy became a central characteristic of celebrating the Sabbath (*Gen. Rab.* 100:7).

26. E.g., *t. Ketub.* 1:1; *b. Šabb.* 12b; see further Westerholm and Evans, "Sabbath," 1031–32. Keeping it was meritorious (e.g., later, *Pesiq. Rab.* 52:4), just as disobeying it was a grievous sin (*Jub.* 1:10).

27. One could also kill a threatening animal (*y. Šabb.* 14:1, §2); other peoples had also observed holy days that disallowed offensive warfare (e.g., Xen. *Hell.* 6.4.16; Thucyd. 5.54.2–4; 5.75.5; 5.82.2–3; 8.9.1; Ovid *Fasti* 3.811–12). (On war's necessitating reinterpretation of the Sabbath laws, see Nikiprowetzky, "Sabbat.")

28. *m. Pesaḥ.* 6:2 (Akiba); *t. Pisha* 5:1; with regard to warfare, Jos. *Life* 159, 161. The later practice of a Sabbath goy (cf., e.g., *Deut. Rab.* 1:21; for sheep tending, *t. Šeb.* 2:20; *y. Šeb.* 3:3, 34c) would not have been viewed favorably (CD XI, 2; *m. Šabb.* 16:8; *t. Šabb.* 13:9; cf. Exod 20:10; Deut 5:14).

29. Sanders, *Jesus to Mishnah*, 13; cf. Falk, *Jesus*, 149, on *t. Šabb.* 17:14; see further, e.g., *m. Yoma* 8:6; *t. Šabb.* 12:12–13; *y. 'Erub.* 10:11; *Ma'aś. Š.* 2:1, §4; *Šabb.* 6:3; further discussion in Keener, *Matthew*, 357–58. Later rabbis preferred death to Sabbath violation if, to pagans, the latter would imply apostasy (*b. Sanh.* 74b).

expected that the Sabbath and all festivals be devoted partly to religious observance and partly to relaxation.[30]

Under later rabbinic rules, which may or may not reflect earlier Pharisaic ideals, Sabbath violation was, in theory, worthy of death.[31] Nevertheless, under the same rules it would have been impossible to have found someone sufficiently guilty of Sabbath violation to warrant execution in practice.[32] The Essenes observed the Sabbath more strictly than others,[33] probably sharing the view of *Jubilees* that death was appropriate for even minor infractions such as intercourse with one's wife (*Jub.* 50:8) or fasting (50:12–13) on the Sabbath.[34] Nevertheless, in practice they commuted the biblical death sentence for its violation to seven years of excommunication.[35]

Despite some pagan hostility toward Jewish Sabbaths,[36] some Christians, probably especially Jewish believers in Jesus, continued to observe the Sabbath centuries later,[37] just as many Jewish and Gentile followers of Jesus, convinced that the teaching remains scriptural, continue to do today. Nevertheless, some later rabbinic texts stereotype sectarians, probably most of them Christian, as challenging the Sabbath,[38] suggesting that correct interpretation and practice of the Sabbath remained a major issue of controversy between many of Jesus's followers and many of their Jewish contemporaries.

Should we infer from Luke's mention of the Sabbath day's journey that his ideal audience continued to keep the Sabbath? It is not clear that Pauline churches expected this behavior of Gentiles (Rom 14:5–6; Col 2:16),[39] but Diaspora God-fearers would know the Sabbath and probably knew some customs surrounding it; Jewish believers continued to observe it, perhaps with some Gentiles (Rom 14:5).[40] Certainly, Luke can refer to common Jewish festivals such as the Sabbath (twenty-seven times), Passover (Acts 12:4; Luke 2:41; 22:1, 7, 8, 11, 13, 15), Pentecost (Acts 2:1; 20:16), and the Day of Atonement (27:9) without explanation, and sometimes he sounds as if Paul observed such festivals with other believers (cf. 20:6; perhaps 20:16), a not implausible scenario historically (cf. 1 Cor 16:8). Most Gentile Christians, whether as slaves or as other workers, would not have the liberty to stop work on the seventh day

---

30. Le Cornu, *Acts*, 716, citing *b. Pesaḥ.* 68b. The Sabbath should be joyful (*y. Ber.* 2:6, §3), as festivals normally were (e.g., Dion. Hal. *Epid.* 1.255; for joy during festivals, see further comment on Acts 2:1).

31. E.g., *y. Meg.* 1:6, §2.

32. Sanders, *Jesus to Mishnah*, 18–19.

33. See CD X, 14–XI, 18, prohibiting talk of work (X, 19) and lifting dust (XI, 10–11); cf. Jos. *War* 2.147–49, prohibiting even defecation; *Jub.* 50:1–13 and comments in Finkelstein, *Making*, 205–11; 4Q251 frg. 1; 4Q265 7 I, 6–9); those who forgot the Sabbath were apostate (1Q22 I, 7–8; *Jub.* 1:10). Some scholars argue that the Scrolls represent broader Jewish tradition before Akiba (Kimbrough, "Sabbath"), but parallels in Philo may suggest that the more lenient customs, though not universal, predate the Tannaim (see Belkin, *Philo*, 192–203).

34. Contrast pagans who associated the Sabbath and fasting (e.g., Mart. *Epig.* 4.4.7; Suet. *Aug.* 76; Strabo 16.2.40; cf. further Whittaker, *Jews and Christians*, 70; Sevenster, *Anti-Semitism*, 130–32), perhaps confusing the Sabbath with Yom Kippur.

35. See Sanders, *Jesus to Mishnah*, 18; Sanders, *Judaism*, 367, citing CD XII, 3–6.

36. As laziness (e.g., Hor. *Sat.* 1.9.68–69; Juv. *Sat.* 14.96, 105–6; Tac. *Hist.* 5.4) and ridiculous superstition (e.g., Sen. Y. *Ep. Lucil.* 95.47; see further Whittaker, *Jews and Christians*, 63ff.).

37. See, e.g., *Apost. Const.* 7.36.1–7 (*OTP* 2:682–83); *CPJ* 3:16, §457d. Others, of course, rejected the practice (e.g., *Barn.* 15.8; Ign. *Magn.* 9.1; Justin *Dial.* 10; *Diogn.* 4.1, 3).

38. E.g., *Exod. Rab.* 30:9 (recounting a purportedly late first- or, at the latest, early second-century C.E. episode, but the tradition is probably later); cf. *b. Taʿan.* 27b.

39. Though some argue that even these passages support continuing Sabbath observance (see Weiss, "Sabbath in Corpus").

40. The Sabbath itself appears in the creation narrative and hence could be construed as a universal expectation for humanity, including Gentiles (Gen 2:2–3), though the rabbis did not so construe it.

of every week, but they surely knew that it was the Jewish Sabbath (perhaps ideally applicable universally; see Gen 2:2–3). Compare comment at Acts 20:7.

b. The Upper Room (1:13)

One might suppose that the entire group was "staying" in one upper room, but Luke means only that they "habitually met there."[41] Even if some were staying there, certainly the women of Acts 1:14 were not staying there along with the men of 1:13, and it would be impossible for the 120 of 1:15 all to sleep there. Since upper rooms were typically approached from the outside by steps, those who entered would not need to disturb residents of the ground floor.[42]

i. Large Upper Rooms

The home that welcomed them was certainly an exceptional one. Most people who lived in the cities of the empire were confined to crowded *insulae*, or tenements;[43] they would not own their own upper room.[44] Further, very few upper rooms could have accommodated so many people (cf. 9:37, 39; the one in 20:8 is large but probably not this large).[45] Upper-city Jerusalem, however, had large homes rather than tenements, with central courts in Hellenistic fashion, and many of the homes included their own immersion pools.[46] Yet few Jerusalem homes even in the upper city would hold more than fifty people, though a courtyard (which obviously would not occur in an "upper room" but could occur in the same compound) with a house or homes built around it could have accommodated more.[47]

This is not to suggest that Luke is architecturally naive; he shows no sign of defensiveness that he strains his credibility (and is expending it on a nonmiraculous report at that). Not all homes were designed the same way; potentially a home could have an upper floor as large as the lower one, with members of the family living in each.[48] More important, it is not clear that all the people were present during the entire day, and the 120 may represent a larger number than was usually gathered at one time, perhaps for a special meeting (1:15). It is doubtful that we should think of banqueters reclining on couches at this point;[49] most of us with experience among the poor in the Majority World can testify that many impoverished churches and mosques there cram more people sitting (cf. 2:2), and certainly standing, into a room than we in the

41. Barrett, *Acts*, 87 (citing the "periphrastic tense").

42. See Foakes-Jackson, *Acts*, 6; Safrai, "Home," 731 (also commenting on cases of joint ownership of the building, 730–31). In Roman homes, constructed to welcome and impress guests, decorations show that even upper floors were not purely private (Balch, "Families," 265).

43. Blue, "Influence," 480 (in n. 21 he suggests that homes in urban areas were probably about 3 percent). This extrapolates from cities that we know best, especially Rome; there may have been some regional variation. See further discussion at Acts 18:3; 20:8.

44. Upper stories in such tenements lacked plumbing and hence were often filthy (Carcopino, *Life*, 39–40), but upper stories are not "upper rooms" (despite the possible utility of some tenements' long hallways; see comment on Acts 12:12–13; 20:8).

45. On the usual small size of upper rooms, see Jdt 8:5; more fully, Safrai, "Home," 731.

46. Avigad, *Jerusalem*, 83, 139, 142; Stambaugh and Balch, *Environment*, 97. Upper-city Jerusalem's mikvaot were very much like those found elsewhere (Sanders, *Judaism*, 222–29, esp. 223).

47. Bishop, *Apostles*, 32–33; Witherington, *Acts*, 211, following Blue, "House Church," 119–22, esp. 131n44. For similar estimates in Corinth, varying according to the seating and the rooms used, see Jeffers, *World*, 81; Murphy-O'Connor, *Corinth*, 156–57; Thiselton, *Corinthians*, 861 (twenty to thirty people could squeeze into a triclinium, or fifty into a large villa).

48. Lysias *Or.* 1.9 (in *Murder of Eratosthenes*), although this is a significantly earlier Greek source.

49. A house could have a second-floor *triclinium* (see the diagram in White, "Pater *familias*," 461), but such a room was not meant to accommodate large numbers.

West would think possible. (It is also possible that large meetings like this one were not held in the upper room, although we cannot gather that perspective solely from the flow of the narrative.)

External evidence also indicates that a large number of sages had gathered in an upper chamber to make many decrees in the generation before Jerusalem's fall; tradition claims that this included both Shammaites and Hillelites (*m. Šabb.* 1:4; *t. Šabb.* 1:16).[50] Other sources speak of elders and sages in an upper room in Yavneh a generation after Jerusalem's fall[51] or of sages reclining in an upper room of a home in Jericho in R. Gamaliel II's time (end of the first century C.E.).[52] Other traditions also report sages meeting and sometimes voting in upper rooms of homes.[53] An inscription shows that synagogues could include upper rooms (ὑπερῷα); at least some other early Christians also worshiped in them (Acts 20:8).[54]

II. Which Upper Room?

The definite article might suggest that this was a well-known upper room.[55] The reader of Luke-Acts will infer that it is probably the same upper room that hosted the Last Supper (Luke 22:11–12) and perhaps was also the site of a resurrection appearance (24:33–36).[56] Whereas Jesus took the disciples to the Mount of Olives to pray after leaving that upper room (22:39–40), here they gather in an upper room after leaving the Mount of Olives (Acts 1:12) and praying (1:14). The upper room of Luke 22 was "large" and "furnished"; the home included at least one servant, since, in a home without a servant, a woman would generally be carrying the water (22:10). (Then again, the number of servants seems limited. If the household had several servants, a woman presumably would have been carrying the water.)[57]

Given the relative unlikelihood that Jesus had many followers among the elite from the very beginning, it is possible that this home is that of John Mark's mother (see Acts 12:12–13), as later tradition suggests.[58] If this were the case, however, one might expect Luke to mention it here, allowing him to introduce some characters earlier.[59] Even if the earliest passion tradition obscured the owner's name to protect the owner, Luke's Pauline connection (and Paul's Markan connection) should have made this

---

50. Some later traditions also speak of sages meeting in upper rooms as early as the time of Hillel the Elder (perhaps early first century); *t. Soṭah* 13:3; *y. 'Abod. Zar.* 3:1, §2; *Hor.* 3:5, §3; *Soṭah* 9:16, §2. On the sages meeting in an upper chamber, see also Le Cornu, *Acts*, 30.

51. Also in *b. Sanh.* 11a; *Soṭah* 48b; *y. 'Abod. Zar.* 3:1, §2; *Hor.* 3:5, §3; *Soṭah* 9:16, §2.

52. E.g., *b. Ber.* 37a; *Soṭah* 48b; *Sanh.* 11a. Later estimates of R. Gamaliel II's academy (students on eighty or three hundred benches; *y. Ta'an.* 4:1, §14) are exaggerated (cf. the sukkah to avoid having them cramped, in *y. Sukkah* 2:1, §3). Guria's house in Jericho appears also for the times of Hillel (*t. Soṭah* 13:3; *b. Sanh.* 11a) and his school (*b. Soṭah* 48b).

53. E.g., R. Tarfon (early second century) with the elders in Nitzeh's upper room in Lydda (*b. Qidd.* 40b; *Šabb.* 29b; cf. *y. Sanh.* 3:5, §2); in Aris's home in *y. Ḥag.* 1:7, §4.

54. Riesner, "Synagogues in Jerusalem," 206, citing also Strack and Billerbeck, *Kommentar*, 2:594–95, for teachers meeting there (as do most commentators, e.g., Lake and Cadbury, *Commentary*, 10); cf. the Theodotus inscription (discussed at Acts 6:9). For prayer (Acts 1:14) in upper rooms, see, e.g., Dan 6:10; the special case in Acts 9:37–40; but since upper rooms were common, we should perhaps not press the connections too far.

55. Longenecker, *Acts*, 56.

56. For the upper room of Luke 22:12, despite the different term, see, e.g., Dunn, *Acts*, 15–16; Parsons, *Departure*, 197; D. Williams, *Acts*, 35.

57. On women drawing water, see Eurip. *El.* 56–57, 309; Safrai, "Home," 752; cf. Eickelman, *Middle East*, 163. On multipurpose single servants, see Luke 17:7–8; Bailey, *Peasant Eyes*, 114–15; Ael. Arist. *Def. Or.* 380, §127 (on παιδαγωγοί).

58. Longenecker, *Acts*, 56; Fitzmyer, *Acts*, 213.

59. Then again, Luke fails to mention the kinship of Mark and Barnabas (Col 4:10). But it is not clear that Luke completely suppresses Mark (see comment on Acts 13:13; 15:37–39), and so antipathy to the household should not be a factor in their exclusion here.

information available to him. Further, gatherings this large would not have escaped notice, making it less likely that the more secretive gatherings in time of persecution in Acts 12 would have occurred in the same home.

Some scholars argue for the traditional site of the Cenacle, in spite of the obvious objection that Jerusalem was destroyed in 70 C.E. In favor of their position, second-century evidence exists for a Christian presence in Aelia Capitolina; given the obstacles that Christians must have faced living there, their commitment to locating their heritage could allow for the traditional claim. Granted, the visible remains are late medieval, but the location might be roughly accurate.[60]

This argument is debatable but not impossible. Exiles returning a generation or two after Jerusalem's first destruction by conflagration still could remember and discern the remains of many sites (Neh 2:13–15; 3:1–31; cf. 7:4; 11:21). The case is similar in most cases of war devastation today.[61] In upper-city Jerusalem, where homes were larger and more distinct, someone might be able to locate at least an approximate area; certainly, everyone knew where the Temple Mount was.[62]

Still, the fire was severe in this area,[63] and the argument for continuity with this site appears much more difficult than for some other traditional locations. Apparently, no complete buildings survived the destruction of 70,[64] and archaeologists have differed over even whether the legion stayed in Jerusalem at this time (cf. Jos. *War* 7.5).[65] Epiphanius's claim of Jewish Christians assembling in this location in Jerusalem (Epiph. *De mens.* 14) appears reasonable, but this is much more modest than the identification with the Pentecost site first attested in Byzantine times and the site of the Last Supper attested in the fifth century.[66]

c. The List of Apostles (1:13)

Jesus undoubtedly selected twelve as representatives[67] for the righteous remnant of the eschatological people of God, in a manner analogous to the twelve select leaders in 1QS VIII, 1.[68] (See further comment at Acts 1:26.) Thus, selecting a twelfth apostle to restore the symbolic value of leaders for Israel's remnant (Acts 1:15–26)

60. Murphy O'Connor, "Cenacle," 303–4, 310–12. Less persuasively, Murphy O'Connor doubts the Christian flight to Pella (316–17; cf. Brandon, *Zealots*, 284; Lüdemann, "Successors"; Aune, *Prophecy*, 312). By contrast, most scholars appear to still accept the basic claim in Euseb. *H.E.* 3.5.3 (e.g., Reicke, *Era*, 216; Lohse, *Environment*, 49; idem, *Mark's Witness*, 79; Sowers, "Circumstances"; Cole, *Mark*, 203; Schoeps, "Ebionitische Apokalyptik"; Pritz, *Nazarene Christianity*, 122–27; for some possible archaeological support, see Smith, "Sarcophagus"). Pella does not fit Mark 13:14 closely enough to be based on it (or vice versa).

61. After troops burned much of Dolisie, Congo, my wife and some other returning refugees readily located ruins of their homes (or, failing remains, at least the plots of land), even in areas that had been densely populated and severely scorched. In their case, people recognized their districts, and concrete and metal markers remained on the sites of their homes.

62. Archaeologists dispute the precise site of the temple proper; cf., e.g., Kaufman, "Temple"; Cornfeld, *Josephus*, 364, 426; McRay, *Archaeology*, 113; Vogt, "Tempel."

63. See, e.g., Avigad, *Jerusalem*, 120–39; idem, "Burnt House" (on the skeletal forearm, 67, 71–72).

64. Geva, "Searching." Of course, Luke 21:6 (Mark 13:2) is hyperbolic; some stones were left standing on others (Danker, *New Age*, 198; Kaufman, "Eastern Wall," 115; Sanders, *Figure*, 257). The western retaining wall of the temple survived, and later rabbis counted it indestructible (*Num. Rab.* 11:2; *Song Rab.* 2:9, §4; *Lam. Rab.* 1:5, §31; *Pesiq. Rab.* 15:10).

65. Geva, "Searching" (against); Bar, "Aelia Capitolina" (for, but uncertain exactly where).

66. Skarsaune, *Shadow*, 190–91; cf. Le Cornu, *Acts*, 31.

67. Contrary to some who share this perspective, however, "their significance" may well be "evocative and not constitutive"; see Richardson, *Israel*, 61.

68. See Harrington, *God's People*, 39; Sanders, *Jesus and Judaism*, 104; cf. Jervell, *Luke and People of God*, 82; in Luke-Acts most fully, see the case in Fuller, *Restoration*, 239–64 (who interprets Israel's restoration mostly spiritually through the apostolic mission); cf. 1QM II, 1; V, 2; esp. (with 1QS VIII, 1) 4Q259 II, 9. For the eschatological hope for the twelve tribes, see Sanders, *Judaism*, 291 (citing, e.g., 1QM II, 2–3; 11QT[a] VIII, 14–16; LVII, 5–6).

fits well into this context of the Spirit and Israel's restoration (1:6–8).[69] The reason for a list of these names, however, invites further exploration.

i. Name Lists

Starting from Homer's catalogue of ships (*Il.* 2.484–877), catalogues (e.g., of gods; genealogies; chains of proofs) became a common Greek literary form.[70] Lists of heroes' names were common, and their variants often suggest older tradition.[71] Readers in later centuries could refer back respectfully to such lists (Philost. *Hrk.* 6.3; 7.2) and expand on them by means of traditions and literary imagination (6.3); this tendency may have aided the growth of traditions about apostles in later centuries. Ancient literature also sometimes included lists of disciples (e.g., Iambl. *V.P.* 23.104),[72] whether the most prominent (35.251), a chain of successors who passed on the early tradition (36.265–66; m. *'Ab.* 1:1–12), or a list of all known disciples' names (Iambl. *V.P.* 36.267).

ii. Historical Tradition

The designation "the twelve"[73] undoubtedly is authentic tradition (given the embarrassment caused by Judas, not to mention Q material such as Matt 19:28//Luke 22:30, which did not suit typical Gentile Christians' theology).[74] The term was established tradition well before the writing of the Gospels (1 Cor 15:5) despite the likelihood that those who passed on the tradition knew that one of Jesus's own disciples betrayed him (cf. possibly 1 Cor 11:23;[75] the criterion of embarrassment). The variations in the lists among NT documents are slight, but the variations probably testify to the idea of a group of "twelve" more widely known than a standardized list of names.[76] (Thus Luke both here and in Luke 6:16 has "Judas son of James" rather than Mark's "Thaddeus.")[77] Since Luke mentions the "twelve" again only in Acts 6:2 and does not even mention "the apostles" after the Jerusalem council (15:6, 22, 23; 16:4), his primary interest in them seems historical rather than hagiographic.[78]

The list of apostles here[79] is identical to the list in Luke 6:14–16 except for sequence and the obvious omission of Judas.[80] The changes in sequence are also minimal; James and John here intervene between Simon and his brother Andrew because the three

---

69. See Turner, *Power*, 301.

70. Reitz, "Catalogue," 6–7 (citing, e.g., Virg. *Aen.* 7.641–817; 10.120–45). In historical works, see, e.g., the list of ten generals on Samos in Androtion *Atthis* frg. 38. More generally, cf. genealogies and tribal lists in the OT. For vice and virtue lists, see comment on Acts 15:20.

71. E.g., 2 Sam 23:8–39; 1 Chr 25:1–7; Hom. *Il.* 3.161–242; Ap. Rhod. 1.23–228; Val. Flacc. 1.352–483; cf. Gordon, *Near East*, 110.

72. For lists of disciples, see Davies and Allison, *Matthew*, 2:150, cite m. *'Ab.* 2:8; Diog. Laert. 8.46.

73. On the twelve apostles in Luke-Acts, see, e.g., Pesch, *Apostelgeschichte*, 1:92–97.

74. Sanders, *Jesus and Judaism*, 11 ("almost indisputable"), 98–101 (esp. refutation of Vielhauer, 99–100); Witherington, *Christology of Jesus*, 126–27; Meier, "Circle of Twelve"; Ehrman, *Prophet*, 186–87; Charlesworth, *Jesus within Judaism*, 137; on the embarrassment, Zwiep, *Judas*, 47.

75. Whether this verse refers to Judas's betrayal (Fee, *Corinthians*, 549, given the Last Supper context) or not (Hays, *First Corinthians*, 198; Smith, *Symposium*, 188, citing Rom 4:25; 8:32; perhaps Isa 53:6, 12b) is debated.

76. Sanders, *Jesus and Judaism*, 101. Such a standardized list would be difficult, in any case, in the earliest period, given the frequent use of multiple names (see comment on Acts 1:23).

77. Luke might follow Q here, Matthew (Matt 10:3) preferring Mark on this point; either way, Luke likely has genuine tradition (cf. John 14:22). Although the lists could include different persons at this point, they could also reflect differing traditions of the names of the same person; on the great frequency of persons bearing multiple names in antiquity, see comment on Acts 1:23.

78. Hengel and Schwemer, *Between Damascus and Antioch*, 25.

79. Linked with seven copulatives (had all been linked, it would be polysyndeton, on which see comment on Acts 15:20); but not all are so linked, and hence the names are divided into four groupings (the first containing four names; the next, two; the third, two; and the last, three). The first four are the most prominent.

80. Barrett, *Acts*, 87, might read too much into the repetition here; one would not expect all Luke's audience to unwind the first scroll to find all the names or (without deliberate memorization) to recall

had become a special group (Luke 8:45, 51; 9:28; cf. Mark 3:16–17; 14:33; though cf. Mark 13:3).[81] Although pairs of brothers figure in Greek hero stories and lists,[82] our sparser gospel tradition makes less of their joint activities (cf. Luke 5:10; 9:54; Mark 10:35, 41). Beyond that, only Bartholomew and Thomas change places.[83] The following narrative (Acts 1:15–26) will explain the omission of Judas.

III. SIMON PETER

The mention of Peter first suggests his influential position (also Luke 6:14; Mark 1:29; 3:16; 13:3). Peter, who appears outspoken, often functions as spokesman for all the disciples,[84] is part of Jesus's intimate circle,[85] and is recognized as a leader (Luke 22:31–32; cf. Mark 14:37).[86] Hebrew burial inscriptions attest that biblical names were common in this period, and hence Jesus's circle included three persons named James (lit. "Jacob"), four Simons (similar to the biblical Simeon), three Judases, and so forth.[87] Patriarchal names were dominant in Diaspora Judaism, and Hasmonean names (though some of these were also patriarchal) in first-century Palestine.[88]

"Simon" occurs in Palestinian (e.g., *CIJ* 2:117, §890; 2:126, §905) and Diaspora Jewish (e.g., 1:117, §165; possibly 1:138, §197) inscriptions and was one of the most common Jewish names in Egypt (see *CPJ* 1:29; 3:191–92). "Simon" was perhaps the most popular masculine name of the period,[89] requiring a distinguishing name to accompany it (such as "Peter"). A Greek name (e.g., Lysias *Or.* 3.1, §96), it was readily identified with the patriarchal "Simeon" (see comment on Acts 15:14).[90] "Peter" functions as a nickname, and nicknames normally signified something about the person.[91] It translates the Aramaic *Kepha*, or "Rocky"; this was not a personal name in this period, though later it was common among Christians (and used as the baptismal name of a Jewish convert to Christianity).[92]

---

all the names sequentially until hearing Luke-Acts many times. On the apostles in Luke-Acts, cf. Bovon, *Theologian*, 359–67.

81. With Dunn, *Acts*, 16; Johnson, *Acts*, 34. Some sages apparently divided their disciples by respective levels of attainment (Iambl. *V.P.* 18.80–81).

82. E.g., the sons of Boreas in Dio Chrys. *Or.* 4.117–18 (cf. perhaps, but not likely, Mark 3:17). Other scholars have compared the Dioscuri (on which see comment on Acts 28:11; for the comparison, see, e.g., Derrett, "Co-rescuers"), though some are unconvinced (e.g., Mitchell, "Homer," 252). In family-dominant cultures, brothers can also act in pairs or groups—in Hebrew epic (e.g., Gen 34:25; 37:12, 23; 1 Sam 17:18; the sons of Zeruiah in 2 Sam 2:18; 3:39; 16:10; 19:22) and in contemporary real life.

83. If Luke wishes us to suppose that the names are grouped by twos as ministry teams (cf. Luke 10:1; but this is uncertain), these two could have switched on occasion (but this is also uncertain).

84. Luke 8:45; 9:20, 33; 12:41; 18:28; Acts 1:15; 2:14; for similar character, cf. Luke 22:54; 24:12; Mark 1:36; 8:29, 32; 9:5; 10:28; 11:21; 14:29, 31.

85. Luke 8:51; 9:28; 22:8; cf. 24:34; Mark 5:37; 9:2; 14:33; 16:7.

86. Peter's role is not always positive (Luke 22:34, 58–61; cf. 9:33), but he grows (Acts 10:17–23). For Peter's developing characterization as an agent of God's message in Luke-Acts, see Wells, "Characterization."

87. Dalman, *Jesus-Jeshua*, 28. Given the few extant traditions about most of the disciples, the production of two similarly named persons to harmonize divergent traditions (as in Diod. Sic. 4.4.1–5; Arrian *Alex.* 2.16.1–3; 4.28.2; *Ind.* 5.13) is unlikely here.

88. See Williams, "Names," 107–9.

89. Fitzmyer, *Essays*, 105–12.

90. See Brown, *Death*, 915.

91. On nicknames, see, e.g., Dion. Hal. *Ant. rom.* 7.2.4; Gen 29–30; cf. the "Goliath" family in Hachlili and Killebrew, "Byt glyt"; and by contrast, "Samuel the Small" in *y. Soṭah* 9:13, §2. Less relevant is that converts sometimes changed their names (Horsley, "Name Change"; proselytes with Jewish names in *CIJ* 1:384, §523 [also in Bamberger, *Proselytism*, 234]; Dominus Flevit inscription 31 in Meyers and Strange, *Archaeology*, 68; Finegan, *Archeology of New Testament*, 247–48; *m. Yad.* 4:4; *Sipre Deut.* 253.2.2; *b. Ber.* 28a [but cf. *b. Šabb.* 33b]), *pace* Bagatti, *Church*, 237 (who assumed that these were Jewish converts to Christianity). Parents could name children symbolically, but often for events in the parents' own lives (Gen 29:32–35; 41:51–52; cf. Job 42:14).

92. Williams, "Names," 104. The name was not common (Meier, *Matthew*, 182; for a possible occurrence in 4Q130 8–9, see Charlesworth, "Peter"; but William Whiston's "Peter" in Jos. *Ant.* 18.156 should

IV. OTHER NAMES

As one would expect in an authentic list of names, some of the names were much more common than others; our extant evidence for ancient names is nowhere close to complete, though it is surely representative for the more common names.

"John" and its variant forms appear commonly enough.[93] "Andrew" is a rare name, so far attested in first-century Palestine on only two ossuaries, never in the first-century Diaspora, and only rarely in the Diaspora outside the first century.[94] Some scholars argue that "Thomas" appears as a first name in the sixth and seventh centuries and was not so used by first-century Jews.[95] Most likely it is a nickname, meaning "twin."[96] The name "Philip" is much better attested, though it was not particularly popular, for first-century Jews in Palestine.[97] We lack clear Jewish examples of the name "Bartholomew," but it makes sense as "son of Tolmai" or "son of Talmai."[98] "Matthew" and variants such as "Mattathiah" and "Matthiah" (Acts 1:23) were very common among Palestinian Jews in the first century but very rare in the Diaspora.[99]

Readers would understand "James of Alphaeus" probably as "James, son of Alphaeus." The formula appears elsewhere—for example, Μαρία ἡ τοῦ ἱερέως (CIJ 1:291, §375), which probably means "Maria, [daughter] of the priest," and Ἰωσήπου Σίμωνος (2:112, §880), presumably "of Joseph, Simon's [son]."[100] Different individuals with the same name (see further comment on Acts 1:23) were confused frequently enough that later writers sometimes tried to distinguish earlier people with the same name (who sometimes were probably not distinct).[101] Because "James" (lit. "Jacob," Ἰάκωβος) was a common name[102] and two of the Twelve shared it, one needed to supply patronyms or epithets to distinguish them or others who also shared the name.[103] Apart from James "of Alphaeus" and Alphaeus, Levi's father, in Mark 2:14, the only attestation for James's father's name appears in a few other Aramaic names with *halaf*-roots.[104] Given the name's rareness, the Alphaeus who is father of Levi might also be father of James. But if so, if Luke's and Mark's Levi (Mark 2:14; Luke 5:27) is Matthew's "Matthew" (Matt 9:9), Luke seems unaware of the connection; he points to no clear connection between Matthew and James in his lists.

---

read Πρῶτον); for discussion of the figurative sense behind the nickname, relevant to Matt 16:18, cf. Keener, *Matthew*, 426–27.

93. E.g., *CPJ* 1:132–33, §7; 1:246–47, §133, lines 35, 39; *CIJ* 2:312, §1367; 2:358, §1429; 2:391, §1468; Luke 8:3; see Ilan, "Lhbdly ktyb."

94. Williams, "Names," 97.

95. Ibid., 103. But see *CIJ* 2:74, §825 (194 C.E., Dura-Europos); it was, in any case, uncommon.

96. Williams, "Names," 103. See "Didymus," which bears the same meaning (John 11:16; 20:24; 21:2; comments in Keener, *John*, 1225; "Didymus" or "Didymas" appears, e.g., in the name "Arius Didymus" and in P.Oxy. 115). (That his parents could have assigned him a title as a name also cannot be ruled out.)

97. Williams, "Names," 98–99.

98. Ibid., 94 (though even "Tolmai" is rare, 94–95).

99. Williams, "Names," 91–92 (they never appear in Egypt or Cyrene); cf., e.g., *CIJ* 2:270, §1276 (Jerusalem).

100. Also *CIJ* 2:117, §890; 2:126, §905; 2:128, §911; 2:137, §932; 2:171, §986; 2:391, §1468; 2:445, §1538. Cf. the same practice in Lucian *Anach.* 39; *True Story* 2.7.

101. E.g., for "Heracles," cf. Arrian *Alex.* 2.16.1–3; 4.28.2; *Ind.* 5.13; Appian *Hist. rom.* 6.1.2; Philost. *Vit. Apoll.* 2.3. For others, see Val. Max. 3.3.ext. 3; Iambl. *V.P.* 5.25; Philost. *Hrk.* 26.16; Libanius *Anecdote* 3.29.

102. See, e.g., Jos. *Life* 96; *CPJ* 2:137, §235; 3:179; *CIJ* 1:267, §340; 2:117, §890; 2:155, §967; 2:186, §1017; 2:212, §1161; 2:391, §1467; 2:414, §1505; Williams, "Names," 86.

103. E.g., "the less" in Mark 15:40; cf. the analogous method of distinguishing the two Ajaxes of Homeric fame (e.g., Philost. *Hrk.* 23.21; 32.33; 33.39; 35.1).

104. Williams, "Names," 94. An Aramaic inscription from Capernaum mentions a *"Halphai"* alongside the more common *"Zebidah"* and *"John"* (*CIJ* 982; Hemer, *Acts in History*, 221). "Alpheios" does appear as a Gentile name, notably for a river in, e.g., Ovid *Metam.* 5.573–641; Libanius *Narration* 3.

Josephus, ossuaries, and two disciples among the Twelve with the name attest the great popularity of the name "Judas" among first-century Palestinian Jews.[105]

Simon's surname, "Zealot," translates an Aramaic word (קנאה) transliterated Καναναῖος in Mark 3:18; Matt 10:4;[106] this might indicate that he had belonged to, or resembled a member of, the sort of revolutionary group later associated with the "Zealot" revolutionaries.[107] But whereas "Zealot" could mean a particular kind of "revolutionary" to an audience after the first Jewish revolt (66–70), it is doubtful whether most people employed the term this way in the earliest period when Aramaic (the source of Mark's designation) was the primary language.[108] Alternatively, since we lack certain evidence for this title for a group of revolutionaries before 66 C.E.,[109] it may thus simply indicate that he was "zealous" in the law (see comment on Acts 22:3).

Excursus: Zealots

Evidence seems to tell against a *unified* revolutionary movement in first-century Palestine.[110] The term "Zealots" applies strictly only to some, rather than to most, early Jewish revolutionaries; Josephus seems to reserve the title for a limited group.[111] Indeed, Josephus employs the title primarily in his *Jewish War* and, apart from *War* 2.651, does not employ the title in this sense until *War* 4 (of the *War*'s seven books).[112] Horsley and Hanson see the Zealots as peasant brigands in contrast to more educated levels of resistance.[113]

Josephus portrays the revolutionaries as "brigands," endeavoring to marginalize them from the mainstream Jewish population. Some modern scholars view the brigands before the Jewish revolt in the light of modern studies of social bandits.[114] The revolutionaries and bandits of Jesus's day may have had some support from Galilean villagers; at least Cumanus thought so (*War* 2.228–29).[115] But it is not clear to what extent Galilean peasants really supported the goals of such bandits, especially in the

---

105. Williams, "Names," 89–90. In the Diaspora, see *CIJ* 1:15, §12; 1:26, §33; 1:84, §121; 1:85, §122; 1:270–71, §345; 1:271, §346; 1:272, §347; 1:272, §348; 1:273, §349; 1:274, §350; 1:274–75, §351; 1:455, §636 (unless it means "a Jew"); 1:479, §668; 2:46, §791.

106. Most scholars acknowledge this; e.g., Gundry, *Matthew*, 183; Smith, *Parallels*, 1; Cullmann, *State*, 15; idem, *Peter*, 22n24; Bruce, *History*, 93; Filson, *History*, 52; Klausner, *Jesus of Nazareth*, 284n11. The rabbis used *qannaim* more broadly than for only Zealots (cf. Salomonsen, "Remarks").

107. Cf. Barrett, *Acts*, 87 (citing Jos. *Ant.* 18.23). The epithet must be significant in some respect because Simon alone receives it (Witherington, *Christology of Jesus*, 98); France thinks that although the term did not connote a revolutionary this early, it might have already depicted the sort of zeal for God's rule that led to the later party (*Matthew*, 177), perhaps rooted in the model of Phinehas (Num 25:7–13; 1 Macc 2:23–27, 50; cf. Ps 106:28–31; 1QHᵃ VI, 13–15; see further comment on Acts 22:3). I treat the debate on the title's usage further in Keener, *Matthew*, 58–60.

108. Horsley and Hanson, *Bandits*, passim; Davies and Allison, *Matthew*, 2:156; cf. Witherington, *Christology of Jesus*, 97–98.

109. See Foakes-Jackson and Lake, "Zealots," 425; see the excursus below. Least plausible is the suggestion of Fitzmyer, *Acts*, 214–15, and others that this apostle *later* joined the Zealots after 66 C.E.

110. Mason, *Josephus and New Testament*, 206; Borg, *Conflict*, 27–28; idem, *Vision*, 90; cf. Kingdon, "Zealots."

111. Now widely held: Horsley and Hanson, *Bandits*, 214–17; cf. 190–243; Baumbach, "Zeloten"; Smith, "Zealots"; Borg, "Zealot"; idem, *Conflict*, 35–36; Sanders, *Judaism*, 281–83.

112. The sense elsewhere (Jos. *Ant.* 12.271; 20.47; *War* 2.444, 564; *Life* 11; *Ag. Ap.* 1.162) is different.

113. Horsley and Hanson, *Bandits*, 220–41; cf. Crossan, *Jesus*, 217.

114. Horsley and Hanson, *Bandits*, 190, distinguish the Sicarii themselves from peasants and social bandits, relating them to a line of teachers of resistance (194–97). They suspect that Judas the Galilean may have advocated martyrdom rather than violence (197–98), but this is unclear.

115. Note, however, that the villagers *could* not have caught everyone (cf. Deut 21:1).

Lower Galilee, whence Jesus came (see comment on Acts 9:31);[116] one should also allow for the impact of some degree of urban unrest.[117] Nevertheless, many bandits may have circulated among the peasantry.[118]

Much of this brigandage before the first revolt may have been "prepolitical" rather than aimed at an overthrow of Roman domination, as the objective became toward the beginning of the Jewish War.[119] Brigandage was common in antiquity and inevitably warranted execution if the brigands were captured.[120] Yet revolution was always a possibility. Many dissatisfied persons opted to work within the system, but many likewise hoped for its overthrow eschatologically or otherwise.[121] Even Josephus informs us that some of these fancied themselves kings (*Ant.* 17.285), suggesting that the authorities could view the line between revolutionary and messianic sentiment as thin (see Luke 23:2).

Although some Pharisees may have opposed the revolutionary ideal,[122] many of the revolutionaries, though distinct from other Pharisees, seem to have carried out a basic Pharisaic ideology in a more militant manner.[123] Sanders is surely right that the Fourth Philosophy was "largely Pharisaic in opinion" and its "members would accept no master but God (*Antiq.* 18.23; *War* 2.118)."[124] Most of their ideas were probably widespread in early Judaism,[125] and eschatological expectation probably fueled all levels of Jewish resistance.[126] Both resentment against Rome[127] and confidence that God would defend those loyal to him[128] were also widespread. Josephus disparages "brigands" of all sorts except in the one case where he need not do so, the speech he creates for Eleazar.[129]

Witherington points out that some Pharisees did "basic training" (Jos. *Life* 11–21) and that revolutionary leaders could send Pharisees in charge of military contingents (*Life* 197).[130] In the earlier *Jewish War*, when the material is still sensitive, Josephus

116. *Pace* Crossan, *Jesus*, 304–5; Horsley and Hanson, *Bandits*, 48–50, 69–70; Oakman, "Peasant," 131. Horsley and Hanson, *Bandits*, 71, citing Jos. *Ant.* 14.168, contend that the common people asked for justice against Herod when he killed the bandits, but Josephus seems to refer to *relatives*. Villagers did protect bandits who robbed a servant of Caesar (p. 72, citing Jos. *Ant.* 20.113–17; *War* 2.228–31), and *War* 2.253 may also be relevant; but Josephus himself does not indicate that the "inhabitants" ravaged by the brigands were nobles. The drowning of nobles is significant (*War* 1.314–16, 326; *Ant.* 14.431–33), but *Ant.* 20.255–56 does not explicitly differentiate "Jews" as gentry from the "masses." *War* 2.235–38 may well be relevant, but one wonders whether the elders in *Ant.* 14.167 are peasants, since the speaker is a Pharisee. The nuancing of Crossan, *Jesus*, 170 (their social location between the powerful and the powerless), may be helpful.

117. Cf. Donaldson, "Bandits."

118. Cf. Horsley and Hanson, *Bandits*, 77–85.

119. Ibid., xiii–xiv, 250–51; Crossan, *Jesus*, 194; Horsley, *Galilee*, 259. Josephus's sources regarding brigands appear weak for 6–44 C.E., though he reports some uprisings (cf. also Mark 15:27), but after 44 he supplies many reports of bandits with heavy followings (*War* 2.228, 235, 238, 253; *Ant.* 20.121, 124, 161; Horsley and Hanson, *Bandits*, 66–69).

120. Lewis, *Life*, 204.

121. Sanders, *Judaism*, 35–43.

122. Davies, *Introduction*.

123. Simon, *Sects*, 44; cf. Neusner, *Beginning*, 26–27; see esp. Jos. *Ant.* 18.4, 9, 23–25. Falk, *Jesus*, 57–58, 120–25, even decides (too narrowly) that the Zealots were Shammaites.

124. Sanders, *Judaism*, 13–14; cf. 280–84, 408–11. Hengel, *Zeloten*, saw them as a religiously motivated movement; Giblet, "Mouvement," believes that they saw themselves as more religious than political. Though assuming specific religious beliefs, the nationalists did not represent an organized religious group (Salomonsen, "Debat"). Applebaum, "Zealots," regards the revolutionary movement as a natural response to the Roman situation. Evidence at Masada indicates the Sicarii's religious commitment (Cornfeld, *Josephus*, 489, 499).

125. Horsley and Hanson, *Bandits*, xv.

126. Cf. ibid., 19, 76. For priestly elements of resistance, see, e.g., Goodblatt, "Priestly Ideologies."

127. Horsley and Hanson, *Bandits*, xv; Borg, *Conflict*, 36–47.

128. Sanders, *Judaism*, 241.

129. Ibid., 6–7.

130. Witherington, *Christology of Jesus*, 83. Josephus may have assumed command of many brigands himself; see the evidence in Horsley, *Galilee*, 266–67.

plays down both Pharisaic involvement in the revolt and Jewish involvement more generally, but in the later *Antiquities of the Jews*, a revolt as early as 6 C.E. appears part of a larger movement toward the revolution (Jos. *Ant.* 18.9–10, 23–25; Acts 5:34–35). Menahem in the revolt of 66–70 was descended from Judas the Galilean in the earlier revolt (Jos. *War* 2.433), and Josephus admits the revolutionaries' theological commitments (*Ant.* 18.4–5, 23); in all, the evidence may not support the early use of the title "Zealot," but it does support the continuing existence of simmering revolutionary sentiments through the early first century.[131]

d. The Women and Siblings (1:14)

Luke often balances genders in his narrative where his information allows. The women, in general, hark back to the Gospel (Luke 8:2–3), especially to the passion and resurrection narratives (23:49, 55; 24:5, 10), providing a line of continuity and also an example of consistent faithfulness not found with the male apostles. The mention of Mary, in particular, connects the beginning of Luke's second volume with the beginning of his first (Luke 1:27). Jesus's "brothers" (naturally related to Mary) appear only briefly but may offer an alternative form of leadership (or at least contribute that of James) that is never clarified in Acts (cf. Acts 12:17).

I. MARY AND THE OTHER WOMEN

Some Greek philosophic schools included women (see introduction, ch. 18, sect. 2.j), although even in these schools they remained a minority. Thus Iamblichus, after listing all known names for male disciples of Pythagoras (218 of them, and where each was from), lists the best-known women from the movement (seventeen in number; Iambl. *V.P.* 36.267). Although Luke's focus in the first two chapters of Acts is on the apostles,[132] especially Peter, because of his theme, he pauses to explicitly mention the women present, as he often does (Acts 2:18; 5:14; 8:3, 12; 9:2; 17:4, 12; 22:4).

By referring to Mary, "Jesus's mother," in his introduction, Luke recalls the first two chapters of his first volume, which also evoke Jewish piety. Because the Holy Spirit overshadowed her in Luke 1:35, her reception of the Spirit may function paradigmatically for female servants (δούλας, Acts 2:18, a term elsewhere reserved in Luke-Acts for Mary alone, Luke 1:38, 48).[133] But while Mary fills a special role in Luke (Luke 1:42, 48),[134] her role is qualified in 2:48–50; 8:19–21; and 11:27–28;[135]

131. Wright, *People of God*, 179–80; Witherington, *Christology of Jesus*, 84–87. For anti-Roman polemic even in Qumran documents, see, e.g., Atkinson, "Polemics."

132. On this basis, Blanco Pacheco, "María y el Espíritu," argues that Acts 1:14 is not a text for Mariology (contrast, e.g., Montes Peral, "Dios"). Still, Mary's prominence in Luke's first volume's introduction gives her a significant role in Luke's work, as scholars often note (e.g., Crocetti, "Madre," though offering textually unwarranted eucharistic connections); Luke's opening chapters connect tightly with the story that follows (see at length Ó Fearghail, *Introduction*).

133. That Mary is among those whom Luke uses paradigmatically as prototypical Christians is generally agreed; see Syreeni, "Paradigms," 36; following Räisänen, *Mutter*. For discussions of Mary in the NT, see, e.g., Gaventa, *Mary*; for continuing interest in the early second century, see, e.g., Ign. *Eph.* 7.2; 18.2; 19.1; *Trall.* 9.1. But some subsequent approaches blended more elements of Greco-Roman ideology (e.g., Görg, "Göttin"; cf. Bernabé Ubieta, "Esposas"; Koester, *Introduction*, 1:188).

134. One should not read too much into the use of a beatitude in Luke 1:48, since it was a common literary form (see comment on Acts 20:35).

135. The beatitude in Luke 11:27 was a common form of praising someone, often a mother or ancestor, by blessing another (cf. 1:42; *Jub.* 25:19; 2 *Bar.* 54:10–11; *m. ʾAb.* 2:8; *t. Ḥag.* 2:1; *ʾAbot R. Nat.* 13, §32 B; *Pesiq. Rab Kah. Sup.* 6:5; *b. Ḥag.* 14b; *y. Ḥag.* 2:1, §4; *Pesiq. Rab.* 37:2; Petron. *Sat.* 94; Mus. Ruf. 16, p. 104.26;

she too is a disciple. When Luke mentions "Mary," he must specify which Mary he has in view, having mentioned several in his own work (hence "Jesus's mother" here). Here he does use the fuller Jewish name "Mariam" (i.e., the Hebrew "Miriam"), which refers to Jesus's mother except in Luke 10:39, 42 (1:27, 30, 34, 38, 39, 46, 56; 2:5, 16, 19, 34), but Jesus's mother could also be simply "Maria" (1:41), a name shared with Mary Magdalene (8:2; 24:10) and with one or two mothers (Luke 24:10; Acts 12:12). "Maria" (also meaning "Miriam") is one of the most common Jewish names of the period, appearing both in Jerusalem (e.g., *CIJ* 2:247, §1214; 2:274, §1284) and in the Diaspora.[136] It was apparently not popular (despite the name of Moses's sister) until Mariamne, a Hasmonean princess executed (and, in the eyes of many Judeans, martyred) by her husband, Herod the Great. After her death, the popularity of the name exploded.[137] In its various forms, "Mary" was "easily the most popular woman's name in 1st-century Palestine" across all social levels;[138] the commonness of the name in Luke simply reflects its commonness in his genuine Palestinian tradition.

Luke distinguishes Mary from the other women perhaps partly because of her special role but, more to the point, because he did not mention her presence, or that of Jesus's brothers, at Jesus's final Passover in Jerusalem (unless she is designated "mother of James" in Luke 24:10, but this would be a strange description after the emphasis on her bearing Jesus in Luke 1–2).[139] On the basis of their omission in the Synoptic passion narrative, some scholars suggest that Mary and Jesus's brothers simply came to Jerusalem "to claim his body, as family members should."[140] But given the length of the journey, the Sabbath's beginning on Friday evening and the discovery of the empty tomb early Sunday morning, they might have received the resurrection report at the same time as the crucifixion report had they stayed in Galilee for that Passover. Alternatively, James's resurrection appearance (1 Cor 15:7) could have drawn them to Jerusalem. So could have the apostles' brief return to Galilee, suggested above (see comment on Acts 1:4).

More important, it is not clear that they would not have been in Jerusalem; if the family regularly made the relatively short journey from Galilee for Passover (Jos. *Life* 269; cf. Luke 2:41; John 2:13; 7:10), would they have avoided the city at the height of Jesus's career? If Paul's list of resurrection appearances is chronological, it seems plausible that James was near Jerusalem, like the recipients before and after him (1 Cor 15:5–8), though this suggestion is not provable.[141] The apparently independent tradition in John (John 19:25) suggests Mary's presence, though many scholars question John's historical veracity (especially because he varies so far from the Markan story line, followed by Matthew and Luke).[142] The brothers' apparent

Men. Rhet. 2.8, 412.20–22; Musaeus *Hero* 138–39; cf. also sources in Danker, *New Age*, 140; Dalman, *Jesus-Jeshua*, 231; Manson, *Sayings*, 88).

136. See *CIJ* 1:15, §12; 1:96, §137; 1:290–91, §374; 1:291, §375; 1:374, §511; 1:416, §§564–65; 2:443, §1535; cf. "Marina" in *CIJ* 1:292, §376. It can also be a Latin name (Judge, *Rank*, 13, 36n18).

137. Williams, "Names," 107.

138. Ibid., 90–91.

139. Unless (this is less likely) we should think of either the resurrection or James's subsequent prominence as inviting the title. The names of her children (Matt 27:56; Mark 15:40; 16:1) are compatible with those of Jesus's siblings (Mark 6:3), but these were common names.

140. Malina, *Anthropology*, 99.

141. Paul's later experience (1 Cor 15:8) was not in Jerusalem (Gal 1:16–17); the Gospels also suggest that geographic distance no longer posed a barrier to the risen Christ (e.g., Luke 24:31).

142. I have argued for John's reliability both in general (Keener, *John*, 3–52, esp. 29–34, 40–42) and on this point (1143), but I also recognize that John does not follow the same sorts of historiographic methodology as Luke.

lack of association with Jesus's followers at that time could suggest either that they did not come or that the standard passion tradition had reason to omit their presence; but their presence cannot be ruled out. In any case, Luke's failure to mention Mary in his passion narrative requires him to explicitly note her presence here in addition to "the women."[143]

Codex D, which seems to betray an antifeminist bias at other points, wrongly assumes that "the women" here are the apostles' wives.[144] But the apostles' wives are nowhere else mentioned in Luke-Acts (though Peter's wife is implied in Luke 4:38).[145] For one who approached Acts after having recently heard Luke's Gospel, the identity of "the women" would have been clear enough. They undoubtedly are those who appeared at the end of Luke's Gospel:[146] Mary Magdalene, Joanna, and Mary mother of James (Luke 24:10); also the women who followed from Galilee (23:55), who probably would be Mary Magdalene, Joanna, and Susanna (8:2–3); and *other* women (24:10; perhaps not specifically named by Luke or preserved in his oral sources because they were lower in status or simply forgotten).

The presence of these women may not be significant by itself; women certainly attended synagogues, and (against some scholars) we lack clear evidence for their segregation there.[147] Moreover, although later rabbinic tradition exempted women from some prayer requirements incumbent on observant men,[148] they were expected to participate in other prayers, such as the Tefillah, Mezuzah, and the after-meal benediction (*m. Ber.* 3:3).[149] The significance is less in their presence than in their mention alongside members of the Twelve, a mention that reminds us of Luke's consistent practice in telling of women's as well as of men's responses to Jesus (e.g., Luke 8:2; Acts 5:14; 8:3, 12; 9:2; 17:4, 12; 22:4).

Even if Mary occupies a special place in Luke's story, this need imply nothing concerning his perspectives on women in general. A few "mythic women" attained heroic roles in Greek tragedy without thereby abolishing the system that restricted Athenian matrons to the domestic sphere.[150] It is therefore important to survey Luke's treatment of women in general before coming to conclusions about Luke's perspectives on gender. Although this commentary briefly surveys women in business and as converts in Acts 16:13–15 and women working alongside husbands in 18:3, Luke's perspective on women is treated especially in our introduction, chapter 18 (particularly sects. 1, 4),[151] which argues, contrary to some, that Luke's perspective on women is strongly favorable, more so than that of most of his contemporaries.

---

143. By placing her among the disciples, Luke may defend Jesus's honor by showing a new family to care for her (so Malina and Neyrey, "Honor and Shame," 64), but the same verse mentions Jesus's brothers, who could have done the same.

144. González, *Acts*, 27.

145. With Witherington, *Acts*, 113.

146. Cf. similarly Reimer, *Women*, 232–33; Johnson, *Acts*, 34; González, *Acts*, 27.

147. Brooten, "Segregated"; idem, *Women Leaders*, 103–38; Safrai, "Synagogue," 939; idem, "Segregated"; idem, "Place of Women"; cf. Seager, "Synagogue," 170–71; *pace*, e.g., May, "Synagogues," 14; Swidler, *Women*, 89–90. On women active in the synagogues, see also Manns, "Femme." A few ancient cults excluded women, notably (with a few exceptions) Mithraism (Klauck, *Context*, 141, 148); it may have been customary to segregate genders informally in some settings (cf., e.g., Iambl. *V.P.* 9.50), just as women were restricted from entering the Court of Israel in the temple (cf. Safrai, "Temple," 867).

148. See discussion below.

149. Le Cornu, *Acts*, 881.

150. Willner, "Oedipus Complex."

151. Originally that discussion was an excursus here, but it became too long to justify digressing so long from the text.

II. JESUS'S BROTHERS

Jesus's brothers here must include James (Acts 12:17; 15:13; 21:18; Gal 1:19; cf. Jas 1:1; Jude 1);[152] though he is not named here, Acts 12:17 introduces him as if he is already known to Luke's audience. Luke is able to take for granted some knowledge among his audience (cf. likewise 1 Cor 15:7; Gal 2:9, 12).[153] His presence here prefigures his leadership role later in the book.[154] Despite his later role (and Paul's apparent mention of him as an "apostle," Gal 1:19), no prominence is accorded him here; he cannot be numbered among the Twelve in Acts 1:15–26 because he was not a witness of Jesus's ministry (1:21–22).[155] (This was due to his own hostility, according to a tradition not likely to have been invented; see Mark 3:21, 31–35; John 7:5).[156]

Over the centuries, commentators have advanced various views regarding the identity of Jesus's brothers. Jerome defended Mary's perpetual virginity, arguing that there are different kinds of brothers.[157] Barrett summarizes the views as follows:

1. The Helvidian (i.e., Helvidius's) view: sons of Mary and Joseph after Jesus[158]
2. The Epiphanian (i.e., Epiphanius's) view: "sons of Joseph by an earlier marriage"[159]
3. The Hieronymian (i.e., Jerome's) view: cousins, sons "of Mary's sister"
4. A more recent view: cousins from Joseph's side, brought up as foster brothers

Although any of these views is possible, Barrett concludes, with the majority of scholars, that "the most natural meaning of ἀδελφός is blood-brother, that foster-brother is not impossible, and that cousin is very improbable."[160]

Jesus taught that disciples must be prepared to risk alienating and losing the support of their families for the sake of the kingdom (Luke 14:26; 18:29; 21:16), including by caring for the needy more than for near kin who were not so needy (14:12).[161] Jesus had treated his own family accordingly, ranking discipleship above family ties (8:19–21; cf. 18:22–30); that his family now followed him (Acts 1:14) might encourage others who had to make similar sacrifices (cf. 16:31–32). Luke's contemporaries probably would have found perfectly credible the portrait of a great sage's not being

152. On the "brothers of the Lord," who achieved a special role in ministry alongside the apostles (1 Cor 9:5), see, e.g., Lightfoot, *Galatians*, 247–82. Tradition claims that another relative of Jesus succeeded James (Malina and Pilch, *Acts*, 108, rightly notes Euseb. *H.E.* 3.32).

153. With Barrett, *Acts*, 103. Whether this is the James of Luke 24:10 may be disputed—"Jacob" and "Mary" were both common names in this period (Williams, "Names," 86, 90–91)—but the statement is not clear enough by itself to explain the abruptness of Acts 12:17.

154. Larkin, *Acts*, 44, also sees their inclusion as emphasizing "the link between the church and Israel"; this is true, but the apostles serve the same function (cf. comment on Acts 1:13, 26).

155. Eisenman, *Maccabees*, 38, regards this passage as "a probably Lucan counterfeit of James' episcopal election," but Luke makes no effort to disguise James's leadership (Acts 12:17; 15:13–21; 21:18–19) in the period in which Paul speaks of it (Gal 1:19; 2:9, 12), and Paul mentions James apart from the "twelve" and "all the apostles" (1 Cor 15:7).

156. Cf. C. Williams, *Acts*, 58; Dunn, *Acts*, 16. Perhaps his "inside" perspective on the material of the infancy narratives, through Mary, may have contributed to his later role, but that he, rather than Joses, Judas, and Simon (Mark 6:3), achieves this role might suggest leadership ability (his mention before the others may well also rank him second in age to Jesus).

157. Jerome *Against Helvidius* 16–18 (Pelikan, *Acts*, 45–46).

158. Cf. Tertullian in Vicastillo, "Hermanos."

159. This view is first attested in the mid- to late second century (*Prot. Jas.* 9.2; 19.1–20.3; Thiselton, *Corinthians*, 681–82).

160. Barrett, *Acts*, 90; also Thiselton, *Corinthians*, 681–82; see esp. and most fully Meier, *Marginal Jew*, 1:318–32. Mary's perpetual virginity probably originated from *Prot. Jas.* 19.3 (Blomberg, *Matthew*, 57).

161. The Gospel recognizes that brothers often divide over earthly matters such as inheritance, but Jesus disapproves of this (Luke 12:13; 15:27–28).

believed by his brother (cf. John 7:3–5) but the brother's being won over by the sage (cf. later Philost. *Ep. Apoll.* 44–45).

e. Joined for Prayer (1:14)

Although not unique to Luke's work,[162] prayer is a regular theme in Luke-Acts.[163] Indeed, many interpreters have argued that prayer is viewed as the method through which God accomplishes his purposes and directs history.[164] In Acts, it appears in 2:42; 3:1; 4:24; 6:4, 6; 7:59–60; 8:15; 9:11, 40; 10:2, 4, 9, 30–31; 12:5; 13:3; 14:23; 16:13, 16, 25; 20:36; 22:17; 27:29; 28:8.

This passage specifically links the prayer with waiting for the coming of the Spirit, as often in Luke-Acts (Luke 3:21–22; 11:13 [contrast Matt 7:11]; Acts 4:31; 8:15; 13:2).[165] Early Judaism understood the divine spirit as an aspect of God and agent of God's activity (see introduction, ch. 15, sect. 5, excursus), so by praying to receive the Spirit, the petitioners in this passage are, in a sense, praying to receive God himself (for such prayers, cf. John 14:13–17; Porph. *Marc.* 13.226–27). Jesus had taught about the kingdom (Acts 1:3) and the Spirit (1:4–5) earlier in this context, and these two themes occur again immediately afterward (1:6, 8). Now the disciples are praying for precisely these promised blessings.

A prayer for the coming of the Spirit (1:14) was also a prayer for the coming of the kingdom (esp. Luke 11:2, 13) because it was the Spirit who would empower the witnesses to take the gospel to the ends of the earth (Acts 1:8), something that would precede Jesus's return and Israel's restoration (1:6, 11).[166] Prayer precedes the coming of the Spirit also in 4:31 (which includes prayer for signs and consequent boldness) and 8:15 (for the Spirit) and seems implied in 9:17 (cf. 9:11) and 19:6 (laying on hands could accompany prayer, as in 6:6; 13:3; 28:8). (Although Luke likes this pattern, he does not impose it on his material; 13:52 does not mention it, and 10:44 does not allow for an immediately preceding prayer for the Spirit, though the intense prayer experiences of both Cornelius and Peter directly led to it [10:2–4, 9, 30–31].)

Some scholars think that a particular *place* of prayer is in view here, in view of the definite article.[167] The term προσευχή, employed here, frequently functioned as a designation

---

162. E.g., prayer (Tob 3:2–6, 11–15; 8:5–8, 15–17) and praise (11:14–15; 13:1–7) are regular motifs in Tobit (Harrington, "Prayers"); for prayer in Josephus, see Jonquière, *Prayer in Josephus*; Urbanz, "Gebet"; at Qumran, e.g., sources at Acts 3:1; in Jewish sources in Greek, see van der Horst and Newman, *Prayers*; in Paul, see, e.g., sources at Acts 16:25.

163. See, e.g., Bovon, *Theologian*, 400–403; Trites, "Prayer Motif"; Karris, *Saying*, 74–83; Liefeld, *Acts*, 87–88; Plymale, *Prayer Texts*; Han, "Prayer"; Jesudasan, "Prayer"; Green, *Thirty Years*, 268–73; Thielman, *Theology*, 142–46; Puskas and Crump, *Introduction*, 137–38; Osborne, "Prayer," 253–57 (on Acts); on spirituality, Walton, "Spirituality." For redactional evidence in the Gospel, see Mediavilla, "Oración de Jesús"; further on Jesus as the model intercessor in Luke-Acts, see Crump, *Jesus the Intercessor*; Lane, *Gentile Mission*, 64–67; Roth, "Pray-er"; Viljoen, "Intercessor"; for some prayers in Acts, Caballero Cuesta, "Oración en Iglesia."

164. See, e.g., O'Brien, "Prayer in Luke-Acts"; Trites, "Prayer Motif"; cf. also Smalley, "Spirit, Kingdom, and Prayer." In more recent history, some see a pattern between prayer and revivals in various parts of the world (see, e.g., Koch, *Zulus*, 319).

165. For the connection between prayer and the Spirit in Acts, see also, e.g., Hull, *Spirit in Acts*, 48; Richard, "Pentecost," 135; Hur, *Reading*, 270. Twelftree, "Prayer," nuances the discussion by pointing out that the Spirit comes in Luke-Acts to prayerful people, not necessarily to those praying specifically for the Spirit (noting the lack of direct object for αἰτοῦσιν in Luke 11:13).

166. Probably even the "bread" of Luke 11:3 (omitted in 11:11–12 but found in Matt 7:9) points especially to desperate need (Luke 11:5–8) for the Spirit (11:13). Talbert, *Acts*, 11, compares also prayer concerning imminent testing (Luke 11:4; 21:36; 22:46) and Jesus's return (18:1–8).

167. E.g., Lake and Cadbury, *Commentary*, 10–11; Bruce, *Acts*[1], 74. Some see even the entire phrase προσκαρτεροῦντες . . . τῇ προσευχῇ as referring to a place or at least (more likely) the action of meeting (Thornton, "Continuing Steadfast").

for Jewish prayerhouses, which were clearly gathering places.[168] These were always specifically Jewish; on only one occasion do we know of Gentiles using the term, and even then they applied it to a specifically Judaizing group.[169] The title more common in Palestine, as regularly in the NT (even for the Diaspora) is "synagogue" (συναγωγή),[170] but this difference in nomenclature should not lead us to think that prayer was a marginal activity there (cf. Jos. *Ag. Ap.* 1.209).[171] Perhaps in Jerusalem prayer was held more frequently in the temple, minimizing the need for synagogues to perform this function.[172] This possible practice cannot, however, be assumed for all of Palestine (Matt 6:5; Jos. *Life* 277, 293). Although Josephus's audience is a Diaspora audience, it remains significant that he calls a Galilean assembly hall a προσευχή (*Life* 277); this was a large building that may have held the entire citizen assembly on this occasion (*Life* 277–78). But the term functioned more in some parts of the empire than in others; "prayerhouse" is most common in Egypt but appears rarely in Rome, where (as in Palestine) συναγωγή is dominant.[173] (On synagogues, see the excursus at Acts 6:9–10.)

Against the suggestion that Luke thinks of a particular place of prayer, we should remember that this title for prayerhouses was used mainly in the Diaspora, yet Luke, even when writing of the Diaspora, uses the term συναγωγή. Further, the definite article appears at points where a *place* cannot be in view (e.g., Acts 6:4); in the one place in Acts where the phrase may mean a meeting place for prayer, it can appear either with or without the article (16:13, 16). The phrase for "continue in prayer" (προσκαρτερέω τῇ προσευχῇ) is one that recurs in 2:42 and 6:4 (cf. also Rom 12:12; Col 4:2), indicating that this devotion to prayer continued to characterize the apostles (for whom it was a major priority, Acts 6:4) and was meant to characterize the Christian community as a whole (2:42).[174]

That the believers acted with "one mind" (ὁμοθυμαδόν) suggests a theme that runs through Acts (2:46; 4:24; 5:12; 15:25; see further comment on Acts 2:46).[175] Indeed, their unity offers an inclusio framing the section regarding their preparation for the outpouring of the Spirit (2:1). The emphasis on unity is not of course unique to Luke; it was a common one in the Pauline churches as well (e.g., Rom 12:4–6; 1 Cor 1:10; 12:12–13; Eph 4:3–4, 13; Phil 1:27; 2:1–5; Col 3:14)[176] and fits the Greco-Roman rhetorical and moralist emphasis on concord or harmony.[177] To act

168. E.g., *CPJ* 1:239–40, §129, line 5 (218 B.C.E.); 1:247–49, §134, lines 18, 29 (late second century B.C.E.); *CIJ* 1:495, §683 (80 C.E.); 1:497, §684; Ptolemaic inscriptions (2:367, §1440; 2:368, §1441; 2:369, §1442; 2:370–71, §1443; 2:371, §1444; 2:375–76, §1449); Juv. *Sat.* 3.296 (*proseucha*); perhaps *CIJ* 1:525, §726; 2:360, §1432; 2:361, §1433. This usage is regularly cited, e.g., Deissmann, *Studies*, 222; Boring, Berger, and Colpe, *Commentary*, 324.

169. Levinskaya, *Diaspora Setting*, 207–25; Levinskaya, "Gentile Prayer House?"

170. Cf., e.g., Cohen, *Maccabees*, 66.

171. On prayer, see Sanders, *Judaism*, 203.

172. Falk, "Prayer Literature," 277–78 (noting that Philo and Josephus focus on Scripture study in pre-70 C.E. synagogues). Urman, "House of Assembly," tries to distinguish between community centers and houses of study (but how many communities could afford both?).

173. Applebaum, "Organization," 490. Schubert, "Sacra Sinagoga," suggests that rabbinic Judaism's spread made the difference, but the term may appear as late as the sixth century C.E. (if *CIJ* 1:476, §662 refers to this).

174. The verb προσκαρτερέω implies continuing attention to a matter (Acts 8:13; 10:7; Rom 13:6); Jeremias applies it to "observance of the regular hours of prayer" (*Prayers*, 79).

175. For recipients of the gospel, Acts 8:6; used negatively for anti-Christian mobs in 7:57; 18:12; 19:29; otherwise negatively in 12:20. It usually implies unity (Walton, "Ὁμοθυμαδόν," esp. 104–5). On the church's unity in Acts, see further Thompson, "Unity."

176. Brodie's suggestion ("Division and Reconciliation") that Luke depends on 1 Corinthians here fails to recognize the wider topos in ancient moral discourse.

177. In speeches, see, e.g., Dio Chrys. *Or.* 32.37; 34.17–19; 38 passim; 40.35–38; 48.14; Philost. *Vit. Apoll.* 6.38; see esp. Mitchell, *Rhetoric of Reconciliation*, 60–64; in early Stoicism, see, e.g., Erskine, *Stoa*, 59.

"as one" also emphasized unity, acting in concert, in the Hebrew Bible (e.g., in Judg 20:1, 8; 1 Sam 11:7; 2 Sam 19:14; Ezra 3:1; Neh 8:1).

2. Establishing Leaders and Their Testimony for the Future (1:15–26)

The appointing of leaders for the movement's future, despite its modest numbers so far, indicates confidence in Jesus's promise. These leaders would shepherd the massively growing church[178] but also functioned as witnesses (Acts 1:8), repositories, and guardians of the tradition for the rest of the church (cf. 1:21–22).[179] Like prayer (1:14), establishing the church's future testifying leadership is a preparation for Pentecost, an act of faith. Even more generally, the church's leadership is important for Luke (e.g., 6:3–5; 14:23).

Many scholars recognize that an important issue in this section is the choosing of a twelfth apostle because of the emphasis on Israel's restoration.[180] That Jesus originally chose twelve as the nucleus of a reconstituted or remnant community of Israel is widely accepted.[181] The Qumran community also had a group of twelve leaders meant to signify an eschatological nucleus of the righteous remnant of Israel. The restoration of the Twelve here thus fulfills a theological purpose for Luke's audience and for the earliest apostolic community.[182]

The analogy with Qumran may be significant here more generally. In the Qumran scrolls, members of the sect appear to constitute the members of God's covenant, those eligible for salvation.[183] Although they did not usually apply the name "Israel" exclusively to themselves, they viewed themselves as a "miniature Israel," with Levites, priests, and Israelites, and as the fulfillment of Israel's history.[184] Certainly, they portray themselves repeatedly as the "remnant."[185]

Some commentators believe that Luke inserts the account of restoring the apostolic number (1:15–26) into the previously existing story of disciples waiting for (1:14) and experiencing (2:1–4) Pentecost.[186] This may well be true in terms of arrangement (the story does interrupt the flow of the narrative), though digressions were standard fare in ancient literature, including in Acts (see 11:30–12:25).[187] Yet even if Luke has inserted the account, it would not mean that Luke invents this

---

178. Rowe, "Authority," 106–7, counters those who use anthropological equality to deconstruct all authority roles, noting that leadership (in some form) remains a functional necessity in communities, as history attests.

179. Naturally, Luke, as a historian, emphasizes the importance of eyewitness testimony; but while the language of witness in this sense is particularly emphatically Lukan and Johannine, the appeal to eyewitness testimony seems to have been an emphasis of early Christianity more generally (1 Cor 15:5–8, 15; cf. 2 Pet 1:16; John 4:39; 15:27; 1 John 1:2; 4:14; Rev 1:2). Given the early date and the character of the testimony preserved, we have good reason to take it seriously, as much historical Jesus scholarship notes; see, e.g., Theissen, *Gospels*; Theissen and Merz, *Guide*; Charlesworth, "Archaeology"; Bauckham, *Eyewitnesses*; Keener, *Historical Jesus*; in greatest detail, the recent four-volume work, Holmén and Porter, *Handbook*.

180. Pao, *Isaianic Exodus*, 123–29; see discussion in Butticaz, *Identité*, 67–86.

181. E.g., Borg, *Conflict*, 70; Sanders, *Jesus and Judaism*, 98–101, 104; Bruce, "Jesus," 75.

182. Harrington, *God's People*, 39; Sanders, *Jesus and Judaism*, 104; cf. Jervell, *Luke and People of God*, 82.

183. Sanders, *Paul and Judaism*, 242; see further 243–44.

184. Ibid., 245–47; also Vermes, *Jesus and Judaism*, 117; Flusser, *Judaism*, 49; cf., e.g., 4QpNah 3–4 IV, 3. In the eschaton, the sect will be Israel because all will have chosen their sides, but ultimately it is the Gentiles who will be destroyed (Sanders, *Paul and Judaism*, 249, 254). Samaritans also viewed themselves as the true Israel (Bowman, *Documents*, ii).

185. With Jeremias, *Theology*, 171–72 (citing CD I, 4–5; II, 6; 1QH^a XIV, 8; 1QM XIII, 8; XIV, 8–9; cf. also 1QH^a XIV, 11; 4Q163 4–6 II, 11; 4Q174 1 II, 2; 4Q268 1 12; 4Q393 3 7; 4Q491 8–10 I, 6; 4Q537 1 + 2 + 3 1).

186. E.g., Boismard and Lamouille, *Actes*, 2:13.

187. See comment on Acts 1:18. For narrative asides in Acts, see Sheeley, *Asides*, 119–35; in ancient historiography, 56–78.

tradition; inserting preexisting material into new frameworks was common rhetorical practice.[188]

Historically, there is no reason to doubt Luke's claim that the early Christians sought another apostle, who turned out to be Matthias, to fill up again the number of the twelve chief witnesses.[189] Luke might have reasons to wish to bring the number back to twelve, but then again, so would the earliest church, on whose traditions he depends. Early Christians would have hardly invented a betrayer among the Twelve (Luke 22:47); at the same time, after the betrayal the official number (if not the actual number) remains "the Twelve" in our earliest sources (1 Cor 15:5), inviting the sort of scenario Luke describes here. Unless Matthias was a Palestinian Jew specially honored by Luke's Diaspora community (which is unlikely, especially since he nowhere appears in Acts again) or that of his source, it is unlikely that Luke would have invented a story about such a secondary figure[190] (even apart from such an invention's inconsistency with Luke's normal historiographic practice; see introduction, chs. 6–7). Further, most groups would have recognized the importance of replacing leadership as quickly as possible for the sake of the group's efficient functioning.[191]

Some think that Luke views the believers as wrong to choose another apostle because they still misunderstood Jesus's teaching, as in Acts 1:6.[192] But this is not Luke's perspective. Although it is likely true that the apostles wished to raise their number to twelve to prepare for the kingdom, we should not forget that in Luke (and Q) it was the reliable character Jesus who promised them this (Luke 22:30); further, Peter maintains this restoration expectation even when he preaches the gospel after Pentecost (Acts 3:21–26), and Paul also affirms a hope shared with the twelve tribes (26:6–7). The qualifications for membership in the Twelve in 1:21–22 are sensible (see comment there), and by these conditions, neither James nor Paul (the most frequent candidates proposed by those dissatisfied with Matthias) qualifies.[193]

Many church assemblies in Acts addressed controversial issues (Acts 6:1; 11:2–3; 15:1–7; 21:21–22); the matter of choosing Judas's successor, however, seems not so much controversial as necessary to prepare a united witness for the time when the Spirit would come (2:14). Peter speaks confidently and articulately (a far cry from his character as narrated before the resurrection), developing his argument from Scripture. The lot oracle (see comment on Acts 1:26) also suggests that the disciples acted in accord with God's purposes. Some scholars contrast the peaceful meetings of the church in Luke's narratives with the more chaotic scenes of assemblies hostile to the apostolic message.[194]

188. See, e.g., Theon Progymn. 4.73–79; 5.388–441.

189. For historical tradition here, see, e.g., Rengstorf, "Election of Matthias," 180; Gundry, *Matthew*, 553; Pervo, *Acts*, 49 (noting the minor role of the "Twelve" in Acts and that in free composition Jesus might have chosen Judas's successor); cf. even Haenchen, *Acts*, 163.

190. C. Williams, *Acts*, 59.

191. E.g., Xen. *Anab.* 3.1.38.

192. Dunn, *Acts*, 17–18; Rengstorf, "Election of Matthias," 191 (though he still affirms that Luke does expect the kingdom, 192). Rius-Camps and Read-Heimerdinger, "Reconsideration," view Codex Bezae as critical of the apostles replacing Judas to forestall the rivalry of Jesus's brothers. But whatever the Western text's approach, any suggestion that Judas's replacement here was an apostolic mistake (others suggest that they should have waited for Paul, e.g., Blaiklock, *Acts*, 53) runs counter to the portrayal of the positive apostles in the opening of Acts (certainly in most early textual tradition).

193. Barrett, *Acts*, 103.

194. See Pervo, "Meet Right." Such literary contrasts are not relevant, however, to the question of historical genre. Although such a contrast would serve an apologetic purpose, it is intrinsically likely that even disagreeable meetings of the church would be less violent than the mob scenes on which Luke focuses for the movement's enemies. Yet it is likely that some such (nonchurch) mob scenes historically occurred (cf. public

a. The Setting (1:15)

Peter takes the lead role, as Jesus had promised (Luke 22:32; cf. Matt 16:18) and as fits Peter's very visible personality in the Gospel (Luke 5:4–10; 8:45; 9:20, 33; 12:41; 18:28; 22:33–34, 54–62; 24:12, 34) and his being named first (5:10; 6:14; 8:51; 9:28, 32; 22:8; Acts 1:13). (Luke's portrayal comports well with our other historical tradition: Peter's role as leader of the disciples in the early church fits the unanimous testimony of our early sources.)[195] Jesus had given Peter a special resurrection appearance (Luke 24:34; cf. 1 Cor 15:5); Peter was also first among the Twelve (Luke 6:14), and his family had reason for gratitude to Jesus from early in Jesus's public ministry (4:38–39).[196] But Peter also admitted his sinfulness (5:8), would be tested in a special way (22:31–34), and denied Jesus (22:54–62), allowing for character development; likewise, he must learn in Acts (Acts 10:28) and provide a suitable comparison for Paul the converted sinner (9:4).

That Peter "stood" to address the assembly fits the standard ancient practice for speaking in assemblies (e.g., 1 Cor 14:30),[197] and its mention is characteristic of Luke's style (Acts 5:34; 11:28; 13:16; 15:5, 7; 17:22; 23:9; 25:18; 27:21).[198] "In those days" is a regular Septuagintal and Semitic idiom[199] that also appears elsewhere in Luke-Acts (e.g., Luke 1:5, 39; 2:1; 6:12; Acts 6:1; 7:41; 11:27). Peter speaking "in the midst" may recall Jesus's role, which would be natural, given Peter's leadership among the disciples (Luke 22:27; esp. 24:36; cf. 2:46; 4:30; for Paul "standing" in the "midst," Acts 27:21); it probably, however, represents simply Luke's characteristic style (Luke 4:35; 5:19; 6:8; 8:7; 10:3; 17:11; 21:21; 22:55; 23:45; Acts 1:18; 2:22; 4:7; 17:22, 33; 23:10).

That those gathered here are called the "crowd" (ὄχλος) may provide connections with Jesus's speeches in the Gospel.[200] "One hundred twenty" appears elsewhere as a round number, for example, for the minimum population of men in a village to warrant its own judicial assembly (according to some rabbis, m. Sanh. 1:6).[201] It may

---

punishments in 2 Cor 11:24–25, especially stoning; "dangers in the city" in 2 Cor 11:26; perhaps 1 Cor 4:11). Annen, "Heilige Geist," applies this section (and Acts 6:1–7 and 15:1–35) to church leadership principles.

195. See further Schnabel, *Mission*, 395–98. Cf. 1 Cor 1:12; 3:22; Gal 1:18; esp. 1 Cor 9:5; 15:5; Gal 2:9.

196. Teachers were not to show favoritism too quickly (Philod. *Crit.* col. 13b), but they often had a disciple outstanding above the rest (e.g., *m. 'Ab.* 2:8; cf. Tilborg, *Love*, 246).

197. E.g., Xen. *Anab.* 5.1.2, 5; 6.4.12; 6.6.11; *Cyr.* 7.5.55; Plut. *Cic.* 16.3; Tac. *Ann.* 16.29; an orator who had to deliver a speech sitting, hence limiting bodily expression, was disadvantaged (Pliny E. *Ep.* 2.19.3). For rabbinic sources (where the situation is more complex), see discussion at Acts 13:16.

198. It appears less frequently with Jesus, probably because Luke knows the different Palestinian Jewish custom for teachers (cf. Luke 4:20; 5:3; cf. *Pesiq. Rab Kah.* 18:5). Some later texts indicate that only ordained rabbis sat to teach whereas disciples stood (*'Abot R. Nat.* 6 A; *Gen. Rab.* 98:11). Jesus was not "ordained" in the rabbinic movement, but some differences in practice may have existed among Pharisees of Jesus's day, in any case (cf. *t. Ber.* 1:3; *Sipre Deut.* 34.5.3).

199. In the LXX, e.g., Exod 2:11; Judg 17:6; Neh 13:15, 23; Esth 1:2; Zech 8:6, 23; Jdt 1:5; 6:15; 8:1; 1 Macc 1:11; 2:1; 9:24; 11:20; 13:43; 14:13; *Pss. Sol.* 17:44; 18:6; elsewhere, e.g., *1 En.* 105:1; Luke edits the phrase in Joel 4:1 LXX in Acts 2:17.

200. See Tannehill, *Luke*, 143–66 (who regards the term as synonymous with λαός, with its LXX connections, 143); but the Evangelists, including Luke, use "crowds" in quite varied ways (157–58; Sanders, *Jesus and Judaism*, 289). For the varied (and fickle) character of the crowds in ancient texts, see Meeks, *Moral World*, 57.

201. Some commentators (e.g., Lake and Cadbury, *Commentary*, 12; Karris, *Invitation*, 28; Marshall, *Acts*, 64) cite *m. Sanh.* 1:6 as primary background here for establishing a new community; but Luke's audience would not be familiar with a single rabbinic tradition (unless it attests to a wider conception). This estimate may relate to rabbinic tradition about the number of elders who returned from exile with Ezra (see Danby, *Mishnah*, 446n5; Strack, *Introduction*, 9). Bede *Comm. Acts* 1.15 (Martin, *Acts*, 15–16) emphasizes that it is a triangular number (with 15 as its base); although this could be relevant in an apocalyptic passage (Rissi, *Time*, 76; Bauckham, *Climax*, 390–94, 402), it is improbable in historical narrative (cf. Keener, *John*, 1232–33). Some ridiculed Pythagoreans' excess interest in such matters (Lucian *Phil. Sale* 4).

relate to the sort of standard quorum attested in Qumran literature, which also had about ten members per (priestly) leader (1QS VI, 3–4; CD XIII, 1–2; cf. 1QSa II, 22); scholars who object to this sort of connection note that Luke's count probably includes women (Acts 1:14), which Jewish quorums would not typically count.[202] Further, Qumran, in at least some periods,[203] probably did not include women,[204] especially if (as many still think) the primary residents there were Essenes.[205] Those who suggest that it simply represents an estimate of about ten times as many believers as apostles may also be correct;[206] this would indicate the participation of all the community rather than a decision from the top (cf. 6:3, 5).

Luke includes a parenthetical remark[207] about the number of disciples, perhaps preparing for the greater growth of the church to come (2:41; 21:20). The large number of disciples here[208] is not surprising, given other traditions (see comment below); despite Mark's (and Luke's) focus on the Twelve, Luke is aware of a much larger number of disciples. He earlier reports the sending of the seventy-two (or seventy; Luke 10:1, 17);[209] after the resurrection, he mentions the eleven "and all the others" (24:9).

Nor is the evidence limited to Luke; indeed, he emphasizes the more limited group of the "Twelve" more than our other sources do. If Paul reports that more than five hundred witnessed the risen Jesus on a single occasion (1 Cor 15:6), there is no reason to doubt that more than a hundred may have remained in Jerusalem at this time, especially if we take seriously Luke's report that Jesus ordered his disciples to stay in Jerusalem (Luke

202. Witherington, *Acts*, 120; Barrett, *Acts*, 96. "Names" (ὀνομάτων) here functions as a metonymy for people (as in Rev 3:4; 11:13), perhaps reflecting Semitic or LXX influence (Barrett, *Acts*, 96, citing Num 1:18; 26:53, 55), though also in the papyri (Deissmann, *Studies*, 196). When Luke or his sources restrict a count to males, he is generally explicit (Luke 9:14; Acts 4:4); his male address (Acts 1:16) may function more inclusively (see 2:14, 22, 29, 37).

203. The practice may have changed from one period to another (Marx, "Racines"). The cemetery includes a small minority of female skeletons (Harrison, "Rites," 28; Dupont-Sommer, *Writings*, 65; Bengtsson, "Kvinnor") or nearly one-third (Elder, "Question"); women may have lived there only during particular periods (cf. Atkinson, "Women"; Cross, *Library*, 97). But while some argue that they were from the community (Taylor, "Cemeteries"), recent discussion suggests that they may date to many centuries after the original community vanished (Zias, "Cemeteries"; Beall, "Essenes," 345; suggested as a possibility already by Cross, *Library*, 97).

204. Cf. CD XII, 1–2 (for Jerusalem). Many assume Qumran celibacy and that all were males (e.g., Desprez, "Groups"; Thiering, "Source"; Gusella, "Therapeutae"). Others suggest that only the *Manual of Discipline* excludes them (Bernstein, "Women"; cf. Bengtsson, "Kvinnor") and note that women appear elsewhere in the documents (e.g., Hübner, "Zölibat"; Strugnell, "Wives"; Davies and Taylor, "Testimony"; Elder, "Question"; cf. Baumgarten, "4Q502"; 1Q28a I, 7–11; 4Q270 7 I, 12–13). The conflicting evidence may comport with literary evidence for both celibate and married Essenes (Cohen, *Maccabees*, 152). Further, the *Damascus Document's* ideology need not represent the practice of its producing community (Grossman, "Reading"). Some think that the community excluded women for purity reasons (Buchanan, "Purity," 399–405) or because of eschatological urgency (cf. van der Horst, "Celibacy") or the eschatological holy war in particular (Steiner, "Warum asketisch?").

205. Ancient sources claim that Essenes (still the majority view about the source of Qumran's sectarian documents, although debated) were mostly celibate (Philo *Hypoth.* 11.14; Pliny E. *N.H.* 5.15.73; Jos. *Ant.* 18.21; *War* 2.120), but Josephus mentions that some did marry (*War* 2.160). Probably, some groups of Essenes were celibate and others married (with Chapman, "Marriage," 211–15; Cohen, *Maccabees*, 152), though Hellenistic depictions of Essenes may draw on philosophic models (cf. Deming, *Celibacy*, 89–91) and conceptions (cf. Stowers, "Self-Mastery," 534).

206. Witherington, *Acts*, 120. Some scholars compare the rabbinic minyan (see *b. Ber.* 6ab; *Meg.* 23b; *y. Meg.* 4:4, §5) to suggest ten males per apostle (Malina and Pilch, *Acts*, 25).

207. See on "parenthesis" (Latin *interpositio* or *interclusio*) Black, "Oration at Olivet," 87 (citing Quint. *Inst.* 9.3.23); Aune, *Dictionary of Rhetoric*, 337; Rowe, "Style," 147; Blass, Debrunner, and Funk, *Grammar*, §465.

208. An approximation, as Luke characteristically indicates by using ὡσεί (cf. Acts 2:41; 10:3; 19:7; Luke 3:23; 9:14, 28; 22:41; 23:44).

209. Matson, *Conversion Narratives*, 29–31, thinks that Luke may have created the mission of the seventy-two as a paradigm for the later Gentile mission; he is probably correct about its paradigmatic function (31–38), but as argued above, the large number of disciples is multiply attested.

24:49; Acts 1:4). Luke's numbers here are plausible enough; a well-known teacher at a given time might easily have about a hundred students[210] and, over the course of some years, more disciples and many more adherents.[211] Schools for Greek boys could hold 60 to 120 students[212] and "ranged from a handful to two hundred in both grammar and rhetorical schools."[213] Associations in antiquity generally ranged from ten to twenty on the lower end to one to two hundred on the higher end.[214] Given Jesus's ministry of healing, he probably had hundreds of followers among the Galilean festal pilgrims.

Peter's initial sermon had a respectable hearing that prefigures his greater ministry to come (Acts 2:41). This portrayal, while credible (as noted above), also would play well to Luke's audience; an orator visiting a town needed to attract sufficient numbers for his initial audition or risk shame.[215] One could address a large crowd in a usual place of prayer (cf. Jos. *Life* 277–78), as undoubtedly happened regularly in ancient synagogues. Peter may have addressed this (presumably mostly Galilean) assembly in Aramaic,[216] though neither Luke nor any oral informants who could have communicated the substance to him had reason to show interest in or highlight it. His address, "Men, brothers" (Ἄνδρες ἀδελφοί),[217] need not imply that on this occasion the women (Acts 1:14) were absent (cf. discussion about women's participation in some Jewish gatherings above; comment on Acts 1:16 below); the masculine address was common rhetoric for addressing public assemblies (see comment on Acts 2:14) and appears even where gender-mixed audiences may be presumed (2:14, 22, 29).[218]

b. Scripture on Replacing a Fallen Leader (1:16–20)

That one of Jesus's own intimate disciples betrayed him would have been an embarrassment to the rest of his followers.[219] Following the regular practice of Jesus in the Gospel, however, Peter reaches into Scripture for principles addressing their situation. In 1:18–19, Luke interrupts this part of the speech temporarily to digress about Judas's sorry end, vindicating God's purpose in the situation.

i. Judas's Apostasy and God's Plan (1:16)

Judas's apostasy may have been an embarrassment in natural terms but could be explained as part of God's plan, just as Jesus's crucifixion itself was (2:23). That the

---

210. Philost. *Vit. soph.* 2.11.591. Pythagoras allegedly had about eighty (Diog. Laert. 8.1.39). Even as an itinerant, Apollonius allegedly had thirty-four (until persecution reduced the number to eight, somewhat closer to Jesus's inner circle; Philost. *Vit. Apoll.* 4.37).

211. Over the course of his life, Pythagoras allegedly had 235 whose names were allegedly preserved in the tradition (Iambl. *V.P.* 36.267), with allegedly six hundred adherents (on some level) in a particular city (Iambl. *V.P.* 6.29, if original), and at times spoke to crowds (not disciples) of more than two thousand (*V.P.* 6.30). By contrast, Diogenes the Cynic had none (as distinct from the sophists; Dio Chrys. *Or.* 4.14).

212. Jeffers, *World*, 254.

213. Watson, "Education," 311. All the schools of Bethar had at least five hundred in *y. Taʿan.* 4:5, §10, but this is part of a rabbinic hyperbole.

214. Klauck, *Context*, 43.

215. Winter, *Left Corinth*, 37, noting that a small number such as seventeen was too few to succeed (citing Aristides *Discourse* 51.29; Russell, *Declamation*, 77n16).

216. C. Williams, *Acts*, 60. By contrast, the speech of Acts 2:17–39 would have to have been in Greek to be intelligible to most of those reported gathered in Acts 2:9–11.

217. Knowling, "Acts," 63, plausibly suggests that the title indicates "the solemnity of occasion"; but cf. Acts 2:14–15. On "brother," see 9:17.

218. Although one could argue that Acts 3:12 may address a crowd beyond the Court of Women (cf. 4:4), this suggestion would not fit the likeliest geography of the temple (3:2), and whatever one concludes about Acts 3, the converts in 2:41 cannot be restricted to males.

219. Estrada, *Followers*, 37, indeed, contends that Luke promotes the apostles in Acts' opening chapters in part "to blot out the effect of Judas' betrayal of Jesus," which "had serious social implications, especially on the honour and reputation of the apostles as a group." On the embarrassment, see also Zwiep, *Judas*, ch. 5.

speaker (Peter) also denied Jesus in the passion narrative may underline the difference made by the resurrection.

It is helpful here to digress momentarily to comment on Peter's address to his associates. There is some question as to whether the title "men" is intended gender exclusively here (because the text employs a form of ἀνήρ rather than a form of the more gender-inclusive ἄνθρωπος).[220] Some scholars have proposed that Peter treated the gathering like a synagogue and hence have suggested that the title is not gender-inclusive;[221] but synagogues were not gender-segregated in this period, at least not so far as our sources indicate.[222] Possibly because many people of status in the empire still regarded the public sphere as male, Luke protects the public image of the movement by emphasizing a male decision-making body here.[223] But this solution is too narrow for Luke's usage, since the phrase used here appears in other speeches, even to clearly gender-mixed groups (e.g., 2:29, 37).[224] Luke instead simply employs the conventional vocative for such speeches. For discussion of the traditional title "men," see comment on Acts 2:14; on "siblings," see comment on Acts 9:17.

When Peter speaks of Judas as a guide to those who arrested Jesus, Luke's audience would think of the fuller account of this betrayal in Luke 22:3–6, 21–22, 47–48. Treachery or betrayal was considered one of the most heinous offenses in antiquity, a breach of sacred trust.[225] Most ancients regarded with disgust traitors against their own peoples;[226] such behavior was worthy of death[227] and invited the hatred of even one's family.[228] Disloyalty to friends likewise remained despicable (e.g., *Rhet. Alex.* 36, 1442.13–14). In particular, to injure or kill those with whom one had eaten at table was a terrible offense from which all but the most wicked would normally shrink;[229] such behavior was held to incur divine wrath.[230] Those who eat together at table should not even betray friendship by slandering one another.[231] This experience was a matter of shame and hardly likely to have been invented by the later church.[232]

220. Beck, "Women," 281, attributes this usage to Luke's "androcentric bias," despite acknowledging that the use is traditional. On gender issues, see comment on Acts 1:14; esp. our introduction, ch. 18.

221. See Ellingworth, "Men and Brethren."

222. See esp. Brooten, "Segregated"; Brooten, *Women Leaders*, 103–38; see further comment on Acts 1:14.

223. Cf. Vander Stichele, "Gender," 314, following D'Angelo, "ANHP Question," 52.

224. Nevertheless, Luke's usage might still be apologetic, emphasizing respect for male hearers and hence responding to objections from those sensitive to Eastern cults reputed to undermine traditional family values; cf. Keener, *Paul*, 140–42; discussion in our introduction, ch. 13, sect. 3. Thus Acts 7:2, e.g., includes titles clearly meant to defer to elite audience members' honor. If so, however, Luke balances this with a contrasting gender-inclusive emphasis in his narrative (which likewise welcomes elite and poor alike). "Men and brothers" is specifically Lukan (fourteen times in Acts; elsewhere derivative from Acts unless *1 Clem.* 14.1, 37.1, 43.4, and 62.1 are independent; Pervo, *Acts*, 51).

225. E.g., slaying a person whose trust one gained through feigned friendship, as in Corn. Nep. 14 (Datames), 11.3–5.

226. Xen. *Hell.* 1.7.22; Cic. *Fin.* 3.9.32; Val. Max. 1.1.13; Sen. E. *Controv.* 7.7.intro.; Babr. 138.7–8. This was despicable to the gods (Virg. *Aen.* 6.621) and usually even to those who benefited from the betrayal (Livy 1.11.6–7; 5.27.6–10; though not always, Livy 4.61.8–10).

227. E.g., Quint. Curt. 4.1.33.

228. Livy 2.5.7–8; Corn. Nep. 4 (Pausanias), 5.3.

229. E.g., Hom. *Il.* 21.76; *Od.* 4.534–35; 11.414–20; 14.404–5; Hesiod *W.D.* 327; Eurip. *Cycl.* 126–28; *Hec.* 25–26, 710–20, 850–56; *Heracl.* 1034–36 (even in subsequent generations!); Cic. *Pis.* 34.83; by seeking the host's wife, Ovid *Her.* 17.3–4. On kindness due a host, see Cic. *Verr.* 2.2.47.117; Ap. Rhod. 3.377–80; Ovid *Metam.* 1.144; 10.225–28; Livy 25.16.6. This principle included providing protection from enemies (Ovid *Metam.* 5.44–45; Corn. Nep. 2 [Themistocles], 8.3).

230. Hom. *Od.* 21.26–28; Livy 39.51.12. Nevertheless, some warned that too much trust even of friends could prove dangerous (Hesiod *W.D.* 370–72).

231. Aeschines *Embassy* 22, 55. For a guest to act unkindly was deceptive treachery (Catull. *Carm.* 64.176).

232. On its presumable historicity, see, e.g., Robbins, "Meal," 30; cf. also probably 1 Cor 11:23, although the meaning is debated. Later polemic against Christians honored Judas (*Toledot Yeshu*; see Heindl, "Rezeption").

The Holy Spirit testified about Jesus through prophets in advance, just as the new prophetic movement would do retroactively (Acts 1:8; 2:17–18; cf. 1 Pet 1:10–12); the Spirit's scriptural testimony is elucidated in Acts 1:20. By citing David as the psalmist,[233] Luke may add to the comparison with the righteous sufferer a specific connection with David's household (see 2:30); that is, if such a psalm applied to anyone, it would certainly apply to the Davidic king.[234] David offers both inspired prophecy (Luke 20:42–44; Acts 2:25; 4:25) and a limited messianic model (cf. Luke 6:3; Acts 13:22, 34; 15:16).

To attribute Judas's apostasy to God's plan reinterprets the shame of this event in a manner analogous to that in which early Christians reinterpreted the shame of the cross (e.g., 1 Cor 1:17–25; 2:2; see comment on Acts 2:23).[235] This seems evident also from Luke's use of δεῖ, which often in Luke-Acts connotes divine necessity;[236] one may compare especially the necessity of Scripture's fulfillment, including regarding Jesus's passion, in Luke 24:44.[237]

The involvement of God's plan also reduces the apparent shame and incongruity of a disciple of God's chosen betraying him.[238] This is a real issue of cultural honor and shame that must be addressed. Pupils occasionally became antagonists (Eunapius *Lives* 493); more often they turned out poorly and so reflected badly (in popular opinion) on their teachers (e.g., Alcibiades with Socrates).[239] One could somewhat exonerate a leader blindsided by others' unscrupulousness by attributing his naiveté to a benevolent disposition (e.g., Cic. *Quint. fratr.* 1.1.4.12),[240] but obviously, this approach would not work for a prophet such as Jesus. God's salvation-historical plan explains the case with Jesus.

Emphasizing that Judas belongs in the category of a traitor rather than merely a failed disciple may help alleviate the shame. States treated traitors as among the worst of criminals (Xen. *Hell.* 1.7.22), and betrayal of intimate friendships was no

233. "Through David's mouth" also appears in Acts 4:25. This phrasing does not evoke God's speaking to David through God's mouth (and fulfilling it by his hand; 1 Kgs 8:15, 24; 2 Chr 6:4, 15) but rather the broader divine speech through the "mouth of prophets" (Luke 1:70; Acts 3:18, 21), phraseology in Zech 8:9 (and less positively, 1 Kgs 22:22–23; 2 Chr 18:21–22).

234. Psalms figure prominently in early Christian interpretations of Jesus's passion, including in Luke's theology (see Jipp, "Messiah"). Cf. Ps 2:1–2 in Acts 4:26; Ps 31:5 (LXX 30:6) in Luke 23:46 (here undoubtedly reflecting early Palestinian tradition; see discussion in Stauffer, *Jesus and Story*, 142; Stanton, *Jesus of Nazareth*, 37); a clear allusion to Ps 22:18 (LXX 21:19) in Luke 23:34; a possible allusion to Ps 69:21 (LXX 68:22; the relevant term appears only four times in the LXX) in Luke 23:36; a possible allusion to Ps 38:11 (LXX 37:12) or perhaps 88:8 (LXX 87:10) in Luke 23:49.

235. God's will and purposes are a recurrent theme in Acts' speeches (see Soards, *Speeches*, 184–89; Squires, *Plan*; Bock, *Theology*, 122–28). Tannehill thinks that it echoes Luke 24:44 and hence allows Peter to carry forward Jesus's role as interpreter (*Acts*, 20); the motif, however, is pervasive.

236. Soards, *Speeches*, 187–88; Cosgrove, "Divine dei" (though it is not a technical term). Other NT writers often employ the term similarly.

237. Cf. Acts 17:3; the passion in Luke 9:22. Δεῖ functions as a rhetorical authenticating device in Luke-Acts, invoking divine necessity (Rothschild, *Rhetoric of History*, 185–212). For prediction and fulfillment as an authenticating device in ancient historiography, see 142–84.

238. For the importance of rhetorical authentication where historical narratives seemed improbable, see Rothschild, *Rhetoric of History*, 97 (citing Josephus, Lucian, and Philostratus).

239. For behavior reflecting (positively or negatively) on teachers, see, e.g., Aeschines *Tim.* 171–73; *t. 'Ed.* 3:4; *'Abot R. Nat.* 27 A; 34, §76 B; Mark 2:18, 24; Alciph. *Court.* 7 (Thaïs to Euthydemus), 1.34, ¶¶6–7; cf. Daube, "Responsibilities," 3–4. For apologetic distancing of a teacher's behavior from that of a wayward disciple, cf. Ael. Arist. *Def. Or.* 336, §111D; and especially the case of Alcibiades (Xen. *Apol.* 19; *Mem.* 1.2.12–18, 26; Plut. *Alc.* 7.3).

240. It was a shame to trust foolishly and experience betrayal; but because it was impossible to trust no one (Polyb. 8.36.1–9), one should simply be as careful as possible, gaining pledges and, where relevant, hostages, and if one was still betrayed, the shame belonged to the betrayer alone (8.36.4).

less awful.[241] Some also felt that those who were once good but became bad merited greater punishment.[242]

11. Judas's Portion (1:17)

Peter begins by noting that Judas the traitor had received the same privileges of calling that the other eleven had; Judas is described as being "numbered"[243] with them for their "service" and "lot" (see below). In the context of Luke's entire work, Judas's failure to persevere sounds a warning to other would-be disciples (Luke 8:12–13; 9:62; Acts 8:20–24; 14:22; 20:26–30), though it was also possible to sin yet be restored (Luke 22:32; Acts 8:22–24).[244] In its immediate context, though, it has created a problem that must be resolved. Most Jews thought of apostasy as a particularly heinous crime,[245] yielding severe divine punishment;[246] when possible, it would yield human punishment as well.[247]

Peter describes the apostolic calling here as a "service" (διακονίας) in which Judas once shared (also in Acts 1:25). Luke elsewhere refers to such "service" as the sort of work done by women (Luke 4:39; 10:40) and slaves who wait on tables (12:37; 17:8), a role Jesus himself filled (22:26–27). The apostles ultimately must relinquish literally waiting on tables (Acts 6:1–2), but only so that they can devote themselves to "serving" the message (6:4).[248]

Peter also describes this calling in terms of a "portion" or "lot" (κλῆρον) in the service. This description reinforces the fact that possessors of the office were chosen by divine purpose,[249] including the betrayer. Just as God "allotted" to Levites[250] their specific duties (see 1 Chr 24:5, 7, 21; 25:8–9, 13–14), God also assigned particular roles to Jesus's various disciples; one tenth of the 120 disciples here might be allotted to apostleship, as the lot determined which tenth of the people would abandon their land to resettle Jerusalem (Neh 11:1).[251] God gave the Levites the "lot" of their ministry rather than land (Deut 10:9; 18:1–2; cf. also Num 18:21; Deut 12:12; 14:27, 29);[252] likewise, God was the one who chose Jesus's witnesses for a special calling that left little room for unjust "wages" (Acts 1:18; cf. Luke 12:13–48, esp. 12:41–42; Acts

241. E.g., Lysias Or. 6.23, §105; 8.5–6, §112; Char. Chaer. 5.6.2; Corn. Nep. 14 (Datames), 6.3; 11.5; Sir 22:21–22; Test. Jud. 23:3; this remained true even if one's life was at stake (Babr. 138.7–8). The deeper the level of intimacy, the more that trust was a duty, and the more terrible its betrayal (Cic. Rosc. Amer. 40.116). Refusing to betray a friend or spouse was honorable (Athen. Deipn. 15.965F, item 25; Sen. E. Controv. 2.5.intro.); conversely, treachery and betrayal warranted death (Val. Max. 9.6). See further comment at Acts 12:19; 13:13; with reference to Judas as a "guide," cf. perhaps Luke 6:39.

242. E.g., Thucyd. 1.86.1; 1QS VII, 18–23; Heb 6:6; 2 Pet 2:20–21; b. Pesaḥ. 49b.

243. Johnson, Acts, 35, suggests that this phrase recalls the cognate noun that first appears in Luke when Satan entered Judas (Luke 22:3).

244. Cf. Jas 5:19–20. On perseverance in Luke-Acts, see esp. Brown, Apostasy. The involvement of Satan with both Judas (Luke 22:3) and Peter (22:31) in the same context suggests that only Jesus's intercession preserved Peter from a similar fate (22:32).

245. E.g., 1 Macc 2:15; Pss. Sol. 17:15; 4 Macc 9:24.

246. So, e.g., Ezek 33:12–13, 18; 1 En. 91:7; Jub. 15:34; cf. Apoc. Pet. 5.1–2 (Ethiopic); perhaps 4Q163 6–7 II, 4–7 (though part is illegible). Some Jewish groups lamented much of Israel's apostasy (e.g., 4Q501 line 3); some viewed it as characteristic of the end time (e.g., Test. Iss. 6:1; 2 Thess 2:3).

247. E.g., 1QS VII, 22–24; 3 Macc 7:14–15; Burkert, "Craft," 18; R. Meir in t. Demai 2:9.

248. As Paul also does later (Acts 20:24; 21:19). Cf. similarly Tannehill, Acts, 22. The term applies to economic contributions in Luke 8:3 and Acts 11:29; 12:25; this usage provides a suitable contrast to the greed probably implied by Judas's "wage" (Acts 1:18). It apparently applies to servant-disciples in 19:22.

249. For "portion" and predestination, see, e.g., Jub. 11:17.

250. For a comparison with OT Levites, see also Johnson, Acts, 35; Witherington, Acts, 122.

251. The context of this passage also speaks of "overseers" for the people (Neh 11:9, 14, 22; see Acts 1:20).

252. Cf. also Pss 16:5 (15:5 LXX, κληρονομίας); 119:57; 142:5, though these are not κλῆρος in the LXX. Appeals to late Targumim for the wording (cf. Marshall, Acts, 64) are unnecessary.

3:6; 1 Cor 4:11). Money could not purchase a "lot" in God's calling (Acts 8:21), and the one who betrayed his calling for land would be left with desolation on his land (1:20).[253] Judas abandoned his "portion" (1:17); thus the next apostle would need to be chosen by "lot" (1:26).[254] (The scriptural argument in 1:17, 20, may resemble an incomplete syllogism.)[255]

III. JUDAS'S GORY END (1:18–19)

Luke adds an explanatory aside here to inform the reader what has happened to Judas since his betrayal in Luke 22:47–48 and Jesus's prediction that a terrible fate awaited him (22:21–22).[256] Just as the *Iliad* uses digressions to catch the reader up on earlier parts of the Trojan War (such as Calchas and Iphigeneia) and the *Odyssey* uses them to survey what has transpired since the close of the *Iliad*, Luke uses a digression here, probably to inform the reader what has happened since the end of his Gospel or at least since his last mention of Judas. Digressions were common practice among ancient historians, as among many modern ones.[257] This was also true in other genres.[258] Luke often avoids them but sometimes inserts them at seemingly awkward moments (here and Acts 2:7–11),[259] perhaps for emphasis.

As scholars often note,[260] disembowelment or bowel pains were considered a particularly painful and appropriate way for a wicked person to die[261] (e.g., Agrippa's stomach pains, Jos. *Ant.* 19.346–50, though not elaborated in Acts 12:23). But they also provide a graphic image for a terrible death that is not limited to the wicked (e.g., 2 Sam 2:23; 3:27; 20:10, 12).[262] Historians were not above reporting the later suffering of an evil character in the account as just deserts for evil behavior.[263] The gruesome reports of Judas's death here and in Matt 27:5 help conform his death "to that of other notoriously evil men, such as Herod the Great or Nadan in the story of Ahikar."[264] Judas's death, like that of Herod (Acts 12:23) and Ananias (5:5), warns Luke's audience of the dangers of opposing the kingdom.[265]

---

253. The radical apostolic values concerning ministry and possessions (cf., e.g., Acts 3:6; Luke 12:41–42) also recall earlier prophetic values (cf., e.g., 2 Kgs 5:26–27).

254. Scholars frequently note this connection; e.g., Johnson, *Acts*, 35; Witherington, *Acts*, 122.

255. On enthymeme in this broader sense, cf. Vinson, "Enthymemes," 119–22, 131.

256. Bruce, *Commentary*, 48–49. For asides in Acts, see Sheeley, *Asides*, 119–35; in ancient historiography, 56–78. Astonishingly, Pervo, *Dating Acts*, 310, apparently attributes even the aside to Peter, then counts this attribution against early tradition.

257. E.g., Xen. *Hell.* 7.4.1; Thucyd. 1.24.1ff. (digressing from 1.23.6); Polyb. 3.2.7; 3.9.6; 3.39.1; 3.59.9; 31.30.4; 6.1.2; 6.50.1; Sall. *Catil.* 5.9–13.5; Livy 9.17.1–9.19.17 (apologizing in 9.17.1); Val. Max. 4.8.1 (with 4.7.ext. 2b); Jos. *Ant.* 20.224–51; Arrian *Ind.* 6.1; Tac. *Hist.* 2.2; cf. also Eigler, "Excursus" (noting Polyb. 18.35); Aune, *Environment*, 102 (citing Josh 5:4–7; 1 Sam 9:9; 2 Kgs 14:6–7; 7:6–7; 17:23–41; 1 Macc 8:1–16).

258. In other narratives, e.g., Hom. *Od.* 19.392–468 (Harvey, *Listening*, 58, following Whitman, *Homer*, 253); Corn. Nep. 16 (Pelopidas), 3.1; Jos. *Life* 336–67; Plut. *Alex.* 35.8; Photius *Bibl.* 166.109a (on *Ant. Diog. Thule*). Among rhetoricians, both in theory (Cic. *Or. Brut.* 40.137–38; *Brut.* 93.322) and in practice (e.g., Max. Tyre 19.1 [from 18.9]; Dio Chrys. *Or.* 12.38; 36.1–6); see "excursus" in Quint. *Inst.* 4.3.1–17. See also comment on Acts 1:15–26. In other genres, Dion. Hal. *Lysias* 13; Cic. *Fin.* 2.32.104; *Att.* 7.2; *Or. Brut.* 43.148; Sen. E. *Controv.* 2.1.35–36; Pliny E. *N.H.* 28.1.1 (for *N.H.* 28–32); Mus. Ruf. 1, p. 34.34; Jos. *Ag. Ap.* 1.57; Philost. *Hrk.* 20.1 (cf. 18.6–19.9); 53.2–3.

259. Aune, *Environment*, 130.

260. E.g., Barrett, *Acts*, 98.

261. E.g., Judg 3:21–22; Jos. *War* 1.81, 84; 5.385; 7.453; *Ant.* 9.101–3.

262. E.g., Hom. *Il.* 4.525–26; 20.418–20; 21.180–81; b. *Ḥul.* 56b–57a.

263. E.g., Xen. *Anab.* 5.1.15–16; see esp. Allen, *Death of Herod*, 155–95, on the retribution theme in apologetic historiography (155–71 for Diodorus Siculus; 171–82 for Dionysius of Halicarnassus; 182–95 for Josephus).

264. Lake, "Death of Judas," 25. Van de Water, "Punishment," compares the Wicked Priest's demise.

265. Dunn, *Acts*, 19. For judgment in Acts, see, e.g., Morris, *Cross in New Testament*, 112–13.

That the field is "of blood" (1:19) reinforces the goriness of Judas's end (1:18), although "Field of Blood" is from tradition (see discussion below). It may also draw attention to Judas's bloodguilt,[266] a concept that Luke elsewhere reflects (Luke 11:50–51; Acts 5:28; though he does not explicitly associate this language with Judas as Matthew does in Matt 27:4, 6, 8). Jewish sources sometimes spoke of God's bringing "like" punishments, analogous to the crimes, in Scripture (Exod 1:22; 7:20; 12:29; 14:27–28; Prov 26:27) and very frequently in early Jewish tradition.[267] Gentiles, too, understood the concept.[268]

IV. The Tradition (1:18–19)

Multiple accounts emphasize Judas's terrible end. Yet Matthew's version of Judas's demise differs at key points from Luke's and also from another early version in Papias.[269] Is it possible to reconcile these accounts or at least to find a core of common tradition? Papias claims that Judas was so inhumanly (we might add, supernaturally) swollen that not even his head could pass where a wagon would, until worms and pus emerged from every part of his body, leading to terrible pain (frg. 24).[270] This account appears later, sounds less plausible, and may derive from garbled oral traditions based on the earlier accounts reported in Matthew and Luke.[271]

Thus we focus especially on the differences between Matthew's and Luke's accounts. Judas's hanging in Matthew recalls especially Ahithophel, who betrayed King David (2 Sam 17:23; Jos. Ant. 7.229).[272] Davies and Allison doubt Matthew's account for this reason but Acts' account even more, noting that "the bursting of the bowels must be reckoned a conventional fate for the wicked."[273] But as noted above, convention could supply a reason for historians to emphasize a tradition without their having composed it.

The comparison with other gory accounts remains relevant even if it is Judas's corpse that experiences this disfigurement (rather than Judas, alive, experiencing a painful end). But the sources suggest that historical as well as novelistic disembowelments happened, including to people whose enemies would be happy to report this end for them. Further, *if* at least Matthew's tradition that Judas died by suicide is correct (certainly disputed but explaining his quick disappearance),

---

266. Ray, *Irony*, 64, notes the irony: Judas took money for betraying Jesus, and the field that he bought with it led to Judas's own death.

267. E.g., Sir 27:25–27; 2 Macc 4:38; 9:5–6; 13:7–8; *L.A.B.* 44:9–10; 1QpHab XI, 5, 7, 15; XII, 5–6; 4Q181 1 1–2; *Jub.* 4:32; 35:10–11; 37:5, 11; John 9:2; Matt 26:52; *m. 'Ab.* 2:6/7; *Sipre Deut.* 238.3.1; *'Abot R. Nat.* 27, §56 B; *b. 'Abod. Zar.* 17b, bar.; *Ber.* 5a; *Sanh.* 108b; *y. Ḥag.* 2:1, §3; *Gen. Rab.* 53:5; *Tg. Rishon* on Esth 1:11; some other sources in Bonsirven, *Judaism*, 110. A rabbi would not even face execution without God having found at least a minor transgression (*Mek. Nez.* 18.55ff.).

268. Diod. Sic. 20.62.2; see also Demosth. *Zenoth.* 6. The principle also applied to executions by rulers (e.g., Diod. Sic. 20.101.3; Aul. Gel. 7.4.4) or heroes (Apollod. *Bib.* 3.16.1; *Epit.* 1.2–3). Cf. sorcerers' death by sorcery in Kenyan Luo tradition (Whisson, "Disorders," 289).

269. Various scholars include Papias's version in the comparison at least briefly (e.g., Lake, "Death of Judas," 25; Fitzmyer, *Acts*, 219).

270. From Apollinaris of Laodicea (*AF*, ed. Holmes, 582–85). Talbert, *Acts*, 15, compares the grotesque deaths depicted in Jos. *War* 7.451–53 and in *Ahiqar* (though the latter may belong only to later versions; see J. M. Lindenberger in *OTP* 2:498).

271. On the whole, it sounds closer to Luke's account than to Matthew's (Witherington, *Acts*, 121). MacDonald, "Papias," even argues for Luke's dependence on Papias.

272. See further Meier, *Matthew*, 338; Gundry, *Matthew*, 553; Brown, *Death*, 656–57; Davies and Allison, *Matthew*, 3:560 (for parallels in the betrayal sequence of the passion tradition, 565, though they regard this tradition as pre-Matthean, 566).

273. Davies and Allison, *Matthew*, 3:560 (citing 2 Chr 21:18–19; 2 Macc 9:7–12; Bel 27; Jos. *Ant.* 17.168–69; *War* 7.452–53; *Ahiq.* 8; *Acts Thom.* 3.33; Theodoret *Hist. Rel.* 1.10, on Arius); cf. also Fitzmyer, *Acts*, 219–20 (adding Jos. *War* 1.656–65).

both Matthew and Luke provide plausible pictures of how such a suicide could have occurred (though Matthew's report represents the more common method). Hanging constituted a common form of suicide,[274] though many considered it a particularly dishonorable method (as opposed to falling on one's sword; cf. comment on Acts 16:27).[275] Jumping to one's death was less common but appears as a form of suicide at times (e.g., Cic. *Scaur.* 3.4);[276] it could be presented as one method of suicide alongside of (but not compatible with) hanging (Lucan *C.W.* 2.154–58).[277]

Although full harmonization appears historically implausible here, I admit that the conflict between the two accounts should not be overstated.[278] Contrary to what some scholars suppose, it is not impossible to harmonize Matthew's depiction of hanging with Luke's depiction of bowels bursting; stranger "contradictions" in oral sources have, in fact, been verified as stemming from accurate facts.[279] This congruency is not likely to be found in the occasionally proposed harmonization that the weak, makeshift rope broke during the suicide attempt or that, as an ancient tradition proposed, someone cut him down before he died.[280] Such incidents were not, of course, impossible or unknown. Thus the elder Seneca describes theoretically a person who hangs himself from a tree unsuccessfully because someone cuts the noose, saving him against his will (Sen. E. *Controv.* 5.1; cf., similarly, 8.1). Such a reconstruction is possible but not likely; ancient texts describe such an occurrence—but it is most prominent in comic descriptions of "losers" who could not even commit suicide successfully.[281] Had Judas met his end in a *failed* suicide attempt, Matthew and Luke might well have both wished to capitalize on it!

Much more plausibly, *if* Judas hanged himself from a tall tree or building in the sort of rocky field natural in Judean hill country, his innards *might well* spatter (assuming that the tree was tall)[282] when someone cut or (less likely) untied the rope

274. E.g., Soph. *Oed. tyr.* 1237–66; Eurip. *Hel.* 136, 200–202; *Hipp.* 776–81, 802; frg. 1111; Ap. Rhod. 1.1063–65; Polyb. 33.5.2; Cic. *Scaur.* 6.10–11; Ovid *Her.* 3.38; Pliny E. *N.H.* 16.45.108; Quint. *Decl.* 270 intro; 289 intro; Aul. Gel. 15.10.1–2; Hermog. *Inv.* 4.13.209.

275. Livy 42.28.11–12; Plut. *Themist.* 22.2; cf. also sources in Talbert, *Matthew,* 300. Romans denied burial to those who hanged themselves (see Livy, LCL, 12:372n1, citing Servius on *Aen.* 12.603; cf. Jewish tradition in Stauffer, *Jesus and Story,* 209). One might reconsider suicide by hanging lest one bring reproach on one's family for excess misfortune (Tob 3:10). Judas likely had no sword (though cf. Luke 22:38).

276. Also, e.g., Alciph. *Fish.* 11 (Glaucippê to Charopê), 3.1, ¶4; *y. Kil.* 9:3, §3.

277. It was hardly the only alternative; Ap. Rhod. 3.789–90 lists poison alongside hanging (though this is for a sorceress).

278. When we examine differing accounts with elements of common tradition, we normally seek the most plausible reconstruction that makes best sense of the extant data, as, e.g., in Suet. *Otho* 8.1–2; Tac. *Hist.* 1.80–82; Plut. *Otho* 3.3–7. Cf. Keener, "Otho," 344.

279. Eddy and Boyd, *Legend,* 424 (citing Bogart and Montell, *Memory,* 77, a work on method in oral historiography), compare two "contradictory" accounts of an 1881 lynching: in one, the men hang "from a railroad crossing," and in the other, from a pine tree. But the historians found "old photographs that showed the bodies hanging *at different times from both places*"; after being lynched in one place, they were hanged again in another. These particular oral-history accounts proved more reliable than our modern critical resistance to harmonization. For one suggestion of harmonization, see Peterson, *Acts,* 124. Such language polarizes binary thinkers quickly; strangely, one reviewer focused on my brief concession regarding some efforts at harmonization in my *Historical Jesus,* 331, ignoring the context (331–32) in which I personally take a different approach.

280. So Apollinaris of Laodicea, in the fourth century (Papias frg. 18 [*AF* 583]).

281. Apul. *Metam.* 1.16; cf. Petron. *Sat.* 94. Cf. the attempted hangings in Eurip. *Andr.* 811–13; Ovid *Metam.* 10.378–81. Enraged mobs also occasionally dragged a corpse with a noose around its neck (Val. Max. 7.8.5), regarding natural death an inadequate price (cf. posthumous hanging in the OT, Deut 21:22–23; Josh 8:29; 10:26), but this is not what Matthew states (Matt 27:5).

282. "Pour out" (ἐκχύννω) often refers to blood (Luke 11:50; Acts 22:20), a fitting contrast to Jesus's death, which Judas occasioned (Luke 22:20), but σπλάγχνον, though elsewhere in the NT used figuratively,

(or it eventually broke).[283] (This assumes that the body was cut down before it decomposed or before it was picked apart by scavengers; in view of Judean piety, this assumption is likely,[284] again assuming that the corpse was found, as it probably would have been if near Jerusalem.) Others have suggested the possibility of the body's being torn down and opened by wild dogs, fitting both versions.[285] Luke or his source would then report the gorier fate of Judas's corpse rather than his actual mode of death (even if he were cut down in part to avoid the shame of hanged corpses; Deut 21:23; 2 Sam 21:10). Nevertheless, it is not clear how many details Matthew and Luke knew of about Judas's death, about which both writers share some common tradition.

Luke (no less than Matthew) has theological reasons for his report. Noting its appropriate description of the fate of corpses of the wicked (dishonored and a matter of insult [πτῶμα ἄτιμον; ὕβριν]), Luke may allude to Wis 4:18–19, which claims that God will cast the wicked headlong (πρηνεῖς).[286] We should not forget how well this depiction of Judas's end fits Herod's abdominal destruction (Acts 12:23; cf. the stomach pains in Jos. *Ant.* 19.346, 348, 350). Yet the accounts of Matthew and Luke, though plainly independent, share much information in common. One may compare and contrast some details as follows:

Matt 27:5–8	Acts 1:18–19
Judas as the betrayer	Judas as the betrayer
The priestly elite used Judas's wages to buy a field (27:6–7)*	Judas acquired† a field (1:18), which was the "wage" of his injustice (1:18)
Judas hanged himself (27:5)	He fell and his abdomen ruptured (1:18)
(Apparently the story remained widespread; 27:8)	Judas's sorry end became widely known (1:19)
This occasion prompted naming the field "Field of Blood" (27:8)	This occasion prompted naming the field "Field of Blood" (1:19)

*One could argue that they bought this particular field for burial because it was already defiled by Judas's blood, but objective support for this reconstruction would depend on the tradition in Acts. Goulder, *Type and History*, 176, derives the purchase of the field in Acts 1:18 from Jer 32 (Jer 39 LXX), but this suggestion will not work as well for those who regard Matthew as independent from Luke.

†Κτάομαι usually carries the sense "buy" in Luke (Acts 8:20; 22:28; cf. Luke 18:12; but not in Luke 21:19); the term appears elsewhere in the NT only rarely (only Matt 10:9; 1 Thess 4:4). Rare words here indicate nothing about sources; λακάω and πρηνής appear nowhere else in Luke-Acts, but they appear nowhere else in the NT either. Parsons, *Acts*, 33, contrasts Judas's purchase of a field with believers selling fields (Acts 4:34; cf. 5:3, 8) and Peter's forsaking all (Luke 18:28).

Clear parallels exist between the two accounts; certainly, "Field of Blood," for which Luke cites an Aramaic expression, is not his own invention.[287] The story apparently spread widely; although Luke probably uses this claim to emphasize how divine

---

may apply to all the abdominal organs (LSJ). A hanged corpse would not literally fall headfirst, but see comment below.

283. Λακάω suggests the violence (cf. BDAG) and perhaps sound of the landing (cf. LSJ, λάσκω), but nothing necessarily about its subject's consciousness. The verb recurs in Apollinaris of Laodicea's quotation of this passage (Papias frg. 18.1), its only use in the Apostolic Fathers.

284. See Deut 21:23.

285. Packer, *Acts*, 25–26.

286. Apart from the unrelated uses in 3 Macc 5:43, 50; 6:23, this is the only use of πρηνής in the LXX, and Acts 1:18 is its only use in the NT. A hanged corpse (in Matthew's version) when cut down would not literally fall headfirst (possibly in Luke's). This term in Acts could suggest either a symbolic allusion by Luke here or that his tradition or interpretation is irreconcilable with Matthew on this point; but the term may also have a range of potential meaning not limited to "headfirst" (see BDAG).

287. The site traditionally designated as the location may have been a Sadducean tomb complex, perhaps belonging to Annas (Ritmeyer and Ritmeyer, "Akeldama"). "*Their* language" in 1:19 might highlight the contrast with those soon speaking the languages of other locales (2:11). "That is" appears in midrash (Rom 10:6–8; Bekken, *Word*, 79–81), but is also appropriate outside it (Acts 19:4), including for translation (Matt 27:46).

vengeance spread fear of the Lord (as in Acts 5:11, 13),[288] Matthew also implies this account's circulation by mentioning that the field's name remained for at least a generation.[289] Gossip probably spread quickly in cities such as Jerusalem;[290] whether the reports were true or false, they were widespread and apparently accepted by Matthew's and Luke's sources without protest. In Matthew's account, the land is, in a sense, desolated, thereafter useful only for the unclean activity of burial (Matt 27:7);[291] in Acts, it is implied that the land becomes "desolate" and will not again be lived in (Acts 1:20).

Further, the common tradition also indicates that the wage paid for his betrayal bought this field and that Jerusalemites came to call the field "Field of Blood" in relation to Judas, who also (probably implied in both accounts) met an early and terrible death. Some other details may cohere but are not fully clear: since Acts 1:18–19 is a parenthetical aside,[292] Judas's death need not have occurred before Peter's speech, but on the whole, it seems more likely to have done so (at least in the story world, in view of 1:20, 25) and hence probably within a month and a half of Jesus's betrayal. Likewise, in Matthew's account, the suicide seems to follow Jesus's arrest fairly closely (Matt 27:3), though this could be Matthew's narrative tidiness (cf., e.g., Matt 21:12–22 with Mark 11:12–25). Thus in both sources Judas *appears* to have died relatively quickly after Jesus's betrayal, though this is not absolutely clear. And if he died so quickly and we do not attribute this to a surprising coincidence, Matthew's explanation of remorseful suicide is at least plausible.

The major differences are (1) whether Judas obtained the field himself (Acts 1:18 vs. Matt 27:7)[293] and (2) how he met his end (Acts 1:18; Matt 27:5). It is possible that in the former case Luke's report stems from his (or his sources') abbreviation of a longer account that could have included the high priests[294] or that the priests, counting "the money as legally belonging to Judas," could have "bought the field in his name."[295] (Because of Judas's "unclean" death there, the owner might have been willing to sell it for a burial plot.) Although such an explanation is plausible, a larger question remains over one of the accounts: how would Matthew's tradition have access to conversation that transpired between Judas shortly before his decease and high priests who remained hostile to the Christian movement (see discussion of unreported scenes in comment on Acts 25:14–22)?

If Acts focuses on the gory fate of Judas's corpse, which bloodied the land, rather than on his mode of death, the other difference between the accounts is explained. But if one must choose one account or the other, Luke's account better explains the clearly traditional title "Field of Blood" than does Matthew's (since Judas presumably would have had to hang himself with rope, not with nails).[296]

---

288. On "like-for-like" punishment, see, e.g., Sir 27:25–27; 2 Macc 4:38; 9:5–6; 13:7–8; 1QpHab XI, 5, 7, 15; XII, 5–6; 4Q181 1 1–2; *Jub.* 4:32; and comment above.

289. It was most likely near but outside Jerusalem, especially if one thinks of burials there (Matt 27:7).

290. See, e.g., Stambaugh, *City*, 139–40; comments on Acts 19:10, 29.

291. Suicides were not buried with others (Le Cornu, *Acts*, 42–43), just as the condemned were often buried separately (Stauffer, *Jesus and Story*, 209, citing *t. Sanh.* 9:8–9; *m. Sanh.* 6:7; *Sanh.* 45b, bar.).

292. Much larger parenthetical narratives often appear in ancient sources (on parenthetical "episodes," see Anderson, *Glossary*, 50).

293. Regularly observed, e.g., Boismard and Lamouille, *Actes*, 2:202.

294. Luke often does abbreviate his material, sometimes obscuring connections that might otherwise be clear to us.

295. Bruce, *Acts*[1], 77 (noting that this is "a common explanation"). Cf. Xen. *Anab.* 5.3.9 (though this is money dedicated to a deity, who may have had little other use for it).

296. Though Sen. E. *Controv.* 10.3.intro. speaks of a daughter who hangs herself, then (10.3.3) one describes her (presumably for rhetorical effect) as writhing in her blood (cf. Judg 4:19–21 with 5:26–27, the latter taking poetic liberties); and Matthew links the name to the price of innocent blood (Matt 27:6–8; cf.

Still, the differences between the two accounts underline their independence, hence highlighting the substantial tradition that they share, as Benoit points out: "This tradition, vaguer in Acts, more precise in Matthew, is especially well authenticated on those points where the two agree independently, namely on the violent death of Judas following his crime, and on the connection between his death and a certain 'field of blood' which was well-known in Jerusalem."[297] On the whole, Luke's historiography seems generally more careful than Matthew's,[298] though this observation does not determine the accuracy of the respective traditions on which they depend at a given point (though Luke appears to depend on a source that claims that Judas's end was "widely" known in Jerusalem; Acts 1:19). Matthew might use midrashic wordplay to expand on details (especially the "Field of Blood"),[299] but common details are too striking to be coincidence.

v. Applying the Fate of the Psalms' "Enemy" (1:20)

Luke often looks for general patterns and principles in Scripture (as in Acts 7; see comment there). As Israel's hymnbook, the psalms were commonly quoted and remembered; they constitute the most popular work at Qumran (though one might readily expect this of a monastic sect).[300] If the psalmist could speak of the righteous sufferer,[301] this role would apply to Jesus par excellence (cf. Acts 3:14; 7:52).[302] Thus it is not surprising that Peter quotes two verses both applicable generally to the wicked who persecute the righteous (Pss 69:25 [68:26 LXX]; 109:8 [108:8]). Because Jewish interpreters frequently applied the psalms to King David, it made sense to early Christians to apply them to the Davidic king par excellence (cf. Acts 2:30, 34); depictions of the psalmist's enemies thus become appropriate for the enemies of the Messiah and his people (cf. Acts 4:25–27).[303] If these verses applied to oppressors of the righteous generally, then "how much more" (*qal vaomer*, a "light to heavy" argument) ought they to apply to Judas, betrayer of the righteous one.[304]

In contrast to faithful disciples who did not seek to accumulate wealth (Luke 12:13–48; Acts 3:6; 20:33–35), Judas's "wage" bought what became a "Field of Blood"

Derrett, "Akeldama," who suggests compensation for blood). The claim that the common tradition indicates "an aetiological story" (Johnson, *Acts*, 36) is not likely; the tradition was young, and the site would not likely have attracted pilgrims.

297. Benoit, *Jesus*, 1:206–7 (concluding his analysis, 189–207); cf. others more briefly, e.g., Chance, *Acts*, 41.

298. Some regard Matthew as more accurate here (e.g., Benoit, *Jesus*, 1:206–7); others prefer Luke (e.g., Gundry, *Matthew*, 555–56; cf. Keener, *Matthew*, 657–60).

299. See Longenecker, *Exegesis*, 150; cf. Burkitt, *Gospel History*, 125; Hill, *Matthew*, 348; Lindars, *Apologetic*, 118; for Jer 18–19, cf. Meier, *Matthew*, 339; Gundry, *Matthew*, 556; Upton, "Potter's Field." Manns, "Mort de Judas," sees both Luke's and Matthew's accounts as employing midrashic elements; but this is far less characteristic of Luke, though he often explains events in light of Scripture (e.g., Luke 22:37; 24:27, 44–47; Acts 1:16; 13:27).

300. See Flint, "Psalms and Hymns," 850. Among the "books" of Scripture, Luke distinguishes Psalms (Acts 1:20; Luke 20:42); Isaiah (Luke 3:4; 4:17, 20; cf. Acts 8:28–30); and the "minor" prophets (Acts 7:42). Luke situates this biblical text in the very center of 1:15–26 (Marguerat, *Actes*, 57).

301. Developed in wisdom texts, including Wisdom, as well as in the NT (Miranda, "Schicksal"; dependent on Wisdom, see, e.g., Matt 27:43). The theme of righteous sufferers appears in Mesopotamian, not exclusively Israelite (cf. Job), wisdom (*ANET* 434–35; Kramer, "Variation"; idem, "Literature," 281).

302. Christians elsewhere applied psalms of righteous sufferers to Jesus, e.g., Ps 41:9 in John 13:18; Ps 69:9 in John 2:17 and Rom 15:3. Hays, *Conversion*, 107, finds Christ himself praying in "Davidic" psalms headed by the LXX superscription εἰς τὸ τέλος, which Christians may have interpreted eschatologically. On early Christian reapplication of psalms, cf. also Grant, "Singing."

303. Cf., e.g., Bruce, *Commentary*, 48.

304. With Longenecker, *Exegesis*, 97; idem, *Acts*, 60; cf. Bock, *Acts*, 87, emphasizing the "principle"; Miura, *David*, 159–60. For typological use of Ps 22 and Ps 69 for Jesus as the righteous sufferer, see, e.g., Gundry, *Use*, 210. More fully on the use of Ps 22 in the passion narratives, see Brown, *Death*, 1455–64.

(Acts 1:18–19)—making his dwelling place desolate (1:20). In the OT, the Levites' "lot" or "portion" was to serve God's sanctuary rather than be given land (see comment on Acts 1:17); Judas chose land over God's "lot," and so his land became desolate. Now, as his new property is "vacant," so is his office among the apostles.[305]

The selected texts are particularly useful for the point. Both are laments crying for deliverance from enemies;[306] both pray for the wicked to lose what they have owned, which allows one to link them by means of a common key thought.[307] Early Christians regularly applied Ps 69 to Jesus's passion—for example, 69:9 in John 2:17 and Rom 15:3; Ps 69:21 in Matt 27:34; and Ps 69:22 in Rom 11:9.[308] The persecuted one there is also called the Lord's servant (παιδός, Ps 69:17 [68:17 LXX]),[309] which allows for midrashic connections with Isaiah's servant (see comment on Acts 1:8; 8:32–33). Luke adjusts the Septuagintal wording—for instance, making it singular to apply to Judas but retaining even words elsewhere rare in Luke (e.g., ἔπαυλις, which is a NT hapax legomenon despite its frequency [thirty-seven times] in the LXX).[310] While Judas's ministry office remains available (Ps 109:8), the land he exchanged for that office (Acts 1:18) will remain desolate (Ps 69:25; Acts 1:20a). Luke plays on what Judas gave up, which is now available to another, in return for the worthless thing he received (see the play on τόπον, "place," in Acts 1:25).

The LXX's use of ἐπισκοπὴν for Ps 109:8's (LXX Ps 108:8) פקדתו ("office") works well for Luke's application to an office of ministry.[311] Luke applies the title ἐπίσκοπος to the elders who shepherd their fellow Christians (Acts 20:28; cf. 1 Pet 2:25 for Christ as shepherd and overseer), a usage that seems to have become technical in Pauline churches at some point (Phil 1:1; 1 Tim 3:1–2; Titus 1:7). Making his household "desolate" (ἔρημος, Acts 1:20, from Ps 69:25)[312] may play on Judas's lack of heirs or lack of inheritance (cf. κλῆρον in Acts 1:17) to give them: to make a household desolate was to prevent it from having heirs to carry on the line.[313]

If Peter addressed this crowd in Aramaic,[314] Luke could quote in Greek the verses that Peter would have quoted in Hebrew. The problem with this suggestion is that the two verses might be connected by an implicit *gezerah shevah* based on the way they begin in Greek: γενηθήτω (Ps 69:25 [68:26 LXX]) and γενηθήτωσαν (Ps 109:8 [108:8]). To this, one might respond that Peter may have spoken in Greek, as undoubtedly in Acts 2, 3, and 10, or that the *gezerah shevah* is unclear (it is at least subtle, since Luke omits the relevant part of the second quotation), or that the *gezerah shevah*'s very subtlety points to a more complete source on which Luke here depends. As to whether we

---

305. With, e.g., Johnson, *Acts*, 40.

306. E.g., Fitzmyer, *Acts*, 225–26; note the similar structure and content in Miura, *David*, 156.

307. Jewish interpreters commonly linked texts on the basis of common key words (e.g., *Mek. Pisha* 5.103; *Mek. Nez.* 10.15–16, 26, 38; 17.17 [Lauterbach, 1:41; 3:75–77, 130]; *b. Ber.* 9a; 35a; *B. Qam.* 25b; *Giṭ.* 49a; *Ker.* 5a; *Qidd.* 15a; 35b; *Menaḥ.* 76a; *Naz.* 48a; *Nid.* 22b–23a; *Roš Haš.* 3b; 34a; *Sanh.* 40b; 51b; 52a; *Šabb.* 64a; *Tem.* 16a; *Zebaḥ.* 18a; 49b–50b; see more fully Keener, *John*, 305, 1184). In the LXX, both of these verses begin with the aorist passive imperative of γίνομαι; there is no such connection in the Hebrew.

308. Commentators (e.g., Johnson, *Romans*, 178) regularly note that it is widespread in early Christian usage.

309. See Moessner, "Script," 223.

310. On adaptation for Acts, cf. Steyn, *Septuagint Quotations*, 62. For adapting texts for new contexts, see comment at Acts 2:17; cf. Stanley, *Language of Scripture*, 291.

311. With, e.g., Johnson, *Acts*, 36. The term ἐπίσκοπος appears in the LXX for a leader (Num 31:14; 2 Kgs 11:15, 18; 12:11; 2 Chr 34:12, 17; Neh 11:9, 14, 22; Isa 60:17; 1 Macc 1:51), borrowed from familiar Greek usage; see more fully comment on Acts 20:28. The shift in mood might represent "assimilation to the mood of the previous citation" (Marshall, "Acts," 530).

312. Luke changes the psalm's perfect passive participle to an adjective, perhaps for connection with his other uses of ἔρημος but probably simply to smooth the style (he employs the verb only at Luke 11:17).

313. Isaeus *Apollod.* 43–44 (οἶκος . . . ἐξερημῶσαι); *Menec.* 35, 43.

314. C. Williams, *Acts*, 60.

should expect Luke to have reproduced Peter's very Scripture texts, see the discussion of ancient speeches in our introduction, chapter 8. On the one hand, it is not impossible that some members of the earliest church would have remembered Peter's texts on this significant occasion; on the other, it would be within Luke's prerogative as a historian to supply the kinds of verses Peter would most plausibly be thought to have offered. On the whole, I think the implicit *gezerah shevah* probably does point to pre-Lukan tradition (it is not typical of Luke's own method of handling Scripture); if even this detail actually goes back to Peter, he likely would have given the speech in Greek.[315]

The title "Scripture" borrows standard nomenclature (as early as *Let. Aris.* 155, 168).[316] The quotation formula "as it is written" appears already even in Scripture itself[317] but grew more popular in time in the Qumran scrolls[318] and elsewhere.[319] A formula resembling "as it is written" also remained common in later rabbinic[320] and related[321] texts; these are instructive but are sometimes less close than the earlier Qumran examples.[322] Sources also often employed formulas such as "it is said."[323] Naturally, "it is written" became common in early Christian literature.[324] Although, as we have seen, some of these citation formulas are quite early, Greek use of citations may have disposed Jewish people to their abundant use of them in this period.[325]

"It is written" is common in Luke-Acts, whether for laws cited by Luke (Luke 2:23), commands cited by disputants in the narrative (cf. 4:4, 8, 10; 10:26; 19:46; Acts 7:42; 23:5), prophecies concerning John (Luke 3:4; 7:27), or messianic prophecies (24:46), including Davidic psalms (Acts 13:33) or prophecies about David's house (15:15). Other similar quotation forms also became common, though many are less common in early Christian usage. "It is written" is naturally much rarer in Greek literature,[326] which preferred verbs of speech to verbs of writing, even when appealing to written texts.[327] (Fulfillment-formula quotation forms, of the type common in Matthew, are

315. Witherington, *Acts*, 125, adds another approach: early Jewish exegetes frequently mixed text types according to which fit their argument best, including using the LXX when writing in Hebrew.

316. Hadas, *Aristeas*, 161, n. on *Let. Aris.* 155, sees this as the earliest use of the title; but cf. LXX 1 Chr 15:15; 2 Chr 30:5, 18; Ezra 6:18. Later, cf. *m. 'Ab.* 3:9–11; 5:1, 27; 6:2, 6, 7.

317. Referring to the law of Moses, it appears in, e.g., Josh 8:31; 2 Kgs 23:21; 2 Chr 23:18; 25:4; 31:3; 35:12; Ezra 3:2, 4; 6:18; Neh 8:15; 10:34, 36; Dan 9:13. Cf. 2 Sam 1:18 (referring to Jashar).

318. E.g., CD I, 13; V, 1; VII, 10; XI, 18, 20 (כי כתוב); 1QS V, 15, 17; VIII, 14. Cf. 1QM XV, 5–6, possibly quoting the Book of the War (but the text is quite fragmentary here). On the formulas and their resemblance to NT forms, cf. Fitzmyer, *Essays*, 7–16; idem, "Christianity in Light of the Scrolls," 252–53.

319. E.g., *Test. Zeb.* 3:4; *m. Git.* 9:10; *Sanh.* 10:1; *Mek. Pisha* 1.76–77; *Sipre Deut.* 56.1.2b; *y. Meg.* 1:5, §1; *Sukkah* 2:10, §1; 3:5, §1; *Ta'an.* 3:11, §5; *3 En.* 5:14; 18:7, 18, 24; 28:4, 9, 10; 31:2. Cf. "as it is written" (*Jub.* 50:12; *Test. Levi* 5:4) and "it is written" (*Jub.* 4:5; 5:18; 32:28; 33:10, 12) in the heavenly tablets. Cf. Deissmann, *Studies*, 249–50, for the legal use of such a phrase in Hellenistic papyri.

320. E.g., *m. 'Ab.* 6:10; *Git.* 9:10; *Sanh.* 10:1; *Mek. Pisha* 1.76 (וכתוב); 1.77 (וכתיב); *Sipre Deut.* 56.1.2b; *y. Meg.* 1:5, §1; *Sukkah* 2:10, §1; 3:5, §1; *Ta'an.* 3:11, §5; *Gen. Rab.* 1:4; *Num. Rab.* 19:8; cf. Sandmel, *Judaism*, 112 (noting the Gemara's *ka-katúv*); Bultmann, *Tradition*, 45.

321. In the semirabbinic apocalypse *3 Enoch*, for biblical quotations by the narrator (*3 En.* 5:14; 18:7, 18, 24; 23:1–18; 24:1–23; 28:4, 9, 10; 31:2; 35:4, 5; 38:2, 3; 40:3, 4; 42:3, 5, 6; 44:9; 46:13; 48A:3, 6; 48B:2; 48C:9–12; 48D:4; cf. 43:3; 48A:7) or heavenly beings (2:4, except A and E texts).

322. So Fitzmyer, "Quotations." The rabbis' "it is written" usually literally translates "it is said," but "written" appears in 4Q266 11 3–6 (Alexander, "IPSE DIXIT," 120).

323. For "said" instead of "written," see, e.g., CD IV, 19–20; XIX B, 15; 1QpHab VI, 2; *m. 'Ab.* 1:18; 2:13; *Mek. Pisha* 1.70–71; *'Abot R. Nat.* 36 A; cf. related formulas in 1QM XI, 5–6; CD IV, 13; V, 8; VI, 7–8, 13; VII, 8, 14; VIII, 9, 14; IX, 7–9; X, 16.

324. Outside the NT, see *1 Clem.* 4.1; 14.4; 29.2; 36.3; 39.3; 46.2; 48.2; 50.4, 6; Ign. *Eph.* 5.3; *Magn.* 12.1; *Phld.* 8.2; *Barn.* 4.14; 11.1; 14.6; 16.6; *Herm.* 7.4; Papias frg. 2.1.

325. Cf. Bovon, *Studies*, 115. In Roman court settings, citing laws, see, e.g., Quint. *Decl.* 315.3, 5 (*Scriptum est*).

326. Deissmann, *Studies*, 249–50, argues for its legal character in early Hellenistic papyri.

327. Alexander, "IPSE DIXIT," 119.

much rarer.)[328] As Fitzmyer notes, most of the "explicit quotations introduced by such formulas in Acts are found in the early chapters which deal specifically with the early Jewish Christian church."[329]

c. A New Apostle (1:21–26)

Peter now lists the qualifications, based on his exposition of Scripture (1:20), for Judas's replacement among the twelve foundational witnesses. In response, the community provides the best-qualified candidates, and the lot decides which of the two is God's choice.

i. The Qualifications (1:21–22)

Lists of qualifications were common in antiquity (e.g., 1 Tim 3:2–4; see comment on Acts 6:3). Certainly, witnesses had to be credible morally (Cic. *Flacc.* 15.34); such a restriction probably could already be safely assumed, however, among those who had persevered in following Jesus. The statement of qualifications also fits a comparable OT account of supplementing leadership (Exod 18:21).[330]

Luke here implies that this gathering of 120 (probably mostly Galilean) Jews included many original disciples besides the Twelve. This is not surprising, given other sources about Jesus's followers (1 Cor 15:6). Since the apostles had to be witnesses (Acts 1:8), choosing those who had spent the most time with Jesus was important so that they could guarantee and interpret the message about him.[331] Eyewitness sources were considered the best, and those further removed from the witnesses were considered weaker (e.g., Sen. Y. *Nat. Q.* 4.3.1).[332] Although Peter's language specifies that the witness be from the "men" who had accompanied them,[333] the new apostle's maleness is probably assumed rather than emphasized;[334] in the cultures most relevant to both Peter and Luke's audience, male testimony was nearly always accepted most highly,[335] a point relevant to the issue of "witnesses" here. Further, as noted at Acts 16:13 and the introduction, chapter 18, too much cross-gender association among leaders could play into hostile accusations. Moreover, one could argue that while Peter is a mostly reliable character, Luke does allow him to retain some views that he undoubtedly historically held at this point, without necessarily endorsing those views.[336] Finally, we should not think that Peter's description here excludes from all important leadership roles anyone who does not fit it; otherwise,

328. Fitzmyer, *Essays*, 55 (arguing against B. Gärtner on this point).

329. Fitzmyer, "Christianity in Light of the Scrolls," 253.

330. Cf. Talbert, *Acts*, 22, who also compares the setting apart of leaders in Exod 18:25; Num 27:22–23; and (perhaps implicitly) Acts 1:26.

331. See Clark, "Role," 177–80. For varied language in such summaries of Jesus's ministry, cf. Mussies, "Variation."

332. See further Jos. *Life* 357; *Ag. Ap.* 1.45–56; our introduction, ch. 4, sect. 1.d; comment on Acts 1:8.

333. Vander Stichele, "Gender," 313, sees maleness as a criterion for the new apostle here.

334. Certainly, there was at least one woman among the early "apostles" as Paul uses the term (Rom 16:7; so Chrys. *Hom. Rom.* 31; Bruce, *Mind*, 262; Dunn, *Theology of Paul*, 587; Fàbrega, "War Junia[s]?"; see discussion in Bauckham, *Women*, 172–81; possibly as itinerant missionaries [as in Lung-Kwong, *Purpose*, 29; MacDonald, "Role of Women," 163]), though none among the Twelve (how Luke usually defines "apostles").

335. E.g., Jos. *Ant.* 4.219; *Sipra VDDeho.* pq.7.45.1.1; Justin. *Inst.* 2.10.6 (though contrast the earlier Gaius *Inst.* 2.105); see further Buckland, *Roman Law*, 92, 293; Schiemann, "Intestabilis," 875; Wegner, *Chattel*, 120–23; outside forensic settings, cf., e.g., Avianus *Fables* 15–16. Women did testify under some circumstances (cf., e.g., Davies and Taylor, "Testimony"; Rothstein, "Testimony").

336. E.g., contrast Peter's confession in 10:28 with the implications of his theology in 2:17, 39. Admittedly, Luke later confronts Peter's approach to Gentiles more forcefully than he addresses his view of gender, but the gender implications of 2:17–18 and their fleshing out elsewhere (cf. 21:9) might be relevant here.

it would exclude Paul and Barnabas (accepted as apostles at least in Acts 14:4, 14) and James (cf. 15:13; 21:18).[337]

That Jesus went "in and out among" them is Semitic idiom for association and freedom of movement, often long and close (in 9:28, perhaps only close).[338] Those who "accompanied"[339] Jesus and the Twelve presumably are those who participated in his journeys, including Luke's long travel narrative (Luke 9:51–19:44) and Jesus's final journey (23:49, 55), which had brought most of Peter's listeners there ("Galileans," Acts 1:11; 13:31).[340] If we may judge by Luke's more expansive descriptions of events in his "we" narratives, he valued the testimony especially of companions.

Luke could recount Jesus's story accurately because he had investigated how it happened "from the beginning" (Luke 1:3),[341] presumably by depending on those who were eyewitnesses (1:2) "from the beginning" (Acts 1:21; cf. John 15:27).[342] Thorough historians liked to address their topics "from the beginning" (ἀπ᾽ ἀρχῆς, Diod. Sic. 4.8.5). (In biographical literature, this often means starting with the person's adulthood or public career.)[343] For many early Christians, "the beginning" of the gospel story was Jesus's introduction by John (Mark 1:1–4; John 1:19–37; Acts 10:37; 13:24).

The outline of the gospel story to which they are witnesses (Acts 1:22) includes the part of the story that Luke's Gospel covers after the introductory infancy narratives; early Christians often started the narration with John's ministry, even when they also rooted it in prior Scripture (Acts 10:37; 13:24; Mark 1:1, 4; John 1:19–37). Although their testimony includes all of Jesus's ministry (Acts 10:39), its focus is Jesus's resurrection (Luke 24:46, 48; Acts 1:22; 2:32; 3:15; 4:33; 5:31–32; 10:40–41; 13:30–31).[344] The ministry of John the Baptist is attested outside the NT, in Josephus, as is widely noted.[345] We may note in passing the contrast between the status of the new apostle and the fate of Judas (Acts 1:18).[346]

337. See Gaventa, *Acts*, 71. Paul includes among the apostles also James (Gal 1:19; cf. 1 Cor 15:7) and apparently his own coworkers, Silvanus and Timothy (1 Thess 2:6; on Timothy, see, e.g., Ambrosiaster *Comm.* [CSEL 81:190; Bray, *Corinthians*, 187]; *pace* Bruce, *Thessalonians*, 31).

338. E.g., Num 27:17; Deut 31:2; 1 Sam 18:13, 16; 29:6; 2 Sam 3:25; 1 Kgs 3:7; 2 Chr 1:10; with Lake and Cadbury, *Commentary*, 14. Cf. also Deut 28:6, 19; Josh 14:11; 1 Sam 29:6; 2 Kgs 19:27; Ps 121:8; Isa 37:28; Jer 17:19; 37:4; *Jub.* 35:6; CD XI, 10; Acts 9:28; John 10:7; *m. Mid.* 1:3.

339. Of thirty uses of συνέρχομαι in the NT, more than half (sixteen) occur in Acts, though only two in the Gospel.

340. See Tannehill, *Acts*, 23.

341. In the case of Luke 1:3, this may include the infancy narratives (traditions from James and ultimately Mary); cf. Acts 26:4 for Paul's background. Ancient historians such as Herodotus and Thucydides consulted with family members for information (Byrskog, *History*, 82–83), and Byrskog argues persuasively that early Christians would have regarded Jesus's relatives, including James and Mary, as authoritative sources (83–90).

342. Johannine literature also speaks of the "beginning" of believers' own experience of the good news (1 John 2:7, 24; 3:11; 2 John 5–6).

343. E.g., Plut. *Caes.* 1.1–4; Jos. *Life* 1–12; also *Life of Aesop* in Drury, *Design*, 29; see Burridge, *Gospels*, 197–98.

344. Smith, "Comparison of Tradition," 174–75, presses this emphasis to the exclusion of teaching (against Gerhardsson), but one wonders if Luke's *emphasis* should be pressed so far (as against, e.g., Matthew's); the sayings material in the Gospel suggests that even Luke would have been less restrictive than Smith thinks. Cf. Eddy and Boyd, *Legend*, 286–91.

345. See Abrahams, *Studies* (1), 30–35; Meier, "John the Baptist"; Webb, *Baptizer*. One should discount, however, the Slavonic additions between Jos. *War* 2 and *War* 3 (LCL, 3:644–45).

346. For the importance of comparing characters, cf. the prominence of *synkrisis* in rhetoric (e.g., Hermog. *Progymn.* 8, "On Syncrisis," 18–20). For an extensive and helpful contrast between Peter and Judas, see Parsons, *Acts*, 31–32.

II. The Candidates (1:23)

That they put forward two candidates who met the qualifications may suggest a practice in which disciples would put forward candidates they thought best for apostolic ratification (see comment on Acts 6:3; cf. Deut 1:13), in this case (for numerical reasons) narrowed down further and ratified by divine choice (Acts 1:26). (Where assemblies consisted of newer disciples, founding leaders apparently selected the leaders themselves [14:23; cf. Titus 1:5].) Luke has not introduced these individuals before, but a reader might infer that they probably belonged to the seventy/seventy-two whom Jesus had already sent on an earlier occasion (Luke 10:1).[347]

Not surprisingly, "Joseph" was a very common name (cf., in Luke-Acts alone, Luke 1:27; 3:24, 30; 23:50; Acts 4:36; 7:13–14),[348] requiring here some distinguishing epithets.[349] Historians often concerned themselves with distinguishing various historic people with the same name (sometimes distinguishing *too* thoroughly, when only a single person was actually in view).[350] Multiple names appear frequently in ancient business documents and even funerary inscriptions.[351] In Roman Asia, for example, the use of two or more names was normal (often with such phrases as "x, who is also y").[352] Nicknames are widely attested[353] and were especially common in Palestine "because so many people tended to have the same first name."[354] Regardless of the historic origin of double names in the Hebrew Bible, they were generally accepted as part of a venerable and seamless tradition by the apostolic period;[355] thus Horeb was Sinai (Exod 3:1; 19:11; 24:13) and Jethro was probably Reuel (2:18; 3:1; 4:18; 18:1–12; Num 10:29).[356]

Cornelius Nepos opines that in human history only one Aristides displayed such integrity as to merit the title *Justus* ("the just"; Corn. Nep. 3 [Aristides], 1.2), but this claim is certainly hyperbolic.[357] The name and the nickname are both common (e.g., Acts 18:7; Col 4:11). (Roman surnames often sounded like nicknames because the surnames originally began as nicknames; see Plut. *Cic.* 1.2.)[358] Apparently,

347. The number may be symbolic for the nations, as the number of the twelve is for Israel, or it might allude to the number of elders who received the Spirit with Moses; see the discussion at Acts 6:3.

348. E.g., in Jerusalem, *CIJ* 2:281, §1291; Luke lacked reason to include Caiaphas's first name. "Joseph" was the only non-Hasmonean name as popular as Hasmonean ones in first-century Palestine (Williams, "Names," 108–9; it appears widely across social levels in Palestine and the Diaspora, Williams, "Names," 89).

349. On epitheton, see Anderson, *Glossary*, 52–53.

350. E.g., Polyb. 9.24.5; Dion. Hal. *Din.* 1; Plut. *Themist.* 32.1, 5; Philost. *Vit. soph.* 1.483; in mythology, e.g., Ajax (Philost. *Hrk.* 23.21; 32.33; 33.39; 35.1); "Heracles" (Arrian *Alex.* 2.16.1–3; 4.28.2; *Ind.* 5.13; Appian *Hist. rom.* 6.1.2); Plato (philosopher vs. comic poet, Hor. *Sat.* 2.3.11); and others (Arrian *Alex.* 2.16.4). Cf. Symm. *Ep.* 1.2.2; two people named John Eck in Luther's day (in Bainton, *Stand*, 182).

351. E.g., P.Oxy. 494.32; 1273.3, 49; *CPJ* 2:140, §§248–49; 2:143, §261; 2:145, §§269–70; 2:146, §274; 2:147, §275; 2:147, §276; 2:151, §298; 2:153, §304; 2:154, §311; 2:156, §321; 3:9, §453; *CIJ* 1:24, §30; 2:111, §879.

352. Matthews, "Names, Greek," 1023.

353. On nicknames, see, e.g., Dion. Hal. *Ant. rom.* 7.2.4; Philost. *Hrk.* 14.4; Gen 29–30; cf. the "Goliath" family in Hachlili and Killebrew, "Byt glyt"; and by contrast, "Samuel the small" in *y. Soṭah* 9:13, §2.

354. Williams, "Names," 106. In the Diaspora, Jews made less use of alternative, ethnic-specific names than Egyptians did (Williams, "Alternative Names").

355. Double names were also standard in the culture (e.g., *CIJ* 1:24, §30; 2:111, §879; *CPJ* 2:143, §261; Leon, *Jews of Rome*, 107, 111; Acts 1:23; Wilkinson, *Jerusalem*, 47–48).

356. The Hebrew term translated "father-in-law" may also allow "brother-in-law" or another relative in some of these cases. Cf. also "Jacob" and "Israel"; "Elohim" and "YHWH" (though variant names also occur in Egyptian inscriptions and other ancient sources; see Kitchen, *Orient*, 121–22). For dual names in Bronze Age Mesopotamia and the Levant, see Cole, "Numbers," 355.

357. Cornelius Nepos himself notes another figure surnamed "the good" (19 [Phocion], 1.1).

358. Most people had one name, but Roman citizens had three names (see comment on Acts 13:9), just as some Greeks had surnames (Appian *Hist. rom.* pref. 13). In Rome's Jewish inscriptions, Latin users had

Jesus's younger brother James eventually took the surname "the Just."[359] Since Joseph Barsabbas was Galilean (Acts 1:21, 23), he may have acquired the nickname near Greco-Roman Tiberias,[360] or "Justus" may transliterate a later Latin translation of the Hebrew הצדיק, "the righteous one," "one of several honorific nicknames" in Palestinian Judaism (for Jesus, cf. Acts 3:14; 7:52; 22:14).[361] Rare in Cyrene and Egypt, the name is more common in Greece, Gaul, and Asia Minor;[362] but whatever Justus's possible earlier experience abroad, the aorist ἐπεκλήθη argues against this being a nickname later appended from missions work abroad. As a nickname rather than a given name, it is suitable enough even in Palestine.

The Aramaic nickname "Barsabbas" means "son of the Sabbath" and would have been applied to someone born on the Sabbath (cf. 15:22; like various "Sabbath" compounded names found in both Palestine and the Diaspora).[363] According to a second-century tradition, which Papias attributed to one of Philip's daughters, Barsabbas was unharmed when he drank poison.[364] "Matthias" and "Mattathias" were common names (e.g., 1 Macc 2, passim; 16:14), though apparently not so common among the disciples as to require a surname here.[365]

III. GOD'S CHOICE (1:24)

The recognition that God knows the heart is used to support the Spirit's testimony to the genuineness of Gentile conversions in Acts 15:7–8.[366] Dunn argues that the use of the same language both here and in that passage highlights the contrast between that incident, empowered by the Spirit, and this one before Pentecost.[367] But the use of the same language more likely suggests continuity than contrast, at least in this case; Jesus cites God's knowledge of hearts to condemn the Pharisees for valuing merely what is externally valuable (Luke 16:15).[368] It was natural to appeal to this principle in depending on God to reveal the appropriate leader (1 Sam 16:7).[369]

---

double and triple names far more often than Greek (Leon, *Jews of Rome*, 111–13), though Semitic names are rarely combined with others (107).

359. Euseb. *H.E.* 2.23.4–7; *G. Thom.* 12 (*NHL* 119); cf. Klausner, *Jesus of Nazareth*, 41.

360. For the name in Palestine, see, e.g., *CIJ* 2:135, §928; 2:143, §946; 2:169, §983; 2:171, §986; 2:235, §1197; 2:253, §1233; Jos. *Life* 36, 338, 346, 350, 357–60, 410.

361. Williams, "Names," 104; cf. Bruce, *Commentary*, 50. It appeared primarily as a nickname there, not as a first or second name.

362. Williams, "Names," 104; cf. Hemer, *Acts in History*, 221–22. For Diaspora Jews, see, e.g., *CIJ* 1:8, §3; 1:15, §13; 1:88, §125; 1:160, §224; 1:172, §240; 1:175, §245; 1:279, §357; 1:279, §358; 1:280, §359; 1:366–67, §502; 1:393, §533; 1:427, §583; 1:478, §666; 1:481, §670.

363. Williams, "Names," 101–2; cf. Carter and Earle, *Acts*, 22; cf. the Jerusalem ossuary in Yamauchi, *Stones*, 121.

364. Papias frg. 3.9 (*AF*) (= frg. 6 in ANF 1:154); Euseb. *H.E.* 3.39.9; cf. Mark 16:18. Noted also in Fitzmyer, *Acts*, 226–27.

365. Also 3Q15 II, 5; Jos. *Ant.* 17.151; *Life* 7; *Let. Aris.* 47; *CIJ* 2:309, §1361; 2:309, §1362a; 2:310, §1362b; Luke 3:25–26; see also comment on "Matthew" at Acts 1:13. Some note the unlikely later legend of Matthias's martyrdom in Ethiopia (Blaiklock, *Acts*, 53).

366. Outside these two passages, the only other use of the term in the earliest Christian texts is *Herm.* 31.4, which may reflect Luke's terminology.

367. Dunn, *Acts*, 21. Barrett, *Acts*, 94, also contrasts pre- and post-Pentecost guidance, though affirming the legitimacy of Matthias's choice.

368. Cf. perhaps God's knowledge of the future state of hearts in Luke 2:35.

369. Closer to the wording is 1 Kgs 8:39 (//2 Chr 6:30), where, at the temple's dedication, Solomon prays that God will answer people's prayers according to the integrity of their hearts. Some find temple themes in Luke's following context; the following context of 1 Kgs 8:41–43 also addresses the welcoming of Gentiles in God's house (a point prefigured in Acts 2:5–11). But the idea is frequent enough (1 Chr 28:9; Prov 24:12; Jer 12:3), and Acts may borrow the language without emphasizing the context. (Acts 2:39 offers a covert allusion to the Gentile mission, but not as covert as this one would be.)

God's omniscience, particularly concerning hearts, is widely cited in early Christianity (e.g., Rom 8:27; 1 John 3:20; Rev 2:23; *Acts Paul* 3.24). It is also emphasized in Greco-Roman antiquity in general[370] (where some high gods knew[371] or saw[372] all things) and especially in ancient Judaism.[373] This omniscience also entailed knowledge of persons' hearts[374] (as, again, often for the highest deities among the Gentiles),[375] so that God "who knows" or "searches" the heart (Ps 7:9; Jer 17:10) became a familiar designation for God in later texts.[376] Long before the first century, Jewish people called God the ἐπίσκοπος (and synonyms), the one who oversees all things,[377] especially concerning human hearts.[378] That God sees yet remains unseen seems to have become a popular saying.[379]

The assembly's prayer[380] indicates that they are depending on God to provide the right replacement for Judas. The Lord's "choosing" Matthias (Acts 1:24) provides continuity with his "choosing" other apostles in 1:2 (cf. Luke 6:13).[381] Acts repeat-

370. The gods have access to all knowledge (Mus. Ruf. 1, p. 32.17–18; tongue-in-cheek, cf. Lucian *Phal.* 1.1). Thales opined that one should guard the purity of one's mind, since the gods know all thoughts (Val. Max. 7.2.ext. 8; Diog. Laert. 1.36). I draw here from Keener, *John*, 532.

371. E.g., Hom. *Od.* 4.468; 13.417; 20.75; Pindar *Pyth.* 3.28; Xen. *Cav. Com.* 9.9; Plut. *Isis* 1, *Mor.* 351E; Athen. *Deipn.* 5.218F; Mus. Ruf. 1, p. 32.17–18; Max. Tyre 3.1; Philost. *Hrk.* 16.4. Cf. the claim for Caesar in Ovid *Pont.* 4.9.125–28; a hero in Philost. *Hrk.* 43.3; the function of oracles in Aune, *Prophecy*, 68. At one point, a mortal suggests that the gods know all things (Hom. *Od.* 4.379), but the deity, who does not know, must refer him to another (4.382–93) who does know (4.472–80).

372. E.g., Hom. *Il.* 3.277; Hesiod *Theog.* 514; Aeschylus *Eum.* 1045; *Suppl.* 139, 210, 303–5; Ap. Rhod. 2.1123, 1133, 1179; cf. Aristoph. *Birds* 1058; Ovid *Metam.* 13.852–53.

373. E.g., Jos. *Ag. Ap.* 2.181, claiming that all Jews agree; Sir 39:19; Bar 3:32; Sus 42; *Let. Aris.* 210; *Sib. Or.* 1.151; 3.12; *1 En.* 9:5; 39:11; 84:3; CD II, 9–10; *2 Bar.* 21:8; cf. *Tg. Ps.-J.* on Gen 3:9; 16:13; *Tg. Neof.* 1 on Gen 1:9; "God of knowledge" in 4Q504 4 4; 4Q510 1 2; 4Q511 1 7.

374. 4Q180 2–4 II, 5–10 (explaining Gen 18:21); 4Q299 3 II, 10–11; *1 En.* 63:3; *Pss. Sol.* 9:3; 14:8; 17:25; *Let. Aris.* 132–33, 189; Jos. *Ag. Ap.* 2.166; *Ant.* 4.41; Philo *Prov.* 2.35; *Test. Jud.* 20.3–4; *Test. Zeb.* 5:2; *Test. Naph.* 2:4–5; *t. B. Qam.* 7:2; *y. Roš Haš.* 1:3, §§39–42; *Exod. Rab.* 21:3; 43:3; 46:3. See also the sixth-century C.E. synagogue inscription in Carmon, *Inscriptions*, §185, pp. 85, 188–89; numerous targumic references in Lane, *Hebrews*, 103.

375. See, e.g., Hesiod *W.D.* 267; Eurip. *El.* 1176; Xen. *Cyr.* 5.4.31; *Mem.* 1.1.19; Epict. *Diatr.* 2.14.11; Val. Max. 7.2.ext. 8.

376. E.g., *PGM* 4.3046–48; Philo *Spec. Laws* 3.52; Rom 8:27; *t. Sanh.* 8:3; *b. Ber.* 58a (attributed to Ben Zoma); *Gen. Rab.* 67:8; *Exod. Rab.* 14:3; *Acts Paul* 3.24 (*Paul Thec.* 24); cf. Marmorstein, *Names*, 73, 79, 86. One finds similar designations in other societies (e.g., Mbiti, *Religions*, 39), and the monotheistic emphasis continues in Islam, where Allah is All-knowing (Qur'an 3.73; 4.128, 130, 177; 5.54, 97; 24.64; 36.78; 49.16; 57.3; 58.7; 64.4), the Knower (e.g., 4.11, 17, 26, 32, 35, 70, 104, 111; 6.3, 13, 18, 60, 74; 8.71; 9.15, 16, 28, 60, 106, 110; 12.6, 83; 17.17; 31.28; 49.13; 67.14), seer (40.44; 67.19), seer or knower of deeds (33.9; 34.11; 48.24; 49.17; 57.4; 58.3, 13; 63.11; 64.2, 8), knower and seer (17.96), Watcher over all things (33.52; witness of all, 33.55; 34.47; 58.6), knower of all hidden and invisible things, especially hearts (5.116; 9.78; 13.9; 16.19; 32.6; 34.48; 39.46; 42.24; 49.17; 50.16; 57.6; 59.22; 60.1; 62.8; 64.4, 18; 72.26; 84.23; including sins, 25.58; sincerity, 29.3, 11; secrets, 33.54); hears and sees all (e.g., 4.134, 135, 148; 5.76; 7.200; 40.20, 56; hearer and knower, 8.17, 42, 61; 24.21, 60; 26.220; 29.5, 60; 31.28; 44.6; 49.1; 58.1); knows hearts (5.7; he knows what humans do, 11.123); is Knower, wise (22.52; 24.18, 38–39; 33.1; 34.1; 48.4; 43.84; 49.8; 60.10), mighty and wise or knower (35.2; 36.37; 39.1; 40.2, 8; 41.12; 42.3, 50; 43.9; 45.2, 37; 46.2; 48.7, 19; 57.1; 59.1, 24; 62.1, 3; 64.18).

377. E.g., Wis 7:23; 2 Macc 7:35; *Let. Aris.* 16; *Sib. Or.* frg. 1.3, 4; 1.152; 2.177. God watches especially the ways of the righteous; e.g., *Test. Benj.* 4:3; 6:6; *4 Bar.* 7:35. Greeks also spoke of chief deities as ἐπίσκοποι of all human life (e.g., Theon *Progymn.* 11.194; Epict. *Diatr.* 1.14.1, 9; 1.30.1; cf. Xen. *Cyr.* 8.7.22; Ap. Rhod. 2.1123, 1133, 1179; Callim. *Hymns* 3 [to Artemis], line 39; Plut. *Isis* 51, *Mor.* 371E; Xenophanes in Diog. Laert. 9.2.19; Ps.-Callisth. *Alex.* 1.33; Porph. *Marc.* 12.205–6).

378. E.g., *m. 'Ab.* 2:1; Wis 1:6; among Greeks, Callim. *Aetia* 3.85.15.

379. E.g., Plut. *Isis* 75, *Mor* 381B; *PGM* 13.62; Ps.-Euripides in "Fragments of Pseudo-Greek Poets," *OTP* 2:828; Philo *Creation* 69.

380. Haenchen, *Acts*, 162, suggests that the prayer was uttered in unanimity. For discussion, see comment on Acts 4:24–30.

381. Also Lake and Cadbury, *Commentary*, 15; Crowe, *Acts*, 6–7.

edly stresses the divine plan (see comment on Acts 2:23); dependence on God's omniscience here supports the choice that will occur in Acts 1:26.

The Spirit uses various forms of guidance after Pentecost; although drawing lots is not one of them,[382] we should certainly not question its value in Acts 1. Luke's first narrative in the Gospel includes God's directly selecting Zechariah by lot (Luke 1:9)[383] before sending those with prophetic ministry (1:15–17, 67); his first narrative in Acts after recapitulating the Gospel's ending includes a leader selected by lot before the prophetic empowerment of the church (Acts 2:17–18). The parallel use of lots suggests analogous divine superintendence in both cases.

Do the disciples here invoke Jesus as "Lord" in prayer (cf. 1 Cor 16:22; 2 Cor 12:8–9), or do they address God the Father?[384] Luke frequently uses "Lord" for Jesus (e.g., Acts 2:21, 36; 4:33; 9:10–11, 15, 17, 27–28; 11:16, 17, 20; 15:11; 16:31; 19:5, 13, 17; 20:21, 24, 35; 21:13; 22:10; 26:15; 28:31), including in the immediate context (1:21), sometimes even in prayer (7:59–60).[385] Further, Jesus "chose" the other eleven (Acts 1:2; Luke 6:13), and so it is reasonable to suppose that he does the choosing here (Acts 1:24). Yet Luke regards the title as applicable to both (see Luke 20:42; Acts 2:34) and hence also applies the title to Jesus's Father (e.g., Luke 1:16, 32; 2:22–24, 29; 4:8; Acts 4:26), including in prayer (Luke 10:21; Acts 4:24). Perhaps the analogous prayer in Acts 4:24–30 shifts the weight in favor of addressing the Father, since that prayer addresses the Father in the second person and speaks of the Son in the third.

iv. Judas's Place (1:25)

Historians, like rhetoricians in legal settings, commonly imputed motives, though someone who disagreed could attribute the imputation to malice (as in Plut. *Mal. Hdt.* 25, *Mor.* 861DE). One may contrast the typical positive eulogies offered for the fallen in classical Athens and elsewhere.[386]

Because Judas abandoned his apostleship and service (see comment on Acts 1:17 regarding the latter), someone else would take that "place" (τόπον)[387] while he would go to his own "place" (τόπον).[388] Judas abandoned his calling for land (Acts 1:18), leaving the literal land desolate (1:20a; cf. Matt 27:7) but his oversight position available for another to take (Acts 1:20b). His "place," then, is, in the first case, his office but, in the second, the field he bought, where he met his gory end.[389] "His

---

382. Bede *Comm. Acts* 1.26 warns against inferring too much from their use here.

383. This is not a purely modern observation; Bede *Comm. Acts* 1.26 (trans. L. Martin, 20; Martin, *Acts*, 18) also compares the use of lots in the case of Zechariah in Luke 1.

384. See Lake and Cadbury, *Commentary*, 15, who settle on the Father (though noting that καρδιογνῶστα applies to Christ in the later *Apost. Const.* 3.7.8). Ladd, *Young Church*, 50–51, and Talbert, *Acts*, 21, apply it to Jesus. (Talbert helpfully compares Luke 10:2; but his examples of Jesus's knowing hearts in 5:22 and 7:39–40 seem less compelling than Acts 15:8; see comment on Acts 1:24 above.)

385. Jesus is also often "Lord" in the Gospel (e.g., Luke 2:11; 6:5, 46; 7:13, 19; 10:1, 41; 11:39; 12:42; 13:15; 22:61; 24:3, 34); vocatives can mean "Sir," but surely after the resurrection, they convey something more (Acts 1:6).

386. E.g., Thucyd. 2.34.8–2.46.2; *b. Šabb.* 153a; Lebram, "Literarische Form," on 4 Macc 3:19–18:24; see fuller comment in the section "Mourning" of the excursus "Burial and Mourning Practices and Stephen's Death" at Acts 8:2.

387. Sinaiticus's reading κλῆρος also makes good sense of the context (Acts 1:17, which it may reflect), but τόπον (𝔓⁷⁴ A B) has wider geographic distribution and appears the likelier reading here (Metzger, *Textual Commentary*, 288). "Lot" and "place" appear synonymous in 1QS II, 23 (Barrett, *Acts*, 103).

388. Gaventa, *Acts*, 70, suggests a connection between his "turning aside to go" and similar movement in Luke 22:3–4 (after Satan entered Judas, he "went"). Though not impossible, this connection does not appear strong.

389. Going to one's "place" can mean going home (Gen 30:25; 1 Sam 2:20; cf. Exod 18:23; 1 Sam 14:46). Johnson, *Acts*, 37, notes that it sometimes applies to "one's place of final destiny" (citing Tob 3:6; *1 Clem.*

own [ἴδιον] place" contrasts with the disciples who left their "own" (ἴδια) property to follow Jesus (Luke 18:28; cf. Acts 4:32) and possibly with the new community whom the apostles received in return (Acts 4:23; 24:23; cf. Luke 18:29–30).[390]

v. "The Eleven" (1:26)

The primary emphasis of Acts 1:15–26 is the selection of a twelfth apostle to prepare for Israel's renewal and restoration.[391] Why was it necessary to restore the number from "eleven" (Luke 24:9, 33) to twelve?[392] Though only one answer stands out above the rest, one could offer many possible associations with the number twelve. Twelve was a significant number throughout the ancient Mediterranean world.[393] Classical Greek religion had twelve chief deities on Olympus, often called simply the "twelve gods" (δώδεκα θεοί).[394] The number remained from tradition even though some specific members of the pantheon changed over the centuries[395] (a potential explanation for divergent lists of the Twelve if multiple names were not so common). Ancients regularly noted the twelve signs of the zodiac,[396] and some referred to them simply as "the twelve" (e.g., Aratus *Phaen.* 703, 740).[397] Persians appointed twelve leaders over their groups, following the pattern of their twelve tribes.[398] Rabbis spoke of "the twelve" with reference to the twelve biblical "minor prophets."[399]

Yet despite various significations attached to the number twelve in various circles, for Luke and other biblically informed early Christians, it surely carried the same connotations for which Jesus presumably chose it. Twelve naturally could symbolize the twelve tribes of Israel, and many contemporary interpreters understood other references to "twelve" in this manner (even the twelve signs of

---

5:4; Ign. *Magn.* 5.1; but Tob 3:6 refers to death and Ignatius probably depends on Acts 1:25); Witherington, *Acts*, 122, and Barrett, *Acts*, 103, read it as a euphemism for hell (cf. Luke 16:25). For death (but applicable to all persons), cf. Eccl 3:20; 6:6.

390. Note also the contrast with Peter's own "other place" in Acts 12:17 (in Land, *Diffusion*, 177, 226). Acts 28:30 does not fit the pattern, but it was the most coherent way for Luke to say what he needed.

391. With, e.g., Pao, *Isaianic Exodus*, 123–29.

392. Pythagoreans provoked much ancient numerical symbolism (cf. Laroche, "Numbers"; Menken, *Techniques*, 27–29), and their influence was known (e.g., Plut. *E Delph.* 8, *Mor.* 388C), though Israel's "twelve tribes" certainly predate Pythagoras.

393. E.g., Rome's Law of the Twelve Tables (Tac. *Ann.* 3.27); twelve servants in *Jos. Asen.* 3:2/3 (cf. seven in 2:6); *Test. Ab.* 2:5 A.

394. E.g., Aristoph. *Knights* 235; Menander *Kolax* E232; *Fabula Incerta* 8.11, 172; Alciph. *Court.* 18 (Menander to Glycera), 2.3, ¶8; Polyb. 4.39.6; Apollod. *Bib.* 3.14.2; Lucian *Parl. G.* 15; Paus. 1.3.3; Libanius *Descr.* 25.5; see further Guthrie, *Greeks and Gods*, 110–12; Phillips, "Twelve gods." Cf. a group of twelve deities in Livy 22.10.9 (Purcell, "Consentes Di"); Romans used twelve rods to symbolize the two consuls (Val. Max. 1.1.3).

395. Aune, "Religion," 919; Kearns, "Religion, Greek," 1301.

396. E.g., Pliny E. *N.H.* 2.3.9; Petron. *Sat.* 35; cf. the twelve elements of heaven in *PGM* 36.19.

397. Cf. zodiacal associations with the twelve tribes in, e.g., Philo *Mos.* 2.112, 124–26; *Rewards* 65; *Pesiq. Rab Kah.* 16:5; *Pesiq. Rab.* 4:1; 29/30A:6. Cf. later Mithraic and Christian associations with the zodiac (Deman, "Mithras and Christ," 517, including the twelve apostles; in Mithraism, Beck, "Zodiac"; Campbell, *Iconography*, 44–90). Some Jews connected temple symbolism (Philo *Heir* 221–25; *QE* 2.73, 79; Jos. *War* 5.217) or the priest's breastplate (Philo *Mos.* 2.123–24; Jos. *Ant.* 3.186) with the zodiac; cf. also the later synagogue zodiacs (e.g., *CIJ* 2:212–13, §1162; 2:240–42, §1206; 2:242, §1207; Narkiss, "Elements," 186; May, "Synagogues," 9; Shanks, "Zodiac"; Hachlili, "Zodiac"; idem, "Zodiac in Art"; Gutmann, "Beth Alpha," 299; Weiss, "Mosaic"; Meyers, "Synagogues," 106), presumably depicting God over creation (cf. Philo *Dreams* 2.112; *Sib. Or.* 13.69–71; *Tr. Shem* passim; rabbis would have understood these monotheistically; Miller, "Rabbis"; as also in early Christianity, Oster, "Windows"). Arator *Acts* 1 (Martin, *Acts*, 16) compares the constellations even here!

398. Xen. *Cyr.* 1.2.5 (for Xenophon's firsthand knowledge of Persia, see Xen. *Anab.* passim). Division into twelve tribes appears elsewhere (cf. Gen 17:20; 25:16; cf. Noth, *History*, 85–97); Alexander could also divide his army into twelve parts (Arrian *Alex.* 5.29.1).

399. E.g., *y. Meg.* 1.9, §12.

the zodiac).[400] Jesus undoubtedly selected twelve[401] as representatives[402] for the righteous remnant of the eschatological people of God,[403] in a manner analogous to the twelve select leaders in Qumran texts (e.g., 1QS VIII, 1–2; 4Q259 II, 9),[404] as is widely noted.[405]

That the title "the twelve" remained for Paul even after Judas's death (1 Cor 15:5) suggests a representative function for the number.[406] The church that was built on this foundation of the twelve leaders of Israel's remnant represents the true heir of God's ancient promises.[407] The twelve apostles may be viewed as akin to the twelve patriarchs (cf. Rev 21:12, 14) or to the princes of the tribes (cf. Num 2:3–29; 7:11, 18–78; 17:6), who would rule over the tribes at the time of their eschatological restoration (Luke 22:30//Matt 19:28).[408] In Luke's perspective, in contrast to the unfaithful leaders of Israel in Acts 3–5, the apostles become the true leaders for Israel, who should have been followed by the Jewish people.[409] (Less significant for Luke but perhaps significant to some in his audience was the effectiveness of this number of witnesses; legal documents typically settled for half as many.)[410]

It was common to refer to groups of leaders by their number. In classical Athens, the Eleven (cf. Acts 1:26; 2:14; Luke 24:9, 33) were the police magistrates supervising prison and executions.[411] The Thirty were a group of tyrants who held power in Athens for a time;[412] in David's kingdom, a group with the same numerical title (and varied membership) represented David's elite military corps (2 Sam 23:13, 18–19, 23–24; 1 Chr 11:11, 15, 20, 25; 12:4, 18; 27:6). Athens also knew another group, the Four Hundred, who appear rather frequently in the sources considering how quickly they fell from power.[413] In addition, Athens had a ruling council called the Six Hundred

---

400. E.g., Philo *Mos.* 2.112, 124–26; *Rewards* 65; *Pesiq. Rab Kah.* 16:5; *Pesiq. Rab.* 4:1; 29/30A:6; cf. Jos. *War* 5.217.

401. Although Luke may use an estimate in Acts 19:7 ("about" twelve) to evoke the original twelve (paralleling Paul with Jesus), the allusion in his clearer "the twelve" (6:2; Luke 8:1; 9:1, 12; 18:31; 22:3, 47) is surely to the twelve tribes (Acts 7:8; 26:7; Luke 22:30).

402. Contrary to some who share this perspective, however, "their significance" may well be "evocative and not constitutive"; see Richardson, *Israel*, 61.

403. E.g., Jeremias, *Theology*, 234–35. Thus they mark Jesus's movement as a renewal movement within Judaism (e.g., Charlesworth, *Jesus within Judaism*, 138), a frequent scholarly understanding of the earliest Jesus movement (cf., e.g., Horsley, "Movements").

404. Cf. also 1QM II, 1–3; 4Q159 2–4 3–6; 4Q164 1 4–5. For "twelve" in Qumran and other literature, see also Geyser, "Tribes," 392.

405. See Bruce, "Jesus," 75–76; Harrington, *God's People*, 39; Sanders, *Jesus and Judaism*, 104; cf. Jervell, *Luke and People of God*, 82, 89.

406. Jeremias, *Theology*, 234; Sanders, *Jesus and Judaism*, 99–101.

407. The tradition of the Twelve—which is older than any given list of the names themselves—is a nearly certain bedrock tradition going back to the historical Jesus (Sanders, *Jesus and Judaism*, 11, 98–101; Witherington, *Christology of Jesus*, 126–27; Ehrman, *Prophet*, 186–87; Charlesworth, *Jesus within Judaism*, 137). (In contrast to the slight variations in the canonical lists, one may compare the forms in the Apostolic Church Orders and the *Epistula apostolorum* [Lake, "Twelve," 41].)

408. Bauckham, "James," 430 (citing the views of Spencer and Daube, not his own). For the eschatological hope for the twelve tribes, Acts 26:7; see Sanders, *Judaism*, 291 (citing, e.g., 1QM II, 2–3; 11QTᵃ VIII, 14–16; LVII, 5–6).

409. Clark, "Role," 173–77, esp. 174.

410. Six in, e.g., P.Col. 270.1.25–28; *BGU* 1273.36–40; P.Cair.Zen. 59001.48–52; P.Eleph. 1.16–18; P.Tebt. 104.34–35.

411. E.g., Isaeus *Nicost.* 28; Lysias *Or.* 10.16, §117; 13.86, §138; 11.5, §119; 14.17, §141; 15.3, §144; Xen. *Hell.* 1.7.10; 2.3.54; Lucian *Indictment* 5. See also MacDowell, "Eleven." Cf. Allison, *Jesus*, 69.

412. E.g., Xen. *Mem.* 4.4.3; *Hell.* 2.3.11; Dio Chrys. *Or.* 43.8; Plut. *Lys.* 21.1–2; Paus. 1.29.3; Philost. *Vit. soph.* 1.16.501; see at greater length Gagarin, "Thirty Tyrants" (also noting a board called "the Ten"); Rhodes, "Triakonta."

413. Lysias *Or.* 13.70, §136; Thucyd. 8.68.2; 8.70.1; 8.86.1; 8.92.2, 6; 8.93.1–2; Xen. *Hell.* 2.3.30, 45; Plut. *Alc.* 26.2; 27.1; Philost. *Vit. soph.* 1.15.498. On the Four Hundred, see further Andrewes and Rhodes,

(which replaced the Five Hundred).[414] Rome had groups of cultic officials called the Fifteen, the Seven, and so forth.[415] "The Ten" referred to the board of *decemviri*;[416] "the Fifteen" to the fifteen priests in Rome guarding the Sibylline Books.[417] Rome's *centumviri* (lit. "100 men")[418] was a court that had 105 men during the republic but 180 during the empire.[419] Luke himself speaks of the "seven" (Acts 21:7) and "the seventy-two" (or "the seventy"; Luke 10:17).[420]

Paul may refer to the "twelve" as a group (1 Cor 15:5) even after the betrayal (which he probably knows, 11:23); groups once named for numbers (such as the Hundred) retained these names even when the actual membership numbers fluctuated.[421] (Some early church fathers felt that Matthias must have been chosen before Jesus's ascension, so that the number remained twelve during the resurrection appearances, as in 1 Cor 15:5;[422] but in view of ancient usage for defined groups this interpretation is not strictly necessary.) Some ancients did feel that an official number of members in a small group of leaders could function as an average, with more or fewer persons at different times in practice, depending on who was most qualified.[423] Roughly ten or twenty was an acceptable size for a small group[424] and an acceptable number for a core group of disciples.[425]

vi. Lots (1:26)

The casting of "lots" here does not refer to a vote;[426] that the κλῆρος "fell" underlines its literal sense here (cf. LXX 1 Chr 26:14; Esth 3:7; Jonah 1:7; Ezek 24:6).[427] Lot oracles (usually answering yes/no questions or other binary choices as here) were common in antiquity and more dominant even at Delphi than the Pythia's responses.[428] Most cities of Lycia and Pisidia had dice oracles for their citizens to consult in city

---

"Four Hundred"; they were replaced by the Five Thousand (Thucyd. 8.86.3–6; 8.92.11; 8.93.2). Cf. also the Eleans' "Three Hundred" (Xen. *Hell.* 7.4.31) and the Ten Thousand (Xen. *Hell.* 7.4.33); two groups of "three hundred" (Rhodes, "Triakosioi").

414. E.g., Dio Chrys. *Or.* 50.2 (and see H. L. Crosby, LCL, 4:314n1); *IG* 2² .3277 (Sherk, *Empire*, §78A, p. 115); *IG* 2² .3449 (Sherk, *Empire*, §42F, pp. 80–81). Massilia's senate was also called "the Six Hundred" (Val. Max. 2.6.7e). For Athens's Five Hundred, see, e.g., Lysias *Or.* 13.86, §138; in a later period, constituting their councilors that year, see Paus. 1.3.5.

415. Tac. *Ann.* 3.64.

416. E.g., Suet. *Aug.* 36. Cf. the board of five (*quinqueviri*; e.g., Pliny *Ep.* 2.1.9).

417. E.g., Suet. *Jul.* 79.3.

418. See, e.g., Pliny *Ep.* 2.14.1; 4.16.1; 4.24.1; 5.9.5; 6.12.2; 9.23.1.

419. Nicholas, "Centumviri," 309; Pliny *Ep.* 6.33.3.

420. On the textual variant, see Metzger, *Textual Commentary*, 150–51; further sources in our introduction, ch. 15, sect. 3.a.i. If the number prefigures the Gentile mission as the Twelve suggests the mission to Israel, the association of seventy with the nations is significant, but see discussion our introduction, ch. 15, sect. 3.a.i.

421. E.g., Cic. *Agr.* 2.17.44; Statius *Silv.* 1.4.24 (see J. H. Mozley in LCL, 1:49 n. *f*); 4.4.43; 4.9.16; Suet. *Aug.* 36; *Vesp.* 10; *Dom.* 8.1; *Passienus Crispus*; *Rhet.* 6; cf. 2 Sam 23:23, 39.

422. Origen *Comm. 1 Cor.* 4.77; Chrys. *Hom. 1 Cor.* 38.5; cf. Oecumenius in *Pauluskommentare* (Bray, *Corinthians*, 150).

423. See Philost. *Vit. Apoll.* 3.30, on the "eighteen" Brahman sages at the king's court.

424. This was close to the lowest limits for associations (Klauck, *Context*, 43).

425. Philost. *Vit. Apoll.* 1.19 notes that Apollonius had seven disciples at one point; in 5.43, he has thirty and selects the ten most suitable to accompany him.

426. Cf. classical Athenian use of ostraca for voting (Deissmann, *Light*, 52, 55; MacDowell, "Ostracism"), but the usual Greek appointment of Athenian officials by lot reduced the Roman problem of "electoral corruption" (Eder, "Elections," 897). For some jurors chosen by lot, cf. Max. Tyre 16.4; for lots selecting the roles for participants in sacred dramas, see Smith, *Symposium*, 117.

427. Cf. Fitzmyer, *Acts*, 228; Barrett, *Acts*, 105.

428. Aune, *Prophecy*, 25, 30; cf. Parker, "Oracles"; Kauppi, *Gods*, 21–24 (for the relationship with Acts 1:15–26, see 25–27). Lots were apparently important among the Germans as well, where a priest (for the state) or a father (for a family) would distinguish slices of branch by runes and spread them over a cloth (Tac. *Germ.* 10).

centers.[429] Early Greek leaders cast lots for guidance;[430] Greek myth claimed that Zeus, Poseidon, and Hades divided their realms by lot.[431]

More relevant here is the use of lots for choosing public officials. Various classical Athenian officials were chosen by lot.[432] Democracies in particular, but also other Greek cities, used lots to distribute, with a minimum of conflict, public offices "among those who were equally eligible."[433] The use of lots is also well documented in Ptolemaic and Roman Egypt.[434] In the Roman Republic, Romans could evade partisan politics by drawing lots (*sortes*).[435] Romans did not use lots for selecting normal magistrates but did use them for selecting judges and vestal virgins and for dividing duties of consuls or praetors.[436] Romans used lots to determine where governors would be sent[437] and which sphere of office each praetor would take (Cic. *Verr.* 1.8.21).[438]

Lots could be used to decide who would lead in battle (Xen. *Cyr.* 6.3.34), which general would go to war (Val. Max. 1.5.3), which positions the legions would take in battle (Tac. *Hist.* 2.41; cf. Judg 20:18), which members of a disgraced cohort would be beaten to death (Tac. *Ann.* 3.21), who might be sacrificed (Quint. *Decl.* 384), and whose property would have to be sold (Val. Max. 6.3.4).[439] Lots selected the pairs for wrestling or the pancratium in the Olympic Games (Lucian *Hermot.* 39). If necessary, they could be used to decide whose court trial would come first (Quint. *Decl.* 250 intro) or even which brother would go into exile to leave the kingdom to the other (Vell. Paterc. 1.1.4).

Ancient Israel used lots to choose workers for special duties (1 Chr 24:7; 25:8; see comment on Acts 1:17);[440] Judas had earlier received a "lot" by Jesus's choice (Acts 1:17). The members of the Qumran community also viewed their membership as

429. Mitchell, *Anatolia*, 2:13; cf. discussion in Toner, *Culture*, 44–46. "Many of the major oracular sanctuaries" in antiquity had lot oracles (Nollé, "Lot"). Numbered stones or small shaped objects could be used (Stumpf, "Tessera," 313). For the ancient Near Eastern practice, see, e.g., Horowitz and Hurowitz, "Urim" (suggesting multiple draws, with a white stone signifying "Yes" and a black stone "No"); and Kitz, "Terminology" (shaking items onto the ground, summarized in Hubbard, *Joshua*, 403). For lots in some cultures today, see, e.g., Werbner, "Truth," 200–201; Rives, *Religion*, 57, compares the I Ching in traditional Chinese culture.

430. See Hom. *Il.* 7.171, 175; Pliny E. *N.H.* 33.4.12; cf. marriage partners in Eurip. *Aeolus* hypothesis 29–32; frg. 24a. MacDonald, *Imitate Homer*, 105–19, compares the selection of Matthias with the portrayal of the selection of Ajax to fight Hector in *Il.* 7; this comparison illumines some common cultural selection procedures, but we should note that they are hardly limited to Acts and Homer.

431. E.g., Heracl. *Hom. Prob.* 41.5; Lucian *Dance* 37.

432. See, e.g., Jones and Rhodes, "*Epistatēs*." Some (apparently often including archons) obtained offices in Athens by lot (Plut. *Arist.* 1.8).

433. Rhodes, "Lot," 816.

434. Ameling, "Lot" (for land lots, inheritance, liturgies, etc.).

435. See Rosenstein, "Sorting Out the Lot"; earlier among Greeks, see *Rhet. Alex.* 2.1424a.13–14. Penner, "Discourse," 96n94, compares Acts 1:26 with Roman use of lots for political offices; although this is but one possible comparison, it is a useful one.

436. Kierdorf, "Lot," 818 (also noting the tribes to which freedpersons were assigned). For other duties, see, e.g., Tac. *Ann.* 4.56.

437. Cic. *Quint. fratr.* 1.1.9.27; Vell. Paterc. 2.59.2; Pliny *Ep.* 2.12.2; 4.9.2; Suet. *Vesp.* 4.3; but cf. Tac. *Ann.* 3.58, 71.

438. The senate may have occasionally made exceptions for some reputed for extraordinary virtue (Val. Max. 8.15.4); sometimes, in praetors drawing lots for provinces, the matter could be rigged (Cic. *Fam.* 5.2.3).

439. For military use of oracles, see, e.g., Hdn. 8.3.7; for the Delphic oracle, Nilsson, *Cults*, 124–27; earlier in the ancient Near East, see, e.g., *ANET* 274–75, 277, 281, 292, 416, 449–50; *ARMT* 13.23, 114 in Moran, "Prophecy," 17; Craghan, "Mari," 48; Ross, "Prophecy," 17; van der Toorn, "Oracle de victoire"; Craigie, *Ugarit*, 35; cf. Hayes, "Oracles," 81–82. The pious would consult deities before acting (Xen. *Cyr* 1.5.6, 14; 1.6.2; 1.6.44; *Anab.* 6.3.18; 1 Sam 23:2–4; 2 Sam 5:23); they might wait for favorable omens (Xen. *Anab.* 6.4.16–25; 6.5.2, 8; Plut. *Arist.* 17.6–18.2). Others might ignore or reinterpret them (Val. Max. 1.6.6; 3.7.ext. 6; Suet. *Jul.* 59; 77; *Tib.* 2.2).

440. In Josephus, see, e.g., *Ant.* 6.62. Brug, "Lottery or Election?" thinks that the OT background supports lots here, though he doubts that the use of lots here is as clear as most commentators suggest.

ordained by divine lot (1QS V, 2–3; VI, 16; 1QM I, 5).[441] At the command of priests, the lot (הגורל) determined rank in the community (1QS XI, 7).[442]

Jewish people also believed that lots could give them divine direction.[443] In Jewish tradition Noah divided the land for his three children by lot (*Jub.* 8:10–11); Israel divided some of the land by lot (e.g., Josh 14:2; 18:6, 8, 10; Ezek 45:1);[444] priests and Levites received their duties by lot (e.g., 1 Chr 24:5, 31; 25:8; 26:13–14),[445] as Luke knows (Luke 1:9); lots determined the cities for Levites (e.g., 1 Chr 6:61–65) and who would settle in Jerusalem (Neh 11:1).[446] Later Jewish texts even use biblical texts as lot oracles of a sort.[447]

In the ancient world, lots also were used in punishments, as in determining which two prisoners would fight each other to the death (Polyb. 3.62.7, 9), which tenth of a shamed company would be beaten to death (6.38.2–3), and who would be executed first (*'Abot R. Nat.* 38 A). Of course, lots could be manipulated, as was probably the case in Josephus's suspicious survival in *War* 3.388–89; as the general, he may have "supervised" while those demanding suicide eliminated themselves.[448]

Not everyone agreed with the use of lots. Socrates reportedly opposed choosing public officials by lot, noting that one would not choose a helmsman or builder this way (Xen. *Mem.* 1.2.9). Some opined that, despite the false tradition that Zeus and Pluto drew lots for Olympus and Hades, Zeus had in fact merited Olympus by his power (Callim. *Hymns* 1 [to Zeus], lines 60–66). But most people did believe that lots revealed the divine will (e.g., Xen. *Cyr.* 6.3.36; 7.1.15). On fate and providence, see the excursus at Acts 2:23. Here, as suggested above, the lots (toward the beginning of Luke's second volume) positively evoke the lots through which Zechariah was chosen for his duties in the temple (toward the beginning of his first volume, Luke 1:8–9); in both cases God performs his purposes.

The lots may have been stones or pottery fragments shaken in a container, with Matthias's being the first to emerge.[449] Barrett notes that "the usual method of casting lots" entailed collecting "names . . . in a vessel" and letting "one . . . fall out."[450] Commentators suggest that either cloth bags or vessels could be used.[451] The lots used for matching competitors at the Olympics may be instructive. Lucian reports: "A silver urn dedicated to the god is placed before them. Into this are thrown small lots, the size of beans, with letters on them. Two are marked alpha, two beta, two gamma, and so on in the same way, if there are more competitors, two lots always having

441. Le Cornu, *Acts*, 50, adds 1Q28a I, 16.
442. See Driver, *Scrolls*, 520 (also the suggestion that Essenes appointed leaders by lot, though Jos. *War* 2.123 need not be so construed).
443. E.g., by revealing Achan as the transgressor (Josh 7:14; Jos. *Ant.* 5.43; *b. Sanh.* 11a; 43b; *Num. Rab.* 23:6) or (some thought) by determining the order of suicide (Jos. *War* 7.396). Some thought the Urim and Thummim worked by one of the stones shining supernaturally (*Ant.* 3.215; 1Q29; 4Q376; see Abegg, "Introduction to 1Q29," 178). Lots may have even been used casually, as a form of gambling (e.g., *Lam. Rab.* 1:6); God would be sovereign in Israel's favor, as with Purim (Esth 3:7; 9:24–32; *Esth. Rab.* 7:11).
444. Also *b. Zebaḥ.* 119b; *Num. Rab.* 21:9; one view in *Gen. Rab.* 98:2.
445. Also Jos. *Ant.* 7.367; *b. Ta'an.* 27b. The rabbis differ on whether the priestly courses did certain things during certain parts of the Feast of Sukkoth by lot or by turn (*t. Sukkah* 4:15–16). Priests cast lots regarding sacrifices (*b. Šabb.* 148b; 149b; *Ta'an.* 28a, using Neh 10:34; *b. Sukkah* 55b; *Menaḥ.* 20b; 106b; *Tamid* 26a; 28a; 30a; 32b).
446. Cf. also lots in the Day of Atonement ritual (Lev 16:8; *m. Yoma* 4:1; *b. Yoma* 37a; 39b; *Menaḥ.* 59b).
447. Van der Horst, "Bibliomancy," citing as possibilities 1 Macc 3:48; 2 Macc 8:23; and esp. *b. Ḥul.* 95b; *Ḥag.* 15ab; *Ta'an.* 9a.
448. For the suspicion, see also Cornfeld, *Josephus*, 241.
449. Witherington, *Acts*, 126.
450. Barrett, *Acts*, 105; for some reason, he doubts that this is the form of lot here.
451. Conzelmann, *Acts*, 12 (citing Prov 16:33 for the former; Livy 23.3.7 for the latter).

the same letter. Each of the competitors comes up, offers a prayer to Zeus, puts his hand into the urn, and picks up one of the lots." A guard keeps the competitors from examining the letters they have drawn; then a guard or one of the judges inspects the lots and matches them.[452]

Sometimes minor characters provide new options for readers, bridges through which the implied audience can better identify with the story.[453] Thus the opportunity for a disciple unnamed in the Gospel (and perhaps unknown to Luke's ideal audience) to serve may invite his implied audience to feel welcome to participate (even if not among the Twelve, cf. Acts 5:13) in the story—the way Gentiles may identify with the Diaspora Jewish crowds in 2:5–11; more with the bicultural ministers in Acts 6–8; and still more with Gentile converts and evangelists to Gentiles in later chapters. Given qualifications in 1:21–22 that limit the 120 present (1:15), it would be reasonable for Luke's ideal audience to surmise that Matthias and Joseph may also have participated in the mission of the seventy-two (or seventy) earlier in Luke's narrative (Luke 10:1).[454]

452. Lucian *Hermot.* 40 (LCL, 6:337). Greek letters functioned as numerals.

453. See Malbon, "Importance of Minor Characters."

454. This tradition about Matthias is reported in Euseb. *H.E.* 1.12.3 (Fitzmyer, *Acts*, 227; Barrett, *Acts*, 102). Some (Barrett, *Acts*, 102) read Euseb. *H.E.* 3.29.4 as if Clement of Alexandria claimed that Matthias later became inappropriately ascetic; but Luke might not make so much of Judas's replacement if he knew of such a tradition in his day.

THE EVENT OF PENTECOST
(2:1–13)

This passage focuses on the fulfillment of the promise of empowerment to speak God's message. In the larger context of Luke's work, Jesus's followers are empowered for mission toward the beginning of Acts just as Jesus was toward the beginning of Luke's Gospel. Given Luke's emphasis on the Gentile mission, this is cross-cultural empowerment (Acts 1:8), proleptically foreshadowed by the Spirit-empowered disciples speaking other languages (2:4) and by the Jewish hearers from many nations (2:5–13). The Spirit leads to proclamation (2:14–40), and the ideal end result of this Spirit-empowered mission is a community living out the ideals of the kingdom (2:41–47).[1]

1. The Passage's Message

Here I focus especially on the empowerment of the Spirit, which, like the multicultural mission, was introduced in Acts 1:8 (and Luke 24:47, 49). I will also touch on the multicultural emphasis of this passage briefly at Acts 2:4 and more fully at Acts 2:5–13, and focus more on this chapter's prophetic dimension at Acts 2:17–18. (For the temporal relationship of this empowerment vis-à-vis conversion, see the discussions at Acts 1:4–5; 2:38–39; and 8:14–17 and some of the discussion of the Spirit in the introduction, ch. 15, sect. 5.a.)

a. The Spirit's Empowerment

This passage focuses on the fulfillment of the promise of empowerment to speak God's message. Although 1:8 explicitly associates the empowerment for proclaiming God's message only with the apostles, this passage demonstrates that the empowerment is provided for all Jesus's followers (see esp. 2:38–39 and comment there). This empowerment is to speak God's own message (like prophets of old, 2:17–18) across cultural boundaries (2:4–11) and hence ultimately to form the church across such boundaries (as the struggle to embrace the Gentile mission in the rest of Acts emphasizes and as 2:5–11 foreshadows).

This coming of the Spirit is therefore especially "prophetic" empowerment (explicit in 2:17–18); Scripture often and ancient Judaism even more regularly (though neither exclusively) associate God's Spirit with prophecy and other mighty works often done via prophets (see the excursus at Acts 2:17). This empowerment also proleptically fulfills end-time promises (wind, 2:2; fire, 2:3; the Spirit; "the last days," 2:17; cf. 1:6–11). Eschatological and following Jesus's exaltation, this empowerment attests Jesus as the risen one who baptizes in the Holy Spirit (Luke 3:16) and hence as God's own vizier, the promised Messiah, Israel's rightful Lord (Acts 2:36). All those who

---

1. I treated various material in Acts 1–2 in much more cursory fashion in Keener, *Spirit*, 190–213.

turn to Christ receive the same gift of the Holy Spirit (2:38–39) and consequently can participate in the life of the ideal community (2:41–47), a community that will carry on the same lifestyle that characterized Jesus and his early followers (sacrificial lifestyles; common meals; signs and wonders; and the word spreading everywhere).[2]

In contrast with some approaches that treat Luke's interests as merely historically descriptive (or, worse yet, merely novelistically entertaining; see introduction, ch. 2), Luke is presumably interested in calling the church of his own day to depend on the same empowerment of the Spirit that he reports. Because he associates the Spirit with signs, witness, and church growth, it seems unlikely that he conceives of the Spirit's coming as simply a theoretical theological designation with no expectation of experiential effects in the life of the church. Because Luke believes that the outpouring of the Spirit yields an eschatological empowerment (2:17), it is hardly plausible that he would relegate this eschatological experience only to the past.[3] He presumably believes that it is available for those who seek to experience God's gift, like his characters who sought the outpouring of the Spirit in prayer and faith (1:14; 4:31; cf. 8:15; 9:11–12, 17; 10:4; 13:2–4; Luke 11:13) and/or received this experience through the mediation of those who were known to be strong in it (Acts 8:17; 9:17; 19:6). Why else would he emphasize this point so often?

Luke presents the outpouring of the Spirit as the direct result of the ascension (2:33), the proof that Jesus is the one authorized to pour out God's Spirit and hence Lord and Christ (2:34–36). Here is the central theological pivot of Luke's transition between the two volumes: as Jesus has ascended, he has sent the Spirit to his witnesses to carry on the mission (1:8–11). Whereas the initial commission focuses on selected apostolic witnesses (1:2, 8, 24; 10:41; later, cf. 9:15), the Pentecost event theologically democratizes the empowerment and commission for all believers (2:39; cf., e.g., 8:4, though such references are comparatively rare, since they are incidental to Luke's more biographic focus on key narrative figures).[4] Again, all these elements are factors supporting Luke's expectation that the experience he reports is paradigmatic for and continues in his day: Jesus remains exalted as Lord and Christ; the mission remains in progress; and the promise of the empowering Spirit is for all believers past and present (2:39).[5]

The pivotal place of Pentecost in Luke's larger narrative structure is not difficult to discern. Just as Jesus began his public ministry only after being anointed by the Spirit (Luke 4:18; Acts 10:38), so also his followers must be empowered for their

2. The signs and wonders, with the consequent spreading of the word (and mention of corporate prayer and economically sacrificial lifestyle) are dramatically exemplified in Acts 3:1–4:4.

3. Others also note that the eschatological emphasis allows Luke to highlight the *present* availability of the Spirit and incipient salvation (e.g., Kilgallen, *Commentary*, 18; see further discussion below). For the continual repeatability of (a prominent dimension of) the Pentecost experience (based on its repetition elsewhere in Acts' narrative), see Kim, "Mission," 49–74, esp. 53–62 (for other narratives in Acts, 63–74).

4. Luke's Scripture already suggested this ideal democratization, esp. in Num 11:29 (cf. 11:16–17, 25) and, above all, Joel 2:28–29, which Luke cites (see further discussion below).

5. Some scholars have objected to this portrait on theological grounds or argued on such grounds that Luke would not expect prophetic phenomena that he associated with the Spirit to continue after his own day; his view of the eschatological character of the present interim time, however, renders such theological considerations suspect. At one time, many Christians believed that Matt 28:18–20 was limited to the Twelve; few hold this today, because most recognize that Matthew's work is meant to function prescriptively as well as descriptively (see, e.g., Keener, "Matthew's Missiology"). Analogously, some hold that the commission to witness (though given directly to the apostles in Acts 1:8) remains valid today, yet they appear less enthusiastic to affirm the empowerment on which it is predicated in 1:8, even though it is more explicitly for the entire church (2:38–39) than is the call to witness in 1:8 and even though Jesus forbade his followers to begin their mission without it (1:4–5). This approach appears to me dependent on a modern theological system rather than on Lukan theology.

designated ministry (Acts 1:8).[6] Jesus was anointed at his baptism while praying (Luke 3:21–22); he announces that he will "baptize" his followers with the Spirit in a manner analogous to water baptism (Luke 3:16; Acts 1:4–5; 11:15–16), an event that again comes in the context of prayer (Acts 1:14). The gift of the Spirit is the promise with which the Gospel closes (Luke 24:47–49) and Acts opens (Acts 1:4–8), and the final element of the Gospel's conclusion (Luke 24:53) is continued in the final element of the Pentecost narrative proper (Acts 2:46–47). Jesus's public ministry opens with an Isaiah text explaining his empowerment and mission (Luke 4:18–19); his apostles' public ministry opens with a text from Joel explaining the church's empowerment and mission (Acts 2:17–18).[7]

What is their mission introduced in this passage? The explicit Scripture text focuses on prophetic empowerment (2:17–18), that is, empowerment to proclaim the word of the Lord. Throughout Acts, the Spirit's activity often includes "charismatic" phenomena characteristic of OT prophets (including the gift of prophecy proper; e.g., 11:27; 13:1); it is also attested on multiple occasions by the charismatic phenomenon of praise in languages unknown to the speaker (2:4; 10:46; 19:6). But prophecy, or inspired speech, in the most general sense is proclamation of the "word of the Lord," which in Acts includes the inspired gospel (e.g., 8:25; 12:24; 13:49). The heart of this calling, as defined in 1:8, is "witness" to all nations; that is, all the forms of inspired speech and activity reflect or evoke the central commission of proclaiming God's central message of salvation in Christ, the climax of God's plan in salvation history (or, to put the matter differently, the climax of Luke's understanding of Israel's story). Inspired speech in other languages (2:4) offers a particularly apt illustration of the Spirit's empowerment to cross cultural barriers in articulating this testimony, and the Diaspora Jews from a range of nations (2:5–11) prefigure the fulfillment of the mission to come. Various ideals set forth by Jesus in the Gospel (e.g., Luke 12:33) are fulfilled in the Spirit-inspired community (e.g., Acts 2:44–45).

Christian scholars in a variety of cultures and traditions seek to reapply Luke's Pentecost interest to the church today.[8] In terms of "reception history," many have applied Luke's description as a model in subsequent "revivals" in history,[9] such as calls to apostolic poverty and sharing (some monastic movements such as the Franciscans; other critics of clerical wealth, such as Wycliffe and some of his contemporaries and successors),[10] signs and wonders (twentieth-century Pentecostal and charismatic healing revivals; contemporary healing revivals in a number of nations; Third Wave

6. See fuller discussion at Acts 1:4–5, 8. Luke reserves the term "anointed," however, for Jesus, probably because he alone is the Christ, i.e., the "anointed" (king). (Contrast 2 Cor 1:21; 1 John 2:20, 27.)

7. Jesus's teaching about their empowerment in advance also echoes the servant mission of Isaiah; see comment on Acts 1:8.

8. For sample applications in various contexts, see, e.g., Chempakassery, "Jerusalem Pentecost"; Bediako, "African Culture," 120; Forrester, "Pentecost" (addressing, e.g., castes); on Acts 2:17–21, Prema, "Paradigm"; Lloyd-Jones, *Christianity*; nonviolent direct action in Alexander, "Action." Note also artistic appropriations of Pentecost from the sixth through the sixteenth centuries, in Hornik and Parsons, "Perspectives."

9. For lack of better terminology, I borrow "revival" from the discipline of U.S. religious history and contemporary studies of global Christianity (cf., e.g., Blumhofer and Balmer, *Revivals*; McClymond, *Encyclopedia of Revivals*; Harrell, *Possible*; Robeck, *Mission*; Burgess, *Revolution*; Roberts, *Revival*; Dermawan, "Study"; Lee, "Korean Pentecost"; Longkumer, "Study"; McGee, "Revivals in India"; Shaw, *Awakening*; Wiyono, "Timor Revival"; York, "Indigenous Missionaries"). I employ it in the sense of a religious renaissance or awakening, not in the more specific sense of the North American form that came to be called revival meetings. Others (e.g., Dunn, *Jesus and Spirit*, 192) have offered sociological comparisons with such movements; see further discussion below.

10. E.g., Evans, *Wycliffe*, 155, 226.

practices), or other beliefs or practices.[11] Contemporary readers could also emphasize that the Spirit's empowerment is available to all believers (not just to the apostles or leaders, although Luke's narrative as a whole does focus on extraordinary activity through particular individuals).[12] They could further point out that the Spirit in Acts is a dramatic end-time gift to speak and live out God's message and therefore invites Jesus's followers to model sacrificial caring for one another, worship, and joyful sharing of their experience of Christ with others.

b. The Spirit Inaugurates the Age to Come

Acts 1:4–8 (see comment there) suggests that the disciples must understand the Spirit's coming as a piece of realized eschatology—that is, that some of the end-time promise is being fulfilled in their time, before Jesus's return. It remains to be fully consummated; because the king will come twice, the kingdom he has already established among his followers is yet to be fulfilled to the extent that all his enemies are placed beneath his feet (Luke 19:27; 20:43; Acts 2:35).[13] But he already reigns at the Father's right hand (2:34–35), and the realized element of his eschatology is explicit (Acts 2:17).

In view of this eschatological association, potent signs of the end time in 2:2–4 are not surprising. Some of these signs may well also recall the Sinai theophany (or theophanies in general), but both their accumulation and their interpretation in Peter's speech (which associates the event with "the last days," 2:17) also indicate the eschatological character of the event. The "wind" of 2:2 recalls the promised wind of Ezekiel, which would raise the dead and/or reestablish God's people (Ezek 37:5–10).[14] The "fire" undoubtedly prefigures the fiery end-time judgment on the wicked that John the Baptist prophesied (Luke 3:9, 16–17; cf. 17:29). Luke explains the disciples' Spirit-inspired worship in languages they do not know (Acts 2:4) as a form of the end-time outpouring of the Spirit of prophecy (2:16–18).

Many scholars have thus recognized in Acts 2 the inbreaking of the new, messianic era for which most Palestinian Jews yearned and prayed.[15] C. F. Sleeper, for example, remarks, "From the structure of Acts 1 and 2, it is clear that Luke understands the gift of the Spirit at Pentecost as the beginning of the age of the Spirit."[16] Although it is certainly true that Luke also emphasizes continuity with earlier divine activity

11. Some such events may parallel Pentecost without deliberately echoing it. For example, in November 1994, an unexpected "experience of the Spirit" during prayer in Nieuw Nickerie, Suriname, excited and united the small number of believers there across all denominational lines. In the resultant enthusiasm, several hundred residents—reportedly more than the entire number of local conversions over the previous century—were converted the same day, and a mass people movement began (Norwood, "Colloquium," 24–26; also confirmed by Dr. Douglass Norwood, interview by author, Philadelphia, June 6, 2006; Norwood was an eyewitness and participant). Cf. also early twentieth-century children's experiences in the Adullam orphanage in China (Baker, *Visions* [12th ed.], esp. 9–14) and those in Pandita Ramabai's home for orphan brides in India.

12. On Luke's outpourings indicating the church's prophetic empowerment, see, e.g., Boxall, "History and Spirit."

13. See, e.g., Keener, "Pentecost," 360.

14. Ezekiel 37:1–14 applies to individual resurrection in the end time at least as early as 4Q385–386 (see Dimant, "Resurrection"). Ruthven's argument for Isa 59:19 here (in view of 59:21; "Covenant," 36–38) would also fit an eschatological/restoration context; his insightful connections with the rare βίαιος and (contextually) the Spirit might suggest that Isa 59 also informs Acts 2:2.

15. E.g., Ridderbos, "Speeches of Peter," 12; Barclay, "Acts ii.14–40," 198–99; Cadbury, "Eschatology," 300; Bruce, *History*, 206; Ladd, *Young Church*, esp. 34–52; Heuthorst, "Apologetic Aspect." Cf. further Hunter, *Gospel according to Paul*, 36; Cullmann, *Worship*, 21; Hernando, "Function," 251. But Grässer, "Parusieerwartung," 119–22, regards it as more "churchly" than eschatological (cf. idem, *Forschungen*, 312–15). The eschatology here must be "realized" eschatology, in any case.

16. Sleeper, "Pentecost and Resurrection," 390.

(including salvific continuity),[17] Acts 2, linked theologically with Jesus's exaltation that precedes it, constitutes a turning point in the history of salvation.

The two ages appear frequently in apocalyptic literature, especially by the late first century,[18] and also inform the Qumran literature from before the rise of the Jesus movement.[19] Later rabbis often contrasted the present age with the age to come,[20] often with an eschatological inversion that would exalt Israel,[21] an image already clear in some earlier texts.[22] The coming age would follow the resurrection of the dead;[23] "eternal life" was thus technically the life of the coming age (Dan 12:2).[24]

Treating Acts 2 as the opening scene of a new era allows for a parallel with the opening of Luke's Gospel, which also announced a new stage in salvation history. Witherington points to the parallel structure (for the parallel between Jesus and the church here, see more fully the discussion above on Acts 1:4–5):[25]

Luke 3–4	Acts 2
John promised that the coming one would baptize in the Spirit and fire (3:16)	Jesus does baptize in the Spirit (1:4–5; 2:4, 16–18, 38–39); tongues of fire (2:3)
The Spirit came at Jesus's baptism (3:21–22)	The Spirit comes; is promised to believers at their baptism (2:38)
Jesus's mission program from Isa 61 (Luke 4:18–19)	The church's mission program from Joel 2 (Acts 2:17–21)

c. Covenant Renewal and the Pentecost Festival

It would not be surprising if Luke (like John, who emphasizes Jewish festivals) made some connections between the festival he mentions (Acts 2:1) and the events that occurred there. Luke's audience may have even expected this; Greek orators often lectured at festivals on the subject of the festival.[26] But the likelihood of any particular allusions to the festival has so far eluded scholarly consensus.

Some scholars have pointed to parallels between Essene traditions about the Jewish festival of Pentecost (Shavuot) and Acts 2:1–13,[27] parallels that, undeveloped and

17. See rightly Turner, *Power*, 346–47, 353, on this point (he correctly differs from Dunn, who underestimates disciples' faith in Luke's first volume; 329–30).

18. E.g., *1 En.* 71:15; *4 Ezra* 6:9; 7:50, 113; 8:1–2; *2 Bar.* 15:8; *Gr. Ezra* 1:24; see further Ferch, "Aeons"; cf. Novello, "Nature." After judgment would come an era of worldwide peace, even in *Sib. Or.* 3.367–80 (see discussion of backgrounds in Collins, "Sibylline Oracles," 320, 358–59); for the end of this age or the beginning of the next, cf. *1 En.* 16:1; *4 Ezra* 4:26–27, 36; 6:20; 7:31, 47, 112–13; 8:52; *2 Bar.* 59:8; 69:4; 73:1; 83:7; 85:14.

19. See 1QS IV, 16–17; 4Q215a 1 II; Pryke, "Eschatology," 48–49. On the evil of the present era, see, e.g., CD VI, 10, 14; XII, 23; XV, 7, 10; 4Q215a 1 II, 4; 4Q266 3 I, 6; 3 II, 20; 4Q270 7 II, 13; 4Q271 2 12; 4Q301 3 8; 4Q509 205 2; 4Q510 1 6–7; on its approaching end, e.g., CD IV, 8–12; 4Q266 3 I, 2–4.

20. E.g., *m. ʾAb.* 4:17; *t. Ber.* 6:21; *Sipre Deut.* 31.4.1; 34.4.3; 48.7.1; *Pesiq. Rab Kah.* 4:1; *y. Ḥag.* 2:1, §16; *Gen. Rab.* 1:10; 53:12; 59:6; 66:2; 90:6; *Lev. Rab.* 2:2; 3:1; *Deut. Rab.* 2:31; 3:4; *Song Rab.* 2:2, §6; *Pesiq. Rab.* 21:1; *Tg. Ps.-J.* on Gen 25:32.

21. E.g., *t. Taʿan.* 3:14; *Sipre Num.* 115.5.7; *Sipre Deut.* 32.5.10; *Pesiq. Rab Kah.* 6:2; 9:1; *b. Yoma* 87a; *Gen. Rab.* 95 MSV; *Exod. Rab.* 30:19; *Lev. Rab.* 36:2; *Deut. Rab.* 1:20; *Eccl. Rab.* 4:6, §1; *Pesiq. Rab.* 16:6; cf. *ʾAbot R. Nat.* 22, §46 B; for Moses, in *Sipre Deut.* 29.2.3; *Exod. Rab.* 47:3 (Moses enters it at death in *ʾAbot R. Nat.* 12 A); for others, *t. Peʾah* 1:2–3; *Sipre Deut.* 307.3.2–3; *ʾAbot R. Nat.* 39 A; 44, §123 B; *b. Šabb.* 30b; *Ḥag.* 12b; *Gen. Rab.* 66:4; *Lam. Rab.* 1:5, §31; 3:3, §1; 3:18, §6; 3:22, §8; *Pesiq. Rab.* 25:2.

22. The conception is basically the same as in *2 Bar.* 15:8.

23. Schiffman, "Crossroads," 140 (citing *b. Sanh.* 90a, bar.); cf. *L.A.E.* 51:2.

24. Cf., e.g., *Gen. Rab.* 59:6; 90:6; Buchanan, *Consequences*, 138–39; see fuller comment on Acts 13:46.

25. Witherington, *Acts*, 128–29 (which I have modified for use here); cf. Rackham, *Acts*, xlvii; Goulder, *Type and History*, 61 (suggesting that the parallels emphasize that Christ continues to live in his church).

26. Men. Rhet. 1.3, 365.30–366.1; subjects for epideictic consideration include the object of the festival's honor (often divine; 366.6) but also matters such as the location and the distance from which pilgrims come (366.8–10), which Luke does treat.

27. See Grappe, "Récit de la Pentecôte" (depending on, e.g., *Jub.* 6:15–22; 1QHᵃ XIV, 8–22; 1Q34).

perhaps unnoticed by Luke, could suggest authentic Palestinian tradition.[28] Others have drawn parallels with targumic traditions about Pentecost,[29] which may also be relevant to the (very uncertain) degree to which our current Targumim reflect earlier traditions.

Many have suggested specific parallels to a Sinai theophany.[30] Some of these potential parallels were available without scholars' recourse to citing late or sectarian documents: storm, fire, and a gift from heaven appear in the biblical Sinai theophany (Exod 19:18–20).[31] Fitzmyer thus suggests the following among verbal allusions to Exod 19–20 here: "together" (Acts 2:1; Exod 19:8), "sounds" (Acts 2:2, 6; Exod 19:16; "from heaven," Acts 2:2, cf. Exod 20:22), and fire (Acts 2:3; Exod 19:18).[32] Others have found additional elements of Jewish interpretations of Sinai (e.g., Philo *Decal.* 33–46) in the Pentecost narrative.[33] Thus some compare the gift of the Spirit (or other features of the narrative) with the theophany and gift of Torah at Sinai, though interpreters divide over whether Luke recognized it.[34]

Such comparisons do not depend specifically on links between Sinai and the Jewish festival of Pentecost in Jewish tradition, but a number of scholars have also suggested such links.[35] Certainly, the book of *Jubilees* in the second century B.C.E. already links Pentecost with covenant renewal (*Jub.* 6:17).[36] In time, this theme developed more fully into a festival commemorating the giving of the law,[37] surely by the third century C.E.[38] God gave the Torah in the third month (Exod 19:1);[39] with a bit of exegetical ingenuity, Pharisees seem to have adjusted the time to correspond with the Feast of

28. Noack, "Pentecost in Jubilees," 90–91 (though weighing too much on the date).

29. See esp. Potin, *Fête de la Pentecôte*; idem, "Fête de la Pentecôte."

30. E.g., Kremer, *Pfingstbericht*, 238–53; Jervell, *Apostelgeschichte*, 133, 138; Pervo, *Acts*, 61; more extensively, Wenk, *Power*, 246–51. Wenk fits this perspective into his view of the Spirit as involving covenant renewal and not just prophetic empowerment (252–53), though (as noted below) Jewish people of this period linked Pentecost with covenant renewal even when they did not link it with Sinai. He also argues that this anticipates a new exodus (254). Estrada, *Followers*, 192–96, treats covenant renewal more generally, then (196–200) treats evidence for influence from Sinai traditions. Others regard the echoes as merely probable (e.g., Arrington, *Acts*, 20) and sometimes note (6–7) that Luke's *explicit* text (Joel in Acts 2:17–28) addresses prophetic empowerment rather than inward renewal (e.g., not citing Ezek 36–37). Although the explicit text suggests Luke's emphasis, however, these options are not mutually exclusive.

31. Cf. Neh 9:12. One might also biblically link the Spirit's coming with renewal in the Torah (Ezek 36:14), a context fruitfully mined by Luke's hero Paul (2 Cor 3:6–8), though biblical associations with the Spirit's coming are many and only the wind (Acts 2:2; Ezek 37:9–10) points to this specific context.

32. Fitzmyer, *Acts*, 234; cf. O'Hagan, "Pentecost."

33. Kremer, *Pfingstbericht*, 241–46 (for Philo; 240–41 for Josephus; 246–48 for Targumim; 248–51 for rabbis); Potin, "Fête de la Pentecôte"; Lövestam, "Apostlagärningarnas arende"; Delcor, "Bundesfest und Pfingstfest"; Talbert, *Acts*, 25, 229. See further comment below. Menzies, *Empowered*, 193–98, thinks that commonalities with Philo reflect merely common theophany traditions.

34. E.g., Wedderburn, "Redaction in Acts 2.1–13"; Chmiel, "'Sociophonie' de la fête"; Berends, "Celebrate at Pentecost?" (citing also Sinai-Pentecost connections in Ps 68); R. Williams, *Acts*, 40; Witherington, *Acts*, 131; Turner, *Power*, 267, 279–89, esp. 282–85 (linking it to a prophet-like-Moses Christology); Hamm, *Acts*, 18; Wright, *Acts*, 22. Some compare the use of Ps 68 in Eph 4:7–8 (e.g., Weiser, *Apostelgeschichte*, 78). Cf. the eschatological Torah of Isa 2:3; but the warning in Keener, *John*, 358–59.

35. Christian interpreters of Acts have linked Pentecost and the giving of Torah at least as early as Augustine (so Gaventa, *Acts*, 74).

36. *Jub.* 6:32–38. Cf. Wintermute, "Introduction," 39, on the Sinai era in *Jubilees* (though the figures of Testuz on which he depends may be questioned); Patte, *Hermeneutic*, 149. Luke is naturally interested in covenant renewal (cf. Luke 22:20; Talbert, *Acts*, 27).

37. Scholars frequently cite the alleged connection between Pentecost and Sinai (e.g., Goulder, *Type and History*, 150; Bruce, *Commentary*, 54), usually citing *b. Pesaḥ.* 68b; *Tanḥ.* 26c; cf. also *Exod. Rab.* 31:16.

38. Le Cornu, *Acts*, 59, cites *t. Meg.* 4[3]:5; *y. Meg.* 26a; *b. Meg.* 31a; *Pesaḥ.* 68b (and for earlier hints, 2 Chr 15:10ff.; Pss 50:2f.; 81:3f.; 99:7; *Jub.* 14:20; 1QS I, 16ff.; II, 1ff.; 4Q280; 4Q86; 4Q287).

39. Cf. also *L.A.B.* 11:1; *Pesiq. Rab Kah.* 12:20.

Pentecost.[40] Later Jewish Pentecost liturgy celebrated God's gift of Torah to Israel.[41] Many scholars believe that Luke had this understanding of the giving of Torah, or at least of covenant renewal, in mind.[42]

Complicating some of these connections (although, again, not necessarily Sinai allusions unrelated to the specific Jewish festival of Pentecost), scholars debate the date of the specifically law-giving connection with Pentecost.[43] Associations with the triennial cycle of readings, in which Exod 19 was read on the festival, may have influenced this interpretation of Pentecost[44] (though it is possible that they instead reflect it).[45] Probably later rabbis developed this specific connection, which was then recognized by fourth-century Christians (including Jerome and Augustine) as well.[46] Barrett points out that Qumran's annual covenant renewal (1QS I, 8–II, 19) does not specifically mention Pentecost and that the annual renewal in *Jub.* 6:17 connects Pentecost's covenant renewal more with Noah than with Moses.[47] Given the connections between Qumran's calendar and *Jubilees*,[48] however, it seems likelier than not that Qumran's covenant renewal period coincides with Pentecost.[49] Yet even by itself, *Jubilees* is clear enough that some associated the feast with covenant renewal. Granted, that renewal is in Noah's day; but it is not limited to Noah (*Jub.* 15:1–2, 11), the setting suggests more (1:1), and *Jubilees* portrays the patriarchs as keeping Torah in advance (at least much more than Genesis does).[50] Thus the tradition that the law was given at Sinai may well be later than Luke and his tradition; it does, however, provide external attestation for the much earlier (pre-Christian) and probably Essene tradition relating Pentecost to covenant renewal.[51]

Despite the probable antiquity of these traditions for covenant renewal on Pentecost in some circles, most of Second Temple Judaism probably celebrated the festival

40. See Dupont, *Salvation*, 36; cf. 2 Chr 15:10–14.

41. Jacquin, "Worte in der Erziehung." Pentecost and Yom Kippur are the only two festivals whose prayers explicitly appear among the fragments of festival prayers at Qumran (4Q507–509; Abegg, "Liturgy: Qumran," 649).

42. Foakes-Jackson, *Acts*, 10; Goulder, *Type and History*, 151; Hull, *Spirit in Acts*, 53–55; Cocchini, "Evoluzione della festa"; Le Déaut, "Savu'ot"; Weinfeld, "Giving of Law"; Harrelson, *Cult*, 25; Dunn, *Baptism*, 48; Zehnle, *Pentecost Discourse*, 62; Fitzmyer, *Acts*, 233–34; Giesen, "Verheissungen" (for covenant renewal).

43. Carter and Earle, *Acts*, 28; Sleeper, "Pentecost and Resurrection," 390; Isaacs, *Spirit*, 130–31 (though she does think that the new Sinai is in view; cf. comment on Acts 2:2–3); Barrett, *Acts*, 111; Schreiber, "Aktualisierung"; Menzies, *Empowered*, 190–93.

44. Cf. Charnov, "Shavuot."

45. Cf. sources cited in Dunn, *Baptism*, 48 (they argue that the reading predates the first century, which is more questionable; cf. Zehnle, *Pentecost Discourse*, 116–18).

46. Cocchini, "Evoluzione della festa" (citing *b. Pesaḥ.* 68b; cf. *t. Meg.* 4:5), suggesting that Luke drew on the earlier covenant renewal image.

47. Barrett, *Acts*, 111.

48. Commonly noted; e.g., Fritsch, *Community*, 70; Marcus, "Scrolls," 12. Qumran need not have composed *Jubilees*, but it found it congenial (Noack, "Qumran and Jubilees," 196–98); conservatives may have preferred this older solar calendar as against the newer lunar calendar imposed by the Seleucid hellenizers or the Hasmoneans (VanderKam, *Studies in Jubilees*, 283–84; cf. Rivkin, "Pseudepigraph," who argues that the Pharisaic movement established the new calendar; and Zeitlin, "'Jubilees' and Pentateuch," 224, and idem, "Jubilees, Character," 8–16, who thinks that the lunar calendar was established by the Hasmonean period). Scholars have debated an additional twenty-eight-days-per-month tradition supposedly preserved in *Jubilees* (suggested by Rook, "Tradition"; opposed by Baumgarten, "Problems"). Questionably early dating of rabbinic tradition has driven some of the discussion.

49. See Flusser, *Judaism*, 48; Noack, "Pentecost in Jubilees," 89; Black, *Scrolls*, 92; Harrelson, *Cult*, 25; Bruce, *History*, 208; see esp. VanderKam, "Covenant." For additional support, see Vermes, *Scrolls*, 205; possibly 2 Chr 15:10–12; Turner, *Power*, 281–82, adds 4Q266 17–18.

50. See Schultz, "Views of Patriarchs," 45. The culpability of some behavior, however, is reduced because the law was not yet revealed (*Jub.* 33:15–16).

51. In favor of this tradition's antiquity, see, e.g., Weinfeld, "Giving of Law"; Parker, "Apokatastasis," 58–61.

especially as "but a wheat-harvesting festival."[52] More important for our purposes, Luke provides few clear indications linking the day of Pentecost with Sinai, fewer than one would expect if Luke recognized and hence wished to make use of such a connection.[53] (The elements that could evoke Sinai in Acts 2:2–4 can evoke other associations—especially eschatological ones—no less easily, even cumulatively; see comments on these verses.) Indeed, Luke even omits obvious potential Pentecost allusions such as "firstfruits" (which Pauline churches could have applied to the three thousand initial converts; cf. Rom 16:5; 1 Cor 16:15).[54] To Luke, the particular festival mentioned may have had no more specific significance to his narrative than the crowds and short interval between it and Passover.[55] Luke's source or sources may have been among the many who looked for deeper connections with Israel's past. Thus some scholars reasonably attribute the new Sinai or other covenant renewal associations to the source rather than to Luke himself.[56] This attribution would support our observations concerning Luke's dependence on some prior material, discussed below.

d. An Authentic Pentecost Tradition?

Luke makes his theology of Pentecost clear enough, but does he depend on historical tradition? Some scholars point to Luke's literary skill in the narrative and suggest a weaving together of oral traditions with Septuagintal, Pauline, and other sources here.[57] But as noted earlier in this commentary, even the freest retelling of sources can still convey their information, and so Lukan characteristics do not by themselves indicate how much pre-Lukan information is or is not present.

Some scholars have expressed skepticism about the Pentecost event because it is not mentioned elsewhere,[58] but this argument is of very limited value because "Acts is the only Christian historical narrative" that covers this early period.[59] Even for others who knew about an initial experience of the Spirit among the disciples, the proliferation of early Christians' other experiences of the Spirit (e.g., Acts 4:31) may have also relativized the prominence of Pentecost for some writers.[60] Nevertheless, other early Christian writers do speak of God's having poured out his Spirit (Rom 5:5; Titus 3:5–6) and presuppose that at some point God began to lavish his Spirit on the church in a way dramatically greater in magnitude than God's people

---

52. Safrai, "Temple," 893; cf. also idem, "Religion," 810; Menzies, *Empowered*, 190–93.

53. Cf. O'Toole, "Davidic Covenant of Pentecost" (emphasizing 2 Sam 7:12–16 instead); Menzies, *Development*, 229–44; Strauss, *Messiah*, 145–47; Bock, *Acts*, 131–32. Estrada, *Followers*, 200–203, interacts with Menzies's argument but ultimately doubts that one should use differences to ignore what he views as compelling similarities (203–4, following Max Turner in finding an evocation of Sinai, despite differences because the event is a different one).

54. Cf. Hull, *Spirit in Acts*, 51 (who sees the term as already implicit in the festival). Not surprisingly, Romans also prayed during a "harvest of the first-fruits" (*primitias pomorum*, Pliny E. *N.H.* 28.5.23).

55. Cf. Wilson, *Gentile Mission*, 126–27; Barrett, *Acts*, 111 (citing also Calvin); Gaventa, *Acts*, 74 (also mentioning Calvin on the crowds). Menzies, *Empowered*, 193–98, doubts any Sinai connections in Acts 2, attributing commonalities with various sources to common theophany traditions. Against those who appeal to a Sinai connection with Ps 68:19 (67:19 LXX), he argues (198–201) that it lies behind Eph 4:8 but not Acts 2:33–34.

56. E.g., Knox, *Acts*, 62. While acknowledging Luke's thorough compositional activity in the narrative, some find clear "memory of the theophany on Mount Sinai and traces of Jewish traditions connected with that theophany" (Dupont, *Salvation*, 35).

57. See esp. White, "Pentecost Event."

58. Lüdemann, *Acts*, 54, is skeptical because Peter's speech quotes the LXX rather than Hebrew, but if this is a problem (despite Peter's presumable knowledge of Greek), it would only show that Luke exercises a historian's liberty to compose a speech or part of a speech (perhaps in conjunction with Luke's linguistic limitations), nothing about the event to which the speech is attached.

59. Witherington, *Acts*, 129.

60. See Twelftree, *People*, 65–83.

had experienced before (Rom 7:6; 8:2–4; 14:17; 2 Cor 3:3–18; Gal 3:2–5, 14; 4:6, 29; 5:18, 22–23; Eph 2:18–22; 3:5; 1 Pet 1:11–12; Heb 2:4; 6:4). This dramatic experience of the Spirit must have begun at *some* point early in the Jesus movement's existence, however Luke or other writers may have arranged their sources to express it. The possible connections between Pentecost and covenant renewal, never developed in Acts itself, may suggest that Luke draws on a theologically fuller source or sources that he does not develop, and the Pentecost after Jesus's passion was certainly very early in the movement's history.[61]

In favor of a historical event behind Acts 2, Dunn provides several points, not all of equal direct weight but which I regard as cumulatively convincing, at least in view of Luke's approach to Acts' genre (see our introduction, chs. 2–8):[62]

1. Early Christians were pervasively and unusually charismatic (e.g., Rom 8:2–16, esp. 8:9; Heb 2:4; 1 Pet 1:12; 1 John 3:24), and most such movements start in group ecstasy or enthusiasm.
2. Despite friction, Paul acknowledged Jerusalem as the center (Rom 15:19, 25–27; Gal 2:1–2); as the founding center, it was the likeliest source for the experience that characterized all known forms of early Christianity.
3. Pentecost is a reasonable date:
   a. A longer delay might have strained group cohesion too severely.
   b. Pentecost was the next major pilgrim festival after the Passion Passover, and Christians adopted it (cf. Acts 20:16; 1 Cor 16:8).
   c. Paul associates the Spirit with "firstfruits" (Rom 8:23), which characterized that festival.[63]
4. Dunn finds echoes of an established Pentecost tradition:
   a. The Spirit was "poured out" (Acts 2:17–18, 33; 10:45) in Rom 5:5; Titus 3:6.
   b. Conversion appears as baptism in the Spirit in 1 Cor 12:13,[64] language also familiar to us from Acts 1:5.

In favor of the Pentecost date, one may add that the church's close association of the gift of the Spirit with believers' conversion (e.g., Rom 8:9; Gal 3:3) and apparently Christ's exaltation (Rom 8:11; 1 Pet 3:18), in addition to the experience's pervasiveness in early Christianity, suggests a date shortly after Jesus's resurrection. By themselves, these factors could suggest an experience even *earlier* than the one Luke mentions; but Luke himself connects the experience theologically with Christ's exaltation and believers' conversion (Acts 2:33, 38), so he must have strong reasons for separating the events in his narrative as much as he does.[65]

Likewise, the widespread early Christian experience of prayer in "tongues" (cf. 1 Cor 14:18) started at some point (before the Corinthian church experienced it);

61. Although I think that Luke may wish an implicit comparison between Peter's Pentecost speech here and Paul's in Acts 22, his mere hints of Pentecost in the latter case (explicit only at 20:16) suggest that he does not invent Pentecost information where he does not have it.

62. Dunn, *Acts*, 22–23; see, at greater length, idem, *Jesus and Spirit*, 135–56.

63. Also Hull, *Spirit in Acts*, 52. Though cf. also the resurrection, 1 Cor 15:20, 23. Still, the connection is interesting, especially since Luke himself makes little of the Pentecost connection (perhaps less than his sources).

64. The Q material about Spirit baptism (Matt 3:11//Luke 3:16) also fits the church's pervasive experience of the Spirit. The traditional identification of water baptism and Spirit baptism (e.g., Richardson, *Theology*, 352) goes too far for Luke (cf. Acts 10:47–48; nevertheless, they may be ideally simultaneous [cf. discussion at Acts 2:38], and the former probably signifies the latter).

65. Especially given his failure to exploit allusions to the festival (some of which may be presupposed in his source), unless he simply needed a festival and picked the next one after Passover.

Luke's omitting mention of it on a few occasions (Acts 4:31; 8:17–18; 9:17; 13:52), despite its usefulness to his emphasis (see comment on Acts 2:4), might suggest that he mentions it only where he has a specific tradition that it occurred, including here.[66] (It may have also sometimes occurred even when Luke does not mention it—as some scholars think, in 8:17–18; compare 9:17 with 1 Cor 14:18, and note that despite 1 Cor 14, Luke does not mention it in Corinth.) Some others cite the recurrence of such phenomena in periods of revivalistic intensity in subsequent eras to support their plausibility in Acts.[67] Indeed, reports of such phenomena in revivalistic settings around the world today further reinforce the account's plausibility.[68] Many conclude that, whatever legendary accretions or literary embellishments the narrative may include, Acts 2 preserves a genuine tradition of ecstatic phenomena in the earliest church.[69]

Not all arguments for prior tradition prove equally compelling. Some who are skeptical of sources elsewhere find too much Aramaic influence in Acts 2 to suppose it Luke's own composition.[70] Others have suggested doublets with other passages, which in turn could suggest variant sources based on earlier tradition.[71] Some suggest that Luke weaves together various different traditions here, such as echoes of a Sinai event at Pentecost, preaching to pilgrims in Jerusalem, and a tradition about glossolalia.[72] But while Luke's implicit genre invites us to test historical plausibility at relevant points, where possible, and to observe some specific examples of Aramaisms, Luke has mostly composed Acts 2, like the rest of Acts, in his own style. Because we lack other accounts concerning this earliest period of the church, his theology will be easier to locate here than his sources are. (The one likeliest exception is where fertile connections with Jewish Pentecost traditions exist, which Luke fails to develop or emphasize.) But given the arguments above, it seems likely that he does have sources, perhaps oral informant(s) from during his stay in Judea (cf. 21:8, 15–18; 27:2).

e. Compatible with John's Tradition of Receiving the Spirit?[73]

The Fourth Gospel also reports an initial reception of the Spirit toward the church's inception, but at a different time and under different circumstances. In John 20:22, Jesus breathes on the disciples at his first resurrection appearance among them as a

---

66. Forbes, *Prophecy*, 72–74, thinks Paul's language for "tongues" a shorthand for the clearer and more original "other tongues" found in Acts 2:4. Still, "other" here is typically Lukan (eight times in Matthew; once in Mark 16:12; once in John; though twenty-seven times in Paul; forty-eight times in Luke-Acts).

67. E.g., Dodd, *Preaching*, 58; cf. the comparison with "cross-cultural manifestations of . . . glossolalia" in Levine, *Misunderstood Jew*, 53–54. For examples of ecstatic physical phenomena in revival movements, see, e.g., Dunn, *Jesus and Spirit*, 192; Wolffe, *Expansion*, 57–59; Vidler, *Revolution*, 238; emotional arousal in millenarian movements, cf. also Gager, *Kingdom*, 21. See, e.g., among seventeenth-century Huguenots, in Spittler, "Glossolalia," 339; Rosen, "Psychopathology," 235–37; ecstasy in various U.S. revivalist movements (Rosen, "Psychopathology," 239–41). One may also compare phenomena of religious emotion as widely as the trembling of many early Friends (Cross and Livingstone, *Dictionary of Church*, s.v. "Quaker," 1363; Moore, "Quakerism," 338 [noting its rapid decline]; a small number of more unusual phenomena in Hudson, *Religion*, 45; Rosen, "Psychopathology," 232–34) and the celebratory worship of the Latino (e.g., Maynard-Reid, *Worship*, 180–81) and the African-American (66–68, also noting its African roots) religious experience.

68. Cf., e.g., Gibbs, "Launching of Mission," 21 (based on experiences with the Pentecostal Methodist Church in Chile); Tarr, "Power," 9–10 (based on his experience in Burkina Faso).

69. E.g., Conzelmann, *Theology*, 37–38. Cf. Knox, *Acts*, 62: "there is no reason to doubt" the occurrence of glossolalia and "a new stage in the life of the Church" on Pentecost; cf. van Halsema, "Betrouwbaarheid" (despite the reasons).

70. Knox, *Acts*, 82.

71. Harnack, *Acts*, 179.

72. Wedderburn, "Redaction in Acts 2:1–13"; Lincoln, "Interpretation of Luke's Pentecost."

73. The accounts are not strictly susceptible to harmonization (Barrett, *Acts*, 74), at least as a single event.

group, telling them to receive the Spirit. This image is modeled after Gen 2:7[74] and presumably implies the formation of a new creation, perhaps (in Pauline terms) in the new Adam. In contrast to the Fourth Gospel's presentation, the narrative of Acts separates the giving of the Spirit from Jesus's resurrection temporally (though not theologically) by several weeks (Acts 1:3–5).[75] Some scholars think that Luke and John view the same event but with differing theological emphases.[76] Does this mean that "Pentecost" actually happened before Pentecost (i.e., Luke has invented the setting)?[77] Or do John and Luke refer to distinct events? Or has John invented the setting to include the event before his narrative closes?

Because I believe that John takes many more symbolic theological liberties with his story than does Luke, my John commentary addresses this question somewhat more fully than does the treatment here, which rehearses some of my discussion and conclusions there.[78] I believe that there may have been historical experiences behind both reports but that Luke is accurate about a subsequent setting for the Spirit's empowering the church for mission. John also depicts the experience he reports as empowerment for mission (John 20:21–23), but I believe that because John ends his narrative long before Pentecost, he makes the earlier event the narrative fulfillment of his Gospel's promises about the Spirit (even if John himself may have viewed this event as proleptic). Since Luke connected the resurrection, exaltation, and gift of the Spirit theologically (Acts 2:33), he had no reason to invent the temporal disjunction among these events.

The question whether John intends John 20:19–23 as an equivalent to Luke's Pentecost presupposes the question whether he uses Luke's version (or, more likely, a widespread tradition behind Luke's version) of Pentecost.[79] Although other early Christian writers attest the Spirit empowerment of early Christianity (e.g., Rom 5:5; Titus 3:5), they do not comment on the time at which it occurred. As already noted, early Judaism connected Pentecost with covenant renewal.[80] Some scholars have therefore concluded that Luke connects the outpouring with specific aspects of that festival;[81] but Luke himself does not emphasize the connection much in Acts 2.[82] As noted, I believe that this lack of explicit connection probably suggests that the tradition of the church's experience on its first Pentecost predates Luke. But does John know, ignore, deny, or replace this tradition?

Some scholars argue that John retains a distinction between Easter and a later Pentecost, perhaps by John 20:22 symbolically pointing forward to the historical Pentecost.[83] Proponents of this position note that Luke and John may employ their

74. See Turner, *Gifts*, 90–92; Keener, *John*, 1204–5; Haenchen, *John*, 2:211; Sanders, *John*, 433; Dunn, "Spirit," 703; Ellis, *Genius*, 293; Wojciechowski, "Don"; O'Day, "John," 846; Cook, "Exegesis," 8. Like Acts 2:2, it may also echo Ezek 37, but this connection (probably implied in John 3:8) is less clear here.

75. Robinson, *Studies*, 166. For the theological link between the Spirit and Jesus's resurrection, see, e.g., Giesen, "Verheissungen."

76. E.g., Alvarez Valdés, "Espírito Santo."

77. Although John is even more interested in some festivals than Luke is, John often employs festivals in his narrative in a very different way than Luke does (as I suggested in Keener, "Festivals").

78. Keener, *John*, 1196–1200.

79. The question of John's knowledge of the Synoptics is controversial in current Johannine scholarship (see, e.g., Smith, *John among Gospels*); my own view (in summary form) is that John *wrote* independently of other Gospels, except in his passion narrative, yet could not have helped but have *known* of them (especially Mark).

80. *Jub.* 6:17; Noack, "Pentecost in Jubilees," 89; Le Déaut, "Savu'ot."

81. E.g., Williams, *Acts*, 40.

82. See comments in Keener, *Spirit*, 193.

83. E.g., Holwerda, *Spirit*, 133 (who sees this as a distinctly apostolic gift, voiding the narrative of its prescriptive function); Carson, *John*, 648–55; Rossum, "Pentecost." The verb for Jesus's breathing on the disciples means

language for "receiving the Spirit" in different manners[84] and that both experiences are historically compatible, John's being either a symbolic or a less substantial impartation.[85]

Although such arguments are historically plausible, they do not settle John's theological purpose. Some scholars argue too much in contending that because John does not describe the Spirit's *activity* beginning in this passage, the disciples have not yet received the Spirit in the sense promised earlier in the Gospel.[86] Whatever truth this contention may represent in terms of pre-Johannine tradition, suggesting that John intends to communicate a lesser impartation than the better-known Pentecost, it ignores the nature of his narrative. This passage is not the appropriate place for John to demonstrate the Spirit's new activity but to introduce the Spirit's coming.[87]

Others show that John 20:19–23 fulfills specific promises of the final discourse, especially the promise of the Spirit (14:16–17, 27) and Jesus's promise that after he went away, he would return to them (14:18–19, 22).[88] Other allusions include the fulfillment of "peace" (14:27; 20:19, 21) and "rejoicing" (16:20–24; 20:20),[89] and the language of rebirth or re-creation in Jesus's breathing on them also recalls earlier Johannine pneumatological motifs (3:3, 8; 20:22).[90] Empowerment for mission (20:21, 23) fits Jesus's earlier promises (15:26–27; 16:7–11).[91] The fulfillment of Johannine motifs in John 20 is nearly as clear as that between Luke 24:49 and Acts 2:4.[92] Thus some write that this passage and Acts 2 ultimately represent the same event.[93]

Turner presents the strongest case for distinguishing the two events,[94] to which I here respond. First, he argues that Jesus's glorification (a prerequisite for the Spirit's coming, John 7:39) is not complete by 20:22 because the ascension remains future

more than mere exhalation (Turner, *Gifts*, 90–92), but whether *John* might use Jesus's breathing symbolically is a different question from whether Jesus is portrayed as acting merely symbolically in the narrative world.

84. With Turner, "Concept"; see also others, including Keener, *Giver*, 137–69.

85. See Aug. *Tract. Jn.* 74.2.2–3 (Martin, *Acts*, 24); Chrys. *Hom. Jn.* 86; Origen *Cels.* 7.51; Menoud, "Pentecôte"; Horton, *Spirit*, 127–33; cf. Ladd, *Theology*, 297. On the symbolic view, see Burge, *Community*, 117–18, who notes, however, that it does not work on the level of Johannine theology. Barrett, *Acts*, 74, objects to Origen's distinction of the two events in terms of quantity (*Cels.* 7.51) by noting that the Spirit is personal; but this may read later trinitarian theology (or even John's Paraclete) into passages that are more functional than ontological in description. The Spirit's functional empowerment in various ways may be distinguished (cf. Keener, *Spirit*, passim, esp. 214–16).

86. Turner, "Concept," 28–34, esp. 34.

87. John can assume that those familiar with his discourses will expect the fulfillment of all long-range promises related to the Paraclete's activity, based on short-range fulfillments implied in the text, the same way readers of Mark can anticipate resurrection appearances even if none are narrated in that Gospel itself.

88. See Bartlett, "Coming," 73; Beare, "Spirit," 96; cf. de Jonge, *Jesus*, 174. By contrast, Menzies, "John's Place," distinguishes the regenerative and prophetic strands of the Spirit's coming (the latter focusing on the Paraclete passages) in John's Gospel (esp. 43–50). My own dissertation independently identified both of these strands in John (Keener, "Pneumatology," passim; see esp. 324–25, in the conclusion), but I believe that this passage fulfills (at least proleptically) both the regenerative (John 20:22, echoing Gen 2:7) and prophetic (John 20:21; cf. 20:23) strands.

89. Cf., e.g., Beare, "Spirit," 96; Lightfoot, *Gospel*, 335.

90. Hatina, "Context," also employs *Tg. Onq.* on Gen 2:7 and *Tg. Neof.* on Gen 2:7 to argue for genuine rather than merely symbolic eschatological fulfillment here.

91. The Spirit is available after Jesus's glorification (John 7:39), especially his death and resurrection. Because I doubt that the ascension-glorification is, in fact, complete in 20:25 (cf. 20:17; this is a primary objection of Turner, *Gifts*, 94), the text allows a subsequent impartation, but I do not believe that it *requires* it; Jesus has already "gone away" and returned (14:18–20; 16:7, 16–22).

92. With Ashton, *Understanding*, 425.

93. E.g., Chevallier, "Pentecôtes."

94. Turner, *Gifts*, 94–97; he summarizes (92–94) Brown's and other arguments for identifying the two.

(20:17).[95] I agree that the ascension remains future,[96] but would argue that for the purposes of John's theological point, Jesus was "lifted up" sufficiently on the cross for the Spirit to be "given" proleptically (and symbolically) already in 19:30. Second, Turner argues that Jesus will not be present when he provides the Spirit, since 16:7 says he will "send" the Spirit to them after his departure. I believe that this argument reads too much into the wording; Jesus "goes" at his death and returns at the resurrection (16:16–22), and so sending the Spirit in his *absence* would technically place the Spirit's coming *before* the resurrection.[97] Third, Turner states that the Paraclete is a *substitute* or *replacement* for Jesus's presence (14:16–17), yet Jesus continues appearing to the disciples after 20:22 (20:26–29; 21:1). Again, I would argue that this weights the meaning of replacement too heavily; after all, the Spirit also replaces Jesus's presence in Acts (Acts 1:8–11), but this does not preclude a very rare subsequent resurrection appearance (9:3–4).[98] Fourth, for Turner, that the disciples remain behind locked doors in John 20:26 seems too anticlimactic to fulfill the glorious promises of John 14–16. I do believe that Turner here identifies a strand of dissonance in John's narrative, created by the historical experience of a later Pentecost, before recounting which his narrative must end. That dissonance does not, however, negate the fact that in this short encounter (20:19–23), nearly every promise associated with the Spirit's coming appears at least proleptically.

Some of Turner's observations may suggest legitimate complexities or incongruities in John's language. These in turn may suggest that John is aware of a subsequent Pentecost event and lays emphasis on an earlier event that also provided an encounter with the Spirit.[99] On the level of Johannine theology, however, this event ties together diverse elements of the Johannine promise of the Spirit, fulfilling a function theologically analogous to Pentecost in Acts: the promised Spirit has come, so the church must live in the empowerment thus provided.

Given the connections that I believe existed among early Christian communities (see introduction, ch. 6, sect. 2.d), I do think it likely that John knew of a story of Pentecost such as appears in Acts, whether through pre-Lukan tradition or tradition stemming from Acts. Even if John and his audience knew the tradition of Pentecost, however, John need not be directly adapting or reacting against the Pentecost tradition in his narrative. John completes his Gospel in either chapter 20 or chapter 21;[100] if he is to narrate any fulfillment of Jesus's Paraclete promises, which provide continuity between the missions of Jesus and his followers, he must do so here. Further, John's theology necessitates a close connection between the passion/resurrection and the giving of the Spirit (John 7:39); indeed, he may report a proleptic "giving of the Spirit" at both Jesus's death (19:30) and his first resurrection appearance to the gathered disciples

---

95. One could also note that the disciples, by abandoning Jesus, have not yet met the condition of John 14:15; but one could respond that their remaining together (20:19) fulfilled part of the command (cf. 13:34; 1 John 2:19; Acts 2:1).

96. Keener, *John*, 1193–95.

97. The language of "sending" deliberately parallels the Father's sending the Son, without necessary reference to distinction in location; it simply involves delegated authority and mission (as in John 20:21, 23).

98. We might expect overlap even more in John, for whom the cross and exaltation are theologically a single event, than in Luke, whose scheme of salvation history is more chronological.

99. Turner, *Gifts*, 100–102, thinks that John sees the Spirit as a single "gift" that arrived in "two chronological stages," yet denies that these need be paradigmatic for subsequent Christian experience. I see the possibility of subsequent experiences in Acts (esp. Acts 8:14–17; treated in Keener, *Gift*, 157–68) but also doubt that John speaks to the question directly.

100. I am among those who argue for John 21 as an integral part of the Fourth Gospel (Keener, *John*, 1219–22; see also Brant, *John*, 278).

(20:22).[101] Even if the giving of the Spirit in the tradition behind 20:22 represents merely a symbolic or partial impartation, it must bear in John's narrative a full theological weight *equivalent* to the experience Luke narrates at Pentecost.[102]

If its Johannine literary function (in terms of its full theological weight) is in some sense symbolic, however, one need not seek a chronological harmonization with Acts 2.[103] As Gary Burge emphasizes, Luke-Acts itself provides a similar chronological situation: because Luke must end his Gospel where he does, he describes the ascension as if it occurs on Easter (Luke 24:51) even though he will soon inform or remind his readers that it occurred only forty days afterward (Acts 1:3, 9). Likewise, "knowing his Gospel would have no sequel," the Fourth Evangelist theologically compressed the historical "appearances, ascension, and Pentecost into Easter. Yet for him, this is not simply a matter of literary convenience. . . . John weaves these events into 'the hour' with explicit theological intentions."[104]

f. The Event and the Pattern

To summarize the comparison with John, the Johannine "Pentecost" (John 20:19–23) shares some common features with Luke's Pentecost, but their primary relationship is their mutual affirmation that Jesus imparted or sent the Spirit shortly after his resurrection. John's report is far less dramatic and does not occur in the era of Christ's exaltation, but John completes his account before the promised exaltation (20:17, on the likelier interpretation) and hence presses into this event the narrative fulfillment of Christ's promises concerning the Spirit. It is possible that historically the disciples experienced a foretaste in 20:22 that was fulfilled more dramatically on a later occasion (Luke, at least, allows for multiple fillings; e.g., Acts 2:4; 4:8, 31). But for those who must choose one account or the other and regard Luke's as too dramatic: Luke seems more likely to report the events as he has them from his tradition than does John. John takes significant liberties with the way he reports his events, especially in several symbolic adaptations in the passion narrative,[105] whereas Luke follows, where we can test him (especially in his use of Mark), the procedures of a good Hellenistic historian (see introduction, chs. 3–8, esp. 6–7).

Yet Luke reports the Pentecost experience not merely as a matter of historical interest but because for him it set the normative pattern for the church. This is not to say that all the phenomena of Pentecost would be repeated on subsequent occasions (he never reports the wind or fire again) but to contend that, for Luke, the church's experience was (or should be) pervasively charismatic; as Richard Hays puts it, it was to be not so much an expression of "early catholicism"[106] as of "early pentecostalism."[107]

The Pentecost experience is repeated (Acts 4:31–35), including beyond Jerusalem for other groups (8:15–17; 10:44–47; 19:6), suggesting that it is

---

101. Cf. Swetnam, "Bestowal."

102. Cf., e.g., Strachan, *Gospel*, 228; Bultmann, *John*, 692; Michaels, *John*, 335; Brant, *John*, 276 ("John's streamlining of events achieves a unity of action"). See more fully the evidence in Burge, *Community*, 123–31.

103. E.g., Dunn, "Spirit," 704.

104. Burge, *Community*, 148.

105. E.g., Jesus gives Judas the sop (John 13:26; contrast Mark 14:20); he appears to be executed on Passover (John 18:28; contrast Mark 14:14); he carries his own cross (John 19:17; contrast Mark 15:21).

106. Referring here of course to traditional usage in NT scholarship, not to what became the Roman Catholic Church.

107. Hays, *Moral Vision*, 135. Fee, *Paul, Spirit, and People*, 95, thinks that the Spirit was much more an experiential matter for Pauline Christians than for most second- and third-generation Christians today. For an emphasis on the likely pervasiveness of tongues in early Christianity, see, e.g., Jewett, *Romans*, 73 (following, among others, Smith, "Glossolalia").

paradigmatic.[108] As Luke repeats the Cornelius story and Paul's conversion each three times, emphasizing key turning points for the Gentile mission, he repeats glossolalia (a sign useful for Luke's emphasis on cross-cultural speech, 1:8) three times (2:4; 10:46; 19:6). But whereas the other repetitions allude back to a key event, the repetition of this sign from the Pentecost narrative evokes that narrative through a repeated experience. Luke thus treats the Pentecost experience as paradigmatic (as in 2:38–39).[109]

2. Signs of Pentecost (2:1–4)

In 2:1 the believers remain united, presumably in prayer, continuing the thought of 1:14. That is, the preparation for Pentecost (1:12–2:1) is complete. The signs confirming the subsequent coming of the Spirit include wind (2:2), fire (2:3), and the miraculous ability to worship God charismatically in languages they have not learned (2:4). While these signs evoke earlier biblical theophanies, they are also eschatological in character (the last so specified in 2:17), confirming that the eschatological Spirit promised by Joel has come. The climactic sign, worship in other tongues (2:4), confirms that they have been empowered to speak God's message across cultural and linguistic barriers (cf. 1:8). This sign is significant enough to bear repeating in some other narratives about the Spirit's coming (10:44–46; 19:6).

a. United at Pentecost (2:1)

The unity of Jesus's followers here continues the thought of 1:14 (from which 1:15–26 digressed and elaborated). It also foreshadows and prepares for the fuller ideals of community realized after the Spirit's outpouring (2:41–47).

Some scholars think that the disciples united here include only the participants from 1:13–14 (the apostles, women, and Jesus's brothers) and not the rest of the 120 from 1:15.[110] Jacques Dupont, for example, links "all" in 2:1 with the same term in 1:14 (where it refers to the eleven), but πᾶς is a difficult term to build a case on by itself, occurring more than twenty times in the first two chapters of Acts (and roughly 170 times total in Acts). He argues further that the title "Galileans" (2:7) restricts them to the Twelve; although this language certainly applies to the apostles (1:11; 13:31), it is likely that most or all of the 120 were also Galileans (Luke 23:49, 55; Acts 1:21–22).[111] He further notes that Luke mentions only the other eleven at Peter's side (Acts 2:14, 37); the Twelve speak because they are the witnesses, and the promise to the witnesses was (he argues) only to the apostles (Luke 24:49; Acts 1:4–5, 8).[112] But as argued above on Acts 1:4–5 and 1:8, the promise applies to all believers (2:39); although perhaps only the Twelve would stand to minister

---

108. Richard, "Pentecost." (Johnson, *Acts*, 14, lists the same five accounts of the Spirit's "outpouring.")

109. This is not to suggest that he expects glossolalia on every occasion (see comment on Acts 8:15–17) or that he is concerned only with "initial experiences" (see 4:8, 31; 13:9).

110. Estrada, *Followers*, 204–8, goes so far as to limit it to the Twelve, viewing them as the primary subject of Acts 1–2. The apostles (1:2) do receive the promise (1:8), but others join them in prayer (1:14), with still more remaining with them at least on some occasions (1:15). Since the promise is ultimately for all (2:38–39) and since people are sometimes filled with the Spirit after prayer elsewhere in Acts (4:31; cf. 9:11, 17; 10:30; Luke 11:13), one should infer that at least those continuing in prayer with the apostles (Acts 1:14) also received. (On other occasions of prayer, Spirit-filled persons could pray for others rather than for themselves [as in 8:15], but those who needed the Spirit themselves prayed and received themselves.)

111. Dupont, *Salvation*, 37.

112. Ibid., 38; Lake and Cadbury, *Commentary*, 17.

on Pentecost, Dupont himself admits that the women and Jesus's brothers of 1:14 received the Spirit (hence not the Twelve alone).[113]

The "all" of 2:1 must include the Twelve (1:13, 26; cf. 2:14), the women, and Jesus's brothers (1:14), and presumably some others as well; the total number present some of the time rose at least to as high as 120 (1:15). Many argue that we would also have to suppose more than twelve disciples together in 2:1 who will be filled with the Spirit at 2:4; more than twelve languages are spoken (2:5–11).[114]

The preceding context fills in the meaning of the disciples being "together" as one (2:1). The groups mentioned above were certainly devoting themselves to united prayer (1:14). The wording of 2:1 (ἐπὶ τὸ αὐτό) probably suggests a deliberate allusion to 1:15[115] and hence that most of that number continued to be present at this time.[116] The expression ἐπὶ τὸ αὐτό occurs six times in Luke-Acts, most frequently in this context (Luke 17:35; Acts 1:15; 2:1, 44, 47; 4:26).[117] The emphasis is not so much on their common location ("in one place," e.g., GNB; JB; NASB; NEB; NIV; NKJV; NRSV; RSV; RV) as on their concerted activity or unity (e.g., Goodspeed; Moffatt; TWENTIETH CENTURY).

This phrase reinforces the "together" in ὁμοῦ (which derives its sense of "unity" from ὁμός ["one and the same, common, joint," LSJ], as does ὁμοθυμαδόν in Acts 1:14 and 2:46).[118] Ancient teachers emphasized public unity and concord.[119] (Writers and speakers emphasized the need for unity for the state,[120] for armies,[121] for families,[122] and so forth, and the dangers of disunity;[123] they might also praise those who made peace.)[124] Idealizations of some periods in Israel's history emphasize their unity and brotherly love (*Jub.* 46:1; cf. perhaps Ps 133:1–3). Although festivals did not always generate unity,[125] some Jewish traditions emphasized the unity achieved when the people of Israel gathered for their pilgrim festivals (e.g., *Sipre Deut.* 168.2.4).[126] Their

113. Dupont, *Salvation*, 37. Estrada, *Followers*, 206–7, acknowledges that the gift is for all believers but contends that it could have come to the apostles first. Yet Acts 1:14 mentions more persons than the apostles, even if we ruled out the 120 in 1:15, and so Luke does not clearly portray the gift as initially coming to the apostles exclusively. Cf. also "those with them" in Luke 24:33.

114. See, e.g., Menzies, *Development*, 208n4. Contrast Dupont, *Salvation*, 37 (as noted above, because "all" echoes Acts 1:14). Estrada, *Followers*, 207, counters plausibly that the apostles need not have each spoken only one language over the course of their speaking (he regards it [208n66] as a "hearing" miracle anyway). Estrada's objection is viable if (as he contends) we have other reason to limit the sense of "all" here; otherwise, however, the multiple languages tend to support more speakers.

115. Thus Acts 1:15–26 is a deliberately bracketed digression, not an interpolation.

116. Estrada, *Followers*, 205–6, objects that it refers to the same place, not the same people. But why would the number of people gathered in the place be lower (indeed, down to only the apostles) on Pentecost?

117. Acts 4:26 is a quote of Ps 2:2 LXX; elsewhere in the NT, the expression appears only at Matt 22:34; 1 Cor 7:5; 11:20; 14:23, but it occurs fifty-one times in the LXX (e.g., Neh 4:8; 6:2, 7).

118. The word ὁμοῦ appears nowhere else in Luke-Acts or in the NT outside John (but means "together" there: John 4:36; 20:4; 21:2); in the LXX, it appears mainly in the Maccabean literature (2 Macc 8:14; 10:15; 11:7, 9; 13:12; 3 Macc 3:26; 4:13; 5:5, 21; 4 Macc 8:29; 13:13; 15:12), except for Wis 7:11; Sir 22:23.

119. E.g., Iambl. *V.P.* 7.34; 9.45; see further Keener, *John*, 1061–62; for the theme as a rhetorical topos, see comment on Acts 15:25.

120. E.g., Dion. Hal. *Ant. rom.* 7.53.1; Livy 2.33.1; 5.7.10; 24.22.1, 13, 17; Sen. Y. *Ep. Lucil.* 94.46; Mus. Ruf. 8, p. 64.13; Max. Tyre 16.3; Men. Rhet. 2.3, 384.23–25; some thinkers even applied this globally (cf. Whitacre, *John*, 417; Keener, *Revelation*, 341). In early Christianity, cf. 1 Cor 1:10; 11:18–19; Phil 2:1–2; 4:2.

121. Babr. 85.

122. Val. Max. 2.6.8.

123. E.g., Hom. *Il.* 1.255–58; Livy 2.60.4; 3.66.4; Sall. *Jug.* 73.5; Hdn. 8.8.5; Babr. 44.7–8; 47.

124. E.g., Hom. *Od.* 1.369–71; Iambl. *V.P.* 7.34; 9.45.

125. They could become occasions of unity or of discord (Dio Chrys. *Or.* 40.26–27), though presumably designed for the former purpose.

126. It also evokes the mythic unity that later tradition attributed to Israel in the wilderness (*Mek. Bah.* 1.108–12 [Lauterbach, 2:200]). Those who emphasize Sinai echoes in the Pentecost narrative often draw attention to Israel's unanimity at Sinai in Tannaitic tradition (Dupont, *Salvation*, 38–39).

unity forms an inclusio around the selection of Matthias (Acts 1:15–2:1) and hence helps prepare for Pentecost. The subject of their unity was prayer and restoration of their leadership structure to prepare for empowerment and mission.

I. THEIR LOCATION

Where were the disciples meeting? The evidence seems almost evenly divided between the temple[127] and a private home, presumably the one with the upper room.[128] They frequently met in the temple (Luke 24:53; Acts 2:46; 5:12) but also "from house to house" (Acts 2:46). (The "entire house" in 2:2, mentioned here, might sound like neither the temple *nor* the upper room.[129] People would stand, not sit, while worshiping in the temple; nevertheless, the term for "sitting" in 2:2 could refer to meetings in temple courts as easily as to the upper room.)[130] The likeliest background also fails to settle the issue: not only in Jerusalem but throughout the Greco-Roman world, private associations, including religious associations, could meet "in an area of a public temple, in a rented hall or in a private house," with "poorer groups" meeting in "corner cafes."[131]

If we favor preceding context (most important to first-time readers) over following context (available also to later readers), the allusion to the disciples' unity together (cf. 1:15) may imply the upper room of 1:13 (in which case they may have rushed from there into the temple, still praising God; for a state that might invite such a rapid transition, see comment on Acts 2:13, 15). By contrast, the narrative that follows implies that either they were in or at some point they enter the temple courts. Nowhere else in Jerusalem could they have drawn a crowd sufficient to produce three thousand converts, whereas the Temple Mount could fit about seventy-five thousand people.[132] (A transition from upper room to temple, perhaps abbreviated out of Luke's narration of an event, is plausible; any home large enough to host huge numbers in an upper room, 1:15, would have to have been in the upper city near the Temple Mount. Yet the street leading to the temple would undoubtedly be thronged with pilgrims, slowing entrance.)

In either case, Luke has omitted a transition that would have explained a location change. (Luke has clearly omitted details between 2:4 and 2:5, which may allow for the disciples to run a short distance and begin attracting crowds in the temple.)[133] If it were unified, the narrative of Acts 2 would make more sense as the narration of a meeting in the temple courts; but why would Luke, given his emphasis on the church's meeting in the temple, omit stating this explicitly? Luke has reason to emphasize both house meetings and the early Christians' experience in the temple; perhaps he leaves the matter ambiguous for this very reason, allowing connections with both (cf. 1:13). Then again, perhaps his sources are ambiguous, or, even likelier, given the wealth of other material that must be covered here, he telescopes his material. In any case, the possible shift in location is less germane to his point than that for at least most of

127. E.g., Bruce, *Commentary*, 56; Hengel, "Geography of Palestine," 37.

128. Dunn, *Acts*, 24; cf. Spencer, *Acts*, 32 (who sees a deliberate *contrast* with the temple here); Witherington, *Acts*, 131. Bishop, *Apostles*, 32–33, suggests that 9:00 a.m. was too early to be in the temple courts; but the temple opened for sacrifices and prayers much earlier than this (see comment on Acts 3:1).

129. The phrase does not specify which house; Luke speaks of the "whole household" in Acts 7:10; 18:8 (cf. Titus 1:11; Heb 3:2, 5, the Hebrews texts alluding to Num 12:7; "whole household" also appears in 1 Sam 22:15; 1 Kgs 16:11; 2 Kgs 9:8). "Whole house" can refer to the temple (1 Kgs 6:10, 22; Ezek 41:19) or other buildings (1 Kgs 7:1; 2 Kgs 20:13).

130. See Barrett, *Acts*, 113–14.

131. Jeffers, *World*, 77.

132. See Blue, "Influence," 483.

133. Blue, ibid., is among those who suggest this change in venue.

this scene they are now in public, presumably in the temple courts. A house with a large enough upper room to hold so many people would have been in the upper city, closer to the temple courts than the lower city was (see comment on Acts 1:13). See further comment on Acts 2:2.

II. The Festival

Whatever connections with the gift of the Spirit Luke's sources may have seen in the festival, Luke mentions Pentecost for two especially clear reasons: he thereby shows that, as Jesus had promised, the disciples did not have long to wait for the gift of the Spirit (1:5), and he explains why so many Diaspora Jews were present to recognize the languages spoken (2:5–12).

Those who wanted to attract attention for their claims or activities most naturally sought it at festivals;[134] this suggests that Luke's ideal audience might infer that the timing of the Spirit's coming in this narrative is providential. For example, condemned criminals were often executed at festivals to provide optimum pedagogic and deterrent value to the crowds.[135] The period of the Eleusinian Mysteries constituted the most crowded of Greek festivals yet afforded some recreation (Philost. *Vit. Apoll.* 4.17). Gentiles flocked to their festivals to enjoy contests, merchandise, and arts and crafts;[136] a festival was a major affair that relieved the monotony of survival, a communal celebration with religious and social sanction.[137]

Pentecost (by this period, the standard title for the Feast of Weeks in Greek texts)[138] was one of the great pilgrimage festivals, and as such, it would have been heavily attended.[139] Although many ancient estimates of festival attendance may be exaggerations (certainly, later rabbinic estimates were),[140] the crowds at some modern festivals do suggest that numbers could be massive.[141] Throughout the Mediterranean world, local festivals in prominent urban centers hosted many pious visitors as well as local citizens.[142] Well-to-do Greeks and Romans also visited sanctuaries as tourists; given the Greek and Latin graffiti on pharaonic monuments in Egypt,[143] it is reasonable to guess that the Jerusalem temple's grandeur may have even drawn a few Gentile tourists, though pilgrims would constitute the vast majority of visitors. (Pliny the Elder called Jerusalem "by far the most famous city of the East and not of Judaea only.")[144]

134. E.g., Lucian *Peregr.* 1.

135. Cf. Jeremias, *Theology*, 78; Hill, *Prophecy*, 52; Stauffer, *Jesus and Story*, 209; *m. Sanh.* 11:4.

136. E.g., Dio Chrys. *Or.* 27.5; for athletic competitions and theatrical performances, see Rives, *Religion*, 113. Jewish people also sought relaxation during festivals (Le Cornu, *Acts*, 716).

137. For the "festivity" of ancient festivals, see, e.g., Apoll. K. Tyre 39; Diog. Laert. 2.68; Libanius *Descr.* 5 (esp. 5.1, 6); 29 (esp. 29.1–2, 7–9, 12); for Sukkoth, *m. Sukkah* 5:1; *b. Sukkah* 51ab, 53a; in earlier times, cf. Murray, *Splendor*, 184; Heidel, *Genesis*, 71. Gentile cities expected all their citizens to participate in cultic festivals (Rives, *Religion*, 56).

138. Olson, "Pentecost," cites Tob 2:1; 2 Macc 12:31–32; Jos. *Ant.* 3.252; *War* 1.253.

139. E.g., Jos. *War* 1.253; 2.42 (though anger fueled the gatherings in this instance); *Ant.* 17.254; cf. 3.252–54; 13.252. On pilgrimage for festivals, see Safrai, "Temple," 898–904 (guessing [898] tens of thousands). Josephus's numbers are internally consistent (i.e., proportionate), and some allow more than a million (Byatt, "Population Numbers"; cf. also Foakes-Jackson and Lake, "Background of Jewish History," 1), but 2,700,000 Passover pilgrims (Jos. *War* 6.425) is clearly exaggerated (Avi-Yonah, "Geography," 109).

140. Some texts (*t. Pisha* 4:15; *Lam. Rab.* 1:1, §2) claim more than six million Jewish visitors for every Passover.

141. Cf. Jochim, *Religions*, 152, on an annual festal season when Peikang, Taiwan, receives five hundred thousand to a million visitors, that is, up to 5 percent of Taiwan's population.

142. E.g., Xen. Eph. *Anthia* 1.2. Sometimes large numbers at festivals unexpectedly overtaxed available resources (see Lucian *Peregr.* 19). On Greek pilgrimage, see Corvisier, "Pèlerinages."

143. Spawforth, "Tourism."

144. Pliny E. *N.H.* 5.15.70 (LCL, 2:273, 275). He refers to its former state, writing after its destruction (5.15.73; hence perhaps to glorify the Roman conquest).

Although Scripture demanded the attendance of all Israelite males at these festivals (Exod 23:17; 34:23; Deut 16:16; see also Philo *Spec. Laws* 1.69–70),[145] first-century Jews seem to have applied the requirement only within the Holy Land itself (cf. Jos. *Ant.* 4.203), a concession demanded by practical realities. Nevertheless, many Diaspora Jews did come (Jos. *War* 5.199), though many who came from distant lands could come only very rarely.[146] Some sources suggest that more Diaspora Jews attended Pentecost than Passover because of the difficulties of traveling earlier in the season (see comment on Acts 27:9; cf. 20:6, 16).[147] Those who did come for Passover and made the long and time-consuming trip only once during their lives may well have often stayed for Pentecost seven weeks later (see comment on Acts 2:5).

The festival appealed to a diverse variety of Jewish groups, though not all understood it in the same way.[148] Various Jewish groups argued for different dates for the festival,[149] but Philo's agreement with the tradition also attributed to the Pharisees[150] suggests a generally held date for most of Second Temple Judaism. Certainly, Luke, who refers to the Diaspora crowds gathered (Acts 2:9–11), assumes the common dating of Pentecost.

Luke's expression (συμπληροῦσθαι) for the day "having arrived," or the waiting period (cf. 1:4–5) "having been completed," is probably a biblicism suggesting the momentous nature of the occasion, since Luke earlier uses the term in connection with Jesus's impending ascension (Luke 9:51; elsewhere in the NT, only 8:23).[151] The term suggests the day's arrival, not its completion (Acts 2:15).[152]

b. Life-Giving Wind (2:2)

The wind here reflects a common element of biblical storm theophanies, indicating a revelation of the awesome, one true God. It probably evokes especially Ezek 37: God's promised life-giving breath, or his Spirit.

i. The House

As suggested above, the "entire house" mentioned here sounds neither like the temple (though it was a "house") nor the upper room (see comment on Acts 2:1).[153]

---

145. A tradition also preserved in later rabbinic literature (*Eccl. Rab.* 1:7, §8); for the tradition of crowds at such festivals (and miraculous space to prostrate themselves), see, e.g., *b. Yoma* 21a.

146. Sanders, *Judaism*, 130 (suggesting that "it is doubtful that many came more than once in their lifetime"); Safrai, "Relations," 191; idem, "Pilgrimage to Jerusalem," 12–21.

147. Hull, *Spirit in Acts*, 55–56; also *Song Rab.* 7:2, §2. (Others think Pentecost less popular because it was shorter, Parker, "Apokatastasis," 58–61; available evidence is quite limited, Noack, "Pentecost in Jubilees," 92.) Many Diaspora Jews, however, would have celebrated the festival locally (*CIJ* 2:36, §777, Pentecost in Hierapolis); there is no Diaspora emphasis, however, in the temple scene following Acts 20:16.

148. E.g., *Jub.* 6:32–38; 22:1–9 (though Zeitlin, "Jubilees, Character," 5–7, emphasizes *Jubilees'* alteration of Genesis). Some think that the rabbis may deliberately play down Pentecost because of Essene and Christian emphasis (Noack, "Pentecost in Jubilees," 88–89).

149. See, e.g., *Jub.* 6:32–38 (emphasizing the right calendar); for the Sadducees, see Belkin, *Philo*, 217 (citing *m. Menaḥ.* 10:3; *t. Roš Haš.* 1:15; *b. Menaḥ.* 65a); Dupont, *Salvation*, 36; Fitzmyer, *Acts*, 233; cf. *m. Ḥag.* 2:4; *Megillat Taanit* 1.

150. Belkin, *Philo*, 217–18 (citing Philo *Spec. Laws* 2.162, 176).

151. The specific term appears nowhere in the LXX, though the cognate noun συμπλήρωσις appears in 1 Esd 1:55 [ET 1:58] and 2 Chr 36:21 for the fulfillment of the divine promise, and the cognate verb πληρόω can function in this manner (e.g., Jer 36:10 LXX = Jer 29:10; cf. again 2 Chr 36:21); cf. also συντελεῖσθαι in Acts 21:27.

152. Cf. Dupont, *Salvation*, 36; Haenchen, *Acts*, 167n2 (comparing Gen 25:24 with Luke 1:57; 2:6; 2:21–22; and Lev 8:33 with Luke 9:51); Bruce, *Acts*[1], 81; Knowling, "Acts," 71 (citing Exod 7:25; Jer 29:10); Aubert, *Motif*, 55; cf. the thought in Gal 4:4.

153. Early Pentecostals probably associated it with the upper room (given the application to the upstairs room at Azusa Street; in Menzies, *Anointed*, 52; also the Upper Room Mission, 75–76; Robeck, *Mission*, 94–95, 202–4, 315–18 and passim).

The term "house" cannot decisively settle the question of the location;[154] the temple or tabernacle is a (specially designated) house in Luke 6:4 and 19:46 (quoting Isa 56) and Acts 7:46–47; but the term also appears in *contrast* to the temple (Luke 1:23; Acts 2:46; 5:42), and Luke's emphasis on house meetings makes that sense more likely (Acts 2:46; 5:42; 20:20). One could think that the wind "filled" the "whole household" (18:8), except that Luke gives no indication of that metaphor for the church in the immediate context.[155]

Perhaps Luke deliberately leaves the location ambiguous because he emphasizes both the importance of the temple early in Acts and of the house meetings (cf. 2:46 and 5:42 for both).[156] Especially if the original venue was a house, the ambiguity may allow his probable temple allusion to the wind's "filling the house" here, as smoke filled God's "house" in Isa 6:4 (cf. the fire of Acts 2:3; cf. also Ezek 43:5).[157] The cloud of God's glory filled the tent in Exod 40:34–35 and God's "house" in 1 Kgs 8:10–11 at their dedications—appropriate to a reappropriation of the temple for God's kingdom here. But while the noise filled the house in Acts 2:2, those inside it were filled with the Spirit in 2:4, perhaps making them like the temple of old.[158]

II. Spirit and Wind

As in 4:31, God provided objective, external phenomena to confirm the internal empowerment taking place when he filled the church with the Spirit. Yet Luke is "reserved in his description," simply speaking of phenomena "like" wind and "like" fire,[159] just as he spoke of the Spirit coming on Jesus as "like" a dove (Luke 3:21–22). Luke does not tone down his accounts (as Josephus did with some biblical accounts) or accommodate skeptics as much as some other Hellenistic historians (see introduction, ch. 9, sect. 4.a),[160] but he does practice some of the reserve that many considered appropriate to the genre.

If Luke identified the Spirit with wind or fire, he might view the Spirit as a "substance," as in Hellenistic sources.[161] But Luke's pneumatology is more Jewish and biblical,[162] and he intends only a comparison; the *sound* fills the house and is merely

154. Lake and Cadbury, *Commentary*, 17. Haenchen, *Acts*, 168n1, does note, however, that Luke's preferred term for the temple is ἱερόν (twenty-two times); Jos. *Ant.* 8.65 uses οἶκος for the temple and its chambers, but Josephus usually uses ναός.

155. The "women" and "brothers" of Acts 1:14 would provide household imagery only if we took "women" as "wives" (which I have argued is unlikely) or accepted the unlikely textual variant there.

156. The "house" might provide a paradigm for Christian experiences in homes/familial settings, like the outpouring in Acts 10:44 (10:22, Cornelius's house). But Luke does not emphasize that as the mandatory setting; it is not specified in Acts 8 or 19.

157. See Hull, *Spirit in Acts*, 57; Spencer, *Acts*, 32; Beale, "Descent." Dupont, *Salvation*, 41, compares also Exod 19:18.

158. Whether Luke might also allude to a spiritual temple/house (Eph 2:20–22; 1 Pet 2:5; Rev 3:12) is uncertain, though he seems aware of this image (Luke 19:40, 44–47). For a plausible and well-articulated case for the descent of the eschatological temple here, see Beale, "Descent" (idem, "Temple," arguing for the temple contexts of texts often used to illumine this passage).

159. Witherington, *Acts*, 132. This paucity of description militates against this passage's being a good illustration of ekphrasis (*pace* Parsons, *Acts*, 37–38; Escobedo, "Lens," 134–38, despite insights).

160. Cf. also Keener, *Miracles*, 87–96.

161. Hull, *Spirit in Acts*, 58–59 (comparing Philo *Flight* 32; Nemesius *De Natura hominis* 30, 40). On the Stoics, see Long, *Philosophy*, 155–58, 171; Chevallier, *Ancien Testament*, 41–42; Büchsel, *Geist*, 45–49, esp. 47. Philo's Jewish background prevented complete assimilation to Stoic conceptions here (Scott, *Spirit*, 58–59; Isaacs, *Spirit*, 19), but the blending of Jewish and Stoic sources is evident even in Wisdom of Solomon (Chevallier, "Souffle," 43–46, esp. 45–46).

162. See, e.g., Keener, *Spirit*, 7–8, 10–13, with the emphasis on the prophetic Spirit in Luke-Acts (e.g., Acts 2:17–18); see our introduction, ch. 15, sect. 5, and esp. the excursus there on the background for Luke's conception of the Spirit.

compared with a wind (ὥσπερ in Acts 2:2 and especially ὡσεὶ in 2:3).[163] Wind was stereotypically unpredictable or unstable (Catull. *Carm.* 70.4; John 3:8). Naturalists viewed wind as "air flowing in one direction" (Sen. Y. *Nat. Q.* 5.1.1 [LCL])[164] or caused by celestial objects moving opposite the earth's motion,[165] but most people saw supernatural connections behind it.[166] Luke's ἄφνω, "suddenly," was appropriate for storms (cf. Prov 1:27) as well as (more often) other calamities (cf. Acts 16:26).

The theophanic storm images of wind and fire would not be lost on even the most recent pagan converts to the churches: citing a wide range of ancient sources, P. W. van der Horst concludes that "wind and especially fire (often on the head) are frequently regarded as signs of divine presence."[167] Similarly, a deity might breathe (πνεύσῃ) strength into one or both sides in a battle (Hom. *Il.* 19.159). Greeks also could associate breezes and scents with a hero's apparition.[168] Some Greek thinkers also allegorized Poseidon as a πνεῦμα (wind or breath) in the sea; a second-century C.E. Middle Platonist even identifies him with the cosmic soul.[169] Biblical allusions, however, supply the dominant background here.

Luke uses a rare term here for "wind," one that connects especially with God's gift of the breath of life in the LXX and in Luke's other usage of it (Acts 17:25), which alludes to Gen 2:7.[170] The more common term for "wind" and "breath" in Greek (including the LXX, πνεῦμα; and likewise with the Hebrew equivalent) provides obvious associations with God's "Spirit," which is the same term (cf. John 3:8; Ezek 37:9–10).[171] Early Israelite writers may have distinguished spirit, breath, and wind more as various nuances of a connected concept,[172] but in Greek the connections function more like paronomasia or related forms of wordplay,[173] though probably not as a deliberate rhetorical device.[174] The very different narrative of the Johannine

163. Hull, *Spirit in Acts*, 59; Johnson, *Acts*, 42.

164. For further empirical observation and related speculation about the winds, see, e.g., Sen. Y. *Nat. Q.* 5.16.1–5.18.2; Vitruv. *Arch.* 8.2.5–6. Williams, "Winds," suggests moralizing applications in Seneca's discussion of winds.

165. Pliny E. *N.H.* 2.45.116; see further 2.44.114–15.

166. Personifying them or viewing them as under the gods (e.g., Virg. *Aen.* 1.56–59; Val. Flacc. 8.322–27; Plut. *Bride* 12, *Mor.* 139DE; cf. Käppel, "Notos"; Rives, *Religion*, 16; ancient Near Eastern weather deities in Schwemer, "Weather gods") or under the true God's dominion (e.g., *1 En.* 4:3; 18:1–5; 34:2–3; 76:4; Rev 7:1; *Jos. Asen.* 12:2; *Sib. Or.* 1.195; *Gen. Rab.* 24:4; *Lev. Rab.* 15:1; *Tg. Jon.* on 1 Kgs 19:11–12).

167. Van der Horst, "Parallels to Acts," 49–50, citing Hom. *Il.* 18.225–27; Eurip. *Bacch.* 757–58; Cic. *Div.* 1.53.121; Ovid *Fasti* 6.634–36; Virg. *Aen.* 2.680–84; 8.680–81; Iambl. *Myst.* 3.2.3.6; Livy 1.39.2; 25.39.16; Pliny E. *N.H.* 2.241; Apul. *De deo Socr.* 7 (and several more). For some analogous modern claims, see below.

168. Philost. *Hrk.* 3.2–5; 10.2; 11.3 (see Maclean and Aitken, *Heroikos*, xxvii).

169. Max. Tyre 4.8; and comments in Trapp, *Maximus*, 39 (who contrasts earlier sources, Chrysippus in Cic. *Nat. d.* 1.40 and Diogenes of Babylon frg. 33).

170. The term πνοή appears elsewhere in the NT only at Acts 17:25, where it refers to human "breath" as a gift of God (and alludes directly to Gen 2:7); in the LXX (twenty-four times), it refers especially to the breath of life. For the Gen 2:7 allusion in John 20:22, see Turner, *Gift*, 90–92; Keener, *John*, 1204–5. Later Targumim interpreted God's breath into Adam as endowment with speech (*Tg. Ps.-J.* on Gen 2:7; *Tg. Neof.* on Gen 2:7; probably analogous to the Spirit of prophecy's frequent effects). The comparison with the divine wind or Spirit at creation (Gen 1:2; Walaskay, *Acts*, 34) seems less convincing.

171. Cf. Dupont, *Salvation*, 40; Longenecker, *Acts*, 66; Dunn, *Acts*, 24–25; Fitzmyer, *Acts*, 235. For wind as πνεῦμα, see, e.g., Philost. *Hrk.* 31.9.

172. See Keener, "Spirit," 484–87.

173. On which see *Rhet. Her.* 4.21.29–22.32; Quint. *Inst.* 8.3.11–12; 9.3.66–67; Rowe, "Style," 132; Anderson, *Glossary*, 93, 127; idem, *Rhetorical Theory*, 283–85; cf. Blass, Debrunner, and Funk, *Grammar*, §488; for "Spirit" and "wind," see Keener, *John*, 555–57 passim. As noted above, writers could use the wind to illustrate unpredictability (Catull. *Carm.* 70.4; John 3:8; cf. as something difficult to trace in *Pesiq. Rab.* 23:8). Some diverse cultures link "spirit" with "wind" (Kaplan and Johnson, "Navajo Psychopathology," 205; Egyptian language in Görg, "Wehen") or "wind" with the divine (Mbiti, *Religions*, 70).

174. Theorists advised its sparing use, mainly for lightening speech (Anderson, *Rhetorical Theory*, 283–84, cites Cic. *Part. or.* 72; Quint. *Inst.* 8.3.11–12; *Rhet. Her.* 4.29–32).

"Pentecost" also alludes to the biblical picture of a breath or wind imparting God's Spirit (John 20:22).[175] But by also describing it as sudden and violent, Luke pushes this "breath" into the category of a strong wind (cf. Exod 14:21).[176] Such strong and stormy winds were common in the Judean hill country, including Jerusalem.[177]

Some scholars have argued that John the Baptist's "Spirit and fire" (Luke 3:16// Matt 3:11) originally alluded to the wind and fire of the threshing floor (Luke 3:17// Matt 3:12),[178] though this interpretation is not likely in the Gospels or even in early Judaism, where "Holy Spirit" has a standard sense.[179] But even though it is unlikely that John or the Gospels that report his saying think only of a wind, a wordplay in the original saying is plausible. Such a wordplay would illustrate the principle emphasized here, namely, the connection naturally drawn between wind and Spirit.

III. BIBLICAL ALLUSIONS

A more specific connection between wind and Spirit, however, is likelier. In accordance with the pervasive biblical allusions in Luke-Acts, it is best to understand Luke's ideal audience as at least biblically literate Gentile converts and as probably including a substantial core of Jewish Christians and God-fearers with a background in understanding the Scriptures (see introduction, ch. 12, sect. 2). The stormy images of wind and fire (Acts 2:2–3) recall various theophanies in ancient Israel (cf., e.g., Exod 3:2; 2 Sam 5:24; Job 38:1; Pss 29:3–10; 97:2–5; 104:3; Isa 29:6; 30:27–28; 66:15; Ezek 1:4),[180] perhaps including the pillar of cloud and fire (as noted above; Exod 13:21–22; 14:24; Num 14:14; Neh 9:12, 19; Wis 18:3; 2 Esd 1:14),[181] and scholars cite especially the following: Sinai (Exod 19:16, 19; Deut 4:11; cf. Ps 68:16–18; Hab 3:3–15; Jos. Ant. 3.79–81), smoke filling the house in Isa 6:4 (cf. Exod 19:18; 40:34–38; 2 Chr 7:1–3), and possibly 1 Kgs 19:11–12 (though in this case God's voice to Elijah contrasts with the storm and earthquake and comes as a gentle blowing, 19:12).[182] Fire and wind also appear together at Elijah's ascension (2 Kgs 2:11), offering Luke a fitting potential allusion since it would recall Jesus's departure (for the Elijah allusion there, see comment on Acts 1:9–11), reinforcing the allusion to the passing on of Jesus's Spirit (like Elijah's in 2 Kgs 2:9–10).

In view of the disciples' eschatological expectations in the context (see Acts 1:3–8, esp. 1:6) and the explicitly eschatological interpretation of this event (2:17), the disciples would have experienced this theophany at least partly as an eschatological event (though, with the advantage of retrospect, Luke transmutes their experience

175. Recalling Gen 2:7 but possibly implying Ezek 37 as well in the light of John 3:8; see more fully Keener, John, 555–58, 1204–5.
176. Exodus 14:21 LXX uses the most common term for wind but adds βιαίῳ. Cf. ἄφνω (in the NT, solely Lukan, found in Acts 16:26; 28:6) in Prov 1:27; and βία or βίαιος with πνεῦμα in Ps 48:7; Isa 11:15; Wis 5:11; 7:20 (cf. 13:2; 17:17, where wind is linked with violent waters). For fire and storm, Conzelmann, Acts, 13, adds 4 Ezra 13:10.
177. Bishop, Apostles, 31. The rainy season was over by Pentecost, but such winds could bring heat and sand (31–32); winds could be violent whether at sea (e.g., Acts 27:4–15) or in the desert (e.g., Sall. Jug. 79.6; Jer 13:24; Hos 13:15).
178. So Bruce, "Matthew," 84; Flowers, "En pneumati"; cf. Dunn, "Spirit," 695; Isa 4:4; Mal 3:2. Barnard, "Matt. III.11," 107, suggests the image of a fiery stream (which appears in many Jewish texts).
179. See Keener, Matthew, 127n157.
180. In early Jewish sources, also Jub. 1:3; L.A.E. 25:3; 4 Ezra 3:19; cf. 13:27; at the law-giving at Sinai, L.A.B. 11:5; 23:10; 32:7; God's greatness over these elements in 4 Ezra 4:5, 9; 2 Bar. 48:4; m. 'Ab. 5:8.
181. Some in the first century C.E. thought of a fiery pillar as a type of whirlwind (Pliny E. N.H. 2.50.133–34).
182. E.g., Knowling, "Acts," 72; C. Williams, Acts, 62; O'Hagan, "Pentecost"; Stronstad, Charismatic Theology, 58; Barrett, Acts, 113; Spencer, Acts, 32 (focusing on Isa 6); Gaventa, Acts, 74; Escobedo, "Lens," 140 (fire in Exodus as God's presence). The Isaiah connection fits the context of mission (Rigato, "Evento").

into the realized eschatology of the spreading of the gospel; cf. Isa 52:7).[183] Biblical storm theophanies could also prefigure a future revelation of God's power (Isa 66:15; cf. 2 Thess 1:7–10). At some point (not necessarily before Acts), Jewish tradition connected the divine breath of Gen 2:7 with the eschatological wind of the Spirit in Ezek 37.[184] Jewish people expected an eschatological "wind" of the Spirit to bring the breath of life into the slain of Israel (Ezek 37:14). Ezekiel's "dry bones" prophecy in this context figured prominently in Jewish end-time thought, especially among eschatologically oriented sects.[185] Many commentators recognize Ezek 37 as a primary background for the image here.[186]

The "noise" (ἦχος)[187] might allude to the Sinai theophany (Exod 19:16–19, especially φωνή with ἤχει in 19:16);[188] it may be noteworthy that outside of Luke's usage (here and in Luke 4:37; 21:25), the NT uses this Greek word only once, in a description of the revelation at Sinai (Heb 12:19).[189] It might also allude to Ezek 37:7, which directly precedes the wind of 37:9–10; in Ezekiel, the noise refers to the rattling of bones preparing for the resurrection.[190] That the noise came "from heaven" fits the Sinai parallel (Exod 20:22; Deut 4:36) as well as Luke's general cosmology (cf. Luke 3:22; Acts 1:11; 11:9 and comment at Acts 11:9 about the *bat qol*).[191] (The phrase "from heaven" was also good Jewish[192] and even pagan[193] language for "from God" but was usually figurative.)

c. Eschatological and/or Theophanic Fire (2:3)

Though less common than simply "flames," the expression "tongues of fire"[194] is common in Jewish texts,[195] perhaps because fire licks and "devours."[196] It appears to be idiomatic, applicable in the Qumran scrolls even to flashes of brilliance from the Urim or Thummim when God answers.[197] Still, Luke probably employs this

183. Cf. Abri, "Meaning of Pentecost"; O'Hagan, "Pentecost"; Boismard and Lamouille, *Actes*, 2:101.

184. *Gen. Rab.* 14:8; Grassi, "Ezekiel xxxvii.1–14," 164; a link between "breathe" in Gen 2:7 and Ezek 37:9 is also logical on midrashic hermeneutical assumptions. On the relevance of Gen 2:7, see comment above.

185. See 4Q386; 4Q388; 4Q385 frg. 2 (for wind, see lines 7–8); also see Diaspora frescoes at Dura-Europos (Philonenko, "Ossements desséchés"); for Ezek 37 and the hope of the Spirit's raising the dead, e.g., *Sipre Deut.* 306.28.3; *y. Šeqal.* 3:3; *Gen. Rab.* 96:5; *Exod. Rab.* 48:4.

186. E.g., Grassi, "Ezekiel xxxvii.1–14," 164; Bruce, *Commentary*, 54; Longenecker, *Acts*, 66; Gibbs, "Launching of Mission," 21.

187. Applicable to storms or waves, as in Acts 2:2–3 (cf. Luke 21:25; Pss 65:7; 77:16; Jer 51:16, 42; Sir 46:17), or praises or musical instruments (Pss 42:4; 150:3; Amos 5:23; Dan 3:7, 10, 15; Wis 19:18; Sir 50:18).

188. Dupont, *Salvation*, 39 (noting also Philo *Decal.* 33, and φωνή in Acts 2:6; Philo *Decal.* 46; Exod 20:18); Johnson, *Acts*, 42; cf. Jos. *Ant.* 3.81.

189. Also Dupont, *Salvation*, 39. It is revelatory in the later *Herm.* 22.4.

190. Cf. the sound reviving the dead at Sinai in *Tg. Ps.-J.* on Exod 20:15/18. Earlier and more relevant, cf. the tradition of a noise on a later Pentecost in Jos. *War* 6.299, but there it signifies the Lord's withdrawal from the temple.

191. Cf. Dupont, *Salvation*, 40.

192. E.g., Dan 4:26; 3 Macc 4:21; *1 En.* 6:2; 1QM XII, 5; Rom 1:18; Luke 15:18; *m. 'Ab.* 1:3; *t. B. Qam.* 7:5; *Sipra Behuq. pq.* 6. 267.2.1; 79.1.1; *b. Taʿan.* 14b; *Pesaḥ.* 66b; *ʿAbod. Zar.* 18a, bar.; *Moʿed Qaṭ.* 17a; *B. Qam.* 76a.

193. Fronto *Eloq.* 1.3 warns against waiting for eloquence to fall, like the Palladium, *de caelo*, "from heaven."

194. On various translations of γλῶσσαι here, see Steyn, "Γλῶσσαι."

195. Hull, *Spirit in Acts*, 58; Haenchen, *Acts*, 168n2; Conzelmann, *Acts*, 13 (citing Isa 5:24 MT; *1 En.* 14:9–10, 15; 71:5; 1Q22; 1Q29 1 3; 2 3; 4Q375–376); cf. *Gen. Rab.* 59:4. Menzies, "Occurrences," notes that these occurrences became most common in the Merkabah tradition, appropriate for heavenly revelation in Acts 2:4.

196. Cf., e.g., LXX Isa 10:17; 26:11; 30:27; Jer 21:14; also cf. Heb 10:27; Jas 5:3; even more often the cognate in Lev 9:24; 10:2; Num 11:1; 16:35; 21:28; 26:10; and passim in the LXX; Rev 11:5. To some extent the metaphor may have lost its figurative force, but the image apparently remained.

197. E.g., 1Q29 1 3; 2 2; 4Q376 1 II, 1.

particular fire idiom here to emphasize the connection with Acts 2:4:[198] just as noise filled the house (2:2) but the Spirit the disciples (2:4), so here divine tongues of fire fall on the disciples (2:3) but the Spirit empowers their tongues (2:4). The fire divides among them; the term here for dividing (διαμεριζόμεναι) is particularly Lukan,[199] perhaps conceivably evoking sharing (2:45; cf. Luke 22:17) but probably simply indicating the individuation of the gift (cf. 1 Cor 12:27 and the distinct languages in Acts 2:9–11). Jewish teachers could also envisage fire dividing up to rest on different individuals.[200]

Fire was a common element of theophanies (see Deut 4:24; Heb 12:29; see further above on Acts 2:2),[201] including the Sinai theophany (Exod 19:16, 18; Deut 4:12, 15; Heb 12:18).[202] Less relevant is that later Jewish teachers occasionally imagined fire falling as at Sinai during the most intense study of Torah.[203] In Philo, the Sinai fire itself became an understandable voice that was miraculously heard at the same volume regardless of distance (Philo *Decal.* 32–35, 46–47; cf. later *Tanḥ.* 26c); many commentators suggest that Luke drew on these traditions or reflects the same approach to interpretation.[204] Admittedly, although Philo wrote before Luke and later rabbis who support his version must depend on a common tradition of interpretation, we cannot be sure how pervasive the extrabiblical elements were among Diaspora Jews in Luke's day or among Palestinian Jews in the time of Luke's source or sources. Yet the approach of Philo and other midrashists is a logical inference from an overliteralistic interpretation of both the Hebrew text and the LXX;[205] since Luke does not

198. Cf., e.g., Dupont, *Salvation*, 41; Fitzmyer, *Acts*, 238; Chance, *Acts*, 48. Rhetoric welcomed continuity of metaphors; see the later Hermog. *Inv.* 4.10.200 on Demosth. *Or.* 4.49. Levison, *Filled*, 329–30, connects fire with inspiration in Greek sources (cf. also Jer 20:9).

199. Not referring to fire (Luke 11:17–18; 12:52–53; 22:17; 23:34); elsewhere in the NT, only for the dividing of Jesus's garments (Matt 27:35; Mark 15:24; John 19:24; as in Luke 23:34).

200. In *Sipra Sh. M.D.* 99.5.7, for judgment. Some scholars cite God's voice dividing into seven and then seventy at Sinai, in third-century rabbinic tradition (Dupont, *Salvation*, 42), but the parallel might be too distant, despite possible Sinai allusions in the context.

201. Here, see, e.g., Rackham, *Acts*, 18 (citing Exod 3:2–4; Virg. *Aen.* 2.682–84); Hull, *Spirit in Acts*, 58; Johnson, *Acts*, 42. Fire was sacred to the Persians (Quint. Curt. 3.3.10; 4.13.12; cf. later among Zoroastrians, Yamauchi, *Persia*, 447) and viewed as divine (Hdt. 1.131; Lucian Z. *Rants* 42; Max. Tyre 2.4). Some Stoics viewed God as the primal fire (Sen. Y. *Ben.* 4.8.1; Hippol. *Ref.* 1.3); Jews recognized God as consuming fire (Deut 4:24; 9:3; Isa 30:27, 30; Heb 12:29; *Exod. Rab.* 30:19; *Pesiq. Rab.* 11:7), and Torah could be associated with it (*Song Rab.* 5:11, §6; cf. *Song Rab.* 1:10, §2).

202. Dupont, *Salvation*, 41; Johnson, *Acts*, 46; Conzelmann, *Acts*, 13. For an earlier, personal theophanic revelation to Moses at Sinai, see Luke 20:37; Acts 7:30. Like subsequent Lukan reports of outpourings of the Spirit, most modern popular revival reports that include tongues and other Pentecost-type phenomena omit the tongues of fire, but reports of fire or fire-like phenomena do appear; e.g., Wacker, *Heaven*, 93 (citing W. W. Hall's claim in 1924); Sung, *Diaries*, 109 (while others were seeing or hearing angels; March 27, 1937), 140–41 (secondhand but leading to many conversions; January 1935); Synan, *Voices*, 137–38 (June 20, 1905, in the Indian revival at Pandita Ramabai's home for orphan brides, also noted in Ma, "Mission," 24; Jones, "Fire," 214; McGee, *People of Spirit*, 74; idem, "Regions Beyond," 84; cf. also Bartleman, *Azusa Street*, 35); Liardon, *Generals*, 400; cf. also the globe of fire above the head of St. Martin of Tours (Gardner, *Healing Miracles*, 72), and the visible cloud of glory in Clark, *Impartation*, 213; the bright light from heaven seen by many during the 1939 Presbyterian revival in the Hebrides (Peckham, *Sounds*, 107); the rushing wind in an early American Methodist revival noted in Wigger, *Saint*, 301 (if the witness intends the expression literally); "an audible wind" in the 1930s Shandong revival (with Southern Baptist participation; Bays, "Revival," 173); another on Aug. 27, 1970, in the Solomon Islands revival (Koch, *Gifts*, 22; idem, *Zulus*, 50); on Sept. 26, 1965, a rushing wind and visible fire at the beginning of the Timor revival in Indonesia (Tari, *Wind*, 24–25; idem, *Breeze*, 6).

203. E.g., *b. Ḥag.* 14b; *y. Ḥag.* 2:1, §9; cf. the child expositor of mysteries consumed by fire in *b. Ḥag.* 13a.

204. E.g., Isaacs, *Spirit*, 131; Zehnle, *Pentecost Discourse*, 117; Conzelmann, *Acts*, 13; Boring, Berger, and Colpe, *Commentary*, 311; Le Cornu, *Acts*, 59–60 (citing also *Mek. Bah.* 9; *Exod. Rab.* 5:9; 34:1); Neudecker, "Volk"; cf. Klauck, *Magic*, 8; Chance, *Acts*, 48.

205. The LXX ἑώρα (Exod 20:18; cf. Deut 4:12; perhaps 5:24) is the third singular imperfect active indicative of ὁράω, not the verb to be expected with φωνήν (but one that fits the other objects).

normally handle Scripture in this midrashic manner, it is plausible that he depends here on prior tradition.

Fire also applied to judgments, including end-time judgments.[206] Because of its association with the Spirit here (Acts 2:4), Luke's informed audience would quickly connect the fire with Luke 3:16,[207] which was originally a promise of end-time judgment.[208] Although this fire may function proleptically for purification (Luke 12:49–50), it symbolizes the eschatological judgment that is the converse of baptism in the Spirit (3:16).[209] Jesus's coming to cast fire on the earth,[210] conjoined with his own baptism of suffering (12:49–50), might suggest the fire baptism of judgment for all who do not accept his vicarious judgment in the cross.[211] (The image of a river of fire, found in Jewish sources,[212] also attested in pagan sources,[213] is probably not as directly relevant.)

Just as the Spirit descended on Jesus in a visible way (Luke 3:21–22), so here a fiery association with the Spirit (alluding to the same context, 3:16) descended on the disciples. One could argue that "appeared" (ὤφθησαν) is visionary language (Acts 16:9; cf. 7:2),[214] but Luke uses it for angelic encounters (Luke 1:11; 22:43; Acts 7:30, 35) and Jesus's glory, whether at the transfiguration (Luke 9:31) or after his resurrection (Luke 24:34; Acts 9:17; 13:31; 26:16; cf. Acts 1:3). Likewise, when the Spirit descended in form "like" a dove (Luke 3:22), the appearance was symbolic but not for Luke only a personal "vision."[215]

d. Spirit Filling and Tongues (2:4)

As noted above, Luke has an important reason to emphasize tongues when addressing the coming of the Spirit. Luke's particular emphasis regarding the Spirit is empowerment for cross-cultural prophetic witness (Acts 1:8), and nothing could

206. For judgments, see, e.g., Isa 26:11; 66:15–16, 24; CD II, 4–6; *1 En.* 103:8; *Sib. Or.* 4.43, 161, 176–78; 2 Thess 1:6–7; *Exod. Rab.* 15:27; see further Davies and Allison, *Matthew*, 1:310; Keener, *Matthew*, 128–29.

207. Johnson, *Acts*, 42; Barrett, *Acts*, 114. Cf. Boismard and Lamouille, *Actes*, 2:101, who connect it with division in Luke 12:49–53; but for 12:49–50 as Jesus's baptism of fire (experiencing judgment for others), cf. comment below. Some have identified the Spirit and fire (Pelagius *Comm. Rom.* on 6:3 [de Bruyn, 96; Bray, *Romans*, 154]), but while they are one eschatological gift, the repentant "wheat," in the context in Q, receive the Spirit, and the "chaff" the fire (Matt 3:10–12; Luke 3:9, 16–17).

208. See, e.g., Keener, *Spirit*, 127; Menzies, *Development*, 137–44.

209. On judgment in Acts 2:3–4, see Charette, "Tongues as of Fire"; cf. Isa 28:11 (a judgment passage) in 1 Cor 14:21.

210. Likely judgment (cf., e.g., Tannehill, *Luke*, 251, though he does not see it as necessarily final judgment; for the graphic language here, cf. idem, *Sword*, 145), perhaps on Israel (cf. Witherington, *Christology of Jesus*, 121–22).

211. I read Luke 12:49–50 with Luke 3:16; see Robinson, *Studies*, 161; Dunn, *Baptism*, 42. Cf. also Mark 10:38 (on which cf. Robinson, *Studies*, 160–61; Lampe, *Seal*, 39; Lane, *Mark*, 380–81).

212. Cf. Davies and Allison, *Matthew*, 1:316, who cite Dan 7:10; 1QHᵃ XI, 29–36; *1 En.* 67:13; *Sib. Or.* 2.196–205, 252–54 (probably a Christian interpolation); 3.54 (against Rome), 84–87; *4 Ezra* 13:10–11. See also 4Q385 4 11; 4Q405 15 II, 2–3; 20 II, 10; *1 En.* 14:19; 17:4–5; 67:7; 71:1–2, 6; *3 En.* 33:4; *Lam. Rab.* 3:23, §8; *Pesiq. Rab.* 20:4; for the lake of fire, e.g., *1 En.* 14:22; Rev 19:20; 20:10, 14–15; cf. *Pesiq. Rab Kah.* 5:3 (though these are literally just "realms" of fire).

213. E.g., Virg. *Aen.* 6.735–42. It can depict torment in Tartarus, as in, e.g., Virg. *Aen.* 6.551; Lucian *Dial. D.* 450 (24/30, Minos and Sostratus 1); Sil. It. 13.836, 871; 14.61–62.

214. Cf. Dunn, *Acts*, 25; Miller, *Convinced*, 170–71. Johnson, *Acts*, 45, emphasizes αὐτοῖς, hence to "the disciples, not the crowd"; but this argument begs the question as to who was gathered in the "house" at that moment. Historians and others reported as true a special solar phenomenon at one of Augustus's entries into Rome (in 44 B.C.E.; Vell. Paterc. 2.59.6; Sen. *Nat. Q.* 1.2.1; Suet. *Aug.* 95), though this report is explicable in terms of a natural phenomenon interpreted as a portent. For halo or halo-like claims, see, e.g., Pliny E. *N.H.* 36.70.204; a glorious deity (Mithras) in *PGM* 4.696–99; but Jewish portraits of angels and others may be more relevant (e.g., *4 Ezra* 10:25; *2 En.* 1:5; 19:1; 22:4; 26:2–7; *3 En.* 14:5; 18:25; 22:5; 26:7; Rev 10:1).

215. In Mark 1:10, Jesus saw the heavens opened and the Spirit descending; Luke leaves this ambiguous (Luke 3:21), even more than Matt 3:16 (though Matthew's voice sounds more public, 3:17).

better symbolize empowerment to cross such barriers than the ability to speak, by the Spirit's inspiration, in languages one has not learned. Luke repeats this sign on two other strategic occasions in Acts (10:46; 19:6). In contrast to the question of miracle cures, which I have been able to relegate to a separate book,[216] I must explore the question of the possible background and meaning of tongues in more detail here (below).

Even more often than tongues, Luke emphasizes the experience of being "filled" with the Spirit, sometimes for the same individual on multiple occasions (cf. 4:8, 31; 9:17; 13:9). This experience fulfills the promise of the Spirit's coming announced in 1:4–5, 8 and further interpreted in 2:17–18, 38–39 (for further comment, see discussion of those passages).

1. Filled with the Holy Spirit

In 2:2, a noise "filled" the house; now in 2:4, the disciples are "filled" with the Spirit, producing a different kind of sound (2:6). Luke's language here could be intelligible even to some uninstructed Gentiles. One inspired to speak authoritatively for a deity might be compared with someone "full of the deity" (*plena deo*, Sen. E. *Suas.* 3.5–7).[217] Speaking figuratively, a third- or fourth-century C.E. orator could comment that Apollo at Delphi and elsewhere "was filling the prophet with the mantic spirit" (ἐπλήρου τὴν προφῆτιν μαντικοῦ [τοῦ] πνεύματος, Men. Rhet. 2.4, 390.23–24).[218] Figuratively, a teacher could "fill" (διαπιμπλὰς) his disciples "as with nectar" (Eunapius *Lives* 458); Iamblichus's disciples could approach him as a spring to fill themselves (*Lives* 460).[219]

Yet Luke shares with his audience a more central common background in Scripture. In Scripture, the phrase "filled with the Spirit" applied to the Spirit's gifting for skills, whether in sacred craftsmanship (Exod 31:3; 35:31), for leadership (Deut 34:9), or for prophecy (Mic 3:8).[220] In Sirach, the righteous person is filled (ἐμπλησθήσεται) with the Spirit of understanding when God wills, and pours out wise sayings (Sir 39:6).[221] In view of the parallels with the Elijah succession narrative in Acts 1:8–11, it could also be instructive that Elisha is "filled with" Elijah's spirit in Sir 48:12.[222]

Luke employs the biblical phrase "filled with the Spirit" frequently, especially for an experience enabling prophets and prophetic inspiration (Luke 1:15, 41, 67)[223] and for power for Christian proclamation, both for apostles (Acts 4:8; 9:17; 13:9) and

216. Keener, *Miracles*.

217. For the image of being "seized" by a spirit in inspiration in another language, cf. the descriptions of the Pythia in comment on Acts 16:16.

218. Cf. Philost. *Hrk.* 7.3 (μαντικῆς σοφίας ἐμφοροῦνται). Because these examples stem from the third or early fourth century, the possibility exists that some of their religious language reflects the influence of Christian vocabulary (note especially προφῆτιν, though the "mantic" language is not used for Christian prophecy in any extant first-century sources.

219. Eunapius is late enough that it could potentially (though need not) reflect Christian influence.

220. Thus the Pentecost experience stands in continuity with earlier biblical experience (cf. Fuller, *Gospel*, 173–74; Haya-Prats, *Believers*, 5–6n6). *'Abot R. Nat.* 43 B links a few of these texts midrashically (Le Cornu, *Acts*, 63).

221. In *Test. Job* 41:5 (*OTP* 1:861)/41:7 (Kraft, 74), one could speak evil because "filled [ἐμπλησθείς] by Satan" (cf. Acts 5:3); cf. a nonhuman filling with an "evil spirit" in *Test. Ash.* 1:9.

222. Whoever seeks the law will be filled with it (Sir 2:16; 35:15 [32:15]). A successor being filled with the Spirit through his predecessor also appears in Deut 34:9, mentioned above.

223. Hull, *Spirit in Acts*, 69, suggests that the fillings in Luke 1 were temporary but *prefigured* Pentecost (a likely premise, given the fillings' relative locations at the beginnings of the respective books). *Herm.* 43.9 associates being filled with the prophetic spirit with an angel, different from most early Christian usage (though cf. Rev 1:1; some would add 1 Cor 14:32); contrast being filled with the devil's spirit in *Herm.* 43.3.

others (4:31; 13:52).[224] Christians could experience multiple fillings (4:8, 31; 9:17; 13:9), though Luke might restrict the term "baptize" only to the initial experience.[225]

This narrative democratizes the widespread prophetic filling of the Spirit in Num 11:16–17, 25 even further, fulfilling Moses's prayer that all God's people would be filled with the Spirit (Num 11:29).[226] (Some later Jewish interpreters also connected Num 11:29 with Joel 2:28, indicating that Joel's outpouring constituted the answer to Moses's prayer.)[227]

Luke describes most of his work's major characters at some point as being "filled with" or "full of" the Spirit (e.g., Luke 1:15, 41, 67; 4:1; Acts 4:8; 6:3; 7:55; 9:17; 11:24; 13:9) and hence speaking God's message or doing signs and wonders. In this way they stand in continuity with the prophets and are rejected for the same reasons (Luke 6:22–23; 11:47–51; Acts 7:51–52).[228] Luke also employs the related phrase "full of the Spirit," probably to describe those who are already or regularly equipped by the Spirit for their tasks (Luke 4:1; Acts 6:3, 5; 7:55; 11:24).[229]

11. Introductory Comments on Tongues Speaking Here

Although this commentary addresses tongues speaking in more detail (even proportionately) than most, it can survey only some of the questions involved. The secondary literature on tongues (both ancient and modern) is now enormous, extending to far more than a thousand sources.[230]

Luke portrays tongues speaking as Spirit-inspired speech, a fulfillment of the eschatological promise of the prophetic Spirit (Acts 2:17–18).[231] Luke emphasizes tongues because inspired speaking in languages that one has not learned serves as a powerful theological sign and narrative confirmation of empowerment for cross-cultural witness (1:8).[232]

The term for "speaking" (ἀποφθέγγομαι) in tongues often applied to oracular speech,[233] but it also applied to any other kind of formal utterances.[234] Egyptians allegedly sought prophetic portents in the crying out (the cognate φθέγγομαι) of children (Plut. *Isis* 14, *Mor.* 356E),[235] but the same term can refer to wicked speech

224. Its clearest non-Lukan, early Christian usage applies to inspired worship (Eph 5:18–20), perhaps in contrast to the Mysteries, or at least to drunken banquet songs (see Keener, *Paul*, 259–63).

225. Witherington, *Acts*, 133; Keener, *Gift*, 157–68.

226. With Faw, *Acts*, 51 (who less convincingly connects the scoffers of Acts 2:13 with Joshua's "opposition" in Num 11:28). For Num 11 in Acts 2, cf. also Cotton, "Significance," esp. 3; Leeper, "Gift," esp. 25, 28–29, 36–37; Williams, "Old Testament Pentecost"; Menzies, "Sending," 98–99; Stronstad, "Baptized," 171–72, noting significant parallels (esp. the transfer and dissemination of the Spirit); note also Edward Barber in 1648 (in Barr, Leonard, Parsons, and Weaver, *Acts*, 110).

227. Lake and Cadbury, *Commentary*, 22 (citing *Midr. Pss.* 14:6).

228. Tannehill, *Acts*, 32–33.

229. See Menzies, *Power*, 169. He notes (166) the frequent LXX idiom "πλήρης + subjective genitive of quality." Calderón, "Llenura," similarly suggests "filling" for inspired speech and "full" for virtue.

230. Cf. esp. Mills, *Glossolalia: Bibliography*, with more than 1,150 entries already in 1985.

231. Even in 1 Cor 12–14, some scholars associate tongues with realized eschatology (Snyder, *Corinthians*, 180).

232. See Keener, "Tongues," 177–78, 180–81; idem, "Holy Spirit," 171; earlier, *Gift*, 180. For a survey of various understandings of the theological implications that Luke finds in tongues, see Choi, "Personality," 158–60.

233. Cf. Dupont, *Salvation*, 51. Knowling, "Acts," 72–73, cites LXX usage for prophetic speech (1 Chr 25:1; Ezek 13:9, 19; Mic 5:12; Zech 10:2; but contrast Ps 59:7 [58:8 LXX]); also Palma, "Ἀποφθέγγομαι." Cf. Philo *Heir* 259; Jos. 117; *Mos.* 1.175–76; 2.253, 263; (using a cognate) mental inspiration in Porph. *Marc.* 26.417–18; magical gibberish in Semitic languages in Lucian *Alex.* 13.

234. Forbes, *Prophecy*, 163; e.g., *Test. Dan* 5:2 (cognate); Porph. *Marc.* 15.255–56 (cognate); probably the cognate in Acts 4:18. For speaking in angelic dialects, *Test. Job* 48:3; for wisdom as *figurative* prophecy, Diogenes *Ep.* 21; for speaking divine mysteries, Eunapius *Lives* 469; for uttering an apothegm, Diog. Laert. 1.88.

235. The term refers to the crying out, not to the prophetic aspect (covered by μαντικήν).

(Wis 1:8).[236] Its occurrences in Acts beyond 2:4 (Acts 2:14; 26:25; the only other uses in the NT corpus) could connote inspiration (see comment on Acts 26:24–25) but need not do so. Ancients sometimes understood prophecy as a deity speaking through a person's mouth,[237] though the text here emphasizes human cooperation (noting that *they* spoke with the Spirit's inspiration).[238]

That they "began" to speak in tongues may underline the durative (as opposed to punctiliar) nature of their experience (cf. comment on Acts 1:1), but it may be simply a "redundant auxiliary," following a Semitic or semitized Koine construction.[239] Luke elsewhere often uses "began" with verbs of speech (with λέγω, Luke 3:8; 4:21; 7:24, 49; 11:29; 12:1; 13:26; 20:9; Acts 11:4; cf. also, e.g., Luke 1:64; 5:21; 13:25; 23:2, 30; Acts 24:2).

III. Proposed Jewish Settings for Tongues

Scholars have proposed various backgrounds for understanding early Christian glossolalia or Luke's interpretation of it.[240] Some appeal here to the tradition that the heavenly flame at Sinai accommodated the languages of the audience (Philo *Decal.* 46) or that the law was promulgated in seventy languages at Sinai (*b. Šabb.* 88b).[241] If Luke (or his sources) knew such traditions, he would have had every reason to allude to them with his mention of tongues (they suit his theology), but because his narrative is rich with diverse biblical nuances and because we do not know whether this tradition was available to him, we cannot conclude firmly whether this tradition is in view.[242]

Some early Christians seem to have shared the early Jewish ideal, evident at Qumran, of participation in the heavenly worship or liturgy[243] (cf. Col 2:18;[244] Rev 4:8–11;

236. This cognate generally means simply "utter" (e.g., *Test. Dan* 5:2, speaking truth; *Test. Job* 18:4 [*OTP* 1:846]/18:5 [Kraft, 40]).

237. E.g., Ovid *Metam.* 6.159–62; Max. Tyre 9.1 (on δαίμονες); Aune, *Prophecy*, 47; see the excursus on prophecy at Acts 2:17–18. Cf. Jer 1:9 (though this may simply represent a Hebrew expression for telling another what to say; 2 Sam 14:3, 19); cf. also Luke 1:70; Acts 1:16; 3:18, 21; 4:25 (perhaps 15:7, though indirectly); 2 Chr 36:21–22; Ezra 1:1; 1 Esd 1:57; 2:1; Athenag. *Plea* 7.

238. The imperfect ἐδίδου presumably means that the Spirit was supplying the utterance progressively as they were speaking it. But it is probably also causative in function (see here Parsons and Culy, *Acts*, 25, on this use of δίδωμι). Cf. God's "giving" speech in association with the Spirit in Isa 59:21 (Ruthven, "Covenant," 40–41).

239. E.g., Bruce, *Acts¹*, 82.

240. See one survey of proposed backgrounds (both Jewish and pagan) in Klauck, "Von Kassandra."

241. E.g., Moule, *Messengers*, 24; Bruce, *Commentary*, 59–60; Weiser, *Apostelgeschichte*, 84; Crowe, *Acts*, 9–10; Witherington, *Acts*, 131; D. Williams, *Acts*, 45; Talbert, *Acts*, 26. See also *Exod. Rab.* 5:9; *Tg. Ps.-J.* on Exod 20:15/18 (and the numerous sources cited in M. Maher's translation, 219, including *Mek.* on Exod 20:18, 2.267; on 19:16, 2.218; and Philo *Decal.* 33, 46).

242. The tradition is late (Barrett, *Acts*, 111) and is not explicitly connected with Pentecost (Conzelmann, *Acts*, 16).

243. For Sabbath worship, see, e.g., 4Q400–407; 4Q504 1–2 VII, 4–6; 11Q17; for humans participating, see 1QS XI, 8; Lincoln, *Paradise*, 149; Vermes, *Religion*, 128; Newsom, "Songs," 1138. For humans among angels (or vice versa) in sacred matters, cf. 1QS XI, 7–8; 1QSb III, 25–27; IV, 24–26; 1QM VII, 4–6; XII, 1–2, 8–9; 4Q181 1 3–4; elsewhere, *Jub.* 30:18; 31:14; *Test. Job* 33:2–3. Others also celebrated angelic worship (e.g., Pr Man 15; *L.A.B.* 19:16; *2 En.* 19:1–3; *Tg. Ps.-J.* on Exod 14:24) and its connection with Israel's worship (*Sipre Deut.* 306.31.1; cf. Lincoln, *Paradise*, 112).

244. Some view the problem in Col 2:16–18 as Judaizing angel-worshipers (Hengel, *Acts and History*, 121; Schweizer, *Colossians*, 159; Kraabel, "Judaism in Asia Minor," 145), since angel veneration is known (Smith, *Magician*, 69), as are claims of angel mediation (e.g., *1 En.* 99:3; 104:1; *2 En.* 33:10; cf. Le Déaut, "Intercession") or revelations (e.g., Rev 1:1; *b. Ber.* 51a; *Ned.* 20ab). Angels could well invite invocations (e.g., later, *PGM* 7.1012–13; 35.1–42; *CIJ* 2:91, §850; cf. Cohen, *Maccabees*, 84) or requests for revelation (e.g., Lesses, "Speaking with Angels"). By the fourth century, councils opposed Christians' worshiping angels in Anatolia (Kraabel, "Judaism in Asia Minor," 144–45). (The issue here could simply be pride in visions of angels; Yates, "Worship.") Others have argued plausibly that the problem is the Colossian believers' supposed involvement in the angelic liturgy (Francis, "Humility," 178–80; Carr, *Angels*, 70), but one wonders why this would appear problematic. It probably appears in Rev 4–5; later, cf. Robinson, "Testament."

5:8–14).[245] In one document from Qumran, different angels apparently lead the heavenly worship on successive Sabbaths in different languages.[246] Because these angels are called "princes,"[247] it is possible that they are understood as angels overseeing the nations whose languages they employ (cf. Dan 10:13, 20–21; 12:1).[248] The angels of this document might also be, and are at least linked to, priests of the heavenly sanctuary (cf. Rev 15:6).[249]

The clearest examples of speaking in angelic languages in early Jewish sources are *Apocalypse of Zephaniah* and, probably earlier and most important, *Test. Job* 48–51.[250] Thus Job gave his daughters sashes that God had given him (*Test. Job* 46–47) and by which he had been healed (*Test. Job* 47). Then all his daughters spoke ecstatically in the language of angels (*Test. Job* 48–50). Job's daughters each praised (ηὐλόγησαν)[251] God in their special dialects (διαλέκτῳ, 52:7 [*OTP* 1:867]/52:3 [Kraft, 84]).[252] Still, one wonders about the nature of these dialects, since the hymns were recorded as if intelligible (51:4). More problematic, in contrast to the Qumran texts above, these sources may be late enough to betray Christian influence[253] (or Jewish Christian authorship).[254] Possibly some Christians believed that they prayed in heavenly, angelic languages (1 Cor 13:1),[255] though the context of Paul's reference there may suggest merely hyperbole (13:1–3).[256]

245. For the song of the living creatures and/or the Trisagion, see also 4Q405 20 II, 7–11; *1 En.* 39:12; *2 En.* 21:1; *3 En.* 1:12; 20:2; 22B:7; 27:3; 34:2; 35:5; 38:1; 39:1; 40:1–3; *Apoc. Ab.* 18:3–5; *Exod. Rab.* 29:9; for a survey of sources, cf. Böttrich, "Liturgie"; Hayward, "Chant" (regardless of conclusions about temple worship); Aune, *Revelation*, 303–7; Oesterley, *Liturgy*, 67–68; cf. also 4QSamª (Warren, "Trisagion"); *Test. Ab.* 3:3; 20:12 A; *Num. Rab.* 4:20; *4 Bar.* 9:3; Incant. Text 33.5; *1 Clem.* 34.6; *Test. Adam* 1:4; 4:8; Origen's interpretation in Pritz, *Nazarene Christianity*, 22. Walker, "Thrice-Holy," 133; idem, "Disagion," 171, improbably favors a disagion in the earliest mss of Rev 4:8. Later Christian forms seem to follow Jewish patterns (e.g., Oesterley, *Liturgy*, 142–47; Flusser, "Roots").

246. See 4Q403 1 I, 1–3, 5–6.

247. 4Q403 1 I, 1, 21, 26, 31; 1 II, 11, 20, 24.

248. E.g., Deut 32:8 lxx; *Jub.* 15:31–32; 35:17; *Mek. Shir.* 2.112ff. (Lauterbach, 2:20); *Sipre Deut.* 315.2.1; *Pesiq. Rab Kah.* 23:2; probably Sir 17:17; for further detail, see discussion of Acts 16:9.

249. 4Q403 1 II, 19–20 (reconstructed), 22, 24 (but apparently 1 I, 23 in Hebrew reads "prince" rather than "priest"); also 4Q400 1 I, 19–20; 4Q511 35 2–5; on worship in the heavenly sanctuary, see also Heb 8:1–6; 9:23–24; *Pesiq. Rab Kah.* 1:3; *Pesiq. Rab.* 20:4; cf. Davila, "Macrocosmic Temple"; for heavenly archetype temples, see Buchanan, *Hebrews*, 134–35; in Judaism, Lane, *Hebrews*, 205 (following Cody, *Sanctuary*); Wilcox, "Pattern."

250. E.g., Boring, Berger, and Colpe, *Commentary*, 310; U. B. Müller (as cited in Aune, *Prophecy*, 414n237). Many view *Testament of Job* as the most plausible of proposed backgrounds (e.g., Talbert, *Corinthians*, 90). Some patristic sources understand glossolalia as angelic languages (Parmentier, "Zungenreden"; Talbert, *Corinthians*, 90, citing *Asc. Is.* 8).

251. The text may also add "glorified" (ἐδοξολόγησαν).

252. Horsley, *Corinthians*, 181, compares with Paul's tongues inspired vocal sounds in Philo (citing *Spec. Laws* 4.49), but while the mind is displaced, the "revelation" (δήλωσιν [4.49]) is probably intelligible. Philo's understanding of ecstasy and displacement of the mind probably is relevant to 1 Cor 14:14 (see Pearson, *Terminology*, 43; Horsley, *Corinthians*, 181).

253. Spittler, "Introduction," 834 argues that *Test. Job* 46–53 (and perhaps *Test. Job* 33) was added to an earlier Jewish work by Montanist redactors seeking earlier precedent for glossolalia. This proposal seems speculative (especially if we lack data for Montanist glossolalia), but so are other proposals. Some date the entire work to the first century b.c.e. (McNamara, *Judaism*, 91); Jacobs, "Motifs," also thinks it pre-Christian, and Rahnenführer, "Testament des Hiob," explains the parallels with the nt from the lxx. Certainty, however, remains elusive.

254. See Forbes, *Prophecy*, 45–47, 182–87. The work appears in a sixth-century list of apocryphal Christian works, the *Decretum Gelasianum de libris recipiendis et non recipiendis* (Schneemelcher, "Introduction," 46–49, esp. 48).

255. E.g., Fee, *Corinthians*, 598, 630; Conzelmann, *Corinthians*, 221n27; Hill, *Prophecy*, 136; Hengel, *Jesus and Paul*, 94; Wicker, "Defectu," 148. Witherington, *Acts*, 135, thinks that Acts 10:46 and 1 Cor 14, in contrast to Acts 2, are angelic tongues (cf. Storms, "View," 220–21). From *Test. Job* 52, Spittler surmises that Paul's "languages of angels" is not a wholly new idea ("Testament of Job," 1191), but see comment above.

256. With Horsley, *Corinthians*, 176 (noting that Paul often uses angels hyperbolically; 1 Cor 4:9; Gal 1:8; 4:14); Keener, *Corinthians*, 108; cf. Forbes, *Prophecy*, 61. Many thought that angels spoke Hebrew anyway (see, e.g., Yahalom, "Angels"). The idea of worship in heavenly languages (such as angelic languages used in

If Spirit-inspired use of other languages in early Judaism is uncertain, Spirit-filled praise in one's own language is not. More important, ancient Israel already affirmed Spirit-filled worship (1 Chr 25:1, 3)[257] and linked it with prophecy (e.g., 1 Sam 10:5; 2 Sam 23:3–4; 2 Kgs 3:15; Pss 12:5; 46:10; 95:9–11).[258] Jewish sages recognized that only the praise inspired by indwelling wisdom was sent from the Lord (Sir 15:9–10). Some Jewish traditions also speak of Spirit-inspired prayers and worship (Sib. Or. 3.489–91; L.A.B. 32:14).[259] (Compare the connection between music and inspiration also in Hellenistic experience,[260] and the occasional prayer to an inspiring deity to effect in the worshiper praise worthy of the deity.)[261] Ancient Israel could also envision praising God among the nations (Pss 18:49; 96:3, 10; 108:3). Corporate prophetic speech also appears (1 Sam 10:5; 19:20–24).[262] These backgrounds, which are widespread but indicate praise inspired in the speaker's own, rather than another, language, shed light on the early Jesus movement's use of tongues, although they do not explain it.[263]

iv. Greek Paganism

Unfortunately for our quest, most ancient parallels seem less compelling than the stronger (and probably often somewhat derivative) modern parallels sometimes proposed. Philostratus claims that Apollonius understands all languages without having studied them, because he learned the (Pythagorean) language of silence (Vit. Apoll. 1.19, 21).[264] This third-century attribution of dramatic linguistic powers to a mystic sage is not, however, duplicated in historical sources for individuals or groups.

Egyptian religious tradition focused on sacred language; since hieroglyphs were considered sacred by the Roman period, understanding such hieroglyphs mattered little, compared with simply reproducing them in any variety of combinations.[265] Greek letters could be combined in the same incomprehensible, magical way, probably drawing from the example of the Egyptian ritual tradition.[266] Thus Lucian tells of a false

magic, Reitzenstein, Religions, 31) is probably later and not relevant here (Forbes, Prophecy, 154–56). Given the angels-of-nations concept, "tongues of angels" could even refer to humanity's languages (cf. Severian of Gabala in Pauluskommentare 265, in Bray, Corinthians, 130–31).

257. This inspired worship probably generated many of the psalms in the Psalter (2 Chr 29:30); in the priestly perspective of the Chronicler, national revivals normally included revivals of cultic worship (1 Chr 6:31–32; 15:16, 28–29; 16:4–6, 41–42; 23:30; 2 Chr 8:14; 20:18–22, 28; 29:25; 30:27; 31:2; 35:2–5; Ezra 3:10–11; Neh 12:24, 27–47).

258. For the renewal and intensification of this in early Christianity, see John 4:23–24; Phil 3:3; further discussion in Keener, John, 616–17.

259. Also Test. Job 51:4 (OTP)/51:3 (Kraft); 52:12/52:6; Mek. on Exod 14:31 and 15:1 (cited in Smith, Parallels, 64); later, y. Soṭah 5:4, §1; Pesiq. Rab. 9:2; Tg. Jon. on 1 Sam 2:1; 19:23–24; on 2 Sam 22:1; 23:1; cf. Sib. Or. 3.306; Did. 10.7. Turner, Power, 357, is correct that Jewish texts emphasized charismatic prophecy more than praise.

260. E.g., L.A.B. 32:14; Pesiq. Rab. 9:2; Max. Tyre 38.2; Philost. Hrk. 7.5–6; 54.3, 12–13; Iambl. Myst. 3.9; prophesying in song, Dion. Hal. Ant. rom. 1.31.1; Sib. Or. 3.489–91; cf. Pindar frg. 150 (from Eustath. Com. Il. 1.1); Ovid Her. 21.232; Fasti 6.8; Philost. Hrk. 25.8; Guthrie, Orpheus, 36. Apollo was also linked with music (e.g., PGM 2.81–87). For music and inspiration generally, see Pilch, Flights, 83–86.

261. Men. Rhet. 2.17, 437.25–26 (cf. esp. δύναμιν, line 26); 437.31–438.1 (though these are much like requests to the Muse or Apollo, who is invoked here, for other kinds of inspiration).

262. The assumption that all such corporate speech (albeit likely ecstatic in the broader sense; see 19:6) involves babbling (e.g., Neil, Thessalonians, 129; though apparently differently in Neil, Acts, 73) apparently reads some later phenomena into earlier texts. For prophetic groups outside Israel, see, e.g., Huffmon, "Prophecy," 107; Paul, "Prophets," 1160; in Israel, Gordon, Near East, 214; Paul, "Prophets," 1155–56.

263. Most scholars (e.g., Schnabel, Mission, 400) do not think that tongues per se occurred in early Judaism.

264. In Vit. Apoll. 1.20, Philostratus claims that Arabs purport to understand birds' language and omens.

265. Frankfurter, Religion in Egypt, 254; cf. Engels, Roman Corinth, 105 (on Apul. Metam. 11).

266. Frankfurter, Religion in Egypt, 255–56. On the problem of diglossia among Greeks, see Browning, "Greek Diglossia."

prophet who uttered senseless syllables in a language "like Hebrew or Phoenician," making people think he had magical powers (*Alex.* 13).[267] It is possible, though not proven, that these practices may have influenced the compositions of angelic names in the later Jewish mystic texts.[268] Many scholars think that the early Christian experience of tongues originated in such magical syllables or in unintelligible ecstatic speech, attested in both Egypt and Greece.[269] The extant early Christian understandings of the experience, however (in Luke and Paul), do not reflect this background, and the experience probably (as Luke suggests) initially predates the expansion of Christianity into a Diaspora setting where such a background could make sense. At best, then, this context sheds light on how some Gentile Christians may have understood the experience.

Although many scholars have accepted other scholars' proposed parallels, careful investigation of the claims limits the concrete values of these parallels. Supposed parallels between tongues (with interpretation, as in Paul) and Delphic incoherency translated by a prophet[270] misunderstand the nature of the Delphic experience; the Pythia spoke ambiguous, obscure oracles, not incoherently (see comment on Acts 16:16).[271] Her supposed glossolalia is "a product of modern scholarly imagination,"[272] an example of an early Christian idea now read back into its environment. Mystery cults offer no parallels to tongues.[273]

As suggested above, once the other evidence has been weighed, the magical papyri may offer the most concrete parallels for unintelligible speech.[274] Yet the strings of nonsense syllables found in magical papyri are mostly from the third century or later; more decisively, they are incantations and invocations, not understood as genuine language, not revelatory, and not inviting "interpretations."[275] Appeal to gnostic[276] and Montanist "tongues" would be anachronistic,[277] but there are no clear parallels there anyway.[278] Greco-Roman religion thus offers no sufficient explanation for

267. Boring, Berger, and Colpe, *Commentary*, 310; also in Grant, *Religions*, 96; cf. similarly Xen. Eph. *Anthia* 1.5; the Magus in Lucian *Men.* 9. Forbes, *Prophecy*, 162–64, also shows that this example fits the broader magical usage (comparing Lucian *Men.* 7–9; see esp. *Men.* 9).

268. Alexander, "Introduction," 234 (citing mystics' speech during trances as in Hekalot Rabbati 18:4); cf. Scholem, *Gnosticism*, 33.

269. Reitzenstein, *Religions*, p. 300; Moffatt, *First Corinthians*, 208, 214; Mills, "Utterances and Glossolalia"; van Halsema, "Betrouwbaarheid"; Johnson, *Acts*, 42 (citing Cic. *Div.* 1.32.70–71; Plut. *Obsol.* 14 and 40, *Mor.* 417C, 432CF; Apul. *Metam.* 8.27); cf. Aune, *Prophecy*, 199; Klauck, *Context*, 230; discussion in Frenschkowski, "Zauberworte"; Pliny E. *N.H.* 28.4.20.

270. E.g., Moffatt, *First Corinthians*, 208; Spittler, *Corinthian Correspondence*, 68; Ruble, "Tongues," 16; cf. Héring, *First Corinthians*, 128; Dormeyer and Galindo, *Apostelgeschichte*, 42.

271. Forbes, *Prophecy*, 103–19, esp. 104–6 for terminology and 107–19 for the phenomena; Aune, *Prophecy*, 31; Fontenrose, *Delphic Oracle*; Sourvinou-Inwood, "Delphic oracle," 445; Witherington, *Corinthians*, 54–55; cf. Maurizio, "Pythia's Role."

272. Aune, "Magic," 1551.

273. See Forbes, *Prophecy*, 124–48; Ruble, "Tongues," 15.

274. Williams, "Glossolalia as Phenomenon"; cf. Smith, "Pauline Worship."

275. Forbes, *Prophecy*, 153–54; Aune, "Magic," 1550–51. On these *voces magicae*, see, e.g., Aune, "Amulets," 114; Rives, *Religion*, 163 (on 164 noting that some also contained "garbled forms of genuine Egyptian or Hebrew words").

276. E.g., Wire, *Prophets*, 141–42 (tentatively comparing *Allogenes* 53.36; *Zost.* 52.17; 118.18–21; 127.1–5).

277. As are some modern parallels (to modern glossolalia) offered, some of which are closer than others (e.g., Couture, "Glossolalie et mantra," compares Hindu mantras, though noting differences); cf. apparently analogous possession phenomena today in non-Christian religions (Martinez and Wetli, "Santeria").

278. The few examples of heavenly languages in later Gnosticism are not applied to people (Forbes, *Prophecy*, 156–60), and no ancient source associates tongues with Montanism (160–62). The primary analogy with Montanism involves its prophetic character (see, e.g., Kim, "Montanism," who argues that its detractors misrepresented it).

"tongues"—as a phenomenon understood as inspired "languages"—such as we find it in our earliest Christian sources.[279]

Ecstatic speech and behavior, by contrast, were a common element in ancient prophetism and many forms of worship. Prophets and other divinely possessed persons were thought to act in ways normally considered insane.[280] Certainly, the possession trance described for the Pythian priestess fits here (e.g., Lucan *C.W.* 5.97–101); this also applies to Sibylline prophecy (Virg. *Aen.* 6.77–102) and to (not usually prophetic) Bacchic frenzy (Eurip. *Bacch.* 298–99). In many ancient conceptions, inspiration displaced the mind.[281] (See further the excursus on prophecy at Acts 2:17.)

Ecstatic experience appears in Hellenistic Judaism as well.[282] Thus, in some Hellenistic Jewish works,[283] notably in Philo,[284] inspiration displaces mental activity, as in Greek mantic activity. Whether early Christian tongues were "ecstatic" depends on how one defines "ecstatic"[285] and on one's further conclusions about the nature of ancient Christian tongues (which, like modern tongues, may have varied in form from one church and individual to another). Paul does allow that tongues do not come from the mind (1 Cor 14:14)[286] yet expects (in contrast to pagan possession trance) the individual believer to maintain control of responses (14:32); also distinctively, for Christian (in contrast to pagan Greek) prophecy, he appears to insist on the need for an accompanying rational component (14:2–3).[287] If Christian prophecy differed from many pagan analogues at this point, we cannot generalize about tongues when we lack sufficient clear pagan claims about speech inspired in other languages.

Tongues speaking was thus a highly unusual phenomenon outside Christian circles in the first century. Further, tongues are one of the most distinctive aspects of the Pentecost narrative; whatever light may be shed on them from later Jewish traditions, Luke's prophetically inspired praise in languages unknown to the speaker[288] does not appear in the OT. (Prophetically inspired praise is common enough, as noted above, but at least in the sources dated securely before Luke's writing, the inspiration always extends to one's own language, not, by a linguistic miracle, to languages one has not learned.) Tongues came, then, in a sense, unexpectedly.[289] But in exceptional circumstances, God's Spirit could move people to speak under inspiration even when

279. Forbes, *Prophecy*, 103–65 passim; Aune, "Magic," 1549–51; Winter, *Left Corinth*, 181; Turner, "Experience," 30–31.

280. E.g., Ovid *Metam.* 2.640. See further Otto, *Dionysus*, 94, 97, 144.

281. Ael. Arist. *Def. Or.* 34–35, §11D; see further Graf, "Ecstasy," 800; Aune, *Prophecy*, 47; see comment on Acts 26:24.

282. E.g., Pearson, *Terminology*, 43. See further discussion of ecstasy in the excursus on prophecy at Acts 2:17–18.

283. See, e.g., *Sib. Or.* 12.295–96 (third century C.E.); on *L.A.B.*, see Piñero, "Mediterranean View." But even the rabbis denied that prophecy was from one's own mind (e.g., *Num. Rab.* 18:12), just as Philo did (e.g., *Spec. Laws* 1.65; 4.49).

284. See, e.g., Horsley, *Corinthians*, 181 (comparing Plato *Phaedr.* 243E–245C with Philo *Heir* 259, 264–65; *QG* 3.9; *Mos.* 2.188–91); Martin, *Body*, 97–100; Garland, *1 Corinthians*, 638–39. This fits Philo's Hellenistic anthropology (Dillon, *Middle Platonists*, 174); though some doubt that Philo embraced the mantic view fully (Burkhardt, "Inspiration der Schrift"; but Philo may have believed in *various* forms, Winston, "Types of Prophecy"; Levison, "Types of Prophecy"); Philo often uses it as an analogy for experience of the sublime (e.g., *Creation* 71; *Drunkenness* 146).

285. See also Turner, "Experience," 31–32.

286. Isaacs, *Spirit*, 75, compares this with Hellenistic ecstasy.

287. With, e.g., Collins, *Corinthians*, 501. Some knew and approved of "controlled" inspiration (e.g., Dio Chrys. *Or.* 1.56), and some later Christian leaders expected this (Chrys. *Hom. 1 Cor.* 29.2; Severian of Gabala in *Pauluskommentare* 262 [Bray, *Corinthians*, 118]).

288. The phenomenon in both Luke and Paul (with Turner, "Experience," 32).

289. Cf. Bruner, *Theology*, 164 (though applying this prescriptively, which may not be Luke's intent; cf. 1 Cor 12:31; 14:1, 5).

they did not desire to do so (1 Sam 19:20), and so, from earlier Israelite history, one could anticipate, in a sense, that some such unexpected experience could occur (also Acts 10:46).

v. Tongues in Early Christianity

Apart from Luke, we know of tongues in first-century sources only through Paul (1 Cor 12:10, 28, 30; 13:1, 8; 14:2–6, 13–14, 18–23, 26–27, 39),[290] and Luke writes about Paul's life presumably because he and his audience belong to the Pauline circle of churches (see our introduction, ch. 7; cf. ch. 12, sect. 3). Paul mentions the phenomenon only in 1 Corinthians, but Barrett is undoubtedly correct that since Paul himself spoke in tongues much (14:18), "it is difficult . . . to believe that anyone in personal contact with the Pauline mission was unfamiliar with the phenomenon."[291] Nor does its absence outside Paul and Luke suggest that tongues did not occur outside the Pauline churches; even Paul mentions them only incidentally, because of the Corinthians' abuse,[292] yet he places them within the sphere of a wider array of gifts, many of which do in fact appear (also, generally, incidentally) elsewhere in early Christianity, such as expectation of supernatural healing (e.g., Jas 5:14–16; cf. Mark 16:17–18) and miracles (e.g., Rev 11:5–6; cf. Jas 5:17–18). If we omit incidental references, we draw the boundaries of acceptable evidence too tightly for investigation, given the small amount of evidence left, mostly in occasional documents.

As Forbes notes, tongues were widespread enough to continue for some time over a wide geographic area.[293] Mark 16:17 was accepted by the time of Irenaeus, and thus probably provides second-century evidence for the phenomenon.[294] Irenaeus (*Her.* 5.6.1; Euseb. *H.E.* 5.7.6) claimed that the gift continued in his day;[295] to argue the contrary from its omission in Justin Martyr is to prefer an argument from silence to explicit evidence[296] (especially when we consider how much else Justin omits).[297] Tertullian, before he became a Montanist, also argued that tongues continued among the orthodox (*Marc.* 5.8);[298] Novatian (*De Trinitate* 2.9) and Ambrose (*The Holy Spirit* 2.150) spoke of tongues in the present tense, in the very

290. And perhaps Mark 16:17 if it refers to glossolalia (as it may) rather than to restoration of mutes' speech (Isa 32:4; 35:6) and *if* the tradition behind this later addition to Mark's Gospel stems from the first century. (Farmer, *Verses*, even offers a skillful argument that the passage might be Markan, but few scholars have followed him.)

291. Barrett, *Acts*, 116. Others in addition to Barrett (e.g., Downing, *Cynics*, 220–21) infer that it was widespread in his churches, noting other gifts (e.g., Gal 3:5; 1 Thess 5:19–20). Spirit-inspired prayer also appears elsewhere in early Christianity (Jude 20), where it is self-edifying as in 1 Cor 14:4, although even for Paul Spirit-inspired prayer cannot be restricted to tongues (14:13–19, 26).

292. Without the Corinthians' abuse, our knowledge of early Christian practice of the Lord's Supper would be likewise severely curtailed (e.g., Richardson, *Theology*, p. 364).

293. Forbes, *Prophecy*, 75–84. Some also link it with the later practice of *jubilatio* (Parmentier, "Zungenreden").

294. Forbes, *Prophecy*, 76–77. That is, as noted above, unless this tradition refers to mute tongues miraculously speaking in the eschatological time (Isa 35:6; cf. use of the context for Jesus's messianic ministry, Luke 7:22).

295. Forbes, *Prophecy*, 78–79. Cf. also Palma, "Glossolalia," 42; Ruble, "Tongues," 18; contrast Rogers, "Tongues" (scholarly but polemical).

296. Forbes, *Prophecy*, 77–78. For continuing prophecy in Justin, see *Dial.* 82; exorcism, *Dial.* 85; miracles, *Dial.* 35.8 (on which see Williams, *Justin Martyr*, 71n3).

297. Contrast Justin's almost complete silence on the Fourth Gospel (excepting perhaps *1 Apol.* 61) with other sources that are not much later (Keener, *John*, 93; cf. Braun, *Jean*, 136–44; Osborn, *Justin*, 137; Barnard, *Justin Martyr*, 60–62).

298. Forbes, *Prophecy*, 79–80 (also expressing doubt that Montanists, as a rule, spoke in tongues). For exorcism, cf. Tert. *Spect.* 26. Cf. also Origen in Robeck, "Charismata," 120.

period when John Chrysostom and Augustine thought that the gift had finally died out.[299] These later traditions also challenge the assumption of some modern scholars[300] that Luke's church must have no longer known what genuine tongues experiences were.[301]

Paul speaks in various texts about God's generous benefactions or gifts (χαρίσματα, Rom 12:6; 1 Cor 1:7; 12:4, 9, 28, 30–31; cf. Eph 4:8–11; 1 Tim 4:14; 2 Tim 1:6).[302] A non-Pauline text (unless one defines "Pauline" so broadly as to make nearly all NT evidence Pauline) also uses for such gifts language very similar to Paul's, whether it is dependent on Paul or both are dependent on a common source (1 Pet 4:10–11).

Paul's theological emphasis on "tongues" is quite different from Luke's, but it is likely (against many)[303] that he is interpreting the same phenomenon;[304] it is virtually inconceivable that the two writers would independently coin the same obscure phrase for two entirely different phenomena. Although some Corinthian Christians overemphasized tongues (perhaps in response to Paul's earlier sharing the value of his own experience, 1 Cor 14:5, 18), Paul presents tongues as one gift of the Spirit among many (12:10, 28, 30; 13:1, 8; 14:1–40).[305] They are a form of praying with one's spirit as opposed to one's mind and hence are preferably balanced by interpretation (14:13–16). In contrast to Luke's generally corporate picture of the experience, Paul emphasizes the private devotional use of tongues (14:4, 18–19) unless they are accompanied with an inspired interpretation (12:10, 30; 14:5, 13, 26–28).[306] Luke associates them with worldwide evangelism, but Paul does not clearly do so,[307] and Luke associates them with prophetic speech more fully than does Paul.[308]

But whereas their emphases differ, they almost certainly are interpreting the same phenomenon. For both writers, those who speak in tongues offer their own prayer, but they are led by God's Spirit (Acts 2:4, they spoke by the Spirit's gifting; 1 Cor 12:4–11; 14:2, 14). Likewise, both see the gift as prayer and praise (Acts 2:11; 10:46; 1 Cor 14:2, 14–17).[309] Both also recognize that the gift may accompany or produce ecstatic or at least abnormally joyful speech or behavior during its use (Acts 2:13; 1 Cor 14:23). In both cases, prophecy and tongues are closely connected or paralleled (Acts 2:16–18; 19:6; 1 Cor 14, passim).[310]

299. Forbes, *Prophecy*, 80–84. For the long duration of Christian tongues speaking in late antiquity, see, e.g., Ruble, "Tongues," 17–25; Carson, *Showing Spirit*, 165–68; cf. Wimber, *Power Evangelism*, 157–74.

300. E.g., Goulder, *Type and History*, 77.

301. Forbes, *Prophecy*, 50n14. As Bovon, *Theologian*, 237, notes, the Spirit's early activity was remembered (with Dunn) but continued to function in Luke's own day (with Schulz).

302. See, e.g., Turner, *Gifts*, 182–302, esp. 262–67; Schatzmann, *Charismata*, passim, esp. 1–13; Fee, *Presence*, 146–261, but esp. 32–35, 886–95; Carson, *Showing Spirit*, passim; Keener, "Gifts."

303. E.g., Polhill, *Acts*, 99.

304. E.g., Harnack, *Acts*, 153–54; C. Williams, *Acts*, 63; Faw, *Acts*, 319–20; Robeck, "Tongues," 943; possibly (on Luke's source before he adapted it), Stagg, "Glossolalia," 41. Most patristic authors identified the two (Kovacs, *Corinthians*, 229n1).

305. Given its portrait in Acts, supplemented by 1 Corinthians, it was probably common in early Christianity (with, e.g., Neil, *Acts*, 73), though best attested in the sphere of the Pauline mission.

306. See, e.g., Forbes, *Prophecy*, 52–53 (though rightly noting that the different emphasis is not a contradiction in substance).

307. Wolff, "Λαλεῖν γλώσσαις," 190–91.

308. Ibid., 195–99; but Wolff's conclusion that Luke therefore no longer was acquainted with tongues (199) infers too much from the differences. Paul is defining prophecy more narrowly than Luke but nevertheless accepts tongues as a form of inspired speech.

309. Cf. perhaps eschatological worship (e.g., *1 En.* 39:7; *Sib. Or.* 3.715, 726; *t. Pisha* 8:22; *b. Ta'an.* 31a; *Sanh.* 91b; *Eccl. Rab.* 1:11, §1) if realized eschatology is in view. For the connection between praise and the Spirit in Luke-Acts, see, e.g., Cullen, "Euphoria"; Shelton, *Mighty in Deed*, 85–101 (note esp. 87–92 on Luke 10:21).

310. See esp. Bornkamm, *Experience*, 38–39 (though he also rightly underlines the contrast in 1 Cor 14).

Although Paul plays down tongues to counter the Corinthian overemphasis on the gift, his own perspective regarding them is positive: they are, after all, a divine benefaction (χάρισμα) from the Spirit (1 Cor 12:4, 10), and Paul prays in tongues himself (14:18).[311] Though inferior to vernacular prophecy in the public assembly if uninterpreted, they are useful for edifying oneself (14:4), as a form of prayer to God from one's spirit (14:2, 14, 16–17).[312] Indeed, in one of the rare texts where another NT writer uses the characteristically Lukan phrase "filled with the Spirit," the result emphasized is especially worship (Eph 5:18–20, including "songs from the Spirit," 5:19).[313]

Lukan "tongues" (esp. Acts 2:4)	Pauline "tongues" (1 Cor 12–14)
"Tongues" (γλῶσσαι), i.e., "languages" (2:4)	"Tongues" (γλῶσσαι), i.e., "languages"* (13:1; 14:10–11)
Tongues are inspired by the Spirit (2:4, 17–18)	Tongues are a gift from the Spirit (12:7–11)
The speakers apparently do not know the languages (2:4)†	The speakers do not know the languages (14:13–15)
They are understandable (when some who recognize the languages are present [2:8–11], but apparently not in other cases, when no one is present who knows the languages [10:46; 19:6])	They are understandable (to those with supernatural interpretation [12:10, 30; 14:13])
They are not intelligible to those who do not recognize the languages (2:13; cf. 10:46; 19:6)	They are not normally intelligible (without a supernatural interpretation [14:2, 9–11, 19, 23])
They apparently function as inspired praise (2:11; cf. 10:46)‡	They function as praise (14:15–17) and prayer (14:2, 14–15)§
They can be associated with (though distinguishable from) other speech gifts, such as prophecy (19:6), and are related to prophetic speech (2:17–18)	They can be associated with (though distinguishable from) other speech gifts, such as prophecy (12:10; 14:2–6, 22–33, 39–40)‖
Tongues speech belongs to a larger sphere of the Spirit's activity (e.g., visions and dreams, 2:17–18; cf. 2:43)	Tongues speech belongs to a larger sphere of the Spirit's activity (e.g., healings and miracles, 12:8–10, 28–30)
Tongues, at least on this occasion, function as a sign to unbelievers (2:11–13)	Tongues can function as a sign to unbelievers (14:22)
The emotion of tongues speech leads to some outsiders assuming the speakers' drunkenness (2:13)#	The emotion of tongues speech leads to outsiders assuming madness (14:23)**
The gift of tongues speech is God's choice, not always mediated through human agency (2:4; 10:44–46), though such agency is possible (cf. 19:6)	Tongues speech, like other gifts, is God's sovereign choice (12:10–11), though individuals can apparently seek for gifts (12:31; 14:1, 39)

*In Paul, it is often "a tongue" (sing.; 1 Cor 14:2, 4, 9, 13, 14, 19, 26, 27), because he addresses individuals, whereas Luke describes a group. But where Paul addresses a group (and sometimes when he addresses individuals), he also is aware of the plural usage (1 Cor 12:10, 28, 30; 13:1, 8; 14:5, 6, 18, 22, 23, 39).

†They did not learn them; they are "other" languages; this is unexpected for Galileans (Acts 2:7), and only the foreigners are said to understand the meaning (2:9–11).

‡Note that Acts 10:46 employs καί, but in contrast to 19:6, not τε . . . καί.

§For their function as praise, see Levang, "Content." Some would argue that they can also fulfill other functions (see, e.g., Aker, "Tongues"), but whatever one's conclusions on this point, praise and prayer are the explicit and dominant functions specifically and clearly mentioned by Paul.

‖Paul divides the gifts differently than Luke would (1 Cor 12:8–10, 28–30), though probably in an ad hoc way (cf. 14:6, 26; Rom 12:6–8), but the association remains; both are inspired speech.

#The implication of an affective component comports well with Paul's prayer "with my spirit" (1 Cor 14:14–15; in that context, prayer "with my mind" apparently refers to interpretation, 14:13, 16–19).

**Cf. also the analogy in 1 Cor 14:11.

311. With, e.g., Ramsay, *Teaching*, 338; Pearson, *Terminology*, 45; Caird, *Apostolic Age*, 61; Spittler, "Limits," 260–61n12; Stendahl, *Paul*, 113; Dunn, *Jesus and Spirit*, 245; Martin, *Worship*, 181; Hays, *First Corinthians*, 234; MacDonald, "Glossolalia"; Richardson, "Order and Glossolalia"; it is difficult to see how one could speak of a *bad* χάρισμα from God. For more negative appraisals, see, e.g., Fuller, "Tongues"; Fabbro, "Prospective"; cf. Horn, "Speaking in Tongues"; Van Elderen, "Glossolalia."

312. Self-edification is not negative for Paul, simply not the primary goal of corporate worship, with Carson, *Showing Spirit*, 102n89; Fee, *Corinthians*, 653; in contrast to Bruner, *Theology*, 298.

313. On filling with the Spirit in Luke-Acts and in Pauline literature (Eph 5:18), see, e.g., Holman, "Spirit-Filled."

The idea that Luke and Paul depict unrelated phenomena requires too many random coincidences to be deemed plausible. Nevertheless, there are also differences, especially in theological application:

Lukan "tongues" (esp. Acts 2:4)	Pauline "tongues" (1 Cor 12–14)
Hearers understand tongues (but only at Pentecost, not in 10:46; 19:6)*	Hearers would not (normally) understand the tongues (14:2, 16–19, 23)
Tongues are not abused in the instances described in Acts, which are positive†	Tongues are abused in the instances presupposed in 1 Corinthians, although Paul affirms this experience as a divine gift (12:10; 14:26), especially valuable for private use (14:2, 4); he practices it privately (14:18), and he warns against forbidding its public use if it is accompanied by interpretation (14:39)
Multiple speakers apparently speak in tongues simultaneously, in group worship (2:4; 10:46; 19:6)‡	Those who speak in tongues should do so one at a time, allowing for interpretation of each (14:27–28)
Tongues are a sign of power to witness to the nations (1:8)§	Tongues are one among many gifts (among the less useful in public), useful especially for private prayer
Tongues begin in (2:5–11) and attest (10:45–46) the Spirit's multicultural work	Paul addresses the use of tongues in a more homogeneous setting of Corinthian house churches (cf. 14:23)‖
Tongues seem to accompany the inauguration of the Spirit's activity where they occur, i.e., toward the beginning of believers' experience with the Spirit (2:4; 10:44–46; 19:6)	Tongues are one among many gifts (among the less useful in public), useful especially for private prayer
Luke does not use the analogy of the body and its members or speak of spiritual "gifts" (focusing instead on the "gift" of the Spirit)#	Paul speaks of diverse gifts of grace (ideally especially as enablements for service to others) or of the Spirit in the context of a body with many members (Rom 12:4–8; 1 Cor 12:4–30)

*This difference is not significant because it relates to the different settings: Pentecost included hearers from all regions (Acts 2:9–11), divinely arranged for the first occurrence of tongues speech, whereas the same would not be expected in the average house church.

†This is a difference of situation.

‡Cf. this pattern possibly for prophetic speech in 1 Sam 10:5–6, 10; 19:20–24; perhaps 1 Chr 25:1–6.

§See further Keener, "Tongues," esp. 180–83. This emphasis constitutes the heart of the theological distinction. Paul nowhere even explicitly addresses a special empowerment to witness to the nations, though he recognizes the importance of the Spirit in his own ministry of Christ to the Gentiles (Rom 15:16–19; cf. Gal 3:14; Isa 42:1).

‖The Spirit's activity more generally does, however, attest the Spirit's multicultural work (Gal 3:5, 14).

#Luke nowhere employs χάρισμα (which, outside Pauline literature, appears in the NT only at 1 Pet 4:10; cf. 1 Clem. 38.1; Ign. Pol. 2.2; Smyrn. intro) and always employs "gift" (δωρεά) for the Spirit (Acts 2:38; 8:20; 10:45; 11:17).

It is possible to subsume these differences under two basic categories: setting and theological emphasis. The first differences above relate to the situation; it is possible that multiple speakers in group praise also involve a situation distinct from the normal edifying course of a house church meeting or that Paul's instructions about sequential use relate specifically to abuses in Corinth.

The dramatic difference, however, is the theological emphasis, that is, the purposes for which Luke and Paul employ their treatment of tongues speech. Paul's interest in his passage is in the practical function of the gift in personal and especially corporate worship; Luke's interest is the theological meaning of inspired prayer in other people's languages, which relates directly to the thrust of his work (Acts 1:8). That one in limited space omits what the other includes is not a contradiction and does not even prove that Luke, though belonging to a Pauline circle of churches, never employed Paul's language on the matter (although we also cannot be sure that he did so). But Luke's emphasis does control most of the theological differences: because tongues function as a sign of power to witness to the nations (1:8), they are particularly useful to Luke, who emphasizes them especially as an inaugural activity and in a multicultural setting. Tongues speaking serves a more exalted narrative function for Luke, as symbolic proof of the church's empowerment to proclaim Christ across cultures.

Some scholars think that for Paul, at least, tongues are merely ecstatic gibberish lacking genuine linguistic content, rather than genuine languages.[314] This is what many writers mean by "glossolalia," which some also suggest early Christians construed as angelic languages; but this modern usage can easily prejudice the discussion of what Paul and Luke meant by the Greek terms from which the compound is derived. As argued below, this practice may represent one form of modern glossolalia, but it is not clear that this represents what Paul understood by the phenomenon (or how all modern tongues speakers understand or experience some other forms of modern glossolalia).

VI. STUDIES OF MODERN CHRISTIAN GLOSSOLALIA

Although the analogy is incomplete, scholars examining the ancient phenomenon (which is available to us only secondhand) often take into account modern examples.[315] Concrete ancient evidence (such as textual evidence in Paul) must always take precedence, but analogies from anthropological and other field data might prove useful here, as elsewhere, to try to fill lacunae in our knowledge, thereby improving the "educated" element in our educated guesses.[316] The recorded phenomena for comparison are certainly much more complete today than those available for pre-Pentecostal commentators; whatever the relevance of the modern parallels, they would challenge the perplexity of a commentator in 1876, who complained, "The phenomenon here described is mysterious . . . wholly unknown in modern times"[317] (a complaint not completely true, however, even in his own day).[318]

Although fuller treatment of Pentecostal and charismatic Christian analogies appears below, I offer first brief comments on some proposed or potential non-Christian analogies to glossolalia and on Christian examples treated in the same anthropological studies. Given the existence of various forms of inarticulate sounds and glossolalia even in a variety of contemporary religious movements,[319] one would expect some ancient parallels to the phenomenon, though we are surprisingly hard pressed to find explicit evidence for them.

314. E.g., Hill, *Prophecy*, 97; cf. Foakes-Jackson, *Acts*, 11. Many distinguish Acts 2 from Paul and from Acts 10 and 19, though with various views of the later events; e.g., Hull, *Spirit in Acts*, 60–65; Turner, *Gifts*, 226; idem, *Power*, 357; Fitzmyer, *Acts*, 239; Witherington, *Acts*, 134. In my view, however, it is only the absence of those who know the languages that clearly distinguishes the later occurrences in Acts from 2:4.

315. Williams, "Ecstaticism," urges that even studies of ancient ecstatic prophecy should take into account modern tongues speaking; cf. Dunn, "Reconstructions," 302; Horrell and Adams, "Introduction," 42.

316. Thus, e.g., some anthropologists have compared their observations of West African apostolic "Holy Spirit" sects with Acts (see Field, "Possession," 10). Ma, "Manifestations," compares the Pentecostal experience of a traditional people in northern Luzon, Philippines. Likewise, Miller and Yamamori, *Pentecostalism*, 218, compare modern Pentecostal experience with Acts 2 and activity during the U.S. Great Awakenings.

317. Abbott, *Acts*, 37, suggesting only the possibility of the Irvingite use of tongues in 1831–33, which might, he thought, be due to "a mere nervous affection."

318. Anderson, *Pentecostalism*, 19–37, esp. 24–25, 36–37; for pre-Pentecostal tongues elsewhere, e.g., Hunter, "Portrait," 83–84; Blumhofer, "Portrait," 96; Cavaness, "Women," 26; Hinson, "History of Glossolalia," 57–66; Satyavrata, "Perspectives," 205 (the Indian revival of 1860); Jacobsen, *Thinking in Spirit*, 16; McGee, *Mission*, 91; Ma, "Mission," 24, 31–32 (in Asia); Cragg, *Reason*, 195 (Catholic Jansenists); Mullin, *Miracles*, 70–71 (incidents known to Horace Bushnell); negatively, among some early Anabaptists, Williams, *Radical Reformation*, 133. Cf. *possibly* even Charles Finney when he "bellowed out the unutterable gushings of [his] heart" (Finney, *Memoirs*, 20; for another person, 305), although this experience may be construed differently.

319. See Spittler, "Glossolalia," 336–37.

Glossolalia sometimes appears in trance states in various traditional societies today,[320] often in conjunction with change of pitch[321] and even changes in the brain state.[322] On occasion these utterances in trance states also have been said to constitute xenoglossy, often attributed to the activity of a foreign spirit.[323] In Kalabari possession, spirits often speak "a fairly standard 'water-people's language'"[324] or a neighboring language (which the speakers claim not to understand), or stutter in Kalabari.[325] In a traditional Zulu treatment, smoke inhalation removes spirit-illness and invites speech "in 'foreign' tongues appropriate to the medicine administered," which Western hearers may regard as simply meaningless sounds.[326]

Some controversial instances of xenoglossy have been cited for mediums in the Western world,[327] including for various ancient languages supposedly unknown to the mediums[328]—claims that have in some cases been disproved and in others remain at least disputed.[329] It has been argued that the famous case of "Rosemary," popularly attributed to reincarnation, was in fact learned behavior, improving as the coaching in "ancient Egyptian" improved.[330] Obviously, such claims differ markedly from the early Christian experience as understood theologically by Luke.

Modern anthropological studies of (usually) Christian glossolalia across various cultures, languages, and religions have generally noticed patterns of altered states of consciousness with physical and emotive effects, including "hyperarousal dissociation."[331]

---

320. See, e.g., Tippett, "Possession," 145, 151, 162; Shorter, *Witchdoctor*, 177 (though noting that these are known and simply secondary languages); idem, "Spirit Possession," 112 ("meaningless gibberish, or words of a foreign language" they know), 118 (similarly, noting that one who knew the supposed language verified instead that it was unintelligible); Gray, "Cult," 181–82; Bourguignon, "Self," 50; Freston, "Transnationalisation," 211; Naipaul, *Masque*, 121. The case of spirit possession in Abdalla, "Friend," 38, includes foreign intonation.

321. E.g., Tippett, "Possession," 162. Others also report dramatic changes during trance states: e.g., Oesterreich, *Possession*, 19–22; Ising, *Blumhardt*, 104–5, 168, 169, 171–72, 174–75, 178, 183; Shorter, *Witchdoctor*, 177; Greenfield, *Spirits*, 83; Grof, "Potential," 144; Wilson, "Miracle Events," 275.

322. See, e.g., Goodman, *Speaking in Tongues*, 8, 58–86, 153–54.

323. E.g., nineteenth-century Chinese reports in Nevius, *Demon Possession*, 58, also cited in Tippett, "Possession," 153–54; cf. a case in 1902 Tanzania, difficult to otherwise explain, in Shorter, *Witchdoctor*, 183 (his "parapsychology" classification is not an explanation); a possessed person who knew no English speaking English in York, *Missions*, 185 (himself the eyewitness); alleged strange tongues in some nuns' possession ca. 1611 (Rosen, "Psychopathology," 231); the illiterate George Lukyns speaking Latin during possession (exorcised by Methodists in 1788; Rack, "Healing," 148); the possessed speaking what hearers took to be Italian or French in Ising, *Blumhardt*, 181; other reports, sometimes naturally explicable, in Kreiser, "Devils," 63–64; Krings, "History," 55–58; Wilson, "Miracle Events," 275; Oesterreich, *Possession*, 208; Hickson, *Heal*, 65 (in 1921); Koch, *Zulus*, 55; cf. perhaps the secret language of some shamans' spirits in Eliade, *Shamanism*, 347, 440; Scherberger, "Shaman," 60, 62.

324. Horton, "Possession," 29, noting that it often includes Kalabari words with substituted syllables or lengthened forms.

325. Horton, "Possession," 29. Cf. also the "Water Doctor" spirit, speaking Ibo (Horton, "Possession," 30); regional languages allegedly not known to the speaker in Southall, "Possession," 242.

326. Lee, "Possession," 132 (following Sundkler, *Bantu Prophets*, 23). Lee notes ("Possession," 133) that "English" and "Indian" tongues are now supplanting the older "foreign" tongues.

327. Griffiths, "Xenoglossy," 141–42 (on a séance on February 27, 1924, that convinced Welsh writer Caradoc Evans); alleged Greek expressions from a deceased person who had known Greek through some mediums who claimed not to know it (McClenon, *Events*, 194–95; cf. archaic English style in 195–96).

328. Griffiths, "Xenoglossy," 142–48.

329. Ibid., 147 (an instance of the Latin's being borrowed from a novel); somewhat less convincingly, 148, attributed to "cryptomnesic recitative xenoglossy, in which a subconscious and latent memory of words in a foreign language becomes activated."

330. Ibid., 148–65, esp. 152–63, noting irregular syntax (151, 155, 162–63), mixing with other languages (157), mixing different phases of the language (159; this might suit a spirit that lived through the entire period rather than an individual reincarnation), and improvement with better coaches (164–65).

331. Goodman, *Speaking in Tongues*, 8, 58–86, 153–54 (cf. idem, "Glossolalia," 238). Many charismatics would, however, strongly differentiate themselves from many of the groups she studied, such as modalist Pentecostals. Cf. also allegedly "neurotic" associations with spirit possession in some groups, Ward and

(We should, however, be careful about drawing too wide a net: in most charismatic circles that I have observed, the "trance state" cited in some sources simply does not occur during prayer in tongues, although prayer in tongues may exert a calming or emotional influence.)[332] Some have also noticed common patterns of glossolalia in diverse cultural and linguistic settings, though there are also some strictly stereotyped forms within the groups.[333] Although it has not, to my knowledge, been studied as extensively by anthropologists, some Christians working with hard drug users have reported that use of glossolalia also can seriously reduce the pain of drug withdrawal and can greatly increase the probability of long-term recovery.[334]

Some studies of modern tongues have focused on nonlinguistic patterned speech; such free vocalization could be understood, at most, as "coded" language, adding vowels to break the speech "into arbitrary bits."[335] Some Pentecostal theologians also define tongues as "pneumatic speech" with intelligible (perhaps affective) content but not human languages.[336] Various linguistic studies of glossolalic speech suggest that it functions as "free vocalisation" that, on the one hand, comes short "of the complex suprasegmental sound-patterning associated with natural language," yet, on the other, proves more phonologically structured than what occurs "in comparable phenomena like baby talk and schizophrenese."[337] Clusters of sounds resemble the sorts of words and groups of words known in other languages, but they are not coherent enough at a semantic level for full language.[338] This may suggest a nonpropositional communication by the speaker that is heavily dependent on formulaic implicatures.[339]

Beaubrun, "Possession" (albeit with a very small sample size); cf. also Preus, "Tongues" (polemically). More subjectively, many claim an experience of spiritual reality in the forms of glossolalia best known to them (e.g., Wink, "Write," 5).

332. Cf. also similar reservations (from others with significant exposure to the experience) in Turner, "Experience," 32; Malony, "Debunking," 109; Tarr, *Foolishness*, 360–61, 368, 410 (though he affirms the nonrational character of prayer in tongues).

333. Goodman, "Glossolalia," 237–38. She notes that the intonation rises in intensity, peaks, then recedes quickly; I have heard public utterances like this in some Pentecostal circles, but the pattern does not fit most of the glossolalia I hear used by individuals in private prayer.

334. Wilkerson, *Cross*, 154–68 (regarding Teen Challenge, the success rate of which has been supported by other studies); and, regarding Jackie Pullinger's work in Hong Kong, Storms, *Guide*, 145–46; Pullinger, *Dragon*, 83, 149, 158–60, 166, 169, 173, and esp. 174; external corroboration in sociologists Miller and Yamamori, *Pentecostalism*, 99–105, esp. 104, 109 (against any supposition of their starting with favorable bias, see 99, 147). Testimonies of deliverance from addiction also appear elsewhere (e.g., Wacker, *Heaven*, 65; Khai, "Pentecostalism," 269). I myself have observed glossolalia's utility in dealing with severe pain in one instance. Apart from mention of tongues, religion can also facilitate addiction recovery; cf., e.g., Flynn et al., "Dependence"; Mohr et al., "Integration"; Benda, "Factors"; Walsh et al., "Transcendence" (gambling addiction); Winkelman, "Spirituality" (altered states of consciousness induced by shamanic drumming). For whatever reasons, studies suggest that religious disinterest correlates significantly with substance abuse (see Schoeneberger et al., "Abuse"), and both religiosity (Wills, Yaeger, and Sandy, "Effect") and particular religious values (Kendler and Liu, "Dimensions") correlate with lower substance abuse (cf. also lower alcohol consumption among religious Israeli youth, Schiff, "Shadow").

335. Carson, *Showing Spirit*, 84–86 (adapting Poythress, "Analyses of Modern Tongues-Speaking," 369, 375–76). Coding might function as a way to preserve the privacy of the experience (cf. 2 Cor 12:4), whether because of God's ineffability (cf. Shibata, "Ineffable"), because of the sacred character of the revelation, as with secrets in the Mysteries (e.g., Paus. 1.14.3; Lucian *Fisherman* 33; *Men.* 2; Callim. *Aetia* 3.75.8–9), indescribably sublime heavenly experience (Plut. *Isis* 78, *Mor.* 383A), or other sacred secrets (e.g., Philost. *Vit. Apoll.* 6.11; *Hrk.* 2.10–11; 44.2–4), or because of other factors.

336. Williams, *Renewal Theology*, 2:215–16, 221–22. Cf. the Anglican thinker C. S. Lewis, *Transposition*, 9–19, who is cited as affirming that the phenomenon could be babbling, but useful when energized by the Spirit.

337. Hilborn, "Glossolalia," 111.

338. Ibid., 112; Wacker, *Heaven*, 52. Hilborn, "Glossolalia," 112–13n6, notes one study where a speaker's structures belonged not to a language the speaker knew but to some other known languages.

339. Hilborn, "Glossolalia," 114, 128–29; for "decoding," cf. 131. If the speech is to God, as in 1 Cor 14:2 (113), partial implicatures could symbolize a larger communication. Hilborn, 132–45, goes beyond the code

Scholars sometimes suggest that if something like this phenomenon happened on the day of Pentecost, Luke may have partly or fully redacted "an incomprehensible ecstatic speech" experience into a language miracle.[340] But whatever the actual nature of the phenomenon, it is highly doubtful that Paul understood it as nonlinguistic babbling any more than Luke did.[341] Certainly, Paul believes, as Luke does (Acts 2:4), that the tongues are unknown to the speakers (1 Cor 14:2) and sometimes perhaps to anyone on earth (13:1).[342] The term γλῶσσα *means* "language," whether earthly or heavenly (13:1), and Paul compares the problem of untranslated tongues to other forms of untranslated speech (14:11). G. B. Caird warns that the experience's very distance from that of most modern scholars should caution us to attempt "to enter into a sympathetic and imaginative understanding of it, if we are to have an accurate picture of primitive Christianity." From Acts and Paul, he argues, "there can be no doubt . . . that glossolalia gave the normal impression of articulate utterance and not of hysterical raving."[343]

No consensus exists on even the psychological character of modern glossolalia. Modern psychological literature reflects diverse understandings or approaches of different psychological schools.[344] For a few samples among many various views (not all of them mutually exclusive): some envision it as a pathological, "delusional" speech act (more common earlier);[345] some find elements enigmatic;[346] some view psychopathological explanations as too simplistic;[347] some have found it in both pathological and helpful forms;[348] some have compared its unpatterned form to early childhood speech[349] or a release from the unconscious;[350] and some view it as religious emotion.[351] Some treat it as universally a dissociative state;[352] others[353] disagree, suggesting more

---

model of language to relevance theory's contention that evidence of speaker intention is paramount (cf. also the summary in Cartledge, "Tongues-Speech," 217–18). Hilborn seems to lay more emphasis on the act than on the phonological content, and I am not convinced that this is quite right; the sounds might communicate through inference the way musical rhythm, keys, etc., can communicate, in some (neurophysiological) ways cross-culturally but in most ways within the framework of particular cultural expectations (not necessarily the speaker's own). Following Goodman, Malina and Pilch, *Acts*, 28, emphasize tongues "not as language but as communication" (see also idem, *Letters*, 119–20).

340. Lüdemann, *Christianity*, 41; cf. Hull, *Spirit in Acts*, 60–65; Hanson, *Acts*, 63–64; Griffiths, "Xenoglossy," 142 (following Williams, *Tongues*, 25–45); Klauck, *Magic*, 7–8; Stagg, "Glossolalia," 41; Conzelmann, *Acts*, 15 (who also supposes, p. 160 on 19:6, that Luke "no longer has any exact knowledge of what speaking in tongues really was"; see the sound critique of this view in Pervo, *Acts*, 63); Marguerat, *Actes*, 69; allowing the possibility, Levison, *Filled*, 323. Barrett, *Acts*, 115, thinks that Acts 2:4–12 sounds like languages yet 2:13 "suggests something more like Pauline glossolalia."

341. See rightly, e.g., Garland, *1 Corinthians*, 584; Palma, *Spirit*, 146–47; Calderón, "Lenguas."

342. Some interpret "tongues of angels" literally, whether from Paul's or from the Corinthians' perspective (e.g., Fee, *Corinthians*, 598; Witherington, *Acts*, 135), but the phrase is probably hyperbolic (cf. 1 Cor 13:1–3; Horsley, *Corinthians*, 176; Keener, *Corinthians*, 108).

343. Caird, *Apostolic Age*, 54.

344. E.g., psychoanalytic, Godin, "Moi perdu"; role theory, Holm, "Role Theory."

345. Cf. Dor, "Bobon." Pathological approaches are much less common today than in the early twentieth century; e.g., Klausner, *Jesus to Paul*, 274–75, viewed tongues in psychopathological terms.

346. Godin, "Moi perdu."

347. Samarin, "Variation."

348. Cf. Pattison, "Research on Glossolalia," 84.

349. Oates, "Study" (allowing that it can be useful); cf. Theissen, *Erleben*, 200.

350. Thiselton, *Corinthians*, 970–88, esp. 984–85, 988 (favoring Theissen's approach perhaps too much).

351. Cf. Thrall, *Letters*, 98; for tongues as positive emotional expression, see also Wright, *Acts*, 24. Miller and Yamamori, *Pentecostalism*, 147, positively compare healthy nonrational "forms of expression and communication that bubble up out of the inner depths," such as "laughing, crying, or dreaming." They treat prayer in tongues as presaging postmodern holistic sensibilities by drawing body and emotion into worship (142).

352. Goodman, "Style of Discourse." Cf. parallels with Tourette's syndrome, associated with evil, in Womack, "Coprolalia"; cf. temporary changes in the temporal lobe in Persinger, "EEG profiles."

353. Samarin, "Explanations."

social explanations.[354] Some help explain tongues as social empowerment (by allowing individuals to transcend their social limitations)[355] or a form of "resistance discourse."[356]

Unfortunately, most of these studies focus on particular groups and hence do not distinguish among various forms of glossolalic speech in various circles;[357] this factor may account for some of the differences in conclusions. Yet a historical survey of psychological approaches suggests that hermeneutical frameworks figure heavily in many of these interpretations:[358] early studies often treated tongues speaking as pathological;[359] empirical studies in the 1960s, challenging traditional assumptions and biases, proved much more positive;[360] and the most recent research has overturned most of the early research's negative claims.[361]

Even if we assume a static interpretation of the modern phenomenon of ecstatic tongues (despite the unsettled debate surrounding it),[362] reading it back even into 1 Corinthians faces two obstacles: first, we cannot be certain that the modern phenomenon described in these studies is necessarily the same as Paul's (or as that of other groups of glossolalists who may not fit this pattern).[363] More clearly problematic, we cannot assume that Paul so *understood* the phenomenon; many (possibly most) modern Pentecostal Christian glossolalists, in fact, assume (on the basis of their reading of Paul) that they are speaking languages that they do not know.[364] Dunn notes that, rightly or wrongly, "if such claims can be made with such conviction in the twentieth century, it is more readily conceivable that they were made at the time of the first Christian Pentecost."[365] Luke or Paul could have coined some term to

354. Samarin, "Making Sense"; for a positive social role, cf., e.g., Griffith, Young, and Smith, "Elements." Some tests suggest the ability to emulate tongues as learned behavior (Spanos et al., "Learned Behavior"; cf. "glossolalic training," used to improve nonverbal sensitivity, Gutierrez and Wallbrown, "Sensitivity").

355. Poloma, "Glossolalia," esp. 172.

356. Smith, "Resistance Discourse" (suggesting [on 110] that it is thus ideally suited for Pentecostals as "the religion of the urban poor"); idem, *Thinking*, 123–50. Cartledge, "Tongues-Speech," 233–34, suggests the utility of this insight for modern middle-class glossolalists. Hine, "Glossolalia," 221–22, considers it learned behavior associated with personal changes (noting that it is more characteristic of those converted to it than of those raised with it).

357. Though I have witnessed clear distinctions (e.g., between possession and nonpossession phenomena). See further Turner, "Experience," 32, who complains that those who view it as ecstatic often draw this conclusion from "ecstatic glossolalia today, without paying attention to the far greater stream of modern tongues-speech which is definitely non-ecstatic" (cf. 1 Cor 14:28).

358. See Kay, "Glossolalia," 204: "Early research on glossolalia was almost uniformly hostile, though with honourable exceptions, and this must reflect the value systems inherent within early psychology.... More recent investigation has been friendly, theologically informed and deliberately interdisciplinary."

359. So ibid., 178–80. It may be relevant that in contrast with most approaches today, a number of earlier social scientists were expressly hostile to religion more generally (Smith, "Secularizing Education," 111–53; cf. Marsden, *Soul of University*, 163).

360. Kay, "Glossolalia," 180–85. Hine, "Glossolalia," 212–14, 217–18, shows that the earlier pathological view does not fit the fuller data available by the 1960s; she argues (218) against attributing it to suggestibility or hypnosis and (219) against attributing it to deprivation. Goodman, "Glossolalia," 238, even cites "an extensive study" (Vivier, "Glossolalic") showing "that the glossolalist is of significantly better mental health" than a socially analogous nonglossolalist as a result of helpful "after-effects" of dissociation.

361. See esp. Kay, "Glossolalia," 204–5; for a nonpathological reading, see also Malony, "Debunking," 104–8. Wacker, *Heaven*, 293n50, also notes that many or most recent studies do not view the practice as pathological (citing Williams, *Tongues*, 129; Malony and Lovekin, *Glossolalia*, ch. 5, esp. 93); cf. also Huber and Huber, "Psychology," 134–37.

362. See discussion above.

363. Following Goodman, *Speaking in Tongues*, some seem firm in identifying ancient and modern tongues (cf. Meeks, *Urban Christians*, 119, 232n27), which may be correct (certainly, we lack closer analogies). Yet there may have been different kinds of (and understandings concerning) glossolalia then as today (Barrett, *Acts*, 116).

364. See, e.g., the views reported in Hollenweger, *Pentecostals*, 342.

365. Dunn, *Jesus and Spirit*, 151 (who thinks that some on Pentecost did think that they recognized "words and phrases spoken by the disciples in their ecstasy"), 243 (on Paul).

describe an excited expression of language, or nonlinguistic, ecstatic babbling; but "languages" (γλῶσσαι) would hardly be the appropriate one![366]

VII. OTHER TONGUES AS FOREIGN LANGUAGES

The phrase "other tongues" probably connotes foreign speech (as confirmed by the hearers' "own tongues" in Acts 2:11). Forbes has proposed that even Paul's language for "tongues" is a shorthand for the clearer and more original "other tongues" found in Acts 2:4.[367] He may be right, though we should note that "other" (ἕτερος) is typically Lukan (forty-eight times in Luke-Acts; eight times in Matthew; never in the original text of Mark, though once in Mark 16:12; once in John; twenty-seven times in Paul).[368] Luke may have borrowed the particular phrase for foreign speech from Isa 28:11 LXX, which Paul had already applied, by analogy, to Christian tongues speaking (1 Cor 14:21);[369] if so, this Isaiah passage may have influenced early Christian usage (or at least usage in the Pauline circle of churches) more widely.

Some scholars grant that Luke claims that the disciples spoke genuine languages or dialects, yet doubt that Luke assumes a miracle of speech unknown to the speakers. Because Hebrew was a holy language for Judeans, some propose that the disciples spoke "other" languages (Acts 2:4) as merely "profane" ones (already known to the speakers).[370] But it is unlikely that the disciples spoke Hebrew on a regular basis.[371] A supporter of the "profane languages" position might respond that many Palestinian Jews who spoke Greek or Aramaic in other settings probably recited traditional prayers and psalms in Hebrew and that prayer is certainly relevant to the nature of speech here (1:14). Granted, but Mark 14:36 and 15:34 suggest that not even the historical Jesus always prayed in Hebrew (though, if Mark reports Jesus's actual practice, Matthew hebraizes the latter occasion, Matt 27:46).[372] Hebrew would be no more mandatory for prophecy.[373]

Far more problematic, Luke provides no indication that diglossia was in view or that one should expect the disciples to have spoken only Hebrew on this or another occasion. Luke is happy to specify an original Jewish language (Aramaic or, some think, Hebrew) when this is in view (Acts 21:40; 22:2; 26:14). Luke does not think of the disciples as limited to any Semitic language: they quote the LXX; they also clearly knew some Greek, without which communication within the Jerusalem church would have become unintelligible (without tongues) by the time of Acts 6 (see comment on Acts 6:1). Further, one holding this view must discount the explicitly parallel (10:46) passage where Cornelius's household cannot be expected to have *ever* spoken much Hebrew (10:1–2).[374] (This is not to mention that the view must discount the relevance

---

366. For some similar conclusions on tongues being understood as languages, cf. Forbes, *Prophecy*, 50, 56–72; Gundry, "Ecstatic Utterance?"; Cartledge, "Glossolalia."

367. Forbes, *Prophecy*, 72–74. The use of "other" (ἕτερος) at 1 Cor 12:10, however, simply substitutes for the ἄλλος in front of other gifts in the verse as a stylistic preference (cf. 12:9), distinguishing recipients of gifts.

368. Dupont, *Salvation*, 50.

369. "Another tongue" appears also in Sir prol. 20, in explaining the need for a translation.

370. Zerhusen, "Judean *diglossia* in Acts 2?" (cf. also idem, "Tongues in 1 Cor 14"); Crystal, "Applied Sociolinguistics." (See further refutation of Zerhusen in Garland, *1 Corinthians*, 584n12.) Some also claim that "tongues" meant simply "archaic language"; see the refutation in Forbes, *Prophecy*, 60–61.

371. See, e.g., Horsley, *Galilee*, 247–49; more extensive discussion at Acts 21:40.

372. The change from Mark's ἐλωΐ to ἠλί in Matt 27:46 could reflect such concerns (though the latter had also come into Aramaic) or be included to explain (probably correctly, *pace*, e.g., Cope, *Scribe*, 104) how listeners thought they heard "Elijah" (*Eliyahu*; Jeremias, *Theology*, 5n2; cf. Anderson, *Mark*, 346; Keener, *Matthew*, 682).

373. Cf., e.g., *Sibylline Oracles*; or in Judea, Josephus's claims for his own; or the Aramaic portions of Daniel.

374. One can hardly aver that most of the gathering (Acts 10:24) was Jewish (see 11:1, 3, 18). As for the cases being parallel, Peter says so explicitly (10:47; 11:15–16), and it is hardly plausible to assign a wholly

of Paul's evidence, despite his similarly unusual use of the same term γλῶσσα, and Paul's emphasizing that the languages spoken were unknown to the speakers [1 Cor 14:13, 14, 19, 27–28].)

Most important, this view renders implausible Luke's mention of *each* language in Acts 2:8, which Luke goes on to elaborate specifically in 2:9–11; such elaboration makes little sense if Luke meant only the lingua franca of the eastern Mediterranean (Greek) and Middle East (Aramaic; or Latin, the lingua franca of the West).[375] The use of λαλέω and γλῶσσα in 2:11 explicitly recalls the same terms in 2:4. In the context of Acts, this event was a *sign* of the reception of the Spirit, which would hardly merit specific mention (esp. in 10:45–47 and 19:6) if the persons inspired spoke merely their own languages as they had before the inspiration. This proposal seems an attempt to circumvent Luke's cross-cultural use of tongues in his story.

But while Luke seems clear that the disciples spoke in diverse languages representing a wide geographic range, he does not settle our logistical questions of how this phenomenon might have occurred. On the historical level, probably only a minority of Jews in these different nations would have been familiar with most local dialects; most Jews settled in the cities and spoke the lingua franca of their regions, whether Greek, sometimes Latin, or the eastern or western dialects of Aramaic.[376] Indeed, even in Rome more Jews retained Greek than communicated among themselves in Latin.[377] Luke himself, knowledgeable of Diaspora Judaism, must know this.

Nevertheless, Luke is clear that the hearers understood at least enough of what the disciples were saying to recognize that they were praising God (2:11). Recognition and some level of understanding languages with which one has some familiarity (which requires recognition of key words, not perfect comprehension) is *far* more easily obtained than a speaking knowledge of a language.[378] Luke was aware of Jews (cf. 14:19) in the vicinities of places where local dialects were still spoken (cf. 14:14) and probably expected many to recognize at least some of the local languages from regions where they resided. This would be especially the case for those who did not live in large Jewish enclaves (e.g., Alexandria) and hence did some business with local residents (cf., e.g., 18:3, though in Corinth the languages were Latin and Greek). Further, Luke can employ these representative provenances of Diaspora Jews as a symbol of ethnic universalism even if only some representatives among them recognize other languages (just as he can employ them in this manner even though they are not Gentiles).

new meaning to "tongues" in the context of the Spirit's outpouring in Acts 10, a meaning different from what an ordinary reader would expect from the last usage, also in the context of the Spirit's outpouring, in Acts 2.

375. For this critique, see also, e.g., Witherington, *Acts*, 133.

376. Knox, *Jerusalem*, 33. Abbott, *Acts*, 37, thus thought (in 1876) of different dialects of Greek but further apart than French and German; the subsequently published papyri refute the possibility of such divergent dialects of Greek spoken over this geographic range in the Koine period. Earlier Greek dialects would cause trouble for Greek interpreters (see Forbes and Browning, "Glossa") but were not as different as, for example, German is from French or other Romance languages (early Greeks thought of these Greek dialects as a common language), and by the late Hellenistic period, a universal Koine emerged (with Attic eventually emerging as a literary language; see Davies, "Greek language," 653–54). Luke's omission of the Greek mainland from the languages in Acts 2:9–11 also confirms that in his view the disciples are not simply speaking various forms of Greek.

377. Leon, *Jews of Rome*, 75–77; Lung-Kwong, *Purpose*, 105–6; Noy, "Writing." Most Jewish papyri from Egypt are in Greek (or, in the earlier Elephantine papyri, Aramaic), but this was common in the Ptolemaic and Roman periods in cities or Hellenistic nomes.

378. In view of the other evidence, I take the mention of "their own dialects" Acts (2:6) and "dialects in which they were born" (2:8) as a loosely worded reference to local dialects of the locations in which they were born rather than to their own mother tongues; such loose wording is neither uncommon nor uncharacteristic of Luke. (Similarly, "Simon of Cyrene" probably employs a geographic designation, though he was Jewish and his own language probably Greek.)

Some scholars suggest a hearing miracle rather than the disciples speaking in various languages; even some early interpreters held this view.[379] But some of the suggested background for this position is based on a misinterpretation of ancient texts.[380] More important, this proposal does not match what Luke himself says.[381] Luke reports their speaking "other languages" before mentioning that anyone hears them (2:4), and emphasizes that the Spirit enables them to speak this way; further, the gift recurs later as a supernatural sign with no indication that such hearing took place (10:45–46; 19:6).[382] Moreover, in his work, Luke emphasizes not so much the Spirit producing receptivity in crowds[383] but God working through those who are agents of his Spirit (4:8, 31; 6:3, 10; 10:38; 13:9–11; 21:4, 11). As Max Turner notes, Luke "would not wish to suggest that the apostolic band merely prattled incomprehensibly while God worked the yet greater miracle of interpretation of tongues in the *un*believers."[384]

VIII. MEANING AND FUNCTION OF TONGUES IN ACTS

Whatever aspect of charismatic tongues anyone else in the early church (such as Paul) emphasized, Luke derives considerable symbolic mileage from them. He emphasizes that the Spirit empowered witnesses, and hence ultimately the church, to cross cultural barriers with their prophetically inspired message. What better symbol of this cross-cultural empowerment for mission could have been available than the phenomenon of tongues, which he understands as inspired speech in languages the speakers had not learned?[385] (Although tongues seem to have functioned as prayer and worship and although Luke does not depict peoples from different cultures praying this way simultaneously, one might guess that it would also serve an equalizing function in the joint worship of believers in Jesus who did not share a common language.)

That Luke emphasizes tongues is no surprise; as Barrett notes, "Speech is in Acts the characteristic mark of the Spirit's presence, sometimes in glossolalia (2.4; 10.46; 19.6), sometimes in prophecy (2.17, 18; 11.27; 13.1–3; 21.(4), (9), 10, 11), sometimes in proclamation (e.g., 4.31)."[386] As the Spirit's activity often produced prophetic speech in

379. E.g., Bede *Comm. Acts* 2.6. We might compare divinely altered perception of a person (Luke 24:16), but in that case the reality is temporarily obscured, whereas here the focus of the miracle is cross-cultural empowerment (cf. Acts 1:8). Young, "Miracles in History," 119, reports a modern hearing miracle, as does Anna Gulick (interview, March 11, 2011: she understood a sermon in Gaelic despite complete unfamiliarity with it). Reports of these are infrequent, however, and much less frequent than claims of speaking miracles.

380. The purported evidence for a hearing or speech miracle in *Hom. Hymns* 3.156–64 (to Delian Apollo) (e.g., Burkert, *Religion*, 110; Ruble, "Tongues," 15, citing Martin, *Glossolalia*, 78) is not even clearly miraculous but probably refers to "singing in dialect" (Forbes, *Prophecy*, 119–23; van der Horst, "Parallels to Acts," 52–53, following Allen, Halliday, and Sikes, *Hymns*, 225), though ancients would have understood selective revelation (3 Macc 6:18; cf. John 14:22; Acts 10:41) and hearing one sound in various languages (scholars cite *Tanḥ.* 26c, whose tradition is of uncertain date).

381. Note, e.g., objections in Haenchen, *Acts*, 168n5 (*pace* Wendt, *Apostelgeschichte*; Wikenhauser, *Apostelgeschichte*, 34); Hull, *Spirit in Acts*, 61; Bock, *Acts*, 97.

382. Faw, *Acts*, 319. It is clear in Acts 10:46 that Luke intends the same phenomenon as on Pentecost, in view of 10:47; 11:15 and especially with the γάρ providing 10:46 as the explanation for their recognition in 10:45. Witherington, *Acts*, 134, emphasizes that in 2:6, "in his language" modifies speaking, not hearing.

383. One might propose Acts 5:32 and 7:51, but even these texts could refer to the Spirit's working through agents.

384. Turner, *Gifts*, 222–23.

385. Keener, *Questions*, 69; idem, *Gift*, 180; idem, "Tongues," 177–78, 180–81, 183–84; cf. Wrede, *Secret*, 232; Lenski, *Acts*, 62–63; Wikenhauser, *Apostelgeschichte*, 38; Hanson, *Acts*, 63–64; Fitzmyer, *Acts*, 239; Watson, *Gentiles*, 68–69; York, *Missions*, 80, 185–86 (for a missiological perspective; following Richardson, *Eternity*, 156–57); and esp. Ladd, *Young Church*, 56; Dupont, *Salvation*, 52, 59; Stendahl, *Paul*, 118–19; Kilgallen, *Commentary*, 16; Kim, "Mission," 37–40.

386. Barrett, *Acts*, 2:lxxxiv, also claiming that although Luke accepted the Spirit's activity in moral renewal, he emphasized instead "showier" phenomena (which Barrett considers "shallower," but which certainly make for a livelier narrative, an important consideration for one writing a narrative work).

ancient Israel, so now it produced "prophetic speech," but "of a peculiar kind."[387] Luke explicitly uses tongues to identify the activity of the Spirit of prophecy (2:17–18), albeit with a particular emphasis on crossing cultural boundaries. Presumably, the prophetic aspect of the Spirit's empowerment that he articulates in general includes and could be evidenced by any speech inspired by the Spirit or perhaps by prophet-like miracles as well, provided they testified about Jesus. But in view of his likely thesis statement at 1:8, Luke's primary concern is not simply prophetic speech in general but especially prophetic speech that extends to other peoples (promoting what scholars typically call the "Gentile mission," which, however, does not end once the initial Jewish-Gentile barrier has been surmounted in 8:27–39 or 10:23–48). We shall revisit this question further below.

Thus tongues are a sign of prophetic empowerment for the continuing cross-cultural mission. In contrast to this portrayal of the apostles early in Acts, Luke, toward the beginning of his first volume, reports a priest who initially disbelieved the divine message and was struck mute (Luke 1:20). When he was later filled with the Spirit, however, even he prophesied the divine message (1:67).[388] More in parallel with the scene here, Jesus, filled with the Spirit, foreshadows the Gentile mission (4:1, 14, 24–27). Tongues thus offer one kind of prophetic speech (Acts 2:16–18).

IX. Tongues as Evidence of Spirit Baptism?

Some scholars believe that tongues speaking was rare by Luke's day. M. D. Goulder pointed out that Acts stresses tongues only at vital points. Contrasting this selectivity with the likelihood that tongues speaking may have occurred each week in Corinthian assemblies in the 50s, Goulder draws from the relative paucity of Luke's descriptions the conclusion that by Luke's day the experience was merely a memory of a special phenomenon of earlier times.[389] Against this interpretation of the evidence, we should note that tongues speaking continued (albeit presumably much less than in Corinth in the 50s) in the late second century[390] (see further discussion above, under "Tongues in Early Christianity").

More critically, in a monograph the length of Acts, which offers no detailed descriptions of what took place during early Christian worship (Acts 2:42, 46 is a general summary, not a detailed description), we should not expect (and do not find) *any* description of tongues speech during house assemblies, in contrast to Paul's depiction of Corinth. What we do find are several descriptions of corporate experiences of the Spirit, three of which include tongues speaking. This represents three-quarters of the descriptions pertaining to groups experiencing the outpouring of the Spirit for the first time. This representation suggests that those who interpret these events as signs that tongues were long since past read too much into Luke's silence on such matters. Their observation of tongues occurring at significant junctures is, however, close to accurate; it would be more accurate, however, to claim that the *Spirit* (rather than simply tongues) is poured out at significant junctures, since this would include even the Samaritan "Pentecost," where tongues speaking is not narrated (8:17). Luke reports the junctures most relevant to his account of the church's cross-cultural expansion; he does not imply that such activity, once demonstrated in a new group of people, thereafter ceased simply because Luke then focuses on its reception among a different group of people!

387. Bruce, *Commentary*, 56.
388. Cf. Spencer, *Acts*, 32–33.
389. Goulder, *Type and History*, 77.
390. Forbes, *Prophecy*, 75–84. I have dated Acts only about a decade earlier than Goulder, but even the later dating would render tongues speaking within memory of many Christians even if (and this is unlikely) the practice never extended into the 60s. This conclusion invalidates any attempt to extrapolate Luke's knowledge (and hence context) from his allegedly "rare" notice about tongues.

Many scholars of global religion today estimate the size of the Pentecostal and charismatic bloc of the Christian church at nearly half a billion now (especially strong in the Majority World),[391] by some estimates more than a quarter of global Christianity;[392] most recognize that these movements account for a high proportion of Christianity's growth globally.[393] In view of these factors, it seems myopic (though not uncommon)[394] to interact with the often comparatively obscure views of various individual scholars yet fail to at least mention questions already raised by some scholars (and an increasing number of commentary users) from the Pentecostal tradition.[395] Their interpretation provides a significant example of recent reception history of the text. Moreover, these circles also provide a particularly useful contemporary analogy for helping us to understand some of the social dynamics involved in revival movements such as earliest Christianity;[396] although such analogies are never fully adequate,[397] they do check modern scholars' sometimes too ready assumptions about what members of the earliest Jesus movement "could have" thought or experienced.

Views on tongues, in fact, varied in early Pentecostalism.[398] Although tongues as the "initial physical evidence" of Spirit baptism became the dominant view in

391. For a more nuanced and cautious discussion of the figures, see Anderson, *Pentecostalism*, 11.D. Barrett defines "charismatic" much more broadly than I do; by his definition, he estimated more than 600 million by 2000, or nearly 30 percent of world Christianity ("Statistics," 813); statisticians have estimated 614 million for 2010 (Johnson, Barrett, and Crossing, "Christianity 2010," 36; cf. Johnson and Ross, *Atlas*, 102); Sanneh estimates almost 590 million for 2005 (and a projected nearly 800 million by 2025; *Disciples*, 275); in 1994, Harvey Cox already accepted an estimate of 410 million (Cox, *Fire*, xv). For Pentecostalism in the Majority World, see, e.g., Yong, *Spirit Poured*, 33–80; for its growth in much of Asia, see, e.g., Ma, "Challenges," 195–96; idem, "Theology"; Yung, "Pentecostalism"; Anderson, "Face"; in Africa, e.g., Maxwell, *African Gifts*, 6–7. For the rapid expansion of Pentecostal missionaries from the Majority World, see, e.g., Pate, "Missions," 244–46; for one perspective on the movement's growth, see Wagner, "Perspective," 266–68.

392. See Johnson, Barrett, and Crossing, "Christianity 2010," 36; Cox, "Foreword," xxi (a quarter); Hanciles, *Beyond Christendom*, 121 (at 27.4 percent); Barrett, Johnson, and Crossing, "Missiometrics 2007," 32 (29 percent of church attenders); cf. Tomkins, *History*, 245. Historian Robert Bruce Mullin observes that already by the end of the twentieth century there were "more Pentecostals worldwide" than mainline Protestants (Mullin, *History*, 211).

393. See Tomkins, *History*, 220: "the fastest-growing form of Christianity ever"; see likewise Sweeney, *Story*, 153. Sociologist Peter Berger contends that Pentecostalism "accounts for something like 80 percent of its [evangelical Protestantism's] worldwide growth" (Berger, "Faces," 425, also viewing it as a major force in cultural globalization).

394. Some scholars (e.g., Dunn, *Baptism*; Menzies, *Development*; Parsons, *Acts*, 49–50) explicitly do engage the claims of the Pentecostal tradition (whether agreeing or disagreeing), but the discipline of church history has understandably been much quicker to acknowledge the significance of, and sometimes profit from, discussion with Pentecostalism (with considerable attention from Walter Hollenweger, Grant Wacker, Edith Blumhofer, and a large number of others) than has biblical studies. For some sociological reasons for the academy's slowness to attend to global Pentecostalism until recent decades, see Maxwell, *African Gifts*, 10–11.

395. As Hollenweger, "Dialogue," 207, notes, "so far the theological contributions of Third World Pentecostals have been largely ignored," partly for linguistic and cultural reasons and partly because the majority of adherents are poor and their theologies are not contained in official documents. Nevertheless, Pentecostal scholarship has been coming into its own (with numerous publishing scholars and multiple mainstream scholarly journals). Acts 2 is naturally foundational for Pentecostal theology; see, e.g., Leeper, "Gift." For a Pentecostal (vs. cessationist) approach to interpreting Acts, see, e.g., Elbert, "Themes."

396. In addition to the usual studies of such movements, Summers, "Approach," uses sociology and anthropology to compare modern charismatic phenomena with those reported in Paul. Cf. also Miller and Yamamori, *Pentecostalism*, 218.

397. Sometimes they derive from models in Acts (a derivation that, however, at least reveals that some find such models workable); charismatic and Pentecostal theologies are also diverse (most mainline and academic Pentecostals, e.g., reject the obviously non-Lukan "prosperity" theology common in some popular charismatic circles and also some culturally shaped ecstatic behaviors found in some earlier Pentecostal circles, such as appear in, e.g., Wacker, *Heaven*, 53, 100–102) but concur on the centrality of the Spirit's activity and the continuing value of spiritual gifts, including prayer in tongues.

398. I use the modern definition of "Pentecostal"; late nineteenth-century Holiness movements applied the title to the Spirit's activity before widespread use gave the title a new sense in the early twentieth century

Pentecostalism, many influential early Pentecostal proponents of tongues (e.g., Agnes Ozman, F. F. Bosworth, Minnie Abrams, and, according to many, even Azusa Street leader William Seymour) apparently denied or came to deny that tongues speaking was a necessary evidence of the seminal experience of the Spirit described in Acts.[399] This perspective was probably even more prevalent outside the United States.[400] Some other early Pentecostal leaders wished to place the focus of the movement elsewhere than on tongues.[401]

Tongues as the "initial evidence" of baptism in the Spirit became the dominant view among classical Pentecostals,[402] however, despite dissent from some of its leading figures.[403] This might be a minority view among global charismatics and certainly is so among charismatics in most traditional denominations.[404] Although speaking in tongues has occurred frequently through Christian history,[405] the idea that tongues function as evidence of Acts' experience of baptism in the Spirit appears to be more recent.[406] It might occur in one nineteenth-century movement (Edward Irving's Catholic Apostolic Church in the 1830s)[407] but mostly stems from the early twentieth-century Pentecostal movement.

(cf., e.g., Bebbington, *Dominance*, 210). Some of these groups offered the most vigorous opposition to the new movement in the early period (see, e.g., Walsh, "Signs").

399. Robeck, "Seymour," 81–89; McGee, "Hermeneutics," 108–10; idem, *Miracles*, 135 (Abrams); Wacker, *Heaven*, 41; Opp, *Lord for Body*, 152 (on Bosworth); Williams, "Acts," 219 (on Seymour); Alexander, *Fire*, 130–31 (Seymour); cf. Robeck, *Mission*, 178; Jacobsen, *Thinking in Spirit*, 10; Kalu, *African Pentecostalism*, 20 (on Abrams). Seymour may have played down the role of tongues rather than denied their inclusion in Spirit baptism (Jacobsen, *Thinking in Spirit*, 78; Tarr, *Foolishness*, 379–80); in keeping with his Holiness background, he connected tongues more closely to ethics (see Brathwaite, "Tongues").

400. In the early period, note esp. Pandita Ramabai (Burgess, "Evidence," 33–34; McGee, "Hermeneutics," 107–8; Hudson, "Strange Words," 67; Burgess, "Pandita Ramabai," 195) as well as Minnie Abrams, mentioned above. Many Pentecostal movements in Europe and Latin America are less insistent on tongues than are many other traditional Pentecostals (Spittler, "Glossolalia," 339).

401. Blumhofer, *Sister*, 208–14. In fact, many Pentecostal leaders and scholars have emphasized from the beginning that the focus should not be tongues but empowerment (Wyckoff, "Baptism," 450, and sources he cites; Jacobsen, *Thinking in Spirit*, 75–80 [esp. on Seymour], 190–91, 287, 289, 354).

402. See, e.g., Jacobsen, *Thinking in Spirit*, 62, 84, 95–98, 288–90; Johns, "New Directions"; Horton, *Spirit*, 157, 216–19, 259–60. This view was pioneered by Charles Parham (Jacobsen, *Thinking in Spirit*, 19, 48–49) and provided a definite social marker distinguishing Pentecostals from their Holiness kin (288; cf. this function of the early restorationist rhetoric, Nienkirchen, "Visions"), though preoccupation with such "evidence" may reflect modernist epistemological assumptions (Smith, *Thinking*, 124n1). It has been estimated that perhaps 35 percent of Pentecostals have prayed in tongues (Lederle, "Evidence," 136; cf. McGee, "Hermeneutics," 107; though the more recent and extensive figures in *Landscape Survey*, 55, are closer to 50 percent), statistics probably comparable to first-generation Pentecostals as well (Wacker, *Heaven*, 41). For various current Pentecostal and other perspectives on the doctrine (not all the traditional versions), see, e.g., the various articles in *Asian Journal of Pentecostal Studies* 1 (1998) (Menzies, "Tongues"; Cruz, "Response"; Macchia, "Groans"; Ling, "Response"; Hunter, "Aspects"; Clark, "Evidence"; Lim, "Critique"; Turner, "Tongues") and 2 (1999) (Ma, "Sign"; Gladstone, "Sign Language"; Chan, "Glossolalia"; Plüss, "Evidence"; Lim, "Reflection"; Dionson, "Doctrine"; Menzies, "Issue"; Chan, "Response"; Menzies, "Universality"; Turner, "Responses"; and esp. bibliography in Flokstra, "Sources").

403. See McGee, "Hermeneutics," 107–10; Jacobsen, *Thinking in Spirit*, 293, 314–15, 395n4. Doctrinal freedom on issues secondary to the gospel characterized early Pentecostalism (see Lederle, *Treasures*, 29–31, esp. 29; see also Hollenweger, *Pentecostals*, 32, 331–36).

404. Lederle, "Evidence," 131ff.

405. E.g., Anderson, *Pentecostalism*, 24–25, 36–37; Hinson, "History of Glossolalia," 57–66.

406. Some interpreters of recent centuries may have also emphasized baptism in the Spirit more than previously on account of their movements' emphases; see comment on Acts 1:4–5.

407. Dorries, "Irving and Spirit Baptism" (Irving viewed speaking in tongues as a prominent sign of Spirit baptism; see also Strachan, *Theology of Irving*; cf. Synan, *Voices*, 85–87); for a very brief survey of the movement, see Bundy, "Irving," and the many sources cited there. That glossolalia occurred in the movement is widely acknowledged (see Wacker, *Heaven*, 51). The movement's final "apostle" died in 1901, the year that Charles Parham began preaching tongues as the "Bible evidence" of Spirit baptism (albeit with little known likelihood of direct contact).

Recent as the emphasis may be, it is grounded in a genuine observation about the text and Luke's overall narrative pattern, one that some earlier interpreters may have overlooked precisely because it was so foreign to their own experience. (This despite the fact that some of the earliest Christian interpreters apparently did recognize the pattern.)[408] Both the early classical Pentecostals and their modern scholars who associate tongues with Spirit baptism observed a genuine feature of Luke's story. Robert Menzies, for example, accurately notes that Luke closely connects tongues with "inspired speech, of which tongues speech is a prominent form, possessing a unique evidential character."[409]

The observation of this connection is hardly limited to Pentecostals. James D. G. Dunn, who is known for challenging classical Pentecostalism by identifying Spirit baptism with conversion-initiation rather than with a subsequent experience, has noted, "It is undoubtedly true that Luke regarded the glossolalia of Pentecost as an external sign of the Spirit's outpouring." Luke used tongues the same way in 10:45–46 and 19:6, and Dunn thinks that, most likely, tongues occurred in 8:17, though it is not mentioned.[410] (I allow the opposite argument in 8:17, at least regarding what information was available to Luke. But in both cases we admittedly argue from silence, lacking sufficient concrete evidence for a more explicit judgment.) Since these passages exhaust the "initial" fillings that are *described* in Acts (9:17 predicts but does not describe Paul's), Dunn recognizes that the case "that Luke *intended* to portray 'speaking in tongues' as 'the initial physical evidence' of the outpouring of the Spirit" makes far more sense than most scholars have noticed.[411]

Yet Dunn nevertheless demurs from the classical Pentecostal conclusion: Luke's intention is to demonstrate the Spirit's presence through tongues, not to "teach" that tongues will always accompany the Spirit (Luke does, after all, omit its mention in 8:17).[412] Most interpreters here agree with Dunn's conclusion, based on the very limited evidence we have in Acts: Luke regarded tongues as one verbally inspired manifestation of the prophetic Spirit among several, along with praise (2:11; 10:46), prophecy (19:6; cf. 2:17–18), and boldness (4:8, 31).[413] Such expressions underline the prophetic character of the empowerment. Likewise, as noted further below, tongues speech evidences the experience of baptism in the Spirit (i.e., reveals its purpose and function), not the individual recipients of this baptism; it thus need not occur on every occasion to maintain its symbolic function.[414]

408. Severus of Antioch, in *Cat. Act.* 10.44 (Martin, *Acts*, 140), doubted that miracles and such evidences remained necessary in his own day, but he contended that in apostolic times, "those who received holy baptism both spoke with tongues and prophesied in order to prove that they had received the Holy Spirit." Cf. Aug. *Retract.* 1.13.7 (PL 32:604–5, cited in Kelsey, *Healing*, 185); McDonnell and Montague, *Initiation*, 314 (cited in McGee, "Miracles and Mission").

409. Menzies, *Empowered*, 254. From this he further infers that those who receive the gift of the Spirit "should *expect* to manifest tongues" (255). Stronstad, "Baptized," 188, noting signs accompanying Spirit empowerment earlier in salvation history, argues that tongues are the distinctive sign for baptism in the Spirit.

410. Dunn, *Jesus and Spirit*, 189.

411. Ibid., 189–90. Cf. Catholic scholar Haya-Prats, *Believers*, 120: "Luke presents glossolalia as the typical manifestation of the Spirit."

412. The logical distinction between premise *a* necessarily leading to conclusion *b* and the reverse (*b* leading to conclusion *a*) would not have been lost on ancient thinkers (e.g., Hermog. *Issues* 51.16–22; 52.1–4; Porph. *Ar. Cat.* 90.12–91.12; cf. another sort of distinction in Epict. *Diatr.* 1.8.14).

413. Dunn, *Jesus and Spirit*, 190–91; cf. similarly Turner, *Power*, 446–47 (who is also skeptical that early Jewish sources expected *any* particular "initial evidence," 448–49); Talbert, *Acts*, 33, 99; Twelftree, *People*, 98–99 (any ecstatic or supernatural manifestations). Cf. Nigerian Baptist scholar Caleb Olapido, who notes that when Yoruba Christians are filled with the Spirit, "ecstatic utterances are common" (*Development*, 108, 112–13, in Barr, Leonard, Parsons, and Weaver, *Acts*, 133).

414. Of course, prophetic empowerment should presumably lead at least to prophetic witness, and cross-cultural empowerment should lead to participation in cross-cultural witness. Luke does often report prophetic

Nevertheless, that Luke is able to report as many instances of tongues accompanying Spirit baptism as he does (but does not invent it where he cannot report it) suggests that, historically, the verbal phenomenon sometimes or often accompanied the spiritual experience (cf. Aug. *Bapt.* 2.16.21; cf. 4.22.30; *Tract. Jn.* 6.18). (Paul's evidence leaves little historical doubt that tongues speaking occurred.) More important, it suggests that Luke drew a connection, viewing tongues as a frequent and theologically normal (though not necessarily mandatory) sign of the Spirit's special empowerment for cross-cultural ministry. That is, Luke emphasizes a prophetic empowerment with a typically cross-cultural focus.

Luke's theological use of the motif allows us to develop this observation further. We should note that the primary manifestations of the Spirit reported by Luke, especially in key, paradigmatic texts, are vocal (1:8; 2:4, 17–18). Luke does not focus on every aspect of the Spirit's activity mentioned by other early Christian writers (including his hero Paul; though he does not deny such aspects); he focuses on inspired speech flowing from the prophetic Spirit (2:17–18). At the same time, Luke has a reason for emphasizing a particular form of inspired speech, namely, tongues, where he can (which is why I am more skeptical than Dunn, though not dogmatically so, that Luke found it in, or felt free to infer it for, his source for Acts 8): this particular form of prophetic speech provides the most obvious symbol of people empowered to cross cultural and linguistic barriers with the gospel, which fits Luke's emphasis (1:8).

Tongues speaking itself is not simply one sign among many, only arbitrarily connected with Spirit baptism. Rather, it is intrinsically connected with Luke's emphasis on the Spirit's empowerment to proclaim Christ cross-culturally (1:8).[415] It may not be necessary to evidence the cross-cultural facility of every individual recipient, but in Luke's narrative it does evidence the character of Spirit baptism itself, explicating for Luke the *nature* of that empowerment.

Some historians have noted that some nineteenth-century Holiness advocates initially sought the "gift of tongues" because they believed it relevant to missionary endeavor.[416] Following this expectation, many of Pentecostalism's early exponents understood tongues as a form of missionary xenoglossy,[417] a view attested also among

---

evidences of this empowerment at the time of the experience, and classical Pentecostals would infer that this narrative pattern suggests a pattern for individual Christian experience. Whether it is normative for each individual, however, remains open to debate, views varying depending on what we make of the incidents where Luke does not report any charismatic phenomena at the moment of reception. (That no other documents from the Pauline circle treat tongues as evidence or address a subsequent experience for prophetic empowerment may also invite the question as to how strongly Luke could have insisted on this paradigm in his circle of churches. Pentecostal scholars could, however, respond by emphasizing Luke's distinctive theological contribution; genre; and that this objection argues from silence.) Each side, in a sense, argues what to make of certain cases of silence, but if tongues (and other prophetic speech) are used to explicate the nature of the experience, they could maintain their function without our inferring that they occur on every occasion when an individual receives the experience. It is possible that charismatic phenomena at the point of experience represent for Luke an *ideal* pattern; but Luke does not impose his ideal patterns strictly (compare, e.g., Acts 2:38 with 10:44–48).

415. See Keener, "Tongues." Although no NT writer makes the connection, it is possible that some would have found texts such as Zeph 3:9 useful: God would ultimately purify their lips (from deception, 3:13) so that all peoples could call on YHWH's name.

416. E.g., Anderson, *Pentecostalism*, 33–34; McGee, *Miracles*, 61–76; and some sources in the following note on early Pentecostal views of xenoglossy.

417. See McGee, "Hermeneutics," 102; idem, "Strategy," 52–53; Goff, "Theology of Parham," 64–65; Jacobsen, *Thinking in Spirit*, 25, 49–50, 74, 76, 97; Robeck, *Mission*, 41–42, 236–37, 243, 252; see esp. McGee, "Shortcut"; idem, "Logic"; Anderson, "Signs," 195–99. Before Pentecostalism, some evangelical missions advocates, such as A. B. Simpson, the early Christian and Missionary Alliance, and three members of the famous "Cambridge Seven," sought missionary tongues, apparently in most cases without success (McGee, "Radical Strategy," 77–78, 80–83).

some church fathers.[418] (There are oral[419] and written[420] reports of such xenoglossy occurring in isolated modern cases, although a number of scholars have suggested alternative explanations for many of the purported cases.)[421] Although most early Pentecostals fairly quickly abandoned the "missionary tongues" view after it failed the empirical test,[422] the early Pentecostal teacher Charles Parham insisted on it to the end, criticizing others for abandoning it.[423] Early Pentecostals continued to embrace

418. See esp. Parmentier, "Zungenreden"; Talbert, *Corinthians*, 90 (citing Iren. *Her.* 5.6.1; Chrys. *Hom. 1 Cor.* 29, on 12:1–11; though noting that this is less common than the glossolalia interpretation, Iren. *Her.* 5.6.1; Tert. *Marc.* 5.8).

419. Dr. Derek J. Morphew, interview, November 12, 2007, Corona, California, stated that in ca. 1975 an elder in the church that he pastored came up wide-eyed after Derek's wife, Karin, gave an utterance in tongues in the church. The elder, who had grown up in Italy and whom they knew well and for a long time, recognized the Portuguese dialect and told her what she had said (very similar to the interpretation). Pastor David Workman, interview, April 30, 2008, Wynnewood, Pennsylvania, stated that his mother, without much formal education or any exposure to French, was understood to be praising God in an old dialect of French. He also noted that about fifteen years before our conversation a friend of his had prayed for someone in Mexico who apparently knew no English and the person began praising God in glossolalia—in this case, fluent English. My wife tells of a well-known Congolese minister when she was young, Daniel Ndoundou (on whom see Keener, "Ndoundou," but not including this oral claim), who was said to have preached in Swedish in Sweden without knowing the language. My student Leah Macinskas-Le (interview, April 25, 2010) reported that her mother, who is Jewish, many years ago became a believer in Jesus through glossolalia that she recognized as fluent Hebrew. Most "firsthand," my friend Leo Bawa, from Nigeria, tells me of his own temporary ability to understand and speak some local tribal languages (Aug. 10, 2009).

420. E.g., Tarr, *Foolishness*, 401–3 (about ten cases, some with considerable supporting evidence, especially cases where Tarr, a linguist, was one of the eyewitnesses); Mansfield, *Pentecost*, 50 (another's prayer in perfect French, attested by the author, a French major); Warner, *Evangelist*, 256–57, noting a woman who, according to Romanians present, spoke Romanian for twenty-five minutes (267n13 offers the source in an interview with the woman's son; also noted in Liardon, *Generals*, 69); Prather, *Miracles*, 166–71 (esp. 168; the speaker was as surprised as the hearer [169], whose life was permanently changed [171]; Prather, a journalist, knows the persons involved); Gardner, *Healing Miracles*, 142–43 (a Pentecostal tongues utterance in a Western church that proved a dramatic message in Sinhalese to visiting missionaries); Yeomans, *Healing*, 119 (understood "a little" by the author); Woodworth-Etter, *Miracles*, 110; see also some possibly relevant examples in McGee, "Shortcut" (some after minimal acquaintance with a language; citing, e.g., "Tarry"; "Gift of Tongues"; Goforth, *Goforth*, 87–88); McGee, "Radical Strategy," 78–79, 84–85 (including pre-Pentecostal missionary claims in the 1880s and 1890s); Sithole, *Voice*, 53, 90, 103; cf. 137, 183. In many instances in early Pentecostalism and subsequently, it was believed that genuine xenoglossy was recognized in prayer (see, e.g., McGee, *People of Spirit*, 24, 46–47, 57, 61, 64, 75; Robeck, *Mission*, 268–69; Lindsay, *Lake*, 25, 27; Blumhofer, "Portrait," 96, 99; Sherrill, *Tongues*, 19, 20, 42–43, 45, 90–91, 93, 94, 95, 96–97, 99–100; Synan, *Voices*, 60, 76–77, 84, 101–2; Alexander, *Fire*, 126–27; Gardner, *Healing Miracles*, 38; most extensively, about twenty-five cases in Harris, *Acts Today*, 108–30 [on 7 he refers to his earlier book with seventy-five cases]); earlier, cf. the view of Margaret Macdonald in 1830 (Gardner, *Healing Miracles*, 97). Others have reported its occurrence today (e.g., Stibbe, *Prophetic Evangelism*, 75; Olson, *Bruchko*, 152), sometimes after very minimal acquaintance with a language (Wagner, *Wave*, 102–4 [cited in McGee, "Shortcut," 123]; Rutz, *Megashift*, 38, 90–91; Synan, *Voices*, 147; analogously, learning how to read by inspiration, Rutz, *Megashift*, 88–89; cf. Rumph, *Signs*, 124–28, though after exposure to words]). For a reported case of independent yet identical "interpretations" of tongues in two different languages, see Pullinger, *Dragon*, 69–70 (the second interpreter did not know the first's language).

421. Hilborn, "Glossolalia," 115–16, on some tested incidents; Wacker, *Heaven*, 47–48. Hudson, "Strange Words," 61, suggests that most accounts are based on snippets here and there recognized by hearers (which could be random) or the sorts of sounds speakers could have heard before and unconsciously verbalized (one so inclined could offer the same proposal regarding the Diaspora hearers' perception at Pentecost). Griffiths, "Xenoglossy," 147, dismisses modern Pentecostal claims for xenolalia but offers the discussion only two paragraphs (the article's focus being mediums).

422. E.g., Wacker, *Heaven*, 47–51; McGee, *People of Spirit*, 77–78; Hudson, "Strange Words," 61–63; Anderson, "Points," 167; Ma, "Eschatology," 100 (noting Goff, *Fields*, 16). Noted leader G. B. Cashwell apparently left the movement in part because xenolalia failed in mission (Alexander, *Fire*, 141). Note especially the shift in the Indian mission context, after which Garr emphasized that the point was not tongues themselves but how they symbolized baptism in the Spirit (McGee, "Calcutta Revival," 138–39). The xenolalia interpretation "was already waning by 1906," shortly after the movement's beginning (McGee, "Strategies," 204).

423. Anderson, *Pentecostalism*, 190.

both power for mission and tongues speaking, but with the latter as a more symbolic sign of the former. Yet whereas most no longer claimed a direct "missionary" function for tongues, we may observe today that the doctrine's first advocates had at least noticed a genuine connection that most subsequent interpreters (including most Pentecostals) have missed: the connection in Luke's theology between tongues speech and the empowerment for global mission.[424]

The aspect of Spirit baptism on which Luke focuses is empowerment for cross-cultural mission; although tongues speaking provides a key illustration of this empowerment in Acts when Luke has it available, the focus is prophetic inspiration to communicate Christ's message cross-culturally.[425] Nor is recognition of this association limited to modern interpreters. As John Chrysostom noted, the Corinthians exalted tongues because it was the first spiritual gift on Pentecost; but it was first "because it was a sign that they were to go everywhere, preaching the gospel."[426] Similarly, the Venerable Bede believed that Acts 2:3–4 "indicated that the holy church, when it had spread to the ends of the earth, was to speak in the languages of all nations."[427]

Thus I would argue that Luke does in fact use tongues as evidence of baptism in the Spirit and in one sense would argue this more strongly than most traditional Pentecostals: tongues is not an arbitrary evidence but is highlighted because it is intrinsically related to the point of what Luke means by baptism in the Spirit.[428] In this case, reception history draws our attention to an important feature of Luke's narrative pattern that we might easily have missed. At the same time, we need not go as far as traditional Pentecostals in believing that Luke expected tongues on every occasion when a person was initially filled with the Spirit, even given Luke's emphasis. Tongues is a sign that attests the *nature* of the experience, not necessarily an exclusive, mandatory sign of every *individual's* reception of that experience.[429] Yet without insisting that Luke would have doubted the Spirit baptism of believers who had not

424. McGee, *Miracles*, 102, notes that this emphasis continued. Global mission has remained a central issue in Pentecostal theology (with Ma, "Studies," 62–63); this emphasis has undoubtedly spurred Pentecostalism's massive growth over the course of the twentieth century.

425. Cf. at greater length Keener, *Questions*, 66–76, esp. 69; and esp. idem, *Gift*, 177–85, esp. 180; and idem, "Tongues."

426. Chrys. *Hom. 1 Cor.* 35.1 (Bray, *Corinthians*, 138); on the Corinthians exalting it as the first gift, see also Theodoret *Comm. 1 Cor.* 251. Theodoret (*Comm. 1 Cor.* 240) believes that these gifts were common in former days and reproves the Corinthians for abusing the gifts by showing off instead of edifying the church.

427. Bede *Comm. Acts* 2.3A (Martin, *Acts*, 22). Cf. Aug. *Hom. 1 John* 6.10; Leo the Great *Sermons* 75.2 (Martin, *Acts*, 23): in Acts 2:4, "the particular voices of each distinct people become familiar in the mouth of the church." Origen *Comm. Rom.* on Rom 1:14 (CER 1:128, 130; Bray, *Romans*, 28) concludes that Paul received all peoples' languages (1 Cor 14:18). Cf. Wesley on tongues at Pentecost as a foretaste of peoples of all languages worshiping God (Wesley, *Notes*, 396, cited in McGee, *Miracles*, 61). Much more recently, see, e.g., Packer, *Acts*, 27: "The gift of tongues (*glossolalia*) was symbolic of the world-wide work they were to do (1:8)."

428. See more fully Keener, "Tongues." Although I have had significant exposure to Pentecostal (as well as non-Pentecostal) arguments over the years, which, in addition to my experience, stimulated my interest in the subject, my church and teaching affiliations are not Pentecostal. I mention this only to observe that no institutional constraints demand my conclusions (they might in fact prefer different ones if any); my conclusions have developed over nearly three decades of grappling with arguments on both sides. Both sides have read the passages in light of their corporate experience and interpretive traditions, but it appears to me that Pentecostals and many charismatics have noted a phenomenon genuinely rooted in the text.

429. It is difficult, in any case, to demonstrate from the text that Luke believed that it must occur in every case, since he did not make (but could have made) any point of it by indicating the pattern on every occasion. It would be less difficult to make a case that he regarded it as a normal and common mark of the experience. Some classical Pentecostals understandably counter that Luke does not report baptism on all occasions, leaving readers to infer it from other occasions where it is reported; but Acts 2:38 creates a strong expectation of baptism (which explicitly occurs at 2:41; 8:12, 38; 9:18; 10:48; 16:15, 33; 18:8; 19:5) whereas the expectation formed by Luke's pattern with tongues is weaker, the pattern, though genuine, appearing explicitly in just three instances.

evidenced it by tongues, one may nevertheless accept a central biblical insight of early Pentecostalism regarding the association of tongues with the Spirit's cross-cultural empowerment in Luke's narrative.

3. The Diaspora Crowd's Responses to Signs (2:5–13)

The scene with disciples speaking in "other" tongues by the Spirit's inspiration opens directly into a mention of the crowds that recognized these tongues (2:5–13) and that the apostles evangelized through their common linguistic ground with them (2:41). It also offers a list of the linguistically diverse hearers' locations (2:9–11).

a. The Crowd (2:5–8)

Luke often uses the literary technique of a divided crowd (e.g., 17:18, 32), usually implying that one group is more receptive to the message than the other (17:32–34; 23:7–9). If Luke uses this technique the same way here as he often uses it, then the Diaspora Jews may be among Peter's most receptive hearers in 2:37–41, just as Gentiles are in 13:48–50 (or probably Stoics in 17:32–34; Pharisees in 23:7–9). They may thus serve also as a bridge for audience identification.[430]

Luke treats the crowds, from a literary standpoint, like a chorus in Greek plays: as Dunn notes, these crowds, like a chorus, have a representative function (for the nations, though they remain Jews). Perhaps like a chorus, a subgroup within the chorus provides some comic relief (2:13).[431] The "crowds" appear frequently in Luke-Acts (πλῆθος, as here, more than twenty times; ὄχλος, as in 1:15, more than sixty times; see comment on Acts 1:15). In ancient aristocratic ideology, the "crowds" were untrustworthy; the masses were easily misled by demagogues, those who appeal to the ignorant masses rather than the wise elite.[432] Trained philosophers often expressed the same sentiments concerning the philosophically uninformed masses.[433] An urban elite might suspect that visitors to the festival would prove particularly susceptible to such deception; centuries earlier a Greek writer mocked urban demagogues who through flattery seduced country folk unaccustomed to their ways.[434] In contrast to ancient aristocratic ideology, Luke's crowds are often willing to learn (e.g., Luke 1:10; 3:10; 4:42; 5:1; Acts 8:6; 11:24, 26), a welcome contrast to the Jerusalem aristocrats (e.g., Acts 4:1–2), though sometimes easily stirred up (16:22; 17:8, 13).[435]

Orators at festivals discussed how far people had traveled to attend a festival, "for what is much sought after has value" (Men. Rhet. 1.3, 366.9–10 [Russell and Wilson,

---

430. Cf. this function for minor characters in Malbon, "Importance of Minor Characters."

431. Dunn, *Acts*, 26.

432. E.g., Aristoph. *Frogs* 419, 1085–86; Isoc. *Ad Nic.* 48; Xen. *Hell.* 2.3.27, 47; Arist. *Pol.* 3.6.4–13, 1281a–1282b; 4.4.4–7, 1292a; 5.4.1–5, 1304b–1305b; 6.2.10–12, 1319b; *Rhet.* 2.20.5, 1393b; Diog. Laert. 6.42; Polyb. 6.3–4; Diod. Sic. 10.7.3; 15.58.3; Dion. Hal. *Ant. rom.* 7.8.1; 7.31.1; 7.56.2; 8.31.4; 9.32.4; 10.18.3; Livy 3.71.5; 6.11.7; 22.34.2; Appian *Hist. rom.* 2.9; 3.7.1; 7.3.18; 11.7.40; *Bell. civ.* 1.5.34; Phaedrus 1.14.10–13; Plut. *Cic.* 33.1, 3–4; *Cam.* 31.2; *Praising* 16, *Mor.* 545C; *Statecraft* 5, *Mor.* 802DE; Max. Tyre 6.5; 27.6; Ael. Arist. *Def. Or.* 189, §57D; 201–2, §§61D–62D; Philo *Creation* 171; Jos. *Ant.* 4.223; 6.36. On Dio Chrysostom's mistrust of the mob, see Barry, "Aristocrats."

433. E.g., Epict. *Diatr.* 1.18.10; 1.2.18; 1.3.4; 1.18.4; 2.1.22; 4.8.27; Sen. Y. *Ep. Lucil.* 66.31; 108.7; Marc. Aur. 11.23; Mus. Ruf. frg. 41, p. 136.22–26; Max. Tyre 1.7–8; 33.1; Iambl. *V.P.* 31.200, 213; Porph. *Marc.* 17.291–92; 30.475; Diogenes the Cynic in Diog. Laert. 6 passim.

434. Aristoph. *Acharn.* 371–73.

435. The "crowds" play a less hostile role in Jesus's crucifixion in Luke (Luke 23:4, 48) than in Mark 15:11, 15. Luke's term in Acts 2:6 refers to God's people more often than the other Greek term (Acts 4:36; 6:5; 15:12, 30).

73]). They also might comment on the vast numbers who came (366.24), "as at the Hebrews' festival in Palestine, where they gather in great numbers from many nations" (366.26–28 [Russell and Wilson, 73]). Luke is not offering an epideictic oration on the greatness of the Pentecost festival, but he uses the same sort of expected appreciation for the festival and its pilgrims' interest to show the greatness of the event of the Spirit's coming.

The Diaspora Jews in the crowd are astonished (Acts 2:7, 12),[436] a familiar response in Luke-Acts to miracles (Luke 2:18, 33; 8:25; 9:43; 11:14; 24:12, 41; Acts 3:12; 7:31) and other divinely orchestrated phenomena (Luke 1:21, 63; 4:22; 20:26; Acts 4:13). Two terms for their reaction are used here: the term ἐξίστημι appears eleven times in Luke-Acts (about 65 percent of the NT uses);[437] the term θαυμάζω appears in Luke-Acts eighteen times (about 42 percent of the NT uses).[438] The reader can hardly miss the point, which reinforces the "confounding" or "confusion" of the audience in Acts 2:6.[439] Such amazement constituted a normal response to God's wonders.[440] It does not always guarantee faith (cf. 13:41), but it is often its prelude.[441] See fuller comment on Acts 3:12.

By asking what "this" (τοῦτο) phenomenon means, the crowds allude back to "this" (ταύτης) sound (2:6, referring to the disciples speaking in other languages in 2:4) and prepare for Peter's explanation (2:16, τοῦτο): "this" sound of other languages fulfills Joel's promise of Spirit-inspired speech in the eschatological time (Acts 2:17–18).[442]

The crowds heard the disciples declaring God's greatness (μεγαλεῖα, 2:11); Luke elsewhere uses a cognate of this term for an amazed crowd's reaction to God's greatness (Luke 9:43; cf. Acts 19:27), and another cognate for exalting God (Luke 1:46 [cf. Acts 19:17]; conjoined with tongues speaking in Acts 10:46).[443] Praising God's mighty deeds appears also in Ps 150:2 (though the LXX uses a different word), in a context that includes the "sound" (ἤχῳ) of the praise (150:3; cf. Acts 2:2) and praise from all with the "breath" of life (Ps 150:6; cf. Acts 2:2).[444] In view of Acts 10:46 and (if we may admit it as evidence) the use of tongues for prayer and worship in Paul (1 Cor 14:14–17), it seems likely that the crowds heard the disciples worshiping God.[445]

436. Van der Horst, "Parallels to Acts," 54, cites Hdt. 8.135 as a parallel for astonishment when hearing an unexpected language. When recounting this narrative, an ancient reader would probably dramatize the amazement by (Shiell, *Reading Acts*, 172) turning his "hand upward," bringing his "fingers into the palm one by one, beginning with the little finger, and then" opening the "palm in reverse order (Quint. *Inst.* 11.3.100)."

437. Except in Acts 8:9, 11 (where it applies to Simon's acts), it always applies to God's acts, such as miracles (Luke 8:56), the resurrection (24:22), Saul's conversion (Acts 9:21), the Spirit on the Gentiles (10:45), and Peter's deliverance (12:16).

438. Emotions of various kinds feature prominently in Acts; Pauw, "Influence of Emotions," provides more than a hundred examples. The LXX, earlier than Luke, uses θαυμάζω fifty-seven times, but often for horror.

439. The verb so applies to groups of people, typically hostile, in Acts 9:22; 19:32; 21:27, 31 (together constituting 100 percent of NT uses). Of four uses of the cognate noun in the LXX (the other three in 1 Samuel), the first is Gen 11:9—the Babel passage (the only NT use being Acts 19:29).

440. E.g., *1 En.* 26:6; *Sib. Or.* 1.32; *Test. Ab.* 3:12; 6:8; 7:10 A.

441. Cf. Dupont, *Salvation*, 53.

442. The demonstrative pronoun by itself would not need to carry so much weight if the context did not support it (it occurs in 1,262 verses of the NT corpus, 425 in Luke-Acts, and twenty-six times in the first two chapters of Acts), but the context does support it (and ancient interpreters could find it significant at times, e.g., *y. Meg.* 1:5, §3).

443. For exalting God's "great deeds" (μεγαλεῖα), see also Ps 70:19 LXX (Ps 71:19 ET); Sir 18:4 (cf. also Tob 13:6); for God displaying these works, see Deut 11:2; Sir 17:8; 33:8; 43:15; 2 Macc 3:34; 7:17.

444. See God's "great" or "mighty acts" (τὰ μεγαλεῖα) in, e.g., Deut 11:2; Sir 17:10; 18:4; 36:7 [36:10]; 42:21; 3 Macc 7:22. Cf. "the mighty one" as a divine title (Gen 49:24; Josh 22:22; Pss 50:1; 132:2, 5; Isa 10:34; 49:26; 60:16; Sir 46:5; *4 Ezra* 6:32; 9:45; 10:24; *2 Bar.* 21:3, 4; 25:4; 32:1, 6; 34:1; 44:3, 6; 46:1, 4; 47:1; 48:1, 38; 54:1, 11; 55:6; 56:2–3); the "mighty one" does "great things" in Luke 1:49.

445. With also Turner, *Gifts*, 223; idem, *Power*, 271–72 (citing also songs about mighty acts in Exod 15:1–18, 21; Judg 5:2–31; Luke 1:46–55, 68–79); idem, "Experience," 32; for various possible uses of tongues, cf. Forbes, *Prophecy*, 91–99. The same expression, μεγαλεῖα τοῦ θεοῦ, appears in *Test. Job* 51:4 (*OTP* 1:867)/51:3

Recipients of a benefactor's favor were expected to honor the benefactor with public recognition, a common understanding in a milieu in which the emphasis on public praise for benefactors was more intelligible than it sometimes is for Western society.[446] It is also relevant that "God's mighty acts" are what Luke's history is about;[447] the Spirit-empowered disciples engage in precisely an activity most significant to Luke, who undoubtedly trusts the Spirit in an analogous manner for his own literary task.

b. Were the Diaspora Jews Visitors or Residents?

Whether these crowds were visiting for the festival season (perhaps since Passover, but some perhaps new) or Diaspora Jews who had settled in Jerusalem makes a difference for how we understand following chapters. If they had settled in Jerusalem, the Jerusalem church had a sizable number of Hellenist converts (Acts 6:1) from the start. This would also mean that these Diaspora converts did not all immediately return to share their faith in the Diaspora (cf. 11:19).[448]

The evidence is somewhat ambiguous but probably favors residents over visitors. Many scholars conclude that these Diaspora Jews had taken up permanent residence in Jerusalem, because of a term that normally suggests this in 2:5 (κατοικοῦντες).[449] Luke does, indeed, usually employ the term in this manner.[450] Peter addresses the crowd as Judean men and residents of Jerusalem (2:14), but since "residents" here presumably means what it meant in 2:5, it does not settle whether he addresses short- or long-term residents. The term appears twenty-one times in Luke-Acts, and in almost every case, it could mean a long-term resident, quite often for resident *alien* communities, though in many of these cases the long-term element may be incidental to the term's meaning.[451] Yet against reading the term as necessarily requiring long-term residents, Luke uses the same term for "residents" of Mesopotamia present for the festival in 2:9.[452]

Archaeological evidence confirms that a large population of Diaspora immigrants settled in Jerusalem (see comment on Acts 6:1), though this information does not settle the case of the individuals mentioned here.[453] In support of their being long-term residents, only the Romans are designated as "visiting" (2:10),[454] though these could be set apart because of the narrative's geographic goal (28:14–31). By contrast, some scholars argue that the Romans may be set apart not because of their geography but because of their citizenship, distinguishing them from provincials[455] (a view that might

---

(Kraft), though it could depend on Acts (but cf. also Tob 12:22); there it involves inspired worship; cf. also Ael. Arist. *Or.* 40.12 and 37.27 (of Greek deities; van der Horst, "Parallels to Acts," 54).

446. See deSilva, *Honor,* 142.

447. With Hengel and Schwemer, *Between Damascus and Antioch,* 20.

448. Cf. Dupont, *Salvation,* 55.

449. E.g., Knowling, "Acts," 73; Dupont, *Salvation,* 55; Johnson, *Acts,* 43 (though contrast his apparently opposite position on 381); Witherington, *Acts,* 135; Dunn, *Acts,* 26; Klauck, *Magic,* 9; Judge, *First Christians,* 444.

450. See Luke 11:26 (taking up residence); Acts 1:20; 7:2, 4, 48; 17:24, 26; for those "living in Jerusalem" (at the time of the event depicted but presumably normally long-term), see Luke 13:4; Acts 1:19; 4:16; 13:27; in Judea, Acts 11:29; in Damascus, 9:22; 22:12; in Lydda, 9:35; in Asia, 19:10; in Ephesus, 19:17. Still, 7:2, 4, may suggest temporary (though lengthy) residence as aliens.

451. Luke's usage could be distinctive; κατοικέω appears four times in Matthew, never in Mark, three times in Pauline literature (Eph 3:17; Col 1:19; 2:9), ten times in Revelation (the largest number outside Luke-Acts in the NT), and, as noted above, twenty-one times in Luke-Acts.

452. Reinhardt, "Population Size," 259; cf. Noack, "Pentecost in Jubilees," 91. They may be long-term residents of Mesopotamia, but the point is that they cannot be both long-term residents of Mesopotamia in 2:9 and long-term residents of Judea in 2:5.

453. Witherington, *Acts,* 135; cf. Safrai, "Relations," 194–95.

454. Johnson, *Acts,* 44; Dunn, *Acts,* 26.

455. Hanson, Acts, 64; Judge, *Pattern,* 55.

require some adjustment to the various attempts to make sense of Luke's geographic arrangement, below; he might count Rome as their "place" but does not seem to do so for the Roman citizen Paul, 21:39; 22:3). That Peter addresses Jerusalemites and Judeans (2:14; though "Israelites" in 2:22 may expand this address) and holds his audience partially culpable for Jesus's crucifixion (2:23; cf. 3:17; in contrast to Diaspora Jews in the audience of 13:27–28) seems to militate against visitors being the *primary* audience.

Perhaps the ambiguity of the evidence (though generally favoring "residents," especially on the basis of Luke's normal usage) suggests that some Diaspora Jews present fell into either category, and Luke simply does not sacrifice the space to explain this detail; he could use either group to foreshadow the later Diaspora mission. Certainly, there must have been many visitors for the festival (see more extended comment on this point at Acts 2:1), and perhaps Luke would have included temporary residents who stayed for the seven weeks after Passover among his κατοικοῦντες.

Whether or not the Diaspora Jews whom Luke emphasizes here were visiting Jerusalem or had settled there, their sojourn in the Holy City would have signaled their piety (see comment on Acts 6:1), which Luke makes explicit (εὐλαβεῖς). In the NT corpus, only Luke uses the term εὐλαβής, and three of his four uses modify ἀνήρ or ἄνδρες (2:5; 8:2; 22:12; the exception uses ἄνθρωπος, for Simeon, Luke 2:25).[456] Although he employs a term with a related semantic range for God-fearers (εὐσεβής, Acts 10:2, 7; cf. σέβομαι in 13:43, 50; 16:14; 17:4, 17; 18:7), Luke never applies this particular term of piety to people here; here their Jewishness is explicit.[457]

Their symbolic value for Luke's narrative is clearer: as Diaspora Jews with linguistic and cultural contexts abroad, they prefigure the Gentile mission for which the Spirit is empowering the disciples (Acts 1:8; 2:39).[458] Some national histories or foundation narratives report strife consequent on intermarriages or other ethnic mixing[459] but also portray founders ready to welcome all foreigners.[460] Luke, with his Diaspora and mostly Gentile audience, has even greater reason to portray the Jewish Jesus movement's welcome to foreigners. (Some scholars compare the Diaspora Jews here with the "mixed multitude" of Exod 12:38,[461] but aside from the ethnic difference, the Diaspora Jews here play a more unambiguously positive role in Luke's narrative.)[462]

Many readers today view the globalization of Christianity, the church's global multiculturalism, or the Christian mission's sensitivity to indigenous languages and cultures as a theological extension of Pentecost.[463] It seems likely that Luke would

456. The cognates εὐλάβεια and εὐλαβέομαι appear only in Heb 5:7; 11:7; 12:28 (like Luke, this author is skilled in good Hellenistic Greek).

457. With Bruce, *Acts¹*, 83; idem, *Commentary*, 60–61.

458. E.g., Shenk and Stutzman, *Communities*, 19. This is true even though the speech proper is addressed to Israel (Acts 2:14, 36; cf. Tannehill, *Acts*, 27).

459. Balch, "ΜΕΤΑΒΟΛΗ ΠΟΛΙΤΕΙΩΝ," 167 (citing Dion. Hal. *Ant. rom.* 1.60.1–3; 1.64.2; 1.89.3–4; 2.30.2; and noting the frequent rejection of intermarriage, 168–70). On intermarriage, see comments on Acts 16:1–3.

460. Ibid., 173.

461. Le Cornu, *Acts*, 66.

462. The mixed multitude in Exodus probably should be understood as turning out badly (Num 11:4); cf. Keil and Delitzsch, *Exodus*, 30. On the mixed multitude, see also comment on Acts 7:41.

463. E.g., Bediako, "African Culture," 120 (for translation in the vernacular); González, *Months*, 18; Solivan, *Spirit*, 112–18; Míguez-Bonino, "Acts 2," 163–64; cf. Keener, "Acts 2:1–21," 526–27; idem, "Diversity"; Marguerat, *Actes*, 81; at length, cf. Harms, *Paradigms*. This application was also important in the early twentieth-century Azusa Street Revival's application of Acts (e.g., Robeck, *Mission*, 88, 137–38; testimony in Horton, *Corinthians*, 66n29; cf. Synan, *Movement*, 80, 109–11, 165–69, 172, 178–79, 182–83, 221; idem, "Seymour," 778–81; idem, "Legacies," 148–49; Lovett, "Holiness-Pentecostalism," 83; Daniels, "Differences"; Jacobsen, *Thinking in Spirit*, 63, 260–62). Ethnic and class reconciliation is a natural application of the passage (e.g., Yong, *Spirit Poured*, 94, 169–73; Park, *Healing*, 130–32; Keener, "Acts 2:1–21," 526–27; Williams, "Acts," 219–20

have viewed such approaches, had he known of them, as a legitimate application of his perspective.

c. Lists of Nations, Languages (2:9–11)

Although in most instances Acts appears to employ "all" with "nations" or "Gentiles" literally (Acts 10:35; 14:16; 15:17; 17:26; cf. Rom 1:5; 15:11; Gal 3:8), in Acts 2:5 "every nation" is presumably hyperbolic.[464] Nevertheless, it may also be missiologically and eschatologically representative (Luke 24:47; Rom 16:26; Col 1:23).[465] Thus the list in Acts 2:9–11 omits some obvious locations, such as Greece and Macedonia (though Jews lived there; cf. 17:1–5, 10–13, 17; 18:4–17). Ancient writers could employ such lists[466] for rhetorical effect; thus, for example, Pseudo-Callisthenes provides a list of ten hostile nations arrayed against Alexander, plus "all the other great nations of the East."[467]

People naturally considered "Galilean" the antithesis of "cosmopolitan" (cf. Luke 22:59); this prejudice made these Galileans' apparent universal linguistic proficiency appear all the more astonishing (Acts 2:8).[468] Some Jewish texts also specify that Galileans failed to distinguish their gutturals properly.[469]

I. ARRANGEMENT

The nations begin in the east; then the list mentions the Holy Land, then turns north, south, west (Rome), and (for the final two, which break the literary pattern as well) circles back to summarize some others. The fifteen nations apparently circle around Jerusalem; Luke moves counterclockwise in the first half of his list, then shifts.[470] According to one more complex suggested pattern, we may count the third group, including Egypt and Libya as well as Rome, as west, with a return toward Judea by way of the sea (hence including Crete) and concluding with Arabia.[471] The geography keeps circling back to Jerusalem, as the theological "center" of the earth (see comment on Acts 1:8, proleptically fulfilled here). The nations to the north are in Asia Minor,

---

[noting also failures]) and was so applied at Azusa Street (Yong, *Spirit Poured*, 183; cf. Bartleman, *Azusa Street*, 54: "The 'color line' was washed away in the blood"); though the racial status quo quickly reasserted itself (see Alexander, *Fire*, 110–58, esp. 137–40), and violent response from Jim Crow segregationists motivated some changes (cf. Bosworth, "Beating"). The emphasis was likewise natural in early Indian Pentecostalism, although again the ethnic or caste status quo often quickly reasserted itself (Yong, *Spirit Poured*, 56–57); for ethnic reconciliation in a different renewal setting in India in 1921, see Hickson, *Heal*, 62, 64, 66. In South Africa, see LaPoorta, "Unity," cited in Tarr, *Foolishness*, 379–80.

464. On hyperbole, see, e.g., *Rhet. Alex.* 11, 1430b.16–19; *Rhet. Her.* 4.33.44 (but cf. 2.20.32); Cic. *Or. Brut.* 40.139; Anderson, *Glossary*, 122–24; Rowe, "Style," 128; Porter, "Paul and Letters," 579; Watson, "Speech," 203; e.g., Luke 18:25; Matt 23:24; Fronto *Ad M. Caes.* 2.3.3.

465. "Under heaven" (ὑπὸ τὸν οὐρανόν) reiterates the emphasis on all nations (the phrase appears in Acts 4:12; Col 1:23; in a different sense, in Luke 17:24) and would be familiar to Luke's ideal audience (see Exod 17:14; Deut 4:17; 25:19; 29:19; Eccl 1:13; 3:1; Dan 7:27; 9:12; 2 Macc 2:18; worded slightly differently, Gen 6:17; 2 Kgs 14:27); see esp. Deut 2:25; 4:19; Dan 7:27.

466. On lists in general, see Anderson, *Glossary*, 111–12 (s.v. συναθροισμός); also comment on Acts 1:13. Although Luke does not use copulatives for the entire list, he uses many (cf. Anderson, *Glossary*, 103, s.v. πολυσύνδετον); he probably omits a few simply for stylistic variation (cf. Acts 1:13; 15:20).

467. Ps.-Callisth. *Alex.* 1.2 (Dowden, 655). This novelist, writing about events half a millennium earlier, adapts much more freely than I suggest of Luke; he in fact omits the nation that Alexander did face historically on the occasion.

468. Also Dunn, *Acts*, 27; cf. Bruce, *Acts¹*, 84. Meyers and Strange, *Archaeology*, 168, suggest also urban snobbery toward rural Galileans; see discussion of urban-rural social boundaries in our introduction, ch. 17, sect. 2, and brief discussion of Galilee at Acts 9:31.

469. Dibelius, *Jesus*, 40; cf. Talbert, *Acts*, 25–26 (citing *b. ʿErub.* 53ab; *Meg.* 24b).

470. See Dunn, *Acts*, 26; cf. Marguerat, *Actes*, 78–79.

471. Bauckham, "James," 419–20. Gaventa, *Acts*, 75, largely follows Bauckham, "James," 417–27.

and some appear in Paul's ministry (though Luke skips Greece). Like *1 En.* 26–36 (and presumably any derivative early Jewish sources), Luke may list nations in four groups starting in the east and moving counterclockwise.[472] If Luke's arrangement is not exact at all points, we should recall that he likely had no maps to consult (though some maps did exist; see introduction, ch. 17, sect. 1.a).

Other texts use the four points of the compass to relate the Diaspora to Jerusalem (Isa 11:12; 43:5–6; 49:12; Zech 2:6).[473] This arrangement could suggest a Judean source,[474] but it could as easily suggest dependence on biblical geography that articulated a Judean perspective.

II. Specific Pre-Lukan Sources?

Lists of nations appear widely, although not all of them purport to be or represent universal geography. Just as biblical prophets uttered oracles against nations (e.g., Amos 1:3–2:6; Jer 46:1–51:64), so also did some postbiblical oracles; some of these included summaries of nations to be destroyed (e.g., 1QM II, 10–16; *Sib. Or.* 3.515–19). But universal lists are less frequent.

Dibelius thinks that the catalogue of nations, as well as the sermon, was likely composed by the author.[475] Others consider it difficult for this view to explain why Luke lists precisely the nations he does and in this sequence, and thus suggest that Luke depends on a prior source.[476] W. Knox suggests that Luke's source contained twelve nations, one for each apostle; Luke then added Rome because of his focus, and either Luke or a "not very intelligent copyist" added Cretans and Arabians.[477] Others also argue for an original list of twelve, which they identify with the twelve signs of the zodiac (a view no longer considered likely; see discussion below), arguing for a pre-Lukan list of twelve nations in Acts 2:9–11 (instead of the current fifteen).[478]

Although Luke has arranged the first twelve differently from the few that follow, this *might* represent Luke's choice of arrangement as easily as his redaction of a source. It was not uncommon to vary a structure at its end; cf. how Matt 5:11–12 departs from the structure of 5:3–10; or the sets of variations in 2 Cor 6:4–10;[479] or the opposed paradigms of Ps 1:1–3 and 4–5, followed by the summary of 1:6. Metzger points to the catalogue's "rhythm and structure, disclosed partly by the author's use of connectives (καί and τε καί)," and observes that even the apparently dissonant "coda" at the end, "Cretans and Arabs," "has many parallels in other examples of what can be called the catalogue-form."[480] Luke may have varied the structure in Acts 2:10–11 to draw attention to Rome (cf. 28:14–31) and proselytes (cf. 6:5; 13:43).[481] If Luke deliberately marks off the first group of twelve, he may call attention to the multiplied ministry of the apostles the way he possibly did by mentioning the 120 in 1:15.

---

472. Bauckham, "James," 419.

473. Ibid. (citing also 4Q448 II, 3–6; *Pss. Sol.* 11:2–3); Bauckham suggests (423) that as Luke 2:1 focuses on Rome, Acts 2:9–11 makes Jerusalem the center. For Jerusalem as the center, see comment on Acts 1:8; Keener, *John,* 729–30.

474. Knox, *Jerusalem,* 32.

475. Dibelius, *Studies in Acts,* 1:15.

476. E.g., Fitzmyer, *Acts,* 240.

477. Knox, *Jerusalem,* 32.

478. E.g., Conzelmann, *Acts,* 15.

479. Fitting rhetorical convention; see Keener, *Corinthians,* 188; Cic. *Sest.* 1.1; Val. Max. 7.1.1; Max. Tyre 3.2.

480. Metzger, "Astrological Geography," 132.

481. Luke may also have wished to draw attention to Crete (Acts 27:7, 12–13, 21) and perhaps even Arabs (cf. 9:20–22, though Luke omits Paul's Arabian excursions there, known to us from Gal 1:17); but then why not include "Asia" and "Phrygia" here (2:9–10)?

III. ZODIACAL OR MORE GENERAL LISTS OF NATIONS?

For a period of time many scholars believed that Luke's list adapted an astrological list of nations under the twelve signs of the zodiac. The list compared with Luke's list was from Paul of Alexandria, toward the end of the fourth century, but was based on earlier sources.[482] (Critics condemned zodiacal geography as inaccurate, but Ptolemy made it difficult to falsify by claiming that groups were dispersed among various zodiacal regions.)[483]

Excursus: Astrology[484]

Before dismissing the zodiacal interpretation (although I will ultimately do so for other reasons), it is important to recognize that astrology was widely accepted in Greco-Roman antiquity. Many people in this era regarded astrology as a plausible science.[485] Originating in the East, astrology spread in the Hellenistic era;[486] it met some initial resistance in Rome,[487] but it eventually became pervasive.[488] Despite some intellectual detractors[489] and political concerns,[490] astrology was, by this period, widely known and used.[491] People used it, for example, to predict the weather.[492] On a cosmic level, however, it was bound up with the concept of fate.[493] Because the place of the stars at one's birth could determine one's destiny,[494] horoscopes became common,[495] reflecting earlier Eastern usage.[496]

482. E.g., Conzelmann, *Acts*, 15; Hill, *Prophecy*, 95; Grant, "Christian and Roman History," 15.
483. See Hübner, "Ptolemaic View."
484. This excursus serves not only the present passage but other comments on astrology in the work, e.g., at Acts 13:6–7. On the zodiac historically, see Hübner, "Zodiac" (esp. 939–42).
485. Koester, *Introduction*, 1:377–78.
486. See, e.g., Diod. Sic. 2.29.1–2.31.9 (in Grant, *Religions*, 60); Avi-Yonah, *Hellenism*, 39; Rochberg-Halton, "New Evidence"; idem, "Elements"; for pre-Christian works on cometary theory, see Keyser, "Cometary Theory." Astrology did exist earlier among Greeks in more general fashion (Hom. *Il.* 22.26–31), but organized Babylonian interest in stars may predate even this (see, e.g., "Temple Program," *ANET* 333).
487. E.g., Val. Max. 1.3.3. But cf. even Cic. *Cat.* 3.8.18; Varro *L.L.* 7.2.14; Hor. *Odes* 2.17.17–25; Ovid *Fasti* 2.79; 3.711–12; 5.417–19; 6.788.
488. Its dominance in later centuries naturally affected Gnosticism (e.g., Burkitt, *Church and Gnosis*, 30–33) and eventually Mandaism (Drower, *Mandaeans*, 73–99) as well.
489. E.g., Sext. Emp. *Math.* 5 (because of Skepticism); Pliny E. *N.H.* 2.5.22; 2.6.28–30 (though he allows that stars can injure people, 2.41.108); Tac. *Hist.* 1.22; Aul Gel. 14.1; Lucian *Astr.* (if genuinely from Lucian); cf. at least selective disapproval in Xen. *Mem.* 1.1.11–14; Petron. *Sat.* 76; Pliny *Ep.* 2.6.28–30; 2.20.3, 5; Soranus *Gynec.* 1.10.41; naturalistic explanations in Sen. Y. *Nat. Q.* 1.1.5. Epicurus rejected the stars' power (Long, *Philosophy*, 41–42); Stoic views about cosmic sympathy (Murray, *Stages*, 178) and order in the universe (cf. Sen. Y. *Dial.* 1.1.2), however, disposed Stoics more favorably toward astrology than some; on Stoic interest, see Mastrocinque, "Choices," 381.
490. E.g., Tac. *Ann.* 2.32; 3.22; 4.58; 12.52; 16.14–15, 30–31; Suet. *Tib.* 36; *Nero* 36; cf. MacMullen, *Enemies*, 128–62.
491. E.g., Mart. *Epigr.* 9.82.1; Juv. *Sat.* 6.579; see further Klauck, *Context*, 231–49. E.g., comets predicted the future (Ptolemy *Tetrab.* 2.9.90–91).
492. E.g., Aratus *Phaen.* passim, esp. 1140–41, 1153–54.
493. E.g., Sen. Y. *Ep. Lucil.* 88.14–15; Suet. *Tib.* 69; Vett. Val. 5.9.2 (in Grant, *Religions*, 60–62); *Test. Sol.* 8:3; cf. Nilsson, *Piety*, 110–15; Murray, *Stages*, 124–27; Koester, *Introduction*, 1:156–59, esp. 159. Those supporting free will in late antiquity had to argue against causative astrology (e.g., Plot. *Enn.* 2.3; 3.1; though he allows for predictive astrology, 3.3.6).
494. E.g., Ptolemy *Tetrab.* 3.1.106; Ps.-Callisth. *Alex* 1.12.
495. E.g., P.Oslo 6; P.Oxy. 1476; *PGM* 4.651; 62.52–75; *PDM* Sup. 183–84; another in Sherk, *Empire*, §159, p. 202; cf. Lewis, "Horoscope."
496. For more than thirty Babylonian horoscopes from the first three centuries B.C.E., see Rochberg-Halton, "Horoscopes."

Astrology often overlapped with astronomical uses[497] (such as navigation[498] or attempted agricultural applications[499]) and eventually appeared among academic disciplines.[500]

A wide range of Jewish sources know and approve of astrology in some form.[501] Astrology became widespread in Hellenistic Judaism;[502] its discovery was sometimes attributed to Enoch.[503] Josephus accepts the idea that astrology was effective for the emperor Tiberius (*Ant.* 18.216–17).[504] Philo allowed that stars could predict the future, since God ordained them as signs (*Creation* 58–59).[505] More ambiguously, he could allow celestial bodies as proximate causes (*Creation* 58, 113) but ultimately only under God's sovereign will (*Creation* 46). They were not divine (Philo *Spec. Laws* 1.13), and although Philo links sacred objects with heavenly bodies (e.g., *Heir* 221), in some places he sounds opposed to astrology (*Rewards* 58).[506] It was, for him, useful only as a form of meteorology, offering predictions for navigation and agriculture.[507] Some other people apparently took astrology further, as a method of achieving power and gratification.[508]

Palestinian Judaism also imbibed astrological influence.[509] Astrological interest, including horoscopes,[510] appears in the Qumran literature, and such interest grew in later sources;[511] astrology was supposed to predict the future accurately.[512] Some later rabbis seem to have used astrological information[513] and also used imagery

---

497. See, e.g., Pliny E. *N.H.* 2.112.247; Krafft et al., "Astronomy." Astrologers' astronomy was not always accurate; e.g., Mars is red because its proximity to the sun makes it hot (Ptolemy *Tetrab.* 1.4.18). Some viewed the earth as cylindrical (Plut. frg. 179 [Euseb. *P.E.* 1.7.16]) or spherical (Diog. Laert. 7.1.144; 9.9.57), but spheres were considered perfect shapes.

498. E.g., Polyb. 9.15.7; see further comment on Acts 27:20.

499. E.g., Virg. *Ecl.* 3.41–42; *Georg.* 1.204–58; Pliny E. *N.H.* 18.54.200; 18.57.207–18.58.219; *Tr. Shem* passim; disapproved in *Sipra Qed. pq.* 6.203.2.1; *Sipre Deut.* 171.4.1. Not only storms, etc. (Pliny E. *N.H.* 18.69.278–79), but particular celestial bodies can damage crops (18.69.280–83; cf. 2.40.107); Pliny the Elder believed that stars could cause paralysis (2.41.108), and some rabbis believed that constellations could ripen fruits (*Gen. Rab.* 10:6).

500. E.g., Men. Rhet. 1.3, 360.18–19. Ptolemy treats it as self-evidently a science (*Tetrab.* 1.1.1).

501. See one survey in Charlesworth, "Astrology." For other kinds of signs in the heavens, see, e.g., *1 En.* 80:2–5; further comment on Acts 2:20; Keener, *Matthew*, 100–102, 568.

502. E.g., Ps.-Eup. in Euseb. *P.E.* 9.17.9; Philo *Creation* 112–13; Jos. *Ant.* 1.69; Ness, "Astrology." The naming of constellations and other celestial bodies or patterns (Job 38:32; *Sib. Or.* 5.207–9, 517–27; *CIJ* 2:90–91, §849), however, need not imply the acceptance of astrology (as is clear in *Sib. Or.* 13.69–71; cf. 3.221–22, 227–28, 713).

503. Ps.-Eup. in Euseb. *P.E.* 9.17.8–9. Also in Palestinian Judaism (*Jub.* 4:17; Milik, "Écrits préesséniens," 93–94).

504. For Tiberius's dependence on an astrologer, see Tac. *Ann.* 6.21.

505. Like Stoics, Philo also allowed sympathy in nature (*Creation* 117).

506. Abram did not know God as an astrologer (Philo *Abr.* 77).

507. Knox, *Gentiles*, 64. Like Josephus (*Ant.* 1.156), he recognized that God controlled the irregular movements in the heavens.

508. See Carroll, "Analysis," with a preliminary dating before 200 C.E.

509. See, e.g., Greenfield and Sokoloff, "Omen Texts." See comments on the zodiac in Palestinian Judaism at Acts 1:26. Later Babylonian Amoraim even suggested that all substances were linked to constellations (*Gen. Rab.* 10:6).

510. See, e.g., VanderKam, "Wisdom." Some have connected astrological material at Qumran with Enochic astronomy (esp. *1 En.* 72–82; cf. Böttrich, "Astrologie"; cf. *2 En.* 11–16; *3 En.* 17). For Qumran astrology, cf., e.g., 4Q186; 4Q416 frg. 1; 4Q561; Wise, "4Q318"; Greenfield and Sokoloff, "Astrological Text"; Schmidt, "Astrologie"; Lehmann, "Light on Astrology" (though he views rabbinic opposition to astrology as normative, against 4Q186); Toepel, "Planetary Demons"; Allegro, "Cryptic Document."

511. Astrology influenced rabbinic thought especially in the third through fifth centuries, particularly in Babylonia (Wächter, "Astrologie"). Still later, see, e.g., Goldstein and Pingree, "Almanacs."

512. E.g., *Gen. Rab.* 63:2; *Exod. Rab.* 20:8; *Lev. Rab.* 36:4 (on horoscopes); *Deut. Rab.* 4:5; *Eccl. Rab.* 1:14, §1; *Pesiq. Rab.* 43:1.

513. E.g., *y. Ber.* 9:2, 2; *b. Šabb.* 156a (R. Hanina, at length); cf. Stieglitz, "Names." Mars was said to rule at particular times of the week (*b. Šabb.* 129b).

from the zodiac and seven planets.[514] Some thought that astrology could often accurately predict the future, though it was inadequate and God shows himself truly in control.[515] Sometimes pagan astrology even revealed Israel's sufferings (*Num. Rab.* 20:7). But later rabbis generally agreed that astrology could not control Israel, which was under God's dominion;[516] God freed Abraham (and hence his descendants) from the power of fate and the stars.[517] Both earlier[518] and later[519] sources often condemned using astrology; certainly, the form of astrology that worshiped stars was condemned.[520]

The view that zodiacal geography ultimately stands behind Luke's list is not meant to claim that Luke intended to evoke the zodiac (and certainly not astrological notions of fate or prediction) but that he or his source borrowed the list from one that depended on zodiacal regions of the cosmos to arrange the nations of humanity. Paul of Alexandria's list and its alleged parallels (in different sequence) in Acts are as follows:[521]

Sign	Zodiacal list of Paul of Alexandria	Acts 2:9–11
Ram (Aries)	Persia	Parthians, Medes, Elamites
Bull (Taurus)	Babylonia	Mesopotamia
Twins (Gemini)	Cappadocia	Cappadocia
Crab (Cancer)	Armenia	Pontus (contiguous region in Acts 18:2; 1 Pet 1:1)
Lion (Leo)	Asia	Asia
Virgin (Virgo)	Hellas, Ionia	Phrygia and Pamphylia*
Scales (Libra)	Libya, Cyrene	Parts of Libya near Cyrene
Scorpion (Scorpio)	Italy	Romans
Archer (Sagittarius)	Cilicia, Crete	Cretans
Ibex (Capricorn)	Syria	Judea
Water carrier (Aquarius)	Egypt	Egypt
Fish (Pisces)	Red Sea, India	Arabians

*In this view, Luke avoids mentioning Greeks yet; Phrygia, however, is on the *opposite* side of Asia from Hellas.

514. E.g., *Pesiq. Rab Kah.* 23:8; *Pesiq. Rab.* 20:1–2; 27/28:1; 40:7; perhaps *b. Šabb.* 146a. The constellations were assumed to be a matter of simple astronomy (e.g., *b. Ber.* 58b–59a; *Gen. Rab.* 100:9), following the science of the era. For the lampstand (as earlier in Philo and Josephus, e.g., Jos. *Ant.* 3.182, 186), see, e.g., *Tg. Ps.-J.* on Exod 39:37; 40:4. But for problems in Jewish calendation and astronomy, see Amadon, "Calendation."

515. E.g., *Mek. Pisha* 2.44ff. (Lauterbach, 1:19); *Pesiq. Rab Kah.* 4:3; *b. Ber.* 63b; *y. ʿAbod. Zar.* 2:2, §5; *Roš Haš.* 3:8, §§1–2; *Eccl. Rab.* 7:23, §1; *Pesiq. Rab.* 14:8; see also Cohen, "Structural Analysis." The planets were inactive during the flood (*Gen. Rab.* 25:2); the stars had to prostrate themselves before God before shining (*Exod. Rab.* 45:2); God created the signs of the zodiac (*Pesiq. Rab.* 53:2); and God controlled stars' movements (*Lev. Rab.* 23:8).

516. E.g., *Pesiq. Rab.* 20:2 (mostly); Montefiore and Loewe, *Anthology*, 113–14, §§297–98.

517. E.g., *b. Ned.* 32a; *Šabb.* 156ab; *Gen. Rab.* 44:10, 12; *Exod. Rab.* 38:6 (recalling an exaltation that appears earlier but without astrological connections, as in *Apoc. Ab.* 20:2–5 or *Test. Ab.* 9:8–15:2 A); on Abraham and astrology, see also *b. Yoma* 28b; *Gen. Rab.* 43:3. In earlier sources, too, Abram was once an astrologer and rejected astrology (*Jub.* 12:17; 13:16–18; Ps.-Eup. in Euseb. *P.E.* 9.17.8; Philo *Abr.* 77; *t. Qidd.* 5:17; see Mayer, "Abrahambildes," 123–25), but later pagan texts, undoubtedly influenced by assimilated Jews, appreciate Abraham's astrology (Siker, "Abraham"; Gager, *Anti-Semitism*, 110; Stern, *Authors*, 2:173).

518. See, e.g., *1 En.* 6:7, Gr^Sync-a; 8:3 (see comments in Nickelsburg, "Apocalyptic," 405); *Jub.* 8:3 (cf. Jacobus, "Curse"); *L.A.B.* 4:16. See perhaps also *Sent. Syr. Men.* 292–93.

519. E.g., *y. Šabb.* 6:9, §3; *Gen. Rab.* 44:12; 87:4; *Deut. Rab.* 8:6. Among Christians, e.g., *Did.* 3.4 (associating it with idolatry); Aug. *Tract. Jn.* 6.17.2; Hippol. *Ref.* Bk. 2.

520. E.g., *Gen. Rab.* 6:1; *Pesiq. Rab.* 15:1. Later some accepted synagogue decorations (as in later synagogue zodiacs), provided no worship was involved (*Tg. Ps.-J.* on Lev 26:1).

521. Zehnle, *Pentecost Discourse*, 121; similarly but slightly differently (Rome as a redaction), see Conzelmann, *Acts*, 15.

Supporters of this view suggest that the divergences from Acts may stem from Luke's use of a variant source or that he chose names most useful for his story line in Acts.[522]

The evidence for this view, however, is questionable. Contrary to the suggestions of some,[523] the phrase "under heaven" offers no support to the astrological interpretation; the idiom was frequent and unrelated to astrology,[524] and its rare occurrences elsewhere in Luke and the NT corpus simply indicate the gospel's universality (Acts 4:12; Col 1:23). Since a 1970 article by Bruce Metzger, few scholars have followed the astrological geography view. The parallels are not close enough (only five nations are the same in both lists);[525] the parallels that are present also exist in other lists of nations not related to the zodiac. Luke's and Paul of Alexandria's lists may simply reflect more widespread usage. Barrett opines that the zodiacal view may now be safely dismissed as "impossible."[526]

The zodiacal lists simply resemble the more general form of lists of nations representing regions that together composed all nations.[527] Romans, for example, often used such lists to celebrate the emperor's reign or military prowess; some scholars have plausibly suggested that Acts 2:9–11 serves an analogous propagandistic function, but in this case to critique and offer an alternative to imperial ideology.[528] Ad hoc lists could also include mention of the locations from which visitors to a widely attended festival came (Dio Chrys. Or. 9.5, with six locations named). Jewish people as well as Gentiles used such lists, developing their original model in Gen 10.[529]

Barrett regards the closest parallels as "accounts of the distribution of Jews throughout the world" (not coincidentally, what Luke claims to be writing about here). These parallels do not depend on a common source but reflect a similar form; Luke may have used Diaspora Jewish lists as a model.[530] By all ancient accounts, the Jewish people were widely dispersed.[531] Luke here intends all the lands of the Diaspora.

iv. Table of Nations in Genesis 10

Luke's elaboration of regions here underlines a pervasive emphasis in his work. By enumerating the lands from which Diaspora Jews came, Luke prepares his audience for the dispersal of the word of God to those places. In so doing, he alludes to all humanity in a manner similar to the way he did in his Gospel. Immediately after Jesus received the Spirit (Luke 3:21–22), Luke listed generations back to Adam, the

---

522. Zehnle, Pentecost Discourse, 122.

523. E.g., Grant, "Christian and Roman History," 15.

524. E.g., LXX Gen 6:17; Exod 17:14; Prov 8:28; Eccl 3:1; Job 1:7; 2:2; Dan 7:27; 9:12; van der Horst, "Parallels to Acts," 52, cites also Plato Tim. 23C; Ep. 7.326C. Most relevant are the references to "all peoples under heaven" in Deut 2:25; 4:19 (Marshall, "Acts," 532).

525. Metzger, "Astrological Geography."

526. Barrett, Acts, 121; cf. also Fitzmyer, Acts, 242.

527. Cf., e.g., Macrob. Sat. 5.15.3 (van der Horst, "Macrobius," 225); van der Horst, "Parallels to Acts," 53–54, also cites Quint. Curt. 6.3.3; Ps.-Callisth. Alex. 2.11.2; Xen. Cyr. 6.2.10; Dio Chrys. Or. 9.5, 12; 33.40; Arrian, FGH 156; Darius's Behistan inscription 1.6; Xerxes's Daiva inscription 19–28 (cf. also Fitzmyer, Acts, 240).

528. Gilbert, "List"; idem, "Propaganda," 247–53; Reid, "Resistance Discourse," 44. This is a much closer literary analogy than the Achaemenid parallels suggested by Taylor, "List," though these underline the antiquity of the form. One might compare conquest lists in Josh 12 and ancient Egyptian and other ancient Near Eastern sources (see examples in Younger, Conquest Accounts; Kitchen, Reliability, 168–74, esp. 174), but these samples were less "universal" than here.

529. Johnson, Acts, 43, cites Sib. Or. 3.160–72, 205–9; L.A.B. 4:3–17; Philo Embassy 281–82; Flacc. 45–46, though noting that no theory of selection has been proven.

530. Barrett, Acts, 122 (citing Jos. Ag. Ap. 2.282; War 2.398; 7.43; Ant. 14.114–18; Philo Flacc. 45–46; Embassy 281–82); also Dunn, Acts, 26.

531. See esp. Kraft, "Judaism on Scene," 82–83 (citing, in addition to the sources above, e.g., Sib. Or. 3.271–72; Jos. Ant. 15.39); Stern, "Diaspora," 117–22.

progenitor of humanity; here, after recounting the parallel gift of the Spirit in Acts, he lists the nations with the same universal allusion to all humanity.[532]

Luke must have known broader frontiers of the world than he lists.[533] The Roman world had trade ties with India and China in the east and Africa far to the south. Greek sages often commented on their counterparts in India, the famous gymnosophists.[534] They also spoke regularly of Scythians in the far north(east);[535] Rome controlled Gaul and fought with Germans, and Claudius had conquered Britannia.[536] Luke omits distant Ethiopia, but clearly *knows* about it, correctly reproducing even the title of the queen as it appeared in Greco-Roman sources of his day (Acts 8:27). Why does Luke limit his geographic horizons here? One reason may be that he is citing the Jewish Diaspora, but then why not include Ethiopia, where the Jewish message had obviously reached (8:27)? A more complete reason may be that he draws on a list updating names from the table of the nations in Gen 10.[537]

The first and best-known table of nations in the Bible, hence the prototype for most other Jewish lists and the most obvious single table of nations known to Luke's ideal audience, was Gen 10.[538] This list of nations is followed almost immediately by the tower of Babel narrative, in which God miraculously scatters the languages (Gen 11:7–9).[539] In the context of Luke's table of nations, God also scatters languages, but in this case for the opposite purpose, one framed by divinely sanctioned unity (Acts 1:14; 2:1, 46).[540] Luke will not list all seventy nations from Gen 10; instead he provides samples, updating the names for his list.[541] Updating the names of the nations was common even in paraphrases of Gen 10;[542] some later Targumim thus include (by coincidence of selection, but probably also analogy of method) many names that Acts includes, such as Phrygia,[543] Asia,[544] Italy,[545] the Cappadocians,[546] the

---

532. Johnson, *Acts*, 47.

533. Palestinian Judaism also had access to contemporary Greek geographical views (cf. *Jub.* 8:12; 1QM X, 13).

534. See discussion at Acts 1:8 for India, China, and other "ends of the earth."

535. See comment on Acts 8:27.

536. See, e.g., Caesar's *Gallic War*; Tacitus's *Agricola* and *Germania*. Some had reportedly sailed north of Germany and Denmark (Pliny E. *N.H.* 2.67.167).

537. Also Goulder, *Type and History*, 153–54; Parsons, *Acts*, 39. But even some of these included distant lands such as India (e.g., *Tg. Ps.-J.* on Gen 10:7).

538. For the table-of-nations tradition in Second Temple Judaism, see Scott, "Horizon," 507–22; idem, "Geographical Perspectives," 412–13; in Acts, idem, "Horizon," 525–27. See further Bechard, *Walls*, 171–231 (173–209 on Jewish use; 209–31 in Acts); Scott, *Nations*.

539. Following the Babel narrative, Genesis lists the chosen line of Seth; Luke also recounts the success of the church after his Babel analogy (Acts 2:41–47), though this may be coincidental (he does not develop any parallels).

540. Ironically, Paul might challenge abuse of tongues in Corinth by the political commonplace that "common language is needed for concord" (Mitchell, *Rhetoric of Reconciliation*, 172; cf. Witherington, *Corinthians*, 275; Dio Chrys. *Or.* 39.3); Luke uses tongues to symbolize cross-cultural unity.

541. See, e.g., Goulder, *Type and History*, 153–54, 158; Moule, *Messengers*, 24. For the continuing tradition of the seventy nations, see, e.g., *Jub.* 44:34; *3 En.* 2:3; 29:1 (cf. 30:2); *Pesiq. Rab Kah.* 2:7; 28:9; *b. Šabb.* 88b; *Sukkah* 55b; *y. Meg.* 1:9, §1; *Gen. Rab.* 39:11; *Lev. Rab.* 2:4; *Tg. Ps.-J.* on Gen 11:8; *Tg. Rishon* on Esth 2:22; the incantation in Deissmann, *Light*, 262. Luke may play on twelve (Luke 9:1) and seventy (depending on the variant reading of Luke 10:1) elsewhere.

542. E.g., *Tg. Neof.* 1 on Gen 10:2–14; *Tg. Ps.-J.* on Gen 10:2–14; *Tg. 1 Chr.* 1:5–17. On updated lists (in various ways) in *Jub.* 8–9 and Jos. *Ant.* 1.120–47, see Scott, "Horizon," 521–22. For that matter, the language in the current text of Gen 10 may represent updating over earlier traditions (cf. Yamauchi, *Stones*, 43).

543. *Tg. Neof.* 1 on Gen 10:2; *Tg. Ps.-J.* on Gen 10:2.

544. *Tg. Neof.* 1 on Gen 10:3; *Tg. Ps.-J.* on Gen 10:2.

545. *Tg. Neof.* 1 on Gen 10:4.

546. *Tg. Neof.* 1 on Gen 10:14; *Tg. Ps.-J.* on Gen 10:14.

Medes,[547] Arabians,[548] as well as obvious choices such as Egypt and Libya.[549] More significantly, Acts 2:9–11 shares about half the names found in Josephus's updated table (*Ant.* 1.122–47).[550]

Luke's probable allusion to Gen 10 (whatever other samples he may have added) here underlines his very likely allusion to the tower of Babel in the context.[551]

v. A Reversal of Babel (Gen 11:1–9)

Many scholars understand Acts 2 as a reversal of the Babel story and believe that Luke patterned his narrative after it;[552] some ancient commentators made the same connection.[553] Such an approach would certainly fit Luke's theme of mission transcending cultural and linguistic barriers.[554] Others object that although the connection may be a legitimate theological inference to draw for Luke's sources or others,[555] the text gives no indication that Luke made the connection.[556] Barrett regards the Babel narrative as more important background here than the alleged connection with "giving of Torah" at Sinai[557] but thinks that Luke apparently "makes no attempt to call it to his readers' mind."[558]

Does Luke in fact make "no attempt" to allude to Babel? Or does he make subtle allusions even in the narrative's structure? If we surmise that the table of nations in Gen 10 informs Luke's list of nations (as it did most Jewish lists of nations), an allusion to Babel in Gen 11:1–9 in the same context seems likely.[559] This suggestion becomes more likely when we consider that Babel represents the only scattering of languages in the OT and hence the only *potential* background for Luke's story shared by all his ideal audience. (Certainly, the Babel story, as part of the very popular book

547. *Tg. Ps.-J.* on Gen 10:2.

548. *Tg. Ps.-J.* on Gen 10:6.

549. *Tg. Ps.-J.* on Gen 10:6–7. They also include Greece (*Tg. Neof.* 1 on Gen 10:4; *Tg. Ps.-J.* on Gen 10:4), which Luke does not.

550. Scott, "Horizon," 529.

551. With, e.g., ibid., 530. Davis, "Acts 2," finds plausible allusions to Gen 10–12 in Acts 2.

552. E.g., Moule, *Messengers*, 23; Carter and Earle, *Acts*, 33; Kirby, *Ephesians*, 117 (citing another commentator in 1904); Bruce, *Commentary*, 64; Stendahl, *Paul*, 117; Hill, *Prophecy*, 95; Shenk and Stutzman, *Communities*, 19; Dominy, "Spirit, Church, and Mission"; Smith, "Hope after Babel?"; Spencer, *Acts*, 32–33; Chéreau, "Babel à la Pentecôte"; Venter, *Reconciliation*, 155; Turner, "Experience," 32; Kim, "Mission," 40; Nasrallah, "Cities," 557; Pervo, *Acts*, 61–62; Asamoah-Gyadu, "Hearing"; Wackenheim, "Babel"; Green, "Acts," 739; cf. B. H. Carroll (1916) in Barr, Leonard, Parsons, and Weaver, *Acts*, 120.

553. Cyril Jer. *Cat. Lect.* 17.16–17 (Martin, *Acts*, 24); Arator *Acts* 1 (Martin, *Acts*, 26); Bede *Comm. Acts* 2.4 (trans. L. Martin, 29; also Martin, *Acts*, 23); see other patristic sources in Marguerat, *Actes*, 81n45. Early Pentecostals also read their experience as a reversal of Babel (Anderson, *Pentecostalism*, 44).

554. See, e.g., Keener, "Tongues," 181–82. González, *Acts*, 39, emphasizes here a "second Babel" with a new scattering, underlining appreciation for cultural diversity as opposed to a demand for uniformity (e.g., by causing everyone to understand Aramaic). Cf. more fully Wagenaar, "Kumba." Similarly, Macchia, "Babel," envisions a partial reversal but a partial analogy: "a promise/fulfilment relationship between these events, in which only the folly and threat of Babel is reversed at Pentecost but not God's providential will and purposes" (51).

555. For this connection in the church's theology (whether or not Luke noticed it), see, e.g., Cloete and Smit, "Name Called Babel." Arrington, *Acts*, 20, treats the allusion as a strong but uncertain possibility; Marshall, "Acts," 532, finds evidence for a deliberate connection weak but allows that such canonical connections may be helpful to modern readers.

556. Polhill, *Acts*, 105. Dunn's objection (*Acts*, 24; cf. also Willimon, *Acts*, 32) that "Luke evidently did not think of the tongues as a single language" presses details more than most biblical allusions require.

557. Barrett, *Acts*, 112, 116; cf. 119: "confounded" could suggest Babel, but the phrase is common even in Acts.

558. Ibid., 112.

559. Also Goulder, *Type and History*, 158; Scott, "Horizon," 530. Compare unity of mind in Acts 1:14; 2:46 with "one tongue and voice" in the LXX of Gen 11:1; "every nation under heaven" in Acts 2:5 with "all the earth" in Gen 11:1, 8; the elaboration of Mesopotamian peoples not emphasized elsewhere in Luke-Acts in Acts 2:9 with Gen 11:2, 9; perhaps the honoring of Jesus's name (Acts 2:21, 38) with those honoring their own in Gen 11:4 (a deliberate contrast with 12:2). It is also Scripture's seminal "language miracle."

of Genesis, was widely told and retold[560] and was reapplied for new settings.[561] Even the very story of the scattered languages at Sinai, to which many scholars appeal, probably alludes to Babel—rabbinic haggadah tended to borrow other stories for Moses and the law[562]—and even if it was widely known in the first century, it would not have been as widely known as the biblical story of Babel.)

When the author of the Qumran *War Scroll* refers to a "confusion of tongues" (1QM X, 14, בלת לשון), we know that he refers to Babel because this mention follows the creation of Adam and his seed and it parallels scattering. Luke's use of a table of nations and his mention of scattered languages seem similarly transparent. Whatever the date of the triennial Jewish lectionary readings,[563] at least some of them reflect earlier traditions, and so it would probably not be a coincidence if we concluded on other grounds, with some, that the cycle's first year used Gen 11 as a reading for Pentecost.[564] As a possible God-fearer or one in touch with early Jewish Christians who kept the Feast of Pentecost (cf. Acts 20:16), Luke may have been familiar with such a tradition or depended on a written or oral source that reflects such a tradition. Even if the lectionary connection is pure coincidence, however, the Babel allusion in this narrative is clear enough. At least some Jewish people could envision an eschatological reversal of Babel (cf. *Test. Jud.* 25:3).[565]

Differences are clear, of course. God scattered nations at Babel for trying to deify themselves (Gen 11:4), paralleling Adam's revolt and his expulsion from the garden (3:5, 22–23).[566] By contrast, the disciples at Pentecost were waiting in obedience to a divine command (Acts 1:4–5); instead of trying to reach heaven, they were waiting for their Lord, who *had* ascended to heaven (1:9–11), to send them the Spirit. In Gen 11:7, God descended to confound the transgressors (the wording reflects their rebellion in 11:3–4), but at Pentecost God descends, in one sense, in a different way (Acts 2:33). In Genesis, God descended and scattered tongues to prevent unity; in Acts, the Spirit descends and scatters tongues to create multicultural unity (1:14; 2:1, 42, 44–46).

Luke employs the verb συνεχύθη for the crowd's response in 2:6; although this is not Luke's sole use of συγχέω (9:22; 19:32; 21:27, 31),[567] it is likely an allusion to the Babel narrative, which employs the cognate noun σύγχυσις, "confusion," as a Greek translation for "Babel" (Gen 11:9; the noun's other three LXX uses all appear in 1 Samuel, two in the same passage).[568] The verb appears some fifteen times in the

---

560. For later Jewish comments on the Babel narrative, see, e.g., Jos. *Ant.* 1.116–18 (with the "Sibyl" quoted as describing it in 1.118); *L.A.B.* 7; *Sib. Or.* 3.98–107; 8.4–5; 11.9–13; *y. Meg.* 1:9, §1; cf. the incantation in Deissmann, *Light*, 262.

561. Inowlocki, "Rewriting," finds such a rewriting, for a Gentile audience, in Josephus (who here, as elsewhere, opposes tyranny and prefigures God's judgment on Jerusalem).

562. See, e.g., comments on Acts 7:20.

563. See, e.g., Safrai, "Synagogue," 927 (doubting any fixed sequence in the early period); Perrot, "Lecture de la Bible" (some principles of later lectionaries used even if the cycle was not yet in use); Patte, *Hermeneutic*, 37 (dating uncertain, since *Tanḥ.* 7 is a late source). Refuting lectionary theses for the Gospels, see Morris, "Lectionaries"; idem, *Lectionaries*, passim, esp. 16 (noting that they are too late for relevance to Jesus). Second-century Christians may not have been interested in Jewish lectionary readings (Morris, *Lectionaries*, 25, citing Justin *1 Apol.* 67).

564. See Charnov, "Shavuot"; cf., cautiously, Moule, *Messengers*, 23.

565. Cf. the end of Babel's curse in the day of judgment (*Jub.* 10:22), but we should probably not read much into this. Plutarch apparently borrows a hope for future world unity from Persian eschatology (Boring, Berger, and Colpe, *Commentary*, 309–10, cite Plut. *Isis* 47); cf. Rev 5:9; 7:9.

566. Some later rabbis emphasized that God invited their repentance (*Gen. Rab.* 38:9).

567. Possibly Acts 19:32 and 21:27, 31 could also evoke Babel (cf. Hamm, *Acts*, 91, contrasting ἐκκλησία in Acts 19:32, 39, 41), though that appears much less likely than here and, so far as I can discern offhand, could be defended only by way of allusion to Luke's usage here.

568. With, e.g., Hamm, *Acts*, 18–19.

LXX,[569] but of these, the earliest uses and those clustered most closely together are Gen 11:7 and 9, referring to the confusion of languages; the same verb appears, referring to Babel, in Wis 10:5.[570] Here it is the audience rather than the language that is confused, but in view of other allusions, this is likely an additional example (perhaps inverting the identity of those confused, to highlight reversal).

vi. Proleptic Universalism

Jesus promised that the Spirit would enable the disciples to take the gospel to the nations (Acts 1:8), and throughout the book the Spirit continues to thrust the witnesses across previously foreboding cultural barriers (8:29; 10:19; 11:12). Although the mission is not completed in Acts 2 (or, for that matter, at the end of Acts 28), Luke provides, at Pentecost, a narrative foretaste of the Spirit's equipping the church to reach all nations. Granted, at this stage in the narrative, Peter's audience remains a Jewish one, but throughout Acts, Diaspora Jews become the link for God-fearers and eventually Gentiles; Paul himself regularly starts with synagogue communities (13:5, 14; 14:1; 16:13; 17:1, 10, 17; 18:4; 19:8; 28:17). Thus the Twelve begin to fulfill their commission to announce the gospel to every nation, "beginning from Jerusalem" (Luke 24:27); as Jacques Dupont puts it, "The Church was born universal."[571] Scholars have long recognized the proleptic universalism here;[572] see also comment on Acts 2:17, 39.

I noted earlier some likely Sinai allusions in the text of Acts (cf. 2:2–3; some others find the allusion in 2:33, 38) and that some also cite Jewish traditions linking the Pentecost festival with law-giving and with God's voice being divided into seventy streams for all the nations. An allusion to these other Jewish traditions, which are of uncertain date, is less secure, but it is not impossible. At least as early as the second century, some Jewish teachers believed that God offered Torah to the other nations before offering it to Israel but that the other nations rejected it.[573] If this tradition was widely known in Luke's day, it is possible that his hearers would have found here a sort of universalistic reversal of Sinai, in which the message is now spread among the nations. It is not clear to what extent Gentile converts in Pauline churches would have been familiar with extrabiblical traditions (cf. 1 Tim 1:4; Titus 1:14), but at least the Jewish nucleus probably knew some (cf., e.g., 1 Cor 10:2–4; 2 Tim 3:8).

d. Particular Nations in 2:9–11

As noted above, Luke portrays the disciples as praising God in various languages, many of which are recognized by Jewish people and proselytes at the festival. Summarized below is some information on each of the groups Luke mentions, although

569. Gen 11:7, 9; 1 Sam 7:10; 1 Kgs 20:43; Amos 3:15; Mic 7:17; Joel 2:1, 10; Jonah 4:1; Nah 2:5; 1 Macc 4:27; 2 Macc 10:30; 13:23; 14:28; Wis 10:5.

570. Philo uses the verb frequently but, apart from *Special Laws*, nowhere so often as in *On the Confusion of Languages* (*Conf.* 1, 84, 152, and esp. 168, 182, 189, 191), about 15 percent of his uses; he employs the cognate noun sixteen times there (*Conf.* 1, 9, 43, 109, 158, 183, 184, 187, 188, 191, 192, 195, 198), more than 48 percent of his uses. Josephus does not employ the verb, but he twice uses the noun for Babel in *Ant.* 1.117 (about 9 percent of his uses).

571. Dupont, *Salvation*, 58.

572. E.g., Dibelius, *Studies in Acts*, 106; Foakes-Jackson, *Acts*, 11; Robinson, *Studies*, 167. Bruce, *Commentary*, 64, suggests that the narrative also reverses local expectations that Diaspora pilgrims would be the ones worshiping in various languages. Aune, *Environment*, 130, sees the list (Acts 2:7–11) as an "awkward insertion" (by Luke) into the surrounding context; be that as it may stylistically, Luke makes it theologically crucial.

573. *Mek. Bah.* 5 (in Urbach, *Sages*, 1:532); *Sipre Deut.* 343.4.1; later, *b. ʿAbod. Zar.* 2b; *Pesiq. Rab Kah.* 2:1; 12:10; *Pesiq. Rab Kah. Sup.* 1:15; *Exod. Rab.* 17:2; 30:9; *Num. Rab.* 14:10; *Pesiq. Rab.* 15:2; 21:2/3; 30:4; cf. *Pesiq. Rab Kah.* 2:7; 12:20. See discussion in Keener, *John*, 398 (on John 1:11).

his greater emphasis is on their cumulative import. Many local languages remained in use in this period,[574] although we need not suppose that representatives of every locality listed here heard languages mutually exclusive of all other localities.

I. PARTHIANS

Many Jews had never returned to Palestine after the Babylonian exile.[575] The names from Parthia through Mesopotamia (which Parthia controlled) recall not simply the farthest points east but the places of the longest exile.[576] Given "the constant communication and travel between Jerusalem and the eastern diaspora," the gospel surely reached Mesopotamia in Paul's lifetime,[577] though this is not Luke's story to tell.[578]

Parthia was on the overland silk route from China, and so many Parthian Jews took advantage of the connections with fellow Jews in the Roman Empire to work in the highly profitable silk trade. Indeed, "the earliest Christian apostles to Edessa and elsewhere in the Parthian empire were Jewish silk merchants."[579] Parthian Jews' loyalty to a temple in the Roman Empire before 70 C.E. and Judeans' ethnic ties with many Jews in Parthia adversely affected their treatment in both the Parthian and Roman empires.[580]

The Parthians were among the most feared enemies of Rome.[581] Though the river Euphrates appears throughout Roman literature as the general boundary between the Roman and the Parthian empires,[582] Rome's and Parthia's boundaries shifted periodically (especially in Armenia).[583] The threat remained a live one in the first century, though Parthians themselves usually did not want trouble with Rome, a formidable empire.[584] The discordant note that the mention of Parthian Jews might strike among some of Luke's audience might serve a rhetorical function similar to that served in the Jerusalem church by Peter's ministry to Cornelius's household (Acts 11:3–18), challenging traditional prejudices and hostilities. In any case, the "ends of the earth"

---

574. See, e.g., the documentation in Shiell, *Reading Acts*, 12–14; the brief observation of Toner, *Culture*, 1. Naturally the official languages dominate epigraphic and literary sources, but the language of markets and ethnic enclaves, reflecting mother tongues from the countrysides, may have been more diverse.

575. As commentators regularly note here (e.g., Bruce, *Acts¹*, 84).

576. Excluding a small outpost such as Elephantine in Egypt. On Babylonian and Parthian Jewry, see Stern, "Diaspora," 170–79.

577. Bauckham, "East Rather Than West?" 180 (citing also Jas 1:1).

578. Luke focuses on the Roman Empire, particularly the Aegean region and Rome, in order to be relevant to his ideal audience (see our introduction, ch. 12, sect. 3); only at points do we receive brief examples of where the larger mission must have carried others (e.g., Acts 1:8; 8:27).

579. Neusner, *Sat*, 32. Stark, *Cities*, 39, estimates Edessa's population at seventy-five thousand, a sizable community by ancient standards.

580. Neusner, *Sat*, 48. For an example of concern about Parthia, see *1 En.* 56:5 in Bruce, *Commentary*, 61n21; for massacres of Babylonian Jews, see Jos. *Ant.* 18.310 (for a Roman audience).

581. Cf., e.g., Sall. *Mith.* 1–23; Hor. *Sat.* 2.1.15; *Odes* 1.19.12; 2.13.18; Lucan *C.W.* 2.552–53; 10.48–51; Mart. *Epig.* 2.53; Suet. *Jul.* 44.3; *Aug.* 8.2; *Nero* 57.2; Tac. *Hist.* 1.2; Hdn. 6.3.2 (Persia); for Jewish fears, *1 En.* 56:5–7; *Sib. Or.* 4.139; 5.438 (they tried to seize Judea in 40 B.C.E., Tac. *Hist.* 5.9). For their strength, e.g., Fronto *Ad verum imp.* 2.3. On Parthia in general, see Pliny E. *N.H.* 6.29.112–6.31.141.

582. E.g., Cic. *Fam.* 8.10.1–2; Appian *Hist. rom.* pref. 9; 12.15.105; 12.17.116; Lucan *C.W.* 8.354–58; Sen. Y. *Nat. Q.* 1.pref. 9; Pliny E. *N.H.* 6.29.119; Tac. *Ann.* 12.11; 15.9; Suet. *Calig.* 14; Char. *Chaer.* 5.1.3; Hdn. 4.10.2; Jos. *War* 1.5, 179–80; 7.105; *Sib. Or.* 4.119–20, 124; *b. B. Meṣi'a* 28a; cf. Virg. *Georg.* 4.561; Rev 9:14; 16:12; earlier, for Persia, cf. Plut. *Alex.* 29.4; Ps.-Callisth. *Alex.* 2.9.

583. See, e.g., van Wickevoort Crommelin, "Euphrates," 188; for Armenia's frequently shifting status as a border kingdom, see, e.g., Tac. *Ann.* 13.34, 37; 15.24; Suet. *Jul.* 44.3; *Aug.* 21.3; *Tib.* 41; Ps.-Callisth. *Alex.* 2.9. Some provinces beyond the Euphrates and the Danube were annexed in the second century (Fronto *Pr. Hist.* 10).

584. E.g., Jos. *Ant.* 20.69–73; Suet. *Aug.* 21.3; Fronto *Pr. Hist.* 14; cf. Cic. *Fam.* 3.8.10; Hor. *Ep.* 2.1.256; *Odes* 1.12.53; 1.21.13–16; 3.5.3–4; 4.4.25–27; *Epodes* 7.9–10; Plut. *Pomp.* 70.3. Cf. Parthians as peaceful in Augustan art (Rose, "Parthians"); peace discussions in Jos. *Ant.* 18.101–2; as possible hosts for a fugitive Nero (Suet. *Nero* 47.2) and as allies of Vespasian (*Vesp.* 6.4).

(1:8) could not be completed in the East without their evangelization, and Christians had to be more committed to evangelism than to the stability or preeminence of whatever kingdom in which they happened to live (a theme that we would not expect Luke to develop fully, given his apologetic).

II. MEDES AND ELAMITES

"Medes" and "Elamites" here indicate other peoples of the East along with the Parthians. Because by this period the Medes existed not as an empire but merely as a collection of tribes in Parthia, Luke's source for the name is probably biblical: the Jewish Diaspora had gone there (2 Kgs 17:6; 18:11).[585] Josephus derived the "Medes" from "Madai" in Gen 10:2 and 1 Chr 1:5 (*Ant.* 1.124). They are mostly coupled with the Persians[586] and are associated with greater "Asia" in contrast to Europe.[587]

Though the Elamites were now part of Parthia, they "often asserted their autonomy,"[588] but like the Medes, they probably represent simply an example of the eastern Diaspora. Elamite was among the languages into which later rabbis ruled it lawful to translate the Esther scroll.[589]

III. RESIDENTS OF MESOPOTAMIA

The title "Mesopotamia"[590] appears twenty-one times in the LXX, nineteen times in Josephus,[591] and often elsewhere. In the LXX it was common Greek usage for Aram-naharaim or Paddan-Aram (e.g., Gen 24:10; 25:20).[592] Some scholars have estimated about a million Jews still in exile in the Mesopotamian region and Parthia.[593] The largest concentration of Parthian Jews was in Babylonia; the second largest was in northern Mesopotamia (related to the Assyrian exile).[594] For Luke, this was the very region from which Abraham hailed (Acts 7:2; cf. Jdt 5:7–8); like others, it was among the nations that would be blessed in Abraham's seed (cf. Acts 3:25).

IV. JUDEA

Some scholars have estimated about 2.5 million Jews in Palestine, including Judea, in this period.[595] Because Judea is not the Diaspora and Judeans would not be surprised to hear Galileans speaking their language, some have emended Ἰουδαίαν to Ἰουάν,[596] but this speculation is unlikely, presupposing more than a mere scribal change. Others

585. Fitzmyer, *Acts*, 240–41. But cf. the general usage in Jos. *Ant.* 20.74; *War* 7.246.

586. As in Esth 1:9; Dan 5:28; 6:8, 12, 15; Jdt 16:10; 1 Macc 1:1; 2 Esd 1:3; Jos. *Ant.* 10.113, 244, 272; 11.33, 203; 12.257; *Ag. Ap.* 1.64; *Test. Naph.* 5:8; *Sib. Or.* 4.62; 5.147, 441; 4Q550e 1 4. For the Parthians and Medes, see *1 En.* 56:5.

587. Jos. *Ag. Ap.* 1.64; cf. also *Ant.* 10.74. For ancient Media, see, e.g., Young, "Media."

588. Fitzmyer, *Acts*, 241.

589. Le Cornu, *Acts*, 67, citing *b. Meg.* 18a, bar. This language, written in cuneiform, has no close linguistic analogues today (Le Cornu, *Acts*, 67; Vallet, "Elam," 423).

590. On Mesopotamia, see Pliny E. *N.H.* 6.30.117–20. Pliny thinks that the Assyrians had few cities until Macedonian times (6.30.117). On the history of Mesopotamia, see Nissen and Oelsner, "Mesopotamia," esp. (for this, the Parthian, period, 141 B.C.E.–226 C.E.) 744–45.

591. Jos. *Ant.* 1.152, 187, 244, 276, 278, 281, 285, 341, 342; 2.173, 177, 213; 8.61; 12.149, 393; 13.184; 18.310, 339; *War* 4.531. Cf. also nine uses in Philo (*Posterity* 76; *Conf.* 65, 66; *Prelim. St.* 70; *Flight* 48–49; *Abr.* 188; *Mos.* 1.264, 278).

592. Cf., e.g., *Jub.* 9:5; 27:12; 29:12; 44:18; 1QM II, 10; 4Q496 II, 3.

593. De Ridder, *Discipling*, 10n33 (following Grayzel, *History of Jews*, 138). Babylonian Jews were probably also open to oracles, but the testimony in *Sib. Or.* 3.809–10 is Hellenistic.

594. Stern, "Diaspora," 170–71.

595. De Ridder, *Discipling*, 10n33 (following Grayzel, *History of Jews*, 138). On Jews in Syria and Phoenicia, see Stern, "Diaspora," 137–42.

596. Knox, *Jerusalem*, 32.

have suggested, more plausibly, that "Judeans" was added to the original list;[597] but one wonders why a redactor would add it as well. If "residents" in Acts 2:5 might include short-term residents between the festivals, then perhaps Luke means here Diaspora Jews who had settled in Judea (cf. 6:9); but then why distinguish them at all? Perhaps it distinguishes them from "residents" of Mesopotamia, but the matter is not easily resolved.

Hengel suggests that "Judea" stands for "greater Judea," including all of Syria, according to its eschatological extent.[598] This proposal would allow it to fit easily between Mesopotamia and Cappadocia, but Luke nowhere else uses "Judea" in this sense; there is also no reason to believe that Luke would appeal to eschatological boundaries here. Perhaps Luke simply wants to prevent his audience from forgetting that Judeans were also present, although they would be less likely to recognize the foreign languages being spoken.

v. Cappadocia, Pontus, and Asia

Cappadocia,[599] which became a province under Tiberius through his treachery,[600] apparently had a large Jewish population.[601] It was to the east of greater Phrygia,[602] north of the Taurus Mountains north of Cilicia. The LXX claimed that the Philistines originated there (Amos 9:7). Josephus notes that Herod's family had close ties with a king of Cappadocia,[603] and often follows a famous writer, one Strabo of Cappadocia.[604] Cappadocia was also near Pontus.[605]

The region of Pontus was closely connected with Cappadocia (as noted above) and Bithynia.[606] For Jews in Pontus, see Acts 18:2 (cf. perhaps 1 Pet 1:1). Luke may mention it because, when listing Jews in Asia Minor, one might mention Pontus to show how far north they had penetrated (Philo *Embassy* 281).[607] He may also prepare for his mention of Aquila's place of origin (Acts 18:2), though Luke could well have mentioned Pontus anyway. Located in the north of Asia Minor, it was less romanized in this period than was the western coast;[608] it also was less educated (at least in Roman terms).[609] In time it had a significant church (1 Pet 1:1; Pliny *Ep.* 10.96.6).[610]

597. Fitzmyer, *Acts*, 241.

598. Hengel, "Liste"; translated as idem, "List."

599. For a summary of 1990s archaeological publications on Cappadocia and Isauria, see Mitchell, "Archaeology," 186–88; on Cappadocia, see further Sullivan, "Cappadocia"; Edwards, "Cappadocia." Cappadocia was less urbanized than the rest of Anatolia in this period (Mitchell, *Anatolia*, 1:98). Pliny E. *N.H.* 6.3.8–6.4.14 deals with Cappadocia (24.102.162 also mentions a plant from there that supposedly could make lions lie on their backs).

600. Tac. *Ann.* 2.42.

601. On Jews in Cappadocia and nearby Armenia, see Stern, "Diaspora," 153; cf. Bruce, *Commentary*, 62; Harrill, "Asia Minor," 135; perhaps 1 Pet 1:1. Some Cappadocian Jews apparently settled in Joppa (Hemer, *Acts in History*, 223, cites *CIJ* 2:128, §910; 2:137, §931).

602. Jos. *Ant.* 16.23; *War* 4.632; Pliny E. *N.H.* 5.41.145; 5.42.146. Cappadocia could be grouped with other Asian regions to its north and south (Jos. *War* 2.368) but also with Armenia on its east (7.18), placing it among the easternmost, hence less romanized, parts of Asia Minor.

603. Jos. *Ant.* 16.11, 74, 131, 261, 269, 302, 309, 325, 357; 17.350; 18.139; *War* 1.446, 499–501, 530, 553; 2.114.

604. Jos. *Ant.* 13.286; 14.35, 104, 111, 138; 15.9; *Ag. Ap.* 2.84.

605. For the geographic relationship, see Hemer, "Address"; Ramsay, "Roads and Travel," 402. Pontus was, in fact, formed from part of old Cappadocia (Strabo 12.1.4).

606. For the Bithynian connection, see, e.g., Strabo 17.3.25. On Pontus, see further Sullivan, "Pontus."

607. See further Stern, "Diaspora," 153; Harrill, "Asia Minor," 135.

608. For associations with peoples considered less romanized, see Jos. *Ant.* 19.338; *War* 2.366; *Ag. Ap.* 1.64.

609. Lucian *Alex.* 17. A Pontic inscription also critiques religious quacks as Lucian does (Grant, *Paul*, 58–59).

610. Nevertheless, some later claimed that the numbers of Christians were sparse in central Pontus (Basil *On the Holy Spirit* [Pruche, 511–13], in Grant, *Paul*, 59).

Some scholars estimate about a million Jews in all Asia Minor (including the Roman province of Asia).[611] Philo speaks of many Jews in all the cities of Asia (*Embassy* 245), though (as will be evident below in the discussion of some towns of Asia's interior) this is an exaggeration; still, they seem to have clustered in major cities. The Roman province of Asia figures prominently in the narratives of (and commentary on) Acts 18–20.

VI. Phrygia and Pamphylia

There were large Jewish communities in Phrygia[612] (see further Acts 14:1; cf. Phrygia in 16:6; 18:23). Josephus claims that Phrygians descended from Thugrames, son of Gomer, son of Japheth (*Ant.* 1.126). Jews elsewhere knew that some Jews lived in Pamphylia (Philo *Embassy* 281; 1 Macc 15:23).[613] Luke may mention the area to highlight it here because it will reappear in Acts 13:13; 14:24; 15:38; 27:5.

VII. Egypt

Although Greek was the dominant language in urban Egypt (see comment on Acts 21:38), the Egyptian language endured (though by the second century sometimes written in a combination of demotic and Greek scripts).[614] The claim that more Jews lived in Alexandria than in Palestine[615] is almost certainly an overstatement, but no one doubts that many Jews lived in first-century Egypt (Jos. *Ant.* 14.116–18).[616] Some scholars have estimated about a million Jews in northern Egypt, especially around Alexandria, in the first century.[617] These estimates, too, may be high; Philo, who had every reason to exaggerate, claimed a total of a million Jews in Egypt from its borders with Libya and Ethiopia (*Flacc.* 43).[618] Nevertheless, a substantial portion of the residents of Egypt, especially Alexandria (where the proportion was perhaps a third), was Jewish. Two of Alexandria's five districts were Jewish, with only a few Jews living in the other parts (Philo *Flacc.* 55).

Despite the cultural distance between members of Alexandria's hellenized elite (such as the Middle Platonist Philo) and the average Palestinian sage, Egyptian Jewry was deeply influenced by events in Judea. After Luke's day, Egyptian and Cyrenian Jews later joined their own revolt, and Alexandrian Greeks crushed them more brutally than Romans had crushed the revolt in Judea, virtually obliterating Alexandrian Jewry.[619] Subsequent Christian presence in the city would therefore be primarily Gentile. See further comments on Acts 6:9 and especially on Acts 18:24. Although Luke focuses his narrative on the spread of the message in the northern Mediterranean world, it is clear that the Christian movement spread also in Alexandria, where it later became a significant force.

---

611. De Ridder, *Discipling*, 10n33 (following Grayzel, *History of Jews*, 138). For Jews in Asia, see, e.g., Jos. *Ant.* 16.160; Philo *Embassy* 245; Stern, "Diaspora," 143–55; further on Ephesus in comments on Acts 18–19.

612. See Jos. *Ant.* 12.147; Stern, "Diaspora," 149–50; Kraabel, "Judaism in Asia Minor," 61ff. (for syncretism, see, e.g., 81–86, 142, 146); Bruce, "Lycus Valley"; cf. Meyers and Kraabel, "Remains," 191; in general, Harrill, "Asia Minor," 134–35. On Phrygia, see, e.g., Bruce, "Phrygia."

613. See, e.g., Stern, "Diaspora," 148. For Pamphylia, Carroll, "Pamphylia."

614. This evolved into Coptic, which long persisted until replaced, after centuries of Islamic rule, with Arabic even in the churches, which retained a very limited role for Coptic (Emmel, "Coptic Language").

615. Sandmel, *Judaism*, 257.

616. On Jewish people in Egypt, see Stern, "Diaspora," 122–33; comment on Acts 18:24.

617. De Ridder, *Discipling*, 10n33 (following Grayzel, *History of Jews*, 138).

618. See Foakes-Jackson and Lake, "Dispersion," 151. Later rabbis permitted the use of Coptic as a translation language for the Esther scroll (*b. Meg.* 18a, bar.; so Le Cornu, *Acts*, 67).

619. See Sherk, *Empire*, §129, pp. 169–73. The line between Jewish Philo and Christian Clement of Alexandria may suggest some hidden continuities, but whatever of a Jewish presence reemerged must have been initially at best a shadow of its former existence.

viii. Libya around Cyrene

Well-known locations in Cyrenaica included the Ammon oracle (ca. four hundred miles from Cyrene) and the Pentapolis (the Five Cities). The five most prominent cities were "Benghazi [Latin *Berenice*], Arsinoe, Tolmeita [*Ptolemaide*], Marsa Sousah [Apollonia] and Cyrene itself" (Pliny E. *N.H.* 5.5.31).[620] The Five Cities were not close to each other; by ancient estimates, from Arsinoë to Benghazi was forty-three Roman miles, Ptolemais was twenty-two miles farther, and so forth. Cyrene was eleven miles from the sea but had a harbor there (5.5.32).

Cyrene's Jewish population originally came especially from Egypt, which adjoined Libya (Jos. *Ant.* 14.118; *Ag. Ap.* 2.44).[621] Cyrene was connected with Egypt not only geographically; the Ptolemies even subdued it as part of their Egyptian dominion (though the Romans divided them again; Strabo *Geog.* 17.1.5). (Substantial evidence testifies to the Jewish presence not only in Cyrene but in much of Roman Africa farther west.)[622]

Some scholars have estimated that there were about one hundred thousand Jews in Cyrenaica in this period.[623] They made up one of the four groups of people among whom Cyrene was divided (Strabo, according to Jos. *Ant.* 14.115). Cyrenian Jews appear frequently in ancient sources (Acts 6:9; 11:20; 13:1; Luke 23:26; Mark 15:21; Jos. *Ant.* 16.169; cf. 1 Macc 15:23; 2 Macc 2:23). Jews experienced repression from Greeks in Cyrenian Libya in the time of Herod the Great and Augustus (Jos. *Ant.* 16.160, 162). Like the Jewish community in Egypt, many Jews around Cyrene ultimately revolted, leading to their destruction (Jos. *War* 7.437).[624]

Romans generally looked down on Libyans in Rome, apparently because many were descended from prisoners of war and hence were of servile or freed status (Plut. *Cic.* 26.4). But inhabitants of Macedonia and Achaia (where we locate most of Luke's audience) probably would have thought of Libyans simply as North Africans near Egypt.[625] One of the most familiar accounts would have been Alexander's visit to the famous oracle of Zeus at Ammon.[626] Educated Greeks also knew that much of Libya was fertile and produced horses and goats in addition to providing elephants, ostriches, and other creatures that northern Mediterranean peoples regarded as exotic.[627] In the late first century, Arrian claimed that Cyrene was in a more desert part of Libya yet itself was "well-watered with groves and meadows," with animals and fruits of many kinds (Arrian *Ind.* 43.13).

620. Trans. H. Rackham, LCL, 2:241.
621. That Cyrene was in "Libya" was widely known (*Sib. Or.* 5.198). For a summary of archaeological data about Cyrene, see Yamauchi, "Cyrene in Libya"; for early Christianity there, Oden, *Christianity*.
622. Hemer, *Acts in History*, 222, notes at least 124 inscriptions not included in *CIJ*. For archaeological evidence on Roman Africa, especially Carthage, see Mattingly and Hitchner, "Roman Africa"; this area was largely Carthaginian before Roman conquest (Strabo 3.2.14).
623. De Ridder, *Discipling*, 10n33 (following Grayzel, *History of Jews*, 138); on Cyrenian Jewry, see further Foakes-Jackson and Lake, "Dispersion," 151; Stern, "Diaspora," 133–37; most fully, Applebaum, *Jews and Greeks in Cyrene*, esp. 130–200. On Cyrene generally, see, e.g., Gasque, "Cyrene."
624. For earlier civil strife there, see Jos. *Ant.* 14.114; for Jewish animosity probably in the early second century c.e., *Sib. Or.* 5.198.
625. By Greek and Greco-Jewish standards, inner Libya's residents were also dark skinned (*Sib. Or.* 11.289), though not as much as "Ethiopians" (see comment on Acts 8:27).
626. Cf. Pindar *Pyth.* 4.16; Diod. Sic. 17.51.1–2; Plut. *Alex.* 27.5–11; S. *Kings*, Alexander 15, *Mor.* 180D; Lucian *Dial. D.* 395 (12/14, Philip and Alexander 1); Ps.-Callisth. *Alex.* 1.30; Olmstead, *Persian Empire*, 511; apparently transferred to the Caesars (P.Fouad 8, in Sherk, *Empire*, §81, p. 123). On the oracle, see also, e.g., Pindar *Hymns* frg. 36 (from scholion on *Pyth.* 9.53). Egyptian Jews rejected the claim (*Sib. Or.* 5.7; 11.197–98; 12.7). On some pagan sanctuaries in Cyrene, see Rose, "Return to Cyrene."
627. Polyb. 12.3.1–6; by the empire, most of the "exotic" creatures would come from trade farther south.

IX. Visitors from Rome, both Jews and Proselytes

Apart from "Cretans and Arabs" in Acts 2:11, Rome holds the climactic geographic position here—fitting for a work that narrates the movement of the gospel from Jerusalem to Rome. Some scholars estimate about one hundred thousand Jews in Italy, with half of them in Rome, in the first century (see further comment on Acts 28:17);[628] others estimate closer to half this designated figure for Rome.[629] There were already Jews in Rome in the second century B.C.E., but many more came as slaves because of Pompey's triumph in the first century B.C.E.[630] We know the names and locations of various Jewish communities in first-century Rome.[631]

If this passage refers to Diaspora Jews who have come from Rome and not merely Roman citizens from various locations,[632] it could help explain why Paul finds (in both Acts and Romans) an established Christian community there,[633] though some of his ministry colleagues had also been working there (Rom 16:3–5, 7, 9, 12). Rome also had many proselytes, more than xenophobic Romans appreciated;[634] sincere proselytes made pilgrimage to Jerusalem, just like other Jews,[635] as one might also infer from this passage in Acts. Luke's term for "proselyte" here could mean "resident alien" (as often in the LXX), but its contrast with "Jews" in the same line indicates the more technical sense of "convert" here.[636]

Whereas the Antioch mission, with its more lenient approach to Gentile conversion, planted churches in Asia and Greece, the Roman church (with its initial interest in circumcision, food laws, and holy days; see Rom 2:25–29; 14:1–23) probably was founded directly by Judeans from Jerusalem. The probable circumstances that prompted Claudius's expulsion (see comment on Acts 18:2) suggest that Jesus's followers reached Rome before that time (at the least, controversies about the Christ disrupted the Jewish community there at that time). Porphyry's alleged later claim that Jewish law reached Rome under Caligula or afterward (Aug. *Ep.* 102.2) must refer, if accurate, to Christians (since the Jewish community more generally arrived, as we noted, much earlier).[637] These strands of evidence probably support the idea that the Christian message reached Rome before Claudius. Certainly, the church was well established in Rome long before Paul's arrival there (Acts 28:14–15; Rom 16:3–16), and Jerusalem had the largest evangelized Jewish population with strong ties to Rome (cf. Acts 28:21).[638]

Luke would have reason to highlight both Rome and proselytes, the former because it is the geographic goal of this volume (28:16–31) and the latter because proselytes offer a narrative transition toward Gentiles even more effective than "Hellenist" Jews (6:5; cf. 13:43).[639]

---

628. De Ridder, *Discipling*, 10n33 (following Grayzel, *History of Jews*, 138); Jewett, *Chronology*, 37.

629. E.g., Brändle and Stegemann, "Formation," 120, estimating some twenty thousand. Both estimates are within at least the same order of magnitude; estimates range from ten thousand to sixty thousand (Levinskaya, *Diaspora Setting*, 182). On Rome and population figures, see comment on Acts 28:16–17.

630. Bruce, *Commentary*, 63.

631. See comment on Acts 28:17.

632. For Roman citizens, see Judge, *Pattern*, 55; idem, *First Christians*, 444 (citing inscriptions regarding groups of Roman citizens outside Rome, though these normally involved long-term residents); Hanson, *Acts*, 64 (Acts 16:21, 37–38; 22:25–29; 23:27).

633. Stambaugh and Balch, *Environment*, 162; Das, *Debate*, 25.

634. See comment on Acts 16:20; cf. Juv. *Sat.* 3.60–63.

635. See Safrai, "Relations," 199–200.

636. With, e.g., Fitzmyer, *Acts*, 243. On "converts," see, e.g., Keener, *John*, 445–46, 542–44.

637. Hengel and Schwemer, *Between Damascus and Antioch*, 257–58.

638. For Jerusalemite ties with Rome, see, e.g., the synagogue of freedpersons in Acts 6:9; Theodotus's father's Roman gentilic name; and early Aramaic-speaking Jewish community in Trastevere (cf. Hengel and Schwemer, *Between Damascus and Antioch*, 258).

639. On the significance of proselytes and God-fearers among hearers in Acts 2:11; 13:43, cf., e.g., discussion in Koch, "Proselyten."

x. Cretans and Arabs

This closing coda need not be an afterthought but has parallels in other catalogues.[640] Although geographic designations in Luke's list that will recur later in Acts do not follow the precise sequence of their later appearance,[641] it may be significant that Crete appears toward the end of the book. A sizable Jewish community lived in Crete (Titus 1:10–14);[642] see further comment on Acts 27:7.[643]

In this period the Greek term that is rendered "Arab" applied especially to the Nabateans, on which see much fuller comment on Acts 9:23; Nabatea, with its capital at Petra, was "then at the height of its power under Aretas IV (9 B.C.–A.D. 40)"[644] and extended from the Red Sea in the south to the Euphrates in the north.[645] Jerusalem had considerable trade with the Nabateans (*Let. Aris.* 114, 119), and Jews were making converts among some Arab tribes as far south as modern Saudi Arabia at least by the second and third centuries C.E.[646] Various forms of languages related to proto-Arabian existed in the vicinity of Judea and could have been known by Jewish people living in these areas.[647]

e. Hecklers in the Crowd (2:13)

Not all members of the crowd are Diaspora Jews who understand bits of the disciples' praises. Here, as elsewhere in Acts, God's activity divides the crowd (Acts 14:1–2; 17:12–13; 19:9; 28:24; cf. 17:32), and as on some other occasions, it is those of lower status (here Diaspora Jews) who accept the message (cf. 4:1–4),[648] although ultimately its recipients are broader (2:41; cf. 6:1).

Mockery was so common that ancient rhetoricians remarked on appropriate rhetorical ways to implement it.[649] Sometimes hecklers interrupted speakers with questions or objections.[650] Public questions sometimes set the agenda for teachers'

---

640. Metzger, "Astrological Geography," 132. Hengel, "Liste" and "List," applies it to "Greater Judea's" immediate eastern and western neighbors, but Cyprus would fit better than Crete here.

641. The larger blocs may appear in roughly those areas: perhaps Galileans (Acts 1:11; 2:7); Judea (2:9, 14); in Asia Minor (should we count Pontus in 18:2?), Asia (2:9; 6:9; 16:6; 19:10), Phrygia (2:9; 16:6; but perhaps Acts 14), and Pamphylia (2:10; 13:13); with Romans (2:10) and Cretans (2:11) toward the end (but in reverse order). But this apparent pattern does not account for Cyrene (2:10; 6:9; 11:20; 13:1).

642. See also Philo *Embassy* 282; 1 Macc 15:23; van der Horst, "Jews of Crete"; cf. also the later *IC* 1.5.17 (in Hemer, *Acts in History*, 222–23). It may be only coincidence that Cretan Jews appear in literature often in the context of being deceived, sometimes by fellow Jews (Jos. *War* 2.103; *Ant.* 17.327; Titus 1:10–14), and Cretans in general had a reputation for dishonesty (e.g., Lucian *Lover of Lies* 3; *Sacr.* 10; Winter, *Wives*, 149; commentaries on Titus 1:12, and, e.g., Dibelius, *Studies in Acts*, 49). Some Jews there were also well-to-do (Jos. *Life* 427).

643. For a suggested connection between Cretans and Arabs, see Scott, "Horizon," 529–30.

644. Bruce, *Acts*[1], 86.

645. Bruce, *Commentary*, 64.

646. E.g., Guillaume, *Islam*, 12. For Idumean and Perean Arab converts here, see Grafton, "Arabs."

647. Le Cornu, *Acts*, 67. Some scholars argue from inscriptions that the later classical Arabic, the Arabic of the Qur'an, apparently dates to a generation after Muhammad, when conquests had invited loanwords, in Muslim-controlled Syria (Koren and Nevo, "Approaches," 104–5). (Late seventh-century coins and inscriptions with Qur'an quotations differ from the current text, which, some also hold, suggests that standardization occurred later; Cook, *Muhammad*, 74.)

648. González, *Acts*, 37, speaks of "the disadvantage of the advantaged"; because the locals expect to understand, they cannot recognize their own linguistic limitations and hence fail to appreciate the miracle.

649. See, e.g., Anderson, *Glossary*, 78 (a "sneering remark" with the "drawing together of the nostrils"), 126.

650. E.g., *Rhet. Alex.* 18, 1432b.35–40; 1433a.14–25; Caesar *C.W.* 2.33 (favorably); Cic. *Or. Brut.* 40.138; *Prov. cons.* 8.18; Sen. E. *Controv.* 3.pref. 4–5; Plut. *Lect.* 4, *Mor.* 39CD; 11, *Mor.* 43BC; 18, *Mor.* 48AB; *Demosth.* 6.3; 8.5; Cic. 16.3; Dio Chrys. *Or.* 15.26–32; Aul. Gel. 8.10; 16.6.1–12; 18.13.7–8; 20.10.1–6; Pliny *Ep.* 3.9.25; 3.20.3–4; 9.13.19–20; Lucian *Dem.* 14; *Z. Rants* 41; Diog. Laert. 7.1.19; Philost. *Vit. soph.* 2.30.623; Eunapius *Lives* 460; cf. also *'Abot R. Nat.* 6 A.

lectures on a given occasion.[651] In this case, some complain that the disciples are drunk, just as on a later occasion one charges Paul with madness for his impassioned speech (26:24), perhaps due to apparent inspiration (cf. 26:25, employing the verb for "utter" used in 2:4).

1. Ecstatic Behavior?

The outsiders' misunderstanding, and hence mockery (cf. elsewhere 17:18; 26:24), fits the disciples' inspiration. Even Paul, who prayed in tongues devotionally (1 Cor 14:18), believed that outsiders would judge tongues-speaking believers insane if no interpretation was provided (14:23).[652] (He also may have depicted his private devotional life as being what outsiders would consider "out of his mind" [2 Cor 5:13].)[653] Although Paul believed that the pneumatic aspect of believers' personalities can be controlled for the greater public good (1 Cor 14:32) and hence he would not identify tongues with pagan possession trance,[654] he probably allowed for more exuberant aspects of speech or behavior (cf. perhaps 1 Cor 14:14–18, 23–25) that were unwelcome in, for example, the somber ritual of Roman civic cults.[655]

It is probably also no coincidence that Paul (or, according to some readings, his disciple) contrasts being "filled with the Spirit" with drunkenness (Eph 5:18);[656] the same contrast is probably implied in Luke 1:15. Ecstasy could also be associated with drunkenness, or "Bacchic" frenzy;[657] this is most prominent in ancient portrayals of frenzied maenads, women followers of Dionysus.[658] Occasionally it was thought that Bacchic frenzy could produce mantic prophecy (Eurip. *Bacch.* 298–99);[659] occasion-

651. E.g., Mus. Ruf. 3, p. 38.25–26; 4, p. 42.34–35; 14, p. 90.24–25 (cf. 14, p. 96.4); 16, p. 101.20–21; 17, p. 106.20–21.

652. Others also cite 1 Cor 14:23 here (e.g., Zehnle, *Pentecost Discourse*, 119; Barrett, *Acts*, 125), and John Chrysostom also drew the connection (*Hom.* 36, PG 61:305–9; in Kovacs, *Corinthians*, 236); for outsiders construing tongues in terms of pagan ecstasy, cf. also Smit, "Tongues." Ecstasy in the Cybele cult could generate temporary "madness" (Ovid *Fasti* 4.236, 243, 245–46); mystic revelations could produce (*b. Ḥag.* 14b) or, more often, resemble (2 Kgs 9:11) madness; see further comment on Acts 26:24.

653. So the language was used (e.g., Dio Chrys. *Or.* 17.21; Alciph. *Fish.* 12 [Charopê to Glaucippê], 3.2, ¶1); cf. Keener, *Corinthians*, 184.

654. First Corinthians 12:2–3 refers not to tongues but to pagan prophetism, and Paul clearly ruled out prophetic possession trance for believers (14:32). See discussion at Acts 2:4.

655. See, e.g., Pliny E. *N.H.* 28.3.11; 28.5.25; Klauck, *Context*, 30. It is possible that the unknown language alone would accomplish this, but an unintelligible utterance might simply lead outsiders to suppose that members of the cult recited in their sacred language (e.g., Hebrew; such was my own assumption during my first naive experience with tongues and interpretation in a modern Pentecostal meeting in Massillon, Ohio, on November 2, 1975).

656. The connection with Eph 5:18 is also noted by others (e.g., Talbert, *Ephesians*, 129, also citing 1 Sam 1:12–18). Some view Dionysiac ecstasy as the background in Eph 5:18 (Rogers, "Background," esp. 257; cf. Leonard, "Status," 318; Kroeger, "Cults," 34). We should note, however, that the NT never uses the usual Greek terms for possession by the Spirit (Nock, "Vocabulary," 134).

657. E.g., Strabo 10.3.13; Dio Chrys. *Or.* 27.2; van der Horst, "Parallels to Acts," 55. Associated with the Bacchic cult, e.g., Val. Max. 1.3.1; Lucian *Gout* 38; Dio Chrys. *Or.* 32.58–59; Arrian *Alex.* 5.2.7; *Orph. H.* 50.8; Tert. *Apol.* 6.10; Klauck, *Context*, 107; Guthrie, *Orpheus*, 32–33; Burkert, *Religion*, 109–11, 292; idem, *Mystery Cults*, 112–13; Martin, *Religions*, 93–94; Otto, *Dionysus*, 54. Dionysus could madden one with drunkenness as a punishment (e.g., Plut. *Par. St.* 19, *Mor.* 310B).

658. See, e.g., Apollod. *Bib.* 2.2.2; Philo *Plant.* 148; Statius *Theb.* 7.649–51; 9.479–80; Plut. *Rom. Q.* 112, *Mor.* 291AB; Lucian *Dial. G.* 247 (22/18, Hera and Zeus ¶1); *Dion.* 1–4; Otto, *Dionysus*, 94; cf. Lucian *Dial. G.* 272 (2/22, Pan and Hermes ¶4); Klauck, *Context*, 120. In artwork, e.g., Philost. Elder *Imag.* 1.18; 2.17; Callistr. *Descr.* 2. Allusions to Euripides's scene of tearing apart Pentheus are many (Lucian *Sat.* 8; *Peregr.* 2).

659. Although mantic (associated with Apollo) and initiatory (associated with Dionysus) ecstasies were usually distinct (cf., e.g., Dio Chrys. *Or.* 32.56–58; Iambl. *Myst.* 3.25), they sometimes overlapped (Philost. *Hrk.* 7.3) or were confused (so Aune, *Prophecy*, 21, 42; cf. Lucan *C.W.* 1.673–95) in antiquity. For the usual categories (following Plato), see Plut. *Dial. L.* 16, *Mor.* 758EF; Graf, "Ecstasy," 800–801. For prophetic frenzy, see the excursus at Acts 2:17–18 on prophecy, especially the nature of pagan prophecy.

ally Apollo and Dionysus are thus linked.[660] (Particular Greek deities were portrayed as "frenzied";[661] worshipers of Cybele were also known to become frenzied.)[662]

Many commentators thus find in Acts 2:13's accusation of drunken-like behavior a suggestion of behavior or speech that is ecstatic;[663] at the least (a qualification offered only because "ecstatic" has been subject to too wide a range of definitions), it suggests an extremely atypical exuberance. Various ancient writers contrast divine enthusiasm with the kind caused by alcoholic intoxication[664] or use inebriation as a symbol of divine intoxication.[665] A few circles even used literal drunkenness to induce religious ecstasy.[666] The type of frenzy associated with the maenads could be associated with simple drunkenness.[667] Perhaps relevant to exuberant behavior, some claimed that a measure of wine would also make dancing easier (Eurip. *Cycl.* 124, 156).[668]

Excursus: Wine and Excessive Drinking

Drinking wine of various expenses and qualities was pervasive in Greco-Roman antiquity, but many moralists frowned on drunkenness, and even many who sometimes became drunk recognized its often harmful effects. Only a few moralists in antiquity counseled abstinence, most regarding moderation as sufficient. Ancient wine was, however, limited in its alcohol content (distillation not yet having been developed) and was normally watered down except when intoxication was the object.

1. Wine

Not only Judean but more generally Mediterranean practice is relevant here, given the broader world of Luke's audience and even that of Peter's audience within the narrative (which includes Diaspora Jews). Although Greece and Italy used beer, it was more popular in Egypt and northern Europe; Greece and Italy preferred wine.[669] Wine was a basic staple in the Mediterranean world, drunk with meals by all social

660. E.g., Plut. *E Delph.* 9, *Mor.* 388E; Men. Rhet. 2.17, 446.4–6; cf. further Detienne, "Polythéisme"; Otto, *Dionysus*, 202–8. Orpheus and Apollo are also connected (Men. Rhet. 2.17, 443.3–6; Philost. *Vit. Apoll.* 4.14), and Orpheus and Dionysus (Guthrie, *Orpheus*, 42–48, 258).

661. E.g., *Orph. H.* 11.21; 18.17; 27.13.

662. Val. Flacc. 7.635–36; Strabo 10.3.13; Lucian *Alex.* 13; probably Sen. Y. *Dial.* 7.26.8; but contrast Dio Chrys. *Or.* 1.56.

663. E.g., Caird, *Apostolic Age*, 60.

664. Iambl. *Myst.* 3.25.

665. Especially Philo; e.g., Philo *Creation* 71; *Alleg. Interp.* 3.82; *Drunkenness* 147; *Dreams* 2.190; *Flight* 166; *Contempl.* 84; Isaacs, *Spirit*, 50. For the contrast between physical and spiritual inebriation (cf. Eph 5:18), see later Cyril Jer. *Cat. Lect.* 17.19 and Eastern and Western Christian mysticism (Pelikan, *Acts*, 50).

666. See Epict. *Diatr.* 2.20.17 (on the Galli); Graf, "Ecstasy," 801; Huffmon, "Prophecy," 112. In Hellenism, drunkenness could be used to induce ecstasy, but not for oracles (Forbes, *Prophecy*, 282).

667. Lucian *Dion.* 5.

668. Dancing frequently occurred at banquets (e.g., Hom. *Od.* 18.304–5; Eurip. *Heracl.* 892–93; Xen. *Symp.* 2.1; Babr. 80.1–2), although the dancers were usually the entertainers; communal dancing was common, however, at celebrations (*Song Rab.* 7:1, §2; *Eccl. Rab.* 10:19, §1), notably at weddings (Dion. Hal. *Epid.* 2.260–61; Men. Rhet. 2.7, 409.11–13) and certain festivals (Lucian *Sat.* 4; *t. Sukkah* 4:4; *Lam. Rab.* proem 33; Safrai, "Religion," 812); a circumcision party in *y. Ḥag.* 2:1, §9. It could also be associated with Dionysus worship (Eurip. *Bacch.* 62–63; Arrian *Ind.* 7.8).

669. Gutsfeld, "Beer"; Burkert, "Symposia," 8; Cary and Haarhoff, *Life*, 94–95 (this is not to discount wine use in Hellenistic Egypt; e.g., P.Tebt. 118). For the history of wine, see Forbes, *Technology*, 3:106–25; on its preparation, see 3:70–78. Palestinian Jews also knew locally produced date "beer" (Broshi, "Date Beer").

classes.[670] It was a necessary part of wedding banquets.[671] Many kinds of wine were used;[672] Romans often considered Falernian the best.[673] Wine was associated with the deity Dionysus (the Roman Bacchus), as allusions in ancient literature regularly attest;[674] some ancients considered drunkenness unbecoming except at Dionysus's feasts.[675]

Although wine was supposed to be sold undiluted,[676] it was rarely drunk straight;[677] it was normally diluted with a larger amount of water.[678] Some scholars estimate this as commonly one to three parts water for every part wine;[679] others, two parts wine to five of water or one part to three.[680] Greeks counted the failure to dilute wine backward and barbaric;[681] drinking unmixed wine could lead to violence.[682] People not only could alter the water content or the type of wine but also sometimes added various substances to adapt the effects; sometimes it was said that people added toxins,[683] even hemlock.[684]

Most ancients did not object to moderate drinking.[685] Romans valued recreational use of wine among friends.[686] Moderate drinking freed a person to laugh, sing, and dance, in contrast to excessive drinking, which exposed matters better not discussed in public.[687] Moralists who warned against excessive drinking might suggest drinking moderately as a remedy.[688] Many praised the benefits of wine.[689] Wine could help one forget the day's toils, relax, and rejoice.[690] Most people approved of even heavy drinking for festivals;[691] drinking could last for days.[692]

---

670. So, e.g., Paterson, "Wine."

671. See, e.g., John 2:3 (and Keener, *John*, 498–501); Men. Rhet. 2.7, 408.32–409.1.

672. On viticulture and various kinds of wine, see Pliny E. *N.H.* 14. In Jewish sources, see *b. ʾAbod. Zar.* 30a; Paul, "Wine."

673. E.g., Ovid *Pont.* 4.2.9; Catull. *Carm.* 27.1; Fronto *Ad verum imp.* 1.1.4; cf. Fronto *Fer. als.* 3.2.

674. E.g., Pindar *Encomia* frg. 124; Apollod. *Bib.* 3.5.1; Hor. *Odes* 1.18; Ovid *Pont.* 4.2.9; Sil. Ital. 11.285; Plut. *Table* 3.2.1, *Mor.* 648E; Dio Chrys. *Or.* 64.20; Phaedrus 4.16; Lucian *Icar.* 27; Ach. Tat. 4.18.5; *Orph. H.* 47.1; 50.1; Athen. *Deipn.* 4.148bc; 15.675BC; *Gr. Anth.* 4.3.132–33; 6.257. Bacchus was, naturally, popular in a wine-producing area such as Pompeii (Massa, *Pompeii*, 108).

675. So Diog. Laert. 3.39 (on Plato).

676. E.g., Theophr. *Char.* 30.5.

677. Unless one wished to achieve drunkenness quickly (cf. Catull. *Carm.* 27.1; Athen. *Deipn.* 14.653E). But this led to foolish behavior (Ap. Rhod. 1.473; Anacharsis *Ep.* 3.1–3). Rabbis had blessings over both forms of wine, allowing handwashing with the undiluted form (*t. Ber.* 4:3).

678. E.g., Lucian *Lucius* 47.

679. Forbes, *Technology*, 3:98.

680. Smith, *Symposium*, 32. Hesiod recommended one part wine to three parts water (*W.D.* 596; Athen. *Deipn.* 10.426C), but for various other mixtures, see, e.g., Athen. *Deipn.* 10.426DE, 430A; for one part wine to two parts water, Pliny E. *N.H.* 23.25.51.

681. Smith, *Symposium*, 32 (with sources); cf. Theophr. *Char.* 4.6; Avi-Yonah, *Hellenism*, 137. It resembled the behavior of Scythians (Athen. *Deipn.* 10.427AB, 432A), reputed for their heavy drinking (Hdt. 6.84). Mediterranean peoples also associated drunkenness with Germans (Tac. *Germ.* 22) and Ethiopians (*b. Qidd.* 49b); each place had its own customs regarding wine (*Esth. Rab.* 2:13).

682. E.g., Diod. Sic. 4.4.6.

683. So Ruck, "Mystery," 42; Wasson, Hofmann, and Ruck, *Eleusis*, 89–90. Against Ruck, "Mystery," 47, however, narcotics were probably not used in the Eleusinian rites (Burkert, *Mystery Cults*, 108–9; Klauck, *Context*, 96; cf. Schulze, "Intoxicating substances," 880).

684. Pliny E. *N.H.* 14.28.138. As early as Hom. *Od.* 4.219–26, Greeks wrote of drugs mixed in wine (here from Egypt, perhaps magical).

685. E.g., Socrates in Xen. *Symp.* 2.24–26; Plato in Aul. Gel. 15.2.4–5.

686. See, e.g., Fleming, "Savoring."

687. Plut. *Table* 3.intro., *Mor.* 645A.

688. E.g., Crates *Ep.* 10.

689. E.g., in Athen. *Deipn.* 2.36–37.

690. E.g., Tibullus 1.7.39–42; Sir 34:27–28 [31:27–28]; cf. Prov 31:4–7. On peasants wanting to forget their toils, see MacMullen, *Social Relations*, 27; some thinkers regarded drunkenness and other aspects of wild partying (gluttony and promiscuity) as mere diversions from the depressing existence of the philosophically unenlightened (Max. Tyre 36.4).

691. Tibullus 2.1.27–30; forgiving even drunkenness there, Libanius *Descr.* 5.12; 29.10. Even the gods were supposed to banquet, in various ancient cultures (Burkert, "Symposia," 10–11).

692. E.g., during Saturnalia (Statius *Silv.* 1.6.8; Lucian *Sat.* 2, 25).

2. Objections to Drunkenness

The mockers in 2:13 are not complimenting the disciples. Ancients knew well the negative effects of drunkenness.[693] One writer claimed that drunkenness was the worst of all harms to humanity.[694] Many warned that drunkenness or wine (emblematic for drunkenness) could be dangerous.[695] Wine could enslave persons,[696] so that they were no longer masters of their own bodies or minds.[697] An intensely self-disciplined person might maintain sobriety, avoiding much alcohol;[698] it is reported that all of Spartan society followed this noble regimen.[699] Excessive drinking parties were known as one way to squander one's wealth.[700]

Health was a further consideration in avoiding excess alcohol.[701] Some, following the general Roman tradition that simplicity was healthier, complained that people were neglecting water, which was healthier than wine and easier to procure.[702] Someone who became too drunk might still have a hangover two days later;[703] in a more dangerous drinking bout, it was said that forty-one persons died afterward, including the winner.[704] A tyrant who drank too much at a feast precipitated his sickness and ensuing death.[705] One in ill health might hasten or precipitate his death by drinking undiluted wine.[706]

Many philosophers opposed drunkenness;[707] Stoics could even insist that the (ideal) wise person may drink but will not become drunk, since it leads to raving.[708] Stoics could also opine that a person who becomes addicted to alcohol develops the psychological illness of loving wine.[709] To control one's drinking, one Stoic suggested, one should first develop the discipline of abstinence, then test oneself with small quantities.[710] Craving wine, like craving sex or other things, was foolish, one thinker opined;[711] once such individual vices become pervasive in society, they are

693. O'Brien and Rickenbacker, "Alcoholism."
694. Athen. *Deipn.* 10.443.
695. E.g., Eurip. *Cycl.* 678; Pliny E. *N.H.* 14.28.137–48; Max. Tyre 25.6; a writer in Athen. *Deipn.* 10.443E.
696. E.g., maxims of Menander 2, 5 in *SPap* 3:260–61.
697. So Dion. Hal. *Ant. rom.* 7.11.3 (with fatal consequences).
698. E.g., Suet. *Jul.* 53; cf. Vell. Paterc. 2.41.1–2 (contrasting Caesar favorably with Alexander). Cf. also Augustus's sparing use of alcohol in Suet. *Aug.* 77.
699. Xen. *Lac.* 5.4–7.
700. Plut. *Alc.* 16.1; *Luc.* 39.1–2. Those who inherit (as opposed to those living by flattery) should maintain sobriety (Plut. *Educ.* 17, *Mor.* 13A).
701. Diluting it, Plutarch said, removed its harmfulness without removing its benefit (*Poetry* 1, *Mor.* 15E; *Table* 1.4.3, *Mor.* 621CD). For protection against drunkenness (magically), see Pliny E. *N.H.* 30.51.145; for a plant helpful for dissipating drunkenness, see 24.92.148.
702. Pliny E. *N.H.* 14.28.137 (for various dangers and problems with excessive drinking, see 14.28.137–48). Cicero jested that he might be prosecuted for drinking too much water, as a way of criticizing another's use of wine (Plut. *Cic.* 27.2). One should avoid drunkenness before conceiving (Iambl. *V.P.* 31.211). Although some considered wine a (relative) luxury (4Q416 2 [+ 4Q417] II, 19–20), it was pervasive.
703. Alciph. *Farm.* 30 (Scopiades to Cotion), 3.32.
704. Plut. *Alex.* 70.1. Alexander himself contracted a fever from an entire day of drinking on another occasion (75.3) and reportedly eventually drank himself to death (75.4); Alexander Jannaeus contracted a quartan fever for three years after overdrinking (Jos. *Ant.* 13.398).
705. Diod. Sic. 15.74.2.
706. Philost. *Vit. soph.* 2.10.588.
707. E.g., Sen. Y. *Ep. Lucil.* 58.33; 83; *Dial.* 7.12.3. It kills by pleasure (*Dial.* 1.3.2).
708. Arius Did. *Epit.* 2.7.11m, pp. 88–89.34–39 (esp. 34); Diog. Laert. 7.1.118. Stories about the early Stoic Zeno suggest that he might have disagreed (Diog. Laert. 7.1.26).
709. Arius Did. *Epit.* 2.7.10e, pp. 62–63.20–23 (cf. 2.7.5f, pp. 30–31.31). For the disease concept of alcoholism in late antiquity, see further Keller, "Disease Concept." Lovers of wine should take special precautions against overindulgence (Plut. *Poetry* 11, *Mor.* 31C).
710. Epict. *Diatr.* 3.12.11.
711. Dio Chrys. *Or.* 66.1, 7.

issues of public order.[712] A few even practiced and/or advocated abstention, such as Pythagoras and his followers.[713]

Jewish writers also warned against drunkenness;[714] in small quantities or well diluted, wine was beneficial, but it was deemed harmful in excess.[715] Some noted that one ought not to pray while drunk (though rabbis differed over whether such a prayer was valid).[716] Some commended even abstinence because it kept one far from the temptation,[717] though most accepted even drinking parties so long as participants maintained self-control.[718] The early Christians also valued sobriety, which in some contexts clearly included avoiding drunkenness (Rom 13:13; Eph 5:18; 1 Tim 3:3, 8; Titus 1:7; 2:3; 1 Pet 4:3); Luke undoubtedly shared this perspective, though like others he presupposes rather than argues it (cf. Luke 12:45).

Excess drinking is regularly associated with shameful loss of control;[719] it makes people commit offenses that they would not commit when sober,[720] and actions that a sober person found shameful a drunk person would not.[721] This could lead to embarrassing behavior at banquets,[722] to inability to make one's way out properly,[723] to losing one's presence of mind and ability to discern,[724] to mistakes in one's activity,[725] to criminal acts,[726] or even to acts considered worthy of death, such as blasphemy.[727] It clearly affected and even confused the mind,[728] and one could speak of wine as mind-numbing arrows[729] or as driving a person into temporary insanity.[730] Drunkenness afforded satirists

712. Dio Chrys. *Or.* 32.91.

713. Iambl. *V.P.* 3.13; Philost. *Vit. Apoll.* 2.7, 36 (also citing Indian Brahmans for this, 3.40); 6.11. This appears more mildly in Diog. Laert. 8.1.9, 19.

714. E.g., Tob 4:15; 1QpHab XI, 13–14; 4QpNah 3–4 IV, 4–5; Jos. *Ag. Ap.* 2.195, 204; Philo *Flacc.* 4, 136; *Mos.* 2.162 (though cf. *Plant.* 139–42, 174, 177); *Test. Jud.* 16:1; *Sipra Sh. par.* 1.100.1.2–3 (where R. Judah hyperbolically suggests capital punishment); *Pesiq. Rab Kah.* 4:4; *b. Pesaḥ.* 113b; *Gen. Rab.* 43:6; *Lev. Rab.* 12:1–5 (though cf. the Lord drinking in *Pesiq. Rab.* 16:3!). Cf. also the warning in *Ahiq.* 2.9–10 (so Syr. A; Syr. B has only 2.9; Arabic is 2.12–13), though its focus is one's drinking companions.

715. E.g., Sir 31:25–31 [34:25–31]; *Sent. Syr. Men.* 52–58; *Test. Jud.* 16:1; *'Abot R. Nat.* 37 A; *b. Ker.* 13b. Rabbis sought to quantify the amount of wine the drinking of which constituted drunkenness (*y. Ter.* 1:6); sages could drink wine well, but not the ignorant (*Gen. Rab.* 89:8).

716. So *y. Ter.* 1:6.

717. *Test. Jud.* 16:3; *Iss.* 7:3. Naturally, priests in the temple had to practice abstinence (Lev 10:9; Ezek 44:21; Jos. *Ag. Ap.* 1.199).

718. *Test. Naph.* 1:2.

719. E.g., Demosth. *Con.* 7; Hor. *Sat.* 1.3.90–91; Sen. Y. *Dial.* 5.37.1; Dio Chrys. *Or.* 32.55. It was thought to change a person by warming one internally (Plut. *Statecraft* 3, *Mor.* 799B; cf. Cic. *Tusc.* 5.41.118; Sen. Y. *Dial.* 4.20.2; Pliny E. *N.H.* 14.7.58; Char. *Chaer.* 4.3.8; Athen. *Deipn.* 5.185C); for wine's power to control, see, e.g., 1 Esd 3:17–24. Dionysus would stir those who consumed his wine immoderately to act indecorously (Dio Chrys. *Or.* 27.2).

720. Sen. Y. *Ep. Lucil.* 83.19–20. Cf. the story of Noah (*Jub.* 7:7; Jos. *Ant.* 1.141; *Gen. Rab.* 36:4; *Num. Rab.* 10:2); also Eve in *Num. Rab.* 10:8.

721. Sext. Emp. *Pyr.* 1.109; Mart. *Epigr.* 3.16.3; 3.48.5–10. Thus one lawgiver on an island with much wine doubled all penalties for crimes committed when drunk (Diog. Laert. 1.76; also in the third-century B.C.E. P.Hal. 1.193–95).

722. E.g., Plut. *Table* 3.intro., *Mor.* 645A; Dio Chrys. *Or.* 27.2; *Sipre Deut.* 43.8.1.

723. Polyb. 31.13.8; cf. many trampled when fleeing a banquet drunk in Polyb. 14.4.9–10. Better to leave early, Isocrates suggested, if one had to attend at all (*Demon.* 32); a banqueter unable to defend himself would need to at least be able to flee (Polyb. 8.30.6).

724. E.g., Libanius *Encomium* 5.14; *b. Pesaḥ.* 110b; *y. Ter.* 1:6.

725. So, e.g., Val. Max. 6.2.ext. 1 (judging); Phaedrus 4.16 (creation); Anacharsis *Ep.* 3.1–3.

726. E.g., breaking up someone's property (Aeschines *Tim.* 59–61).

727. Plut. *Alc.* 19.1.

728. E.g., Isoc. *Demon.* 32; Anacharsis *Ep.* 3.1–3; Aul. Gel. 15.2.4–5; Philost. *Vit. Apoll.* 2.36; *Song Rab.* 2:4, §1. It weakens both mind and body in Lucret. *Nat.* 3.476–83; Val. Max. 9.1.ext. 1; that a physician condemns it (in Plato *Symp.* 176D) does not surprise us.

729. Pindar *Encomia* frg. 124.

730. Plut. *Isis* 6, *Mor.* 353C; Heracl. *Hom. Prob.* 35.3. The continuing practice might produce long-term insanity (Hdt. 6.84).

an opportunity for mockery,[731] and more serious writers an opportunity for other criticisms.[732] Some philosophers, though, opined that drunkenness was acceptable for wise persons who would not drivel[733] or lose control of their tongue.[734] Not drinking by itself but loss of control thereby was the problem.[735]

Positively, wine could make people open up, talk more, and become more intimate;[736] it revealed one's true identity, as opposed to what one pretended to be.[737] But such loss of normal reserve had necessary drawbacks. Drinkers made promises they would not offer (or keep) when sober;[738] they also often grew loud.[739] Their loose tongues could reveal secrets[740] and otherwise get them in trouble;[741] one might make someone drunk to learn his secrets.[742] If one corrected a servant when drunk, it could be assumed that one so spoke only because drunk.[743]

Because wine could make one sleep,[744] it could make one vulnerable to dangers;[745] even those who remained awake might become unable to defend themselves.[746] Those who were drunk were vulnerable to slayers;[747] one could deliberately get someone drunk to subdue him[748] or escape his custody.[749] Drunkenness and partying were thus bad military discipline.[750] Soldiers or guards who fell asleep were thus easily killed.[751] Conversely, drunk soldiers were also dangerous where they should not be.[752] A leader given to too much drunkenness would neglect proper military and political duties[753] and make foolish decisions;[754] it was said that Alexander mocked his drunken father, Philip, for thinking he could invade Asia when he could not even cross from one couch to another.[755]

731. E.g., Mart. *Epig.* 3.82.
732. E.g., Suet. *Tib.* 42.1.
733. So Epicurus *Symposium*, according to Diog. Laert. 10.119.
734. So Zeno (acknowledging that his feet might trip) in Diog. Laert. 7.1.26. A sophist with a weakness for wine nevertheless "controlled" it so well that he could study before sleeping (Philost. *Vit. soph.* 2.11.591). Philo warned that if compelled to be drunken, one should not relinquish moral self-control (*Flight* 32).
735. *Test. Iss.* 7:3; *Test. Jud.* 14:7–8.
736. Hor. *Ep.* 1.5.16–20; Plut. *Table* 3.intro., *Mor.* 645AC; cf. Plut. *Dinner* 12, *Mor.* 156C.
737. E.g., Plut. *Table* 3.intro., *Mor.* 645A; Athen. *Deipn.* 10.427EF.
738. E.g., Mart. *Epig.* 12.12; cf. Mark 6:22.
739. Dio Chrys. *Or.* 30.35–36.
740. Char. *Chaer.* 4.3.8.
741. Philost. *Hrk.* 18.5.
742. Jos. *Life* 225.
743. Diog. Laert. 1.92.
744. E.g., Hor. *Sat.* 2.1.9; Ovid *Her.* 14.42; Tibullus 1.2.1–2; Libanius *Encomium* 2.17; further soporific substances could be added (Pliny E. *N.H.* 24.51.88; 28.79.260). To deaden pain, see Prov 31:6–7; Tibullus 1.2.1–2. Wine created unnatural dreams not susceptible to normal interpretations (*y. Ma'aś. Š.* 4:6, §5).
745. Ovid *Her.* 14.42. Humorously, drunkenness could put to sleep an entire company, rendering them susceptible to the theft of expensive napkins (Alciph. *Paras.* 10 [Stemphylochaeron to Trapezocharon], 3.46, ¶¶2–4).
746. Polyb. 8.30.6.
747. E.g., Livy 33.28.2; Jdt 13:2, 15; *L.A.B.* 43:6 (Samson).
748. E.g., Hdt. 1.211–12.
749. E.g., Jos. *Life* 388. See esp. the Cyclops (e.g., Hom. *Od.* 9.105–542; Eurip. *Cyclops* 488–94; Apollod. *Epit.* 7.6–7); many drew the moral from the story (e.g., Eurip. *Cyclops* 678; Crates *Ep.* 10; Athen. *Deipn.* 1.10E).
750. Livy 23.18.12; Tac. *Hist.* 2.68; cf. Hom. *Il.* 6.264–65.
751. E.g., Xen. *Cyr.* 7.5.21; Polyb. 8.27.1; 11.3.1; Dion. Hal. *Ant. rom.* 7.11.3; Jos. *Ant.* 18.370; Plut. *Cam.* 23.6; Xen. Eph. *Anthia* 1.13.
752. E.g., Tac. *Hist.* 1.80.
753. Polyb. 20.8.2, 4.
754. 1 Kgs 20:16; cf. Herodotus's characterization of Persian leaders (Hdt. 1.133, although at least he allows them to evaluate the decisions after becoming sober; cf. Esth 1:10; 2:1).
755. Plut. *Alex.* 9.5. Historically, Philip's drunkenness elicited criticism from contemporaries (e.g., Demosth. *Olynth.* 2.18–19).

Drunkenness often produced violence;[756] it was said that Alexander, drunk, speared to death his friend.[757] It also facilitated sexual license,[758] for which specified reason some Jewish sources warn against it[759] and early Romans forbade it to women.[760] Aristophanes thus calls it "Aphrodite's milk."[761] Enough wine might loosen one's inhibitions sufficiently to perform sexual activities openly instead of privately.[762] Sometimes it yielded both violence and sexual license in the raping of women or boys.[763]

However it was viewed, drunkenness was commonplace at symposia.[764] Cultic festivals were occasions of celebration throughout the eastern Mediterranean world, at which times strangers met each other and dined together.[765] Although this spirit of celebration undoubtedly included its share of excessive drinking in many cities, Jewish people would not approve of drunkenness at their festivals, certainly not at Pentecost in the temple.

That women as well as men received the Spirit (Acts 1:14; 2:17–18) and may have also appeared intoxicated could have increased the offense. Although women's inebriation may have been considered scandalous (see relevant comments above), it was known in urban areas.[766] Drunkenness in the temple, whether involving men or women, would be offensive. Even knowledge that the disciples were praising God (probably in the temple courts) may not have softened the accusation much: as noted above, later rabbis even declared that a drunken person should not pray.[767]

3. Inebriation as Positive

The matter was different if the inebriation was mystical rather than physical. Granted, drunkenness could symbolize improper thinking and behavior (as often in the NT; e.g., 1 Thess 5:6–8).[768] But it also provided a metaphor for divine inebriation (especially for the writings of the Hellenistic Jewish philosopher Philo[769] but perhaps also for some others).[770] P. W. van der Horst cites many other texts that compare ecstasy to

756. E.g., Eurip. *Cycl.* 534; Aeschines *Tim.* 59; Lysias *Or.* 3.6, §§96–97; 3.11, §97; Diod. Sic. 4.4.6; Philo *Contempl.* 40–47; Lucian *Dial. G.* 248–49 (22/18, Hera and Zeus ¶2); Diogenes *Ep.* 20. People who could drink without any violence were considered exceptional (Tac. *Germ.* 22).

757. Plut. *Alex.* 51.1–6.

758. Cf. Hor. *Odes* 1.18; Val. Max. 4.3.ext. 3a; 9.1.8; Lucian *Nigr.* 15; *True Story* 2.46; Char. *Chaer.* 4.3.8; Athen. *Deipn.* 15.668B; discussion in Winter, *Wives*, 153. Courtesans might use it to loosen up (Aelian *Farmers* 9 [Chremes to Parmenon]), and its potential for sexual mixing discredited early Dionysiac Mysteries in Rome (Diod. Sic. 4.4.1). Gluttony and sexual license, as two expressions of the lack of self-control, are likewise often linked (e.g., Corrington, "Defense"; Winter, *Left Corinth*, 82–85; Mus. Ruf. 4, p. 44.16–18; 1 Cor 6:13). The phallic deity Priapus was also associated with Dionysus (Diod. Sic. 4.6.1–2).

759. Sir 19:2; *Test. Jud.* 14:1–8.

760. So Val. Max. 2.1.5b. One husband allegedly cudgeled his wife to death for drinking wine (6.3.9).

761. Athen. *Deipn.* 10.444D.

762. Alciph. *Court.* 13, frg. 6, ¶¶11–18, esp. 18 (though this is fictitious).

763. Polyb. 6.7.5.

764. Smith, *Symposium*, 36.

765. E.g., *Apoll. K. Tyre* 39; Libanius *Descr.* 29.8; cf. Mikalson, "Festivals." Festive occasions also demanded, where possible, bright and colorful garments (Cary and Haarhoff, *Life*, 97).

766. E.g., Sen. Y. *Ep. Lucil.* 95.20–21.

767. *Y. Ter.* 1:6.

768. E.g., Max. Tyre 3.7; Hermog. *Inv.* 4.10.200.

769. E.g., Philo *Creation* 69–71; *Alleg.* 3.82; *Drunk* 146–47; *Dreams* 2.190; *Flight* 166; *Contemp.* 84.

770. Fitzmyer, *Acts*, 243–44, cites Job 32:19 (in light of 32:18; 33:4), which is unclear but possible. An allusion to Joel's wine (Joel 1:5) in light of Peter's quotation in Acts 2:17–21 is also possible (Evans, "Prophetic Setting," 217; see also below), but we should note that Joel does not connect drunkenness with inspiration. Prophesying from drunkenness was, however, a negative biblical image (Isa 28:7; Mic 2:11; differently and not related, Jer 23:9 and Amos 2:12).

drunkenness.[771] Bacchic revelry (Βακχεία) could also blend with frenzied worship of the Anatolian mother goddess (Strabo 10.3.13). (Frenzy was common in the cult of the mother goddess,[772] though one sage claims that one who truly received prophecy from her uttered it not as most do but calmly.)[773] But while some popular cults used alcohol and frenzy, this did not occur in cults focused on oracles.[774]

Moreover, one newly taken with philosophy might depict himself as "enraptured and drunk with the wine" (ἔνθεος καὶ μεθύων) of the philosopher's words.[775] (His colleague, however, corrects him: that is not inebriation but "sobriety and temperance.")[776] Although the apostles' interlocutors in the narrative world use the charge of drunkenness as an insult, the informed audience, aware of the disciples' pneumatic inspiration, should instead understand it positively.

11. Sweet Wine

Many scholars suggest freshly made wine here, which was still fermenting (cf. Isa 49:26); this usage would fit the eschatological fresh but sweet wine (γλυκασμόν) of Joel 4:18 LXX (3:18 ET) and Amos 9:13 LXX, as well as Greek literature in general.[777] In business documents, "sweet wine" (γλεῦκος) was often unfermented must.[778] Yet Pentecost was well more than half a year after the most recent grape vintage,[779] and most wine would no longer be "new" (cf. Job 32:19; Luke 5:37–38; Mark 2:22; Matt 9:17). (The Qumran *Temple Scroll* does associate new wine with a second Feast of Weeks, fifty days after the Pentecost festival of grain firstfruits presupposed in this narrative.)[780] Some means of preserving wine's sweetness did, it is true, exist, and so some "new wine" could remain.[781] One could preserve unfermented must by storing it in cold water until winter (Pliny E. *N.H.* 14.11.83).[782] But the season for wine is probably beside the point here; we should remember that Luke attributes these words to hecklers who are mocking, not claiming that the disciples have literally become drunk on long-stored fresh wine!

771. Van der Horst, "Parallels to Acts," 55 (Plut. *Rom. Q.* 112, *Mor.* 291B; *Obsol.* 40, *Mor.* 432E; *Dinner* 4, *Mor.* 150C; Lucian *Nigr.* 5; Iambl. *Myst.* 3.25; cf. wine inducing ecstasy in Eurip. frg. 265; Macrob. *Sat.* 1.18.1).

772. E.g., Ovid *Fasti* 4.237–46; Livy 38.18.9; Strabo 10.3.13; Val. Flacc. 7.635–36; Sen. Y. *Ep. Lucil.* 108.7; Epict. *Diatr.* 2.20.17; Juv. *Sat.* 2.110–16; Lucian *Alex.* 13; *Lucius* 37; *Gout* 30–32; *Syr. G.* 51; Iambl. *Myst.* 3.10. Cf. further comment in Burkert, *Mystery Cults,* 36.

773. Dio Chrys. *Or.* 1.56 (with "self-control and moderation," ἐγκρατῶς καὶ σωφρόνως).

774. Forbes, *Prophecy,* 282.

775. Lucian *Nigr.* 5 (LCL, 1:104–5); cf. *Nigr.* 37.

776. Lucian *Nigr.* 6, νήφειν τε καὶ σωφρονεῖν (LCL, 1:104–5).

777. Cf. also Song 5:16 LXX; Jos. *Ant.* 2.64; Philost. *Hrk.* 1.4; Lake and Cadbury, *Commentary,* 20 (citing Lucian *Lover of Lies* 39, which Barrett, *Acts,* 125, takes as referring only to indigestion); Bruce, *Acts¹,* 87 (citing usage as early as Aristotle); see the term in LSJ. Contrast the sour wine in Luke 23:36.

778. See Mayerson, "Translations"; BDAG.

779. With, e.g., D. Williams, *Acts,* 47. The vintage was August-September in Egypt (Lewis, *Life,* 125) and Palestine (Hepper, *Plants,* 99); likewise, in autumn in the northern Mediterranean (Longus 1.28; 2.1), including September in Italy (Gutsfeld, "Wine," 662). On viticulture, see sources from Columella's *On Trees*; Theophr. *Caus. Plant.*; Pliny the Elder's *Natural History*; and others in Keener, *John,* 989, 993–98.

780. 11QTᵃ XIX, 9–XXI, 10 (esp. Maier, *Temple Scroll,* 80n). Likewise Fitzmyer, *Acts,* 235, on 11QTᵃ XIX, 11–14 (with XVIII, 10–13; XXI, 12–16), who even suggests that Luke "alluded to the Pentecost of New Wine when speaking more properly of the Pentecost of New Grain." Malina and Pilch, *Acts,* 30 (cf. 230), jest that some of the festal visitors "have their calendar mixed up." Luke could be mocking the mockers (cf. comment on Acts 17:18), but this solution does not seem obvious enough to be deemed likely.

781. Lake and Cadbury, *Commentary,* 20; Bruce, *Acts¹,* 87 and Bruce, *Commentary,* 65 (citing Cato E. *Agr.* 120 for storage in a sealed container in a cool pond); Bishop, *Apostles,* 34 (citing a twentieth-century Palestinian village practice of adding sugar to new wine to preserve it).

782. Likewise, storing wine cool in the ground prevented its turning to vinegar (Pliny E. *N.H.* 14.26.131–35).

Yet "new wine" did not lend itself to drunkenness as easily as more fermented wine.[783] Sweet wines were "heavy" in the stomach,[784] but they did not make the head "heavy."[785] By contrast, intoxication seems to be the primary point here. If Luke imported the wider semantic range of γλυκύς and its cognates into the narrower γλεῦκος, he could mean by "sweet" wine any wine mixed with honey or other sweetener, available at many banquets.[786] To attribute unusual usage to an author should, however, be a solution of last resort, not a convenient way for modern interpreters to elude a problem. Some wines were both fairly sweet and months removed from the vintage: Italians prized especially sweet white wines, darkened and aged for years (the aging sometimes accelerated by storage in warm locations).[787] One could serve wine that was both "sweet" (ἡδύς; possibly "pleasant") and "old" (παλαιός; Lucian Lucius 3).

The key may be how *much* of the new wine the disciples are accused of drinking; when wine was not watered down[788] and/or was drunk in sufficient quantity, a person could become drunk even if the alcohol content otherwise seemed low.[789] Luke's term for "full of" (a NT hapax legomenon) contrasts with his normal term for being filled with or full of the Spirit (Acts 2:4); it can be used with anger (3 Macc 5:1) or with glutting or satiating oneself. The hecklers may thus be mocking the disciples as being not only drunk but having made do with weaker wine to this effect by means of gluttony. (Pagan writers often condemn gluttony and overindulgence,[790] which was common behavior;[791] Jewish and Christian writers also condemned it.)[792] Because

783. Aelian *Farmers* 8 (Opora to Dercyllus).

784. Plut. *Table* 3.7.3, *Mor.* 656B. For sweet wine being thicker and with less aroma, see Pliny E. *N.H.* 14.11.80; on sweet wine more fully, 14.11.83–85.

785. Athen. *Deipn.* 2.45e, βαρύνει (citing Hippocr. *Diet* 2.332; Hippocrates also uses sweet wine medicinally, e.g., *Use of Liquids* 5).

786. Cf., e.g., Le Cornu, *Acts*, 88. Cf. spices in Mark 15:23; 3 Macc 5:2, 10; Pliny E. *N.H.* 14.15.92; sweet spiced wine in Eunapius *Lives* 463; honey in Pliny E. *N.H.* 13.20.113; esp. 22.53.113–22.54.115; honey in aged wine in Athen. *Deipn.* 10.432C.

787. Paterson, "Wine," 1622; for stored, aged wine cf., e.g., Sen. Y. *Ep. Lucil.* 114.26. The sweet wine (ἡδυοίνους) of Philost. *Hrk.* 17.2 may be due to the kind of vine or the care of cultivation.

788. Wine was often diluted with two to four parts water per every part wine (Ferguson, *Backgrounds*, 80; cf. Plut. *Bride* 20, *Mor.* 140F; Philost. *Hrk.* 1.6; *Sipra Sh. par.* 1.100.1.3; b. *'Abod. Zar.* 30a; *Num. Rab.* 10:8; see esp. various mixtures in Athen. *Deipn.* 10.426CE, 430A). See the excursus on wine and excess drinking, above. Wine was supposed to be sold unmixed (Mart. *Epig.* 1.56; 9.98; cf. Theophr. *Char.* 30.5; but one said blessings over either mixed or unmixed wine, t. *Ber.* 4:3); water, of course, was normally cheaper (Mart. *Epig.* 3.56; Hor. *Sat.* 1.5.88–89).

789. Drinking wine that was too strong, however, served as a mark of ignorance (Theophr. *Char.* 4.6); drinking undiluted wine was viewed as dangerous (Ap. Rhod. 1.473; Diog. Laert. 7.7.184; 10.1.15; Apul. *Metam.* 7.12; Plut. *Poetry* 1, *Mor.* 15E; *Table* 1.4.3, *Mor.* 621CD; Diod. Sic. 4.4.6; Philost. *Vit. soph.* 2.10.588; Athen. *Deipn.* 10.427AB, 432A). Though one might devote undiluted wine to Dionysus, one might dilute wine dedicated to Zeus (as in Diod. Sic. 4.3.4). To become drunk at parties, mixers could dilute the wine less (Ferguson, *Backgrounds*, 80; cf. Catull. *Carm.* 27; Athen. *Deipn.* 14.653E) or add various herbal toxins (Ruck, "Mystery," 42; Wasson, Hofmann, and Ruck, *Eleusis*, 89).

790. See, e.g., Xen. *Cyr.* 1.2.8; *Lac.* 5.4–7; *Mem.* 2.1.1; Eurip. *Cycl.* 334–35; Aeschines *Tim.* 42; Arist. *Pol.* 1.1.12, 1253a; Pindar *Ol.* 1.52–53; Polyb. 12.8.4; Sall. *Sp. Caes.* 8.2; *Rhet. Her.* 4.28.39; Val. Max. 9.1.ext. 1; Sen. Y. *Ep. Lucil.* 60.4; Mus. Ruf. 4, p. 44.18; 16, p. 104.18; 18A, p. 112.6–7, 29; 18B, p. 116.4–22, 25–33; 18B, p. 118.4–5, 9, 16–19; Pliny E. *N.H.* 11.119.284; 28.14.56; Epict. *Diatr.* 2.9.4; Plut. *M. Cato* 9.5; Dio Chrys. *Or.* 32.90; 77/78.28; Aul. Gel. 6.16; Max. Tyre 7.7; 25.5–6; 36.4; Diog. Laert. 1.104; 2.34 (Socrates); Iambl. *V.P.* 31.203; Philost. *Vit. soph.* 1.20.512–13; *Vit. Apoll.* 1.7; Porph. *Marc.* 33.506; Babr. 34; Longus 4.11; Ach. Tat. 2.23.1. This includes those who vomit to make room for more (e.g., Hipponax frg. 42; Sen. Y. *Ep. Lucil.* 108.15), though people valuing decorum viewed drunken vomit in public as shameful (Cic. *Phil.* 2.25.63; *Sipre Deut.* 43.8.1). Satirists often targeted gluttony (Mart. *Epig.* 2.40.1–8; 3.17.3; 3.22.1–5; 5.70, 76; 7.20; 11.86; 12.41; Juv. *Sat.* 2.114).

791. See, e.g., Smith, *Symposium*, 36; Ruscillo, "Gluttony." Cf. Suet. *Claud.* 33.1 (but contrast *Jul.* 53).

792. E.g., Rom 16:18; 1 Cor 6:13; Phil 3:19; Matt 11:19; *Syr. Men. Epit.* 6–8; 4 Macc 1:3; *Test. Mos.* 7:4; *Apoc. Elij.* 1:13. See esp. Philo on the "belly" (*Creation* 157–59; *Spec. Laws* 1.148, 192; 4.91; *Dreams* 2.155; *Alleg. Interp.* 3.159, 161, 221; *Migr.* 66; Rhodes, "Diet").

such fresh (and less alcoholic) wine was also, presumably, cheaper, they might also be implying "that the Christians have been getting drunk as cheaply as possible."[793]

Many ancient texts associate "sweetness" with pleasant speech (e.g., Prov 16:21, 24; 27:9)[794] or God's message;[795] thus eloquent speech is "honeyed,"[796] and a voice may be "honey-voiced."[797] But it is likely the "inspiring" value of wine, rather than the pleasantness of its taste (compared with a pleasant message), that is in view here. For inebriation as negative, and spiritual inebriation as positive, see the excursus on wine above.

Why would Luke employ such a potentially ambiguous image? First, sweet wine could recall a restoration context that prepares for the imminent Joel quotation of Acts 2:16–21: after judgment on wine and other resources, God would pour out his Spirit (Joel 2:28 [3:1 LXX]), and there would be an eschatological abundance of sweet wine, milk, and water (3:18 [4:18 LXX]).[798] Unfortunately, the terminology in Joel 3:18 is not close enough (γλυκασμόν) or distinctive enough (cf., e.g., Amos 9:13) to suggest this allusion except in retrospect. More important, Luke's ideal audience might recall that Jesus compared kingdom joy to new wine (Luke 5:37–39; slightly expanded from Mark 2:22).[799] Whereas the hecklers within the narrative might envision Jesus's followers becoming drunk on sweet new wine, Luke's audience instead recognizes a joy that previous structures could not contain.

793. Barrett, *Acts*, 125 (citing Lucian *Ep. Sat.* 22 for the implication of γλεῦκος as cheap wine).

794. E.g., Hom. *Il.* 1.249 (a model for some later quotations); Val. Max. 1.7.ext. 3; Pliny *Ep.* 4.3.3; Lucian *Portr.* 13; Philost. *Vit. soph.* 1.8.490; 1.21.521; 1.22.522; 2.1.561; 4Q372 3 5; cf. Sen. E. *Controv.* 3.pref. 3. Some enjoyable kinds of content make speech "sweeter" (Dio Chrys. *Or.* 33.10; Men. Rhet. 2.4, 388.13–14, 27; 392.18); for songs, Pindar *Isthm.* 2.3; *Paeans* 6.59; 8.78.

795. So Wisdom or God's message in Prov 24:13–14; Ps 119:103; Ezek 3:3; God's message mixes sweet and bitter in Rev 10:9–10; cf. philosophic wisdom in Dio Chrys. *Or.* 33.16; the claim about truth in Egyptian religion in Frankfurter, *Religion in Egypt*, 53–54.

796. Herodas *Mimes* 3.93.

797. *Thebaid* frg. 4 (from Plato *Phaedr.* 269A); cf. Pindar frg. 152.

798. Locusts ravage the crops (Joel 1:4), including new wine (1:10), leaving no "sweet wine" (though the LXX has here simply οἶνος) for the drunkards (1:5). If Israel turns to God, however, God will send new wine and other fertility (2:19, 22, 24), making up for what the locusts had destroyed (2:23). After this, the Spirit will be poured out (2:28 [3:1]), and eschatological wine will be available (3:18 [4:18]). The wine press of judgment (3:13 [4:13]) is probably not relevant here. Cf. also Evans, "Prophetic Setting," 217.

799. Some ancient commentators also relate this to Jesus's promise of new wine with new wineskins; e.g., Bede *Comm. Acts* 2.13 (who contends that the mockers ironically speak truth); cf. Cyril Jer. *Cat. Lect.* 17.18 (Martin, *Acts*, 26).

PETER'S CALL TO REPENTANCE (2:14–40)

The speech uses some judicial rhetoric (see especially the indictment, Acts 2:23, 36), though its conclusion (and perhaps overall purpose) is deliberative (2:37–40);[1] such mixed genres were common. Though it includes some clearly early and possibly distinctively Palestinian elements, Peter's speech reflects some forms of argumentation known to rhetoricians;[2] Luke does not portray Peter as a poor speaker (4:13). When, in the larger context of Luke-Acts, one recalls that Jesus called Peter not as a member of the educated, hellenized urban elite of Jerusalem or even as a traditional scribe but as a Galilean fisherman, one recognizes the remarkable character of his transformation.[3] Jesus had promised that Peter would become a fisher of people (Luke 5:10); Peter's success glorifies not himself but his mentor (Acts 4:13).[4]

Nevertheless, this speech does not follow Hellenistic rhetorical patterns the way most speeches in later sections of Acts do; Peter probably had relatively little exposure to rhetoric, and none of Luke's audience would have expected otherwise. Regardless of how much information they had available, Hellenistic historians worked hard to offer speeches at least suitable to the speakers. When reporting speakers of an earlier era, for example, they often archaized their speech; since Peter is a Jewish Scripture expositor, Luke uses a style heavily shaped by the LXX.[5]

1. Structure

Though the speech purports to be a spontaneous composition, it reflects the sort of careful structure that could be marred by even minor changes at points (cf. Cic. *Or. Brut.* 70.232). The speech's end echoes its beginning, in good rhetorical fashion, on two points: baptism in Jesus's name (Acts 2:38) fulfills "calling on the Lord" (2:21), and the promise of the Spirit (2:38) alludes to Joel's quoted words in 2:17–18 (as well as to Jesus's words known to Luke's informed audience, albeit not Peter's—what "the

---

1. Cf. similarly Soards, *Speeches*, 31; Witherington, *Acts*, 138. The "refutation" of Acts 2:15 is not limited to forensic speech but also appears in deliberative speech (e.g., Rufus Rhetor 39 in Anderson, *Glossary*, 124) and certainly in any speech interrupted by hecklers. Certainly, it is not an epideictic "festival speech" (on which cf., e.g., Aune, *Dictionary of Rhetoric*, 145), though unprepared hearers might have expected a few of these.

2. See, e.g., Kurz, "Rhetoric in Christological Proof." Because the rabbis derived many of their argumentative midrashic techniques from Hellenistic rhetoric, however (see Lieberman, *Hellenism*, 47–82; Hengel, *Judaism and Hellenism*, 1:80ff.; Levine, *Hellenism*, 113–16; for examples, see, e.g., Arist. *Rhet.* 2.23.4–5, 1397b), we cannot isolate these techniques as purely Diaspora products.

3. John Chrysostom contrasts Peter's boldness with his previous denials of Jesus (*Hom. Acts* 4, in Martin, *Acts*, 28).

4. The wording of Mark 1:17 would have made Jesus's involvement in the transformation even clearer, but Luke changes it, perhaps to avoid a potentially negative misconstrual of fishing (Marshall, *Luke*, 206).

5. With Witherington, *Acts*, 137–38.

Father promised" in 1:4–5). The *peroratio* (closing exhortation) of 2:40 echoes the end of 2:21 ("saved").[6] Many ancients criticized those who wished to speak without training (cf. 4:13)[7] or preparation,[8] though people also praised those quick-witted in debate[9] and skillful in spontaneous composition.[10] While not fitting all conventions of Greek rhetoric, Luke's summary depiction of Peter's spontaneous speech should impress Luke's audience.

One simple way to structure the speech is to see the addresses in 2:14, 22, 29, and 37 as structural markers.[11] Such markers seem reasonable if 2:29 marks the transition from laying out Scripture evidence to appealing to present circumstances. An analogous shift appears in 13:26 (cf. 13:16).

This speech also displays what appears to be a certainly elaborate chiastic pattern in one section (2:22–36).[12] Granted, chiasmus has often (perhaps usually) been overdone (often choosing nonrepresentative points and radically asymmetrical blocks of material to fit the pattern),[13] but this particular occasion appears to be a legitimate instance of the inverted parallelism technique. A simple chiasmus may simply invert word order in the second of two successive clauses[14] and in many cases may be accidental, but the pattern is much larger and more deliberate here.

Such an extensive inverted parallelism was not as common as with many other forms of parallelism, but it does occur. The label "chiasmus" is first attested in Hermogenes (*Invention* 4.3),[15] but the practice is much older[16] and is often noted by classicists in classical texts;[17] it is clear at points in Homer[18] as well as in the biblical tradition.[19] Thus it could have been recognized and appreciated by the rhetorically astute in the first century.[20] Chiasmus serves a purpose, as John Harvey notes: "Chiasmus serves to make ideas memorable. In so doing, it may perform any of three functions: (1) emphasis, (2) comparison, or (3) contrast."[21]

The chiastic pattern some have pointed out here corresponds at so many points (and with far fewer gaps between elements than in many of the proposed chiastic

---

6. Witherington, *Acts*, 139. Such an *inclusio*, or verbal bracketing, was a common literary technique; see, e.g., Luke 15:24, 32; Matt 5:3, 10; 1 Cor 12:31; 14:1; Catull. *Carm.* 52.1, 4; 57.1, 10; Pliny *Ep.* 3.16.1, 13; Harvey, *Listening*, 66–67, 75–76, 91–92, 102–3, 289; Aune, *Dictionary of Rhetoric*, 229; Rowe, "Style," 130; Porter, "Paul and Letters," 579, 582.

7. Xen. *Mem.* 4.2.6.

8. Sen. E. *Controv.* 10.pref. 3; Quint. *Inst.* 10.7.21.

9. Sen. E. *Controv.* 10.pref. 2.

10. Philost. *Vit. soph.* 1.24.529. Cf., e.g., Sen. E. *Controv.* 4.pref. 7; Pliny *Ep.* 2.3.1; Suet. *Gramm.* 23; Tac. *Dial.* 6; Lucian *Prof. P.S.* 20; Philost. *Vit. soph.* 1.482; see further discussion at Acts 14:15–17.

11. Gaventa, *Acts*, 73.

12. See Bailey, *Poet*, 65–66, along with his other literary insights there; more modestly, Parsons, *Acts*, 44.

13. Often they are "in the eye of the beholder" (Witherington, *Christology of Jesus*, 6). Bailey, *Peasant Eyes*, xix, xx, himself sounds this warning, noting that Bullinger's abuse for a time discredited pursuit of chiasmi altogether. See the four test cases in Harvey, *Listening*, 104–17, with Gen 6:3–9:16 (113–14) being the likeliest.

14. Rowe, "Style," 137; Harvey, *Listening*, 286. Rhetoricians did not emphasize such simple structures, but they are clear in texts (Aune, *Dictionary of Rhetoric*, 94).

15. Harvey, *Listening*, 98. Note the verb twice in Hermog. *Inv.* 4.3.181; the genuine author is unknown.

16. In the LXX, see, e.g., Prov 10:17; Job 30:15 (Lee, "Translations: Greek," 780); cf. the comparison with *commutatio* in *Rhet. Her.* 4.28.39 (Black, "Oration at Olivet," 87).

17. See, e.g., Dewey, *Debate*, 206n123; Kennedy, *New Testament Interpretation*, 28–29; esp. Harvey, *Listening*, 61–82.

18. Harvey, *Listening*, 64–65, taking an extensive example from Hom. *Od.* 11.171–203 (ABCD-D′-C′-B′-A′).

19. Like other forms of parallelism (e.g., Albright, *Yahweh*, 4ff.), chiasmus appears in the ancient Near East and the Hebrew Bible (Kitchen, *World*, 97; Harvey, *Listening*, 83–96) as well as in early Jewish texts (*OTP* 1:850 n. *a*, on *Test. Job* 25; Vellanickal, *Sonship*, 38–39, on 1QHᵃ XI, 7–12).

20. See Stock, "Chiastic Awareness."

21. Harvey, *Listening*, 99. Chiasmus may draw attention to the relationship between lines parallel to each other (Gutt, *Relevance Theory*, 59).

structures in the NT) that even if one found some possible breaks in the pattern, it would not call it into question.[22]

A This one . . . you *crucified* and killed (Acts 2:23)
B But God *raised* him up . . . (2:24)
C *David says* + Psalm 16 quote involving right hand (2:25–28)
  a. Men, brothers, b. it is necessary to speak c. to you boldly (2:29)
D the patriarch *David died* . . . (2:29)
E Being therefore a *prophet*, and knowing (2:30)
F that God had sworn an *oath* to him (2:30)
G that he would set one of his descendants *upon his throne* (2:30)
H he foresaw and spoke (2:31)
I of the *resurrection* of Christ (2:31)
J that he was not abandoned to *Hades* (2:31)
J' nor did his flesh see *corruption* (2:31)
I' This Jesus God *raised up* (2:32)
H' of that we are all *witnesses* (2:32)
G' Being therefore exalted *at the right hand of God* (2:33)
F' having received from the Father the *promise* of the Holy Spirit (2:33)
E' he has poured out this [*phenomenon*] which you see and hear (2:33)
D' For *David* did *not ascend* into the heavens (2:34)
C' But *he himself says* + Psalm 110 quote involving right hand (2:34–35)
  c. Assuredly therefore b. let it be known to a. all the house of Israel (2:36)
B' that God has made him *Lord and Christ* (2:36)
A' this Jesus, whom you *crucified*[23] (2:36)

The weakest points in this proposed parallelism are probably B, E, F, H, and J, but Luke's explicit connection among the Spirit, prophecy, and witness (1:8; 2:17–18) may also support E and H. If we link A with J (questionable), B with I (stronger), C with H (likely), D with G (likely), and E with F (possible), the weaker points of the chiastic structure are strengthened, yielding an even more complex literary structure of double chiasmus:[24]

Death	Resurrection	Witness	Enthronement	Coming of Spirit
You crucified>	God raised>	David says>	David died (not enthroned)>	Prophet knew>
<Hades	<resurrection	<Saw and spoke	<His throne	<(God swore)
Corruption>	God raised>	We are witnesses>	Exalted to the right hand>	Promise of the Spirit>
You crucified	<God made him Lord and Christ	<(David said)	<David did not ascend	<Spirit poured out

Not every element works at every point, but the cumulative force of much of the structure seems compelling. In most proposed chiasmi, observed "patterns" simply involve repetition of themes without particular concern for sequencing, but in this case, for the programmatic speech of Acts, a strong argument can be made for deliberate, large-scale patterning. Ancient readers would not expect someone to compose

22. Cf., e.g., the Heb. version of Ps 155 in 11Q5 XXIV, which is a *partial* acrostic; line 5 begins with b, line 7 with g, and "then (roughly) each line following with the subsequent letters" (Michael O. Wise in *DSSNT* 449).
23. Slightly adapted, but mostly reproduced, from Bailey, *Poet*, 65–66.
24. Ibid., 67.

such an extended structure extemporaneously,[25] but some might perhaps attribute it to inspiration,[26] which might perhaps be implied here (see comment on Acts 2:14).

Careful literary design does not exclude historical tradition in the speech. The following points offered by James D. G. Dunn in support of authenticity might indicate only that Luke knows basic tradition from early Christianity, but they would also prove consonant with the idea that the sermon reflects someone's genuine reminiscences of the heart of Peter's Pentecost speech:

1. The composition throughout fits principles of Jewish midrash (completing Joel's quotation in 2:39).[27]
2. The Joel passage was widely used and hence certainly part of early Christian preaching (Rom 10:13; Titus 3:6), as was Psalm 110.
3. The eschatology ("last days" in 2:16–20) is not a primary Lukan emphasis in Acts.
4. Some aspects of "primitive" Christology appear: Nazarene (2:22); a man attested by signs (2:22); "Messiah" is a title (2:33).[28]

Some scholars object that Peter's use of a quotation from Joel cannot be primitive, since this would imply that the church already knew its place in the events of the end time.[29] This objection, however, misses the frequently cited point that the early Christians, believing that the Messiah had come, were more apt to recognize that they were in the end time (cf. 1:6) than they were to recognize the likelihood of a delay in its consummation.

Authenticity of essential substance does not mean that a speech is verbatim or that a historian would feel inhibited in creatively filling in where needed (see introduction, ch. 8); it certainly does not imply that the speech was preserved and transmitted to Luke in Aramaic, as some have suggested.[30] It is unlikely that Peter originally preached the sermon in Aramaic, in any case. Granted, some of Peter's hearers in 2:9–11 (especially the Mesopotamians in 2:9) spoke various dialects of Aramaic, but most of his hearers (especially from Asia, Egypt, and Rome) would find Aramaic unintelligible; the LXX quotes also support a sermon in Greek.[31] Granted, even if Luke's source did not use the LXX, he could have reframed the text in that more familiar form. But Peter on a regular basis probably could speak passable Greek (see comment on Acts 21:37, 40), if not yet at this point the carefully constructed rhetoric of Acts 2, and so his use of arguments that depend on Greek cannot be used against basic authenticity.[32] Some themes recur in Peter's speeches in Acts, but these speeches have different emphases suiting their different settings.[33]

25. Though skill in oral patterning could begin early (Harvey, *Listening*, 77, citing Quint. *Inst.* 2.4.15).

26. Cf. Dion. Hal. *Thuc.* 34, who doubts that Thucydides was "inspired" (θεοφορήτων) in view of his rhetorical inadequacies.

27. Cf. also Ellis, "Midrashic Features."

28. Dunn, *Acts*, 27–28; cf. further Dupont, "Don de l'Esprit"; Turner, "Spirit of Christ and Christology," 184–86; idem, *Power*, 268–69; Bonnah, *Spirit*, 275. Cf. also God appointing him as Lord and Christ (2:36).

29. Lindars, *Apologetic*, 37, arguing against views such as in Dodd, *Preaching*, 59 (though Lindars accepts much early tradition in the speech; *Apologetic*, ch. 2).

30. Cf. C. Williams, *Acts*, 60, for Aramaic. By contrast, Lüdemann, *Acts*, 54, rejects the authenticity of both speech and event because of LXX quotations, which expects too much of ancient historians.

31. Lake and Cadbury, *Commentary*, 20, though they are probably wrong to think that Luke's play on "Lord" would have worked only in Greek (the Syriac translation to which they appeal represents its own milieu, not that of the primitive church).

32. *Pace* Haenchen, *Acts*, 185.

33. See Tannehill, "Functions of Peter's Speeches"; idem, *Shape*, 169–84.

2. Introducing the Speech (2:14–15)

Peter, backed up by the other apostles, deflects the hecklers' charge before developing his biblical explanation of the event. This is "a witty aside to the audience" and hence would presumably employ a vocal inflection implying irony.[34]

a. Peter's Peers, Posture, and Tone

Given the ancient characterization of inspired speech (or being "full of a deity") as rapid, Luke's audience might imagine, and the lector might dramatize, a rapid delivery style.[35] If following the usual rhetorical custom, the ancient public reader of Acts would imitate Peter's presumed gesture, "the common gesture of address," as Peter was ready to speak.[36]

Although Peter gave the speech, the "eleven" (cf. 1:26) stood with him.[37] Possibly they already act, in proleptic fashion, as the proper judges of Israel's twelve tribes, foreshadowing the fulfillment of Jesus's prediction in Luke 22:29.[38] Certainly, their stand together fits the model of joint ministry in Luke-Acts, where only Jesus ministers without peer (cf., e.g., Luke 10:1; Acts 6:3; 13:2; 14:23; 15:6, 22–23, 40; 20:17, 28–30).[39] Peter refers to the group as a whole when he claims that they are "all" witnesses (Acts 2:32).

That they "took their stand" (also 5:20; 17:22; 25:18; 27:21)[40] presents them in the regular posture for a Hellenistic orator or other public speakers.[41] One who was seated would rise to speak,[42] a practice helpful both visually and acoustically. In this period rules for when to stand or sit when expounding Torah or reciting prayers were not yet standardized (*t. Ber.* 1:3; *Sipre Deut.* 34.5.3).[43]

That Peter "raised his voice" (again in Acts 4:10) is a frequent idiom in the LXX but also appears in Greek from the classical era forward.[44] One would expect Peter to project his voice loudly to address more than three thousand people; although we have grown dependent on sound systems today, there is no reason to doubt such a scenario.[45] Charles Spurgeon (in the Tabernacle, in the late nineteenth century) and Aimee Semple McPherson (at Angelus Temple, in the early twentieth) preached to many thousands in their acoustically designed megachurches without voice amplification.[46]

---

34. Shiell, *Reading Acts*, 171, citing Cic. *De or.* 2.57.270–71.

35. See Shiell, *Reading Acts*, 174.

36. Ibid., 172.

37. That is, "eleven *besides* Peter," the usual Lukan and Hellenistic, rather than classical, sense of the construction (Haenchen, *Acts*, 178n2, following Blass, Debrunner, and Funk, *Grammar*, 118–19, §221).

38. So Fitzmyer, *Acts*, 234. The comparison with "an Ignatian bishop with his crescent of attendant presbyters" (Pervo, *Acts*, 75) does not seem very relevant, though it might make sense on Pervo's dating.

39. Their support also confirms that Peter's speech is on behalf of the Christian community of "witnesses," not for himself alone. Cf. Aeschines *Tim.* 29: only one who upholds the city's "common interests" (κοινά) should address the citizen assembly.

40. These are aorist passive participles of ἵστημι, which also appears in this form in Acts 11:13; Luke 18:11, 40; 19:8 and nowhere else in the NT.

41. With Haenchen, *Acts*, 178n1; Fitzmyer, *Acts*, 251.

42. E.g., Xen. *Anab.* 5.1.2, 5; *Cyr.* 7.5.55; Dion. Hal. *Ant. rom.* 7.47.1; Cic. *Verr.* 2.4.64.142; *Rosc. Amer.* 1.1; 22.60; Virg. *Aen.* 11.342; Plut. *Cic.* 16.3; *Coriol.* 16.2; Tac. *Ann.* 16.29; Pliny *Ep.* 9.13.18; Lucian *Peregr.* 31; *'Abot R. Nat.* 6 A; 1 Cor 14:30 (though cf. Suet. *Rhet.* 6 for an exceptional case).

43. See more fully Keener, *Matthew*, 164; comment on Acts 13:16.

44. Soards, *Speeches*, 139 (on the LXX); Fitzmyer, *Acts*, 251 (citing Demosth. *Cor.* 291; *Fals. leg.* 336; Philost. *Vit. Apoll.* 5.33).

45. Even in Galilee, some natural acoustic settings existed that would amplify one's voice range (Crisler, "Acoustics," 134–37); the temple steps could have functioned similarly.

46. Edith L. Blumhofer, personal correspondence, April 18, 2006. Likewise, John Sung preached to thousands without amplification (Sung, *Diaries*, 112).

Since these sites were designed for acoustics, an outdoor analogy might work better for Peter's preaching here (perhaps from the steps to the Court of Women, in the outer court). Benjamin Franklin, skeptical of reports about George Whitefield's audiences, experimented and discovered that as many as thirty thousand people could hear him at a time.[47]

Had the tongues speaking (2:4) and probably ecstatic behavior (2:13) not attracted attention, Peter's hearing might have been smaller; so many noises competed for attention at festivals that it was difficult for any one speaker to command attention.[48] That Peter "uttered" (ἀπεφθέγξατο) his words may suggest inspiration (see 2:4),[49] though the term is applicable for any sort of solemn pronouncement (see comment on Acts 2:4). Teachers often lectured in temples, and there is no reason to believe that the Jerusalem temple was an exception.[50] At least in the Hellenistic world, public speakers often gave speeches at festivals,[51] and the more effective of them may have drawn significant crowds.

Both the objection and Peter's response reflect the familiar challenge-and-riposte scenario of ancient public speech.[52] Often speakers made points, for the entertainment of the audience, at their adversary's expense.[53] Peter instead deflects the mockery with a potentially humorous response that does not shame the hecklers.[54] This reflects the rhetorical desire to win over parts of the audience one may need,[55] not any deficiency in the boldness expected of an orator;[56] Peter has a more serious target in mind for explicit denunciation after his speech has turned to a more serious note (2:23). The transition to 2:16 sounds abrupt,[57] but we should keep in mind that this is a speech summary, not a complete speech (cf. 2:40).

b. The Address

Speakers in Acts address crowds appropriately as "men of Galilee" (1:11), "men of Judea" (2:14) or "of Israel" (2:22; 3:12; 5:35; 13:16; 21:28), "men of Athens" (17:22), and "men of Ephesus" (19:35); although Luke has varied the expression less than he could have, it was a common form of address. Peter's address to "Judean men" and

47. Noll, *History*, 93. (Conversely, in some locations in Africa I have found it difficult to project my voice for even a thousand people in a closed space without a sound system—but undoubtedly in part because I have been spoiled by my modern Western dependence on technology.)

48. Dio Chrys. *Or.* 27.5–7 complains that such competition virtually silenced philosophers (esp. *Or.* 27.7); although this would not likely be true of teachers in the Jewish temple, only the most popular (cf. Luke 19:47–20:1) would gather large crowds.

49. Bruce, *Acts¹*, 88; cf. Lake and Cadbury, *Commentary*, 21; Haenchen, *Acts*, 178n4; Marguerat, *Actes*, 87; Parsons, *Acts*, 41 (comparing also the "sound" in Acts 2:6, 14). Certainly, Acts 2 emphasizes preaching empowered by the Spirit as well as the message about Jesus (cf. Dyk, "Teologia").

50. Cf. *'Abot R. Nat.* 38 A; *b. Pesaḥ.* 26a; Mark 12:35; Luke 19:47; 20:1; 21:37; John 7:14, 28; 8:20; 18:20; more sources in Liefeld, "Preacher," 191; Safrai, "Temple," 905.

51. See Men. Rhet. 1.3, 365.27–29. Cf. possibly Libanius *Descr.* 29.1, but this could refer to discussions about festivals afterward.

52. Cf., e.g., Malina and Rohrbaugh, *Gospels*, 141; deSilva, *Honor*, 29–31; for examples, see Pliny *Ep.* 1.5.5–6 and passim in ancient literature.

53. E.g., Xen. *Cyr.* 2.2.16; Cic. *De or.* 2.58.236; *Fin.* 4.26.73; Plut. *Demosth.* 11.4. This method sometimes, as in Cicero's case, made enemies unnecessarily, contrary to Cicero's own advice in *Or. Brut.* 26.88–90 (though more mildly, cf. *Brut.* 43.158; 93.322).

54. Scholars sometimes note the comic nature of the interchange (Dunn, *Acts*, 28; Pelikan, *Acts*, 53); on humor in Acts, cf. Goldingay, "Comic Acts?"; Grassi, *Laugh*.

55. See comment on Acts 7:51–53 (although Stephen rejects the convention). Even Cicero is more restrained with someone whom he cannot afford to alienate (Cic. *Mur.* 29.60).

56. For orators' expected boldness, see comment on Acts 4:13.

57. An abrupt change of subject can be acceptable in rhetoric (see Rowe, "Style," 145; Porter, "Paul and Letters," 582).

"residents of Jerusalem"[58] ought not to be pressed as if Peter welcomes all Jerusalemites to listen but only adult males from the rest of Judea. Thus classical Athenian orators regularly addressed their audiences as ὦ ἄνδρες or (very often) ὦ ἄνδρες Ἀθηναῖοι, or occasionally other combinations with ἄνδρες, especially ἄνδρες δικασταί (men who are judges or jurors),[59] as in Aeschines,[60] Isaeus,[61] Lysias,[62] Demosthenes,[63] and military speakers in Xenophon.[64] In classical Athens, an honorable man in public addressed only "men," who constituted citizen assemblies and could vote in them; when women and aliens were present, a speaker might even be obliged to omit a salutation.[65] But Jerusalem is not classical Athens, and it is reasonable that an honorable man in other settings (e.g., theaters, amphitheaters, and synagogues) might retain the convention of explicitly addressing only adult males even though others might be welcome to listen and profit.[66]

The custom of explicitly addressing "men" hardly died out in classical Athens; one addressing assemblies elsewhere employed the same language. In the late first century, Dio Chrysostom still addresses his audiences as "men of" various locations: "men of Rhodes" (ἄνδρες Ῥόδιοι, 31.8); "men of Tarsus" (34.37); Apameans as simply "men" (ὦ ἄνδρες, 35.1); "men of Nicomedia" (38.1, 5, 21, 30); "men, citizens" for Prusans, his fellow citizens (40.1; 44.1; 45.1; 50.1; simply "O men" in 46.1, 5). We read addresses to "men of Athens" (Lucian Dem. 11) and to jurors as "men of the jury" (ὦ ἄνδρες δικασταί; Lucian Hall 32);[67] when all Ephesus attends Apollonius's lecture, he addresses his hearers as ὦ ἄνδρες (Philost. Vit. Apoll. 8.26).

In using ἄνδρες rather than the normally more gender-neutral ἄνθρωποι, Luke simply employs the language considered appropriate in his era's rhetorical culture.[68] The vocative plural for ἄνθρωπος appears in biblical Greek, the Apostolic Fathers, and Josephus only at Prov 8:4. By contrast, the vocative plural for ἀνήρ appears thirty-two times in the NT (albeit twenty-nine of them in Acts),[69] seven times in 1 Esdras (1 Esd 3:18, 24; 4:2, 12, 14, 32, 34), as many as three times elsewhere in the LXX (Jer 4:4; 19:3; 4 Macc 8:19), four times in 1 Clement (1 Clem 16.17; 37.1; 43.4; 62.1), and fourteen times in Josephus.[70] This is the usage we would have to expect

58. The term "residents" here, whatever else it means, must at least include the Diaspora Jews, some of them possibly pilgrims, subsumed under the same term in Acts 2:5.

59. Isaeus Pyrr. 1; Astyph. 16; Euphil. 10; Hagnoth. 1 (frg. 1); Demes. frg. 6; Eumath. frgs. 18, 20; Lysias Or. 14.32, §142; 14.41, §143; 15.1, §144; 17.1, §148; 18.1, §149; 18.20, §151; Demosth. Aphob. 1.1, 3, 4; Fals. leg. 4.

60. E.g., Aeschines Embassy 1, 4, 7, 55, 80, 87, 88, 108, 129, 135; Ctes. 179; Tim. 38, 41, 51, 69, 70.

61. Isaeus Menec. 17, 38, 44; Pyrr. 65; Nicost. 1–2, 13, 14, 21, 27; Dicaeog. 5, 29, 34, 35, 38, 41; Philoct. 9, 12, 39, 51; Apollod. 37; Ciron 1, 7, 21; Astyph. 6–7, 14, 26, 28, 34, 35; Aristarch. 1–3, 8, 11–12, 14, 18–19, 22; Hagnias 12, 37, 38; Cleon. 24–25, §37; 29, §37.

62. E.g., Lysias Or. 1.1, 11, 17, 34, 37, 47 (Murder of Eratosthenes); 6.41, §106 (equivalent to simply Ἀθηναῖοι, 6.50, §107).

63. E.g., Demosth. Fals. leg. 3, 4, 62, 64, 67.

64. E.g., ἄνδρες σύμμαχοι (to allies), Xen. Cyr. 5.3.30; 6.1.6; ἄνδρες φίλοι (to friends or soldiers), 5.5.44; 7.1.29. Later, see "men of Athens" in Hermog. Inv. 1.1.96 (twice), 97, 98, 99; 1.5.107; 2.7.124; 4.1.171.

65. As in Demosth. Epitaph. 1 (see DeWitt, "Demosthenes," 7:6–7 n. a).

66. In conservative circles, even private conversations with women were discouraged (Eurip. El. 343–44; Theophr. Char. 28.3; Val. Max. 5.3.10–12; Livy 34.2.9; 34.4.18 [but cf. 34.5.7–10]; Sir 9:9; 42:12; John 4:27; m. ʾAb. 1:5; Ketub. 7:6; t. Šabb. 1:14; b. Ber. 43b, bar.; ʿErub. 53b), and the common use of the address suggests that speakers sometimes politely ignored women's public presence. Perhaps it was considered poor taste to seem to address other men's wives; perhaps it was simply convention.

67. See further Lucian Indictment, passim, e.g., 21, 30, 33, 34; Tyr. 1; Disowned 1, 6, 11, 14, 15, 18.

68. Indeed, he can occasionally use ἄνδρες to include women (Acts 17:34; so Bock, Acts, 572); Greek could also use the term to mean "person" generally (BDAG). Augustine explicitly addressed "men" in mixed audiences (MacMullen, Second Church, 97–98).

69. Luke accounts for a disproportionate share of the use of ἀνήρ in the NT; but what counts here is the plural use in speeches, and Luke has the majority of speeches following good Greek form.

70. Jos. Ant. 4.177; 6.20; 8.227; 11.38, 169; 14.172; 15.127, 382; 18.320; War 2.211; 3.472; 6.328; 7.323; Life 141.

unless Luke had a deliberate program of gender inclusivity unexpected for his era (in contrast to our own) and one that took precedence over rhetorical acceptability for his apologetic target audience.

The use of the masculine might presuppose an androcentric society, but it did not necessarily exclude female hearers from being present (see clearly, e.g., Acts 25:23–24); a later philosopher regularly speaks of the wise ἀνήρ (e.g., Porph. *Marc.* 32.497), even when writing to exhort his *wife*.[71] When Zeus addresses the deities of heaven as ὦ ἄνδρες θεοί (Lucian Z. *Rants* 15), both genders are apparently present (Aphrodite is there, Z. *Rants* 10). Following a useful rhetorical strategy, Peter shifts from the more formal "men" in Acts 2:14, 22 to build more rapport with "men and brothers" in 2:29; the audience's response of "men and brothers" in 2:37 is a sign of his effectiveness.[72] Rhetorical histories often created different, appropriate introductions for different speakers; Luke lacked either desire or ability to do so for his précis summaries.

Rhetoricians sometimes advised calling attention to important points in advance.[73] Peter's invitation for his audience to "hear" him (also 2:22; 4:10; 7:2; 13:16, 40; 15:13; 22:1; 26:3) has a long history of rhetorical precedent, both Jewish[74] and Gentile.[75] "Let it be known" (2:14) reflects daring speech, typically confronting Israel (4:10; 13:38; 28:28);[76] it may seem daring by implying the speakers' ignorance (generally not complimentary; see comment on Acts 17:23).[77] (Of course, Peter had no rhetorical training at all [cf. 4:13], but rhetorical texts at least provide us an objective control for understanding speech conventions of the era.)

Speakers often took the subject of their *exordium* from the nature of the case before them and used it to attract hearers' attention, inform them, and secure their favor.[78] Before Peter can explain what the disciples' speaking in tongues means (2:16–21) and its consequences for the audience (2:22–40), he must briefly answer (hence dispense with) the hecklers' objection (2:15). Peter would have many hearers at this time of day. Undoubtedly, they were on the Temple Mount (see discussion on Acts 2:1), and the temple courts would have been "quite busy"[79] at about 9:00 a.m.,[80] when Peter

---

71. He expressly emphasizes that gender as a bodily matter is irrelevant (Porph. *Marc.* 33.511–12).

72. Witherington, *Acts*, 138–39. For building rapport, see, e.g., Kennedy, *New Testament Interpretation*, 36.

73. See, e.g., the more elaborate form of προπαρασκευή in Anderson, *Glossary*, 104–5 (citing Quint. *Inst.* 9.2.17); less elaborately, Porter, "Paul and Letters," 582 (on Phil 1:12).

74. E.g., Luke 14:35; 18:6; Mark 4:3, 9, 23; 7:14; Matt 11:15; Jas 2:5; Gen 4:23; 23:6, 8; 27:8, 43; Exod 18:19; Deut 4:1; 5:1; Josh 3:9; Prov 1:8; 4:1, 10; Job 13:6, 17; Sir 3:1; 6:23; 16:24; 23:7; 31:22; Bar 2:16; 3:2, 4, 9; 4:9; Jdt 5:5; 7:9; 8:11, 32; 14:1; Tob 6:13, 16; *Test. Dan* 1:2; *Test. Jud.* 20:1; *Test. Iss.* 6:1. The proposed allusion specifically to Joel 1:2 here (Evans, "Prophetic Setting," 217) is thus forced.

75. E.g., Xen. *Anab.* 5.1.8; *Rhet. Alex.* 19, 1433b.19–23; Cic. *Mil.* 2.4; Philost. *Hrk.* 8.1; Epict. *Diatr.* 2.19.12; 3.24.68.

76. These are the only four occurrences of γνωστόν with ἔστω in early Christian literature. The phrase can hardly be daring in its LXX occurrences, all to the king (1 Esd 2:18; Ezra 4:12, 13; 5:8), but it does appear dramatic.

77. But rhetoricians also appreciated using wit to set hearers at ease; see Anderson, *Glossary*, 126 (citing Theon *Progymnasmata* (*RG* 2:99); Demet. *Style* 128; Cic. *De or.* 2.216–89; 3.205; *Or. Brut.* 138; Quint. *Inst.* 6.3).

78. Montefusco, "Exordium," 272 (for the subject, citing Arist. *Rhet.* 1415a 26f; Cic. *De or.* 2.321; for the purpose, citing Cic. *Inv.* 1.20; *Rhet. Alex.* 1436a 33ff.).

79. In the words of Blue, "Influence," 483.

80. Calculating Jerusalem sunrise in this season at around 6:00 a.m. Public business started early; in Rome, clients approached their patrons starting around dawn (e.g., Hor. *Sat.* 1.1.9–10; *Ep.* 2.1.103–5; Mart. *Epig.* 3.36.1–3); senators also could assemble at daybreak (Cic. *Fam.* 1.2.4; Plut. *Cic.* 15.3; 19.1); even schools started then (Watson, "Education," 311–12); in summer, Romans counted "late morning" as before 8:00 or 9:00 a.m. (Carcopino, *Life*, 152). For early schedules for much of Mediterranean life, see further Keener, *John*, 1098.

was speaking. Given the temple's morning offering and prayers, the day was already well under way.[81] If the synagogue's three hours of prayer known to us in later sources were observed in this period, the disciples and other Jews may have been praying at this hour (2:15), as at the sixth (10:9) and ninth (3:1) hours when prayer was held,[82] although this cannot be certain[83] (see comment on Acts 3:1).

c. The Third Hour

Days and nights were rounded to quarters, and hence the most common hour designations in Luke-Acts are the third hour (Acts 23:23),[84] the sixth hour (Luke 23:44; Acts 10:9), and the ninth hour (Luke 23:44; Acts 3:1; 10:3, 30).

Different peoples calculated hours from different chronological points: Babylonians between sunrises; Athenians between sunsets; the Roman and Egyptian official day, from midnight to midnight; but most ordinary people from sunrise to sunset, though such day lengths changed with the seasons.[85] The days here would be calculated from sunrise; this was common practice and also the standard Judean practice.[86] Although most people would have simply estimated time based on the position of the sun in the sky, sundials could be very precise.[87]

As suggested in Acts 2:15, however, the favored time for drunkenness was evening banquets. (Peter here assumes this obvious premise, which would complete his argument that they are not drunk.)[88] Scholars estimate mealtimes for some ancient Mediterranean cultures. Normally the major Roman meal (the *cena*) started around the ninth hour, which began (depending on the length of the day) between 2:31 and 3:46 p.m. by modern reckoning in summer or between 1:20 and 2:13 p.m. in winter and lasted for at least two and a half hours; it could last after dark and, for Greeks, often lasted "well after dark."[89] The wealthy might begin normal meals at the tenth hour and more formal banquets at the ninth (Mart. *Epig.* 4.8); those maligned as particularly decadent might start even at the seventh (Hor. *Sat.* 2.8).[90]

Although such hours supposedly allowed banqueters to finish before dark,[91] evening banquets sometimes lasted into the night (Rom 13:12–13; 1 Thess 5:7).[92] Thus we read in many texts of people partying into the night, walking home drunk in the dark,

---

81. On nonfestival days, work typically began after prayers at dawn; children also began school early and returned home by noon (Safrai, "Education," 954).

82. Oesterley, *Liturgy*, 125 (attested in the *Apostolic Tradition*, Tertullian, Origen, and Cyprian).

83. Note the prudent caution of Falk, "Prayer Literature," 274. Commentators usually note that on normal days Jews did not breakfast until 10:00 a.m. (Lake and Cadbury, *Commentary*, 21; Munck, *Acts*, 17; Bruce, *Acts¹*, 89; Barrett, *Acts*, 135). Greek practice varied in different periods (Dion. Hal. *Lit. Comp.* 3; Walter Miller, LCL 1:19n1 to Xen. *Cyrop.*; Keener, *John* , 1230; for this period, see esp. Smith, *Symposium*, 20–21).

84. Cyril Jer. *Cat. Lect.* 17.19 (Martin, *Acts*, 28) connects the third hour in Acts 2:15 with that in Mark 15:25; although this is not impossible, we should note that Luke omits the latter time description. Luke does not symbolically reinscribe time the way that John may do.

85. So Pliny E. *N.H.* 2.79.188.

86. Le Cornu, *Acts*, 93; Jeremias, *Parables*, 136n21; e.g., *Exod. Rab.* 41:7. Apart from legal contracts, Romans counted from sunrise as well; noon was VI (not XII) on their sundials (Morris, *John*, 158n90). Calculating from midnight (cf. Walker, "Hours") was not the norm.

87. For pocket sundials (though rare), see Casson, *Travel*, 176–77; for water clocks, see comment on Acts 24:4. Some scholars have argued that a particular device found at Qumran is a detailed sundial (Albani and Glessmer, "Instrument de mesures"; Hollenbach, "Roundel"), but others have demurred (Levy, "Bad Timing").

88. On enthymemes as (by one definition) incomplete syllogisms, see Vinson, "Enthymemes," 119. On the category of time in refutations as relevant here, see Parsons, *Acts*, 42 (citing Theon *Progymn.* 93–94).

89. Smith, *Symposium*, 21. Vitruv. *Arch.* 6.4.1 expects dining after dark in winter.

90. Stambaugh, *City*, 200–201.

91. This was important, since the streets were often not safe (Jeffers, *World*, 31).

92. E.g., Alciph. *Paras.* 10 (Stemphylochaeron to Trapezocharon), 3.46, ¶2; Statius *Silv.* 2.4.6; Sen. Y. *Ep. Lucil.* 95.21; Tac. *Ann.* 3.37; see further Winter, *Left Corinth*, 189.

and so forth.[93] Admittedly, it was exceptional for a person to leave a night banquet so late that he would come across another who had started the day early (Dio Cass. 69.18). One who partied till midnight and (having drunk too much) could not get up the next morning was subject to ridicule (Lucian *Hermot.* 11). All-night parties appear in connection with weddings (Xen. Eph. *Anthia* 1.8) and festivals (5.1, 7; Libanius *Descr.* 5.9). On other occasions, however, all-night revels could be subject to ridicule or criticism.[94]

Thus lazy banqueters (and even a few people considered efficient in their daily business) might spend most of their night in banquets, sleeping over the hangover until noon.[95] Staying up as late as one wished and sleeping in as long as one wished were marks of excessive leisure, though tolerable for rulers (*m. Ber.* 1:2),[96] the retired (Pliny Y. *Ep.* 3.1.4; 7.3.2),[97] and those on vacation (9.36.1).[98]

If some condemned late-night partying, it was in any case thought better (and far more common) than partying during the day (2 Pet 2:13).[99] The few people who were said to start drinking in the morning and continue through the day were considered exceptional and viewed quite negatively.[100] Lucian satirizes the wine deity Dionysus as drunk even early in the day (Lucian *Parl. G.* 4). That the Germans reveled in the day as well as the night without shame was considered unusual enough to be noteworthy (Tac. *Germ.* 22).[101] Some Jewish sages contended that morning sleep (as well as noon wine) would exclude a person from the coming world (*m. 'Ab.* 3:10). Those who banqueted all day were viewed as lazy even if they slept at night (Dio Chrys. *Or.* 8.13).

Before modern lighting, sleep schedules often followed sunlight. Many felt that night was properly for sleeping[102] and that a disciplined person should rise early;[103] sleeping at night and being awake during the day were considered universal customs.[104] But not all nocturnal activity was condemned. Staying up after dark to write letters or speeches by lamplight was not, of course, attributed to laziness.[105] Some Gentile intellectuals[106] and Jewish teachers studied at night,[107] especially those who had to work during the day.[108] A biographer who mentions that Pythagoras was awake at night hastily explains

93. Stambaugh, *City*, 201, citing Pliny *Ep.* 3.12; Prop. *Eleg.* 3.10.25–26; 4.8; Petron. *Sat.* 73.6; 78.6–7.

94. E.g., Sen. E. *Controv.* 2.1.15; Philo *Cher.* 92–93; Suet. *Jul.* 52.1; *Tib.* 42.1; *Tit.* 7.1; Libanius *Descr.* 6.6. Partying at night could be said to dull the senses (Livy 39.15.9). Toner, *Culture*, 151, cites emperors' public nocturnal parties and the criticisms they invited (citing Suet. *Calig.* 18; Tac. *Ann.* 14.20–21).

95. Plut. *Alex.* 23.5 (of Alexander); Sen. Y. *Ep. Lucil.* 83.14 (who would have normally considered this behavior lazy; 122.1–2; cf. Seneca Elder *Controv.* 1.pref. 8); Aul. Gel. 7.10.5; Philo *Cher.* 92–93; cf. also Carcopino, *Life*, 151. Hangovers could include headaches and belching (e.g., Alciph. *Farm.* 30 [Scopiades to Cotion], 3.32, alleging that the hangover lasted two days).

96. Le Cornu, *Acts*, 93.

97. Pliny held a generally high view of the privileges of retirement (*Ep.* 4.23.3).

98. In *Ep.* 9.36.1, Pliny woke about sunrise, per his habit, but remained in bed afterward.

99. Cf. also Kelly, *Peter*, 340 (rightly citing Eccl 10:16; Isa 5:11; *As. Mos.* 7:4).

100. Dion. Hal. *Demosth.* 12 (quoting Demosth. *Con.* 3). Van der Horst, "Parallels to Acts," 56, and Fitzmyer, *Acts*, 251, appropriately cite Cic. *Phil.* 2.41.104. The sailors in Xen. Eph. *Anthia* 1.13 apparently were drunk the night before.

101. A Roman who so behaved invited criticism (Sen. E. *Controv.* 2.6.9).

102. Dio Chrys. *Or.* 3.81; Fronto *Fer. als.* 3.8–9 (cf. *Ad M. Caes.* 1.5.1). Sleep's appropriate time was night (Sil. It. 4.88–89; excepting the afternoon siesta during midday heat, see Keener, *John*, 592; comment on Acts 26:13).

103. Dio Chrys. *Or.* 52.1 (where he rises at the first hour, apparently late for him); cf. Quint. Curt. 3.2.15.

104. Artem. *Oneir.* 1.8. Keener, *John*, 1098–99, surveys sources on early rising.

105. Fronto *Ad M. Caes.* 4.5.3 (letters); Ker, "Nocturnal Writers" (speeches and books; Quint. *Inst.* 10.3.26). But people more often studied in the morning (Vitruv. *Arch.* 6.4.1).

106. Cic. *Att.* 7.7; 13.26, 38; Plut. *Demosth.* 8.4; 12.5–6, though Philost. *Vit. soph.* 1.21.518 seems to view it as unusual (and one worked by night so he could study by day; Val. Max. 8.7.ext. 11).

107. E.g., 1QS VI, 6–7; t. *Šabb.* 1:13; b. *'Abod. Zar.* 3b; *Ber.* 43b, bar.; *'Erub.* 18b; 65a; *Tamid* 32b; *Pesiq. Rab Kah.* 7:4; *Exod. Rab.* 47:5; *Lev. Rab.* 19:1; *Num. Rab.* 15:16; Safrai, "Home," 745; Schnackenburg, *John*, 1:366.

108. Safrai, "Education," 964–65.

that this was due to his attention to astronomy, not partying.[109] Sometimes one reads of individuals who simply experienced difficulty sleeping at night.[110] Ancient literature attests a wide variety of causes for sleeplessness then, as today.[111]

3. Biblical Explanation for the Event (2:16–21)

Peter's argument will be that the disciples' inspired praise in other languages (Acts 2:4) represents the promised eschatological prophetic gift (2:17–18); this being the case, the eschatological time has arrived (2:17), the time of salvation in which this gift is available to all who call on the Lord's name (2:21, 39).[112] The longest component in Peter's attempt to persuade will be a midrashic argument contending that the "Lord's" name on which they must call (in baptism) is Jesus (2:24–36, esp. 2:38).

In 2:16, Peter begins to interpret the phenomenon of speaking in tongues for his audience.[113] Peter comments on "this" (τοῦτο, 2:16), referring back to the crowd's question about "this" (2:12),[114] which presumably referred in turn to "this" (ταύτης) sound (2:6, referring to the disciples' speaking in other languages in 2:4): "this" sound of other languages fulfills Joel's promise of Spirit-inspired speech in the eschatological time (Acts 2:17–18).[115] Like the Paul of the epistles,[116] Luke and the apostles he cites read their own time in light of Scripture, as a time of fulfillment.

Most scholars recognize the quotation from Joel (Acts 2:17–21) as programmatic for Acts in the same way that Isaiah's quotation about Spirit and mission was for the Gospel (Luke 4:18–19).[117] Functioning programmatically, this passage conditions

109. Iambl. *V.P.* 25.112.

110. E.g., Suet. *Aug.* 78.1–2 (Augustus); Fronto *Ad am.* 2.2. The case of Claudius (Suet. *Claud.* 33.2) may relate to banquets (33.1) and women (33.2).

111. Lack of sleep could stem from self-discipline (Xen. *Mem.* 2.1.1; Dion. Hal. *Ant. rom.* 9.64.2; Livy 23.18.12; Sallust *Catil.* 54.4; *Jug.* 85.33; Sen. E. *Controv.* 1.pref. 17; Vell. Paterc. 2.41.2; 2.88.2; Mus. Ruf. 18B, p. 120.4; Sil. It. 9.4–5; Quint. Curt. 3.2.15; Plut. *Cic.* 36.3; Pliny *Ep.* 3.5.8–9; Iambl. *V.P.* 28.153; Libanius *Maxim* 1.4, 10, 13, 17; 2.12; *Encomium* 5.12; *Anecdote* 2.10; 3.30–31, 35), literary activity (Cic. *Att.* 13.26, 38; Ker, "Nocturnal Writers"), contemplation (Philost. *Vit. Apoll.* 7.30), Torah (Ps 119:55, 148; 1QS VI, 7–8; *Gen. Rab.* 17:5) or repentance (*Jos. Asen.* 18:4 MSS), sickness (Hippocr. *Reg. Ac. Dis.* 1–2; *Prorr.* 1.135–36; Fronto *Ad am.* 2.2; *Ad M. Caes.* 5.58 [73]), lovesickness (Ach. Tat. 1.6; *PGM* 101.5–7), jealousy (Plut. *Themist.* 3.3–4), fear (Pub. Syr. 359; Plut. *Alex.* 31.4; Sil. It. 13.256–57; cf. the eve of battle in Quint. Curt. 4.13.23; 7.8.2), anxiety caused by vice (Plut. *Virt.* 2, *Mor.* 100F), concern for others (Pliny *Ep.* 7.5.1; Fronto *Ad M. Caes.* 3.16.1; Symm. *Ep.* 1.48; perhaps 2 Cor 11:27–28), or other anxiety (Hom. *Il.* 2.2–3; Aristoph. *Lys.* 27; Livy 40.56.9; Plut. *Cic.* 35.3; *Alex.* 31.4; Ps 102:7); hunger (Libanius *Invect.* 6.16); mourning (Hom. *Il.* 24.4–6; Ovid *Metam.* 14.423–25; *Tristia* 3.8.27) or joyful reunion (*Jub.* 31:24); withholding of sleep for torture (Aul. Gel. 7.4.4; Cic. *Pis.* 19.43; Val. Max. 9.2.ext. 1); idleness during the day (*m. 'Ab.* 3:4); or hardships (Xen. *Anab.* 3.1.11; 7.6.36; Arrian *Ind.* 34.7; Gen 31:40; perhaps 2 Cor 11:26–27; Char. *Chaer.* 1.2.3).

112. Cf. Lampe, "Wolves," 256; Lindars, *Apologetic*, 361; differently, Zehnle, *Pentecost Discourse*, 27–28 (who thinks that Acts 2:25–32 establishes Jesus's messiahship, and 2:33–35 his lordship). Turner, *Power*, 346–47, is probably correct that the Spirit continues the salvation the disciples already had before Pentecost; but I think Luke emphasizes the soteriological dimension of the Spirit less than Turner believes (cf. Cho, *Spirit and Kingdom*, 51).

113. Johnson, *Acts*, 53–54, contrasts expectations that priests at oracular shrines interpret ecstatic speech; but note questions above regarding the nature of the speech's unintelligibility (comment on Acts 2:4). As Acts 2:15 answers the complaint in 2:13, so 2:16–18 agrees with the affirmation in 2:11 (cf. Parsons, *Acts*, 42).

114. With, e.g., Pesch, *Apostelgeschichte*, 1:119.

115. For this use of the demonstrative pronoun, see comment on Acts 2:12. Haenchen, *Acts*, 179, notes that "prophecy, elsewhere distinguished from the gift of tongues, is here identified with it to facilitate the scriptural proof."

116. See Hays, *Echoes*, 170–72 (similar to the Qumran scrolls, but the latter do not regard "the decisive eschatological event" as having happened already; but cf. Aune, *Cultic Setting*).

117. Many scholars parallel Jesus's opening speech in Luke 4:18–27 with Peter's in Acts 2:17–40 (e.g., Zehnle, *Pentecost Discourse*, 128; cf. Neirynck, "Luke 4,16–30," 376–78, among other comparisons). For these

how we should read most later "references to the Spirit in Acts."[118] Choice of a new explicit programmatic passage for his second volume does not nullify the use of Isa 61 in his first volume, as if Isaiah's eschatological justice emphasis were meant to be forgotten. The outpouring of the Spirit actually has social implications and effects (Acts 2:44–45; 4:32–35), but this is not Luke's central focus in this volume (cf. 6:2–4). Moreover, in view of Luke 24:45–49, Isaiah remains implicitly in view in Acts 1:8, which summarizes the theme and plot of Acts. What all these "programmatic" texts have in common is God's Spirit empowering God's agents for their mission.

Greeks as well as Jews valued quotations from ancient authorities (albeit from different authorities);[119] Aristotle opined that ancient witnesses (the poets) were better than recent ones because they were universally known and not susceptible to corruption (Arist. *Rhet.* 1.15.13, 17, 1375b). In the broader urban world, hearers expected orators to demonstrate mnemonic proficiency,[120] and introducing appropriate literary allusions was a sign of intellectual respectability.[121]

Quoting the words of prophets, however, was more authoritative than simply citing a text from the amorphous Greek literary "canon"; it was God speaking.[122] Thus Peter can say, "God says" (λέγει ὁ θεός), a Septuagintal expression (2 Sam 23:3; Isa 40:1; 41:14; 44:6) equivalent to the more pervasive "The Lord says."[123]

a. Comparisons to Pesher Application (2:16)

Commentators most frequently cite parallels to the kind of exegesis found here in the Qumran scrolls,[124] where the pesher application of texts to the present time is most obvious.[125] The writers of the Qumran scrolls did not necessarily deny a historical meaning relevant to an earlier generation (e.g., 1QpHab II, 3–4)[126] but insisted that it also held a special meaning relevant to the final generation, that is, their own time (e.g., 2.5–6).[127]

---

as key passages, see also Baarlink, "Bedeutung." Ruthven, "Covenant," treats Isa 59:19–21 as programmatic (noting in "Covenant," 34, that I prefer Joel 2). The strength of Ruthven's case is the many details he finds paralleled (e.g., geographic universality in Isa 59:19; some motifs are widespread, but cumulatively, the recurrence of the rarer samples, such as βίαιος, suggests at least that this passage informed Luke's pneumatology). But even if this text offers a framework, it is an implicit one that cannot function as programmatic in the same way the explicit Joel text does.

118. Johnson, *Function*, 41.

119. See also, e.g., Black, *Rhetoric of Gospel*, 128.

120. E.g., Sen. E. *Controv.*, passim; Eunapius *Lives* 502; see more fully our introduction, ch. 8, sect. 2.c.iii.

121. See comment on Acts 17:28.

122. E.g., 4Q158 1–2 11–12 (with Gen 32:32); *Let. Aris.* 155; *m. Soṭah* 9:6; *t. Soṭah* 12:2; *Mek. Shir.* 6 (Lauterbach, 2:43–44); *Esth. Rab.* 10:5; Rom 9:17; Matt 19:4–5 (with Gen 2:24); *1 Clem.* 56.3.

123. Peter might prefer "God" here so as not to confuse the midrashic application that he will draw from Acts 2:21, but it is probably simply for stylistic variation (cf. 7:7).

124. E.g., Tiede, *Prophecy*, 89; on this technique in the Qumran scrolls, see Dimant, "Pesharim"; Brooke, "Pesharim"; idem, "Interpretation" (comparing and contrasting Qumran and NT approaches); Aune, *Dictionary of Rhetoric*, 347–50; Longenecker, *Exegesis*, 31, 38–45; Fitzmyer, "Quotations," 325–30; Brownlee, "Interpretation," 60–62 (on 1QpHab); Lim, "Orientation" (also on 1QpHab); Patte, *Hermeneutic*, 211ff.; cf. more briefly Sandmel, *Judaism*, 101; Moule, *Birth*, 61–62; Nickelsburg, *Literature*, 127; Mickelsen, *Interpreting*, 23. Some think that the pesharim were even publicly performed (Snyder, "Naughts and Crosses"; though the analogies may be too late for relevance).

125. E.g., *pesher* or *pishro* in 1QpHab I, 2 (cf. I, 6, 8, 11, 13, 15); II, 5, 8, 12 (cf. II, 1, 15); III, 4, 7 (cf. III, 9); IV, 5, 10, 14; V, 3, 7, 9 (cf. V, 16); VI, 3, 6, 10 (cf. VI, 16); VII, 4, 7, 10, 15; VIII, 1, 8, 16; IX, 4, 9 (cf. IX, 16); X, 3, 9, 15; XI, 4, 12; XII, 2, 7, 12; XIII, 1. On pesher exegesis, see, e.g., Brooke, "Pesharim"; cf. Harries, "Trends"; even with reference to dreams, Finkel, "Pesher."

126. Likewise 4Q166 I–II (for Hosea's generation).

127. Also, e.g., 4Q167 frg. 2. Some pesharim, in fact, inverted the original sense of the text (see Silberman, "Unriddling," 342).

As Fitzmyer notes, early Christians shared with Qumran "the common conviction that they are living in the 'end of days' (1QpHab 2:5; 9:6; 1QSa 1:1; 4QpIsᵃ A:8; 4QFlor 1:2, 12, 15, 19; CD 4:4, 6:11; etc.; cf. Acts 2:17; ...). This conviction enables both groups to refer sayings of the Old Testament prophets and writings to events or tenets in their own history or beliefs."[128] Longenecker finds examples of pesher interpretation in Peter's speeches in Acts (and in 1 Peter), in contrast to Paul's speeches and letters.[129] But he believes that whereas Qumran's eschatology was mainly proleptic and anticipated, early Christians believed that the messianic era had arrived because Jesus was in fact the Messiah.[130] Pesher thus supplies some interpreters with one background for christocentric interpretation.[131] The approach is much more common in Luke's Petrine sermons than in, for example, Paul;[132] not distinctively Lukan, it might reflect Luke's knowledge of early apostolic preaching.[133]

"Pesher" sorts of interpretation might also appear in some other sects considered peripheral to common Judaism.[134] But pesher methods also bear resemblance to interpretive techniques of the later rabbis, probably reflecting some more widespread principles.[135] Certainly, the rabbis were able to apply many prophetic promises specifically to the messianic era (cf. also Acts 3:18, 24).[136] Abraham saw not only Egyptian bondage in Gen 15:13 but also the four kingdoms (*Gen. Rab.* 44:17).[137] Likewise, "Esau" in the biblical text could become Rome (*Gen. Rab.* 63:9).[138] For that matter, the point of *all* midrash was "to make yesterday's text (which is the word of God for all time) meaningful and nourishing for today."[139] Even Josephus is ready to loosely apply biblical prophecies of a coming king, applying them to Vespasian (*War* 6.312–13).

b. Adapting Joel's Text (2:17)

We should not think that Luke's slight changes to the text of Joel[140] reflect ignorance of the text's correct wording, either on his own part or attributed by him to Peter.

128. Fitzmyer, "Christianity in Light of the Scrolls," 251. Cf. similarly Bruce, "Exposition," 97.

129. See Longenecker, *Exegesis*, 100, 105, 130–31, for a number of examples (though see also our introduction, ch. 8). For a "pesher" Petrine perspective, cf. esp. 1 Pet 1:10–12.

130. Longenecker, *Exegesis*, 95. On partly realized eschatology at Qumran, see Aune, *Cultic Setting*; but nowhere in Greco-Roman antiquity, outside early Christianity, do we see the pervasive expectation of prophetic phenomena even on a local congregational level.

131. See Black, "Christological Use."

132. Longenecker, *Exegesis*, 30–31, 100–101.

133. Cf. ibid., 105.

134. Cf. the later Karaites (Wieder, "Exegesis among Karaites," 77, 102–3). Even pagan writers sometimes used a "this was that" sort of statement to explain the fulfillment of an obscure prophecy (Virg. *Aen.* 7.128, *haec erat illa*). Brownlee, "Comparison with Sects," 68, compares Qumran's pesher technique with the Therapeutae's purported allegorical methods; but this stretches definitions considerably, even allowing for Philo's bias.

135. Cf. perhaps, e.g., *Pesiq. Rab.* 21:1. Some (Wright, "Midrash," 418–22; Brooke, "Pesher") treat pesher under the broader rubric of midrash, although (see Horgan, "Prophecies," 251) there are some clear differences. Miura, *David*, 150, finding "pesher" too loosely defined, prefers the label "typological prophetic" for the sorts of interpretations of psalms found in Acts 1–4.

136. Often noted among NT interpreters after Dodd, *Preaching*, 21.

137. On the four kingdoms, cf., e.g., 2 *Bar.* 39:7; *Sipre Deut.* 320.2.3; 317.4.2; *Gen. Rab.* 44:17; *Tg. Neof.* 1 on Gen 15:12.

138. For Esau as Rome in the Amoraim, e.g., *b. Mak.* 12a; *y. Taʿan.* 4:5, §10; *Pesiq. Rab Kah.* 5:14; *Pesiq. Rab Kah. Sup.* 5:3; *Gen. Rab.* 78:3; 83:4; *Exod. Rab.* 1:26; 18:12; 23:6; *Lev. Rab.* 13:5; 23:6; *Num. Rab.* 11:1; 14:1; *Eccl. Rab.* 11:5, §1; *Pesiq. Rab.* 12:25; 13:2; 15:20; perhaps also 4 *Ezra* 6:9. See further discussion in Hayward, "Pseudo-Jonathan" (on *Tg. Ps.-J.* to Gen 27:31); Freedman, "Jacob"; Butterweck, "Begegnung." The tradition is not likely known to the author of Ps.-Philo *Biblical Antiquities* (which is fairly positive toward Edom; see Zeron, "Swansong"), but it probably originated no later than the early second century C.E. (cf. Hadas-Lebel, "Jacob et Esaü").

139. Wright, "Midrash," 133–34. Although ancients could take into account historical settings (see our preface), they read them with less historical distance than is customary today (see Bryan, *Preface*, 50–51).

140. Noted by others, e.g., Mufwata, *Extrémités*, 28–31.

Jewish teachers of Torah peppered their expositions with numerous biblical allusions, and most changes in quotations appear to have been deliberate.[141] If we object that Luke portrays Peter earlier as an unlearned fisherman, we may betray class prejudices: whereas fishermen were not among the urban elite, they were better off economically than rural peasants (the majority of Galilee)[142] and hence probably had some of the boyhood schooling in Torah that Jewish people were famous for worldwide.[143] Further, Luke presents Jesus's education as more than sufficient (Luke 4:16–17); Joel may well be among the texts in the Prophets that Luke implies that Jesus taught his disciples (24:44–45).[144] It is doubtful that Luke himself (in contrast to Paul) had advanced formal training in Scripture; some particularly Judean elements may suggest that Luke depends on an earlier Christian source (though possibly an oral one).

Peter adds to Joel's text at various points to bring out the implications, especially that this is the eschatological gift of prophecy and hence that the eschatological time of fulfillment of the promises has come (cf., similarly, Jesus's explanation about Isa 61:1–2 in Luke 4:21).[145] Jewish interpreters reworded textual allusions where it suited them or where they regarded their interpretation as a reasonable inference.[146] Qumran texts sometimes altered the biblical text to adapt it to their purpose (e.g., 1QpHab XII, 1–10; V, 8–12).[147] Sometimes Jewish interpreters read the letters differently so as to give an eschatological application (*Sipre Deut.* 357.5.11). Greeks and Romans also felt free to adapt quotations,[148] whether to update archaic language,[149] improve language, or make the text more relevant. Accidents of memory could of course produce inexact quotations, but often they were deliberate.[150]

On page 876 is a comparison of Joel 3:1–5 LXX (2:28–32 ET) and Acts 2:17–21, 39, with the changes emphasized.

Some of these changes are more critical and rhetorically strategic than others. The most significant seem to include: (1) emphasis on the gift's eschatological character (though already in Joel), (2) emphasis on the prophetic nature of the gift (though already in Joel), (3) an ethnically universalized application (not in Joel) in Luke's later context ("far off" in Acts 2:39, and the larger context of Acts),[151] and (4) an emphasis on the present fulfillment (not in Joel) by linking the earthly "signs" with 2:22. Luke probably presupposes that his ideal audience will catch at least some of

141. Cf., e.g., revocalization (e.g., Brownlee, "Light," 32), but writers could also update language (Cic. *Brut.* 17.68–69), conflate quotations (Max. Tyre 41.3), or make strategic changes in the text (see below). The rabbis did not permanently alter the biblical text, however (on earlier *soferim*, cf. Lieberman, *Hellenism*, 28–37), in contrast to Qumran scribes (Heger, "Exegesis").

142. Freyne, *Galilee, Jesus*, 241; cf. *ILS* 7486; Wilkinson, *Jerusalem*, 29–30; Hengel, *Property*, 27. Cf. the "hired servants" in Mark 1:20.

143. See Stern, *Authors*, 1:8–11, 46, 50, 93–96, 131–33; Hengel, *Judaism and Hellenism*, 1:255–61.

144. On the historical level, those who emphasize parallels with other "charismatic" sages sometimes doubt that Jesus often expounded texts; but it appears in every stratum of gospel tradition, and it is tenuous to discount such evidence on the assumption that Jesus functioned *only* as a signs prophet (see Keener, *Matthew*, 53–56).

145. Because Luke often plays down future eschatology, Dunn (*Acts*, 28) attributes this change to Luke's source. But it is *realized* eschatology, which also appears in the Qumran scrolls (on which see Aune, *Cultic Setting*).

146. E.g., Silberman, "Unriddling," passim; Roth, "Subject Matter of Exegesis," 64–65.

147. See Lim, "Orientation."

148. E.g., Philost. *Vit. soph.* 2.13.594 (quoting Eurip. *Herc. fur.* 1406; probably an example of educated people demonstrating their knowledge by their quotations).

149. E.g., Cic. *Brut.* 17.68–69.

150. Lucian *Critic* 32, closing his essay by loosely quoting Eurip. *Bacch.* 386ff. without concern for the meter (since his essay defends his diction, he would hardly close with an obvious mistake).

151. Cf. Doeve, *Hermeneutics*, 114; van de Sandt, "Fate of Gentiles," thinks that Luke knew the context and deliberately transformed its expectation.

Joel 3:1–5 LXX	Acts 2:17–21, 39
3:1: and it will be that *after these things* I will *also* pour forth from my Spirit on all flesh	2:17: and it will be that *in the last days,** says God,† I will pour forth from my Spirit on all flesh
and your sons and your daughters will prophesy	and your sons and your daughters will prophesy
and your elders will dream dreams and your young men will see visions	and your young men will see visions and your elders will dream dreams [*clauses reversed*]‡
3:2: And in those days I will pour forth from my Spirit on *the* male and female slaves	2:18: And in those days I will pour forth from my Spirit on *my* male and female slaves,§ *and they will prophesy*‖
3:3: And I will grant wonders in the heaven and on the earth: blood and fire and smoky vapor	2:19: and I will grant wonders in the heaven *above* and *signs* on the earth *below*:# blood and fire and smoky vapor
3:4: the sun will be turned to darkness and the moon to blood, before the great and obvious day of the Lord comes!	2:20: the sun will be turned to darkness and the moon to blood, before the great and obvious day of the Lord comes!
3:5: and it will be that everyone who calls on the Lord's name will be saved	2:21: and it will be that everyone who calls on the Lord's name will be saved**
because in Mount Zion and in Jerusalem will be survivors (those saved), just as the Lord said	[*No parallel*]††
and good news will be announced [εὐαγγελιζόμενοι] to those whom the Lord has called [or summoned; προσκέκληται]	2:39: to as many as the Lord our God will call [προσκαλέσηται]

*Luke reinforces the eschatological nature of the gift already indicated by Joel's context.
†Luke or his source adds, "says God," to clarify the speaker but perhaps also so that Luke can "specify the promise as that of the Father (cf. Luke 24:29; Acts 1.4)" (Turner, *Power*, 270).
‡Luke does emphasize visions more than dreams; he may also emphasize or appeal to honorable youth (cf. Acts 5:6, 10; 7:58; 20:9; 23:17–18, 22), but this cannot be certainly ascertained from the slight change.
§Luke emphasizes that the recipients of God's Spirit (Acts 2:38–39) will be his servants, like the prophets; see below.
‖Luke hereby underlines the emphasis on prophecy already in Joel; commentators naturally recognize frequently Luke's redaction here (Menzies, *Development*, 221, 224).
#The addition of "signs" allows for Luke's application to Jesus's ministry in Acts 2:22. Luke's hermeneutic here resembles that which earlier in his work allows salvation both from physical enemies (Luke 1:71) and by forgiveness (1:77).
**Peter stops here to explain the name on which they are to call (Acts 2:34–38).
††Although Peter had reason to stop with calling on the Lord's name (above), his omission of the specifically Israel-centered part of the quotation seems significant in view of the fact that he could have appropriately picked it up, with what follows it in Joel, in Acts 2:39. At the same time, his preaching does produce a remnant in Jerusalem, presumably (though not explicit here) on the Temple Mount.

these changes (though, for all their biblical literacy, most of any writer's audience are not perfectly "ideal"; the clear verbal connection in 2:22 might catch more attention than Luke's redaction of Joel).

Luke may well also hope that some of his ideal audience will recall the term in the Septuagintal context that he elsewhere uses for preaching the good news (εὐαγγε-λιζόμενοι, Joel 3:5 LXX [at 2:32 ET]; a form of the verb appears twenty-five times in Luke-Acts), which would apply to Peter's preaching to the crowds. Luke omits that wording, however, whether because he or his tradition knows that it is not in the Hebrew or because he could midrashically assume it.[152] (Then again, it is not impossible that Luke overlooked the connection, surprising as this would be; he could easily have inserted it into Acts 2:39, and he also fails to use this verb anywhere between Luke 20:1 and Acts 5:42.)

Some later rabbis characteristically (and *possibly* also polemically) applied this passage in Joel to knowledge of Torah by connecting it midrashically with Ezek 36:26.[153] More important, they also recognized that this passage applied to the messianic era

152. Cf. also Johnson, *Acts*, 61.
153. *Deut. Rab.* 6:14. If 1QS IV, 21 alludes to Joel 2:28–29 (which is possible, given the eschatological pouring of the Spirit; but cf. also Isa 32:15; 44:3; Ezek 39:29), others connected the two passages even earlier. For Christian and rabbinic polemic (especially in the Amoraic period), see Keener, *John*, 194–214, esp. 194–207; for early Jewish applications of Ezek 36, see *John*, 551–52.

or the age to come;[154] it could be fulfilled only when the Messiah, resurrection, and other events of the end time arrived. The relatively scant attention paid to the passage in the earliest rabbinic sources could represent a polemical response to early Christian claims that Christians possessed the Spirit, though this is not clear.[155]

Litwak argues that Joel's passage provides continuity between Israel's story and Luke's story in Acts,[156] defining the prophetic church as the prophetic community of God's people.[157] As Hays shows for Paul, early Christian readings are sometimes ecclesiocentric[158] (and here also pneumatological), not exclusively christocentric (although the Spirit's outpouring here has a decisive significance not only for the community's identity but regarding that of Jesus, Acts 2:32–36). Eschatology here provides a line of continuity with promises to Israel; this continuity has apologetic value, both in relation to Jewish detractors and probably Roman courts, in identifying Christ's followers as heirs of the biblical covenant.

c. Last Days and Eschatological Fulfillment (2:17)

One of these additions is at the beginning of Peter's quotation of Joel, to underline the eschatological character of the era in which he is now speaking (in view of the coming of the Messiah and the Spirit). Peter substitutes "In the last days" for Joel's "afterward," simply bringing out the implications of the context that he does not go on to cite (cf. Joel 4:1 LXX [3:1 ET]).[159] This offers a sort of inclusio with the conclusion of 2:18, "in those days" (which does appear in Joel).[160] "In the last days" (and related expressions such as "last times") was a biblical phrase for the period of Israel's restoration, which Jewish hopes now fixed in the eschatological time (Isa 2:2; Hos 3:5; Mic 4:1; Dan 2:28).[161] This title for the eschatological period of restoration also applied to a period of great suffering just before that restoration (Jer 23:20; 30:24; Ezek 38:16; Dan 10:14);[162] it would be a period of apostasy for the insincere (e.g., ἐν ἐσχάτοις καιροῖς, Test. Iss. 6:1).[163] Christian texts likewise mention an eschatological period

154. Lake and Cadbury, Commentary, 22 (citing Midr. Pss. 14:6); Davies, Paul, 216 (on Num. Rab. 15:25); Zehnle, Pentecost Discourse, 29–30. Luke might sometimes assume the postbiblical history of interpretation in his exegesis (cf. Sanders, "Isaiah 61 to Luke 4"). Menzies, Empowered, 94–98, 232–43, notes the connection between the Spirit and eschatology in rabbinic sources but rightly emphasizes its lateness.

155. On possible rabbinic polemic against early Christian prophetic experience, see Keener, Spirit, 20–23, 26–27; idem, John, 203–7; idem, "Pneumatology," 77–94; Bamberger, "Prophet," 306–7.

156. Litwak, Echoes, 155.

157. Ibid., 156. Luke thus uses Joel regarding "the creation of a new community of God's people" (168–73). On Luke's relating this outpouring to the new community's identity formation, see also Wenk, Power, 252–53.

158. Hays, Conversion, 187.

159. With, e.g., Ridderbos, "Speeches of Peter," 13; Horton, Spirit, 146. Greco-Roman audiences would also be familiar with the practice of adapting quotations to clarify their intention (Stanley, Language of Scripture, 291; cf. 335, 337, 342–44).

160. In chiastic fashion, the nearest element is "I will pour out my Spirit," with gender diversity next and diversity of age in the center. "These days" recurs in Acts 3:24 in a realized eschatological sense (cf. perhaps 1:15; 13:41; but such expressions are not intrinsically eschatological [cf. 5:37; 7:41; 9:37]).

161. Also 11Q13 II, 4; 1 En. 27:3–4 (after the final judgment); cf. 4Q509 II, 19; 2 Bar. 76:5; Test. Zeb. 8:2; 9:5. Jewish interpreters would also so understand Deut 4:30; 31:29; cf. others' restoration in Jer 48:47; 49:39. The "last days" or "last generation" is a natural feature of the pesharim (e.g., 1QpHab I, 2; II, 5–6). Cf. also comment in Patte, Hermeneutic, 138.

162. Also 1Q22 I, 7–8; 4QpNah 3–4 III, 3; 4Q162 II, 1 in its context; 4Q163 23 II, 3–11; 4Q176 12 + 13 I, 9; 4QMMT C 21–22; Test. Dan 5:4; Test. Zeb. 9:5; Test. Iss. 6:1; cf. Sib. Or. 5.74; Apoc. Elij. 1:13. Writers could also apply the phrase to a person's "last days," i.e., on one's deathbed (Test. Dan 1:1).

163. See also 1Q22 I, 7–8; 4QpNah 3–4 III, 3; 4Q162 II, 2–7; 4Q390 1 7–9; 1 En. 91:7; 3 En. 48A:5–6; 4 Ezra 14:16–18; Sib. Or. 5.74; Test. Naph. 4:1; Test. Dan 5:4; Test. Zeb. 9:5; Sipre Deut. 318.1.10; b. Sanh. 97a; Pesiq. Rab Kah. 5:9. Cf. perhaps 4Q501, line 3.

of suffering and apostasy (1 Tim 4:1;[164] 2 Tim 3:1; 2 Pet 3:3; cf. Mark 13:9–13; Rom 8:22; 1 John 2:18). As a time of final suffering, the last days prefigured the final "day of the Lord"; as a time of Israel's restoration, they were identical with it or followed it. Thus the phrase roughly means "the eschatological time."

Early Christians consistently viewed this eschatological time as their own (Acts 2:17; 1 Tim 4:1; 2 Tim 3:1; Heb 1:2; Jas 5:3; 1 Pet 1:20; 2 Pet 3:3; Ign. *Eph.* 11.1), as in the Qumran scrolls (e.g., 4Q162 I–II, esp. II, 1–10; 4Q163 23 II, 10–11). The Qumran scrolls used their pesher interpretation (psalms, etc.) to apply much of Scripture to the special situation of the last days, a special era of fulfillment (e.g., 4Q162 I–II; 4Q176 12 + 13 I, 7–9; 4QpNah 3–4 IV, 3; see also *1 En.* 108:1); Peter does the same, believing the time of fulfillment has come (Acts 3:18–26). God would expose the wickedness of Israel's compromising leaders in the end time (4QpNah 3–4 III, 3).

Thus commentators often note that, from Luke's perspective, the church has entered the eschatological era.[165] Some doubt that we should make much of Luke's alteration, given the signs of the new era already in the birth narratives.[166] But the Davidic kingdom announced at the beginning of the Gospel (Luke 1:32, 69) enters a new phase with Jesus's exaltation (Acts 2:33–36), and the issue of eschatology suffuses the context (1:6–7).

Greeks and Romans did not share Jewish ideals about an ultimate end time,[167] but some had looked for a restoration of a golden age[168] (especially popular a century earlier as Romans celebrated Augustus's era, e.g., Virg. *Ecl.* 4.4–25;[169] Calpurnius Siculus 42–45). Many Roman texts refer to a primeval golden age;[170] in the golden age of Cronus, there was no poverty, the earth brought forth without effort, and rivers flowed with wine, milk, or honey.[171] Greeks as early as Hesiod (*W.D.* 109–26, esp. 110–20) spoke of a golden race,[172] and the idea of a golden age appears often in both Greek and Roman literature.[173]

After the Augustan era, however, many had grown disillusioned with the idea that the empire, full of corruption, had ushered in such an era.[174] Many implied a present decline from the glorious Augustan age,[175] although some spoke of a few individuals

164. Wilson, *Pastoral Epistles*, 16, thinks that 1 Timothy employs "last days" in the Lukan manner.

165. E.g., Stagg, *Acts*, 59.

166. Menzies, *Empowered*, 180.

167. One could cite the Stoic idea of cyclical cosmic conflagration (see comment on Acts 3:19–21) or Greco-Asian and Egyptian anti-Roman oracles, but even these do not accept Judaism's common linear concept of time with an ultimate judgment.

168. E.g., Winslow, "Religion," 239. On the new era here in contrast to imperial propaganda (in light of Joel's original context of deliverance), see Reid, "Resistance Discourse," 44.

169. Though some think that Virgil actually doubted a renaissance and viewed the golden race as morally ambiguous (Barker, "Golden Age"). Virgil might be ironic in *Ecl.* 8.27–28, where he declares that in the coming era, griffins will mate with mares and the deer drink alongside hounds.

170. E.g., Tibullus 1.3.35ff.; Sen. Y. *Ep. Lucil.* 90.5; 115.13; Fronto (Naber, 214, §3; LCL, 1:46–47); Max. Tyre 36.1–2.

171. Lucian *Sat.* 20, remarking on the views of the poets. For the lack of animal sacrifice then, see discussion in Ullucci, "Sacrifice."

172. For the full depiction of decline in Hesiod, see *W.D.* 110–201; later, also Ovid *Metam.* 1.89–312 (gold in 1.89–90; silver in 1.113–15; bronze in 1.125–27; etc.; cf. 15.111–13); Babr. prol. 1–4. *Sib. Or.* 1.65–124 similarly speaks of different races of people.

173. Fowler and Fowler, "Golden age" (citing, e.g., Aratus *Phaen.* 100–114; Ovid *Metam.* 1.89–112; cf. *Aetna* 9–16 (*Minor Latin Poets*, LCL, p. 358); Athen. *Deipn.* 6.267e–270a).

174. Some (e.g., Harrison, *Grace*, 226–34, 351–52, on imperial beneficence) nevertheless see the Augustan motifs as relevant to the mid-first century. Certainly Velleius maintains Augustan utopianism ca. 30 C.E. (e.g., Vell. Paterc. 2.89.3).

175. E.g., Sen. Y. *Ep. Lucil.* 95.14, 18 (cf. 97.1, 10); Tac. *Dial.* 12, 28–29; on literary decline, cf. Laistner, *Historians*, 103. Cf. also the long-standing theme of decline in Greco-Roman (Cic. *Sest.* 1.1; Sen. E. *Controv.*

recovering that primitive life in the present (cf. comment on Acts 2:44–45).[176] Even without reference to a primeval age or future hope, many Greeks and Romans recognized the need of their own times, considering them degenerate by comparison with those of their heroic ancestors.[177] (Of course, as in many other periods in history, elders sometimes also complained that the morals and discipline of the younger generation had declined from their own day.)[178]

Jewish people also hoped for a restored Eden, paralleling the end time with the primeval beginning.[179] Because Acts 2:44–45 may evoke the image of utopian communities, Luke's "last days" (recalling biblical prophecies about the future restoration and its ideal bliss) might recall, for some, utopian hopes. Luke's primary horizon, however, is Scripture, which often employs the phrase; his usage here indicates a partly (cf. 1:6–8) realized eschatology through the present activity of the eschatological Spirit. For Luke, both the expected end-time evils and the future utopia beyond it can partly coexist because the future hope is partly realized in the Spirit-empowered church, in anticipation of the kingdom's consummation.

Peter's "last days" fits the expectation that the disciples had entered an interim era between the first and the second comings of the Messiah (see comment on Acts 1:6–7), called to testify to the nations by the eschatological gift of the Spirit (see comment on Acts 1:8).[180] Although it is not clear that later first-century Christians struggled over the parousia's "delay" nearly so much as scholars have suspected (see comment on Acts 1:6–8), the earliest disciples probably did not expect an interval sufficiently long enough to anticipate two distinct comings.[181] Luke's portrayal here is realistic: even though Luke writes for a later generation, his Peter still appears to anticipate (or at least hope for) a quick repentance and restoration of Israel (3:19–21).

If the Messiah had come, his followers were necessarily in the last days in some sense. Many early Christians struggled with overrealized eschatology, undoubtedly partly due to future linear eschatology's incompatibility with Greek thought (e.g., 1 Cor 15:12; 2 Thess 2:2; 2 Tim 2:18), but the very affirmation that the Christ had come constituted the basis for a realized eschatology alongside a future one. This "already/not yet" tension is a major feature of Paul's theology;[182] many scholars

---

1.pref. 6; 2.7.1; 10.pref. 7; Plut. *Sulla* 1.3; cf. Laistner, *Historians*, 22, 53–54; Judge, *First Christians*, 52–58; Roller, "Past," 227–28) and Egyptian literature (Frankfurter, *Religion in Egypt*, 247); Augustus may have allowed this theme because it was applied against his rivals (Judge, *First Christians*, 55–56). Many averred that the people of the past were superior (Hom. *Il.* 12.381–82; Dio Chrys. *Or.* 31.75; Crosby in LCL, 3:80–81n1, also cites Lucian *Teacher of Rhetoric* 9; Themistius *Or.* 22.281a; Plato *Laws* 10.886C; Lucret. *Nat.* 2.1157ff.; Sen. Y. *Ep.* 90.44; cf. the express demurral in Vell. Paterc. 2.92.5).

176. E.g., Diogenes in Max. Tyre 36 passim.

177. Xen. *Mem.* 3.5.9–13; cf. Babr. 126; esp. Romans (e.g., Pliny *Ep.* 3.3.5; 8.5.1; 8.14.4–6; Tac. *Hist.* 3.51; earlier, Sall. *Catil.* 6.6–13.5; with additional observations on Sallust in Feldherr, "Translation"); even as early as Hom. *Il.* 12.381–82. Tacitus so portrays even the rhetorical situation (*Dial.* 1) despite oratory's revival in his era. The longevity of pre-Abrahamic ancestors also mostly declined progressively in Gen 5 (Hartman, "Thoughts," 30).

178. Pliny *Ep.* 2.14.2–13.

179. For the eschatological Eden, see, e.g., *4 Ezra* 8:52; *Test. Dan* 5:12; *Test. Levi* 18:10–12 (from a Christian interpolation); cf. 1QH^a XIV, 16–17; esp. in later rabbis (*m. 'Ab.* 5:20; *Sipra Behuq. pq.* 3.263.1.5; *b. Ber.* 28b; *Šabb.* 104a; *Ta'an.* 31a; *Tamid* 32b; *Tem.* 16a; *Yoma* 87a; *y. Pe'ah* 1:1, §8; *Exod. Rab.* 7:4; *Lev. Rab.* 32:1; *Num. Rab.* 13:2; *Tg. Neof.* 1 on Gen 3:24); on the *Endzeit* as the *Urzeit*, see, e.g., *Sipra Behuq. pq.* 1.261.1.6; Rev 22:1–3; *Barn.* 6.13; Russell, *Apocalyptic*, 280ff.; Arrington, *Aeon Theology*, 77–81; Mattill, *Last Things*, 5–6; Rissi, *Time*, 4.

180. For the entire period from Pentecost to the parousia as eschatological here, see, e.g., Cullmann, *Time*, 156; Johnson, *Function*, 44; Kent, *Jerusalem to Rome*, 32.

181. See Dodd, *Preaching*, 33.

182. See, e.g., Wikenhauser, *Mysticism*, 207; Howell, "Dualism"; Dunn, *Theology of Paul*, 466–72.

also see it in Jesus's teaching about the kingdom (see further comment on Acts 1:3, 6–8).[183]

The Spirit's presence marks out the eschatological people of God (or remnant of God's people),[184] God's "slaves" (Acts 2:18). The Spirit identifying God's people appears widely in early Christianity (e.g., Rom 8:9, 14–17; Gal 3:2–5, 14; 4:29; Eph 4:30; 1 John 3:24; 4:13; 5:7).

The Spirit as an eschatological gift attested clearly that the eschatological time had dawned, and functioned as a primary apologetic tool for the early Christians[185] (who seem to have explained the interval between comings partly by citing Ps 110:1 and the model of a salvific interval between redemption and inheritance in the exodus, e.g., Rom 8:23; Eph 1:14).[186] If its unique possession of the Torah[187] or of prophetic endowment[188] identified Israel as the elect in some other early Jewish circles, the Jesus movement's distinctive possession of the prophetic Spirit could be used to identify Christians as the elect remnant.[189]

> Peter explained that this marvelous power to speak in other tongues . . . was the outward sign of the fulfilment of Joel's prophecy that God would pour out his Holy Spirit on all his people. In Joel this promise was associated with the Day of the Lord; Peter asserts that this event has now occurred in history. It results from the fact that God had exalted the crucified Jesus, had enthroned him at his right hand, thus inaugurating his messianic reign; and the outpouring of the Holy Spirit upon his people was nothing less than the blessing of the messianic age.[190]

The apologetic would be difficult to refute for those who considered visions,[191] prophecies,[192] or other prophetic activities to be signs that a person had received the Holy Spirit. (The natural polemical response would be to qualify the value of such signs: sometimes they were merely tests of faith [Deut 13:3] or were performed through sorcery.)[193] Such an apologetic would have made no sense had Luke believed that the eschatological era of the Spirit had ceased (see comment on Acts 2:4). Instead of focusing on explaining the parousia's delay, Luke viewed his own era as continuing in the last days, presumably seeking to fulfill the mission of Acts 1:8 before Christ's return (see comment on Acts 1:6–8). No one could read Luke's "last days" as a tem-

183. See further Aune, "Delay," 5:93–94; in NT theology in general, Kümmel, *Theology*, 149; Ladd, *Theology*, 322; Minear, *Kingdom*, 147; Ridderbos, *Paul and Jesus*, 67. Ladd, *Kingdom*, 36, finds its roots in the OT prophets.

184. With, e.g., Dodd, *Preaching*, 59; Jervell, *Unknown Paul*, 96–121; cf. Litwak, *Echoes*, 168–73; the covenant renewal theme in Wenk, *Power*, 252–53.

185. So, e.g., Lampe, "Wolves," 255–56, who notes it in other early Christian literature as well. On Luke's relating this outpouring to the new community's identity formation, see Wenk, *Power*, 252–53.

186. I argued for this exodus interpretation in Keener, *Background Commentary*, 429–31, 542. Later writers appealed to other arguments to justify two comings (see Justin *1 Apol.* 52; cf. Tert. *Apol.* 21.15), e.g., typology based on the two goats (Justin *Dial.* 111; Tert. *Adv. Jud.* 14; cf. *Barn.* 7.6–10; Williams, *Justin Martyr*, 80n3).

187. Cf., e.g., Herford, *Pharisees*, 158; cf. 175.

188. Cf., e.g., Kohler, *Theology*, 37, 323–41.

189. Cf. later Justin *Dial.* 82, claiming that Israel's prophetic gifts had been transferred to the church.

190. Ladd, *Theology*, 345. Cf. R. Williams, *Acts*, 43: the apostles' prophetic speech functions as the sign that the last days have arrived. For the Spirit as eschatological foretaste, see also, e.g., Cadbury, "Eschatology," 300; Ridderbos, "Speeches of Peter," 12; comment on Acts 1:6–8.

191. So *y. Šeqal.* 3:3.

192. See our introduction, ch. 15, sect. 5, excursus part 3; or, e.g., Keener, *Spirit*, 10–13.

193. For Christians' healing miracles in rabbinic sources, see Herford, *Christianity*, 50–51, 54–56, 211–15; Bagatti, *Church*, 95–96, 106–7; Manns, "Jacob." Although rabbinic sources do not recite the charge of sorcery against miracles of Jesus or his movement before the late second century (Flusser, *Judaism* 635), Sanders, *Jesus and Judaism*, 166, rightly notes that the charge must be early, stating, "Why answer a charge that was not levelled?" (Matt 12:24; cf. John 8:48); cf. Betz, *Jesus*, 58.

porary event in Jerusalem that had given way to a cessation of signs and revelations in Luke's own day, unless they viewed the "last days" as a failed experiment.

d. "All Flesh" and All the Last Days

Luke clearly believes that prophetic empowerment should characterize the entire church. His focus is on this empowerment to speak for God in terms of apostolic, cross-cultural evangelism (1:8), but clearly the empowerment extends beyond the apostles (2:38–39).[194] Joel's prophecy applies not just to the apostles as the primary witnesses (1:8; cf. 1 Pet 1:12; Heb 2:4) but to all who became Jesus's followers (Acts 2:38–39). That Christians as a whole constituted a prophetic community[195] is implied by some other early Christian writers (e.g., Rev 19:10; probably also 11:18).[196]

Both Luke (cf. Acts 11:27; 15:32; 21:9–10) and Paul (1 Cor 12:28–29; 14:29, 32; Eph 4:11) reserve the title of prophet for specific individuals (though in Paul it applies to any who prophesy, 1 Cor 14:29–32). For Paul, perhaps all Christians can prophesy in principle (1 Cor 14:24, 31), though in practice only some are prophets (12:29), and it is a good gift for others (or the community) to seek (14:1, 5, 39; cf. 12:31).[197] Luke, whose narrative emphasizes disciples' role in the world more than in the church, focuses on disciples' prophetic witness for Christ, proclaiming the prophetic "word of the Lord" (e.g., Acts 4:31; 6:7; 8:25; 12:24; 13:49; 15:35, 36; 19:10, 20). Perhaps depending on Israel's role as witnesses in Isaiah (Isa 43:10, 12; 44:8) or in Joel, some streams of early Jewish thought may have also envisioned all God's people as prophets in the end time.[198]

Although Peter would not so understand it at this point in the story, Luke undoubtedly interprets "all flesh" as referring not simply to the men and women, young and old, and servants stated in Joel 2:28–29 but to people from all nations.[199] Luke may expect his informed audience to recall another programmatic quote that defined John's mission: through his mission, "all flesh" would see God's salvation (Luke 3:6; Isa 40:5);[200] because Luke quotes beyond his source (Mark 1:3 in Luke 3:4, quoting Isa 40:3), he surely knows the Isaian context (on which see comment on Acts 1:8). This mission quotation is Luke's only other use of "all flesh" (or, for that matter, any other use of σάρξ in Luke-Acts except in discussing Jesus's resurrection, Luke 24:39; Acts 2:26, 31). Moreover, Luke will complete his allusion to Joel in Acts 2:39, where he augments it with an allusion to Isa 57:19, confirming (given its function in Luke's narrative) that Luke understands the prophecy as applicable to Gentiles.[201] As Luke's narrative continues, the

194. Apostolic signs often echo prophetic signs in the OT, but Acts, despite its focus, does not limit even these to apostles (Acts 6:8; 9:12, 17–18) and certainly not to the twelve who are usually called apostles (e.g., 13:11; 14:3; 15:12; 19:11–12; 28:8–9). Further, Luke treats the continuance of prophecy in the narrower sense as normal, a continuing sign of the eschatological blessing on the church (albeit not expressed by all individuals; 11:27; 13:1; 21:9, 10; cf. 13:2; 20:23; 21:4).

195. Cf. also Hill, *Prophecy*, 99; Cruz, "Hermeneutics."

196. See Keener, *Revelation*, 305; Hill, "Prophecy in Revelation," 414; Bruce, "Spirit in Apocalypse," 337; idem, *Time*, 103; contrast Aune, *Prophecy*, 197, 206. It is likely also implied in Rev 11:3–6, although this is a notoriously difficult passage (Keener, *Revelation*, 289–93).

197. Cf. Forbes, *Prophecy*, 252–55.

198. *Sib. Or.* 3.582–83 (προφῆται; in view of 5.584–89, this may include wise counsel to avoid idolatry); cf. also, earlier, 1 Chr 16:22; Ps 105:15.

199. E.g., Marshall, *Acts*, 73n3; York, *Missions*, 82; Meek, *Mission*, 107–8. They appear in Joel's context only as Israel's enemies, not Israel's converts (Joel 3:2–14, 17, 19, 21), but Luke apparently places Joel's message in the larger picture he draws from Isaiah.

200. The LXX helpfully adds seeing God's "salvation" to seeing his glory; Luke may prefigure this LXX addition in Luke 2:30.

201. See Pao, *Isaianic Exodus*, 230–32.

Spirit clearly is poured out on Gentiles (10:45).[202] The Spirit on the Gentiles is a very different eschatological vision than the best of Gentiles being subjugated to slavery.[203]

Luke surely means his programmatic use of Joel as theologically prescriptive and not merely historically descriptive; that is, he believes that the church of his day continues, or should continue, to experience the outpouring of the Spirit. Luke must view the promise as valid for all believers in his day, given his appeal to a text referring to "all flesh" (Acts 2:17) and his emphasis that the gift was for their descendants, even those far away (2:39).

The idea that such empowerment or its prophetic expressions had ceased in his day, or was scheduled to cease before the Lord's return, is one that could not have occurred to Luke. For Luke, such activity characterizes the eschatological era in which the church lives; Luke would hardly emphasize that this era was inaugurated on Pentecost and then expect us to infer, without clear evidence, that the era would be phased out before its consummation at Christ's return.[204] God would hardly pour out his Spirit, then pour it back again![205] Indeed, such a conclusion would have played into the hands of those who questioned whether the eschatological Messiah had even come, and would undermine Luke's entire apologetic and theology of fulfillment.

Further, Luke presents the interim messianic era of Christ's reign at the Father's right hand (2:34–35) as in continuity with God's activity in Scripture. If this eschatological era continued "biblical" experience, then it is relevant that despite ebbs and flows, prophetism was always active in biblical history (3:18, 21, 24); those who received the message would, indeed, be "children of the prophets" as well as of Abraham (cf. 3:25).[206] For that matter, Christian prophecy did continue in later centuries,[207] and later opponents of Christianity continued to attack it.[208]

e. Surmounting Gender and Other Barriers

Joel's prophecy declared the eradication of any gender barrier in the Spirit of prophecy. Although some women prophesied in the OT (Exod 15:20; Judg 4:4; 2 Kgs 22:14; Isa 8:3), Luke more explicitly balances women and men in this gift (Luke 2:25–27, 36; Acts 21:9).[209] In this period, respectable women did not typically speak publicly to groups including men (see introduction, ch. 18, sect. 3). People would have to make exceptions for inspired speech, however, and Luke certainly does emphasize women's participation in inspired speech here.[210]

202. For the echo of Acts 2's Joel quotation in Acts 10:45, see, e.g., Mufwata, *Extrémités*, 61. See my comment at Acts 10:45.

203. On different visions for Gentiles in the future, see Donaldson, *Paul and Gentiles*, 52–74.

204. Cf. similarly Paul's expectation of prophecy until Christ's return in 1 Cor 13:8–13, which I discuss briefly in Keener, *Corinthians*, 109–10.

205. That is, in modern theological terms, Luke cannot be a cessationist regarding this prophetic gift of the Spirit. For this passage and the expectation of continuing signs, see also Menzies, "Paradigm."

206. It is more likely that the idea of prophecy's cessation derived from reading into the NT the observed experience of Christians in some subsequent eras, where prophecy was either rare or demonstrably errant. Even this observation must be balanced, however, by the frequency of prophetic phenomena in many other eras of Christian history, including its current frequency in charismatic circles and especially in some regions of the world.

207. See, e.g., Shogren, "Prophecy."

208. See, e.g., Cook, *Interpretation*, 77–79.

209. Thus, e.g., Chrys. *Hom. Acts* 5 (*NPNF* 11:33) emphasizes that the gift is now available to both genders, in contrast to being limited to a few women in the OT. Some scholars have, by contrast, supposed that Luke relegates women's prophetic voice mostly to the OT era and does not present it as the norm of the new community (e.g., Reid, *Choosing*, 206), but such an inference runs directly counter to the one programmatic statement in Luke-Acts that specifically mentions women.

210. Luke does not explicitly challenge the public/private divide, which was an ancient custom difficult to violate while retaining an honorable hearing (although he makes use of ways in which it was already breaking down); his emphasis on inspired speech for God, however, relativizes that divide's importance.

Prophetesses appear in Hellenistic literature, although some are tragic victims of their escape from Apollo. Apollo gifted Cassandra prophetically but cursed her with no one believing her prophecies.[211] The Sibyl likewise received immortality without perpetual youth;[212] Romans did heed books of Sibylline oracles, however.[213] That some of the prophecies were forged was known.[214] (There is also a strong Jewish Sibylline tradition, naturally purified of polytheism.)[215] Dio Chrysostom claims to have met a woman who prophesied accurately by the mother of the gods yet without ecstatic raving.[216] In late antiquity a source claims a young woman astonishingly accurate in her revelations.[217] Some oracular centers, such as Apollo's oracle at Delphi, employed a mantic priestess.[218] Germans were said to depend on women for prophecies.[219]

Much more relevant, however (especially in view of the explicit citation of Scripture here), are biblical traditions about prophetesses. Far fewer in number than male prophets in ancient Israel (as one would expect in most patriarchal societies), they nevertheless appear, sometimes prominently: Miriam (Exod 15:20), Deborah (Judg 4:4), Huldah (2 Kgs 22:14; 2 Chr 34:22), and Isaiah's wife (Isa 8:3).[220] Most Jewish sources continued to recognize Deborah as a prophetess.[221] Although the biblical picture of Huldah is wholly favorable, attitudes toward her in Jewish literature range from positive to negative.[222] Some rabbinic sources amplified the number of biblical prophetesses (adding Sarah, Hannah, Abigail, and Esther) but continued to attribute to them the negative traits they attributed to women in general.[223] In some sources, the matriarchs became prophetesses.[224] See further discussion on prophetesses at Acts 21:9.

Paul certainly expected women to engage in prophetic gifts (1 Cor 11:5).[225] Some later Christian writers, both "orthodox" and sectarian,[226] sought to reduce biblical

---

211. E.g., Sen. Y. *Troj.* 34–37.

212. E.g., Ovid *Metam.* 14.129–53; cf. Statius *Silv.* 5.3.175. On the Sibyls, see further, e.g., Strabo 14.1.34; Dio Chrys. *Or.* 35.2; Juv. *Sat.* 3.3; Ant. Diog. *Thule* 111a; Heraclitus *Ep.* 8; overpowered by prophetic frenzy in Virg. *Aen.* 6.77–102. Eventually, other women besides Sibyl could be Sibylla (Diod. Sic. 4.66.6).

213. E.g., Dion. Hal. *Ant. rom.* 10.2.5; 12.9.1; Cic. *Verr.* 2.4.49.108; Livy 4.25.3; 5.13.5; 7.27.1; 10.8.2; 22.36.6–9; 22.57.4–6; 36.37.4; 40.19.4; 41.21.10; 45.16.6; Strabo 12.5.3; 17.1.43; Val. Max. 1.5.ext. 1; Tac. *Ann.* 15.44; Plut. *Caes.* 60.1; Appian *Hist. rom.* 7.9.56; 9.2; Aul. Gel. 1.19; Dio Cass. 48.43.5. On the pagan Sibyl tradition, see further Bouquet and Morzadec, *Sibylle*; Pigeaud, *Sibylles*; a summary of both in Roessli, "Vies."

214. Tac. *Ann.* 6.12; Plut. *Cic.* 17.4; Lucian *Peregr.* 30–31; Dio Cass. 57.18.5. Those deemed legitimate could be interpreted so as to justify almost any decision (cf., e.g., Cic. *Rab. Post.* 2.4).

215. See *Sib. Or.* passim (on which see Collins, *Sibylline Oracles*; more briefly, idem, "Oracles"); Jos. *Ant.* 1.116–17; cf. *Herm.* 1.2.4; Justin *1 Apol.* 20; Theoph. 2.36; Tert. *Apol.* 19.1.

216. Dio Chrys. *Or.* 1.54–56. Although this could be a literary device, there is no more reason to doubt it than Dio's other stories of exile.

217. Eunapius *Lives* 468, 470.

218. See Aune, *Prophecy*, 28 (contrasting Apollo's sanctuary at Claros); see further comment on Acts 16:16.

219. Tac. *Germ.* 8; cf. also the frenzied women prophesying in Britain in Tac. *Ann.* 14.32.

220. Also a false prophetess in Neh 6:14. For prophetesses at Mari, see Moran, "Prophecy," 29ff.; Paul, "Prophets," 1159–60.

221. *L.A.B.* 33:1; *Tg. Jon.* on Judg 4:4; 5:3, 7, 9. Some scholars think that Josephus diminishes Deborah's role (Feldman, "Roncace's Portraits"), but others differ (Roncace, "Portraits"). Certainly, Josephus neglects to mention her judging Israel (*Ant.* 5.201), a point that might not have played well to a Hellenistic audience.

222. Van der Horst, "Graf." Huldah's prophesying is restricted to women (*Pesiq. Rab.* 26:1/2), despite the biblical account (2 Kgs 22:12–15; 2 Chr 34:22–23).

223. See Bronner, "Prophetesses through Rabbinic Lenses" (on *b. Meg.* 14b).

224. E.g., *Gen. Rab.* 67:9 (in the name of a Tanna); 72:6.

225. Some concur that Paul permitted women's vertical speech (to and from God) but argue that he did not permit horizontal speech (cf. Vander Stichele, "Silence"; Sigountos and Shank, "Public Roles"), a pattern that might fit the larger culture. Even if one accepts this perspective, however, the vertical was of higher authority (1 Cor 12:28; cf. Pelser, "Women," 94–95; Spencer, *Beyond Curse*, 106–7; Bilezikian, *Roles*, 177). On the involvement of both genders, cf. Theissen, *Erleben*, 200 (citing also *Testament of Job*).

226. E.g., Origen *Comm. 1 Cor.* 4.74.6–16 (Bray, *Corinthians*, 146); Montanist oracles in *Cat. Cor.* 14.36 (Bray, *Corinthians*, 147).

claims about women's prophesying, reflecting broader trends in the church (and society) of late antiquity; some others, however, preserved the notion of spiritual gifts not distributed according to gender.[227]

It is unlikely that Peter himself envisions eradication of a gender barrier here; he did not yet even envision eradication of the ethnic barrier on which Luke focuses his account (Acts 10:14, 28).[228] But Luke expects the ideal audience to recognize some ethnic implications of Peter's speech that Peter would not have recognized ("all flesh" in 2:17; "afar off" in 2:39), and may therefore invite readers to consider other implications as well.[229] Luke's narrative confirms the charismatic gender egalitarianism of his programmatic statement here, reporting prophetesses as well as prophets (Acts 21:9; Luke 2:36).[230] A significant measure of functional charismatic egalitarianism could exist without disrupting social hierarchy, a hierarchy reflected in Luke's culture and his sources, including in his picture of early church offices (e.g., Acts 6:3; 15:7, 13; perhaps 20:30; but cf., again functionally, 18:26). Whether Luke would have recognized a summons to still further egalitarianism in the principle he espouses here is difficult to infer from the narrative of Acts;[231] at the least, we can say that Luke's positive attention to women presses beyond that of many of his male contemporaries (see more fully discussion on Acts 1:14). Some church fathers recognized from Acts that spiritual gifts (such as tongues) were given to women as well,[232] and subsequent readers have long drawn from the Joel quotation a justification for women's ministry.[233]

227. Cf., e.g., Theodoret *Comm. 1 Cor.* 245 (Bray, *Corinthians*, 122), citing Acts.

228. See Spencer, *Acts*, 37 (who thinks that gender barriers would be the "logical next step"). Still, Peter was probably already more comfortable with Galilean women in mixed company at this point than with Gentiles.

229. Cf. Gaventa, *Acts*, 60: "the prophecy of Acts 2 stands only partially fulfilled," but like other prophecies in Acts, this one will be fulfilled.

230. As Kanyoro, "Mission," 63, points out, most of Luke's narrative is theologically inclusive: all are told to wait (Acts 1:4), to be witnesses (1:8), filled (2:4); whoever calls will be saved (2:21). Rigato, "Valore inclusivo," also reads gender inclusiveness from the "all" in 2:1–4. As some Pentecostal theologians emphasize, many Pentecostals have also viewed their own gender-egalitarian tendencies in this light (Yong, *Spirit Poured*, 190–94); in early Pentecostalism, see Wacker, *Heaven*, 158–65 (but for countervailing cultural and traditional tendencies, 165–76); Alexander, "Conscience," 59 (William J. Seymour's affirmation of women ministers, without their baptizing or ordaining); McGee, *Miracles*, 135 (on 136–37 noting the decline in the next generation); Alexander, *Fire*, 294 (initial freedom, declining with institutionalization); for a range of information about women leadership in Pentecostalism more generally, see Alexander and Yong, *Daughters*; for the prominence of women's missionary roles among Indian Pentecostals and charismatics, see Pothen, "Missions," 191–92, 255; for Pentecostal women in ministry in the Philippines, see Ma, "Women," 136–42; in Africa, see Kalu, *African Pentecostalism*, 161–62; in the pre-Pentecostal healing movement (with limitations), see, e.g., Curtis, "Character," 40; among U.S. Latino/a Pentecostals, see Espinosa, "Healing in Borderlands," 140. Some estimate that Pentecostalism has been the largest historic force for inaugurating women's ordination and promoting it worldwide (Powers, "Daughters," 313; also cited in Richards, "Factors," 98; cf. Sweeney, *Story*, 147). Miller and Yamamori, *Pentecostalism*, 208–9, note many women on pastoral staff worldwide, but their case studies located fewer as head pastors. In Ecuadorian Pentecostalism, whereas men claim more revelations in dreams, women report far more visions and prophecies (Castleberry, "Impact," 142, also noting women's typically greater diversity in charismatic experience in Abell, *Experience*; Brusco, *Machismo*; McDonnell, *Renewal*); at least in that culture, women feel less inhibited in expressing religious feeling (Castleberry, "Impact," 144). For Pentecostalism, despite its limitations, empowering Colombian women, see Brusco, "Gender."

231. Cf. Paul, who makes egalitarian statements (1 Cor 7:2–4, 12–16; 11:5, 11–12; Gal 3:28; Eph 5:21) and functions, in some respects, as an egalitarian with women colleagues (Rom 16:1–7, 16; Phil 4:2–3; Col 4:15) but does not usually directly confront the social hierarchy (1 Cor 11:3–16; 14:34–35; Eph 5:22). I believe that he would have readily relinquished gender hierarchy in a different social situation (see Keener, *Paul*, passim; idem, "Subversive Conservative"), but this conclusion rests on hermeneutical extrapolation (since we have no NT texts addressing such situations). Ramsay, *Pictures*, 7–8, thinks Luke similar to Gal 3:28 here, acknowledging a gap between ideal calling and the current actuality of church and society.

232. E.g., Theodoret *Comm. 1 Cor.* 245.

233. E.g., nineteenth-century African Methodist Episcopal evangelist Julia A. J. Foote (see Anderson, "Reading Tabitha"), Holiness and Pentecostal advocates (Powers, "Daughters," 318) such as Phoebe Palmer (Everts

The gift is not only for both male and female but for "young and old," and Luke illustrates this principle: Simeon and Anna are aged (Luke 2:26, 36–37), but Philip's daughters are virgins and hence likely teenagers (Acts 21:9). Following good Hebrew form, Joel encompassed entire ranges by listing opposite extremes; "young" and "old" together mean people of all ages.[234] On "youth," see comment on Acts 7:58. Some pagans used children's words at play to divine the will of deities,[235] but this was analogous to the flight of birds or other forms of divination. More relevant illustrations would be the use of Jeremiah as a youth (Jer 1:6–7), and especially Samuel as a boy (1 Sam 2:11, 18, 26; 3:4–19), as well as probably more numerous aged prophets, such as Moses (Deut 34:7) and Ahijah (1 Kgs 14:4–6).[236]

Joel's prophecy also challenged the class barrier, mentioning God's enabling Israel's servants to prophesy (Joel 2:29).[237] But while Luke certainly is interested in confronting such barriers (note especially the emphasis on the poor in his Gospel), he changes the wording to provide a different theological nuance also relevant to his interests.[238] These prophets are all God's own "slaves." God's prophets were often called his servants in Scripture[239] (as were David,[240] Moses,[241] the patriarchs,[242] and Israel as a whole),[243] though John the Baptist had implied that he was not worthy to be even Christ's slave (Luke 3:16).[244]

---

and Baird, "Palmer," 147, 151), Baptist A. J. Gordon in 1894 (Wacker, *Heaven*, 160), and others (Kisau, "Acts," 1303; Shillington, *Introduction*, 114–16; Williams, "Acts," 218, 220; cf. Cox, *Fire*, 123–38, esp. 138; Flattery, *Spirit*, 2:210). For an eighteen-year-old woman's prophetic outlet in 1560, see Midelfort, "Possession," 127–28; for the roles of women in other periods of religious revival, see, e.g., Roxburgh, "Impact," 191–92, 203–4.

234. Gen 17:24–25; Exod 10:9; Deut 28:50; Josh 6:21; 1 Sam 5:9; 2 Chr 36:17; Esth 3:13; Job 29:8; Ps 148:12; Isa 20:4; Jer 6:11; 31:13; 51:22; Lam 2:21; Ezek 9:6. Pseudo-Hermogenes lists children and the aged among those who, with women, needed advocates to speak for them in court (*Method* 21.437).

235. E.g., Dio Chrys. *Or.* 32.13; Plut. *Isis* 14, *Mor.* 356E; Xen. Eph. *Anthia* 5.4; also Aug. *Conf.* 8.12; cf. Matt 21:16; for children in ancient religion, see Mantle, "Roles"; idem, "Addendum." For an old man interpreting dreams, see Hom. *Il.* 5.150.

236. Children have also proved susceptible to revival phenomena (cf. their presence at Cane Ridge; Wolffe, *Expansion*, 59; Wacker, "Living," 426–27). Modern Christians in societies less influenced by the Western tradition of antisupernaturalism also report children having visions (some ten-year-olds in Yangon, Myanmar, in Khai, "Pentecostalism," 270, noting that the pastor's theological training had predisposed him against it but that he was compelled by the unexpected phenomena to accept it; elsewhere in Holder, "Revival"; Ma, "Vanderbout," 135; Anderson, "Signs," 201; Baker, *Visions*; Koch, *Zulus*, 207 [children's prophecies in Indonesia], 208–16 [a Zulu girl's accurate visions], 217–18 [prophecy through a Zulu child]); traditional cultures also report preteen children being possessed (Southall, "Possession," 242).

237. Shiell, *Reading Acts*, 172, suggests that readers were often slaves and that a slave reading a passage about the Spirit poured out on slaves would intensify the "rhetorical effect." Although this observation is plausible, we cannot be certain how often in congregations the reader would be a slave or if Luke anticipated this as a regular occurrence.

238. So also Philip, *Pneumatology*, 213, emphasizing that Luke thereby limits "all flesh" to believers (rather than all humanity).

239. 2 Kgs 9:7, 36; 10:10; 14:25; 17:13, 23; 21:10; 24:2; Ezra 9:11; Isa 20:3; Jer 7:25; 25:4; 26:5; 29:19; 35:15; 44:4; Dan 3:28; 6:20; 9:6, 10; Amos 3:7; Zech 1:6; later, cf. 'Abot R. Nat. 37, §95 B.

240. 2 Sam 3:18; 7:5, 8, 19–21, 25–29; 1 Kgs 3:6; 8:24–26, 66; 11:13, 32, 34, 36, 38; 14:8; 2 Kgs 8:19; 19:34; 20:6; 1 Chr 17:4, 7, 17–19, 23–27; 2 Chr 6:15–21, 42; Pss 78:70; 89:3, 20; 132:10; 144:10; Isa 37:35; Jer 33:21–22, 26; Ezek 34:23–24; 37:24–25; later, cf. 'Abot R. Nat. 43, §121 B.

241. Exod 14:31; Num 12:7–8; Deut 34:5; Josh 1:1–2, 7, 13, 15; 8:31, 33; 9:24; 11:12, 15; 12:6; 13:8; 14:7; 18:7; 22:2, 4–5; 1 Kgs 8:53, 56; 2 Kgs 18:12; 21:8; 1 Chr 6:49; 2 Chr 1:3; 24:6, 9; Neh 1:7–8; 9:14; 10:29; Ps 105:26; Dan 9:11; Mal 4:4; later, cf. 4Q378 22 2; *L.A.B.* 30:2, *famulum*; 'Abot R. Nat. 43, §121 B.

242. Cf. Gen 26:24; Exod 32:13; Deut 9:27; Ps 105:6; 2 Macc 1:2; *Jub.* 31:25; 45:3; *Test. Ab.* 9:4 A; *2 Bar.* 4:4; 'Abot R. Nat. 43, §121 B.

243. Lev 25:42, 55; Deut 32:43; Isa 41:8–9; 42:1, 19; 43:10; 44:1–2, 21; 45:4; 48:20; 49:3; Jer 30:10; 46:27–28; Ezek 28:25; 37:25; *2 Bar.* 44:4; t. B. Qam. 7:5; 'Abot R. Nat. 43, §121 B; *Gen. Rab.* 96 NV; y. Qidd. 1:2, §24; cf. Tob 4:14 MSS.

244. For this meaning of this Q saying, see, e.g., Keener, *Matthew*, 130.

The title is certainly appropriate for those empowered by the Spirit to speak God's message. Although "servant" was not a position of high status relative to the master, a servant of a powerful person could wield more social status than some aristocrats.[245] Some people became slaves of Caesar voluntarily, for example, to advance their career.[246] To be slaves of God himself would thus constitute the highest of all human honors; not surprisingly, biblical prophets issued God's orders to kings (albeit as messengers). (On slavery in general, see the excursus at Acts 12:13.)

Luke's model for God's female slave (δούλη) is Mary embracing God's call (Luke 1:38, 48) through the gift of his Spirit (1:35). (As the only explicit Spirit-empowered "servant" from the previous generation to be present for Pentecost [Acts 1:14], Mary may indeed constitute the primary model for all God's servants here.) For a male slave (δοῦλος) of God, Luke provides as a seminal example Simeon (Luke 2:29), who had the Spirit on him (2:25–27) and accordingly prophesied about Christ (2:29–35). As Mary asked that she might fulfill her role as God's servant (1:38), so all the believers request boldness as God's servants in Acts 4:29; in response, they are filled with the Spirit and speak God's word boldly (4:31). The title "slaves" applies to all believers but especially to those with the greatest responsibilities (Luke 12:37, 43–48; 17:7–10; 19:13, 15, 17; 20:10–11; cf. 14:17, 21–23; Acts 16:17).

Excursus: Prophecy (2:17–18)

Through his allusion to Elijah and Elisha in Acts 1:9–11, Luke has already emphasized that the disciples receive the Spirit of prophecy; the allusion to the mission of Isaiah's Spirit-empowered servant in 1:8 also involved Spirit-empowered speaking for God. But Joel's prophecy is much more explicit.

For further discussion of the Spirit, including the Spirit's relationship to prophecy, see the lengthy treatment (including of early Jewish pneumatology) in our introduction, chapter 15, section 5, which also emphasizes the pervasive early Jewish association between the Spirit and prophecy, the phenomenon probably most widely linked with the Spirit. Here, however, I address issues especially regarding early Jewish views of prophecy in more detail.[247] Although placed at Acts 2:17–18, this excursus serves the many references to prophets and prophetic phenomena in Acts; comments on pagan prophecy here are relevant for Acts 16:16.

1. Ancient Israelite and Ancient Near Eastern Antecedents

Because the focus in this commentary is on historical setting and because most readers of NT commentaries are already very familiar with the biblical prophetic tradition, this survey of Israelite prophetism will focus on Israel's broader prophetic milieu. Because entire books address Israelite prophetism, these few paragraphs represent

245. Cf. Martin, *Slavery*, 47–49. Even a person of great rank might call himself a "slave" before one of greater rank (e.g., Char. *Chaer.* 5.2.2).
246. E.g., Horsley, *Documents*, 3:7–9, §1 (on P.Oxy. 3312.99–100). For the exalted status of Caesar's slaves, see Epict. *Diatr.* 1.19.19; 4.7.23; cf. further Sherk, *Empire*, §47, pp. 89–90. Slaves in Caesar's household often preferred that status to freedom (Dixon, *Roman Mother*, 19, citing Suet. *Gramm.* 21).
247. In this excursus, I have developed Keener, *Spirit*, 6–48.

only a brief summary of some themes to set the stage for a discussion of prophetism in the early Christian period; not every feature can be mentioned. Yet because early Christians' primary textual models for prophecy were found in Israel's Scripture, it is inappropriate to simply jump to early Jewish or Greco-Roman oracular traditions without at least mentioning ancient Israelite prophetism.

The Hebrew term for prophet (נביא) refers to a divine spokesperson and is widely attested in Semitic languages;[248] another term used in the early Israelite period, "seer," is also attested elsewhere.[249] Even "man of God"[250] is attested elsewhere; Hittites used it for those who through dreams could provide answers from the deity.[251] Israel's "sons of the prophets" may refer to trainees within a prophetic guild.[252] The value of divinely guided prediction was widely accepted.[253]

Some scholars compare the prophets' role as divine messengers to that of other authoritative messengers in the milieu.[254] The common prophetic phrase "This is what YHWH says" was also a common messenger formula of the era (e.g., Exod 5:10; Josh 22:16; 2 Kgs 18:19, 28).[255] A comparable messenger formula appears at Mari, when the prophets speak outside the temple.[256] A royal messenger stood in the court of the great king (the suzerain ruler)[257] and then, as his ambassador, might deliver his message to a vassal king (as Israelite prophets often delivered messages to Israel's king). This formula seems to fit particularly well Aramaic suzerainty treaties and messages to vassal kings in the period of the Israelite monarchy[258] and lends itself well to the covenant lawsuit imagery of some of the prophets.[259]

In contrast to Israel's prophetic experience, most Mesopotamian "prophetism" was simply divination, though carried out by "seers." The Hittites received revelation in ecstasy and dreams, but they viewed as more reliable divination in the form of extispicy (entrails), augury (movement of birds), and (possibly) a "lottery" by female soothsayers.[260] Traces of nondivinatory prophecy are comparatively scarce not

248. The original background of the term may be "the called one" (see Albright, Yahweh, 208–9; Holladay, "Statecraft," 30), though whether it is a genuine passive or its sense is active remains debated (e.g., Lewis, Prophets, 9).

249. Ross, "Prophecy," 4; cf. Lindblom, Prophecy, 85–86. It was an earlier (cf. 1 Sam 9:9) Israelite term for a visionary, though a "vision" could be simply a word from YHWH (1 Sam 3:15 [but cf. 3:10]); "seers" were prophets (Isa 29:10; Amos 7:12) or diviners (Mic 3:7); cf. 2 Sam 24:11ff.; 2 Kgs 17:13; 1 Chr 29:29; 2 Chr 9:29; 12:15; 29:30.

250. More than seventy uses, including 1 Sam 2:27; 9:6–10; 12:22; 13:1–31; 17:18, 24; 20:28; 2 Kgs 1:9–13; 4:7–8:11; 13:19; 2 Chr 11:2; 25:7–9.

251. Kitchen, World, 118; Huffmon, "Prophecy," 105n8; cf. ANET 394–96.

252. Cf. the analogous use of "son" in scribal guilds (Chiera, Clay, 165–66).

253. See, e.g., Admonitions of Ipuwer (twenty-third to twenty-second century B.C.E.); Prophecy of Neferti (ca. 1990 B.C.E.); Kitchen, "Background," 6–7.

254. Prophets were also understood as messengers in early Judaism; see Mek. Pisha 1.87 (Lauterbach, 1:8); 'Abot R. Nat. 37, §95 B; Keener, John, 315.

255. The last reference, to an Assyrian official, is paralleled in Assyrian records of negotiations (Yamauchi, Stones, 77).

256. See Moran, "Prophecy," 24–25. "By the hand of" in Israelite prophecy (cf. 1 Sam 28:6; 1 Kgs 16:7, 12, 34; 2 Kgs 9:36; 17:13; 2 Chr 10:15; Neh 9:30; and seventeen times attributed to Moses) is also paralleled in the Zakir inscription (Ross, "Prophecy," 4).

257. For the image in Yahwistic prophetism, cf. Cross, Myth, 186–89. For the covenant as suzerain-vassal treaty, see, e.g., Kline, Treaty.

258. Holladay, "Statecraft," 34 (cf. also 31–32, esp. 32nn14, 16). See also possible "messenger" names in Ross, "Prophecy," 5–6 (also Mal 1:1 in the LXX; Lewis, Prophets, 82).

259. See Rabe, "Prophecy," 127; cf. Weinfeld, "Patterns," 187–88; on the form, see also Ramsey, "Speech-Forms" (though I doubt the cultic use); Blenkinsopp, "Reproach"; cf. also the covenant format in Tucker, "Prophetic Speech" (though he may push the point too far).

260. Gurney, Hittites, 158–59. Likewise, although Greeks were not limited to divination, it characterized Greek practice far more than that of ancient Israel (Lange, "Seers").

only among the Hittites but also at Ugarit, Hamath, and elsewhere, with divination predominating.[261]

Mari provides better parallels to the forms of Israelite prophetism, though it is going too far to suggest that the activity originated there.[262] (Still, even at Mari, divination was used for the final evaluation of prophetic claims.)[263] In addition to Mari, Egyptian prophetic literature offers a parallel to Israelite prophetism,[264] especially where its emphasis on justice overlaps with that of the writing prophets starting in the eighth century B.C.E.[265] That Israel's prophets sometimes traveled or worked in bands (e.g., 1 Sam 10:5; 19:20; 2 Kgs 2:3, 5, 7; 4:38; 6:1) is also not unique, since prophets at Mari sometimes acted in concert.[266]

Often seers in the ancient Near East served the function of political legitimation or to confirm impending victory in military campaigns.[267] Apparently, a truce was established with a rival Egyptian dynasty on the basis of a prophetic message,[268] and Akkadian oracles contain optimistic prophecies concerning Esarhaddon's successes.[269] Omens by seers (probably diviners) affected the actions of armies from Mari.[270] This practice may have had a magical function in weakening the enemy;[271] certainly Hittites and Egyptians used ritual accusation and execration oracles.[272] Oracles against nations were thus not necessarily delivered to those nations; an oracle against Babylon at Mari was given to the king of Mari, not to that of Babylon.[273] Israel also had its share of oracles to the nations (e.g., Isa 13–23; Amos 1:3–2:6), prophetic insight before battles (e.g., 1 Sam 23:2, 4; 30:8), and other prophecies that had military significance (e.g., 2 Kgs 6:8–14). Military use of divination[274] continued in the Greek and Roman spheres.

Prophecies also validated royal enthronements and reinforced political perspectives.[275] This was also the case in Israel (e.g., 2 Sam 7:12–16; Ps 2:7–9). Naturally,

261. Lindblom, *Prophecy*, 31. Rainey, "Kingdom," 123, concurs but notes several rare references in Akkadian found at Ugarit. For divination in more recent cultures, see, e.g., Mbiti, *Religions*, 89, 218, 232–33, 328; Shorter, *Witchdoctor*, 94; Saoyao, "Practices," 77–78.

262. Some suggest that Israel's prophetic style as a whole originated with Mari (Bright, *History*, 88–89; more cautiously, Ross, "Prophecy," 11–12), but the usage probably predates Mari (cf. Pettinato, *Archives*, 319n12; Kitchen, *World*, 47) and may have been widespread in the milieu. (Mobile prophets unattached to the local sanctuary might also appear at Ebla [cf. Pettinato, *Archives*, 119].) Prophetism appears even in many preliterate cultures; what should be sought in the milieu is the forms rather than the concept.

263. Moran, "Prophecy," 22–24; Huffmon, "Prophecy," 109; Paul, "Prophets," 1160.

264. With Lindblom, *Prophecy*, 31.

265. For the moral emphasis, see, e.g., Scott, *Relevance*, 57–58; McCown, *Genesis*, 213–15. Though Heschel, *Prophets*, 465–66, offers contrasts even here (such as the Israelite focus on justice for the poor more than on lamenting the demise of prosperity).

266. Huffmon, "Prophecy," 107; Paul, "Prophets," 1155–56, 1160.

267. Victory oracles constituted one of the most common kinds of oracles in Assyria, at Mari, and in Israel (van der Toorn, "Oracle de victoire").

268. "The Instruction for King *Meri-Ka-Re*" (*ANET* 416).

269. *ANET* 449–50.

270. Pritchard, *East*, 1:261. Moran, "Prophecy," 17, notes that *ARM* 13.23, 114 from Mari "predict either victory over Babylon or at least deliverance from its threat."

271. Hayes, "Oracles," 81, compares the Balaam oracle.

272. Ibid., 85–86, 91. Its connection with the royal coronation ritual, however (90–91), is not demonstrable.

273. Hayes, "Oracles," 84–85; Paul, "Prophets," 1160; Craghan, "Mari," 48; cf. 1 Kgs 22:12. Oracles against nations in Amos, Isaiah, Jeremiah, and Ezekiel (and probably even those against cities, e.g., in Mic 1) need not have been delivered to those nations (e.g., Isa 37:21; though there may have been exceptions when the opportunity arose; 2 Kgs 8:7–8; Jer 27:3).

274. E.g., Xen. *Cyr.* 6.4.12–13; Ps.-Callisth. *Alex.* 1.2–3; Hdn. 8.3.7 (on Italians); cf. also Kearsley, "Octavian."

275. Ross, "Prophecy," 9; Wilson, "Early Prophecy," 10; *ANET* 446–48. At Mari, extant oracles focused on the king's activity, whereas the interests of local shrines predominate in the outlying areas (Moran, "Prophecy," 17–18; cf. Lindblom, *Prophecy*, 30); many of Israel's extant prophecies address kings, though this is surely

prudent ancient Near Eastern prophets typically gave favorable oracles concerning kings (cf. 1 Kgs 22:10–13; 2 Kgs 8:10);[276] some were likely even on the government payroll,[277] as apparently sometimes in Israel (1 Kgs 22:23; 1 Chr 25:5; 2 Chr 18:22; 29:25; 35:15; cf. Jer 37:19). (Although Israel's prophets could address anyone on any subject [e.g., Num 11:25–29; 1 Sam 9:6, 20; 10:5], the interest of the biblical writers in God's purposes in history led to a frequent mention of prophecies to kings, both positive and negative.)

Nevertheless, kings were bound to obey the words of the gods through the prophets, unfavorable though they might be. Thus even Assyrian kings took military actions based on oracles,[278] and in some cases at Mari, prophets even dared pronounce judgment on rulers.[279] Certainly, in Israel in normal times, prophets exercised authority over kings in their role as YHWH's messengers, even when their messages were harsh; they also enjoyed prophetic immunity from being harmed for their words.[280]

Despite some oracular forms shared with various surrounding cultures, Israelite prophecy was distinctive in many respects.[281] Thus, for example, despite some parallels with Mari prophetism, there are significant differences.[282] Many of Israel's prophets address moral issues and reprove rulers for personal morality, exposing themselves to ridicule or death for the message, in contrast to extant prophecies from surrounding cultures.[283] The lengthy succession of countercultural prophets over the period of several centuries is also missing elsewhere.[284] Most distinctive, of course, is that Israel's prophets spoke for a different deity: they spoke for only one God, indeed a universal God with absolute and exalted moral interests.[285] We turn now to approaches

---

due to the large-scale focus of the preserved books (cf., e.g., 1 Sam 9:6–9; 1 Kgs 17:14). Roman divination continued to affect political perspectives (cf. Ripat, "Omens").

276. Moran, "Prophecy," 29–54.

277. Huffmon, "Prophecy," 105. At Mari they were connected with the royal court but were generally not on the royal payroll (so Hayes, "Prophetism," 409).

278. ANET 281, 284ff.; Pritchard, East, 1:192, 196, 198. In Mesha's Moabite inscription, see ANET 320 (Pritchard, East, 1:209–10).

279. Hayes, "Prophetism," 404–5. Many were simply conditional as threats, but some others were absolute (Craghan, "Mari," 46). On the usual view, most Egyptian judgment oracles (e.g., ANET 441–46) seem to have been issued after the fact.

280. See, e.g., 1 Sam 10:8; 15:1, 18–19; 1 Kgs 11:29–39; 12:22–24; 13:4; 14:4; 18:13, 22; 19:15–16; 2 Kgs 3:14; 4:13; 9:1–2; 13:14; 1 Chr 16:22 [the patriarchs]; 2 Chr 20:20; 25:16. The word of a prophet was God's message (1 Sam 4:1; 2 Sam 24:18–19); at least at the beginning of dynasties, they anointed kings (1 Sam 13:14; 16:13; 1 Kgs 1:34, 45 [but cf. 1:39]; 12:15; cf. 2 Kgs 8:13). For judgment oracles, see, e.g., 2 Sam 24:11–13; 1 Kgs 13:21–22; 14:5–16; 16:2–7; 20:42; 21:19–24; 2 Kgs 1:16; 5:7; 7:2; 2 Chr 2:16). On immunity, one may compare that granted to heralds throughout Mediterranean and Middle Eastern antiquity (see 2 Sam 1:15; 18:20, 22; Hom. Il. 17.694–96; Eurip. Heracl. 272; Xen. Anab. 5.7.18–19, 34; Apollod. Epit. 3.28–29; Polyb. 15.2; Dion. Hal. Ant. rom. 8.43.4; Diod. Sic. 4.10.3–4; 36.15.1–2; Jos. Ant. 8.220–21; Appian Hist. rom. 12.12.84; Arrian Ind. 34.4; 35.1; Dio Cass. 19.61; Ps.-Callisth. Alex. 1.35, 37); their office was held sacred (Hom. Il. 1.334; 7.274–82; 8.517; Aeschines Tim. 21; Cic. Phil. 13.21.47; Hdn. 6.4.6).

281. Pfeiffer, Ras Shamra, 44.

282. Mari prophecy was more mechanical than in, e.g., Hosea (Buss, "Prophecy," 338); Scott, Relevance, 58, distinguishes the biblical prophets' urgent message from the repetitious form in pagan cults. Paul, "Prophets," 1160, lists seven contrasts: Mari prophets' demands were cultic or political, not ethical; the primary agenda with the king was favor for the cult; Mari prophecy does not speak of the deity's being involved in history; at least twice, the king would make the final decision (ARM 2.90; 3.40); the lock or fringe is missing in Israel (though cf. its identifying value in 1 Sam 15:27; 24:11; 1 Kgs 11:30); omens had to authenticate the oracle (perhaps the most significant contrast); and there was no prophetic succession.

283. See Kitchen, World, 116–18. Egyptian sermons on social ills would be closest in content, but they seem to have been mostly composed safely after the judgments they predict, sometimes to extinct dynasties.

284. Scott, Relevance, 57 (though his scheme, 59–62, appears somewhat subjective); esp. Heschel, Prophets, 472.

285. Heschel, Prophets, 471–73, esp. 471; Craghan, "Mari," 52. On moral and other contrasts between YHWH and other deities, see comment on Acts 14:15–17. The prophetic conflict between YHWH and

to prophecy in early Judaism and its Greco-Roman context (although some further comments about Israelite prophecy will appear below at relevant points).

2. Departure of the Spirit and Cessation of Prophecy

Although the rabbis emphasized the cessation of prophecy more than others, it is an exaggeration to claim that only they believed that prophecy had ceased.[286] Most early Jews of the Maccabean and later eras allowed that prophecy continued in some form but not through official "prophets" on the same level as in the era of earlier Israel.

a. Prophecy's Cessation Generally

Some scholars have traced the belief that prophecy had ended to late in the OT period,[287] but stronger arguments have been made for this belief's arising in the "intertestamental" period. Hill, for example, arguing for the "intertestamental" period, points to the use of pseudonymity in apocalyptic texts[288] and argues that no prophets appear who speak with the authority of OT prophetic messengers.[289] Aside from the activities of prophets chronicled in Josephus (below), Hill's arguments depend ultimately on assuming that prophetic authority would be conveyed by the same genre conventions in all periods, which does not hold true even in the OT itself.[290]

There are, however, indications that prophecy no longer maintained the role it once had and that some parts of Judaism did not believe that prophets continued in the biblical sense. First Maccabees 9:27 speaks of the cessation of prophecy, and 4:45–46 and 14:41 speak of the coming of a prophet as a future expectation.[291] Against some scholars,[292] "prophet" in Scripture normally connoted inspired authority, and so there is no reason to assume a new definition here. First Maccabees 14:41 need not relegate prophets only to the end time, but it does clearly indicate that none were known or acknowledged in that time and that Simon's divinely given leadership ability was not regarded as making him a prophet.

Josephus contends that there has been no exact succession of prophets since the time of Artaxerxes, which was why no books had been accorded canonical authority

---

Baal is distinctive (see Buber, *Faith*, 70–75), perhaps because of the exclusivism of YHWH's cult (but cf. the political struggle in the era of Akhenaton). (Parallels might also appear in the imposition of foreign cults, though Yahwism's exclusivism amplified the reaction.)

286. As in Sandmel, *Judaism*, 174–75.

287. Hill, *Prophecy*, 21, citing the view, based on "Zech. 13.4–6; Mal. 4.5–6 and perhaps Ps. 74.9." The problem with using such texts to make such a case, of course, arises if one suspects that Zechariah and Malachi may be claiming to *be* prophecy, even if postexilic prophetic form often differed from preexilic forms (much less poetry, etc.).

288. Ibid., 22. See further 25, 71.

289. Ibid., 25.

290. Hill explicitly excludes the *Sibylline Oracles* from consideration, though he does not think this changes the case at all. Despite the purely hellenized form of these oracles, however, they are spoken with full authority, and Sibylline pseudonymity was a literary convention meant to increase, not decrease, one's prophetic authority. On change in OT prophecy, see Haran, "Continuity and Change"; but cf. Paul, "Prophets."

291. Hill, *Prophecy*, 22. Aune contends here that 1 Macc 4:45b–46 refers to a future *clerical* prophet, not a prophet like the OT prophets, but offers no evidence to support this position (*Prophecy*, 105). He suggests that 1 Macc 9:27 means only that the ancient kind of prophets no longer appeared, and that 14:41 does not speak of a future prophet but was meant only to restrain an idealization of the Hasmonean program and, again, refers only to clerical prophecy related to the priesthood (*Prophecy*, 105). Aune may be right (against some scholars) that the future prophet is not eschatological, but he offers no convincing reason to assume that the intended readers of 1 Maccabees should have taken "prophet" in any other than the conventional sense.

292. E.g., Hill, *Prophecy*, 22.

since that time.[293] Josephus does report continuing prophetic phenomena, but he fails to associate them, unlike prophetic activity from the biblical period, with πνεῦμα.[294] Moreover, although prophecy continued, the *title* "prophet" belongs only to the past and to the future. Josephus used the term "prophets" for his own time only when he spoke of "false prophets."[295]

Other texts also seem to imply that prophets are no more in the present time (*2 Bar.* 85:3; perhaps John 8:53); Sir 36:14–16 probably implies an eschatological restoration or multiplication of prophecy (36:14, λόγια) and perhaps prophets (36:15–16).[296] *Fourth Ezra* 12:42 suggests that "Ezra" alone remained. Some scholars argue that examples of continuing prophecy appear especially in circles believing that the end time was at hand.[297]

Of course, while there may have existed in various circles a belief that prophets no longer existed as they had in biblical times, no one denied that revelatory experiences continued to be possible.[298] But biblical prophecy was seen as different from postbiblical prophecy; thus, in Josephus and Philo, "πνεῦμα is confined to prophecy in the biblical period," giving a special role to the canon.[299]

b. Cessation of Prophecy in the Rabbis

If the concept of the prophetic Spirit's departure already existed in early Judaism in some sense, the rabbis certainly developed it further after 70 C.E.[300] The Holy Spirit might have departed from Israel after Elijah was taken up to heaven[301] or (with minor exceptions) in the time of Jeremiah,[302] but the usual rabbinic timing associated with the Holy Spirit's departure was the death of the last of the biblical prophets.[303] Some later rabbis dated the departure of the Holy Spirit to the destruction of the temple,[304] but the net effect was the same: the Spirit of prophecy had ceased to be available in their own time. This departure has been widely noted by modern scholars.[305] Some

293. Jos. *Ag. Ap.* 1.41. For more on the cessation of prophets in Josephus, see Leiman, "Josephus and Canon"; Bamberger, "Prophet," 305.

294. Best, "Use of Pneuma by Josephus," 222–25; Isaacs, *Spirit*, 49.

295. See Aune, "Προφήτης"; cf. also Hill, *Prophecy*, 26, 28. For the eschatological prophets in Josephus (regarded by him as false prophets), see Aune, *Prophecy*, 81. But while Josephus dismisses false eschatological prophets and their signs, he accepts authentic oracles and omens; see Kee, *Miracle*, 178–79. The Qumran texts may contrast true inspiration by the Spirit with false prophets (CD VI, 1; 4Q266 3 II, 9; 4Q267 2 6; 4Q269 4 I, 2; 6Q15 3 4), as also in *Herm.* 43.2, 7, 12.

296. Although prophets and prophecy were added to older scriptural examples in Sirach (Sir 46:1), I am not aware of any emphasis on current prophetism in the book.

297. See Sommer, "Prophecy," 36. We should note, however, that a view may be widespread without being universal (see examples below).

298. See esp. Grudem, *Prophecy*, 21–23, for references on the cessation of prophecy, but see 24–33 on the continuation of revelatory experiences understood to be different from OT prophecy.

299. Isaacs, *Spirit*, 51.

300. That most rabbis associated the Spirit with past revelation does not mean that the rabbis had no surrogates for prophecy. In fact, they stressed that the prophetic function had been subsumed under their task of expounding the written Scriptures. Controversy with pneumatic sects—particularly the most pneumatic, early Christianity—may be an additional reason for emphasizing the quenched Spirit.

301. *t. Soṭah* 12:5.

302. *Pesiq. Rab Kah.* 13:14. For its diminution after the first temple's destruction, see *b. Yoma* 21b; *Eccl. Rab.* 12:7, §1.

303. E.g., *t. Soṭah* 13:3; *b. Sanh.* 11a, bar.; *Soṭah* 48b, bar.; *Yoma* 9b; *Song Rab.* 8:9, §3; cf. *Ḥul.* 137b; *Gen. Rab.* 37:7.

304. *Num. Rab.* 15:10; *Song Rab.* 8:9, §3, both anonymous.

305. See esp. Davies, *Paul*, 208–15, who provides the appropriate qualifications; Bamberger, "Prophet," 306; Leivestad, "Dogma"; Hill, *Prophecy*, 33–35. This view is commonly held; e.g., Rivkin, *Revolution*, 86; Patte, *Hermeneutic*, 119; Barrett, *Spirit*, 123.

note that by relegating prophecy to the past, the rabbis also reduced competition with their own role as interpreters of past revelation.[306]

This does not mean that revelations were not available, since the heavenly voice (*bat qol*) functioned as a surrogate for the Spirit of prophecy.[307] But this substitute was at best an inferior one, and there was thus sometimes an expectation of a future time when the prophetic Spirit would be restored. The giving of the Spirit had been associated with the eschatological salvation of Israel in the Hebrew prophets[308] and was similarly associated with eschatology in early Christianity.[309] Lack of emphasis on an eschatological role for the Spirit in Diaspora Jewish texts fits the lack of eschatological emphasis in Diaspora Judaism.[310] Its apparent absence from Palestinian Jewish texts, apart from the writings of the Qumran covenanters,[311] leads some scholars to suppose that the doctrine was not widespread in early Judaism.[312] This is, however, almost an argument from silence, given the relative scarcity of references to the Spirit in early Judaism and the fact that there is not an abundance of Palestinian Jewish literature, apart from the Scrolls, from this period. Although rabbinic texts do not stress eschatology to the extent that the documents of the Qumran covenanters do, some later texts do occasionally suggest an eschatological return of the Spirit that corresponds to the belief that it had departed for the present time.[313]

3. The Continuance of Prophecy

Although some people allowed that prophecy had ceased, this was not the general view outside rabbinic circles.[314] Perhaps prophets had ceased in some sense or the Spirit had departed, but prophetic activity continued. Josephus says that John Hyrcanus had the gift of prophecy; he also attributes this power several times to the Essenes.[315] He also claimed to possess the gift himself, in the form of prediction of the future.[316] And although Joshua ben Hananiah (Jesus son of Ananias, prophesying shortly before Jerusalem's demise) may

306. Greenspahn, "Prophecy."
307. E.g., *t. Soṭah* 13:3; *b. Sanh.* 11a; *Yoma* 9b; *Soṭah* 48b. See comment on Acts 10:13.
308. Cf., e.g., Chevallier, *Ancien Testament*, 31–32; Ma, *Spirit*, 175–78, 210–11. For associations with the new covenant in the OT, see Chevallier, *Esprit de Dieu*, 84–85; in early Judaism, 85–88.
309. Cf., e.g., *Esprit de Dieu*, 220–22; Dunn, "Kingdom," 36.
310. Isaacs, *Spirit*, 84. She refers mainly to Philo, of whom the statement is undoubtedly true, and Josephus, who had good apologetic reasons not to stress the eschatological side of Judaism. But we may observe here *Sib. Or.* 4.46, possibly from the Hellenistic period (also 4.189–90, probably ca. 80 C.E.), although, in context, "spirit" may mean simply "life" at the resurrection.
311. Coppens, "Don," 209, emphasizes that the Spirit is eschatological in the Qumran scrolls, linking it with the new-creation idea.
312. Isaacs, *Spirit*, i, 84–86.
313. See, in some detail, Davies, *Paul*, 208–17; Menzies, *Development*, 104–8; idem, *Empowered*, 94–98, 232–43 (rightly emphasizing the texts' lateness); cf. Jeremias, *Theology*, 80–81; idem, *Parables*, 117, 126; Freedman, "Pottery," 23. The presence of the Holy Spirit on Israel in the first exodus (*Mek. Shir.* 7.17–18 [Lauterbach, 2:55]; cf. *Ruth Rab.* 2:1), perhaps related to the idea of God's Shekinah among Israel at that time, might also allow for such an endowment at a future new exodus.
314. Sandmel, *Judaism*, 174, as above; Aune, *Prophecy*, 4–6; Levison, "Withdraw"; Knox, *Jerusalem*, 36. Foerster, "Geist," 117–18, thinks that the view that the Holy Spirit ceased with the last prophets was found mainly in rabbinic texts addressing certain situations and thus that it was not a dogmatic construct.
315. Jos. *War* 1.78–80; 2.159 (though the latter applies also to biblical interpretation, perhaps along the lines of the Qumran pesharim); cf. *War* 1.68–69; *Ant.* 15.374–79; 17.346 in Isaacs, *Spirit*, 49; Aune, *Prophecy*, 145; more extensively, Gray, *Figures*, 80–111. Aune argues that the prophecy in Jos. *War* 2.159 is noneschatological and very Hellenistic, and therefore probably inauthentic (*Prophecy*, 145); but Josephus could have hellenized the form himself.
316. See in Gray, *Figures*, 35–79; Isaacs, *Spirit*, 48; Hill, *Prophecy*, 26–27, on Jos. *War* 3.351–54; cf. an analogous claim of prediction in Cic. *Fam.* 6.6.7. Today prophecy is often associated with prediction of the future, but while this sense was included in ancient literature (Plut. *E Delph.* 6, *Mor.* 387B; Heraclitus *Ep.* 5;

not have received the title "prophet," his actions and message certainly characterize him as one.[317] It is thus fair to conclude that although Josephus distinguished contemporary prophecy, in some sense, from its biblical form, he accepted its continuance.[318] Similarly, even if Philo felt that prophecy had ceased with the biblical period, he felt that inspiration continued and that he availed himself of it.[319] If this is not quite as explicit as Josephus's use of προφητ- roots for the present period, it is nonetheless typical Greek language for inspiration as well as Philo's own language for the inspiration of ΟΤ prophets.[320]

Despite (again) the lack of the prophetic title (even for the Teacher of Righteousness), prophecy also may have continued in the Qumran sect, who believed that the Spirit guided their activities.[321] Prophecy and even the presence of the Spirit continued in early Judaism, particularly in apocalyptically oriented sects.[322] Still, even in Qumran texts, the present revelatory dimension of the Spirit is relegated especially to wisdom and insight into the Scriptures.

Some scholars have also argued that prophecy continued in rabbinic Judaism. Abrahams, for instance, notes that Maimonides believed that prophecy belonged to good men,[323] and argues that the prophetic office was transferred to the sages.[324] This much is true; but when Abrahams argues that although prophets had gone, the Holy Spirit continued to work in human experience,[325] his argument rests more on a theological interpretation of rabbinic literature as a whole than on the normal usage of the language of "Holy Spirit" in that literature.[326]

Likewise, Aune notes that among the rabbis there were exceptions to the view that prophecy had ceased,[327] yet fails to emphasize the extent to which these examples represent a minority opinion. Further, in early Jewish texts, one can sometimes predict the future without necessarily being a prophet (especially on one's deathbed, as in some rabbinic examples),[328] and not all predictions are prophetic.[329] Admittedly, Johanan ben Zakkai is

---

Socrates *Ep.* 1; 6; *Sib. Or.* 3.822 [both future and past]; rabbinic references in Bowman, "Prophets," 107), it was not the standard or only sense of the term.

317. See Jos. *War* 6.300–309, and esp. the study of him in Noack, *Jesus Ananiassøn*; Aune, *Prophecy*, 135–37. Cf. also on John the Baptist in Josephus, presented as, but not termed, a "prophet" (Aune, *Prophecy*, 130).

318. See Gray, *Figures*, 7–34, esp. 34.

319. Isaacs, *Spirit*, 48, cites Philo *Abr.* 35; cf. *Migr.* 34–35; *Cher.* 27; *Dreams* 2.252; she also notes that corybantic frenzy thrusts ascetics into the wilderness in *Names* 39; moreover, the LXX translators are inspired in *Mos.* 2.37.

320. Of interest here is Baer, *Categories*, 55–64, 96–98, for an important discussion of divine inspiration as divine impregnation in Philo. He also addresses Philonic texts, fewer in number but nevertheless significant, in which divine inspiration also enables one to throw off sense perception and thus become "virgin" or asexual; this might connect the prophetic Spirit with the purifying aspect of the Spirit, but (especially if the latter was primarily Essene) the latter may have been unknown to Philo.

321. Hill, *Prophecy*, 40–41 (though depending on 1QpHab II, 1–2, a reconstructed text that could be interpreted otherwise; and on the assumption that the Teacher authored many of the *Hodayot*).

322. Aune, *Prophecy*, 104; see earlier idem, *Cultic Setting*.

323. Abrahams, *Studies* (2), 126; he also believed, as Abrahams points out, that prophecy would be restored in the messianic age.

324. Ibid., 126; addressed in more detail below.

325. Ibid., 127–28; cf. also Abelson, *Immanence*, 268.

326. Although there are several references to its presence on the community gathered for Pesach; see in Urbach, *Sages*, 1:576.

327. Aune, *Prophecy*, 104. He provides (375n12) a partial list of modern scholars who have also come to this conclusion.

328. E.g., R. Eliezer ben Hyrcanus in *'Abot R. Nat.* 25 A (a connection also evident in, e.g., Plato *Apol.* 39); see also Xen. *Apol.* 30; Tac. *Ann.* 6.46, 48; perhaps Vell. Paterc. 2.71.2; further, Malina and Rohrbaugh, *John*, 221–22). In early Judaism outside the rabbis, see much more often testamentary literature. Jesus's passion predictions likely have historical foundations (see, e.g., Tan, *Zion Traditions*, 57–80, esp. 79–80, 221–22; Keck, *Jesus*, 118; Keener, *Historical Jesus*, 283–302, esp. 288–89).

329. Rabbi Eliezer ben Hyrcanus, Aune points out, was said to have predicted suffering just before Messiah's coming (*m. Soṭah* 9:15 and other references in Aune, *Prophecy*, 145), but this was part of Judaism's

said to predict the future,[330] which does suggest prophetic insight; this probably reflects the sort of miraculous powers attributed to past rabbis, similar to R. Simeon ben Yohai's ability to disintegrate disrespectful people with a harsh look.[331] (Miraculous powers could safely be attributed to past guardians of the tradition without opening the field up to charismatic challengers of that tradition.) The downplaying of current prophecy may "reflect an apologetic attempt to undermine the prophetic claims of the early Christians"[332] and, to a lesser extent, other prophetic movements that could challenge the epistemological hegemony and thus authority of the rabbinic movement.[333]

We should keep in mind, however, what was noted above: even where prophecy continued, it was rarely seen in the same terms as OT prophecy. Josephus and Philo do not associate current inspiration with the Spirit;[334] Qumran documents associate prophecy and the Spirit only with the past.[335] The Qumran community might emphasize the Spirit's presence because it believed that it lived at the threshold of the new age and thus could experience some of the power of that age in advance.[336] Boring suggests that prophecy was likewise, by definition, eschatological; this was true both in groups "that affirmed the presence of the prophetic Spirit (e.g., Qumran) and those that denied it (many streams of rabbinic tradition)."[337] The early Christians seem to be noteworthy in overcoming "this reluctance to apply the designation to contemporary figures";[338] see, for example, Acts 11:28; 21:9–11.

eschatological tradition by Eliezer's time (e.g., 1QM XV, 1; Sib. Or. 3.213–15; Test. Mos. 7–8; 4 Ezra 6–8 passim; 2 Bar. 26:1–30:24; in later rabbis, e.g., m. Soṭah 9:15; b. Sanh. 97–99) and could thus be viewed as appropriate to a wisdom teacher, not necessarily a prophet.

330. Aune, Prophecy, 144, citing y. Šabb. 16:15d. Although the tradition may depend on Josephus's account of his own insight, the focus here is on the extent to which the view existed in rabbinic tradition, not on the antiquity of this particular tradition.

331. B. Šabb. 34a; Gen. Rab. 79:6; Pesiq. Rab Kah. 11:16; later transferred to R. Johanan and others (b. B. Bat. 75a; Pesiq. Rab Kah. 18:5; cf. "the rabbis" in b. B. Meṣiʿa 85a). Is this more related to the evil-eye idea also found in the Greco-Roman world (Plut. Table 5.7.1–6, Mor. 680C–683B; Pleas. L. 5, Mor. 1090C) or to the idea that the pious man can summon forth divine fire (besides Elijah in 1 Kgs 18:38; 2 Kgs 1:10, 12; Liv. Pr. 21:2 [Schermann, §33], cf. Rev 11:5; Jos. Asen. 25:6–7; Test. Ab. 10:11–12; 14:11 A; 12:3–4 B; and perhaps y. Ḥag. 2:1, §4)? Cf. other images of fire falling in judgment (Lev 10:2; Num 16:35; 1QM XVII, 2–3; Jos. Ant. 4.55–56; Luke 9:54; Rev 20:9) or fire falling on altars (Exod 40:34; Plut. Aem. Paul. 24.1) or during esoteric Scripture expositions (e.g., y. Ḥag. 2:1, §4) to validate divine authorization.

332. Aune, Prophecy, 104; Glatzer, "Study," 115–17, 121–22 (an already-existing tendency greatly augmented in reaction to the charismatic/prophetic activity of early Christianity). Schäfer, Vorstellung, 89–114, treats the quenching of the Spirit and eschatological renewal, and (on 116–33) those texts in which the Spirit is still available to the pious, suggesting that Christians may have used the presence of the Spirit as a polemic; Reif, "Review," 158, reiterates Urbach's view that the rabbis were reacting against early Christianity and argues that Schäfer presents no evidence to substantiate his view as better. It is not unlikely, however, that the polemic would have been operating in both directions.

333. One may wonder if Mekilta's emphatic denial of Baruch's possession of the gift of prophecy (Mek. Pisha 1.148–66 [Lauterbach, 1:14–15]) is not intended against the circles that produced 2 Baruch in the early second century. Likewise, Enoch was extolled in the rabbinic mystical tractate 3 Enoch as well as in other Enoch literature; Ps.-Eupolemus (OTP 2:881); 1Qap Gen^ar II, 19; Test. Ab. 11:3–9 B; Jub. 4:23, 10:17 (see further VanderKam, "Traditions"); but early Amoraim, seeking to refute minim, argued that Enoch died and was either wicked or ambivalent (Gen. Rab. 25:1).

334. Isaacs, Spirit, 49.

335. E.g., 1QS VIII, 16; 4Q381 69 4; cf. 4Q481a 2 4. This might be a coincidence due to the limited texts available, in view of Josephus's emphasis on Essene prophecy.

336. Aune, Prophecy, 81, 104; see his earlier treatment of realized eschatology in idem, Cultic Setting, esp. ch. 2, "The Present Realization of Eschatological Salvation in the Qumran Community," 29–44. Cf. Chevallier, "Souffle," 38–41, who contrasts the Qumran writings with rabbinic literature and suggests that the presence of the Spirit in the Qumran writings is due to their partly realized eschatology. Much of early Christianity may have shared a view similar to the Qumran perspective.

337. Boring, Sayings, 111. Rabbinic association of the Spirit with the future seems primarily late and probably a peripheral emphasis (cf. Menzies, Empowered, 94–98).

338. Aune, Prophecy, 195.

4. Recipients of the Spirit and/or Prophecy

Jewish literature (especially the more abundant but post-NT rabbinic texts) often speaks of those who were worthy to receive various gifts from God, even if those gifts were sometimes withheld due to the unworthiness of their generation. For instance, in the essentially rabbinic mystical treatise called 3 *Enoch*, R. Ishmael, being descended from Aaron, is "worthy to behold the chariot";[339] likewise, some Amoraim felt that those who did good deeds were worthy to receive the Shekinah.[340]

Although Qumran texts speak of the Spirit as a current blessing for the community (e.g., 4Q509 V, 15–16), some other groups would not have agreed. Rabbi Nehemiah argued that as a reward for their faith, the people of Israel had been worthy of having the Holy Spirit rest on them.[341] Rabbi Eliezer used to say that the Holy Spirit would rest on one who cleaved to God's presence;[342] an Amora claimed that whoever taught Torah was worthy to receive the Spirit.[343]

But usually the Holy Spirit or Spirit of prophecy was not easily acquired.[344] There are a number of rabbinic stories about pious rabbis who were worthy to receive the Holy Spirit but who could not because their generations were unworthy of its effects.[345] This story is told, for instance, of Hillel and Samuel Hakaton: "Elders went into the upper room in the house of Gedaya in Jericho. An echo went forth and said to them, 'There are among you two who are worthy of receiving the Holy Spirit, and Hillel the Elder is one of them.' They gazed upon Samuel the Small."[346] Similarly, Israel acquired her prophets on account of merit.[347]

Related to this is the idea that the Holy Spirit was quenched in Israel because of Israel's sins.[348] This accords with the more common image of the removal of

339. 3 *En.* 2:4 (*OTP* 1:257), basing the case on Ps 144:15. Cf. Manoah's doubt of his worthiness to see the angel in *L.A.B.* 42:5 (he does, however, get to see him, 42:6–7).

340. *B. B. Bat.* 10a; *Num. Rab.* 12:21. *'Abot R. Nat.* 14 A; 28, §57 B, attribute this worthiness for the Shekinah to thirty of Hillel's eighty disciples (rec. A claims that their generation was unworthy, as below).

341. *Mek. Besh.* 7.135ff. (Lauterbach, 1:252–53). *Exod. Rab.* 5:20 suggests from Num 11 that because of the elders' merit, they received the Holy Spirit and so were made prophets. *'Abot R. Nat.* 11, §28 B, probably refers to *prophets* worthy to have the Holy Spirit rest on them.

342. *Sipre Deut.* 173.1.3 (Neusner, 2:50). Rabbi Yudan in *Song Rab.* 1:1, §9 declares that whoever publicly teaches the Torah merits the Holy Spirit resting on him. One of the Amoraim by the name of R. Aha also linked obedience to reception of the Holy Spirit (*Lev. Rab.* 35:7), although, in general, the Spirit was not so easily received (contrast Rom 5:5; Gal 3:2). For rabbinic references to the Holy Spirit's continued availability for the worthy, see also Glatzer, "Prophecy," 122–24.

343. *Song Rab.* 1:1, §9. For Torah obedience leading to the Spirit, Davies, "Spirit in Mekilta," 98 (idem, *Paul*, 207, 218), cites *m. Soṭah* 9:12, 15; *t. Soṭah* 13:2; *b. 'Abod. Zar.* 20b; *Yoma* 9b; *Soṭah* 48b; *Sanh.* 11a; *Lev. Rab.* 35:7; *Song Rab.* 1:8; *Mek. Besh.* 7.

344. See, e.g., Urbach, *Sages*, 1:577–78.

345. Simeon ben Azzai pointed out that prophecy was acquired only for the sake of Israel and is not due to personal merit, *Mek. Pisha* 1.148–66 (Lauterbach, 1:14–15); all the prophets were thus intensely nationalistic in their Judaism (*Mek. Pisha* 1.105–6 [Lauterbach, 1:10]). For a treatment of mainly Amoraic texts following this tendency, see Bowman, "Prophets," 213–15, and for the nationalistic context of the rabbinic view of prophecy in general, 205–20; Glatzer, "Prophecy," 130–36. Glatzer, "Prophecy," 136, suggests that this is in part due to a polemic against Christian ideas of the church as a new Israel; but it may also indicate a community response to Roman oppression, an alternative to the apocalyptic paradigm.

346. *Y. 'Abod. Zar.* 3:1, §2 (Neusner, 33:114); this was repeated in the upper room at Yavneh with Samuel the Small, all eyes turning to R. Eliezer as the other; also in *y. Hor.* 3:5, §3; *Soṭah* 9:16, §2; in simpler form (but in a later collection), *Song Rab.* 8:9, §3; with thirty of Hillel's eighty disciples, according to "Our rabbis," in *b. Sukkah* 28a; with the Shekinah in place of the Holy Spirit, *b. Soṭah* 48b. For other references to the linking of obedience to Torah with reception of the Holy Spirit, see Davies, "Spirit in Mekilta," 98; idem, *Paul*, 207, 218; Urbach, *Sages*, 1:577–78.

347. *Sipre Deut.* 176.1.1; 176.2.2; R. Akiba in *Mek. Pisha* 1.137–41 (Lauterbach, 1:13); the gift of prophecy was also acquired thus; so *Mek. Pisha* 1.58–113 (Lauterbach, 1:5–11); R. Isaac in *b. Sanh.* 39b.

348. *T. Soṭah* 14:3; cf. also Eph. 4:30; third-century *Test. Sol.* 26:6.

the Shekinah, God's presence, because of sin.[349] In any case, current generations were less worthy than the generations of great prophetic figures of the past, and the rabbis thus found fewer examples of the possession of the Holy Spirit in their own time.[350]

The Tannaim could amplify Moses's prayer that all Israel be prophets,[351] and the Amoraim could connect this with Joel and, echoing Joel, argue that all Israel would be prophets.[352] But this adds little to the picture of an eschatological prophetic community already found in Joel and perhaps implied by the reception of the Spirit in some of the other prophets, and it does not indicate an emphasis on even the eschatological availability of the Spirit in rabbinic Judaism.

Other circles in early Judaism may have been more open to the current availability of the Spirit. In Wis 7:27, for instance, we read that Wisdom "enters into holy souls, making them God's friends and prophets" (NEB). Philo, in *Heir* 259, argues that prophecy is available to every ἀστείῳ, "worthy man."[353]

Among the Qumran covenanters, as Flusser points out, "the Holy Spirit was bestowed upon all the Elect, but not to the same degree." But only the elect had the Holy Spirit, and this distinguished them from anyone else.[354] The presence of the Spirit was also felt to mark off the early Christians as a unique community, as Aune points out: "In early Christianity, the presence of the Spirit within the community was the central phenomenon which convinced Christians that the eschaton had in some decisive way arrived in the person of Jesus of Nazareth."[355]

5. The Nature of Prophecy

It is helpful to look at the way pagan circles and a variety of Jewish circles, including rabbinic sources, understood prophecy as occurring. This examination may offer at least some insight into how early Christians and their contemporaries interpreted some of the early Christian charismatic experience.

349. E.g., *Sipra Qed. pq.* 8.205.2.1, par. 206.2.6; *Sipre Num.* 1.10.3; *Sipre Deut.* 258.2.3, 320.2.1; *b. Ber.* 5b; *Roš Haš.* 31a; *Yoma* 21b; *Šabb.* 33a; 139a; *y. Sanh.* 8:8, §1; *Deut. Rab.* 5:10; 6:14; *Ruth Rab.* 1:2. The Presence withdrew because of sin but was restored because of merit: *Gen. Rab.* 19:7; *Song Rab.* 5:1, §1; *Pesiq. Rab Kah.* 1:1. On merit and the Presence, see *Sipre Deut.* 305.3.1; 312.3.1; 355.6.1; *Gen. Rab.* 60:12; *Exod. Rab.* 45:5; *Num. Rab.* 19:20; *Song Rab.* 4:5, §2; 7:6, §1; *Pesiq. Rab.* 10:2.

350. Adding more prophets to the biblical narrative was much less problematic; e.g., *y. Meg.* 1:5, §3; *Pesiq. Rab Kah.* 16:3; cf. references in Bowman, "Prophets," 205; *Jos. Asen.* 22:13 (Levi as προφήτην); 23:8; *Herm. Vis.* 2.3.4 (and comments by E. G. Martin in *OTP* 2:463–65). That patriarchs should be prophets (expanding Gen 20:7) (see Philonic references in Hill, *Prophecy*, 32) should not surprise us.

351. *Sipre Num.* 96.3.1 (Neusner, 2:109); but it remains a wish, as in Num 11:26.

352. See *Num. Rab.* 15 in Davies, *Paul*, 216; cf. Aune, *Prophecy*, 193; Abrahams, *Studies* (2), 127. But this tradition is late and does not appear to have been a common topic of discussion in our texts.

353. Hill, *Prophecy*, 32.

354. Flusser, *Judaism*, 54; cf. also Coppens, "Don," 209, who notes that it characterized the community. Tannaim cited Hillel for the tradition, mentioned above, that the Holy Spirit rested on the community of festal pilgrims gathered for Pesach (*t. Pesaḥ.* 6:13; *y. Pesaḥ.* 6:1; *b. Pesaḥ.* 66a, in Urbach, *Sages*, 1:576). Davies, *Paul*, 200–204, regards the OT teaching of the Spirit, most frequently observed in terms of prophecy, to be associated with the community for the growth of the community. Presumably, however, the prophetic practices mentioned in 1 Sam 10:5; 19:20 suggest that much prophecy was carried on that was never published because generally only the larger community-oriented prophetic message (and more specific samples of it) were valued by the communities that preserved them.

355. Aune, *Realized Eschatology*, 103. He does not, however, feel that all Christians were regarded as potential prophets (idem, *Prophecy*, 195, 206, esp. on Revelation); this may be affected in part by the various levels of meaning given to the terms "prophets" and "prophecy" in the early Christian literature (cf. 1 Cor 14:29–32).

a. Non-Jewish Sources

Pagan sources could regard prophecy as highly accurate, whether by outstanding individuals[356] or by stationary oracle cults.[357] Jewish sources allowed a few[358] pagan prophets (especially Balaam) some knowledge,[359] but none had revelation at all close to the genuine revelation given to Israel's prophets.[360] Pagans sometimes complained about false prophets and spurious oracles among them;[361] in the ancient Near East, some required confirming signs,[362] and sometimes a king took a lock of hair or fringe of the prophet's garment, perhaps to hold him legally accountable for his message.[363]

As in the ancient Near East in the OT period,[364] so in the Mediterranean world of more recent times,[365] divination was an extremely common practice. Sacrificial divination in Babylonia involved the correspondence between the deity and his possessions in a mystic sense.[366] Through divination, Greeks and Romans sought to discern the "will and mood of the gods" so they could seek to change or accommodate them safely.[367] Divination had the approval of Pythagoras,[368] Platonists,[369] and Stoics[370] despite some opposition.[371] Literature of the early Roman Empire is replete with the

356. E.g., Arrian *Alex.* 4.13.5; Philost. *Vit. Apoll.* 8.26.

357. E.g., Dio Chrys. *Or.* 13.9–10; Xen. Eph. *Anthia* 1.6. See comments in Nagy, "Prologue," xxix; Maclean and Aitken, *Heroikos*, xxxix.

358. Far fewer than in Israel (*Exod. Rab.* 32:3; *Lev. Rab.* 2:9).

359. E.g., *Sipre Deut.* 343.6.1.

360. E.g., *Gen. Rab.* 52:5; 74:7; *Lev. Rab.* 1:13.

361. E.g., Thucyd. 2.21.3; cf. fabricated omens in Philost. *Hrk.* 31.5. Naturally, this was still truer of skeptics such as Lucian: *Alex.* 9; *Peregr.* 30–31; *Dial. G.* 244 (18/16, Hera and Leto 1); *Dem.* 37. A Byzantine text calls Apollo a false prophet (Lucian *Patriot* 5), a view also articulated in *Sib. Or.* 4.4–6. On false prophets, see further comment on Acts 13:6.

362. Weinfeld, "Patterns," 179–80. Cf., e.g., Isa 7:11, 14; 20:3. At Mari, omens provided the final say on a prophecy (Moran, "Prophecy," 22–24; Huffmon, "Prophecy," 109).

363. In public prophecies; Moran, "Prophecy," 19–21; Hayes, "Prophetism," 407–8; Malamat, "Revelations," 225–27; Craghan, "Mari," 542–43.

364. Especially the Mesopotamian *baru* diviners (called "seers" because they read the omens; Lawrence, "Roots of Divination," 55), but the practice was widespread; cf. Gen 44:5; "*Taanach*, No. 1" (fifteenth century B.C.E.; *ANET* 490); Assyrian "Hymn to the Sun-God" (ca. 668–633 B.C.E.; *ANET* 388); Hittite "Investigating the Anger of the Gods" (*ANET* 497–98); "The Telepinus Myth" (*ANET* 128); AQHT C (ii) (*ANET* 153); Akkadian text ("Akkadian Observations on Life and the World Order" [*ANET* 434]); Wilson, "Early Prophecy," 10; Long, "Divination"; Mendenhall, "Mari," 18; Gurney, *Aspects*, 45–46; idem, *Hittites*, 158–59; Lindblom, *Prophecy*, 31; cf. Reiner, "Fortune-Telling." For modern divination, cf., e.g., Gelfand, "Disorders," 161.

365. Among pre-Roman Arabs, Philost. *Vit. Apoll.* 1.20; Greeks, Hdt. 1.47ff.; Paus. 3.11.5; 6.2.4; Burkert, *Religion*, 111–14; Martin, *Religions*, 40–50; Heschel, *Prophets*, 454–56; Scythian, Hdt. 4.68–69; Romans borrowed much from the Etruscans (Briquel, "Divination: Rome," 576–77; cf. Mastrocinque, "Choices," 384, 388); on Roman divination, see Rosenberger, "*Nobiles*," 298–302; in the late republic, e.g., Cic. *Inv.* 1.53.101; in early imperial Rome, MacMullen, *Enemies*, 128–62; paid specialists in the Roman army, Horster, "Professionals," 337. It could take the form of augury (as in Plut. *Rom. Q.* 72, *Mor.* 281B), examination of flames (Apul. *Metam.* 2.11), dream divination (Artemidorus *Oneirocritica*), and a variety of other forms (see Aune, *Prophecy*, 23, for one breakdown of categories, following K. Latte). Divination functioned essentially on the principle of sympathetic magic. See Stogiannos, "Πνευμα Πυθωνα," for a review of the data (in Greek).

366. Lawrence, "Roots of Divination," esp. 52.

367. Rives, *Religion*, 27.

368. Diog. Laert. 8.1.20, 23.

369. Max. Tyre 8.7 (see Trapp, n. 33). For Maximus, prophecy was akin to one's intellectual faculties (Max. Tyre 13, esp. 13.2–3).

370. Cic. *Div.* passim (refuting Stoic arguments); *Nat. d.* 1.20.55–56; 2.3.7–2.4.12, esp. 2.4.12; 3.6.14; Diog. Laert. 7.1.149; cf. Sen. Y. *Nat. Q.* 2.34.1–2. Stoics believed that the gods knew the future because it had already occurred, history being cyclical (Chrysippus frg. 1192, in Boring, Berger, and Colpe, *Commentary*, 312) and that exclusively the virtuous person exercised true mantic gifts (Arius Did. *Epit.* 2.7.11s, pp. 98–99.16–23). They viewed the mantic art as following rules that help one interpret signs from the gods (2.7.5b.12, pp. 24.32–27.2).

371. Certain Cynics (Diog. Laert. 6.2.24; Diogenes *Ep.* 38) and less defined opponents (cf. Artem. *Oneir.* 1.pref.). Some sought to stigmatize diviners in classical Greece to reduce their political effects (Carastro,

Roman use of omens.[372] Sailors depended on omens for good sailing;[373] the pious used divination before battles,[374] and others neglected it to their peril.[375] Besides the examination of entrails,[376] omens could be inferred from birds,[377] from trees,[378] and so forth.[379] Some ancients even used sieves (though most doubted their authenticity).[380] For the use of lots in divination, see comment on Acts 1:26.[381]

Oracular prophetism, however, maintained an important place as well. Despite a reputed decline of some of the great oracular centers[382] and the fact that the Romans tended to be much less interested in prophetism than the Greeks,[383] prophecy also flourished in the eastern Mediterranean, for example, in Egypt;[384] sometimes it was defended by intellectuals.[385] Perhaps connected with antecedents such as Mari through neo-Assyrian and other models,[386] ecstatic prophecy was found in some[387] Greek oracles apparently from the Archaic period on.

"Tirésias"). Naturally, the most solid opposition would be encountered in Jewish sources: Hecataeus in Jos. *Ag. Ap.* 1.203–4 (*OTP* 2:919); *Sib. Or.* 3.224–26 (probably second century B.C.E.); *Asc. Is.* 2:5; 11QT^a LX, following Deut 18; *Sipra Qed. pq.* 6.203.2.1; *Sipre Deut.* 171.5.1; 172.1.2–4; cf. Smelik, "Witch."

372. See, e.g., Val. Max. 1.4.1–7; 1.4.ext. 1–2 on auspices; 1.5.1–9 and 1.5.ext. 1–2 on omens; 1.6.1–13 and 1.6.ext. 1–3 on prodigies; 1.7.1–8 and 1.7.ext. 1–10 on dreams; 1.8.praef.–1.8.12 and 1.8.ext. 1–19 on miracles. Among others, Augustus took omens seriously (Suet. *Aug.* 92.1; cf. Vespasian, Suet. *Vesp.* 5; contrast Tiberius in Suet. *Tib.* 63.1); Julius did not (Suet. *Julius* 59, 77), to his doom (*Julius* 81.2–4; Vell. Paterc. 2.57.2). Omens were consulted even to ensure that weddings proved auspicious (Quint. *Decl.* 291.5).

373. Philost. *Hrk.* 1.2; cf. comment on Acts 27:10.

374. Xen. *Cyr.* 1.5.6, 14; 1.6.2; 1.6.44; *Anab.* 6.3.18; 6.4.16–25; Plut. *Arist.* 17.6–18.2; 1 Sam 23:2–4; 2 Sam 5:23.

375. E.g., Val. Max. 1.6.6; 3.7.ext. 6; Suet. *Tib.* 2.2.

376. See, e.g., Val. Flacc. 1.28–29; Sen. Y. *Nat. Q.* 2.34.1–2; Fronto *Ad verum imp.* 2.8 (also from ants and bees); Char. *Chaer.* 8.2.9; Collins, "Mapping"; Frateantonio, "Haruspices."

377. E.g., Hom. *Od.* 2.159; Soph. *Antig.* 998–1002; Ap. Rhod. 1.66; Sen. Y. *Nat. Q.* 2.34.1–2; as in Plut. *Rom. Q.* 72, *Mor.* 281B; Dio Chrys. *Or.* 34.4–5; Plut. *Alex.* 27.2; Fronto *Ad verum imp.* 2.1.11; Iambl. *V.P.* 13.62; Diog. Laert. 8.1.20 (on Pythagoras); *Sib. Or.* 1.95; 3.224 (against it); *Sipra Qed. pq.* 6.203.2.1 (forbidding it).

378. Pliny E. *N.H.* 17.38.241–45.

379. Cf. the use of flames (Ap. Rhod. 1.436–39; Apul. *Metam.* 2.11), saucers (*PGM* 4.3209–54, though this is supposed to be an appearance), or cups (Gen 44:5; Sarna, *Genesis*, 223). Egyptian magic introduced special rituals (*PGM* 4.934), but some ancients considered witchcraft a despicable means to achieve these ends (Lucan *C.W.* 6.425–34; and esp. 430–34; 1 Sam 28:6–10; cf. Smelik, "Witch").

380. Lucian *Alex.* 9 (and LCL, 4:186–87n2).

381. Some Jewish divination existed (cf. 4Q318; *b. Sanh.* 101a), although those who viewed it as divination naturally disapproved (cf. Deut 18:10, 14; Isa 47:13).

382. See Plutarch *Obsolescence of Oracles*; cf. Lucan *C.W.* 5.139–40; Bremmer, "Divination: Greek," 573; Theissen, *Miracle Stories*, 268; Parke, *Oracle*, 381; Grant, *Gods*, 63. (Oracles had long been connected with temples; Gilg. 7.4.45–48 [*ANET* 87]; Lindblom, *Prophecy*, 31; Wilson, "Early Prophecy," 10; Holladay, "Statecraft," 13, 17; Huffmon, "Prophecy," 109, 111, 114; Kitchen, *World*, 119; Parke, *Oracle*, 370–71; Grant, *Gods*, 38.) They were still widely consulted (Collins, *Sibylline Oracles*, 5; Nilsson, *Piety*, 166; Aune, *Prophecy*, 51). They were still respected enough, however, that oracles could be useful in a court dispute; see Quint. *Inst.* 5.11.41–42 (this depended entirely on what side one argued; see 5.7.36). It may have been primarily their political use that declined (Rives, *Religion*, 57); this use had, of course, been strongest in the classical period; Nilsson, *Cults*, 123–42.

383. Hill, *Prophecy*, 11. The Romans were, of course, fascinated by Sibylline oracles, but in contrast to those of the Greeks, their cults concentrated more on divination (such as augury) than on prophetic inspiration (see further Salles, "Pythies et sibylles").

384. Oracular prophecy may have even grown in the first three centuries C.E. (Lewis, *Life*, 98). For Greco-Egyptian prophecy, cf. *CPJ* 3:119–21, §520 (dated to the third century C.E. on paleographic grounds), probably reflecting the Potter's Oracle (which Aune, *Prophecy*, 76–77, thinks reflects the *Sitz* of ca. 130 B.C.E.); cf. Deissmann, *Studies*, 235–36. Strabo 17.1.43 claims that even in Egypt, with its oracle of Ammon, oracles were in decline because of the Roman satisfaction with Sibylline oracles and the Tyrrhenian prophecies based on divination. Arrian *Alex.* 2.3.3 claims that the mantic gift was hereditary among the Telmissians.

385. E.g., Plutarch (Mackay, "Plutarch," 99–101; for divination, 101–2; for portents, 103–4).

386. See Parke, *Sibyls*, appendix 3, "Ecstatic Prophecy in the Near East," 216–20.

387. For the variety among different cults on this point, see Parke, *Sibyls*, 219; idem, *Oracles*, 85, 256–57.

Oracles could take questions.[388] In older Egyptian processions, images of deities on the priests' shoulders "answered" oracular questions by movement, since the priests who carried them (as many as eighty) moved however the god moved them.[389] At some oracles, inquirers experienced the deity's revelation in different forms.[390] In Israelite prophetism, "inquiring of a deity"[391] need not always mean that a question was put to the deity as in Hittite divination.[392]

Prophetic activity in pagan sources is often ecstatic; we observe this even in our earlier sources. We find prophetic ecstasy in late second-millennium B.C.E. Palestine in the Egyptian "Journey of Wen-Amon to Phoenicia," where an ecstatic, seized with some violent motion, prophesies to the king of Byblos.[393] At Mari, prophecy given in trances was institutionalized,[394] and as sometimes in Israel,[395] prophets could be designated by a term that otherwise denoted madmen.[396] Dependence on ecstatic inspiration continued into a late period.[397] Religious ecstasy was induced by various means, including intoxication, dancing,[398] ascetic fasts,[399] and even self-inflicted pain.[400] Although music was sometimes employed in Israelite prophetism,[401] some other forms

388. E.g., Statius *Silv.* 5.3.172–75; Max. Tyre 8.3.

389. Frankfurter, *Religion in Egypt*, 147, citing Diod. Sic. 17.50.6.

390. Paus. 9.39.11 (on Trophonius's oracle). For further documentation on oracles, see comment on Acts 16:16.

391. With pagan deities, e.g., Deut 12:30; 1 Sam 28:7; 2 Kgs 1:2–3; Isa 19:3; but it was often used with YHWH (e.g., 2 Kgs 1:16; 3:11; 8:8; 22:13; cf. 1 Kgs 22:5; 2 Kgs 19:2; esp. 1 Sam 9:9).

392. Huffmon, "Prophecy," 105, who suggests a connection with the Mari cult title of a prophet as an "answerer."

393. *ANET* 26, including n. 13; see Albright, *Yahweh*, 212; cf. Gordon, *Near East*, 159n19. Other examples of ecstatic prophecy among the Hittites and pre-Islamic nomads exist; see in Paul, "Prophets," 1156. Egyptians did not necessarily have high regard for the possessed; a "man who is in the hand of the god" is classed with the blind and lame in "The Instruction of Amen-em-opet" 25 (*ANET* 424), where it refers to someone insane.

394. Haran, "Continuity and Change," 181; Huffmon, "Prophecy," 111–12; cf. the possible evidence of Ebla here in Pettinato, *Archives*, 253. This is relevant even if the ecstasy was controlled and not a full ecstasy, as some have suggested due to the forms of the prophecies (Moran, "Prophecy," 27–28).

395. Cf. 2 Kgs 9:11; Jer 29:26; Hos 9:7. Some contrast earlier ecstatic prophets with later literary ones (Gordon, *Near East*, 159n19, 214; cf. 221); this, however, underestimates the measure of continuity in Israelite prophetism (Paul, "Prophets," 1160ff.), though some changes occurred (see Haran, "Continuity and Change"). The rise of prophetic literacy need not diminish ecstasy.

396. Albright, *Yahweh*, 212; Malamat, "Revelations," 210–11; cf. Paul, "Prophets," 1159; Lindblom, *Prophecy*, 31; Gordon, *Near East*, 206. For a modern study of the psychological state suggested by the possession trance, see, e.g., Nussbaum, "Phenomena." Possession trances are documented in a variety of cultures (e.g., among traditional Australian aborigines in Berndt, "Role," 269) and sometimes associated with madness (Mbiti, *Religions*, 227); see fuller discussion in the excursus on possession at Acts 16:16.

397. See, e.g., Mithraic inspiration in *PGM* 4.738–39.

398. Plut. *Dial. L.* 16, *Mor.* 759AB (LCL, 9:364–65), describes the use of dance in "Bacchic orgies and Corybantic revels" and compares this behavior to the Pythia's inspiration; cf. *Table* 1.5.2, *Mor.* 623B; *Orph. H.* 52.7 (cf. 40.15); cf. Burkert, *Religion*, 166; Martin, *Religions*, 61; Otto, *Dionysus*, 143–45; Huffmon, "Prophecy," 112. Dancing can be used to stimulate trance states in various societies; see Eliade, *Rites*, 69; Mbiti, *Religions*, 106; sources in Keener, *Miracles*, 793–94; cf. the use of music in Gelfand, "Disorders," 156, 162.

399. Fasting could prepare the way for revelations in *2 Bar.* 20:5; 43:3; *Herm.* 1.2.2, 3.1, 10 (but cf. 1.3.13); also part of the initiation for the Lesser Mysteries of Eleusis (Mylonas, *Eleusis*, 241) and perhaps also the Greater Mysteries (258). On fasting and revelations, see the commentators on ταπεινοφροσύνη in Col 2:18, esp. Francis, "Humility," 168–71; Lincoln, *Paradise*, 111. In early Judaism, fasting could be used for mourning (e.g., *2 Bar.* 5:7; *Test. Zeb.* 4:1–3; cf. Apul. *Metam.* 2.24) or to intensify prayer (cf. Tob 12:8; 2 Macc 13:12; *Test. Benj.* 1:4–5; cf. *Did.* 1.3), but the rabbis strictly regulated fasting to avoid ascetic practices harmful to the body or dishonoring to the joy of the Sabbath (*t. Kip.* 4:1–2; *Ta'an.* 2:12, 14; *y. Ta'an.* 3:11, §3; 4:3, §2; *Ned.* 8:1, §1). Tribal religions sometimes use fasting to gain requests from deities (e.g., Fox, "Witchcraft," 181), and in initiatory rites (Eliade, *Rites*, 67).

400. See Lindblom, *Prophecy*, 5, 8–9, 43, 58–60; cf. Paul, "Prophets," 1156; 2 Kgs 18:28–29; Zech 13:4–6.

401. E.g., Exod 15:20; 1 Sam 10:5; 2 Kgs 3:15; cf. Hab 3:19; 1 Chr 25:1–6. Lindblom, *Prophecy*, 99, suggests that Canaanite models affected Israel here; probably the association between music and prophecy was more pervasive (cf. musical inspiration in Pilch, *Flights*, 73–88).

of religious arousal employed by its neighbors were prohibited to Israel; nevertheless, ecstatic Israelite prophecy also existed in this period.[402]

Mantic prophecy was normally through one "possessed" by the deity.[403] Although a rationalistic Plutarch could detect the natural faculties of the Pythia in her prophesyings,[404] prophetic possession was often thought to virtually eliminate any human elements[405] and could be associated with μανία or μαίνομαι[406] and sometimes involve self-mutilation.[407] Possession could occur in the context of various cults,[408] but Aune questions whether all such possession was prophetic in nature;[409] theories of inspiration extended to music[410] and poetry,[411] law,[412] and other disciplines, and

402. Cf. Schmid, "Geistwirkungen"; Aune, *Prophecy*, 86–87; for connections between Israelite and Mari models, see Holladay, "Statecraft," 11–12; Bright, *History*, 88–89; cf. Pettinato, *Ebla*, 319n12. Wilson, "Ecstasy," 323–25, finds further cases of ecstasy based on more subtle phraseology in the prophets; Parker, "Possession Trance," views the experience as only marginal in Israelite prophetism. More recent studies challenge some earlier ones (see Michaelsen, "Ecstasy"). Levison, *Filled*, 154–77, emphasizes especially Greek ecstasy as background for early Jewish and Christian experience.

403. E.g., Arrian *Alex.* 4.13.5–6; Lucan *C.W.* 1.673–95; Plut. *Table* 1.5.2, *Mor.* 623B; Philost. *Hrk.* 7.3. But Sen. Y. *Ep. Lucil.* 28 recounts the possession in Virg. *Aen.* 6.78–79 and regards it as folly.

404. Plut. *Or. Delphi* 7, *Mor.* 397C; but cf. Theon in *Or. Delphi* 21, *Mor.* 404E. Aune, *Prophecy*, 4, does not think that the Pythia experienced mantic frenzy, but this is not the view of Plutarch (*Dial. L.* 16, *Mor.* 759B; cf. Lucan's description of her rapturous trance, cited by Reitzenstein, *Religions*, 71; Plato *Phaedr.* 47). For the reputed authority and accuracy of this oracle, see Isoc. *Paneg.* 31; Hdt. 1.47ff., 65–67, 86; Plut. *Gk. Q.* 12, *Mor.* 293E; 19, *Mor.* 295DE; *Borr.* 3, *Mor.* 828D; *Thes.* 36.1; *Lyc.* 6.5; *Solon* 4.2; Diog. Laert. 8.1.21; cf. 5.91; Strabo 9.3.2, 11–12; Mart. *Epig.* 9.42.4; it also posed questions to early Christianity, Justin *1 Apol.* 18; Min. Fel. *Oct.* 26.6; cf. Acts 16:16.

405. So, e.g., Iambl. *Myst.* 3.4–6; for the Trojan Cassandra, as late as the sixth century C.E., see *Gr. Anth.* 2.189–91 (cf. lines 42–44); some felt that inspiration raised a matter beyond reproach (Libanius *Confirmation* 1.1). See Aune, *Prophecy*, 47–48. That prophesying was not always irrational (Aune, *Prophecy*, 39) is not reason to presume that it could not have been uttered ecstatically. For possession and prophecy in later societies, see, e.g., Evans-Pritchard, *Religion*, 96, 303; on possession trance more fully, see the excursus at Acts 16:16.

406. Chevallier, *Ancien Testament*, 40, from Plutarch; Lucian *Alex.* 12; see the perception of Cassandra in Eurip. *Alexander* frg. 62g. Athena puts madnesses (μανίαισι) in men's souls in *Orph. H.* 32.6, but line 9 shows that she does this only to the wicked, giving prudence to the good. The etymological relationship with μάντις proposed by Plato may be correct, but it does not indicate the view of all diviners in antiquity (Aune, *Prophecy*, 35); mantic frenzy was more common for peripheral intermediaries than for those in central cults (21).

407. Lucian *Syr. G.* 51; Apul. *Metam.* 8.27–28 (the Phrygian music in 8.30 could suggest Cybele, but a differentiation is made in 9.9–10); cf. 1 Kgs 18:28.

408. E.g., the cult of Cybele (Guthrie, *Orpheus*, 118); on ecstasy in this cult, see Burkert, *Religion*, 178; cf. Menander *Theophoroumene* 27; *Orph. H.* 27.11; Lucret. *Nat.* 2.618–20; Juv. *Sat.* 3.63; Dio Cass. 48.43.4. For ecstasy as divine possession in the Mysteries, see, e.g., Hill, *Prophecy*, 10–11; cf. Aune, *Prophecy*, 47.

409. Aune, *Prophecy*, 21; also Forbes, *Prophecy*, 282; Aune thinks that Livy has wrongly associated the two for several cults (*Prophecy*, 42). Plato had distinguished various kinds of inspiration, as Plutarch, nearer our period, also points out (*Dial. L.* 16, *Mor.* 758EF). Although possession was common in allusions to the Bacchae (e.g., Euripides *Bacchanals*; Plut. *Par. St.* 19, *Mor.* 310B; cf. Grant, *Gods*, 65; Martin, *Religions*, 93–94; Burkert, *Religion*, 292), the only author I have found who *consistently* links Bacchic or corybantic frenzy with prophetic inspiration is Philo: *Op.* 71; *L.A.* 3.82; *Plant.* 148; *Contempl.* 84.

410. Music and prophecy were associated in the figure of Orpheus, according to Linforth, *Arts of Orpheus*, 166; Guthrie, *Orpheus*, 21. Likewise, Apollo, the god of prophecy (a prophet himself, Cic. *Tusc.* 1.47.114; Epict. *Diatr.* 3.1.18; *Orph. H.* 34.4; cf. 11.21; 18.17; 27.13; 28.4; Lucian *Z. Cat.* [LCL, 2:76–77]; Dionysus in Eurip. *Bacch.* 298–99, μάντις), was also associated with music, Lucian *Amber* (LCL, 1:77); Dio Chrys. *Or.* 32.56–57; Marc. Aur. *Med.* 11.11; Artem. *Oneir.* 2.35; *Gr. Anth.* 2.266–70. There was also a high degree of assimilation among Orpheus, Dionysus, and Apollo, Plut. *E Delph.* 9, *Mor.* 388E–389A; Burkert, *Orphism*, 8; Guthrie, *Orpheus*, 36, 42–48, 113; Linforth, *Orpheus*, 171; Detienne, "Polythéisme"; Otto, *Dionysus*, 202–8.

411. Plato, *Ion* 533E (he compares this with Bacchic possession in 533E–534A); for oracular singers in Plato, see Aune, *Prophecy*, 38. Although they were divinely possessed, in Plato's thought, their words still had to be judged and interpreted by nonpossessed governors; see Tigerstedt, "Idea," 64–66, 72. Plutarch associates poetry with inspiration (*Poetry* 1, *Mor.* 15E; cf. *Or. Delph.*, *Mor.* 394D–409D). Hesiod in Lucian *Conversation with Hesiod* 7 (LCL, 6:234–35) argues that the Muses inspired him and other poets (his interlocutor dissents). Horace entreats the Muses for inspiration in *Odes* 1.26; cf., e.g., 2.12.13; 3.1.3–4; 3.14.13–15; 4.8.29; 4.9.21; Juv. *Sat.* 7.10, 36–39; Frey in *CIJ* 1:cxxiii (a pagan sarcophagus with the Muse Urania teaching music to the spouse, reused by Roman Jews); Philo *Plant.* 129.

412. For the inspiration of lawgivers (divine sanction for laws had been important as early as Hammurabi), see Hadas, *Aristeas*, 194, on *Let. Aris.* 240.

they do not by any means all involve possession in the form in which it is found in some varieties of prophetism. But that ecstasy was seen as an acceptable phenomenon in Greek religion, at least for certain kinds of people in certain contexts, is commonly agreed upon.[413]

Lucan claims that inspiration opened the Pythia's lips, erupting like a volcano (*C.W.* 5.97–101); only the divine frenzy proved that she was not fabricating her words (5.148–57). Then Apollo forces himself on her, invading her body and replacing her thoughts; her head tosses, her hair bristles, things are overturned, the fire of Apollo's wrath tortures her from within, yielding frenzy, foaming lips, inarticulate panting and groans, wailing, and finally articulate speech (5.165–93). Lucan composed this description as poetry, and we should not read too much into it. Archaeology shows that despite literary references, no "mephitic vapors" beneath the Delphic tripod inspired the Pythian priestess.[414] Nevertheless, neither should we attribute her possession altogether to Lucan.[415] Although lacking Lucan's elaborate description, both earlier and later sources indicate that she is possessed by a spirit[416] and goes into mad ecstasy[417] at this site, and abundant anthropological parallels leave no necessary reason to dispute such a claim (see comment on Acts 16:16).

One woman is said to have predicted the future in song, possessed by a spirit.[418] Likewise, the Galli of the Great Mother met the Romans, prophesying in frenzy that the Romans would win a battle;[419] another priest ecstatically but correctly prophesied a victory while seized by prophetic inspiration.[420] Unable to shake off the overpowering of Apollo, the Cumean Sibyl prophesied, words bursting forth in her frenzy.[421] Another prophesied "madly," overpowered by a divine fire within her.[422] Some people may have used magical means to induce trances.[423]

Prophecies, like other means of divine communication,[424] were often obscure.[425] For Greeks, inspiration did not always guarantee freedom from all error;[426] there were levels of inspiration, later poets sometimes being less inspired than earlier poets.[427] But one could also prophesy as the deity's mouthpiece;[428] *daimones* might speak through human bodies like a piper producing music through a pipe.[429] Thus, for Philo, a prophet

---

413. E.g., Hadas, *Aristeas*, 34, 36; Wikenhauser, *Mysticism*, 76–77; Boring, *Sayings*, 82–83.

414. Cary and Haarhoff, *Life*, 317; Klauck, *Context*, 187.

415. As some appear to do: Klauck, *Context*, 187–88, noting that it depends solely on Lucan *C.W.* 5.116–20, 161–74, 190–97, and that Lucan himself claims that this possession was more powerful than ever before (*C.W.* 166–67). Also others (e.g., Witherington, *Corinthians*, 278–79).

416. Val. Max. 1.8.10; Max. Tyre 8.1; see further comment on Acts 16:16.

417. Plut. *Dial. L.* 16, *Mor.* 759B (regaining tranquility afterward); Ael. Arist. *Def. Or.* 34–35, §11D.

418. Dion. Hal. *Ant. rom.* 1.31.1.

419. Livy 38.18.9.

420. Aul. Gel. 15.18.2.

421. Virg. *Aen.* 6.77–102.

422. Ovid *Metam.* 2.640–41.

423. *PGM* 4.850–929, including both Jewish and pagan elements.

424. Cf. the Jewish portrayal of astrology in, e.g., *y. 'Abod. Zar.* 2:2, §5.

425. E.g., Dio Chrys. *Or.* 10.23–27; 13.9; Philost. *Hrk.* 28.11–12; Klauck, *Context*, 189. See comment on Acts 21:4.

426. E.g., compare Philost. *Hrk.* 25.4, 8 with 24.1–2; 25.10–17; see also Lucian *True Story* 2.32; perhaps Hierocles *How Should One Behave toward the Gods?* (Stobaeus *Anth.* 1.3.53; criticizing Homer *Il.* 9.497); Libanius *Refutation* 1.1; 2.1; cf. Rives, *Religion*, 28. Cf. even *Gen. Rab.* 91:6 (though this is after the departure of the Spirit of prophecy), though the rabbis would have treated canonical revelation differently (see discussion on their own replacement of the prophetic function with exegesis). Yet some Gentiles did contend that inspiration guarded against error: e.g., Libanius *Confirmation* 1.1 (the poets' voice but the Muses' content); 2.1.

427. Dio Chrys. *Or.* 36.34–35.

428. E.g., Ovid *Metam.* 6.159–62; cf. discussion in Aune, *Prophecy*, 47.

429. Max. Tyre 9.1.

might speak not from himself but only from God,[430] and the Jewish *Sibylline Oracles* declare that the oracles derive from compulsion.[431]

Although Greeks believed in mantic inspiration, their terminology differed notice-ably from examples in the NT corpus. Greeks rarely used προφήτης and its cognates before the NT period except for a position in the hierarchy of oracular centers; early Christianity was much more directly influenced by the use of the LXX, which originally borrowed this term and its cognates innovatively to translate Hebrew terms for the prophets and their inspiration.[432] The familiar Greek oracular term μάντις appears nowhere in the NT (the cognate verb only in Acts 16:16, for pagan spirit possession), and in the LXX without exception refers to pagan divination (Josh 13:22; 1 Sam 6:2; Mic 3:7; Jer 29:8 = 36:8 LXX; Zech 10:2).[433] Not only the terminology but the practice was usually, though not always, different:

1. Greeks and Romans believed that most inspired prophecy belonged to past eras,[434] and hence they emphasized divination.
2. They practiced most contemporary prophecy in oracular shrines with priesthoods.
3. Most of this prophecy consisted of answers to questions posed at the shrines.[435]

b. Nonrabbinic Jewish Literature

We often conceptualize the character of ancient Israelite prophecy too nar-rowly. Although we often think of prophecy as spontaneous at the time of delivery, the prophecies could be written (Jer 36:4–8) or otherwise received beforehand.[436] Again contrary to our usual expectation, prophets sometimes even prophesied to themselves,[437] perhaps revealing one of the forms in which the "word of the Lord" came to the prophet. Prophets often had to act before knowing the full intent of the Lord (e.g., 13:6–7; 35:2, 14).

The understanding of prophecy developed in early Judaism. Perhaps following the example of Saul and David, who were both anointed with the Spirit of prophecy before they could become kings,[438] or translating the Platonic notion of a wise man/philoso-pher as the ideal ruler, one source suggests that prophets will rule in the eschatological

430. So Philo *Spec. Laws* 1.65; 4.49. Cf. similarly, e.g., *Num. Rab.* 18:12. Philo may have allowed for two forms of prophecy: ecstatic and noetic (the latter through reason; Winston, "Types of Prophecy"); Philo may have viewed Moses's ecstasy as milder than Balaam's (Levison, "Types of Prophecy"). Some think that Philo merely used Greek language for inspiration but did not envision ecstasy (Burkhardt, "Inspiration der Schrift"), but this is unlikely. Ps.-Philo's *Biblical Antiquities* may also envision the Spirit displacing the prophet's mind during inspiration (Piñero, "Mediterranean View").

431. E.g., *Sib. Or.* 2.1–5; 3.1–7, 295–99, 489–91; 11.315–18; 12.295–96.

432. See Forbes, *Prophecy*, 188–217. Callan, "Prophecy," suggests that the LXX applies it to nontrance activity, in contrast to Greek usage.

433. As also the verb (Deut 18:10; 1 Sam 28:8; 2 Kgs 17:17; Mic 3:11; Jer 27:9; Ezek 13:6, 23; 21:21, 23, 29; 22:28) and μαντεία (Num 23:23; Deut 18:10, 14; 2 Kgs 17:17; Isa 16:6; 44:25; Jer 14:14; Ezek 13:7–8, 23; 21:21, 23; Mic 3:6); μαντεῖον functions thus in Num 22:7 and Ezek 21:27 (ET 21:22), with Prov 16:10 being exceptional because it is figurative.

434. Some ancients also perceived oracles as declining in their days (cf. Plut. *Obsol.* 5, *Mor.* 411F; the opposite of Acts 2:17–18), or respect for inspiration as declining (Callim. *Iambi* 3.193). This fits the general pattern of early Judaism as well, except, of course, that they did not replace it with formal divination.

435. Forbes, *Prophecy*, 288–308.

436. E.g., 1 Sam 8:6–7; 9:17; 15:10, 16; 2 Sam 7:4–5; 12:1, 25; 24:11–12; 1 Kgs 12:22; 13:1; 14:5; 16:1; 19:15–16; 21:17–19; 2 Kgs 1:3–4; Jer 28:12–13.

437. E.g., 2 Sam 23:2; Hos 1:2; cf. Pss 12:5; 46:10; 91:14; Jer 27:2.

438. 1 Sam 10:6, 10; 16:13–14. Cf. the Spirit-moved leaders of Israel in the book of Judges (Judg 3:10; 6:34; 9:23; 11:29; 13:25; 14:6, 19; 15:14).

time.[439] The prophetic anointing could thus be envisioned in terms of divine wisdom to lead, even if the initial experience (as in 1 Sam 10:5–11) might be particularly ecstatic.

Although prophecy was not always conceived as ecstatic,[440] most of our references in Diaspora-oriented Jewish texts do include an ecstatic element. This fits the ecstatic component often found in non-Jewish sources concerning mantic prophecy (Gentile divination was not ecstatic, but in its most blatant forms, it was forbidden in Israel).[441] (The differences between Israelite and other ancient Near Eastern prophecy have frequently been pointed out.)[442]

The acceptance of the place of the ecstatic in the Hellenistic world no doubt provided a context in which this aspect of Israelite prophetism would be developed. A Jewish Sibyl, perhaps in late first-century B.C.E. Egypt, writes that all will pronounce her a true seer (μάντιν), though someone might call her "a messenger with a frenzied spirit" (μεμανηότι θυμῷ ἄγγελον),[443] and she complains that she must prophesy with frenzy.[444]

In Pseudo-Philo's *Biblical Antiquities*, a holy spirit (*spiritus sanctus*) came upon Kenaz and "put him in ecstasy" (*extulit sensum eius*), so that he prophesied (*prophetare*),[445] and when he had finished speaking, "he was awakened, and his senses came back to him."[446] Likewise, in *4 Baruch*, Abimelech (Ebedmelech) the Aethiopian fell into "a great trance" (μεγάλη ἔκστασις) and only awoke sixty-six years later.[447] The charismatic sashes that enabled Job's daughters to sing in angelic languages altered their minds to think in heavenly ways.[448] Apocalyptic visionaries could also have rapturous experiences modeled on those of OT prophets such as Ezekiel, who saw the throne-chariot.[449]

Hellenistic Jewish images of ecstatic inspiration are most pronounced in Philo. Following Plato[450] as well as OT forms,[451] "Philo interpreted corybantic frenzy as a sign of true inspiration"; thus he treats a prophet as "an ecstatic, totally possessed by

---

439. *Sib. Or.* 3.781–82, probably from second-century B.C.E. Alexandria; cf. *Gen. Rab.* 73:5.

440. Cf., e.g., the angel of the Lord with the prophetic-messenger formula in *L.A.B.* 38:3. Greek literature could sometimes use προφήτης as a spokesperson for a view, e.g., Diogenes *Ep.* 21, or μαντεύομαι (not used of Christian prophecy in the NT) as a metaphorical extension of predicting nonsupernaturally, e.g., Ach. Tat. 1.9.5, 7. Epict. *Diatr.* 1.17.29 uses the μαντείαν as a parable of the philosopher; cf. 2.7.1–3 for Epictetus's distaste for the real thing; and, more qualified, *Encheir.* 32.3.

441. See, e.g., Jos. *Ag. Ap.* 1.203–4; *Sib. Or.* 3.224–26; *Asc. Is.* 2:5; *Sipra Qed. pq.* 6.203.2.1; *Sipre Deut.* 171.5.1. It could be a capital offense (11QTᵃ LX, 18–19; LXI, 2, repeating Deut 18:10–11, 20) and exclude one from the coming world (*'Abot R. Nat.* 36 A).

442. E.g., Heschel, *Prophets*, 465–66; Paul, "Prophecy," 1160; on prophetic succession, Scott, *Relevance*, 57–62; Heschel, *Prophets*, 472–73; for Mari, Buss, "Prophecy," 338; Craghan, "Mari," 52; Heschel, *Prophets*, 471–72; for Greek versus Jewish prophecy, cf. Büchsel, *Geist*, 43–44.

443. *Sib. Or.* 11.316–18 (*OTP* 1:442; Greek text, Geffcken, 187–88).

444. *Sib. Or.* 11.320–24. Cicero concluded from pagan Sibylline use of acrostic that the form (which is Hellenistic, not classical) indicated deliberate, rather than ecstatic, thought (Parke, *Sibyls*, 139), but while there may not have been first-person speech or the same kind of possession as with the Pythia (219), the Sibyl portrays herself in the extant Jewish and Christian oracles as irresistibly moved.

445. *L.A.B.* 28:6 (*OTP* 2:341; Latin text, Kisch, 195).

446. *L.A.B.* 28:10 (*OTP* 2:342).

447. *4 Bar.* 5:8; also 5:12 (both Kraft, 22–23). The story of a long nap also circulated concerning Epimenides (who lived ca. 600 B.C.E.), as reported by Diog. Laert. 1.109 and Honi the Circle-Drawer, grandson of his more famous namesake, in *y. Ta'an.* 3:9, §4. Washington Irving had some Germanic and ultimately Mediterranean roots for his "original" American tale of Rip Van Winkle.

448. *Test. Job* 48–50 (though some have attributed this section to Christian influence, perhaps from the Montanist period). Philo's description of the worship of the Therapeutae in *Contempl.* 84, compared with Bacchic rites of strong drink, includes apparently inspired singing. For inspired singing elsewhere, see *Mek.* on Exod 14:31–15:1 (in Smith, *Parallels*, 64); *y. Soṭah* 5:4, §1; *Pesiq. Rab.* 9:2; *L.A.B.* 32:14. It is possible that in Judaism this related to the heavenly (*Test. Ab.* 20:12–13 A; *2 En.* 17:1 A and J) or eschatological (*Sib. Or.* 3.715, second century B.C.E.; *b. Ta'an.* 31a; *Sanh.* 91b; *Num. Rab.* 15:11; *Eccl. Rab.* 1:11, §1; *Pesiq. Rab.* 21:1) worship.

449. See, e.g., Russell, *Apocalyptic*, 160.

450. Isaacs, *Spirit*, 49 (citing Plato *Tim.* 71D; *Ion* 533D, 543C, and Philo *Heir* 264; *Spec. Laws* 4.49; *QG* 3.9).

451. Isaacs, *Spirit*, 51 (citing 1 Sam 10:10–12).

God and His helpless instrument."[452] He speaks of prophets experiencing an ecstasy of heavenly love, the whole mind "snatched up in holy frenzy by a Divine possession";[453] this divine frenzy could provide prophetic dreams and be described as possession by some philosophic principle;[454] the heir of God's good things is the ecstatic soul that leaves even itself:[455] "Higher than our reasoning, and in very deed divine, arising by no human will or purpose but by a God-inspired ecstasy [ἀλλ᾽ ἐνθέῳ μανίᾳ]."[456] Philo observes that "a prophet possessed by God will suddenly appear and give prophetic oracles. Nothing of what he says will be his own, for he that is truly under the control of divine inspiration has no power of apprehension when he speaks but serves as the channel for the insistent words of Another's prompting."[457]

The prophets are often seized with ecstasy (ἐνθουσιάζει), so that they are full of God and their understanding departs.[458]

> So while the radiance of the mind is still all around us, when it pours as it were a noonday beam into the whole soul, we are self-contained, not possessed. But when it comes to its setting, naturally ecstasy and divine possession and madness [ἔκστασις . . . ἔνθεος . . . μανία] fall upon us. For when the light of God shines . . . this is what regularly befalls the fellowship of the prophets. The mind is evicted at the arrival of the divine Spirit, but when that departs the mind returns to its tenancy. Mortal and immortal may not share the same home. And therefore the setting of reason and the darkness which surrounds it produce ecstasy and inspired frenzy.[459]

Abraham had this ecstatic, prophetic experience in Gen 15:12;[460] Moses also began his prophetic career (προφητείας) by possession (ἐνθουσιασμόν);[461] and Philo himself would sometimes become full (πλήρης), so influenced by corybantic frenzy (ἐνθέου κορυβαντιᾶν) that he would be unconscious of what he had written.[462] As Hill points out, such language is "almost entirely derived from non-biblical Greek."[463]

Josephus, himself also not alien to ecstatic prophetic experience,[464] tells of a man who for seven years did nothing but cry, "Woe to Jerusalem!" ignoring pain and opposition;[465] Bamberger comments on the natural association of Joshua's actions with madness.[466] Further, Josephus "not only describes the prophetic experience in terms of possession,[467] but translates the πνεῦμα θεοῦ of 1 Kgdms 10:6 as γενόμενος ἔνθεος."[468]

452. Isaacs, *Spirit*, 49–50, citing Philo *Heir* 69, 249, 266.

453. Philo *Plant.* 39 (LCL, 3:232–33).

454. Philo *Migr.* 190.

455. Philo *Heir* 68–69.

456. Philo *Flight* 168; cf. 2 Pet 1:21.

457. Philo *Spec. Laws* 1.65 (LCL, 7:136–37), using ἐνθουσιῶν.

458. Philo *QG* 3.9. In *QG* 4.138, every true prophet was called "seer" or "beholder" because of the eye of the soul. Contrast Aune, *Prophecy*, 150, who makes Philo's allowance for an ecstatic to be aware of his surroundings a contrast with *L.A.B.* 28.

459. Philo *Heir* 264–65 (LCL); cf. 1 Cor 14 (the parallel between Philonic and Pauline language was originally pointed out to me by Prof. Dale Martin).

460. Philo *Heir* 249, 258–59.

461. Philo *Mos.* 2.258; cf. 1.201. This is especially effective when he is about to leave his body (2.288).

462. Philo *Migr.* 35. On Philo's own experience, see Aune, *Prophecy*, 147.

463. Hill, *Prophecy*, 32–33. One may contrast the NT literature, for whatever reason: Nock, "Vocabulary," 134. For a lengthy treatment of prophets moved by the divine Spirit in Philo, see Wolfson, *Philo*, 2:11–59.

464. Cf. Jos. *War* 3.353.

465. Jos. *War* 6.300–309.

466. Bamberger, "Prophet," 305, citing *b. B. Bat.* 12b for a similar association of prophecy with madness after the temple's destruction.

467. Isaacs, *Spirit*, 50, cites *Ant.* 6.222–23; 4.118.

468. Isaacs, *Spirit*, 50, citing *Ant.* 6.56, 76.

This general picture of inspiration carried over into at least some forms of early Christianity. One may compare the second-century C.E. *Odes of Solomon*:

> As the [wind] moves through the harp
> and the strings speak,
> So the Spirit of the Lord speaks through my members,
> And I speak through his love.[469]

Yet early Christians argued that prophets could control their inspiration, in contrast to pagan prophets, who were moved against their will.[470]

All of this may suggest that the common later rabbinic understanding of the nature of prophecy differed from the popular Jewish perspective that had prevailed outside Pharisaic ranks before a certain brand of Pharisaism rose to prominence over Palestinian and later, in a further developed form, over much of Mediterranean and Parthian Jewry. Although ecstatic phenomena and equivalents of prophecy occurred among rabbis, this experience is viewed with caution by most of the other rabbis. They might be cautious for the same reasons that rabbinic Judaism did not allow much room for the Spirit of prophecy in the present and barely addressed other functions of רוח הקודש, the Holy Spirit.

c. Prophecy in the Rabbis

That prophecy was a heavier task than prayer could be simply assumed by a Tanna arguing his case in the second century C.E.[471] Prophets had the authority to tell Israel which site God had chosen and to tell kings what they were to do.[472] Perhaps like the rabbis who had to temporarily circumvent the letter of the law to fulfill its purpose (cf. Hillel's *prozbul*), prophets might temporarily supersede the letter of the law: "'Him you shall heed': Even if he should instruct you to violate one of the religious duties that are listed in the Torah, as did Elijah on Mount Carmel, in a case of emergency obey him."[473] There are, of course, serious limitations on the extent to which this exception was allowed to be taken.[474]

The sages essentially took over the role once granted to the prophets.[475] A story is told of a Tanna who applies the words of Amos 7:14 to himself. When R. Eliezer accurately predicts that a disciple will die that week, other rabbis ask whether he is a prophet. He responds, "I am not a prophet nor the disciple of a prophet"; he simply

---

469. *Odes Sol.* 6:1–2 (*OTP* 2:738). Even Hellenistic magical divination seems to have influenced some strands of early Christianity, as in the *Shepherd of Hermas* (see Aune, *Prophecy*, 17, 211, 303, following Reiling, *Hermas*). At the same time, one should be cautious not to read in influences arbitrarily; cf. Forbes, "Inspired Speech"; Hill, *Prophecy*, 9, 29–30 (who goes too far, however, in denying the influences).

470. 1 Cor 14:32; Severian of Gabala in *Pauluskommentare* 262, 270 (Bray, *Corinthians*, 118, 144); Chrys. *Hom. 1 Cor.* 29.2.

471. *Mek. Pisha* 1.38–40 (Lauterbach, 1:4).

472. *Sipre Deut.* 62.1.1–2; 70.1.3; 157.1.1; *Gen. Rab.* 73:5. Of course, prophets functioned as messengers of the suzerain King Yahweh to his vassal kings of Israel in the OT as well, and so they executed a calling of higher authority than that of kings in the eyes of the Deuteronomic historians. Cf. Holladay, "Statecraft," 31–34; and, on the court of Yahweh, Cross, *Myth*, 186–87.

473. *Sipre Deut.* 175.1.3 (Neusner), on Deut 18:15–22. This principle may have appeared relevant during Jesus's proclamation of the imminent kingdom (Keener, *Historical Jesus*, 208, 235).

474. See *t. Sanh.* 14:13; even more so, *Sipra Behuq. pq.* 13.277.1.12.

475. It has been argued that sages replaced the temple also (Rosenfeld, "Sage and Temple"). Similarly, prophecy becomes especially teaching in the church fathers (though they did not exclude revelations); see Bray, *Romans*, 305, 311, citing, e.g., Origen *Comm. Rom.* on 12:6 (CER 5:60); Diodore of Tarsus, on Rom 12:6, in *Pauluskommentare* 106.

predicted on the basis of the tradition of the sages.[476] Although Eliezer's authority is in the tradition, his denial of filling a prophet's role is worded in the same terms as Amos's denial of *his* role as a prophet, as if to suggest that the authority of the sages' tradition is comparable to that of the prophets.

Although in some texts the prophets could be regarded as higher than the sages,[477] in others sages are comparable to but higher than prophets,[478] and in still others sages are considerably higher than prophets.[479] Indeed, Bamberger writes, "The scholar had replaced the prophet; as R. Abdimi of Haifa put it, 'prophecy has been taken from the prophets and given to the sages.' A Babylonian comment on this remark declares that the scholar is more important (*'adif*) than the prophet."[480]

Cohen notes that prophets moved in the direction of "apocalyptic seers, mystics, healers, and holy men," but prophetic authority shifted to the scribes.[481] The rabbis could view themselves as, in some sense, successors of the prophets.[482] (Similar institutional or academic domestication of prophetic roles appeared in some Gentile circles as well.)[483]

This was perhaps only natural, given the fact that Torah was normative whereas there could be both true and false prophets.[484] Torah was sometimes assumed to be a step above prophecy.[485] Most often, however, no contrast was made between prophets and interpreters of Torah.[486] Just as the heavenly court or academy could be portrayed in terms mirroring the earthly academy,[487] so the prophets could be seen in anachronistic terms as sages.[488] Moses was the father of all the prophets,[489] and thirty prophets were among the eighty-five elders of Israel debating whether Esther's "new" laws could already be found in the Torah.[490] In this respect, they were not different from other prominent OT figures, such as Hezekiah, whom Akiba regarded

476. *Sipra Sh. M.D.* 99.5.6 (Neusner, 2:135); again in *Pesiq. Rab Kah.* 26:6/7. A similar use of Amos 7:14 by an Amora is noted in *b. Ber.* 34b; *Yebam.* 121b, by Hill, *Prophecy*, 34–35.

477. *Y. Sanh.* 10:1, §9, placing sages directly below prophets, prophets directly below Moses, and Moses directly below God. For Apollinaris of Laodicea, on Rom 12:6, in *Pauluskommentare* 76–77 (Bray, *Romans*, 311), as for Paul (1 Cor 12:28), prophecy is the greatest gift next to apostleship.

478. *Y. Sanh.* 11:4, §1: their teachings are more stringent than those of the prophets, and they may be accepted without signs, unlike the prophets. This is also taught in the *y. Berakot* reference noted by Jeremias, *Jerusalem*, 241–42.

479. *Y. Hor.* 3:5, §1: Sages are above kings, kings above high priests, high priests above prophets, and so on.

480. Bamberger, "Prophet," 306, citing *b. B. Bat.* 12a; cf. also Urbach, *Sages*, 1:306.

481. Cohen, *Maccabees*, 23; cf. Hengel, *Judaism and Hellenism*, 1:206. Cf. Urbach, *Sages*, 1:578: in the rabbinic period, "prophecy evolved into a mystic experience."

482. E.g., *'Abot R. Nat.* 1 A. This is often observed: Aune, *Prophecy*, 104; Hill, *Prophecy*, 34–35; Urbach, *Sages*, 1:306, 564–65, 578 (although disagreeing with the proposed connection between the fixed law and the cessation of prophecy, p. 566).

483. Among Gentiles, cf. Val. Max. 7.2.ext. 1a: Socrates's wisdom was like an earthly *oraculum*; likewise, a Cynic could claim (Lucian *Phil. Sale* 8) to be a sort of prophet. Earlier, Egyptian scribes foretold the future (P.Beatty 4, in Simpson, *Literature of Egypt*, 1; cf. Frankfurter, *Religion in Egypt*, 240), and priests interpreted the will of the gods (Dunand, *Religion en Égypte*, 123); on Egyptian oracles, see Frankfurter, *Religion in Egypt*, 145–97.

484. A false prophet (like a bad disciple) speaks what he did not hear (*t. Sanh.* 14:14–16; cf. *Sipre Deut.* 177.1.1).

485. E.g., by the early Amora R. Levi, in *Pesiq. Rab Kah.* 14:4 (though cf. 24:7); cf. Aune, *Prophecy*, 124; Glatzer, "Prophecy," 119–20, 126–30.

486. *'Abot R. Nat.* 4 A; 6, §19 B, predicates Johanan ben Zakkai's "prophecy" to Vespasian on Scripture interpretation (Isa 10:34).

487. Besides eighteen references cited in Keener, "Heavenly Court," see *'Abot R. Nat.* 32 A; *y. Sanh.* 1:1, §4, 11:5, §1; *Pesiq. Rab Kah.* 24:11; cf. 11QMelch and explanation in Kobelski, "Melchizedek," 123; *Test. Ab.* 12:11 A; 10:8 B (a heavenly judge); *3 En.* 2:4; 5:10–12; 16:1; 18:16 (?); 28; 29:1; 30:1–2; for prophetic and apocalyptic tradition, cf. Couturier, "Vision du conseil."

488. E.g., *Tg. Jon.* on 1 Sam 19:23–24; 2 Kgs 6:1; 9:1, 4.

489. *Sipre Deut.* 306.24.2. A true prophet must do as Moses did: *Sipre Deut.* 83.1.1.

490. Third-century Amora R. Samuel bar Nahman in R. Jonathan's name, in *y. Meg.* 1:5, §3. For the divergent data on whether prophets could make innovations in the law, see Bowman, "Prophets," 263–74.

as a teacher of Torah to all Israel.[491] The rabbis tended to regard the OT prophets as creative transmitters of Torah and did not oppose the two,[492] following a tendency in early Judaism that did not originate with them.[493]

As in nonrabbinic sources,[494] prophetic enablement could be described as having God's words put in one's mouth,[495] although the same expression came to be used for Torah study.[496] But while the general rabbinic conception of prophecy would be less ecstatic than that of Philo and Josephus (as noted), there are indications that prophecy was not limited to Torah study and exposition, as may be indicated by the contrast between the prophet par excellence of Israel and the prophet par excellence of the nations:

> But there is quite a difference between the prophecy of Moses and the prophecy of Balaam. Moses did not know with whom he was talking, but Balaam knew. . . . Moses did not know when [God] would speak with him, until he actually was spoken with, while Balaam knew full well. . . . Moses would speak with [God] only standing up. . . . But Balaam was spoken with when he had fallen. . . . To what is the matter comparable? To the case of the king's butcher, who knows precisely how much the king is spending on his table.[497]

There are also indications of mystical, revelatory experiences by certain rabbis.[498] The experiences attributed to R. Ishmael in *3 Enoch*[499] and the earlier and more likely authentically based accounts[500] of R. Akiba's ascent to paradise in Tannaitic tradition[501] suggest that these experiences, similar to those described in apocalyptic literature,[502]

491. *Sipre Deut.* 32.5.12.

492. Davies, "Aboth," 129–37. Thus the words of Isa 51:16, "My words in your mouth," applying in some contexts to prophecy, could be taken to apply to the study of Torah in *y. Ta'an.* 4:2, §13; *Meg.* 3:6, §2 (in *Sipre Deut.* 176.3.1, however, it is used prophetically).

493. Cf., e.g., 2 Macc 2:1–3; Hill, *Prophecy*, 27–28, on Josephus; Aune, *Prophecy*, 124, on Maccabean texts.

494. *L.A.B.* 11:2; *Jub.* 8:20.

495. *Sipre Deut.* 176.3.1, on Deut 18; see Jer 1:9. This phrase can be used in the OT simply for teaching another what to say, as in Exod 4:15; 2 Sam 14:3.

496. *'Abot R. Nat.* 24 A; *y. Ta'an.* 4:2, §13; *Meg.* 3:6, §2.

497. *Sipre Deut.* 357.18.2 (Neusner, 2:461), citing Num 24:16; Deut 5:28; Num 24:4. For the inability to control prophetic inspiration, see the references in *Ecclesiastes Rabbah* cited by Bowman, "Prophets," 207. On *b. B. Bat.* 15b, comparing Moses and Balaam, see the extended discussion in Bowman, "Prophets," 108–14; for the contrast between the two in Philo *Mos.* 1.263–99, see Feldman, "Balaam." Jewish writers often regarded Balaam as the greatest of the Gentile prophets or philosophers (Jos. *Ant.* 4.104; *Gen. Rab.* 65:20, 93:10; *Lam. Rab.* proem 2; *Pesiq. Rab Kah.* 15:5; in *Num. Rab.* 20:19, the Holy Spirit spoke with him); he was the only one who could explain to the nations what was happening at Sinai (*Sipre Deut.* 343.6.1; *Pesiq. Rab.* 20:1); but God kept him from cursing Israel against his will (Jos. *Ant.* 4.104; cf. *Exod. Rab.* 4:3; 20:5; 27:3), though he found another strategy to carry out his purpose (Jos. *Ant.* 4.104; *Sipre Deut.* 252.1.4; *y. Sanh.* 10:2, §8; cf. *Ta'an.* 4:5, §10). He is repeatedly considered wicked (Philo *Conf.* 159; *Mos.* 1.48; *b. Ber.* 7a; *'Abod. Zar.* 4a; *Sanh.* 105b–106a; *Exod. Rab.* 30:20; *Num. Rab.* 20:6; *Pesiq. Rab.* 20:1; 41:3) and is contrasted with Moses (*Sipre Deut.* 357.18.1–2, above; *Exod. Rab.* 32:3; *Num. Rab.* 14:20; *Eccl. Rab.* 2:15, §2) and Abraham (*m. 'Ab.* 5:19; *Gen. Rab.* 55:8). Later rabbinic polemic uses him as a type or name for Jesus (Herford, *Christianity*, 65ff.).

498. Schäfer, *Vorstellung*, may not conclusively demonstrate his case that the Holy Spirit's continued activity in rabbinic texts originates from mystical sources (Reif, "Review," 158), but these sources do seem to be the center of revelatory activity in extant rabbinic texts.

499. See P. Alexander's comments in *OTP* 1:229–38 for broader connections.

500. Bonsirven, *Judaism*, 135, comments on *t. Ber.* 3:5, 7 (that Akiba would spend hours in fervent prayer and would be left in one part of the room and be found in another) that rapturous or ecstatic experiences may be in view here, but *b. Ber.* 31a suggests that he was moved around "on account of his many genuflexions and prostrations." The latter *could* be an attempt to play down mysticism but is more probably the realistic explanation for his movement.

501. See esp. *t. Ḥag.* 2:3–4; *b. Ḥag.* 14b; *y. Ḥag.* 2:1, §§7–8; *Song Rab.* 1:4, §1. Visions of heaven became standard fare in the apocalypses; besides Enoch's tour, see later employment of the theme in *L.A.E.* 25:3–4; *Apoc. Zeph.* 5:6; *Gr. Ezra* 5:20; *Apoc. Sed.* 9:1; cf. Moses in *Sipre Deut.* 357.6.6.

502. P. Alexander, in *OTP* 1:235, suggests the "tempting" possibility "that Merkabah mysticism" was originally part of the apocalyptic stream of experience "and that it was the events of the years A.D. 70–135

were not foreign to the rabbis.[503] At the same time, the dangers of such mystical revelations were not to be underestimated;[504] esoteric teachings on the laws of creation[505] and on the throne-chariot,[506] which could border on the mystical vision of God, were to be communicated only privately;[507] some matters were, in the words of a first-century visionary, ἄρρητα (2 Cor 12:4).[508]

Was this reticence to publicly communicate these teachings due to the dangers of misappropriation by nonrabbis or inauthentic legitimation of the mystical experiences of those outside rabbinic circles? Or could these mystical experiences have included some eschatological elements that would pose threats to rabbinic Judaism's interpretive hegemony? Rabbi Akiba's support of Bar Kokhba could lend credence to this last alternative, although his mysticism and his messianism could have been unrelated.[509] Whatever the particular reason, certain forms of revelation no longer could function as adequate sources for communal knowledge, and the prevailing image of prophets sanctioned in rabbinic Judaism was as interpreters of the already-given Torah in accordance with the confines of developing rabbinic tradition.

---

in Palestine which brought about a reorientation of apocalyptic and gave rise to a more or less independent Merkabah movement." Hellenistic ascents may have provided a model, but Jewish ascent traditions were not uncommon, and they were often associated, e.g., with Moses to receive Torah (*b. Šabb.* 88b; cf. *Exod. Rab.* 42:4; *Pesiq. Rab.* 20:4; Aristob. frg. 4 [Euseb. *P.E.* 13.13.5, in *OTP* 2:840–41]; *L.A.B.* 12:1). Meeks, *Prophet-King*, 122–25, 141, 205–11, 241–46, 295–98; Nicholson, *Death*, 98; and others see a polemic against Moses's ascent in the Fourth Gospel; for an early view that this is a polemic against Jewish mystic ascent traditions, see Odeberg, *Gospel*, 72.

503. Scholem, *Gnosticism*, 11–12, argues that the early Jewish mystics lived near the center of rabbinic Judaism, not near its fringes. The date of the materials is difficult to decide; Halperin, "Merkabah Midrash," finds traces as early as the LXX; Goodenough, *Symbols*, 1:221 (cf. also 8:17; 12:198) thinks that Jewish mysticism was common, especially in the more Hellenistic circles, until halakic Judaism became dominant, and he finds evidence for this in Philo (idem, *Introduction*, 134–60). Neusner, "*Merkavah* Tradition," thinks that the earlier Merkabah traditions were expanded and made more complex with time.

504. Cf. Basser, "Democratize"; Urbach, *Sages*, 1:193. Various Jewish mystical texts show varying degrees of emphasis on responsibility to the mystic's community; see Chernus, "Individual." Such ascents could be read in light of the myth of invading heaven in OT traditions (Halperin, "Ascension"), and some of the motifs may have come from Gnosticism in the Amoraic period (Schultz, "Angelic Opposition"). Abelson, *Immanence*, 340–56, strikes a balance between rabbinic Judaism's use and its restraint of mystical tendencies.

505. E.g., *t. Ḥag.* 2:1, 7; *b. Ḥag.* 15a; *y. Ḥag.* 2:1, §15; *Gen. Rab.* 1:5, 10; 2:4; *Pesiq. Rab Kah.* 21:5; cf. *2 En.* 24:3 A (rec. J is similar); perhaps 1QHᵃ IX, 11, 13 (in Casciaro Ramírez, "Himnos").

506. E.g., *t. Ḥag.* 2:1. After a child understood the reading of Ezekiel and was instantly consumed by fire, some rabbis wished to suppress Ezekiel (*b. Ḥag.* 13a; cf. Jerome's report of a Jewish tradition that the beginning of Ezekiel was not to be read, in Scholem, *Trends*, 42); when R. Johanan ben Zakkai refused to teach the "Work of the Chariot" to R. Eleazar ben Arak, R. Eleazar then expounded it himself, and all the trees caught fire, bringing R. Johanan's commendation (*b. Ḥag.* 14b); a disciple of a rabbi expounded a chapter in the "Work of the Chariot" without the rabbi's permission and was struck with a skin disease (*y. Ḥag.* 2:1, §§3–4). Throne mysticism appears to exist in the Dead Sea Scrolls; see Dupont-Sommer, *Writings*, 333–34; Vermes, *Scrolls*, 210–11; Gaster, *Scriptures*, 285–88; Patte, *Hermeneutic*, 290, on the angelic litany. *Test. Job* 33:9 uses similar language, but of *Job's* throne; the allusion in *L.A.E.* 25:2–3 (cf. *Apoc. Mos.* 33:2) may conflate Ezekiel's and Elijah's chariots.

507. An opinion is cited in which Torah should be taught only privately (*b. Sukkah* 49b), but this is normally reserved for certain esoteric teachings (*b. Pesaḥ.* 119a; *Ḥag.* 13a; *Pesiq. Rab.* 22:2). In *b. Šabb.* 80b, a certain Galilean (his place of origin may be significant) was going to lecture publicly on the chariot passage and so died before he could.

508. This may have associations with the language of the Mysteries (e.g., Lucian *Lex.* 10; Apul. *Metam.* 11.23; cf. *Orph. H.* 30.3, 7; Burkert, *Mystery Cults*, 9; Lincoln, *Paradise*, 82; Dibelius, "Initiation," 65; Aune, *Prophecy*, 65; and commentaries on 2 Cor 12:4, such as Martin, *Corinthians*; Furnish, *II Corinthians*; and Barrett, *2 Corinthians*), though it thereby acquired a broader religious semantic range (e.g., Philost. *Vit. Apoll.* 1, §1), and the idea is already found in first-century Judaism (Philo *Worse* 175–76; *Cher.* 48; Jos. *Ag. Ap.* 2.94 [of the law]; cf. P. Alexander, *OTP* 1:246–47, for the concept among Merkabah mystics).

509. Not all eschatology would have direct political implications, some of it being quietistic; but apparently eschatology and messianic hope in general were somewhat discredited or thought to threaten political instability, for they are, for whatever reason, toned down in the Tannaitic literature.

d. Inspiration of Works in Antiquity

Inspiration was desirable for both utterances and literature[510] and was often invoked. Inspiration was important, especially for epic poets, who needed divine help to write as omniscient narrators. Sometimes this poetic inspiration could be compared with being a prophet.[511] Most frequently, narrators and poets invoked a Muse or Muses to help them.[512] Some invoked Apollo to enable them to tell their stories well.[513] As the imperial cult progressed, some invoked the emperor instead of the Muses or other deities.[514] An orator who wished to seem particularly dependent on divine aid might invoke Hermes as patron of oratory, Apollo as guide of the Muses, along with the Muses as his own guide,[515] or might invoke the Muses and Apollo but add "Persuasion" rather than Hermes.[516] (Apollo was often associated with poetic and musical inspiration.)[517] Although invoking divine help was especially conventional for poetry, it was acceptable for history as well.[518]

Those writing religious texts normally expected assistance from deities.[519] A gardener about to praise a Greek hero invokes that hero's aid in recalling and recounting the stories about him.[520] Iamblichus opines that Pythagorean commentaries were "composed perfectly with heaven-sent knowledge."[521] Some also applied the language of inspiration to speech from a God-directed mind.[522] Philosophers could also argue that one needed divine inspiration to understand divinely inspired philosophy.[523]

f. Luke and the Spirit of Prophecy

Luke underlines the importance of prophecy in the Joel quotation by reiterating it explicitly at the end of Acts 2:18,[524] so that in Greek it frames the list of the classes that would prophesy. Luke thus also explicitly emphasizes prophecy at both points in 2:17–18 where he mentions the outpouring of the Spirit.

Luke also connects the Spirit especially with prophecy and prophetic types of activity;[525] Jesus appears as a Spirit-anointed (Luke 4:18; Acts 10:38) prophet (Luke

---

510. Cf. the idea of prophetic scribes as early as P.Beatty 4 (Simpson, *Literature of Egypt*, 1).

511. E.g., *vates* in Ovid *Fasti* 6.5–8.

512. E.g., Pindar *Nem*. 3.1–5; frg. 150 (from Eustath. *Com. Il.* 1.1); Callim. *Aetia* 1.1.1–38; Musaeus *Hero* 1. For the Muses' help, cf. also Max. Tyre 38.2; cf. Schmeling, "Spectrum," 21; on the Muses more generally, see, e.g., Walde, "Muses."

513. E.g., Val. Flacc. 1.5–7; Statius *Ach*. 1.9.

514. Val. Max. 1.pref.; see Wardle, *Valerius Maximus*, 68.

515. Ael. Arist. *Def. Or*. 19, 5D–6D. He claimed that he needed the help especially because he would be arguing against a popular view of Plato (20, 6D). For deities of speech in general, see Dubourdieu, "Divinités de la parole."

516. Dio Chrys. *Or*. 1.10.

517. E.g., Pliny E. *N.H.* 37.3.5; Fronto *Eloq*. 1.13; Marc. Aur. 11.11; cf. Statius *Theb*. 6.355–56; Men. Rhet. 2.17, 440.32–441.1. For prophecy more generally, e.g., Aristoph. *Birds* 716; Dio Chrys. *Or*. 13.9; Men. Rhet. 2.4, 390.23–24; comment on Acts 16:16; for Apollo and music, e.g., Dion. Hal. *Epid*. 1.256; Dio Chrys. *Or*. 32.56–57; Artem. *Oneir*. 2.35; *Gr. Anth*. 2.266–70.

518. Pliny *Ep*. 8.4.5.

519. See, e.g., Egyptian books in Frankfurter, *Religion in Egypt*, 240.

520. Philost. *Hrk*. 25.18.

521. Iambl. *V.P.* 29.157 (Dillon and Hershbell, 173).

522. Porph. *Marc*. 20.329, ἔνθεος.

523. Iambl. *V.P.* 1.1.

524. Speakers sometimes repeated a word or phrase for stylistic purposes (Anderson, *Glossary*, 37, on διλογία), but the point here is emphasis (cf. *diaphora*, as described in Rowe, "Style," 133–34, citing Demosth. *Fals. leg*. 186; Cic. *Phil*. 12.6.14; also Porter, "Paul and Letters," 580, on Rom 3:21–26).

525. See Menzies, *Development*, esp. 205–77 (on Acts).

4:24; 13:33; 24:19), and now the church is empowered prophetically as well (Acts 2:17–18). In view of the parallels with Elijah and Elisha in 1:8–11 (also emphasized in the programmatic text for the Gospel, Luke 4:25–27), this would include the sorts of signs associated with those prophets (see comment there; and on "power" in Acts 1:8).[526] This fits the ministry of apostles (2:43; 5:12; 14:3; 15:12) and others in Acts (6:8; 8:6, 13). But by quoting the Joel text in full (Luke has the prerogative of omitting part of it, as he does with part of Joel 2:32), Luke also appears to assume that visions and dreams remained part of the church's experience.[527] But whereas Matthew emphasizes dreams (Matt 1:20; 2:12–13, 19, 22; 27:19), Luke's narrative usually emphasizes the more spectacular visions (Acts 9:10, 12; 10:3, 17–19; 26:19 [= 9:3–6]; Luke 1:22; cf. Acts 7:55; 22:14),[528] perhaps guarding against Aristotelian-type objections to dreams.[529] Even those that occur at night are typically "visions" (Acts 16:9; 18:9), language with OT precedent (Gen 46:2; Job 4:13; Dan 7:7, 13). Luke reports them much more often in Acts than in the Gospel, presumably in part because God's own Son—the primary protagonist of the Gospel—would not need any.[530]

Prophecy is crucial for Luke's apologetic and the church's mission. As Hengel and Schwemer point out, "It is impossible to overestimate the importance of earliest Christian prophecy, as the most important phenomenon of the charismata given by the Spirit, for the extension of the new Jewish-eschatological movement."[531] For a Jewish audience, it constituted decisive evidence that God was fulfilling his eschatological promises.[532] Prophecy was far more common among early Christians (who apparently experienced the gift regularly in congregational meetings, 1 Cor 14:26, 29–31; 1 Thess 5:20) than in other movements in the Greco-Roman world; people could seek information regularly from divination or oracles, but the idea of all members of a movement being potentially prophets is unusual.[533]

Prophetic figures such as Agabus and Philip's daughters function much like their ancient Israelite counterparts and demonstrate that the church continues the prophetic anointing of the OT. Acts also portrays the broader activity of christocentric testimony (Acts 1:8) as inspired speech, undoubtedly one reason that "the word of the Lord" in Acts, as in Paul, normally refers to the good news (e.g., 4:31; 8:25; 12:24; 19:10, 20). In the broadest sense of prophetic inspiration,[534] the entire church carries forward this task by its experience with the Spirit and consequent empowerment for

526. Turner, *Power*, 105–14, 118, addresses the association between the Spirit and miracles in early Judaism, though the evidence is (compared with prophecy proper) not very wide.

527. Cf. Aune, *Cultic Setting*, 91.

528. He does not repeat the exact term ὅρασις (cf. Rev 4:3; 9:17; ninety-five times in the LXX; thirteen times in the Apostolic Fathers, 2 *Clem.* 1.6; 7.6; 17.5; *Herm.* 5.1; 8.2; 18.3–5; 19.2, 4; 20.1; 21.1; 22.1), but we may take ὀπτασία (Luke 1:22; 24:23; Acts 26:19; elsewhere in NT, only 2 Cor 12:1; in the LXX, in a nonvisionary sense, at Esth 14:16; Sir 43:2, 16; Mal 3:2; in the Apostolic Fathers, visionary in *Mart. Pol.* 5.2; 12.3) and ὅραμα (Acts 7:31; 9:10, 12; 10:3, 17, 19; 11:5; 12:9; 16:9–10; 18:9; elsewhere in the NT only at Matt 17:9, but some thirty-eight times in the LXX; and in the Apostolic Fathers, *Herm.* 10.3; 12.3; 18.6; 22.3; 23.2) as equivalent.

529. Luke never repeats the exact terms for "dream" here (elsewhere in early Christian texts, only Jude 8; but the verb appears perhaps seventeen times in the LXX, and the noun appears sixty-seven times in the LXX).

530. See Koet, "Divine Communication," 756–57.

531. Hengel and Schwemer, *Between Damascus and Antioch*, 236.

532. Ibid.

533. Extrasocial groups such as the Galli (castrated priests who experienced ecstasy) are not comparable except in the broadest sense (and in ancient depictions, castration is more characteristic of their ecstasy than prophecy is, in any case; see comment at Acts 8:27).

534. For diverse forms of early Jewish prophecy, see Cousland, "Prophets and Prophecy," 833–35. The democratization of the Spirit within the church (language employed by others, e.g., Ma, "Empowerment," 39; Marguerat, *Actes*, 88) resembles the "sectarian" emphasis of Qumran literature on the Spirit's pervasiveness among the Qumran covenanters.

spreading the gospel. Because Luke himself retells the gospel narrative in particularly great detail, he undoubtedly views himself as an inspired historian as well, standing within a Jewish line of tradition on this theological matter.[535] That Luke would accept prior claims of accurate prophetism in early Christianity (rather than composing them novelistically) is entirely plausible on the principle of historical uniformity, since such claims remain common today as well (albeit primarily in popular sources).[536]

Excursus: Dreams and Visions (2:17)

Sometimes writers conflated the language for visions and dreams;[537] followers of Isis sometimes experienced visions in the night.[538] Vision claims are not infrequent in antiquity.[539] The Greek world knew magical means of seeking for revelations,[540] and some intellectuals emphasized visionary ascents to the higher realm[541] as well as sometimes soul travel out of the body.[542] (Some shamanic circles in various cultures also claim disembodied soul travel.)[543] Paul himself sidesteps the question of whether

535. On this Jewish tradition, see Hall, "History," 13–46; idem, *Revealed Histories*; cf. Hill, *Prophecy*, 27; Braun, "Prophet"; Mason, *Josephus and New Testament*, 20–21. Greeks were more explicit about inspiration claims in epics (e.g., Gordon, *Civilizations*, 224–25).

536. Sometimes accurate to the detail; see, e.g., Anderson, *Pentecostalism*, 71–72; Deere, *Power of Spirit*, 36–37, 133, 210–12; Alexander, *Signs*, 121; Gutierrez, *Milagros*, 76–77; Koch, *Zulus*, 219–20, 232, 234–35, 240–41; McKenna, *Miracles*, 6–7, 9–13, 23; Pytches, *Come*, 97–100; Storms, *Convergence*, 52, 60, 64, 66, 76–80, 86–87; idem, *Guide*, 37–38, 44–47, 81–85, 94, 100; Stibbe, *Prophetic Evangelism*, 1–5, 14–17, 49–50, 59–60, 62–64, 66–67, 70, 107, 129–30, 134–35, 159, 163, 166, 167, 195; Baker and Baker, *Enough*, 27; Moreland and Issler, *Faith*, 198–99; Best, *Supernatural*, 54–57, 92–93, 101–2, 107, 109–11, 125, 127–28, 199; cf. Pullinger, *Dragon*, 129. Storms also points to occasions in history (here Charles H. Spurgeon's ministry) where the phenomenon occurred by other names (*Guide*, 89–90, citing Spurgeon, *Autobiography*, 2:226–27; also in Storms, "View," 201–3). For accurate non-Christian prophecy, see, e.g., Ashe, *Miracles*, 165–66; Kibicho, "Continuity," 381; Harner, *Shaman*, 97–98; Salamone, "Bori," 18; Grindal, "Heart," 72; Scherberger, "Shaman," 60; Turner, "Advances," 36; McClenon, *Events*, 135; Montefiore, *Miracles*, 41–42, 51–52.

537. E.g., Plut. *Alc.* 39.1–2; *Cim.* 18.4; *Demosth.* 29.2; *Sulla* 9.4. A "dream" parallels a "vision" in Baal h. I AB (iii–iv) (*ANET* 140). On dreams and visions, see also Keener, *Miracles*, 870–84; esp. Pilch, *Flights*.

538. Apul. *Metam.* 11.13, 19. Cf. also *1 En.* 90:39–40.

539. See, e.g., Strelan, *Strange Acts*, 136–43; Rives, *Religion*, 102. Chance, "Prognostications," 220n4, points to the presence of dreams and visions in Xen. Eph. *Anthia* (though not proportionate to their appearance in Acts).

540. *PGM* 4.930–1114, esp. 934; 77.1–24, specifically 1–5; Aune, *Prophecy*, 45; cf. Toner, *Culture*, 142, on *PGM* 7.727–39. Egyptian priests entreated the supreme deity to manifest himself to them (Plut. *Isis* 9, *Mor.* 354D); others could also plead for visions of the deceased (Philost. *Hrk.* 33.36). Cf. also fasting or ascetic means (e.g., Reitzenstein, *Religions*, 42; Francis, "Humility," 168–69; Lincoln, *Paradise*, 111; see further comment on Acts 13:2).

541. Platonic philosophers embraced such mysticism (e.g., Plut. *Isis* 77, *Mor.* 382D; Philo *Spec. Laws* 3.1–2; Max. Tyre 11.10; Porph. *Marc.* 7.131–34; 10.180–83; 16.267–68; 26.415–16; for Philo, Sterling, *Ancestral Philosophy*, 31–32; Winston, "Philo's Mysticism"; for Plotinus, see Case, *Origins*, 93–94), though especially in later Platonism (see MacMullen, *Enemies*, 108). Some thinkers parodied visionary ascents (Lucian *Icar.* passim).

542. E.g., with Hermotimus (Pliny E. *N.H.* 7.52.174; parodied in Lucian *Fly* 7), as a metaphor for rational ascent (Max. Tyre 26.1; 38.3); or more commonly (Russell, *Apocalyptic*, 166); during sleep (Lucret. *Nat.* 4.916–24); likewise, the soul of one dying might travel around the world, then reenter the body to proclaim such sights (Max. Tyre 10.2). Cf. cosmic tours in apocalypses (e.g., in Bauckham, "Visiting"; *L.A.B.* 19:10).

543. E.g., Eliade, *Rites*, 95; Prince, "Yoruba Psychiatry," 92; Mbiti, *Religions*, 220; Rasmussen, "Shaman's Journey," 308. Many peoples attribute possession trance to the soul's absence (Bourguignon, "Distribution," 7–9), and Greeks sometimes attributed it to the mind's displacement (see comments on ecstasy in the excursus on prophecy at Acts 2:17). For shamanic journeys to heaven, see also Scott, "Ascent," 448. Among some other peoples, part of one's soul travels regularly, and the rest does during sleep (Schmidt, "Psychiatry," 140; for part of the spirit leaving the body in sleep, see also Lucret. *Nat.* 4.916–24); or soul travel occurs after death (Mbiti, *Religions*, 208–9).

one of his more extraordinary revelatory experiences was bodily or out of the body, perhaps to accommodate Corinthian sentiments (2 Cor 12:2).[544]

Visions were especially important in so-called apocalyptic literature, often characterized by visions (cf., e.g., Enoch recounting his visions to his son in *1 En.* 83:1).[545] Indeed, "apocalypses" in the narrowest sense, by definition, involve visions and revelations, often including cosmological speculation (e.g., *1 En.* 72–82). They may form part of the background for early Jewish mysticism.[546] In contrast to assumptions that the pseudepigraphic experiences must reflect only fabrication, the heavenly visions in ancient Jewish apocalyptic and mystic sources show some parallels with shamanic sky journeys in various cultures.[547]

Jewish literature often reports visions,[548] most of which (outside the broader selection in apocalyptic literature) concern the heavenly throne-chariot[549] or throne[550] (and by implication, the Lord). Although the rabbinic evidence is late, the roots of such speculation in some form are much earlier.[551] (Such speculations were considered potentially quite dangerous and hence to be passed on only secretly.)[552] Although most reported visions occur in altered states of consciousness that we might call trance states (so also, e.g., Acts 10:10; 11:5), some "visions" in Acts report no prior trance state, probably functioning more like "apparitions."[553]

Cross-cultural studies show that altered states of consciousness are a frequent phenomenon; indeed, brain research suggests that the human brain is open to such experiences.[554] In fact, from dreams during REM sleep to sleepwalking, occurrences

544. Some early Jewish apocalyptic texts allowed the spirit to be caught up (*1 En.* 71:1; cf. also Russell, *Apocalyptic*, 166); but the Jewish approach was more commonly "in the body" (Furnish, *II Corinthians*, 525; e.g., Ezek 2:2; 3:14, 24; 8:3; 11:1, 24; Wis 4:11; *1 En.* 39:3; 87:3; *Test. Ab.* 8:2–3 B), and so Paul's allowance of "out of the body" may constitute a concession to Corinthian sentiments.

545. See fuller discussion in Keener, *Revelation*, 31–32.

546. Rowland, "Visions in Apocalyptic Literature," 154.

547. See Pilch, "Sky Journeys," focused esp. on the author of *1 Enoch* (106–10; idem, *Flights*, 66–70).

548. *Test. Jud.* 3:10 adds extrabiblical visions to those Jacob had in Scripture. For visions of heavenly paradise, see, e.g., *L.A.E.* 28:3–4; *Apoc. Mos.* 22:3; *Apoc. Zeph.* 5:6; *Gr. Ezra* 5:20; *Sipre Deut.* 357.6.6. But these are closely related to visions of God's throne (cf., e.g., *t. Ḥag.* 2:3–4; *b. Ḥag.* 14b, bar.; *y. Ḥag.* 2:1, §7; *Song Rab.* 1:4, §1).

549. See, e.g., *3 En.* 1; Scholem, *Trends*, 44. In contrast to apocalypses, Hekhalot texts (like magical texts) provide instructions for the journey (Himmelfarb, "Ascent"). God might make the patriarchs his chariot (*Gen. Rab.* 47:6; 69:3; 82:6); for other chariots, cf. *L.A.E.* 25:2–3; *Apoc. Mos.* 22:3; 33:2.

550. See, e.g., *1 En.* 14:24–25; 15:1; for Moses's mystic ascents, see Meeks, *Prophet-King*, 122–25; Lincoln, *Paradise*, 118. The goal was to behold God (Arbel, "Understanding"). On heavenly ascent in general, see Segal, "Ascent in Judaism"; comment on Acts 1:9–11.

551. Some scholars suspect some Merkabah speculation even in the LXX (Halperin, "Midrash"); more clearly, it appears in Qumran scrolls (cf. Davila, "4Q534"; Dimant and Strugnell, "Vision"), as generally noted (e.g., Dupont-Sommer, *Writings*, 333–34; Gaster, *Scriptures*, 285–88; Patte, *Hermeneutic*, 290; Vermes, *Religion*, 128); also in *L.A.E.* 25:3. Some Jewish people disapproved of such activities (cf. Jos. *Ag. Ap.* 2.191), which probably penetrated later rabbinic circles only gradually. For the tradition's development, cf., e.g., Neusner, "*Merkavah* Tradition."

552. See *t. Ḥag.* 2:1, 3–6; *b. Ḥag.* 13a, bar.; 14ab (including 14b, bar.); *Šabb.* 80b; *y. Ḥag.* 2:1, §§3–4, 7–8; *Song Rab.* 1:4, §1; Scholem, *Trends*, 42, 52–54; idem, *Gnosticism*, 14; Lieber, "Angels"; on suggested secret transmission, see, e.g., Séd, "Traditions secrètes." The rabbis wanted to keep such material from the masses (Basser, "Merkavah Narrative") and may have tried to play down such speculation (Basser, "Democratize"). Pythagoreans who leaked secrets of the sect also faced divine judgment (Iambl. *V.P.* 18.88; 34.247).

553. E.g., Acts 9:3–4 (though called a "vision" in 26:19, and despite a scholar's suggestion of a "road trance"; see comment there). Cf. 10:3 (though called a "vision"; although some forms of intense prayer [10:30] could create a hypnotic state, reciting Jewish liturgy presumably would not have done so). For Luke's use of vision as symbolic or nonphysical reality, contrast 12:9 with secondhand vision claims in Luke 1:22; 24:23.

554. So Pilch, *Visions*, passim, esp. 158–59; idem, "Trance Experience"; Malina and Pilch, *Acts*, 185–87; idem, *Letters*, 331–33. Although alternative explanations merit more consideration, Beauregard and O'Leary, *Brain*, argue that such mystic experiences reflect genuine connections with the primordial ground of being (e.g., 293–94). Strelan, *Strange Acts*, 131, suggests that ancients were less concerned than moderns to distinguish

of psychomotor epilepsy, and possession trance, a continuum of altered states of consciousness overlaps at some points with "normal" life.[555] Although such phenomena do not all involve identical external causes, they do suggest that the common wiring of human nervous systems allows for similar symptoms due to a variety of causes, typically experienced by the nervous system as something analogous to emotional stresses.[556] In religious contexts, various cultures often construe such altered states positively.[557]

This excursus focuses more on dreams here because they appear more frequently in the sources, probably because people dream far more regularly than see visions; but note further the apparition examples discussed at Acts 1:3. Many ancients believed that dreams provided them divine direction.[558] (For dreams at healing sanctuaries, see comment in the introduction, ch. 9, sect. 3.a.i.) Whether in Greece and Macedonia,[559] Rome,[560] Egypt,[561] Carthage,[562] the East,[563] Palestine,[564] among Diaspora Jews,[565] among later rabbis,[566] or in magical papyri,[567] people often believed that dreams conveyed divine messages. So compelling was trust in dreams' warnings that they could be employed to bolster an army's courage;[568] a fabricated dream

---

visual from visionary sight; although this was probably true in some cases, many ancient writers would have recognized the distinction.

555. Bourguignon, "Introduction," 14; for psychomotor epilepsy, Prince, "EEG," 122–24; for sleepwalking, 124–25; for hysterical fugue states, 125–27; cf. Pilch, *Flights*, 26.

556. Whether in humans suffering battle fatigue or in experimental dogs overwhelmed by stresses, the nervous system may collapse (Prince, "EEG," 129). Cathartic release of emotion, or at a more extreme level, emotional collapse, seems to reset human emotional circuits; whether in ecstasies during Wesley's preaching (June 15, 1739) or in the course of brainwashing techniques, emotional collapse yields a suggestible state, to which some also compare possession trance (Prince, "EEG," 130). (Prince himself [132] thinks that ecstasies in Wesley's meetings were caused by suggestion, lacking neurophysiological causes as in some other cases. But other studies have shown that intense religious emotion can produce altered neurophysiological states [see, e.g., Goodman, *Speaking in Tongues*; on mystical "call" trances, cf. Lewis, *Ecstatic Religion*, 37–44].) Prince, "EEG," 133–34, notes neurophysiological changes due to rhythmic drumming (as in West Africa and Haiti) and in "photic driving," "light flashing at or near the alpha rhythm of the brain."

557. Ludwig, "Altered States," 88. Cf. Goodman, *Trance Journeys*; idem, *Ecstasy*; Pilch, *Flights*.

558. See generally Croy, "Religion, Personal," 927; Theissen, *Erleben*, 138. On Greek and Roman dreams, see also Miller, *Convinced*, 23–39 (noting both acceptance and criticism); Bovon, *Studies*, 145–49; on Jewish dreams, Miller, *Convinced*, 40–61; Bovon, *Studies*, 149–52; on post-NT Christian dreams up through Augustine, 155–61 (e.g., *Acts Thom.* 154; *Acts John* 48).

559. Hom. *Il.* 1.63; 5.150; Eurip. *Philoctetes* frg. 789b.3; Xen. *Anab.* 3.1.11; 4.3.8; 6.1.22; *Cav. Com.* 9.9; Paus. 4.19.5–6; 9.26.4; Longus 1.7; 2.23, 26–27; 3.27; 4.35; Appian *Hist. rom.* 11.9.56; 12.12.83; Quint. Curt. 4.2.17; Arrian *Alex.* 2.18.1; Babr. 136.3–4; Ach. Tat. 1.3.2; 4.1.4; 7.12.4; Char. *Chaer.* 1.12.5; 2.9.6; 3.7.4; 4.1.2; 5.5.5–7; 6.2.2; 6.8.3; Libanius *Narration* 13; cf. *Orph. H.* 85–87; Epidaurus inscriptions; Hadas, *Aristeas*, 184–85; Reinhold, *Diaspora*, 35; Oberhelman, "Dreams"; Mackay, "Plutarch," 104–6; Hanson, "Dreams and Visions"; Martin, *Religions*, 48–50; idem, "Artemidorus."

560. Tac. *Ann.* 2.14; Marc. Aur. 1.17.8; van der Horst, "Macrobius," 221–22; cf. Virg. *Aen.* 4.556–57; 7.415–20; Ovid *Metam.* 9.685–701; 15.653–54.

561. Ezek. Trag. *Exag.* 68–89; *Sib. Or.* 3.293; Philo *Migr.* 190; Deissmann, *Light*, 154; Lewis, *Life*, 99; Wright, *Archaeology*, 53.

562. Dio Cass. 13, frg. in Zonaras 8.22.

563. Hdt. 1.34, 107, 127; Quint. Curt. 3.3.2–3 (but probably a non-Persian literary invention).

564. Jos. *War* 1.328; 2.116; *Life* 208–10; for a fuller comparison between dreams in Josephus and Luke, see Vogel, "Traumdarstellungen" (on Josephus, esp. 136–45). Some dreams in *Jubilees* are from Scripture (e.g., *Jub.* 14:1; 29:6; 39:16; 40:1–3, 12; 44:2; cf. 29:3), but others were added (27:1; 35:6; 41:24); cf. extrabiblical dreams in *Test. Levi* 8:18; *Test. Naph.* 7:1 (but biblical ones in *Test. Zeb.* 3:3; *Test. Gad* 2:2); in apocalyptic sources, see, e.g., *1 En.* 13:8; 85:1; 90:42; *4 Ezra* 11:1; 12:35; 13:1, 15, 19, 53; 14:8.

565. *Sib. Or.* 3.293; *Let. Aris.* 192, 315.

566. *'Abot R. Nat.* 40 A; 46, §§128–29 B; *Pesiq. Rab Kah.* 5:2; *b. B. Bat.* 10a; *Ber.* 55a–58a; *Ḥag.* 14b; *Gen. Rab.* 17:5; 44:17; 89:5–6, 8; *Lev. Rab.* 3:5; 34:12; *Eccl. Rab.* 1:1, §1; 3:2, §2; 5:2, §1; 5:6, §1; *Lam. Rab.* 1:1, §§16–18; Zeitlin, "Dreams"; Alexander, "Dreambook."

567. *PGM* 4.2076–80, 2444–45, 2625, 3172; *PDM Sup.* 117–30.

568. E.g., Quint. Curt. 4.2.17.

reportedly precipitated an innocent man's execution,[569] and some warned of false dream-tellers and interpreters.[570]

God revealed things to biblical heroes in Jewish tradition as well,[571] and later stories amplified the frequency of such revelations.[572] Later rabbis believed revelatory dreams could be secured through fasting (y. *Ketub.* 12:3, §7) or their ill pronouncements revoked through fasting (*Pesiq. Rab Kah.* 28:2).[573] Ancients also emphasized dreams experienced in a sacred place. The ancient Near Eastern practice of incubation—receiving a dream by sleeping in a temple[574]—continued in the Hellenistic and Roman periods.[575]

Sometimes dreams were prophetic but required an interpretation (Plut. *Cim.* 18.3; see comment on Acts 16:10); others might be interpreted easily (Plut. *Demosth.* 29.2).[576] Some people were particularly skillful in dream interpretation; sometimes, as here, they might be "old men" (Hom. *Il.* 5.150). Some Jewish traditions implied that although God spoke to pagan rulers in dreams, they needed pious Jewish interpreters to help them understand.[577] For more on dream interpretation, see comment on Acts 16:10.

Though the majority of people did not consult professional dream interpreters, dreams were embraced and acted on very widely in antiquity.[578] Oft-repeated dreams could prove particularly persuasive.[579] Pagan dreams are often cited as premonitions of the dreamers' imminent deaths[580] or of another's death.[581]

Still, people realized that not all dreams were divine revelations, and those who were more skeptical excluded most dreams from being revelations.[582] What one had been thinking about during the day could cause dreams.[583] Orators could invent "dreams" for effect,[584] even noting that they could be caused by eating particular kinds of food.[585]

569. Dio Cass. 60.14.4–15.1; cf. Appian *Hist. rom.* 12.2.9.

570. Juv. *Sat.* 6.542–47; *Lam. Rab.* 1:1, §§14–15; cf. Virg. *Aen.* 5.636.

571. E.g., Gen 28:12; 37:5–9; Dan 2:19; cf. Jos. *Ant.* 2.13–16, 63–73.

572. E.g., 1Qap Gen^ar XIX, 14–23; *Jub.* 27:1–3; 32:1; 41:24; Ezek. Trag. *Exag.* 68–89; Jos. *Ant.* 2.216–19; 6.38; 7.147; *L.A.B.* 9:10; 42:3; *4 Ezra* 10:59; *Test. Ab.* 4:8 A; 4:16; 6:1–2 B; *L.A.E.* 23:2/*Apoc. Mos.* 2:2; Endres, *Interpretation*, 207.

573. Fasting for revelations appears in a variety of texts (e.g., *Herm.* 1.3.10; see comment on Acts 13:2).

574. Cf. Gen 15:12–13; 1 Sam 3:3–4; 1 Kgs 3:4–5; Keret in KRT A (i) (*ANET* 143); Aqhat in AQHT A (i) (*ANET* 150).

575. E.g., Diod. Sic. 1.25.3–4; 1.53.8; Paus. 1.34.5; 2.27.2; Hdn. 4.8.3; Grant, *Religions*, 16, 38; Oepke, "ὄναρ," 223–24; Grant, *Gods*, 66–67; cf. Rousselle, "Cults"; in Josephus, Gnuse, "Temple Experience."

576. The fauns supposedly inspired both prophecies and sleep (Fronto *Eloq.* 1.13).

577. Gen 40:8; 41:16, 25, 28; Dan 2:27–28; Jos. *War* 2.111–13; *Ant.* 17.345–48. See Gnuse, "Dream Interpreter in Foreign Court."

578. Bowersock, *Fiction as History*, 77–98 (including Galen 16.222); see further Hanson, "Dreams and Visions" (who also notes literary forms for dream or vision reports).

579. E.g., Apul. *Metam.* 11.19 (Isis calling Lucius to her priesthood).

580. Xen. *Cyr.* 8.7.2; Plut. *Alc.* 39.1–2; *Sulla* 37.2.

581. Aeschylus *Pers.* 176–99; Fronto *Bell. parth.* 6. When a preacher in Congo known for signs and wonders died, my future wife, then studying in France and unaware that he was passing, dreamed that he had stopped to say farewell; she later learned that many others had similar dreams when he died.

582. Sir 34:1–8 [31:1–8]; *Let. Aris.* 213–16; Jos. *Ag. Ap.* 1.207–8; Hom. *Od.* 19.559–67; Hdt. 7.12–19; Arist. *On the Soul; On Prophecy in Sleep;* Artem. *Oneir.* 1.1; Hdn. 2.9.3; cf. *b. Hor.* 13b; Cic. *Div.* 2.58.119–2.72.150; Diog. Laert. 6.2.43; probably Polyb. 33.21.1–2 (see LCL, 6:290–91). See further discussion esp. in Miller, *Convinced*, 29–36.

583. Artem. *Oneir.* 1.1. White, *Artemidorus*, 67–68n6, provides many parallels to this conception.

584. Men. Rhet. 2.4, 390.4–10 allows orators to invent dream-revelations for effect (cf. the value of *visiones* in Quint. *Inst.* 6.2.29, though he applies this to emotive, descriptive language, e.g., 6.2.32).

585. Plut. *M. Cato* 23.4. Thus a king's prophets might claim to interpret a dream that he had in fact made up (Char. *Chaer.* 6.8.3; cf. Dan 2:9; of course, political expediency could dictate the outcome of many prophecies, as in 1 Kgs 22:13).

Some considered dreams less likely to be true during autumn[586] but more common in spring and autumn and especially when lying on one's back.[587] Some dreams were even intended or regarded as divine deceptions.[588]

Biblical dreams typically differed from many of their counterparts in who delivered the message. Pagan[589] and Jewish[590] dreams often included apparitions of deceased persons; like the biblical tradition, however, the NT writers generally limited apparitions to angels (though cf. discussion on Acts 16:9).[591] Matthew stresses revelation through dreams more than do other extant first-century Christian writers (Matt 2:12, 13, 19, 22; 27:19), though Luke includes almost as many (Acts 16:9–10; 18:9–10; 23:11; 27:23–24).[592] See some further discussion at Acts 16:9–10.

Although in the West consideration of dreams is often relegated to the realm of Jungian psychotherapists[593] and (perhaps more helpfully) neurologists, the divinatory or prophetic use of dreams and visions continues to play a role in many societies and religions, including Asian and African Christianity.[594] (Such claims also appear in the West[595] and belong to foundational periods of even some fairly conservative Christian movements.)[596] Some scholars report that in some regions, large numbers or even most of those converted to Christianity today testify to being converted through dreams or visions.[597] My wife, a second-generation Christian from central Africa, collected

---

586. Alciph. *Farm.* 2 (Iophon to Eraston), 3.10, ¶3; Plut. *Table* 8.10, *Mor.* 734D.

587. Pliny E. *N.H.* 28.14.54.

588. Hom. *Il.* 2.20–21; Virg. *Aen.* 5.893–96; *Vit. Aes.* 33; P.Paris 47; cf. the prophecy in 1 Kgs 22:22–23. 4Q560 1 I, 5 is an incantation to protect against dreams, apparently recognizing that not all are from God.

589. E.g., Hom. *Il.* 23.65, 83–85; Eurip. *Hec.* 30–34, 703–6; Virg. *Aen.* 1.353–54; 2.268–97, 772–94; 4.351–52; 5.721–23; Ovid *Metam.* 11.586–88, 635, 650–73; Plut. *Sulla* 37.2; *Br. Wom.*, *Mor.* 252F; Apul. *Metam.* 8.8; 9.31; cf. Hom. *Od.* 4.795–839; 19.546–49; Appian *Hist. rom.* 8.1.1; Arrian *Alex.* 7.30.2.

590. *'Abot R. Nat.* 40 A; *Pesiq. Rab Kah.* 11:23; *y. Ḥag.* 2:2, §5; *Ketub.* 12:3, §7; *Sanh.* 6:6, §2; *Eccl. Rab.* 9:10, §1; to my knowledge, the earliest Christian example is *Acts Paul* 11.6.

591. Greek tradition also allowed for apparitions of deities, not restricted to incubation (see, e.g., Plut. *Luc.* 10.2–3; 12.1; *Sulla* 9.4; 28.6).

592. On Luke's dream and vision reports, see esp. now Miller, *Convinced*; for a survey of Lukan scholarship on dreams and visions, see 81–90.

593. Shorter, *Witchdoctor*, 152–53, notes Jung's "big dream" (Jung, "Symbolic Life," 556), that Freud conceded his inability to explain accurate premonitory dreams (Freud, *Interpretation*, 61), and that some have argued for genuine precognition in some dreams (citing Dunne, *Experiment*, 37ff., 50, 59; and esp. Rycroft, *Innocence*, 36).

594. For examples in Myanmar, Khai, "Pentecostalism," 269, 270; popular-level claims about dreams in China, Sung, *Diaries*, 9–10, 15–16, 28, 55, 99, 102, 109, 110, 189–90; Yun, *Heavenly Man*, 32, 35, 135, 137, 178, 180, 181, 189, 197, 305–6, 315, 341; about visions, 58, 60, 68–69, 73, 103, 108–9, 122–23, 124, 254; for children in early twentieth-century China, see also Baker, *Visions* (new ed.), passim; visions in Timor, Indonesia, e.g., Wilkerson, *Beyond*, 76, 78, 81 (also on a popular level); in the Philippines, Ma, "Manifestations." In Africa, see Evans-Pritchard, *Witchcraft*, 137, 378–86; Shorter, *Witchdoctor*, 149–61, esp. 152–54); in African Christian movements, see, e.g., Gornik, *Word*, 29–30, 58, 60, 64–65, 269; Adeyemo, "Dreams"; Dayhoff, "Machava"; idem, "Mthethwa"; idem, "Mucavele"; idem, "Vilakoti"; Fuller, "Harman"; idem, "Taiwo"; Gaiya, "Gindiri"; Koschorke, Ludwig, and Delgado, *History*, 221 (on Isaiah Shembe), 222; Magaji and Danmallam, "Magaji"; Manana, "Magaji"; Menberu, "Abraham"; Odili, "Okeriaka"; Quinn, "Kivebulaya" (on an Anglican, 1864–1933); Sundkler, "Worship," 552–53; Wodi, "Wodi"; Kalu, *African Pentecostalism*, 288; Baker and Baker, *Enough*, 21, 58–59, 62–65, 72, 76, 142, 157, 182; idem, *Miracles*, 173; Clark, *Impartation*, 208.

595. In early modern Pentecostalism, see, e.g., McGee, *People of Spirit*, 269; more recently in the West, e.g., Rumph, *Signs*, 83–90; Deere, *Voice*, passim; Williams, *Signs*, 141–42; Storms, *Convergence*, 60–61, 64, 78–80; Stibbe, *Prophetic Evangelism*, 95; Baker and Baker, *Enough*, 49–50, 55, 181; idem, *Miracles*, 31, 199; Moreland and Issler, *Faith*, 198–99; Clark, *Impartation*, 120, 145–48, 200; dreams in Pullinger, *Dragon*, 28, 106, 123, 135; visions, 29, 200, 232; dreams in Jackson, *Quest*, 176, 335; visions, 70–71, 298.

596. E.g., they were common in early evangelicalism (Noll, *Rise*, 267), a movement in the twentieth century traditionally shyer concerning extrabiblical "revelation."

597. E.g., Moreland, *Triangle*, 169; Moreland and Issler, *Faith*, 151–53; cf. Becken, "Healing Communities," 233; Guthrie, "Breakthrough," 26; Morgan, "Impasse," 61; Stibbe, *Prophetic Evangelism*, 5–6, 17–20 (in the West, 101–2), 98 (a vision; in the West, 104–5); for some examples claiming conversions through visions or

---

in her journal many examples of Christians' dreams and visions that were taken very seriously and often proved (albeit in retrospect) strikingly accurate.[598] In such settings people may use the predictive element as a warning rather than assume an unalterable future; the retrospective component may be used to interpret dreams and presumably to distinguish "accurate" (more apt to be revelatory) from "inaccurate" dreams.

g. Other Eschatological Imagery

Luke includes other imagery, the fuller interpretation of which is possible through surveying the language of the biblical prophets as a whole. The Spirit's being "poured," cosmic signs, the "day of the Lord," and salvation all evoke Israel's future hope, understood by this period in eschatological terms.

i. Pouring Out (2:17–18)

The language of "pouring out" God's Spirit (Acts 2:17) probably originated as a Hebrew idiom comparing one's spirit or heart with fluid (1 Sam 1:15; Isa 29:10; Lam 2:11); the same idiom applies to wisdom's (Prov 1:23) or God's (Isa 32:15; 44:3; Ezek 39:29; Zech 12:10) Spirit in a number of passages.[599] (Luke follows the LXX in literally rendering the MT's "my Spirit" as "from my Spirit";[600] some scholars take this to imply "a material concept of Spirit,"[601] but it may simply emphasize a finite measure that does not exhaust the supply.)[602]

This image fits nicely with the water metaphor of "baptism in the Holy Spirit" (on which see Acts 1:5). The other references to pouring out the Spirit in Acts (2:33; 10:45) naturally refer back to the Joel quotation, and the Pauline references (Rom 5:5; Titus 3:5–6) may do the same.[603]

---

auditions, see, e.g., Kwan, "Argument," 499; Filson, "Study," 150; Knapstad, "Power," 82–83; Burgess, *Revolution*, 250; Chesnut, "Exorcising," 181–82 (apparently; Brazil); Kim, "Healing," 273; Bush and Pegues, *Move*, 53, 62; Yun, *Heavenly Man*, 50; regarding dreams, Filson, "Study," 154; Knapstad, "Power," 87–88; Bush and Pegues, *Move*, 54, 62; Pope-Levison, *Pulpit*, 51. Ekechi, "Factor," 294, notes the influence of a vision on corporate conversion in 1873 Onitsha. For dreams and healings (or prescriptions), see, e.g., Shorter, *Witchdoctor*, 153–54; Zempleni, "Symptom," 119; Bush and Pegues, *Move*, 51, 61. Many Catholic and Protestant clergy are called to ministry through dreams (in Africa, see Sundkler, *Bara Bukoba*, 98, cited in Shorter, *Witchdoctor*, 153; e.g., Burgess, *Revolution*, 160; in Latin America, Marostica, "Learning," 210; in Asia, Kim, "Healing," 275; Yohannan, *Revolution*, 127–28; in the West, Tallman, *Shakarian*, 147); dreams also sometimes recruit priests in traditional religions (e.g., Verger, "Trance," 51, though noting that this was not the most common method) or portend possession (Colson, "Possession," 73).

598. Such dreams and visions included another person's vision of her leaving the country and inadvertently returning during danger in the airport, twenty years before the event took place—and the visions of others, when she was in her country, that she would eventually marry a U.S. minister. (Not Pentecostal, she belonged to her country's major Protestant church.) Shorter, *Witchdoctor*, 160–61, cites an example of what he took to be accurate African precognition through a dream. For possibly veridical experiences, see Pilch, *Flights*, 166–68.

599. Also 1QS IV, 21 and 4Q509 V, 15–16, which speak of God pouring out his "spirit of holiness" or "holy spirit" (as in Acts 2:33; 10:45; Rom 5:5; but "holy spirit" appears in the OT only at Ps 51:11 and Isa 63:10–11); *1 En.* 91:1; cf. the metaphor for other divine attributes (justice poured out in Isa 45:8; 1QM XII, 10). In Joel 2:29, the Hebrew may play on the sound of the words for "pour" and "female servant," but the Greek offers no echo of this.

600. Otherwise rare in the LXX and the Greek NT.

601. Barrett, *Acts*, 136. Cf. the material conception of "Spirit" in Stoicism (e.g., Long, *Philosophy*, 155–58, 171; Chevallier, *Ancien Testament*, 41–42; see discussion in our introduction, ch. 15, sect. 5, excursus part 1); for Stoics, all existent things had substance (Arius Did. *Epit.* 2.7.5a.5–6), including virtues, mind, and soul (2.7.5b.7, pp. 20–21.28–30).

602. Cf. Num 11:17, where the Hebrew agrees. Steyn, "Ἐκχεῶ," suggests that something other than the Spirit is being poured out from the Spirit, but this thoughtful interpretation (while otherwise feasible) does not seem to fit the widespread OT background or the analogous passages in Acts.

603. With, e.g., Dunn, *Romans*, 1:253. Whether from Joel or from other OT fluid images for the Spirit, they probably do not stem solely from baptism in this period (unless we date Titus 3 quite late), for which

ii. Cosmic Signs (2:19–20)

In Acts 2:19, Luke adds "signs" to Joel's "wonders."[604] The likeliest reason is to prepare the reader for the description of Jesus's ministry in terms of "miracles, wonders and signs" in 2:22[605] and hence to show that the eschatological era of the Spirit and salvation has arrived, revealed also by the continuing signs in Acts (2:43; 4:16, 22, 30; 5:12; 6:8; 8:6, 13; 14:3; 15:12).[606] This offers an explicit literary connection in the immediate context (in fact, at the outset of Peter's explanation of the text from Joel).

The heavenly darkness at Jesus's death[607] probably also constitutes a partial fulfillment here (Luke 23:44–45)[608] and prefigures the eschatological cosmic signs (21:11, 25–26) some indefinite time after Jerusalem's fall (21:20–23).[609] Turner also suggests that the Pentecost event itself constitutes a "wonder from heaven" (cf. Acts 2:33–34);[610] this would certainly make sense of the signs on the day of Pentecost as well (2:2–4).[611] In particular, the "fire" of 2:19 could readily point to the fire of Pentecost in 2:3.[612]

Undoubtedly, Joel anticipated more graphic cosmic phenomena than Luke's realized eschatological application suggests[613] (and presumably, Luke himself would re-

---

immersion provided a more natural analogy than pouring (on the character of early Jewish baptismal analogies, see Keener, *John*, 442–47, 549; in view of ancient mikvaot, it is beyond question that immersion was favored in the earliest period). They might reflect a common tradition of interpretation. The image could also be a banquet image for pouring wine, offering continuity with the image of Acts 2:13 (as Hermog. *Inv.* 4.10.199–200, finds in Demosth. *Or.* 3.31; 4.49), but Luke would know the water imagery for the Spirit in the prophets (a motif developed esp. by John; see Keener, *Spirit*, 135–89).

604. Although this is pleonastic, the LXX pairs these two terms twenty-six times, always placing σημεῖα first (cf. also Lake and Cadbury, *Commentary*, 23; Turner, *Power*, 273). In Acts, however, "signs" appears before "wonders" in 4:30; 5:12; 14:3; and 15:12; but "wonders" appears first in 2:19, 22, 43; 6:8; and 7:36. They may function interchangeably for Luke (see Menzies, *Development*, 222; in Byzantine lexicography, cf. Remus, *Conflict*, 48). Various functional synonyms existed for "miracles" (cf., e.g., θαυμαστόν in *Test. Ab.* 18:6 A; cf. Tob 12:22).

605. The rhetorical compilation of all three terms appears rarely (2 Cor 12:12; Heb 2:4).

606. With, e.g., Lake and Cadbury, *Commentary*, 23; Lampe, "Miracles," 173; Stanton, *Jesus of Nazareth*, 16, 72; Juel, *Promise*, 61; Zehnle, *Pentecost Discourse*, 34; Turner, *Power*, 273; Johnson, *Function*, 44–45n1; Johnson, *Acts*, 49; Barrett, *Acts*, 138 (citing Acts 2:43); Jervell, *Apostelgeschichte*, 145; Chance, *Acts*, 53; Menzies, "Paradigm," 214; Peterson, *Acts*, 143. The LXX connects the language most often with Moses and the exodus (with Acts 7:36; Johnson, *Function*, 45; Johnson, *Acts*, 50). Sloan, "Signs," 161, adds the climactic sign of Jesus's resurrection (cf. 2:24–32; cf. also perhaps Luke 11:29–30, though it lacks explicit connection with the resurrection, in contrast to Matt 12:39–40).

607. Already objecting to the gospel tradition some two decades after the event, one Thallus reportedly attributed the darkness to a coincidental eclipse, which Julius Africanus (ca. 221) disputes (see, e.g., discussion in Goguel, *Life*, 91–92; Bruce, *Documents*, 113; Allison, "Thallus," 405 [with translation, 405–6]; Evans, "Non-Christian Sources," 454–55). An unanticipated solar eclipse for three hours (most last a few minutes at most, like one eclipse for under two minutes in 29 c.e., Brown, *Death*, 1041–42) is improbable, but the report suggests that Diaspora Christians were circulating this tradition of the passion narrative even before the early 50s. Although Luke employs language often associated with eclipses, clouds could account for the earliest tradition's darkness (cf. Mark 15:33).

608. Barclay, "Acts ii.14–40," 198; Juel, *Promise*, 61. Cf. earlier Bede *Comm. Acts* 2.20, for whom the prophecy is partly fulfilled (the sun was darkened at the cross, but the moon was not obscured during Passover season).

609. Turner, *Power*, 273. In view of Luke 21:25–28, Marshall, "Acts," 535, opines that the "wonders in heaven" may remain future.

610. Turner, *Power*, 274.

611. Cf. Borg, *Conflict*, 217.

612. The "blood" specifically applies to the moon in Acts 2:20, but if Luke presses realized eschatology even into such details (which seems somewhat more unlikely than likely), he might think also of Jesus's blood (Luke 22:20, though this is not a characteristically Lukan emphasis), whether as a sign (22:44) or as an invitation to judgment (cf. 11:50–51).

613. Dunn, "Demythologizing," 297, complains that Peter "treats the cosmic spectacle language of Joel 2 as little more than apocalyptic sound-effects."

serve the full impact of Joel's promise for the completed day of the Lord, which he also expects here). Eschatological signs in the heavens are common in early Jewish texts.[614]

Nevertheless, readers could grasp present as well as eschatological fulfillments of such language.[615] Because Joel refers to judgment, his "smoky clouds" may be war language (cf. Joel 2:2, 10; 3:15; for Luke, wars continue in the time preceding the end, Luke 21:9, 20–24). One could speak of a dust cloud rising from a marching army[616] or its hasty retreat,[617] clouds of dust rising to heaven from a battle,[618] or a "cloud" of arrows overshadowing the sky.[619] Even a cloud of dark birds obscuring the sky before battle was a negative omen.[620] Fierce battle could stir dust clouds that shrouded the sky and sun, the latter expressing "sympathy."[621] Given the context in Joel, he may have also envisioned locusts;[622] Romans viewed clouds like locusts as an omen as well.[623] Joel has just depicted the day of YHWH (Joel 2:1) as a day of darkness and clouds (2:2), with the sky darkened by the locust invasion (2:10) in the terrible day of YHWH (2:11).[624]

Many ancients understood that the moon passing in front of the sun caused a solar eclipse.[625] Some viewed eclipses simply as purely natural phenomena[626] and complained about the superstition of those terrified by them.[627] Nevertheless, even some who, like Pliny the Elder, treated eclipses as natural phenomena[628] noted their apparent function as portents.[629] Darkness during the day, as happened to those near the erupting Mount Vesuvius, terrified bystanders (Pliny *Ep.* 6.20.13–14); in that case many prayed (6.20.14–15), but many thought that the whole world (6.20.17), including their gods (6.20.15), was perishing.[630]

614. E.g., *1 En.* 80:1–5; 91:16; *4 Ezra* 5:4–5; 7:38–42; *Sib. Or.* 3.82–92; 5.29–31, 211–13. Sunlight is blotted out in *Sib. Or.* 3.800–804; 5.476–84, 512–31; *Test. Mos.* 10:5.

615. For cosmic catastrophe language used within history, see, e.g., Judg 5:4; Ps 18:4–19; Jer 4:23–28; *Sib. Or.* 3.286–92; 4.57–60; Petron. *Sat.* 124.

616. Sall. *Jug.* 53.1; Sil. It. 4.94; Ps.-Callisth. *Alex.* 2.13; Ezek 38:16; 3 Macc 5:48; with regard to the Assyrian army, see Gordon, *Civilizations*, 260.

617. Hom. *Il.* 16.374–75.

618. Virg. *Aen.* 12.407–8, 463.

619. E.g., Aristoph. *Wasps* 1084; Val. Flacc. 2.522; Val. Max. 3.7.ext. 8 (where a Spartan thus quips he will fight in the shade); Sil. It. 2.37; 9.11–12, 311–12; Ps.-Callisth. *Alex.* 2.16.

620. Tac. *Hist.* 3.56. Cf. the disaster involved when clouds cover the sun too long in the earlier "*Prophecy of Nefer-Rohu*" (*ANET* 445).

621. Ps.-Callisth. *Alex.* 1.41 (Dowden, 684).

622. In Joel 1–2, locusts appear to be depicted as an invading army; in Joel 3, they may foreshadow a genuine war.

623. Livy 42.2.5.

624. Darkness and clouds also characterize the day of YHWH in Ezek 30:3; Zeph 1:14–15.

625. Diog. Laert. *Lives* 7.1.145–46; 10.96; Pliny E. *N.H.* 2.6.47; Dio Cass. *R.H.* 60.26.1–5; Livy 44.37.6–7.

626. E.g., Heracl. *Hom. Prob.* 57.6; Philost. *Hrk.* 33.6; cf. Hübner, "Eclipses," 791–92; the alleged prediction of Thales in Hdt. 1.74. Most people, however, did view unexpected darkness as the activity of deities (Plut. *Tim.* 28.2), and leaders who knew the natural cause of lunar eclipses might accommodate superstition (as the "opiate of the people," so to speak) to manipulate them (see Quint. Curt. 4.10.5–7).

627. E.g., Polyb. 9.19.1; Val. Max. 8.11.ext. 1; Sen. Y. *Nat. Q.* 7.1.2 (also Plut. *Superst.* 8, *Mor.* 169B in van der Horst, "Parallels to Acts," 56); some used unexpected darkness for advantage (Polyb. 7.16.3). Some attributed sickness (Manetho frg. 84) or various astrological effects (Ptolemy *Tetrab.* 2.9.89–90).

628. Pliny E. *N.H.* 2.6.43; 2.7.47 (the moon or earth obstructing the sun); 2.9.53–55 (earlier views); 2.10.56–57 (their cyclic nature).

629. Pliny E. *N.H.* 2.30.98; 2.31–32.99 (in a larger context of portents, 2.33.100–2.37.101). He also believed that solar eclipses could generate epidemics (36.69.202).

630. This was more terrifying than a normal eclipse, which did not obscure sunlight totally (Pliny *Ep.* 6.20.18). Most Gentiles regarded sun and moon as deities (Rives, *Religion*, 16; cf. Plut. frg. 213); for the sun, see for Persia, e.g., Hdt. 1.131; Quint. Curt. 4.13.12; Olmstead, *Persian Empire*, 477 (cf. Ps.-Callisth. *Alex.* 1.36; Parthians in Hdn. 4.15.1); for Phoenicians, Ptolemy *Tetrab.* 2.3.66; for Syrians, Tac. *Hist.* 3.24.5; for Rome, Tac. *Ann.* 15.74; Plut. *Pomp.* 14.3 (cf. Cic. *Resp.* 6.17.17; Pliny E. *N.H.* 2.4.12–13; among Greeks,

Eclipses were generally thought to represent frightening omens, both in Jewish[631] and other Greek and Roman sources.[632] For some rabbis, the sun turning red signified impending war; its blackness signaled famine and pestilence (*t. Sukkah* 2:6). An eclipse could predict trouble for the emperor (Philost. *Vit. Apoll.* 4.43) or a coming revolution (8.23). In a case of war, of course, combatants had to determine for which side the eclipse portended disaster.[633] An imminent assassination was symbolized by the moon's being stained with blood (Suet. *Dom.* 16.1). Dreams (cf. Acts 2:17) of such phenomena portend harm except for those attempting to escape something (Artem. *Oneir.* 2.36).[634] But for Jewish people, the darkened sun and moon could signal the terrifying eschatological judgment (*Sib. Or.* 5.346–49).

iii. The Day of the Lord (2:20)

The "day of the Lord" appears often in the prophets, including Isaiah (Isa 13:6, 9; 58:13), Ezekiel (Ezek 13:5; 30:2–3), the briefer prophets (Amos 5:18, 20; Obad 15; Zeph 1:7, 14; Mal 4:5), and most notably in Joel (Joel 1:15; 2:1, 11, 31; 3:14).[635] Postbiblical early Jewish references seem rarer.[636] References to "that day" in which God will judge (e.g., Isa 2:11, 17, 20) would increase the list.[637]

Early Christians also spoke of "the day of the Lord" (1 Thess 5:2; 2 Thess 2:2; 2 Pet 3:10; cf. *Barn.* 15.4); the "day of God" (2 Pet 3:12; Rev 16:14); "the day of the Lord Jesus" (1 Cor 5:5; 2 Cor 1:14); "the day of the Lord Jesus Christ" (1 Cor 1:8); "the day of Christ Jesus" (Phil 1:6); or "the day of Christ" (Phil 1:10; 2:16). The christological applications (especially "the day of the Lord Jesus") are most significant here, in view of the identification of the "Lord" of this context (Acts 2:21) with Jesus in 2:38. Luke himself reports Jesus's predicting "the days of the Son of Man" (Luke

Soph. *Oed. tyr.* 660–61; Dio Chrys. *Or.* 3.57, 73; Dion. Hal. *Epid.* 1.256; *Orph. H.* intro lines 3–4; Philost. *Vit. Apoll.* 2.38; 7.10, 31 (cf. Jos. *Ag. Ap.* 2.265); allegedly Paeonians in Max. Tyre 2.8; allegedly India in Philost. *Vit. Apoll.* 2.24, 32, 43; 3.15; earlier, the *Hymn to the Aton* (*ANET* 369–71); *Hymn to the Sun-God* (*ANET* 387–89); 2 Kgs 23:11; Ezek 8:16 (cf. "Mystery of Horses"; Gordon, *Near East*, 249; *Jos. Asen.* 6:2/5). The sun could also be identified with Apollo (Heracl. *Hom. Prob.* 6.6; 8.4–5; Max. Tyre 4.8; Men. Rhet. 2.17, 438.12–13; 442.30; 445.31–446.9), but Helios was considered divine himself, as in Lucian *Dial. G.* 278–80 (24/25, Zeus and Helios 1–2). For Jewish opposition, see, e.g., *t. Suk.* 6:6; *Sipre Deut.* 318.2.1–2; *Pesiq. Rab Kah.* 5:1; *y. Suk.* 5:5, §3; they personified the sun, but more like an angel (cf. *1 En.* 41:5–6; 72:2–37; 75:4; *3 En.* 17:4). On moon deities, see Becker, "Moon deities"; Röllig, "Moon deities"; and Lieven, "Moon deities"; Druids in Pliny E. *N.H.* 16.95.250; supposedly Ethiopians in Heliod. *Eth.* 10.4; in the Mediterranean world, in myth, e.g., Ovid *Fasti* 4.374; Statius *Ach.* 1.619–21; Lucian *Dial. G.* 231 (19/11, Aphrodite and Selene 1); cf. Godwin, *Mystery Religions*, 69; perhaps Isis in Plut. *Isis* 52, *Mor.* 372D. For witchcraft and the moon, see, e.g., Ovid *Her.* 6.85; Philost. *Vit. Apoll.* 8.7; Heliod. *Eth.* 6.14; for the moon more like an angel, see, e.g., *2 En.* 16; *3 En.* 17:5.

631. E.g., *t. Sukkah* 2:5–6; *Gen. Rab.* 28:1; *Tg. Ps.-J.* on Deut 28:15. Eclipses predicted evil for the world, but especially for Israel (*b. Sukkah* 29a), but when occupied with Torah, Israel did not need to fear them (*t. Sukkah* 2:6). The sun's being darkened (by whatever means) expressed judgment in the OT prophets (Isa 13:10; Ezek 32:7; Amos 5:18, 20; 8:9; cf. Mic 3:6; Zeph 1:15), including in Joel (Joel 2:2, 10, 31; 3:15).

632. E.g., Aristoph. *Peace* 414; Xen. *Hell.* 1.6.1; Thucyd. 2.28.1; Polyb. 29.16.1–3; Diod. Sic. 20.5.5; Livy 25.7.8; Plut. *Caes.* 69.3–4; *Aem. Paul.* 17.5; Arrian *Alex.* 3.7.6; 3.15.7; Philost. *Hrk.* 33.5; Hermog. *Inv.* 1.1.98; see discussion in Grafton, "Eclipses"; Hübner, "Eclipses," 790. In Diog. Laert. 4.64, a lunar eclipse signified nature's sympathy for the decease of a great man.

633. Plut. *Alex.* 31.4; Arrian *Alex.* 3.7.6; Quint. Curt. 4.10.2–6.

634. Ovid depicts witches who could cover the sky with clouds (*Am.* 1.8.9–10), turn the moon and stars blood-red (1.8.11–12), draw down the moon (*Her.* 6.85), and darken the sun (6.86).

635. In the short run, such days meant days of God's reckoning and judgment (Everson, "Days of Yahweh," 337), but in the distant future, the judgments blended together as a single event (see Ladd, *Kingdom*, 36).

636. With also Ladd, *Theology*, 555. Cf. "the day of the Lord's judgment" in *Pss. Sol.* 15:12; *Gr. Ezra* 3:3 for the "great day" of God's revelation; a time of judgment in *b. Roš Haš.* 16b; *Soṭah* 3b; *'Abod. Zar.* 18a.

637. E.g., Isa 2:12; Jer 46:10; Ezek 7:19; Lam 1:12; 2:1; cf. Ezek 30:9; Zech 14:1.

17:22, 26), probably equivalent to the less ambiguous Jewish phrase "the days of the Messiah" (see comment on Acts 3:24).

IV. SALVATION (2:21)

"Salvation" for Luke (Acts 2:21, 40, 47; 4:12) includes both the eschatological kingdom for Israel (e.g., Luke 1:69, 71; 2:11; Acts 13:23, 26) and individual spiritual deliverance (e.g., Luke 8:12; 9:24; 13:23; Acts 11:14; 15:11; 16:30–31), presumably including participation in that kingdom (cf. Luke 19:9–10; Acts 5:31; 13:47; 15:1; on Luke's use of soteriological language, see more fully comment on Acts 27:20).[638] The horn of salvation in David's house (Luke 1:69)[639] includes salvation from enemies (1:71, 74); John, called to announce this salvation (1:76–77), proclaimed this message of salvation (3:6) and hence warned of either eschatological fiery destruction or the Spirit (3:16). For Luke, the former fate remains future (cf. Acts 2:35), but the latter is realized proleptically through the gift of the Spirit (1:6–8). This "salvation" is based on the forgiveness of sins (Luke 1:77; 3:3), which is also true of Israel's ultimate salvation (Acts 3:19). Thus salvation is available in the present (2:40, 47; 4:9, 12; 5:31; 7:25; 13:23; 15:11; 28:28) though consummated in the future;[640] individuals can participate in it in the present era, even while awaiting the corporate experience when Israel turns to the Messiah and God confirms his kingdom of peace and justice on earth.

In Joel's quotation, "all" who call on the Lord will be saved (Acts 2:21). Although one would not expect such a frequent term as πᾶς in 2:21 to carry heavy semantic weight (161 Times in Acts alone), it is noteworthy that the term is central to Paul's midrash on the same text (see Rom 10:11–13). It fits Luke's implications in "all [πᾶσαν] flesh" (Acts 2:17, part of the same quotation), in "all [πᾶσιν] who are far away" (2:39), and perhaps "every [παντός] nation under heaven" (2:5). Whether or not Peter recognizes it at this point (cf. 10:28), his own Spirit-inspired preaching already foreshadows for Luke (in the context of the whole story of Acts) the ultimate inclusion of the Gentiles (2:21, 39; perhaps also "first" in 3:26).[641]

h. Calling on the Lord's Name (2:21)

The expression "call on the Lord's name" was familiar in Jewish texts, where it concerned especially praying to him,[642] as in the later Targum on this verse (Tg. Joel 3:5), or praise (Jdt 16:1). Luke's term for "call upon" (ἐπικαλέω) could also apply to a formal appeal to Caesar (as in Acts 25:11–12, 21; 26:32; 28:19), but it is the Lord who could grant true deliverance.

I. PETER'S POINT AND THE LORD'S "NAME"

Peter's sermon expounds at length on this final line from Joel, arguing that the Lord's name on which his hearers must call in this salvific era is Jesus (2:21, 34, 38).[643] Thus

638. For a chronological bibliography (especially 1953–76) on Luke's soteriology, see Bovon, *Theologian*, 239–41; for a review of views, see 242–66 (with conclusion and synthesis, 263–66); see also Stenschke, "Salvation"; Witherington, *Acts*, 821–43; Barnett, "Salvation," 1072–73; Luter, "Savior (*DLNTD*)," 1082.

639. Cf. the fifteenth benediction of the Amidah ("the 'blessing of David'"), which contains the phrase "who causes the horn of salvation to sprout" (Le Cornu, *Acts*, 726).

640. Cf. Ridderbos, "Speeches of Peter," 28; Bovon, *Theologian*, 263 (for whom it is more often present).

641. With, e.g., Bayer, "Preaching," 268; Meek, *Mission*, 108–9.

642. E.g., Gen 4:26; 12:8; 13:4; Pss 79:6 (78:6 LXX); 99:6 (98:6); *Let. Aris.* 226; *Gen. Rab.* 39:16. Cf. also *Test. Mos.* 1:18 (literal reading). "Calling on" (ἐπικαλέω and cognates) could be used for invoking divine heroes (e.g., Philost. *Hrk.* 31.7; 53.6, 11, 16) or divine kings (Jdt 3:8). A later Targum interprets Joel's "calling on the name of the Lord" as *prayer* in his name (*Tg. Joel* 3:5). For connection with Acts 10:34, see Marguerat, *Actes*, 89.

643. Lake and Cadbury, *Commentary*, 22; Knowling, "Acts," 81; van Unnik, "Anathema," 123; Kilgallen, *Commentary*, 18; cf. Juel, "Use of Psalm 16," 544–45 (on which of the two "Lords" of Ps 110:1 must they call?).

Peter concludes by exhorting them to call on the Lord's name by baptism in Jesus's name (2:38).[644] After this Peter completes his Joel quotation, picking up later in Joel's sentence after the point where he broke off to begin expounding the last line he had quoted (2:39; see also comment there).[645] Cultic invocation of Jesus's name appears elsewhere in Acts (22:16) and early Christianity (e.g., Rom 10:9, 13; cf. 1 Cor 1:2; 12:3; Phil 2:11); in this context, Jesus's name is necessary for salvation (Acts 4:12), and in the immediate context, he is "Lord" (2:36).[646]

Peter can link one κύριος with another (Acts 2:34; Ps 110:1) in part because the LXX does not distinguish them[647] but also perhaps because most Jews refused to pronounce the divine name. This tradition of not pronouncing God's name already existed in the NT era, as is clear, for example, from Josephus (*Ant.* 2.276)[648] and the Qumran scrolls;[649] uttering the Name could lead to permanent exclusion from the community, regardless of the reason (1QS VI, 27–VII, 1). An earlier sage warned against both "swearing by" (ὀμνύων) and naming (ὀνομάζων) God (Sir 23:9–10). A Semitic text from third-century C.E. Palmyra in Syria changes the divine name YHWH (יהוה) to Adonai (אדוני) in the Shema, according to its public pronunciation (*CIJ* 2:69–70, §821).[650] A Diaspora Jewish text, probably pre-Christian, compares the difficulty of truly hearing God's name to the impossibility of seeing him.[651]

Later rabbis insisted that the name should be spelled out fully for use in the sanctuary and Aaron's benediction;[652] in the provinces, however, a euphemism should be used.[653] The divine name was powerful,[654] and strictly pious hearers might rend their garments when hearing it blasphemed.[655] Later variations in the forms of the divine name may reflect ignorance of the original pronunciation.[656] As well as safeguarding the name's sanctity against false oaths, it also guarded against exploitation for magic

644. Recognized, e.g., by Turner, *Power*, 272.

645. Cf., e.g., Dunn, *Acts*, 27; Costa Grillo, "Discourso de Pedro"; Marshall, "Acts," 536, 543; Haenchen, *Acts*, 184n5; Dupont, *Salvation*, 22; Zehnle, *Pentecost Discourse*, 34; Pao, *Isaianic Exodus*, 231–32.

646. Cf. Hurtado, *Become God*, 161n29. On the implied invocation in Rom 10:9, see, e.g., Stuhlmacher, *Romans*, 154.

647. For the absence of the Tetragrammaton in the LXX, see, e.g., Dodd, *Bible and Greeks*, 3ff. Howard, "Tetragram," argues that some pre-Christian Greek manuscripts used the divine name in Aramaic or Paleo-Hebrew letters or transliterated it as IAΩ; for Greek transcriptions of the Tetragrammaton, see Deissmann, *Studies*, 321–36. The originals, however, simply translated the divine name as κύριος (Rösel, "Translation of Name"). IAΩ and "El" appear together as a single name in *Apoc. Ab.* 17:13.

648. Cf. the prohibition against verbatim recitation of the sacred Ten Commandments (Jos. *Ant.* 3.90). Cf. the ineffability of God in such philosophic thinkers as Philo and Justin (Shibata, "Ineffable").

649. Cf. 4Q462 1 7 (which uses four dots instead of the divine name; *DSSNT* 401); Qumran's use of Paleo-Hebrew letters for the divine name may reflect a similar fence (Siegel, "Employment," compares the rabbinic proscription of erasing the divine name; see also Green, "Rabbinic Production"). The Tetragrammaton appears, e.g., in 4Q185 (Vermes, *Scrolls*, 258).

650. See, e.g., Hurtado, *Lord Jesus Christ*, 108–18; more briefly, Keener, *John*, 297–98. For similar respect, cf. Paleo-Hebrew for the divine name in 4QIsa^c (Green, "Rabbinic Production").

651. *Sib. Or.* 3.17–19.

652. *M. Soṭah* 7:6; *Yom.* 3:8, 6:2; *Sipre Num.* 39.5.1; cf. Marmorstein, *Names*, 39; it is said that it was gradually used more quietly to prevent abuse (*y. Yoma* 3:7). *Let. Aris.* 98 speaks of the sacred name inscribed on Aaron's miter; in later texts, it was engraved on Israel's weapons at Sinai (*Song Rab.* 5:7, §1; 8:5, §1). Use in the sanctuary might be quite early (cf. Lemaire, "Scepter," suggesting its inscription on a Solomonic priestly scepter).

653. *Sipre Num.* 39.5.2; cf. Urbach, *Sages*, 1:127. Benedictions should not be written lest the name be burned in a fire (*b. Šabb.* 115b, bar.). On keeping the name secret, see also, e.g., *Eccl. Rab.* 3:11, §3; failure to revere the name's mystery invited judgment (*Pesiq. Rab.* 22:7).

654. On the divine name's power, see Urbach, *Sages*, 1:124–34; Moore, *Judaism*, 1:378, 426. His name created and destroyed worlds (*Pesiq. Rab.* 21:7). Much earlier, see its power in Artapanus in Euseb. *P.E.* 9.27.24–26.

655. So, e.g., *b. Sanh.* 60a, bar. (most opinions). It constituted blasphemy only if the divine name was used (*m. Sanh.* 7:5; cf. Lev 24:11, 16).

656. E.g., *Lad. Jac.* 2:18 (perhaps third century, though the editor dates it earlier). Some apparent permutations, however, simply reflect Egyptian ritual use of the "seven vowels" (Demet. *Style* 2.71).

(the permutations of YHWH's name in magical texts indicate the extent to which magicians desired to discover the name; see fuller discussion on Acts 19:13).

God's name could be associated with his presence.[657] The title "the name" in fact became a surrogate for repeating the divine name;[658] early Christians transferred this use of the "name" from the Father to Jesus,[659] and some scholars think that the frequent early Jewish Christian "name of Jesus" formula reflects this usage.[660] If we ask how it is possible for Luke to portray Peter as already exhibiting such a christological understanding so early in the second volume, we must remember how Luke has prepared for Peter's understanding within his narrative. Starting from John's proclamation of the coming baptizer in the Spirit (Luke 3:16// Matt 3:11), Luke has provided clues about Jesus's role.[661] Luke probably also expects his audience to infer Peter's further learning during the forty days of resurrection appearances in Acts 1:3.

II. THE TITLE "LORD"

"Lord" was a frequent title for pagan deities, but for the earliest Jewish followers of Jesus, it was especially a divine title in the LXX.[662] (See further comment in the introduction, ch. 15.) For Luke, God the Father is "Lord" (Acts 2:20, 39; 3:19–20, 22; 4:25–26, 29), but Christ also receives this title by exaltation (1:21; 2:36; 4:33; 5:14; 9:1; Rom 10:9–13; 2 Cor 4:5; Phil 2:9–11); Jesus receives faith (Acts 3:16) and prayer (7:59) and is the world's judge (10:42; 17:31).[663] Contrary to what some scholars would expect, most of the uses of "Lord" for Jesus in Acts appear in the first half of the book and hence are attributed to the Jerusalem church[664] (despite Luke's frequent portrayal there of that earliest community's probably more distinctive features, such as "servant"). For the title, the earliest Christians probably depended on Jesus's use of Ps 110:1 (Luke 20:42);[665] it is not clear that the passage was in widespread messianic use earlier,[666] but it is fairly clear, given the potential non-Davidic reading of Jesus's ancestry in the passage, that the later church did not invent the account for Jesus.[667]

Some scholars have suggested that the Hellenistic church deified Jesus, thereby allowing LXX statements about the "Lord" to be applied to him.[668] But apart from

657. Longenecker, *Christology*, 43ff. (citing Deut 12:11, 21; 14:23–24; 16:2, 11; 26:2; Neh 1:9; Ps 74:7; Isa 18:7; Jer 3:17; 7:10–14, 30). Longenecker (42) also cites evidence for pre-Christian use of the "name" as a "quasi-hypostatic" medium of revelation.

658. See, e.g., Jeremias, *Theology*, 10 (comparing [n. 1] even Samaritan usage to the modern period); rabbinic use of *ha-Shem* in Bietenhard, "ὄνομα," 268–69; Bonsirven, *Judaism*, 7 (citing, e.g., *m. Yoma* 3:8). Cf. perhaps in Semyaza's name in *1 En.* 6:3. Philo used it also as a name of the Logos (*Conf.* 146; also noted by Longenecker, *Christology*, 43).

659. See discussion in Longenecker, *Christology*, 43–45.

660. Longenecker, "Christological Motifs," 533–36.

661. See discussion of this saying in, e.g., Keener, *Historical Jesus*, 169.

662. Nock, *Christianity*, 32–33; Hunter, *Gospel according to Paul*, 65; Hengel, *Acts and History*, 105. Pace, e.g., Conzelmann, *Theology*, 83, who takes too little account of the *Marana tha* title (though acknowledging it, 82); see, e.g., Howard, *Criticism*, 162; Ladd, *Criticism*, 210.

663. Ladd, *Young Church*, 50–51; idem, *Theology*, 339. The later rabbinic distinction between "Lord" as God of mercy and "God" as judge (e.g., *Sipre Deut.* 26.5.1; Moore, *Judaism*, 1:387; the distinction might be earlier; cf. Rösel, "Theologie") reflects the same method of exegesis that allowed distinctions at least of attributes.

664. Ladd, *Theology*, 338.

665. Ibid., 341.

666. Longenecker, *Exegesis*, 73, argues that some were interpreting it messianically; but it was not a pervasive messianic text (see comment on Acts 2:34).

667. Gundry, *Use*, 200; Witherington, *Christology of Jesus*, 190–91; Keener, *Matthew*, 532; pace Weeden, *Mark*, 133.

668. Bultmann, *Theology*, 1:124.

hypotheses about christological evolution, the direction of influence was almost certainly the opposite; Gentile Christians would embrace Judaism's monotheism before or simultaneous with, not after, Judaism's Scriptures. More concretely, the most Jewish NT sources (e.g., John and Revelation) are the most emphatic about Christ's deity in the NT corpus; the idea of their borrowing from Greek Christianity is unlikely.[669]

Though recognizing the connection in Peter's exegesis in the context, Dunn thinks Luke presents Jesus only as "a plenipotentiary representative of God."[670] But Luke's interpretation of Scripture elsewhere (see Luke 3:4; cf. 3:16–17) suggests that Luke himself affirms the divine Christology[671] held by much of the early church, certainly by his generation (see Rom 9:5; Titus 2:13).[672] Certainly, from an early period,[673] Aramaic-speaking Christians invoked Jesus as "Lord" (1 Cor 16:22).[674] Divine language from the OT appears in the parousia imagery of 1 Thessalonians, probably the earliest extant Christian document.[675] Moreover, the application of Septuagintal language for God to Jesus must have happened within two decades of the resurrection at the latest (Rom 10:9–13; 1 Cor 8:6; Phil 2:10).[676] Contrary to frequent traditional scholarly opinion, Jesus's deity is affirmed in a variety of first-century Christian sources.[677] Although variations may have existed within early Jewish monotheism, the consistent theme was the worship of only one God; by worshiping Jesus, early Christians innovated.[678] (Second-century Christians used explicitly divine language more often,[679] and pagans also recognized that this was the Christians' view.)[680]

669. See at length Keener, *John*, 298–310; briefly idem, *Matthew*, 66–68; idem, *Revelation*, 42. Paul affirmed Jesus's deity while believing that he remained within the Jewish monotheism of his day (see Wright, *Founder*, 63–72).

670. Dunn, *Acts*, 29. Cf. biblical divine language applied to Michael and Melchizedek in the Qumran scrolls (Hengel, *Son*, 80, citing also Philo *Dreams* 1.157 for the archangel Logos as κύριος); cf. also the Messiah as a representative of God in 4Q174 (on the interpretation of Schreiber, "König"; cf. Le Cornu, *Acts*, 130, on the Messiah and others bearing God's name in *b. B. Bat.* 75b).

671. On "Jesus-devotion" in Luke-Acts, see Hurtado, *Become God*, 160–62; on Luke's predicating analogous claims about Jesus and God, see O'Toole, *Christology*, passim; for Luke's divine use of "Lord" and "Savior" titles for Jesus already in his first volume's infancy narrative, see Rowe, "Trinity"; cf. also comment on Jesus's "theophany" at Acts 9:3; the Isaiah background for Acts 1:8. Hays, "Category or Methodology," also suggests it from Isa 35:4, a plausible (though uncertain) intertextual echo associated with Isa 35:5 in Luke 7:22. Cf. also Jesus's unity with the Father (Luke 10:22) and equivalent statements about both the Father and the Son (noted in Langner, *Hechos*, 48).

672. See further Mark 1:3–4, 7–8; later, Revelation and John; Keener, *John*, 298–310; Harris, *Jesus as God*, passim. Gathercole, *Son*, argues that the Synoptic writers all accept the Son's preexistence.

673. Probably already Jesus's first Galilean followers; the more hellenized, bilingual urban churches of Jerusalem and Antioch (cf. Acts 6:1, 9; 11:19–20) may have spoken more Greek.

674. E.g., Hunter, *Message*, 41; Dunn, *Theology of Paul*, 247–48; Hengel, *Acts*, 105; Longenecker, *Christology*, 121–24; Fee, *Corinthians*, 839; Ladd, *Criticism*, 210. Some regard the original meaning of the term as ambiguous (Simon, *Stephen and Hellenists*, 66; cf. Vermes, *Jesus the Jew*, 114–20), but a use in early Christian liturgy (eschatological, eucharistic, or both, e.g., Robinson, *Studies*, 154–57; idem, *Coming*, 26–27; Conzelmann, *Corinthians*, 300–301; Cullmann, *Christology*, 201–2; Hunter, *Gospel according to Paul*, 65; cf. *Did.* 10) would constitute a divine invocation (Fee, *1 Corinthians*, 838–39; Ladd, *Theology*, 341, 416–17; for divine usage elsewhere, cf. Marmorstein, *Names*, 62–63; Betz, *Jesus*, 108; Bruce, *Apostle*, 117).

675. Cf. Glasson, *Advent*, 161–83; Robinson, *Coming*, 140; Bruce, *Thessalonians*, 73; *1 En.* 91:7.

676. See arguments in, e.g., Hengel, *Son*, 77; Keener, *John*, 302–3; Pitto, "Señor."

677. See Keener, *John*, 302–7; esp. Hurtado, *Lord Jesus Christ*, passim; cf. also Eddy and Boyd, *Legend*, 91–132, for a telling response to those who attribute such ideas purely to Hellenistic influence. Even Q has a "high" Christology, venerating Jesus (Hurtado, *Lord Jesus Christ*, 217–57).

678. See Hurtado, "Monotheism."

679. E.g., Ign. *Eph.* 7; *Rom.* 3; Justin *2 Apol.* 13; Iren. *Her.* 3.19; cf. Justin *1 Apol.* 67; from ca. 230 C.E., Tzaferis, "Inscribed." Cf. also *1 En.* 48:5–6 (depending on the translation).

680. Lucian *Peregr.* 11; Pliny *Ep.* 10.96.7.

4. Narration about Jesus's Death and Resurrection (2:22–24)

a. Appealing to Jesus's Signs (2:22)

The repetition of an invitation to "hear" (though not using the same terms; Acts 2:14, 22)[681] frames the introductory citation of biblical authority, which functions as the basis for the exhortation proper starting here. An invitation to continue listening was not unusual; Cicero, for example, points out that his audience has listened to him carefully in earlier speeches, and he encourages them to keep listening in this manner (*Verr.* 2.3.5.10).[682] Perhaps Peter also uses this invitation to underline the importance of what he is about to say,[683] or is preparing the audience for the shocking statement to follow.[684]

That Peter opens his exposition with mention of Jesus sets the tone for what will follow.[685] If this verse provides such a transition (expounding Acts 2:19), this would explain its absence from the chiastic structure that some scholars have suggested for 2:23–36 (see comment above, in the section on *structure* beneath "Peter's Call to Repentance [2:14–40]"). Some doubt that Luke's generation would usually describe Jesus as "a man attested by God," suggesting that this is a primitive trait. But while it may not have been the common language of Nicene Christianity two and a half centuries later, Luke does not appear to have been involved in serious christological controversy, and he felt free to use such language alongside his divine Christology probably implied in 2:38 (see 10:38).[686] "Man" (ἄνδρα) may link Jesus with Peter's hearers in the same verse (ἄνδρες). Nazareth was an insignificant village (John 1:45)[687] but, for this reason, provides a suitable geographic epithet distinguishing this Jesus from his many contemporaries bearing the same name.[688]

If Acts 2:22 is transitional, we should note that the signs it mentions are central to the Gospel's narrative before the passion (taken up in 2:23) and provide a sort of "proof" for Peter's argument. That signs and wonders provide a primary attestation to Jesus is a major emphasis in Luke-Acts (cf. the summaries in Luke 7:22; Acts 10:38; suggested in Luke 4:18).[689] This is also true for the apostles (Acts 2:43). The primary theological background for early Christian usage is the story of Moses, who prefigures the apostolic ministry (2 Cor 3:7–18). Because Luke is here expounding

---

681. Ἀκούω appears with the impv. in Acts 2:22; 7:2; 13:16; 15:13; 22:1; and προσέχω in 5:35; 20:28; cf. 1 Tim 4:13. On the transitional function of this repetition from Acts 2:14, see also Marguerat, *Actes*, 90.

682. Also see Philost. *Hrk.* 8.1; 9.1; 19.3; 20.2; 23.2; 25.18; 40.1; 53.4.

683. A technique often used in amplification, inviting hearers' attention (Men. Rhet. 2.1–2, 372.19–20).

684. Cf. *prodiorthōsis* in Rowe, "Style," 142 (citing Demosth. *Cor.* 199; Livy 39.37.17); and *proparaskeuē*, 146 (citing Hyperides *Euxenippum* 23; Cic. *Clu.* 4.11). In Paul, cf. Porter, "Paul and Letters," 581–82 (citing 2 Cor 11:1, 16, 21, 23; Phil 1:12).

685. When transitioning to a new section of a speech, orators often tried to signal their new topic explicitly (Men. Rhet. 2.1–2, 372.14–18).

686. The language need not be understood in an adoptionist manner (Ridderbos, *Paul and Jesus*, 38–39, comparing Rom 1:3–4); Bede *Comm. Acts* 2.22–23 suggests that Peter starts at a more basic level than "Son of God." For a perhaps more convincing feature of primitive Christology, see Acts 2:36.

687. With an estimated population of about five hundred (Strange, "Nazareth," 113; Stanton, *New People*, 112; Horsley, *Galilee*, 193), though more may well have lived in the surrounding countryside. Earlier estimates ranged from about sixteen hundred to two thousand (Meyers and Strange, *Archaeology*, 27, 56; cf. Finkelstein, *Pharisees*, 1:41; Stauffer, *Jesus and Story*, 54). By contrast, an estimate of one hundred (Malina and Rohrbaugh, *Gospels*, 37) is too low; Nathanael may dismiss Nazareth, but at least he has heard of it (John 1:46). Archaeological evidence for an early Christian presence there is ambiguous (Skarsaune, *Shadow*, 191–92).

688. Designating people according to hometowns was conventional (e.g., Pliny *Ep.* 3.21.5; Mark 15:43; John 11:1) and appears in Luke-Acts (Luke 8:2; 24:10). The tradition that Jesus hailed from there is multiply, independently attested (Theissen and Merz, *Guide*, 164–65), and no one would invent an origin there.

689. Cf., e.g., Achtemeier, "Perspective on Miracles."

the Joel quotation, he views these signs as proofs that the eschatological, messianic era has arrived in part (Acts 2:19; see more fully comment there).

The pairing of signs and wonders (2:19, 22, 43; 4:30; 5:12; 6:8; 14:3; 15:12) appears elsewhere in early Christian texts (Rom 15:19; 2 Cor 12:12; Heb 2:4) but in all of them would probably still evoke for informed readers the OT story of Moses. The pairing is common in the OT,[690] yet the textual evidence is overwhelming that this pairing was rooted especially in the exodus story and Moses's prophetic leadership role.[691] Jesus's and the apostles' works indicated that a new era of salvation had dawned.

One would not expect Diaspora Jewish visitors or even Jerusalemites to be as familiar with Jesus's signs as Galileans were, but Luke elsewhere assumes that word spread widely about Jesus's passion (Luke 24:18; Acts 26:23, 26) and his miracles (Luke 9:6–9; 23:8). For more on Luke's use of signs, see our introduction, chapter 9.[692] Peter appeals to the audience's own knowledge of the veracity of his statement, a common rhetorical technique (cf. Acts 10:37; 20:18, 34; 26:26).[693]

b. Jesus's Death and God's Plan (2:23)

In contrast to many speeches in Acts (some of which are "interrupted" after the narratio), this speech follows the advice of some rhetoricians to keep the narration (here 2:22–24) as concise as possible while sneaking "conviction unnoticed past the listener's senses" (Dion. Hal. *Lysias* 18 [LCL]).

i. Divine Purpose and Luke's Plot

This passage fits the fulfillment-of-prophecy theme and summarizes the Gospel's plot as a part of God's larger plan in salvation history.[694] Oracles[695] and the designs of a deity[696] or fortune[697] often functioned as a plot-moving device. Novelists could use oracles as literary devices to lay out, in nugget form (and somewhat ambiguously), the plot of events that would follow,[698] or use oracles as events to move the plot forward by directing characters in the story.[699]

Such devices, however, were hardly limited to novels. Prophecy and fulfillment constitute a plot-moving device in Hellenistic historiography,[700] including in

---

690. Later signs (Esth 10:9 LXX; cf. Dan 4:37 LXX; Wis 8:8); prophetic tokens (Isa 8:18; 20:3); those of false prophets (Deut 13:1–2; cf. Mark 13:22; 2 Thess 2:9); also of God's judgments (Deut 28:46). Continuing signs followed the model of those in the exodus (Jer 32:20 [39:20 LXX]). The partial parallel (characterizing magicians) in Philost. *Vit. Apoll.* 8.7 might depend on the by-then-widespread currency of Christian usage.

691. Acts 7:36; LXX Exod 7:3, 9; 11:10; Deut 4:34; 6:22; 7:19; 11:3; 26:8; 29:3; 34:11; Pss 77:43 [ET 78:43]; 104:27 [105:27]; 134:9 [135:9]; Jer 39:20–21 [32:20–21]; Wis 10:16; Bar 2:11.

692. For more on signs in general in ancient literature, see Keener, *John*, 253–75.

693. E.g., Aeschines *Embassy* 44, 56; Matt 26:65; 1 Thess 2:1; cf. comment at Acts 20:18; 26:26. Recounting what the audience knows is believable though not always interesting (Gorg. *Hel.* 5).

694. For a 1948–78 bibliography concerning God's plan, salvation, history, and eschatology in Luke-Acts, see Bovon, *Theologian*, 1–8.

695. E.g., Apollod. *Epit.* 5.10.

696. E.g., Char. *Chaer.* 1.1.3.

697. E.g., Ach. Tat. 1.3.2; Char. *Chaer.* 1.13.4; 8.1.2.

698. Xen. Eph. *Anthia* 1.6–7; after noting this reference, I subsequently discovered that Chance, "Prognostications," not only highlights this very text but elaborates on it at length. In Israelite historiography, see 2 Sam 12:10–12 (cf. esp. 16:21–22).

699. Ps.-Callisth. *Alex.* passim, e.g., 1.30, 33; Apoll. K. *Tyre* 48; in Virgil's epic, see Bonz, *Past as Legacy*, 192.

700. Squires, *Plan*, 121–29; Walbank, "Fortune," 350–54 (noting that sometimes Tychē functions as a goddess, and sometimes as luck). Prediction (with its fulfillment) functioned as an authenticating device in Hellenistic historiography (Rothschild, *Rhetoric of History*, 142–84; although common in epics, it appears in historians, p. 97). Outside Greek writers, note, e.g., the foreshadowing function of omens for Caesar's death in Vell. Paterc. 2.57.2; Suet. *Jul.* 81; predictions to Sulla in Vell. Paterc. 2.24.3; Alexander's "fortune" advances

Josephus.[701] No one could escape Fate;[702] some who mocked or sought to circumvent oracles nevertheless suffered the predicted fate.[703] Various historians viewed as tragic the way Fate acted in human lives.[704] Acts is full of programmatic prophecies, though Acts 1:8 is the most obvious.[705] Luke uses the fulfillment of prophecy (including prophecies of Jesus and other reliable characters, not just Scripture) as part of the theme of God's plan, which the entire story presupposes.[706] This theme provides a "functional counterpart" to the Greek concept of Fate.[707]

God's will and purposes are a recurrent theme in Luke-Acts, especially in the speeches of Acts.[708] The emphasis on God's purposes is especially clear in Luke's use of δεῖ, often (though not exclusively) pointing to God's will,[709] whether emphasizing obedience to it (Luke 2:49; 4:43; 12:12; 13:33; 19:5; Acts 1:21; 5:29; 9:6, 16; 19:21; 23:11)[710] or God's fulfilling his own plan (Luke 21:9; Acts 27:24, 26), usually regarding the passion (Luke 9:22; 13:33; 17:25; 22:37; 24:7, 26, 44; Acts 17:3; cf. 1:16; 3:21).[711] Acts 2:23 does not use this frequent Lukan term for divine necessity, instead using three more explicit (though less frequent) terms. First, Luke uses ὁρίζω, which (with its cognate προορίζω) usually designates God's determination, especially concerning Jesus's passion (Luke 22:22; Acts 2:23; 4:28) or exalted status (Acts 10:42; 17:31).[712]

Second, he uses here βουλή ("counsel"), which can refer to God's salvation-historical plan (Luke 7:30; Acts 13:36; 20:27) and specifically to the passion (Acts 4:28, the verse most closely recalling 2:23).[713] The divine purpose included God's plan in the OT (13:36); God's purpose in the gospel contrasts starkly with the human plan to oppose it (cf. 5:38),[714] which coincided in the cross (Luke 23:51; Acts 2:23; 4:28).

---

the plot in Quint. Curt. passim (the degree of Fortune's role in his success was a favored topic of debate in antiquity; see Baynham, *Alexander*, 104–11, as cited in idem, "Reception," 290); the succession of prophetic revelations provides an interpretive framework for the narratives of Samuel through Kings, ultimately offering theodicy concerning the exile (cf. 2 Kgs 21:12–15).

701. Squires, *Plan*, 129–37.

702. Demosth. *Cor.* 289 (citing an epitaph); Quint. Curt. 4.6.17.

703. On inescapable fate (sometimes fulfilled in the attempt to avert it), see, e.g., Soph. *Oed. tyr.* passim; Apollod. *Bib.* 2.4.4; 3.5.7; 3.12.5; Diod. Sic. 15.74.3–4; Val. Max. 1.8.ext. 8–9; Lucian *Z. Cat.* 12; Babr. 136; Libanius *Narration* 41; 1 Kgs 22:30, 34–35; cf. Plut. frg. 21 (LCL, 15:98–99), from his lost *Is Foreknowledge of Future Events Useful?* Zeus's will could be fulfilled even through human folly (compare Hom. *Il.* 1.5 with 1.1–2).

704. In Thucydides, see Grene, *Political Theory*, 75–79; common elsewhere, e.g., Vell. Paterc. 2.53.3. For the danger of ignoring portents, see, e.g., Tac. *Hist.* 1.86; Suet. *Otho* 8.3.

705. See Johnson, *Acts*, 12 (citing Acts 3:22; 11:27; 13:46–47; 19:21; 20:25; 21:11; 23:11; 27:22; 28:28).

706. See Squires, *Plan*, 137–54. Promise-fulfillment is a major theme in Luke-Acts, though not necessarily *the* major one (Talbert, "Promise and Fulfillment").

707. On "Fate," see, e.g., Robertson and Dietrich, "Fate"; cf. Purcell, "Fortuna/Fors."

708. Soards, *Speeches*, 184–89; Jackson, "Churches," 103–9; in surrounding chapters, cf. also Taylor, *Atonement*, 18. Preaching both conveys and fulfills God's plan (see Ferreira, "Plan").

709. Cosgrove, "Divine ΔΕΙ"; Soards, *Speeches*, 187–88; Liefeld, *Acts*, 93–94; Bass, "Necessity," 51–53. Noting the use of necessity in rhetorical argumentation (53–58), Bass helpfully explores its function in Luke-Acts (59–68).

710. Or obligation to it (Luke 13:16; 18:1; Acts 4:12; 16:30; 20:35), often as stated in Torah (Luke 11:42; 22:7; cf. Acts 15:5; 26:9); cf. other kinds of obligation (Luke 15:32; Acts 19:36; 24:19; 25:10, 24; 27:21).

711. For the necessary "passion" of Paul and his converts, cf. Acts 9:16; 14:22; perhaps 19:21; 23:11; 27:24. For connections between Petrine preaching in Acts and Luke 24, see esp. Dupont, "Discours de Pierre et chapitre XXIV."

712. Also his plan in human history (Acts 17:26); Luke does not, however, reserve the term exclusively for divine decisions (11:29).

713. Luke also uses the term for human actions (Luke 23:51; Acts 5:38; 27:12, 42; the similar compounding in Luke 23:51 and Acts 5:38 is Lukan style). Cf. the use of βουλή for God's plan in history elsewhere in Greek-speaking Judaism (e.g., *Sib. Or.* 1.216, 282; 3.571–74, esp. 571, 574).

714. Cf. perhaps also Acts 27:12, 42, though these uses might not be theologically significant for Luke.

Finally, he uses πρόγνωσις, which appears nowhere else in Luke-Acts but indicates divine foreknowledge (also in 1 Pet 1:1–2; Jdt 9:6).[715]

Most sections of the Gospel reveal explicitly divine activity (the work of the Spirit; the fulfillment of Scripture; divine agents such as angels; miracles) moving the story forward.[716] Here God's sovereignty stands even behind the very political powers that brought about Jesus's death. In contrast to some Palestinian Jews before the war of 66–70, Luke does not advocate violent resistance against the powers in the face of their selective repression, but recognizes that God is free to use them to further his good purposes. God is sovereign and knows in advance what believers will face; thus, when he wills, he can provide warnings of impending suffering (Acts 20:23; 21:4, 11), assurance of safety (cf. 18:10; 23:11; 27:34; Luke 21:16–19), or even miraculous deliverance (Acts 12:7–11; cf. 5:19; 16:26). God can provide promises that his agents will bear witness, without guaranteeing for them the response (Acts 23:11; 27:24). Although God can answer prayer with deliverance from a ruler (12:5–11; cf. 2 Thess 3:2), we read of prayer for boldness in the face of opposition rather than a prayer against these rulers (Acts 4:26–30; cf. Eph 6:19–20; Col 4:3–4; 2 Thess 3:1–2). Yet God clearly works in the narrative to guard his people (Acts 21:31–32; 25:3–5) as well as to work through their suffering. God can also blind the resistant (28:26–27) and open others' hearts (16:14) and doors of ministry (14:27; cf. 11:21). Whether in the forefront or in the background of Luke's narrative, Israel's God is accomplishing his purposes and promises.

Excursus: Providence, Fate, and Predestination

Although Luke's idea of providence depends on the monotheistic Jewish under-standing of God, it also resembles Hellenistic historians' articulation of providence. Moreover, even Jewish and Christian debates about predestination and free will were very much shaped (at the very least, in the questions they addressed) by ideas debated in the Greco-Roman milieu. It is therefore helpful to survey some Greco-Roman conceptions of Fate and related ideas before examining predestination.

1. Fate and Fortune

Providence and fate play a major role in Hellenistic historiography,[717] including in monotheistic historians such as Josephus[718] and Luke.[719] Indeed, no less "naturalistic" a historian than Polybius defines the historian's task as simply showing how Tychē (Τύχη), Chance or Fortune, ordered all the matters of the world toward her purpose (Polyb. 1.4.1–2).[720] He also opined that it was the task of historians to report Fortune's activity so that later generations would know not to fear its caprices (2.35.5).

715. Luke uses the cognate verb for previous knowledge on a human level in Acts 26:5 (as in 2 Pet 3:17; Jdt 11:19), but others apply it to God (Rom 8:29; 11:2; 1 Pet 1:20; to wisdom in Wis 8:8).

716. Squires, "Plan."

717. Squires, *Plan*, 15–17, 38–46 (esp. Dionysius of Halicarnassus); Hengel, *Acts*, 50–51; Peterson, "Fulfillment and Purpose"; Squires, "Plan," 38; Aune, *Environment*, 134; Balch, "Genre," 10–11; Meister, "Herodotus," 269. Cf., e.g., Fortune in Polyb. 1.4, 58, 62; Diod. Sic. 1.1.3; 31.4.1; Dion. Hal. *Ant. rom.* 6.21.1.

718. Squires, *Plan*, 18–20, 46–52; Chapman, "Josephus," 321. On fate in Josephus's depiction of Ahab's death in 1 Kgs 22 (which resembles Greek stories of failed attempts to avert fate), see Begg, "Death of Ahab."

719. See Squires, *Plan*, 20–36, 52–77.

720. This included observing causal connections (Polyb. 1.4.3).

Many attributed Rome's rise to Fortune.[721] Most Hellenistic historians,[722] including Josephus[723] and (perhaps) Luke,[724] temper determinism or fate with free will. Luke's emphasis on necessity is "not entirely deterministic, but rather serves to reinforce the personal will of God in much the same way as we find in Josephus."[725]

Such approaches to fate were widespread. Greek and Roman historians followed an emphasis on Fate already present "in Greek epic and dramatic poetry."[726] In common Greek and Roman thought, even the gods could not contradict Fate, no matter how much they might wish to do so (Virg. *Aen.* 7.314–15).

a. Popular Views about Fate

Many scholars have argued that common people in the ancient world felt insecure,[727] were fearful about fate, and were pervaded with a cosmic pessimism;[728] Gilbert Murray titled this period "the age of the failure of nerve."[729] Yet this attitude, including its preoccupation with immutable fate, was surely more characteristic of late antiquity (with its new profusion of demons, increase in astrology, and so forth) than the early empire. Some recent scholars have pointed out that an emphasis on enslavement to fate has been overstated.[730] Such reservations rightly must be taken into account; nevertheless, the evidence more generally for individual and corporate concerns about fate is widespread already long before Luke's day.[731] Thus, for example, Fortune often became tutelary goddess of cities being founded in the Hellenistic era.[732]

In common understanding, Fate or Fortuna (Tychē) controlled everything;[733] nothing could resist her will,[734] and she did with persons as she wished.[735] Fortune controlled the station in life in which one was born;[736] it could act toward a person with apparent hostility[737] or help a person.[738] Fate killed Patroclus (Hom. *Il.* 16.849)

---

721. E.g., Plutarch (Swain, "Plutarch"; see esp. Plut. *Fort. Rom.*, *Mor.* 316C–326C, allowing also for many Romans' virtue; cf. similarly, *Fort. Alex.*, *Mor.* 326D–345B); for Fortune favoring Rome in a war, e.g., Diod. Sic. 31.4.1. Cf. Sallust *Cat.* 10.1 in Feldherr, "Translation," 385.

722. Squires, *Plan*, 154–60.

723. Ibid., 160–66.

724. See ibid., 166–85. Luke may be less interested in the philosophic problem of free will, since Jewish ideals of God's sovereignty did not necessarily contradict it (see the discussion of free will below).

725. Ibid., 185 (while also noting that his language ranks him closer to popular Stoic usage than does that of Dionysius or Diodorus). Cf. the exploration in Mainville, "Liberté" (emphasizing God's direction).

726. Aune, *Environment*, 134.

727. Probably more pervasive across more centuries was economic insecurity (Grant, "Economic Background," 114); also relevant to our period is social instability (Lee, "Unrest").

728. E.g., Case, *Origins*, 92; Whittaker, *Jews and Christians*, 210. Some argue that pessimism also characterized Palestine in this period (Davies, *Paul*, 13). Many argue for a rising popularity of personal religions from the East, as against the state cults (Carcopino, *Life*, 121–27).

729. Murray, *Stages*, 155. The evidence characterizes the third century more than the first, however.

730. Denzey, "Enslavement" (against Cumont, E. R. Dodds).

731. See, e.g., Hor. *Odes* 2.17.16; 3.24.6 (Necessity); *Carm. saec.* 25. On Fate, see further, e.g., Frede, "Fate" (including on philosophic theories, 367–68).

732. Nilsson, *Piety*, 94.

733. Demosth. *Epitaph.* 21 ("lord over all," in a funeral oration); Thales in Diog. Laert. 1.35 (Necessity); Heraclitus in Diog. Laert. 9.1.7 (Destiny); Democritus in Diog. Laert. 9.7.45 (Necessity); Plut. *Aem. Paul.*, e.g., 36.1; Alciph. *Farm.* 4 (Eupetalus to Elation), 1.25; Lucian *Z. Cat.* 1.

734. Aeschylus *Suppl.* 1046–47; Char. *Chaer.* 2.8.4; Apul. *Metam.* 9.1.

735. E.g., Sen. Y. *Dial.* 6.16.5; Apul. *Metam.* 10.13.

736. Cic. *Inv.* 1.25.35 (though he believed that nature's demands were higher than Fortune's, *Off.* 1.33.120). Epicureans, by contrast, simply attributed station in life to chance (Lucret. *Nat.* 1.455–58).

737. E.g., Ach. Tat. 6.3.1; cf. Galen *Grief* 23b–24a.

738. E.g., Sen. Y. *Dial.* 7.23.2; Juv. *Sat.* 12.63–65; Ach. Tat. 1.3.2; 4.1.3; 7.13.1. Cf. Horace's portrayal of Fortune (*Odes* 1.7.25; 1.31.10; 1.34.14–16; 1.37.11–12; 2.1.3; 4.14.37; *Epodes* 4.6) and Fate (favorably in *Odes* 3.9.12; 4.2.38). Apollonius was pleasing to the Fates (Philost. *Vit. Apoll.* 4.1).

and Hector (16.853);[739] it was also responsible for others' deaths in battle[740] or in general.[741] Many burial inscriptions complain that Fate is unavoidable.[742] Storytellers could evade having to explain improbabilities by attributing unexpected acts to Fortune.[743]

Lucian, satirizing inconsistent views in Greek religion, notes that one cannot avert fate; the very attempt to do so would bring it to pass (*Z. Cat.* 12).[744] Therefore, why pay fees for oracles, since foreknowledge cannot change anything (*Z. Cat.* 13)?[745] Josephus follows this Greek idea in his portrayal of Ahab's death: fate let the false prophet seem more convincing, because even with foreknowledge one cannot escape from fate (*Ant.* 8.409, 419).[746]

Many Hellenistic cities, as already noted, had Fortune as a tutelary deity;[747] she was patron deity of Syrian Antioch, for example.[748] Romans worshiped Fortuna as a goddess;[749] the cult of Tychē was thus influential, for example, in Roman Corinth.[750] The Roman high priest sacrificed to and invoked the Fates in a public ritual;[751] individuals might also call on them.[752] Some sources assimilate Zeus, as the supreme deity, to Fate or Fortune.[753] Certainly, for Stoics, Fate could be understood as identical to the supreme deity.[754] (One writer claimed that if we simply followed wisdom, we would need no goddess of Fortune, but probably meant this in hyperbolic praise of wisdom.)[755] When something happens to which the gods *surely* would have objected, such as Julius Caesar's death, the reader is reminded that the gods had to submit to Fate (e.g., Ovid *Metam.* 15.808–9).[756]

739. Fate produced the Trojan War (Philost. *Hrk.* 25.3).

740. E.g., Virg. *Aen.* 11.43 (Fortuna); *Test. Sol.* 8:7. Others also spoke of battle deaths' randomness (2 Sam 11:25).

741. Hor. *Odes* 4.13.22–23; *Epodes* 13.15; Sil. It. 3.134–35; Quint. *Inst.* 6. pref. 1–2; Sen. Y. *Apocol.* 3; Prop. *Eleg.* 2.28.25.

742. E.g., Horsley, *Documents*, 4:20–21, §5; 4:25, §6; 4:33–34, §9; see also Sherk, *Empire*, §168G, p. 217 (including, e.g., *CIL* 2.4314).

743. Philost. *Hrk.* 2.10–11.

744. That attempts to avert prophecies lead to their fulfillment appears elsewhere (e.g., 1 Kgs 22:30–35; Babr. 136; Val. Max. 1.8.ext. 9; Lucian *Z. Cat.* 12).

745. On this point, biblical oracles differ, since they are often warnings (2 Kgs 20:1–6; Jonah 4; Jer 18:7–10), as in some other cultures (e.g., Walton, "Genesis," 121). Greek philosophers affirmed divine foreknowledge (see Boyd, "Motivations," contesting their view).

746. Likewise, Fortune conspired to bring about Germanicus's death (Jos. *Ant.* 18.54).

747. Nilsson, *Piety*, 94; on her importance as a goddess for the Hellenistic world, see Tarn, *Civilisation*, 340.

748. Stambaugh and Balch, *Environment*, 146. In the Roman period, she was patron deity of Caesarea in Judea; see Carmon, *Inscriptions*, §211 (English, 100; Hebrew, 216).

749. See Graf, "Fortuna." Fortuna was more an abstraction than personalized (Lind, "Abstraction").

750. Engels, *Roman Corinth*, 99. We know that Fortune was also among the gods worshiped at Ephesus (*I. Eph.* 1237; 3817.1) and Pisidian Antioch (*I. Eph.* 1238).

751. Sherk, *Empire*, §11, p. 21.

752. So Apul. *Metam.* 6.28.

753. Aeschylus *Suppl.* 1046–49; Pindar *Pyth.* 5.122–23; Dio Chrys. *Or.* 64.9; Max. Tyre 4.8; cf. Zeus as guide of Fate in Paus. 8.37.1; Zeus decreeing all things together with the Fates in Epict. *Diatr.* 1.12.25. But in Hom. *Od.* 1.32–43, Zeus attributes some bad fortune to human malice rather than to divine choice; in Max. Tyre 5.1, bad things come not from the gods but from chance; Ael. Arist. *Def. Or.* 336, §111D, opines that human misdeeds come from human rather than divine choices.

754. Klauck, *Context*, 353.

755. Juv. *Sat.* 14.315–16. This is likely hyperbole, since no one envisioned wisdom eliminating chance; cf. the contrary view in a fragment from 4–5 c.e. in *SPap* 3:190–91: life is determined by fortune (τύχη), not by wisdom (φρόνησιν). But Epicurus felt that Fortune affected the wise little, in view of their dependence on reason (Diog. Laert. 10.144.16).

756. For Fate ruling even the gods, see also Hom. *Il.* 18.94–96; Hdt. 1.91; Sen. Y. *Dial.* 1.5.8; Tarn, *Civilisation*, 350–51; Ferguson, *Backgrounds*, 116. But in Sil. It. 17.374, 385, "omnipotent" Jupiter fates something according to his word to Juno (which depends on Fate).

Although rhetoricians could praise a person's good fortune,[757] most people lamented Fortune's fickleness or even caprice; it could bring good and bad to the same people at different times.[758] (Some nevertheless entreated Fortune for help.)[759] Some complained of Fate's cruelty;[760] others (undoubtedly far fewer) responded that people ought not to complain about what happens, since we were born not to govern life but to submit to Fate.[761] It is noble, some thought, to remember the fickleness of Fortune.[762] (Romans did envision another side, personified as good luck,[763] and might praise Fate for their benefits.)[764] Certainly, one ought not to ridicule another's misfortune, recognizing that "fate is common to all."[765]

b. Philosophic Notions of Fate

Whether everything was foreordained in advance or whether Fortune and chance act randomly could be disputed;[766] others debated whether Fate and Nature were identical.[767] The question of whether the world was ruled by providence was an ongoing debate between Stoics and Epicureans.[768]

Some intellectuals criticized the popular attribution of everything to Fortune.[769] Some, such as Epicureans, ridiculed the consistency of belief in Fate, noting that it eliminated personal responsibility.[770] (Some did, in fact, attribute their own misdeeds to fortune,[771] which is, obviously, not how proponents of Fate understood their teaching.)[772] Logically, they might argue, there is no need to honor lesser gods

757. Men. Rhet. 2.11, 420.29–31 (though this is a funeral oration, avoiding future shifts of fortune).

758. Polyb. 29.21.1–6, 9; Dion. Hal. *Ant. rom.* 9.25.3; Terence *Moth.* 406; Corn. Nep. 10 (Dion), 6.1; 13 (Timotheus), 4.1; Val. Max. 7.1. praef.; Pliny E. *N.H.* 2.5.22; 7.41.133–7.43.141; Tac. *Hist.* 4.47; Apul. *Metam.* 7.2. Some doubted fickleness in deities (Max. Tyre 5.3); some complained that at least death freed them from fate (Men. Rhet. 2.9, 414.9–10). Some spoke of Necessity (Hor. *Odes* 3.1.14–15) or Fortune (Dio Chrys. *Or.* 64.8) as "impartial," but many viewed it as randomness (cf. Mart. *Epig.* 4.21, regarding the gods not avenging).

759. So Apul. *Metam.* 6.28.

760. Polyb. 29.21.1–6; Hor. *Odes* 2.6.9; *CIL* 11.1421 (in Sherk, *Empire*, §19, p. 34); Lucan *C.W.* 1.114; cf. "Necessity" as a "grim goddess" (Hor. *Odes* 1.35.17). This is frequent in novels with happy endings (Ach. Tat. 5.11.1; Char. *Chaer.* 5.1.4; 5.5.2; Apul. *Metam.* 7.16).

761. Plut. *Apoll.* 18, *Mor.* 111E.

762. Polyb. 38.21.2–3.

763. See Schaffner, "Felicitas," 377. Earlier Greeks also believed that Fortune could bestow *good* things on people (e.g., Isoc. *Paneg.* 26).

764. Petron. *Sat.* 29 (ridiculing Trimalchio); *ILS* 1980 (from Ravenna) in Sherk, *Empire*, §178H, p. 238.

765. Isoc. *Demon.* 29.

766. Lucan *C.W.* 2.10–13; see also Plut. *Fate, Mor.* 568B–574F, which distinguishes fate from providence and (against Stoicism) notes interruptions in the causal chain. Max. Tyre 5.4 differentiates four causes: divine providence, destiny stemming from necessity, human activity, and Fortune dictated by chance. Allowing for why astrology does not always work, Ptolemy *Tetrab.* 1.3.11–12 distinguishes between irresistible and more resistible forces (though he does allow the forces to affect moral behavior, 3.13.159; 4.7.194).

767. Aul. Gel. 13.1. Some ancients doubted that they were (e.g., Cic. *Off.* 1.33.120), whereas for Stoics they would be interwoven (Marc. Aur. 2.3; Murray, *Philosophy*, 40–41).

768. Quint. *Inst.* 5.7.35; cf. Hippol. *Ref.* 1.19. As Marc. Aur. 4.2 summarizes it, "Either Providence or Atoms." Later philosophers often sided with the Stoics (e.g., Iamblichus *Letter* 8 frg. 4, in Stobaeus *Anth.* 2.8.45).

769. Pliny E. *N.H.* 2.5.22–25, esp. 22. Some responded that Fortune was all the worthier of praise for such control (Dio Chrys. *Or.* 64; cf. also *Or.* 63; 65).

770. So Lucian *Dial. D.* 410–11 (27/19, Aeacus and Protesilaus 1–2); 451 (24/30, Minos and Sostratus 2).

771. E.g., Aeschylus *Lib.* 910–11 (Clytemnestra killing Agamemnon, and consequently Orestes killing her); others noted in Dio Chrys. *Or.* 64.2; also for protagonists' acts (Char. *Chaer.* 2.8.4); cf. passion blamed on Fate or Fortune (Gorg. *Hel.* 6; Prop. *Eleg.* 1.6.30). Blaming behavior on fate was a way to evade responsibility (Max. Tyre 13.8–9).

772. For Cleanthes, only bad doings were not predestined (Long, *Philosophy*, 181); by contrast, some attributed misdeeds to fate and good behavior to choice (Plot. *Enn.* 3.1.10). Some offered a balance: most people shared the moral depravity of tyrants but lacked their "fortune" to indulge such depravity (Mus. Ruf.

if everything, including those gods, is controlled by Fate.[773] They also noted that it was difficult to harmonize the role of the three mythical Fates[774] with Destiny (Εἱμαρμένη) and Fortune (Τύχη).[775] Some writers less opposed to Fortune nevertheless observed the inconsistency of praising Fortune for victories and crucifying generals for failures.[776]

Stoics, by contrast, embraced Fate.[777] Some Cynics mocked Fortune, saying they had nothing and hence could suffer nothing from its vagaries.[778] Stoics and many Cynics[779] were more apt to seek to cooperate with Fate, though, again, by holding nothing as permanent. Early Stoics treated Fate as endless causation, ruling all things.[780] For Stoics closer to Luke's era, order in the universe demonstrated providence.[781] The Stoic trust in fate was not easily falsifiable, at least not by popular misapplications of the teaching to personal aspirations. Thus, when Galba was assassinated, someone challenged Musonius's belief in providence (πρόνοια); he answered that his faith in providence never rested on Galba.[782] For Pythagoras, Fate controlled everything individually and as a whole.[783] Middle Platonists also accepted divine providence[784] and viewed anything under the power of fate as inconsequential.[785]

c. Fate and Astrology

Fate was often closely connected with astrology.[786] The stars either predicted the future or, in the harder deterministic approach, controlled it.[787] In the more pessimistic approach, astrology simply provided the freedom for knowing the unalterable future so that one could accept it willingly.[788] For discussion of astrology more generally, see the excursus at Acts 2:9–11.

---

frg. 23), or destiny controls by decreeing that the self-controlled should succeed and those who indulge passions should fail (Plut. *Poetry* 6, *Mor.* 23DE).

773. Lucian *Z. Cat.* 5–7, 19. Contrast other thinkers, e.g., Iamblichus *Letter* 11.1 (Stobaeus *Anth.* 1.1.35).

774. The Fates appear in many texts, e.g., Lycophron *Alex.* 584, 716; Mart. *Epig.* 4.73; Juv. *Sat.* 9.135–36; Philost. *Vit. Apoll.* 4.1; 8.31; and passim; in more detail, Apollod. *Bib.* 1.3.1. See discussion in Henrichs, "Moira" (124–25 on the goddesses; 125–26 for "cult, myth, and iconography").

775. Lucian *Z. Cat.* 2.

776. Val. Max. 2.7.ext. 1 (on the Carthaginians). For victories depending on Fortune's favor, see, e.g., Dion. Hal. *Ant. rom.* 6.21.1; Virg. *Aen.* 9.282; Fortune predicted Philip's rule over Greece (Plut. *Demosth.* 19.1). Fortune helped both Athens (Demosth. *Philip.* 4.38) and Philip (*Ep. Philip* 15).

777. See likewise Πρόνοια, Providence, in Epict. *Diatr.* 1.6; 3.17; Marc. Aur. 2.3; 12.1.1. One should submit to whatever happens, for it is not an evil (Epict. *Diatr.* 3.17). On Necessity in the philosophers, see Hübner, "Necessity."

778. Dio Chrys. *Or.* 64.18 (Dio disapproving).

779. E.g., Crates *Ep.* 35.

780. Cic. *Top.* 15.59; Diog. Laert. 7.1.149 (citing Chrysippus *De fato*; Posidonius in Chrysippus *De fato* 2; Zeno and Boethus in Chrysippus *De fato* 1). On causation in Stoicism, see Long, *Philosophy*, 163–70.

781. Sen. Y. *Dial.* 1.1.2 (cf. 12.8.3); Epict. *Diatr.* 1.6.1. Belief in providence in human affairs also appears in Chrysippus in Aul. Gel. 7.1. By contrast, Cicero *De fato* argues that chance explains events as well as fate does. Romans honored Providence; Cicero's discussion of Stoic providence affected Augustan propaganda (Schlapbach, "Providentia").

782. Mus. Ruf. frg. 47, p. 140.

783. Diog. Laert. 8.1.27.

784. Trapp, *Maximus*, 267–68, on Max. Tyre 34.

785. Porph. *Marc.* 30.470–76.

786. See, e.g., Apul. *Metam.* 11.22; Tarn, *Civilisation*, 350–52; Nilsson, *Piety*, 110–15; Murray, *Stages*, 124–27; Grant, *Hellenism*, 11; Lohse, *Environment*, 229–30; MacMullen, *Enemies*, 141; Koester, *Introduction*, 1:156–59, 380; Croy, "Religion: Personal," 929–30. On control by the seven planets, see, e.g., Stob. *Ecl.* 1.5.14 (in Grant, *Religions*, 62–63).

787. For prediction but not determinism, see, e.g., the Neoplatonist Plot. *Enn.* 2.3; 3.1; 3.3.6.

788. Klauck, *Context*, 247, citing second-century Vett. Val. 5.9.2 (220.19–221.5 Kroll) = 5.6.9–11 (209.34–210.14 Pingtree); also in Grant, *Religions*, 60–62.

Various philosophers argued against fortune-telling from astrology;[789] some thinkers denied any connection between stars and mortals.[790] Some thought that astrologers could predict people's imminent deaths;[791] charlatans, naturally, exploited this expectation. Pliny claims that his enemy, Regulus, used astrology to gain the trust of a dying matron by promising hope; after she had added him to her will, she then died, cursing him (as Pliny plausibly imagines) for his deception.[792] Even Stoics, who accepted the reality of Fate and hence could accept astrology,[793] could criticize worrying over astrology if it reflected the decrees of Fate, which one could not change anyway.[794] Epicurus, naturally, doubted the power of the stars altogether.[795]

d. Judaism on Fate and Providence

A central understanding of God shared by most Jews was his sovereignty.[796] God was sovereign over human hearts,[797] and hence it was good to pray for God to order one's heart aright.[798] The Hebrew Bible already regularly affirmed God's sovereignty over history,[799] but Jewish writers in Greek took over Greek ways of conceptualizing such understandings.[800] Thus God's plan would be fulfilled by a strong "necessity,"[801] and Jewish people often spoke of God's Πρόνοια, his "Providence."[802] Some Diaspora Jews even spoke of the Μοῖραι, the "Fates."[803]

Josephus emphasizes divine providence, even borrowing Hellenistic historiography's term "Fortune" to express God's purposes in history.[804] That God showed Daniel the future in advance adequately refutes Epicurean denials of providence, Josephus insisted (*Ant.* 10.277–78). Although Josephus recounts some social causes for the war, the primary cause remains God's plan.[805] No mortal, he points out, may escape "destiny" (Jos. *War* 6.84). Fate let the false prophet seem more convincing than the true one so that Ahab would die (*Ant.* 8.409); even foreknowledge does not allow one to escape fate (8.419). Fortune devised the appropriate time for Germanicus's tragic murder (18.54).

---

789. E.g., Favorinus in Aul. Gel. 14.1.

790. Pliny E. *N.H.* 2.6.28–30.

791. E.g., Mart. *Epig.* 9.82.1.

792. Pliny *Ep.* 2.20.3, 5.

793. Cf., e.g., Murray, *Stages*, 124–27; Albright and Mann, *Matthew*, 14.

794. Sen. Y. *Ep. Lucil.* 88.14–15. For an example of such inconsistent fear while believing in astrology and fate, see, e.g., Suet. *Tib.* 69.

795. Long, *Philosophy*, 41–42.

796. E.g., *Let. Aris.* 17, 195, 210, 227, 239, 244, 255, 266–72, 287; Wis 7:15–16; *Test. Mos.* 12:4; *Test. Job* 37 (a praiseworthy attribute of Job is faith in God's sovereignty); *2 En.* 33:7.

797. E.g., Gen 13:6–9; 36:6–7; Deut 29:4; Prov 21:1; Jer 32:40; *Let. Aris.* 231, 237–38, 243, 246, 252, 267, 270–72, 274, 276, 278, 282, 290; *Sib. Or.* 1.304.

798. 1 Kgs 3:9; *Let. Aris.* 251, 256. For repentance, see the fifth benediction of the Amidah in Oesterley, *Liturgy*, 63; cf. Rom 2:4.

799. Such notions hardly need depend on Greek thought (cf. similar notions in some unrelated traditional societies, e.g., Mbiti, *Religions*, 47, 52).

800. See, e.g., ἀνάγκη in Wis 19:4; προνοίας in 3 Macc 4:21.

801. So ἀνάγκη in *Sib. Or.* 3.571–72.

802. E.g., in protecting God's people (*Sib. Or.* 5.227) and destroying their enemies (5.324). Jews could view philosophers' recognition of providence as agreement with their own faith (*Let. Aris.* 201). This term was also applied to rulers (see comment on Acts 24:2).

803. *Sib. Or.* 5.215, 230, 245 (probably late first to early second century C.E. Egypt). In *Sib. Or.* 1.294, the "Fates" are enemies overcome by the just rule of Noah's sons. *Test. Sol.* 8:3 names Clotho (one of the Fates) as the third of the astrological powers.

804. Aune, *Environment*, 108; Attridge, "Historiography," 327.

805. Bilde, "Causes."

Most important, Josephus uses εἱμαρμένη to distinguish his three "sects" (13.171–73).[806] For the Essenes, fate governs everything[807] (at least according to Josephus);[808] they thus appear as deterministic as the early Stoa. Sadducees reject fate, attributing everything to human choice;[809] they thus appear like the religiously skeptical Epicureans. The Pharisees, whose mediating position Josephus undoubtedly favors, believe that God and fate rule everything, yet also allow a measure of free will.[810] In this way, Jewish philosophic options mirror those of Josephus's Hellenistic ideal audience, commending to them the relevant forms of Judaism (most would have rejected the Saducean/Epicurean option). But for Josephus, fate expresses God's plan and does not overrule it. Thus he mocks Greek myths in which fate rules over even Zeus.[811]

Philo likewise argues for God's providence in human affairs.[812] But while Philo acknowledges causes and effects, he denies blind Fate or Necessity; God, not Fate, rules the universe.[813] Rejecting Stoic determinism, he may opt for the relative free will doctrine of many philosophic contemporaries rather than an absolute free will doctrine such as found in Epicureanism.[814] His understanding of providence, arguing against that of the Stoics, also differs from that of Platonism; he believed that God expressed providence in his care for individuals whom God favored.[815]

The Jewish king Agrippa I (known elsewhere for his Judean sympathies; see comment on Acts 12:3) commissioned a coin depicting the goddess Fortune, who was considered protectress of Caesarea.[816] Just as fate decreed deaths, so at the Feast of Trumpets God declared who would die and be born.[817] "Fate" could be used, in fact, to refer to "death."[818] A second-century Christian writer who accepted the notion of destiny could subordinate it to God.[819] Even the use of "destiny" in the *Manual of Discipline* may reflect Hellenistic influence.[820] It is also said that the concept of providence is common in the sages, although the particular term for it (*hashgaha*) is later.[821]

806. Martin, "*Heimarmene*," argues that Josephus uses popular astrological (more than Stoic) language and that Josephus views Israel as freed from fate to freely obey God.

807. Jos. *Ant.* 13.172. This may influence Josephus's view about their foretelling the future accurately (*War* 2.159).

808. Despite the heavy predestinarian outlook of the sectarian Qumran scrolls, scholars generally argue that even these accept both predestination and free will; see, e.g., Vermes, *Scrolls*, 52; Price, "Light from Qumran," 17; Driver, *Scrolls*, 558–62; Brown, *Essays*, 151–54; Sanders, *Judaism*, 251; Nötscher, "Schicksalsglaube."

809. Jos. *War* 2.164–65; *Ant.* 13.173.

810. Jos. *War* 2.162–63; *Ant.* 18.13; so also *Ant.* 13.172 (except there he attributes only some actions to fate); cf. discussion in Klawans, "Fate." The rabbis did embrace both poles (*m. 'Ab.* 3:16, at least as most commonly interpreted); see also, e.g., Urbach, *Sages*, 1:268–69. Josephus might compare the Pharisees with Platonists here (Pines, "Model," even thinks that Josephus used a text that also stands behind Apul. *De Platone et eius dogmate* 1.12.205–6).

811. Jos. *Ag. Ap.* 2.245.

812. See fragments of Philo's *On Providence* in LCL, 9:458–507.

813. Philo *Heir* 300–301.

814. See Sterling, *Ancestral Philosophy*, 135–50, esp. 149–50; Winston, *Freedom*, 14–15 (also the responses by Dillon and Eisenberg); cf. idem, "Freedom" (emphasizing determinism and rejecting absolute free will).

815. Wolfson, *Philo*, 1:180.

816. Carmon, *Inscriptions*, §211 (English, 100; Hebrew, 216). Although we lack evidence for a cult of Tychē there, she is prominent on many coins, often assimilated to the Roman Fortuna or Dea Roma (Gersht, "Tyche").

817. *L.A.B.* 13:6. This idea is developed much more elaborately in later Jewish tradition.

818. *Sib. Or.* 1.40; 11.221 (possibly first-century B.C.E. Egypt). For "fate" as God's judgment, see 3.502, 513, 517.

819. *Sent. Sext.* 436 (noting [436a] that it does not generate faith and [436b] that it "does not control God's grace"); this source apparently accepts both God's choice (*Sent. Sext.* 1–2) and that of his followers (*Sent. Sext.* 5).

820. So Dombrowski, "Misfortune."

821. Urbach, *Sages*, 1:256.

2. Alternatives to Fate

Philosophers often asserted free will, in whole (e.g., the Epicureans) or in part (e.g., the Stoics), to address the practical problems created by determinism. On a popular level, some resorted instead to cultic solutions.

a. Free Will

Although ordinary people in most societies act as if they have a measure of moral choice (admittedly constrained by circumstance),[822] it was no longer possible to take this for granted. Many thinkers reacted against the growing dominance of Fate and cosmic fatalism in popular circles by emphasizing free will.[823] Some scholars argue that thinkers misreading Aristotle's philosophy of choice in light of Stoic determinism highlighted the tension between free choice and determinism, especially in the second century C.E. and later.[824] The question was, however, a long-standing one. Thus Cicero admits that circumstances affect behavior but nevertheless insists that the will is free;[825] Plutarch emphasizes reason and free choice against the rule of Fortune.[826]

For Stoics, freedom was simply choosing to accommodate fate willingly;[827] yet first-century Stoics viewed this freedom as real.[828] For Epictetus, the divine spark within the soul conferred such freedom;[829] for Seneca, the very knowledge that all had been predetermined gave him freedom to follow God's plan voluntarily rather than under compulsion.[830] Even an early Stoic such as Chrysippus may have viewed Fate as compatible with human control of decisions.[831]

Epicureans argued for total freedom, contending that "atoms" "swerve" and hence the course of matter is not determined;[832] arguing against a long chain of causality, they denied Stoic determinism.[833] Middle Platonists could affirm human freedom yet accept the accuracy of prophecy by viewing the latter as conditional.[834] Later Platonists likewise argued that people were free to choose their moral course.[835] Various other writers in late antiquity accepted both Fate and free choice.[836]

822. Cf., e.g., the consensus assumption of modern psychology, despite diversity on many points (Patterson, *Theories*, 640ff., 653).

823. For one survey of the range of solutions to the apparent contradiction between Fate and free will, see Dihle, "Liberté" (covering philosophers, gnostics, and orthodox Christian thinkers).

824. Bobzien, "Conception." For freedom of the will in Aristotle, see, e.g., Arist. *E.E.* 2.6.1–11, 1222b–1223a.

825. Cic. *Fat.* passim. Stoics, of course, emphasized that submission to Fate was how one could express freedom of the will; thus, e.g., a dying wise man escapes necessity by wishing to do what it requires of him (Sen. Y. *Ep. Lucil.* 54.7).

826. Plut. *Chance* [Περὶ τύχης], *Mor.* 97C–100A. He also argues that, contrary to some accusations, Homer does not deny human choice (Plut. *Coriol.* 32.4–5).

827. See Klauck, *Context*, 375; Murray, *Philosophy*, 44.

828. They affirmed both causality (with teleology and providence) and human will (see Long, "Freedom"), the universal causal principle dwelling in each person's share in the Logos (194).

829. E.g., Epict. *Diatr.* 1.17.27; on human freedom, see further, e.g., 1.6.40; 4.6.5. Some argue that Epictetus's slave background influenced his emphasis on freedom (Oldfather, "Introduction to Epictetus," vii–viii), but the emphasis was hardly limited to him (see, e.g., more than fifty sources besides Epictetus in Keener, *John*, 750–51), though some later Stoics quoted him (Marc. Aur. 9.36).

830. E.g., Sen. Y. *Dial.* 1.5.6.

831. Aul. Gel. 7.2.

832. Lucret. *Nat.* 2.225–50; on randomness cf. also 1.958–1115. Randomness may occur in particle physics today (regarding theological implications, cf. Polkinghorne and Beale, *Questions*, 42; but cf. also Thurs, "Quantum Physics"), although, of course, these particles are not Epicurean "atoms."

833. Lucret. *Nat.* 2.251–60. Motions begin in the mind, which then acts on the body (2.261–65).

834. Max. Tyre 13.5. Scholars debate the emphasis that Philo gives to each, but no one debates that he includes both free and deterministic elements.

835. Plot. *Enn.* 3.1. Traveling a mediating course, he rejects control by the stars (2.3, arguing that Soul controls) yet accepts stars and other signs for divination because of the universe's unity and correspondence (3.3.6).

836. E.g., Iambl. *V.P.* 32.218.

In the determinist mood of late antiquity, Christians and Jews had to qualify determinism to allow enough free will for moral responsibility.[837] Before it became a widespread philosophic issue in popular culture, Judaism already assumed free will.[838] Early in the first century, Philo already was grappling with how to articulate the balance,[839] as already noted; he uses free will to distance human sin from divine responsibility, yet his portrayal of God's sovereignty may owe more to philosophic determinism than to the concept of God's gracious election.[840] In the late first century, Josephus characterizes questions of God's sovereignty and human choice as a lively discussion among different Judean sects.[841]

Contrary to Josephus's verdict about the Essenes, most readers of the Qumran scrolls allow that the sectarians who authored them affirmed both predestination and free will (see esp. 1QS IX, 17–18).[842] The consensus throughout rabbinic literature embraced both providence and free choice.[843] One commonly cited saying, probably from early second-century tradition, is that despite God's foreknowing everything, people retain freedom of choice (m. 'Ab. 3:15).[844] A number of early church fathers, faced with the dominant philosophic questions of their era, also argued for free will.[845]

b. Liberation from Fate

Many religious responses to Fate evolved in late antiquity. Some deities, such as Isis,[846] were also associated with Fortune or with deliverance from it. "I conquer fate," Isis was portrayed as saying. "It is to me that fate listens."[847] She extended Lucius's

837. Cook, *Dogma*, 151–52, 156.

838. E.g., *Pss. Sol.* 9:4; for human freedom and responsibility in several Jewish pseudepigraphic works, see Segalla, "Problema." Some scholars argue that Ben Sira affirmed free will against some contemporary notions (Boccaccini, *Judaism*, 105–9); others, that he balanced the predestinarian character of earlier wisdom tradition with moral responsibility in a manner analogous to Stoics (Winston, "Determinism"); others still, that he used the Stoic idea of providence without its deterministic associations (Kaiser, "Rezeption"); yet others doubt that Sirach knew Stoicism at all.

839. On the deterministic side, see, e.g., Winston, *Freedom*; idem, "Freedom"; on the free-will side, see Wolfson, *Philo*, 1:424–62. See brief discussion above on Philo.

840. Carson, "Sovereignty in Philo."

841. Jos. *Ant.* 13.171–73; *War* 2.162–65.

842. E.g., Vermes, *Scrolls*, 52; Brown, *Essays*, 151–54 (though noting internal contradictions due to their view of double predestination); Sanders, *Judaism*, 251. Nötscher, "Schicksalsglaube," rightly notes that this was a practical coexistence of ideas, not a theoretical resolution of the two.

843. E.g., *Sipre Deut.* 312.1.1–2; 319.3.1. Moore, *Judaism*, 1:454ff.; Urbach, *Sages*, 1:268–69 (for astrology, 276–77). Later rabbis reacted even against the moral determinism of the fall, though perhaps partly because of Christian exploitation of the fall (Hayman, "Fall").

844. This is a common explanation, in any case (e.g., Moore, *Judaism*, 1:454ff.; Bonsirven, *Judaism*, 17, 100). While צפוי probably means "foreseen" (see Jastrow, *Dictionary*, 1296), הרשות, often taken here as "freedom," can mean authority or power to rule, often used for pagan governments such as Rome; the phrase could thus refer to God's sovereignty over the nations. But see also 'Abot R. Nat. 39 A.

845. Justin *Dial.* 141; *1 Apol.* 43; Tatian *Or. Gks.* 11 (arguing against Fate, 8–10); *Ps.-Clem. Hom.* 12.3–4 (rejecting Fate as an abdication of moral responsibility); 13.1–2 (rejecting random chance and hence, by implication, Epicureanism). Later, see Severian of Gabala in *Pauluskommentare* 232 (Bray, *Corinthians*, 23); John of Damascus *The Orthodox Faith* 2.29 (Oden and Hall, *Mark*, 69); Chrysostom argued against God's gift coercing the human will (Hall, "Chrysostom," 56–57). Part of Justin's concern was apologetic against the gnostic predestinarian perspective (Chadwick, *Early Church*, 77). Islam emphasized the other, absolute predestinarian side (e.g., Qur'an 28.68). Focusing on grace, many Western church fathers came to emphasize a stricter predestination, as in Ambrosiaster (Bray, "Ambrosiaster," 36–37) and the later Augustine, after a long shift (see Bright, "Augustine," 76–78; Reasoner, *Romans*, 71–72, 97, 100, 106; Roach, "Choice"; contrast earlier Augustine *On Romans* 62; *To Simplician* 1.2.1; 10; Bray, *Romans*, 244, 249, 254, 257). Denzey, "Beast," 193–95, associates the form of early Christian willingness to face martyrdom with the Stoic ideal of asserting freedom in the face of Fate.

846. Dunand, *Religion en Égypte*, 70–71.

847. Horsley, *Documents*, 1:20, §2; also in Grant, *Religions*, 133 (second century C.E.). See also Reitzenstein, *Religions*, 64–65.

days beyond the Fates' decrees.[848] Some scholars think that Artemis of Ephesus also functioned in this manner.[849]

Many have argued that people looked to the Mysteries to liberate them from astrological bondage.[850] Astrologers such as Firmicus Maternus resented the Mysteries.[851] Mithraic incantations associated with astrology also hailed the Fates;[852] Mithraism raised initiates above the control of the stars and the planets.[853] Some of these sources are much later than our period, at a time when astrological influences were becoming much more pervasive.[854] But it is likely that some sought freedom from determinism earlier.

Some philosophers emphasized that their reason was, or naturally moved, in the heavens, among or above the stars[855] and hence above concerns with astrology and fate. Being raised above the world in transcendental thought allowed one to look down on it objectively.[856] In some Mysteries, at least in a later period, initiates were raised to the deity's celestial home and hence freed from the power of fate.[857] Some Jewish thinkers eventually adopted a similar solution in which Israel was exalted in Abraham and thus above the stars.[858]

3. Early Jewish Predestination

Some segments of early Judaism included a heavy predestinarian element.[859] This is especially evident in the Qumran scrolls and related literature.[860] That is not surprising, since Josephus emphasizes the Essenes' predilection toward predestination (though he overschematizes their view); his Sadducees deny it, whereas his Pharisees affirm both human choice and divine sovereignty.[861] The Qumran sectarians could confess that humans are too sinful to go in the right way without God's help (1QS XI, 9–10). They also seem to have accepted double predestination, contrasting the "lot" of the community with that of Belial (1QM I, 5).[862] Their view of God's sovereignty extended

848. Apul. *Metam.* 11.6. Her providence delivered him from Fortune (11.12, 15, 25).

849. So Arnold, *Power*, 21; Trebilco, "Asia," 317–18.

850. So, e.g., Knox, *Gentiles*, 101; Nock, *Conversion*, 99–102; Caird, *Apostolic Age*, 17; Avi-Yonah, *Hellenism*, 40–41; Dahl, *Studies*, 17; Tinh, "Sarapis and Isis," 113.

851. See Bram, "Fate," 326–30.

852. *PGM* 4.662–73 (here, seven Fates).

853. Sheldon, *Mystery Religions*, 33–34. Mithras worked with Isis in ordering planetary destiny (Apul. *Metam.* 11.22).

854. Also, some ideas associated with salvation in the Mysteries were in fact more widespread (see, e.g., Gasparro, *Soteriology*, 98).

855. See Engberg-Pedersen, *Paul and Stoics*, 59, 63; cf. Plato *Phaedr.* 248AB, 248E–249A; Val. Max. 4.1.ext. 2; Sen. Y. *Nat. Q.* 1.pref. 7, 17; Max. Tyre 7.5; 11.10; 25.6; Porph. *Marc.* 6.103–8. Cf. their critics in Plato *Theaet.* 174A; Alciph. *Farm.* 11 (Sitalces to Oenopion, his son), 3.14; Ps.-Callisth. *Alex.* 1.14; Philost. *Hrk.* 1.2.

856. Philo *Spec. Laws* 3.1–2.

857. Cf. Klauck, *Context*, 136; Angus, *Mystery-Religions*, 51; Knox, *Gentiles*, 101. Cf. perhaps ascent rituals in some other cultures (Eliade, *Rites*, 77–78).

858. E.g., *Gen. Rab.* 44:12 (cf. 48:12); *Exod. Rab.* 38:6. Cf. Israel's exaltation in *Test. Mos.* 10:8–9; Abraham's in *Apoc. Ab.* 20:2–5 (without mention of astrology). Cf. perhaps an earlier analogous solution for believers exalted in Christ in Eph 1:20–2:6.

859. See, e.g., Sterling, *Ancestral Philosophy*, 44–56. Even in the LXX (see Carson, *Sovereignty*, 42–44). Carson, *Sovereignty*, 74, argues that apocalyptic literature tends to de-emphasize election; in a different sense, however, determinism features heavily in apocalyptic (Arrington, *Aeon Theology*, 74–77).

860. E.g., 1QS X, 1ff.; 1QH[a] X, 13; 4Q180 1 2; *1 En.* 1:1–3, 8; 5:7–8; 25:5; 38:4; 48:1, 9; 50:1; 58:1; 61:4, 12; 93:2; *Jub.* 11:17; cf. *Test. Job* 4:11/9. They probably go beyond the OT (see Carson, *Sovereignty*, 83).

861. Jos. *Ant.* 13.172–73; 18.3; *War* 2.162–64. Despite Josephus's presentation of the Essenes (*Ant.* 18.18), even the Scrolls do not deny all free will (Nötscher, "Schicksalsglaube"; Driver, *Scrolls*, 558–62; Marx, "Prédestination"; Sanders, *Judaism*, 251).

862. For double predestination, see also 11Q13 II, 8, 12.

to nature (1QS X, 1–5), apparently the experience of testing (4Q298 1 III, 8), and the workings of all ages (4Q180 1 2).

In *1 Enoch*, those "born in darkness" who were *not* "of the generation of light" will be thrown into darkness, whereas the righteous will shine forever (*1 En.* 108:11–14).[863] In the Similitudes, it sounds as if Enoch is personally predestined for eternal life.[864] Philo believed in God's providential care for individuals whom God favored,[865] but this is more closely related to his general determinist outlook[866] than to an emphasis on God's gracious election of Israel.[867]

Early Jewish sources emphasize particularly the chosenness of Israel (Deut 4:37; 10:15)[868] or (especially in the Dead Sea Scrolls) its righteous remnant;[869] the latter conception is particularly relevant for early Christian applications to Jewish believers plus their Gentile adherents.[870] The Qumran sectarians could note, "You chose a people for yourself";[871] Israel could cry, "You chose us as your own."[872] The Qumran scrolls often link predestination with God's special favor toward Israel, often emphasizing God's goodwill toward the elect.[873] The emphasis on chosenness continues in the rabbis;[874] God also chose Abraham[875] and the other patriarchs.[876]

Yet as noted above in greater detail, most Jewish groups affirmed human responsibility alongside God's sovereignty,[877] at least when it became an issue in dispute in the determinist mood of late antiquity.[878] Later rabbinic theodicy explained, for example, that Israel also chose God.[879] In contrast to some systems then and later, most Jews probably viewed predestination and human responsibility as compatible. Early Christians probably shared the same conviction.[880] See also comment on Acts 1:26.

We may conclude that ancient audiences would have readily grasped the idea of God's "predetermined plan" and that such a conception was, even when articulated

---

863. Though in *1 En.* 108:11 some of them may have been "born" in darkness, with sufferings. Many ancients viewed character as inborn, not changed (Pindar *Ol.* 13.12; also 11.19–20), but others recognized that character changed (Val. Max. 6.9.pref.–6.9.9; cf. 2 Chr 24:17–22).

864. *1 En.* 37:4; 39:8–9. Cf. the use of "chosen one" in, e.g., 39:6; 45:3–4; 48:6, 9; 51:3; 53:6; 55:4; 61:8, some for an exalted personage.

865. Wolfson, *Philo*, 1:180.

866. See Winston, *Freedom*; idem, "Freedom." By contrast, Wolfson, *Philo*, 1:424–62, argues more for free will in Philo.

867. Carson, "Sovereignty in Philo."

868. See, e.g., Neh 9:7; Jer 33:24; Sir 46:1; 2 Macc 1:25; *Jub.* 1:29; 22:9–10; *2 Bar.* 48:20. See further Sanders, *Paul and Judaism*, 84–106, 329–33, 362–64, 389–90; Wright, *People of God*, 259–68.

869. 1QS I, 10; II, 5; IX, 14; XI, 7; 1QM X, 9–10; XII, 1, 4; XV, 1–2; XVII, 7; 1QpHab V, 3; IX, 12; X, 13; 4QpPs 37 frg. 1; 4Q164 1 3; 4Q171 II, 5; III, 5; IV, 14; 4Q174 1 I, 19; 1 II, 2; 4Q381 46 5; 4Q504 1–2 III, 9. See further Sanders, *Paul and Judaism*, 257–70.

870. For individual Gentiles becoming part of the chosen people, see *Jos. Asen.* 8:9/11; for application of the title to believers in Jesus, e.g., Col 3:12; 2 Thess 2:13; *1 Clem.* 50.7.

871. 1Q34; and 1Q34bis 3 II, 5.

872. 4Q504 1–2 III, 9–10.

873. Flusser, *Judaism*, 32–33.

874. *Mek. Pisha* 1.135ff.; *Shir.* 9.118ff.; *Gen. Rab.* 1:4; cf. Urbach, *Sages*, 1:524–41; Sanders, *Paul and Judaism*, 88–107; on foreknowledge, see, e.g., Marmorstein, *Names*, 154. On an individual level, it is possible that some rabbis accepted predestination of the righteous but not of the wicked (*y. Ber.* 1:5, §7); one who suffered Persian persecution accepted the corporate predestination of the Persians for damnation (*b. Ber.* 8b). God foreknows what he will do but relates to humans in their time (*'Abot R. Nat.* 37 A).

875. Neh 9:7; *Apoc. Ab.* 14:2; *Num. Rab.* 3:2.

876. E.g., 4Q266 11 11; 2 Macc 1:25; *Jub.* 19:18; 22:10; *Num. Rab.* 3:2.

877. E.g., *Pss. Sol.* 9:4; *Sipre Deut.* 319.3.1; cf. Boccaccini, *Judaism*, 105–9; Wolfson, *Philo*, 1:424–62; Urbach, *Sages*, 1:268–69; Bonsirven, *Judaism*, 17, 20, 100. Cf. conditional promises, e.g., Gen 18:19.

878. See discussion above.

879. *Sipre Deut.* 312.1.1–2; *Num. Rab.* 14:10.

880. For both God's sovereignty and human responsibility in Paul's letters, see, e.g., Lee, "Tension." For John, early Christianity, and its Jewish setting, see esp. the thorough study of Carson, *Sovereignty*.

in terms shared by a Hellenistic audience, also thoroughly at home in a Jewish setting such as Acts here portrays. Some perspectives on predetermination, however, were closer than others; Jewish notions of providence were much closer than pagan notions of arbitrary fate.

II. Jesus's Death

Luke's theology does not neglect the cross even if he emphasizes (especially in the theologically pregnant speeches) the resurrection. Despite the reservations of many as to whether Luke has much of a theology about Jesus's death, scholars have explored Luke's theology of the cross. One scholar argues that Luke alludes to imagery from Wisdom of Solomon to help explain Jesus's death as the righteous sufferer.[881] This view might appear as developed as the views of some other early Christian writers, but it would indicate, at the least, a coherent theology of the cross.[882]

Although Luke does not articulate an explicit doctrine of propitiatory atonement as it appears in some other writers (e.g., Rom 5:6–10; 1 John 2:2; 4:10),[883] it is not correct to say that he neglects any soteriological significance to Jesus's death.[884] Jesus's blood inaugurates a new covenant (Luke 22:20); Luke also draws on Isaiah's Servant "Songs" in relation to Jesus's passion (Luke 22:37; Acts 8:32–33). To suggest that Luke would reject the theology drawn from Isaiah's servant by his Christian contemporaries simply because he does not cite the particular lines stressing atonement (cf. Mark 10:45; 14:22–24; Luke 22:27) seems more an argument from silence than would the presumption that he accepted the widely held early Christian view regarding the context he cites.[885] He does not react against this view, and so silence cannot be construed as rejection.

Luke's emphasis, however, lies elsewhere, especially on the resurrection, which gives the cross its divinely informed meaning.[886] Because he writes a narrative and not an argumentative treatise, Luke often focuses on Christ's death as part of God's salvific plan.[887] God's sovereignty in Jesus's death (joined with the resurrection that

---

881. See Doble, *Paradox*, e.g., 160, comparing Wis 2:16 and arguing that Luke 23:47 should be translated "righteous" (its usual sense in Luke-Acts, 93–160) rather than merely "innocent."

882. Doble, *Paradox*, 243, also concluding here that because Luke echoes Wisdom's model of δίκαιος in his passion narrative, "his readers may infer that Luke probably intended to affirm that Jesus's death stood in God's plan of salvation as *that willing act of faithful response to God's call which turned the ages.*"

883. If we factor in early Christian references to Christ's dying for sins (e.g., Rom 5:6–10; 1 Cor 15:3) and other sacrificial language (1 Cor 5:7; 11:23–25; Heb 7:27; 9:25–26, 28; 10:10–12) as allusions to sin or atonement offerings (or that value attached to paschal sacrifices), the theme is abundant in Paul, in whose circle of churches Luke presumably moved (otherwise, why would he write so much on Paul?). See comment on Acts 8:32–33.

884. Most scholars note Luke's lack of *emphasis* on this point, but they divide over the reason for it (see Bovon, *Theologian*, 164–65, for survey). For Luke's seeing salvific significance in the cross, cf. Zehnle, "Salvific Character"; Fuller, "Theologia Crucis"; for atonement by Jesus's death in Luke's theology, see Peterson, *Acts*, 75–79; for vicarious atonement in Acts 20:28, Parsons, *Acts*, 300.

885. For the servant and atonement in these verses in Mark, see Keener, *Matthew*, 487–88, 630–31; for sacrificial language in Jesus's words at the Last Supper, see, e.g., Jeremias, *Eucharistic Words*, 220–22; McNamara, *Targum*, 129. In view of Isaiah and Maccabean texts, there is no need to doubt that even Jesus could have believed in substitutionary atonement (see, e.g., Morris, *Preaching*, 34); rabbis also believed in vicarious atonement (see Kim, "Atonement," 145; cf. idem, "Targum Isaiah 53"; other Jewish sources in idem, "Concept of Atonement"); Greeks also understood dying for others and expiatory sacrifice (Hengel, *Atonement*, 9, 19), though the language of propitiation in select early Christian documents echoes especially Jewish sources (see Kim, "Hellenistic Thought," 115–16).

886. On this resurrection preaching, see, e.g., Longenecker, *Wine*, 108–9; Morris, *Cross in New Testament*, 130–34.

887. Cf. Moessner, "Script." The inversion of the tragedy into victory was part of early Christian preaching, but it fits Luke's emphasis on God's inverting humanly planned outcomes (see Grassi, *Laugh*, passim).

followed it in Acts 2:24) would encourage those who followed his model according to God's plan (e.g., 7:59–60; 14:22; 20:24).

Excursus: The Cross and Crucifixion

Although the cross became a badge of honor for some Christians through identifying with Christ (e.g., Gal 6:14), it remained a shocking scandal for outsiders (e.g., 1 Cor 1:17–18; Gal 5:11; 6:12).[888] The cross represented shameful execution by slow torture, a penalty reserved for low-class criminals and slaves.

The cross required little explanation for Luke's audience; it was well known in their world, though undoubtedly less common in Achaia, Macedonia, and the province of Asia in this period than in more troublesome provinces such as Judea.[889] Jesus's crucifixion by the Romans outside Jerusalem is an "almost indisputable" historical fact;[890] early Christians would not have invented the crucifixion. The full horror of this mode of execution (see discussion below) remained vivid enough in the first century that all four evangelists hurry quickly by the event itself, Matthew, for example, "disposing of it in a participial clause."[891] (It was established rhetorical practice to hurry most quickly over points that might disturb the audience.)[892]

Although some features of crucifixions remained common, executioners could perform them in a variety of manners, limited only by the extent of their sadistic creativity.[893] Thus, for example, one man is bound to a fig tree and anointed with honey so that the ants devour him, but this, too, is called a cross (*cruciatum*).[894] Before the Roman conquest, following Hellenistic[895] and Persian[896] practice, Jewish executions had also adopted hanging by crucifixion.[897] Though this was then read back into earlier times (*L.A.B.* 55:3), Israelites originally hanged corpses posthumously[898] and only till nightfall, limiting the shame (Deut 21:23; *m. Sanh.* 6:4). It was the Romans, however, who popularized the practice most fully.[899]

Executioners usually tied victims to the cross with ropes but in some cases hastened their death by also nailing their wrists (Acts 2:23; cf. John 20:25; Col 2:14).[900] The

---

888. On ancient crucifixion generally, see, e.g., Hengel, *Crucifixion*; briefly, e.g., Green, "Crucifixion."

889. For its use in Judea, see, e.g., Jos. *Ant.* 19.94; 20.102; *War* 2.75, 253; this often degenerated into blatant abuse (e.g., *War* 2.306, 308).

890. Sanders, *Jesus and Judaism*, 11. I have borrowed much of the material from Keener, *Matthew*, 678–79; idem, *John*, 1135–36, but have woven in additional information omitted in those briefer works.

891. Bruce, "Matthew," 328.

892. Theon *Progymn.* 5.52–56.

893. Hengel, *Crucifixion*, 25. For different shapes of crosses and the likeliest for Jesus (a four-armed cross), see Brown, *Death*, 948; Blinzler, *Trial*, 248–49. Positions varied, but for evidence for one possibly common position, see Tzaferis, "Crucifixion," 52–53. For the torture entailed, see also Scott, *Customs*, 364–65; Brown, *Death*, 946–47. Crosses thus became a metaphor for suffering (Sen. Y. *Dial.* 1.3.10; Apul. *Metam.* 7.16; 8.22; 9.31; 10.9; 11.23); crucifixion apparently symbolizes suffering for one's sins in Sen. Y. *Dial.* 7.19.3.

894. Apul. *Metam.* 8.22; cf. Prometheus's fetters (Mart. *Epig.* 7; Lucian *Z. Cat.* 8; also Lucian *Prom.* 1–2, 4, 9, 17, and passim).

895. E.g., Jos. *Ant.* 12.256, where it was used against Jews resisting hellenization.

896. Esth 9:25; de Vaux, *Israel*, 159. Alexander used hanging in Persia (Arrian *Alex.* 6.30.2).

897. E.g., Jos. *War* 1.97; *Ant.* 13.380; 4QpNah 3 + 4 I, 7–8; 11QTª LXIV; *Sipre Deut.* 221.1.1; *y. Sanh.* 6:6, §2; perhaps *Exod. Rab.* 20:10.

898. Cf. Gen 40:19; *m. Sanh.* 6:4.

899. Ironically Livy claims that Romans were the most humane of peoples with the mildest of punishments (1.28.11)!

900. See Artem. *Oneir.* 2.56; Plaut. *Most.* 2.1.12–13; *m. Šabb.* 6.10; Lane, *Mark*, 564; Allison, *Jesus*, 392–93; cf. Luke 24:39; for ropes alone, cf., e.g., Xen. Eph. *Anthia* 4.2. Cf. Diod. Sic. 25.5.2 (if προσηλόω

nails were typically five to seven inches long, enough to penetrate both the wrist and well into the wood of the cross.[901] One being executed on the cross could not swat flies from one's wounds, nor could one withhold one's bodily wastes from coming out while hanging naked for hours and sometimes days.[902] The upright stakes were normally ten feet at the highest, more often closer to six or seven feet so that the person hung barely above the ground, with a seat (*sedile*) in the middle;[903] animals sometimes assaulted the feet of the crucified. Romans could employ high crosses to increase visibility for significant public executions (Suet. *Galba* 9.1), and Jesus may have been slightly higher than usual.[904]

Crucifixion was treated as appropriate for cases of treason against the majesty of the emperor or for revolutionaries, that is, for political cases.[905] This is undoubtedly the basis for Jesus's crucifixion, since he is called "king of the Jews" (Luke 23:38; Mark 15:26; Matt 27:37; John 19:19), a charge his followers would hardly dare invent in the first-century Roman world (especially in the reign of Tiberius) unless all were deliberately suicidal.[906] Although the charge against Jesus was undoubtedly political, it put him in the company of other despised groups.[907] Vindictive conquerors sometimes used crucifixion to punish prisoners of war for resistance or war crimes.[908] Avenging Tyre's long resistance, Alexander sold its women and children into slavery and crucified its men.[909]

Crucifixion was considered an apt penalty for wayward slaves;[910] when a general crucified Roman deserters, a narrator decides not to describe more, since Romans disgracefully "suffered the punishment of slaves."[911] Slaves could be crucified by cruel masters;[912] those who killed their masters were automatically liable to crucifixion.[913] Slaves were generally much more susceptible to crucifixion than free persons (certainly more than Roman citizens; see comment on Acts 16:37); in an attempted murder where a slave was only an accomplice, a noble might be banished

---

here means "nail," as it often does). Perhaps also the skeleton recovered at Givat ha-Mivtar (Bruce, "Trial," 18), though original reports about the ankle nail(s) have been revised (Stanton, *Gospels*, 148; Kuhn, "Gekreuzigten"); on the wrists, see Yamauchi, "Crucifixion," 2; Tzaferis, "Crucifixion," 52; but this is still debated (McRay, *Archaeology*, 204–5). Since our sample size for crucifixion skeletons is one out of thousands crucified, we dare not infer too much from it.

901. Whitacre, *John*, 457.

902. Klausner, *Jesus of Nazareth*, 350; cf. also Malina and Rohrbaugh, *John*, 264.

903. Blinzler, *Trial*, 249; Reicke, *Era*, 186.

904. Especially given the branch in John's Gospel (John 19:29; cf. Mark 15:36). See further Blinzler, *Trial*, 249; Brown, *Death*, 948–49, guesses seven feet. Romans preferred to crucify criminals along the most-traveled roads to derive the optimum warning benefit (Quint. *Decl.* 274.13).

905. Cf. Blinzler, *Trial*, 213–14; Overman, *Crisis*, 387; Brown, *Death*, 968. This is its usual function in Josephus and hence probably in Judea (Harvey, *History*, 13; e.g., Jos. *War* 2.241, 253).

906. With, e.g., Harvey, *History*, 13–14; Stanton, *Gospel Truth?*, 173. Certainly, it remained for centuries an apologetic problem vis-à-vis the empire's elite (Cook, *Interpretation*, 50–53, 107–8; cf. Lucian *Peregr.* 11).

907. On the *shame* of crucifixion, see, e.g., Polyb. 1.86.6; 8.21.3; Pliny E. *N.H.* 36.24.107–8; Deut 21:23; cf. probably Hor. *Sat.* 2.7.46–47; Epict. *Diatr.* 3.26.22.

908. E.g., Polyb. 1.86.4; 8.21.3 (though posthumous, after various other disgraces); Diod. Sic. 2.1.10; 25.5.2; cf. Caesar's crucifixion of his former pirate captors, Vell. Paterc. 2.42.3; Plut. *Caes.* 2.4; Suet. *Jul.* 4, 74.1. Carthaginians also allegedly crucified their generals if they mismanaged campaigns (Val. Max. 2.7.ext.1).

909. Diod. Sic. 17.46.4; Quint. Curt. 4.4.17.

910. Terence *Andr.* 622–24; Cic. *Verr.* 2.5.66.169.

911. Val. Max. 2.7.12 (LCL, 1:191). On the event, Shackleton Bailey in LCL, 1:190n13, refers here also to Livy 30.43.13.

912. Sen. E. *Controv.* 3.9 excerpts; Mart. *Epig.* 2.82; Juv. *Sat.* 6.219–24; Quint. *Decl.* 380 intro. The authors' editorial perspective probably suggests general disdain for such cruelty.

913. Sen. Y. *Clem.* 1.26.1 (against a cruel master); Xen. Eph. *Anthia* 4.2 (though the false accuser is ultimately crucified instead). Slaves who acted as informers, betraying their masters to Antoninus, were crucified after the latter's demise (Hdn. 5.2.2).

but a slave crucified.[914] Like others, a slave might be left to hang so that the animals could eat him.[915]

Crucifixion could be employed as an example for the most awful sort of death.[916] Needless to say, crucifixion was meant to be, and was understood as, a horrifying, shameful mode of execution; not the sort of event disciples would create for the Lord they proclaimed, it was one preachable only in light of the resurrection.

III. Responsibility for the Cross

This verse summarizes one aspect of Luke's passion narrative (Luke 22–23).[917] Israel as a nation bears corporate guilt for Jesus's death—but the most explicit mention of this situation shares Israel's guilt with the Gentiles (Acts 4:27) and emphasizes (4:28), as does 2:23, that all this happened according to God's plan.[918] Luke emphasizes both God's plan and human responsibility, just as he emphasizes both Israel's failure and that Israel continues to belong to God.[919]

Peter charges especially Jerusalemites with Jesus's death (2:23, 36; cf. 3:15; 4:10). Presumably, he does so because of the participation of the crowds (Luke 23:13, 18, 21, 23), though Luke does not emphasize them (Luke 23:13; cf. Mark 15:11, 15) and they elsewhere appear more ambiguously in his passion narrative (Luke 22:2, 6; 23:27). Historically, hostile crowds probably would have consisted more of Judeans than of Galileans, who knew Jesus better; but theologically, Peter generalizes the sin to "men of Israel" (Acts 2:22). In charging his own Jerusalemite persecutors, Stephen more broadly denounces Israel's history (7:52), but the narrative is explicit that he does so as a law-abiding Jew (like Jesus or the Qumran sectarians who made similar charges; see comment there). Law-abiding Jews might denounce their nation's disobedience to the God of Israel, but they recognized that the history of Gentiles was even worse. Such charges, even isolated from the narrative of Luke-Acts, are hardly anti-Semitism (see further our introduction, ch. 14, sect. 1):[920] biblical prophets often denounced Israel as a whole (e.g., Isa 1:10; Ezek 16; Amos 2:6–3:2; 5:21–27), and Jewish people understood well the notion of corporate responsibility and its demands for atonement or restitution (e.g., 1 Sam 15:2–3; 2 Sam 21:1, 6), including for any sort of bloodguilt near a town (Deut 21:1–9).[921] The primary function of Peter's charges in Acts 2:23 and 3:13–15 is

914. Apul. *Metam.* 10.12. Earlier, a Carthaginian spy was maimed and released, but twenty-five slaves charged with conspiring were crucified (Livy 22.33.1–2). Even if only some slaves were judged guilty, all would be crucified (Char. *Chaer.* 4.2.7). A writer who sounded critical of the emperor was killed and his servant copyists crucified (Suet. *Dom.* 10).

915. Llewelyn, *Documents*, 8:1–3, §1.

916. Diod. Sic. 34/35.12.1; Cic. *Verr.* 2.5.66.169; Sen. Y. *Ep. Lucil.* 101.10–12; Lucian *Fisherman* 2; Apul. *Metam.* 3.9; 6.32; Char. *Chaer.* 3.3.12.

917. Gaston, "Anti-Judaism and Passion Narrative," thinks Luke's passion narrative more anti-Jewish than the rest of his Gospel and Acts. Yet Luke is far less harsh than Matthew (Matt 27:25; though both follow Q in Matt 23:34–36; Luke 11:49–51), perhaps because Matthew engages in greater intra-Jewish polemic.

918. On the historical question, see Keener, *John*, 1068–76, esp. 1073–76; on the Sanhedrin trial (in Luke, perhaps an informal hearing), see Keener, *Matthew*, 644–46 (with 613–16). Some take the account in Jos. *Ant.* 18.64 as omitting a Jewish trial, but this interpretation is at best unclear (Bammel, "Trial," 433) even if the passage's authenticity were not in question.

919. Gaventa, *Acts*, 47.

920. Cf. Wilch, "Jewish Guilt" (rejecting the notion that these passages are anti-Jewish).

921. In their ancient Near Eastern setting, cf. *ANET* 154 (Aqhat), 167 (Hamm. 23); Moyer, "Purity," 120 (citing *KUB* 13.2.3.9ff.); Pfeiffer, *Ras Shamra*, 43–44. Among Greeks, cf., e.g., Xen. Eph. *Anthia* 4.2; the Spartans in Hdt. 7.133–37; Dio Chrys. *Or.* 76.5; for corporate responsibility elsewhere, see, e.g., Mbiti, *Religions*, 269.

ultimately not forensic (to convict; though perhaps 7:52 functions this way); it is deliberative, to call for repentance.[922]

Although the crowds share the guilt, however, the leaders are the primary target of Peter's long-term preaching (4:10–11; 5:30; Luke 24:20; cf. Acts 3:17; 13:27), and they recognize this charge (Acts 5:28).[923] Peter's allusion to the "builders" who rejected the cornerstone (4:11) confirms this by alluding to a parable of Jesus that the leaders also recognized as directed against them (Luke 20:19).

Ultimately Peter will mitigate the culpability of the people and even of the leaders by noting their ignorance of what they were doing (Acts 3:17; see comment there), though some responsibility remains. Most important, Diaspora preaching charges Jerusalemites as a whole (13:27), not the scattered Jewish people as a whole,[924] with the offense and implies consequent judgment (cf. also Luke 13:33–35 and its implication of Jerusalem's judgment).[925] This cannot be construed as anti-Semitism, and Peter's words here can be pressed into anti-Semites' service only by isolating them from the larger context of Peter's preaching in Acts. Granted, Pilate "and the Gentiles" (presumably the Roman system of governance) also remain culpable (Acts 4:27), but less so because they had less direct knowledge of Scripture and hence less responsibility to recognize its Messiah than those who handed him over (3:13; 13:27–28).

Peter claims that they have killed Jesus by the hands of the "lawless," a fitting title for Romans and other Gentiles who did not acknowledge God's law (cf. 3 Macc 6:4, 9, 12–13).[926] This linked Jesus's opponents with lawlessness, just as Stephen's preaching reverses the charges of lawlessness against him (Acts 6:11–14; 7:51–53).[927] To those who prided themselves on obedience to Torah, the charge of lawlessness would be deeply offensive and shaming.[928]

That they acted by the "hands" of the lawless might also evoke passages in which one person sought to kill another "by the hand" of someone else, covering up his own guilt (1 Sam 18:25; 2 Sam 12:9).[929] The theme of secondhand responsibility for mur-

---

922. Cf. Matera, "Responsibility for Death"; Valentino, "Homiletical Charge." Once appropriated by Gentiles and generalized to all Jews and Jews alone (cf., e.g., Justin *Dial.* 17), however, such words became ominous. Later, however, Bede *Comm. Acts* 2.22–23 argues that Peter first makes them aware of their guilt, then afterward preaches salvation to them (an approach similar to Paul in Rom 1–8).

923. Historically, they undoubtedly bore its onus; the likeliest text of Josephus attributes the charges against Jesus to the local elite (*Ant.* 18.64; with Evans, "Non-Christian Sources," 466).

924. Cf. Walton, "Acts," 29, contrasting the "you" responsibility in Jerusalem (Acts 2:23, 36; 3:13–17; 4:10) with the "they" responsibility in the Diaspora (10:39; 13:27–29).

925. Cf., by contrast, Haenchen, *Acts*, 183: "That specifically the pious diaspora Jews (2.5!) are charged with this guilt is from a literary point of view inept."

926. Lake and Cadbury, *Commentary*, 23, see the background in the Hebrew רשעים, which the LXX often renders by (when singular) ἄνομος (e.g., 1 Sam 24:14; 1 Kgs 8:32; 2 Chr 24:7; Prov 10:2) and which rabbis called the Romans. Bruce, *Acts¹*, 91, suggests this as a mark of historical tradition, since Luke would hardly have designated the Romans thus (cf. introduction, ch. 13); yet if not, he certainly did not mind retaining it.

927. The term ἄνομος appears elsewhere in Luke-Acts only at Luke 22:37, where it applies to those executed with Jesus; it is rare in the NT in general. The term would be useful in polemic; Greek could use cognate terms for savage, anarchic behavior (e.g., Diod. Sic. 4.70.3; 33.14.1; 34/35.12.1; 36.6.1; 36.11.1) or unjust treatment (Dion. Hal. *Ant. rom.* 8.4.2), and anti-Judaic traditions even applied the label to Israel's customs (Diod. Sic. 34.35.3). Greeks also opined that lawlessness merited vengeance from the gods (e.g., Demosth. *Neaer.* 126).

928. This was a charge that sectarian communities regularly leveled against those outside (Overman, *Gospel and Judaism*, 17–18), including Qumran (1QpHab VII, 1–5; Overman, *Gospel and Judaism*, 24–25), *1 En.* 99:10–12, and *Psalms of Solomon* (*Gospel and Judaism*, 26–27). In *2 Baruch*, the law reveals who is wicked (41:3; 51:4; 54:14; *Gospel and Judaism*, 27), as in *4 Ezra* (9:36–37; *Gospel and Judaism*, 27–28).

929. Acting "by the hand" of another was a familiar Semitic idiom (e.g., Lev 16:21; 1 Sam 11:7; 2 Sam 3:18; 11:14; 2 Kgs 14:27; Ezra 1:8; Ps 77:20; Prov 26:6; Jer 19:7; 29:3; Ezek 30:12). Bruce, *Acts¹*, 91, cites the Aramaic idiom ביד, but the LXX translation of the Hebrew is sufficient; on the Semitism, see, e.g., Blass, Debrunner, and Funk, *Grammar*, 117, §217.

der appears elsewhere in ancient texts as well.[930] Biblical tradition could also remind Peter's hearers in the story world and Luke's ideal audience that whatever anyone meant for evil, God could use it as part of his plan for good (Gen 45:5, 8; 50:20).[931]

c. Released from Death's Power (2:24)

Although Jesus's death is pivotal, it is his resurrection over which the speech "lingers" (Acts 2:24–36). Dwelling on a point was one way to emphasize it.[932] As is universally noted, resurrection is a theme in the speeches in Acts (3:15; 4:10; 5:30; 10:40; 13:30–37; 17:31; 23:6; 24:15, 21; 26:23; summaries in 4:2, 33; 17:18). The theme is not, of course, distinctively Lukan, but Luke elaborates resurrection narratives (Luke 24) much more fully than Matthew or (especially) Mark.

The "pangs of death" echoes the LXX; thus one could speak of ὠδῖνες θανάτου (2 Sam 22:6; Pss 17:5 LXX [18:4 ET]; 114:3 [116:3]) or the equivalent ὠδῖνες ᾅδου (Ps 17:6 [18:5]).[933] The image, as this text stands, might be of Hades travailing to give birth to Jesus's resurrection and ultimately that of his followers,[934] but the figurative extension of "pangs" for other traumatic sufferings was by now widespread,[935] even for an era of the end time.[936] (The idea of suffering immediately preceding the end is even more frequent, though usually without the expression "pangs.")[937]

Another question is more vexing. Why does Luke speak of these pangs being "loosed" (λύσας) and of Jesus not being "held in death's power" (where Luke translates differently than the LXX)? The Greek term λύω often meant "to destroy," which could make sense of death's power over Jesus (cf. Job 5:20 LXX; Hos 13:14),[938] but it also

930. For the theme of secondhand murder, see also 1 Kgs 21:19; Quint. *Decl.* 305.12; Philost. *Hrk.* 34.6–7; cf. Amos 4:1. Cf. also Philost. *Hrk.* 31.7, where indirect murder is "all but by his own hand" (Maclean and Aitken, 97).

931. God's sovereign use even of testing and hardship appears elsewhere in ancient literature, e.g., Rom 8:28; *b. Ber.* 60b; *Lev. Rab.* 5:4; *Did.* 3.10; cf. esp. 4Q298 1 III, 8 (if one adopts the reading "predestined testings"); in the OT, see Eichrodt, "Faith in Providence," 19–20. Stoics also believed that bad could be used for good in wise people's lives (Sen. Y. *Dial.* 1.3.1; *Ep. Lucil.* 98.3; Mus. Ruf. frg. 27; esp. Epict. *Diatr.* 3.20.11), including by God (Epict. *Diatr.* 3.24.113); cf. also the Roman saying "Perhaps it is for the best" (Cic. *Fam.* 13.47.1), also used by R. Nahum of Gimzo (*b. Ta'an.* 21a).

932. Cf. ἐπιμονή in Anderson, *Glossary*, 53; lingering to elaborate in Hermog. *Inv.* 4.4.185–86. On resurrection in Peter's speeches in Acts, see Anderson, *Raised*, 197–233 (in Acts 2, esp. 202–9).

933. Ὠδίς can refer metaphorically to any kind of anguish (Exod 15:14; Deut 2:25; Jer 8:21; Ezek 7:4 LXX [7:7 ET]; Nah 2:10), comparable to the trauma of childbirth (1 Sam 4:19; 2 Kgs 19:3; Job 39:1–2; Ps 47:7 LXX [48:6 ET]; Isa 13:8; 21:3; 26:17; 37:3; 66:7; Jer 6:24; 13:21; 22:23; 27:43 LXX [50:43 ET]; Hos 9:11; 13:13; Mic 4:9; Sir 7:27; 4 Macc 15:7, 16; 16:7–8; *Pss. Sol.* 3:9). Possibly some would have also applied to Jesus's death the more universal travail implied in the rabbinic "birth-pangs of the Messiah" (so Bruce, *Commentary*, 71n56; on these "birth-pangs," see, e.g., Keener, *Matthew*, 567).

934. Rackham, *Acts*, 29 (the Hebrew has a more natural sense, but the Greek is more "picturesque"); Mattill, *Last Things*, 32; cf. Barrett, *Acts*, 143, though he prefers dependence on the LXX here.

935. "Birth pangs" draws on OT judgment language (Ps 48:6; Isa 13:8; 21:3; 26:17; 42:14; Jer 4:31; 6:24; 13:21; 22:23; 30:6; 31:8; 48:41; 49:22, 24; 50:43; Hos 13:13; also Glasson, *Advent*, 175; cf. further 1QHᵃ XI, 8, 12; XIII, 30–31; 4Q429 1 IV, 3).

936. So Morris, *Apocalyptic*, 23; Lane, *Mark*, 459; Ladd, *Theology*, 201–2; Keener, *John*, 1044–45; cf. *1 En.* 62:4; *b. Sanh.* 98b; *Šabb.* 118a; see OT origins for eschatological travail, for the Messiah and/or the community, in Isa 26:17–19; 66:7–8; Mic 5:2–4; cf. Isa 9:6. See particularly 1QHᵃ XI, 3–18, esp. XI, 7–12, but applications have varied: some scholars have applied it to the bringing forth of the Messiah himself (Brownlee, "Messianic Motifs," 209; cf. Gordis, "'Begotten' Messiah," 194; Thiering, "Suffering"); others think this, at most, possible (Brown, "Messianism," 71–72) but, at best, unclear (Baumgarten and Mansoor, "Hodayot," 188) or unlikely (Silberman, "Language," 106); some view it as eschatological but not messianic (Brown, "Deliverance"), as the travail of the Teacher of Righteousness (Feuillet, *Apocalypse*, 111), or as the birthing of the community (Black, *Scrolls*, 151; Pryke, "Eschatology," 50–51; Vellanickal, *Sonship*, 38–39).

937. E.g., CD IV, 12–13 A; 1QM XV, 1; 4Q162 I–II; 4Q215a 1 II; 4QMMT C 21–22; *Jub.* 23:13; *4 Ezra* 6:24; 8:63–9:8; 13:30; *2 Bar.* 26:1–29:3; *m. Soṭah* 9:15; see further documentation at Acts 14:22.

938. Cf. Marshall, *Acts*, 75.

could mean "to loose" or "to free" (as from bonds, e.g., 3 Macc 6:27; Luke 13:15–16; Acts 22:30). The sense "to loose" would work well with a Semitic original here. The Hebrew חבל could be vocalized to mean either "bonds" or "pangs," and the LXX often used ὠδῖνες to translate both meanings.[939] Thus, even though Luke borrows wording from the LXX (cf. Pss 18:4–5; 116:3),[940] he preserves an exposition that presupposes knowledge of the Hebrew text.

Some scholars suggest that Luke borrowed the LXX's wording without catching the original speaker's nuances (which may have been intended more along the lines of Pss 18:4–5 and 116:3).[941] Because some examples of being "bound" with pangs appear in Greek literature, the mixed metaphor could possibly be "merely fortuitous in an original Greek composition."[942] Likewise, the phrase "held in its power" was a familiar expression for subduing (κρατέω with ὑπό).[943] Most likely, however, "loosing the pangs of death" does reflect an author (perhaps more likely Luke's source than himself) who was aware of both potential nuances of the triconsonantal Hebrew root behind the LXX translation and alluded to this knowledge by his wording even though speaking or writing in Greek. In its present form, the full expression appears only in a text in the Apostolic Fathers likely dependent on Acts.[944]

5. Jesus as Lord in Light of Scripture about His Resurrection (2:25–36)

Although Luke does not spell out the array of Jesus's texts concerning his resurrection in Luke 24:44–47 (apart from allusions in the wording there and in Acts 1:8), he offers samples of such teaching in the speeches in Acts. In Acts 2:25–36, Peter makes an argument from Scripture that the risen one is the Lord (2:25–31, 34–35), an argument from the testimony of eyewitnesses and the Spirit's present confirmation that Jesus has risen (2:32–33), with the resulting conclusion that Jesus is the Lord (2:36).

a. Psalm 16 and Jesus's Resurrection (2:25–28)

Deliverance from the "pangs of death" (2:24; cf. Pss 18:4–5; 116:3) invited contemplation of another psalm that addressed deliverance from death (Ps 16).[945] Peter will then expound this psalm by recourse to another one, depending, in this instance, especially on psalms language to interpret psalms.[946] "Right hand," explicitly in Acts 2:25 (Ps 16:8 ET [15:8 LXX]) and probably implicitly in the context (Ps 16:11 [15:11]), provides for the link (by means of *gezerah shevah*) with Ps 110:1 in Acts 2:34.[947] (I

---

939. Lake and Cadbury, *Commentary*, 23 (citing 2 Sam 22:6; Job 21:17; 39:3; Pss 18:4–5; 116:3; Isa 13:8; 26:17; Jer 13:21; Hos 13:13); Le Cornu, *Acts*, 112.

940. This implicit use of psalm language fits the seven explicit quotations from Psalms in Acts, which conform mostly to the LXX (with a few variations; Dupont, *Salvation*, 104–5).

941. Doeve, *Hermeneutics*, 171; Bruce, *Acts¹*, 92; Bruce, *Commentary*, 71n56; the LXX translator probably misunderstood the Hebrew (Haenchen, *Acts*, 180). Likewise, "the Aramaic חבלא means both 'rope', 'cord' and 'pain'!" (Doeve, *Hermeneutics*, 170).

942. See Lindars, *Apologetic*, 39 (noting both possibilities). Λύω appears with ὠδῖνες in Job 39:2; Poly. *Phil.* 1.2 (Lake and Cadbury, *Commentary*, 23; but Polycarp is directly quoting Acts 2:24, albeit in the Western text).

943. Josh 18:1; Jdt 5:18; 1 Macc 15:33; 2 Macc 15:37; 3 Macc 1:1; with personification, 4 Macc 2:9.

944. Poly. *Phil.* 1.2 (see discussion in our introduction, ch. 10, sect. 4).

945. Some have found in this section other verbal reminiscences of Ps 16 besides the quotation (cf. Steyn, *Septuagint Quotations*, 112–13). On Ps 16 here, see many studies, including Rese, "Funktion," 73–76; Kaiser, "Promise in Psalm 16"; Constant, "Psaume 16 dans discours."

946. Psalms was one of the most widely quoted sections of Scripture in Qumran texts, after Isaiah and the Pentateuch (Fritsch, *Community*, 45).

947. Longenecker, *Exegesis*, 97. On *gezerah shevah*, see comment on Acts 13:34.

suggest the implicit connection with Ps 16:11 [15:11] because it refers directly to *God's* right hand, as in Ps 110 but not in Ps 16:8.)[948]

i. The Psalm's Meaning

Exactly how Luke understands the original sense of Ps 16 is a matter of dispute. According to one view, the ultimate righteous sufferer's deliverance from death encouraged David that death would not separate him from God.[949] According to another, although the psalm originally referred to simply restoration of health, its eschatological rendering in the LXX allowed its early Christian application.[950] Later rabbis did interpret the passage eschatologically, and a late midrash (*Midr. Pss.* 16:9) even applies it, in some sense, to the Messiah;[951] on a different psalm, one text (*b. Sukkah* 52a, bar.) claims that David already prophesied the Messiah's eternal life (Ps 2:7–8).[952]

At the least, the psalmist spoke of deliverance from death (probably beforehand), and if the principles in the psalms of righteous sufferers applied to Jesus par excellence, so did the vindication they usually promised (see comment on Acts 1:20). As one commentator on the psalms observes, even though the psalmist had no prediction of a messiah's resurrection in mind, "the New Testament teaching of the resurrection from the dead and the thoughts which here occupy the mind of the psalmist are based on the same fundamental conviction, namely, an unshakable belief in the life-giving power of God."[953]

This much of the argument would work for modern as well as ancient readers; some of the sermon's connections, however, follow a hermeneutic that most modern readers would find uncomfortable. We might tolerate the *gezerah shevah* on the premise that similar language among the psalms might convey related ideas (or at least evoke related feelings); but Luke further tightens the application to Jesus by appealing to the psalm's authorship by David, who might speak not only for himself but for the promised seed he knew about.

Luke follows the traditional ascription of the psalm to David (see Ps 15:1 LXX); some early Jewish tradition ascribed to David, indeed, 3,600 psalms (11Q5 XXVII, 4)

948. With also Johnson, *Acts*, 52.

949. Kaiser, "Promise in Psalm 16"; cf. Constant, "Psaume 16 dans discours" (who suggests that Peter developed a nucleus of significance already present from Ps 16:9–10); Marshall, *Acts*, 77 (David's own hope, but Peter claims that David cannot exhaust or complete its meaning). Miura, *David*, 153, connects David with Jesus as righteous sufferers both delivered in hope, with hope of enthronement. Miura, *David*, 144, notes that Qumran and Targums treated psalms as prophetically "transcending their immediate context"; David's voice became the Messiah's in *Tg. 2 Sam* 22. Thus (Miura, *David*, 151–52) a typological prophetic use of psalms fits the use in Acts 1–4 and some other texts (e.g., Rom 15:3, 8–9, citing R. Hays).

950. Schmitt, "Zeugnis der Auferstehung"; cf. "hope" in God in Ps 15:1 LXX. Psalmists could plead for deliverance from destruction while alive (cf., e.g., the postbiblical Ps 152:4); Ps 16 may pray to avoid premature death (Marguerat, *Actes*, 91). Dahood, *Psalms*, 1:91, thinks (to my mind, implausibly) that the psalmist expected complete avoidance of death, like Elijah; he notes Ugaritic parallels for the grant of eternal life. Litwak, *Echoes*, 175–79, argues against reading promise fulfillment here, instead suggesting a revisionary reading based on Jesus's experience.

951. Lake and Cadbury, *Commentary*, 23–24; Bruce, *Commentary*, 71; cf. the interpretive traditions in Miura, "David as Prophet." Trull, "Interpretation," argues that Peter (rightly) viewed Ps 16:8–11 as a specifically messianic prophecy. Some others see it as open to messianic interpretation (given the assumption that the audience will so understand it; Bellinger, "Psalms and Acts," 134–36) through midrashic linking of Psalms texts (Bellinger cites Juel, "Use of Psalm 16"; idem, *Messianic Exegesis*, 146–49). Fenske, "Aspekte," emphasizes a christological hermeneutic. The later Targumim may illustrate the propensity of other Jewish interpreters to highlight messianic readings (see Shepherd, "Targums").

952. Le Cornu, *Acts*, 114.

953. Weiser, *Psalms*, 178; for the hint of eternal life here, see also Knight, *Psalms*, 1:78. Kilgallen, "Use of Psalm 16:8–11," contends that Luke argues from Ps 16 that God's love for his holy one logically necessitates the resurrection (Acts 2:27, 31; 13:35); Genuyt, "Écritures," emphasizes the connection between faith in Scripture and resurrection here.

plus other special songs (XXVII, 5–10), all by means of divine prophecy (XXVII, 11). Jewish people naturally spoke of the Holy Spirit's inspiring David to write such songs.[954]

The original psalm, however, is surely Levitical (or at least uses Levitical metaphor; cf. Deut 10:9; 1 Chr 25:8): as with the Levites, God is the psalmist's portion (Ps 16:2, 5) because of his heritage (16:6); further, he need not pour libations for the wicked (16:4; cf. Lev 23:37; Num 28:31; 1 Chr 29:21). Thus (unless Ps 16:7–11 was originally a separate psalm) "saints" (16:3)[955] and "holy one" (16:10) could refer to priests in the temple.[956]

By itself, priestly imagery would not affect the validity of the *gezerah shevah* with Ps 110; indeed, 110:4 also uses priestly imagery (albeit for the Davidic ruler), and the Lord at the right hand is a shield or protector in both cases (16:8; 110:5). Both psalmists also find a place at God's right hand (16:11; 110:1). It would affect only the specific argument that the psalm *must* apply to a Davidic descendant (Acts 2:29–31, 34). But the work of Psalms as a whole was attributed especially to David, who in a sense authorized them (1 Chr 25:1; 2 Chr 29:25), and as some Jewish interpreters could apply prophecies broadly to the messianic era (see comment on Acts 3:19–21, 24),[957] Luke readily follows the early Christian christocentric hermeneutic.

Some scholars suggest that Luke may also use another implicit *gezerah shevah*: the psalmist cries for God to preserve the life (ψυχή) of his holy one (ὅσιος) from death both in Ps 16:10 (15:10 LXX) and in 86:2 (85:2); the holy one in 86:2 is God's "servant" (δοῦλος), which invited messianic connections (89:3, 20, 39; cf. Isa 42:19; 49:3, 5, 7).[958] These midrashic steps are logical, and some ancient interpreters probably would have made them. But the objections against presupposing this midrashic process here are compelling: the argument is too complex (requiring two different links, neither of which is stated); the term ὅσιος is too pervasive to make a specific link obvious (seventy-six times in the LXX, twenty-six of them in the psalms);[959] and finally, it is not the means by which Peter in the story world arrives at the link between the psalmist and the Messiah. More plausible would be a link with the ὅσια of David in Isa 55:3 because Luke clearly notes this connection, although much later in his account (Acts 13:34–35; see comment there).

II. THE LORD'S PRESENCE AND RIGHT HAND (2:25)

Perhaps because Luke understands God as continually "present" with Jesus, he omits Jesus's cry on the cross, "Why have you forsaken me?" (Mark 15:34; Ps 22:1), while including a promise of paradise the same day (Luke 23:43).[960] It is even

---

954. E.g., *Lev. Rab.* 5:5; *Esth. Rab.* 10:5. For the Spirit inspiring other Scripture, see, e.g., *Sipre Deut.* 355.17.1; *Tg. Qoh.* 1:4; 3:11–12; 4:15; 9:7; 10:7, 9; see discussion of inspiration in the excursus at Acts 2:17–18. It was natural to portray Scripture speaking in the present tense (e.g., Rom 9:17; *3 En.* 48A:7; *t. Soṭah* 12:2; *Mek. Shir.* 6 [Lauterbach, 2:43–44]; *Sipra A.M. par.* 8.193.1.7; *pq.* 11.191.1.3); Luke usually reduces Mark's historical presents (cf. Dion. Hal. *2 Amm.* 12 for a rhetorician's critique of inconsistency in verb tenses).

955. *Pace* Dahood, *Psalms*, 1:87–88, who compares Canaanite deities (thinking them the object of libation in Ps 16:4, p. 86).

956. Cf. Aaron as God's holy one (albeit using ἅγιον) in Ps 106:16 (105:16 LXX).

957. E.g., David's prophecy in *Tg. Jon.* on 2 Sam 23:1 (applied to the Messiah's coming in *Tg. Jon.* on 2 Sam 23:3; Solomon's prophecy concerning this in *Tg. Jon.* on 1 Kgs 5:13).

958. Juel, "Use of Psalm 16," 549 (also noting that *Midrash on Psalms* links Pss 16:10 and 86:2). Less relevant in this context is the application of the "holy one" (albeit using ἅγιος) title to God himself (e.g., 71:22; 78:41; 89:18; Isa 1:4; 5:19, 24; 10:17, 20 and passim; *1 En.* 1:2; 93:11; 97:6; *Sib. Or.* 3.709; *Sipra Behuq. pq.* 3.263.1.5, 8; *Pesiq. Rab Kah.* 4:2).

959. Cf. also in Jewish (especially funerary) inscriptions: e.g., *CIJ* 1:37, §55; 1:267, §340; 1:71, §100; 1:78, §111; 1:111, §154; 1:253, §321; 1:282–83, §363; 1:468, §652; cf. the Latin equivalent in 1:166, §233.

960. Haenchen, *Acts*, 181; Barrett, *Acts*, 145; Miura, *David*, 153; cf. Parsons, *Acts*, 45. Cf. the similar approach of John (John 16:32), perhaps suggesting that some Christians felt compelled to respond to what they would have regarded as a misinterpretation of Mark 15:34 (Keener, *John*, 1048).

possible that some ancient interpreters would understand the "always" as implying Jesus's preexistence[961] if they had other reasons to find it there; but the text by itself is not clear enough to support this inference (and Luke nowhere else emphasizes this teaching).[962]

Not only Luke (Luke 20:42; 22:69; Acts 5:31; 7:55–56) but other NT authors affirm that Christ is at the Father's right hand, presumably usually dependent on Ps 110 (Mark 12:36; 14:62; Rom 8:34; Eph 1:20; Col 3:1; Heb 1:3, 13; 8:1; 10:12; 12:2; 1 Pet 3:22; Mark 16:19). The idea was thus one of the most pervasive in early Christianity. (That many of these texts apply it to Christ's supremacy over angelic powers may suggest a major issue of contention in a Hellenistic Jewish context where the Logos alone ruled the other powers.[963] It may be relevant that some Jewish sources, perhaps as early as the second century, speak of angels who sought to prevent Moses's ascent to receive the Torah.)[964] Since one can hardly be at another's right hand and have that person at one's own right hand (unless each faces the other, not the usual arrangement of thrones), the language of the "right hand" is metaphor in both psalms (Pss 16:8, 11; 110:1, 5). Although seating to the left of the person of highest status was a great honor at a banquet (because one reclined on one's right elbow; cf., e.g., Luke 16:22–23),[965] seating by a throne was a different matter. Most ancients associated the left hand with dishonor;[966] for example, in the Qumran scrolls, gesturing with the left hand invited the punishment of reduced rations for a time (4Q266 10 II, 13–14). Being at a king's left hand was still a position of honor (cf. Xen. Cyr. 8.4.3; Mark 10:37–40), but in early Christian imagery, the right hand was better in general.[967] In some texts δεξιά connotes "favorable" (Aratus Phaen. 6, 8), and the right hand was generally more honorable than the left.[968]

In Jewish sources, the queen normally held the position at the king's right hand;[969] the favorite would also hold such a position near God's (Sir 12:12) or the Messiah's (Mark 10:37, 40) throne.[970] In late rabbinic tradition, God reserved a place for Moses beside him in the heavenly court;[971] more relevant is the observation that divine wisdom sits by God's throne in Wis 9:4. Once exalted, a person might rule the emperor's

---

961. So apparently Witherington, *Acts*, 148–49.

962. But neither can we assume, with Conzelmann ("Luke's Place," 308), that his silence polemicizes against it! Hengel, *Jesus and Paul*, 46, excepts preexistence Christology from the majority of NT Christology that probably predates Paul's conversion; identification with the divine Lord in Acts 2:21–38 warns against ruling out preexistence for Luke without specific grounds to do so.

963. Eph 1:20; Heb 1:3, 13; 1 Pet 3:22; on the Hellenistic Jewish setting, see Keener, *John*, 375, 378.

964. See Schultz, "Angelic Opposition."

965. Xen. Cyr. 8.4.3 probably refers to the banquet pattern (unless it suggests an alternative arrangement); these positions were also subject to change (8.4.5). The right hand is probably better in Sir 12:12. One's closest associates would be on either side of one (b. Ber. 46b); in rabbinic sources, the center was most important and the right hand second (Lachs, *Commentary*, 337, citing m. Yoma 3:9; t. Sanh. 8:1; b. Yoma 37a; Midr. Pss. 18).

966. On preference for the right side, see, e.g., Plut. Rom. Q. 78, Mor. 282E; the left side is physically weaker (Eccl 10:2); in one Jewish tradition, the angel on the right of the throne recorded good deeds while the one on the left recorded evil ones (Test. Ab. 12:8–12 A); see other examples in Davies and Allison, *Matthew*, 3:424.

967. E.g., Luke 22:69; Mark 14:62; Matt 25:31. Cf. help by God's right hand, e.g., Exod 15:6, 12; Pss 17:7; 18:35; 20:6; 21:8; 44:3; 48:10; 60:5; 63:8; 118:15–16; Isa 41:10; 45:1; 48:13 (though some of these may connote the generally greater strength of the right arm).

968. Artem. Oneir. 1.2; b. Šabb. 61a; Num. Rab. 12:3; Midr. Pss. 17:8.

969. 1 Kgs 2:19; Ps 45:9; 1 Esd 4:29–30; cf. Tg. Rishon on Esth 2:17; cf. Tac. Ann. 12.37 (presented as an unusual case; cf. 12.56; 13.5).

970. Note more generally the priority of the right in Gen 48:13–18; 1 Chr 6:39 (6:24 LXX); 1 Esd 9:43; 2 Chr 18:18; Neh 8:4. Johnson, *Acts*, 52, compares also God's right hand as a source of power (e.g., Exod 15:6; Ps 118:16); Lake and Cadbury, *Commentary*, 25, note that Rashi cites a midrash on Ps 118:16, where God uses his right hand to raise the righteous dead.

971. Tg. Ps.-J. on Deut 5:31.

assembly, seated at his right hand.[972] Greeks could speak of Athena seated by the right hand of her father, Zeus.[973]

A temporary seat at a ruler's right hand was a position of honor,[974] but this was still more the case if the seat was permanent.[975] The position at the right hand of the throne invested its holder with delegated authority to act for the ruler. Aelius Aristides praises Athena by claiming that she sits "at the right hand of her father," Zeus; then he adds that she "receives [ἀποδέχεσθαι] his orders [ἐντολάς, commandments] for the gods."[976] (Later rabbis said that the righteous or the scribes would get to stand at God's right hand in Ps 16:11.)[977]

iii. Joy and Hope (2:26)

The theme of joy here (and in Acts 2:28) is probably deliberate; Luke could have skipped this part of the quotation or, without skipping (which he seems disinclined to do in Luke 3:4–6 and Acts 8:32–33; 28:26–27), at least omitted the end of the quotation in Acts 2:28 (though the part about God's presence there reinforces the same idea in 2:25, which supports the emphasis on the exaltation to God's right hand in 2:33). Such rejoicing characterizes the early church following Pentecost (2:47). The theme of joy (using ἀγαλλιάω, as here, and other terms) surrounds momentous events in the infancy narrative (Luke 1:14, 44, 47, 58; 2:10); miracle working (10:17; 13:17); suffering in hope of divine vindication (Luke 6:23; Acts 5:41);[978] and celebrating eternal life (Luke 10:20; Acts 8:8, 39; 13:48, 52; 16:34), others' conversions (Luke 15:5–10, 32; Acts 11:21–23; 15:3), and other good news (Acts 12:14; 15:31). It could be empowered by the Holy Spirit (Luke 10:21; Acts 13:52) and is associated with the resurrection in Luke 24:41, 52.

In this context, that the psalmist's "flesh" would "dwell in hope" may also suggest the resurrection (cf. Acts 23:6; 24:15; 26:6–7; 28:20).[979] Here the LXX wording, which Luke follows exactly at this point (κατασκηνώσει ἐπ' ἐλπίδι), proves fortuitous; the Hebrew spoke only of "dwelling safely."[980] That the "tongue" also celebrates may be exemplified in the context's glossolalic speech as well (2:4), though it need not be limited to that (Luke 1:64).

iv. Hades and Decay (2:27)

This is a key text; Luke repeats it in his explanation in Acts 2:31 and reuses it in another sermon at 13:35. That Jesus was no longer in "Hades" (emphasized again in

972. Εἰς τὸν δεξιόν, Eunapius Lives 462.

973. Pindar frg. 146, from scholion on Il. 24.100; quoted also in Plut. Table 1.2.4, Mor. 617C; cf. Ael. Arist. Or. 37.4–7 (Hymn to Athena).

974. E.g., Suet. Nero 13.2, where Nero offers the seat to Tiridates of Armenia.

975. According to the gospel tradition, such seats were coveted (Mark 10:37).

976. Ael. Arist. Or. 37.4–7 (Hymn to Athena), LCL; in Pindar Odes, LCL, 2:378–79, Race's note on Pindar frg. 146. Also cited in van der Horst, "Parallels to Acts," 57.

977. Pesiq. Rab Kah. 27:2.

978. Cf. Maccabean warfare μετ' εὐφροσύνης (1 Macc 3:2; the term appears in the NT only at Acts 2:28; 14:17 but 162 Times in the LXX).

979. Eschatological hope also appears in Luke 24:21, though the speakers have abandoned it. Pervo, Acts, 83, argues that "resurrection of the flesh" with reference to Jesus is a distinctively Lukan idea, not attested elsewhere until Ignatius (esp. Smyrn. 3.2–3; cf. Eph. 7.2; Magn. 1.2; Smyrn. 12.2); early Jewish parallels (for resurrection generally) suggest, however, that Luke did not originate the notion, and certainly other early Christians affirmed "bodily" resurrection of some sort (cf., e.g., sources in Keener, John, 1175–77).

980. Though Luke's composition (and probably the communication of his informant) was probably Greek, Lake and Cadbury, Commentary, 24, infer too much in favor of such from this example; Jewish teachers often practiced a utilitarian text criticism that allowed them to adopt LXX readings when these supported their argument (see comment on Acts 2:17).

2:31) simply means that he was no longer dead, but it provided a fitting rhetorical contrast with his exaltation to heaven (2:34).[981] The term ᾅδης refers to the realm of the dead (Luke 16:23) and hence is frequently poetically coupled with "death" not only in the psalms (Pss 6:5; 18:5; 49:14; 55:15; 89:48; 116:3) and other Hebrew poetry (Job 33:22; 38:17; Prov 2:18; 5:5; 7:27; Song 8:6; Isa 28:15, 18; Hos 13:14; Hab 2:5) but also in Hellenistic Jewish literature.[982]

That the second line repeats or develops the substance of the first is good Hebrew parallelism, but it could also prove intelligible to Greek hearers.[983] The NT employs δια-φθορά only in Acts 2:27, 31 and 13:34–37, that is, in its expositions of Ps 16:10 (though the term appears twenty times in the LXX).[984] Whereas the soul was in Hades, it was the body that would decay. Even if Hades were a metaphor for nonexistence (not its typical usage in ancient texts), the experience of death for the body here, though parallel and related, does not appear identical to that for the soul. Although Luke's audience probably would not have paused long over it, how would they have heard this distinction?

Greeks for centuries and, later, Romans regularly differentiated soul and body,[985] often emphasizing the immortality of the former[986] (although many differed on this).[987] Some Greek thinkers denigrated the body, even regarding it as a tomb from which one might be released at death.[988] Contrary to common scholarly opinion, however,[989] early Judaism often accepted this differentiation between the soul and the body. Such differentiation does not surprise us in Josephus (*Ag. Ap.* 2.203) and other hellenized sources,[990] but it also appears in many sources traditionally viewed as less hellenized.[991] Jewish sources,

981. For this antithesis, see Luke 10:15//Matt 11:23; cf. Ps 139:8 (138:8 LXX); Job 7:9; 11:8; Amos 9:2.

982. Wis 16:13; Sir 14:12; 28:21; 48:5; 51:6; *Pss. Sol.* 18:2; Rev 1:18; 6:8; 20:13–14; cf. *Test. Ab.* 19:7 A. For the realm of the dead as the "gates of Hades," see Hom. *Od.* 14.156; Hesiod *Theog.* 773; Eurip. *Hipp.* 56–57, 1447; *Hec.* 1; Diog. Laert. 10.126; Char. *Chaer.* 4.1.3; *Orph. H.* 18.15) likewise the house (e.g., Hom. *Il.* 15.251; 20.336; 21.48; 22.52, 213, 425, 482; 23.19, 71, 74, 103, 179; 24.246; *Od.* 14.208; 20.208) or realm (e.g., Soph. *Ajax* 635; Eurip. *Alc.* 25, 73, 436–37, 457, 626; *El.* 142–43; *Herc.fur.* 610, 619; *Heracl.* 218, 912–13, 949; *Hipp.* 895; *Andr.* 414; Ap. Rhod. 2.609; 3.810) of Hades; see Keener, *Matthew*, 428–29. Considerable continuity exists among Mesopotamian and Egyptian (Lieven, "Underworld"), Greek (Johnston, "Underworld"), and Roman (Käppel, "Underworld") conceptions of the netherworld.

983. Cf. the more general sense of *synonymia* (as opposed to the technical usage) in Rowe, "Style," 133; Porter, "Paul and Letters," 580.

984. Cf. also Steyn, *Septuagint Quotations*, 184. The cognate verb appears sixty-two times in the LXX and five times in the NT, but bears a different sense.

985. E.g., Arist. *N.E.* 1.12.6, 1102a; Lucret. *Nat.* 3.370–95; Marc. Aur. 5.13; 6.32; Diog. Laert. 3.63; Heraclitus *Ep.* 9; Diogenes *Ep.* 39; Plut. *Plat. Q.* 3.1, *Mor.* 1002B; Sext. Emp. *Pyr.* 1.79; *Gr. Anth.* 7.109. Some allowed the distinction only for humans (Sall. *Catil.* 1.2, 7), others also for animals (Arist. *Pol.* 1.2.10, 1254a; Diog. Laert. 8.1.28).

986. Plato *Laws* 8.828D; *Phaedo* 64CE; *Phaedr.* 245C; *Rep.* 10.611BC; Arist. *Soul* 1.4, 408b; Hdt. 2.123; Cic. *Senect.* 20.78; *Tusc.* 1.14.31; Dion Hal. *Ant. rom.* 8.62.1; Sen. Y. *Dial.* 12.11.7; *Ep. Lucil.* 57.9; Plut. *Div. V.* 17, *Mor.* 560B; Diog. Laert. 8.5.83; Plot. *Enn.* 4.7–8; Philo *Virt.* 67. Some popular thought drew from the "shades" of earlier myth (Hom. *Od.* 11.204–24, 487–91).

987. Most notably, Epicureans viewed the soul as mortal (Lucr. *Nat.* 3.417–829; Diog. Laert. 10.124–25); Stoics also accommodated their view of the soul's afterlife to their view of the eventual cosmic conflagration (Sen. Y. *Dial.* 6.26.7). Many inscriptions are pessimistic.

988. Plato *Cratyl.* 400BC. Even when the specific language is absent, the concept is frequent: Plato *Phaedo* 80DE; Epict. *Diatr.* 1.1; 1.8–9; 1.9.11–12, 16; 3.13.17; 4.7.15; Arrian *Alex.* 7.2.4; Plut. *Isis* 5, *Mor.* 353A; Marc. Aur. 3.7; 4.5, 41; 6.28; 9.3; Plot. *Enn.* 1.5.3; cf. 4 *Ezra* 7:96; *Diogn.* 6.7–8.

989. Many mid-twentieth-century NT scholars, more familiar with the Hebrew Bible than with early Judaism, made a leap from most of the era of ancient Israel to early Judaism that is simply unjustifiable in this case in light of the ancient literature itself.

990. *Let. Aris.* 236; *L.A.B.* 3:10; *Test. Ash.* 2:6; *Test. Naph.* 2:2–3; *Test. Job* 20:3; *Apoc. Ezek.* 1–2. Often "soul and body" together signified the whole (e.g., 2 Macc 7:37; 14:38; *Let. Aris.* 139; *Test. Sim.* 2:5; 4:8).

991. E.g., *1 En.* 102:5; *t. Sanh.* 13:2; *b. Ber.* 10a; 60b; *Yoma* 20b, bar.; *Lev. Rab.* 4:8; 34:3; *Deut. Rab.* 2:37; *Pesiq. Rab.* 31:2. See esp. the Hellenistic dualistic language in *Sipre Deut.* 306.28.3; later, *Gen. Rab.* 14:3; *Eccl. Rab.* 6:6–7, §1.

both those traditionally regarded as more hellenized[992] and other sources, also usually embraced the immortality of the soul;[993] this seems to have posed little conflict, for much ancient Jewish thought, with the doctrine of the resurrection. Some even used various forms of the Greek idea of the body as a tomb.[994]

v. Ways of Life and God's Presence (2:28)

On the "gladness" of his presence, see comment on Acts 2:26. The "presence" reinforces Acts 2:25, and together they emphasize that Jesus was not only alive again but at the Father's right hand (2:33), fulfilling Ps 110:1 (Acts 2:34–35). Luke might leave out the final "stich of the last verse" he cites (addressing God's right hand) to save the exaltation for the second part of his argument (Ps 110:1 in Acts 2:33);[995] his argument would have been easier for less biblically literate readers to follow, however, had he made the connection explicit by including the line.[996]

Luke might envision the "ways of life" as the "ways of the Lord" (Luke 1:76; 3:5; Acts 13:10), although the LXX expression may refer to safe, as opposed to dangerous, behavior (Prov 5:6; 6:23; 10:17; 12:28; 15:24; cf. 4:10; 16:17; 21:21), applicable to the "two ways" tradition (Jer 21:8; Matt 7:14).

b. Jesus, Not David, Is the Exalted King (2:29–36)

Peter here argues that David, having died and been buried yet not having ascended, fulfills neither Ps 16 (Acts 2:29–31) nor Ps 110 (Acts 2:34–35). Rather, both the apostles as eyewitnesses and the outpoured Spirit attest that Jesus has risen and ascended to God's right hand (Acts 2:32–33); therefore Jesus is both the "Lord" of Ps 110:1 and the "Christ," the ultimate Davidic king.

i. David Died and Was Buried (2:29)

That David (in contrast to, e.g., Moses or Ezra) died, as Peter notes, was not disputed; one late tradition suggests that his body did not experience decay,[997] but it is unlikely that Luke needs to polemicize against this idea here. He simply underlines the point that the Scripture, which must be fulfilled, had not applied literally and fully to David and hence must apply to someone else of whom David would have spoken. Peter points out the obvious: the tomb is in plain view among them, and David has not vacated it.[998] (Peter's stating the obvious is intended either as humorous or as boldness seeking to avoid the appearance of disrespecting the deceased; he prefaces it with, "I may say boldly," which can mean "Do not be offended if I point out"[999]—depending on whether he meant his preface literally or ironically.)

---

992. E.g., Philo *Alleg. Interp.* 1.1; *Abr.* 258; Jos. *Ant.* 17.354; 18.14, 18; *War* 1.84; 2.154, 163; 7.341–48; *Test. Ab.* 1:24–25 A; 4:9; 9:10 B; *Jos. Asen.* 27:10/8; *Apoc. Mos.* 13:6; 32:4; 33:2.

993. E.g., *1 En.* 22:7; *4 Ezra* 7:78; *Gen. Rab.* 14:9. Some traditions allowed the destruction of both soul and body for the wicked at the final judgment (*t. Sanh.* 13:4; cf. 1 Macc 2:63); Sadducees reportedly denied immortality (Jos. *Ant.* 18.16).

994. Philo *Dreams* 1.138–39; cf. Wis 9:15; Jos. *War* 2.154–55.

995. Zehnle, *Pentecost Discourse*, 34.

996. Just as he quotes the line of Joel 2:32 that he will expound; or just as Hebrews involves an explicit midrash on Ps 110 (Heb 1:13; 5:6, 10; 7:1–10).

997. Noted in Barrett, *Acts*, 146 (following Strack and Billerbeck, *Kommentar*, 2:26; *Der. Er. Zuṭ.* 1). The nondecay of patriarchs sounds like the sort of hagiography popular also among Christians in late antiquity.

998. Witherington, *Acts*, 146; Barrett, *Acts*, 146.

999. With Johnson, *Acts*, 51 (citing Ael. Arist. *Or.* 6.2); cf. Anderson, *Glossary*, 94. On preparing hearers for a shocking statement, see comment on Acts 4:9–10; on παρρησία (often rendered "boldness"), see comment on Acts 4:13 (also Keener, *John*, 705–6).

A teacher who wanted to argue that a psalm (or any other text) applied in a way other than what it seemed to claim literally could begin by showing that the apparent literal meaning was not fulfilled (e.g., *y. Ber.* 2:1, §5). Because the passage (if interpreted of bodily resurrection)[1000] cannot apply literally to David, it applies naturally and especially to Jesus.[1001] In many texts, "David" would have been naturally construed as a title for the messianic ruler from David's line (Jer 30:9; Ezek 34:23–24; 37:24–25; Hos 3:5; cf. Jer 23:5; 33:15–30; Amos 9:11; Zech 12:7–13:1), and this is how the sermon argued the psalm should be applied. This hermeneutic would have sounded plausible on the premises used by some rabbis; we may compare a later tradition that gave as the reason for David's biblical claim to be "afflicted" that he foresaw that Ahaz, Manasseh, and Amon would be his descendants; he called himself "king" because he foresaw Asa, Jehoshaphat, and Hezekiah (*Pesiq. Rab Kah.* 27:3). Simeon ben Laqish, a third-century Amora, inferred that David spoke not of himself but of Manasseh, his descendant, when he mentioned the "destitute" man in Ps 102:18 (also *Pesiq. Rab Kah.* 27:3).

Clearly Luke understood the importance of tombs to Judeans (Acts 7:16; 13:29; Luke 11:47; 23:53–55), but this importance pervaded antiquity. Luke is not, however, theologically impressed with them (Luke 11:48), recognizing also their associations with uncleanness (11:44)[1002] and evil spirits or ghosts (8:27).[1003]

In the broader culture of Mediterranean antiquity, tombs were sacred and hence often linked with temples.[1004] Like Greeks,[1005] Jewish people venerated tombs of past heroes (see, e.g., Jos. *War* 4.531–32; cf. *Ant.* 16.179–82). Indeed, tombs of famous persons were, like temples, tourist attractions (Paus. 2.7.2; 8.41.1); though new tombs were normally constructed outside the walls of ancient cities, some had tombs of famous leaders in public places, even in a marketplace (ἀγορά, Plut. *Themist.* 32.3).

David's tomb was near Jerusalem (1 Kgs 2:10; 2 Chr 32:33),[1006] and its traditional site, apparently still known after the exile (Neh 3:16), continued to be so in the first century.[1007] Some rabbis suggested that the tombs of David and Huldah (unlike any others) were allowed to remain in Jerusalem because of their antiquity or because (one suggested) subterranean streams carried away the uncleanness.[1008] Judean care for

1000. A hermeneutical presupposition for approaching biblical texts, shared by the Pharisees (*Sipre Deut.* 329.2.1; *b. Sanh.* 90b; *Gen. Rab.* 20:10; *Eccl. Rab.* 9:5, §1; cf. 4 Macc 18:19; *b. Pesaḥ.* 68a) and the early Christians (Luke 20:37–38; cf. Lachs, *Commentary*, 361; Davies and Allison, *Matthew*, 3:233). One later rabbi went so far as to say that all texts implied the resurrection if one simply had the ingenuity to find it there (*Midr. Tannaim* on Deut 32:2, in Moore, *Judaism*, 2:383; *Sipre Deut.* 306.28.3).

1001. Cf. Strauss, *Messiah*, 131–47. Miura, *David*, 144–45, notes that since contemporary Jewish expectations could apply the psalm to David himself (cf. "David redivivus" in *Tg. 2 Sam* 23:3), Peter demonstrates that it applies instead to Jesus.

1002. For the uncleanness of tombs, see *m. Naz.* 3:5; 7:3; *t. B. Bat.* 1:10–11; *Kelim B. Qam.* 3:7; *Šeb.* 3:13; *Mek. Pisha* 1.83–84; *'Abot R. Nat.* 41 A; for warning markers, probably in view in Luke 11:44, see *m. Mo'ed Qaṭ.* 1:2; *Ma'aś. Š.* 5:1; *Šeqal.* 1:1; *b. B. Meṣi'a* 85b; *y. Mo'ed Qaṭ.* 1:2, §7.

1003. E.g., *PGM* 101.1–3; Nineham, *Mark*, 153; Alexander, *Possession*, 29; cf. *Jub.* 22:17; *'Abot R. Nat.* 3 A; *Test. Sol.* 8:9; Apul. *Metam.* 2.20; Lewis, *Life*, 96.

1004. E.g., Plut. *Themist.* 9.4.

1005. Veneration of holy persons' and ancestral tombs is an ancient practice in the Middle East (Diod. Sic. 17.17.3; Dion. Hal. *Ant. rom.* 8.24.6; 11.10.1). Cf. Koester, "Heroes," 261. For the character of funerary monuments in this period, see Cormack, "Funerary Monuments."

1006. Also *'Abot R. Nat.* 35 A; *t. B. Bat.* 1:11.

1007. Jos. *Ant.* 7.392–94; 13.249; 16.179–83; *War* 1.61. Josephus's passages indicate various attempts to pilfer it, but these would not affect Peter's point that the tomb, and perhaps David's remains, were available for public verification of his death. Some add later reference to Jerome *Ep.* 46.

1008. *T. B. Bat.* 1:11; *'Abot R. Nat.* 35 A. That many of David's descendants were buried in his city (e.g., 1 Kgs 11:43; 15:24; 22:50; 2 Kgs 8:24; 9:28; 12:21; 15:38; 2 Chr 9:31) might be taken to mean in its vicinity. On the Huldah tradition (and its absence in *Lives of the Prophets*), see van der Horst, "Graf." Moving tombs

prophets' tombs seems to have particularly flourished around Jesus's time.[1009] Notable monuments for others who were deceased also appear in this period.[1010]

Not all alleged tomb sites were correct (some cities and regions even had competing sites for a famous person's tomb).[1011] The site of David's tomb is lost to us today; today's traditional site on Mount Zion is from late Roman times and was not identified as David's tomb before the tenth century;[1012] excavation reports suggest that it might even be a Jewish-Christian synagogue.[1013] According to one tradition of uncertain (but probably Amoraic) date, David died on Pentecost (*y. Ḥag.* 2:3, §4),[1014] but this datum is probably irrelevant to the connection in Luke-Acts, which emphasizes the Davidic Messiah, in any case (Luke 1:27, 32, 69; 2:4, 11; 3:31; 18:38–39; 20:44; 13:22–23, 34–36; 15:16).

II. DAVID PREDICTED CHRIST (2:30–31)

Peter emphasizes that David spoke not of himself but in his role as a prophet. Probably many Jewish teachers would have shared the assumption that prophets spoke especially of the messianic era (see comment on Acts 3:24). Jewish people agreed that the Holy Spirit inspired the psalms.[1015] Widespread agreement on this point could obviate the point of stating it, but it serves a subsidiary purpose for Peter in the story world and especially for Luke: as the Spirit inspired prophets to testify of Jesus in advance, now the Spirit was inspiring Jesus's witnesses to testify for him after the events had occurred (1:8; 2:17–18; cf. 1 Pet 1:10–12); the proposed chiastic parallel between this point and its analogue in the outpouring of the Spirit (Acts 2:33), if accurate, would further reinforce this emphasis. For the promise in the psalms of God's endorsing David's lineage, see also Pss 89:26–29; 132:11–12.[1016]

That the Spirit inspired David in song (indeed, here an inspired canonical psalm) provides more than sufficient reason for calling him a prophet (cf. 2 Sam 23:1–2; 2 Chr 29:25). Other Jewish texts expanded the list of prophets (Tob 4:12; Sir 46:1), and some included David among them.[1017] When the Spirit left Saul for David, Josephus emphasizes, David prophesied (Jos. *Ant.* 6.166).

God's promise to David of a seed from his own loins echoes especially Ps 132:11; though the LXX has ἐκ καρποῦ τῆς κοιλίας, Luke's adaptation is neither unusual nor, likely, significant.[1018] As is often noted, the Qumran scrolls apply this psalm

---

or their contents was almost universally abhorrent (cf., e.g., Sen. E. *Controv.* 4.4, excerpts, intro.; Callim. *Aetia* 3.64), but a Second Temple period inscription suggests that the bones of at least some kings were moved (Carmon, *Inscriptions*, §255, pp. 120, 252).

1009. Jeremias, *Theology*, 146n2; Schweizer, *Matthew*, 442–43.

1010. Jos. *Ant.* 18.108; 20.95; Carmon, *Inscriptions*, §255, pp. 120, 252.

1011. This was to be expected especially with the rise of tomb veneration in late antiquity; see Philost. *Vit. soph.* 1.25.543; further discussion at Keener, *John*, 98.

1012. See Lake and Cadbury, *Commentary*, 24; Riesner, "Synagogues in Jerusalem," 201; Fitzmyer, *Acts*, 257.

1013. See Pixner, "Church of Apostles."

1014. Also noted in Lake and Cadbury, *Commentary*, 24, following Strack and Billerbeck, *Kommentar*, 2:619.

1015. For Scripture in general, e.g., 4 Ezra 14:22; *Sipra VDDen. par.* 1.1.3.3; 5.10.1.1; *Sipra Behuq. pq.* 6.267.2.1; *Sipre Deut.* 355.17.1–3; 356.4.1; also, on inspiration of worship and song, see comment on Acts 2:11; on inspiration in general, see the excursus at Acts 2:17–18.

1016. Cf. Ps 2:7–9; Isa 9:7; 16:5; Jer 23:5; 33:15, 17, 21–22; Ezek 34:23–24; 37:24–25; Hos 3:5; Amos 9:11; Zech 12:8. For David's rule in the world to come even in much later sources, see *Midr. Pss.* 57:3. God's covenant with David directly involved his descendants (with Miura, *David*, 146).

1017. 11Q5 XXVII, 11; *Sipre Deut.* 1.1.4; cf. Jos. *Ant.* 7.391. Also Philo *Agr.* 50 (though he leaves the psalmist anonymous); cf. Moffatt, *Hebrews*, 3; Miura, *David*, 128–29; esp. Daly-Denton, "Prophet."

1018. Cf. Lake and Cadbury, *Commentary*, 25; Bock, "Scripture and Realisation," 50. The term ὀσφῦς appears sixty-two times in the LXX, occasionally referring to the place of one's seed, as here (Gen 35:11; 37:34); but καρπός τῆς κοιλίας is more common (Gen 30:2; Deut 7:13; Ps 132:11; Prov 18:20; Lam 2:20; Hos 9:16;

about David's descendants messianically (4QFlor 1 I, 7–13).[1019] The Davidic emphasis is much larger in Luke than in his mentor (in extant Pauline literature, only at Rom 1:3; 2 Tim 2:8) or in Johannine literature (Rev 3:7; 5:5; 22:16; cf. John 7:42); it is more comparable to the emphasis in Mark and Matthew.[1020] Yet, outside references shared with Mark, Luke's Davidic Christology is not pervasive in his first volume, but especially prominent in the infancy narratives with their emphasis on Israelite piety.[1021] Jesus later cites the example of David (Luke 6:3–4; Mark 2:25–26) as he cites other examples; like Saul hunting David, Herod Antipas wants to kill Jesus (Luke 13:31–32), but the comparison, if intended at all, is not explicit. Luke retains some Davidic acclamations from Mark (Luke 18:38–39, as in Mark 10:47–48) but omits the crowd's acclamation from Mark 11:10 in Luke 19:38. Davidic expectation figures more prominently in the infancy narratives: Joseph was the son of David (Luke 1:27; 2:4; 3:31); Jesus will have the throne of his ancestor David (1:32), though this is later qualified as one greater than David, as David's Lord (20:41–44; Acts 2:34–35). Salvation would come in David's household (Luke 1:69).

That God "swore" to David might recall other divine oaths to the ancestors (Luke 1:73), which appear more prominent in biblical tradition.[1022] But God also swore to David the promise of his kingship (cf. 2 Sam 3:9) and his continuing seed (Ps 132:11, paraphrased here; also Ps 89:3–4, 35–36, 49; cf. Isa 55:3). Luke is not alone in his interest in this; Hebrews emphasizes both the oath to the patriarchs (Heb 6:13, 16) and the promise of Ps 110:4 (Heb 7:21), perhaps the "two immutable" promises of Heb 6:18. The promised "throne" of David recalls Luke 1:32 (in addition to Ps 132:11), but in view of Ps 110:1, this throne is an exalted throne at God's right hand, as his vice-regent (Acts 2:34).[1023]

"Throne" stands for kingdom (and is heavenly, in any case, 7:49), but in view of the emphasis on "sitting" at God's right hand (from Ps 110:1 in Acts 2:34; cf. 2:33), ancient hearers might visualize the thrones with which they were familiar. The throne, with its backrest and armrests, was unique among ancient seats and was normally reserved for images of rulers and deities; the legs often ended in animal paws[1024] (perhaps primarily as a display of lavish wealth). But God's throne was not comparable to earthly ones, and its image was developed elaborately beyond earthly parallels in early

---

Mic 6:7). The psalms elsewhere use καρπός for offspring only in Pss 21:10 and 127:3. Luke's "swore *with an oath*" is pleonastic (Mickelsen, *Interpreting*, 195).

1019. Johnson, *Acts*, 52; Witherington, *Acts*, 146; it is also connected with 2 Sam 7:12–13 there (Barrett, *Acts*, 147).

1020. For one comparison with Qumran (which sometimes de-emphasizes the Davidic Messiah), see Ruzer, "Unhappy." Josephus, while playing down messianism, certainly emphasizes the Davidic dynasty (Höffken, "Rolle"), perhaps foreshadowing the Herodian dynasty. For Davidic messianic connections in early Judaism and Luke-Acts, see Miura, *David*.

1021. Kilgallen, "Assumptions," emphasizes especially Luke 1:35 as informing how we should read Peter's speech. Matera, *Theology*, 63, notes that the Gospel's Christology (Luke 1:32–33) is completed only in the apostolic preaching in Acts. For the Davidic kingdom in Luke-Acts, see also Neubrand, *Völker*, 166–82.

1022. See Gen 24:7; 26:3; Exod 13:5, 11; 32:13; 33:1; Num 14:16, 23; 32:11; Deut 1:8; 4:31; 6:10, 13, 18, 23; 7:8, 12, 13; 8:1, 18; 9:5, 27; 10:11; 11:9, 21; 13:17; 19:8; 26:3, 15; 28:9, 11; 29:13; 30:20; 31:7, 20; 31:21, 23; 34:4; Josh 1:6; 21:43, 44; Judg 2:1; 1 Chr 16:16; Ps 105:9; Jer 11:5; 32:22; Bar 2:34; Sir 44:21; Wis 18:22. On the judicial function of oaths, cf. briefly Anderson, *Glossary*, 84–85; Keener, *Matthew*, 192–95.

1023. This throne is exalted (cf. Acts 7:49); God will also cast down rulers from their thrones (Luke 1:52) and establish the Twelve on thrones over Israel's tribes (22:30). The vice-regent role seems equivalent to that assigned to humanity in Gen 1:26–28, though there appears no hint of this text here.

1024. Hurschmann, "Furniture," 623 (on Greek furniture; Roman furniture was comparable, 624); idem, "Throne," 628. For animal decorations associated with thrones, cf., e.g., 1 Kgs 10:20; Rev 4:6.

Jewish literature.[1025] For Jesus to take David's throne *in heaven*, however, redefines the traditional Jewish expectation of Davidic rule.[1026]

Prophets often "foresaw" the future (Acts 2:31); indeed, in Jewish tradition, many patriarchs and prophets foresaw future eras. For example, various Jewish traditions emphasized that Abraham saw the future or at least some aspects of it in his vision in Gen 15:12–21.[1027] Later rabbinic tradition emphasized the future vision of the patriarchs Abraham, Isaac, and Jacob;[1028] thus, for example, Abraham foresaw the temples and all the kingdoms to come.[1029] Similarly, Jacob foresaw the temple's destruction and restoration and all the rabbinic academies,[1030] as well as some other revelations,[1031] although tradition was more ambivalent about Jacob's visions.[1032] In one source, Jacob prophesied to each tribe what it would experience until the days of the Messiah.[1033] Such traditions are late, but they develop an early nucleus that God revealed the future history of Israel to Jacob (*Jub.* 32:21). Others also receive such visions, such as Adam,[1034] Joseph,[1035] Amram,[1036] Moses,[1037] and R. Meir.[1038]

One late tradition suggests that David's body did not experience decay;[1039] Greek myth also spoke of substances (the gods' nectar and ambrosia) used to temporarily prevent a corpse's decomposition.[1040] The widespread belief in David's tomb could have countered such a supposition here, but it is unlikely that if this belief about David was known in the first century, it was widespread enough to invite Peter's polemic. Rather, he simply addresses the obvious: the incorruptible one is not David.

1025. E.g., *1 En.* 14:18–20; *2 En.* 1a.4; 20:3; 22:2; *3 En.* 33:4; *Test. Levi* 5; *b. Ḥag.* 13a; *Tg. Ps.-J.* on Gen 27:1. God is sometimes "the one seated on the throne" (e.g., Sir 1:8; 40:3; *Test. Mos.* 4:2; seated in heaven in *CIJ* 2:54, §802); cf. Zeus's throne (Hom. *Il.* 8.442; Virg. *Aen.* 10.116), as also Hera (Eurip. *Hel.* 241) and Artemis (Hom. *Il.* 9.533).

1026. Cf. Tuckett, "Christology," 162, noting that this royalty would not entail a revolt against the empire. Tuckett (164) contends that the character of Jesus's messiahship (exalted to heaven) differs from earlier expectations but that Luke is presenting earlier Christian Christologies rather than articulating his own.

1027. *4 Ezra* 3:14; *2 Bar.* 4:4; *L.A.B.* 23:6; *Apoc. Ab.* 9–32; *Gen. Rab.* 44:12. In Philo, Abraham encounters the Logos (*Migr.* 174 in Argyle, "Philo," 38; on Philo here, cf. more fully Philo *On the Change of Names* in Urban and Henry, "Abraham").

1028. E.g., *b. B. Bat.* 16b–17a, bar.

1029. E.g., *Pesiq. Rab Kah.* 5:2; *Gen. Rab.* 44:15, 22; 56:10; *Exod. Rab.* 51:7; *Lev. Rab.* 13:5; *Pesiq. Rab.* 15:2; cf. *2 Bar.* 4:4. The future vision of the patriarchs appears a favorite emphasis of *Genesis Rabbah*'s editors, but the earliest tradition refers especially to Abraham; "he went into the days" (Gen 24:1, lit.) may have provided a natural basis for rabbis assuming that Abraham saw the future world (e.g., Dodd, "Background," 334).

1030. *Gen. Rab.* 69:7; 97 NV; Joseph also wept for the destruction of the first and second temples (*Gen. Rab.* 93:10). In a tradition newly created in the third century, many biblical heroes saw a new world, but this may refer to their change in status (*Gen. Rab.* 30:8).

1031. He also foresaw Joseph's survival (*Tg. Ps.-J.* on Gen 37:33, opposite MT!), Jephthah's victory in Gilead (*Tg. Ps.-J.* on Gen 31:21), and Samson (*Gen. Rab.* 98:14). In earlier texts, Jacob receives a revelation apparently of the temple (4Q537 1–2; so Adam in *2 Bar.* 4:3); that Wisdom revealed God's reign to Jacob (Wis 10:10) may be relevant, though eschatologically oriented Jewish interpreters seem to have done little with this work.

1032. Some Tannaim felt that he lost his prophetic sight in Gen 48:10 (*Gen. Rab.* 97 MSV). In the Targumim (McNamara, *Targum*, 140), although Jacob looked for the messianic redemption (*Targum Neofiti*), he could not see it even in a vision (*Ps.-J.* on Gen 49:1).

1033. *Num. Rab.* 13:14, extrapolating from the tradition in Gen 49 (cf. *Testaments of the Twelve Patriarchs*). More simply, Jacob simply saw the Lord (i.e., the archangel) in Philo *Dreams* 1.157. *Tg. Neof.* 1 on Gen 49:1 allows him an eschatological revelation that he then forgot (cf. similarly *Tg. Ps.-J.* on Gen 49:1).

1034. *2 Bar.* 4:3; 'Abot R. Nat. 31 A; 42, §116 B; *b. Sanh.* 38b; *Gen. Rab.* 21:9; 24:2; *Pesiq. Rab.* 23:1.

1035. *Tg. Ps.-J.* on Gen 45:14.

1036. 4Q544 1 10–12; 4Q547 4 8.

1037. *Sipre Deut.* 357.5.11.

1038. *Num. Rab.* 9:20.

1039. Noted in Barrett, *Acts*, 146.

1040. Hom. *Il.* 19.37–39; 23.184–87.

III. Appeal to Testimony (2:32–33)

Peter next appeals to two forms of eyewitness: first, the apostolic eyewitnesses' testimony that Jesus rose and ascended (Acts 2:32) and, second, the eyewitness recognition of his audience members themselves that the eschatological Spirit has been poured out among them (2:33). Peter's bold claim, "We are witnesses," recurs frequently in the Petrine speeches in Acts (3:15; 5:32; 10:39).[1041] (On the witness motif at greater length, see comment on Acts 1:8.) The disciples were compelled to testify of what they had seen (cf. 4:20); other Jewish texts also indicated that one should testify of what one had seen of God's works (2 Macc 3:36). At various points in Acts, preachers announce Jesus as "this Jesus" (Acts 1:11; 2:32, 36; 9:22; 17:3), usually emphatically while citing powerful evidence.[1042] Eyewitness claims were, of course, significant "proofs" in rhetoric.[1043] But the crowds themselves were now also witnesses, seeing and hearing supernatural events (2:33).

Pentecost is connected theologically with Luke's recapitulation and ascension narrative. F. S. Spencer points out the following connections:

1. Visible supernatural phenomena accompany both (1:10–11; 2:2).
2. Prophecy in one (1:4–5, 8) is fulfilled in the other (2:1–13, 17–18).
3. The Galilean provenance of the disciples (1:11; 2:7) contrasts with the universal mission (1:8; 2:5).
4. Although Peter and the Twelve lead (1:2, 13, 15–26; 2:14, 37, 42–43), the entire community participates (1:15, 23–26; 2:41, 44–45), including women (1:14; 2:17–18).[1044]

Luke might even connect the ascension with Pentecost by analogous wording in Luke 9:51 and Acts 2:1,[1045] if this is not coincidental. Certainly, Luke closely connects the giving of the Spirit with the ascension (2:33).

Luke uses the expression "seen and heard" with both components together, but if we are to press specific distinctions into them, "seen" could refer to the tongues of fire if they were continuing (2:3); "heard" certainly refers to the Galileans' speaking other languages (ἀκούω in 2:6, 8, 11). Allusions to these two senses naturally occur together elsewhere in ancient literature[1046] (Acts 7:34), including for divine revelations.[1047] But the terms' conjunction is a frequent Lukan idiom: it usually applies to hearing and seeing signs (Luke 2:20; 7:22; 10:24 [Q Matt 13:15]; Acts 8:6; 22:14) and invites testimony (Luke 2:20; 7:22; Acts 4:20; 22:15).[1048] Probably Luke derived

---

1041. In Petrine literature, the term "witness" (frequent in the NT) applies to Peter in 1 Pet 5:1 (but also to the elders in Asia Minor); the concept might also appear in 2 Pet 1:16.

1042. Johnson, *Acts*, 27, compares "this Moses" (Acts 7:35), which derives from the tradition of his rejection (7:40; Exod 32:1, 23). "This man" applies to Jesus (Acts 2:23; 3:16), but the various forms of demonstrative that comprise it are common in Acts (twenty-five times). Rhetoric could employ repetition to underline a point (cf. Rowe, "Style," 133–34, on diaphora).

1043. With, e.g., Black, *Rhetoric of Gospel*, 128.

1044. Spencer, *Acts*, 23–24. The clearest of these is the second point, which may be further amplified by subpoints.

1045. Zwiep, *Ascension*, 184.

1046. Longus 2:30, ὅσα εἶδεν . . . ὅσα ἤκουσεν. In early Christian texts, e.g., John 3:32; 5:37; 8:38; Rom 11:8; 15:21; 2 Cor 12:6; Phil 1:30; 4:9; Jas 5:11; 2 Pet 2:8; 1 John 1:1, 3; *1 Clem.* 28.1; *Mart. Pol.* 9.1; also the oft-repeated formula in 1 Cor 2:9; *1 Clem.* 34.8; *2 Clem.* 11.7.

1047. E.g., Jer 23:18; Ezek 40:4; 44:5; Jos. *Ant.* 1.284; 2.275; Lucian *Icar.* 2 (and cf. *Men.* 14); Max. Tyre 8.2; Rev 8:13; 22:8.

1048. When used separately, the terms can also convey celebrating miracles (e.g., Luke 19:37), but their combination is emphatic.

the combination, consciously or unconsciously, especially from his Isa 6 quotation (Luke 8:10, 18; Acts 28:26–27; cf. Luke 10:24), though most of his own uses are more positive.

IV. CHRIST'S EXALTATION (2:33)

On the theological level, the Spirit's outpouring stems from Christ's exaltation (Acts 2:33).[1049] That Luke does not identify these moments precisely chronologically but allows more than a week between them (probably because of his historical sources) fits his willingness on other matters to let his narrative record stand in tension at points with his theological declarations. (For example, 2:38–39 tightly connects the gift of the Spirit with conversion theologically, but in 8:14–17 the Samaritan believers experience the Spirit after their conversion; see discussion of this matter at Acts 1:4–5.) In the same way, Jesus's resurrection and exaltation are theologically united as God's vindication of Jesus; the few weeks between them are irrelevant to the point. Christ's exaltation after the cross (also 5:31) also fits the divine pattern of God's exalting those who humble themselves, whether in the OT (e.g., Ps 138:6; Isa 2:11–12, 17; 57:15; Ezek 21:26) or Luke's and other early Christian texts (Luke 1:52; 14:11; 18:14; cf. Acts 7:9–10; 13:17; Phil 2:8–9).[1050]

If Jesus is in God's presence (Acts 2:25, 29), Peter can infer for his hearers that Jesus is in heaven. Peter here anticipates his dependence on the more explicit Ps 110:1 in Acts 2:34–35. If Jesus is already enthroned at the Father's right hand, then he has begun his messianic reign, and hence "the messianic age has begun and the messianic blessings have been given."[1051] Jesus receives royal authority at his exaltation (Luke 20:17, 42–43; 22:69; Acts 2:30–36), and the apostles also begin their eschatological positions of leadership (Luke 22:30; Acts 1:15–26).[1052] The outpouring of God's Spirit constitutes proof that the disciples' lord, Jesus, was reigning—hence risen.[1053]

Jesus's position here is familiar in terms of a viceroy or vizier.[1054] Sometimes this position could apply to a son installed or functioning as coregent (cf. 1 Kgs 1:35–37, 46);[1055] thus, for example, Titus dictated letters and "edicts in his father's name" and publicly read his speeches (Suet. *Titus* 6). A son or other favorite might also have special access to gaining a supreme ruler's favors for friends.[1056] Jesus's being at the Father's right hand to reign indicates that the kingdom has been inaugurated in some sense (Acts 1:3), though in some sense it remains not yet (1:6; 3:19–21). (On the "right hand" as a special position of honor, including at a throne, see comment at Acts 2:25.)

1049. As often noted; e.g., cf. Talbert, *Mediterranean Milieu*, 133. On Christ's exaltation in early Christian literature (including the Apostolic Fathers), see deSilva, "Exaltation"; for the ascension, see discussion at Acts 1:9–11.

1050. Cf. the same idea in Sir 11:5–6; 'Abot R. Nat. 11 A; 22 B; b. 'Ab. 6:4, bar.; 'Erub. 13b; Gen. Rab. 1:5; Der. Er. Zuṭ. 9 (following Moore, *Judaism*, 2:274; Lachs, *Commentary*, 368). Czachesz, "Logic," draws attention to the humiliation/exaltation pattern in Luke-Acts.

1051. Ladd, *Theology*, 337.

1052. See Tannehill, *Luke*, 269.

1053. On the connection with Jesus's death and resurrection, see also Kilgallen, "Pentecost."

1054. On Joseph and this post in ancient Egypt, cf., e.g., ANET 212–14 (esp. 213), 252, 412–14; Bright, *History*, 39; Smith, *Education*, 24; with regard to Joseph, Wright, *Archaeology*, 53; Yamauchi, *Stones*, 47; Thompson, *Archaeology*, 45.

1055. On ancient coregencies, see, e.g., Diod. Sic. 31.19.6 (in this case, his equal); Tac. *Ann.* 1.2; Bright, *History*, 52; Gordon, *Near East*, 63.

1056. Xen. *Cyr.* 1.3.14; 1.4.1.

v. The Spirit-Giver (2:33)

Jesus "pours out" the Spirit here, a clear allusion to God's pouring out the Spirit in 2:17–18 (the only other passage in Luke-Acts that uses ἐκχέω).[1057] Jewish texts also speak of God's pouring out wisdom (Sir 1:9) as his gift (1:10; cf. Acts 2:38); wisdom was often portrayed as water.[1058] This connection is relevant because wisdom sits by God's throne (Wis 9:4) and a stream of wisdom teaching did identify God's Spirit with his wisdom.[1059] But the closest parallel must be the one most explicit in the text; the allusion to Acts 2:17–18 indicates that Joel 2:28–29 is the primary background, whatever other images may contribute.[1060] If Jesus as God's agent pours out God's Spirit (cf. also Luke 3:16), he fulfills an explicitly divine role (cf. divine agency in Acts 5:32; 15:8).

"The promise of the Spirit" (i.e., the promised Spirit)[1061] in Acts 2:33 is "from the Father";[1062] this notice links the promise even more clearly with "the Father's promise" in Luke 24:49. Already in Luke 11:13 Jesus teaches that the Father will "give" the Spirit.[1063] In view of this connection, it is not surprising that this promise is also called the "gift" of the Spirit (Acts 2:38–39; Luke reserves the term "gift" for the Spirit, 8:20; 10:45; 11:17).

vi. Luke's Christology in 2:33

If Jesus is the Spirit-baptizer (Luke 3:16), he takes on a divine role in light of the OT, where only God can pour out God's Spirit (Isa 44:3; Ezek 39:29; Joel 2:28–29).[1064] The present verse (Acts 2:33) is among the most important for understanding Luke's Christology and pneumatology and their relationship with each other.[1065] This is a particularly key text for the work of Max Turner, one of the leading scholars on Lukan (and early Christian) pneumatology. Using this text and others, he rightly points out that Luke does not present an absentee Christology, with Jesus's return indefinitely deferred (*pace* Conzelmann); Jesus is enthroned as Messiah (as Luke 1–2 predicted)

1057. The variant form ἐκχύνω (ἐκχύννω) in Acts 10:45 is in the passive (ἐκκέχυται), not specifying who pours out the Spirit, but it is clear that this "gift" (δωρεά, 10:45) is from God (11:17; meanwhile 11:16, like 1:5, uses the passive for a prophecy earlier applied to Jesus [Luke 3:16]).

1058. Philo *Flight* 166; *Worse* 117; *Sib. Or.* 1.33–34; cf. Sir 24:21. Analogously, the rabbis identified the Torah with water, in m. 'Ab. 1:4; 2:8; *Mek. Vay.* 1:74ff.; *Bah.* 5:99; *Sipre Deut.* 48.2.7; 306.19.1; 306.22–25; 'Abot R. Nat. 18 A; cf. b. Ta'an. 7a; B. Qam. 17a; 82a; Gen. Rab. 41:9; 54:1; 69:5; 70:8–9; 84:16; 97:3; Exod. Rab. 31:3 (Wisdom); 47:5; Song Rab. 1:2, §3; as a well, Sipre Deut. 48.2.7; Pesiq. Rab Kah. 24:9; for heresy as bad water, m. 'Ab. 1:11; Sipre Deut. 48.2.5.

1059. See Wis 9:17; cf. 1:6–7; 7:22; for Philo, Isaacs, *Spirit*, 54–55; cf. also Keener, *John*, 963–64.

1060. Cf. Philo's depiction of the Logos as continually flowing from God, bringing order to creation (*Dreams* 2.249; cf. *Immut.* 155–58), which was probably modeled on Ganymede as Zeus's winepourer (Dillon, "Ganymede as Logos").

1061. See Johnson, *Acts*, 52, arguing for the epexegetical genitive, since the Spirit was promised (Luke 24:49); he notes that it fulfills also the "promises" to the patriarchs (1:55, 73; Acts 3:13, 25; 7:17) and that the gift of the Spirit "realizes the blessings promised to Abraham (Acts 2:39; 7:17; 13:23, 32; 26:6)" (in the present age, see also Eph 1:3; Gal 3:14; cf. Hag 2:5). As in Gal 3:14, the Spirit in the community's experience allows a rereading of the traditional promise (cf. Hays, *Echoes*, 110).

1062. Luke emphasizes God as Jesus's Father more often than as the disciples' Father (few of the latter examples appear in specially Lukan material; see Mowery, "God the Father," 132).

1063. See Tannehill, *Luke*, 239. Cf. also verbs of "receiving" with the Spirit in Acts. For God "giving" the Spirit in the LXX, see Haya-Prats, *Believers*, 5n6, citing 2 Kgs 19:7 and especially Num 11:29; Isa 42:1; Ezek 11:19; 36:26–27; 37:6, 14.

1064. For one consideration of the role of Acts' pneumatology in articulating Acts' Christology, see Larkin, "Spirit and Jesus" (esp. 138–39).

1065. Its centrality is frequently acknowledged; e.g., Mainville, "Jésus et l'Esprit"; idem, "Messianisme," esp. 327, recalling the connection between Jesus's identity and the Spirit as early as Luke 1:35. Bauckham, *Crucified*, 49–51, also shows the midrashic links among Isa 6:1; 52:13; 57:15; and sometimes Ps 110:1 in early Christianity (cf. John 12:38–41; Heb 1:3), perhaps facilitating the link with Ps 110 and divine Christology here.

and now reigns in his church by the Spirit.[1066] Instead of an "absentee Christology," Luke has a pervasive Christology "of soteriological omnipresence."[1067]

When analyzing the activity of the Spirit in ancient Jewish literature, Turner isolates a "messianic" use of the Spirit (Isa 11:2), which he sees as important in descriptions of Jesus and the Spirit in Luke-Acts.[1068] By relating the Spirit to Jesus in the way Jewish people had understood the Spirit's relationship to God (Acts 2:17–18, 33; 16:7; cf. Luke 3:16), Luke further "takes the reader beyond anything Judaism conceived of the messiah."[1069] Luke thus portrays Jesus as the "Lord of the Spirit," who gives God's Spirit in Acts 2:33; such a role necessarily involves a "high," even divine Christology (Luke 3:16).[1070] Having affirmed a high and present Christology, however, he denies (against Dunn) the paradigmatic function of Jesus's earthly empowerment by the Spirit.[1071] The latter conclusion must follow from the former premise only if Luke accepted "earthly paradigm" and "heavenly Lord" as mutually exclusive categories, but Luke does not.

Although Turner is largely right in what he affirms, he is surely mistaken in what he denies here. The risen Christ clearly holds a unique status,[1072] but the earthly Jesus also functioned as a model for disciples in Acts, as the strong parallels between the two works demonstrate.[1073] Luke's Jesus was more than a prophet, but Luke does not force his audience to therefore reject Jesus's prophetic status or his dependence on the Spirit for activities that are not solely messianic (e.g., Acts 10:38). Disciples are not messiahs, but Jesus's ministry is paradigmatic for the church's, and the programmatic statement of Luke 4:18–19 is related to, though distinct from, the programmatic statement of Acts 2:17–18 (see comment on Acts 1:4–5, 8; 2:17–18).

Scholars cite various analogies on which Luke might draw for describing Jesus as the one whom God has delegated to provide the gift of the Spirit.[1074] Given the possible associations between Pentecost and the law-giving in Jewish tradition (noted in the introduction to Acts 2, at "Covenant Renewal and the Pentecost Festival," above),[1075] many scholars see a background in Moses's ascending on the mountain (and, in some

1066. See Turner, *Power*, 296–97.

1067. Ibid., 305 (following O'Toole, *Unity of Theology*, chs. 2–3). Cf. Dodd, *Preaching*, 22, 26: one element of the kerygma is that the Spirit in the church is "the sign of Christ's present power and glory" (also Ladd, *Theology*, 329).

1068. E.g., Turner, *Gifts*, 17–18; idem, *Power*, 114–18; for the Spirit and the Messiah in Isa 11, see Ma, *Spirit*, 211 (he distinguishes [213] the prophetic and leadership aspects of the Spirit except where, as in Isa 42:1–3 and 61:1, a single figure integrates both). I would argue that Turner's approach here risks confusing categories; what the Spirit does and whom the Spirit anoints are distinct ways of categorizing the evidence. Thus, e.g., the Spirit of prophecy does not cease to be the prophetic Spirit simply because it is on the Messiah. But this potential confusion does not diminish the importance of the evidence he cites (and Turner also provides questions about my own categorization of the evidence in "Review," 70–71).

1069. Turner, *Power*, 277–78 (quote, 277); idem, "Spirit of Christ and Christology" (esp. 190); idem, "'Divine' Christology," 436. I agree with Turner on the christological implications of such a pneumatology (Keener, *Matthew*, 130); cf. also Acts 16:7; Rom 8:9; Phil 1:19; 1 Pet 1:11.

1070. For the special power for Israel's renewal involved in Jesus's enthronement, see Turner, *Power*, 268, 290–97; for the Spirit's acting as Jesus's executive power, see Turner, *Power*, 303; for divine Christology, see Buckwalter, "Saviour," 107–23, esp. 115.

1071. See Turner, "Jesus and Spirit in Perspective"; idem, *Gifts*, 35; idem, *Power*, 188–266, esp. 212, 266. Contrast, e.g., Crowe, *Acts*, xxi, for whom 2:33 itself simply adds irony to the parallel (Jesus now gives to the disciples as the Father anointed him).

1072. The Gospels themselves mostly reveal a higher Christology (or greater homage) after the resurrection (see Hurtado, "Homage").

1073. See Goulder, *Type and History*; Talbert, *Patterns*; Tannehill, *Acts*; see also our introduction, ch. 16.

1074. Cf. Elisha's receiving Elijah's spirit because of the latter's ascent (Sir 48:12).

1075. E.g., Jacquin, "Worte in der Erziehung"; see further the introduction to Acts 2; comment on Acts 2:2–3.

Jewish traditions, to heaven)[1076] to receive the law as a gift for Israel.[1077] (For the law as a "gift," see comment on Acts 2:38; it is identified with the "promise" in 2:39 and hence also here. For Jewish haggadah on Moses's ascent, including its heavenly extent, see comment on Acts 7:38; compare also comment on ascents at Acts 1:9–11.) Thus Jesus here "received" the promise of the Spirit as Moses "received" inspired oracles to pass on (7:38).[1078] In support of such a Moses analogy, some scholars find a specific echo of Ps 68:18, which Jewish interpreters associated (perhaps rightly) with Sinai and which later Jewish tradition may have used as a reading on Pentecost.[1079] Some early Christians, at least, applied this verse from the psalms to Christ's triumphant exaltation to offer a multifaceted gift to his church (Eph 4:8). Jewish literature also portrays Wisdom[1080] as a divine gift (4Q185 1–2 II, 8–11), including in a context where God "pours out" (ἐξέχεεν) wisdom (Sir 1:9–10) as God pours out his Spirit in this verse. If there are Moses parallels here, they are not very explicit; nevertheless, they would fit the "prophet like Moses" Christology of Acts 3:22–23 and 7:37.[1081]

Some others see only a Davidic promise here (cf. Ps 89:19), based on the immediate context in Acts 2:25–34; David's promise seems to be the most explicit background of Jesus's enthronement, even if it offers no other striking parallels here.[1082] It is possible that Luke draws on several backgrounds to varying degrees.[1083]

VII. The Exalted Lord of Psalm 110 (2:34)

In 2:29–31, Peter shows that David, being dead and buried, could not fulfill the promise of resurrection or incorruption he finds in Ps 16; after attesting Jesus's exaltation in Acts 2:32–33, he produces another key text that David, not having ascended, could not fulfill (2:34–35). Peter continues his argument that the promise could not fully apply to David himself (see comment on Acts 2:29 for this kind of argument); he claims that it is self-evident that Ps 110:1, with which Peter links Ps 16, *cannot* apply to David (both because David did not ascend and because he speaks of his Lord).

Jewish tradition attributed ascensions to several biblical characters (see comment on Acts 1:9–11), but so far as our extant sources reveal, David was not one of them. Peter did not need to respond to potential objections that the psalm applied to others, since probably no one nonmessianic candidate was widely cited in his day. In the mid-second century, Justin refutes the supposed Jewish claim that the psalm referred to Hezekiah (Justin *Dial.* 33), but Jewish sources themselves (and these later than Justin) suggest at most that a later rabbi proposed that Hezekiah was the Messiah.[1084]

1076. E.g., Aristob. frg. 4 (Euseb. *P.E.* 13.13.5); Philo *QE* 2.46; *Sipre Deut.* 49.2.1; *b. Šabb.* 88b; *Exod. Rab.* 28:1; 41:5; 47:5; *Lev. Rab.* 1:15; *Pesiq. Rab.* 20:4; 47:4; *3 En.* 15B:2; cf. *L.A.B.* 12:1. Some scholars think that the rabbinic emphasis on Moses's ascent might respond to Christian claims for Jesus (cf. Van de Water, "Moses' Exaltation"); others, that the Christian claim might respond at times to claims about Moses (cf. Meeks, *Prophet-King*, 295–97; Keener, *John*, 562–63).

1077. E.g., Turner, *Power*, 267, 279–89.

1078. For the parallel, see Johnson, *Acts*, 46 (though, for what it is worth, Luke uses ἐδέξατο in Acts 7:38 and λαβὼν in 2:33).

1079. See Turner, *Power*, 288; Dupont, "Don de l'Esprit"; idem, *Salvation*, 35; Lincoln, *Paradise*, 158. It applies to Moses's ascension in later texts, e.g., *Exod. Rab.* 28:1; *Ruth Rab.* 2:3; *Pesiq. Rab.* 20:4; 21:7; 47:4. Marshall, "Acts," 541, suggests that if such an allusion is present, it may reflect Luke's tradition rather than Luke's own allusion, since he makes nothing of it (cf. Strauss, *Messiah*, 145–47).

1080. Identified with Torah in Sir 24:23; 34:8 [31:8]; 39:1; Bar 3:29–4:1; 4 Macc 1:16–17; *Sipre Deut.* 37.1.3; later, *Gen. Rab.* 17:5; 31:5; 44:17; *Lev. Rab.* 11:3; 19:1; *Eccl. Rab.* 1:4, §4; *Pesiq. Rab.* 20:1; see more fully Urbach, *Sages*, 1:198–99, 287; Hengel, *Judaism*, 1:169–71; Keener, *John*, 354–55.

1081. Cf. Turner, *Power*, 302.

1082. Cf. Steyn, *Septuagint Quotations*, 120–21.

1083. Cf. Turner, *Power*, 267.

1084. See Williams, *Justin Martyr*, 15 (citing *b. Sanh.* 99a).

More commonly, the psalm may have been applied to the Messiah; the rabbinic tradition applying it to Abraham (e.g., *Midr. Pss.* 110)[1085] is probably polemic against the exaltation of Melchizedek (cf. Ps 110:4; Gen 14:18–20) in some circles that they considered heterodox (cf. 11QMelch; Heb 7:4–10).[1086]

Some scholars have suggested that Ps 110 may have been one of the readings during the Pentecost festival;[1087] whether or not this is the case, its use was pervasive in early Christianity in many contexts without direct relation to Pentecost (Mark 12:36; Luke 20:42; 22:69; Eph 1:20; Col 3:1; Heb 1:13; 8:1).

Because "Lord" is not a title of Jesus in other speeches in Acts, some have regarded its presence here as a late addition.[1088] Yet the church's use of the title "Lord" for Jesus was certainly dominant well before Luke wrote (and before the later speeches in Acts would have occurred); it is Paul's primary title for Jesus and appears in every part of early Christianity (including Jas 2:1, though James barely addresses Christology elsewhere).[1089] Its absence in most speeches could suggest that Luke believed that this Christology evolved gradually in the early church (which would contradict Luke 20:41–44 and Acts 2:34–35); more likely, it suggests that he doubted that the earliest Christians preached the title directly to new hearers without explaining it (contrast the speech to believers, e.g., Acts 11:16; 15:26; 20:19, 21, 24, 35; 21:13). Even here there are exceptions (22:10, 19; 26:15; cf. 10:36). (For other details of the "Lord" title, especially with regard to God, in addition to those noted here, see comment on Acts 2:21.)

Even as a title for the Messiah, "Lord" is hardly a post-Lukan development; the pre-Christian work called the *Psalms of Solomon* speaks of the "Lord Messiah" (χριστὸς κύριος,[1090] *Pss. Sol.* 17:32) and probably is interpreting Ps 110:1, since the pseudepigraphic psalm goes on to identify the Messiah's king as the "Lord himself" (κύριος αὐτός, 17:46). That is, the basic line of interpretation was established even before Jesus; Christian sources differ from this pre-Christian tradition only in associating this title with Jesus's deity (see Acts 2:21, 38).

Some scholars argue that the earliest church used Ps 110 to describe the resurrection but only in later times (probably in the Hellenistic church) applied it to Jesus's lordship.[1091] Others think that Luke-Acts depicts people calling Jesus "Lord" in more than a respectful way only after the resurrection and hence faithfully reports historical tradition even when it does call Jesus "Lord."[1092] But the title even before the resurrection is significant for Luke, if not for those in the narrative world; it is our theological reading of Luke-Acts, rather than grammar, that decides what characters mean by the vocative form of "Lord" on the larger Lukan level.[1093] Against the view that the earliest church applied Ps 110 only to Jesus's resurrection, the psalm itself describes the

1085. Also *b. Ned.* 32b; *Gen. Rab.* 46:5; *Lev. Rab.* 25:6; the connection is noted by some commentators (e.g., Buchanan, *Hebrews*, 121). Cf. the application of Ps 45:8 to Abraham (*Pesiq. Rab Kah.* 16:4; *Gen. Rab.* 39:6; 49:9; *Lev. Rab.* 10:1; *Pesiq. Rab.* 29/30A:4 [but contrast Isaiah in 29/30A:5]; 33:3 [also Isaiah]).

1086. In view of the probable use in *Pss. Sol.* 17:32, 46, the proposal of Bodendorfer, "Rechten," that the Abraham interpretation precedes the Davidic Messiah interpretation cannot be sustained.

1087. Delcor, "Bundesfest und Pfingstfest."

1088. Robinson, *Studies*, 141 (he excludes [n. 7] 10:36 because it uses "Jesus Christ" as a name and hence betrays a later stage).

1089. See further Longenecker, *Christology*, 120–36; Keener, *John*, 297–98.

1090. The reading χριστὸς κυρίου is an emendation. Cf. Luke 2:11; Rom 16:18; Col 3:24.

1091. Loader, "Christ at Right Hand."

1092. Longenecker, *Wine*, 97–99.

1093. The vocative κύριε appears about twenty-five times (the exact count depends on textual variants) before the resurrection (including uses in parables) and about fifteen times afterward (including addresses to the Father in prayers).

exaltation and lordship (at least kingly lordship) but not directly the resurrection.[1094] Against weakening the title's christological content on the Lukan level, that "Lord" was a Jewish as well as Hellenistic title is clear from the LXX.[1095]

In support of the antiquity of Ps 110 in the early church[1096] is that its usage is pervasive. (This is an argument based on probability, not certainty, since a later idea could easily be deemed useful widely enough to spread in the church of its era; but were Christ's exalted lordship a later idea, it should not have spread with less resistance than Paul's refusal to demand Gentile circumcision, and it certainly should not have spread from Gentile to Jewish circles.) Whereas one of the few obvious allusions to Ps 110 in extant non-Christian Jewish literature from before about 200 C.E. is the *Testament of Job* (*Test. Job.* 33:3), where it is applied to Job's exaltation (in a nondivine way), it is prevalent in early Christianity. Bauckham counts twenty-one quotations or allusions scattered throughout the entire NT corpus (except John, who could not be accused of denying the exalted Christology other Christians found there).[1097] The Christians also consistently used the text in an exalted manner.[1098]

The Christian application went beyond contemporary usage. Thus Ps 110:4 (the Melchizedek priesthood) is at the heart of the extended midrash in Heb 5:6–7:28,[1099] but Heb 1:13 applies Ps 110:1 in the context of verses on Christ's deity making him greater than the angels (three texts in Heb 1:6, 8–9, 10–12). Although biblical tradition recognized that at least some people could reign under God (Gen 1:27; Dan 7:13–14), many Jews would have viewed Jesus's exaltation to God's own throne to participate in his rule as threatening monotheism.[1100]

"My lord" who is addressed in the original psalm could be the psalmist's king (cf. Acts 25:26),[1101] but if one assumes Davidic authorship for the psalm, as most first-century hearers would have done, "my Lord" becomes someone greater (Luke 20:41, 44).[1102] (A midrashic connection to Ps 16:2 also suggests the deity of "my lord," as it is

---

1094. But Judaism sometimes connected resurrection with exaltation (*1 En.* 62:14–16; *2 Bar.* 51:5, 10; *Test. Benj.* 10:6, 9; cf. Dan 12:1–3; so Marshall, *Acts*, 160, following Anderson, "Resurrection," 171).

1095. See more fully Longenecker, *Christology*, 130–32; and discussion at Acts 2:21.

1096. Its messianic use seems to be pre-Pauline (see Hays, *Conversion*, 109).

1097. Second-century Christianity continues the usage; e.g., Justin *Dial.* 32; *1 Apol.* 45.

1098. Bauckham, *Crucified*, 29–30. For divine use of Ps 110:1, cf. also Marshall, *Origins*, 97–111; Hanson, *Unity*, 154; for the most extensive survey, see Hay, *Glory at Right Hand*.

1099. On Melchizedek's exalted, sometimes supernatural, status, see 11QMelch; *2 En.* 71–72; Philo *Alleg. Interp.* 3.82; see further de Jonge and Van der Woude, "11QMelchizedek," esp. 321; Kobelski, "Melchizedek," esp. 120, 138–39; Carmignac, "Melkisédeq"; Laubscher, "Angel of Truth"; Caquot, "Jubilés" (his role in *Jubilees* prefiguring 11QMelch); Puech, "Manuscrit"; Fitzmyer, "Melchizedek"; idem, *Essays*, 221–67; McNamara, "Melchizedek"; Schniedewind, "Melchizedek"; Longenecker, *Christology*, 113–14, 117–18. There is a lacuna at this place in *Jubilees* (*Jub.* 13:22–27), whether because the Maccabees used Melchizedek as a model (Charles, *Jubilees*, lxxxviii) or, likelier, because some exalted him too highly (cf. Fitzmyer, *Apocryphon*, 174–75); some think that *Jubilees* used Melchizedek as a model for the priesthood (Caquot, "Livre"). Apparently various marginal groups used Melchizedek (Vivian, "Movimenti"; Garuti, "Melchisedek"; but specific links with Hebrews [cf. Longenecker, "Melchizedek Argument"; Carmignac, "Melkisédeq"; Yadin, "Melchizedek"] are questionable [Cockerill, "Melchizedek"]) whereas later rabbis claimed that Abraham displaced him (e.g., *b. Ned.* 32b); but cf. his exalted role again in *Pesiq. Rab Kah.* 5:9; *b. Sukkah* 52b; *Song Rab.* 2:13, §4; *Pesiq. Rab.* 15:14/15. Qumran may use him as a Messiah figure (Sabugal, "1QRegla"; Rainbow, "Melchizedek"); some have even argued that Qumran sectarians viewed their Teacher of Righteousness as Melchizedek incarnate (Tantlevskij, "Melchizedek"), though I am not persuaded.

1100. Bauckham, *Crucified*, 28–29. Cf. *m. Sanh.* 4:5; *Sipre Deut.* 329.1.1; *b. Sanh.* 38ab (mainly third century but with some second-century tradition); *Pesiq. Rab.* 21:6; *3 En.* 16:2 (but cf. 12:5); perhaps also *b. Menaḥ.* 110a (purportedly Tannaitic); Justin *Dial.* 55, 63; further discussion in Keener, *John*, 203.

1101. If one does not take reigning at the right hand literally, with reference to God's heavenly throne, but as an earthly vizier.

1102. Cf. the abundance of exalted figures in early Judaism, noted in Bock, *Blasphemy*, 112–83. Miura, *David*, 146, notes the irrelevance of the figures David addressed as "my lord" (Saul, 1 Sam 24:7, 9, 11; 26:17–19;

addressed directly to God.)[1103] This fits the exposition here, where this "Lord" bears the specific divine name on which hearers must call to be saved (Acts 2:21, quoting Joel). The assumption of the second lord's divinity in Ps 110:1 helps explain why even most biblically literate Gentiles would understand that the divine name stands behind the LXX's κύριος cited in Acts 2:21. For Luke, this interpretation of the psalm goes back to Jesus (Luke 20:41–44) and would have been among the teachings Jesus provided his disciples (24:27, 44–45).

VIII. UNTIL HIS ENEMIES BECOME HIS FOOTSTOOL (2:35)

The remainder of the quotation in Acts 2:35 is hardly simple decoration; it carries theological weight for Luke. It is significant that Luke (who also expands on a Markan quotation in Luke 3:4–6) includes more of the Ps 110 quotation than does Mark (Mark 12:44; followed by Matt 22:44), both in Luke 20:43 and in Acts 2:35 (only Heb 1:13 and 10:13 also include the rest). Although Luke's primary point in quoting Ps 110 is Christology, the rest of 110:1 also supports the eschatology he establishes in Acts 1:6–8 and 2:17–18. In this eschatology, Jesus's present reign is an interim period until its consummation (1:6–7; 3:21). The "horn of salvation" in David's house (Luke 1:69) would bring "salvation" from enemies (1:71, 74)—presumably the "enemies" here made into his footstool.[1104] Jesus's reign was heavenly, his enemies earthly (especially likely if early Christians linked Ps 110:1 with Isa 66:1 by means of *gezerah shevah*; cf. Acts 7:49). Jesus has left earth to receive a kingdom but will return (Luke 19:12)[1105] at the time of his enemies' subjugation (cf. 19:27), ending the interim period and establishing the kingdom (cf., perhaps similarly, 1 Cor 15:24–26).[1106]

First-century readers would still understand the metaphor of enemies being made a footstool.[1107] Prisoners had long been symbolically "trampled underfoot,"[1108] as lavishly illustrated, for example, by Egyptian royal sandals with bound prisoners portrayed on the soles[1109] or by royal footstools with images of them bound.[1110] In classical Athens, people could claim ownership of objects, and hence seize them, by stepping on them;[1111] this seems to reflect a wider practice in antiquity.[1112] In addition to corporate enemies

---

and Achish, 1 Sam 29:8). Thus he suggests (146–47) a historical application to Solomon (1 Chr 29:23 LXX; 1 Kgs 1:48; 5:3–4 [LXX 5:17–18]), with applicability in principle to the Messiah (147–48).

1103. Apart from Ps 110:1, this is one of only two other uses of "my lord" in the canonical corpus of Psalms (cf. also Ps 151:3 LXX).

1104. Some people used backless footstools to sit on (Hurschmann, "Furniture," 623; cf. Jas 2:3), but linked with a throne, they were for resting feet (Acts 7:49).

1105. The historical model for Luke 19:12 could be Herod (Ladd, *Kingdom*, 21) or Archelaus (Kodell, *Luke*, 92–93; Schweizer, *Matthew*, 471; Young, *Parables*, 166; Reicke, *Era*, 133; Jeremias, *Parables*, 59), though the situation it envisions could also be illustrated more generally (cf., e.g., *Apoll. K. Tyre* 24; perhaps *Pesiq. Rab.* 21:9). Luke 19:14 fits both Herod (cf. Reicke, *Era*, 92–93) and Archelaus, both of whom were hated.

1106. Eph 1:20–21 (cf. also 6:12) apparently interprets the psalmist's enemies as present spiritual powers; "this age and the age to come" alludes both to Jesus's present exaltation and to the psalm's coming time of enemies under his feet.

1107. See van der Horst, "Parallels to Acts," 57 (citing Ovid *Fasti* 4.857–58; *Tristia* 4.2.44; *Pont.* 9.12–13; Virgil *Aen.* 10.495–96; Bömer, *Kommentar*, 282–83). The image of treading down enemies is even more widespread (e.g., Job 40:12; Pss 60:12; 108:13; Isa 25:10; 28:3; 41:25; 63:2–3, 6; Lam 1:15; Zech 10:5; Mal 4:3; Sen. Y. *Ep. Lucil.* 94.56).

1108. After slaying Tiamat, Marduk stood on her carcass (earth; *Enuma Elish* 4.104, in Heidel, *Genesis*, 40–41); ancient Near Eastern art portrays conquerors stepping on their victims' backs (Kitchen, *Orient*, 164; Pfeiffer, *Ras Shamra*, 60).

1109. Ritner, *Mechanics*, 119–36, esp. 123–24; cf. Niehaus, *Themes*, 67, 73.

1110. Hayes, "Oracles," 90–91 (referring [90n36] to Tutankhamen's footstool). In Quint. Curt. 5.2.15, Alexander uses his enemy's table as a footstool.

1111. See Thür, "Embateuein."

1112. At Nuzi, a buyer claimed ownership by placing a foot on the ground (de Vaux, *Israel*, 169, comparing also Pss 60:8; 108:9).

of their people, many individuals had personal enemies in their own town (sometimes creditors)[1113] and might take advantage of unstable situations to kill them.[1114] The idiom of those under one's feet being subjected would be especially clear in light of Scripture (1 Kgs 5:3 [LXX 5:17]; Pss 8:6 [8:7]; 47:4 [46:5]; 18:38 [17:39]).

IX. CONCLUSION: LORD AND KING (2:36)

Speakers commonly provided a final summation (κεφάλαιον, as in Heb 8:1) of their argument,[1115] and Luke provides this in Acts 2:36. The proclamatory "Let all the house of Israel know" fits such a climax.[1116] Jesus is the "Lord" of 2:21 (Joel) by way of 2:34–35 (Ps 110). He is "Christ" as in Acts 2:31—that is, the king from David's line, climaxing the Davidic emphasis in the sermon. As Barnabas Lindars notes, "The argument of the 'Resurrection speech' can be summarized in v. 36: the Resurrection proves that Jesus is both Lord, the literal fulfiller of Ps. 110, and Christ, the literal fulfiller of Ps. 16."[1117] Peter may use ἀσφαλῶς emphatically, underlining the appropriateness of how his conclusion follows from his established premises (cf. Acts 21:34; 22:30; 25:26; Luke 1:4).[1118] Peter has narrated certain truth in his speech just as Luke has in his two-volume work (Luke 1:4).[1119]

That Jesus is Messiah (i.e., Israel's king) and that he is Lord at God's right hand are truth claims that demand universal allegiance; that is, they demand the response of all humanity. Israel should accept its king, but Samaritans and Gentiles should also submit to this true lordship.[1120] "King," however, was a dangerous title in the Roman world (cf. Acts 17:7), whereas "Lord" could be construed in less political, purely religious terms.

Although Bultmann doubted that "Lord" by itself could function as a divine title, it is widely attested in extrabiblical texts in Greek, Hebrew, and Aramaic; given the argument it climaxes (see 2:21, 38), it surely functions as a divine title here.[1121] (See fuller discussion of this point at Acts 2:21.)

But together with the title "Christ," it emphasizes Jesus's kingship and hence that he fulfills Israel's hope and that Israel must embrace him as their rightful ruler.[1122] In

1113. E.g., Sen. E. *Controv.* 5.2; for creditors, see Thucyd. 3.81.2, 4. In a culture emphasizing greetings, some teachers defined as a personal enemy a person who has not spoken to you for a month (Abrahams, *Studies* [2], 213); personal enmity was also intelligible even in the setting of Galilean villages (Horsley, "Ethics"; Freyne, *Galilee, Jesus*, 154).

1114. E.g., Thucyd. 3.81.2, 4; cf. Sen. E. *Controv.* 10.1.intro. Although Luke uses philosophic language at points, he is far from offering a Stoic discussion of "enemies" as merely negative "externals" (Arius Did. *Epit.* 2.7.5e, pp. 30–31.12–13), though Stoics did speak of the senseless as enemies of the gods (2.7.11k, pp. 84–85.28–33).

1115. Isaeus *Cleon.* 48 (out of 51 paragraphs); Aeschines *Tim.* 196; *Rhet. Alex.* 36, 1443b.15–16; 1444b.21–35; 37, 1445b.21–23; Cic. *Fin.* 5.32.95–96; *Or. Brut.* 40.137; Polyb. 39.8.3; Dion. Hal. *Demosth.* 32; *Thuc.* 55; Mus. Ruf. 6, pp. 54.26–56.11, esp. 54.26; 56.7–11; Ael. Arist. *Leuct. Or.* 5.43–44; Hippol. *Her.* 10.1; see further Anderson, *Rhetorical Theory*, 181–82; comment on Acts 28:30–31.

1116. Concluding statements sometimes even took the form of exclamations (see Rowe, "Style," 148, on epiphonema; cf. Porter, "Paul and Letters," 583). "Know therefore" or "see therefore" was natural in argumentation (e.g., Epict. *Diatr.* 1.11.39).

1117. Lindars, *Apologetic*, 46.

1118. As with the usage in Acts 16:23 and Mark 14:44, the cognates can also apply to something being secure, whether a prison (Acts 5:23; 16:33–34) or a certainty that something is true (Wis 18:6; Heb 6:19); cf. Knowling, "Acts," 89.

1119. Gaventa, *Acts*, 79.

1120. Whether as members of the "commonwealth" of Israel (see Brawley, "Commonwealth") or as spiritual proselytes (see discussion at Acts 15).

1121. See Fitzmyer, *Acts*, 260 (he also refers to his fuller expositions in idem, *Luke*, 200–204; idem, *Wandering Aramean*, 115–42); Buckwalter, "Saviour," 107–23, esp. 107.

1122. To the extent that this challenged the temple hierarchy that abetted Jesus's death, it would have sounded political; but the situation was a special one for Israel (Acts 3:19–21), not relevant to Gentile politics (Luke 20:35).

Hebrew idiom, one could "appoint" or "install" someone to an office (especially, to "place" them, שׂים, e.g., Exod 1:11; 1 Sam 8:1; or to "give" them, נתן, e.g., 1 Sam 12:13; 1 Kgs 1:48; 2:35; 2 Kgs 8:6; 2 Chr 2:11; 9:8), though the LXX rarely uses ποιέω to express this.[1123] The language of "appointing" refers to status, not ontology, and hence is appropriate for Jesus beginning only at his exaltation.[1124] This sort of "Messiah-designate-until-enthroned" Christology seems to have been an early one in the church.[1125]

Although the language ("appointed him Lord") may not be the preferred language of later generations of Christians (a realization that might favor primitive tradition here), neither does it reflect an early tradition incorporated by Luke that remained inconsistent with the Christology articulated in the rest of the sermon. As Tannehill notes, "The connections indicated show that Acts 2:36 should not be separated from the rest of the speech as a fragment of an early adoptionist Christology that conflicts with the narrator's views."[1126] The Christology of Acts 2:36 seems designed, in fact, to close the sermon it follows (a "summation," as suggested above).[1127]

In accordance with the "appropriateness" expected for speeches in ancient histories (see introduction, ch. 8), preaching Jesus as "Messiah" seems to be an appropriate emphasis in many sermons to Israel in Acts, generally missing in sermons to Gentiles (2:36; 3:18–20; 5:42; 8:5; 9:22; 17:2–3; 18:5, 28; 26:22–23).[1128]

Excursus: Messiahship[1129]

How would Luke's first audience understand the claim about Jesus's being "Christ"? There was no single interpretation of messiahship in the first century, but at the heart of most messianic expectation was an ultimate Davidic ruler associated with the eschatological restoration of Israel.

1. Views of Messiahship

The prophets had foretold an eschatological king and/or dynasty descended from David,[1130] a theme that continued in early Judaism.[1131] Because the king was the

---

1123. It is not impossible Greek; cf. Plut. *Alex.* 27.4, where it was given (δίδωσιν) to Alexander to be "lord" (κυρίῳ).

1124. Rowe, "Continuity," argues that the real shift in Acts 2:36 relates to human perception of Jesus's identity (see Luke 1:43; 2:11).

1125. Longenecker, *Christology*, 66–73; Polhill, *Acts*, 111; cf. Keener, *Matthew*, 262–63. Foundations for most of NT Christology (such as *Marana tha*) probably predate Paul's conversion (Hengel, *Jesus and Paul*, 30–47). Zehnle, *Pentecost Discourse*, 68–69, nuances it differently: rather than a Messiah-designate, there were different stages in the status of messiahship (Luke 2:26).

1126. Tannehill, *Acts*, 38; cf. Witherington, *Acts*, 149.

1127. For a survey of various views on Christology (esp. 1948–77) in Luke-Acts, see, e.g., Bovon, *Theologian*, 109–97 (on messiahship, see 187–88; on "Lord," 189–92).

1128. Longenecker, *Wine*, 93–94.

1129. Adapted from Keener, *John*, 283–91; see further Fitzmyer, *One*.

1130. E.g., Isa 9:7; Jer 23:5. That the eschatological ruler would be a restoration after the Davidic rule had been cut off was suggested by preexilic prophets (Jesse's "stump" in Isa 11:1; Amos 9:11 [on the authenticity of the latter, see discussion at Acts 15:16–18).

1131. *Pss. Sol.* 17:21; 4Q252 V, 1–4; *b. Sanh.* 97b–98a; *y. Sukkah* 5:1, §7; *Gen. Rab.* 88:7; *Song Rab.* 2:13, §4; *Pesiq. Rab.* 15:14/15; *Tg. Jer.* 30:9; the inscription in Yardeni, "Scroll." See Fitzmyer, *Essays*, 113–26; Longenecker, *Christology*, 109–10; Kee, *Community*, 126, esp. on the Dead Sea Scrolls.

"anointed one,"[1132] Jewish people often granted the eschatological anointed king, the king par excellence, the articular title "the Messiah," which came into the LXX regularly as "the Christ" (as "the anointed one" normally did in what we would regard as nonmessianic usages as well).

The Gospels provide the impression that Palestinian Jews in general understood the term "Messiah" and expected his coming. Given the term's inadequacy in the Diaspora and in later Christian Christology (son of David Christology is far less prominent than wisdom, lord, and other Christologies), it is unlikely that the Gospels would have simply invented this usage. Yet our first-century evidence on the issue is disparate; some of it, especially texts directed toward Diaspora audiences, makes minimal use of the term. But this lack of use may say more about our sources than about first-century Palestinian Judaism's messianic expectations.

Josephus's omission of messianic data is understandable; writing for a Diaspora readership, seeking to minimize Judaism's revolutionary involvement, he has reason to play down messiahs and messianic ideals among the people that could have political implications.[1133] Josephus may have even toned down David's revolutionary activity and ancestry for the Messiah.[1134] He elsewhere suppresses Jewish ideas that would present them badly to the Romans and undoubtedly does the same with messiahship, "though certain of the persons whom he describes as brigands and deceivers must really have been messianic pretenders."[1135] Yet the nature of such messiahs varied: not all such messiahs were necessarily associated with militant resistance. If the Samaritan prophet, Theudas, or the Egyptian prophet were messianic figures, they looked instead to a miraculous divine intervention to establish God's reign.[1136]

The failed Bar Kokhba revolt of 132–35 C.E. led to Hadrian's establishment of pagan Aelia Capitolina on the site of Jerusalem, and the Romans flayed alive R. Akiba, one of the primary sources for the Mishnaic tradition of R. Judah ha-Nasi's academy, which edited the Mishnah. It should therefore not surprise us that the earliest rabbinic texts generally preserve a much more cautious approach to messianism, where it has not been suppressed altogether, than later texts that have returned to contemplation on biblical prophecies about the Son of David.[1137] Such skepticism is reported of R. Johanan ben Zakkai, who survived the destruction of 70 C.E.: finish what you are doing before going out to greet a messianic claimant.[1138] But even in the late second century, rabbis still reportedly hoped for the coming of the Messiah.[1139]

Other texts, however, emphasize messianic hopes.[1140] For example, the fourteenth and fifteenth benedictions of the Amidah, probably rooted in the pre-70

1132. A concept that made more sense in some ancient Near Eastern (especially Egyptian and Hittite) than in Hellenistic settings; see de Vaux, *Israel*, 104; cf. *ANET* 338 (though this is merely ritual anointing).

1133. Cf., e.g., Witherington, *Christology*, 83.

1134. Cf. Feldman, "David."

1135. Kraeling, *John the Baptist*, 52. Some professed signs prophets also sought kingship in broader Mediterranean culture (Diod. Sic. 34/35.2.5–6, 22–23).

1136. See Freyne, *Galilee, Jesus*, 194–95, on Jos. *Ant.* 18.85–87; 20.97–98, 169–71; *War* 2.261–66; Acts 5:36; 21:38; cf. also Crossan, *Jesus*, 158–68. Horsley and Hanson, *Bandits*, 110–31, do, however, point out that popular attempts to rule often focused on commoners rather than on a revived Davidic dynasty.

1137. Cf. Moore, *Judaism*, 2:346. Rivkin, "Messiah," 65, contrasts the set belief in the world to come and the resurrection with the greater flexibility on messianic belief after the revolt.

1138. *'Abot R. Nat.* 31, §67 B.

1139. *Sipre Deut.* 34.4.3 (resurrection in the messianic era); *y. Ketub.* 12:3, §13 (R. Meir); speculation flourished again in the Amoraic period (e.g., *b. Meg.* 12a); the Davidic Messiah remained later (e.g., *Tg. Jer.* 30:9). Aberbach, "Hzqyhw," thinks that "Hezekiah" was sometimes a code name for R. Judah when some still thought him the Messiah.

1140. For groups that emphasized biblical messianic hopes, see Horsley and Hanson, *Bandits*, 102–10. 4Q521 2 II, 1, suggests a global or even cosmic (though this may be hyperbole) role for the Messiah.

period,[1141] long for the restoration of David's house.[1142] Likewise, *Pss. Sol.* 17:32, a pre-Christian source, declares hope in the coming king; the context envisions a warrior messiah (17:21–25). A variety of other Jewish sources from this period (*4 Ezra*; *2 Baruch*; *Testaments of the Twelve Patriarchs*) address the Messiah and often connect him with the final judgment.[1143] Both *4 Ezra* 13 and the Similitudes of Enoch suggest a preexistent individual Messiah of some sort who will destroy the wicked.[1144]

The Davidic Messiah was, by the definition of the type, a future ruler ordained by God with political (not merely spiritual) rule.[1145] Nevertheless, views about this Messiah diverged widely. Qumran's "messianic" expectation apparently encompassed two major eschatological anointed figures, a Davidic Messiah and a high priest (e.g., 1QSa II, 11–17; cf. 4Q174 1 I, 11–12).[1146] The Hasmoneans had combined priesthood and kingship in the same persons,[1147] a combination to which the Zadokite priests who founded the Qumran community strenuously objected.[1148] Thus this separatist priestly community emphasized an "anointed" priest as well as a king (cf. Zech 4:14; 6:13).[1149] Other texts less clearly connected with the Essene movement also stress the role of the future priest.[1150]

In the earliest texts associated with the sort of movement we find at Qumran, Levi and Judah probably fulfill a special role because these two tribes constituted most of Israel as the community knew it,[1151] but only a salvific figure from Judah is mentioned.[1152] The ruler would come from Judah, not from what the sectarians viewed as the corrupt priestly Hasmonean line.[1153]

After this period, however, scholars divide on the interpretation of the Qumran texts. Some contend that they support one messiah,[1154] others that they support two

1141. There is debate as to how widespread or regular their recitation was in this period (see comment on Acts 3:1), but they are surely some of the earliest samples of postbiblical Jewish prayer that we have.

1142. Horsley and Hanson, *Bandits*, 109. In a later period, redemptive work suggested genealogical correctness rather than Davidic descent as being primary; cf. Kaufmann, "Idea."

1143. See Wittlieb, "Bedeutung."

1144. Collins, "Son of Man."

1145. Wächter, "Messianismus," stresses this political aspect of Jewish expectations, distinguishing them from the early Christian view, defined by Jesus's mission. That Jesus did not inaugurate an earthly kingdom in any conventional sense is one of the primary objections to his messiahship in contemporary Jewish scholarship; cf. Berger and Wyschogrod, *Jewish Christianity*, 18–19; Klausner, *Jesus of Nazareth*, 414; Borowitz, *Christologies*, 21.

1146. Evans, "Messianism," 701–2, finds thirty Qumran texts describing "anointed" individuals, with the royal Messiah probably in CD XII, 23–XIII, 1; XIV, 19 (= 4Q266 10 I, 12); XIX, 10–11; XX, 1; 1QS IX, 11; 1QSa II, 11–12, 14–15, 20–21; 4Q252 V, 3–4; 4Q381 15 7; 4Q382 16 2; 4Q458 2 II, 6; 4Q521 2 II, 1; 4Q521 8 9. The "firstborn" of 4Q369 1 II, 6–7 probably evokes biblical messianic language.

1147. E.g., 1 Macc 14:41–42, with the functions of ruler, priest, commander, and possibly prophet sought for Simon Maccabee.

1148. See the Wicked Priest of 1QpHab VIII, 8–10; IX, 4–7; XI, 4–6; XII, 5; and the role of Zadokites in the community. The view that the Teacher of Righteousness is modeled after Judas Maccabee (Eisenman, *Maccabees*, 35) has not garnered much support.

1149. Evans, "Messianism," 703, lists OT precedent for the two messiahs (Jer 33:15–18; Hag 2:1–7; Zech 4:11–14; 6:12–13; 4Q254 4 alludes to Zech 4:14).

1150. *Test. Reub.* 6:8; *Test. Jud.* 21:1–2; compare *Test. Sim.* 5:5 with the Qumran *War Scroll*. On Melchizedek as eschatological priest, see Puech, "Manuscrit."

1151. See *Jub.* 31:12–17 and 31:18–20; cf. similarly *Test. Iss.* 5:7; *Test. Dan* 5:4, 10; *Test. Naph.* 5:3–5; 8:2. Schniedewind, "King," roots the dual messianic expectation in the Chronicler's ideal leadership pattern (esp. 1 Chr 17:14).

1152. *Jub.* 31:18–20; see Noack, "Qumran and Jubilees," 201.

1153. See Charles, *Jubilees*, xiv (although we may date Jubilees somewhat earlier than he [xiii] suggests).

1154. Higgins, "Priest," 333; idem, "Messiah," 215–19; Laurin, "Messiahs," 52. LaSor, *Scrolls*, 152ff., argues that the Hebrew idiom supports one Messiah, rabbinic scholars seeing two because of their talmudic background; although there may be more than one "anointed one," only one is eschatological. *Test. Benj.* 11:2 seems to support a figure from both Judah and Levi (perhaps reflecting a Jewish-Christian desire to derive

messiahs,[1155] and yet others that diversity of opinion existed within Qumran or its documents[1156] or that different documents portray different stages in the community's development of eschatological thought.[1157] The *Manual of Discipline* (1QS IX, 11) does conjoin the expectation of a prophet with that of "the Messiahs of Aaron and Israel"; the *Damascus Document*, however, consistently employs the singular, lending credence to the possibility of diverse views in the texts.[1158]

"Anointed," however, may apply to any figure for a leading office, which diminishes the conflict.[1159] One "anointed" figure is the rightful high priest (in contrast with the wicked one in the temple), and so only the other anointed figure is the eschatological king.[1160] Still, the Qumran evidence may suggest diverse approaches to messianism: the possibly single Messiah of Aaron and Israel in the *Damascus Document* could suggest that at some point the community's greatest expectation was a Levitic rather than a Davidic anointed one.[1161]

The rabbinic idea of two messiahs,[1162] however, derives from different exegesis and probably arises independently from later circumstances.[1163] Sufficient OT basis existed to provide midrashic proofs for a suffering Messiah,[1164] but it is probably only after

one of Jesus's parents from Levi; cf. Luke 1:5, 36). The Scrolls conflate various anointed figures (e.g., 4Q174 1 I, 10–13; 4Q252 V, 3; 11Q13 II, 15–20).

1155. Aune, *Prophecy*, 123 (citing *Test. Reub.* 6:5–12; *Test. Levi* 18:2–9; 1QS IX, 10–11; 1QSa II, 12–17; cf. CD XIX, 10–11; XX, 1); Villalón, "Deux messies," 53–63, esp. 63; Burrows, *More Light*, 297–311 (or perhaps three, 311); Jóczwiak, "Mesjanizm" (or even three); de Jonge, "Anointed," 141–42; Brown, "Messianism," 54–66. In "Theory of Development," 56, Brown still thought there were probably two messiahs, but he noted that not all texts were clear or represented the same period.

1156. Smith, "Variety"; Abegg, "Messiah."

1157. Longenecker, *Christology*, 114; Driver, *Scrolls*, 468–69; Priest, "Mebaqqer"; cf. Priest, "Messiah." Wcela, "Messiah(s)," finds in the *Damascus Document* (CD XII, 23–XIII, 1; XIV, 19; XIX, 10–11; XX, 1; cf. VII, 17–21) one military messiah with a priest who could be an Aaronic messiah (342); 1QS IX, 11 has two messiahs, but often a priestly companion to the Messiah is in view, and the *Damascus Document* probably sees both as one individual (347). Cf. Smith, "Begetting," 224, who thinks that both anointed ones may be "survivals of the same figure" but is not certain that either is eschatological or messianic.

1158. CD XII, 23–XIII, 1 (albeit with an emended misspelling of משיח); XIV, 19 (not all of the word is clear, but the relevant ending is); XX, 1; also the warrior Messiah of 1QM XI, 7–8. Puech, "Apocalypse," considers 4Q521 an "apocalypse messianique" (but contrast Bergmeier, "Beobachtungen"); García Martínez, "Textos," finds a messianic king (4Q252, 285, 521), priest (4Q540), and heavenly figure (4Q246). See Mitchell, "Deliverer," on 4Q175 (suggesting that the fourth figure is messianic).

1159. LaSor, "Messiahs," 429; Gaster, *Scriptures*, 392; Bruce, *History*, 122. Stefaniak, "Poglądy," thinks that Qumran stressed eschatology more than messianology; this is probably right, unless the Messiah was a righteous Teacher redivivus.

1160. Silberman, "Messiahs," 82, questioning whether the expectation is even eschatological in the final sense. Perhaps the title originally applied to the first Teacher of Righteousness.

1161. Cf. the priest's precedence to the "Messiah" in 1Q28a II, 19–20; "Moses God's anointed ['messiah']" in 4Q377 1 II, 5; 1Q22 I, 11–12 even adds Eleazar to Joshua in Deut 31:7, to couple priest and ruler figures; see also the "anointed priest" in 4Q376 1 I, 1. Some late rabbis also spoke of a priest "anointed for battle," i.e., an eschatological priest to accompany the troops, along with the Davidic Messiah (*b. Yoma* 73b; *Song Rab.* 2:13, §4).

1162. For the suffering and triumphant messiahs, see, e.g., *3 En.* 45:5; for a suffering Messiah, see, e.g., the various views offered in *b. Sukkah* 52a; *y. Sukkah* 5:2, §2; *Pesiq. Rab.* 31:10; 34:2; 36:1–2, and see data listed in Torrey, "Messiah"; for a Messiah suffering for Israel's sins, cf. *Pesiq. Rab.* 36:1–2; 37:1; for a servant Messiah, cf. *2 Bar.* 70:9. The doctrine of two messiahs continued in ninth-century Karaite doctrine (possibly from Essene roots?); cf. Wieder, "Messiahs."

1163. Driver, *Scrolls*, 465–66, notes the different exegesis but thinks that the rabbinic picture could shed light on the Scrolls, a proposition that takes too little account of the relative dates of the traditions. Kuhn, "Messias," 208, points out that the Scrolls subordinate the political messiah to the priestly one, but rabbinic literature offers no parallel to this (though *Jub.* 31 and some other texts might).

1164. E.g., Dan 9:26, which is probably messianic in the context of 11Q13 II, 18; see Rosenberg, "Messiah," who (less accurately) predicates the prominence of Qumran's Levitic messiah on the decease of the Davidic one. Brownlee, "Servant," argues that 1QIsaᵃ applies the Suffering Servant of Isa 52–53 to the "anointed" community as a whole (he and Reider, "MSHTY," debate the Hebrew back and forth on 27–28). Justin argues from the failure of the Bar Kokhba revolt that the rabbinic tradition of a suffering Messiah (Messiah ben Joseph) in addition to the triumphant warrior Messiah (Messiah ben David) arose.[1165] (The proposed slain Messiah in 4Q285 5 4[1166] has been rejected by most scholars.)[1167]

2. Jesus and Messiahship

Some doubt that Jesus's earliest followers considered him a Messiah, but this skepticism rejects, in favor of a hypothesis argued virtually from silence, all the explicit testimony that remains extant.[1168] Others suspect that Jesus drew on 2 Sam 7 and other passages that lent themselves to a messianic interpretation.[1169] Given the environment in which Jesus ministered, he had to know that his teachings about the kingdom and some of his actions would lead to speculation about his messianic character.[1170]

The earliest strands of the Jesus tradition indicate that Jesus taught that his disciples would have a role in the messianic kingdom, which would naturally imply that he attributed to himself the role of Messiah.[1171] His disciples claimed him to be Messiah; his execution as king indicates that others believed that he considered himself Messiah.[1172] It is inherently likelier that Pilate and the disciples shared a common source for this idea in Jesus than that the disciples derived it from Pilate or that Pilate received it from renegade disciples who affirmed something their teacher denied. (That Pilate did not crucify Jesus on this charge is implausible. Given the persecution that this could and did create for them, the disciples would hardly have simply *invented* the charge that Jesus was crucified as "king"—that is, for high treason against the emperor.) That Jesus is the common source is, in fact, what our only extant sources claim.

E. P. Sanders thus thinks that many scholars have been too cautious about assuming that Jesus believed he was a king:[1173]

> Jesus taught about the *kingdom*; he was executed as would-be *king*; and his disciples, after his death, expected him to return to establish the *kingdom*. These points are indisputable.

---

the Scriptures for a suffering Messiah and in his account persuades Trypho (Justin *Dial.* 39; 90.1; Higgins, "Belief," 304, regards Trypho's concession as unusual).

1165. So Vermes, *Jesus the Jew*, 140; Yamauchi, "Concord," 165–66 (this seems more reasonable than Berger's attribution of the doctrine to typology; cf. Berger, "Themes"). If a tradition of testing the Messiah existed (e.g., Bar Kokhba by his sense of smell, *b. Sanh.* 93b), it may have arisen the same way (Rivkin, "Meaning," 397, thinks instead that the Pharisees used this tradition in their opposition to Jesus). But Mitchell, "Messiah in Targums," argues for a pre-Christian suffering Messiah (and even views the figure's death as atoning, in idem, "Atonement").

1166. E.g., Tabor, "Messiah" (among others).

1167. Vermes, *Religion*, 211n1; idem, "Forum"; idem, "Messiah Text"; Bockmuehl, "Messiah"; Abegg, "Hope"; Martone, "Testo"; Abegg, "Introduction to 4Q285"; Evans, "Messianism," 703. Collins, "Servant," doubts that 4Q541 (on a suffering sage/priest) is messianic.

1168. For one example of this extreme approach, see Mack, *Lost Gospel*, 4–5. Did later Gentile Christians assign Jesus to a category that they could hardly have created, when they often failed to comprehend even what "anointed one" meant in Judaism?

1169. Davies and Allison, *Matthew*, 2:594–601.

1170. Marshall, *Origins*, 54–56; Witherington, *Christology of Jesus*, 272–73.

1171. Sanders, *Jesus and Judaism*, 234; cf. Beasley-Murray, "Kingdom," 27–32.

1172. Sanders, *Jesus and Judaism*, 321–22. Jesus's execution as a royal pretender leads many scholars to this conclusion (e.g., Witherington, *Christology of Jesus*, 104, 116; Stanton, *Gospel Truth?*, 173–87).

1173. Sanders, *Figure*, 242, suggests that Jesus's view of his royalty may not have been that he was a messiah but rather that he was God's eschatological viceroy. These figures, however, are easily coalesced.

Almost equally indisputable is the fact that the disciples thought that they would have some role in the kingdom. We should, I think, accept the obvious: Jesus taught his disciples that he himself would play the principal role in the kingdom.[1174]

The Gospels suggest that Jesus's view of his kingship was not the common political or military understanding but instead that his disciples and enemies may have misconstrued him. Nevertheless, Jesus and his disciples at least found in the diverse concepts of messiahship a nucleus appropriate for defining his mission.[1175] Just as Qumran adapted its messianic and eschatological vision, Jesus's disciples would have been forced to do the same.[1176]

Why was Jesus reticent to announce his messiahship publicly during most of his ministry? Various factors explain this far better than the idea that the disciples invented his messiahship after his crucifixion or inferred it from Pilate. If Jesus knew anything at all about the political situation in Jerusalem, he would know that a public messianic claim would lead to his immediate execution; in Mark it does.[1177] Further, "self-boasting" was rejected in the Mediterranean world.[1178] Our limited information on first-century potential messianic claimants may suggest a reticence to declare their identity prematurely; most apparently felt they had to produce some evidence of their messiahship before publicly claiming kingship.[1179] Many teachers, both Greek and Jewish, also kept some esoteric or secret teachings private among a small circle and sometimes revealed it reticently even to them.[1180]

"Messiah" was a Jewish category, not a Gentile one, so the suggestion that the title was invented by later Gentile Christians can be rightly deemed hopeless. "Christ" was a natural way to translate "Messiah" in Greek[1181] and so translates "anointed one" (not just in the royal sense) regularly in the LXX. But because this term in regular Greek usage simply meant "ointment"—an image wholly unintelligible to most Greeks[1182]—

1174. Sanders, *Jesus and Judaism*, 307. The same conclusion is argued from a variety of data; cf., e.g., Chilton, "Announcement," 168. Raymond Brown likewise concludes that some of Jesus's followers may have thought him the Messiah but that he responded ambivalently because his mission defined the term differently than the popular title would suggest (Brown, *Death*, 473–80; cf. Marshall, *Origins*, 89–90).

1175. Founders of most ancient schools provided for their perpetuity (see Culpepper, *School*, 123; Sanders, *Jesus and Judaism*, 20–22), and the same would naturally be true for Jesus (see Flusser, *Judaism*, 35). Although Jesus's apocalyptic orientation could be cited against his intention for a continuing movement, his choice of twelve favors his plan for the church (Borg, *Conflict*, 70; Sanders, *Jesus and Judaism*, 104).

1176. Klein, "Messianism," 201, relates Jesus to the priestly and royal messiahs at Qumran, but I argue here from analogy only that messianic concepts were gradually adapted to the communities and social situations that they addressed.

1177. See Rhoads and Michie, *Mark*, 87; cf. Aug. *Tract. Jn.* 113. Times can dictate discretion; a pagan who claimed his teacher divine had to be very discreet when Christian emperors were in power (Eunapius *Lives* 461). Such observations are hardly new; Chrys. *Hom. Jn.* 3 recognizes the messianic secret and thinks that it was the model for Paul's missions strategy in Acts 17:31.

1178. See, e.g., Isoc. *Nic.* 46 (*Or.* 3.36); Plut. *Praising* 15, *Mor.* 544D; Quint. *Inst.* 11.1.17–19; Lyons, *Autobiography*, 44–45, 68–69; on the relevance of avoiding self-boasting to Jesus's mission, see also Neyrey, "Shame of Cross," 127; Keener, *Matthew*, 262. Even later "divine men" (see the brief discussion in our introduction, ch. 9, sect. 3.a.ii; also my *Miracles*, 51–58) were often coy about revealing their divinity (e.g., Philost. *Ep. Apoll.* 44), especially to outsiders (see, e.g., Philost. *Vit. Apoll.* 7.32; 8.5).

1179. See Witherington, *Christology of Jesus*, 265–67. For documentation on various reasons for the "messianic secret," see Keener, *Matthew*, 261–63.

1180. See full documentation in Keener, *Matthew*, 378–79; also Eunapius *Lives* 371–72, 468. Suspense was a rhetorical technique (e.g., Cic. *Verr.* 2.5.5.10–11), but it is less relevant here.

1181. Outside the LXX, however, Diaspora Judaism rarely used the term; even *Sib. Or.* 2.45 is a Christian interpolation. The most obvious exception would be disputes about "Chrestus" in Rome cited by Suetonius (see above on Gentile backgrounds), but if this refers to Jesus, the title could have been introduced mainly by Christians.

1182. Meeks, *Urban Christians*, 94; Hooker, *Message*, 13, 65; Ladd, *Criticism*, 96.

Paul in the Gentile mission normally uses it as Jesus's surname rather than as a title,[1183] in contrast to the more primitive usage in the Gospels.[1184]

The closing reference to Peter's hearers crucifying their own king recalls the statement of responsibility in Acts 2:23 (see comment there) and invites the sort of response that follows in 2:37. The plural pronoun "you" is emphatic in 2:36, underlining the guilt of Peter's hearers. The accusation of carrying the guilt of unjust blood is no small matter (cf. 20:26): crucifixion was such a shameful event (see the excursus on crucifixion, above) that those who could might avenge it also by crucifixion (Polyb. 1.86.4, 6). The purpose of the accusation is to summon the hearers to a response; an emphatic "you" likewise appears in the promise in Acts 2:39 for all who do turn to the Lord.[1185] Those who sought to persuade audiences could appeal to their reason (λόγος), as Peter has already done (2:22–36), or to their good character (ἦθος), or to their emotions (πάθος).[1186] Peter shames his hearers' character but appeals to their emotions by charging them with the expected Messiah's bloodguilt (2:23); their emotional response is evident in 2:37. Appeals to self-interest or a sense of honor or advantage[1187] were also important in persuasion, and Peter certainly provokes their interest on this count (2:37–40).

6. The Response and the Promise (2:37–40)

Conscience-stricken over their people's corporate failure in rejecting and killing their own graciously God-given king, the crowd asks what to do (2:37)—that is, in order to be saved (the issue raised in 2:21). Peter summons them to repentance ("turning" to God, as in the prophets) and to call on Jesus's name in a baptism involving such repentance. God's promise to them, and to all those whom their repentance proleptically foreshadowed, was the Holy Spirit (2:38–39).

a. The Crowd's Response (2:37)

Like other ancient writers, Luke often employs the literary technique of interruption of speeches (7:53; 10:44; 17:32; 26:24).[1188] In Luke's case, such interruptions help him to conceal the unrealistic conciseness required by his space constraints.[1189] Although novels sometimes employed such interruptions,[1190] they did so because of verisimilitude imitating reality; such interruptions appear in various genres.[1191] Certainly, interruptions were common in real speeches.[1192] Hecklers might interrupt

---

1183. Morris, *Romans*, 37.

1184. Ladd, *Theology*, 140–41.

1185. Tannehill, *Acts*, 36 (also noting pronouns for Israel placed first in clauses in Acts 3:25–26; 13:26, 46).

1186. Aune, *Environment*, 199 (citing Arist. *Rhet.* 1.2.3; 2.4–7; Quint. *Inst.* 6.2.9–12). For ἦθος (*ēthos*), see further comment on Acts 24:11, 14–17; for πάθος (*pathos*), see further comment on Acts 20:19.

1187. Aune, *Environment*, 199 (citing Quint. *Inst.* 3.8.1; Cic. *De or.* 2.81.333–37).

1188. See Aune, *Environment*, 127 (citing Jos. *War* 1.629; 2.605; 3.485; 7.389; Hdn. 2.5.8; Ach. Tat. 8.1.2; 8.7.1; 8.11.1); Soards, *Speeches*, 138 (following Dibelius).

1189. Horsley, "Speeches," 610.

1190. E.g., *Apoll. K. Tyre* 48–49 (where the speaker finishes the speech before the hearer, who should have reacted earlier, cries out; cf. a similar suspension of reaction in Gen 44:18–45:1).

1191. Cf. Acts 22:22; Jer 36:16. Parsons, *Acts*, 47, cites references from histories (Appian *Bell. Civ.* 3.51–61; Quint. Curt. 6.9.2–24; 7.1.10–40; Tac. *Ann.* 16.31).

1192. E.g., Livy 3.40.5; Cic. *Prov. cons.* 8.18; *Or. Brut.* 40.138.

speeches, often seeking to promote the heckler's honor at the expense of the speaker's shame (Lucian *Dem.* 14).[1193] See fuller comment at Acts 2:13.

The interruption here, however, is carefully positioned. Whereas in some of his speeches Luke completes only the *narratio* (the early narrative element), in a few he displays the full skeleton of the argument that he wishes to include at a few points. Here he allows Peter to complete the speech and even provide a brief summary; the "interruption" is actually a full response.[1194]

The crowd's question is a familiar one in Luke-Acts (Luke 3:10; Acts 16:30), though taken from tradition at least in Luke 18:18.[1195] In each case, the question concerns what is required for salvation. The apostolic response in Acts 16:31 (not unexpectedly from Paul) is faith in the Lord Jesus; in Luke 3:11, from John the Baptist, it is divesting oneself of possessions beyond what is needed for life, to serve others' needs.[1196] Jesus's requirement in Luke 18:22 is also that of giving all one's possessions to the poor; this requirement is derived from Mark 10:21, but Luke's earlier inclusion of John's requirement indicates that Luke intends no mere historical description of a demand for a rich ruler but an example for all followers of Jesus. Jesus's answer to the question of Luke 10:25 (in 10:26–37) involves caring for one's neighbor across ethnic and cultural barriers.[1197] The lifestyle of those responding to the summons here (Acts 2:44–45; cf. 4:32–35) suggests that the wording in texts such as Luke 3:11 may be hyperbole, but it also suggests that it runs against the grain of Theophilus's and probably Luke's milieu. This background will invest Peter's call to repentance (Acts 2:38) with new meaning: true repentance produces a lifestyle of radical simplicity and care for others' needs. Genuine faith in Jesus (16:31) saves, but such genuine commitment to Jesus as "the Lord" (τὸν κύριον) will entail following Jesus's teaching (perhaps increasingly as one learns its specific content), including what Luke has reported concerning the poor.

Describing the responses of a rhetorician's or philosopher's audience often revealed the effectiveness of the speaker's skill or message.[1198] When Curio's speech won his hearers over, they showed their fervor by interrupting his speech to affirm him (Caesar *C.W.* 2.33). Failure to applaud or otherwise display appreciation for a speech could prove offensive (Pliny *Ep.* 6.17.1–4); crowds often applauded the debater they thought was winning (Lucian *Z. Rants* 41).

Although the very deep emotional response described here ("struck to the heart") produces a favorable behavioral response, Luke provides two other occasions where,

---

1193. For other interrupting questions and objections, see, e.g., *Rhet. Alex.* 18, 1432b.35–40; 1433a.14–25; Sen. E. *Controv.* 3.pref. 4–5; Plut. *Lect.* 4, *Mor.* 39CD; 11, *Mor.* 43BC; 18, *Mor.* 48AB; *Demosth.* 6.3; 8.5; *Cic.* 16.3; Dio Chrys. *Or.* 15.26–32; Aul. Gel. 8.10; 16.6.1–12; 18.13.7–8; 20.10.1–6; Pliny *Ep.* 3.9.25; 3.20.3–4; 9.13.19–20; Diog. Laert. 7.1.19; Philost. *Vit. soph.* 2.30.623; Eunapius *Lives* 460.

1194. Luke indicates that Peter said more on the occasion than his skeleton summary of and examples from the speech could recount (2:40; see comment there). Nevertheless, the position of the interruption makes sense of both Luke's arrangement for his own audience and the sequence of events within the narrative world: the audience response presupposes the completion of Peter's narration of the passion, and audience interaction also renders more plausible a significant response to Peter's deliberative conclusion.

1195. Noted also in Nave, *Repentance*, 36–37. Johnson, *Function*, 184, rightly notes the connection between the question and the Lukan demand for sharing possessions (Luke 3:11; Acts 2:44–45), which seems soteriologically significant (cf. Keener, "Reconciliation," 127–29).

1196. This requirement is for the crowds in general; for those in a position to exploit others, John demands dealing justly (Luke 3:14–15).

1197. For Luke, ultimately pointing to cross-cultural sharing, as in Acts 11:29, and the Gentile mission. Jesus's response presupposes a sound exegesis of Lev 19:18 in light of its context (in addition to *gezerah shevah*) in Lev 19:34: Israelites must love strangers in the land, among whom the parable implicitly includes Samaritans.

1198. Malherbe, *Moral Exhortation*, 57 (citing Lucian *Nigr.* 3–7, 35–37; *2 Clem.* 19; *Herm. Mand.* 3.3; 12.4).

by contrast, the emotional response provoked deadly hostility (Acts 5:33; 7:54).[1199] Moreover, although the depicted response to Peter's Pentecost speech favorably portrays the revivalistic origins of the Jerusalem church, it also offers a foil to the harsh response to Paul's "Pentecost" speech in 22:22 in different times some three decades later. Luke does not present favorable responses as the invariable response to faithfulness.

b. Repentance and Baptism (2:38)

Just as John, the forerunner, preached a baptism symbolizing or effecting repentance (Luke 3:3; Acts 13:24; 19:4), so now does Peter. One Jewish use of baptism in antiquity was as an act of conversion (as part of the process of conversion), although Jewish people traditionally applied this function of immersion only to Gentiles. Peter here demands a conversion no less radical, but from members of his own people who must likewise turn to Israel's God and the divinely appointed king, Jesus.

i. Repentance[1200]

Gentiles did not speak much of moral repentance in light of religion. Joining a new mystery cult simply supplemented one's previous religious experience;[1201] polytheism was inclusive. Philosophers understood conversion to philosophy,[1202] but it was not, of course, a turning toward the one God of Israel.

In Acts 2:38 and 3:19, Peter preaches repentance like the OT prophets calling Israel to return (see 3:19; cf. 5:31; 8:22).[1203] In the immediate context, the people of Israel must repent for their corporate responsibility for Jesus's death (2:23); but in its fuller Lukan context, the summons to repentance is appropriate for all humanity (e.g., 17:30; 20:21; 26:20), though, in the story world, Peter and his companions do not yet recognize this point (11:18). The biblical prophets summoned Israel to "turn" or "return" to the Lord (e.g., Isa 55:7; Jer 3:12, 14, 22; 4:1; 25:5; 26:3; Ezek 14:6; 18:21, 23, 30; Hos 14:1; Joel 2:12–13; Mal 3:7), which could even be summarized as their message (Zech 1:3–4).[1204] Individuals also needed to turn from wickedness to righteousness (Ezek 33:14–16, 19), that is, change their lifestyle, not merely indulge in guilty feelings.[1205]

1199. For an intense emotional response, *Jos. Asen.* 6:1 uses κατανύσσομαι, as here (except there conjoined with ψυχή).

1200. For a thorough survey of background concerning repentance in Greek and Greco-Jewish sources, relevant to Luke-Acts, see Nave, *Repentance* (for the lexical background, see 39–144); for one survey of Luke's theology of repentance, see Tannehill, *Shape*, 84–101. On conversion in Acts, see Talbert, *Mediterranean Milieu*, 135–48 (comparing Jewish and Greco-Roman elements of conversion and concluding [147–48] that the components of conversions are comparable, though the object [i.e., Jesus] differs).

1201. See Burkert, *Mystery Cults*, 14.

1202. See comment on Acts 17:30. Against Luke's term referring to merely intellectual change without emotions, however, see thoroughly Nave, *Repentance*, 40–70 (esp. 48–66).

1203. Bayer, "Preaching," 262–67; on the OT prophetic tradition informing the NT usage of repentance, see, e.g., Goppelt, *Theology*, 1:34–36; Ladd, *Theology*, 38–39. For the commonly held view of Semitic rather than Greek background, see, e.g., Filson, *History*, 100; but while this difference may be true at the conceptual level, it is not necessarily true at the lexical level. Nave, *Repentance*, 74–118, skillfully shows that Jewish sources in Greek tend to use the particular term employed here with a semantic range similar to some other Greek sources (involving changed thinking and behavior that allowed for reconciliation, but not translating *shuv*). Unlike Nave, however (*Repentance*, 203n262), I view the close association of the two aorist imperatives in 3:19 as communicating mostly equivalent force, and hence retain the prophetic conceptual background for the preaching of prophetic figures like Peter here. On the demand for repentance in Luke-Acts, see Morris, *Cross in New Testament*, 109–12.

1204. Applied to Egypt in Isa 19:22.

1205. Though some philosophers did believe that sharp regret could serve the moral function of goading a person to moral improvement (Fredrickson, "Hardships," 172–76).

Occasionally the LXX uses μετανοέω to express turning to the Lord (Jer 8:6; 38:19 LXX [31:19 ET]; Joel 2:13; perhaps Isa 46:8),[1206] though it uses ἀποστρέφω (cf. Acts 3:26) far more frequently.[1207] The noun μετάνοια appears even more rarely (five times, all but one in the Apocrypha), though it seems to have more of a consistent association with turning from sin (esp. in later sources, Sir 44:16; Wis 11:23; 12:10, 19).[1208] Apparently, however, usage had shifted by the first century; ἀποστρέφω appears just nine times in the NT (only twice in Luke-Acts) whereas μετάνοια and μετανοέω together appear fifty-two times, with a fairly consistent range of usage, including in Luke-Acts.

Early Judaism heavily emphasized the value of repentance, from Qumran[1209] to the rabbis[1210] to others.[1211] Israel as a whole needed to turn to God;[1212] the fifth benediction of the Amidah requests that God turn Israel to repentance.[1213] Many believed that corporate repentance could hasten the judgment.[1214] The need for repentance also applied to individuals. Although some Jewish traditions denied that the righteous like Abraham needed repentance,[1215] most acknowledged that all people have sinned[1216] and all need repentance.[1217]

For the later rabbis, repentance would atone for lighter transgressions, whereas it suspended judgment for most heavier ones until the Day of Atonement could atone for them.[1218] One should repent a day before one's death—that is, always be

1206. See also Pr Man 7 (8 employs the noun), 13; Wis 5:3; Sir 17:24; 48:15.

1207. This verb appears an estimated 431 Times in the LXX with a variety of meanings. Apart from the later Apocrypha, the LXX applies μετανοέω more often to God changing his mind than to people (e.g., Jer 4:28; Amos 7:3, 6; Joel 2:13–14; Jonah 3:9–10; 4:2; Zech 8:14).

1208. That is, in these cases it means more than simply changing one's mind (as in, e.g., Arius Did. Epit. 2.7.11m, pp. 96–97.5–7); in some Greek sources, the term involved remorse (see Marc. Aur. 8.10; Char. Chaer. 3.3.11; Danker, Corinthians, 110). Some date Wisdom in the first century C.E., eliminating three of the five LXX exceptions; but I think a first-century B.C.E. date more likely (cf. Sandmel, Judaism, 71–76; Rost, Judaism, 59; Holmes, "Wisdom," 1:520–21).

1209. CD II, 5; X, 3; XV, 7; XX, 17; 1QS III, 1, 3; V, 1; VII, 19; 4Q171 II, 3–4; 4Q257 III, 2, 4; 4Q266 2 II, 5; 4Q269 1 2; 4Q400 1 I, 16; 4Q461 1 10; 4Q512 frg. 70, 71.2; 4Q525 10 6; 11Q10 XXVII, 4.

1210. E.g., m. 'Ab. 4:13, 22; 5:21; 'Abot R. Nat. 39 A; Sipre Deut. 30.1.2; Pesiq. Rab Kah. 24 passim; 25:3; Pesiq. Rab Kah. Sup. 3:2; b. Yoma 86ab; Exod. Rab. 31:1; Lev. Rab. 15:4; Deut. Rab. 2:24; Eccl. Rab. 7:14, §1; Song Rab. 5:16, §1; 8:6, §2; Pesiq. Rab. 44:7; 47:1; Tg. Isa. 57:19; cf. b. Roš Haš. 16b. Some rabbis placed its creation before the world (b. Pesaḥ. 54a; Gen. Rab. 1:4; Midr. Pss. 90:3; 93:2); it was available to Adam (Gen. Rab. 1:4; he refused it in Num. Rab. 13:3) and to the generation of Babel (Gen. Rab. 38:9).

1211. See, e.g., Sir 18:21 (though using ἐπιστροφήν); 17:24; 44:16; Pss. Sol. 9:7; Let. Aris. 188; Jub. 34:21; 1 En. 40:9; 50:3–5; Test. Iss. 6:3; Test. Reub. 1:9; 2:1; Test. Sim. 2:13; Test. Jud. 15:4; 19:2; 23:5; Test. Zeb. 9:7; Test. Gad 5:6–8; 6:3, 6; 7:5; Test. Jos. 6:6; Test. Ab. 11:10; 12:13 B; 4 Bar. 8:12; cf. Herm. 2.4.2. Repentance is personified in Jos. Asen. 15:7/6–7. For repentance in Judaism, see also Montefiore and Loewe, Anthology, 315–33; Urbach, Sages, 1:462–70; Le Cornu, Acts, 122–29 passim; for another survey of the literature (arguing that later rabbis are more lenient than earlier sources such as Philo, Josephus, and the earliest Christians), see Bell, "Teshubah"; cf. also Petuchowski, "Teshuvah." For John the Baptist's message of repentance, see Taylor, Immerser, 106–11.

1212. E.g., Hos 14:1–2; Tob 13:6.

1213. Oesterley, Liturgy, 63. God granted repentance (Wis 12:19; Rom 2:4), although in some texts this means that God gives space for repentance (cf. 2 Pet 3:9). Vermes, Religion, 192, suggests that John's and Jesus's repentance was personal as opposed to the corporate repentance found in Qumran liturgy (e.g., 1QS I, 24–26), but the personal decision on entrance into that community (e.g., III, 9–11; V, 8, 13–14; acknowledged in Vermes, Religion, 192n8) is, in fact, more analogous.

1214. See comment on Acts 3:19.

1215. Pr Man 3:8; cf. Test. Ab. 10:14 A (but contrast 9:3); 'Abot R. Nat. 14 A.

1216. 1 Kgs 8:46; 1 Esd 4:37–38; Sir 8:5; Test. Ab. 9:3 A; 1 En. 40:9; 4 Ezra 8:35; see further Moore, Judaism, 467–69; Bonsirven, Judaism, 114. Some later Amoraim observed that repentance even one day before death could spare the wicked hell (Ruth Rab. 3:3; Eccl. Rab. 1:15, §1).

1217. Sanders, Paul and Judaism, 174–80; Montefiore and Loewe, Anthology, 315–33.

1218. M. Yoma 8:8; t. Kip. 4:7. For repentance atoning or partly atoning, see, e.g., Pss. Sol. 3:9–10 (or 3:8, in a different enumeration; using different wording); y. Šebu. 1:6, §5; Num. Rab. 14:10.

ready to stand before God in the judgment.[1219] Death atoned for sin, with or without repentance, but the three most serious sins required repentance as well as death.[1220] If a person kept committing a sin after repentance, however, his or her repentance was not held to be genuine.[1221] According to some views, God received even Manasseh's repentance (despite angelic opposition),[1222] though other rabbis denied it.[1223]

God established repentance as the way to deal with (ἐπί) sins (Wis 12:19). Repentance could lead to the hope of eternal life (*1 En.* 40:9). Proselytes also "repented," turning from their former Gentile way of life;[1224] conjoined with a dramatic immersion, the model of John's preaching (Luke 3:8), and Luke's overall emphasis on welcoming Jews and Gentiles on the same terms, the present repentance evokes this dramatic sort of turning of life rather than merely an initial sample of periodic penitence. For Luke, repentance involved conversion and a new way of life.

In Luke-Acts "repentance" is both the content (Luke 3:3, 8; 5:32; 13:3, 5; 24:47; Acts 3:19; 5:31; 13:24; 17:30; 19:4; 20:21; 26:20; cf. 8:22) and the appropriate response (Luke 10:13; 11:32; 15:7, 10; 16:30–31; Acts 11:18) to kingdom preaching. The term is barely used otherwise.[1225] Because God's "kingdom" was his reign (see comment on Acts 1:3, 6), those who turned to embrace his reign were accepting a new king. Just as Luke's mention of faith in various soteriological passages in Acts (e.g., 8:12–13; 10:43; 11:17; 13:39, 48; 15:9, 11; 16:31; 26:18) informs his understanding of repentance, so repentance informs his understanding of faith: genuine faith in Jesus as Lord requires acknowledgment of his lordship and beginning to adjust to its practical demands (cf. 6:7; 20:21).[1226] Luke's particular wording in each case may be appropriate to the speakers (see introduction, ch. 8, sect. 2.b); the summons to "believe in the Lord Jesus" is characteristically Pauline language (see, e.g., Rom 4:24; 5:1; 10:9; though cf. also Peter in Acts 11:17; 15:11).[1227]

As noted above on 2:37, the various answers in Luke-Acts to the question of how to be saved (Acts 16:30; Luke 3:10; 18:18) infuse the content of repentance here with special meaning: both faith in Jesus as Lord (Acts 16:31) and radical sacrifice of possessions on behalf of others (Luke 3:11; 18:22). That the believers expressed repentance in these ways is clear in Acts 2:44–45, where "those who were believing" (οἱ πιστεύοντες, present active participle, 2:44) were sacrificing

1219. M. *'Ab.* 2:10; *'Abot R. Nat.* 15 A; 29, §62 B; *b. Šabb.* 153a; *Midr. Pss.* 90:12. Repentance was always efficacious before death (*Test. Ab.* 10:14 A) and even shortly before the end of the age (*1 En.* 50:3–5; but not if one waited too long, *4 Ezra* 7:82; 9:11; *2 Bar.* 85:12). The gates of repentance were always open (*Deut. Rab.* 2:12; *Lam. Rab.* 3:43–44, §9; though many rabbis demurred about apostates like Manasseh).

1220. B. *Šebu.* 13a, bar.

1221. M. *Yoma* 8:8–9; *'Abot R. Nat.* 39, 40 A; *Pesiq. Rab.* 44:1. Repentance destroys disobedience (*Test. Gad* 5:7; cf. 2 Cor 7:10; later, against the evil impulse, *Lev. Rab.* 9:1). But this was nothing like the later Christian rule allowing only a single repentance (e.g., *Herm.* 2.4.1)!

1222. E.g., *Pesiq. Rab Kah.* 24:11; *Tg. 2 Chr.* 33:12–13. Surely his repentance is viewed favorably in 2 Chr 33:12–15; Pr Man 7–8.

1223. Most rabbis in *Num. Rab.* 14:1. For a survey of rabbinic approaches to Manasseh's repentance, see Hoffer, "Manasseh's Repentance." Cf. Elisha ben Abuyah in *Eccl. Rab.* 7:8, §1.

1224. *Jos. Asen.* 9:2; 15:7; *Pesiq. Rab Kah.* 12:20; cf. Acts 14:15; 1 Thess 1:9; perhaps also Philo *Virt.* 175–82 (if Bekken, *Word*, 85–90, is correct about the application to both Jews and Gentiles).

1225. The clearest exception involves personal reconciliation (Luke 17:3–4).

1226. I say "beginning" because learning remained necessary (e.g., Acts 10:14; 11:2–3, 18; 15:5).

1227. Cf. Gal 3:22; Eph 1:15; Phlm 5; also Jas 2:1; Paul blends repentance and faith in Acts 20:21. Whether the difference in Acts is the speaker or, more importantly (in view of Petrine uses in 11:17; 15:11), relevance to the Gentile mission (cf. Luke 7:9), within the narrative world Peter may grow in articulating the message of saving faith. Yet this growing articulation should not be overplayed into a theological tension; Luke hardly implies that the Lord Jesus, who is the object of faith in Acts, articulated the message inadequately in Luke's Gospel.

("were selling," ἐπίπρασκον, imperfect active indicative, 2:45) their goods to meet others' needs.

The "forgiveness of sins" is explicitly associated especially with repentance in Acts (e.g., 3:19; 5:31; 11:18).[1228] Jesus's final recorded Lukan command to his disciples was to preach repentance for the forgiveness of sins in Jesus's name to all nations, starting (as they do here) from Jerusalem (Luke 24:47). Early Jewish sources often emphasize God's forgiveness[1229] and pray for it.[1230] But forgiveness normally required confession and repentance.[1231]

II. BAPTISM[1232]

Scholars debate to what extent the forgiveness of sins is also associated with baptism, and the grammatical debate can become quite involved.[1233] Given the various texts surveyed above, it seems that "for forgiveness" is linked more often with repentance (though the grammar alone could not decide this), which is never missing when baptism and forgiveness are both mentioned (Luke 3:3; Acts 2:38) or even when forgiveness is mentioned without baptism. For Luke, however, baptism is not dissociated from repentance but constitutes an act of repentance; under normal circumstances, one does not separate the two (Luke 3:3; Acts 13:24; 19:4).[1234]

John's mission was to bring Israel to forgiveness (Luke 1:77); he preaches a *baptism* of repentance for the forgiveness of sins (3:3) when he preaches repentance (3:8).[1235] Thus preaching repentance in Jesus's name (ἐπὶ τῷ ὀνόματι, 24:47) is concretely expressed by summoning the repentant to baptism in Jesus's name (ἐπὶ τῷ ὀνόματι, Acts 2:38), and baptism figuratively "washes away sins" (22:16).[1236] As in contemporary Judaism (below), a baptism of repentance was an act of conversion, though early Christians invited Jews as well as Gentiles to submit to it.[1237]

1228. With, e.g., Bruce, *Commentary*, 77; Dunn, *Acts*, 33; Bock, *Acts*, 144.

1229. E.g., *Jub.* 22:14; 1QH^a VI, 24; *Exod. Rab.* 52:2.

1230. E.g., 4Q504 4 6–7; also the sixth benediction of the Amidah (Oesterley, *Liturgy*, 63); for a later discussion of prayer on the eve of Yom Kippur, see, e.g., *Lev. Rab.* 3:3.

1231. E.g., *Jos. Asen.* 11:18; *Sipra Behuq. pq.* 8.269.2.1; *Tg. Ps.-J.* on Lev 16:30; 1 John 1:9; for confession, see also, e.g., *Pss. Sol.* 9:6; *b. Sanh.* 43b; further comment at Acts 7:60.

1232. For studies of baptism relevant to Acts, see Mattill and Mattill, *Bibliography*, 290–93, §§4039–87; for a more recent but brief survey of views, see Powell, *Acts*, 74–75 (usefully highlighting, among others, Giles, "Exponent," 194–205; Beasley-Murray, *Baptism*, 93–122).

1233. E.g., McIntyre, "Baptism and Forgiveness" (some of whose other points are stronger), cites the rule of concord to separate baptism and forgiveness in Acts 2:38, but Camp, "Reexamining Concord," responds that ἕκαστος can serve as a plural pronoun. Grammar alone will not easily decide the theological point here. That εἰς in 2:38 may mean "for the purpose of" (cf., e.g., Dana and Mantey, *Grammar*, 104, §111.i) is far likelier than Mantey's theologically determined "because of" (see Wallace, *Grammar*, 369–71, following Marcus, "*Eis*"; idem, "Elusive *eis*," 44; against Mantey, "Causal Use of *eis*"; "*Eis* Again"). Moule, *Idiom Book*, 70, has "*with a view to*, or *resulting in*."

1234. My concern here is exegetical only. That is, I am not addressing theological questions about how the church should deal with those incapable of being baptized (the oft-cited thief on the cross in Luke 23:42–43 might be relevant, though one could readily counter that the example precedes Christian baptism). More relevant is the spiritual conversion of Cornelius's household before baptism (Acts 10:47). In view of the latter case, Luke probably would not attribute to baptism any mechanical efficacy for spiritual transformation (against such efficacy, see further, e.g., Stonehouse, *Areopagus*, 78, 83–84). But such questions remain peripheral to Luke's central concern here, which is baptism as the standard *act* of conversion, by which one publicly confesses allegiance to Christ (even if one has already received the Spirit).

1235. The continuity between John's practice and the early Jesus movement suggests that Jesus himself approved the use of baptism (cf. John 3:22; 4:1–2; France, "Jesus the Baptist?," 107).

1236. John's baptism prefigures even this element of proclaiming Christ, except that John proclaims the "coming one" (Luke 3:16) and Peter proclaims the one who has already come.

1237. That is, I understand Luke differently than I understand the Fourth Gospel (cf. Keener, *John*, 546–52); although I do not think that Luke presents baptism as itself regenerative (or that he anywhere addresses the question of regeneration, in any case), I do believe that he sees it as the decisive act of conversion (*pace*, e.g.,

In contrast to the wicked in John's preaching (Luke 3:7–9, 17), the repentant (in 3:3, 8, 11–14) would receive the Spirit (3:16). It seems no coincidence, then, that baptism becomes a normal prerequisite for the gift of the Spirit (though God did sometimes sovereignly vary the sequence, as in Acts 10:46–47). Jesus, the model, received the Spirit at his baptism (Luke 3:21–22), and even the expression "baptized in the Holy Spirit" suggests that it is an experience to which both John's baptism in water (3:16) and that of the apostles (Acts 2:41; esp. 10:47) points. (Conversely, Acts 10:44–48 shows that they are ontologically distinguishable,[1238] and 10:47 that water baptism could confirm the more critical experience with the Spirit that God had already granted.)[1239] Baptism was the act of repentance by which one embraced the eschatological gift[1240] and consequent empowerment to share the apostolic mission for cross-cultural testimony. Water baptism was meant to symbolize and (ideally) accompany the gift of the Spirit, however, not to replace it, as if the act were sufficient without the experience (see 10:47; 19:5–6; esp. 8:12–17).[1241] As argued elsewhere in this section, Luke repeats the experience (8:14–17; 10:44–47; 19:6; and even the title "baptized in the Spirit" in 11:16) and expects his audience to continue to experience charismatic phenomena.

Whether Luke had a specific tradition of baptisms on Pentecost (as I believe likely; see comment on Acts 2:41) or simply inferred their occurrence, we have good reason to believe that he was correct. Baptism appears as the accepted initiatory rite in our earliest Christian sources[1242] (e.g., Rom 6:3–4; 1 Cor 1:13–17; 10:2; Gal 3:27) and was used by John the Baptist as a moral purificatory rite before the Christians adopted it (Mark 1:4; Jos. *Ant.* 18.117, βαπτισμῷ). Instead of assuming that this distinctive, single initiatory baptism arose independently among John's and Jesus's followers or that the new urban Jesus movement adapted the former's wilderness baptism without earlier connections, it seems to make more sense to assume a connection by way of Jesus and to believe that it was practiced by the earliest disciples. What is most striking is not the activity of baptism but its use for initiation specifically into the community of Jesus's followers, identifying them as a distinguishable sect within Judaism.[1243] That is, they practiced baptism "in the name of Jesus."

Most Jewish groups, like the Pharisees and the Sadducees, practiced purificatory immersions without requiring an initial one specific to their own order; the Essenes, however, did include a special cleansing for initiates upon entrance into their community,[1244] albeit the first of many such washings.[1245] This renders use of initiatory immersion by Jesus's followers also plausible (though it is also confirmed by more

---

Tanton, "Gospel and Baptism: Acts 2:38"). For views on baptism in Luke-Acts, see, e.g., Bovon, *Theologian*, 377–79.

1238. This prebaptismal experience with the Spirit here is identified as being baptized in the Spirit (Acts 11:16), its "gift" being the same as that of the first Pentecost (10:45, 47; 11:17).

1239. Acts 10:47–48 does not provide a normative alternative model for Luke's audience's practice (it represents only 10 percent of Acts' baptism passages), but it does demonstrate (perhaps incidentally) that water and Spirit baptisms are *ontologically* separable. I recognize that some have critiqued Dunn, *Baptism*, for such a "mediating" position between "sacramentalism" and "Pentecostalism" (Lull, *Spirit in Galatia*, 72–73), but a position is not rendered untenable merely by "mediating."

1240. Cf. Harrington, *God's People*, 41: "Not only a sealing for the eschaton but also the symbolic appropriation of the present salvation proclaimed by Jesus."

1241. Cf. this potential danger in Robinson, *Studies*, 167: since Pentecost, water baptism became "the effective representation" of the Pentecost experience "for every *succeeding* person and generation (Acts 2.39)."

1242. On the basis of its presence in the earliest sources, Meeks, *Moral World*, 99, guesses that baptism as Christian initiation began "very soon after the death of Jesus." Byrne, *Romans*, 189, notes that Paul presupposes familiarity with it in the Roman churches, which he did not found.

1243. On the anthropological significance of baptism as a rite of separation, see, e.g., deSilva, *Honor*, 305.

1244. See, e.g., Brownlee, "Comparison," 58; Brown, "Scrolls," 4.

1245. See, e.g., Jos. *War* 2.150; Ringgren, *Faith*, 221; Milik, *Discovery*, 102–3.

explicit evidence). Jewish Christians, however, at some point transformed John's baptism of Jews, rendering it, whether or not this was already John's intent, as something like proselyte baptism. Now, however, it was applied to Jews as well as Gentiles (as in John's baptism) and hence was probably more radical than that of the Essenes.

Excursus: Proposed Backgrounds for Baptism

Luke's audience would understand the association of baptism with repentance and conversion. Clearly John's baptism forms the primary backdrop for early Christian baptism, including in Luke's own account (Luke 3:3–4). Less familiar to many modern readers is the Jewish conversion baptism that informed the repentance element of John's baptism. Before turning to a discussion of conversion baptism, however, we survey the wider context of ritual lustrations in Jewish and Gentile circles.[1246]

1. Ritual Washings

Ritual lustrations were common throughout the ancient world. In addition to ancient Israel,[1247] ancient Egyptians,[1248] Mesopotamians,[1249] and Hittites[1250] practiced various ritual washings; they also appear in some genetically unrelated or distant societies.[1251] Later Mediterranean models probably also contributed to the development of Jewish purification ideas. Although some philosophers, such as the Cynics, detested the thought behind bodily purifications,[1252] other schools, such as the Pythagoreans[1253] and the Stoics,[1254] valued them as important.

Various temples had their own rules mandating ritual purity,[1255] and the Eleusinian[1256] and Isis[1257] cults used lustrations as preliminary purifications in their initiatory rites;

1246. I borrow most of the material in this excursus from Keener, *John*, 442–47. On proselytes in general, see Keener, *John*, 543–44.

1247. On OT ablutions, see, e.g., Webb, *Baptizer*, 96–108.

1248. Spell 20, part T-1, in the Egyptian *Book of the Dead* (Allen, 36); Moyer, "Purity," 130; Blackman, "Purification," 476; cf. Philo *Mos.* 1.14.

1249. Moyer, "Purity," 130. In the ancient Near East generally, see, e.g., Sallaberger and Felber, "Purification."

1250. Moyer, "Purity," 132; cf. the importance of ritual purity in "Instructions for Palace Personnel to Insure the King's Purity" (*ANET* 207); "Instructions for Temple Officials" 14 (*ANET* 209).

1251. E.g., postpartum purificatory water rituals among Eskimos, in Fiji, and in Uganda (Fallaize, "Purification"); postpartum or postmenstruation rituals among the Nandi and the Ndebele (Mbiti, *Religions*, 169, 172); prenuptial washings in Batoro (182–83), Jewish (Safrai, "Home," 758), and Greco-Roman (Ferguson, *Backgrounds*, 54–55; Batey, *Imagery*, 28) cultures; Hindu water purifications before approaching a deity (Fry et al., *Religions*, 61; and, to a lesser extent, in Shinto tradition in Japan [154]); possibly related Islamic purifications (Guillaume, *Islam*, 88); Mandaeans (Drower, *Mandaeans*, 100–123; cf. Kraeling, *John the Baptist*, 107–9).

1252. Diogenes in Diog. Laert. 6.2.42. Plutarch explicitly condemns only the βαπτισμούς of superstitious religion and magic (*Superst.* 2, *Mor.* 166A).

1253. Cf. Diog. Laert. 8.1.33; Culpepper, *School*, 49 (following Iambl. *V.P.* 71–74).

1254. Diog. Laert. 7.1.119.

1255. E.g., inscription (*SIG*² 566.2–9) from Athena's temple at Pergamum (in Grant, *Religions*, 6). Aune, *Prophecy*, 30, cites the Pythia's ritual bath preceding sacrifice. Ach. Tat. 8.3.2 speaks of a fountain of τὸ ἱερὸν ὕδωρ used for ablutions in the temple of Artemis in Ephesus. Even deities might purify themselves (Ovid *Metam.* 4.479–80).

1256. Epict. *Diatr.* 3.21.14; Mylonas, *Eleusis*, 248; Angus, *Mystery-Religions*, 81–82.

1257. Plut. *Isis* 75, *Mor.* 381D; Apul. *Metam.* 11.1. For such ablutions deriving from older Egyptian traditions, see Wild, *Water*, 129–48. Cf. later blood baptisms in the cult of Cybele (Goodenough, *Church*, 9; cf. Prudentius *Peristephanon* 10.1011–50 in Barrett, *Documents*, 96–97).

some initiatory baths were, however, used to secure pardon from the gods (Apul. *Metam.* 11.23). But in contrast to some earlier scholarship,[1258] most contemporary scholars have rightly observed that such acts were simply preliminary washings and not initiatory of themselves.[1259] It is moreover noteworthy that most standard terms for purification in the Greco-Roman world (καθαρμός, καθάρσιον, κάθαρσις) are missing in the NT.[1260]

The early Jewish practice of ritual washings was widespread in Jewish Palestine long before the time of the Jesus movement, as evidence from Josephus,[1261] coins,[1262] and especially archaeology attests.[1263] Mikvaot, or standard ritual immersion pools, often included steps for descending into the pool and ascending from it, as well as a conduit for water to flow into it from an adjoining pool.[1264] One of the most pervasive Jewish features in excavations of Galilean and Judean sites,[1265] they are in evidence in the Hasmonean[1266] and Herodian[1267] periods and are found at places such as Masada[1268] and Jerusalem.[1269] They were especially common among the well-to-do who lived in upper-city Jerusalem[1270] and on the Temple Mount.[1271] (Jerusalemites may have been more concerned with ritual purity than were the provincials, "who purified themselves mainly for the festal pilgrimages.")[1272] Wandering wilderness pietists such as Bannus frequently washed in the Jordan or other available sources of water (Jos. *Life* 11). Rabbinic texts include many discussions of ritual purification.[1273] The mikveh's waters were thought to cleanse ritual impurity[1274] and so were important for priests,[1275]

1258. E.g., Bultmann, *Christianity*, 158.

1259. Livy 39.9.4; Burkert, *Mystery Cults*, 101; Nock, *Christianity*, 60–62, 133; Wagner, *Baptism*, 71–72, 102–3; Meeks, *Christians*, 152–53. Typical stages of initiation were κάθαρσις (purification), σύστασις (sacrifices), τελετή (initiation proper), and ἐποπτεία. Romans were also "cleansed" (καθαίρονται) by sacrifice (Dion. Hal. *Ant. rom.* 4.22.1–2).

1260. Nock, "Vocabulary," 134. John twice uses καθαρισμός, both times for Jewish lustrations (John 2:6; 3:25).

1261. E.g., Jos. *Ant.* 6.235 (who implausibly reads it into the David narrative); cf. his comments (18.19) on the form of purification used by Essenes at the temple.

1262. Wirgin, *Jubilees*, 27–38, adduces numismatic evidence that may argue for priests' use of holy water for their hands and feet in the Maccabean period.

1263. On the development of mikvaot ideology in an early period see Selkin, "Exegesis," esp. ch. 5 (97–161); for a recent survey of information about Palestinian mikvaot, see Hoss, "Mikwen"; cf. also Štrba, "*Miqveh.*" The Pharisees probably did more to extend it beyond the priesthood than anyone else (e.g., Stambaugh and Balch, *Environment*, 87). On early Jewish ablutions apart from Qumran, see Webb, *Baptizer*, 95–132, esp. 108–32.

1264. E.g., Yadin, *Masada*, 164; Avigad, *Jerusalem*, 142; Bruce, *Thoughts*, 50–51; Kotlar, "Mikveh," 1535.

1265. Reed, "Contributions," 52, counts more than three hundred. In the Judean foothills, see, e.g., in Zissu and Ganor, "Horvat 'Ethri."

1266. Avigad, *Jerusalem*, 85–86; notes in Cornfeld, *Josephus*, 50; probably at Gezer, in Reich, "Mqww'wt"; Netzer, "Mqww'wt."

1267. E.g., Reich, "Miqweh."

1268. Pearlman, *Zealots*, 179, who identified this mikveh as the earliest known at the time of his writing. Zissu, Tepper, and Amit, "*Miqwa'ot*," suggest their presence even at some rural sites.

1269. See Avigad, *Jerusalem*, 139–43. *M. Parah* 3:7 also mentions a place of immersion at the Mount of Olives.

1270. Avigad, *Jerusalem*, 139, 142.

1271. Cf. the Chamber of Immersion (*m. Mid.* 1:9) and, for the immersion of lepers, the Chamber of Lepers (*m. Neg.* 14:8). See Meyers and Strange, *Archaeology*, 55; Mazar, "Excavations," 52; Cornfeld, *Josephus*, 272. The list of "officers" in the temple (*m. Šeqal.* 5:1–2) includes one Nehemiah as "over the water," lit. "trench-digger," and he was "in charge of the aqueduct and the Temple cisterns, and to look after the baths" used for ablutions (Jeremias, *Jerusalem*, 174).

1272. Neusner, *Beginning*, 24–25.

1273. See esp. the Mishnah, the Tosefta, and the talmudic tractate *Miqwa'ot*. The most extensive discussion of this material to date is in Neusner, *Purities*. Miqveh came to be considered a commandment of God (cf. the Amoraic blessing in *b. Ber.* 51a).

1274. *M. Parah* 11:6; *b. Šabb.* 64b; *y. Šebu.* 2:1, §6. The touch of Gentiles could communicate impurity requiring immersion (cf. *y. Šeb.* 6:1, §12, 36c).

1275. E.g., *b. Ber.* 2b, with a purportedly Tannaitic attribution.

menstruants,[1276] and even vessels.[1277] Ritual purity was required before a festival and was achieved mainly through immersion.[1278]

Although such Jewish lustrations and their broader cultural background provide a context for John's and early Christian baptism, however, they cannot define them. John's baptism in the Synoptic tradition was initiatory and eschatological, a baptism of repentance in light of the coming kingdom of God.[1279] Many scholars have suggested Qumran initiatory baptism as the background for John's and early Christian baptism,[1280] but though the sect did practice baptism as part of initiation,[1281] the initial baptism at Qumran was apparently viewed only as the first among many.[1282] Because of the cost and separation entailed in joining the Qumran sect, one could describe Qumran baptism as a repentance baptism;[1283] but again, one's first baptism at Qumran was one among many rather than the primary line of demarcation. Qumran washings probably reflect a particularly meticulous form of early Jewish purification ritual, and the covenanters performed their washings frequently.[1284]

2. Conversion Baptism

Although the Qumran parallel for Jews joining a particular sect in view of the coming judgment supplies a partial context for John's wilderness baptism, it, like Jewish lustrations in general, does little to explain the fully initiatory status of a single baptism as an act of conversion to a new way of life. For this we must turn to the closest Jewish parallel to John's and early Christian baptism, namely, proselyte baptism, a specific and extremely potent form of ritual purification.[1285]

Some scholars argue against proselyte baptism as a source for Christian baptism,[1286] but it has long had its advocates,[1287] and the opinion is increasingly shifting in the

1276. *B. Pesaḥ.* 90b; *Šabb.* 84a; *Yoma* 6b; the importance of this may be underlined by the haggadic illustration on an OT narrative in *Lev. Rab.* 19:6 and the illustration of R. Gamaliel's maidservant in *Pesiq. Rab Kah.* 12:15.

1277. *M. Makš.* 4:6; *Miqw.* 9:5–7, 10; *Sipra Sh. pq.* 9.115.1.6–8; *b. Šabb.* 15b; 34a; 84a; *Zebaḥ.* 22a; *Menaḥ.* 101a; *Bek.* 22a; *Ḥul.* 123a; *y. Ḥag.* 3:8, §§1–3; cf. *m. Ṭehar.* 8:9; CD X, 12; XI, 3–4. Other Eastern cults (such as that of Cybele) also purified vessels (Mart. *Epig.* 3.47).

1278. *B. Pesaḥ.* 59a, bar.; references in Urbach, *Sages*, 1:582–83. Cf. Jdt 16:18 (the people were purified [ἐκαθαρίσθη] before offering sacrifices); cf. John 11:55; also possibly 2:6 with 2:13, if 2:6 prepares for Passover.

1279. See, e.g., Ladd, *Theology*, 38–39.

1280. Fritsch, *Community*, 7; Thiering, "Initiation"; idem, "Cleansing"; Smith, "Baptism"; Brownlee, "Comparison with Sects," 58; Brown, "Scrolls," 4; Bertalotto, "Immersion"; Flusser, *Sage*, 19; cf. Robinson, *Studies*, 16; Jeremias, "Qumran Texts," 68–69; Anderson, *Mark*, 70–71; against Pryke, "John," 483–96; Delmore, "Pratique."

1281. See 1QS V, 8–23 and texts in Josephus cited by Cross, *Library*, 95n96a; see at length Webb, *Baptizer*, 133–62. Wood, "Dip," argues for dipping in ritual purifications; the mikvaot that archaeologists have uncovered argue strongly in favor of immersion as the form of washing, fitting other early Jewish evidence.

1282. Cf., e.g., Jos. *War* 2.150. This has been argued by many scholars, e.g., Driver, *Scrolls*, 496–506; Ringgren, *Faith*, 221; Milik, *Discovery*, 102–3; Pryke, "John," 483–96; Simon, *Sects*, 75. Such purifications were not thought to purify the soul from sin; see Sutcliffe, "Baptism." On ritual purity at Qumran more generally, see, e.g., Bowley, "Purification Texts."

1283. So Black, *Scrolls*, 94. I write from the more traditional perspective that sectarians did live at Qumran and composed the major documents, though I am aware that this position is debated today.

1284. E.g., 4Q512 passim; 4Q414 frg. 12; Oxford Genizah Text C 2–8; Mount Athos manuscript in *DSSNT* 255. The impression that Essenes were meticulous in washings may be gained, e.g., from Jos. *War* 2.129, 150; cf. *Ant.* 18.19. It should be noted, however, that non-Essene Jews in upper-city Jerusalem, who had adequate resources, may have also been more meticulous than their halakah demanded; see Avigad, *Jerusalem*, 142.

1285. Cf., e.g., *y. Qidd.* 3:12, §8.

1286. Beasley-Murray, *Baptism*, 18–31; Anderson, *Mark*, 71; cf. Albright, *Stone Age*, 290.

1287. E.g., Abrahams, *Studies* (1), 42; Montefiore, *Gospels*, 1:8; Rowley, "Baptism"; cf. Taylor, *Mark*, 155; White, *Initiation*, 78–79; Argyle, *Matthew*, 23.

direction of recognizing it as a source, with whatever modifications.[1288] Major differences naturally distinguish John's baptism from proselyte baptism, including the former's public and eschatological orientation and particularly its summoning of Jews as well as Gentiles to turn to Israel's God.[1289] Such differences are genuine and should not be underestimated in distinguishing John's baptism from proselyte baptism. Nevertheless, John's (and hence early Christian) baptism did not arise *sui generis* (which could have rendered its symbolism unintelligible), and Jewish initiatory purification of proselytes would hardly borrow an earlier Christian practice for initiating members (including both Jews and Gentiles). The appeal to Judaism's most widespread once-for-all immersion ritual complements Qumran or other suggested background by providing key elements of the context they omit.[1290]

The conversion ritual provided a clear, symbolic line of demarcation between a proselyte's Gentile past and Jewish present. Although Judaism employed circumcision as the primary sign of entering the covenant,[1291] both circumcision and baptism would have normally been required for new converts to Judaism. Because the Babylonian Gemara reports a debate between early Tannaim R. Joshua and R. Eliezer concerning whether baptism or circumcision by itself would suffice for a valid conversion,[1292] some scholars have held that some authorities accepted baptism without circumcision;[1293] but it is hard to think that R. Joshua could have openly diminished an explicit commandment of the Torah. Other scholars have thus preferred to follow the Palestinian recension of this tradition, where R. Eliezer allows circumcision without immersion (probably under exceptional circumstances) and R. Joshua insists that both are necessary.[1294] On either reading, the sages concurred on that occasion that both circumcision and proselyte baptism were necessary, and other texts reinforce the conclusion that proselyte baptism was a necessary part of conversion.[1295]

It is quite probable that proselyte baptism is pre-Christian. Some scholars have denied this claim, sometimes seeking to argue for the temporal priority of Christian baptism,[1296] but their denial seems difficult to maintain. The relative paucity of references to conversion in general in pre-70 rabbinic traditions, as well as baptism's secondary place to circumcision for males, may explain the relative paucity of pre-70 references to proselyte baptism in particular. Ceremonial washings were so common

1288. Schiffman, "Crossroads," 128; idem, *Jew*, 26; Goppelt, *Theology*, 1:37; Bruce, *History*, 156; Ladd, *Theology*, 41; Meeks, *Urban Christians*, 150; Falk, *Jesus*, 151; cf. Hooker, *Message*, 9; LaSor, "Miqva'ot."

1289. Rowley, "Baptism," 333–34.

1290. That is, those joining the Christian movement could justify their baptisms on the analogy of washings before joining other sects; but the element of conversion, even for Jewish adherents (cf., e.g., Q in Matt 3:9/Luke 3:8), is suggestive, and the lack of subsequent baptisms required by this particular community (as opposed to those invited by Jewish practice more generally) weighs the initiatory baptism much more heavily than at Qumran.

1291. For its importance in Jewish practice, see discussion at Acts 15. Some of those who were spreading Judaism apparently thought that exceptions could be made where Judaism would be brought into more reproach if it was carried out (e.g., Jos. *Ant.* 20.40–42), but this laxity is undoubtedly exceptional (cf. Eleazar of Galilee in Jos. *Ant.* 20.43–44).

1292. B. *Yebam.* 46a.

1293. McEleney, "Conversion"; Gilbert, "Convert"; cf. Lake, "Proselytes," 78–79.

1294. Bamberger, *Proselytism*, 49–52; cf. Nolland, "Proselytes"; in support of this position, cf. *b. Yebam.* 71a. Then again, it is easy to see how the tradition would have been modified to its Palestinian form to conform the tradition to the normative interpretation of the Torah.

1295. T. *'Abod. Zar.* 3:11; *b. Ber.* 47b; *'Abod. Zar.* 57a; *Yebam.* 46ab; *y. Qidd.* 3:12, §8; cf. *t. Zabim* 2:7.

1296. Taylor, "Baptism"; Smith, "Baptism," 13–32; Robinson, *Studies*, 16n12; Légasse, "Baptême"; Meier, *Marginal Jew*, 2:52. Webb, *Baptizer*, 125–27, finds no pre-70 evidence for it and notes that Jos. *Ant.* 20.34–48, where we might expect to find it mentioned, is silent about it. Although this could be a stronger-than-usual argument from silence, it could be omitted simply because immersion was a transculturally common practice and, unlike circumcision in this case, would not risk generating much controversy.

and so unobjectionable in the ancient Mediterranean that one would not expect any particular washing to appear as frequently in conversion literature as circumcision, which provided a comparatively major hurdle for Gentile men to cross.[1297] Lacking explicit support from the Hebrew Scriptures (though naturally inferred from purity considerations there), it may also have been less universal than circumcision,[1298] but references show that it was well enough known to merit allusions even in the Diaspora, and such wide geographical distribution makes it improbable that it rose suddenly with our first references to it in the sources. The antiquity of Jewish proselyte baptism may be argued on several grounds:

1. The Hasmonean mikvaot and references to immersions in the Dead Sea Scrolls make the antiquity and widespread character of Jewish ritual cleansing obvious, and it is almost inconceivable that the transition from the most unclean state to a state of cleanness should not have been marked by such a washing.[1299]

2. At the end of the first century, Epictetus speaks of full converts to Judaism in the Diaspora being βεβαμμένου (perfect of βάπτω) as if this is well known,[1300] and Epictetus was undoubtedly not alone in this knowledge.[1301]

3. *Mishnah Pesaḥ.* 8:8 makes tebillah a matter of dispute between the first-century adherents of Beth Hillel and Beth Shammai;[1302] this point is considerably weakened, of course, if proselyte baptism was not originally in view here,[1303] but Tannaitic tradition in the Tosefta supports the antiquity of the proselyte baptism interpretation.[1304]

4. A possibly first-century Diaspora Jewish text assumes that even Gentiles know the Jewish practice of baptisms in running water when one is turning from sins.[1305]

5. Most other initiation rituals in the ancient Mediterranean (from mystery cults to Qumran) included at least ceremonial washing, even if they viewed it as merely one washing among many (see comments above).

6. Given the facts that later rabbinic Judaism was in a position of far greater power than were the early Jewish Christians in its area of geographical influence and that it usually ignored or condemned their teachings, it would be quite unlikely that it would have borrowed initiatory baptism from the Christians and hardly

1297. For whatever reasons, Judaism attracted Gentile women more frequently than their husbands (cf. Jos. *War* 2.560–61; *CIJ* 1:384, §523; inscriptions in Leon, *Jews of Rome*, 256).

1298. Cohen, "Ceremony," may be correct that until the mid-second century, different people practiced it in different ways. At least in politically sensitive cases such as Izates, some Jews felt circumcision itself unnecessary (cf. Gilbert, "Convert"), though others clearly disagreed (Jos. *Ant.* 20.44).

1299. Cf. similarly Pusey, "Baptism." Also Taylor, *Immerser*, 64–68 (though she on other grounds rejects this as background for John's baptism, 69); for Gentile impurity (because of idolatry), cf., e.g., Acts 10:28; 11:3; *m. Pesaḥ.* 8:8; *'Ohal.* 18:7; Jos. *War* 2.150; *y. Šeb.* 6:1, §12; Safrai, "Religion," 829.

1300. *Diatr.* 2.9.20, despite the interpretation of the Loeb editor. Stern, *Authors*, 541, interprets it correctly.

1301. It might also be implied by Juv. *Sat.* 14.104, who would then be regarding it as a matter of common knowledge in Roman society that after Jews circumcised their converts, they led them to the place of washing. On *Sib. Or.* 4.165 (probably first century), see below; cf. Justin *Dial.* 29.1 for a mid-second-century Diaspora reference.

1302. Schiffman, "Crossroads," 128–31; definite early attestation is not possible here, but "the transmission of this statement in the names of three separate Tannaim may indicate that it was widespread" and probably reflects an authentic early dispute. Cf. Torrance, "Baptism," 154.

1303. Taylor, "Baptism," 196.

1304. See Abrahams, *Studies* (1), 37.

1305. *Sib. Or.* 4.162–65; the text probably dates to ca. 80 c.e., and Collins regards this as Jewish rather than Christian. The association of turning from sin (4.162–64), repentance (4.168–69), and washing in water (4.165) is significant. Some Diaspora circles may have required only washing of hands and feet (*Jos. Asen.* 14:12).

> more likely that it would have developed and approved initiatory baptism on its own once this practice had become associated with the Jewish Christians.[1306]

Other arguments—for instance, that some definite symbol of transition was necessary for women converts—are less substantial but can supplement the case.

Apparently John's baptism historically summoned Israelites to turn to God the same way Jewish people expected Gentile proselytes to do; like the Qumran sect but with a more radical and public symbolism,[1307] John regarded only the true remnant of Israel as prepared for the Lord (see the Q material in Matt 3:9//Luke 3:8), and sought to turn the larger community of Israel to repentance.[1308]

iii. Baptism in Jesus's Name

Baptism "in Jesus's name" distinguishes this baptism from other Jewish immersion practices noted above, with respect to its object. For Luke, baptism in Jesus's name does not involve a ritual formula uttered over an initiate but the new believer's "calling on the name of the Lord" Jesus (see comment on Acts 2:21; 22:16); thus Luke employs with this phrase the verb βαπτίζω in the passive rather than the active voice, employing the active form only when the verb is without the phrase (see fuller discussion below).

Luke presents apostles acting by means of Jesus's name, probably meaning that they were able to perform his works because he had authorized them to do so (Acts 3:6, 16; 4:7, 10, 30; 16:18; cf. 19:13, 17); all who wished to be saved must likewise be so by his name (4:12; 10:43; cf. 15:17), a point relevant to 2:21 and 2:38. Outsiders also recognized that the apostles taught in Jesus's name (4:17–18; 5:28, 40; 9:27–28; cf. 21:13), presumably meaning that they did so explicitly as his followers (probably also relevant to the expression "baptism in Jesus's name"). Acts also speaks of those who called on Jesus's name (2:21; 9:21); as we shall see, this is quite relevant for "baptism in Jesus's name." These examples of Luke's use of Jesus's name employ various prepositions, but as in the case of baptism (see below), the specific prepositions are probably roughly interchangeable.

In Israel's Scriptures, "name" often connoted reputation, so that when God acted "on account of his name," he defended his honor, a matter readily understood in the ancient Mediterranean with its emphasis on honor and shame. "In God's name" could signify a representative's acting on God's behalf (Exod 5:23; Deut 18:19–22; Jer 14:14–15), according to his command (Deut 18:5, 7), or by his help (Ps 118:10–11; Prov 18:10) or using his name for a miraculous act (2 Kgs 2:24). In prayer, which suits this context (Acts 2:21), calling on the deity's name meant addressing him (1 Kgs 18:24–26, 32; 2 Kgs 5:11; Pss 9:2; 18:49); similarly, in 1 Chr 16:2, when

---

1306. Cf. also Rowley, "Baptism," 313; Cohen, *Maccabees*, 53; Schiffman, "Crossroads," 128; White, *Initiation*, 320. Kraeling, *John the Baptist*, 99–100, indicates the widespread acceptance for an early date, noting that "a growing sense of historical proportion showed how impossible" was the view of some early Christian scholars that Judaism took proselyte baptism from the Christians. Rather, later rabbis and early Christians shared a common source in the wider milieu of early Judaism.

1307. For John's baptism as a "prophetic symbolic action," see, e.g., Malina and Pilch, *Letters*, 333.

1308. Some scholars suggest that John the Baptist himself was an Essene (e.g., Betz, "John"); whether he may have been one at one time, he certainly was not one by the time he began his public proclamation (Witherington, *Christology of Jesus*, 36; Pryke, "John"). Qumran sectarians practiced strict separatism from the rest of Israel (see, e.g., van der Minde, "Absonderung"). Further, most commonalities between them also appear in most of the rest of Second Temple Judaism (Taylor, *Immerser*, 15–48), and John's baptism implied the inadequacy of former purifications (99).

David blessed the people in the Lord's name, he apparently was calling on the Lord to bless them. That various early Jewish circles could employ "name" as a polite surrogate for pronouncing the divine name also fits this usage.[1309] (See more extensive comment regarding the "name" at Acts 3:6.)

Perhaps relevant is the Diaspora Jewish formula that God accepts those "who repent in the name of the Most High God";[1310] Christian baptism is distinct by specifying Jesus's name. Although this suggestion is quite possible, we cannot be sure enough that *Joseph and Aseneth* lacks Christian influence to stake too much on it by itself.[1311] Rabbis also later speak of genuine proselytes as converts "in the name of" (for the sake of) heaven (לשם שמים).[1312] Given the diverse strands of evidence, it seems likely (though not certain) that some Jews spoke of Gentiles converting in God's name. In any case, Jewish people were known for "calling on the Lord's name," and the more specific application to Jesus would be striking.[1313] If it parallels invoking the divine name, it fits the context's exalted, divine Christology.

Baptism "in Jesus's name" probably simply specifies Christian baptism as distinct from various Jewish immersion rituals (whether or not some other Jewish people spoke of converts in God's name). People being baptized "in his name" designated whose followers they would be (cf. Paul's ironic response to Corinthian misunderstanding in 1 Cor 1:13–15, which may well presuppose baptism in Jesus's name).[1314] The supposed conflict with the trinitarian formulation in Matt 28:19 (thought to represent a later stage[1315] or different geographic region) misses the fact that both function to identify baptism for followers of Jesus as distinct from other kinds of baptism (and possibly both link Jesus with God in some way). Although there is little direct historical support outside Matthew for that formula's being earlier, we should note, against the common opinion of scholarship, that its affirmation of Jesus's role, though divine, may be more subtle than Luke's baptism solely in the name of Jesus.

Further, whatever the function of Matthew's "baptismal formula," Luke's is not a phrase uttered by a supervisor over one receiving baptism.[1316] As already mentioned, although the verb βαπτίζω appears in both passive and active forms, Luke includes the formula "in the name of Jesus" only with passive uses of the verb (Acts 2:38; 8:12, 16; 10:48; 19:5); this indicates that the formula has to do with *receiving* rather than giving (which essentially meant preaching or supervising) baptism. Further, one who would wash away his sins by baptizing himself was to "call on the name of the Lord" while doing so (22:16). This matches the context of Acts 2: one called on the Lord's

1309. *1 En.* 6:3 (if "Semyaza" means "he sees the Name"); perhaps 1 Chr 13:6 LXX; Jeremias, *Theology*, 10; Longenecker, *Christology*, 43; Bietenhard, "ὄνομα," 268–69. Bonsirven, *Judaism*, 7, cites *m. Ber.* 4:4; *Yoma* 3:8.

1310. *Jos. Asen.* 15:7 (*OTP* 2:227).

1311. It might be helpfully supplemented with the righteous being saved "in the name of the Lord of Spirits" (*1 En.* 48:7, in both Knibb and Isaac), though the Similitudes could be as late as the mid-first century C.E.

1312. See most fully Abrahams, *Studies* (1), 45 (citing the small extracanonical tractate *Gerim* 1:7 and comparing *b. Yebam.* 45b, 47b); cf. De Ridder, *Discipling*, 107. The expression undoubtedly reflects the sentiment that all genuine works should be done for the name of heaven (e.g., *m. 'Ab.* 2:2, 12). Perhaps ἐπί also conveys the sense of the Hebrew *le*, which apparently stands behind the idiom with εἰς in Acts 8:16 (see discussion there); different prepositions simply reflect different Greek ways to translate the underlying Semitic original (see Hurtado, *Lord Jesus Christ*, 201).

1313. Peterson, "Worship," 381–82 (his association with the temple is less plausible).

1314. See Martin, *Worship*, 127; cf. Goppelt, *Times*, 42. The supposed gnostic background (Schmithals, *Gnosticism in Corinth*, 256) inverts chronology, appealing anachronistically to sources in a movement dependent on Christianity; alleged baptism in schismatics' names (cf. Ambrosiaster *Comm.* [CSEL 81:11–12; Bray, *Corinthians*, 11]) may be patristic polemic.

1315. E.g., Grant, *Gods*, 53; Bultmann, *Second Corinthians*, 252.

1316. Cf. Chrys. *Hom. 1 Cor.* 3.6 (Bray, *Corinthians*, 11) regarding its theological function: "The greatness of baptism does not lie in the baptizer but in the one whose name is invoked in the baptism."

name (2:21) by being baptized in Jesus's name (2:38). If 2:38 fulfills Joel's quotation (as most exegetes affirm), then what specifies that a baptism is in Jesus's name is the recipient's confession of faith in Jesus.[1317]

This is not to suppose that early Christians would not have cared who supervised baptisms (which were probably effectively self-dunkings). Apparently second-century Jewish teachers debated whether Samaritans could circumcise Jews (though Jews could circumcise Samaritans), because Samaritans circumcised in the name of, or for the sake of, Mount Gerizim.[1318] There is no indication that one needed to be "ordained" to oversee baptism (cf. 8:38; 9:18), but early Christians probably at least expected Christian commitment for anyone performing Christian acts, including overseeing baptism.

Luke's particular expression varies: is one baptized ἐπί Jesus's name (as here), εἰς his name (8:16; 19:5), or ἐν his name (10:48)? But εἰς and ἐν tended to merge in Koine, so that (in contrast to classical Greek) εἰς with the accusative no longer necessarily implied movement.[1319] Luke was probably unconcerned with the preposition; "what mattered was the name" (see 3:6, 16; 8:12).[1320]

Because Christian baptism especially evokes John's baptism, it is likely Palestinian and early, and its widespread use among various Christian movements also suggests its antiquity.[1321] Semitic expressions behind the prepositions (see comment on Acts 8:16) suggest the same for baptizing in Jesus's name.[1322] This, in turn, suggests that the Jesus movement used it as a line of demarcation within Judaism even from an early period and that the primary line of demarcation was faith in Jesus's exalted status. Although we lack external data to corroborate what was said on the precise occasion Luke describes, the evidence does favor his claim that the "primitive" Jerusalem church used baptism in Jesus's name for converts to its sect, in the process likely affirming Jesus's lordship.

c. The Promised Gift of the Spirit (2:38–39)

Luke recalls earlier teachings about the Spirit through his terms "gift" (cf. Luke 11:13, concerning dependent prayer) and "promise" (Luke 24:49; Acts 1:4; 2:33). By noting that the promise is for others, he makes the proper response for the present crowd (namely, repentance and baptism in Jesus's name) and the gift of the Spirit received at Pentecost (Acts 1:8; 2:4, 17–18) paradigmatic for all subsequent believers. By alluding to "far-off" Gentiles by way of Isaiah's language, Luke also reiterates the prominence of the Spirit for the Gentile mission (cf. 10:44–47).

i. The "Gift" (2:38)

Peter and the apostolic witnesses can preach repentance in Jesus's name in Jerusalem precisely because they have now received God's promise of power for this task (Luke 24:47–49). Those who receive the same gift will likewise spread God's message (cf. Acts 2:47; 8:4).

1317. Judge, *First Christians*, 619, views "a theological confession as the basis for a new movement" as highly unusual, perhaps unprecedented in antiquity. It would probably not have been possible in typical Greco-Roman religion (see Rives, *Religion*, 47–50).

1318. T. ʿAbod. Zar. 3:13; b. ʿAbod. Zar. 27a, bar.; y. Yebam. 8:1, §10.

1319. Mussies, "Greek," 1042. Cf. the confusion of εἰς with ἐπί and πρός (Blass, Debrunner, and Funk, *Grammar*, 112, §207); ibid., 100, also note (introduction preceding §187) that "the dative was exposed to a greater extent than either the accusative or genitive to the encroachment of various prepositions, especially ἐν and εἰς, on the function of the simple case" (the other mentioned cases also having some such exposure).

1320. Barrett, *Acts*, 154; Hurtado, *Lord Jesus Christ*, 201.

1321. Hurtado, *Lord Jesus Christ*, 203.

1322. Ibid., 203.

What Luke emphasizes as included in the gift is more simply ascertained than questions of normative sequence. Complicating any attempt to create a mandatory sequence here, Luke clearly speaks of conversion (repentance and baptism) in this text;[1323] in context, he also clearly associates the gift with prophetic empowerment,[1324] which (elsewhere in Acts; cf. 4:8; 13:9; esp. discussion at Acts 8:14–17) apparently might not occur at the same moment yet was also part of the "gift" of the Spirit. Luke's focus with regard to the gift's content in his narrative is empowerment, not conversion, but most scholars assume that the timing of the gift here is simultaneous with conversion. Noting sequential variations in Acts' subsequent narratives, some scholars have questioned whether this text places any emphasis on simultaneity, which is not explicit,[1325] though the gift at least appears to follow inevitably.

If Luke indicates simultaneity here, he may mean the gift here more broadly than exclusively prophetic empowerment (in my approach, his empowerment emphasis does not eradicate all other elements; Luke 3:16). But whether or not Luke implies a temporal connection here, conversion and the gift of the Spirit are inseparably connected theologically.[1326] In Paul, at least, the gift of the Spirit is, as Gordon Fee puts it, "the chief element of the Christian life, from beginning to end."[1327] Yet this theological connection does not predetermine Luke's subsequent narrative portrayals of prophetic-empowerment experiences, which are his more dominant focus.

Because Luke emphasizes the prophetic-empowerment dimension of the Spirit, he does not identify the experience he emphasizes with conversion at every occurrence in his narrative (see comment on Acts 1:4–5). Granted, the events of Acts 2:38 are theologically a single package; this does not mean, however, that they always occur in the exact sequence as in 2:38.[1328] That is, the sequence seems to be normal rather than normative, allowing "exceptions" (see 8:14–17; 10:44–48).[1329] (Variation was common for literary reasons,[1330] but on such a key point, given Luke's thesis here,

---

1323. On "reception of salvation" (conversion, repentance, etc.), see Bovon, *Theologian*, 267–89. Repentance and baptism themselves might not be simultaneous (cf. discussion in Stonehouse, *Areopagus*, 78, 83–84).

1324. Lake and Cadbury, *Commentary*, 26: "If the words were used in the Jewish sense this would mean 'become prophets.'" Reformed scholar Ned Stonehouse warns that a connection with salvation here would have "a Pelagian flavor" (*Areopagus*, 71) and thus connects the gift of the Spirit with charismatic manifestations, citing Luke's other references to the gift in Acts 8:20; 10:45; and 11:17 (82, 84). Shelton, *Mighty in Deed*, 130, notes the ambiguity here.

1325. Cho, *Spirit and Kingdom*, 140–50 (emphasizing [146–50] the subsequent narratives); Menzies, *Empowered*, 203–4, argues that Acts 2:38 makes repentance and baptism a prerequisite for receiving the prophetic gift but does not indicate the reverse (i.e., it does not make the gift of the Spirit—in the Lukan sense of empowerment—necessary for conversion). Noting the absence of the Spirit directly following baptism in Luke's narratives, Shauf, *Theology*, 155, contends that 2:38 is not a formula, but merely "what they should do and what they should expect." Cf. also Haya-Prats, *Believers*, 148–52 (on the imprecise relationship between water and Spirit baptism) and xvii, 138–41, 192, 237 (on the lack of interest in salvation and sanctification in the pneumatology of Acts).

1326. Presumably, the gift (as the entire sphere of the Spirit's activity in the believer's life) becomes available at conversion whenever some aspects of it (such as empowerment, Luke's emphasis) may be actualized in believers' lives.

1327. Fee, *Gospel*, 98.

1328. See also Witherington, *Acts*, 154; Gaventa, *Acts*, 139. Luke does not clarify inconsistencies regarding baptism because they are beside his primary point (cf. Weatherly, "Purpose").

1329. Dunn, *Baptism*, 55–72, seeks to conform Acts 8 to 2:38, in my view, unsuccessfully; more plausibly, many regard 2:38 as the norm and view divergent cases as exceptions (see Hull, *Spirit in Acts*, 98–99; Turner, *Gifts*, 44–45; Marshall, *Theology*, 177), or view the narrative diversity as normative and 2:38 as a schematization or a prerequisite (Cho, *Spirit and Kingdom*, 140–50; Menzies, *Empowered*, 203–4). For surveys of views concerning receiving the Spirit and the contemporary debate about subsequence in Acts, see Turner, "Significance of Receiving"; Elbert, "Spirit through Lukan Lens."

1330. On literary variation, see, e.g., Aul. Gel. 1.4; Max. Tyre 21.4; Anderson, *Glossary*, 53–54, 114; Nock, "Vocabulary," 137; in LXX, see Lee, "Translations: Greek," 776–77; varied imperatives for attentiveness in Xen.

his variation probably reflects the historically authentic variety of early Christian experience.)

Although the "gift of the Spirit" and "giving the Spirit" are natural Lukan expressions (Luke 11:13; Acts 5:32; 8:18–20; 10:45; 11:17; 15:8, using various Greek terms),[1331] similar language appears elsewhere in early Christianity (John 3:34; 4:10; Rom 5:5; 2 Cor 1:22; 5:5; Eph 1:17; 3:16; 1 Thess 4:8; 2 Tim 1:7; 1 John 3:24; 4:13).[1332] "Giving the Spirit" likewise fits the language of "receiving the Spirit," both in Acts (Acts 1:8; 2:33, 38; 8:15–19; 10:47; 19:2) and elsewhere (John 7:39; 14:17; 20:22; Rom 8:15; 1 Cor 2:12; Gal 3:2, 14; cf. 2 Cor 11:4; Rev 22:17).[1333] Surveying the context of the references in Paul and (for the most part) John suggests that the expression refers to conversion, which initiates a person into a continuing life by the Spirit; by contrast, the context of the passages in Acts suggests especially prophetic empowerment (at least in Acts 1:8; 10:47; and 19:2–6). The language of "gift" might contrast with the common early Jewish expectation that the Spirit was merited only by the most pious.[1334]

Those who emphasize a parallel between Moses's ascent to receive Torah for his people and Jesus's ascension to receive the Spirit for his followers could find a parallel between the "gift" of the Holy Spirit here and the "gift" of the Torah. Jewish texts regularly emphasize that God "gave" the Torah to Israel[1335] and that it was God's "gift."[1336] A rabbinic tradition at least as early as R. Simeon ben Yohai (late second century) speaks of God's three special gifts to Israel on account of its suffering: the Torah, the land, and the world to come.[1337] Jewish literature also portrays Wisdom as a divine gift (4Q185 1–2 II, 8–11), including in a context where God "pours out" (ἐξέχεεν) wisdom (Sir 1:9–10).

Anab. 5.1.8–10; words for "serving" in Xen. *Cyr.* 3.1.36, 41; see esp. Cic. *Or. Brut.* 46.156–57; *Fam.* 13.27.1; cf. Cic. *Brut.* 91.316. For further examples, see Keener, *John,* 244–46, 251, 324–25.

1331. Lindars, *Apologetic,* 57, regards it as exclusively Lukan, which is true insofar as one limits the usage to δωρεά (unless two phrases in Heb 6:4 are synonymous).

1332. Cf. similarly 1 Cor 12:7–8; Eph 4:7–8; Heb 6:4. Given connections between the Spirit and wisdom (Keener, *John,* 961–66), it might be useful to note that Wisdom is God's "gift" (although with different terminology) in Wis 8:21; 9:17.

1333. It seems noteworthy that Luke and other NT writers always use λαμβάνω for "receiving" the Spirit and not δέχομαι (possibly excepting 1 Cor 2:14; 2 Cor 11:4), though they do employ both for "receiving" the word (e.g., Luke 8:13; Acts 8:14; 11:1; 17:11; 1 Thess 1:6; 2:13; Jas 1:21; λαμβάνω appears in the NT six times as often as δέχομαι, though only about 2.5 times as often in Luke). Most of Luke's key verbs with respect to the Spirit ("come," "pour out," "descend," and, distinctive to him in the Gospels, "anoint") have LXX precedents (Haya-Prats, *Believers,* 5–6; note also "fall," Ezek 11:5; Acts 10:44). "Receiving" the Spirit usually appears in the aorist tense in Luke (Haya-Prats, *Believers,* 54–58), a pattern that Haya-Prats, *Believers,* 58–59, attributes to grammatical reasons, OT usage, and emphasis on the moment of reception.

1334. See, e.g., *m. Soṭah* 9:15; *t. Soṭah* 13:2–4; *Mek. Besh.* 7.135ff.; comments in our introduction, ch. 15, sect. 5.a.ii. Rabbis connected Peter's Joel passage, however, with Ezek 36:26 to indicate that the divine presence (i.e., the Spirit) will cause Israel to merit the law.

1335. E.g., Exod 24:12; Lev 26:46; Deut 4:8; Ezra 7:6; Neh 9:13; 1 Esd 9:39; 2 Macc 7:30; Wis 18:4; Sir 45:5, 17; *Sipre Deut.* 305.1.2; the moral law in 4 Macc 2:23 (and perhaps *Sib. Or.* 11.37).

1336. E.g., Jos. *Ant.* 4.318; *Num. Rab.* 19:33; *Pesiq. Rab.* 29/30:2; further on the rabbis' *mattan Torah,* see discussion in Moore, *Judaism,* 1:398; Sandmel, *Judaism,* 182. Whether this analogy is relevant, it is far more so than Greek "gifts" such as Dionysus's "gift" of wine (e.g., Plut. frg. 54, from scholia on Hesiod *W.D.* 368–69, in F. H. Sandbach in Plutarch, *Moralia,* LCL, 15:146–47; Arrian *Ind.* 7.5); various innate gifts like speaking, hunting, intellect, and the like (e.g., Hom. *Il.* 13.730–34; Xen. *On Hunting* 13.18; Cic. *Senect.* 12.40; Val. Max. 7.1.1; Ael. Arist. *Def. Or.* 397, §135D; Iambl. *Letter* 13, frg. 1.3–4, in Stob. *Anth.* 2.2.6); the physician's art (Philost. *Vit. Apoll.* 3.44); or Zeus's gift of wealth (Lucian *Tim.* 37).

1337. *Sipre Deut.* 32.5.10; *b. Ber.* 5a; *Exod. Rab.* 1:1; cf. *Lev. Rab.* 35:8. An early third-century teacher added that God gave the Torah as a gift because Moses kept forgetting it (R. Johanan in *b. Ned.* 38a; *y. Hor.* 3:5, §1; elsewhere, however, mediating Torah was merited, e.g., by Ezra in *y. Meg.* 1:9, §3)—obviously not part of the analogy here!

II. The "Promise" and Those "Afar Off" (2:39)

The "promise" of the Holy Spirit (Luke 24:49; Acts 2:33) must refer to baptism in the Spirit, as it explicitly does in Acts 1:4-5. Luke's language thus connects baptism in the Spirit (1:5), being filled with the Spirit (2:4), the promise of the Spirit, the gift of the Spirit, and receiving the Spirit (2:38-39); as in rhetoric, variation was valuable where it would not impair clarity.[1338] In the larger context of Luke's work, "promise" also involves the eschatological inheritance of God's people (7:17; 13:23, 32-33; 26:6-7); this aspect of the promise theme may cohere with the promise of the Spirit because the Spirit provides a foretaste guaranteeing the eschatological future. This approach would resemble Paul's usage in Galatians, where Paul, like Luke (see comment on "afar off" here), also believed that this promise of the Spirit would apply to Abraham's ethnically Gentile descendants (Gal 3:14; cf. Eph 1:3, 13).

Initially, the promise is to all Israel ("your children"), as in the Scriptures (cf. also Acts 3:20, 25-26). "Your children" may develop "your sons and daughters" in 2:17[1339] (cf. Luke 13:34). But even if Israel, which holds priority, rejects the offer, it remains available for others who will desire it (Acts 13:46; 28:28). (In a sense, Israel's temporary rejection also bought time for more Gentile conversions, since Israel's repentance would usher in Christ's return [3:19-20; Rom 11:25-26].)

"Afar off" (μακράν) likely alludes to Isa 57:19, as scholars often suggest,[1340] and probably refers (on the Lukan level, not that of Peter in the narrative world) to the Gentile mission.[1341] Other scholars have also applied Isaiah's language in that verse to the Gentile mission (Eph 2:17; cf. 2:13).[1342] In context, Isaiah may refer to both Diaspora Jews returning and to Gentiles converting; these nuances would serve Luke's purpose as well.[1343] Some early Jewish interpreters applied the text to proselytes.[1344] One of the other two uses of μακράν in Acts (it appears only ten times in the NT) also suggests that Gentiles are in view here (Acts 22:21; cf. discussion of Isa 57:19 at Acts 10:36). (Later interpreters of Isa 57:19 applied "far off" to those who had recently repented and turned to the law,[1345] but the tradition is probably Amoraic.) Most likely Peter and his hearers within the narrative world would not yet understand the allusion that Luke offers his own informed audience through Peter's words. Many ancients believed that individuals could sometimes speak prophetically in ways they did not understand (e.g., John 11:49-50). Perhaps developing the Greek conception of loss of control in prophecy,[1346] many imagined the possibility of prophecies unintended and unrecognized by the speaker.[1347] They also allowed for literary or rhetorical observations of unintended truth; thus, for example, when a speaker unwittingly said something that sounded like a confirmation of Timarchus's known immorality, the

---

1338. See e.g., Hermog. *Method* 4.416.

1339. Zehnle, *Pentecost Discourse*, 34. Against Jeremias's argument for infant baptism here, "children" means any offspring, even as adults (Barrett, *Acts*, 155).

1340. E.g., Pao, *Isaianic Exodus*, 230; Klauck, *Magic*, 12. The healing in that verse is likely spiritual (as in *Pesiq. Rab.* 44:8).

1341. E.g., Neirynck, "Luke 4,16-30," 378; Hamm, *Acts*, 21; cf. especially now Meek, *Mission*, 110-11 (allowing even Peter's understanding).

1342. Dupont, *Salvation*, 23; Johnson, *Acts*, 58.

1343. Cf. Dunn, *Acts*, 33. Haenchen, *Acts*, 184, mentions God's revelation in Sir 24:32.

1344. Kirby, *Ephesians*, 157, citing *Gen. Rab.* 8:4.

1345. *B. Ber.* 34b; *Tg. Isa.* 57:19.

1346. See discussion of ecstatic prophecy in the excursus at Acts 2:17-18; Keener, *Spirit*, 24.

1347. Plut. *Isis* 14, *Mor.* 356E; Xen. Eph. *Anthia* 5.4; *'Abot R. Nat.* 43, §118 B (biblical examples); *b. Soṭah* 12b (pagans). See further Aune, *Prophecy*, 139, following Strack and Billerbeck, *Kommentar*, 2:546; cf. Jdt. 6:2.

informed audience laughed and spoke of truth prevailing over human intentions (Aeschines *Tim.* 84).[1348]

By concluding that the gift was available to "as many as God calls," Luke clearly echoes the end of Joel 2:32 (3:5 LXX), completing the quotation interrupted in Acts 2:21.[1349] That is, having finished his exposition of "whoever calls on the Lord's name" (2:21) by showing that the name on which his hearers must call is Jesus's (2:38), he concludes the quotation in 2:39. By applying a biblical text about YHWH to Jesus, Luke emphasizes Jesus's deity in this text; that other early Christians interpreted the Joel text similarly (Joel 2:32 in Rom 10:9, 13)[1350] signals that Luke follows an earlier tradition of interpretation. (Both God and those who are saved "call.")[1351]

For Luke, this quotation reinforces the "all flesh" of Acts 2:17, summarizing "your children" plus "those who are far away" earlier in 2:39. With "your children" it points beyond Peter's generation, at least implicitly, to all who call on Jesus for salvation (2:21, 38–39). It is clear from this passage that Luke, as Turner notes, "believed the 'Spirit of prophecy' was still available to all believers." In contrast to the suggestion of some scholars that Luke's circle was no longer charismatic, the warnings of problems in the church in 20:25–35 do not include "a waning of the Spirit."[1352]

d. Summary of Peter's Closing Exhortation (2:40)

Peter "solemnly testifies" to his audience.[1353] Luke elsewhere summarizes speech (Luke 24:27; Acts 1:3; 8:35; 15:12) but here uses a special formula to note it. Speakers could be quite long-winded. Cato spent an entire day speaking, thus preventing Caesar's faction from having the chance to present their case (Plut. *Caes.* 13.1). Cicero complains about Rome's Pompeian law (52 B.C.E.) that allowed each speaker for the defense (of which there could be more than one) only three hours (Cic. *Brut.* 93.324).[1354] Because courts eventually placed limits on the length of one's speech, Albucius preferred to speak in other venues (Sen. E. *Controv.* 7.pref. 8), perhaps even speaking for nine hours at a time.[1355] (See further comment on Acts 24:5.)

In light of long speeches, historians often had to compress their contents,[1356] and some careful writers explicitly noted that they could report only a portion of what was said. For example, a source concludes a report of one of Musonius Rufus's lectures

1348. Cf. Psyche in Apul. *Metam.* 5.6; Saul in 1 Sam 14:39. An accurate societal critic could also be dubbed "oracular" in a figurative sense because he spoke truth (Sen. E. *Controv.* 1.pref. 9).

1349. As is widely agreed (Haenchen, *Acts*, 184n5; Dupont, *Salvation*, 22; Zehnle, *Pentecost Discourse*, 34; Pao, *Isaianic Exodus*, 231–32; Marshall, "Acts," 536, 543). "The Lord God" appears in Luke-Acts especially in the semitized infancy narrative (Luke 1:32, 68) and in Scripture quotations (here and Acts 3:22); it appears some 525 times in the LXX, though missing in our LXX text of Joel 2:32 (i.e., 3:5 LXX).

1350. See esp. Hurtado, *Lord Jesus Christ*, 198–99, who suggests that this belongs to a very early ritual of confessing Jesus (cf. 1 Cor 1:2; 12:3). Paul elsewhere applies earlier biblical language for God to Jesus, e.g., Isa 45:22–23 in Phil 2:10–11. For divine language surrounding Jesus's appearing in 1 Thess 4–5, see Glasson, *Advent*, 161–79; followed also by Robinson, *Coming*, 140–41.

1351. Parsons, *Acts*, 47, notes the wordplay on the cognate terms. The theological compatibility of the two expressions probably also ranks Luke in the dominant stream of Jewish thought, which accepted both divine sovereignty and human responsibility (cf. Jos. *Ant.* 13.172, 297–98; 18.13).

1352. Turner, *Gifts*, 56.

1353. Luke often employs διαμαρτύρομαι (Luke 16:28), including for Peter and his colleagues (Acts 2:40; 8:25; 10:42) and Paul (18:5; 20:21, 23, 24; 23:11; 28:23); it appears sixteen times in the LXX; elsewhere in the NT, it appears once in Paul's undisputed letters (1 Thess 4:6), three times in the Pastorals (1 Tim 5:21; 2 Tim 2:14; 4:1), and once in Heb 2:6.

1354. Cicero was known for his lengthy speaking (e.g., Plut. *Cic.* 12.5).

1355. I read the three trumpet calls in Sen. E. *Controv.* 7.pref. 1 as a figurative reference to three-hour segments; since I myself must teach eight (or as long as fourteen) hours a day in some intensive sessions, I regard this as exhausting but not incredible.

1356. E.g., Thucydides (Kennedy, "Survey of Rhetoric," 15).

thus: "These words [ταῦτα] and others [ἕτερα] like them he then spoke, exhorting and urging his hearers to look upon hardship with disdain."[1357] Xenophon justifies merely summarizing Socrates's words by admitting that Socrates and his friends said more but that he intended not to report the entire trial, instead emphasizing a central point only.[1358] Tacitus recounts some sample arguments as direct speech and then summarizes the effect of "these and similar arguments."[1359] Novels could use the same form: one person exhorted another "with these and many other like words."[1360] Luke's summary in fact uses "a well-known stylistic abbreviatory device," as van der Horst notes.[1361] This "literary device . . . shortens the length of a speech and suggests the transcriptional character of the part 'quoted.'"[1362] Jewish interpreters likewise explained texts on the assumption that biblical narratives merely abbreviated what had really been said.[1363] This does not necessarily mean that Luke knew more of the speech than he reports (any more than that, as many scholars think, he knew less), only that he knew that there was more.[1364]

Writers also often mentioned that they had many more examples available and were providing only a sample (e.g., Mus. Ruf. 10, p. 78.22; 2 Macc 2:24–25; Heb 11:32).[1365] Rhetoricians sometimes noted that they could offer other examples but that they provided only those necessary to demonstrate their case.[1366] Sometimes writers or speakers indicated that they could have provided further evidence of a person's guilt, thereby insinuating greater guilt than they had stated.[1367] Similarly, one could imply a subject's virtue by noting that one lacked sufficient time to recount all the positive examples available.[1368] The same was true of great sufferings,[1369] the teachings of scribes,[1370] or an epideictic treatment of virtue.[1371]

Probably this verse means that Luke skips through many supplementary πιστοί (proofs, arguments; some of which the informed reader may infer from the broader context of Luke-Acts)[1372] and moves quickly "to the *peroratio*, the final exhortation and emotional appeal involving *pathos*": "Save yourselves!"[1373] This restates briefly

1357. Mus. Ruf. 7, p. 58.29–30 (Lutz, 59).

1358. Xen. *Apol.* 22. Thus also Aeschines summarizes to avoid repeating the entirety of an earlier speech (*Embassy* 118). Galba's speech in Tac. *Hist.* 1.15–16 is "to this effect" (LCL, 1:27, 33).

1359. Tac. *Ann.* 11.23–24 ("these and similar arguments" is 11.24).

1360. Ach. Tat. 7.14.4 (LCL).

1361. Van der Horst, "Parallels to Acts," 57 (citing Xen. *Hell.* 2.4.42; Polyb. 3.111.11; 21.14.4); cf. earlier Dibelius, *Studies in Acts*, 178 (citing, besides those above, Appian *Samnite History* 10.6; *Bell. civ.* 3.63.257; followed by Haenchen, *Acts*, 184; Zehnle, *Pentecost Discourse*, 36; Soards, *Speeches*, 138; Barrett, *Acts*, 156; Marguerat, *Actes*, 96).

1362. Aune, *Environment*, 127–28 (citing Arrian *Alex.* 3.9.8; Jos. *War* 1.638; 2.33; 3.383; Longus 1.16). For instructions on abbreviating one's speeches, see *Rhet. Alex.* 22, 1434b.11–18.

1363. E.g., *Gen. Rab.* 55:7 (interpolating Gen 22); 93:8; *Exod. Rab.* 44:5. For the principle of selectivity of rabbis' teachings in rabbinic literature, see Gerhardsson, *Memory*, 174.

1364. Witherington, *Acts*, 156 (who suggests that perhaps Luke's source told him there was more). Even in recent history, extant notes for a genuine three-and-a-half-hour speech may be read aloud in three minutes (Tomkins, *Wilberforce*, 80, 84).

1365. See more fully Keener, *John*, 1214–15, 1241–42.

1366. Dion. Hal. *Thuc.* 55; *Isaeus* 19–20; *Demosth.* 42, 46, 58; *Lit. Comp.* 11.

1367. Lysias *Or.* 2.1, §190; 12.1, §120; 28.1, §179; Aeschines *Tim.* 109; Cic. *Verr.* 2.2.47.118; 2.2.48.118; 2.4.26.57; 2.4.46.102; 2.4.47.105; *Flacc.* 5.12; Plut. *Mal. Hdt.* 1, *Mor.* 854F; cf. Isoc. *Antid.* 140, 310, 320.

1368. Lysias *Or.* 2.2, §190; 2.54, §195; Ovid *Tristia* 2.324; Philost. *Vit. soph.* 2.17.597; 1 Macc 9:22; cf. the difficulty in Diod. Sic. 16.95.5.

1369. E.g., Hom. *Od.* 3.113–17.

1370. *Pesiq. Rab.* 3:2; for Torah learning, *Song Rab.* 1:3, §1.

1371. Philo *Spec. Laws* 4.238; for analogous hyperbole, cf. *Abr.* 1; *Mos.* 1.213; *Dreams* 2.63.

1372. For reading Luke's "other words" in light of Luke-Acts as a whole, see Kilgallen, "Assumptions."

1373. Witherington, *Acts*, 139. On *pathos*, see comment on Acts 20:19.

the speech's central deliberative thrust.[1374] Although Luke, like other early Christian writers, makes abundant use of "salvation" language, the immediate referent of "Save" here and "saved" in Acts 2:47 is Joel's prophecy in Acts 2:21: whoever calls on the Lord's name will be saved.[1375] For Luke (especially in view of his application of Joel's prophecy), this salvation is deliverance from God's eschatological wrath and destruction, available through Christ (4:12; 11:14; 15:1, 11; 16:31). Thus Luke would apply it to his own generation as well as to Peter's.[1376]

For Peter's hearers to save themselves from the generation's wickedness was not, as some later Gentile Christian interpreters would have it, a summons to leave Israel and their Jewishness;[1377] rather, it was a summons to leave their rebellion against God, like a repeated prophetic summons to Israel in the OT. Luke's term γενεά means here a temporal "generation," not (against some popular interpretations) "race" (γένος).[1378] Perhaps in contrast to the pious generation of Jesus's childhood (Luke 1:50–55, 68–79), Jesus held harsh words for his own generation (γενεά, 7:31; 11:30–32), which he called faithless and twisted (διεστραμμένη, 9:41) and evil (11:29). Jesus also condemned it in advance as guilty of his murder (17:25; perhaps Acts 8:33) and hence guiltier than rebellious generations before it (Luke 11:50–51) and destined for judgment (21:32). Luke distinguishes that generation from previous generations (Acts 13:36; 14:16; 15:21). By calling the generation σκολιᾶς ("crooked")[1379] here, he surely alludes to Deut 32:5 (γενεά σκολιά καὶ διεστραμμένη), the same LXX text alluded to in the Jesus tradition in Luke 9:41 (//Matt 17:17; these texts use γενεά and διεστραμμένη).[1380] The crooked generation needed to be straightened to be prepared for the Lord's coming (Luke 3:5; cf. Acts 13:10, using διαστρέφων). (Following the LXX more fully, Paul combines both terms for "twisted" in Phil 2:15.) Deuteronomy 32:5 refers to the rebellion of the wilderness generation; Ps 77:8 LXX (78:8 ET) provides the only other occasion where the LXX employs σκολιός with "generation," and it also depicts the wilderness generation.[1381] Peter's point is an exhortation not to harden their hearts as their ancestors did in the wilderness (Ps 95:8).[1382]

Luke's language here is closest to his earlier description of John the Baptist, who also announced the good news to the people with many "other exhortations" (Luke 3:18),[1383] summoned crowds for a baptism of repentance (3:7–8), and answered their question how to be saved (3:10). Peter thus continues the preaching tradition followed by John, underlining the continuity of salvation history and of the saving message.[1384]

1374. Even transitions ideally restated the point briefly (*Rhet. Her.* 4.26.35, though Luke does not set forth what follows).

1375. With Ridderbos, "Speeches of Peter," 28.

1376. With Sloan, "Signs," 162.

1377. See Hort, *Judaistic Christianity*, 41–42.

1378. See, e.g., Luke 11:30–32, 50–51; 17:25; 21:32; Keener, *Matthew*, 589; the "race" interpretation is mentioned in Cullmann, *Early Church*, 151; Mattill, *Last Things*, 97; in Luke's usage, cf. Luke 16:8.

1379. The term often had moral connotations (e.g., Dio Chrys. *Or.* 80.9; BDAG cites Dio Chrys. *Or.* 58[75].1; Lucian *Indictment* 16; Jos. *Ag. Ap.* 1.179).

1380. Deut 32:5 probably also supplies the language for *Sib. Or.* 1.124. Διαστρέφω elsewhere appears in the NT only at Luke 23:2; Acts 13:8, 10; 20:30.

1381. Commentators regularly note these two LXX passages (Knowling, "Acts," 92; Lake and Cadbury, *Commentary*, 27; Haenchen, *Acts*, 184; Munck, *Acts*, 20).

1382. Such an invitation sounds different as an intra-Jewish critique (as in the psalm or in Peter's preaching) than it would otherwise; indeed, this text remains part of today's regular synagogue liturgy.

1383. Both texts employ παρακαλέω, but this appears twenty-nine times in Luke-Acts.

1384. Tannehill, *Luke*, 49, links the term also with σκολιά in Luke 3:5–6, further connecting Peter with John.

THE LIFE OF THE
EMPOWERED COMMUNITY
(2:41–47)

The goal of the Pentecost experience, with its empowerment for mission, includes a community modeling the ideal, proleptically eschatological lifestyle of the kingdom (cf. comment on Acts 1:3–8; 2:1–4). The community is now much larger than the earlier united nucleus in Acts 1:12–14: the Holy Spirit's activity has brought about church growth. The ideal church offers a pivotal climax and goal of Luke's larger story, though, for Luke, this ideal church cannot be complete until it includes representatives of all nations (1:8).

In this summary section, the Jerusalem community of disciples begins to fulfill Jesus's teachings and model in the Gospel on various points: prayer, continuing signs, eating together, and sharing of possessions (cf. Luke 12:33). Both here and in the Gospel, through explicit quotations and implicit allusions, Luke also grounds this lifestyle in the ideals of community for Israel and the example of its prophets (e.g., Deut 15:7–8; 2 Kgs 4:38–44); he also effectively employs Hellenistic language for the ideal community. Luke himself recognizes that the Jerusalem church experienced conflicts at times (Acts 5:3–4; 6:1), but affirms that the new life of the Spirit experienced as a norm by the earliest Jesus movement epitomizes God's plan. Presumably, he also intends it as a model for Spirit-filled communities of his own day where not restricted by historical particulars (such as meeting in the temple, characteristic of, and possible only for, the Jerusalem church).

Modern movements have noted that conversions without integration into the life of a community are sometimes difficult to sustain; ancient movements were no different in this regard. Ancient sources often report such integration following conversion.[1] Merely "receiving the word" (2:41) did not guarantee perseverance (Luke 8:13; cf. Acts 8:14, 20–23). But just as proselyte baptism meant initiation into the full (or nearly full) life of the community of Israel,[2] so those baptized in Acts 2:41 were initiated into the life of the new community in 2:42–47.

Scholars often are unduly creative in locating chiastic structures, and I do not find many signs of deliberate chiasmus in Acts. Nevertheless, Luke's elaborate chiasmus at 2:22–36 suggests that he is not averse to them at least in his introductory section, and it is possible that we should think of one here:[3]

---

1. See Gallagher, "Conversion and Community" (on *Acts of John*; *Joseph and Aseneth*; Apuleius's *Metamorphoses*).

2. See White, *Initiation*, 70. In contrast to multiple allegiances permitted in Mysteries, Judaism and Christianity were exclusivistic, creating (especially for Christians in Jerusalem and both in the Diaspora) a strong bond (see Gager, *Kingdom*, 131–32).

3. Talbert, *Acts*, 33, conversely offers a chiastic structure that includes shared possessions as part of the common life in Acts 2:44–46, and views apostolic signs (2:43) as the structure's central element. Talbert's structure may be correct; that 2:44–45 (using κοινά) may develop the summary of κοινωνία in 2:42 is, indeed, likely. Luke does

A Effective evangelism (through preaching, 2:41)
  B Shared worship and meals (2:42)
    C Shared possessions (2:44–45)
  B′ Shared worship and meals (2:46)
A′ Effective evangelism (through lifestyle, 2:47)

If so, the sharing of possessions is a central (perhaps because so distinctive) feature of Luke's vision of the early Christian community formed by the Spirit, leading to a wide impact on the society around them.

Excursus: Summary Sections and Statements

Dibelius suggests that historical tradition normally dealt with individual accounts and incidents whereas the larger perspective afforded by summaries belonged to the composers of histories.[4] Witherington suggests that "the use of such summary material, including linking summary remarks, is rather typical of ancient historio-graphical works that were based on research and the use of sources, which were by nature episodic in character."[5] Like Luke, ethnographic historians use summaries to generalize and comment on their descriptions after they describe religious or philo-sophic sects (such as Egyptian priests or Essenes).[6]

Luke's summary statements trace the spread of the message about Jesus in Acts (6:7; 9:31; 12:24; 19:20; 28:31; cf. 13:49; 19:10, 17),[7] as he does, albeit less frequently (perhaps because of more material), for Jesus's ministry in the Gospel (Luke 4:14, 37; 5:15; 7:17).[8] Given Acts' emphasis on spreading the gospel (Acts 1:8) and its conclusion before the task is complete, these summaries invite Luke's audience to participate in the mission.[9] In addition to this narrative function of keeping the focus on the central issue, they may also serve another literary function. In these generaliza-tions, Luke condenses an undoubtedly wider collection of information than he can afford space to narrate.[10] Writers such as Josephus exercised more freedom in their summary statements (see comment on Acts 6:7), and the same is likely the case for Luke, who exercises more creative freedom in introducing or concluding material that he takes over from Mark than in that material's content.[11]

Summary *passages*, by contrast, are more complete than mere summary statements and may depict the regular life of the Christian community.[12] Still, writers could

---

not elaborate apostolic signs so much as the sharing of possessions at this point, but it does fit evangelism (2:41, 47; see comment on "power" at Acts 1:8) and the following narrative (3:1–4:4). Both elements recur in 4:32–35, with apostolic power being located more centrally (4:33), but the emphasis is laid heavily on sharing possessions (4:32, 34–35). If one adopts either chiastic model, at least the A/A′ and B/B′ elements are clear on either view.

4. Dibelius, *Studies in Acts*, 127.

5. Witherington, *Acts*, 159 (following Fornara, *Nature of History*, 47ff.).

6. Sterling, "Athletes of Virtue."

7. The same impression is conveyed in reports within the narrative (e.g., Acts 14:27; 15:3, 12). Many scholars also take several such statements as structural clues for the narrative's movement (see our introduction, ch. 16, sect. 2.a).

8. See Rosner, "Progress," 215–33, esp. 221–23; Weiser, *Apostelgeschichte*, 102; cf. Mark 1:28.

9. See Rosner, "Progress," 232–33.

10. See Witherington, *Acts*, 158 (also noting variations, as in Mussies, "Variation").

11. Witherington, "Editing," 346. Their consistent structure and style in Acts also support this conclusion (Co, "Summaries in Acts").

12. Brehm, "Significance of Summaries."

express considerable freedom in composing summary passages (where selectivity shaped perspective).[13] They appear especially in the earlier chapters of Acts, covering a period where Luke has less access to concrete information. They may thus help make up for limited specific examples while underlining Luke's sense of the whole story.[14] Both summary statements and summary passages appear elsewhere in ancient literature. Speakers sometimes concluded a section by saying, "This is what happened in connection with these events."[15] But often they recapitulated their preceding arguments.[16] Additional summaries were probably more common especially when writers needed to "expand" their material.[17] Occasionally ancient prose writers[18] (and often poets)[19] included some sort of refrain, a recurring line that kept the reader focused on the main point. Though not a refrain in any poetic sense, Luke's repetition of his historical interest in the spread of the message and its movement emphasizes his point analogously.

This first summary section also emphasizes Luke's main point, continued with the next summary in 4:32–35, pausing in between to flesh out the summary with a detailed, dramatic, and, for the life of the community (4:4 implies), significant example.[20] The major summaries of the earliest Jerusalem church (2:42–47; 4:32–35; 5:12–16) thus emphasize the theme of empowered witness as applied to the Jerusalem mission (see 1:8).[21] The summaries of the earliest Christian community (2:41–47 or 2:42–47; 4:32–35; 5:12–16) also serve an apologetic function by emphasizing the community's virtue.[22]

1. Luke's Conversion Report (2:41)

Unless the event was more organized than we are imagining it above, it may have been difficult to make a precise count of the converts on that day. Ancient writers might cite such dramatic conversion reports to indicate the success of their protagonist's preaching; such reports are known about Pythagoras.[23] We should note, however,

13. Josephus's summaries about Jewish "sects" (*War* 2.119–66; *Ant.* 13.171–73; 18.11–25) are driven by ideology and especially apologetic (McLaren, "Josephus' Summary Statements," goes even further).

14. See Witherington, *Acts*, 159. This sense would include the broader story, showing how they fulfilled Jesus's teaching in the Gospel of Luke (e.g., Luke 12:33; 14:33; see Varickasseril, "Portrait"); for Luke's theology of the church as the witnessing community where the Spirit works, see Haacker, "Bild."

15. E.g., Xen. *Hell.* 3.5.25 (the close of *Hell.* 3); 4.8.19 (not the close of a book). Such summary statements were also appropriate in lists of laws (4Q270 7 II, 14–15).

16. E.g., Cic. *Fin.* 3.9.31; *Quinct.* 19.60; 28.85–29.90 (at the end of proofs); Mus. Ruf. 3, p. 42.23–29; 1 Cor 6:20; 10:31–11:1; 14:39–40. On recapitulation, see also Anderson, *Glossary*, 85 (citing *Rhet. Alex.* 20–21); for various methods of recapitulation (not used by Luke), see Anderson, *Glossary*, 22, 24, 39, 51; cf. additional citations in Keener, *John*, 887, 1213.

17. *Rhet. Alex.* 22, 1434b.8–11 (cf. abbreviation in lines 15–17).

18. E.g., Sen. Y. *Nat. Q.* 3.pref. 11, 12, 13, 14, 15, 16; Judg 17:6; 21:25 (cf. 18:1; 19:1).

19. E.g., the wedding invocation to Hymen in Catull. *Carm.* 61.4–5, 39–40, 49–50, 59–60; 62.4–5, 10, 19, 25, 31, 38, 48, 66 (with *io* added, 61.117–18, 137–38, 142–43; 147–48; 152–53, 157–58, 162–63, 167–68, 172–73, 177–78, 182–83); the bridal summons (61.96, 106, 113); invocation to the Fates (64.327, in briefer form thereafter in 333, 337, 342, 347, 352, 356, 361, 365, 371, 375, 381); or a summons to love (*Perv. Ven.* 1, 8, 27, 36, 48, 57–58, 68, 75, 80, 93).

20. Cf. Tannehill, *Acts*, 44 (Acts returns to the theme at Acts 4:32–5:11 and 6:1–6).

21. See Joubert, "Gesigpunt." For parallels among them, see Marguerat, *Actes*, 102.

22. Cf. Sterling, "Athletes of Virtue."

23. Van der Horst, "Parallels to Acts," 58, notes the two thousand converts in Porph. *V.P.* 20 and Iambl. *V.P.* 30. These are from so long after Pythagoras's time that we can no longer ascertain the extent to which they depend on tradition.

that Luke does not provide simply conversion reports in Acts. After each evangelistic sermon in Acts, Luke also reports people's acceptance or rejection (2:41; 4:4; 5:33; 7:54; 8:6, 36; 10:44; 13:44, 48–50; 17:32; 22:22; 28:24, 29).[24]

Many scholars doubt that all three thousand could have been baptized in a single day.[25] Barrett, for example, notes, "Mass baptisms would have been easy at a river . . ., but there were no natural large-scale supplies of water in the city."[26] Although one could wonder about the precision of Luke's information source here, Barrett's argument against it is ill-founded, as we shall see below in view of Jerusalem's water resources. Luke's "in that day" could be hyperbole, but in this case Luke and his sources probably knew the available resources of the Temple Mount better than do most of his modern critics.

a. Jerusalem's Water Resources

To accommodate the thousands of worshipers the temple hosted daily, the Temple Mount must have afforded plenty of baptismal pools.[27] Despite lack of complete excavations, it appears that some, apparently many, mikvaot on the Temple Mount were used before entering the temple area.[28] A number of mikvaot appear in what may be a bath complex for ritual bathing south of the temple.[29] Even the Roman historian Tacitus was familiar with the claim that the temple held many pools as well as cisterns for rainwater (*Hist.* 5.12). (When flowing water was unavailable, mikvaot normally depended on rainwater.[30] For further discussion of mikvaot, see the excursus at Acts 2:38.)

Nor should we suppose that such use would risk exhausting the water supply for mikvaot, even if (and this is not the case) many people's use depleted the pools significantly more than disuse would have. Archaeologists have excavated thirty-four cisterns near the Temple Mount; "the capacity of some of these is as much as 8,000–12,000 cubic metres."[31] If one includes pools[32] such as Bethesda and Siloam (and tradition designated at least Siloam as already useful for ritual immersion),[33]

24. Goulder, *Type and History*, 84. I use much of this material regarding Luke's presentation of the Jesus movement's early growth in Keener, "Plausibility."

25. E.g., Hull, *Spirit in Acts*, 93.

26. Barrett, *Acts*, 159.

27. With, e.g., Taylor, *Immerser*, 63; Adler, "Baths" (interpreting the baths differently than Regev). Cf. Meyers and Strange, *Archaeology*, 25–26.

28. See Reich, "Possible *miqwa'ot*"; Cornfeld, *Archaeology*, 50n229c (on Jos. *War* 1.229), 272; Mazar, "Excavations," 52; Meyers and Strange, *Archaeology*, 25–26, 55; Regev, "Baths"; in later literary sources, cf. *m. Tamid* 1:1; *Mid.* 1:9; *Neg.* 14:8; further comment on Acts 2:38. Others were apparently en route to Jerusalem or at least nearby (e.g., Reich, "'Isawiya"; *m. Parah* 3:7). For the tradition of officers over water resources in the temple, see Jeremias, *Jerusalem*, 171, 174.

29. McRay, *Archaeology*, 106.

30. See *m. Ter.* 5:6; *'Ed.* 1:3; 7:3–4; *Miqw.* 2:3ff.; 3:1–4; 4:1–5; 5:1–6; *t. Miqw.* 2; *'Ed.* 1:3; *Sipra Sh. par.* 9.118.1.1; *b. Šabb.* 16b; 65a; 144b; *Pesaḥ.* 17b; 34b; *Beṣah* 18; *Giṭ.* 16a; *B. Bat.* 66a; *Mak.* 4a; *Bek.* 55b; *y. Ter.* 4:12; 5:7; cf. CD X, 12; more fully, Keener, *John*, 510–11. Even most homes in Herodian Jerusalem had underground cisterns for collecting drinking water (McRay, *Archaeology*, 125).

31. Safrai, "Temple," 884. Some estimate that the subterranean reservoirs beneath the Temple Mount functioned as cisterns holding up to ten million gallons (McRay, *Archaeology*, 123). Proper mikvaot would not use drawn water (see Keener, *John*, 510–11), but the cisterns would accommodate the temple's other needs; I am not aware whether conduits existed between some cisterns and mikvaot here, but some did elsewhere (cf. Avigad, *Jerusalem*, 139; Pearlman, *Zealots*, 180–81; Yadin, *Masada*, 166; Hachlili and Killebrew, "Saga," 44, 46). Cultic precincts in general demanded water supplies (Egelhaaf-Gaiser, "Sites," 211), but Jerusalem's massive temple seems particularly well-endowed.

32. On these other pools in Jerusalem, see, e.g., McRay, *Archaeology*, 122–24; Reich and Shukron, "Brykt hsylwh."

33. *M. Zab.* 1:5; *y. Ta'an.* 2:1, §8; Jeremias, *Jerusalem*, 320.

the amount of water available for baptism is among the least problems to the narrative's plausibility. With a total of 150 *known* immersion pools in Jerusalem, the immersion of three thousand persons in the span of a few hours would not have been difficult.[34]

Likewise, against those who doubt that the 120 disciples of 1:15 could baptize three thousand people,[35] these baptisms would not have been formal ceremonies analogous to modern baptisms (baptismal records, family gatherings, and so forth) or even individual ancient proselyte baptisms. "Baptizing" in this period involved mainly supervision while the people coming for purification immersed themselves; the disciples could, like John, supervise mass baptisms without individual attention (Luke 3:3, 7, 12, 16, 21). Even if only the apostles and a few of their colleagues, a total of perhaps thirty, "performed" the baptisms in thirty mikvaot, they could finish their task in a few hours. Indeed, this view of matters probably assumes more organization than actually occurred in the excited atmosphere of mass conversions;[36] once verbal instructions were issued, mass immersions in response to Peter's command could have occurred with very little supervision at all (though, by analogy with John's baptism and various passages claiming that the apostles "baptized" people, supervision probably remained the norm; Luke 3:7; 7:29–30; Acts 1:5; 8:38; 10:48; 11:16; 19:4).

b. Inflating Numbers

It was common to exaggerate the numbers of, for instance, enemies slain in battle (Xen. *Hiero* 2.16; Livy 3.8.10), or one might exaggerate enemy numbers to mitigate the shame of one's own defeat (Tac. *Hist.* 3.61).[37] Pliny the Younger, who otherwise emphasizes historians' high standards for facts, jests that one correspondent boasts, like historians, of numbers too great to count (*Ep.* 9.16.1). Lucian complains that one particularly ridiculous historian so reduces Roman casualties, and inflates those of the enemy, that no one will take him seriously (*Hist.* 20).[38] Thus Dunn, commenting on this passage in Acts, remarks, "Numbers in ancient historians tended to be more impressionistic (or propagandistic) rather than to provide what we today would regard as an accurate accounting."[39] Some ancient figures would be more concrete (such as reckonings based on the number of men lost if a Roman legion were destroyed), but many were estimates. On the whole, historians were not careless, but even the best of

34. See Grasham, "Archaeology and Baptism." Pools also apparently occurred on roads en route to Jerusalem, for pilgrims (Amit, "*Miqveh* Complex"). Such accommodations proved particularly important just before festivals (cf. John 11:55; for early arrivals for purification, see, e.g., Safrai, "Temple," 876–77, citing, e.g., Jos. *War* 1.229; esp. for corpse impurity, cf. deSilva, *Honor*, 274–75; Sanders, *Judaism*, 134–35).

35. E.g., Barrett, *Acts*, 159. He is also skeptical that the women among the 120 would have participated; but only women would supervise women's immersions, at least insofar as such immersions would have been done in the nude (cf. Meeks, *Urban Christians*, 151), as with mikvaot on the Temple Mount.

36. Conversion could also include emotion in a philosophic setting (cf. the desired response in protrepsis in Plut. *Lect.* 37F–38D in Malherbe, *Moral Exhortation*, 71–72).

37. Cf., e.g., high enemy numbers in Vell. Paterc. 2.23.3; 2.30.5; 2.47.1; 2.110.3 (though Velleius was himself an officer in this war—2.111.3—he would not have compiled the statistics himself); some such large figures, however, must have depended on genuine sources despite their propaganda value (see, e.g., *Res gest.* 1.3; 4.21; *Res gest.* summary). Few rivaled the rabbis in numerical hyperbole, with 80,000 myriads (i.e., 800 million) slain at Betar (*y. Ta'an.* 4:5, §10) or 150,000 schoolchildren (*Lam. Rab.* 3:51, §9); blood flowing to distant lands (*y. Sukkah* 5:1, §7; *Lam. Rab.* 2:2, §4); Gentiles fertilizing their vineyards for seven years with Jewish blood (*b. Giṭ.* 57a). Cf. the growth in Philistine numbers between Judg 16:27 MT and *L.A.B.* 43:8; 150,000 dead in Diod. Sic. 14.76.2.

38. He does, however, inadvertently attest that firsthand records were available; this historian contradicts the officers' reports, which Lucian apparently knows. Yet even firsthand reports are often estimates.

39. Dunn, *Acts*, 34.

them often had only approximations.[40] Sometimes numbers that historians cited did not fit other known data, in which case later historians might critique them (Polyb. 12.17.1–12.22.7) or prefer to blame the scribe rather than the historian (12.4.4–6).[41] Thucydides also complains that he could not provide the numbers for one battle because one side would not reveal them and the other side clearly exaggerated its numbers (Thucyd. 5.68.2).[42]

At the same time, strikingly large numbers do appear frequently in documented historical times; in the most costly war of which Polybius knew (Polyb. 1.63.4, 8), the Romans lost about seven hundred quinqueremes and the Carthaginians about five hundred (1.63.6). No less dramatically, Polybius estimates that about seventy thousand Romans died in the battle at Cannae (3.117.4). Lest anyone question his accuracy, Polybius emphasizes that he is not (like some historians) merely interested in numbers that are simply "plausible"; he discovered an actual list from Hannibal on a bronze tablet (3.33.17–18). We may choose to think that Polybius invented the tablet or, much likelier, that his Carthaginian source did. But given the stakes in the war, these numbers likely bear some semblance to what took place.

Josephus's estimates are inflated;[43] where we can test him most clearly, he is not averse to inflating numbers in the biblical text.[44] He estimates that more than one million in Jerusalem died during the war (*War* 6.420), though he concedes that most were Jews from elsewhere trapped inside (6.421). Although he attributes the information to a census of the high priests in the time of Nero, few take literally his claim that 2,700,000 people showed up for Passovers (6.423–25); increasing the numbers was to Josephus's advantage.[45] Some scholars, however, adjust the figures too far in the opposite direction; Josephus is at least internally consistent.[46] Pliny the Elder, after all, calls Jerusalem the East's "most illustrious city."[47] Where we can compare their estimates on concrete points, Josephus's estimates appear higher than Luke's (see comment on Acts 21:38).[48]

c. Jerusalem's Population

Most scholars reject Luke's figures because the scholars depend on Joachim Jeremias's now outdated estimates for Jerusalem's population (25,000–30,000) instead of newer estimates that range much higher.[49] Jerusalem had expanded beyond its walls

---

40. Rubincam, "Numbers" (evaluating, among others, Thucydides). Thus Quint. Curt. 4.16.26 (LCL, 1:319) reports the number of Persian casualties "so far as the victors could determine their number" (and even here does not match all other sources). Suet. *Aug.* 30 lists higher values for one donation than *Res gest.* 4.21 (which would not underestimate) lists altogether, but in addition to the real possibility that Suetonius misinterpreted his source, his value estimates might account for inflation by his day, or perhaps Augustus may not have calculated the gems and pearls in equivalent sesterces (gold appearing later in the passage).

41. Sometimes scribes did miscopy numbers (e.g., reading VIII as CIIII in Livy 3.3.9; see LCL, 2:251n1).

42. Even Roman legions provided a higher paper strength than their real force; thus a century contained only about sixty troops (see comment on Acts 10:1).

43. As is widely acknowledged (e.g., Feldman, "Introduction," 45–46).

44. Compare Jos. *Ant.* 6.203 with 1 Sam 18:27 MT (though the LXX, if derivative, actually decreases the MT number!).

45. Cf., e.g., Foakes-Jackson and Lake, "Background of Jewish History," 1n3; Avi-Yonah, "Geography," 109.

46. See Byatt, "Population Numbers" (but most think that Byatt estimates too high).

47. Pliny E. *N.H.* 5.70 (Fiensy, "Composition," 214).

48. Where Luke lacked any incentive to inflate; Josephus may have had some, but he may simply have a habit of estimating high.

49. Reinhardt, "Population Size," 237, 240–41 (suggesting 60,000–120,000 in the 30s C.E.); Borg, *Vision,* 173, suggests 40,000–70,000. Even much earlier, F. C. Grant's estimates were triple Jeremias's; estimates are, as some scholars (e.g., Bruce, *History,* 39, warning that Jerusalem was just one square mile; Sanders, *Judaism,* 125) note, difficult. Foakes-Jackson and Lake, "Background of Jewish History," 1, estimated fifty thousand.

in this period,[50] but Jeremias's biggest mistake was his underestimation of population density,[51] which was much greater than the early nineteenth-century Palestinian settlements on which Jeremias based his estimate.[52] Magen Broshi has noted that Roman Jerusalem enclosed about 450 acres, and he estimates about eighty thousand inhabitants.[53] More recent density and area estimates also usually estimate eighty thousand or higher.[54] Herod so increased the city's water supply that the city could have doubled its population[55] and supported at least seventy thousand (though some think that the temple complex consumed so much water that the population remained around forty thousand).[56]

At feast times such as Pentecost, Jerusalem might swell to as many as half a million people, with an estimated thirty thousand from the Diaspora.[57] The Temple Mount was large enough to hold tens of thousands at one time; estimates run as high as two hundred thousand[58] and four hundred thousand.[59] Modern Western interpreters, underestimating population density, tend to dismiss high numbers,[60] but checks exist on our skepticism today. For example, the Sacred Mosque at Mecca, which is 180,000 square meters (i.e., just 36,000 sq. m. more than Jerusalem's Temple Mount), holds five hundred thousand in prayer.[61] Mecca hosted only about 108,000 pilgrims annually before the First World War but with modern transportation now hosts more than two million; and Mecca is smaller and less accessible than was Jerusalem.[62]

Given such estimates, thousands of hearers and a rapid mass movement of three thousand conversions are not at all implausible. Although religious movements can start small, their history demonstrates that some can also multiply at a tremendous rate after a major corporate spiritual experience such as the one suggested in Acts 2.[63] For example, some scholars estimate that early U.S. Methodists grew roughly a thousand

50. Reinhardt, "Population Size," 243.

51. Ibid., 245. Population density in Ostia (435 per hectare) was much higher than in Pompeii (125–156 per hectare; Horsley, *Galilee*, 166); Jerusalem, analogously, was probably heavily populated compared with Galilean towns.

52. Reinhardt, "Population Size," 250.

53. Broshi, "Estimating," 14 (close to double his estimate for the Herodian period, p. 13); cf. also idem, "Population de l'ancienne Jérusalem." Earlier, *Let. Aris.* 105 estimates a compass of forty stadia.

54. Reinhardt, "Population Size," 241–43. Wilkinson, "Population," estimates more than seventy thousand for this period.

55. See, e.g., McRay, *Archaeology*, 122–23.

56. Stambaugh and Balch, *Environment*, 97. It is possible that Rev 11:13 provides one ancient estimate of Jerusalem's population at around seventy thousand (cf. Beasley-Murray, *Revelation*, 177; Aune, *Revelation*, 628). Revelation's apocalyptic use of numbers predisposes it to round the figure to a multiple of seven, but the number could have also been rounded to twelve, so that seventy thousand might provide an estimate, within a few ten thousands, of the population. Even if this inference is correct, however, how accurate can we depend on Revelation's estimate to be, especially if written perhaps two decades after the city's demise?

57. Fiensy, "Composition," 233 (also citing archaeological evidence for the community centers that housed many of them, including the Theodotus inscription). Pervo's denial that Luke could include Diaspora hearers would seem to ignore Acts 2:5–13, but he may mean this objection only to Diaspora hearers in 4:4 (*Acts*, 86–87n115).

58. Witherington, *Acts*, 156.

59. Sanders, *Judaism*, 126.

60. Ancients sometimes did the same with ruined cities (a practice to which Thucydides objected in Thucyd. 1.10.1–2).

61. Sanders, *Judaism*, 126.

62. Ibid., 127.

63. The modern history of revivals readily illustrates the possibility of rapid growth (Wolffe, *Expansion*, 57–62; cf. Noll, *Shape*, 111), as does the rapid proliferation of Christianity (and its particular branches), Islam, and other movements in various parts of the world in the twentieth century.

times over in four decades;[64] one recent revival movement in India grew 3,000 percent in a two-year period;[65] a revival movement in Suriname led to the conversion of perhaps a third of one people group over the course of a decade;[66] and so on. Larger mass conversions occur in various biblically saturated parts of the world today,[67] often with less clear incidents to prompt them than what Luke reports in this narrative.

Such observations do not constitute proof that Luke's report is accurate, but they do challenge the grounds on which many commentators tend to dismiss them. Granted, it is unlikely in the revival atmosphere described in Acts 2[68] that the apostles and their

64. Early Methodists in the United States, under the leadership of Francis Asbury, grew from three hundred in 1771 to three hundred thousand forty years later, i.e., one thousand times over (e.g., Noll, *Rise*, 190); Methodism in England grew from twenty-two thousand in 1767 to 518,000 (more than twenty times over in about eighty years; Bebbington, *Dominance*, 51); for more restrained yet comparable statistics from about 1800 to 1850, see Wolffe, *Expansion*, 70 (about eighteenfold increase in the United States and fivefold in Great Britain); for growth from fourteen thousand to more than a million between 1784 and 1844, see Mullin, *History*, 182–83; one thousand to nearly half a million from 1770 to 1830 in Sweeney, *Story*, 64; twenty Methodist churches in the U.S. in 1770 to nearly twenty thousand ninety years later in Kidd, *Awakening*, 322. For some factors, see Wolffe, *Expansion*, 41; but apart from immigration, such factors could have applied equally to the Jerusalem church as a renewal movement within Judaism. Similarly, a Holiness denomination grew 300 percent in five years after its "pentecost" (Synan, *Power*, 123); Jesuits multiplied five hundred times in their first sixteen years (Mullin, *History*, 138); northern Methodists grew 118 percent in one year (and Presbyterians 34 percent) during the Korean revival of 1907 (Lee, "Korean Pentecost," 81); one Korean church grew from five to 720,000 members in forty years (i.e., multiplied by 144,000; Lim, "Evaluation," 182–83; with a generally "20–30 percent annual growth rate," Lee, "Movement," 518; but in South Korea generally, cf. also Hong, "Leadership," 233–34); Indonesia's Nias church grew from five hundred to 135,000 (i.e., 270 times the original number) in forty years; other Indonesian Christian groups multiplied in the 1960s, with the Timor church baptizing two hundred thousand in two years (York, "Indigenous Missionaries," 249); in South Africa, "African Independent Churches" grew from thirty-two groups in 1913 to more than 3,500, accounting for more than 27 percent of the black population seventy-one years later (Oosthuizen et al., "Introduction," 5; cf. Oosthuizen, "Healing," 73–74; for 35 percent of the indigenous population, idem, *Healer-Prophet*, 1). The Welsh revival of 1904–5 led to nearly one hundred thousand conversions (White, "Revival," 1), including perhaps twenty thousand in a five-week span (a contemporary cited in Hooper, "Awakening," 225). Although absorbing elements of some other movements, Pentecostalism (with charismatics) grew by half a billion (by perhaps high estimates) in one century (see comment at Acts 2:4).

65. Pothen, "Missions," 187 (on the Filadelfia church movement, see more fully 174–94); as in Acts, miracle reports are a major factor in the growth (189–90). Stark, *Cities*, 65–70, insists that sociology supports gradual growth rather than mass conversions, but he does not take into account such rapid people movements often noted in current missiological literature. Pervo, *Acts*, 87, cites Stark's estimate (in Stark, *Rise*, 7–13) against Luke's accuracy here. MacMullen, *Second Church*, 112, argues for a much lower proportion of Christians in the empire (esp. actual church-attending ones) than usually thought, but his estimates reflect archaeological remains (which are always incomplete), more space between worshipers than I would extrapolate from typical Majority World churches today, and, what really matters for our considerations, the later period of ca. 400 C.E. (though his distinction between the faith of the elite and that of the masses is well taken). Movements often begin rapidly and then slow in their growth rate. For higher estimates from literary sources, see Hart, *Delusions*, 184–86, 192.

66. In a single day in November 1994, perhaps eight hundred residents of Nieuw Nickerie, Suriname, were converted—reportedly more than ten times the number of local conversions over the previous century—leading to a mass people movement (from less than 1 percent of the population) that over the following decade converted perhaps 35 percent of the population (Norwood, "Colloquium," 24–26; also Dr. Douglas Norwood, interview by author, Philadelphia, June 6, 2006; Norwood, as mentioned earlier, was an eyewitness of the initial revival).

67. E.g., although the retention rate is not documented, one Reinhard Bonnke crusade in Nigeria claimed one million "decisions for Christ" on the first night (November 2000, with a claim of "hundreds of thousands" of healings; Rutz, *Megashift*, 25–26); even allowing for exaggeration or misunderstanding, the numbers are phenomenal (admittedly in a culture already familiar with Christianity; but the Jerusalem church worked in a familiar environment of Jewish piety). On rapid "people movements," see discussion at Acts 9:35. Contrast the older romantic notions that earliest Christianity's converts were necessarily few (Case, *Origins*, 79).

68. As also noted at the beginning of Acts 2, I borrow "revival" from the discipline of U.S. religious history and contemporary studies of global Christianity (cf., e.g., Blumhofer and Balmer, *Revivals*; McClymond, *Encyclopedia of Revivals*; Harrell, *Possible*; Robeck, *Mission*; Burgess, *Revolution*; Roberts, *Revival*; Dermawan, "Study"; Lee, "Korean Pentecost"; Longkumer, "Study"; McGee, "Revivals in India"; Shaw, *Awakening*; Wiyono,

colleagues made an exact count; numbers rounded to the thousands belong to the realm of estimates, and Luke's sources are more likely to have estimated high than low. But if we accept the description in the narrative that follows (2:42–47), the earliest Christians seem to have had a sense of their enormous numbers, which suggests that the estimate is not only realistic but in the general range.

Still, if the figures are realistic, they imply an extraordinary explosion in the church's membership on Pentecost. To offer a sense of proportion, Josephus, never known to play down numbers, reckons the Essenes at "over 4,000" (*Ant.* 18.20). Although the Jerusalem elite prove hostile to the apostles, Jerusalem's common people respond to them far more favorably in this period (Acts 4:4; 5:13; 6:7), just as the elite opposed Jesus while many of the people followed him.[69] Although this situation apparently changes after the Hellenist reaction against supposed rejection of the law (6:11–14; 8:1) and the increasing conservatism under Agrippa I (12:3), Luke presents the Jerusalem church as again well accepted in Jerusalem in the decade just before the city's destruction, so long as it did not associate too closely with Gentiles or their allies (21:20).[70]

d. Other Features of 2:41

To speak of the converts as three thousand ψυχαί does not invite us to read Middle Platonism or later Christian soteriology into the narrative.[71] The term ψυχή (traditionally translated "soul") has a wide semantic range in Luke-Acts, but in the immediate context, the term applies to people (Acts 2:43); when attached to numbers, it simply provides a count of "people" (7:14; 27:37).[72] That the multitude "welcomed[73] his word" may reflect the language of moral exhortation[74] but certainly also reflects what was, by Luke's day, conventional language of early Christians. Although NT writers nowhere else employ the word ἀποδέχομαι as here, they do use both δέχομαι (Luke 8:13; Acts 8:14; 11:1; 17:11; 1 Thess 1:6; 2:13; Jas 1:21; cf. 2 Cor 11:4) and λαμβάνω (Matt 13:20; Mark 4:16; John 12:48; 17:8) for this activity.

More significant is Luke's expression "the word," which is frequent throughout the Gospel (e.g., Luke 1:2; 3:2; 5:1; 8:11–15) and Acts (e.g., Acts 4:31; 6:2, 4, 7; 8:4, 14, 25; 11:1, 19; 12:24). Jewish people accepted the divinely inspired law as God's word (e.g., Ps 119:9, 11, 16–17, 25, 28, 67, 140), as also the prophetic message (e.g., 1 Sam 3:7, 21; 15:10, 23, 26).[75] Early Christians, empowered by the Spirit of prophecy (Acts 2:17–18), might, not surprisingly, speak this divine "word" like the prophets

---

"Timor Revival"; York, "Indigenous Missionaries"). I employ it in the sense of a religious renaissance or awakening, not in the more specific sense of the North American form that came to be called revival meetings. Some other scholars have also employed these religious models for broad social analogies with features of early Christianity (e.g., Dunn, *Jesus and Spirit*, 192).

69. Cf. Johnson, *Acts*, 17.

70. Cf. also the acceptance of James by pious Jerusalemites in Jos. *Ant.* 20.200–201.

71. Luke does speak of "saving" one's soul or life for eternity (Luke 9:24; 17:33), but this reflects the Jewish doctrine of "eternal life" (see Dan 12:2; *Pss. Sol.* 3:12; *m.* ʾ*Ab.* 2:7; *b. Ber.* 28b; *Lev. Rab.* 13:2; *CIJ* 1:422, §569; 1:474, §661; 2:443, §1536; Keener, *John*, 328–29). Septuagint readers may have read the Greek semantic range into the term (Hartman, "*Psychae*"), and some Diaspora Jewish documents could speak of righteous "souls" being "saved" after death (*Test. Ab.* 11:10 A, though probably based on their previously established trajectories), but Acts' converts are neither disembodied nor dead (cf. LXX Gen 2:7; 12:5; and passim).

72. For ψυχαί as "persons," see further LXX Gen 46:15–27; Exod 1:5; van der Horst, "Parallels to Acts," 58 (who adds to Bauer's list Eurip. *Andr.* 611; *Hel.* 52–53; for a Latin equivalent, Val. Flacc. 7.274; 8.389).

73. For this sense of ἀποδέχομαι, see Luke 8:40; 9:11; Acts 18:27; 21:17; 28:30 (all other Lukan uses except Acts 24:3).

74. Van der Horst, "Parallels to Acts," 58 (citing Plato *Symp.* 194D; *Laws* 642D; *Theaet.* 162E). With the ἀσμένως of later manuscripts he compares Diod. Sic. 12.54.1; 12.57.2; Dion. Hal. *Ant. rom.* 1.82.1.

75. Gerhardsson, *Memory*, 225, thinks that the "word of the Lord" includes not only *kerygma* but *didachē*, in view of Acts 1:21–22; I think that the *kerygma* simply includes the gospel story (which could be both

of old (cf. 1 Thess 2:13; 1 Pet 1:10–12). Luke's language was by now standard in early Christianity, but he may have still thought of Septuagintal usage. If one passage influenced his usage more than any other, it might be Isa 40:8 (used also in 1 Pet 1:25), the end of a passage whose earlier part is important to Luke (Luke 3:4–6).[76]

2. Community Life in 2:42[77]

Luke emphasizes that the church was continuing or persevering in the life depicted here; the various elements are each developed further in Acts 2:43–47.[78] The church's unity in these verses also builds on the earlier reversal of Babel (see comment on Acts 2:6–11); Diaspora Jews are included in this unity (2:9–11).[79] Although it remains debated how many of these Diaspora Jews were festal visitors (cf. comment on Acts 2:6), at least a number probably remained in the Jerusalem church, forming the nucleus of the growing group of "Hellenists" in 6:1.

As comparisons of evangelistic claims and church growth reports reveal today, it is possible to have many "converts" in meetings yet a lack of social reinforcement for, and perseverance in, their new faith afterward. Luke underlines the point that the outpouring of the Spirit produced not simply short-term numbers but long-term results.

Most scholars recognize four elements in the community life (the apostles' teaching, fellowship, breaking bread, and prayers);[80] some see two elements (with breaking bread and prayer together as part of the fellowship);[81] grammatically, one could also divide it into three elements (perhaps each separated by καί, which appears twice,[82] taking fellowship and breaking bread together; contrast Luke's different syntax in the outline in 1:8).

a. Early Church Order?

Some scholars suggest that 2:42 indicates an early pattern for corporate worship, providing the contents (though not a fixed sequence) of a service.[83] Certainly, Christian gatherings were incorporating these elements by the middle of the second century. Thus Justin Martyr speaks of the standard order of service on a Sunday (*1 Apol.* 67):[84]

1. All gather to one place.
2. The writings of the apostles and prophets are read ("as long as time permits").
3. The person presiding instructs and exhorts everyone to imitate these things.

---

taught and announced as good news; see 5:42; 15:35; 28:31). The prophetic connection is fairly explicit in, e.g., Luke 3:2.

76. Possibly, Luke 3:2 alludes to Isa 40:8, but this is by no means clear.

77. For a survey of views concerning Luke's ecclesiology, see Bovon, *Theologian*, 290–308 (chronological bibliography, most complete from 1946 to 1977; and the review of views, 309–408, summarized on 403–8).

78. With Johnson, *Acts*, 58. Thornton, "Continuing Steadfast," suggests that the continuing element of προσκαρτεροῦντες implies meetings; see comment on Acts 1:14 (also for other discussion of προσκαρτεροῦντες) and 2:46.

79. Note also Noack, "Pentecost in Jubilees," 93.

80. E.g., Johnson, *Acts*, 58.

81. Pesch, *Apostelgeschichte*, 1:130; Witherington, *Acts*, 160. This view would accord with the following narrative (Acts 2:43–47).

82. See, however, Stancil, "Evaluation," for an additional καί following κοινωνία.

83. Jeremias, *Sermon*, 20; Prieur, "Actes 2,42 et culte réformé"; cf. less certainly Blue, "Influence," 488. For worship in Acts and earliest Christianity, see earlier studies in Mattill and Mattill, *Bibliography*, 288, §§4008–17, including Macdonald, *Worship*.

84. *ANF* 185–86.

4. All rise to pray.
5. The Lord's Supper
   a. The president offers prayers and thanksgivings.
   b. People assent with "Amen."
   c. The Lord's Supper is distributed and all partake.
   d. Deacons send it to those who are absent.
6. Those who have money and are willing "give what each thinks fit."
7. They leave the collection with the president, who then helps orphans and widows and anyone else in need (the sick, prisoners, travelers, etc.).

Pagans could worship in temples or privately but did not meet together for corporate worship;[85] Christians' models would thus arise from the synagogue and from whatever was distinctive in Christian experience.

But this reconstruction may read too much of later Christians' formal worship experience back into the earliest church (cf. 1 Cor 14:26). Although some of these activities (such as the apostles' teaching and perhaps much of the prayer) may have involved hundreds meeting together in the temple courts (Acts 2:46),[86] many, such as the breaking of bread, would have been practiced in house meetings (2:46), which could afford more informality.

The sharing developed in 2:44–45 may have included apostolic oversight (4:35, 37; 5:2; 6:2), but it would have been an administrative matter (or a personal one when people shared directly, perhaps especially at first) rather than part of a formal worship "service." Prayers together probably continued in both the larger (cf. 2:42; 2:46–3:1; perhaps 4:23–24) and smaller (cf. 12:12) meetings. When meeting in homes, individual[87] Christians probably offered both fixed prayers learned from the synagogue (though not formalized as much as in a later period)[88] and personal (perhaps usually spontaneous) prayers, practiced by other Jews[89] but especially important in the charismatic worship of the early Christians (1 Cor 14:14–16, 26).

b. Apostolic Teaching

Luke may provide examples of the apostles' teaching in Acts 3:11–26; 4:8–12; and 5:29–32, though these messages are directed toward outsiders.[90] He can safely assume in the apostles' teaching the teachings of Jesus already included in his Gospel. Because the apostles' teaching provided the historic link to Jesus's ministry (1:21–22),

85. See Winter, *Left Corinth*, 133–34.

86. Corporate prayer in the temple appears also in the opening scene of the Gospel (Luke 1:10).

87. There is some question as to whether Jews recited prayers corporately in synagogues; probably at least some did, but there was no single standard practice (see discussion in Keener, *John*, 209). Jews did gather together for prayer (Jos. *Life* 277) and probably did pray aloud (as with Gentile prayers; van der Horst, "Prayer"), and fixed prayers did exist; but it is not clear that they prayed these prayers together or in unison.

88. E.g., the parallel between the *Kaddish* and the first stanza of Jesus's model prayer was so obvious that an eighth-century translation of the Lord's Prayer from Latin into Hebrew borrows some of its wording directly from the *Kaddish* (Lapide, *Hebrew*, 8); cf. Bivin, "Prayers"; Petuchowski and Brocke, *Liturgy*; Keener, *Matthew*, 215–16; later adaptations of traditional Jewish formulations in 1 Tim 4:4–5; *Did.* 10.3, 5; *Apost. Const.* passim. At least some fixed prayers (with corporate responses) appear at Qumran and hence before 70 c.e. (Abegg, "Liturgy: Qumran," 648, cites 1QS I, 22–III, 12; 4Q502; 4Q503; Abegg [649] thinks communal prayers also likely in 4Q504; 4Q507–509).

89. E.g., *m.* ʾAb. 2:13; *Ber.* 4:4; see further Sandmel, *Judaism*, 152; Moore, *Judaism*, 2:220–21; Abrahams, *Studies* (2), 84; Johnson, *Prayer*, 61.

90. Karris, *Invitation*, 45. For the emphasis on "teaching" in Acts, in various passages, see Varickasseril, "Shepherding"; Bartel, "Role," 329–30.

it is essential for Luke in emphasizing the continuity between the mission of Jesus and his church.[91]

For Luke's audience, moral "teaching" may have resembled lectures in a philosophic school (cf. 19:9; 1 Cor 14:34–35);[92] for the apostles within his narrative world, it probably most resembled the sort of midrashic exposition with which they would have been most familiar in the synagogues. Some scholars distinguish teaching here from proclamation,[93] which in Acts tends to be especially deliberative (seeking converts),[94] but it is possible that the apostles also "proclaimed" to believers (Acts 20:25). In a synagogue context, even evangelistic preaching would include Scripture exposition (cf. 7:2–53; 13:16–47). The content of "teaching" (διδαχή) could sometimes be evangelistic (5:28; 13:12; 17:19); the cognate verb (διδάσκω) is evangelistic in 4:2, 18; 5:21, 25, 28, but it refers to instruction in 18:25, probably refers to instruction in 11:26; 15:1, 35; 18:11; 20:20; 21:21, includes instruction in 1:1, and is unclear in 5:42; 21:28; and 28:31. By contrast, "proclaiming" (κηρύσσω) was usually evangelistic (8:5; 9:20; 10:37, 42; 19:13; probably 28:31) but represents instruction in 15:21 and possibly in 20:25 (where either meaning is possible but teaching is easier). Their semantic ranges overlap, but like the familiar OT coupling of opposites to indicate a whole, their appearance together (Luke 20:1; Acts 5:42; 28:31) probably implies the full range of activities.

The appearance of the believers' continual learning from the apostles is undoubtedly deliberate and would probably elicit respect in Luke's circle. A first-century Stoic opined that students of philosophy, unlike students in other disciplines, needed more intensive and lengthy training because they had spent their previous lives learning the opposite of the truth.[95]

Jewish hearers might think more specifically of learning God's message in Scripture. Learning Torah was a pervasive element of Palestinian Jewish life, pursued whenever possible.[96] Some scholars have compared the division of devotion here to the more formal and temporal division in 1QS VI, 1–8 (with study, prayer, and meals).[97]

c. Koinōnia

The term κοινωνία, or partnership, can refer to the sort of harmony created by shared purpose (Mus. Ruf. 13B, p. 90.7, 13–16, 19–20) and working together (14,

91. Tert. *Praescr.* 20 emphasizes this more fully: the churches derive from an apostolic foundation and hence are in continuity with the apostles.

92. Outsiders may have often viewed Christians in terms of philosophic schools (see, e.g., Judge, "Scholastic Community": see comment on Acts 17:19); this may also comport with much of Luke's portrayal (see Witherington, *Acts*, 197). Lacking cult, the earliest churches resembled associations, still more philosophic schools, and most of all synagogues (Judge, *First Christians*, 614–15). Apostolic education was Jewish rather than classical (ibid., 703, 705), but Diaspora Christian education mostly utilized the conventional classical models (see comment on Acts 19:9) unless Julian forced Christians to have distinctive schools (ibid., 695–96).

93. E.g., Fitzmyer, *Acts*, 270.

94. That it can also occur in houses (Acts 5:42) may suggest that nonbelievers were welcomed (cf. 1 Cor 14:23); perhaps inquirers sometimes even offered their homes (Acts 10:24).

95. Mus. Ruf. 6, p. 52.29–32; 54.1–2.

96. See Safrai, "Education," 968; cf. Deut 6:7–9. The later rabbinic movement particularly developed this tendency; on the merit of Torah study, cf., e.g., b. *Ḥag.* 15b; y. *Ḥag.* 2:1, §§10–11; *Num. Rab.* 12:4; *Ruth Rab.* 6:4; it equaled all other commandments (*'Abot R. Nat.* 40 A). Although one must practice as well as study (Jos. *Ant.* 20.44; m. *'Ab.* 1:15, 17; 3:9, 17; 5:14; *Sipre Deut.* 32.5.12; *'Abot R. Nat.* 24 A; *Pesiq. Rab Kah.* 12:10; 27:9; b. *'Abod. Zar.* 17b; *Sanh.* 106b; *Yoma* 72b; 86a; *Lev. Rab.* 35:7; *Num. Rab.* 14:10; *Deut. Rab.* 7:4; cf. Sen. Y. *Ep. Lucil.* 20.2; 108.6; Mus. Ruf. 6, p. 52.15–17; 17, p. 108.38–39; Epict. *Diatr.* 2.9.13), some rabbis felt that study took priority as a prerequisite for proper practice (*Sipra Behuq. par.* 2.264.1.4; *Sipre Deut.* 41.2.5–6; *Pesiq. Rab Kah.* 15:5; b. *Qidd.* 40b; y. *Ḥag.* 1:7, §4; *Song Rab.* 2:14, §5).

97. Le Cornu, *Acts*, 146.

p. 92.21–28).[98] Partnership included sharing profit,[99] and early Christians sometimes used the term κοινωνία to refer to sharing with others (Rom 15:26; 2 Cor 8:4; 9:13; Heb 13:16), as also the cognate verb (κοινωνέω, Rom 12:13; 15:27; Gal 6:6; Phil 4:15). Thus the sacrificial sharing described in Acts 2:44–45 (note κοινά, 2:44) expands further on the meaning of the term here; although it may represent only a concrete manifestation of their "fellowship,"[100] the community's "fellowship" was accomplished by sharing their possessions (see comment there).[101]

In light of early Christian teaching, this is not a surprising fruit of Pentecost. Though Luke emphasizes the Spirit's empowerment especially for verbal proclamation, the community effectively evangelizes here through its lifestyle (2:47). The Pauline circle of Christianity emphasized the Spirit's involvement in κοινωνία (2 Cor 13:14; Phil 2:1) and in love (Rom 15:30; Gal 5:22; Col 1:8; 2 Tim 1:7; cf. Rom 5:5; 1 Cor 4:21; 2 Cor 6:6; Gal 5:5–6; 6:1).[102]

d. Breaking Bread

Because "breaking bread" is so closely connected grammatically with "fellowship" here, it seems likely that part of the disciples' sharing of possessions included common meals at the expense of those who could afford the food. It was a daily (Acts 2:46) practice that involved shared use of property in, presumably, especially the more ample homes.

Perhaps it happened most often at the main meal later in the day (which, like other Jewish meals, would start with breaking and blessing bread, as well as wine);[103] otherwise "breaking bread" might refer literally to simply taking bread together, because other meals were simpler and the one food necessary to be able to offer to a guest was bread (Luke 11:5).[104] Probably, however, "bread" functions as a metonymy for a meal, however simple it may have been[105] (see further discussion below). As the most basic staple, "bread" could easily stand for food in general (4:3–4; 7:33; 9:3; 11:3, 5; 14:1, 15; 15:17).

On a literary level, the breaking of bread here very likely alludes to and includes the Lord's Supper (Luke 22:19; cf. 24:30).[106] If, for Luke, the Lord's Supper represented a

98. Aristotle earlier applied the term κοινωνία to the state as a community (*Pol.* 2.1.2, 1260b); cf. the verb cognate for common interest in, e.g., Hierocles *Siblings* (in Stob. *Anth.* 4.84.20); the noun for common nature in Iambl. *Letter* 4.7–9 (in Stob. *Anth.* 3.3.26).

99. In Latin, Cic. *Verr.* 2.3.20.50.

100. See Panikulam, *Koinōnia*, 123–24, 129.

101. With many commentators, including Dupont, *Salvation*, 86–87; Boismard and Lamouille, *Actes*, 2:151–52; Witherington, *Acts*, 160; Finger, *Meals*, 229. The term κοινωνία is associated with sharing goods in the Apostolic Fathers as well (*Did.* 4.8; *Barn.* 19.8; Dupont, *Salvation*, 99).

102. Cf. also Lampe, *Seal*, 51. Haya-Prats, *Believers*, 168–77, is technically correct that Luke explicitly associates the Spirit only with prophetic empowerment in Acts 2, not with the spiritual life of the community; our connection is indirect, but note similar community life following the outpouring of the Spirit in 4:31–35.

103. Cf. Safrai, "Religion," 802. The blessing over the bread stood for "the basic food staple" (Le Cornu, *Acts*, 148); for Jerusalemites' diet, see Bar-Oz et al., "Garbage." For the meal later in the day, cf. the Roman custom in Jeffers, *World*, 39 (on Roman meals more fully, Carcopino, *Life*, 263–75); Keener, *John*, 1230; but esp. (most thoroughly and accurately) Smith, *Symposium*, 20–21.

104. On preparing bread, see Pliny E. *N.H.* 18.27.105–6; on breaking bread to symbolize unity at a wedding, see Quint. Curt. 8.4.27. In *Galilee*, "bread" was often conjoined with fish as well (Matt 14:17, 19; 15:34, 36; Mark 6:38, 41; Luke 9:13, 16; John 6:9, 11; 21:9, 13), but fish might be less a staple for less well-to-do households in Jerusalem. The urban working classes ate especially bread and legumes (Stambaugh, *City*, 200). Derrett, *Audience*, 44, thinks that most people shared from a common dish or pot.

105. On metonymy, see *Rhet. Her.* 4.43; Rowe, "Style," 126; Porter, "Paul and Letters," 578; Black, "Oration at Olivet," 85.

106. The majority view, e.g., Hort, *Judaistic Christianity*, 43; LaVerdiere, "Breaking of Bread"; Witherington, *Acts*, 160; idem, *Meal*, 30; Barrett, *Acts*, 165; see esp. Heil, *Meal Scenes*, 243 ("The ideal table fellowship of the

meal believers shared together in memory of what Jesus had done for them (22:19), then ideally all early Christian meals together may have represented the Lord's Supper or at least been taken in the same spirit (cf. Acts 2:46; 20:7, 11). Meals together appear throughout Jesus's ministry (e.g., Luke 9:17), including with religious (7:36; 14:1) and notoriously sinful (5:30, 33) persons,[107] climaxing in the final meal together (22:14–20), which established the grid through which all common meals afterward (after the resurrection; see 24:41, 43; Acts 1:4a; 2:42, 46; 10:41; 20:7; cf. 16:34; 27:35–36) should be understood. Such meals foreshadowed the eschatological banquet (Luke 14:15), as the Lord's Supper could more explicitly (22:16, 30; cf. Mark 14:25; 1 Cor 11:26).[108]

Many scholars distinguish the breaking of bread in the Lord's Supper from the early Christian *agapē*, or love feast,[109] though most believe that at the earliest stage they occurred together.[110] But given the model for the original Lord's Supper in the Passover meal, where bread and wine (Luke 22:19–20) were simply (as at other meals)[111] notable elements of a meal with far more components, it seems more likely that the earliest version of the Lord's Supper involved eating a meal together (1 Cor 11:20–21, 34)[112] of which the most basic and always present elements (as at any Jewish meal; cf. Luke 7:33) were bread and wine.

e. Common Meals

Common meals as part of a religious bond would not be surprising for disciples who embraced one another as members of the same spiritual extended family (Luke 8:21; 18:29–30).[113] Synagogues were not only places for religious assembly but also

---

Jerusalem believers serves as a *model for the eucharistic celebrations of the audience*"); for a survey, Powell, *Acts*, 75–77; cf. Mattill, *Last Things*, 120 ("more than secular," though the eucharistic nature is unclear). Pelikan, *Acts*, 59–60, allows that the sacramental system developed much later than Acts though the basis exists here; for an argument for eucharistic symbolism in Lukan bread-breaking, see Taylor, "Fraction du pain"; for comparison among community meals throughout Luke-Acts, see Lindemann, "Einheit," 250–53; for a survey of views on the Lord's Supper in Luke-Acts, see Bovon, *Theologian*, 479–83. For earlier studies on the Lord's Supper in Acts, see Mattill and Mattill, *Bibliography*, 288–90, §§4018–38 (including, e.g., Lohmeyer, "Abendmahl"; Menoud, "Actes et l'Eucharistie"; Sloyan, "Concepts"; Thayer, "Discussions"; Weiss, "Herrenmahl"). Against overreading this, see discussion at Acts 27:33–38.

107. Cf. also Luke 6:1; the summary of Jesus's meals with sinners in 7:34; the expectation for Jesus's followers in their mission (10:7); kingdom celebration (15:23, for new converts; cf. 5:38). Without Jesus at the center, however, meals were not specifically virtuous (12:19, 22, 29, 45; 13:26; 17:27–28). Luke's examples of common meals in the Gospel invite believers to cross class, ethnic, and other barriers to share meals (see rightly Finger, *Meals*, 280–81, 286; cf. Ashworth, "Hospitality"), since they belong in common to the family of Christ.

108. Cf. esp. Heil, *Meal Scenes* (on this passage, 235–43), esp. 312 (all Luke's meal scenes foreshadow the eschatological banquet, with the Last Supper in Luke 22:7–38 serving "*as the focal point for all of the other meals in Luke-Acts*"). Some have argued that the communal meal at Qumran foreshadows the messianic banquet (Schiffman, "Communal Meals"; Vermes, *Scrolls*, 47; Harrington, *God's People*, 42); not all have agreed (cf. Driver, *Scrolls*, 506–16, esp. 516); cf. also Tait, "Banquet," who argues that the "messianic banquet" concept (though appearing in Isa 25 and some other sources and common in later rabbis) has been overused; and Smith, "Banquet," who warns against facile assumptions of what the (widespread) image means (see esp. 71 on Qumran).

109. For the love feast, see, e.g., Jude 12; Tert. *Apol.* 39.16.

110. Cf. Jeremias, *Sermon*, 20. In Paul, "the community meal was a full-course dinner" (Smith, *Symposium*, 178); "the Lord's Supper is one and the same with the communal meal" (Smith, *Symposium*, 285, undoubtedly rightly; with also, e.g., Bauckham, *Jude*, 84–85).

111. Cf., e.g., Goppelt, *Theology*, 2:12.

112. Cf. Hort, *Judaistic Christianity*, 43.

113. Cf. particularly Bartchy, "Community," esp. 312, 318, on the kinship connection with shared possessions. Foreign to most Westerners, table fellowship is more intelligible in an Asian context (e.g., Yao, "Barriers," 33–35).

community centers that often included a dining hall and facilities for travelers.[114] Some Diaspora synagogues (Ostia, Delos) provide evidence that local Jews shared common meals, as Josephus also suggests (*Ant.* 14.214–15),[115] though perhaps these reflected the celebration of feasts for the majority who could not afford to make pilgrimage to Jerusalem each year.[116]

Common meals were well known in Greco-Roman society, and not only by those invited to wealthy patrons' banquets. Many urbanites of lower social status "enfranchised" themselves by joining voluntary associations (often trade guilds), which characteristically shared common meals.[117] (This feature does not mean that they breached hierarchical boundaries; patrons of such associations probably acted like other patrons.) Dedicated to patron deities, their meetings were always "marked by festivity rather than solemnity,"[118] and their "regulations stipulate the equitable sharing of the meal and give rules for good behavior at the banquets."[119] Early Pythagoreans, stories of whom figured in the utopias (writings featuring utopias, mentioned in the comment on Acts 2:44–45 below), practiced communal meals, probably of a very frugal sort.[120] The Platonic Academy also shared relatively simple banquets (συμπόσια), which Plato considered essential to proper education.[121]

f. Meals and Relationships

A host who shared a meal with guests was thought to have formed a bond of relationship that never should be taken lightly.[122] Providing food and partaking of what was provided were social obligations; failure on either part could be taken as disrespectful.[123] Symposia strove to reconcile members, making them friends rather than enemies.[124] In Greek etiquette at least, meals involving friends required equality;[125] even in larger banquets, fellow banqueters ought not to speak against one another

114. Blue, "Influence," 476.

115. Ibid., 477.

116. There seems little evidence for this function for Jerusalem synagogues; there the temple filled most needs (Sanders, *Judaism*, 207), although, admittedly, our nonliterary evidence for Jerusalem is limited to the Theodotus inscription, which has guest rooms (Fiensy, "Composition," 233).

117. Pearson, "Associations," 136–37. On common meals in such associations, see, e.g., Harland, *Associations*, 59, 74–83; Rives, *Religion*, 125–26; and (stressing various forms) Ascough, "Commensality." Pearson, "Associations," 138, thinks that Luke might present the church's meetings in ways "reminiscent for his readers" of their own involvement "in various associations," but the "ideal community" view seems to have more in its favor. Like households, voluntary associations undoubtedly affected outsiders' understanding of house churches (Barton, "Values," 1132).

118. Willis, "Banquets," 144; indeed, "one inscription forbids the bringing up of any business matter at the meal, lest it distract from the joy of the occasion" (145).

119. Ibid., 145.

120. See Iambl. *V.P.* 21.98; Culpepper, *School*, 51 (citing Hdt. 4.95; Diod. Sic. 10.5.2). Apparently, however, Pythagoras disapproved of literally "breaking" the bread (Diog. Laert. 8.1.34–35).

121. Culpepper, *School*, 78 (citing Plato *Rep.* 2.372BC; *Laws* 1.639E–641D; Cic. *Tusc.* 5.32.91; 35.100; Diog. Laert. 5.4; Athen. *Deipn.* 5.186B).

122. Cf., e.g., Xen. *Cyr.* 8.2.2–3; 8.7.14; Lysias *Or.* 12.14, §121; 18.10, §150; Plut. *Coriol.* 10.3; Hierocles *Elements of Ethics* 11.17–19; Cic. *Fam.* 13.19.1; 13.25.1; 13.36.1; Corn. Nep. 5 (Cimon), 3.3; *Exod. Rab.* 28:1. This was true even over several generations (Hom. *Il.* 6.212–31; Cic. *Fam.* 13.34.1). This did not prevent many guests, in practice, from complaining about perceived snubs at banquets (cf., e.g., Mart. *Epig.* 3.12, 49; 4.85; 12.28; Juv. *Sat.* 4.24–25, 37–48; Pliny *Ep.* 2.6.1; Lucian *Nigr.* 22; Alciph. *Paras.* 37 [Thermolepyrus to Ocimon], 1.20; Theissen, *Setting*, 156–58).

123. Bailey, *Poet*, 122.

124. Smith, *Symposium*, 55 (citing Plato *Laws* 2.671C–672A).

125. Xen. *Cyr.* 2.1.30; 4.2.38–39; *Mem.* 3.14.1; Plut. *Table* 1.2.3, *Mor.* 616E; 2.10.2, *Mor.* 644AB; Plut. *S. Sp.*, Agesilaus the Great 1, *Mor.* 208BC; Lucian *Carousal* 43; also Pliny *Ep.* 2.6.3–5 (but contrast 9.5.2–3); cf. Saturnalia (Lucian *Sat.* 13, 17, 22). At Jewish festivals, see, e.g., *m. Bik.* 3:4; *t. Bik.* 2:10; at the Lord's Supper, see 1 Cor 11:21–22; Theodoret *Comm. 1 Cor.* 236–37.

or otherwise act in disunity at a meal.¹²⁶ Luke's mention of κοινωνία in a banquet context is not surprising; symposium ethics included κοινωνία, a common sharing not only of food from a common platter and wine but of conversation.¹²⁷

Luke articulates his vision of early Christian unity carefully, in terms meant to exceed the expectations of his contemporaries. Grounding the meal in the same κοινωνία that produced the sharing of possessions in common (as opposed to merely patronal benevolence) contrasts starkly with the usual purpose of meals in the rest of the urban Mediterranean world.¹²⁸ Granted, all meals established a relationship among those who partook, a relationship that made betrayal in such a context all the more heinous (cf. Luke 22:21).¹²⁹ Those who had shared meals were not to even gossip against each other.¹³⁰

But the nature of the relationship was defined by the respective societal positions of the different parties at table. Thus most common meals were shared by members of the same general segment of society; in a romanized setting, a patron might invite clients of lower station, but their seating and meal depended on their status, only those with sufficient status were invited, and the patron reclined apart with the patron's own peers.¹³¹ Jesus specifically challenged this hierarchical notion of shared meals, demanding that those with resources invite those who cannot repay them even in honor (Luke 14:1–14).¹³² Once transplanted to the Diaspora, however, this original transcending of social boundaries might fail (and in fact did fail in Corinth, 1 Cor 11:21).¹³³

Given the informal household setting, entire families would be present, though perhaps not seated together as families. In traditional Greek banquets, women either were excluded or sat rather than reclined; among Romans by this period, women of status often reclined with men, and even some Greek customs were in flux.¹³⁴ The transition was not complete, however, and continued to face resistance.¹³⁵ But early Christians may have had to adapt some customs due to space available in the homes in which they met; although they had some well-to-do homes in upper-city Jerusalem (see comment on Acts 12:12–13), they would need many homes to accommodate

126. Klauck, *Context*, 49 (citing P.Lond. 2710). This behavior represents merely the ideal.
127. Smith, *Symposium*, 54–55 (citing Plut. *Table, Mor.* 614E, 615A, 644C). Luke's depiction of inclusive table fellowship (in contrast to Pharisaic or temple avoidance of impurity) throughout his work (cf. Luke 5:30; 7:34; 15:2; Acts 27:35–36) is significant (see Kim, "Fellowship").
128. If we observe what Luke actually depicts, very few Western churches today, regardless of how sacramental or nonsacramental they may be, genuinely reflect the spirit of the breaking of bread, in the context of shared possessions, that Luke portrays in the earliest church.
129. E.g., Hom. *Il.* 21.76; *Od.* 4.534–35; 11.414–20; 14.404–5; 21.26–28; Hesiod *W.D.* 327; Eurip. *Heracl.* 1034–36; *Cycl.* 126–28; *Hec.* 25–26, 710–20, 850–56; Ap. Rhod. 3.377–80; Cic. *Pis.* 34.83; Ovid *Her.* 17.3–4; *Metam.* 1.144; 10.225–28; Livy 25.16.6; 39.51.12; cf. Derrett, *Audience*, 39.
130. Aeschines *Embassy* 22, 55; also P.Lond. 2710 in Klauck, *Context*, 49; cf. 1QS V, 25; VII, 15–16 (perhaps also 4Q261 f.6.a e.1–2, though the reconstruction depends on 1QS VII).
131. Cf., e.g., Plut. *Table* 1.2.3, *Mor.* 616E; 1.3, *Mor.* 619BF; Juv. *Sat.* 4.15–18; Theissen, *Setting*, 156–58. On seating by rank, see further Smith, *Symposium*, 33, 55–57, 136. A poor and rich person dining together was normally exceptional (e.g., Quint. *Decl.* 301.10).
132. Capper, "Reciprocity," 516–17.
133. Ibid., 514.
134. Smith, *Symposium*, 11 (with 298n27), 42–43, 208–9; Corley, *Meals*, 28–34; cf. Roller, "Horizontal Women." For women earlier sitting rather than reclining, see, e.g., Val. Max. 2.1.2; Killebrew, "Furniture," 359; likewise for children, Xen. *Symp.* 1.8. Most surviving guest lists are predominantly male, but Romans, in contrast to Greeks, allowed women's attendance (Stambaugh, *City*, 207; on the Greek custom, known to Romans, see, e.g., Isaeus *Pyrr.* 14; Cic. *Verr.* 2.1.26.66; Vitruv. *Arch.* 6.7.4–5; cf. Lysias *Or.* 3.6, §97). Wives might begin the banquet but withdraw during the heavy drinking (Corley, *Meals*, 30); perhaps some even stayed for that (Sen. Y. *Ep. Lucil.* 95.21; Winter, *Wives*, 153).
135. Smith, *Symposium*, 44, noting women sitting in Lucian *Symp.* 8; cf. the characterizations reported in Corley, *Meals*, 34–66.

the burgeoning church. Even Greeks had some meals, especially on festive occasions, where the entire family would be present, and when women were full members of clubs, they would have participated in these banquets.[136] Early Christians' dining together in Jerusalem with both men and women from different families[137] would not have been unique, but it would have been noticeable.[138]

That shared meals could appear in Luke's portrait of the early Jerusalem church should not surprise us.[139] Some scholars have compared the Lord's Supper to pagan cult meals[140] or even suggested that the Hellenistic sacramental meals were read back into the Jewish Last Supper tradition.[141] More relevant is that Greek associations of various sorts regularly met for common meals,[142] normally dedicated to the association's patron deity but celebrated with attention on the banquet itself.[143] Some associations gathered for specifically religious purposes,[144] and cultic meals were also standard in pagan festivals.[145]

Greek meal practice did affect contemporary Jewish banquets, including Passover customs,[146] and hence did indirectly influence some customs at the Last Supper; in some respects, the Hellenistic church also assimilated the Lord's Supper to, and interpreted it in the light of, Hellenistic meals.[147] These do not provide the most immediate parallels for the earliest form of the Lord's Supper tradition, however, even for those who view the Lord's Supper as sacramental (rather than simply a common meal) at an early period. Most scholars also recognize that before the spread of Christianity, Hellenistic meals were not sacramental[148] and did not communicate mystical elements of the deity.[149]

But we need not look so far afield from the church's Palestinian Jewish origins. Among these, Qumran provides common meals as well, although it should be noted at the outset that these probably represent one sort among many Jewish common meals and not the decisive background of the early Christian practice. Some have

---

136. Smith, *Symposium*, 208–9. Burton, "Commensality," points to respectable women dining with men even in earlier Greek culture; some banquets (such as at weddings) certainly included them (see Smith, *Symposium*, 40); Greek banquets also had long allowed courtesans (Plut. *Alex.* 38.1; cf. deSilva, *Honor*, 184).

137. Naturally, it was expected within one's own household, whether for Passover or regularly (e.g., *t. Pesaḥ.* 10:4).

138. Smith, *Symposium*, 209.

139. I adapt below the discussion in Keener, *Matthew*, 627–29.

140. E.g., Bousset, *Kyrios Christos*, 131.

141. Bultmann, *Jesus and Word*, 153.

142. Angus, *Mystery-Religions*, 127; Wilken, "Collegia," 280–81; Theissen, *Setting*, 131–32; Willis, *Idol Meat*, 14.

143. Willis, *Idol Meat*, 47–61.

144. E.g., Cic. *Senect.* 13.45; Horsley, *Documents*, 1:5–9; Cole, *Theoi megaloi*, 36–37. For a comparison and contrast with associations (and other groups) here, see Öhler, "Urgemeinde."

145. E.g., Burkert, *Religion*, 107.

146. Bokser, *Description*, 6–7; Smith, *Symposium*, 133–72; cf. Pines, "Darkness"; Levine, *Hellenism*, 119–24. All ancient banquets shared some similarities (see Smith, *Symposium*, 3).

147. Cf. Justin *1 Apol.* 66; Tert. *Apol.* 39.15; Pliny *Ep.* 10.96. Minor assimilation begins as early as the Pauline churches (Guthrie, *Orpheus*, 268; cf. Caird, *Apostolic Age*, 96). Paul's κυριακός, "of the Lord," may allude to typical Roman usage for "imperial" (Deissmann, *Light*, 357). But early attestation of parallels often comes from early Christian writers who interpreted the Mysteries through the grid of their own experience (cf. Campbell, *Iconography*, 323), as an "imitation demoniaque du Christianisme" (Benoit, "Mystères," 79–81), and the rites remained quite distinct (Metzger, "Considerations," 15).

148. A small following of Dionysus (Henrichs, "Identities," 160) and Mithraism (which gained prominence in the empire after Paul; Nock, *Christianity*, 133; Metzger, "Considerations," 13–15) may have been the exceptions that ultimately affected other Mysteries and the later Christian sacramental view. But most now reject Cumont's reading of even later Mithraic liturgy in light of Christian practice (Yamauchi, *Persia*, 517).

149. Nock, *Christianity*, 74; Willis, *Idol Meat*, 18–46, 62; Kane, "Cult Meal," 349–51; *pace* Willoughby, *Initiation*, 85, 136–37, 161; Goodenough, *Church*, 22; Godwin, *Mystery Religions*, 28.

compared to the Lord's Supper these Qumran meals,[150] which may themselves evince some Hellenistic influence.[151] Some think that these meals followed rules for sacerdotal purity,[152] were sacrificial sacred meals,[153] were annual and sacramental,[154] or foreshadowed eschatological meals.[155] But the sacral character may be no more than in most Jewish meals,[156] and the eschatological interpretation also remains unclear: 1QSa's messianic banquet could simply evoke the common practice of the community rather than the latter evoking the former.

The specific proposed parallels between the Qumran meals and the Lord's Supper are not strong.[157] The leader presiding over the meal and blessing bread and wine fits all Jewish meals, as do most other characteristics of the meal.[158] Certainly, special rules obtained in the Qumran order (1QS VI, 4–5, 20–21), but its meals merely show that a concept related to the sacred meal was already present in Palestinian Judaism and that one need not appeal to geographically distant parallels to explain the Lord's Supper. One may also compare the sacred communal meals of the Therapeutae (Philo *Contempl.* 82).[159]

Some scholars think that the Lord's Supper more closely resembles the regular weekly gatherings of the *haburoth*,[160] whose Pharisaic purity rules, some think, may have bound them to eating especially among themselves.[161] Among schools of sages in Palestine, study companions often ate together as well (*'Abot R. Nat.* 18, §40 B), though perhaps partly to save time (14, §34B). But again, are meals of associates or students of the sages distinctive enough as meals to warrant special attention in connection with the Last Supper? Palestinian Jewish families probably celebrated the more common weekly Sabbath kiddush very early;[162] one could also share Sabbath meals in common with other families.[163] Diaspora Jews also apparently assembled for communal meals at times.[164] Luke's Gospel, like the rest of the gospel tradition, indicates that meals together were a standard part of Jesus's lifestyle, undoubtedly carried on in the primitive church.[165] Insofar as those welcomed must have included

150. Fritsch, *Community*, 123–24; Cross, *Library*, 235.

151. Cf. Culpepper, *School*, 168; Donceel-Vouté, "Coenaculum."

152. Gnilka, "Gemeinschaftsmal"; Gärtner, *Temple*, 10.

153. Delcor, "Repas"; cf. 1Qap Gen^ar XXI, 20–22.

154. Groh, "Meal."

155. Harrison, "Rites," 32–33; Schiffman, "Communal Meals"; idem, *Law*, 191–210; Simon, *Sects*, 77–78; Harrington, *God's People*, 41–42; Schniedewind, "1QSa," esp. 1025–26.

156. Sutcliffe, "Meals"; Schiffman, *Law*, 191–97. The meal in 1QS VI is "pure" because it is consecrated by the community and the priestly blessing, but it is not ceremonial food; the text indicates merely that a newcomer cannot partake until he has surrendered his own wealth and labor to the community—preventing free handouts.

157. The claim of some scholars that only men participated at each is based on inference about Qumran practice in general, not just meals, and an inference about the Last Supper that certainly did not obtain in house churches (cf. 1 Cor 11:2–34; 2 Pet 2:13–14 with Jude 12).

158. Van der Ploeg, "Meals"; Driver, *Scrolls*, 506–16; Lach, "Zrzeszenia."

159. Burchard, "Importance," suggests that *Joseph and Asenath* influenced the Lord's Supper, but this view likely overstates the prominence of *Joseph and Asenath* (the date of which is also debated).

160. Oesterley, *Liturgy*, 167.

161. See Neusner, *Beginning*, 27. Against food's being eaten in priestly purity, see Sanders, *Jesus to Mishnah*, 131–254.

162. Oesterley, *Liturgy*, 79, citing *t. Ber.* 5:1. Jeremias, *Eucharistic Words*, 28, doubts this, but one may compare echoes of the kiddush blessing in *Did.* 9.2–3; it is far more likely that the *Didache* betrays Jewish liturgical influence than that it influenced later rabbinic tradition.

163. E.g., *y. B. Bat.* 1:5, §2.

164. Jos. *Ant.* 14.215–16, cf. 14.260–61; Sanders, *Jesus to Mishnah*, 78; idem, *Figure*, 202; Rabello, "Condition," 707.

165. Some view Jesus's meals as also anticipating the eschatological banquet (Becker, "Frohbotschaft"); for the Lord's Supper, see 1 Cor 11:26; Mark 14:25.

the poor (Luke 14:13), such table fellowship probably also figured into the sharing of goods (Acts 2:44–45).[166]

Jeremias contends that Essene meals are more different than similar and that *haburoth* meals are undocumented,[167] preferring a Passover background for the Last Supper (and hence the Lord's Supper).[168] Many of the features of the Last Supper that are distinguishable from regular Jewish meals parallel the Passover meal, a correspondence not surprising in view of the night on which Jesus was betrayed.[169] That Jesus followed the more common practices regarding Passover cannot be proved, but it is likely, especially in view of the correspondences on points that can be tested.[170]

If any more Hellenistic elements appear in the meals, they may fit the environment of urban Jerusalem. Luke's "symposium" section (Luke 14:1–24),[171] however, suggests that he recognized Hellenistic-style banquet customs throughout Palestine,[172] which probably accurately reflects the degree of hellenization by the first century.

g. Logistics of Meals

Greeks and Romans who could afford it had three courses in their banquets: appetizers, the meal proper (δεῖπνον), and finally the "drinking party" (συμπόσιον; Latin *convivium*).[173] Greek-speaking Jews were familiar with this language;[174] Luke uses δεῖπνον (Luke 14:12, 16–17, 24; 20:46).

For dinners (at home or outside), wealthy people in this period apparently wore special clothes that were less formal than day clothes.[175] Some of the poor in the Jerusalem church may have lacked this option, but many probably had a clean garment

166. Cf. commentators cited in Finger, *Meals*, 50, 81.

167. Jeremias, *Eucharistic Words*, 29–36.

168. Many of the Passover traditions are undoubtedly early, although some scholars have over-stated the case (Segal, *Passover*; Finkelstein, "Documents"; Wright, "Midrash," 417; Safrai, "Religion," 809). This does not mean the Haggadah used today; Stemberger, "Pesachhaggada," doubts that any of the Pesach Haggadah predates 70 C.E.; it is also post-first century in Hauptman, "Haggadah"; Manns, "Pâque" (suggesting anti-Christian polemic in it); and in the current consensus more generally (Kulp, "Origins"). Leonhard, "Älteste Haggada," doubts that it predates the tenth century. For one of the earlier extant versions varying from other copies, see Rovner, "Haggadah" (cf. idem, "Corrigenda"). Yet a prayer recorded in Hippolytus's *Apostolic Tradition* adapts tradition preserved in the Passover Haggadah (Kinsella, "Transformation").

169. With, e.g., Thiselton, *Corinthians*, 871–74; Winter, *Left Corinth*, 150; *pace* Smith, *Symposium*, 4, 295n5. See Jeremias, *Eucharistic Words*, although he overstates the case, contending, e.g., that Jewish people drank wine only on special occasions (50–51). Yet even if one merely factors in the regular Sabbath kiddush meals (e.g., *t. Ber.* 3:8; Tannaitic tradition in *b. B. Qam.* 69b; *Pesaḥ.* 102a, bar.; later, *b. Šabb.* 23b; *Taʿan.* 24a; Safrai, "Home," 747; cf. *Jub.* 2:21), which he concedes, they drank quite regularly (cf. blessings over wine in meals in 1QS VI, 4–5; *b. Ber.* 33a; 51a); they drank wine often. He is, however, probably correct to emphasize that of the many kinds of wines available (on which cf., e.g., *b. ʿAbod. Zar.* 30a; Paul, "Wine"), *red* wine was used on Passover, augmenting Jesus's symbolism (*Eucharistic Words*, 53, 290; *t. Pesaḥ.* 10:1).

170. The generally stricter Shammaite school (regarding Passover, e.g., *b. Šabb.* 18b, bar.) prevailed in his day, but our records were preserved by more lenient, rather than stricter, practitioners. Finkelstein, *Making*, 13–120, offers some source-critical suggestions on the Pesach Haggadah; but the current Haggadah is a late composition (as noted above).

171. See Aune, *Environment*, 122.

172. Unless (as is possible in view of his redaction elsewhere) he simply translated local customs into those more intelligible for his audience (and perhaps for himself). For Greek influence on Jewish banquet customs, see Smith, *Symposium*, 133–72.

173. Ibid., 27.

174. See συμπόσιον and cognates in LXX Esth 14:17; 7:7; 1 Macc 16:16; 2 Macc 2:27; 3 Macc 2:25; 4:16; 5:15–17, 36; 6:33; 7:20; Sir 31:31; 32:5; 49:1; δεῖπνον in LXX 4 Macc 3:9; Dan 1:13, 15–16 (the verb cognate appears in Tob 8:1; Prov 23:1; Dan 11:27; Luke uses it in Luke 17:8; 22:20). The uses may not all be technical (cf. Mark 6:39).

175. Croom, *Clothing*, 40.

not soiled by work (cf. Luke 3:11; Matt 22:11–12).[176] Did church members "dress up" for these meals? Perhaps those of lower social station would have done so if invited to banquets among those of higher social station (more plausible in the more spacious homes of the upper city), but for small gatherings among neighbors and peers, the issue seems less likely to have arisen.[177]

Because Jewish people had adopted Hellenistic banquet customs,[178] the ideal setting would be about three reclining couches for up to twelve people, with diners leaning on their left elbows and eating with their right hands.[179] The massive numbers in the Jerusalem church, however, could not have been accommodated only in such settings; they would sometimes meet in poorer homes,[180] and even the larger ones, class issues aside, might not limit their guests to the number that could be reclined comfortably on couches.[181]

Apostolic teaching (Acts 2:42) may have occurred in conjunction with the meal, perhaps after the main course. Greco-Roman banquets (or sometimes the more intimate drinking party that followed) usually included some form of entertainment,[182] whether music,[183] flute girls,[184] pantomimes,[185] dancers,[186] or, for more refined tastes,[187] lectures,[188] readings and recitations,[189] or topics for discussion (philosophic or otherwise).[190]

---

176. Cf. festive garments for imperial festivals (Winter, *Left Corinth*, 276, citing Tert. *Cor.* 13); the best Sabbath garments of those who could afford them (*y. B. Meṣi'a* 2:11, §1; *Pe'ah* 8:8, §2; *Sanh.* 2:1, §4); even many villagers in Egypt had a set of special clothes, distinct from their work clothes, for special occasions (Lewis, *Life*, 69). Some, however, would not have two garments; most did not have two pair of sandals, one reserved for the Sabbath (*y. Šabb.* 6:2, §1). Cf. the possibility of garments being provided at weddings (Bultmann, *Tradition*, 202, cites *b. Šabb.* 152b) or public functions (2 Kgs 10:22); but homeowners could not do this for all guests. Commentators often interpret even Matt 22:11–12 with reference to merely clean clothes (e.g., Jeremias, *Parables*, 187–88; Davies and Allison, *Matthew*, 3:204, citing most early Christian commentators, such as Origen *Hom. Exod.* 11.7; Chrys. *Hom. Matt.* 69.2; Isaac the Syrian [Isaac of Nineveh] *Ascetical Homilies* 2, 76); cf. clean clothes for entering a house of worship (CD XI, 22) and for the Sabbath (XI, 3–5).

177. Wealthy Romans dressed down, wearing for evening banquets less formal clothes than their day clothes (Croom, *Clothing*, 40).

178. See esp. Smith, *Symposium*, 133–72.

179. Jeffers, *World*, 39–40; Cary and Haarhoff, *Life*, 96; Dupont, *Life*, 98–99.

180. On the usual environments for ancient Judean meals, including those of the poor, see further Finger, *Meals*, 122.

181. For such reclining at banquets, see, e.g., Plato *Rep.* 2.372D; Xen. *Anab.* 6.1.4; Sen. Y. *Ep. Lucil.* 47.5; Mart. *Epig.* 3.30.1 (*recumbis*); Ps.-Callisth. *Alex.* 2.14; Athen. *Deipn.* 1.18ab; *Let. Aris.* 181, 183; *t. Ber.* 4:20; *Sipre Deut.* 41.2.5; *Pesiq. Rab Kah.* 6:3; *b. Ber.* 37a; 42b–43a; *Eccl. Rab.* 9:8, §1; more fully, Keener, *John*, 900–901, 915–16. Except for the hellenized elite, most Judeans probably used chairs at ordinary meals (Safrai, "Home," 736–37), reclining at banquets.

182. Even most association meals were festive (Willis, "Banquets," 144).

183. Hom. *Od.* 1.153–55, 325–26; 9.3–6; 17.270–71; Dio Chrys. *Or.* 32.58; Plut. *Table* 1.1.5, *Mor.* 614F–615A; Pliny *Ep.* 1.15.2; 9.36.4; 9.40.2; Athen. *Deipn.* 15.694BC; Sir 32:3; Smith, *Symposium*, 16–17, 136–37. Cf. later singing during the Lord's Supper in Chrys. *Hom. 1 Cor.* 24.3.

184. E.g., Xen. *Symp.* 2.1; Smith, *Symposium*, 16–17, 35; cf. the use of flutes in Val. Max. 2.1.10. A girl's attractiveness sometimes was a consideration (cf. Catull. *Carm.* 13.1–8, though not specifying her fluting).

185. E.g., Pliny *Ep.* 9.17.1; Jones, "Dinner Theater," 185; Stambaugh, *City*, 207. Also acrobatics (Xen. *Symp.* 2.1).

186. E.g., Xen. *Symp.* 2.1; Slater, "Introduction," 3; Stambaugh, *City*, 207; Smith, *Symposium*, 35.

187. Cf. Pliny *Ep.* 9.17.2–3 (objecting to mimes and clowns); Max. Tyre 22.3 (preferring lectures to music; cf. also *Let. Aris.* 286). Mimes tended to be vulgar (Val. Max. 2.6.7b; cf. Philost. *Vit. Apoll.* 4.2; Friedländer, *Life*, 1:218; 2:90–95, esp. 92).

188. E.g., Max. Tyre 22; Slater, "Introduction," 2–3; cf. Lucian *Posts* 35–36; Pogoloff, *Logos*, 264–71. Sages could also offer private instruction to young men at such parties (Arius Did. *Epit.* 2.7.5b.9, pp. 22–23.30–33).

189. Val. Max. 2.1.10; Corn. Nep. 25 (Atticus), 14.1; Pliny *Ep.* 1.15.2; 6.31.13; 9.17.3; Iambl. *V.P.* 21.99; Smith, *Symposium*, 35; Stambaugh, *City*, 207. Cf. comedies (Pliny *Ep.* 1.15.2; 9.36.4; 9.40.2). Sometimes poor clients had to endure patrons' bad recitations (Mart. *Epig.* 3.45).

190. E.g., Plut. *Table* 1.1.5, *Mor.* 614F–615B; 3.intro., *Mor.* 644F; Pliny *Ep.* 3.12.1; 6.31.13; Aul. Gel. 7.13; Philost. *Hrk.* 45.5; cf. Smith, *Symposium*, 37–38, 50–56, 64, 138–39; Friedländer, *Life*, 1:219–20, 224–25;

Among Jewish people, the standard topic of discussion was Torah.[191] Just as all events at a banquet normally occurred in the dining hall, it is likely that prayer (2:42) and other elements occurred in the same room where believers shared their meal.[192]

h. Prayer

Prayer proved to be not only a prelude to Pentecost (1:14) but a continuing part of the community's life. Prayer is one of Luke's primary emphases, but this emphasis also presents an accurate reflection of early Christian life (e.g., Rom 1:9–10; Eph 6:18; Phil 2:3–4; Col 4:2–4, 12; 1 Thess 3:10; 5:17, 25; 2 Thess 3:1; 1 Tim 2:1–2; 5:5; Jas 5:13–18; 1 Pet 4:7).

The corporate prayer meetings in which the largest number of the community's members gathered were probably in the temple (Acts 2:46), the courts of which were expansive enough to house large groups of people, especially in the less crowded intervals between festivals (Luke 24:53; Acts 2:46; 3:1; 5:12). Continual prayer presumably means gathering for regular times of prayer (as illustrated concretely in the following narrative, Acts 3:1),[193] though they may have also maintained a spirit of prayer through the day[194] as in some traditional cultures.[195] Regular prayer times in the temple might best explain Luke's use of the plural here.[196]

3. Awe, Signs, and Wonders (2:43)

This verse is one of a number of miracle summaries in Acts (e.g., 5:12; 8:7; 19:11–12; 28:9).[197] The imperfect tense for fear's "falling" suggests that it continued over a long period of time instead of ending immediately.[198] This event is paralleled with fear following a sign of judgment after the next outpouring of the Spirit in 4:32–35 (5:5, 11), in the summary statement lauding the church's growth in 9:31, and after dramatic events in Paul's ministry (19:17). In each case, the fear suggests that God was glorified and the crowds were now paying attention to the Lord's work through his apostolic agents. Luke uses this description the same way in his Gospel (Luke 1:65; 5:26; 7:16; 8:27; though also for angelic revelations in 1:12; 2:9; and eschatological signs in 21:26).[199]

This response to signs is not surprising, nor that it might prove one contributing factor to the church's continued growth (2:47), as modern parallels from most

---

Pogoloff, *Logos*, 241–42, 255–64. This could also include light teasing (Xen. *Cyr.* 2.2.1; 8.4.6–27). Philosophers needed to make sure that they were influencing instead of being influenced (Epict. *Diatr.* 3.16; *Encheir.* 33.6).

191. Sir 9:15; Ps 154:14 (11QPs^a 154, Hebrew, in *OTP* 2:619; and Syriac, 5ApocSyrPs 2, in *OTP* 2:621); *m. 'Ab.* 3:2–3; cf. *y. Ḥag.* 2:1, §9; 2:2, §5; Safrai, "Education," 968. The rabbis resented idle talk (e.g., *Gen. Rab.* 91:10; *Eccl. Rab.* 1:8, §1), which was antithetical to discussing Torah (*'Abot R. Nat.* 26; 29 A; 32, §68 B; cf. *t. 'Abod. Zar.* 2:6; *y. Ta'an.* 3:11, §4).

192. Smith, *Symposium*, 179.

193. Cf. Plut. *S. Sp., Lyc.* 22, *Mor.* 228D, where unceasing worship involves many sacrifices rather than continuous sacrifice; continual prayer in 1 Macc 12:11 is also simply regular prayer. Other examples also probably refer to praying regularly and frequently rather than to every moment (*Let. Aris.* 196; P.Lond. 42.2–4; *PSI* 209.13–14). Ancients did understand regular prayer (e.g., Fronto *Ad M. Caes.* 5.25 [40]). The same interpretive question may arise in Rom 1:9; 1 Thess 5:17; Poly. *Phil.* 4.3.

194. But *t. Ber.* 3:6 cites Daniel's thrice-daily prayers (Dan 6:11 [ET 6:10]) *against* praying continuously all day long.

195. Cf., e.g., in Mbiti, *Religions*, 83–84.

196. Le Cornu, *Acts*, 147.

197. For comparison among miracle summaries in Luke-Acts, see Lindemann, "Einheit," 248–50.

198. With, e.g., Bruce, *Acts¹*, 100.

199. "Fear" appears with γίνομαι in Luke 1:65; Acts 5:5, 11; as also in LXX Gen 35:5; Exod 20:20; cf. 2 Chr 19:7 (impv.); Lam 3:47.

regions of the modern world suggest. That signs usually produce church growth is a thesis argued extensively by Christiaan De Wet, who complains, "My research has turned up so much material on signs and wonders that are happening and churches that are growing, that it is impossible to use all of it."[200] Ancient Christian missionary accounts offer the same connection between signs and church growth, for example, in stories of Columba.[201] (See further discussion on signs in the introduction, ch. 9; ch. 15, sect. 6.)

That God performed signs and wonders through the apostles is attested from an early period outside Acts (2 Cor 12:12; Heb 2:3–4); see our introduction, chapter 9, especially section 2. Luke informs his audience that many signs were taking place, although he will report only one (a public sign yielding many new believers) in Acts 3:1–10.

4. Sharing Possessions (2:44–45)

A central part of Luke's portrayal of the ideal church is its sharing of possessions.[202] This is the center of the possible chiasm in 2:41–47; more important, the characteristic recurs more elaborately at the next corporate outpouring of the Spirit in 4:32–35, and fulfills Jesus's example and teaching regarding possessions (Luke 3:11; 9:58; 12:33; 14:33). Luke describes "all those who were believing" in Acts 2:44,[203] the bulk of whom would have joined the movement on Pentecost (2:41; cf. 1:15) or afterward (2:47). Their commitment was radical, fitting Jesus's demand for disciples in the Gospel (Luke 12:33; 14:33).

Peter had answered the question about how the hearers should respond to Peter's deliberative message by inviting repentance (Acts 2:37–38). Luke's ideal audience will recognize that equivalent answers to the question entail giving all one's goods to the poor (Luke 3:10–11; 18:18, 22) and (though a first-time hearer would not yet recognize this point) faith in Jesus (Acts 16:30–31). Because Luke describes these people as "believing" and sharing their possessions, he clarifies (without needlessly repeating himself) that they have followed the appropriate pattern for repentance outlined in his larger work.[204]

Arlandson estimates that 15 percent of typical urban populations in antiquity were "expendables," those for whom the rest of society had no use, such as beggars (see comment on Acts 3:2), widows without families, and orphans.[205] Others estimate that the 2 percent at the top of agrarian empires typically controlled half to two-thirds

200. De Wet, "Signs," 92, notes that he checked "over 350 theses, written by people from many different church denominations, covering almost every country in the world," and also interviewed many "missionaries serving in overseas countries."

201. Latourette, *To A.D. 1500*, 344; Tucker, *Jerusalem*, 41.

202. On this passage, see also Hoyt, "Poor in Luke-Acts," 213–22.

203. Luke employs participial forms of πιστεύω nineteen times; the most relevant here is the analogous summary statement in Acts 4:32.

204. My view here contrasts sharply with Phillips, "Role Model," esp. 50, 61–62, who suggests that Luke uses "we" to focus on Paul and distance the reader from the uncomfortable primitive demands in Acts 2:44–45. Tannehill, "Ethics," 117–18, thinks Acts less demanding than the Gospel; though this passage may fulfill Jesus's teaching, the ideal is realized only in the Jerusalem church (119). But whatever Luke's available information beyond the Jerusalem church, it seems evident in light of the Gospel that he presents the Jerusalem church's sacrificial giving as an ideal to be emulated. Admittedly, the emphasis has shifted in Acts; care for the poor remains necessary, but as the work grows larger, it is delegated, less central to the apostolic task than proclamation though apparently usually preparatory for it (Acts 6:2–4, 8; 11:30; 12:25–13:3). Hays, *Ethics*, rightly unites the varied dimensions of Luke's wealth ethics around absolute discipleship, as in Luke 14:33.

205. Arlandson, *Women*, 108–9.

of an empire's wealth; 10 percent at the bottom continually lived in mortal danger; most of the empire fell into the 70 percent category of peasant farmers.[206] Aristocrats and the 5–7 percent retainer class beneath them tended to concentrate in cities, but cities were still full of poor people. The Gospel's emphasis on caring for the poor climaxes in this depiction of the ideal community. (On urban poverty, see also the discussion at Acts 3:2.)

Certainly, those who joined the early Christian community went far beyond the normal entry dues for guilds or associations.[207] In a Dionysiac association, payment of dues was the central requirement of membership, an obligation due the deity; expenses included entrance fees, monthly fees for wine, regular fees for festivals, and fines for inappropriate behavior at banquets.[208] (Associations often voted on prospective members' worthiness, one factor likely being their ability to pay the requisite dues.)[209] But these were mandatory fees to belong to a group, whereas the Jerusalem believers shared their wealth more fully and voluntarily.

a. Hellenistic Utopian Ideals

Luke portrays the church's ideal beginnings in glowing terms that would have been easily recognized by his contemporaries. Christians undoubtedly did help one another, as the residents of Qumran apparently did, but Luke's description of Jesus's followers, like the description of the Essenes in Philo and Josephus, provides Greek utopian allusions.[210] "The writer of Acts seems to have seen the nascent Christian community as fulfilling the hopes, the promises, and the ideals, not only of Deuteronomy, but also of that same Greek Utopianism."[211]

Johnson cites Plato's depiction of earliest Athens (Plato *Critias* 110CD) and notes, "A Hellenistic reader would recognize in Luke's description the sort of 'foundation story' that was rather widespread in Hellenistic literature."[212] Plato's ideal state in the *Republic* was particularly widely known (much more than his more practical *Laws*),[213] and some scholars find here allusions to Plato's utopian ideal in addition to other elements of background.[214]

Ancients who described ideal communities typically shared a common, often idealized language. It included expressions such as μία ψυχή and πάντα κοινά (cf., very closely, Acts 4:32).[215] One could parallel many "examples from late antiquity of

206. Blomberg, *Poverty*, 89–90 (following earlier sociological studies). Toner, *Culture*, 2–3, suggests that most of the roughly 80–85 percent of the empire that lived in the countryside was desperately poor.

207. Pearson, "Associations," 137. Concerned about the church's image regarding money (1 Cor 9:1–18; 2 Cor 2:17; 11:7–9; 12:14–18), Paul demanded less from his churches in this respect than did the surrounding culture (Rom 15:27; 1 Cor 16:1; Gal 6:6).

208. Smith, *Symposium*, 119; cf. Klauck, *Context*, 50 (citing *SIG*³ 1109 = *LSCG* 51).

209. Smith, *Symposium* 119.

210. Mealand, "Utopian Allusions," 99 (but while Mealand allows the possibility of Christians helping each other, the "undoubtedly" is mine; see discussion below). Luke's audience (for whom he provides far more marked biblical than Hellenistic quotations) is less educated in Greek elite thought, but portrayals of such ideals appear in a range of texts.

211. Ibid., 99. Whereas philosophers sought to design utopias, poets were more interested in depicting them (Kytzler, "Utopia," 146).

212. Johnson, *Acts*, 62.

213. Meeks, *Moral World*, 28.

214. Mealand, "Utopian Allusions," 97. Mealand notes that the practices may go back to Pythagoras or Spartans but that Plato popularized the ideal (97–98). Dupertuis, "Summaries," especially highlights these parallels with the *Republic* (most obviously shared possessions, e.g., p. 293) and even thinks that Luke used the *Republic* as a direct literary model (295).

215. Malherbe, *Social Aspects*, 90 (citing Schubert, *Kommunismus*; Plümacher, *Lukas*, 16ff.; and other sources); cf. also Hengel, *Property*, 31.

idealizing descriptions of religious brotherhoods like the Essenes, Therapeutae, Brahmans, Gymnosophists, Egyptian priests, Pythagorean communities, etc."[216] Epicureans sought to demonstrate communal sharing.[217]

Some scholars suggest that Acts' depiction of the primitive church may reflect the image of the primeval, utopian golden age in pagan writers.[218] Many ancients believed that people held property in common during that golden age;[219] it might make sense to expect the same in the church's golden age as well. Writers praised the few philosophers whose lives of simplicity recovered the shared life of the primeval golden age (Max. Tyre 36, passim).[220] Because Jewish visions of eschatological blessing often recycled primeval ideas of paradise (see comment on Acts 3:21), this tradition might be relevant for Luke's Hellenistic audience reading about the eschatological community (see comment on Acts 2:17–18).[221]

But even ideas of past simplicity would not necessarily recall the golden age alone. Many have compared Luke's description of the early Christian community with others' descriptions of the Pythagoreans.[222] Pythagoreans were known for sharing things in common among themselves (Iambl. V.P. 35.257). Their ideal was equality based on their desire to be of "one body and one soul" and calling "that which is mine and that which belongs to another by the same name."[223] Thus they sought to banish what is private and increase what is common, "for all things were common and the same for all, and no one possessed anything privately."[224] Some of this language is almost identical to Acts 4:32; though it should be admitted immediately that these particular quotations derive from an era when NT accounts were in popular circulation, the general portrait of early Pythagoreanism is earlier.

Pythagoras allegedly authored the eventually popular statement that "friends share everything in common [κοινά]" and that "friendship is equality" (φιλίαν ἰσότητα); his disciples reportedly practiced this (Diog. Laert. 8.1.10).[225] Disciples devoted all their resources to the sect once they joined it, and many observers found this model virtuous (Aul. Gel. 1.9.12). Yet even in stories about Pythagoras's followers, holding goods in common was either "short-lived or applied only to the innermost group."[226]

216. Van der Horst, "Parallels to Acts," 58–59 (citing Iambl. V.P. 30; the collections in Festugière, "Nouvelle édition du 'Vita'"; idem, Astrologie, 19–44; van der Horst, Chaeremon, 56ff.; Berger, "Gattungen," 1280).

217. Dorandi, "Epicurean School," 1074.

218. Cf. Capper, "Reciprocity" (who recognizes a possible connection in Acts 2–6, though later chapters of Acts suggest only alms). Cf. Boshoff and van Aarde, "Apokaliptek," contrasting a utopian reading of the Pax Romana with early Christian understanding of the eschatological kingdom.

219. Capper, "Reciprocity," 504–6 (citing Hesiod W.D. 106–201; Plato Rep. 6.499CD; Virg. Georg. 1.125–29; cf. possibly Jos. Ant. 1.53–54); Johnson, Acts, 62 (citing Ovid Metam. 1.88–111).

220. When a gardener, after an allusion to the golden age's utopian economy (Philost. Hrk. 2.1), offers any fruits free of charge (2.2–5), the guest wonders if the gardener is a philosopher (2.6).

221. Beavis, "Kingdom," even seeks to use Hellenistic Jewish appropriation of "utopianism" to better apprehend Jesus's kingdom teaching.

222. E.g., Grant, Gods, 50; idem, Paul, 127; Stambaugh and Balch, Environment, 142; van der Horst, "Parallels to Acts," 59 (citing Iambl. V.P. 30).

223. Iambl. V.P. 30.167 (Dillon and Hershbell, 183).

224. Iambl. V.P. 30.168 (Dillon and Hershbell, 183).

225. The former proverb was often quoted; e.g., Plato Rep. 4.424A, 449C; Arist. N.E. 8.11, 1159b 31; 9.8, 1168b 8; Eurip. Andr. 376–77; Plut. Dial. L. 21, Mor. 767E; Terence Brothers 803–4; Philo Abr. 235; Iambl. V.P. 19.92; and others (many of these cited in Dupont, Salvation, 90; Johnson, Acts, 59). For the latter, see, e.g., Diog. Laert. 8.33 (Thom, "Akousmata," 111).

226. Culpepper, School, 51 (citing Iambl. V.P. 89); see also Iambl. V.P. 18.81. Some question whether Pythagorean communities in the literal sense, as opposed to mere associations of friends, existed (Dillon and Hershbell, "Introduction," 14–16). Nevertheless, Pythagoras approved of giving to others whenever they had needs (Iambl. V.P. 11.55), and his followers reportedly shared possessions even with other Pythagoreans they had never met (33.237–40).

The same might have been true for the Jerusalem community or even Luke's interpretation of it (Acts 5:4), but written sources about the earliest Pythagoreans are generally so much later than the events they describe that we can compare only the ideal descriptions of both communities.

b. Greek Ideals of Common Property

Ancient literature often mentions the ideal of common property.[227] Virgil praises bees for their supposed practice of this ideal (Virg. *Georg.* 4.155–57).[228] In some ideals of romance, the couple shared everything in common.[229] To some degree, groups in the Lipari Islands, Crete, and Sparta had practiced forms of common ownership of goods without citing explicit philosophic underpinnings.[230] Although not in a radical way, country folk were known for sharing their resources with one another because of friendship or love (φιλαλλήλους, Alciph. *Farm.* 29 [Comarchides to Euchaetes], 3.73 ¶2).[231] Some portrayed "noble barbarians" who lacked private possessions and claimed instead to own all the earth (Anacharsis *Ep.* 9, to Croesus).

Educated Hellenistic readers, however, might think most immediately of philosophic schools. Rules of hospitality required the well-to-do to share their resources with guests of equal status, considering this to be treating one's resources as if they were the others', though this was a more or less fictitious (or at least temporary) measure of generosity.[232] (See further discussion on hospitality at Acts 16:15.) Their gifts directly to the poor, however, represented a minimal proportion of their benevolence.[233]

Sharing property could also depict the ideal state (though no real ones that the ancients knew of in recent history).[234] Although Plato's ideal community did not require all members to share everything in common, its guardians did (Plato *Rep.* 6.499CD).[235] Others also understood him as approving a state with minimal selfishness (where "mine" and "not mine" were mentioned infrequently), where people would treat truly significant things as held in common (κοινοῖς, Plut. *Bride* 20, *Mor.* 140DE).

---

227. Klauck, "Gütergemeinschaft"; Dupont, *Salvation*, 88. Van der Horst, "Parallels to Acts," 59 (citing more fully Wacht, "Gütergemeinschaft") lists the most abundant parallels (59–60), including *Pyth. Sent.* 24; Zenobius *Proverbia* 4.79; Iambl. *V.P.* 81, 168; Porph. *V.P.* 20; Eurip. *Orest.* 735; *Phoen.* 243; Plato *Rep.* 424A (cf. 449C; *Phaedr.* 279C); Arist. *N.E.* 8.9, 1159b 31 (cf. 9.8, 1168b 78); Cic. *Off.* 1.16.51; 43.1.5; Sen. Y. *Ep. Lucil.* 90.36–41; Dio Chrys. *Or.* 3.110 (cf. 37.7); Lucian *Sat.* 19; Ael. Arist. *Or.* 27.24; Diog. Laert. 8.10; 10.11 (cf. 6.72); Varro *ap.* Macrob. *Sat.* 1.8.3.

228. Cf. also the ideal applied to mythical creatures in Philost. *Hrk.* 1.5.

229. See Cic. *Off.* 1.17.54; Longus 1.10 (κοινῇ); Mus. Ruf. 13A, p. 88.13–14 (κοινά); 14, p. 94.8–9; Plut. *Bride* 19–20, *Mor.* 140DE (though the husband is then said to "own" everything, *Bride* 20, *Mor.* 140F); esp. *Bride* 34, *Mor.* 143A; cf. Xen. *Oec.* 10.4 (κοινωνήσοντες).

230. Dupont, *Salvation*, 88–89. An assembly (ἐκκλησία) could be a κοινός (common) body of people (e.g., Philost. *Hrk.* 32.33; for the "common" good in 48.8). It fits some cultures' ideals better than others even today; see, e.g., its relevance in an African context in Ukachukwu Manus, "Community of Love."

231. Cf. also the Greek emphasis on relations with neighbors especially in early and rural sources (Osborne, "Neighbours," 617).

232. E.g., Pliny *Ep.* 1.4.3; 6.28.3; cf. Pliny *Ep.* 6.18.3; 6.30.1; 6.32.2; in the setting of a military alliance, Xen. *Cyr.* 5.4.29; Arrian *Alex.* 5.26.8; 1 Kgs 22:4; 2 Kgs 3:7; 1 Macc 12:23.

233. See Hahn, "Alms," 522.

234. Johnson, *Acts*, 62, cites Plato *Rep.* 4.420C–422B; 5.462B–464A; *Laws* 3.679BC, 684CD; 5.744B–746C; 6.757A.

235. Including sharing wives (Plato *Rep.* 5.457, 459; also noted in Sext. Emp. *Pyr.* 3.205; Lucian *Runaways* 18; *True Story* 2.19; *Phil. Sale* 17), which his student Aristotle completely rejected (Arist. *Pol.* 2.1.3, 1261a), as, of course, did early Christians (Tert. *Apol.* 39.11–12; for an exception from a gnostic family, cf. Grant, *Paul*, 50). Diogenes the Cynic also supported sharing wives (Diog. Laert. 6.2.72), as did early Stoics, such as Zeno (7.1.33, 131; modified in Epict. *Diatr.* 2.4.8), but most people would have agreed more with Pindar (*Encomia* frg. 122) that "shared" women are prostitutes. Some cultures were thought to practice group marriage (Hdt. 1.216; Diod. Sic. 2.58.1), as some do today (Grunlan and Mayers, *Cultural Anthropology*, 161; Mbiti, *Religions*, 166).

Cynics lived as simply as possible,[236] sometimes offering a positive model of simplicity to non-Cynics.[237] Essenes went beyond most ideal Greek sects and practiced complete community of goods[238] (see comment on the Essenes more fully below). An early Christian writer concluded that those who share God in common should also share all other things in common (*Sent. Sextus* 228).

Ancient literature often mentions the ideal of common property, but it was usually regarded as fulfilled "only in primeval times, in the Golden Age ... or in Utopias," or in a very select number of groups, especially in legends about the Pythagoreans at their founding and the Essenes.[239] Cynics, Stoics, Pythagoreans, and others regarded sharing all possessions as an ideal for society, though they did not believe that, given human frailty, all of society would practice it.[240]

Early Stoics in principle affirmed sharing all things in common, but while they rejected private property in an ideal society, they seem to have allowed it in their own.[241] The principle of the value of sharing all things in common remained as an ideal of concord;[242] only the wise could practice this form of concord and friendship, which recognized "knowledge of common goods."[243] Stoics in this period viewed wealth as a positive indifferent, since it could be used to support that which is intrinsically valuable.[244] Seneca, a first-century Stoic, suggests, "Let us possess things in common [*habeamus in commune*], for birth is ours in common [*nati sumus*]" (Sen. Y. *Ep. Lucil.* 95.53 [LCL]).[245] Seneca was personally rich, but his theory, at least, appeared noble. The Pythagorean Apollonius allegedly taught the Ephesians that they should share goods in common (Philost. *Vit. Apoll.* 4.2).

Some other philosophers doubted the wisdom of holding property in common; against holding everything in common [κοινωνεῖν] in a city (Arist. *Pol.* 2.1.2, 1260b), Aristotle warned that people cared for their private property most and so property held in common would be the least cared for (2.1.10, 1261b).[246] Epicurus, who shared his goods, reportedly rejected Pythagoras's maxim about sharing goods, claiming that true friendship required trust, and trust did not require common ownership (Diog. Laert. 10.1.11). A comic poet might use the radical proposal of community of goods in Athens for farce (Aristoph. *Ec.* 728–29). In practice, most people with ample resources did not share even the most basic philosophic ideals: "Classical

---

236. E.g., Val. Max. 4.3.ext. 4a; Dio Chrys. *Or.* 64.18; Crates *Ep.* 18, 30; Diogenes *Ep.* 6, 13, 30; Lucian *Dial. D.* 423 (2/22, Charon and Menippus 1); 336–37 (3/2, Dead to Pluto against Menippus the Cynic 1–2); Quint. *Decl.* 283.2–3, 5; Diog. Laert. 6.2.37; 6.5.93; 6.9.104; Max. Tyre 36.5. Yet even the best Cynics recognized that the significance of their lifestyle was the values it reflected rather than merely the simplicity itself (Julian Ap. *Or.* 6.200C–201C in Malherbe, *Moral Exhortation*, 35; Crates *Ep.* 19; cf. Aul. Gel. 9.2.4–5; Plut. *Isis* 3, *Mor.* 352C; Petron. *Sat.* 14; Diogenes *Ep.* 15). On Cynic begging, see comment on Acts 3:2–3. Further on Cynic simplicity, see Desmond, *Praise*.

237. E.g., Dio Chrys. *Or.* 4.8–10; Plut. *Alex.* 14.2–3. (Jewish sages may replace Diogenes in *b. Tamid* 32a; cf. the African king in *Pesiq. Rab Kah.* 9:1.)

238. E.g., 1QS I, 11–13; VI, 22–23; Jos. *Ant.* 18.20; *War* 2.122–25; Philo *Good Person* 76; *Hypoth.* 11.4–5.

239. Van der Horst, "Parallels to Acts," 59 (citing, on the Essenes, Philo *Good Person* 86; *Hypoth.* 11.4, 12 = Euseb. *P.E.* 8.11.4, 12; Jos. *War* 2.122–23; *Ant.* 18.20; Pliny E. *N.H.* 5.73).

240. Capper, "Reciprocity," 507–8.

241. Erskine, *Stoa*, 120–21.

242. Arius Did. *Epit.* 2.7.11b, pp. 64–65.1–9; 2.7.11d, pp. 66–67.1–4; 2.7.11i, pp. 76–77.17–20.

243. Arius Did. *Epit.* 2.7.11m, pp. 88–89.13–16.

244. Arius Did. *Epit.* 2.7.7e, pp. 48–49.7–10.

245. Stoics always work for the good of others, for the common good (*communi bono*; Seneca *Dial.* 8.1.4).

246. He warned that a city with too much in common becomes like a family (Arist. *Pol.* 2.1.4, 1261a); he also addresses various views demanding equality or limitations on inequality with reference to property (2.4.1–2, 1266ab). Aristotle preferred equity (based on social worth) to equality (see, e.g., Meeks, *Moral World*, 36–37). For another defense of private property against "equalizing" all property in a city, see Quint. *Decl.* 261.4–6.

literature is filled with upper-class sneers, unrelieved by any sense of compassion, at the disgusting laziness and squalor and servility of the poor."[247] Such attitudes later translated into charges that Jesus's teachings on possessions reflect merely the wishful ideas of poor people desiring to strip the rich of their property.[248]

c. Friendship Ideals

Other scholars see the ancient language of friendship here.[249] The adage that "friends share all things in common" was widespread,[250] and the idea even more so.[251] This apparently extended even to the sort of "friendship" reflected in military alliances;[252] one could speak (in this case, falsely) of armies belonging to a "friend" through his "partnership" (κοινωνία, Hdn. 3.6.1–2).

Epicurus welcomed all his "friends" (this was how Epicureans viewed each other) to his garden, where they lived together (Diog. Laert. 10.1.10).[253] He believed that friendship was prompted by self-interest but was mutually beneficial, sustained by sharing (κοινωνίαν) in pleasures (10.120).

Stoics claimed that "friendship is a partnership in life"[254] and that the best fellowship stemmed from "equality in partnership."[255] One could help friends most effectively by providing help in their time of need, even before they would request it (Isoc. Demon. 25). When an inferior could not repay a superior in kind, the latter became the former's benefactor and should receive some other kind of return.[256] Greco-Roman literature commonly refers to such unequal patronage as "friendship."[257] (Greeks and Romans also provided benefactions for the poor, with an even wider social gap, but Judaism's emphasis on charity was much greater; see comment on Acts 3:2.)

While such patronage was "friendship," Greeks particularly valued another kind of friendship, in which a friend was "another self," one's equal.[258] In contrast to Aristotle, whose "equality" was merely proportionate,[259] Stoics used equality language

247. Stambaugh and Balch, *Environment*, 114. E.g., on poor lodging for the poor, see Juv. *Sat.* 3.190–211.
248. Mac. Magn. *Apocrit.* 3.1–6 (*Porphyry's* 44–45).
249. Mitchell, "Friendship in Acts 2:44–47," 257, thinks Luke eclectic and dependent on popular expressions of the topos rather than on a particular philosophic school's understanding. For friendship in Cicero, see, e.g., Gruber-Miller, "Relationships"; Fogel, "Friends."
250. Besides citations above, Dio Chrys. *Or.* 3.110 (noting it as an ancient proverb); Sen. Y. *Ben.* 7.4.1; Mart. *Epig.* 2.43.1–2; Plut. *Table* 9.14.2, *Mor.* 743E; *Flatt.* 24, *Mor.* 65AB; Ps.-Phoc. 30; even among fishermen, as in Alciph. *Fish.* 7 (Thalassus to Pontius), 1.7. See further discussion in Keener, *John*, 1010–11.
251. E.g., Eurip. *Andr.* 585 (though contrast 632–35); Corn. Nep. 15 (Epaminondas), 3.4; Diog. Laert. 7.1.124; Libanius *Anecdote* 1.6. Reciprocity in gift-giving was an essential element of much ancient friendship (Marshall, *Enmity*, 1–24).
252. See sources in Keener, "Friendship," 381; idem, *John*, 1007.
253. Cf. also Stambaugh and Balch, *Environment*, 142 (citing Cic. *Fin.* 1.65).
254. Arius Did. *Epit.* 2.7.5l, pp. 34–35.30 (φιλίαν ... κοινωνίαν βίου). Cf. κοινωνία and ὁμόνοια (concord, harmony) in Dio Chrys. *Or.* 40.35–36 (on the heavens).
255. Arius Did. *Epit.* 2.7.5b.2, pp. 14–15.15–16 (ἰσότητος ἐν κοινωνίᾳ).
256. Capper, "Reciprocity," 516.
257. E.g., Dion. Hal. *Lit. Comp.* 1; Val. Max. 7.8.7; Mart. *Epig.* 3.36.1–3; Philost. *Hrk.* 4.3; 10.2; Iambl. *V.P.* 22.101; 33.230; 3 Macc 5:26; Acts 19:31; cf. also Mus. Ruf. 19, p. 122.29; Keener, "Friendship," 381–82; idem, *John*, 1008.
258. Hom. *Il.* 18.81–82; Plato *Laws* 8.837AB; Arist. *E.E.* 7.9.1, 1241b; Arrian *Alex.* 7.14.6; Diog. Laert. 5.31; Iambl. *V.P.* 29.162; 30.167; Jos. *Ant.* 19.317; see Keener, "Friendship," 382–83, esp. 382; idem, *John*, 1008–11, esp. 1008–9. For the "second self," see, e.g., Diod. Sic. 17.37.6; Cic. *Fam.* 7.5.1; 13.1.5; cf. P.Oxy. 32.5–6; Cic. *Fin.* 1.20.70; Sen. Y. *Ep. Lucil.* 95.63.
259. Arist. *Pol.* 3.7.2, 1282b; 5.1.7, 1301b; *N.E.* 8.7.3, 1158b; cf. Diog. Laert. 5.31. Others also adapted equality ideology to aristocracy, against democracy (Pliny *Ep.* 2.12.5–6; 9.5.2–3; Max. Tyre 14.7). Later Stoics seem to have adopted proportionate justice (Arius Did. *Epit.* 2.7.5b.1, pp. 12–13.19–20; 2.7.5b.2, pp. 14–15.8; 2.7.5b.5, pp. 18–19.34–35). Cf. Lucian's spoof on democratic equality in Hades in *Dial. D.* 433 (30/25, Nireus, Thersites, Menippus 2); 436 (8/26, Menippus and Cheiron 2).

for arithmetic equality;[260] early Stoics thus critiqued social inequality,[261] though more recent Stoics had adapted to the political norms of the empire.[262] Equality could characterize an ideal city.[263] Even among equals, friendship involved reciprocity; thus, in a time of need, a fisherman might remind his fellow that he had sent him fish but now needed new oars, basing his request on friends' sharing all things (Alciph. *Fish.* 7 [Thalassus to Pontius], 1.7). Luke thus presents the primitive church as fulfilling the highest Greek aspirations of friendship.

Alan Mitchell finds a great deal of friendship imagery in Luke-Acts,[264] especially in Acts 2:44–47, which he believes challenges ancient friendship ideals of reciprocity.[265] For this reason, he doubts that Greco-Roman utopian ideals affect this passage, since those ideals required abolishing private property (a practice Luke does not advocate here).[266] (Even the claim that early disciples despised possessions and shared all of them in common could be used in polemic against them[267] as well as in apologetic on their behalf.)[268] Rather, Luke shares the views of some *anti*-utopian writers of his day who advocated sharing *without* abolishing private property. Certainly, Luke goes well beyond the traditions of Greek culture; he summons higher-status members to serve others with their possessions without expecting reciprocation, very unlike their contemporaries (Luke 6:34–35; 14:12–14).[269] Mitchell may dismiss too readily the value of the utopian model; if "utopian" models in the strictest sense do not fit the entire church, they certainly fit the ideal call to discipleship (3:11; 12:33; 14:33; 18:22).[270] Nevertheless, he probably rightly highlights the friendship model.

Luke may draw on various models, including models of the ideal community.[271] The "friendship" model would have been the most widely known and recognizable, though Luke stretches this beyond its most common framework. Luke's vision of

260. Erskine, *Stoa*, 118–19.

261. Ibid., 121–22. Pythagoreans likewise associated ideal equality with sharing in common rather than with private property (Diog. Laert. 8.1.10; Iambl. *V.P.* 30.167; cf. Diog. Laert. 8.1.33; 8.2.65). Others opined that it ought to start with sharing at table (Plut. *Table* 1.2.3, *Mor.* 616E; 2.10.2, *Mor.* 644AB; Athen. *Deipn.* 1.12C); some applied equality to democracy (Xen. *Cyr.* 1.3.18).

262. Erskine, *Stoa*, 149, 181.

263. Lucian *Hermot.* 22; Men. Rhet. 1.3, 363.6–7; in the state as a whole, Marc. Aur. 1.14; for equality and justice, see, e.g., Dion. Hal. *Ant. rom.* 10.1.2. Vassiliadis, "Equality," doubts that typical ancient notions of "equality" had much social effect.

264. Mitchell, "Friends by Name," 236–57.

265. Ibid., 237–40. For friendship ideals here, see also Penner, "Discourse," 90–91.

266. Mitchell, "Friends by Name," 240–42; idem, "Friendship in Acts 2:44–47," 260–61. The ancient Israelite ideal of sharing (e.g., Deut 15:10–11) did not eliminate property (cf. esp. Lev 25:13–31, 41), though the sharing naturally required greater emphasis.

267. A point that may militate against the facile assumption that Luke simply invented the description to match philosophic ideals.

268. See the ridicule of Lucian *Peregr.* 13. To avoid offending the rich, Jos. *Ant.* 18.20 might, in fact, tone down the character of the Essenes' communal sharing.

269. Mitchell, "Friends by Name," 243–48; idem, "Friendship in Acts 2:44–47," 264–67. He regards Acts 20:35 as especially countercultural (249). Finger, *Meals*, 231–32 (citing Mitchell, "Friendship in Acts 2:44–47"), suggests that Greek thinkers typically applied the adage about friends sharing everything to friends of the same class; Luke transcends this by speaking of "believers" rather than "friends." As already noted, by this period many also applied "friendship" to socially unequal relationships, but the church's "sharing" across class lines is significant. Luke probably encompasses the socially marginalized in his "poor" of Luke 4:18 (see Green, "Good News," esp. 66–69, 71–72).

270. The Gospel's ideals are more demanding than the narrative of Acts. Kraybill and Sweetland, "Sociological Perspective," attribute this difference to divergent stages in the social movement; Arai, "Gemeindeethik," attributes it to differences between the era of Jesus and that of the church; but cf., more probably, the difference in *genre* between radical sayings and paradigmatic narrative; cf. Keener, *Matthew* (1997), 18; Tannehill, *Sword*, passim.

271. As often argued. Öhler, "Urgemeinde" (noting friendship ideals, community of goods, associations, etc.), argues that Luke's community is intended to *exceed* expectations for ideal communities. Social-identity

the earliest church may also have apologetic value; it resembles Josephus's Essenes, who "pose no political threat."[272] Noting similar language in Josephus's apologetic portrayal of Israel's "constitution,"[273] some scholars even argue that Luke portrays the Christian movement in Acts as an ideal *politeia* equal or superior to the best Greek and Roman models.[274]

d. Qumran Examples

Whereas sharing in common was merely an ideal for most Greek sects, some Essenes (assuming the dominant[275] but disputed[276] view of the identity of Qumran's community) practiced it quite literally, as commentators both on the Qumran scrolls and on Acts regularly observe.[277] (Complete community of property may have been practiced only by the Essenes who lived there, with lesser forms elsewhere.)[278] The sources suggest that the Essene example was widely known, even if infrequently encountered.[279] Their simple life was thought to attract converts (Pliny E. *N.H.* 5.15.73), a point perhaps relevant for comparison here (cf. Acts 2:47). If their view that they lived on the verge of the end time[280] played a critical role in their sharing of possessions, as some scholars argue,[281] this point of comparison also would be relevant for Luke's narrative and the traditions behind it (see comment on Acts 2:17).

Ideal portrayals of the Essenes emphasized their complete sharing of possessions.[282] Philo elaborates at greater length: They are the Jewish equivalent of other exotic sages, such as Persian magi and Indian gymnosophists (*Good Person* 75). They do not care for wealth or land but only for what is necessary to live (*Good Person* 76); they cooperate with neighbors and share (76), and remain poor by choice (77).[283] Their

---

theory helps identify various elements of this community's distinctness from (cf. Acts 2:40) its surrounding culture (so Brawley, "Social Identity," 16–33).

272. Mason, *Josephus and New Testament*, 202.

273. Penner, "Discourse," 91: in Jos. *Ag. Ap.* 2.145–46, "Moses' law promotes piety, *koinonia* in the community, and *philanthropia* toward humanity at large." These "cardinal virtues" are ancient, and Luke and Josephus may both draw on this tradition.

274. Penner, "Discourse," 89–100.

275. With most scholars, e.g., VanderKam, "People"; McRay, *Archaeology*, 359; Beall, "Essenes," 344–46; Fitzmyer, "Essene"; Talmon, "Link"; Lönnqvist and Lönnqvist, "Emergence"; Vermes, *Jesus and Judaism*, 127; Zias, Tabor, and Harter-Lailheugue, "Toilets"; cf. Magness, "Qumran"; Schultz, "Qumran"; earlier, e.g., Cross, "Wrote"; idem, *Library*, 51; Colpe, "Essener"; Strugnell, "Flavius Josephus"; Albright and Mann, "Qumran and Essenes"; Dupont-Sommer, *Writings*, 408–12. See Pliny E. *N.H.* 5.15.73; Synesius on Dio, ch. 1, pp. 35ff. Petav. (H. L. Crosby in Dio *Chrysostom*, LCL, 5:379).

276. Thus many scholars, e.g., Golb, "Manuscripts"; cf. Schiffman, "*Miqsat*"; earlier, e.g., Eisenman, *Maccabees*; Pryke, "Identity." It is possible that a number of scrolls were not from the community (cf. Golb, "Anomalies"; Crown and Cansdale, "Settlement"), though inkwells suggest that writing was done there (Goranson, "Inkwells"). It is also true that there were likely more sects than Josephus reports (Goodman, "Essenes") and more than one kind of Essene.

277. E.g., Fitzmyer, *Essays*, 284–88; Pfeiffer, *Scrolls*, 58–59; Mealand, "Community of Goods at Qumran"; Fabry, "Umkehr und Metanoia" (seeking to compare entrance there with repentance); Klauck, "Gütergemeinschaft"; Witherington, *Acts*, 162; and the extensive treatment in Finger, *Meals*, 146–66. Johnson, *Acts*, 59 cites numerous references (1QS V, 1–3, 14–16, 20; VI, 17–22, 24–25; VII, 24–25; VIII, 22–23; IX, 3–11; CD IX, 10–15; X, 18–20; XII, 6–7; XIII, 14–15; XIV, 20; XX, 7) but notes that sharing in common is based on ritual purity rather than on friendship (1QS IX, 3–11).

278. With, e.g., Jeremias, *Theology*, 223; Haenchen, *Acts*, 234; Vermes, *Jesus and Judaism*, 128; Capper, "Context," 330–31. Thus note the lesser demands in, e.g., CD XVIII, 2–5 (Fritsch, *Community*, 84). Failure to note this difference mars the occasional critique of the notion of Essene communalism (e.g., LaSor, *Scrolls*, 84).

279. Flusser, *Judaism*, 194.

280. See Aune, *Cultic Setting*.

281. Murphy, "Disposition."

282. Jos. *Ant.* 18.20; Philo *Hypoth.* 11.4–5; Pliny E. *N.H.* 5.17.13.

283. Thus they avoid war and slaves (Philo *Good Person* 78). Cf. also *Hypoth.*; on communalism, esp. 11.4–5.

dwelling is shared in common (*Good Person* 85–86). They share the same treasury, earnings, and clothes, and they share meals together (*Good Person* 86). Josephus also remarks (*War* 2.122 [LCL, 3:368–69]),

> Riches they despise, and their community of goods is truly admirable; you will not find one among them distinguished by greater opulence than another. They have a law that new members on admission to the sect shall confiscate their property to the order, with the result that you will nowhere see either abject poverty or inordinate wealth; the individual's possessions join the common stock and all, like brothers, enjoy a single patrimony.

In Qumran texts, a person's property enters the community with him (1QS VI, 22–23). They may have regarded wealth negatively (4Q183 1 II, 4–5). Even outside Qumran, covenanters would care for the poor, presumably in the community (CD VI, 21). Although most people were undoubtedly uncomfortable with those preaching universal abandonment of possessions, they probably often respected those who, like the Essenes, abandoned their own.[284]

Josephus saw parallels between Pythagoras and the Essenes on sharing (*Ant.* 15.371),[285] and some scholars have suggested even direct influence of Pythagorean ideas on the Essenes. Since the discovery of the Qumran scrolls, however, scholars are more apt to think that Josephus exaggerated the Pythagorean comparison and that the similarities reflect more general influence from the milieu.[286] (Some even think that the founders of the Essenes were influenced by the Hellenistic utopias at a number of points.[287] Other Jewish writers may also have adapted the utopian model.)[288] Luke was probably influenced by the language of ideal communities, and if he knew of specific descriptions of Jewish groups such as the Essenes and Therapeutae,[289] he may have regarded them as the closest analogues to his description of the early Christians.

There are, of course, significant differences between the model in Acts, which functioned voluntarily in urban society, and a monastic wilderness community.[290]

284. Jos. *War* 2.122–27; *Ant.* 18.20, 22; Philo *Good Person* 76–87; *Hypoth.* 11.4; Pliny E. *N.H.* 5.15.73; cf. Philo *Contempl.* 34–39.

285. Mealand, "Utopian Allusions," 98. Dupont, *Salvation*, 89, cites also Josephus's comparison of Essenes with Stoics (*War* 2.122). Hellenistic Jews often paralleled Pythagoras's teaching with Judaism (see, e.g., Gorman, "Pythagoras Palaestinus").

286. See the balanced evaluation of Culpepper, *School*, 59–60.

287. Mendels, "Utopia and Essenes." Certainly, Hellenism was felt in Palestine at the time of Qumran's founding, and such philosophic ideals (if not utopias themselves) could have assimilated well with some OT prophetic ideals.

288. E.g., Tcherikover, "Ideology," 64.

289. On the latter, see, e.g., Evans, "Therapeutae." Philo employs them as a model for meditative lives (Bergmeier, "Gottesfreunde"). Philo may have interpreted them through the lens of radical philosophical utopian or anti-utopian communities (see Stowers, "Resemble Philosophy?" 94–95); somewhat, Egyptian priests (cf. Balch, "Families," 267); and perhaps even Hyperboreans (Diod. Sic. 2.47.3). But while some view his depiction as pure fiction (Engberg-Pedersen, "Dream"), others argue that they may have been a genuine community (Beavis, "Therapeutae"; Szesnat, "Virgins"). The Therapeutae appear similar to the Essenes, except including both genders (Gusella, "Therapeutae"); others emphasize differences, viewing them as a small philosophic group (Taylor and Davies, "Therapeutae"). Our limited data about them has long fueled speculation: some early Christians viewed them as Christians (Euseb. *H.E.* 2.17; Pritz, *Nazarene Christianity*, 39; Inowlocki, "*Interpretatio*"); some link *Testament of Job* with the Therapeutae (tentatively, Spittler, "Introduction," 833), but this has been questioned (Collins, "Testamentary Literature," 276); some link Wisdom of Solomon with them (Tantlevskij, "Wisdom," surprisingly finding Qumran parallels), but this is also difficult to prove; some have even linked them with a pagan temple (Moss, "Sect").

290. On differences, cf. Cothenet, "Secte de Qumrân et la communauté chrétienne"; Kim, *Stewardship and Almsgiving*, 234–51.

Both Christians and Qumranites surrendered their property, but it was obligatory on members of the Qumran sect as soon as they entered.[291] Further, Christians continued to use their property until needs arose, requiring them to sell it (Acts 2:45; 4:34–35). Their resources do not become community property but are designated for the poor.[292]

Most Jews would have regarded both groups as extreme; thus a Jewish tradition could complain that only someone ignorant would claim that there was no difference between "mine" and "yours" (*m. 'Ab.* 5:10).[293] Likewise, while helping a neighbor who is poor, one should take heed to avoid falling into the same situation (Sir 29:20, in a context of the dangers of sureties). Nevertheless, Jewish sages acknowledged that one should give what was necessary to meet a person's genuine needs (*Sipre Deut.* 116.5.1–3),[294] and Judaism respected caring for the needy (e.g., Tob 2:14).

e. Ancient Israelite Models

For Luke, Jesus's example in the Gospel lies in the immediate foreground, with Hellenistic friendship and ideal communities in the immediate background. For the earliest Christian community in Acts, Jesus's teaching again would have contributed the nearest model, with reports about wilderness sectarians (see on Qumran, below) providing some likely background as well. But biblically thoughtful readers among Luke's ideal audience, as well as members of the earliest community itself, undoubtedly contemplated models in their Scriptures as well. Although the language and ideal of *koinōnia* fits Hellenistic models, it is also congruent with ideals in biblical law.[295]

Israelites had a different tradition of ancient equality than Greeks, whether in Egypt (*Jub.* 46:1) or, more plainly, in the wilderness (Exod 16:17–18),[296] a tradition some Greek-speaking Jews applied as an example of equality.[297] Greek-speaking Jews readily adopted Greek language of equality as compatible with their own faith.[298] Diodorus Siculus, misunderstanding the Jubilee legislation, claims that Moses divided the land equally (ἴσους) among all its citizens.[299] Although Israel's laws, like other ancient Near Eastern regulations, sought only to restrain and not to abolish selfishness, such equality was also the ideal to which they pointed (Deut 15:4).[300] As Wenk points out, "the renewed prophetic community of Acts" ultimately expressed itself "in terms of a renewed society as anticipated in Joel."[301]

291. See Fitzmyer, "Christianity in Light of the Scrolls," 243 (citing 1QS VI, 19); Pervo, *Acts*, 128n16 (though apparently discarding the Qumran analogy's usefulness entirely).

292. Jeremias, *Theology*, 223. For a broader economic context for first-century Palestine, see Oakman, "Economics."

293. See Hare, *Persecution*, 15–16.

294. As a further example, later rabbis commended the pimp who nevertheless sold his own bed to get a weeping woman's husband out of prison (*y. Ta'an.* 1:4, §1).

295. See Wright, *Ethics*, 194–96. For justice for the poor in the OT, see, e.g., Exod 22:25; Ps 72:13; Prov 14:21; Isa 3:14; Jer 5:28; Ezek 16:49; in the prophets, see, e.g., Gordon, *Near East*, 224.

296. For manna as a background here, see Grassi, *Laugh*, 121.

297. Philo *Heir* 191; 2 Cor 8:14; Jos. *Ant* 3.29.

298. Deut 13:7 LXX (13:6 ET), with friends as equals; *Let. Aris.* 228, 257, 263, 282 (see further Hadas, *Aristeas*, 174, 188n; 201, on *Let. Aris.* 257). Philo employs ἴσος regularly (altogether more than two hundred times; see discussion in Wolfson, *Philo*, 2:393).

299. Except extra for priests (Diod. Sic. 40.3.7).

300. Also van der Horst, "Parallels to Acts," 59; cf. Mealand, "Utopian Allusions," 97.

301. Wenk, *Power*, 313 (more extensively, see the discussion in 259–73). To use Pauline language: although Luke emphasizes some of the Spirit's "gifts" initially, his longer-range interest is in the Spirit's "fruit." In keeping with Luke's own terminology, however, he does not make the connection with the Spirit as explicit in the latter case.

f. Rooted in Jesus's Model

To understand fully the church's sacrificial behavior in Acts, we must understand Jesus's teaching on possessions in the Gospel.[302] The discipleship that the Gospel emphasizes requires using one's resources to serve the poor.[303] Real disciples must forsake their possessions (Luke 14:33), give them to the poor (3:11; 12:33; 18:22),[304] and practically demonstrate that they value other people's welfare more than they value their own resources (16:9–13, 21, 25). Jesus's example likewise teaches such sacrifice, a sacrifice the disciples necessarily shared as they periodically left their families and traveled with him (5:11; 18:28–29; cf. 9:58–62).[305] Whereas the Qumran scrolls reveal their community's "economic communism," Luke's Jesus (and probably the historical Jesus) was more demanding: at least on the ideal level, he sought disciples ready to endure "almost absolute poverty."[306] In practice, his emphasis on charity suggests that disciples might still hold some resources, but Jesus advocated a voluntary renunciation of wealth to demonstrate greater allegiance to God's kingdom (12:33–34; 14:33; 18:22–30; cf. 3:11).[307]

In Jesus's teaching, care for the poor is rooted in the model that fellow Christians belong to one's family (e.g., Luke 8:21; 22:32; see comment on Acts 9:17) and one must act accordingly—even at the risk of alienating one's natural kin (Luke 8:20–21; 14:12, 26; 18:29; cf. 21:16).[308] Those who abandoned worldly connections and advantages would have spiritual kin and their resources to help in time of need (18:30).[309] In contrast to the usual Roman pattern of patrons supplying and clients groveling or praising them,[310] Christians even in a Roman colony would praise God as their patron who provided through other Christians (2 Cor 9:12).[311]

The sharing of goods in Acts (cf. also sharing in Acts 9:36, 39; 11:28–30; 20:33–35; 24:17) thus may fulfill on a literal level what Jesus demanded in an ideal and hyperbolic manner.[312] Because those with resources would share, everyone would have enough, even in the present age (Luke 18:29–30). Similarly, one philosopher opines that he has ample possessions though owning little, because his friends share with him (Socratics *Ep.* 22, to Simmias and Cebes). Others observed that κοινωνία yielded shared resources (Hdn. 3.6.2).

---

302. For a survey of studies on poverty and shared goods in Luke-Acts, see Bovon, *Theologian*, 390–96; see more recently Gillman, *Possessions and Faith*; Kim, *Stewardship and Almsgiving* (for Acts, 218–33); earlier, cf. Cadbury, *Making*, 260–63; Karris, *Saying*, 84–104. Scholars often recognize the connection between Acts 2:44–45 and Luke's teaching elsewhere (e.g., Jervell, *Apostelgeschichte*, 156).

303. E.g., Abraham, "Good News to Poor."

304. Tannehill, "Ethics," 119, finds Luke 14:33 fulfilled in Acts 2:44–45 and 4:32–35 and notes that "sell" and "distribute" (Luke 18:22) recur in Acts 4:34–35.

305. Cf. Hengel, *Property*, 33.

306. Flusser, *Judaism*, 195 (who thinks that Jesus rejected the Essenes' economic separatism because he developed mainstream Judaism's doctrine of love, 196–97); cf. Schmidt, *Hostility to Wealth*, esp. 135–62.

307. See France, "God and Mammon."

308. For the language of family (more than patron-client relations) as dominating Luke's treatment of rich and poor, see Moxnes, "Social Relations," esp. 72. Cf. in this connection the citation of the first encyclical of Pope Benedict XVI in Scholl, *Apostelgeschichte*, 25: "The church is God's family in the world."

309. Cf. Lane, *Mark*, 372; Kee, *Community*, 109–10; Tannehill, *Sword*, 147–52, esp. 148–51; Rhoads and Michie, *Mark*, 92. For an analogy to this kind of "wealth," cf. Socratics *Ep.* 21–22.

310. See discussion above on Acts 2:42.

311. See Danker, *Corinthians*, 143; Keener, *Corinthians*, 214–15; cf. deSilva, *Honor*, 113–14, 127n11. Cf. this model also in *1 Clem.* 38.2 (see comment in Grant, *Paul*, 55); this is a *major* adaptation of patronage.

312. See Tannehill, *Acts*, 45; Kim, *Stewardship and Almsgiving*, 233–34. Bede *Comm. Acts* 2.44 speaks here of love for God generating love for neighbor, principles coherent with Jesus as well (cf. Luke 10:27–28; Mark 12:30–31). Tuckett, *Luke*, 96–97, rightly notes that Luke further radicalizes his already radical sources in the Jesus tradition, but on 100–102 suggests (in my opinion, somewhat less convincingly) that Luke expects a more lenient standard for his own day than for Jesus's. Walton, "Communism," shows the continuity of the charity ethic later in Acts (denying common ownership of property here).

Radically sacrificial disciples demonstrated the effectiveness of their teacher; a later story declared that when Crates gave his property to the citizen body (ἐκκλησία), the rest of the citizens marveled at his teacher Diogenes, who formed people like this (Diogenes *Ep.* 9, to Crates). Jesus certainly called for radical disciples (Luke 5:11; 9:23, 58–62; 14:26–34; 18:22–30). Although Paul is less rhetorically demanding for a different setting,[313] he retains a heavy concern for the poor (Rom 15:26–27; 2 Cor 8–9; Gal 2:10), even at potential risk to himself (cf. Rom 15:30–31), perhaps reflecting the continuing ethos of Jesus's teachings in the early Jesus movement,[314] suggested also in Acts 2:44–45.

Excursus: Possessions[315]

Although Luke does not inveigh against possessions here, he elsewhere makes them (like everything else, Luke 14:26–27) worthless compared with the kingdom (12:31–34) and hence readily sacrificed for the needs of one's family in Christ (18:29–30). Although Luke probably addresses a fairly comfortable urban audience (see introduction, ch. 12; cf. ch. 17, sect. 2),[316] he appears to offer good news for the poor but bad news for the rich (6:20–21, 24–25).[317] His approach to possessions invites brief comparison with some philosophic and other ideal views of possessions (in contrast with the dominant cultural ethos, which was, of course, to acquire as much wealth as possible).

Greek and Roman sages often claimed that wealth was neutral and could be used positively,[318] but many praised the moral blessing of poverty[319] and condemned the danger of wealth.[320] The love of money is folly;[321] wealth is worthless[322] compared to knowledge[323] or virtue,[324] and Stoics regarded only the wise as genuinely wealthy in

313. Cf., e.g., Keener, *Corinthians*, 206.

314. See particularly Longenecker, "Good News," esp. 63–64.

315. I have adapted and expanded some wording in this excursus from Keener, *Matthew*, 229–30.

316. See also Karris, "Poor," 112–25.

317. See Esler, *Community*, 187–89 (he rightly compares this [189–91] with *1 En.* 92–105). On wealth in Jesus's teaching, esp. in Luke, see also Goppelt, *Theology*, 1:79–84, esp. 79–81; on finances in Luke, see Cadbury, *Making*, 260–63; on wealth and poverty in Luke-Acts, O'Toole, "Poverty"; on economic reversal and God's favor for the needy in Luke-Acts, Sampathkumar, "Rich and Poor"; on sharing possessions, esp. Johnson, *Function*; idem, *Sharing Possessions*.

318. Plato *Laws* 9.870AB; Diog. Laert. 6.6.95; Sen. Y. *Ben.* 6.3.1–2; *Ep. Lucil.* 94.7; Arius Did. *Epit.* 2.7.5a.12, 14; 2.7.7e, pp. 48–49.10; 2.7.7f, pp. 48–49.22; cf. Isoc. *Nic.* 50 (*Or.* 3.37). In Plato, see Lodge, *Ethics*, 355–56.

319. Xen. *Symp.* 3.9; Diod. Sic. 10.7.1; Sen. Y. *Ep. Lucil.* 4; 17:4–5; *Dial.* 2.13.3; 5.2.1; 12.10.10–11.2; Lucian *Tim.* 33; Diog. Laert. 6.9.104; Aul. Gel. 9.8. See also Mus. Ruf. 19 in Boring, Berger, and Colpe, *Commentary*, 81–82; Pythagoras in Malherbe, *Moral Exhortation*, 110.

320. Lucret. *Nat.* 5.1105–42; Cato *Distichs* 4.1; Publ. Syr. 58; Sen. Y. *Dial.* 5.33.1; *Ep. Lucil.* 119.9; Pliny E. *N.H.* 33.2.4; Plut. *Educ.* 8, *Mor.* 5D; Phaedrus 4.12.5–8; Sall. *Catil.* 5.8; 52.7; *Jug.* 6.1; Lucian *Tim.* 28; Heraclitus *Ep.* 8. Cf. love of money as the source of all evils (Theon *Progymn.* 3.91–92, 264–66; Ps.-Phoc. 42; 1 Tim 6:10; Diog. Laert. 6.2.50; cf. Sen. Y. *Ep. Lucil.* 110.10; Iambl. *V.P.* 30.171).

321. Dio Chrys. *Or.* 13.13; Diog. Laert. 6.2.24; cf. Plut. *Educ.* 8, *Mor.* 5D; Libanius *Encomium* 3.11.

322. E.g., Mus. Ruf. 1, p. 34.31–33; 17, p. 110.20–22; Sen. Y. *Dial.* 12.11.6; Dio Chrys. *Or.* 79; Lucian *Charon* 12; Diog. Laert. 2.115; Libanius *Invect.* 5.2. A charlatan could thus be "worthy" of mere money (Mus. Ruf. frg. 50, pp. 142, 144).

323. Isoc. *Demon.* 19; Xen. *Mem.* 4.2.9; *Let. Aris.* 8; Sen. Y. *Ep. Lucil.* 108.11; Dio Chrys. *Or.* 79.6; Diog. Laert. 2.115; Fronto *Nep. am.* 2.8; Marc. Aur. 3.6.2; Philost. *Vit. Apoll.* 5.22; *Vit. soph.* 2.1.547; in Plato, cf. Plato *Phaedo* 82BC; Lodge, *Ethics*, 174–247.

324. Hor. *Ep.* 1.1.52; elsewhere, Confuc. *Anal.* 56 (4.11); 79 (15.31). One could invest also in one's children (Val. Max. 4.4.praef.).

what mattered.[325] Most philosophers and moralists stressed the virtue of contentment[326] and valued self-sufficiency.[327] One should avoid pride if wealthy.[328] A first-century Stoic philosopher declared that philosophy teaches not to fear poverty or to seek wealth as if they mattered (Mus. Ruf. 1, p. 34.31–33).[329] After all, one could not take one's wealth in death;[330] the pursuit of wealth itself could, indeed, lead to destruction.[331] Wisdom means having nothing to lose,[332] for fear of loss is as bad as grief of loss,[333] and hence possessions generate anxiety.[334]

In general, Greeks and Romans seem to have preserved respect for the old-fashioned virtues of military discipline and rustic simplicity, both among philosophers[335] and among others.[336] Thus, for example, Cicero warned that Capua's luxury corrupted even rugged Hannibal (Cic. *Agr.* 1.7.20).[337] Moralists often condemned extravagance,[338] squandering,[339]

325. E.g., Cic. *Parad.* 42–52; Arius Did. *Epit.* 2.7.11i, pp. 76–77.12–13; Sen. Y. *Ep. Lucil.* 108.11; Mus. Ruf. frg. 34; Plut. *Flatt.* 16, *Mor.* 58E. Some mocked (and misrepresented) this view (Hor. *Sat.* 1.3.124–25; Plut. *St. Poets* 4, *Mor.* 1058C; Lucian *Phil. Sale* 20; *Hermot.* 16, 81). Some non-Stoics also articulated such ideas (Plato *Phaedr.* 279BC; Porph. *Marc.* 9.167–72; cf. Socratics *Ep.* 21; perhaps Philo *Good Person* 77; [Ps.]-Plut. frg. 28, from scholia on Hesiod *W.D.* 126; Diogenes the Cynic in Max. Tyre 36.5; figurative usage in Pliny *Ep.* 6.32.2; *b. Tamid* 32a).

326. Xen. *Oec.* 2.2–4; Hor. *Odes* 2.18; 3.16; *Ep.* 1.2.55–59; Val. Max. 7.1.2; Mart. *Epig.* 4.77.2; Juv. *Sat.* 14.303–4; Cic. *Tusc.* 5.31.89–5.32.89; Diogenes *Ep.* 46; Publ. Syr. 626; Sen. Y. *Ep. Lucil.* 61.4; 94.43; 104.34; 119.2; Mus. Ruf. 7, p. 56.28; Pliny E. *N.H.* 7.46.151; Epict. *Diatr.* 3.9.15–17; Plut. *L. Wealth* 1–2, *Mor.* 523C–23E; *Coriol.* 10.3–4; Dio Chrys. *Or.* 6; Lucian *Dial. D.* 436 (8/26, Menippus and Cheiron 2); Quint. *Decl.* 268.4 (a speaker treats this as the noblest aspect of philosophy); Aul. Gel. 13.24; Marc. Aur. 5.1, 14; 8.45.1; Diog. Laert. 6.1.11; 10.1.11; Porph. *Marc.* 27.429–34; 28.447–48; Jos. *Ag. Ap.* 2.291–92. In Plato, see Lodge, *Ethics*, 68–72. Basic needs, such as food, mattered more than fineries (Babr. 83; cf. Sir 29:21; 4Q416 2 [+ 4Q417] II, 19–20).

327. E.g., Arist. *N.E.* 1.7.6–8, 1097b; Epict. *Diatr.* 2.2.3; Plut. *Virt.* 3, *Mor.* 101B; Aul. Gel. 2.29.17–20; Marc. Aur. 3.11.2; Socratics *Ep.* 8; Diog. Laert. 6.1.11; Porph. *Marc.* 28.449; 30.469–70; Phil 4:11; 1 Tim 6:6; cf. Sir 29:22–23.

328. Cic. *Off.* 1.26.90; Sen. Y. *Ben.* 6.3.2; Diog. Laert. 1.93; *Let. Aris.* 290.

329. It was said that Democritus donated most of his family wealth to his city so that he might study with less distraction (Val. Max. 8.7.ext. 4).

330. E.g., Isoc. *Demon.* 9; Cic. *Tusc.* 1.38.91 (cf. 1 Tim 6:7); Sen. Y. *Ep. Lucil.* 20.13; Lucian *Dial. D.* 336 (3/2, Dead to Pluto against Menippus the Cynic 1); 337 (3/2, Dead to Pluto against Menippus the Cynic 2); 363–64 (20/10, Charon and Hermes 1); 429–31 (29/24, Diogenes and Mausolus 1–3); Job 1:21; Ps.-Phoc. 110; cf. Wis 7:6.

331. E.g., Val. Max. 7.2.ext. 1a; 9.4.ext. 1; Plut. *Br. Wom.* 22 (Chiomara), *Mor.* 258E; also Sir 31:6 [34:6]; 1 Tim 6:9.

332. E.g., Sen. Y. *Dial.* 2.6.8.

333. Sen. Y. *Ep. Lucil.* 98.6.

334. E.g., Diog. Laert. 4.48; *m. 'Ab.* 2:7.

335. E.g., Sen. Y. *Ep. Lucil.* 87; Mus. Ruf. 1, p. 34.10–12; 6, p. 54.12–15; 9, p. 70.29–31; 18A, p. 112.9; p. 114.21–26; 18B, pp. 118.340–120.7; 19, pp. 120.18–122.32; Dio Chrys. *Or.* 54.3 (on Socrates); Iambl. *V.P.* 16.69; 32.226.

336. Polyb. 31.25.1; 32.13.6–7; Diod. Sic. 33.7.1–5; 38/39.9.1; Dion. Hal. *Ant. rom.* 6.94.2; 6.96.2; Livy 21.4.5–7; 39.40.10–11; Val. Max. 2.5.5–6; Vell. Paterc. 2.78.2; 2.79.1; Quint. Curt. 3.2.15; Plut. *M. Cato* 3.2; Aul. Gel. 1.14; 2.24; 13.24; 15.12.1–4; Corn. Nep. 3 (Aristides), 3.2; 19 (Phocion), 1.3–4; 25 (Atticus), 13.6–7; 14.3; 22.4; Sall. *Catil.* 54.4–5; *Jug.* 85.33; Tac. *Hist.* 2.5, 64; Suet. *Tib.* 18.1–2; Max. Tyre 3.1; cf. Dio Chrys. *Or.* 7.81; 32.22; Philost. *Hrk.* 27.11; 33.14–18, 41–45; Libanius *Declam.* 36.16–17. On the Scythians, see, e.g., Strabo 7.3.7; Croesus *Ep.* 9; on old Romans, Dupont, *Life*, 32–37.

337. Cf. also Roman armies in Diod. Sic. 37.2.1; Tac. *Hist.* 2.69; Alexander's in Plut. *Alex.* 40.2; condemnation of Roman luxury in Vell. Paterc. 2.1.1; 2.10.1; 2.33.4.

338. E.g., Polyb. 31.25.4–5; Corn. Nep. 7 (Alcibiades), 1.4; Sall. *Catil.* 5.8; 52.7; *Jug.* 6.1; Val. Max. 2.6.1; Sen. E. *Controv.* 1.pref. 7–8; Quint. *Inst.* 3.7.24; Sen. Y. *Nat. Q.* 1.17.10; Mus. Ruf. 1, p. 34.8–10; 9, p. 70.11–22, 28; 18B, p. 118.34–36; Mart. *Epig.* 3.62; Plut. *Comp. Arist. Cato* 4.1; Dio Chrys. *Or.* 4.5–6; 33.28; Suet. *Jul.* 43.2; Max. Tyre 36.2; Fronto *Nep. am.* 2.9; Diogenes *Ep.* 38. Some criticized others for (in their view) carrying this critique too far (Pliny *Ep.* 9.12.1–2; Lucian *Peregr.* 19).

339. Aeschines *Tim.* 30, 42, 53, 170; Lysias *Or.* 14.27, §142; 19.10, §152; Diod. Sic. 17.108.4; Alciph. *Farm.* 32 (Gnathon to Callicomides), 3.34, ¶1; Cic. *Sest.* 52.111; *Cat.* 2.4.7; 2.5.10; Hor. *Sat.* 1.2.7–11; Val. Max. 9.1.2; Corn. Nep. 7 (Alcibiades), 1.4; Sall. *Jug.* 16.4; Sen. Y. *Dial.* 4.7.2; Lucan *C.W.* 2.352–91; Mart. *Epig.* 5.32; 9.82; Arrian *Alex.* 7.28.3; Diog. Laert. 6.2.50; Sall. *Catil.* 5.8; 52.7; *Jug.* 6.1; 16.4; Cato *Distichs* 3.21;

greed,[340] and stinginess[341] and praised generosity.[342] Still, some of wealth's ancient critics (such as Philo and Seneca) apparently ignored their own possession of it.[343]

Like Greek views, Jewish views on wealth varied,[344] usually depending on how people used wealth. Some could regard wealth positively, as a sign of blessing,[345] yet many also acknowledged the spiritual dangers of wealth[346] and "love of gain"[347] (a vice also in Greek and Roman tradition),[348] likewise condemning greed.[349] One should love God rather than wealth;[350] sometimes Jewish writers also oppose the uselessness of worldly wealth with the true treasure of the world to come.[351] True wealth could thus include contentment,[352] and poverty could be a blessing.[353] Wisdom was true wealth (e.g., Prov 3:14).[354]

Although the rabbis, like mainstream Judaism in general, never advocated community of goods,[355] first-century Pharisees (though typically[356] economically well-off enough to devote time to study) were known for seeking to live simply,[357] and both Pharisees and their rabbinic successors advocated caring for the poor.[358] Rabbis could

---

Hor. *Sat.* 1.1.101–7; 1.2.62; *Epistle* 1.15.26–27; *Epodes* 1.34; Mus. Ruf. 19, p. 122.12–32; Plut. *Alc.* 16.1; Juv. *Sat.* 1.58–60; Philost. *Vit. soph.* 2.25.610; Athen. *Deipn.* 8.344b; Ps.-Phoc. 138; *Sipre Deut.* 11.1.2; Luke 15:13.

340. E.g., Eurip. *Cycl.* 316; Plato *Laws* 1.649D; Thucyd. 3.82.8; Diod. Sic. 21.1.4a; Hor. *Sat.* 1.1.84–87; *Ep.* 1.18.21–25; Val. Max. 9.4; Sen. Y. *Ep. Lucil.* 110.9; Mus. Ruf. 3, p. 40.27–28; 4, p. 48.9; 14, p. 92.22; 17, p. 108.13; Dio Chrys. *Or.* 17; Max. Tyre 33.4; Hdn. 3.8.8; Iambl. *V.P.* 17.78; *Let. Aris.* 277; Jos. *Ant.* 15.89. Cf., e.g., Achilles's refusal to take plunder (Philost. *Hrk.* 48.5; cf. Gen 14:22–24); by contrast, the oft-told tale of Midas (e.g., Lucian *Ship* 21).

341. E.g., Sen. Y. *Ben.* 6.3.1–2, 4; Dio Chrys. *Or.* 7.91; Diog. Laert. 4.50. Theophrastus (*Char.* 10 passim) makes fun of a stingy character with various examples: for instance, if a household servant breaks a dish, he subtracts its price from the servant's food rations (10.5); no passerby dare seize an olive or date knocked down by the wind on his property (10.8); cf. similarly Theophr. *Char.* 22 passim, on stinginess.

342. E.g., Arist. *N.E.* 4.1.6–14, 1120a.

343. On Philo, cf. Schmidt, "Hostility to Wealth"; Downing, "Philo on Wealth"; Mealand, "Philo's Attitude"; idem, "Paradox"; Phillips, "Revisiting Philo" (arguing that Philo opposes only lack of self-control, not wealth itself); on Seneca, Sevenster, *Seneca*, 200–206.

344. On views of poverty and wealth in intertestamental Jewish literature, see also Blomberg, *Poverty*, 91–103; in the rabbis, Montefiore and Loewe, *Anthology*, ch. 17 (440–50); Abrahams, *Studies* (1), 113–17.

345. *Sib. Or.* 3.783; *Let. Aris.* 204–5; *m. 'Ab.* 4:9; *Qidd.* 4:14; cf. *Sipre Deut.* 352.1.1; *b. Šabb.* 151b; *Ned.* 38a; *Gen. Rab.* 11:4. Money could be used either for good or bad (*y. B. Meṣi'a* 2:5, §2; *Exod. Rab.* 31:3; *Eccl. Rab.* 3:10, §1).

346. Deut 6:10–12; 11:15–16; 32:15; *1 En.* 63:10; 94:8; 96:4; 97:8; 1QS X, 18–19; XI, 2; CD IV, 17; VIII, 5, 7; 4Q183 1 II, 4–5; Sir 31:8–11; *Pss. Sol.* 5:16–17; *Let. Aris.* 211; Jos. *War* 2.122, 250; *Ant.* 4.190; Ps.-Phoc. 42–47; *Test. Jud.* 19:1; *m. 'Ab.* 2:7; *Sipre Deut.* 43.3.1–2, 5; 318.1.1–4.

347. Sir 31:5 [34:5]; *Sib. Or.* 3.189, 234–36, 640–42; Ps.-Phoc. 42–47; *1 En.* 108:8; *Test. Levi* 17.11; *Test. Jud.* 17.1; 18.2; 19.1; Sir 31:5–8; Philo *Spec. Laws* 1.281; cf. *Test. Benj.* 6:2.

348. Xen. *Mem.* 1.2.5; Isoc. *Demon.* 9, 27–28; Plato *Hipparch.* 225A–232C; Longin. *Subl.* 44.6; Sil. It. 11.33–36; Plut. *Br. Wom.* 22 (Chiomara), *Mor.* 258E; Dio Chrys. *Or.* 66.1; Diog. Laert. 4.48; 6.2.50; Theon *Progymn.* 3.91–92; Arius Did. *Epit.* 2.7.5f, pp. 30–31.30; 2.7.10b, pp. 58–59.36; 2.7.10c, pp. 60–61.19; 2.7.10e, pp. 62–63.23.

349. E.g., 4Q416 2 [+ 4Q417] III, 8–12; Ps.-Phoc. 6.

350. *1 En.* 108:8; cf. independently Porph. *Marc.* 14.242–46.

351. *1 En.* 100:6; *m. 'Ab.* 4:1; 6:9; *b. B. Meṣi'a* 114b; *Gen. Rab.* 67:5; *Exod. Rab.* 31:3, 5, 14; 52:3; *Lev. Rab.* 34:4; *Eccl. Rab.* 2:1, §1; cf. Luke 12:34; *Herm.* 1.1.1. For true wealth, see also *b. Šabb.* 25a (in Finkelstein, *Akiba*, 187).

352. Especially *m. 'Ab.* 4:1; cf. also Tob 4:21; *Let. Aris.* 223; Philo *Good Person* 77; 4Q417 1 I, 17–22; Finkelstein, *Akiba*, 187. On contentment, cf. also Galen *Grief* 41–45, 78b–81.

353. It could lead to repentance (*b. Ḥag.* 9b; *Lev. Rab.* 13:4; *Song Rab.* 1:4, §4).

354. Sir 1:24; 41:14; Wis 7:13–14; 8:5; Cambridge Geniza Text, col. F, lines 16–17; cf. also, e.g., 4Q213 6 + 7 3; Philo *Cher.* 48 (cf. 107); Col 2:2; the Torah in *Pesiq. Rab Kah.* 12:11; *b. Šabb.* 88b. Among Gentiles, cf. Vitruv. *Arch.* 6.pref. 1–2; Philost. *Vit. Apoll.* 8.21.

355. Johnson, *Sharing Possessions*, 133.

356. Hillel was said to have started poor (*b. Yoma* 35b).

357. Jos. *Ant.* 18.12; *'Abot R. Nat.* 5 A. The idealization of poverty probably originated among the comfortable (Unsok Ro, "Context").

358. *M. 'Ab.* 1:5.

praise a sage who sold everything to devote himself entirely to study of the Torah.[359] Josephus claimed that many Gentiles admired and wished to imitate Jewish charity practices (*Ag. Ap.* 2.283). Although Judean society prospered in the period depicted here, most individuals had modest lives.[360]

g. How *They Supported the Poor* (2:45)

Luke does not portray possessions as evil in a gnostic sort of way, only as worthless compared with needs within the believers' new family.[361] Thus believers divested themselves of property only as needs arose (which was apparently quite often). The noun κτήματα may refer to fixed property (as in Acts 5:1);[362] ὕπαρξις is rare (elsewhere in the NT only at Heb 10:34) but probably refers to all possessions (cf. the cognate verb in Luke 12:33, 44; 14:33; 16:1; 19:8).[363]

The imperfect tense ("were selling") suggests that members periodically sold their goods when needs arose,[364] rather than immediately on entering the community (this aspect is less demanding than in the Qumran scrolls).[365] Thus they did not all (cf. Acts 5:4) divest themselves of all possessions at conversion but, rather, disavowed their personal ownership of their possessions, along with their lives (Luke 14:26, 33), so as to sacrifice them when "any had need" (Acts 2:45; 4:35). As historian and ethicist Ronald Sider notes, "the text does not suggest that the community decided to abolish all private property and everyone instantly sold everything. Rather it suggests that over a period of time, whenever there was need, believers regularly sold lands and houses to aid the needy."[366]

h. Authenticity

Despite occasional scholarly speculation that the passage lacks historical basis,[367] the history of movements suggests that it is more likely that the church would move away from radical ideals on possessions as it incorporated more members[368] than that it would have invented ideals it never practiced.[369] Some suggest that 2:44–45 and 4:32–35 are doublets of the same source,[370] but current narrative criticism is more apt

---

359. *Pesiq. Rab Kah.* 27:1.

360. Neusner, *Beginning*, 23.

361. Cf. Troeltsch, *Social Teaching*, 1:59, whose generally romantic view nevertheless commends itself here: "The ethic of Jesus is heroic rather than ascetic." In its ideal form, however, the former may appear like the latter. For a survey of the secondary literature on poverty and sharing goods in Luke-Acts, see, e.g., Bovon, *Theologian*, 390–96.

362. Cf. Bishop, *Apostles*, 37 (who notes the long-term hereditary nature of such deeds and the difficulties with absentee landlords). Note BDAG on the shift in meaning.

363. Two-thirds (about forty) of the verb's NT uses are in Luke-Acts (with twelve in Paul, leaving about eight); it appears as a participle (most relevant) twenty-eight times in Luke-Acts, again two-thirds of the NT uses.

364. So likewise in Acts 4:34. When Luke depicts a particular sale, he employs an aorist passive participle (5:4).

365. Dunn, *Jesus and Spirit*, 161; idem, *Acts*, 59; Tannehill, "Ethics," 118.

366. Sider, *Christians*, 76. "If the need was greater than the current cash reserves, they sold property. They simply gave until the needs were met" (ibid.).

367. E.g., Horn, "Gütergemeinschaft" (who speculates that the idea derived from the historic help that Antioch gave Jerusalem in Acts 11:27–30—though, as will be noted there, some think that passage a projection of Paul's collection!).

368. Cf. Kraybill and Sweetland, "Sociological Perspective."

369. Others also offer arguments in favor of its authenticity (e.g., Finger, *Meals*, 244–45, based on what is known of the first-century social environment; also Bartchy, "Community"; Marguerat, *Actes*, 162–63, on Acts 4:32–35; esp. Capper, "Context").

370. Lake, "Communism," 145.

to see "doublets" as repetition for effect, and it seems likely that Luke is emphasizing a repeated effect of the Spirit's outpouring, perhaps increasing the previous level of commitment.[371] The practice in 2:44–45 continues to be presupposed in 6:1–6, comports with the view of caring for the poor in the Letter of James,[372] and may also help explain a continuing emphasis on sharing suggested in Paul's collection(s)[373] and some second-century Christianity.

Although Luke used his rhetorical skill to stylize the events of 2:44–45 in a way pleasing for his Hellenistic readers,[374] in content the Qumran parallels remain closer.[375] The obvious Hellenistic topos in Philo's and Josephus's descriptions of Essenes led W. Bauer in 1924 to doubt that the Essenes really shared possessions; the discovery of Qumran's Manual of Discipline, however, laid such skepticism to rest.[376] Some have even suggested that Essenes who settled in Jerusalem a few decades before (yet maintained contact with wilderness Essenes) may have directly influenced the early Christian practice.[377] Yet even without such direct mediation, early Christians would have known of wilderness ascetics (there were others; cf. Bannus in Jos. *Life* 11) and a life of sacrifice through the example of John the Baptist (Luke 1:80). Parallels with Qumran's communal life probably go back through Jesus's disciples who traveled, ate together, and shared a common purse.[378]

Some also find Semitic idioms in Luke's description, comparing his expression for "together" (ἐπὶ τὸ αὐτό) to an analogous Hebrew term that in the Qumran scrolls means "the community" (cf. 1QS I, 1; III, 7).[379] This argument is more questionable; Luke probably depends on oral rather than written sources here and probably uses his own vocabulary (though in all his writings the phrase admittedly appears only in Luke 17:35; Acts 1:15; 2:1, 44, 47; 4:26; elsewhere in the NT, only Matt 22:34; 1 Cor 7:5; 11:20; 14:23). But other elements may reinforce the idea of pre-Lukan tradition, especially if the primitive Christians' sharing reflected, in part, their probable expectation of Christ's almost immediate return.[380]

Despite Luke's idealized language, he does not create the kind of complete community of goods suggested for Pythagoreans or Qumran Essenes; people sold their goods when their economic resources were needed. Given his apologetic *Tendenz*,

371. Finger, *Meals*, 217–18, plausibly argues that Luke, having narrated the pattern and never informing us of its demise, expects his audience to infer its continuance in the churches.

372. See Blomberg, "Posesiones materiales."

373. Cf. Watson, "Collection," chs. 6–7.

374. Hengel, *Property*, 8.

375. Ibid., 9; Capper, "Reciprocity," 500. Cf. Capper, "Context," 324–25; idem, "Houses," 472, 486.

376. Capper, "Context," 335. Against many detractors today, I continue to find persuasive the thesis, explained by Geza Vermes and others, that the sectarian documents from Qumran reflect Essene thought.

377. Capper, "Context," 341–50, arguing that the Christians probably met especially in the Essene Quarter. Others also suggest Essene and/or Qumran influence (Boismard and Lamouille, Actes, 2:162).

378. Betz, *Jesus*, 73; Munck, *Acts*, 22.

379. Capper, "Context," 336; Witherington, *Acts*, 161–62; Finger, *Meals*, 231. The Hebrew could be rendered differently, and the wording is not close enough to make the inference a strong one. Its occurrences in the first chapters of Acts (Acts 1:15; 2:1, 44, 47; cf. 4:26) constitute half of NT uses (cf. also Luke 17:35; Matt 22:34), but it appears in Paul (1 Cor 7:5; 11:20; 14:23), about fifty times in the LXX, and about thirteen times in the Apostolic Fathers. It is rare, however, in the eloquent Greek of Philo (only at *Rewards* 24) and Josephus (*Ant.* 16.270; *War* 2.346).

380. See Hengel, *Property*, 32 (cf. also 84). But contrast Goppelt, *Times*, 50: because the sacrifice was voluntary (in contrast to Qumran), "the Church did not act out of an enthusiasm arising from an expectation of the imminent end, but" instead on the basis of Jesus's teaching. Koester, "Structure," 215–16, believes that there was an apocalyptic communal group of primitive Christians in Jerusalem, though he thinks little about them authentic.

Luke certainly would not have invented the conflict of Acts 6:1, yet it presupposes a concerted program of sharing such as Luke describes earlier.[381]

Although Luke's description of the early community may be idealized, another idealized (and apologetic) portrait of the churches in the mid-second century suggests that the ideal was not Luke's alone but continued in the life of the church. Justin claims that former pagans, converted to Christianity, continue to share their resources in common and with the needy (Justin *1 Apol.* 14). In the late second century, Tertullian remarks wittily that Christians readily share everything in common except their wives—the one thing, he complains, pagans were most willing to share (Tert. *Apol.* 39.11–12). In antithetical contrast to the apologists' idealized portraits, Lucian ridicules worshipers of "the crucified sophist" as despising "all things indiscriminately" and reckoning everything as "common property," hence easily cheated.[382] Celsus critiqued Christians for their effective appeal to "the socially objectionable classes"[383] as well as to "the unhappy and sinful."[384] Other sources also attest to Christians' continuing commitment to share their resources in the second century and beyond.[385]

Finally, activity such as is described here is not unrealistic in times of fervent religious commitment. Reception history reveals various attempts to evade the text's demands, domesticating them to fit one's context.[386] Yet various renewal movements in history have successfully emulated the radical model of Acts 2:44–45.[387] The behavior is not implausible for such movements, and hence there is no reason to deny an authentic Palestinian tradition behind Luke's report. Insofar as our interest is Luke's application to his audience, however, the Hellenistic parallels remain important.

381. Dunn, *Jesus and Spirit*, 161.

382. Lucian *Peregr.* 13 (LCL, 5:15). Peregrinus, still a Christian at this point, garbs himself as a Cynic and bequeaths all his inheritance to his town in *Peregr.* 15.

383. Cook, *Interpretation*, 84–85.

384. Ibid., 85–87.

385. See Hengel, *Property*, 42–43 (citing Aristides *Apol.* 15.7–8) and 43–44 (beyond the second century). Community of goods, however, did not endure (45).

386. E.g., Augustine employs it as a continuing model for his church (*Ep.* 211.5; Martin, *Acts*, 38); yet it is argued that he mostly emphasized "basic theological claims," neither caring for the poor nor changing the political order (McGee, "Possessions," 166). McGee notes (177) the historical contingency of all the interpretations; but the more sacrificial approaches probably approximate the ideal better than do the preferred cultural assumptions of middle-class interpreters. Finger, *Meals*, 13–14, surveys pre-Reformation interpretations on economic sharing in Acts; views of "magisterial" reformers, 14–18; views of the radical reformers, 18–22; views of (middle-class or elite) critical scholarship, 22–26; socialist approaches, 27–29 (cf. also Williams, "Acts," 221–23, on African-American socialist preacher George Woodbey); early sociological approaches, 29–33; and more recent scholarly approaches, 35–45. As Finger concludes (45), most Western commentators "assume capitalism's superiority to other economic systems, and have profited by it," and many twentieth-century commentators were reacting against political communism.

387. Cf. Wesley in Jennings, *Good News*, 25, 97–117, esp. 111–16; early Moravians (Williams, *Radical Reformation*, 429; cf. 229–33); monastic movements. Peter Riedeman, an Anabaptist (1506–56), argued for communal sharing of goods (still practiced among Hutterites; McGee, "Possessions," 167–68; Williams, *Radical Reformation*, 232, 426–29, esp. 429 for the use of Acts 2:44), although, among Anabaptists, only Hutterites practiced this literally (Finger, *Meals*, 21–22); more recently, the communitarian Jesus Family in China (Anderson, *Pentecostalism*, 135; Zhaoming, "Chinese Denominations," 452–64; Yamamori and Chan, *Witnesses*, 54–62; Wesley, *Church*, 56); some elements in the North American Jesus Movement of the 1960s–1970s (Jackson, *Middle*, 32; Di Sabatino, "Frisbee," 395–96). Cf. John Chrysostom, for whom it was not a model to be imposed but an example of voluntary sharing seeking unity (McGee, "Possessions," 165), yet also a radical prescription (Nassif, "Body," 13). Although without citing this text, cf. John Winthrop, according to Cotton Mather, in Bradley et al., *Tradition*, 121. Blomberg, "Liberation Theology," suggests a synthesis of evangelical appreciation for the historical grounding of radical NT teaching with liberationists' praxis; Miller and Yamamori, *Pentecostalism*, passim, esp. 31–34, 39–128, 211–13, observe an increasing stream of social engagement in global Pentecostalism. Some scholars argue that divine healing beliefs provide social support for impoverished Brazilian Pentecostals (Mariz, *Coping*, in Castleberry, "Impact," 151).

5. Community Life in 2:46–47

The daily meeting in the temple follows Jesus's example when he taught there daily (Luke 19:47; 22:53),[388] and the daily breaking of bread (see comment on Acts 2:42) perhaps follows Jesus's teaching that his followers should pray daily for their bread (Luke 11:3); discipleship also entailed daily acts of sacrifice (Luke 9:23), and the Jerusalem church fed the poor daily (Acts 6:1). Likewise, and perhaps consequently, the number of believers was growing daily (2:47; 16:5).[389] That believers would meet daily, as here, seems the ideal pattern (cf. Heb 3:13; 10:25; *Did.* 4.2), though we cannot be certain that all members met daily or how often this proved feasible in the later Diaspora churches.

a. Unity of Purpose (2:46)

The term ἀφελότης is rare (it appears nowhere else in the NT or LXX), but where it does occur, it can be equivalent to ἁπλότης.[390] Given the context, emphasizing both worship and activity together, perhaps it could imply singleness of heart to the Lord[391] as well as being in unity. Greek texts often emphasize being of one mind (e.g., μιᾷ γνώμῃ in Lysias *Or.* 2.24, §192), as did the early Christians (Rom 15:5; Phil 1:27; 2:2–3). True friendship involves unity of mind (ὁμόνοιαν; Dio Chrys. *Or.* 4.42); this was also the ideal for families (ὁμοφροσύνη; 38.15).[392] Political analogies are also relevant for early Christians; a city should have "singleness of purpose" (ὁμοφρονούσης; 39.3),[393] and a favorite theme of oratory was the ὁμόνοια (*homonoia*) speech, exhorting hearers to concord (see comment on Acts 15:25). If two rival cities were to reconcile, each would share the prosperity of the other (Dio Chrys. *Or.* 38.47–49; see comment on Acts 2:44–45).

Luke presents the early church as holding the virtue of acting ὁμοθυμαδόν, in unity, a consistent theme (Acts 1:14; 2:46; 4:24; 5:12);[394] when members of the church are later divided, the Spirit leads them through dialogue back to this sharing of the same mind (15:25). It is a preferred term of Luke's (though never used in the Gospel); outside Acts, it appears in the NT only at Rom 15:6 (though it occurs thirty-six times in the LXX, especially in Job and the works originally composed in Greek). When the wicked act in concert in this way, they do so to oppress the righteous (Acts 7:57; 18:12; 19:29); the unity of crowds hearing the gospel (8:6) also underlines the effectiveness of Philip's ministry, though the term also applies to a crowd's desperate attempts to seek Agrippa's favor (12:20).

388. Paul also taught daily when able to do so (Acts 17:11; 19:9).

389. Luke was not necessarily consciously weaving all these texts together; it is one of his preferred expressions (see also Luke 16:19; Acts 3:2; he uses it in eleven of the seventeen times it appears in the NT; it appears twenty-two times in the largest form of the LXX and only twice in the Apostolic Fathers [*Did.* 4.2; *Diogn.* 6.9]). But his usage does reveal an emphasis on regularity.

390. Barrett, *Acts*, 171. The latter term's cognates can involve generosity or lack of greed (see Luke 11:34; for discussion, see Keener, *Matthew*, 232–33), relevant to this context (Acts 2:44–45).

391. E.g., 1 Chr 28:9; Wis 1:1; *Pesiq. Rab.* 51:2; cf. Ps 86:11.

392. For unity among family members, relevant to early Christian understanding of their unity, see deSilva, *Honor*, 169–73.

393. See further, e.g., Dio Chrys. *Or.* 39.8.

394. Walton, "Ὁμοθυμαδόν," 104, allows that it may mean "together" in the same location in Acts 2:46, but notes (105) that usually Luke uses it for "unitedly, unanimously, with one impulse, as one person" or "shared passion or commitment, with one heart/mind/purpose." On the church's unity in Acts, see further Thompson, "Unity." For connections between expressions of unity in 2:44–45 and 4:32, see Giroud, "Propre."

The Greco-Roman world had a wide vocabulary for unity, and exhortations to unity constituted a major topos for speeches and the essays of moralists alike.[395] Paul's letters often repeat this exhortation to early Christians, suggesting that they, like everyone else, needed to be called to unity (Rom 15:5–6; 1 Cor 1:10–12; Phil 2:1–5). It often appears in narratives, therefore, in a paradigmatic way, as an ideal inviting imitation. Early Jewish traditions about the exodus emphasize this ideal unity.[396] It also characterized the ideal Pythagorean communities.[397]

b. House Meetings (2:46)

Some scholars suggest that early Christians used public meeting places to evangelize in seeking converts, but houses to disciple the converts (cf. Acts 5:42; 20:20).[398] The meetings from house to house[399] follow Jesus's instructions for expansion (Luke 10:5–7) and form the basis for the later house churches, which became the dominant meeting places for early Christians. Meetings in homes in the Gospel may foreshadow this pattern (5:29; 7:36–37; 8:51; 9:4; 10:5–7; 14:1; 19:5, 9; 22:11),[400] though the idea, in any case, would have seemed less novel to them than to us: apart from community centers (such as synagogues), temple courts, or gathering outdoors, where else would disciples meet? In a familial setting, ancient Israel also used homes for worship and instruction.[401] Crates the philosopher reportedly entered one house after another to admonish those within (Diog. Laert. 6.5.86). In particular, the early Christians practiced their teaching (Acts 2:42) especially in believers' homes.

As basic observation of group dynamics confirms, smaller groups tend to invite more interaction.[402] Meals together of voluntary associations were widely known in antiquity (see comment on Acts 2:42); a Palestinian Jewish form was the *haburah*, probably practiced by Pharisees.[403] Open courtyards amid homes could hold larger numbers of people,[404] but apart from some extraordinarily large homes (cf. 1:13), even the larger homes probably rarely held more than fifty people,[405] although there were likely some exceptions.[406] Even those with wealthy homes tended to host smaller banquets in the dining room; ten or fifteen may have been a common number.[407]

House meetings naturally created an environment of family, especially for Luke's audience in places like Philippi, who were familiar with clients and freedpersons

395. E.g., Men. Rhet. 2.3, 384.23–25; 2.7, 411.15–18; for early Stoics, see Engberg-Pedersen, *Paul and Stoics*, 75 (citing *SVF* 1.263); see further comment on Acts 15:25; or Keener, *John*, 1061–62.

396. *Mek. Bah.* 1.108ff. (Lauterbach, 2:200).

397. Van der Horst, "Parallels to Acts," 58–59 (comparing Iambl. *V.P.* 30).

398. Blue, "Influence," 481–82, 486.

399. Sir 29:24 depicts as difficult moving "from house to house" (ἐξ οἰκίας εἰς οἰκίαν), but there it refers to depending on the hospitality of strangers. Cullmann, *Worship*, 10, reads simply "at home," but here they eat "together." Ignatius's exhortations to unity around the bishop, addressed to a later situation (*Eph.* 5.2; *Magn.* 7.1; *Trall.* 7.2; *Philad.* 4; *Smyrn.* 8.1; 9.1), cannot be applied anachronistically against earlier, less official forms of house meetings.

400. On a symbolic level, see, e.g., Luke 14:23; 15:25.

401. Wright, *Ethics*, 359–60. In antiquity, respect for religion made religious settings less threatening; even city folk invited foreigners to dine with them during festivals (Libanius *Descr.* 29.8).

402. Also more honest interaction (Pliny *Ep.* 5.12.1).

403. Neusner, *Beginning*, 27; Oesterley, *Liturgy*, 167; Lohse, *Environment*, 79; Bruce, *Commentary*, 81. Jewish communal banquets were more broadly recognized (Jos. *Ant.* 14.214; Rabello, "Condition," 707).

404. Some Galilean families whose chambers surrounded a common courtyard formed associations that shared food resources (see Horsley, *Galilee*, 192).

405. Witherington, *Acts*, 211. See comment on Acts 18:2–3 (information on Corinthian homes is well documented).

406. Larger homes in Pompeii could hold more than fifty (Balch, "Houses").

407. Cf. the invited diners in Dio Chrys. *Or.* 17.21.

who formed an extended household and often ate at their patron's banquets.[408] Such relationships were so central that some ancients presented household relationships as paradigmatic or foundational for the state (cf. 1 Tim 3:4).[409]

Like meetings in the temple, the house meetings undoubtedly reflect authentic tradition from the earliest period (even though house meetings also undoubtedly remained the norm in Luke's day). The house church model preceded Paul's church-planting ministry; the Roman church, which he did not found, used it;[410] synagogues often started in homes; and there was no other practical place to meet in difficult times. It is also reasonable to believe that this part of the Jesus tradition is authentic, attested in both Markan (Mark 6:10; Luke 9:4) and Q (Luke 10:5–7; Matt 10:12–14) forms (though Mark might depend here on Q).

c. Meeting in the Temple (2:46)

Unlike the house meetings, a continuing model for Luke's own day, the temple meetings directly reflect only the past (on a post-70 dating of Luke-Acts).[411] Other meetings in the temple must also have been common; it provided the largest available open space in Jerusalem and a natural place for teaching. The massive Jerusalem temple—easily one of the largest in the empire—could host vast crowds in its courts and surrounding areas (e.g., the gallery in Jos. War 2.344). The Temple Mount comprised 1,527,920 square feet, that is, about 35 acres.[412] Ancient cities typically had an acropolis or other prominent area containing public buildings (such as temples and administrative buildings) as well as palaces and homes of the elite; Jerusalem had its upper city and Temple Mount.[413] People congregated especially in a city's public space, including temples;[414] in Jerusalem, this public space would have been the Temple Mount.

Jewish traditions suggest that sages often taught in the temple,[415] and Jesus had set a precedent for the disciples there (Luke 21:37). Temple courts were public locations used by various ancient lecturers,[416] and people typically associated there.[417]

408. Although patronage was especially a Roman model, it was disseminated in colonies (such as Corinth and Philippi) and widely known (overlapping with benefaction in the Greek East). It would be much better known in its technical form to Luke's audience than to the ordinary Jerusalemites he depicts; on differences between patronage and benefaction, and the lack of patronage in relevant Jewish sources, see MacGillivray, "Patronage."

409. See Eurip. El. 386–87; Isoc. Ad Nic. 19; Nic. 41 (Or. 3.35); Cic. Off. 1.17.54; Iambl. V.P. 30.169; Klauck, Context, 56; Meeks, Moral World, 21; Verner, Household, 152; cf. Demosth. Lept. 9; Val. Max. 2.6.6; Mus. Ruf. 8, p. 66.15; Plut. Alex. 9.6; Comp. Arist. Cato 3.1; Dinner 12, Mor. 155D; S. Sp., Lycurgus 21, Mor. 228CD; Philost. Vit. soph. 1.485.

410. Possibly learned from Paul's colleagues (Rom 16:5), but probably not (cf. 16:10–11), since the churches needed somewhere to meet before Paul entered the picture (Acts 18:2).

411. Elliott, "Temple" (cf. discussion of divergent approaches to meals in these spheres in idem, "Purity System"; idem, "Household and Meals"), finds a temple/household contrast in Luke-Acts, with Luke favoring the latter. Aarde, "Houses," counters by postulating broadening rather than replacement (cf. the relation of synagogues to the temple); Esler, "Reply," critiques Aarde. In any case, the coupling of temple and household and of the larger dimension of public and private appears in Luke-Acts.

412. McRay, Archaeology, 102.

413. Rohrbaugh, "Pre-industrial City," 134. Public buildings consumed perhaps half of Rome's total space (Stambaugh, City, 90).

414. Stambaugh, City, 111, 113; for temples as civic space, see, e.g., Libanius Topics 2.8.

415. E.g., m. Ker. 1:7; 'Abot R. Nat. 38 A; 41, §114 B; b. Pesaḥ. 26a; Liefeld, "Preacher," 191–92 (following esp. Büchler, "Open Air"); Safrai, "Temple," 905; Vermes, Religion, 76–77.

416. E.g., Iambl. V.P. 9.50; 21.96; Philost. Vit. Apoll. 4.2; see also Siegert, "Homily," 421n1 (citing Plut. Pythical Dialogues passim; Dio Chrys. Or. 36); Watson, "Education," 310. Educators in Rome often used temples and other public space near the Forum (310); for teaching in various public spaces, see, e.g., Dio Chrys. Or. 20.9.

417. Religious guilds often met in temples, with other guilds also renting or owning rooms within temples' sacred space (temenos; Smith, Symposium, 104, 110).

Pythagoreans, who may have provided part of Luke's utopian model for sharing (see comment on Acts 2:44–45), spent time together especially in temples in the afternoon (Iambl. *V.P.* 21.96).

Although Qumran sectarians felt that an earlier temple establishment had banished them,[418] Pharisees, Sadducees, and most other Jews, despite their differences, shared the temple courts by the first century.[419] Such an image would not be unfamiliar to Diaspora readers; whereas only wealthier associations owned their own buildings, "small associations met in an area of a public temple, in a rented hall or in a private house. Corner cafes might serve as informal clubs for the poorer groups."[420]

d. Jesus's Movement and the Temple (2:46)

Although Jesus may have regarded the temple as facing judgment (Luke 21:5–6), he and the disciples regarded it as an appropriate place for worship and teaching (19:47; 20:1; 21:5, 37–38; 22:53; Mark 12:35; 13:1; 14:49).[421] Some scholars regard this feature as indicating primitive tradition;[422] certainly, it is pre-Lukan, but it does not characterize only the earliest years of the church. Even from Luke's perspective, the members of the Jerusalem church continued to worship in the temple until they fled the city (cf. Acts 21:20, 26). This continued practice (in a period that Luke knows more clearly) must, however, reflect the "primitive" practice; they undoubtedly continued an unbroken tradition from the earliest Jerusalem church instead of representing a departure from a less orthodox prior tradition.[423] Although this tradition is pre-Lukan, it fits Luke's perspective of salvation history. His Gospel begins and ends with scenes in Jerusalem and worship in the temple (Luke 1:9–22; 24:52–53); Acts moves from heritage to mission (Acts 1:8; see our introduction, ch. 13, sect. 2) but without despising that heritage in which Luke has so carefully grounded it.

That the temple would be judged (Luke 19:45–48) but also renewed (cf. 20:17–18; discussion below) allows for the temple to be superseded after 70, yet this could (if the establishment's neglect or rejection of appropriate worship there was among the reasons for its judgment) encourage worship in the temple while it remained.[424] Some scholars suggest that in dominating discourse in the temple in Acts 3 and by challenging the temple authorities in Acts 4–5, the apostles even imply that they, as the leaders for Israel appointed by the Messiah (Luke 22:30), should rule there rather than the politically compromised priestly aristocrats (cf. Acts 4:11; 5:30, 32).[425] If such a proposal overstates the apostles' claims—it is by no means clear that the apostles advocated disrespect or resistance, and even less clear that they expected the leaders

418. See on the "wicked priest," e.g., 1QpHab VIII, 8–12; IX, 9–10; XI, 4–6; XII, 2–8; 4Q171 IV, 8.

419. See Sanders, *Jesus to Mishnah*, 36–37 (citing *m. Parah* 3:7; 4QMMT).

420. Jeffers, *World*, 77.

421. See Sanders, *Jesus and Judaism*, 76, 268; cf. also Dunn, *Partings*, 37–56 on Jesus, and 57–74 on the Jerusalem Christians (minus, in his view, the Hellenists); Reitzel, "Luke's Temple Image" (on the Gospel's temple motif, even if he sometimes presses it too far for structural clues). Jesus apparently protested not the temple but the inadequate respect being shown its sanctity (Mark 11:15–17, esp. 11:16, omitted by Luke; John 2:16–17).

422. E.g., Dawsey, "Luke's Positive Perception."

423. On the temple and various Jewish views toward it, see Chilton, Comfort, and Wise, "Temple"; Wise, "11QTemple"; for various expectations of judgment, see the summary in Keener, *Matthew*, 561–62. Cf. Cousland, "Temples," for Greco-Roman expectations for temples.

424. For a positive picture of worship in the temple in Luke-Acts, see Weinert, "Meaning of Temple." The temple's positive function for prayer could also highlight the paradox of Israel's failure to embrace Jesus (see Holmås, "House").

425. Cf. Clark, "Role," 173–77, esp. 174; Ehrhardt, *Acts*, 19.

to hand over their position willingly (cf. 4:8; 5:41; 23:5)—it nevertheless illustrates how the authorities could have heard the claims the apostles did make. Certainly, by charging the leaders with rejecting and killing God's Messiah, the apostles regarded the "builders" (4:11) as unfit for further leadership (cf. Luke 20:16–18).

The temple at this point serves a positive function,[426] which may reflect the religious fervor of the earliest church; times of rapid expansion can produce optimism about reclaiming lost ground. Mostly tragic stories could have happy endings, and so a "den of robbers" destined for judgment (Luke 19:46; 21:6) might yet be saved.[427] Presumably, Luke's audience knows otherwise, but the primitive Christians' devotion to the temple makes sense in the story world, adds pathos to the ultimate rejection of Paul in the temple and (beyond the narrated story) its promised destruction, and strengthens Luke's perception (and likely the historical reality) of the earliest Jerusalem Christians' fidelity to their biblical heritage.

e. Renewal of Temple Worship

The revival of spiritual temple worship here would evoke for Luke's biblically informed audience grand precedents. Throughout the priestly work of the Chronicler, renewal of temple (or tabernacle) worship accompanied revivals in Israel's history.[428] This worship could involve the prophetic Spirit (1 Chr 25:1–6),[429] and it generated the psalms that became standard in later temple liturgy (2 Chr 29:30). The early Christians thus had good reason to expect (and experience) a renewal of temple worship, whether or not the authorities saw fit to cooperate with their agenda.[430]

Many Jewish people expected a new or renewed temple in this period.[431] This hope naturally stirred more prominently after 70 C.E.[432] but is abundantly attested before that period,[433] especially in the Qumran scrolls.[434] The restoration of the vessels, the ark,[435] and perhaps its manna[436] also imply a renewed, eschatological temple of some sort.[437] Many emphasized a new or renewed temple because they viewed the current

426. For some positive approaches to the temple in Luke-Acts, see Walton, "Perspectives," 136–37; Tomson, "Centrality"; Chance, *Acts*, 118 (as well as Weinert, "Meaning of Temple," as above).

427. Spencer, *Acts*, 40.

428. See 1 Chr 6:31–32; 15:16, 28–29; 16:4–6, 41–42; 23:27, 30; 2 Chr 8:14; 20:20–24; 29:25, 30; 31:2; also Ezra 3:10–11; Neh 12:24, 27–47; implicit also in 2 Chr 35:2–6.

429. Cf. 1 Sam 10:5; 2 Kgs 3:15; Hab 3:19.

430. Some also make a plausible case for spiritual-temple imagery earlier in the chapter (see Beale, "Descent"). One modern Christian renewal movement has envisioned a restoration of temple worship in Acts 15:16; although this is possible (cf. "tabernacle" in 7:43–44), both Amos and Luke probably apply that image instead to a restoration of Davidic rule.

431. See, e.g., Sanders, *Jesus and Judaism*, 78–86; Freyne, *Galilean*, 153–57.

432. E.g., *2 Bar.* 4:3; 32:4; *t. Roš Haš.* 2:9; *Šabb.* 1:13; *y. Ber.* 1:5, §5; *Gen. Rab.* 65:23; *Num. Rab.* 14:8; 15:10; *Lam. Rab.* proem 33; a coin from 132 C.E. (Carmon, *Inscriptions*, 81, 178, §§178–79); cf. probable indications in the sixth-century Beth Alpha mosaic (Dequeker, "Zodiaque"); cf. also the plea for Jerusalem's rebuilding in the fourteenth benediction of the Amidah (Oesterley, *Liturgy*, 65) and surrogate temple features in synagogues (e.g., Friedman, "Features"). Worship may have continued on the site of the temple until 135 (Clark, "Worship").

433. E.g., *1 En.* 90:28–29; Tob 13:10; 14:5; *Sib. Or.* 3.657–60, 702, 772–74. The Aramaic may diverge from the Ethiopic of *1 En.* 91:13, but the reconstruction of the Aramaic is problematic, and so *1 En.* 91:13 probably also refers to the future temple.

434. 11QT^a XXX–XLV; 4Q174 1 I, 2–3; 4Q509 IV, 2, 12; 4Q511 35 3; notes in Maier, *Temple Scroll*, 98–116; Yadin, "Temple Scroll," 41; Lincoln, *Paradise*, 149; Broshi, "Dimensions."

435. Cf. 2 Macc 2:4–7; *2 Bar.* 6:7–9; *4 Bar.* 3:10–11, 19; 4:4; *Liv. Pr.* 2:15 (Schermann, 83) (25, Jeremiah); Rev 11:19; *m. Šeqal.* 6:1–2; *Yoma* 5:2; *t. Kip.* 2:15; contrast Jer 3:16.

436. Cf. *2 Bar.* 29:8; commentaries (including mine) on Rev 2:17; John 6:32–35. For manna in the ark, see Heb 9:4.

437. The Samaritan hope seems to have drawn this conclusion; see Kalimi and Purvis, "Hiding"; cf. Collins, "Vessels"; MacDonald, *Samaritans*, 365; Bowman, *Documents*, 89.

priesthood as impure.[438] These expectations support the plausibility of the earliest Jesus movement sharing some contemporaries' expectations that Jerusalem and the temple would play a central part in God's end-time plan.[439]

Many early Christians valued worship by the Spirit in direct contrast to dependence on the temple liturgy (John 4:20–24)[440] or other Jewish tradition (Phil 3:3; cf. Jude 20). The teaching of a new temple is even more pervasive in early Christianity (Eph 2:18–22; 1 Pet 2:5; Rev 3:12; cf. John 4:23–24) and hence is undoubtedly early.[441] This does not mean, however, that they entirely rejected the current one. Many early Jewish sources that expected destruction of the present temple regarded it as impure and unsuitable for worship,[442] but the image of a present spiritual temple or of spiritual sacrifices was not necessarily incompatible with the literal practice.[443] Unlike sectarians who withdrew from the temple, the earliest Christians met there; like many Jewish sects, however, they resented the abuse of authority they felt the temple authorities practiced.[444] They challenged the leaders without rejecting the validity of the temple institution itself.

This seems also true for the picture in Luke-Acts. In the context of the temple establishment's hostility (Luke 20:1–2), Jesus taught that stones (not in the temple) could cry out in worship to him (19:37–40) whereas Jerusalem's stones would be hurled down (19:41–44). The temple would be judged (19:45–48), but it would be given a new foundation with Jesus himself as the cornerstone (20:17–18; cf. Mark 12:10; Eph 2:20; 1 Pet 2:6–7).[445]

f. Prayer and Worship (2:46–47)

That the disciples were persisting (προσκαρτεροῦντες) in the temple probably indicates not prayer without pausing (cf. Acts 6:4; Rom 12:12; Col 4:2) but "observance of the regular hours of prayer" (see also comment on Acts 1:14; 2:42).[446] These meetings apparently occur more frequently here than later in Acts and in other early

438. Thus in the Scrolls (Flusser, *Judaism*, 43; probably, e.g., also in 4Q176 1 + 2 I, 2–3).

439. See, e.g., Taylor, "Jerusalem and Temple."

440. See discussion in Keener, *John*, 611–18. Taylor, "Temple," 720–21, argues that for Luke, after the rending of the veil, God's presence was available only through the Spirit; the temple's destruction in 70 therefore did not change the situation.

441. Dunn, *Partings*, 75–97.

442. Jos. *War* 6.301; *Test. Mos.* 6:8–9; *Test. Levi* 15:1 (cf. 14:6); cf. the hope of the new temple (*1 En.* 90:28–29; 11QT[a] XXIX, 8–10; Sanders, *Figure*, 262) or judgment on the Jerusalem priesthood (1QpHab IX, 6–7). Jesus, by contrast, did not secede from the temple (hence Sanders, *Jesus and Judaism*, 61–76, doubts that he thought it impure), yet if Jesus predicted its destruction, must he have not thought it impure in *some* way? For criticism of the temple and its cult in some early Jewish sources, see Holmén, *Covenant Thinking*, 280–84; Gathercole, *Boasting*, 205; for the authenticity of early Christian reports of Jesus's prophetic criticism, see Holmén, *Covenant Thinking*, 286–303; Broadhead, "Priests," 141–42; Keener, *Matthew*, 561–62 (and sources cited there).

443. See *Let. Aris.* 170, 172, 234. Philo's emphasis on spiritual sacrifice (sources in Johnson, *Romans*, 189–90) did not lead to rejection of the temple. Even the Essenes seem to have used part of the temple, though not sacrificing there (Jos. *Ant.* 18.19; cf. Davies, "Temple in Damascus Document"; spiritual sacrifices in 1QS IX, 4–5; 4Q403 1 I, 39–40); cf. Sanders, *Judaism*, 53 (differing with Philo *Good Person* 75, who may have assimilated Essenes to Pythagoreans), though some argue that later Essenes substituted their own community as a spiritual temple for observance in the physical one (Kapfer, "Attitudes," viewing the *Manual of Discipline* as later and diverging from the *Damascus Document*).

444. Cf. 1QpHab IX, 4–5; *Test. Levi* 14:1; *2 Bar.* 10:18; Jos. *Ant.* 20.181, 206; Overman, *Crisis*, 329.

445. Cf. Keener, "Human Stones," 34–35. Green, "Demise of Temple," sees the veil's rending (Luke 23:44–49) as a critical transition toward universality. Taylor, "Temple," 716–17, finds in the rending exposure of the temple's emptiness.

446. Jeremias, *Prayers*, 79. Luke likes the term; of its ten NT uses, six are in Acts. For early-morning prayers together following Jewish custom, cf. Manns, "Ante lucem" (citing Wis 16:28; Pliny *Ep.* 10.96), although, for Pliny's urban Christians, meeting before the workday may have also been a factor.

Christian sources (cf. Acts 20:7; 1 Cor 16:2; Heb 10:25), perhaps in part because it was difficult for working Christians scattered throughout a city to gather several times (or even once) a day. Rome, ever wary of potential sedition, prohibited associations from meeting more frequently than once a month; it made an exception for synagogues.[447] Because Christians followed the synagogue pattern, they might initially be able to claim exemption on such grounds even in Rome, and because they met in homes, potential accusers (*delatores*) would probably not recognize or be able to complain about the frequency of their meetings; in a later period, however, their regular meetings (not to mention their title as an ἐκκλησία, which to Greeks often signified a "town meeting") could carry subversive political connotations. For whatever reasons, later Christians seem to have met less frequently than here, but they preserved the memory of religious intensity of the earliest, ideal community.

Although Luke associates "gladness" here especially with food[448] (i.e., especially the home meetings, discussed above), it may also have some relevance for the public meetings. In the psalms, "gladness" could describe celebratory worship of the Lord, often corporate worship in the temple.[449] Many Greek and Roman thinkers argued that wisdom and virtue, rather than bodily pleasure, yielded happiness.[450] Jewish people often connected it with God's commandments[451] and also with prayer (Tob 13:1) and worship (*Jub.* 36:6; *Jos. Asen.* 3:4).[452] The picture of joyful hearts corresponds with the promise of life in Acts 2:26 (cf. comment there) and resolves the picture of stricken "hearts" in 2:37. The picture of the "guilelessness" (ἀφελότητι) of their hearts evokes a virtue.[453]

g. Praise (2:47)

Given the emphasis on honor in the ancient Mediterranean world, "praise" was very important in worshiping deities. More important is that biblical tradition spoke of "praising" the Lord.[454] Early Judaism often emphasized the praise of God,[455] even among superhuman beings.[456] The particular term here, αἰνέω, is characteristically

447. Winter, *Left Corinth*, 134. Many civic cults held public celebrations only once a year (e.g., Philost. *Hrk.* 53.8, 12, 15), but monthly meetings for associations were common (e.g., Smith, *Symposium*, 99, 108, 112).

448. On food and gladness together, see, e.g., Acts 14:17; Deut 12:7, 18; 14:26; 27:7; 1 Kgs 4:20; 1 Chr 29:22; Neh 8:10; Esth 9:19, 22; Ps 104:15; Isa 22:13; 65:13; Jer 15:16; Joel 1:16; 1 Esd 9:54; 4Q545 1 I, 7; *Jub.* 13:27; 22:4; 31:22; 32:7; 36:17; Jos. *Ant.* 5.346; 7.60; *Sib. Or.* 1.73; *Test. Jud.* 15:4.

449. Dunn, *Acts*, 36–37 (citing as examples Pss 42:4; 47:1; 63:5; 100:2). Expressions of "joy," "gladness," etc., appear more than a hundred times in the canonical psalms, sometimes in connection with God's house (Pss 42:4; 122:1). Expressions such as "joy" and "gladness" appear more than thirty times in Luke-Acts but may be connected partly with the temple only here in Luke-Acts. Joyful celebration characterized ancient festivals (Libanius *Descr.* 29.12).

450. Cic. *Parad.* 16–19; *Leg.* 1.23.60; *Tusc.* 5.7.19–20; Mus. Ruf. 7, p. 58.13; 17, p. 108.7; Iambl. *V.P.* 31.196; Sen. Y. *Ep. Lucil.* 23; 27.3–4; 59.10; *Ben.* 7.2.3; *Dial.* 7; also Lutz, "Musonius," 28; Engberg-Pedersen, *Paul and Stoics*, 73. Self-knowledge also yielded full joy (Cic. *Tusc.* 5.25.70).

451. Jos. *Ag. Ap.* 2.189; *Pesiq. Rab Kah.* 27:2; *b. Yoma* 4b; *y. Pesaḥ.* 10:1; *Lev. Rab.* 16:4; *Song Rab.* 4:11, §1; *Pesiq. Rab.* 21:2/3; 51:4; Urbach, *Sages*, 1:390–92; Anderson, "Joy." See further comment at Acts 13:52.

452. The Spirit appears with joy in *y. Sukkah* 5, cited in Montefiore and Loewe, *Anthology*, 203.

453. E.g., Arius Did. *Epit.* 2.7.11m, pp. 88–89.8; cf. BDAG.

454. Using this term, see, e.g., 1 Chr 16:4, 7, 10, 35, 36, 41; 23:5, 30; 29:13; 2 Chr 5:13; 6:26; 7:3; 8:14; 20:19, 21; 31:2; Ezra 3:10–11; Neh 5:13; 12:24, 36; 1 Macc 4:33; 3 Macc 2:8; 5:13; 6:32; Jdt 13:14; Tob 13:17; and many other sources (including some fifty times in Psalms and more than a hundred total times in the LXX). Jewish tradition amplified praise in some cases, e.g., for Abraham (*Jub.* 16:31; *Tg. Neof.* 1 on Gen 21:33). Naturally, Gentiles also praised their deities (e.g., Xen. *Cyr.* 8.1.23; Men. Rhet. 2.17, 445.31–32).

455. E.g., 1 En. 9:4; 1QS X, 10. Cf. eschatological worship in 1 En. 39:7; *Sib. Or.* 3.715, 726; *t. Pisha* 8:22; *b. Sanh.* 91b; *Ta'an.* 31a.

456. E.g., 1 En. 12:3; 39:12; 61:11–13; 1QM XII, 1; 4Q403 1 II, 15; 4Q405 frg. 19; 20 II + 21–22; 4Q405 23 I, 8–10; 4Q511 35 2–5; *Tg. Ps.-J.* on Exod 14:24. For earthly worship connected with the heavenly worship, cf., e.g., *Sipre Deut.* 306.31.1.

Lukan (Luke 2:13, 20; 19:37),[457] soon to recur in response to a dramatic healing (Acts 3:8–9).

An emphasis on daily (2:46) praise also appears in some Greek texts, suggesting the great worthiness of the deity being praised.[458] In the Jerusalem church, such praise could include all individuals offering their own prayers simultaneously, as was frequent in much ancient worship, but probably at least included some corporate singing, as typically in the psalms. Qumran provides many contemporary examples of Judean thanksgiving hymns;[459] Levites sang in the temple, and choruses of priests sang in other temples. (On religious singing, see discussion at Acts 16:25.) That later Gentile churches sang (1 Cor 14:15; Eph 5:19; Col 3:16) and the singing included the specifically Jewish category of "psalms" renders it likely that they continued the practice of the earlier Jerusalem church.[460]

The term for praise here, αἰνέω, is particularly favored by Luke among NT writers, though it is not common even there, but it appears more than a hundred times in the LXX, most prominently in the priestly writings of the Chronicler (nearly twenty times), the psalms (about forty times), and Sirach (sixteen times, though only about two-thirds of the references apply to God himself).[461] Nearly all the texts in Chronicles associate this praise with the house of the Lord (1 Chr 16:4, 7, 10, 35–36, 41; 23:5, 30; 29:13; 2 Chr 5:13; 6:26; 7:3; 8:14; 31:2; cf. 2 Chr 23:12; Ezra 3:10–11; Neh 12:24, 36) or at least the Levites (2 Chr 20:19–21); psalms were used in the temple, and some psalms allude to the temple as an important setting for praise (e.g., Pss 35:18 [34:18 LXX]; 84:4 [83:5]; 100:4 [99:4]; 135:1–3 [134:1–3]; cf. 150:1). It also appears in the prelude to the Spirit's outpouring in Joel (Joel 2:26).

Probably much of the worship of the early Jesus movement was corporate, in the temple, a place of prayer (Luke 2:36–38; 18:10; 19:46; 24:53); this public devotion brought them more favor.[462] That this element is important for Luke, emphasizing the movement's continuity with its Jerusalem heritage, is clear from the repetition of information offered in Luke 24:53;[463] this is the final element of the Gospel's conclusion reiterated in Acts and the only one reiterated after Acts 1:2–12. By reading the psalms or later Jewish liturgy (which reflected earlier patterns of worship), we may reconstruct some of the sorts of praise they would have used. Shaye Cohen emphasizes,

> The most common element in Jewish prayer is praise. In the temple the recitation of the Ten Commandments and the *Shema* was preceded and followed by benedictions (or blessings, in Hebrew *berakhot*; sing. *berakha*). Praise of the deity is universal, but benedictions are a quintessentially Jewish mode of worship, which was adopted by

457. Outside Luke-Acts, only twice in the NT (i.e., Rom 15:11; Rev 19:5), and only two further times in the Apostolic Fathers (*Barn.* 7.1; *Mart. Pol.* 14.3). Nevertheless, it appears 117 times in the largest form of the LXX, particularly prominent in 1–2 Chronicles and in Psalms. The explicit command αἰνεῖτε τὸν κύριον appears five times in Psalms (in other forms of the verb, eight times; the number is higher if anarthrous uses of the object are included or if we include the objects in the dative); with τὸν θεόν, in Pss 147:12; 150:1; Jdt 13:14.

458. See van der Horst, "Parallels to Acts," 60 (Ael. Arist. *Or.* 40.1; Chaeremon Stoicus frg. 10).

459. It is not strictly clear whether they were used liturgically (Schuller, "Thanksgiving Hymns," 1217), but it is improbable that only Christians and Therapeutae sang.

460. Technically, ψαλμός (psalm) was an accepted Greek term, but normally implied harp playing, which was probably not available in all the house churches the way remembered psalms (or newly composed psalms on the biblical model) would be. Early Christian usage follows the LXX, where instruments are not relevant to the definition.

461. E.g., toward God in Sir 17:10, 27–28; 39:14; 51:1, 10, 12, 22 (in God's house, 47:10; 50:18); applied to Wisdom in 24:1; to people in 11:2; 39:9; 44:1; 47:6; and to words in 21:15.

462. See Falk, "Prayer Literature," 272–73.

463. Luke opens and closes the narratives of his Gospel with scenes of the temple (Luke 1:8–22).

Christianity (see the *Benedictus*; Luke 1:68–79; cf. 2 Cor. 1:3; Eph. 1:3; 1 Peter 1:3) and Islam.[464]

Given the church's experience with tongues on Pentecost (Acts 2:4), some of the early Christians' worship, at least in home settings, may have included inspired praise in unknown languages (1 Cor 14:15), though it is likely that at some point already at an early period they may have also sought interpretations (cf. 14:13–16). But orderly liturgical worship could also be charismatic and prophetic (1 Chr 25:1–3), and Luke does not give us much specific insight into the community's worship except by reproducing their use of psalms (e.g., Acts 4:25–26) and other biblical language (e.g., Luke 1:46–55) in prayer.

h. Favor and Growth (2:47)

God had given "favor" (χάρις) before others to the patriarchs, such as Joseph (Acts 7:10; Gen 39:4, 21; 50:4),[465] and to Israel before the Egyptians (Exod 3:21; 11:3; 12:36)—relevant to the eschatological remnant among a larger people. That the early church had favor with its contemporaries at the close of Acts' introductory section parallels Jesus's favor with God and people at the end of Luke's infancy narrative (Luke 2:52), as also (using different language) in his ministry even in Jerusalem (19:48).[466] Reading the Gospel and Acts together, the apostolic church was able to build on the foundation that Jesus laid in his popularity in Jerusalem (20:1, 19, 26, 45; 21:38; 22:2, 6; 24:18–19), now that they proclaimed that his resurrection had vindicated him.

Reporting such favor was appropriate to epideictic depictions of ideal communities. Thus the simple life of the Essenes was thought to attract converts sufficient to replenish their numbers without sexual reproduction (Pliny E. *N.H.* 5.15.73). Historians also reported positively the rapid growth of new colonies.[467] Even Stoics accepted favor; it was ultimately a matter of indifference, but a *positive* one.[468] "Favor" was not a permanent gift, as Jesus's mission reveals (e.g., Luke 4:22, 28; cf. 19:37–38; 23:13, 18; Mark 2:2; 15:11); ancient literature (especially with its aristocratic bias) testifies to how quickly the sentiments of "the masses" changed (cf., e.g., Acts 12:3).[469]

---

464. Cohen, *Maccabees*, 70; cf. also Arbel, "Liturgy: Rabbinic," esp. (on the earliest period) 650–51; Le Cornu, *Acts*, 168. The benediction form was common in Qumran hymns (Cohen, *Maccabees*, 70), though more pervasive in the rabbis (Hoffman, "*Berakhah*"). Many have argued for hymns in the NT (Sanders, *Hymns*, 24–25; Hunter, *Paul*, 37–38; Hengel, *Jesus and Paul*, 78–96; Porter, "Creeds"), though (in my view) the hard evidence appears mainly in Revelation and Luke's infancy narratives, not in Paul's letters.

465. Also *Jub.* 39:4; 40:9; *Test. Jos.* 11:6; 12:3. Other patriarchs, e.g., Gen 18:3; *Jub.* 19:5; perhaps *Test. Jud.* 2:1 (χάριν); Jesus in Luke 4:22. It was a general idiom (e.g., Gen 43:14; 47:25, 29; Num 32:5; Deut 24:1; Ruth 2:2, 10, 13; Esth 2:9, 15, 17; Tob 1:13).

466. For favor with God, see, e.g., Luke 1:30; Acts 7:46; Gen 6:8; Exod 33:12–13, 16–17; 34:9; Num 11:11; Sir 3:18.

467. So Balch, "ΜΕΤΑΒΟΛΗ ΠΟΛΙΤΕΙΩΝ," 165, citing Dion. Hal. *Ant. rom.* 1.3.1, 4; 1.11.3; 1.16.2; 1.23.1; 1.31.3; 1.59.5; 1.64.4; 2.15–17; 2.32.2; 2.36.2, 3; 2.47.1; 2.50.1; 2.62.5.

468. Arius Did. *Epit.* 2.7.7b, pp. 44–45.32–33, on acceptance by others.

469. On the masses, see discussion in Keener, *John*, 732–33; on negative attitudes toward fickleness, see, e.g., Cic. *Fam.* 1.9.11; 5.2.10; Quint. *fratr.* 1.2.2.4; Virg. *Aen.* 4.569–70; 2 Cor 1:17; Plut. *Demosth.* 13.1–2; Cic. 26.7; Pliny *Ep.* 2.11.22; 4.2.1; 8.18.3; Tac. *Hist.* 2.57, 101; 3.73, 84; *Ann.* 12.1, 3 (probably also 15.36); Suet. *Tib.* 67.4; *Claud.* 15.1; 16.1; 39–40; Quint. *Decl.* 352.1; Max. Tyre 5.3; Fronto *Ad am.* 1.19; Hermog. *Issues* 69.3–13; Arius Did. *Epit.* 2.7.11i, pp. 78–79.16–18; Porph. *Marc.* 27.438; Libanius *Thesis* 1.29; on fickle mobs, Livy 31.34.3; Lucan *C.W.* 3.52–56; Corn. Nep. 10 (Dion), 10.2; 13 (Timotheus), 4.1; Tac. *Ann.* 2.41; *Hist.* 1.32, 45; 3.85; 5.8; Max. Tyre 27.6; Ps.-Phoc. 95–96; Philo *Embassy* 120; Jos. *Life* 87, 97, 143–44, 313–17, 333; 1 Sam 18:16; 25:10; 2 Sam 3:36; among "barbarians," Caesar *Gall. W.* 4.5; Jos. *Ant.* 18.47; Tac. *Hist.* 2.29; 3.85. The "crowds" of the Gospel may be identical with the "people" here (Tannehill, *Luke*, 143; cf. 143–66), and those crowds, though favorable in Galilee, appeared less favorable as Jesus drew closer to Jerusalem (157–58).

(The "people" [λαός] are God's people;[470] a glance at the LXX, however, warns that this audience does not always guarantee favor for God's servants [cf. Acts 6:8–14].)[471] Though not permanent, it was a strategic gift to be used wisely while it lasted. Josephus also presents his popularity with the people (despite the enmity of the Jerusalem elite) as positive in his apologetic autobiography (*Life* 250).[472]

Although the apostles played a strategic role (Acts 2:43), the entire church's "favor" with the people seems to have contributed to the continuing conversions; whereas the Spirit's empowerment for preaching had been effective (2:41), the Spirit's empowerment for eschatological living, though less explicit in the text, also is effective (2:46–47).[473]

The mention of those being "saved" alludes to Joel 2:32, quoted in Acts 2:21 (alluded to also in 2:40), suggesting that the term continues to connote the eschatological remnant of Israel.[474] (The present tense of the participle probably says more about continuing conversions, and hence the community's evangelistic effectiveness, than about elements of realized eschatology in Luke's soteriology, though of the latter we find sufficient hints elsewhere.)[475] That the Lord was daily adding these converts to their community indicates the expectation that those being saved were becoming part of the remnant or, in subsequent theological terms, the relevance of soteriology to ecclesiology. Luke makes much use of the term here for "adding" (προστίθημι); of its eighteen occurrences in the NT, thirteen (nearly three-quarters) are in Luke-Acts (for converts also in Acts 2:41; 5:14; 11:24).[476] Luke employs the term both at the beginning (2:41) and conclusion (2:47) of this summary section, underlining the importance of the movement's growth to his focus. The expression for "community" here, ἐπί τὸ αὐτό (lit. "at the same [place]," i.e., "together"), appears in 1:15; 2:1; and 2:44; the LXX uses it for the Hebrew *yahad* in a number of texts, a Hebrew term that in the Qumran scrolls refers to the "community" (1QS I, 1, 12; VIII, 1; IX, 2).[477]

470. Eighty-three of 138 NT uses (about 60 percent) appear in Luke-Acts; for the frequent evocation of LXX connotations, cf. Tannehill, *Luke*, 143. God sometimes gave his "people" "favor" with others (Exod 3:21; 11:3; 12:36; Esth 7:3). The LXX does not, however, by any means restrict the term to Israel, though this is, naturally, its most common application.

471. E.g., Exod 32:1, 3, 6, 7, 21–22, 25, 30–31, 34–35; 33:3; Num 11:1; 16:41; 20:3; 21:4–5; 25:1; also, e.g., *Liv. Pr.* 2:1 (*OTP* 2:386; Schermann, §25, p. 81, on Jeremiah).

472. Local popularity often appears among praises of a person (e.g., Xen. Eph. *Anthia* 1.1; among achievements noted in Vell. Paterc. 2.43.3–4); for the benefits of a good reputation with the people, see 1 Sam 14:45; Prov 22:1; Jdt 8:8; Sir 42:8; Pindar *Nem.* 8.37–39; 1 Tim 3:7; *Sipre Deut.* 1.10.1; *b. Ber.* 17a; Char. *Chaer.* 1.1.10; see comment on Acts 6:3. Van der Horst, "Parallels to Acts," 59, compares here Iambl. *V.P.* 30.

473. Many studies, both more exegetical (Trites, "Church Growth") and more applicational (Brewer, "Group Dynamics," 162–63; cf. Rainer, "Church Growth and Evangelism"; for some other applications, see Roberts, "Resources"), have noted the significance of the group dynamic in evangelism and church growth in Acts.

474. With, e.g., Lake and Cadbury, *Commentary*, 30.

475. Dunn, *Acts*, 37, emphasizes both (comparing 1 Cor 1:21; 15:2); but cf. Lake and Cadbury, *Commentary*, 30; Mattill, *Last Things*, 50 (comparing Luke 13:23; 1 Cor 1:18; but both of these may be corporate expressions for those being converted). The present participle may correspond to the imperfect προσετίθει.

476. An analogous Hebrew construction applies to expanding the community in the Qumran scrolls (e.g., Driver, *Scrolls*, 520, citing 1QS VI, 4; Capper, "Context," 336), which some think supports Semitic tradition here. The LXX uses προστεθήσεται for a convert in Isa 14:1 (see Hort, *Judaistic Christianity*, 42).

477. Johnson, *Acts*, 60.